15th International PEAT Congress (IPC 2016)

Peatlands in Harmony

Oral Presentations

Kuching, Malaysia
15-19 August 2016

Volume 1 of 2

ISBN: 978-1-5108-6213-5

Printed from e-media with permission by:

Curran Associates, Inc.
57 Morehouse Lane
Red Hook, NY 12571

Some format issues inherent in the e-media version may also appear in this print version.

Printed by Curran Associates, Inc. (2018)

International Peatland Society (IPS)
Vapaudenkatu 12
40100 Jyvaskyla Finland

Phone: 358 14 3385 440
Fax: 358 14 3385 410

ips@peatlands.org

Additional copies of this publication are available from:

Curran Associates, Inc.
57 Morehouse Lane
Red Hook, NY 12571 USA
Phone: 845-758-0400
Fax: 845-758-2633
Email: curran@proceedings.com
Web: www.proceedings.com

TABLE OF CONTENTS

TABLE OF CONTENTS

PLENARY & KEYNOTE SESSIONS

Plenary

Keynote

PEATLANDS IN HARMONY

PEATLANDS IN HARMONY

1.1: PEAT CHARACTERISTICS

1.2: GEOCHEMISTRY, HYDROCHEMISTRY & HYDROLOGY

1.3: PEATLAND REMOTE SENSING, AERIAL & SATELLITE IMAGERY

1.4: PEATLAND CONSERVATION & MANAGEMENT

1.5: PEATLAND BIODIVERSITY

1.6: CONSERVATION OF PEATLAND FOREST & WILDLIFE

2.1: PEATLAND CARBON BALANCE, STOCKS, STORAGE & LOSSES

2.2: GHG EMISSION FROM NATURAL & MANAGED PEATLANDS

2.3: PEAT FOREST-WILDFIRE-IMPACT ON ENVIRONMENT & SOCIETY

2.3: PEAT FOREST-WILDFIRE-IMPACT ON ENVIRONMENT & SOCIETY

Bandung Sahari

3.1: RESTORATION OF BOREAL, TEMPERATE & TROPICAL PEATLANDS

3.1: RESTORATION OF BOREAL, TEMPERATE & TROPICAL PEATLANDS

3.2: REWETTING & RE-VEGETATION TECHNIQUES

4.1: PEAT USE, PEATLANDS TECHNOLOGY & AGRO-TECHNOLOGY

5.1: AGRICULTURE & FOREST PLANTATIONS ON PEATLAND

5.2: PEATLAND FORESTRY

5.3: PEATLAND MANAGEMENT: LEGISLATIONS, REGULATIONS & POLICY

6.1: CULTURAL & SOCIO-ECONOMIC ASPECTS OF PEATLAND

6.2: PEATLAND & LOCAL PEOPLE

SPECIAL SESSION 1: SOFT SOIL ENGINEERING

SPECIAL SESSION 2: PEAT FOR HORTICULTURE & ENERGY

SPECIAL SESSION 3: PUBLICALLY MANAGED PEATLAND CARBON STORAGE, ECOSYSTEM SERVICES, AND MANAGEMENT

SPECIAL SESSION 3: PUBLICALLY MANAGED PEATLAND CARBON STORAGE, ECOSYSTEM SERVICES, AND MANAGEMENT

SPECIAL SESSION 4: TROPICAL PEATLAND BIODIVERSITY & CONSERVATION IN SOUTHEAST ASIA

Special Session 5: PEATLAND RESTORATION: THE WAY FORWARD

SPECIAL SESSION 6: ASIA FLUX

SPECIAL SESSION 6: ASIA FLUX

Proceedings

15th International PEAT Congress 2016

Peatlands in Harmony

-Agriculture, Industry and Nature-

ORAL PRESENTATIONS

15th - 19th August 2016

Kuching, Sarawak, Malaysia

Organized by:

MPS
MALAYSIAN PEAT SOCIETY

In partnership with:

IPS
International Peatland Society

15th International
PEAT Congress 2016

Peatlands in Harmony

"Agriculture, Industry and Nature"

15th - 19th August 2016

Kuching, Sarawak Malaysia

Supported by:

Sarawak Government

MPOC Malaysian Palm Oil Council

International Union of Soil Sciences

IUFRO International Union of Forest Research Organizations

Malaysia Convention & Exhibition Bureau

SARAWAK CONVENTION BUREAU

With Thanks to Our Valued Sponsors

Lead Partner :

Ta Ann Holdings Berhad

Rimbunan Hijau Group of Companies

WTK AGRIBUSINESS

Titanium :

PELITA

SAMLING

PEATMAX

Platinum :

SARAWAK OIL PALMS

Diamond :

WEIDA

PT SMART TBK Agribusiness and Food

Gold :

sarawak energy

PALMHEAD GROUP

HGI

MPOC Malaysian Palm Oil Council

Silver :

we make it grow Klasmann Deilmann

SARAWAK TIMBER ASSOCIATION

TURFTECH INTERNATIONAL

Foreword

The theme of the 15th International Peat Congress 2016, 'Peatlands in Harmony' was chosen to highlight the closely linked relationship of the environment, industry and socio-economic factors in relation to peat. It serves as a reminder for all to find balance in social and economic progress with the conservation of the eco-system and biodiversity of peatlands towards ensuring the development of peatland is in harmony with the environment and ecosystem. The congress has striven and driven hard at stringing together industry players, government agencies and policy makers, who are hungry for information as well as enthusiastic researchers and academicians, who are passionate in proving that science is the key to unlocking potentials, solving problems and creating opportunities for the next generation. With the balance of these people, the congress aims at bringing to reality its theme 'Peatlands in Harmony'.

The Scientific Secretariat accepted 332 contributions for oral and poster presentations under six main themes with a major input from Theme 1: Inventory, Biodiversity, Conservation and Functions of Peatlands and Theme 2: Peatlands and Ecosystem Management. A special whole day session on Peat Forest-Wildfire – Impacts on Environment & Society was dedicated under Theme 2 to gather papers related to peat fire that comes at an important time in addressing the haze issue in the region. It has successfully attracted a total of 179 papers from both Malaysia and Indonesia, a huge leap in number for the very first time in the history of the congress. The congress also opened up six other special sessions with two unconventional topics; Soft soil engineering and Asia flux. Soft soil engineering addresses the challenging engineering problems from construction on peat and soft soils whereas Asia flux brings forward a discussion on the potential changes and sustainability/resilience of peatland ecosystems, especially those of tropical peatlands, in terms of terrestrial biosphere-atmosphere exchanges.

Overall, the congress had received an overwhelming request for papers to be included in the oral sessions. However, with the limited number of available rooms and slots, the Scientific Secretariat had had to select the best representative papers. Without the extended members of the Scientific Secretariat, it would have been havoc in the selection and arrangement of all the papers. With this, the congress wishes to thank the extended members of the Scientific Secretariat for giving so much of their time and expertise in making this congress a success.

The Scientific Secretariat
August 11, 2016

ORGANIZING COMMITTEE

Patron

YAB Datuk Patinggi Tan Sri (Dr) Haji Adenan Bin Haji Satem,
Chief Minister of Sarawak

Congress Chairman

YB Tan Sri Datuk Amar Haji Mohamad Morshidi Bin Abdul Ghani
State Secretary of Sarawak

Congress General

Dr Lulie Melling
Tropical Peat Research Laboratory (TPRL)

Secretariat

Nur Azima Busman *(TPRL)*
Priscilla Esther Mikin *(TPRL)*
Immas Janggok *(TPRL)*
Jicqueline Ratai *(TPRL)*
Davina Halpi *(TPRL)*
Jared Jimbau Chabu *(TPRL)*

Treasurer

George Chong Chook Voon *(TPRL)*
Alexson Gura *(TPRL)*
Candy Robun *(TPRL)*

Sponsorship

Dr Lulie Melling *(TPRL)*
Datu Dr Hj. Sulaiman Bin Haji Husaini
(Land Custody and Development Authority)

Scientific Programme

Dr Wan Rashidah Bt Wan A.Khadir
(Forest Research Institut, Malaysia)
Dr Sharon Lau Yu Ling *(TPRL)*
Auldry Chaddy Petrus Rudut *(TPRL)*
Nur Azima Busman *(TPRL)*

Congress Venue

Priscilla Esther Mikin *(TPRL)*
Lo Mei Lieng *(TPRL)*

Excursion

Frederick Haili Teck
(Department of Agriculture)
Mohd Zulhilmy Abdullah *(TPRL)*
Donny Sudid *(TPRL)*

Opening / Closing Ceremony

Dr Sharon Lau Yu Ling *(TPRL)*
Bobbie Yamoh *(TPRL)*
Auldry Chaddy Petrus Rudut *(TPRL)*
Lo Mei Lieng *(TPRL)*
Jared Jimbau Chabu *(TPRL)*

Gala Dinner

Auldry Chaddy Petrus Rudut *(TPRL)*
Bobbie Yamoh *(TPRL)*
George Chong Chook Voon *(TPRL)*

Ice-Breaking

Frazer Midot *(TPRL)*
Chesles Merikan *(TPRL)*

ORGANIZING COMMITTEE

Cultural
Auldry Chaddy Petrus Rudut *(TPRL)*
Sydney Augustine Assom *(Institute of Teachers Education Tun Abdul Razak Campus)*

Exhibition & Poster
Priscilla Esther Mikin *(TPRL)*
Alexson Gura *(TPRL)*
Dr Sharon Lau Yu Ling *(TPRL)*
Auldry Chaddy Petrus Rudut *(TPRL)*

Technical
William Nyigor
(Information and Communication Technology Unit)
Michael Meling *(TPRL)*
Edward Baran Aeries *(TPRL)*
Joseph Wenceslaus *(TPRL)*

Design & Printing
Tiffany Sam *(TPRL)*
Jicqueline Ratai *(TPRL)*
Su Li Yang *(TPRL)*

Protocol
Dato Haji Khir Bin Haji Busrah
(State Protocol and Public Relation Unit)
Bobbie Yamoh *(TPRL)*

Decoration
Donny Sudid *(TPRL)*
Joshua Rengga *(TPRL)*
Aicher Joseph Toyat *(TPRL)*
George Dinggat David Among *(TPRL)*
Su Li Yang *(TPRL)*

Accommodation & Logistics
Lo Kim San *(TPRL)*
Sim Siew Yen *(TPRL)*
Simon Peter *(TPRL)*

Scientific Secretariat

Chairman

Dr Wan Rashidah Wan Abdul Khadir
Forest Research Institute, MALAYSIA

Deputy Chairman

Dr Sharon Lau Yu Ling
Tropical Peat Research Laboratory Unit, MALAYSIA

Members

Prof Lars Lundin
Swedish University of Agricultural Sciences, SWEDEN

Prof Gerald Schmilewski
Klasmann-Deilmann GmbH, GERMANY

Dr Barbara Kalisz
University of Warmia and Mazury in Olsztyn, POLAND

Prof Jürgen Schoenherr
Zittau University of Applied Sciences, GERMANY

Prof Maris Klavins
University of Latvia, LATVIA

Dr Catherine Farrell
Bord na Móna Energy Limited, IRELAND

Dr Roxanne Andersen
University of the Highlands and Islands, UNITED KINGDOM

Dr Leena Larva
Aino Klinikat, FINLAND

Dr Sakari Sarkkola
Natural Resources Institute, FINLAND

Dr Sylvain Jutras
Université Laval, CANADA

Dr Michiel Gerding
Assen, The NETHERLANDS

Prof Jack Rieley
Nottingham University, UNITED KINGDOM

Dr David Wilson
Earthy Matters Environmental Consultants, IRELAND

Prof Son Radu
University of Putra Malaysia, MALAYSIA

Dr Irnayuli R. Sitepu
Indonesia International Institute for Life Sciences, INDONESIA

Dr Nagamitsu Maie
Kitasato University, JAPAN

Dr Tasren N Mahamooth
Advanced Agriecological Research Sdn. Bhd, MALAYSIA

Dr Goh You Keng
Advanced Agriecological Research Sdn. Bhd, MALAYSIA

Dr Dave Siak-Wei Ow
Bioprocessing Technology Institute, SINGAPORE

Prof Che Fauziah Ishak
University of Putra Malaysia, MALAYSIA

Dr Jeyanny A/P Vijayanathan
Forest Research Institute Malaysia, MALAYSIA

Dr Margaret Abat
Department of Agriculture Sarawak, MALAYSIA

Dr Helena Varkkey
University of Malaya, MALAYSIA

Prof Monique Leclerc
The University of Georgia, USA

Dr Pozi Milow
University of Malaya, MALAYSIA

Prof Ryusuke Hatano
Hokkaido University, JAPAN

Prof Takashi Hirano
Hokkaido University, JAPAN

Dr Suwardi
Bogor Agricultural University, INDONESIA

Assoc Prof Dominic Ong
Swinburne University of Technology, MALAYSIA

Dr Ian Singleton
Sumatran Orangutan Conservation Programme, INDONESIA

Dr Kho Lip Khoon
Malaysian Palm Oil Board, MALAYSIA

Assoc Prof Catherine Yule
Monash University, MALAYSIA

An ordinary housefly, if placed within a hollow clear glass globe having a single hole for an outlet, generally escapes tather promptly. But a bee, under like circumstances, seldoms escapes. This ... does not indicate superior wisdom on the part of the fly - quite the countrary. For the fly, dashing hither and thither in planless flight, continues to try to force its way through what must seem to it to be queerly resistant atmosphere.

From the preface to Colloid Chemistry, Vol. III, J. Alexander, 1931

Wonderful are the ways of God
In creation, and the love with which
He guides His creatures' destinies,
Gives them the means by which to strive
For maturity by ordered steps, and reach
The end most fitted for their natures,
His Law is just and easy, and His grace
Is ever ready to help: let us look
To the Eternal Goal, with hearts and souls
Of purity and glorify His name:
For in this changing, fleeting world,
His word is always true, and will remain,
Through all the ages, ever the same.

SURAH 87 - AL A' LA

WTK Group
Harnessing Ingenuity for Sustainable Growth
Principal Business Activities
■ Palm Oil
■ Hotel
■ Property Development
■ Aluminium Foil & Adhesive Tapes Manufacturing
■ Timber
■ Insurance
■ Trading
BANGUNAN HUNG ANN
Bangunan Hung Ann, No. 1, Jalan Bujang Suntong
P. O. Box 256, 96007 Sibu, Sarawak, Malaysia
Phone: +60 84 326155 Fax: +60 84 316180
Website: www.wtk.com.my
Email: info@wtk.com.my

TABLE OF CONTENTS

TABLE OF CONTENTS

PLENARY & KEYNOTE SESSIONS

Plenary

Keynote

Abstract No: A-414

HISTORY OF TROPICAL PEATLAND IN SOUTHEAST ASIA

Furukawa Hisao

Kyoto University, Japan

* *Corresponding author: hisaofurukawa@gmail.com*

SUMMARY

Geohistory of tropical peatlands in Southeast Asia and a historical retrospect of the exploitation are presented.

***Keywords**: Age, stratigraphy, early and modern ways of exploitation.*

INTRODUCTION

Coastal plains of the Malay Peninsula, Sumatra and Borneo bordering the Sunda Sea were, and still are partly, the realm of swamp forests which included mangrove at seaward outskirts, freshwater swamp forests in the tidal zone, and peat swamp forests inland. Under natural conditions, the ground surface is covered by tropical woody peat layers of varying thickness. These peatlands emerged through the Holocene submersion of the vast and flat terrains at the periphery of the former Sunda Land, and the productive tropical rain forests which expanded over the region. The tropical peatlands inhabited only by mammals, apes, birds and reptiles, remained miasmic for long periods against human interferences because of dense forests, high humidity, numberless mosquitoes, often submerged and bumpy ground surface. Now amidst the worldwide industrialism, they are swiftly changing into one of the important agro-industrial bases, and no one cannot deny that industrialism is a powerful engine to make a people richer and more free. On the other hand, we have seen negative effects of industrialism so often. London was famous for its smog by the mid 20th century. Japan in the 1960s to 1970s was an emporium with so many kinds of environmental pollution and induced diseases. These issues were met, and even now are met through dialogs, scientific studies and legislative measures supported by our own accord. Now, as everyone knows, there is a serious discord on the size of CO_2 emission from the drained tropical peatlands. Apparently, too many things are unknown to make a decisive judgment. The critical issue how to balance the economic growth and environment conservation is not only limited to the people and society living there, but also addressed to all of us who live in industrialized countries. This brief historical retrospect aims to understand how the people have been struggling to transform the miasmic lands, the natural and regional assets, into sustainable agro-industrial resources through trials and errors in the past and with ongoing improvements. I would be happy if my speech could make a voice to call for calm, sensible and fair discussions based on ecological and creative perception.

METHODS

Main materials have been collected through field surveys, some in detailed level in Indonesia and reconnaissance level observations in Malaysia, interviews with dwellers, and supplemented with references.

RESULTS AND DISCUSSIONS

Geohistory

A clear model of tropical peat formation has been presented by J. A. R. Anderson, who studied the swamp forests of Sarawak and Brunei. He divides coastal wetlands into freshwater swamp and peat swamp, based on differences in surface structure and degree of flooding. He explains the process of peatland formation as starting from the coastal mangrove clay, which was dated 5,400 years BP, and also how the distinctive saucer-shaped foundation of peat swamp is formed (Anderson, J. A. R., 1964). Our studies in Jambi Province of Sumatra revealed peatland stratigraphy in a bit different mode, which is illustrated in Fig. 1 (Furukawa, H. & Sabiham, S.,1985; Furukawa, H. 1994). We consider as follows: As the sea level rose in the post-glacial age, choked river water flooded over the former ground surfaces in lower reaches, accreting more fluviatile sediments nearby and rather less faraway. This process made the saucer-shaped topography of the foundation and induced the wood debris to be piled up as woody peat in water-saturated conditions. The littoral zone was accreted with mangrove clay, marine clay and tidal flat deposits, which were exposed on the ground as the sea receded, and changed into fresh water swamps of the present tidal zone. The peat on the former ground surface is thicker and older than tidal zone peat.

The lowest part of peat on the former ground surface was dated 6,830 years BP (400-430 cm), 5,710 years BP (700-750cm), and the peat covered by mangrove clay as 5,980 years BP (335-390cm), while tidal zone peat with 100 to120 cm thickness were dated around 1,120 to 1,440 years BP. From the forgoing survey of carbon dating, it seems probable that peat formation started at hypsithermal age, and through recurring fluctuation of sea level, at least two pe ... years BI

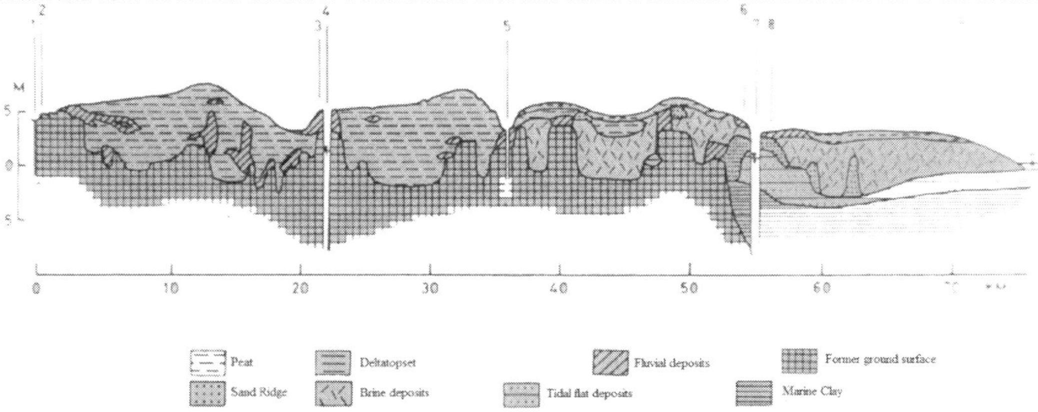

1. Kumpeh River 2. Bangso Village 3. Rantaupangjang Village 4. Batang Hari River 5. Dendang River 6. Teluk Buan 7. Batang Hari River 8. Lambur Village 9. Simburnaik Village

Figure 1: Stratigraphy of peatland in Jambi, Sumatra

The underground structure of peat cannot be observed without digging a deep pit, and we were not able to meet this task in long-distance transect surveys. But, from the experiences of borings with peat sampler we supposed it to be a scaffolding structure: stumps, fallen tree trunks and branches which peat samplers could not penetrate are embedded underground; these would function as posts and beams and the framed space would be filled with water, partly decomposed wood and plant debris, and porridge-like peat mud. A similar depiction has been made by Polak as well:" a brown mash held together by a framework of tree branches and trunks" (Polak, 1975). This structure is quite different from the sphagnum moss peat in the cold temperate region. This assumption has been confirmed at many pit profiles in Sarawak thanks to the painstaking toils by Tropical Peat Research Laboratory Unit. Understanding the peculiar feature of structured tropical woody peat would have a great meaning in predicting the subsidence and decomposition, and be related to the choice of proper measures for water regime control, field maintenance, and cropping performances.

Early exploitation

Tropical peat swamp forest is by no means primeval forest that has never known the ax. It has been frequently touched by man. Close inspection of old aerial photographs reveals countless lines, running through a monotonous texture. While not all can be said to be man-made, man has been into the forest more than might be expected. On walking the ground one finds many narrow paths cut for many aims. There are many paths trodden by collectors of various forest products, such as *jelutung* (*Dyera* spp.) latex, *Agathis* dammar, *nibung* (*Oncosperma* spp.) palm pole, rattan cane of *Calamus* spp. and *Daemonorops* spp., sago starch of *Metroxylon* spp. and many kinds of tropical timbers. Sago logs and timber logs were extracted through man-made ditches and on sledge. This is an old tradition.

Three waves of peatland exploitation in pre- modern and current times

The first known peak of swamp land reclamation emerged in the tidal zone of Kedah-Perlis plain and Johor coast of Malaya in the mid- to late-19th century through the influx of Chinese and Siamese farmers, who drained the waterlogged plain by digging tidal canals. With the increasing demand for gambier, pepper, sago and cassava starch under British colonial rule, their cultivation spread in swamp lands of Malaya in much the same way that sugarcane cultivation had been pushed forward in Province Wellesley in 1840s.The villages opened by the Chinese migrants were located, in the case of Johor, for example, upstream from the coast along the tidal rivers and creeks, just inside the fresh water tidal zone. Agricultural lands were cleared in the swamp forest nearby, and canals were dug between the farms and migrants' villages, and waterways were interlinked to form a network. Tree stumps were uprooted and piled up, covered with soil, incinerated, and the ash spread as fertilizer. The European planters who followed the Chinese discovered that the large tidal range facilitated drainage, and that sugarcane could be transported cheaply through the canal network (Jackson, J. C., 1968). This trend in Malaya, together with the reclamation design based on tidal irrigation and drainage, came to be known by Banjarese pilgrims on their way and by Javanese and Buginese who had permeated to the Malayan states. Banjarese transmitted the reclamation design to the tidal zone peatland around Banjarmasin through 1910s. Banjarese, Javanese and subsequently Buginese farmers further migrated through 1930s to every feasible corner of tidal zone peatlands of Sumatra and Kalimantan. The design was almost same with that mentioned above, and planted wet rice, coconut and rubber. These pre-modern reclamations rarely had water gates other than simple wooden weirs to adjust water level, but mostly still function because their ditches are small and short, at the longest 3 to 4 km from tidal creeks, and fields can be drained and irrigated.

Large scale modern reclamations of peatlands, the second wave, emerged first in the west coast of Selangor State of Malaya. The representative memorial example was Tanjong Karang-Sekinchan Project that started in 1945 and completed the first phase irrigation and drainage works in 1952, succeeded by complimentary phases afterwards, and was integrated into Barat Laut Selangor Irrigation Project that completed in 1995. The project area was located on the tidal zone shallow peat, aiming at two crops a year of wet rice culture, and presently it is surrounded completely by coastal and river bunds equipped with tidal control gates. In this project, the inland peat swamp forest with thick peat was reserved as a catchment for the irrigation, and still sustains. On the other hand, selective logging in deep peat forests had appeared extensively in Malaya and Indonesia. Timber extraction was, after the 1950s, facilitated through installing railway on which small locomotives pulled timbers. Meanwhile in Indonesia, the government started the Transmigration Policy in the late 1960s, when several millions ha of tidal zone peat forests of Sumatra and Kalimantan were transformed into agricultural fields through total logging and drainage. Big and deep drainage canals were cut through between the tidal rivers and creeks, hardly heeding the water level control. The thin peat layers swiftly disappeared, and underlying pyritic sediments were exposed on the ground, releasing a huge amount of sulfuric acid. Soils of reclaimed areas changed from peat to acid sulfate soils. Migrants suffered critical hazards, which, 30, 40 years afterwards now, seem to be mitigated significantly thanks to natural flushing processes. Barren fields are recovering green again.

Figure 1: Miserable rice culture, Jambi, 1983

Figure 2: Vast wasteland in Jambi, 1983

The current third wave, a total transformation of deep peat swamps into plantations for perennial crops such as oil palm and coconut palm, seems to have occurred in the early1980s in Johor State, and soon extended to Sumatra and Kalimantan. In Riau, Jambi, South and Central Kalimantan, selective logging in concession forests changed to the total cutting of forests. Sawmill, plywood, pulp and paper, and palm oil companies sprang up. Soon resources extinguished and enterprises started to make plantations of acacia and oil palm to meet big capacity of the factories. Fire, smoke and haze occurred rampantly. After the early 1990s, deep peat swamps of Sumatra east coast changed into plantations, collaborating with the government's Industrial Tree Plantation Programs. In this last phase, major enterprises started to implement sophisticated water management systems. Drains are not cut through to tidal rivers but segmented with many dams, water gates, sedimentation ponds, and designed so as to drain only the surplus water. From a technical point of view, this system seems to be highly elaborated with regard to the sustainability of the plantations inside concession areas. However, the neighboring shrubs, forests and dwellers' lands are left uncontrolled, and vast areas get dried, easily catch fire in *el nino* years, degraded and abandoned.

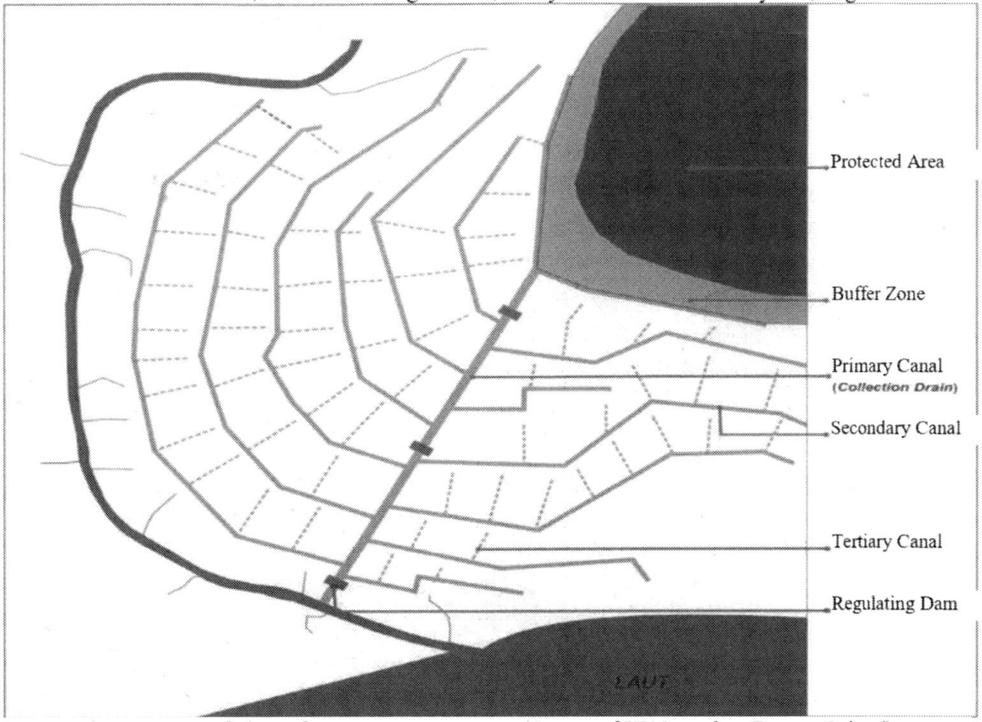

Figure 2: Layout of advanced water management system (Courtesy of PT Mayangkara Tanaman Industri)

The third wave extended to Sarawak as well, particularly in the 3rd National Agriculture Policy spanning from 1998 to 2010. Consequently Sarawak peatlands with thick peat layers have been opened for oil palm plantations, rapidly expanding the number and area. Here, a new catalog was created for enhancing the sustainability. That is the compaction of the peat ground surface by heavy machine after destumping. This treatment diminishes the coarse porosity in the surface layer, makes the bulk density a bit heavier, improves the capillary rise of ground water, and induces the better crop growth on properly moist peat surface. This new technology is widely adopted by many planters.

Figure 3: Collecting Acacia log, Riau, 2014

CONCLUSION

This brief historical retrospect reveals that miasmic tropical peatlands are changing into one of the worldwide industrial nodes through the collaborated toils of the people in this region. It is a fact, it is good. And all of us stand now equally on a new horizon to make our desire reconcilable with the nature.

REFERENCE

1. Anderson, J. A. R. 1964. The structure and development of the peat swamps of Sarawak and Brunei. *Journal of Tropical Geography*, 18: 7-16.
2. Furukawa, H. 1994. *Coastal Wetlands of Indonesia; Environment, Subsistence and Exploitation.* Kyoto: Kyoto University Press.
3. Furukawa, H. and Sabiham, S. 1985. Agricultural landscape in the lower Batang Hari, Sumatra. Part one: Stratigraphy and geomorphology of coastal swampy lands. *Southeast Asian Studies*, 23: 3-37.
4. Jackson, J. C. 1968. *Planters and Speculators.* Kuala Lumpur: University of Malaya Press, pp. 13-30, 130-145.
5. Polak, B. 1975. Character and occurrence of peat deposits in the Malaysian tropics. *Modern Quaternary Research in Southeast Asia*, 1: 71-81.

Abstract No: A-405

BIOMASS RECOVERY IN SECONDARY MIXED PEAT SWAMP FOREST, COASTAL RIAU, INDONESIA

J. Bathgate*, M. Iqbal, Zulnaidi, S. Marpaung

Asia Pacific Resources International Limited (APRIL), Indonesia

**Corresponding author: john_bathgate@aprilasia.com*

SUMMARY

APRIL group operates a half million ha of fiber plantation and restoration licenses on peatland in coastal Riau. Half of this area is mixed peat swamp forest (MPSF) that has permanently been set aside from development. Prior to becoming APRIL's, in an unregulated setting that then prevailed, the MPSF underwent uncontrolled local logging. Stands that have been monitored since 2004 indicate that secondary forest is now recovering structure and biomass. On heaviest disturbed sites *Meranti spp.* have become the commonest trees. Biodiversity is a future goal, for now secondary forest is showing resilience and protected area management is working to secure what remains. Production on 50% of the land, to finance and create a physical barrier around the set-aside 50%, is proving the way to maintain services of nature from a heavily modified landscape.

Keywords: *secondary tropical peat swamp forest, basal area, biomass, biological recovery, Meranti trees, services of nature*

INTRODUCTION

The Kampar natural landscape consists of a central core of pole forest located on a raised plateau, surrounded at lower elevation by mixed peat swamp forest (MPSF). The two types of peat swamp forest occupy similar proportions of the Kampar. Most pole forest is pristine. All MPSF forest, however, experienced licensed selective logging from about 1980; a portion of the large merchantable trees were taken out by light rail. The impacts of this original logging are no longer obvious. From 2000 the MPSF was cut again, severely, by informal loggers. Logs were floated out to the nearest rivers along excavated ditches, of dimensions approximately 2 m deep by 2 m wide. Abandoned ditches continued to drain water from the area until APRIL took up ditch blocking in 2010 (Bathgate and Rachmady, 2012). While logging has greatly reduced structure and biomass of MPSF, vegetation re-growth has been luxuriant and forest fires very few under a rainfall that averages 200 mm per month and exceeds 100 mm for all except for 3 months in most years.

Today, within the Kampar landscape, APRIL manages more than 150,000 ha of lowland MPSF as well as 100,000 ha of the peat dome pole forests. Development has now ceased and nearly half of the Kampar landscape is formally protected, including large areas of heavily modified MPSF. The aim is to protect and restore the landscape to provide services of nature: catchment and riparian function, carbon storage, biodiversity and wildlife refuge. In this paper a small sample of logged MPSF that was originally measured in 2004 is examined with a view to whether the now protected MPSF is recovering biomass.

METHODS

An initial forest inventory took place in 2004 at a time when the informal logging in the study area had largely ceased. 30 bounded plots of 100 m x 20 m dimension were established within disturbed MPSF. Trees were tallied by species in diameter classes of 20-40-60- 20-40, 40-60, 60+ cm diameter at breast height (DBH). In 2016 the 15 plots that remained within forest that had been set aside from development were upgraded to Permanent Sample Plot (PSP). Stems >10 cm DBH were tagged, re-measured for DBH, and samples of tree heights taken. Six sites that received heavier logging than most are reported in this study. Due to limitations with botanic identification, local tree names are used here. One abandoned logging ditch was topographically leveled to indicate the amount of soil subsidence that has occurred. The location of the study area, including PSP and the leveling profile, are shown in Figure 1.

RESULTS

The MPSF plots all occur at about 6 m elevation (above mean sea level) and prior to being logged would likely have had similar biomass to one another. PSP have been allocated to two relative categories, 'disturbed' and 'intact' canopy. These types are compared for the change in density and basal area (BA) of stems >20 cm DBH; smaller stems were not recorded in 2004 (Figure 2). Detailed inventory of 2016 enables the current size structures between forest types to be compared (Figure 3).

Trees >20 cm in the intact type have increased over the observation period by 25% in number and 30% in BA. Most trees tallied in 2004 have survived, increased in girth and contributed to an unmistakable increase in basal area. Canopy gaps are relatively small and are closing over; biomass recovery is underway.

However in the disturbed type, 25% of 40-60 cm trees and all >60 cm trees of 2004 have since died (Figure 2), and many are now on the forest floor. This phase of high mortality, which may or may not have passed, is a lingering 'edge effect' impact from canopy opening by logging. While stand basal area has not increased since 2004, 10-20 cm stems are numerous and contribute to BA (Figure 3). Now, over a decade after the logging, large numbers of small stems are replacing original canopy trees. It is unclear how long it will be before stand biomass accelerates/reaches the levels observed in the intact forest.

Forest composition, in terms of common trees per forest type, is summarized in Figure 5. Gaps in both forest types have developed into a dense secondary canopy of 10-20 m tall pandanus. Pandanus has a growth form that includes adventitious and prop roots, dense spreading canopy and heavy litter formation, and tolerance of flooding (Gunawan *et al.*, 2012). Pandanus can rapidly fill canopy gaps in heavily modified forest. Meranti and other species that would have been present pre-logging as suppressed small stems are now common as poles emerging through the pandanus. Meranti tree species are reported to have relatively fast DBH growth in lowland forest (Bin Kassim). Both Meranti and pandanus tree species are examples of dynamic pioneer populations. In the smaller gaps of the less disturbed forest the small trees are less numerous and of more varied composition than in the heavily disturbed type.

The relationship between tree height and DBH for a sample of canopy and emergent trees from both forest types is shown in Figure 4. The intact forest includes both taller and larger diameter trees and several trees of approximately 35 m tall that are emergent over the canopy. Disturbed forest includes no large emergent trees: these have all been extracted by logging operations or subsequently died.

Figure 6 shows a leveled profile of ground elevation oriented across a log extraction ditch that was abandoned in 2004. Intensified drainage of ground water into the ditch appears to have formed a subsidence valley that is approximately 0.5 m deeper than the surrounding land surface, and extends to about 400 m in each direction from the ditch. During site visits, the soil water depth beside the ditch averaged -42 cm (Sep 2004), -98 cm (Oct 2011) and -70 cm (February 2016). At other plots distant from ditches, ground water depths from -40 cm to +10 cm (flooded) were noted. There are insufficient data to show the effect of ditch drainage on forest condition; however the disturbed type close to ditches does include several fastest growing PSP. Proposed blocking of ditches in all State conservation forest (Hendroyomo 2014 may have some benefit for soil moisture, but the deeper the subsidence valley the more limited the area of peat that is likely to be rewetted.

CONCLUDING REMARKS

Biomass recovery is an established trend in the semi-intact secondary MPSF. Where disturbance has been severe, numbers of small trees have increased and biomass recovery is now expected to follow. High turnover and fast growth of trees in disturbed gaps has been reported for tropical forest (Condit *et al* 1999). Disturbance and slight drainage apparently suit Meranti, which when mature tend to occupy well drained mounds in the undisturbed peat swamps (Shimamura *et al 2005*. It has become the commonest tree of secondary forest. Since monitoring started in 2004, APRIL and stakeholders have succeeded to halt the informal logging. Nearly half of the Kampar landscape is now formally protected and most is being effectively protected on the ground. The evidence from monitoring is that the secondary MPSF is now on the way to recovering structure and biomass. Potentially, APRIL's extensive holdings of secondary MPSF are set to capture considerable carbon through biomass growth in the decades to come.

ACKNOWLEDGEMENTS

Thanks to the many APRIL workers and staff who supported this field project on a number of occasions with track cutting, PSP location, layout, marking and tree measurement, as well as with field accommodation, logistics and data entry. Particular thanks are due to Water Management at Teluk Meranti Estate for the thankless tasks of operating speedboats, cutting tracks and carrying supplies.

REFERENCES

1. Bathgate, J., and Rachmady, R. 2012. *Recent history of a modified peat dome, Coastal Riau, Sumatra.* Abstracts of the 14th International Peat Congress: Stockholm, June 3-8 2012, IPS.
2. Hendroyoma, B. 2015. *Regulation of Ministry of Environment and Forestry on forestry and land fire control.* Regulation S.66, MoEF, Republic of Indonesia
3. Bin Kassim, A. R. (undated). *Tree population dynamics of Shorea spp. in a primary lowland Dipterocarp forest at Pasoh, Peninsular Malaysia.* Geoinformation programme, Forestry and Environment Division, Forest Research Institute, Malaysia.
4. Gunawan, H., Kobayashi, S., Mizuno, K., and Kono, Y. 2012. *Peat swamp forest types and their regeneration in Giam Siak Kecil - Bukit Batu biosphere reserve, Riau, East Sumatra, Indonesia.* Mires and Peat, Volume 10.
5. Condit, E., Ashton, P., Manokaran, N., LaFrankie, J., Hubbell, S. and Foster, R. (1999). *Dynamics of the forest communities at Pasoh and Barro Colorado: comparing two 50-ha plots.* Phil. Trans. R. Soc. Land. B, p1739-1748*c*.
6. Shimamura,T., and Momose, K. 2005. *Organic matter dynamics control plant species coexistence in a tropical peat swamp forest.* Proceedings of the Royal Society B: Biological Sciences, V 272 (1571)

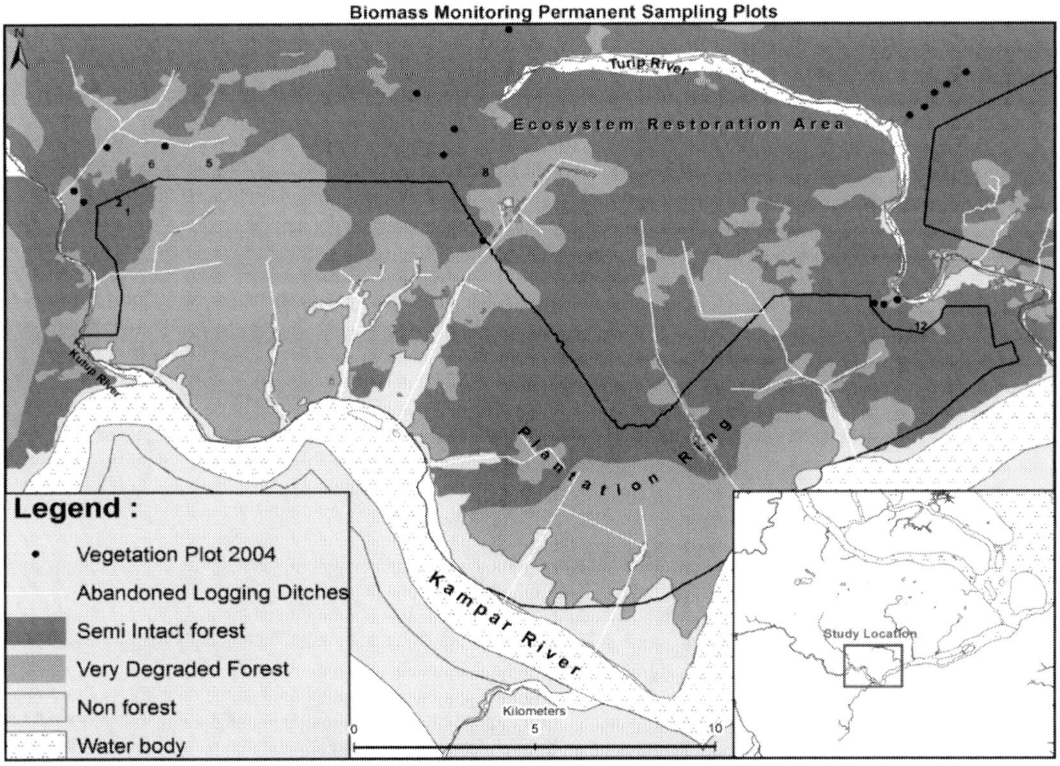

Figure 1: Location of study area

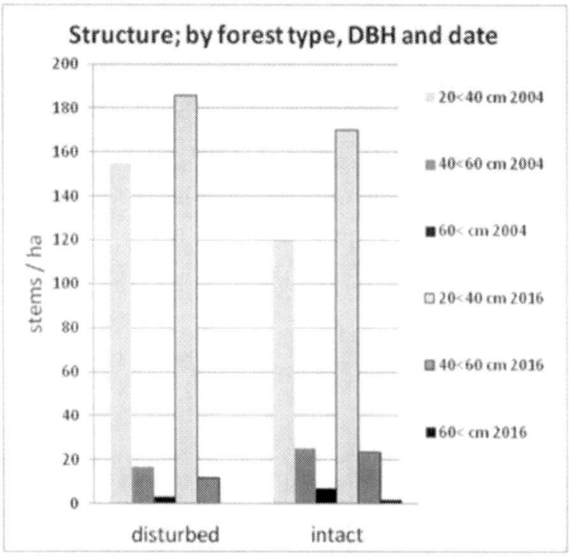

Figure 2: Change in forest structure 2004-2016

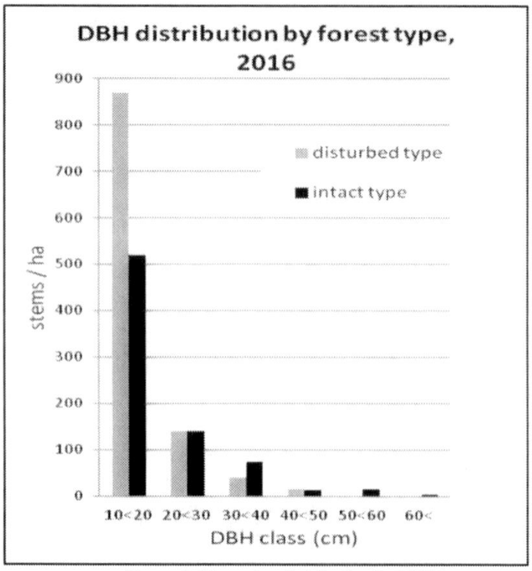

Figure 3: Stem size distribution in 20016

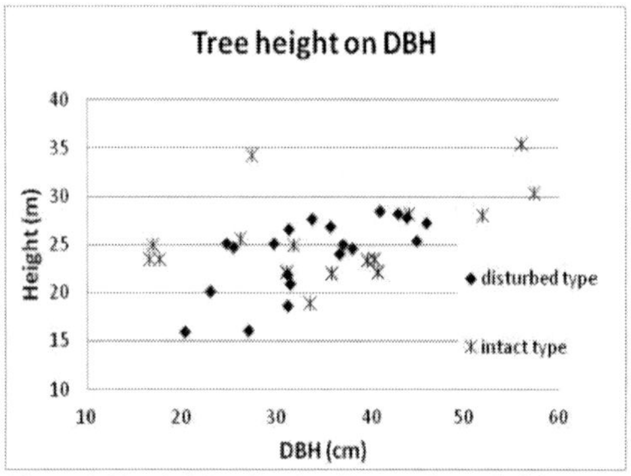

Figure 4: Tree height related to diameter breast height

Common trees in each type, by dbh class - 2016							distance
forest type	10<20	20<30	30<40	40<50	50<60	60< cm	to drain
disturbed	pandan meranti mixed	meranti kelat mixed	gerunggan mixed	mixed	-	-	<100 m
intact	pandan medang balam	medang balam pandan	medung balam kelat	kelat	kelat	mixed	> 1000 m

Figure 5: Table of common trees

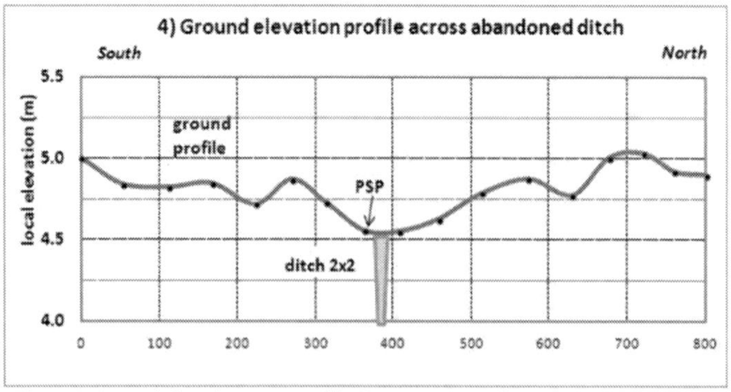

Figure 6: Ground elevation cross profile, Permanent Sample

Abstract No: A-034

CARBON BALANCE OF TROPICAL PEAT SWAMP FOREST

Takashi Hirano

Research Faculty of Agriculture, Hokkaido University, Japan

**Corresponding author: hirano@env.agr.hokudai.ac.jp*

SUMMARY

The features of the carbon balance of tropical peat swamp forest, such as seasonal variation, environmental controls and distrubance effects, are described based on long-term field monitoring of CO_2 flux at three tropical peat ecosystems with different disturbance degrees in Central Kalimantan, Indonesia.

Keywords: *Disturbance, ecosystem, groundwater level, photosynthesis, respiration*

INTRODUCTION

Tropical peat swamp forest (PSF) is a unique ecosystem rich in carbon and water, which is widely distributed in Southeast Asia's coastal lowlands, mainly in Indonesia and Malaysia. The ecosystem has accumulated a huge amount of organic carbon as peat soil over millennia under the condition of high groundwater level (GWL). However, the PSF has been degraded by logging and drainage, and many of PSFs were converted into oil palm and pulpwood plantations during the last two decades. Such human disturbances potentially increase carbon dioxide (CO_2) emissions to the atmosphere through enhanced oxidative peat decomposition and raised risk of peat fires. Moreover, PSF suffers from drought of El Niño-Southern Oscilation (ENSO) quasi-periodically. Therefore, PSF is recognized as a "hot spot" for vulnerable carbon pool in this century. It is essential to quantify the current carbon status of PSF to assess the role of PSF in the regional and global carbon balances. Thus, we have measured net ecosystem CO_2 exchange (NEE) between the atmosphere and PSF using the eddy covariance technique and soil CO_2 efflux (soil respiration: RS) using the chamber technique at three tropical peat ecosystems with different disturbance degrees (almost undrained PSF (UF), drained PSF (DF) and burnt ex-PSF (DB)) (Figure 1) in Central Kalimantan, Indonesia (Hirano et al., 2012) for more than 10 years. Based on the long-term field data from the three sites, the features of the carbon balance of PSF, such as seasonal variation, environmental controls and the effect of disturbance due to human activities and ENSO drought. Although the outflow of dissolved organic carbon (DOC) and methane (CH_4) should be considered for full carbon accounting (Hirano et al., 2009), here the focus is on two large CO_2 fluxes with opposite directions: gross primary production (GPP, ecosystem photosynthesis) and ecosystem respiration (RE). GPP and RE can be partitioned from NEE (= RE – GPP) using an empirical technique. Conventionally, NEE is positive when the ecosystem functions as a net CO_2 source, and vice versa.

Figure 1: Pictures of study sites. a) UF site (Jul. 2004), b) DB site (Apr. 2004), c) DF tower (Oct. 2007) and d) a large canal running between DF and DB sites (Mar. 2001).

HYDROLOGICAL CONTROLS

The carbon balance is strongly affected by local hydrology. In particular, RE and RS are mainly governed by GWL. RE and RS decreased as GWL increased, but increased slightly at shallow GWL near the ground surface, and then decreased sharply if water level rose aboveground (Hirano *et al.*, 2012; Sundari *et al.*, 2012). Large RE and RS at low GWL were caused by the enhancement of oxidative peat decomposition through oxygen (O_2) supply to deeper peat (Hirano *et al.*, 2014). Increase in RE and RS at shallow GWL was attributable to the enhanced decomposition of leaf litter on the ground through wetting (Sundari *et al.*, 2012). Water-saturated peat by flooding suffered from anoxia, and consequently RS was strongly inhibited. Also, GPP was affected by GWL, though it was mainly governed by solar radiation. GPP showed a convex quadratic curve with GWL (Hirano *et al.*, 2012). GPP decrease at low GWL was chiefly due to lower surface conductance (G_s), which corresponds to stomatal opening of vegetation, because of water stress (Hirano *et al.*, 2015). The decrease was more distinct at DB site, where re-growth of fern plants with shallow root systems dominated the site after fire. In contrast, GPP decrease at high GWL was probably caused by slow nutrient mineralization and consequent slow plant nutrient uptake because of poor aeration in water-saturated peat (Mezbahuddin *et al.*, 2014). As a result, NEE increased sharply as GWL decreased, if GWL was lower than a threshold, at which GPP reached a peak on the quadratic curve. The GWL thresholds were -0.3, -0.7 and -0.3 m, respectively, at UF, DF and DB sites (Hirano *et al.*, 2012). The lower threshold at DF site than UF site suggests the adaptation of tree species to the low GWL environment over five years after canal excavation (Hirano *et al.*, 2015; Mezbahuddin *et al.*, 2016). Annual NEE showed a negative linear relationship with minimum monthly-mean GWL at forest sites (UF and DF) (Hirano *et al.*, 2016). In spite of different drainage conditions of the two sites, the relationships were combined into a single significant line ($r^2 = 0.82$). The linearity suggests that 10-cm drawdown of minimum monthly-mean GWL brings about further net annual CO_2 emissions (NEE) of about 50 gC m^{-2} y^{-1} from PSF. At DB site, although no significant relationship was found for NEE, a significant negative relationship of RS with GWL suggests that every 10-cm drawdown of GWL causes additional oxidative peat decomposition of about 90 gC m^{-2} y^{-1} on an annual basis (Hirano *et al.*, 2014).

DISTURBANCE EFFECTS

Recently, tropical PSF has been threatened by several kinds of disturbances due to logging, drainage, fire and ENSO drought. The conversion of PSF into plantations usually accompanies logging and drainage, and frequent fire for land clearing. In ENSO years, the dry season is prolonged, and consequently peat becomes dry to be easily ignited, especially in disturbed PSF with lower GWL. The resultant peat fire frequently becomes out of control and spreads. During large-scale fires, the ground is covered with dense smoke emitted through peat/biomass combustion, and solar radiation is attenuated, but the diffused fraction of solar radiation increases rapidly (Marpaung and Hirano, 2014).

Annual NEE was all positive at the three sites for four years (2004-2008); mean annual values were 174, 328 and 499 gC m^{-2} y^{-1}, respectively, at UF, DF and DB sites (Hirano *et al.*, 2012). Although no significant difference among the sites, net CO_2 emission (positive NEE) increased according to disturbance degrees (drainage and fire). Both annual GPP and RE were significantly larger at PSF sites (UF and DF sites) than DB site. The largest NEE at DB site was largely because of much lower GPP due to less vegetation after fire outbreak. On the other hand, mean annual evapotranspiration (ET) for the same four years was 1529, 1365 and 1197 mm y^{-1}, respectively, at UF, DF and DB sites (Hirano *et al.*, 2015). Annual ET was significantly lower at DB site similarly because of less vegetation (less transpiration). During ENSO drought, RE increased because GWL was lowered. Also, GPP decreased because of water stress and shading by dense smoke emitted from peat fire, whereas increase in diffused solar radiation and higher CO_2 concentration can compensate the shading effect to some extent (Hirano *et al.*, 2012). As a result, net CO_2 emissions increased in ENSO years, even if direct CO_2 emissions through peat combustion were not considered.

ACKNOWLEDGEMENTS

This work was financially supported by JSPS Core University Program, JSPS KAKENHI (Nos. 15255001, 18403001, 21255001 and 25257401), JST-JICA SATREPS Project (Wild Fire and Carbon Management in Peat-Forest in Indonesia), the Asahi Glass Foundation and the Environment Research and Technology Development Fund (2-1504) of the Ministry of the Environment, Japan. Field work was supported by the staff of CIMTROP, University of Palangka Raya.

REFERENCES

1. Hirano, T., Jauhiainen, J., Inoue, T. and Takahashi, H., 2009, Controls on the carbon balance of tropical peatlands. *Ecosystems*, **12**, 873-887.

2. Hirano, T., Kusin, K., Limin, S. and Osaki, M., 2014, Carbon dioxide emissions through oxidative peat decomposition on a burnt tropical peatland. *Global Change Biology*, **20**, 555-565.
3. Hirano, T., Kusin, K., Limin, S. and Osaki, M., 2015, Evapotranspiration of tropical peat swamp forests. *Global Change Biology*, **21**, 1914-1927.
4. Hirano, T., Segah, H., Harada, T., Limin, S., June, T., Hirata, R. and Osaki, M., 2007, Carbon dioxide balance of a tropical peat swamp forest in Kalimantan, Indonesia. *Global Change Biology*, **13**, 412-425.
5. Hirano, T., Segah, H., Kusin, K., Limin, S., Takahashi, H. and Osaki, M., 2012, Effects of disturbances on the carbon balance of tropical peat swamp forests. *Global Change Biology*, **18**, 3410-3422.
6. Hirano, T., Sundari, S. and Yamada, H., 2016, CO_2 balance of tropical peat ecosystems. In Osaki, M. and Tsuji, N. (eds.) *Tropical Peatland Ecosystems*. 329-337.
7. Marpaung, F. and Hirano, T., 2014, Environmental dependence and seasonal variation of diffuse solar radiation in tropical peatland. *Journal of Agricultural Meteorology*, **70**, 223-232.
8. Mezbahuddin, M., Grant, R.F. and Hirano, T., 2014, Modeling effects of seasonal variation in water table depth on net ecosystem CO_2 exchange of a tropical peatland. *Biogeosciences*. **11**, 577-599.
9. Mezbahuddin, M., Grant, R.F. and Hirano, T., 2016, How hydrology determines seasonal and interannual variations in water table depth, surface energy exchange, and water stress in a tropical peatland: Modeling versus measurements. *Journal of Geophysical Research: Biogeosciences*. **120**, doi:10.1002/2015JG003005.
10. Sundari, S, Hirano, T., Yamada, H., Kusin, K. and Limin, S., 2012, Effect of groundwater level on soil respiration in tropical peat swamp forests. *Journal of Agricultural Meteorology*, **68**, 121-134.

Abstract No: A-455

COMMUNICATING PEAT SCIENCE TO SOCIETY

Kalyana Sundram*

Malaysian Palm Oil Council (MPOC), Malaysia

* *Corresponding author: kalyana@mpoc.org.my*

Humanity currently requires all available natural resources, both renewable and non-renewable be managed optimally and sustainably. Peatlands is one such resource and historically mankind has excavated and exploited peat for fuel and use as arable land for agriculture and forestry. Peatlands have vital ecological functions, support biodiversity and functions as a carbon depository. In the process of exploiting peat and its associated natural resources, it is inevitable that land use change and other environmental impacts arise, especially when poorly managed. The cultivation of oil palm has been targeted as a major cause of deforestation and increases in greenhouse gas emissions especially when peatlands are exploited for this agriculture activity. While the scientific community has been quick to rally against palm oil and plays a major role in shaping lay consumer opinions, it begs the question of whether science has done this responsibly and in an unbiased manner. To the lay person, peat today is solely a tropical issue and consumer perception about peat is extremely lopsided largely due to a variety of communication tools used to sell a one-sided story. Science unfortunately does not communicate a balanced picture, especially regarding Europe having exploited its peatlands and literally fueling its economy while providing arable land for Europe's forestry, agriculture and horticulture sectors. Some of these sectors have remained key pillars in Europe's economy. On the other hand peat exploitation in developing countries especially when cultivated under oil palm is highlighted as the curse of the tropics that critically endangers the environment and contributes to GHG emissions and biodiversity losses. Sadly, scientific outputs from most developing countries, even when they meet peer-review standards, are frowned upon unless they agree with established perceptions about the damages brought about due to peat disturbances. If the peat debate is to be managed and won for the overall benefit of mankind, it is highly desirable that scientific experts, legislators, media, industry and lay-consumers engage in unbiased assessment of the facts rather than play on emotions. Thus communicating the correct messages should become the responsibility of all those concerned and involved in the management and exploitation of peat in any part of the world and not just the tropical belts alone.

Keywords: -

Abstract No: A-371

EMISSIONS OF METHANE AND NITROUS OXIDE FROM PEATLANDS

Ryusuke Hatano*

Research Faculty of Agriculture, Hokkaido University

* *Corresponding author: hatano@chem.agr.hokudai.ac.jp*

SUMMARY

Peatland is a significant storage of carbon (C) and nitrogen (N) on the earth surface. Human activities in peatlands influence significantly the emissions of greenhouse gases, carbon dioxide (CO_2), methane (CH_4) and nitrous oxide (N_2O). Methane and N_2O are produced through oxidation-reduction reactions, so their emissions essentially influenced by ground water level. This paper reviews the characteristics of CH_4 and N_2O emissions. There were different trends of CH_4 and N_2O emissions from between tropical peatland and boreal and temperate peatlands. Methane emission increased significantly with the rise of ground water level above -20 cm, and larger in boreal peatland with plant mediated CH_4 emission than tropical peatland with plant mediated oxygen supply. Forest disturbance in tropical peatland increased CH_4 emission. On the contrary, N_2O emission increased with a drop of ground water level below -40 cm. The increase of N_2O emission was significantly lager in tropical peatland than in boreal and temperate peatlands. Nitrous oxide emission increased with N mineralization, and further increased with N fertilizer application. High N_2O emission in tropical peatland was induced by denitrification. Increase of soil nitrate-N (NO_3-N) content in rainy season increased N_2O emission. Maintaining ground water level between -20 and -40 cm minimizes CH_4 and N_2O emissions from peatland.

Keywords: ground water level, methane, nitrogen fertilizer, nitrous oxide, peatland

INTRODUCTION

Peatland has been generated at the rate of 100 to 200 kg C ha^{-1} yr^{-1} of organic matter accumulation for past 10,000 years due to lower microbial decomposition than plant production in wetland. The area is around 4 million km^2 in boreal and temperate region and around 0.4 million km^2 in tropical region. Although the area occupies only 3 % of terrestrial area, it contains 612 Gt C (547 Gt C in northern boreal and temperate peatland, 50 Gt C in tropical peatland) (Yu et al., 2010), accounting for 25 % of total soil carbon.

Wetland is a major source of CH_4. Natural wetland emits 217 Tg CH_4 yr^{-1}, accounting for 63 % of total natural CH_4 emission, and rice paddy field emits 36 Tg CH_4 yr^{-1} accounting for 11% of total anthropogenic CH_4 emission (IPCC, 2013). In wetland, CH_4 is produced in reductive sub soil, is transported to top soil and is emitted from the surface of the soil. However, 90% of CH_4 produced is oxidized during the transportation (Kolb and Horn, 2012). In well drained peatland, CH_4 emission is almost trace (Couwenberg et al., 2010).

On the other hand, wetland is not a source of N_2O, rather a sink of N_2O. This is because of slow N mineralization, low nitrification activity, high denitrification activity in the reductive condition (Kolb and Horn, 2012). But, drained and agriculturally used peatland emits N_2O significantly, and large N_2O emission is recorded in NO_3-N accumulated upland fields in tropical peatland (Takakai et al., 2006, Repo et al., 2009. This is because of denitrification with NO_3-N leaching (Kolb and Horn, 2012).

This paper reviews CH_4 and N_2O emissions from peatland to understand appropriate use of peatland

METHANE EMISSION

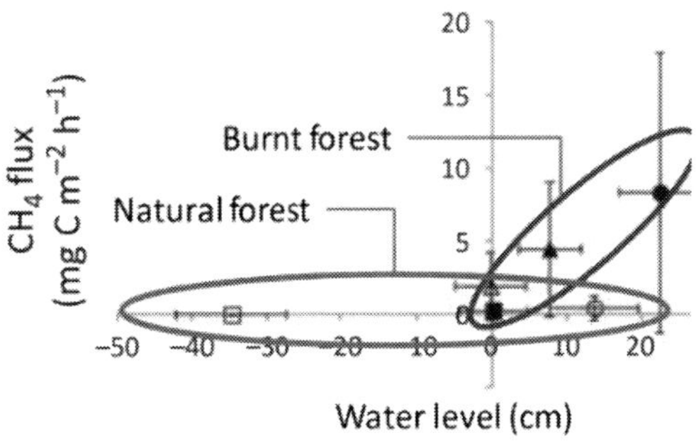

Ground water level is major controlling factor of CH_4 emission. Methane emission increases significantly when ground water level rise above -20 cm (Couwenberg et al., 2010). However, the increase of CH_4 emission is higher in boreal and temperate peatland than in tropical peatland. Recent global model uses 0.2 to 0.25 for the CH_4/CO_2 mole ratio in boreal natural peatland and 0.0052 in tropical natural peatland (Spahni, et al., 2011). This is because of strong oxidizing power in natural tropical peatland induced by the plant mediate oxygen supply through aerial roots (Adji et al., 2014) and fast water flow in well water permeable peat layer (Kelly et al., 2014). Peat fire or clear tree cutting increases CH_4 emission in tropical peatland due to the disappearance of plant mediate oxygen supply and the rise of ground water level with subsidence, while drainage decreases CH_4 emission due to the drop of ground water level (Fig. 1) (Jauhiainen et al., 2008、Adji et al., 2014). On the other hand, vegetation in boreal and temperate wetlands accelerates CH_4 emission. An observation in a thermokarst depression of 63.7 ha in East Siberia for four years from 2006 to 2009 showed that 95.4 ± 5.4 % of total CH_4 emission was emitted from thermokarst pond (60.7 ± 19.2 % of the total area) and plant mediated CH_4 emission from the pond vegetation accounted for 45.4 ± 23.2 % of total CH_4 emission (Desyatkin et al., 2014).

NITROUS OXIDE EMISSION

Natural peatland with high water level is not a source of N_2O due to its low activities of N mineralization and nitrification, high activity of denitrification in reductive condition (Kolb and Horn, 2012). But, by drainage for agricultural use, N_2O emission together with increase of CO_2 emission increases (Mu et al., 2014). Comparing emission data published previously, CO_2 emission was significantly higher in tropical peatland than boreal and temperate peatlands, and increased with N fertilization significantly (3815 ± 2900 and 4822 ± 2313 kg C ha^{-1} yr^{-1} in unfertilized and fertilized boreal and temperate peatlands, respectively, and 7382 ± 3558 and 13001 ± 3027 kg C ha^{-1} yr^{-1} in unfertilized and fertilized tropical peatland, respectively). N_2O emission increased with N fertilization significantly, especially in tropical peatland (4.93 ± 10.04 and 17.76 ± 21.15 kg N ha^{-1} yr^{-1} in unfertilized and fertilized boreal and temperate peatlands, respectively, and 8.08 ± 15.69 and 178.59 ± 218.28 kg N ha^{-1} yr^{-1} in unfertilized and fertilized tropical peatland, respectively).

Furthermore, in all peatlands, CO_2 and N_2O emissions increased with the drop of ground water level, and much larger increase was found in N fertilized peatlands (Fig. 2). Increase of CO_2 emission with the drop of water level was larger in tropical peatland than in boreal and temperate peatlands, and maximum CO_2 emission was found at -80 cm of water level. Increase of N_2O emission with the drop of water level was distinct below -40 cm of water level. Especially in tropical peatland, maximum N_2O emission of 700 kg N ha^{-1} yr^{-1} was found from -60 to -70 cm of water level. There was a significant relationship between mineral N input which is sum of mineralized N (CO_2 emission / CN ratio) and applied fertilizer N) and N_2O emission (Fig. 3). This indicates that increase of peat decomposition with a drop of water level and N fertilizer application increases N_2O emission.

In an upland field of tropical peatland where large N_2O emission was observed, there was a significant relationship between NO_3-N content in top soil and N_2O flux at the water filled pore space more than 60 %, suggesting N_2O emission was caused by denitrification after mineralization and nitrification (Takakai et al., 2006). Soil microbes which are adopted to low pH of tropical peatland and obtain nitrate respiration ability, fungi (*Fusarium oxysporum and Neocosmospora vasinfecta*) (Yanai et

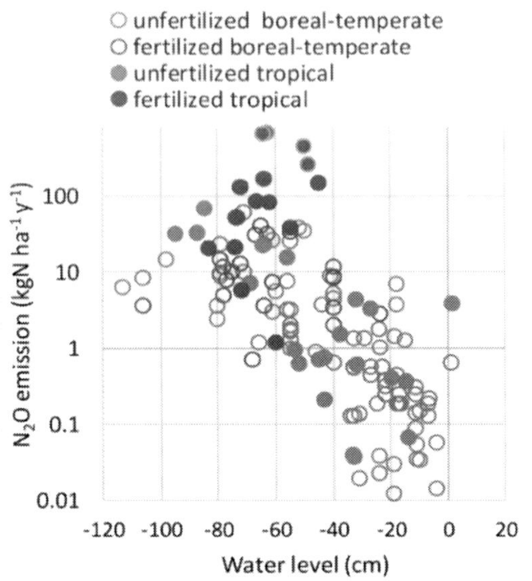

Figure 2: Relationship between N_2O emission and water level in peatlands (modified from Mu et al., 2014 by addition of Melling et al., 2007, Takakai et al., 2006, Toma et al., 2011)

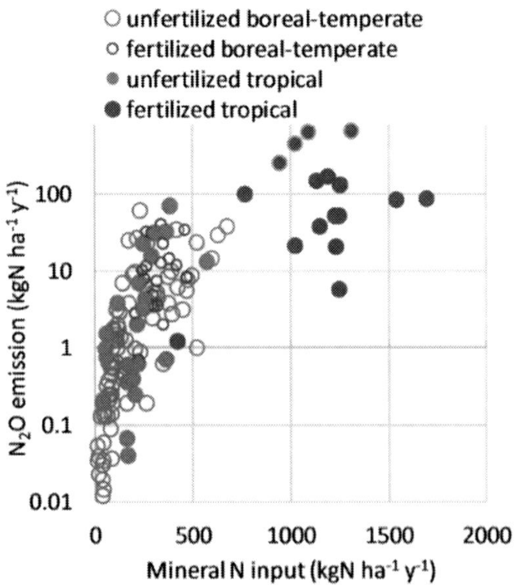

Figure 3: Relationship between N_2O emission and mineral N input in peatlands (modified from Mu et al., 2014 by addition of Melling et al., 2005, 2007, Takakai et al., 2006, Toma et al., 2011)

al., 2007) and bacteria (*Janthinobacterium*) (Hashidoko et al., 2008), were identified.

CONCLUSION

From the findings above, following conclusion can be drawn. Ground water level is major controlling factor of CH_4 and N_2O emissions from peatland. Ground water level above -20 cm increases CH_4 emission. The increase of CH_4 emission is lager in boreal peatland than in tropical peatland. However, in tropical peatland, loss of natural vegetation increases CH_4 emission significantly due to loss of plant mediated oxygen supply. On the other hand, ground water level from -40 to -70 cm stimulates N_2O emission together with CO_2 emission. Nitrogen fertilizer application increases N_2O and CO_2 emissions. The increase of N_2O and CO_2 emissions is larger in tropical peatland than in boreal and temperate peatlands. Overall emission data show the lowest emissions of CH_4 and N_2O are achieved in the range of -20 to -40 cm of ground water level.

REFERENCES

1. Adji FF, Hamada Y, Darang U, Limin SH, Hatano R (2014) Effect of plant-mediated oxygen supply and drainage on greenhouse gas emission from a tropical peatland in Central Kalimantan, Indonesia. Soil Science and Plant Nutrition, 60: 216–230.
2. Couwenberg J, Dommain R, Joosten H (2010) Greenhouse gas fluxes from tropical peatlands in south-east Asia. Glob Change Biol 16:1715–1732.
3. Desyatkin AR, Takakai F, Hatano R (2014) Flood effect on CH_4 emission from the alas in Central Yakutia, East Siberia. Soil Science and Plant Nutrition, 60: 242-253.
4. Hashidoko Y, Takakai F, Toma Y, Darung U, Melling L, Tahara S, Hatano R (2008). Emergence and behaviors of acid-tolerant Janthinobacterium sp. that evolves N_2O from deforested tropical peatland. Soil Biology and Biochemistry, 40: 116-125.
5. IPCC (2013) Climate Change 2013: The Physical Science Basis. Contribution of Working Group I to the Fifth Assessment Report of the Intergovernmental Panel on Climate Change [Stocker, T.F., D. Qin, G.-K. Plattner, M. Tignor, S.K. Allen, J. Boschung, A. Nauels, Y. Xia, V. Bex and P.M. Midgley(eds.)]. Cambridge University Press, Cambridge, United Kingdom and New York, NY, USA, 1535 pp.
6. Jauhiainen J, Limin S, Silvennoinen H, Vasander H (2008) Carbon dioxide and methane fluxes in drained tropical peat before and after hydrological restoration. Ecology, 89: 3503-3514.
7. Kelly TJ, Baird AJ, Roucoux KH, Baker TR, Honorio Coronado EN, Lawson IT, Ríos M (2014) The high hydraulic conductivity of three wooded tropical peat swamps in northeast Peru: Measurements and implications for hydrological function, Hydrological Processes, 28: 3373–3387.
8. Kolb S, Horn MA (2012) Microbial CH_4 and N_2O consumption in acidic wetlands, Frontiers in Microbiology, 3: 1-8.
9. Melling L, Hatano R, Goh KJ (2005) Soil respiration from three ecosystems in tropical peatland of Sarawak, Malaysia. Tellus, 57: 1-11.
10. Melling L, Hatano R, Goh K J (2007) Nitrous oxide emissions from three ecosystems in tropical peatland of Sarawak, Malaysia. Soil Science and Plant Nutrition, 53: 792–805.
11. Mu J, Huang A, Ni J, Xie D (2014) Linking Annual N_2O Emission in Organic Soils to Mineral Nitrogen Input as Estimated by Heterotrophic Respiration and Soil C/N Ratio. Plos One, 9, e96572.
12. Repo ME, Susiluoto S, Lind SE, Jokinen S, Elsakov V, Biasi C, Virtanen T, Martikainen PJ (2009) Large N_2O emissions from cryoturbated peat soil in tundra. Nat.Geosci. 2: 189–192.
13. Spahni R, Wania R, Neef L, van Weele M, Pison I, Bousquet P, Frankenberg C, Foster PN, Joos F, Prentice IC, van Velthoven P (2011) Constraining global methane emissions and uptake by ecosystems, Biogeosciences, 8: 1643-1665.
14. Takakai F, Morishita T, Hashidoko Y, Darung U, Kuramochi K, Dohong S, Limin SH, Hatano R (2006) Effects of agricultural land-use change and forest fire on N2O emission from tropical peatlands, Central Kalimantan, Indonesia. Soil Science and Plant Nutrition, 52: 662-674.
15. Toma Y, Takakai F, Darung U, Kuramochi K, Limin SH, Dohong S, Hatano R (2011) Nitrous oxide emission derived from soil organic matter decomposition from tropical agricultural peat soil in central Kalimantan, Indonesia. Soil Science and Plant Nutrition, 57: 436-451,
16. Yanai Y, Toyota K, Morishita T, Takakai F, Hatano R, Limin S H., Darung U and Dohong S: (2007) Fungal N_2O production in an arable peat soil in Central Kalimantan, Indonesia. Soil Science and Plant Nutrition, 53: 806–811.
17. Yu Z, Loise J, Brosseau DP, Beilman DW, Hunt SJ (2010) Global peatland dynamics since the Last Glacial Maximum. Geophysical Res Letters, 37: L13402.

Abstract No: A-456

KEY AGRO-ENVIRONMENTAL MANAGEMENT OF TROPICAL PEATLAND

Lulie Melling and Auldry Chaddy

Tropical Peat Research Laboratory Unit, Chief Minister's Department, Sarawak, Malaysia

**Corresponding author: luliemelling@gmail.com*

SUMMARY

Sarawak, like many peatland sites throughout Southeast Asia is currently faced by challenges because of the needs for agricultural development to meet its aspiration for socio-economic progress. But, with limited suitable agricultural land, the cultivation of peat swamp, which is abundant in the State, is inevitable. To do this, it necessitates the Government and the associated agencies to develop an environmental sensitive home grown holistic approach to balance the agricultural development in order to mitigate carbon emission problems associated with peat development. This approach takes into account soil processes and interaction between agro-management and environments. The key features of these agro-environmental management approaches, which are based on the principle of drainage, compaction and water management, attempts to integrate agriculture, nature and environment for humankind. The key agro-environmental management of tropical peatland in Sarawak, Malaysia is discussed in this paper. The study was conducted in oil palm plantation on peat (OPP) and undisturbed peat swamp forest (PSF). Compaction of peat is introduced primarily as a means to increase the bulk density and bearing capacity of the peat in order to reduce early palm leaning, decrease the rate of nutrient leaching and optimize the yield. Mechanical compaction has also brought unintended benefits such as decreased soil CO_2 emissions and reduced susceptibility of peat fire outbreaks because the lower soil porosity enhances the capillary rise of water in the soil, keeping the soil moist. The higher soil moisture content due to the higher soil bulk density was also found to decrease soil CO_2 fluxes in cultivated peat as evidenced by the comparisons of compacted and non-compacted peat in OPP as well as OPP versus PSF. Thus, the successful implementation of key agro-environmental management as good agricultural practices on peat lies heavily on good procedural synthesis based on scientific findings, knowledge and understanding of tropical peat.

***Keywords**: drainage, compaction, water management, CO_2, oil palm yield*

INTRODUCTION

Hydrology is an important factor in the formation, functions and resilience of peat swamp ecosystems (Melling and Hatano, 2004; Wosten *et al.*, 2008). Under natural conditions, the accumulation and long-term maintenance of peat carbon requires a continuous supply of organic matter and a decomposition rate lower than its supply. The latter is assumed to be met if water table is equal or near to the peatland surface throughout the year (Ritzema *et al.*, 2002). Thus, most studies reported that the conversion of peatland for agriculture purposes, which involved lowering of water table, would result in the acceleration of peat oxidation and degradation, which release massive carbon dioxide (CO_2) (Hooijer *et al.*, 2011; Page *et al.*, 2011). Using this premise, it has become an entrenched notion that the ultimate solution towards the lowering of peat oxidation and release of CO_2 depends solely on the control of water table (Hooijer *et al.*, 2010; Page *et al.*, 2011; Hergoualch and Verchot, 2011). These authors generally ignored that the lowering of water table in tropical peatlands can occur naturally, especially in Borneo, where the peatlands are of ombrogenous type i.e. receiving water and nutrient through rainfall only. Under this condition, the fluctuation of water table is mainly dictated by the seasonal changes in rainfall pattern. The presumption that water table maintenance is an all cure for GHG issues to some extent reflects the lack of detailed understanding of the ecosystem and dynamics across the wide geographic variation of peatland sites throughout Southeast Asia.

Peat soils in their inherent state have high infiltration capacity and hydraulic conductivity, low soil bulk density and low capillary rise, resulting in lower plant available water (Melling *et al.*, 2008). These peat soil characteristics make reliance on water table alone impractical in water management of peat where loss of water via evapotranspiration and outflow would create moisture deficits, particularly in the top layer of peat above the water table. In fact, effective mitigation of peat oxidation would require a permanent water table equal to or above the peat surface, which is deleterious to the growth and production of terrestrial agricultural crops because they require both sufficient oxygen and water to facilitate optimum metabolic pathways for growth and photosynthesis.

Sarawak has developed an environmental sensitive holistic approach to balance agricultural development and mitigation of carbon emission problems associated with peat development. It takes into account soil processes and interaction between agro-management and environments. This agro-environmental management approach, combining the principle of drainage, compaction and water management, attempts to integrate agriculture, nature and environment for humankind.

In oil palm plantation, drainage is carried out to lower the water table to between 50 and 75 cm below ground surface which is suitable for its deep rooting system (Henson and Chai, 1997). Upon the lowering of the water table, peat compaction is implemented to increase the bulk density and bearing capacity in order to reduce early palm leaning and decrease the rate of nutrient leaching and optimize the yield.

However, the introduction of peat compaction upon drainage in plantation has brought other unintended benefits such as decreased soil CO_2 emissions and reduced susceptibility of peat fire. Thus, this paper discusses the concepts, aim and importance of agro-environmental management of oil palm on peat.

MATERIALS AND METHODS

This study was conducted in an oil palm plantation (OPP) (02° 11' N, 111° 50' E) and a tropical peat swamp forest (PSF) (001°27'N, 111°8'E). Two different sites namely compacted and un-compacted OPP were selected to assess the physical properties, yield and soil CO_2 fluxes.

Monthly measurements of soil CO_2 fluxes since 2008 until 2013 were performed using open bottom cylindrical stainless steel chamber. Water table was measured on a monthly basis using a perforated PVC pipe dip well. Undisturbed core samples were also collected to determine soil bulk density and water-filled pore space (WFPS). Porosity is derived from soil bulk density and particle density (Brady and Weil, 1996). Bunch weight and bunch number were recorded weekly from both compacted and un-compacted OPP and tabulated into monthly data. The average fresh fruit bunch (FFB) at each site was then calculated.

Regression analysis was carried out using SAS 9.2 to determine the relationship between the FFB, soil CO_2 flux and WFPS.

RESULTS

Water table, bulk density, porosity and water-filled pore space (WFPS) of both OPP and PSF are shown in **Table 1**. The levels of mean water table in un-compacted, compacted OPP and PSF were -59.8 cm, -60.7 cm and -15.1, respectively. Bulk density at 5 cm, 10 cm, 25 cm, 45 cm and 60 cm depth for PSF were generally lower than OPP. Bulk density for compacted OPP were higher than un-compacted OPP as a result of drainage and mechanical compaction. The consequent of higher bulk density in compacted OPP were lower porosity at 5 cm, 10 cm, 25 cm, 45 cm and 60 cm depth. Soil moisture expressed as water-WFPS in compacted OPP was higher (83.3%) than in un-compacted OPP (71.3%) and forest (75.1%).

As shown in **Table 1**, FFB from compacted OPP (32.3 t ha^{-1} yr^{-1}) was higher than un-compacted OPP (16.8 t ha^{-1} yr^{-1}). At the same time, mean soil CO_2 flux from compacted OPP (9.5 t C ha^{-1} yr^{-1}) was lower than un-compacted OPP (11.2 t C ha^{-1} yr^{-1}). Highest mean soil CO_2 flux was recorded from the PSF (12.5 t C ha^{-1} yr^{-1}). Fresh fruit bunch increased with WFPS. There was a significantly positive linear relationship between FFB and WFPS (**Figure 1a**). However, a significantly negative linear relationship between soil CO_2 fluxes and WFPS (**Figure 1b**) was obtained indicating that soil CO_2 fluxes decreased with increasing WFPS.

DISCUSSION

The water table at the studied sites was controlled between 50 and 75 cm below the peat surface. This is deemed suitable for the oil palm rooting system as suggested by Henson and Chai (1997). Similar benefit was also observed by Lim et al. (2012) who found that the highest FFB yield was recorded at water table of 50-75 cm, followed by 25-50 cm, 75-100 cm, more than 100 cm and less than 25 cm below the peat surface.

Although the water table was similar for both sites, FFB yields differed by almost 50% between the two sites. FFB yield from compacted OPP (32.2 t ha^{-1} yr^{-1}) was higher than un-compacted OPP (16.8 t ha^{-1} yr^{-1}) (**Table 1**). In unmanaged peat, higher porosity of the peat leads to higher leaching rate of nutrients and lower capacity to retain soil moisture particularly in peat surface (Melling *et al.*, 2008). This affects the availability and efficiency of nutrient uptake by the crop. However, with compaction, peat properties changed through improved bulk density and WFPS (Ball *et al.*, 2008). Higher bulk density upon compaction decreased macropores (>600μm) and increased micropores (3–30 μm) (Kasimir-Klemedtsson *et al.*, 1997). The consequences are higher soil mass per volume and reduced nutrient loss via leaching, resulting in better growth and yield of the crops (Laiho *et al.*, 1999) including oil palm. Thus, FFB yield increased with increasing WFPS (**Figure 1a**).

In this study, soil CO_2 flux from compacted OPP was 15% and 24% lower than un-compacted OPP and PSF, respectively, which was due to the higher bulk density, lower porosity and higher soil moisture in compacted site (**Table 1** and **Figure 1b**) (Melling *et al*., 2005; Melling *et al*., 2012). This agrees with Ruser *et al*. (2006) who found that compaction significantly reduced soil CO_2 fluxes when soil moisture exceeded 70%. Higher moisture in the soil pore space reduced both underground biotic activity and soil gas diffusiveness resulting in lower soil CO_2 fluxes from compacted peat (Ball *et al*., 2008; Castellano *et al*., 2011).

In addition to proper drainage, compaction is one of the most important key for water management in sustaining peat moisture. Studies conducted in an oil palm plantation and natural peat swamp forest revealed that soil CO_2 flux was highest in the tropical peat swamp forest ecosystem even though its mean water table level was higher (Melling *et al*., 2005; Melling *et al*., 2012) (**Table 2**). This indicated that water table was not the dominant factor affecting soil CO_2 flux from oil palm plantation on tropical peatland, which contradicted the findings of Jaenicke *et al*. (2010) and Hergoualch and Verchot (2011). Bulk density and WFPS were observed to be higher in OPP compared with forest ecosystem (**Table 2**). Brigham *et al*. (2000) surmised that larger pore spaces in peat resulted in large losses of stored water while higher bulk density enabled greater water retention even under unsaturated conditions. This probably contributed to better capillary rise which allows water to move upwards to the surface and therefore, improves and sustains the moisture of peat along its vertical profile even in dry spells to meet plant water requirement, which is difficult to achieve through water table control only.

Table 1: Comparison of soil physical properties, oil palm yield and soil CO_2 fluxes between PSF, un-compacted OPP and compacted OPP

Variables	PSF	Un-compacted OPP	Compacted OPP
Mean water table (cm)	-15.1	-59.8	-60.7
WFPS* (%)	75.1	71.3	83.3
Bulk density (g cm^{-3}):			
5 cm	0.15	0.23	0.24
10 cm	0.14	0.11	0.18
25 cm	0.09	0.11	0.13
45 cm	0.08	0.09	0.13
60 cm	0.07	0.09	0.08
Porosity (%):			
5 cm	87.7	88.1	82.4
10 cm	88.3	94.3	87.0
25 cm	92.8	95.1	91.4
45 cm	93.8	97.2	91.7
60 cm	94.0	96.4	94.9
FFB (t ha^{-1} yr^{-1})	-	16.8	32.3
Soil CO_2 flux (t C ha^{-1} yr^{-1})	12.5	11.2	9.5

Table 2: Average water table, WFPS, bulk density, soil CO_2 fluxes of different ecosystems

Ecosystem	Mean water table (cm)	WFPS (%)	Bulk density (g cm^{-3})	Soil CO_2 flux (t C ha^{-1} yr^{-1})	Reference
Forest	-45.3	57.6	0.15	21.9	Melling et al., 2005
Sago	-27.4	78.1	0.16	12.0	
OPP	-60.2	60.4	0.20	16.6	
OPP	-67.6	70.1	0.23	9.0	Melling et al., 2012
SF	-14.7	66.5	0.11	11.2	
PSF	-3.9	70.0	0.11	12.3	

OPP= oil palm plantation; SF = Secondary peat swamp forest; PSF = Natural peat swamp

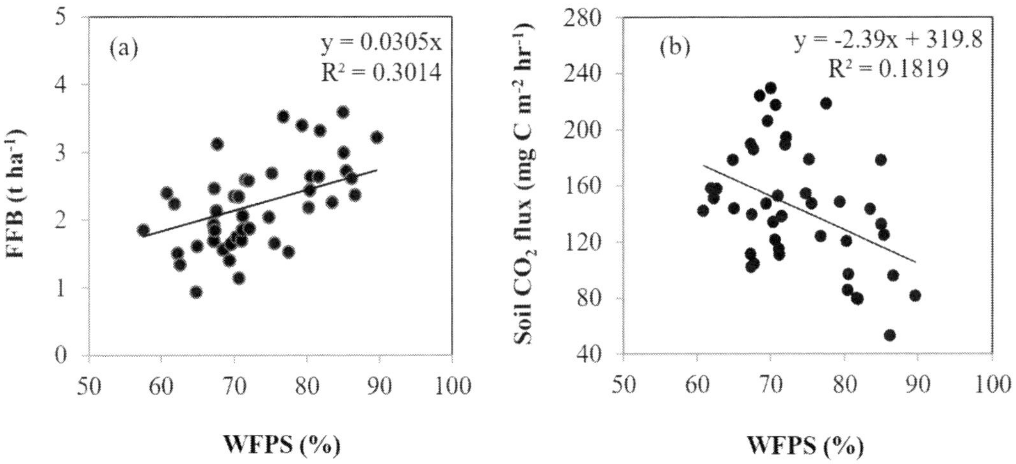

Figure 1: Relationships between (a) FFB, (b) soil CO_2 flux and WFPS

CONCLUSION

The agro-environmental management approach is based on the principle of compaction and water table management. Effective water management can be achieved by apposite compaction procedure and the control of water table. The agro-environmental management for oil palm on tropical peatland improved peat properties, which resulted in higher oil palm yield, reduced soil CO_2 emissions and lower susceptibility of peat fire outbreaks. However, the success of agro-environmental management lies heavily on good procedural synthesis of scientific findings, knowledge and understanding on tropical peat. The promotion and communication of this successful concept should be intensified, preferably with government incentives and incorporate into good agriculture practice certification for oil palm on peat.

ACKNOWLEDGEMENTS

This study was supported by both the Sarawak State Government and Federal Government of Malaysia. Special thanks to those who have contributed towards the completion of this paper.

REFERENCES

1. Ball, B.C., Crichton, I. and Horgan, G.W. (2008). Dynamics of upward and downward N2O and CO_2 fluxes in ploughed or no-tilled soils in relation to water-filled pore space, compaction and crop presence. Soil and Tillage Research 101:20-30.
2. Brady, N. C., and Weil, R. R., (1996). The nature and properties of soil. Prentice- Hall, International, Inc. London.
3. Bridgham, S. D., C.-L. Ping, J. L. Richardson, and K. Updegraff. (2000). Soils of northern peatlands: Histosols and Gelisols. p. 343-370. In J. L. Richardson and M. J. Vepraskas (eds.) Wetland Soils: Genesis, Hydrology, Landscapes, and Classification. CRC Press, Boca Raton, FL, USA.
4. Castellano, M.J., Schmidt, J.P., Kaye, J.P., Walker, C., Graham, C.B., Lin, H. and Dell,C. (2011). Hydrological controls on heterotrophic soil respiration across an agricultural landscape. Geoderma. 162:273-280.
5. Henson, I.E. and Chai, S.H. (1997). Analysis of oil palm productivity. II Biomass, distribution, productivity and turnover of the root system. Journal of Oil Palm Research 9(2):78-92.
6. Hergoualc'h, K., and Verchot, L. V. (2011). Stocks and fluxes of carbon associated with land use change in Southeast Asian tropical peatlands: A review. Global Biogeochemical Cycles, 25(2).
7. Hooijer, A., Page, S., Jauhiainen, J., Lee, W. A., Lu, X. X., Idris, A., and Anshari, G. (2012). Subsidence and carbon loss in drained tropical peatlands.
8. Jaenicke, J., Wösten, H., Budiman, A. and Siegert, F. (2010). Planning hydrological restoration of peatlands in Indonesia to mitigate carbon dioxide emissions. Mitig. 30 Adapt. Strateg. Glob. Change 15:223-239.

9. Kasimir-Klemedtsson, A., Klemedtsson, L., Berglund, K., Martikainen, P. and Silvola, J.. (1997). Greenhouse gas emissions from farmed organic soils: a review. Soil Use Manage. **13**, 245–250.
10. Laiho, R., Sallantaus, T., and Laine, J. (1999). The effect of forestry drainage on vertical distributions of major plant nutrients in peat soils. Plant and Soil, 207(2), 169-181.
11. Lim, K. H., S. S. Lim, F. Parish, and R. Suharto, editors. (2012). RSPO manual on best management practices (BMPs) for existing oil palm cultivation on peat. RSPO, Kuala Lumpur, Malaysia.
12. Melling, L., Goh, K.J., Kloni, A. and Hatano, R. (2012). Is water table the most important factor influencing soil C flux in tropical peatland? Proceedings of the 14th International Peat Congress. Extended Abstract No. 330, 6pp.
13. Melling, L., Goh, K.J., Beauvais, C. and Hatano, R. (2008a). Carbon flow and budget in a young mature oil palm agroecosystem on deep tropical peat. The Planter 84(982), 21-25. Melling, L.,
14. Hatano, R. and Goh, K.J. (2005). Soil CO2 flux from three ecosystems in tropical peatland of Sarawak, Malaysia. Tellus. 57B: 1-11.
15. Melling, L. and Hatano, R. (2004). Peat Soils Study in Maludam. Technical Report-Joint Working Group Malaysia-The Netherlands Development and Management of Maludam National Park. Forest Department Sarawak.
16. Page, S. E., Morrison, R., Malins, C., Hooijer, A., Rieley, J. O., and Jauhiainen, J. (2011). Review of peat surface greenhouse gas emissions from oil palm plantations in Southeast Asia. White Paper, (15).
17. Ritzema, H., and Wösten, H. (2002). Hydrology of borneo's peat swamps. In STRAPEAT Partners Workshop, STRAPEAT Project, Palangka Raya, Kalimantan, Indonesia and Sibu, Sarawak, Malaysia.
18. Ruser, R., Flessa, H., Russow, R., Schmidt, G., Buegger, F. and Munch, J.C (2006). Emission of N_2O, N_2 and CO_2 from soil fertilized with nitrate: effect of compaction, soil moisture and rewetting. Soil Biology and Biochemistry 38:263-274.
19. Wösten, J. H. M., Clymans, E., Page, S. E., Rieley, J. O.,and Limin, S. H. (2008). Peat–water interrelationships in a tropical peatland ecosystem in Southeast Asia. Catena, 73(2), 212-224.

Abstract No: A-457

PLANTING OIL PALM IN PEAT LAND: MY EXPERIENCE, CHALLENGES AND OPPORTUNITIES

Abdul Hamed Sepawi

Sarawak Oil Palm Plantation Owners Association

* *Corresponding author: lsw@taann.com.my*

This paper attempts to provide a comprehensive, albeit compact, account of the development of oil palm plantations on peatland in Sarawak and the prospect it offers. The writer firmly believes that palm oil is the cheapest seed oil to produce oils and that it also has an important role to play in carbon sync for purposes of sequestration of gaseous CO_2 into solid carbon in the form of biomass and this ensures the sustainability of production of the oil it produces. In tracing the course of its development, the writer brings to light some of the major issues and challenges confronting the pioneers who dared to take their dreams to places on which many feared to tread. He shares his experience in planting oil palm on peatland and later efforts to meet the compliance standards set by MSPO and RSPO. Writing in the first person, the writer provides an insightful account of the early years when he was part of a pioneer group who ventured into planting oil palm on peat land. His is a narrative that brings to light an experience that saw him and the pioneer group taking a courageous and bold step in exploiting the potential of peatland. They initiated new planting techniques and scientific innovations that would soon turn peatland once regarded as unconducive to agriculture into arable land for large-scale plantations, where productivity has increased from 12 to 30 tons per hectare per year. The efforts paid dividends. Today, the oil palm industry in Sarawak bears witness to the success story of the planting of oil palm on peatland. But the journey ahead continues to face challenges from unfounded attacks and criticism from NGOs who demonise the palm oil industry in the face of the stiff competition it poses to the seed oil industry of Europe. The writer views the barrage of criticism arising from the competition as reminiscent of genocide acts waged by the Dutch East India Company against inhabitants of the Maluku Islands to exert a monopoly over the spice trade in the region. To the writer, the tactics employed by present-day NGOs to demonise palm oil are no different in their hideousness and patronising attitude. In this context, the palm oil producers must stand united and remain committed to the pursuit of a sustainable palm oil industry.

***Keywords**: -*

Abstract No: A-060

SHIFTING PARADIGMS IN SOUTHEAST ASIAN PEATLAND MANAGEMENT

Marcel Silvius

Wetlands International, The Netherlands

**Corresponding author: marcel.silvius@wetlands.org*

Peat swamps in SE Asia originally covered 27.1 million ha with high biodiversity forests, and until the 1980s they were hardly affected by development. SE Asian peat swamp ecosystems have a very high biodiversity with a high rate of endemism and many threatened species. Currently, outside of Papua and Brunei, there are almost no pristine peat swamp forests left in Indonesia and Malaysia. The remainder has been largely subject to selective logging as well as illegal logging activities, and less than 5% is protected for nature conservation. But even the protected areas have been largely affected by logging and many are drained by logging channels. A recent study by Miettinen *et al.*, 2016 revealed that in 2015, only 29% (4.6 Mha) from the original 15.7 million ha of peatlands in Peninsular Malaysia, Borneo and Sumatra remain covered by peat swamp forest (vs. 41% or 6.4 Mha in 2007 and 76% or 11.9 Mha in 1990). Managed land cover types (industrial plantations and smallholder dominated areas) cover 50% (7.8 Mha) of all peatlands (vs. 33% 5.2 Mha in 2007 and 11% 1.7 Mha in 1990). Industrial plantations have nearly doubled their extent since 2007 (2.3 Mha; 15%) and cover 4.3 Mha (27%) of peatlands in 2015. The majority of these are oil palm plantations (73%; 3.1 Mha) while nearly all of the rest (26%; 1.1 Mha) are pulp wood plantations.

Since the early 1990s the most significant cash crops developed in SE Asia's peatlands are oil palm and Acacia (for pulp-for-paper) plantations. These crops require a minimum of 50 to 60 cm drainage, which results in various environmental impacts, including soil carbon oxidation, soil compaction and subsidence, and increased fire risks. The conversion of peat swamp forests results in significant loses of biodiversity. Whereas the drained land-use of peatlands in Indonesia covers only 6% of the total national agricultural land, the peatland deforestation and peat carbon oxidation (excluding fires) contribute over 50% of the country's national emissions. In Malaysia, peatland degradation related emissions contribute about 25% of national emissions, but have so far not been specified as such in Malaysia's reports to the United Nations Framework Convention on Climate Change (UNFCCC), which mentioned only 3% of the country's emissions to coming from soils.

In latest (second) communication to the UNFCCC Malaysia referred to its reiterated pledge in 2009 to keep at least 50% of its forest area as forest in view of their important role in both adaptation and mitigation from soil and water protection, conservation of biological diversity and regulation of the climate system to carbon sequestration. However, in 2015, only 21.7% of the peat swamp forests remains forested in Peninsular Malaysia (with only 4.6% as pristine forest), 27% in Sarawak (with only 0.5% pristine) and 24.5% in Sabah (with only 1.8% pristine) (Miettinen *et al.*, 2016), whereas these are the key carbon stores of Malaysia.

Globally, SE Asian degraded peatlands cover less than 0.1% of the world's land surface, but contribute about 3% of all global anthropogenic emissions. Peat fires occur frequently, but especially so in very dry years – related to the occurrences of El Niño. In such years, peat fires may ravage through millions of hectares of degraded peatlands, and the related emissions may more than double the emissions from oxidation. The fires and smog have resulted in significant impacts on public health, agriculture, tourism, transport and other major economic sectors, and have affected millions across Indonesia, Singapore and Malaysia, as well as parts of the Philippines and Thailand. A World Bank study on forest fires in 2014 in Riau province estimated that fires caused US$935m of losses relating to lost agricultural productivity and trade. Early estimates by the Joko Widodo administration of damages of the Indonesian haze crisis in 2015 were reported at to be up to 475 trillion rupiah (US$47 billion) (Francis, 2015).

Whereas the impacts of drainage-based peatland use may still be considered by some to be acceptable in view of the high economic value of these cash-crops, there is one more issue which is generally overlooked in peatland development and management planning and policies. This is the impact of peatland subsidence. Almost all peatland areas have the base of the peat soil layer at or below the gravity drainage limit, which is determined by their relative elevation to sea and river levels. This means that the landscapes dominated by drained peat are gradually but surely subsiding to levels at which gravity drainage becomes impossible. Recent studies commissioned by Wetlands International in Malaysia and Indonesia (Hooijer *et al.*, 2015, Hooijer *et al.*, 2016), indicate that over 50% of all peatland areas that are currently under drained land-use will reach that level by the middle of this century, and over 80% towards the end of this century. The high levels and temporal patterns of precipitation in SE Asia and the size of the landscapes affected constrain the options to put in place possible mitigating measures such as used in temperate climate zone, i.e. dikes and pump-operated drainage systems. It means that drained peat land-use in SE Asia, while profitable in the short-term, is inherently unsustainable and will lead in the medium to long-term to significant loss of land and land productivity. Current studies also indicate that now already there are substantial areas affected by increased and prolonged flooding.

To prevent further damages and loss of productivity a paradigm shift in SE Asian peat land management is required. This needs to consider:

a. Full protection and restoration of remaining natural peat swamp forest ecosystems

b. Restoration of hitherto undeveloped concession areas on peat

c. Responsible phasing out of current drainage-based land-use on peat

d. Alternative non-drained utilization options for peatland areas, including paludiculture (commercial use of rewetted peatlands using native perennial peat swamp crop species such as sagu (for starch production), jelutung (Asian rubber), Tengkawang (Illipe nut oil production, Melaleuca (pulp-for-paper) many timber species and rattan (furniture). There are over 100 native peat swamp species with a high economic potential.

e. These options may all be combined with REDD+ business schemes under national and international climate change mitigation mechanisms.

Major investments in these land-use change options are urgently required, in order to stop the disproportionately high GHG emissions from unsustainable peatland use, stop the ongoing creeping disaster of land loss, halt the loss of biodiversity, and to prevent further fire calamities like the one in 2015.

LITERATURE

1. Chan, Francis. "$47b? Indonesia counts costs of haze". *The Straits Times*. 11 October 2015.
2. Hooijer, A., Vernimmen, R., Visser, M., Mawdsley, N., 2015a. *Flooding projections from elevation and subsidence models for oil palm plantations in the Rajang Delta peatlands, Sarawak, Malaysia.* Deltares report 1207384. Deltares, The Netherlands. Available online at: https://www.deltares.nl/en
3. Hooijer, A., Vernimmen, R., Mawdsley, N., Page, S., Mulyadi, D., Visser, M., 2015b. *Assessment of impacts of plantation drainage on the Kampar Peninsula peatland, Riau.* Deltares Report 1207384 to Wetlands International, CLUA and Norad
4. Miettinen J., Chenghua Shi, Soo Chin Liew. 2016. *Land cover distribution in the peatlands of Peninsular Malaysia, Sumatra and Borneo in 2015 with changes since 1990.* Global Ecology and Conservation 6 (2016) 67–78
5. Ministry of Natural Resources and Environment Malaysia. 2015. *Malaysia's Second National Communication (NC2) submitted to the United Nations Framework Convention on Climate Change (UNFCCC).* nc2.nre.gov.my
6. World Bank. 2014. *Indonesia Economic Quarterly. Hard choices.* http://www.worldbank.org/content/dam/Worldbank/document/EAP/Indonesia/IEQ-July14-ENG.pdf

Abstract No: A-059

SUSTAINABLE NUTRIENT MANAGEMENT OF FEN GRASSLAND ON PEAT SOIL

Pickert J., Behrendt A. and S. D. Bellingrath-Kimura

Leibniz Centre for Agricultural Landscape Research, Germany

**Corresponding author: pickert@zalf.de*

SUMMARY

In the past the northeast German lowlands drained peat soils are mainly used as pastures and meadows for milk, beef and energy production. Sustainable utilization of peat soil grassland is highly required, based on an appropriate management of the grass sward itself, water and nutrients. In order to fulfil the quality and quantity requirements of animal production systems, peat soil grasslands need an adequate fertilization with potassium (K) and phosphorus (P) and, in many situations, also with nitrogen (N). In this paper, results of grassland fertilization studies on peat soil are introduced. It is based on several long term field and lysimeter experiments, conducted for N, P and K at the peat soil research station Paulinenaue (northeast Germany) since 1960 and 1991 respectively. The results revealed, that the nutrient type, the fertilizer rate, their reduction, omission or increase, rapidly influenced the nutrient uptake and yield of the grassland sward as well as the nutrient leaching losses. In contrast to the common practice on mineral soils, the soil nutrient content was not helpful for the fertilizer rate determination whereas the optimum K and P content and the dry matter yield of the grass sward were a good indicator for calculating the fertilizer rate. For N, the findings resulted in on farm fertilizer rate recommendations minimizing the trade-off between production and leaching losses.

Keywords: *nitrogen, potassium, phosphorus, nutrient balances, nutrient leaching*

INTRODUCTION

In the past the North German lowlands were dominated by large peat swamps. Particularly since the eighteenth century those areas have been drained and used for agricultural production. Currently, those drained peat soils are mainly used as pastures and meadows for milk and beef production and biomass production for energy plants. Grasslands provide a broad list of ecosystem services, mainly in the fields of production, biodiversity, climate, water and cultural issues (Isselstein and Kayser 2014). While the functions of grasslands for biodiversity and cultural issues are significantly influenced by the historical development and the actual situation within the regions, the task of simultaneously optimizing the production systems and minimizing negative effects on climate and water are globally very similar. Drainage is a precondition for the establishment and use of high yielding and high quality forage grass swards on peat soils, however, this also leads to peat mineralization, causing carbon (C) emissions and leaching of nutrients. The amounts of C emissions are mainly depending on groundwater level and thickness of the peat layer (Figure 1). In comparison to other grassland sites of northeast Germany in the peat soil the N store was higher and the K store was lower, but the leached N and K amounts were higher in peat soils than in mineral soils (Figure 2).

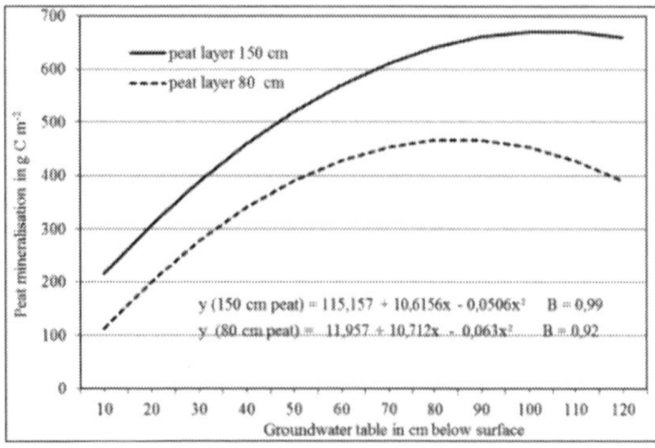

Figure 1: Peat mineralization of two Histosols depending on groundwater table (lysimeter, Mundel 1976)

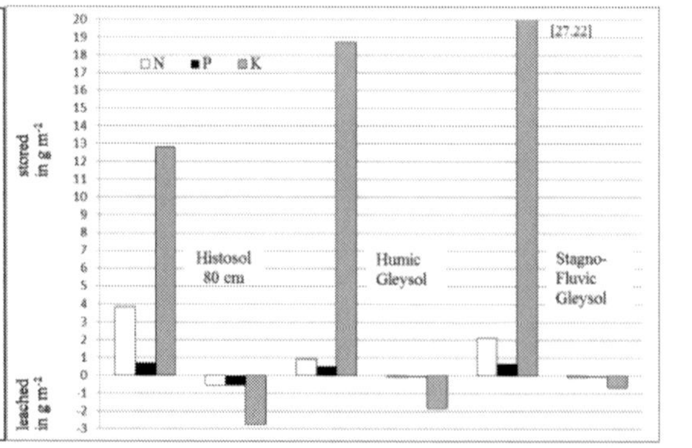

Figure 2: Nutrient stores and nutrient leaching of different European soils under grassland use (lysimeter, N 200, P 48, K 133 kg ha^{-1}, Mundel 1977)

Therefore, more sustainable management systems of drained peatlands are required, particularly including smooth, non-destructive treatments of the grass sward to ensure long-term usability and to avoid frequent ploughing and re-seeding, the limitation of drainage intensity and the adaption of fertilizer rates just to the swards requirements as well. Very often grassland use is characterized by an inappropriate management of nutrients. With particular respect to the soil nutrient storage grasslands on peat soil need an adequate fertilization with K and P and, in many situations, also with N, in order to fulfil requirements of animal production systems in terms of forage quality and quantity. In this paper results of ongoing long term field fertilization experiments and associated lysimeter experiments with N, P and K are reported and integrated into a sustainable nutrient management strategy on peat soils.

MATERIAL AND METHODS

The results presented here originate from the field experimental and lysimeter station Paulinenaue, located in the federal state of Brandenburg, Germany (52.687° N, 12.721° E, 9.2 °C mean annual air temperature, 534 mm mean annual precipitation 1982-2012). It was formed in the Warsaw-Berlin ice marginal valley of the central European last glaciation (Weichsel) and is part of a large, about 550 km² peatland zones. The sandy sediments were covered by 0.3 to 3 m thick peat layers, mainly formed from reed and sedge dominated vegetation. Actually, the soil is a Eutric Histosol of an up to 0.7m thick peat layer with a total C (Ct) content of 30 - 40%, covering about 12m of fluviatile sand. The first draining attempts were executed in the 14th century, followed by several further developments, especially by the construction of a channel and ditches, so from 1718 to 1724, extended in 1882 and between 1907 and 1925. Therefore the area could be used for cattle and sheep grazing and hay production. Between 1958 and 1961 and during the 1970ies and 1980ies, the ditches were again extended and water pumping stations were constructed in order to adjust the ground water table in the grassland site according to the actual demand of the plants (Behrendt 1988). Mean groundwater tables in summer were between 40 cm and 80 cm below and in winter close to the surface.

Two field trials have been conducted on the peat soil with graduated N fertilization from 0 to 480 kg N ha^{-1} (every cut got one third of the total yearly N rate) and constant PK fertilization since 1961 (Kreil 1965, Käding and Werner 1997) and with graduated P and K fertilization (applied in Spring) since 1991 (Schuppenies 1995, Pickert and Schuppenies 2002a). These constitute the experimental bases of our fertilizer studies, over the time periodically analyzed and evaluated with respect to different scientific questions. Both field trials as well as the additionally introduced joined grassland experiment on K and P fertilization on different soils together with other research stations since 1997 (Greiner *et al*,. 2014), are single-factor field plot trials of a complete randomized block design with four replications. They have been managed with three cuts and a harvesting area of at least 10m² per plot. Between 1977 and 2000 the influence of the N fertilization on the soil Ct and total N (Nt) contents in the upper soil layer was analyzed in order to check a potentially negative impact of the N fertilization on the peat soil (Käding *et al.,* 2003). Additionally, experiments at the Paulinenaue Lysimeter Station were conducted to study special questions in terms of peat mineralization and nutrient leaching (Mundel 1976 and 1977, Käding and Hölzel 1996). The lysimeters are consisting of peat and other soil types originating from Paulinenaue and other northeast German grassland sites and can be operated at adjusted groundwater levels with at least four replications. Each has a surface area of 1m² and a depth of 1.5m.

RESULTS AND DISCUSSION

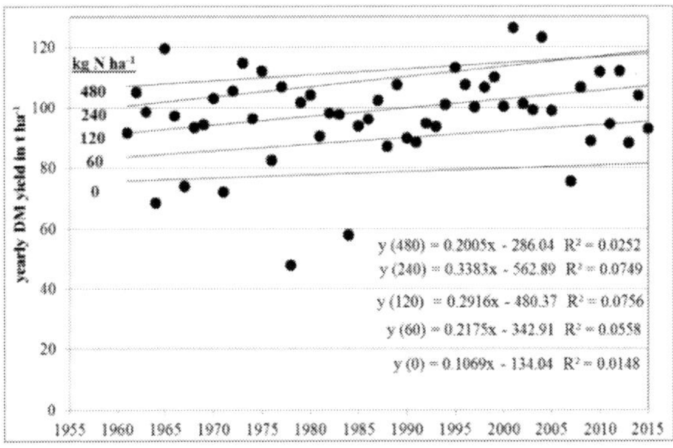

Figure 3: Grassland DM yield on peat soil depending on N rate. (single scores for the annual means over all N rates, 1961 – 2015)

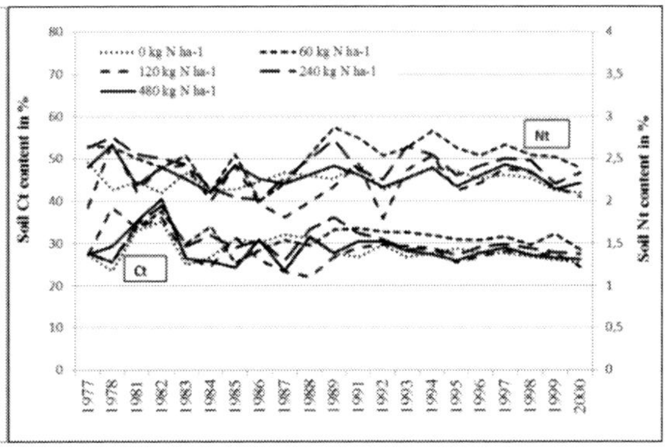

Figure 4: Ct and Nt content in the peat grassland soil depending on the N fertilizer rate from 0 to 480 kg N ha^{-1} (1977 – 2000)

In the grassland experiment with graduated **N fertilization** the dry matter (DM) yield increased with increasing N rates. The yields are characterized by a large variation among the years, but did not decrease over the trial period of 55 years. Without N an annual mean DM yield of almost 8 t ha^{-1} was gained, increasing to 10 t ha^{-1} with 120 kg N ha^{-1}. The effects of the higher N rates on DM yield were rather low but lead to a further increase of 10% up to about 11 t ha^{-1} with 240 kg N ha^{-1}. Any further N increase did not lead to a DM yield increase (Figure 3). The soil Ct and Nt contents were analyzed between year 16 and 39 of the trial. During this period of 23 years the Ct and Nt contents did not decrease. There was no difference between the different fertilizer levels (Figure 4).

At 'normal' fertilizer levels, as shown in Figure 2, only small amounts of N were found in the leachate. When high N fertilizer rates of 750 and 1,500 kg ha^{-1}, corresponding to excreta spots on cattle pastures, were applied in lysimeters for three years, severe N leaching up to 81.9 g m^{-2} could be observed (Table 1).

Table 1 N discharge in the seeping water in depending on the N fertilization (lysimeter, fertilization 1992 – 1994, 1995 no fertilizer; fertilization and discharge data in g m^{-2})

N fertilizer rate*	1992*	1993*	1994*	*1995*	**1992-94***	***1992-95***
0	0,3	0,6	1,2	*1,4*	**0,7**	***0,9***
75	0,6	4,5	20,0	*11,2*	**8,4**	***9,1***
150	6,0	47,3	81,9	*37,7*	**45,1**	***43,2***

On peat soil almost 40% of the DM yield is generated by the 1st cut and 30% in each of the two following cuts. Without N fertilization the DM production per kg N is very high. It amounts to more than 160 kg DM kg N ha^{-1} for the 1st cut and to 130 kg for the 2nd and 3rd cuts and decreases rapidly with increasing N fertilizer rates (Figure 5). At a yearly N rate of 120 kg N ha^{-1} the scope of the lower DM production rates already starts. Due to increasing N contents in the crop the crude protein (XP) yield is also increasing with the N fertilizer rates (Figure 6). With 4 and 2 kg harvested N per kg fertilized N at a fertilizer rate of 60 and 120 kg N ha^{-1} there were high N recovery rates, rapidly approaching 1 kg with further increasing N fertilizer application.

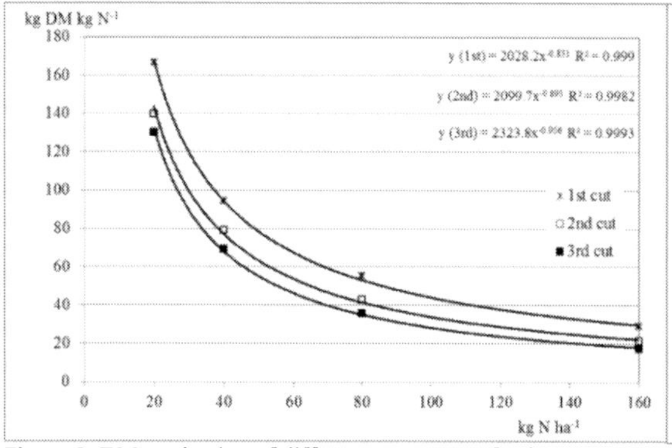

Figure 5: DM production of different cuts on grassland on peat soil depending on the N fertilizer rate (1961-2015)

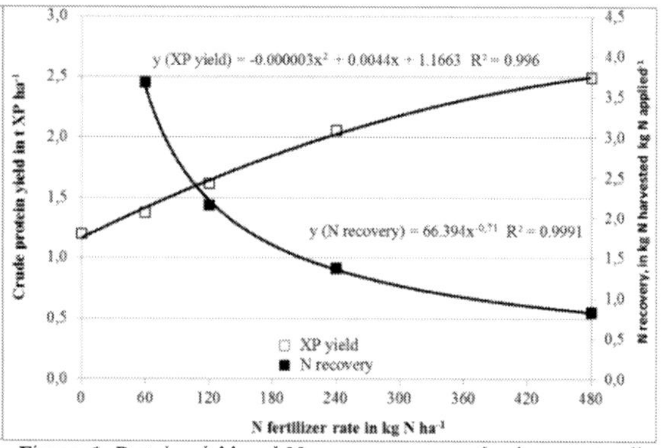

Figure 6: Protein yield and N recovery on grassland on peat soil depending on the N fertilizer rate (1961-2003)

Without **K fertilization** the grassland DM yield on the peat soil at Paulinenaue was declining very rapidly up to 30% within 5 years, independently from the level of N fertilization (Figure 7). On the other hand, in all three N levels the yield was increasing rapidly and reaching the level before the interruption of K fertilization within 2 years after K has been applied again. After 14 years without **P fertilization** almost no decline was observed on different grassland sites. Concerning K, this situation can differ among other typical non peat grassland sites and must be evaluated with respect to the specific soil and ground water conditions. Whereas without K the DM yield on the grassland on peat soil and on the silty loam in the mountains rapidly decreased, there was no yield impact on the silty river plain grassland (Figure 8).

During the trial period the K balance ($K_{applied}$ - K_{yield}) was negative for all N and K fertilizer levels. There was no correlation to the soil K content (Figure 9). The course of K contents in the harvested grass corresponded very well with course of DM yield (Figure 10 vs. Figure 7). If the K content in the first cut was in the range of 18 to 29 g kg DM^{-1} and in the second and third cut in the range of 14 to 21 g kg DM^{-1} the grass swards delivered high yields, if the K content in the first cut was below 10 to 18 g kg DM^{-1} and in the subsequent cuts in the range of 7 to 19 g kg DM^{-1} the grass sward suffered from potassium shortage and delivered only weak yields. In all cuts at P contents of 2.5 to 4 g kg DM^{-1} the grass swards delivered high yields, below the range of 2 to 2.8 g P kg DM^{-1} the grass sward suffered from P shortage and delivered only weak yields.

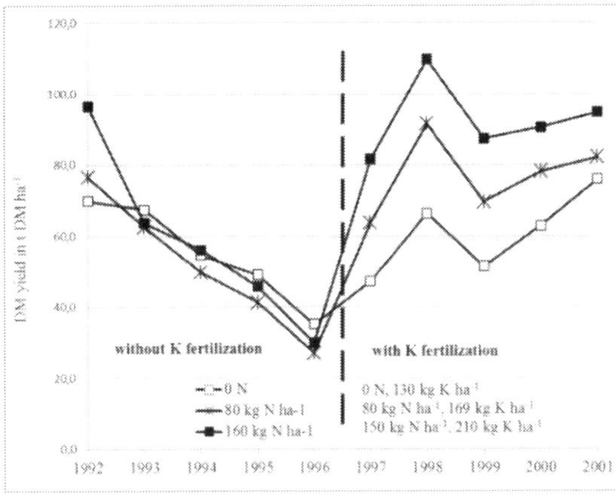

Figure 7: Course of DM yield with and without K fertilization (1992-2001) (Pickert and Schuppenies 2002b)

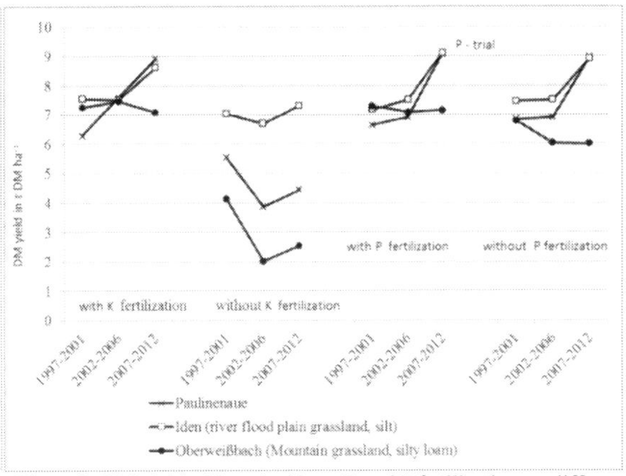

Figure 8: DM yield with and without K and P fertilization on different grassland sites in northeast Germany (1997-2012) (Greiner *et al.*, 2014)

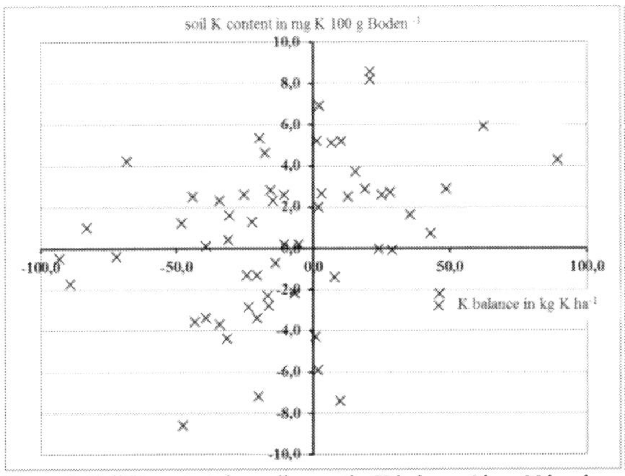

Figure 9: Soil K content depending on the K balance (three N levels, 1992-2001)

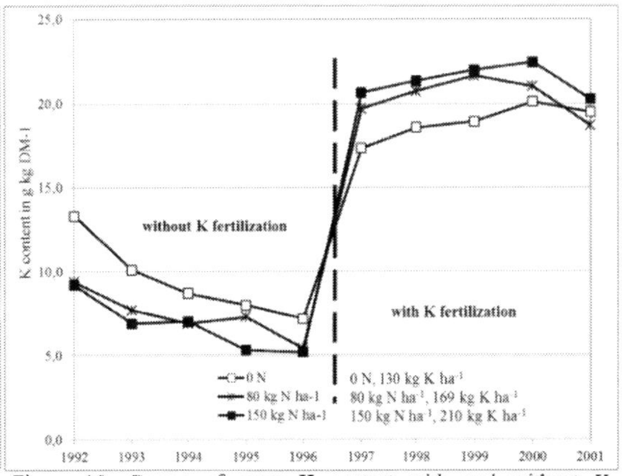

Figure 10: Course of grass K content with and without K fertilization on different grassland sites in northeast Germany (1997-2002)

By supporting a higher uptake with the grass yield a balanced K fertilization helped to minimize N leaching (Figure 5). The N balance is strictly negative, even if fertilized with 160 kg N ha^{-1}. In the opposite, the sole application of N fertilizers dramatically increased the N balances and the risks for N leaching (Figure 12).

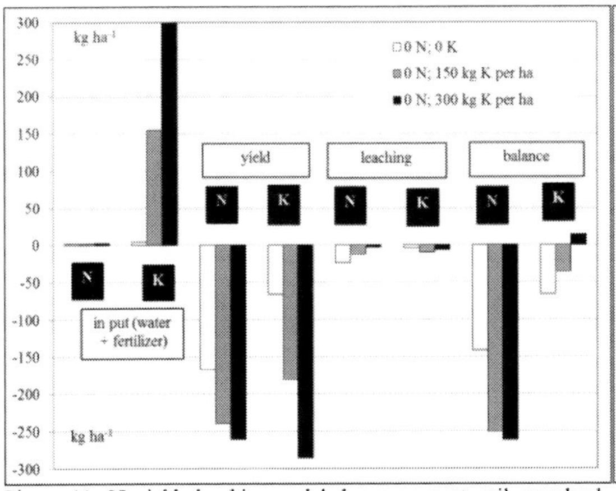

Figure 11: N yield, leaching and balance on peat soil grassland depending on the K fertilizer rate (lysimeter 2003-2008)

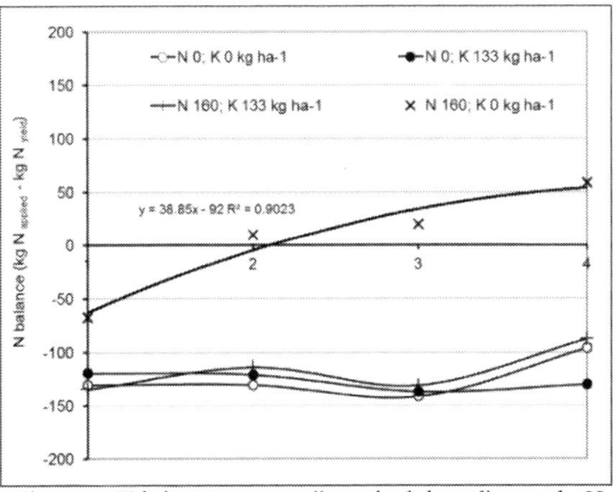

Figure 12: N balance on peat soil grassland depending on the N and K fertilization (mean 2 trials, 4 years each (Pickert and Schuppenies 2002a)

CONCLUSIONS

The results of the long term fertilizer experiments in the field trials and in the lysimeters allow the establishment of a resource efficient nutrient management system for grassland on peat soil under the climatic conditions of northeast Germany, that minimises the trade-offs within the ecosystem services in the fields of production and climate and water protection.

Despite a much greater N uptake by the grass sward, a fertilizer rate of 120 kg N ha^{-1} is sufficient in terms of high yields and efficient nutrient use on peat soil grassland. If there is a particular need, i.e. in years with yield depressions an increase up to 160 kg N ha^{-1} is possible. In that N fertilizer range the soil Ct and Nt content are not affected and there is no risk of N leaching. The difference between the grass sward N uptake of about 300 kg N with a normal yield of 10 t DM ha^{-1} and the N fertilizer rate of 120 to 160 kg N ha^{-1} amounts to 140 to 180 kg N ha^{-1}, that is delivered by the peat soil. Compared to grassland on mineral soils only the half amount of N is needed for the same DM yield. In the new fertilizer regulation in Germany the contribution of the peat soil nutrient store to the nutrient supply of grassland and therefore the reduction of the fertilizer rate is set to 80 kg N ha^{-1} (BMEL 2015). The results show, that this value could be corrected remarkably for the northeast German peat soil grassland.

For K and P on peat soil only the yearly grass uptake in the range of 20 and 3 kg t DM^{-1} (200 and 30 kg ha^{-1} for a grassland yield of 10 t ha^{-1}) should be yearly replaced by fertilization. It does not seem necessary to keep the soil P and K content at a certain level as recommended for mineral soils. By checking the content of P and K in the grass, i.e. together with the laboratory analysis of the nutritive value of the grass silage, it is possible to supervise and optimize the nutrient management system of a farm.

ACKNOWLEDGEMENTS

The authors like to thank Dr Horst Käding and Dr Rudolf Schuppenies, Paulinenaue, for their long-term experimental work in the cited field trials and for the valuable advice during the preparation of the paper.

REFERENCES

1. Behrendt A. (1995) Moorkundliche Untersuchungen an nordostdeutschen Niedermooren unter Berücksichtigung des Torfschwundes, ein Beitrag zur Moorerhaltung. Dissertation, Humboldt-University, Berlin 170 pp.
2. BMEL (2015) Verordnungsentwurf vom 16.12.2015. Verordnung zur Neuordnung der guten fachlichen Praxis beim Düngen, notified according Guideline (EU) 2015/1535
3. Greiner B., Hertwig F., Hochberg H., Priebe R., Riel G. and Schuppenies R. (2014) Auswirkungen einer unterlassenen Phosphor- und Kaliumdüngung – Ergebnisse aus sechzehnjährigen Grünlanddüngungsversuchen. Tagungsband 58. Jahrestagung AG Grünland und Futterbau, Arnstadt, 107-110
4. Isselstein J. and Kayser M. (2014) Functions of grassland and their potential in delivering ecosystem services. *Grassland science in Europe*, 19, 199-214
5. Kreil W. (1965) Ergebnisse von Stickstoffdüngungsversuchen auf verschiedenen Weidestandorten in der DDR. *Tagungsberichte der Deutschen Akademie der Landwirtschaftswissenschaften*. Berlin, Nr. 94, 65-78
6. Käding H. and Hölzel D. (1996) Nährstoffflüsse auf Grünland nach punktförmiger Überdüngung mit Mineraldüngern und Tierexkrementen bei unterschiedlichen Standortbedingungen. Müncheberg, ZALF-Bericht Nr. 26, 67-72
7. Käding H. and Werner A. (1997) Ergebnisse eines 35jährigen N-Düngungsversuches auf Niedermoor in Paulinenaue. *Arch. Acker-Pfl. Boden*. 42, 137-147
8. Käding H., Werner A. and Schalitz G. (2003) Auswirkungen langjähriger N-Düngung auf Standorteigenschaften, Erträge, Stoffgehalte und Vegetationszusammensetzung des Niedermoorgrünlandes. *Pflanzenbauwissenschaften* 7, 13-20
9. Mundel G. (1976) Untersuchungen zur Torfmineralisation in Niedermooren. *Arch. Acker-Pfl. Boden*. 20, 669-679
10. Mundel G. (1977) Die Auswaschung von Nährstoffen in hydromorphen Graslandböden anhand von Lysimeterergebnissen. XIII Int. Grassl. Congr. Leipzig, Sectional Papers, sect. 3-5, 38-43
11. Pickert J. and Schuppenies R. (2002a) Sward composition, N balance and yield on low bog grassland used under fertilizer restrictions by environmental programmes. *Grassland Science in Europe* 7, 832-833
12. Pickert J. and Schuppenies R. (2002b) Veränderungen in Ertrag und Grünlandnarbe bei Kalium-Aushagerung und Wiederaufnahme der K-Düngung auf einem sandunterlagerten Niedermoor in Nordostdeutschland. Tagungsband 46. Jahrestagung AG Grünland und Futterbau, Rostock, 84-87,
13. Schuppenies R. (1995) Die Bedeutung der Kaliumdüngung auf Niedermoorgrünland. Tagungsband 39. Jahrestagung AG Grünland und Futterbau, Weihenstephan, 71-76

Abstract No: A-125

THE RING OF FIRE: TACKLING INDONESIA'S PEATLAND FIRE DYNAMIC

Susan Page[1], Aljosja Hooijer[2], Ronald Vernimmen[2], Jukka Miettinen[3], David Gaveau[4], Morten Rossé[5] and Thomas E.L. Smith[6]

[1]*Dept. Geography, University of Leicester, UK*
[2]*Deltares, The Netherlands*
[3]*Centre for Remote Imaging, Sensing and Processing (CRISP), Singapore*
[4]*Center for International Forestry Research, Indonesia*
[5]*McKinsey & Company, Germany*
[6]*Dept. Geography, King's College, UK*

Corresponding author: sep5@le.ac.uk

SUMMARY

Peatlands are a significant component of the global carbon (C) cycle, yet despite their role as a long-term C sink, they are increasingly vulnerable to destabilisation. The shift from C sink to source is happening rapidly in SE Asia and particularly in Indonesia, where combined pressures of land use change and fire on peatland C dynamics and their environmental and socio-economic consequences are increasingly apparent. The present-day peat fire dynamic of Indonesia is the consequence of a 'perfect storm' of events providing key ingredients for fire activity, namely an abundance of both fuel and ignition sources. We discuss the link between deforestation, drainage, fire and accelerating C emissions. Using data on fires over the period 2010-2015, the location, scale and controls on peat driven C emissions are addressed. The paper concludes by advocating land management options to reduce future fire risk as part of wider peatland management strategies, while acknowledging the substantial governance and political challenges associated with damping down the current fire dynamic.

Keywords: *peat fire, peat swamp forest, tropical peatland, Indonesia, GHG emissions*

INTRODUCTION

Peatlands are a globally important carbon (C) pool. While covering only ~3% of the Earth's land surface, they contain an estimated 500 to 700 Gt (=Pg) of C, likely exceeding that contained in the world's vegetation (500 Gt). In terms of both area (3.6 million km^2) and C storage (400-600 Gt), the most extensive peatlands are found in northern regions of the world, but there are also significant deposits in the humid tropics. Collectively, these cover some 0.4 million km^2 with a total C pool of 80 to 90 Gt (Page *et al.*, 2011). Their greatest extent is in Southeast (SE) Asia (0.25 million km^2; 69 Gt C), with 57 Gt C in Indonesian peatlands and a smaller 9 Gt C in Malaysia. Most peat C has accumulated over long time periods; yet despite their role as a C sink throughout the Holocene, peat C pools are increasingly vulnerable to destabilisation through a combination of land use change, fire and climatic warming. Nowhere is the shift from peatland C sink to C source happening more rapidly than in insular SE Asia where there are combined pressures of land use change and fire on peatland ecosystem C dynamics.

Hydrology plays a critical role in the peatland C cycle. The position of the water table controls the rate at which aerobic microbial decomposition (mineralization) of organic matter, and hence the rate of peat accumulation, can proceed. Under conditions of near permanent waterlogging, the absence of oxygen in the soil profile favours the accumulation of undecayed or partially decayed organic matter facilitating long-term ecosystem C storage, but water table drawdown accompanying anthropogenic land use change increases both the rate of peat mineralization and the risk of fire. It is estimated that drained tropical peatlands contribute almost 70% (~200 Mt C) of global drainage- and fire-derived greenhouse gas (GHG) emissions from organic soils, with a smaller 30% from drained northern peatlands (Biancalani & Avagyan 2014).

In SE Asia, the contemporary peat fire dynamic is the consequence of both an abundance of fuel and of ignition sources. Landscape-scale forest clearance and peat drainage combined with widespread use of fire as a cheap, fast and effective means to clear large areas of forest debris and regrowth have led to an increase in fire activity. It is not only deforested and drained peatlands that are at risk of fire since the fire-resilience of remaining fragments of peat swamp forest has been reduced, placing them at increased risk of ignition. Where peat swamp forest has burnt once, it will undergo secondary succession back to closed forest. But in reality, the standing and dead timber remaining from the first fire will increase the chance of a second fire, placing the ecosystem on a trajectory towards fire-prone scrub with very limited opportunity for forest recovery (Hoscilo *et al.*, 2011).

Although the most severe fires of recent years can be linked to droughts driven by the ENSO climate anomaly (e.g. Page *et al.*, 2002), abnormal weather conditions are not a prerequisite for peat fires. Indeed fires are now a regular feature of every dry season, even those of short duration (Gaveau *et al.*, 2014), and are as much a product of rapid land use change (e.g. Field et al. 2009) as they are of climatic variability. This new fire dynamic means that peat fires in this region can no longer be considered occasional events that result in short-term perturbations of the peatland ecosystem followed by medium-term recovery to a new stable state. With every fire season, they are an intensifying environmental concern with profound implications for GHG emissions, air quality, human health, local livelihoods and regional economies. This short paper reviews the link between fire, land use change and GHG emissions in Indonesian peatlands focusing on the period 2010 to 2015. It presents data on fire location and extent and apportions fire-derived GHG emissions to different land covers. The paper ends by comparing the scale of GHG emissions from peat fires and peat oxidation and considers opportunities for land management options to mitigate these emissions and the risk of future fires.

METHODS

Our approach involved linking burnt area to peat extent, land cover status and fire-derived GHG emissions for the period 2010-2015 (until end of October 2015). Burnt area was obtained from MODIS gridded fire data products. MODIS tiles covering Sumatra, Kalimantan and Papua (results for Papua are not presented here) were processed. One MODIS grid cell covers an area of 1 km^2 (100 ha) but not every fire results in the burning of the whole grid cell. To obtain an estimate of the burnt area within a grid cell, the number of surrounding (neighbouring) cells was considered, on the assumption that the fraction of a cell that had burnt was proportional to the number of surrounding cells that were also 'hotspots' in the same period. For each day, for each fire observation and for each grid cell, the number of neighbouring fire cells was counted and attributed to the centre grid cell; the minimum number being zero and the maximum 8. On an annual basis the maximum number of neighbouring fire cells was determined and the burnt area related to the number of neighbouring cells, starting at 10% burnt area for a fire cell without neighbouring cells (i.e. 10 ha), and increasing by 10% burnt area for each subsequent neighbouring cell. A fire cell with the maximum of 8 neighbouring fire cells was considered to have a conservative 90% burnt area (90 ha); a percentage of 100% burnt area was not applied, as remnant pockets of unburned vegetation are often observed after fires while a small percentage of intensively drained peatland is open water that cannot burn. The burnt area estimate was validated for an area of approximately 6.8 Mha covering part of Central and South Kalimantan (D. Gaveau, unpub. data). The two burnt area products were compared and revealed an acceptable degree of agreement, while acknowledging both errors of omission (under reporting of burnt area) and commission (overestimation). This gave confidence in the accuracy of our MODIS hotspot burnt area method, although additional sensitivity analyses will be performed for additional validation. The burnt area calculated in this way was then overlaid onto maps of peatland extent, using the peat map of BBSDLP (Ritung *et al.*, 2011) and land cover status, using Margono *et al.* (2014) to provide forest/non-forest data over the period 2000-2012, while data on 2010 and 2015 plantation extent (oil palm and pulpwood plantation areas developed or under development) were provided by CRISP (*Miettinen et al.*, 2012, 2016).

Emissions from belowground (peat) fires were calculated using fuel load data from Konecny *et al.* (2016) and GHG emissions factors (CO_2, CH_4, N_2O) from Smith *et al.* (2016). Aboveground (biomass) fuel load values were obtained from IPCC (2006) and corresponding GHG emission factors from Stockwell *et al.* (2014). Using the knowledge of fuel load from recurrent peat fires (Konecny *et al.*, 2016), we accounted for the decrease in peat lost in each subsequent fire, which results in intact peat swamp forest having emissions that are 4.6 times higher (699 t CO_2-e ha^{-1}) than the third fire in a deforested peatland (153 t CO_2-e ha^{-1}), including both peat and aboveground biomass emissions. Given that emissions even from third fires in peatlands are still many times higher than those from fires on mineral soils, it follows that all fires in peatland areas have far higher emissions than fires in other land covers. Further details of the methodologies employed in this study are available in Hooijer *et al.* (2016).

RESULTS

Using our approach, the total burnt area in Sumatra and Kalimantan over 2010-2015 was estimated to be 13 Mha, of which over half occurred as a result of fires during 2014 and 2015 (3 Mha and 3.6 Mha, respectively). There was an increasing trend in annual total burnt area from 2010 to 2015, both in peatland areas and on mineral soils, which may be attributable to the key drivers of land cover change and climate. The proportion of annual burnt area located in peatland in each year averaged ~33% (range 28 - 41%), with peak values of 1.2 Mha of burnt peatland in both 2014 and 2015 (Figure 1).

Within peatland, the area of forest that burnt steadily increased over the 6 year period, reaching a peak of around 227,000 ha in 2014 and 208,000 ha in 2015 (Figure 2). This amounts to the loss of some 0.9 Mha of peat swamp forest as a result of fires over the six year period. Burnt area inside land developed or being developed for industrial-scale plantations shows a similar trend, with around 300,000 ha burning in both 2014 and 2015. The largest burnt area category in all years, however, with pronounced increases in 2014 and 2015, is 'other'; this includes scrub, which may well have burnt during previous fire years, and also smallholder land (main land uses are for growing oil palm and vegetable crops).

In terms of peatland fire GHG emissions (Figure 3), these have risen steadily over the period 2010-2015 with the increase in burnt area. Using our approach, we calculate that the total peat fire emission over the 6 year period is 1700 Mt CO_2-e, which is 78% of the total fire emission of 2200 Mt CO_2-e (for fires on both mineral and peat soils; data not shown). Thus some 78% of the total 6 year emission is from fires on peatland despite these fires

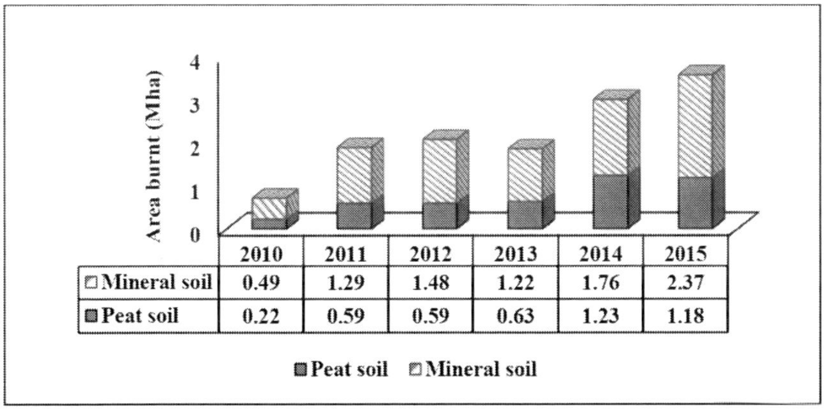

	2010	2011	2012	2013	2014	2015
Mineral soil	0.49	1.29	1.48	1.22	1.76	2.37
Peat soil	0.22	0.59	0.59	0.63	1.23	1.18

Figure 1: Total burnt area (Mha) across mineral and peat soils in Sumatra and Kalimantan between 2010 and 2015; total burnt area over 6 years is 13.05 Mha, with 4.44 Mha on peat soils (34%) and 8.61 Mha on mineral soils (66%).

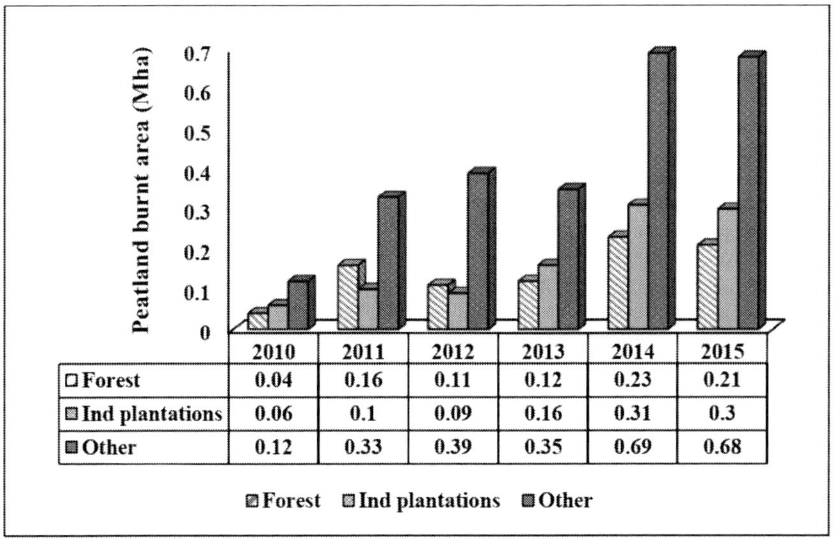

	2010	2011	2012	2013	2014	2015
Forest	0.04	0.16	0.11	0.12	0.23	0.21
Ind plantations	0.06	0.1	0.09	0.16	0.31	0.3
Other	0.12	0.33	0.39	0.35	0.69	0.68

Figure 2: Total burnt area (Mha) and land cover on peat soils in Sumatra and Kalimantan between 2010 and 2015; total burnt area over 6 years is 4.44 Mha, with 0.87 Mha (20%) in forest, 1.02 Mha (23%) in industrial plantations (both developed and under development) and 2.55 Mha (57%) in other land covers

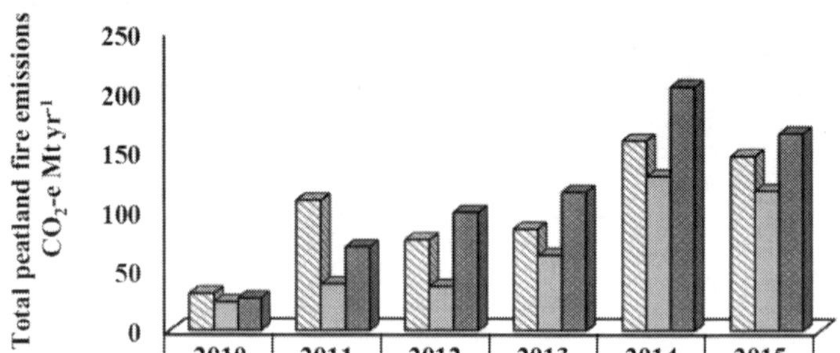

	2010	2011	2012	2013	2014	2015
Forest	31	109	76	85	159	146
Ind plantations	24	39	37	63	129	117
Other	27	70	99	116	204	165

Forest Ind plantations Other

Figure 3: Total annual emissions of greenhouse gases (CO_2, CH_4, N_2O; expressed as CO_2-e Mt) from peatland fires across Sumatra and Kalimantan during 2010-2015. Emissions increase from a total of 82 Mt in 2010 to 492 and 428 Mt in 2014 and 2015, respectively. Total emissions over the 6 year period are ~1700 Mt CO_2-e, of which fires on forested peatland contribute 36%, fires in plantations (both developed and under development) contribute 24% and fires in other land cover categories (scrub and smallholder land) contribute 40%.

occurring on only 34% of the burnt area. Total CO_2-e emission from peatland fires alone is around 500 Mt yr^{-1} in both 2014 and 2015; these are lower estimates than some other assessments, mostly because lower emission factors for recurrent peat fires are applied in our study. It is important to note that these two most recent fire years (2014 and 2015) were in fact likely quite similar in magnitude. This is true when considering the total burnt area (peat and mineral soils) in Sumatra and Kalimantan (3 and 3.6 Mha respectively for 2014 and 2015), the total burnt peat area (~1.2 Mha in both years), and the burnt peat forest area (~0.2 Mha in both years).

DISCUSSION

In pre-disturbance landscapes in SE Asia there was limited risk of accidental ignitions or fire spread since the landscape was resistant to fire. But the new landscapes of fragmented forests and drained peatlands are highly fire-prone. The occurrence of extended droughts associated with ENSO-events undoubtedly exacerbates the intensity of peat fires, but this climatic phenomenon is not, in itself, the root cause. Our results show that there was a large burnt area on peatland in 2014 (a non-ENSO year) just as there was in the subsequent ENSO year of 2015, both resulting in similar GHG and, presumably, smoke emissions. This result concurs with the study by Gaveau *et al.* (2014) on the severity of fires and associated emissions in 2013, which again was a non-ENSO year. Between 2014 and 2015, the location of fires, and hence the impact of air pollution on large centres of population, was different. But while national and international attention focused on the 2015 fire year, the 2014 and indeed the 2013 fire years were also notable. This is an important finding underlining the need for fundamental changes in peatland management practices, regardless of year to year variability in climate.

The scientific evidence on both the drivers of and the amount of GHG emissions from peat fires in insular SE Asia and their local to global consequences is now reasonably well established, yet this knowledge has been inadequately translated into land use policy and land management practices. A study of the 2006 peat fires established that 59% of the fire emissions from Sumatra and 73% of the emissions from Kalimantan originated outside timber and oil-palm concession boundaries (Marlier *et al.*, 2015); our data for 2010-2015 show a similar pattern, at least for land developed or under development for industrial-scale plantations. These results further emphasise that many actors play a part in the 'ring of fire dynamic' with a steady year-on-year decrease in the remaining peat swamp forest through encroaching fires from all sides (both literally and figuratively) and that they all need to be engaged not just in fire fighting but in fire prevention. While some of the largest plantation companies have made commitments to 'zero burning', 'no deforestation', 'no planting on peatland' and working with local communities to reduce fire occurrence (Padfield *et al.* in press), much more needs to be done to remove fire from the most vulnerable landscapes. While all peat landscapes in Sumatra and Kalimantan are now largely deforested, drained and fire prone, there are large differences in the extent and condition of the fragments of remaining peat swamp forest, and also in the condition and management of the non-forest areas, and therefore in the emissions generated by fires in such areas. Some peatland areas produce far more fire emissions than others: first and second fires in peat swamp forest are the greatest emission sources by unit area. Better understanding of these emission hotspots, and their nature, along with a determined effort to engage with all involved in managing fire prone landscapes could improve the planning and implementation of fire mitigation activities.

A comparison of the scale of GHG emissions arising from peat fires and oxidation (the latter estimated using land cover data from Miettinen *et al.* (2016) and IPCC (2014) for CO_2 emission factors) reveals that for 2015, the scale of emissions from both sources were likely comparable in magnitude (428 Mt CO_2-e from fires; 437 Mt CO_2-e from oxidation). Over the full 6 year period, peat fire emissions are estimated at 1696 Mt CO_2-e while peat oxidation emissions are 2621 Mt CO_2-e. Since the latter value can be considered conservative (only CO_2 emissions are accounted for), this comparison stresses the point that mitigating fire emissions is only part of the bigger issue of mitigating the total sum of GHG emissions produced as a result of peatland drainage. Overall, the most effective measure that Indonesia could apply to mitigate the continuation or even further increase of GHG emissions from peatlands would be to prevent fires in the remaining peat swamp forest fragments, and to restore the hydrology of peatland areas that are degraded. This is because forest fires generate the highest emissions per unit area: up ten times or more than fires in other land covers (e.g. Van Leeuwen *et al.* 2014) while the extent of drained peatland makes a major contribution to the high annual value for emissions from oxidation. In remnant forests, successful solutions must focus on the peat itself – i.e. on efforts to keep the peat wet. This will require hydrological interventions on drained peatlands adjoining remnant peat swamp forest in order to restore forest water levels. This will reduce both oxidative and fire emissions but have inevitable economic consequences for stakeholders involved in agricultural production, since high water levels will reduce or even completely halt the productivity of plantation crops. Opportunities do exist, however, to identify and develop alternative plantation crop species that tolerate higher water levels while still providing an economic return.

There are now some 140,000 km^2 of drained peatland across Peninsular Malaysia, Sumatra and Borneo (Miettinen *et al.* 2016); thus the geographical magnitude of managing such 'high emissions' landscapes is daunting. There are technical and economic challenges to be overcome in persuading policy makers and land managers that peat water tables should be maintained at a sufficiently high level to reduce fire risk and oxidative emissions, as well as substantial governance and political challenges, including uncertainties over land rights and weak policy implementation. Addressing the contemporary Indonesian fire dynamic will require a radical shift in human behaviours and practices, but also a fundamental recognition that interventions will require strong and effective political leadership, financial investment, and an honest and transparent commitment from everyone involved in peatland management.

ACKNOWLEDGEMENTS

Norad for funding part of the peatland burnt area work & support to DG from DFID (grant to CIFOR; project no. 203034).

REFERENCES

1. Biancalani R., Avagyan A. (eds) 2014. *Towards climate responsible peatland management practices: Part 1.* FAO, Rome.
2. Field R.D., van der Werf G.R., Shen S.S.P. 2009. Human amplification of drought-induced biomass burning in Indonesia since 1960. *Nature Geoscience* 2: 185–8.
3. Gaveau D.L.A., Salim M.A., Hergoualc'h K., Locatelli B., Sloan S., Wooster M., Marlier M.E., Molidena E., Yaen H., DeFries R., Verchot L., Murdiyarso D., Nasi R., Holmgren P., Sheil D. 2014. Major atmospheric emissions from peat fires in Southeast Asia during non-drought years: evidence from the 2013 Sumatran fires. *Scientific Reports* 4: 6112.
4. Hooijer A., Page S.E., Canadell J.G., Silvius M., Kwadijk J., Wösten H., Jauhiainen J. 2010. Current and future CO_2 emissions from drained peatlands in Southeast Asia. *Biogeosciences* 7: 1505-1514.
5. Hooijer A., Vernimmen R., Miettinen J., Page S.E., van der Werf G., Gaveau D., Smith T., Visser M. 2016. 2010-2015 MODIS hotspot derived peatland burnt area and carbon emission estimates for Sumatra and Kalimantan; trends and priority areas for intervention. Deltares for McKinsey and NORAD.
6. Hoscilo A., Page S.E, Tansey K.J., Rieley J.O. 2011. Effect of repeated fires on land cover change on peatland in southern C. Kalimantan, Indonesia 1973 to 2005. *International Journal of Wildland Fire* 20: 578-588.
7. IPCC 2006. *IPCC Guidelines for National Greenhouse Gas Inventories. Volume 4: Agriculture, Forestry, and Other Land Use.* Available online at http://www.ipcc-nggip.iges.or.jp/public/2006gl/vol4.html
8. IPCC 2014. *2013 Supplement to the 2006 IPCC Guidelines for National Greenhouse Gas Inventories.* Hiraishi, T. et al. (eds). IPCC, Switzerland.
9. Konecny K., Ballhorn U., Navratil P., Jubanski J., Page S., Tansey K., Hooijer A., Vernimmen R., Siegert F. 2016. Carbon emissions from recurrent fires in drained tropical peatlands. *Global Change Biology* 22: 1469-1480.

10. Margono B., Potapov P., Turubanova S., Stolle F., Hansen M. 2014. Primary forest cover loss in Indonesia over 2000-2012. *Nature Climate Change* 2014 doi:10.1038/nclimate2277
11. Marlier M.E., DeFries R.S., Kim P.S., Koplitz S.N., Jacob D.J., Mickley L.J., Myers S.S. 2015. Fire emissions and regional air quality impacts from fires in oil palm, timber, and logging concessions in Indonesia. *Environmental Research Letters* 10: 085005
12. Mietinnen J, Hooijer A., Shi C., Tollenaar D., Vernimmen R., Liew S.C., Malins C., Page, S.E. 2012a. Extent of industrial plantations on Southeast Asian peatlands in 2010 with analysis of historical expansion and future projections. *Global Change Biology – Bioenergy* 4: 908-918.
13. Padfield R. et al. (*in press*) Landscapes in transition: An analysis of sustainable policy initiatives and emerging corporate commitments in the palm oil industry. *Landscape Research*.
14. Page S.E., Siegert F., Rieley J.O., Boehm H-D.V. Jaya, A., Limin S. 2002. The amount of carbon released from peat and forest fires in Indonesia in 1997. *Nature* 420: 61-65.
15. Page S.E., Rieley J.O., Banks C.J. 2011 Global and regional importance of the tropical peatland carbon pool. *Global Change Biology* 17: 798-818
16. Ritung S, Wahyunto, Nugroho K, Sukarman, Hikmatullah, Suparto, Tafakresnanto C, 2011. Peta lahan gambut Indonesia. Skala 1:250.000. Balai Besar Penelitian dan Pengembangan Sumberdaya Lahan Pertanian.
17. Stockwell C., Yokelson R., Kreidenweis S., Robinson A., DeMott P., Sullivan R., Reardon J., Ryan K., Griffith D., Stevens, L. 2014. Trace gas emissions from combustion of peat, crop residue, biofuels, grasses, and other fuels. *Atmospheric Chemistry & Physics* 14: 9727-9754.
18. Smith T.E.L., Yule C., Evers S., Paton-Walsh C., Gan J.Y. 2016. First in situ measurements of tropical peatland fire emissions: new emission factors for GHG reporting. *Proceedings of the IPC, Kuching, August 2016.*
19. Van Leeuwen T., van der Werf G., Hoffmann A., Detmers R., Rücker G., French N., Archibald S., Carvalho Jr. J., Cook G., de Groot W., Hely E., Kasischke E., Kloster S., McCarty J., Pettinari M., Savadogo P., Alvarado, E., Bsochetti L., Manuri S., Meyer C., Siegert F., Trollope L., Trollope W. 2014. Biomass burning fuel consumption rates: a field measurement database. *Biogeosciences*11: 7305-7329.

Abstract No: A-454

WHAT IS THE WAY FORWARD ON INDONESIAN PEATLAND?

Supiandi Sabiham*, Winarna, Heru Bagus Pulunggono, Dian Novarina, and Bandung Sahari

Peat Society of Indonesia, Department of Soil Science and Land Resource, Bogor Agricultural University (IPB), INDONESIA.

**Corresponding author: ssupiandi@yahoo.com*

SUMMARY

Indonesian peatland has now become the global topic in relation with environment problems including land fires, declining massive ecosystem functions, and increasing carbon emission. Agricultural activities on it are currently seen as an irresponsible development which created those environmental catastrophes especially land fires, instead of climatic problem. This was responded by the government policies which prohibit peatland conversion, restrict ground surface water level not more than 0.4 meter for cultivated peatland, and develop peatland restoration program. Peatland cultivation in Indonesia has been started a long time ago since 1910s where Banjarese and Buginese migrated to the tidal zone peatland of Kalimantan and Sumatera. This was followed by transmigration program which reclaimed peatland for crops cultivation in Sumatera and Kalimantan. Unfortunately, poor knowledge and understanding on tropical peatland has brought many negative consequences. There were not enough in depth study whereby. Inappropriate drainage canals were applied on shallow peat layers with underlying potential acid sulfate soil which results in the exposure of pyritic sediments. However, at present with the better understanding on tropical peatland and with better technology, the management peatland has improved. Canal systems with water gate and overflow based on topography information have successfully controlled water level and drained only surplus water. This particularly true for large concession of oil palm and pulp plantations in Riau which have been applying that technology. For provinces where peat is dominant such as Riau, Jambi, and South Sumatera, peatland plays a very important role in alleviating local farmers from poverty and at the same time brings economic benefit for larger community through multiplier effects. For many years, peatland cultivation has provided a huge amount of experiences for people from different education levels, background, and culture to learn that Indonesian peatland is unique and complex. This can not only be seen as a single soil type that should be preserved, but there have been many social, cultural, and economic activities on it since a long time ago that should also be considered. The critical issue now is how to bridge among social, economic, and environment purposes to address sustainable development. Constructive perception, better knowledge and tranquil inputs based on scientific evidences are discussed to build up an appropriate strategy for better future of Indonesian peatland.

Keywords: *peatland, sustainable management, social, economic*

INTRODUCTION

Peatland is now become the global topic in relation with massive utilization for various purposes that is capable of causing environment problems including land fires, declining massive ecosystem functions, and increasing carbon emission. In relation with greenhouse gases emission, alteration of peat for agriculture by lowering of water table is frequently associated with increasing number of carbon dioxide (CO_2) emission (Hooijer *et al.*, 2010; Page *et al.*, 2010; 2011). In fact, lowering water table is also recorded to take place in natural ecosystem where water level of peatland is influenced by seasonal rainfall. Massive release of CO_2 is also predicted to occur during massive land fire on peat in Indonesia along the year 2015. Page *et al.* 2002 has reported that peat fire in Indonesia in 1997 has resulted in massive carbon release that is expected to contribute to global greenhouse gas emission.

Land fire has been recorded to occur by year to year. First record of land fire was documented in 1982-1983 in East Kalimantan (*Dirjen Perlindungan Hutan dan Pelestarian Alam* 1983). Land burning was originally a traditional knowledge in local community to prepare land for cultivating cash crop because it was cheap and believed that burned land will return into fertilized land. The most phenomenal case of land fire was recorded in 2015, where many areas in Sumatera and Kalimantan burned out and created a dangerous air quality which impacted on sickness and death.

Agricultural activities on peat are now seen as an irresponsible development which created land fires along 2015, instead of climatic problem. This is particularly true since many cases of land fires are found in areas where agriculture activities are on peat soil including Riau, Jambi, and South Sumatera. However, it cannot be disregarded that longer dry season due to EL-NINO phenomenon was one reason why fire become massive disaster. Opinion to blame cultivated peat as main driving factor of land fire kept continuing along the year of 2015 until now. This can be seen from many discussions (workshops, conferences, focus group discussion) conducted at various levels from local to international that was then followed by many opinions coming from different people from different background about peat fires on many newspapers and magazines. This was then responded by the Government to take progressive actions and policies to tackle land fire especially on peatland, one of which is the policy to stop planting for both forestry plantation and oil palm on peatland.

Peat cultivation in Indonesia has been started since many years ago. Technology to tackle peatland for agriculture also gradually develops by year to year. Today, many peatland areas are cultivated for various cash crops across islands and successfully help local people to survive and grow. As an example, Riau Province, where massive peatland is found, there are many activities on it including agriculture, social, and culture. In essence, peatland problem is not only about technique, but it should also touch many aspects including culture and local economic situation.

Thus, the purpose of this paper is to discuss about the future shape of peatland in Indonesia by involving current policies, practices, technologies, and socio-economic situation of the local community. Through this analyses, we expect to have a blue print on how tackling today's peat problem to adapt the future.

GOVERNMENT POLICIES TO RESPOND PEATLAND RELATED FIRES

Peatland cultivation is now frequently associated with land fires that result in tremendous environmental catastrophes and health problem. This was then responded by the Government through Ministry Letters 3rd and 5th November that new planting for both oil palm and forestry plantation on peatland is no longer allowed including those are in the approved concession. Main objective of those two letters is to prevent land fire from peatland. These two policies seem to localize fire problem only on cultivated peat with less attention to others. In fact, based on public information available on the website, (see https://fires.globalforestwatch.org), hot spots recorded from peatland along 2015 was found to be lower than 50%, in contrast more than 50% of hot spots were found in mineral soil. About 61% hot spots were found in outside concession. Therefore, more attention should be paid to mineral land.

Increasing concern on the increasing number of degraded peat and the urgency for restoration program for burned peat has triggered the Government, in January 2016, to establish Peat Restoration Agency with the aim to develop restoration program for more than two million burned peat land. In line with above policies, The Ministry of Environment and Forestry has also been pushed for the implementation of President Regulation No 71, which restrict ground water level (GWL) not more than 0.4 meter for cultivated peatland. Peat soil is determined as a broken peat when the GWL is found to be lower than 0.4 meters. Unfortunately, there is no scientific evidence has proved that peat with GWL below 0.4 meter is biologically, physically, or chemically broken. This regulation has called many debates among scientists, growers, and environmentalists regarding why this parameter used as an indicator of broken peat. There should be some prior baseline research to implement the regulation since it will bring some negative consequences on yield loss from suffering plantation with water level cannot be lower than 0.4 meter.

PEATLAND CULTIVATION IN INDONESIA: LEARNING FROM THE PAST, ADAPTING FOR THE FUTURE

Peat (or in Indonesia *Gambut*) was named after *Gambut* Sub-district, near Banjarmasin City of South Kalimantan. In the past, people (especially most of local people), always avoid using peat for settlement and agriculture for many reasons. The main reason is that peat is very acid and its productivity is very low. In the Dutch colonial period, the channel construction to develop the area around the peatland is mainly for improvement of transportation means instead of agriculture. Peatland use for agriculture is often considered as not feasible by the Dutch government. Pons and Driessen (1975) reported that Indonesia peatlands generally have a very low level suitability for agriculture.

However, different story was recorded for Banjarese and Buginese who started to utilize peatland for agriculture in Indonesia since 1910s when they migrated to the tidal zone peatland of Kalimantan and Sumatera. Banjar and Bugis communities implement certain method to manage peatland for agriculture in South and West Coasts of Kalimantan and east coast Sumatra starting from selecting land, making channels, managing water system, cultivating soil, planting, to harvesting, they all do traditionally in a *Handil* system. The *Handil* system is implemented by creating a main channel that is more or less almost perpendicular to the river. Learning from the local people experience, the Dutch government, according to Polak (1949) report, cleared peatlands for agricultural expansion in Lakbok Marsh, West Java. In Pulau Petak Delta, South Kalimantan cleared Sarapat, Tamban and Talaran *Anjirs* (Channel). In addition, the Dutch government at the beginning of the Republic of Indonesia independence has tried to practice the *polder* system (closed irrigation system), designed and implemented by Dr.

H.J. Schophuys in Sungai Utara Upstream, which then is known as the Polder Alabio. All things done have given very significant outomes on the increased agricultural production at the time.

Transmigration program which reclaimed peatland for crops cultivation in Sumatera and Kalimantan was the next era in peat cultivation. Then, with the background of the needs to supply food mainly rice that keeps increasing, in line with population growth on one hand and on the other hand the limited area available in Java, Indonesian government through P4S began to clear swamp land in 1969 to develop agriculture, particularly crop agriculture, which was associated with transmigration program. The number of transmigrant people placed in some locations during the period 1969/1970 – 1999/2000 were 1,150,902 (Tirtosudarmo 2004). However, since early 1980s, the private sectors are also being given the opportunity to clear and develop peatlands for plantation (such as coconut and oil palm plantation), and Industrial Plantation Forest (HTI).

The history of peat management for agriculture in Indonesia cannot be separated from the failure e of 1 million ha peatland project for agriculture in Central Kalimantan in 1996. This project was part of transmigration program developed by the Government under Suharto Rezime. Unfortunately, poor knowledge and understanding on tropical peatland has brought many negative consequences. There were not enough in depth study whereby inappropriate drainage canals were applied on shallow peat layers with underlying potential acid sulfate soil which results in the exposure of pyritic sediments. Today with the better understanding on tropical peatland and with better technology, the management peatland has improved. Canal systems with water gate and overflow based on topography information have successfully controlled water level and drain only surplus water. This particularly true for large concession of oil palm and pulp plantations in Riau which have been applying that technology.

Today, there are now about 14.9 million ha of peatland, 6.5 million ha of which have been altered for many purposes including agriculture. Actually, treating the peat marsh forests properly and correctly according to the peatlands capabilities/bearing capacity, will obtain proven better results. For example, in plantation development (mainly oil palm in some places in in Riau and Jambi, with proper management, the obtained results are satisfied (average production can reach > 22 t TBS ha^{-1}. During peatland management in the field, the primary channels are built with the proper size according to the needs, which are used to supply fresh water and to remove excessive water (drainage). Groundwater level is mapped (on the range ≥40 cm during rainy season until ≥80 cm during dry season) and the channels are continually controlled tightly by making floodgate and runoff construction; secondary (collection drain) and primary (main drain) channels that were built are only to control the peat water level in the field. Similarly, the provision of macro-micro nutrients according to the needs of oil palm growth must be done in proper procedures.

In peatland management, groundwater level is always controlled in order to avoid peat fire. However, the problem is then come from abandon peatland which can continue to cause fire if there is no program of peat fire protection. There are now about 3.5 million ha of abandon peat that needs to be managed to prevent land fire (Wahyunto *et al.*, 2014). Restoration by rewetting is quite tricky since during long dry season water is insufficient to wet the abandon peat. Immature peat of the abandon peatland will not be able to hold water since the capillarity is very poor and this make the abandon peat prone to fire.

SOCIO-ECONOMIC ASPECTS OF PEATLAND CULTIVATION

For provinces where peat is dominant such as Riau, Jambi, and South Sumatera, peatland plays a very important role in alleviating local farmers from poverty and at the same time brings economic benefit for larger community through multiplier effects. Rina dan Noorginayuwati (2013) identified that 90.6% of farmers on peatland (Kalimantan Tengah, Sulawesi Barat, and Riau) riley their live on agriculture. In Central Kalimantan, about 72% of local people living in this province, and farming on peatland is the main livelihood. Those facts indicate that peat for some people is a land that can produce food and money to survive. These lands help people from poverty and teach them to grow and develop culture. Oil palm is another example for local people to survive and to reach the so-called "welfare". Palm oil farmer will have significant benefit since this palm is the most important vegetable oil in the world. For people living on peat, this land is the key to help them to be in the same degree with people from developed country. Herman *et al.* 2009 reported that farmers planting oil palm on peat will still have a significant economic benefit although the capital cost is still higher compared with oil palm on mineral soil.

For provinces, where peat is dominant soil type, there is not much choice except planting cash crop on peatland. The main homework here is that how peat can be well managed to prevent unexpected environment problems such as fire. Updated technology in water management system or peat compaction to maintain soil humidity should be applied to keep the plantation away from fire.

CONCLUSION

For many years, peatland cultivation has provided a huge amount of experience for people from different education levels, background, and culture to learn that Indonesian peatland is unique and complex. This can not only be seen as a single soil type that should be preserved, but since a time ago there have been many social, cultural, and economic activities on it since a long time ago which should also be considered. The critical issue now is how to bridge among social, economic, and environment purpose to address sustainable development. Constructive perception, better knowledge and tranquil inputs based on scientific evidences are needed to be further analyzed to build up an appropriate strategy for better future of Indonesian peatland.

REFERENCES

1. Direktorat Jenderal Perlindungan Hutan dan Pengawetan Alam. 1983. Pengumpulan Pengolahan Analisis Data Masalah Kebakaran Hutan. Departemen Kehutanan Republik Indonesia. Jakarta
2. Herman, F. Agus,dan I. Las. 2009. Analisis finansial dan keuntungan yang hilang dari pengurangan emisi karbon dioksida pada perkebunan kelapa sawit. Jurnal Litbang Pertanian 28(4):127-133
3. Hooijer A, Page S, Canade; JG, Silvus M, Kwadijk J, Wosten H, Jauhinien J. 2010. Current and future CO2 emissions from drained peatlands in Southeast Asia. Biogeoscience 7: 1505-1514.
4. Page S, Rieley JO, Banks C. 2011. Global and regional importance of the tropical peatland carbon pool. Global Change Biol. 17:798-818
5. Page S, Wus R, Bank C. 2010. Past and present carbon accumulation and loss in South East Asian peatland. PAGES News. 18(1): 25-27
6. Page SE, Siegert F, Rieley JO, Boehm HV, Jaya A, Limin S. 2002. The amount of carbon released from peat and forest fires in Indonesia during 1997. *Nature* 420, 61-65 (7 November 2002) | doi:10.1038/nature01131
7. Rina dan Noorginayuwati. 2013. Sosial dan ekonomi petani di lahan gambut. Dalam Lahan Gambut: Pemanfaatan dan Pengembangannya untuk Pertanian. M. Noor, M. Alwi, Mukhlis, D. Nursyamsi, M. Thamrin (Eds). Kanisius. Yogyakarta

PEATLANDS IN HARMONY

PEATLANDS IN HARMONY

PEATLANDS IN HARMONY

Abstract No: A-062

BEST MANAGEMENT PRACTICES FOR SUSTAINABLE DEVELOPMENT OF OIL PALM PLANTING ON PEAT: TH PLANTATIONS BERHAD'S EXPERIENCE

Zainal Azwar Zainal Aminuddin[1], Radin Rosli Radin Suhardi[1], Abd Rashid Sahibjan.[2], Muhammad Pilus Zambri[1] and Khairul Ismadi Ismail[3*]

[1]TH Plantations Berhad, Kuala Lumpur, Malaysia
[2]TH Plantations Berhad, Sarawak Regional Office, Sarawak, Malaysia
[3]TH Plantations Berhad, Agronomy & Innovation Centre, Sarawak, Malaysia

**Corresponding author: ismadi@thplantations.com*

SUMMARY

Claims were made that oil palm development on peat is not sustainable due to the impact on the hydrological balance and emission of greenhouse gases (GHG) which inevitably led to global warming. Conversely, with proper management and maintenance or cultural practices implemented, the sustainability and economic viability of the oil palm planting can be ensured.

Keywords: *oil palm, peat, management practices, sustainable, development*

INTRODUCTION

Peatlands are not only valued for their ecological services (water quality and storage, biodiversity) but, historically, have met human needs for food, energy, construction material, livestock bedding and in arts and health. Continuing unregulated and unmanaged demand for new land for cultivation and construction, along with the ongoing degradation of drained peatlands, will lead to continuous depletion of peatlands and peat resources unless concerted action is taken. Peatlands are managed for many different purposes and drained peatlands are used mostly for agriculture and forestry (Joosten and Clarke, 2002) and also for peat extraction to provide growing media and energy. Peatlands are also 'used' or managed indirectly as a result of other landscape activities, for example, urbanization, mining, reservoir construction, mineral extraction and wind farms. Peatlands are valued for different reasons by a wide range of stakeholders (Joosten and Clarke, 2002).

CHARACTERISTIC AND CLASSIFICATION OF PEAT

Hectarage

Peat soil development will remain an important issue in the cultivation of oil palm in Malaysia and Indonesia. It is estimated that there are about half a million hectares of peatland in Sarawak developed for agricultural purposes and about 330,000 hectares are planted with oil palm. Of this about 43,000 hectares are owned by TH Plantations Berhad with approximately 75% of the land parcel is on deep peat which possess poor physical and chemical properties that requires improvement for successful cultivation of oil palm.

Depth, Horizon and Topography

It is important to determine the peat depth. Peat is considered shallow if it is less than 1.5 metres deep. The depth of peat is generally shallower near the coast and increases inwards, sometimes exceeding more than 20 m deep in Sarawak (Melling *et al.*, 2006).

Physico-Chemical Characteristics of Drained Peat

Volarovich and Churaev (1968) describe peat as a complex, heterogeneous, poly-dispersed system consisting of both true solutions of low and high molecular weight, hydrophobic sols and hydrophilic semi-colloids in a dynamic state of dispersion at equilibrium. The structure of the peat colloids is determined by the chemical composition of the compounds formed during the decomposition of vegetable matter, whereas the coarse-dispersed fraction is composed of plant remains in the form of insoluble and high co-polymers of cellular tissues. Peats can be divided into two categories:

a. High moor peat
   This peat type, comparable to most dome-shaped lowland tropical peats of ombrogenous oligotrophic nature, has a large hydrophilic humic material content (humic acids and hemicellulose). An increasing degree of decomposition results in an increase in hydrophobic components. This explains the stronger irreversible drying in sapric materials than in fibric materials.

b. Low moor peat
   This peat of eutrophic nature is uncommon in the tropics and appears to have a smaller content of hydrophilic materials. The colloid fraction mainly consists of humates of polyvalent metals forming compact coagulated aggregates.

CONSTRAINTS TO OIL PALM CULTIVATION ON DEEP PEAT

a. Low Nutrient Content
   i. Macronutrients – high K requirement
   ii. Micronutrients – Cu and Zn essential
b. Low Bulk Density
   i. Subsidence and shrinkage
   ii. Root exposure
   iii. Leaning / lodging of palm
   iv. Movement and access to palms difficult
c. High Watertable
   i. Needs to be controlled and managed
   ii. Regular desilting of drains
d. High Infrastructure Cost
   i. Drains and roads – expensive to construct / maintain
e. Water control structures (watergate, weirs, tidalgate)

NEW PLANTING FROM JUNGLE

Site Selection

It is important to assess the topography and the drainability of the site especially for planning, development and management purposes. To be successful in planting oil palm on peat based on present technology and experience, it is suggested to avoid certain peat areas such as those with salinity problem, which are difficult or problematic to manage. This will invariably increase the development cost, therefore, it is best not to develop such areas (Lim, 2006).

Perimeter Drain and Main Outlet Drains

To have systematic drainage system for draining out excess water from the field into main water course and to irrigate the field by bringing in water from the main water ways when necessary. Boundary drain is to demarcate the ownership of the property as well act as a security measure of the property. Prior to drain construction, lining should be done. The lining peg should be the centre of the drain. To ensure the right drain size and drain density. To remove all blockages during drain construction and those blockages which are not possible to be dug out should be cut and removed from the drain. To ensure all drains are inter-connected to each other. Drains are to be constructed on flat area.

Land Preparation

Once an area has been selected for oil palm planting, every effort must be made to prolong its economic life span. Peat should be considered as a precious soil resource that must be properly and sustainably managed because once it is destroyed, the damage is often irreversible.

Compaction of the Peat

Compaction has several advantages. Other than increasing the soil bulk density, it increases the soil mass per volume, thus reducing the rate of fertilizer leaching. It also increases nutrient supply (more nutrient per unit peat volume) and help to reduce early palm leaning due to better root anchorage. For effective compaction, it is very important to have a good destumping and also useful to first lower the water level in the field drains to about 90 cm. Avoid rainy seasons when carrying out compaction. The front bucket of the excavator can also be used for compaction of areas not reachable by the tracks. Compaction is done 12 months before initiation of harvesting works to help facilitate the field for mechanisation purposes.

NURSERY PRACTICES ON PEAT

One of the major constraints of raising oil palm seedlings in peat was the availability of suitable planting medium. With the scarcity of mineral soil, peat is often the preferred planting medium choice for polybag filling in every nursery established. From our experience, peat yellow incidences for oil palm seedlings raised in peat planting medium was due mainly to micronutrient deficiencies especially on Fe or iron. This was found to be effectively addressed with the additional application of ferrous sulphate (20% $FeSO_4 \cdot 7H_2O$) included in the nursery manuring regime.

PLANTING DENSITY AND PLANTING DEPTH

Water-table of 90 cm from the peat surface is required during planting. The seedlings are watered thoroughly before leaving the nursery. The root-pruned seedlings shall be lifted carefully from the ground to prevent breakage of the polyethylene (PE) bags, and transported to the designated points. Any seedlings found with damaged PE bags during transportation shall be rewrapped with plastic bag and tied to prevent breakage of the soil-bole. The seedlings should be placed in the inner planting hole of the hole-in-hole formation. The palms collar is to be at the same level with the bottom of the larger hole. The seedlings should be planted on the very same day as delivered to the field. Upon completion of planting, the palm should be in an upright position and firmly placed. Sufficient care must be taken to ensure that there is no breakage of root-bole during planting. It is important that close supervision led by an experienced executive or senior staff is provided.

PALM NUTRITION

Macronutrients and Micronutrients

Provision of essential elements required for normal growth and development of palm includes macronutrients such as nitrogen (N), phosphorus (P), potassium (K), and magnesium (Mg) and micronutrients consists of boron (B), copper (Cu), zinc (Zn). Nitrogen is the primary constituent of amino acids, proteins, enzymes and metabolic processes involved in the synthesis and transfer of energy and also part of the chlorophyll that is responsible for photosynthesis. It also increases leaf area and net assimilation rate and is taken up as NH_4^+ and NO_3^-. Phosphorous is also an essential element for photosynthesis specifically in the formation of oils, sugars, starches, etc. It also encourages blooming and root growth and transformation of solar energy into chemical energy. Potassium helps in building of proteins, photosynthesis, fruit quality and reduction of diseases and increases bunch weight but decreased oil to bunch ratio. Magnesium is a constituent of the chlorophyll in all green plants which converts light energy into biochemical energy during photosynthesis while activating many plant enzymes needed for plant growth. It increases the oil to bunch ratio (thicker mesocarp). Boron aids production of sugar and carbohydrate synthesis and is essential for seed and fruit development and also important for meristematic activity. Copper is necessary for reproductive growth. It aids in root metabolism and helps in the utilization of protein. Zinc is essential for the transformation of carbohydrates and regulates consumption of sugars. It is also a part of the enzyme systems which regulates plant growth.

Peat Acidity

The pH of organic soils is related to the presence of organic compounds, the exchangeable hydrogen and aluminium, iron sulphide and other oxidizable sulphur compounds. In contrast with mineral soils, the presence of organic acids largely determines the acidity, and the presence of mobile or hydrolysable aluminium is less important. The range of acidity in organic materials is very wide. In conditions where there has been infiltration of brackish water the pH can be as high as 7.8 as in the Maldives where peat has developed in the inner part of atolls which had strongly saline initial conditions (Hammond 1971). On the other hand, peat can be very strongly acidic where it contained pyritic materials which have been oxidized upon reclamation. The pH of such peats can reach values of less than 2. Tropical peats of ombrogenous and oligotrophic nature, which include most lowland tropical peats, are commonly acidic or extremely acidic with a pH range in water of 3 to 4.5. Variations within this range are caused either by admixtures of mineral soil which generally increase the pH, or by the specific location in the peat swamp. Surface layers of the dome-shaped peat deposits in the lowlands of Borneo have an average pH of 3.3 for the thickest peat whereas the shallow peat near the edge has an average pH of 4.3.

WATER MANAGEMENT

Water management is an integral part of oil palm cultivation which determines the degree of success of the crop. Water management is crucial in peat where subsidence and peat drying are solely dependent on water retention. Similarly water management in mineral soils would also require close attention.

Objective

a) To achieve and maintain optimum water table at 40 – 50 cm in the field.
b) To retain adequate moisture status in the soil.
c) To avoid irreversible drying and decelerate subsidence.
d) To ensure that water-gates and bunds remain steadfast even during adverse weather i.e. flooding.
e) To improve soil pH

Water management in peat requires the following course of action;

During wet seasons:

a) Main and subsidiary water-gates are to be opened to allow excess water to be drained out into the external water course.

b) Excess water in the main and collection drains must be drained out quickly but to retain at 50 cm from ground level.

c) Backflow of external water must be prevented from entering the estates.

During dry seasons:

a) Timely attention on managing the water-gates and weirs must be given before the onset of dry season to ensure the water level in the collection drain is retained at 40 cm from ground level.
b) In situation of severe water deficit, pumping in non-saline water (< 2.0 dS/m or mS/cm) during high tides may be required.

Optimal Field Water Table

The availability of soil water must be sufficient for good palm growth and high yield. During the development and six months of planting, water table in the field is to be lowered down to about 75 cm below soil surface. The average peat subsidence rate per year (cm yr^{-1}) is equivalent to 0.1 X depth of water table. Therefore, setting up water table at 75 cm resulting subsidence of 7.5 cm/ year. Due to the rapid initial peat subsidence, it is preferred to install temporary stop-offs using logs and soil bags in the initial year. As the palm grow older and to keep the feeder roots active, it is essential to maintain an optimal water table of 40-50 cm in the field. To consistently maintain the field water table at 40-50 cm, construction of stop-offs, weirs and water-gates are essential. Permanent water-gates at strategic locations are to be installed later when the subsidence rate is reduced.

SUBSIDENCE

Irreversible Drying Of Peat

Irreversible drying occurs after periods of intensive drying and is typical of many peat soils. Surface layers of organic materials in many reclaimed and drained peat swamps exhibit this behaviour. After exposure to the sun, the materials become rather like coffee grounds, and are very difficult to re-wet. This may cause severe drought stress in shallow rooting crops.

Water Holding Capacity

The phenomenon of moisture conductivity in peat is no less complex. Investigations into drying indicate that the first drying stage is characterized by the removal of free water and of water from large pores. On further drying, the forces of capillary contraction increase and weakly bound intracellular and immobilized water is squeezed out. The transfer and removal of moisture in microcapillaries brings about a change in the transport mechanism and a reduction in the drying rate.

INTEGRATED PEST MANAGEMENT ON PEAT

Tirathaba Bunch Moth

The caterpillars feed on the surface of maturing fruits causing pitting and scoring on the distal and in the form of a characteristic ring around the remains of the style. In younger bunches, they may bore into the developing fruit causing it either to fall prematurely or develop a hollow centre without a kernel. The larvae form tunnels of silk which mixed with their excreta create the frass that can be found all over the bunch during heavy infestation. The bio-insecticides Dipel ES containing the bacteria *Bacillus thuringiensis* v. *kurstaki.* was used to control *Tirathaba* both in Pusa and Beladin plantation complex. It is a safe product with no demonstrated toxicity for other non-target organism. It preserves other beneficial insects like predatory bugs, wasps, as well as parasitic flies in the plantation. The mode of action of Dipel Es is through stomach poisoning. The larvae will stop feeding and will die within several days after consuming lethal dosage of *Bacillus*.

Leaf Defoliators – Ipm

Bagworms and nettle caterpillars are opportunistic pests that can devastate large areas of oil palm if not detected and treated early. Early detection is achieved by carrying out regular inspection and counting of pest numbers in the field. Action is taken to control the pests by use of selective insecticide application. Indirect biocontrol is achieved by the cultivation of nectariferous plants like *Euphorbia heterophylla, Cassia cobanensis, Antigonon leptopus* and *Turnera subulata* in and around infested fields. These plants encourage populations of parasitoids and predators of bagworms and nettle caterpillars by providing them with nectar and shelter. The increased populations of natural enemies would in turn exert biocontrol on the pests.

Termite

For effective termite control, monthly census on all palms is required. Infested palms should be treated immediately using fipronil (5.0% a.i.) at 2.5 ml / 5 litres water/ palm (Lim and Bit, 2001). Delayed treatment will result in death of the infested palm, when the meristematic region is consumed by the termites.

SOCIAL AND CULTURAL ISSUES

Vendor Development Initiative ("Vdi")

The effort for vendor development has been in practise by THP since it ventured into plantations in the 70s. In line with the Malaysian Government's implementation of its Transformation Programmes and the New Economic Model, the VDI was formally implemented when THP ventured into Sarawak in realising the nation's agenda.

Joint Venture with Local Community

THP provides assistance in terms of financial and expertise, so as not to leave the community's land left undeveloped. This effort started off in Sarawak, whereby a joint venture initiative with the local community enabled the development of their Native Customary Rights (NCR) lands. This smart partnership allows the land owners to enjoy a sustainable future income and it also provides job and business opportunities to the local community.

CONCLUSIONS

Best management procedures that are vital for successful oil palm cultivation of peat specifically on land development, palm nutrition, water management and integrated pest management has led to the implementation of sustainable practices in relation of improving yield performances of oil palm planting in peat which varies with the topography and depends to a large extent on nutritional inputs and on water management. With proper monitoring and supervision, yields comparable to good mineral soil can be obtained and in this respect, overcoming constraints and challenges of oil palm cultivation on peat can be achieved by adhering to strict guidelines on sustainable agricultural practices for oil palm planting in peat.

ACKNOWLEDGEMENT

The authors wish to thank all those who have helped towards the completion of this paper and generously contributed much useful information.

REFERENCES

1. Chapman, D. (2002) Peatlands and environmental change. John Wiley and Sons Ltd.,Chichester, United Kingdom: 300 pp.
2. Lim, K.H. (2006) Challenges and key agro-management practices for sustainable cultivation of oil palm on deep peat. Proc. International Planters Conference, Organised by ISP, 26-28 June 2006, KL: 183-207.
3. Melling, L., Ambak K., Osman, L. and Ahmad H. (1999) Water management for the sustainable utilization of peat soils for agriculture. Paper presented at the International Conference & Workshop on Tropical Peat Swamps, 27 – 29 July 1999. Penang, Malaysia: Preprint.

Abstract No: A-085

CHINA: THE NEXT HUGE PEAT AND GROWING MEDIA MARKET IN THE WORLD

Meng Xianmin[1, 2, 3]

[1]*China National Committee, International Peatland Society, China*
[2]*Peat Industry Association Branch, China Humic Acid Industry Association, China*
[3]*Institute for Peat and Mire Research, Northeast Normal University, China*

**Corresponding author: mengxm3711@163.com*

SUMMARY

The demand for peat for different uses in China is estimated according to the crop area and peat need per ha. The data show that China is one of biggest new potential markets for peat in the world. The total demand of growing media for growing seedlings in China is about 49.51 million cubic meters per year. The total demand for growing media for soilless cultivation including vertical greening, home gardening, roof garden media and growing plants on balconies is about 20.25 million cubic meters per year. The total demand for peat as a soil improver for degenerated greenhouse soils is about 110 million cubic meters each year. The total demand of peat for functional fertilizer is about 72.4 million cubic meters per year. The total estimated peat demand in China is about 250 million cubic meters for all possible applications. Although China is rich in peat resources with a total deposit of 12.4 billion cubic meters, 99% of the total is eutrophic peat, predominantly sedge and reed peat and only 1% oligotrophic peat. In order to meet the estimated demand it will be essential to import *Sphagnum*-based peat. In 2014 more than 1 million cubic meters of *Sphagnum* peat were imported; that equals the annual amount of peat being extracted in China. The total amount of imported peat will reach 10-20 million cubic meters per year within the next 5-10 years. In spite of importing peat and coconut coir, new technologies and modern machinery are needed. This would include the import of sophisticated growing media manufacture technology, manufacture lines and packaging equipment, growing media additives like wetting agents, different types of fertilizers and various devices and equipment for soilless cultivation. Furthermore, in future Chinese manufacturers of growing media will need to certify their products as responsibly sourced and manufactured. These objectives are a huge opportunity y for foreign companies to get involved in setting up a modern Chinese growing media industry. The strategy of the Chinese peat industry is to foster *the* ability of sustainable development, to use *two* peat resources- domestic as well as imported peat, to depend on *three* means, being technology, market and information, to enhance the production of *four* peat product groups, namely growing media, peat-based soil improvers, functional fertilizer and peat-based medical products and treatments and – last but not least – obtain support via *five* essential tools innovation, machinery, peat and growing media standards, quality management and industry management. The main aim of the Chinese peat industry is to reach the production and quality level of western countries in the next 5-10 years.

***Keywords**: peat, growing media, Chinese market, allocation of peat resources, China*

INTRODUCTION

The peat industry of China is emerging and turning a highway 20 years after starting. Together imported *Sphagnum* peat and domestic fen peat have reached a total production of 2 million cubic meters in 2014. Peat use in China is welcomed due to its characteristics of being clean and risk-free in use. The amounts of peat per area of application vary significantly depending on crop types and sown area. Sometimes, governmental politics and public awareness deeply affect the peat market in China. As the economic transition and green development in China are going ahead, peat use in China will receive more and more attention. But although China is rich in eutrophic peat, it unfortunately lacks *Sphagnum* peat which is much more favorable for horticultural applications. Therefore, information on the demand for peat in China in the next 5-10 years and what kind of peat products are needed is very important for the Chinese government to develop a peat industry strategy and for foreign peat companies to expand their peat market in China.

METHODS

All data was collected from the China National Statistical Year book 2014, China Agricultural Statistical Yearbook 2014, the development plan of China watermelon and sweet melon 2014-2020 and the China flower industry yearbook. All data of peat application rates in each unit is based on the averages of different regions. All data regarding the future of the industry comes from the document of the State Council and different ministries.

RESULTS

Demand for Growing Media for the Seedling Industry

In China most growing media are used in seedling nurseries. The most important seedling crops are vegetables (cucumber, tomato, eggplant and pepper), water melon, sweet melon, tobacco, tree, rice and floricultural crops. Amongst these crops, the largest area is used for growing rice seedlings. The application of growing media in rice seedling nurseries is emergent and growth rates are high. Second to rice cultivation is vegetable growing, being a traditional industry with high demands. Seedling nurseries that grow water melon and sweet melon occupy a very large area because both melons are main fruit crops in northern China. In general, the amount of growing media used in seedling nurseries accounts for 95% of the total growing media usage. However, the future demand for professional growing media takes account for a total of 45.91 million cubic meters – the current amount used is 3.50-4.50 million cubic meters. The enormous data gap implies a huge market potential for growing media.

Table 1: Demand of growing media for nursing industry

Types	Area (10^3ha)	Amount (m^3/ha)	Demand(10^3m^3)
Amenities vegetable	2,660	3.8	10,108
Water melon	1,801.5	0.58	1,044.87
Sweet melon	4,100.4	2.4	9,840.96
Tobacco	1,225	0.68	833
Trees	3,850	0.08	308
Rice	30,310	1.5	22,733
Flowers	1,227.1	1.7	1,043
Total			45,910

Greenhouse growing is a main target market for growing media in the seedling industry. The growth trend of greenhouse area presents the dynamic process of demand increase of professional growing media in China. The area of greenhouses was 254.1 thousand ha in 2008, the figure increased up to 696.5 thousand ha in 2014. The demand for growing media in 2008 was 965.6 thousand cubic meter sand 2.64 million cubic meters in 2014, respectively.

The area change of greenhouse locations in geographical terms shows different trends in Northern China, Northeast China, Eastern China, Center China and Northwest China. Northern China, Northeast China and Northern China not only are great in greenhouse area, but also area increase is fast; these three regions represent the main market of growing media for the seedling industry. As Northwest China poses arid, sandy, salinity land, the demand for growing media in that region will increase rapidly as the application of new technologies and financial input will increase.

The Demand for Growing Media for Soilless Culture

Soilless culture is very new industry in China and most soilless cultivation techniques are hydroponics and mineral wool cultures. Vegetable crops in growing media have continued to advance during the last five years. Most growing media used in soilless culture are so called bio-growing media which are made of compost with crop residue. Seldom professional peat-based growing media can be found in soilless culture because the price of imported *Sphagnum* peat is too high and domestic fen peat does not have the needed characteristics.

The total area of soilless culture is not more than 10,000 ha in China at present. Because China is a country with a huge population and land shortage, soilless culture should be extended quickly in near future because of its superiority of land saving, application of new technology and high productivity. If the total area of soilless culture was the same as in Europe, the consumption of growing media in soilless culture would reach 14.25 million cubic meters a year.

Chinese families which live in cities have no real home garden but people grow flowers and green plants indoors. As the quality of living and public awareness of food safety increase, more and more peoples start to home-grow their own vegetables on balconies and on roofs of buildings. Now there are 430 million families living in Chinese cities. It is estimated that in future these families will consume 5 million cubic meters of growing media a year.

The Demand for Peat-Based Soil Improvers

Degradation, fertilization failures and pollution of agricultural soils are serious problems in China. Food safety is highly challenged. The restoration of degraded and polluted soil is urgent and demands for of soil improvement is massive. Attention must be paid to greenhouse soils because relinquishment of crop rotation will cause serious soil compaction, an unbalanced soil nutrient status, soil acidification, soil salinization and accumulation of soil-borne pathogens, pests and weeds. Greenhouses are the main production sites of vegetable and fruits for the Chinese urban population and can make 40-60 thousand Chinese Yuan per ha and year. That is why greenhouse soils are seen as the target market for peat–based soil improvers, although peat is also very efficient in improving arid, saline and sandy soils.

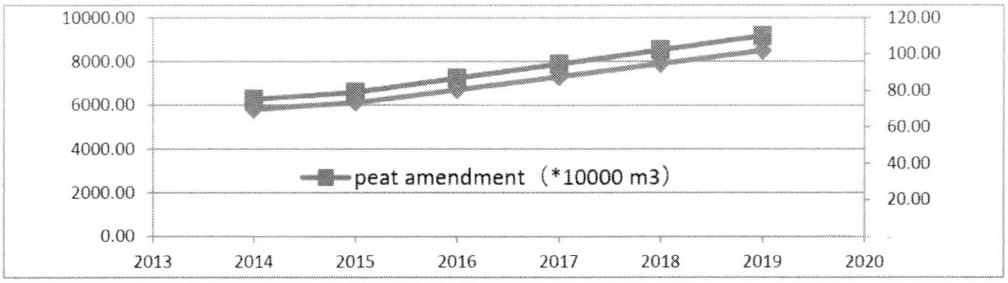

Figure 1: The growth of greenhouse area and demand of soil amendment

In China in 2014 greenhouses covered a total area of 700 thousand ha. By 2019 the total area will be 1.04 million ha. . The amount of soil improvers will increase from 62.6 million cubic meters to 91.6 million cubic meters. Even though compost and organic fertilizer can be used for greenhouse soil improvement, peat-based soil improvers will dominate the market due to their advantageous physical, chemical and biological properties.

Demand for Functional Fertilizer for Peat

Peat-based fertilizers not only supply nutrients but are also effective in dry soil conditions, as diluents of stressed soils and can balance the nutritional status of soils. Peat-based fertilizers can be manufactured as organic-inorganic complex fertilizers, liquid fertilizers, suspension fertilizers and microbiological fertilizers. The total peat demand for the manufacture of peat-based fertilizer is estimated to be about 72.4 million cubic meters.

Table 2: Peat Demand for the manufacture of peat-based fertilizer

Product	Organic fertilizer	Liquid fertilizer	Suspension fertilizer	Microbiological fertilizer
Composition	Peat powder + manure	Fulve acid	Peat powder + inorganic fertilizer	Peat powder + microbial agents
Form	Solid powder	liquid	Suspension slurry	Solid powder
Process	Manure is absorbed by peat then fermented, dried and packaged	Fulve acid is extracted then mixed with macro-, meso-, micro nutrients	Ultrafine grinding of peat, then mixed with fertilizer.	After grinding then spread and absorb micro-agents
Price ¥/ton	600-1,000	30,000-50,000	600-1,000	1,000
Application	Cultivation of organic vegetable and fruit	Vegetables, fruits and grain	Greenhouse	Greenhouse and field farmland
Effect	Increased output, improved quality	Increased output, Improved quality, improved resilience	Increased output, Improved quality, Improved resilience	Improved soil conditions , Better plant growth, reduced disease risk
Market demand	20,00 million tons	1,000 tons	1.20 million tons	10million tons
Peat demand	40.00 million cubic meter	25 thousand cubic meters	2.40 million cubic meters	30million cubic meters

Total Demand for Peat in China

The estimated potential total demand for peat in China is 253.7 million cubic meters per year. The output value of the peat industry is estimated to be about ¥132.6 billion.

Table 3: The total potential demand of peat resource in China

Peat use	Demand (million m^3)	Price (¥/m^3)	Output value (Billion ¥)
Growing media for seedling	45.91	500	22.95
Growing media for soilless culture	14.25	600	8.5
Home garden	5.00	800	4.0
Vertical greening	1.00	600	0.6
Soil amendment	110.00	500	55.0
Functional fertilizer	72.40	500	36.2
Medicine	1.00	38,000	3.8
Energy	5.04	300	1.5
Total	253.70	Total	132.6

DISCUSSION

China's economy is shifting from quantity to quality growth, the government's strategic policy is: innovation, green, open, sharing and coordination. Therefore China ushered in a new era for the peat industry which is a rare and excellent opportunity for all involved. The more applications of peat, the faster peat demand growth of China will be. The overall eat demand is expected to climb up to 10-20 million cubic meters with a growth rate of 20% in the next five years

With this scale of expansion of peat use, peat processing technology and equipment, the demand for peat will grow rapidly. Especially the manufacture technology and processing equipment for growing media, soil improvers, peat-based fertilizers and, application techniques for all peat-based products will receive worldwide attention.

CONCLUSION

The next 10 years will be a rapid growing era of the peat industry in China. This does not only present development opportunities within the Chinese peat industry, but also for the worldwide peat industry. China will openly receive the required quality resources from throughout the world ensuring lowest custom tax and powerful promotion of peat applications. Any entrance of peat resources and interested companies is welcome. As China lacks indigenous resources of woody peat with high contents of humic acids and weakly decomposed *Sphagnum* peat for horticultural applications, imports from

Europe, America and Russia will be the resource strategy that China will engage in. Imported peat will be the predominant constituent of peat products in China, supplemented by domestic fen peat. The main target of the Chinese peat industry is modernization, standardization and value-added peat processing.

ACKNOWLEDGEMENTS AND REFERENCES

1. Bureau of People's Republic of China, China Statistical Yearbook 2014, China Statistics Press.
2. Ministry of Agriculture, Accelerate the implementation of innovation-driven development strategy and reform of agricultural technology system. Document of Agriculture Ministry, No.2015(3)
3. State Council, Accelerating the transformation of agricultural development, Document of State Council,No.2015(59)
4. Ministry of Agriculture, Greenhouse Vegetable Key regional development planning, Document of Agriculture ministry No. 2015(4)
5. Ministry of Agriculture, National Watermelon Industry Development Plan (2015-2020), Document of Agriculture ministry No.2015(5)
6. State Council: "Twelve Five" national strategic of emerging industry development planning, Document of State Council No.2015(5)

Abstract No: A-266

DEGRADED PEATLANDS IN SUMATRA, INDONESIA: HOW LAND RIGHTS INFLUENCE THE ABANDONMENT AND BURNING OF LAND

Kosuke Mizuno

Center for Southeast Asian Studies, Kyoto University

**Corresponding author: spfyn587@yahoo.co.jp*

Peatlands in Sumatra, Indonesia are one of Southeast Asia's last resource frontiers and they are currently being exploited on a large scale, leading to massive fires and carbon emissions. Despite the global implications of this problem, few studies have investigated the social aspects of peatland degradation, limiting our understanding of potential sustainable management regimes for peatland resources. This study focuses on the factors causing land abandonment and fire, key precursors to peatland degradation. Detailed household questionnaires in a village in Riau province investigated village formation and land history, paying particular attention to how land is acquired and the land titling process. Seventy one (71) households that owned 823.3 ha land were surveyed in detail. Of this land, 646.7 ha were peatlands. The reasons for land abandonment were analysed qualitatively and quantitatively. The village surveyed used to be covered by peat swamp forest and started to be occupied by the present Malay inhabitants or their parents in the 1930s. The village landscape has changed drastically since the 1990s when industrial tree plantations started operation in the surveyed area. Currently there are many degraded peatlands in the surveyed village that have been burned and abandoned. However the lands acquired prior to 1984 have not been abandoned, although many of them have experienced fire. The research found that lands with customary land rights such as inheritance and clearing, and also land certified with customary land rights documents have not been abandoned. However, peatland forests that were logged and distributed among villagers, especially after 1995, have since been seriously burned and abandoned. Those lands tend to belong to state forest areas and therefore people tend not to have any documents certifying land rights.

Keywords: *peatland, peatland degradation, land rights, Sumatra, government designated state forests*

Abstract No: A-416

DEVELOPING SUSTAINABLE PRACTICES TO MITIGATE IMPACTS OF CLIMATE CHANGE ON NATURAL AND MANAGED TROPICAL PEATLANDS

Shailendra Mishra[1, 2, 3], Yung Pui Yi[3], Umashankar Shivshankar[1, 3], Daniela Moses[3], Aswandi Idris[4], Stephan Schuster[3] and Sanjay Swarup[1, 2, 3*]

[1]*Metabolites Biology Laboratory, Department of Biological Sciences, National University of Singapore (NUS), Singapore*
[2] *NUS Environmental Research Institute, Singapore*
[3]*Singapore Centre on Environmental Life Sciences Engineering (SCELSE), Nanyang Technological University, Singapore*
[4]*Faculty of Agriculture, University of Jambi, Jambi, Indonesia*

**Corresponding author: sanjay@nus.edu.sg*

SUMMARY

Southeast Asian peatlands are undergoing degradation through drainage and deforestation, accompanied by forest fires. This is occurring at unprecedented rates for agriculture and human settlement purposes. Exposure of carbon-rich peat to air has resulted in enhanced microbial-mediated peat oxidation emitting high levels of potent greenhouse gases (GHGs). Peat oxidation results in land subsidence thus increasing the risk of flooding that can affect the livelihoods of millions of people. The overall aim of this study was to provide an in-depth understanding of how land-use change and peat management practices affect the microbial ecology and physicochemical processes leading to peat oxidation and release of GHGs. We have used molecular marker–based approaches (microbial and metabolic profiles) that revealed the profiles were most influenced by variations in water table and land-use patterns, followed by age of drainage and peat thickness in that order. Plantations with mixed cropping had the least subsidence rates, where land subsidence is a proxy for peat loss by oxidation. We aimed to determine the functional potential of peat microbiome that is associated with peat oxidation from contiguous land-use types: degraded forest, degraded land and oil palm plantation sites. Metagenomic analysis revealed that genes belonging to aromatic compound biosynthesis and degradations were mostly associated with degraded forest and degraded land. *Actinobacteria* and *Firmicutes* were among the most abundant taxonomic groups, demonstrating their linkages in oxidation of tropical peatlands. The overall findings of this study will be useful in peatland management by providing a basis to focus early efforts on hydrological interventions and improving sustainability of oil palm plantations by adopting mixed cropping practices.

Keywords: *Greenhouse gas emissions, Mixed cropping practices, Metagenomics, Peat oxidation, Peat subsidence*

INTRODUCTION

Peatlands are formed by the accumulation of partially decayed vegetation matter over millennial timescales in low-lying areas that are frequently waterlogged due to heavy rainfall or periodic inundation. Peatlands are a highly vulnerable natural resource that cover 50–70% of global wetlands (Gillespie, 2006) and sequester one-third of the world's soil carbon (Freeman *et al.*, 2012). In Southeast Asia, peatlands cover an area of nearly 25 Mha and store approximately 69 Gt of carbon, which is 77% of all the tropical peatland carbon pool (88.6 Gt), of which 65% (57.4 Gt of carbon) is in Indonesia itself, distributed within 23.4 million ha of peatland (Page *et al.*, 2011). Carbon density is relatively high in tropical peatlands compared to temperate or boreal peatlands; this is largely a consequence of deeper peat layers in the former, with peat thickness up to 20m recorded (Page *et al.*, 2002).

Southeast Asian peatlands are undergoing drainage and deforestation, including forest fires at unprecedented rates, making way for commercial plantations of oil palm and Acacia trees. These industrial-scale plantations on deforested, drained and burnt degraded peatland covered over 3.1 million hectares (approximately 20%) of the peatlands of Peninsular Malaysia, Sumatra and Borneo in 2010, an area expected to grow to 6.2 million hectares by 2020. Palm oil is the world's most important vegetable oil in terms of production quantity (USDA – FAS, 2010). In 2009 global palm-oil production amounted to 43.4 million tonnes, of which 47% was produced in Indonesia (USDA – FAS, 2010). The rapid expansion of oil-palm agriculture in Southeast Asia and other tropical regions is testament to an almost insatiable global demand for palm oil and the consequent financial lure to ramp up production. Oil palm has contributed greatly to regional, national, and local economies (Zen *et al.*, 2005). However, this intensive agriculture has impacts on its sustainability mainly due to following reasons: (i) Peatlands under agriculture are undergoing oxidation due to microbial oxidation, leading to physical peat loss, also called subsidence (Mishra *et al.*, 2014); (ii) This peat loss would increase the flooding risk and the synthetic chemical load in the form of fertilizers would also be increased due to a loss of nutrients from the peat; (iii) Peat oxidation will also result in increased GHG emissions, which has resulted in Indonesia becoming one of the major global producers of GHGs.

In the tropics, we have a relatively poor understanding of the relationship of microbial diversity and factors influencing community structure for intact peatlands, as well as peatlands under land-use change. Given both the ecological and economic importance of these peatlands, it is useful to understand the differences among the various land-use patterns in degraded tropical peatland with respect to microbial ecology. Our approach is based on the ability of molecular profiling to capture shifts in community structure and metabolic profiling to reflect the functional outcome of metabolic activities of microbes, plant roots and their exudates, respectively. Using these two microbial profiling approaches, we report the effects of water table depth and oxygen availability, land-use patterns, age of drainage and peat thickness on bacterial diversity in degraded peatlands of Indonesia. Further to this, we have used next-generation sequencing approaches to determine the functional potential of the peat microbiome associated with peat oxidation.

MATERIALS AND METHODS

Site description and sampling

The study area is located in peatlands of the eastern part of Jambi province, Sumatra, Indonesia. The coordinates of sampling locations distributed across two broad areas, referred to as Site A and Site B, were 103°53′52.58′′ E, 1°43′12.47′′ S and 103°49′32.23′′ E, 1°40′58.24′′ S, respectively (described in Mishra et al., 2014). In order to monitor the hydrological parameters, both rainfall and water table depths were measured periodically using rain gauges at strategic locations and dipwells along a transect. At each sampling location, a $1 m^3$ pit was dug. Three equidistant pits were used for sampling in each transect. We collected samples from above and below the water table.

Bacterial community structure (terminal restriction fragment length polymorphism (T-RFLP) analysis)

Bulk peat gDNA was extracted using a ZR Soil Microbe DNA MidiPrep™ extraction kit (Zymo Research Corporation, Irvine, USA) based on the manufacturer's protocol, with minor modifications. TRFLP analysis was performed based on the protocol described in Mishra *et al.*, (2014).

Chemical analysis

The bioavailable extract for microorganisms from peat was used for the analysis of anions, cations and dissolved organic carbon (DOC) based on the protocol described in Mishra *et al.*, (2014). Peat water samples were run through a Solid Phase Extraction cartridge using the protocol described in Mishra *et al.*, (2014).

Data analysis

To analyze the variation in bacterial community structure as well as differences in metabolic functions due to the influence of the analyzed parameters (namely, water table, land-use patterns, age of drainage and peat thickness), multivariate statistical techniques (PRIMER 6, PRIMER-E, Ltd., Plymouth, United Kingdom) were used to calculate distance matrices using Bray–Curtis similarity indices and one-way ANOSIM (Analysis of Similarity) coefficients, following the steps mentioned in Mishra *et al.*, (2014). Similarly, to analyze the influences of geochemical traits on the bacterial community structure, Canonical Correspondence Analysis (CCA) was performed using Canoco (version 4.5 for Windows, PRI Wageningen, the Netherlands).

Metagenome 454 sequencing and data processing

Whole-community metagenomic DNA was extracted as described above from above water table level of samples from three land-use types: (i) degraded forest; (ii) degraded land; (iii) oil palm plantations. The sequencing was performed on a Genome Sequencer (GS) XLR70+ FLX system (Roche Applied Science, Mannheim, Germany) using Titanium chemistry based on methods described earlier (Poinar *et al.*, 2006; Allentoft *et al.*, 2009). The paired read sequences were imported and the paired-end protocol of MEGAN5 was used (Huson *et al.*, 2011) to obtain taxonomic profiles of the three land-use patterns. Annotated taxonomic assignments were linked to functional potential using SEED and KEGG databases.

RESULTS

Peat microbiome and functional potential in different land-use types do not differ qualitatively

Metagenome sequence abundance based annotation indicated that the majority (77 – 81%) of the sequences belonged to bacteria (Table 1). Data for the microbiome from the degraded forest is only shown here. Within microbial communities, *Proteobacteria* was the abundant phyla, followed by *Actinobacteria* and *Firmicutes* (Figure 1: Right panel). *Actinobacteria* was found to be higher (21% of total microbial communities) in abundance in the degraded forest compared to oil palm and degraded land (18% and 15%, respectively). The functional potential based on SEED annotations revealed a higher diverse set of functional categories as 5.756, 5.764 and 5.751, respectively, for degraded forest, oil palm plantations and degraded land (data not shown). Based on associations of different functional categories and geochemical characteristics with different land-use types, it was evident that the electron transfer reactions were mostly associated with oil palm plantations. The genes belonging to aromatic compound biosynthesis and degradations were mostly associated with degraded forest and degraded land. On the other hand, Archaeal-ribosomes/RNA metabolism categories were mostly associated with degraded land.

Table 1: General information for peat microbial metagenome Bp: means base pairs; % non-ACGT = Percentage of bp that are non- ACGT; Transl. reads = Translated reads (in silico); aa = amino acids

	Degraded Forest	Oil palm Plantations	Degraded Land
Reads	1,070,200	1,419,551	996,081
Megabyte (Mb)	425.8 Mb	641.2 Mb	402.3 Mb
Longest assembled contigs	10392 bp	5648 bp	25547 bp
Average read length (bp)	397.9	451.7	403.9
Average GC%	61.6%	61.2%	60.7%
% non-ACGT	0.0175%	0.0162%	0.0249%
% distribution at Kingdom level			
Bacteria	81.1	81.4	76.9
Archaea	10.1	9.6	11.8
Eukaryota	5.0	5.8	7.5
Viruses	0.5	0.5	0.6
Unclassified sequences	0.5	0.4	0.5
Sequences unassigned in MEGAN	2.7	2.2	2.7

Relationship of peat oxidation with land-use pattern

Peat samples from mixed crop plantations, which have a more diverse plant cover than monoculture oil palm plantations, contain more DOC, have a more diverse metabolic profile, support a more diverse microbial community (both oxic and anoxic zone) and importantly experience a lower rate of peat subsidence; a proxy for oxidation-led peat loss (Figure 1: Left panel). However, the peat oxidation rates under these two land-use patterns followed a reverse trend, with higher rates in oil palm sites when compared to sites with mixed crop plantations (Mishra *et al.*, 2014).

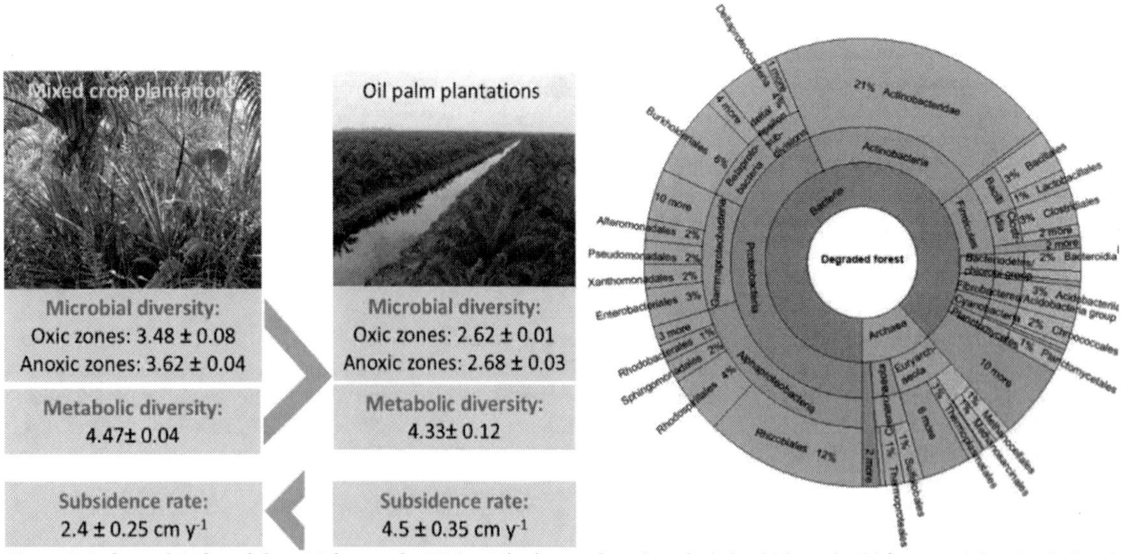

Figure 1: Left panel (*Adapted from Mishra et al., 2014*) - Mixed crop plantations depicting higher microbial taxa and functional diversity compared to monoculture (oil palm), based on Shannon Diversity Index. Right panel- Representative figure of Peat microbiome from land-use type:

DISCUSSION

Bacterial and metabolic markers that represent the complex nature of bacterial communities and metabolic processes of diverse biota, respectively, provided the resolving power to distinguish different habitats. This resolution ranged from the centimeter scale in depth measurements to the kilometer scale, where sites were distributed within the 48 km^2 of the study area. Our findings show that microbial profiles from peatland sites are most influenced by variations in water table and land-use patterns. The ability of microbial markers to distinguish the low- and high- water table sites shows their robustness in capturing differences in community structures despite the differences in the range of fluctuations in water level at these sites. Hence, microbial profiling presents a practical approach to monitor peat responses to both rapid short-term and long-term hydrological changes.

Oil palm plantation monocultures supported the least diverse bacterial communities and had the lowest levels of DOC. On the other hand, mixed crop plantations consisting of up to five plant species only, supported the most diverse bacterial communities and had the highest levels of DOC. In the tropical peatlands of Kalimantan, land conversion from secondary forest to paddy fields (monoculture plantations) led to a decrease in carbon content, together with a decrease in microbial abundance (Hadi *et al.*, 2001), which is consistent with our findings. Carbon levels increased when paddy–soybean rotation cropping was followed by a further decrease in microbial abundance. This possibly underlines the importance of adopting simultaneously mixed plantations rather than sequential crop rotations, as evident in our study. Low bacterial diversity in oil palm plantations, as seen in our study, can be sensitive to environmental pressures, thereby leading to a reduction in the productive period of plantations. These findings provide a good basis to adopt microbial ecology principles to encourage mixed crop planting in the existing plantations, in order to increase their microbial diversity, especially of beneficial microbes, which can lead to sustainable use of these plantations.

The deep sequencing-based approach reveals a more accurate prediction of microbial community abundance and their functional potential. In temperate peatlands, the carbon degradation is reported to be linked with the abundance of certain taxa, such as *Actinobacteria,* among others (Pankratov *et al.*, 2006; Mackelprang *et al.*, 2011; Tveit *et al.*, 2013; Tveit *et al.*, 2014). In the *Sphagnum* peat bogs of Russia, *Actinobacteria* has also been reported to play an important role in aerobic cellulose degradation (Pankratov *et al.*, 2006). A combined metagenomic and metatranscriptomic study on arctic permafrost peatlands (Tveit *et al.*, 2013 and 2014) revealed that *Actinobacteria* seemed to be particularly important, having a metabolic potential for carrying out several of the key steps in soil organic carbon degradation. In tropical peats, as reported in this study, similar abundance of these taxa was found. *Actinobacteria* and *Firmicutes* were the most abundant taxa after *Proteobacteria* in the metagenome data reported here, suggesting its potential role in the carbon degradation of tropical peat. This observation is consistent with the findings from marker-based approach (Mishra *et al.*, 2014), where *Actinobacteria* and *Firmicutes*, were among the predicated abundant species.

CONCLUSION

We conclude that mixed crop plantations, which have a more diverse plant cover than monoculture oil palm plantations contain more DOC, have a high diverse metabolic profile, support a more diverse microbial community and, most importantly, experience a lower rate of peat subsidence; a proxy for oxidation-led peat loss. *Actinobacteria* and *Firmicutes* were among the most abundant taxonomic groups, demonstrating their linkages in oxidation of tropical peat. These findings provide a good basis to adopt microbial ecology principles to encourage mixed crop planting in the existing plantations, in order to increase their microbial diversity, which can lead to sustainable use of these plantations.

ACKNOWLEDGEMENTS

We thank NUS Environmental Research Institute (NERI), Department of Biological Sciences, NUS, and Singapore–Delft Water Alliance (SDWA) for their funding and infrastructure support. We thank Choon Nam Ong for his insightful comments and kind support throughout the program. Lastly, we thank Sugino, research staff from University of Jambi, for his assistance during the field work. The research presented in this work was supported by funding from the National Research Foundation and the Economic Development Board (SPORE, COY-15-EWI-RCFSA/N197-1), NERI (WBS: R-706-000-008-646) and SDWA (R264-001-011-490).

REFERENCES

1. Allentoft, M., Schuster, S., Holdaway, R., Hale, M., McLay, E., Oskam, C., Gilbert, M. T., Spencer, P., Willerslev, E. and Bunce, M.: Identification of microsatellites from an extinct moa species using high-throughput (454) sequence data, *BioTechniques,* 46(3), 195–200, 2009.

2. Gillespie A.: Climate Change, Ozone depletion and Air pollution: Legal Commentaries within the context of Science and Policy, Book publisher: Leiden [u.a.] Nijhoff, p 41, 2006.
3. Freeman, C., Fenner, N., and Shirsat, A. H.: Peatland geoengineering: an alternative approach to terrestrial carbon sequestration, *Philosophical Transactions of the Royal Society A*, 370, 4404–4421, 2012.
4. Hadi, A., Haridi, M., Inubushi, K., Purnomo, E., Razie, F., and Tsuruta, H.: Effects of land-use change in tropical peat soil on the microbial population and emission of greenhouse gases, *Microbes and Environments*, 16, 79–86, 2001.
5. Huson, D. H., Mitra, S., Ruscheweyh, H.-J., Weber, N. and Schuster, S. C.: Integrative analysis of environmental sequences using MEGAN4, *Genome Research*, 21(9), 1552–1560, 2011.
6. Mackelprang, R., Waldrop, M. P., DeAngelis, K. M., David, M. M., Chavarria, K. L., Blazewicz, S. J., Rubin, E. M. and Jansson, J. K.: Metagenomic analysis of a permafrost microbial community reveals a rapid response to thaw, *Nature*, 480(7377), 368–371, 2011.
7. Mishra, S., Lee, W. A., Hooijer, A., Reuben, S., Sudiana, I. M., Idris, A., and Swarup, S: Microbial and metabolic profiling reveal strong influence of water table and land-use patterns on classification of degraded tropical peatlands, *Biogeosciences*, 11, 1727-1741, 2014.
8. Page, S. E., Rieley, J. O., and Banks, C. J.: Global and regional importance of the tropical peatland carbon pool, *Global Change Biology*, 17, 798–818, 2011.
9. Page, S. E., Siegert, F., Rieley, J. O., Boehm, H. D. V., Jaya, A., and Limin, S.: The amount of carbon released from peat and forest fires in Indonesia during 1997, *Nature*, 420, 61–65, 2002.
10. Pankratov, T. A., Dedysh, S. N. and Zavarzin, G. A.: The leading role of actinobacteria in aerobic cellulose degradation in Sphagnum peat bogs, *Doklady Biological Sciences*, 410(1), 428–430, 2006.
11. Poinar, H. N.: Metagenomics to Paleogenomics: Large-Scale Sequencing of Mammoth DNA, *Science*, 311(5759), 392–394, 2006.
12. Tveit, A. T., Urich, T. and Svenning, M. M.: Metatranscriptomic Analysis of Arctic Peat Soil Microbiota, *Applied and Environmental Microbiology*, 80(18), 5761–5772, 2014.
13. Tveit, A., Schwacke, R., Svenning, M. M., and Urich, T.: Organic carbon transformations in high-Arctic peat soils: key functions and microorganisms, *International Society for Microbial Ecology (ISME) Journal*, 7, 299–311, 2013.
14. USDA-FAS Oilseeds: World Markets and Trade (US Department of Agriculture– Foreign Agricultural Service, Washington, DC), *Circular Series FOP* 3-10, 2010.
15. Zen, Z., Barlow, C., and Gondowarsito, R.: Oil Palm in Indonesian Socioeconomic Improvement. A Review of Options. Working Paper. (*Australian National University, Canberra, Australia*), 2005.

Abstract No: A-288

EDDY COVARIANCE MEASUREMENT OF METHANE FLUX ABOVE A PRIMARY TROPICAL PEAT SWAMP FOREST IN SARAWAK, MALAYSIA

Wong Guan Xhuan[1, 3*], Ryuichi Hirata[2], Takashi Hirano[1], Edward B. Aeries[3], Kevin K. Musin[3], Joseph W. Waili[3], Frankie Kiew[1, 3] and Lulie Melling[3]

[1]*Graduate School of Agriculture, Hokkaido University, Japan*
[2]*National Institute for Environmental Studies, Japan*
[3]*Tropical Peat Research Laboratory Unit (Chief Minister's Department), Malaysia*

**Corresponding author: jiaxiang31@hotmail.com*

SUMMARY

Tropical peat swamp forest is one of the world's most important terrestrial ecosystems, in which both swamp forest and peat soil have evolved together over millennia, because it has accumulated huge amount of carbon as peat. In recent years, considerable attention has been devoted to understand the role of this ecosystem in amplifying global warming. Owing to a significant amount of carbon stock, waterlogged, and associated anaerobic conditions, tropical peatlands may represent a potential source of methane (CH_4). However, there are a few studies on CH_4 flux based on periodic measurement, and no study on continuous CH_4 flux measurement in tropical peat swamp forest. Thus, we started CH_4 flux monitoring in 2011 above a primary tropical peat swamp forest in Sarawak, Malaysia, using the eddy covariance technique. Using field data from January 2014 to July 2015, ecosystem-scale CH_4 exchange was assessed. The tropical peat swamp forest showed net emissions of CH_4 with a mean value of 18.1 n mol m^{-2} s^{-1} for 19 months. Monthly mean CH_4 flux was always positive. On the diurnal timescale, CH_4 flux was positive during daytime and night time where peak CH_4 flux occurs in the early morning. The CH_4 emissions from this ecosystem were mainly controlled by groundwater level (GWL) and soil water content (SWC). Both GWL and SWC were positively (both $r = 0.41$ and 0.39, $P < 0.001$) correlated with CH_4 flux.

Keywords: *Peatland, eddy covariance technique, open-path CH_4 analyser, diurnal variation, groundwater level*

INTRODUCTION

Tropical peat swamp forest is a unique dual ecosystem, which consists of both tropical rainforest and tropical peatland that exist in high humidity and acidic waterlogged conditions (Melling *et al.*, 2007). The co-existence of tropical rainforest and peatland has accumulated huge amount of soil carbon over the millennia (Page *et al.*, 2004). It has been estimated that about 44.1 Mha of peatland is distributed in the tropics, of which 24.8 Mha is located in Southeast Asia. The amount of carbon in this region accounts for 11-14% of global peat carbon pool (Page *et al.*, 2011). Being an immense carbon store, tropical peatlands play an important role in the global carbon cycle (Müller *et al.*, 2015).

After carbon dioxide (CO_2) and nitrous oxide, methane (CH_4) is another important greenhouse gas that contributed significantly to global warming. Over a century, CH_4 is 25 times more effective than CO_2 at trapping heat in the atmosphere (IPCC, 2007). Its concentration has increased by 150% since the pre-industrial era and currently contributes to 20% of the enhanced greenhouse effect (IPCC, 2007). Due to the significant amount of carbon stock in the soil, tropical peatlands may represent a potential source of CH_4 (Inubushi *et al.*, 2007).

Measurement of greenhouse gas emissions to the atmosphere has largely relied on the chamber method, especially with closed chamber systems (Yu *et al.*, 2013). The chamber method is particularly suitable for point measuring of trace gas emissions in small scale field experiments, but the spatial and temporal variability induce this method become time consuming and labour intensive for large field scale experiments (Wang *et al.*, 2012). Thus, the tower-based micrometeorological approaches such as the eddy covariance technique have been used to measure greenhouse gas flux with the advantage of representing a larger area in the field (Yu *et al.*, 2013), leading to measurements that are more representative of the ecosystem as a whole. This approach also provides minimal disturbance on the measured ecosystem and possibility to measure long, more or less continuous, time series (Rinne *et al.*, 2007).

In tropical peat swamp forest, however, there are a few studies on CH_4 flux based on periodic measurements by the chamber method (Hirano *et al.*, 2009; Inubushi *et al.*, 2007; Melling *et al.*, 2005), and no study is found on continuous CH_4 flux measurement. Therefore, we have measured CH_4 flux above a primary tropical peat swamp forest using the eddy covariance technique with an open-path CH_4 analyser (LI-7700). Using the continuous data from 1 January 2014 to 31 July 2015, we quantify CH_4 flux on an ecosystem scale, examine its diurnal and seasonal variations and determine the environmental factors that influence CH_4 flux.

MATERIAL AND METHODS

Site description

The study site is a primary tropical peat swamp forest located in Maludam National Park, Sarawak, Malaysia (01°27'14.8"N, 111°8'45.3"E). The forest is classified as Alan Batu Forest dominated by *Shorea albida* with an average height of 30 m and dense understory vegetation (*Pandanus tectorius*). The climate at the study site is equatorial, characterized by consistently high temperature, high humidity, and abundant precipitation throughout the year. Precipitation is generally higher during November-March and the lowest in July-August. Groundwater level (GWL) is typically high and rises aboveground during the wettest period. A 40-m-tall tower was built at the study site with a fetch of 600 to 1000 m in all directions. The topography is almost flat with a elevation of about 8.5-9 m above mean sea level and peat depth of about 10 m.

Measurement of CH_4 flux and environmental variables

Fluxes of energy, CO_2 and CH_4 were measured by the eddy covariance technique using a 3D sonic anemometer/thermometer (CSAT3, Campbell Scientific Inc.), an open-path CO_2/H_2O analyser (LI-7500A, Li-Cor Inc.), and an open-path CH_4 analyser (LI-7700, Li-Cor) installed at the tip of a 1-m-long boom projecting towards the predominant winds from southeast at a height of 41 m. The signals of the sensors were sampled at a frequency of 10 Hz using a data logger (CR3000, Campbell).

In addition, downward and upward shortwave and longwave radiation components were measured at 41-m height using a radiometer (CNR4, Kipp & Zonen). Air temperature and relative humidity were measured at 11 m and 41 m using temperature and relative humidity probes (CS215, Campbell). Wind speed and wind direction were measured at 41 m height using a 3-cup anemometer and wind vane (01003-5, R.M. Young Company Young). Soil temperature was measured at a depth of 10 cm using thermocouple thermometers. Volumetric soil water content was measured in the top 30-cm-thick layer using TDR sensors (CS616, Campbell). Precipitation was measured at 1 m above the ground using a tipping-bucket rain gauge (TE525, Campbell). All the environmental variables were measured every 10 s and recorded every 5 min. Groundwater level (GWL) was recorded on a half-hourly basis using a GWL logger (HOBO, Onset). In this study, data measured from 1 January 2014 to 31 July 2015 were used for analysis.

Data Processing

From eddy covariance raw data, half-hourly mean CH_4 flux was calculated using the Flux Calculator software (Ueyama *et al.*, 2012). The flux values were corrected using the modified WPL equation (LI-COR, 2010). Net ecosystem CH_4 exchange was calculated as the sum of the CH_4 flux and the change in CH_4 storage in the air space below the flux measurement height. To avoid flow distortion by the tower, the CH_4 flux data were excluded when wind direction was within 0° to 30° and 280° to 360°. The stationarity and turbulence conditions of CH_4 flux were checked using the criteria of Foken and Wichura (1996). The threshold to screen out the CH_4 flux data based on the absolute value of skewness and kurtosis were set at 3.6 and 14.4, respectively. The CH_4 fluxes corresponding to relative signal strength indicator (RSSI) values less than 20% (due to rain, signal dropout, instrument malfunction, etc) were filtered out. As a result, 47.9% of CH_4 flux data remained after the quality control.

RESULTS AND DISCUSSION

Seasonal and diurnal variations

Figure 1 illustrates the ensemble averaged normalized daytime (0800 – 1600) cospectra of vertical wind speed and air temperature ($w'T'$) and CH_4 density ($w'CH_4'$) against natural frequency (n). In the inertial subrange, $w'CH_4'$ does not exhibit a slope close to the ideal one (-4/3 power law), and the cospectra loss started at n = 0.2. The high frequency loss of CH_4 flux was corrected using the analytical model of Massman (2000, 2001).

The mean half hourly CH_4 flux from January 2014 to July 2015 was 18.1 n mol m^{-2} s^{-1} whereas the annual mean of CH_4 flux for 2014 was 17.8 n mol m^{-2} s^{-1}. CH_4 flux was positive on a half-hourly basis with a peak of 49.1 n mol m^{-2} s^{-1} in the early morning at around 0800 to 0830 (Figure 2). The seasonal variations in monthly means of measured CH_4 flux is shown in Figure 3. In general, CH_4 flux was higher in the wet season than in the dry season. CH_4 flux was 22.3 and 15.8 nmol m^{-2} s^{-1}, on average, in the wet (October to March) and dry season (April to September), respectively.

The ecosystem-scale CH_4 flux was substantially higher than -0.11 - 0.19 n mol m^{-2} s^{-1} reported by Melling *et al.* (2005) but comparable to 19 n mol m^{-2} s^{-1} reported by Inubushi *et al.* (1998) for mixed peat swamp forest and secondary tropical wetland forest, respectively, which were measured with the closed-chamber technique. Pangala *et al.* (2012) reported that tree stems emit greater amount of CH_4 than the soil surfaces, accounting for 62 - 87% of total ecosystem CH_4 flux from a relatively undisturbed tropical peat swamp forest. During night time, CH_4 was stored in the forest floor, rather than being mixed into the overlying atmosphere. The early morning peak in half-hourly CH_4 flux is due to the flushed out of nocturnally stored CH_4 as turbulent mixing is enhanced after sunrise.

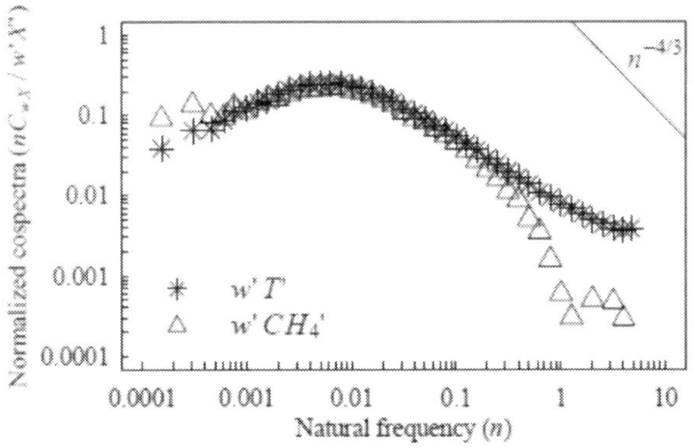

Figure 1: Ensemble averaged normalized daytime cospectra for *w'T'* and *w'CH₄'*; the straight line represents the -4/3 power law.

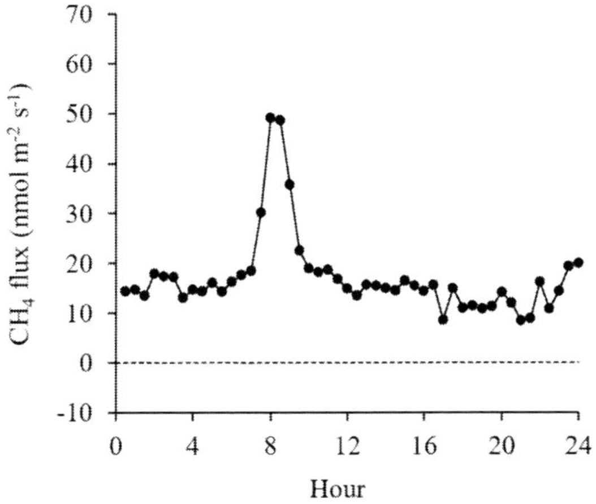

Figure 2: Ensemble-mean diurnal variation in measured CH_4 flux from January 2014 to July 2015.

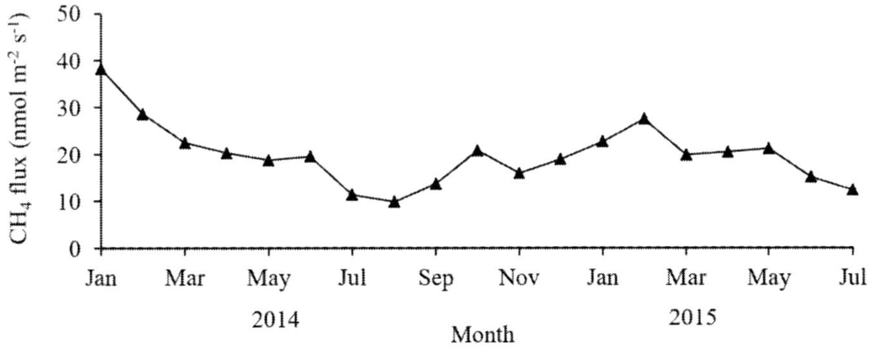

Figure 3: Variations in monthly mean of measured CH_4 flux.

Driving factors of methane flux

Based on the regression analysis, vapor pressure deficit (VPD), air temperature (T_a), soil temperature (T_s), GWL, and soil water content (SWC) showed significant linear relationships ($P < 0.001$) with CH_4 flux on a daily basis. The relationships are positive against GWL and SWC, whereas negative against VPD, T_a, and T_s. Pearson correlation coefficient (r) for GWL was higher than SWC. The influence of GWL on CH_4 flux was most distinct in driest period (July and August) when the GWL was lowest. Figure 4 indicates the linear relationships of CH_4 flux with GWL and SWC. Methanogenesis is the process of microbial CH_4 production under the anaerobic conditions, as a result of fermentation (van Noordvijk *et al.*, 2004). Increase in GWL and SWC would lead to oxygen depletion in the soil and consequently favours the methanogenesis. Thus, the CH_4 emissions from this ecosystem were primarily controlled by GWL and SWC. Generally, there is a positive relationship between CH_4 production and T_s (Wang *et al.*, 1995). However, the T_s was negatively correlated with CH_4 flux in this study (r = - 0.26). This is probably due to the strong negative correlation between SWC and T_s (r = - 0.81).

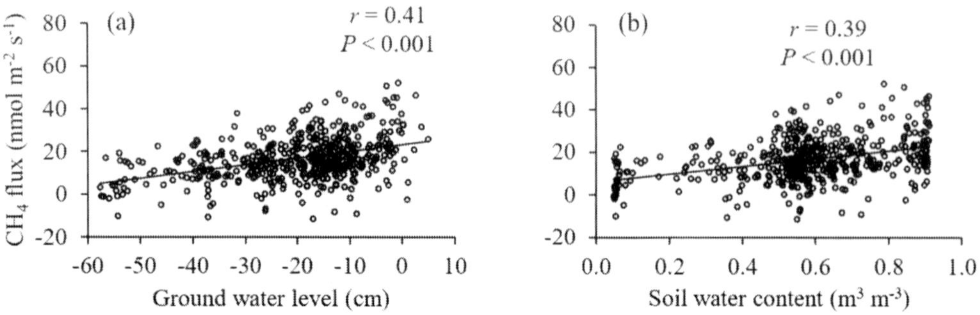

Figure 4: Relationships between CH_4 flux and environmental variables (GWL and SWC) on a daily basis.

CONCLUSION

This study is the first continuous CH_4 flux measurement above the tropical peat swamp forest using eddy covariance technique. The outcomes of this study enable us to have a better understanding of CH_4 flux and its driving factors in tropical peat swamp forest ecosystem. CH_4 flux showed net emissions on an ecosystem scale. The factors influencing the CH_4 emissions from this ecosystem were GWL and SWC.

ACKNOWLEDGEMENTS

This study was supported by both the Sarawak State Government and the Federal Government of Malaysia. We would like to thank the supporting staff of Tropical Peat Research Laboratory Unit for their valuable assistance for the field work. Special thanks to Japan Ministry of Education, Culture, Sports, Science and Technology for the Monbukagakusho scholarship.

REFERENCES

1. Foken, T. and Wichura, B. (1996). Tools for quality assessment of surface-based flux measurements. *Agricultural and Forest Meteorology*, **78**, 83-105.
2. Hirano, T., Jauhiainen, J., Inoue, T., and Takahashi, H. (2009). Controls on the carbon balance of tropical peatlands. *Ecosystems*, **12**(6), 873-887.
3. Inubushi, K. and Hadi, A. (2007). Effect of land-use management on greenhouse gas emissions from tropical peatlands. In *Carbon–Climate–Human Interaction on Tropical Peatland. Proceedings of the International Symposium and Workshop on Tropical Peatland,* (**27**, pp. 29). Yogyakarta.
4. Inubushi, K., Hadi, A., Okazaki, M., and Yonebayashi, K. (1998). Effect of converting wetland forest to sago palm plantations on methane gas flux and organic carbon dynamics in tropical peat soil. *Hydrological Processes*, **12**(13 - 14), 2073-2080.
5. IPCC (Intergovernmental Panel on Climate Change). (2007). *Climate Change 2007: The Physical Science Basis. Contribution of Working Group I to the Fourth Assessment Report of the Intergovernmental Panel on Climate Change* (eds Solomon, S., Qin, D., Manning, M., Marquis, M., Averyt, K., Tignor, M. M. N, Miller, Jr, H. L. and Chen, Z.). Cambridge University Press, Cambridge, UK.
6. LI-Cor, Inc. (2010). LI-7700 open path CH_4 analyzer instruction manual. LI-COR Inc., Lincoln.
7. Massman, W. J. (2000). A simple method for estimating frequency response corrections for eddy covariance systems. *Agricultural and Forest Meteorology*, **104**(3), 185-198.

8. Massuman, W. J. (2001). Reply to comment by Rannik on "A simple method for estimating frequency response corrections for eddy covariance systems". *Agricultural and Forest Meteorology*, **107**, 247-251.
9. Melling, L., Goh, K. J., Uyo, L. J., Sayok, A., and Hatano, R. (2007). Biophysical characteristics of tropical Peatland. In *Proceedings of the Soil Science Conference of Malaysia*, (pp. 17-19). Selangor, Malaysia.
10. Melling, L., Hatano, R., and Goh, K. J. (2005). Methane fluxes from three ecosystems in tropical peatland of Sarawak, Malaysia. *Soil Biology and Biochemistry*, **37**(8), 1445-1453.
11. Müller, D., Warneke, T., Rixen, T., Müller, M., Jamahari, S., Denis, N., Mujahid, A., and Notholt, J. (2015). Lateral carbon fluxes and CO_2 outgassing from a tropical peat-draining river. *Biogeosciences Discussions*, ***12***(13), 10389-10424.
12. Pangala, S. R., Moore, S., Hornibrook, E. R., and Gauci, V. (2013). Trees are major conduits for methane egress from tropical forested wetlands. *New Phytologist*, **197**(2), 524-531.
13. Page, S. E., Rieley, J. O., and Banks, C. J. (2011). Global and regional importance of the tropical peatland carbon pool. *Global Change Biology*, **17**, 798–818.
14. Page, S. E., Wüst, R. A. J., Weiss, D., Rieley, J. O., Shotyk, W., and Limin, S. H. (2004). A record of Late Pleistocene and Holocene carbon accumulation and climate change from an equatorial peat bog (Kalimantan, Indonesia): implications for past, present and future carbon dynamics. *Journal of Quaternary Science*, **19**, 625–635.
15. Rinne, J., Riutta, T., Pihlatie, M., Aurela, M., Haapanala, S., Tuovien J. P., Tuittila, E. S., and Vesala, T. (2007). Annual cycle of methane emission from a boreal fen measured by the eddy covariance technique. *Tellus B*, **59**(3), 449-457.
16. Ueyama, M., Hirata, R., Mano, M., Hamotani, K., Harazono, Y., Hirano, T., Miyata, A., Takagi, K., and Takahashi, Y. (2012). Influences of various calculation options on heat, water and carbon fluxes determined by open-and closed-path eddy covariance methods. *Tellus B*, ***64***, 1-26.
17. van Noordvijk, M., Cadish, G., and Ong, C. (2004). *Below-ground interactions in tropical agroecosystems: concepts and models with multiple plant components* (pp. 212). CAB International, Oxfordshire.
18. Wang, J., Hui, D., Jima, T., Bhattarai, S., Dennis, S., Stockert, C., Smart, D., Sammis, T., Millerd, D., and Reddy, C. (2012). Eddy-covariance and chamber measured greenhouse gas emissions from a commercial cornfield. In *Symposium on Boundary Layers and Turbulence*. Westin Copley Place, Boston.
19. Wang, Z., Kludze H., Crozier, C.R., and Patrik W.H.Jr. (1995). Soil characteristics affecting methane production and emission in flooded rice. In *Climate Change and Rice* (pp. 80-90). Springer-Verlag, Berlin, Heidelberg.
20. Yu, K., Hiscox, A., and DeLaune, R. D. (2013). Greenhouse gas emission by static chamber and eddy flux methods. *Methods in Biogeochemistry of Wetlands*, (pp. 275-285). Soil Science Society of America, Madison.

Abstract No: A-270

FORESTRY USE OF BOREAL PEATLANDS – CHALLENGES AND POSSIBILITIES

Harri Vasander[1*], Meeri Pearson[2] and Raija Laiho[2]

[1]*University of Helsinki, Finland*
[2]*Natural Resources Institute Finland (Luke), Finland*

**Corresponding author: harri.vasander@helsinki.fi*

SUMMARY

Approximately 15 million ha of peatland have been drained to improve forest growth. Most of this area is in Northern Europe, while Finland holds the world record with close to 5 million ha of forestry-drained peatlands. Drainage aims to lower the water-table level, thus extending the rooting zone and improving its oxygen status, and increasing tree growth through improved root functioning. Many peatlands are well suited for forestry because of the relatively high soil nitrogen content, even though the nutrient regime of peatlands varies widely. Yet, since peatlands are highly dynamic ecosystems with an organic soil, they are likely to respond to land use with greater adverse environmental impacts, such as loading of watercourses and release of CO_2 from the soil, than mineral soil sites. Currently, the main targets for both research and political guidance concerning peatland forestry in Finland are to find management options for reducing the harmful impacts, and to identify such areas that should be excluded from active, regulated forestry due to low productivity. Here, we review 1) the potential of continuous-cover forestry (CCF) to reduce harmful environmental impacts, 2) means to improve ecosystem condition with active management, and 3) identification and potential novel uses of low-productive drained peatlands.

Keywords: *drainage, peatland forestry, continuous-cover forestry, restoration*

INTRODUCTION

The aim of draining peatlands for forestry is to increase forest stock and thus raw material for the forest and wood products industry. Forestry in peatlands is most common in Northern and North-Western Europe, especially in some of the Nordic countries (Finland, Sweden, Norway), Baltic countries (Estonia and Latvia) and Russia (Päivänen and Hånell 2012). In addition, peatland forestry has some importance in the United Kingdom, Ireland, Canada and the United States (Minkkinen *et al.*, 2008). It has been estimated that around 15 million ha of peatlands in total have been drained for forestry in the boreal and temperate zones during the last century (Päivänen and Hånell 2012).

Drainage is a prerequisite for peatland forestry in most countries. Drainage is needed to enhance the productivity of the tree stand and alleviate operational limitations of the peatland. Drainage also causes ecological changes in the ecosystem, which affect the carbon sink function and greenhouse gas (GHG) dynamics of the peatland.

In the Nordic countries peatland forestry is extensive: it is based on the use of natural tree stands, and management intensity is high with final cuttings, soil preparations, plantings, and fertilizations. In temperate zone countries, like UK and Ireland, forestry is much more intensive. It is mostly based on plantations on originally treeless peatlands, including, e.g., soil preparation and repeated fertilizations. Often these forest sites are former peat production areas, afforested as an after-use. In both areas, however, the stands are cut and regenerated, either by planting or natural regeneration. Regeneration often involves soil preparation. Continuous cover forestry (in which no clear-cuts take place) has gained more interest lately in the Nordic countries, but is still marginal. The intensity of forestry operations is reflected in stand productivity but unfortunately also environmental impacts.

In Finland, which probably holds the world record in forest drainage, about half (appr. 5.5 million ha) of the mire and peatland area has been drained for forestry since the beginning of 1900s. The proportion of growing tree stock on drained peatlands is about one quarter of the total (Päivänen and Hånell 2012). The economic value of timber growing on drained peatlands in Finland was estimated to be around 11 billion euros in 2013. Both state subsidies and private investments have been used to finance initial and maintenance drainage operations. The crucial questions for the future are: can we continue to grow forests on drained peatlands sustainably and what should we do with those drained peatlands deemed unsuitable for the continued practice of forestry?

Peatlands drained for forestry may be roughly divided into three groups: 1. Productive sites where forestry is profitable, 2. Sites that are low-productive because of nutritional imbalance (high N but low K and/or P in peat), and 3. Sites that is low-productive because of generally insufficient nutrient regime (low N). Common for both 2 and 3 is that their ecosystem services (C sequestration, provision of clean water) are degraded while low or no economic profit is gained. Their future land-use options may differ, however; while type 3 sites are moved from forestry to some other land use, type 2 sites may alternatively be reclaimed for forestry with the aid of ash fertilization (Huotari *et al.*, 2015). In the following, we present possible future scenarios for these different cases.

ALTERNATIVES FOR FORESTRY ON DRAINED PEATLANDS

As of 2014, revamped forest legislation in Finland has permitted alternatives to conventional silvicultural practices. For instance, instead of traditionally intensive forest management aimed at producing even-aged, single-species stands which are then clear-cut upon reaching maturity, forest owners now have the option to practice uneven-aged, continuous-cover forestry (CCF), thereby avoiding stand-replacing clear-cuts. In continuous-cover forestry, trees are, e.g., harvested selectively and/or in small gaps (repeatedly) to advance natural regeneration by creating suitable light conditions, and providing shelter, for seedlings. Thus, the goal is that the forest continually regenerates without clear cutting, soil preparation and planting. The legal possibility of managing forests in an unconventional, less disturbing manner coincides with the changing structure of forest ownership and public attitudes and preferences in Finland which increasingly emphasize other forest-related values (e.g., recreation, conservation, landscape), non-timber forest products, and non-market ecosystem services. While economics are always an important consideration in commercial forestry, ecologically and socially sustainable alternatives to even-aged forest management regimes are pivotal to progression towards a climate-smart, resource-efficient, carbon-neutral society.

Compared to mineral soil forest, peatland forest stands may offer better possibilities for shifting towards continuous-cover forestry. This results from their tree stand history and dynamics. Tree stand structure in undrained peatlands is usually very uneven considering both tree age and size (e.g., Heikurainen 1971). Also, the spatial distribution of trees is often clumped, with open treeless areas surrounded by dense tree stands. After drainage, new seedlings start to grow especially on formerly wet treeless surfaces, which increase the unevenness of the stand structure even further (Sarkkola *et al.*, 2005). As stands age, the size differences of stems decrease but in old mature peatland tree stands, stem number distributions are nevertheless usually broader than in the corresponding mineral soil stands. Even after canopy closure of the dominant tree layer, more undergrowth will arise which further increases stand variation.

In peatland forests the associated environmental benefits of CCF could also be considerable. To prevent the water table from infringing on tree growth, ditch network maintenance (DNM) (i.e., cleaning ditches and making supplementary ditches as necessary) is typically performed once or twice during the stand rotation in the traditional management schemes. However, this practice is harmful to downstream watercourses due to consequent leaching of nutrients, suspended solids and organic matter. At the same time, lowering the water table increases the thickness of the oxygenated peat soil layer, hence accelerating its decay and the release of CO_2 and in some cases also N_2O into the atmosphere. Add commonly applied clearcutting and soil preparation treatments at the end of the stand rotation to the silvicultural equation, and the need for alternative, less intensive management schemes for forestry-drained peatlands is obvious from the environmental point-of-view. From the economic perspective, ditch network maintenance in particular is a costly investment which can "make or break" the forest owner; if applied on sites where it does little or naught to increase stand growth, the overall profitability of peatland forestry is significantly undermined.

Recent research (Sarkkola *et al.*, 2010, 2013) indicates that a tree stand volume of around 100 m^3 ha^{-1} in drained peatland forests may maintain WL deep enough for tree growth, 30-40 cm, via evapotranspiration. Maintaining a continuous cover of forest could thus pre-empt intensive forestry practices like DNM on such sites. If continuous-cover methodology facilitates forestry on drained peatlands without clear-cuts, soil preparation, artificial regeneration and regular ditch network maintenance, while maintaining WL relatively close to the surface, GHG emissions and harmful effects on watercourses may be greatly reduced. This seems a plausible scenario especially for the most nutrient-rich and most productive sites, where the harmful environmental impacts are the strongest. These sites are typically dominated by Norway spruce which tolerates shade and has a large leaf area that facilitates efficient biological drainage through evapotranspiration.

Although legal backing exists for practicing continuous-cover forestry, its practical application by forest managers and owners is hindered in part by the lack of research-based information available. Informational constraints concern, e.g., forest growth and yield, economic productivity, stand structure development and natural regeneration in various conditions, optimization models for uneven-aged, mixed stands, impacts on biodiversity, carbon cycling and storage. Furthermore, as most forests in Finland have thus far been managed as even-aged, there is limited knowledge and experience of how the residual stand responds after transformation cutting aimed at altering the present stand structure from even-aged towards an irregular (uneven-aged) one for the purposes of CCF.

OPTIONS FOR THE MANAGEMENT OF UNPRODUCTIVE DRAINED PEATLANDS

In Finland, there are nearly one million hectares of drained peatlands that are so low in productivity that active forestry is not economically feasible. About 0.5 million hectares are so poor that the landowner will not be obliged to regenerate such sites after cutting, which is otherwise a legal responsibility. This means that in the future around 4 million hectares will remain in more or less active forestry use.

An imbalanced nutrient regime, i.e., high peat N content but low phosphorus (P) and/or potassium (K), may check tree growth especially in originally wet, treeless peatlands where such soil conditions are common. Such imbalances can be remedied with wood ash fertilization, which contains all other nutrients that trees require, and in favorable proportions, except for N which is removed in combustion. In well-targeted sites, ash application increases tree production and reduces the acidity of the soil while increasing base cation reserves, with few harmful side-effects (Huotari *et al.*, 2015). Whether this is economically feasible depends on several factors, such as the potential productivity of the site after fertilization, and the costs of the fertilization operation.

Where low productivity is primarily caused by lack of N, fertilization is, as a rule, not feasible. Such sites are best left out of active forestry. There are different possible scenarios for such sites, which are also valid for the nutritionally imbalanced sites if fertilization is not a feasible option. Restoration to a functional peatland is an option that may mitigate climate change if the usually slightly negative soil C balance of such sites is replaced by C accumulation into peat, as is characteristic of these sites in pristine conditions. Restoration implies active measures, which aim to accelerate the regeneration of peatlands towards the structure and function of natural mires. Energy wood may be harvested before restoration, which may both speed up the regeneration process and provide income for covering the costs of active restoration. Where economic profit is sought, some sites may be suitable for peat extraction, or provide opportunities for producing renewable *Sphagnum* biomass. Present requirements for profitable industrial-scale peat extraction are that the size of the area is at least 20 ha, and the peat layer is at least 1.5 m thick. In addition, the distance to a peat-burning power plant must be reasonable. About 57% of cut-away peatlands have been evaluated to be suitable for forestry, and 20-25% for rewetting (Picken 2007).

As for renewable *Sphagnum* biomass, it has the potential to replace peat as growing medium in horticultural production. It is believed that harvesting of living *Sphagnum* biomass to a maximum depth of max 20-25 cm on poor, forestry-drained drained sites will ensure sufficient *Sphagnum* regeneration thereafter. The rotation time is presumed to be 20-30 years. However, *Sphagnum* species diversity, species suitability as horticultural substrate, and the abundance of cotton grass are critical factors to consider when selecting the appropriate sites for this purpose. The precise amount of suitable sites in Finland is not known. Thus far, only limited experiences of *Sphagnum* farming and its environmental sustainability have accumulated worldwide (Gaudig *et al.*, 2014, Pouliot *et al.*, 2015), mainly from cut-over or bog grassland sites.

CONCLUSIONS

In Finland there is now a boom in bio economy. This also means that there is greater demand for raw materials like wood – also from drained peatlands. The principles of ecologically, economically and socially sustainable development have to be followed when managing forests on drained peatlands. To safeguard the sensitive and dynamic peat soils, logging methods and machinery will also need to be further developed, taking into account the low bearing capacity of these soils.

We must also consider other ecosystem services of peatlands besides wood production. The most important are the maintenance and increase of carbon stocks, regulation of water flow and water quality as well as the maintenance of typical plant, animal and microbe communities in mires and peatlands.

ACKNOWLEDGEMENTS

Tiina ja Antti Herlin Foundation made it possible for HV to join IPS 2016 conference in Kuching, Malaysia.

REFERENCES

1. Gaudig, G, Fengler, F, Krebs, M, Prager, A, Schulz, J, Wichmann, S, Joosten, H (2014) Sphagnum farming in Germany – a review of progress. Mires and Peat 13(8): 1-11.
2. Heikurainen L (1971) Virgin peatland forests in Finland. Acta Agralia Fennica 123: 11-26.
3. Huotari N, Tillman-Sutela E, Moilanen M, Laiho R (2015) Recycling of ash - for the good of the environment? Forest Ecology and Management. doi: 10.1016/j.foreco.2015.03.008
4. Minkkinen K, Byrne KA, Trettin C (2008) Climate Impacts of Peatland Forestry. *In*: Strack M (ed*) Peatlands and Climate Change:* 98-122. Saarijärvi, International Peat Society. 223 pp.

5. Päivänen, J, Hånell B (2012) Peatland ecology and forestry – a sound approach. *Univ. Helsinki, Dept. Forest Sciences Publications* 3: 1-267.
6. Picken P (2007) Geological factors affecting on after-use of Finnish cut-over peatlands with implications on the carbon accumulation. *University of Helsinki, Publications of the Department of Geology D10.*
7. Pouliot, R, Hugron, S, Rochefort, L (2015) *Sphagnum* farming: A long-term study on producing peat moss biomass sustainably. Ecological Engineering 74: 135-147.
8. Sarkkola S, Hökkä H, Laiho R, Päivänen J, Penttilä T (2005) Stand structural dynamics on drained peatlands dominated by Scots pine. Forest Ecology and Management 206: 135-152.
9. Sarkkola, S, Hökkä H, Koivusalo H, Nieminen M, Ahti E, Päivänen J, Laine J (2010) Role of tree stand evapotranspiration in maintaining satisfactory drainage conditions in drained peatlands. Canadian Journal of Forest Research 40(8): 1485-1496. http://dx.doi.org/10.1139/X10-0
10. Sarkkola S, Nieminen M, Koivusalo H, Laurén A *et al.* (2013) Domination of growing-season evapotranspiration over runoff makes ditch network maintenance in mature peatland forests questionable. Mires and Peat 11(2): 1-11.
11. Vasander H, Laine J (2008) Site type classification on drained peatlands. *In*: Korhonen R, Korpela L, Sarkkola S (eds.), *Finland – Fenland. Research and sustainable utilisation of mires and peat.* Finnish Peatland Society and Maahenki Ltd.: 146-151.

Abstract No: A-301

HAZE CONTROL AND THE OIL PALM FARMER – A REVIEW OF POLICY OPTIONS

Khor Yu Leng*, Johan Saravanamuttu and Deborah Augustin

LMC International Ltd, Singapore

**Corresponding author: yuleng@hotmail.com*

SUMMARY

Southeast Asia has arguably seen the worst-ever, certainly the longest, peat-driven haze-smoke pollution between September and November 2015. Over 100,000 fires have burned some two million hectares, apparently worsened by El Nino climatic conditions and the Indonesian electoral cycle. Some 43 million Indonesians were exposed to toxic smog in Kalimantan and Sumatra. Neighbouring countries also endured the haze-smoke drift. This decades-old problem erupted in August 1997, presumably for the expansion of oil palm and other cash crops. This led the Association of Southeast Asian Nations (ASEAN) to sign the 2002 Transboundary Haze Pollution Agreement (ratified by Indonesia in 2014). It gave rise to the Europe-led non-government organisation (NGO) movement for sustainable palm oil. Despite these measures, the problem recurs yearly. We examine the political-economy of the sources and solutions of the problem from the perspective of the palm oil supply chain. Oil palm is a profitable commercial crop established as tolerating peat's wet and acidic conditions. Big companies have often targeted as the land clearing culprits, and many have knuckled down to the Roundtable on Sustainable Palm Oil (RSPO) certification and a few had Indonesian courts impose fines and jail terms for poor fire control efforts. Now, the immediate fire blame is shifting to independent farmers and smallholders as concessionaires have adjusted their practices. Despite the new blame-the-farmer trend, the authorities have started to revoke and freeze concessions. Also, the World Bank reckons that "a few hundred businesses and a few thousand farmers seek to profit from land and plantation speculation practices." We consider various policy options. Reactive policies include boycotts and buying sustainably certified products; these may be counter-productive as expected multi-tier prices, may suppress prices for farmers in the least desired peat zone product origins. Proactive solutions may seek to improve farmer economic outcomes (with consideration of product prices and/or subsidies) and extension services for responsible peat zone development. This paper expands on the authors' work in "Haze Control through the Sustenance of Indonesian Oil Palm Smallholders" in Thinking ASEAN Issue 5 / November 2015, The Habibie Center.

Keywords: *Palm oil, smallholder, Indonesia, air pollution, sustainable development*

INTRODUCTION

The Southeast Asian region has arguably seen the worst ever, certainly the longest, peat-driven haze-smoke pollution in the months of September till November in 2015.[1] Some 43 million Indonesians were exposed continuously to toxic smog in Kalimantan and Sumatra. In neighbouring Singapore and Malaysia, unhealthy to hazardous levels of haze-smoke were recorded causing the closing of schools and great consternation among the public. A number of Singapore retailers have stopped the sale of some products of alleged haze-causing companies (The Straits Times, 2015). This decades-old problem re-erupted in August 1997 when some 8 million hectares of forests were razed due to slash and burn land clearing of land presumably for oil palm crops and other cash crops (Golver and Jessup, 1999)[2]. The 1997 episode led the Association of Southeast Asian Nations (ASEAN) to sign the 2002 Transboundary Haze Pollution Agreement, which Indonesia ratified in 2014.[3]

This paper examines the political-economy of the sources and solutions for the fire-smoke-haze problem from the perspective of the palm oil supply chain. The dominant narrative of the peat fire and the resulting haze is the role of oil palm expansion into peat zones as the agricultural land frontier closes. Oil palm is regarded as a sure-win crop for companies and smallholders. Big companies have reduced fire burn problems in their concession zones

[1] There was already great concern in 2013 when the seasonal haze-smoke saw PSI readings in Singapore peaking at 226, Khor Reports (2013).

[2] The 1997 Operation Haze saw the involvement of Malaysian and Singapore firefighters on Indonesian soil fighting a desperate battle with the fires raging across Sumatra and Kalimantan over 25 days the numbers of hotspots reaching 37,938 in August 1997 and were it not for monsoon rains, the fires may not have doused.

[3] Status of Ratification, http://haze.asean.org/?page_id=187 (accessed 3 Nov 2015)

and the fire are now mostly outside of their boundaries; and many point out that it is hard to control the smallholders who are allowed to use fire under Indonesia regulations. NGOs like Greenpeace cite various problems: oil palm is planted on burnt out land and that in an average year fires cause an estimated 110,000 premature deaths across the region.

The 1997/98 peat fire and haze season gave rise to the Europe-led NGO movement for sustainable palm oil. But despite these efforts, haze-smoke pollution has continued on a yearly basis, due primarily to the burning on peat lands in Sumatra and Kalimantan. In 2015, fires have burnt over 2 million hectares of land, and over 100,000 fires have occurred (Business Times 2015, New York Times 2015a and 2015b). While El Nino climatic conditions exacerbate the situation, scientists consider that it is no longer a controlling factor, given regularity of the problem.[4] Environmental activism is even emerging near the major palm oil processing origins - in Singapore, Kuala Lumpur and Medan. The imperative for growing palm oil under Roundtable on Sustainable Palm Oil (RSPO) and other certifications increases, Indonesian courts have imposed fines and jail terms for poor fire control within concessions, and the immediate fire blame has shifted to independent farmers and smallholders. Despite the blame-the-farmer narrative, the Indonesian government has started to revoke and freeze concessions, and the World Bank reckons that "a few hundred businesses and a few thousand farmers seek to profit from land and plantation speculation practices."

We consider policy options for addressing the peat-haze-smoke problem. Reactive policies include: (i) boycotts – risk being counter-productive, (ii) buying sustainably certified products - of good but still limited reach and expected to create multi-tier prices, with potential to suppress product prices for its less desired peat zone origins and (iii) suing and penalizing companies. We also consider policy options to address a longer-term solution to the problem. Indonesia's attention has turned to the interests and prospects of its oil palm smallholders. Proactive solutions should seek an understanding of and seek to improve farmer economic outcomes (with consideration of product prices and/or subsidies) and service delivery for responsible peat zone development for sustainable agriculture.

DISCUSSION

Palm oil and concerns about "haze free" products

The dominant narrative of the peat fire haze-smoke is the role of oil palm expansion into peat zones as the agricultural land frontier closes. Oil palm is a profitable commercial crop established as tolerating peat's wet and acidic conditions. Its large-scale development on (relatively uninhabited) peat is eased by a lack of native land right claimants.[5] Big companies are often targeted as the culprits behind the land-clearing involving fire, whether they are directly involved in these activities or not.[6] In the past, NGO analysts have placed up to 80% of the responsibility for fires on the corporate players, and only 20 % on small farmers. The 1997/98 peat fire haze-smoke season gave rise to the Europe-led NGO movement for sustainable palm oil. As environmental concerns and the imperative for growing palm oil under RSPO and other certifications[7] increases, and Indonesian courts have imposed fines and jail terms for poor fire control within concessions, the immediate fire blame is shifting to independent farmers and smallholders.

In October 2015, amidst the haze-smoke crisis, there were sudden and unexpected shifts in Indonesia governance and policy over eco-sustainable palm oil. The mandatory Indonesia Sustainable Palm Oil (a re-regulation drive led by a unit of the Ministry of Agriculture and co-funded by the UNDP and others) had a surprise change in leadership. The big business-led Indonesia Palm Oil Pledge (IPOP) was ordered to dilute its efforts. The industry faces sustainability roll-back concerns as the Jokowi administration apparently stepped up concern for smallholder expansion and market access in the face of more restrictive sustainability policies and corporate pledges. Indonesia and Malaysia have also revived palm oil joint-marketing talks.

Consumer concerns are springing up within the region, activated by weeks of haze-smoke disruptions. Medan and Kuala Lumpur (key cities near major palm oil downstream processing and export centers) may join the burgeoning Singapore movement (now centering on boycotts on pulp and paper and heavy scrutiny of palm oil products). Some regional activists talk about "haze-free" products and these points to a difference between regional and international activists. It appears that the former care a bit less about biodiversity and deforestation or carbon stock agendas, which are prioritized by non-resident international NGOs. "Haze free" logically points to the rise of

[4] Universiti Malaya's AEI-JPAS-CARUM Roundtable on Transboundary Pollution, 5 Nov 2015.

[5] Universiti Malaya's AEI-JPAS-CARUM Roundtable on Transboundary Pollution, 5 Nov 2015.

[6] See the works of Helena Varkkey, Varkkey (2015a) which provides such a perspective. Varkkey shared her views on the 2015 haze, Varkkey (2015b).

[7] The Roundtable on Sustainable Palm Oil (RSPO), with the participation of the big integrated palm oil groups, was initiated by WWF. It has become the main certification for palm oil (non-fuel use) favoured by buyers in Europe and other developed markets. But it facing intense competition by apparently lower compliance cost "traceability" alternatives.

jurisdictional-based palm oil marketing efforts as haze-smoke origins are geographically concentrated. This may be at odds with the apparent palm oil "solidarity" reactions of October from national officialdom. Indeed, the 21 October 2015 decision by the Sabah state government (in East Malaysia) for sustainable palm oil within 10 years may trigger other well-positioned sub-national units to do likewise (The Borneo Post, 2015).

Transmigration and small farmers in peat zones

Recent studies have shown that small, independent growers, who have been encroaching on peat lands in Kalimantan and Sumatra, are a major cause of the haze-smoke. Dr Francis Ng, a botanist who was with the UN's FAO and Centre for International Forestry Research in Bogor, suggested that farmers who settled in Kalimantan through Indonesia's transmigration programme of the 1960s and 1970s may be responsible for peat fires (The Malaysian Insider, 2015). There may be literally millions of impoverished transmigrants, mostly Javanese and also locals including Dayaks, who continue to use fire when growing food like rice paddy, vegetables and fruits as well as rubber and oil palm. Lesley Potter (2012) describes the situation for the transmigrant scheme in Lamunti, Central Kalimantan (part of the abandoned mega rice project on 1.4 million hectares of peat) as follows:

...a few years later, the rice was constantly failing and in 2006, all the crops failed. To grow fruit, they had first to burn the peat, but if they tried that in the dry season, the fire just spread and could not be contained. Plants that would grow were bananas, pineapple and rubber. One Javanese farmer noted that to succeed with oil palm, he had to use either chicken manure or commercial fertiliser. It was expensive, but as he had no experience with rubber, he preferred to try oil palm. The problems of the transmigrants included the cost of producing crops with limited capital and inconsistent help from district authorities....(they) had been promised they would receive food for five years, but after three years, it ceased. Local Dayaks were still waiting for the outcome of land claims against the government...

A study by environmental scientists (Marlier *et al.*, 2015) clearly shows that in Sumatra 59% of fire emissions originate from outside timber and oil-palm concession boundaries. While in Kalimantan, non-concession fires play an even bigger role, with fires outside concessions generating 73% of all emissions and 76% of smoke affecting equatorial Southeast Asia has been frequently cited. In fact, recent data from the Global Forest Watch website (for 1 July to 2 November 2015) show that only 10% of fire alerts were on oil palm concession areas (and 26% on pulpwood concession, now driving more Singapore retailers to demand FSC paper products, primarily supplied from Scandinavia). Only 103 of 3,215 of such fires were on RSPO certified concessions. It is good, but its limited reach (RSPO covers about 19% of global palm oil and only about half is bought as such) and the US$1-2 per tonne basic premium versus its US$4-12 per tonne cost is disadvantageous (especially for small farmers facing higher costing than large plantations under its system). Such voluntary international standards suffer policy leakage and disintermediation problems. This point to the important role of national mandatory standards such as Indonesia Sustainable Palm Oil or ISPO.

In view of these findings, this article attempts a new narrative in addressing the yearly recurring haze-smoke problem and argues that it could be controlled to a great extent by addressing the plight and the livelihood of independent oil palm growers and the local peoples supplying produce and casual labour to the plantations. Focusing on the former, these small farmers tend to fall outside the "inti-plasma" (core companies-tied smallholders) management system of the Indonesian palm oil concessions, obvious questions arise. Who drains the peat lands? Why do these farmers still resort to the use of fire after many years of haze-smoke? What are the sources of income? How much income does a 2 hectare oil palm plot generate? What role can the middlemen of farmer supply-chains play? In our view, the haze problem has to be approached holistically in terms of the oil palm industry and, most crucially, from the perspective of *sustaining livelihoods, small farmers and their supply-chain should be seen as part of the solution. In this light, boycotts or other consumer-led efforts that ultimately reduce small farmer incomes may be counter-productive, if farmers are then pushed to use more (peat) land areas to achieve their needed income.*

The prevalence of small farmers in haze zones, as shown by studies, is due in part to transmigration. The practice of moving groups of people in heavily populated areas to less populated areas has intensified during the Suharto years as a means to relieve population density in the inner islands such as Java, Bali, and Madura, alleviate poverty, and spur development in the outer islands (Sri Adhiati and Bobsien, 2001). However, a lack of infrastructure, suitable land, and communal tensions has marred the program's overall ability to reach its development goals.

These problems have not gone unnoticed by the Indonesian government, and a policy shift has occurred. In the new transmigration effort, the Ministry introduced the concept of *Kota Terpadu Mandiri* (KTM) or integrated self-sufficient cities to serve rural economic hinterlands. The new policy targets three types of districts: backward areas; districts close to international borders; and strategic, fast-growing districts of high potential. The 'backward' areas and Central Kalimantan saw the largest numbers of fast-growing settlement sites followed by South Sumatra (BBC Monitoring, 2005). "The majority of the hinterlands of these planned new towns will be covered with oil palm plantations (Kep 293/ MEN/IX/2009). The aim is to largely use independent transmigrants as a labour force for growing the towns. The payment for KTM developments is supposed to be 30% by the central government, 30%

by the district governments concerned and 40% by investors... to eventually create 186 KTMs and resettle 25,000 transmigrant families (100,000 additional workers) per year" (Potter, 2012).

However, surveys show that transmigrants in several new and earlier sites in Kalimantan still face significant difficulties once relocated. Many transmigrants may be relegated to peat zones with no experience or capital to farm on peat with proper development and methods. In Sumatra's peat zones, similar issues are faced by many of its small farmers. Thus, it can be hypothesized that transmigrants who often have little infrastructure support and poor income turn to unsustainable agricultural practices on peat land.

It is evident that increased support for transmigrants and rural communities in general, in the form of extension services is crucial to preventing further use of fire in peat zones. An example of extensive support offered to resettled rural communities exists in Malaysia, where landless settlers were administered by the Federal Land Development Authority (FELDA) in schemes with new rural towns not dissimilar to the KTM concept. Settlers in the early FELDA schemes faced similar problems as their Indonesian counterparts in terms of lack of infrastructure and insufficient incomes. Initially, FELDA settlers were given a house lot and 4 hectares to grow rubber, and eventually oil palm for targeted minimum family income. By 1990, settlers were allocated 7 hectares. However, the average FELDA family of 5 would likely need 10 hectares today. In 1986 costing terms, FELDA spent some US$2.3 billion on settling 120,000 families. Each settlement of 300-500 families had the services of 25-35 onsite staff, mostly agricultural extension services, and one-third on community development (Khor *et al.*, 2015).

Given the yearly haze-smoke problem, there is no escaping question of the need for expanded rural development agencies and extension services for Indonesia's peat zone smallholders and appropriate peat development policies. We have to assume there would not be large-scale relocation (evacuation) of peat zone smallholders and farmers. Adjoining Kalimantan, Sarawak's peat development practices (involving among others, a compaction of porous peat with the benefit of higher yield and incomes) has reportedly resulted in reduced fire outcomes in recent years.[8]

Indonesia's current rapid smallholder development phase has largely been under a corporate neo-liberal framework in which there is a positive role for supply chain middlemen; oil palm fresh fruit bunch (FFB) traders, independent mills and other concession-linked mills. They are integral in buying small farmer oil palm FFB (which needs to be taken to mill within 24 hours for a better quality palm oil). This is not an unsophisticated sector and it can play role as agent of change in promoting decent incomes and better (non-fire) practices by oil palm smallholders and associated rural peoples (supplying labour and food).

CONCLUSION

Going beyond reactive policies vis–à–vis the haze such as: (i) boycotts – risk being counter-productive, (ii) buying sustainably certified products - of good but still limited reach and expected to create multi-tier prices, with potential to suppress product prices for its less desired peat zone origins and (iii) suing and penalizing companies; we suggest several policy measures which would address a longer-term solution to the problem. In October, Indonesia's attention rightly turned to the interests and prospects of its oil palm smallholders. At bottom line, what is required to handle the peat haze-smoke problem are proactive solutions, that is, understanding and improving farmer economic outcomes and service delivery and proper peat zone development for sustainable agriculture. If relative poverty is found to be a problem, a policy intervention to increase rural incomes in peat zones by say 50% (with non-fire and non-expansion achievement indicators) within a suitable physical peat landscape that has been rewetted under effective water table management may be considered. For implementation, this will have to be mediated by business-political networks at national and sub-national level within Indonesia's decentralized political economy and should be well-crafted for this context.

How to pay for it? Welfare economist Ng Yew Kwang asks: "How much compensation would make me indifferent to the (haze) situation?" He postulates that Singaporeans might be willing to forgo 10-15% of their annual salary to make the haze problem go away (The Malaysian Insider, 2013). It is intriguing to consider how much Southeast Asian urbanite might be willing to contribute to really resolve the peat haze-smoke problem at source.

ACKNOWLEDGEMENTS

This paper expands on the authors' work in "Haze Control through the Sustenance of Indonesian Oil Palm Smallholders" in Thinking ASEAN Issue 5 / November 2015, (weblink; http://admin.thcasean.org/assets/uploads/file/2015/11/Thinking_ASEAN_November_2015.compressed.pdf) and we thank The Habibie Center for their permission reproduce this work here. The authors also worked on "The Felda case study" (Khor et al, 2015) for LMC International Ltd. Khor is an economist specializing in palm oil and sustainable supply chains at LMC International Ltd. Saravanamuttu is an independent scholar and a former

[8] Interview with Dr Lulie Melling, Tropical Peat Research Laboratory Unit of Sarawak, 6 Oct 2015.

professor of political science at the Universiti Sains Malaysia at Penang. Augustin is a US based analyst with a recent focus on palm-oil and energy issues. The opinions expressed in this article are personal to the writers and do not reflect the official opinion of the organizations with whom they are affiliated.

REFERENCES

1. BBC Monitoring (2005), "Indonesia's Transmigration Programme Aimed at Border, Outer Island Areas." *BBC Monitoring Asia Pacific (1),* 13 Mar 2006. ProQuest. (Accessed 4 Nov 2015).
2. Business Times (2015), "Burning shame," 21 Oct 2015, http://www.businesstimes.com.sg/infographics/burning-shame (accessed 3 Nov 2015).
3. Golver, David and Jessup, Timothy (1999), *Indonesia's Fires and Haze: The Cost of Catastrophe*, 200 pages, Institute of Southeast Asian Studies, Singapore.
4. Khor Reports (2013), "Great Haze II- Karmic winds of change," 22 June 2013, https://docs.google.com/viewer?a=v&pid=sites&srcid=ZGVmYXVsdGRvbWFpbnxraG9ycmVwb3J0czIwMTF8Z3g6MWJjODhlZjEzNTRkY2ZiZQ (accessed 5 Nov 2015).
5. Khor, Yu Leng, Saravanamuttu, Johan and Augustin, Deborah (2015), "The Felda Case Study," LMC International Limited for the Sustainable Palm Oil Manifesto group, http://www.carbonstockstudy.com/carbonstockstudy/files/94/94ad98bf-119c-47c5-a355-1900822a6e04.pdf (accessed 21 June 2016).
6. Marlier, Miriam E et al. (2015) "Fire emissions and regional air quality impacts from fires in oil palm, timber, and logging concessions in Indonesia," *Environmental Research Letters 10*, IOP Publishing.
7. New York Times (2015a), "Southeast Asia, Choking on Haze, Struggles for a Solution," 8 Oct 2015, http://www.nytimes.com/2015/10/09/world/asia/indonesia-forest-fires-haze-singapore-malaysia.html?_r=0 (accessed 3 Nov 2015).
8. New York Times (2015b), "Rain in Indonesia Dampens Forest Fires That Spread Toxic Haze," 28 Oct 2015, http://www.nytimes.com/2015/10/29/world/asia/indonesia-forest-fire-toxic-haze.html (accessed 3 Nov 2015).
9. Potter, Lesley (2012). "New Transmigration 'paradigm' in Indonesia: Examples from Kalimantan." *Asia Pacific Viewpoint*, Vol. 53, No. 3, December 2012.
10. Sri Adhiati, M.Adriana and Bobsien, Armin (ed.) (2001). "Indonesia's Transmigration Programme - An Update." Jakarta: *Down to Earth*, July 2001, http://www.downtoearth-indonesia.org/sites/downtoearth-indonesia.org/files/Transmigration%20update%202001.pdf (accessed 4 Nov 2015).
11. The Borneo Post (2015), "Sabah to get CPO certified as sustainable palm oil," 5 Nov 2015, http://www.theborneopost.com/2015/11/05/sabah-to-get-cpo-certified-as-sustainable-palm-oil/#ixzz3qffHcZnx (accessed 5 Nov 2015).
12. The Malaysian Insider (2013), "Singapore's losses to haze underestimated, says Nanyang professor," 6 Jul 2013, http://www.themalaysianinsider.com/world/article/singapores-losses-to-haze-underestimated-says-nanyang-professor#sthash.B1UjVjef.dpuf (accessed 20 October 2015).
13. The Malaysian Insider (2015), "Botanist says squatters in Kalimantan could be smoke culprits," 2 Nov 2015, http://www.themalaysianinsider.com/malaysia/article/botanist-says-squatters-in-kalimantan-could-be-smoke-culprits (accessed 3 Nov 2015).
14. The Straits Times (2015), "NTUC FairPrice withdraws 18 products sourced from firm suspected of contributing to haze," 7 Oct 2015, http://news.asiaone.com/news/singapore/ntuc-fairprice-withdraws-18-products-sourced-firm-suspected-contributing-haze (accessed 30 Oct 2015).
15. Varkkey, Helena (2015a), *The Haze Problem in Southeast: Palm Oil and Patronage*, 244 pages, Routledge Malaysian Studies Seriesm Routledge, New York.
16. Varkkey, Helena (2015b), Interview with BFM radio, http://www.bfm.my/helena-varkkey-who-is-profiting-from-the-haze.html (accessed 3 Nov 2015).

Abstract No: A-467

IMPACT OF MINERAL NUTRITION MANAGEMENT ON *GANODERMA* INCIDENCE IN OIL PALM PLANTED ON PEAT SOIL

Pujianto, Achmad W.S, Dafian.P., Syaiful, Suhardi, Putri A.W and J.P Caliman

SMART Research Institute, Indonesia

**Corresponding author: pujianto_smartri@yahoo.com*

SUMMARY

The basal stem rot (BSR) disease of oil palm due to *Ganoderma* fungus is seriously threatening oil palm plantation in Malaysia and Indonesia, as well as part of Africa. Its increases with time and replanting cycles and therefore impact the profitability of the commodity. *Ganoderma* infection is widespread in mineral, peat, acid sulphate soils, etc. Mineral nutrition management on peat soil is undoubtedly an important factor to optimizing the nutrition balance of palms to producing high yield. However, it has been reported on many crops that mineral or organic fertilizers could affect the incidence of the diseases. Generally while some nutrients are favorable for the development of diseases, others seem to provide some protection to the plants. It is known that the equilibrium chemical composition in plants affect their resistance to pest and disease. Reports also mentioned that the change in soil mineral nutrition levels and balance due to fertilizer applications could also affect the soil microbial development, including pathogenic microbe. Here we report the results of a long-term field trial using NPK (3x3x3) fertilizer with 3 replicates was conducted during the period of 1999-2012 in a *Ganoderma* endemic area on peat soil in Riau-Indonesia. The objective of this study was to assess the impact of mineral fertilizer application on *Ganoderma* incidence on mature oil palm as well as on their productivity. The incidence of *Ganoderma* infection was observed regularly in the field by counting the number of dead palms in the treatment plots. The results indicated that the application of Phosphorus (P) and Nitrogen (N) fertilizers increased significantly the percentage of *Ganoderma* incidence; while the application of Potassium (K) fertilizer did not give a significant effect. Based on cumulative 14 years (1999 – 2012) observation the control (without P), the application of 0.45 kg P_2O_5/palm/year and 0.90 kg P_2O_5/palm/year increased the percentage of *Ganoderma* incidence 190 % and 240 % respectively. For N fertilizer treatments, the application of 0.69 kg N/palm/year and 1.38 kg N/palm/year increased the percentage of *Ganoderma* incidence by16 % and 18 % respectively compare to control (without N). The estimated yield loss due to *Ganoderma* incidence recorded during observation (cumulative 1999-2012) on P treatments varied from 6 to 15 ton/ha (0.5 to 1.1 ton/ha/year) and for N treatments varied from 9 to 12 ton/ha (0.7 to 0.9 ton/ha/year) respectively.

Keywords: *Ganoderma, peat, mineral nutrition management*

INTRODUCTION

The basal stem rot (BSR) disease of oil palm due to *Ganoderma* fungus is seriously threatening oil palm plantation in Malaysia and Indonesia, as well as part of Africa with significant yield losses through direct loss of stand, reduce yield of infected palms. Generally, BSR increases with time and replanting cycles impacting the profitability of the commodity. *Ganoderma* infection is widespread in mineral, peat, acid sulphate soils, etc (Idris A S *et al.*, 2001).

Mineral nutrition management on peat soil is undoubtedly an important factor for optimizing the nutrition balance of palms to produce high yield. It has been reported in many crops that mineral or organic fertilizers could affect the incidence of diseases. Generally there are nutrients are favorable for the development of diseases, while others seem to provide some protection to the plants. Mohd Tayeb D. *et al.* (2003) reported highest incidence of Ganoderma occurred when the nitrogen and phosphorus levels were highest. The application of mineral fertilizers in different amount and form not only affect the growth and composition of the plant directly but also has profound effect on microbial activity in the soil and rhizosphere and plant tolerance to root pathogen (Marschner, 1995). Aciego *et al.* (2009) and Rousk *et al.* (2009) reported soil pH has marked effects on microbial biomass, community structure and response to substrate addition, where at low soil pH, fungal species were more dominant in the microbial community.

MATERIAL AND METHOD

The trial was conducted in the field from 1999 to 2011 on peat soil (Typic Tropohemist) in Riau-Indonesia. The planting material was DxP Socfindo planted in 1992 (density 143 palms/ha). The treatments used were: 1). Nitrogen (N), where N0 = 0 kg N/palm/year, N1 = 0.69 kg N/palm/year (1.5 kg Urea/palm/year) and N2 = 1.38 kg N/palm/yr (3.0 kg urea/palm/year). 2). Phosphorus (P), where P0 = 0 P_2O_5/palm/year, P1 = 0.45 kg P_2O_5/palm/year (1.5 kg Rock Phosphate/palm/year) and P2 = 0.90 kg P_2O_5/palm/year (3.0 kg Rock Phosphate/palm/year) and Potassium (K), K0 = 0 kg K_2O/palm/year, K1 = 1.5 kg K_2O/palm/year (2.5 kg MOP/palm/year) and K2=3.0 kg K_2O/palm/year (5.0 kg MOP/palm/year). An incompletely confounded factorial design with 3 replicates was employed. Homogenous fertilizers ($CuSO_4$, $ZnSO_4$ and HGFB) were applied yearly according to the dosage recommended based on foliar analysis. The incidence of *Ganoderma* infection was observed regularly in the field by counting the number of dead palms in the treatment plots. The census for *Ganoderma* incidence was conducted for all palms in every plot (49 palms/plot).

RESULTS AND DISCUSSION

Mineral Nutrition and Ganoderma Incidence

The result showed that, in general, the application of P fertilizer gave significant increasing number of dead palms due to *Ganoderma* attack (p-value < 0.01). During the observation period (1999-2012), the cumulative number of dead palms due to *Ganoderma* infection observed on P0, P1 and P2 was 30 %, 53 % and 73 %, respectively. Compared to control (without P application), the application of 0.45 kg P_2O_5/palm/yr (P1) and 0.90 kg P_2O_5/palm/yr (P2) increased the incidence of *Ganoderma* infection 190 % and 240 % respectively. The field observation also indicated that the appearance *Ganoderma* disease incidence was firstly reported in P2 (approximately 2 years after application), then in P1 (approximately 4 years after application) and P0 (approximately 5 years after application) (Figure 1A). This situation was paralleled with the rise of leaf P content (Figure 3-A).

N fertilizer gave significant effect on *Ganoderma* incidence (p-value < 0.01). An increased dosage of N fertilizer applied increased *Ganoderma* infection on oil palm in this soil. Statistically, the incidence of *Ganoderma* infection found in control (without N application) was significantly lower than that observed in N1 and N2 treatments. N1 and N2 treatments were not significantly different. Compared to the control, the N rates of N1 and N2 increased *Ganoderma* incidence by 16% and 18%, respectively (Figure 1B). The application of N fertilizer increased the leaf N content that may have contributed to the increase in *Ganoderma* infection (Figure 3B).

The application of potassium fertilizer did not give any significant effect on the incidence of *Ganoderma* infection in peat soil (p-value > 0.05). Figure 2A indicated that the incidence of *Ganoderma* infection was observed 4 years after application. 20 years after planting, the number of dead palms due to *Ganoderma* infection was about 54 % in control (K0) compared to 51 % in K1 and 55 % in K2, and the differences was not significant statistically. There was an interaction was a tendency to indicate N and K application on *Ganoderma* incidence (Figure 2B).

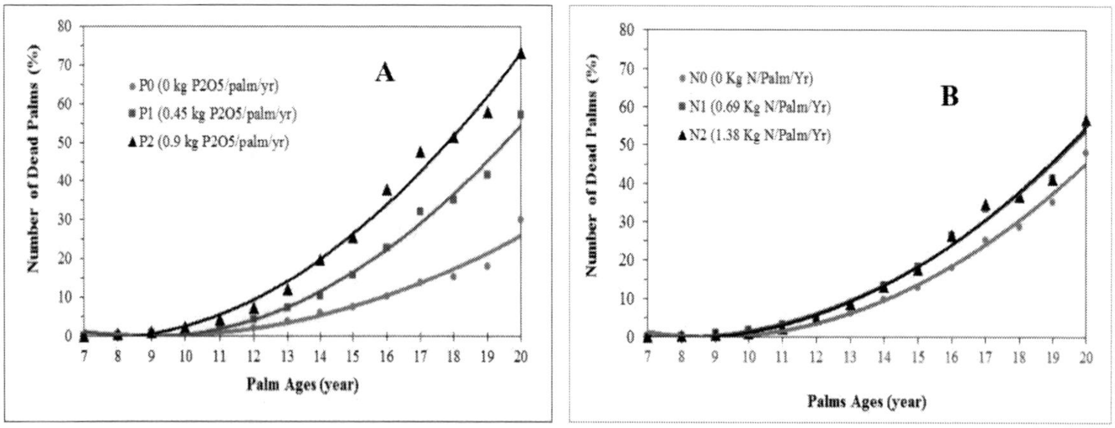

Figure 1: Impact of Phosphorus (A) and Nitrogen (B) application on Number of Dead Palm Due to *Ganoderma* infection in Peat Soil

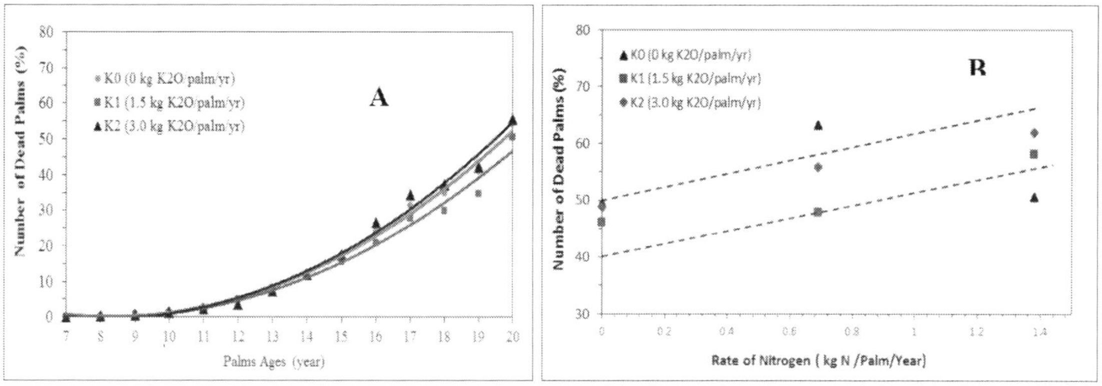

Figure 2: Impact of K Application (A) and N-K Interaction on Number of Dead Palm Due to *Ganoderma* infection in Peat Soil

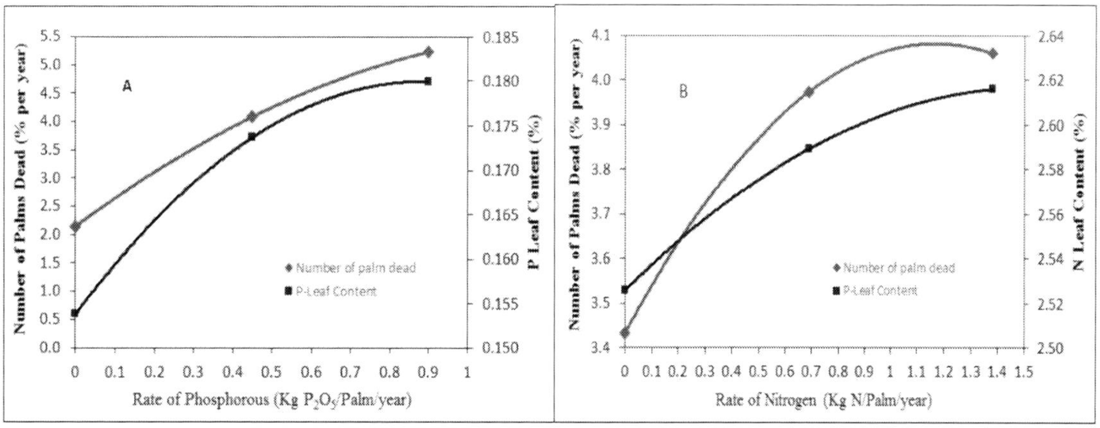

Figure 3: Correlation between The Rate of Phosphorus (A) and Nitrogen (B) With Incidence of *Ganoderma* infection and Leaf Nutrient.

Ganoderma and Oil Palm Yield

The average yield obtained during period 1999 - 2011 with different rates of N, P and K fertilizers can be seen in Table 1. The effect of application of these fertilizers was only significant on bunch weight, while on bunch number and average bunch weight, the effect was not significant statistically.

Table 1: Average Palm Yield Obtained by Different Rate N, P and K Fertilizers during Period 1999 – 2011.

Parameters	Treatments											
	Nitrogen				Phosphorus				Potassium			
	N0	N1	N2	Anova	P0	P1	P2	Anova	K0	K1	K2	Anova
Bunch Weight (ton/ha/yr) *)	19	22	21	Sig	21	22	19	Sig	19	21	21	Sig
Bunch Number (Bunch/ha/yr)*)	1317	1398	1364	NS	1364	1407	1307	NS	1269	1417	1391	NS
Average Bunch Weight (Kg/Bunch)	14.7	15.4	15.2	NS	15.1	15.3	14.8	NS	15.3	14.6	15.1	NS

Note : *) extrapolation based on yield per palm/year and palm density 143 palms/ha; Sig: significant (p-value < 0.01); NS : Not Significant (p-value >0.05).

The estimation of yield loss due to *Ganoderma* incidence on area applied with P and N fertilizers is given in Figures 4 A and B. Based on the number of dead palm observed, the cumulative yield loss (during 14 years) in control (P0) was approximately 6 tons/ha (0.5 ton/ha/yr); while in P1 and P2, the cumulative yield loss estimated was approximately 12 tons/ha (0.9 ton/ha/yr) and 15 tons/ha (1.1 ton/ha/yr) respectively (Figure 4 A). For N application, the cumulative yield loss in control (N0) was approximately 9 tons/ha (0.7 ton/ha/yr) compared to 12 tons/ha (0.9 ton/ha/yr) in N1 and 12 tons/ha (0.9 ton/ha/yr) in N2 treatments. We also observed that the average cumulative yield loss due to *Ganoderma* incidence in K application was approximately 11 tons/ha (0.8 ton/ha/yr).

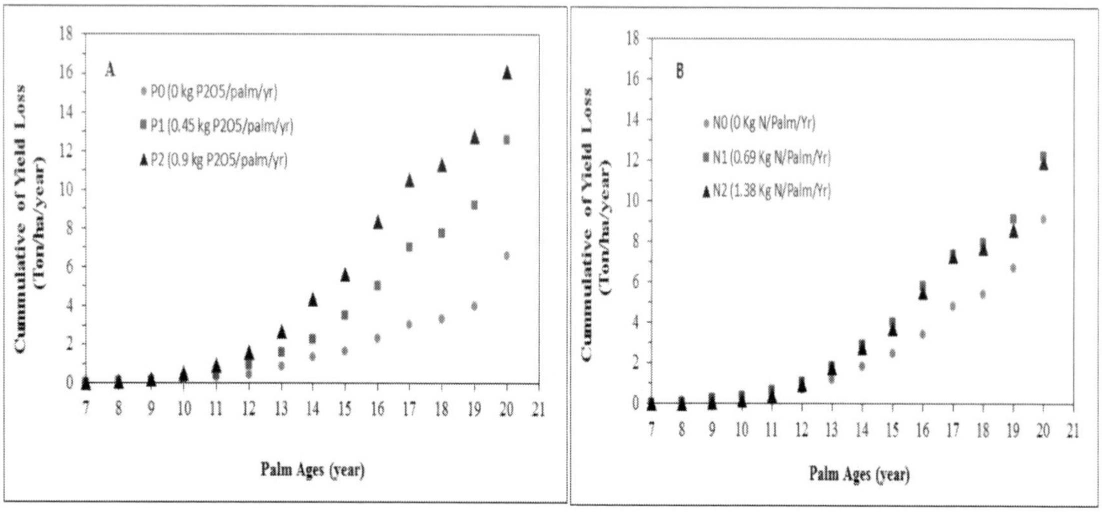

Figure 4: Loss Yield Estimated Due to *Ganoderma* Incidence on Different Rate of Phosphorus (A) and Nitrogen (B) Fertilizers

CONCLUSION

The application of Phosphorus (P) and Nitrogen (N) fertilizers increased significantly the percentage of *Ganoderma* incidence; while the application of Potassium (K) fertilizer was not significant. Based on the cumulative 14 years (1999 – 2012) observation, the application of 0.45 kg P_2O_5/palm/year and 0.90 kg P_2O_5/palm/year increased the percentage of *Ganoderma* incidence 190 % and 240 % respectively compared to the control (without P). For N fertilizer treatments, the application of 0.69 kg N/palm/year and 1.38 kg N/palm/year increased the percentage of *Ganoderma* incidence by16 % and 18 % respectively compared to control (without N).The estimated yield loss due to *Ganoderma* incidence with P treatments varied from 6 to 15 ton/ha (0.5 to 1.1 ton/ha/year), for N treatments varied from 9 to 12 ton/ha (0.7 to 0.9 ton/ha/year) and for K 11 ton (0.8 ton/ha/year) respectively. Further study is required to explain the role of mineral fertilizer and its effect on reduce *Ganoderma* incidence or tolerance in oil palm.

ACKNOWLEDGEMENTS

The authors wish to thank the President Director of PT.Smart.Tbk for permission to publish this paper. The co-operation by FOES Dept. and supporting staff of the Agronomy Dept. of SMARTRI are gratefully acknowledged.

REFERENCES

1. Aciego Pietri JC, Brookes PC (2009) Substrate input and pH as factors controlling microbial biomass, activity and community structure in an arable soil. Soil Biol Biochem 41:1396.
2. Idris AS, , Arrifin D, Watt TA and Swinburne TR (2001) Distribution of species of *Ganoderma* Basal Stem Rot of Oil Palm in Relation to the Environmental Condition in Peninsular Malaysia, In Proc. International Palm Oil Congress., Kuala Lumpur., 20 – 22 august 2001., MPOB .p.385-394.
3. Marschner, H (1995) Mineral Nutrition of Higher Plants, second edition. Academic Press Limited London.,p437.
4. Mohd Tayeb, D, Idris Abu Seman and Mohd Haniff Harun (2003), Reduction of *Ganoderma* Infection in Oil Palm Through Blanced Fertilization in Peat, In Proc. International Palm Oil Congress., Putrajaya Malaysia., 24 – 28 august 2003., MPOB .p.193-218.
5. Rousk J, Brookes PC, Baat E (2009) Constrating Soil pH effect on fungal and bacterial growth suggest functional redundancy in carbon mineralization. Appl. Environ. Microbial 75:1589-1596.

Abstract No: A-391

LET CHINA OPEN THE NEW LIFE ACTIVITY OF PEAT INDUSTRY

Xiancheng Zeng

China Humic Acid Industry Association

**Corresponding author: chaia@126.com*

SUMMARY

Peat, which is given by God to human beings as the natural substrate for the activity of opening the new life, is clean, safe and reliable. And, it is the cradle of nurturing "new life (wise heart) agriculture". Learning from Europe and initiating the new life activity of peat industry will have a brilliant future. In 2014, the peat product sales in China is 5 million m^3, the market demand is 23 million m^3, the expected market demand is 250 million m^3, and fifth year new industries set up is worth of 230 billion Yuan RMB. Base on the current tendency, the development prospect could be seen very well. Basically, we carry forward the new life activity of peat industry, start from the resource allocation involving the "domestic and international" scope, strengthen the deep cooperation of the global peat industry, provide "green product and health services", bring up a glorious future of "peat (substrate reconstruction) → infant care home (pure land and industry) → health products (soul reconstruction) → happy life (the essence of people's livelihood)". In conclusion, the concept of "peat+" is to be built and will accelerate the new rural production pattern of "precision of micro domain agriculture + organic ecological agriculture + customer-friendly health industry". This will not only benefit China, but also benefit the world.

Keywords: *China, peat, industry, new life, activity*

BACKGROUND

China is a big agricultural country, and the majority is about 800 million farmers. Solving the problem of agriculture, country and farmer correctly is a great business to realize national well-off and build of a harmonious society [1]. To carry out the new life activity of peat industry is mainly geared by the needs of agriculture, introduction and digestion the advanced experience from European countries, combining with the development level of agriculture in China. It is of great practical significance to promote the new life activity of peat industry in China. Based on the "one belt, one road" national strategy [2], it will have extremely far-reaching influence on sharing the experience of happy life led by peat health industry with other developing countries.

THE CONNOTATION OF THE NEW LIFE ACTIVITY

At present, agriculture in China is facing five major problems: (1) the area of arable land will only tend to reduce but not increase. (2) the population will only increase but not reduce; (3) people's requirements on the quality of agricultural products is only with the tendency of improve, but not drop; (4) tackling climate change, the development of low carbon agriculture will only be enlarged, but not shrinking; (5) carry out the ecological environment construction, biodiversity can only be strengthened, but not weakening. In this regard, China promotes the new life activity of peat industry, in accordance with the climate change and the climate & smart agriculture. A fresh human-centered life style is able to develop generally by improving the quality of crops and stimulating the public demand. The application of "Peat+" is capable of adjusting the relationship between new agricultural productivity and ecology. Comprehensively creating the new pastoral production mode of "regulated soil remediation + precision of micro domain agriculture + organic ecological agriculture + friendly health industry + open new resources" will gain fruitful achievements.

CHINA PEAT MARKET SPACE CAPACITY

Regarding to the whole world, the annual exploitation quantity of peat is about 64 million cubic meters. Among of which, 50 % is applied in agriculture. Comparatively, the annual exploitation quantity of peat in China is about 1.5 million cubic meters. Among of which, 90% is applied in agriculture, mainly involving the areas of peat resource utilization, professional matrix, peat fertilizer, soil remediation, and water pollution control et al. At present, the total value of out-put in five years of the five largest markets associated with promotion of new life activity in peat industry in China is expected to be 230 billion yuan.

The Comprehensive Utilization of Peat Resources

Aiming to promote the new life activity of peat industry in China, firstly it should meet the needs of peat products. Current peat resources is about 12.4 billion cubic meters in China, only less than 8% of which can be put in use[3]. In addition, the peat is mainly meadow peat with large decompose degree, low fiber content, and worse structure, which cannot reach up with the requirement of "quantity and quality" in the market of China. According to the statistics, the sales volume of peat products in China in 2014 was about 5 million cubic meters. Among of which, the imported peat resources was about 1 million cubic meters, which was far from the market demand of peat products. It is estimated that in the next 5 years, the imported peat resources in China is to be 15 million cubic meters. Assuming 350 yuan for 1 cubic meter, then the entire market is worth 5.3 billion yuan. Therefore, the Chinese market is huge for both domestic protection development and global resources utilization.

Personalized Professional Substrate

In recent years, the agriculture in China has presented a new pattern of diversified development. In addition to the traditional agriculture, facility agriculture, landscape agriculture, home furnishing agriculture become more and more popular. The demand of the substrate is growing, such as the plant nursery, horticulture cultivation and individual cultivation. It is estimated that the nursery substrate annually will attain to 50 million cubic meters for industrial crops including vegetables, flowers, fruits, cotton, rice, tobacco and sugar beet et al. At present, the amount of the peat substrate utilization is nearly 5 million cubic meters. Assuming 300 yuan for 1 cubic meter, the market is about 13.5 billion yuan. In addition, the areas of vertical greening, planting balcony, roof planting will increase the peat substrate demand.

Soil Remediation and Production

The quality of cultivated soil in China is generally low. 70% of the soil has problems [4], and about 26 million hectares of cultivated soil owns different level pollution. Among of which, more than 3.3 million hectares of cultivated soil suffers moderate or severe heavy metal pollution. On condition that 1% of the soil utilizes peat for repairing or reconstruction, assuming 1 hectare with 60 cubic meters of peat soil and consume 500 yuan, accordingly the market is up to 7.8 billion yuan. Even though, it does not include the transformation of saline alkali land, desertification control, hilly land utilization and mine reclamation et al. At present, the soil remediation of peat conditioner in China is mainly applied in the cultivation protection of the sunlight greenhouse, plastic greenhouse, and plastic film mulching. It is expected that, in the next 5 years, the protected area will reach up to 1 million hectares. Assuming soil with 1 hectare is with 0.4 cubic meters of peat soil, and consumes 500 yuan, and only the market of soil remediation is able to reach up to 200 million yuan.

Environment Friendly Peat Fertilizer

Fertilizer is dominating in agriculture in China. Over 50 years of practice has proved that the humic acid fertilizer contributes to the soil safety, fertilizer quality and efficiency, crop nutrition and health as well as the friendly environment. Recently, the Chinese government pushes constructing of ecological civilization significantly. Ministry of agriculture and the Ministry of industry and information introduced "Fertilizer zero growth action plan" [5] and "Fertilizer industry transformation guidance"[6], respectively, so that the demand of humic acid fertilizer can grow rapidly, whose origin is identical to soil. Peat, as an important raw material source of extracting humic acid, exhibits versatile and personalized, including peat humic acid based fertilizer, foliar fertilizer, water solution fertilizer, and organic fertilizer and water conservation fertilizer. Assuming in next 5 years, the demand of peat humic acid fertilizer will exceed 5 million tons, and the output value will attain to 13 billion yuan (Calculated according to 2600 yuan / ton).

Amount of Water Pollution Control

China is a country short of water resources. The per capita water resources are only 2300 cubic meters, accounting for 25 % of the world average level [7]. At the same time, China is also one of the countries with the most serious water pollution. The seven river systems of Liaohe, Haihe River, Huaihe River, Yellow River, Songhua River and the Yangtze River are all suffering different degrees of pollution. Lake (reservoir) rich nutritional problems are still prominent. Moreover, the pollution sources along the coast are increasing [8]. Hence, treatment of water pollution is urgent. Environmental scientists has pointed out that the aquatic humic substances is "scavenger", just as the water "white cells" [9]. Industrial extraction of humic acid, including peat, can be used to regulate water quality, water purification, and optimization of aquatic organisms, sewage pollution reduction and development of the aquatic health breeding. Its application areas and the market development space are huge. Taking the sewage treatment as an example, the total amount of wastewater discharge in 2014 was 71.62 billion tons, accounting for 1/6 of the total amount of the wastewater discharge in the whole world [10]. Among of which, 0.3 % has used humic acid product for water pollution control, and the output value was about 200 billion yuan (about 10 thousand yuan for 1 ton).

THE INNOVATION MODE OF NEW LIFE AGRICULTURAL

As early as nineteenth Century, Holland has introduced peat into the field of horticultural crop breeding and cultivation. In early twentieth Century, the peat industry in Europe developed rapidly, especially agriculture [11]. China has been concentrated in the peat study for 58 years [12], and is still behind the European countries for production and application. Therefore, combing the conditions in China and learning from Europe will obtain fruitful achievement for conducting the new life activity of peat substrate in China.

Precision of Micro Domain Agriculture

Micro domain agriculture is mainly focused on the characteristics of significant differences of agriculture production conditions existing among the geographical location, climate, topography, soil and water in China, including scale and non-scale. Scale refers to the intensive production type of micro domain, including land for growing field crops, factory-like seedling nursery et al. Non-scale focuses on the irregular, asymmetric production region of micro domain, including gardens, roofs, balconies et al. The so-called precision, speaking of the scale cultivation, means to provide the specific cultivation substrate and professional products according to different regions, different crops, different varieties and different consumer groups together with habits. In terms of the individual production, combining "substrate, nutrition, regulating acid, controlling disease and container..." into one subject, peat, one-to-one, point-to-point, to provide a fine and delicate cultivation substrate and professional products, can be accurate to a basin, a tree seedlings, a gram of soil. It is true that a unique precision production in micro agriculture will bloom together in China.

Adjustable Soil Remediation

With more attention being paid to the issue of soil, the market of soil remediation is keeping expanding. In recent years, the Chinese government continued to carry out projects of "soil remediation, improving organic matter, protection and utilization of black land, management of heavy metal land, desert governance, transformation of saline and alkaline land, transformation of low yield farmland, fertile soil engineering, soil testing and formulated fertilization, drought resistant water-saving, fertilizer integration". New technology, new products and new methodology are more and more important. The three significant characteristics of "water retention, fertilizer and breathable conditioning" of peat soil conditioner play major role in remediation of contaminated soil, improving organic matter, desertification, salinization controlling, transformation of low yielding fields et al. Especially in the dry farming, water-saving agriculture, plateau agricultural engineering. Accordingly, facing the problem of soil, developing multiple management products for peat soil, and solving the current problems of widespread soil treatment problem in China are particularly important.

Organic Ecological Agriculture

Now Chinese market is advertising organic agriculture, however, all the 1800 million acres of arable land need fertilizer. In this sense, Chinese agriculture cannot realize the real organic agriculture. Assuming organic ecological agriculture in China, should follow the law of the negation of negation, namely mainly reconstruction of the regional ecological environment. And producing the ecological environment friendly peat agricultural products can solve the issue of mass production organic food with large amount. It must be stressed that the organic matter from the industrial and agricultural by-product might be unsafe, but the organic matter in peat humic acid must be safe [13]. Uniting the peat humic acid and fertilizer into "marriage", the safety inorganic nutrients will be brought into the soil. And the production mode of multi-direction of "soil resources and fertilizer efficiency and crop output and environmental benefits" can be built, which further to achieve comprehensive effect of "moderate investment, high yield, no pollution and good quality", to achieve the organic agricultural production thoroughfare.

Man-Of-The-People Style New Rural

Is it the "garden of Eden"? Just build it! Peat is a natural fine substrate, clean, safe and reliable. Let peat own the features of professional, low carbon, high quality, warm and sweet, beauty. Build the new rural life activity of "infant care home " is urgent. Because of professional, it can create characteristic agriculture, recycling agriculture, stereo agriculture, puzzle agriculture, agricultural landscape; because of low carbon, it can create ecological agriculture, organic agriculture, alternative agriculture, seasonal agriculture, recycling agriculture; because of high quality, it can create a ratio agriculture, personality agricultural, clean agriculture, moral agricultural and self-entertainment agriculture; because of the warm and sweet, it can create a passion agriculture, eldly people agriculture, health agriculture, leisure agriculture, festival agricultural; because of beauty, it can create beautiful agricultural, appearance agriculture, fashion agricultural, decorating agriculture, visual agriculture. All close to the green health of the pastoral life, what an attitude of cherishing people!

Open up New Resources Uncultivated Land

At present, the Chinese people's life has presented a new ordinary state: people's demand for the quality of agricultural products is more and more high. The current situation of China's cultivated land (less area, heavy pollution, low quality) has been unable to meet the needs of the people's high quality of life. However, China has an area of about 1 million square kilometers of sandy land, 33.4 square kilometers of desertification land and shifting of sand dunes, 100 square kilometers of the hills, and rich mining resources, the Gobi desert. Promoting the new activity of the peat industry and developing the new resources is undoubtedly a more direct and more rapid beneficial supplement to the cultivated land resources. Furthermore, there are three advantages: one is the resource does not exist the issue of scrambling land with civilian, so that large area of unified development can be realized; the second is the large area of new resources, abundant types and significant differences, so that depth development can be applied to create a distinctive new cultivated land, benefiting diversified agricultural production needs; the third is new resources are unexplored, so that it is able to monolithic integration by one time, and reconstruction of the regional ecological environment, to achieve accurate, ecological, organic and efficient in whole. These new resources will become the uncultivated land of constructing the new life activity of peat industry truely.

CONCLUSION

We believe that promoting the new life activity of peat industry will create a civilized business, and in turn will create a harmonious life. In the next 5 years, promoting the new life activity of the peat industry, adjusting the regional agricultural productivity the ecological relationships, creating "the garden of Eden" of "precision agriculture of micro domain + organic ecological agriculture + friendly health industry" will become a magnificent picture of new rural production in Chinas. To be concluded, promoting the new life activity of peat industry in China will not only benefit the China, but also benefit the whole world.

REFERENCE

1. The Central Committee of the Communist Party of China, *the State Council. Some opinions on the implementation of the new concept of development to speed up the modernization of agriculture and realize the goal of well-off society in an all-round way.* 2016-1-27.
2. National Development and Reform Commission、Ministry of Foreign Affairs、Ministry of Commerce of People's Republic of China. *Vision and Actions on Jointly Building Silk Road Economic Belt and 21st-Century Maritime Silk Road.* 2015-3-28.
3. Xianmin Meng.China. Peat resources reserves, characteristics and protection utilization countermeasures [J]. *Journal of Natural Resources*, 2006, (1): 567-574.
4. Ministry of Environmental Protection, Ministry of Land and Resources of the People's Republic of China. *A nationwide soil pollution survey report.*2014-4-17.
5. Ministry of Agriculture of the People's Republic of China. *To 2020 fertilizer use zero growth action plan.* 2015-3-18.
6. Ministry of Industry and Information Technology of the People's Republic of China. *On promoting the restructuring of the fertilizer industry development guidance.*2015-7-29.
7. Chunling Zhang, Yicheng Fu, Wenbin Zang *et al.,* Chinese of the shortage of water resources and poverty. *China Rural Water and Hydropower*, 2013(1):1-4.
8. Wen Chen. China water pollution treatment of the Dynamic CGE model construction and evaluation of policy, PhD thesis, *Hunan University*, 2012.
9. Hofrichter M, Steinbuchel, Shengrong Guo (Translator). *Biopolymer*, 2004. Beijing: Chemical Industry Press, 2004.
10. Ministry of Environmental Protection of China. *National environmental statistics bulletin*, 2015-10-29.
11. Linfeng Du, Xiangyang Sun, Yan Shen. The research progress of peat, horticultural substrate. *Northern Horiculture*, 2007(10):10-28.
12. Peat bog Institute, Northeast Normal University,1958. http://baike.baidu.com/link?url=
13. tmcn6zVVLQiU0xinXdXLDc_LwHQflg0Yrnhdu6bfh2maxMGKp1V5VyAhUF_m-Dh8Ol0Xv5dOOR8PJNJ5gJ4Qca
14. Xiancheng Zeng, Shuang Li. let humic acid play an important role in the supplement and promotion of soil fertility. *Humid Acid*, 2014(2):1-8.

Abstract No: A-054

LONG TERM PERPECTIVES FOR WATER MANAGEMENT IN DRAINED PEATLANDS; EXPERIENCES IN PEAT-POLDER SYSTEMS IN THE NETHERLANDS

J. M. Schouwenaars

Wetterskip Fryslan, Regional Water Board, The Netherlands

**Corresponding Author: jschouwenaars@wetterskipfryslan.nl*

SUMMARY

In the Netherlands, many peatlands were drained since the 16th -17th century and used for peat extraction and dairy farming. Since then the rate of land subsidence rates varies between 3 mm – 2 cm per year, depending on local conditions. This requires regular adaptation of water management and hydraulic infrastructure. Different stages of water system (or polder) development can be distinguished. Awareness of the actual stage of development in a drained peatland site enables to predict the next stage in its development. This recognition allows a better decision making on required adaptation strategies such as continuation of the actual agricultural land use, adaptations in agricultural zoning (see Rahmadi *et al.*, 2011) or transformation into e.g. restored wetlands (Schouwenaars, 2011). Based upon historical analyses of water management in the peatland polder systems in the Netherlands, trends in development are described. A typology is presented which may serve to identify the actual stage of development of peatlands after drainage. Drainage will continuously require adaptation measures and creates an increasing dependency on human interventions to reduce risks for flooding. The technical infrastructure becomes more complex and fragmented and the costs for water management increase gradually. The presented typology allows a better understanding on the actual stage of development of a drained peatland at a given site. It also gives a tool to predict the future stages in development.

Keywords: *water management, land subsidence, infrastructure, polder typology*

INTRODUCTION

An important feature of the low lying coastal zone in northwestern Europe is the presence of vast areas with organic peat soils. In the Netherlands, many peatlands were drained since the 16th -17th century and used for peat extraction and dairy farming. Since then the rate of land subsidence rates varies between 3 mm – 1 cm per year, depending on local conditions. (Schothorst (1977), Hoogland *et al.* (2012).

Started with the introduction of the individual windmills and later intensified by better pumping equipment, rates of land subsidence have increased considerably in the second half of the 20th century (see Figure1 and 2)

This process of land subsidence requires regular adaptation of water management and hydraulic infrastructure resulting in a continuous further fragmentation in peatland-poldersystems.

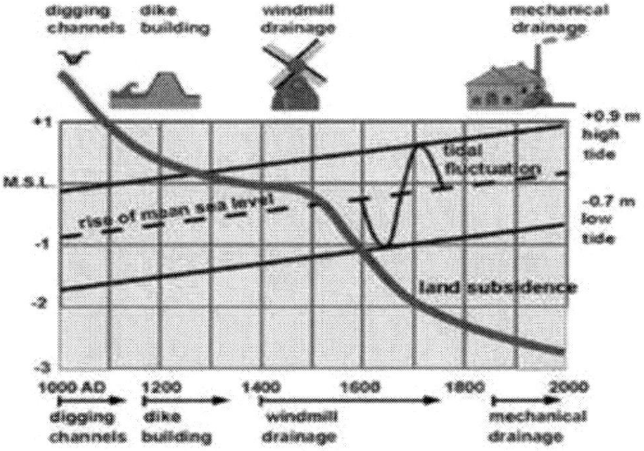

Figure 1: Historical development of drainage and land subsidence in the Netherlands (Atlas van Nederland, 1996)

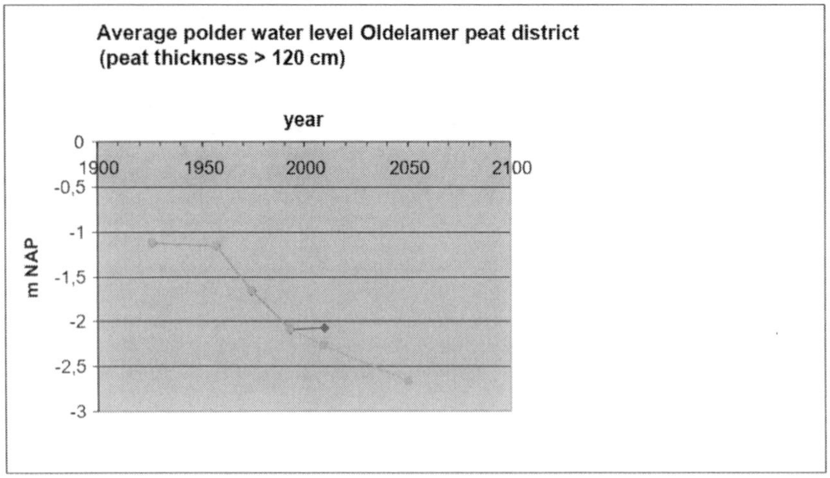

Figure 2: Lowering of polder water levels as a consequence of land subsidence n the Oldelamer peat district (m NAP is meters below sea level) (Hartman *et al.*, 2012)

When the degree of drainage in different parts of the polders is different, either in time or in intensity, also land surface levels will start to differ. Once this process has started, it is hardly possible to scale up the polders again. Here, the creation of larger polders units with a common water level, would lead to unacceptable differences in drainage levels and farming conditions. On the contrary, high rates of land subsidence in some parts of these peatlands urged to install pumps in these lower parts in the polders. In this way, these parts with lower water levels were isolated from the original polder and so called sub-polders were created. An illustration of the consequences of this process of fragmentation is presented in Figure3 and Figure 4.

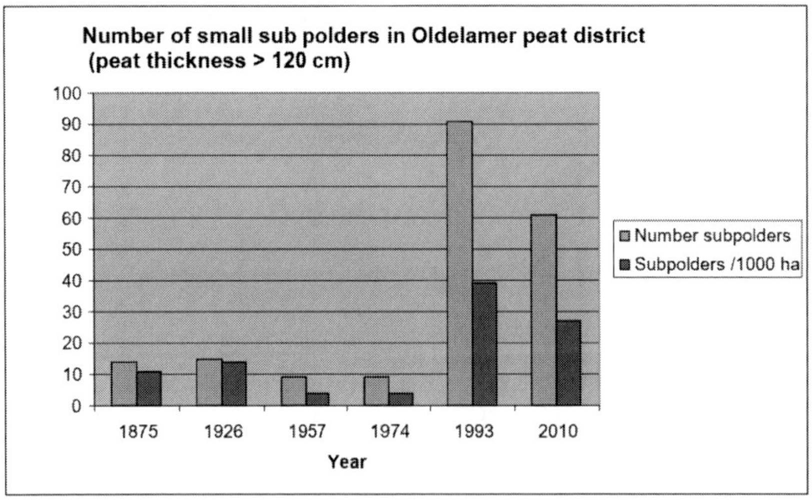

Figure 3: Fragmentation of the polder system in Oldelamer peat district as a consequence of land subsidence (Hartman *et al.*, 2012)

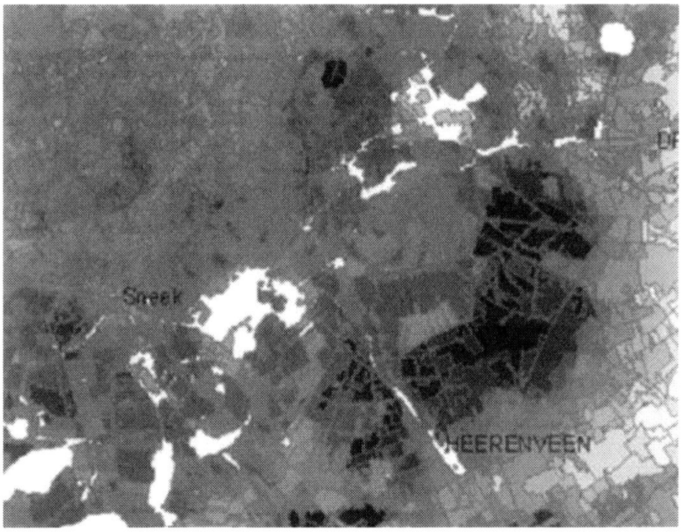

Figure 4: Fragmentation of the peat-polders systems in Fryslan, where in during the 20st century the average polder size has reduced from ca. 100 ha to only 20 ha

INCREASING COSTS FOR WATER MANAGEMENT

Land subsidence resulted in the necessity to construct dikes to prevent the lower parts to get flooded by water from the canal (or boezem) system. In contrast to what is commonly expected it are not the extra pumping costs but the high costs for dike construction and maintenance that cause the major increase in costs for water management in peat-polder systems. This is illustrated in Table 1.

Table 1: Extra costs for water management in peat-polders in the Netherlands over 200.000 ha and cumulative for the period 2010-2050; van den Born *et al.* 2016)

extra pumping costs	€ 0, 4 million
extra dams (and weirs)	€ 24, 8 million
larger dike constructions	€ 178, 1 million
Total	**€ 203, 3 million ***

* The total increase corresponds with ca. € 1000 per ha in 40 years, which equals an average of € 25 / ha/yr. Hence, the costs increase annually with € 1,25 per ha.

The actual annual costs for water management in the peatlands in the Netherlands vary from € 200 per ha per year (in the Fryslan peat district) to more than € 500 per year per ha (as estimated for the Utrecht peat district by van den Born *et al.*, 2016). For Fryslan, the increase of costs for water management due to land subsidence is estimated at ca.1% per year (Hartman *et al.*, 2012).

Hence, it is obvious that in these peatlands the normal process of upscaling driven by technology and cost effectiveness, -which is notable in most polders - is seriously hampered by the process of further fragmentation caused by land subsidence. Schouwenaars (2002) describes the specific problems related to land subsidence and fragmentation in the Echten polder in Fryslan.

DAIRY FARMING IN PEATLAND POLDER SYSTEMS

In the Fryslan peat district with a total area of 80.000 ha almost 70% is used for agriculture. Intensive drainage facilitates at the ca. 1000 dairy farms offer suitable conditions with forage production rates of ca. 10.000 kVEM per ha per year. For an average farmer this represents a production value of ca. € 1800 per ha per year. (Provincie Fryslan 2014, Factsheets Veenweidevisie)

The far reaching impact of intensive drainage for agriculture is the high oxidation rate of the peat soils. As a consequence in 2050 in almost half of the total peat area (i.e. 35.000 ha) the remaining peat layers have a thickness less than 0.4 m. (In the Dutch Soil Classification System soils with less than 40 cm of peat in the top 80 cm are no longer classified as peat soils).

Van den Born *et al.* (2016) present figures for production rates on peat soils in the Netherlands varying form 9.3 ton dry matter for intensive farming to 5.5 ton dry matter for extensive farming.

A NEW TYPOLOGY FOR DEVELOPMENT STAGES IN PEATLAND POLDER SYSTEMS

In historical analyses of polder development in Fryslan a logical sequency can be observed for stadia in development or adaptation of polder and boezem systems. In Table 2, some elements of this typology are presented, based upon a general theoretical analysis of the development of polder systems and illustrated by the specific analysis of the Tzummerpolder as presented in Schouwenaars (2011).

Table 2: Summary of development stages in peatland polder systems, adapted from the Tzummerpolder study after Schouwenaars (2011)

Development stage	**Period (year A.D.)**	**Type Code [1,2]**	**features**
Phase 1a: **Empolderment** *Phase 1b:* **Upscaling of polders**	1000-1100 1150-1500	S1 S1-D1 S1-D2	Small dikes with sluices closed dike-ring with sluices Larger dike rings with an inner boezem (Westergo)
Phase 2: **Enlargement of the boezem system**	1200-1300 1505	S2-D2	Damming of Marne and Middelzee estuaries and creation of a larger outer boezem system for Westergo. Construction of Oude Bildtdijk as new sea defence for Westergo, no longer a sea defence along former Middelsee.
Phase 3a: **Construction of dikes along the boezem** *Phase 3b*: **Upscaling polders and reduction length of dikes along boezem**	1800 – 1950 1900 - present	S2-D2-Bp1 S2-D2-Bp2	Construction of dikes along the boezem inside the polder systems. The discharge canal system of the Tzummerpolder is interconnected with those of neighbouring polders and parts of the inner boezem are no longer essential, enabling removal of dikes
Fase 4a: **Pumping of inner boezem and polders** *Fase 4b:* **Up saling of pumped polder systems**	1850 - 1900 1920	S2-D2-Bp2-M1 S2-D2-Bp2-M2	Construction of windmills in the Tzummerpolder Steam engine pump near Tzum, enabling further combination with drainage of neighbouring polders
Fase 5a: **Creation of sub-polders and further fragmentation induced by subsidence**	From 1900 onwards	Mp1, Mp2 etc.	Construction of sub-polders
Fase 6a: **Partial pumping of the boezem system** *Fase 6b:* **Complete pumping of the boezem system**	1928 1968 Planned 2020 planned in 2030	Bm1-S2-D2-Bp2-M2 Bm1-D2-BP2-M2	Construction of steam pumping station in Lemmer Construction electric pumping station in Stavoren Construction pumping station in Harlingen Construction pumping station Lauwersoog

1. Letters refer to the type of construction. **S** is Sluice; **D** is Dike; **Bp** is inner Boezem inside polder; **M** is pumped (either wind- or fuel driven); **Bm** is boezem system with pumps;
2. Numbers refer to the development stage. The number 1 is used for the first constructions, number 2 for the first upscaling phase, number 3 for the following upscaling phase etc.

CONCLUSIONS

Drainage will continuously require adaptation measures and creates an increasing dependency on human interventions to reduce risks for flooding. The technical infrastructure becomes more complex and fragmented and the costs for water management increase gradually.

Different stages of water system (or polder) development can be distinguished. Awareness of the actual stage of development in a drained peatland site enables to predict the next stage in its development. This recognition allows a better decision making on required adaptation strategies such as continuation of the actual agricultural land use or transformation into e.g. restored wetlands.

The presented typology allows a better understanding on the actual stage of development of a drained peatland at a given site. It also gives a tool to predict the future stages in development.
It will contribute to a better analysis of expected developments in water management and to be prepared in time for implementation of adaptation measures.

REFERENCES

1. G.J. van den Born, F. Kragt, D. Henkens, B. Rijken, B. van Bemmel, G. Renes en S. van der Sluis (PBL) 2016. Bodemdaling Laagveen in Nederland; Bouwstenen voor afweging rond bodemdaling in landelijk en stedelijke gebieden (Land subsidence in peatlands in the Netherlands; a cost -benefit analysis)
2. Hartman, A, Schouwenaars,J. M., Moustafa, A. 2012. De kosten voor het waterbeheer in de veenweidegebied van Friesland. *H2O* / 12 - 2012 p.25-28 (Costs for water management in the peatland district of Fryslan)
3. Hoogland T, van den Akker J.J.H., Brus DJ, 2012. Modeling the subsidence of peat soils in the Dutch coastal area. *Geoderma* 171-172: 92-97.
4. Provincie Fryslan, 2014. Factsheets veenweidevisie.
5. Rahmadi *et al.* 2011. Effects of climate change and land subsidence on water management zoning in tidal low lowlands, case study Telang I South Sumatra In: Proceedings International Seminar-workshop on Integrated Lowland Development and Management, Palembang, Indonesia, 18-20 March 2011.
6. Schouwenaars, J.M. 2002. Waterlevels in the Echten polder; improving agriculture and reducing land subsidence risks. In: Steenvoorden J. *et al.* Agricultural Effects on Ground and Surface Waters; Research at the Edge of Science and Society (Proceedings of a symposium held at Wageningen, October 2000). IAHS Publ. No. 273, p. 169-176.
7. Schouwenaars. J.M. 2006. Land subsidence in drained peatlands and their long term perspectives for ecological restoration. In: 5th European Conference on Ecological Restoration: "Land use changes in Europe as a challenge for restoration: ecological, economical and ethical dimensions", Greifswald, Germany, 22-25 August 2006. - [S.l.]: [s.n.], 2006 - p. 158. (abstract)
8. Schouwenaars,J.M., 2011. Adaptation of polder systems to sea level rise and land subsidence in Fryslan in the period 1000-2000. Paper Congress International Commission on Irrigation and Drainage (ICID) Groningen 2011
9. Schothorst C.J, 1977. Subsidence of low moor peat soils in the western Netherlands.
Geoderma 17, 265–291.

Abstract No: A-287

MANAGING PEATLAND- REGULATING CONTROLLED OPEN BURNING IN SARAWAK

Peter Sawal* and Tsai Koh Fen

Natural Resources and Environment Board, Malaysia

**Corresponding author: petrs1@nreb.gov.my*

SUMMARY

Traditionally, peatlands in Sarawak are only utilised and harvested for timber and non-timber forest products. However, with the advent of scientific, technological innovations and good management practices it is possible to develop these problematic peatlands into major economic crops such as oil palm, sago and other cash crops. The native land owners are also riding on the bandwagon in developing their customary peatlands for cash crops such as oil palm to enhance their socio-economic livelihoods. The opening up of rural peatlands provides impetous for infrastructure, public utilities and telecommunications development to many inaccessible coastal settlements and other rural areas. Recognising the significant roles of peatlands for biodiversity conservation, storage of organic carbon and balancing the emission of GHG, the State of Sarawak has undertaken proactive and integrated approach in peatland ecosystems to prevent their irreversible degradation. Environmental elements are incorporated in the State's development policies, enhanced institutional capacity to enforce environmental regulations and collaboration in scientific peat research to help ensure that peat resources are sustainably managed. The State has also adopted the Canadian Fire Danger Rating System to manage biomass disposal in plantation development, including peatland development, through a controlled open burning permit system. This system has been effective in controlling haze pollution from local sources, as the open burning permit will only be issued during favourable weather conditions.

Keywords: *good management practices, irreversible peat degradation, controlled open burning, Fire Danger Rating System, socioeconomic livelihoods.*

INTRODUCTION

The State of Sarawak has earmarked oil palm (*Elaeis guineensis*) as one of the main agriculture crops for socio-economic transformation of its rural population and to achieve the State's vision of a developed state and a high income economy by 2030. The State is targeting to develop 2.0 million hectares of oil palm plantation by 2020 and to date more than 1.3 million hectares have been planted, including about 400,000 hectares of peatlands. The development of peatlands as the new growth frontier provides the impetous for much need infrastructure and amenity development such as roads, telecommunications and water supply for the rural communities. Many native customary land (NCL) owners are taking the opportunity of market access in developing their once idle and marginal NCR lands, including peatlands, with oil palm to enhance their socio-economic status, children's education and participating in nation building.

BACKGROUND

Traditionally, peatlands have been the source of timber and non-timber forest products, and food, providing sustainable livelihoods for rural communities. Peat swamp forests have high biodiversity of plants and animals. They have hosted numerous mammals, including the famous proboscis monkey (*Nasalis larvatus*) and the elusive red-banded langur (*Presbytis melalophos cruciger*). They have also been home to endangered and rare reptiles, for example, the Malayan false gharial (*Tomistoma schlegelii*), the Asia soft-shell turtle (*Amyda cartilaginea*) and other diverse aquatic animals. To date, the State has set aside about 105,563 ha of peat swamp forests (PSF) as Totally Protected Areas (TPA) under the National Parks and Nature Reserves Ordinance (1997) and other peatlands having high biodiversity conservation values will also be gazetted as TPA in the near future. The remaining peatlands, especially State land and NCR, have been identified for economic development to enhance the living standard of the present and future generations.

There are numerous reports on potential environmental issues associated with development of peatlands, such as peat subsidence, flooding, degradation of terrestrial and aquatic ecosystems, and carbon emission from uncontrolled peat fires (Sawal, 2003; Mamit and Sawal, 2003). In Sarawak, development of peatlands is regulated under the Natural Resources and Environment Ordinance, 1993 (Chapter 84, Law of Sarawak 1958), whereas development of industries such as oil palm mills are regulated under the Federal Environmental Quality Acts (DOE, 1974). Though peatlands were once considered marginal and problematic soils good management practices have not only increased crop productivity but also reduced potential environmental problem associated with peat development. For example, maintaining high water table and using compaction help to improve aeration in the crop root zone, increainge soil bulk density, soil surface load-bearing capacity and water filled pore space. The availability of modern technology and equipment, better understanding of peat dynamics, nutrition and proper water management has enabled developers and land owners to develop problematic deep peat for oil palm, sago and other agricultural crops (Mutert, E. *et al.*, 1999). The recently established Tropical Peat Research Laboratory (TPRL) Unit of the Sarawak Government is a testimony of the State's endeavour to protect and manage its peat resources through holistic research on peat dynamics and potential for lasting benefits to Sarawak as well as global communities.

TRANSBOUNDARY HAZE POLLUTION

In Sarawak, smoke haze pollution from peat fires is very much under control due to strict enforcement and effective fire prevention strategies. Nevertheless, from the month of June to September every year, the dry south westerly brings over these hazardous smoke haze, the State is experiencing transboundary smoke haze pollution from Kalimantan, Indonesia which severely affects the health and socio-economic activities of the State. As seen in Figure 1, transboundary haze as represented by thousands of hotspots (Figure 1) in Kalimantan, Sumatera and Sulawesi are causing severe air pollution in Southeast Asia region (ASMC, 2015). During this period, the correspondingly air quality throughout the State arc also showing downward trends from good to unhealthy levels. Smoke haze which are made up of fine particles, with diameter of less than 10 micron, resides longer in the atmosphere and travel thousands of kilometers. As reportedly in both printed and electronic media, unregulated development and uncontrolled peat burning for oil palm plantation are main sources of smoke haze pollution.

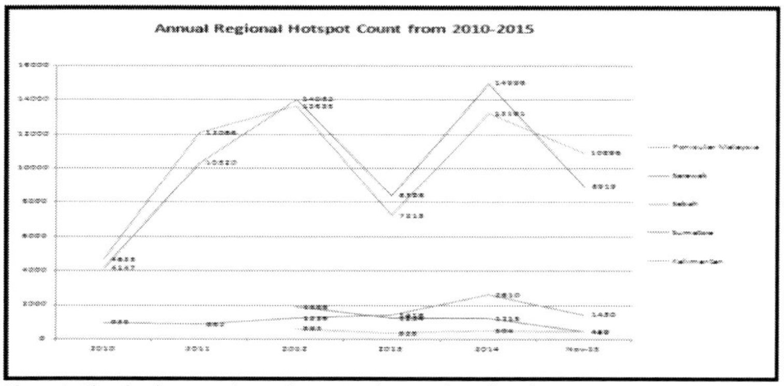

Figure 1: Showing hotspots detected over Southeast Asia regions in 2015

This perennial transboundary haze pollution has immeasurable impact on the livelihood and socio-economic activities of the people of Sarawak. Hundreds of schools were forced to close affecting hundred thousand of students when air quality reaches unhealthy level (API above 100) thereby disrupting classes and outdoor activities. Poor visibility are causing disruption to air flights affecting mobility and reduction in tourist arrival, cancellation of sports and outdoor activities and spiked in respiratory related illness. As an example, when Kuching International Airports (KIA) was closed on 20th October 2015, thousands of passengers were stranded as commercial planes were not able to take off or land at KIA due to low visibility. Indirectly, haze pollution also affects economic and business sector, additional costs for health care, especially for asthma related ailments and crop productivity (NREB, 2015).

FIRE DANGER RATING SYSTEM

During the haze episode in 1997-98, when the State of Emergency was declared over Sarawak due to deteriorating air quality where API readings breached 400 (hazardous level). Following this incident, the State of Sarawak gazetted the Natural Resources and Environment (Fire Danger Rating System) Rules 2004 with the objective of regulating open burning activities in Sarawak and reducing haze pollution from local sources. Under this Rules, land owners or developers are required to apply for Open Burning Permits (OBP) of they wish to manage and dispose of their biomass through open burning (Figure 2). This OBP requirement, however, does not include rural farmers who are free to continue practicing their traditional subsistence livelihood in their respective NCR lands. This has proven to be effective in managing biomass through controlled open burning in both mineral and peat soils in Sarawak (NREB, 2004).

The Natural Resources and Environment Board (NREB), Sarawak will process and issue the necessary permits if they meet the set criteria based on FDRS, adopted from the Canadian Fire Danger rating System, such as favourable weather condition, proper staking of biomass for burning with adequate fire break, trained fire-fighting team, and adequate firefighting equipment and machines to suppress any potential fire outbreak. No OBP will be issued and the approved OBP will be revoked if the weather condition becomes unfavourable, such as:

- *Fire Weather Index (FWI) readings exceed value 7 (high fire hazard);*
- *API readings exceed 100 (unhealthy level); and*
- *Upward trends of hotspots detected locally and across the border.*

To ensure that permit holders comply with the terms and approval conditions, as in Figure 3, the NREB will monitor and carry out site supervision during burning operations. The NREB's Centre for Remote Environmental Monitoring (CREM) will carry out desktop verification on all hotspots over Sarawak (as detected by NOAA18 satellite), to determine their legality, i.e., whether the hotspot located within or outside the EIA approved development areas or the source of hotspots are from OBPs issued by the NREB. The NREB have also established a Geographical Environmental System or GeoEnviron which stores digitized information of all EIA approved projects, including maps and progress of development (NREB, 2014).Thereafter, ground verification will be carried out to determine the exact location of burned areas (Figure 4) and as provided in the law (NREB, 1997), any cases of illegal open burning or violation to terms and approval conditions of the OBP, an Investigation Paper (IP) will be produced for further action. The NREB will seek the support and cooperation from the Royal Malaysian Police and the State's Attorney General Chambers to determine the necessary following up actions, either to:

- Issue directives and reminder letters to require the conduct of remedial and rehabilitation works;
- Issue Offer to Compound for non-compliance to approval conditions; or
- Proceed with Court prosecution for repeated offences or serious breaches of approval conditions.

While strict enforcement acts as a deterrent to would be offenders, the NREB also implement soft enforcement initiatives through environmental outreach programmes which are aimed to seek cooperation and support of all stakeholders to ensure no open burning is carried out during drought period. Through the NREB's Haze Watch Report, public and relevant stakeholders will be updated on the latest environmental quality such as regional hotspots count, Air Pollutant Index (API) and Fire Weather Index (FWI) for various regions in Sarawak. The State also established Hotline access for public to report any cases of environmental pollution or to report directly to enforcement agencies on any information pertaining to environmental pollution for follow up actions.

THE ACHIEVEMENT

The adoption of FDRS in Sarawak has proven to be successful in abating illegal open burning and effectively reducing smoke haze pollution from local sources. As seen in Figure 5, the numbers of hotspots detected over Sarawak during the past few years are strictly under control, as evident from fewer numbers of hotspots than those in other Southeast Asia regions such as Peninsular Malaysia, Kalimantan and Sumatera. In 2015, only 439 hotspots were detected in Sarawak including 110 hotspots from controlled open burning activities regulated by the NREB. Six (6) hotspots were identified to be illegal open burning and the rest were from subsistence farming activities by local NCR land owners. In comparison, there were more than 1,430 hotspots in Peninsular Malaysia, 10,890 and 8,919 hotspots detected over Kalimantan and Sumatera, respectively.

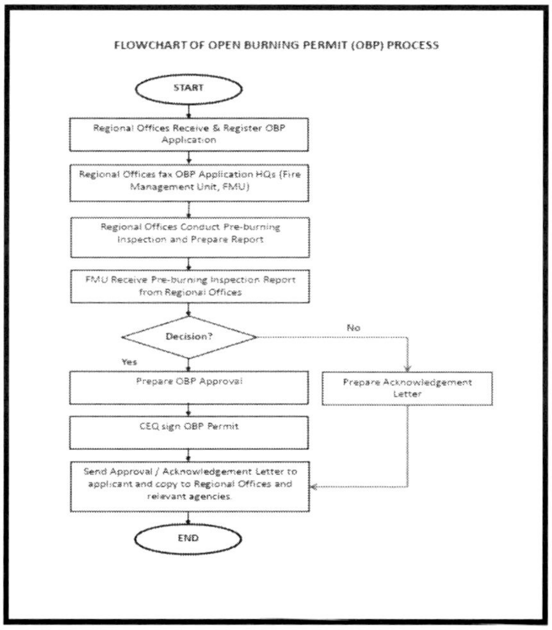

Figure 2: Flowchart for processing of Open Burning

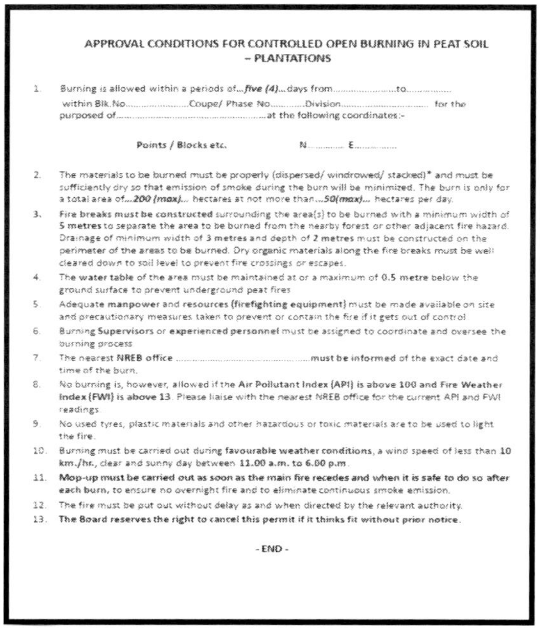

APPROVAL CONDITIONS FOR CONTROLLED OPEN BURNING IN PEAT SOIL – PLANTATIONS

1. Burning is allowed within a periods of...*five (4)*...days from........................to................ within Blk.No......................Coupe/ Phase No.............Division.................................. for the purposed of..at the following coordinates:-

   Points / Blocks etc. N............ E.............

2. The materials to be burned must be properly (dispersed/ windrowed/ stacked)* and must be sufficiently dry so that emission of smoke during the burn will be minimized. The burn is only for a total area of...*200 (max)*... hectares at not more than...*50(max)*... hectares per day.
3. **Fire breaks must be constructed** surrounding the area(s) to be burned with a minimum width of **5 metres** to separate the area to be burned from the nearby forest or other adjacent fire hazard. Drainage of minimum width of **3 metres** and depth of **2 metres** must be constructed on the perimeter of the areas to be burned. Dry organic materials along the fire breaks must be well cleared down to soil level to prevent fire crossings or escapes.
4. The **water table** of the area must be maintained at or a maximum of **0.5 metre** below the ground surface to prevent underground peat fires
5. Adequate **manpower** and **resources (firefighting equipment)** must be made available on site and precautionary measures taken to prevent or contain the fire if it gets out of control
6. Burning **Supervisors** or **experienced personnel** must be assigned to coordinate and oversee the burning process
7. The nearest **NREB office** ....**must be informed** of the exact date and time of the burn.
8. No burning is, however, allowed if the **Air Pollutant Index (API) is above 100 and Fire Weather Index (FWI) is above 13**. Please liaise with the nearest NREB office for the current API and FWI readings
9. No used tyres, plastic materials and other hazardous or toxic materials are to be used to light the fire.
10. Burning must be carried out during **favourable weather conditions**, a wind speed of less than **10 km./hr.**, clear and sunny day between **11.00 a.m. to 6.00 p.m**.
11. **Mop-up must be carried out as soon as the main fire recedes and when it is safe to do so after each burn,** to ensure no overnight fire and to eliminate continuous smoke emission.
12. The fire must be put out without delay as and when directed by the relevant authority.
13. **The Board reserves the right to cancel this permit if it thinks fit without prior notice.**

- END -

Figure 3: Approval conditions for OBP in peat soil Permit development

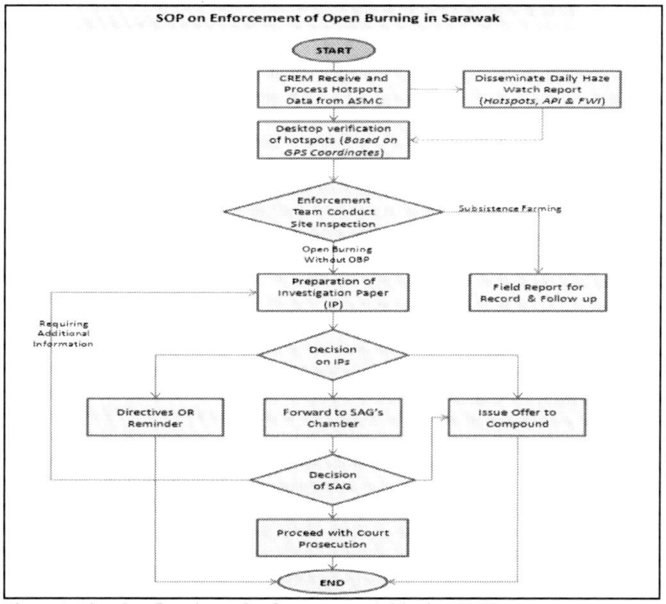

Figure 4: Showing flowchart of enforcement activities by NREB

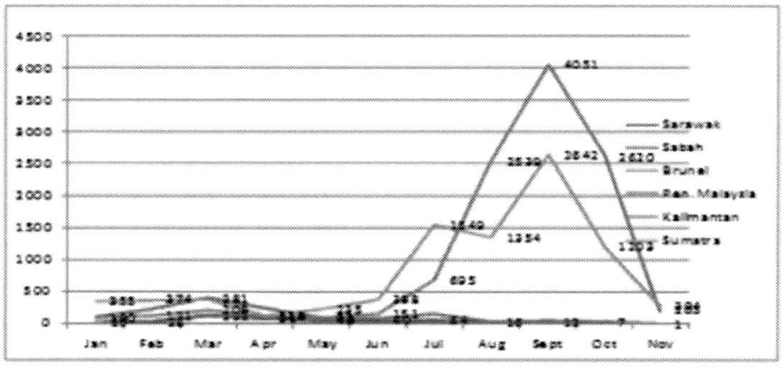

Figure 5: Showing hotspots detected over Southeast Asia regions in 2015

CONCLUSION

Collective and integrated efforts of all stakeholders are equally responsible in ensuring minimal smoke haze from local sources, which include:

- Proactive monitoring and enforcement (both ground and aerial surveillance)
- Prompt fire suppression and water bombing by Rescue and Fire Fighting Department;
- Cloud seeding by the Meteorological Department;
- Construction of tube wells, check dams and watch towers in fire prone areas; and
- Dissemination of information on danger of open burning and the impact haze pollution to human health in printed and electronic media.

Sustainable development can only be achieved if equal attention is given to integrate social-cultural, ecological and environmental integrity in the planning and implementation of economic development. The State of Sarawak is confident that the use of modern technology and innovation, better understanding of peat dynamics and good management practices are able to transform marginal and problematic deep peat soils for development of important commercial crops. The application of FDRS has enable the State of Sarawak to effectively regulate open burning practices and the strict enforcement helps to reduce incidence of illegal open burning.

In the long term, the State Government is committed to adopt integrated management and enforcement of open burning in Sarawak through various initiatives which include; the enforcement of zero open burning by 2020, regulating open burning for commercial activities in NCR areas, adoption of polluter pay principle, provide incentives for companies who adopt zero burning, construction of more Air Quality Monitoring Stations in many strategic and urban areas, and the support of individuals and local communities as enforcement agent to help curb incidence of illegal open burning (HPT, 2015).

REFERENCES

1. ASMC (2015). Asean Specialised Meteorological Centre, Singapore.
2. DOE (1974). Environmental Quality Acts 1974. Department of Environment (DOE) Malaysia
3. HPT (2015). High Performance Team Retreat at Kota Kinabalu Sabah, Malaysia from 15-18 March, 2015. HPT, Jabatan Ketua Menteri Sarawak.
4. Mamit, J.D. and Sawal, P. (2003).Environmental Issues in Peatland Development. Paper presented at Seminar on Integrated Peatland Management for Sustainable Development organised by Sarawak Development Institute, 2003. Corporate Media Sdn Bhd
5. Melling, L., Chua, K.H. and Lim, K.H. (2008). Agro-Management of Peat Soils Under Oil Palm in Sarawak. A paper presented at the seminar on Agronomic Principles and Practices of Oil Palm Cultivation. 13-16 October 2008, Sibu, Sarawak.
6. Mutert, E.; Fairhurst, T.H. and H.R. von Uexküll (1999). Agronomic Management of Oil Palms on Deep Peat. Better Crops International Vol. 13, No. 1, May 1999.
7. NREB (1994). Natural Resources and Environment (Prescribed Activities) Order 1994. Natural Resources and Environment Board, Sarawak.
8. NREB (1997). Natural Resources and Environment (Compounding of Offences) Rules, 1997. Natural Resources and Environment Board, Sarawak.
9. NREB 2014: Two decades of Environmental Stewardship in Sarawak. A commemorative publication in conjunction with the 20th Anniversary of the Natural Resources and Environment Board, Sarawak.
10. NREB (2004). Natural Resources and Environment (Fire Danger Rating System) Rules 2004. Natural Resources and Environment Board, Sarawak.
11. Sawal, P. (2003). Threats to peat swamp forests of Sarawak. Report JWG/RAM/02, Joint Working Group Malaysia-The Netherlands. Forest Department Sarawak, Kuching, Malaysia/Alterra, Wageningen, The Netherlands.
12. NREB (2015). Cabinet Information Paper on the Transboundary Haze Pollution in Sarawak. Natural Resources and Environment Board (NREB) Sarawak

Abstract No: A-322

MICROBIAL BIODIVERSITY AND ECOSYSTEM FUNCTIONING IN MALAYSIAN PEATSWAMP FORESTS

Catherine M. Yule[1*], Steven Y.K Aw[1], Wilhelm W.H. Eng[1], Han Ming Gan[1], Sui Mae Lee[1], Cheryl Ong[1], Kuan Shion Ong[1], Chin Chin Too[1] and Alex Keller[2]

[1]*Monash University Malaysia*
[2]*University of Wuerzburg, Germany*

* *Corresponding author: catherine.yule@monash.edu*

Southeast Asian tropical peatswamp forests support distinctive microbial communities that differ from those of other wetlands, including temperate peatlands. The microbes control the decomposition of plant matter, and consequently their activities are crucial to the formation of peat and sequestration of carbon in peat layers up to 25 m deep. Metagenomic studies indicate that up to 80% of the microbes are novel species or strains, underscoring the enormous gap in our microbial taxonomic knowledge. The extreme, nutrient poor, acidic environment fosters strong competition for niches and scarce nutrients among microbes resulting in the evolution of antibiotics and anti-biofilm agents to overcome competitors, and also nutrient-acquiring enzymes (e.g. to decompose cellulose and lignin under acidic conditions). The microbial communities vary with peat depth and also with respect to the rhizospheres of different tree species. At the surface Acidobacteria, commonly associated with acidic soil, are abundant as well as Proteobacteria (*e.g.Rhodopseudomonas* known for lignin degradation; *Burkholderia* which produces antimicrobial compounds) and also *Actinobacteria*. The activity of microbial enzymes involved in C, N and P cycling is mainly confined to the peat surface where senescent leaves fall. Archaea (Crenarchaeota) are uncommon in surface peat, but dominate deeper (> 20 cm), older, anaerobic peat layers where microbes are less abundant and less metabolically active. The anaerobic blackwater – acidic, low nutrient water with high levels of toxic compounds (tannins, humic acids and phenols leached from newly fallen leaves) and the tough, toxic leaves of the flora (their source of nutrition) exert a potentially strong selective pressure on the microbial community and the diversification of their genomic potential. Slow detrital decomposition typical of pristine peatswamps results in the accumulation of peat but when these conditions no longer prevail (e.g. due to drainage, logging and conversion to oil palm plantations) peat inevitably breaks down.

***Keywords**:-*

Abstract No: A-144

PEATLAND RESTORATION IN RUSSIA FOR FIRE PREVENTION AND CLIMATE CHANGE MITIGATION: THE EXPERIENCE OF A LARGE SCALE REWETTING PROJECT

Andrey Sirin[1*], Gennady Suvorov[1], Aleksandr Maslov[1], Maria Medvedeva[1], Anastasiya Markina[1], Dmitry Makarov[1], Anna Vozbrannaya[1], Natalya Valyaeva[1], Olga Tsyganova[1], Tamara Glukhova[1], Tatiana Minayeva[2], Marcel Silvius[2], Jozef Bednar[2], Arina Schrier[2], Hans Joosten[3], John Couwenberg[3], Inga Gummert[3] and Jan Peters[4]

[1]*Institute of Forest Science, Russian Academy of Sciences, Russian Federation*
[2]*Wetlands International, The Netherlands*
[3]*Greifswald University, Germany*
[4]*Michael Succow Foundation, Germany*

**Corresponding author: sirin@proc.ru*

Since 1990 large areas of peatlands that were drained for agriculture and used for peat extraction in the European part of Russia were left abandoned, with CO_2 emissions and high fire risks. Re-wetting could return peat soils to their original waterlogged state to prevent their vulnerability to fires and peat oxidation, and to bring back important ecosystem services such as biodiversity habitat and water regulation. The project "Restoring Peatlands in Russia – for fire prevention and climate change mitigation" financed under the International Climate Initiative (ICI) by the German Federal Ministry for the Environment, Nature Conservation, Building and Nuclear Safety (BMUB), is aimed to prove approaches for climate change mitigation and adaptation restoration of several dozen thousand hectares of drained abandoned peatlands. The activity is linked to the governmental programme (2010-2013) of rewetting of more than 70 thousand hectares of fire vulnerable transformed peatlands, which Moscow Province started after severe fires in 2010. The project task is to assess the effectiveness of measures for the large scale rewetting and to answer: whether large scale activities effective for GHG reduction; could be integrative goals achieved including habitat restoration for biodiversity conservation and climate change mitigation; how an integrated ecosystem based approach to peatlands restoration is compatible with stakeholders' interests and national legislation in Russia; are available methods of GHG reduction evaluation compatible?; etc. Different methods based on remote sensing techniques were developed to map peatlands related to different land categories, assess and monitor their conditions and fire hazard status, prioritize them for restoration and test the effectiveness of restoration measures applied, evaluate areas used to bind emission factors and carbon data, and evaluate rewetting effectiveness both for fire prevention and GHG assessment. The scientific and practical results of this large-scale project could be expanded to other restoration projects, help further development of methodologies for GHG inventories under UNFCCC and IPCC, and support integration of restoration projects into an economically derived climate change mitigation and adaptation national programs.

***Keywords**: restoration, rewetting, mitigation, GHGs, boreal zone*

Abstract No: A-256

PEATLAND UTILIZATION WITH SECURE AND SUSTAINABLE MANAGEMENT: CASE STUDY IN OIL PALM AND TIMBER FOREST PLANTATIONS IN SUMATRA

Supiandi Sabiham*, Winarna, Heru Bagus Pulunggono, Dian Novarina, and Bandung Sahari

Peat Society of Indonesia, Department of Soil Science and Land Resource, Bogor Agricultural University (IPB), Jln. Meranti, IPB Campus Darmaga-Bogor 16880, Indonesia

**Corresponding author: ssupiandi@yahoo.com*

Peatland utilization for plantations requires aerobic condition at the upper peat layer and groundwater level (GWL) conditions at a certain depth to support plant growth while maintaining peat stability. These conditions can be managed by maintaining water levels in the canals. However, it has been claimed that drained peatland introduces oxygen into the peatland surface which then promotes the decomposition of peat materials resulting in carbon (C) emission as an indicator of the degree of peat stability. In addition, drainage of peatland is also thought to influence vegetation cover in certain places which could increase the risk of peat fires. In order to investigate the problems mentioned above, we tried to analyze the use of peatland in relation to three environmental-issues: deforestation, C-emission, and peat fires. The results indicate that peatland utilization for plantations has mostly been expanded into degraded forest and agricultural cropland. Primary peatforest in fact was only used for plantations in a very few cases. More than 70% of plantations have been developed on agricultural cropland and about 28% of them have replaced the previous disturbed peatforest. Moist peat having a water content higher than a critical water content (CWC) could be categorized as hydrophilic peat; in such conditions C-emission and the risk of peat fire significantly decrease. CWC of peat in the upper layer varies from 150 to 270% (w/w) depending on the degree of peat decomposition and the depth of GWL. Maintaining GWL at the depth of up to 80 cm from peat surface is suggested for utilizing peatland with secure and sustainable management.

Keywords: *peatland, sustainable management, groundwater level, peat decomposition*

Gap in pagination due to unavailable paper.

Page 96

Abstract No: A-373

ROOT RESPIRATION DRIVES PATTERNS OF TOTAL SOIL CO_2 FROM CULTIVATED TROPICAL PEATLANDS

Manning, F. C.[1*], Kho, L. K.[2], Hill, T.[3], Mohd. Haniff Harun[2], Zulkifli Hashim[4] and Teh, Y.A.[1]

[1]*University of Aberdeen, UK*
[2]*Tropical Peat Research Institute, Biological Research Division, Malaysian Palm Oil Board, Selangor, Malaysia*
[3]*University of Exeter, UK*
[4]*Agronomy and Geospatial Technology Unit, Biological Research Division, Malaysian Palm Oil Board, Selangor, Malaysia*

**Corresponding author: frances.claire.manning@gmail.com*

SUMMARY

Draining tropical peatlands for agriculture may change the carbon dynamics of the soil. To determine the corresponding rates of peat oxidation, soil respiration can be used, but must be partitioned into its autotrophic and microbial peat oxidation components. The systematic planting of oil palm plantations allows for this if spatial sampling strategies are employed. In this study, soil respiration and root biomass were sampled at increasing distances away from oil palm, into three different surface microforms (harvest path, frond pile, cover crops). Both variables were greatest by the palms and lowest further away from the palms, allowing for root biomass to be used as a predictor of peat oxidation rates. Soil respiration could also be up-scaled spatially to determine plot scale estimates of total soil respiration. Soil respiration showed high variability in estimates and so large sample sizes are encouraged in order to accurately estimate peat oxidation from cultivated peat soil.

Keywords: *peat oxidation, soil respiration, root biomass, tropical*

INTRODUCTION

Cultivated peat soils have been reported to produce higher carbon dioxide (CO_2) emissions than under natural vegetation (Kasimir-Klemedtsson *et al.*, 1997; FAO 2015). Peat soil plays an important role in the carbon (C) cycle, storing approximately 329 – 525 Gt C globally (Immirzi *et al.*, 1992). The majority of peatlands can be found in temperate and boreal zones, with only ~ 11 % of peatland area found in the tropics (Page *et al.*, 2011). Despite being a geographically smaller area, tropical peatlands have been estimated to store between 15 – 19 % of the total peat carbon budget (Page *et al.*, 2011). According to FAOSTAT, during 1990 – 2012 tropical peats produced 45.5 % of the CO_2eq emissions associated with cultivated peat soils (FAO 2015). It is therefore important to consider the different sources of CO_2 in agricultural peat soils in order to minimise CO_2 emissions.

Agricultural cultivation of peat soils can produce CO_2 emissions due to increased peat oxidation if the water table depth is artificially lowered (Kasimir-Klemedtsson *et al.*, 1997; Jauhiainen *et al.*, 2005; Hirano *et al.*, 2009; Hooijer *et al.*, 2012). This is due to increasing the volume of peat available for microbial communities to decompose. Some estimates of peat oxidation rates from temperate cultivated peat soils have been found between the ranges of 1 and 40.3 Mg CO_2 ha^{-1} yr^{-1} (Kasimir-Klemedtsson *et al.*, 1997; Schils *et al.*, 2008). The range of peat oxidation rates estimated from cultivated tropical peat soils is between 7 and 100 Mg CO_2 ha^{-1} yr^{-1} (Melling *et al.*, 2005, 2013; Farmer *et al.*, 2014; Dariah *et al.*, 2013; Hooijer *et al.*, 2012; Jauhiainen *et al.*, 2012). This large range of values is in part due to environmental variations at the time of measurement, such as different water table depths. However it may also be due to differences in sampling strategy.

It can be very difficult to determine rates of peat oxidation, due to other sources of CO_2 confounding measurements. For example, taking measurements of soil respiration not only provides rates of peat oxidation, but also includes root respiration and mycorrhizal respiration. Different methods have been developed to partition out peat oxidation rates, including creating root-free soil zones with root exclusion collars, or using C isotope analysis. Unfortunately, these methods are not always practical. For instance, root exclusion collars can alter the soil bulk density when they are installed, and have been found to have an altered water balance due to both the absence of roots and the collar acting as a barrier for drainage, and isotope analysis can be expensive.

Plantations offer a unique opportunity for partitioning peat oxidation rates from soil respiration. Due to the crops being planted strictly in ordered rows, root density would be expected to vary considerably within the plantation. Therefore it may be possible to determine rates of peat oxidation from 'root-free' soil zones. Once soil respiration has been effectively partitioned into autotrophic respiration and peat oxidation, it is then possible to consider how plantation management can impact peat oxidation rates.

This work aims to consider the spatial variation of both soil respiration fluxes and root biomass in an oil palm plantation on peat soil. The distribution of root biomass will be used to partition out autotrophic and peat oxidation rates from soil respiration. Soil respiration will be estimated at plot level using area-weighted up-scaling to accurately estimate the CO_2 footprint from oil palm plantations.

METHODS

The study sites for this project were two oil palm estates near Bintulu, Malaysia. The palms were six years old when the study began.

To understand the spatial dynamics in soil respiration, six palms were considered for analysis within a 1 ha plot. Soil respiration measurements were made using an EGM-4 (PP systems). Soil respiration measurements were made at 11 distances away from the palm, along three transects through different land use microforms (harvest path, frond pile and cover crop). Soil respiration measurements were also made at 4.5 m from the palm, in the middle of three palms.

Soil cores of 10 cm diameter by 30 cm were extracted directly below where the soil respiration measurements had been taken. Roots were separated from the soil using the method of Metcalfe *et al.* (2008). Here roots were collected in 10 minute intervals for 50 minutes. The cumulative root masses were extrapolated using log fits and total estimates of root mass were considered at 24 hours – under the assumption that all of the roots would have been collected by then if they had been picked manually for 24 hours.

Soil respiration and root density were considered at different distances from the palm. The relationship between root density and soil respiration was used to estimate peat oxidation fluxes. Soil respiration measurements were also scaled up to plot level using area weighted up-scaling techniques.

RESULTS

Initial analyses have shown that soil respiration fluxes were greater by the palm and lower further away from the palm (Figure 1). Very high variations in soil respiration estimates were seen between 0 and 1.5 m from the palm.

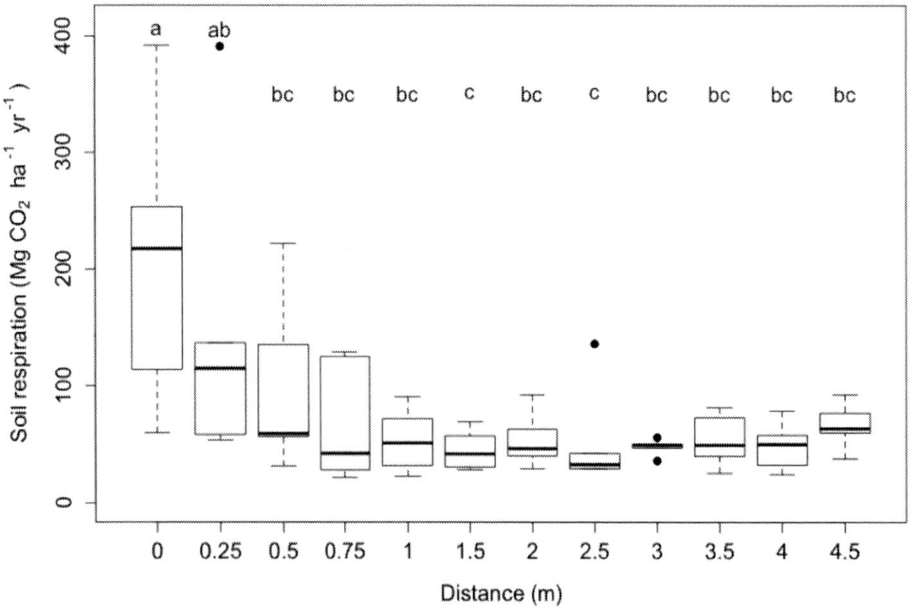

Figure 1: Soil respiration at increasing distances from the oil palm

Similarly, root biomass showed considerable spatial variation within oil palm plantations (Figure 2). Here very high and variable estimates of root biomass were present next to the palm and much lower estimates of root biomass were found further than 1.5 m from the palm. Roots were always present in the soil.

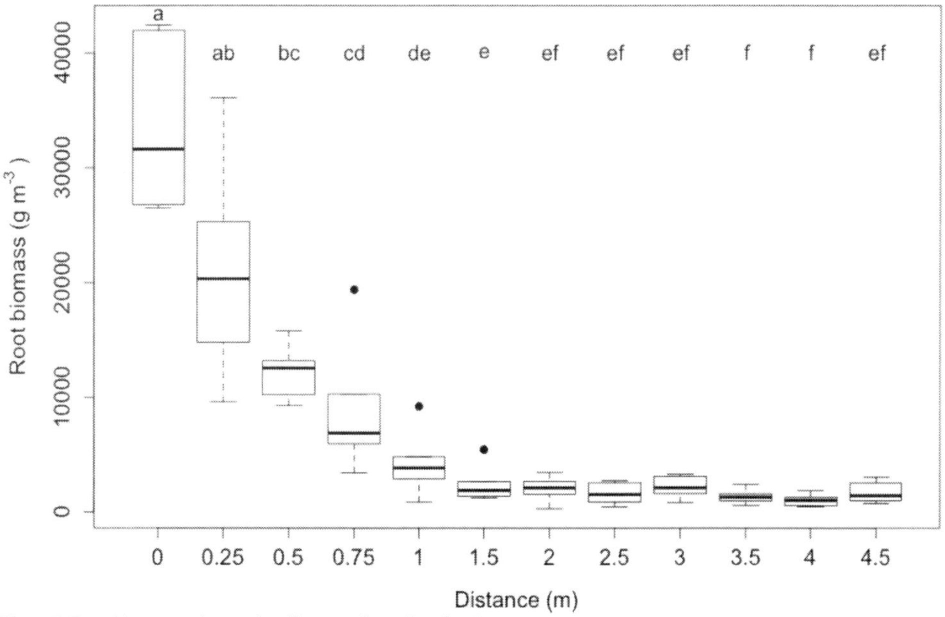

Figure 2: Root biomass at increasing distances from the oil palm.

Peat oxidation was estimated between 26.54 and 52.09 Mg CO_2 ha^{-1} yr^{-1} using linear interpolation of soil respiration against root biomass. Area-weighted up scaling estimated total soil respiration to be 76.23 Mg CO_2 ha^{-1} yr^{-1} at plot level, giving estimates of autotrophic respiration between 24.14 and 49.69 Mg CO_2 ha^{-1} yr^{-1}. Soil respiration estimates varied significantly depending surface microform with much greater estimates in the cover crops than either the harvest path or under the frond pile.

DISCUSSION

Soil respiration fluxes vary considerably in oil palm plantations on peat soil, which can make determining rates of total soil respiration and peat oxidation difficult, in part due to the need for large sample sizes for accurate measurements. Preliminary data presented here shows a high range in total soil respiration fluxes both at different distances from the palm, and within each distance class. The spatial variation of root biomass, also presented here, can be used to explain some of the variation in total soil respiration, as large soil respiration fluxes were present next to the palm where the majority of the roots can be found, and lower soil respiration fluxes were measured further away from the palm where the lowest root biomass estimates were measured. It is therefore important to consider distance from palm as a factor when sampling for total soil respiration, peat oxidation or autotrophic respiration from plantations.

Peat oxidation rates of 26.54 and 52.09 Mg CO_2 ha^{-1} yr^{-1} presented in this study fall within the range of measurements determined by Melling *et al.* (2005; 2013), Dariah *et al.* (2013) and Farmer *et al.* (2014) but are lower than estimates by Hooijer *et al.* (2012). The water table depth at the time of measurement for this study was 0.35 cm, whereas the water table depth at the time of study for Hooijer *et al.* (2012) was 0.73 cm The lower estimate presented in this study may be due to a lower water table depth and thus a smaller volume of soil available for bacteria to oxidise.

Surface microform also showed a difference in soil respiration rates, with more respiration being present in the cover crop area than the bare harvest path. The frond piles also had slightly more soil respiration than the harvest path. This increase in soil respiration may be due to increased carbon inputs from the live vegetation and decomposing fronds and not from increased rates of decomposition. Surface vegetation protects peat and prevents peat oxidation, so it is not advisable to remove the vegetation in order to reduce carbon emissions (Dawson and Smith 2007).

CONCLUSIONS

Soil respiration has been shown to have high but systematic variation in oil palm plantations on peat soil. It is therefore possible to use the planting scheme to engineer experiments that naturally partition total soil respiration into autotrophic and heterotrophic components, based on the variability in root density and therefore autotrophic respiration. We recommend that future studies consider the distance from palm in sampling designs in order to accurately represent areas of high and low root biomass.

Similarly, total soil respiration varies in the different surface microforms, due to carbon inputs from living vegetation. In order to accurately represent total soil respiration in plantations, these microforms need to be considered, to take the carbon fluxes from decomposing shrubby vegetation or old fronds into account.

ACKNOWLEDGEMENTS

I would like to acknowledge the Malaysian Palm Oil Board, Sarawak Oil Palm Berhad and the Natural Environment Research Council, UK, for providing the funding for this project.

REFERENCES

1. Dariah, A., Marwanto, S. and Agus, F. (2014) Root- and peat-based CO2 emissions from oil palm plantations, *Mitigation and Adaptation Strategies for Global Change*, 19: 831-843.
2. Dawson, J.C. and Smith, P. (2007) Carbon losses from soil and its consequences for land-use management. *Science of the Total Environment*, 382: 165-190.
3. FAO (2015) Emissions – Agriculture / Cultivation of Organic Soils. http://faostat3.fao.org/browse/G1/GV/E {Accessed 06.02.2016}
4. Farmer, J. (2014) Measuring and modelling soil carbon and carbon dioxide from Indonesian peatlands under land use change, PhD Thesis, University of Aberdeen, Scotland, 2014.
5. Hirano, T., Segah, H., Harada, T., Limin, S., June, T., Hirata, R. and Osaki, M. (2007) Carbon dioxide balance of a tropical peat swamp forest in Kalimantan, Indonesia. *Global Change Biology*, 13: 412-425.
6. Hooijer, A., Page, S., Jauhiainen, J., Lee, W.A., Lu, X.X., Idris, A., and Anshari, G (2012) Subsidence and carbon loss in drained tropical peatlands, *Biogeosciences*, 9: 1053-1071.
7. Immirzi C.P., Maltby, E. and Clymo, R.S. (1992) The global status of peatlands and their role in carbon cycling. A report for Friends of the Earth by Wetlands Ecosystems Research Group, Department of Geography, University of Exeter, UK. Friends of the Earth, London.
8. Jauhiainen, J., Takahashi, H., Heikkinen, J. E. P., Martikainen, P. J., and Vasander, H. (2005) Carbon fluxes from a tropical peat swamp forest floor. *Global Change Biology*, 11: 1788–1797.
9. Jauhiainen, J., Hooijer, A., and Page, S. E. (2012) Carbon dioxide emissions from an Acacia plantation on peatland in Sumatra, Indonesia. *Biogeosciences*, 9: 617–630.
10. Kasimir-Klemedtsson, Å., Klemedtsson, L., Berglund, K., Martikainen, P., Silvola, J. and Oenema, O. (1997), Greenhouse gas emissions from farmed organic soils: a review. *Soil Use and Management*, 13: 245–250.
11. Melling, L., Hatano, R., and Goh, K. J. (2005) Soil CO_2 flux from three ecosystems in tropical peatland of Sarawak, Malaysia. *Tellus B*, 57: 1–11.
12. Melling, L., Soo Yun Tan, C., Goh, K. J, and Hatano, R. (2013) Soil microbial and root respirations from three ecosystems in tropical peatland of Sarawak, Malaysia. *Journal of Oil Palm Research*, 25: 44-57.
13. Metcalfe, D.B., Williams, M., Aragão, L.E.O.C., da Costa, A.C.L., de Almeida, S.S., Braga, A.P., Gonçalves, P.H.L., de Athaydes Silva Junior, J., Malhi, Y. and Meir, P. (2007) A method for extracting plant roots from soil which facilitates rapid sample processing without compromising measurement accuracy. *New Phytologist*, 174: 697-703.
14. Page, S.E., O.Rieley, J. and Banks, C.J. (2011) Global and regional importance of the tropical peatland carbon pool. *Global Change Biology*, 17: 798-818.
15. Schils, R., Kuikman, P., Liski, J., Van Oijen, M., Smith, P., Webb, J., Alm, J., Somogyi, Z., Van den Akker, J.J.H., Billett, M., Emmett, B., Evans, C., Lindner, M., Palosuo, T., Bellamy, P., Jandl, R. and Hiederer, R. (2008) CLIMSOIL, Review of Existing Information on the Interrelations Between Soil and Climate Change. http://ec.europa.eu/environment/soil/publications_en.htm

Abstract No: A-365

SARAWAK'S APPROACH TO SUSTAINABLE DEVELOPMENT

Sudarsono Osman

Ministry of Resource Planning and Environment Sarawak

* *Corresponding author: sudarsono@sarawak.gov.my*

Sarawak is blessed with abundant natural resources and rich biodiversity. Home to lush tropical rainforests and diverse species of fauna and flora, it is not surprising that Sarawak's main economic drivers are its oil and gas, palm oil and timber, in that order. Because of its dependence on these resources, there is a need to sustainably manage and develop them without compromising the quality of the environment: hence, the *Sarawak Land Use Policy*. This paper will articulate the *Land Use Policy* as the guideline for sustainable development in Sarawak. This policy apportions the hectarage of land to be used for forestry (7 MHA or 57%) with Permanent Forest (6 MHA) and Totally Protected Areas (1 MHA); agriculture (4 MHA or 32%); and the rest for settlement and other miscellaneous uses. Permanent forests serve as production forest to ensure a sustainable timber industry that generates employment for communities mainly in the rural areas. Timber harvesting is carried out in accordance with the principles of sustainable forest management. *Totally Protected Areas* meanwhile comprised National Parks, Nature Reserves and Wildlife Sanctuaries for the conservation of flora and fauna and the environment as a whole, taking into consideration current issues of global warming and climate change. In 1997 the Sarawak Government enacted the Sarawak Biodiversity Centre Ordinance with the aim of protecting and developing its rich biological resources for the benefit of mankind and bringing mutual benefit to the indigenous communities through *Access Benefit Sharing*. Sustainable development is a delicate balance between the need for economic growth and social, political and environmental considerations. All approved developments are required by law to carry out an *Environmental Impact Assessment (EIA)* for approval by the NREB before development projects may commence. Also, there is a conscious drive to diversify Sarawak's economy base to become less reliant on its natural resources.

Keywords: -

Abstract No: A-334

THE CO-FIRING EXPERIENCE: THE USE OF PEAT AND BIOMASS FOR ELECTRICITY GENERATION IN IRELAND

Charles Shier

Bord na Móna, Ireland

**Corresponding author: Charles.Shier@bnm.ie*

SUMMARY

Peat has been used as an energy source for power generation in Ireland since the 1950s. However, peat produces electricity with a comparatively high carbon footprint. This paper discusses the experience of using biomass co-fired with peat in a condensing, bubbling fluidised bed power plant in Ireland as a means of mitigating the carbon emissions. It describes Ireland's underlying climate and energy policy; it examines the sources and types of biomass utilised for co-firing and highlight the key quality parameters; and it explores some of the limitations imposed by the Irish regulatory environment. The European Union's approach to biomass sustainability is discussed, and the greenhouse gas emissions created by the supply chains of the main biomass types utilised to date are quantified. The paper also examines some of the challenges associated with the co-firing of peat and biomass in the years ahead.

Keywords: *peat, biomass, co-firing, electricity, sustainability*

INTRODUCTION

Energy policy in Ireland has supported the use of indigenous peat for the generation of electricity since the 1950s. The production and use of local peat fuel has contributed to the security of energy supply and it has also had a major positive socio-economic impact on the Irish Midlands region. Ireland currently has three peat-fired condensing generating stations with a combined gross electrical output of 378 MW. These stations operate as baseload generators and require 3.1 million tonnes of milled peat, or 23.7 PJ of primary energy, per annum. However, recognising that the use of peat as a primary energy source leads to comparatively high carbon emissions, the Irish Government sought a pragmatic way to mitigate these emissions and introduced a target of 30% co-firing with biomass materials for the peat stations by 2015.

In line with the rest of the European Union (EU), Ireland has a long term goal to reduce its carbon emissions by at least 80% by 2050. This will be achieved by a progressive decarbonisation of the energy sector, with the gradual phasing out of peat and coal, and ultimately also natural gas, in favour of renewable energy sources (DCENR, 2015). As a member of the EU, Ireland has been given a mandatory target to ensure that 16% of its final energy consumption is supplied from renewable energy sources by 2020, as its contribution towards an overall 20% EU renewable energy objective.

The use of biomass as a co-fuel not only reduces carbon emissions, but it also leads to the production of dispatchable renewable electricity. While Ireland has an excellent renewable energy source in the form of wind, which in 2015 contributed 20% of our electricity mix, biomass is capable of delivering dispatchable, synchronous power and also of providing a greater range of electricity system services. This paper describes Bord na Móna's experience of co-firing peat with biomass at the Edenderry power station over the period since 2008, it explores the emerging issue of biomass sustainability and it discusses some of the challenges that lie ahead.

CO-FIRING EXPERIENCE

The Edenderry power station is a 128 MW, bubbling fluidised bed, condensing generating unit that was commissioned in 2000. Following biomass co-firing trials in 2002, the commercial co-firing of biomass with peat commenced in 2008, and a range of biomass materials have been utilised over the intervening years. Suitable biomass materials fall into three main categories:

a) Forest Materials – woody residues arising directly from activities such as harvesting or thinning; or indirectly from sawmills and other wood processors; or treated materials such as wood pellets;

b) Energy Crops – purpose grown, short-rotation, woody species such as willow (*Salix*) and poplar (*Populus*), or high-yielding grass species such as *Miscanthus* or Reed Canary Grass (*Phalaris*);

c) Agro-industrial Residues – co-products produced by the food- or feed-manufacturing industry, such as almond shells, sunflower husk pellets, shea nut pellets and palm kernel shells.

The Edenderry power station was designed to utilise milled peat with an optimum moisture content of around 50%. While the bubbling fluidised bed technology is capable of handling a wide range of biomass materials, with moisture contents ranging from 10% to 60%, it is important to ensure that an adequate moisture balance is maintained in the boiler combustion zone. This is achieved by fuel scheduling and mixing through an intermediate buffer store which can hold over two days' fuel supply.

Quality control of the biomass materials used is extremely important, particularly in relation to potential boiler corrosion and fouling problems. In order to manage the quality issue, Bord na Móna has developed a Biomass Materials Register which uses a simple 'Traffic Light' system as an initial materials screen. This register has been compiled from numerous laboratory analyses of a wide range of biomass materials, and it classifies the materials into three categories: ok for use (green); maybe (amber); and not suitable (red). Biomass specifications have also been developed for different material classes, with particular attention paid to particle size, chlorine content and ash melting behaviour.

In general, forest-based woody materials present very few problems, provided that the leaves or needles are left in the forest. Materials derived from the family Poaceae, such as *Miscanthus x giganteus* or *Phalaris arundinacea*, can be difficult to manage, principally due to their high and varying chlorine content. Edenderry station has managed this problem by limiting the proportion of such materials in the daily biomass materials mix. Agro-industrial residues need to be examined on a case-by-case basis, and samples are analysed to confirm suitability prior to purchase and shipping.

Unlike some of its European neighbours, Ireland does not have a large forest base. Recent inventories indicate that coniferous and broadleaved forests cover around 750,000 ha, or just 11% of the land surface. Many of the Irish forests are quite young, with over half (56%) being less than 20 years old. The total standing volume is just under 100 million m^3, and annual roundwood production is forecast to increase steadily from the current 3.1 million m^3 over the next decade. The proportion of wood fibre potentially available for energy use, including recycled wood, is estimated to increase from 1.1 million m^3 today to round 1.7 million m^3 by 2028 (Phillips, 2011). There will be competition for this energy fraction, especially if the Irish Government introduces incentives to promote the use of renewable heat in commercial and industrial installations.

In the agricultural sector, the majority of Ireland's farmland is under permanent grassland, with around 352,000 ha, or 8% of the farmed area, under cereals and other crops. The Irish Department of Agriculture introduced a Bioenergy Scheme, which provided grant aid for the establishment of willow (*Salix*) and *Miscanthus* energy crops, in 2007. Bord na Móna also promoted the establishment of short rotation coppice willow for a number of years, and offered prospective growers long-term offtake contracts. Despite these initiatives, the area planted with energy crops has remained quite modest, with a maximum of 2,400 ha under Miscanthus and 1,020 ha planted with willow.

The lack of an adequate supply of indigenous biomass has meant that we have had to import a range of biomass materials to co-fire with peat at the Edenderry power plant over the past eight years. The principal materials imported include wood pellets, sunflower husk pellets, shea nut pellets and palm kernel shells. An overview of the balance between indigenous and imported biomass utilised, along with the greenhouse gas (GHG) emissions avoided and the renewable electricity produced, is presented in Table 1.

Table 1: Biomass utilised for co-firing at Edenderry Station, CO_2 emissions avoided and renewable electricity produced: 2008-2015

	Biomass Materials Used		**GHG Emissions**	**Renewable**
Year	**Indigenous (TJ)**	**Imported (TJ)**	**Reduction (t CO_2)**	**Electricity (GWh_e)**
2008	145.6	1.6	16,951	15.2
2009	511.2	2.0	59,126	51.9
2010	683.2	170.0	93,229	84.4
2011	903.1	227.1	126,525	112.4
2012	1,268.1	250.4	169,781	147.6
2013	908.8	1,060.4	220,290	193.8
2014	1,053.2	1,251.1	260,920	229.9
2015	884.9	804.0	188,922	168.9

The use of biomass instead of peat at Edenderry station has resulted in a considerable reduction in emissions of carbon dioxide, and also a significant contribution to Ireland's renewable electricity supply. Both of these positive impacts were lower in 2015, when Edenderry station had a prolonged outage for boiler and turbine renovation.

IRISH REGULATORY IMPACTS

In Ireland, peat-generated electricity qualifies for priority dispatch and receives support through a 'public service obligation' levy on electricity consumers for the first 15 years of a peat station's life. After that, it must survive in the electricity market. However, the peat stations were designed to operate as baseload plants, running constantly throughout the day. While they can ramp output up and down, they are not suited to the stop/start regime that would be required for a merchant plant operating in a market like Ireland's, which has a high proportion of intermittent generation from wind.

In order to achieve a more stable operating regime, the Edenderry station has registered as a 'Hybrid Plant' in the Irish single electricity market (SEM). Hybrid Plants, which must use a renewable energy source for part of their energy input, are accorded priority dispatch. The market regulator has decided that, in order to qualify as a Hybrid Plant, a generating station must:

a) Produce at least 10% of its output from renewable energy sources; and

b) Emit fewer carbon emissions than an appropriate reference thermal plant deemed to be displaced. The carbon emissions threshold has been set at 0.7445 tonnes CO_2/MWh up until the end of 2016 (SEMC, 2013).

Biomass as an energy source is generally more expensive than competing fossil fuels. This additional cost has been recognised by the Irish Government and a series of supports have been introduced for electricity generated from bioenergy sources, including biomass combustion, biomass combined heat and power (CHP) and anaerobic digestion (DCENR, 2012). The support tariffs for renewable electricity produced from energy crops and from other types of biomass co-fired with peat are indexed in line with the increases in the Irish consumer price index, if any, and the current tariffs are published on the Irish Department of Communications, Energy and Natural Resources' website (DCENR, 2016).

BIOMASS SUSTAINABILITY

Within the European Union, biomass as a fuel has been classified as 'carbon neutral', i.e. carbon emissions from the combustion of biomass materials are deemed to be reabsorbed by the re-growing plants. This carbon neutral status has been challenged by a number of environmental NGOs, especially in relation to biomass supply chain emissions, land use change and the impacts on both vegetation and soil carbon stocks. The small-scale and local use of biomass for domestic heating is generally regarded as satisfactory, but the large-scale use of biomass for electricity generation has raised concerns, particularly when the biomass used is imported from overseas.

The European Commission first addressed the sustainability of solid biomass in 2010, when it issued a non-binding recommendation on sustainability requirements to Member States (EC, 2010). The sustainability recommendation included:

a) A methodology for calculating supply chain greenhouse gas emissions;

b) A stipulation that wastes, secondary biomass and forestry and agricultural crop residues shall be considered to have zero life-cycle GHG emissions up to the process of collection of those materials;

c) A fossil fuel comparator of 198 gCO_{2eq}/MJ of electricity, against which biomass used for the production of electricity must be compared; and

d) Typical and default emission values for solid biomass pathways.

The Commission's position was updated in a report on sustainability requirements in July 2014, which included an updated GHG emission accounting methodology and a revised fossil fuel comparator of 186 gCO_{2eq}/MJ of electricity that takes account of the likely evolution of the European single electricity market (EC, 2014). The Commission also indicated to Member States that:

"......it is considered to be good practice for existing bioenergy installations to achieve GHG savings of at least 70% compared to the fossil fuel comparators."

Bord na Móna has quantified the GHG emissions associated with the supply chains for the main indigenous and imported types of biomass used at Edenderry power station. This analysis was carried out using the bioenergy pathway methodologies and the default GHG emission values published by the Joint Research Council (JRC, 2014.) The JRC methodology assumes a standard electrical conversion efficiency of 25%. In quantifying the emissions for Edenderry station, we have used the plant's actual conversion efficiency when co-firing of 35.5%. The percentage GHG emission savings, against peat and against the EU fossil fuel comparator (FFC), are presented in Table 2.

Table 2: Percentage GHG emission savings from using different biomass materials at Edenderry Station

Biomass Type	**Biomass Supply Chain Emissions ($gCO_{2\,eq}$/MJ)**	**Biomass Electricity Emissions ($kgCO_{2\,eq}$/MWh_e)**	**GHG Savings compared to:**	
			Peat (%)	**EU FFC (%)**
Indigenous				
Woodchips - forest residues	6.0	60.8	94.6%	90.9%
Woodchips - thinnings	5.6	56.8	95.0%	91.5%
Woodchips - sawmill resid.	4.5	45.6	96.0%	93.2%
Willow Chips	8.6	87.2	92.3%	87.0%
Wood Pellets	4.0	40.6	96.4%	93.9%
Imported				
Nut Shells - Europe	5.6	56.8	95.0%	91.5%
Agri-pellets - Europe	11.8	119.7	89.4%	82.1%
Wood Pellets - Europe	12.6	127.8	88.7%	80.9%
Palm Kernel Shells - Asia	16.8	170.4	84.9%	74.6%

However, biomass supply chain greenhouse gas emissions are not the only sustainability issue. The illegal harvesting and supply of timber for energy purposes; the sustainability of forest management techniques; the impact of biomass use on biodiversity and on soils with high carbon stocks, including peatlands and wetlands; the potential for direct and indirect land use change; and the socio-economic impact of biomass supply on the local population, are all causes for concern.

In February 2015 the European Commission launched an Energy Union package, which included a framework strategy for energy resilience coupled with a forward-looking climate change policy. As part of this package, the Commission proposed a new approach to the use of renewable energy, including a review of the Renewable Energy Directive 2009/28/EC, and a new policy for sustainable biomass and biofuels that will apply in the period after 2020. The first step in this process began with a public consultation on the existing sustainability policy and the need for additional measures, which was instigated in February 2016.

Bord na Móna expects that, following negotiations with the Member States and the European Parliament, a new bioenergy policy will be introduced in Europe from 2020. This policy is almost certain to include harmonised sustainability criteria for solid biomass that will have to be satisfied in order for any electricity or heat generated from biomass to qualify for Governmental support, or to count towards a Member State's overall renewable energy output.

CHALLENGES FOR THE FUTURE

Looking ahead, there are a number of challenges that both the Edenderry power station and the other two peat-fired plants in Ireland will face in the coming years:

a) Surviving in a progressively lower carbon world. While the co-firing of biomass with peat serves to reduce a power station's net carbon emissions, and leads to the generation of dispatchable renewable electricity, public and environmental pressures could mean that the proportion of biomass that needs to be used is likely to increase as the average carbon intensity of the power sector diminishes;

b) Procuring enough biomass at a commercially viable price. Biomass demands from both the heating and the electricity sector in Ireland will exceed the available indigenous resource. Increased global competition for biomass may serve to push up the price of internationally traded biomass materials;

c) The priority dispatch/renewable support conundrum. The carbon emissions limit, which peat stations will have to achieve to continue to qualify as a Hybrid Plant, may be reduced as the Irish generating fleet changes over time. However, support for biomass co-firing in Ireland is limited at present to 30% of a plant's installed capacity;

d) Tighter sustainability criteria. An increase in the expected GHG emission savings, beyond the proposed 70%, or a lowering of the European fossil fuel comparator for electricity, will serve to rule out certain types and sources of biomass. To help mitigate this risk, Bord na Móna will be examining and quantifying the actual biomass supply chain emissions, rather than using the JRC default values;

e) Lower combustion emission limits. New, non-CO_2 emission limits have been introduced from 2016 for large European power plants by the EU Industrial Emissions Directive 2010/75/EU. These limits will be reduced further by the Best Available Techniques (BAT) Reference Document for Large Combustion Plants (LCP BREF) process currently under way. Capital investment in enhanced flue gas treatment facilities may be required to enable existing plants meet the new emission limit values for SO_x, NO_x, HCl, HF and particulates.

CONCLUSION

The co-firing experience at Edenderry station has been a positive one over the past eight years. The bubbling fluidised bed technology has proven to be very robust and capable of utilising a wide range of biomass materials in combination with milled peat. We have managed to obtain adequate volumes of suitable biomass materials at an acceptable price. Along the way, significant emissions of CO_2 have been abated, and the plant has produced a considerable amount of renewable electricity that contributes towards Ireland's renewable energy target. Looking ahead, there are a number of challenges that the peat stations in Ireland will have to overcome in order to continue to co-fire with a mixture of peat and biomass.

REFERENCES

1. DCENR (2012). Renewable Energy Feed-in Tariff: A Competition for Electricity Generation from Biomass Technologies 2010-2015. 35pp. Department of Communications, Energy and Natural Resources, Irish Government, Dublin.
2. DCENR (2015). Government White Paper: Ireland's Transition to a Low Carbon Energy Future 2015-2030. 122pp. Department of Communications, Energy and Natural Resources, Irish Government, Dublin.
3. DCENR (2016). The current tariffs for renewable electricity produced by biomass combustion, including co-firing, are published on the Department of Communications, Energy and Natural Resources' website at: www.dcenr.gov.ie/energy/en-ie/Renewable-Energy/Pages/Refit-Schemes-Landing-Page.aspx
4. EC (2010). Report from the Commission to the Council and the European Parliament on Sustainability Requirements for the use of Solid and Gaseous Biomass Sources in Electricity, Heating and Cooling. COM/2010/0011. 19pp. The European Commission, Brussels.
5. EC (2014). State of Play on the Sustainability of Solid and Gaseous Biomass used for Electricity, Heating and Cooling in the EU. SWD/2104/259. 33pp. The European Commission, Brussels.
6. JRC (2014). Solid and Gaseous Bioenergy Pathways: Input values and GHG Emissions. Joint Research Centre, Science and Policy Report EUR 26696. 250pp. European Commission, Brussels.
7. Phillips, H. (2011). All Ireland Roundwood Production Forecast 2011-2028. 37pp. COFORD, Department of Agriculture, Fisheries and Food, Irish Government, Dublin.
8. SEMC (2013). Criteria for the qualification of Hybrid Plant for priority dispatch in the SEM. 19pp. Decision Paper SEM/13/006, SEM Committee, Commission for Energy Regulation, Dublin.

Abstract No: A-187

TOWARDS ATTAINING HIGH YIELDS AND LONG TERM SUSTAINABILITY OF SECOND GENERATION OIL PALM REPLANTS ON PEAT IN NORTH SUMATERA, INDONESIA – THE ASIAN AGRI EXPERIENCE

Manjit Sidhu[1*], Mukesh Sharma[2], Abdul Aziz[1], Arusman Limbong[3], Simon Sihotang[3] and Bukit Sanjaya[3]

[1]*April-Asian Agri Group R&D, Bahilang Estate, North Sumatra, Indonesia*
[2]*April-Asian Agri Group R&D, RGE-TC, Riau, Indonesia,*
[3]*Asian Agri Sumatra, Medan, North Sumatra, Indonesia*

**Corresponding author: manjit_singhsidhu@asianagri.com*

SUMMARY

Asian Agri's planting of Gen-1 oil palms on peat commenced in 1991. Due to lack of experience with peat, inadequate drainage and zero soil compaction, initial FFB yields were poor peaking at 24 mt/ha, 11 years after planting. Thereafter, FFB yields started to decline and by 18 years, average yield was less than 15 mt/ha. This rapid deterioration in yield was attributed to a significant loss in palm stand due to *Ganoderma* infection and toppling over of palms due to peat subsidence. In view of uneconomical yields, early replanting with superior Gen-2 DxP progenies commenced in 2006. Right from the start, proper land preparation protocol and BMP's for peat were adopted to ensure that history would not repeat itself. Peat compaction was undertaken to minimise future palm leaning and toppling. Greater emphasis and importance was placed on drainage and water management in order to ensure retention of optimum water levels (40-60 cm) throughout the year and minimise peat subsidence. As *Ganoderma* infection was the pre-dominant factor in reducing palm stand in the Gen-1 plantings, a four stage IPM system was introduced to minimise infection risk in the Gen-2 replants. This included intensive land preparation with a certification scheme, planting varieties with a higher disease tolerance, protection with an effective bio-agent and early detection and removal of newly infected palms. IPM was also used for managing other potential pests with emphasis on establishment of an Early Warning System combined with cultural and biological control methods to limit use of chemical pesticides. As nutrition plays a critical role in achieving high sustainable yields, a network of fertilizer trials were also laid down to re-determine the macro and micro nutrient requirements of the Gen-2 progenies on well decomposed peat. Early yields of the Gen-2 replants have been very promising and were 47% higher than Gen-1 plantings over the first 6 years of evaluation. In the earliest 2006 replant, FFB yields of 27 mt/ha have been achieved within 8 years after planting.

Keywords: *Oil palm, peat, sustainability, second generation*

INTRODUCTION

Asian Agri has 6 estates in the Labuhan Batu District of North Sumatera, totalling 22,547 ha of which 19,529 ha (87%) are on peat. Four of the six estates are contiguous and located partly on a peat dome of variable depth. Approximately 9%, 31% and 47% of the peat is shallow (< 1m), moderately deep (1-3 m) or deep (> 3 m), respectively.

All six estates were established from heavily logged over forest and planting of first generation (Gen-1) oil palms on raw fibrous peat commenced in 1991 and continued until 2000. However, due to rapid planting of large acreages, coupled with lack of experience and full understanding of peat, mistakes were made in land preparation. Drainage was not well planned and often inadequate and no compaction of peat was undertaken prior to planting. In addition, the " hole in hole " planting technique was only utilized on a limited scale due to the high water table.

In view of the above constraints, initial fresh fruit bunch (FFB) yields were poor especially on deep peat, peaking at 24.4 mt/ha, at 11 years after planting. Better yields ranging from 26-28 mt/ha were recorded in moderately deep to shallow peat plantings. In general, FFB yields started to decline 13-14 years after planting and by 18 years, average yields were less than 15 mt/ha.

The rapid deterioration in yield was attributed primarily to a significant loss in palm stand due to high *Ganoderma* infection and to a lesser extent, termite attack. Toppling or lodging-over of palms due to peat subsidence and periodic flooding of low lying sections of the peat basin were also contributing factors to loss of palm stand and productivity. After just 15-18 years, in many fields, the initial palm stand of 148-150 palms/ha had been reduced to 70-80 palms/ha.

In view of uneconomical yields, early replanting with superior second generation (Gen-2) DxP progenies was carried out with the hard lessons learnt from the earlier failure kept in mind. Right from the start, proper land preparation protocol and best management practices (BMP's) for peat were adopted to ensure that history would not repeat itself.

Replanting was initiated in 2006 (228 ha) but major replanting only commenced from 2010 onwards. Up to end 2014, a total of 12,649 ha had been successfully replanted.

Unlike the Gen-1 plantings, peat compaction was undertaken in the Gen-2 replants to improve bulk density and anchorage, as a counter measure to minimize palm leaning and toppling. Compaction to a depth of 15 cm was achieved by the use of wide tracked excavators making two runs over the area designated for planting rows and harvesters paths.

Greater emphasis and importance was placed on drainage and all aspects of water management. Peat soil depth maps, topography surveys and drain ability assessments were used to guide drainage planning and improve on the existing water management master plan. To minimise flooding and water logging, new field drains were constructed at 1:8 ratio (drains: planting rows) and where ever necessary, their intensity increased to 1:4. For better water retention, additional weirs (drain blocks) were installed in collection drains for every 20 cm drop in water table elevation. Prior to onset of the dry season, temporary weirs were also installed in main drains and water levels in collection drains raised to ± 20 cm from ground surface. This was to ensure that water levels remained in the optimum 40-60 cm level for as long as possible during the dry season. Water level poles (WLP) were also installed in each collection drain for weekly water level monitoring and the data used for implementing appropriate responses. Subsidence poles (SP) were also installed in represented locations to further monitor the impact of water levels and other factors on peat subsidence.

As *Ganoderma* infection was a predominant factor in reducing palm stand in the Gen-1 plantings, a four stage integrated disease management (IDM) system was introduced to minimize the infection risk and impact of the pathogen on the Gen-2 replants (Figure 1).

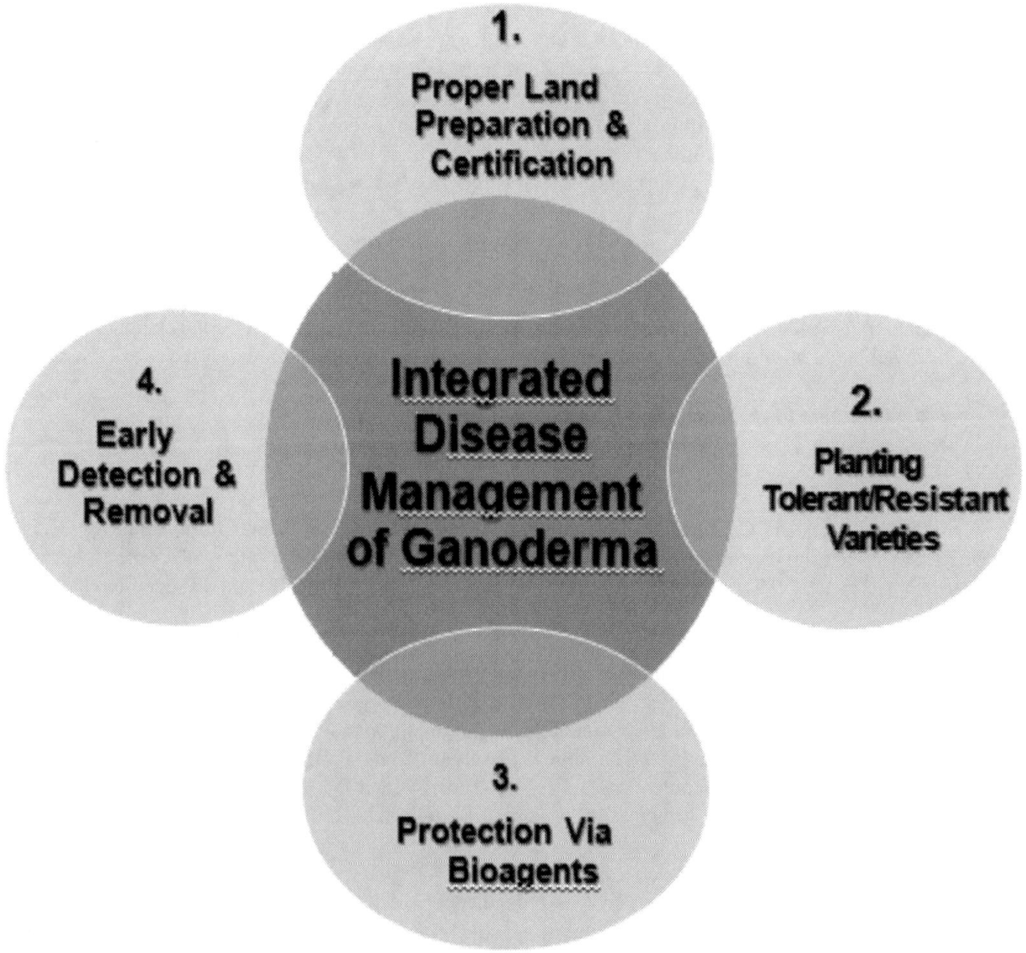

Figure 1: Integrated disease management scheme used in Asian Agri Estates

Stage one involves intensive land preparation with the objective to reduce the residual disease inoculum in the soil. Six months prior to replanting, all identified *Ganoderma* infected palms and dead stumps are dug out to ensure there are no "miss-outs" during the main felling phase. During the latter phase, all remaining palms are felled and their trunks and boles shredded into 10 cm diameter chips by a wide-tracked excavator fitted with a modified chipping bucket. The shredded chips are then spread out in a single layer to facilitate decomposition. Large holes (1.5m width x 1.5m length x 1.0 m depth) are also dug to excavate the remnants of the bole and large roots. The large holes are kept open for a month to expose any residual inoculum to natural UV light prior to being refilled with clean soil. The field is left fallow for a period of six months prior to planting. Planting is only permitted after a field has been certified suitable by a special QC team (certification scheme).

Stage two involves the planting of oil palm varieties with a higher disease tolerance. Both internal and external sources of planting materials are utilized. Since 2011, Asian Agri Research and Development department has screened a total 2,695 DxP progenies and 40 progenies to-date have been identified to have moderate tolerance to *Ganoderma* infection (Figure 2).

Figure 2: Genetic Screening for *Ganoderma* Resistance

Stage three involves the inoculation and protection of oil palm seedlings with an effective bio-agent. AA R&D has identified and isolated a total of 128 endophytic *Trichoderma* strains which are currently undergoing systematic evaluation in the laboratory, nursery and field for their protective and curative properties. To-date, 4 strains (ET 501, ET 531, ET 537, ET 5119) show good potential, of which ET 501 is being used commercially in AA estates. Inoculation of oil palm seedlings is done in 3 stages i.e. pre-nursery stage, main nursery stage and in the planting holes during field planting of the seedlings.

Stage four of the IDM program involves conducting regular census and early removal of infected palms to prevent build-up of inoculum and spread of the disease. Irrespective of infection levels, a minimum of one census round per annum is carried out in all fields and the census frequency being increased with increasing levels of infection (Table 1). Once an infected palm is detected, it is immediately uprooted. A large hole (1.5m x 1.5m x 1.0m) is dug to remove remnants of the bole and roots. The newly dug hole is left exposed for a month before it is filled with clean soil. The uprooted bole and trunk is cut into five even portions (manual) or shred into 10 cm diameter chips (mechanical) and left in the inter rows to decompose.

Table 1: *Ganoderma* Census Frequency

Ganoderma Infection Category	Infection Level per Block (30-35 ha)	Census Frequency
Low	Zero infection	1 round/annum
Medium	1-2 palms	2 rounds/annum (6 monthly interval)
High	> 2 palms	3 rounds/annum (4 monthly interval)

Integrated Pest Management (IPM) is also used for managing other potential pests of oil palms planted on peat such as *Oryctes* beetles, termites, *Tirathaba* bunch moth, slugs, rats and other leaf defoliators. Main emphasis is given to the establishment of an early warning system (EWS) together with cultural and biological control methods in order to limit the use of chemical pesticides. The latter includes the planting of beneficial plants along collection roads as habitats for natural enemies, the use of light and fruit traps for trapping moths of leaf defoliators, as well as pheromone traps for controlling the rhinoceros beetle. Barn owls are reared and used for rat control. Naturally occurring viruses and fungi (*Cordyceps, Beauvaria*) are routinely collected, propagated and re-sprayed into the fields to contain outbreaks of leaf defoliators (nettle caterpillars, bagworms), whilst pathogenic isolates of the muscadine fungus, *Metarhizium anisopliae* is currently being evaluated by R&D as a potential tool for Rhinoceros beetle control. Whenever chemical pesticides have to be used, spraying is restricted to specific target sites (e.g. palm Spears for *Oryctes* control) or via selective application techniques (trunk injection, root infusion) to ensure minimum disruption to the eco-system.

As nutrition plays a critical role towards achieving high yields and sustainability of oil palm on peat, two factors required consideration. First, a change in soil fertility due to maturation and mineralization of the peat over time (> 20 years) and nutrient inputs via recycling of the biomass of the Gen-1 plantings (zero burn). Second, the possibility of differential nutrient requirements and optimum nutrient levels of the Gen-2 replants in contrast to Gen-1 planting materials. In view of the above, a network of fertilizer trials has recently been established to determine the macro and micro nutrients requirement of the Gen-2 DxP progenies. For the meantime, available information from in-house Gen-1 trials and the industry, as well as field nutrient surveys are being used to adjust fertilizer programs to maximize palm growth and yields and minimize negative impact on the environment (nitrification and eutrophication).

Another critical factor towards achieving sustainability on peat is improving executive and supervisory staff knowledge, awareness and technical competency on all aspects of peat management (e.g. BMP's suitable for peat, water management, peat subsidence, GHC emission etc). In Asian Agri, this is being done through information and technology transfer via a detailed SOP, field clinics, advisory visits as well as attending relevant workshops, seminars and conferences.

Early yields of the Gen-2 replants have been very promising and are approximately 51% higher than Gen-1 plantings over the same period of time (7 years). In the earliest replant (OP 2006), FFB yields of 27.7 mt/ha have been achieved within 9 years after planting (Table 2).

TABLE 2 : COMPARATIVE PERFORMANCES OF GEN-2 X GEN-1 PLANTING MATERIALS ON PEAT

Planting Materials	Year of Planting	Ha	Average yield/ha (mt ffb)																			
			Palm age (years)																			
			3*	4	5	6	7	8	9	10	11	12	13	14	15	16	17	18	19	20	21	22
Gen-1	**1991-2000**	**11,718**	**5.1**	**8.5**	**12.7**	**16.1**	**19.7**	**21.3**	**22.9**	**23.6**	**24.4**	**24.2**	**23.0**	**21.6**	**20.2**	**18.5**	**15.6**	**14.5**	**14.5**	**15.0**	**13.6**	**10.6**
Gen-2	2006	228	11.3	19.7	23.7	23.3	25.6	27.3	27.7													
	2010	1,417	11.2	18.4	25.2																	
	2011	2,356	10.7	21.1																		
	2012	2,245	11.6																			
	2006-2012	**6,246**	**11.1**	**20.1**	**25.0**	**23.3**	**25.6**	**27.6**	**27.7**													

* 4-8 months harvesting

Abstract No: A-388

VULNERABILITY OF CO_2 EXCHANGE IN TROPICAL PEAT ECOSYSTEMS: A CASE STUDY FROM SARAWAK, MALAYSIAN BORNEO

Angela C. I. Tang[1], Paul C. Stoy[1], Kevin K. Musin[2], Edward B. Aeries[2], Joseph Wenceslaus[2], Ryuichi Hirata[3] and Lulie Melling[2]

[1]Department of Land Resources and Environmental Sciences, Montana State University, USA
[2]Tropical Peat Research Laboratory, Chief Minister's Department, Malaysia
[3]Center for Global Environmental Research, National Institute for Environmental Studies, Japan

**Corresponding author: atchiemac@gmail.com*

SUMMARY

Tower-based eddy covariance measurements of CO_2 concentration within and above the canopy were made to quantify the seasonal and inter-annual variations in the net ecosystem CO_2 exchange (NEE) of a tropical peat swamp forest in Sarawak, Malaysia (1°27'55"N, 111°9'20"E). NEE was estimated to be 631, 512, 184 and 358 g C m^{-2} y^{-1} for 2011, 2012, 2013 and 2014, i.e. the forest was a net source of CO_2 to the atmosphere during all four years of measurement. The inter-annual variation in NEE was largely driven by the variation in GPP of the tropical peat forest, which was strongly influenced by vapor pressure deficit (VPD).

Keywords: *net ecosystem CO_2 exchange (NEE), tropical peat swamp forest, eddy covariance*

INTRODUCTION

Southeast Asia's peat swamp forests are globally salient ecosystems, storing on the order of 77% of the world's tropical peat carbon and 11-14% of the world's peat carbon. Thus, tropical peatlands in Southeast Asia are a vital component of the global terrestrial carbon pool and quantifying the surface-atmosphere exchange of carbon dioxide in tropical peat forests is critical for understanding its sustainability.

The net ecosystem exchange of CO_2 (NEE) has rarely been measured in tropical peat forests to date, and existing measurements reveal net carbon losses to the atmosphere. The tropical peat forest ecosystem in Kalimantan, Indonesia was a slight sink of CO_2 or close to balance in the first half of the dry season, but emissions increased during beginning of the wet season (Hirano *et al.*, 2007). In addition, the annual sum of NEE in an ENSO year was 220 and 289 g C m^{-2} y^{-1} higher than the two following consecutive years, mainly attributed to a reduction in PPFD caused by dense smoke emitted from large fires. The CO_2 emissions from a peat swamp forest floor in Kalimantan were highest during the dry season due to the lower water table and thicker oxic peat layer (Jauhiainen *et al.,* 2005). On the other hand, Melling *et al.* (2005) showed substantial variability in soil CO_2 efflux from three peat ecosystems of Sarawak in Malaysia; the annual soil CO_2 efflux at forest ecosystem differed from oil palm ecosystem by 33% and sago ecosystem by 63%.

Despite the noteworthy characteristic of tropical peat, relatively little is known on how vulnerable this carbon pool is to changes in the soil-vegetation-atmosphere continuum. To shed light on the paucity of this information, an eddy covariance tower erected in a protected peat swamp forest in Sarawak, Malaysia was instrumented to continuously measure the exchange of CO_2 between the forest ecosystem and atmosphere. The objective of the present paper is to quantify the seasonal and inter-annual variability of NEE, and to analyze the role and relative importance of environmental drivers in determining this variability.

MATERIALS AND METHODS

Site description

The study was carried out in a tropical peat swamp forest in Maludam National Park in the Betong Division of Sarawak, Malaysia. The Park is the largest protected peat swamp forest in Sarawak, and is bordered on the north by Saribas River and on the south by Lupar River. The canopy has an average height of 25 m and emergent trees can exceed 30 m. A 40 m tower was erected in the southern part of the forest and was instrumented to continuously measure fluxes and meteorological variables (1°27'55"N, 111°9'20"E). Dominant over story vegetation includes *Shorea albida*, *Gonystylus bancanus* and *Stemonurus* spp (Anderson 1972).

Measurements of fluxes and micrometeorological variables

NEE was measured continuously using the eddy covariance (*EC*) technique over four years from 2011 to 2014. The EC system consisted of a LI-7500A open-path CO_2/H_2O analyzer (LI-COR Inc., Lincoln, NE, USA) coupled to a CSAT3 three-dimensional sonic anemometer (Campbell Scientific Inc., Logan, UT, USA), which measured the concentrations of CO_2 and water vapor, and the three components of wind speed. Signals from these sensors were recorded at a frequency of 10 Hz using a CR3000 Data logger (Campbell Scientific). A LI-820 closed-path CO_2 analyzer (LI-COR) was deployed to measure the vertical profile of CO_2 concentration at six levels within and above the canopy: 0.5, 1, 3, 11, 21 and 41 m. Net radiation was measured at 41 m using a CNR4 net radiometer (Kipp & Zonen, Delft, The Netherlands). Two LI-190SB quantum sensors (LI-COR) were likewise mounted at 41 m and pointed downward and upward to measure incident and absorbed photosynthetic photon flux densities (PPFD). Air temperature and relative humidity were measured at 11 and 41 m using CS215 temperature and relative humidity probe (Campbell Scientific). The tower was also equipped with a 3-cup anemometer and wind vane (01003-5 R.M. Young Co., Traverse, MI, USA) at 41 m to measure wind speeds and wind directions. Rainfall was collected by a TE525MM tipping-bucket rain gauge (Texas Electronics, Dallas, Texas, USA) 1 m above the ground surface in an open area. Soil temperature was measured with platinum resistance thermocouples at 5 and 10 cm below the ground surface. Volumetric soil water content was measured at a depth of 30 cm using CS616 time domain reflectometry (TDR) (Campbell Scientific, Logan, UT, USA). All meteorological variables were continuously recorded using CR3000 and CR1000 data loggers at a sampling frequency of 5 min and averaged over each 30 min period except groundwater level (*GWL*), which was monitored on a half-hourly basis using a water level logger (DL/N 70 STS Sensor Technik Sirnach AG, Sirmarch, Switzerland).

Data processing, gap filling and uncertainty analysis

Post-processing calculations were performed using the Flux Calculator software (Ueyama, 2012), and these include spike removal, double rotation (Wilczak *et al.*, 2001), time-lag corrections, frequency response corrections (Massman, 2000, 2001) and density fluctuation corrections (Webb *et al.*, 1980).

NEE was calculated as the sum of eddy flux (F_c) and the storage flux (F_s). The F_s was inferred from vertical CO_2 concentration (c) profiles as (Aubinet *et al.*, 2001):

$$F_s = \frac{P_a}{RT_a} \int_0^h \frac{\partial c(z)}{\partial t} dz \quad (1)$$

where P_a is the atmospheric pressure, R is the molar gas constant and T_a the air temperature (K).

A threshold of friction velocity (u^*) was derived to discard underestimated nighttime flux data during stable periods when *PPFD* was less than 5 μmol m^{-2} s^{-1}. We used the atmospheric stability threshold after Novick *et al.* (2004), which requires near-neutral atmospheric stability for nighttime data acceptance. The atmospheric stability defined as $\zeta = (z - d)/L$, where z is the measurement height of the sonic anemometer and L is the Obukhov length. In this study, the lower limit of 0.1 m s^{-1} was accepted as the u^* threshold as determined by a sensitivity analysis of annual NEE to the u^* threshold.

To fill the gaps in the half-hourly NEE, we used the Mitscherlich model:

$$NEE = -(\beta_M + \gamma_M)\left(1 - \exp\left(\frac{-\alpha_M PPFD}{\beta_M + \gamma_M}\right)\right) + \gamma_M \quad (2)$$

where α_M is the initial slope of the light response curve, β_M is the gross ecosystem productivity (GEP) at light saturation, and γ_M, the intercept parameter at zero light, represents the ecosystem respiration, RE. Parameters were fit using least squares regression for observations using seven-day moving windows. The gross primary productivity (GPP) is the difference between the estimated RE and the observed NEE: GPP = RE + NEE.

We applied the approach of Richardson *et al.* (2006) to estimate the random uncertainty of NEE. Random errors were inferred using paired daily-difference approach in which a measurement pair was selected only if the mean half-hourly PPFD for two successive days differed by less than 75 μmol m^{-2} s^{-1}, air temperature differed by less than 3°C, and wind speed differed by less than 1 m s^{-1}. Random uncertainty was propagated through the gap filling routines by perturbing the input flux observations with a random value drawn from a normal distribution multiplied by the afore-calculated random errors. This procedure was iterated 100 times for each day, and 100 gap filling models were fit for each day using least squares regressions. Missing NEE data were filled using the mean of the 100 models.

RESULTS AND DISCUSSIONS

The annual pattern of rainfall in Sarawak is characterized by two seasons: the dry season typically lasts from April to September and the wet season lasts from October to March (Figure 1). In brief, 2013 and 2014 were warmer and drier than 2011 and 2012. The mean annual air temperature above the canopy increased from 26.6 °C in 2011 to 27.09 °C in 2014. The annual cumulative PPFD was 4.7% greater in 2013 (6152 MJ m^{-2} y^{-1}) than in 2011 (5877 MJ m^{-2} y^{-1}), whereas comparable cumulative PPFD was observed in 2012 and 2014 (6015 and 6017 MJ m^{-2} y^{-1}). The mean annual water table depth was lowest in 2014 (-11.3 cm), followed by -5.3 cm in 2011, -2.5 cm in 2012 and above ground at 3.2 cm in 2013.

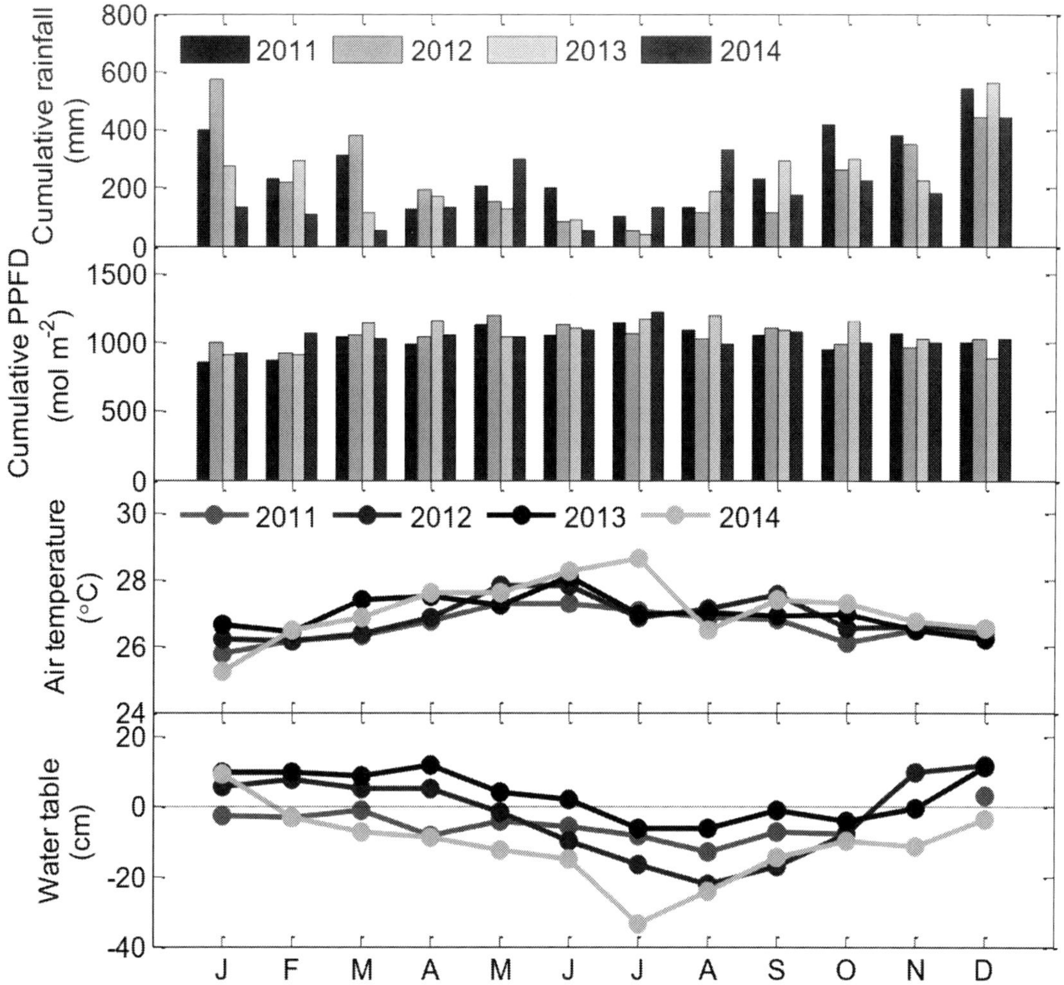

Figure 1: Seasonal variations in monthly sums of rainfall, monthly sums of photosynthetic photon flux densities (PPFD), monthly means of air temperature and water table from 2011 to 2014.

Rainfall was highest in 2011 (3890 mm) and NEE was negative (indicating a carbon sink) during the wet season until mid-June, after which the increasing vapor pressure deficit (VPD) and declining water table depth coincided with a large C loss event of >500 g C m^{-2} over a three month period (Figure 2). Meanwhile, the monthly sum of PPFD in May increased by 14% compared to April 2011; the mean air temperature and daytime VPD increased respectively by 0.6°C and 0.15 kPa from April to May. Notwithstanding higher PPFD in the dry season, higher temperature induced an increase in VPD, which could limit GPP through stomatal closure. These environmental conditions together led to a lower net CO_2 uptake.

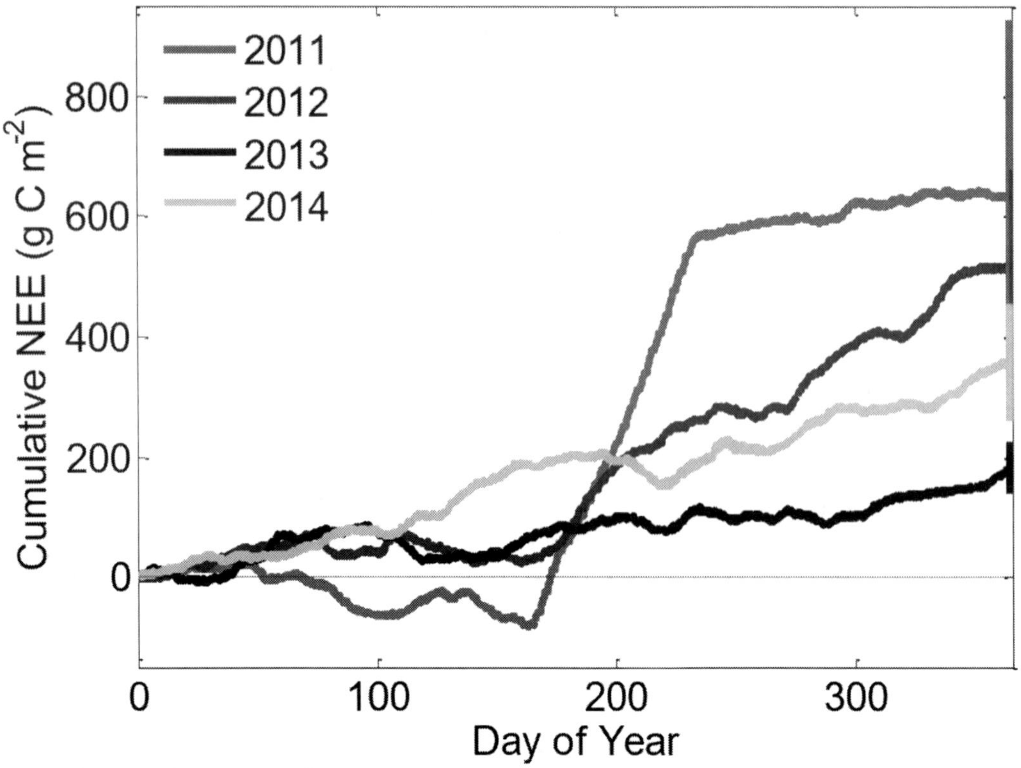

Figure 2: The cumulative sum of NEE for 2011, 2012, 2013 and 2014. Uncertainty bars represent one standard deviation from the sum of one-year study period.

Rainfall in 2012 and 2013 was close to the long-term average (2798 mm) and the cumulative NEE in these two years were similar until early July. The rates of C loss then increased and coincided with decrease in radiation, PPFD, and water table depth and increase in wind speed, noting that the mean daytime VPD increased from 0.66 kPa in April to 0.9 kPa and 0.98 kPa in May and June, respectively. This further suggests that VPD demonstrated lagged effects on CO_2 uptake and the impacts of water stress on GPP that warrant further investigation. 2014 experienced the lowest rainfall (2272 mm) but rates of C loss similar to the average of the other three years.

Table 1: Annual NEE, RE and GPP for 4 years between 2011 and 2014

Year	NEE ($g\ C\ m^{-2}\ y^{-1}$)	RE ($g\ C\ m^{-2}\ y^{-1}$)	GPP ($g\ C\ m^{-2}\ y^{-1}$)
2011	631	2550	1919
2012	512	2789	2277
2013	184	2684	2500
2014	358	3216	2858
Mean	421 ± 194	2810 ± 288	2389 ± 394

The cumulative sum of NEE during the study period is shown in Table 1. Annual NEE varied from 184 g C m^{-2} y^{-1} to 631 g C m^{-2} y^{-1}, with a four-year average of 421 ± 194 g C m^{-2} y^{-1}. Annual GPP increased linearly from 2550 g C m^{-2} y^{-1} in 2011 to 3216 g C m^{-2} y^{-1} in 2014, whereas inter-annual RE variation was not evident except for annual RE in 2014 which increased with annual GPP. At the annual timescale, GPP was clearly more important in modulating inter-annual variance in NEE particularly during the dry season. These findings demonstrate the critical role of plant-water relations, even in the tropical peat forests of Borneo which are amongst the wettest in the world, for regulating the exchange of carbon dioxide between the land surface and the atmosphere.

ACKNOWLEDGEMENTS

This research is supported by both the Sarawak State Government and the Federal Government of Malaysia. We would also like to thank Professor Takashi Hirano, Graduate School of Agriculture, Hokkaido University, Japan for his invaluable advice and assistance in this study.

REFERENCES

1. Anderson, J. A. R. (1972). *Synoptical Key for the Identification of the Trees of the Peat Swamp Forests of Sarawak*. Forest Department, Sarawak.
2. Aubinet, M., Grelle, A., Ibrom, A., Rannik, Ü., Moncrieff, J., Foken, T., Foken, T., Kowalski, A. S., Martin, P. H., Berbigier, P., Bernhofer, C., Clement, R., Elbers, J., Granier, A., Grünwald, T., Morgenstern, K., Pilegaard, K., Rebmann, C., Snijders, W., Valentini, R., & Vesala, T. (2000). *Estimates of the annual net carbon and water exchange of forests: the EUROFLUX methodology* (Vol. 30, pp. 113-175).
3. Hirano, T., Segah, H., Harada, T., Limin, S., June, T., Hirata, R. and Osaki, M. (2007). Carbon dioxide balance of a tropical peat swamp forest in Kalimantan, Indonesia. *Global Change Biology* 13, 412-425.
4. Jauhiainen, J., Takahashi, H., Heikkinen, J. E., Martikainen, P. J., & Vasander, H. (2005). Carbon fluxes from a tropical peat swamp forest floor. *Global Change Biology*, *11*(10), 1788-1797.
5. Massman, W. J.: 2001, 'Reply to comment by Rannik on "A simple method for estimating frequency response corrections for eddy covariance systems"', Agric. For. Meteorol.107, 247-251.
6. Massman, W. J. (2000). A simple method for estimating frequency response corrections for eddy covariance systems. *Agricultural and Forest Meteorology*, *104*(3), 185-198.
7. Melling, L., Hatano, R., & Goh, K. J. (2005). Soil CO2 flux from three ecosystems in tropical peatland of Sarawak, Malaysia. *Tellus B*, *57*(1), 1-11.
8. Novick, K. A., Stoy, P. C., Katul, G. G., Ellsworth, D. S., Siqueira, M. B. S., Juang, J., & Oren, R. (2004). Carbon dioxide and water vapor exchange in a warm temperate grassland. *Oecologia*, *138*(2), 259-274.
9. Richardson, A. D., Hollinger, D. Y., Burba, G. G., Davis, K. J., Flanagan, L. B., Katul, G. G., Munger, J. W., Ricciuto, D. M., Stoy, P. C., Suyker, A. E., Verma, S. B., & Wofsy, S. C. (2006). A multi-site analysis of random error in tower-based measurements of carbon and energy fluxes. *Agricultural and Forest Meteorology*, *136*(1), 1-18.
10. Ueyama, M., Hirata, R., Mano, M., Hamotani, K., Harazono, Y., Hirano, T., Miyata, A., Takagi, K., & Takahashi, Y. (2012). Influences of various calculation options on heat, water and carbon fluxes determined by open-and closed-path eddy covariance methods. *Tellus B*, *64*.
11. Webb, E. K., Pearman, G. I., & Leuning, R. (1980). Correction of flux measurements for density effects due to heat and water vapour transfer. *Quarterly Journal of the Royal Meteorological Society*, *106*(447), 85-100.
12. Wilczak, J. M., Oncley, S. P., & Stage, S. A. (2001). Sonic anemometer tilt correction algorithms. *Boundary-Layer Meteorology*, *99*(1), 127-150.

THEME 1
INVENTORY, BIODIVERSITY, CONSERVATION & FUNCTIONS OF PEATLANDS

1.1: PEAT CHARACTERISTICS

Abstract No: A-072

BRITAIN'S HIGHEST BOG: CAN WE UNLOCK ITS SECRETS?

Olivia M. Bragg[1*], Philip J. Basford[2], Andrew R. Black[1], Graeme M. Bragg[2], Jane K. Hart[2] and Kirk Martinez[2]

[1]*University of Dundee, United Kingdom*
[2]*University of Southampton, United Kingdom*

**Corresponding author: o.m.bragg@dundee.ac.uk*

SUMMARY

The Glenfeshie Mòine Mhór (Great Moss) is Britain's highest bog, the largest bog in the Cairngorm Mountains (Scotland) and a water source area for the River Spey. The area was managed primarily for sport hunting for about two centuries, but deer numbers have been heavily reduced in the last decade to allow regeneration of natural woodland and the return to more natural condition of all ecosystems including peatland. However, it may not be realistic to expect spontaneous improvement in peatland condition and ecosystem services provision in the harsh environment of the Mòine Mhór, which retains snow cover for more than half the year and differs floristically from lower-altitude bogs. To understand whether and where management intervention may be required, we need first to understand how the system works at scales ranging from microform to macro tope, and from sub-catchment to whole-system level. Multi-disciplinary condition and process studies (involving various collaborators) are in progress, with a current emphasis on stream flow generation and fluvial carbon loads. This presentation develops two sub-themes. First, ground survey and GIS analysis are used to address the questions: what are the special features of this bog; what is the nature and extent of degradation; and what are the implications for water delivered to the outflow streams? Secondly, a striking feature is the bare peat patches which were favourite resting places for deer on warm, dry summer days. The occurrence of seasonally extreme surface conditions seems a likely factor in preventing their recolonisation by bog plants now. Information about these conditions that cannot readily be accessed through direct observation, originating from temperature sensors and delivered at 60-minute intervals *via* a low power internet link, is explored in this context. Finally, we discuss aspects of the suitability of our investigation methods for remote and intermittently accessible field sites such as the Mòine Mhór.

***Keywords**: Bare peat, Cairngorms, environmental sensor network, Internet of Things, Vegetation*

INTRODUCTION

The Glenfeshie Mòine Mhór ('Great Moss' in the Gaelic language) occupies a plateau of siliceous Dalradian country rock (Thomas *et al.*, 2004), about 3 km across, at the south-western corner of the Cairngorm Mountains in Scotland. It has been described as the largest expanse of peatland in the Cairngorms National Park and the highest ('raised') bog in Britain (900–950 m a.s.l.). Located within the privately owned Glenfeshie Estate, the centre of the plateau (57° 01′ 58″ N, 03° 48′ 51″ W) lies approximately 600 m above and 5.5 km distant from the Estate office at Carnachuin on the left bank of the River Feshie (Figure 1). It is usually snow-covered for half of the year (November to May), with snow patches often persisting through June. Access at any time of year is constrained by the logistics of fording the notoriously flashy River Feshie and most of the plateau is in mobile phone shadow. The site has considerable interest for nature conservation, being included within the Cairngorms Site of Special Scientific Interest (SSSI) (SNH 2016) and Special Area of Conservation (SAC) (JNCC 2016).

Glenfeshie was managed for sport hunting - primarily stalking of Red Deer (*Cervus elaphus*) - from the early 19th century, and deer stocking levels of 35–40 km^{-2} were usual until 2006. Since then the density of deer has been substantially reduced, to ~1 km^{-2}, to promote the return of native woodland and more natural ecosystems in general. After two centuries of heavy use by deer in summer, the most striking features of the Mòine Mhór are the expanses of bare peat dissected by an extensive system of erosion channels feeding into headwaters of the Feshie, which is in turn a tributary of the River Spey. It is not immediately clear how severely ecosystem services such as water quality maintenance, carbon cycling and support of wildlife have been impaired, or whether it is realistic to expect spontaneous improvements in condition of the peatland without further management intervention.

Here we report some early results from on-going studies that aim to inform future management of the Mòine Mhór. At macro scale we make first estimates of the extent of peatland on the plateau and how much of it still retains vegetation cover, in the context of the implications for river water quality. At micro scale we investigate the environment of the bare peat surfaces with a view to assessing their suitability for recolonisation by plants. For this site, the unpredictability of access poses a major risk to successful implementation of field-based investigations, making efficient use of fieldwork time a priority and remote observation techniques highly attractive. We conclude with some comments about the effectiveness of our methods in this context.

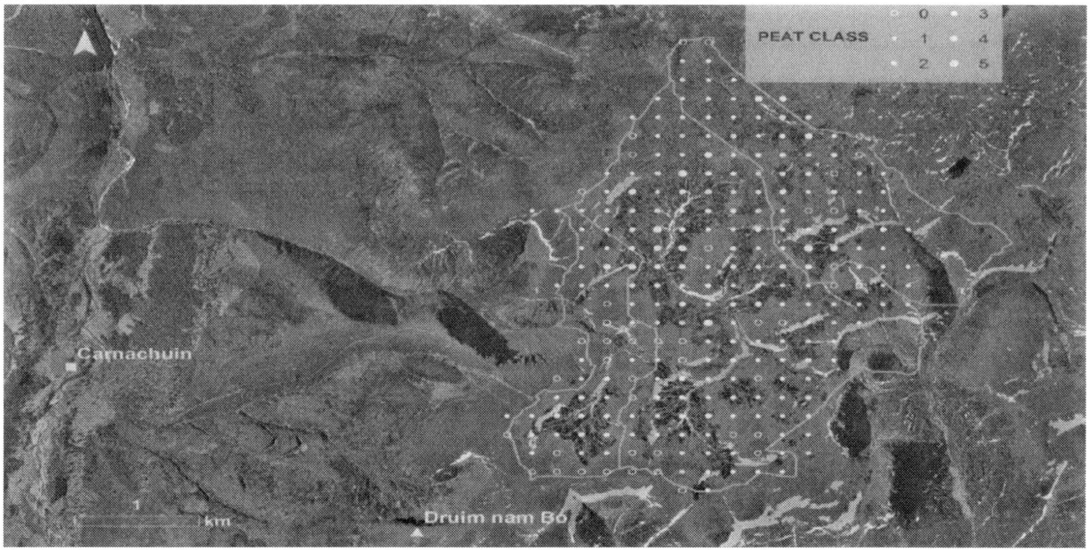

Figure 1. Aerial view of the Mòine Mhór plateau and River Feshie (flowing south–north at left side of image). Cyan polygons divide the plateau between three stream catchments, namely (from west to east) Allt Garbhlach, Coachan Dubh and Allt Sgairnich. Locations of survey quadrats are indicated by yellow points whose sizes reflect peat thickness (key to classes: 0 = no peat, 1 = 1–30 cm, 2 = 31–60 cm, 3 = 61–90 cm, 4 = 91–120 cm, 5 = 121–150 cm). The locations of Carnachuin and Druim nam Bo are also shown. Aerial imagery: Ordnance Survey, Licence No. 100030994. Catchment boundaries derived from OS Terrain 5 DTM [ASC geospatial data], Scale 1:10000, Tiles: nn89ne, nn89se, nn99sw, nn99nw, Updated: 24 March 2015, Ordnance Survey (GB), Using: EDINA Digimap Ordnance Survey Service, <http://digimap.edina.ac.uk>, Downloaded: 2015-08-04 21:44:16.33.

METHODS

A 200 m × 200 m grid of waypoints (defined in six-figure British National Grid co-ordinates, i.e. to 1 m precision) covering the approximate area of the Mòine Mhór plateau and catchment was generated in Microsoft Excel and uploaded to a hand-held GPS with integral camera (Garmin GPSMAP® 62sc). In the field, an observer navigated to each waypoint in turn. At each location a 0.5 × 0.5 m quadrat was laid on the ground, a geotagged vertical photograph of the quadrat was captured using the GPS and, if the observer had botanical knowledge (219/279 quadrats), a list of plant species occurring within the quadrat was recorded. A soil auger or metal probe was then used to determine the thickness of peat (defined as soft organic sediment ≥ 1 cm thick) at the centre of the quadrat. The field data were transcribed into an Excel spreadsheet, then converted to an ArcGIS feature class to which the geotagged quadrat photographs were spatially joined. This facilitated viewing of individual quadrat photographs in conjunction with a base map or aerial photograph, i.e. in their spatial context within the site. The quadrat photographs could then be reviewed and attributed with additional information as required. For present purposes the pertinent attributes are peat thickness and whether more than 50 % of the quadrat was occupied by bare peat.

Catchment boundaries were generated from Ordnance Survey Terrain 5 DTM (digital terrain model) data using the Spatial Analyst 'Hydrology' tools in ArcGIS 10.2.2. After removing small imperfections such as isolated 'sinks' from the data using the 'Fill' tool, flow direction and flow accumulation rasters were generated. Pour point features were placed near the lowest point of each focus stream, then located accurately as pixels in the flow accumulation raster using the 'Snap Pour Point' tool. The generated pour point raster was used in conjunction with the flow direction raster to derive catchment (Watershed) rasters which were then converted to polygons.

Peat temperatures were measured on an expanse of bare peat in the southern (upstream) part of the Allt Garbhlach catchment (Figure 1) using ten temperature sensors (1-Wire DS18B20 digital thermometer; Maxim Integrated Products, San Jose, CA, USA). Five of the sensors (Cluster 106B) were installed horizontally, supported by a strip of plastic mesh, at 10 cm depth intervals in the wall of a 5 cm × 5 cm pit excavated in a small degraded peat hagg using a Malcolm peat sampler (Cuttle & Malcolm 1979), after which the excavated peat was carefully re-packed around them. The remaining sensors (Cluster 106A) were pushed vertically into the ground (to a depth of approximately 1 cm) at intervals of ~20 cm along a transect starting in, and running perpendicular to, a shallow runoff channel on the bare peat surface. The two sensor clusters form part of an environmental sensor network (ESN; Hart & Martinez 2006) that covers the south-western part of the Mòine Mhór plateau. Each sensor cluster is wired to a MSP430-based node running the Contiki operating system (Dunkels *et al.*, 2004). The captured data are stored in flash memory, encoded using protocol buffers to save space. They are fetched hourly *via* an 868 MHz low-power (20 mW) radio network (G.M. Bragg *et al.*, in press) which uses 6LowPAN and CoAP. Once on the micro-PC (border router) at Carnachuin, they are sent *via* the Estate's internet connection to the database server where they are unpacked and loaded into a database for previewing and export for analysis.

RESULTS

In total, quadrats were recorded at 279 GPS waypoints. Of these, 184 (66 %) were on vegetated peat, 51 (18 %) were on bare peat and 44 (16 %) had no peat. Where present, the thickness of the peat layer ranged from >0 to 143 cm (mean 30 cm) (Table 1). The average peat thickness across all quadrats was 25 cm. Rather than accommodating a single expanse of peatland, the Mòine Mhór plateau turned out to consist of a series of knolls topped with *Racomitrium lanuginosum* heath on extremely shallow mineral soils and flanked by *Nardus stricta* grassland. It is probably above the altitude limit for *Calluna vulgaris* but other dwarf shrubs (e.g. *Empetrum* and *Vaccinium* species) were found, as well as *Rubus chamaemorus* growing on isolated *Sphagnum fuscum* cushions. Peatland is more or less confined to basins between the knolls which together form the headwater catchments of three streams, namely Allt Garbhlach (1.64 km^2), Coachan Dubh (5.98 km^2) and Allt Sgairnich (2.88 km^2) (Figure 1). The total number of quadrats recorded within the three stream basins was 237. When assigned to their respective catchments, the data for the 237 quadrats indicated that the relative extents of non-peatland (12–14 %) and vegetated peat (65–68 %) were similar for Coachan Dubh and Allt Sgairnich, whereas 31 % of the Allt Garbhlach catchment had no peat layer and only 55 % was covered by vegetated peat. Whilst 20–21 % of the Allt Garbhlach and Allt Sgairnich peatland had no plant cover, 26 % of the Coachan Dubh peat layer lacked vegetation. Overall, the fraction of bare peat cover *per* catchment was 14 % for Allt Garbhlach, 18 % for Allt Sgairnich and 23 % for Coachan Dubh (Table 1). These figures might provide a first basis for prioritisation of different parts of the plateau for any management intervention driven by peat erosion / water quality considerations.

Example segments of the peat temperature data delivered by Sensor Clusters 106A and 106B are shown graphically in the upper two panels of Figure 2; the lower two panels show concurrent data from an independently operating Campbell CR1000 automatic weather station (Campbell Scientific, Shepshed, UK) located on the Druim nam Bo ridge (Figure 1) that delivers data by conventional telemetry. The data period chosen runs for 21 days from 00:00 hrs on 07 November 2015, and illustrates the transition from autumn to winter conditions on the plateau. A further point of interest is that the first two Atlantic storms to be named (Abigail and Barney) by British Isles meteorologists passed over the UK during this time, and the example record ends as the third (Clodagh) was approaching (Met Office 2016). Up to and including 12 November, peat surface temperature was above 0 °C and followed the more or less diurnal fluctuations in air temperature. The coincident drop in barometric pressure and peak in air temperature that day can be linked to Storm Abigail, which delivered the heaviest rainfall of the period as well as the first dusting of snow on the summits (visible in webcam images of Druim nam Bo captured from Carnachuin around 10:00 hrs on the 13th). Thereafter, the temperature of surface peat fell to ~ 0 °C and the diurnal fluctuations ceased, presumably due to presence of snow and/or ice. The peak in air temperature that preceded Storm Barney during the 15th/16th was mirrored (only) at the three surface peat sensors located highest in the microtopography, suggesting that concave parts of the bare peat surface remained frozen. The next warming event detected on the peat may have been due to insolation on the 19th, as it hardly shows in the air temperature record. This time, four peat-surface sensors responded, perhaps indicating a lower thaw line than previously. Certainly, it appears that the sensor locations were differentially exposed to frosting in the early hours of the 21st as only three sensors indicated cooling. Conversely, when the next warm air mass arrived on the 26th, all surface sensors responded in a sequence that can be interpreted in terms of melt water moving through the channel and snow at other levels requiring time to melt. The '106B' data indicate that subsurface peat cooled quite steadily from the 12th onwards, although the sensors at 10 cm and 20 cm depth showed some responses (with time lags) to warming events at the surface.

Table 1: Summary characteristics of the peat layer of the Mòine Mhór plateau and catchments, as indicated by the quadrat data (see text for details).

		Allt Garbhlach	Coachan Dubh	Allt Sgairnich	All quadrats
catchment	area (m^2)	1643277	5984334	2878267	
	number of quadrats	36	145	56	279
	% without peat	31	12	14	16
	% with vegetated peat	55	65	68	66
	% with bare peat	14	23	18	18
peat	mean thickness (cm ± SD)	29 ± 32	30 ± 30	32 ± 34	30 ± 31
	maximum thickness (cm)	105	143	128	143
	% of peat area bare	20	26	21	22

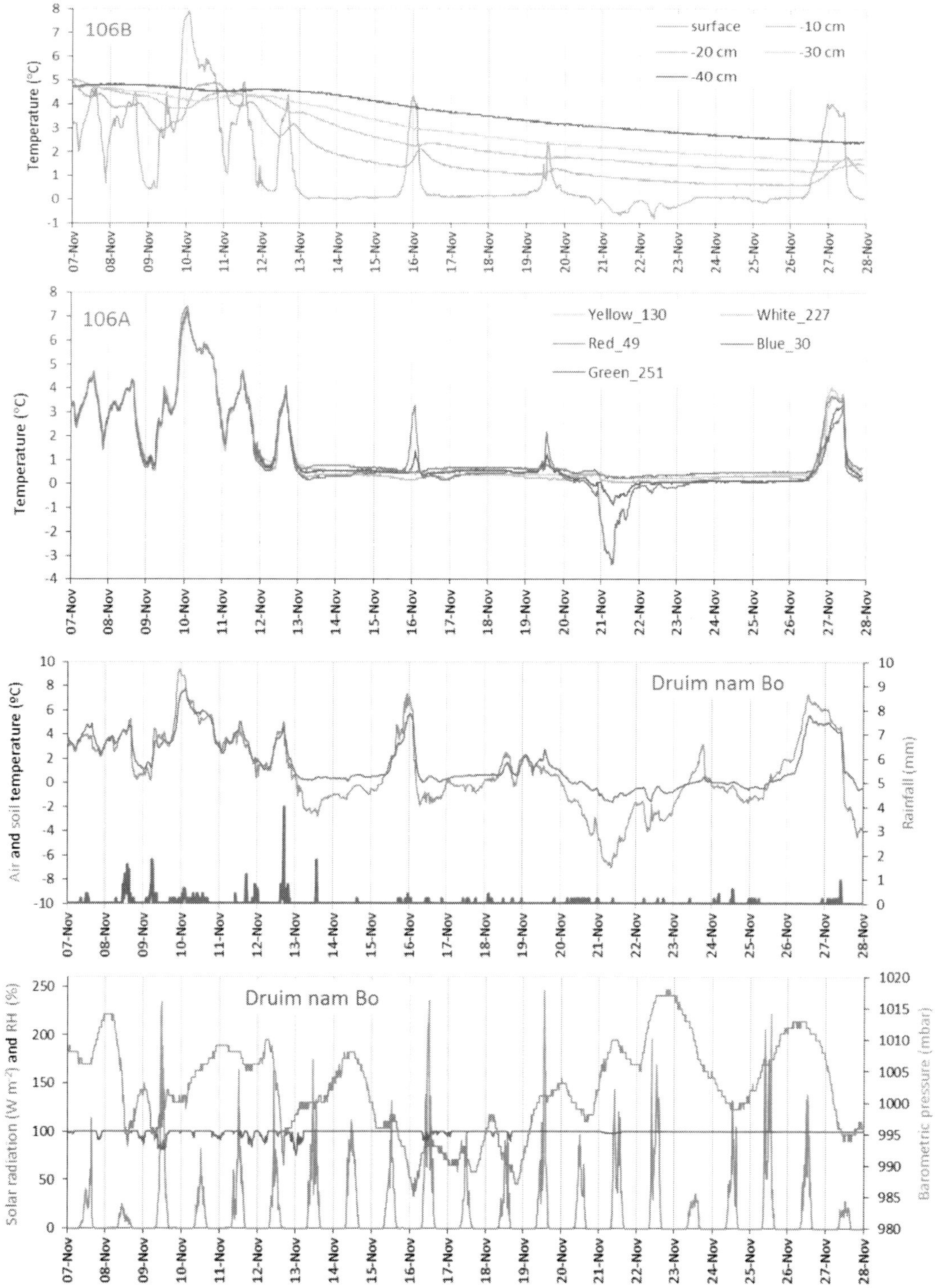

Figure 2. Environmental data for the 21-day period 07–27 November 2015 (the x-axes start at 00:00 hrs on 07 November). The data are peat temperatures from Sensor Clusters 106A and 106B (upper two panes; interval between consecutive records 20 minutes) and information gathered by the (telemetric) Wildland automatic weather station (Campbell CR1000) on Druim nam Bo (lower two panes; interval between consecutive records 15 minutes; RH = relative humidity). Notable weather events during this period were the UK's first two named storms, Abigail and Barney, which tracked over northern Scotland on 12–13 and 17–18 November, respectively, followed by Clodagh on 29 November (Met Office 2016). The sensors in Cluster 106A were positioned in surface peat along a transect (described in the text) in the following order: White_227 (lowest, in channel) - Yellow_130 - Green_251 - Blue_30 - Red_49 (highest, on the side of a peat hagg). The 'surface' sensor of Cluster 106B was located near the centre of a small degraded hagg.

DISCUSSION AND CONCLUSIONS

The use of geotagged photographs was effective in expediting the peat/vegetation survey under circumstances of limited field time, species-poor plant communities and multiple observers with different skill levels; although there were instances where it was not easy to distinguish between graminaceous species in photographs that were not accompanied by field species lists. Nonetheless, the use of geotagging improves on the approach of e.g. Gilbert & Butt (2009) by removing the need for meticulous logging of photograph locations in the field. The intended even coverage of the stream catchments with sampling points was largely but not entirely achieved, firstly because some grid locations were too steep for observers to access safely, and secondly because the data and GIS resources needed to definitively generate the catchment boundaries were not in place before the seasonally determined time window for fieldwork. Now that the photographs have been captured there is potential to re-use them in interpretation of remotely sensed imagery of the site, which would effectively increase the fraction of ground sampled from $< 6.25 \times 10^{-4}$ % (0.25 m^2 *per* 40,000 m^2) to 100 %. The above consideration of just a segment of the peatland data captured *via* the ESN confirms the immense potential of this approach for remote data collection across inaccessible field sites in telemetry shadow under hostile conditions. It is difficult to imagine how such data could otherwise have been gathered on the Mòine Mhór through such a meteorologically eventful period. The environmental sensor network is ideal for investigations in locations like this where there is very limited mobile phone signal, as it allows the network to 'hop' from node to node to reach the field site and provides a 'live' data feed.

ACKNOWLEDGEMENTS

We thank Sangita Pandit Karki for recording part of the GPS grid; and Sebastian Bader, Emma Bryder, Arthur Fabre, Daniel Playle and Tyler Ward for their wide-ranging contributions to establishing and maintaining the Glenfeshie ESN. Sue Jones (Wildland Limited) and Kevin Down (ESRIUK) assisted with GIS resources and analysis; and Alan Long and Craig Phillips provided technical support for fieldwork. Development of the Glenfeshie ESN was funded by NERC 'Technology Proof of Concept' research award NE/L012405/1 "Using Internet of Things technology to aid in Earth and Environmental Science Research". We particularly thank Wildland Limited for permitting and supporting our research, and Wildland's Director of Conservation Thomas MacDonnell and Glenfeshie Estate staff for their valued assistance with the practicalities of site access.

REFERENCES

1. Bragg, G.M., Martinez, K., Basford, P.J. & Hart, J.K. (in press) 868MHz 6LoWPAN with ContikiMAC for an Internet of Things environmental sensor network. *Proceedings of the SAI Computing Conference 2016*, July 13–15, London, UK, 6 pp.
2. Cuttle, S.P. & Malcolm, D.C. (1979) A corer for taking undisturbed peat samples. *Plant and Soil*, 51, 297–300.
3. Dunkels, A., Gronvall, B. & Voigt, T. (2004) Contiki - a lightweight and flexible operating system for tiny networked sensors. *Proceedings of the 29th IEEE International Conference on Local Computer Networks*, Tampa, Florida, USA, 455–462.
4. Gilbert, J.A. & Butt, K.R. (2009) Evaluation of digital photography as a tool for field monitoring in potentially inhospitable environments. *Mires and Peat*, 5(05), 1–6.
5. Hart, J.K. & Martinez, K. (2006) Environmental Sensor Networks: A revolution in the Earth System Science? *Earth Science Reviews*, 78, 177–191.
6. JNCC (2016) *Cairngorms*. Web page, Joint Nature Conservation Committee, Peterborough and Aberdeen, UK. Online at: http://jncc.defra.gov.uk/protectedsites/sacselection/sac.asp?EUCode=UK0016412, accessed 14 Mar 2016.
7. Met Office (2016) *UK Storm Centre*. Web page, The Meteorological Office, Exeter, UK. Online at: http://www.metoffice.gov.uk/uk-storm-centre, accessed 14 Mar 2016.
8. SNH (2016) *Site Details for Cairngorms*. Web page, Scottish National Heritage, Inverness, UK. Online at: http://gateway.snh.gov.uk/sitelink/siteinfo.jsp?pa_code=288, accessed 14 Mar 2016.
9. Thomas, C.W., Gillespie, M.R., Jordan, C. & Hall, A.M. (2004) *Geological Structure and Landscape of the Cairngorm Mountains*. Scottish Natural Heritage Commissioned Report No. 064 [ROAME No. F00AC103]. SNH, Edinburgh, UK, 128 pp.

Abstract No: A-246

DEVELOPMENT OF ANALYSIS METHODOLOGY OF TECHNICAL INDICATORS OF PEAT AND RELATIONSHIP BETWEEN THESE INDICATORS, PEAT PROPERTIES AND FIELDS OF USE

Mall Orru[1, 2, 3, 4], Ingo Valgma[1], Vivika Väizene[1] and Fred Rusanov[1]

[1]*Departmant of Mining, Tallinn University of Technology, Tallinn, Estonia*
[2]*Geological Survey of Estonia, Tallinn, Estonia*
[3]*Eesti Turbaliit, Tallinn, Estonia*
[4]*Mikskaar AS, Tallinn, Estonia*

**Corresponding author: mall.orru@ttu.ee*

SUMMARY

Peat is one of the most important mineral resources of Estonia, 2.37 billion tons, extracted from 1.0 to 1.2 million tons per year. It is exported to 100 countries. It is necessary to analyze the sustainability of peat mining, develop innovative new uses (balneology, activated carbon, peat wax, humic substances, fertilizers, etc). So far, the peat is limited to only heating purposes and horticultural use. Analysis of botanical composition and chemical characteristics of peat provide opportunities for dividing peat layers according to different qualities and possible uses. In Estonia, more than 40,000 peat samples have been collected. Their botanical composition, degree of humification, pH, natural moisture and ash content were determined. Also calorific value, content of trace elements, as well as formation and genesis of peat were described. All the Estonian peat samples have been analyzed using similar methods. Samples have been collected throughout the whole peat sequence. Analysis results give possibilities to determine different quality classes of peat for raw materials and alternative use. It is also important to complete models and maps, where peat layers with different composition of organic matter can be found. The article gives the opportunity and ideas to solve the problems set by the research nationally and internationally

Keywords: *peat characteristics, different peat quality classes, peat alternative use. Peat utilization indicators*

INTRODUCTION AND PEAT INVESTIGATION MATERIALS FOR COMPILING THE DATABASE

Mires and peatlands are an important landscape element in Estonia, covering 1,009,101 hectares (22.3% of territory). Peat reserves amount to 2.37 billion tons (Orru *et al.*, 1992; Orru, 1995). The development of mires and accumulation of peat in the territory of the present-day Estonia started soon after the retreat of continental glacier, first in upland Estonia (Orru, 2010). Considering that peat deposits have formed under variable geological conditions and water regime, their properties (species association, content of mineral and organic matter, chemical composition, the amount and quality of peat reserves) are variable as well.

Peat is among the most important mineral reserves of Estonia, and has long traditions of extraction and utilization. Traditionally peat is used as fuel, in horticulture and as litter. In Estonia annually, 1.1-1.2 million tons of peat is extracted from about 2,000 hectares. Horticultural peat is mostly used in market-gardens of foreign countries, and peat is exported to 100 countries (Orru, Nurme, 2014)

In peat extraction it must be considered that the accompanying establishment of drainage systems affects the technical characteristics of peat (degree of humification, pH, natural moisture content, content of mineral matter (ash content), content of organic matter, mineralization of top peat layers). The above assumption is based on factual data and 1200 laboratory analyses collected within the revision of residual peat reserves carried out at the Geological Survey of Estonia in 1992-1997 (Ramst, 1997). This is important factual information obtained in the process of the above study and must be scientifically systematized. Hydrochemical and hydrogeological investigations for delimiting the buffer zones and elaborating protective measures"(Loigu, Orru & Lode 2008) was carried out. Within the above project, the groundwater level in undrained area bordered with peat production field was measured and the quality of groundwater (pH, temperature, electro conductivity, oxygen content, oxygen saturability) in the water of the peat deposit was assessed, which suggests that similar method could be used also for defining peat layers with different properties (Kink *et al.*, 1998, Orru *et al.*, 2013). Naturally, peat layers with variable structure and association of species have different chemical and physical electric parameters.

Changes of peat properties take place in the process of peat extraction, storing and processing ,where in the result of draining of a peat deposit, its biological and chemical balance is shifted, which favors mineralization of the top layers and sometimes self-combustion of peat (Ranneklev and Gislerod, 2002).

In Estonia, humic substances have been studied in three peat deposits and using the newest laboratory methods (Orru, 2010). The primary results have been positive (Orru *et al.*, 2011) and have attracted interest also internationally (Orru *et al.*, 2010). This peat is good for balneological purposes and successfully used in spas, clinics, exported to many countries. In the Department of Mining, the balneological peat research gives good results and after that it is popularized to use in domestic conditions (Orru, *et al.*, 2013).

In the process of the revision of peatlands carried out by the Geological Survey of Estonia in 1972-1987 (Orru *et al.*, 1972-1987), more than 40, 000 samples of peat were collected (Orru, 2008), their botanical composition, degree of humification, pH, natural moisture content was determined, and the formation and genesis of peat was described (Orru, 1997). Uniquely, in Estonia, large number of peat samples has been analyzed by similar method (Orru & Orru, 2003; Orru & Orru, 2006). The samples have been collected from the whole peat sequence in both, as harvested and natural areas. In many countries only visual assessment is used in peat investigations. In Estonia the botanical composition was determined by microscope, all plant species have been determined starting from Preboreal up to today. It is valuable information on impact of postglacial climate and human activity on environmental changes. In the last two decades in Estonia peatlands investigations have focused on the inventory of vegetation. Practically peat-focused research has not been done in the last 25 years.

In Estonia, the inventory of peatlands was completed in 1987 and in the next 25 years most of the obtained data of peat technical analysis have not been systematized and scientifically analyzed. However, the character of both ecological and water regime depends firstly on the character of the peat layers since in less plant species are found in raised bogs, in comparison with fens The properties of peat determine can provide information on its field of utilisation and quality classes, and the price forecasting. Systematization of the existing extensive factual material (ca 40,000 determinations) allows distinguishing the raw material of different groups and classes within the whole sequence.

However, there are also several perspectives that can be developed in the future. About 40,000 determinations of the peat types and composition of peat by plant species by entire peat sequence (from late Preboreal until present) are stored at the Depository of Manuscript reports of the Geological Survey of Estonia. In further investigations, this material could be used, for instance, for assessing the climate changes during the Holocene as well as the antrophogenic influence.

In Estonia the topic is essential for compiling the concept of utilization and protection of peatlands, and internationally for the programme Strategy for Responsible Peatlands Management. To solve these problems, which are mentioned in the stated article, the Department of Mining set up new project to compile peat characteristics database.

METHODS AND WORKING HYPOTHESES

1. Working hypothesis is that geobotanical inventories of peatlands should be done simultaneously with peat deposit investigations and to prove the allegation that the character of vegetation of a peatland largely depends on the properties of peat. The latter is closely related to water regime and quality. That hypothesis is supported by before done results (Peatlands mapping-1972-1987). It is necessary to analyze the sustainability of peat mining and different fields of use.
2. The development of a new research method, which supports the hypothesis that the peat properties depend on genesis, hydrological regime and climate conditions. Hypothesis are mostly based on technical properties of peat (species associations, pH, ash content, degree of humification, natural moisture content), which are collected prior to peat investigations. The representative factual data (40000 analyses) and experience obtained can be used for successful execution in the future. It gives possibility to determine peat different quality classes of raw materials and alternative use (balneology, active carbon, peat wax, humic substances, etc). It is important to compile models and maps, where we can find peat layers with different organic matter composition. Proof of the hypothesis is mainly by statistical analysis, as well as laboratory and field studies. This hypothesis is the first to be introduced in Estonia and internationally.
3. Proving the hypothesis that draining alters the density of peat, as well as its properties and quality. This hypothesis will be used as foundation and peat sample materials for study peat layers density.
4. Considering the results of earlier investigations of peat properties and water regime, the planned research will provide a new method which enables distinguishing of the prospective peat deposits of highest quality which will be shown on the map. The new method will be economically efficient since minimal amount of new analyses will be required.
5. Assessing the actual mineralization level of top layers of a peat deposit in the result of draining (peat production area, paleudified field, forest). Will be used soil, forest, water and etc maps, LIDAR system for compiling models of mineralized peat layers.

6. Results of research have been used as solutions in Estonia and internationally.

RESEARCH METHODS

The research methods are based mostly on statistical analysis of existing data (40,000 analyses and field observation results), theoretical discussions and computer modeling. The data are stored at the Depository of Manuscript Reports of the Geological Survey of Estonia and are accessible for the public. Most of these data has been collected by the author M. Orru.

DISCUSSION AND RESULTS

The most important discussion to find results is:

1. The relationship between peat properties and genesis of peat deposit
2. The relationship between technical characteristics of peat, enabling assessment of the peat quality classes, modelling the configuration of drained peat deposits and carry out statistical analysis. The humic substances, wax and bitumen rich peat layers for further chemical processing will be evaluated.
3. Sustainable and environmental use of peat deposit will be recommended
4. The results will be applied also in teaching.
5. The elaborated calculation methods and modelling of the configuration of drained areas can be used in the future for solving several peat extraction problems.
6. Based on the results of the research, the valuable peat layers suitable for raw material in the chemical industry can be recommended. Based on the results of the planned research, these valuable peat layers can be contoured and preserved for the time when improved modern equipment can be used for their extraction.
7. The research enables to apply more sustainable peat extraction technologies and foster interdisciplinary cooperation.
8. Peat is one of Estonia's major natural resources, and its integrated use instead of using it just for fuel or horticulture, will enable preserving peat's most valuable resources for future utilization and simultaneous sustainable preservation of these deposits.

CONCLUSION

The properties of peat determine also its field of utilisation and quality classes, and forecasting of its price. Systematisation of the existing extensive factual material (ca 40000 determinations) allows distinguishing the raw material of different groups and classes within the whole sequence.

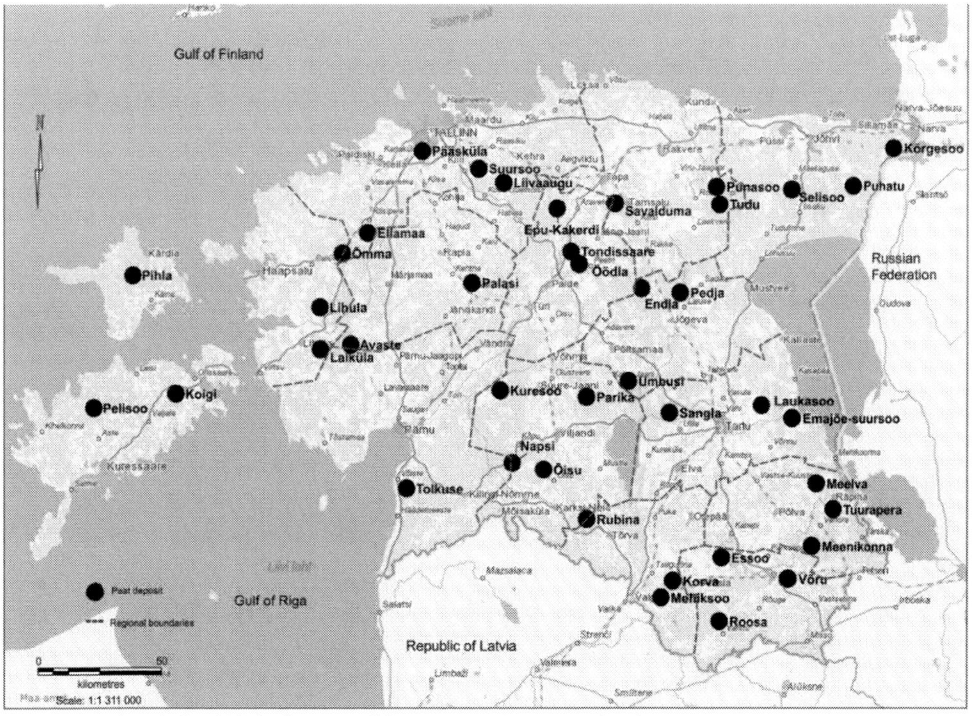

Figure 1: Peat deposits in which the first stage of the peat properties were analyzed

This research is part of the project B36 Extraction and processing of rock with selective methods - mi.ttu.ee/separation, SA Archimedes European Regional Development Fund project No. 3.2.0501.11-0025 (2012 – 2015) "Sustainable and environmentally acceptable oil shale mining", Estonian Science Foundation project No. ETF9018 "Mine collapses in NE Estonia – detection, identification and causes" and Estonian Science Foundation project No. ETF8999 "Tectonics of the continental and offshore territory of Estonia and its structural evolution in Proterozoic and Phanerozoic".

ACKNOWLEDGEMENTS

I would like to acknowledge the technical support of Mr. M. Aarniste and colleague M. Peetermann in the preparation of this paper.

REFFERENCE

1. Kink, H., Andresmaa, E. & Orru, m. 1998. *Eesti soode hüdrogeoökoloogia [Hydrogeoecology of* Estonian *Mires*]. Estonian Academy Publishers, Tallinn, 128 pp. [in Estonian, with English summary].
2. Loigu, E., Orru, M., & Lode, E. 2008. Soode hüdrokeemilised ja hüdrogeoloogilised uuringud puhvertsoonide piiritlemiseks ja kaitsemeetmete välja töötamiseks.
3. [Peatlands hydrochemical and hydrogeological investigations for delimiting the buffer zones and elaborating perspective measures], 92pp. Tallinn University of Technology [in Estonian].
4. Orru, M., Širokova, M., Veldre, M., 1992. Eesti turbavarud (Estonian peat resources). Geological Survey of Estonia, Tallinn, 146pp. (in Estonian with English summary).
5. Orru, M. 1995. *Eesti turbasood [Estonian Mires*]. Geological Survey of Estonia, Tallinn, 240 pp. [in Estonian, with English summary].
6. Orru, M. 2010. *Dependence of Estonian peat deposit properties ans landscape types and feeding conditions*. 121 pp. Tallinn University of Tehnology. Tallinn.
7. Orru, M., Allikvee, H., Veldre, M. & Širokova, M. 1972-1987. Eesti NSV turbasoode otsingulis-hinnangulised tööd aastatel 1972-1987 [Exploration-assesment of Estonian SSR. Manuscripts at Depository of Manuscriptsreports of Geological Survey of Estonia]. Estonian Geological Survey of Estonia, Tallinn [in Estonian, with Russian summary]
8. Orru,M., Orru, H., 2003. Kahjulikud elemendid Eesti turbas *(Trace elements in Estonian peat)*. Geological Survey of Estonia, Tallinn, 144 pp. (in Estonia with English summary).
9. Orru, M., Orru, H., 2006. Sources and distribution of trace elements in Estonian Peat. Global and Tlanetary Changes, 53, 249-258.
10. Orru, M., Übner, M., Orru, H., 2011. Chemical properties of peat in three peatlands with balneological potential in Estonia. In Estonian Journal of Earth Science 60/1.
11. Orru, M., Väizene, V., Pastarus, J-R., Sõstra, Ü., Valgma, I., 2013. Possibilities of oil shale mining under the Selisoo mire of Estonia oil shale deposit. In Environmental Earth Science, 1 – 11.
12. Orru, M., Milvek, H., Väizene, V., 2013. Chemical properties of peat with balneological potential in Estonia. In Programm the 5 th International Conference on Medical Geology, 41-41.
13. Orru, M., Nurme, M., Milvek, H., Rahe, T., 2014. Mõtteid turba tulevikust (Peat alternative use in the future). XXII April Geological Conference, in thesis, 48-49.
14. Ramst, 1997. Lõppes Eesti turbatootmisalade inventeerimine (The inventory work of Estonian peat production areas has been finished). Eesti Turvas, ½ 17-19 (In Estonian, with English summary).
15. Ranneklev, S. B., Gislerod, H., R., 2002. Horticultural Peat- Detection of Self- Heating. In Peat in Horticulture (Rochefort, L., Schmilevski, G. ed.). pp. 135-141.

Abstract No: A-044

EFFECTS OF CARBON SUBSTRATE LABILITY ON TROPICAL PEAT MINERALIZATION UNDER AEROBIC AND ANAEROBIC CONDITIONS

Jyrki Jauhiainen[1*], Hanna Silvennoinen[2, 3], Mari Könönen[1], Suwido Limin[4] and Harri Vasander[1]

[1]Department of Forest Sciences, University of Helsinki, Finland
[2]Norwegian University of Life Sciences (UMB), Department of Plant and Environmental Sciences, Norway
[3]Norwegian Institute for Agricultural and Environmental Research (Bioforsk), Norway
[4]University of Palangka Raya, CIMTROP, Indonesia

**Corresponding author: jyrki.jauhiainen@helsinki.fi*

SUMMARY

Extensive draining at tropical ombrotrophic peatlands in Southeast Asia has made them global 'hot spots' for greenhouse gas emissions. Here, we present the first data on how management practises affect carbon (C) mineralization processes at these soils. We compared the peat carbon mineralization potentials of pristine forest to those of drained fire affected soils, with and without additional labile substrates (glucose, glutamate and NO3- N) and in oxic and anoxic conditions by dedicated *ex situ* experiments. Carbon mineralization (CO_2 and CH4 production) rates were higher in the forest peat, which contains more labile C due to higher input via vegetation. Production rates decreased with depth in peat profile together with decreasing availability of labile carbon. Consequently, the increase in C mineralization rates after labile substrate addition was relatively modest from forest site as compared to the reclaimed site and from the top layers as compared to deeper layers. Methanogenesis had little importance in total carbon mineralization. Surprisingly, oxygen availability was not an ultimate requirement for substantial CO_2 production rates. Flooding of these sites will therefore reduce, but not completely cease, peat carbon loss. Reintroduced substantial vegetation and fertilization in degraded peatlands can enrich recalcitrant peat with simple C and N compounds and thus increase microbiological activity. This outcome reinforces the importance of decomposition-resistant litter types and sufficient litter allocation in the maintenance of ombrotrophic tropical peat carbon store regardless of the land management type.

***Keywords**: anoxia, decomposition resistance, land use, labile carbon*

INTRODUCTION

The fate of dead organic matter in tropical peatlands, like in any ecosystem, depends on the amount and characteristics of deposited litter and on the microbial community decomposing the substrate. Temperature, moisture and oxygen availability are recognized as important decomposition process controls in tropical peat (Adji *et al.*, 2014; Jauhiainen *et al.*, 2014), but the position of the groundwater table (GWT) is a simplified environmental factor mostly applied to explain gaseous emissions from peat decomposition (IPCC 2014).

Litter at the peat swamp forest is largely composed of woody debris, coarse and fine roots, and leaf litter. It is rich both in cellulosic and more complex ligneous substrates (Miyajima *et al.*, 1997). Close to the peat surface, where oxic conditions are most likely present, peat-forming organic polymers (litter) are largely decomposed in aerobic processes by bacteria and fungi. Lignin is more resistant to decomposition than cellulose (Harmon *et al.*, 2009). Over time, the proportion of decomposition-resistant organic substrates in the peat increases and these substrates are located for progressively longer periods in the water-saturated (anoxic) conditions further away from the surface (Harmon *et al.*, 2009). Deforested, drained and abandoned land is a common reclaimed tropical peatland (use) type, in which recurrent wildfires typically keep the vegetation biomass low and add on peat loss by progressively consuming topmost peat. Litter input rate is low in such degraded lands, and aerobic and anaerobic decomposition processes continue consuming aged (recalcitrant) peat materials resurfaced by fires. Litter in these replacement vegetation types (such as ferns) is typically formed from less decomposition-resistant substrates (e.g. Miyajima *et al.*, 1997; Yule and Gomez 2009).

There is demand for converting abandoned and degraded peat areas into active use. Substantial vegetation cover formed in successful reforestation in degraded peat will increase labile C input rates from the root systems, and a start of N fertilization increases markedly labile N availability in cropping lands and plantations. Increase in control over peat water tables will likely alter unsaturated peat profile O_2 conditions compared to peatlands in abandoned conditions.

We established *ex situ* microcosm experiments to provide the first data on tropical peat decomposition rates under controlled oxic and anoxic conditions with differing labile C and N availability. Peat from undrained peat swamp forests represents the original land use and peat from clear-felled, drained, burned landforms the opposing extreme in converted land use types. Samples were taken from close to the peat surface (often facing oxic conditions), from variably water-saturated conditions, and from deeper layers that is typically water-saturated, anoxic environment.

METHODS

Our study sites were in the upper catchment of Sabangau River, 20 km southeast of Palangka Raya city in Central Kalimantan, Indonesia. Sampling sites included undrained peat swamp forest (PF) and clear-felled, drained, fire affected degraded land (DL). We chose three vegetation-free subplots at the sampling sites from typical low surfaces along microtopgraphy at about 20-m distances for the study. Possible recently deposited leaf litter on the top of surface was removed and peat samples were collected from 0–10 cm, 20–30 cm and 100–130 cm depths.

In the laboratory, all visible live root materials were removed from peat. Peat heterotrophic gas production and closed headspace gas composition were monitored in microcosm environments. A setup of microcosms and gas chromatograph (GC) was prepared for conducting the experiments. A robotized GC facilitated the high-frequency analyses of CO_2, CH_4, N_2O, NO, N_2 and O_2 of each sample headspace. Gas concentration analytics was conducted using the GC (Model 7890A, Agilent), equipped with 20-m wide-bore Poraplot Q column, 30-m 5Å mole sieve, 2 HayeSep columns for backflushing water, a thermal conductivity detector (TCD), an electron capture detector (ECD), a flame injection analyzer (FID) and a NO chemiluminescence analyzer. Gas samples (2 ml) were taken with an autosampler, and fed with a peristaltic pump to sampling loops further proving the GC (0.25 ml loop) and the NO-analyser (0.5 ml). For further details of the incubation system, please see Molstad *et al.* (2007). During laboratory incubation and analysis, the vials were held at laboratory temperature at ~ 22 °C or standing in a water bath at 25 °C. For the gas production rate calculations, CO_2 and CH_4 data was divided into condition sequences found in the headspace, e.g., during and after O_2 or NOx reduction.

<u>Experiment A – C mineralization in sudden anoxic conditions.</u> Peats in this experiment describe the soil microbiological functions without added C or nutrients. The experiment was conducted in 'sudden anoxic' conditions in order to simulate conditions where O_2 depleted from peat. Approximately 8 g of field-moist peat was added into a 120-ml vial, which was filled with water to 50 ml, and sealed by butyl-rubber stopper with an aluminium seal. O_2 was removed from the vials by repeated evacuation and helium-flushing, and a replicate set was also amended with 10% C_2H_2 for separately reported denitrification dynamics and N_2 production (report *in prep.*). The data obtained from the replicate C_2H_2-amended samples was used in this study to determine the accurate point where CO_2 production by denitrification ceased. Incubation lasted 145 hours, and gas concentrations were monitored at 5-hour time intervals.

<u>Experiment B – Impact of nitrate addition on C mineralization.</u> We determined the peat respiration dynamics in optimal NO_3^- concentrations over time in peat slurries where oxic conditions develop into anoxic conditions. Approximately 8 g of field-moist peat was set into a 120-ml glass vial and KNO_3 was added to reach a 0.1 mM NO_3^- concentration. The applied concentration of 0.1 mM NO^{3-} (given as KNO_3) was based on the optimal level for achieving maximum denitrification rates in anoxic conditions in surface and deeper peat samples at both sites (report *in prep.*). The vials were filled to 40 ml with water and sealed. Each vial was evacuated and washed thoroughly with helium to remove O_2 and N_2 from the peat and the vials were supplemented to 0.25% O_2 in the headspace, and a set of replicate samples was also amended with 10% C_2H_2. Incubation lasted 44 hours and gas concentrations were monitored in 3-hour time intervals.

<u>Experiment C – Impact of labile C and NO3⁻-N addition on C mineralization.</u> This experiment studied how heterotrophic CO_2 production benefits from C addition in the presence of added NO^{3-}-N in oxic and anoxic conditions. The slurry experiment was conducted with added glucose or glutamic acid, such that the amount of added C on sample DW basis was equal in both treatments. This experiment included peats from the top and deepest sampling depths in both sites. Approximately 8 g of field-moist peat was set into a 40-ml glass vial. Glucose or glutamate (as sodium glutamate) was added to reach an added 20% C concentration on g g^{-1} DW basis in each vial. All vials were supplemented with 0.1 mM NO^{3-} on g g^{-1} DW basis, filled to 40 ml with water, and sealed. Two sets of vials were prepared, half of which were supplemented with 0.25% O_2 and used for studying gaseous C dynamics, and the other half with 10% C_2H_2 in addition to O_2. Incubation lasted 67 hours and gas concentrations were monitored at 3.5-hour time intervals.

RESULTS

Anaerobic CO_2 production rates from peat decomposition in anoxic conditions (Experiment A) were fastest in the upper peat layers, and the forest peat CO_2 production rates from all three depths were higher in comparison to the rates of degraded land peat (Table 1). CO_2 accumulated linearly in the degraded land peat slurries, whereas an increase in peat CO_2 production after the reduction of NOx at 20 hours (N dynamics *in prep.*) was very pronounced in the forest top peat. Peat samples from both sites showed clearly lower peat anaerobic respiration rates at the deepest sampling depth than in the peat layers above. After the reduction of nitrogen oxides, CO_2 production rates were fastest in the two upper forest peat layers and the slowest in the two deepest degraded land peat layers. The lowest forest peat layer produced CO_2 approximately as fast as the top layer of the degraded land. The CO_2 production in the top forest peat was 6.5 × higher than that in the degraded land top peat. Peat CH_4 production was generally smaller than CO_2 production, also in the sudden anoxic conditions (Table 1). Methane production in the slurries without added substrates showed a very clear vertical distribution as the CH_4 production was highest in the top peat and decreased with sampling depth in the peat profiles. The average CH_4 production rate in the top forest peat was *ca.* 400 × faster in comparison to the rate in the degraded land top peat layer, whereas the slow CH_4 production rates in the two deepest forest peat layers were relatively close to values in all peat layers of degraded land.

Table1: Forest (PF) and degraded land (DL) peat CO2 and CH4 production rates (Ave±SE, N = 3) during the main gas sphere conditions for respective depths between the sites, and numbers for various phases in gas space conditions) within the experiment.

Experiment	Site and depth	CO2 production rate (µg g^{-1}DW h^{-1})			CH4 production rate (µg g^{-1}DW h^{-1})
		During reduction of	During reduction of	After reduction of NO_x	After reduction of O2
No amendments	PF (0–10 cm) PF	– –	1.583±0.304	5.885±1.217	1.93^{-2}±0.78^{-2}
(Experiment A)	(20–30 cm) PF	– –	0.876±0.078	1.730±0.433	5.92^{-4}±3.83^{-4}
Optimal NO3$^-$ (Experiment B)	(100–130 cm)	– –	0.464±0.035	0.888±0.043	7.91^{-6}±3.54^{-6}
Optimal NO3$^-$	DL (0–10 cm)		0.786±0.120	0.898±0.146	4.59^{-5}±0.83^{-5}
and glucose	DL (20–30 cm)		0.398±0.181	0.327±0.138	2.11^{-5}±1.09^{-5}
(Experiment C) Optimal NO3$^-$	DL (100–130		0.215±0.069	0.224±0.077	1.54^{-5}±0.40^{-5}
and glutamate	PF (0–10 cm)	9.345±0.593	2.368±0.227	–	1.15^{-3}±0.15^{-3} –
(Experiment C)	DL (0–10 cm)	1.664±0.248	0.413±0.067	–	(*
	PF (0–10 cm) PF	7.725±0.122(**	2.638±0.001	59.498±3.197	1.05-2±2.30-4 (**
	(100–130 cm)	5.488±0.573	2.595±0.464	2.944±0.898	7.33^{-5}±1.05^{-5}
	DL (0–10 cm)	4.206±1.293 (**	1.373±0.324 (**	1.042±0.606(**	5.45^{-5}±2.47^{-7}
	DL (100–130	5.355±0.413	2.341±0.840	0.870±0.052	2.24^{-4}±1.26^{-4}
	PF (0–10 cm) PF	9.821±0.874 (**	2.922±0.319	3.499±0.312	3.10^{-2}±0.07^{-2}
	(100–130 cm)	3.044±0.271	0.744±0.047	–	3.75^{-5}±2.05^{-5}
	DL (0–10 cm)	3.520±0.061	1.746 (10 (***	1.082±0.332	6.62^{-5}
	DL (100–130	6.572±0.359	2.890±1.306	0.470±0.030	–(*

(* Non-detectable amount of CH4 produced, (** Only 2 samples, (***O2 and NO_x were exhausted simultaneously in 2 sample series.

Nitrate addition on C mineralization resulted in relatively small differences in the top peat layer CO_2 production rates supplemented with 0.1 mM NO^{3-} and set to developing anoxic conditions (Experiment B) when compared with the rates in respective peats without added substrates set in sudden anoxic conditions (Experiment A) (Table 1). The CO_2 production rate in the top forest peat with added NO^{3-} was nearly 2 × faster after O_2 reduction than the rate in sudden anoxic conditions, but the production rate in the degraded land peat with added NO^{3-} and developed anoxic conditions was only approximately half of the rate detected in sudden anoxic conditions. CH_4 production in degraded land peat remained practically non-existent in samples supplied with NO^{3-}. Labile C (glucose and glutamate) combined with the NO^{3-}-N addition (Experiment C) resulted in higher peat CO_2 production rates in most samples compared to rates in the peat without added substrates (Experiment A) (Table 1). Proportionally the highest difference in peat CO_2 production rates between the peats with and without added substrates occurred in the deepest sampling depth, where the CO_2 production rates were from 2.1 to 13.4 × faster in degraded land peat and 1.6 to 5.6 × faster in forest peat during and after the NOx reduction stages. Glucose and NO^{3-} addition to forest top peat resulted in the maximum CO_2 production rate found in the present study (59.5 ± 3.2 µg $_g$-1 h-1 in the 'post-NOx reduction stage') and this rate was 10 × faster than the respective rate in peat without added substrates. Both forest land top peat CO_2 production rates in labile C^- and N supplemented samples were otherwise quite close, i.e., with a maximum of 1.7 × faster, to the CO_2 production rates detected in peat without added substrates. CO_2 production rates in degraded land top peat supplemented with glutamate was 2.1 × faster than the rate in peat without added substrates. The highest impacts of glucose and glutamate additions on CH_4 production were apparent in the two deepest peat layers. Glucose addition to the deepest layer resulted in a 9.2 × faster CH_4 production rate in forest peat and a 14.6 × faster rate in degraded land peat in comparison to rates detected in peat slurries without added substrates (Table 1). Comparatively, the glutamate addition yielded a 4.7 × faster CH_4 production rate in the forest deepest peat. CH_4

production rates in top peat layers for both sites remained similar both without added substrates and with added labile C and N.

DISCUSSION

Forest top peat (without added substrates) expressed the highest CO_2 production potential in both oxic and anoxic conditions and the highest CH_4 production potential in anoxic conditions. In peat swamp forests, tree dominated vegetation continuously deposits senesced leaves, and coarse and fine woody debris onto the peat surface and into the rooting zone. This recently deposited litter is rich in both cellulosic and complex ligneous structural substrates (Miyajima *et al.*, 1997), but decomposition-resistant lignin-rich substrates increase proportionally downwards in the peat profile due to faster depletion of more simple cellulosic compounds (Harmon *et al.*, 2009). In peats from this forest site, holocellulose content on DW basis decreased from 10% in the topmost peat to 2% at 80 cm depth and Klason lignin content increased from 68% to 72%, respectively (see Könönen *et al.* this volume). Our results from the forest site support these findings in substrate composition as peat samples already from a depth of 20–30 cm below the forest floor surface resulted in clearly lower CO_2 and CH_4 production potentials, and even more so at the deepest peat sampling depth.

In clear-felled burned peatland, the lack of notable recent carbon inputs, recurrent fires and mineralization have created conditions where the content of relatively easily decomposable carbon substrates is low in the surface peat, and this was largely supported by the GHG production rate results. Therefore, the fastest CO_2 and CH_4 production rates in degraded land peat (without added substrates) in all three sampling depths were comparable with the values for the two lowest peat layers of the forest site. Klason lignin content of 76–82% in degraded land peat is higher than the highest content in forest peat (max. 72%) in peat profile down to the permanently water-saturated peat, and the topmost peat holocellulose content of 1% on DW basis in degraded land is only a fraction of the content (10%) in topmost forest peat (see Könönen *et al.* this volume). It is striking that the anaerobic CO_2 production (and CH_4 production) decreases rather than increases with depth in degraded land. This could be explained by microbial adaptation and differences in preferred carbon donor, where denitrifiers, Fe^{3+} & Mn^{4+} & $SO4^{2-}$ reducers and methanogens may not be able to oxidize some C compounds that are easily decomposable by aerobic respiration. Alternatively, anabolic and catabolic metabolism could be limited by other nutrients besides carbon or by the electron acceptor rather than the donor.

Both of the abovementioned assumptions are supported by the results from the slurry Experiment C where the addition of nitrate together with glucose and glutamate increased anaerobic CO_2 production slightly in the top peat but by several times in the deepest peat layer samples from both sites. Labile C addition in anoxic conditions in degraded land peat enhanced CO_2 production practically only in the deepest peat layer, which suggests that the microbial community in the degraded land surface peat is able to process labile C in anoxic conditions and produce CO_2 when such substrates become available. Experiment C showed that deeper peat layers lack labile C and N substrates and thus CO_2 (and CH_4) production can increase due to increase in available substrates. In Experiment C, where CO_2 (and CH_4) production rates of deepest layer peats in both sites (representing the aged materials protected from oxic conditions) were enhanced in the presence of labile C and N sources compared to the respective rates in peat without added substrates. Varying GHG production responses in more heterogenic forest top peat may be a result of proportionally modest experimental labile substrate addition (in experiment C) in comparison to concentrations of comparable substrates readily contained in the samples. Labile C (glucose and/or glutamate) together with nitrate addition increased CH_4 production only in the deepest peat layers at both sites. The modest CH_4 production difference between labile C-supplemented peat and peat without added substrates in the forest top peat layer implies that the forest surface peat has the highest potential for CH^{4-}production (among the studied peats) in anaerobic conditions, that is likely typical condition at both sites during wet season. Hardwood lignin compounds can partially degrade under anoxic conditions, and the decomposition potential in such substrate remains low (Arai *et al.*, 2014). High Klason lignin content in the studied peats (see Könönen *et al.* this volume) partly explains slow CH4 production rates. In degraded land top peat, CH_4 production rates in anoxic conditions differed modestly which likely indicates a low capacity of the methanogenic population in the surface peat. In contrast, comparable CH_4 production rates of the deepest sampled peat in both sites with added labile C can be regarded a sign of preserved comparable methanogenic populations despite of the difference in land management type.

In developing anoxic conditions (Experiments B and C), CO_2 production rates in slurries were generally fastest in the presence of O_2 (during the O_2 depletion stage) and later the rates became proportionally smaller in anoxic conditions. Unexpectedly, CO_2 production rates remained at a notable level in anoxic conditions. The percent decrease (%-change) in the CO_2 rates from oxic to anoxic conditions was 46–76% in forest deep peat, 66–72% in forest top peat (excluding the even higher rate change in the case of glucose addition), 52–77% in degraded land top peat and 56–93% in degraded land deep peat, respectively. A large disproportion between the CO_2 and CH_4 emission rates in anoxic conditions in the present study peats (with and without added substrates) suggest that CH_4 production from acetate is probably not a notable contributor to CO_2 production in anaerobic conditions. CO_2 production in low O_2 availability could be explained by the accumulation of fermentative low-molecular-weight alcohols and acids and subsequent oxidation coupled with the reduction of inorganic terminal electron acceptors, such as NO^{3-}, Mn^{4+}, Fe^{3+}, and $SO4^{2-}$ (e.g., Lipson *et al.*, 2010; Corbet *et al.*, 2015), or humic substances in water could also form both a suitable energy source and an organic electron acceptor in anoxic conditions (Kane *et al.*, 2013).

CONCLUSION

This study indicated that substantial organic matter decomposition occurs in both oxic and anoxic conditions in tropical peat. Although flooding the soil surface can potentially reduce peat C loss, it cannot completely inhibit it because decomposition-producing CO_2 and CH_4 can continue in anoxic conditions. This outcome strengthens the importance of vegetation in regulation of peat carbon storage as it forms the only peat matter adding source both in undrained and drained conditions. Decomposition potential in degraded peat substrate persists although continued reduction in deposited litter amount and recurrent fires can lead to decrease in GHG production from the surface peat. Both aerobic and anaerobic decomposition processes in such aged and decomposition-resistant peat can be induced by an increase in available labile C and N substrates. Change from open and degraded peatlands to forested areas in ecological restoration and to plantations will likely enhance the heterotrophic C emissions from peat due to increases in rhizosphere productivity and labile N availability. These peat deposits are likely best secured by favouring anoxic conditions, which slow heterotrophic GHG release, and by maintaining high GWT and growing flood-tolerant tree species that deposit high amounts and proportions of woody litter below the peat surface.

ACKNOWLEDGEMENTS

Our study was part of the Academy of Finland-funded project RETROPEAT (253933). Peatlanders prize money awarded by the University of Helsinki, Alfred Kordelin Foundation, and Tiina ja Antti Herlin Foundation made it possible for us to join IPS 2016 conference in Kuching, Malaysia.

REFERENCES

1. Adji FF, Hamada Y, Darung U, Limin SH, Hatano R (2014) Effect of plant-mediated oxygen supply and drainage on greenhouse gas emission from a tropical peatland in Central Kalimantan, Indonesia. Soil Science and Plant Nutrition 60:216–230.
2. Arai H, Hadi A, Darung U, Limin SH, Hatano R, Inubushi, K (2014) A methanotrophic community in a tropical peatland is unaffected by drainage and forest fires in a tropical peat soil. Soil Science and Plant Nutrition 60:577–585.
3. Corbett JE, Tfaily MM, Burdige DJ, Glaser PH, Chanton JP (2015) The relative importance of methanogenesis in the decomposition of organic matter in northern peatlands. Journal of Geophysical Research Biogeosciences 120: 280–293.
4. Harmon ME, Silver WL, Fasth B, Chen H, Burke IC, Parton WJ, Hart SC, Currie WS, Lidet (2009) Long-term patterns of mass loss during the decomposition of leaf and fine root litter: an intersite comparison. Global Change Biology 15:1320–1338.
5. IPCC (2014) Drained Inland Organic Soils. In: 2013 Supplement to the 2006 IPCC Guidelines for National Greenhouse Gas Inventories: Wetlands. Hiraishi T, Krug T, Tanabe K, Srivastava N, Baasansuren J, Fukuda M, Troxler TG (eds). IPCC, Switzerland, 353 p.
6. Jauhiainen J, Kerojoki O, Silvennoinen H, Limin S, Vasander H (2014) Heterotrophic respiration in drained tropical peat is greatly affected by temperature – a passive ecosystem cooling experiment. Environmental Research Letters 9:105013.
7. Kane ES, Chivers MR, Turetsky MR, Treat CC, Petersen DG, Waldrop M, Harden JW, McGuire AD (2013) Response of anaerobic carbon cycling to water table manipulation in an Alaskan rich fen. Soil Biology and Biochemistry 58:50–60.
8. Lipson DA, Jha M, Raab TK, Oechel WC (2010) Reduction of iron (III) and humic substances plays a major role in anaerobic respiration in an Arctic peat soil. Journal of Geophysical Research 115:G00I06.
9. Miyajima T, Wada E, Hanba YT, Vijarnsorn P (1997) Anaerobic mineralization of indigenous organic matters and methanogenesis in tropical wetland soils. Geochimica et Cosmochimica Acta 61:3739–3751.
10. Molstad L, Dörsh P, Bakken LR (2007) Robotized incubation system for monitoring gases (O2, NO, N2O N2) in denitrifying cultures. Journal of Microbiological Methods 71:202–211.
11. Yule C, Comez L (2009) Leaf litter decomposition in a tropical peat swamp forest in Peninsular Malaysia. Wetl Ecol Manag 17:231–241.

Abstract No: A-223

HETEROGENEITY IN PEAT DECOMPOSITION EVALUATED BY FOURIER TRANSFORM INFRARED MICRO-SPECTROSCOPY

Mizuki Morishita* and Masayuki Kawahigashi

Department of Geography, Tokyo Metropolitan University, Tokyo, Japan

**Corresponding author: morishita-mizuki@ed.tmu.ac.jp*

SUMMARY

Peat decomposition is locally processed at the micro scale, owing mainly to the diversity of redox condition because of the heterogeneous distribution of micro-pores in peat. In this study, we evaluated this heterogeneity in peat decomposition in order to obtain useful data on the peat decomposition process. To this end, we differentiated types of peat micro-fragments to describe the diversity of decomposed states in peat. The differentiation was based on their chemical structural analysis using Fourier transform infrared (FTIR) micro-spectroscopy and multivariate analysis. Based on the results of this analysis, the observed peat fragments were classified into five types. The transition of the frequency of each classified fragment type indicated heterogeneity in peat decomposition. Conversely, the bulk analysis was unable to estimate such parameter.

Keywords: *Peat decomposition; FTIR micro-spectroscopy; organic matter*

INTRODUCTION

Peat decomposition is caused by aeration processes mainly due to human impacts, such as drainage for cultivation or afforestation (Moore, 2002; Kroetsch *et al.*, 2011). Peat decomposition has been involved in agricultural activities for over a century (Lohila *et al.*, 2014); this peat degradation changes wetlands from carbon sinks to sources of CO_2 leading to alterations in wetland ecosystems. The study of the peat decomposition process represents a key to understanding the mechanisms of decrease in sequestered soil carbon and past environmental change in wetland systems. In this respect, the evaluation of the degradation state of peat is an effective means to understand the process of peat decomposition. Spectroscopic methods have been used to study the decomposed state of peat. Fourier transform infrared (FTIR) spectroscopy is a useful method to assess the state of decomposition or humification of organic materials (Prasad *et al.*, 2000; Biester *et al.*, 2014). However, these methods have considerable limitations when applied to decomposed peat. This is because decomposed organic substances (humic substances) are composed of ill-defined mixtures and their spectra represent the summation of responses of many different organic components (MacCarthy and Rice, 1985). For this reason, spectroscopic analyses using bulk samples might be inappropriate for detailed evaluations of the properties of decomposed peat.

Additionally, peat has diverse redox conditions in micro-scale, and peat decomposition is therefore considered to be processed locally. This is mainly due to the considerable heterogeneity in the distribution of micro-pores, which renders the surrounding environment oxidative after water drainage. This heterogeneity would also be the key to understand the state of peat decomposition. However, it is difficult to detect such heterogeneity using spectroscopic analysis, because of the limitation of bulk sample methodology, as mentioned earlier.

Hence, we applied Fourier transform infrared (FTIR) micro-spectroscopy as a screening tool to examine the heterogeneous properties of peat. FTIR micro-spectroscopy has been achieved by coupling a microscope with an FTIR spectrometer. This method allows us to analyze the chemical structure of peat micro-fragments by selecting them individually at the microscopic level. By using this technique and multivariate analysis, we tried to classify the state of decomposition of peat micro-fragments based on the chemical structural properties of each peat fragment. In addition, we intended to characterize the composition of peat micro-fragments based on the frequency of each cluster. By comparing these compositional patterns between peat samples at different degrees of decomposition, we proposed to evaluate heterogeneity in peat decomposition.

The aim of this study is to evaluate heterogeneity in peat decomposition, which provides new aspects for studies on the peat decomposition process and improves the limitations of current spectroscopic methods using bulk samples. To this end, we proposed (1) to represent the diversity of the state of decomposition of peat micro-fragments and (2) to characterize the heterogeneity in peat decomposition.

MATERIALS AND METHODS

Soil samples and analysis

Soil samples were taken from buried peat horizons distributed on Sagami Plain, Japan (35°23′31″N; 139°10′04″E). Field observations revealed the presence of large amounts of undecomposed plant tissues, known as fibric peat, in the deeper organic horizon (70–80cm). The soil color of this horizon was brownish black (5YR 2/2). In contrast, the upper peat horizon (50-60cm) was composed of well-decomposed sapric peat with a blacker color (10Y2/1). To investigate the transition of decomposed state between these horizons, intermediate peat soil samples were collected from depths of 60 and 70 cm, together with sapric peat from depths of 50 and 60 cm and fibric peat from depths of 70 and 80 cm. Peat samples were air-dried followed by sieving through 2-mm screen. Peat samples were characterized using the humification index (Kaila, 1956), C/N ratio, bulk density, and ash content as indicators of decomposition.

FTIR micro-spectroscopy

Peat fragments were fixed in a KBr pellet to obtain the fine FTIR spectra from a peat fragment in the microscope's field of view. FTIR absorbance was recorded from each peat fragment in a 70 × 70 μm aperture in a fixed range of wavenumber from 700 cm^{-1} to 4000 cm^{-1} with 2-cm^{-1} intervals using IR Prestige-21 and AIM-8800 (Shimazu, Kyoto). Scans were repeated 100 times to enhance the signal-to-noise ratio. Approximately 50 fragments were measured using five pellets at each sampling depth. Differences in relative absorption intensities between the measurements were corrected by normalizing each spectrum as described by Artz *et al.* (2008). Normalization of the spectrum enables comparison of each measurement via the correction of differences in Infrared (IR) transmittance due to sample thickness. The normalized intensities at all wavenumbers of the spectra of peat samples were averaged to obtain the mean IR spectra of samples from each horizon. The specific absorption bands were assigned based on previous reports, mainly those of Niemeyer *et al.* (1992), Artz *et al.* (2008), and Biester *et al.* (2014).

Statistical classification of fragments

The classification of peat fragments was performed by using Ward's method of cluster analysis in the IBM SPSS Statistics program version 21 (IBM, New York). Characteristic absorption intensities, which were observed at around 832, 915, 1040, 1125, 1160, 1227, 1266, 1331, 1375, 1424, 1463, 1510, 1600, 1636, 2852, 2922, and 3400 cm^{-1}, were extracted from the normalized spectra as variation for clustering analysis. After clustering, the mean IR spectra of each cluster were gained.

RESULTS AND DISCUSSION

Averaged spectra of peat fragments at each depth

The mean IR spectra were obtained by averaging all spectra from peat fragments at each horizon (Figure1). Some absorption bands were assigned as functional groups of organic compounds, such as lignin (832, 1227, 1227, 1266, 1375, 1463, 1510, and 1600cm^{-1}), polysaccharides (1040, 1125, and 1160 cm^{-1}), and silicate ion (915 cm^{-1}). They were weakened and broadened in the spectrum of peat from 50 to 60 cm in depth compared to those of organic compounds in the deeper horizon. The decreasing intensity of specific absorption suggested that degradation of peat in the upper horizon was greater than that in the deeper horizon. However, differences in spectra between the horizons appeared to be small. Similar small differences between depths were also observed in the range of the C/N ratio (19.2– 21.1) and in the humification index (18.4–21.6). These small differences among peat horizons can be attributable to evaluation using the averaged data without accounting for the heterogeneous structure of peat.

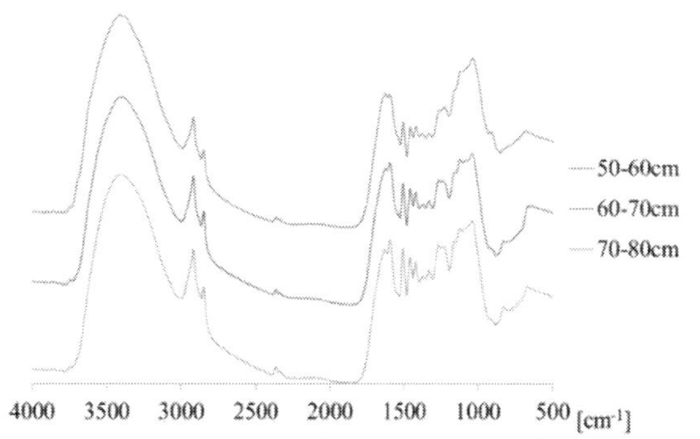

Figure 1: Mean IR spectra of peat fragments in each depth

Classification of peat by cluster analysis

Cluster analysis divided the studied samples into five groups (Figure2). Averaged IR spectra in each cluster group are shown in Figure3. The spectrum of the Group I was characterized by many sharp peaks corresponding to the structure of polysaccharides (1040, 1125, and 1160 cm^{-1}) and lignin (832, 1227, 1227, 1266, 1375, 1463, 1510, and 1600cm^{-1}). Group I was mainly composed of low-decomposed plant materials. Group II was characterized by weaker peaks than those of Group I. Group III was distinguished from the previous two clusters by the broadening of three small peaks corresponding to polysaccharides (1040, 1125, and 1160 cm^{-1}) into a single peak. These polysaccharide bands were almost indistinguishable in Group IV due to the presence of broader of peaks than those in Groups I, II, and III. The spectrum of Group V showed broad absorption of peaks. Additionally, Group V was characterized by a shoulder band at 915 cm^{-1}, identified as a silicate ion-specific feature (Asapo and Coles, 2012). These results suggested that FTIR micro-spectroscopy can differentiate five types of peat micro-fragments based on their chemical structural properties. Furthermore, the difference in peak intensities between the spectra of each cluster was more obvious than in the averaged spectra of peat at each depth (Figure1). This indicates that peat intrinsically has a wide range of structural heterogeneity, which is difficult to understand by any spectral analyses using bulk samples.

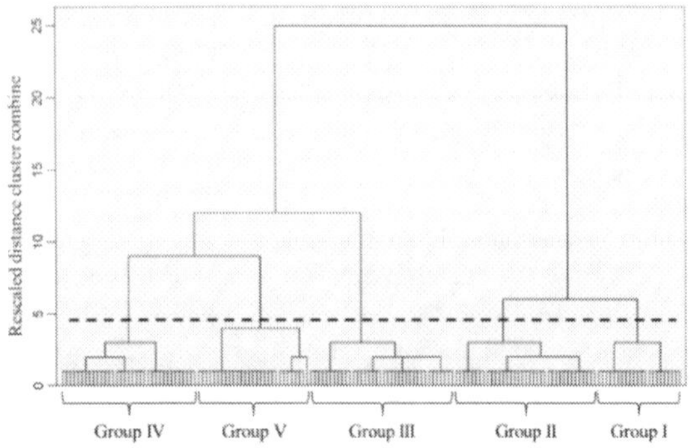

Figure 2: The dendrogram given by a cluster analysis.

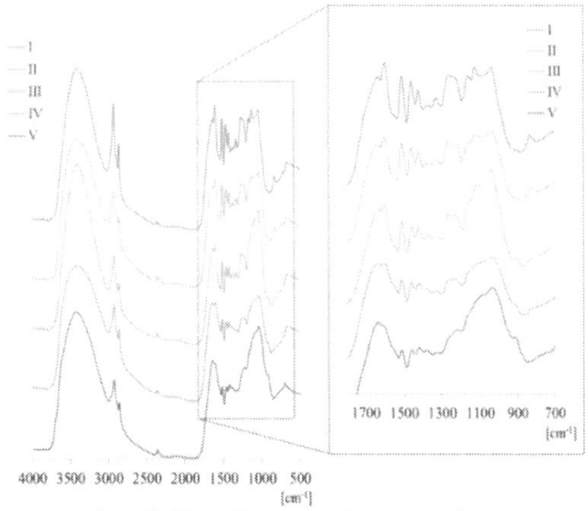

Figure 3: Mean IR spectra of peat on each group.

Cluster composition of decomposed peats

Cluster composition for each sampled depth is shown in Figure 4. At 70–80 cm depth, over 80% of the fragments belonged to cluster Groups I, II and III. Similarly, around 70% of the fragments 60 -70 cm in depth were classified into the Groups I to III, while less than 40% of peat at 50-60 cm depth was classified in these groups. On the other hand, Groups IV and V occupied over 60% of the peat in the horizon 50-60 cm depth. The proportions in each Group proved that peat is a mixture of micro peat fragments existing in a variety of chemical structural degradations. Additionally, given the degree of decomposition of each depth (see Figure4), vertical compositional differences between horizons represented the heterogeneous progress of peat decomposition in each horizon.

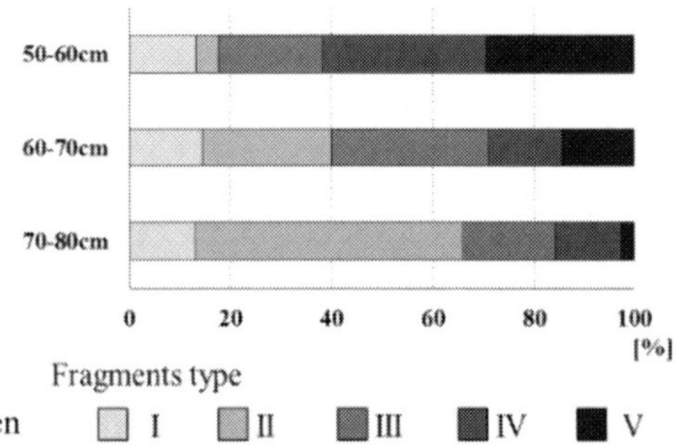

Figure 4: Chemical structural diversities of peat depending on classified types at each depth.

CONCLUSION

The microscopic and chemical structural differentiation of peat fragments clearly revealed the diversity of peat micro-structure, as shown in the spectra (Figure3 and Figure4). In addition, heterogeneity in peat decomposition was indicated by the compositional differences in peat fragment types at each depth (Figure4). These results are novel in that they quantitatively represent the heterogeneity in peat characteristics. A further advantage of the classification of heterogeneous properties is that it can evaluate decomposition state better than bulk analysis can.

ACKNOWLEDGEMENT

The authors would like to thank Dr. Kamiyama from the Agricultural Research Institute of Kanagawa Prefecture for providing the opportunity to collect soil samples and land use information.

REFERENCES

1. Artz, R.R.E., Chapman, S.J., Jean Robertson, A.H., Potts, J.M., Laggoun-Défarge, F., Gogo, S., Comont, L., Disnar, J.-R., Francez, A.-J, 2008. FTIR spectroscopy can be used as a screening tool for organic matter quality in regenerating cutover peatlands. *Soil Biology & Biochemistry*. 40, 515–527.
2. Asapo, E.S., Coles, C.A., 2012. Characterization and Comparison of Saprist and Fibrist Newfoundland Sphagnum Peat Soils. *Journal of Minerals and Materials Characterization and Engineering*. 11, 709-718.

3. Biester, H., Knorr, K.-H., Schellekens, J., Basler, A. Hermanns, Y.-M., 2014. Comparison of different methods to determine the degree of peat decomposition in peat bogs. *Biogeosciences*. 11, 2691-2707.
4. Kaila, A. 1956. Determination of the degree of humification in peat samples. *Journal of the Scientific Society of Finland* 28: 18-25.
5. Kroetsch, D.J., Geng, X., Chang, S.X., and Saurette, D.D., 2011. Organic soils of canada: part 1. Wetland organic soils. *Canadian Journal of Soil Science*. 91, 807-822.
6. Lohila, A., Aurela, M., Tuovinen, J.P., and Laurila, T., 2004. Annual CO_2 exchange of a peat field growing spring barley or perennial forage grass. *Journal of Geophysical Research: Atmospheres*. 109.
7. MacCarthy, P., Rice, J.A., 1985. Spectroscopic methods (other than NMR) for determining functionality in humic substances, in: Aiken, G.R., McKnight, D.M., Wershaw, R.L., and MacCarthy, P. (Eds.), *Humic Substances in Soil, Sediment, and Water: Geochemistry, Isolation and Characterization*. John Wiley and Sons, New York, pp. 527-559.
8. Moore, P.D., 2002. The future of cool temperate bogs. *Environmental Conservation*. 29, 3–20.
9. Niemeyer, J., Chen, Y., Bollag, J.-M., 1992. Characterization of Humic Acids, Composts, and Peat by Diffuse Reflectance Fourier-Transform Infrared Spectroscopy. *Soil Science Society of America Journal. 56,* 135-140.
10. Prasad, M., Verhagen, J.B.G.M., Aendekerk, T.G.L., 2000. Effect of peat type and ph on breakdown of peat using fourier transform infrared spectroscopy. *Communications in Soil Science and Plant Analysis*. 31, 2881–2889.

Abstract No: A-109

VULNERABILITY OF SOIL ORGANIC MATTER IN ANTHROPOGENICALLY DISTURBED ORGANIC SOILS

Annelie Säurich*, Bärbel Tiemeyer, Michel Bechtold, Axel Don and Annette Freibauer

Thünen-Institute of Climate-Smart Agriculture, Braunschweig, Germany

**Corresponding author: annelie.saeurich@ti.bund.de*

SUMMARY

Drained peatlands are hotspots of carbon dioxide (CO_2) emissions from agriculture. However, there is a high variability of the magnitude of CO_2 for disturbed peat soils and little is known about the soil properties and drivers causing these differences in CO_2 emissions. While the instantaneous driving factors for carbon cycling such as temperature and moisture are well studied for both genuine peat and mineral soil, there is a lack of information concerning the role of soil organic matter quality and in general for soil types at the boundary between organic and mineral soils. Our study aims to identify drivers for the vulnerability of soil organic matter to decomposition in anthropogenically disturbed organic soils, especially those near the boundary to mineral soils. Recently agricultural soils in Germany were sampled in an 8x8 km² grid following standardized protocols in the course of the German agricultural soil inventory. From this large sample pool, we selected 120 soil samples from more than 80 sites covering a broad range of soil and site characteristics. As reference sites, three anthropogenically undisturbed peatlands were sampled as well. All samples were sieved through 2 mm, incubated at standardized water content and examined in three replicates using an automated incubation device. CO_2 production was measured as basal respiration and to determine the microbial biomass via substrate induced respiration (SIR) after glucose addition. To determine the equilibrium values of the basal respiration, an exponential model was fitted to the measured data using the Differential Evolution Adaptive Metropolis (DREAM) algorithm. Surprisingly, preliminary results of basal respiration showed that rates of CO_2 production per unit soil organic carbon (SOC) are on average higher for soils at the boundary of mineral and organic soils than for SOC-rich peat soils, while presenting a high variability in the low SOC content range. Analysis of the metabolic coefficient indicated that soils with lower SOC content, higher pH and narrower C:N ratio seemed to have higher bioavailability and more efficient turnover of carbon, whereas the carbon pool of soils with wide C:N ratios seems to be more stable. We conclude that an increasing transformation of organic matter increases the vulnerability of organic matter but cannot explain the large variability in observed mineralization rates.

INTRODUCTION

A lot of former natural peatlands have been influenced and strongly altered by anthropogenic impacts like drainage and fertilization to use the soil for agricultural production. Employment of extensive drainage leads to aeration of the peat layer which optimizes conditions for microbial oxidation of soil organic carbon (SOC) and therefore increases emissions of carbon dioxide (CO_2) to the atmosphere (Kechavarzi *et al.*, 2010). However, the variability of CO_2 emissions is high for disturbed peat soils and little is known about the soil properties driving this variability. While the driving factors for carbon cycling are well studied for both genuine peat and mineral soil (e.g. Brake *et al.*, 1999; Ausec *et al.*, 2009; Kechavarzi *et al.*, 2010; Don *et al.*, 2013; Beare *et al.*, 2014), there is a lack of information about the influence of soil properties on SOM decomposition in soil with high SOC content, in particular in soils at the boundary between organic and mineral soils. Such soils can be of very contrasting origin and develop either from natural processes (e.g. Humic Gleysols) or due to anthropogenic management. The latter type of soils results from former SOC-rich peat layers that were strongly altered by intensive mineralization or by incorporation of mineral soil either by mixing with layers underlying the peat or by surface application of mineral soil.

The study examined 120 samples of soils under cropland and grassland use from all over Germany ranging from almost mineral soil (72 g kg^{-1}) to carbon rich peatlands (up to 560 g kg^{-1}). Our experiments aim to determine soil and peat characteristics that are drivers for soil respiration rates of anthropogenically disturbed organic soils. Furthermore, we would like to answer the question whether there are any critical thresholds of SOC concentrations beyond which the carbon-specific respiration rates or drivers of decomposition change. We hypothesize that basal respiration increases with SOC content but that CO_2 production rates per unit SOC are higher in peat samples than in samples with mineral particles on which SOC can be stabilized.

METHODS

Sites

The German agricultural soil inventory represented the sample basis for our study. Following standardized protocols the soil inventory has sampled agricultural soils in Germany in an 8x8 km^2 grid. From this pool of more than 3000 sites we selected 120 samples of soil horizons from 81 sites. The basic criteria were i) SOC of at least 72 g kg^{-1} (equals 15 % soil organic matter), ii) representing the whole range of basic soil properties (Tab. 1) and iii) sampling depth > 10 cm to avoid disturbance caused by living roots. The final selection was based on cluster analysis to optimally cover the parameter range in Table 1, as well as land use, peat type and geographical position. Land use of our final set of samples comprised croplands (20 %) and grasslands (80 %). Additionally three anthropogenically undisturbed peatlands were sampled as reference sites. These were bog peat, transition bog peat and fen peat.

Table 1: Range of soil properties of selected soil samples

parameter	min	max
SOC (g kg^{-1})	72	568
total nitrogen (g kg^{-1})	2	29
C:N-ratio (-)	10	80
bulk density (g cm^{-3})	0.06	1.41
pH (-)	2.5	7.4
sand content (%)*	0	95
clay content (%)*	2	70

*Only determined for samples with SOC < 190 g kg^{-1}

Incubation

The soil samples were incubated aerobically under optimum moisture and constant temperature conditions to determine basal and substrate-induced respiration (SIR), the latter being converted to microbial biomass.

Preliminary experiments showed that dried samples (40°C) are reusable for measuring soil respiration after a reasonable pre-incubation time as follows: dried, 2 mm sieved soil samples were moistened to a standardized water content of 60 % water-filled pore space and afterwards stored in darkness under aerobic conditions for 7 days at 6°C, following 7 days at 23°C. After 14 days the soil samples were prepared for the incubation in the "Heinemeyer" device (Heinemeyer *et al.*, 1989). Divided in three 20 g dry wt. replicates each sample was put loosely in an acrylic glass tube (25 x 4 cm ID) and enclosed at both ends with polystyrene foam stoppers. Inside the automated incubation device, humidified outside air flew through 24 independent lines, containing the soil samples, at flow rates between 160 and 180 ml min^{-1}. An infrared CO_2 gas analyzer (ADC, UK) measured CO_2 concentrations in differential mode, comparing the concentration in the sample line to the outside air. Each replicate sample was measured hourly for an incubation time of at least 40 h or until stable basal respiration was reached.

For estimation of the active microbial biomass using the SIR method of Anderson and Domsch (1978), the soil samples were amended with a mixture of 100 mg glucose and 100 mg talcum using an electronic stir for 30 s. The addition of inert talcum improved handling and distribution of the glucose. The mixture was then incubated again in the Heinemeyer device for 6 hours to obtain the maximal initial respiratory response of the microbial biomass (Anderson *et al.*, 1995). SIR was transcribed to microbial biomass as follows: SIR-C_{mic} (µg g^{-1} soil) = µl CO_2 g^{-1} soil h^{-1} x 30 (Kaiser *et al.*,1992). To quantify the efficiency of microbial respiration per unit biomass the metabolic or respiratory quotient qCO_2 (mg CO_2-C h^{-1} g^{-1} biomass SIR-C_{mic}) was calculated (Brake *et al.*, 1999). This metabolic quotient describes whether microorganisms use the carbon substrate for their energy metabolism or for growth.

DREAM algorithm

To determine proper equilibrium values of the basal respiration, we fitted an exponential model to the measured data, instead of using the less accurate traditional method of determining a mean value of the last ten measured data points. In this analysis, all three replicates were simultaneously fitted. The uncertainty of the basal respiration rates was inferred as well in a statistically sound manner. For fitting, we used the iterative Markov Chain Monte Carlo (MCMC) method. This method is basically a Markov chain that generates a random walk through the high-probability-density region in the parameter space, separating behavioral from non-behavioral solutions following the probability distribution (Vrugt *et al.*, 2009). The Differential Evolution Adaptive Metropolis (DREAM) algorithm is an efficient MCMC sampler that runs multiple Markov chains simultaneously for global exploration of the parameter space. Thereby DREAM uses a differential algorithm for population evolution and a metropolis selection rule to decide whether a population of candidate points is accepted or not. After the burn-in period the convergence of individual chains is checked using the Gelman and Rubin (1992) diagnostic R-statistics, that examine the variance between and within chains (Vrugt *et al.*, 2008; Vrugt *et al.*, 2009a).

RESULTS & DISCUSSION

As expected CO_2 production rates increased with SOC content (not shown). However, the relation was only weak, indicating that SOC alone is not sufficient to explain basal respiration rates. Surprisingly, CO_2 production rates per unit SOC were highest and most variable for soils with low SOC content (Fig. 1a). These high respiration rates at low SOC content, contradict our hypothesis of carbon stabilization on mineral surfaces. Figure 1b shows the dependence of basal respiration on the C:N ratio and indicates that wide ratios seem to prevent high respiration rates while maximum CO_2 production rates per unit SOC occur at C:N ratios of 10 to 20. These differences are possibly originating from different peat substrates or fertilization. Low C:N ratios also occur in highly humified SOC. However CO_2 production rates per unit SOC were not correlated with other soil properties like total nitrogen, pH or dry bulk density (Tab. 2).

Our data further shows a positive correlation between microbial biomass and total nitrogen content which, as expected, indicates the important nutrition function of nitrogen (Fig. 1c). As observed for the CO_2 production rates per unit SOC, the relation of microbial biomass and C:N ratio (not shown) shows the highest scatter for narrow C:N ratios. In addition to these two soil properties, the results of the microbial biomass indicated significant dependence on SOC, dry bulk density and pH (Tab. 2). Furthermore, the relation between CO_2 production rates per unit SOC and microbial biomass (Fig. 1d) reveals a strong correlation and gives an idea about magnitude and variability of the metabolic quotient.

Overall, it can be noted that the CO_2 production rates per unit SOC of the reference samples fit surprisingly well into the results of their disturbed counterparts. Few exceptions are samples of very young, hardly degraded top layers of undisturbed peatlands that have noticeable higher values of microbial biomass and hence increased production of CO_2. However, samples from increasingly degraded and deeper (> 50 cm) peat layers present results that are similar to the samples from organic soils under agricultural use. The metabolic quotient of the samples from undisturbed peatlands was almost constant (11.8 ± 2.13 mg CO_2-C h^{-1} g^{-1} biomass SIR-C_{mic}) despite the highly varying peat properties. This suggests that the metabolic quotient may represent a relatively stable ecosystem property as the only common feature of these peat samples was the permanent water saturation of the soils. This has to be further studied in a larger ensemble of samples.

Table 2: Matrix of Pearson correlation coefficients between soil and microbial properties without reference sites

	Basal respiration	Microbial biomass	Metabolic quotient
SOC	-0.31**	0.28**	-0.45*
total nitrogen	-0.04	0.53*	-0.44*
C:N-ratio	-0.35*	-0.19	-0.07
bulk density	0.05	-0.33*	0.34*
pH	0.16	0.29**	-0.08

* $p < 0.001$, ** $p < 0.01$

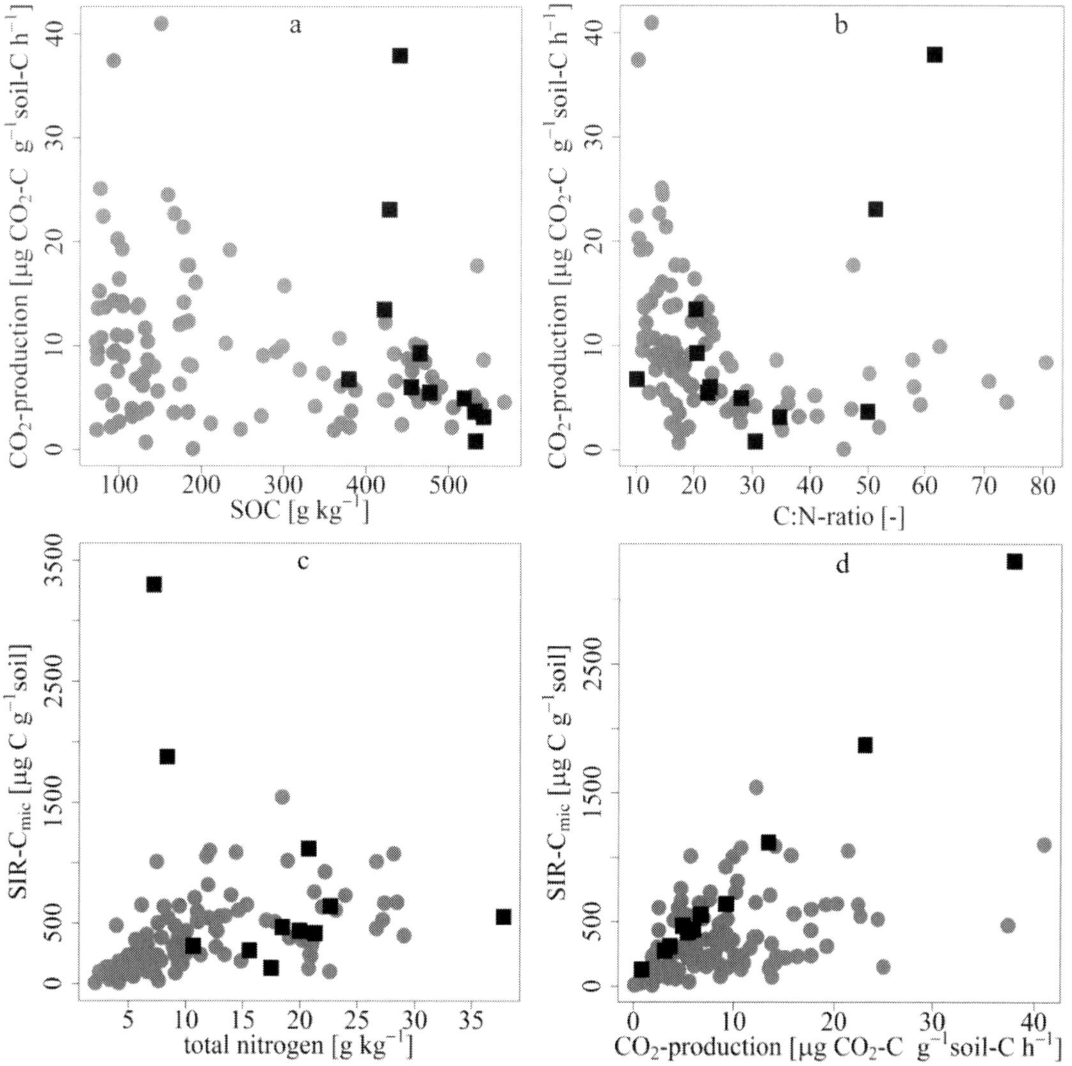

Figure 1: Relations between a) CO_2 production rate per unit SOC and soil organic carbon (SOC) b) CO_2 production rate per unit SOC and C:N-ratio c) substrate induced microbial biomass and total nitrogen and d) substrate induced microbial biomass and CO_2 production rate per unit SOC for the samples of the German agricultural soil inventory (grey circles) and anthropogenically undisturbed peatlands as references (black squares)

CONCLUSION AND OUTLOOK

The results of basal respiration and microbial biomass showed that soils with lower SOC contents, higher pH (6-7) and narrower C:N ratio have a lower metabolic quotient, which may indicate a better availability and more efficient use of carbon. Basal respiration rates per g SOC of soils at the boundary between mineral and organic soils showed to be at least as high as respiration rates of SOC-rich peat soils while presenting a high variability in the low SOC content range. Furthermore, our results indicated that the carbon pool of soils with wide C:N ratios seem to be more stable.

Given the first analysis of the preliminary results presented here, we consider it important to try to distinguish between two causes of decreased SOC content in organic soils: transformation and mineralization or anthropogenic mix with mineral soil, e.g. with deep ploughing. Additionally, it is planned to investigate the potential influence of land use change at the sites, and to analyze $\delta^{13}C$, $\delta^{15}N$ and the H/C and O/C ratio of the samples to get further information about the transformation stage of the soil organic matter.

REFERENCES

1. Anderson, J.P.E. & Domsch, K.H., 1978. A physiological method for the quantitative measurement of microbial biomass in soils. *Soil Biology & Biochemistry*, 10, pp.215–221.
2. Anderson, T.-H. *et al.* 1995. Methoden zur quantitativen Bestimmung und Charakterisierung der mikrobiellen Biomasse des Bodens. *Landbauforschung Voelkenrode. Sonderheft*
3. Ausec, L., Kraigher, B. & Mandic-Mulec, I., 2009. Differences in the activity and bacterial community structure of drained grassland and forest peat soils. *Soil Biology and Biochemistry*, 41(9), pp.1874–1881.
4. Beare, M.H. *et al.* 2014. Estimating the organic carbon stabilisation capacity and saturation deficit of soils: a New Zealand case study. *Biogeochemistry*, 120(1-3), pp.71–87.
5. Brake, M., Höper, H. & Joergensen, R.G., 1999. Land use-induced changes in activity and biomass of microorganisms in raised bog peats at different depths. *Soil Biology and Biochemistry*, 31(11), pp.1489–1497.
6. Don, A., Rödenbeck, C. & Gleixner, G., 2013. Unexpected control of soil carbon turnover by soil carbon concentration. *Environmental Chemistry Letters*, 11(4), pp.407–413.
7. Gelman, A. & Rubin, D.B., 1992. Inference from Iterative Simulation Using Multiple Sequences. *Statistical Science*, 7(4), pp.457–511.
8. Heinemeyer, O. *et al.* 1989. Soil microbial biomass and respiration measurements: An automated technique based on infra-red gas analysis. *Plant and Soil*, 116, pp.191–195.
9. Kaiser, E.A. *et al.* 1992. Evaluation of methods to estimate the soil microbial biomass and the relationship with soil texture and organic matter. *Soil Biology and Biochemistry*, 24(7), pp.675–683.
10. Kechavarzi, C. *et al.* 2010. The role of soil moisture, temperature and nutrient amendment on CO_2 efflux from agricultural peat soil microcosms. *Geoderma*, 154(3–4), pp.203–210.
11. Vrugt, J. a. *et al.* 2009. Accelerating Markov Chain Monte Carlo Simulation by Differential Evolution with Self-Adaptive Randomized Subspace Sampling. *International Journal of Nonlinear Sciences and Numerical Simulation*, 10(3), pp.273–290.
12. Vrugt, J. a. *et al.* 2009a. Equifinality of formal (DREAM) and informal (GLUE) Bayesian approaches in hydrologic modeling? *Stochastic Environmental Research and Risk Assessment*, 23(7), pp.1011–1026.
13. Vrugt, J. a. *et al.* 2008. Treatment of input uncertainty in hydrologic modeling: Doing hydrology backward with Markov chain Monte Carlo simulation. *Water Resources Research*, 44, pp.1–52.

1.2: GEOCHEMISTRY, HYDROCHEMISTRY & HYDROLOGY

Abstract No: A-181

CHANGE OF WATER CHEMISTRY (DISSOLVED ORGANIC CARBON) WITH FREQUENT PEAT FIRES IN INDONESIAN PEATLAND

Masayuki Itoh[1*], Hiroshi Nishimura[1], Satomi Shiodera[1], Takashi Hirano[2], Osamu Kozan[1] and Haris Gunawan[3]

[1]Kyoto University, Japan
[2]Hokkaido University, Japan
[3]Riau University, Indonesia

**Corresponding author: masayukiitoh@yahoo.co.jp*

SUMMARY

Tropical peat swamp forests in Southeast Asia had been considered to be one of the most important parts of larger ecosystems due to the huge amount of carbon stock. Yet, recent rapid and intensive deforestation to procure timber and land preparation for commercial plants or crops (oil palm or Acacia plantations) have induced fundamental changes in the material cycling. Especially, frequent peat fires occur in every dry period especially in Indonesia, which changes the environment fundamentally and emit huge amount of greenhouse gases. We focused on the effects of human impacts on groundwater chemistry in the degraded peatland area in East part of Sumatra Island and Central Kalimantan, Indonesia by comparing with the observation in intact peat swamp forest and secondary forest with no fire experiences. We analyzed both the quantity and quality of dissolved organic and inorganic matters in peatland groundwater and canal water. Our results suggest that frequent peat fires had great effect on change in water chemistry in both quality and quantity aspects especially of dissolved organic carbon.

***Keywords**: tropical peatland, groundwater, dissolved organic carbon, peat fires, drainage*

INTRODUCTION

Tropical peat swamp forest is a tropical moist forest where waterlogged condition prevents the decomposition of dead woods and leaves. In Southeast Asia, peat swamp forest is one of the typical landscapes that regulate material cycling. According to a recent report, tropical peatland area encompasses 441,025 km^2 in which account for approximately 11% of global peatland area and in Southeast Asia alone, consist of 247,778km^2 or 56% of the total area of tropical peatland (Page *et al.*, 2011). These forests are known to be ecological dominance of terrestrial and aquatic biodiversity (Yule, 2010). Nevertheless, a recent statistic showed that these highly disturbance-sensitive forests were massively explored, declining 5.1 Mha or 42% of the total current intact peat swamp forests compared to those in last two decades (Miettinen and Liew 2010).

Under social and economic pressure, recent rapid and intensive deforestation to procure timber and convert land for more commercial plants or crops (oil palm or rubber plantations) (Koh *et al.*, 2009) have caused fundamental changes in land use pattern and material cycling. Carbon sequestration rates in tropical peatlands exceed 80 g C m^2 yr^{-1} (Page *et al.*, 2004) and is now decreasing due to intensive drainage following land conversion. The extensive anthropogenic activity in the form of deforestation for valuable logs and land conversion to agro-industrial plantations expedites peat fire following ground water drainage (Figure 1). The prolonged periods of annual drought and flood further result in the instability of soil condition physically and chemically.

Lowering of water table by constructing drainage canals allows the surface of peat to turn into aerobic condition. This increases decomposition rates. Aerobic respiration by microbe increases oxygen concentration in peat. This induces the increase in larger amount of carbon emission as CO_2 (e.g. Freeman *et al.*, 1992) and dissolved organic carbon (DOC). As a result, peat can be easily oxidized, releasing a large amount of DOC (Freeman *et al.*, 2001; Clair *et al.*, 2002). Recently, in Central Kalimantan, Indonesia, Moore *et al.* (2013) showed that fluvial DOC discharge from disturbed peat swamp forest was 50% larger than that from an intact forest. They also showed that the carbon which was discharged from disturbed forest contained old carbon. This indicates the impact by human activity on the material cycling in peat swamp forests.

In addition, over several millennia, fire has been of common feature in the tropical peatland. However, within the past three decades, catastrophic fires seem to occur more frequently than ever, particularly during extended periods of drought in association with El Niño events (Yulianti *et al.*, 2012) and also being tightly linked to the change of land-used types in these recent years, such as oil palm plantation conversion when slash and burn techniques is always the option as the cheapest mean of land clearing (Langner and Siegert 2009). Under such situation, this paper discusses the impact of land use changes and repeated fire effect on water chemistry (especially carbon concentration) in Indonesian tropical peatland.

METHODS

Site description and hydrological features

The study was conducted in the East part of Sumatra Island and Central Kalimantan in Indonesia. At the site in Sumatra, repeated fire in peat swamp forest changed the environment from swamp forest to degraded bare land. A degraded peatland field was selected (hereafter: DP; Photo 1a) which experienced fire three times in 2002, 2004, and 2007, located in Riau province. An unburnt but drained secondary forest situated in the next village was also made (hereafter UBD). The number of water sample collected depended on the groundwater level at each sampling time and location. Groundwater from wells in undrained peat swamp forest was collected (hereafter: UF), drained peat forest (DF), and drained burnt area (DB) in Central Kalimantan. Water table levels were taken manually using a water-level indicator and continuously monitored by water level sensor. Precipitation was also measured in both sites.

Water collection and analysis

Water samples were collected from canals and piezometers; 1 m depth to measure water chemistry. *In situ* measurements of pH and electrical conductivity (EC) were carried out. To measure dissolved organic carbon (DOC) concentrations and total dissolved nitrogen (TDN), the water samples were first filtered using glass-fiber filters (GF/F; nominal particle retention, 0.7 μm; Whatman, UK). Then, DOC and TDN concentrations were determined using a total organic carbon (TOC) analyzer (TOC-V; Shimadzu, Japan). To examine the quality difference in dissolved organic matter (DOM), the excitation emission matrix (EEM)s were acquired on Aqualog (Horiba Scientific) with the following settings: Ex = 240 to 600 nm at every 3-nm interval, Em = 212 to 619 nm at every 3 nm interval, bandpass = 5 nm and integration time = 0.1 s. EEMs were corrected for any instrument bias, and inner filter corrections were applied using the absorbance values. Blank subtraction of ultrapure water was carried out to remove Raman scattering effects and a solvent effect.

RESULTS AND DISCUSSION

Here, the results of Riau site are presented. Seasonal variations in daily rainfall (DP site), water table levels, and DOC concentrations at DP and UBD sites are shown in Figure2. The study site has rainy and dry season that is affected by the inter-tropical convergence zonal phenomenon, in which the area experiences a rainy season and two dry seasons throughout a year. During the experimental period, high amounts of precipitation were recorded from November to December 2013 and low amounts from January to May 2014.

Groundwater level in DP site decreased below 120 cm in February 2014 when no rainfall was recorded for two months. In contrast, the groundwater level increased up to soil surface in December 2014 (data not shown). This indicated that the groundwater level fluctuated more than 120 cm at this site. DP site is located adjacent to a canal flowing from the Acacia plantation area. Therefore, in addition to the effect of natural increase of water table level, water management of the plantation might affect the groundwater level at the site. The mean values of DOC concentration in groundwater ranged from 43.5-74.3 (mean 60.6) mg C/L in DP site and from 49.4-94.5 (mean 76.0) mg C/L in UBD site, respectively. There were no significant differences ($P=0.15$) for DOC concentrations between these two sites. The highest DOC concentration at DP site was observed during the driest period of February 2014.

Although there were no significant differences in DOC concentration between DP and UBD sites, the quality of the DOC was different. Figure 3 shows the three dimensional fluorescence spectra of water collected from burnt drained peat (DP; left) and unburnt drained secondary forest (UBD; right) sites. In both sites, peak was identified at excitation/emission wavelengths (Ex/Em) of 350/430–450 nm, while another peak was identified at Ex/Em of 300/330 nm in only DP site. This difference between sites suggested that the change in DOM quality before and after peat fires, or deforestation (Itoh *et al.* unpublished). Nevertheless, the current data is insufficient to prove the notion, more samplings are now underway. The presentation will include the results from Central Kalimantan site.

CONCLUSION

Preliminary observation in Riau Province, Sumatra, Indonesia, suggested that the impacts of human activities such as forest clear-cutting and peat burning have changed the ecological condition in tropical peatland area in these few decades. Such changes in groundwater quality may be irreversible to original state or may take decades to restore to nearly natural condition. This study also urges the need to have more studies to access the ecological and economic impact in degraded peatlands.

ACKNOWLEDGEMENTS

We thank Mr. Ahmad Muhammad; Mr. and Mrs. Nur for supporting our research. This work was supported by the Ministry of Education, Culture, Sports, Science, and Technology for Science Research (15H05625), Global Environment Research Fund (4-1504), Ministry of Environment, Japan, and the Institutional Collaboration Feasibility Studies, Research Institute for Humanity and Nature (RIHN), Japan.

REFERENCES

1. Clair, T.A. *et al.* (2002) Gaseous carbon dioxide and methane, as well as dissolved organic carbon losses from a small temperate wetland under a changing climate, Environmental Pollution 116, S1, S143–S148.
2. Freeman, C. *et al.* (1992) Fluxes of CO_2, CH_4 and N_2O from a Welsh peatland following simulation of water table draw-down: potential feedback to climatic change
3. Freeman, C. *et al.* (2001) Export of organic carbon from peat soils, Nature, 412, 785
4. Koh, P.K. *et al.* (2009) Conversion of Indonesia's peatlands. Frontiers in Ecology and the Environment 7 (5), 238–238.
5. Langner, A., and Siegert, F. (2009) Spatiotemporal fire occurrence in Borneo over a period of 10 years. Global Change Biology 15: 48-62.
6. Miettinen, J., and Liew, S. C (2010) Degradation and development of peatlands in Peninsular Malaysia and in the islands of Sumatra and Borneo since 1990. Land Degradation & Development 21: 285-296.
7. Moore, S. *et al.* (2013) Deep instability of deforested tropical peatlands revealed by fluvial organic carbon fluxes, Nature, 493, 660–664
8. Page, S. E. *et al.* (2004) A record of late Pleistocene and Holocene carbon accumulation and climate change from an equatorial peat bog (Kalimantan, Indonesia): implications for past, present and future carbon dynamics. J. Quat. Sci. 19, 625–635
9. Page, S. E. *et al.* (2011), Global and regional importance of the tropical peatland carbon pool. Global Change Biology 17: 798–818.
10. Yule, C. M. (2010) Loss of biodiversity and ecosystem functioning in Indo-Malayan peat swamp forests. Biodiversity and Conservation 19: 393-409.
11. Yulianti, N., *et al.* (2012) Recent forest and peat fire trends in Indonesia: The latest decade by MODIS hotspot data. Global Environmental Research 16: 105-116.

Figure 1: Anthropogenic activities in the form of deforestation and land-used conversion cause ground water drainage in peatland. Intensive drought and raining season could result in wildfires (left) and flood (right).

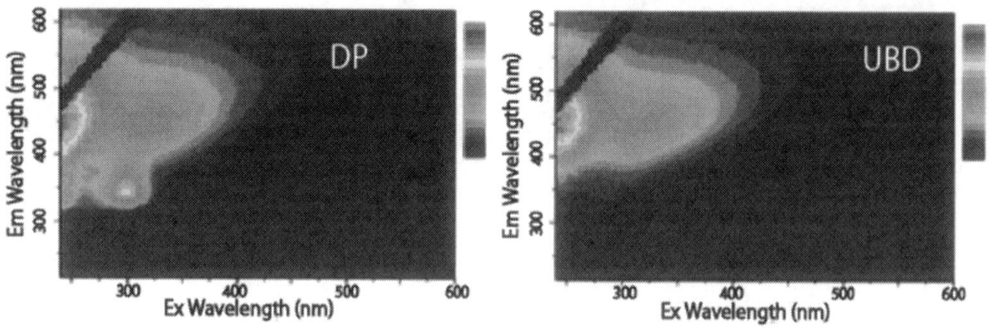

Figure 2: Three dimensional fluorescence spectra of water collected from burnet drained peat (DP; left) and unburnt drained secondary forest (UBD; right) sites. Ex and Em indicate both excitation and emission, respectively (Itoh unpublished).

Abstract No: A-074

COASTAL PEAT MASS MOVEMENT AND ITS EFFECT ON THE TERRESTRIAL CARBON DISCHARGE TO THE OCEAN IN BENGKALIS ISLAND, INDONESIA

Koichi Yamamoto[1*], Muhammad Haidar[1, 4], Ariyo Kanno[1], Motoyuki Suzuki[1], Yoshihisa Akamatsu[1], Noerdin Bashir[2], Sigit Sutikno[3], Mu Hardi[3] and Syawal Satibi[3]

[1]*Yamaguchi University, Japan*
[2]*Politeknik Bengkalis, Indonesia*
[3]*University of Riau, Indonesia*
[4]*Badan Informasi Geospasial, Indonesia*

**Corresponding author: k_yama@yamaguchi-u.ac.jp*

SUMMARY

Multi temporal high resolution satellite imagery was used to identify the peat-coastal setback of Bengkalis Island, Indonesia. Shuttle Radar Topography Mission DEM was used to estimate the geomorphology of the peatland. Multi temporal topographic survey using RTK-GPS, peat core samplings, and ground water level measurements were conducted to clarify the geomorphology change and carbon storage of the peatland. Recent coastline change and long term coastline change were analyzed with high resolution satellite images; SPOT-6 and WorldView3. The average annual setback changed from 11.93 m to 23.37 m. Over the long term, average annual setback was 14.46 m. The results reveal that total erosion extent was 478 ha between 2000 and 2015, which represents a peat volume loss of 21.7 Mm^3 which correspond to a total carbon loss of 1.27 Mt C. Bog bursts in Bengkalis Island coast was observed in the rainy season caused by extensive rainfall. Following the bog burst, the peat mass was eroded to the sea.

Keywords: *peat failure, bog burst, Sumatra, Indonesia*

INTRODUCTION

In the northern part of Bengkalis Island, the peat swamp forest has collapsed and fallen to the sea (Fig. 1). The situation is quite serious as well as strange because peat swamp forest is generally established behind the coast in the peat swamp model of the Anderson (1964). The coastal peat cliff is about 5 m higher than the mean sea level. In the 1950s, a mangrove coast was a likely feature at that time (U.S. Army Map Service, 1955). However, in recent satellite images, the mangrove has gone, and the coast been eroded till 1988. Long term coastline setback and peat mass movements were observed in Bengkalis Island, Indonesia. In Bengkalis Island, Riau Province has faced a coastal erosion problem for more than thirty years. Vast areas of the peat swamp forest have been used for palm oil production since 2002. The objective of this study was to provide an estimate of how much the land area and carbon storage in the terrestrial region have been reduced in the last 15 years.

METHODS

Our study area is Bengkalis Island, Indonesia (Fig. 2), which is located 8 kilometers off the coast of the main island Sumatra and lies along the west side of Malacca strait. The total land area is roughly 900 km^2, of which more than 70% is covered by peat soils with a thickness more than 1 m. The peat deposit on Bengkalis Island contains 3.0×10^9 m^3 of peat (Supardi *et al.*, 1993). The island is almost flat and has a maximum surface elevation of approximately 10-15 m above mean sea level. Low-lying and swampy, the island has high precipitation, is sparsely populated, and is mostly unfit for cultivation. It stretches northwest-southeast for about 68 km; its width east-west is about 19 km. It consists of 4 main peat domes which are typical of tropical peatland morphology. We concentrated our study area on the western side of the island that is currently dominated by palm oil plantations. In order to cover the study area with a time series of high-resolution satellite images for the short term erosion analysis, a total of five satellite scenes from ALOS PRISM, SPOT 6, and World View 3 were used (Fig. 3). ALOS PRISM images were recorded on March 24 2010, and March 27 2011, while the SPOT 6 images were captured on January 27 2013, and September 18, 2013. For the latest image, we used World View 3 recorded on April 2 2015. We used SPOT 6 images recorded on September 18 2013 as a master image for geometric correction. In order to preserve the original pixel value, nearest neighbor was applied for resampling the pixel value following affine method that used to rectify the image. Five ground control points obtained from in-situ measurement by using static GPS were used for rectifying the master image, producing a RMSE of 1.11 m. The other four images were rectified based on the master image by employing image to image rectification, producing a RMSE of less than 1.85 m. For long term erosion, Landsat images were used to obtain the annual erosion and annual setback between 2000 and 2015. Terrestrial carbon loss was calculated by the procedure shown in Fig. 4.

Fig. 1: Erosion of the peat coast in Bengkalis Island, Indonesia. Peat swamp forest (left) and palm oil plantation (right)

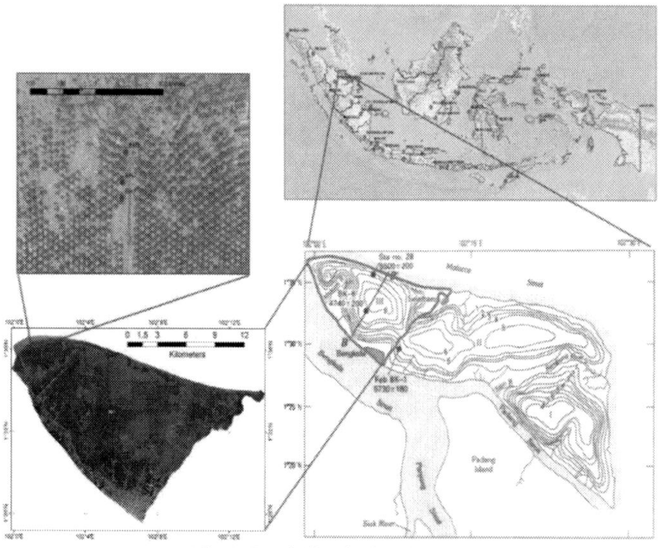

Fig. 2: Bengkalis Island, Indonesia

Fig. 3: Coastal erosion process of the northern part of the Bangkalis Island, Indonesia.

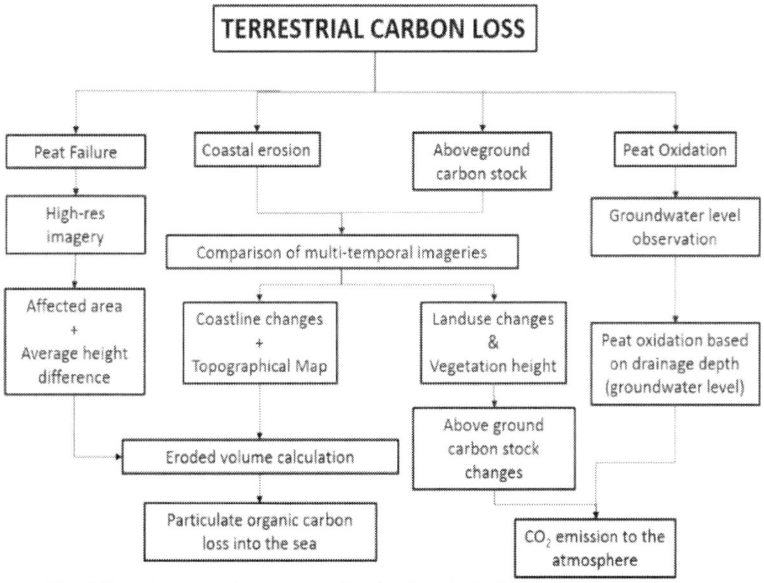

Fig. 4: Procedure to evaluate terrestrial carbon loss in the Bangkalis Island, Indonesia.

RESULTS

We collected peat soil samples from 17 locations in Bengkalis Island that represent various types of land use. Vertical distribution of organic carbon and nutrients were analyzed from sample points located in oil palm plantations and forests. The highest carbon content (57.85%) was found in the forest located on the northern side of oil palm plantation. Even though this forest was affected by a waterway constructed inside the oil palm plantation, it had the highest carbon content among the sample locations. Conversely, the lowest carbon content (40.8%) was located in the small holder oil palm plantation. This area was recently burned for land clearing. Low carbon content might be correlated with the burning activity. To analyze the coastline changes, we employed two images of ALOS prism recorded in March 2010 and March 2011, two images of SPOT 6 recorded in January and September 2013, and one image of World View 3 recorded in April 2015.

Table 1: Annual rate of coastal erosion (ha/year) and setback (m/year).

Time	Erosion		
	Annual (ha/year)	Affected coast length (m)	Average annual setback (m/year)
Mar 2010- Mar 2011	37.79	20807	18.16
Mar 2011- Jan 2013	22.58	18924	11.93
Jan 2013 -Sep 2013	23.5	9903	23.73
Sep 2013-Apr 2015	25.88	12666	20.43
May 2000-May 2015	31.88	22038	14.46

The results in Table 1 shows that the highest annual erosion rate occurred during March 2010 to March 2011, it was caused by the length of affected coastline is long (more than 20 kilometers). In other words, the coastal erosion occurred alongside the coastline. The highest rate of coastal setback occurred during January to May 2013 because the erosion process only occurred at a certain location where massive erosion was observed. This process is closely linked to the peat failure phenomena that occurred near the coastline. In the long term period, coastal erosion somehow showed the average value of the short term. In both short term (2010-2015) and long term (2000-2015). The height points were extracted on the vegetation-free area in SRTM DEM. Based on these points we interpolate by using the nearest neighbor method to derived topographic map. The topographic transect was measured using RTK GPS at 4 survey lines to validate the topographic map. The result of topographic map indicates the morphology of tropical peatland which is in the shape of peat dome. The difference between RTK GPS and topographical map is 0.95 meter in average. Since there is a time gap between the RTK measurement and SRTM observation, the difference between both elevations might be attributed to subsidence process. Another possible explanation is that it was caused by the bush or necromass that cover the open area.

CONCLUSION

Over the past 15 years, Bengkalis Island has experienced a massive loss of terrestrial carbon owing to coastal erosion, deforestation, and peat oxidation. Although peat failure only occurred in the past year on a massive scale, it is the highest contributor to the annual carbon loss. Nearly 50 % of the annual carbon loss came from peat failure. The peatland of Bengkalis islands is facing threats from the over exploitation of natural land resources. This study had revealed that the carbon loss is dominated by particulate organic carbon from coastal erosion and peat failure. This general conclusion was based on the following result: 1) Annual coastal erosion has decreased in the past four years, in contrast to the annual setback that has increased in the past two year. Furthermore, the total erosion extent is 478 ha along 22 km of coastline area in the past 15 years. This represents a peat volume loss of 21.7Mm^3 which correspond to a total carbon loss of 1.28 MtC. In the past year, the peat failure process has occurred on a massive scale and contributes significantly to the carbon loss. In fact, the peat failure contributed to 2.89 Mm^3 of total eroded volume that represents a carbon loss of 0.21 Mt C in the past year. There was no significant different between LULUCF and vegetation height aboveground carbon stock derived method. The difference is less than 3 %. The lowering of groundwater table has contributed the CO_2 emissions of 0.357 Mt per year. This phenomenon occurred due to the construction of artificial drainage in oil palm plantation.

The conservative method of carbon accounting for climate change mitigation only considers the carbon dynamics from land use change and peat oxidation. This study case has shown that other factors (coastal erosion and peat failure) also contribute significantly to terrestrial carbon loss.

ACKNOWLEDGEMENT

This research was supported by JSPS KAKEN 26303015.

REFERENCES

i. J.A.R. Anderson (1964) The structure and development of the peat swamps of Sarawak and Brunei, Journal of Tropical Geography, 18 (1964), pp. 7–16

ii. Supardi, Subetkty, A. D., and Neuzil, S.G., 1993, General geology and peat resources of the Siak Kanan and Bengkalis ISland peat deposits, Sumatra, Indonesia, in Cobb, J. C., and Cecil, C. B., eds., Modern and Ancient Coal-Forming Environments: Boulder, Colorado, Geological Society of America Special Paper 286

Abstract No: A-358

DISSOLVED GREENHOUSE GASES IN PEAT-DRAINING RIVERS IN SARAWAK, MALAYSIA

M. Müller[1*], D. Müller[2], T. Warneke[2], T. Rixen[3], J. Notholt[2], N. Denis[1], E. Sia[1] and A. Mujahid[4]

[1]*Swinburne University of Technology Sarawak Campus, Faculty of Engineering, Computing and Science, Jalan Simpang Tiga, 93350 Kuching, Sarawak, Malaysia*
[2]*Institute of Environmental Physics, University of Bremen, Otto-Hahn-Allee 1, 28359 Bremen, Germany*
[3]*Leibniz Center for Tropical Marine Ecology, Fahrenheitstr. 6., 28359 Bremen, Germany*
[4]*Department of Aquatic Science, Faculty of Resource Science and Technology, University Malaysia Sarawak, 94300 Kota Samarahan, Sarawak, Malaysia*

* *Corresponding author: mmueller@swinburne.edu.my*

Southeast Asian peat soils are a globally important carbon pool, but are currently undergoing severe disturbance due to anthropogenic activities such as deforestation and conversion into palm oil plantations. Peatland degradation usually increases carbon loss through direct emissions to the atmosphere and via riverine export, however, most of the data has been collected in temperate regions and information on tropical rivers is largely lacking. This presentation will provide an overview of recent work in several peat-draining rivers in Sarawak. We have for example measured dissolved greenhouse gases (GHG; CO_2, CH_4, N_2O) using Fourier Transform InfraRed (FTIR) spectroscopy as well as dissolved organic carbon (DOC), particulate organic carbon (POC) and inorganic nutrients over the course of several years and seasons. Results show that while those rivers are sources of GHG to the atmosphere, the level of emission was lower than expected. The occurrence of methanotrophs as well as short residence times are likely the main reasons behind the low emissions.

***Keywords**:-*

Abstract No: A-029

EFFECTS OF WATER TABLE FLUCTUATIONS ON DISSOLVED ORGANIC CARBON CONCENTRATIONS IN AN OIL PALM PLANTATION IN TROPICAL PEATLANDS

Wendy Lim[1], Adesiji Richard Adeolu[2, 5], Fitriah Azizan[3], Alexander Kiew Sayok[1*], Thamer Ahmed Mohammad[2], Nik Norsyahariati Nik Daud[2], Rory Padfield[3], Stephanie Evers[4] and Zuriati Zakaria[3]

[1]*Department of Hydrology and Soil Science, Institute of Biodiversity and Environmental Conservation, Universiti Malaysia, Sarawak, 94300 Kota Samarahan, Sarawak*
[2]*Department of Civil Engineering, Faculty of Engineering, Universiti Putra Malaysia, 43400, UPM Serdang, Malaysia*
[3]*Department of Water and Environmental Management, Malaysian-Japan International Institute of Technology, Malaysia*
[4]*School of Bioscience, University of Nottingham, Malaysia Campus*
[5]*Presently Department of Civil Engineering, Federal University of Technology, P.M.B 65, Minna, Niger State, Nigeria*

**Corresponding author: ksalexender@ibec.unimas.my*

Peatlands are the largest source of soil carbon and some other major soil nutrients. The continuous functioning of these ecosystems as the source of these nutrients depends largely on peatland drainage which helps to lower the peatland water table levels for sustainable peatland agricultural production. Excessive peatland drainage has caused dissolved organic carbon (DOC) loss as a result of lowered water table levels. This study, therefore, investigated the impacts of fluctuations in water table levels on DOC concentrations. The study was undertaken in four blocks of oil palm of different ages which were further sub-divided into eight sampling plots. Samples were taken from each of the study plots for 16 months on a bi-monthly basis from the installed tube wells (piezometers) and were analyzed for temperature, pH and DOC. The study showed that DOC has positive and strong correlations with water table levels in four of the eight sampling points with weak correlation in the remaining plots. Average water table levels ranged from -27.16 cm during the wet period to -90.8 cm during the dry period. DOC concentrations ranged from 18.60 mg l^{-1} during the dry period to 250.50 mg l^{-1} during the wet period when water table levels were expected to rise. These concentrations are much higher than those from studies in temperate countries and elsewhere in the tropics. While water table levels serve as proxy, to some extent, for DOC concentrations, other hydrological elements like rainfall, ambient air temperature except evaporation were observed to correlate strongly and positively with DOC concentrations.

***Keywords**: tropical peatlands, oil palm plantations, water table levels, dissolved organic carbon, peatland drainage*

Abstract No: A-084

LANDSCAPE HETEROGENEITY OF DISSOLVED ORGANIC CARBON (DOC) CONCENTRATIONS WITHIN TROPICAL PEAT LANDSCAPES AND LINKS TO HEAVY METAL MOBILISATION

Stephanie Evers [1*], Paul Williams [2], Rory Padfield [3] and Alexander Kiew Sayok[4]

[1] *University of Nottingham Malaysia Campus, Jalan Broga, 43500 Semenyih, Selangor, Malaysia*
[2] *Queens University Belfast, University Road Belfast, BT7 1NN, Northern Ireland, United Kingdom*
[3] *Malaysia-Japan International Institute of Technology, Universiti Teknologi Malaysia, Jalan Semerak, 54100, Malaysia*
[4] *Universiti Malaysia Sarawak, Jln Meranti, 94300 Kota Samarahan, Sarawak, Malaysia*

**Corresponding author: Stephanie.Evers@nottingham.edu.my*

Tropical peatlands are globally significant carbon stores. To date, many studies have shown the impact of conversion of peat swamp forests (PSFs) into agriculture and the associated C emission from peat soils with clearance and drainage. Yet losses from fluvial carbon have so far received little attention. Fluvial C plays an important role as a transfer pathway of carbon between the terrestrial, freshwater and eventually marine C pools. However in addition to this, it forms a vector for mobilisation of micronutrients such as Iron (Fe) and other trace elements, between those same pools. Yet the heterogeneity of fluvial C concentrations in relation to land use type has not been addressed in any detail, nor has the role of these low oxygen, low pH, dissolved organic carbon (DOC)-rich 'blackwaters' in mobilising and transporting heavy metals within tropical peat catchments in relation to this landscape heterogeneity. Here we present data on DOC concentrations across peat drainage systems in Selangor, Peninsular Malaysia and link these data to seasonality, landscape heterogeneity and heavy metal concentration gradients. Links to rice and oil production and potential implications to catchment food safety are made.

***Keywords**:-*

Abstract No: A-094

METHANE FLUXES FROM A TROPICAL PEATLAND IN BRUNEI DARUSSALAM

A. Hoyt[1*], S. Pangala[2], L. Gandois[3], A. Cobb[4], F. M. Kai[4], X. Xu[5], V. Gauci[2], Y. Mahmud[6], A. S. Kamariah[7], J. A. Eri[8] and C. F. Harvey[1]

[1]*Massachusetts Institute of Technology, Parsons Laboratory, USA*
[2]*Department of Environment, Earth & Ecosystems, The Open University, United Kingdom*
[3]*Université de Toulouse, UPS, INP, EcoLab (Laboratoire Ecologie fonctionnelle et Environnement), France*
[4]*Singapore-MIT Alliance for Research and Technology, Singapore*
[5]*Department of Earth System Science, University of California Irvine,, USA*
[6]*Brunei Heart of Borneo Centre, Brunei Darussalam*
[7]*Universiti Brunei Darussalam, Brunei Darussalam*
[8]*Brunei Forestry Department, Brunei Darussalam*

**Corresponding author: aahoyt@gmail.com*

SUMMARY

Emissions of methane (CH_4) from tropical wetlands are highly uncertain. Although tropical peatlands are warm, wet, anoxic environments, limited CH_4 emissions have been observed. We examine CH_4 production and transport in a pristine tropical peatland in Borneo to determine the rate and carbon source of CH_4 production. First, we use the ^{14}C composition of dissolved CH_4, dissolved inorganic carbon (DIC) and dissolved organic carbon (DOC) within the peat porewater to identify the source of CH_4 production. In contrast to the peat, which ages with depth to nearly 3000 cal BP, DOC is of contemporary origin throughout the peat column, to depths of 4.5m. The ^{14}C content of CH_4 and DIC are nearly identical, and are intermediate between the DOC and peat ^{14}C content. Thus, despite the presence of modern C throughout the peat profile, peat decomposition is an important source of CH_4 production. Next, we use the $\delta^{13}C$ of CH_4 and DIC to identify the mechanism of CH_4 production. Within the peat profile, CH_4 and DIC concentrations increase with depth and DIC becomes increasingly enriched in ^{13}C. The $\delta^{13}C$ of CH_4 is relatively uniform with depth, resulting in a $\delta^{13}C$ fractionation between DIC and CH_4 of 55-70‰ ($\alpha_C CO_2\text{-}CH_4$ = 1.06-1.07). This fractionation suggests CO_2 reduction is the dominant pathway for CH_4 production at the site. These trends are similar to those observed in northern peat bogs. Finally, we use information on site hydrology, CH_4 and DIC concentrations, isotopic compositions and fluxes to build a model of CH_4 production and transport. This model allows us to partition CH_4 losses from the peat due to diffusion, tree-mediated transport, and lateral transport. We find that lateral transport of dissolved CH_4 may be a more important pathway than previously considered.

INTRODUCTION

Southeast Asia is home to the world's largest proportion of tropical peatlands (Page *et al.* 2011). In these ecosystems, anaerobic conditions allow carbon to accumulate over thousands of years. Across Southeast Asia, these forested peatlands are rapidly being drained and deforested, releasing stored carbon to the atmosphere (Hooijer *et al.* 2012; Miettinen *et al.* 2012). Tropical peatlands play an important role in the global carbon cycle, and can be sources of both carbon dioxide (CO_2) and methane (CH_4) to the atmosphere (Couwenberg *et al.* 2010; Hooijer *et al.* 2010).

Tropical peatlands would seem to offer ideal conditions for methanogenesis; they are warm, wet, organic-rich environments. However, tropical peatlands are reported to have much lower CH_4 fluxes than temperate and boreal peatlands. These fluxes range from negligible at low water levels to up to 3 mg $CH_4/m^2/h$ at high water levels (Couwenberg *et al.* 2010). One possible reason for the low CH_4 fluxes is that environmental conditions, such as the organic substrate (e.g. high lignin content) in tropical peatlands may be unfavorable to methanogens (Calvert *et al.* 1991; Gandois *et al.* 2013, 2014). Morphological adaptations by trees that transport oxygen into the root zone may also suppress methane production (Adji *et al.* 2014). Alternatively, aerobic oxidation near the peat surface may consume most of the produced CH_4 before it escapes the peat, resulting in lower apparent CH_4 production rates.

Existing data on CH_4 emissions from tropical peatlands comes from studies based on chamber measurements, which predominantly capture diffusive fluxes (Adji *et al.* 2014; Arai *et al.* 2014; Furukawa *et al.* 2005; Hadi *et al.* 2001, 2005; Inubushi *et al.* 1998, 2005; Jauhiainen *et al.* 2005; Melling *et al.* 2005). Focus on these diffusive fluxes neglects the importance of other possible CH_4 pathways. For example, in addition to aerobic oxidation near the peat surface, CH_4 could be oxidized anaerobically (Gupta *et al.* 2013; Smemo & Yavitt 2011) at the peat-clay interface where sulfate concentrations are higher. Alternatively, CH_4 could leave the peat through ebullition, tree transport (Pangala *et al.* 2013) or lateral transport (Figure 1). Despite the importance of hydrology in peatland carbon cycling and the documented importance of advection in peatlands (Chanton *et al.* 2008; Corbett *et al.* 2013), advection of dissolved gas is not considered a primary CH_4 transport pathway (Chanton 2005). As a result, advective transport of dissolved CH_4 has never been quantified from a tropical peatland, but could play an important role in CH_4 cycling.

Here we use measurements of CO_2 and CH_4 in a pristine tropical peatland to assess the relative roles of different transport pathways. We present data on dissolved gas concentrations and isotopic compositions. We use this data to inform a reactive transport model that considers both vertical and lateral transport in a peatland. We then quantify the relative fluxes of diffusive and advective pathways under a range of scenarios and find lateral transport is the dominant transport pathway at this site. Finally, we use the isotopic composition of the dissolved gases to provide insight into the source and production pathway for methanogenesis.

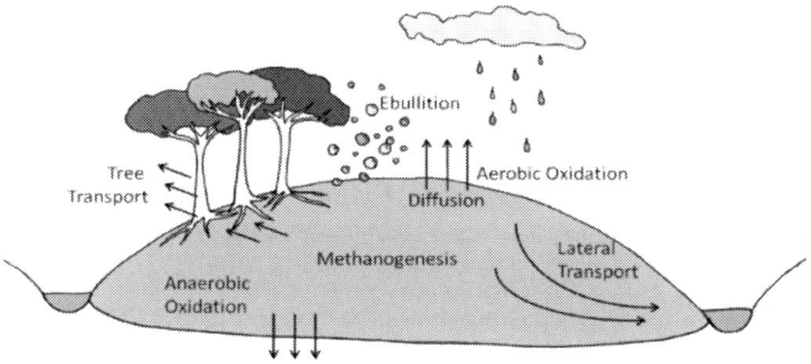

Figure 1: Chamber measurements capture diffusive methane (CH_4) fluxes from the peat surface. There are many alternative CH_4 transport pathways.

METHODS

Study site - Samples were collected from the Mendaram peat dome in the Ulu Mendaram Conservation Area, Belait District, Brunei Darussalam, on the island of Borneo. This is a pristine peat swamp forest characterized by *Shorea albida* (Anderson 1983). Porewater samples were collected from the pristine sites I and III as described in Gandois *et al.* (2014).

Porewater sampling and analysis - Porewater was sampled from throughout the peat profile to capture trends with depth from the surface to 5.5m deep in the peat. Sampling was conducted using a portable Inox pushpoint piezometer (MHE products, USA) and PVC sampling wells. Samples were collected to determine the concentrations of the major elements, dissolved organic carbon (DOC), dissolved inorganic carbon (DIC) and dissolved CH_4 concentrations, and for isotopic analysis. pH and electrical conductivity were also measured.

$\delta^{13}C$ and ^{14}C isotope analysis- Porewater gases for ^{14}C analysis of CO_2 and CH_4 were collected in April and August 2014. Porewater was pumped using a peristaltic pump and flushed through a sealed 1L glass bottle for 1-4 hrs to accumulate sufficient gas volume, with timing depending on concentration. Dissolved gases were trapped in the bottle as they degassed. CO_2 and CH_4 were separated during analysis. Collected gases were transferred via syringes to pre-evacuated serum vials sealed with butyl rubber septa. ^{14}C analysis was conducted at University of California Irvine. Samples for analysis of ^{14}C content of DIC were analyzed at NOSAMS and collected following the standard NOSAMS protocol.

RESULTS

Model Description & Performance - Existing models of CH_4 production and transport within the catotelm represent various subsets of the following processes: methanogenesis, methane oxidation, diffusive transport, ebullition and vertical advection (Steinmann *et al.*, 2008; Shoemaker & Schrag, 2010; Corbett *et al.*, 2013). However, none of these models includes lateral advection. We present a new model which accounts for both downward and lateral advection of porewater and dissolved gases. It uses a steady-state 1D reactive transport model with a non-uniform vertical velocity to capture the both vertical and lateral advection as well as diffusive transport. It generates not only concentration profiles, but also models the profiles of $\delta^{13}C$ and $\Delta^{14}C$ of both CO_2 and CH_4. By modelling ^{12}C, ^{13}C and ^{14}C individually, we capture the fractionation caused not only by methanogenesis, but also as a result of advective and diffusive transport. The steady-state model successfully replicated the observed concentration profiles and $\delta^{13}C$ of CO_2 and CH_4 measured in the peat profile within the variability of the measurements. These fits were achieved using parameters based on literature values and data from the site. The only free parameter was the CH_4 production rate, which was adjusted to 0.045 mol/m^3/yr in order to match the observed CH_4 concentrations.

Methane, CO_2 and DOC concentrations - Despite significant spatial heterogeneity, CH_4 concentrations in all samples increased with depth, from <0.1mM near the surface to maximum concentrations of 1.5mM just above the mangrove peat boundary. A decrease in concentrations was observed in the deepest samples from the mangrove peat, which has a substantial mineral fraction and higher sulfate concentration. There was significant spatial heterogeneity. Short-term temporal heterogeneity was not as dramatic; repeat sampling in the same location after a few days later showed only small changes in the concentration.

$\delta^{13}C$ of CH_4 and DIC - The CH_4 and DIC both became increasingly enriched in ^{13}C with depth. Shallow DIC at 10-20cm had a $\delta^{13}C$ signature of -26‰ to -27‰, similar to that of the vegetation, dissolved organic matter and peat (-28‰ to -31‰) (Dommain *et al.* 2015; Gandois *et al.* 2014) . Deeper samples were increasingly enriched, to a maximum of +2.0‰ at 5.5m. The $\delta^{13}C$ of CH_4 was much more depleted, but followed a similar trend, with values ranging from -90‰ to -70‰, with the most depleted values near the surface. The $\delta^{13}C$ fractionation between DIC and CH_4 was relatively uniform with depth, ranging from 55-70‰ ($\alpha_C CO_2$-CH_4 = 1.06-1.07). This apparent α_C is within the range typical of the CO_2 reduction pathway (Chanton *et al.* 2005; Whiticar 1999).

Radiocarbon dates - We used the ^{14}C content of peat, DOC, DIC, and dissolved CH_4 to identify the carbon source for methanogenesis. Consistent with the gradual accumulation of organic matter, the peat ages with depth to nearly 3000 cal BP (Dommain *et al.* 2015). In contrast, DOC is of contemporary origin throughout the peat column, to depths of 4.5m, indicating flushing of the peat profile with recharge originating as rainwater on the peat surface (Gandois *et al.* 2014). The ^{14}C content of CH_4 and DIC are nearly identical, and are intermediate between the DOC and the peat ^{14}C content. CH_4 and CO_2 are of contemporary origin near the surface and increase in age with depth to over 1500 years at 4.5m. Throughout the profile, the ages of CH_4 and CO_2 from the same sample were within 15% of each other, with CH_4 at most depths slightly older than the CO_2. The ages of the CO_2 were also similar to DIC ages sampled at the same location one year earlier. Samples taken at different times all followed the same depth trends.

DISCUSSION

Importance of lateral transport

Aquatic fluxes are a new and important consideration for the tropical peatland carbon budgets, which has not been as extensively researched as that of northern peatlands. Recent work has demonstrated the importance of lateral fluxes of DOC in tropical peatlands (Gandois *et al.* 2013; Moore *et al.* 2011; Moore *et al.* 2013). However, dissolved gas fluxes have not been quantified in tropical peatlands. Our data suggests the additional importance of including dissolved gas fluxes in the carbon budget.

Our results suggest that lateral flux of dissolved CH_4 plays an important role in tropical peatlands. This is consistent with the hydrology of these peat domes. Coastal peatlands in Southeast Asia experience large amounts of precipitation, much of which runs off the peat surface or flows through the upper few centimeters of the peat. However, some also flows into the deep peat itself, as documented by the presence of DOC of contemporary origin present in the deep peat (Corbett *et al.* 2013; Gandois *et al.* 2014). This downward flow is eventually obstructed by the underlying marine clay, which is relatively impermeable to flow. In order to maintain downward flow from the peat surface in the presence of an impermeable boundary, lateral flow must occur. This flowing water carries dissolved gases with it, which are then released to adjacent streams.

The lateral flow of water and dissolved CH_4 in the peat is controlled by the recharge rate into the peat. The relative importance of diffusive and lateral CH_4 fluxes therefore depends on the rate of water recharging the shallow peat. Figure 2 captures this dependence over a range of recharge rates, assuming a constant rate of CH_4 production. In the absence of recharge, CH_4 concentrations build up within the peat profile, leading to higher diffusion rates. Alternatively, if the peatland experiences rapid flushing, dissolved CH_4 will be transported laterally, immediately following production, leading to negligible diffusive fluxes.

In the Mendaram peat dome, the lateral flux of CH_4 dominates. At our calculated recharge rate of 0.2m/yr, we expect ~20 times more CH_4 to be transported laterally out of the peat column than out of the surface through diffusion (Figure 2). This suggests that current estimates significantly underestimate the amount of CH_4 produced by tropical peatlands. However, the fate of this CH_4 is still unknown. This dissolved CH_4 will be transported to the margins of peatlands, most commonly rivers or drainage canals. There we expect it to degas to the atmosphere or potentially be oxidized before it is released. Further measurements are required to determine the importance of this pathway as a source of methane to the atmosphere.

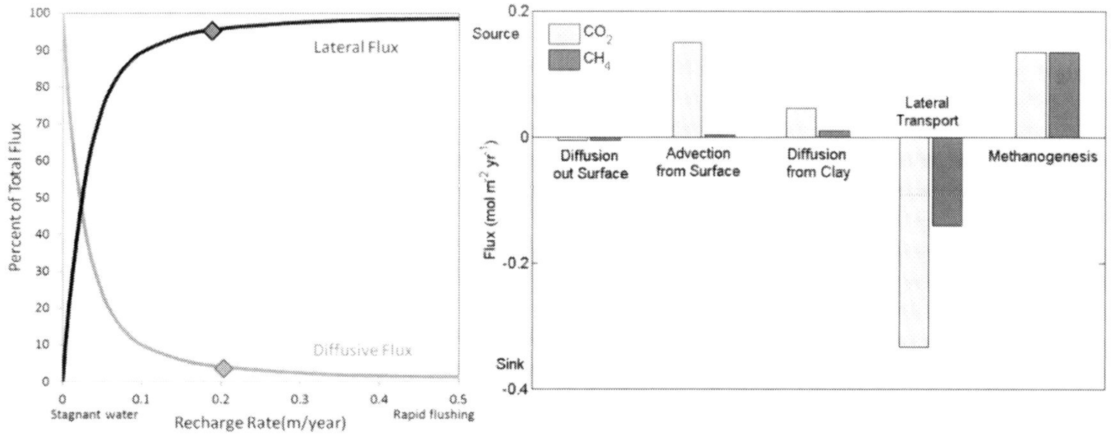

Figure 2: (a) Dependence of lateral and diffusive flux on recharge rate. Diamonds show recharge value of 0.2m/yr appropriate to our site.
(b) Modeled production and fluxes of carbon dioxide (CO_2) and methane (CH_4) show the important role of vertical advection and lateral transport.

CONCLUSION

We found that only a small fraction of the CH_4 produced in the deep peat escapes by diffusion, with other pathways playing a more important role. We collected field data and used it to improve our understanding of CH_4 production and transport within a tropical peat dome. We used the carbon isotopic composition of CH_4 and CO_2 to determine the source and pathway of CH_4 production. We coupled these findings with a model based on the site hydrology to evaluate the production and transport of CH_4 within the peat. Our results show that advection plays an important role in tropical peatlands, and that only a small proportion of the CH_4 produced in the deep peat diffuses out the peat surface. At this site, flow is much greater than production, so an order of magnitude more CH_4 is transported through the system by lateral transport than by diffusion. As a result, current estimates of CH_4 production in tropical peatlands are likely to be significantly underestimated. However, shallow porewater CH_4 data suggests that oxidation plays an important role in the root zone. Much of the CH_4 transported laterally is likely oxidized before it reaches the atmosphere. More detailed seasonal data on oxidation is required to fully evaluate the CH_4 fluxes to the atmosphere from tropical peatlands. Finally, although near-surface processes such as tree transport are not assessed here, they are anticipated to further increase total CH_4 fluxes from the ecosystem. A focus on chamber measurements means that current studies may account for <10% of the total CH_4 produced in the peat. This highlights the important role of hydrology in governing the carbon cycle in tropical peatlands.

ACKNOWLEDGEMENTS

We thank Pudek ak Zulkiflee and Boy ak Incham for their extensive help in the field. This research was partially supported by the National Research Foundation Singapore through the MIT-Singapore Alliance for

Research and Technology, the MIT Environmental Solutions Initiative, and the National Science Foundation under grant numbers 1114155 and 1114161.

REFERENCES

1. Adji, F. F., Y. Hamada, U. Darang, S.Limin, and R. Hatano. 2014. *Soil Science and Plant Nutrition* 60: 216–30.
2. Anderson, J.A.R. 1983. *Ecosystems of the World 4b*, 181–99.
3. Arai, H., A. Hadi, U. Darung, S. Limin, R. Hatano, and K. Inubushi. 2014. *Soil Science and Plant Nutrition* 60(4): 577–85.
4. Calvert, G.D., J.R. Durig, and J.S. Esterle. 1991. *International Journal of Coal Geology* 17(2): 171–88.
   Chanton, J. P., P. H. Glaser, L. S. Chasar, D. J. Burdige, M. E. Hines, D. I. Siegel, L. B. Tremblay, and W. T. Cooper. 2008. *Global Biogeochemical Cycles* 22(4).
5. Chanton, J.P., L.Chaser, P. Glaser, and D. Siegel. 2005. *Stable Isotopes and Biosphere-Atmosphere Interactions*, eds. L.B. Flanagan, J.R. Ehleringer, and D.E. Pataki. San Diego, CA:Elsevier-Academic Press, 85–105.
6. Chanton, J.P. 2005. *Organic Geochemistry* 36: 753–68.
7. Corbett, E.J., D.J. Burdige, M.M. Tfaily, A.R. Dial, W.T. Cooper, P.H. Glaser, and J.P. Chanton. 2013. *Global Biogeochemical Cycles* 27(4): 1163–74.
8. Couwenberg, J., R. Dommain, and H. Joosten. 2010. *Global Change Biology* 16(6): 1715–32.
9. Dommain, R., A.R. Cobb, H. Joosten, P.H. Glaser, A.F.L. Chua, L. Gandois, F.M. Kai, A. Noren, K.A. Salim, N.S.H. Su'ut, and C.F. Harvey. 2015. *Journal of Geophysical Research: Biogeosciences*
10. Furukawa, Y., K. Inubushi, M. Ali, A.M. Itang, and H. Tsuruta. 2005. *Nutrient Cycling in Agroecosystems* 71: 81–91.
11. Gandois, L., A.R. Cobb, I.C. Hei, L.Lim, K.A. Salim, and C. F. Harvey. 2013. *Biogeochemistry* 114: 183–99.
12. Gandois, L., R. Teisserenc, A.R. Cobb, H.I. Chieng, L.B.L. Lim, A.S. Kamariah, A. Hoyt, and C.F. Harvey. 2014. *Geochimica et Cosmochimica Acta* 137: 35–47.
13. Gupta, V., K.A. Smemo, J.B. Yavitt, D. Fowle, B. Branfireun, and N. Basiliko. 2013. *Environmental Science & Technology* 47(15): 8273–79.
14. Hadi, A., M. Haridi, K. Inubushi, E.Purnomo, F. Razie, and H. Tsuruta. 2001. *Microbes and Environments* 16(2): 79–86.
15. Hadi, A., K. Inubushi, Y. Furukawa, E. Purnomo, M. Rasmadi, and H. Tsuruta. 2005. *Nutrient Cycling in Agroecosystems* 71(1): 73–80.
16. Hooijer, A., S. Page, J. Jauhiainen, W.Lee, X. Lu, A. Idris, and G. Anshari. 2012. *Biogeosciences* 9: 1053–71.
17. Hooijer, A., S. Page, J.G. Canadell, M. Silvius, J. Kwadijk, H. Wösten, and J. Jauhiainen. 2010. *Biogeosciences* 7(5): 1505–14.
18. Inubushi, K., A. Hadi, M. Okazaki, and K. Yonebayashi. 1998. *Hydrological Processes* 12: 2073–80.
19. Inubushi, K., S. Otake, Y. Furukawa, N. Shibasaki, M. Ali, A.M. Itang, and H. Tsuruta. 2005. *Nutrient Cycling in Agroecosystems*: 93–99.
20. Jauhiainen, J., H.Takahashi, J.Heikkinen, P.Martikainen, and H.Vasanders. 2005. *Global Change Biology* 11: 1788–97.
21. Melling, L., R. Hatano, and K.J. Goh. 2005. *Soil Biology and Biochemistry* 37(8): 1445–53.
22. Miettinen, J., C. Shi, and S.C. Liew. 2012. *Frontiers in Ecology and the Environment* 10(3): 124–28.
23. Moore, S., V. Gauci, C. D. Evans, and S. E. Page. 2011. *Biogeosciences* 8: 901–9.
24. Moore, S., C.D. Evans, S.E. Page, M.H. Garnett, T.G. Jones, C. Freeman, A. Hooijer, A.J. Wiltshire, S.H. Limin, and V. Gauci. 2013. *Nature* 493: 660–63
25. Page, S.E., J.O. Rieley, and C.J. Banks. 2011. *Global Change Biology* 17(2): 798–818.
26. Pangala, S.R., S. Moore, E.R.C. Hornibrook, and V. Gauci. 2013. *New Phytologist* 197(2): 524–31.
27. Smemo, K.A., and J.B. Yavitt. 2011. *Biogeosciences* 8(3): 779–93.
28. Whiticar, M.J. 1999. *Chemical Geology* 161(1-3): 291–314.

Abstract No: A-193

ONCE THE TREES HAVE GONE: EVALUATING CHANGES IN WATER QUALITY IN RESTORED BLANKET BOG OF THE FLOW COUNTRY, SCOTLAND

Roxane Andersen[1*], Richard Taylor[1], Paul Gaffney[1], Neil Cowie[2] and Alan Youngson[1]

[1]*Environmental Research Institute, University of the Highlands and Islands, UK*
[2]*Royal Society for the Protection of Birds (RSPB) Scotland, UK*

**Corresponding author: roxane.andersen@uhi.ac.uk*

INTRODUCTION

Covering over 4000 km^2, the Flow Country peatlands of Caithness and Sutherland are Europe's largest blanket bog. It is the UK's single largest terrestrial carbon store. It is also home to a wide range of designated species, including rare breeding waders (Lindsay *et al.*, 1988). What's more, it is at the source of many Atlantic salmon (*Salmo salar)* rivers; hence supports sports fishing – a critical income for rural areas in the Highlands.

In an attempt to improve productivity and grazing, a lot of hill drains were dug in those upland peatlands in the early 20th century. A more radical land-use change was initiated in the 1950s due to post-war timber shortages and, fuelled by tax-incentives, by the 1980s, around a fifth of all UK peatlands were covered in coniferous plantations. In the Flow Country, trees were planted in blocks altogether covering approximately 680 km^2, leading to the fragmentation of a once open landscape (Stroud *et al.*, 1987). Growing concerns about the impact on biodiversity and the potential losses of carbon (Cannell *et al.*, 1992) caused by this disturbance led to the first large-scale forest-to-bog restoration initiative. Between 1997and 2012, drains were blocked over 150 km^2 and trees were removed from 50 km^2 in the Flow Country.

Documenting the detrimental impact of afforestation on wader populations in adjacent open bog (Wilson *et al.*, 2014) led to changes in policy, whereby forestry needs to be removed to create buffer areas around designated peatland sites, and further planting on peat >40 cm is not permitted (FCS 2015). Recently, the Scottish Government pledged financial support to peatland restoration, with the expectation that this could contribute to meeting the reduction in greenhouse gas emission targets (Chapman *et al.*, 2012) and biodiversity and habitat directive targets (SNH peatland strategy).

Finally, with most plantations coming to the end of their growth rotation period (ca. 40 years) and now being ready for harvest, forest-to-bog restoration is likely to be a significant land-use change over the coming decade. Where initially small trees were rolled into furrows and collector drains blocked, as the trees got bigger over time, restoration methods had to change. Methods like whole tree harvest, mulching and brashing involve more machinery, which creates more initial disturbance. Sedimentation, pH alterations and metal pollution brought about by forestry and by forest-to-bog restoration could all impact freshwater biology (Ramchunder *et al.*, 2009) but this impact is poorly documented thus far. An overall better understanding of the consequences, timescales and extent of changes caused by restoration of afforested peatlands is needed to further inform management options.

Here we present our current understanding of how some of the key ecosystem processes respond to restoration. We present evidence gathered across a range of sites in the Flow Country and beyond to 1) evaluate how water quality changes over time following restoration and 2) assess the impact of restoration methods on known Atlantic salmon (*Salmo salar*) spawning sites. By documenting the short- and long-term impact of forest-to-bog restoration on ecosystem functions, we aim to provide sound evidence to support policy development, but also to feedback to practitioners which can improve the effectiveness of restoration.

METHODS

We conducted a small study in the Dyke River, a tributary of the Halladale River located in Surtherland, Scotland. The Dyke River and a number of burns and streams which feed it are known habitats for Atlantic salmon. In autumn 2014, 10 pre-identified Salmon spawning sites, known as "redd" sites, in the Dyke River were covered with a slab to prevent spawning. They were divided as follows: four spawning sites were located upstream of a forestry plantation in an area of blanket bog (upstream), three sites were within a section of the plantation where restoration management was ongoing (forest-to-bog) and three sites were downstream of the restored area, still in the plantation (downstream) (Fig 1). Artificial arrays divided in tiers (75cm, 175cm and 275cm) were set up in the stream bed at each site while sediment baskets were set up in the upstream and downstream sites only. We measured pH, dissolved oxygen (DO), electrical conductivity (EC) and sediment accumulation periodically between

November 2014 and March 2015, covering the length of Salmon egg incubation and hatching. This also covered the period during and immediately after management, which included tree felling and harvest as well as drain blocking.

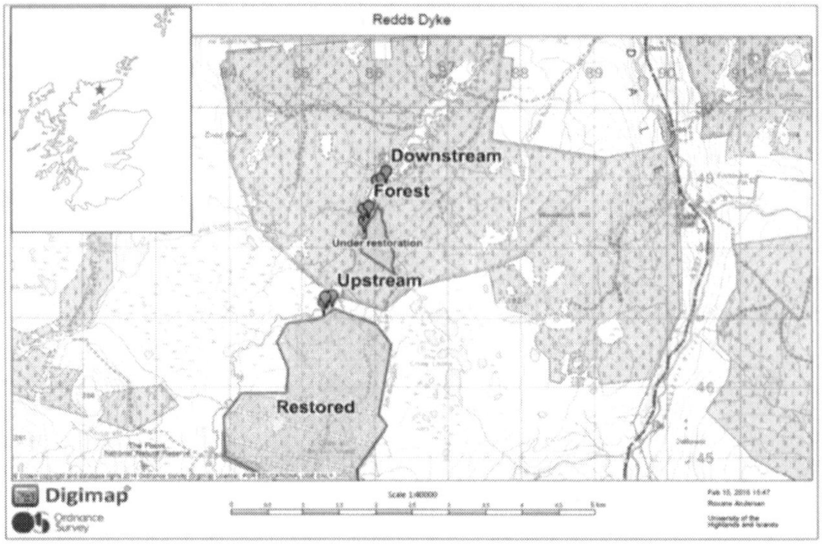

Figure 2: Map of the sampling locations: four sampling points upstream of the Dyke forest, receiving water from open bog and restored (2003-2004) area, three sampling points receiving water from the area under restoration and three points downstream, receiving water from forestry.

All the water samples were taken in the same stretch of river, hence are not independent from each other and this spatial auto-correlation can be modelled and taken into account in the comparison of sites. To do so, we constructed an asymmetric eigenvector map (AEM) and created a matrix of spatial variable describing the spatial connectivity between each sampling point as dictated by the direction of the flow (upstream to forest to downstream) (Blanchet *et al.*, 2010). We then used a redundancy analysis (RDA) to test whether any of the spatial variables generated were significantly related to the four physico-chemical parameters. This allowed us to understand whether a sampling point was likely to be influenced by what happened upstream of it and if so, how far the effect was likely to extend to. We also used redundancy analysis to assess whether stage height was related to the physico-chemical parameters. As it was significantly related, we then tested how the chemical parameters varied across depths within sites over time once the influence of stage height had been taken into account.

RESULTS AND DISCUSSION

Summary of impact from restoration on water and water courses

Many studies have looked at the impact of drainage and/or drain blocking on stream properties (e.g. Ramchunder *et al.*, 2009), but fewer have looked at the impact of tree removal and drain blocking combined. Some studies have shown increases in sediment load and water run-off following conifer afforestation; a consequence of the mechanical (e.g. digging) and the physical disturbances (e.g. cracking, drying) of the peat mass and the mineral soil underneath (Ratcliffe and Thompson, 1988; Ramchunder *et al.*, 2009; Clarke *et al.*, 2015). The disturbance associated with restoration could trigger similar responses. A notable impact of forest-to-bog on water quality is the increased nutrient (N, P) concentration and export related to decomposition of brash and needle litter left on site (Table 1). This impact has been noted both in the pore water (Asam *et al.*, 2014) and in stream water in catchments where restoration work was undertaken (Smith, 2015, O'Driscoll *et al.*, 2014a, Rodgers *et al.*, 2010; Clarke *et al.*, 2015), but usually subsides after two to four years. O'Driscoll *et al.* (2014b) suggested that buffer areas between forestry and rivers could be a potential option to reduce phosphorus (P) load and potential harm to freshwater organisms. As well as nutrients, in some cases, increased metal (Al, Fe) concentrations and exports have been observed (Müller *et al.*, 2012) and have been related to changes in pH and organic matter, and to chemical composition of the peat.

Table 1: Summary impacts of forest-to-bog restoration on pore and stream water chemistry DOC = Dissolved Organic Carbon, P = Phosphorus, N = Nitrogen, SRP = Soluble Reactive Phosphorus,

Variable impacted	Pore water	Receiving burns and streams
DOC	[DOC] in shallow afforested peat	Export depends on catchment properties
P	↑ [P] during the first 2-4 years as needles and brash decay	↑ Export total and SRP during first 2 years; Buffer zone method could be used efficiently in peatland forestry to moderate ↑ [P] concentrations
N	↑ [N] and mineralisation rates	↑ NO_3 export
Suspended solids (SS)	N/A	↑ total SS during peak flow events, substantial ↑ SS during windrowing
Metals	↑ [Al], [Mn]	Export of Fe and Al; dependent on peat characteristics Changes in seasonal cycles of biologically active (C, Si, P) and organically complexed (Fe, Al) elements.
References	*Asam et al., 2014; Gaffney et al., 2014; Müller & Tankere Müller, 2012;Smith 2015*	*Vinjinli, 2012; Asam et al 2014; Rodgers et al 2010; Clarke et al., 2015; O'Driscoll et al., 2014a; Müller & Tankere Müller, 2012; Müller et al., 2015*

Influence of connectivity

In this case, we found that the spatial connectivity between the 10 sampling sites was not significantly related to the water chemistry parameters measured ($F=0.28$, $p=0.99$). A possible explanation is that each stretch of the river sampled receives water from different subsidiary burns but also from near-surface through flow and overland flow, thereby creating a dilution effect. This is the case in many other UK rivers which drain areas of upland blanket peat (Holden and Burt, 2003). Thus, it seems that the immediate influence of those micro-catchments may be important in determining the chemistry of a given sampling location. Similar results have been observed by Shah (2015) in a study looking at the impact of afforestation on water chemistry in the Halladale River, in which the Dyke River flows.

Differences in chemistry between sites

For EC, DO and pH, the three sites presented the same behaviour over time, which suggests that restoration management (felling and drain blocking) has little or no influence on the water quality over the very short term (months). The temporal patterns were similar across depths (only surface data shown). For EC and DO, the values were highest in January and February in all sites. The pH values were inversely related to stage height (Fig. 2), with higher pH at low stage heights and vice-versa. The opposite trend was observed for EC and DO. It is known that during low flows, acidity can be neutralized by calcium carbonate ($CaCO_3$) in streambed sediments (Miller *et al.*, 2001).

Differences in sediment load between sites

The mass of the sediments in the sediment basket also appeared more influenced by the season and inherent catchment characteristics than by management. Generally, there was a decrease in sediments in both sites (upstream and downstream) over time, with proportionally greater reductions in the downstream site. Overall, the upstream sites, which mostly drain open blanket bog and older restored sites, received more sediments than the downstream sites, which drain afforested and restored sections (Fig. 3). This could be related to sediment traps installed along the collector drains as part of the restoration management, which appear to effectively mitigate any potential impact of the machinery and the physical disturbance.

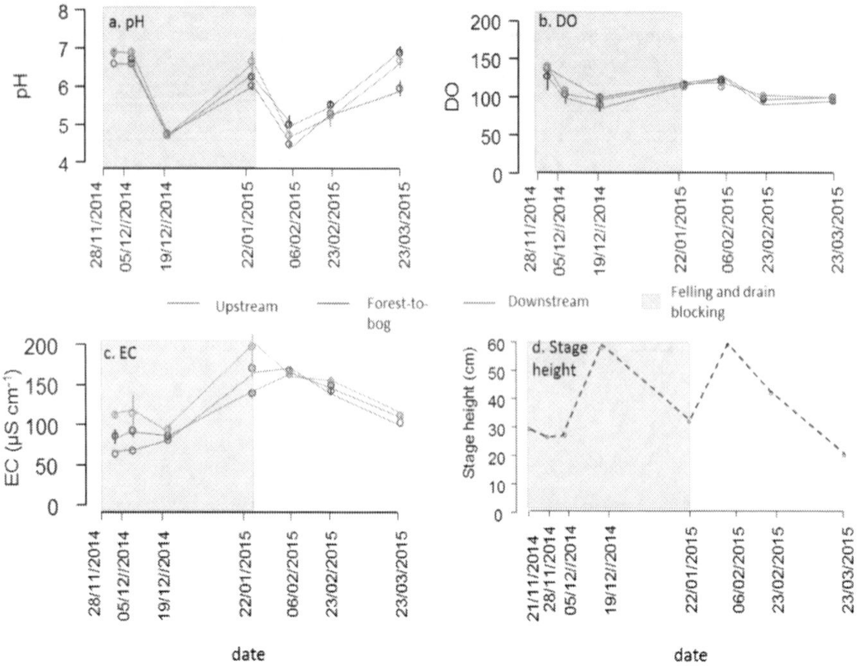

Figure 3: Temporal trends for a) surface pH, b) surface oxygen (DO), c) surface electrical conductivity (EC) and d) Stage height (height of water in the river) measured in the River Dyke in sites upstream, within and downstream of the restoration work between November 2014 and March 2015. Samples were taken prior, during and after the restoration work.

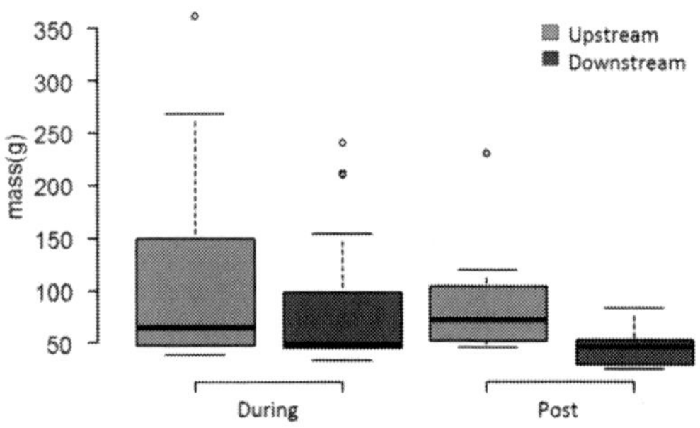

Figure 4: Changes in sediment mass in the Dyke river bed in sites upstream and downstream of restoration work between November 2014 and March 2015. Samples were taken during and post management (felling and drain blocking).

CONCLUSION

While there are documented impacts of forest-to-bog restoration on the water quality both *in situ* and in receiving water course, our study demonstrates no immediate impact of management on sediment load on the river bed, nor on EC, DO and pH in the river Dyke at known spawning sites. We noted that compared to open and older restored bog, forested areas could increase the sediment export but sediment traps appear effective at reducing the load associated with management and disturbance. We also observed an influence of seasonality on the physico-chemistry of the river associated with stage height, and a notable influence of the micro-catchment properties, which might have been misinterpreted if we had not had a control-impact design.

In summary, short-term changes associated with management are likely to be catchment-specific and influenced by local climatic conditions. From a freshwater biodiversity perspective, management should aim to minimise and mitigate short-term changes/impacts for example through installing sediment traps. In any case, it may be argued that short-lived ecosystem changes resulting from disturbance and improved water quality arising from restoration may still be better than longer-term chemical and physical alteration to water courses caused by continued forestry plantations. Further research should aim to assess the direct responses of freshwater organisms to forest-to-bog restoration management, and understand the hydrological processes driving the chemical changes at a wider catchment scale and over longer time-periods.

REFERENCES

1. Asam, ZZ., Nieminen, M., O'Driscoll, C., O'Connor, M., Sarkkola, S., Kaila, A., Sana, A., Rodgers, M. Zhan, X., & Xiao, L. (2014). Export of phosphorus and nitrogen from lodgepole pine (*Pinus contorta*) brash windrows on harvested blanket peat forests. Ecological Engineering, 64, 161-170.
2. Blanchet, F. G., Legendre, P., & Borcard, D. (2008). Modelling directional spatial processes in ecological data. Ecological modelling, 215(4), 325-336.
3. Cannell, M. G. R., Dewar, R. C., & Pyatt, D. G. (1993). Conifer plantations on drained peatlands in Britain: a net gain or loss of carbon? Forestry, 66(4), 353-369.
4. Chapman, S., Artz, R., & Donnelly, D. (2012). Carbon Savings from Peat Restoration. ClimateXChange enquiry, (1205-02), 1-17.
5. Clarke, J., Kelly-Quinn, M., Blacklocke, S., & Bruen, M. (2015). The effect of forest windrowing on physico-chemical water quality in Ireland. Science of Total Environment, 514, 155-169.
6. Forestry Commission Scotland. (2014) Forestry on peatland habitats: Supplementary guidance to support the FC Forestsand Peatland Habitats Guideline Note (2000).
7. Gaffney, P., Andersen, R., Taggart, M., Hancock, M., Robinson, R. (2014). Aquatic measures in the Dyke forest, prior to forest-to-bog restoration. Book of Abstracts, Flow Country Research Conference II: Looking forward. 4-7 March 2014, Thurso (Scotland).
8. Holden, J. and Burt, T.P. (2003). Hydrological studies in blanket peat: the significance of the acrotelm catotelm. Journal of Ecology, 91, 86–102.
9. Lindsay, R., Charman, D. J., Everingham, F., O'reilly, R. M., Palmer, M. A., Rowell, T. A., & Stroud, D. A. (1988). The flow country: the peatlands of Caithness and Sutherland.
10. Miller, J.D., Adamson, J.K. and Hirst, D. (2001) Trends in stream water quality in environmental Change Network upland catchments: the first 5 years. Science of the Total Environment, 265, 27–38.
11. Müller, F.L., Chang, K.C., Lee, C.L., & Chapman, S.J. (2015). Effects of temperature, rainfall and conifer felling practices on the surface water chemistry of northern peatlands. Biogeochemistry, 126(3), 343-362.
12. Müller FL, Tankéré-Muller SP. (2012). Seasonal variations in surface water chemistry at disturbed and pristine peatland sites in the Flow Country of northern Scotland. Science of the Total Environment, 435: 351-362.
13. O'Driscoll, C., O'Connor, M., de Eyto, E., Poole, R., Rodgers, M., Zhan, X., Nieminen, M. and Xiao, L. (2014a). Whole-tree harvesting and grass seeding as potential mitigation methods for phosphorus export in peatland catchments. Forest Ecology and Management, 319, 176-185.
14. O'Driscoll, C., O'Connor, M., de Eyto, E., Rodgers, M., & Xiao, L. (2014b). Creation and functioning of a buffer zone in a blanket peat forested catchment. Ecological Engineering, 62, 83-92.
15. Ramchunder, SJ, Brown, LE, & Holden, J. (2009). Environmental effects of drainage, drain-blocking and prescribed vegetation burning in UK upland peatlands. Progress in Physical Geography, 33(1), 49-79.
16. Ratcliffe, DA. and Thompson, DBA. (1988): The British uplands: their ecological character and international signifi cance. Oxford: Blackwell.
17. Rodgers, M., O'Connor, M., Healy, M. G., O'Driscoll, C., Nieminen, M., Poole, R., Muller, M. and Xiao, L. (2010). Phosphorus release from forest harvesting on an upland blanket peat catchment. Forest Ecology and Management, 260(12), 2241-2248.
18. Smith, B. (2015) Assessment of carbon and nutrient export from a peatland windfarm construction site. Doctoral Thesis, University of Glasgow, Scotland.
19. Shah, NW, Nisbet, TR., Broadmeadow, SB., (2015) The Effects of Conifer Afforestation on a Sensitive Freshwater System – the Upper Halladale Catchment. Book of Abstracts, Flow Country Research Conference III: Taking stock. 27-30 October 2015, Thurso (Scotland).
20. Stroud DA, Reed TM, Pienkowski MW, Lindsay RA (1987). Birds, bogs and forestry The peatlands of Caithness and Sutherland, Nature Conservancy Council, Peterborough.
21. Vinjili, S. (2012). Landuse change and organic carbon exports from a peat catchment of the Halladale River in the Flow Country of Sutherland and Caithness. PhD Thesis, University of St Andrews.
22. Wilson JD, Anderson R, Bailey S, Chetcuti J, Cowie NR, Hancock MH, Quine CP, Russell N, Leigh S, Thompson D. (2014) Modelling edge effects of mature forest plantations on peatland waders informs landscape-scale conservation. Journal of Applied Ecology, 51: 204-213.

Abstract No: A-289

PROFILING WATER TABLE DEPTH AND SOIL MOISTURE IN A DRAINED PEAT SWAMP HOSTING OIL PALM

Susan Waldron[1*], Stephanie Evers[2], Ralph Burton[3] and Rory Padfield[4]

[1] *School of Geographical and Earth Sciences, University of Glasgow, Glasgow, G12 8QQ, Scotland*
[2] *University of Nottingham Malaysia Campus, Kuala Lumpur, Malaysia*
[3]*National Centre for Atmospheric Science (Weather), Environment; School of Earth and Environment, University of Leeds, Leeds LS2 9J, United Kingdom*
[4]*Malaysia Japan International Institute of Technology (MJIIT), University of Technology Malaysia, Kuala Lumpur, 54100, Malaysia*

**Corresponding author: Susan.Waldron@glasgow.ac.uk*

Oil palm is a crop highly valued for its oil. Land conversion to host oil palm is proceeding rapidly due to the economic value in supplying the food and biofuels market. Large and adjacent plantations are transforming the landscape globally, but particularly in Malaysia where the footprint of plantation area has increased by 900% since 1975. Malaysia currently accounts for 39% of world palm oil production and 44% of world exports. For this, areas of native tropical forests have been cleared and drained, including those on peatland swamps, such that national forest cover in oil palm producing areas has declined considerably over the same period. This change in land use is contentious and the scientific community is responding to provide a science base for environmental impacts to support decision-making. For example, multiple organizations are seeking to understand the carbon footprint and changes in biodiversity of such land use change; soil gas effluxes are being measured and atmospheric chemistry changes have been observed. Crucial in many of these processes is how wet the soil is and so the position of the water table. At a drained peat body in South Selangor hosting one of the regionally oldest plantations we installed a grid of 10 pressure transducers to measure water table depth and soil moisture probes at -5 and – 70 cm, all logging every 30 minutes. We have collected data since June 2014, allowing assessment of not only annual but inter-annual variation. Already we know that the water table can be as low as -120 cm, and soil moisture at -70 cm can be less than at the surface. This research suggests that for a considerable part of the year, the site is being over-drained, so revision of management practices and policy is strongly recommended.

***Keywords**:-*

Abstract No: A-081

THE IMPACT OF LAND COVER CHANGE ON THE HYDRAULIC CONDUCTIVITY IN TROPICAL PEATLANDS

Sofyan Kurnianto[1*], James T. Peterson[2], John Selker[3], J. Boone Kauffman[1] and Daniel Murdiyarso[4]

[1]*Dept. of Fisheries and Wildlife, Oregon State University, USA*
[2]*US Geological Survey, Oregon Cooperative Fish and Wildlife Research Unit, Department of Fisheries and Wildlife, Oregon State University, USA*
[3]*Biological and Ecological Engineering Dept., Oregon State University, USA*
[4]*Center for International Forestry Research, Indonesia*

**Corresponding author: Sofyan.Kurnianto@oregonstate.edu; kurnians@oregonstate.edu*

SUMMARY

Hydraulic conductivity is one of the most important parameters that describe peat properties related to water movement through the peat profile. In the application of peat hydrology, the information about saturated hydraulic conductivity is required to estimate the amount of water needed to maintain the saturation condition in the peat dome and is also required to simulate the peat water table depth and groundwater flow. However, some uncertainties regarding hydraulic conductivity in the tropical peatlands especially those related to the effect of peat swamp forest conversion on hydraulic conductivity remain. Hydraulic conductivity was estimated at four different land cover types in West Kalimantan, Indonesia. We utilized the slug test method to estimate the hydraulic conductivity at three depths (1.0, 3.5, and 6.0 m) and interpreted the data based on the Bouwer and Rice (1976) approach. In total, 324 wells were installed in 21 sites including five sites in shrubs, five sites in oil palm plantations and eight sites in forests and three sites in recently burnt forest with six replications for each site. The results show that forested peatlands have higher conductivity with an average of 0.63 ± 0.36 m d^{-1} (mean ± s.e.) compare with oil palm of 0.20 ± 0.13 m d^{-1} and shrubs of 0.16 ± 0.08 m d^{-1}.
The relationship between hydraulic conductivity land cover types, measurement depth and peat properties such as carbon concentration, loss on ignition, bulk density, and degree of decomposition, were assessed using hierarchical linear models. Results depicted that hydraulic conductivity was likely be the best explained by the measurement depth, bulk density, and forests-non forests land cover. However, carbon concentration and loss on ignition provided a very small portion for explaining the variability of hydraulic conductivity.

Keywords: *hydroecology, permeability, forest conversion, eco-hydrology, peat properties*

INTRODUCTION

Hydraulic conductivity is an important parameter that describes the ability of water to flow through a soil profile. In the application of peat hydrology, information about saturated hydraulic conductivity is required to estimate the amount of water needed to maintain the saturation condition in the peat dome (Dommain *et al.*, 2010). Hydraulic conductivity is a characteristic parameter required to simulate the depth of water table in tropical peatlands *(Wösten et al.*, 2006). Kelly *et al.* (2014) suggested that the saturated hydraulic conductivity in tropical Peruvian peatlands varied among different types of peat in minerotrophic and ombrotrophic systems. However, few studies have examined how the hydraulic conductivity of peatland varies with land cover types. In addition, the relationship between peat properties, degree of decomposition, and saturated hydraulic condition remain unclear. Therefore, we estimated the saturated hydraulic conductivity at different land cover types to address the following research questions:

1. What is the effect of the land cover on the saturated hydraulic conductivity?
2. What are the relationships between peat properties and hydraulic conductivity?
3. Do the relationships between peat properties and the hydraulic conductivity differ with land cover?
4. What is the distribution of hydraulic conductivity within the peat column?

We hypothesize that hydraulic conductivity in forests is higher than other land cover types because forested peat is less disturbed due to the human activities. Therefore, peat forest would have lower bulk density and more porosity than any land cover types and eventually higher hydraulic conductivity compare to peat underlain other land cover types. To answer these questions, we used hierarchical linear models to statistically evaluate the relationship between hydraulic conductivity, land cover, peat properties, and their interaction. Outputs from these models including the estimated model coefficients and measures of uncertainty that can be used to assess the relative importance of peat properties and land cover types on saturated hydraulic conductivity.

METHODS

Research design

The field research was conducted in Ketapang, West Kalimantan, Indonesia that could be classified as the coastal peatland because its distance to the coast is less than 20 km. To assess the effect of land cover type on the saturated hydraulic conductivity (later identified as K_s), measurements were performed in 21 sites across four different land cover types comprising eight sites in forests, three sites in recently burnt forests, five sites in shrubs, and another fives sites oil palm plantation.

At each site, a 120 m long transect was installed with six plots set at 30 m intervals. Wells were established at each plot within a circle of 2-m diameter along a line that was perpendicular to the transect and K_s was measured at three depths: 1.0, 3.5, and 6.0 m. If the peat depth in a plot was less than 6.0 m, the deepest measurement was taken above the mineral layer. For shrub and oil palm plantation sites, transects were set perpendicular to drainage canals with the first plot set 20 m away from the canals.

To study the influence of the peat properties on K_s, peat samples were collected for each plot and depth where K_s was measured. The peat samples, then, were transferred to the soil laboratory of Bogor Agricultural University for peat analysis, such as carbon concentration (C), bulk density (BD), and loss on ignition (LOI). The degree of humification was determined in the field qualitatively following the Von-Post method.

Data analysis

K_s calculation

The saturated hydraulic conductivity, K_s was analyzed with the Bouwer and Rice (1976) method using

$$K_s = \frac{r_c{}^2 \ln\left({}^{R_e}/_{r_w}\right)}{2L}\frac{1}{t}\ln\frac{H_0}{H_w},$$

where H_o is the initial head change and H_w is the head change over time. Since K_s, r_c, R_e, r_w and L are constant, the value of $\frac{1}{t}\ln\frac{H_o}{H_w}$ should be constant and can be estimated by fitting a straight line in a plot of the relationship between time, t, and log (H_w/H_0). The term $\ln\left({}^{R_e}/_{r_w}\right)$ was calculated as:

$$\ln\left({}^{R_e}/_{r_w}\right) = \left(\frac{1.1}{\ln\left({}^{H}/_{r_w}\right)} + \frac{A + B.\ln\left({}^{(m-L)}/_{r_w}\right)}{{}^{(L-d)}/_{r_w}}\right)^{-1}$$

and in the case of a well fully penetrating an aquifer, $\text{Ln}\left({}^{R_e}/_{r_w}\right)$ was determined using

$$\ln\left({}^{R_e}/_{r_w}\right) = \left(\frac{1.1}{\ln\left({}^{H}/_{r_w}\right)} + \frac{C}{{}^{(L-d)}/_{r_w}}\right)^{-1},$$

where A, B, and C were dimensionless values based on the chart governed by Bouwer and Rice (1976).

Statistical model

We initially evaluated the relationship between peat properties and land cover types on the tropical peatland K_s by using linear regression models. However, the K_s measurements were taken in 21 sites in which six plots were nested within each site and three K_s measurements were made at different depths in each plot. Because the measurements at a site or plot were potentially dependent, we examined residuals from the preliminary analyses and found strong site-level dependence. To account for the spatial dependence related to sites and plots within sites, we use hierarchical linear models (Bryk and Raudenbush 2002) to evaluate the factors related to K_s.

We use a systematic approach to evaluate the relationship between land cover and peat properties on the K_s. Prior to analyses, land cover was coded as a binary variable (0 and 1) for each type and depth predictors were standardized to a mean of zero and standard deviation of one to facilitate model fitting. We then developed a global model that contained all of the variables potentially related to K_s including: C, BD, LOI, measurement depth, and land cover type and used it to determine the random effects that best accounted for the spatial dependence. To do this, we use the global model and evaluated different combination of random effects that included intercept and slopes that varied normally among sites and among plots nested within sites. The model with the best approximating random effects was considered that with the lowest Akaike Information Criteria (AIC; Akaike 1973) with the small-sample bias adjustment (AICc; Hurvich and Tsai 1989). We then used these random effects to identify the factors that best explained variation in K_s by fitting all possible combinations of predictors (21 models). The relative plausibility of each model was estimated by calculating AICc and model weights using the procedures detailed in

Burnham and Anderson (2002). All of the statistical analysis in this study was performed by using R software with the MuMIn package (Barton, 2015) for the AIC analysis.

RESULTS AND DISCUSSION

K_s varied greatly both within and among sites. It ranged from about 0.001 to 10 m/d (Figure 1). The high variability of K_s was observed at all of the sites. The outliers, points located outside of the boxplots tails, also occurred consistently at all of sites. The skewness of K_s, however, was slightly different among land cover types in which forests tended to have right skewness, whereas K_s in oil palm plantations and shrubs skewed to left.

The best approximating random effects for explaining spatial dependence included an intercept and slope for measurement depth that varied among sites. The most plausible hierarchical model for predicting K_s contained the measurement depth, forests land cover, and the interaction between depth and forests land cover. This model was similar to next the best approximating K_s model that contained LOI. Using the model weights and the 1/8 criteria suggested by Royall (1977) for evaluating strength of evidence, only two additional candidate models were considered plausible models for predict K_s and they contained BD, and C as the explanatory variables.

The model selection criterion indicated that the most-likely model to explain variation in K_s did not contain the peat properties. Rather, variation in K_s was best explained by position within the peat column and whether the land cover was forest or non-forest. Saturated hydraulic conductivity was negatively related to depth of measurement indicating K_s decreased downward within a peat column. The random effects also indicated that average K_s and the relationship between K_s and depth varied among sites suggesting a strong spatial component to the relationship. The forest main effect accounted for 14% of the variation in average K_s among sites and the interaction between depth and forest accounted for 12% of this variation. This interaction also was negative, indicating that the effect of land cover decreased with depth. However, the random effects also indicated that there was substantial variability in K_s that could not be explained by the components in the best model.

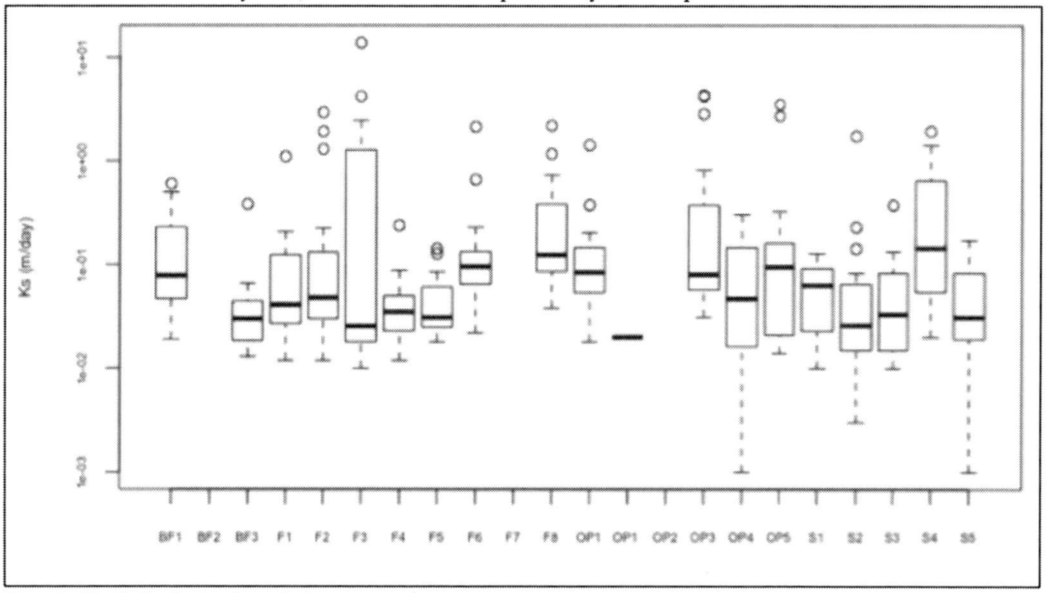

Figure 1: The K_s distribution for each site.

Model selection criteria also indicated that bulk density was a plausible explanation for variation in K_s within and almond sites. Bulk density was, on average, negatively related to Ks. However, the relationship varied greatly among sites and confidence limits for the parameter estimates included zero indicating a lack of precision of the estimate. Model selection criteria also indicated little to no evidence that K_s was related to other properties of peat, LOI and C, which was further supported by very small effect sizes (slopes), i.e., 0.009 and 0.001.

A hierarchical model containing depth of measurement, forests land cover, the depth and forests land cover interaction, and bulk density was also tested to assess the sensitivity of model estimates to the changes in the coefficients. By varying the bulk density and depth coefficients -50% to 50%, the response of K_s depicted the different patterns. The changes in K_s were greater for the peat with higher bulk density. Conversely, in the lower bulk density, the model coefficient perturbation was not really affected hydraulic conductivity. For the depth coefficient, K_s measured close to the surface were more sensitive to changes in the model coefficient than in the deeper peat (Figure 2).

CONCLUSION

The study shows that there was a substantial variability in K_s both within and among sites. The hierarchical model could be used to evaluate the relationship between the peat properties, land cover types and vertical distribution of saturated hydraulic conductivity by incorporating the nested measurement design implemented in this study. In general, hydraulic conductivity was decreased vertically from the peat surface to the deeper position. Forest conversion to other land cover types was likely reduced the peat hydraulic conductivity. However, the relationship among peat properties and hydraulic conductivity was weaker presumably due to the large variability within sites and plots. The parameters in the best approximating model also were unable to account for this predictable spatial variation even when models included all of the predictor variables.

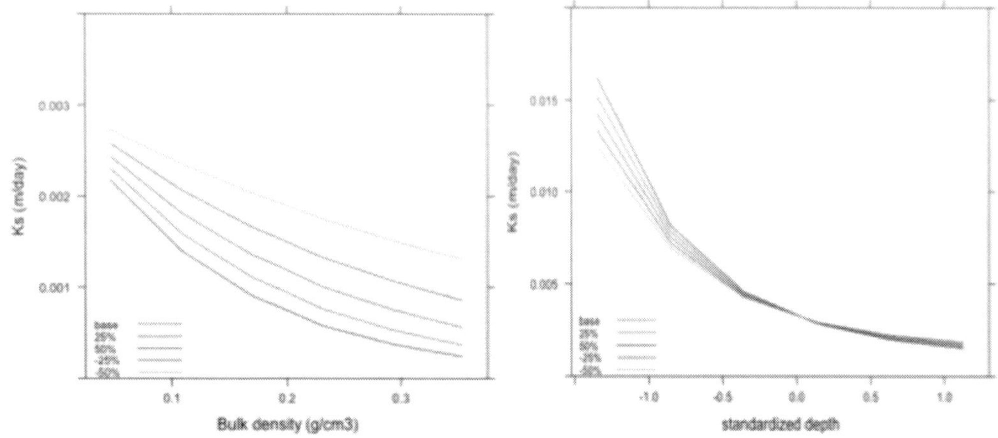

*Figure 2: Plots of the relationship between saturated hydraulic conductivity and bulk density (left) and depth (right) using the equation of log (Ks) = -2.514 – 0.084Depth + 0.17Forest -2.076BD – 0.607Depth*Forest for each varying bulk density coefficient (left) and depth coefficient (right) while keeping the remaining coefficient at the average value.*

ACKNOWLEDGMENTS

The study was supported by the funding from the United States Agency for International Development under the project Kalimantan Wetlands and Climate Studies (KWACs). Part of this study was also funded by Sustainable Wetlands Adaptation and Mitigation Program (SWAMP).

REFERENCES

1. Akaike, H. 1973. Information theory and an extension of the maximum likelihood principle. *Pages* 267-281 *In* Second International Symposium on Information Theory. B.N. Petrov and F. Csaki, *editors*. Akademiai Kiado, Budapest, Hungary.
2. Barton, K. 2015, 'Package MuMIN'. http://cran.r-project.org/web/packages/MuMIn/index.html
3. Bouwer H, Rice R (1976) A slug test for determining hydraulic conductivity of unconfined aquifers.pdf. *Water Resource Research*, **12**, 423–428.
4. Bryk, A. S., and S. W. Raudenbush. 2002. Hierarchical linear models: applications and data analysis methods, 2nd edition. Sage, Newbury Park, California.
5. Burnham, K. P., and D. R. Anderson. 2002. Model selection and inference: an information-theoretic approach. Springer-Verlag, New York.
6. Dommain R, Couwenberg J, Joosten H (2010) Hydrological self-regulation of domed peatlands in south-east Asia and consequences for conservation and restoration. *Mires and Peat, Article*, **6**, 1–17.
7. Kelly TJ, Baird AJ, Roucoux KH, Baker TR, Honorio Coronado EN, Ríos M, Lawson IT (2014) The high hydraulic conductivity of three wooded tropical peat swamps in northeast Peru: measurements and implications for hydrological function. *Hydrological Processes*, **28**, 3373–3387.
8. Hurvich, C. M., and C. Tsai. 1989. Regression and time series model selection in small samples. Biometrika 76:297-307.
9. Royall, R.M. 1997. Statistical evidence: a likelihood paradigm. Chapman and Hall, New York.
10. Wösten H, Hooijer A, Siderius C, Rais DS, Idris A, Rieley J (2006) Tropical Peatland water management modelling of the Air Hitam Laut catchment in Indonesia. *International Journal of River Basin Management*, **4**, 233–244.

Abstract No: A-192

USING LAKE SEDIMENTS IN ESTIMATING POSSIBLE ENVIRONMENTAL IMPACTS OF PEAT PRODUCTION: CASE STUDIES FROM FINLAND

Tuija Vähäkuopus[1], Tommi Kauppila[2], Jari E. Mäkinen[2], Antti E. K. Ojala[3] and Samu E. Valpola[1]

[1]Geological Survey of Finland, Kokkola, Finland
[2] Geological Survey of Finland, Kuopio, Finland
[3]Geological Survey of Finland, Espoo, Finland

**Corresponding author: tuija.vahakuopus@gtk.fi*

SUMMARY

Since the early 2010's, the impact of environmental loading of peat production in lakes and waterways has been widely discussed in Finland. The scarcity of scientific evidence related to influx of allochthonous carbon and the rate of sedimentation in lakes and rivers affected by peat production activities has been a problem and partially prevented a detailed scientific discussion on the topic. In order to provide unbiased data, the Geological Survey of Finland (GTK) launched a sedimentological research project on this topic in 2013. The goal is to compare data from several pairs of lakes on the same catchment, the other lake affected by water coming from peat production area, and the other without any connection to peat production areas. The lakes that are possibly affected by peat production have been chosen using different spatial methods, with a wide geographical coverage over Finland in mind. So far, totally 21 pairs of lakes have been investigated. Four of these lakes were selected for long core sampling. For ensuring a good geographical coverage, another set of 10 lake pairs will be studied during summer 2016. The total amount and areal distribution of sediment was evaluated with echo soundings. Sediment quality, chemical and physical properties, as well as testacean communities were studied from short cores, and the recent sedimentation rate was estimated using a proper dating method (e.g. ^{137}Cs). The description of the long-term sedimentation and natural changes in the study lakes history will be carried out from a long core samples using biostratigraphy and proper dating methods (e.g. ^{14}C, palaeomagnetic dating). Altogether, these results will increase our understanding on if and how peat production activities affect sedimentation rates in lakes and rivers throughout Finland.

Keywords: *lake sediments, peat production, environmental impact, Finland*

INTRODUCTION

Since the early 2010's, the impact of environmental loading of peat production in lakes and waterways has been widely discussed in Finland. Recent legislative actions have emphasized the need for the protection and monitoring of aquatic systems under the influence of peatland use. The scarcity of scientific evidence related to influx of allochthonous carbon and the rate of sedimentation in lakes and rivers affected by peat production activities has been a problem and partially prevented a detailed scientific discussion on the topic. In order to provide unbiased data, the Geological Survey of Finland (GTK) launched a sedimentological research project on this topic in 2013. The goal is to compare data from several pairs of lakes on the same catchment, the other lake affected by water coming from peat production area, and the other without any connection to peat production areas.

MATERIALS AND METHODS

The lakes have been chosen using different spatial methods with several different data in use. The lakes that are possibly affected by peat production are confirmed to be located in the catchment of a peat production area as documented by the environmental permits of peat production. During selection, a perspective on a wide geographical coverage over Finland was used. So far 21 pairs of lakes were investigated of which four lakes were selected for long core sampling. For ensuring a good geographical coverage, another set of 10 lake pairs will be studied during summer 2016 (Fig. 1).

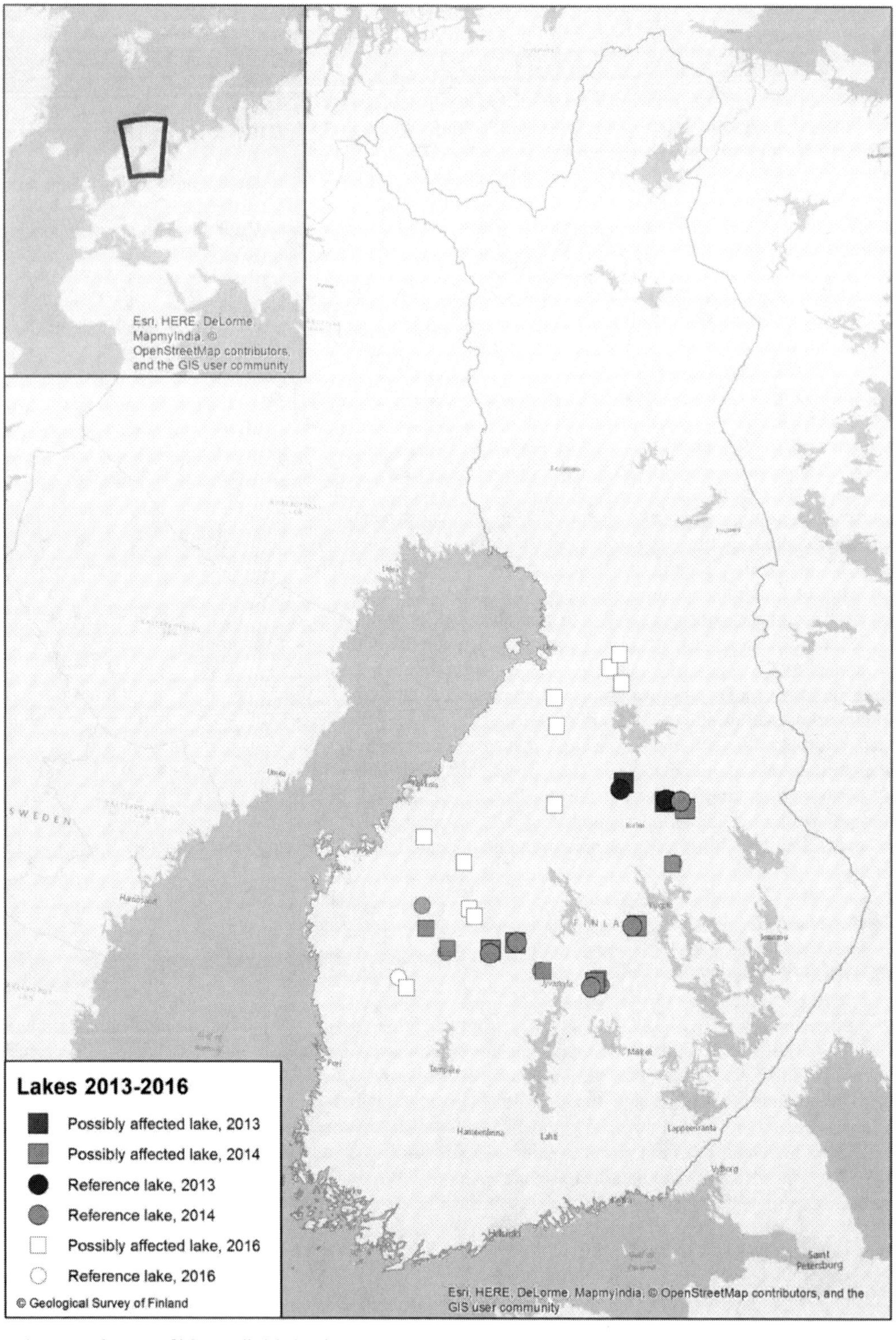

Figure 1: Index map of lakes studied during the years 2013-2016.

A wide variety of physical and chemical analyses have been undertaken to verify the changes in the quality of the sediments and sedimentation history of study lakes. The general characteristics of the lakes and their watersheds have been collected from both reference and possible peat production impacted lakes. Lakes (whenever possible) were surveyed with a sediment penetrating (24 kHz) echo sounder (with MeriData MD 500 Echo sounder and MDSC data collection software) to produce 3D information on the spatial distribution and amounts of soft post-glacial sediments in the basins. The processing and interpretation of sediment units and their boundaries was done with the MDPS Software. Sediment coring from the deepest parts of the lakes or other suitable locations with thick gyttja sections was done with heavy piston gravity corer (PP-corer) and Limnos gravity corer for long and short sediment sections, respectively. The coring method was selected based on objectives of proxy analyses from the sediments. Dating of the cores was done with the ^{137}Cs. Chemical and physical analyses were performed, of which sediment chemical composition was used to obtain information on past land use changes and other stressors that may have affected the lakes (Kauppila *et al.*, in prep.). Physical analyses included e.g. sediment water and dry matter contents and the results from these studies was used together with carbon concentrations and dating results to estimate (apparent) carbon and dry matter accumulation rates for certain periods (Kauppila *et al.*, in prep.). Where possible, testacean communities were also studied.

PRELIMINARY RESULTS

The results from the 2013 and 2014 lake pair cores are under compilation. The results from the echo sounding studies and gyttja coring from the remaining lakes can be expected during the summer 2016 (see Fig. 2). Some complimentary sedimentological results are also expected during the summer 2016. A study compiled by Kauppila *et al.*, (in prep) from one lake pair where results have been obtained earlier will be published later this year. According to the manuscript of Kauppila *et al.*, it seems that the peat production has not affected the distribution and the thickness of lacustrine sediments in Lake Martinjärvi (possibly affected lake) when compared to the reference lake. When the relative increase in coring site-specific carbon and dry matter accumulation was compared, the relative increase was higher in the reference lake, meaning that it eliminates the influence of any differences in sedimentation efficiency between the lakes (Kauppila *et al.*, in prep). As conclusions the manuscript states that peat production has not resulted in excessively thick lake sediment deposits in the impacted lake and when the recent increases in apparent carbon accumulation were compared between the peat mining impacted and the reference lakes, no significant differences were found.

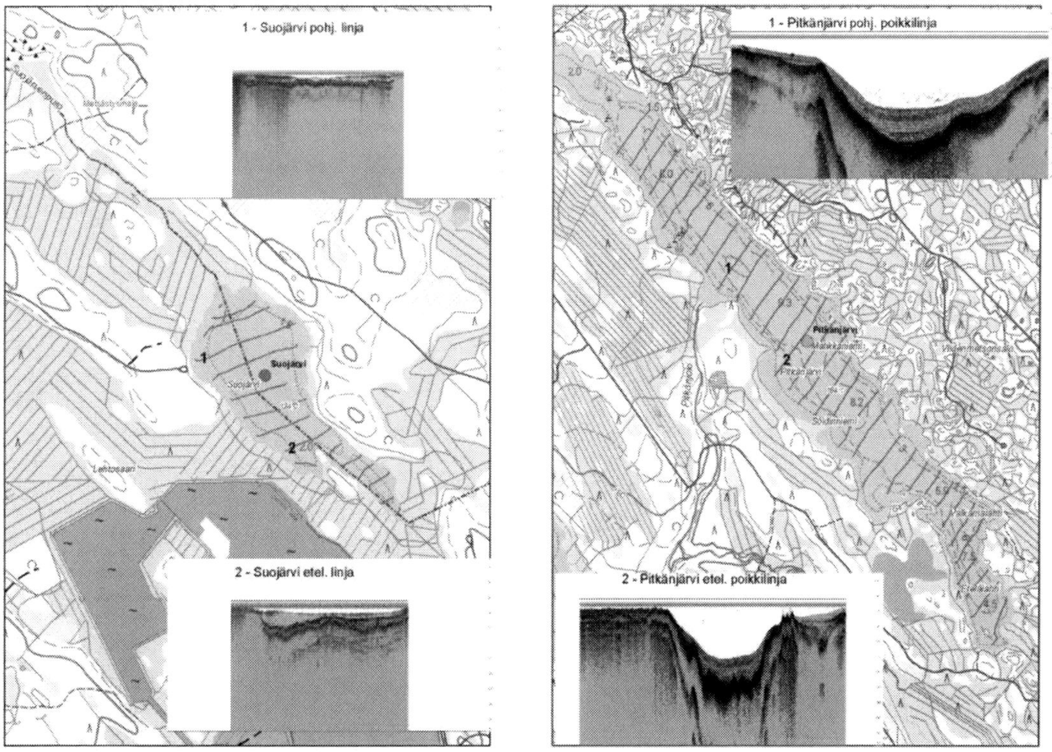

Figure 2: Examples of Echo soundings and profiles from lake Suojärvi (possibly affected lake) and Pitkänjärvi (reference lake), which were surveyed year 2014.

REFERENCES

1. Kauppila, T., Ahokas, T., Nikolajev-Wikström, L., Mäkinen, J., Meriläinen, J., and Tammelin, M. (in prep.). Aquatic effects of peat mining and peatland forest drainage - a comparative sediment study of two adjacent lakes in Central Finland. Manuscript in preparation.

1.3: Peatland Remote Sensing, Aerial & Satellite Imagery

Abstract No: A-021

BIOMASS SITUATION OF MAWAS REGION IN CENTRAL KALIMANTAN BETWEEN 2007 AND 2015 USING LiDAR- AND TerraSAR-X DATA

Viktor Boehm[1*], Michael Schlund[2], Veraldo Liesenberg[3] and Steffen Kuntz[2]

[1]*Kalteng Consultants, Munich, Germany*
[2]*Airbus Defence & Space, Friedrichshafen, Germany*
[3]*Santa Catarina State University, Brazil*

**Corresponding author: viktorboehm@t-online.de*

SUMMARY

Southeast Asian tropical peat swamp forests (PSF) are important for their large carbon stock storage and rich biodiversity. Therefore, the key importance of PSF to ecological processes, their resilience for forest degradation and logging highlights the need for a comprehensive forest monitoring in which LiDAR- and SAR technology may play an important task. Small-footprint LiDAR transects were acquired in August 2007 and 2011 using the Riegl system. The research transects are located at the Mawas Reserve in Central Kalimantan, Indonesia. The transects encompass an ecological peat dome gradient ranging from the river system to the peat dome. The transects faced in the past different forest degradation intensities. Our main objectives were to map changes in the vertical structure of the PSF with the multi-temporal LiDAR, in order to identify both sources and sinks of carbon across the peat dome-shaped gradients. In addition, TerraSAR-X time series were analyzed, whereas TerraSAR-X is a X-band SAR providing consistent and high repetitive coverage due to time and weather independent acquisitions. Subtle changes in the forest canopy are detected with TerraSAR-X due to the high-resolution and radiometric stability. The analysis of TerraSAR-X data between December 2010 and October 2015 show forest logging activities mainly close to the forest edges and channels, where the loggers can transport the logs easily. Analysis of changes between January 2015 and October 2015 resulted in high forest disturbances exceeding the forest disturbance from the four previous years due to possibly increased illegal logging, but also to forest fires in 2015. Further research is needed in order to quantify forest degradation in larger regions in the Central Kalimantan.

INTRODUCTION

Tropical lowland ombrogenous peat lands in Southeast Asia are known for their rich biodiversity and huge amounts of stored carbon. In recent years, large natural areas of this endangered ecosystem have been converted into oil palm and rubber plantations. Hence, forest remnants are currently threatened by extensive drainage, logging, hunting and strong peat fire as in 2015. Remote sensing data can provide useful information in such environments for hydrological and wildfire modeling, retrieval of biophysical parameters and the management of natural resources. Multi-temporal airborne Light Detection and Ranging (LiDAR) data acquired in August 2007, and August 2011 were used to characterize the peat swamp forest in Central Kalimantan, Indonesia.

In this study our main objectives were: a) to characterize ground-measured and LiDAR-derived biophysical properties of PSF and b) information from TerraSAR-X data to present an approach to carbon change assessment.

MATERIALS AND METHODS

Study area description

The study area encompasses two LiDAR transects in Mawas test sites located in Central Kalimantan, Indonesia (Fig. 1). The Mawas area is located at the northeast part of block E of the Ex-Mega Rice Project (EMRP) (Figs. 1a, 1b) between river Kapuas and towards river Barito. Mawas km238 (south of equator) transects were partially damaged by peat fires during the El Niño Southern Oscillation weather effect in 1997 (Page *et al.*, 2002, Usup *et al.*, 2004, Hajnsek *et al.* 2009).

The test sites are relatively flat. Estimates conducted by Jaenicke *et al.* (2008) using GIS techniques showed that the peat thickness varies from 0 to 18m at Mawas sites.

The monsoon occurs between November and April and the average annual rainfall and air temperature are 2500mm and 25°C respectively (Usup *et al.*, 2004). The selected LiDAR transects consist of altered primary forest patches, in which trees have been already selectively logged until the end of the 1990s. However, drainage channels (main and secondary) from the Ex-Mega Rice Project at Mawas are still being used for illegal logging activities up to date.

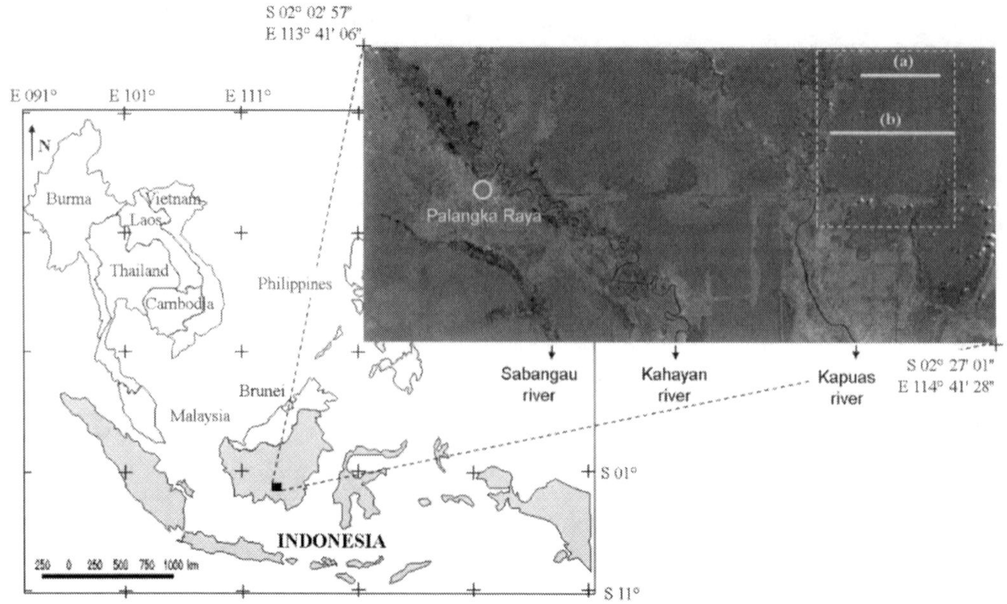

Figure 1: Location of the study area in Central Kalimantan, Indonesia. The yellow circle shows the location of the Palangka Raya city. The solid yellow lines indicate the LiDAR transects a) and b).

LiDAR acquisition and preprocessing

The LiDAR transects were surveyed twice by Kalteng Consultants and Milan Geoservice GmbH from August 5 to 7, 2007, and August 4 to 5, 2011, using a Laser Scanner System Riegl LMS-Q560. It was attached to a Bell 206 helicopter for the first flight and a BK117 helicopter on the second flight. The nominal height was in average 530 m for both surveys. A differential global positioning system (DGPS) reference station was mounted at the airport of Palangka Raya city considering an elevation of 25.0 m or 82 feet. The position and orientation of the LiDAR system on the helicopter was measured by an Inertial Navigation System (INS) and a differential GPS located on the tail boom respectively on the cockpit roof with 256 Hz. A complete description of the LiDAR survey can be found in Boehm *et al.* (2008, 2013).

TerraSAR-X acquisitions and preprocessing

The LiDAR transects were continuously monitored by the space borne SAR (synthetic aperture radar) satellite TerraSAR-X (partially as an acquisition of the close formation of TanDEM-X/TerraSAR-X). The acquisition dates used in this study are December 21, 2010, April 21, 2011, January 18, 2013, October 07, 2014, November 20, 2014, January 03, 2015 and October 16, 2015. The data were acquired in StripMap mode with a resolution of 3 m in HH polarization. All images were co-registered and the intensity ratio of image pairs was calculated. Changes were detected on basis of the known distribution function of intensity ratio (Weihing *et al.* 2010, Poncet *et al.* 2014). Changes detected by TerraSAR-X in forest areas are mainly related to forest canopy disturbance due to the high resolution and low penetration depth of the SAR sensor. Therefore, any disappeared tree crown in the forest canopy can be reliably detected identifying even small scale logging or other disturbances. In order to assess the degree of forest disturbance, forest extent at the initial monitoring date December 21, 2010 was assessed with the SAR data using the amplitude and interferometric coherence of TanDEM-X with an accuracy of about 90% (Schlund *et al.* 2014). A regular grid with a grid cell size of 1 ha within the forest area was created and the proportion of changes within each 1 ha grid cell was calculated in order to estimate the degree of forest disturbance.

RESULTS AND DISCUSSION

Forest disturbance maps based on TerraSAR-X time series analysis showed mainly low to medium disturbance during the acquisitions of December 21, 2010 and January 03, 2015. Main parts of the Mawas area were low disturbed, whereas this could be assumed as natural mortality. However, forest disturbances generally increase to the forest edges. A large patch of medium to high forest disturbance was detected in south-eastern part of Figure 2 left. It could be assumed that the forest disturbance in these areas exceeded the natural mortality. The medium to high forest disturbance was mainly detected at forest edges and close to the canals, where logs could be transported easily. It is worth noting, that Mawas is a conservation area where the forests are supposed to be under protection. The forest disturbance map between the acquisitions of January 03, 2015 and October 16, 2015 revealed a substantial increase in the forest disturbance compared to the previous acquisitions.

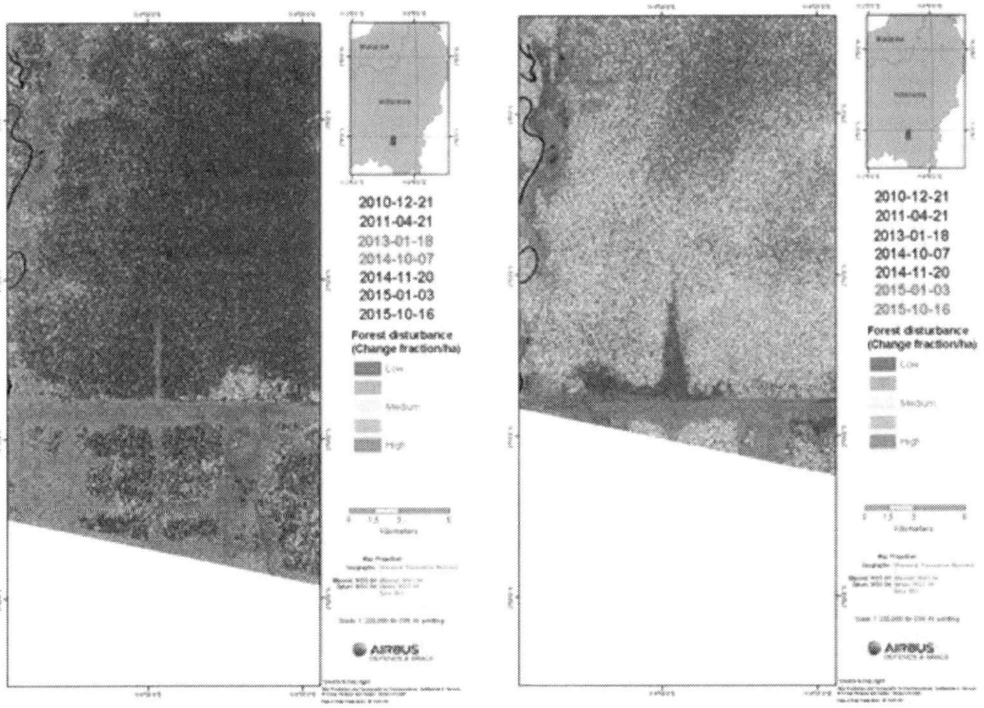

Figure 2: Forest disturbance maps based on TerraSAR-X time series analysis (examples of forest disturbance between 2013-01-18 and 2014-10-07 (left) & 2015-01-03 and 2015-10-16 (right))

This could be due to the fact that the recent El Niño resulted in droughts and increased fire risks. Therefore, the substantial increase of forest disturbance between January 2015 and October 2015 compared to the four previous years could be related to possibly increase illegal logging, but also to forest fires. High forest disturbances were still mainly observed at the edges of the forests, whereas in contrast to the previous year's medium to high disturbance could be observed in the interior of the forest area (Figure 2 right). This suggests that those disturbances were mainly related to extensive droughts and higher fire risk in 2015. An exact answer of the forest changes related to illegal logging or forest fires would show an additional SAR image from July or August 2015.

LiDAR results

The averaged tree height varied widely over the selected transects (Figs. 3, 4, Table 1). This might be due to different intensities of past log intervention to the forest that may explain part of the heterogeneity in the roughness and the variations of tree height among the selected transects. While Mawas km228 has faced less intervention by forest logging, Mawas km238 experienced strong intervention by selective logging through different concession companies until 1997 (Boehm and Siegert, 2004). In such forest logging practices, the large trees are harvested what directly implies on large gaps in the canopy besides the damage of neighbours' trees that further causes a drastic loss in the amount of organic matter inputs. Thus, harvesting practices also includes the construction of small railways and channels to bring the logs out from the forest. These leads to significant changes of the peat floor heterogeneity and their eco-hydrological function. The forest disturbances are still visible on the LiDAR derived products (i.e. CHM and DTM) as well as based on the visual interpretation of Landsat images (Fig. 1).

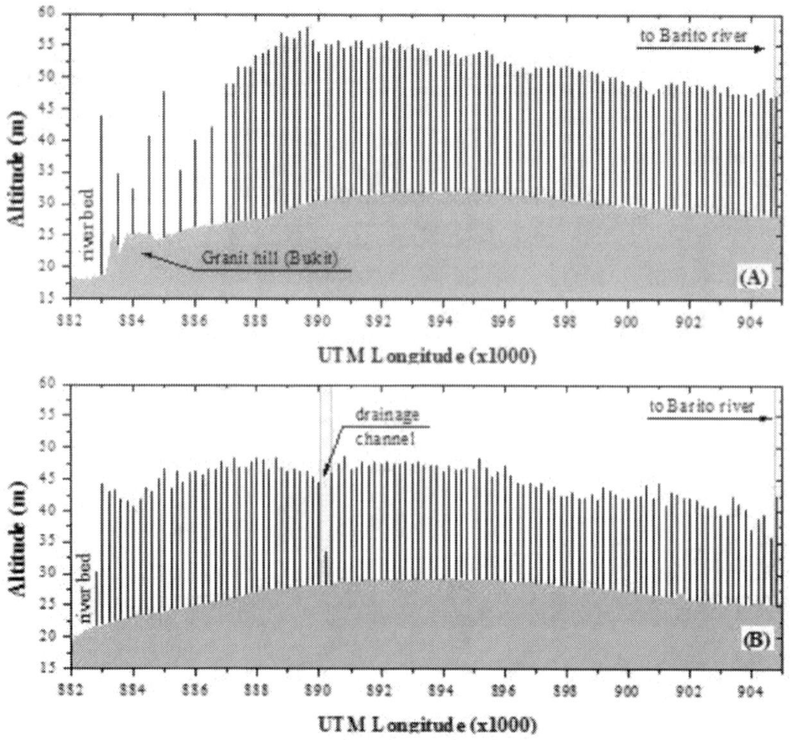

Figure 3: LiDAR derived digital terrain model (DTM) profiles and LiDAR derived canopy height model (CHM) parameter dominant tree height overlaid over the DTM for Mawas km228 south of equator (A) and Mawas km238 (B). Results are based on LiDAR measurements acquired in 2007. Each vertical bar is a 1-ha sample plot.

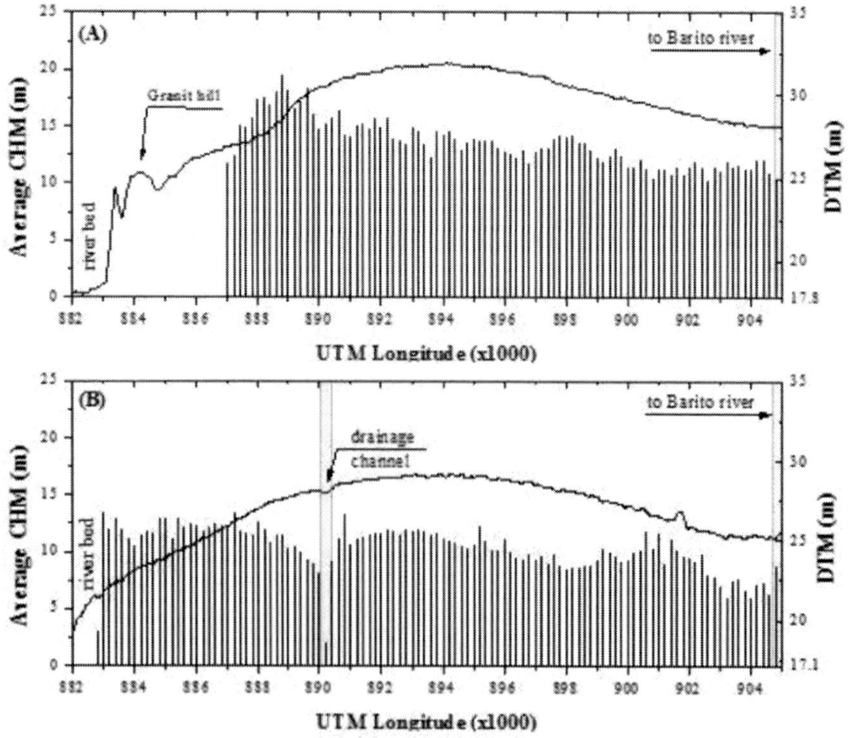

Figure 4: LiDAR derived digital terrain model (DTM) profile and separately LiDAR derived canopy height model (CHM; average tree height) for Mawas km228 (A) and Mawas km238 (B). Results are based on LiDAR measurements acquired in August 5-7, 2007. Each vertical bar is a 1-ha sample plot.

Table 1: Averaged LiDAR derived DTM and CHM parameters for the selected transects in Central Kalimantan

Test Site's Name	**Mawas**		**Mawas**	
UTM Latitude	km 228		km 238	
LiDAR derived DTM parameters				
	2007	2011	2007	2011
River level (m)	17.8	17.8	17.1	17.1
Altitude of the peat dome (m)	**32**	**32**	**29**	**29**
Max. slope (m/km)	2.41	2.90	1.41	1.57
Average slope (m/km)	0.62±0.57	0.63±0.60	0.61±0.37	0.55±0.41
Hummocks roughness (m)	0.73±0.33	1.16±0.22	1.42±0.53	1.12±0.38
Nominal transect length (km)	23		23	
LiDAR derived CHM parmeters				
	2007	2011	2007	2011
Dominant tree height (m)	21.8±2.3	24.6±1.6	18.8±2.5	19.1±2.4
Averaged tree height (m)	13.5±1.8	16.1±1.5	10.9±1.6	13.1±1.6
Maximum tree height (m)	28.3±3.5	32.1±3.4	25.6±3.9	27.4±3.9
Number of sample plots	75		91	
Past activity log	slight		heavy/moderate	

CONCLUSIVE REMARKS

The results lead to the conclusion that degraded PSF might result in dramatic changes to the eco-hydrological function of the peat domes requiring management counteractions in this endangered ecosystem. The effect of forest logging activities on PSF environments and their effects on climate change should also be investigated and confirm whether this disturbance may increase the flux of CO_2. Since peat swamp degradation may enhance peat respiration more than net primary production, more and more areas will become carbon sources rather than carbon sinks, which may have an impact on climate change. In the coming years, as indicated by political support for Reducing

Emissions from Deforestation and forest Degradation (REDD) long-term monitoring of the peat domes will be crucial to quantify changes in carbon stocks of the PSF, and to evaluate forest growth response to climate and land use change in which LiDAR measurements and SAR-data can play an important task.

TerraSAR-X alone has limited capabilities of estimating biomass. However, the combination of LiDAR with high capabilities for forest biomass estimation could be seen as high potential and effective. Usually the aerial coverage and repetition frequency of LiDAR is limited. The biomass could be estimated and changes of that biomass are frequently monitored on a large scale with space borne SAR sensors like TerraSAR-X. In addition, the space borne monitoring could support future planning and sampling of LiDAR acquisitions by indicating hot spot areas.

ACKNOWLEDEMENTS

The third author was supported by the Brazilian Council for Scientific and Technological Development (CNPq, 290043/2007-7) during his PhD research at TU Bergakademie Freiberg (TUBAF). The LiDAR data and their derived products were processed by Kalteng Consultants. The TanDEM-X and TerraSAR-X images were provided by the German Aerospace Center (DLR). The TerraSAR-X study was supported by Airbus Defence and Space, Friedrichshafen.

REFERENCES

1. Boehm, H.-D.V., Siegert, F., 2004. The impact of logging on land use change in Central Kalimantan, Indonesia. International Peat Journal, 12, 3-10.

2. Boehm, H.-D.V., Frank, J., 2008. Peat Dome Measurements in Tropical Peatlands of Central Kalimantan with a high-resolution Airborne Laser Scanner to achieve Digital Elevation Models. In: Proceedings of 13th International Peat Congress, 8-13 June 2008, Tullamore, Ireland, Section 5: Tropical Peatlands.
3. Boehm, H.-D.V., Liesenberg, V., Limin, S., 2013. Multi-Temporal Airborne LiDAR-Survey and Field
4. Measurements of Tropical Peat Swamp Forest to Monitor Changes. IEEE Journal of Selected Topics in Applied Earth Observations and Remote Sensing, VOL. 6, No. 3, June 2013, 1524-1530
5. Hajnsek, I., Kugler, F., Lee, S.K., Papathanassiou, K.P., 2009. Tropical-forest-parameter estimation by means of Pol-InSAR: The INDREX-II campaign. IEEE Transactions on Geoscience and Remote Sensing, 47(2), 481-493.
6. Jaenicke, J. Rieley, J.O., Mott, C., Kimman, P., Siegert, F., 2008. Determination of the amount of carbon stored in Indonesia peatlands, Geoderma, 147(3-4), 151-158.
7. Page, S., Siegert, F., Rieley, J.O., Boehm, H.-D.V., Jaya, A., Limin, S., 2002. The amount of carbon released from peat and forest fires in Indonesia during 1997. Nature, 420(6911), 61-65.
8. Poncet, F. von, Schlund, M., Kuntz, S., 2014. Synergy of TanDEM-X bistatic data & TerraSAR-X to map the state and evolution of forest degradation. In ForestSAT 2014, November 4, 2014 – November 7, 2014, Riva del Garda, Italy.
9. Schlund, M., Poncet, F. von, Hoekman, D.H., Kuntz, S., Schmullius, S., 2014. Importance of bistatic SAR features from TanDEM-X for forest mapping and monitoring. Remote Sensing of Environment, 151, 16-26.
10. Usup, A., Hashimoto, Y., Takahashi, H., Hayasaka, H., 2004. Combustion and thermal characteristics of peat fire in tropical peatland in Central Kalimantan, Indonesia. Tropics, 14, 1-19.
11. Weihing, D., Poncet, F. von, Schlund, M., Lang, O., 2010. Change analysis with TerraSAR-X. In: Wagner W., Székely, B. (eds.): ISPRS TC VII Symposium – 100 Years ISPRS, Vienna, Austria, July 5–7, 2010, IAPRS, Vol. XXXVIII, Part 7B.

Abstract No: A-177

COMBINATION OF PALSAR-2 AND SPOT-6 IMAGES FOR ESTIMATING ABOVEGROUND BIOMASS OF PEAT SWAMP ECOSYSTEM IN MALAYSIA

Hamdan Omar*, Norsheilla Johan Chuah, Ismail Parlan, Abd Rahman Kassim and Samsudin Musa

Forest Research Institute Malaysia (FRIM), Malaysia

**Corresponding author: hamdanomar@frim.gov.my*

SUMMARY

Aboveground biomass (AGB) is one of the key parameters important for carbon accounting in a forest ecosystem. However, estimating this parameter by using remote sensing approach has been challenging as it is constrained by various limitations, especially in tropical region. Spaceborne optical and radar systems have the potential in obtaining AGB reliable estimates but several issues such as cloud cover, dense and complex stand structure, and saturation of signals at certain biomass level still remain unanswered. Peat swamp forest, one of the forest types in Malaysia, is centric as it known to store a large amount of biomass carbon and plays a significant role in balancing terrestrial carbon cycle. A study was conducted to investigate the possibility of combining both optical and radar to improve accuracy of AGB estimation in the peat swamp forest. Optical Satellite Pour l'Observation de la Terre (SPOT-6) and Phased Array type L-band Synthetic Aperture Radar (PALSAR-2) data that have been acquired in year 2015 were used in this study. Peat swamp forest in Pekan, Pahang which is the biggest patch of peat swamp forest in Peninsular Malaysia was selected as the study area. It covers 107,203 ha comprised entirely of peat swamp forest. A number of sample plots were established on the ground and the AGB was measured. Regression models were produced correlating the measured AGB and several variables derived from both satellites data. The study found that the best performing regression model was from the combined modified vegetation-water index (MVWI) with horizontal-vertical (HV) polarized backscatter. The combination of optical and radar systems data has countered limitations of each other and improved the estimate. This approach was therefore suggested to obtain better accuracy in estimating AGB in a large area of peat swamp forest.

***Keywords**: Peat ecosystem, aboveground biomass, remote sensing*

INTRODUCTION

Peat swamp forest and its ecosystem play a significant role in the climate change because they serve as sinks of carbon and store carbon more compared to other forests. Due to the rising climate change issue, the information on peat swamp forest is become vital. There are also interest and rapidly increasing need on carbon stocks (and CO_2) information at a national level in line with international initiatives such as Kyoto Protocol (1997), Reducing Emissions from Deforestation and Forest Degradation and forest conservation (REDD+) (2007), host by United Nations Framework Convention on Climate Change (UNFCCC) and national policies related to climate change (National Forestry Policy (1978), National Energy Policy (1979), National Policy on Biodiversity (1998), National Policy on Environment (2002). Among others, REDD+ program is now is attracting most attentions from the governments including Malaysia.

However, the question of how to measure carbon stock in the forests as well as carbon emissions resulted from the deforestation are crucial and should be answered before the REDD+ can be implemented. There is a tradeoff between the cost and the accuracy of the methods. In some countries, the need for a high level of precision requires the use of fine-resolution remote sensing imagery (e.g. to detect forest degradation or small-scale deforestation), imagery repeated over time (e.g. to overcome cloud cover limitations) or imagery that requires significant expertise to process (e.g. analyzing radar images), all of which come at a cost. Similarly, ground measurements, crucial to verify and measure carbon stocks, are time consuming and relatively expensive at a large scale, such as a national inventory (Gibbs *et al.* 2007).This project is therefore proposed as an initial idea to examine the use of remote sensing technology in providing carbon stock information with optimized cost and accuracy.

In many parts of the world, especially in tropical region, the frequent cloud conditions often restrain the acquisition of high-quality remotely sensed data by optical sensors. The acquisition of cloud-free, wall-to-wall optical satellite images in tropical countries is almost impossible (Hamdan *et al.* 2014a). Thus, synthetic aperture radar (SAR) data become the only feasible way of acquiring remotely sensed data within a given timeframe because the SAR systems are independent of cloud coverage, weather and light conditions. Due to this unique feature compared with optical sensor data, the SAR data have been used extensively in many fields, including forest-cover identification and mapping, discrimination of forest from other land covers and forest biomass estimation (Hamdan *et al.* 2015).

In the context of biomass estimation, optical systems have been facing problems and limitations in tropical forests (Asner 2001; Lu 2006). It has been proven that spectral reflectance and vegetation indices alone are not reliable indicators of biomass in tropical forests and that the direction of their relationship was also inconsistent (Foody *et al.* 2003). Spectral reflectance was also not sensitive to the spatial variation of biomass higher than 150 Mg ha^{-1} (Steininger, 2000). The poor performance of optical remote sensing methods in the tropics has been mainly attributed to the multi-layered closed canopy structure of tropical forest.

SAR, on the other hands estimates biomass in different manner. The capability of SAR system to penetrate through the canopy has contributed to the advancements of modern forestry. Among many SAR systems available, L-band has the most potential for forest biomass estimation as it carries mainly information about larger components of vegetation such as trunks and branches (Wolter and Townsend, 2011). While L-band SAR system offers some advantages in estimating forest biomass, the saturation problem is common in the data. It means that the sensitivity of the returned signal (i.e. backscatter intensity) will cease at certain threshold of biomass. This has been identified as a critical challenge in the last decade (Shi *et al.* 2012). The saturation levels depend on the polarization and the structure of the forests such as the size, density and distribution of the branches and leaves (Hamdan *et al.* 2014b). The relatively low saturation level causes dramatic limitations on the applicability of radar methodology for biomass estimation in tropical forests that typically have high levels of biomass.

Several studies have shown that the integration of optical and SAR data for biomass estimation is promising due to the complementary strengths of the sensors. Studies (e.g. Hamdan *et al.* 2014c) also indicated that the range of validity of SAR signals can be extended by including optical data into canopy scattering models for biomass estimation. Multiple regression models were also used to estimate forest biomass for this purpose.

Realizing the importance of biomass estimation in the tropical forests as well as issues and limitations on the methodology, this study is therefore conducted. It aims to evaluate the capability of both optical and SAR systems in estimating aboveground biomass (AGB) of peat swamp forest in Peninsular Malaysia, simultaneously to investigate the synergy by integrating both of them.

MATERIALS AND METHODOLOGY

The Study Area

The study area is located at the south-east part of Pahang in Peninsular Malaysia. The south-east Pahang peat swamp forest (SEPPSF), located at Pahang state is the largest peat swamp forest complex in Peninsular Malaysia and is believed to be the mainland Asia's largest and intact peat swamp forest. It covers an area of 107,203 ha and comprises four Forest Reserves, namely Pekan, Kedondong, Nenasi and Resak. It harbors unique flora and fauna, provides benefits and services of national interest and supports the livelihood of the aborigines (Orang Asli) communities. Figure 1 shows the location of the study area.

Satellite Images

Two sets of satellites images, which are SPOT-6 and PALSAR-2 (Phased Array type L-band Synthetic Aperture Radar) onboard Advance Land Observing Satellite (Alos-2) were used in this study. Both images were acquired in year 2015. The SPOT 5 HRG image has a spatial resolution of 5 m and contained four wavelength bands; green (Band 1; 0.50 – 0.59 μm), red (Band 2; 0.61 – 0.68 μm), near infra-red (Band 3; 0.79 – 0.89 μm) and shortwave infra-red (Band 4; 1.58 – 1.75 μm). The digital numbers (DN) were first converted to top of the atmosphere (TOA) reflectance by using historical empirical line method (HELM) (Clark *et al.* 2010). For the PALSAR-2 data, the Level 1.5 Fine Beam Dual images were obtained from Japan Aerospace Exploration Agency (JAXA). It was a geometrically corrected and has a resolution of 6 m. The dual-polarized L-band images were converted from 16-bit digital number to the normalized radar cross section (NRCS) that read the data in backscattering coefficient also known as sigma-naught, with units in decibels (dB) (Shimada *et al.* 2009).

Methodology

There are two major activities involved in the study, namely ground data collection and satellite image processing. A total of 48 sampling plot were established in year 2014. All trees stands measuring diameter at breast height (dbh) of 10 cm and above were measured. The allometric function of trees and the calculation of aboveground biomass (AGB) was calculated based on mass per hectare, which gives the units of Mg ha^{-1}. Aboveground biomass comprises all the living aboveground vegetation, including stems, branches, twigs and leaves. It is the most important pool of carbon of all types of forests. In this study, allometric equation from Chave *et al.* (2005), which is specified for peat swamp forest types was adapted. The AGB of a tree can be expressed as

$$AGB = 0.65*\exp(-1.239 + 1.98*\ln(D)+0.207*\ln(D)^2-0.0281*\ln(D)^2 \quad (1)$$

where D is diameter at breast height (dbh) of the measured tree.

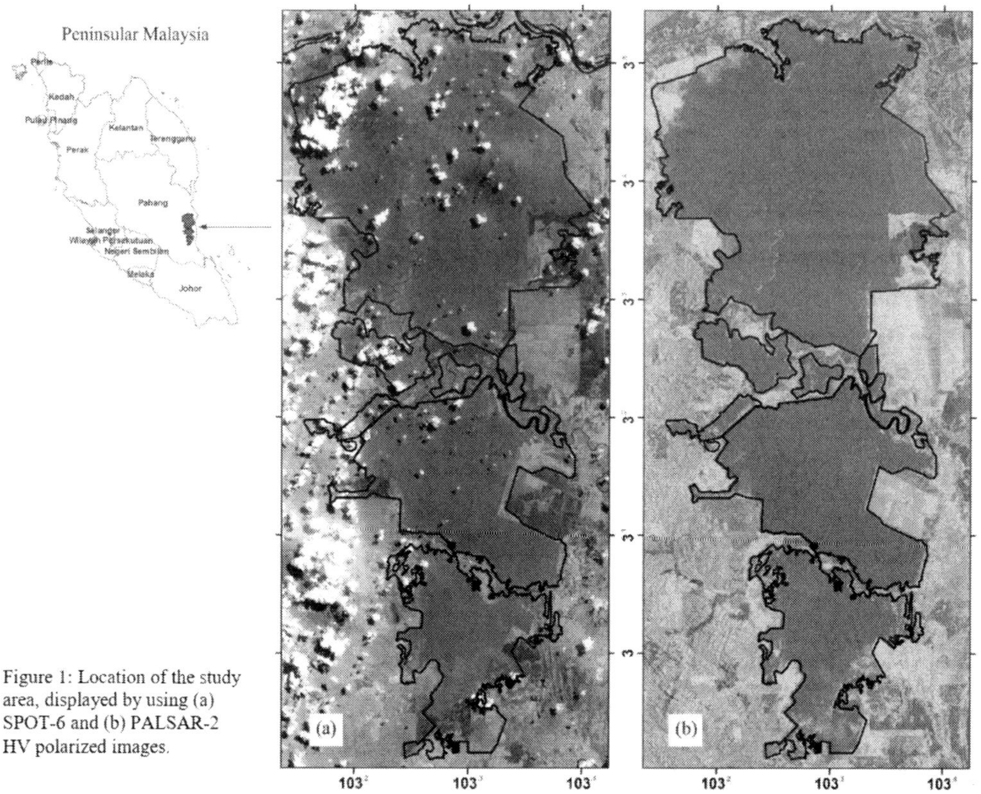

Figure 1: Location of the study area, displayed by using (a) SPOT-6 and (b) PALSAR-2 HV polarized images.

Several images variables were derived from both SPOT-6 and PALSAR-2 data and the pixel values extracted were correlated with the measured AGB on the ground. The microwave energy transmitted that penetrates the forest canopies is largely dependent on the size and orientation of canopy structural elements, such as leaves, branches and stems. It also depends on the polarimetry of the wave. PALSAR-2 has two polarizations, horizontal (HH) and vertical (HV) polarimetry. Studies e.g. Lucas *et al.* (2010); Hamdan *et al.* (2015) found that only HV responded well in estimating AGB of a natural forest. Therefore only HV polarization was used in this study to investigate their correlations.

SPOT-6 in the other hands was used to produce two indices, which are normalized difference vegetation index (NDVI) and normalized difference water index (NDWI). NDVI is a spectral indicator that is commonly used to detect and measure conditions of vegetation. Whereas NDWI is a satellite-derived index from the Near-Infrared (NIR) and Short Wave Infrared (SWIR) channels. The SWIR reflectance reflects changes in both the vegetation water content and the spongy mesophyll structure in vegetation canopies, while the NIR reflectance is affected by leaf internal structure and leaf dry matter content but not by water content. The combination of the NIR with the SWIR removes variations induced by leaf internal structure and leaf dry matter content, improving the accuracy in retrieving the vegetation water content (Ceccato *et al.* 2001). The amount of water available in the internal leaf structure largely controls the spectral reflectance in the SWIR interval of the electromagnetic spectrum. SWIR reflectance is therefore negatively related to leaf water content (Tucker, 1980).

These image variables in this study to predict the AGB. Instead of using the variables individually, a manipulation has been applied. A modified vegetation-water index (MVWI) has been produced from the NDVI and NDWI of the SPOT-6 images. This was then combined with HV backscatter from PALSAR-2 with exponential function to produce a new image variable, namely combined optical and SAR variable (COSV). All image variables that were used in the study is summarized in Table 1.3

Table 1: Summary of image variables used in the AGB predictions

Image Variables	Formula	Description	Source
NDVI	$\frac{NIR - R}{NIR + R}$	Normalized Difference Vegetation Index. Related to changes in amount of green biomass, pigment content and concentration and leaf water stress etc.	Huete (1988)
NDWI	$\frac{NIR - SWIR}{NIR + SWIR}$	Normalized Difference Water Index is a remote sensing based indicator sensitive to the change in the water content of leaves.	Gao (1996)
HV	PALSAR-2 HV	HV backscatter of PALSAR-2 sensor presented in sigma-naught values.	-
MVWI	NDVI × NDWI	Enhancement of normalized vegetation and water indices to extract plant component of peat swamp forest.	This study
COSV	$e^{(HV*MVWI)}$	Combination of indices derived from optical data with PALSAR-2 HV polarization to enhance forest height and biomass of peat swamp forest.	This study

RESULTS AND DISCUSSION

The models used AGB as independent variable to observe the sensitivity of the backscattering coefficients to the AGB. The model was generally written in logarithmic form as $y=a\times ln(x)+b$, where x and y denote AGB and image variables, respectively.

The study has produced a number of models according to the image variables derived. All variables can be used for biomass estimation in the study area with certain degrees of accuracies. Obviously COSV that was derived from the combination of optical and SAR gave relatively higher coefficients of determination (R^2) with RMSE of about 52 Mg ha^{-1} compared to the other variables in a single regression. Table 2 summarizes the models that were produced with accuracies of the estimated AGB and Figure 2 show.

Table 2: Summary of linear regression models developed from the image variables.

Image variables	Model coefficient		R^2	RMSE
	a	*b*		(Mg ha^{-1})
NDVI	0.11211	- 0.2536	0.1429	98.76
NDWI	0.11811	- 0.4123	0.1233	93.21
MVWI	0.07261	- 0.3117	0.1552	71.42
HV	4.29740	- 39.015	0.2257	62.70
COSV	0.14561	- 0.7136	0.3653	51.94

Referring to the Table 2, the last model, which incorporated both SPOT-5 and Alos PALSAR images, surprisingly gave better accuracy compared to the use of SPOT-6 and PALSAR-2 variables alone. The R^2 has slightly increased and thus the RMSE has also decreased. It is therefore proven that the integration of optical and SAR systems could give a better accuracy and potential in estimating biomass in tropical forest. The effect of the combination was also appear on the image and can be seen clearly from visual interpretation as shown in Figure 3.

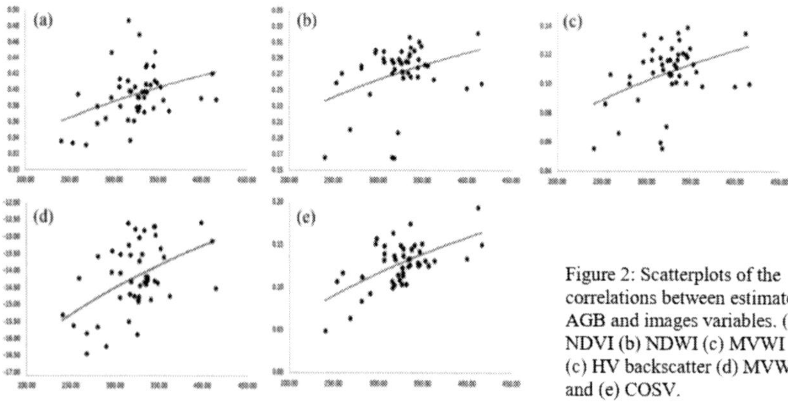

Figure 2: Scatterplots of the correlations between estimated AGB and images variables. (a) NDVI (b) NDWI (c) MVWI (c) HV backscatter (d) MVWI and (e) COSV.

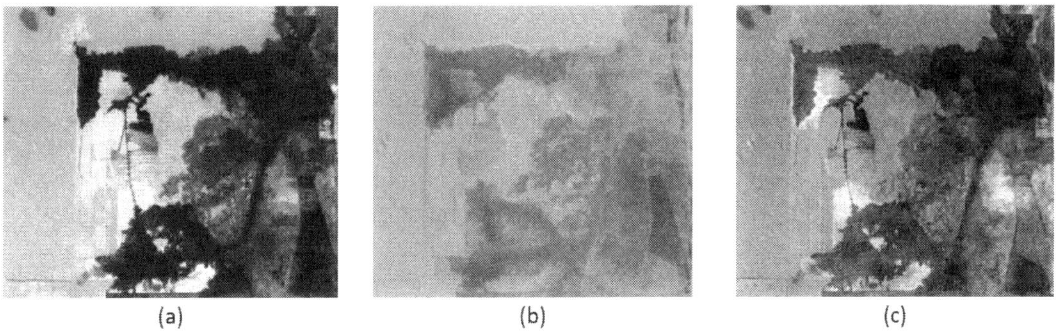

Figure 3: Image variables that were used for AGB prediction, which are (a) MVWI, (b) HV polarization, and (c) combination of MVWI and HV images. The enhancement technique has produced an image with more pixel variation that is able to represent real condition of trees composition on the ground.

The distribution and total AGB in the study area was estimated based on the best correlation model produced. It was found that the AGB in the study area ranged from 68 to 583 Mg ha^{-1} with an average of 352.47±51.94 Mg ha^{-1}. From these figures, it was estimated that the total AGB stored in the study area was about 37,785,841 Mg. The results were validated by using 8 independent plots to measure the overall reliability of the estimate. Figure 3 shows the scatterplots, which include the values of measured AGB on the ground against the predicted AGB from the estimation model. The result shows that the model has slightly underestimated the AGB. Finally, the model was used to produce a spatially distributed AGB in the study area as depicted in Figure 4.

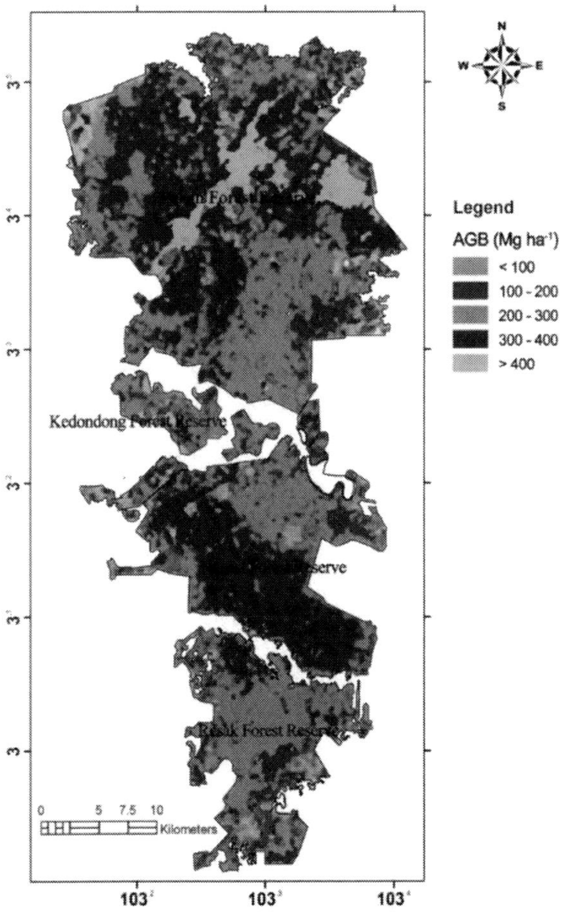

Figure 4: Spatially distributed map of AGB estimated in the study area.

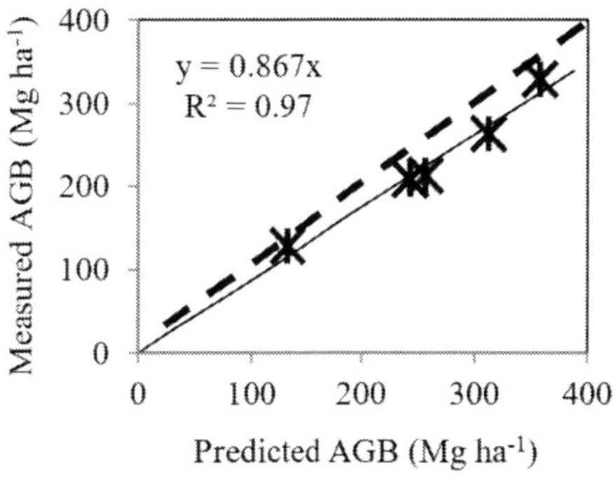

Figure 3: Correlation between measured and predicted AGB in five independent validation plots. The dashed line represents perfect agreement between measured and predicted AGB, indicating that the developed model has underestimated the AGB.

CONCLUSION

The study has successfully investigated the potential benefits that can be obtained from incorporating both optical and SAR systems in the forest biomass estimation. It was found that the combination of indices derived from SPOT-6 with backscattering from HV polarization of PALSAR-2 gave the best accuracy of estimation. Although the issue on saturation is not discussed in details in this study, the results indicated that the optical and SAR systems are compliment to each other, which have potential to overcome saturation problem. Both systems can play significant roles in estimating and monitoring biomass of tropical forest and are still relevant instead of advancements made in remote sensing technology. It is therefore suggested that a combination of optical and SAR remote sensing data supported by extensive field sampling can be used to monitor biomass in tropical forests. Empirically derived biomass estimation models combined with comprehensive sample plots would be of useful for monitoring purposes in REDD+ and other similar activities aiming to promote preservation of biomass in tropical forest ecosystems.

REFERENCES

1. Asner, G.P. (2001). Cloud cover in Landsat observations of the Brazilian Amazon. *International Journal of Remote Sensing*, 22: 3855 – 3862.
2. Foody, G.M., Boyd, D.S. & Cutler, M.E. (2003). Predictive relations of tropical forest biomass from Landsat TM data and their transferability between regions. *Remote Sensing of Environment*, 85: 463 – 74.
3. Ceccato, P, Flasse, S, Tarantola, S, Jacquemond, S, and Gregoire, J.M. (2001). Detecting vegetation water content using reflectance in the optical domain. *Remote Sensing of Environment*, 77: 22–33.
4. Clark B, Suomalainen J & Pellikka P. 2010. A comparison of method for the retrieval of surface reflectance factor from multi temporal SPOT HRV, HRVIR, and HRG multispectral satellite imagery. Canadian Journal of Remote Sensing 36: 397–411.
5. Gao, B.-C. 1996. NDWI - A normalized difference water index for remote sensing of vegetation liquid water from space. *Remote Sensing of Environment*, 58: 257-266.
6. Gibbs, H.K., Brown, S, O'Niles, J. & Foley, J.A. (2007). Monitoring and estimating tropical forest carbon stocks: making REDD a reality. *Environmental Research Letter*, 2: 13 pp.
7. Hamdan, O, Mohd Hasmadi, I & Ismail, H. (2014a). Advance and challenge of remote sensing in assessing tropical forest biomass of Malaysia. *The International Forestry Review*, 16(5): 217.
8. Hamdan, O, Mohd Hasmadi, I, Khali Aziz, H, Norizah, K. & Helmi Zulhaidi, M.S. (2014b). Factors affecting L-band Alos PALSAR backscatter on tropical forest biomass. *Global Journal of Science Frontier Research* 14(3): 51-63.
9. Hamdan, O, Mohd Hasmadi, I. & Khali Aziz, H. (2014c). Combination of SPOT-5 and ALOS PALSAR images in estimating aboveground biomass of lowland dipterocarp forest. *IOP Conf. Series: Earth and Environmental Science*, 18: 012016. 6 pp.
10. Hamdan, O, Mohd Hasmadi, I, Khali Aziz, H, Norizah, K. & Helmi Zulhaidi, M.S. (2015). Determining L-band saturation level for aboveground biomass assessment of dipterocarp forests in Peninsular Malaysia. *Journal of Tropical Forest Science*, 27(3): 388 – 399.
11. Huete, A.R. (1988). A soil-adjusted vegetation index (SAVI). *Remote Sensing of Environment*, 25: 53-70.
12. Lu, D. (2006). The potential and challenge of remote sensing-based biomass estimation. *International Journal of Remote Sensing*, 27: 1297 – 1328.
13. Shi, J.C., Du, Y., Du, J.Y., Jiang, L.M., Chai, L.N., Mao, K.B., Xu, P., Ni, W.J., Xiong, C., Liu, Q., Liu, C.Z., Guo, P., Cui, Q., Li, Y.Q., Chen, J., Wang, A.Q., Luo, H.J. & Wang, Y.H. (2012). Progresses on microwave remote sensing of land surface parameters. *Science China Earth Science*, 55 (7): 1052 – 1078.
14. Shimada, M., Isoguchi, O., Tadono, T. & Isono, K. (2009). PLASAR Radiometric Calibration and Geometric Calibration. *IEEE Transaction on Geosciences and Remote Sensing*, 3: 765 – 768.
15. Steininger, M.K. (2000). Satellite estimation of tropical secondary forest abovgeround biomass data from Brazil and Bolivia. *International Journal of Remote Sensing*, 21: 1139 – 1157.
16. Tucker, C.J. (1980). Remote sensing of leaf water content in the near infrared. *Remote Sensing of Environment* 10: 23-32.
17. Wolter, P.T. & Townsend, P.A. (2011). Estimating forest species composition using a multi-sensor fusion approach. *Remote Sensing of Environment*, 115: 671 – 691.

Abstract No: A-140

LOCATING AND DELINEATING PEATLANDS AND ORGANIC SOILS IN THE TROPICS

Alexandra Barthelmes[1*], Uwe Ballhorn[2] and John Couwenberg[1]

[1]*Greifswald University, Department for Botany and Landscape Ecology, Germany*
[2]*RSS Remote Sensing Solutions GmbH, Germany*

**Corresponding author: alex.barthelmes@greifswaldmoor.de; ballhorn@rssgmbh.de*

SUMMARY

Deforestation and drainage of organic soils stop their ability to sequester carbon and lead to the emission of huge amounts of greenhouse gases both through microbial oxidation and fire. The development of oil palm plantations is one of the main trigger for clearance and drainage of organic soils in the tropics. Drained peatlands are - even when emissions from peat fires are excluded - responsible for 5% of the global anthropogenic greenhouse gas emissions, which is almost double the amount of CO_2 emissions from aviation (Wetlands International 2015). Rewetting drained peatlands has therefore a large GHG mitigation potential. According to the High Carbon Study (Raison *et al.* 2015; Barthelmes *et al.* 2015), all tropical organic soils with more than 20% soil organic matter or more than 12% soil organic carbon and 15 cm depth of the organic layer should be excluded from development. This study outlines the state-of-the-art information and introduces practical guidance on locating and delineating organic soils (incl. peatlands) in West Africa and Southeast Asia, where expansion of oil palm plantations is expected. Unfortunately, adequate geospatial data on location, extent and land use of peatlands and organic soils are not available and incomplete for West Africa and Southeast Asia. Illustrating examples from Indonesia and Sierra Leone, the use of legacy soil and suitable proxy data (e.g. hydromorphic soils, wetlands, wetland vegetation, depressions, floodplains), and up-to-date remote sensing approaches on different scales will be illustrated to identify organic soils in the Tropics. Mapping for the local (concession) scale needs to be accompanied by a thorough field survey, whereas the indication of large tracks of organic soils as 'no-go' areas for oil palm plantations at regional scale may be done using legacy data and remote sensing solely.

***Keywords**: peatland mapping, tropics, high carbon study, remote sensing, legacy soil maps, proxy*

INTRODUCTION

Current estimates indicate that the total area of tropical peatland is in the range of 30-45 million ha (approximately 10-12% of the total global peatland resource), constituting one of the largest near-surface pools of terrestrial organic carbon (Solomon *et al.* 2007, Sorensen 1993). Deforestation and drainage of peatlands stop their ability to sequester carbon and lead to the emission of huge amounts of greenhouse gases both through microbial oxidation and fire (Page *et al.* 2002, Ballhorn *et al.* 2009, Hooijer *et al.* 2010, 2012). Especially in the tropics, conventional land use systems are degrading land, water and biodiversity on a large scale. Concurrently, the rising global demand for biofuels (e.g. palm oil), raw materials and other exportable agricultural products enhance deforestation (DeFries *et al.* 2010, Foley *et al.* 2011). The establishment of oil palm plantations is one of the main trigger for the development of organic soils and peatlands. Overall, an urgent need exists to identify the location of peatlands and organic soils, to protect them against any drainage, and to rewet already drained areas in order to decrease greenhouse gas emissions and to prevent hazardous peat fires.

The High Carbon Consulting Study 5 ('Practical guidance on locating and delineating peatlands and other organic soils in the tropics', cf. Barthelmes *et al.* 2015) defined a carbon threshold that automatically excludes all tropical organic soils with more than 20% soil organic matter or more than 12% soil organic carbon and 15 cm depth from the development for oil palm. This approach merely has to identify the presence of a peat layer of 15 cm depth and can refrain from assessing the total carbon stock of peatlands and other organic soils (cf. Raison *et al.* 2015). This study focused on West Africa, Indonesia and Papua New Guinea, where the expansion of oil palm is expected in near future.

Unfortunately, geospatial data on location and extent of peatlands and organic soils is very rare in most countries of the tropics. Also the rapidly developing remote sensing technologies do not manage to fill this gap, because the large diversity of peatlands worldwide and the multitude of land use types prevent the extrapolation of local results to the global scale. High quality remote sensing based peatland mapping use among others LiDAR technology at local scale - that implies high costs. Therefore, continental and global peatland mapping continues to depend on the aggregation of already existing, local and national data (Montanarella 2014). We give the methodology how to derive organic soil maps for sub-national/regional scale and concession/local scale while integrating existing soil and proxy data and using up-to-date remote sensing.

METHODS

The identification of peatlands and organic soils can be conducted while integrating already existing geospatial data (cartography) under consideration of landscape ecological constrains of their genesis, and/or the use of remote sensing technology. The mapping of larger tracks of peatlands and organic soils might rely on cartography and/or remote sensing, whereas the exact delineation of them at local or concession scale needs a sound ground survey.

A - Cartography

The approach is mainly based on the extensive collation of geo-data and other information. Considering the lack of available data on peatland and organic soil distribution it is appropriate to include proxy data, that indicate areas characterized by persisting high water levels (e.g. wetlands, hydromorphic soils, wetlands vegetation) as suitable environments for the development of organic soils (cf. Barthelmes *et al.* 2015).

Spatially explicit soil and proxy information is available in great numbers in open access online archives, e.g.:

1. ISRIC (World Soil Information; http://eusoils.jrc.ec.europa.eu/esdb_archive/eudasm/indexes/access.htm);
2. JRC (Joint Research Centre; http://eusoils.jrc.ec.europa.eu/esdb_archive/eudasm/indexes/access.htm;
3. FAO Corporated Document Repository (http://www.fao.org/documents/en/docrep.jsp);
4. SPHAERA (Base de données Sphaera du service Cartographie; http://www.cartographie.ird.fr/sphaera/)

While evaluating the collated data, the understanding of underlying concepts and definitions and the identification of relevant terms is crucial. For example, synonyms for areas with possibly organic soils in West Africa are Marigot, Bas-Fonds, Boli, Fadama, Poto-Poto, Loluda, Vida and Uswalo. Much more terms are relevant if considering divers proxy data (cf. Barthelmes *et al.* 2015). Proxy data that appreciates the landscape ecological constraints of peatland and organic soil occurrence are, e.g. Digital Elevation Models or a Topographic Wetness Index. The available maps often display organic soils or suitable proxy information at small scale or cover only parts of the considered area or country. Therefore, it is necessary to to downscale low resolution information to high resolution organic soil probability maps (using additional proxy data as e.g. wetland and wetland vegetation or topographical maps), and to extrapolate spatially restricted peatland/organic soil information to adjacent areas. These procedures are described in detail in Barthelmes *et al.* (2015). Furthermore, two decision support trees are provided for the identification of peatlands and organic soil areas for different scales while predominantly using legacy maps and available proxy data.

B – Remote Sensing

Since most tropical peatlands are highly inaccessible, field mapping of peatlands is a considerable challenge, at regional, national and global scales (Ballhorn *et al.* 2011, Jaenicke *et al.* 2008). The combination of field measurements and remote sensing could provide map products on peatland extent with an optimal balance of covering a region comprehensively, reasonable accuracy and quantifiable uncertainties (Lawson *et al.* 2014).

Lawson *et al.* (2014) identified four key factors that distinguish tropical peatlands from surrounding terra firme (dry-land) forest and that are detectable with the help of airborne and space born remote sensing data: (a) low diversity of vegetation, (b) distinctive vegetation structure, (c) distinctive topography, and (d) high water tables. Which key features of tropical peatlands can theoretically be detected by which sensor type and which sensor in practice is feasible to detect certain key features is address in Barthelmes *et al.* (2015).

Generally, the optical imagery from medium spatial resolution sensors (e.g. on board the Landsat satellites) has been the primary and most successful tool for peatland mapping. It is recommend to use multiple remote sensing products in combination (including passive and active sensors; 'Multisensor approach', Lawson *et al.* 2014).

any tropical peatlands are degraded by e.g. drainage, forest clearance, or fire and lose most of their key features for remote sensing based mapping. Therefore, the acquisition of remote sensing data from pre-degradation stages is essential. LiDAR data imply high costs and are generally only available as discrete point measurements or thin stripes of data, rather than a full coverage. To interpolate between LiDAR measurements other data sources are needed (e.g. L-band RADAR and/or field inventory data on forest structure; e.g. Mitchard *et al.* 2012). As with every remote sensing approach, also peatland distribution mapping from remote sensing needs to be validated with ground reference data.

Barthelmes *et al.* (2015) recommend remote sensing approaches to identify peatlands and organic soils at a sub-national / regional scale and to derive peatland and organic soil maps at local/concession scale.

RESULTS

Carthography

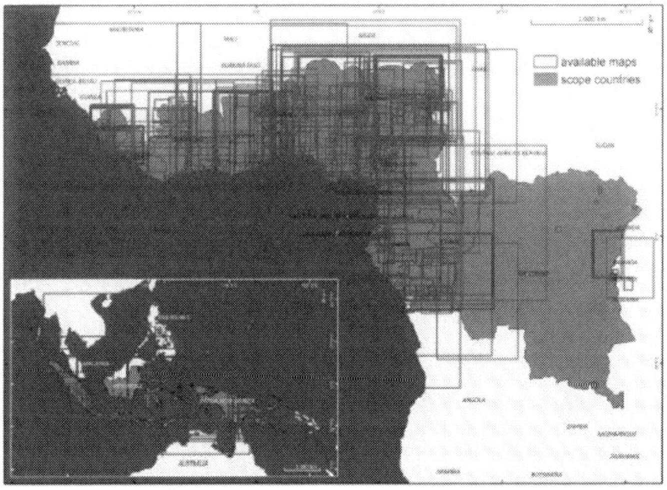

Figure 1: Suitable maps for the indication of organic soils or useful proxies available for West Africa, Indonesia and Papua New Guinea (cf. Barthelmes *et al.* 2015).

A surprisingly large amount of predominantly legacy soil and proxy maps could be collated and analysed.

Figure 1 shows all maps that are useful for the indication of organic soils or suitable proxies as e.g. hydromorphic soil, wetlands, wetland vegetation or inundated areas for West Africa, Indonesia and Papua New Guinea.

A - Mapping example from cartography (Coastal organic soils in Sierra Leone)

Similar to Southeast Asia, organic soils prevail in West Africa along the coastlines in lagoons, river deltas and other estuarine environments. The integration of available data led under use of satellite imagery to the identification of areas with organic soils at sub-national/regional scale. Sierra Leone has undergone a reconnaissance land survey carried out by the FAO in the 1970s. The elaborated map 'Land Systems o Sierra Leone' at scale 1:500,000 indicate land systems with 'highly organic soils' or 'organic top soils' in estuarine swamps and alluvial plains (land systems 'Tasso' and 'Torma Bum'; Figure 2A; cf. Barthelmes *et al.* 2015). Figure 2 shows the data integration to derive an organic soil probability map (Figure 2D).

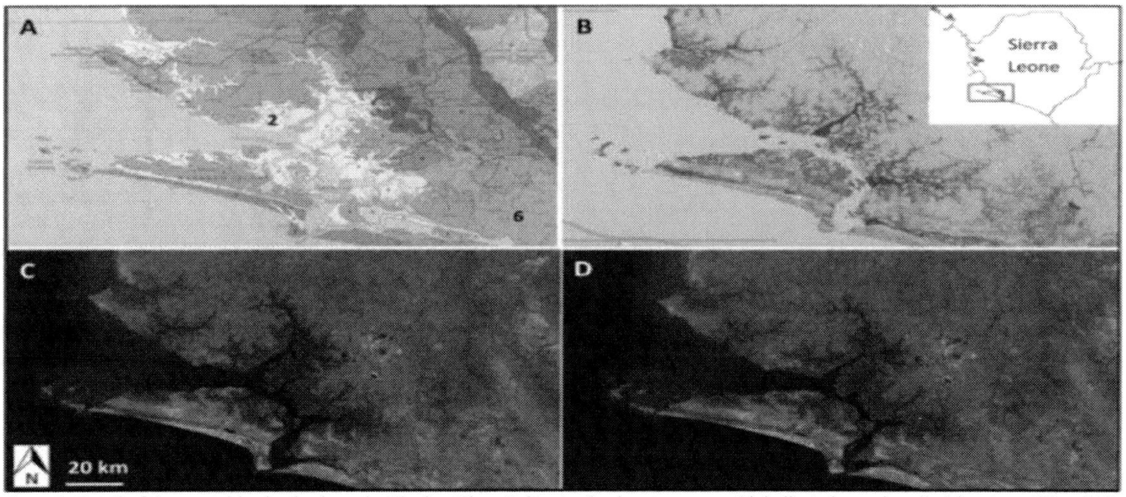

Figure 2: Detail of the coastal lowlands along the Sherbro River Delta: A - land system map with indicated organic soils (signatures '2' and '6'; Birchall & Bleeker 1980); B - remote sensing derived wetland map (cf. Gumbricht 2012); C - satellite image of the area; d) delineated organic soil map (red).

B - Mapping example from remote sensing

To improve the local accuracy of the Wetland International peatland map (Wahyunto *et al.* 2004) different information sources (airborne LiDAR data, aerial ortho photos, historical satellite imagery and the different land cover maps) were compared visually in an iterative integral approach. This approach not only mapped one peatland key feature but as many as possible. No field data for validation of the mapping results were available.

Figure 3 demonstrates the multisensor approach. The upper three images display Landsat satellite data (bands 5, 4, 3; spatial resolution of 30 m) from a subset of the investigated peatland area in Central Kalimantan (years 1991, 1997 and 2000). The first lower image displays a RapidEye image (bands 3, 2, 1; spatial resolution of 5 m) of the area (year 2010). Superimposed is the Wetland International peatland map (brown outline; Wahyunto *et al.* 2004). These first four images clearly demonstrate the importance of historical imagery as considerable land cover change occurred within this area, which complicates peatland mapping. The second lower figure displays how the use of SRTM elevation data (90 m spatial resolution; lighter grey are areas of higher elevation) can be used to enhance this peatland map (yellow outline). Finally the last figure shows to what detail airborne LiDAR elevation data (DTM; one meter spatial resolution; here also lighter grey represents areas of higher elevation) can contribute in improving this peatland map even more (red outline).

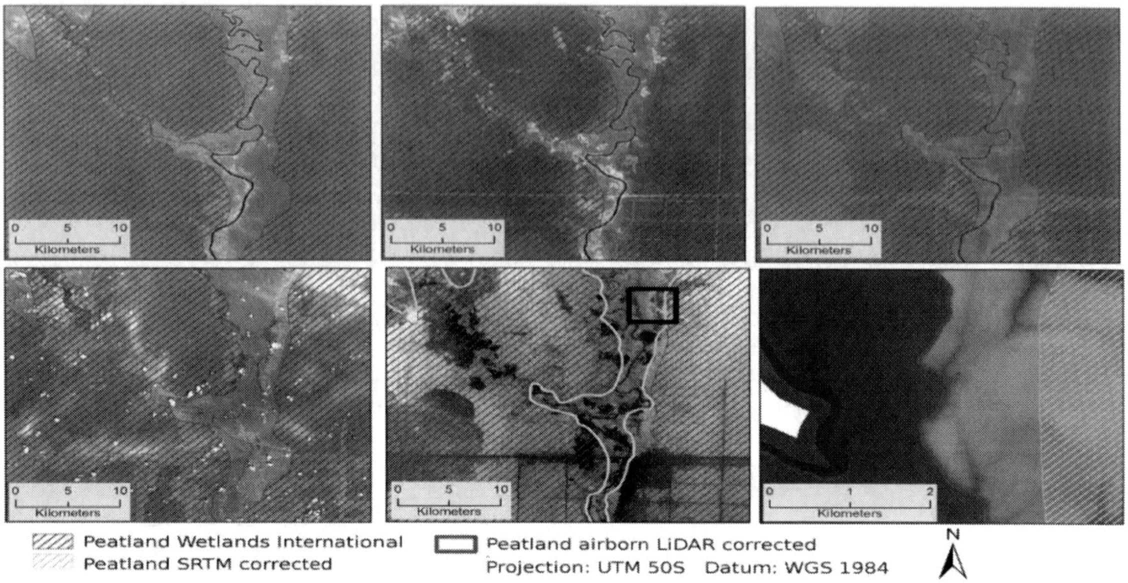

Figure 3: Example of how an existing peatland map (Wetlands International) can be enhanced through the integration of different remote sensing sensors (multi-senor approach), especially airborne LiDAR data.

DISCUSSION

For the identification of peatlands and organic soils with the cartographic approach, it has to be kept in mind that several of the maps are older than 30 years and that organic soil occurrences may have disappeared due to e.g. flooding of reservoirs, or that they may have expanded due to terrestrialization processes in shallow lakes or turned into mineral soils in decades of drainage-based land use. Landscape ecological knowledge of organic soil and peatland constraints and occurrences is needed to interpret these older maps while using modern satellite imagery. The general accuracy of soil and proxy maps provided from online archives is often good, if considering the position of recognizable landmarks as rivers, lakes or mountains in the landscape - which can be assessed using satellite imagery in the GIS software. The maps derived by this method can be regarded as a first indication of areas with high probability of organic soil occurrence. If the background data are reliable, the mapping results are convincing, and organic soils are identified in corresponding landscape settings, this approach can be applied for delineating 'no-go' areas for development at sub-national/regional scale.

To map peatlands and organic soils at local/concession scale the additional use of remote sensing is necessary, at best following the multisensor approach inclusive airborne LiDAR. It is important to note that peatland detection and delineation based on remote sensing data is more or less an iterative process through incorporating different sensors types. The interpreter has to be an expert with a deep background in tropical peatland ecology, have local knowledge of the area under investigation and have a profound understanding of the different remote sensing sensors applied. As with every remote sensing approach, also peatland distribution from remote sensing needs to be validated with ground reference data. Especially in tropical peatlands ground reference data collection is often difficult (accessibility) and expensive. Therefore ground truthing campaigns need to be planned carefully to maximize the output.

CONCLUSION

Increasing land use pressure, growing populations and degradation of agricultural land endanger peatland and organic soil to become developed, especially for oil palm plantations. Therefore, it is necessary to locate them prior drainage and clearance take place. The integration of the huge amount of already existing information like legacy maps on peat, organic soil or suitable proxies enables in many areas of West Africa, Indonesia and Papua New Guinea the identification of larger tracks of organic soils or at least of permanent inundated areas that likely include organic soils. Available remote sensing data and derived tools, like Digital Elevation Models and Topographic Soil Wetness Index enhance the organic soil area delineation, and enables downscaling and extrapolation in case of only small scale maps for a certain area, or their incomplete coverage.

On local/concession scale, the multisensor approach including airborne LiDAR, accompanied by sound field surveys can deliver high quality peatland and organic soils maps. However, cost constraints might hamper the implementation of this approach for assessing extensive tropical lowlands.

ACKNOWLEDGEMENTS

This work has been supported by a group of growers, traders, end users and key stakeholders in the palm oil industry in the framework of the High Carbon Study (http://www.carbonstockstudy.com/home).

REFERENCES

1. Ballhorn U, Siegert F, Mason M & S Limin 2009. Derivation of burn scar depths and estimation of carbon emissions with LiDAR in Indonesian peatlands. Proceedings of the National Academy of Sciences of the United States of America 106: 21213-21218.
2. Ballhorn U, Jubanski J, & F Siegert 2011. ICESat/GLAS data as a measurement tool for peatland topography and peat swamp forest biomass in Kalimantan, Indonesia. Remote Sensing 3: 1957-1982.
3. Barthelmes A, Ballhorn U & Couwenberg J. 2015. Consulting Study 5: Practical guidance on locating and delineating peatlands and other organic soils in the tropics. The High Carbon Stock Science Study, Malaysia.
4. Birchall CJ & Bleeker P 1980. Land Systems Sierra Leone. Land Resources and Survey Project SIL/73/002 FAO UNDP-MANR. United Nations Development Programme, FAO, Freetown.
5. Bonn A, Allott T, Evans M, Joosten H & R Stoneman R 2016. Peatland restoration for ecosystem services. Cambridge University Press, Cambridge.
6. DeFries RS, Rudel T, Uriarte M & M Hansen. 2010. Deforestation driven by urban population growth and agricultural trade in the twenty-first century. Nature Geoscience 3: 178-181.
7. Gumbricht T 2012 Mapping global tropical wetlands from earth observing satellite imagery. Working Paper 103. CIFOR, Bogor, Indonesia.
8. Hooijer A, Page SE, Canadell JG, Silvius M, Kwadijk J, Wösten H & Jauhiainen J 2010. Current and future CO_2 emissions from drained peatlands in Southeast Asia. Biogeosciences 7: 1505-1514.
9. Jaenicke J, Rieley JO, Mott C, Kimman P & Siegert F 2008. Determination of the amount of carbonstored in Indonesian peatlands. Geoderma 147: 51-158.
10. Joosten H & D Clarke D 2002. Wise use of mires and peatlands – Background and principles including a framework for decision-making. International Mire Conservation Group / International Peat Society. Saarijarven Offset Oy, Saarijarvi, Finland.
11. Koohafkan P, Nachtergaele F & J Antoine 1998. Wetland characterization and classification for sustainable agricultural development. Proceedings of a Sub-Regional Consultation, Harare, Zimbabwe, 3-6 December 1997, FAO/Subregional Office for Southern and East Africa, Harare (Zimbabwe).
12. Lawson IT, Kelly TJ, Aplin P, Boom A, Dargie G, Draper FCH, Hassan PNZBP, Hoyos-Santillan J, Kaduk J, Large D, Murphy W, Page SE, Roucoux KH, Sjögersten S, Tansey K, Waldram M, Wedeux BMM & Wheeler J 2014. Improving estimates of tropical peatland area, carbon storage and greenhouse gas fluxes. Wetlands Ecology and Management, doi:10.1007/s11273-014-9402-2.
13. Mitchard ETA, Saatchi SS, White LJT, Abernethy KA, Jeffery KJ, Lewis SL, Collins M, Lefsky MA, Leal ME, Woodhouse IH & Meir P 2012. Mapping tropical forest biomass with radar and spaceborne LiDAR - overcoming problems of high biomass and persistent cloud. Biogeosciences 9: 179-191.
14. Page SE, Siegert F, Rieley JO, Böhm HDV, Jaya A & S Limin 2002. The amount of carbon released from peat and forest fires in Indonesia during 1997. Nature 420: 61-65.

15. Parish F, Sirin A, Charman D, Joosten H, Minayeva T, Silvius M & L Stringer (eds.) 2008. Assessment on peatlands, biodiversity and climate change: Main Report. Global Environment Centre (Kuala Lumpur) and Wetlands International, Wageningen, 179 p.
16. Raison J, Atkinson P, Chave J, DeFries R, Joo GK, Joosten H, Navratil P, Siegert F 2015. HCS+, A new pathway to sustainable oil palm development, draft extended summary. Available at: http://www.carbonstockstudy.com/carbonstockstudy/files/f6/f63fcf9e-10e1-47f8-bfbd-3b9e01505cec.pdf.
17. Solomon S, Qin D, Manning M, Chen Z, Marquis M, Averyt KB, Tignor M & HL Miller (eds) 2007. The physical Science Basis. Contribution of Working Group I to the Fourth Assessment Report of the Intergovernmental Panelon Climate Change. Cambridge, United Kingdomand New York, USA, 996 p.
18. Sorensen KW 1993. Indonesian peat swamp forests and their role as a carbon sink. Chemosphere 27: 1065-1082.
19. UNEP 2011. Oil palm plantations: threats and opportunities for tropical ecosystems. UNEP Global Environmental Alert Service (GEAS), Thematic Focus: Ecosystem Management and Resource Efficiency; available at: http://www.unep.org/pdf/Dec_11_Palm_Plantations.pdf
20. Wahyunto, Heryanto B & HBDF Widiastuti 2006. Peta Sebaran Lahan Gambut, Luas dan Kandungan Karbon di Papua/Maps of Peatland Distribution, Area and Carbon Content in Papua, 2000-2001. Wetlands International - Indonesia Programme
21. Wildlife Habitat Canada (WHC), Bogor, Indonesia.

Abstract No: A-197

REMOTE SENSING AS A TOOL FOR MAPPING AND EVALUATING PEATLANDS AND PEATLAND CARBON STOCK IN NORTHERN FINLAND

Janne Kivilompolo*, Eija Hyvönen, Maarit Middleton, Jukka Turunen, Samu E. Valpola and Tuija Vähäkuopus

Geological Survey of Finland (GTK), Finland

**Corresponding author: janne.kivilompolo@gtk.fi*

SUMMARY

The rates of greenhouse gas fluxes in northern peatlands are a sum of complex interactions between climate, temperature, hydrology, geochemistry, biochemistry and vegetation. Global change is predicted to have impacts on temperature and precipitation patterns, and therefore on peatland hydrology and vegetation. The resulting changes may act as a major triggering mechanism for greenhouse gas release. Thus understanding the species associations as a function of increasing trophic level and surface moisture would be important, as are spatial representations of species associations as inputs into models of greenhouse gas emissions. Remote sensing methods would become valuable in interpreting the vegetation structure and possible changes on northern peatlands. Geological Survey of Finland (GTK) has launched a prestudy to define the available cost-efficient remote sensing datasets to improve the regional scale peat resource and peatland site type mapping. Methods and datasets used would include pre-existing nationwide airborne radiometric data, LiDAR data and Landsat dataset, as well as the GTK's peat database (e.g. 1.7 million peat corings). Also, the benefits of spaceborne synthetic aperture radar and optical data with higher spatial and spectral resolutions are investigated. The National Forest Inventory database could be linked to new datasets in order to achieve a more detailed regional peatland site type distribution and resource information. The developed method will enable a cost-efficient mapping, resource and nature value evaluation of peatlands, especially in scarcely populated northern latitudes. This work is essential in responsible peat and peatland management and needed in questions related to carbon balance and in reconciliation of conservation and other land use activities.

***Keywords**: remote sensing, peat, peatland, Northern Finland*

INTRODUCTION

The main challenge in mapping and estimating the volume of peat reserves in northern peatlands in Finland is the high number and large areal distribution (Fig. 1 and 2). These areas are partially difficult to reach, and therefore the traditional peatland mapping has been either impossible or too expensive to carry out in these regions, and the amount of data is insufficient or there is no data available at all.

Practically only possible methods to carry out a peatland mapping program is using free or low-cost satellite data combined with airborne nationwide LiDAR data. In Finland the European wide CORINE landcover classification by Finnish Environment Centre (SYKE) and Finnish National Forest inventory by Natural Research Institute Finland (LUKE) already utilize satellite remote sensing datasets such as Landsat. These mapping products include peatlands, wetlands, forests, open forests soils, bedrock outcrops and water bodies. However, the idea is to withdraw more detailed information of peatland site types from the satellite data by utilizing additional satellite datasets and calibration of the remote sensed data by information in the peatland inventory database by the GTK which retains the site types and traditional coring data.

POSSIBLE METHODS

Optical and thermal remote sensing satellite methods have proven potential in interpolating the vegetation structure between fields plots through image interpretation a (aerial photographs, thermal, imaging radar, optical multispectral datasets). For example, the multispectral optical remote sensing data has been used effectively for classification of northern peatlands. Poulin *et al.* [2002] used a supervised per-pixel classification approach to distinguish thirteen different habitats within individual peatlands in Southern Quebec, Canada, from Landsat ETM+ data. The success in classification of peatlands with remote sensing is mainly determined by the level of class detail (number of classes and their ecological description) with which the dataset is processed. Mineral soils (uplands) can be well (80-90% accuracy) distinguished from peatlands with VIS-SWIR and imaging radar data and derivatives of a digital elevation model data. When the number of classes increases to the level of wetland site type or to high number of biotopes and higher resolution data is used (digitized aerial photographs, light detection and ranging: LiDAR, airborne hyperspectral data, SPOT satellite imagery, Landsat), overall classification success usually decrease to 60-80 %. However, it is also demonstrated that processing high spatial resolution optical satellite data into less detailed wetland classes can produce results with low classification accuracy. Application of airborne hyperspectral data in northern Finland showed that eutrophic fens could be mapped accurately along with bogs, fens and swamps (Middleton *et al.*, 2012).

Also, cases of successful application of Synthetic aperture radar (SAR) in satellite platforms have been reported on peatland classification worldwide (Touzi *et al.* 2007). SAR is sensitive to top soil moisture which provides a complimentary parameter to optical datasets, and concurrent use with optical data has shown to improve classification of northern peatlands (Grenier *et al.* 2007). The Sentinel-1A satellite carries a C-band Synthetic Aperture Radar (SAR) and was launched in 2014 by the European Space Agency as the first operational Copernicus mission. Data acquired by the Sentinel-1 C-SAR sensor is considered as a potential data for peatland site type classification as it available from the northern latitudes, and may be a significant data source used in the process.
Possibilities of unmanned aerial vehicles (UAV) technology must also be taken into account in the evaluation of the potential methods used in the remote sensing program of the northern boreal peatlands in Finland. Although these data acquisition platforms are rather small and the operating range is limited they may carry cameras and measuring devices. This may provide fast and cost efficient way to acquire spatial data but especially calibration data, for hyperspectral and satellite imagery. The value of this kind local scale data, collected from areas not easily reached by other data collecting methods, will be significant.

The significance of this work is related to the complementing the peatland inventory data in northern Finland (see Fig. 3) and the evaluation of the peatland site types, biodiversity and the peat resource itself. However, the importance of the estimation of the total carbon stock of Finland is increasing rapidly. The questions related to the possible climate change and its effects on the changes of the carbon storage of Finnish peatlands need to be answered when considering the wise use of peat and peatlands.

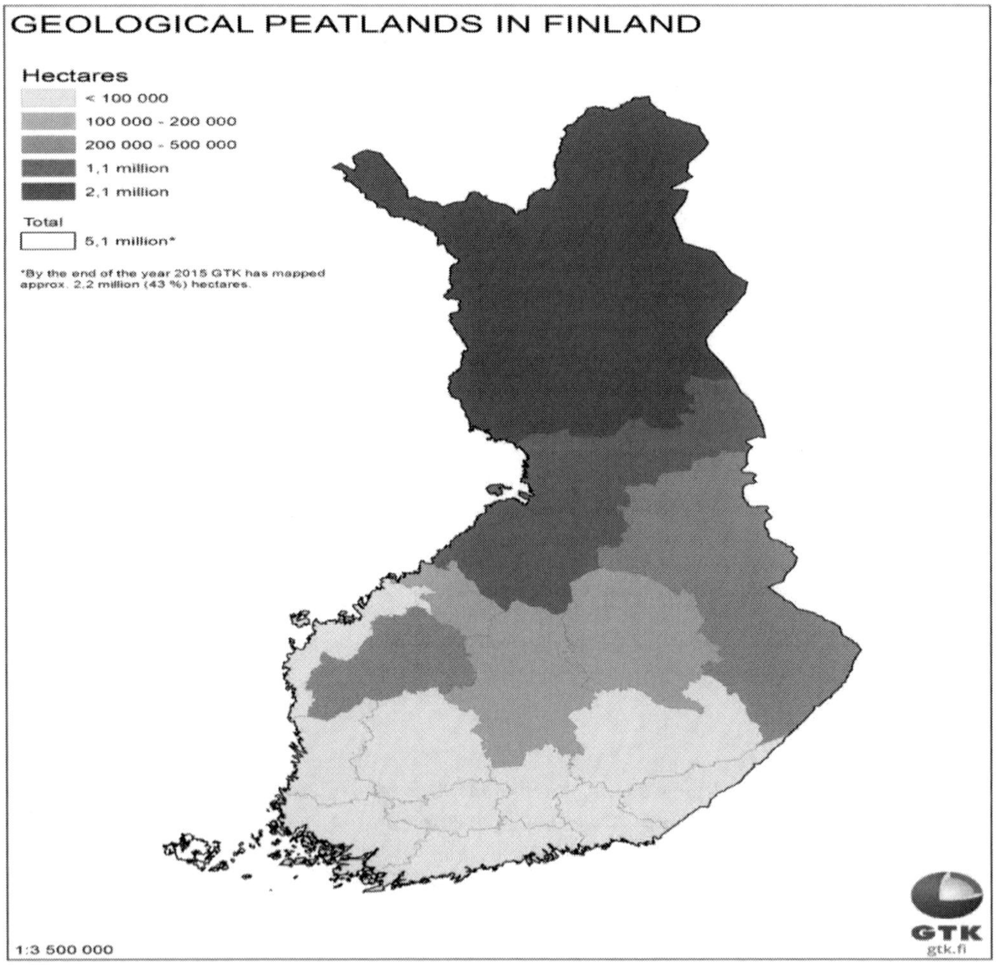

Figure 1: The amount (hectares) of geological peatlands in different provinces of Finland.

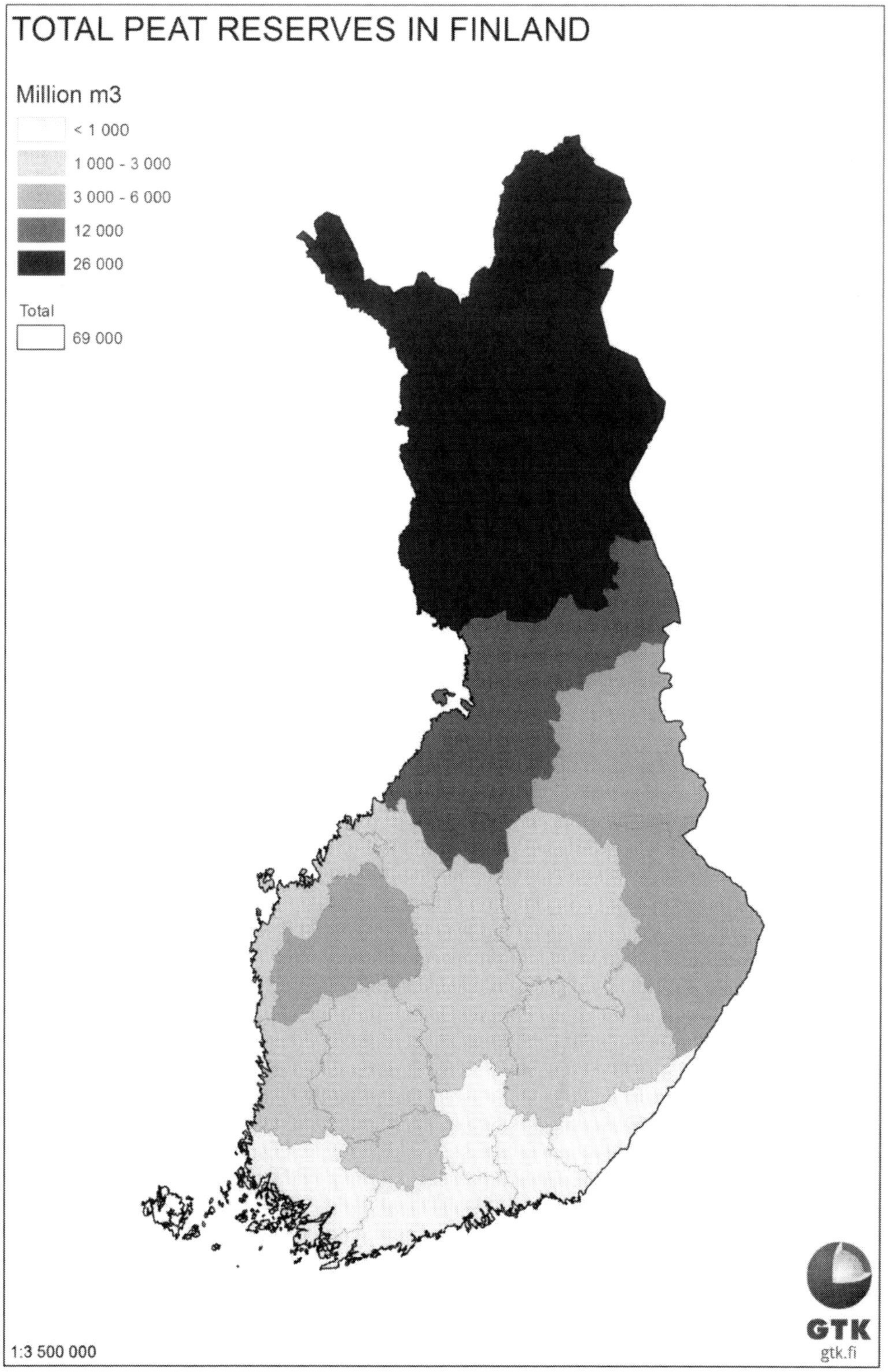

Figure 2: The amount (million m^3) of peat (*in situ*) in different provinces of Finland.

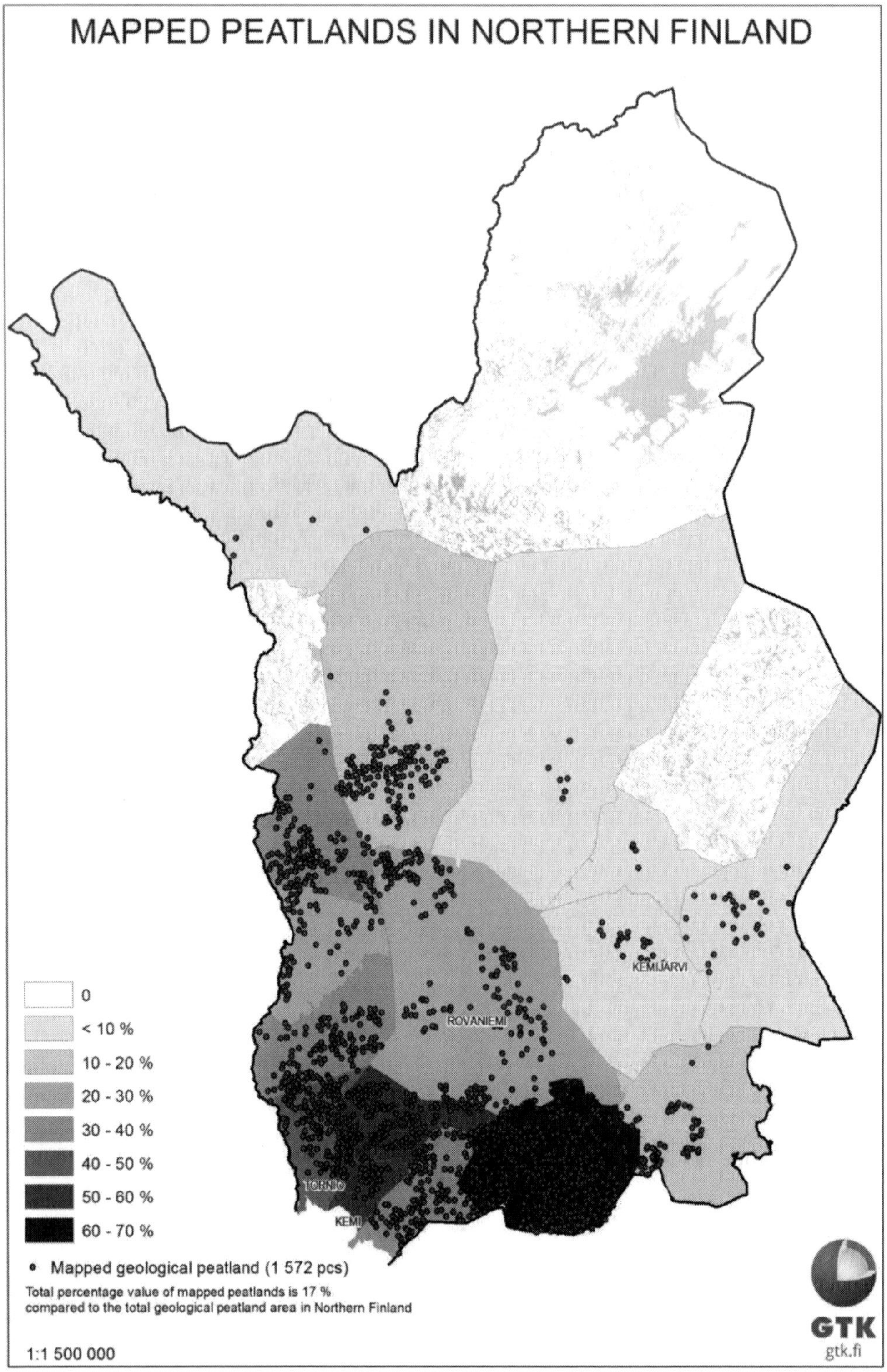

Figure 3: Percentage value of mapped peatlands in different municipality compared to their total peatland area.

REFERENCES

1. Grenier, M., A. M. Demers, S. Labrecque, M. Benoit, R. A. Fournier and B. Drolet (2007), An object-based method to map wetland using RADARSAT-1 and LandsatETM images: test case on two sites in Quebec, Canada. *Can. J. Rem. Sens.,33,* 28-S45.
2. Poulin, M., D. Careau, L. Rochefort and A. Desrochers (2002), From satellite imagery to peatland vegetation diversity: How reliable are habitat maps? *Cons. Ecol., 6,* 3016.
3. Touzi, R., A. Deschamps and G. Rother (2007), Wetland characterization using polarimetric RADARSAT-2 capability. *Can. J. Rem. Sens., 33,* 56-S67.
4. Middleton, M., Närhi, P., Arkimaa, H., Hyvönen, E., Kuosmanen, V., Treitz, P. and Sutinen, R. (2012). Ordination and hyperspectral remote sensig approach to classify peatlands biotopes along soil moisture and fertility gradients. *Remote Sensing of Environment 124,* 596-609.

Abstract No: A-204

UTILIZATION OF DISCRETE-RETURN AIRBORNE LIDAR FOR IDENTIFICATION OF SMALL CANALS IN THE CLOSED-CANOPY OF PEAT SWAMP FOREST IN CENTRAL KALIMANTAN INDONESIA

Solichin Manuri[1*], Baba Barkah[2], Hans-Erik Andersen[3], Bruce Doran[1] and Cris Brack[1]

[1]*Fenner School of Environment and Society, The Australian National University, Australia*
[2]*Borneo Orangutan Survival Foundation, Indonesia*
[3] *USDA Forest Service, Pacific Northwest Research Station, University of Washington, USA*

Corresponding author: solichin.manuri@gmail.com

SUMMARY

Peat swamp forests of South East Asia have contributed the largest portion of global greenhouse gas emissions, due to causes associated with forest resource extraction, including logging, land conversion to agriculture and fires. Accurate mapping of actual and historical infrastructure in peat swamp forests, in particular illegal roads and canals, is crucial for peat land management planning on hydrological restoration and forest protection activities. However, identifying these features using optical satellite imageries is still problematic, even using high resolution satellite imagery or aerial photos. They are often very narrow and covered by closed-canopy forests. Our study aims at identifying small canals and logging roads in peat swamp forest in Central Kalimantan using discrete airborne lidar data. These logging trails and small canals are associated with historical or illegal timber extraction. We used a lidar-derived spatial data layer (relative density model (RDM)) characterizing patterns in the 3-D forest canopy volume, and a normalized digital terrain model (DTM) generated from 2.8 pulse m^{-2} density lidar data for assessing existing logging trails and small canals. We visually digitized the logging roads and small canals from the models and compared the results with field measurement using GPS.

***Keywords**: ALS, digital terrain model, relative density model, peat swamp forest*

INTRODUCTION

Tropical peatlands play a crucial role in global carbon dynamics. In the last several decades, peatlands in South East Asia have contributed the largest portion of global greenhouse gas emissions, due to logging, land conversion to agriculture and fires (Hooijer *et al.* 2010; Page *et al.* 2002). More than 80% of South East Asia peatlands are located in Indonesia and stored more than 55 Gt of soil carbon (Jaenicke *et al.* 2008; Page *et al.* 2011). This amount is comparable to the carbon flux from global tropical deforestation over a century (Cramer *et al.* 2004). Given the fact that current rate of deforestation is hardly slowing down (Hansen *et al.* 2013; Miettinen *et al.* 2011), this could be a major concern in climate change mitigation efforts as this massive terrestrial carbon stock would likely be emitted.

Development of transportation networks allowing access to the forests increase human activities and thus forest degradation. During 1997-1998 drought, fire occurrences become more likely in more deforested areas and degraded forests (Siegert *et al.* 2001). This is because most of direct causes of fires were associated with human activities in land uses and forest resource extraction (Dennis *et al.* 2005). Starting from the early1980s, most of the pristine peat swamp forests in Sumatra and Kalimantan were managed under timber concession rights using selective cutting schemes, then followed by small scale illegal logging (Posa *et al.* 2011; Sorensen 1993) or government resettlement programs (Dennis *et al.* 2005). For large companies and government projects, establishing railways or large canals for accessibility were possible. While illegal loggers often developed transportation routes smaller in width, requiring small and portable tools such as chainsaw or machete. The small canals could be only 0.5 – 2.5 meter wide (Franke *et al.* 2012). Thus identifying small canals using optical satellite imageries is still problematic, even using high resolution satellite imagery or aerial photos.

The identification of canal and road networks in the existing peat swamp forests are not only useful for monitoring forest degradation but also for forest protection and hydrological restoration planning (Jaenicke *et al.* 2010). Canals constructed for accessibility and log transport are normally left open or abandoned in the dry season or when no more commercial timber is remaining. The canals drain the water from the peat dome to the adjacent rivers, which lower the water table and become susceptible to fires (Turetsky *et al.* 2015). Drainage also increases peat oxidation and carbon emissions (Wösten *et al.* 1997). Rewetting of the drained peatlands, through canal blocking, is an effective way to reduce fire risks and carbon emissions (Page et al, 2009). The position and the length of canals are important information for selecting and prioritising which canals to be blocked. Our study aims at identifying small canals and logging roads in peat swamp protection forest in Central Kalimantan using discrete-return airborne lidar data and compare with field measurement using GPS tracks.

MATERIALS AND METHODS

Study Site

Our study site is located at the northern part of the ex Kalimantan Forest Carbon Partnership (KFCP) project area (114° 23.5' – 114° 40.3' E; 1° 56.0' to 2° 30.1' S). in Central Kalimantan Indonesia The study site encompasses 75,342 ha of tropical peat swamp forest with a range of degradation levels. The forest was selectively logged by timber concessionaires in the 1990s and by small-scale illegal logging to the present day. The percentage of forest cover in the study site is much larger than the southern part of the ex KFCP area.

Lidar Data

Lidar data sets were provided by the KFCP project. The calculated pulse density was 2.8 pulse.m^{-2}. All datasets were captured using Optech ALTM 3100 and Optech Orion M200 instruments mounted in Pilatus Porter fixed wing aircraft. Data were collected by the same vendor during the period of 15 August – 2 October 2011. The vendor provided a 1- meter resolution lidar-derived digital terrain model (DTM) for the KFCP area. Ground points were classified by the vendor. The vertical accuracy of the raw lidar data and the DTM product were 0.14 m and 0.18 m, respectively (Ballhorn *et al.* 2014).

GPS measurement

To validate the result from lidar analysis, we used a field measurement data provided by the Borneo Orang Utan Foundation (BOSF). A BOSF team of 5 person conducted the measurement in April 2014 in the south eastern part of the study site using small boat, about 2 years after lidar data acquisition (BOSF, 2014). The team measured position, length, width and direction of the canals using handheld Garmin GPS, compass, and cloth tape. The canal length, depth and width varies between 0.5 km – 10 km, 1 m – 3.8 m and 1.5 m – 3.8 m, respectively. Most of the surveyed canals were constructed in 1990s, none of them were constructed after lidar data collection. Some canals were abandoned or blocked by previous projects and thus inaccessible.

Lidar and spatial correlation analysis

We used FUSION v3.42 to process all point cloud lidar data (McGaughey 2014). The FUSION "Cover" algorithm was used to compute the relative density models (RDM). We generated 5-m RDM for the study sites to identify logging trails. The calculation method of RDM was described in (Andersen *et al.* 2014; D'Oliveira *et al.* 2012). We used ArcGIS 10.3 desktop for additional pre- and post-processing. We generated normalized DTM with high resolution (1 meter). The normalized DTM was generated to identify pixels that abruptly different with the neighbours (Manuri et al, under review). We visually digitized canals and logging trails in the study site.

We evaluated the accuracy of lidar-derived canals identification using ground measurement data. Due to the inaccuracy of the handheld GPS for canals mapping, we buffered the lidar-derived canals with 15 m distance from both sides. We spatially compared by overlaying and intersecting the buffered canals and GPS-measured canals. We calculated the total length of the actual canals that fall into the 15-m buffer zone of lidar-derived canals. Unfortunately, we did not evaluate the logging trails result due to the absence of ground measurement data.

RESULTS AND DISCUSSION

Lidar-derived Models based on ground and aboveground point cloud were used to identify small canals and old logging trails. We found that canal detection using only DTM for was more difficult (Figure 1a) than using normalized DTM (Figure 1b). In the relatively flat peat swamp forest, DTM shows a smooth increase of the elevation towards the centre of peat dome. Small canals were very hard to identify in the DTM. The normalized DTM, on the other hand, was able to differentiate micro depressions. Long and narrow depressions were identified as potential canals.

Figure 1: A DTM map from the eastern part of the study area depicting a very flat elevation (a), the normalized DTM showing terrain depressions (b) and the normalized DTM superimposed by digitized (yellow lines) and field-measured (red lines) canals (c).

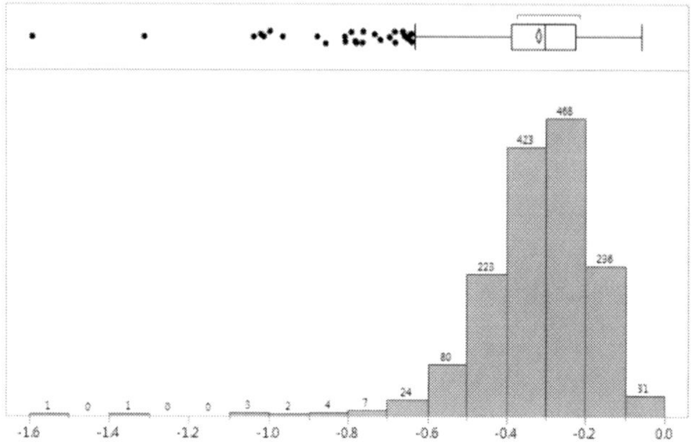

Figure 2: Frequency distribution of depression depth data (in meter) from random points along digitized canals.

We successfully identified small canals (Figure 1c) and old logging trails in the study site using lidar-derived datasets, with total length of 520 km and 276 km, respectively (Table 1). From the comparison analysis, we found that more than 76% of the actual canals were also identified in our digitized canals (Table 1, Figure 1c). Potential reasons for this include the fact that some parts of the canals are very narrow with the size could be only 0.5 – 1 m width (Franke et al). Thus our 1-m resolution DTM data will be unable to capture this very small terrain variation. Closed canopy forest also reduce the possibility of lidar to penetrate to the ground. Most of the canals were built in 1990s for timber transportation and abandoned (BOSF, 2014). At some points, the team that conducted the field survey faced challenges in accessing some canals and was forced to walk in the canals instead of using a boat. The canals were possibly closed due to biomass accumulation from dead vegetation.

Table 1: Summary data of lidar-derived canals and comparison with field-measurement data

	Total digitized from lidar data (m)	density (m/km2)	Total measured in the field (m)	Intersected with 15-m buffer zone of lidar-derived data (m)	% intersected
small canals	520,557	691	50,502	38,570	76.4

The normalized DTM is simply calculating the depth of depression, which is the vertical difference between canal bank and water level (as lidar can not penetrate water) or ground level if not inundated. Thus it is not the depth of the canals. The deepest depression identified in the study area was -4.7 meter, and most depressions were near large canals and rivers. Most of the digitized small canals had depression depths between 0.1 – 0.5 meter

(Figure 2). Given the vertical accuracy of the DTM is 0.18 m (Balhorn, 2009), many shallow depressions may not be detected.

Due to the low impact of the small scale logging in peat swamp forests, monitoring using medium resolution of optical-satellite imageries is still difficult (Franke et al, 2012). This study found that 5-m RDM can be used for detecting logging trails. Figure 3 shows the results of detailed mapping on canals and logging trails using airborne lidar over large area of closed canopy tropical peat swamp forest.

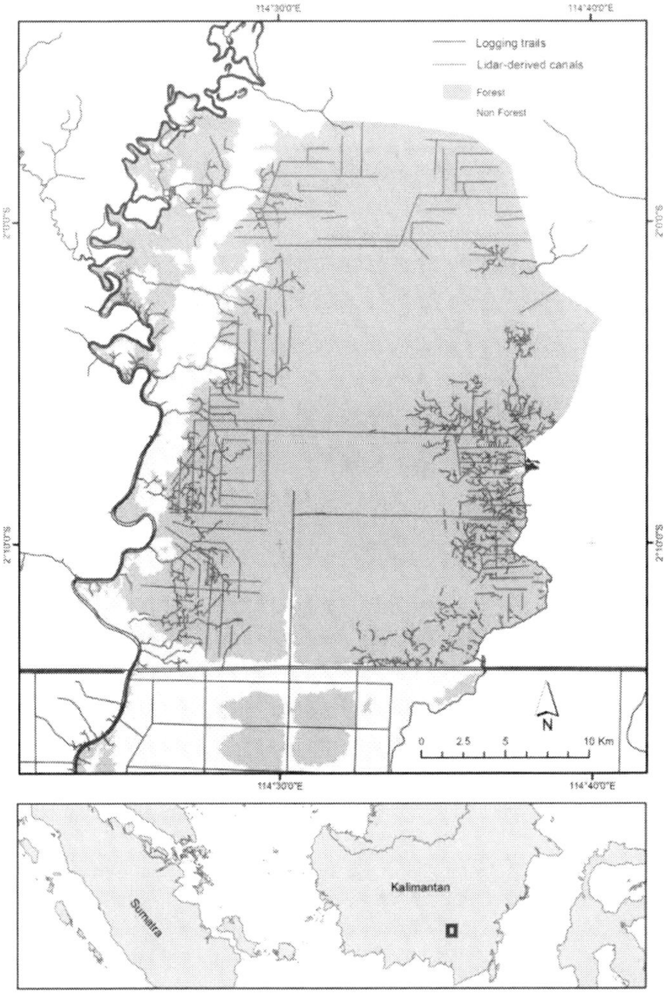

Figure 3: Map depicting old logging trails (red line) and small canals (thin blue line) in the study site

CONCLUSION

Detailed mapping of small canals and logging trails in closed canopy peat swamp forests is feasible using airborne discrete lidar data. The difficulty in identifying narrow canals, even with high resolution aerial photogrammetry, can be overcome using 2.8 m-density airborne lidar. The high resolution normalized DTM, generated using lidar data, was used for identifying small canals with good accuracy.

ACKNOWLEDGEMENTS

The study was supported by Silva Carbon. We thank KFCP-AusAid project and the Indonesian Ministry of Environment and Forestry for providing the lidar dataset.

REFERENCES

1. Andersen, H.-E., Reutebuch, S.E., McGaughey, R.J., d'Oliveira, M.V., & Keller, M. (2014). Monitoring selective logging in western Amazonia with repeat lidar flights. *Remote Sensing of Environment, 151*, 157-165

2. Ballhorn, U., Navratil, P., Jubanski, J., & Siegert, F. (2014). Lidar survey of the Kalimantan Forests and Climate Partnership (KFCP) project site and EMRP area in Central Kalimantan, Indonesia. . *Technical Working Paper. Kalimantan Forests and Climate Partnership*
3. BOSF (2014). Orangutan and peat forest conservation and community development in Mawas, Central Kalimantan. Progress report submitted to USAID IFACS. The Borneo Orangutan Survival.
4. Cramer, W., Bondeau, A., Schaphoff, S., Lucht, W., Smith, B., Sitch, S., Institutionen för naturgeografi och, e., Lunds, u., Naturvetenskapliga, f., Lund, U., Faculty of, S., Dept of Physical, G., & Ecosystems, S. (2004). Tropical forests and the global carbon cycle: impacts of atmospheric carbon dioxide, climate change and rate of deforestation. *Philosophical Transactions of the Royal Society of London. Series B: Biological Sciences, 359*, 331-343
5. D'Oliveira, M.V.N., Reutebuch, S.E., McGaughey, R.J., & Andersen, H.-E. (2012). Estimating forest biomass and identifying low-intensity logging areas using airborne scanning lidar in Antimary State Forest, Acre State, Western Brazilian Amazon. *Remote Sensing of Environment, 124*, 479-491
6. Dennis, R.A., Mayer, J., Applegate, G., Chokkalingam, U., Colfer, C.J.P., Kurniawan, I., Lachowski, H., Maus, P., Permana, R.P., & Ruchiat, Y. (2005). Fire, people and pixels: linking social science and remote sensing to understand underlying causes and impacts of fires in Indonesia. *Human Ecology, 33*, 465-504
7. Franke, J., Navratil, P., Keuck, V., Peterson, K., & Siegert, F. (2012). Monitoring Fire and Selective Logging Activities in Tropical Peat Swamp Forests. *IEEE Journal of Selected Topics in Applied Earth Observations and Remote Sensing, 5*, 1811-1820
8. Hansen, M.C., Potapov, P.V., Moore, R., Hancher, M., Turubanova, S.A., Tyukavina, A., Thau, D., Stehman, S.V., Goetz, S.J., Loveland, T.R., Kommareddy, A., Egorov, A., Chini, L., Justice, C.O., & Townshend, J.R.G. (2013). High-Resolution Global Maps of 21st-Century Forest Cover Change. *Science, 342*, 850
9. Hooijer, A., Page, S., Canadell, J., Silvius, M., Kwadijk, J., Wösten, H., & Jauhiainen, J. (2010). Current and future CO2 emissions from drained peatlands in Southeast Asia
10. Ichsan, N., Vernimmen, R., Hooijer, A., & Applegate, G. (2013). KFCP Hydrology and Peat Monitoring Methodology
11. Jaenicke, J., Rieley, J.O., Mott, C., Kimman, P., & Siegert, F. (2008). Determination of the amount of carbon stored in Indonesian peatlands. *Geoderma, 147*, 151-158
12. Jaenicke, J., Wösten, H., Budiman, A., & Siegert, F. (2010). Planning hydrological restoration of peatlands in Indonesia to mitigate carbon dioxide emissions. *Mitigation and Adaptation Strategies for Global Change, 15*, 223-239
13. McGaughey, R. (2014). FUSION/LDV: software for LIDAR data analysis and visualization. USDA Forest Service. *Pacific Northwest Research Station*
14. Miettinen, J., Shi, C., & Liew, S.C. (2011). Deforestation rates in insular Southeast Asia between 2000 and 2010. *Global Change Biology, 17*, 2261-2270
15. Page, S.E., Rieley, J.O., & Banks, C.J. (2011). Global and regional importance of the tropical peatland carbon pool. *Global Change Biology, 17*, 798-818
16. Page S, Hoscilo A, Wösten H, Jauhiainen J, Silvius M, Rieley J, Ritzema H, Tansey K, Graham L & Vasander H (2009) Restoration ecology of lowland tropical peatlands in Southeast Asia: current knowledge and future research directions. *Ecosystems* **12**: 888-905.
17. Page, S.E., Siegert, F., Rieley, J.O., Boehm, H.-D.V., Jaya, A., & Limin, S. (2002). The amount of carbon released from peat and forest fires in Indonesia during 1997. *Nature, 420*, 61-65
18. Posa, M.R.C., Wijedasa, L.S., & Corlett, R.T. (2011). Biodiversity and Conservation of Tropical Peat Swamp Forests. *BioScience, 61*, 49-57
19. Siegert, F., Ruecker, G., Hinrichs, A., & Hoffmann, A.A. (2001). Increased damage from fires in logged forests during droughts caused by El Niño. *Nature, 414*, 437-440
20. Sorensen, K.W. (1993). Indonesian peat swamp forests and their role as a carbon sink. *Chemosphere, 27*, 1065-1082
21. Turetsky, M.R., Benscoter, B., Page, S., Rein, G., Guido, R.V.D.W., & Watts, A. (2015). Global vulnerability of peatlands to fire and carbon loss. *Nature Geoscience, 8*, 11
22. Wösten, J., Ismail, A., & Van Wijk, A. (1997). Peat subsidence and its practical implications: a case study in Malaysia. *Geoderma, 78*, 25-36

1.4: PEATLAND CONSERVATION & MANAGEMENT

Abstract No: A-269

HISTORY AND FUTURE OF SCIENTIFIC RESEARCH ON OZEGAHARA MIRE, CENTRAL JAPAN

Toshio Iwakuma[1*], Kazuyuki Inubushi[2] and Mitsuru Sakamoto[3]

[1]*Hokkaido University, Japan*
[2] *Graduate School of Horticulture, Chiba University, Chiba, Japan*
[3]*University of Shiga Prefecture and Nagoya University, Japan*

**Corresponding author: toshio.iwakuma@nifty.com*

Ozegahara is the largest alpine mire (650 ha in area, 1,400 m a.s.l.) in Japan. The mire, together with upstream Lake Ozenuma and mountains in the catchment area, was designated as part of Nikko National Park for its scenic beauty in 1934. There had been a plan to build a reservoir covering the whole mire for hydroelectricity and water supply, causing a controversy over the protection of nature. The first comprehensive scientific research on Ozegahara Mire was conducted in 1950-1952 by a group of meteorologists, geologists, limnologists, geochemists and biologists, revealing its rich boreal flora and unique insect fauna. Soon after, the area was designated as a natural monument. The second scientific investigation was carried out in 1977-1979 to collect supplementary data to the first one, followed by the third in 1994-1996. The results indicated that the peat accumulation started at the bases of mountains about 9,000 years ago. About 6,000 to 2,700 years ago, backswamp areas of meandering rivers in the main basin had been covered with peat forming a landscape similar to the present: a mire of fen and bog complex with more than 1,500 pools. The mire and its catchment area are now protected as a Special Protection Zone of Oze National Park. The past research demonstrated several changes of the mire ecosystem, e.g., changes of pool vegetation, pool water dissipation, withering of riparian trees due to a river channel shift, increased nitrogen-fixing shrubs, and frequent disturbance by wild deer. Recent climate changes such as warmer summers and intensified rainfall events might have affected the mire ecosystem directly and indirectly. Further research on Ozegahara Mire is needed to detect the recent changes, to clarify the causes, to predict possible future changes, and to evaluate ecosystem services.

***Keywords**: mire, conservation, peat, long-term change*

Abstract No: A-404

OBSERVATIONS ON BIOMASS AND BIOGEOCHEMISTRY OF RAIN-FED PEAT DOME POLE FOREST, RIAU, SUMATRA

J. Bathgate*, D. Probosaputro and M. Iqbal

APRIL Group, Indonesia

**Corresponding author: john_bathgate@aprilasia.com*

SUMMARY

APRIL group operates a half million ha of fiber plantation and restoration concessions on coastal peatland in Riau. Half the area has been permanently set aside for nature, including extensive areas of pristine peat dome pole forest (PDPF) that grows on the raised surface of large ground-water domes. Permanent sample plots (PSP) established in PDPF have gained 16-32% in basal area (BA) since 2008, raising a question of where in a rain-fed organic landscape the minerals for biomass expansion have come from. Physical and chemical analysis indicates that mineral stores in the peat topsoil are relatively small while litter stores are more substantial. Rain while quite clean is abundant; quantities of cations sampled in rainfall appear to be adequate to have supplied the observed expansion of biomass. Soil drainage and subsidence may have stimulated biomass growth of one fastest grown PSP but not of a second one. Other potential sources of nutrient are air borne particulate haze that reaches nuisance levels each dry season, and guano from roosting fruit bats. Historical disturbance and subsequent recovery of PDPF cannot be ruled out. If biomass expansion on extensive ground water domes of Kampar is taking place it could prove important for biomass carbon capture and storage.

***Keywords**: peat dome pole forest, ground water dome, rain fed, geochemical inputs, basal area, canopy expansion*

INTRODUCTION TO STUDY AREA

A feature of the peat landscape of coastal Riau is the sight of extensive areas of stunted pole forest or semi-open 'padang' scrub, growing on the raised surface of large ground water domes. A peat dome pole forest (PDPF) dome can be 30 km plus diameter with the ground surface elevated 10 m plus above mean sea level. Pole forest grows to about 20 m tall and Padang to half that. The short stature of vegetation is widely attributed to a limited supply of nutrient for a raised, convex landform that is free from groundwater geochemical (Brady, 1991). Nutrient inputs are limited to atmospheric sources like rain and dust. Nutrient scarcity pushes the vegetation to invest in roots for more thorough scavenging of nutrients, in turn feeding peat deposition and dome growth, until some limit is reached (Whitten, 1987). However, little experimental data from tropical peat domes has been gathered, in part due to difficulty of access to vast tracts of dense vegetation.

The study area is sited on the periphery of a large raised dome located on the Kampar Peninsular, 30 km from the coast (Figure 1). Like nearly all PDPF within APRIL concessions, it has been permanently set aside from development to provide services of nature. Beyond the natural forest, at lower elevation, is Acacia fiber plantation growing on peat. The local hydrology looks to be influenced by the large ground water dome. During the El Nino of 2015, the water table (WT) was of near uniform depth across this landscape extending from 2 km inside the pole forest until 2 km inside the plantation.

METHODS

The PDPF composition, structure and growth have been monitored periodically from 2008 until 2015 with 2 permanent sample plots (PSP) located in the study area (Figure 1). Additionally, soil subsidence and water table depth have been measured quarterly since August 2007 starting two months after PVC dip-well poles were installed. There is a pole at each PSP plus 5 more spaced between them and a final one located 400 m beyond PSP 2. In 2007 the peat depth was 11.5 m at both sites; PSP 1 was elevated at 12.3 m and PSP 2 at 13.0 m AMSL. Each PSP is 100 x 20 m in size. Trees 10.0 cm and larger in DBH were numbered with alloy tree tags in 2008, and in 2015 additional trees that had acquired 10.0 cm DBH were also tagged. These trees had DBH measured at 5 cm below the tag nail in 2008, 2011 and 2015. Tree tip height was also measured in 2015 on 10 trees per PSP of size that spanned the range of DBH.

Soil bulk density (BD) was sampled in 2015 at depths of 0-15, 15-30, 30-50, 50-75 and 75-100 cm using a cylindrical corer, replicated at 5 points within each PSP. Soil chemical analysis was done on a composite 0.5 kg sample aggregated from 5 separate locations from each depth within each PSP. Also in 2015, five 0.5 kg samples of fresh litter were taken from each PSP in order to determine chemical composition. To determine litter mass, five separate litter samples were taken each of 0.10 m^2 in area. No litter mass was sampled from the PSP prior to 2015, however in 2004 numerous samples of 0.10 m^2 area were taken from PDPF at similar elevation, 10-11 m AMSL, from another position on the same dome.

RESULTS

Since 2007the WT depth of PSP 1 has ranged from -54 cm to -86 cm; soil surface has subsided a mean of 4.6 cm p.a. PSP 2 WT has ranged +2 cm (flooded) to -54 cm; subsidence has been 0.0 cm. Soil and litter mass values, chemical content and that of rain and groundwater are summarized in Figure 2. There is no difference in BD with soil depth or between PSP; all samples measured 0.05 g /ml. Apart from PSP 2 having slightly lower Cu concentration than PSP 1, soil chemical values of the two PSP soils were similar as was vegetation composition. Litter samples averaged 240 g oven dry (OD) per 0.10 m^2 for PSP 1 and 370 g per 0.10 m^2 for PSP 2, with no chemical differences between them. Litter sampled during landscape survey in 2004 from a similar elevation to the study site averaged 200-250 g per 0.10 m^2 area. This observation suggests that PDPF litter tends to be uniform in mass and so is unlikely to have supplied nutrients to enable a rapid expansion of standing forest.

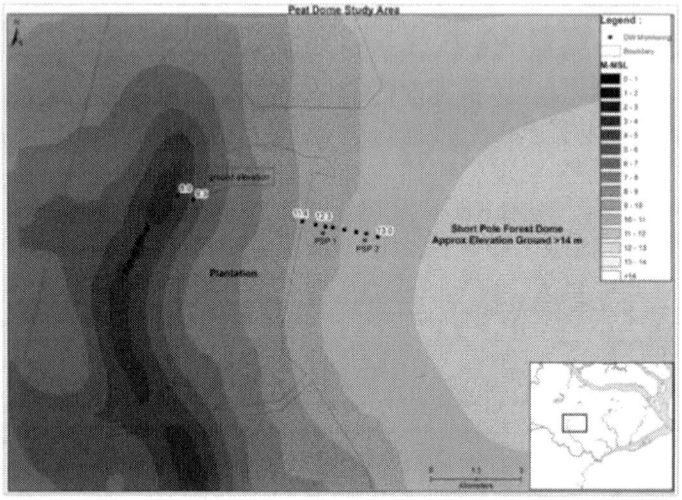

Figure 1: Study area location

PSP dominant tree species and their DBH increments are summarized in Figure 3. A marginal difference in mean DBH between the two PSP may be due to a wind toppled slight gap in PSP 2 having become surrounded by slightly fatter trees. DBH increment for all trees has averaged 0.4 cm p.a. at PSP 1 and 0.2 cm p.a. at PSP 2. Tree tip heights are given in Figure 4. The tree canopy of both PSP is near uniform in height and closure; it conforms to a single-tier model.

Total stem density and basal area by species of each PSP are summarized in Figure 4. In 2007 PSP 1 had 232 trees; in 2015 30 trees had grown in to the 10.0 cm minimum DBH size and 11 original trees had died. Corresponding numbers for PSP 2 are 206, 39 and 20.

The PSP each have 31 identified species; *Calophyllum ferrugineum, Sgzygium ochneocarpum, Campnosperma coriaceae* and *Shorea teysmanniana* are the most abundant trees in both PSP. A slight difference is that in PSP 1 these four trees contribute less to total BA, i.e. species diversity is better spread in PSP 1 (Figure 5). Stand BA has been taken as an index of biomass. There was a procedural issue that some trees in 2008 were estimated to be <10.0 cm DBH rather than measured; had they been >10.0 cm but not tagged in 2008 then stand growth 2008-16 would have been overestimated. Accordingly two estimates of 2008-2015 stand increment have been made; to include and to exclude stems that grew in to the >10.0 cm DBH threshold. Of the two the more conservative estimate of increment has been used in the concluding discussion.

To investigate nutrient inputs in rain, rainfall samples were collected following a published standard, 6 weekly between November 2015 and April 2016, at a canopy opening that occurs 200 m from PSP 1. Rainfall chemistry is included in Figure 2. While clean, rain does contain cations and N possibly in sufficient concentration such that the 2,400 mm p.a. rainfall may have supplied the theoretical quantity required for stand growth.

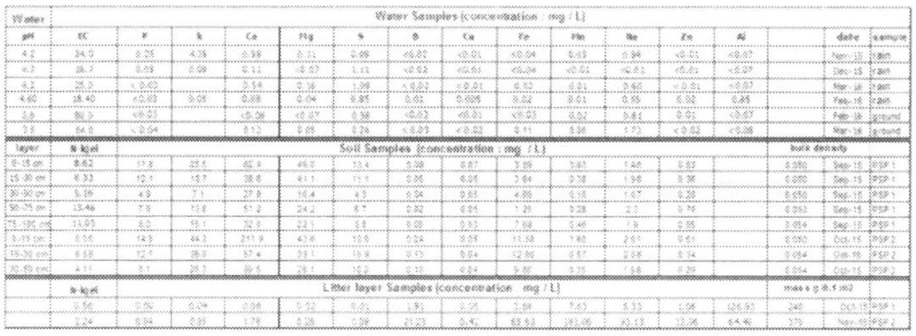
Water Samples (concentration : mg / L)
Soil Samples (concentration : mg / L)
Litter layer Samples (concentration : mg / L)

Figure 2: Chemical analyses of Soil, Litter, Water

Dominant Tree Species	PSP 1 2008 BA m2/ha	PSP 1 mean DBH gro cm p.a.	PSP 2 2008 BA m2/ha	PSP 2 mean DBH gro cm p.a.
Shorea uliginosa	0.95	0.50	0.01	0.50
Ormosia sumatrane	0.95	0.51	1.50	0.35
Campnosperma coriaceae	3.15	0.55	1.80	0.22
Shorea teysmanniana	0.50	0.67	5.60	0.32
Calophyllum ferrugineum	4.05	0.58	4.10	0.27
Mangifera cf. havilandii	1.15	0.00	0.03	0.10
Syzygium sp.	1.85	0.19	0.05	0.00
Sternonurus secundiflorus	0.50	0.09	-	-
Tetramerista glabra	2.00	0.06	1.30	0.10
Knema sp.	0.25	0.05	0.15	0.16
Garcinia eugeniifolia	0.60	0.03	0.50	0.02
Combretocarpus rotundatus	0.40	0.05	0.60	0.21
BA of 12 dominant sp.	**16.35**	**0.36**	**15.64**	**0.23**

Figure 3: Dominant Spp. basal area & DBH increment

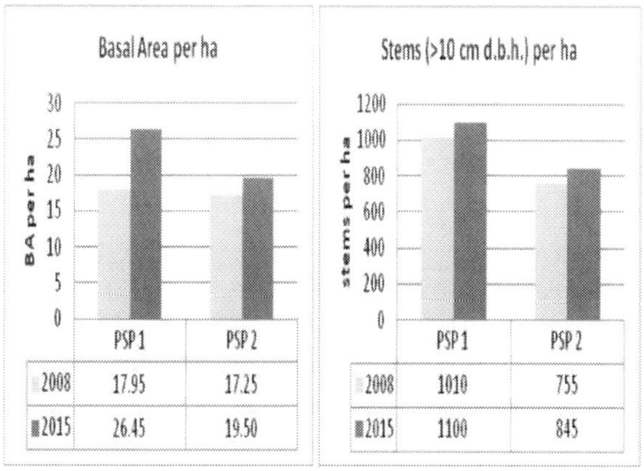

Figure 4: Basal Area and Density of PSP

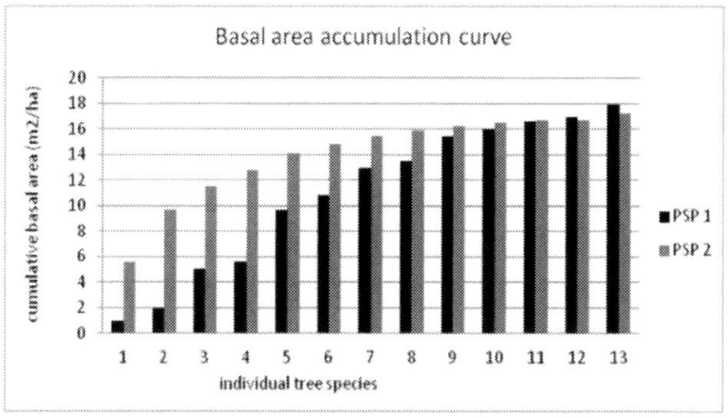

Figure 5: Cumulative Basal Area as index of diversity

CONCLUDING DISCUSSION

Taking a conservative approach that excludes trees grown into the >10.0 cm BDH class trees subsequent to 2007 measurement, PSP 2 gained 16% BA while PSP 1 has gained 32% BA, over the 7.1 year interval. Such a large increment for PSP 1 raises a question of from where came the scarce Ca, k, Mg and other cations required for this magnitude of biomass expansion.

Figure 2 includes indicative values for soil cations contained in the upper 1 m of the soil profile. Cation concentrations are higher in soil layers above 30 cm depth than they are below 30 cm deep. This is consistent with cation supply being added to the soil profile from above, via leaf and litter fall, or from canopy and stem flow, i.e. being rain fed, while being leached from the deeper soil profile by water movement. At both PSP a thick dense mat of live roots separates the surface litter layer from the peat deposit below. The latter is comprised of dead roots, as per observation by Brady (1997). PSP 1 stand has achieved twice the increment as PSP 2 stand, despite both stands growing on soil containing the similar concentration and total quantity of soil cations. This suggests a dominant source for cation supply may not depend on the soil.

PSP 1 total biomass is estimated to be around 100 T /ha; Siregar *et al* (2012) found that *Acacia* plantation on peat soil, similar in total biomass to our current study, contained 68 kg /ha of minerals. Indicatively, a 3% p.a. expansion of that vegetation would require 2 kg / ha p.a. of minerals. The product of soil chemical concentration and subsidence rate in the PDPF are quite inadequate to have supplied that amount. Chuyong *et al* (2002) found that rainfall supplied the majority of minerals, including K, for central African rainforest. Likens *et al* reported that rainfall supplied up to 20 kg / ha p.a. of nutrients to tropical forest systems. While biomass analysis and ground water chemistry study is required to be certain, indications are that PDPF biomass gain reported here could have been sustained by rain fed inputs of minerals.

Another source of minerals may be dry deposition of dust and ash from seasonal biomass burning (Lieu, 2014). Slash and burn local agriculture is common practice in the region, e.g. in vicinity of Kampar River 25 km away. Another potential input is mineral rich bat guano. Large colonies have been observed roosting in *Bintangur* dome forests of offshore islands, and clumps of a few pole trees damaged apparently by roosting bats have been noted in the study area dome. Gumal (2004) describes large colonies of Malaysian fruit bats that favor and reuse many times certain roost trees. Finally, the drainage and subsidence measured at PSP 1 could have contributed to mobilizing nutrients from surface stores in the dome soil and may help account for the greater stand increment at this slightly modified site.

Importantly, if the magnitude of stand increment measured at PSP 2 can be confirmed, biomass stores of Kampar landscape may be accumulating atmospheric CO_2 at a significant rate. There are some half million ha of PDPF on the Kampar; a 10% increase in biomass per decade might capture in the order of one million T of CO_2 p.a.

ACKNOWLEDGEMENTS

Many employees of Pt. RAPP contributed to this study over several years; particular thanks to Water Management staff and workers of Madukoro estate for essential field support to collect soil samples, tag and measure forest vegetation and provide boat transport in arduous conditions. Thanks also to Sahat Marpaung for data entry.

REFERENCES

1. Brady, M. 1997. Organic matter dynamics of coastal peat deposits in Sumatra, Indonesia. Thesis for degree of Doctor of Philosophy, Faculty of Graduate Studies, The University of British Columbia
2. Butler, J. 2015. Indonesian forest fires have been burning since August. The Huntington Post, Australia, 02/11/2015
3. Gumal, M., 2004. Diurnal home range and roosting trees of a maternal colony of Pteropus natunae in Sedilu Sarawak. Journal of Tropical Ecology, Volume 20/Issue 03, May 2004
4. Lieu, W. J. 2014. Seasonal tropical rain forest of Xishuangbanna South West China
5. Likens, G., and Bormann, F., 1995. Biogeochemistry of a forested ecosystem. Springer-Verlag, NY
6. Chuyong, G., Newbery, D., and Songwe, N. 2004. Rain input, throughfall and stem flow of nutrients in a Central African rain forest dominated by ectomycorrhizal forest. Biogeochemistry 67
7. Siregar, S., and Sunarto 2012. *Acacia crassicarpa* biomass development and nutrient accumulation on Riau Peat, Indonesia. APRIL Forestry R&D Technical Report, May 2012

Abstract No: A-027

RESTORING PIG DAMAGED PEAT ECOSYSTEMS IN THE WALPOLE WILDERNESS WESTERN AUSTRALIA

Karlene Bain[1, 2*], Elizabeth J. Edmonds[1] and David M. Edmonds[1*]

[1] *Walpole-Nornalup National Parks Association, Australia*
[2] *Python Ecological Services, Australia*

**Corresponding author: draconis@wn.com.au; jacksplace@westnet.com.au;*

SUMMARY

The Walpole Wilderness is an important component of an internationally recognised biodiversity hotspot in southwest Australia. The Wilderness contains numerous peatlands, many of which are wetlands of national significance and contain critical habitat for a rich diversity of threatened, endemic and relictual taxa. Despite significant control efforts, feral pigs have damaged large areas of peat following fire. Their activities aerate the peat, resulting in accelerated decomposition, acidification and the rapid mobilisation of toxic heavy metals. This project investigates the effectiveness of field techniques available for the stabilisation and recovery of peatlands damaged by feral pigs. The practicalities of attempting to reduce aerobic decomposition of the disturbed peat and to restore vegetation for habitat and peat deposition processes were investigated. With extensive community involvement, a range of remedial techniques were trialled. Fencing was effective at excluding feral pigs, but oxidation and decomposition processes continued well after the removal of pigs. Mulching and planting techniques were the most effective at stabilising the peat substrate, reducing oxidation rates and re-establishing vegetation. A natural mulch layer of <30mm was sufficient to reduce surface aeration, strengthen the peat substrate and provide micro-niches for natural plant growth. Outcomes from this project have potential application for the recovery of peat ecosystems following disturbance from aerating processes such as feral pigs and fire.

Keywords: *oxidation, decomposition, mulching, re-vegetation*

INTRODUCTION

Feral pigs have damaged large areas of peat in the Walpole Wilderness. In many instances, fire is the main predisposing factor that allows the pigs ingress into the peat system. The damages consist of deep and widespread digging, extensive disruption and mixing of soil profiles, complete loss of vegetation and in some cases little sign of vegetation recovery after 15 years. Without active intervention, there is a high likelihood that these peatlands will collapse and species that have persisted for millions of years will become extinct as their mesic refuges disappear. This paper reports on the outcomes of field rehabilitation trials to determine whether:

1. Further damage from feral pigs can be effectively prevented within affected peatlands
2. Rehabilitation efforts can reduce aerobic decomposition processes to levels that are comparable with nearby unaffected peatlands, and
3. Vegetation can be restored in damaged peatlands for habitat and peat deposition processes.

STUDY AREA AND METHODS

The study area comprises two peatlands located in the Walpole Wilderness, Western Australia (Figure 1). The study sites are known to be important habitat for 14 species of conservation significance, a threatened ecological community and 12 Gondwanan relictual taxa. The area of the peatlands is 38 ha and 22 ha respectively, but these relatively small areas are connected with other peatlands in a patchy and extensive system. The peatlands are naturally ephemeral but have experienced below average rainfall for the past seven years resulting in significantly lowered groundwater levels. These conditions, along with fire damage, have contributed to the severity of damage caused by increased feral pig activity.

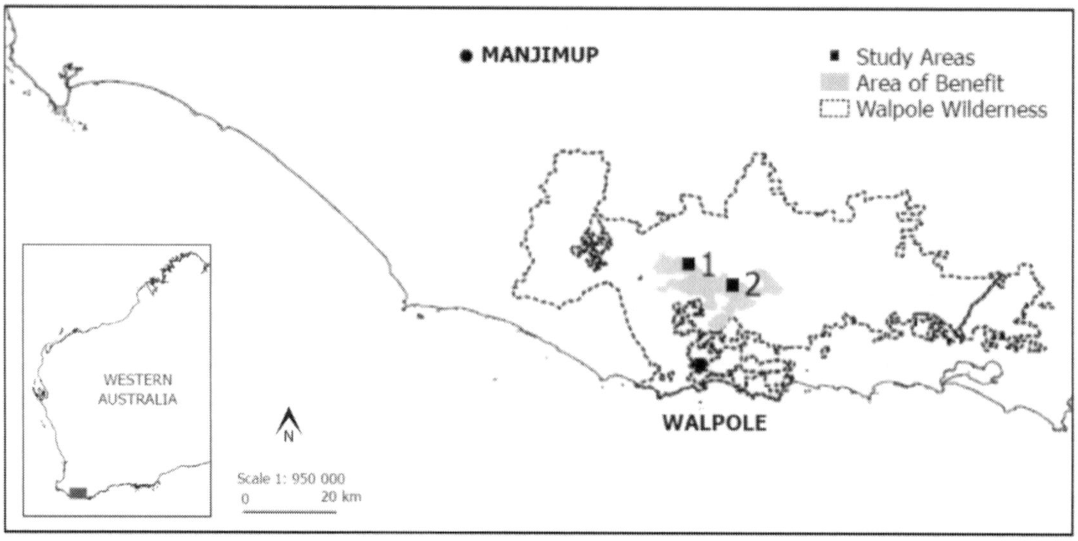

Figure 1: Map showing location of trial sites and an estimation of broader areas of peat and riparian vegetation that will benefit from the project.

Fencing of disturbed areas to exclude feral pigs was undertaken to prevent further damage, allow natural revegetation of areas and prevent disruption of the treatment plots. Fencing in Study Area 1 began in 2001 (0.7 ha), 2010 (0.6 ha) and in March 2015 (4.4 ha) - giving a total fenced area of 5.7 ha. A proportion of Study Area 2 was also fenced in 2012 (3.0 ha).

A total of five remedial treatments (mulching, planting, mulching and planting, disturbed control and undisturbed control) were trialled based on existing techniques for acid sulfate soil remediation (Rosicky *et al.* 2002, Schuman and Joosten 2008, Fraser *et al.* 2012). For each of the treatments, 12 replicates were allocated throughout the two study areas. Surface disturbance techniques were not trialled due to a drought conditions during the trial period.

For each treatment site, sediment and water samples were collected monthly for four months prior to and for 12 months following application of the treatments. Sediment samples at the surface and at 20 cm depth were tested in the field for pH and conductivity. Groundwater samples were collected from piezometers installed within each of the treatment sites and measured for water level, temperature, pH and conductivity. Every three months additional sediment and groundwater samples were sent for laboratory analysis (Table 2). Vegetation plots, photo points and erosion pins were established to record seedling recruitment and survival, percentage vegetation cover and soil loss.

Two threatened species were used as indicators that the peatlands were still providing functional habitat: 1. *Reedia spathaceae* was mapped and the number of seedlings, mature plants and their relative health recorded at the beginning and end of the project; 2. Calling males of *Spicospina flammocaerulea* were surveyed as an indicator of a breeding population.

Community members were actively involved throughout the study with a total of 2425 volunteer hours committed by a broad range of volunteers, local business, government organisations and school groups. The total cost of labour alone in the recovery efforts implemented in this study is estimated at approximately $90,500 (AUD).

Table 2: Physical and biotic factors and analyses used to assess the condition of peatlands being targeted for rehabilitation treatments.

Factor	Analyses undertaken
Soil	Electrical Conductivity at 25°C, Total Soluble Salts, pH KCl, Titratable Actual Acidity, sulfidic - Titratable Actual Acidity, Chromium Reducible Sulfur, Net Acid Soluble Sulfur, acidity - Net Acid Soluble Sulfur, Sulfidic - Net Acid Soluble Sulfur, KCl Extractable Sulfur, HCl Extractable Sulfur, ANC Fineness Factor, Net Acidity (sulfur units), Net Acidity (acidity units), Liming Rate
Water	Electrical conductivity at 25°C, Total Dissolved Solids at 180°C, Acidity as CaCO3, Aluminium, Arsenic and Iron
Vegetation	Digital cover estimation techniques for percentage cover of vegetation, plot based counts of the number of seedlings (alive and dead), number of mature plants (alive and dead), number of different species present and number of invasive species present.
Erosion	Temporal change in substrate surface level as measured from erosion pins.
Threatened species	Persistence and recorded reproduction for *Reedia spathaceae* and *Spicospina flammocaerulea*

RESULTS AND DISCUSSION

Prevention of further damage through fencing

The use of fencing to exclude feral pigs was effective at preventing additional damage to the peat systems as evidenced by a lack of new pig activity within the fenced areas. This resulted in modified chemistry of the groundwater associated with disturbed sites. In particular, sites that had been historically damaged by feral pigs and were subsequently fenced had a significantly lower conductivity, acidity from CaCO3 and concentration of aluminium than sites that were outside of the fence and still being exposed to feral pig activity ($p=0.001$, $p=0.02$ and $p=0.000$; Figure 2). This suggests that there were lower levels of total dissolved solids, acid discharge and oxidation reactions in the sites where pigs had been physically excluded.

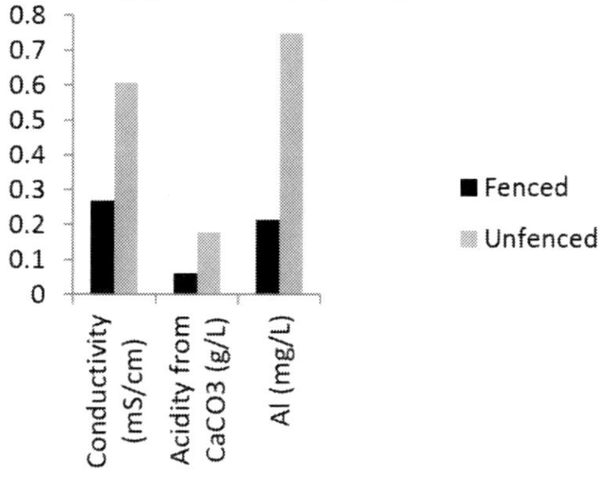

Figure 2: Groundwater parameters sampled in sites disturbed by feral pigs that were found to be significantly different between fenced and unfenced areas.

Reduction in aerobic decomposition through remedial treatments

Although many of the treatments used introduced alkalinity, none were effective in readjusting the pH of the sediments into a range that was completely comparable with the undisturbed sites. Treatments involving mulching came closest, with a significant increase in alkalinity recorded in the top 10 cm of the sediments. This resulted in the field pH of the treatments becoming more similar to those recorded in the undisturbed sites and this was a sustained trend (Figure 3). As the mulch layer continues to decay, the Titratable Actual Acidity (TAA) and pH of the treated sites are likely to reach levels that are more and more comparable with the undisturbed sites over time.

Interestingly, the addition of mulch to treatment sites resulted in a significant increase in the concentration of Aluminium in the groundwater for the first three months following treatment. During these months, an initial decrease in soil pH was also recorded (Figure 3). The short-term decrease in soil pH is likely to have been a result of acids and salts trapped beneath the mulch layer. When soil pH drops, aluminium becomes soluble and a small decrease in pH can result in a large increase in soluble aluminium (Baldwin and Fraser 2009), as seen here.

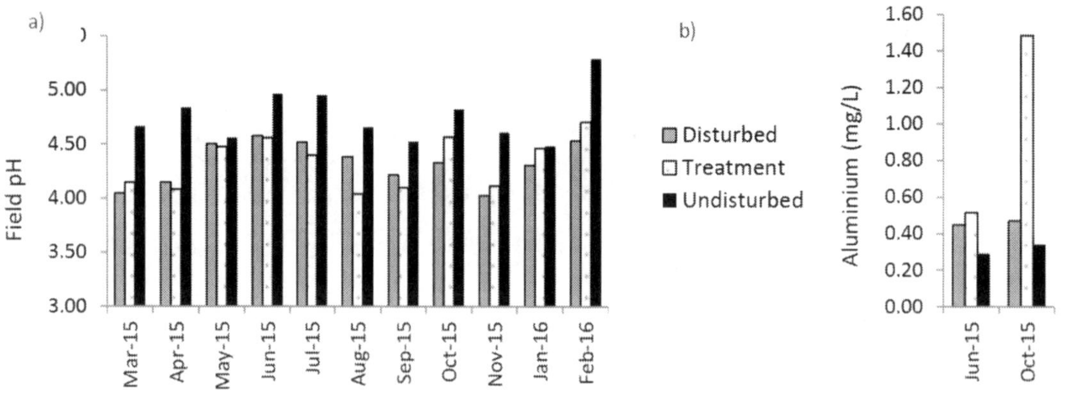

Figure 3: Effects of treatment on a) the field pH of surface soil (p=0.006) and on b) the concentration of Aluminium in the groundwater (p=0.021).

In addition to reducing acidity, the mulch formed a physical barrier between the exposed sediment and the air, which reduced availability of oxygen for oxidation processes. This physical barrier also provided a stable surface for the sediment that prevented further collapse of the substrate as a result of erosion, native fauna movement and human activity (Figure 5). There were observably higher levels of moisture in the sediment below the mulched areas and these treated sites provided a micro-niche for establishing seedlings that was moist, cool and shaded.

While the planting of seedlings didn't result in an effective readjustment of the pH within the duration of this project, the plant material, and particularly the sedge material, is expected to contribute to long-term organic matter accumulation within these peatlands. Over time, the dead and dying plant rhizomes and roots will also serve as a source of carbon for the deposition processes within the peatlands.

There was also a significant effect of time that was independent of treatment on conductivity (p=0.033), titratable actual acidity (p=0.000) and KCl extractable sulfur (p=0.002), which is not surprising given the natural drying and wetting processes that these peatlands are subject to on an annual basis and the associated oxidation processes. To completely avoid these fluctuations and keep the peatlands in a state of deposition, it would be necessary to keep the sediments perpetually inundated. However, these systems are naturally ephemeral and it is not our desire to modify the natural balance of deposition and decomposition, only to return balance where this has been disrupted by feral pigs.

Restoration of vegetation

The expectation that seedling survival would be linked to acidity has not been demonstrated by the results of this study. Acidity levels initially increased in areas where active treatments were undertaken, however seedlings still survived in these sites, which suggests that acid is not the limiting factor for plant establishment in areas that have been affected by feral pigs. Pig activity disturbs the substrate profile, accelerates desiccation processes and contributes to large exposed areas of black soil. The effect of these processes on soil moisture and temperature were not explored in this study, but are worthy of future consideration. This study did demonstrate that the survival of seedlings can be enhanced through the use of mulch and the protection of regenerating areas from further feral pig activity. In all cases, the survival rate for planted and naturally recruiting seedlings outside of the fenced areas was nil due to the pigs returning to areas they had previously disturbed and working outwards from these areas.

Persistence of threatened species

The extent of *Reedia spathacea* did not change during the project however plants within the fenced area remained healthy whilst many plants outside the fence died as a result of sustained pig activity. Plants outside of the fence also showed marked signs of chlorosis as a result of stress or desiccation processes associated with pig activity. A survey undertaken of *S. flammocaerulea* within the breeding period located five calling males in a single pool on the edge of the peatland. This study confirmed the persistence of these species in areas that have been fenced to exclude feral pigs, and within the fence their populations appear to be healthy and breeding, despite drying climatic conditions and other potential stressors such as fire. Outside of the fenced areas however, the feral pig activity has contributed to significant loss of habitat and an associated significant decline in the abundance and condition of individuals. This highlights the effect that unmanaged feral pig activity can have on threatened species, particularly those that have restricted distributions, limited dispersal capacity and specific mesic habitat requirements.

CONCLUSION

There are number of options available for rehabilitating peatlands where the decomposition processes have been unnaturally accelerated. The efficacy of the various approaches will depend on the nature of peatland, the extent of the problem and the resources available to tackle the issue. This project has highlighted some of the practical difficulties faced in the management of peatlands in the Walpole Wilderness. The only effective remedial option here appears to be the combination of fencing, mulching and planting, all of which are expensive and labour intensive processes. Preventing the damage in the first instance is of utmost importance. Proactive management of the interactive threats of fire and feral pigs is critical to the long-term conservation of the peatlands and the huge diversity of unique species and communities that depend upon them.

ACKNOWLEDGEMENTS

This study was supported by the Western Australian Government's Natural Resource Management Program and undertaken by volunteers and partners of the Walpole Nornalup National Parks Association. We would like to thank our project partners, the WA Department of Parks and Wildlife, the WA Department of Corrective Services and the Walpole Op Shop, whose technical support, field labour and donations made this project possible.

REFERENCES

1. Baldwin, D. S., and Fraser, M. (2009). Rehabilitation options for inland waterways impacted by sulfidic sediments - a synthesis. *Journal of Environmental Management* 91, 311-319.
2. Fraser, M. A., Baldwin, D. S., Rees, G. N., Silvester, E. J., and Whitworth, K. L. (2012). Rehabilitation options for inland waterways impacted by sulfidic sediments - Field trials in a south-eastern Australian wetland. *Journal of Environmental Management* 102, 71-78.
3. Rosicky, M.A., Sullivan, L.A. and Slavich, P.G. (2002). *Acid sulfate soil scalds: How they occur and best management practices for their revegetation*. NSW Agriculture and Acid Sulfate Soils Management Advisory Committee, Wollongbar, NSW.
4. Schumann, M. and Joosten, H. (2008) *Global Peat land Restoration Manual*. Institute of Botany and Landscape Ecology, Greifswald University, Germany.

Abstract No: A-284

THE SPRUCE AND PEATLANDS RESPONSES UNDER CLIMATIC AND ENVIRONMENTAL CHANGE (SPRUCE) EXPERIMENT

R.K. Kolka[1, 2*] and P.J. Hanson[1]

[1]*Oak Ridge National Laboratory*
[2]*USDA Forest Service Northern Research Station, United States*

**Corresponding author: rkolka@fs.fed.us*

Spruce and Peatland Responses under Climatic and Environmental Change, or SPRUCE, is an ambitious ecosystem-level experiment that is testing the response of high-carbon northern peatland ecosystems to increased temperatures and elevated carbon dioxide. The experiment is being conducted in a black spruce bog in northern Minnesota at the Marcell Experimental Forest (MEF). The study is supported by the Department of Energy and is a collaboration between Oak Ridge National Lab, the USDA Forest Service and numerous other scientists from across the globe. Peatlands are an ecosystem considered especially vulnerable to climate change, and anticipated to be near their tipping point with respect to their carbon balance, especially at the southern margin of their range. Responses to warming and interactions with increased atmospheric CO_2 concentration are anticipated to have important feedbacks on the atmosphere and climate. SPRUCE provides a platform for testing mechanisms controlling the vulnerability of organisms, biogeochemical processes and ecosystems to climatic change. The manipulation is evaluating the response of the existing communities to a range of warming levels from ambient to +9°C, with and without elevated CO_2, provided via large, modified open-top chambers. Both direct and indirect effects of these experimental perturbations are being analyzed to develop and refine models needed for full Earth system analyses. Whole ecosystem heating began in 2015 and elevated CO_2 treatments will commence in June 2016. Here we will discuss the development and experimental design of SPRUCE and initial results on soil, plant and water processes we have at this time.

***Keywords**:-*

1.5: PEATLAND BIODIVERSITY

Abstract No: A-101

N_2O EMITTERS FROM DIFFERENT HABITATS, BOREAL PEATS AND TROPICAL PEATS AND COMPARISON OF THEIR PHYSIOLOGICAL TRAITS

Yasuyuki Hashidoko*, Yanxia Nie and Sharon Y. L. Lau

Graduate School/Research Faculty of Agriculture, Hokkaido University

**Corresponding author: yasu-h@abs.agr.hokudai.ac.jp*

SUMMARY

Eubacterial nitrous oxide (N_2O) emitters inhabiting (a) boreal peat in North Europe, (b) an Andisol corn farm in northern Japan, and (c) tropical peat in South East Asia were investigated. After isolation of active N_2O emitters, their response to pH (range 3-8), supplemental sucrose, and 10% acetylene were compared. Active N_2O emitting bacteria, *Burkholderia phenazinium* SF-E2 and *Pseudomonas* sp. SC-H2 isolated from *Sphagnum fuscum* and *S. capillifolium* respectively in degrading palsa mires, showed an optimum pH for N_2O emissions around neutral rather than at acidic levels. *B. phenazinium* SF-E2 showed almost no response to supplemented sucrose. In contrast, *Pseudomonas* sp. SC-H2 clearly accelerated N_2O emissions under supplementation with 0.02% sucrose. *Pseudomonas* sp. SC-H2 possess the *nosZ* gene and displayed a 4-times increase in N_2O production upon exposure to 10% acetylene gas. Conversely, eubacterial N_2O emitters isolated from reclaimed tropical peat soils (e.g. *Janthinobacterium* sp. A1-13 and *Burkholderia* sp. 112-30B-5S) showed significantly high responses to supplemented sucrose (50-80 fold increase in N_2O production), but their optimal pH for N_2O emissions was acidic (pH 4.0-5.0). They did not show a positive response to the 10% acetylene due to the missing *nosZ* gene. Similarly, *Pseudomonas* spp. from the Andisol corn farm soils in the cold-temperate zone showed intermediate behaviors between emitters that originated from the boreal and tropical peatlands. It is most likely that the emergence of active N_2O emitters in the boreal and tropical peat ecosystems is due to high disturbance of the ecosystems by human activity and climate change.

***Keywords**: N_2O emitter; N_2O emitting hotspot; denitrifier; N_2O reductase; nosZ gene*

INTRODUCTION

Nitrous oxide (N_2O) is a greenhouse gas that is 300 times active per mole equivalent of carbon dioxide (CO_2) (Metz *et al.*, 2007). Almost 60% of global N_2O emissions are related to agriculture including farming soils and cattle manure, and the widespread use of nitrogenous fertilizers in agricultural soil is a major cause of in N_2O emission (Galloway *et al.*, 2004; Reay *et al.*, 2012). A recent report demonstrated that nearly 70% of the N_2O emissions from agricultural soils are due to the process of denitrification by soil microorganisms (Metz *et al.*, 2007). Biological denitrification known as nitrate respiration uses nitrate (NO_3^-) and other oxygenated nitrogen molecules (NO_2^-, NO, and N_2O) as electron acceptors for degradation of organic compounds under anaerobic conditions. In the process of denitrification, N_2O is the final electron acceptor to be reduced into nitrogen (N_2) gas by N_2O reductase. Hence, some N_2O reductase-malfunctional or *nosZ* gene-missing denitrifiers often emit N_2O actively (Philippot *et al.*, 2011; Shiina *et al.*, 2014).

Some hotspot areas of N_2O emission have been found, in which reclaimed tropical peatlands, boreal peatlands disturbed by cryoturbation, and volcanic Andisol farmlands are recognized as particular active ones (Takakai *et al.*, 2006; Repo *et al.*, 2009; Takeda *et al.*, 2012). Using culture-based N_2O emission assay in a gellan gum soft gel medium, hyper-active N_2O-emitting eubacteria have been identified from those hotspot areas. Thus, saprophytic and facultatively anaerobic eubacteria of denitrifiers were characterized as hyper-active N_2O emitters. In this paper, we show the physiological and metabolic traits of the N_2O emitting eubacteria isolated from three different N_2O emission hotspots sites, compare their N_2O emitting potential and behaviors, and further discuss their similarity and unique characteristics in these different ecosystems.

MATERIALS AND METHODS

Samples

Sphagnum mosses (approximately 50 g as living tissues) were collected from mires in Joensuu (62°47′N, 30°58′E) and Kirpisjarvi (60°26′N, 8°28′E), Finland, in early September 2010 and 2014. Soil samples (approximately 10–50 g as raw soil) were collected at Hokkaido University Shizunai Livestock Farm in Hokkaido, Japan (42°26′N, 142°28′E) in November 2011 and April 2012. Tropical peat soils were collected in 2008-2010 from Riau (0°10′S, 102°9′E) and Central Kalimantan (0°09′N, 101°34′E) in Indonesia, and Sarawak (02°08′N, 111°54′E), Malaysia. Screening and identification of N_2O emitters were performed by means of culture-based N_2O emission assay and homology search on 16S rRNA gene sequence as described previously (Nie *et al.*, 2016).

N_2O emission assay for N_2O emitters

To investigate the main causative microorganisms of N_2O production, culture-based N_2O emission assays were used as previously reported (Nie *et al.*, 2016). As mineral N for the substrate of N_2O production, an excessive concentration of $(NH_4)_2SO_4$ (2.4 g L^{-1}) or KNO_3 (3.6 g L^{-1}) was added to Winogradsky's mineral solution separately with 0.01% (w/v) $CaCO_3$ (Takeda *et al.*, 2012) followed by adjustment to pH 5.0 with H_2SO_4. To the resulting solution previously filtered on a 0.45-μm pore membrane, 0.3% gellan gum powders were added and heated over 100 °C for 15 min to liquefy it. After cooling, 10.0 mL medium was placed in a 30-mL gas chromatographic vial (Nichiden-Rika Glass Co., Kobe, Japan) with a sealed butyl rubber plug and a screw cap septum and autoclaved at 121 °C for 15 min. The headspace volume of the vial was 22.6 mL (Hara *et al.*, 2009). The medium used in the preliminary culture-based N_2O emission assay contained no additional sugar (N_2O emitters from tropical peat), or contained 0.05-1.0% sucrose.

A 100 μL aliquot of bacterial cell suspension was inoculated to 10.0 ml soft gel medium and vortexed for 1 min. The incubation condition was generally at 20-25 °C for 7 days in the dark. A 1 mL volume of the sampled headspace gas was injected to a gas chromatograph (GC) (Shimadzu GC-14B, Kyoto, Japan) equipped with an electron capture detector (ECD) (Shimadzu ECD-2014) kept at 340 °C using a 1 m Porapak N column (Waters, Milford, MS, USA) at 60 °C, with a carrier gas of Argon with 5% methane (CH_4).

Optimal conditions for N_2O production

To evaluate the effect of supplemented sucrose on N_2O emissions, sucrose at different concentration (0.03-1.0% w/v) was added to the medium for the N_2O emission assay. After a 7-day-incubation at 20 or 25°C in the dark, the headspace gas was analyzed by ECD-GC as described above. In addition, pH values of the media were altered in the range f3 to 8 with 1 M H_2SO_4 or 1 M KOH solution, and the amount of N_2O in the headspace gas was also measured in the same manner.

Acetylene blocking assay

To investigate the effect of acetylene on N_2O emitters, pure acetylene gas (2.25 mL) was injected into the headspace. After incubation for 5-7 days, the amount of N_2O in the headspace gas was measured.

Detection of nosZ gene by PCR

Among denitrifying N_2O emitters, the *nosZ* gene was searched by PCR, using a primer set *nosZ-1111F* (5′-STA CAA CWC GGA RAA SG-3′), *nosZ-661F* (5′-CGG CTG GGG GCT GAC CAA-3′), *nosZ-1527R* (5′-CTG RCT GTC GAD GAA CAG-3′), and *nosZ-1773R* (5′-ATR TCG ATC ARC TGB TCG TT-3′) (Scala and Kerkhof, 2006). *NosZ912F* (5'-CGT CCC CGG CCT CGT GTA-3') and *NosZ1853R* (5'-GAG CAG AAG TTC GTG CAG TAG TAG GG-3') (Sanford *et al.*, 2012) were as described in our previous paper (Nie *et al.*, 2016). PCR amplicons assignable as *nosZ* fragments were sequenced followed by the homology search on the DNA database (NCBI).

RESULTS

N_2O emitters from disturbed boreal peat mosses

Boreal peatlands that have been disturbed by cryoturbation and accelerated permafrost defrosting due to current global warming are known to be one of the most active hotspots of N_2O emissions (Repo *et al.*, 2012). In our investigation in a Finnish boreal boreal peat ecosystem, *Burkholderia* spp. and *Pseudomonas* spp. were isolated as leaf epiphytes from *Sphagnum fuscum* and *Sphagnum capillifolium* of upland-adaptable sphagnum mosses, and some of the eubacteria in the North European subarctic tundra showed a potent dominant N_2O emitting capability. These eubacterial N_2O emitters of phylum *Proteobacteria,* widely inhabiting soil, rhizosphere, phyllosphere of agriculture crops, and farm soils in tropical, subtropical, temperate, and cold-temperate zones, acted as potent denitrifiers. The denitrifiers did not have the ability to reduce N_2O into N_2 gas, known as the final step of the denitrification process. In comparison with eubacterial N_2O emitters isolated from different ecosystems other than boreal peatlands, the eubacterial N_2O emitters in disturbed boreal peatlands showed relatively unique traits for N_2O emissions in responses to several environmental factors.

The active N_2O emitting bacteria from the boreal peat; *Burkholderia phenazinium* SF-E2 and *Pseudomonas* sp. SC-H2, isolated from *Sphagnum fuscum* and *S. capillifolium* in degraded palsa mires respectively, showed an optimum pH for N_2O emissions around neutral rather than at acidic levels. *B. phenazinium* SF-E2 showed almost no response to sucrose supplementation, in which N_2O emissions increased by only 2.5 fold, while supplementation of

100 mg L^{-1} caffeic acid led to an obvious acceleration of N_2O emissions (0.45 μg $vial^{-1}$ day^{-1}, 30 fold higher than the control). Both increased pH and phenolic compounds stimulated N_2O in the culture-based N_2O emission assay, and these conditions are probably provided in nature by the disruption of boreal peat ecosystems along with sphagnum peat degradation (Nie *et al*., 2015).

In contrast, while unresponsive to caffeic acid, N_2O emissions by *Pseudomonas* sp. SC-H2 were accelerated (16 fold higher than the control) under supplementation with 0.02% sucrose. This N_2O emitter possessed the *nosZ* gene and showed 4-times increase in N_2O production upon exposure to 10% acetylene gas (known as acetylene blocking assay to measure the activity of N_2O reductase). Effective blockage of N_2O reduction by acetylene gas suggests that *Pseudomonas* sp. SC-H2 is a hyper-active denitrifier at neutral pH. As a large amount of minerals and ammonia are released during degradation of sphagnum peat, and the ammonium cation (NH_4^+) is biologically oxidized to nitrate anion (NO_3^-), *Pseudomonas* sp. SC-H2 may act as remediators for an ecosystem by maintaining the C:N balance in the soil (Mu *et al*., 2012; Lau *et al*., 2014).

N_2O emitting Burkholderia spp. from tropical peatlands reclaimed for agriculture

A powerful eubacterial N_2O emitter, *Burkholderia* spp. were commonly found in tropical woody peatland ecosystems distributed throughout South East Asia, particularly those reclaimed without proper soil and water table management (Hashidoko *et al*., 2010; Jauhiainen *et al*., 2012). These dominant N_2O emitters inhabit the medium to strongly acidic tropical peat soils and show an acid-tolerant trait, and more importantly, are often denitrifiers that actively emit N_2O as the final electron acceptor. In tropical peatlands utilized for crop production, substrate (NO_3^- or NH_4^+) and some essential minerals (Fe, Mo, and S) necessary for denitrification and/or nitrification processes are provided by several types of fertilizers (ash, chemical fertilizers, manure, river sediments, etc.).

From one of the most active N_2O emission hotspots in the world (Takakai *et al*., 2006), order *Burkholderiales* of class *Betaproteobacteria* (e.g. genera *Burkholderia* and *Janthinobacterium*) were commonly isolated and characterized as major eubacterial N_2O emitters. All the N_2O emitters of *Burkholderia* isolated from the tropical peat soils showed hyper-active N_2O emissions (maximum 643 μg d^{-1} $vial^{-1}$) in the culture medium containing 0.3-1.0% sucrose and 0.03-0.2% NO_3^- (Hashidoko *et al*., 2008). This clear response of the N_2O emitters to supplemented sucrose are due to their oligotrophic nature; an important metabolic trait of denitrifiers.

Many N_2O emitters of *Burkholderiales* isolated from tropical peat soils are acid-tolerant eubacteria, and adaptable to nutrient-poor, medium to strongly acidic tropical peat soil (pH 3.0~4.5). Some *Burkholderia* spp. could survive in an acidic medium of less than pH 3.0. Therefore, we have speculated that frequent isolation of *Burkholderia* spp. was probably due to malfunctionality of N_2O reductase or complete loss of the enzyme in the acidic environment. N_2O reductase is highly susceptible to acidic conditions and loses its enzymatic activity in acidic conditions (Bergaust *et al*., 2010). Hence, denitrifiers in acidic soil often cause active N_2O emissions when the substrate (NO_3^-) was sufficient in the soil.

Two active N_2O emitting *Burkholderia* spp. selected from Riau, Indonesia and from Sarawak, Malaysia were subjected to genome sequencing using a second generation DNA sequencer, and it was directly evidenced that both *Burkholderia* spp. lost the N_2O reductase gene (*nosZ*). Thus, tropical peat soil under medium to strongly acidic conditions led to a defect of *nosZ* gene encoding the large subunit of N_2O reductase because N_2O reduction in acidic environment is neither effective nor costless. N_2O used as the final electron acceptor in the denitrification process is not an effective substrate because the catalytic enzyme N_2O reductase is highly susceptible to acidic conditions, and does not function in acidic soils. Hence, *nosZ*-missing denitrifiers are frequently isolated as powerful N_2O emitters.

N_2O emitting Pseudomonas spp. from vitric Andisol corn farmland

Ten strains of *Pseudomonas* denitrifiers were isolated from pre-tilled and post-harvest vitric Andisol corn farm soil (Nie *et al*., 2016). Using a combination of several universal primers (2 forward and 2 reverse primers, and a pair for atypical *nosZ* gene), PCR assay for detection of *nosZ* gene revealed that four out of ten strains harbored the *nosZ* gene. However, acetylene-blocking assay showed relatively weak N_2O reductase activities in the *nosZ*-harboring *Pseudomonas* denitrifiers. The remaining six *nosZ*-missing strains of *Pseudomonas* denitrifiers showed negative responses in the acetylene-blocking assay. This suggested that freeze-thawing conditions of the pre-tilled Andisol corn farm soils led to a suppression of N_2O reductase activity.

In a report by Qin *et al*. (2014), the optimal temperature of N_2O reductase ranged from 35-45 °C, relatively high compared to other enzymes associated with denitrification (e.g. nitrate reductase), and activity was drastically decreased below 20 °C (Qin *et al*., 2014). Thus, relatively low temperatures in the Andisol corn farm (Hokkaido, Japan, 42°25'N, 139°29'E) in winter may have caused a loss of the N_2O reductase activity in the *Pseudomonas* denitrifiers. They were typical oligotrophs and actively emitted N_2O in the 0.5% sucrose-supplemented medium for N_2O emission assay.

The response of *Pseudomonas* N_2O emitters to pH (range 3.2 to 7.6) was opposite to those isolated from tropical peat soils. In the acidic soils (3.2-5.5), N_2O emission was almost zero, but at more neutral conditions (5.5-7.6), N_2O constantly accumulated in the headspace, and maintained high levels of concentration (Nie *et al*., 2016).

CONCLUSION

In comparison of N_2O emitting potentials among the soils that we have examined, the tropical peat soils from the lands reclaimed for agricultural use and managed by fertilization of nitrogen and minerals showed relatively high N_2O emitting potentials (Hashidoko *et al.*, 2010). Similarly, the vitric Andisol from the corn farmland of sufficiently fertilized showed relatively active N_2O emission potential than the soils from the corn farmland without fertilization and from the pasture without tillage (Nie *et al.*, 2016). In the case of the boreal peatlands, *Sphagnum* mosses sampled from the degrading palsa mires along with increasing pH of the stagnant water tended to show relatively high N_2O emitting potentials. Thus, it is most likely that the emergence of active N_2O emitters in the terrestrial ecosystems is due to high disturbance of soil conditions mainly by human activity and global warming impact. Almost all of the denitrifying N_2O emitters that we have isolated from the global N_2O emission hotspots were mostly incomplete denitrifiers, which are missing the enzymatic activity of N_2O reductase or the *nosZ* gene itself.

ACKNOWLEDGEMENTS

We thank Dr. Suwido H. Limin (Palangkaraya University, Indonesia), Prof. Christopher H. Wijaya (Bogor Agriculture University, Indonesia), Dr. Lulie Melling (Tropical Peat Labo., Sarawak, Malaysia), Prof. Seiji Kondo (The Field Science Center for Northern Biosphere, Hokkaido University, Japan), and Dr. Teemu Tahvanainen (East Finland University, Finland) for their assistance in our soil sampling. This study was supported by Grants-in-Aid A (no. 20248033 and 26252058 to Y.H.), and B (26304042 to Y.H.) presented by the Japanese Society for the Promotion of Science (JSPS).

REFERENCES

1. Bergaust L, Mao YJ, Bakken LR, and Frostegard A. Denitrification response patterns during the transition to anoxic respiration and posttranscriptional effects of suboptimal pH on nitrous oxide reductase in *Paracoccus denitrificans*. ***Applied and Environmental Microbiology*, 76**, 8285–8285 (2010).
2. Galloway JN, Dentener FJ, Capone DG, Boyer EW, Howarth RW, Seitzinger SP, Asner GP, Cleveland CC, Green PA, Holland EA, Karl DK, Michaels AF, Porter JH, Townsend AR, and Vörösmarty CJ. Nitrogen cycles: past, present, and future. ***Biogeochemistry*, 70**, 153–226 (2004).
3. Hashidoko Y, Takakai F, Toma Y, Darung U, Melling L, Tahara S, and Hatano R. Emergence and behaviors of acid-tolerant *Janthinobacterium* sp. that evolves N_2O from deforested tropical peatland. ***Soil Biology and Biochemistry*, 40**, 116–125 (2008).
4. Hashidoko Y, Takeda H, Darung U, Melling L, and Hatano R. Genetic analysis of active N_2O-emitting bacteria from tropical peat soils for their nitrous oxide reductase gene. 19th World Congress of Soil Science, Soil Solutions for a Changing World, Brisbane, Australia, Abstract Paper, 86–88 (2010).
5. Hara S, Hashidoko Y, Desyatkin RV, Hatano R, and Tahara S. High rate of N_2 fixation by East Siberian cryophilic soil bacteria as determined by measuring acetylene reduction in nitrogen-poor medium solidified with gellan gum. ***Applied and Environmental Microbiology*, 75**, 2811–2819 (2009).
6. Jauhiainen J, Silvennoinen H, Hämäläinen R, Kusin K, Limin R, Raison RJ, and Vasander H. Nitrous oxide fluxes from tropical peat with different disturbance history and management. ***Biogeosciences*, 9**, 1337–1350 (2012).
7. Lau SYL, Hashidoko Y, Takahashi N, Hatano R, Melling L. Correlation between mineral nitrogen contents and vertical distribution of N_2O emission potentials in tropical peat soils are inverted in 2-year- and 10-year-cultivated oil palm plantations in Sarawak, Malaysia. ***Journal Journal of Agricultural Science & Technology B*,** 4, 787–796 (2014).
8. Metz B, Davidson OR, Bosch PR, Dave R, and Meyer LA (eds), IPCC. 2007. Climate Change 2007. Mitigation of Climate Change. Contribution of Working Group III to the Fourth Assessment Report of the Intergovernmental Panel on Climate Change. Cambridge University Press, United Kingdom and New York, NY, USA.
9. Mu Z, Huang A, Ni J, and Xie D. Linking annual N_2O emission in organic soils to mineral nitrogen input as estimated by heterotrophic respiration and soil C/N ratio. ***PLoS ONE*, 9**, e96572 (2012).
10. Nie Y, Li L, Isoda R, Hatano R, Wang M, and Hashidoko Y. Isolation of nitrous oxide (N_2O)-emitting *Pseudomonas* denitrifiers having lost their N_2O-reductase activity from dent corn Andisol farmland, an active spot of N_2O emission in Hokkaido, Japan. ***Microbes and Environments*,** 31, 93–103 (2016).
11. Nie Y, Li L, Wang M, Tahvanainen T, and Hashidoko Y. Nitrous oxide emission potentials of *Burkholderia* species isolated from the leaves of a boreal peat moss *Sphagnum fuscum*. **Bioscience, Biotechnology and *Biochemistry*,** 79, 2086–2095 (2015).

12. Philippot L, Andert J, Jones CM, Bru D, and Hallin S. Importance of denitrifiers lacking the genes encoding the nitrous oxide reductase for N_2O emissions from soil. ***Global Change Biology,*** **17**, 1497–1504 (2011).
13. Qin SP, Yuan HJ, Hu CS, Oenema O, Zhang YM, and X. X. Li. Determination of potential N_2O-reductase activity in soil. ***Soil Biology and Biochemistry***, **70**, 205–210 (2014).
14. Reay DS, Davidson EA, Smith KA, Smith P, Melillo JM, Dentener F, and Crutzen PJ. Global agriculture and nitrous oxide emissions. ***Nature Climate Change,*** **2**, 410–416 (2012).
15. Repo ME, Susiluoto S, Lind SE, Kinen S, Elsakov V, Biasi C, Virtanen T, Martikainen PJ. Large N_2O emissions from cryoturbated peat soil in tundra. ***Nature Geoscience,*** **2**, 189–192 (2009).
16. Sanford RA, Wagner DD, Wu Q, Chee-Sanford JC, Thomas SH, CruzGarcía C, Rodríguez G, Massol-Deyá A, Krishnani KK, Ritalahti KM, Nissen S, Konstantinidis KT, Löffler FE. Unexpected nondenitrifier nitrous oxide reductase gene diversity and abundance in soils. ***Proceedings of the National Academy of Sciences, USA,*** **109**, 19709–19714 (2012).
17. Scala DJ and Kerkhof LJ. Nitrous oxide reductase (*nosZ*) gene-specific PCR primers for detection of denitrifiers and three *nosZ* genes from marine sediments. FEMS Microbiol. Let. 162, 61–68 (1998).
18. Shiina Y, Itakura M, Choi H, Saeki Y, Hayatsu M, Minamisawa K. Relationship between soil type and N_2O reductase genotype (*nosZ*) of indigenous soybean bradyrhizobia: *nosZ*-minus populations are dominant in andosols. ***Microbes and Environments,*** **29**, 420–426 (2014).
19. Takakai F, Morishita T, Hashidoko Y, Darung U, Kuramochi K, Dohong S, Limin SH, Hatano R. Effects of agricultural land-use change and forest fire on N_2O emission from tropical peatlands, Central Kalimantan, Indonesia. ***Soil Science and Plant Nutrition***, **52**, 662–674 (2006).
20. Takeda H, Takahashi N, Hatano R, and Hashidoko Y. Active N_2O emission from bacterial microbiota of Andisol farmland and characterization of some N_2O emitters. ***Journal of Basic Microbiology***, **52**, 477–486 (2012).

Abstract No: A-448

COMPARISON OF MACROFUNGAL DIVERSITY BETWEEN PEAT SWAMP FOREST AND OIL PALM SMALLHOLDING IN PENINSULAR MALAYSIA

Siti Noor Shuhada Rajihan[1], Sabiha Salim[1*], Frisco Nobilly[3] and Badrul Azhar[2]

[1]Faculty of Forestry, Universiti Putra Malaysia, Malaysia
[3]Faculty of Agriculture, Universiti Putra Malaysia, Malaysia

[*]Corresponding author: sabiha@upm.edu.my

SUMMARY

The North Selangor Peat Swamp Forest is the second largest peat swamp forest ecosystem in Peninsular Malaysia. Changes in land use of peat swamp forest to oil palm agriculture can alter the macrofungal diversity. This study aimed to quantify the macrofungal diversity at three different landscapes; peat swamp forest, monoculture oil palm smallholding and polyculture oil palm smallholding. Five microclimate characteristics were studied, namely, air temperature, humidity, soil pH, soil moisture and wind speed. Substrates availability and vegetation structure such as canopy closure and canopy cover were also measured. A total of 45 plots were established using 9 transect lines in the study area. In January 2016 during rainfall season, a total of 608 macrofungal cluster recorded belongs to 56 families and 81 genera. The number of morphospecies and macrofungal cluster collection were higher ($P \leq 0.001$) at peat swamp forest than smallholding regardless monoculture or polyculture. For peat swamp forest under higher percentage of canopy cover, canopy closure and variety of substrate availability, the macrofungal diversity production increase with humidity and soil moisture but, decreased in air temperature, wind speed and soil pH value. For smallholding, due to lower percentage of canopy cover, canopy closure and also constrain in substrate availability, morphospecies richness and macrofungal abundance decreased with microclimate factor of humidity and soil moisture but increase in air temperature, wind speed and also soil pH value. Therefore, forest land cover contributes to suitable microclimate factors which are important for macrofungal diversity.

Keywords: *Macrofungal, Ecology, Peat swamp forest, Smallholding*

INTRODUCTION

North Selangor Peat Swamp Forest (NSPSF) is the second largest peat swamp forest in Peninsular Malaysia after South-East Peat Swamp Forest in Pahang. It consists of Raja Musa Reserve Forest and Sg. Karang Forest, covers approximately 73,593.03 ha (Rengasamy *et al.*, 2013). Since 2008, forest fire occurs extensively and degraded the forest area and reduced 1,231 ha and more of the forest area (Yule & Gomez, 2008).

Currently, oil palm plantations have surrounded at least 60% of the NSPSF perimeter (Azhar *et al.*, 2011). Recently, conversion of certain NSPSF area to plantation could change the biodiversity, this includes the fungi community that is important for plantation ecosystem. According to the previous reports, respond on macrofungal diversity information from the tropics is still lacking, especially in agricultural plantation, which creates a large knowledge gaps in fungal diversity knowledge in Malaysia. To date, little is known about the effects of forest conversion to oil palm agriculture on fungal diversity. Therefore, we aimed to quantify the macrofungal diversity based on its morphological characteristics at three different landscapes.

MATERIALS AND METHOD

We conducted macrofungal diversity inventories in three different landscapes; peat swamp forest, monoculture smallholding and polyculture smallholding during wet season in January 2016. We used systematic sampling with random starting point (Morrison *et al.*, 2008). A total of 45 circular plots were established using nine transect lines in the study area. Each transect was established 50 m away from the edge of both peat swamp and oil palm plantation. To avoid overlapping, sampling plots were distanced 50 m apart from each other. The geographical coordinates of the sampling point were mapped using a geographic positioning device (GPS II Plus, Garmin Ltd., Olathe, Kansas).

Within 20 m radius from the point centre, *in*-situ inventory and identification was carried out with the use of keys as guidelines (Kirk *et al.*, 2008). The specimens were next photographed and labeled before collection. We focused our sampling on basidiomycetes and ascomycetes with visible sporocarps. Their substrates were also recorded namely, branch with a diameter more than 2.5 cm, twigs with a diameter less than 2.5 cm, fallen leaves, fruit shells (López-Quintero *et al.*, 2012), living trees, trunks and soil (Gibertoni *et al.*, 2007). At each transect, we recorded the environmental factors, including air temperature, humidity, soil pH, soil moisture and wind speed. We also measured the vegetation characteristics such as canopy cover and closure. These factors may affect the occurrence of macrofungal diversity.

We performed one-way ANOVA to compare the number of family and genus between landscapes. Analysis of similarities (ANOSIM) was conducted to investigate the species compositional difference between landscapes. All of the statistical analysis data were conducted in Genstat version 12 software (VSNI, Hemel, Hempstead, UK).

RESULTS AND DISCUSSION

A total of 608 collections of macrofungal morphospecies clusters, from 81 genera belonging to 56 families were recorded. Our One-way ANOVA Tukey's comparison analysis present a statistical significant difference of morphospecies richness and habitat (F=38.19, $P \leq 0.001$). Our results show that morphospecies richness in forest landscape was greater than oil palm plantation smallholdings (Figure 1.a).

Analysis on the collection of macrofungal cluster, also shows a highly significant difference between habitat (F=16.06, $P \leq 0.001$). More than half of the total assemblage macrofungal were originated from the NSPSF (Figure 1.b). Result from previous study at Southern Brazil also reported on similar findings where macrofungal diversity in forest land, outnumbered macrofungal diversity in the oil palm smallholding (Paz *et al.*, 2015).

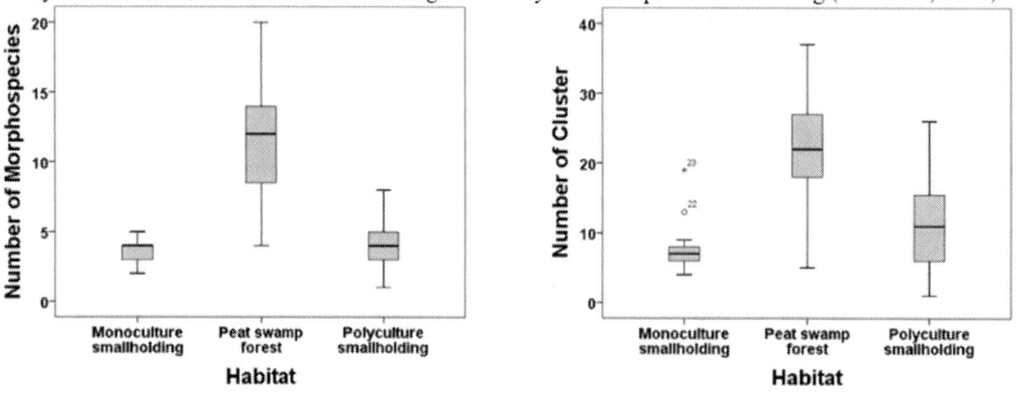

(a) (b)

Figure 1: (a) Mean analysis of variance between number of morphospecies richness collection and type of habitat, and. (b) Mean analysis of variance between macrofungal cluster and type of habitat.

The NSPSF had a denser canopy cover and more intense canopy closure compared to the smallholdings plantation with average of 98.13% (Figure 2.a) and 89.97% (Figure 2.b), respectively where various of tree composition were present inside the peat swamp forest. Due to this reason, various type of substrates such as coarse woody debris are available which explains high assemblage in macrofungal cluster collection at the NSPSF especially saprotrophic fungi of agarics (eg., *Inocybe* sp.) and polyporales (eg., *Trametes* sp.). Due to dense canopy cover also the air temperature of the NSPSF is low (Figure 3.a) and the humidity is high (Figure 3.b). This condition is favorable for the fungi to grow and with a closed canopy the wetter condition of this habitat is retained and resulted in low wind speed (Figure 3.c) but high soil moisture content (Figure 3.d) and is acidic (Figure 3.e) prior to peat swamp nature. Vegetation structure characteristics (eg., canopy cover and canopy closure) determine the distribution and occurrence of macrofungi (Villeneuve *et al.*, 1989; Laganá *et al.*, 1999; Senn-Irlet & Bieri, 1999; Moreau & Coutecuisse, 2003; Bonet *et al.*, 2004; Calado *et al.*, 2009). The modification in vegetative structure would change the original condition of microclimatic variables, mainly the temperature and moisture which function to provide suitable environment for the fungi to grow (Belsky *et al.*, 1989; Belsky, 1994).

Meanwhile, production of macrofungal communities is found more at polyculture smallholding compared to monoculture smallholding, with 24 and 21 morphospecies for polyculture and monoculture respectively. This could be due to different management practices (Paz *et al.*, 2015) and also change in microclimate. Polyculture smallholding comprised of three different crops namely, oil palm, coconut tree and banana, provides denser canopy cover of 81.63 % and higher percentage of canopy closure with 72.50% which result in lower temperature (Figure 3.a), and higher humidity (Figure 3.b) and provide a suitable condition for the fungi to grow. Prior to the vegetative structure, monoculture smallholding, records lowest percentage of canopy cover and canopy closure with 79.73% and 70.67% respectively. Thus, the climate is drier compared to other landscapes.

Nevertheless, during our study, we found similar macrofungal morphospecies in the monoculture and polyculture smallholdings. *Schizophyllum commune* and *Ganoderma* sp. were found to be the two most dominant morphospecies found in oil palm smallholdings (Table 1). Some of the fungi were found to be having the ability to adapt to dry condition such as *Schizophyllum commune* (Lodge & Cantrell, 1995) even though the substrate is limited. This is because, fungi are able to adapt to current condition and withstand water stress (Dighton, 2003). Based on the results, it was also found that *Ganoderma* sp. growing on oil palm and coconut trunk was more frequently occurred in polyculture compared to monoculture oil palm and, smallholding. This could be due to the polyculture oil palm management practice. The villagers cut these trees into a few portion and left them to rot at the sites. Wound on the trunk that remains open are vulnerable to microorganism including fungi communities (Hushiarian *et al.*, 2013).

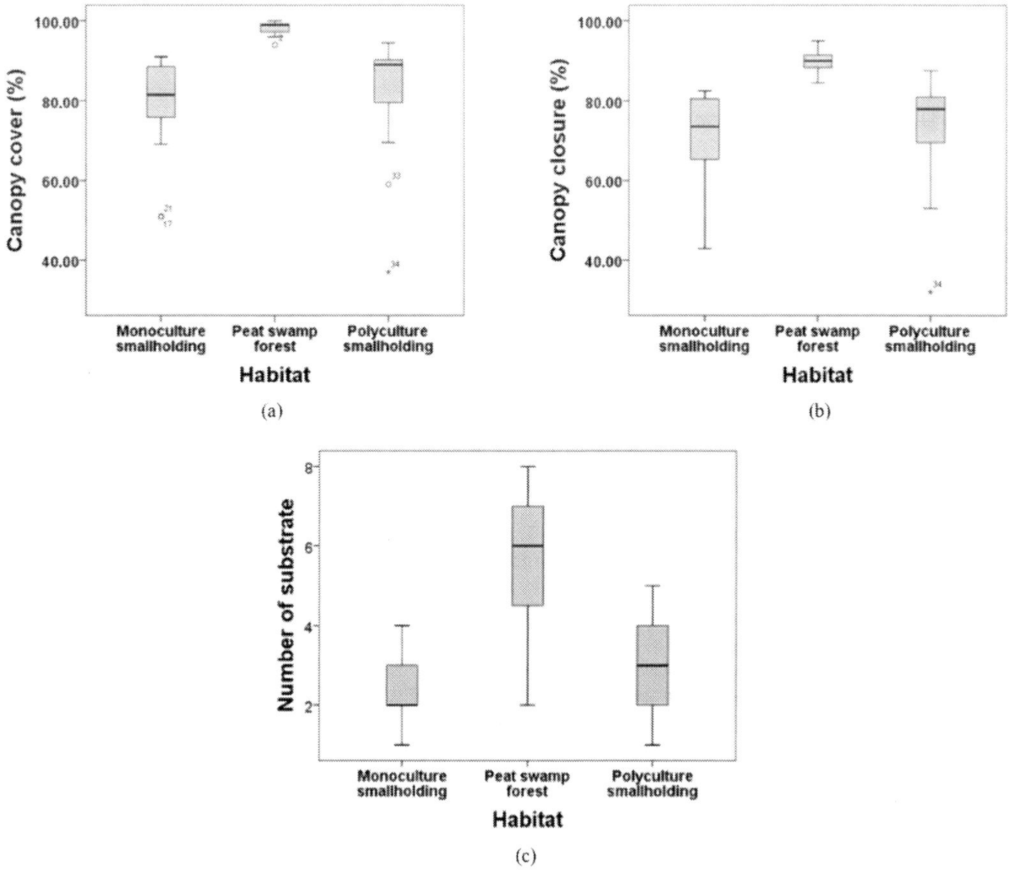

Figure 2: (a) Canopy cover (b) Canopy closure (c) Number of substrates and type of habitat

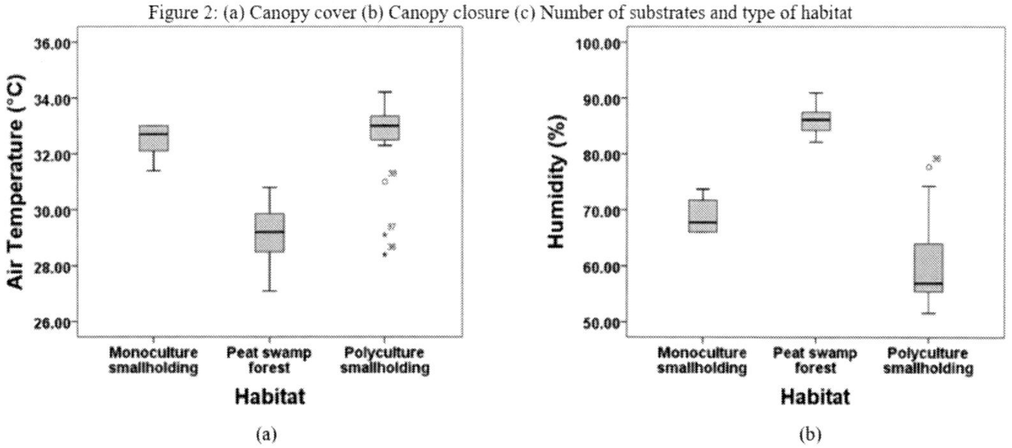

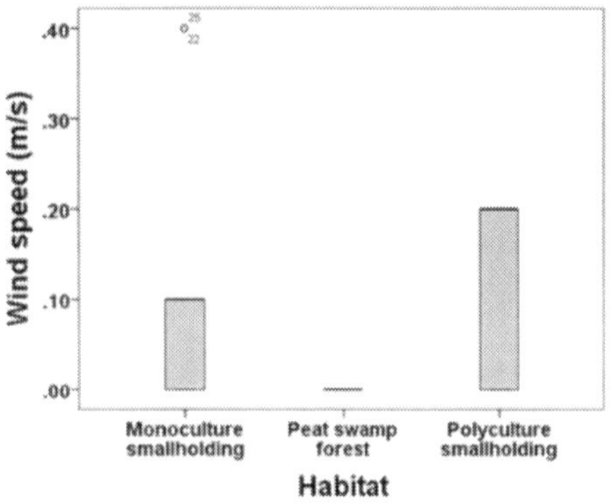

(c)

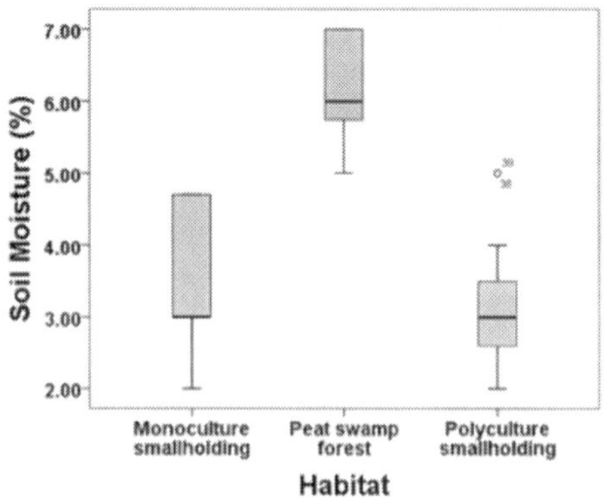

(d)

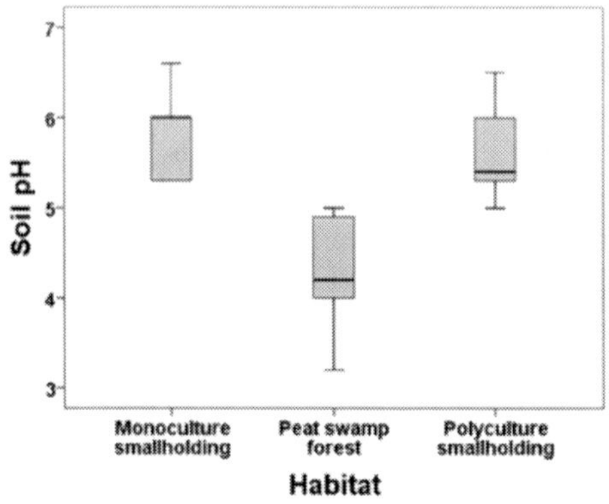

(e)

Figure 3: Boxplot on the mean readings of environmental data of. (a) Air temperature, (b) Humidity, (c) Wind speed, (d) Soil moisture, (e) Soil pH and type of habitat

Table 1: Morphospecies dominating all three different habitats

Habitat	Total morphospecies	Morphospecies	Family	Contribution (%)
Peat swamp forest	**61**	*Inocybe* sp.	Inocybaceae	25.11
		Marasmius rotalis	Marasmiaceae	18.20
		Mycena sp. 1	Mycenaceae	11.95
		Marasmiellus sp.	Marasmiaceae	9.40
		Bjerkandera adusta	Meruliaceae	6.72
		Marasmius sp. 1	Marasmiaceae	5.71
		Trametes sp. 3	Polyporaceae	3.36
		Coriolopsis sp. 1	Polyporaceae	2.46
		Tetrapygros nigripes	Marasmiaceae	2.31
		Trametes sp. 2	Polyporaceae	1.33
		Auricularia sp.	Auriculariaceae	1.18
		Trametes sp. 1	Polyporaceae	1.16
		Dichomitus sp.	Polyporaceae	1.14
				90.04%
Monoculture smallholding	**21**	*Schizophyllum commune*	Schizophyllaceae	63.96
		Ganoderma sp. 3	Ganodermataceae	13.95
		Marasmiellus sp.	Marasmiaceae	7.33
		Entoloma sp.	Entolomataceae	2.85
		Mycena sp. 6	Mycenaceae	2.67
				90.75%
Poly-culture smallholding	**24**	*Ganoderma* sp. 3	Ganodermataceae	31.20
		Schizophyllum commune	Schizophyllaceae	28.88
		Entoloma sp.	Entolomataceae	17.77
		Marasmiellus sp.	Marasmiaceae	11.01
		Trametes sp. 1	Polyporaceae	3.84
				92.71%

CONCLUSION

Forested landscape provides suitable microclimate condition for macrofungal diversity growth. Nevertheless, further study is needed especially on biodiversity-friendly agricultural management practice and its influence on macrofungal diversity. This study provides baseline information about macrofungal diversity in both forestry and agricultural landscapes. The information is useful to highlight the conservation value of those landscapes for macrofungi.

REFERENCES

1. Azhar, B., Lindermayer, D. B., Wood, J., Fischer, J., Manning, A., McElhinny, C., & Zakaria, M. (2011). The conservation value of oil palm estates, smallholdings and logged peat swamp forest for birds. *Forest Ecology and Management*. 262(12), 2306-2315.
2. Belsky, A. (1994). Influence of trees on savanna productivity: test of shade, nutrients, and tree-grass competition. *Ecology*. 75, 922-932.
3. Belsky, A. J., Amundson, R. G., Duxbury, J. M., Riha, S. J., Ali, A. R. & Mwonga, S. M., (1989). The effects on their physical chemical, and biological environments in a semi-arid savanna in Kenya. *Journal of Applied Ecology*. 26, 1005-1024.
4. Bonet, J., Fischer, C. & Colinas, C. (2004). The relationship between forest age and aspect on the production of sporocarps of ectomycorrhizal fungi in *Pinus sylvestris* forests of the central Pyrenees. *Forest Ecology and Management*. 203, 157-175.
5. Calado, M., Lauro, R. & Santos-Silva, C. (2009). Influence of different management practices in the macrofungal communities of a cork oak stand after an extended drought period, in Southern Protugal. *Boletin de la Sociedad Micológica de Madrid*. 33, 237-253.
6. Dighton, J. (2003). *Fungi in Ecosystem Processes*. Marcel Dekker, Inc. New York, United States of America.
7. Gibertoni, T. B., Santos, P. J. P. & Cavalcanti, M. A. Q. (2007). Ecological aspects of *Aphyllophorales* in the Atlantic Rain Forest in Northeast Brazil. *Fungal Diversity*. 25, 49-67.
8. Hushiarian, R., Yusof, N. A. & Dutse, S. W. (2013). Detection and control of Ganoderma boninense: strategies and perspectives. *SpringerPlus*. 2(1), 555.
9. Kirk, P. M., Cannon, P. F., Minter, D. W. & Stalpers, J. A. (2008). *Ainsworth & Bisby's Dictionary of the Fungi, 10th edn.* Cabi International. Wallingford.
10. Laganá, A., Loppi, S. & De Dominicis, V. (1999). Relationship between environmental factors and the proportions of fungal trophic groups in forest ecosystems of the central Mediterranean area. *Forest Ecology and Management*. 124, 145-151.
11. Lodge, D. J. & Cantrell, S. (1995). Fungal communities in wet tropical forests: variation in time and space. *Canadian Journal of Botany*. 73, 1391-1398.
12. López-Quintero, C. A., Straastsma, G., Franco-Molano, A. E. & Boekhout, T. (2012). Macrofungal diversity in Colombian Amazon forests varies with regions and regimes of disturbance. *Biodiversity and Conservation*. 21, 2221-2243.
13. Moreau, P. A. & Courtecuisse, R. (2003). Ecologie des Basidiomyce` tes dans les tourbie`res: quels facteurs expliquent la re´partition des carpophores?. *Bulletin of the Geobotanical Institute, ETH*. 69, 31–44.
14. Morrison, M. L., Block, W. M., Strickland, M. D., Collier, B. A. & Peterson, M. J. (2008). Wildlife Study Design, 2nd edition. Springer.
15. Paz, C. P., Gallon, M., Putzke, J. & Ganade, G. (2015). Changes in macrofungal communities following forest conversion into plantations in Southern Brazil. *Biotropica*. 47(5), 616-625.
16. Rengasamy, N., Hyrul, I. M. H., Nurhayati, H., Mangsor, H., Aszhar, A. & Zanidah, H. (2013). The socio-economic survey on importance of peat swamp forest ecosystem to local communities adjacent to Raja Musa Forest Reserve. Paper presented at *North Selangor Peat Swamp Forest, Scientific Biodiversity Expedition Proceedings 2013*. 28 November 2013. Hotel Quality, Shah Alam, Selangor Darul Ehsan.
17. Senn-Irlet, B. & Bieri, G. (1999). Sporocarp succession of soil-inhabiting macrofungi in an autochthous subalpine Norway spruce forest of Switzerland. *Forest Ecology and Management*. 124(2-3), 169-175.
18. Villeneuve, N., Grandtner, M. & Fortin, J. (1989). Frequency and diversity of ectomycorrhizal and saprophytic macrofungi in the Laurentide Mountains of Quebec. *Canadian Journal of Botany*. 67, 2616-2629.
19. Yule, C. M. & Gomez, L. N. (2008). Leaf litter decomposition in a tropical peat swamp forest in Peninsular Malaysia. *Wetlands Ecology and Management*. 17 (3), 231-241. Doi: 10.1007/s11273-008-9103-9.

Abstract no: A-422

EXPLORING NOVEL MICROBIAL LIGNOCELLULOSIC ENZYMES FROM INDONESIA PEATLAND AND HERBIVORES FOR CONVERSION OF OIL PALM EMPTY FRUIT BUNCH TO BIOFUEL

Amadeus Pribowo[1*], Irnayuli Sitepu[1], Ezra Wijaya[1], Victor De Vries[1] and Kyria Boundy-Mills[2]

[1]*Bioentrepreneurship Program, Indonesia International Institute for Life Sciences, Jakarta*
[2]*Phaff Yeast Culture Collection, University of California Davis, USA*

**Corresponding email: Amadeus.pribowo@i3L.ac.id*

SUMMARY

As the world's number one producer of palm oil, the palm oil industry in Indonesia produces more than 30 million metric tonnes of empty fruit bunches (EFB) every year. Currently, most of these biomass residues have little value or go to waste. These biomass residues can be converted into a number of value-added products, such as biofuels. On the other hand, a large part of Indonesian microbial biodiversity remains unknown to science due to minimum research funds and capabilities in Indonesia. The objective of this study is to explore Indonesia's biodiversity and to find novel enzymes that can improve the efficiency of converting Indonesia's abundant biomass residues into biofuels. We target microbial communities living in peat swamp forests and herbivore guts, that are likely sources of novel lignocellulose-degrading enzymes. Bioinformatic and metagenomics are used to identify and screen for lignocellulosic enzymes that can improve the bioconversion process from Indonesia's microbial biodiversity. Culturable microbes are isolated, purified, identified and screened for active enzymes using synthetic substrate and oil palm empty fruit bunch hydrolysate; and for the ability to convert hydrolysate to biofuel. The long term goal of the study is to promote the development of biorefineries by identifying new enzymes that can lower the cost of bioconversion, and new microbes that can facilitate the production of new products from biomass residues.

Keywords: Biodiversity, biomass, residue, metagenomic, biorefinery,

INTRODUCTION

Lignocellulose is the most abundant form of biomass, with an annual world production of around 170 billion metric tons (Amidon & Liu, 2009). Indonesia alone, as the world's number one producer of palm oil produces more than 30 million metric tons of empty fruit bunches biomass every year. Currently, most of these biomass residues have little value or go to waste. These biomass residues can be converted through biochemical pathways into a number of value-added products, such as liquid fuels, chemicals, electricity, and fibers, that can substitute for products currently derived from fossil fuels. The conversion of lignocellulosic biomass into this range of value-added products is known as the biorefinery concept. However, woody plant biomass that is composed mainly of cellulose, hemicelluloses and lignin is recalcitrant to natural degradation. Lignin is essentially the largest contributor to biomass recalcitrance (Strachan *et al.*, 2014). It is the cement that binds plant materials together and is the most abundant aromatic component of higher plant cell walls, such as woody plants including ferns (T K Kirk & Farrell, 1987). Biomass recalcitrance has made it a challenge for research especially in microbial breakdown.

Conversion of biomass into simple sugars requires a large amount of enzymes to accelerate the degradation process. Consequently, this use of a high amount of enzymes increases the cost of the bioconversion process. Over the past 10 years, intense research efforts have focused on trying to lower the cost of enzymes in the bioconversion process. There are generally three strategies that have been proven effective in lowering the enzyme costs: reducing the cost of enzyme production, improving the efficiency of individual enzymes through genetic and protein engineering, or creating a more efficient enzyme mixture by enhancing the synergistic activities of the individual enzyme components in the mixture. Arguably, most of the improvements in the efficiency of enzyme mixtures, and the resulting decrease in the cost of using enzymes, have been achieved through the last strategy. In recent years, many new enzymes with novel activities have been identified and characterized to have synergistic effects with classic cellulolytic enzyme mixtures during the bioconversion process.

Both Indonesia and Malaysia are countries of mega-biodiversity. Our research aims to develop Indonesia's capacity in biodiversity research to facilitate exploration of Indonesia's biodiversity both using metagenomic and culturable microbes in order to identify new enzymes and microbes that can enhance the efficiency of the bioconversion process as well as to build a culture collection to facilitate ex-situ conservation of Indonesia's microbial diversity. The long term goal of the study is to promote the development of biorefineries by identifying new enzymes that can lower the cost of bioconversion, and new microbes that can facilitate the production of new products from biomass residues.

The microbial diversity of Indonesia's peat swamp forests and of herbivore guts are chosen for our study as potential environmental pools that harbor lignocellulosic enzymes. Peat is partially decomposed biomass material that gets accumulated over years and is typically enriched in lignin and humic acid (Factors, 2015). The high proportion of lignin in peat may naturally promote the selection of microbial communities that can degrade or modify lignin. On the other hand, buffaloes, unlike cows, are known to be able to thrive on a diet of low quality feed (Bilal *et al.*, 2006). Therefore, buffaloes likely harbor gut microflora that can efficiently break down cellulose and hemicelluloses, enabling the herbivores to extract nutrients from this low quality feed. Therefore, microbial communities thriving in peat and buffalo gut are ideal sources to find novel enzymes that can improve the efficiency of the bioconversion process.

Both bioinformatics and metagenomics approaches will be used to identify new enzymes from the microbial diversity in these two ecosystems as these approaches allow for an assessment of the total genetic diversity in an environmental sample. Bioinformatics approach is used to evaluate and identify new enzymes that can improve the bioconversion process from Indonesia's biodiversity in peat soil and buffalo manure. Metagenomics are used to explore the total genetic diversity of enzymes present in an environmental sample. In addition, culturable microbes are also isolated and screened for active enzymes using synthetic substrates such as pure cellulose and oil palm empty fruit bunches as a representation of a real lignocellulosic biomass.

METHODS

Field sampling and microbial isolation

Environmental samples are gathered from two different environments: peat swamp and herbivore manures. Buffalo and cow manure were collected from PT. Sumber Alam Ciapus (SAC), Bogor. SAC center breeds buffaloes and cows with the focus on commercial breeding of spotted buffaloes. Eleven fresh manure samples from seven buffaloes and four cows were collected; pH and temperature of the manure were measured. Each sample was split into three different categories: crude samples, metagenomic analysis, and culturable microbes. All three are preserved at -80°C. To isolate culturable microbes, environmental sample is dissolved in phosphate buffer saline solution and 50μL slurry was plated on three types of media, potato dextrose agar (PDA) with chloramphenicol, rose bengal chloramphenicol agar (RBCA), and 1/10 strength nutrient agar (NA) with cycloheximide. These media allow isolation of filamentous fungi, yeast and bacteria, respectively. The plates are incubated at room temperature (24°C) until visible colonies are observed. Each different colony is purified on pure PDA without chloramphenicol and preserved at -80°C for further use. Filamentous fungi, yeast and bacteria are identified to species level by ribosomal sequencing using standard methods (Golomb *et al.*, 2013; Kumar & Shukla, 2005; Weisburg *et al.*, 1991). For the yeast species, the taxonomy term "aff." indicates that the strain belongs to a novel species that is most closely related to the species (Garay *et al.*, 2016). Peat swamp sampling and sample processing are currently ongoing.

In addition, both oil palm EFB and peat will also be used to enrich for microbes that can degrade lignin. EFB and peat will be added to the growth media as carbon sources at concentrations of 10 g/ml. Microbes will be grown at 50°C and growth will be monitored daily. After sufficient growth has been achieved, supernatants will be collected and analyzed for biomass conversion, enzymatic activities, and protein content. In addition, the microbes will be collected along with the biomass pellet.

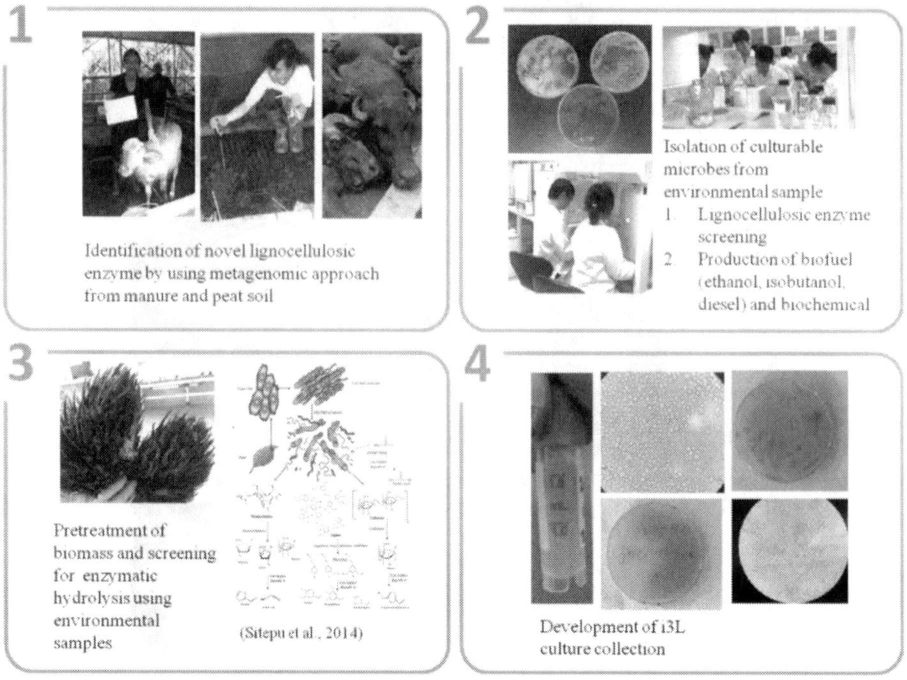

Figure 5: Microbial isolations from environmental samples and EFB pretreatment scenario

Pretreatment and enzymatic hydrolysis of oil palm empty fruit bunch

Hydrolytic efficiency of novel enzymes identified from the environmental samples will be tested on oil palm EFB. Oil palm EFB was obtained from 4-year old oil palm trees planted in Goaboma village, Monterado, district Bengkayang in West Kalimantan. Prior to enzymatic hydrolysis, the EFB will be pretreated with formic acid: water : HCl organosolvent to allow liberation of lignin, cellulose and hemicelluse (Figure 2) (Ferrer *et al.*, 2011). The liberated polymers are then subjected to enzymatic reaction (Sitepu *et al.*, 2014a), using native and commercial enzyme Novozymes Cellic® CTec2 to degrade the polymer into monomer or dimer molecules that will be fed to microbes for biofuel conversion.

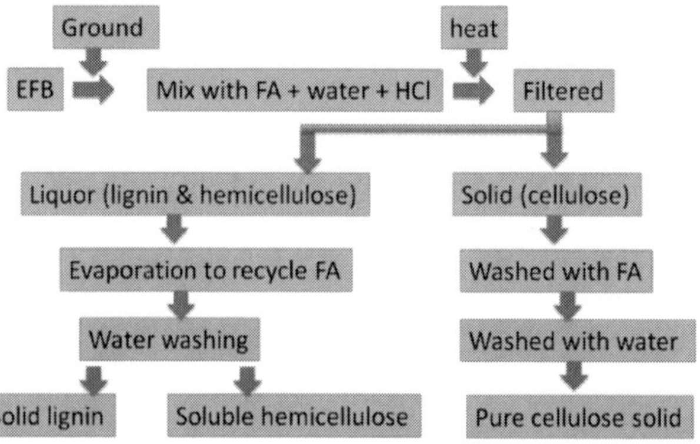

Figure 6: Pretreatment of EFB using organosolvent following methods by Ferrer *et al.* (Ferrer *et al.*, 2011)

Bioinformatic and metagenomics

In house database is generated to gather information from available database about known ligninolytic and cellulolitic enzymes and the microbes that synthesize them. A separate local database is prepared for known microbes and enzymes of Indonesia origins that have been studied and published online. Then, the two databases are linked to map out all possible enzymes that may present in these microbes found in Indonesia. Potential microbes are prioritized for screening against lignocelluloses substrate. In line with this activity, metagenomic analysis from manure and peat soil will be conducted to screen for enzymes from environmental samples (Figure 3).

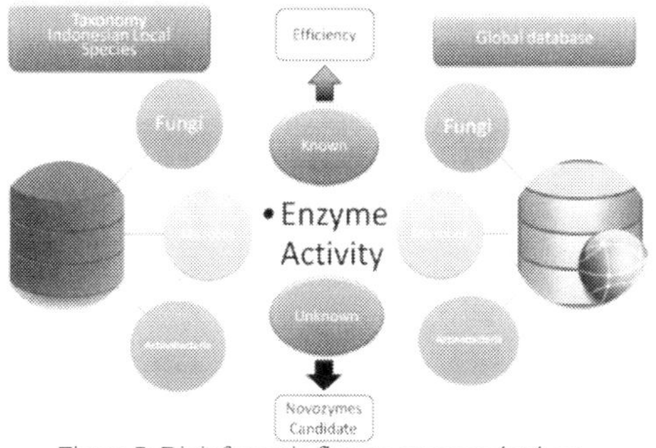

Figure 7: Bioinformatic flow to generate database

Conversion of hydrolysate to fuel

Hydrolysate that is generated from oil palm EFB is fed to microbe for bioconversion to biofuel. In this case, oleaginous yeasts collected from the environmental samples are tested for growth and lipid accumulation in EFB hydrolysate. Candidates that show high growth are scaled up to get enough material to investigate intracellular lipid accumulation following protocols described in Sitepu *et al.* (Sitepu *et al.*, 2014b)

RESULTS AND DISCUSSION

This section provides preliminary results of the study. All the activities outlined in the methodology section are still ongoing and more data/results are still gathered.

We selected environmental samples that would likely harbor diverse microbes that can break down lignocelluloses and/or convert biomass to biofuel. The taxon composition of culturable microbes is presented in Figure 4. Isolation of microbes from the environmental sample is ongoing. Colony morphology observation indicated diverse filamentous fungi, yeast and bacteria present in this sample (Figure 5). Identification of the microbe using ribosomal sequencing is ongoing.

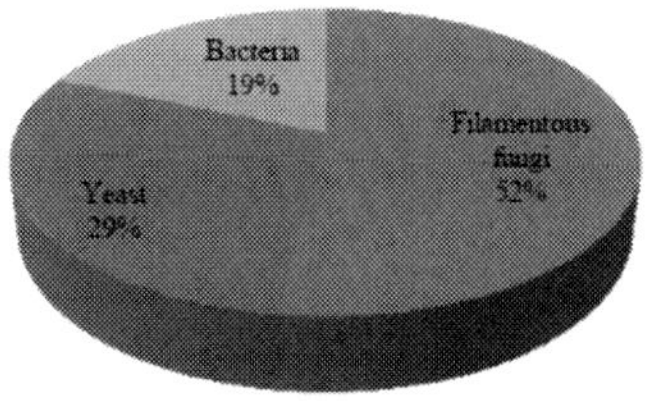

Figure 8: Ratio of filamentous fungi, yeast and fungi isolated from environmental samples

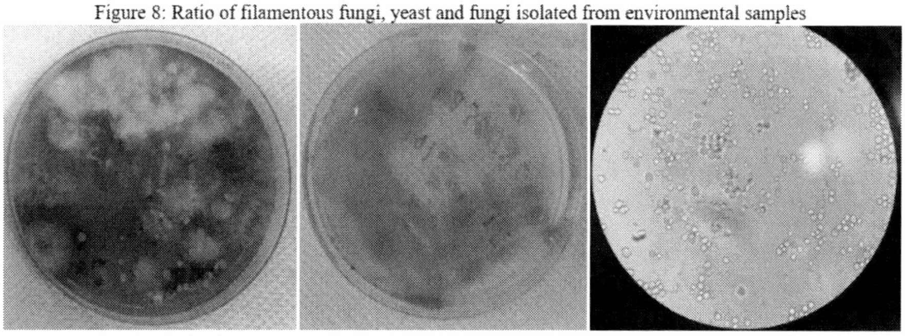

Figure 9: A. Different colonies of microbes grown in RBCA media; B. Yeast grown on PDA; C. Yeast cells under microscope with 1000X magnification

TENTATIVE CONCLUSIONS

The rich biodiversity of Indonesia's microbes serve as potential source for accelerating degradation of biomass and conversion of the biomass into valuable chemicals such as biofuel. Our preliminary results indicated that environmental samples collected from buffalo manure harbor diverse microbes and they are currently investigated for their ability to bioconvert oil palm empty fruit bunch to biofuel.

ACKNOWLEDGMENTS

The study is funded by USAID Partnership for Enhanced Engagement in Research Grant ID# 4-146. Microbes used in this study are collected from PT Sumber Alam Ciapus, Bogor, and a peat swamp in Riau, Indonesia. We would like to thank i3L undergraduate students for their technical assistance, Sanjeevini Pertiwi, Florencia Dewanto, Jeremy Gunawan, Joshua Viryawan, Nurulfitri Wisetyaningsih, and Margaret. Technicians Felic Fanusi, Ester Yusmarina and Sanjaya M Waani are thanked for laboratory and/or field sampling assistance.

REFERENCES

1. Amidon, T.E., Liu, S. 2009. Water-based woody biorefinery. *Biotechnology Advances*, **27**(5), 542-550.
2. Ferrer, A., Vega, A., Ligero, P., Rodriguez, A. 2011. Pulping of empty fruit bunches (EFB) from the palm oil industry by formic acid. *BioResources*, **6**(4), 4282-4301.
3. Golomb, B.L., Morales, V., Jung, A., Yau, B., Boundy-Mills, K.L., Marco, M.L. 2013. Effects of pectinolytic yeast on the microbial composition and spoilage of olive fermentations. *Food microbiology*, **33**(1), 97-106.
4. Kumar, M., Shukla, P.K. 2005. Use of PCR Targeting of Internal Transcribed Spacer Regions and Single-Stranded Conformation Polymorphism Analysis of Sequence Variation in Different Regions of rRNA Genes in Fungi for Rapid Diagnosis of Mycotic Keratitis. *Journal of Clinical Microbiology*, **43**(2), 662-668.
5. Sitepu, I.R., Garay, L.A., Sestric, R., Levin, D., Block, D.E., German, J.B., Boundy-Mills, K.L. 2014a. Oleaginous yeasts for biodiesel: Current and future trends in biology and production. *Biotechnology Advances*, **32**(7), 1336-1360.
6. Sitepu, I.R., Jin, M., Fernandez, J.E., da Costa Sousa, L., Balan, V., Boundy-Mills, K.L. 2014b. Identification of oleaginous yeast strains able to accumulate high intracellular lipids when cultivated in alkaline pretreated corn stover. *Applied microbiology and biotechnology*, 1-13.
7. Strachan, C.R., Singh, R., VanInsberghe, D., Ievdokymenko, K., Budwill, K., Mohn, W.W., Eltis, L.D., Hallam, S.J. 2014. Metagenomic scaffolds enable combinatorial lignin transformation. *Proceedings of the National Academy of Sciences*, **111**(28), 10143-10148.
8. T K Kirk, a., Farrell, R.L. 1987. Enzymatic "Combustion": The Microbial Degradation of Lignin. *Annual Review of Microbiology*, **41**(1), 465-501.
9. Weisburg, W.G., Barns, S.M., Pelletier, D.A., Lane, D.J. 1991. 16S ribosomal DNA amplification for phylogenetic study. *Journal of Bacteriology*, **173**(2), 697-703.

Abstract No: A-374

IMPACT OF FIRE ON MICROBIAL DIVERSITY AND COMMUNITY STRUCTURE IN MALAYSIAN PEATLANDS

Catherine M. Yule[1*], Stephanie Evers[2], Thomas Smith[3], Han Ming Gan[1], Chin Chin Too[1] and Wilhelm W.H. Eng[1]

[1] *School of Science, Monash University Malaysia*
[2] *School of Biosciences, University of Nottingham Malaysia Campus*
[3] *Department of Geography, King's College London*

* *Corresponding author: catherine.yule@monash.edu*

Microbial communities of regional peatlands are poorly known. We used 16S rRNA gene sequencing to assess impacts of fire and degradation on microbial diversity and community structure in peatlands in Peninsular Malaysia. We analysed microbes in surface peat samples from a relatively pristine peat swamp forest (North Selangor PSF) and compared them with surface peat samples from actively burning, degraded peat on the west coast (near Pekan PSF). We then analysed samples from the burning site after we dried them in an oven for 24 hrs at 60° C to determine the effects of further heating and drying (as would be expected to happen to peat near a fire). We also measured environmental parameters such as peat pH, organic carbon, nitrogen and phosphorus. Next Generation Sequencing results indicated that in surface PSF peat Proteobacteria was the dominant phylum, followed by Acidobacteria. The microbial community composition was significantly impacted by fire and also by laboratory heating and drying. Degradation and burning caused a marked decrease in most Acidobacteria, apart from Koribacteraceae. But Koribacteraceae were almost eliminated by laboratory burning and drying. Burning resulted in a significant increase in relative abundance of Actinomycetales, Acidimicrobiales and Crenarchaeota (but the latter two groups were then strongly negatively impacted by laboratory heating and drying). Further heating caused a decrease in Rhodospirillaceae (Proteobacteria), but an increase in relative abundance of Micrococcaceae (Actinobacteria) and also *Bacillus* and *Alicyclobacillus* (Firmicutes). *Bacillus* endospores have been shown to be highly resistant to heat and desiccation in extreme terrestrial environments. Similarly *Alicyclobacillus* are soil-dwelling bacteria that are tolerant of acidity (pH 2.0 to 6.0) and high temperatures (up to 70 °C). Changes in microbial communities caused by peat fires will impact the functioning of microbes with respect to litter decomposition, soil nutrient cycling and greenhouse gas emissions.

Keywords: -

Abstract No: A-330

SPECIES COMPOSITION AND ENVIRONMENTAL FACTORS OF GRASSLANDS DEVELOPING ON THE BURNT PEATLANDS IN SUMATRA, INDONESIA

Satomi Shiodera[1*], Kazuo Yabe[2], Masayuki Itoh[1], Osamu Kozan[1], Tika Dewi Atikah[3] and Joeni Setijo Rahajoe[3]

[1]*Center for Southeast Asian Studies (CSEAS), Kyoto University, Japan*
[2]*Sapporo City University, Japan*
[3]*Research Center for Biology, Indonesian Institute of Sciences (RCB-LIPI), Indonesia*

* *Corresponding author:sshiodera@gmail.com*

SUMMARY

In Sumatra, peat fire is a serious problem for the last two decades. It is a major cause of degradation that leads to loss of biodiversity and carbon stocks in peat swamp forests. After peat fire, grasslands will develop in the early successional stage there. To understand the relationship between grassland vegetation and environmental factors, field observations were conducted in Riau province, Sumatra, Indonesia. Fifty-one 2 × 2 m plots in the various grassland communities were set-up which spent several years after peat fire disturbance. Species compositions and coverage rates of all species in each plot were checked. The ground water levels were measured on October/December (wet season), 2014 and February (dry season), 2015. Groundwater sample was collected at the same time. In situ pH and electrical conductivity (EC) were measured by a compact pH and EC meter, respectively. In the laboratory, dissolved organic carbon (DOC) and total dissolved nitrogen (TDN) concentrations were determined using a total organic carbon (TOC) analyzer. Forty five plant species were found from our plots (total 204 m2). There were only a few tree species were found in site that experienced fire, although many kinds of forb and grass species were found. They were seventeen forbs, eight grasses, nine ferns, nine shrubs and two trees. Dominant families were *Asteraceae*, *Cyperaceae* and *Poaceae*. Species composition seems to be decided by the groundwater level and water quality.

Keywords: *forest degradation, recovery, environmental impact assessment, anthropogenic disturbance, forest management*

INTRODUCTION

Most of the tropical peatlands (24.8 Mha, 56 %) are found in the Southeast Asia region (47 % in Indonesia, 6 % in Malaysia, 3 % in Papua New Guinea, with small pockets and remnants in Brunei, Myanmar, the Philippines, Thailand and Vietnam) (Page *et al.* 2011). Tropical peat swamp forests are unique ecosystems, because of their extreme acidic, anaerobic and nutrient poor conditions. They support diverse forms of flora, fauna and microbes with manyendemic and endangered species. Anderson (1963) recorded 927 species of flowering plants and ferns in the peat swamp forests of Borneo. Most of tree families that are present in lowland dipterocarp forests are also presented in peat swamp forests, but many of species in peat swamp forests are specific to this habitat (Yule 2010, Rahajoe *et al.* 2016). The tropical peatland ecosystems sustain distinctive biodiversity and ecosystem values (Riely and Page 2005), and important refuges for many endangered species including orangutans. At the same time, tropical peatlands are one of the largest sink of organic carbon. The carbon is stored not only in the living biomass, but also in the peat soil. In Southeast Asia, their high carbon density results in a large regional peat carbon store of 68.5 Gt, equivalent to 77 % of the tropical and 11 – 13 % of the global peat carbon pools (Page *et al.* 2011). Indonesia has the largest stock of tropical peat carbon (57.4 Gt, 65%). This data is used to provide revised estimates for Indonesian forest soil carbon pools of 77 Gt, and total forest carbon pools (biomass plus soil) of 97 Gt. Peat carbon contributes 74 % to the total forest soil carbon pools in Indonesia. However, Indonesia is also the third largest emitter of greenhouse gases from peat fires. However, all regional peatlands are threatened by either logging, drainage, agricultural conversion (mostly to oil palm, as well as rice, rubber, coconut and pineapple), fire or other human activities. In Sumatra, peat fire has been a serious problem since the last decade. Peat fire is a major cause of peatland degradation that leads to loss of biodiversity and carbon stock in peat swamp forests. Analysis using Satellite Pour l'Observation de la Terre (SPOT) image clarified that less than 4 % of peatland areas remain covered by intact peat swamp forests (PSFs), while 37 % are covered by PSFs with varying degree of degradation, and over 20 % is considered to be a un-managed degraded landscape, occupied by ferns, shrubs and secondary growth in Sumatra and Kalimantan (Miettinen *et al.* 2010). Peat swamp forests are sustained in the sensitive balance among deep water tables, canopy cover and leaf litter inputs (Yule 2010), causing difficulties in forest recovery after fire.

In other words, this type of landscape is highly susceptible to further degradation and very difficult to regenerate into forest (Page *et al.* 2009, Shiodera *et al.* 2016). In this study, the impact of fire disturbance to peatlands was evaluated The various grassland communities which developed after peat fire, and the relationships between species composition and some environmental characteristics were compared.

METHODS

Research sites

This study was conducted in Riau Province, Sumatra, Indonesia. In this area, repeated occurrence of peat fire changed peat swamp forest to degraded bare land. Degraded peatlands which experienced peat fire around there (35° N, 136° E; 190–255 m above sea level). The study site has rainy and dry seasons affected by the inter-tropical convergence zone, which usually results in a rainy season (November - December) and two dry seasons (January - May and June - September) (Baum *et al.* 2007) in a year in the area.

Vegetational research on the burnt sites

The research period was from October, 2014 to March, 2015. To understand the relationship between vegetational types and environment factors, field observations were conducted in Tanjung Leban and some neighboring villages. Fifty-one 2 × 2 m plots in the various grassland communities were set-up which spent several years after peat fire disturbance. Species components and coverage rates of all species in each plot were checked. The species identification was conducted by researchers and engineering officials in the Research Center for Biology, Indonesian institute of Science (RCB-LIPI), by comparing the samples in the herbarium one by one.

Measurement of soil water contents and analysis of groundwater samples

The ground water levels were measured manually using water-level indicator in December 2014 (wet season) and February 2015 (dry season). Piezometer was inserted in the soil for 1.0 m depth to measure subsurface groundwater levels and collect the groundwater samples at each plot. In situ Ph and electrical conductivity (EC) were measured using a compact pH meter (LAQUA, Twin pH; HORIBA, Kyoto, Japan) and EC meter (LAQUA, Twin Cond, HORIBA, Kyoto Japan), respectively. Then, water samples were filtered, through glass-fiber filters (GF/F; nominal particle retention, 0.7 μm; Whatman, UK). In the laboratory, dissolved organic carbon (DOC) concentrations and total dissolved nitrogen (TDN) concentrations were determined using a total organic carbon (TOC) analyzer (TOC-V; Shimadzu, Japan).

RESULTS AND DISCUSSION

Forty five (45) plant species were found from the study plots (total 204 m2). Four (4) types of vegetations were identified namely *Pennisetum*, *Blechnum*, *Scleria* and *Stenochlaena* (Figure 1). However,there were only a few tree species, but many kinds of forb and grass species were found in sites that experienced fire . There were seventeen (17) forbs and eight (8) grasses, nine (9) ferns, nine (9) shrubs and two (2) trees. Dominant families were Asteraceae (seven species), Cyperaceae (four species) and Poaceae (four species). Two (2) tree species, *Elaeis guineensis* Jacq (oil palm) and *Acacia crassicarpa* A.Cunn ex Benth, were planted by local people for commercial use or natural regeneration after seed dispersal by birds. Seedlings or saplings of other tree species were not found. There were only four (4) shrub species, which were light-demanded species. Many *Asteraceae* species were found, however the coverage was less than 0.01 % in each plot. In contrast, the coverage of some Cyperaceae and Poaceae species were very high. Fern species also separated into higher and lower coverage species. The higher coverage fern species were *Stenochlaena* sp. (Blechnaceae), *Pteridium* sp. (Dennstaedtiaceae) and *Blechnum orientale L.* (Blechnaceae). As for the grass species, *Pennisetum polystachyum* (L.) Schult. (Poaceae) and *Imperata cylindrica* (L.) Rausch. (Poaceae) also showed higher coverage in the sites. The groundwater depth and quality were different with each vegetational type (Table 1).

CONCLUSION

Species composition seems to be influenced by the level of the groundwater table and water quality in the burnt grassland in peatlands in Indonesia.

ACKNOWLEDGEMENTS

We are grateful to the Research Center for Biology, Indonesian institute of Science (RCB-LIPI) for the permission to conduct our research. We also thank Mr. Ahmad Muhammad, Dr. Haris Gunawan, Riau univercity; Mr. and Mrs. Nur for supporting our research. This work was supported by the Institutional Collaboration Feasibility Studies

"Toward the Regeneration of Tropical Peat Land Societies: Establishment of an International Research Network and Proposal of its Future", Research Institute for Humanity and Nature (RIHN), Japan.

Figure 1: Various vegetation after peat fire (left; *Blechnum orientale L. (Blechnaceae)*, center, *Cyperaceae*, right; *Pennisetum polystachyum (L.) Schult.(Poaceae))*.

Table 1. The environmental factors of each vegetational site. The values in parenthesis are standard deviation in each site.

Site name (Dominant species)	Ground water level (cm)	Soil water contents (%)	pH	EC (μS/cm)	TOC (mg/l)	TDN (mg/l)
***Pennisetum* sites**	-74.86 (22.9)	5.48 (3.3)	4.16 (0.4)	90.9 (14.7)	27.98 (3.1)	0.38 (0.1)
***Blechnum* sites**	-27.64 (12.7)	9.98 (3.7)	3.95 (0.4)	96.5 (18.1)	26.45 (2.8)	0.38 (0.0)
***Scleria* sites**	-33.24 (24.8)	32.21 (14.5)	3.84 (0.3)	111.2 (26.2)	23.90 (4.0)	2.97 (3.8)
***Stenochlaena* sites**	-60.16 (13.5)	3.1 (1.9)	3.8 (0.1)	86.2 (9.8)	33.43 (1.2)	0.40 (0.0)

REFERENCES

1. Anderson J (1963) The flora of the peat swamp forests of sarawak and brunei. Including a catalogue of all recorded species of glowering plants, ferns and fern allies. *The Gardens' Bulletin Singapore*, 29: 131 – 228
2. Baum, A., Rixen, T. and Samiaji, J., 2007, Relevance of peat draining rivers in central Sumatra for the riverine input of dissolved organic carbon into the ocean, Estuarine, *Coastal and Shelf Science* 73: 563-570.
3. Joeni Setijo Rahajoe, Laode Alhamd, Tika Dewi Atikah, Bayu A Pratama, Satomi Shiodera and Takashi S. Kohyama, 2016, Floristic diversity in the peatland ecosystem in Central Kalimantan, *Tropical Peatland Ecosystems*, eds. Mitsuru Osaki and Noriyuki Tsuji, pp. 167-196, Springer Japan.
4. Miettinen, J., and S. C. Liew. 2010. Degradation and development of peatlands in Peninsular Malaysia and in the islands of Sumatra and Borneo since 1990. *Land Degradation & Development* 21: 285-296.
5. Page, S.E., Rieley, J.O. and Banks, C.J. 2011, Global and regional importance of the tropical peatland carbon pool. *Global Change Biology* 17: 798–818.
6. Page S, Hoscilo A, Wosten H, Jauhiainen J, Silvius M, Rieley J, Ritzema H, Tansey K, Graham L, Vasander H, Limin S. 2009. Restoration ecology of lowland tropical peatlands in southeast asia: Current knowledge and future research directions. *Ecosystems*, 12: 888-905
7. Rieley JO, Page SE (2005) Wise use of tropical peatlands: Focus on southeast asia. Alterra, The Netherlands
   8. Satomi Shiodera, Tika Dewi Atikah, Ismail Apandi, Tatsuyuki Seino, Akira Haraguchi, Joeni Setijo Rahajoe and Takashi S. Kohyama, 2016, Impact of peat-fire disturbance to forest structure and species composition in tropical peat forests in Central Kalimantan, Indonesia, in *Tropical Peatland Ecosystems*, eds. Mitsuru Osaki and Noriyuki Tsuji, pp. 197-212, Springer Japaan.
8. Yule, C. M. 2010. Loss of biodiversity and ecosystem functioning in Indo-Malayan peat swamp forests. *Biodiversity and Conservation* 19: 393-409.

1.6: CONSERVATION OF PEATLAND FOREST & WILDLIFE

Abstract No: A-341

CONSERVATION IN THE PRODUCTION AREAS: AN OPPORTUNITY TO CONSERVE WILD CAT SPECIES IN KAMPAR PENINSULAR, RIAU PROVINCE, INDONESIA

Donny Gunaryadi[1], Petrus Gunarso[2*], Ryan Avriandy[1], Irene Margareth Romaria Pinondang[1], Andi Arya Fajar Art Christ[1], Safrina Ayu Trisnawati[1], Nugraha Putra Maulana[1], Husnul Fikri[1], Ahmad Dani[1] and Muhammad Iqbal[2]

[1]*Fauna Flora International-Indonesia Programme, Indonesia*
[2]*Riau Ecosystem Restoration, Indonesia*

**Corresponding author: petrus_gunarso@aprilasia.com*

ABSTRACT

The Kampar Peninsula in Riau is a unique ecosystem and shown its unique distribution of biodiversity. Although the peninsula was categorized as production forests since the eighties, the degradation of the core of Kampar Peninsula considered as lowest in the region. To assess the richness of wildlife in Kampar Peninsula, Biodiversity assessments have been conducted by collaborating partner, Fauna & Flora International-Indonesia Programme using camera trap in the landscape. Biodiversity richness of this lightly degraded area is significant. Five species of wild cats of Sumatra were found in the landscape including the charismatic Sumatran Tiger and a rare species of the flat-headed cat. Several large mammals species such as, sunbear, sambar deer and bearded pig were found in the area as well as several unique and endemic species of birds, reptiles and amphibians. Based on this initial finding and the existence of top predator in the region, and its potential of recording new species, the biodiversity richness in the whole Kampar Peninsula appears to be potentially high and its conservation status most likely more significant than the neighbouring designated conservation areas.

***Keywords**: Kampar Peninsula, peatland, tiger, flat-headed cat, camera trap, restoration.*

INTRODUCTION

The Kampar peninsula which part of the largest peatland forest for Riau, provided important ecosystem services such as the storage of carbon stocks which potentially ranged from 2.14 to 2.68 billion tonnes, preservation of water resources and flood reducer (Tropenbos International Indonesia Program, 2010). Since 1980es, the peninsula converted into logging concession then followed by massive industrial production forest. The role of industrial forest plantation in the peat dome of the peninsula discouraged past massive logging operation in the area. Although extensive canals have been developed for small scale illegal logging operation exist, the remoteness and intensive effort to stop illegal practices had shown positive results. Under the moratorium status, large track of peat dome in the peninsular is now designated as ecosystem restoration concession.

Riau ecosystem Restoration Riau (RER) is a not for profit programme formed by APRIL in 2013 with an area of about 150,000 hectare. RER has the purpose of restoration protection and conservation of peat swamp forest ecosystem in the area of Kampar Peninsula as a response to the program from the Ministry of Environment and Forestry-Republic of Indonesia to protect 2.6 million hectares of forest through ecosystem restoration forest concession system (IUPHHK-RE). Three of the four concessions under the supports of the RER had obtained a license of IUPHHK-RE which are PT. Gemilang Cipta Nusantara (20.265 ha), PT. Sinar Mutiara Nusantara (32.830 ha) and PT. The Best One Uni Timber (39.412 ha). RER's restoration, protection and conservation efforts is very important as RER concessions and HCV areas covered more than 30%, beyond legally required (Tropenbos International Indonesia Program, 2010).

A survey of fauna using a surveillance camera has many advantages especially in the tropical forests which might inaccessible terrain by observers. The survey uses a camera trap proved to find a cryptic species which might be hard to be found with other methods, besides the use of camera trap by pairing in the right scheme can provide information on ecological aspects of wildlife by examining their pattern of activity, detection of occupancy or even wildlife density in a landscape (O'Brien *et al.*, 2003).

METHODS

Biodiversity surveys using camera trap have been implemented during March-December 2015 in three APRIL concessions, PT. GCN, PT. SMN and PT. TBOT. This survey aims to figure out basic data and identifying the biodiversity that exists in those three concessions. Camera trap (the Bushnell Trophy Cam type HD 2014) being deployed systematically in the grid cell sized 2 x 2 km, there is a grid cell of each camera which setup in single or paired. The survey targeted a 500 trapday/100 km^2. In each survey grid, one camera station was selected based on the possibility of getting pictures of wildlife, such as a location which has scent marks, scats and former footprint of predation or at least is a wildlife trails. In each station, the camera was mounted on a tree at the height of 40-50 cm with the distance of 4-6 m from the midpoint of animal active tracks where the animal is expected to pass through. The setting of camera trap was divided into two, a video mode with duration of 10 seconds on a single station and a photo mode on the pair stations with the 10 seconds time interval. The camera was activated 24 hours per day with the duration of at least 25 trapdays.

The camera trap data were organized and analysed using a program developed by Sanderson & Harris (2013). The analysis was conducted using total trapdays, the number of pictures and the number of independent pictures (O'Brien *et al.*, 2003). Diversity index was analysed using R version 3.2.3 program, with Biodiversity R package (Kindt, 2016) and script from Gardener (2014). The diversity index used was Shannon index (Krebs, 1999) which enables us to see the richness and composition of species in a community. Species richness was estimated using Richness estimator with a permutation of 1000 times and the results of Jackknife 1 (Tobler *et al.*, 2008).

RESULTS

Camera Trap Survey Effort

A nine (effective) months of camera trap installations accumulated 11.385 trapdays and 14.504 pictures of animals. The number of installation stations for each concession area was PT. GCN 50 stations of 50 stations, PT. SMN 74 stations of 80 stations, PT. TBOT 96 stations of 100 stations (Table 1). Approximately 20% of the installed camera traps suffered physical and electronical damage, such as taking pictures continuously causing the duration of the installation to become very short due to lack of memory card space which in turn made the camera incapable of recording pictures, malfunctioning sensors, and the quality of the resulting image not being representative for identification due to its color (blurred or damaged).

Table 1: Summary of camera trap deployment inthree concessions.

Consession	Total picture		Duration		Duration	Total trap days	Total Station	Distance of camera trap deployment (Km)			
	Total	Independent	Start	End				Min	Mean	Max	Covered area (Km^2)
PT. GCN	1,662	415	3/26/15	6/22/2015	89	1,460	50	0.37	1.33	2.69	189
PT. SMN	4,140	1217	4/12/15	8/31/2015	142	5,948	74	0.70	1.37	2.16	301
PT. TBOT	8,252	1804	9/15/15	11/20/2015	67	3,977	96	0.46	1.48	2.32	354

The camera trap survey results show the existence of a predator species that occupy the peat forests in the RER. The five predator species of the Felidae family in this area are the marbled cat, the flat-headed cat, the leopard cat, the clouded leopard and the sumatran tiger (Figure 1.). Two of which were Sumatran tiger and flat-headed cat as the charismatic species, which categorized as critically endangered and a wetlands specialist.

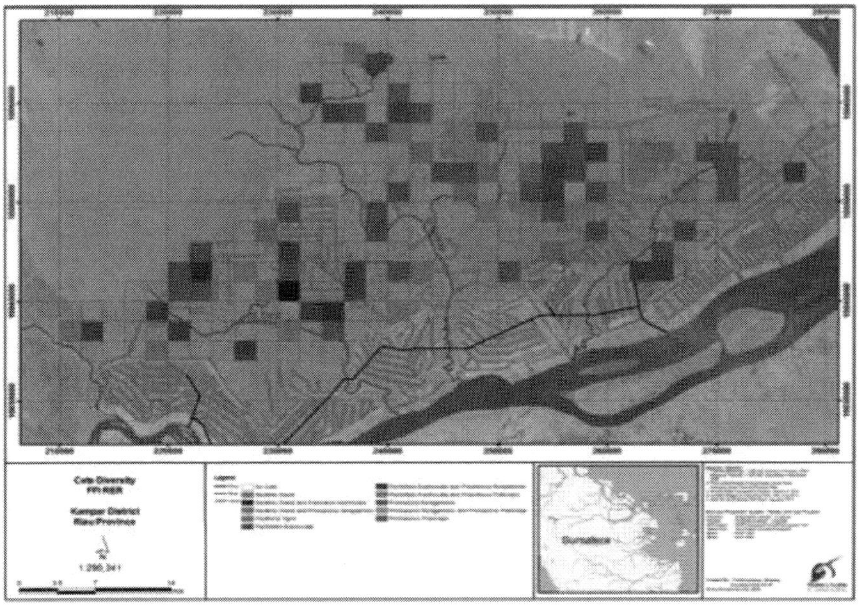

Figure 1: Spatial overlap map of Felidae

Animal Species Richness

As many as 37 species recorded by camera trap in PT. GCN, covering 21 mammals, 13 aves, and three reptiles. The PT. SMN concession acquired 47 species, consisting of 28 mammals, 18 aves, and one reptile, whereas in the area of PT. TBOT consession found 52 species of fauna comprising 30 mammals, 18 aves, and four species of reptiles (Figure 2). The whole number of species being caught by camera traps on RER as much as 75 species of 34 mammals, 35 aves and 6 reptiles. As many as 20% of that were protected wildlife species by either government regulations as well as the red list of IUCN

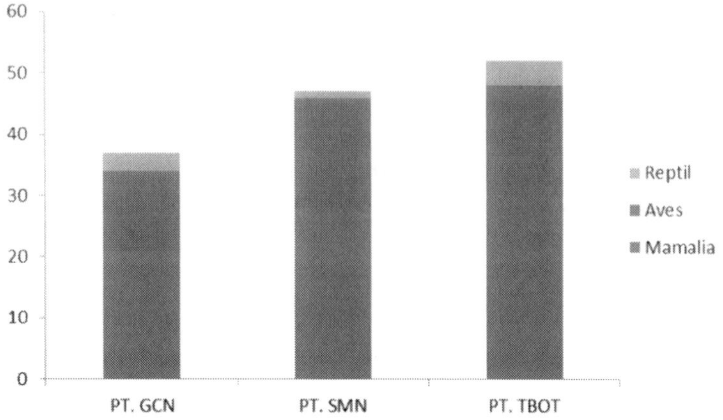

Figure 2: Species richness in three cncessions.

DISCUSSION

The discovery of the flat-headed cat in the region confirmed the study conducted by Wilting *et al* (2010) that the Kampar peninsula is one of the largest habitats on Sumatra for flat-headed cat. This implies an important role for maintaining the sustainability of the landscape for flat-headed cat in Sumatra. Indonesia has nine species of wildcats, seven of which are in Sumatra (Nowell & Jackson, 1996). Golden cats (Catopuma temminckii) and fishing cats (Prionailurus viverrinus) were not found in this survey. This is due to the Golden cats being commonly found in mountains (900-2500 > mdpl) (Griffiths, 1996; W Pusparini *et al.*, 2014). As for the fishing cat, there has not been a valid confirmation about its existence in Sumatra to this day (Duckworth & Shepherd, 2009; Sanderson, 2009).

The discovery of flat-headed cats in this area have already been predicted by previous studies (Wilting *et al.*, 2010), which states that Riau has the widest wingspan habitat for flat-headed cats in Sumatra, and since flat-headed cat are wetland specialists. This species, therefore, can be considered as a flagship for wetland habitats, particularly in peat swamp forests of the Kampar peninsula. Moreover, the existence of large predators have an impact on the health of an ecosystem in that area (Miller *et al.*, 2001). The tiger is one of the top predators found in the RER, a tiger will prey on smaller animals or those equivalent to its size, so do other predators (Karanth & Nichols, 2002). The tigers' ability to prey on a variety of species of different sizes can guarantee their survival in nature. Declining populations of animals they prey on can reduce the abundance of tigers in a location (Karanth & Nichols, 2002). A total of 10 prey animals were recorded in the RER. Bearded pigs are a large size prey animal in the RER, while medium-sized prey consists of monkeys and long-tailed macaques, small-sized prey animals include the mouse-deer, squirrels, forest mice, squirrels, mouse-type mices, and black partridges.

Table 2 provides a comparison of photographic rate between wildcats in the Sumatra region, and it shows that RER possesses the most number of wildcat species in comparison to other similar areas of study. One of the reasons for this was most likely due to the camera trap efforts having longer duration and wider coverage. It should be noted that the camera traps installed in this study were designed to maximize the chances of capturing tiger images, so other smaller mammals, in this case the marbled cats, leopard cats and flat-headed cats were less likely caught on these camera traps. If further studies were conducted where the camera trap installation designs are maximized for capturing smaller cats, then the photographic rate of smaller cats in this area would most likely increase.

Table 2: Photographic rates comparison among landscape in Sumatra.

Area Total trap days	RER[a] 11.385	Kerumutan[b] 1.868	Semenanjung kampar southwest[b] 1.132	Bukit Barisan NP[c] 34.166	Gunung Leuser NP[d] 3.452
Neofelis diardii	0.16	0.05	0.71	0.15	0.41
Panthera tigris	0.02	0.70	-	0.16	N/A
Pardofelis marmorata	0.21	0.21	-	0.1	0.23
Prionailurus bengalensis	0.57	0.05	0.71	0.08	0.2
Prionailurus planiceps	0.04	-	-	-	-

[a] This Study , peat.
[b] (Sunarto *et al.*, 2015), peat.
[c] (McCarthy *et al.*, 2015), mineral.
[d] (Wulan Pusparini *et al.*, 2014), mineral.

CONCLUSION

a) Camera traps installed in concession areas were able to detect a number of important cryptic species which cannot be obtained using other methods. Those cryptic species are five wildcats and pangolin from the mammalian taxonomy.
b) RER in Kampar peninsula indicate a higher number of mammal species diversity compared to other lowlands in Sumatra, especially species of wetland specialists.
c) Flat headed cats as wetland habitat specialist can be promoted as a flagship species for the protection of the Kampar peninsula peat swamp, especially in the concession areas.

ACKNOWLEDGEMENTS

This study was supported by Riau Ecosystem Restoration. It was undertaken with cooperation with the Fauna Flora International Indonesia Program, the staff of PT. GCN, PT. SMN & PT. TBOT. We thank our FFI field staff, RER estate manager, rangers and others who helped this camera trap survey under the dense and rugged terrain of peat swamp forest in Kampar Peninsula.

REFERENCES

1. DUCKWORTH, J. & SHEPHERD, C.R. (2009) Does the fishing cat inhabit Sumatra? *Cat news*.
2. GARDENER, M. (2014) Community Ecology. Analytical Methods Using R and Excel.
3. GRIFFITHS, M. (1996) The large cats of Gunung Leuser National Park. *Leuser: A Sumatran Sanctuary. Van Schaik CP & Supriatna J.(Eds). Yayasan Bina Sains Hayati Indonesia, Depok, Indonesia*, 317–320.
4. KARANTH, K.U., NICHOLS, J.D., KUMAR, N.S., LINK, W.A. & HINES, J.E. (2004) Tigers and their prey :
5. Predicting carnivore densities from prey abundance.
6. KINDT, R. (2016) Package ‘ BiodiversityR ’. *R project*.
7. KREBS, C.J. (1999) Ecological Methodology. Benjamin/Cummings.
8. MILLER, B., DUGELBY, B., FOREMAN, D., DEL RIO, C.M., NOSS, R., PHILLIPS, M., *ET AL.* (2001) The importance of large carnivores to healthy ecosystems. *Endangered Species Update*, 18, 202–210.
9. O’BRIEN, T.G., KINNAIRD, M.F. & WIBISONO, H.T. (2003) Crouching tigers, hidden prey: Sumatran tiger and prey populations in a tropical forest landscape. *Animal Conservation*, 6, 131–139.
10. PUSPARINI, W., WIBISONO, H.T., REDDY, G. V, TARMIZI, T. & BHARATA, P. (2014) Small and medium sized cats in Gunung Leuser National Park, Sumatra, Indonesia. *Cat News*, 8, 4–9.
11. SANDERSON, J. & HARRIS, G. (2013) Automatic data organization, storage, and analysis of camera trap pictures. *Journal of Indonesia Natural History*, 1
12. TOBLER, M.W., CARRILLO-PERCASTEGUI, S.E., LEITE PITMAN, R., MARES, R. & POWELL, G. (2008) An evaluation of camera traps for inventorying large- and medium-sized terrestrial rainforest mammals. *Animal Conservation*, 11, 169–178.
13. TROPENBOS INTERNATIONAL INDONESIA PROGRAM (2010) Buku I: Data dan informasi dasar penilaian menyeluruh nilai konservasi tinggi Semenanjung Kampar.
14. WILTING, A., CORD, A., HEARN, A.J., HESSE, D., MOHAMED, A., TRAEHOLDT, C., *ET AL.* (2010) Modelling the species distribution of flat-headed cats (Prionailurus planiceps), an endangered South-East Asian small felid. *PloS one*, 5, e9612. Public Library of Science.

Abstract No: A-394

ORANGUTAN CONSERVATION IN SARAWAK, MALAYSIA

Oswald Braken Tisen* and Sundai Silang

Sarawak Forestry Corporation, Sarawak, Malaysia

**Corresponding author: oswaldtisen@sarawakforestry.com*

SUMMARY

Traditionally, orangutan ranges through most of southern part of Sarawak. Today, orangutan has a limited distribution in Sarawak with main population in the Batang Ai National Park (BANP) – Lanjak Entimau Wildlife Sanctuary (LEWS) complex. Smaller population occurs in the peat swamp forest of the Sedilu – Sebuyau and Gunung Lesong complex. Orangutan research in Sarawak began with collections and body measurements by Alfred Russel Wallace in 1855. It was more than a hundredth year later, in 1958 that any serious efforts taken to conserve the specie by listing it as protected under the Wild Life Protection Ordinance. Rehabilitation efforts begin in 1963 in Bako National Park was unsuccessful. A concerted rehabilitation program was introduced in Semenggoh in 1975. By 1990, there was a growing population of semi-wild orangutan in Semenggoh – result of a successful rehabilitation program. Semenggoh being too small for more release thus the rehabilitations program was later moved to Matang Wildlife Centre in 1998. With continuing threats to orangutan in the wild, future research focus on the genetic viability of existing populations and identification of the resources required to sustain them in their natural habitat. Population estimates and updating of threats to the species also assist management authority to develop and implement strategic conservation initiatives.

Keywords: *Bornean orangutan, distribution, rehabilitation, peat swamp, Sarawak*

INTRODUCTION

The orangutan (*Pongo spp.*) is the largest ape in Asia. In earlier times, they covered a much larger area as fossil orangutans have been found in stone-age excavation from southern China to Borneo and Java (Frey 1978). At present, the natural population can only be found on the islands of Sumatra and Borneo with an estimated population of 6,600 and 54,000 respectively (Wich *et al.* 2008). More than a decade ago, the orangutans at the two islands were recognized as different species, namely *Pongo pygmaeus* in Borneo and Pongo abelii in Sumatra (Zhi *et al.* 1996; Warren *et al.* 2000; Groves 2001). Bornean orangutans are further divided into three sub-species; *Pongo pygmaeus pygmaeus* (in Western Borneo), *Pongo p. morio* (Northern Borneo) and *Pongo. p. wurmbii* (Southern Borneo) (Groves 2001). Orangutans have become increasingly rare during the last decades and are now confined to areas of suitable habitat on the island of Sumatra and Borneo.

ORANGUTAN HISTORY AND DISTRIBUTION IN SARAWAK

There are at least three large regions in Borneo that have never recorded an existence of orangutan. One of the regions is between Rajang River in Sarawak and Padas River in south-western Sabah, except for some upland records near the Kalimantan border (Payne and Francis 1985). Historically, the distribution of orangutan in Sarawak is mainly occurred in the south-western part of state. Harrison (1949) noted that there was a population of orangutan near Binatang (now Bintangor) but the area was heavily settled by Dayaks and Chinese before 1871. There were also few reports of orangutan occurred in other areas such as in Ulu Sungai Daro near Bintangor, Ulu Sungai Pasin in Sarikei district and from Sungai Assan and Sungai Naman southeast of Sibu near the Rajang River (Schaller 1961). Today, the area has been heavily cultivated and widely populated and no orangutan has been found to occur in these areas. In the northern part of Sarawak, the evidence of orangutan was found in Niah cave in Bintulu Division (Hooijer 1960; von Koenigswald 1958). For the last 50 years there has been no record of orangutan made within Bintulu Division

Studies have shown that the main population of orangutan in Sarawak (Figure 1) occurred in Sri Aman and Sibu divisions mainly in the areas between the upper Batang Ai and Lanjak Entimau (Blouch 1997; Gurmaya and Silang 2002; WCS unpublished report).

In 1992 Meredith conducted field studies in Batang Ai National Park (BANP) and estimated that there were about 360 individual orangutans in the area. The study also found that the species was concentrated in the southern and eastern parts of the park (Meredith, 1993). The following years (1993 and 1994) a field studies conducted by Blouch (1997) in Lanjak-Entimau Wildlife Sanctuary (LEWS) showed that there were about 1,000 orangutans in the sanctuary with the highest density of 1.73 individuals/km^2 recorded at the southern part of the area. It was speculated that the reason could be due to the lower intensity of human disturbance in the southern region. In 2001, Gurmaya and Silang (2002) conducted a field studies in BANP and LEWS. The orangutan density based on medium-age nest analysis for BANP-LEWS complex was 0.7 ind/km^2. Their findings also indicated that the orangutans in LEWS are still concentrated at the southern part for LEWS, meanwhile for BANP were in the southern and eastern parts of the park.

In 2013, a survey was conducted by SARAWAK FORESTRY Corporation (SFC), FDS (Forestry Department Sarawak), WCS (Wildlife Conservation Society) and BA (Borneo Adventure) in Ulu Menyang, further south of BANP (Forestry Department Sarawak unpublished report). The result showed that there was substantial orangutan population occurred in the area with 995 orangutan nests were recorded. A total of 22 sightings of orangutan were made during the survey. The Ulu Menyang area is covered by a mosaic old secondary forest and virgin forest. In 2014, another survey was carried out by the same team (SFC, FDS, WCS and BA) in the area call Ulu Telaus (between Engkari River and Batang Ai River) located at the south-western part of BANP. The survey recorded 53 orangutan nests which showed that there were orangutans in this area (progress report in preparation). In 2014, a helicopter survey was carried out by SFC in Ulu Sebuyau National Park (USNP) and Sedilu National Park (SNP) (Sarawak Forestry Corporation unpublished report). These two national parks with a total area of more than 24,000 ha occurred in the peat swamp area in the lower part of Batang Lupar River. A total of 151 orangutan nests were spotted with 75 nests in USNP and 27 nests in SNP. The other 49 nests were located outside the national parks. This survey recorded more nest as compared to study by Silang *et al.* (2010) at the north-eastern part of USNP, mainly at the upper part of Sebuyau River which recorded only 13 nests.

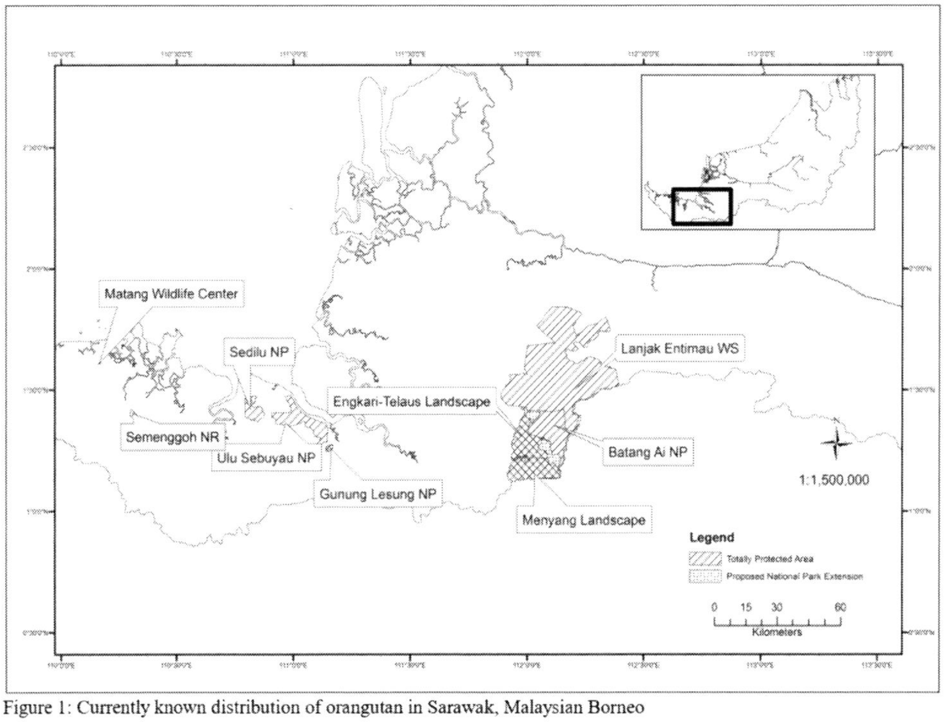

Figure 1: Currently known distribution of orangutan in Sarawak, Malaysian Borneo

RESEARCH AND CONSERVATION OF ORANGUTAN IN SARAWAK

The conservation of orangutan in the state started when there is a concern about the continued decline of the species population which prompted the colonial government of Sarawak to form the *Maias Protection Commission* in 1959 (Harrisson, 1961). The Commission's task was to make a census of the orangutan population in Sarawak and to make recommendations for its protection. According to the Commission's report there were probably 700-900 orangutans in Sarawak at that time. Even in those early days they identified rapid development and increasing human population, coupled with collection of orangutan for zoos and other institutions abroad, as the main culprits for the rapid decline in the population. Forested areas which harbour oangutan were recommended for protection but it was acknowledged that this would be difficult since forests were earmarked for logging which is a more lucrative activity. Harrisson (1961) attributed the disappearance of orangutan from the Balai Ringin and Sabal area to the opening of the Kuching-Simangang (now Sri Aman) road which opened the area to extensive logging and hunting activities. In order to better protect the species and to ensure their survival in the future, the state government has set aside nearly 2,000 -km^2 of forest for the protection of orangutan. These include the BANP and LEWS complex which is the largest totally protected areas (1,687 km^2) solely for the protection and conservation of orangutan (Figure 1).

Research on orangutan in Sarawak probably started by Alfred Russel Wallace with his report on the body measurements of specimens he shot at Simunjan in 1855 (Wallace 1869). He was the first person to record body measurements of the animal. Wallace reported that adult orangutan vary little in height (4 feet 1 inch to 4 feet 2 inches tall), the extent of the outstretched arms varied from 7 feet 2 inches to 7 feet 8 inches and the width of the face from 10-13.5 inches. Wallace also described the habits of orangutan and their preferences towards the unbroken virgin forest in his book *The Malay Archipelago: the land of the orangutan and the bird of paradise*. Apart from studies on orangutan population and its distribution, there were also other studies that focus on behaviour of the species.

Wesley (2001) studied the activity budget of semi-wild orangutan at Semenggoh Wildlife Rehabilitation Centre (SWC). The study showed that there was no significant difference in terms of time spent moving, foraging, nesting and fighting between disturbed and less disturbed area, except for resting and sleeping activities. The study also found that orangutan prefers more secure and less human presence to rest and sleep. Husen (2001) in his study found that the semi-wild orangutan in SWC foraged actively in the evening and this could be due to the food provided to them on a feeding platform in the morning. A study on nesting ecology of semi-wild orangutan in SWC by Mohd-Rahmantullah (2001) found that the animals tend to build nests at between 15 and 25 m on the trees top and reuse of old nests are more frequent. Silang *et al* (2006) conducted a study in BANP looking at potential fruit trees for orangutan in the area. The study recorded a total of 1,570 fruit trees from two areas (Lubang Baya and Batang Ai sites) comprised of 89 species, 44 genera and 24 families. The five most dominants families are Sapindaceae, Fagaceae, Euphorbiaceae, Moraceae and Myrtaceae. In terms of species, the most abundant fruit trees found in the area were *Nephelium daedaleum* (Kedabang), *Trigonopleura malayana* (Sedi) and *Prunus beccarii* (Enteli) with 127, 122 and 111 trees respectively. Their study showed that there was no significant different ($p>0.05$) in term of fruit trees species diversity between Lubang Baya and Batang Ai sites.

In Sarawak the orangutan has been listed as Totally Protected Animals under the Wild Life Protection Ordinance 1998, where a person who hunts, kills, captures, sales or in possession of any recognizable part or derivative of the animal shall be guilty of an offence and the penalty will be imprisonment for two years and fine of thirty thousand ringgit. Besides that, orangutan had also been listed in Appendix 1 under CITES, where trade is banned for the species. Past and current research on orangutan in Sarawak has contributed to the effective conservation and management of orangutan in the state.

REHABILITATION WORK AND ACTIVITIES

The first orangutan rehabilitation project in Sarawak was initiated by Barbara Harrisson in 1960s, in the Bako National Park. The idea was to rehabilitate the confiscated orangutan so that they could be released back to the forest. The rehabilitation work ended abruptly and the orangutans were transfer to Sepilok which had just been opened (Harrisson, 1987). In the 1970s Sarawak received many confiscated or surrendered orangutans and other wildlife species which later brought about the idea to establish a wildlife rehabilitation centre in the state. The animals were sent to the Forestry Department Sarawak to undergo the rehabilitation program and Semenggoh Nature Reserve was chosen as a strategic place due to its locality and suitability of habitat in the area.

SEMENGGOH WILDLIFE CENTRE

In 1975, Semenggoh Wildlife Rehabilitation Centre (SWC) was officially established to cater for rehabilitation of orangutans and other wildlife species in Sarawak. The SWC is located near to Kuching about 30 minutes' drive from the centre of the town. The centre is located within the 653 hectares Semenggoh Nature Reserve of tropical rainforest. The main function of SWC now is to manage the semi-wild orangutans that live within the Semenggoh Nature Reserve. Besides that, it also caters for research, environmental education and ecotourism activities. The facilities in SWC include information and activity centres, kitchen, administrative centre, trails and staff accommodation. Since its establishment, SWC has cared for about 700 animals (protected and non-protected species) in the period between 1975 to the end of 1997 (Abang & Onuma, 1997).

Until 1991 the centre had released 17 individuals of the 42 confiscated orangutans to the Semenggoh Nature Reserve. Six (6) orangutans which had never been included in the rehabilitation training because of their big size and they had been kept in captivity for so long. For safety reasons, it was decided that these animals were kept in the cage for education purposes. To date, 27 individual orang utans live in Semenggoh Nature Reserve as free ranging animals.

MATANG WILDLIFE CENTRE

The Matang Wildlife Centre (MWC) was established in 1998 as a sister facility to SWC. The centre is located about 35km from Kuching, within the tropical forest of Kubah National Park with a total area of approx. 2200 ha. Since 1998, the function of orangutan and other wildlife rehabilitation activities were carried out at MWC and the SWC is only caters for free ranging or semi-wild orangutans. The MWC initially starting with 4 orangutans and all of them were transferred from SWC. Since then all newly confiscated orangutans were sent to MWC. To date, the centre had trained fourteen orangutans and of these numbers, eleven had been release to the forest area within the Kubah National Park. Record showed that only four orangutans occasionally return back to the centre for supplementary food. The others had never return to the centre although there were signs of them (*e.g.* old nest) in the place where they were previously released.

ORANGUTAN BORN AND MORTALITY IN THE REHABILITATION CENTRE

Altogether a total of 25 orangutans were born in SWC and MWC in the period between 1979 and 2014. In SWC, all babies were born in the wild, whereas in MWC most of the babies were born in captivity. The birth intervals for free ranging orangutans in SWC were observed to be between 3 and 5 years.

To date, the centres had recorded eighteen deaths, which were mainly occurred in SWC during the early days of the establishment of the centre. The main causes of the death were mainly due to diseases. Most of the confiscated orangutans that were sent to SWC during that time were in poor conditions or under nourishment because they were not properly kept or fed by the owners. There were few cases where orangutan died due to electrical shock and other natural causes. Mortality rate among infants that were born as semi wild animal in the centres was low probably due to the natural care by their semi-wild mother orangutans.

CONCLUSION

From the conservation effort carried out by the state, the government had established Totally Protected Area (TPA) specifically for the protection of the species and these include the Batang Ai National Park, Lanjak-Entimau Wildlife Sanctuary, Ulu Sebuyau National Park and Sedilu National Park. In Sarawak, orangutan conservation played a vital role in ensuring the survival of the species. Conservation in the future will focus on human factor such as awareness program especially for the communities living in the areas surrounding orangutan habitat range. Continuous monitoring will be carried out as part of the conservation program for the species to monitor the population status, movement patterns, threats etc. More research should be encouraged on genetic diversity through DNA analyses. Local graduates should be encouraged to undertake research on the orangutan to produce more local experts in this field. Generally, conservation efforts that had been carried out in Sarawak have contributed significantly to the better management of the species in the state.

REFERENCES

1. Abang, M.A.T. & Onuma, M. 1997. Review of activities at Semenggoh Wildlife Rehabilitation Centre. Forest Department Sarawak (unpubl. report).
2. Blouch, R. A. 1997. Distribution and abundance of orangutans (*Pongo pygmaeus*) and other primates in the Lanjak Entimau Wildlife Sanctuary, Sarawak, Malaysia. *Tropical Biodiversity*. 4(3): 259-274.
3. Frey, R. 1978. Wildlife management in Southeas Asia. *Biotrop Special Publication* Vol.8: 199-217.
4. Groves, C. (2001): Primate taxonomy. Smithsonian Institution Press, Washington.
5. Gurmaya, K.J. and Sundai, S. 2002. Development of Lanjak Entimau Wildlife Sanctuary as a totally protected area. Phase III. ITTO Project PD 16/99 Rev.2 (F).: A study of habitat conditions, populations, and distribution of orangutan in Lanjak Entimau Wildlife Santuray and Batang Ai National Park, Sarawak, Malaysia. International Tropical Timber Organization, Yokohama, Japan and Forest Department Sarawak. Malaysia.
6. Harrisson, T. 1949. Large mammals of Borneo. *Malayan Nature Journal* IV (2): 70-76
7. Harrisson, B. 1961. Orangutan - what chances of survival? *The Sarawak Museum Journal* 10 (17-18): 238-261.
8. Hooijer, D. A. (1960). The orangutan in Niah Cave pre-history. The Sarawak Museum J. 9 (15-16): 408-421.
9. Husen, A. Z. (2001). Foraging ecology of semi-wild orangutan at Semenggoh Wildlife Rehabilitation Centre, Sarawak. Undergraduate Thesis. Universiti Malaysia Sarawak. Kota Samarahan (unpublished).
10. Meredith, 1993 Meredith, M. E. 1995. A faunal survey of Batang Ai National Park, Sarawak, Malaysia. *The Sarawak Museum Journal* 48 (No. 69 New Series): 133-155.

11. Mohd-Rahmantullah (2001) Mohd-Rahmantullah, M. H. 2001. *Nesting ecology of semi-wild orangutans at Semenggoh Wildlife Rehabilitation Centre, Sarawak.* Thesis (undergraduate), Universiti Malaysia Sarawak, Kota Samarahan.
12. Payne, J and Francis C. M. 1985. A field guide to the mammals of Borneo. The Sabah Society, Kota Kinabalu, Sabah, Malaysia.
13. Schaller, G. B. 1961. The Orangutan in Sarawak. *Zoologica*. 46 (6): 73.
14. Silang, S., Laman, C.J. and Demies, M. (2006). Orangutan Habitat Monitoring: Fruit Trees for Orangutan in Batang Ai National Park. *Hornbill Vol. 8,* 177 - 189.
15. Silang, S., Wahab, T., Dagang, P. and Robi, N.J. (2010). A Preliminary Checklist of Terrestrial Fauna in the Ulu Sebuyau National Park. Paper presented in the Sarawak Biological Resources Forum, 29-31 March 2010, Kuching, Sarawak, Malaysia.
16. Wallace, A. R. 1869. *The Malay Archipelago: the land of the orang-utan and the bird of paradise.* London: Macmillan and Co.
17. Warren, K.S., Nijmian, I.J., Lenstra, J.A., Swan, R.A., Heriyanto & den Boer, M. (2000). Microsatellite DNA variation in Bornean orangutans (Pongo pygmaeus). Journal of Medical Primatology 29(2): 57-62.
18. Wesley, M. N. 2001. *Activity budget of mother-infant pairs of semi-wild orangutans at Semenggoh Wildlife Rehabilitation Centre.* Thesis (undergraduateO Universiti Malaysia Sarawak, Kota Samarahan.
19. Wich, S.A., Meijaard, E., Marshall, A.J., Husson, S. Ancrenaz, M., Lacy, R.C., van Schaik,C.P., Sugardjito, J., Simorangkir, T., Traylor-Holzer, K., Doughty, M., Supriatna, J., Dennis, R., Gumal, M., Knott, C.D. & Singleton, I. (2008). Distribution and conservation status of the orang-utan (Pongo spp.) on Borneo and Sumatra: how many remain? Oryx 42(3): 329-339.
20. von Koenigswald, G.H. 1958. Remarks on the prehistoric fauna of the great cave at Niah. *Sarawak Museum Journal* VIII (12): 620-625
21. Wildlife Conservation Society (WCS)-Malaysia Program. (unpublished). Orangutan nest count surveys at the proposed extension areas of Lanjak-Entimau Wildlife Sanctuary and Batang Ai National Park. Final Report prepared on 26 August 2013.
22. Zhi, L., Karesh, W. B., Janczewski, D. N., Frazier-Taylor, H., Sajuthi, D., Gomber, F., Andau, M., Martenson, J. S. and O'Brien, S. J. 1996. Genomic differentiation among natural populations of orangutan (Pongo pygmaeus). *Current Biology.* 6(10): 1326-1336.

Abstract No: A-051

THE TERRESTRIAL FAUNA COMPOSITION OF THE PEAT SWAMP FOREST OF ULU SEBUYAU NATIONAL PARK, SARAWAK, MALAYSIA

Sundai Silang[1*], Oswald Braken Tisen[1], Wong Ting Chung[1] and Kalyana Sundram[2]

[1]*Sarawak Forestry Corporation, Malaysia.*
[2]*Malaysian Palm Oil Council, Selangor Darul Ehsan, Malaysia*

**Corresponding author: sundai@sarawakforestry.com*

SUMMARY

The Ulu Sebuyau National Park (USNP) is located on the lower Batang Lupar river covering areas of mainly peat swamp forests in the Samarahan and Sri Aman Divisions of Sarawak, Malaysia. Surveys of terrestrial fauna were carried out from August to October 2014 and from September to October 2015 in the eastern and north-western parts of the park which consisted of logged-over peat swamp forests. The surveys concentrated on four faunal groups; primates, small mammals, birds and amphibians. Methods employed during the surveys included line transects, mist-netting and live-trapping. Survey results recorded five primate species, seven small mammal species, 72 bird species and 16 amphibian species. Orang Utans are still found in the area as evidenced by nests seen during aerial surveys. Two hornbill species, Black Hornbill (*Anthracocerosmalayanus*) and Bushycrested Hornbill (*Annorhinusgaleritus*) were also recorded. The recording of two undescribe frog species (*Hylaranasp* and *Microhylasp*) and the rare false gharial (*Tomistomaschlegelii*) added to the excitement of the survey teams. Results of the surveys unearthing the arrays of species, some new and some endangered and rare show the importance of the peat swamp ecosystem albeit disturbed, in sustaining these species. More studies are therefore recommended.

***Keywords**: Peat swamp, primates, small mammals, birds, amphibians, Ulu Sebuyau, Sarawak*

INTRODUCTION

Realising that conservation of the complex (Ulu Sebuyau-Sedilu-Gunong Lesong National Parks) would be a humongous task and that SARAWAK FORESTRY would require all the assistance it could garner especially corporate partners. Subsequently, SARAWAK FORESTRY was in active discussion with Malaysian Palm Oil Council (MPOC) to collaborate in a project that aims to collect basic information on orangutan and other wildlife species in the two selected sites. The principal objective of the project is to ensure the long term survival of orangutans in the state of Sarawak as the areas in the Complex are crucial peat swamp forests habitats of orangutans. The project would also show that the state of Sarawak, contrary to the belief of some vocal and partisan environmental NGOs, that peat swamp forests are indiscriminately converted to oil palm plantations or other monocultures. It is crucial to collect basic information on the biodiversity particularly orangutan and what other resources in the complex. More importantly the recent information gathered from the locals that indicated orangutans are still found both inside and outside the national parks is verified by ground-truthing. The first phase of this project required SARAWAK FORESTRY to provide the relevant expertise and manpower to collect basic information on orangutan and other wildlife species in the national parks and to furnish a progress report to MPOC.

STUDY AREA

The Ulu Sebuyau National Park (USNP), gazetted in 2010, is located at the lower part of the Batang Lupar River with an area about 18,300 hectares (Figure 1). The park is a logged-over area, logging having ceased in 2010. The whole study site is a secondary forest habitat with natural regeneration of disturbed forest patches. Generally, the area is flat and low-lying peat land that is prone to flooding and persistent water retention. In this area, even during the dry season, the peat remains water logged with pools found throughout the study site. The USNP can be accessed by boat through Sg. Sebuyau and by land from Kg. Kepayang in Simunjan District.

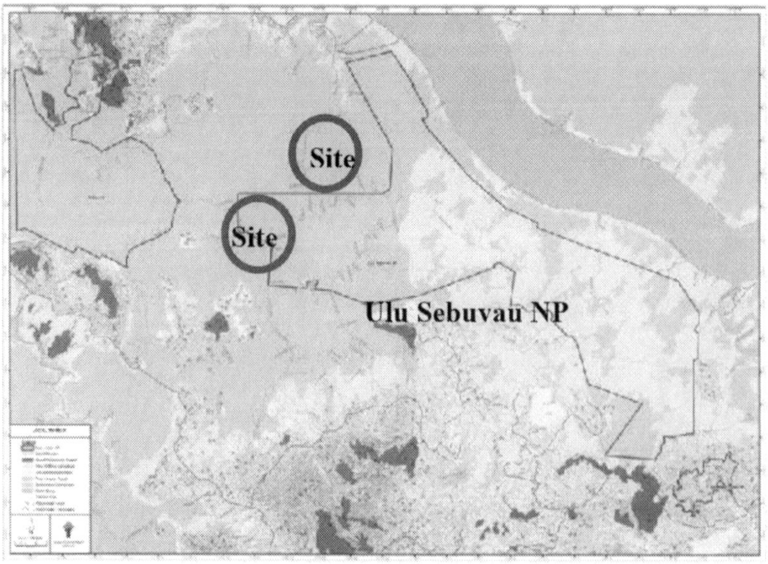

Figure 1: Map of Ulu Sebuyau NP and location of study site (red circle)

METHODOLOGY

Field surveys were conducted at two (2) study sites as shown in Figure 1. The first survey was conducted from August to October, 2014 at Site I. The second survey was carried out from September to October 2015 at Site II. The data collections were conducted based the standard method as stated below:

Line Transect

For primate and large mammals, survey was conducted using line transect method. Altogether, five (5) transects were established with three transects at Site I and another two (2) transects at Site II. Each transects were 4 km in length running parallel to the other transects at 1 km apart. At Site I, transect was in the east-westerly direction, meanwhile at Site II, transect was in north-south direction. The surveys were done following the trail and the walking speed was about 1 km per hour. Line transect survey was carried from early morning to late afternoon. In this study, survey by boat was also conducted along Sungai Sebuyau and surveys were conducted in the evening around 1700 hours to 1900 hours when weather permitted. The observer will record all animals or nests observed on both side of transect. Animal detections were based on direct sighting and call heard during the survey. Parameters including species, number of individuals and way of detection of animal observed will be recorded. For the orangutan nest survey, parameters such as nest age, nest height and nest coordinates were recorded. In this the study, aerial survey using a helicopter was also carried out to determine the present and distribution of orangutan nest throughout the study areas.

Live Trapping

The survey method used for small mammals' data collection was the 'capture-marked-and-release' method. Live traps measuring 20cm x 20cm x 56cm long were used in this study. Live traps were placed on the ground and also above ground (stumps, dead logs or branches). The traps were placed on both sides along the transect line at 20m intervals for 1km. There were 50 station comprised of 2 traps per station. Ripe bananas were used as bait in this study. The traps were checked at 0800 hours every morning during the study period. Each individual captured were anaesthetized with chloroform and parameters such as location, trap number, height of capture, weight, head and body length, tail length [from anus to end of tail], hind foot length, ear length, sex, reproductive condition and species were recorded. Identification of species was based on *A Field Guide to the Mammals of Borneo* by Payne and Francis (1985).

Mist Netting

The birds study was carried out by way of mist-netting and line transect survey. These methods were used as a tool to monitor bird species composition and distribution. Mist netting involves the operation of an array of mist nets in an area over a period of time. The nets were left open from 0600 hours until 1700 hours. Mist-nets were checked at two-hourly intervals and all captured birds were collected. Bird survey using line transect method requires an observer to walk along a fixed transect for several kilometers. For all birds caught, morphometric details such as age (adult or juvenile), breeding condition (brood patch, etc.), moult, parasite load and general physical condition (weight, fat deposits) were assessed by the study team. Leg bands were fixed on the birds before release. All birds caught or observed during the study were identified up to species level based on field guides book: *The Birds of Borneo* by Smythies (1981), *A Field Guide to the Birds of South-East Asia* by Robson (2002) and *A Pocket Guide to the Birds of Borneo* by Francis (2005) were used for the identification of the birds.

Stream Line Transect

Standard method for frog inventory (Heyer *et al.*, 1994) using stream line transect method was applied for field sampling within the selected stream.Sampling of adult amphibians involved visual and acoustic searching using headlights and catching the animals by hand along transect. A minimum length of 500m transects was established along the selected stream during the day. Samplings were carried for at least two hours between 6.00 pm to 10.00 pm. Environmental data such as stream width, nature of substrate, percentage of canopy cover, distance from transect or streams where individual was caught were recorded for species reference. All amphibians caught were weighed (+/- 0.1g), measured (snouth-urostyle length+/- 0.1mm) and identified to species level. Each amphibian identified was photographed (dorso-lateral view, ventral view and head/eyes close-up) for documentation of body colours, eye colour, and other features. All captured frogs were released at the same habitat on the next day.

Camera Trapping

Camera trapping method was also been applied to large mammals study. Altogether, six camera traps were deployed in October 2015. The distance between each camera was at least 1 km radius. The trapping was carried from October until December 2015.

RESULTS AND DISCUSSION

Orangutan and Other Primates

Five primate species were recorded during the survey and these were Orangutan (*Pongo p. pygmaeus*), Proboscis monkey (*Nasalislarvatus*) Cross-marked leaf monkey (formerly known as Banded leaf monkey) (*Presbytischrysomelas*), Pig-tailed macaque (*Macacanemestrina*) and Long-tailed macaque (*M. fascicularis*) (Table 1). During this survey, the Cross-marked leaf monkey was the only primate not encountered during the 2014 study in Site I. Amongst the primate species, the Long-tailed macaque is the most common primate in the area. This was anticipated because the study area is a secondary forest and the macaque was known to survive well in disturbed habitat. Furthermore, Long-tailed macaque is a common primate species found in peat swamp forest and also in the coastal habitat.

Table 1: List of primate species found in Site I and Site II of MPOC project in UluSebuyau NP

No.	Common name	Scientific name	Site II	SiteI
1	Orangutan	*Pongop. pygmaeus*	√	√
2	Proboscis monkey	*Nasalislarvatus*	√	√
3	Cross-marked leaf monkey	*Presbytis c.chrysomelas*	√	*
4	Pig-tailed macaque	*Macacanemestrina*	√	√
5	Long-tailed macaque	*Macacafascicularis*	√	√

*no observation

Aerial and line transect surveys conducted in 2014 and 2015 recorded a total of 159 orangutan nests. Of all these nests, 75 nests were observed within the Ulu Sebuyau NP, 27 nests within Sedilu NP and 57 nests were found outside the national parks (Figure 2). In this study, no population estimate was done due to lack of data obtained during the line transect survey.

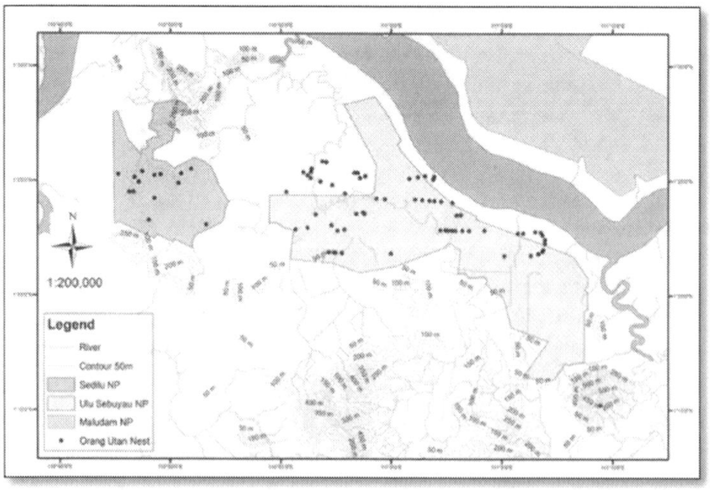

Figure 2: Orangutan nest (black dots) recorded during the aerial and line transect surveys in 2014 and 2015

Avifauna

A total of 71 species of birds representing 25 families were recorded from the study sites. Site II in Ulu Sg. Sebuyau area site recorded 54 species as compare to only 40 bird species in Site I (Sg. Kepayang). Family Timaliidae recorded the most abundance birds with 12 species, followed by family *Nectariniidaeand Pycnonotidae*, with both families recorded 7 species respectively. From the study, it was discovered that in Site II, one bird species *Setorniscriniger*or Hook-billed bulbul is listed as vulnerable IUCN Red List 2015 status. This study also recorded several species of particular interest and this including two totally protected species (Black Hornbill *Anthracocerosmalayanus* and Bushy-crested Hornbill *Annorhinusgaleritus*) listed in the Wild Life Protection Ordinance 1998.

Amphibians

Altogether a total of 280 individuals frog comprised of six families, eleven genera and sixteen species were recorded from this study. The most common amphibian was the Rhacophoridae family with five species and the least anurans belongs to the families of Megophryidae and Microhylidaewith only one species respectively. The Rhacophoridae family was also the dominant anurans in the area with 162 individuals sampled. Meanwhile the Bufonidae was the less common anurans with only 8 individuals which only recorded at Site II. This study also recorded one endemic species the *Limnonectes paramacrodon* or Masked Frogwhich is also listed as near threatened (NT) under the IUCN Red List 2015. The study also managed to record a rare amphibian species, the frilled tree frog (*Kurixalusappendiculatus*) in the study at Site II.This study also had recorded two potential new anurans species. These undescribe species *Hylarana*sp and *Microhyla*sp were recorded at Site I in Sungai Kepayang area of Ulu Sebuyau NP. For the identification purpose 4 life specimens (two specimens for each species) were sent to IBEC/UNIMAS for further species identification.

Mammals

Trapping for small mammals using live trap was conducted only at Site I. A total of 500 traps/night (100 traps x 5 (total trapping days)) managed to record few small mammal species as stated in Table 2. Mueller's Rat (*Sundamymuelleri*) was the most species captured with a total of 12 individuals. For camera trapping activity, species recorded including Sambar deer, Mouse deer and Wild boar. The two deer were elusive specie and not easy to detect using line transect survey method. In this study, the small mammals such as rats and squirrels were not detected using camera trapping techniques. There is no specific explanation to this but experience from other similar studies showed that rodents are not easy to be detected using camera trapping as compare to live trapping technique.

Table 2: List of small mammals captured using live traps at Site I, Sungai Kepayang area in UluSebuyau NP

No.	Family	Common Name	Scientific Name	No of ind.
1.	Tupaiidae (Treeshrew)	Lesser Treeshrew	*Tupaia minor*	1
2.		Slender Treeshrew	*Tupaiagracilis*	1
3.		Painted Treeshrew	*Tupaiapicta*	1
4.	Muridae	Mueller's Rat	*Sundamymuelleri*	12
5.		Malaysian Field Rat	*Rattustiomanicussabae*	1
6.		Dark Tailed tree Rat	*Niviventercremoriventer*	1
7.		Ricefield Rat	*Rattusargentiventer*	1

Crocodile

River survey to determine the present of false gharial (*Tomistomaschlegelii*) was conducted for Sg. Kepayang only at Site I. During this survey, only one hatchling of the species was spotted along Sg. Kepayang. Other evidences found during the survey were including foot print and body track at the puddles that were observed along the survey areas, which the locals believed to be the basking sites of *Tomistoma* species. In Site II, although there was no survey done for crocodile species but few sightings were made on this species especially in the upper part of Sg. Sebuyau during the study in 2015.

CONCLUSION

The surveys confirmed the presence of the endangered orangutan sub-species *Pongopygmaeuspygmaeus* at Site I and Site II which is located outside of USNP. This also indicated that the Site II area is part of the orangutan habitats that occurred in the Ulu Sebuyau area. The surveys also recorded other endangered species such as the Proboscis Monkey and the False Gharial. The False Gharials were found mainly up river of Sungai Sebuyau and Sungai Kepayang in the USNP.

This study also recorded birds of particular interest. These were two species of hornbills, Black Hornbill (*Anthracocerosmalayanus)* and Bushy-crested Hornbill (*Annorhinusgaleritus)*. Amphibian study managed to record one endemic species, the *Limnonectesparamacrodon* or Masked Frog and one rare amphibian species, the Frilled Tree Frog (*Kurixalusappendiculatus*). The study also recorded two undescribed species, the *Hylarana*sp and *Microhyla*sp which at the moment was only found in USNP and Maludam NP. The short span of time and the limited funding have resulted in gaps in data and information pertaining to some aspects and components of the project. These would therefore warrant further studies and injection of more funding to plug the gaps in data and information of the whole complex.

REFERENCES

1. Francis, C.M. 2005. *A Pocket Guide to the Birds of Borneo*. The Sabah Society, Kota Kinabalu.
2. Heyer, W. R., M.A. Donnelly, R.W. Mcdiarmid, L.-A. C. Hayek, & M.S. Foster, (eds.). 1994. *Measuring and Monitoring Biological Diversity Standard Methods for Amphibians.Biological Diversity Handbook Series*. Washington & London, Smithsonian Institution Press.
3. IUCN Red List 2015. The IUCN Red List of Threatened Species. Version 2015-4. http://www.iucnredlist.org/search
4. Myer, S. 2009. *A Field Guide to the Birds of Borneo*. London: New Holland.
5. Payne, J. and Francis, C.M. 1985. *A Field Guide to the Mammals of Borneo*. The Sabah Society, Kota Kinabalu, Sabah, Malaysia.
6. Robson, C. 2002. *A Field Guide to the Birds of South-East Asia*. New Holland Publishers (UK) Ltd, London.
7. Smythies, B.E. 1981. *The Birds of Borneo. 3rd edition*. The Sabah Society & The Malayan Nature Society, Kota Kinabalu, Sabah.

Abstract No: A-171

WETLANDS AS KEYSTONE ECOSYSTEMS: CONSERVATION CORNERSTONES IN DYNAMICALLY-CHANGING LANDSCAPES

David Alexander Locky

MacEwan University, Edmonton, Alberta T5W 4H3, Canada

Corresponding author: lockyd@macewan.ca

SUMMARY

Ecosystems are interconnected to each other in a web of patches, some of which may be more important regionally than others. These are as keystone ecosystems, ecosystems which have an impact on the landscape inordinate to their size or distribution. Keystone ecosystem evolved from the antecedent keystone species concept and the associated keystone processes model. While these concepts share similar characteristics as with keystone species, the keystone ecosystem concept requires refinement. Wetlands were first introduced as keystone ecosystems in Alberta by Locky (2011). In addition to functioning as distinct ecosystems unto themselves, wetlands are critical conduits between upland and aquatic ecosystems on a heterogenous landscape. Wetlands, like other keystone ecosystems, influence the landscape by two primary but not mutually exclusive pathways: shaping landscape disturbance regimes and providing limited resources on the landscape (DeMaynadier and Hunter 1994). They can survive fire and often remain unlogged, both cases equally providing reliable oases in seas of disturbance. Their resilience on the landscape places them in the role of conduits between different ecosystem types. Peatlands similarly modify and store carbon. Important facets of keystone wetlands as keystone ecosystems include values and societal benefits related to conservation, like carbon storage. However, it is clear that the strong functional linkages between wetlands and other landscape types suggest that negative consequences of wetland loss and impairment are exported far beyond geographic boundaries. Addressing wetland losses and conserving existing wetlands through policy provides value far and above the spatial extent on the landscape (Stoneman *et al.* 2016). When identified and mapped, keystone ecosystems can provide politicians, managers, planners, and the public useful information about critical ecosystem components (Stohlgren *et al.* 1997). Uniquely, this is where ecology and management become one. The planning process can be fortified with knowledge of keystone ecosystems. Conversion and or loss of critical functions and values can thus be avoided, particularly for long-term planning. In the case of Alberta, wetlands are found in all of the province's biomes and provide a wide range of ecosystem functions and properties. Wetlands have been subjected to a variety of anthropogenic impacts, including climate change (Locky 2011, 2012, Stoneman *et al.* 2016). Conservation and enhancement of wetlands leverages ecological and societal benefits far above the areal extent of the wetland and far beyond a wetland's borders.

Keywords: *conservation, function, keystone ecosystem, peatland, policy, value, wetland*

INTRODUCTION

The antecedent concept of keystone ecosystem is keystone species which was first by Paine (1966) during his work on the role of *Pisaster* in intertidal communities. The removal of this top predator but non-dominant species, from the community led to the collapse of the system, reducing diversity from 15 to 8 species. The keystone species concept emphasizes direct control processes like competition and predation rather than indirect processes like nutrient cycling in the control of biodiversity. There are also keystone guilds or groups of species that fill various roles, including fruit trees providing fruit to frugivores in seasons with less resources, and certain mammals and birds critical to dispersal of certain seeds and other organisms providing critical landscape disturbances, like beavers and alligators (see review in DeMaynadier and Hunter 1997). Keystone processes are those that are fundamental to the maintenance of an ecosystem (Vold and Buffet 2008). These could include fire in maintaining open ponderosa pine forests and grasslands in B.C.'s dry interior or pollination in maintaining biological productivity (Kevan 1991). Similarly, ecosystems which have a positive impact on the landscape inordinate to their size or distribution are called keystone ecosystems.

Examples of keystone ecosystems include wild coffee ecosystems (Goel *et al.* 2001), coastal temperate rainforests (Moola *et al.* 2004), riparian areas (Naiman *et al.* 2005), estuaries (Pojar 2003), some lakes and other aquatic ecosystems (Ocean Partners, Internet), mangroves (National Geographic 2001), freshwater deltas (Lesak 2014), and coral reefs. Using coral reefs as an example, while our understanding of their role as a keystone ecosystem is incomplete, there is evidence that coral reefs provide a keystone role within the marine environment (Hagedorn and Spindler 2014). While they only encompass 0.2% of the earth's surface over one-quarter of all marine life exists on a coral reef at some point during their life cycle. The proportion of coral reefs threatened with extinction has exceeded that of terrestrial ecosystems (Hagedorn and Spindler 2014). Additionally, coral reefs are among the oldest and most diverse of ecosystems. Wetlands only cover approximately 6% of the earth's surface, of which half are peatlands, but unlike coral reefs, are found in most terrestrial biomes in some form.

Locky (2011) first highlighted wetlands as keystone ecosystems in Alberta using function and value in terms of their limited proportional representation on the landscape; wetlands are found in every biome within the province and likely contribute services and value inordinate to their size on the landscape. Specific attributes and properties of wetlands as keystone ecosystems have yet to be quantified and qualified.

METHODS

Using Locky (2011, 2012) and the literature and white papers, this research attempts to fortify the concept of wetlands as keystone ecosystems using examples from Alberta and elsewhere.

RESULTS AND DISCUSSION

Wetland conservation has been recently gaining worldwide momentum and scientific evidence supports the dual paradigm of wetlands as providing ecological function and economic value (Stoneman *et al.* 2016). Determination of function and value are elusive qualities for many ecosystems. Costanza *et al.*'s (1997) seminal manuscript outlining the value of the world's ecosystem services and natural capital highlights the significance of ecosystem services and values of wetlands relative to other ecosystem types. The research suggests that wetlands are worth more than most other of the earth's ecosystems, approximately \$20,000/ha/year.

While not all wetlands perform all functions nor do they perform all functions equally well, it is well known that valued wetland functions include flood control, groundwater recharge/discharge, sediment and nutrient retention, climate change mitigation, biodiversity reservoirs, wetland products, recreation and tourism, and cultural/heritage value (Locky 2011). The presence of keystone ecosystems on the landscape sustain natural ecosystem process and scarce resources (adapted from Stohlgren *et al.* 1997, deMaynadier and Hunter 1997). They are the parts of the landscape that have high diversity, distinctive species compositions, and/or distinctive ecological processes that are beneficial to many other species and/or ecosystems. Keystone ecosystem presence and arrangement often determines the nutrient balance of a region (Blaschke 2005) in addition to a vast array of other functions and values.

As wetlands are generally minor components on the landscape wetlands fulfil the criteria of being critical keystone ecosystems (Locky 2011, 2012) that function as conservation cornerstones.

Keystone Species, Processes, and Ecosystems

DeMaynadier and Hunter (1997) first introduced the keystone ecosystem concept as a means to capture biotopes having greater importance to the biological structure and function than the average landscape unit. Thus, the definition is extended such that species in ecosystems is upscaled to the role of ecosystems on the landscape. Like keystone species, the concept of keystone ecosystems can be vague and inconsistent. Similarly, as many species have been non-rigorously identified as keystone around the world to the point of meaning 'important-for-something', vis-a-viz functional importance vs. keystoneness (Hurbert 1997), even less rigour has been applied to identifying keystone ecosystems. Indeed, Mouquet *et al.* (2013) outline that while some communities in nature contribute disproportionately to regional dynamics, the concept of keystone ecosystem needs to be refined. This is important to understand species interactions in space and ultimately, produce a better understanding of the consequences of habitat loss.

Keystone Ecosystem Mechanisms

Ecosystems are linked to each other in complex web of interconnected patches and a minority of these may be more important regional than others, functioning as keystone ecosystems (Mouquet *et al.* 2013). Keystone ecosystems influence landscapes by two primary mechanisms: 1) shaping landscape disturbance regimes or 2) providing a limiting resource on the landscape. Many key aspects of wetland could simultaneously fit within both of these categories, i.e., are not mutually exclusive, but I have separated them into disturbance regimes and provision of limiting resources for convenience.

Disturbance Regimes

Many wetlands, including forested peatlands, are left on the landscape during logging operations. The author's work in boreal Canada as related to Locky and Bayley (2007) strongly demonstrated how these remnant peatlands, at times completely encircled by clear-cut forest, appeared to maintain perfect hydrological function with intact plant communities for at least 12 years post-harvest (Figure 1A). The resilience is due to the complex hydrological connections which maintain the wetland function. These remnant forested wetlands are literally oases in a sea of cut forest, resilient to adjacent landscape disturbances while themselves providing resources to vertebrates, invertebrates, and possibly other organisms that may have been displaced by the disturbance.

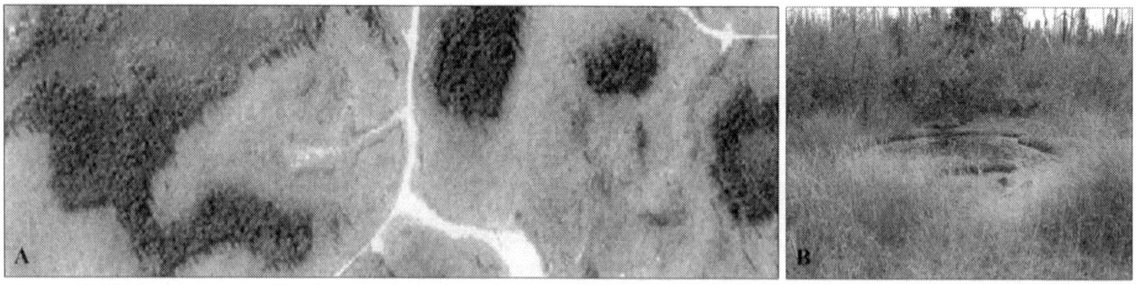

Figure 10: Wetlands as oases to disturbance on the landscape in Canada. A: Forested wetlands left on a logged landscape in boreal Manitoba. B: Spring slope fen in midst of fire-impacted landscape on boreal Alberta. Image A by Lousiana-Pacific Ltd, Image B by D.A. Locky.

Many wetlands can survive forest fires and eventually function as oases for organisms in a greatly changed landscape. Spring slope fens are found intermittently in the Boreal Plains forest of western can. Often very small in nature, their unique hydrology allows them apportions a degree of reliability unseen in other wetland and aquatic ecosystems. Despite their small size it is not uncommon that they survive forest fires virtually intact (Figure 1B). Similar to self-sustaining peatland remnants in logged forests, these sites function as oases for various organisms on the landscape.

During the drought of the 2000s in western Canada, ducks which would normally be breeding in the now dry prairie potholes migrated north to still wet boreal marshes as part of the peatland complexes (Author's observations, Abraham 2014). This is referred to as waterfowl displacement. In this case, one wetland type was providing relief for the loss/degradation of another wetland type. Riverine and lacustrine wetlands can provide relief from disturbance by their ability to buffer the adjacent landscape from the effects of not only high water levels, but low water levels.

Provision of Limiting Resources

Wetlands provide a plethora of limiting resources to adjacent ecosystems/organisms. Not unlike coral reefs (Hagedorn and Spindler 2014), coastal marshes like *Spartina* salt marshes providing primary productivity and nursery habitat (Pomeroy and Wiegert 1981), springs wetlands Keystone ecosystem presence and arrangement often determines the nutrient balance of a region (Blaschke 2005).

Of particular importance are riparian ecosystems near streams, lakes and wetlands as they cover a relatively small area yet support a disproportionately large number of species (Naiman *et al.* 2005). In many parts of the world, such as the boreal zone, riparian areas are comprised primarily of wetlands (Locky 2011).

Ephemeral wetlands are increasingly being accepted as critical landscape components (Cohen *et al.* 2015), with diverse and important flora (Zedler 2003, Deil 2005). Ephemeral wetlands have been well-known to provide critical refugia in drier landscapes such as the vernal pools in California (Zedler 2003). However, the importance of ephemeral wetlands as providing critical services is less accepted in other jurisdictions where they may be just as important as more permanent wetlands (Locky 2011, Stoneman *et al.* 2016).With respect to disturbance regimes, wetlands provide critical refugia to organisms during natural (and non-natural) disturbance events such as fire (Bergeron 1991) and logging (Locky and Bayley 2007).

Figure 11: Ephemeral wetlands (dark patches) in late spring in southern Alberta, Canada. These wetlands provide an important source of habitat for invertebrates and vertebrates and function as recharge conduits for ground water. Image by D.A. Locky.

Wetlands also store resources of significance to humans: carbon. For example, Alberta's peatlands hold 11% of Canada's soil carbon and sequester more carbon than the forests and the value of this carbon is of strategic economic importance (Anieski 1998). Peatland conservation plays a potential role in ameliorating climate change

Conservation Cornerstones

The proportion of coral reefs threatened with extinction has exceeded that of terrestrial ecosystems (Hagedorn and Spindler 2014) and this is arguably similar to the case of wetlands. Research has shown that when keystone ecosystems are lost from the landscape matrix there may be serious consequences for the whole region (Erikson 2014). For example, it is estimated that as of 1999, the cumulative value of Alberta's lost wetlands was \$45.7B (Wilson *et al.* 2001). Like keystone species, conservation of keystone ecosystems plays a critical role in maintaining integrity of the larger landscape (deMaynadier and Hunter 1994). Lost wetlands represent a potential lost legacy far great than their extent on the landscape given their status as keystone ecosystems. As keystone ecosystems, wetlands are truly conservation cornerstones.

CONCLUSION

Ecosystems are linked to each other in complex web of interconnected patches. Some of these patches may be more important regional than others, functioning as keystone ecosystems. Wetlands are ideal keystone ecosystems that influence landscapes by shaping landscape disturbance regimes or providing a limiting resource on the landscape. Enhancement of wetland protection and conservation will leverage the benefits of their keystone function, thus wetlands are critical conservation cornerstones.

REFERENCES

1. Abraham, K.F. 2014. Waterfowl in Ontario's Boreal Region: Looking back, looking forward. Report prepared for Ducks Unlimited Canada. Kingston, Ontario. 97 pp.
2. Anielski, M. 1998. In Search of the Carbonic Truth: Carbon Accounting. Anielski Management Inc. Edmonton, AB.
3. Bergeron, Y. 1991. The influence of island and mainland lakeshore landscapes on boreal forest fire regimes. Ecology 72: 1980-1992.
4. Blaschke, T. 2005. The role of the spatial dimension within the framework of sustainable landscapes and natural capital. Landscape and Urban Planning 75:198-226.
5. Cohen, M.J., I.F. Creed, L. Alexander, N.B. Basu, A.J.K. Calhoun, C. Craft, E. D'Amico, E. DeKeyser, L. Fowler, H.E. Golden, J.W. Jawitz, P. Kalla, L. K. Kirkman, C.R. Lane, M. Lang., S.G. Leibowitz, D.B. Lewis, J. Marton, D.L. McLaughlin, D.M. Mushet, H. Raanan-Kiperwas, M.C. Rains, L. Smith, and S.C. Walls. Do geographically isolated wetlands influence landscape functions? Proceedings of the National Academy of Sciences 113: 1978-1986.
6. Costanza, R., d'Arge, R., de Groot, R. S., Farber, S., Grasso, M., Hannon, B., Limburg, K., Naeem, S., O'Neill, R. V., Paruelo, J., Raskin, R. G., Sutton, P. and van den Belt, M. (1997), "The value of the world's ecosystem services and natural capital". Nature 387(6630): 253–260.
7. Deil, U. 2005. A review on habitats, plant traits and vegetation of ephemeral wetlands – a global perspective. Phytocoenologia 35: 533-706.
8. DeMaynadier, P. and M.J. Hunter 1994. Keystone Support. BioScience 155: 44-429.
9. DeMaynadier, P. and M.J. Hunter 1997. The Role of Keystone Ecosystems in Landscapes. In Boyce, M.S. and Haney, A. (eds). Ecosystems Management: Applications for Suitable Forest and Wildlife Resources. Yale University Press, New Haven, MA.
10. Eriksson, B. 2014. Biodiversity at the ecosystem level: structural variation among food webs in temperate and tropical areas. Bachelor's Thesis. Linköping University, Department of Physics, Chemistry and Biology, Biology. Linköping University, The Institute of Technology.
11. Hagedorn, M. and R. Spindler. 2014. The Reality, Use, and Potential for Cryopreservation in Coral Reefs. *In* Reproductive Sciences in Animal Conservation. Edited W.V. Holt, J.L. Brown, and P. Comizzolo. Springer, New York.
12. Hurlbert, S.H. 1997: Functional importance vs keystoneness: reformulating some questions in theoretical biocenology. Australian Journal of Ecology 22: 369-382.
13. Lesak, Lance. 2014. An Arctic Ecosystem. Available at http://nwtresearch.com/sites/default/files/ari_50th_newsletter_0.pdf. Accessed March 27, 2016.

14. Locky, D.A. and S.E. Bayley. 2007. Effects of logging in the southern boreal peatlands of Manitoba, Canada. Canadian Journal of Forest Research 37: 649-661.
15. Locky, D.A. 2011. Wetlands, Land Use, & Policy: Alberta's Keystone Ecosystem at a Crossroads. Policy position paper published by the Alberta Institute of Agrologists, Edmonton, Alberta.
16. Locky, D.A. 2012. The challenge of managing a keystone ecosystem: Cumulative impacts in a peatland-dominated landscape in Alberta, Canada. Extended Abstract published in the Proceedings of the Annual Conference of the International Peat Congress, June 3 - 8, 2012, Stockholm, Sweden.
17. Moola, F.M., D. Martin, B. Wareham, J. Calof, C. Burda, and P. Grames. 2004. The coastal temperate rainforests of Canada: The need for ecosystem-based management. Biodiversity 5:9-15.
18. Mouquet, N., D. Gravel, F. Massol, and V. Calcagno. 2013. Extending the concept of keystone species to communities and ecosystems. Ecology Letters 16: 1-8.
19. Naiman, R.J., H. Décamps, M.E. McClain and G.E. Likens. 2005. Riparia: ecology, conservation, and management of streamside communities. Academic Press. 430pp.
20. National Geographic. 2001. Northwest Mexican Coast Mangroves, Wildworld Ecoregion Profile. Available at http://www.worldwildlife.org/ecoregions/na1401. Accessed March 27, 2016.
21. Paine, R. 1966. Food web complexity and species diversity. American Naturalist 100: 65-75.
22. Pojar, J. 2003. Biodiversity in the CIT Region. Available at: https://www.for.gov.bc.ca/tasb/slrp/citbc/b-Biodiv-CITReg-02Apr04.pdf. Accessed March 27, 2016.
23. Goel, T.W., M. Denich, D. Teketay, and P.L.G. Vlek. 2001. Human impacts on the coffee *arabica* genepool. Edited by V. Ramanatha Rao, A.H.D. Brown, and M. Jackson. Ed. *In* Managing Plant Genetic Diversity. CABI Publishing, New York.
24. Stohlgren, T.G., M.B. Coughenour, G.W. Chong, D. Binkley, and A. Kalhan. 1997. Landscape analysis of plant diversity. Landscape Ecology 12:155-170.
25. Stoneman R., C. Bain, D. Locky, N. Mawdsley, M. McLaughlan, S. Kumaran-Prentice, M. Reed, and V. Swales. 2016. Chapter 19: Policy Drivers for Peatland Conservation. In Peatland Restoration and Ecosystem Services: Science, Policy, and Practice. A. Bonn, T. Allot, M. Evans, H. Joosten, and R. Stoneman (Eds.). Ecological Review Series, Cambridge University Press, UK.
26. Vold, T. and D.A. Buffett (eds.). 2008. Ecological Concepts, Principles and Applications to Conservation, BC. 36 pp. Available at: www.biodiversitybc.org.
27. Wilson, S., M. Griffiths, and M. Anielski. 2001. The Alberta GPI accounts: Wetlands and Peatlands. Report No. 23. Pembina Institute for Appropriate Development. Drayton Valley, AB.
28. Zedler, P.H. 2003. Vernal pools and the concept of "isolated wetlands". Wetlands 23: 597-607.

THEME 2
PEATLANDS & ECOSYSTEM MANAGEMENT

2.1: PEATLAND CARBON BALANCE, STOCKS, STORAGE & LOSSES

Abstract No: A-328

CALCULATION OF CARBON BALANCE IN *ACACIA* CRASSICARPA PLANTATION ON TROPICAL PEATLAND IN INDONESIA

Muhajir Utomo[1*], Basuki Sumawinata[2], Suwardi, Darmawan[2], Gunawan Djajakirana[2] and Dian Novarina[3]

[1]*Faculty of Agriculture, Lampung University, Indonesia*
[2]*Department of Soil Science, Faculty of Agriculture, Bogor Agricultural University, Indonesia*
[3]*APRIL, Indonesia*

* *Corresponding author: mutomo2011@gmail.com*

Methodologies for calculating carbon balance in peatland are various, reflecting differences in consideration of the factors contributing to the net emission or net sequestration. Among the published methodologies, measured carbon fluxes are considered as a source of carbon release with no exception of the flux originating from respiration. On the other hand, the forest cut as well as the following harvest of planted species are totally calculated as carbon loss, neglecting the drop back of root, litter, dead plant, and the potential harvest which remains on the land. At the landscape scale, the count may be in error if it is assumed that the forest cut and the harvest take place over a homogeneous time span for all the managed area. This study applied an approach in calculating the carbon balance in *Acacia crassicarpa* planted peatland by taking into consideration all the shortcomings mentioned above. The approach includes CO_2 flux from bare land as the source of carbon release and calculation of sequestration by summing the carbon components which enter into the soil from 1) falling trees subtracted of those that decomposed up to the time of harvest, 2) litter falls subtracted of those that decomposed up to the time of plantation harvest, 3) plant roots over a plantation period, 4) plant parts that were left behind in the field after harvest, 5) left-over or residual wood which has not been taken to the mill for technical or economic considerations, and 6) wild understory plants that naturally grew underneath the *Acacia crassicarpa* stand. The results showed that CO_2 flux from the bare peatland was around 11 tons C-CO_2 ha^{-1} $year^{-1}$;, that is lower than the sequestration for one plantation rotation. It can be concluded that the *Acacia crassicarpa* plantation on peatland produces a positive value in the carbon balance calculation.

***Keywords**: CO_2 emission, falling trees, litter fall, CO_2 sequestration*

Abstract No: A-136

CARBON CYCLE IN SAGO PALM CULTIVATION SYSTEM IN TROPICAL PEATLAND

Akira Watanabe[1*], Shuhei Makabe[2], Ho Ando[3], Ken-ichi Kakuda[3], Sudid Donny[4], Zulhilmy Abdullah Mohd[4] and Lulie Melling[4]

[1]*Graduate School of Bioagricultural Science, Nagoya University, Nagoya, Japan*
[2]*Agricultural Research Institute, Ibaraki Agricultural Center, Ibaraki, Japan*
[3]*School of Agriculture, Yamagata University, Yamagata, Japan*
[4]*Tropical Peat Research Laboratory Unit, Chief Minister's Department, Sarawak, Malaysia*

**Corresponding author: akiraw@agr.nagoya-u.ac.jp*

SUMMARY

Sago palm (*Metroxylon sagu* Rottb.) is a high starch producing plant that can grow in a peat soil without intensive drainage. With such characteristics, sago palm is recommendable cash crop in tropical peatland. In this study, carbon (C) cycle in a sago palm cultivation system in Sarawak, Malaysia, was investigated to evaluate the potential of the system as C sink. For this purpose, the rate of C supply from sago palm to soil as litter, accumulation of C as aboveground biomass of sago and weeds, rate of sago litter decomposition on soil surface, and carbon dioxide (CO_2) and methane (CH_4) fluxes from soil were measured in one or two sago palm gardens managed by native farmers. The rate of annual C supply from sago palm was estimated to be 3–4 t C ha^{-1} y^{-1}. The amount of C accumulated as aboveground biomass of sago palm showed a large variation between the two gardens, 1–4 t C ha^{-1} y^{-1}, due to the difference in the proportion of sago palms in the trunk formation stage. The CO_2 and CH_4 fluxes from soil (at 1 m distance from sago cluster) measured manually ranged from 6–9 t C ha^{-1} y^{-1} and -2 to 27 kg C ha^{-1} y^{-1}, respectively. The CO_2 fluxes may be affected by root respiration because those were higher than the CO_2 flux recorded at the centre of four palms using a soil respiration monitoring system.

***Keywords**: Carbon Cycle, Litter Decomposition, Sago Palm, Tropical Peat*

INTRODUCTION

Peatland is a huge natural carbon (C) pool formed by the accumulation of partially decomposed plant material. In Southeast Asia, peatland that occupies 25 million ha (Page *et al.*, 2011) is a potential land source for producing food and energy sources balanced with increasing human population. However, due to high groundwater level, drainage is pre-requisite to facilitate plant root respiration for producing crops in peatland. The intense drainage may affect the decomposition of peat material and subsidence and (Blodau, 2002). In addition, characteristics of tropical peat soil, such as low pH (3–5; Purwanto *et al.*, 2002), high C/N ratio (14–49; Yonebayashi *et al.*, 1994; Purwanto *et al.*, 2005), and low plant-available nutrient contents (Miyamoto *et al.*, 2009), are unfavourable for most of the crops.
Sago palm (*Metroxylon sagu* Rottb.) is worthy of attention as a rare crop that can grow on tropical peat soil without intense drainage of groundwater. The growth of sago palm is divided into two stages of the rosette stage, when leaves emerge near the ground surface, and trunk formation/elongation stage. Trunk body accumulates 160–180 kg per plant of starch (on a dry weight basis; Yamamoto *et al.*, 2003). Total leaf area of sago palms reaches 100 m^2 per plant and fronds with 8–10 m length are deposited on soil periodically (Nakamura and Goto, 2015). Based on this with a high photosynthetic rate (max 130 mg CO_2 m^{-2} h^{-1}; Miyazaki, 2015) and the similarities in carbon dioxide (CO_2) and methane (CH_4) fluxes between a sago palm plantation and neighbouring forest (Watanabe *et al.*, 2008), it was expected that sago palm cultivation system can function as C sink. The objective of the present study was to evaluate the C accumulation potential of sago palm cultivation system in tropical peatland. For this purpose, the amount of C supplied from sago palm to soil as litter, rate of decomposition of sago litter C on soil, C (CO_2 and CH_4) flux from soil to the atmosphere, and rate of accumulation of plant biomass C (sago and weeds) as well as soil C pool were measured in sago palm gardens managed by native farmers.

MATERIALS AND METHODS

Field experiments were conducted in two sago palm gardens (SG1, SG3) in Mukah, Sarawak, Malaysia (Figure 1). Two fields were different in the thickness of peat layer (SG1 < SG3) and the proportion of sago palms in the trunk

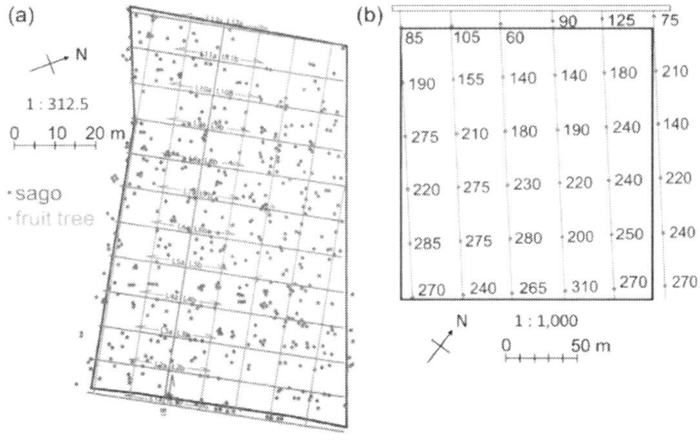

Figure 1: Distribution of sago palms in SG1 (a) and distribution of the thickness (cm) of peat layer in SG3 (b).

formation/elongation stage (SG1 < SG3). Unfortunately, SG3 was burned down by the flame spread from a distant field in the third year and the palms used for monitoring growth were lost.

Number of fronds and plant height were recorded for each 10 palms in the rosette and trunk elongation stages at an interval of 6 months for 3 years (Sep. 2011–Sep. 2014). For the palms in the trunk elongation stage, the trunk length and trunk girth at a height of 130 cm were also measured. As a new frond emerges inside of existing fronds, one of fronds was marked and the rate of frond emergence and that of litter fall (a, plant^{-1} y^{-1}) were estimated from the increase and decrease in the number of inner and outer fronds of the marked one. The rate of C supply to soil (Y, t C y^{-1} ha^{-1}) was obtained by multiplying a by the average amount of C in a litter (b) and the number of palms in a unit area. The b value was obtained using 10 samples. Aboveground biomass was estimated for each 5 palms in the rosette and trunk elongation stages by weighing total fresh weight and determining the water and C contents of pieces for all the leaflets, rachises, and petioles, and trunk.

Rate of decomposition of litter C was estimated from the change in the amount of C in fronds placed on the soil surface in the frame of 4 m x 4 m ($n = 8$). Total fresh weight of frond samples was measured in the field once a half year. A portion of leaflet, rachis, and petiole were brought back to the laboratory, and the water and C contents were determined. This experiment could be done only in SG3 because soil surface in SG1 was frequently submerged even in dry season. Litter bag method using nylon bags with 5-mm mesh was also applied.

Weed biomass was estimated using the quadrat method. Weeds in a 2 m×2 m frame were harvested, separated into fens and others, and total fresh weight and the fresh and dry weights as well as C content of a portion of them were determined in dry and wet seasons ($n = 10$).

CO_2 and CH_4 fluxes were measured 3 times in 2013–2014 at various points in the sago gardens using the closed chamber method. A stainless pipe (20 cmφ × 20 cm height) was placed on soil with the bottom approximately 8 cm below the soil surface ($n = 10$). After 1 h, the top of pipe was closed with an acrylic plate and fastened. Gas samples were collected at 0, 10, 20, and 30 min after enclosure through a W-shaped butyl rubber cap, which was installed in the acrylic plate beforehand, into 30-mL vacuumed glass vials using a double-ended needle. Soil temperature and soil moisture content at 5 cm depth were also recorded. CO_2 and CH_4 concentrations in the samples were determined using a gas chromatograph equipped with a flame ionization and thermal conductivity detectors. CO_2 flux in SG3 was also monitored for a 6-month period using an automatic soil respiration analyzer (ACE-001/L).

RESULTS AND DISCUSSION

The number of fronds ranged from 5–11 or from 5–17 for the plants in the rosette and trunk elongation stages, respectively, which did not increase during the monitoring period. The dry weight of a frond was 1.9±0.5 kg before trunk formation and 2.9±0.9 kg after trunk formation, and the rate of litter fall was in the range of 4.3–6.4 y^{-1} for both growth stages in the two gardens. Based on these values with C content, it was estimated that the rate of C supply from sago palm to soil was 2.9–3.8 t C ha^{-1} y^{-1}.

An increase in the plant height of the sago palms in the rosette stage with time was unclear, as was the case of the number of fronds. Trunk length increased at a rate of 1.1 (SG3) –1.2 (SG1) m y^{-1}, while trunk girth did not change significantly. Thus, the rate of C accumulation as the aboveground biomass of sago palms was determined mainly by the change in trunk length. Based on the relationship between the amount of trunk C (136–215 kg plant^{-1}) and trunk length (8–12 m) in SG1 (n = 5) with the number of sago palms in the trunk elongation stage, annual C accumulation as aboveground biomass of sago palms was estimated to be 3.7 t C ha^{-1}. Similar data could not be obtained for SG3 due to the fire. An application of the SG1 data to the rate of trunk elongation and the number of plants rate in SG3 gave the annual C accumulation of 0.8 t C ha^{-1}. Since the number of sago palms in the rosette stage in SG3 is 4 times of that in SG1, the annual C accumulation in SG3 will be larger than that in SG1 within a few years.

Figure 2 shows the change in sago litter left on the soil surface in the in-situ decomposition experiment in SG3. By regressing the variation in the percentage of residual sago litter C with time to an exponential equation (Figure 2b; r^2 = 1.00), the rate constant of litter decomposition and annual C loss were estimated to be 0.105 $month^{-1}$ and 72%, respectively. Combination of the rate of litter decomposition with the rate of litter fall and stand density of sago palms in the rosette and trunk elongation stages gave the rate of sago litter C accumulation in SG3, 1.9 t C ha^{-1} y^{-1}. However, as the litter fragments that were too small to be collected was regarded as 'decomposed' in this experiment, the C loss rate might be overestimated. The C accumulation rate as was estimated using the data from the litter bag experiment was 3.0 t C ha^{-1} y^{-1}. However, decomposition of litter in the nylon mesh bag might be slower than that deposited directly on the soil surface because of insufficient contact with soil. Thus, real C accumulation rate may be distributed between 1.9–3.0 t C ha^{-1} y^{-1}. Assuming that the rate of litter decomposition was similar between SG1 and SG3, the rate of accumulation of sago litter C in SG1 was estimated to be 1.5–2.5 t C ha^{-1} y^{-1}.

Figure 2: Comparison of sago litter at the onset of in-situ decomposition experiment and after 13 months (a) and variation in percentage of residual litter C in SG3 (b).

In both sago gardens, major weed was fen. Weed species observed in SG1 other than fens included *Areca catechu*, *Scleria sumatrensis*, *Brachiaria mutica*, *Macaranga gigantean*, and *Punicum maximum* and those in SG3 included *Macaranga gigantean* and *Hevea brasiliensis*. Weed biomass C derived from fens ranged from 58–480 and 210–790 kg C ha^{-1} in SG1 and SG3, receptively. Weed biomass C derived from the other species ranged from 30–44 and 9–60 kg C ha^{-1} in SG1 and SG3, respectively. Total weed biomass C (Figure 3) fluctuated in the range of 61–510 kg C ha^{-1} in SG1 and 390–800 kg C ha^{-1} in SG3. The smallest value in SG1 was due to weeding by the owner. When weeds in the same plots were harvested twice with an interval of 1 year, total weed biomass C at the second harvest was equivalent to 68–73% of that at the first harvest. Thus, the influence of the fluctuation in weed biomass C on the whole C budget in the sago palm cultivation system was small.

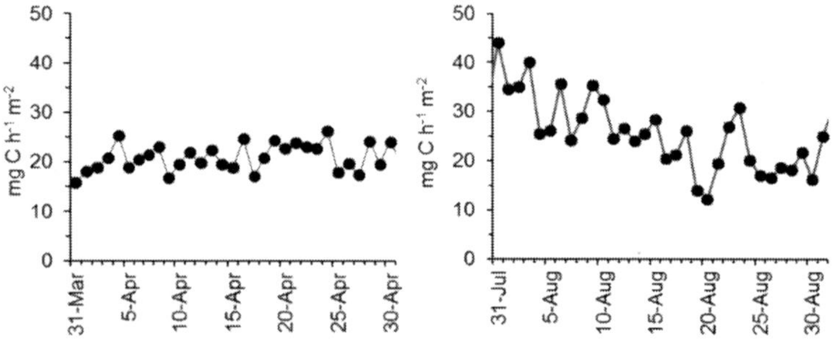

Figure 3: Weed biomass C in sago palm gardens (n = 10). Data in September 2013 was obtained at the plots where weeds were harvested in October 2012.

CO_2 flux measured using the closed chamber method ranged from 10–205 mg C h^{-1} m^{-2}. There were no differences between September and March and between the sites. CH_4 flux differed between SG1 and SG3. The CH_4 flux in SG1 ranged from -3 to 1220 μg C h^{-1} m^{-2} with positive mean values, while that in SG3 ranged from -65 to 93 μg C h^{-1} m^{-2} with negative mean values. The CO_2 and CH_4 emissions were estimated to be 6.1–8.5 t C ha^{-1} y^{-1} and -1.5–27 kg C ha^{-1} y^{-1}, respectively. These results suggest that the amount of C emitted from soil was comparable to the sum of the increase in the above biomass C of sago palms and the amount of sago litter C accumulated in soil in SG1. In SG3, C output as CO_2 emission from soil was larger than the sum of C input, 2.3–3.3 t C ha^{-1} y^{-1}. CO_2 flux recorded on the automatic soil respiration analyzer (Figure 4) was small compared with those measured manually, and the average value, 20 mg C h^{-1} m^{-2}, suggested that the C output did not exceed the C input. Since gas samples for estimating CO_2 and CH_4 fluxes were collected at 1 m distance from a sago cluster while the automatic soil respiration analyzer was installed at the centre of 4 palms (ca 5 m distance from the sago clusters), CO_2 fluxes measured manually may be affected by root respiration.

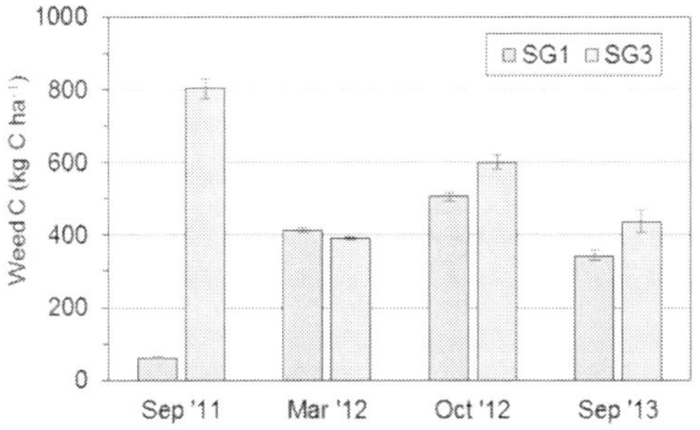

Figure 4: Variation in CO_2 flux from SG3 soil measured twice a day (11 a.m. and 11 p.m.) using the automatic soil respiration analyzer in April and August 2013.

CONCLUSION

The present study showed that the C accumulation in sago palm cultivation system depends on the accumulation of sago litter C and the increase in aboveground biomass C of sago palms in the trunk elongation stage. Total amounts of C accumulated can be comparable with the CO_2 emission from soil, and the rate of sago litter C accumulation can also be comparable with the rate of soil organic C decomposition. Therefore, the regulation of palms population in the trunk elongation stage is suggested to maintain large C input in sago plantation on tropical peatland.

ACKNOWLEDGEMENTS

This research was supported by a Grant-in-Aid for Scientific Research from the Japan Society for the Promotion of Science (No. 24405029). We wish to thank staff members of Tropical Peat Research Laboratory Unit for their technical assistance and support in the field work.

REFERENCES

1. Blodau, C. 2002. Carbon cycling in peatlands–A review of processes and controls. *Environmental Reviews* **10**,111–134.
2. Miyamoto, E., Matsuda, S., Ando, H., Kakuda, K., Jong, F.-S., and Watanabe, A. 2009. Effect of sago palm (*Metroxylon sagu* Rottb.) cultivation on the chemical properties of soil and water in tropical peat soil ecosystem. *Nutrient Cycling in Agroecosystms* **85**, 157–167.
3. Miyazaki, A. 2015. Photosynthesis. In: The Sago Palm—The Food and Environmental Challenges of the 21st Century. Ed. The Society of Sago Palm Studies, p. 129–132, Kyoto Univ. Press, Kyoto, Japan.
4. Nakamura, S. and Goto, Y. 2015. Leaf. In: The Sago Palm—The Food and Environmental Challenges of the 21st Century. Ed. The Society of Sago Palm Studies, p. 66–75, Kyoto Univ. Press, Kyoto, Japan.
5. Page, S.E., Rieley, J.O., and Banks, C.J. 2011. Global and regional importance of the tropical peatland carbon pool. *Global Change Biology* **17**, 798–818.
6. Purwanto, B.H., Kakuda, K., Ando, H., Jong, F.-S., Yamamoto, Y., Watanabe, A., and Yoshida, T. 2002. Nutrient availability and response of sago palm (*Metroxylon sagu* Rottb.) to controlled release N fertilizer on coastal lowland peat in the tropics. *Soil Science and Plant Nutrition* **48**, 529–537.
7. Purwanto, B.H., Watanabe, A., Jong, F.-S., Kakuda, K., and Ando, H. 2005. Kinetic parameters of gross N mineralization of peat soils as related to the composition of soil organic matter. *Soil Science and Plant Nutrition* **51**, 109–115.
8. Watanabe, A., Kakuda, K., Purwanto, B.H., Jong, F.-S., and Ando, H. 2008. Effect of sago palm (*Metroxylon sagu* Rottb.) plantation on CH_4 and CO_2 fuxes from a tropical peat soil. *Sago Palm* **6**, 10–15.
9. Yamamoto, Y., Yoshida, T., Goto, Y., Nitta, Y., Kakudam K., Jong, F.-S., Hilary, L.B., and Hassan, A.H. 2003. Differences in growth and starch yield of sago palms (*Metroxylon sagu* Rottb) among soil types in Sarawak, Malaysia. *Japanese Journal of Tropical Agriculture* **47**, 250-259.
10. Yonebayashi, K., Pechayapisit, J., Vijarnsorn, P., Zahari, A.B., and Kyuma, K. 1994. Chemical alterations of tropical peat soils determined by Waksman's proximate analysis and properties of humic acids. *Soil Science and Plant Nutrition* **40**, 435–444.

Abstract No: A-053

CARBON STOCKS AND EMISSIONS FROM DEGRADATION AND CONVERSION OF TROPICAL PEAT SWAMP FORESTS IN WEST KALIMANTAN, INDONESIA

Imam Basuki[1*], J. B. Kauffman[1], Daniel Murdiyarso[2, 3] and Gusti Anshari[4]

[1]*Dept. of Fisheries and Wildlife, Oregon State University, USA*
[2]*Center for International Forestry Research, Indonesia*
[3]*Bogor Agricultural University, Indonesia*
[4]*Tanjungpura University, Indonesia*

**Corresponding author: imambasuki1974@gmail.com*

SUMMARY

High rates of land cover change and deforestation in tropical peat swamp forests over the past few decades had been judged to increased peat decomposition rates and carbon (C) emissions from peatlands, yet this had been supported by little information. Our main objective was to estimate the C emission resulting from peat swamp forests (PSF) degradation into logged PSF (LPSF) and conversions into the adjacent wet shrub (WS) and oil palm plantation (OP) of the Pematang Gadung peat dome, Ketapang, Indonesia. We tested if degradation and conversion of PSF increase the peatlands' potential C emissions. C emission was measured using the C stock difference methods, comparing aboveground and belowground C stocks of LPSF, WS and OP with the PSF. PSF and LPSF have significantly higher aboveground C stocks (122 and 96 Mg C ha^{-1}, respectively) than WS and OP (12 and 7 Mg C ha^{-1}, respectively). Our results indicated that the loss of the PSF trees is a major driver of ecosystem's C loss. The significant loss of trees and other aboveground carbon stocks directed to a clear negative impact of land cover change on peatlands' role in sequestering atmospheric C. Potential CO_2 emissions of non-PSF sites were significantly higher than the PSF sites. Our study showed that PSF conversion to other land uses comes at a great cost in terms of significantly reduced function in sequestering greenhouse gas emissions. The high rates of deforestation of PSF, and subsequent high greenhouse gas emissions point to the relevance for inclusion of PSF in appropriate climate change mitigation and adaptation strategies.

Keywords: *Land cover change; tropical peat swamp forests; oil palm plantation; CO_2 emissions; climate change.*

INTRODUCTION

Tropical peatland ecosystem has among the largest ecosystem C stocks on earth (Page et al., 2011). Tropical peatlands comprise about 10% (44 Mha) of the global peatland (400 Mha), in which Indonesia alone has about 50% (21 Mha) (Murdiyarso et al., 2009). Indonesia contains the largest area of peat in the tropical zone, where about 6.8 Mha are located in Borneo island (Radjagukguk in Rieley and Page 1997; Murdiyarso et al., 2009). Undisturbed tropical peatlands have been shown to store huge quantities of carbon (C) in peats ranging from 824 to 7,888 Mg C/ha (Murdiyarso et al., 2009; Warren et al., 2012). The C stock of tropical peatlands range from 81.7 to 91.9 Gt or about 15-19% of global peat carbon stock (610 Gt), in which Indonesia contain 57 Gt (Verwer & Meer 2010; Page et al., 2011).

Rates of land cover change in tropical wetlands over the past few decades have exceeded that of upland tropical forests (Hergoualc'h & Verchot 2011). Recent estimate suggests that Indonesia shows highest increase of forest loss that is more than 1,000 km^2/year (Hansen et al., 2013). Deforestation and forest degradation, including forest conversion to oil palm (*Elaeis guineensis)* plantations, are the main human disturbances to peat forest ecosystems (Fearnside 2000). Peat forests mainly converted into oil palm, food crops and timber plantation (Murdiyarso et al., 2009; Hergoualc'h & Verchot 2011). Conversion of tropical peat forest involves cutting trees, burning and/or developing drainage canals (Anshari et al., 2010; Hooijer et al., 2010). This conversion likely increases peat decomposition rates and C emissions from peatlands (Kauffman et al., 2009; Murdiyarso et al., 2010; Hergoualc'h & Verchot 2011). We need to understand impacts of land cover change on the dynamics of peat forests' C in order to inform decision making in climate change mitigation and adaptation strategies.

Emission from peatland in South East Asia has never been estimated using the C stock difference method in a synchronic experiment (Hergoualc'h & Verchot 2013). This study is among the first that combines intensive field measurements of tropical peatlands' carbon stocks to provide accurate estimates of the fate of stocks and emissions.

Our main objective of this study was to estimate the changes on carbon stocks and emissions resulting from forest degradation and conversions of peat swamp forests into the adjacent wet shrubs and oil palm plantations of the Pematang Gadung peat dome, Ketapang, Indonesia. While total carbon stocks information has been reported for the peat swamp forest regions of Kalimantan (Murdiyarso et al., 2009) and of Sumatera, Indonesia (Suwarna et al., 2012) we know of no studies that have measured total carbon stocks associated with the land cover change and their emissions.

Our specific research questions included: What are the carbon stocks of the peat swamp forests (PSF) of the Pematang Gadung peat dome? How do they differ between relatively intact PSF and logged PSF? What are the carbon stocks of wet shrubs (WS) and oil palm plantations (OP) that were formed on sites previously occupied by PSF? And finally, what are the potential emissions that could arise from degradation of PSF to LPSF and from conversion of PSF to WS and OP?

METHODS

The study area is located in Pematang Gadung, Ketapang, Indonesia in the province of West Kalimantan. The Pematang Gadung is a coastal peat dome (34,651 ha) in between the Pawan and Pesaguhan Rivers that flow on the northern and the southern end of the peat dome, respectively. The rainfalls in the region averages 2000 mm per year and mean annual temperature is 27.5°C. Elevation ranges from 11-22 m above sea level.

All forests (5 relatively intact - Peat Swamp Forests/PSF and 5 highly - Logged Peat Swamp Forests/LPSF) were transition between peat swamp and low pole forests with a mean canopy height of 15 m (Page et al., 1999) and occurring around the center of the peat dome. In addition to the forests, we sampled five wet shrubs (WS) and five oil palm (OP) smallholder plantation. The OP plantations were surrounded by the WS and LPSF. Based upon observation on satellite imageries and interviews with local people, the forests were logged since about 25 years before sampling (in 1988) and wet shrub were formed about 19 years before sampling. All wet shrubs had frequently been burned during the dry month's period. The five oil palm plantations were one (1), two (2) and three (2) years old, that were established following burning for land clearing and canalization.

We selected research sites based on field observation, discussion with local experts and analyses on some Landsat images. Considerations include availability of PSF and other land cover types that were previously converted from the PSF, as well as sites' relative position within the peat dome. We studied the ecosystem carbon stocks and structure of 20 different coastal peatlands including five PSF sites, five LPSF sites, five WS sites, and five OP plantations. In order to ensure the sequential changes of land cover types (from forests to WS and OP plantation), we paired each forest site with the others in a close distance. We have five pairs of cover types (PSF – LPSF – WS – OP).

Ecosystem C stocks (above-and belowground) were measured, in each site, following methodologies outlined by Murdiyarso et al. (2009) and Kauffman and Donato (2012). Nested to each forest, wet shrub and oil palm site, six plots were established 30 m apart along a 150 m transect positioned in a perpendicular direction from the riverine ecotone and drainage canal. At each plot, we collected data necessary to calculate total C stocks derived from standing tree biomass, downed wood (dead wood on forest floor), understorey and litter fall, and peat to the depths of the mineral soils.

RESULTS

Aboveground C stocks ranged from 5 Mg/ha in the OP site to 139 Mg/ha in the PSF site. There were significant differences when comparing the PSF to the LPSF, WS and OP sites. The OP was the lowest in aboveground C stocks, with a range from 5 to 11 Mg/ha. In peat swamp forests there was high variation in the total aboveground carbon pools, with a range of 103-159 Mg C/ha among PSF sites and 57–90 Mg C/ha among LPSF sites.

Mean peat carbon stocks at PSF was 3925 Mg C/ha, at LPSF was 3,784 Mg C/ha, at WS was 3,372 Mg C/ha, and at OP was 3,655 Mg C/ha.

The mean ecosystem carbon stock for the PSF sites was 4,024 Mg C/ha, the LPSF was 3,768 Mg C/ha, the WS was 3,147 and the OP was 3,135. At PSF sites, peat carbon pools comprised a mean of 96 % of the total ecosystem pool with range of 95% at the PSF2 site to 97 % at the PSF4 site. At LPSF sites, peat carbon pools comprised a mean of 97 % of the total ecosystem pool with range of 93% to 98%. At all WS and OP sites, peat carbon pools comprised a mean of 99% of the total ecosystem pool.

We examined potential greenhouse emissions on a CO_2 equivalence (CO_2e) basis arising from conversion of PSF to LPSF, WS and OP. In 25 years, the mean potential emission from PSF conversion to LPSF was 938 Mg CO_2e ha^{-1}. The mean potential emission from PSF conversion to WS was 3,215 Mg CO_2e ha^{-1}. The mean potential emission from PSF conversion to OP was 2,132 Mg CO_2e ha^{-1}.

DISCUSSION

Our results indicated that the loss of the PSF trees is a major driver of ecosystem's C loss. The significant loss of trees and other aboveground carbon stocks directed to a clear negative impact of land cover change on peatlands' role in sequestering atmospheric C.

We found that there was a mean loss of 3,215 Mg CO_2e ha^{-1} and 2,132 Mg CO_2e ha^{-1} from the peat carbon pools when PSF are converted to WS and WS+OP, respectively. In contrast, few changes in soil carbon were noted with upland tropical forest conversion. For example, Kauffman et al. (1998) did not find significant differences in either soil C concentration or mass when comparing surface soil carbon in Amazon tropical forests and the converted areas.

Kauffman et al. (2015) argued that the loss in carbon stocks from mangrove conversion was 7-fold that of emissions from dry forests and 3-fold greater than emissions from Amazon forest to pasture conversion. This study shows that the carbon stocks lost from PSF conversion to wet shrub, dominated by grasses and ferns, is significantly greater than emissions from Amazon forest and mangrove to pasture conversion (1,464 Mg CO2e ha^{-1} for 30 years).

We have reported that C emission occurs in peatland ecosystem when the peat swamp forests are degraded and converted into LPSF, WS and OP. This is important because at the peat dome scale, the annual emissions of LPSF, WS and OP are equal to an annual loss of many hectares of PSF's standing C stock.

CONCLUSION

Our study shows that PSF conversion to other land uses comes at a great cost in terms of large quantities of greenhouse gas emissions. The large carbon stocks, high rates of deforestation of PSF, and subsequent high greenhouse gas emissions points to the relevance for inclusion of PSF in nationally appropriate climate change mitigation and adaptation strategies. Tropical peatlands may be bundled with national level mitigation actions and participated by relevant stakeholders.

ACKNOWLEDGMENTS

We wish to thank Randi Ade Chandra, Samsudin and community of Sungai Pelang village, for assistance in the field. We also wish to thank Flora Fauna Indonesia, IFAC USAID, Yayasan Palung, and International Animal Rescue, for collaborating during the research preparation. Dr. Iswandi Anas and Mrs. Asih Karyati of the Biotechnology Laboratory, Bogor Agricultural University for carbon analysis. Funding this study was possible through funding provided by the United States Agency for International Development - The Kalimantan Wetland and Climate Studies Project.

REFERENCES

1. Anshari, G.Z., Afifudin, M., Nuriman, M., Gusmayanti, E., Arianie, L., Susana, R., Nusantara, R.W., Sugardjito, J. and Rafiastanto, A., 2010. Drainage and land use impacts on changes in selected peat properties and peat degradation in West Kalimantan Province, Indonesia. *Biogeosciences*,*7*(11), pp.3403-3419.
2. Fearnside, P.M., 2000. Global warming and tropical land-use change: greenhouse gas emissions from biomass burning, decomposition and soils in forest conversion, shifting cultivation and secondary vegetation. *Climatic Change*, *46*(1-2), pp.115-158.
3. Hansen, M.C., Potapov, P.V., Moore, R., Hancher, M., Turubanova, S.A., Tyukavina, A., Thau, D., Stehman, S.V., Goetz, S.J., Loveland, T.R. and Kommareddy, A., 2013. High-resolution global maps of 21st-century forest cover change. *Science*, *342*(6160), pp.850-853.
4. Hergoualc'h, K. & Verchot, L. V., 2011. Stocks and fluxes of carbon associated with land use change in Southeast Asian tropical peatlands: A review. *Global Biogeochemical Cycles*, 25.
5. Hergoualc'h, K. and Verchot, L. V., 2014. Greenhouse gas emission factors for land use and land-use change in Southeast Asian peatlands. *Mitigation Adaptation Strategy Global Change*, 19, pp.789-807.
6. Hooijer, et al., 2010. Current and future CO_2 emissions from drained peatlands in Southeast Asia. *Biogeosciences*, 7(5), pp.1505–1514.
7. Kauffman, J.B., Cummings, D.L. and Ward, D.E., 1998. Fire in the Brazilian Amazon 2. Biomass, nutrient pools and losses in cattle pastures. *Oecologia*,*113*(3), pp.415-427.
8. Kauffman, J.B., Hughes, R.F. & Heider, C., 2009. Carbon pool and biomass dynamics associated with deforestation, land use, and agricultural abandonment in the neotropics. *Ecological applications : a publication of the Ecological Society of America*, 19(5), pp.1211–22.
9. Kauffman, J.B. and Donato, D., 2012. *Protocols for the measurement, monitoring and reporting of structure, biomass and carbon stocks in mangrove forests* (No. CIFOR Working Paper no. 86, p. 40p). Center for

International Forestry Research (CIFOR), Bogor, Indonesia.
10. Kauffman, J.B. et al., 2015. Carbon stocks of mangroves and losses arising from their conversion to cattle pastures in the Pantanos de Centla, Mexico. *Wetlands Ecology and Management*, pp. 1-14.
11. Murdiyarso, D., Donato, D., Kauffman, J. B., Kurnianto, S., Stidham, M., and Kanninen, M., 2009. *Carbon storage in mangrove and peatland ecosystems*, Working Paper 48, Center for International Forestry Research, Bogor, Indonesia, 2009. 40p.
12. Page, S. E., Rieley, J. O., and Banks, C. J., 2011. Global and regional importance of the tropical peatland carbon pool. *Global Change Biology*, 17. pp 798–818.
13. Rieley, J.O. & Page, S. E., 1997. *Biodiversity and Sustainability of Tropical Peatlands*. Proceedings of the
14. International Symposium on Biodiversity, Environmental Importance and Sustainability of Tropical Peat and Peatlands, Held in Palangka Raya, Central Kalimantan, Indonesia, 4-8 September 1995. Samara Pub.
15. Rieley, J.O. et al., 2008. Tropical Peatland: Carbon Stores, Carbon Gas Emissions and Contribution to Climate Change Processes. In M. Strack, ed. *Peatlands and Climate Change*. pp. 148–181.
16. Suwarna U., Elias, Darusman D, Istomo., 2012. Estimation of Total Carbon Stocks in Soil and Vegetation of Tropical Peat Forest in Indonesia. *Jurnal Manajemen Hutan Tropika* (2): 118-128.
17. Verwer, C. and van der Meer, P., 2010. Carbon pools in tropical peat forest. *Alterra Report, 2108*.
18. Warren, M.W. et al., 2012. A cost-efficient method to assess carbon stocks in tropical peat soil. *Biogeosciences*, 9(11). pp.4477–4485.

Abstract No: A-315

CONTRIBUTION FROM ROOT RESPIRATION AND LITTER DECOMPOSITION TO CARBON FLUX IN TROPICAL PEATLAND

Marissa Permatasari Jayaputra*, Darmawan, Basuki Sumawinata and Gunawan Djajakirana

Faculty of Agriculture, Bogor Agricultural Institute. Indonesia

**Corresponding author: marissa_permatasari@yahoo.com*

SUMMARY

There are several components of carbon flux from peatland, i.e. peat decomposition, root respiration and exudates, and litter decomposition. It is important to know the magnitude of the contribution from each component. Lacking knowledge of contribution from these components may lead people to simply assume that the carbon emission from tropical peatland merely comes from the decomposition of the peat itself. To get the certainty in measuring net carbon emission, therefore it is necessary among others to measure the contribution of root respiration and litter decomposition of planted species on peatland. *Acacia crassicarpa* is the main species that is being cultivated on Indonesian peatland as a source for pulp industries. For this reason, this research was conducted in one of the *A. crassicarpa* plantation on peatland in Jambi, Sumatra. Measurement of CO_2 flux from plots of no root no litter and no root with litter were carried out simultaneously with measurement from the plot of no treatments where the chambers were placed on the peatland surface under the *A. crassicarpa* at natural condition. The root-free plots were obtained with sorting out all roots in a specified manner. The measurement of carbon flux was carried out continuously every week for about a year. Comparison of the results obtained from the plot with roots and those from the plot of no roots did not show a significant difference. It was due to inappropriate technique applied in blocking roots to penetrate back into root-free peat mass of the plot. A clear difference was found between the results of no roots with litter and those of no roots no litter. The difference was detected after several weeks in that the plot with litter has higher flux indicating the flux of the plot with litter includes CO_2 released from litter decomposition that increasing with time. At week 50 the difference between both plots was account to about 65 $g/m^2/day$, meaning that the contribution of the litter decomposition within 50 weeks was happened constantly at around 14% of the total carbon flux.

Keywords: *Acacia crassicarpa, carbon flux, peat decomposition , root respiration*

INTRODUCTION

The contribution of diverse sources to the global CO_2 flux from soils of various ecosystems is very important for the construction of the global, regional and local C balance. A review by Kuzyakov (2006) revealed that over the last view decades, various methods allowing the separation of several CO_2 sources and the calculation of their contribution to total CO_2 flux from soil have developed and used. However the basic assumptions and principles of these methods, and the results obtained, all differ from one to another. The review further concluded that the separation of root-derived CO_2 is still a challenging area to investigate more. Similar situation is happening for the separation of CO_2 flux by decomposition of plant residues.

On the other hand during the last decade numerous publications on the claimed increasing global warming show that Indonesian peatland is massively considered as one of the main sources. The publications says that basically when peatland is changed from its natural condition into any manmade land use, such as that for *A. crassicarpa* plantation, it would then contribute significant emission of greenhouse gases especially of carbon in the form of CO_2. Classical chamber method measurement of CO_2 of different conditions of Indonesian peatland has therefore ever been and still commonly used to get the values of CO_2 flux such as reviewed by Page *et al.* (2011). From the data compiled in the review it was evidenced that the measurement rarely set to separate the CO_2 flux from decomposition of peat mass from those respiration- and plant residue decomposition- derived CO_2. With this situation, the measured data should not be totally considered as the rate of the emitted CO_2 contributing to the greenhouse gas increase in the atmosphere. Unfortunately this misleading is continuously running.

This paper is aimed to show and discuss our results of one year weekly closed chamber measurement carried out in an *A. crassicarpa* planted peatland in Sumatra. The measurement was set to partition the contribution of root respiration and litter decomposition on the CO_2 flux in the plantation system.

METHODS

Data presented here were part of data collected during a research project on carbon dynamics in tropical peatland planted forests conducted in Sumatra. In the research project, CO_2 flux from plots of no root no litter and no root with litter were measured, as well as from the plot of no treatments where the chambers were placed on the peatland surface under the *A. crassicarpa* stand at natural condition. These data however, were not specifically elaborated in the book report written by the research team (Sumawinata *et al.*, 2014).

To get the root-free plot of, the roots were sorted out from peat mass collected from a pit of 3 m x 2 m square up to a depth of 40 cm. The pit square wall was covered with an iron plate and the roots and root free-peat soil mass were then put back into the pit. The use of iron plate wall was to block living roots to penetrate back into the root-free peat mass. Litter was put back onto the surface of the half square mimicking the natural litter so then a plot of no roots and no litter and a plot of no roots with litter were ready. After a week conditioning then the weekly measurement of CO_2 flux by close chamber method was started until the weeks 50 paralleled with the measurement on the natural condition plot. It started when the stand age was 3-year old. Each plot consisted of three replications (three points of close chamber base). The chambers were made in 30 cm x 30 cm x 30 cm sizes of acrylic sheets of 0.5 cm thick covered with aluminum sheets. The gas samples were analyzed for their CO_2 concentration using a CO_2 infrared gas analyzer (IRGA).

The plots of measurement were located within an *A. crassicarpa* plantation compartment in a plantation area on the peatland in Jambi, Sumatra. The peat in this area is categorized as a moderately deep having depth of about 1.5-3 m. The *A. crassicarpa* stand was of second rotation of planting since the area converted into plantation from a logged over peat swamp forest.

RESULTS

Characteristics of peat in the measurement area are presented in Table 1. The peat is tropical peat originated from woody materials of the forest trees. Chemically (Table 1), it is poor of bases and has low pH and and low ash content. Physically (data no shown) it has very low bulk density and dominated by coarse fraction of peat mass especially at depths of deeper than 50 cm. The peat mass meets the category of "fibric" in term of the decomposition stage. The big difference of water content between that at depths of more than 40 cm and that at shallower depth is related to the depth of water tablel that was at around 40 cm when the samples was taken.

Table 1: Characteristics of peat in the measurement location in Jambi, Sumatra

Depth	Water content	Ash content	pH	C	N	S	C/N	Bases (%)				Micro elements (ppm)			
cm	.......(%).......			.........(%)........				Ca	Mg	K	Na	Fe	Mn	Cu	Zn
0-5	356	6.53	3.46	48.12	1.98	0.02	24.36	0.23	0.03	0.02	0.02	990.9	34.85	8.00	16.95
5-10	388	4.26	3.45	50.38	1.87	0.03	27.01	0.18	0.04	0.02	0.03	1,014,1	32.63	10.18	16.75
10-20	439	2.82	3.53	52.02	1.55	0.03	33.47	0.17	0.04	0.01	0.02	774.5	8.38	9.72	13.70
20-30	350	2.22	3.40	52.08	1.87	0.02	27.91	0.08	0.06	0.02	0.07	744.4	4.17	6.81	22.17
30-40	453	1.76	3.51	52.96	1.46	0.02	36.17	0.02	0.07	0.01	0.02	648.2	4.01	9.77	11.58
40-50	823	1.38	3.82	53.90	1.35	0.03	39.87	0.01	0.06	0.01	0.09	458.1	Tr	8.19	8.28
50+	1310	1.11	3.84	54.07	1.33	0.02	40.62	0.03	0.06	Tr	0.12	455.2	0.24	9.20	10.69

Note: Tr - trace

The results of the CO_2 flux measurements are presented in Figures 1, 2 and 3. Figure 1 shows the results of the measurements on the plots that before the close chamber measurements carried out were made to a condition that roots (actually the fine roots) within the peat mass up to a depth of 40 cm were removed and the existed litter was either removed as well or left to exist (put back on). Figure 2 shows the minus roots plots data shown in Figure 1 are plotted again together with those of the results derived from the measurements carried on the non-treated plots (natural condition of plantation). Figure 3 shows the weekly accumulation data of the individual weekly data shown in Figure 1.

The data in Figure 1 show that, regardless the fluctuation of the data, there is a trend that the CO_2 flux from the no roots no litter plot was bit lower than that of no roots with litter. This fact different is clearer when the data are plotted in the way as shown in Figure 3. The fluctuation indicates a correlation of the flux with water table depth.

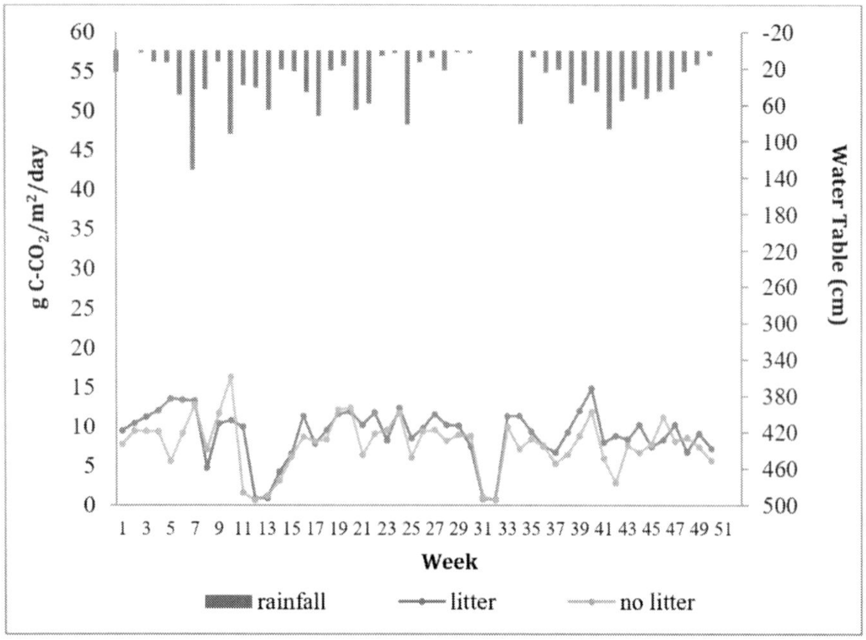

Figure 1: Weekly CO_2 flux in 3-year old (2nd-rotation) *A. crassicarpa* in moderately-deep peatland in Jambi-Sumatra, plots of no roots no litter and of no roots with litter

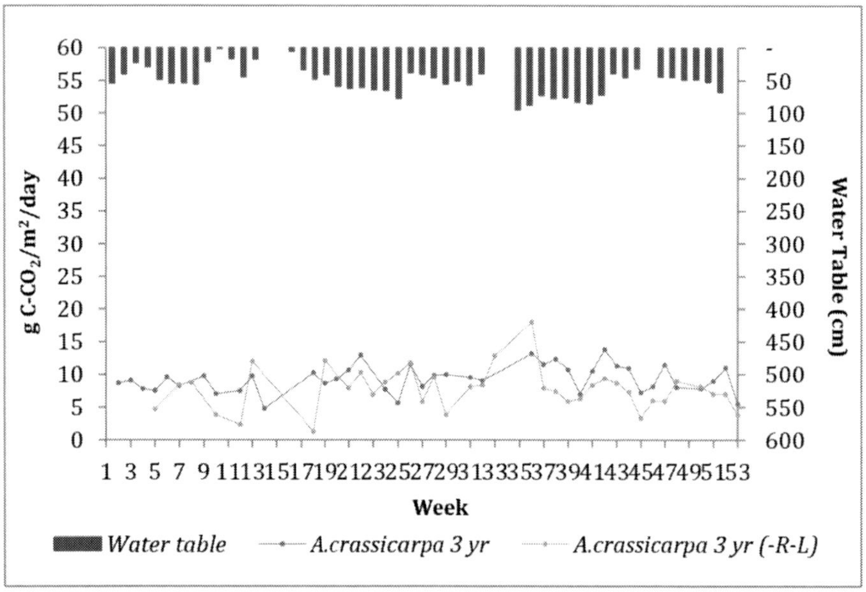

Figure 2: Weekly CO_2 flux in 3-year old (2nd-rotation) *A. crassicarpa* in moderately-deep peatland in Jambi-Sumatra, plots of no treatment and of no roots no litter

Data in Figure 2 show that the flux of the plots of no roots is also somewhat lower than that of the untreated plot. However the graph show an intensive fluctuation during the one year measurement and hence difficult to conclude confidently that with no roots the flux will be certainly lower and therefore the obtained data cannot be used to figure out a certain value for use in any prediction model.

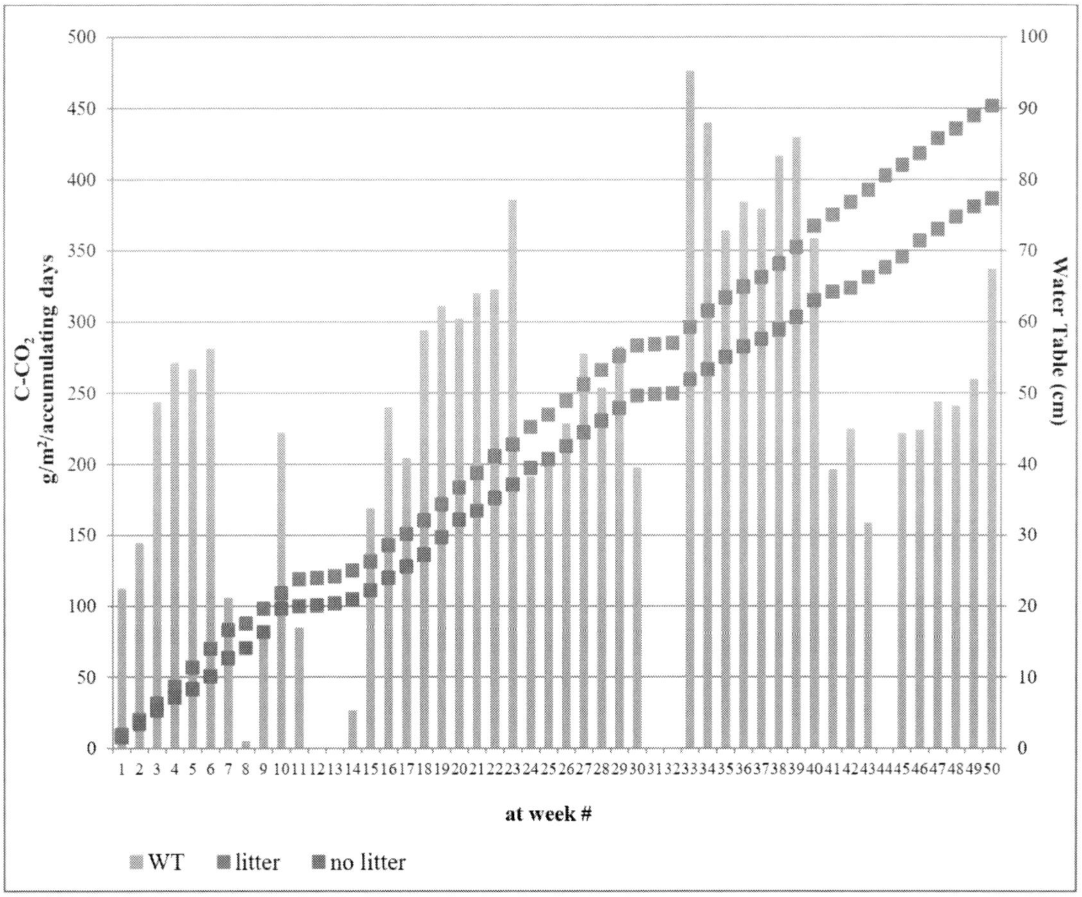

Figure 3: Accumulated CO_2 flux during 50 weeks in 3-year old (2nd-rotation) *A. crassicarpa* in moderately-deep peatland in Jambi-Sumatra, plots of no treatment and of no roots no litter

Data of no roots plots in Figure 3 show that during the one year measurement in accumulation the difference between CO_2 flux of no litter and with litter is quite significance. The graph shows that at week 50 the flux count to about 450g C-CO_2/m^2/50 weeks for the plot with litter and about 390g C-CO_2/m^2/50 weeks for the no litter plot.

DISCUSSION

The difference of no litter with of with litter derived CO_2flux is somewhat clear evidenced in this study and the gap in accumulation is quite significant. Suggesting that for field measurement to get real data of peat decomposition derived flux only, the exclusion of litter is a must. In addition the data obtained for this study point may be useful for in any further study to quantify the contribution of litter decomposition on the total flux.

Comparison of the flux data obtained for the root excluded plots with those for the untreated plot did not show a clear effect of the excluding root treatment. Considering the way the roots were excluded at the plot preparation, there is no doubt that the manner was correct. But the way to block roots from penetrating back into the peat mass by covering the pit wall was not effective. In the following weeks after the blocking the living roots extending and penetrated into the root-excluded peat mass in the plot from the bottom edge of the iron plate. Probably the height of the iron plate was not enough hence the bottom edge the plate inside the peat was not deep enough to hinder the root to propagate that way.

CONCLUSION

The findings in this study confirmed that excluding litter in close chamber measurement of CO_2 flux to get the flux of peat decomposition derived only is must and the way how to do is easy. However the root exclusion measurement is not that easy.

ACKNOWLEDGEMENT

Thanks to APP and Sinar Mas Forestry, Indonesia for supporting this study.

REFFERENCES

1. Kuzyakov, Y. 2006. *Sources of CO_2 efflux from soil and review of partitioning methods*. Soil Biology & Biochemistry, 38(2006): 425-448.
2. Page, S. E., R. Morrison, C. Malins, A. Hooijer, J.O. Rieley, and J. Jauhiainen. 2011. *Review of peat surface greenhouse gas emissions from oil palm plantations in Southeast Asia* (ICCT White Paper15). Washington: International Council on Clean Transportation.
3. Sumawinata B, Darmawan, Djajakirana G, Suwardi. 2014. *Carbon Dynamics in Tropical Peatland Planted Forests*. Bogor, Institut Pertanian Bogor Press. pp 172.

Abstract No: A-049

EFFECT OF DRAINAGE ON THE CARBON LOSS FROM SOIL ECOSYSTEMS IN TROPICAL PEATLANDS OF CENTRAL KALIMANTAN

Siti Sundari[1*], Takashi Hirano[2] and Hiroyuki Yamada[2]

[1]*Research Center for Biology, Indonesian Institute of Science (LIPI), Indonesia*
[2]*Research Faculty of Agriculture, Hokkaido University, Japan*

**Corresponding author: ssundari1977@gmail.com*

SUMMARY

Effect of drainage on the carbon loss from soil ecosystems in tropical peatlands had been conducted at two tropical peat swamp forests in Central Kalimantan, undrained forest (UF) and drained forest (DF) sites from July 2010 to December 2011. Carbon loss was assessed by the summation of soil respiration (RS) and groundwater dissolved organic carbon (DOC) flux. Field data in 2004 and 2005 were used to make an empirical model to calculate RS from July 2010 to December 2011, while DOC flux through groundwater from July 2010 to December 2011 was calculated by multiplying groundwater DOC concentration by groundwater flux. Cumulative RS at the UF and DF sites were estimated at 599 and 640 gC m^{-2}, respectively, for six months in 2010. Annual RS in 2011 at the UF and DF sites were 1427 and 1256 gC m^{-2} y^{-1}, respectively. Cumulative groundwater DOC flux at the UF and DF sites were estimated at 14 and 52 gC m^{-2}, respectively, for six months in 2010. Annual groundwater DOC flux in 2011 at the UF and DF sites were 33 and 94 gC m^{-2} y^{-1}, respectively. Carbon loss from soil ecosystems at the UF and DF sites were summed up to 613 and 692 gC m^{-2}, respectively, for six months in 2010. Carbon loss in 2011 at the UF and DF sites were 1460 and 1350 gC m^{-2} y^{-1}, respectively. Carbon loss from soil ecosystems at the DF site was larger than that at the UF site in 2010, suggesting a drainage effect. However, it was larger at the UF site than at the DF site in 2011. The discrepancy in carbon loss from soil ecosystems between 2010 and 2011 was due to interannual variation in groundwater level (GWL) that affected RS that contributes much larger to the carbon loss from soil ecosystems than groundwater DOC flux.

***Keywords**: carbon loss, dissolved organic carbon, drainage, soil respiration, tropical peatlands*

INTRODUCTION

Tropical peatlands are widely distributed at the mainlands of East Asia, Southeast Asia, the Caribbean and Central America, South America and Southern Africa. The largest area of tropical peatlands occurs in Southeast Asia, where they are found in Indonesia (predominantly Sumatra, Kalimantan and West Papua), Malaysia (Peninsular Malaysia, Sarawak and Sabah), Brunei and Thailand (Rieley and Ahmad-Shah, 1996). In Southeast Asia, Indonesia has the largest peatland area about 20 million ha, 80% of the total peatlands in this area (Page *et al.*, 2010). However, peatland ecosystems have been devastated by logging, land development and management since the 1970's. Peat degradation occurs most rapidly and extensively in Indonesia, where 47% of tropical peatlands are located (Page *et al.*, 2011). There, peat is degraded by fires, drainage and deforestation of swamp forest (Couwenberg *et al.*, 2010; Hergoualc'h and Verchot, 2011; Hooijer *et al.*, 2010; Murdiyarso *et al.*, 2010). Burning of peat releases CO_2 intensively but occasionally, whereas drainage raises CO_2 emissions steadily through accelerated aerobic peat and deforestation simply halts CO_2 uptake by trees. Therefore, under such anthropogenic pressure, tropical peatlands present the threat of switch from a role as a global carbon sink to a role as a huge carbon source to the atmosphere (Hirano *et al.*, 2009).
The main controlling factors in several variations of soil respiration (RS) may depend on the type of ecosystems and climate (Luo and Zhou, 2006). Furukawa *et al.* (2005) made monthly measurement in Sumatra using the chamber technique and reported that RS in a drained forest was three times larger than that in an undrained forest. Jauhiainen *et al.* (2005) showed microtopographical difference in RS from hummocks and hollows of the forest floor in Central Kalimantan. The RS was almost independent of GWL on hummocks, where it decreased as GWL rose on hollows. Hirano *et al.* (2009) showed that CO_2 emissions from tropical peatlands ecosystems were strongly controlled by GWL in the undrained and drained peat swamp forests in Central Kalimantan. In the undrained forest, soil CO_2 flux sharply decreased when GWL rose above -0.2 and 0.1 m for hollows and hummocks, respectively. The sharp decrease suggests that the contribution of surface RS to total soil CO_2 flux is large. In the drained forest, soil CO_2

flux increased as GWL decreased below -0.7 m probably because the fast aerobic decompositions continued in lower peat.
Dissolved organic carbon (DOC) is defined as the organic matter that is able to pass through a filter (filters generally in size 0.45 μm). The DOC is the main form in which organic carbon is transported downwards into the subsoil where it can be mineralized, stabilized or further leached to the groundwater. Peat soils are a major source of DOC to surface waters. DOC is an important component of the carbon cycle within peat soils and peat soil are a vital store of terrestrial carbon. The DOC flux is important on watershed scale through river flow because in the flux of DOC will result in a significant regional redistribution of terrestrial carbon and DOC loss would be important for determining peatlands carbon balances (Moore *et al.*, 1997; Billet *et al.*, 2004). Moore *et al.* (2011) analysed concentration of DOC and particulate organic carbon (POC) of river water sampled from the source to the mouth of the Sebangau River in Central Kalimantan during the dry and wet seasons in 2008/2009 and estimated an annual total organic carbon (TOC) flux. This equates to a fluvial TOC flux per unit area over the entire Sebangau catchment of 88 gC m^{-2} y^{-1}, with annual DOC flux and POC flux were estimated at 83 and 5 gC m^{-2} y^{-1}, respectively.
Methane (CH_4) emissions are restricted to high water levels when methanogenesis occurs under anaerobic conditions closed to the surface and re-oxidation of methane is limited. In comparison to temperate and boreal peatlands, CH_4 emissions from tropical peatlands are low (Couwenberg *et al.*, 2010). Low CH_4 emissions from tropical peatlands relate to the poor substrate quality of the peats (high polyphenol contents, e.g. lignin). Although CH_4 is produced under anaerobic conditions, the global warming potential (GWP) of the CH_4 flux was small in the tropical peatlands (Hirano *et al.*, 2012). In areas of tropics which are expected to experience reduced rainfall and more prolonged drought, peatlands may become less important source of atmospheric CH_4. Therefore, the contributions of CH_4 and POC could be neglected to the total carbon loss from soil ecosystems in tropical peatlands of Central Kalimantan because their contributions were small, so the total carbon loss from soil ecosystems in tropical peatlands was assessed by the summation of RS and DOC flux (Sundari, 2012). The purposes of this study are to assess carbon loss from soil ecosystems from July 2010 to December 2011, evaluate the effect of drainage on the carbon loss from soil ecosystems, and compare the contribution of soil respiration and groundwater DOC to the carbon loss from soil ecosystems in tropical peatlands.

METHODS

Study site
This study was conducted at two tropical peat swamp forests in Palangkaraya, Central Kalimantan. The two peat swamp forest sites were located near each other, with Sebangau River between them. In Central Kalimantan, a large peatland area was deforested and drained during the late 1990's, mainly to develop farmlands according to a national project, Mega Rice Project (MRP). However, the project was terminated in 1999 consequently a vast peatland was left. One site was an undrained peat swamp forest (UF) in Sebangau area. The other was a drained peat swamp forest (DF) in Kalampangan area (Hirano *et al.*, 2012; Sundari *et al.*, 2012).

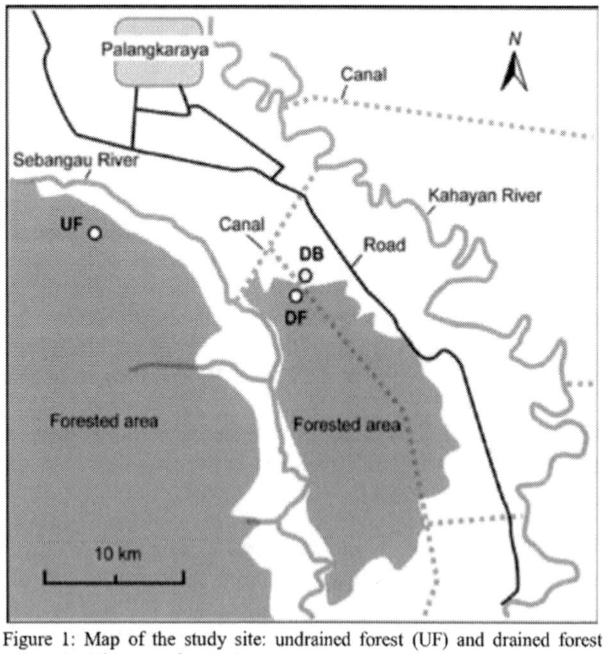

Figure 1: Map of the study site: undrained forest (UF) and drained forest (DF) in Central Kalimantan, Indonesia (Hirano *et al.*, 2012).

The UF site (2.32°S, 113.90°E) had been logged selectively until the late 1990s, so that it is an almost secondary forest. Although no large canal has been excavated in this area, a network of small canals for illegal logging remains influencing forest hydrology. The peat depth of UF was 2–3 m. A 35-m-high tower was built at the site in 2004 for flux measurement. The soil surface was covered with thick debris, mainly comprising leaf litter. Few herbaceous plants existed on the soil surface. The DF site (2.35°S, 114.14°E) is a secondary forest remaining in Block C of the MRP. The forest had also been selectively logged until the end of the 1990s. The peat depth of DF was 4 m. A large canal (25 m wide x 3.5-4.5 m deep) that was excavated in 1996 and 1997 has function effectively to facilitate drainage of the forest. A 50-m-high tower was built for flux measurements. The condition of soil surface resembled those at the UF site (Hirano *et al.*, 2012; Sundari *et al.*, 2012).

Soil respiration

RS in the UF and DF sites from July 2010 to December 2011 was calculated from GWL using an empirical model, which was made using field data in 2004 and 2005 (Sundari *et al.*, 2012). The equation that was used to calculate RS in the UF and DF sites was based on the relationship between the spatially averaged RS and GWL.

In the UF site: When GWL > -0.1 m, RS = 3.53 – 9.83 GWL

When GWL < -0.1 m, $RS = 4.66 + 0.5\ GWL + 2.11\ GWL^2$

In the DF site: $RS = 4.03 + 2.41\ GWL + 1.69\ GWL^2$

Groundwater dissolved organic carbon flux

DOC flux through groundwater was calculated by multiplying groundwater flux by groundwater DOC concentration. Ground water flux was obtained using a single tank model which was based on a premise that water flux has been increased in proportion to water content in the tank (Sugawara *et al.*, 1983). Groundwater level and evapotranspiration data were used to calculate groundwater flux. Groundwater level was measured continually every 10 minutes at three wells in the UF and DF sites, and evapotranspiration was measured on towers at the two sites. Groundwater samples were collected every two weeks from July 2010 to December 2011 at three wells in the two sites and analysed for groundwater DOC concentration using Total Organic Carbon (TOC) analyser (Sundari *et al.*, 2012; 2013).

Carbon loss

Carbon loss from soil ecosystems at the UF and DF sites was estimated by the summation of RS and groundwater DOC flux from July 2010 to December 2011.

RESULTS

The results of annual soil respiration (RS), groundwater dissolved organic carbon (DOC) flux, and total carbon losses were specifically described for the UF and DF sites. The data were available for six months in 2010 and 2011, respectively in Table 1 and Table 2.

Table 1: Cumulative soil respiration, groundwater DOC flux, and total carbon loss for six months in 2010

Site	RS (gC m^{-2})	Groundwater DOC flux (gC m^{-2})	Carbon loss (gC m^{-2})
UF	599	14	613
DF	640	52	692

Table 2: Annual soil respiration, groundwater DOC flux, and total carbon loss in 2011

Site	RS (gC m^{-2} y^{-1})	Groundwater DOC flux (gC m^{-2} y^{-1})	Carbon loss (gC m^{-2} y^{-1})
UF	1427	33	1460
DF	1256	94	1350

Table 1 showed that cumulative RS, cumulative groundwater DOC flux and carbon loss for six months in 2010 were larger at the DF site than at the UF site. These results were due to a drainage effect. Drainage to lower groundwater level potentially increases CO_2 emissions from soil through the enhancement of aerobic peat decomposition and DOC production leaching through groundwater flow (Sundari, *et al.*, 2012; 2013). Contrarily, table 2 showed that annual RS and annual carbon loss in 2011 were larger at the UF site than at the DF site, although the annual groundwater DOC flux was larger at the DF site than at the UF site. The drainage effect did not influence the carbon loss from soil ecosystem in 2011 because the RS in 2011 at the UF site was larger than that at the DF site (Table 2). It means that the drainage effect also did not influence the RS in 2011. These results related to the comparison between soil respiration and groundwater dissolved organic carbon to the carbon loss from soil ecosystems at the both sites. It showed that the contribution of soil respiration was much higher than that of groundwater dissolved organic carbon flux to the carbon loss from soil ecosystems.

DISCUSSION

The assumption of RS is greater at the DF site than at the UF site because of the enhancement of peat decomposition under aerobic condition by drainage is relevant to the result of cumulative RS for six months in 2010. However, the assumption is not relevant to the result of annual RS in 2011 because it was larger at the UF site than at the DF site. The result in 2011 showed that the effect of drainage which lowering GWL do not support the annual value of RS at the DF site, although peat decomposition is expected, in theoretical terms, to be greater in the DF site. This discrepancy was probably due to the difference in forest productivity at the both sites (Sundari *et al.*, 2012). The UF site retains a relatively intact peat swamp forest, whereas the DF site is secondary peat swamp forest which had been drained and illegal logged for many years, so that the forest productivity was higher at the UF site than that at the DF site. According to this result, effect of drainage was unable to explain the difference in annual RS between the two forest sites in 2011. This fact indicates a large contribution of surface soil and litter to RS and to soil CO_2 efflux (Hirano *et al.*, 2009). Therefore, flooding duration is a key determinant of annual RS at the UF site. When GWL is underground, lowered GWL slows litter decomposition because of desiccation of the litter, but it facilitates the decomposition of deeper peat through enhanced aeration. Conversely, elevated GWL increases litter decomposition but decreases deeper peat decomposition. In fact, RS can be regarded as including two components that are oppositely affected by GWL. Therefore, lowering of GWL does not necessarily increase RS (Muhr *et al.*, 2011; Page *et al.*, 2011). Furthermore, the peat decomposition in deeper soil profile would have increased more under unsaturated conditions than the RS decrease in surface soil and litter decomposition attributable in desiccation.

The groundwater DOC fluxes in the both years at the DF site were higher than at the UF site, suggesting a drainage effect that influences the production of DOC at the DF site through the enhancement of peat decomposition by increasing the aerobic zone. The DOC was produced during the decomposition of organic matter in soil and also is used as a substrate for microbial activity which involves the production of DOC which resulted in higher DOC production and groundwater DOC concentration. In addition, much water was out of the drained peatlands increased the groundwater flux at the drained forest site, consequently groundwater DOC flux became high. The groundwater DOC flux directly related to the amount of water flowing through peat soil, so it enhanced in the high water flow.

Cumulative carbon loss in 2010 and annual carbon loss in 2011 were larger at the UF site than at the DF site because of a large contribution of RS in 2010 an in 2011, respectively, to the total carbon loss from soil ecosystems in tropical peatlands. It also showed that the contribution of RS was much larger than that of groundwater DOC flux to the total carbon loss in both years. This fact supports that RS is one of the largest fluxes in the global carbon cycle which produces CO_2 in the soil and transports CO_2 from the soil to the atmosphere. This result suggested that mostly carbon losses from soil ecosystems were much larger to the atmosphere than leaching through ground water flow in the form of DOC because the components of soil respiration are attributable to the heterotrophic respiration by decomposers and autotrophic respiration by roots and mycorrhizas. Hirano *et al.* (2009) and Sundari *et al.* (2012) showed that CO_2 emissions from tropical peatlands ecosystems in Central Kalimantan were chiefly affected by groundwater level (GWL). The discrepancy in carbon loss from soil ecosystems between 2010 and 2011 was due to interannual variation in GWL that affected soil respiration at the both sites. Hooijer *et al.* (2012) investigated in detail the parameters involved in subsidence and carbon loss in tropical peatlands of Riau and Jambi. They concluded the investment in water management is needed to achieve water levels that reduce subsidence and reduce carbon loss, while at the same time protecting forest and peat resources in the surrounding peatland.

CONCLUSION

Carbon loss from soil ecosystems in tropical peatlands was assessed by the summation of soil respiration and groundwater dissolved organic carbon flux. Cumulative carbon loss, soil respiration, and groundwater dissolved organic carbon for six months at the drained peat swamp forest were greater than at the undrained peat swamp forest. Annual groundwater DOC flux in 2011 was also larger at the drained peat swamp forest than at the undrained peat swamp forest. These results suggested a drainage effect. However, annual carbon loss and soil respiration in 2011 were greater at the undrained peat swamp forest than at the drained peat swamp forest, and showed that drainage effect was unable to explain this result because of the difference in forest productivity between undrained peat swamp forest and drained peat swamp forest. Additionally, the contribution of soil respiration was much larger than that of groundwater dissolved organic carbon flux to the total carbon loss from soil ecosystems in tropical peat swamp forests of Central Kalimantan.

ACKNOWLEDGEMENTS

This work was supported by JSPS Core University Program, JSPS KAKENHI (Nos. 15255001 and 18403001), JSPS A3 Foresight Program (Carbo East Asia), JSPS Institutional Program for Young Researcher Overseas Visits and JST-JICA Project (Wild Fire and Carbon Management in Peat-Forest in Indonesia). Mr. Kitso Kusin, Dr.

Suwido Limin and staffs in CIMTROP, Palangkaraya University for their kind helps in the field investigation. The members of Laboratory of Plant, Soil and Plant Litter Ecology in Research Center for Biology, Indonesian Institute of Sciences (LIPI) in Cibinong for kind help in DOC analysis.

REFERENCES

1. Billett MF, Palmer SM, Hope D, Deacon C, Storeton-West R, Hargreaves KJ, Flechard C, and Fowler D (2004), *Linking land-atmosphere-stream carbon fluxes in a lowland peatland system*. Global Biogeochemical Cycles, 18, 1-12.
2. Couwenberg J, Dommain R, and Joosten H (2010), *Greenhouse gas fluxes from tropical peatlands in Southeast Asia*. Global Change Biology, 16, 1715-1732.
3. Furukawa Y, Inubushi K, Ali M, Itang AM, and Tsuruta H (2005), *Effect of changing groundwater levels caused by land-use changes on greenhouse gas fluxes from tropical peatlands*. Nutrent Cycling in Agroecosytems, 71, 73-91.
4. Hergoualc'h K and Verchot LV (2011), *Stocks and fluxes of carbon associated with land use change in Southeast Asian tropical peatlands*. A review. Global Biogeochemical Cycles, 25, doi: 10.1029/2009GB003718.
5. Hirano T, Jauhiainen J, Inoue T, and Takahashi H (2009), *Controls on the carbon balance of tropical peatlands*. Ecosystems, 12, 873-887, doi: 10.1007/s10021-008-9209-I.
6. Hirano T, Segah H, Kusin K, Limin S, Takahashi H, and Osaki M (2012), *Effects of disturbances on the carbon balance of tropical peat swamp forests*. Global Change Biology, 18, 3410-3422, doi: 10.1111/j.1365-2486.2012.02793.x.
7. Hooijer A, Page S, Canadell JG, Silvus M, Kwadijl J, Wosten H, and Jauhiainen J (2010), *Current and future CO_2 emissions from drained peatlands in Southeast Asia*. Biogeosciences, 7, 1505-1514, doi: 10.5194/bg-7-1505-1010.
8. Hooijer A, Page S, Jauhiainen J, Lee WA, Lu XX, Idris A, and Anshari G (2012), *Subsidence and carbon loss in drained tropical peatlands*. Biogeosciences, 9, 1053-1071, doi: 10.5194/bg-9-1053-1012.
9. Jauhiainen J, Takahashi H, Heikkinen JEP, Martilainen PJ, and Vasander H (2005), *Carbon fluxes from a tropical peat swamp forest floor*. Global Change Biology, 11, 1788-1797.
10. Luo Y and Zhou X (2006), *Soil respiration and the environment*. Elsevier, Inc. San Diego, California, USA, 92-93.
11. Moore S, Gauci V, Evans CD, and Page SE (2011), *Fluvial organic carbon losses from a Bornean blackwater river*. Biogeoscience, 8, 901-909, doi: 10.5194/bg-8-901-2011.
12. Moore TA and Shearer JC (1997), *Evidence for Aerobic Degradation of Palangka Raya Peat and Implications for its Sustainability*. In: JO Rieley & SE Page (eds) Tropical Peatlands, Samara Publishing Limited, Cardigan, 55-72.
13. Muhr J, Hohle J, Otieno DO, and Borken W (2011), *Manipulative lowering of the water table during summer does not affect CO_2 emissions and uptake in a fen in Germany*. Ecology Application, 21(2), 391-401.
14. Murdiyarso D, Hergoualc'h K, and Verchot LV (2010), *Opportunities for reducing greenhouse gas emissions in tropical peatlands*. Proceeding of the National Academy Sciences, USA, 107, 19655-19660.
15. Page SE, Wust R, and Banks CJ (2010), *Past and present carbon accumulation and loss in Southeast Asian peatlands*. PAGES News 18 No.1, 25-27.
16. Page SE, Rieley JO, and Banks CJ (2011), *Global and regional importance of the tropical peatland carbon pool*. Global Change Biology, 17, 798-818.
17. Rieley JO, and AA Ahmad-Shah (1996), *The vegetation of tropical peat swamp forests in tropical lowland peatlands of Southeast Asia*. Proceeding of a Workshop on Integrated Planning and Management of Tropical Peatlands, IUCN, Gland, Switzerland, 55-73.
18. Sugawara M, Watanabe I, Ozaki E, and Katsuyame Y (1983), *Reference manual for the tank model*. National Research Center for Disaster Prevention, Tokyo, 165-172.
19. Sundari S (2012), *Soil respiration and dissolved organic carbon efflux in tropical peatlands*. Graduate School of Agriculture, Hokkaido University, Sapporo, Japan, 45-47.
20. Sundari S, Hirano T, Yamada H, Kusin K, and Limin S (2012), *Effect of groundwater level on soil respiration in tropical peat swamp forests*. Journal of Agricultural Meteorology, 68(2), 121-134.
21. Sundari S, Hirano T, Yamada H, Kusin K, and Limin S (2013), *Effects of fires and drainage on dissolved organic carbon leaching in tropical peat swamp forests*. Proceeding of International Symposium on Wild Fire and Carbon Management in Peat-Forest in Indonesia, Bogor, Indonesia, 36-42.

Abstract No: A-222

EXACT MEASUREMENT OF PHOTOSYNTHETIC CARBON ACCUMULATION RATE IN SPHAGNUM COMMUNITY

Akira Haraguchi

Faculty of Environmental Engineering, The University of Kitakyushu, Japan

*Corresponding author: sphagnummire@hotmail.com

Sphagnum plants are major peat forming plants in circumpolar mires and they fix and store atmospheric carbon in peat. Due to water saturation of peat as well as hardly biodegradable substance in Sphagnum plants, Sphagnum peat can be an effective persistent carbon pool. Despite the importance of Sphagnum plants in global carbon dynamics, the carbon fixation rate of the Sphagnum community or photosynthetic activity of Sphagnum plants has not yet been accurately determined. Sphagnum leaves have a layered distribution, not only in a population but also within one individual plant. Thus the photosynthetic response to light shows a community type curve, i.e. the response curve did not saturate within the usual light condition of the actual Sphagnum community. Consequently, the response curve for individual leaves of vascular plants could not be applied to the photosynthetic response of Sphagnum plants. Live shoots of Sphagnum plants continue to senesced litter and form further peat, and so CO2 release by biodegradation of litter and peat should also be included when evaluating the carbon exchange rate between the Sphagnum community and the atmosphere. I attempted to measure exact photosynthetic rates of Sphagnum plants by considering the layered structure of the photosynthetic parts of the shoot as well as respiration of litter and peat, by separating shoot, litter and peat. CO2 release rates from litter and peat were much lower than the respiration rate of live shoots, and the carbon exchange rate between a live shoot and the atmosphere can be a good approximation. However the CO2 release from litter fluctuated largely and sometimes the rate was extremely high depending on the condition, and then the rate was not negligible. I tested the effect of water table and temperature on CO2 release rate from litter. Further exact measurements of photosynthetic rate of Sphagnum plants will improve the advanced model for estimating atmospheric carbon fixation rate and peat accumulation rates in circumpolar peat mires.

Keywords:-

Abstract No: A-071

FLUVIAL ORGANIC CARBON LOSSES FROM OIL PALM PLANTATIONS ON TROPICAL PEAT, SARAWAK, SOUTHEAST ASIA

Sarah Cook[1*], Susan E. Page[1], Mick Whelan[1], Chris D. Evans[2], Vincent Gauci[3] and Kho Lip Khoon[4]

[1]*University of Leicester, United Kingdom*
[2]*Environment Centre Wales, Centre for Ecology and Hydrology, United Kingdom*
[3]*The Open University, Dept. of Environment, Earth and Ecosystems, United Kingdom*
[4]*Tropical Peat Research Institute, Biological Research Division, Malaysian Palm Oil Board, Malaysia*

**Corresponding author: sarah.cook11@hotmail.com*

SUMMARY

The conversion of tropical peatlands into oil palm plantations can result in significant perturbations to the terrestrial carbon cycle. However, dependable estimates of gaseous and fluvial carbon losses from oil palm plantations are few (Evans *et al*., 2014). Here, we present preliminary data that quantify the effect of establishing oil palm plantations on tropical peat fluvial organic carbon losses. The study focuses on two oil palm estates in Sarawak, Malaysia and nearby stands of peat swamp forest. Concentrations of dissolved and particulate organic carbon in the water draining these areas is being monitored at weekly to bi-monthly intervals, allowing a comparison between these two land covers.

Keywords: *fluvial organic carbon, oil palm plantations, tropical peatlands, Southeast Asia*

INTRODUCTION

The tropical peatlands of Southeast Asia are important stores of carbon. They hold approximately 69 GtC, equivalent to 14% and 77% of the global and tropical peat carbon pools, respectively (Page *et al*., 2011). These ecosystems are currently experiencing significant degradation in the form of deforestation, drainage and burning, to convert them into other land-uses (Miettinen *et al*., 2011). One example is the conversion of tropical peat swamp forest (PSF) into oil palm plantation (OPP), which is increasing throughout Southeast Asia (Miettinen *et al*., 2011). Predictions suggest that OPP expansion is likely to double or triple from 3 million ha to 6-9 million ha by 2020, across Peninsular Malaysia, Borneo and Sumatra (Miettinen *et al*., 2012a), with further studies suggesting that approximately 23% and 93% of Malaysian peat could be under oil palm by 2020 and 2030, respectively (Miettinen *et al*., 2012b).

The conversion of PSF to OPP requires significant land modifications, mainly drainage and deforestation, exposing previously saturated peat layers to aerobic conditions and promoting rapid organic matter decomposition (Evans *et al*., 2015). This leads to perturbations to the terrestrial carbon cycle; often converting these natural sinks into sources. Estimates suggest that CO_2 emissions from the conversion of PSF to OPP contributes between 33 to 100 Mg $CO_{2\text{-eq}}$ $ha^{-1}yr^{-1}$ (Germer & Sauerborn., 2008; Hooijer *et al*., 2010) and accounts for approximately 16% and 32% of the total land-use emissions from Indonesia and Malaysia, respectively (Agus *et al*., 2013).

There is increasing interest in the importance of fluvial carbon losses in the global carbon cycle. At present only one study (Moore *et al*., 2013) has reported on the considerable losses of dissolved organic carbon (DOC) from degraded tropical peatlands experiencing little management. However, the study was based on a limited number of field sites and so more data are needed in order to understand the dynamics of DOC in more intensively managed peatlands with controlled drainage.

DOC is both biologically and chemically reactive (Evans *et al*., 2015). The labile carbon fractions can be metabolized by in-stream fauna, and subsequently oxidized, leading to indirect atmospheric carbon dioxide (CO_2) emissions (Evans *et al*., 2015). In addition, the more recalcitrant constituents of DOC are also believed to be broken down via photochemical processes, so may actually be more 'reactive' than the labile component as a result of this process (Evans *et al*., 2015). Consequently, the degradation of DOC into its gaseous metabolic products, and subsequent efflux from peatland surface waters, could represent a hidden and important contributor to atmospheric greenhouse gas emissions.

The aim of this study is to address the knowledge gap surrounding fluvial carbon losses from oil palm plantations established on tropical peat. The results will be used to help identify all carbon emissions from land-use change, as well as potentially contributing to derivation of IPCC Tier 2 emissions factors. Collectively these will allow Malaysia to monitor, report and verify their land-based greenhouse gas emissions in a more effective way.

METHODS

The study sites are located within the Malaysian province of Sarawak and are concentrated within the Sebungan (SE) and Sabaju (SA) oil palm estates. These two estates are situated east of the coastal town of Bintulu between Latitudes 3°07.81' N and 3°14.91'N and Longitudes 113°18.72' E and 113°32.19'. The estates range in age from mature (established 2007, 9 years old) to immature (established 2010, 6 years old). Main and collection drains are being monitored (sampling frequency 1-2 weeks) over a 12-month period in four main plantation study areas: Sebungan (SE), Sabaju 1 (SA 1), Sabaju 3 (SA 3) and Sabaju 4 (SA 4). Nearby stands of peat swamp forest are also being monitored, allowing a comparison between these two land cover types.

The concentrations of both dissolved (DOC) and particulate organic carbon (POC) in the water draining both estates and forest sites are being quantified. Within the OPP estates, water samples are collected from a combination of i) "mini catchments"- collection drains, draining water from individual plantation blocks of a known area and ii) "large catchments"- main drains, draining water from multiple plantation blocks of a known area.

A combination of salt dilution gauging and stage recording is being used to generate rating curves for individual channels, allowing discharge measurements and DOC and POC fluxes to be generated throughout the sampling period. These data will be used to calculate total organic carbon (TOC) fluxes (g C m^{-2} yr^{-1}) for the "mini" and "large" catchments based on their areas. Eventually these estimates can be up-scaled to give an amount for the whole plantation area.

RESULTS

The investigation is currently on-going. Initial results from the first 5 months of the study are presented below. At present, the majority of the fluvial carbon lost is in DOC form (72.8 - 93.1% of TOC: Figure 1). In the plantation main drains and collection drains, respectively (Figure 2), the initial mean DOC concentrations range from 28.9 to 43.7 mg l^{-1} and 23.6 to 43.3 mg l^{-1}. DOC concentrations are variable across all plantation study sites with the highest concentrations found within Sebungan and the lowest within Sabaju 3. DOC concentrations within the forest sites are also variable ranging from 32.2 to 46.7 mg l^{-1}. Based on current DOC concentration data and available discharge measurements, average weekly fluxes from the plantation collection drains range from 0.02 to 0.07 t C $week^{-1}$ ha^{-1}. The lowest fluxes are found within Sebungan and the highest within Sabaju 1 and 3.

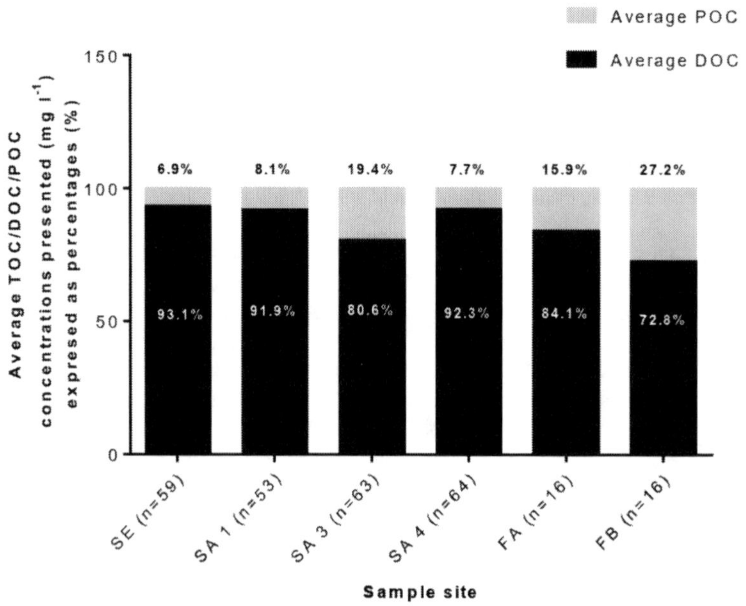

Figure 1: Average TOC concentration from August – October 2015 from all study sites, split into its two components; DOC (black) and POC (grey). Where: SE= Sebungan plantation, SA 1-SA 4= Sabaju 1 to 4 plantations and FA and FB= forest sites.

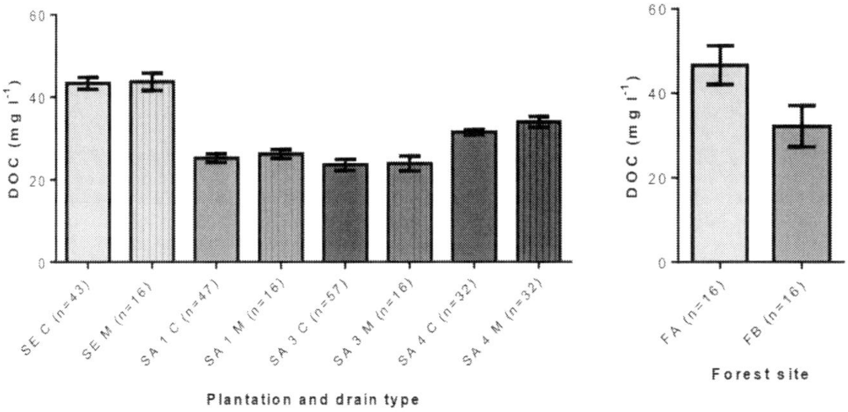

Figure 2: DOC concentrations from the plantation sites (left), where c= collection drain and m= main drain and the forest sites (right), from August – December 2015. Bars display the standard error of the mean

DISCUSSION

The observed contribution of DOC to TOC is consistent with data reported by Moore *et al.* (2013). DOC concentrations are wide ranging across all sites. On-going data collection across both the wet and dry season will help to identify any consistent data trends and allow a fuller picture of temporal DOC dynamics to be established. DOC concentrations from the plantation sites compare well with those reported by Moore *et al.* (2013) for a severely drained and degraded peat swamp forest (48.3 mg l^{-1}). Further work to delineate drainage areas will allow load estimates to be derived, and relationships between management and DOC loss to be evaluated.

ACKNOWLEDGEMENTS

This study is sponsored and supported by the Malaysian Oil Palm Board and Sarawak Oil Palms Berhad, along with the Natural Environment Research Council (NERC), UK and AXA Research Fund.

REFERENCES

1. Agus, F., Gunarso, P., Sahardjo, B.H., Harris, N., van Noordwijk, M., Killeen, T.J, 2013. Historical CO_2 emissions from land use and land use change from oil palm industry in Indonesia, Malaysia and Papa New Guinea. In: Killenn, T.J & Goon, J (eds.). 2013. *Reports from the Technical Panels of the 2nd Greenhouse Gas Working Group of the Roundtable on Sustainable Palm Oil (RSPO).* 65-88 pp. RSPO, Kuala Lumpur, Malaysia.
2. Evans, C.D., Page, S.E., Jones, T., Moore. S., Gauci, V., Laiho ,R., Hruška, J., Allott, T.E.H., Billett, M.F., Tipping .E., Freeman,C., Garnett, M.H, 2014. Contrasting vulnerability of drained tropical and high-latitude peatlands to fluvial loss of stored carbon. *Biogeochemical Cycles*. DOI: 10.1002/2013GB004782
3. Evans, C.D., Renou-Wilson, F., Strack, M, 2015. The role of waterborne carbon in the greenhouse gas balance of drained and re-wetted peatlands. *Aquatic Sciences*. DOI:10.1007/s00027-015-0447-y
4. Germer, J and Sauerborn, J, 2008. Estimation of the impact of oil palm plantation establishment on greenhouse gas balance. *Environment, Development and Sustainability* 10: 697-716
5. Hooijer, A., Page, S.E., Canadell, J.G., Silvius, M., Kwadijk, J., Wosten, H., Jauhiainen, J, 2010. Current and future CO2 emissions from drained peatlands in Southeast Asia. *Biogeosciences* 7:1505–1514
6. Miettinen, J., Hooijer, A., Shi, C., Tollenaar,D., Vernimmen, R., Liew, S.C., Malins , C., Page, S.E, 2012a. Extent of industrial plantations on Southeast Asian peatlands in 2010 with analysis of historical expansion and future projections. *Global Change Biology Bioenergy* 4: 908-918
7. Miettinen, J., Hooijer, A., Tollenaar, D., Page, S., Malins,C., Vernimmen, R., Chi, C., Liew, S.C, 2012b. Historical Analysis and Projection of Oil Palm Plantation Expansion on Peatland in Southeast Asia. *White Paper Number 17*. International Council on Clean Transportation, Washington DC
8. Miettinen, J., Shi, C., Liew, S.C, 2011. Deforestation rates in insular Southeast Asia between 2000 and 2010. *Global Change Biology* 17: 2261–2270

9. Moore, S., Evans, C.D., Page, S.E., Garnett, M.H., Jones, T.H., Freeman,C., Hooijer, A., Wiltshire, A., Limin,S., Gauci, V, 2013. Deep instability of deforested tropical peatlands revealed by fluvial organic carbon fluxes. *Nature* 493: 660-664
10. Page S. E., Morrison, R., Malins, C., Hooijer, A., Rieley, J. O., Jauhiainen, J, 2011. Review of peat surface greenhouse gas emissions from oil palm plantations in Southeast Asia. *White Paper Number 15.* International Council on Clean Transportation, Washington DC

Abstract No: A-379

MAPPING THE DEPTH AND CARBON STOCK FOR PEATLAND IN MERANTI, RIAU INDONESIA

Dian Novarina[1*], Rudiyanto[2], Budi Indra Setiawan[2] and Muhajir Utomo[3]

[1] *Asia Pacific Resources International Limited (APRIL), Indonesia*
[2] *Bogor Agricultural University (IPB), Indonesia*
[3] *Lampung University (Unila), Indonesia*

* *Corresponding author: novarinad@gmail.com*

Accurate estimates of below ground carbon stocks in peat land strongly depend on the peat depth, bulk density and carbon content of peat. The range values of bulk density and carbon content are well known, while peat depth is quite variable depending on locations. This study was addressed at mapping peat depth and estimation of belowground carbon stocks in Meranti, Palawan Regency, Riau Province, Indonesia. Two regression models, artificial neural networks (ANN) and support vector machine (SVM), were compared in modelling and mapping of peat depth. The peatland was delineated according to peatland hydrological unit (PHU) bounded by rivers. The digital elevation and nearest distance to rivers, used as covariates, were derived from DEM SRTM 1 arc (about 30.7 m) and Euclidian distance to rivers, respectively. Peat depth observations were obtained from field transect surveys. Based on training results, while ANN (RMSE = 0.68 m and R^2 = 0.92) is superior to SVM (RMSE = 0.85 m and R^2 = 0.88), both models show excellent agreement. The peat depth map resulting from ANN seemed influenced by nearest distance to river rather than elevation; conversely the shape of the peat depth map by SVM is similar to elevation rather than nearest distance to river. The range estimates within the 90% confidence interval are 99.635 to 125.553 Mt (x10^6 tonne) with the best estimates of 112.594 Mt for ANN; while SVM resulted in slightly higher estimates ranging between 121.472 to 153.071 Mt (x10^6 tonne) with the best estimate of 137.272 Mt.

Keywords: -

Abstract No: A-019

SENSITIVITY OF HIGH ALTITUDE PEATLANDS TO CHANGES AND THEIR SUSTAINABLE MANAGEMENT IN THE HINDU-KUSH HIMALAYAN REGION

Wu Ning

International Centre for Integrated Mountain Development (ICIMOD), GPO Box 3226, Kathmandu, Nepal

**Corresponding author: nwu@icimod.org*

Peatlands in the Hindu Kush Himalayan (HKH) region are present in diverse forms including floodplain marshes, wet meadows, seasonal waterlogged areas and forest swamps. As one kind of the most important wetlands in this high altitude region, they are a kind of ecosystem interface between terrestrial and aquatic habitats encompassing water, soil and organisms that are adapted to the unique wet environment, making it one of the most productive and sensitive. The dynamics of an ecosystem interface are particularly sensitive to rapid changes in climate and anthropogenic impacts, thus they could be a good indicator to use in environmental monitoring. In the HKH region peatlands with an extent of about 20-25% of the total wetland are sources of energy, fodder and food for local communities, play an important role as aquifers and provide habitat for diverse species of flora and fauna. However, these valuable ecosystems are facing multiple stresses from a variety of drivers such as changes in land use, over-extraction of resources, pollution, and environmental change, including climate change. Large areas of peatlands have been opened up for the cultivation of crops and plantations or drained out for livestock grazing. These changes have created new economic opportunities and contributed to strengthening food security. However, the environmental impact of these changes has become a source of deep concern. Currently, the scientific, technical and political debate has been focused on the assessment of the greenhouse gas (GHG) emissions resulting from peatland utilization and their production potential. Although the significance of high altitude peatlands as the source of methane and sink for carbon in the HKH region has been identified, the relative contributions of peatlands to atmospheric methane levels are highly uncertain. At present the urgency in addressing the challenges and enhancing cooperation for better understanding and management of these unique ecosystems has been noted in many national, regional and global forums. In this report the author addresses the distribution of peatlands, carbon storage, GHG emission features and their sustainable management with case-studies in the HKH region including the Tibetan Plateau.

***Keywords**: greenhouse gas emission, carbon storage, sustainable management*

Abstract No: A-207

THE EFFECT OF LAND USES ON SELECTED PEAT PROPERTIES THAT CONTROL CARBON STORAGE IN A MASSIVELY DRAINED TROPICAL PEAT DOME

Gusti Z. Anshari[1, 3], Evi Gusmayanti[2, 3] and M. Afifudin[4]

[1]*Soil Science Department, Faculty of Agriculture, Tanjungpura University, Indonesia*
[2]*Agrotechnology Department, Faculty of Agriculture, Tanjungpura University, Indonesia*
[3]*Magister of Environment, Graduate Studies of Tanjungpura University, Indonesia*
[4]*Regional Development Agency (Bappeda), Indonesia*

**Corresponding author: gzanshari@live.untan.ac.id, gzanshari@gmail.com*

SUMMARY

Tropical peats in Indonesia are important for carbon storage, but land use changes cause substantial decline of carbon stock. This study aims to assess impacts of land uses on selected peat properties that importantly control carbon stock. The study site is located in a massively deforested and drained peat dome, presently called Rasau Jaya in West Kalimantan Province, Indonesia. This peat dome was firstly logged in early 1970, drained and converted into agriculture development in 1972. Land uses consist of secondary forest (DF), open peat (BF), and oil palm plantation (OP). A total of 160 peat samples, each 100 cm^3, were analyzed. Research variables consist of bulk density (BD), Total organic carbon (TOC) and total nitrogen (TN). We also analyzed organic matters through loss on ignition (LOI). Then, C/N ratio, C and N densities (CD and ND) were calculated. We used one-way ANOVA to assess mean differences of these variables following land uses (sites) and control sections of peat thickness. If results of ANOVA showed significant, we used Games-Howell post-hoc tests, with a set of orthogonal contrasts. Results of this research show that land uses generally does not significantly alter peat properties, but leads to increases in CD and ND, in particular, on oil palm plantations due to substantial increases of bulk densities. Vertically, peat properties in the surface and sub-surface tiers (0-100 cm and 100-200 cm) are highly significantly different from the below and bottom tiers (200-300 cm and >300 cm). We recommend monitoring carbon stock in the upper 200 cm thickness section, as this section suffers most from anthropogenic land use changes in tropical peats.

Keywords: *Land use changes, Tropical peat degradation, Carbon storage, Human disturbances*

INTRODUCTION

Tropical peats are mainly found in Indonesia. The extent of tropical peats in Indonesia are estimated to be around 20 millions hectares, which store 50 to 57 Gt C (Jaenicke *et al.*, 2008; Page, Rieley, and Banks 2011). Most of these peats have been disturbed, converted and drained for agricultural development. Peats belong to organic soils (Histosols), and store a large amount of organic carbon. Most of tropical peats in Indonesia are logged, drained and converted into agricultural uses. These disturbances are detrimental, as tropical peats become sources of CO_2 emission to atmosphere, and substantially reduce Carbon stock in tropical peats. This study aims to assess impacts of land uses on selected peat properties that control C stock in a disturbed and drained peat dome used for agriculture development.

STUDY SITE

This study site is located in Rasau Jaya peat dome, about 53,000 Ha, in West Kalimantan Province, Indonesia (See Figure 1). We recorded that human disturbances on this peat dome firstly occurred in 1970 in the form of timber harvesting. Then, the government of Indonesia drained and converted this peat into agriculture development in 1972. At that time, knowledge on tropical peats was very poor. Tropical peatlands were treated as a marginal land for agriculture. Drainage is common practice in order to lower water table and to enhance peat soil fertility.

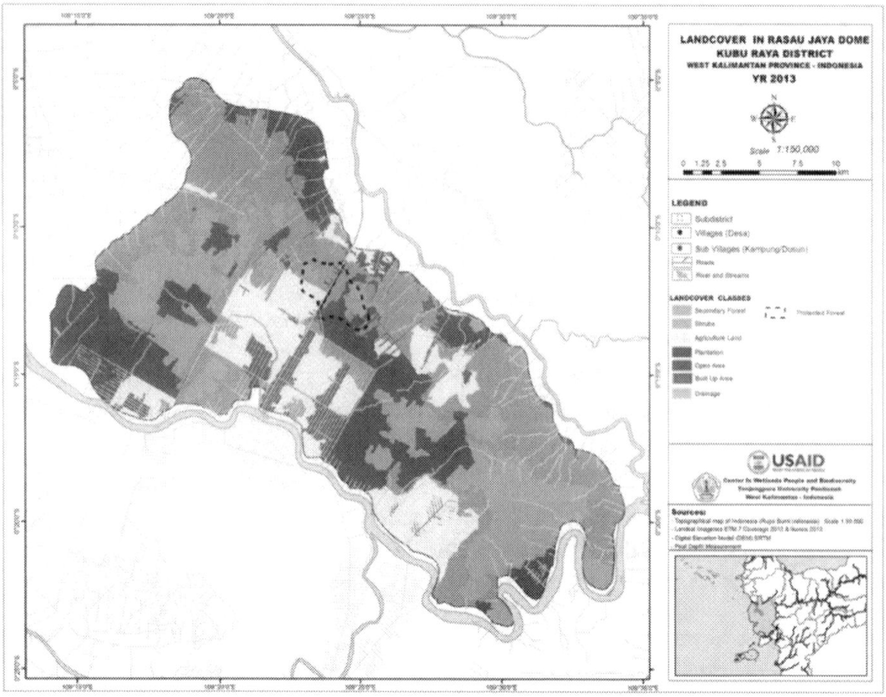

Figure 12: A map of Rasau Jaya peat dome, which is located in the upper Kapuas River of West Kalimantan Province, Indonesia

METHODS

We collected peat samples from two transects that cross over South to North, and East to West directions of Rasau Jaya peat dome. We investigated 22 peat core samples. We measured a total of 160 subsamples, consisting of 20 oil palms (OP), 57 degraded secondary forests (DF), and 83 open peats dominated by ferns (BF). We measured peat thickness with a Russian peat auger. Coring was done until reaching a mineral substratum. Samples were carefully collected for laboratory analyses. This fieldwork was done in five months, from September 2012 until February 2013. In addition, these subsamples were categorized into four thickness sections, consisting of surface tier (0-100 cm); sub-surface tier (100-200 cm); below tier (200-300 cm), and bottom tier (>300 cm). Research variables consist of bulk density (BD), total organic carbon (TOC), total nitrogen (TN), and organic matter content or loss on ignition (LOI). We also calculated C/N ratio, and carbon and nitrogen densities (CD and ND). BD is defined as a product of dry weight of peat samples (grams) by intact sample volume (cm^{-3}). CD and ND are products of BD ($g\ cm^{-3}$) multiplied by TOC (%) and TN (%), respectively.

LOI and BD were measured by gravimetric technique (Agus *et al.*, 2011) (Anshari 2010; Anshari *et al.*, 2010) (Heiri, Lotter, and Lemcke 2001) TOC and TN were measured by high temperature combustion with CHNS analyzer (Anshari 2010; Anshari *et al.*, 2010; Warren *et al.*, 2012). We used one-way ANOVA and Games-Howell contrast comparisons to present and interpret research results.

RESULTS AND DISCUSSION

Table 1 shows that values of TOC, TN and LOI in oil palm are slightly lower than in open peat and degraded forest sites. CD and ND in oil palm are high due to high BD value. Low TOC and TN concentrations in OP suggest C loss due to decomposition. Decomposers use Nitrogen, which is also absorbed by plants when it is available on soils. TOC is converted into CO_2 gas, and other forms of soluble carbon compounds are dissolved in water. Low LOI strongly indicates C loss and high decomposition rate. High BD values on OP indicate peat compaction, consolidation, and shrinkage of organic particles. Based on ash content differences, it is estimated that percentages of chemical decomposition that leads to C emission are about 40%. It is assumed that all of ash contents are purely originated from the conversion of organic matters, and there is no external input of inorganic matters into the peats. Significant decomposition of carbon is detected by lowering TOC concentration and LOI, as shown on OP site.

Results of Levene tests on these variables, except CD, show that variances of all variables are highly significanty different. As expected, data distribution of these variables is not normal. Accordingly, Brown-Forsythe

ANOVA was applied rather than traditional ANOVA and identified significant differences of these variabel among peat thickness sections.

Table 3: Summary results of TOC, TN, C/N, BD, LOI, CD and TN on Oil Palm (OP), Open Peat (BF), and Degraded Secondary Forest (DF)

. Variables	OP (n=20)		BF (n=83)		DF (n=57)		Total (n=160)	
	Mean	SD	Mean	SD	Mean	SD	Mean	SD
TOC (%)	49.63	10.87	53.99	8.79	43.67	10.31	52.80	9.67
TN (%)	0.98	0.28	1.12	0.30	1.10	0.39	1.10	0.33
C/N Ratio	52.59	9.86	50.60	10.29	51.74	14.65	51.26	11.93
BD (g cm^{-3})	0.16	0.08	0.12	0.08	0.13	0.10	0.13	0.08
LOI (%)	86.37	16.18	92.41	15.15	90.26	17.22	90.72	16.10
CD (kg m^{-3})**	74.16	21.37	56.55	21.49	60.90	22.99	60.30	21.58
ND (kg m^{-3})*	1.50	0.74	1.14	0.42	1.22	0.50	1.22	0.51

Note: * and ** indicate landuse significantly affected variables at 0.05 and 0.01 level

It is important to note that mineralization or low content of organic matters on OP affect an increase of carbon density (CD) (See Table 2). An average value of ash free CD on OP must be lower than the present calculation, and is estimated to be about 64 kg m^{-3}.

Table 4: Results of Contrast Test for Carbon and Nitrogen Densities

Contrast	t-stat	df	p-value	t-crit
	Carbon Density (kg m^{-3})			
C1 (OP vs BF+DF)	3.07**	157	0.00	1.98
C2 (BF vs DF)	-1.20	157	0.23	1.98
	Nitrogen Density (kg m^{-3})			
C1 (OP vs BF+DF)	2.68**	157	0.01	1.98
C2 (BF vs DF)	-0.98	157	0.33	1.98

Note: ** indicate contrast is significant at 0.01 level

Table 2 presents a summary result of contrasts following thickness section groups. Generally, variables fluctuated at the upper thickness (< 200cm), and relatively constant at the bottom sections. Lower TOC and TN in the surface indicate decomposition rate of organic matter and mineralization occur more rapidly leading to carbon loss through emission and nitrogen loss through plants root retrieval. Further, decomposition and compaction due to physical disturbace increase BD in the suface.

Table 5: Summary results of TOC, TN, C/N, BD, LOI, CD and TN on thickness section group

No	Variables	Thickness Section Group									
		0-100 cm (n=15)		100-200 cm (n=25)		200-300 cm (n=40)		>300 cm (n=80)		Total (n=160)	
		Mean	SD	Mean	SD	Mean	SD	Mean	SD	Mean	SD
1	TOC (%)**	38.55	14.25	42.35	12.70	56.91	2.56	56.69	1.75	52.80	9.67
2	TN (%)**	0.83	0.42	0.81	0.42	1.08	0.22	1.25	0.22	1.10	0.33
3	C/N Ratio**	51.00	11.82	59.64	16.38	54.85	10.83	46.89	8.62	51.26	11.93
4	BD (g cm^{-3})**	0.25	0.12	0.22	0.10	0.10	0.03	0.09	0.03	0.13	0.08
5	LOI (%)**	68.66	22.29	77.55	18.14	97.36	3.88	98.18	6.43	90.72	16.10
6	CD (kg m^{-3})**	81.44	23.51	81.79	19.98	55.46	18.18	52.04	15.58	60.30	21.58
7	ND (kg m^{-3})**	1.72	0.84	1.47	0.54	1.05	0.43	1.13	0.35	1.22	0.51

Note: ** indicates peat thickness section significantly affected variables at 0.01 level

Table 3 presents that all of investigated peat properties are significantly differences following control sections of surface (0-100 cm), sub-surface (100-200 cm), below (200-300 cm) and bottom (> 300 cm) tiers. Values

of TOC and LOI in surface and sub-surface are lower than bottom and below tiers (Figure 2). In contrast, values of BD and TN are high and low in surface, respectively (See Figure 2).
Table 4 presents results of contrast tests on peat thickness sections. It shows that the surface and sub-surface tiers (Contrast D3) are all indifferent for all variables. However, combinations of the surface and sub-surface tiers contrasted to below tier (200-300 cm) show highly significant differences, except for C/N ratio (See Contrast D2). The combinations consisting of all tiers are all highly different from the bottom tier (Contrast D1). This analysis strongly pinpoints impacts of disturbances on tropical peats that cause substantial changes in surface peats, i.e., the surface tier (0-100 cm) and the sub-surface tier (100-1200 cm). Major changes in these tiers are lower values of TOC, TN and LOI, and substantial increases of BD in both surface and sub-surface than in the below and bottom thickness tiers (see Table 3 and Figure 2).

Table 6: Results of Contrast Tests on Peat Thickness Sections

No	Variables	Contrast		
		D1	D2	D3
		(0-100 + 100-200 + 200-300 cm) vs >300 cm	(0-100 + 100-200 cm) vs 200-300 cm	0-100 cm vs 100-200 cm
		q-stat		
1	TOC (%)	10.07** (q crit 1% = 4.825)	10.25** (q crit 1% = 4.818)	-1.20 (q crit 5% =3.870)
2	TN (%)	23.88** (q crit 1%= 4.624)	4.76** (q crit 1% = 4.666)	0.26 (q crit 5% = 3.854)
3	C/N Ratio	-6.27** (q crit 1% = 4.544)	-0.23 q crit 5% = 3.725)	-2.73 q crit 5% = 3.806)
4	BD (g cm^{-3})	-10.56** (q crit 1% = 4.797)	-9.89** (q crit 1% =4.798)	1.16 (q crit 5% = 3.881)
5	LOI (%)	9.67** (q crit 1% = 4.808)	9.64** (q crit 1% = 4.895)	-1.80 (q crit 5% = 3.917)
6	CD (kg m^{-3})	-7.12** (t crit 1% = 2.608)	-6.47** (t crit 1% = 2.608)	-0.06 (t crit 1% = 2.608)
7	ND (kg m^{-3})	-4.37* (q crit 5% = 3.811)	-5.56** (q crit 1% = 4.747)	1.48 (q crit 5% = 3.940)

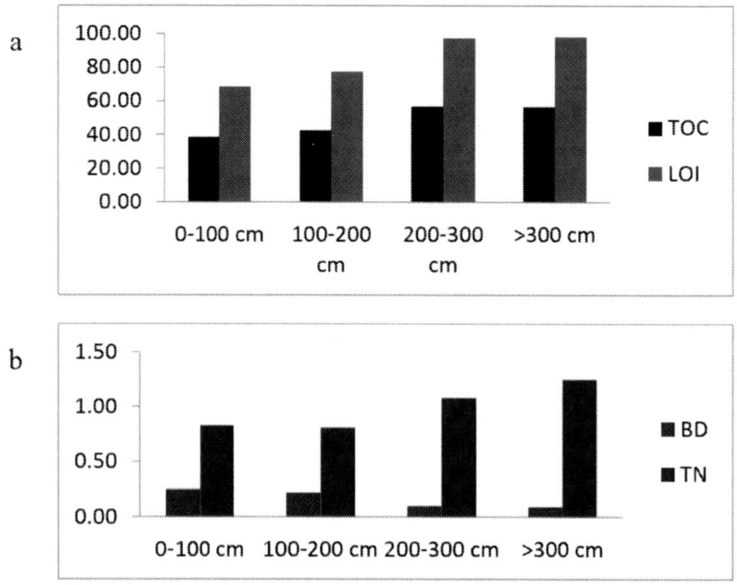

Figure 13: The average values of TOC and LOI (a); BD and TN (b) by peat thickness tiers

This study strongly shows that anthropogenic disturbances on tropical peats affect significant property changes on the upper section of peat thickness. This information is very important, as it will be useful for monitoring peat properties and carbon stock changes. It is also important to note that mineralization of peats would augment carbon stock due to an increase of bulk density, but significant reduction of total organic carbon.

CONCLUSION

This study highlights both natural and anthropogenic Carbon properties in tropical peats. Anthropogenic disturbances cause substantial changes of peat properties up to 200 cm thickness. This study concludes that monitoring Carbon stocks in disturbed and drained peats for agriculture must cover the upper 200 cm thickness. Bulk Density (BD) is the most important factor that control the amounts of C storage and emission

ACKNOWLEDGEMENTS

We would like to express our sincere thanks for M.Nuriman, Eka Kurnia, Idriss, Ilham, who did very laborious fieldwork, and many of villagers who helped as field workers. We also thank Charley Harvey, Alison Hoyt and Laure Gandois from MIT, USA for their cooperation. This research is financially supported by USAID and NSF through PEER program, under NSF grant number: 1114161 for Gusti Anshari, Evi Gusmayanti, and M. Afifudin. Further information is available at http://sites.nationalacademies.org/pga/peer/index.htm

REFERENCES

1. Agus, Fahmuddin, Kurniatun Hairiah, Anny Mulyani, and World Agroforestry Centre. 2011. *Measuring Carbon Stock in Peat Soils: Practical Guide.*
2. Anshari, M. Afifudin, M. Nuriman, E. Gusmayanti, L. Arianie, R. Susana, R. W. Nusantara, J. Sugardjito, and A. Rafiastanto. 2010. "Drainage and Land Use Impacts on Changes in Selected Peat Properties and Peat Degradation in West Kalimantan Province, Indonesia." *Biogeosciences* 7 (11): 3403–19. doi:10.5194/bg-7-3403-2010.
3. Anshari, Gusti Z. 2010. "Carbon Content of the Freshwater Peatland Forests of Danau Sentarum." *Borneo Research Bulletin* 41: 62–73.
4. Heiri, Oliver, André F Lotter, and Gerry Lemcke. 2001. "Loss on Ignition as a Method for Estimating Organic and Carbonate Content in Sediments : Reproducibility and Comparability of Results," 101–10.
5. Jaenicke, J., J. O. Rieley, C. Mott, P. Kimman, and F. Siegert. 2008. "Determination of the Amount of Carbon Stored in Indonesian Peatlands." *Geoderma* 147 (3-4): 151–58. doi:10.1016/j.geoderma.2008.08.008.
6. Page, Susan E., Rieley, J., and Banks, C. 2011. "Global and Regional Importance of the Tropical Peatland Carbon Pool." *Global Change Biology* 17: 798–818. doi:10.1111/j.1365-2486.2010.02279.x.
7. Warren, M. W., J. B. Kauffman, D. Murdiyarso, G. Anshari, K. Hergoualc'h, S. Kurnianto, J. Purbopuspito, *et al.* 2012. "A Cost-Efficient Method to Assess Carbon Stocks in Tropical Peat Soil." *Biogeosciences* 9 (11): 4477–85. doi:10.5194/bg-9-4477-2012.

2.2: GHG EMISSION FROM NATURAL & MANAGED PEATLANDS

Abstract No: A-178

CHALLENGES AND OPPORTUNITIES FOR EDDY-FLUX MEASUREMENTS OF CO_2 EMISSIONS OF OIL PALM ON PEAT

M. Y. Leclerc[1*], G. Zhang[1], H. Nahrawi[1], J. Nur Maisarah[2], H. Mos[2], M. Law[2], M.H. Haniff[2], K. Norman[2] and Y.M. Choo[2]

[1] *The University of Georgia, United States*
[2] *Malaysian Palm Oil Board*

**Corresponding author: moniqueleclerc@moniqueleclerc.org*

This paper reports on the opportunities and challenges of measuring the total net ecosystem exchange from managed tropical oil palm plantations in Southeast Asia. In contrast with other methods used to link CO_2 emissions to point measurements, be they of either water table level or of temporal and spatial grab sampling measurements, the eddy-flux method offers a method which provides *in situ* and continuously a spatial and temporal integration of the net ecosystem exchange at the plantation scale. This confers it the enormous advantage of providing net ecosystem exchange accounting for carbon uptake and respiration simultaneously. The method however must be used with care and a fundamental knowledge of micrometeorology for these measurements to be robust. Some of the challenges involved in day-to-day site selection planning and data analysis interpretation involves the limitation of often small oil palm plantations. Small blocks surrounded by spatial heterogeneities in adjoining land surfaces, whether they arise from tropical forested lands, oil palm plantations of different ages or recent clearings, lead to high surface albedo contrasts. This paper uses lessons learned from experience garnered from other flux measurements in other ecosystems. It also highlights some of the basic uncompromising physical principles to make robust, scientifically credible flux measurements. This paper also addresses how such violations of the principles of eddy-covariance assumptions cannot be easily remedied or corrected without a costly relocation of flux towers. This paper proposes guidelines to ensure that measurements of net ecosystem exchange from 'realistic' operational oil palm plantations are robust.

***Keywords**:-*

Abstract No: A-194

CHARACTERIZING PEAT PALM FOREST DEGRADATION IN THE PERUVIAN AMAZON FROM SPACE AND ON THE GROUND

K.Hergoualc'h [1*], V.H. Gutierrez-Velez [2], J. van Lent [1] and L.V. Verchot[1]

[1]Center for International Forestry Research
[2]Columbia University

**Corresponding author: k.hergoualch@cgiar.org*

Peru has the second largest area of peatlands in the Tropics. Little, however, is known of how the biogeochemical cycle of its peat forests can be affected through anthropogenic intervention. The most representative land cover on peat is a *Mauritia flexuosa*-dominated palm swamp forest which has been under human pressure over decades due to the high demand for the *M. flexuosa* fruit often collected by cutting down the entire palm. Degradation of these carbon-dense forests can severely affect emissions of greenhouse gases and contribute to climate change. The objectives of this research were to assess the impacts on soil trace gas fluxes and biomass carbon stocks of peat palm swamp forest degradation and to explore the potential of remote sensing methods combined with field measurements to map the distribution of peat palm swamp forest according to degradation levels. Results suggest a shift in forest composition from palm- to woody-tree dominated forest following degradation. We also found that human intervention in peat palm swamp forest can translate into substantial reductions in tree carbon stocks with a decrease in initial biomass (above- and below-ground) stocks (118.3 ± 1.1 Mg C ha^{-1}) by 26 and 44% following medium and high degradation. Preliminary results suggest high and low soil CH_4 and CO_2 emission rates on average, as compared to Southeast Asian peat swamp forests whereas N_2O emissions are of the same magnitude. Degradation seems to disturb soil respiration mainly through micro-climatic changes induced by reduced canopy cover. The analysis indicates a good potential to discriminate areas of peat palm swamp forest with different levels of degradation from other land covers, suggesting the feasibility of monitoring peat palm swamp forest degradation using remote sensing analyses.

***Keywords**: -*

Abstract No: A-276

COMPARISON OF THE CARBON DIOXIDES FLUXES UNDER PEAT SOIL BETWEEN TEMPERATE AND TROPICAL REGION UNDER INTENSIVE AGRICULTURE PRODUCTION

Ahmad Suhaizi Mat Su[1, 3*], Ahmad Husni Mohd. Hanif[2] and Viacheslav I. Adamchuk[3]

[1]*Department of Agriculture Technology, Faculty of Agriculture, Universiti Putra Malaysia, Malaysia*
[2]*Department of Land Management, Faculty of Agriculture, Universiti Putra Malaysia, Malaysia*
[1,3]*Department of Bioresource Engineering, Macdonald Campus of McGill University, Canada*

**Corresponding author: asuhaizi1@gmail.com*

SUMMARY

Agriculture production under peat soil (organic soil) is a significant contributor to carbon dioxides (CO_2) emission worldwide. Agriculture activities under organic soil are categorized as one of the anthropogenic activities for global climate change and greenhouse gases (GHG) contributors. Organic soils are used for specialty crops as green vegetables and onions in Canada, pineapple and oil palm in Malaysia. The aim of this study was to compare the two growing environments in terms of CO_2 fluxes emission and potential strategies for management strategy improvements. Thus, in Canada, the gas was manually sampled at 15-min for an hour duration from multiple stationary installed non-steady state chambers (NSS) design. In Malaysia, two different chambers were used namely; NSS and CO_2 Draeger gas detection tube chambers were used to measure the CO_2 fluxes for 30-min duration. In results it was found that the mean CO_2 fluxes under tropical region is higher than in temperate area due to continuous warm and humid climate. This result helps in the understanding of the different factors contributing to the CO_2 flux variation and differences between these two regions. Good management practices should be taken into account to ensure the sustainability of the peat soil under intensive agriculture practices.

Keywords: *Carbon dioxides, non-steady state chamber, organic soil*

INTRODUCTION

Mitigation of GHG *i.e.* CO_2 - from the soil is important in reducing the impact from climate change. Microbial activities in the soil play a vital role in releasing or consuming these three gases, and thus are significant in the global GHG cycle. Modelling techniques of GHG estimation from anthropogenic, terrestrial and aquatic components mark the effects on quantification of flux data. Quantifying spatial and temporal variations of the GHG emission is necessary in accessing the potential impact of different agriculture practices on global warming. Consequently, methods used to calculate fluxes of trace gases directly affect the localized or global scale emission estimation and validation (Asman *et al.*, 1999). Draining the organic soil for agriculture purposes increase potential GHG gases, mainly CO_2 fluxes. Draining process exposed the organic soil layer to the decomposition, which allows more oxygen to enter the soil profile. The estimation of the GHG base on soil physical characteristic in rich organic soil is not new. Howard and Howard (1993) found non-linear relationship between soil moisture and CO_2 flux production using wide range of agriculture soil types, including the peat soil. Intensive cultivation under rich organic soil profoundly increase and decrease certain GHG fluxes and emissions. The mineralization of the organic soil very much depend on the soil moisture and temperature. Increase in climatic temperature, reduced the organic matter content of soils. Conseqently, increase the potential GHG emissions (The Leirós *et al.*, 1999). The actual measurement of the estimated value will be valuable for the IPCC standard and as for now just based on the inaccurate studies and not from a crop specific and too generalized. Direct measurement of the CO_2 fluxes for the temperate and tropical region from cultivated cropland on peat soil is needed. Therefore, the aim of this study is to compare the two growing conditions of temperate versus tropical climates in terms of CO_2 fluxes emission and discuss potential strategies for management strategy improvements under peat soil cultivation.

METHODOLOGY

Study location under organic soil in Canada was located at Sherrington, Quebec, Eastern Canada. This location was intensively cultivated for vegetable production. The growing season begin from late spring (May) until the end of November. The water table below soil surface was about at 1 m depth and due to the crop water requirement, the schedule irrigation is normally took place for 8 mm water for one hour sprinkler irrigation. About 24 NSS gas chambers were installed at three different locations with 4 replicates chambers per location. Each chamber location was geo-referenced using Garmin eTrex Legend handheld GPS (Garmin International Inc., Olathe, KS, USA). The gas measurement was done through the gas extraction from a NSS gas chamber (figure 1) made from a flexi-glass frame with size (W x L x H): 0.556 x 0.556 x 0.140 m, and vented to avoid pressure perturbations. The gas samples were collected at least once per week throughout the growing season. All gas samples were extracted using a 20 ml syringe from the headspace. For each sampling event, five gas samples were taken at 15 minutes intervals, thereby totalling one hour. All samples were then injected into 12 ml vacuumed exetainers (Labco, Wycombe, UK) fitted with an extra 60 mil (60 mil equal to 1/16th of an inch or 0.0625 inches) of Teflon-silicon septa (National Scientific, Rockwood, TN, USA). All samples were brought immediately to the Soil Ecology Research Laboratory of Macdonald campus, McGill University, where they were stored in a temperature controlled location, and analyzed for the three main trace GHG gases, N_2O, CH_4 and CO_2 concentrations, using a customized Bruker-Varian 450 gas chromatograph (Bruker, Bremen, Germany). These five gas concentrations allowed the flux to be calculated based on median flux estimated using a simple linear regression method. The median slope of the flux was used during the data processing in the MATLAB is to i) remove bias imposed by outlier data, ii) calculate fluxes of trace gases, and iii) estimate total GHG cumulative diurnal emissions under various agriculture practices. A median slope technique was used to disregard outliers of gas measurements taken in a short sampling period. This approach provided an efficient and integrated method to process large datasets for GHG emission estimation.

While in Malaysia, the study sites were located at Simpang Renggam, Johor, Malaysia in pineapple and oil palm areas. The test sited was about 1 acre each and about 200 m distance to each other. The palm was at 8 years old during the measurement, and 10 months for pineapple. Both areas were established with an open drainage and the water table was about sub meter depth. During the gas sampling at each crop type, a total of 24 CO_{2}- samples were collected (2 site x 2 replicated chambers x 2 times gas measurement x 3 sampling time of the year). This resulted of 48 gas samples for both sites. The CO2 from the peat was captured using the NSS closed chamber design and the gas was detected using the CO_2 Draeger Gas detection tube (Kitigawa, Japan). The cylinder shape chamber was about 15 cm diameter and 15 cm height. The chamber was deployed at 7.4 cm height from the soil surface. After 30-min a gas fluxes emitted, a 100 mL gas was drawn using a syringe from the headspace and then transferred through an opened CO_2 Draeger gas detection tube for flux level measurement. The CO_2 level was read as in percentage which was indicated by the color change from the purple to pink.

Figure 1: Method of gas collection. (a) Non-steady state chamber design under vegetable production, and (b) Close chamber design under pineapple and oil palm plantation.

RESULTS AND DISCUSSION

The results of the CO_2 fluxes (figure 2) indicated that the emission is higher in tropical organic soil i.e. under oil palm and pineapple rather than under vegetable production. The result indicated that the average CO_2-C fluxes was about 5, 7 and 2.4 g m^{-2} d^{-1} fluxes for pineapple, oil palm and vegetable productions (table 1). Higher CO_2 fluxes in the tropical region compared to the eastern temperate region may be due to the continuously hot and humid weather condition. Since most of the sampling was conducted during the day, the fluxes presented may require more data for statistically robust comparison purposes. Moreover, for the temperate climate area the vegetable production only took place for about a half of the year as compared to the perennial crop.

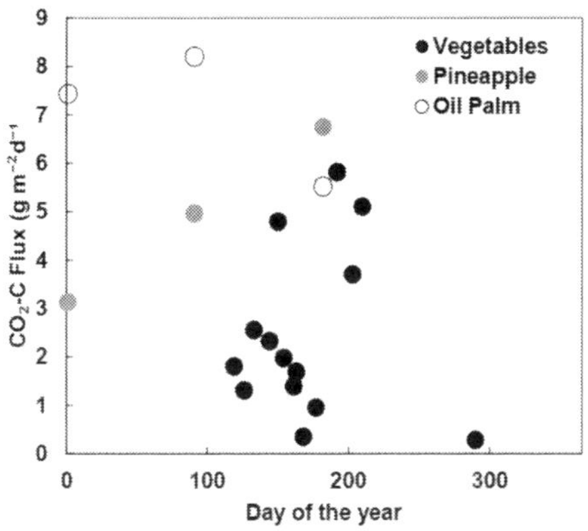

Figure 2: Compare the degree of the CO2 fluxes under different crop, over the number of day in the year.

Table 1: A descriptive statistics of the CO2

Parameter	Pineapple	Oil palm	Vegetable
	CO_2-C (g m^{-2} d^{-1})		
Max	6.8	8.2	5.8
Average	5.0	7.1	2.4
Median	5.0	7.4	1.9
Min	3.1	5.5	0.3

This result presents an initial understanding of the CO_2 fluxes level during the growing season under organic soil production. One of the most important sampling strategies that need to be done is by considering the field heterogeneity. Both locations either in Canada and Malaysia were not based on the field spatial variability consideration upon the sampling location. High root respiration during the gas measurement under pineapple and oil palm is the susceptible factors that may have contributed to the observed high CO_2 fluxes. Thus, more further studies are required to investigate for hot and low spot for the CO_2 emission rather than directly measured at any location. Such an approach can be achieved by mapping the soil electrical conductivity to characterize the field heterogeneity.

SUMMARY

Overall, it was observed that the mean CO_2 fluxes under oil palm cultivation are higher than in other cropping system. However, the cumulative CO_2 fluxes in the tropical region may be higher due to the hot and humid weather as compared to the temperate region. This result helps in the understanding of different factors contributing to CO_2 flux variation and differences between these two regions. Good management practices should be taken into account to ensure the sustainability of the peat soil under intensive agriculture practices

ACKNOWLEDGEMENTS

The authors acknowledge the data contribution from Hafsah Nahrawi, and Agriculture and Agri-Food Canada (AAFC) – Agricultural Greenhouse Gases Program (AGGP).

REFERENCES

1. Asman, W. A. H., Andreae, M. O., Conrad, R., Denmead, O. T., Ganzeveld, L. N., Helder, W, and Trumbore, S. (1999). How can fluxes of trace gases be validated between different scales? In *Approaches to scaling of trace gas fluxes in ecosystems* (Vol. 24, pp. 85-97). Elsevier Amsterdam.
2. Howard, D. M., and P. J. A. Howard. "Relationships between CO~ 2 evolution, moisture content and temperature for a range of soil types." *Soil Biology and Biochemistry* 25 (1993): 1537-1537.
3. Leiros, M. C., Trasar-Cepeda, C., Seoane, S., & Gil-Sotres, F. (1999). Dependence of mineralization of soil organic matter on temperature and moisture. *Soil Biology and Biochemistry*, *31*(3), 327-335.

Abstract No: A-105

EFFECT OF FOREST TYPE ON DECOMPOSITION RATE AND GREENHOUSE GAS FLUXES OF TROPICAL PEAT SOIL AFTER CONVERSION INTO AN OIL PALM PLANTATION

Faustina Elfrida Sangok[1, 2]*, Nagamitsu Maie[3], Lulie Melling[2] and Akira Watanabe[1]

[1]*Graduate School of Bioagricultural Sciences, Nagoya University, Chikusa, Nagoya, Japan*
[2]*Tropical Peat Research Laboratory Unit, Chief Minister's Department, Sarawak, Malaysia*
[3]*School of Veterinary Medicine, Kitasato University, Aomori, Japan*

**Corresponding author: faustina270187@gmail.com*

SUMMARY

The effect of forest type on the decomposability and greenhouse gas fluxes of tropical peat soils after conversion to an oil palm plantation was evaluated through a field incubation experiment of peat soils from three representative types of primary forest in Sarawak, Malaysia, namely Mixed Peat Swamp (MPS), Alan Batu (ABt), and Alan Bunga (ABg). Carbon dioxide (CO_2) and methane (CH_4) fluxes were measured on a monthly basis for 36 months. The CO_2 and CH_4 fluxes ranged from 78–625 mg C m^{-2} h^{-1} and -67–653 µg C m^{-2} h^{-1}, respectively. Both of CO_2 and CH_4 fluxes were larger in the order ABg > ABt > MPS, which corresponded to the relative abundance of *O*-alkyl C derived mainly from polysaccharides in soil organic matter (SOM). Rate of decomposition of peat was almost constant during the 3-year period, and annual decomposition rate was estimated to be 0.033 y^{-1} for MPS, 0.048 y^{-1} for ABt. and 0.066 y^{-1} for ABg.

Keywords: *decomposition, greenhouse gas, tropical peat, vegetation*

INTRODUCTION

In Malaysia, peatland has been actively converted to agricultural land, of which 25% was oil palm plantation (Lim *et al.*, 2012). The conversion of tropical peatland to an oil palm plantation may accelerate soil organic matter (SOM) decomposition (Murayama and Bakar, 1996) and promote greenhouse gas (GHG) fluxes (Jaenicke *et al.*, 2008). Change in groundwater table due to drainage is considered to have a significant effect on carbon dioxide (CO_2) and methane (CH_4) fluxes (Melling *et al.*, 2005; Watanabe *et al.*, 2009). However, the rate of SOM decomposition may also differ depending on the composition and chemical structure of SOM. Peat in Southeast Asia generally develops to dome shape, leading to the transition of forest types from the edge to the interior (Page *et al.*, 1999). It is expected that the quality and sensitivity to the environmental change vary among SOM accumulated in different types of forests. The objective of the present study was to evaluate the effect of forest type on the rate of SOM decomposition and the GHG fluxes after the conversion to an oil palm plantation, based on a field soil incubation experiment.

MATERIALS AND METHODS

Three soil samples of 20–40 cm depth were collected from Mixed Peat Swamp (MPS; 1° 25' N, 111° 07' E), Alan Batu (ABt; 1° 27' N, 111° 08' E), and Alan Bunga (ABg; 1° 27' N, 111° 09' E) zones in the Maludam National Park, Sarawak, Malaysia, in August 2012 and Dominant tree species in the MPS site included *Gonstylus bancanus, Dactylocladus stenostachys, Copaifera palutris, Shorea platycarpa, Shorea scabrida,* and *Shorea uliginosa*. Although dominant tree species in the ABg and ABts sites was same, *Shorea albida*, ABg is characterized by an even upper story with canopy at 50–60 m high while ABt site had a non-uniform forest crown. Annual mean soil temperature at 5 cm depth and annual mean groundwater table were in the ranges of 25.7°C (MPS) to 27.1°C (ABg) and -17 cm (MPS) to -7.3 cm (ABg), respectively.

The soil samples were transferred to an oil palm in Sibu, Sarawak (2° 09' N, 111° 53' E), instantaneously, and packed in the PVC pipes with a plastic net attached at the bottom after removing large roots and mixing thoroughly. Four soil-packed pipes and an empty pipe that have a flange and two lateral holes were connected as are shown in Figure 1. The pipes packed with different soil samples were installed at the same point with 1 m distance between two pipes and the distance from a nearest oil palm tree was 3–4 m. CO_2 and CH_4 fluxes as well as environmental variables, including soil temperature and moisture at 5 cm depth and groundwater table, were monitored once a month for 3 years since October 2012. The gas samples collected were brought back to the laboratory, and the concentrations of CO_2 and CH_4 were determined using gas chromatographs equipped with a thermal conductivity detector (6890N, Agilent, Santa Clara, CA, United States) or a flame ionization detector (7890A, Agilent), respectively.

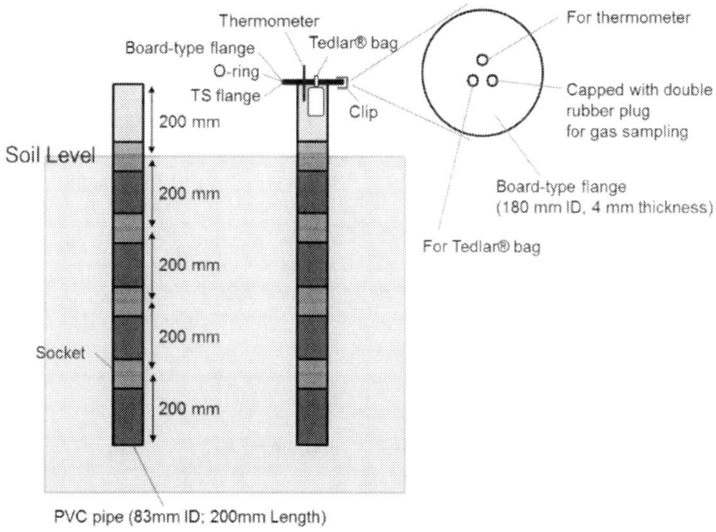

Figure 1: Design of field incubation experiment of peat soil samples collected from different types of forests.

SOM in the three soils was characterized using ^{13}C NMR spectroscopy. Ramp cross polarization (CP)/magnetic angle spinning ^{13}C NMR spectra with phase-adjusted spinning side bands (PASS) sequence (Ikeya and Watanabe, 2016) were recorded on ECA 700 spectrometer (JEOL, Tokyo, Japan) with the number of data accumulation, 2080–4160. C composition was estimated from the relative intensity of signals from major C functional groups. Soil pH, total C and total nitrogen (N) contents, and loss on ignition (LOI) were determined by using a pH meter (Metrohm 827, Metrohm, Herisau, Switzerland), NC analyzer (Sumigraph NC-22, Sumica Chemical Analysis Service, Osaka, Japan), and a thermal gravimetric analyzer (TGA 701, Leco, St. Joseph, MI, USA).

Rate constant of soil organic C (SOC) decomposition was estimated by regressing cumulative CO_2-C emissions to exponential decay model. One-way ANOVA was used to analyze the difference in the rate of SOC decomposition and GHGs fluxes among the three peat soil samples. The significance of the difference between the forest types was determined using Fisher Least Significance Difference (LSD).

RESULTS

The physico-chemical properties of the soil samples are shown in Table 1. All of the soils are very acidic with pH in the range of 3.6 to 3.7, while LOI describes the organic matter content of the soil samples in the range of 98 to 99%. Total C and total N contents were in the range of 520–535 g kg^{-1} and 13–20 g kg^{-1}, respectively. C/N ratio increase from MPS soil (27) to ABg soil (40).

Table 1 Physico-chemical properties of Maludam peat soil samples

Soil sample	pH (2:5)	LOI (%)	Total C (g kg^{-1})	Total N (g kg^{-1})	C/N ratio
MPS	3.6	98	535	20	27
ABt	3.7	99	523	16	33
ABg	3.6	99	520	13	40

Table 2 shows the C composition as was estimated from the NMR spectra. The %*O*-alkyl C was larger in the order ABg (37%), ABt (32%), and MPS (26%) and %aromatic C was also larger in the ABg soil (33%) than in the other two soils (27%). The order of %alkyl C was opposite as MPS (33%), ABt (27%), and ABg (21%), and %carboxyl C also tended to be smaller in the ABg soil (9%) compared to the other two soils (13%).

Table 2: C composition of Maludam peat soil samples

Soil sample	%alkyl C (0–45 ppm)	%*O*-alkyl C (45–110 ppm)	%aromatic C (110–160 ppm)	%carboxyl C (160–190 ppm)	%ketone C (190–220 ppm)
MPS	33	26	27	13	1
ABt	27	32	27	13	2
ABg	21	37	33	9	1

The monthly CO_2 flux ranged from 95 to 480, 78 to 592, and 138 to 625 mg C m^{-2} h^{-1}, for the MPS, ABt, and ABg soils, respectively. The total CO_2 emission during the 3-year period was larger ($P < 0.05$) in the order ABg, ABt, and MPS (Figure 2). CO_2 flux the ABt and ABg soils was correlated negatively with groundwater table (-99.0–16.2 cm), while none of the three soil showed significant correlations between CO_2 flux and soil moisture content (54%–85%) or soil temperature. The monthly CH_4 flux ranged from -67 to 402, -60 to 607, and -20 to 653 µg C m^{-2} h^{-1}, for the MPS, ABt, and ABg soils, respectively. The total CH_4 emission during the 3-year period was also larger ($P < 0.05$) in the order ABg, ABt, and MPS (Figure 2). A positive correlation was observed between CH_4 flux and groundwater table in all three soils type ($r = 0.37$-0.44; $P < 0.05$). The rate constant of SOM decomposition was estimated to be 0.033 y^{-1}, 0.048 y^{-1} and 0.066 y^{-1} for the ABg, ABt, and MPS soils, respectively.

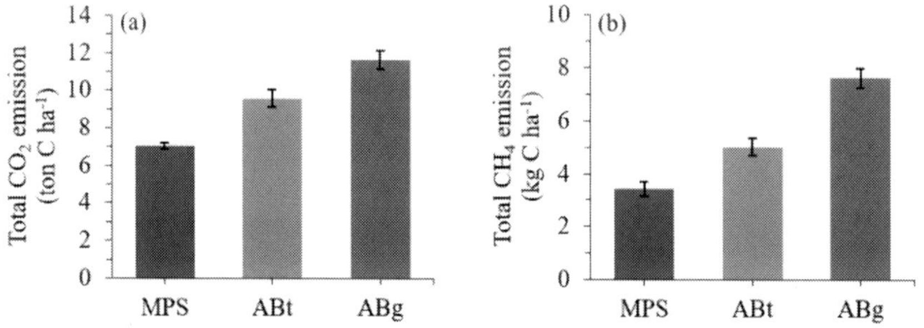

Figure 2: Total emissions of CO_2 (a) and CH_4 (b) for 3 years from peat soils developed under different types of forests.

DISCUSSION

The variation of CO_2 and CH_4 fluxes from the three peat soils suggested the difference in SOM stability under the environmental conditions in the oil palm plantation, i.e. higher temperature and lower groundwater level compared to those in natural forests. However, temperature change may be a minor or insignificant factor in tropical peatland, because the increase in soil temperature was the largest for the MPS soil that emitted the smallest amount of CO_2 and CH_4. No correlation between GHG fluxes and soil temperature supported it. Numerous studies have reported the relationship of lower groundwater table and higher CO_2 flux in temperate peatland (e.g., Dinsmore *et al.*, 2009; Berglund and Berglund, 2011). Similar trend has also been observed in tropical peatland (Furukawa *et al.*, 2005; Melling *et al.*, 2013). There are spatial variations in groundwater level in the Maludam National Park and it is higher in the order ABg > ABt > MPS. The change in groundwater level after installation in the oil palm plantation was more drastic in the same order, which is a possible cause of the difference in CO_2 emission among the three soils.

Another possible cause is the difference in the composition of SOM. CO_2 emission was larger in a soil that contains a larger amount of *O*-alkyl C, which is derived mainly from polysaccharides such as cellulose and hemicellulose. Greater decomposability of *O*-alkyl C than alkyl C in peat SOM has been recognized (e.g., Purwanto *et al.*, 2008; Leifeld *et al.*, 2012). While the seasonal variation in CH_4 flux shows a not so tight relationship with that in groundwater table, total CH_4 emission from the three Maludam soils was higher in the same order as total CO_2 emission (Figure 2). The amount of labile SOM determines the rates of development of reducing conditions after water saturation and supply of substrates for methanogenesis. Thus, the decomposability of peat SOM could also be the major factor of CH_4 flux in the oil palm plantation.

CONCLUSION

The conversion of the tropical peat forest to oil palm plantation can cause the annual SOC loss of 3–6%. Variations in the rate of SOM decomposition and GHG fluxes among the three soils from the different types of forests were confirmed, which was possibly due to the variations in the extent of groundwater level change and the composition/structure of SOM, in particular the relative abundance of polysaccharides. As the independency of SOM quality from the groundwater level is still unknown, direct effect of tree species on the composition/structure of tropical peat SOM should be examined.

ACKNOWLEDGEMENTS

This research was supported by a Grant-in-Aid for Scientific Research from the Japan Society for the Promotion of Science (No. 24405029). The authors wish to acknowledge staff members of Tropical Peat Research Laboratory Unit and the oil palm plantation company for their contribution to this research.

REFERENCES

1. Berglund O, Berglund, K. Influence of water table level and soil properties on emissions of greenhouse gases from cultivated peat soil, Soil Biology and Biochemistry, 2011;43:923–931.
2. Dinsmore KJ, Skiba UM, Billet MF, Rees RM. Effect of water table on greenhouse gas emissions from peatland mesocosms. Plant Soil 2009; 318:229-242.
3. Furukawa Y, Inubushi K, Ali M, Itang AM, Tsuruta H. Effect of changing groundwaterlevels caused by land-use changes on greenhouse gas fluxes from tropical peat lands. Nutrient Cycling in Agroecosystems 2005; 71:81-91.
4. Ikeya K, Watanabe A. Application of ^{13}C ramp CPMAS NMR with phase adjusted spinning sidebands (PASS) for quantitative estimation of carbon functional groups in natural organic matter. Analytical and Bioanalytical Chemistry 2016; 408: 651–655.
5. Jaenicke J, Rieley JO, Mott C, Kimman P, Siegert F. Determination of the amount of carbon stored in Indonesian peatlands. Geoderma 2008; 147:151–158.
6. Leifeld J, Steffens M, Galego-Sala A. Sensitivity of peatland carbon loss to organic matter quality. Geophysical Research Letters 2012; 39: L14704.
7. Lim KH, Lim SS, Parish F, Suharto R (Eds). RSPO Manual on Best Management Practices (BMPs) for existing oil palm cultivation on peat. 2012;pp 5, RSPO, Kuala Lumpur, Malaysia.
8. Melling L, Hatano R, Goh KJ. Soil CO_2 flux from three ecosystems in tropical peatland of Sarawak, Malaysia. Tellus 2005; 57B:1–11.
9. Melling L, Tan CSY, Goh KJ, Hatano R. Soil microbial and root respirations from three ecosystems in tropical peatland of Sarawak, Malaysia. Journal of Oil Palm Research 2013; 25 (1):44-57.
10. Murayama S, Bakar ZA. Estimation of in situ decomposition by measurement of CO_2 flux. Japan Agricultural Research Quarterly 1996; 30:153–158.
11. Page SE, Rieley JO, Shotyk ØW, Weiss D. Interdependence of peat and vegetation in a tropical peat swamp forest. Philosophical Transections B 1999; 354:1885–1897.
12. Purwanto BH, Watanabe A, Jong FS, Kakuda K, Ando H. Kinetic parameters of gross N mineralization of peat soils as related to the composition of soil organic matter. Soil Science and Plant Nutrition 2005; 51:109–115.
13. Watanabe A, Purwanto BH, Ando H, Kakuda K, Jong FS. Methane and CO_2 fluxes from an Indonesian peatland used for sago palm (*Metroxylan sagu* Rottb.) cultivation: Effects of fertilizer and groundwater level management. Agriculture, Ecosystem and Environment 2009; 134:14–18.

Abstract No: A-102

ESTIMATING CO_2 FLUX FROM BARE LAND IN A PEAT ISLAND USING ARTIFICIAL NEURAL NETWORK MODEL

Yudi Chadirin[1*], Satyanto K. Saptomo[1], Rudiyanto[1], Budi I. Setiawan[1], Kazutoshi Osawa[2], Dian Novarina[3] and Muhajir Utomo

[1]*Department of Civil and Environmental Engineering, IPB, Indonesia*
[2]*Department of Environmental Engineering, Utsunomiya University, Japan,*
[3]*PT April Management, Indonesia*
[4]*Faculty of Agriculture, University of Lampung, Indonesia*

**Corresponding author: gooday926@yahoo.com*

SUMMARY

Temperature and soil moisture are cofounded factors that has influence on CO_2 soil emission while rainfall increase in soil moisture. These parameters were varied and easy to change by time and affected on CO_2 soil emission. A continuous measurement of CO_2 emission provides the accumulated emission more accurately but needs expensive instrument. Meanwhile, the measurement of soil moisture and temperature could be conducted with simpler and cheaper instruments. Thus it's a need to figure out the CO_2 emission from peat with low cost based on environmental biophysics to predict CO_2 emission based. The objective of this study was to develop an artificial neural network model to predict CO_2 emission from peat in tropical region based on environmental biophysics data. Environmental biophysics data such as soil temperature, soil moisture, its gradients and rainfall were used as covariates for the model. The model was trained based on continuous field measurement on bare peatland. CO_2 emission had positive correlation with soil temperature but had negative correlation with soil moisture and rainfall. Result showed that ANN model could predict CO_2 emission from bare peatland with R^2 and RMSE are = 0.71 and 0.49 for training and 0.5 and 0.76 for testing respectively. We proposed that this model can be used to figure out the CO_2 emission from peatland in low cost and conducted in simple measurement.

***Keywords**: artificial neural network, bare peatland, CO_2 emission, temperature gradient, soil moisture gradient*

INTRODUCTION

CO_2 flux as result of soil respiration is an important component of carbon budget in consideration for sustainability management for peat land. Soil respiration is affected by variety of biotic and abiotic factors, such as soil temperature, soil moisture, amount and quality of carbon stored, precipitation, soil properties and soil management activities (Rustad *et al*., 2000; Raich and Tufekcioglu, 2000; Hui and Luo, 2004; Carrasco *et al*., 2006; Davidson and Janssens, 2006; Borken *et al*., 2002; Shen *et al*., 2008). Soil respiration is changing by temporal and spatial variation (Shen *et al*., 2008; Epron *et al*., 2004) and small changes in soil respiration may strongly affect soil carbon sequestration (Raich and Schlesinger, 1992). Thus, it is important to conduct long term and continues measurement. A long term and continues measurement produced accumulative CO_2 flux that more accurate than extrapolation (Chadirin *et al*., 2015). However a long term and continues measurement of CO_2 flux need complex measurement system and expensive instrument. Therefore it is important to obtain good estimates of soil respiration from simple, cheap, long-term measurement. Artificial neural network (ANN) is one of promising method for estimating CO_2 flux from micrometeorological data (Melesse and Hanley, 2009) and soil carbon budget from soil C content, temperature, and moisture level (Alvarez *et al*., 2009). In this study, we developed an artificial neural network model top CO_2 flux from bare land in peat island in tropical region based on soil temperature, moisture and precipitation

METHODS

This research was conducted in Pulau Padang, a peat island located on eastern of Sumatera Island. The location of observation is a bare field that was dedicated for monitoring station, at a site of pulpwood plantation. CO_2 flux and environmental biophysics parameters were measured and monitored automatically in monitoring station. Electrical conductivity, moisture and temperature of soil were measured by using sensor Decagon 5TE. Depth of water level in peat was measured by CTD-10. Those sensors were connected to data logger (Decagon, EM50) for recording the measurements data. Data were recorded in 15 minutes interval. Weather condition was measured and monitored by using Automatic Weather Station (Davis, Vantage Pro 2). This instrument measured solar radiation, wind speed and direction, precipitation, air temperature and humidity and recorded in 15 minutes interval, too. A Licor Li-8100 Automatic Soil CO_2 Emission Measurement System (Licor, USA) was set up on bare peat in the monitoring station to measured and monitored CO_2 flux from bare peat. The system includes mechanical chamber and gas analyzer unit. This measurement system was powered by solar panel. Soil emission was measured from area that covered by mechanical chamber and the gas analyser unit controlled the movement of chamber. Measurement of CO_2 was set to be conducted hourly with 3 times replication. The hourly average CO_2 emission was obtained as average from those replications.

We proposed ANN model to predict CO_2 flux based on measurement of soil moisture and temperature and also precipitation. The ANN consists of three layers: input, hidden and output layers. Input layer has 5 nodes for inputs (covariates), hidden layer has 6 hidden nodes and CO_2 flux as a single output layer. The Sigmoid function was used as activation function in each node. Before the data were used in the calculation, the data were linearly normalized into 0 to 1 for input and 0.2 to 0.8 for output. The optimization of weights that connected between nodes in different layers was performed using the feed-forward back propagation learning method (Hecht-Nielsen, 1989). Learning rate and momentum were set equal to 0.9 and 0.8, respectively. Training process was terminated when iteration reached 10000.

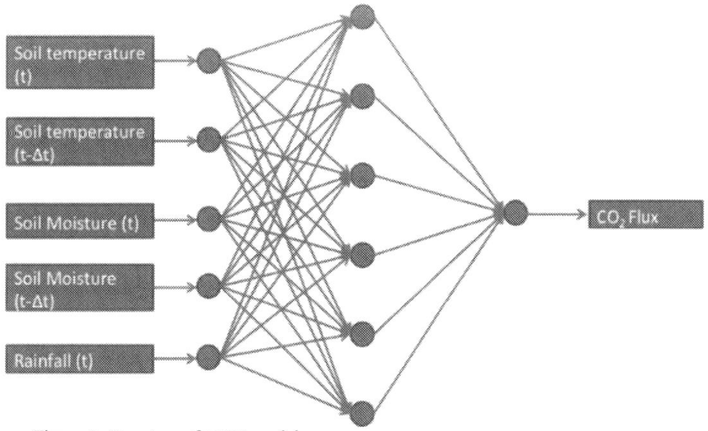

Figure 1: Structure of ANN model

RESULTS AND DISCUSSION

The ANN model shows that the CO_2 flux modeled from soil temperature, moisture and rainfall showed a good agreement with the observed values (Figure 2). The CO_2 flux model has same pattern with observed value. The shape of the curve of CO_2 emission flux following the change in soil temperature in form a sinusoidal curve which is generally highest during the day and lowest at night. CO_2 flux decreased dramatically when soil moisture increased from 0:23 became 0:28 cm^3/cm^3 volumetric water content (VWC). It caused by rain, where the soil pores filled with water so that the aeration is reduced and lowering microorganism activity. The influence of soil moisture and temperature had variability to soil respiration. Temperature affected soil respiration either as independent factor or as cofounded factors (Saiz *et al.*, 2007; Davidson *et al.*, 1998). As independent factor, soil temperature has positive correlation (R^2=0.24) and had negative correlation with soil moisture (R^2=0.09) and precipitation (R^2=0.001). Thus we applied soil moisture, temperature and precipitation as ANN model to estimate CO_2 flux. In this study, soil respiration had different rate at same temperature, thus the gradient soil moisture and temperature was applied as input parameters together with soil moisture and temperature itself.

The ANN model was trained using hourly inputs and output diurnal data. The ANN model performance between training and testing were evaluated by RMSE and R^2. Figure 3 shows that the performance of ANN model was better at training (R^2=0.71 and RMSE=0.49) compared to testing (R^2=0.5 and RMSE=0.76). The accuracy of the model at testing was lower than training because the baseline data for CO_2 flux decreased from 4.1 $mmol/m^2/s$ to 0.38 $mmol/m^2/s$. Then it resulted the model overestimated at testing.

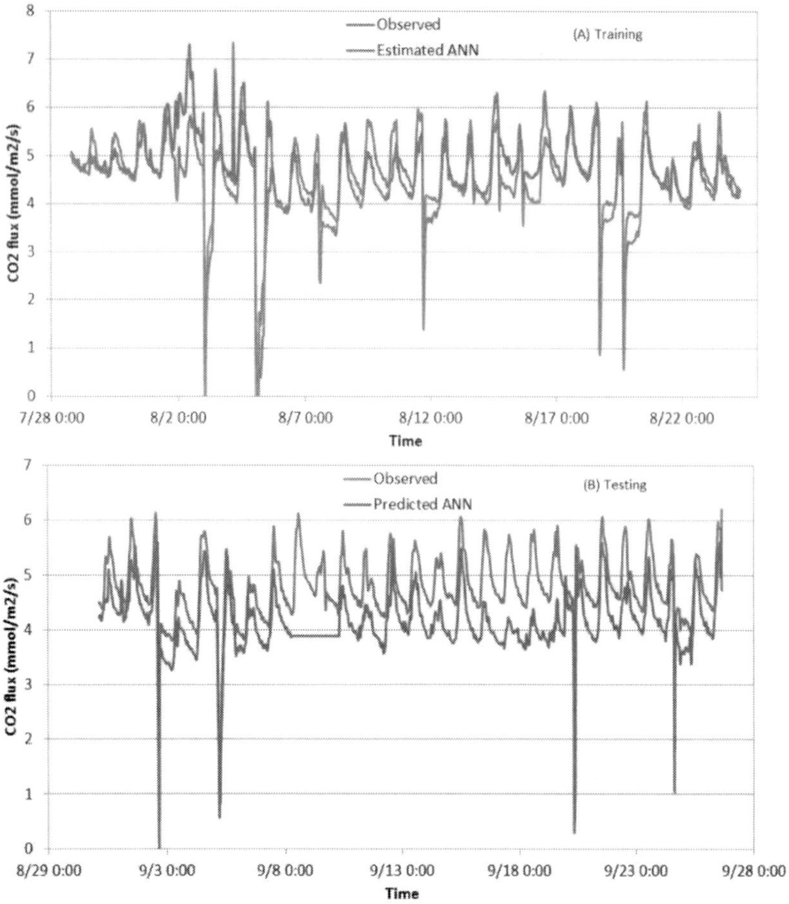

Figure 2: Predicted CO_2 flux based on ANN model for (A) training and (B) testing

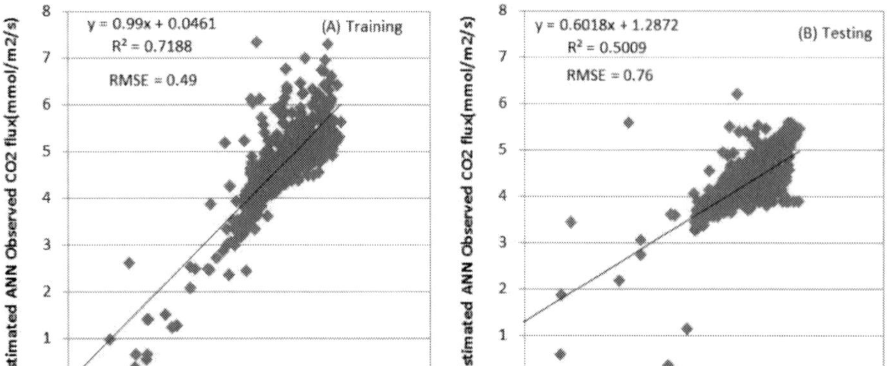

Figure 3: Agreement between observed and predicted CO_2 flux from ANN model for (A) training and (B) testing

CONCLUSION

The applicability of ANN to CO_2 flux model from environmental biophysics data was studied in range of dry condition for bare peat land. Soil moisture, temperature, precipitation and it`s gradient were used as cofounded factor for ANN model to obtain higher correlation compare to its as independent factor for CO_2 flux estimation. We proposed that this model can be used to figure out the CO_2 emission from bare land in peat island with low cost and conducted in simple measurement.

REFERENCES

1. Borken, W., Xu, Y.-J., Davidson, E.A., Beese, F., 2002. Site and Temporal Variation of Soil Respiration in European Beech, Norway Spruce, and Scots Pine Forests. Global Change Biology 8, 1205–1216.
2. Carrasco, J. J., N. C. Jason, and J. W. Harden (2006), *Modeling Physical and Biogeochemical Controls Over* Carbon *Accumulation in A Boreal Forest Soil*, Journal of Geophysical Research, 111.
3. Chadirin, Y., Saptomo, K.S., Setiawan, B.I., Osawa, K., and Novarina, D., 2015. CO_2 Emission from Bare Peat Land Using Continues Measurement. Advances in Environmental Biology, 9, 180-183
4. Daniel Epron, Yann Nouvellon, Olivier Roupsard, Welcome Mouvondy, André Mabiala, Laurent Saint-André, Richard Joffre, Christophe Jourdan, Jean-Marc Bonnefond, Paul Berbigier, Olivier Hamel, 2004. *Spatial and Temporal Variations of Soil Respiration in A Eucalyptus Plantation in Congo, Forest Ecology and Management*, 202: 1–3, 149-160.
5. Davidson, E. A., and I. A. Janssens (2006), T*emperature Sensitivity of Soil Carbon Decomposition and Feedbacks to Climate Change,* Nature, 440, 165 – 173
6. Hecht-Nielsen, R., 1989. *Theory of the Backpropagation Neural Network.* Proceedings of International Joint Conference on Neural Networks Vol 1, 593–605.
7. Hui, D., and Y. Luo (2004), *Evaluation of Soil CO_2 Production and Transport in Duke Forest Using A Process-Based* Modeling *Approach*, Global Biogeochemical Cycles, 18.
8. Lloyd, J., and J. A. Taylor. 1994. "On the Temperature Dependence of Soil Respiration". Functional Ecology 8 (3). [British Ecological Society, Wiley]: 315–23.
9. Raich, J. W., and A. Tufekcioglu (2000), *Vegetation and Soil Respiration: Correlations and Controls,* Biogeochemistry, 48, 71–90.
10. Raich, J.W., Schlesinger, W.H., 1992. *The Global Carbon Dioxide Flux in Soil Respiration and Its Relationship to Vegetation* and *Climate.* Tellus, 44B, 81–99.
11. Rustad, L. E., R. G. Huntington, and R. D. Boone (2000), *Controls on Soil Respiration: Implications for Climate* Change, Biogeochemistry, 48, 1–6.
12. Shen, W., G. D. Jenerette, D. Hui, R. P. Phillips, and H. Ren (2008), *Effects of Changing Precipitation Regimes on Dryland Soil Respiration and C Pool Dynamics at Rainfall Event, Seasonal and Interannual Scales*, Journal of Geophysical Research, 113.

Abstract No: A-118

GREENHOUSE GAS (GHG) BALANCE OF BIOMASS GROWN FOR BIOGAS PRODUCTION ON REWETTED AGRICULTURAL FEN PEATLAND

Poul Erik Lærke*, Tanka P. Kandel, Sandhya Karki and Lars Elsgaard

Aarhus University, Department of Agroecology, Blichers Allé 20, DK-8830 Tjele, Denmark

**Corresponding author: poule.laerke@agro.au.dk*

Rewetting has been recommended to reduce CO_2 emission and to restore the carbon sink function of drained peatland. Paludiculture, the combination of peatland rewetting and biomass production, has gained interest as a possible land use option without losing agricultural land. Biogas production is one possible option if grass biomass is produced in paludiculture. However, more knowledge on suitable crops and their effects on the GHG balance is needed. With intact soil cores (mesocosms) we have shown that the GHG emission from cultivation of reed canary grass (RCG) under controlled conditions can offset the GHG emission from a drained peat soil if the water table is raised close to the soil surface and at the same time produce 12 Mg ha^{-1} DM per year in two cuts. To support these findings, a new field experiment was initiated in 2015. The water levels of four plots established with RCG in 2013 on a fen peat soil were raised to soil surface by pumping water back from the ditch. Emissions of CO_2, CH_4 and N_2O were measured bi-weekly with opaque chambers and NEE of CO_2 was assessed with temperature controlled transparent chambers. Two cuts of the biomass in 2015 yielded 13.8 Mg ha^{-1} DM and the NEE from March to October 2015 showed that more than 20 Mg ha^{-1} CO_2 was taken up by the ecosystem. However, in the same period 18.8 Mg ha^{-1} CO_2 eq of CH_4 and 2.7 Mg ha^{-1} CO_2 eq of N_2O were emitted. Based on these preliminary results from the first year of rewetting we can conclude that peat degradation at this agricultural field was reversed but high emission of the stronger GHG CH_4 maintained the field as a GHG source.

Keywords: *paludiculture, wetland, methane, nitrous oxide, carbon dioxide*

Abstract No: A-273

GREENHOUSE GAS EMISSIONS FACTORS FOR DRAINED AND REWETTED BOREAL, TEMPERATE AND TROPICAL PEATLANDS

J. O. Rieley[9*], D. Wilson[1], D. Blain[2], J. Couwenberg[3], C. D. Evans[4], D. Murdiyarso[5, 6], S. E. Page[7], F. Renou-Wilson[8], A. Sirin[10], M. Strack[11] and E-S. Tuittila[12]

[1]*Earthy Matters Environmental Consultants, Donegal, Ireland*
[2]*Environment Canada, Gatineau, Canada*
[3]*University of Greifswald /Greifswald Mire Centre, Greifswald, Germany*
[4] *Centre for Ecology and Hydrology, Bangor, Wales*
[5]*Center for International Forestry Research, Bogor, Indonesia*
[6]*Bogor Agricultural University, Bogor, Indonesia*
[7]*University of Leicester, Leicester, England*
[8]*University College Dublin, Dublin, Ireland*
[9]*University of Nottingham, Nottingham, England*
[10]*Institute of Forest Science, Russian Academy of Sciences, Uspenskoe, Russia*
[11]*University of Waterloo, Ontario, Canada*
[12] *University of Eastern Finland, Joensuu, Finland*

**Corresponding author: jack.rieley@btinternet.com*

SUMMARY

Organic soils store an estimated 610 Gt of carbon (C) worldwide, an amount equivalent to >70% of the current mass of C in the atmosphere. Organic soils have been drained for forestry, crop production, grazing, water supply, peat extraction and other human-related activities and account for around 10% of all greenhouse gas (GHG) emissions from the agriculture, forestry and other land use sectors (AFOLU). In addition, drainage increases the vulnerability of organic soils to fire which can lead to considerable additional GHG emissions in all climate zones, particularly from tropical organic soils. Rewetting by blocking drainage ditches, construction of bunds or disabling drainage pump facilities can have several objectives, such as nature conservation, GHG emissions reductions, leisure activities or paludiculture. This paper describes the methods and scientific approach used in the IPCC Wetlands Supplement to derive the Tier 1 emission factors (EFs) for the full suite of GHG and waterborne C fluxes associated with rewetting of organic soils and compares these values with data published since that time.

Keywords: *Peatland, carbon dioxide, emission factors, fire, methane, nitrous oxide, peat, rewetting. IPCC*

INTRODUCTION

Drained organic soils are a significant source of greenhouse gas emissions (GHG) to the atmosphere accounting for around 10% of all GHG emissions from the agriculture, forestry and other land-use sectors (AFOLU) (Smith *et al.*, 2014). In addition, drainage increases the vulnerability of organic soils to fire (Turetsky *et al.*, 2015), which can lead to considerable additional GHG emissions, particularly from tropical organic soils (Page *et al.* 2002). Furthermore, waterborne carbon (C) losses may also be accentuated following drainage (Evans *et al.*, 2015). Rewetting of drained organic soils may reduce GHG emissions and waterborne C losses and could be included in mitigation strategies (IPCC 2014a). While emissions from some drained organic soils are reported annually by Annex 1 countries under the UNFCCC Kyoto Protocol, emissions or removals (i.e. C uptake) from rewetted organic soils have not been included thus far owing to an absence of data and a lack of methodological guidance. The IPCC 2013 Wetlands Supplement provides methodological guidance for countries to report GHG emissions/removals from the rewetting of organic soils in their national inventory submissions. This paper expands on the work related to rewetted organic soils. We examine the robustness of the emission factors by comparing the Tier 1 values in the Wetlands Supplement with data published since that time.

METHODS

While the C contained in the woody biomass pool may be substantial in treed peatlands, particularly in the tropics, it is outside the scope of this paper and readers are directed to methodologies contained in the 2006 IPCC Guidelines (IPCC 2006. In organic soils C fluxes are generally small relative to the total stock and are problematic to measure in a stock based approach. Therefore, net CO_2 emissions or removals from organic soils are more accurately measured directly as a flux. Emissions (and removals) of the other main GHGs in the land use sector; CH_4 and N_2O, are commonly approached as fluxes. These are here denoted as CO_2-C and CH_4-C and N_2O-N to be consistent with those used in the 2006 IPCC Guidelines. The net C stock change of rewetted organic soils results from net gains or losses of C resulting from the balance between CO_2 and CH_4 emissions /removals and includes both on- and off-site components (Eq.1).

$$\Delta C_{rewetted\ org\ soil} = CO_2\text{-}C_{rewetted\ org\ soil} + CH_4\text{-}C_{rewetted\ org\ soil} \qquad \textbf{Eq. 1}$$

CO_2 EMISSIONS/REMOVALS FROM REWETTED ORGANIC SOILS

In organic soils, it is difficult to distinguish between the different C pools[9]. Living non-woody biomass (mosses, sedges, grasses) can be hard to separate from the dead litter derived from it, and the litter can be hard to separate from the (organic) soil. The default emission factors presented in this presentation are all derived from published direct flux measurements (eddy covariance (EC) towers and/or static chambers) over organic soils with moss and/or herbaceous and/or dwarf shrub vegetation (in tropical peatland EC towers are over and under forest canopy or on other land uses). Whereas some publications attempt to assess changes in the above ground biomass pool separate from the other pools, most combine all pools together. Therefore, we defined the term $CO_2\text{-}C_{composite}$ in Eq. 2, which integrates all CO_2 fluxes from the soil and the above- and belowground vegetation components other than trees.

$$CO_2\text{-}C_{rewetted\ org\ soil} = CO_2\text{-}C_{composite} + CO_2\text{-}C_{DOC} + CO_2\text{-}\ C_{fire} \qquad \textbf{Eq. 2}$$

CH_4 EMISSIONS/REMOVALS FROM REWETTED ORGANIC SOILS

Methane (CH_4) emissions/removals from rewetted organic soils result from (a) the balance between biochemical CH_4 production and oxidation and (b) emissions of CH_4 produced by the combustion of soil organic matter during fire (Eq. 3).

$$CH_4\text{-}C_{rewetted\ org\ soil} = CH_4\text{-}C_{composite} + CH_4\text{-}C_{fire} \qquad \textbf{Eq. 3}$$

The probability of fire occurrence in rewetted organic soils is likely to be low if the water table position is near the surface, although possible soil emissions from fires are included in Eq. 3 for completeness.

N_2O EMISSIONS FROM REWETTED ORGANIC SOILS

The emissions of N_2O from rewetted organic soils are controlled by the quantity of nitrogen available for nitrification and denitrification, and the redox potential.

$$N_2O_{rewetted\ org\ soil}\text{-}N = N_2O\text{-}N_{composite} + N_2O\text{-}N_{fire} \qquad \textbf{Eq. 4}$$

Published data are currently insufficient to develop default N_2O emission factors for the burning of organic soils (see Chapter 2, IPCC 2014a), therefore $N_2O\text{-}N_{fire}$ of Eq. 4 is not considered further here.

DERIVATION OF EMISSION FACTORS

An extensive literature review was conducted to collate all GHG (CO_2, CH_4, N_2O) and DOC studies that were available at the time the Wetlands Supplement was prepared (i.e. 2013) for (1) rewetted organic soils (includes rewetted, restored and wet managed sites) and (2) natural/undrained organic soils (to be used as a proxy for rewetted soils, see criteria below). No studies exist on rewetted tropical sites with the water table close to the surface. A detailed database of annual GHG fluxes was then constructed to evaluate the main drivers of GHG dynamics in rewetted organic soils. When available, the following parameters were extracted from the literature source and included in the database for analysis: climate zone as defined by IPCC (2006), nutrient status, mean water table level (*MWTL*), median water table level (as well as minimum and maximum values), soil pH, thickness of the organic soil layer, C/N ratio, degree of humification, soil moisture, soil bulk density, plant cover and species or functional groups, previous land use and time since rewetting. However, non-annualized CH_4 flux values were used for tropical sites as annual data from those sites are scarce and seasonality is either absent or relates to a wet and dry season only.

[9] The six pools in AFOLU are (1) aboveground biomass, (2) belowground biomass, (3) dead wood, (4) litter, (5) soil and (6) harvested wood products

DATA TREATMENT

In the database, flux values were standardised to the following units; t CO_2- C ha^{-1} yr^{-1}, kg CH_4-C ha^{-1} yr^{-1} and t C ha^{-1} yr^{-1} (for DOC). For multi-year studies from the same site, annual flux estimates were averaged over the years. Emission factors (t C ha^{-1} yr^{-1}) were calculated as flux means, with 95% confidence intervals calculated for each of the categories.

COMPARISON WITH DRAINED ORGANIC SOILS

In order to assess the impact of rewetting on GHG dynamics in organic soils, the emission factors derived in Chapter 2, IPCC Wetlands Supplement (IPCC 2014a) for drained land use categories were compared to the emission factors derived here for their rewetted counterparts. The net GHG emissions, based on the global warming potential (GWP; t CO_2-eq ha^{-1} yr^{-1}) of each gas, for the land use categories under drained and rewetted conditions were calculated. CH_4 and N_2O fluxes were converted to CO_2 equivalents according to their GWP on a 100-year timescale including climate–carbon feedbacks: CH_4 = 34 and N_2O = 298.

RESULTS

Data entries for CO_2 and CH_4 were relatively evenly spread between the boreal and temperate zones, while no CO_2 entries and only a small number of CH_4 entries (11) were recorded for the tropical zone. N_2O entries were mainly found in the temperate and boreal zones, while DOC entries were found for all three climate zones. In most cases, the data could be further disaggregated by nutrient status (i.e. nutrient poor (bog), nutrient rich (fen)), with the exception of tropical data, and DOC entries.

Undrained Sites as Proxies

The relationship between *MWTL* and CO_2/CH_4 fluxes was very similar for undrained and rewetted sites in the boreal and temperate climate zones and we concluded that undrained sites can, for the purposes of emission factor calculations, act as proxies for rewetted sites with the same mean *MWTL*, and hereafter we combined the two datasets. Moreover, we also used tropical undrained organic soils as a proxy for tropical rewetted organic soils for the derivation of CH_4 and N_2O emission factors.

Emissions Factors

CO_2-$C_{composite}$

The CO_2-$C_{composite}$ values varied considerably across climate zones and nutrient status. Boreal nutrient rich sites showed the highest annual CO_2 removals at 0.55 tonnes C ha^{-1} yr^{-1} and temperate nutrient rich sites showed the highest annual emissions at 0.50 tonnes C ha^{-1} yr^{-1}. Boreal and temperate nutrient poor sites showed CO_2 removal values of 0.34 and 0.24 tonnes C ha^{-1} yr^{-1} respectively. Uncertainty with the CO_2-$C_{composite}$ values was lowest for boreal nutrient rich sites (±40%) and highest in the temperate nutrient rich sites (±242%).

CH_4-$C_{composite}$

The lowest emissions were observed in the boreal nutrient poor and tropical sites (41 kg CH_4-C ha^{-1} yr^{-1}) and the highest emissions were seen in the temperate nutrient rich sites (216 kg CH_4-C ha^{-1} yr^{-1}). Associated uncertainty was very high across all groups.

CO_2-C_{DOC}

Most data on DOC processing indicate that a high proportion is converted to CO_2 in headwaters, rivers, lakes and coastal seas. A value of 0.9 is proposed for $Frac_{DOC\_CO2}$ with an uncertainty range of 0.8 to 1 (IPCC 2014, Evans *et al.*, 2015).This resulted in CO_2-C_{DOC} values of 0.08, 0.24 and 0.51 tonnes C ha^{-1} yr^{-1} for the boreal, temperate and tropical zones, respectively.

N_2O-$N_{composite}$

As the sample sizes were low, it was not possible to derive a robust N_2O-$N_{composite}$ value disaggregated by nutrient status. Values for the boreal and temperate zones were very similar (0.06-0.07 kg N ha^{-1} yr^{-1}). Average emissions from the tropical zone were higher at 0.94 kg N ha^{-1} yr^{-1} but displayed very high uncertainty owing to the very small sample size (n=5) and the inclusion of a single high data point (Melling *et al.*, 2007).

Comparison with Drained Organic Soils

CO_2 emissions decreased considerably following rewetting of drained organic soils. In contrast, CH_4 emissions were much higher following rewetting and were also characterised by very high variability. N_2O emissions were considerably reduced following rewetting.

DISCUSSION

With the exception of temperate nutrient rich organic soils, all rewetted organic soils were estimated to be net CO_2 sinks, although the inclusion of the most recent data suggests that CO_2 emissions from temperate nutrient rich soils may be much lower than those derived from the original dataset, with many studies indicating a net CO_2 sink. Data on net CO_2 fluxes from successfully rewetted tropical organic soils are completely lacking, and data on the CO_2 balance of undrained tropical organic soils are also scarce. Although C accumulation data for undrained tropical peatlands indicate a net-sink, the re-establishment of such a sink after rewetting may present a considerable challenge. As such, the default emission factor of 0 t CO_2-C ha^{-1} yr^{-1} probably applies to best case rewetting scenarios only.

The removals of CO_2 in rewetted organic soils are in sharp contrast to the high emissions associated with drained organic soils. Moreover, our derived values for DOC losses are lower than those reported for drained organic soils (Evans *et al.*, 2015). In addition, N_2O emissions in rewetted soils were very low across all climate zones, although rewetting does result in strongly increased CH_4 emissions following the reversal of drainage. However, rewetting in general represents a significant climate change mitigation action as a result of (a) the considerable decrease in CO_2 emissions and (b) the accompanying reduction of N_2O emissions (with its high global warming potential) relative to drained organic soils.

UNCERTAINTIES

Considerable uncertainty is attached to individual data points used in the derivation of the emission factors as most of the studies in the database are generally of a short duration (1-2 years) and do not take into account the longer-term natural variation, a feature captured in long-term datasets. The large uncertainties associated with the derived emission factors indicate that individual rewetted and undrained sites may differ considerably in terms of their current abiotic and biotic conditions and resulting vegetation cover.

REFINEMENT OF EMISSION FACTORS

GHG fluxes in rewetted organic soils are controlled by a wide range of external and internal factors, which include the prevailing climate, nutrient status, water table position, previous land use history, time since rewetting, absence or presence of vegetation and vegetation composition. However, in seeking to determine the overarching driver(s) of GHG exchange for rewetted organic soils, the exercise here was constrained by the quantity of available data for rewetted sites and by the quality of ancillary data in published studies.

Time since rewetting

Available datasets from rewetted organic soils generally cover a period of 10 years or less after rewetting and for this reason it is difficult to identify clear temporal patterns in GHG fluxes and determine with accuracy the transition time required to fully capture the changes following rewetting (Wilson *et al.*, 2013).

Vegetation composition

Numerous studies have indicated the important role of vegetation in the regulation of GHG fluxes in both undrained and rewetted organic soils. The presence of aerenchymous shunt species, for example, has a significant effect on CH_4 efflux from organic soils (Levy *et al.*, 2012).

Water table levels

The relationship between water table and CO_2/CH_4 emissions/removals was evident in this study. As the water table is one of the main controls on GHG cycling, future emission factors (i.e. country specific) could be derived and disaggregated by water table level provided sufficient ancillary data are available. Drainage ditches have been shown to be "hotspots" of CH_4 emissions within the wider drained landscape (Cooper *et al.*, 2014) but few data are available on CH_4 emissions from ditches that remain after rewetting or that are filled in during rewetting activities.

INFORMATION GAPS AND ONGOING ISSUES

While the number of GHG studies on organic soils has steadily increased over the last few decades this work has highlighted the existence of some research gaps, in particular the paucity of GHG data from the tropical climate zones, as well as specific issues associated with rewetting.

Tropical data

Rewetting as a management practice is in its infancy in the tropics and there are no published flux measurement data from successfully rewetted tropical organic soils from which to derive emission factors. Therefore, a default emission factor for rewetted tropical organic soils was developed based on surrogate data. If the peat becomes persistently waterlogged, CO_2 fluxes should be near zero from a biochemical perspective. However, it is much more difficult to rewet tropical peat and maintain a stable water table than boreal and temperate peat soils given that the hydraulic conductivity of tropical peat is extremely high (Page *et al.*, 2008). Furthermore, there is also a tendency to flooding during the wet season and near drought in severe dry periods, such as in El Niño years. Moreover, several studies in Southeast Asia have indicated that there could still be sizeable C emissions from former agricultural lands even if these were essentially wet (Hooijer *et al.*, 2012, Jauhiainen *et al.*, 2012) and it could take some considerable time for ecosystem C dynamics to approach those typical of undrained organic soils. Additional research on rewetting techniques and associated GHG fluxes will be needed as a basis for higher tier emission factors. Furthermore, reliable data on GHG fluxes from organic soils in Africa, the tropical Americas or other tropical regions outside Southeast Asia are very rare and virtually nothing is known about the effects of rewetting.

Fire

Due to high moisture contents, organic soils in intact ecosystems are protected to some degree from burning (Turetsky *et al.*, 2015), although fires do occur on undrained organic soils. It can be assumed that the probability of fire occurrence in rewetted organic soils is likely to be small if the water table position is maintained at or near the surface, although there may still be a major risk of fire affecting trees in tropical regions where the temperature is high, even if the water table is near the peat surface.

Waterborne pathways

An understanding of the fate of DOC leaked from organic soils is still poor. Large parts are returned to the atmosphere as CO_2 (or CH_4) or transferred to long-term C stores, such as the deep ocean or marine sediments (Abrams *et al.*, 2016) and the use of alternative values for the conversion factor $Frac_{DOC\_CO2}$ (where sufficient evidence is available) may be more appropriate.

CONCLUSION

Rewetting of organic soils results in a decrease in CO_2 and N_2O emissions, DOC losses and GHG emissions based on the global warming potential but also leads to an increase in CH_4 emissions. However, the GHG emission factor estimates derived in this paper are subject to uncertainty as a consequence of the lack of data for some climate zones and land use categories, and the wide variation in GHG emissions/removals inherent with organic soils in general. Future research should focus on the information gaps that have been highlighted here, with particular emphases given to determining the transient period following rewetting, reducing uncertainty through the derivation of country specific emission factors and, perhaps most critically given the high emissions associated with drainage, the quantification of GHG emissions/removals in rewetted tropical organic soils.

REFERENCES

1. Abrams, J. F., Hohn, S., Rixen, T., Baum, A. & Merico, A. (2016) The impact of Indonesian peatland degradation on downstream marine ecosystems and the global carbon cycle. *Global Change Biology,* 22(1): 325-337.
2. Cooper, M. D. A., Evans, C. D., Zielinski, P., Levy, P. E., Gray, A., Peacock, M., Norris, D., Fenner, N. & Freeman, C. (2014) Infilled Ditches are Hotspots of Landscape Methane Flux Following Peatland Re-wetting. *Ecosystems*: 1-15.
3. Evans, C., Renou-Wilson, F. & Strack, M. (2015) The role of waterborne carbon in the greenhouse gas balance of drained and re-wetted peatlands. *Aquatic Sciences*: doi:10.1007/s00027-015-0447-y.
4. Hooijer, A., Page, S., Jauhiainen, J., Lee, W. A., Lu, X. X., Idris, A. & Anshari, C. (2012) Subsidence and carbon loss in drained tropical peatlands. *Biogeosciences,* 9: 1053-1071.

5. IPCC. (2006) *IPCC Guidelines for National Greenhouse Gas Inventories. Prepared by the National Greenhouse Gas Inventories programme*. Eggleston H. S., Buendia L., Miwa K., *et al.*, IGES, Japan.
6. IPCC. (2014a) *2013 Supplement to the 2006 Inter-Governmental Panel on Climate Change Guidelines for National Greenhouse Gas Inventories: Wetlands*. IPCC, Switzerland.
7. Jauhiainen, J., Hooijer, A. & Page, S. E. (2012) Carbon dioxide emissions from an Acacia plantation on peatland in Sumatra, Indonesia. *Biogeosciences,* 9(2): 617-630.
8. Levy, P. E., Burden, A., Cooper, M. D. A., Dinsmore, K. J., Drewer, J., Evans, C., Fowler, D., Gaiawyn, J., Gray, A., Jones, S. K., Jones, T., McNamara, N. P., Mills, R., Ostle, N., Sheppard, L. J., Skiba, U., Sowerby, A., Ward, S. E. & Zieliński, P. (2012) Methane emissions from soils: synthesis and analysis of a large UK data set. *Global Change Biology,* 18(5): 1657-1669.
9. Page, S. E., Siegert, F., Rieley, J. O., Boehm, H.-D. V., Jaya, A. & Limin, S. (2002) The amount of carbon released from peat and forest fires in Indonesia during 1997. *Nature,* 420: 61-65.
10. Page, S., Hoscilo, A., Wösten, H., Jauhiainen, J., Silvius, M., Rieley, J., Ritzema, H., Tansey, K., Graham, L., Vasander, H. & Limin, S. (2008) Restoration Ecology of Lowland Tropical Peatlands in Southeast Asia: Current Knowledge and Future Research Directions. *Ecosystems,* 12(6): 888-905.
11. Smith, P., Bustamante, M., Ahammad, H., Clark, H., Dong, H., Elsiddig, E. A., Haberl, H., Harper, R., House, J., Jafari, M., Masera, O., Mbow, C., Ravindranath, N. H., Rice, C. W., Robledo Abad, C., Romanovskaya, A., Sperling, F. & Tubiello, F. (2014) Agriculture, Forestry and Other Land Use (AFOLU). In: Edenhofer O., Pichs-Madruga R., Sokona Y., *et al.* (eds.), *Climate Change 2014: Mitigation of Climate Change. Contribution of Working Group III to the Fifth Assessment Report of the Intergovernmental Panel on Climate Change*. Cambridge University Press, Cambridge, United Kingdom and New York, NY, USA, pp. 811-922.
12. Turetsky, M. R., Benscoter, B., Page, S., Rein, G., van der Werf, G. R. & Watts, A. (2015) Global vulnerability of peatlands to fire and carbon loss. *Nature Geoscience,* 8(1): 11-14.

Abstract No: A-123

ROOT EXUDATES AND CARBON EMISSIONS FROM TROPICAL PEATLANDS

Nicholas T. Girkin[1], Nick Ostle[2], Benjamin L. Turner[3] and Sofie Sjogersten[1]

[1]*School of Biosciences, University of Nottingham, Nottingham, UK*
[2]*Lancaster Environment Centre, Lancaster University, Lancaster UK*
[3]*Smithsonian Tropical Research Institute, Ancon, Republic of Panama*

SUMMARY

Plant root exudates represent a large, labile carbon (C) input to tropical peatlands, but their contribution to methane (CH_4) and carbon dioxide (CO_2) emissions remain poorly understood. Peat under two contrasting vegetation types, the palm *Raphia taedigera* and the broadleaf evergreen tree *Campnosperma panamensis*, from a coastal peatland in Panama, were incubated anaerobically and received daily C additions for two weeks. C was added as a combination of three sugars or four organic acids, with the effects on CH_4 and CO_2 production measured over 40 days. C additions significantly increased CH_4 and CO_2 production under both vegetation types, although emissions were significantly greater under palms. Addition of organic acids was also associated with increases in pH and dehydrogenase activity, likely due to changes in microbial populations. Taken together, these results indicate that regular additions of root exudates are associated with increased fluxes and microbial activity, depending on composition, may enhance C mineralisation.

Keywords: *Methane, root exudates, tropical, wetland*

INTRODUCTION

Tropical forested peatlands are a globally important C store that is under significant threat from climate and land use changes (Page *et al.*, 2011). While it is known that CH_4 and CO_2 fluxes can differ significantly between different vegetation types (Wright *et al.*, 2013), the mechanisms responsible for these differences remain poorly understood.

Plants can release significant quantities of photosynthetically derived C into the rhizosphere as root exudates, which play an important role in regulating plant–microbial interactions (Shi *et al.*, 2011). Exudates consist primarily of sugars, organic acids, and amino acids (Walker *et al.*, 2003). Root exudates contain low concentrations of C compared to inputs from decaying plant material, but their labile nature means that they are rapidly utilised by the microbial community (Kuzyakov and Domanski, 2000).

While sugars are generally considered to be the dominant exudate in grasslands and agricultural systems, low molecular weight organic acids are more significant components of forest soil profiles, often present at two to three times the concentration of sugars (Smith, 1976, Grayston and Campbell, 1996, Shi *et al.*, 2011). However, most studies of root exudates have been conducted on agricultural plants such as maize (Baudoin *et al.*, 2003, Henry *et al.*, 2008) or wheat ((Kuzyakov and Cheng, 2001), within grasslands (Fu and Cheng, 2002, Bird *et al.*, 2011) or in temperate or boreal forest species (Fox and Comerford, 1990, Shi *et al.*, 2011). Few studies have examined tropical forests or peatlands.

We carried out an anaerobic incubation study of tropical peats from two contrasting plant successional communities dominated by the palm *R. taedigera* and a broadleaf evergreen tree, *C. panamensis*. After two weeks incubation at 30°C, peats were treated with a combination of three sugars (glucose, fructose and sucrose) and four organic acids (acetic acid, formic acid, malic acid and oxalic acid) for two weeks. We quantified total CH_4 and CO_2 production and changes to pH and microbial dehydrogenase activity.

METHODS

Subsurface peat samples were collected from Bahia Almirante (09° 18' 13.00"N, 82° 21' 13.80"W) from a mixed forest stand located 600 m from the coast. Samples were collected under three *C. panamensis* trees and three *R. taedigera* palms within 0.5 m of the nearest tree. 7.5g of dry weight equivalent soil were water saturated and sealed in 48 replicate 120 mL glass serum bottles after flushing with N_2 to generate anaerobic conditions. Microcosms were incubated at 30°C for two weeks prior to the first addition of root exudate compound solutions to allow the establishment of the microbial communities.

In the absence of root exudate profiles for *R. taedigera* and *C. panamensis*, the selection of substrates was based on several criteria. Across all ecosystems fructose, glucose and sucrose have consistently been identified as the most abundant sugars in root exudates (Smith, 1976, Jones, 1998, Shi *et al.*, 2011) Acetic acid is the most important substrate for methanogenesis in peatlands (Ferry, 1992, Lloyd *et al.*, 1998). Previous incubation experiments have highlighted that malic acid can have a significant priming effect on CO_2 fluxes (Chowdhury *et al.*, 2014). Furthermore, malic acid, alongside oxalic acid, was amongst the most commonly occurring organic acids in the root exudates of several forest species (Smith, 1976; Grayston and Campbell, 1996, Jones, 1998, Strobel, 2001). Formic acid has previously been detected in high concentrations in forest soils (Fox and Comerford, 1990) and is also an additional substrate for methanogenesis in peat (Ferry, 1992).

Sugars and organic acids were added in combination over a 14 day period at concentrations of 0.1 mg, 0.2 mg, and 0.3 mg C g^{-1} day^{-1} dissolved in 1 mL deionised water. Additions at these concentrations closely match rates reported previously and mimic the gradual release of exudates over time (Baudoin *et al.*, 2003, Henry *et al.*, 2008).

Sugar additions consisted of a C input of 0.1 mg g^{-1} dry soil day^{-1} of equal quantities of fructose, glucose and sucrose. Organic acid additions (AFMO) comprised a C input of 0.2 mg g^{-1} dry soil day^{-1} of acetic, formic, malic and oxalic acids. Combined sugars and organic acids (SAFMO), sugar and acetic acid (SA), sugar and formic acid (SF), sugar and malic acid (SM), and sugar and oxalic acid (SO) were added at a C input of 0.3 mg g^{-1} dry soil day^{-1}, with sugars comprising 0.1 mg and organic acids comprising 0.2 mg. A 2:1 ratio of organic acids to sugars matched reported ratios in forest exudate profiles (Smith, 1976, Grayston and Campbell, 1996, Shi *et al.*, 2011).

C additions began 14 days after the preparation of the microcosms to establish background rates. Headspace gas samples were collected weekly and analysed by gas chromatography. The potential rate of gas production, expressed as µg CO_2 g^{-1} or µg CH_4 g^{-1}, was calculated assuming the linear accumulation of gases in the headspace over time (Hogg *et al.*, 1992).

Soil pH and dehydrogenase activity were measured after 14 days (prior to treatment) and after 40 days at the conclusion of the experiment. Dehydrogenase activity, one of the principle components of soil enzymatic activities was assessed using the reduction of 2,3,5-triphenyltetrazolium chloride to triphenylformazan (Ohlinger, 1995) and was used as an indicator of microbial populations and activity. Analysis of variance was performed using the Residual Maximum Likelihood method (REML) in GenStat (v15.1.). Rates of CH_4 and CO_2 were logged to comply with the requirements of REML. Differences in dehydrogenase activity and pH were analysed by two-way ANOVA.

RESULTS

For both *R. taedigera* and *C. panamensis*, the addition of sugars and organic acids significantly enhanced CH_4 production ($p < 0.05$) (Figure 1A). The greatest cumulative CH_4 fluxes for *R. taedigera* were recorded under SAFMO treatment with an increase of 243.8% to 1075.1 µg CH_4 g^{-1} compared to the control.In contrast under *C. panamensis* the maximum measured CH_4 fluxes were recorded under AFMO treatment, an increase of 139.24% to 748.2 µg CH_4 g^{-1} compared to the control. SO and SF treatments showed a decrease in CH_4 flux of 19.8% and -47.9% under *R. taedigera*, but under *C. panamensis* only SF caused an inhibitory effect (-26.6%). Only the inhibitory effect from the SF treatment was found to be significant ($p > 0.05$). There was a significant difference in cumulative CH_4 fluxes between *R. taedigera* and *C. panamensis*, with mean fluxes higher under *R. taedigera* ($p < 0.05$).

All sugar and organic acid additions significantly enhanced CO_2 compared to the control ($p < 0.05$) (Figure 1B). The greatest flux for *R. taedigera* was associated with SAFMO addition, with an increase of 434.4% to 3212.7 µg CO_2 g^{-1}. For *C. panamensis* the greatest flux was recorded for SO addition with a 566.3% increase to 3304.8 µg CO_2 g^{-1}. There was no significant difference between these treatments. In contrast to results for CH_4 fluxes, SF treatments significantly enhanced CO_2 fluxes compared to the control. There was a significant difference in cumulative CO_2 fluxes between *R. taedigera* and *C. panamensis*, with mean fluxes higher under *R. taedigera* ($p < 0.05$).

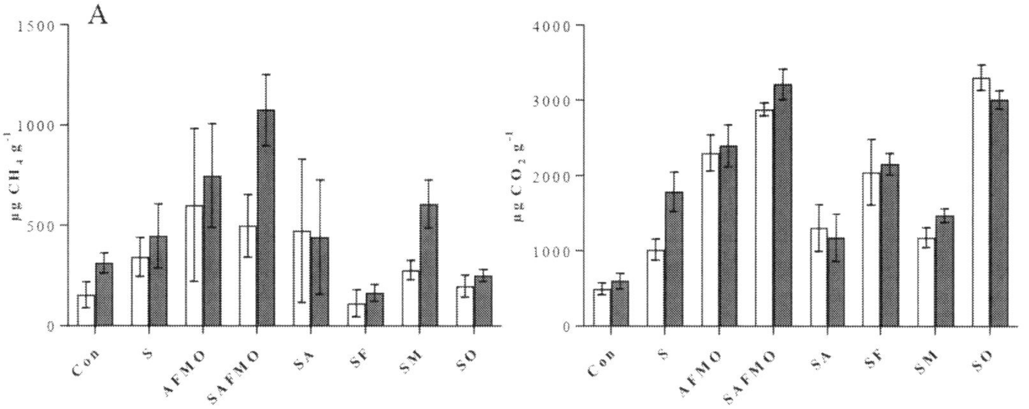

Figure 1: A.Total CH_4 production for *C. panamensis* (white) and *R. taedigera* (grey) after 40 days. B. Total CO_2 production for *C. panamensis* (white) and *R. taedigera* (grey) after 40 days. Con = Control, S = sugars, AFMO = organic acids, SAFMO = sugars + organic acids, SA = sugars + acetic acid, SF = sugars + formic acid, SM = sugars + malic acid, SO = sugars + oxalic acid. Error bars equal 1 SEM.

There was no significant difference in peat dehydrogenase activity after 14 days, prior to root exudate addition ($p > 0.05$). At the conclusion of the experiment sugar and SM additions did not significantly increase dehydrogenase activity compared to the control ($p > 0.05$). All other treatments significantly enhanced dehydrogenase activity ($p < 0.05$) (Figure 2A). There was no significant difference in dehydrogenase activity between *R. taedigera* and *C. panamensis*, although mean activity was greatest under *R. taedigera* ($p > 0.05$). Greatest dehydrogenase activity was measured under SF for both *R. taedigera* (1345.0 mg TPF g^{-1} h^{-1}) and *C. panamensis* (1097.0 mg TPF g^{-1} h^{-1}).

All additions affected soil pH: sugar addition significantly decreased pH from 5.3 to 4.5 ($p < 0.05$) (Figure 2B). SM additions also lowered pH to 4.9 but not significantly ($p < 0.05$). All other treatments significantly increased pH, with the greatest increase occurring under SO additions, to pH 7.4 ($p < 0.05$). Soil pH was greater under *R. taedigera* but did not differ significantly from *C. panamensis* ($p > 0.05$).

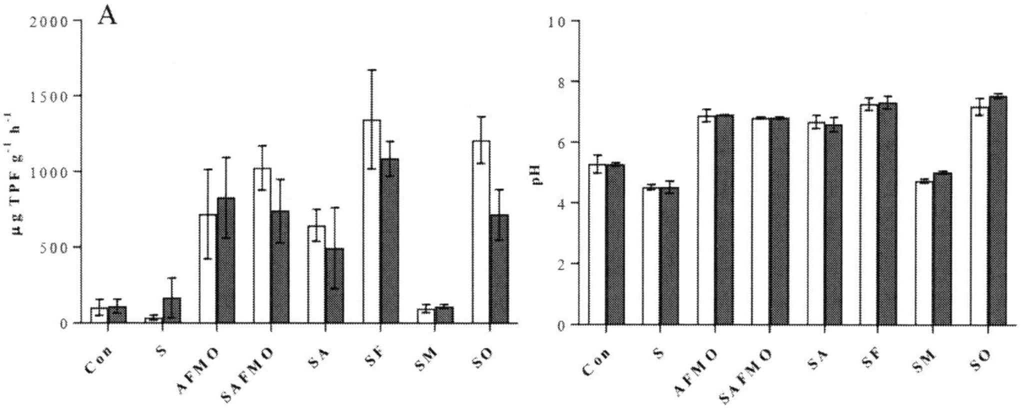

Figure 2: A. Dehydrogenase activity, B. pH. *C. panamensis* (white) and *R. taedigera* (grey) after 40 days. Con = Control, S = sugars, AFMO = organic acids, SAFMO = sugars + organic acids, SA = sugars + acetic acid, SF = sugars + formic acid, SM = sugars + malic acid, SO = sugars + oxalic acid. Error bars equal 1 SEM.

DISCUSSION

Differences in *in situ* surface CH_4 and CO_2 fluxes between *R. taedigera* and *C. panamensis* may be associated with the different decomposition rates previously reported for peats formed from both species (Wright *et al.*, 2013). *R. taedigera* surface litter decomposes more rapidly than *C. panamensis* litter, although the effect varies with depth and plant tissue (Hoyos-Santillan *et al.*, 2015). The extent of the response differed between peat types: the same addition of 0.1 mg C per day of sugars elicited a greater increase in CH_4 production from *C. panamensis* of 122.3% compared to 43.0% for *R. taedigera*. Responses of this nature have previously been reported when labile C was added to bulk soil and the rhizosphere, with differences ascribed to differing bacterial communities (Baudoin *et al.*, 2003).

Despite being identified as the most significant substrate for methanogenesis in peatlands, after 40 days CH_4 and CO_2 production under SA addition did not differ significantly from sugar addition alone, despite the total C input being higher (0.3 mg C g^{-1} day^{-1} compared to 0.1 mg C g^{-1} day^{-1}). Previously the addition of acetic acid alone has been found to trigger greater peat mineralisation than the addition of the same concentration of glucose or fructose (Hamer and Marschner, 2002).

SF and SO additions were found to have an inhibitory effect only on CH_4 production but not on CO_2 production. In the case of SO, this effect was only observed for *R. taedigera*. Organic acid additions have previously been reported to have an inhibitory effect, with negative responses observed in changes to bacterial taxa diversity and abundance (Shi *et al.*, 2011). This effect may be driven by the direct inhibition of microbial activity through the presence of specific organic acids. Alternatively the SA, SF and SO responses may arise through a competition effect, with taxa that utilise organic acids as a C source being outcompeted by other more rapidly growing microorganisms that are better able to respond to changes in environmental conditions, such as the increase in soil pH (Figure 2b) (Paterson *et al.*, 2007).

Differences in hydrolytic enzymatic activity have previously been reported along a plant successional gradient that included *R. taedigera* and *C. panamensis* in Bocas del Toro (Sjogersten, 2010) but no significant difference were observed on this occasion between species. Sugar addition did not significantly increase dehydrogenase activity compared to the control despite being associated with significant increases in CH_4 and CO_2 production. This may be because sugars are more readily utilised than organic acids and thus their effects are seen more quickly, with enzyme activity only being measured after the activity in sugar treated peats had declined: in an arable ecosystem, sugar and amino acid amendments triggered the activation of the soil microbial communities in less than a minute (Jones and Murphy, 2007). It is likely that sugar treatments induced fewer changes in the microbial community than organic acids as the latter stimulated a reduced group of specialised microorganisms (Landi *et al.*, 2006). Sugar additions have previously been found to increase dehydrogenase activity when added at the same concentration (Shi *et al.*, 2011), although this difference may be because activity was measured two weeks after the last addition of root exudates by which time changes in dehydrogenase activity stimulated by sugars may have declined.

All organic acid additions, with the exception of SM, increased pH significantly compared to the control. The lower dehydrogenase activity recorded for SM may be associated with the lower pH (Trevors, 1984). Increases in pH have previously been reported after organic acid additions, and such changes have been associated with significant shifts in microbial communities (Shi *et al.*, 2011) and increases in CH_4 (Wang *et al.*, 1993) and CO_2 production (Yan *et al.*, 1996). However, pH and dehydrogenase activity were not found to be significant determining factors for CH_4 and CO_2 production ($p > 0.05$).

CONCLUSIONS

Peats from contrasting vegetation types differ significantly in their responses to labile C addition. Greater increases in CH_4 and CO_2 fluxes were measured from soils under *R. taedigera* compared to *C. panamensis*. These differences are of significance due to the continued conversion of many peatlands to oil pal plantations. This is likely to be because of the different composition of the peat types and differences in the initial microbial communities (Hoyos-Santillan *et al.*, 2015). While low C concentration sugar additions were associated with greater CH_4 and CO_2 fluxes than some higher C organic acid treatments, enzyme activity and pH were generally higher under organic acid addition. This is likely to be associated with longer term changes in microbial composition and may lead to later increases in fluxes through increased C mineralisation.

ACKNOWLEDGEMENTS

This research was funded by a NERC ENVISION DTP grant. We thank Eric Brown for field assistance and the staff at the Smithsonian Tropical Research Institute in Bocas del Toro for logistical support.

REFERENCES

1. BAUDOIN, E., BENIZRI, E. & GUCKERT, A. 2003. Impact of artificial root exudates on the bacterial community structure in bulk soil and maize rhizosphere. *Soil Biology & Biochemistry,* 35, 1183-1192.
2. BIRD, J. A., HERMAN, D. J. & FIRESTONE, M. K. 2011. Rhizosphere priming of soil organic matter by bacterial groups in a grassland soil. *Soil Biology & Biochemistry,* 43, 718-725.
3. CHOWDHURY, S., FARRELL, M. & BOLAN, N. 2014. Priming of soil organic carbon by malic acid addition is differentially affected by nutrient availability. *Soil Biology & Biochemistry,* 77, 158-169.
4. FERRY, J. G. 1992. Methane from Acetate. *Journal of Bacteriology,* 174, 5489-5495.
5. FOX, T. R. & COMERFORD, N. B. 1990. Low-Molecular-Weight Organic-Acids in Selected Forest Soils of the Southeastern USA. *Soil Science Society of America Journal,* 54, 1139-1144.
6. FU, S. L. & CHENG, W. X. 2002. Rhizosphere priming effects on the decomposition of soil organic matter in C-4 and C-3 grassland soils. *Plant and Soil,* 238, 289-294.

7. GRAYSTON, S. J. & CAMPBELL, C. D. 1996. Functional biodiversity of microbial communities in the rhizospheres of hybrid larch (Larix eurolepis) and Sitka spruce (Picea sitchensis). *Tree Physiology,* 16, 1031-1038.
8. HAMER, U. & MARSCHNER, B. 2002. Priming effects of sugars, amino acids, organic acids and catechol on the mineralization of lignin and peat. *Journal of Plant Nutrition and Soil Science-Zeitschrift Fur Pflanzenernahrung Und Bodenkunde,* 165, 261-268.
9. HENRY, S., TEXIER, S., HALLET, S., BRU, D., DAMBREVILLE, C., CHENEBY, D., BIZOUARD, F., GERMON, J. C. & PHILIPPOT, L. 2008. Disentangling the rhizosphere effect on nitrate reducers and denitrifiers: insight into the role of root exudates. *Environmental Microbiology,* 10, 3082-3092.
10. HOYOS-SANTILLAN, J., LOMAX, B. H., LARGE, D., TURNER, B. L., BOOM, A., LOPEZ, O. R. & SJOGERSTEN, S. 2015. Getting to the root of the problem: litter decomposition and peat formation in lowland Neotropical peatlands. *Biogeochemistry,* 126, 115-129.
11. JONES, D. L. 1998. Organic acids in the rhizosphere - a critical review. *Plant and Soil,* 205, 25-44.
12. JONES, D. L. & MURPHY, D. V. 2007. Microbial response time to sugar and amino acid additions to soil. *Soil Biology & Biochemistry,* 39, 2178-2182.
13. KUZYAKOV, Y. & CHENG, W. 2001. Photosynthesis controls of rhizosphere respiration and organic matter decomposition. *Soil Biology & Biochemistry,* 33, 1915-1925.
14. KUZYAKOV, Y. & DOMANSKI, G. 2000. Carbon input by plants into the soil. Review. *Journal of Plant Nutrition and Soil Science-Zeitschrift Fur Pflanzenernahrung Und Bodenkunde,* 163, 421-431.
15. LANDI, L., VALORI, F., ASCHER, J., RENELLA, G., FALCHINI, L. & NANNIPIERI, P. 2006. Root exudate effects on the bacterial communities, CO_2 evolution, nitrogen transformations and ATP content of rhizosphere and bulk soils. *Soil Biology & Biochemistry,* 38, 509-516.
16. LLOYD, D., THOMAS, K. L., BENSTEAD, J., DAVIES, K. L., LLOYD, S. H., ARAH, J. R. M. & STEPHEN, K. D. 1998. Methanogenesis and CO_2 exchange in an ombrotrophic peat bog. *Atmospheric Environment,* 32, 3229-3238.
17. OHLINGER, R. 1995. Dehydrogenase activity with the substrate TTC. *In:* SCHINNER, F., OHLINGER, R., KANDELER, E. & MARGESIN, R. (eds.) *Methods in Soil Biology.* Springer.
18. PAGE, S. E., RIELEY, J. O. & BANKS, C. J. 2011. Global and regional importance of the tropical peatland carbon pool. *Global Change Biology,* 17, 798-818.
19. PATERSON, E., GEBBING, T., ABEL, C., SIM, A. & TELFER, G. 2007. Rhizodeposition shapes rhizosphere microbial community structure in organic soil. *New Phytologist,* 173, 600-610.
20. SHI, S. J., RICHARDSON, A. E., O'CALLAGHAN, M., DEANGELIS, K. M., JONES, E. E., STEWART, A., FIRESTONE, M. K. & CONDRON, L. M. 2011. Effects of selected root exudate components on soil bacterial communities. *Fems Microbiology Ecology,* 77, 600-610.
21. SJOGERSTEN, S. C., A. W.; LOPEZ, O.; TURNER, BENJAMIN, L.; 2010. Biogeochemical processes along a nutrient gradient in a tropical ombrotrophic peatland. *Biogeochemistry,* 104, 147-163.
22. SMITH, W. H. 1976. Character and Significance of Forest Tree Root Exudates. *Ecology,* 57, 324-331.
23. STROBEL, B. W. 2001. Influence of vegetation on low-molecular-weight carboxylic acids in soil solution - a review. *Geoderma,* 99, 169-198.
24. TREVORS, J. T. 1984. Effect of Substrate Concentration, Inorganic Nitrogen, O-2 Concentration, Temperature and Ph on Dehydrogenase-Activity in Soil. *Plant and Soil,* 77, 285-293.
25. WALKER, T. S., BAIS, H. P., GROTEWOLD, E. & VIVANCO, J. M. 2003. Root exudation and rhizosphere biology. *Plant physiology,* 132, 44-51.
26. WANG, Z. P., DELAUNE, R. D., MASSCHELEYN, P. H. & PATRICK, W. H. 1993. Soil Redox and Ph Effects on Methane Production in a Flooded Rice Soil. *Soil Science Society of America Journal,* 57, 382-385.
27. WRIGHT, E. L., BLACK, C. R., TURNER, B. L. & SJOGERSTEN, S. 2013. Environmental controls of temporal and spatial variability in CO_2 and CH4 fluxes in a neotropical peatland. *Global Change Biology,* 19, 3775-89.
28. YAN, F., SCHUBERT, S. & MENGEL, K. 1996. Soil pH increase due to biological decarboxylation of organic anions. *Soil Biology & Biochemistry,* 28, 617-624.

Abstract No: A-046

SPATIAL DISTRIBUTION OF GHG SINKS AND SOURCES IN FORESTRY-DRAINED BOREAL PEATLANDS

Mari Parkkari*, Miia Parviainen, Paavo Ojanen and Anne Tolvanen

Natural Resources Institute Finland (Luke), Finland

**Corresponding author: mari.keranen@luke.fi*

SUMMARY

Boreal peatlands contribute significantly to the global carbon store and have a major role in global greenhouse gas (GHG) balances. The peatland drainage for forestry purposes has an effect on CO_2, CH_4 and N_2O fluxes and thereby on GHG balances. In Finland, there is a remarkable area of drained peatlands, which indicates that decisions made for future peatland uses have effects on GHG emissions at a larger than national scale. Identification of reliable measures of GHG balances is needed to estimate whether suitable conditions for GHG sinks may be generated through peatland management. As extensive GHG data is expensive to acquire, alternative methods to obtain data from larger areas are needed. Statistically-based spatial models provide a cost-efficient approach for mapping and analysing GHG balances. The aim of this study is to explore the possibility of modelling and mapping the GHG balances of CO_2, CH_4 and N_2O in forestry-drained boreal peatlands using different environmental datasets, Geographic Information Systems (GIS) and spatial modelling method Maxent. With the aid of spatial methods it is possible to produce prediction maps showing the locations of GHG sinks and sources and identify the environmental factors controlling the GHG balance. The visual presentations are important not only for researchers but also for land use management and political decision making, since they help to implement climate-friendly land use options in critical geographical locations.

***Keywords**: peatlands, drainage, greenhouse gas, spatial modelling, GIS*

INTRODUCTION

Peat soils have a notable effect on greenhouse gas (GHG) balance (Frolking *et al.*, 2006; Gorham, 1991). In Finland, more than half of the 9 million ha of originally pristine mires have been drained for forestry (Finnish Forest Research Institute, 2009), which has led to changes in the greenhouse gas balance (Maljanen *et al.*, 2010; Minkkinen *et al.*, 1999; Nykänen *et al.*, 1998). The changes, however, are diverse and the balance is affected by various environmental factors. Some sites are sinks of GHGs after the drainage whereas some are sources (Lohila *et al.*, 2011; Maljanen *et al.*, 2010; Ojanen *et al.*, 2010). It is a challenge to identify the suitable locations for GHG sinks, but the identification is nevertheless important for climate friendly peatland management (Mander *et al.*, 2010).

The spatial distribution of GHG fluxes in various ecosystems has been presented in previous studies (e.g. Ernfors *et al.*, 2008; Huang *et al.*, 2013; Leppelt *et al.*, 2014; Mander *et al.*, 2010; Petrescu *et al.*, 2010; Xiao *et al.*, 2008; Zhu *et al.*, 2013). Both Petrescu *et al.* (2010) and Zhu *et al.* (2013) presented the distribution of CH_4 fluxes from northern wetlands with the spatial resolution of 0.5 °. Petrescu *et al.* (2010) used process-based models to estimate the CH_4 emissions, whereas Zhu *et al.* (2013) created a statistical model to extrapolate flux measurements for their study area.

Ernfors *et al.* (2008) presented the distribution of N_2O emissions from drained organic forest soils in Sweden based on soil CN ratio. Brocks *et al.* (2014) estimated N_2O emissions from agricultural soils in Germany, by combining flux measurements with spatially explicit data on land use, climate and soil properties. Mander *et al.* (2010) estimated the distribution of CH_4 and N_2O emissions from rural lands in Estonia based on land use. Leppelt *et al.* (2014) used statistical models to estimate the N_2O fluxes from European organic soils and to identify the important drivers within different land use types, presenting the distribution with 1 km^2 grids.

The distribution of fluxes has also been estimated using remote sensing based variables (e.g. Huang *et al.*, 2013; Jägermeyer *et al.*, 2014; Xiao *et al.*, 2008). For example, Huang *et al.* (2013) studied the distribution of soil respiration in Tibetan alpine grasslands with a resolution of 25 ha. They used remote sensing based vegetation indices as explanatory variables in the model. Xiao *et al.* (2008) estimated the net ecosystem exchange of different ecosystems in USA with the spatial resolution of 1 km^2. They used remote sensing variables as explanatory variables to upscale from the tower measurements to continental level.

The need for a reliable extrapolation method has been expressed in several studies (e.g. Klemedtsson *et al.*, 2005; Mander *et al.*, 2010; Ojanen *et al.*, 2010). The spatial models that cover a spatial distribution of an ecological phenomenon (Jørgensen, 2008) have proved valuable for generating, for example, biogeographical information that can be applied across a broad range of fields and scales (e.g. Austin & van Niel, 2011; Elith & Leathwick, 2009; Guisan and Zimmermann, 2000; Zimmermann *et al.*, 2010). Spatial modelling has been utilized mostly in species distribution studies (e.g. Arundel, 2005; Parviainen *et al.*, 2008; Thuiller *et al.*, 2008; Williams *et al.*, 2009) and for example Maxent modelling has been designed particularly for species distribution modelling (Phillips *et al.*, 2006). The same modelling method could be used to identify the controlling environmental conditions and the locations of sinks and sources of GHGs.

The aim of this study is to explore the possibility of modelling and mapping the GHG balances (CO_2, CH_4 and N_2O) of forestry-drained boreal peatland soils using environmental information and Maxent modelling technique. We use Geographic Information Systems (GIS) and different available environmental datasets as sources of explanatory variables. In this paper, we present the study setting and some preliminary results.

METHODS

Study area

The study was performed in total of 809 363 grids of 25 ha situated in the zones of aapa mires and raised bogs in Finland, excluding the northernmost part of Finland because of the lack of measured GHG data. Advantages of the grid approach are the possibility to split the study areas objectively into comparable sampling units and the opportunity to utilize GIS and RS data as a source of explanatory variables. Most of the study area belongs to the boreal zone and only the southernmost part belongs to the hemi-boreal zone (Ahti *et al.*, 1968). The mean annual temperature in Southern Finland is ca. +5 °C and in Northern Finland ca. −2 °C. Annual precipitation is between 400 and 750 mm (FMI).

GHG data

The GHG fluxes used in this study has been measured between May and October in 2007 and 2008 from 68 peatland sites drained for forestry in Finland (Figure 1). All sites were drained at least 20 years before the GHG measurements. The momentary fluxes of CH_4, N_2O and heterotrophic respiration were measured and based on the measurements, yearly balances of CH_4, N_2O and CO_2 were estimated (see Ojanen *et al.* 2010 for more details of CH_4 and N_2O and Ojanen *et al.* 2013 for CO_2). We used these balances for the modelling and created separate models for sinks and sources of each GHG both in aapa mire and in raised bog zones (excluding N_2O sink in raised bog zone). The data was treated as presence only in the creation of the model, but as presence/absence in the evaluation of the models.

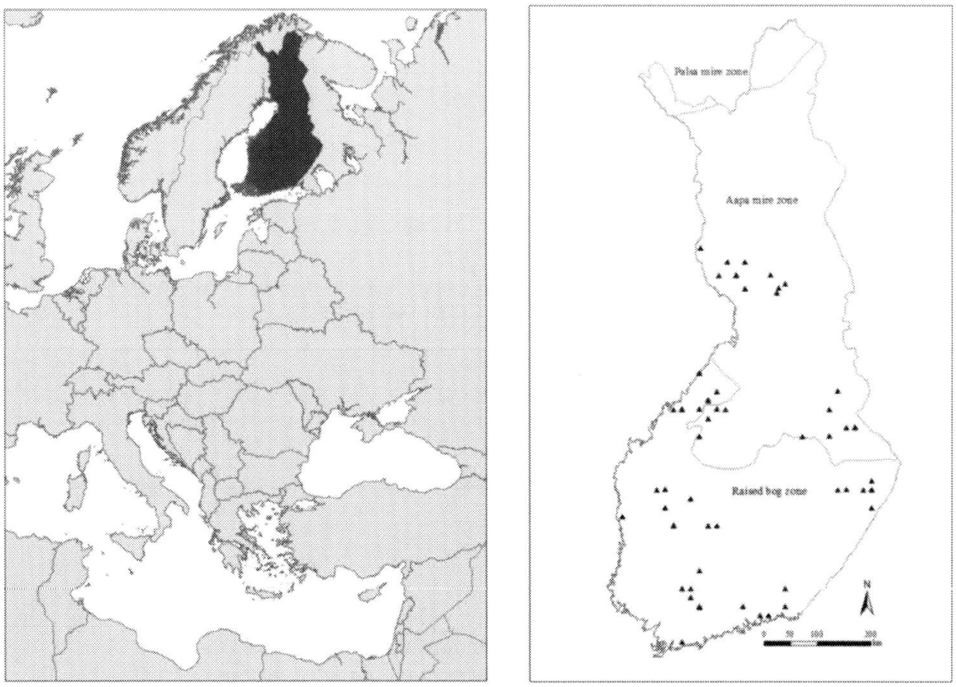

Figure 1: The location of GHG measurement sites (triangles) in Finland in northern Europe.

Environmental variables

The environmental variables used in this study were selected to represent important ecological gradients that may influence the GHG balances. In total, 13 environmental variables were calculated at 25 ha resolution: the mean summer temperature (Finnish Meteorological Institute FMI), water balance (FMI), land surface temperature (Landsat TM 5), wetness component derived from Tasseled Cap transformation (Landsat TM 5), soil adjusted vegetation index SAVI (Landsat TM 5), topographical wetness index (Digital Elevation Model), root biomass, mean diameter of trees and proportion of drained peatland types in the grid cells derived from Multi-source National Forest Inventory (MS-NFI) of Finland (Natural Resources Institute Finland Luke). Distinct sets of environmental predictors were used depending on the modelled GHG balance. The correlations between variables were tested to minimize the effect of multicollinearity in the multivariate study setting.

Modelling procedure

For the modelling, we used Maxent (Maximum Entropy), which applies the principle of maximum entropy to predict the potential distribution of phenomenon of interest from presence-only data and environmental variables (Phillips *et al.*, 2006). High predicted environmental suitability indicates the locations where environmental conditions are similar to those, where modelled phenomenon is known to occur. Maxent uses generalising approach, rather than discriminating, so it can utilise training data with limited occurrence information (Phillips *et al.*, 2006). It has been observed to achieve better discrimination capability compared to other modelling techniques (e.g. Phillips *et al.*, 2006; Wisz *et al.*, 2008). We composed the models using linear, quadratic and hinge features and 4-fold cross validation with random seed.

The performances of the models were evaluated by calculating AUC (area under the curve of a receiver operating characteristic plot ROC) (Fielding & Bell, 1997) value and implementing visual interpretations of the predictions maps. AUC value indicates the discriminations ability of the models which refers to the ability to separate the potential locations of sinks and sources from each other. The discriminating ability was considered as low if AUC < 0.7, fair if $0.7 <$ AUC < 0.8, good if $0.8 <$ AUC 0.9 and excellent if AUC > 0.9 (Swets 1988). Finally, we calculated the AUC value with SPSS (IBM SPSS Statistics 22) for sinks using the locations of sources as absence data and for sources using the locations of sinks as absence data. We evaluated the models visually.

PRELIMINARY RESULTS

The AUC values ranged from 0.506 (CH_4 sink in raised bog zone) to 0.824 (CH_4 source in raised bog zone). The variables that contributed the most in the models varied between different models (Figure 2). The proportion of *Vaccinium vitis-idaea* (Ptkg) and Dwarf shrub drained peatland types (Vatkg) were the most important variables in three models.

For some gases, the predicted suitable locations are different for sinks and sources (for example CO_2 in aapa zone) but for some models predict suitable environmental conditions in same areas. Especially the suitable locations for CH_4 sinks and sources in raised bog zone overlapped greatly.

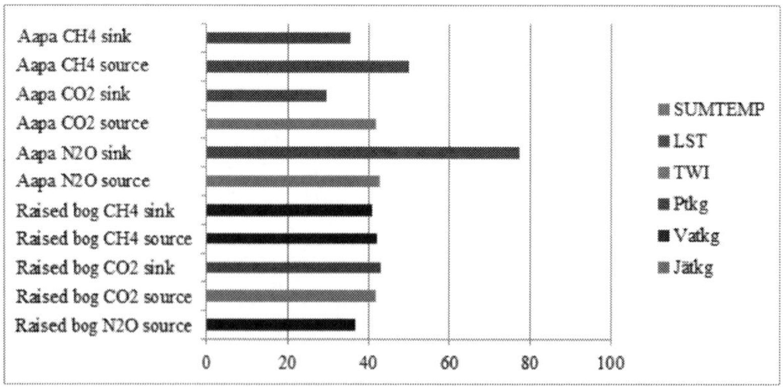

Figure 2: The relative contributions of the most important environmental variable in each model. SUMTEMP mean summer temperature, LST land surface temperature, WAB water balance, TWI topographic wetness index, Ptkg *Vaccinium vitis-idaea* type, Vatkg Dwarf shrub type and Jätkg *Cladina* type

DISCUSSION AND CONCLUSIONS

The performance of the models varied from low to good based on AUC values (Swets 1988). The model for source of CH_4 in raised bog zone achieved the best discrimination ability whereas the model for sink of CH_4 in the same zone had the weakest ability. The visual interpretation revealed that predicted sinks and sources overlapped especially in the case of CH_4 in raised bog zone. This may be explained by rather coarse resolution of the study (25 ha); there can be both potential sinks and sources of a GHG in the same grid and thus it may cause uncertainty to the models. Also Huang *et al.* 2013 noticed the problem with heterogeneity in their study of 25 ha. However, because some of the environmental data have coarse spatial resolution, the use of smaller modelling scale would not bring extra information.

The variables describing the proportions of different drained peatland types contributed to the models because they are proxies of for example nutrient conditions of a grid and thereby affect also the vegetation, tree growth and GHG fluxes. The variables describing the small-scale conditions seemed to work better than variables of a large scale. However, we underline that these are preliminary results so the models need to be further calibrated and the results should be evaluated with more than AUC value and visual interpretation.

Spatial models combined with environmental data have been used to acquire distribution data of ecological phenomena and in this study we found out that they could be utilized also in studying the distribution of GHG balances. To our knowledge, Maxent has not been previously utilized in this kind of GHG study. Our study provides new insights to identify GHG sinks and sources in a landscape scale resolution. With the information of the GHG distribution, land use management can be used as a tool to maximize carbon sequestration and help to mitigate climate change.

ACKNOWLEDGEMENTS

We warmly thank the Maj and Tor Nessling Foundation, University of Helsinki and Natural Resources Institute Finland (Luke) for the contributions to this research. The Maj and Tor Nessling Foundation provided a personal scholarship for M. Parkkari and University of Helsinki provided the GHG data. The study is part of the EU LIFE+ - project LIFE Peat Land Use (LIFE12 ENV/FI/000150).

REFERENCES

1. Ahti, T., Hämet-Ahti, L. & Jalas, J. (1968). Vegetation zones and their sections in northwestern Europe. *Annales Botanici Fennici*, 5, 169–211.
2. Arundel, S. T. (2005). Using spatial models to establish climatic limiters of plant species' distribution. *Ecological Modelling*, 182, 159–181.
3. Austin, M. P. & van Niel, K. (2011). Improving species distribution models for climate change studies, variable selection and scale. *Journal of Biogeography*, 38, 1–8.
4. Brocks, S., Jungkunst, H. F. & Bareth, G. (2014). A regionally disaggregated inventory of nitrous oxide emissions from agricultural soils in Germany - a GIS-based empirical approach. *Erdkunde*, 68, 125–144.
5. Elith, J. & Leathwick, J. R. (2009). Species Distribution Models: Ecological Explanation and Prediction Across Space and Time. *Annual Review of Ecology, Evolution, and Systematics*, 40, 677–697.
6. Ernfors, M., von Arnold, K., Stendahl, J., Olsson, M. & Klemedtsson, L. (2008). Nitrous oxide emissions from drained organic forest soils – an up-scaling based on C:N ratios. *Biogeochemistry*, 89, 29–41.
7. Fielding, A. & Bell, J. (1997). A review of methods for the assessment of prediction errors in conservation presence/ absence models. *Environmental Conservation*, 24, 38–49.
8. Finnish Forest Research Institute (2009). *Finnish Statistical Yearbook of Forestry*. Finnish Forest Research Institute, Vantaa, Finland, 452 p.
9. FMI Finnish Meteorological Institute. <*http://en.ilmatieteenlaitos.fi/normal-period*>. Cited 3.3.2016.
10. Frolking, S., Roulet, N. T. & Fuglestvedt, J. (2006). How northern peatlands influence the Earth's radiative budget: Sustained methane emission versus sustained carbon sequestration. *Journal of Geophysical Research*, 111, 1–10.
11. Gorham, E. (1991). Northern peatlands: Role in the carbon cycle and probable responses to climatic warming. *Ecological Applications*, 1, 182–195.
12. Guisan, A. & Zimmermann, N.E. (2000). Predictive habitat distribution models in ecology. *Ecological Modelling*, 135,147–186.
13. Huang, N., He, J-S. & Niu, Z. (2013). Estimating the spatial pattern of soil respiration in Tibetan alpine grasslands using Landsat TM images and MODIS data. *Ecological Indicators*, 26, 117–125.
14. Jägermeyer, J., Gerten, D., Lucht, W., Hostert, P., Migliavagga, M. & Nemani, R. (2014). A high-resolution approach to estimate ecosystem respiration at continental scales using operational satellite data. *Global Change Biology*, 20, 1191–1210.
15. Jørgensen, S. E. (2008). Overview of the model types available for development of ecological models. *Ecological Modelling*, 215, 3–9.
16. Klemedtsson, L., von Arnold, K., Weslien, P. & Gundersen, P. (2005). Soil CN ratio as a scalar parameter to predict nitrous oxide emissions. *Global Change Biology*, 11, 1142–1147.

17. Leppelt, T., Dechow, R., Gebbert, S., Freibauer, A., Lohila, A., Augustin, J., Drösler, M., Fiedler, S., Glatzel, S., Höper, H., Järveoja, J., Lærke, P. E., Maljanen, M., Mander, Ü., Mäkiranta, P., Minkkinen, K., Ojanen, P., Regina, K. & Strömgren, M. (2014). Nitrous oxide emission budgets and land-use-driven hotspots for organic soils in Europe. *Biogeosciences*, 11, 6595–6612.
18. Lohila, A., Minkkinen, K., Aurela, M., Tuovinen, J.-P, Penttilä, T., Ojanen P. & Laurila, T. (2011). Greenhouse gas flux measurements in a forestry-drained peatland indicate a large carbon sink. *Biogeosciences*, 8, 3203–3218.
19. Maljanen, M., Sigurdsson, B. D., Guðmundsson, J., Óskarsson, H., Huttunen, J. T. & Martikainen, P. J. (2010). Greenhouse gas balances of managed peatlands in the Nordic countries – present knowledge and gaps. *Biogeosciences*, 7, 2711–2738.
20. Mander, Ü., Uuemaa, E., Kull, A., Kanal, A., Maddison, M., Soosaar, K., Salm, J-O., Lesta, M., Hansen, R., Kuller, R., Harding, A. & Augustin, J. (2010). Assessment of methane and nitrous oxide fluxes in rural landscapes. *Landscape and Urban Planning*, 98, 172–181.
21. Minkkinen, K., Vasander, H., Jauhiainen, S., Karsisto, M. & Laine, J. (1999). Post-drainage changes in vegetation composition and carbon balance in Lakkasuo mire, Central Finland. *Plant and Soil*, 207, 107–120.
22. Nykänen, H., Alm, J., Silvola, J., Tolonen, K. & Martikainen, P. J. (1998). Methane fluxes on boreal peatlands of different fertility and the effect of long-term experimental lowering of the water table on flux rates. *Global Biochemical Cycles*, 12, 53–69.
23. Ojanen, P., Minkkinen, K., Alm, J. & Penttilä, T. (2010). Soil-atmosphere CO_2, CH_4 and N_2O fluxes in boreal forestry-drained peatlands. *Forest Ecology and Management*, 260, 411–421.
24. Ojanen, P., Minkkinen, K. & Penttilä, T. (2013). The current greenhouse gas impact of forestry-drained boreal peatlands. *Forest Ecology and Management*, 289, 210–208.
25. Parviainen, M., Luoto, M., Ryttäri, T. & Heikkinen, R. (2008). Modelling the occurrence of threatened plant species in taiga landscapes, methodological and ecological perspectives. *Journal of Biogeography*, 35, 1888–1905.
26. Petrescu, A. M. R., van Beek, L. P. H., van Huissteden, J., Prigent, C., Sachs, T., Corradi, C. A. R., Parmentier, F. J. W. & Dolman, A. J. (2010). Modeling regional to global CH_4 emissions of boreal and arctic wetlands. *Global Biogeochemical Cycles*, 24, 1–12.
27. Phillips, S., Anderson, R. & Schapire, R. (2006). Maximum entropy modeling of species geographic distributions. *Ecological Modelling*, 190, 231–259.
28. Swets, K. (1988). Measuring the accuracy of diagnostic systems. *Science*, 240, 1285–1293.
29. Thuiller, W., Albert, C., Araújo, M. B., Berry, P. M., Cabeza, M., Guisan, A., Hickler, T., Midgley, G. F., Paterson, J., Schurr, F. M., Sykes, M. T. & Zimmermann, N. E. (2008). Predicting global change impacts on plant species' distribution: Future challenges. *Perspectives in Plant Ecology, Evolution and Systematics*, 9, 137–152.
30. Williams, J. N., Seo, C., Thorne, J., Nelson, J. K., Erwin, S., O'Brien, J. M. & Schwartz, M. W. (2009). Using species distribution models to predict new occurrences for rare plants. *Diversity and Distribution*, 15, 565–576.
31. Wisz, M., Hijmans, R., Li, J., Peterson, A., Graham, C., Guisan A. & NCEAS predicting species distribution working group (2008). Effects of sample size on the performance of species distribution models. *Diversity and Distributions*, 14, 763–773.
32. Xiao, J., Zhuang, Q., Dennis, D. D., Law, B. E., Richardson, A. D., Chen, J., Oren, R., Starr, G., Noormets, A., Ma, S., Verma, S. B., Wharton, S., Wofsy, S. C., Bolstad, P. V., Burns, S. P., Cook, D. R., Curtis, P. S., Drake, B. G., Falk, F., Fischer, M. L., Foster, D. R., Gu, L., Hadley, J. L., Hollinger, D. Y., Katul, G. G., Litvak, M., Martin, T. A., Matamala, R., McNulty, S., Meyers, T. P., Monson, R. K., Munger, J. W., Oechel, W. C., Paw, K. T., Schmid, H. P., Scott, R. L., Sun, G., Suyker, A. E. & Torn, M. S. (2008). Estimation of net ecosystem carbon exchange for the conterminous United States by combining MODIS and AmeriFlux data. *Agricultural and Forest Meteorology*, 148, 1827–1847.
33. Zhu, X., Zhuang, Q., Qin, Z., Glagolev, M. & Song L. (2013). Estimating wetland methane emissions from the northern high latitudes from 1990 to 2009 using artificial neural networks. *Global Biogeochemical Cycles*, 27, 592–604.
34. Zimmermann N.E., Edwards T.C., Graham C.H., Pearman P.B. & Svenning J-C. (2010). New trends in species distribution modelling. *Ecography*, 33,985–989.

Abstract No: A-372

SURFACE-ATMOSPHERE EXCHANGE IN TROPICAL PEAT FORESTS *VERSUS* OTHER TROPICAL FORESTS: A FLUXNET SYNTHESIS

Paul C. Stoy[1, 2*], Tobias Gerken[1, 3], Rong Yu[4, 5], Benjamin Ruddell[5] and FLUXNET contributors

[1]*Department of Land Resources and Environmental Sciences, Montana State University, USA*
[2]*Institute on Ecosystems, Montana State University, USA*
[3]*Department of Meteorology, The Pennsylvania State University, University Park, USA*
[4]*University of Nebraska*
[5]*Arizona State University*

* *Corresponding author: paul.stoy@gmail.com*

SUMMARY

Tropical peat forests are largely found in Southeast Asia and - like tropical forests globally - are subject to multiple threats including deforestation and hydrologic disturbances. How might these changes impact the globally important exchanges of carbon, water, and energy between the land surface and the atmosphere? A comparative study of tropical peat forests *versus* other tropical forests has not been undertaken to date. Here, I conduct a synthesis of surface-atmosphere exchange observations from tropical forests in the FLUXNET database. Available observations – of which there are few – indicate that tropical forests are usually carbon sinks, but tropical peat forests tend to be carbon sources. This discrepancy can be explained by differences in ecosystem respiration (carbon loss) rather than gross primary productivity (carbon uptake). Tropical peat forests have higher gross primary productivity than most other tropical forests measured to date, but ecosystem respiration is among the highest of any global ecosystem. The causes for this discrepancy are unclear. Tropical peat forests must have been long-term carbon sinks to accumulate carbon in peat, yet this peat is also likely the source of carbon losses to the atmosphere. Observations of carbon losses from tropical peat forests are often attributed to hydrological disturbances, but it is unclear how widespread this phenomenon is and if even relatively undisturbed tropical peat forests are now carbon sources. Tropical peat forests also differ from most other tropical forests in the surface-atmosphere exchange of water and energy. For example, the ratio of sensible to latent heat flux (the Bowen ratio) tends to increase as a function of net radiation in tropical forests, but the response of the Bowen ratio to net radiation in tropical peat forests is more muted. Such responses of ecosystem water and energy flux to available energy have implications for convective precipitation dynamics and ecosystem hydrology. By placing tropical peat forests in the context of other tropical forests, we can gain a richer understanding of their unique function and gain a stronger appreciation of their role in providing critical ecosystem services.

***Keywords**:-*

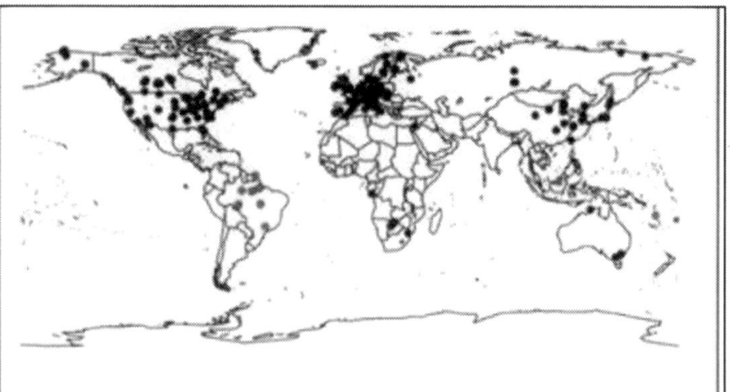

Figure 1: A global map of eddy covariance towers in the LaThuille FLUXNET database with tropical forest ecosystems in red.

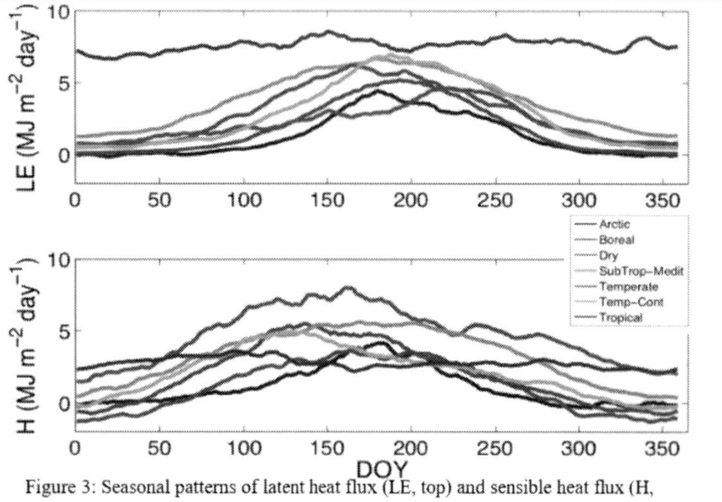

Figure 3: Seasonal patterns of latent heat flux (LE, top) and sensible heat flux (H, bottom) from different climate zones from eddy covariance observations in the LaThuille FLUXNET database. The day of year (DOY) was adjusted by half a year for ecosystems in the Southern Hemisphere to match their Northern Hemisphere counterparts.

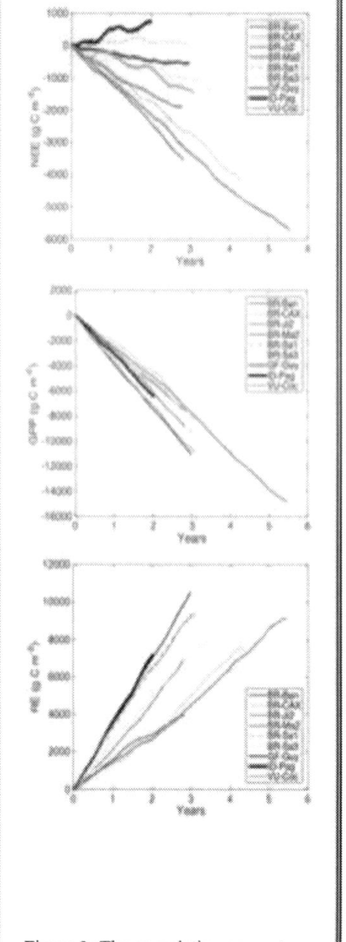

Figure 2: The cumulative sum net ecosystem exchange of CO2 (NEE, top), gross ecosystem productivity (GPP, middle), and ecosystem respiration (RE, bottom) across different tropical ecosystems of differing measurement length.

RESEARCH RESULTS

Eddy covariance observations in the LaThuille FLUXNET datasbase (Figure 1) are publically open for analyses, but only contain ten tropical forest sites of which only one, Palangkaraya in Indonesia (ID-Pag), is a tropical peat forest (Hirano *et al.*, 2012). This limits our ability to compare tropical forest and tropical peat forest ecosystems against other global ecosystems, but important insights can still be gained.

First and foremost, ID-Pag is the only tropical forest in the FLUXNET database with positive net ecosystem exchange of CO2 NEE, indicating a net carbon loss to the atmosphere (Figure 2). The reason for this difference is that the rate of ecosystem respiration (RE) is highest at ID-Pag (alongside a tropical rainforest in Guyana, Gf-Guy), but carbon uptake via gross ecosystem productivity (GPP) at ID-Pag is similar to the mean GPP of other ecosystems. In other words, GPP rates that are characteristic of other tropical forests and RE rates that are amongst the highest of any global ecosystem are the reason for the positive NEE over the two years of available measurements at ID-Pag. These observations are cause for alarm given the substantial C stocks of this and other tropical peat forests (Hirano *et al.*, 2007; Hirano *et al.*, 2008; Hirano *et al.*, 2012).

The effects of the biosphere on the climate system are not of course limited to CO2 exchange. Ecosystems influence atmospheric processes and *vice versa*, and connections between the two are changing as a result of anthropogenic influences (Luyssaert *et al.*, 2014). Energy exchange between the biosphere and atmosphere via latent heat (LE, *i.e.* evapotranspiration in energy flux units) and sensible heat (H) are critical for determining atmospheric moisture content and boundary layer development, and thereby precipitation processes.

Tropical ecosystems are characterized by the highest LE of any global ecosystem (Figure 3), although temperate forests have similar LE during their peak growing season on average. The lack of seasonality in tropical ecosystems – at least compared to most non-tropical ecosystems – results in a situation where H can be relatively high (during the non-growing season in ecosystems with greater seasonality of net radiation) or low (Figure 3). How might these energy fluxes influence precipitation?

Precipitation processes in tropical ecosystems are often limited by vertical atmospheric motions that bring moisture-rich air from the surface to the top of the atmospheric boundary layer (Badiya Roy and Avissar 2002). These vertical motions are driven largely by H in areas with limited topography. A simple analysis of the Bowen ration (, simply the ration between H and LE) and available energy (via the net radiation, Rn) reveals that ID-Pag partitions relatively less energy into H than most other tropical ecosystems during the mid-day conditions that are characterized by higher Rn (Figure 4), suggesting potentially that water vapor flux from peat ecosystems limits H under high radiation loads.

To begin progress on understanding the role of the biosphere to atmospheric processes across different tropical forest ecosystems, we can apply techniques from information theory (Ruddell *et al.*, 2013). Namely, the transfer entropy (T') - the amount of information passed from one time series to another as inferred by a process network (Ruddell and Kumar 2009a; Ruddell and Kumar 2009b) - can quantify the importance of H to precipitation across different tropical ecosystems (Figure 5). T' between H and precipitation decreases across all tropical forest ecosystems during the (typical) dry season, indicating a potential shift between H and LE in determining precipitation dynamics, and interestingly H at ID-Pag has a smaller influence on precipitation than most other tropical forest ecosystems. A number of mechanisms may underlie these findings, which require additional research attention. Fortunately, new releases of eddy covariance data via the worldwide consortium of researchers in FLUXNET provide further opportunity to place tropical forest ecosystems in a global context in order to better-appreciate their critical role in the Earth system.

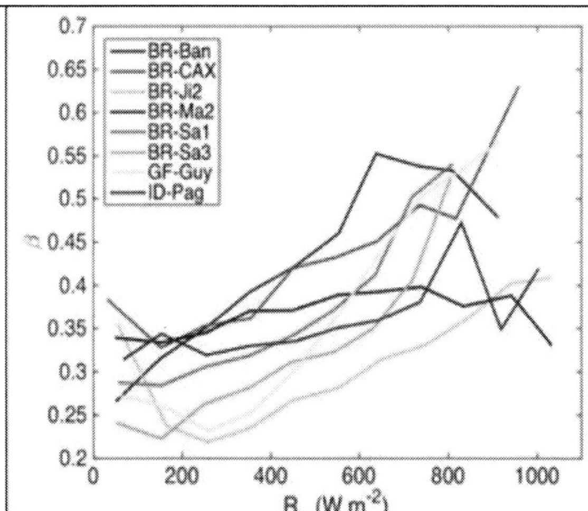

Figure 4: The response of the Bowen ration (the ration between sensible and latent heat flux) as a function of net radiation (R_n) for different R_n bins across eight tropical forest ecosystems in the LaThuille FLUXNET database.

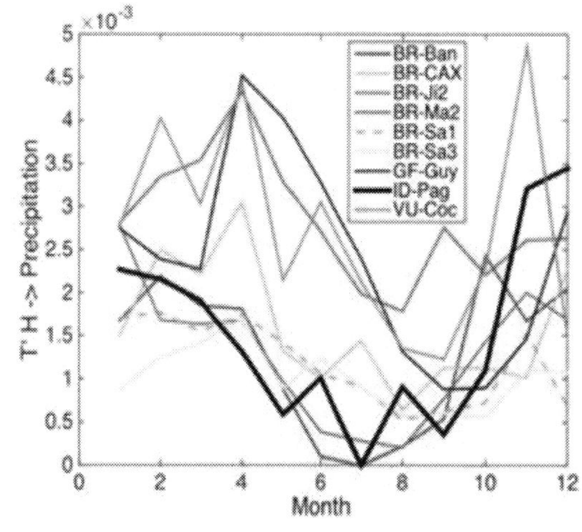

Figure 5: The transfer entropy (T') between sensible heat flux (H) and precipitation for monthly time steps calculated following Ruddell and Kumar (2009a) across tropical forest ecosystems in the LaThuille FLUXNET database.

REFERENCES

1. Badiya Roy S, Avissar R (2002) Impact of land use/land cover change on regional hydrometeorology in Amazonia. J Geophys Res 107:doi: 10.1029/2000JD000266.
2. Hirano T, Jauhiainen J, Inoue T, Takahashi H (2008) Controls on the Carbon Balance of Tropical Peatlands. Ecosystems 12:873–887. doi: 10.1007/s10021-008-9209-1
3. Hirano T, Segah H, Harada T, *et al.* (2007) Carbon dioxide balance of a tropical peat swamp forest in Kalimantan, Indonesia. Glob Chang Biol 13:412–425.
4. Hirano T, Segah H, Kusin K, *et al.* (2012) Effects of disturbances on the carbon balance of tropical peat swamp forests. Glob Chang Biol 18:3410–3422.
5. Luyssaert S, Jammet M, Stoy PC, *et al.* (2014) Land management and land-cover change have impacts of similar magnitude on surface temperature. Nat Clim Chang 4:389– 393.
6. Ruddell BL, Brunsell NA, Stoy PC (2013) Applying information theory in the geosciences to quantify process uncertainty, feedback, scale. Eos, Trans Am Geophys Union 94:56.
7. Ruddell BL, Kumar P (2009a) Ecohydrologic process networks: 1. Identification. Water Resour Res 45:1Ð22. doi: 10.1029/2008WR007279
8. Ruddell BL, Kumar P (2009b) Ecohydrologic process networks: 2. Analysis and characterization. Water Resour Res 45:1Ð14. doi: 10.1029/2008WR007280

2.3: PEAT FOREST-WILDFIRE-IMPACT ON ENVIRONMENT & SOCIETY

2.3: PEAT FOREST-WILDFIRE-IMPACT ON ENVIRONMENT & SOCIETY

Bandung Sahari

Abstract No: A-421

2015 SEVERE PEAT FIRES AND AIR POLLUTION NEAR THE FORMER MEGA RICE PROJECT AREA IN CENTRAL KALIMANTAN, INDONESIA

Hiroshi Hayasaka[1*] and Alpon Sepriando[2]

[1]*NPO Hokkaido Institute of Hydro-climate, Sapporo, Hokkaido, Japan,*
[2]*Indonesian Agency for Meteorology, Climatology and Geophysics, Palangkaraya, Indonesia*

**Corresponding author: hhaya05@me.com*

SUMMARY

Severe air pollution due to biomass burning occurred again in Indonesia during the 2015 super El Niño. In this report, air pollution data measured at Palangkaraya, near the northern part of the Mega Rice Project (MRP) area in Kalimantan, are analyzed in conjunction with fire and precipitation data, and satellite imagery. During super (very strong) El Niño conditions in 2015, the dry season lasted about 150 days from late May to late October, with low precipitation (=1.0 mm day^{-1}; average precipitation in dry season = 3.9 mm day^{-1}). Forest and peat fires became active around mid August, about three months after the onset of the dry season, followed by a period of severe air pollution (Hazardous level: PM10 > 420×10^{-6} g m^{-3}) starting in mid-September and lasting through late October. These time-lags between the dry season, fires, and air pollution period, suggest that biomass fuel needs about three months to become dry enough to start active fires, and that peat underground needs about four months to become ignitable dry peat. After severe peat fires began in late September, highest daily and hourly PM10 concentrations (3,010 and $3{,}760 \times 10^{-6}$ g m^{-3} respectively) were observed on October 20, 2015. These fire and air pollution occurrence tendencies suggest that peat fires are a main source of air pollution.

Keywords: *Peat fire, PM10, MRP, MODIS, El Niño*

INTRODUCTION

In Southeast Asia (SEA), El Niño is typically associated with drought. This has helped fuel some of the worst wildfires on record in Indonesia in 2015 (OCHA 2015) during super (very strong) El Niño conditions. The total burnt area in Indonesia during the previous super El Niño in 1997–1998 was estimated at about 40,000 km^2 (Siegert and Hoffmann 1998). Thus, vegetation and peat fires in Kalimantan, Indonesia, were very active under El Niño and quasi-El Niño conditions, especially in recent years (2002, 2004, 2006, 2009, 2014, and 2015). These recent active fires may suggest vulnerable conditions in forests and peatlands in Kalimantan. The sources of particulate matter (PM) are mainly forest and peat fires. The Indonesian fires of 1997 released pyrogenic aerosols of around 55×10^{12} g PM10 into the atmosphere, the equivalent of around one-third of the global annual anthropogenic emissions of primary particles (Heil *et al.*, 2006). Indonesia also formally admitted to releasing a very large amount of CO2 emissions from fires and deforestation (Yulianti 2013). From 2001 to 2010 in Palangkaraya, maximum peak concentrations of particulate matter (PM10), SO2, CO, and O3 were observed on October 14, 2002 during a moderate El Ni–o event, and their values reached 1905, 85.8, 38.3, and 1003×10^{-6} gm^{-3}, respectively. Photochemical smog also occurred (Hayasaka *et al.*, 2014).

In this report, air pollution data (PM10) measured at Palangkaraya, near the northern part of the MRP area in Kalimantan, are analyzed in conjunction with fire and precipitation data, and satellite imageries, to discuss precipitation during the dry season under El Ni–o conditions, fire (hotspot) occurrence tendency during the dry season, occurrence tendency of PM10, and air pollution sources.

METHODS

Study area

Figure 1 shows a detailed map of the study area in the Mega Rice Project (MRP), called "MRP+" in this paper. MRP+ covers the MRP area and its vicinity, including the Sebangau National Park (1.75Ð3.5°S, 113.5Ð115°W). MRP+ was chosen as the study area simply because MRP+ is major peatland in Central Kalimantan, and is the highest hotspot density area in Indonesia. Deforested peatlands, abandoned after the MRP, became major sources of air pollution because of the large accumulation of peat.

Palangkaraya is located in Central Kalimantan, as shown by a circle (2.207°S, 113.917°E) in Figure 1. The distance from the nearest coastline is about 100 km, and the average altitude is only around 10 m. The MRP was built on tropical swamp forest areas on the eastern and southern sides of Palangkaraya. Before the disturbance, the tropical swamp forest could hold enough water to stay wet even in the dry season. However, the newly constructed 4,000-km-long MRP canal system built for irrigation facilitated not only illegal logging, but also loss of water through drainage from most of the peatlands in the MRP area. This is one of the reasons for severe fire occurrence in the MRP area.

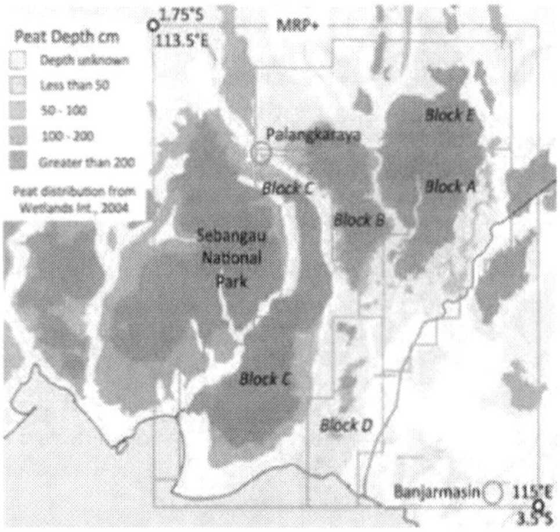

Figure 1: Peatland distribution in study area (MRP+) (Original Map from Global forest watch and Wetland Int. 2004

Air pollution, PM10 data, and weather data

The air pollution (PM10), precipitation, and visibility were measured hourly by the Palangkaraya weather station of the Indonesian Agency for Meteorology, Climatology, and Geophysics (BMKG) at Palangkaraya International Airport (Tjilik Riwut, 2.224°S, 113.946°E). In our previous paper, we used air pollution data from the Air Quality Management System and Regional Center at Palangkaraya. Unfortunately, most of their gas analyzers were broken in 2011. In this paper, we used PM10, precipitation, and visibility data from BMKG to evaluate air pollution.

RESULTS AND DISCUSSION

Peat fires in 2015 during super El Niño

The number of daily hotspots (NASA EARTHDATA) in Kalimantan and the study area (MRP+), and the precipitation at Palangkaraya, are shown in Figure 2 using double Y-axes. Only a few precipitation events were observed from August to late October. Average daily precipitation during the dry season (Day Number (DN) = 154–298) in 2015 was 1.0 mm day^{-1}. September was a rainless month.

Under the very dry (drought) conditions created by a super El Niño, the number of hotspots began to increase in mid-August (Figure 2). The two-month time lag between late May (beginning of dry season in 2015) and August (beginning of active fires) suggests that the biomass needs a drying period after the wet season to become combustible biomass. From mid-September, the number of daily hotspots exceeded 2000. The maximum number of daily hotspots observed in October 14, 2015 (DN = 287) was 2890. This fire activity suggests that the biomass becomes highly combustible in mid-September. In particular, deep peat fires could begin because the underground water level becomes lowest just before the rainy season begins in October, when the amount of ignitable peat becomes largest. The number of hotspots in MRP+ also increased from around mid-August (see Figure 2). The ratio of number of hotspots in MRP+ to those in Kalimantan also gradually increased, as seen in Figure 2. One of large ratios was 0.573, at one of largest hotspot peaks at DN = 266. The large ratio suggests peat fire activity in MRP+ due to a large peat area in the MRP. After the rainy season started in late October, the number of hotspots in MRP+ became nearly zero (Figure 2). This suggests only a large amount of precipitation could suppress peat fires.

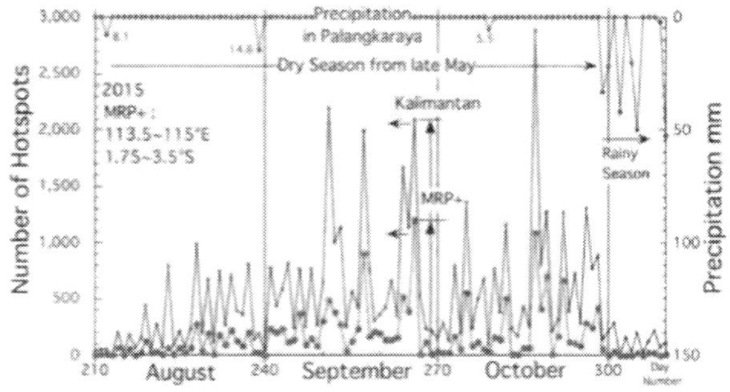

Figure 2: Number of daily hotspots and precipitation in Kalimantan and study area (MRP+)

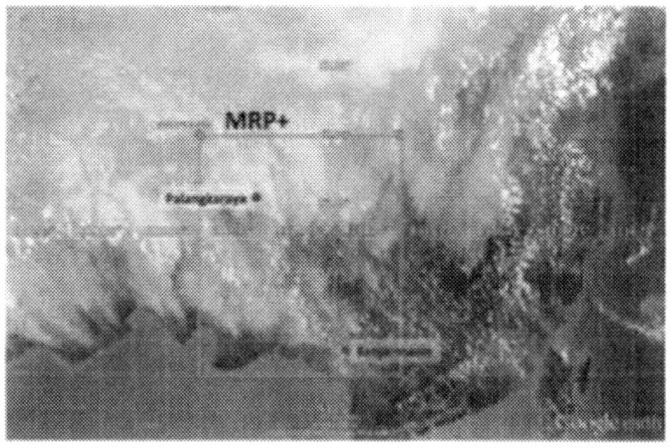

Figure 3: Satellite imagery (MODIS on Aqua) for daily hotspot peak day (DN = 287, October 14, 2015)

Satellite imagery in Figure 3 clearly shows the fire situation in Central, South, and East Kalimantan on a hotspot peak day on October 14, 2015 (DN = 287, Figure 2). A strong southeasterly wind in Figure 3 activated fires on the peatlands. In particular, fires southeast of Palangkaraya emitted a dense haze (Figure 5). Most of these fires were located on peatlands in Block A, B, and C of the MRP (Figure 1). In contrast, the number of fires in the pristine forests in the northern part of Sebangau National Park (south of Palangkaraya, Figure 1) was nearly zero.

Severe air pollution in 2015 during super El Nibo

PM10, and minimum and average visibility measured at Palangkaraya are plotted in Figure 4. Minimum and average visibility gradually decreased with fire activity in MRP+ (Figure 2). The daily maximum PM10 was 3245 $\times 10^{-6}$ gm^{-3}, observed on October 21, 2015 (DN = 294). The hourly maximum PM10 was 3761 $\times 10^{-6}$ gm^{-3} and was also observed on the same day (DN = 294). The minimum and average visibility on this day (DN = 294) were nearly zero (hourly data varied from 10 to 150 m). A severe air pollution period (Hazardous level (API > 300): PM10 > 420 $\times 10^{-6}$ g m^{-3}) began in mid-September (about four months after the dry season started) and lasted until late October. Very severe air pollution (>1000 $\times 10^{-6}$ gm^{-3}) occurred beginning in late September. This severe air pollution just before rainy season also suggests that the main source of air pollution was peat.

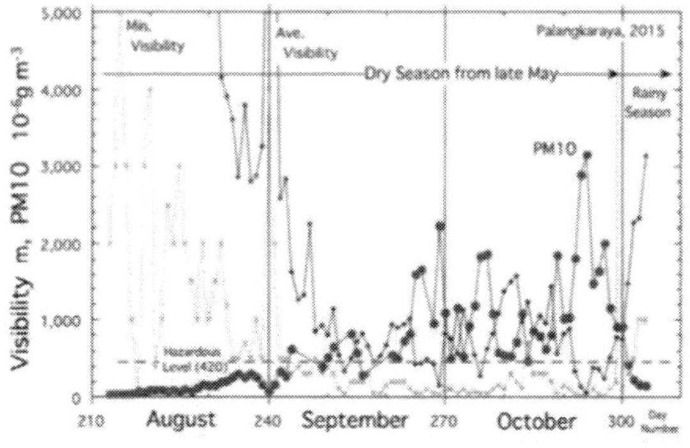

Figure 4: PM10, minimum and average visibility measured at peak Palangkaraya.

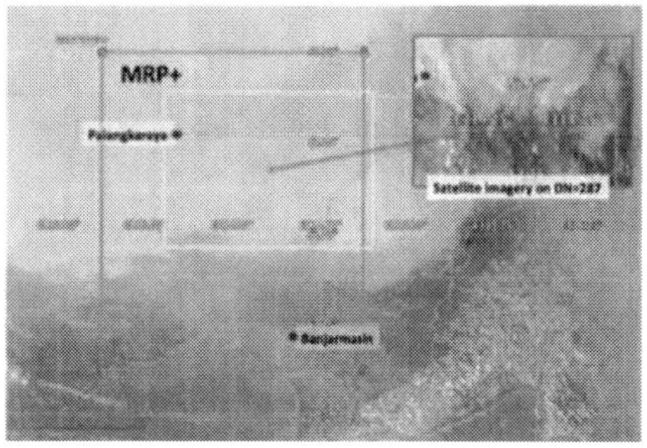

Figure 5: Satellite imagery (MODIS on Aqua) for daily hotspot day (DN = 294, October 21, 2015)

To explain the several days difference between the hotspot peak day (DN = 287 in Figs. 2 and 4) and PM10 peak day (DN = 294 in Figure 4), satellite imagery on DN = 294 is shown in Figure 5.

The satellite imagery in Figure 5 clearly shows that a thick haze covers more than 60% of the northern part of the MRP+ area. Because of the thick haze and underground peat fires, the number of hotspots in Kalimantan and MRP+ was small, 724 and 101 respectively. The worst air pollution occurring at the end of the dry season or just before the rainy season suggests that the air pollution source is peat because the underground water level becomes lowest at the end of the dry season, and this makes deep (<40 cm) peat highly combustible (Usup A *et al.*, 2004). This tendency was also found in the 2002 air pollution at Palangkaraya. Previous studies reported that the worst air pollution in 2002 occurred on October 14, 2002 during a moderate El Niño event, and about 10 days before the onset of the rainy season.

CONCLUSION

In this report, air pollution data measured at Palangkaraya, near the northern part of the Mega Rice Project (MRP) area in Kalimantan are analyzed in conjunction with fire and precipitation data, and satellite imagery. The analysis results clearly showed: (1) In 2015, MRP area has about five months of dry weather, from late May to

October. (2) The dry season during an El Niño event becomes very dry compared with average precipitation (=3.9 mm day^{-1}). (3) During the 2015 super El Niño, the dry season was longer and very dry. The dry season lasted about 150 days, from late May to late October with lower precipitation (=1.0 mm day^{-1}, ratio to average = 1/3.9). (4) Forest and peat fires became active around mid-August, about three months after the dry season started. The number of daily hotspots in MRP+ exceeded 200 beginning in mid-August. (5) Severe fires began around mid-September, about four months after the dry season started. Although hotspot detection was interrupted by dense haze from fires, the number of daily hotspots in MRP+ exceeded 500 several times beginning in mid-September. (6) A period of severe air pollution (Hazardous level (API > 300): PM10 > 420 × 10^{-6} g m^{-3}) also began in mid-September (about four months after the dry season started) and lasted until late October. (7) The second largest hotspot peak (1,100 hotspots) was observed on October 14, 2015. (8) Several days after the second largest hotspot peak day, the highest daily and hourly PM10 concentrations (3,010 and 3,760 × 10^{-6} g m^{-3} respectively) were observed On October 20, 2015. (9) In our previous report (Hayasaka H *et al.*, 2014), a maximum peak in PM10 concentration in the ten-year period from 2001 to 2010 was 1905 × 10^{-6} g m^{-3}, and was observed on October 14, 2002 during a moderate El Niño. (10) Both PM10 peaks in 2002 and 2015 occurred in October simply because the amount of ignitable dry peat increased at the end of dry season, when the underground water level reached a deepest level.

From the above results and discussion, we recommend strong conservation measures of peatlands in the MRP+ area in Central Kalimantan. In particular, we suggest limiting the construction of irrigation canals, which contribute to further development and subsequent drying of the land. Drastic land use/land management planning, including re-wetting, should be developed based on scientific knowledge, and carried out using modern technology.

ACKNOWLEDGEMENT

This study was partly supported by The Environment Research and Technology Development Fund 4-1506, Ministry of Environment, Japan.

REFERENCES

1. Hayasaka H et al. (2014) Peat-fire-related air pollution in Central Kalimantan, Indonesia, *Environmental Pollution*, http://dx.doi.org/10.1016/j.envpol.2014.06.031
2. NASA EARTHDATA, Fire Information for Resources Management System, https://firms.modaps.eosdis.nasa.gov/download/
3. Heil A Langmann B and Aldrian E (2006) Indonesian peat and vegetation fire emissions, *Mitigation and Adaptation Strategies for Global Change*, http://dx.doi.org/10.1007/s11027-006-9045-6.
4. OCHA (United Nations Office for the Coordination of Humanitarian Affairs) (2015), El Niño in Asia, http://www.unocha.org/el-nino-asia-pacific
5. Siegert F Hoffmann AA (1998) Evaluation of the 1998 forest fires in East-Kalimantan (Indonesia) using multitemporal ERS-2 SAR images and NOAA-AVHRR data. Proceedings of The International Conference on Data Management and Modeling Using Remote Sensing and GIS for Tropical Forest Land Inventory, Jakarta, Indonesia, 26-29 October 1998. Also available on http://smd.mega.net.id/iffm/n&r0.htm.
6. Usup A et al. (2004) Combustion and Thermal characteristics of peat fire in tropical peatland in Central Kalimantan, Indonesia, *Tropics* 14–1, 1–19.
7. Yulianti N (2013) The Influence of Precipitation Patterns on Recent Peatland Fires in Indonesia. PhD thesis. Graduate School of Engineering, Hokkaido University.

Abstract No: A-278

DEGRADED PEATLANDS, GROUND WATER LEVEL AND SEVERE PEAT FIRE OCCURRENCES

Erianto Indra Putra[1, 2*], Mark A. Cochrane[1], Yenni Vetrita[1, 3], Laura Graham[4] and Bambang Hero Saharjo[2]

[1]*South Dakota State University (SDSU), USA*
[2]*Bogor Agricultural University (IPB), Indonesia*
[3]*Indonesian National Institute of Aeronautics and Space (LAPAN), Indonesia*
[4]*Borneo Orangutan Survival Foundation (BOSF), Indonesia*

**Correspondence Author: erianto.putra@sdstate.edu*

SUMMARY

Tropical peat fires occur nearly every year, but burning conditions are aggravated during droughts in Indonesia. Severe dry conditions in degraded peatlands may increase peat susceptibility to fire, creating suitable conditions for peat fires to be ignited. Ground water level (GWL) has been used as a key indicator for determining fire activity in peatlands. We studied the fire situation on 2011-2012 in a portion of the ex-Mega Rice Project (MRP) area, Central Kalimantan to get better understanding of this critical issue. Further analyses using TRMM data and the changing GWL from 460 dipwells set up at Block A and E of MRP area showed a time-lag between the lowest precipitation and the lowest GWL at this area, pointing out the high risk of future fires in the area due to the loss of the peat's future ability for absorbing and storing water. Terra/Aqua MODIS hotspot data, combined with Landsat imagery showed that most of fires occur in areas with GWL less than -20 cm, indicating that fire is coincident with lower GWL. This result also strongly illustrates the importance of maintaining high GWL, of more than 5 cm, to reduce fire risk and prevent degraded peatlands from experiencing surface peat fires and further devastating deep peat fires.

***Keywords**: peat fires, degraded peatland, ground water level, precipitation*

INTRODUCTION

Indonesia holds the largest tropical peatland areas, comprising approximately 50% of world's total tropical peatlands. Of the total of 14,905,574 ha of Indonesian peatland area, 32% is in Kalimantan and peatland in Central Kalimantan accounts for 56% (Ritung *et. al.*, 2011). An ambitious Mega Rice Project (MRP) in Central Kalimantan was initiated by Indonesian Government, in 1996, to convert 1.4 million hectares of peatland there to fields for cultivating rice and promoting transmigration. Over 4,000 km of channels were dug to open up the area, but with inadequate consideration of topography and peatland hydrology (Siegert, *et. al.*, 2001), this project just exacerbated the problem when the over drained peatland became more vulnerable to fire. Fires commonly occur in this area annually during the dry season (July-September), but burning conditions are aggravated during pronounced *El Niño* years when the peatlands there are subjected to extremely severe dry conditions.

Ground water level (GWL) has been used as a key indicator for predicting fire occurrences in Central Kalimantan's degraded peatland (Putra et. al 2008, Usup *et. al.* 2004, Wosten et. al. 2008). Putra *et al.* (2008) revealed that more than 99% of fires in the Ex-MRP area occurred when the GWL was below the soil surface. Furthermore, recurrent fires in the Ex-MRP area may result to the decreasing of peatland capacity for retaining and absorbing water from precipitation, lowering ground water levels further and making the area more susceptible to fire, particularly in the dry season. To get a better understanding of this critical issue, we studied the recent fire situation in a portion of the ex-Mega Rice Project (MRP) area by linking the situation with GWL and precipitation.

METHODS

In this study, we are using monthly GWL data from 460 dipwells in upper part of Block A and the bottom part of Block E of the Ex-MRP area (Figure 1). These dipwells were established in 2010 within the Kalimantan Forest and Climate REDD+ demonstration project (KFCP). The GWL were monitored monthly during the period of January 2010-January 2013 using the blow-straw method (Ichsan *et al.*, 2014). In this study, we examine the relationship between ground water level, rate of precipitation and fire occurrences during 2011 - 2012. IDW (Inverse Distance Weighting) multivariate interpolation technique is used to figure the ground water level surrounding each dipwell point. We used monthly TRMM (Tropical Rainfall Measuring Mission) data from NASA and JAXA to illustrate precipitation patterns in the study area. Monthly TRMM precipitation data is derived from GES-DISC NOAA (http://mirador.gsfc.nasa.gov/). Terra/Aqua MODIS active fire data from NASA-EOSDIS (https://earthdata.nasa.gov/) is used to explain fire occurrences and tendency in the area.

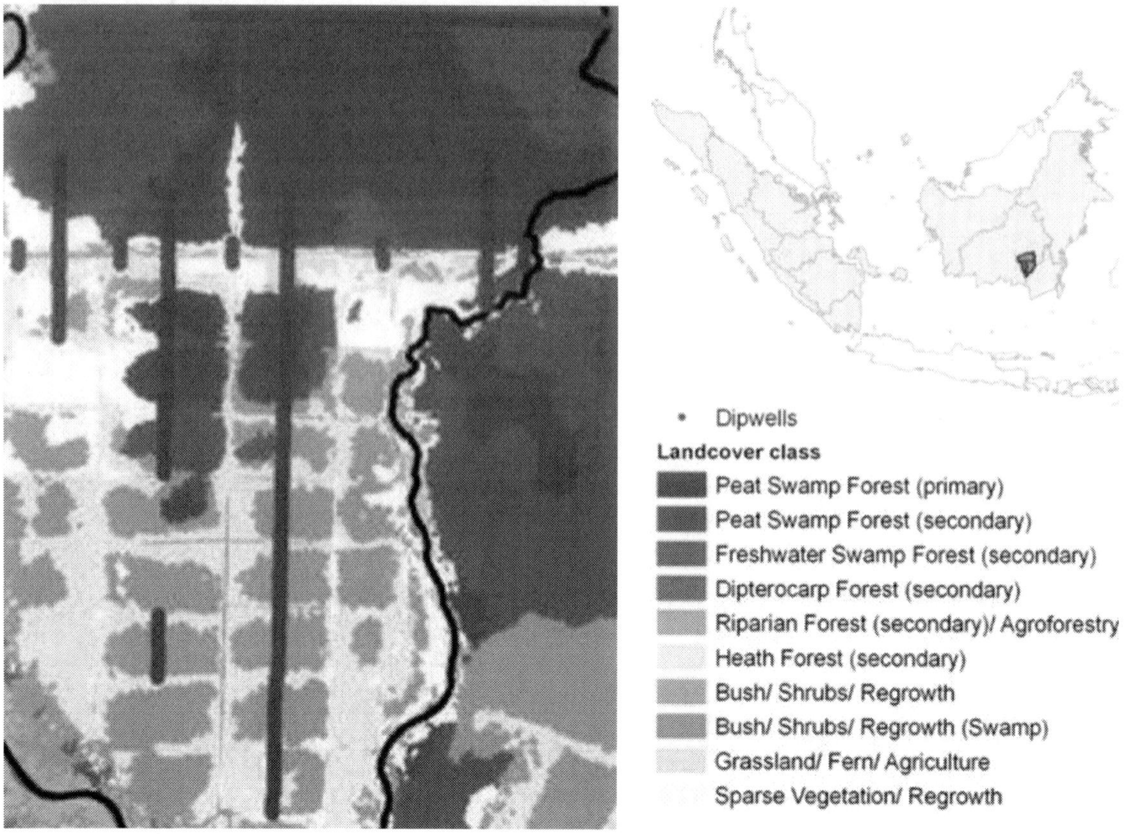

Figure 1: Location of dipwells at the Ex-MRP area, Central Kalimantan (Ichsan *et al.*, 2014)

RESULTS AND DISCUSSION

The Tropical Rainfall Measuring Mission (TRMM) is a joint mission between NASA and the Japan Aerospace Exploration (JAXA) Agency to study rainfall for weather and climate research. The TRMM dataset became the space standard for measuring precipitation, and led to research that improved our understanding of tropical cyclone structure and evolution, convective system properties, lightning-storm relationships, climate and weather modeling, and human impacts on rainfall (Braun, 2016). Northern part of Block A and southern part of Block E of Ex-MRP area covers four TRMM pixels, thus we have four different precipitation regions for the study area (Figures 2 and 4).

All of the regions experienced similar precipitation patterns in 2011 and 2012 (Figure 4), with peak dry season between July and September, and the lowest precipitation in August. Previous studies (Aldrian and Susanto 2003, Putra *et al.*, 2008, Usup *et al.*, 2004) have defined dry and wet seasons in Central Kalimantan by using the monthly rainfall variation. Figure 4 clearly shows a U-shaped monthly precipitation pattern with a trough reaching minimum in August. Similar findings were found by Putra and Hayasaka (2010), revealing that the dry periods in the Ex-MRP area remains the same in June – October each year, with the peak in August. Low precipitation dries the degraded peatland in the MRP area, increasing its susceptibility to fire, and creating suitable conditions for peat fires to be ignited. Figure 5 illustrates that peat fires are found mainly during the dry periods between July – October.

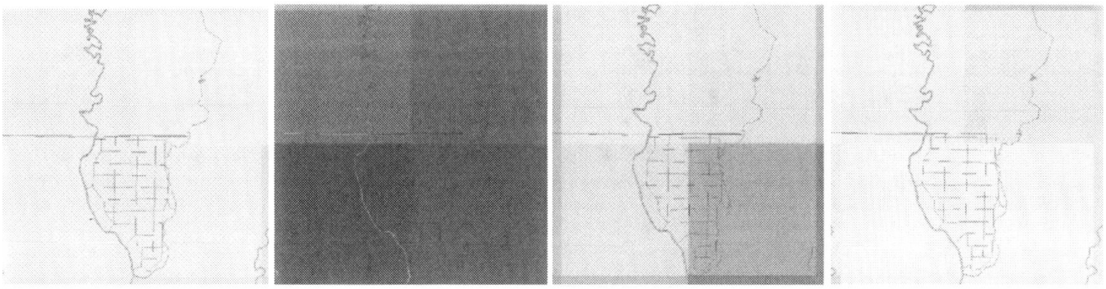

July 2012 August 2012 September 2012 October 2012

Figure 2: Monthly precipitation surrounding area, July – October 2012. The graduated color indicates precipitation rates; dark blue for lowest precipitation (0-10 mm), yellow for moderate rain (30-40 mm); light blue and green indicates precipitation rate between lowest and moderate.

Peatland areas at the northern part of Block A experienced severe dry conditions during the dry periods of July – October, as shown by the red and orange colors in Figure. 3. These areas have suffered from almost yearly peat fire occurrences since 2001, except 2008 (Figure. 4).

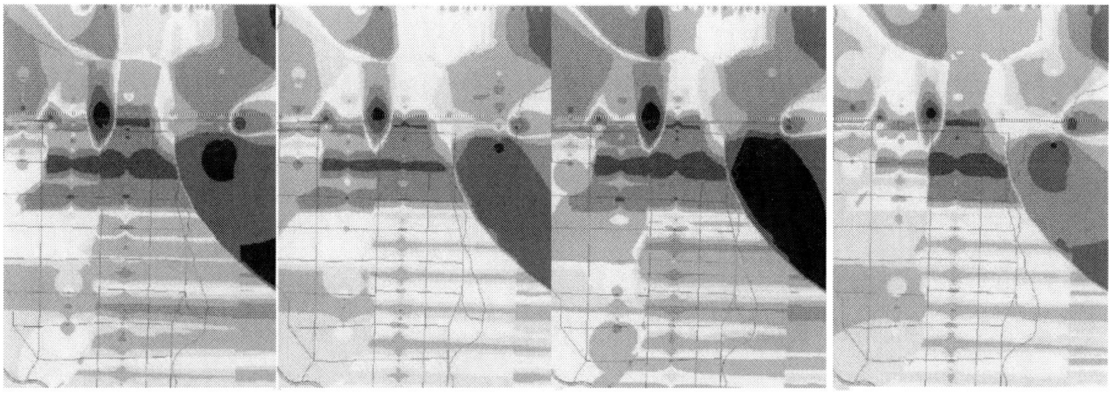

July 2012 August 2012 September 2012 October 2012

Figure 3: Change of ground water level from July – October 2012. Red color indicates deep GWL (more than 30 cm below peat surface); dark blue color for positive GWL; light blue, yellow and orange indicates GWL between 0 (peat surface) and -30 cm (30 cm below peat surface).

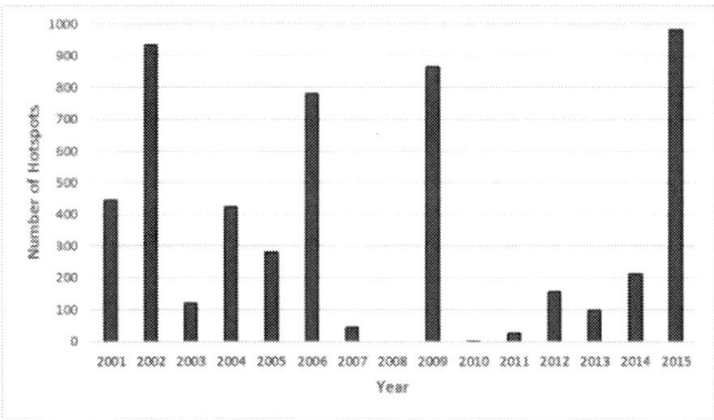

Figure 4: Number of hotspots detected by Terra/Aqua MODIS Satellite in study area, 2001 - 2015

In its natural condition, peat swamp forest is always inundated with water. The peat acts as a natural sponge, retaining moisture at times of low rainfall but, because it is normally waterlogged already, with a very limited capacity to absorb additional heavy rainfall during periods such as a tropical monsoon (UNDP, 2006). GWL in the study area now remains in deficit for the whole of the year (Figure 5) which can be considered unnatural for the system and can explains the severe dry condition of peat in the area.

There was a month time-lag between the lowest precipitation and the lowest GWL both in 2011 and 2012 (Figure 5). Lowest precipitation is found in August, while the lowest GWL occurred in September. GWL starts to increase in October after having continuous high precipitation that starts in September. This time-lag may indicate that peat capacity in absorbing and retaining water from rain water droplets has been substantially decreased, suggesting that ground water levels in the area will recover only after having plenty water supplies from continuous precipitation.

Figure 6 shows that the peat fire occurrences in the study area coincide with the precipitation curve. Fires occur following precipitation patterns with little or no rainfall during the dry period. A large number of peat fires tends to start three months after the start of the decreased of precipitation. In 2011, precipitation decreased gradually from May and reached the lowest point in August, creating the necessary dry conditions for fires to ignite. Equally, a large number of fires began to occur in July and became numerous during August and September. The end of the fire season occurred during October in 2011 and 2012, after having peak fire periods in September. A large numbers of fires started during August 2012, three months after the commencement of decreasing precipitation patterns during June 2012. These peat fire occurrence tendencies may indicate that peat in the study area is still quite dry into the beginning of the wet period, after suffering from severe dry conditions for prolonged dry periods, thus maintaining conditions where ignition may easily occur.

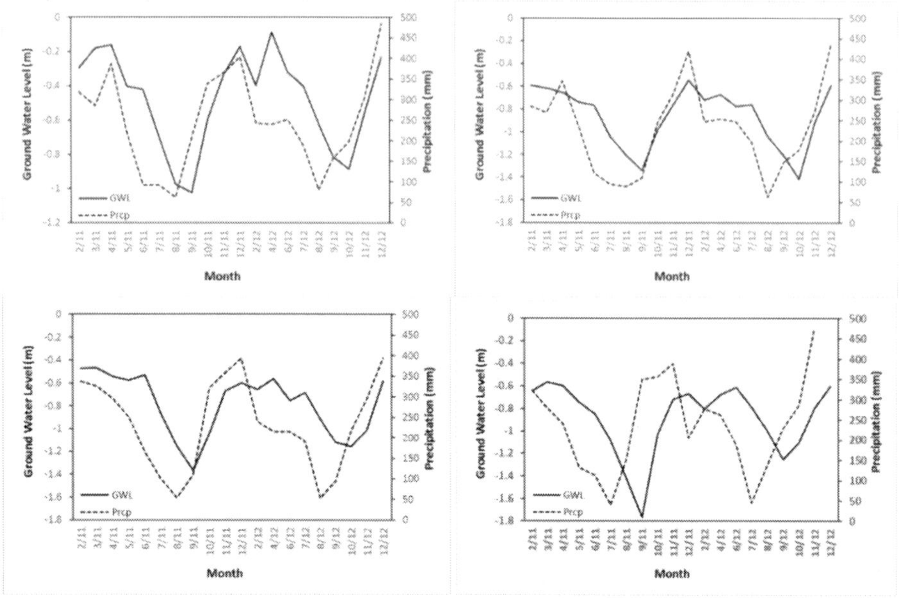

Figure 5: Ground water level and precipitation patterns at four TRMM pixels in the study area, 2011 - 2012

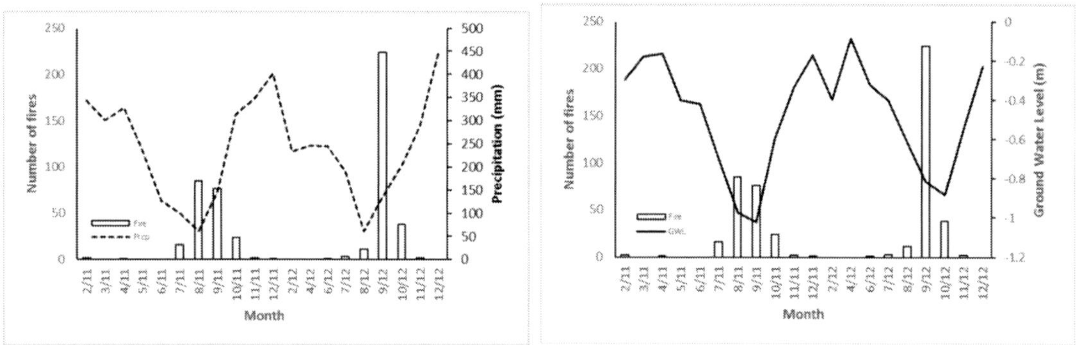

Figure 6: Relationships between number of fire occurrences and precipitation (left), and with GWL at study area (right), 2011 – 2012.

Figures 6 (right) and 7 illustrate the relationships between fire occurrences and GWL, suggesting that the low GWL accelerated conditions where fires ignite with ease. In 2011, a large number of fires started occurring in July when the mean GWL dropped to – 69.9 cm, while in August 2012 fires began with a mean GWL of -61.7 cm (Figure 5). Numbers of fires in 2011 greatly expanded to more than 80 in August and September when the area was subjected the lowest GWL of -1 m. The same phenomenon was observed in 2012 when fires spread quickly after the GWL reached its minimum at -80 cm.

Usup *et al.* (2004), Wosten *et al.* (2008) and Putra *et al.* (2011) suggested critical ground water level of 40 cm below peat surface to prevent fire. However, our findings suggest that shallower GWL below peat surface should be maintained to prevent peat fire occurrences in dry-degraded peatlands. Figure 6 (right) shows that fires are also found during GWL conditions between 15 and 30 cm below the peat surface, such as in February 2011 (-30 cm), March 2011 (-16 cm) and December 2011 (-17 cm).

Most of the fires occurred with shallow GWL conditions of 25 – 30 cm below the peat surface (Figure 7), but fire occurrences with GWL of less than 5 cm below peat surface may strongly suggests that degraded peatlands are very vulnerable to fires even under relatively moist conditions, and therefore degraded peatlands should be maintained in wet conditions with critical GWL of less than 5 cm below peat surface, to prevent the area from experiencing surface peat fires. Dry conditions of degraded peatland create suitable condition for the fire to burn downward into deeper peat layers and ignite deep peat fires, resulting to devastating peat fires in the area.

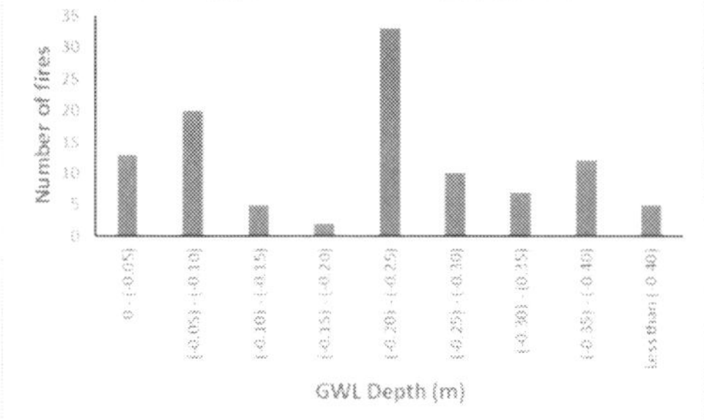

Figure 7: Number of selected peat fires on each GWL depth, September 2012

CONCLUSION

This study reveals that the peatlands in the northern part of Block A and southern part of Block E of Ex-MRP have been changed to degraded peatlands that are very vulnerable to fire. A time lag between lowest precipitation and lowest GWL strongly indicates that peatlands here have lost the capacity to effectively absorb and retain water from rain water droplets, keeping them in drier conditions than natural for most of the year, and therefore maintaining conditions where ignitions may easily occur. Numerous fires found starting during shallow GWL conditions strongly illustrate the importance of maintaining high GWL, of less than 5 cm below the surface, to reduce fire risk and prevent degraded peatlands from experiencing surface peat fires from human impact that may escalated to devastating deep peat fires.

ACKNOWLEDGEMENTS

The research was funded by NASA (NNX13AP46G). The authors wish to thank KFCP for sharing the hydrology data from the project, and the KFCP Hydrology field team for its collection.

REFERENCES

1. Aldrian E, Susanto RD. 2003. Identification of three dominant rainfall regions within Indonesia and their relationship to sea surface temperature. *International Journal of Climatology* 23: 1435-1452, 2003.
2. Braun SA. 2016. TRMM – Tropical Rainfall Measuring Mission. http://trmm.gsfc.nasa.gov.
3. Ichsan N., Hooijer A, Vernimmen R, Applegate GB. (2014) KFCP Hydrology and Peat Monitoring Methodology. Scientific Report, Kalimantan Forests and Climate Partnership, Indonesia.
4. Putra EI, Hayasaka H, Takahashi H, Usup A. 2008. Recent Peat Fire Activity in the Mega Rice Project Area,Central Kalimantan, Indonesia. Journal of Disaster Research Vol.3 (5): 1-8, 2008
5. Putra EI, Hayasaka H. 2011. The effect of the precipitation pattern of the dry season on peat fire occurrence in the Mega Rice Project area, Central Kalimantan, Indonesia. Tropics Vol. 19 (4): 145 – 156, 2011
6. Ritung, S., Wahyunto, K. Nugroho, Sukarman, Hikmatullah, Suparto, dan C.Tafakresnanto. 2011. Peta Lahan Gambut Indonesia Skala 1:250.000. Balai Besar Litbang Sumberdaya Lahan Pertanian. Bogor, Indonesia
7. Siegert, FH, Boehm DV, Rieley JO, Page SE, Jauhiainen J, Vasander H, Jaya A. 2001. Peat fires in Central Kalimantan, Indonesia: fire impacts and carbon release. Proc. of the International Symposium on Tropical Peatlands, pp. 142-154, 2001.
8. UNDP. 2006. Malaysia's Peat Swamp Forests Conservation and Sustainable Use. Kuala Lumpur.
9. Usup A, Hashimoto Y, Takahashi H, and Hayasaka H, Combustion and thermal characteristics of peat fire in tropical peatland in Central Kalimantan, Indonesia, Tropics Vol.14 (1):1-19, 2004.
10. Wosten JHM, Clymans E, Page SE, Rieley JO, Limin SH. 2008. Peat-water interrelationships in a tropical peatland ecosystem in Southeast Asia. Catena 73: 212-224, 2008.

Abstract No: A-259

DETAILED ANALYSES OF EMISSIONS FROM PEAT COMBUSTION ACROSS BIOMES

Adam C. Watts[1, 2*], Hans Moosmüller[2], Vera Samburova[2], Andrey Y. Khlystov[2], Madhu Gyawali[2], Deep Sengupta[2], Chiranjivi Bhattarai[2], Reddy L. N. Yatavelli[3], Rajan K. Chakrabarty[4], Ian J. Arnold[2], Barbara Zielinska[2], Joe D. Knue[2], Judith Chow[2], John G. Watson[2], Xiaoliang Wang[2], L.-W. Anthony Chen[5], Anna Tsibart[6] and Guenter Engling[2]

[1]*Division of Atmospheric Sciences, Desert Research Institute, USA*
[2]*Desert Research Institute, USA*
[3]*California Air Resources Board, USA*
[4]*Washington University, USA*
[5]*University of Nevada, USA*
[6]*Lomonosov State University, Russia*

**Corresponding author: adam.watts@dri.edu.*

SUMMARY

The multifaceted impacts of fires in peatlands have attracted global attention and concern in recent years. Documenting the nature and effects of combustion products from peatlands has been a particularly active area of work, although detailed analyses of emissions are still needed. Our research includes a focus on the chemical composition and the physical and optical properties of particulate matter emissions from peatland fires. We will present detailed emissions work conducted across a wide range of peatland fuels from boreal, subtropical, and tropical peatland ecosystems. Although many similarities exist, we will highlight important differences in combustion emissions observed across the climatic range of our fuel sources and describe some of their implications. Also, we will discuss some of our initial efforts to address challenges facing future emissions research, such as proposing criteria by which to prioritize fuels for detailed emissions analysis.

Keywords: *fire; smoldering, emissions, carbon, atmospheric science*

INTRODUCTION

With carbon stocks rivaling those of Earth's atmosphere (5-6 x 10^{17} g; Gorham 1994, Page *et al.*, 2011), the organic soils in peatlands represent one-fifth to one-third of the planet's terrestrial organic carbon. The importance of these ecosystems in the global carbon cycle is therefore highly significant, despite peatlands occupying only 2-3% of the Earth's terrestrial surface (Yu 2012). The significance of peatlands includes economic, agricultural, and ecological values, and this study relates to the multi-scale importance of fire in peatlands from the standpoint of carbon, climate, and air quality.

Peatlands generally accumulate organic carbon due to wet conditions under which decomposition is slower than biomass production. Therefore, fire in these ecosystems is a very infrequent occurrence, with naturally-ignited fires (*i.e.*, from lightning) recurring only on the order of every 100-1000 years in many of the tropical, temperate, and boreal biomes. When fires do occur, they can be categorized generally into two types: surface fires, which burn aboveground vegetation and, due to high soil moisture, are characterized by short duration, low intensity, and low to moderate severity; and ground fires, which occur during periods when soil moisture is sufficiently low to permit fires to become established in the organic soils of peatlands (Watts and Kobziar 2013). These ground fires, where smoldering combustion of peat soils can result in considerable loss of soil via combustion over extended periods (Rein *et al.*, 2008), and the effects from their emissions, are the focus of this study. (Here, the term "peatland fire" is used to refer to the smoldering ground fires that occur in peatlands.)

At local scales—at the site of a peatland fire and within a distance of 100km, the extended duration of these fires, their production of smoke during nighttime when winds are generally calm, and the difficulty of extinguishing them lead to health concerns from their impacts on air quality (Rappold *et al.*, 2011). At global scales and over long time scales, emissions from peatland fires are a concern for their potential to contribute to global climatic change, both because of the magnitude of emissions and the nature of those emissions. For example, the infamous 1997-1998 fires in Indonesia were estimated to have released carbon emissions equivalent to 13-40% of annual fossil fuel emissions for that year (Page *et al.*, 2002). Also, previous studies have identified smoldering as a major contributor of aerosols and particulates compared to flaming combustion, owing to less efficient combustion and lower temperatures encountered during smoldering (Hadden 2011). Peatland fires can emit up to six times more aerosols per unit carbon consumed than flaming grassland fires (Page *et al.*, 2004). While much is known about the gaseous emissions, the properties and climatic impacts of particulate matter from these fires is an understudied topic. Since the identification of optical properties of aerosol organic carbon (OC) from combustion two decades ago, increasing efforts have focused on the enhanced potential of radiative forcing impacts of aerosol emissions from wildfires (See *et al.*, 2007). These organic compounds, which strongly absorb solar radiation in the low-visible and UV wavelengths, are called brown carbon (BrC; Gyawali *et al.*, 2009, Chakrabarty *et al.*, 2010, Moosmüller et al., 2009) or black carbon (BC). Black carbon (BC) aerosol has been identified as the major light-absorbing and warming agent, influencing radiative forcing directly by as much as 17 ± 30 W/m^2 after a flaming boreal fire (Oris *et al.*, 2013; Randerson *et al.*, 2006). The implications are that not only do peatland fires potentially contribute to altered climate, but that the nature of their emissions cause these fires to have a greater impact on climate per unit of carbon emitted than do other types of wildland fires. Furthermore, the contribution from smoldering combustion of organic soils to global releases of terrestrial carbon to the atmosphere may increase under scenarios of warming and drying climatic conditions (Solomon *et al.*, 2007). However, science still lacks a good understanding of the nature and properties of emissions from peatland fires, especially in regards to the variation that may exist among the emissions from fires in different peat biomes.

In a series of studies, we have conducted detailed analyses of particulate emissions from the combustion of peats found in multiple climatic regions where peatlands occur, in order to compare the chemical, physical, and optical properties of these emissions.

METHODS

Peat samples were collected from three locations: Siberia, Russia, and Alaska, USA (intended to represent boreal and arctic ecosystems), and Florida, USA, (representing temperate-subtropical biomes). These samples were burned at moisture levels approximating those found during droughts and under which peat soils will support combustion. Samples were burned at the DRI biomass combustion facility within insulated containers to simulate field conditions in which surrounding peat soils provide insulation, trapping heat and gases near the site of smoldering combustion. Aerosol emissions were characterized for optical properties with three-wavelength photoacoustic spectrometer and nephelometer (Droplet Measurement Technologies, Inc., CO).

We compared the optical properties of peat samples collected in three biomes at multiple moisture levels to determine whether peat source or fuel moisture content was more important to emissions optical characteristics. Aerosol absorption and scattering coefficients, measured at three wavelengths (405, 532, and 870 nm) were analyzed for single scattering albedo (SSA) and absorption Ångström coefficients (AAC) (405-870 nm).

RESULTS

As expected, low molecular weight Polycyclic aromatic hydrocarbons (PAHs), such as naphthalene, methylnaphthalenes, are mostly present in the gas phase, while high molecular weight PAHs (*e.g.* retene, dimethylphenanthrene) are present in the particle phase (Figure 1). The chemical analysis of emissions constituents revealed similar levels of many compounds compared to needles from Ponderosa pine (*Pinus ponderosa*); a well-characterized fuel from the western U.S. However, all three peat fuels produced considerably higher emissions in the particle phases compared to either pine needles or *Bromus tectorum*; a fine grass that burned rapidly and efficiently in tests (Figure 1).

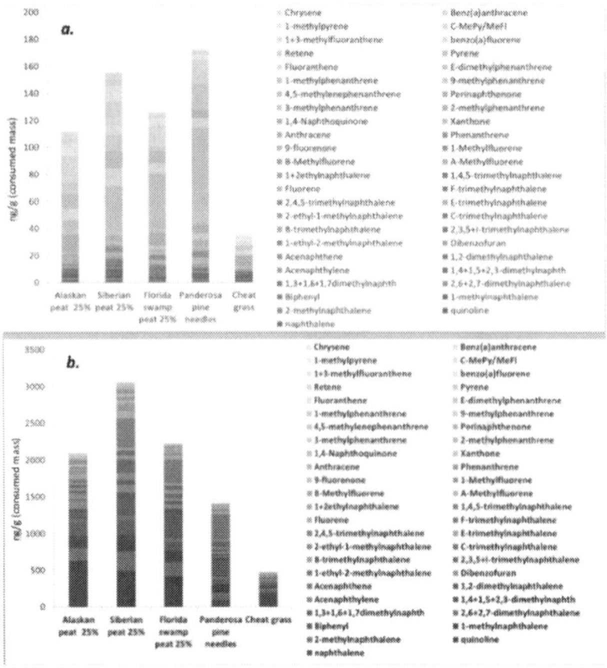

Figure 1 (left): Constituents of gaseous-phase (*a*) and particle-phase (*b*) emissions from Alaskan, Siberian, and Florida peat samples, as well as Ponderosa pine and cheatgrass, two wildland fuels found extensively throughout the western United States which burn primarily in the flaming phase.

Figure 2 (below): Particle size distributions from smoldering combustion of Alaskan peat at two different moisture contents (25% and 50% by mass dry weight). This graph illustrates the effect of moisture content on particulate emissions seen in all three peats.

Particle size distributions counted from emissions of smoldering peats indicated an effect of moisture level on particulates, with drier samples emitting more aerosols in the 100nm size class (Figure 2). Compared with reported values for many other common wildland fuels, emissions from the four peats measured in this study displayed similar values for single scattering albedo, with values in the 0.9-1.0 range at 405nm (Figure 3). However, observed values for absorption Ångström coefficients (405-870 nm) were substantially higher for peats than for other fuels. Furthermore, our observations appear to indicate that as moisture content of a peat sample decreased, AAC values for their emissions increased.

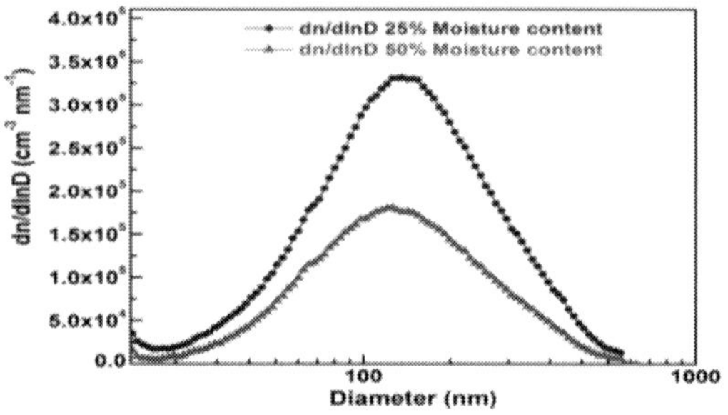

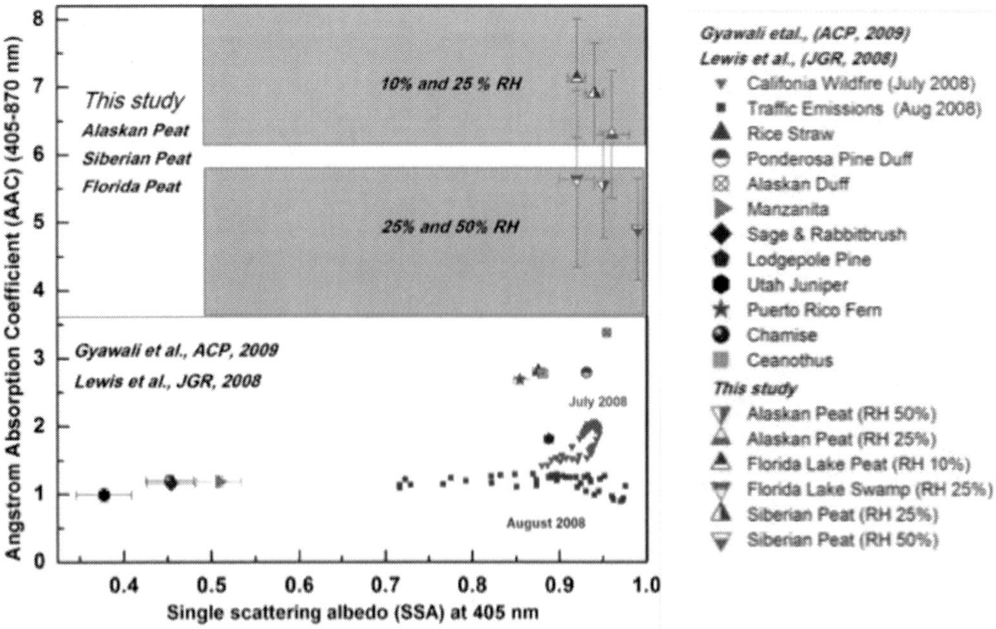

Figure 3: Optical characteristics of peat emissions examined in this study compared with those of other fuels measured by Gyawali *et al.* (2009) and by Lewis *et al.* (2009).

DISCUSSION

Our findings show that BrC from smoldering peat fires in the Boreal region could give rise to significant absorption in the shorter wavelengths and ultraviolet regions of the solar spectrum. This strong absorptivity of the aerosols could drive the net forcing values in the positive (warming) over bright surfaces. The common understanding has been that BC constitutes the light-absorbing aerosol type from boreal forest fires (Randerson *et al.*, 2006) while OC are light scattering in nature and help offset the BC warming effects. However, our results show that OC could further amplify the warming effects of BC over this region, especially since 47% of incoming solar energy is distributed between 400 nm and 700 nm.

CONCLUSION

This study highlights the importance of evaluating optical properties of particulate emissions from peatland fires from various sites under different moisture contents, because understanding the effects of location and moisture on emissions characteristics could potentially enhance the accuracy in the predicted radiative forcing contribution from peat fires and other biomass emissions. We plan to expand our analysis to include more sites and environmental parameters, in order to better characterize the impacts of peatland fires on the global climate. Objectives for these future efforts will be 1) to link understanding of terrestrial carbon emissions from peat/smoldering fires with radiative forcing so that we can better understand the mechanisms driving climate change; 2) to understand how emissions species partitioning may change due to varying environmental factors; and 3) to eventually couple models of emissions and forcing potential with climate change scenarios downscaled to biomes where large deposits of organic soils occur.

ACKNOWLEDGEMENTS

This material is based on work supported by U.S. National Science Foundation Grant AGS1455215, NASA ROSES Grant NNX15AI66G, and the Division of Atmospheric Sciences and Wildland Fire Science Center at the Desert Research Institute, Reno, NV USA. A. Watts also acknowledges support from the Nevada Governor's Office of Economic Development.

REFERENCES

1. Chakrabarty, R., H. Moosmüller, L. Chen, K. Lewis, W. Arnott, C. Mazzoleni, M. Dubey, C. Wold, W. Hao, and S. Kreidenweis 2010. Brown carbon in tar balls from smoldering biomass combustion. Atmospheric Chemistry and Physics 10: 6363-6370.
2. Gorham, E., 1994. The future of research in Canadian peatlands – a brief survey with particular reference to global change. Wetlands 14, 206–215
3. Gyawali, M., W. Arnott, K. Lewis, and H. Moosmüller (2009), In situ aerosol optics in Reno, NV, USA during and after the summer 2008 California wildfires and the influence of absorbing and non-absorbing organic coatings on spectral light absorption, Atmospheric Chemistry and Physics *9*(20), 8007-8015.
4. Hadden, R. M. 2011. Smouldering and self-sustaining reactions in solids: an experimental approach. Ph.D. Dissertation, University of Edinburgh. 143 pp.
5. Moosmüller, H., R. K. Chakrabarty, and W. P. Arnott 2009. Aerosol light absorption and its measurement: A review. Journal of Quantitative Spectroscopy and Radiative Transfer. 110: 844-878.
6. Oris, F., H. Asselin, A. A. Ali, W. Finsinger, and Y. Bergeron. 2013. Effect of increased fire activity on global warming in the boreal forest. Environmental Reviews. 22: 206-219.
7. Page, S., R. Wüst, D. Weiss, J. Rieley, W. Shotyk, and S. H. Limin 2004. A record of Late Pleistocene and Holocene carbon accumulation and climate change from an equatorial peat bog (Kalimantan, Indonesia): implications for past, present and future carbon dynamics. Journal of Quaternary Science 19: 625-635.
8. Page, S., Rieley, J. O. & Banks, C. J. 2011. Global and regional importance of the tropical peatland carbon pool. Global Change Biology 17: 798–818.
9. Rappold, A.G., S.L. Stone, W.E. Cascio, L.M. Neas, V.J. Kilaru, M.S. Carraway, J.J. Szykman, A. Ising, W.E. Cleve, J.T. Meredith, H. Vaughan-Batten, L. Deyneka, and R.B. Devlin. 2011. Peat bog wildfire smoke exposure in rural North Carolina is associated with cardiopulmonary emergency department visits assessed through syndromic surveillance. Environmental Health Perspectives 119: 1415-1420.
10. Randerson, J. T., H. Liu, M. G. Flanner, S. D. Chambers, Y. Jin, P. G. Hess, G. Pfister, M. Mack, K. Treseder, and L. Welp 2006. The impact of boreal forest fire on climate warming. Science 314: 1130-1132.
11. Rein, G., N. Cleaver, C. Ashton, P. Pironi, and J.L. Torero. 2008. The severity of smouldering peat fires and damage to the forest soil. Catena 74: 304-309.
12. See, S. W., R. Balasubramanian, E. Rianawati, S. Karthikeyan, and D. G. Streets 2007. Characterization and

source apportionment of particulate matter < or = 2.5 micrometer in Sumatra, Indonesia, during a recent peat fire episode, Environmental Science and Technology 41: 3488–3494.

13. Solomon, S., D. Qin, M. Manning, Z. Chen, M. Marquis, K. Averyt, M. Tignor, and H. Miller 2007. The physical science basis. Contribution of working group I to the fourth assessment report of the intergovernmental panel on climate change, 235-337.
14. Watts, A.C., and L.N. Kobziar. 2013. Smoldering combustion and ground fires: ecological effects and multi-scale significance. Fire Ecology 9: 124-132.
15. Yu, Z. 2012. Northern peatland carbon stocks and dynamics: A review. Biogeosciences 9: 4071–4085.

Abstract No: A-114

DETECTION AND CHARACTERIZATION OF LOW TEMPERATURE PEAT FIRES DURING THE 2015 FIRE CATASTROPHE IN INDONESIA USING A NEW HIGH-SENSTITIVITY FIRE MONITORING SATELLITE SENSOR (FIREBIRD)

Elizabeth C. Atwood[1, 2], Sandra Englhart[2*], Eckehard Lorenz[3], Werner Wiedemann[2] and Florian Siegert[1, 2]

[1]*GeoBio Center, Dept. Biology II, Ludwig-Maximilians-Universität Munich, Germany*
[2]*RSS Remote Sensing Solutions GmbH, Germany*
[3]*Institute of Optical Sensor Systems, German Aerospace Center (DLR e.V.), Germany*

**Corresponding author: englhart@rssgmbh.de*

SUMMARY

Vast and disastrous fires occurred on Sumatra and Borneo during the 2015 dry season, pushing Indonesia into the top 5 carbon emitting countries. The region was affected by a very strong El Niño-Southern Oscillation (ENSO), similar to or even stronger compared with the last severe event in 1997/98. Fire dynamics in Central Kalimantan, Borneo, were investigated using an innovative sensor offering higher sensitivity at a finer spatial resolution (160 m) than previously available. The sensor is onboard the TET-1 satellite, which together with a second satellite (BIROS, planned launched May 2016) form the German Aerospace Center (DLR) FireBird mission. TET-1 images (acquired every 2-3 days) were used to detect fires continuously burning for almost three weeks in the protected peatlands of Sebangau National Park and surrounding areas with active logging and oil palm concessions. TET-1 detection capabilities were compared with MODIS active fire and Landsat burned area algorithms. Fire dynamics, including propagation speed and area burned, were investigated and possible causes for fires were explored. We show that TET-1 has improved detection capabilities over MODIS in monitoring small, low intensity peatland fire fronts through thick smoke and haze. Analysis of fire dynamics revealed that the largest burned areas resulted from fire front lines started from multiple locations. The highest propagation speeds measured, in excess of 200 m/day, were over peat deeper than 2 m. Fires were found to occur most often in concessions that contained drainage infrastructure but had not yet been cleared. Benefits of implementing this sensor system to improve current fire management techniques are discussed. Near real-time fire detection together with enhanced fire behavior monitoring capabilities will also advance analysis of fire impact on tropical peatlands, greenhouse gas emission estimations as well as design of measures to prevent and mitigate severe fire events in the future.

Keywords: *peat fires, high sensitivity fire monitoring, fire dynamics, FireBird, Sebangau*

INTRODUCTION

The fires that swept across Indonesia during the latter half of 2015 were catastrophic on many levels. Costs incurred from the fires to the Indonesian government are estimated to be in excess of USD $16 billion (World Bank 2015), signifying 1.9% of the national gross domestic product. Greatly reduced air quality in Southeast Asia is a consequence of major forest fires (Hyer & Chew 2010), and the resulting smoke cloud, coined the 2015 Southeast Asian Haze, spread across several countries. The islands of Sumatra and Borneo were especially heavily impacted, with poor air quality causing a state of emergency to be declared in six Indonesian provinces. Initial emission estimates from the 2015 fires amount to 1.75 billion metric tons of CO2 equivalents (World Bank 2015), pushing Indonesia into the world's top 5 CO2 emitting countries (www.globalfiredata.org).

The peatlands on Borneo, covering 16-27 million ha, constitute more than half of all tropical peatlands worldwide (Page *et al.*, 2009). In recent decades, these peat swamp forests have been degraded through both industrial and illegal logging, industrial plantation activities and infrastructure from development projects such as the Mega Rice Project (Miettinen *et al.*, 2012). Drainage infrastructure, such as canals, contribute to lowering the water table (Konecny *et al.*, 2016), which is then compounded by drought periods coinciding with climatological events such as El Niño-Southern Oscillation (ENSO) (Page *et al.*, 2009). On Borneo, slash-and-burn techniques often result in fires spreading into surrounding un-slashed peat swamp forests. Peatland fires are characterized by low intensity burning, which can spread into peat deposits up to 0.5 m below the surface. Combined with slow propagation speeds of less than 2 m/day, peatland fires can burn for long periods of time, are very difficult to extinguish and produce large amounts of particulate matter, CO and other gas compounds (Usup *et al.*, 2004). Peatland and forest fires in Indonesia during the 1997/98 ENSO event are estimated to have produced 0.2-0.4 Pg C, accounting for at least 10%

of the global total carbon production due to forest fires (Taylor 2010).

Many questions remain regarding better fire management practices to help avoid catastrophic fire events in Indonesia such as those in 1982/83, 1997/98 and recently in 2015. Remote sensing systems have been utilized for over three decades to support monitoring efforts, which include NOAA-AVHRR, GOES-VAS, ERS-ATSR, TRMM-VIIRS, and MODIS on the EOS Terra and Aqua satellites. Most sensors saturate between 300-340 K, the exception being one MODIS band (4-µm low-gain) which saturates at 500 K. Low sensor saturation inhibits detection of very large fire events (Zhukov *et al.*, 2006). While MODIS was to date best able to overcome this limitation, its 1-km pixel resolution hinders detection of initial fire fronts or multiple small fires.

The sensor onboard the Technology Experiment Carrier (TET-1) saturates at 900 K, improving detection of smoldering to intense large-area fires (Zhukov *et al.*, 2006). This, together with the sensor's 160-m spatial resolution, could improve active fire monitoring and allow measurement of fire dynamic behavior previously not possible.

We explore whether TET-1 can provide improved fire detection capabilities than hereto existing systems, thus offering the basis for an improved early-detection fire management system. Focus is paid to fire dynamics (propagation speed, area burned) over different ground and vegetation types, as well as fire occurrence in and around concession areas.

METHODS

The study area covered the Sebangau National Park as well as neighboring oil palm concessions and degraded areas. Datasets for peat depth, primary forest cover and concessions were accessed from Global Forest Watch. Oil palm plantation concession extent was updated based on Landsat-8 imagery and classified as "Plantation", "Small-plot agriculture", "Recently cleared", "Drained not cleared" or "Concession area not converted".

TET-1 images were provided by the DLR Institute of Optical Sensor Systems in Berlin. MODIS hotspot data (MCD14) were accessed through the Fire Information for Resource Management System (FIRMS). Detection of large fire events is hindered by a low sensor saturation temperature (Zhukov *et al.*, 2006), and while MODIS has until now offered the highest sensor saturation range, the 1-km pixel resolution limits detection capabilities of small fires and fire dynamics. An initial comparison with the MODIS hotspots product suggests that TET-1 can provide improved detection of small fire fronts through thick smoke and haze (Fig 1). Landsat-7 and -8 images from June-Dec. 2015 were accessed from GloVis and atmospherically corrected.

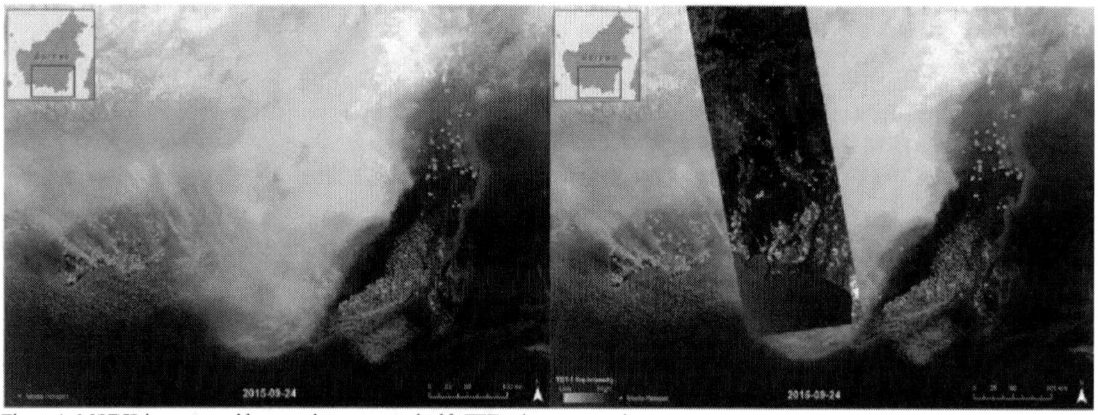

Figure 1: MODIS imagery and hotspot data compared with TET-1 imagery overlay.

MODIS Aqua true color (RGB: 1, 4, 3) images from Sept 24th, superimposed with same day MODIS hotspot data (MCD14, red dots) and TET1 gray-scale midwave infrared (MWIR) acquisition. MODIS hotspot data are under-detecting low intensity fire fronts visible in TET-1 imagery (fire intensity indicated by yellow gradient).

Classification of active fires and burned areas

Hierarchical object-based image analysis (OBIA) is a recently developed technique that evaluates spectral band information combined with spatial context and pattern recognition algorithms. Both TET-1 and Landsat images were classified with eCognition software (Trimble Navigation Ltd.).

Comparison TET-1 and MODIS active burning fire detection capabilities

MODIS hotspot data were controlled for temporally as well as spatially, since TET-1 acquisitions did not consistently cover the study area. *Areas of Interest (AOI) selection and measuring fire dynamics*: Fire AOI's were selected dependent upon a series of TET-1 detected active burning fire pixels covering at least three separate dates. For each AOI, fire front propagation speed was measured by comparing the location of a fire front from one date to the next. Area burned within each fire AOI was quantified from the TET-1 and Landsat classification results.

RESULTS

TET-1 comparison with MODIS: Hotspots data were clearly outperformed by the TET-1 data (Table 1). From Sept. 24th to Oct. 23rd , MODIS detected less than half of that by TET-1 (resp., 109,000 ha and 225, 469 ha) because thick haze hampers the detection of active fires.

Table 1: Comparison MODIS and TET-1 Active Burning Fire Detection Capabilities.

Sensor	Revisit time (days)	Spatial resolution (m)	Detected fire pixels	Estimated area (ha)
MODIS hotspots	0.5	1,000 x 1,000	1,090	109,000.00
TET-1	2-3	160 x 160	88,074	225,469.44

Fire front analysis and area burned:

Comparing TET-1 active burning fire pixels over successive dates revealed interesting fire propagation dynamics (Fig 2). Previous fire scars (purplish areas) and changes in logging infrastructure (rails and canals) are evident from the Landsat imagery from 1991 and 2015 (Figure 2a, b). The outer fire front from each TET-1 image is displayed as a colored fire isochrome with the respective image acquisition date indicated (Figure 2b). TET-1 MWIR data from different points within the series are also presented. One can observe fire propagation speed over previous fire scar areas being either greatly slowed (along the northern border) or the fire becoming no longer detectable (along the western and southern borders).

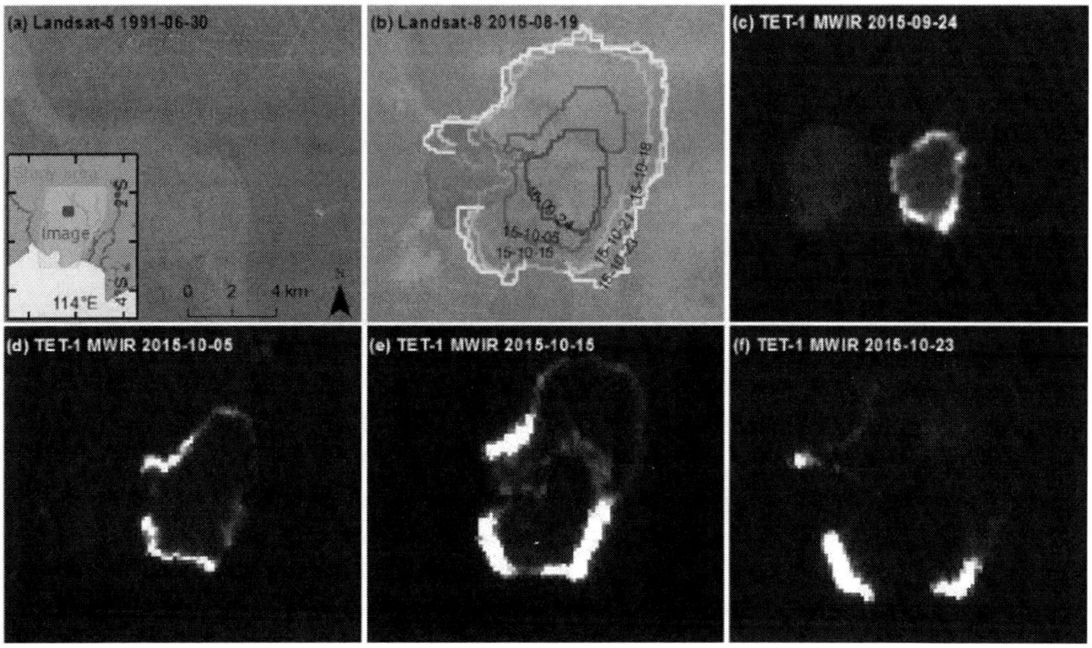

Figure 2: Fire ring front time series.

(a) Landsat-5 imagery (false color: 5, 4, 3) from June 30th, 1991, showing historical logging railway infrastructure and burn scars (purple color).
(b) Landsat-8 imagery (false color: 9, 5, 4) from Aug. 19th, 2015, overlain with TET-1 detected isochromes. Recently burned area prior to fire event is located along the western fire edge. Original TET-1 midwave infrared (MWIR) imagery is shown for Sept. 24th (c), Oct. 5th (d), Oct. 15th (e), and Oct. 23rd, 2015 (f).

Fire dynamic measurements:

The most common fire form observed was a long fire line discerned to have started from either a single or multiple points (resp., 6 and 7 AOIs), the other form was a fire ring spreading from a central location (3 AOIs). Highest fire propagation speeds (> 200 m/day) occurred over peat > 2 m deep. Average propagation speed reduced with decreasing peat layer depth. AOIs with the heaviest fire damage (representing burned areas from 9,948-23,367 ha) resulted from fire lines started from multiple sources. *Fire prevalence in relation to different levels of concession usage*: By normalizing by area, we observed that fires occurred most frequently in concession areas that are "Drained not cleared" (13.5%). Fires were found to occur least often in "Small-plot agriculture" (3.2%) and "Plantation" areas (4.1%).

DISCUSSION

TET-1 detection of burning fire pixels consistently outperformed the MODIS hotspot algorithm (Table 1). While MODIS, with saturation at 500 K and daily global coverage, has been and continues to be a workhorse of global fire detection, the coarse 1-km spatial resolution detracts from the sensor's capability to capture fine fire structures (Zhukov *et al.*, 2006). The ability of the TET-1 sensor to measure these dynamics is demonstrated well in Fig 1, where multiple smaller fire fronts were not being detected by the MODIS hotspot algorithm.

Analysis of fire occurrence in different concession usage areas revealed that fires occur most often in plots with installed drainage infrastructure but have not yet been cleared. Since fire is the technique of choice to quickly and cheaply clear slashed areas, the frequent occurrence of fire within the "Drained, not cleared" areas is not surprising. Fires were often first detected in previously burned areas which then spread into surrounding primary forest.

Previous disturbance increases the susceptibility to fire. For instance, many fires have started in logged over areas. Logging creates gaps in the canopy, which dries out the forest microclimate and thus increases the temperature of the peat surface. Whereas drainage causes a decrease in the water table which can result in shrinkage and irreversible drying out of the peat. This study shows that peatland fires in the study area follow drainage, selective logging and old burn scars.

Efficient and effective fire management is difficult on many levels, and a key component for improvement will depend upon the best fire monitoring system possible. Early detection of small fires, before they become fire fronts many kilometers long, will greatly improve firefighting response efficiency. Fig 3 shows how fires first detected in September then, over 2 weeks, spread and connect with one another to form fire fronts over 10 km long. The MODIS hotspot algorithm failed to detect fires over the image extent on both days. The estimated burned area within Fig 3 is 15,992 ha (from Landsat). The most common fire form observed over the study were fire lines, emphasizing how early detection of small fires, before they have the chance to expand, is essential to improving fire management as it is impossible to fight the fires once they have grown to a huge fire front.

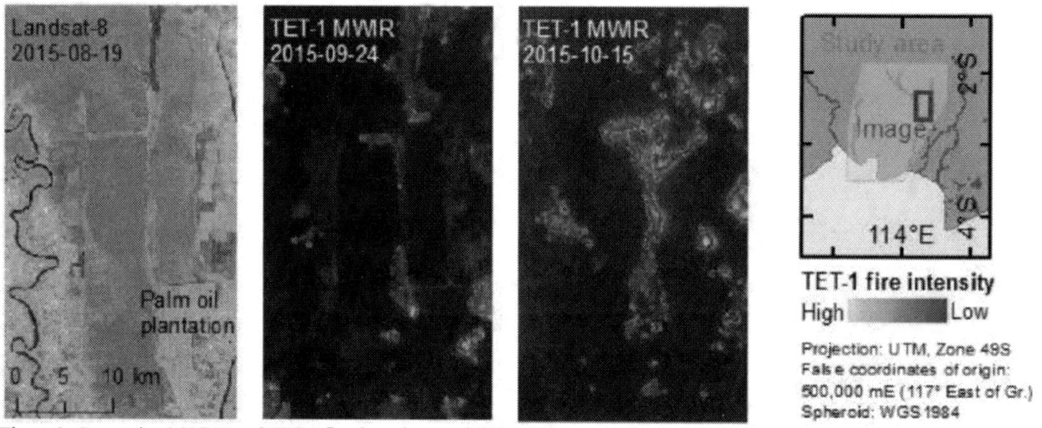

Figure 3: Comparing MODIS and TET-1 fire detection capabilities during rapid fire front expansion over 2 weeks.

Landsat-8 (false color: 6,5,4) image from Aug. 19th, and TET-1 midwave infrared (MWIR) images from Sept. 24th and Oct. 15th, 2015, with TET-1 detected active fire pixels overlaid in red-yellow gradient. Location of image within study area indicated in the inset, no MODIS hotspots were detected within image extent on either day.

CONCLUSION

This study demonstrates the improved fire detection capabilities of TET-1 compared to existing systems. Given the sensor's high saturation (900 K) and finer spatial resolution (160 m), TET-1 fire detection capabilities proved double that of MODIS. The FireBird mission offers an opportunity to build upon existing sensors with a system capable of providing more detailed information on fire occurrence and previously not possible fire dynamic measurements. Monitoring of fire damage extent using sensors working in the VNIR, such as Landsat and Sentinel-2, provide estimates of burned area at even finer spatial resolution (down to 10 m) but are limited by waiting for relatively cloud and haze free images (Hoscilo *et al.*, 2011). Early fire detection through smoke and haze provides valuable information for fire control management, and the financial as well as social costs incurred by the fall 2015 fires present clear motives for improving current fire control management strategies.

Fire dynamic measurements revealed that fires tended to spread most quickly over peat > 2m deep. Fire front lines many kilometers long were the most common form observed. We found that fires occurred with the highest frequency in concession areas containing drainage infrastructure but had not been cleared prior to the fire event. Fires were observed to often begin in areas previous burned and then spread into neighboring primary forest.

TET-1 will be joined this year by BIROS, expanding the FireBird constellation and thus reducing time between acquisition dates. Expansion of the FireBird fleet is in discussion, which would enable near real-time fire detection and support improved organization of firefighting activity by enabling efforts to be focused on fires while they are still small and easily contained. We have here demonstrated not only how a FireBird sensor can improve hereto existing monitoring systems, but also how detected fire dynamic data can be used to help design measures to reduce risk of fire. This information will be useful for government agencies, fire managers and monitoring groups concerned with preventing such catastrophes in the future.

ACKNOWLEDGEMENTS

The authors would like to first and foremost thank Peter Navratil and Kristina Konecny for providing essential support during the development and analysis of this project. Both Julianna Freitas Santos and Moritz Altenbach provided much appreciated help during data processing. R. Richter provided advice for the atmospheric correction processing. Funding was provided by DLR and Remote Sensing Solutions RSS GmbH. We kindly acknowledge the use of data from (MODIS) LANCE FIRMS operated by the NASA/GSFC/Earth Science Data and Information System (ESDIS) with funding provided by NASA/HQ, (Landsat) NASA Goddard Space Flight Center and USGS, and (TET-1) the DLR Institute of Optical Sensor Systems.

REFERENCES

1. Hoscilo A, Page SE, Tansey KJ, Rieley JO (2011) Effect of repeated fires on land-cover change on peatland in southern Central Kalimantan, Indonesia, from 1973 to 2005. *International Journal of Wildland Fire,* 20. 4, 578.
2. Hyer EJ, Chew BN (2010) Aerosol transport model evaluation of an extreme smoke episode in Southeast Asia. *Atmospheric Environment,* 44. 11, 1422–1427.
3. Miettinen J, Hooijer A, Shi C *et al.* (2012) Extent of industrial plantations on Southeast Asian peatlands in 2010 with analysis of historical expansion and future projections. *Global Change Biology Bioenergy,* 4. 6, 908–918.
4. Page S, Hoscilo A, Langner A *et al.* (2009) Tropical peatland fires in Southeast Asia. In: *Tropical Fire Ecology: Climate Change, Land Use, and Ecosystem Dynamics.* Cochrane MA (ed.), Springer, Berlin. pp. 263–287. Taylor D (2010) Biomass burning, humans and climate change in Southeast Asia. *Biodiversity and Conservation,* 19. 4, 1025–1042.
5. Usup A, Hashimoto Y, Takahashi H, Hayasaka H (2004) Combustion and thermal characteristics of peat fire in tropical peatland in Central Kalimantan, Indonesia. *Tropics,* 14. 1, 1–19.
6. World Bank (2015) *Indonesia Economic Quarterly: Reforming Amid Uncertainty.* Dec. 2015, Jakarta, 54 pages. Zhukov B, Lorenz E, Oertel D, Wooster M, Roberts G (2006) Spaceborne detection and characterization of fires during the bi-spectral infrared detection (BIRD) experimental small satellite mission (2001–2004). *Remote Sensing of Environment,* 100. 1, 29–51.

Abstract No: A-361

DRIVERS OF RECURRENT PEATFIRE IN RIAU AND SOUTH SUMATERA, INDONESIA

Oka Karyanto[1*], Ismail[1], Ari Susanti[1], Satyawan Pudyatmoko[1] and Trias Aditya[2]

[1]*Faculty of Forestry, Universitas Gadjah Mada, Indonesia*
[2]*Department of Geodetic Engineering, Universitas Gadjah Mada, Indonesia*

**Corresponding author: okka@ugm.ac.id*

SUMMARY

Riau province once has been blessed with about 4 million Ha peat forest, making it one of the largest peatland countries in Indonesia. Responding to economic development, most of the peat forests have been largely drained and the province has been among the most prone to recurrent peat fire area. There has been much debates on the patterns and root of causes (drivers) of peat fire, causing effort to curb recurrent peat fire are daunting task and even becoming an inconclusive high tension of public debates. There has been much ambiguity on the drivers and the triggers. Poor availability of evidence of the peat fire patterns and their drivers making efforts to suppress the recurrent peatfire and its policy intervention has never been effective. Using different techniques of remote sensing, we present here a number of evidences that peatland in Riau becoming more vulnerable to recurrent peatfire due to expanding large scale peatland drainage, intensified peatland-human interaction and poor peatland governance. We found also a similar pattern in a near areas in province of South Sumatera, to make confident that recurrent peatfire is a merely consequence of a systemic impact following adoption of paradigm of development to put peatland as among central farming areas to provide a globally traded commodities like crude palm oil (CPO) and pulp and paper.

INTRODUCTION

Recent frequent & recurrent peatfires in Indonesia and its impacts throughout the region has caused an escalating political economy discourse as to clarify the drivers (Ref). Many claims on poor peatland governance such as encroachment by peasants as trigger for recurrent peatfire have resulted many suspects have been jailed and has somehow left many discourse on the biophysical factor that driving recurrent peatfire for example there is somehow a little confidence that disturbance on peatland in humid tropical forests makes them more vulnerable to fire. As commonly found that peatland disturbance has drying effect of the opened canopy and greater amounts of dead woody debris (Cochrane, 2001; Siegert *et al.*, 2001). Drained peatland areas with degraded vegetation become extremely vulnerable to annual fires that further degrade these ecosystems (Hoscilo *et al.*, 2011). Occasional but catastrophic fires on peatland can release immense quantities of carbon into the atmosphere from peat combustion (Page *et al.*, 2002; Heil *et al.*, 2006).

Indonesia has about 20 million Ha of peatland, making as a country with the greatest area for tropical peatland. Due to market pressure that heavily influences the development paradigm, in the last decades, about half of the peatland have been drained for cultivating export-oriented commodities like palm oil and pulp and paper, using species that are not adapted to water-logging. Within only less than two decades, Riau (which more than half of its areas ca. 4 million Ha once were peatforest) has experienced massive ecosystem change from previously being 'frequently inundated and moist -ecosystem' into human-made 'drained-ecosystem'. This is due to peatforest conversion and draining into plantations (palm oil, pulp-paper, whether at large scale owned by concessionaires or at smallholder scale). Furthermore, a large scale dried peat (biomass) material which has been left-behind could easily turn to be massive fire fuel during the dry seasons. This making Riau landscape has shifted into (peat) fire vulnerable ecosystem on the historical record. Its vulnerability has been increasing due to climate extremities and continuous extension of the drained areas.

Recurrent peatfire in across peatland in Indonesia has been worsening recently and with its regional haze impacts has a very sensitive political consequence domestically and internationally. Hence, many interpretation on as to why this severity is always increasing, making as a counter-productive in developing an effective policy intervention. The objective of this paper is to demonstrate using remote sensing data that onset and rapid increasing frequency of peatfire (and its recurrency) is due to conversion of peatforest and draining for establishing monoculture farming system. This is strongly linked and merely a consequence to the policy for regional development adopted by the peatland provinces.

MATERIALS AND METHODS

We used spatial plan map to delineate the peatland designated for non-conservation areas in order to demonstrate that these areas are then been drained (canal infrastructure were built) making them vulnerable to the recurrent peatfire as they are subjected into disturbances (forest conversion, peatland draining and its corresponding intensive management). Using a historical analysis of Landsat imageries, we did manual peatforest classification (2000, 2005 and 2010) superimposed corresponding annual hotspot to ascertain that non-disturbed peatforest are not vulnerable to peatfire. Manual canal mapping was done using available optical and when the cloud-smog were too bad, we used different SAR imageries. Hotspot datasets from MODIS sensor for the year of 2014 and 2015 within both study areas (province of Riau and South Sumatera) were collected from NASA data server[10]. Regardless the confidence level, all hotspot were taken into account as suggested by Zubaidah., *et al.* (2014). From canal location, a buffer zones were established, ranging from zone of "within canal[11]" to 10 km with interval of 1 km. Buffer zone of "within canal" refers to areas surrounded by canal (land-locked) with distance less than 1 km. From each buffer zone, the quantities of hotspot were summed, and the proportions of the quantity relatively to the total hotspot within study area were calculated. Nonetheless, due to uncomplete canal network map in the northern part of Riau province, this area was excluded from the hotspot computation. In addition, the calculation of quantity and proportion for hotspot with confidence level above 70 % were also performed. Due to similar results, the graphics are unseen in this paper. The computation of hotspot in buffer zone is aimed to proof that hotspot were caused by canalization (peatland drainage) and the draining impact has extended beyond to the canal.

RESULTS AND DISCUSSION

Figure 1 shows rapid increase in palm oil plantation in Riau. FAO report also showed that global demand for CPO is double in 2050, making further pressure to the remaining forest and peatland in the tropics, as we saw in Riau province as among the fastest expansion areas for palm oil plantation, including on the peatland. A similar trend is also found in global demand in pulp-paper products which also trigger new expansion on pulp-paper plantation in the drained peatland.

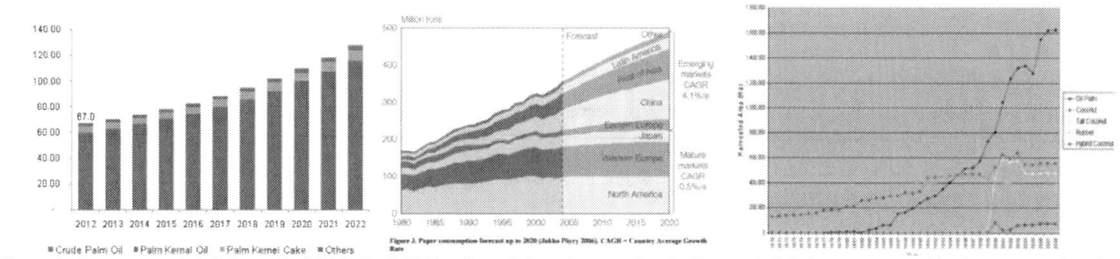

Figure 1: Increase on global demand of CPO, FAO 2011 (*above-left*), pulp-paper Jaacko Poyry 2013 (*above-centre*) and its impact on a drastic increase of palm oil plantation area in Riau which also include on peatland-Ministry of Agriculture GOI 2009 (*above-right*)

In 2013, a total 15 m Ha palm oil plantation produce 65 m ton palm mesocarp + kernel oils, whilst global demand in 2018 will be increasing at 77 m ton (FAO) and further increase at 93-156 m t by 2050 (Corley, 2009). Continuous pressure to increase productivity and additional land conversion to satisfy increasing global demand, where Riau among the place where this further expansion is very possible. We saw this global market demand has coincidence and thus we believed that it has triggered these large scale peatland draining, as shown by Figure 2. These peatland draining has been justified by the government spatial plan to further drain peatland, in order to response global demand of CPO-pulp paper and its related new investments. These well-ordered extensive and intensive canal infrastructure typically developed by large concessionaires (pulp and palm oil plantations) have concentrated in the non-conservation peatland areas as previously designated by the government (as shown by outside of the red-polygon (non-conservation areas), indicating compliance of the those expanding peatland drainage to the existing spatial planning. This clearly shows that the peatland drainage have been mostly expanding due to commercial farming by large concessionaires on non-conservation areas designated by the government.

[10]https://earthdata.nasa.gov

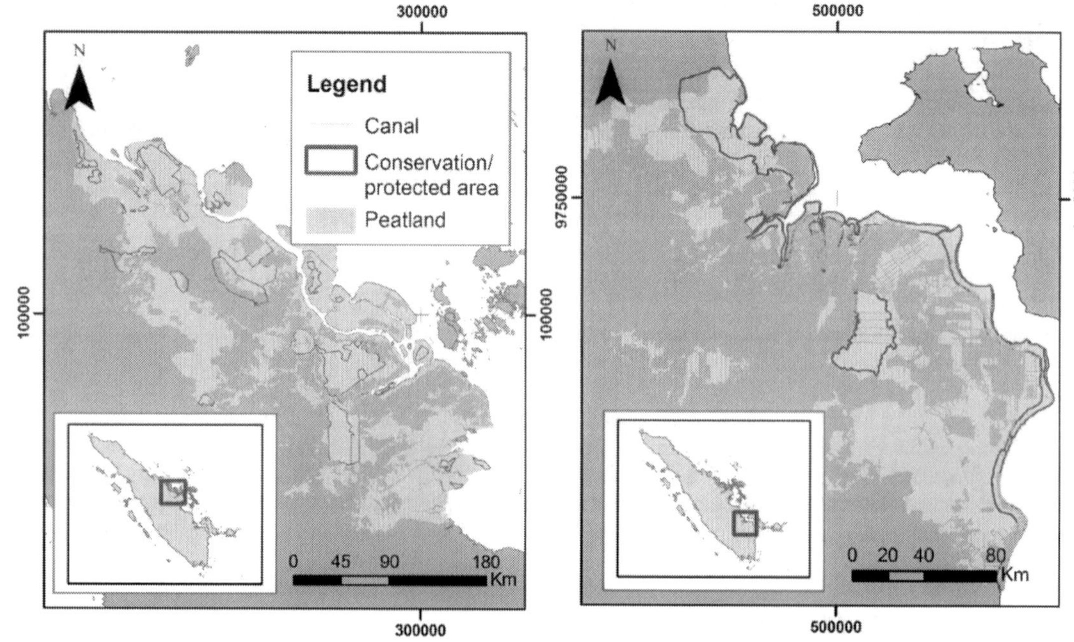

Figure 2: Spatial plan and peatland drainage areas of Riau and South Sumatera Provinces. See the canal infrastructure (yellow) did not encroach the designated conservation-protected areas (red line polygons)

Such global market has put a pressure on the development of many frontiers areas in Indonesia ie. peatland areas that previously relatively untouched. Global demand on CPO and pulp-paper has made those peatland as a new area for large scale farming on drained peatland since the plant species being cultivated are not tolerant to water-logging condition. This developmental scenario on peatland has been justified by current legislation designated by both at central and at local (provincial and district) levels to support new livelihood and new economic era. As spin off impacts, this intensive farming on drained peatland has also attracts further new large scale migrants and investments, making peatland ecosystem previously were relatively unoccupied by settlement, now becoming among centre for agro-politan areas including pressure from human populations who seek for new livelihood. Under poor land governance and government policies which prefers providing licences for large scale companies and do not offer equitable opportunity of peatland access for smallholders and the locals, we see a dramatic sporadic peatforest encroachment.

Both small-scale and large-scale peatland drainage infrastructure have severely impacted on peatland water status, as shown in Figure 3 which is respectively borrowed from Sumawinata *et al.* (2012) and Hooijer *et al.* (2011) papers who worked in closely with pulp plantation companies in Indonesia. It is very obvious that the so called ecohydrology, a sophisticated technology adopted by the companies to maintain water level in across drained peatland landscape have failed to achieve the target water level ie. it drops mostly below 1 m during peak of dry seasons, making them very vulnerable to recurrent peatfire, worsening during the El Nino years. This vulnerability of water level drop on peatland against recurrent peatfire have been clearly demonstrated by few monitoring data shown by Osaki *et al.* (2011) and Saharjo *et al.* (2012) in Figure 3b.

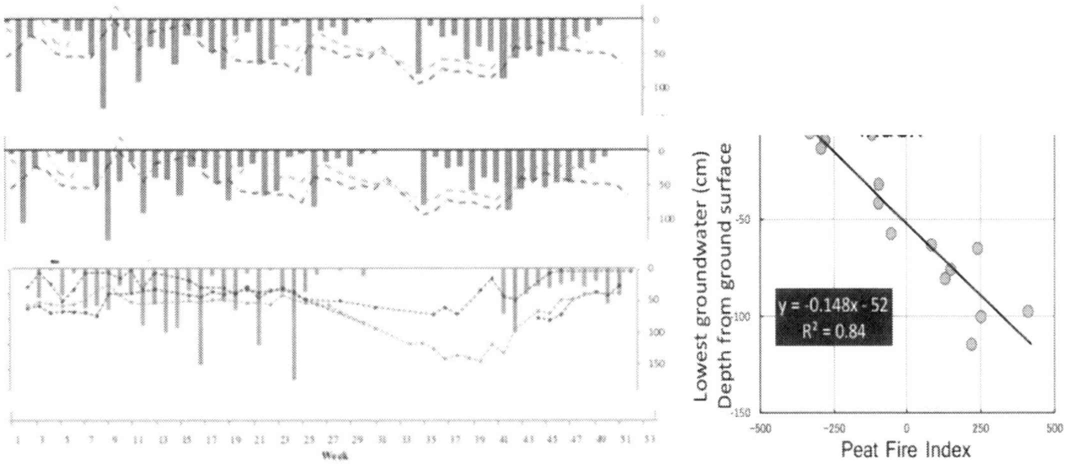

Figure 3: Left-Dropped water level (*dashed lines*) on drained peatland during peak of dry season in a pulp-paper plantations in three provinces in Sumatera in a year monitoring, see the water level in cm below peatsurface that could drop below 150 cm during the peak of dry seasons even under on so called ecohydrological technology management (after Sumawinata *et al.* 2013) and right- increased peatfire index under low water level (drought condition-after Takahashi 2012)

Peatfire occurs under dry atmospheric condition worsen during extreme weather events, such as ENSO (El Niño–Southern Oscillation) events and prolonged droughts, make areas more prone to fires. This background will be triggered by large-scale developments, such as oil palm and timber plantations, also make the landscape more prone to fire by degrading the land through logging and drainage and left dead aboveground biomass prone to fire. When peatlands are excessively drained, as happens in plantation developments, upper layers dry up and become prone to fire. The repeatedly burned vegetation is more prone to fire as the peat becoming hydrophobic hence vulnerable to fire.

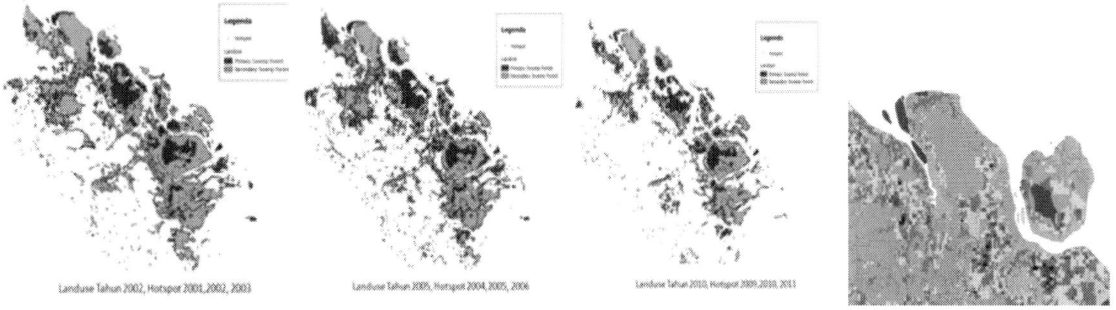

Figure 4: No 1 - 4 (from left-to-right) Historical hotspot patterns in Riau province :2001-2003 (1), 2004-2006(2) and 2011 (3) super-imposed on 2010 land cover indicating that hotspot were mostly on peatland especially associated with peatforest conversion. Negligible hotspot was detected in less-disturbed undrained peatforest. Hotspot were detected by MODIS and land cover were generated from Landsat (dark green is primary forest and light green is secondary or plantation forest or plantation forest). No (4) shows that the peatfire from the surrounding drained peatland have been encroaching its core undrained peatforests.

It is very clear from Riau analysis 2000 to 2010 (Figure 4) that hotspot have been obviously absence in the less-disturbed (non-drained) peatforest, confirming that peatfire is not natural peatforest phenomena. However following draining of the surrounding forest, fire could start to invade the edge of undrained secondary forest.

We have calculated how close interaction between peatland drainage and occurrence of the hotspots including the corresponding footprints areas beyond the drained peatland. It is clearly shown that the hotspot were mostly concentrated on the drained peatland areas, but the impact of draining on the hotspot could be as far as 5 km beyond the outer of canal infrastructure (Figure 5), possibly caused by an evidence of high hydraulic conductivity of very porous material such as these peatland which has ability to suck the water from the areas of undrained peatalnd. It was previously reported that the lateral ground water movement across the peatland (not in the canal) per day could reach as far as 125 m (*Hooijer pers commun*, 2014), questioning the effectiveness issue of canal blocking system as the way to retain the water within the drained peatland areas. That reported value of hydraulic conductance is rather greater than have been previously reported since the plantations are usually located on the peatdome (not shallow peatland).

Our manual canal digitations would have possibly missed the small canals developed by smallholders (who plant rubbers for the last few decades and the closed canopy have prevented us to digitize the canals). If so, our calculation result could be interpreted as impacts of large scale peatland drainage.

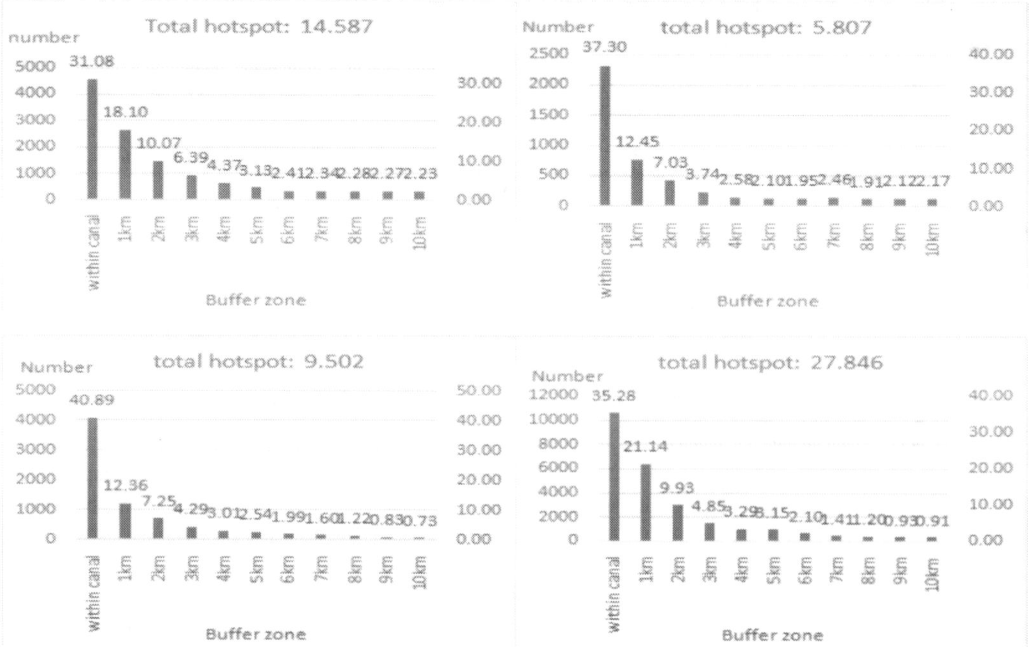

Figure 5: Hotspot occurrence in various distances from canal in Riau (above) and South Sumatera (below) provinces (2014-left and 2015-right) indicating that most of the hotspots were within the canals and the footprint of the hotspots has extended beyond few km away from the outermost canals.

Palm oil expansion expansion on drained peatland in Sumatera has followed its benchmark in Sarawak, Malaysia but why such massive and recurrent peatfire have not occurring in the similar drained tropical peatland areas like in Sarawak? It was reported that from the climatic condition, Sarawak has rarely exposed to the pronounced dry months, in contrast to eastern coasts of Sumatera peatland (Vernimmen *et al.*, 2012).

By pointing out that it is peatland drainage that mostly drives the recurrent peatfire, we also acknowledge social driver that frequently triggers peatfire ie. due to contesting peatland access. Most of peatland in Riau and South Sumatera has been designated for large scale concessionaire and the remaining areas are strictly prohibited for use ie. deep peatland (moratorium under the Presidential Instruction 10/2011), leaving a limited action space for the locals (Riau Forest Watch, 2014). This has triggered a tenurial conflicts recorded in Riau which the trend has rapidly increased from 79,100 Ha in 2012 to 171,645 Ha in 2013 (Scale Up, 2014) which ignites peatfire under poor peatland governance.

CONCLUSION

It is clearly demonstrated that extensive and intensive peatland drainage has respond global demand increase for CPO and pulp paper products that attract large scale investments and been justified by the provincial spatial plan. Peatland drainage has been the most dominant driver for recurrent peatfire at least in two provinces Riau and South Sumatera, and the impact of the peatfire has extended up to few km away from the outmost canals. This understanding should provide a strong basis for effective policy for improving peatland management in Indonesia.

Based on sustainable peatland management principles peatland should be minimum disturbed, always kept moist and never been opened, we could propose policy intervention to minimize peatfire such as improving spatial planning to protect peatforest from conversion thus any developments involving large-scale land-use change take place only on land that is already degraded/deforested non peatland. Peatland drainage should be highly regulated and be transparence for spatial planning and independent monitoring for restoration of peatland hydrology beyond frequently claimed ecohydrological engineering so peat will be moist throughout the year (wet peat does not burn).

REFERENCES

1. Anderson IP and M. Bowen R. 2000. *Firezone and the threat to the wetlands of Sumatera, Indonesia* EU MoF GoI
2. Applegate G, Chokkalingam and Suyanto.2001. *The Underlying Causes and Impacts of Fires in South-east Asia.* Final Report. CIFOR 2 International Centre for Research in Agroforestry (ICRAF)

3. ADB (1999). *Causes, extent, impact and costs of 1997/98 fires and drought. Final report, Annex 1 and 2. Planning for fire prevention and drought management project. Asian Development Bank TA 2999-INO.* Fortech, Pusat Pengembangan Agribisnis, Margules Pöyry,Jakarta, Indonesia.
4. Applegate, G. B. (1994). *Concession Allocation and Management. In: Forestry Sector Policy Analysis, Working Paper No.3, Forestry Sector Study, Ministry of Forestry, Indonesia.* Asian Development Bank 1994.
5. Dennis R. 1999. A Review of Fire Projects in Indonesia (1982-1998). CIFOR
6. Heil, A. (2007). *Indonesian Forest and Peat Fires: Emissions, Air Quality, and Human Health.* PhD thesis, Max Planck Institute for Meteorology, Hamburg, Germany
7. Hooijer A, S. Page, J. G. Canadell, M. Silvius, J. Kwadijk, H. Wosten, and J. Jauhiainen. 2010. Current and future CO2 emissions from drained peatlands in Southeast Asia. *Biogeosciences*, 7, 1505–1514
8. Jaakko Pöyry: World paper markets up to 2015. Know-how wire magazine, June 2003. Jaakko Pöyry Ltd
9. Karyanto *et al.* 2014. Sustainable Peatland Management Recommendation. Indonesia Centre for Climate Change
10. Langner, A., J. Miettinen and F. Siegert (2007). *Land cover change 2002–2005 in Borneo and the role of fire derived from MODIS imagery. Global Change Biology* **13**: 2329-2340. DOI: 10.1111/j.1365-2486.2007.01442.x.
11. Miettinen J and Liew SC. 2010. *Status of Peatland Degradation and Development in Sumatra and Kalimantan.* AMBIO. 39:394-401 DOI 10.1007/s 13280-0 10-005 1-2.
12. Nurruddin AA, Leng HM and Basarudin F. 2006. *Peat moisture and water level relationship in a tropical peat swamp forest.* Journal of Applied Sciences 6 (11) 2517-2519.
13. Page, S. E., A. Hoscilo, A. Langner, K. J. Tansey, F. Siegert, S. H. Limin and J. O. Rieley (2009). Tropical peatland fires in Southeast Asia. In: M. A. Cochrane (Eds). *Tropical Fire Ecology: Climate Change, Land Use and Ecosystem Dynamics.* Springer-Praxis,Heidelberg, Germany. pp. 263-287.
14. Potter, L. and J. Lee. 1998. *Oil Palm in Indonesia: its Role in Forest Conversion and the Fires of 1997/98.* A report for WWF, Indonesia Programme. Jakarta, Indonesia.
15. Sumawinata, B, Suwardi and Munoz CP.2013. Emission of CO2 and CH4 from plantation forest of Acacia crassicarpa on peatland in Indonesia. International Peat Symposium, Stockholm
16. Vernimmen RRE, Hooijer A., Mamenun, E. Aldrian, and A. I. J. M. van Dijk. 2012. *Evaluation and bias correction of satellite rainfall data for drought monitoring in Indonesia* Hydrol. Earth Syst. Sci., 16, 133–146, 2012
17. Wösten, J. H. M., E. Clymans, S. E. Page, J. O. Rieley and S. H. Limin (2008). Peat–water interrelationships in a tropical peatland ecosystem in Southeast Asia. *Catena* **73**: 212-224. DOI: 10.1016/j.catena. 2007.07.010.
18. Zubaidah, A., Vetrita, Y., &Khomarudin, M. R. (2014). MODIS hotspot validation over Sumatra and Kalimantan based on remote sensing data SPOT-4 in 2012. *Jurnal Penginderaan Jauh* (11), 1-14.

Abstract No: A-427

FIRE PREVENTION THROUGH COMMUNITY ENGAGEMENT - THE FIRE FREE VILLAGE PROGRAM

Craig Tribolet* and Sailal Arimi

Asia Pacific Resources International Limited (APRIL), Indonesia

**Corresponding author: craig_tribolet@aprilasia.com*

SUMMARY

Fire and smoke haze are issues high on the agenda currently largely as a result of catastrophic fires in 2015, associated with one of the strongest El Nino phenomena on record. Early indications are that fires during the 2015 El Nino damaged a larger area than 1997. APRIL, as a forest manager in Riau Province, Sumatra has an influential role across the Riau landscape and has developed an enviable reputation for their fire suppression capability. But even the best fire suppression capability is only reactive with little influence on the root causes behind forest and land fires. In late 2014 APRIL undertook a comprehensive root cause analysis and developed a range of programs designed to stop the fires before they start. This 'fire prevention through community engagement strategy', titled the Fire Free Village Program, has successfully reduced burnt area by 90%. This paper outlines that prevention strategy, the engagement framework and the processes that lead to a reduction in burnt area by more than 90% across the nine pilot villages.

***Keywords**: Fire Management, Fire Prevention, Fire Free Village*

INTRODUCTION

The concept of fire management has an important role in the ongoing discussion of forest and land fires that impact Indonesia and its neighbours each year. Fire management includes Prevention, Preparation, Suppression and Recovery. The focus until recently has been very strongly on Suppression but it is critical that the discussion be broadened to include the other three parts.

Fire Prevention is a critical first step – stopping the fires before they start. Key to developing a prevention framework is accepting, without fault, a number of the key challenges that are specific to the Indonesian context, namely:

- Fire is the cheapest and most accessible land preparation tool;
- Poverty and short term decisions play a significant role in community decision making;
- There is often not a viable, sustainable alternative to fire.

The Fire Free Village Program (FFVP) includes two broad aspects – Fire Aware Communities (FAC), an initial community engagement process and Fire Free Villages (FFV) which is focused on the delivery of operational capability.

The ability to fine tune the program to meet local requirements, sharing control of the decision making process and taking a patient and open approach while engaging with communities appear to be making an important contribution to positive fire management outcomes. Working closely with communities on fire prevention has been a very successful strategy for APRIL. APRIL has rapidly expanded this prevention program in 2016 and is actively liaising with a range of other stakeholders to share this fire prevention process and on the broader implementation of the 'Fire Free Village' program.

METHODS

The recent history of fire management in Indonesia has been very strongly focused on fire suppression rather than fire prevention. This is problematic because it tends to be reactive and as a result has little influence on the key causes of fire.

Part of developing sustainable solutions is determining the root cause of the problem. In the case of landscape fires there has been a lack of analysis of root cause – either due to a lack of available data, lack of understanding of fire management or concerns relating to the political ramifications. However APRIL fire incident data leaves no room for doubt, nearly 80% of fires are related to burning for an agricultural outcome. The unfortunate reality is that local communities play a key role in this burning despite the limited long term viability of this as a large scale land preparation process.

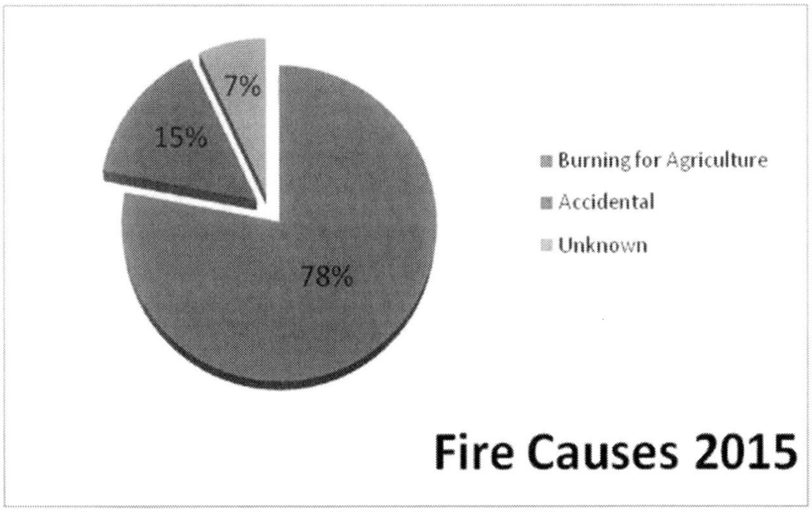

Fire Causes for 2015, Source: APRIL2015

The project team developed a Project Manual that clearly structures a process for problem formulation, and assists in identifying causation as well as understanding impacts and effects. Once a clear root cause is established it is possible to start a constructive conversation around sustainable solutions and developing outputs that will assist in solving the problem. From this problem analysis it was immediately obvious that the solution must include a strategy to meet with and discuss the challenge of inappropriate fire use with local communities.

Given limited resources it was also important to prioritize locations where the risk of fire is highest. APRIL developed a Risk Map process that integrates information including recent fire history, village locations, roads and rivers as well areas where there is known land tenure conflict or other illegal forest activity (hunting and logging for example). A spatial Risk Map provides a clear indication not only of where the risk is highest and also some guidance on the underlying causation.

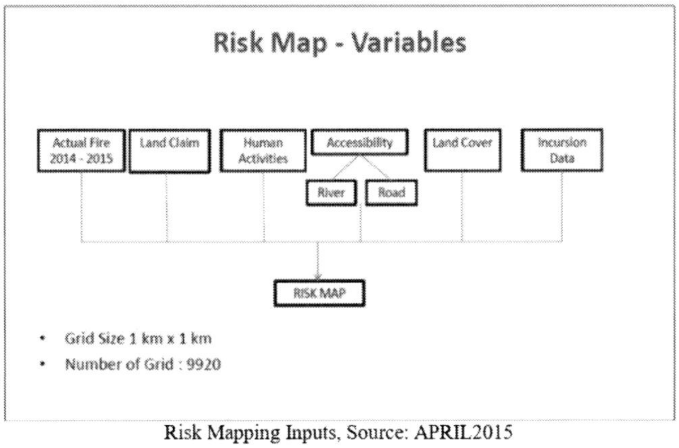

Risk Mapping Inputs, Source: APRIL2015

RESULTS

Fire suppression is important in the fire management cycle but it is reactive – firefighting treats the symptoms of the problem. Only effective fire prevention can change the cycle of burning and it necessarily includes local communities as key stakeholders. The problem analysis revealed that one of the key issues was a lack of understanding of fire, its broader environmental impact as well as access to sustainable alternatives. The annual wet and dry seasons provided a very difficult environment for small scale farmers who were often working to prepare areas of 2 hectares or less. Unfortunately unmanaged fires, often associated with cheap slash and burn practices, routinely damage much larger areas than this.

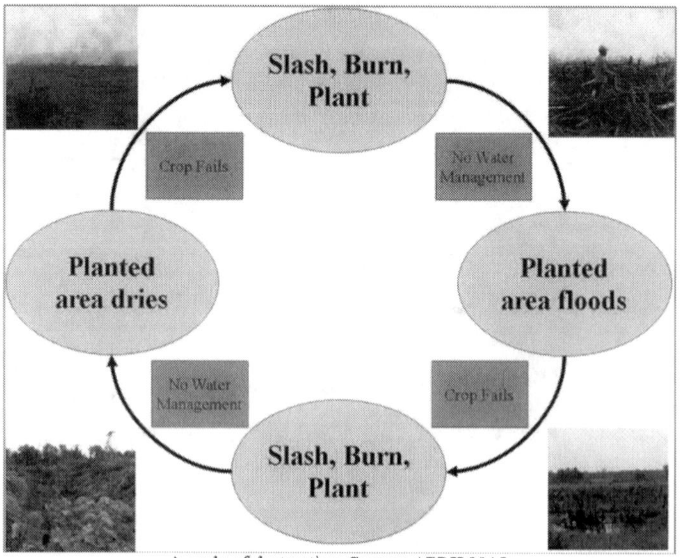

A cycle of destruction. Source: APRIL2015

Identifying the destructive impact of this cycle of slash and burn is not new. However, it is not enough to identify the causes and lecture communities on what they need to do to prevent fires. Communities must be willing to be involved and take responsibility as a group for fire management. Engagement is destined to fail if government agencies and big companies do not share the decision making process with local people and allow communities to engage in developing their own solutions. The FFVP takes a respectful and patient approach to developing community capability, acknowledges that communities are not homogeneous and that peoples needs will develop and evolve over time.

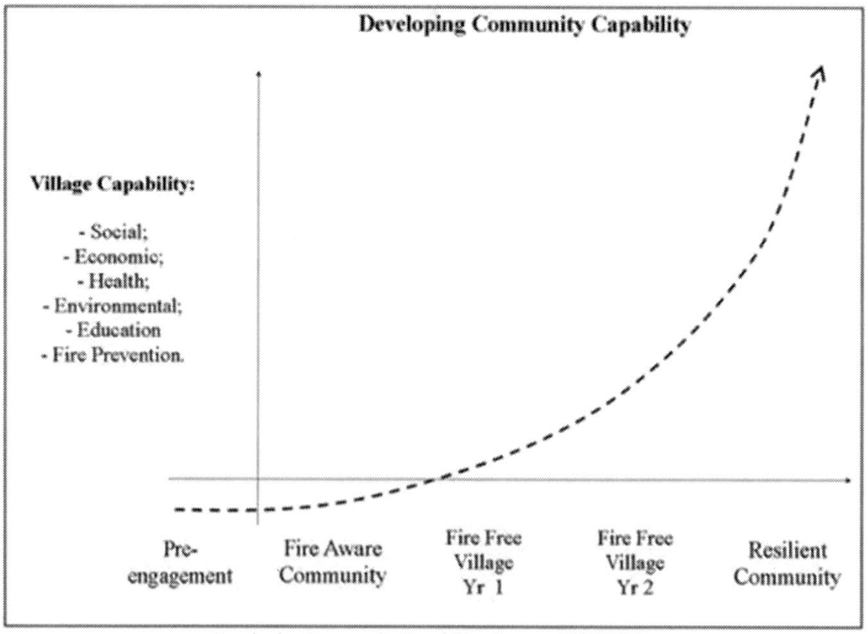

Developing Community Capability, Source: APRIL2015

The concept of developing capability at the community level is a key part of the Fire Free Village Program and the initial results of the pilot program should provide optimism for other fire management activities. In a short period the Program was able to reduce burnt area within community controlled lands by 90% as well as provide a range of sustainable tools and alternatives to using unmanaged fire as a land preparation tool.

DISCUSSION

The FFVP provides five key platforms to support the development of fire management in local communities:

i. Incentive Rewards for No Burning;
ii. Village Crew Leaders;
iii. Agricultural Assistance (mechanical site preparation and agricultural education);
iv. Community Awareness;
v. Haze Monitoring.

Local communities play the lead role in determining how they will apply each of these with guidance and support from the APRIL Fire Prevention team.

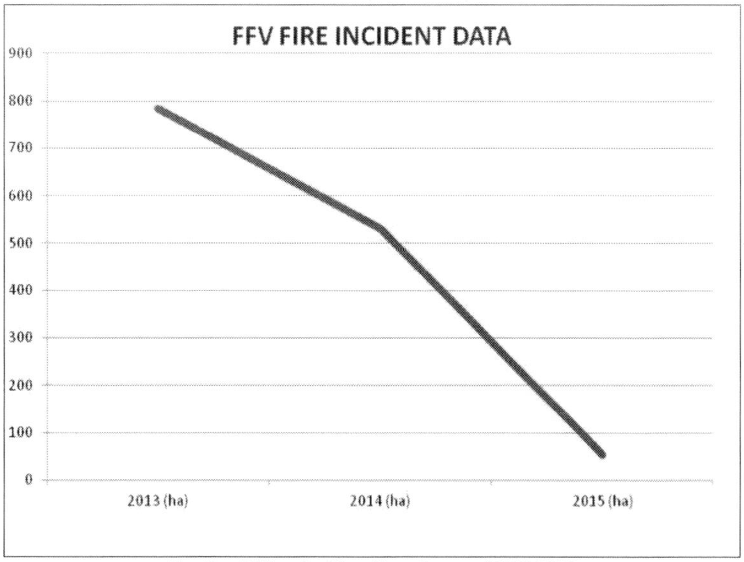

Fire Free Village Incident Data, Source: APRIL2015

Some communities may not be ready for a sophisticated discussion around fire prevention and as a result may be introduced to the concept through the Fire Aware Communities (FAC) program which has developed a package of fire awareness programs for local schools and community groups.

CONCLUSION

The FFVP has shown significant success in applying the 'prevention through engagement' strategy with local communities. APRIL is expanding their own program in 2016 as well as sharing the engagement process with a range of other landscape partners through the Fire Free Alliance – which allows companies and government agencies to develop their own community fire prevention programs based on the FFVP model.

It is important that the process understand and engage with the root causes behind landscape fires, in particular the lack of community access to sustainable agricultural alternatives. Success relies on an engagement process that is respectful of communities, is flexible enough to meet their unique challenges and can deliver prevention focused outputs without blame.

Abstract No: A-112

FIRE-CLIMATE-ECOSYSTEM INTERACTIONS RELATED TO CARBON ACCUMULATION RATES OF PEATLANDS IN JAMBI, SUMATRA (INDONESIA) DURING THE PAST 12,000 YEARS

Siria Biagioni[1*], Kartika Hapsari[1], Valentyna Krashevska[2], Marife D. Corre[3], Peter M. Reimer[4], Yudhi Achnopha[5], Asmadi Saad[5], Tim C. Jennerjahn[6], Supiandi Sabiham[7], Edzo Veldkamp[3] and Hermann Behling[1]

[1] *Department of Palynology and Climate Dynamics – Albrecht-von-Haller Institute for Plant Sciences, Georg-August-University of Göttingen, Göttingen, Germany*
[2] *J.F. Blumenbach Institute of Zoology and Anthropology, Georg-August-University of Göttingen, Göttingen, Germany*
[3] *Soil Science of Tropical and Subtropical Ecosystems, Büsgen-Institute, Georg-August-University of Göttingen, Göttingen, Germany*
[4] *Department of Biological Science, Goshen College, Goshen, Indiana, United States*
[5] *Department of Soil Science, University of Jambi, Jambi, Indonesia*
[6] *Department of Biogeochemistry and Geology, Leibniz Center for Tropical Marine Ecology (ZMT), Bremen, Germany*
[7] *Department of Soil Science and Land Resource, Bogor Agriculture University (IPB), Bogor, Indonesia*

**Corresponding author: siria.biagioni@gmail.com*

The largest tropical peatlands are found in Southeast Asia and their global importance as terrestrial carbon reservoirs is well documented. Despite that, little is known on the response of these peatland ecosystems to long-term climatic variability. Particularly needed is an understanding of the long-term fire regime and rainfall pattern changes linked to the *El Niño* Southern Oscillation (ENSO) and the Indian Ocean Dipole (IOD). Valuable insights into the response of peatlands to climate change can be obtained from palaeo-record reconstructions. We present palaeoecological data from two peatland cores located in the Jambi Province, Sumatra, Indonesia. The Jaw SPT core from an inland peat dome (8,000 years since peat initiation) and Sungai Buluh core (12,000 years since peat initiation) from a freshwater coastal peatland, are representative of the two main types of peatlands in the Jambi Province. We investigated the relation of reconstructed vegetation community phases (pollen and spores data), palaeohydrology (testate amoebae), fire regime history (macro-charcoal peak analysis), humification (peat characteristics) and the long-term apparent carbon accumulation rates (LORCA) with the reconstructed climatic and sea-level changes for Southeast Asia. We inferred ecosystem disturbances from $\delta^{15}N$ and pioneer pollen and spore taxa. Preliminary results indicate that vegetation dynamics were an important driver of changes in LORCA. At both sites, the fire magnitude increased from 2,000 years ago, simultaneously with an increase of *El Niño* and IOD. However, the comparison between LORCA and fire regime indicates that the overall carbon storage function was not affected at the centennial time scale. Our study highlights the potential of using palaeo-reconstructions to investigate fire ecology in the Southeast Asian peatlands and the effect of climate on these ecosystems at the centennial to millennial time scale.

***Keywords**:-*

Abstract No: A-132

FIRST *IN SITU* MEASUREMENTS OF TROPICAL PEATLAND FIRE EMISSIONS: NEW EMISSION FACTORS FOR GREENHOUSE GAS REPORTING AND HAZE FORECASTING

Thomas E L Smith[1*], Catherine M Yule[2], Stephanie Evers[3], Clare Paton-Walsh[4], and Jing Ye Gan[2]

[1]*King's College London, Department of Geography, UK*
[2]*Monash University Malaysia, School of Science, Malaysia*
[3]*University of Nottingham Malaysia Campus, School of Biosciences, Malaysia*
[4]*University of Wollongong, School of Chemistry, Australia*

**Corresponding author: thomas.smith@kcl.ac.uk*

INTRODUCTION

Tropical peat swamp fires in Southeast Asia are a major source of greenhouse gases (GHGs), responsible for climate change; and reactive gases and aerosols, responsible for poor regional air quality affecting hundreds of millions of people (Table 1). Approximately 90% of seasonal haze in Southeast Asia is due to fires burning on peatlands. Despite such damaging impacts, very little is known about the makeup of peatland fire emissions. Current estimates of total emissions from tropical peatland fires, including the important GHGs CO_2 and CH_4, use emission factors derived from one study where a single peat sample was burned in a laboratory. Here, we present the first emission factors to be measured *in situ* at active peat fires burning on degraded peatlands in southeast Pahang, Peninsula Malaysia.

Between 22 July and 22 August 2015, 232 active fire hotspots were detected by MODIS in a tropical peatland region south of Kuantan, Malaysia (Figure 1). During this fire episode, we embarked on a field campaign to measure gaseous emissions at fires in this region using open-path Fourier transform infrared spectroscopy (OP-FTIR). We successfully deployed at eight fires burning in degraded tropical peat. Spectra of infrared light passing through an open-path (10–40 m) through ground-level smoke released from these fires were collected using an infrared lamp and a field-portable FTIR system (Figure 2). The IR spectra were used to retrieve mole fractions of 14 different gases present within the smoke (including CO_2 and CH_4), and these measurements used to calculate emission factors of the various gases emitted by the burning (Table 2). We discuss possible causes for inter-site variability in emissions, and implications of these emission factors for greenhouse gas accounting and haze forecasting.

Table 1: A selection of gas species emitted by peat combustion; their direct/indirect impacts; and the main control on emissions of each species (Modified Combustion Efficiency, MCE; and peat Nitrogen content).

Major compounds	Direct impacts	Secondary impacts	Main control on emissions
CO_2	Climate change		MCE
CH_4	Climate change	Photochemical smog (haze)	MCE
CO	Ozone formation, illness	Photochemical smog (haze)	MCE
NMHCs (C_2H_2, C_2H_4, C_2H_6)	Illness	Photochemical smog (haze)	MCE
VOCs (CH_3OH, CH_3COOH, HCOOH)	Illness/cancer	Photochemical smog (haze)	MCE
N_2O	Climate change	Ozone depletion	MCE and peat N-content
NO, NO_2	Ozone formation, acid rain	Photochemical smog (haze)	MCE and peat N-content
NH_3, HCN	Illness/cancer	Photochemical smog (haze)	MCE and peat N-content

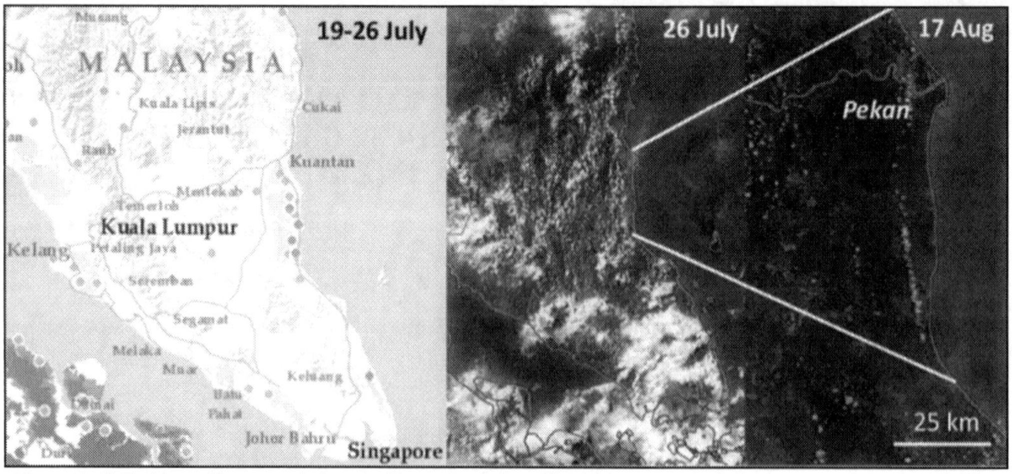

Figure 1: (left) Map of hotspots during the fire outbreak in mid-July (green areas indicate areas of peat), taken from http://fires.globalforestwatch.org/; (centre) MODIS hotpots & visible imagery showing fire hotspots on 26 July 2015 & their associated smoke plume; (right) fire hotspots on 17 August south of Pekan.

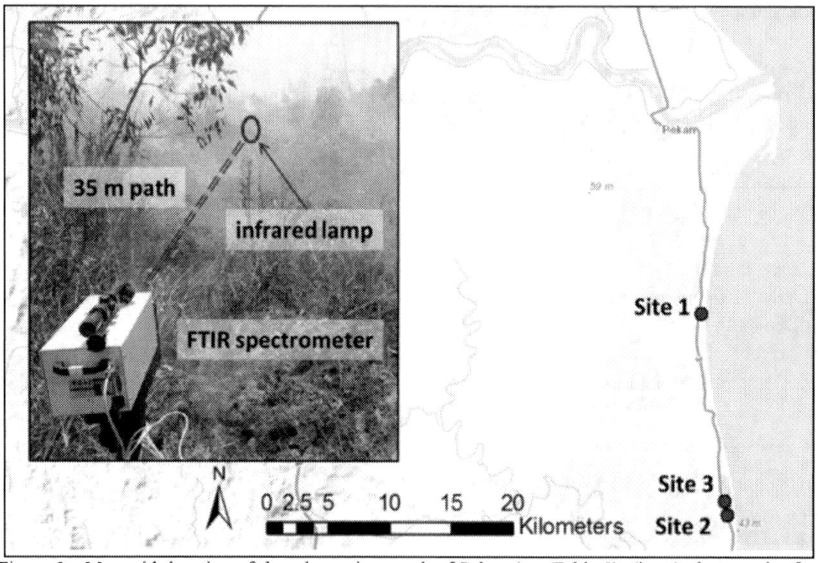

Figure 2: Map with location of three burn sites south of Pekan (see Table 2); (inset) photograph of a typical OP-FTIR setup at Site 2 using a 35 m path between the FTIR spectrometer and infrared lamp.

Table 2: *Site characteristics and results from analysis of peat samples and OP-FTIR-derived MCE for each of the eight burns measured for this paper.*

Burn	Site	Lat (°)	Long (°)	Path (m)	Temp (°C)	Pressure (hPa)	Bulk density (g cm^{-3})	Soil moist (%)	N (%)	C (%)	MCE
P1	1	3.361	103.420	17	34	1008	0.63 ± 0.03	24 ± 0.0	-	-	0.82
P2	1	3.361	103.420	12	36	1011	0.46 ± 0.20	20 ± 1.3	-	-	0.77
P3	2	3.221	103.440	35; 29	40	1008	0.28 ± 0.09	33 ± 0.1	0.69	20.9	0.83
P4	2	3.221	103.440	23; 13	38	1009	0.31 ± 0.10	31 ± 0.1	0.58	18.3	0.79
P5	3	3.231	103.437	20; 12	40	1010	0.25 ± 0.05	41 ± 0.6	1.75	43.3	0.79
P6	2	3.221	103.440	17	40	1010	0.38 ± 0.04	29 ± 1.2	0.51	23.2	0.75
P7	3	3.231	103.437	12; 11; 10	34	1011	0.41 ± 0.11	16 ± 0.3	1.76	41.1	0.78
P8	2	3.221	103.440	11; 11	34	1011	0.37 ± 0.10	28 ± 0.9	1.02	24.3	0.79

Abstract No: A-031

FLAMING PEAT: SYNERGISTIC EFFECTS OF FIRE AND FOREST CLEARANCE ON TROPICAL PEAT SWAMP FORESTS

Lydia E. S. Cole[1,4*], Shonil A. Bhagwat[2,4] and Katherine J. Willis[1,3,4,5]

[1]*Oxford Long-term Ecology Laboratory, Department of Zoology, University of Oxford, United Kingdom*
[2]*Department of Geography, Faculty of Social Sciences, the Open University, United Kingdom*
[3]*Department of Biology, University of Bergen, Norway*
[4]*Biodiversity Institute, Oxford Martin School, Department of Zoology, University of Oxford, United Kingdom*
[5]*Royal Botanical Gardens, United Kingdom*

**Corresponding author: lydcole@gmail.com*

SUMMARY

Recent burning in the tropical peat swamp forests of Southeast Asia, linked with anthropogenic land-use change, has resulted in widespread environmental degradation across the region. Yet little is known about the long-term natural fire regime in these landscapes. Using fossil pollen and charcoal data from three peat cores collected from Sarawak, Malaysian Borneo, we looked at the incidence and impact of local and regional fire on coastal peat swamp forests over the last 7000 years. Results show that burning has occurred in these wetland ecosystems throughout their history. However, prior to the Colonial era *c.* 1839, when human presence in the peat swamp forest was comparatively limited, neither local nor regional burning significantly impacted on the forest vegetation. After the mid-19th Century, at the onset of intensified land-use change, fire incidence elevated significantly within these coastal peat swamp forests. Although fire does not correlate with past vegetation changes in these ecosystems, the long-term data reveal that open vegetation, a proxy for human forest clearance, does to a greater extent. However, results suggest that human activity may be strongly influencing and acting synergistically with fire in the recent past, leading to the enhanced degradation of these peatland ecosystems. These findings support present-day concerns about the increase in fire incidence and combined impacts of fire and human disturbance on peat swamp forests, with serious implications for biodiversity and global climate change.

***Keywords**: fire, burning, peat swamp forest, long-term ecology, anthropogenic disturbance*

INTRODUCTION

The peat swamp forests of Southeast Asia, covering an area of 25 million ha, hold *c.* 12% of the total carbon stored in the world's peatlands (Page *et al.*, 2011). The performance of these peat swamps as a carbon sink relies on a tight interrelationship between the landscape, vegetation and hydrological conditions (Page *et al.*, 1999; Dommain *et al.*, 2010; Posa *et al.*, 2011), making the forest component of this ecosystem vital for its maintenance. Despite this, peat swamp forests are being lost at a rapid pace: in Southeast Asia between 2000 and 2010, 56% were converted to plantations (Miettinen *et al.*, 2012a), in addition to the area lost through logging and other development (Koh *et al.*, 2011). In particular, fire is considered one of the most important drivers of land-use change and vast areas of these tropical peat swamps burn every year (Razali *et al.*, 2010; Phua *et al.*, 2012), especially on the island of Borneo (Langner & Siegert 2009; Hoscilo *et al.*, 2011).

Burning has increasingly affected the peat swamp forests of Southeast Asia in the last two to three decades (Taylor 2010) and is claimed to be one of the most insidious threats to peat-swamp habitats (Razali *et al.*, 2010), as well as to all rainforest ecosystems (Laurance 2003). However, natural fires, predominantly caused by lightning strikes, have constituted an important part of the ecosystem dynamics in these tropical peat swamps (Taylor *et al.*, 2001), by creating gaps in which succession can occur. A study of peat swamp forests in Western Kalimantan suggests that fire has been a component of the landscape for at least the last 30,000 years (Anshari *et al.* 2001), and in Singapore, for the last 23,000 years (Taylor *et al.*, 2001).

Small-scale forest burning by humans, largely as part of shifting cultivation practices (Haberle *et al.*, 2001), has been recorded in forests in Sarawak from the early Holocene (Hunt & Premathilake 2012). More recently however, fires are reported to have increased in frequency, magnitude and impact in peat swamp forests in eastern Kalimantan (Hope *et al.*, 2005), in Australasia over the last few centuries (Mooney *et al.*, 2011), and across other areas of Southeast Asia in the last two or three decades (Taylor 2010). How much recent fire frequency has increased relative to historical levels, and what impact it has had in shaping ecosystem dynamics in the peat swamp forests of Sarawak, is still poorly understood.

This study aimed to investigate the patterns of fire, both local and regional in scale, in Sarawak's coastal peat swamp forests, using a long-term ecological approach. The overall objective was to determine the change in frequency and magnitude of fire through time in these ecosystems, and how/if this has influenced forest composition. Through reconstructing past burning regimes and vegetation change from fossil records contained in three sedimentary sequences extracted from peatlands on the coast of northern Borneo, this study addressed two key research questions: (i) What is the natural fire regime in these swamps, and how has it changed through time?, and (ii) How do the changing fire regimes impact the peat swamp forest vegetation?

METHODS

The State of Sarawak contains the greatest proportion of Malaysia's peat swamp forests, covering an area of approximately 3000 km^2 or 2% of the State (Miettinen *et al.*, 2012b), and of its deforested peatlands, which extend over an additional 11% (FAQ, 2012). Until recently, the peat swamp forests of Sarawak were denounced as "marginal wastelands" (Sawal, 2003), of little use except in the absence of alternative land. As such, large-scale conversion has occurred (Miettinen *et al.*, 2012a), predominantly for agricultural production (Koh *et al.*, 2011), where fire is commonly used to clear the forest vegetation (Wooster *et al.*, 2012).

Sedimentary cores were extracted using a hand-held coring device, from three peatlands across the Miri and Batu Niah Districts of north-east Sarawak: Deforested Peatland from Senadin, Kuala Baram (04°30'47"N, 114°2'47"E), an area of degraded peatland covering >50 km^2; Peat Swamp Fragment from Sungai Dua Forest Reserve (04°21'24"N, 114°0'21"E), a *c.* 2 km^2 fragment of secondary peat swamp forest; and Converted Peatland from Sungai Niah (03°52'4"N, 113°42'43"E), an agriculture-forest matrix of *c.* 1 km^2. Though these three sampled sites cover a relatively narrow geographical range of 80 km along the coast of northern Borneo, since there is limited variation in climate, geology and land-use across the region, they are sufficiently representative of the coastal peat swamp ecosystems of Sarawak, and to an extent, of Borneo and parts of Southeast Asia.

Using standard palaeoecological techniques (Bennett & Willis, 2001), the sedimentary cores were analysed at set intervals through the sequences for fossil pollen, microfossil and macrofossil charcoal and mineral magnetic material (magnetic susceptibility). Once counted, fossil pollen grains were divided into different ecological groups, defined as follows: total PSF (TotPSF), which encompasses all peat swamp forest (PSF) associated taxa; the mature PSF community (PSF); the pioneer PSF community (PSF+); taxa of degraded peatlands (DP); taxa of other forests (OF); coastal vegetation (CV), and open vegetation, comprising taxa which dominate open-canopied areas of greater spatial and temporal scale than tree-fall gaps, for example Poaceae, Cyperaceae and ferns (both of monolete and trilete morphologies). This latter ecological group is used as an indicator of human impact. A size-class analysis of fossil charcoal, *i.e.* differentiating between macrofossil and microfossil charcoal was performed to investigate changes in local and regional fire regimes, respectively, in each site through time (Whitlock and Larsen, 2002). To determine the age-depth relationship of the sedimentary cores, samples containing organic material suitable for ^{14}C dating were extracted from each and analysed with AMS radiocarbon dating techniques, at the ^{14}Chrono Centre in the Archaeology and Palaeoecology Department, at Queen's University Belfast, and the SUERC AMS Laboratory, at the NERC Radiocarbon Facility.

KEY RESULTS

i. What is the natural fire regime in these coastal peat swamps? How has it changed towards the present day?

Fire has been present in all three sites through time (Figure 1). Fluctuations in macrocharcoal and microcharcoal levels vary within and between cores, though there are two distinct phases of elevated magnitude and frequency of burning: between *c.* 2800 and 1800 Cal. yr BP and from *c.* 200 Cal. yr BP to the present.

ii. How do the changing fire regimes impact the peat swamp forest vegetation?

Peat swamp forest is the baseline vegetation at all three sites over the late Holocene period that these coastal swamps have been present, dominating the vegetation profile. Since the inferred onset of peat swamp development (varying in each core), the percentage of pollen from the total PSF ecological group (aggregate dark and light green components on the pollen sum diagram, Figure 1) has been relatively constant in each site through time, fluctuating *c.* 80%. However, in the Peat Swamp Fragment and Converted Peatland sites, the total PSF proportion declines in the last *c.* 500 years. The indicator group of disturbance within the peat swamp forest, PSF+, does not appear to follow a pattern within or across sites, thus demonstrating internal dynamism throughout the past. Open vegetation levels in all sites remain low until *c.* 200 Cal. yr BP, with the exception of an anomalous peak in the Peat Swamp Fragment prior to 2000 Cal. yr BP. This notable increase in open vegetation taxa suggests that there was a higher incidence of open-canopied areas in the vicinity of these sites in the last several hundred years.

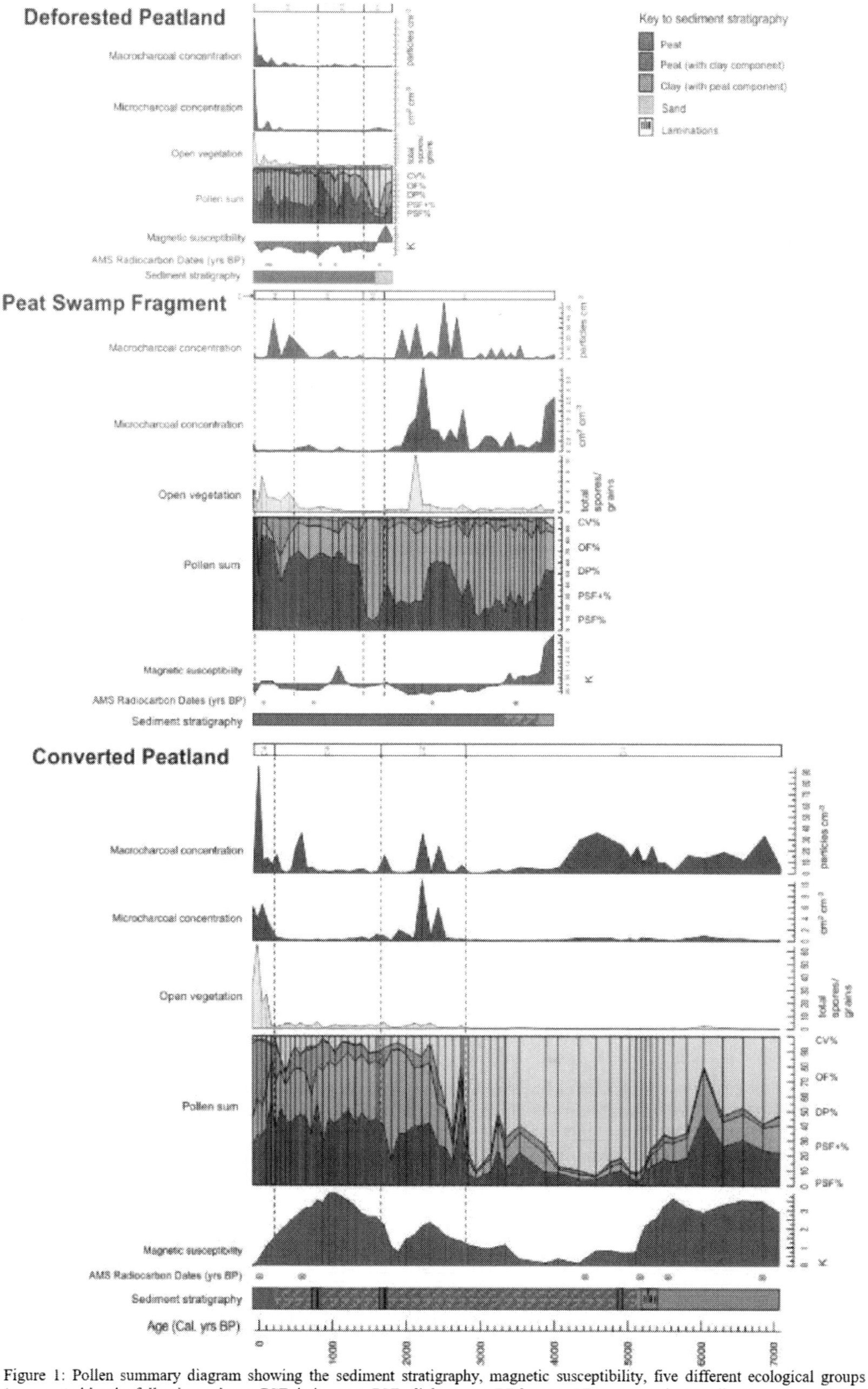

Figure 1: Pollen summary diagram showing the sediment stratigraphy, magnetic susceptibility, five different ecological groups (represented by the following colours: PSF dark green, PSF+ light green, DP brown, OF orange and CV yellow), open vegetation (light grey) and macrocharcoal and microcharcoal (red) for the Deforested Peatland, Peat Swamp Fragment and Converted Peatland sites. Cores have been adjusted to enable their chronological correspondence against one timescale. Significant pollen zones are shown for each. TotPSF% comprises the sum of PSF% and PSF+%, and is represented by the division between PSF+% and DP%.

DISCUSSION

This investigation found there to be no consistent fire regime across the three studied peat swamp forest ecosystems on the coast of Sarawak over the last 2000 to 7000 years. It also demonstrates that fire has not had a significant impact on either internal peat swamp forest vegetation communities or ecological change within the wider landscape through time. Rather, patterns of burning appear to be predominantly idiosyncratic and drivers of vegetation change predominantly anthropogenic.

(i) What is the natural fire regime in these coastal peat swamps? How has it changed towards the present day?

Results from this study demonstrate that fire has been present throughout the past within these coastal peat swamp forests, in accordance with findings from elsewhere in the region (Anshari *et al.*, 2001; Taylor *et al.*, 2001). However, there is no apparent 'natural' or predictable baseline local or regional burning regime. Instead, evidence suggests that there were two notable episodes of increased fire across sites, overlaying a background of heterogeneity. The first episode, between *c.* 2800 and 1800 Cal. yr BP, coincides with a period of climatic drying in the Tropics that is reported to have occurred in the interval 2000 – 3000 Cal. yr BP (Selvaraj *et al.*, 2007; Woodroffe *et al.*, 2003). The latter episode, from *c.* 200 Cal. yr BP to the present, is likely to have resulted from increased human interaction with and impact on Sarawak's coastal peat swamp forests. Until several hundred years ago, local fires (those within peat swamp forest) would predominantly have been driven by natural disturbances such as lightning strikes, especially during dry climatic periods, *i.e. El Niño* years (Hope *et al.*, 2005). Human disturbance would have been minimal (Sawal, 2003), restricted to activities such as subsistence sago cultivation. Within the last 200 years however, the coincidence of data showing dramatic increases in the magnitude and frequency of local and regional fire (and open areas), with the reporting and documenting of increased human interaction with Sarawak's coastal peat swamp forests, suggests that humans were responsible for these elevations in burning. Significant landscape exploitation by people, in a great part through the use of fire, is likely to have started after Colonial Rule was established in Sarawak approximately 170 years ago. More recently, further and more dramatic increases in the burning of peatlands have been recorded in Sumatra (Miettinen *et al.*, 2012c) and across Southeast Asia (Van Eijk *et al.*, 2009).

(ii) How do the changing fire regimes impact the peat swamp forest vegetation?

Results from this study suggest that fire has not caused significant disturbance to these three coastal peat swamp forests through time. Even during episodes of elevated burning in the past, for example during the hypothesised dry phase between *c.* 2800 - 1800 Cal. yr BP, there is no decline in the peat swamp forest or apparent impact on the vegetation within these ecosystems. In terms of internal peat swamp forest dynamics through time, the fluctuation between mature and pioneer taxa does not correlate with fire incidence, again suggesting that, in general, burning has not played a significant role in the regeneration of these ecosystems. Since anthropogenic burning is hypothesised to have only started in the last two centuries, it appears that the natural burning regimes in each site, which have been predominantly idiosyncratic, have not had a significant negative impact on these peat swamp forests.

In conjunction, the results from the three studied sedimentary cores strongly suggest that fire has been present in tropical peat swamp forests for thousands of years and that it is not the most prominent driver of long-term or recent changes in coastal peat swamp forest vegetation, contrary to the common concern expressed in the literature on the sustainable management of tropical peat swamp forests today (for example Razali *et al.*, 2010; Miettinen *et al.*, 2012c). Instead, human impact has had the most influence on internal peat swamp forest dynamics and peat swamp forest decline, and this disturbance has manifested only in the last *c.* 200 years. In reality however, it is likely that forest clearance, drainage and fire occur simultaneously and act synergistically in these landscapes, exacerbating impacts, reducing forest regeneration potential and thus jeopardizing the resilience of these peat swamp forests. Management implications The causes of fire are complex, and include underlying cultural, political and socio-economic conditions, not simply environmental or climatic factors (Stolle *et al.*, 2003; Langner & Siegert, 2009; Carlson *et al.*, 2012), such as the recent *El Niño* event. The interaction between different drivers of disturbance requires further investigation when considering management interventions. If recent elevated trends in burning can be prevented, predominantly through halting forest clearance and drainage, this and other studies (e.g. Hope *et al.*, 2005) provide evidence that peat swamp forests are resilient to less frequent and less intense fire. However, in the face of current conversion rates and future land-use planning in the region (Miettinen *et al.*, 2012a), potential disturbance by fire must be a central consideration in the more sustainable management of these carbon-rich ecosystems.

ACKNOWLEDGEMENTS

Authors would like to thank Samantha Jones, Kho Lip Khoon and several kind reviewers, and acknowledge NERC, the NERC Radiocarbon Dating Facility (Radiocarbon Analysis Allocation Number 1565.0411) and SUERC Dating Lab for their financial support with this project.

REFERENCES

1. Anshari, G., P. Kershaw, A. & Van Der Kaars, S. (2001). A Late Pleistocene and Holocene pollen and charcoal record from peat swamp forest, Lake Sentarum wildlife reserve, West Kalimantan, Indonesia. *Palaeogeography, Palaeoclimatology, Palaeoecology*, 171, 213–228.
2. Carlson KM, Curran LM, Ratnasari D, et al. (2012) Committed carbon emissions, deforestation, and community land conversion from oil palm plantation expansion in West Kalimantan, Indonesia. *Proceedings of the National Academy of Sciences of the United States of America*, 109, 7559–7564.
3. Dommain, R., Couwenberg, J. & Joosten, H. (2010). Hydrological self-regulation of domed peatlands in south-east Asia and consequences for conservation and restoration. *Mires and Peat*, 6, 1–17.
4. Haberle, S.G., Hope, G.S. & Van Der Kaars, S. (2001). Biomass burning in Indonesia and Papua New Guinea: Natural and human induced fire events in the fossil record. *Palaeogeography, Palaeoclimatology, Palaeoecology*, 171, 259–268.
5. Hope, G., Chokkalingam, U. & Anwar, S. (2005). The stratigraphy and fire history of the Kutai Peatlands, Kalimantan, Indonesia. *Quaternary Research*, 64, 407–417.
6. Hoscilo, A., Page, S.E., Tansey, K.J. & Rieley, J.O. (2011). Effect of repeated fires on land-cover change on peatland in southern Central Kalimantan, Indonesia, from 1973 to 2005. *International Journal of Wildland Fire*, 20, 578–588.
7. Hunt, C.O. & Premathilake, R. (2012). Early Holocene vegetation, human activity and climate from Sarawak, Malaysian Borneo. *Quaternary International*, 249, 105–119.
8. Koh, L.P., Miettinen, J., Liew, S.C. & Ghazoul, J. (2011). Remotely sensed evidence of tropical peatland conversion to oil palm. *Proceedings of the National Academy of Sciences of the United States of America*, 108, 5127–5132.
9. Langner, A. & Siegert, F. (2009). Spatiotemporal fire occurrence in Borneo over a period of 10 years. Global Change Biology, 15, 48–62. Laurance, W.F. (2003). Slow burn: the insidious effects of surface fires on tropical forests. *Trends in Ecology & Evolution*, 18, 209–212.
10. Miettinen, J., Shi, C., Tan, W.J. & Liew, S.C. (2012a). 2010 land cover map of insular Southeast Asia in 250-m spatial resolution. *Remote Sensing Letters*, 3, 11–20.
11. Miettinen, J., Shi, C. & Liew, S.C. (2012b). Two decades of destruction in Southeast Asia's peat swamp forests. *Frontiers in Ecology and the Environment*, 10, 124–128.
12. Miettinen, J., Hooijer, A., Wang, J., Shi, C. & Liew, S. (2012c). Peatland degradation and conversion sequences and interrelations in Sumatra. *Regional Environmental Change*, 12, 729–737.
13. Mooney, S.D., Harrison, S.P. & Bartlein, P.J. (2011). Late Quaternary fire regimes of Australasia. *Quaternary Science Reviews*, 30, 28–46.
14. Page, S.E., Rieley, J.O. & Banks, C.J. (2011). Global and regional importance of the tropical peatland carbon pool. *Global Change Biology*, 17, 798–818.
15. Page, S.E., Rieley, J.O., Shotyk, Ø.W. & Weiss, D. (1999). Interdependence of peat and vegetation in a tropical peat swamp forest. *Philosophical Transactions of the Royal Society B: Biological Sciences*, 354, 1885–1887.
16. Phua, M.-H., Tsuyuki, S., Soo Lee, J. & Ghani, M.A.A. (2012). Simultaneous detection of burned areas of multiple fires in the tropics using multisensor remote-sensing data. *International Journal of Remote Sensing*, 33, 4312–4333.
17. Posa, M.R.C., Wijedasa, L.S. & Corlett, R.T. (2011). Biodiversity and conservation of tropical peat swamp forests. *BioScience*, 61, 49–57.
18. Razali, S.M., Nuruddin, A.A., Malek, I.A. & Patah, N.A. (2010). Forest fire hazard rating assessment in peat swamp forest using Landsat thematic mapper image. *Journal of Applied Remote Sensing*, 4, 043531.
19. Sawal, P. (2003). Threats to Peat Swamp Forest of Sarawak. Malaysia/The Netherlands Joint Working Group on Sustainable Forest Management, Kuching, Malaysia, Available from: http://www.alterra.wur.nl/NR/rdonlyres/78164A36-BDC0-471F-BB80-08D10A55F689/135280/JWGRAM05.pdf.
20. Selvaraj, K., Chen, C.T.A. & Lou, J.-Y. (2007). Holocene East Asian monsoon variability: Links to solar and tropical Pacific forcing. *Geophysical Research Letters*, 34, L01703.
21. Stolle, F., Chomitz, K.M., Lambin, E.F. & Tomich, T.P. (2003). Land use and vegetation fires in Jambi Province, Sumatra, Indonesia. *Forest Ecology and Management*, 179, 277–292.

22. Taylor, D. (2010). Biomass burning, humans and climate change in Southeast Asia. *Biodiversity and Conservation*, 19, 1025–1042.
23. Taylor, D., Yen, O.H., Sanderson, P.G. & Dodson, J. (2001). Late quaternary peat formation and vegetation dynamics in a lowland tropical swamp; Nee Soon, Singapore. *Palaeogeography, Palaeoclimatology, Palaeoecology*, 171, 269–287.
24. Van Eijk & et al. (2009). Regeneration and restoration of degraded peat swamp forest in Berbak NP, Jambi, Sumatra, Indonesia. *Malayan Nature Journal*, 61, 223–241.
25. Whitlock, C. & Larsen, C. (2002). *Charcoal as a Fire Proxy*. In: Tracking Environmental Change Using Lake Sediments: Developments in Paleoenvironmental Research (eds. Smol, J.P., Birks, H.J.B., Last, W.M., Bradley, R.S. & Alverson, K.). Springer Netherlands, pp. 75–97.
26. Woodroffe CD, Beech MR, Gagan MK (2003) Mid-late Holocene El Niño variability in the equatorial Pacific from coral microatolls. *Geophysical Research Letters*, 30, 10–1.
27. Wooster, M.J., Perry, G.L.W. & Zoumas, A. (2012). Fire, drought and El Niño relationships on Borneo (Southeast Asia) in the pre-MODIS era (1980-2000). *Biogeosciences*, 9, 317–340

Abstract No: A-317

IS PEATLAND UTILIZATION THE MAIN CAUSE OF LAND FIRE IN INDONESIA?

Moch. Riza Kasfari*, Yudha Asmara Adhi, Basuki Somawinata and Bandung Sahari

Indonesian Palm Oil Association, Indonesia

Corresponding author: riza.kasfari@gmail.com

SUMMARY

In recent years, land fire has been occurred across islands in Indonesia. Peatland utilization is frequently associated with this land fire due to its susceptibility to fire during dry season. However, no scientific analysis has ever been reported to answer this rumor. Here, we present data analysis of spatial distribution of land fire in Indonesia and the status of fire on peat. Data was extracted from public domain reports between 2013 and 2015 including from Global Forest Watch Fires (GFWF), Sipongi (under the Ministry of Environment and Forestry) and LAPAN (Indonesian National Institute of Aeronautics and Space). Analysis was based on high confidence fires only across 33 provinces. Our analysis shows that during 2013-2015, fire alerts were found to be higher in 2015 than 2014 and 2013 with 48499 hot spots, 29512 hotspots and 11664 hot spots respectively. Higher number of hot spots in 2015, especially between September and November may relate to El Nino effects indicated by longer dry season. During 2015, fire alerts were found to be higher in South Sumatera and Central Kalimantan (based on data from GFWF and Sipongi) compared to other provinces. However, in 2013 and 2014, highest number of fire alerts was concentrated in Riau. Fire distribution pattern was found to be similar among 2015, 2014 and 2013 with fire alerts in non-concession area higher than in concession area with percentage 61%, 59 % and 58% respectively. Fire alerts on peat were found to be lower than on mineral soil (49%:51%) between 2013 and 2015. Those findings clearly show that land fires increased by year to year, and the main cause of land fires should be well identified and solved. There is not enough reason to blame peat cultivation as main cause of land fire since more than half of burned area was on mineral soil.

INTRODUCTION

Land fire in Indonesia is now becoming global issue due to its tremendous negative impact on ecosystem destruction and human health. First record of land fire was documented in 1982-1983 in East Kalimantan, where fire was mostly triggered by human activities, such as burning land for agriculture (Dirjen Perlindungan Hutan dan Pelestarian Alam 1983). Land burning was the traditional knowledge in local community to prepare land for agriculture in Sumatera and Kalimantan because it was cheap and believed that burned land will turn into fertilized land. For plantation, land clearing using burning method was not allowed by law. However, land fire was still recorded to occur by year to year. The most phenomenal case of land fire was what happened in 2015, where many areas in Sumatera and Kalimantan burned out and created dangerous air quality which impacted on sickness and death. There is no doubt that land fire brings many negative impacts not only on ecosystem, but also human health. Haze was recorded much higher than normal for more than one month.

Peatland cultivation especially for oil palm was suspected as main factor triggering land fire in many places and become global issue. This case was responded by the Government with some regulations to stop cultivating oil palm on peat. Unfortunately, no scientific analysis has ever been reported to answer the question "does peat land cultivation trigger land fire in Indonesia?" Blaming peat cultivation as main factor of land fires without any depth analysis will lead to misleading decision. This particularly true since there are many social and economic activities on peat for many years ago. Land fires in a certain area can be well detected and identified with available satellite. Hotspots information is open access to public. Here, we present data analysis of spatial distribution of land fire in Indonesia and the status of fire on peat based on open access data (public domain information).

MATERIAL AND METHODS

We used public domain information to develop hot spot spatial distribution analysis to study pattern of Indonesia land fires. Hotspot is a certain size of area which shows a certain degree of temperature which are found to be higher than other surrounding areas. These hotspots that can be detected by specific satellite. In this analysis we used hotspots resulted from Satellite NOAA and Terra/Aqua MODIS that can be downloaded from open access websites: (a) Terra/Aqua MODIS, NASA (https://earthdata.nasa.gov/data/near-real-time-data/firms), (b) Global

Forest Watch Fires (https://fires.globalforestwatch.org). Hotspots from Satellite MODIS with confidence level ≥ 80% were selected for analysis since lower confidence level does not represent fires. Hotspots distribution across 33 provinces were analyzed to identify which provinces are more vulnerable to fire and why. Hotspots pattern between 2013 and 2015 were also monitored. Hotspots in relation to land-use including forestry plantation, logging concession, and oil palm plantations were analyzed to study the relationship between land-use and fires.

RESULTS AND DISCUSSION

From the hotspot pattern, land fire significantly increased from 2013 to 2015. Highest hotspot number was found in 2015 covering 48.499 hotspots (See Figure1). Hotspot pattern was found to be different for different year. In 2014, hotspot number reached the peak in two different time periods, February-March and September-October. However, in 2013, peak of fire was found in June. In 2015, hotspots started to increase from August and reached fantastic number in October (See Fig 2). The differences in hotspots number from 2013 to 2015 may relate to many aspects such as climate, water scarcity, and human error. Longer dry season as an effect El-nino is predicted as climatic factor triggering land fire in 2015. Unfortunately, in many discussions, peat cultivation is frequently blamed as the main cause of national land fire. This was then responded by The Government to launch regulation to stop planting oil palm on peatland. However, data show different facts. Riau is one of province recognized to have biggest peat soil in Indonesia. Riau was recorded to become province with highest hotspot number both in 2013 and 2014 which contributed to 52% and 30% of national land fires respectively (See Fig 3a and 3b). However, in 2015, this pattern has changed. Riau only contributed about 5% of national land fires. Higher number of land fires was recorded in Sumatera Selatan and followed by Kalimantan Tengah which contributed 28% and 23% of national land fires respectively (See Fig 3c). Land fire was mostly found to occur in non-concession area. This pattern was similar in 2013, 2014 and 2015 which contributed 59%, 58%, and 61 % respectively (See Fig 4). Oil palm plantations only contributed less than 12 % of national land fires. More than half of national land fires occur in mineral soil, and fires on peatland covered 47% of national land fires (See Fig 5). This data clearly shows that blaming peat cultivation for crop is a misleading perspective that leads to an appropriate decision.

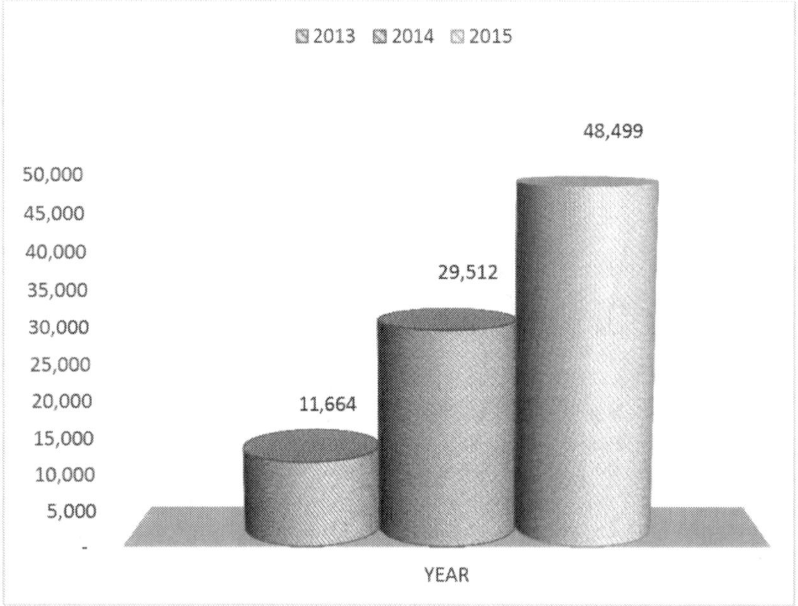

Figure 1: Hotspot number from 2013 to 2015

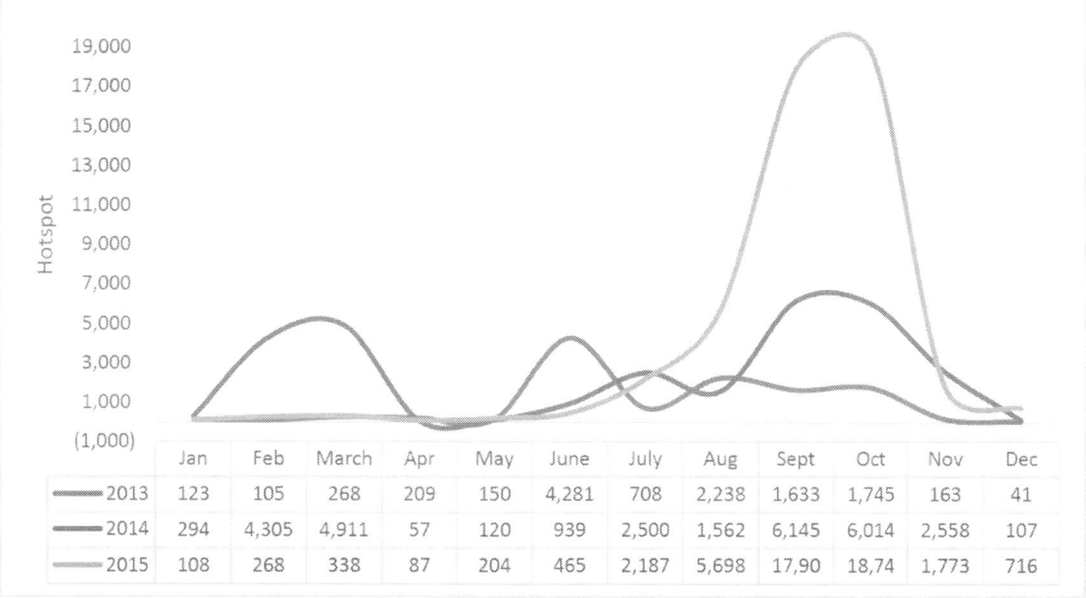

	Jan	Feb	March	Apr	May	June	July	Aug	Sept	Oct	Nov	Dec
2013	123	105	268	209	150	4,281	708	2,238	1,633	1,745	163	41
2014	294	4,305	4,911	57	120	939	2,500	1,562	6,145	6,014	2,558	107
2015	108	268	338	87	204	465	2,187	5,698	17,90	18,74	1,773	716

Figure 2: Temporal hotspot dynamic pattern from 2013 to 2015.

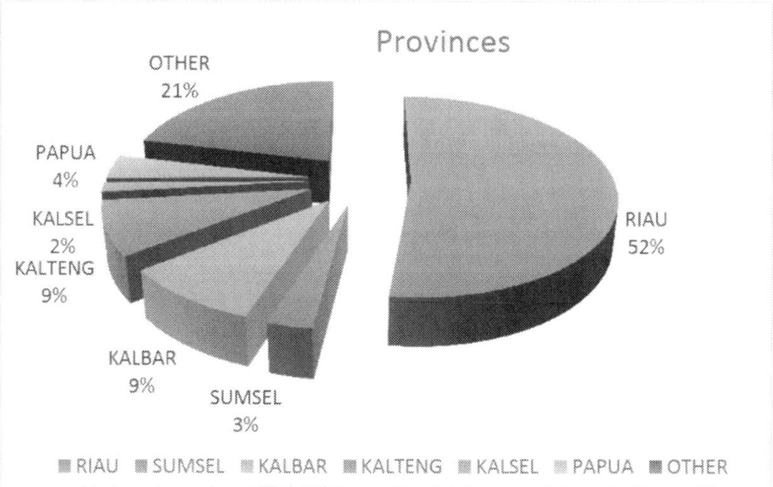

Figure 3 (a): Spatial distribution of national hotspots in 2013

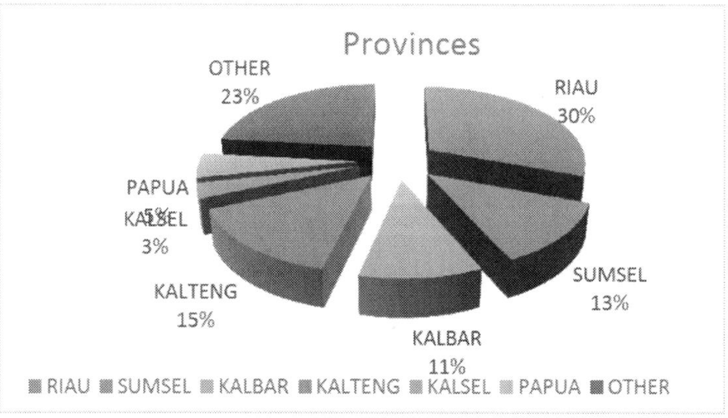

Figure 3 (b): Spatial distribution of national hotspots in 2014

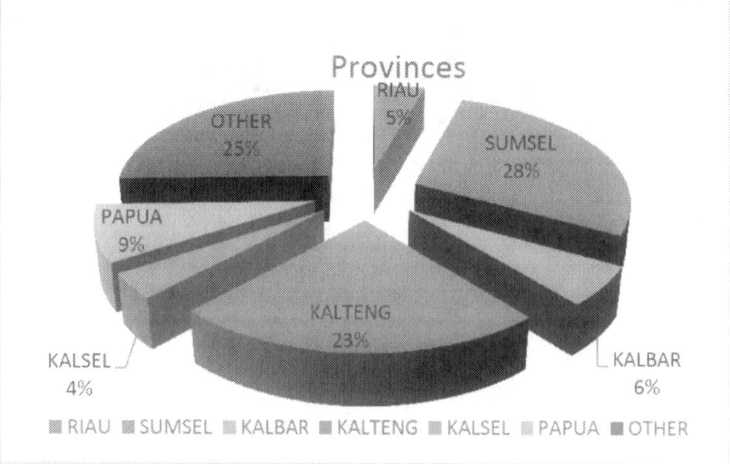

Figure 3 (c): Spatial distribution of national hotspots in 2015

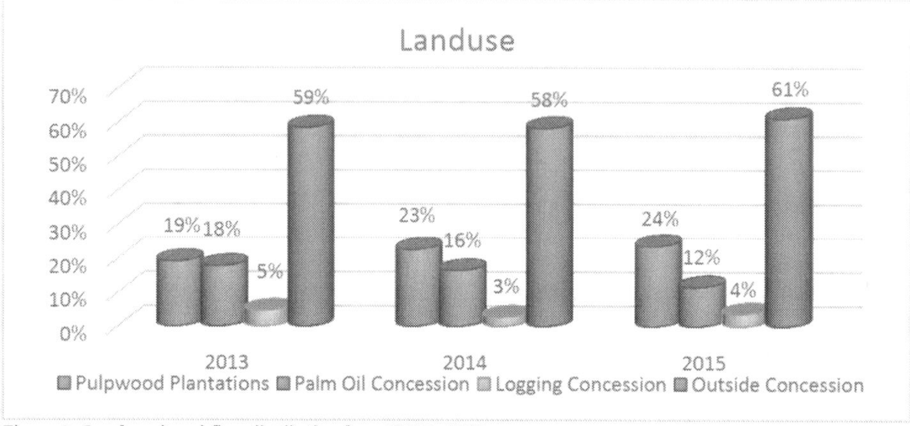

Figure 4: Land-use based fires distribution from 2013 to 2015

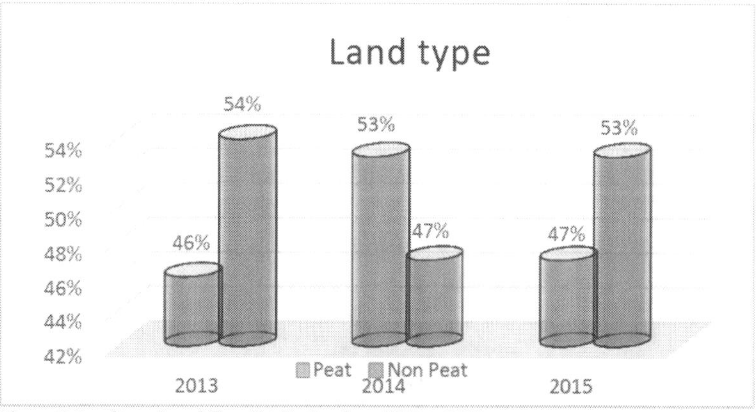

Figure 5: Land type based fires distribution from 2013 to 2015.

REFERENCES

1. Direktorat Jenderal Perlindungan Hutan dan Pengawetan Alam. 1983. Pengumpulan Pengolahan Analisis Data Masalah Kebakaran Hutan. Departemen Kehutanan Republik Indonesia. Jakarta.
2. Global Forest Watch Fires. https://fires.globalforestwatch.org.
3. Tim Menteri Negara Lingkungan Hidup Republik Indonesia dan UNDP. 1998. Kebakaran Hutan dan Lahan di Indonesia. Jilid 1. Dampak, Faktor dan Evaluasi. Kantor Menteri Negara Lingkungan Hidup. Jakarta
4. Suratmo, F.G., S. Manan, O. Rachmatsah dan E. Husaeni. 1996. The Central Forest Fire Management in Indonesia. Strengthening National Forest Fire Management Capacity. In cooperation between FAO and Facultas of Forestry, IPB. Bogor.

Abstract No: A-057

HAZE AND PEATLANDS: THE TOP THREE CHALLENGES OF TACKLING SMOULDERING MEGAFIRES

Guillermo Rein

Imperial College London, United Kingdom

**Corresponding author: g.rein@imperial.ac.uk*

One again, peat fires raged in 2015 in Indonesia and their extent was staggering. They emitted in excess of 1.6 Gton of CO_2 equivalent. In fact, if peat fire emissions were considered, Indonesia would be the 3rd or 4th highest emitting country in the world. Smouldering fires are the largest and longest burning fires on Earth and take place in Indonesia, Siberia, Alaska, Florida and Australia, to name a few. Peat megafires destroy essential peatland ecosystems, and release very large quantities of CO_2, CO and CH_4, making up 15% of annual global greenhouse gas emissions. Moreover, the burning of deep peat affects older soil carbon that has not been part of the active carbon cycle for centuries to millennia, and thus creates a positive feedback to the climate system. Given the scale of the problem, relatively little action is being taken. After 15 years of research on the topic, I have identified the three major challenges hampering global action: Scientific Understanding is poor: There are still large gaps in our knowledge of how smouldering fires ignite and spread, which impedes development of any successful mitigation strategy. Poor scientific knowledge even leads to disastrous confusion between flaming and smouldering combustion. Non-existent technologies: Smouldering fires are routinely fought across the globe with techniques that were developed for flaming fires. These techniques are ineffective. For instance, aerial tankers do nothing to stop smouldering fires, and satellite monitoring substantially underestimates the size of peat fires. Topic fragmented among disciplines: Smouldering fires are an intrinsically multidisciplinary theme requiring collaboration by combustion scientists, ecologists, atmosphere scientists and biochemists. These three challenges must be overcome before effective mitigation strategies can be implemented. While the largest fires on Earth continue releasing naturally stored carbon into the atmosphere, we are failing to protect both people and the planet.

Keywords: -

Abstract No: A-170

MUTUAL INTERDEPENDENCE BETWEEN REWETTING, AFFORESTATION AND FIRE PROTECTION IN TROPICAL PEATLANDS

Hidenori Takahashi[1]*, Bambang Setiadi [2] and Mitsuru Osaki [3]

[1]*Hokkaido Institute of Hydro-climate, Japan*
[2]*National Research Council of Indonesia, Indonesia*
[3]*Hokkaido University, Japan*

**Corresponding author: nana77hihc@gmail.com*

SUMMARY

Peat surface moisture was significantly higher in the forest comparing that of grass land. This high moisture in the forest will be important for prevent easy igniting of surface peat. To control the carbon emission by peat fire and microbiological decomposition from tropical peatlands, the efficiencies of rewetting peatlands by rising groundwater level, controlling peat fire by firefighting, recovering forest were evaluated with some outcomes of the JST-JICA SATREPS project "Wild Fire and Carbon Management in Peat-Forest in Indonesia". Carbon emission by peat fire after the rising groundwater level with dam construction is estimated to be 76% of that before dam construction. The extinguish rate by firefighting is directly affected on the decreasing rate of carbon emission from peatlands. Using relationship between the net ecosystem CO2 exchange (NEE) and groundwater level (Hirano, *et al.*, 2012), the amount of carbon emission from the un-drained forest was estimated to be decreased to 27% by rising the annual mean groundwater level from 0.2 m to 0.1 m.

***Keywords**: groundwater level, canopy density, peat moisture, carbon emission*

INTRODUCTION

Soil moistures of surface layer in tropical peatland are different with the canopy density of trees at the sites. And the moisture has a relationship with the occurrence of peat fire (Adi Jaya *et al.*, 2011). The one dimensional tank models were applied to estimate the difference of surface peat moisture in open grass land and dense forest. The surface peat moisture in open grass land has been dried by evapotranspiration from surface layer in three month after the last rainfall. But the surface peat moisture in the forest was not so dry (Takahashi, *et al.*, 2013). The higher moister content of surface peat layer in the forest means that forest recovery on peatland is one of keys for pear fire prevention.

Rewetting of peatland by rising groundwater level is the most important and basic method for peat fire prevention (Takahashi *et al.*, 2011). The most of peat fire is caused by human carelessness. The extinction of fire in early stage is the most important to prevent the surface fire spread to peat fire.

The outline of scenario of carbon management is mentioned and the reduction of carbon emission from peatlands was roughly estimated in this paper.

THE EFFECT OF FOREST CANOPY ON PREVENTION OF PEAT FIRE

Peat moisture in the fields

i. <u>Study sites for peat moisture measurement</u>

Two sites with different surface cover and land use were set-up for measurement of peat surface moisture in the tropical peatland of Central Kalimantan. The first site was a peat swamp forest (NF) without large effect of canal in the Sebangau Nature Laboratory. The second site was the open grass land area with small tree cover after peat fire (OG).

ii. <u>Measurement of peat moisture</u>

Measurement of peat moisture was carried out using DL6 with Theta Probe (ML2x) sensor. The sensor was buried in peat at depth of 5 cm.. The data was recorded at 1 hour interval. The groundwater level logger(DL/N70 STS) was deployed at the same locations. The measurement was conducted for 2 years, starting from 1st June 2011 until 13 August 2013.

iii. Annual change of the surface peat moisture in the fields

Moisture of surface peat layer in the forest is clearly higher than that in the grassland during dry season in 2011 and 2012 (Figure1). The dry seasons in both years were not so longer than that in 2009 then the moisture of the surface peat in grassland was not lower than 0.4. But the surface peat moisture in the open grassland OG was decreased very soon after rainfall. On the other hand, it in the forest, NF, was decreased slowly. The difference of the decreasing speed of peat moisture in both sites was caused by the difference of strength of solar radiation on the ground surfaces. From this result, we can conclude that the forest canopy has an important role to keep the surface peat in wetter condition.

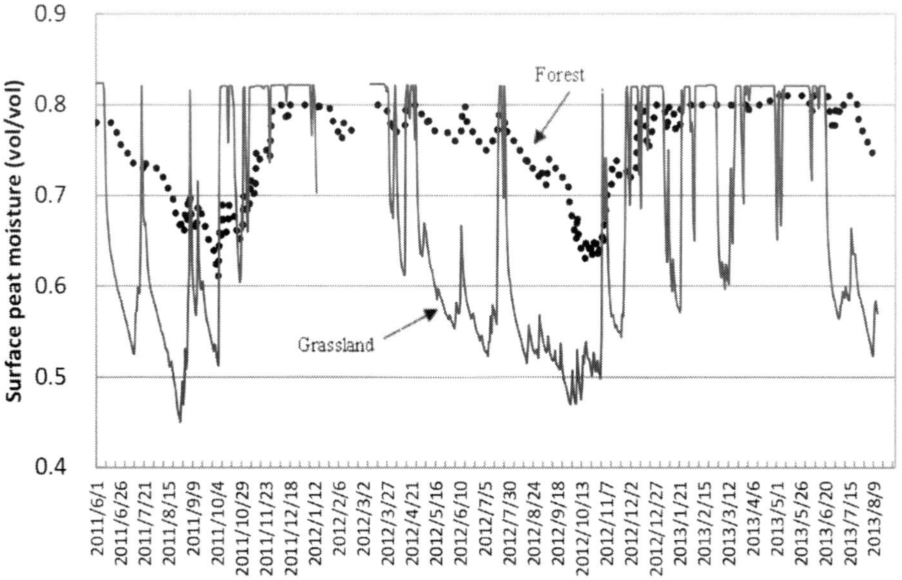

Figure 1: Annual changes of the moisture of surface peat layers in a grass land and forest

Peat moisture and ignition

The dry bulk density of tropical peat in the basin and dome area is 98.4±22.3 kg m^{-3} (Shimada *et al.*, 2001). The dry bulk density of 100 kg m^{-3} was used to convert the peat moisture from the gravimetric density to volumetric/bulk density. According to Jaya *et al.*, (2012), analyzing the relationship between number of fire spot observed by MODIS and peat moisture in a forest revealed that the critical moisture of peat for ignition was around 0.15 in volumetric moisture. The probability of ignition of the upper sphagnum also increases at around 0.15 in volumetric moisture (Babrauskas, 2003). From the moisture behaviors of surface peat layers in the forest and the open grassland, the forest canopy is very important to keep the surface peat in wet and to prevent the surface peat ignition

CONTROLS OF CARBON EMISSION BY REWETTING AND FIRE MANAGEMENT

The rising of groundwater level by construction of dams in the canal

Ishii *et al.* (2012) conducted very precise measurements of water level in the canal, groundwater level in the peat dome in the north of block C, the Mega Rice Project area. The effect of dam construction on the groundwater level was calculated using MODFLOW model. The groundwater level near the center of the target area, where was the top of peat dome, rose around 1 m at near the canal and 0.2 m at 400 m far from the canal after dam construction. The effect of rising groundwater level on the carbon emission was evaluated using the relationship between the annual lowest groundwater level and the amount of carbon emission from MRP area shown in Figure 2.

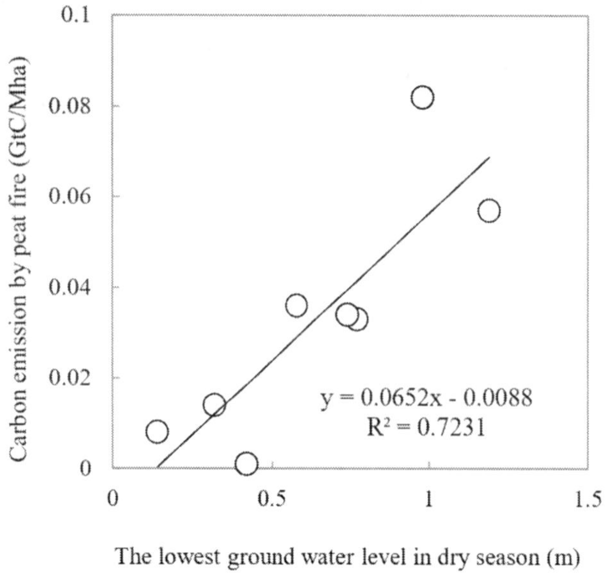

Figure.2: The amount of carbon emission by peat/forest fire relating to the annual lowest groundwater level in a peat swamp forest in Central Kalimantan. Groundwater level was measured at the site in the Sebangau National Park, named Plot-1b and located 2°19'15.80"S, 113°54'4.10"E in coordinate. The amount of carbon emission was estimated using the number of fire spot in the Mega Rice Project area by Dr. Indra Putra.

The effect of rising groundwater level on carbon emission by fire was estimated for the area 1 km far from the canal. The area was divide into 4 zones namely Zone A: from the canal to 100 m far from canal, Zone B: from 100 me to 200 m, Zone C from 200 m to 500 m and Zone D from 500 m to 1000 m. The mean groundwater level I each zone was used the values along the line $X_0 - X_0$' in Figure 3. The amount of carbon emission was calculated by using the regression formula shown in Figure 2 and Table 1.

The amount of carbon emission after dam construction in Zone A decreased to 46.4% of that before dam construction. The ration of carbon emission after the dam construction was 66.0% in Zone B, 71.8% in Zone C, 90.6% in Zone D.

Around 50% of carbon emission by peat/forest fire in the area from canal to 200 m far from canal can be decreased by dam construction. Most of peat/forest fire is generally occurred in the area along road and canal with human errors. Decreasing of carbon emission by fire in the zone along the canal will make a ripple effect on carbon emission far from the canal.

Table 1: Controls of carbon emission from peatland by peat/forest fire with dam construction and firefighting activity

	Changes of annual lowest groundwater level by dam construction				Fire fighting Extinction rate (%)		
Zone (m)	Dam	GWL (m)	C-loss (Gt/Mha)	C-loss (%)	50	70	100
A (100)	before	2.0	0.122	100			
	after	1.0	0.056	46.4	23.2	13.9	0
B (100)	before	1.9	0.115	100			
	after	1.3	0.076	66.0	33.0	19.8	0
C (300)	before	1.2	0.069	100			
	after	0.9	0.050	71.8	35.9	12.5	0
D (500)	before	1.2	0.069	100			
	after	1.1	0.063	90.6	45.3	27.2	0
Total (1000)	before		0.792	100			
	after		0.597	76.0	38.0	21.8	0

The firefighting effect on reduction of carbon emission by peat/forest fire

Pear fire occurs generally from surface fire near the canals and roads, which burns the grass and organic materials on the ground with human mistake. Therefore, the area from canal or road to 200 far from them is very important area for peat/forest fire control. Generally, fire in urban area is control by the fire service of local government whereas fire in forest area is control by firefighting team belong to the forest management bureau. Peat/forest fires occur mostly in the abandoned land which experienced peat/forest fire before. However, the severity of peat forest fire is beyond the abilities of both local government and forest bureau firefighters to control. The firefighting activity by people in local community is the most important, useful and effective for fighting on peat/forest fire. In general, the most important action for firefighting is the initial fire extinguishing. The compact firefighting system which was handled by local people is useful for the initial fire extinguishing (Takahashi *et al.*, 2013).

The effect of firefighting on carbon emission by peat/forest fire was classified to three ranks; 50%, 70% and 100% (Table 1). The peat/forest fires more than 200 m from the canal and road are mostly caused by the spreading fire from the area near canal and road. So if 50% the peat/forest fire is extinguished by local firefighting team, 50% of carbon emission will be decreased. In the case of the firefighting effects 70% and 100%, the carbon emission by peat/forest fire will be decreased with same way.

CONCLUSION

Three activities, forest recovery, rewetting and firefighting, for reduction of carbon emission from tropical peatlands were evaluated and concluded as follows:

1. Forest recovery is necessary and important to prevent the surface layer of peatland become dry and reduce the fire risk. Rising of groundwater level by constructing dams is remarkably effective in the area from canal to 200 m far from canal which also reduced the carbon emission due to peat/forest fire by 50% of that without dam.
2. Firefighting by local community on the peat/forest fire is also very important to prevent the fire spreading. If 50% of peat/forest fire in the area from canal to 200 m far from the canal is extinguished, the carbon emission by peat/forest fire will be decreased to 50% of that without firefighting.

ACKNOWLEDGEMENTS

Results shown in this paper were mainly obtained from SATREPS (Science and Technology Research Partnership for Sustainable Development) project entitled as "Wild fire and carbon management in peat-forest in Indonesia" founded by JST (Japan Science and Technology Agency) and JICA (Japan International Cooperation Agency).

REFERENCES

1. Babrauskas V (2003) Ignition handbook. Fire Science Publishers, Issaquah, USA.
2. Jaya Adi, Takada Masayuki, Hirano Takashi, Mishima Yoshio, Inoue Takashi, and Takahashi Hidenori, 2012: Moisture behavior of surface peat layer in areas of different surface cover and different ground condition during dry season in Central Kalimantan. Proceedings of International Symposium on Wild Fire and Carbon Management in Peat-Forest in Indonesia,
3. Kamiya M. and Kawabata S., 2003: Physical properties of peat in Central Kalimantan. *Proceedings of the International Symposium on Land management in Southeast Asia, Bali*, 2002, 341-345.
4. Shimada, S., Takahashi, H., Haraguchi, A. and Kaneko, M, 2001: The carbon content characteristic of tropical pets in Central Kalimantan, Indonesia: Estimating their special variability in density, Geochemistry, 53, 249-267, 2001.
5. Takahashi H., Yonetani Y. and Miyasaka H. 1998: Micrometeorological aspects of tropical peat swamp forest and farmland in Central Kalimantan, Indonesia. *Proceedings of the International Workshop on Environmental Management of Wetland Ecosystem in Southeast Asia* (Eds. Tokura, S.), 41-46.
6. Takahashi Hidenori, Usup Aswin, Hayasaka Hiroshi, Limin H. Suwido, 2003: Estimation of ground water level in a peat swamp forest as an index of peat/forest fire. *Proceedings of the International Symposium on Land management in Southeast Asia, Bali*, 2002, 311-314.
7. Takahashi Hidenori, Jaya Adi and Limin H.Suwido, 2013: Compact fire extinguishing system for firefighting teams of villages in peatland area of Central Kalimantan. *Proceedings of International Symposium on Wild fire and Carbon Management in Peat-Forest in Indonesia,* Palangka Raya, 2012, 203-206.
8. Usup Aswin, Hashimo Yoshihiro, Takahashi Hidenori and Hayasaka Hiroshi, 2004: Combustion and thermal characteristics of peat fire in tropical peatland in Central Kalimantan, Indonesia. *TROPICS*, **14(1)**, 1-19.

Abstract No: A-180

NATIONAL RESPONSES IN THE CONTEXT OF ASEAN DEVELOPMENTS OVER PEAT FIRES AND HAZE

Helena binti Muhamad Varkkey

Department of International and Strategic Studies, University of Malaya, Malaysia

**Corresponding author: helenav@um.edu.my*

SUMMARY

The recent haze episodes of 2013 and 2015 have been especially severe, with serious consequences on the day-to-day lives of Indonesians living closest to the fires and in neighbouring countries. With satellite imagery and news reports pinpointing sustained peat fires as a major source of the haze, national and regional responses have, more than ever, focused on peatlands. At the ASEAN level, on-going efforts to address peat and haze issues focus around two documents, namely the ASEAN Agreement on Transboundary Haze Pollution (ATHP) 2002 and the ASEAN Peatland Management Strategy (APMS) 2006-2020. This paper analyses the latest national responses within the context of these documents, particularly on the 2013 Haze Monitoring System (HMS) and the soon-to-be-established ASEAN Coordinating Centre for Haze (ACCH). Two responses are of particular interest, namely Singapore's Transboundary Haze Pollution Bill (THPB) 2014, and Indonesia's recent ratification of the ATHP. Singapore's THPB ties in closely to ASEAN's HMS as it needs accurate land maps so that Singaporean prosecutors can correctly assign blame. The HMS is however constrained as concession maps are available on a case-by-case basis only, which is augmented by Indonesia's repeatedly delayed One Map Initiative. Indonesia for its part has finally ratified the ATHP and this has renewed regional interest in the establishment of the ACCH in Riau, which, due to its location close to some of the most severe peatfires, is hoped to encourage more local ownership of the issue. However, Indonesia has announced that it needs at least another three years before a marked reduction of haze episodes. Indonesia's three-year timeline does still fall within the timeframe of the APMS, so the document should be a useful tool to inform developments of Indonesia's fire and peat policy in the years to come.
Keywords: *ASEAN, transboundary haze, peatland management, fire monitoring, Haze Monitoring System*

INTRODUCTION

The recent transboundary haze episodes of 2013 and 2015 have been especially severe, with serious consequences on the day-to-day lives of Indonesians living closest to the fires and in neighbouring countries, especially Malaysia and Singapore. Singapore experienced its worst haze ever on record in June 2013, with its Pollution Standards Index (PSI) reaching 401, ranked as extremely hazardous. In September 2015, an emergency was declared in Riau, Sumatra, the worst-hit Indonesian province that was close to the epicentre of the fires. And during the same period in Malaysia, schools were closed in three states and the federal territory for several days as air quality worsened.

Satellite imagery captured during these two haze episodes detected hundreds of hotspots in Kalimantan, Sumatra, and to a lesser extent Peninsular Malaysia and Sarawak. The majority of these hotspots were on peatland areas, and plumes of smoke rising out of these areas were clearly visible (NASA, 2015). Peat fires are notoriously hard to put out, as they often spread over vast distances on the surface and penetrate into the peat underground. These smouldering fires emit thick, sooty smoke that can travel far distances in the atmosphere. One study has indicated that about 80% of the regional haze consists of smoke from peat fires (Reddington *et al.*, 2014). With satellite imagery and news reports pinpointing sustained peat fires as a major source of the haze, national and regional responses have, more than ever, focused on peatlands. Hence, the purpose of this paper is to analyse the latest national responses within the context of regional peat and haze initiatives.

METHODS

This research is qualitative in nature. Media and archival research was the main methods of data collection used for this paper. Triangulation of data from these two sources was essential in better understanding the circumstances surrounding particular pieces of information, and also to verify the accuracy of the information obtained. Media (mainly newspaper) research was a very important primary resource for this study, as the publicity from haze events meant that there was extensive coverage of the matter in the media. Therefore, there was a substantial amount of newspaper articles written around the time of haze events that were useful as primary sources for this research. Archival research proved important for obtaining official Indonesian, Malaysian and Singaporean government documents, ASEAN documents and documents published by relevant organizations. Especially useful also were non-governmental publications and company annual reports.

RESULTS

At the ASEAN level, on-going efforts to address peat and haze issues focus around two documents, namely the ASEAN Agreement on Transboundary Haze Pollution (ATHP) 2002 and the ASEAN Peatland Management Strategy (APMS) 2006-2020. This paper analyses the latest national responses within the context of these documents, particularly on the 2013 Haze Monitoring System (HMS) and the soon-to-be-established ASEAN Coordinating Centre for Haze (ACCH). Two responses are of particular interest, namely Singapore's Transboundary Haze Pollution Bill (THPB) 2014, and Indonesia's recent ratification of the ATHP.

Regional initiatives

The ATHP, which was adopted by all ASEAN member countries in 2002 and brought into force in 2003, was meant to provide legally binding support to an earlier ASEAN document, the Regional Haze Action Plan (Florano, 2003). Hence, the ATHP is notable for being one of the few legally binding ASEAN environmental agreements to be entered into force (ASEAN Secretariat, 2004). The Agreement's stated objective, under Article 2, is 'to prevent and monitor transboundary haze pollution as a result of land and/or forest fires which should be mitigated, through concerted national efforts and intensified regional and international cooperation' (ASEAN Secretariat, 2002).

However, up till late 2014, the ATHP remained ratified by only nine ASEAN states, with the Philippines being the ninth country to ratify in early 2010. Indonesia held off ratification till 16 September 2014. During this time, the effectiveness of the ATHP was severely crippled, in the following ways:

1. ASEAN-level initiatives have not been able to address sensitive issues like influencing Indonesian land and forest policy and the implementation of laws. Article 9 of the Agreement does call for the development of appropriate policies to curb activities that may lead to land and/or forest fires (ASEAN Secretariat, 2002), however this is only applicable to ratified states.
2. As part of the ATHP mechanism, if a serious forest fire was spotted by the ASMC, neighbouring states could activate fire-fighting services and move in, without having to write in to the receiving government to get diplomatic clearance for aircrafts and permission from local fire services for each new case (Khalik, 2006). However, this clause was only applicable if both countries have ratified the treaty.
3. Non-ratification has also delayed the establishment of the ACCH and its dedicated Secretariat, which was supposed to be for the purposes of facilitating cooperation and coordination among the parties in managing the impact of land and/or forest fires in particular haze pollution arising from such fires (ASEAN Secretariat, 2002). Currently, the ASEAN Secretariat in Jakarta, which acts as an interim coordination centre, is crippled by its limited staff and location far away from the fires.

The APMS was also designed to provide support to an earlier ASEAN project, the ASEAN Peatland Management Initiative 2002 (Ramirez, 2013). It was developed to provide a common framework for peatland management in the region in the period 2006–2020. There are four main objectives to the strategy, namely:

1. To enhance understanding and build capacity on peatland management issues in the region
2. To reduce the incidence of peatland fires and associated haze
3. To support national and local level implementation activities on peatland management and fire prevention
4. To develop a regional strategy and cooperation mechanisms to promote sustainable peatland management (ASEAN peat, 2016)

As part of the APMS, ASEAN Member Countries with significant peatlands are to develop complementary National Action Plans (NAPs) on Peatlands. The NAPs are to provide the respective countries with their national focus, and identify agencies involved, funds and requirements for implementing activities towards the sustainable management of peatlands (ASEANpeat, 2016). Currently, two projects are being implemented to support the implementation of regional and national strategies for sustainable management of peatlands in Southeast Asia and the incorporation of peatland management into policies and plans related to forest and land-related resources. These two complementing projects are the Rehabilitation and Sustainable Use of Peatland Forests in Southeast Asia (APFP Project) and the Sustainable Management of Peatland Forest in Southeast Asia (SEApeat Project) (www.peat-portal.net) (Ramirez, 2013).

National responses

i. Indonesia

The guidelines provided by the APMS proved useful to Indonesia when it was able to submit its Nationally Appropriate Mitigation Action (NAMA) plan on Sustainable Peatland Management to the United National Framework Convention on Climate Change (UNFCCC) in January 2010 (Thamrin, 2011). Thanks in part to this effort, Indonesia has managed to secure substantial international funding for national peatland management efforts, namely from the Global Environment Facility (GEF) Trust Fund (GEF Trust Fund, 2014) and from the Ministry of Environment, Japan in collaboration with the Global Environmental Centre (GEC). A feasibility study carried out after one year of the Japan-GEC collaborative project showed positive results, with a projection of 227,500t-CO2/yr GHG reduction estimation at the 10,000 hectare project site area (Motoda, 2010).

In terms of the ATHP, it was mentioned above that Indonesia delayed ratification of the ATHP for over a decade. Finally in September 2014, the outgoing President Susilo Bambang Yudhoyono announced Indonesia's ratification of the instrument as one of his final acts in office. Indonesia's ratification of this treaty was received with much fanfare by the other ASEAN countries, and marked renewed goodwill over collective action to mitigate haze.

ii. Singapore

Singapore on the other hand had a quite different set of responses to the ASEAN initiatives as compared to Indonesia. Singapore proposed to ASEAN the establishment of a HMS in 2013 to further operationalize the ATHP, especially in terms of the implementation of land and forest policies and laws. The HMS was conceptualised as a platform for open-access digitized land-use maps and concession maps of fire-prone areas that cause haze, to act as a deterrent to errant companies (National Environment Agency, 2014).

This was meant to complement another Singaporean initiative that was put into force the following year, which was the THP, which provides for criminal and civil liability for any Singaporean or non-Singaporean entity causing or contributing to transboundary haze pollution in Singapore (Parliament of Singapore, 2014).The THPB makes it a criminal offence when an entity engages in conduct, or authorizes any conduct which causes or contributes to haze in Singapore. A penalty of up to SGD 300,000 can be imposed, and this may be increased up to SGD 450,000 if the entity has deliberately ignored requests by authorities to take appropriate action to prevent, reduce, or control the pollution. Affected parties may also bring civil suits against errant entities (Parliament of Singapore, 2014). The Bill is unique for its application of extra-territoriality; it covers the operations of all Singapore and non-Singapore entities whose activities outside of Singapore contribute to haze pollution in the city-state. Since proving what happens abroad is difficult, evidential presumptions relating to causation (linking open burning elsewhere and wind direction with the presence of haze in Singapore) and culpability (based on ownership and occupation of land) help to give teeth to this Bill.

DISCUSSION

Indonesia

In terms of peatland management in particular, it was hoped that the ratification of the ATHP would mean that there could be more candid and open discussion and consultation at the ASEAN level over the previously deemed 'too sensitive' issues of land policy, peatland in particular. However, ratification does not mean that the earlier three limitations mentioned in the previous section will automatically be resolved. Out of the three points, the one with the most positive outlook is the final one, on the ACCH. Hope for the first two, including that pertaining to peatland policy, may be overstated. This is because, in the nature of other ASEAN agreements, the ATHP was also vague and lacking in various hard-law instruments such as strong dispute-resolution or enforcement mechanisms (Nguitragool, 2011, p. 357), or any provisions for dispute settlements through international courts or other arbitration tribunals (Tan, 2005, p. 664). This means that Indonesia still cannot be called to task if they should refuse to cooperate on these two points, despite ratification. Indeed, none of the ASEAN countries did so during the recent 2015 haze episode.

However, there is much hope for the third point on the ACCH. Shortly after Indonesia's ratification, ASEAN Environmental Ministers renewed discussions for the establishment of the ACCH in Riau (ASEAN Secretariat, 2015). The centre's new location in Riau is hoped to fuel more awareness and ownership of the fire problem in the Riau administration, in addition to coordinating information and cooperation efforts around the region (ASEAN Secretariat, 2002). This dedicated ACCH in Riau should be better able to:

1. Establish and maintain regular contact with the respective National Monitoring Centres regarding the data, including those derived from satellite imagery and meteorological observation, relating to land and/or forest

fire, environmental conditions conducive to such fires; and air quality and levels of pollution, in particular haze arising from such fires;
2. Facilitate co-operation and co-ordination among the Parties to increase their preparedness for and to respond to land and/or forest fires or haze pollution arising from such fires;
3. Facilitate co-ordination among the Parties, other States and relevant organizations in taking effective measures to mitigate the impact of land and/or forest fires or haze pollution arising from such fires; and
4. Respond to a request for or offer of assistance in the event of land and/or forest fires or haze pollution resulting from such fires by transmitting promptly the request for assistance to other States and organizations; and co-ordinating such assistance, if so requested by the requesting Party or offered by the assisting Party (ASEAN Secretariat, 2002).

Singapore

Even though ASEAN formally adopted Singapore's HMS idea at the 14th Sub-Regional Ministerial Steering Committee on Haze (National Environment Agency, 2014), this was not without significant watering-down, as is the fate of many ASEAN agreements. Indonesia (and Malaysia as well) cited privacy and legal concerns of making maps publicly accessible. Indonesia also argued that its own One Map Initiative was underway, so there was no need for this additional platform which would essentially serve the same purpose. With these reservations, ASEAN adopted the HMS with maps to be shared on an ad-hoc, government-to-government basis only, much to Singapore's disappointment.

Singapore, as well as other ASEAN observers, expressed concern that this lack of transparency severely damaged the credibility of this system, and other actors not privy to the maps will continue to view the HMS, and by extension the governments with suspicion. And while it is exemplary that Indonesia is taking unilateral effort with the One Map Initiative, problems related to its decentralization process (Austrin, Alisjahbana, & Darusman, 2014), where local governments can now apply to change forest classification areas every five years, has meant that forest classifications are changing at a much more rapid rate, often faster than maps can be updated. This has drastically slowed down the One Map Initiative.

The TPHB importantly allows for reliance on satellite imagery, meteorological information, and maps as evidence (Chua & Ee, 2014). This was why Singapore placed high hopes on the HMS to provide accurate land maps, so that Singaporean prosecutors can correctly assign blame. Furthermore, such maps can also be used by companies to defend itself by proving the fires were caused by natural disaster or by parties not under its direction. However, the watering down of the HMS and the repeated delay of Indonesia's One Map Initiative makes identifying errant companies problematic. Because of this, Singapore's National Environment Agency (NEA) would need to work closely with their counterparts in Indonesia to build a case against these companies (Tay & Chua, 2014). However, Indonesia has thus far shown a weak track record; clearing land through burning is prohibited in Indonesia but authorities have so far only successfully prosecuted a handful of companies for starting such fires. Hence, the effectiveness of the TPHB as a plausible tool to mitigate peatfires and haze remains to be seen.

Following the haze episode in 2015, Singapore's NEA requested information from the Indonesian government to provide details of companies it suspects of causing haze pollution. Following this, the NEA has sent Preventive Measure Notices to four Indonesian companies pursuant to Section 9 of the THPB, requesting them to:

1. Deploy fire-fighting personnel to extinguish or prevent the spread of any fire on land owned or occupied by them
2. Discontinue, or not commence, any burning activities on such land
3. Submit to NEA any plan of action to extinguish any fire on such land or to prevent its recurrence (MEWR, 2015)

The information provided by these companies are hoped to assist the NEA in its investigations under the THPB. However, it is obvious that the effectiveness of the Bill is reliant on the cooperation of the alleged perpetrator, as a result from the watering down of the HMS mechanism.

CONCLUSION

In 2014, the author attended a NGO Roundtable on Environment, Sustainability and Climate Change, where discussants pointed out that a common weakness in a lot of the ASEAN initiatives on peat fires and haze is that while many initiatives like the ATHP and HMS are useful to be applied when the fires occur, they were not preventive in nature. The discussants noted that it was important for the haze to be framed as not merely a fire problem, but more broadly as a land use issue, and specifically as a peatland management issue. When peatland disturbances occur, fires, whether accidental or intentional, will become more likely.

While initiatives like the APMS can be considered more preventive, usually these types of initiatives are not given as much attention or importance, either from the government or even the media, as compared to the more reactive ones as discussed above. A good example is the fanfare involved around Indonesia's long-awaited ratification of the ATHP, while the peatland management projects on-going under the APMS remain relatively unknown in ASEAN circles. Furthermore, for such preventive measures, participating countries often rely on external assistance as seen above, and are often not proactively involved in the preventive action. This becomes a problem when fire and haze events actually do occur, where governments are suddenly thrust into action in unfamiliar (peat) soil.

Indonesia has announced that it needs at least another three years before a marked reduction of haze episodes. Indonesia's three-year timeline does still fall within the timeframe of the APMS, which ends in 2020. Herein lies an opportunity for Indonesia, under the fresh leadership of Joko Widodo, to change the country's hitherto reactive approach to peat fire and haze management to a more preventive approach, as outlined in the APMS. The APMS should be a useful tool to inform developments of Indonesia's fire and peatland management policy in the years to come, not only for Indonesia, but for the region as a whole.

ACKNOWLEDGEMENTS

The author would like to acknowledge the Singapore Institute of International Affairs, the Habibie Centre in Jakarta and ISEAS-Yusof Ishak Institute in Singapore for hosting various dialogue sessions that enabled me to engage with other scholars in the field to gain a better understanding of current issues, and also as a platform for feedback and critique of my ideas for this article.

REFERENCES

1. ASEAN Secretariat. (2002). *ASEAN Agreement on Transboundary Haze Pollution* Kuala Lumpur.
2. ASEAN Secretariat. (2004). *4: Transnational Issues*. Paper presented at the ASEAN Annual Report.
3. ASEAN Secretariat. (2015). *Declaration on ASEAN Post-2015 Environmental Sustainability and Climate Change Agenda*. Kuala Lumpur.
4. ASEANpeat. (2016). Regional Policy Framework. *Peatlands in Southeast Asia.* Retrieved from http://www.aseanpeat.net/index.cfm?&menuid=42
5. Austrin, K., Alisjahbana, A., & Darusman, T. (2014). *Indonesia's Forst Moratorium: Impacts and Next Steps*. Retrieved from
6. Chua, G., & Ee, D. (2014, 21 February). Govt seeks feedback on law on haze. *The Straits Times*.
7. Florano, E. R. (2003). Asssesment of the "Strengths" of the New ASEAN Agreement on Transboundary Haze Pollution. *International Review for Environmental Strategies, 4*(1), 127-147.
8. GEF Trust Fund. (2014). *Project Identification Form (PIF)*.
9. Khalik, A. (2006, 14 October 2006). ASEAN ups pressure on haze as lawmakers bicker. *Jakarta Post*.
10. MEWR. (2015). SIngapore send notices to four Indonesian companies and seeks information from SIngapore-Listed APP [Press release]
11. Motoda, T. (2010). *MOEJ/GEC Feasibility Study (FS) Programme for New Mechanisms*. Retrieved from Japan:
12. NASA. (2015). Smoke Blankets Indonesia. *Image of the Day.* Retrieved from http://earthobservatory.nasa.gov/IOTD/view.php?id=86681
13. National Environment Agency. (2014). *Factsheet on Transboundary Haze Pollution*. Singapore.
14. Nguitragool, P. (2011). Negotiating the Haze Treaty. *Asian Survey, 51*(2), 356-378.
15. Parliament of Singapore. (2014). *Transboundary Haze Pollution Bill No. 18/2014*.
16. Ramirez, N. E. (2013). ASEAN Peatlands Management Strategy 2006-2020: Promoting sustainable management of peatlands in Southeast Asia. *ASEAN Biodiversity*(January-April), 14-16.
17. Reddington, C. L., Yoshioka, M., Balasubramanian, R., Ridley, D., Toh, Y. Y., Arnold, S. R., & Spracklen, D. V. (2014). Contribution of vegetation and peat fires to particulate air pollution in Southeast Asia. *Environmental Research Letters, 9*(9), 094006. Retrieved from http://stacks.iop.org/1748-9326/9/i=9/a=094006
18. Tan, A. K. (2005). The ASEAN Agreement on Transboundary Haze Pollution: Prospects for Compliance and Effectiveness in Post-Suharto Indonesia. *N.Y.U. Environmental Law Journal, 13*, 647-722.
19. Tay, S., & Chua, C. W. (2014, 21 February). To end the haze problem, both penalties and cooperation are needed. *TODAY*.
20. Thamrin, S. (2011). *Indonesia's National Mitigation Actions: Paving the Way towards NAMAs.* Paper presented at the CCXG/Global Forum on Environment Seminar on MRV and Carbon Markets, Paris.

Abstract No: A-357

PEAT FIRE ECONOMY AND ACTOR NETWORK IN SUMATRA: AN ANALYTICAL APPROACH

Herry Purnomo[1, 2*], Bayuni Shantiko[1] and Harris Gunawan[3]

[1]Center for International Forestry Research (CIFOR), Indonesia
[2]Bogor Agricultural University (IPB), Indonesia
[3]University of Riau, Indonesia

* *Corresponding author: h.purnomo@cgiar.org*

SUMMARY

Peat fires have become a local, national and global concern. The health issues and economic disruption caused by haze from peat fires have been enormous. Estimated economic losses from fires in 2015 were in excess of USD 16 billion. This paper focuses on the political economy of forest and land fires in Riau It highlights how fires break out, the actors involved, rent seeking activities, and the social networks associated with forest and land fires. It identifies the actors involved through surveys and value chain analyses, while their roles and relationships with other actors are analyzed using social network analyses. We found that some actors obtained enourmous benefit from fires. The economic power is the determining factor in how these actors influence decision-making processes and their implementation to work in their own interests through their network patronage.

***Keywords**: peat, fire, actor, economy, network*

BACKGROUND

The health issues and economic disruption caused by haze from forest and land fires have been enormous. In 2015 the cost of fire and haze was estimated USD16 billion (The World Bank 2015). In 2012, forest fires in Riau released 1.5 to 2 billion tonnes of carbon emissions in a week - equivalent to 10 percent of Indonesia's total annual emissions (Moss 2015). Singapore and Malaysia complained about trans-boundary haze from Indonesia causing disruptions to tourism, health and the economy.

The Indonesian government has tried to overcome the problem of forest and land fires. The President committed to stop Indonesia producing haze from forest and land fires in 2015. Can this commitment be achieved? How can the Ministry of Environment and Forestry, local governments, the business community and civil society organizations create a quick and accurate response to overcome forest and land fires? This paper focuses on the political economy of forest and land fires in Riau as input for our collaboration to overcome them. It highlights how fires break out, the actors involved, rent seeking activities, and the social networks associated with forest and land fires.

POLITICAL ECONOMY ANALYSIS AND METHODS

Political economy is generally defined as a study that views politics as a crucial factor in determining economic outcomes (Drazen 2000). Forest and land fire-related projects have long been carried out in various provinces in Indonesia, with and without bilateral cooperation, and a number of technical, economic, social and political recommendations have been generated (Dennis 2009). The failure to understand the political economy (Dauvergne 2009) of actors and patronage have often resulted in failed attempts to resolve the problem of forest and land fires (Varkkey 2013). Key patrons in forest fires comprise businesses and political ruling elites at the local, national and global levels. Incongruence between the causes of fires and proposed management solutions occurs in countries all over the world. In Indonesia and Brazil the underlying cause of fires is social-politic problems, whereas action plans prioritize technical research into firefighting. This hampers efforts to overcome the problem of forest and land fires (Carmenta 2011).

Value chains analyses were used to understand how added value and benefits are distributed between each actor along production and marketing value chains. Per actor added value can be calculated using benefit and cost analyses. The roles of actors in forest fire occurrences can be determined independently, or based on their relationships with other actors. Each actor has a particular role to play, and is not necessarily reliant on its relationship to others (Borgatti 2013). The roles of actors in the context of how they are related and connected to other key actors were analyzed using a Social Network Analysis (SNA). Actors may be highly capable of analysis or might be practitioners, but if they are disconnected or isolated from a network, they have no significant role. Rent seekers often sit in important positions in networks; another underlying problem causing land and forest fires.

FIRE ECONOMY

Cleared land (cut and slashed) was worth USD 665/ha and sold in the form of two-hectare blocks. Added value for land consisted of the following: 26% for farmer groups in the land clearing phase; 4% gained by claimers for their efforts in claiming the land; 6% of the total value of the land for marketing, including travel, communications and other costs; and 13% of the total value of the land gained by village officials for land administration documents; with the organizers of farmers groups gaining the highest value at 51%. Based on information on the ground, there were no clear patterns for benefit sharing between farmer group organizers and other organizers. However, the organizers of farmers groups usually gained more benefits than any others.

When buyers bought only cleared (cut and slashed) land, they would be responsible for land preparation. They might burn it or use mechanized tools to prepare the land. The marginal cost for land preparation would benefit the buyers. Higher values were obtained from 'ready-to- plant' land, which had already been slashed and burned. Local people call this mode of trading '*terima abu*' (receiving the ashes). The distribution of benefits for actors involved in '*terima abu*' is shown in Figure 1. The trading value was USD 856/ha. Farmer group organizers promised their members would gain parts of the land for free or at a reduced price. This cost about 0.2% of the total value. The farmer group organizers gained 57% of the total value or around USD 486 per hectare.

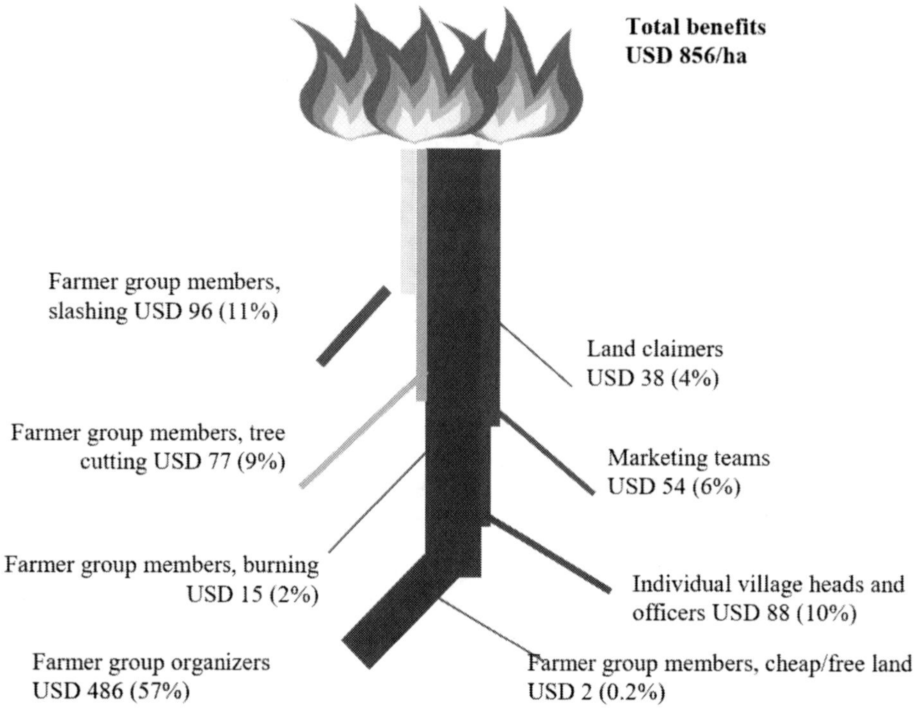

Figure 1: Added value for 'ready-to-plant' land per hectare

'Ready-to-plant' land was not only sought by palm oil investors but also by small-scale investors for horticultural purposes. It was easier for small-medium investors to buy 'ready-to-plant' land due to its lower price and its flexibility in managing growing costs. Other investors, preferring to choose more practical means and quicker profits, were willing to pay USD 3077 /ha for ready-to-harvest oil palm plantation land. Around USD 992 or 32% of the total value was allocated for planting and growing costs for 3-4 years. Laborers received around 7% and 5% of the total value respectively for land clearing and planting. Benefits gained by individual village heads and sub-district officials amounted to 3% of the total value. Land block letter or 'certificate' holders would only gain 1% of the total value, an extremely small amount for those not involved in group management. Farmer group organizers carried out management, administration and marketing processes and gained the largest share at 51% of the total value.

ACTOR NETWORK

Stakeholders in forest fires are related to one another in various contexts, i.e. information exchange, economic transactions, kinship, political affiliation, ethnicity or religion. Each of these relations can be independent or mutually reinforcing. Centrality determines the importance of actors in the network, which is measured by degrees of connectivity and betweenness. The degree of centrality measures the quantity of relations, such as information received or sent out from each node or actor, while betweenness measures an actor's role as the shortest path (geodesic link) between two other actors.

Degrees for centrality in land transaction and fire information networks are shown in Figure 2. Higher degrees are indicated by larger circles. There are four actors having high degrees of connectivity, namely: village governments, sub-district governments, district governments and advocacy groups. Connectivity is the amount of received information (in-degree) or outgoing information (out-degree). The lowest degree belongs to farmer group members, which indicates they are the most isolated actors in forest fire information traffic.

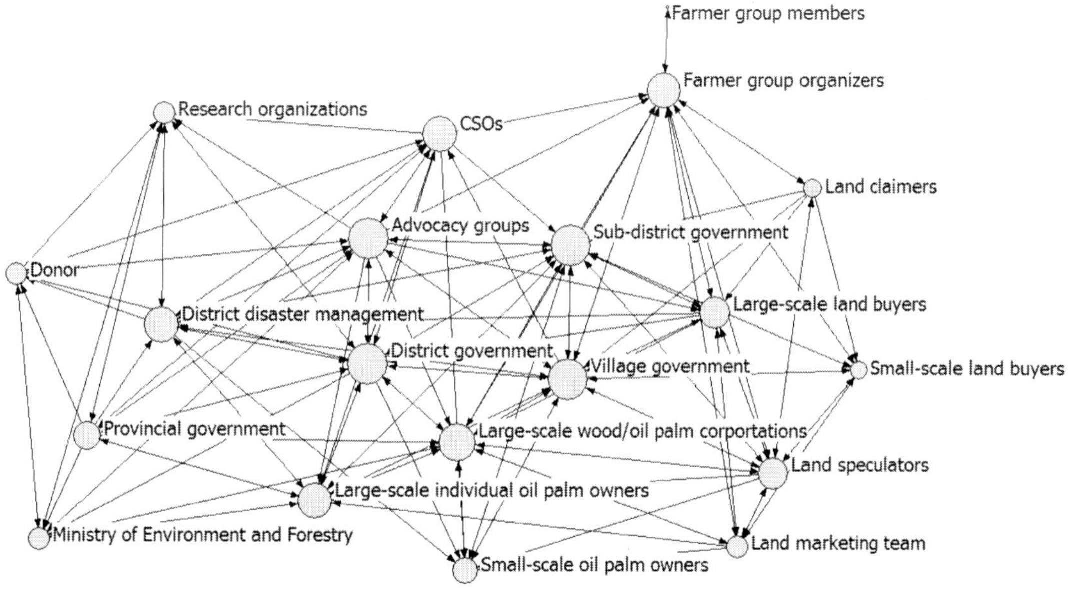

Figure 2: Centrality information network for land transaction and fire stakeholders

The crucial roles of actors in linking information between other actors are shown in Figure 3. Larger circles indicate a greater role in becoming information hubs between actors in land transactions and fires. Farmer group organizers and advocacy groups are the two most important actors in linking with other actors. Farmer group organizers became central hubs for other actors in land transactions connected to fires. Figure 5 shows groups of actors based on their *Euclidean* distances, The Euclidean distance between two stakeholders is equal to the square root of the sum of the squared differences between them.

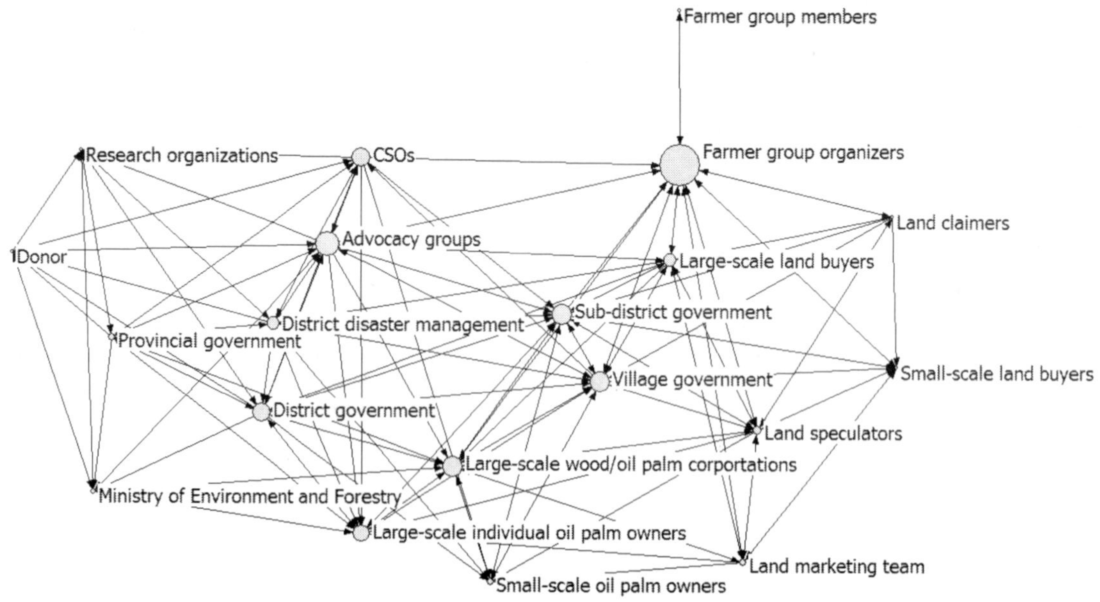

Figure 3: Betweenness information network for land transaction and fire stakeholders

DISCUSSION

The large amounts of economic rent involved bring negative impacts for natural resource development. There are illegal aspects to the accumulation and pursuit of economic rent. The burned areas are land and a state forest area, the use of which is regulated by brings about losses for society and the majority of people. The economic rent surrounding fires will be legal when they occur only on privately owned land and are supported by law. A zero burning policy is advocated by many stakeholders, while others doubt it is possible (Tacconi *et al.*, 2008). In some parts of Indonesia, traditional, limited and controlled burning remains an integral part of land clearing law. Land claims occurring in the lead up to forest fires are often carried out illegally. Illegal economic rent is a livelihood source for some sections of communities as well as people at the local and national levels.

The magnitude and amounts of economic rent involved indicate that fires generate huge earnings for certain people, particularly for elites ruling farmer groups for their contributions in land clearing, and for oil palm investors for their contribution in developing areas in the aftermath of fires. Putting a stop to forest and land fires will mean ending the economic rent for such people. Legality, economic and social approaches are crucial in order for this to happen. The legality approach alone is not enough for tackling forest and land fires. The distribution of economic rent also shows actors interested in policy development and the implementation of fires. Actors who benefit from fires will have net incentives for them to continue. As long as fires create more economic value than REDD+ or PES, then those actors will not feel incentivized to overcome or tackle fires.

Policy interventions should focus on central actors in land transaction and fire information networks, namely local governments (village, sub-district and district) and advocacy groups. The information networks position them as the most important actors playing roles in preventing and overcoming fires. Elites ruling farmer groups are the most important actors in linking whole networks. At the same time, these ruling elites are also the biggest recipients of economic rent from land clearing for oil palm plantations. In other words, in order to create effective efforts for preventing and overcoming forest and land fires we must start from the network core that involves these ruling elites.

ACKNOWLEDGEMENT

This research was conducted with financial assistance from DFID KNOWFOR UK under the project entitled 'The political economy of fire and haze' http://www.cifor.org/fire-and-haze/.

REFERENCES

1. Borgatti SP, Everett MG and Johnson JC. 2013. Analyzing Social Networks. Sage Publications UK.
2. Carmenta R, Parry L, Blackburn A, Vermeylen S, Barlow J. 2011. Understanding human-fire interactions in January 2015)

3. Dauvergne. P. 1998. The political economy of Indonesia's 1997 forest fires. Australian Journal of International Affairs, 52:13-17.
4. Dennis R. 2009. A review of fire projects in Indonesia (1982-1998). Bogor: CIFOR.
5. Drazen A. 2000. Political economy in macroeconomics. http://press.princeton.edu/chapters/s6819.html (accessed 10 Augues 2015)
6. Moss C. 2015. Hilangnya lahan gambut mengemisi karbon senilai 2.800 tahun dalam sekejap mata: Riset. http://blog.cifor.org/26501/hilangnya-lahan-gambut-mengemisi-karbon-senilai-2-800-tahun-dalam-sekejap-mata-riset#.VXKQjc-qqko (accessed 12 July 2015)
7. The World Bank. 2015. Indonesia Economic Quarterly: Reforming amid uncertainty. December 2015. http://pubdocs.worldbank.org/pubdocs/publicdoc/2015/12/844171450085661051/IEQ-DEC-2015-ENG.pdf (accessed 15 January 2016)
8. Varkkey H. 2013. Oil palm plantations and trans-boundary haze: Patronage networks and land licensing in Indonesia's peatland. Wetlands, 33:679-690.
9. Tropical forest regions: a case for interdisciplinary research across the natural and social sciences. Ecology and Society 16(1): 53. [online] URL: http://www.ecologyandsociety.org/vol16/iss1/art53/ (accessed 10

Abstract No: A-351

PEAT FIRE SUSCEPTIBILITY IN SARAWAK, MALAYSIA IN THE CONTEXT OF CLIMATE CHANGE

Zulfaqar Sa'adi and Shamsuddin Shahid

Faculty of Civil Engineering, Universiti Teknologi Malaysia (UTM), Malaysia

**Corresponding author: zulfaqar19863@gmail.com*

SUMMARY

Fire has the potential to disturb the carbon stored in peats, which globally account near to the total amount of carbon in the atmosphere. Therefore, peat fire risk management is important for carbon emission reduction, particularly in the context of global climate change. Though peat in tropics is naturally fire resistant as they maintain high moisture, it has been reported that human activities including plantation development, agriculture, and logging, have made tropical peatlands more vulnerable to burning. Peat ignition probabilities may increase in a warm climate and therefore, fire susceptibility of peatlands may increase due to global warming. The objective of the present study is to assess the changes in fire susceptibility of the peatlands of Sarawak, Malaysia due to the changes in climate. The peat fire index (PFI) proposed by Takahashi using a one-dimensional water balance equation with rainfall and evapotranspiration as the components. Monthly total rainfall and temperature data at six locations for the time period 1981-2014 were employed to calculate the historical PFI. An ensemble of six global circulation model (GCM) simulations of Coupled Model Intercomparison Project phase 5 (CMIP5) namely, BCCCSM1-1, CanESM2, MIROC5, MIROC-ESM, MIROC-ESM-CHEM and NorESM1-M under two Representative Concentration Pathways (RCP) scenarios, namely, RCP4.5 and RCP8.5 were used for climate downscale at the points of interests using support vector machine (SVM). Projected climate was then used to assess the future changes in PFI compared to historical period in the study area. The results show high uncertainty in the projection of peat fire susceptibility in the region due to climate change. It is expected that projected PFI in the region can be used to assess the peat fire risk as well as in operational fire management and development of early warning system.

***Keywords**: Tropical peatlands, peat fire index, climate change, risk assessment, uncertainty.*

INTRODUCTION

Peatland fire is an annual phenomenon in Borneo island (Yong and Peh 2014; Yulianti Nina, Barbara Betrixia *et al.*, 2014). In the last three decades, the region has suffered from large events of peat fire in 1982/83, 1990, 1991, 1994, 1997/98, 2005/2006, 2009, and 2012-2015. Peat fire is considered as one of the major causes of the deforestation of tropical peat swamp in Malaysia and Indonesia (Razali, Nuruddin *et al.*, 2010). The peat fires cause severe damage to soil and consequently, the whole agro-ecosystem (Yulianti Nina, Barbara Betrixia *et al.*, 2014). (Miettinen, Shi *et al.* (2010) used land-cover maps and active fire detection based on satellite imagery to evaluate the rates and spatial distribution of peat land deforestation in Southeast Asia for the time period 1990-2010, and reported that the deforestation in the region is strongly associated with fire activity. Therefore, actions toward combating the peat fires are very important for long-term conservation of peat swamps, protect peat agro-ecology and biodiversity, and the livelihood of the people (Yong and Peh 2014). Development of peat fire index (PFI) for assessment of vulnerability of peat land to fire is considered as one of the options to mitigate peat fire. Mitigation measures based on vulnerable zones identified using PFI can minimize the losses of peat layers, reduce emission, and prevent the high cost of peat land fire suppression. Furthermore, the index can be used to assess the possible changes in peat land fire vulnerability due to climate change. (McLaughlin and Webster 2014) reported that future dry conditions due to climate change may potentially increase peat land susceptibility to fire. Therefore, knowledge of these changes should be useful for climate change vulnerability and adaptation assessments for peat swamps

Number of studies has been carried out to assess the peat fire vulnerability using peat fire index.. (Yulianti Nina, Barbara Betrixia *et al.*, 2014) developed a Geographic Information System (GIS) data base of Peat land Fire Risk Index (PFRI) for Central Kalimantan of Indonesia that can be used as fire early warning system. Khomarudin *et al.* (Khomarudin, Vetrita *et al.*, 2013) conducted a study to characterize peat fire hotspots from Terra/Aqua MODIS data, field survey, haze detection, and the burnt area mapping. They reported that the fires spot can be analyzed by the hotspot characteristics and the haze detection. Seitawan *et al.* (Setiawan, Mahmud *et al.*, 2004) identified the peat swamp forest fire hazard areas by integrating GIS-grid-based and multi-criteria analysis.

They concluded that proposed method can provide valuable information about the locations most likely to be affected by fire. However, all the methods mentioned above are mostly based on satellite remote sensing data, which is often very time consuming and need to high computational skill to identify peat fire risk zones.

The objective of the present study is to assess fire susceptibility of the peatlands of Sarawak, Malaysia using climatic parameter. The PFI) proposed by Takahashi is used. The study can provide a too quick assessment of peat fire vulnerability which in turn may help in adopting necessary mitigation measures.

DATA AND METHODS

Rainfall data from 24 locations in Sarawak were used in the present study for computation of peat fire index (Figure 1). Daily rainfall data of the stations were obtained from Drainage and Irrigation Department (DID) of Malaysia. The daily data was converted to monthly total. The temperature data for four locations available in open source database are collected from the website. Time periods of data used for the study are different for different locations. PFI is estimated using whole data available at a location. As the spatial variation of temperature in Sarawak is not very high, temperature data from the nearby location is used.

The peat fire index (PFI) proposed by Takahashi is used in the present study. Takahashi method uses a one-dimensional water balance equation with rainfall and evapotranspiration as the components using the following equation (Hayasaka, Noguchi *et al.* 2014):

$$I_{pf} = \int_{June}^{Nov} G_w dt = c \int_{June}^{Nov} (P_r - E_t)\, dt \qquad \text{Equation 1}$$

Where, P_r is precipitation and E_t is evapotranspiration estimated from mean temperature.

Hayasaka *et al.* (Hayasaka, Noguchi *et al.* 2014) derived Takahashi's PFI from monthly rainfall data and established the linear relationship to the annual lowest groundwater level and hotspots observed by MODIS and reported that it can be used for the early warning of peat fire in tropical peat lands.

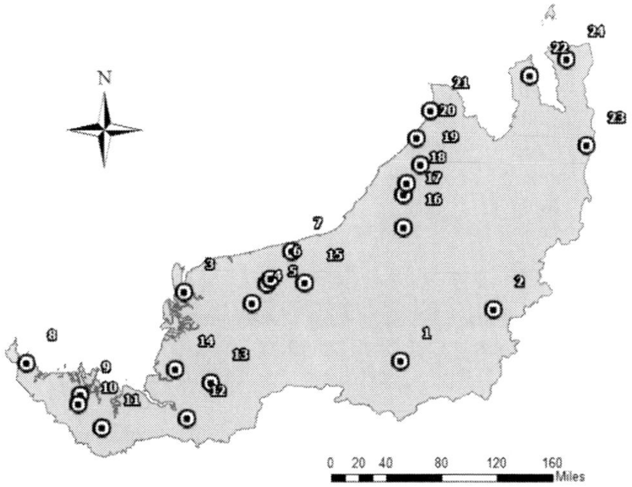

Figure 1: Location of rain gauge stations used for computation of Peat Fire Index (PFI)

RESULTS

The time series of PFI at four locations are shown in Figure 2. Negative values of PFI indicate the possible occurrence of peat fire in that year. Therefore, the number of years with negative PFI to total number of years used for the study indicates the frequency of possibility of peat fire.

The graphs in Figure 2 shows number of negative PFI years vary widely from one station to another. However, negative PFI in years 1982 and 1997 is found common in most of the stations. Hot weather and low rainfall due to El-nino caused peat fire in those years. Literature reviews suggested that peat fire burned the rainforests in the summer of 1997. Prolonged air pollution in the region due to peat fire affected the health of tens of millions of people. It also severely affected the peat ecosystem in the region (Brauer and Hisham-Hashim 1998). The PFI used in the present study is able to detect those years efficiently. This indicates the potential of Takahashi's PFI index to detect peat fire vulnerable zones.

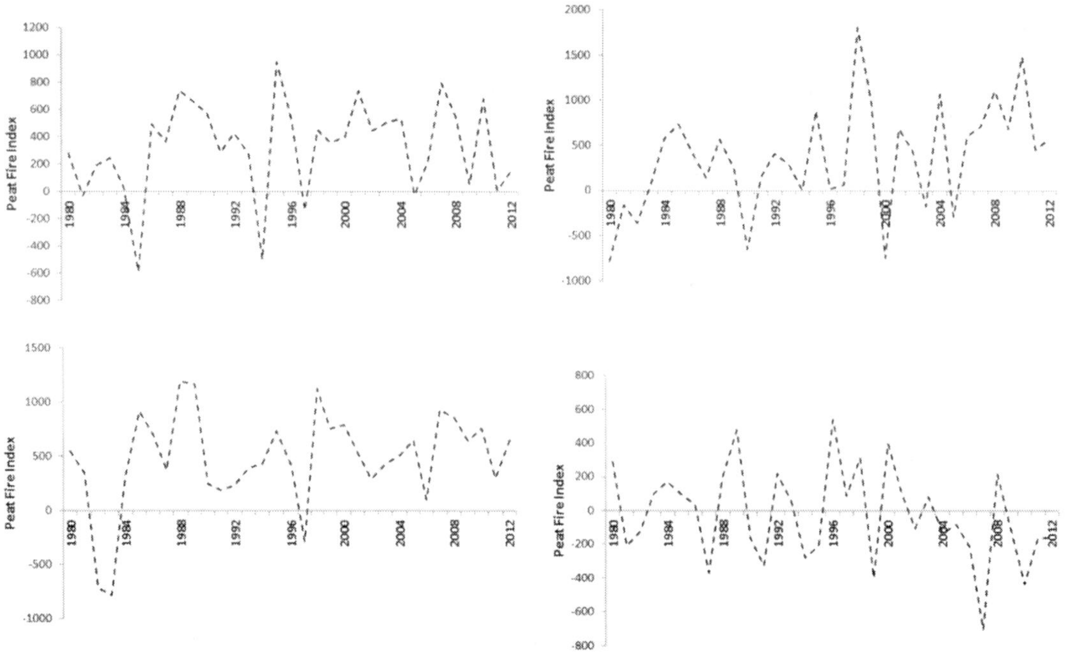

Figure 2: Time series of PFI at four locations in the study area

Analysis of frequency of occurrence of peat fire through fitting of frequency distribution curves to PFI reveals that return period of peat fire events in the study area varies from 5 to 15 years. Spatial analysis of return period of peat fire shows no particular pattern in peat fire vulnerability zones.

CONCLUSION

A PFI index that uses climatic parameters namely, rainfall and evapotranspiration for the estimation of peat fire vulnerability at a point are used in this study. The study reveals that PFI used in the present study is able to identify the historical peat fire years effectively, which means that it can be used for assessment of peat fire vulnerability in Sarawak. The study can be extended further in future for assessment of the impacts of climate change on peat fire vulnerability in the study area.

REFERENCES

1. Brauer, M. and J. Hisham-Hashim (1998). "Peer Reviewed: Fires in Indonesia: Crisis and Reaction." Environmental Science & Technology **32**(17): 404A-407A.
2. Hayasaka, H., I. Noguchi, *et al.* (2014). "Peat-fire-related air pollution in Central Kalimantan, Indonesia." Environmental Pollution **195**: 257-266.
3. Khomarudin, R., Y. Vetrita, *et al.* (2013). Lesson learnt of the forest/land fire occurrences in Riau Province to enhance the monitoring methodology The 34th Asian Conference on Remote Sensing. Denpasar, Bali, Indonesia. **34**.
4. McLaughlin, J. and K. Webster (2014). "Effects of Climate Change on Peatlands in the Far North of Ontario, Canada: A Synthesis." Arctic, Antarctic, and Alpine Research **46**(1): 84-102.
5. Miettinen, J., C. Shi, *et al.* (2010). "Influence of peatland and land cover distribution on fire regimes in insular Southeast Asia." Regional Environmental Change **11**(1): 191-201.
6. Razali, S. M., A. A. Nuruddin, *et al.* (2010). "Forest fire hazard rating assessment in peat swamp forest using Landsat thematic mapper image." J. Appl. Remote Sens. **4**(1).
7. Setiawan, I., A. R. Mahmud, *et al.* (2004). "GIS-grid-based and multi-criteria analysis for identifying and mapping peat swamp forest fire hazard in Pahang, Malaysia." Disaster Prevention and Management: An International Journal **13**(5): 379-386.
8. Yong, D. L. and K. S.-H. Peh (2014). "South-east Asia's forest fires: blazing the policy trail " Fauna & Flora International 2014.
9. Yulianti Nina, Barbara Betrixia, *et al.* (2014). A Satellite-Based Early Warning System for Peatland Fires Toward Sustainable Palm Oil in Indonesia.

Abstract No: A-138

PEATLAND FIRES IN RIAU, SUMATRA: STAKEHOLDERS' PERCEPTIONS OF A "WICKED PROBLEM"

Rachel Carmenta[1], Aiora Zabala[2] and Jacob Phelps[3]

[1]*CIFOR*
[2] *University of Cambridge, United Kingdom*
[3]*Lancaster University, United Kingdom*

**Corresponding author:*

Indonesia's peatland fires, and resulting haze, represent a leading environmental concern, not only within those fire affected areas of Indonesia, but regionally and globally. These fires embody the challenges of "wicked problems": existing solutions have largely failed; the problem involves interdependencies and multiple drivers at different scales, and is often understood and explained in a number of different and contested ways. Yet, popular solutions to fire are often simplistic, short term and technology-driven. Further, widespread "finger-pointing" about the causes of fire (e.g., between communities and corporates), fails to reflect the complexity of the issue, causes discord, and impedes productive problem-solving. Policy instruments that do not engage with the underlying motivations of agents, or that do not capture the complexity of the problem, are unlikely to result in desired behavioural change. We contextualize problem-solving efforts with on-the-ground insights of how different actors experience and explain large fire events in Indonesia's Riau Province. This study draws on the results of perceptions surveys with a purposive sample of diverse actors in Riau (e.g., corporate actors, small farmers, absentee investors, domestic and Singaporean decision-makers). As part of a q-method enquiry, participants responded to a broad range of statements related to three dimensions of fire: its benefits, burdens, and preferred solutions. Respondents prioritized statements, revealing their underlying viewpoints and preferences. Using factor analysis, we identified how groups of perspectives are shared between stakeholders and construct distinct discourses. We map out and interpret the distinct discourses on 1) the benefits and burdens and 2) the solutions to the peatland fires in Riau. Further, we are able to examine which stakeholder groups, with different levels of power and interests are populating which discourse. Such insight identifies areas of agreement and those of contention, serving as a boundary object to facilitate negotiation and consensus-building within challenging policy debates.

***Keywords**: peat fires, perceptions survey, 9 – method enquiry*

Abstract No: A-119

QUANTIFICATION AND CHARACTERIZATION OF PEAT FIRES AND RELATED FIRE-EMISSION FACTORS FROM TROPICAL PEATLANDS

Grahame Applegate[1*], Bambang H. Saharjo[2], Bob Yokelson[3], Kevin Ryan[4], Andrew P.Vayda[5], Tim Jessup[6], Sulistyo[7], Erianto Indra Putra[2, 8], Laura Graham[7*] and Mark Cochrane[8]

[1]*University of the Sunshine Coast, Australia*
[2]*Bogor Agriculture University (Institut Pertanian Bogor), Indonesia*
[3]*University of Montana, USA*
[4]*Independent Fire Scientist, USA*
[5]*Rutgers University, USA*
[6]*Formerly AusAID advisor for the Kalimantan Forests and Climate Partnership; current address, Global Green Growth Institute, Jakarta, Indonesia*
[7]*Research and Policy Coordinator of the Project*
[8]*Borneo Orangutan Survival Foundation, Indonesia*
[9]*Project Team Leader, South Dakota State University, USA*

**Corresponding author: grahame.applegate@gmail.com*

SUMMARY

Peatland fires are a major contributor to Indonesia's greenhouse gas emissions in recent decades, particularly in previously drained and burnt areas during El Niño events, as witnessed in 2015. Despite the estimated magnitude of these emissions, peat and peatland fires still lack verified field data, methods and models. Peat fire emissions are still not fully incorporated within the Indonesian National Carbon Accounting System (INCAS) as part of its carbon Monitoring, Reporting and Verification (MRV). This NASA-funded joint Indonesia and USA project is based in the Ex-Mega-Rice Project, within the BOS-Mawas Area in Central Kalimantan. It builds upon the extensive investments and research of the previous Kalimantan Forests and Climate Partnership (KFCP) REDD+ demonstration project. The current project is developing the necessary fire emissions factors and expertise to implement operational annual peatland fire emission quantification capabilities to complement the existing peat decomposition-related emissions monitoring capacity for the area. The project has developed improved fire evaluation methods and information, and ground-to-remote calibrations for detecting fires, determining what can burn, mapping burned areas, quantifying relevant emission factors and estimating the volume and mass of consumed biomass. The project will through field data collection integrate fire-related human actions with fire scene analyses to ascertain when, where, how, and under what surface fuel load conditions are likely for initiating peat fires. The project is working directly with villages, district, provincial and national governments, Central Kalimantan's Environmental Agency and INCAS to ensure the methods, data and applications of the analyzed results are quickly and appropriately integrated into carbon models and fire management activities in Indonesia.

***Keywords**: Peat fires, peat emission factors, tropical peat land, MRV, peat fire evaluation*

INTRODUCTION

Peatland fires are a major contributor to Indonesia's greenhouse gas (GHG) emissions, particularly in drained areas, and in first and second burn areas during El Niño–Southern Oscillation ENSO events. Despite the volume of these GHG emissions, peatland fires emission factor are not currently incorporated accurately within the Indonesian National Carbon Accounting System (INCAS), implemented by the Indonesian Government's carbon Monitoring, Reporting and Verification (MRV).

This NASA-funded project is a partnership between Bogor Agriculture University or *Institut Pertanian* Bogor and South Dakota State University, with a number of Indonesian collaborating institutions and builds upon extensive investments in peat and fire research, since 2009, developing technical capacity, data collection, and site infrastructure development, completed as part of the Kalimantan Forests and Climate Partnership (KFCP) REDD+ demonstration project, which concluded in June 2014. The NASA project is conducting the necessary fire research and expertise to implement operational annual peatland fire emission quantification capabilities within INCAS to complement the existing decomposition-related emissions monitoring capacity for the BOS-Mawas Area in Kapuas District in Central Kalimantan, Indonesia.

Quantification of the amounts of GHGs, aerosols and smoke particulates emitted in peat fires are critical elements for properly assessing their global climate effects and impacts upon local health. However, the IPCC GHG accounting guidelines (IPCC 2006; 2014) provide very little guidance for estimating such emissions from peat fires. Few studies have quantified the chemistry and climate relevant emissions from burning tropical peat and, have all been conducted in laboratory settings. In undisturbed tropical peat forests, peat carbon stocks are relatively stable, protected by anaerobic conditions underground. However, disturbance, especially drainage, even in the absence of fire, leads peat soils to suffer from compaction and aerobic conditions, allowing bacterial decomposition that emits an estimated 86 Mg/ha/yr of CO_2 (Hooijer *et al.,* 2009); or roughly 26 Mg/ha/yr of soil carbon. Although episodic, and varying in area each year (Ballhorn *et al.*, 2009), peat fires are estimated to oxidise between 100 and 600 Mg ha^{-1} of carbon from peatlands (Konecny *et al.,* 2016). Monitoring fires that penetrate into the peat is of particular interest and difficult because of the quantity and form of emissions that result from these burns, yielding disproportionate impacts on human health and global climate. The purpose of this paper is to provide an overview of the project and present some initial outputs although, detailed results and subsequent discussions are not presented.

OBJECTIVES

Peat fires require sustained high temperatures and fuel moisture levels below 130% at the fire front (Usup *et al.,* 2004) to be maintained. Factors controlling peat burning are the moisture level, mineral content of the fuels, organic composition, bulk density, flow permeability, and the presence of sufficient cracks or channels for sufficient oxygen flow. While the basic characteristics and processes of peat fires and emissions have been documented, much of the human influences and quantification of emissions are still to be determined.

The Project which spans three years from 2013 to the end of 2016 is located in the BOSF–Mawas Area in Kapuas District, Central Kalimantan, Indonesia and has the following objectives:

- To work with trained field teams to regularly monitor the vegetation, fuel loads and hydrology and to also investigate actual fires by recording biophysical characteristics and social aspects of surface and peat fires supported by remotely sensed data, to provide essential details that could indicate what relevance, if any, they had for explaining the ignition of episodic deep-peat fires.
- Investigate and document causal connections between biophysical and social elements of the fire dynamic and the chains of bio-physical events leading to deep-peat fires.
- To quantify the chemistry and climate-relevant emissions from burning peat and develop fire emission factors for the various vegetation types on peatlands using in-situ whole air sampling and filter collections. These will be used to support laboratory analyses of smoldering peat and burning vegetation that have quantified CO_2, CH_4, and many other important gases.
- To determine fuel loads for the various peatland vegetation types, changes in land cover and number of surface fires based on burn scar maps using Landsat Imagery from 1990-2015.
- To develop models that will provide estimates of the changes in peat elevation and volume in degraded peatlands using field based plot measurements, along with Landsat Imagery and LIDAR to determine changes in peat elevation (building on methods and measurements developed during the KFCP Project) along with ground water hydrology.
- To socialize the results and to provide outreach material for stakeholders, including establishment of appropriate links to INCAS for integration of project findings into Indonesia's MRV process.
- To strengthen Indonesian ability to accurately estimate GHG emissions from peatlands as a significant factor in Indonesia's overall emissions from the forests and land sectors.

METHODOLOGY

Vegetation Monitoring

This work is designed to facilitate estimation and description of biomass, forest structure, composition, type of vegetation and rates of regeneration, by monitoring a series of Forest Monitoring Plots (FMP) established by KFCP in 2009 across a range of locations in the study site (Graham *et al.*, 2014a). There are eight locations representative of the range of forest types spread throughout the study site, with five locations associated with a canal and three locations in relatively undisturbed, closed-forest, both logged and unlogged. Each location contains three rows of plots perpendicular to the canal and parallel to the hydrology transects. Along each row, four plots were established, at 50 m, 100 m, 400 m and 700 m from the canal, making a total of 96 plots. The plots in each location comprise a set of 'nested quadrats of different sizes to facilitate the monitoring of seedlings, saplings, poles and trees. There are also heavy fuel load (Graham *et al.,* 2014b), hydrology and peat depth data for each location.

Hydrology Monitoring

The hydrology monitoring follows the methodology and protocols developed in KFCP (Ichsan *et al.*, 2014) and focuses on the 60 km of transects and the monitoring of over 300 dipwells (on the peat dome) and 31 staff gauges located in the canals and rivers where they intersect with the transects. The transects are monitored twice per year; at the peak of the dry season when water levels are lowest and at the peak of the wet season when water levels are highest. Monitoring is concentrated on transects in the highly degraded part of the peat dome (Block A) and around the large east-west canal (SP1 canal). Subsidence data, is not monitored as there is already an extensive set of analysed subsidence data from KFCP.

Fire Monitoring

The Fire Scene Evaluation Form (FSE) and accompanying Manual, is a scientific field-practice that has been developed for the Project by experienced fire and social scientists to ensure consistency and accuracy. The Form and its 79 questions and measurements involves the recording of biophysical data (including field weather and environmental conditions, measurements of basic fire characteristics, area burnt, fuel and peat characteristics with a focus on peat fires) and social data (land tenure and related governance, human actions and causal mechanisms of fire ignitions). When coupled with landscape scale GIS data and more detailed human actions data, this information then enables evaluators to create models of area-specific peatland and peat fire dynamics, and related carbon emissions. The Form is designed to be completed by those with competent field skills to undertake a replicable evaluation of different fires and locations. In some instances, the evaluators need to make some decisions, judgements and interpret the environmental conditions.

In order to obtain accurate and consistent results, a Manual has been developed which provides the necessary methodologies and descriptions to undertake the FSE. In some cases where questions are not 'quantifiable', possible answers are provided in the form of photos or illustrations. Since the field conditions during or after the fires are not always easy to characterise, the Form is designed with a 'Confident, Quite Confident, Some Confidence' rating that the evaluators can use to enable all questions to be answered with a proviso from the evaluators that some questions can only be answered based on a 'best guess' rather than certain data. Furthermore, many questions are accompanied with a request for a photograph (the photo code written on the form) so that those with more experience can later cross-reference visual evidence and answers on the Form.

Human Actions

This activity was designed to utilise interdisciplinary research techniques involving both the biophysical and social science disciplines to better understand the causal connections between human actions and biophysical characteristics of surface fires which transitions from surface to peat fires in tropical peatlands. The methodology involves village interviews and obtaining observational data to identify causal linkages between anthropogenic ignitions and the establishment of peat fires. In contrast to other interdisciplinary wildfire research projects (Vayda 2013), the social data obtained has been designed to be specific enough to be combined with bio-physical evidence from fire scenes for descriptions of when, where, how, and under what conditions fires have occurred and, critically, whether or not they have ignited large fuels like logs and stumps or light fuels such as ferns. From these descriptions, conclusions will be drawn about the likelihood of different fires or types of fires causing subsequent peat fires.

A Project database is being developed (SDSU-IPB Peat Fire Database) in Access, building upon the KFCP vegetation database. The database holds the hydrology, vegetation, FSE, fuel and social data. All data locations are uniquely coded, with GPS data recorded, so that spatial cross-analysis across the data subsets is possible, allowing for landscape, interdisciplinary results and models.

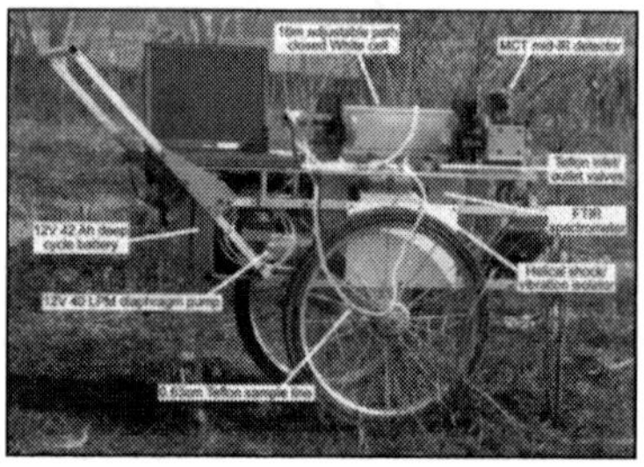

Figure 1: UM off-road FTIR, flask, filter lab.

Quantification of Emissions from Peat and Peat Swamp Forest Fires

A battery-powered, off-road Fourier Transform Infrared Spectrometer (FTIR) and Whole Air Sampling (WAS) system with an on-board filter collection laboratory was used along with two photoacoustic extinction meters (at 405 and 870 nm) in the 2015 fire season for field measurements of the trace gas and aerosol emissions from smouldering peat (Figure 1; Akagi *et al.*, 2013). The instrument suite can accurately measure and analyse ~90 gas species and aerosol mass, chemistry, and optical properties. Many of the dominant emissions are reactive species that could only be measured accurately in-situ by the FTIR. These field samples will allow comprehensive field/laboratory comparisons and the development of reliable algorithms to derive quantitative estimates for real fires of the numerous chemical species that are currently only measureable in the laboratory. Based on these results, comprehensive field-derived emission factors for peat burning under ambient conditions will be determined. This will better constrain the quantity of carbon emissions by chemical species, allowing better estimates of the global warming potential (GWP), health effects and atmospheric chemistry and climate impacts.

Notably, the filter collection and PAX systems allow the determination of emission factors (g/kg fuel burned) for concomitant scattering/cooling aerosols at the same time as the warming greenhouse gases. Among the gases measured in the laboratory and field were many precursors for secondary formation of more scattering aerosols and ozone, which is another powerful GHG formed in smoke plumes after emission. A key product of this research will be the comprehensive emission factors that will be calculated for surface and subsurface peat burning to specify the amount of compound per kg peat burned (dry mass basis) for all the chemical compounds measured using the carbon mass balance method.

Peat Fire Research & Modelling Annual Emissions

Quantifying peat-fire carbon emissions is challenging due to their location, depth of burning and rate of spread which results from the interplay with climate, weather, land use (human actions), land cover, drainage, disturbance history, fire type, peat depth and composition. Hence, the answer lies in determining the surface area burned, available fuel fraction at a given location through time and the amount of fuel consumed per unit area. Peatlands are extensive, remote, and are difficult landscapes to navigate, so remotely sensed data is used for modelling regional fire dynamic in the project area and annual emissions. Modelling of annual emissions will be based on a probabilistic model based upon satellites, existing Landsat-based annual land use and fire history data sets from 1990-2010 (Ballhorn *et al.*, 2009), fire history data from 2010-2016 and on peat fire measurements for MC%, rate of spread and volume of peat consumed (Graham *et al.*, 2016).

Tropical Rainfall Measuring Mission (TRMM) data has been found to be highly accurate for drought detection in Indonesian lowlands (Vernimmen *et al.*, 2011). Although the scale of the data do not allow for detailed rainfall measurements within project area, the data provide excellent coverage and estimation of precipitation across the entire basin, thereby driving the depth of the water table that largely controls peat flammability. TRMM data will be used to calibrate the hydrological field data and monitor peat flammability.

The MODIS active fire product is a useful tool for monitoring fire, but there are additional challenges for detection of fires in tropical regions that result from gaps in orbital overpasses in equatorial regions, low intensity nature of many surface and peat fires, and general masking issues related to clouds and smoke (Cochrane 2013). The Terra morning overpass MODIS satellite will mainly be used for monitoring fires but will also use the proximity and persistence of fire detections on the ground to parameterize the vulnerability of mapped surface fires to potential peat fires burning into the ground surface.

Land cover change and burn scar mapping with Landsat has long been used for land cover change mapping. Spectral Mixture Analyses (SMA) techniques using Landsat imagery have been shown capable of mapping understory fires in tropical closed canopy forests (Cochrane and Souza 1998). The project will use similar techniques to develop the land cover and fire scar mapping through to 2016.

In parts of the project area, a limited Lidar dataset was collected in 2007 along several transects using a small footprint (0.25m) pulse system and used to provide an initial estimation of burn depths (average 0.33 +/- 0.18 m) within the peatlands (Ballhorn *et al.*, 2009). A second full waveform, dataset for the same areas was collected in the 2011 season by KFCP and a third Lidar data collection was undertaken in 2014 by the Project on the same transects as used previously, greatly facilitating comparability within the dataset. Changes to the elevation of the peat and volumes from differential Lidar data will be estimated using these data sets.

Data from current Peat Moisture Content determined at the peat fire front undertaken in the Project along with water table depths, will be used to determine when peat fire ignitions are likely to occur. Peat-fire spread will be modelled using current measurements being undertaken by the project (Graham *et al.*, 2016), with rate of spread of deep peat fires based on results by Usup *et al.* (2004) and Graham *et al.* (2016). Hence using field based plot measurements, along with Landsat Imagery and LIDAR changes in peat elevation and volume along with ground water hydrology will be used in the model (based also on methods and measurements developed within the BOSF-Mawas Area (Ballhorn *et al.*, 2009).

Improved emissions estimates will be made based on comprehensive emission factors derived from integration of field and laboratory based emissions analyses. Once validated, the ignition/spread/emissions model will be used to provide annual emissions estimates for the 1997-2016 time periods.

Strengthening Capacity, Socialisation and Integration into Indonesia's MRV

The Project involves many scientists from Indonesia to promote capacity building, training, sharing data for INCAS and to facilitate collaboration with other Indonesian institutions. The Project plans to present methods and initial results at two Workshops each year; one in the District and another in the Provincial capital. The Workshops provide the opportunity for presentations by the Project as well as researchers undertaking studies in similar topics. In association with the Workshops, the project has held 'hands on" field days, for water table depth determination, peat sampling, vegetation monitoring. These have been well attended with positive feedback.

In 2012, the Indonesian National Carbon Accounting System (INCAS) implemented the Indonesian Carbon Accounting and Reporting Model (ICARM) for Kalimantan. As the initial estimates of GHGs modelled for peatlands was limited, the project collaborated with INCAS to develop recording system to incorporate fire-related carbon emissions based upon the project's modelled and validated peat consumption amounts and the field and laboratory verified emission factors for in-situ peat combustion. To ensure this will be possible, the output formats have been designed in association with INCAS staff so data produced by the Project can be readily used by INCAS for its peat fire emissions estimates.

CONCLUSION

The Project is in its third year, and has been able to monitor three fire seasons, the last one in 2015, being the longest and driest during the period of the Project. In addition, the 96 vegetation plots were able to be remeasured and water table and ground water measured across the area in the middle of each dry and wet season for the past three years. In 2015, the battery-powered, off-road Fourier Transform Infrared Spectrometer (FTIR) for sampling gasses from peat fires along with a Whole Air Sampling (WAS) system, filters and PAX for particulate was deployed with results to be published in mid-2016 and presented at the mid-year Workshop. The emission modelling is on-going and the human actions component has completed the field based interviews with results being available in mid-2016. It is anticipated that the 2016 fire season will also be monitored using the FSE Forms and a pre fire season workshop held in the District in mid-2016.

ACKNOWLEDGEMENTS

The research was supported and funded by NASA. The authors acknowledge the support of the Ministry of Forestry, Indonesia in close cooperation with the Kapuas District Government and the Central Kalimantan Provincial Government. We also acknowledge the field team from BOSF who have undertaken most of the vegetation, hydrology and fire monitoring activities and assisted in the village interviews for the human causes studies.

REFERENCES

1. Akagi, S. K., Yokelson, R. J., Burling, I. R., Meinardi, S., Simpson, I., Blake, D. R., McMeeking, G. R., Sullivan, A., Lee, T., Kreidenweis, S., Urbanski, S., Reardon, J., Griffith, D. W. T., Johnson, T. J., and Weise, D. R. (2013) Measurements of reactive trace gases and variable O_3 formation rates in some South Carolina biomass burning plumes, *Chemistry and Physics,* **13**: 1141-1165.
2. Ballhorn, U., Siegert, F., Mason, M. & Limin, S. (2009) Derivation of burn scar depths and estimation of carbon emissions with LIDAR in Indonesian peatlands. *Proceedings of the National Academy of Sciences of the USA*, **106**: 21213-21218.
3. Cochrane, M.A. (2013) Satellite-based active fire detection. Working Paper. Indonesia-Australia Forest Carbon Partnership, (http://www.iafcp.or.id/publication/detail/87/Satellite-basedactive-fire-detection), 13p.
4. Cochrane, M.A., and Souza, C.M. (1998) Linear mixture model classification of burned forests in the eastern Amazon. *International Journal of Remote Sensing,* **19**: 3433-3440.
5. Hooijer, A., Page, S., Canadell, J.G., Silvius, M., Kwadijk, J., Wosten, H.,Jauhiainen, J. (2010) Current and future CO2 emissions from drained peatlands in southeast Asia. *Biogeosciences,* **7**: 1505-1514.
6. Ichsan, N., Hooijer, A., Vernimmen, R. Applegate, G.B. (2014) KFCP Hydrology and Peat Monitoring Methodology. Scientific Report, Kalimantan Forests and Climate Partnership, Indonesia.
7. IPCC, (2006) IPCC Guidelines for National Greenhouse Gas Inventories. Guidelines for National Greenhouse Gas Inventories, Prepared by the National Greenhouse Gas Inventories Programme (Eggleston HS, Buendia L, Miwa K, Ngara T, Tanabe K *eds*). Published: IGES, Japan.
8. IPCC (2014)2013 Supplement to the 2006 IPCC Guidelines for National Greenhouse Gas Inventories: Wetlands, Hiraishi, T., Krug, T., Tanabe, K., Srivastava, N., Baasansuren, J., Fukuda, M. and Troxler, T.G. (eds). Published: IPCC, Switzerland.
9. Konecny, K., Ballhorn, U., Navrati, P., Jubanski, J., Page, S.E., Tansey, K., Hooijer, A., Vernimmen,R., and Siegert, F. (2016) Variable carbon losses from recurrent fires in drained tropical peatlands. *Global Change Biology* doi: 10.1111/gcb.13186.
10. Graham, Laura L. B., Susanto, T.W., Xaverius, F., Eser, E., Didie, Thomas, A., Salahuddin, Mahyudi,A., and Applegate, G.B. (2014a) KFCP Vegetation Monitoring: Rates of change for forest characteristics, and the influence of environmental conditions, in the KFCP study area. Scientific Report, Kalimantan Forests and Climate Partnership, Indonesia.
11. Graham, Laura L. B., Manjin, S., Juni, E.T., Waldram, M., Massal, F., Ichsan, N., Fatkhurohman and Applegate, G.B. (2014b) KFCP Heavy Fuel Load Assessment: Line Intersect Method and Heavy Fuel Load Results. Kalimantan Forests and Climate Partnership, Indonesia.
12. Graham, Laura L. B., Applegate, G.B., Putra, E.I., Ryan, K., Cochrane, M. (2016) Field research methodologies for collecting peat fire data to enhance understanding of tropical peat fire events. Paper

presented at 15th International PEAT Congress, 15-17 August, 2016, Kuching, Malaysia.
13. Putra, E., Hayasaka, H., Takahashi, H. Usup, A. (2008) Recent peat fire activity in the Mega Rice Project area, central Kalimantan, Indonesia. *Journal of Disaster Research,* **3**: 334-341.
14. Usup, A., Hashimoto, Y., Takahashi, H., Kayasaka, H. (2004) Combustion and thermal characteristics of peat fire in tropical peatland in central Kalimantan, Indonesia. *Tropics,* **14**.
15. Vayda, A.P. (2013) Causal explanation for environmental anthropologists. In: *Environmental Anthropology: Future Trends* (Kopnina H, Ouimet ES *eds*), London: Routledge, pp. 207-224.
16. Vernimmen, R., Hooijer, A., Mamenun, A.E. (2011) Evaluation and bias correction of satellite rainfall data for drought monitoring in Indonesia. *Hydrology and Earth System Sciences Discuss,* **8**: 5969-5997.

Abstract No: A-239

RECURRENT BURNT PEAT: POTENTIAL POSITIVE FEEDBACK FOR PEAT FIRES

Ahmad Ainuddin Nuruddin[1], Dayang Nur Sakinah Musa[2] and Luqman Chua[1]

[1]*Institute of Tropical Forestry and Forest Products (INTROP), Universiti Putra Malaysia, Malaysia*
[2]*Faculty of Forestry, Universiti Putra Malaysia, Malaysia*

Corresponding author: a_ainuddin@yahoo.com

SUMMARY

Peat swamp forest is a unique ecosystem with multiple functions such as timber, non-forest products and wildlife. Lately, many studies have shown the importance of peat swamp forest as provider of ecosystem services such as flooding mitigation and carbon storage. However, overexploitation of peat swamp forest has led to forest degradation and occurrences of forest fires. Repeated fires at the burnt peat have led to further deterioration of the peat areas. Hence the need to understand the flammability of the peat and factors which encourage repeated burnings. The aims of the study were to characterise the peat and to determine the relationship between the fuel thermal characteristics of the repeated burnt peat swamp forest. Peat samples were collected in compartment 99 for burnt area, and compartment 1 for unburnt area. The peat samples from both areas were obtained in February, 2014. These samples were collected using an auger at two layers of peat, i.e., at the surface and 1.5m depths. Peat samples were analyzed for thermal characteristics using Thermo Gravimetric Analyzer (TGA). It was found that the peat from repeated area was more thermally stable compared to unburnt area. This show that burnt peat thermal characteristics has been transformed to encourage further burning.

INTRODUCTION

Peat swamp forest is a unique ecosystem with multiple functions such as timber, non-forest products and wildlife. Lately, many studies have shown the importance of peat swamp forest as provider of ecosystem services such as flooding mitigation and carbon storage. However, overexploitation of peat swamp forest has led to forest degradation and occurrences of forest fires (Ainuddin *et al.*, 2006). Forest fire occurrence is usually due to several reasons combining and may be severe if not being controlled entirely (Lailan *et al.*, 2004). It is considered as one of the factors which alter the environment and deterimine vegetation. The burning of a large scale biomass will directly change the landscape and vegetation composition (Ainuddin and Goh, 2010) which give rise to succession process to start. Tsoi (2009) stated that the implication of biomass burning will affect the chemical composition in the atmosphere as well as global carbon cycle. Species such as *Macaranga spp. and Imperata cylindrica* can dominate the burned areas. The loss of high value timbers, herbs, habitat and wildlife are totally inevitable once fire occurs.

Fuel characteristics are essential in understanding the dynamics of forest fire as the availability and fuel composition must be known. The fuel physical characteristics can be done by determining the species of the fuel available in the forest as well as the fuel load. Determination of its fuel moisture content (FMC) is significant to address the flammability, flame and rate of spread (ROS) of that particular fuel. The calorific values of the fuel will indicate the energy released during combustion. The higher calorific value, the potential of the species for fuel is higher. The fuel characteristics will contribute to the flammability of each fuel type. Flammability is defined as the ability of a matter to be ignited and burned which consist of three main elements: ignitibility, combustibility and sustainability (Gill and Zylstra, 2006). All these three elements are the summary of all the forest fuel characteristics. Therefore, there is a need to obtain this information in order to manage, control and suppress the spread of devastating fire in repeated burnt peat swamp forest.

METHODOLOGY

Raja Musa Peat Swamp Forest has a tropical climate (16 m above sea level) with mean annual rainfall of over 200 cm per year and average temperature of 28°C. The peat substrate is several meters deep, and is continually waterlogged with the forest floor flooded during rainy season. The water is acidic (pH 3–4). The vegetation is dominated by *Macaranga pruinosa*, with other abundant vegetation includes ferns (*Stenoclaena palustris*, *Nephrolepis biserrata*, *Asplenium longissimum*, *Dicranopteris* sp.), palms (*Pinanga* sp., *Ptychoraphis* sp., *Korthalsia* sp.), Pandanus (*Pandanus helicopus*), trees (*Macaranga hypoleuca*, *Campnosperma coriaceum*, *Ixora grandiflora*, *Cryptocarya impressa*, *Parartocarpus venosus*, *Aglaia odorata*), also climbers (*Pternandra galeata* and *Shorea platycarpa)* (FPDM, 1999).

Four (4) plots of 400m^2 (20m X 20m) were established in burnt and unburnt areas. From the plots, four (4) subplots are established (5x5m) and samples were obtained peat depth from 2 depths; surface and 1.5 m depth. These samples were taken back to the laboratory for further analyses for peat thermal properties.

The peat samples were oven dried at the Soil laboratory, Faculty of Forestry. They were oven-dried at the temperature of 60°C until the constant weight is attained (Chen and Twilley, 1999). Subsequently, the samples were grinded to pass through 40-mesh sieve size, and were sent to the laboratory of the Institute of Tropical Forestry and Forest Products (INTROP), Universiti Putra Malaysia. The thermal properties of the peat were determined through the TGA. The TGA was conducted using TGA Q500 V20.13 at 10 degree/minute up to 1000°C. The results of TGA were plotted using TA universal analysis.

RESULTS AND DISCUSSION

Thermogravimetric Analysis (TGA) was conducted for the samples taken from the surface and at the depth of 1.5m of both burnt and unburnt plots. The study found that the surface area of burnt area had higher mean residue left compared to 1.5m depth of peat (Figure 1). At the surface of burnt area, the mean residue left was 67.12% while at 1.5m depth; the residues left were 33.57%. However, for the unburnt area, the residue at 1.5m depth was higher compared to the surface with mean of 32.54% and 25.533% , respectively. Generally, the study found that residue left in the burnt area was higher compared to the unburnt area. Based on the results, it showed that the burnt area was more thermally stable at the surface, and the stability was gradually reduced below the ground. Generally, the study found that the residues for both the suface and at 1.5m depth of burnt area was higher compared to the unburnt area. This indicates that it was more thermally stable in the burnt than in the unburnt area of the RMFR peat swamp forest.

Table 2 shows the process of thermogravimetric analysis for pyrolysis of burnt and unburnt area for two depths; surface and 1.5m depth. From the analysis, it was found that in burnt peat, the pyrolysis started at 360.32°C (42.73 min) for surface while 262.15°C (26.23 min) for 1.5 depth. For the unburnt area, surface peat pyrolysis started at 281.84°C (35.5 minutes) while peat from 1.5m depth, pyrolysis started at 253.29°C (11.95 min). Therefore, the unburnt area took shorter time for the pyrolysis process to complete compare to the burnt area, and it was significant difference between the surface and 1.5m depth during starting of pyrolysis process. However, the surface took longer time to complete the process compared to 1.5m depth.

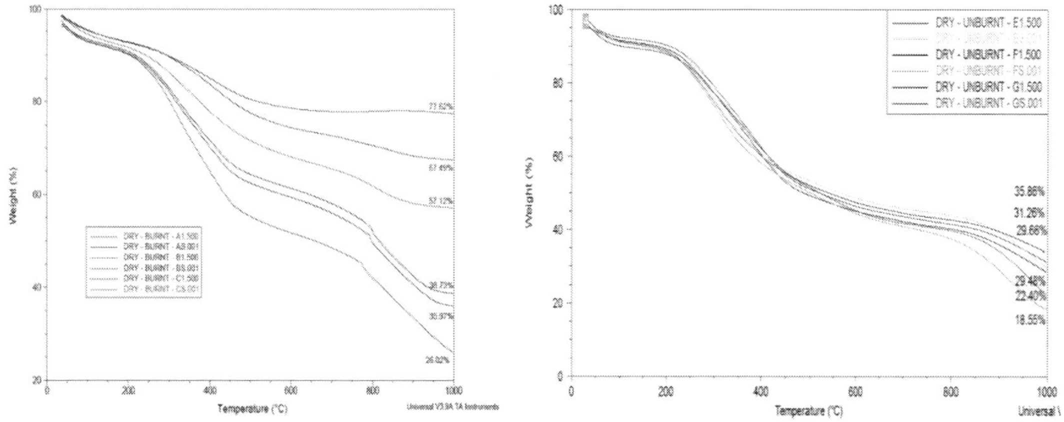

a. Burnt b. Unburnt

Figure 1: Thermogravimetric analysis of burnt and unburnt peat.

Table 1: Mean of residues on burnt and unburnt peat.

	Plots	Residues (%)	Residues (mg)
Burnt	Surface (mean)	67.410	3.285
	Standard error	5.918	0.604
	1.5m Depth (mean)	33.573	1.598
	Standard error	3.859	0.143
Unburnt	Surface (mean)	25.533	1.301
	Standard error	3.259	0.173
	1.5m Depth (mean)	32.540	2.340
	Standard error	1.853	0.489

Table 2: Thermogravimetric analysis process of burnt and unburnt peat.

Area	Depth	Pyrolysis (°C / min)	
		Start	End
Burnt	Surface Mean± Standard Error	360.320±23.632/ 60.513±6.702	548.407±33.441/ 103.263±6.528
	1.5 Depth Mean± Standard Error	262.153±3.963/ 46.053±0.803	394.507±53.816/ 72.280±10.731
Unburnt	Surface Mean± Standard Error	281.837±2.952/ 49.807±0.625	459.357±6.502/ 85.313±1.299
	1.5m Depth Mean± Standard Error	253.293±5.900/ 44.253±1.184	314.773±23.631/ 56.200±4.529

CONCLUSION

The study shows that there were changes to the thermal characteristics of burnt peat. TGA shows that it has more residues with longer time for pyrolysis process. This shows that burnt peat is more thermally stable and transformed to enhance further burning. This study suggests that the thermal characteristic of burnt peat can influence the fire behavior of the recurrent burnt peat areas.

REFERENCES

1. Ainuddin, N. A and Goh, K. 2010. Effect of forest fire on stand structure in Raja Musa Peat Swamp Forest Reserve, Selangor, Malaysia. Journal of Environmental Science and Technology. 3:56-62.
2. Ainuddin, N.A., Hoo M.L. and Faridah, B. 2006. Peat moisture and water level relationship in a tropical peat swamp forest. Journal of Applied Science. 6(11):2517-2519
3. FDPM, 1999. Sustainable Management of Peat Swamp Forest in Peninsular Malaysia: Resource and Environment. Vol. 1. (ed: , Chin, T. Y. and Havmoller, P.) Forestry Department of Peninsular Malaysia. 238 pp.
4. Gill and Zylstra. 2006. Flammability of Australian Forest. Australian Forestry. Vol 68 2:88-94
5. Lailan, S, Ainuddin, A.N., Jamaluddin, B., Lai, F.S. and Mohd Rashid, M.Y. 2004. The effects of climatic variations on peat swamp condition and peat combustability. Jurnal Manajemen Hutan tropika. Vol X N0. 1:1-14.
6. Tsoi, 2009. The natural factors that are responsible for forest fires in the sourthern Far East. Geography and Natural Resources 30:136-140.

Abstract No: A-147

SOURCES OF ANTHROPOGENIC FIRE IGNITIONS ON THE PEAT-SWAMP LANDSCAPE IN KALIMANTAN, INDONESIA

Megan E. Cattau[1, 2, 3], Mark E. Harrison[2, 3, 5], Iwan Shinyo[2, 3], Sady Tungau[2, 3], María Uriarte[1] and Ruth DeFries[1]

[1]*Department of Ecology, Evolution, and Environmental Biology, Columbia University, New York, USA*
[2]*Orangutan Tropical Peatland Project, Palangka Raya, Central Kalimantan, Indonesia*
[3]*Center for the International Cooperation in Sustainable Use of Tropical Peatlands (CIMTROP), Universitas Palangka Raya, Palangka Raya, Central Kalimantan, Indonesia*
[5]*Department of Geography, University of Leicester, Leicester, UK*

**Corresponding author: megan.cattau@gmail.com*

SUMMARY

Fire disturbance in Southeast Asian tropical peat swamps have become more frequent and extensive in recent decades. These fires compromise a variety of ecosystem services, notably mitigating global climate change through carbon storage, and cause severe health, ecological, and economic impacts. Key to understanding and managing fire in the region is identifying the land use / land cover (LULC) classes associated with fire ignitions. We assess the oft-asserted claim that industrial-scale oil palm concessions and smallholder farms near settlements are the primary ignition sources in a peat-swamp forest area in Central Kalimantan, Indonesia, equivalent to around a third of Kalimantan's total peat area. We use the MODIS Active Fire product from 2000-2010 to evaluate fire origin and spread on the LULC classes of legal oil palm concessions, non-forest (a relatively heterogeneous mixture that includes fern-dominated, shrub/bushland, bare peat, plantations including smallholder and very young oil palm outside legal concession boundaries, and degraded forest), and forest, as well as in relation to settlement proximity. Most fires (70%) originate in non-forest, compared to legal, industrial oil palm concessions (18%), and relatively few (5%) are within 5 km of settlements. Moreover, most fires started within oil palm concessions and close to settlements stay within those boundaries (90% and 88%, respectively). Similarly, a small proportion of fire detections in forest originate from oil palm concessions (2%) and within close proximity to settlements (2%). However, fire ignition density in oil palm (0.055 ignitions km^{-2}) is comparable to that in non-forest (0.060 ignitions km^{-2}), which is approximately ten times that in forest (0.006 ignitions km^{-2}). Ignition density within 5 km of settlements is the highest at 0.125 ignitions km^{-2}. Thus, although fire in oil palm is important, these results refute the claims that most fires originate in oil palm concessions and that fires escaping from oil palm concessions and settlements constitute a major proportion of fires in this study region. However, there is a potential for these land use types to contribute more substantially to the fire landscape if their area expands as projected. Effective fire management in this area should target not just legal oil palm concessions, but also non-forested, degraded areas where ignitions are most likely to occur.

Keywords: *disturbance, fire, human-environment coupled system, ignitions, Indonesia*

INTRODUCTION

Peatland fires in Indonesia have been following pantropical trends of increased frequency and severity in recent decades (Meijaard and Dennis, 1997). During El Niño phases, there is increased likelihood of drought in Southeast Asia and, thus, an increased incidence of fire (e.g., Page *et al.*, 2002; Wooster *et al.*, 2012). Extreme fire events would not exist without anthropogenic influence on the landscape, as fire is increasing in tandem with land use change and increased population density (Field *et al.*, 2009). Carbon emissions from fires in peatlands are particularly high, as peat is extremely rich in belowground organic carbon. An estimated 0.81-2.57 Gt C were released from Indonesia's peatlands during the 1997/98 fire season alone due to peat and vegetation combustion (Page *et al.*, 2002), equivalent to 13-40% of the mean annual global carbon emission from fossil fuels (van der Werf *et al.*, 2004). Fires in the 2015 dry season were the most severe since 1997/98. Peat fires in Indonesia are consequently a major cause of smog and particulate air pollution (Hayasaka *et al.*, 2014; Reddington *et al.*, 2014), with serious consequences for human health (Marlier *et al.*, 2013). In addition, peatland fires are responsible for habitat loss and degradation, driving wildlife declines (Jaafar and Loh, 2014; Yule, 2010), as well as high economic costs (Varma, 2003). Given the variety and severity of the consequences of tropical peatland fires, particularly those in Indonesia, it is of global interest to understand this disturbance regime and reduce fire occurrence.

Ignitions in Indonesia, as in many parts of the tropics, are primarily of anthropogenic origin (Bowen *et al.*, 2000), through either accidental or deliberate fires. Thus, a key component to understand changing fire regimes is to identify the sources of fire ignitions and the land use / land cover (LULC) classes associated with fire ignitions. Who is responsible for ignitions in Indonesia is highly contested, and reports of the ignition sources are many and varied (Dennis *et al.*, 2005; Page *et al.*, 2009). Although some large-holders do clear land mechanically, most land is cleared in Indonesia through use of fire (Stolle *et al.*, 2003), and people use fire as a management tool to clear debris and reduce pests. Because fires set for clearing can 'escape' beyond their intended boundaries, both large and small holders have been held responsible (e.g., Page *et al.*, 2009; Stolle *et al.*, 2003), as is often the case in rainforest fires more generally (Goldammer, 1991). In this study, for what we believe to be the first time, we disentangle fire detections from individual fire ignitions to discern the origin of fires in a peat-swamp forest landscape in Central Kalimantan, Indonesia. In so doing, we assess the oft-asserted claim that escaped fires from oil palm concessions and from smallholder farms near settlements are the primary sources of fire, through addressing the following questions:

1) In which LULC classes do fires, in particular the longest and hottest fires, originate and to which LULC classes do they spread?,
2) What proportion of fires, in particular the longest and hottest fires, escape from oil palm concessions and settlements into other surrounding LULC classes?, and
3) Do fire ignitions occur disproportionately in proximity to oil palm concessions and settlements? Are these fires longer in duration or hotter than fires occurring away from oil palm concessions and settlements?

METHODS

Study Site

We analyze fire ignitions in an area of lowland tropical peat-swamp forest in Central Kalimantan, Indonesia (Figure 1). The study area consists of the Sabangau-Katingan Forest and the recently degraded failed agricultural development called the Mega Rice Project (MRP), representing a combined total of ~2.5 Mha of the total 6.8 Mha of lowland peatland in Kalimantan. Currently, tens of thousands of families live along the Katingan, Sabangau Kahayan, Kapuas, and Barito Rivers that border the area. There are several oil palm concessions located throughout.

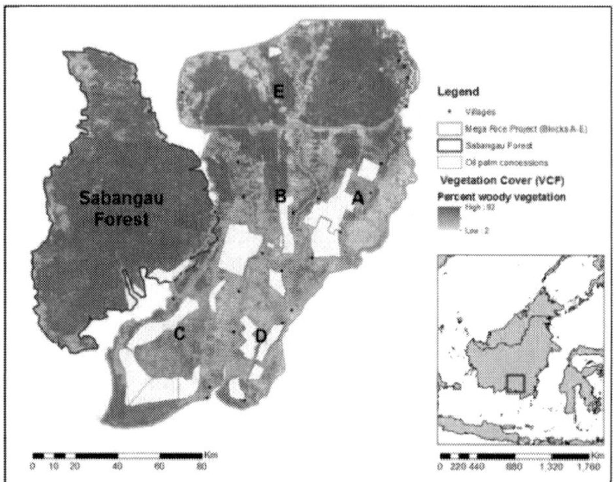

Figure 1: The study area: lowland peat-swamp forest in Central Kalimantan, Indonesia, consisting of the failed Mega Rice Project (pink borders; letters indicate administrative zones) and the adjacent Sabangau Forest (yellow border), including the percent woody vegetation, legal oil palm concession boundaries, and major villages and settlement locations. Inset: Location within Indonesia.

Data

Fire detections at the 1 km^2 resolution across the study area from 2000-2010 are obtained from the Moderate Resolution Imaging Spectroradiometer (MODIS) Active Fire Detections, extracted from MCD14ML. We create a LULC layer at the annual temporal resolution consisting of oil palm concessions, forest, and non-forest classes. Oil palm concession boundaries for this LULC layer according to the Indonesian Ministry of Forestry are obtained from the Global Forest Watch portal. The forest and non-forest classes for this LULC layer are based upon tree cover derived from the MODIS Vegetation Continuous Fields (VCF) Collection 5 product, which contains proportional estimates of woody vegetation at the 250 m^2 resolution. VCF is aggregated to the 1 km^2 resolution, and a forest binary layer is created by thresholding VCF at 55 percent woody vegetation to designate tree cover based upon the range of VCF values of areas known to be tree cover in the study area. Classification accuracy of the forest binary layer is assessed using GPS points collected in the field in forest (50 points) and non-forest (50 points) in 2009, and accuracy is over 95%. Finally, settlement locations, or points indicating the center of major villages and cities, obtained from Simon Husson of OuTrop, are used to calculate distance from settlement across the study area.

Analysis

Data analysis covers the period from 2000-2010. The MODIS Active Fire Product indicates the presence of a fire within a 1 km^2 area, but not the exact location or size of a particular fire. Thus, it is challenging to determine if proximal fire detections are spatially contiguous or if they represent isolated fires. We assign all fire detections to a particular fire event using two methods: the single-pixel technique, in which fire detections from successive days that occur within a given pixel are assigned to the same fire and thus fires are restricted to a 1km^2 area, and the neighborhood-pixel technique, in which fire detections from successive days that occur within a given pixel or the eight adjacent pixels are assigned to the same fire using hierarchical clustering. We consider the earliest fire detection in each fire event to be the ignition for that fire event. Fire events with a duration and/or maximum heat (fire radiative power (FRP)) within the top decile of fires are considered "high-impact," because these factors affect the fires' potential environmental damage.

1) In which LULC classes do fires, in particular the longest and hottest fires, originate and to which LULC classes do they spread?

For each fire event, we identify the LULC class in which the ignition occurs and calculate how many fire detections are associated with fires started on each LULC class. We determine the density of ignitions per LULC class by normalizing the number of ignitions in each LULC class to the area of that class in the entire study region for each year.

2) What proportion of fires escape from oil palm concessions and settlements into other surrounding LULC classes?

We identify fires that escape from oil palm concessions by isolating fires that start within oil palm concessions and burn outside the concession boundaries at some point during the burn. Similarly, we identify fires that escape from settlements by isolating fires that start near settlements (5km threshold) and burn outside that boundary at some point during the burn.

3) Do fire ignitions occur disproportionately in proximity to oil palm concessions and settlements?

To analyze the influence of increased anthropogenic activity around settlements and outside of oil palm concessions on fire activity, we evaluate if the number of ignitions and the severity of fires (i.e., fire duration or the maximum FRP) varies as a function of the fire ignitions' distance from oil palm concessions or from settlements. After assessing exploratory plots, we fit models of the number of fire ignitions as a function of distance from oil palm concessions and from settlements (binned into 50m increments). We fit exponential regression models for distance from oil palm concessions because we expect anthropogenic ignitions to be highest near concession borders (due to expansion of the concession itself, clearing for smallholder plots, or accidental fires where workers are regularly frequenting) and then decrease as distance from concession increases (due to increased cost of travel from the concession). For distance from settlements, we fit Ricker functions of the form $y{\sim}ax\ exp\ (-bx)$, where y is the number of ignitions and x is the distance from settlements. We select a Ricker model because we expect the number of ignitions to start at zero due to an aversion to burn very close to the village, increase to a peak, and then decrease back to zero as the cost of travelling from the settlement increases with distance. We estimate the parameter b and calculate $1/b$, the distance from settlements at which ignitions peak.

RESULTS

1) In which LULC classes do fires, in particular the longest and hottest fires, originate and to which LULC classes do they spread?

Non-forest and oil palm concessions have a comparable density of ignitions, which is about ten times the density of ignitions in forest (Table 1). However, by far the majority of fire detections are associated with fires that start on non-forest (70.0% for all fires and 70.3% for high-impact fires). Non-forest is also the primary LULC class on which ignitions occur for fires that burn forest (46.4%). Fire detections associated with fires started on oil palm constitute 17.5% of all detections (17.9% for high-impact fires), and most fires that burn oil palm concessions are started on the concessions themselves. The density of fire ignitions in forest is low, and fire detections associated with fires starting on forest constitute only 7.3% of all detections (6.5% for high-impact fires). The percent of detections associated with fires that are started close to settlements, which could occur on oil palm concessions, non-forest, or forest, is negligible (0.2-5.0% for all fires and 0.1-3.4% for high-impact fires). However, although the overall contribution of ignitions near settlements is low, the density of ignitions near settlements is high - just over twice that of non-forest and oil palm for all fires, and approximately 1.5 times that of non-forest and oil palm for high-impact fires.

Table 1: The percent of fire detections associated with fires that start on each land use / land cover (LULC) class and density of fire ignitions (ignitions km^{-2}) that are located in each LULC class. Numbers for high impact fires are in parentheses.

Land use / land cover class	Non-forest	Oil palm concession	Forest	Within 5km	Within 4km	Within 3km	Within 2km	Within 1km
Density of ignitions (ignitions km^{-2})	0.060 (0.010)	0.055 (0.010)	0.006 (0.001)	0.125 (0.015)	0.096 (0.011)	0.077 (0.008)	0.058 (0.006)	0.051 (0.008)
Percent of detections	70.0 (70.3)	17.5 (17.9)	7.3 (6.5)	5.0 (3.4)	2.9 (1.8)	1.8 (1.2)	0.6 (0.2)	0.2 (0.1)

2) What proportion of fires escape from oil palm concessions and settlements into other surrounding LULC classes?

A minority of fires (10.5% of all fires, 37.3% of high-impact fires) that are started within oil palm concessions escape the concession into other LULC classes, and a minority of fires (12.2% of all fires, 44.1% of high-impact fires) that are started near settlements escape. Although some fires, and particularly high-impact fires, do escape from oil palm concessions and from settlements, they constitute only a small percent of total fires in the study area (1.8% of all fires, 6.8% of high-impact fires and 1.2% of all fires, 3.0% of high-impact fires, respectively). Furthermore, these escaped fires do not serve as a notable ignition source for forest fires; only 1.5% of forest fire detections are associated with fires that were ignited in oil palm concessions and 2.4% with fires that were ignited close to settlements.

3) Do fire ignitions occur disproportionately in proximity to oil palm concessions and settlements?

The number of ignitions of all fires and high-impact fires decreases exponentially with increasing distance from oil palm concessions (adjusted $R^2= 0.59$, $p<0.001$). When we explore the relationship between the number of ignitions and distance from settlements, we find that the Ricker model fits the data well, including at the extremes, and that the number of ignitions increases farther from settlements, peaks at 7.2 (±0.2) km from settlements, and then decreases. Fire duration and maximum FRP do not have a clear relationship with either distance from oil palm concessions or from settlements.

DISCUSSION

Our results provide only limited support to the claim that fires occurring on or escaping from industrial-scale oil palm concessions and settlements are major contributors to fire in this study region during our study period. The vast majority of fire detections is associated with ignitions that occur in non-forested areas, a relatively heterogeneous mixture that includes fern-dominated, shrub/bushland, bare peat, plantations including smallholder and very young oil palm outside legal concession boundaries, and degraded forest. A relatively low but still substantial percentage of detections are associated with ignitions that occur on oil palm concessions, and very few with ignitions that occur in close proximity to settlements. The majority of fires started within concessions or near settlements is confined to those boundaries, and ignitions in these land use classes contribute very little to fires that burn in forest.

While there is potential for oil palm concessions from converted degraded land to reduce fire prevalence on the landscape if ignitions on oil palm concessions can be reduced relative to degraded areas, this is not currently the case; ignition density in oil palm was on par with that in degraded areas, both of which were substantially higher than in forests. Although fires that have escaped from oil palm concessions currently constitute a small percentage of fires in the study area relative to fires on degraded non-forest areas, our findings nevertheless support concerns about the contribution of oil palm companies to emissions and hazardous smog in the region (e.g., Marlier *et al.*, 2015; Stuart, 2012). Furthermore, our results likely underestimate the number of ignitions attributable to oil palm companies and overestimate the contribution from other LULC classes, as our oil palm category includes only those plantations found within the reported boundaries of legal oil palm concessions.

Our findings that there is a detectable pattern in the number of fire ignitions as a function of distance from oil palm concessions and settlements suggest that these LULC classes influence the fire regime through increased anthropogenic activity around them, plus escaped fires from these LULC classes. The extent to which these ignitions will result in high-impact fires depends upon both the flammability of the landscape and the capacity for management interventions. If the peat is relatively undrained and inundated close to the surface, the forest is intact, and fire-fighting resources are available, an ignition is much less likely to turn into a high-impact fire than if the land is degraded from canal development and unmanaged. Our results indicate that fire reduction efforts are needed in these degraded areas, through both capacity building and awareness raising, to increase the success of management interventions, plus landscape restoration to reduce the predisposition of the landscape to burning. Additionally, because the density of ignitions is high in oil palm concessions and within 5km of settlements, it is clear that these land use types have the potential to contribute substantially to the fire landscape if they continue to expand, and peat and fire management practices do not improve, particularly if fragmentation and/or climate change leave the landscape even more predisposed to burning.

Our results support previous research that most fires occur in non-forest or degraded areas (including oil palm in Gaveau *et al.*, 2014; Miettinen *et al.*, 2007) by showing both that the majority of fires are ignited in non-forest, and highlighting that fires actually start in non-forest rather than merely just occur in non-forest (with the possibility that ignition started there or elsewhere). Management to reduce ignitions in degraded non-forest areas, in addition to reducing the probability of continued burning when ignitions do occur, will be pivotal in reducing fire across the landscape. This is also key to preventing forest fires and the associated loss of habitat, as we found that the majority of forest fires start in non-forest.

CONCLUSION

Results of this research, which uses remotely sensed data and modeling to analyze where fires originate and spread in tropical peat-swamp forest in Central Kalimantan from 2000-2010, indicate that most fires (70%) originate in non-forest areas, and refute the claim that fires occurring on or escaping from oil palm concessions and settlements constitute the major proportion of fires in this study region during 2000-2010. We find that only 18% of fires are ignited on oil palm concessions, and that most fires that start on oil palm concessions stay on the concession (90%). Similarly, few fires start within 5km of settlements (5%) and most stay within those boundaries (88%). However, we do find a detectable pattern of fire ignitions around oil palm concessions and settlements, and a high density of ignitions within them (0.055 ignitions km^{-2} and 0.125 ignitions km^{-2}, respectively), suggesting that increased anthropogenic activity around these land use classes contributes to fire activity, and that the expansion of settlements or concession areas could substantially increase fire on the landscape, if peat and fire management is not improved. Effective fire management should therefore target not just legal oil palm concessions or areas around settlements, but should also focus strongly on non-forested, degraded areas and illegal oil palm plantations – and in particular those near legal oil palm concession boundaries and outside the immediate vicinity of settlements – where ignitions are most likely to occur.

ACKNOWLEDGEMENTS

We thank the United States Indonesia Society (USINDO), The Explorer's Club, the Center for International Forestry Research (CIFOR), StOLT Foundation, The American Indonesian Exchange Foundation (AMINEF), and the Fulbright Program for financial and other support. We also thank the DeFries lab at Columbia University and Dr. Bénédicte Bachelot for feedback that improved this paper substantially, and Simon Husson for providing settlement data. We thank the staff and volunteers at the Orangutan Tropical Peatland Project, which works in partnership with the Center for International Cooperation in Sustainable Management of Tropical Peatland (CIMTROP). We thank the University of Palangka Raya for ongoing support and the Ministry of Research and Technology (RISTEK) for permission to conduct research in Indonesia.

REFERENCES

1. Bowen MR, Bompard JM, Anderson IP, Guizol P, Gouyon A. Anthropogenic fires in Indonesia: A view from Sumatra. In: Forest Fires and Regional Haze in Southeast Asia--Eaton P, Radojevic M, eds. (2000) New York: Nova Science. 41–66.
2. Dennis R, *et al.* Fire, People and Pixels: Linking Social Science and Remote Sensing to Understand Underlying Causes and Impacts of Fires in Indonesia. Human Ecology (2005) 33:465-504.
3. Field RD, van der Werf GR, Shen SSP. Human amplification of drought-induced biomass burning in Indonesia since 1960. Nature Geosci (2009) 2:185-188.
4. Gaveau DLA, *et al.* Major atmospheric emissions from peat fires in Southeast Asia during non-drought years: evidence from the 2013 Sumatran fires. Sci. Rep. (2014) 4.
5. Goldammer JG. Tropical wild-land fires and global changes: Prehistoric evidence, present fire regimes, and future trends. In: Global Biomass Burning: Atmospheric, Climatic, and Biospheric Implications--Levine JS, ed. (1991) Cambridge: MIT Press. 83-91.
6. Hayasaka H, Noguchi I, Putra EI, Yulianti N, Vadrevu K. Peat-fire-related air pollution in Central Kalimantan, Indonesia. Environmental Pollution (2014) 195:257-266.
7. Jaafar Z, Loh T-L. Linking land, air and sea: potential impacts of biomass burning and the resultant haze on marine ecosystems of Southeast Asia. Global Change Biology (2014) 20:2701-2707.
8. Marlier ME, *et al.* Fire emissions and regional air quality impacts from fires in oil palm, timber, and logging concessions in Indonesia. Environmental Research Letters (2015) 10.
9. Marlier ME, *et al.* El Niño and health risks from landscape fire emissions in southeast Asia. Nature Climate Change (2013) 3:131–136.
10. Meijaard E, Dennis R. Forest fires in Indonesia: bibliography and background information (1997) Amsterdam, The Netherlands: World Wide Fund for Nature.
11. Miettinen J, Andreas L, Siegert F. Burnt area estimation for the year 2005 in Borneo using multi-resolution satellite imagery. International Journal of Wildland Fire (2007) 16:45-53.
12. Page S, *et al.* Tropical peatland fires in Southeast Asia. In: Tropical Fire Ecology: Climate Change, Land Use, and Ecosystem Dynamics--Cochrane MA, ed. (2009) Germany / Chicheser, U.K.: Springer/Praxis. 263-287.
13. Page SE, Siegert F, Rieley JO, Boehm H-DV, Jaya A, Limin S. The amount of carbon released from peat and forest fires in Indonesia during 1997. Nature (2002) 420:61-65.
14. Reddington CL, Yoshioka M, Balasubramanian R, Ridley D, Toh YY. Contribution of vegetation and peat fires to particulate air pollution in Southeast Asia. Environmental Research Letters (2014) 9:094006.

15. Stolle F, Chomitz KM, Lambin EF, Tomich TP. Land use and vegetation fires in Jambi Province, Sumatra, Indonesia. Forest Ecology and Management (2003) 179:277-292.
16. Stuart H. Indonesia Fires, Singapore Smog Likely Caused By Palm Oil Companies (2012) (accessed August 1, 2015, (Type of Medium).
17. van der Werf GR, *et al.* Continental-scale partitioning of fire emissions during the 1997 to 2001 El Niño/La Niña period. Science (2004) 303:73-76.
18. Varma A. The economics of slash and burn: A case study of the 1997/1998 Indonesian forest fires. Ecological Economics (2003) 46:159-171.
19. Wooster MJ, Perry GLW, Zoumas A. Fire, drought and El Nino relationships on Borneo (Southeast Asia) in the pre-MODIS era (1980-2000). Biosciences (2012) 9:317-340.
20. Yule C. Loss of biodiversity and ecosystem functioning in Indo-Malayan peat swamp forests. Biodiversity and Conservation (2010) 19:393-409.

THEME 3
PEATLANDS AFTER-USE, RESTORATION & REHABILITATION OF EX-PRODUCTION PEATLANDS

3.1: RESTORATION OF BOREAL, TEMPERATE & TROPICAL PEATLANDS

3.1: RESTORATION OF BOREAL, TEMPERATE & TROPICAL PEATLANDS

Abstract No: A-168

A PARTNERSHIP BETWEEN TWO PROTECTED PEATLANDS: GREAT DISMAL SWAMP NATIONAL WILDLIFE REFUGE, VIRGINIA, USA AND SEBANGAU NATIONAL PARK, CENTRAL KALIMANTAN, INDONESIA

Chris Lowie[1], Frederic C. Wurster[1*], Sean Lawlor[2], Jason Riley[2], Adib Gunawan[3] and Noviyanti Nugraheni[3]

[1]*U.S. Fish and Wildlife Service, Great Dismal Swamp National Wildlife Refuge, Suffolk, VA, USA*
[2]*U.S. Department of the Interior, International Technical Assistance Program, Reston, VA, USA*
[3]*Republic of Indonesia, Ministry of Environment and Forestry, Sebangau National Park, Central Kalimantan, Indonesia*

**Corresponding author: fred_wurster@fws.gov*

SUMMARY

The designation of two protected areas from opposite ends of the world as sister protected areas, provides many benefits. It allows for the exchange of knowledge and information that may impact ecosystems in both protected areas. It provides inspiration to protected area staff, motivated by the shared challenges and encouragement of their partners around the globe. A sister protected area arrangement is an effective training and capacity building mechanism, especially when exchange visits are sustained over time. It can be used to enhance visitation and environmental education when interpreted in such a way that it links the purpose of a particular protected area to issues of global conservation. Finally, it serves as a reminder that the cause of conservation cannot be advanced by one protected area, or one country, but must be a common effort of all mankind.

***Keywords**: peatland, protected area, Sebangau National Park, Great Dismal Swamp, partnership*

INTRODUCTION

The creation and restoration of protected areas is a key tool in the global conservation of peatlands. National parks, wildlife refuges, and other types of conservation areas allow for the permanent protection of high-priority peat resources and the long-term, intensive management required to restore degraded peatlands back to productive ecosystems.

Indonesia and the United States are partnering to improve restoration and management efforts at two protected forested peatlands: Great Dismal Swamp National Wildlife Refuge in Suffolk, VA, USA and Sebangau National Park, Central Kalimantan, Indonesia.

GREAT DISMAL SWAMP NATIONAL WILDLIFE REFUGE

The Great Dismal Swamp National Wildlife Refuge (NWR) is the largest intact remnant of a vast peatland that once covered more than 400,000 ha of southeastern Virginia and northeastern North Carolina. Formal protection of this resource began in 1973 when a local forest production company donated 20,000 ha to The Nature Conservancy. The land was later conveyed to the United States Fish and Wildlife Service to establish the Great Dismal Swamp NWR in 1974. Since its establishment, additional acquisitions have expanded the refuge's land area to 45,300 ha (Figure 1).

The soils of Great Dismal Swamp NWR play a critical role in supporting its forested wetland communities. Organic soils predominate and are divided into two taxonomic classes: Typic Medisaprists and Terric Medisaprists. The peat is composed of material from woody plants, has little mineral content, and has been accumulating in the Dismal Swamp for about 8,000 to 9,000 years. Maximum peat depths approach 3m in places but are typically closer to 1.0 – 1.5m in much of the swamp. Partially decomposed layers of logs and stumps are buried in the decomposed organic material.

Within the refuge, construction of 240 km of canals and their attendant spoil bank roads have combined to form the single most significant alteration to the swamp's water regime. The Refuge is currently focused on research and restoration of the hydrologic processes to be managed for the benefit of wildlife and people.

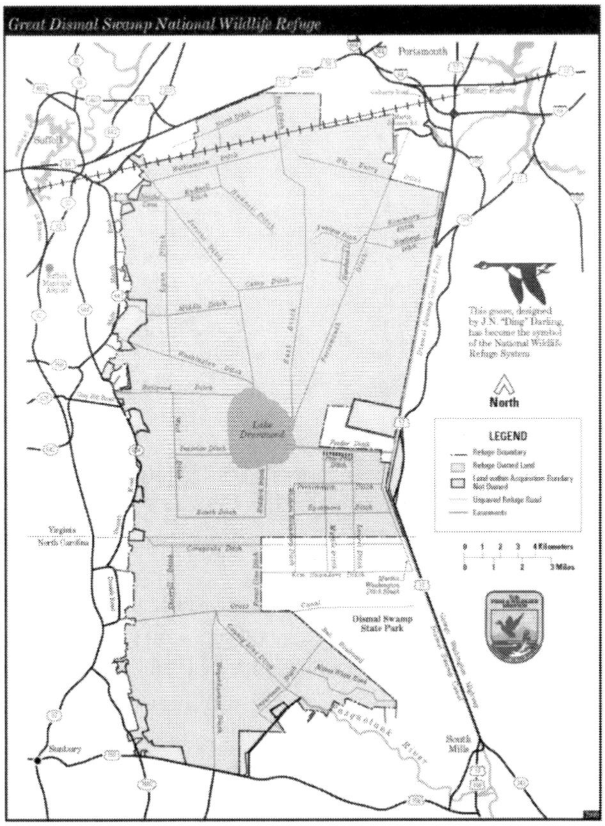

Figure 1: Great Dismal Swamp National Wildlife Refuge, Suffolk, VA USA

SEBANGAU NATIONAL PARK

Sebangau National Park protects 568,700 ha of forested peatland between the Katingan and Sebangau Rivers in the southern portion of Central Kalimantan Province, Indonesia (Figure 2). The park constitutes one of the largest relatively intact tropical peat-swamp forests in Kalimantan and hosts an estimated 6,900 orangutans – the largest orangutan population in any protected area in Indonesia. The park protects an ecosystem characterized by its rich biodiversity including more than 300 plant species, 200 bird species, and 35 species of mammals including the primates: orangutan (*Pongo pygmaeus* sp.), proboscis monkey (*Nasalis larvatus*), and agile gibbon (*Hylobates albibarbis*), as well as a number of diverse fish and reptile species including the estuarine crocodile (*Crocodylus porosus*). This species richness is largely dependent upon the canopy provided by the tropical peat swamp forest and the underlying peat layer which ranges from 1m – 12m in thickness.

Sebangau was designateded a National Park in 2004 following several decades of legal and illegal logging. An extensive network of drainage canals, constructed to support logging activities, continues to drain the underlying peat soils. Since 2004, the Ministry of Environment and Forestry has worked to restore the park through rewetting of the peatland, reforestation, and working with local communities to protect the park's biodiversity.

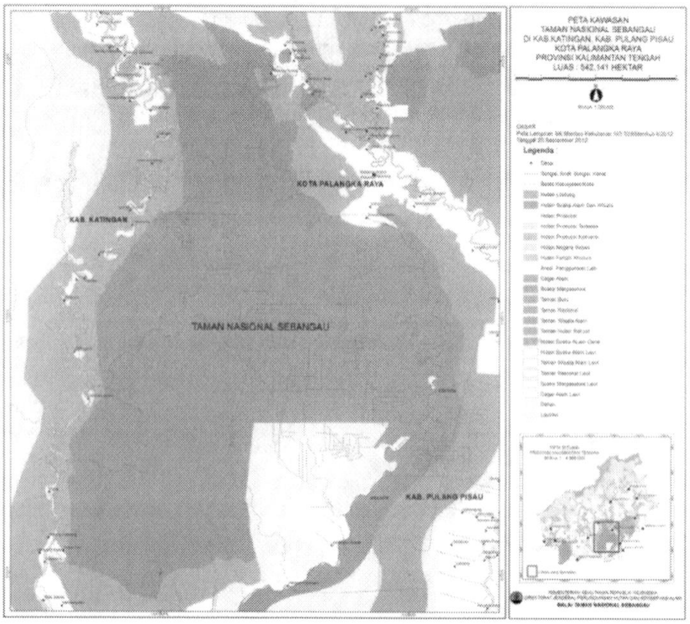

Figure 2: Sebangau National Park, Central Kalimantan, Indonesia

SISTER PROTECTED AREA AGREEMENT

Great Dismal Swamp and Sebangau are uniquely similar protected areas. Both sites protect significant forested peatlands that have been subjected to damaging logging practices. Extensive networks of drainage canals, constructed to facilitate logging, have altered the hydrology of both peatlands and contribute to an increase in ground fire severity and frequency. The staff at Great Dismal Swamp and Sebangau are working closely with non-governmental partners and local universities to develop approaches for restoring hydrologic processes and suppress severe ground fires at their respective protected areas. This work is important to managers at both sites because both are home to high-profile endangered species. Sebangau National Park is a haven for orangutans. Great Dismal Swamp is home to a diverse array of wildlife, including the most dense black bear population in Virginia and several endangered species, such as the red-cockaded woodpecker, northern long-eared bat, and canebrake rattlesnake.

In 2013, the Indonesian government requested assistance from the Unites States Agency for International Development (USAID) to provide support to national parks in Indonesia. This request led to a five year (2013-2018), $1.5 million program to provide government-to-government technical assistance and training to protected area staff in Indonesia: *Strengthening Indonesia's National Parks and Wildlife Protection*. An initial assessment of the Indonesian parks identified priority needs in peatland hydrologic restoration and management.

USAID solicited support from the U.S. Department of Interior, International Technical Assistance Program (ITAP) to partner with Indonesia's Ministry of Environment and Forestry to implement the five-year program. Technical assistance and training will be accomplished through natural resource assessments, training workshops, technical consulting, U.S.-based training internships, and scientific exchanges between DOI experts and Indonesian protected area staff.

The idea for the partnership began to take root in February 2015, when Great Dismal Swamp hydrologist, Fred Wurster, participated in a training and assessment team sent to Sebangau by ITAP. The team trained Sebangau park staff on basic peatland hydrology and hydrological restoration techniques. This workshop included case studies from Great Dismal Swamp and the Everglades National Park as well as exercises in water quality sampling. The team spent a few days in the field with workshop participants to demonstrate field techniques for analyzing soil pits, assessing peat cores, and installing shallow groundwater monitoring wells (Figure 3). In addition, the team took time to visit the village of Habaring Huarung, to learn about the challenges of community development in villages surrounding the park. Engaging these local communities is an essential part of the protected area management strategy at Sebangau.

In late March of 2015, DOI-ITAP staff invited several Indonesian colleagues to visit the Great Dismal Swamp National Wildlife Refuge (Figure 4). A group of nine staff from two Indonesian National Parks, including Sebangau, and senior officials from the Ministry of Environment and Forestry made the trip to Suffolk, Virginia. The group undertook three days of classroom and field based activities to learn more about Great Dismal Swamp's restoration efforts, which were recently profiled in The Nature Conservancy magazine (http:/www.nature.org/magazine/archives/the-great-dismal-swamp.xml), and earned the 2013 National Environmental Leadership Award for "Refuge of the Year". The Indonesian delegation also studied wetland management techniques at nearby protected peatlands at Alligator River National Wildlife Refuge and Pocosin Lakes National Wildlife Refuge in northeast North Carolina.

Figure 3: Great Dismal Swamp Hydrologist, Fred Wurster, instructing on well installation at Sebangau National Park – February 2015 (image: Mark Flora)

Figure 4: Participants at Great Dismal Swamp National Wildlife Refuge - March 2015, Suffolk, Virginia, USA (image: Cindy Lane).

When the managers realized how similar their resources and challenges were, they agreed to pursue a "Sister Protected Areas Partnership". The goals of the partnership include:

1. Enhance understanding of and capacity for peatland management.
2. Enhance understanding of hydrological restoration and monitoring activities.
3. Develop and support a wildlife- and hydrological-based nature tourism.
4. Exchange of knowledge and experiences on recovery of endangered species and biodiversity conservation.
5. Organize scientific exchanges that result in improved natural resource management techniques.
6. Enhance capacity for database management.
7. Other programs of mutual interest.

A year of successful cooperation culminated in the signing ceremony in January 2016 in Palangkaraya, Central Kalimantan (Figure 5). This arrangement became the first relationship of its kind between the two countries. Following the signing ceremony, Great Dismal Swamp staff conducted a workshop on Visitor Services, Tourism Planning and Ecotourism.

Figure 5: Chris Lowie (Great Dismal Swamp NWR Manager) and Adib Gunawan (Sebangau National Park Manager) with commemorative plaque during the signing ceremony, Palangkaraya, Indonesia – January 2016 (image: DOI-ITAP collections)

CONCLUSION

To date, accomplishments of the Sister Protected Areas Partnership include, 72 staff trained, three major assessments, and three sister protected area exchanges. For the next five years, the Great Dismal Swamp and Sebangau staff will continue to exchange ideas on hydrologic restoration, peatland management, wildfire prevention, endangered species protection, ecotourism, and community outreach. This bilateral collaboration is expected to strengthen the capacity of both protected areas and will contribute to a broader understanding of peatland management. In addition, the project is expanding in 2016 to protected areas in Aceh and Papua Provinces.

Abstract No: A-451

THE IUCN-UK PEATLAND PROGRAMME AND THE YORKSHIRE PEAT PARTNERSHIP

Rob Stoneman

Yorkshire Wildlife Trust, United Kingdom

**Corresponding author: Rob.stoneman@ywt.org.uk*

The United Kingdom (UK) straddles the British Isles, islands that lie off the western reaches of the Eurasian mainland. With a temperate air and ocean flow lapping onto the shores of the UK, these islands are marked by an intensely temperate and oceanic climate. In winter, warmed by the Gulf Stream that circulates past the British Isles from the Caribbean to the Arctic, temperatures only infrequently fall to below zero degrees centigrade. Likewise, summer temperatures are depressed the Atlantic such that over 20°C days are considered warm. Cloudiness and rain are the norm rather than the exception although England and Scotland have a marked rainfall variation from west to east; parts of Cumbria on the west coast of England have annual rainfall totals of over 3,000mm; just 400 km SE in Cambridgeshire, rainfall can be as low as 500mm. In short, much of Britain experiences a mild wet climate – the ideal conditions for peat formation.

British peatlands are commonly sub-divided into bog (rain-fed only) and fen (rain and ground-water fed), although fenland systems show greater variation in vegetation and chemistry depending on the nature of the groundwater (Wheeler and Proctor, 2000). In turn, bogs are commonly subdivided into two very distinct types of peatlands: (1) Lowland raised bogs, which were always a rare habitat and have been highly damaged or completely removed through peat cutting and conversion to agricultural land. These peatlands normally form through ecological succession from lakes through a wet woodland and fen stages. (2) Upland and western blanket bog where peat forms directly on saturated ground as a result of a hyper-oceanic climate in which rain falls on over 150 days per year. These bogs literally blanket the landscape. Whilst many of these peatlands have been heavily modified through burning, grazing, drainage and air pollution, blanket bog still forms one of Britain's largest extents of semi-natural habitat with large areas forming the UK's only recognisably wilderness areas in, for example, the Flow Country in north-east Scotland and the Isle of Lewis north-west of the Scottish mainland.

Peatlands in the UK have long been regarded as a waste-land, areas of land ripe for 'improvement', mainly for agriculture, recreational shooting and to mine peat, originally as a domestic fuel and more recently for horticultural peat-based growing media. Lindsay (1993) noted that peatlands were a 'Cinderella' habitat – one of Britain's most important habitats but mostly over-looked despite their importance for wildlife, for their cultural value in many parts of Britain and other 'ecosystem services'. Such thinking was brought to the fore by a Consortium of Non-Governmental Organisations (NGOs) leading a campaign to conserve peatlands. High profile nature conservation cases during the 1980s and 1990s highlighted the issue, including a campaign to remove tax breaks for tree planting that had blighted the Flow Country during the 1980s (the tax break was reversed in 1988) and to stop peat extraction at Thorne and Hatfield Moors, Yorkshire (peat extraction ceased in 2002). The European Habitats Directive, brought into English and Welsh law through the 1994 Habitats Regulations, was another major driver for the conservation of peatlands in that the Directive identified both raised and blanket bog as well as certain types of fen for designation as Special Areas of Conservation.

In the uplands, the Peak District National Park, through their *Moors for the Future* Project, began work to restore highly damaged blanket bog in the Southern Pennines of England – pioneering work that began to look at landscape scale restoration. In the lowlands, progress was more fragmented, although in Scotland, the Scottish Wildlife Trust led on the development of a strategy to conserve their lowland raised bogs (Stoneman, 1993). Elsewhere restoration work was on a site-by-site basis.

This fragmented situation led a group of restoration practitioners, peatland scientists and policy makers to gather together at a workshop in London in 2008. The workshop concluded that there was an overwhelming need for a programme of actions to deliver large scale peatland restoration across the UK with a focus around the conservation quartet of partnership, science, policy and practice. A key driver for this programme was the recognition of the multiple benefits of peatland including their role in helping to mitigate climate change. Based on this consensus, the Peter De Haan Charitable Trust provided funding for a three year programme of work. Subsequently, this programme was adopted by the IUCN-UK Committee as this provided an effective umbrella for the NGO, Government and the scientific community to come together. Short-term funds have enabled the programme to extend to 2018.

The programme had five original aims: (1) to inform policy and legislation; (2) to champion peatlands and their plight particularly to decision-makers; (3) to improve knowledge and understanding; (4) to improve information sharing across the peatland community and (5) to promote good practice particularly amongst the land management community and identify economic opportunities for better land management. Some of the more notable successes are highlighted here to demonstrate progress.

A particularly important aspect of the programme was to bring together and informally coordinate the peatland conservation community. The programme provided a common platform to meet, inform each other and share ideas. Over the last six years, the programme has run five conferences across the UK – in Bangor (Wales), Durham and York (England), Stirling and Inverness (Scotland) – held numerous workshops and developed a shared web-resource (http://www.iucn-uk-peatlandprogramme.org) to publish common materials. This work is critical as it has helped build a momentum around the benefits and need for peatland restoration across the country and given individuals and organisations the confidence and information to be more ambitious.

Significantly, this better coordinated community of peatland conservationists were brought together in a Commission of Inquiry (Bain *et al.*, 2011) to gather together up-to-date knowledge from science, policy and practice and provide an authoritative assessment of the available evidence, based on peer-reviewed scientific consensus. The inquiry process commissioned 12 topic based reports as well as engaging hundreds of people through two of the conferences (at Durham University in 2010 and Stirling University in 2011) and an open public inquiry held in Edinburgh. A core panel of experts coordinated the Inquiry supported by an Advisory Panel drawn from land management, scientific and Government organisations and agencies. The Inquiry drew out the core ecosystem service benefits of peatlands – as one of Britain's most important carbon stores, the largest remaining semi-natural habitat in the UK, a source for 70% of Britain's drinking water and as national treasures in terms of their archive of environmental and cultural change. It recognised that many peatlands were highly damaged such that the peat is wasting away contributing to greenhouse gas emissions rather than absorbing and storing carbon from the atmosphere. It set out the cost-effectiveness of peatland restoration, noting that the more damaged a peatland becomes, the greater the cost to Society. Crucially, the Inquiry built a consensus that recognised that peatlands in good condition should be conserved and damaged peatlands restored in turn requiring effective Government policy, necessary funding and coordinated action. The UK has about 2.3 million ha of blanket and raised bog, of which 1.8 million is damaged in some way. The Inquiry set a target of 1 million ha of peatland in conservation management by 2020.

In addition to the Inquiry publication, the IUCN-UK Peatland Programme has enabled a variety of other publications. After a land manager workshop that exposed an issue around the identification of moorland into upland heath and blanket bog (two rather distinct habitats that require different management interventions to conserve), the programme facilitated the Field Studies Council to publish a simple field guide to Sphagnum mosses (O'Reilley and Tratt, 2011). The programme also published two publications to demonstrate restoration success that highlight restoration case-studies both in the UK (Cris *et al.*, 2011) and internationally (Cris *et al.*, 2014). In addition, as part of the Programme's commitment to improve understanding, a series of topic briefings were published on specific issues[12]. More recently, the special symposium of the British Ecological Society and the Peatland Programme formed the basis of a review of peatland restoration and ecosystem services (Bonn *et al.*, 2016). Likewise, the programme has updated the Bog Management Handbook (Brooks and Stoneman, 1997) that was originally published as part of the Scottish Lowland Raised Bog Project. The new version can be found as a freely available on-line resource[13].

The IUCN-UK Peatland Programme has also been responsible for developing the Peatland Code. This is a mechanism by which businesses can help fund peatland restoration projects. The code is a voluntary standard that quantifies carbon emission reductions of restored peatlands designed to ensure environmental credibility so that businesses can invest in pre-selected projects with confidence that their funds will return clear carbon benefits, enabling them to meet corporate social responsibility targets.

All this work has helped to facilitate a step-change in Government policy and action. Significantly, at the IUCN-UK Peatland Programme York Conference in 2012, the four Environment Ministers of the United Kingdom[14] signed a joint letter setting out a statement of intent "*to protect and enhance the natural capital provided by peatlands in the UK and British Overseas Territories*." The letter set out four critical intentions: (1) land management policies to protect peatlands; (2) funding through agri-environment schemes; (3) development of private funding mechanisms to support peatland restoration and (4) a commitment to further research.

An example of this increased Government and private commitment to peatland conservation is drawn from Yorkshire, where the charity Yorkshire Wildlife Trust (YWT) has spearheaded the Yorkshire Peat

[12] See: http://www.iucn-uk-peatlandprogramme.org/resources/iucn-briefing-notes-peatlands

[13] See http://www.iucn-uk-peatlandprogramme.org/resources to access links to the on-line version

[14] Nature conservation policy operates under devolved governance within the UK, *i.e.* it is devolved to Northern Ireland, Wales, Scotland and England.

Partnership. This programme was developed in 2009 by scoping out the scale of the issue across Yorkshire. Of the 70,000 ha of upland blanket bog across the region, over 40,000 ha are highly damaged, having been drained, burnt and over-grazed by sheep to the point that much of the peatland resource is characterised by areas of bare peat, deep drainage gullies and a network of cut drains, most of which were cut using agricultural subsidies from the 1960s to 1980s.

To help restore this damage, YWT developed a partnership of organisations ranging from National Park Authorities and Government Agencies to landowner interests and private companies, such as Yorkshire Water. A team of restoration officers were developed who could undertake surveys, set out restoration management plans, liaise with land-owners/managers, develop funding agreements, let and manage contractors to undertake restoration work and facilitate a substantial regulatory and administrative requirement to enable peatland restoration.

Over the last six year, the team has surveyed over 37,000 ha of peatland, undertaking over 21,000 individual surveys of vegetation, damage characteristics and peat depth. This has enabled over 23,000 ha of peatland to come into restoration management involving the damming of thousands of kilometres of drain through the installation of around 300,000 dams.

The £12 million of funds for this work come from a range of sources although the most important funding mechanism is the rural development programme of the Common Agricultural Policy that can fund environmental improvements on farmed (in this case grazed) land. Yorkshire Water, recognising the significant benefits that could accrue in terms of water quality, have also invested substantial funds to restore peatlands in drinking water catchments whilst further funds have derived from Government Agencies – the Environment Agency and Natural England – and charitable sources.

The Yorkshire Peat Partnership represents a substantial restoration initiative but is just one of many big peatland restoration projects across the UK. To the south of the Yorkshire partnership area is the even more expansive work of the Peak District National Park; to the north it is the North Pennines Area of Outstanding Natural Beauty team that takes the lead. There is a long way to go before the million ha target set by the IUCN-UK peatland programme is reached but substantial progress is being made. Our longer-term aim is to bring all 1.8 million ha of peatland into conservation management of some form. If the UK is able to return its peatlands from systems that emit carbon to the atmosphere to a system that absorbs carbon then that sends a strong signal to the world community that peatland conservation can make a substantial difference in the battle to resolve catastrophic climate change.

REFERENCES

1. Bain, C.G., Bonn, A., Stoneman, R., Chapman, S., Coupar, A., Evans, M., Gearey, B., Howat, M., Joosten, H., Keenleyside, C., Labadz, J., Lindsay, R., Littlewood, N., Lunt, P., Miller, C.J., Moxey, A., Orr, H., Reed, M., Smith, P., Swales, V., Thompson, D.B.A., Thompson, P.S., Van de Noort, R., Wilson, J.D. and Worral, F. (2011) *IUCN UK Commission of Inquiry on Peatlands*. IUCN UK Peatland Programme, Edinburgh.
2. Bonn, A., Allot, T., Evans, M., Joosten, H. and Stoneman, R. (2016) *Peatland Restoration and Ecosystem Services – Science, Policy and Practice*. Cambridge University Press.
3. Brooks, S. and Stoneman, R. (1997) *The Bog Management Handbook*. The Stationary Office, Edinburgh.
4. Cris, R. Buckmaster, S. Bain, C. Reed, M. (Eds) (2014) *Global Peatland Restoration – Demonstrating Success*. IUCN UK National Committee Peatland Programme, Edinburgh.
5. Cris, R., Buckmaster, S., Bain, C. and Bonn, A. (Eds.) (2011) *UK Peatland Restoration – Demonstrating Success*. IUCN UK National Committee Peatland Programme, Edinburgh.
6. Lindsay, R. (1993) Peatland conservation – from cinders to Cinderella. In: Barber, K (ed) Biodiversity and Conservation, 2, pp. 528-540.
7. O'Rielly, J. and Tratt, R. (2011) *Sphagnum mosses in Bogs*. Field Studies Council.
8. Stoneman, R. (1997) Towards a Scottish raised bog conservation strategy. In: Parkyn, L., Stoneman, R. and Ingram, H. (eds) *Conserving Peatlands*. CAB International.
9. Wheeler, B.D. and Proctor, M.C.F. (2000) Ecological gradients, subdivisions and terminology of north-west European Mires. *Journal of Ecology*, 88, 187-203.

Abstract No: A-121

DESIGNING TARGETED INTERDISCIPLINARY RESTORATION ACTION PLANS FOR ASIA'S DEGRADED TROPICAL PEAT SWAMP FORESTS

Laura L. B. Graham[1], Jenny Pickerill[2] and Susan E. Page[3]

[1]*Borneo Orangutan Survival Foundation, Indonesia,*
[2]*Sheffield University, UK,*
[3]*University of Leicester, UK.*

**Corresponding author: l.l.b.graham.02@cantab.net*

SUMMARY

Between 1985 and 2006 about 47% of tropical peat swamp forest (TPSF), mainly found in South East Asia, became degraded. The degradation of tropical peatlands can lead to large GHG emissions, through logging, drainage and burning. Consequently numerous peatland rehabilitation programs are at the early stages of development across Indonesia. Unfortunately, relevant ecological and social data to base these upon are limited and interdisciplinary case-studies even more so. This study explored the social and ecological factors affecting the regeneration of a degraded TPSF in Central Kalimantan, Indonesia. An ecological investigation revealed that seed rain, animal-dispersal, flooding, increased light levels and lowered soil nutrient and mycorrhizae levels had become forest regeneration barriers, whilst seed banks, drought and competition with invasive species had not. In the adjacent village, focus groups and interviews revealed other factors influencing forest regeneration; the community's lack of livelihood options, their dependency on the forest, the lack of funding for restoration and their dislike of 'outsiders'. Not all factors were negative however; the community's ecological knowledge and their attitude towards restoration were positive. Social and ecological data were equally important in understanding the factors influencing the landscape. Furthermore, the data were closely linked and were often combined to better explain each factor. This study therefore describes how to select appropriate methods by which to collect ecological and social data within a degraded tropical peatland location through a process called 'anticipation and engagement'. It then proposes a new methodology for integrating these two disciplines in order to describe the factors influencing regeneration. The social and ecological data are combined to explain the factors using the categorizations: 'negative', 'potential negative', 'in-active', 'positive', and 'compound'. These factors can then be used to develop an appropriate and targeted site-specific restoration action plan.

Keywords: *Restoration action plan, regeneration barriers, tropical peatlands, interdisciplinary, degradation*

INTRODUCTION

Ecological restoration (ER) is the practice of assisting a degraded ecosystem in its recovery of health, integrity and sustainability. Restoration ecology (RE) is the science which supports the practice of ER. ER and RE are relatively new, with a dramatic increase in the number of studies and applications in the last 20 years. This field of science and practice offers great potential in overcoming the problems of land exploitation, loss of ecosystem services (ES) and climate change (Alexander *et al.* 2011). The science and practice of ER encompasses ecology, sociology, politics, geography and economics, amongst other disciplines and all must be investigated and combined to facilitate the design and implementation of appropriate restoration action plans (RAPs) (Tongway & Ludwig 2011). Interdisciplinary science, however, is complex and still in the early stages of development, resulting in a socio-ecological gap with contemporary ER activities having access to few case-study examples of interdisciplinary methods (Clewell & Aronson 2013).

One RE methodology is the exploration of regeneration barriers existing at a specific site and consideration of how to overcome these barriers (Holl *et al.* 2012). These can then be used to help design and implement a RAP for the specific location together with all stakeholders, and to monitor progress (Tongway & Ludwig 2011). The regeneration barriers and appropriate RAP are site-specific reflecting site natural history, disturbance history and sociology (Holl *et al.* 2012). Given the vast areas of degraded land across the globe, landscape-restoration has become an important topic of research and practice (Manning *et al.* 2006). There is a need for large-scale solutions and transferability of data, and yet the site-specific nature of regeneration barriers creates a challenge: how this work can be undertaken in a way that is successful and also has a wide-scale impact?

Indonesia supports the world's largest area of tropical peat swamp forest (TPSF) (Page *et al.*, 2011). Following Indonesian independence in 1945, an authoritarian regime was established (1966-1998) who prioritized economic growth through commercialization of the country's natural resources, which left many local communities feeling exploited and abused (Tsing 2005). In the last 15 years, democracy has been established, corruption is being challenged and repair of land exploitation is starting to be addressed (Ricklefs 2008). Indonesia's TPSFs, however, continue to be degraded at a rapid rate through logging, burning, drainage or conversion to agricultural use, and only 4% of the TPSF in Sumatra and Kalimantan is still in an intact condition, with 37% classified as degraded forest (Mietinnen & Liew 2010). TPSF provides important ES; biodiversity support, hydrological regulation and particularly, carbon storage (Page *et al.*, 2011). In light of recent developments in international policy targeting climate change, especially REDD+ (Alexander *et al.*, 2011), the restoration of Indonesia's tropical peatlands and its TPSF has become a topic of international interest. Restoration, however, requires intimate knowledge of an ecosystem's processes, and the study of TPSF has only developed in the last 30 years with, at present, little of that knowledge being applied to ecosystem restoration (Page *et al.*, 2009).

The aim of this study was, firstly, to investigate regeneration barriers, both ecological and social, at the local scale influencing the recovery of a specific site, then secondly, to consider whether these data or methods could be applied at a landscape-scale. The study explored how the ecological and social disciplines might be bridged during this process. It considered new methods and approaches to facilitate inter-disciplinarity in a multi-faceted practice and the transferability of methods in a science governed by its site-specific nature. The aim of this paper is to present briefly the ecological and social findings from this study, then to address the larger question of how this information was combined to create an interdisciplinary RAP and how these methods might be transferred.

METHODS

The ecological study took place in the TPSF within the Sabangau peat dome, Central Kalimantan, Indonesia. These forests were previously continuous and undisturbed but during recent years concessional and illegal logging and fires have resulted in areas near the river becoming severely degraded. Kereng Bangkirai is the closest village to the ecological study site, and the location of the community study Fig. 1).

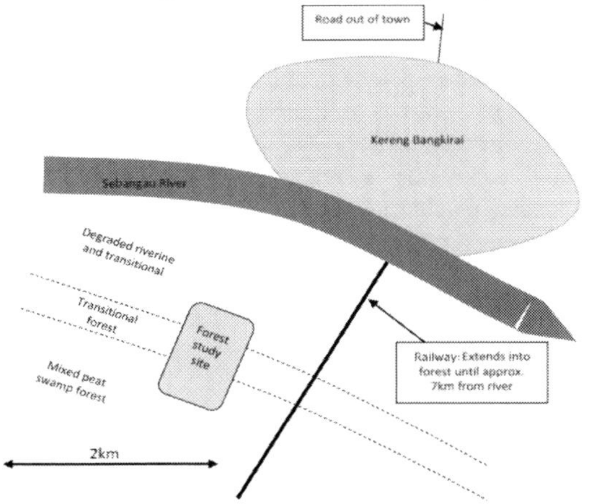

The ecological component comprised of five 600 m transects running parallel to the forest edge, encompassing a gradient of forest degradation: the natural forest (representing the control or reference site approx. 1 km within the forest), closed-canopy disturbed forest (50 m inside the forest), the forest edge, open-canopy disturbed forest (50 m outside the forest) and degraded forest (200 m outside the forest). Vegetation study plots were established in each FZ which showed increasing environmental degradation in all recorded attributes - species diversity and composition, forest dynamics, forest structure and productivity.

Figure 1: Map of the forest study site, river, access railway and Kereng Bangkirai.

Within each of these FZs, the following ecological conditions were selected, based on other tropical RE studies and a review of TPSF ecology, and then studied for one year: seed rain, seed dispersal, seed bank (representing the process of seedling recruitment), nutrient availability and pH of the peat, water table, light intensity, competition with herbaceous vegetation and mycorrhizal availability (representing the process of seedling survival and growth), with 5-8 replication points in each FZ for each condition. These conditions were analysed in comparison to the natural forest to determine if they differed significantly. Seedlings of three native TPSF early-succession species, *Dyera polyphylla, Shorea balangeran* and *Combretocarpus rotundatus,* were cultivated and transplanted into 32 mixed seedling plots in each forest zone. Eight plots per FZ were the control or natural environmental conditions plots. Eight plots had slow-release nutrient tablets added to each seedling. Eight plots were provided with shade cover and eight plots had the non-tree vegetation regularly cleared from the plots, i.e. competition removed. The survival and growth of the seedlings was recorded for seven months, and these data were analysed to investigate the impact of the seedling treatments in relation to the control seedlings and in relation to the FZ for each species. Analysis was carried out using ANOVA or Mann-Whitney U tests.

The social component of the study focused on understanding what the 'local community' (defined as residents of Kereng Bangkirai who regularly use the adjacent degraded study site) saw as barriers preventing natural regeneration, and how these might be alleviated. Focus groups and interviews were conducted to discuss past, present and future uses, changes and concerns about the land and forest surrounding their village. At the time of study (2009) Kereng Bangkirai had a population of approximately 5550. The total number of participants involved in the activities was 154, or 2.8% of the village. Three topics were covered, one topic per meeting: Topic 1: History of the land - historical uses, events, ownership and access, in particular which led to the land's degradation. Topic 2: Present uses of the land, both degraded and non-degraded, and Topic 3: Future of the land: concerns and hopes. Within these topics, sub-themes were addressed; physical barriers to recovery of the land, issues relating to land ownership, land rights and access, issues of social tension, and conflict over land-use. These topics and the methods were flexible such that new directions could be taken as the discussions proceeded. The activities were recorded and transcribed and analysed, and as the topics progressed so did recurrent themes or factors perceived to be influencing the regeneration of the forest.

During the data collection, maximum opportunity for cross-transfer of knowledge from the ecological study site and the village, with regard to the emerging barriers, was provided. Having one focal researcher at the heart of the study, dealing with the both the 'ecological' and 'social' aspects, allowed themes and concepts to flow across the so-called 'socio-ecological gap', so that the findings evolved as a whole rather than two halves. N.B. For more details on all the ecological and social methods including an in-depth description of the participants, their gender, age, religion, occupations etc., discussion on the community's social structure and, mine and the facilitators' positionality, and related potential trust, biases and impacts upon the social data see Graham (2013).

RESULTS

The ecological results revealed some distinct differences in the environmental conditions between the NF and the disturbed FZs; seed rain and the number of tree species in the seed rain were reduced in the more disturbed FZs, and a lower percentage of the seeds that did reach the FZs arrived through animal dispersal. %-orgC, %N and Total-P values for the surface peat were reduced in some of the disturbed FZs, however pH was unaffected by level of degradation. In both the wet and dry seasons, the water table in the disturbed FZs was higher than in the NF, resulting in issues of flooding but not drought. Light levels significantly increased in the disturbed FZs, although this effect was somewhat ameliorated by the ground-cover vegetation; but even beneath this cover, the light levels were still greater than under the canopy cover created by the forest. The ground cover of pandan and lianas reduced outside the forest whilst cover of sedges increased, and overall non-tree vegetation ground cover was greater outside the forest. Finally, levels of mycorrhizae in the degraded FZs appeared to be below optimal levels for the species investigated. The impact of forest degradation on seedling survival and growth further indicated alterations to the environmental conditions. Providing nutrient additions to the seedlings improved the growth of two of the three tree species planted in some of the disturbed zones; shade cover was advantageous to only one species outside the forest; removal of invasive ground cover vegetation either had no effect or actually reduced survival of one species and the growth of another; finally, mycorrhizal inoculation improved nutrient uptake in two species of seedlings, and, given the higher colonisation levels of the inoculated seedlings, the results suggest some additional advantages (Graham 2013).

The social results revealed several regular themes that explained how the community engaged with the landscape and which, in their view, were impacting upon the regeneration of the area. Key themes are described below, for the complete list see Table 1, with further detail provided in Graham (2013).

- *Importance of the forest:* This was the most recurrent theme: The forest provided the community with most of their livelihoods: logging, fishing, jelutong, gemur etc. It was the source of many of their foods, timber and medicines. It linked to their culture, identity, tradition, heritage, and sense of well-being.
- *High awareness of ecology:* Their knowledge of the forest and ecology was very high. They described the water, atmosphere and soil and how this was affected by different forest qualities. They had knowledge on tree and animal species, and their habits and seasons, which allowed them to work year-round in the seasons of the forest.
- *Feelings of being observers:* Most of the degradation was perceived as coming from external forces. The community felt they were not to blame for what happened to their land and felt overwhelmed and pushed out.
- *Outsiders:* Strong resentment was felt towards 'outsiders', perceived as people or groups that came to the area, exploited a resource, then left again. They acknowledged that they themselves had partaken in some of the degradation activities, but they felt it was due to an increased competition and need that resulted from outsiders.

- *Feelings of lack of options*: The community tried to maintain their forest livelihoods with the few resources that were left. They were aware their activities were no longer sustainable, that the money they made was only just sufficient and with general prices rising, they struggled to make ends meet.
- *Attitude towards restoration:* They were extremely motivated towards restoring the forest, and saw the restoration and subsequent management as a long-term solution to their current situation. They had suggestions for how to bring this about, but did not feel financially or authoritatively empowered to do it. They said they would want to be involved in all the activities, and that the commitment, the period of commitment and recipients of future benefits should be made clear from the start.
- *Relationship with government:* They were honest about the ways they felt the government had not managed the area well, regarding the logging, illegal logging and fires. Despite this, they looked to the government as the main potential source of funding for restoration and to provide the laws and authority necessary to bring about restoration.

DISCUSSION

The ecological results presented above could form the basis of the 'usual' ecological component of a restoration action plan (RAP) for this specific site. These findings do not stand-alone, however, as the social factors should also be incorporated. Furthermore, as this study progressed, it became apparent that the 'active' regeneration barriers only told half of the story. Some factors which might have been regeneration barriers, were in fact only potential or inactive barriers. Equally there were factors that could have a positive impact on regeneration. These factors are just as important to include in a RAP. In order to successfully combine social and ecological data, and to show the array of factors influencing the degraded landscape, new terminology was needed (Table 1). All the factors found to be affecting this landscape could now be categorised within this new terminology, with the ecological and social components of each combined (Table 2), and a more targeted RAP could be designed.

Table 1: A summary of the terminology developed in this study to describe the factors influencing the regeneration of the degraded landscape.

Factor	Definition
Negative	Also called regeneration barriers, these are factors acting upon the degraded area such that they would need to be directly removed or overcome in order for regeneration to take place.
Potential negative	Factors causing some degree of negative impact on regeneration, or which may become active negative factors based on an external trigger.
In-active	Factors that have neither a negative nor a positive effect on regeneration, and as such, would not need to be addressed in restoration activities.
Positive	Factors shown to support regeneration activities, and awareness of these factors and their incorporation into a RAP would be advantageous.
Compound	Factors that are may not be negative or positive, but which are complex, affected by numerous events and as yet unresolved. Awareness of the factors would be needed when designing an RAP.

Regeneration barriers, or, as proposed here influencing regeneration 'factors', can have ecological, social, economic and political components, which develop both pre- and post-disturbance. The result is that although the regeneration factors for one site may be known, one cannot then simply extrapolate these barriers to other sites. Whilst it would therefore be inappropriate to try to develop a one-for-all RAP, one can instead stream-line the route by which these factors are identified. This can be done by the method used in this study - 'anticipation and engagement'. 'Anticipation' refers to using the available literature and local knowledge to outline the most likely regeneration factors at a specific site, whilst 'engagement' refers to exploring these potential factors directly in the location and with the community. As used in this study, this results in a comprehensive overview of the factors influencing the site, enabling the next step to be facilitated, that of developing a RAP.

Given the large area of degraded TPSF in SE Asia, the desire to have a one-for-all RAP is tempting, especially with the increased application of landscape-scale restoration theory (Manning *et al.*, 2006). However, this study argues that by over-looking the local-scale, by side-stepping true engagement with each study-site, the success of restoration can be compromised. This study endeavoured to show a stream-lined method to determining the regeneration factors that need to be incorporated in a RAP for a particular site. The method of anticipation and engagement would, in the space of one year of study, facilitate an economical, appropriate and long-lasting RAP.

CONCLUSION

This study could have been a discreet exploration into the specific regeneration barriers for this particular site. It was, however framed within a bigger context, of developing methods which incorporate both social and ecological factors, thus creating a holistic RAP. The division of ecological and social factors is somewhat arbitrary as they overlap on numerous occasions. The separation of these combined ecological and social factors into negative, potential, inactive, positive and compound factors provides a more functional and holistic route to guiding the development of a RAP.

Table 2: All the factors found in this study to be affecting the regeneration of the forest, described by their factor type and their ecological and social dimensions.

Factor	Factor type	Ecological dimension	Social dimension
Seed dispersal	Negative	Present	Present
Flooding	Negative	Present	Present
Nutrient availability	Negative	Present	Present
Lack of options/money	Negative	Absent	Present
No funding for restoration	Negative	Absent	Present
Outsiders	Negative	Absent	Present
High light intensity	Negative	Present	Present
Fire	Negative	Not studied	Present
Mycorrhizae availability	Potential	Present	Absent
Selecting transplant species	Potential	Present	Present
Drought	Potential	Present	Present
Community's dependence on the forest	Potential	Not studied	Present
Community's ideas for forest restoration	Potential	Absent	Present
Community's desire manage the restoration	Potential	Absent	Present
Seed banks	Inactive	Present	Absent?
Competition with non-tree vegetation	Positive	Present	Present
Community's attitude to the forest	Positive	Not studied	Present
Community's awareness of the state of the forest	Positive	Not studied	Present
Community's forest and restoration knowledge	Positive	Absent	Present
Community's attitude to restoration	Positive	Absent	Present
Community's relationship with the government	Compound	Absent	Present
Logging	Compound	Not studied	Present
Issues of access and ownership	Compound	Absent	Present

ACKNOWLEDGEMENTS

CIMTROP for research facilitation; all field assistants; the Wildlife Conservation Society, Rufford Foundation and British Ecological Society for funding; Kereng Bangkirai participants for their time, patience and honesty.

REFERENCES

1. Alexander, S., Nelson, C. R., et al. (2011) Opportunities and challenges for ecological restoration within REDD+. Restoration Ecology 19: 683–689
2. Clewell, A. F. and Aronson, J. (2013) *Ecological restoration: Principles, values and structure of an emerging profession*. 2nd Edition. Island Press, Washington.
3. Graham, L. L. B. (2013) Restoration from Within: An interdisciplinary methodology for tropical peat swamp forest restoration, Indonesia. PhD thesis submitted to the University of Leicester.
4. Holl, K. D. (2012) Chapter 9: Restoration of tropical forests. In: van Andel, J. and Aronson, J. (2012) *Restoration Ecology: The New Frontier*. Second edition. Wiley-Blackwell Press.
5. Manning, A. D., Lindenmayer, D. B. and Fischer, J. (2006) Stretch-goals and backcasting: approaches for overcoming barriers to large-scale ecological restoration. Restoration Ecology 14: 487–492.
6. McManus, P. (2006) Mangrove Battlelines: culture/nature and ecological restoration. Australian Geographer 37: 57-71

7. Miettinen, J. and Liew, S. C. (2010) Degradation and development of peatlands in Peninsular Malaysia and in the islands of Sumatra and Borneo since 1990. Land Degradation and Development 21: 285-296
8. Page, S.E., Hoscilo, A., Wosten, H., Jauhiainen, J., Ritzema, H., Tansey, K., Silvius, M., Graham, L., Vasander, H., Rieley, J. and Limin, S. (2009) Ecological restoration of lowland tropical peatlands in Southeast Asia – Current knowledge and future research directions. *Ecosystems* 12: 888-905
9. Page, S. E., Rieley, J. O. and Banks, C. J. (2011) Global and regional importance of the tropical peatland carbon pool. Global change biology 17: 798-818
10. Ricklefs, M. C. (2008) A *modern history of Indonesia since c.1200*. Fourth edition.
11. Tongway, D. J. and Ludwig, J. A. (2011) *Restoring disturbed landscapes: Putting principles into practice*. Island Press, Washington, USA.
12. Tsing, A. L. (2005) Friction: An ethnography of global connection. Princeton University Press.

Abstract No: A-417

DOES HYDROLOGICAL RESTORATION AFFECT GREENHOUSE GASES EMISSION AND PLANT DYNAMICS IN *SPHAGNUM* PEATLANDS?

F. Laggoun-Défarge[1*], S. Gogo[1], L. Bernard-Jannin[1], C.Guimbaud[2], R. Zoccatelli[3], J. Rousseau[4], S. Binet[1], B. D'Angelo[1], F. Leroy[1], N. Jozja[3], F. Le Moing[1] and C. Défarge[1,3]

[1]*ISTO, University of Orléans/CNRS/BRGM, France.*
[2]*LPC2E, University of Orléans/CNRS, France.*
[3]*CETRAHE, University of Orléans, France*
[4]*SNE, 41200 Romorantin-Lanthenay, France.*

**Corresponding author: Fatima.Laggoun-Defarge@univ-orleans.fr*

SUMMARY

The C-sink function of peatlands is mainly controlled by soil waterlogging and *Sphagnum* moss dominance. La Guette peatland (Sologne, France) was drained for decades by a road ditch resulting in vascular plant (*Molinia caerulea*) invasion. Hydrological restoration was undertaken in 2014 and vegetation experiments were set up. In both downstream and upstream stations, three treatments (n=4) were conducted: "control" with intact vegetation, "bare peat", and "*Sphagnum*" (bare peat seeded with *Sphagnum*). Our aim was to assess the effect of such actions on plant community diversity and CO_2/CH_4 fluxes. In each plot, gas fluxes and plant cover were measured. 18 months after the restoration work, "bare peat" and "*Sphagnum*" plots were quickly colonised by *Eriophorum angustifolium* (up to 90%), *Rynchospora alba* (up to 10%), *Trichophorum cespitosum* (up to 60%). In both stations, control plots functioned as C sinks with lower CH_4 emissions and higher ecosystem respiration compared to the other treatments. However, at peak biomass the latter treatments tended to act as sinks for CO_2 in 2015 than in 2014 suggesting that plant cover, higher in 2015 than in 2014, is a crucial determinant for CO_2 fluxes. Although vegetation colonisation is proceeding fast, two years do not appear to be sufficient to trigger a C sink function in restored peatlands.

***Keywords**: CO_2 and CH_4 fluxes, Molinia caerulea, peat organic matter, plant removal experiments, water table.*

INTRODUCTION

Northern hemisphere peatlands are estimated to contain about 300-400 Pg C as peat, corresponding to about 30% of the world's soil C stock in an area accounting for only 3-5% of the land surface. This C-sink function is largely controlled by the low rate of organic matter (OM) decomposition due to hydrological conditions that favour soil waterlogging, combined with the dominance of vegetation that produces decay-resistant litter, i.e. *Sphagnum* mosses that hampers microbial decomposition (Holden, 2005), resulting in a net accumulation of OM as peat. In Western Europe, due to a high anthropogenic pressure, e.g. hydrological disturbances (i.e. drainage), peat cutting and nutrient amendment, many peatlands are invaded by vascular plants at the expense of *Sphagnum* mosses (Francez & Vasander, 1995; Berendse *et al.* 2001; Bubier *et al.* 2007). It has been shown that drainage or increased air temperature can have direct negative effects on *Sphagnum* productivity by increasing evapotranspiration (Gerdol 1995; Weltzin *et al.* 2001). In the same way, vascular plants can gain a competitive advantage due to improved soil oxygenation (Buttler *et al.*, 2015) that also favors also greenhouse gases (GHG) emission (mainly CO_2). Careful attention is thus needed to understand how a change in plant species cover due to altered hydrological conditions can affect belowground interactions that largely control GHG (CO_2, CH_4) emissions and C stocks in peatlands. Nowadays several ecological engineering actions are being undertaken to restore peatland functioning. Our study aimed to assess the effect of such actions undertaken in a disturbed peatland (La Guette, France) on plant community diversity and GHG (CO_2, CH_4) fluxes. Hydrology has been monitored since 2010 and several environmental variables (e.g. vegetation, GHG emission), from the hydrological restoration of the peatland, i.e. 2014.

MATERIALS AND METHODS

The La Guette peatland (150m a.s.l., 47°19N, 2°16'E, 20 ha, Figure 1), located in the Sologne forest (Neuvy-sur-Barangeon, France) is a transitional fen composed of moss patches (*Sphagnum cuspidatum* and *S. rubellum*) and of *Calluna vulgaris* and *Erica tetralix*. The mean annual precipitation and temperature is 883 mm and

11°C respectively. Two sub-hydrological systems (upstream and downstream sub-watersheds) characterise the site (Binet *et al*, 2013). The peatland has been invaded by *Molinia caerulea* and *Betula spp* for 30 years with an acceleration of the invasion in the recent decades (Gogo *et al.*, 2011). This was partly caused by a road ditch at the outlet that accelerated the peatland drainage. In February 2014, we undertook hydrological restoration in the downstream sub-watershed to raise the water table level and to promote the soil rewetting. This consisted in building thresholds composed of eight trenches dug in the peat soil and filled with sand and bentonite. In addition, manipulative experiments were initiated in two experimental stations: 1) within the downstream sub-watershed impacted by the restoration work and 2) within the upstream one supposedly non-affected by the restoration work. In each station three treatments were applied, each in four replicates: A) control (intact plots), B) bare peat (vegetation and first 5 cm of peat removed), and C) *Sphagnum* treatment (bare peat with *Sphagnum capitula* spread to accelerate C accumulating vegetation recolonisation). In each station (12 plots of 2m x 2m each), we measured CO_2 and CH_4 fluxes about once a month at the peak biomass using a closed static chamber (diameter of 30.5 cm, height of 30 cm), with a GMP343 Vaisala probe for CO_2 fluxes and with SPIRIT, a portable infrared laser absorption spectrometer for CH_4 fluxes (see D'Angelo *et al.*, 2016 and Gogo *et al.*, 2011 for CO_2 and CH_4 measurements respectively). Plant species abundance was measured with a 50-50 cm gridded frame placed above a permanently marked subplot. Water table level was monitored since 2010.

RESULTS AND DISCUSSION

Effect of the restoration on the peatland hydrology

The water table depth was monitored since 2010 in two piezometers: WO and DO located in the downstream and the upstream sub-watershed respectively.

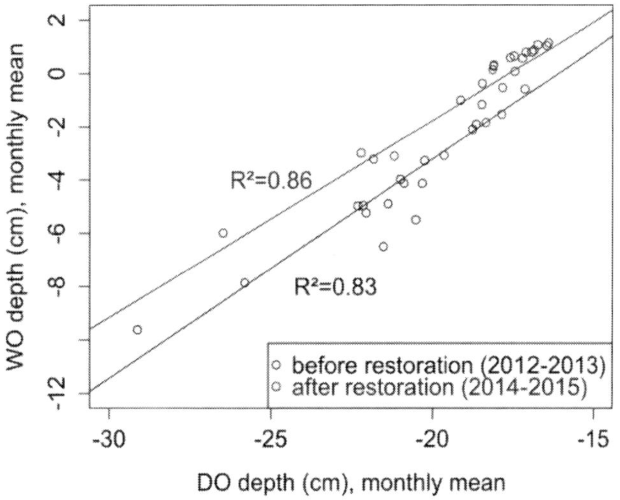

Figure 1: Relationship between the monthly water table depth in WO and DO piezometers before and after the hydrological restoration

To assess the specific role of the restoration, we analysed the relationship between monthly water table depth in WO and DO for two periods: the two years preceding the restoration (2012-2013) and the two following years (2014-2015) (Figure 1). The results indicated a strong linear correlation between water table depths in the two piezometers. This correlation was different for the two periods analysed: for the same water table depth in DO, the water table depth in WO was higher for the period after the restoration. This could indicate that restoration work led to an increase in the water table depth in the downstream sub-watershed since the water table depth in the upstream sub-watershed remained unchanged. However, a longer dataset chronicle is needed to confirm this tendency.

Influence of treatments on gas fluxes

On the whole, when the results of the 2 stations are pooled, differences in net ecosystem exchange (NEE), ecosystem respiration (ER) and CH_4 fluxes were observed between treatments (Figure 2). During the growing season (May to September), ER was found to be higher in the control plots, where the water table depth was lower (8 cm below the surface in average) than in the other two treatments (1 cm above the surface in average). In the same period, a negative NEE was recorded in these plots which thus acted as a sink for CO_2. The bare peat and the *Sphagnum* plots exhibited low CO_2 fluxes in 2014 and did not have a marked positive or negative CO_2 balance, in contrast to 2015 where they tended to act as a sink for CO_2 at peak biomass. This suggests that plant colonisation, higher in 2015 than in 2014, is a crucial determinant for CO_2 fluxes. In the same plots, higher CH_4 fluxes were measured during the growing season compared to the controls (Figure 2), probably in relation with the high water table depth recorded during the two years (data not shown).

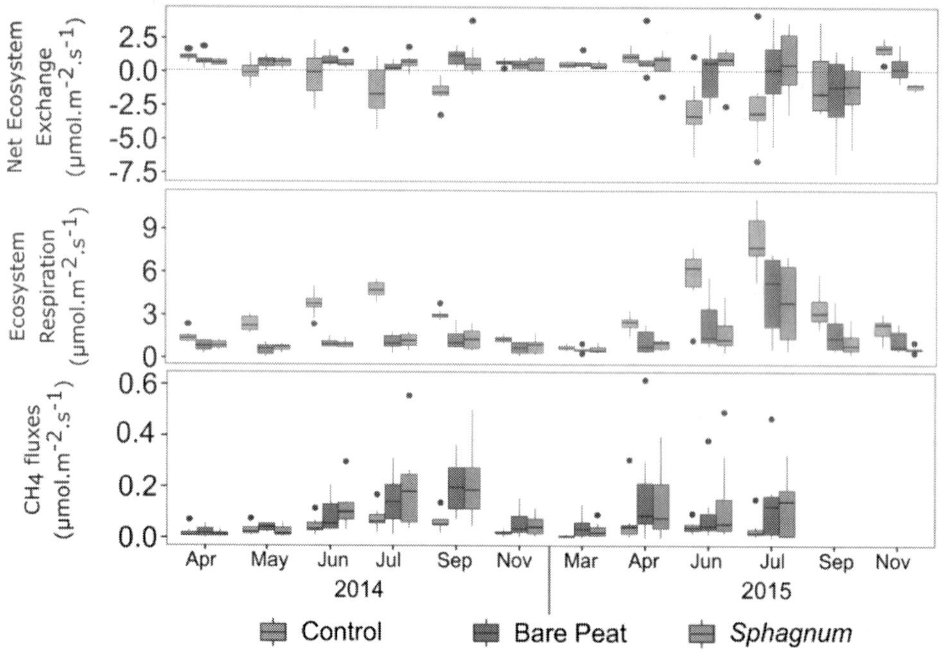

Figure 2: Net ecosystem exchange, ecosystem respiration and CH4 fluxes for the three treatments (control, bare peat and Sphagnum) in upstream and downstream stations (the two stations were pooled: n=8)

Influence of treatments on plant species cover

A plant removal experiment was performed to renew the vegetation and increase the moisture of surface peat. 18 months after the restoration work, "bare peat" and "*Sphagnum*" plots were quickly colonised by *Eriophorum angustifolium* (up to ca. 90%), *Trichophorum cespitosum* (up to ca. 60%) and *Rynchospora alba* (up to ca. 10%) (Figure 3). Considering all the vascular plants, it appeared that in bare plots, the abundance of *E. angustifolium* and *T. cespitosum* was higher during the growing season of 2015 as compared to 2014. Similarly, vascular plant cover became more heterogeneous in *Sphagnum* plots during the 2015 growing season compared to 2014. It is worth noting that in these plots, *Sphagnum* moss abundance increased at the beginning of the first growing season (May and June 2014) and remained roughly constant thereafter. Overall, this seemed to be related to the degree of wetness of microhabitats (Price & Whitehead 2004). The plant species cover in the control plots was almost constant in 2014 and 2015 and was dominated by *M. caerulea* and *E. tetralix* at peak biomass.

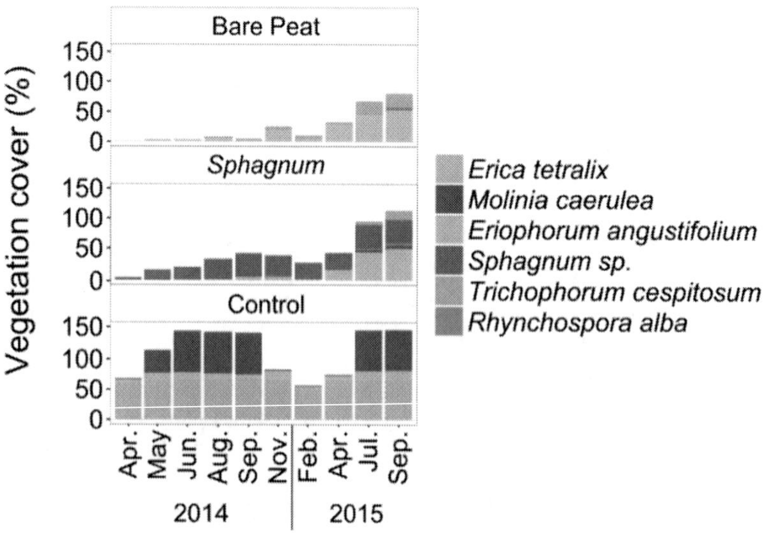

Figure 3: Vegetation cover (%) in the three treatment plots (bare peat, *Sphagnum* and control, mean of replicates)

CONCLUSION

The hydrological restoration carried out in La Guette peatland had an impact on the water table dynamics in the downstream sub-watershed. The treatments have been shown to affect CO_2 and CH_4 emissions and vegetation cover. Although a longer period of monitoring is needed to better assess the impact of hydrological restoration on gas emission, the first hints of the positive effect of the restoration work were detected, namely decreased water table fluctuations and the return of typical acidic fen vegetation.

ACKNOWLEDGEMENTS

This work was funded as part of the CARBIODIV project, Labex VOLTAIRE (ANR-10-LABX-100-01) and the French Peatland Observatory (SNO Tourbieres).

REFERENCES

1. Berendse, F., Van Breemen, N., Rydin, Hå., Buttler, A., Heijmans, M., Hoosbeek, M.R., Lee, J.A., Mitchell, E., Saarinen, T. & Vasander, H. (2001) Raised atmospheric CO_2 levels and increased N deposition cause shifts in plant species composition and production in Sphagnum bogs. *Global Change Biology*, 7, 591–598.
2. Binet, S., Gogo, S. & Laggoun-Défarge, F. (2013) A water-table dependent reservoir model to investigate the effect of drought and vascular plant invasion on peatland hydrology. *Journal of Hydrology*, 499, 132–139.
3. Bubier, J.L., Moore, T.R. & Bledzki, L.A. (2007) Effects of nutrient addition on vegetation and carbon cycling in an ombrotrophic bog. *Global Change Biology*, 13, 1168–1186.
4. Buttler, A., Robroek, B.J.M., Laggoun-Défarge, F., Jassey, V.E.J., Pochelon, C., Bernard, G., Delarue, F., Gogo, S., Mariotte, P., Mitchell, E.A.D. & Bragazza, L. (2015) Experimental warming interacts with soil moisture to discriminate plant responses in an ombrotrophic peatland. *Journal of Vegetation Science*, 26, 964–974.
5. D'Angelo, B., Gogo, S., Laggoun-Défarge, F., Le Moing, F., Jégou, F., Guimbaud, C. (2016). Soil Temperature Synchronisation improves representation of diel variability of Ecosystem Respiration in *Sphagnum* Peatlands. *Agricultural and Forestry Meteorology*, 223, 95-102.
6. Francez, A.-J. & Vasander, H. (1995) Peat accumulation and peat decomposition after human disturbance in French and Finnish mires. *Acta oecologica*, 16, 599–608.
7. Gerdol, R. (1995) The growth dynamics of Sphagnum based on field measurements in a temperate bog and on laboratory cultures. *Journal of Ecology*, 83, 431–437.
8. Gogo, S., Guimbaud, C., Laggoun-Défarge, F., Catoire, V., Robert, C. (2011) In situ quantification of CH_4 bubbling events from a peat soil using a new infrared laser spectrometer, Note. *Journal of Soils and Sediments*, 11, 4, 545-551.
9. Gogo, S., Laggoun-Défarge, F., Delarue, F. & Lottier, N. (2011) Invasion of a *Sphagnum*-peatland by Betula spp and Molinia caerulea impacts organic matter biochemistry. Implications for carbon and nutrient cycling. *Biogeochemistry*, 106, 53–69.
10. Holden, J. (2005) Peatland hydrology and carbon release: why small-scale process matters. *Philosophical Transactions of the Royal Society A*, 363, 2891–2913.
11. Price, J.S. & Whitehead, G.S. (2004) The influence of past and present hydrological conditions on *Sphagnum* recolonization and succession in a block-cut bog, Quebec. *Hydrological Processes*, 18, 315 – 328.
12. Weltzin, J.F., Harth, C., Bridgham, S.D., Pastor, J. & Vonderharr, M. (2001) Production and microtopography of bog bryophytes: response to warming and water-table manipulations. *Oecologia*, 128, 557–565.

Abstract No: A-067

ENHANCING REFORESTATION IN DEGRADED TROPICAL PEATLANDS IN CENTRAL KALIMANTAN

Maija Lampela*, Jyrki Jauhiainen and Harri Vasander

Department of Forest Sciences, University of Helsinki, Finland

**Corresponding author: maija.lampela@gmail.com*

SUMMARY

Tropical peatlands of Southeast Asia are great terrestrial carbon stores and major hot spots of biodiversity. Main peat forming ecosystem is peat swamp forest (PSF). Currently peat swamp forests are converted to plantations and agriculture with breath-taking pace. Aside from conservation, active restoration is also needed on degraded areas to conserve both biodiversity and the remaining peat deposits. Our work searches practical and affordable techniques for reforestation of degraded peatlands. Our study site was clear-felled open, drained and several times burnt deep peat area in the so-called Ex-Mega Rice area in Central Kalimantan, Indonesia. We chose five native PSF tree species (*Shorea balangeran, Dyera polyphylla, Alstonia pneumatophora, Dacryodes rostrata* and *Campnosperma squamatum*) known to have potential for reforestation. Seed material acquired from local forests was grown in a field nursery. At the age of 6-11 months seedlings were planted in the field in three replicate locations characterized by differing wetness conditions. We tested three treatments: weeding (3 intensities), mounding and fertilizing, and their combinations to study the best practices to enhance seedling success. Growth and mortality of the seedlings and environmental variables (water table, temperature) were monitored for two years. Effects of treatments and environmental variables on the growth were tested with mixed-effect models and on mortality rates with Cox regression. We conclude that fertilizing had most clear positive effect both on growth and mortality in tested species whereas mounding decreased mortality but the effects on growth were ambiguous. Weeding had slight positive effect both on growth and survival in most cases. Water table position had effect both on growth and mortality but the results differed substantially between species. When labor and material costs are taken into account, our results can derive species-specific best option for reforestation scheme for these five species on degraded tropical peatlands.

Keywords: *tropical peatland, reforestation, restoration*

INTRODUCTION

Tropical peatlands of Southeast Asia are one of the great terrestrial carbon sources. Main peat forming ecosystem, peat swamp forest (PSF) has been, until recently, one of the last relatively untouched wilderness inhabiting one of the most diverse flora and fauna on the Earth. During the last decades peat swamp forests have been converted to plantations and agriculture with increasing intensity. Drainage and removal of forest cover have caused loss of biodiversity, progressive decrease in carbon stores and these damages are reinforced by fire outbreaks during dry seasons.

In the autumn 2015, prolonged and wide-spread fires in the Indonesian and Malaysian archipelago covered again large areas in Southeast Asia to thick haze. This "worst environmental disaster of the century" (Meijaard 2015 and Monbiot 2015) brought the situation of the tropical peatlands to the international awareness. To amend the devastating situation, Indonesian government has taken measures to ban all new development in peatlands and start restoration of the drained areas (Letter of Instruction no S.661 /MenLHK-Setjen/Rokum/2015). Aside from conserving the remaining peatlands, active restoration will be needed in the degraded peatlands. In the clear-cut and several times burnt areas there is not a need only for the hydrological restoration, but also for the reforestation. This study searches for practical techniques for reforestation of these degraded tropical peatlands. This is done by testing how five native species seedlings responded to selected silvicultural practices in a planting trial on a degraded tropical peatland area. The tested practices were fertilizing, mounding and weeding. Full analysis of the results is yet to come and thus we present here the preliminary findings.

METHODS

The study was conducted in the degraded peatland in the Ex-Mega Rice area block C, in the Kalampangan zone (2°19'S 114°01'E), near Palangka Raya, Central Kalimantan. The former peat swamp forest was drained, clear-cut and it had burnt several times. The peat depth in the area was approximately 4 m. The vegetation on the area consisted of ferns, bushes and sparse small trees. The mean annual rainfall was approximately 2500 mm and the mean temperature was 26 °C (Hirano *et al.*, 2014).

We chose five native PSF species (*Shorea balangeran, Dyera polyphylla, Alstonia pneumatophora, Dacryodes rostrata* and *Campnosperma squamatum*) known to have potential for reforesting degraded peat areas. Seeds were collected from the local forests and seedlings were grown in a field nursery near the Kalampangan village. After 6-11 months in the nursery, the seedlings were planted in the start of rainy season in November 2012 in the field in three replicate locations characterized by differing wetness conditions. We used three treatments: weeding (3 intensities: no weeding, moderate weeding, total weeding), mounding (40 cm high constructed mounds filled with peat material from the site) and fertilizing (organic manure from local farms, applied once at planting), and their combinations to study the best practices to enhance seedling success. Height and mortality of the seedlings was monitored for two years. Water table was monitored with automated loggers in all three replicate locations. Soil temperature and soil properties (chemistry and physical properties) were monitored with regular measurement campaigns. For each separate species, effects of the treatments and environmental variables on the growth were tested with linear mixed-effect models and on mortality rates with Cox regression models.

RESULTS

Based on the preliminary findings, *Shorea balangeran* was had the best results both in growth and survival, followed by *Dacryodes rostrata* with more modest results for the three remaining species (Figure 1).

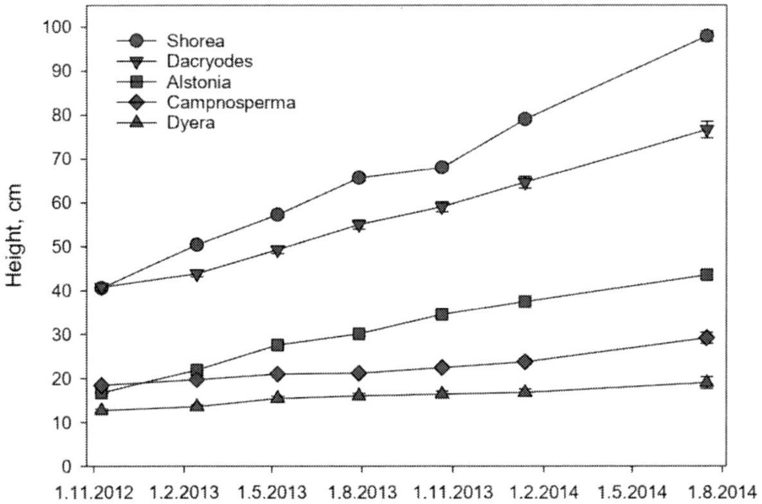

Figure 1: Height of the species without any treatments during the first 1.5 years after planting

Fertilizing had most clear positive effect both on growth and survival in tested species (Figure 2). Mounding decreased mortality in most cases but the effects on growth were mixed. Weeding had slight positive effect both on growth and survival in most cases. Water table position had effect both on growth and mortality but the results differed substantially between species. Two years after planting in October 2014 all the sites were caught by fire and most of the seedlings were killed and the measurements had to be terminated.

DISCUSSION

Drained, clear-cut and several times burnt tropical peatlands are extremely harsh environments for any vegetation. After removal of trees, repeated fires and heavy rainfall eroding the surface peat, the nutrient pool especially in deep peat areas, such as in Kalampangan zone in this study, is practically non-existing (Könönen *et al.*, 2015). The water table change between wet and dry seasons can be up to 2 meters. Flooding can rise 50 cm above the soil surface in places in wet season whereas the water table can be 1.5 m deep in the dry season. This sets high demands for both flood and drought tolerance of the plants. Based on our findings, species like *Shorea balangeran* and *Dacryodes rostrata* may well be able to overcome these conditions and establish viable stands over time. Fertilizing as a one-time investment seems to have clear positive effect on the onset of stand establishment and should thus be considered. Mounding is a labor intensive and more costly technique and even if it might reduce the mortality in the early stages, based on this study we cannot anticipate if it would enhance future success of the seedling or not. Weeding needs to be done several times and is also labor intensive. Based on the somewhat contradicting results depending on the species and sites, we may suggest that the shelter provided by the existing vegetation (mostly ferns) may in some cases be beneficial, as well as the decrease of the competition and increased light availability achieved by weeding. When labor and material costs are taken into account, comparing the results of these techniques can derive species-specific best option for reforestation scheme on degraded tropical peatlands.

Figure 2: Moderate weeding and fertilized *Shorea balangeran* 1.5 years after planting

CONCLUSION

Even in the very harsh conditions in the deep peat areas, with right species and techniques, the reforestation of degraded tropical peatlands can be successful. Nevertheless, the main concern should be in securing the stands from burning, which in turn needs local commitment for responsible use of fire. The chance for success can further be enhanced with hydrological restoration, where permanently elevated ground water table can reduce the susceptibility for fires.

ACKNOWLEDGEMENTS

We thank our Indonesian partner Center for International Cooperation in Sustainable Management of Tropical Peatland (CIMTROP), their staff and field workers. This study was funded by the Ministry for Foreign Affairs of Finland STEM project and RETROPEAT (253933) project of the Academy of Finland.

REFERENCES

1. Hirano T, Kusin K, Limin S, Osaki M. 2014. Carbon dioxide emissions through oxidative peat decomposition on a burnt tropical peatland. *Global Change Biology* 20, 555–565
2. Könönen M, Jauhiainen J, Laiho R, Kusin K, Vasander H. 2015. Physical and chemical properties of tropical peat under stabilised land uses. *Mires and Peat* 16, 08
3. Meijaard E. 2015. Erik Meijaard: Indonesia's Fire Crisis — The Biggest Environmental Crime of the 21st Century. *JakartaGlobe* (internet newspaper), October 23, 2015. http://jakartaglobe.beritasatu.com/opinion/erik-meijaard-indonesias-fire-crisis-biggest-environmental-crime-21st-century/
4. Monbiot G. 2015. Indonesia is burning. So why is the world looking away? *The Guardian* (internet newspaper), October 30, 2015. http://www.theguardian.com/commentisfree/2015/oct/30/indonesia-fires-disaster-21st-century-world-media

Abstract No: A-066

GREENHOUSE GAS FLUX HETEROGENEITY ACROSS A TEMPERATE LOWLAND FEN UNDER RESTORATION MANAGEMENT

Emma Brown[1, 2], Andrew Smith[2], David L. Jones[2] and Chris Evans[1]

[1] *Centre for Ecology and Hydrology, Bangor, UK*
[2] *School of Environment, Natural Resources and Geography, Bangor University, UK*

**Corresponding author: emmbro@ceh.ac.uk*

SUMMARY

Natural peatlands function as a carbon (C) sink and long term C store. However, past management has led to substantial net losses of stored C across the UK, other areas of northern Europe and more recently in tropical peatlands. Degraded peatlands are being targeted for restoration to reduce current emissions and restore their original C sink potential. This study investigates GHG flux heterogeneity across a partially degraded lowland fen on the west coast of the UK, where a tall fen, short fen and former improved pasture were subjected to management interventions, including burning, hand-cutting and excavation. The upscaling of chamber measurements to annual budgets found the tall fen acted as a net sink of C throughout the study period, whilst the short fen acted as a net source of C following intervention. The opposing response in GHG fluxes from the tall and short fen following intervention has implications for the management of degraded fens and highlights the importance of taking into consideration initial conditions in restoration decisions.

***Keywords**: peatland, restoration, greenhouse gas flux*

INTRODUCTION

Natural peatlands act a net sink of atmospheric carbon and long term C store due to the imbalance of ecosystem respiration (R_{ECO}) and gross primary productivity (GPP). Globally, peatlands contain a third of the terrestrial C store, whilst covering only 3% of the Earth's surface (Gorham, 1991). Past management of peatlands, predominately involving drainage for agriculture and extraction, has led to substantial net losses of stored C. The drainage of peatlands affects the hydrological function of the soil, increasing aeration and thus favouring higher ecosystem respiration rates which (provided they are not accompanied by a larger increase in gross primary productivity) lead to net CO_2 emissions. In contrast, drained peatlands are associated with lower CH_4 emissions due to the increased opportunity for methane oxidation within the aerobic layer of the soil. In order to reduce emissions, degraded peatlands are increasingly being targeted for restoration, with the aim of restoring their original C sink potential as well as achieving favourable nature conservation status (Lunt *et al.*, 2010). The restoration of peatlands can also provide other benefits such as increased biodiversity, as well as emission reductions being included in national GHG reporting to meet targets to the UN Framework Convention on climate change (IPCC, 2013). Within the UK, studies of restoration effects on GHG fluxes have predominately focused on upland blanket bogs, with little focus on lowland fen peatlands. The aim of this study is to investigate the effects of restoration interventions, namely burning, hand-cutting and excavation, on the CO_2 and CH_4 fluxes across a UK lowland fen.

METHODS

The study area is located within the Anglesey Fens Special Area of Conservation, on the west coast of the UK (53°31' N, 4°29' W) and experiences a temperate maritime climate. The study site, Cors Erddreiniog is a partially degraded lowland fen covering an area of 289 ha, and comprises of a tall fen, a short fen and an excavated area of former improved pasture, hereafter referred to as 'restored pasture'. The site underwent a series of restoration interventions as part of the Anglesey and Llyn Fens LIFE project (LIFE07 NAT/UK/000948) in 2012 which aimed to restore favourable or recovering conditions through burning, hand-cutting and excavation. A total of 12 measurement plots were established across Cors Erddreiniog encompassing the tall and short fen, restored pasture and the different interventions applied (Table 1): at both the tall and short fen, some areas underwent burning and hand-cutting, whilst some areas remained as unmanaged controls. At the restored pasture where the nutrient enriched topsoil associated with the former pasture land was removed in 2012, bare soil and recolonising plots were identified, together with a grassland control plot which did not undergo excavation.

Table 1. Site description

Measurement plot	Dominant vegetation (no. collars)	pH	Electrical conductivity ($\mu S\ cm^{-1}$)	Organic matter (%)	Mean water table depth (mm)
Tall fen - control	*Cladium mariscus* (3)	5.94	81	69.9	-80
	Phragmites australis (3)	5.73	83	70.6	-60
Tall fen – burnt	*Phragmites* (4)	5.65	92	84.6	64
Tall fen – hand cut	Grassland (4)	5.92	118	83.0	-39
Short fen – control	*Sphagnum* hummock (3)	6.67	73	89.7	-102
	Brown moss hollow (3)	6.77	142	84.1	10
	Juncus species (3)	6.75	142	90.5	-47
Short fen – burnt	*Phragmites australis* (4)	6.76	218	75.6	-83
Short fen – hand cut	Grassland (4)	6.70	126	74.0	-61
Restored pasture – grassland	Grassland (3)	7.45	148	35.6	-97
Restored pasture – recolonising	Short sedges e.g. Black-bog rush (3)	7.36	184	64.5	1
Restored pasture – bare soil	Bare soil (3)	7.30	318	31.5	-115

CO_2 and CH_4 flux measurements were carried out approximately every 4 weeks from March 2014 – March 2015 using a static chamber approach and portable field gas analyser (Los Gatos UPGGA). In addition to GHG flux measurements, environmental variables were measured simultaneously including soil temperature, photosynthetically active radiation (PAR), water table depth (WTD) and air pressure. GHG fluxes were calculated based on the change in gas concentration in the chamber headspace over time. Here, the atmospheric sign convention is followed: the uptake of C from the atmosphere to the ecosystem is defined as negative fluxes, whilst fluxes of C from the ecosystem to the atmosphere are defined as positive fluxes.

Annual flux estimates of R_{ECO}, GPP and CH_4 were initially calculated for each collar using the entire 12 month dataset, however this gave a high sensitivity to outliers and consequently data was pooled by vegetation group to produce more robust models. GPP was modelled using a Michaelis-Menten relationship with PAR, with the addition of 10cm soil temperature as an explanatory variable which improved the model fit. R_{ECO} was modelled using the Arrhenius type model by Lloyd and Taylor (1994) using 10cm soil temperature as the single explanatory variable. Annual methane fluxes were modelled using multiple linear regression using 10cm soil temperature, PAR and WTD. Annual flux estimates were converted to CO_2-equivalents using the 100 year global warming potential (GWP) of 25 for methane, according to Forster *et al.* (2007).

The differences between measured CO_2 and CH_4 fluxes from measurement plots were identified using the Kruskal-Wallis test, whilst the correlations between C fluxes and environmental variables were determined using Kendall Tau statistic. All data processing and analysis was carried out using the statistical programme R (R Development Core Team, 2009).

RESULTS

CO_2 fluxes

CO_2 fluxes were significantly correlated with temperature at all measurement plots, with a greater net sink of CO_2 observed at higher temperatures. Lower water table levels were correlated with a greater net sink of CO_2 at all plots within the short and tall fen ($p < 0.05$), however only the intervention plots at the restored pasture demonstrated this relationship. An increase in PAR was associated with a greater net sink of CO_2 at all plots, except for tall fen-burnt intervention plot ($p < 0.05$). R_{ECO} and GPP showed a clear seasonal pattern during the study period, with the greatest fluxes occurring between May and September.

Within the tall fen, the control and intervention plots all acted as net sinks of CO_2 throughout the study period, with the *Cladium* dominated collars (tall fen-control) acting as the greatest net sink (figure 1). The short fen-control plot acted as a net sink of CO_2, however the short fen-intervention plots both acted as a net CO_2 source. Within the tall and short fen, no significant differences were observed in measured NEE fluxes between the control and intervention plots as a whole. At the vegetation level, the *Cladium* dominated collars (tall fen-control) acted as a greater net sink of CO_2 compared to tall fen-hand cut plot ($p < 0.05$). Ecosystem respiration was higher in the short fen-hand cut plot compared to the short fen-control plot ($p < 0.05$), with further investigation at the vegetation level showing differences arose between the *Juncus* collars ($p < 0.05$) and brown moss collars ($p < 0.01$) with the hand-cut plot.

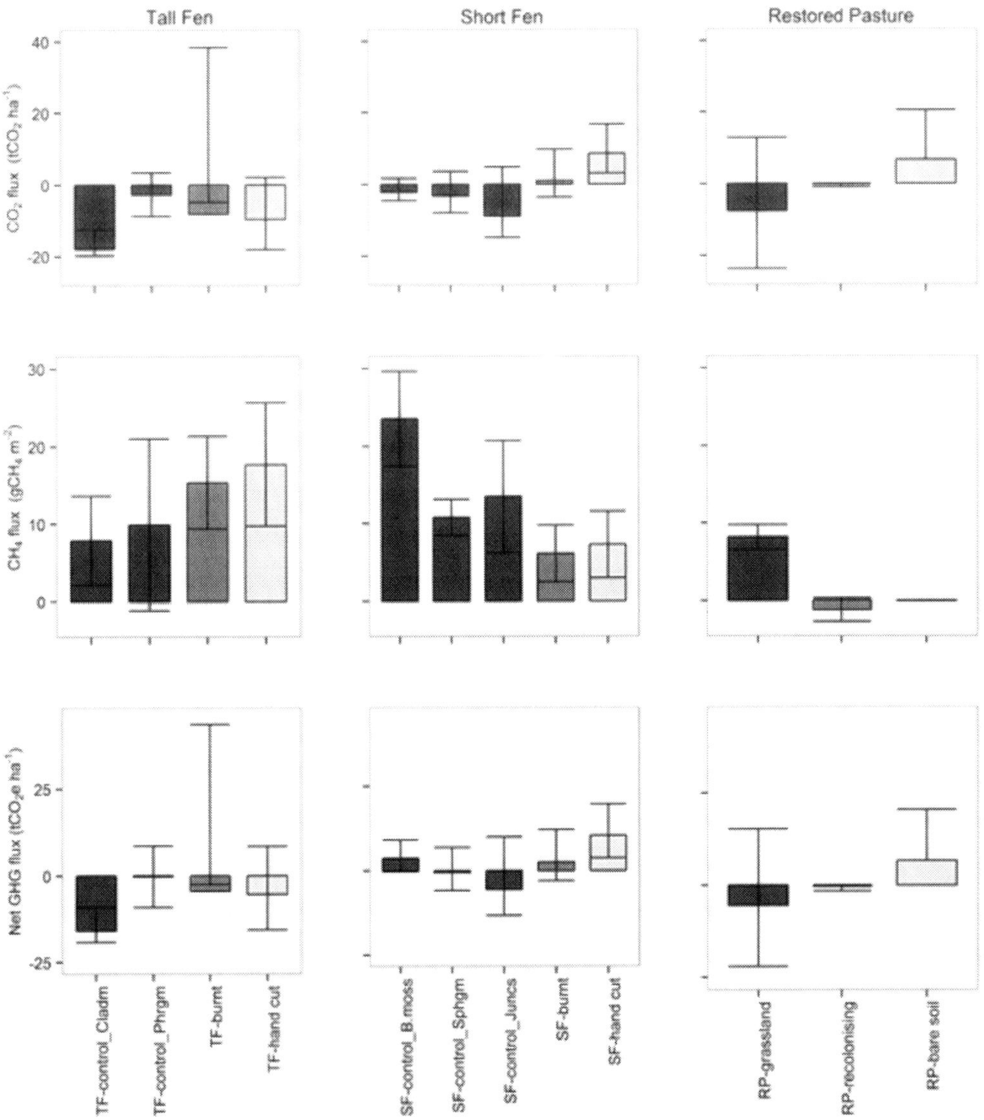

Figure 1. Top row: Annual net ecosystem exchange; Middle row: annual methane fluxes; Bottom row: annual net GHG flux (in CO_2-equivalents), for the vegetation groups at measurement plots.

Within the restored pasture, the bare soil plot acted as a net source of CO_2, whereas the control and recolonising plots were CO_2 sinks, though the latter was negligible. The restored pasture-control plot acted as a significantly greater CO_2 sink compared to the restored pasture intervention plots ($p < 0.01$).

CH_4 fluxes

At all measurement plots higher methane fluxes were observed at higher temperatures ($p < 0.05$), as found with CO_2 fluxes. Methane emissions were only significantly correlated with water table depth at the short fen plots, and within the tall fen control plot, where higher CH_4 emissions were associated with a water table closer to the surface. Methane fluxes had a similar but less pronounced seasonal pattern to CO_2 fluxes, with the greatest CH_4 fluxes from April to September.

All plots acted as a net source of CH_4 throughout the study period, with the highest fluxes originating from the short fen control and tall fen intervention plots (figure 1). Within the tall fen and the short fen, no significant differences were observed between the control and intervention plots, however when considered at the vegetation level tall fen-burnt had higher CH_4 fluxes compared to *Cladium* collars at tall fen-control ($p < 0.01$).

Methane fluxes were higher from the restored pasture control plot compared to the restored pasture intervention plots ($p < 0.01$), with no difference observed between the bare soil and the recolonising plots.

Net GHG flux (in CO_2-equivalents)

The tall fen control and intervention plots both had a negative net GHG flux (i.e. a net cooling effect). Overall, the short fen-control plot also had a negative GHG flux, however the brown moss collars had a positive GHG flux (i.e. net warming effect) driven by high CH_4 emissions, along with both short fen intervention plots. The restored pasture control plot had a net cooling effect, with the restored pasture recolonising having a negligible GHG flux and the restored pasture bare soil having a net warming effect.

DISCUSSION

Model Performance

Model performance was rated using the thresholds outlined by Hoffman *et al.* (2015) including; mean absolute error, coefficient of determination (r^2), percent BIAS and Nash-Sutcliffs model efficiency, with all models achieving at least a satisfactory fit of modelled v. measured fluxes. The only threshold to not meet this satisfactory criteria was the RSR (RMSE-observations standard deviation ratio) for modelling R_{ECO} at the restored pasture bare soil, however no other model provided an improved fit so the Lloyd and Taylor model was used. A common limitation of modelling annual fluxes from chamber measurements is the bias towards daytime measurements, which leads to not measuring at the full temperature and PAR range. In this study, all flux measurements were carried out between 10:00 – 16:00 and consequently modelling could have benefitted from diurnal campaigns to capture conditions outside of these hours, or using partial shading of chambers to create a range of PAR conditions (e.g. Elsgaard *et al.*, 2012). However, the logistical demands of measuring GHG fluxes using chamber based approaches meant it was not possible to intensify measurements.

GHG fluxes

The lack of studies on GHG fluxes from semi-natural lowland peatlands means there are few values in the literature to compare this study to. Studies on GHG fluxes from permanent grassland on peat soils in Europe predominantly show a net loss of C, with extensively managed grasslands having an annual NEE of -0.9 (0.70) tC ha^{-1} (Renou-Wilson *et al.*, 2014) to 6 (3.8) tC ha^{-1} (Görres *et al.*, 2014), a range also found by Elsgaard *et al.* (2012) across permanent grasslands in Denmark (-1.5 tC ha^{-1} a^{-1} to 10.9 tC ha^{-1} a^{-1}). In terms of vegetation at Cors Erddreiniog, the hand cut intervention plots are most similar to the extensively managed grasslands from the literature, with short fen-hand cut NEE values falling within the range above, and the tall fen-hand cut plot acting as a marginally greater CO_2 sink (-2.67 tC ha^{-1} a^{-1}). CO_2 and CH_4 fluxes have been measured at a rewetted fen in NE Germany for *Phragmites* dominated stands, with NEE values ranging from -2.25 to 1.64 tC ha^{-1} a^{-1} and CH_4 fluxes of 1 to 23 gCH_4 m^{-2} a^{-1} over the two years of the study (Günther *et al.*, 2013 and Günther *et al.*, 2015). The annual NEE and CH_4 fluxes from *Phragmites* dominated collars in this study fall within the ranges reported by Günther *et al.* (2013; 2015), except for the NEE from the tall fen-burnt plot which acts as a marginally greater CO_2 sink (-3.05 tC ha^{-1} a^{-1}). Generally the difference in GHG fluxes between the tall and the short fen appear to be linked to productivity, with the tall fen accumulating more biomass over the year, and therefore acting as a stronger C sink compared to the short fen.

Intervention effect

The net radiative effect across the restored pasture varies from a net cooling effect from the control plot, to neutral (recolonising plot) to a net warming effect from the bare soil. Following topsoil removal, the bare soil acts as a net source of C as no photosynthesis can occur, however as vegetation establishes and primary productivity begins to dominate, net sequestration occurs. The vegetation in the recolonising plots has been developing for approximately 2 years before measurements commenced and this study suggests the net source of C following excavation may be short lived if the bare soil is able to recolonise, either naturally or from an imported seed bank. Further research would be required to account for inter-annual variability of fluxes and to assess the magnitude of fluxes once the vegetation is fully established. Measurements before, during and after excavation would also be desirable to identify when the recolonising plots switched from a net source to net sink, and into the future to quantify long term effects on GHG fluxes. Further to this, quantification of the topsoil removed would enable the exported C to be accounted for and a net ecosystem carbon balance to be produced.

The differences in net radiative effect between the tall fen and short fen control plots are predominately vegetation driven, with the *Cladium* collars in the tall fen-control having significantly greater ecosystem respiration and productivity compared to the brown mosses and *Juncus* collars of the short fen-control ($p < 0.01$). Within the tall fen and short fen, the same pattern emerges with the net GHG emissions (in CO_2 equivalents) becoming increasingly positive from control to burnt to hand-cut plots, although the range in net GHG emissions at the site level within the tall fen is small (-8.13, -7.36, -5.34 t CO_2e ha^{-1} respectively). At the short fen, the increase in net GHG emissions observed could be explained by the difference in ecosystem respiration, with the short fen-hand cut plot having significantly greater R_{ECO} compared to the brown moss and *Juncus* collars of short fen-control ($p < 0.05$) and the short fen-burnt plot having greater R_{ECO} compared to the brown moss collars ($p < 0.05$).

CONCLUSION

This study produces annual CO_2 and CH_4 flux estimates for a partially degraded UK lowland peatland which has undergone a range of interventions including hand-cutting, burning and excavation. This study suggests that following restoration through topsoil removal, the C sink function can return to peatlands within a few years, provided there is the opportunity for recolonization, however further research is required to determine the magnitude of this C sink, effects of inter-annual variability and therefore long-term success. Although the differences observed in GHG fluxes between measurement plots here are predominately vegetation driven, soil conditions also play a key role in determining whether there is a net sink or release of C. This has important implications for restoration management decisions as the response of GHG fluxes following intervention can differ depending on initial conditions.

ACKNOWLEDGEMENTS

This study is financed by a studentship from the Natural Environment Research Council. We would like to thank Natural Resource Wales as site owners of Cors Erddreiniog and members of the DEFRA Lowland Peat project for their support.

REFERENCES

1. Elsgaard, L., Görres, C.-M., Hoffmann, C. C., Blicher-Mathiesen, G., Schelde, K., & Petersen, S. O. (2012). "Net ecosystem exchange of CO2 and carbon balance for eight temperate organic soils under agricultural management". *Agriculture Ecosystems & Environment*, 162, 52-67.
2. Forster P, Ramaswamy V, Artaxo P, Berntsen T, Betts R, Fahey DW, Haywood J, Lean J, Lowe DC, Myhre G: Changes in atmospheric constituents and in radiative forcing. In *Climate Change 2007: The Physical Science Basis Contribution of Working Group I to the Fourth Assessment Report of the Intergovernmental Panel on Climate Change.* Edited by Solomon S, Qin D, Manning M, Chen Z, Marquis M, Averyt K, Tignor M, HL H. Cambridge, UK and New York, USA: Cambridge University Press; 2007.
3. Gorham, E. (1991). "Northern peatlands: role in the carbon cycle and probable responses to climatic warming". *Ecological applications,* 1(2), 182-195.
4. Görres, C. M., Kutzbach, L., & Elsgaard, L. (2014). "Comparative modeling of annual CO2 flux of temperate peat soils under permanent grassland management". *Agriculture Ecosystems & Environment*, 186, 64-76.
5. Günther, A., Huth, V., Jurasinski, G., & Glatzel, S. (2015). "The effect of biomass harvesting on greenhouse gas emissions from a rewetted temperate fen". [Article]. *GCB Bioenergy*, 7(5), 1092-1106.
6. Günther, A. B., Huth, V., Jurasinski, G., & Glatzel, S. (2013). "Scale-dependent temporal variation in determining the methane balance of a temperate fen". *Greenhouse Gas Measurement and Management*, 1-8.
7. Hoffmann, M., Jurisch, N., Borraz, E. A., Hagemann, U., Droesler, M., Sommer, M., & Augustin, J. (2015). "Automated modeling of ecosystem CO2 fluxes based on periodic closed chamber measurements: A standardized conceptual and practical approach". *Agricultural and Forest Meteorology*, 200, 30-45.
8. IPCC, 2013: Climate Change 2013: The Physical Science Basis. Contribution of Working Group I to the Fifth Assessment Report of the Intergovernmental Panel on Climate Change [Stocker, T.F., D. Qin, G.-K. Plattner, M. Tignor, S.K. Allen, J. Boschung, A. Nauels, Y. Xia, V. Bex and P.M. Midgley (eds.)]. Cambridge University Press, Cambridge, United Kingdom and New York, NY, USA, 1535 pp.
9. Lunt, P., Allot, T., Anderson, P., Buckler, M., Coupar, A., Jones, P., Labadz, J., Worrall, P., & Evans, M. (2010). "Impacts of peatland restoration". *Draft Scientific Review for the IUCN UK Peatland Programme's Commission of Inquiry into Peatland Restoration*
10. R Development Core Team: R version 2.9. 2. Vienna, Austria: R Project for Statistical Computing; 2009.

Renou-Wilson, F., Barry, C., Mueller, C., & Wilson, D. (2014). "The impacts of drainage, nutrient status and management practice on the full carbon balance of grasslands on organic soils in a maritime temperate zone". *Biogeosciences*, 11(16), 4361-4379.

Abstract No: A-092

MODELLING THE IMPACT OF MARGINAL CUTTING ON RAISED BOG TOPOGRAPHY AND CONSERVATION

Alister Best[1, 2] and Raymond Flynn[1]

[1] *School of Planning, Architecture and Civil Engineering, The Queen's University of Belfast, David Keir Building, Stranmillis Road, Belfast BT9 5AG.*
[2] *RPS Group, Elmwood House, 74 Boucher Road, Belfast BT12 6RZ.*

**Corresponding author: abest04@qub.ac.uk*

SUMMARY

Irish peatland conservation programmes need to be implemented sustainably and in accordance with the law. Any approach needs to consider not only legal and technical issues, but also the social and financial elements of conservation and restoration strategies. Article 6.3 of the EU Habitats Directive provides a mechanism allowing on-going human activity within Natura 2000 areas, protecting priority habitats, provided these do not conflict with site conservation objectives (COs). Allowing continued localised peat cutting on SACs, containing active raised bog and degraded raised bog, requires a robust site characterisation strategy to predict changes in hydrological supporting conditions and their impact on site-specific COs. Profiling peat properties across uncut peatlands, when coupled with geotechnical and hydrogeological first principles, provides information necessary for predicting impacts of continued localised marginal turf cutting on raised bog topography and on the hydrological conditions needed to support active raised bog. Use of these data subsidence simulations, employing principles of conservation of organic and inorganic matter, combined with equations of groundwater flow and outputs from ground penetrating radar, permit bog profiles to be modelled, while taking natural subsurface variability into account. Application of this model to Clara Bog, Co. Offaly has simulated changes in bog topography, including the recent development of areas of standing water, while also generating changes in peat properties arising from turf cutting and marginal drainage. On-going field data collection and application of the approach will demonstrate its value for predicting impacts of localised cutting and drainage on raised bog hydrological supporting conditions and the confidence with which it may be applied for determining site suitability for continued cutting. Successful application has the potential to identify suitable sites for continued cutting and help address needs of local stakeholders, while also meeting Habitats Directive requirements

Keywords: *peatlands, modelling, subsidence, conservation*

INTRODUCTION

Western European peatlands have experienced significant ecological impacts over the past 100 years due to pressure from a growing population and an increasing demand for resources in the shape of farmland, fuel and horticulture, forestry and wind farm development (Joosten & Clarke 2002).

In Ireland the utilization of peatlands for human resource requirements has resulted in a dramatic loss of once widespread peatlands. For the example of raised bogs, once covering over 300,000 ha of Ireland, only 16% remain uncut, of which only 0.4% (1210 ha) of the original area is active (peat accumulating) raised bog (ARB) (Ryan 2007 & National Raised Bog SAC Management Plan 2014). These Irish sites, containing ARB, represent some of the last remnants of this habitat in the Atlantic region of the EU.

Recent research indicates that peatlands may play an important role in areas such as climate change, flood management, as well as acting as areas of special interest for flora and fauna (Schouten 2002). As remaining Irish bogs are sites of European and international importance (National Raised Bog SAC Management Plan 2014) there have been increased efforts to protect these peatlands over the last 20 years. As a consequence ARB, defined as the living, actively peat accumulating upper layer of a bog, has been identified as a priority Annex I habitat within the EU Habitats Directive (1992). Degraded Raised Bog (DRB), which is bog habitat no longer actively peat accumulating but is still capable of natural regeneration following restoration measures, is also protected. Across Ireland a network of special areas of conservation (SACs), now aim to conserve ARB and DRB (Habitats directive 1992 & National Raised Bog SAC Management Plan 2014).

Legislation protecting bog sites can generate wider social impacts. In Ireland the conservation of these habitats often causes discord with stakeholders whose turbary rights (rights to harvest peat for fuel) are affected, especially where alternative relocation peat cutting sites are not available. This can place peat cutters at odds with legislators wishing to implement site specific conservation objectives (SCCOs) for SACs. The EU Habitats Directive provides legislation to resolve this issue through Article 6(3), which provides a mechanism allowing on-going human activity within protected (Natura 2000) areas, containing priority habitats, provided these do not impact on SSCOs.

Allowing continued localised peat cutting on sites, containing active and degraded raised bog, requires an appropriate assessment of the potential risks to these priority habitats. A robust site characterisation strategy is thus required to predict changes in hydrological supporting conditions and their impact on SSCOs. However, the hydrological and geotechnical properties of peatlands can be affected by drainage thereby complicating prediction of anticipated impacts to raised bog ecohydrology. The process is further hindered by a lack of understanding on how changes in peat properties impact the conservation status of protected sites.

This paper summarises work undertaken to evaluate the impact of marginal cutting and drainage on peat properties, using a combination of geophysical, geotechnical and hydrological investigation techniques.

THEORY

Previous research has aimed to model restoration potential in Irish raised bogs using hydrological and topographical data by employing point measurements, set out on a 100mx100m grid, to determine slope and flow path length as indicators of restorability (van der Schaaf 2002). LiDAR survey data provides higher resolution topographic data and can be used to refine existing models to more accurately predict restoration potential (National Raised Bog SAC Management Plan 2014, Mackin *et al.*, 2015). This approach thus permits estimation of the amount of active raised bog that could be restored (DRB). The approach has proven to work well in selected Irish raised bogs, which typically require a surface slope of between 0.2% and 0.6% for peat accumulating habitats to survive.

Kool *et al.* (2006) suggest that subsidence of peatlands is not necessarily detrimental to carbon storage. If the water table remains high during subsidence the peat can continue to accumulate under anaerobic conditions and carbon will not be lost to the atmosphere through oxidation. Evidence of this mechanism can be seen in subsidence hollows on raised bogs across Ireland, such as that shown in Figure 5 on Clara Bog, Co. Offaly. Although subsidence hollows can be regarded as potentially large and very healthy areas of a bog, they can also reflect/indicate the impact of drainage causing more widespread ecological problems. If subsidence can occur without significant loss of carbon, as indicated by Kool *et al.* (2006), organic matter content can be considered constant during subsidence and thus provide a tool to assess impacts of drainage on raised bog topography and ecohydrology. This constancy is described as the principal of Conservation of Organic Matter and may be expressed mathematically as follows:

Organic Matter % x Peat Depth (at location A) = Organic Matter % x Peat Depth (at location B)

Using this principle, mathematical models may be generated to predict impacts of peat subsidence on organic matter content due to drainage.

METHODS

Moneybeg Bog (Moneybeg) forms part of the Moneybeg Clareisland Bogs SAC that contains areas of ARB and DRB. Although extensive areas of Moneybeg have been impacted by subsidence due to marginal cutting, it also has areas proposed for consideration under Article 6(3) of the Habitats Directive thus required a thorough assessment of the impacts of proposed cutting on Annex I habitats. Investigations headed up by RPS consulting engineers on behalf of National Parks & Wildlife Service (NPWS) have included:

- A desk study, collating earlier reports and remote sensing data, provided a detailed overview of the condition of the site. Evaluation of groundwater vulnerability, subsoil, bedrock, ecotopes, existing drains and surface drainage flow paths provided an understanding of the regional hydrological and hydrogeological setting of the bog.
- An initial site investigation verified the information provided by remote sensing, while a hydrochemical survey of the drainage network surrounding the bog was completed.
- Existing geological maps provided no indication of peat thickness or substrate. Reconnaissance coring at 15 locations (2 at Clareisland and 13 at Moneybeg) provided an initial indication of spatial variation in peat thickness and substrate composition.
- Further focused coring was performed at 62 locations in six zones, five of which broadly corresponded to areas where continued peat cutting was proposed. Continuous samples were collected for the entire peat depth profile at each coring location using a 50mm diameter stainless steel Russian auger. The final depth

of peat was noted and, when possible, the substrate recovered and described. A total 1505 samples were analysed for water content. The coring locations on Moneybeg Bog are indicated in Figure 1.

- Ground penetrating radar (GPR) surveying was carried out along elected lines, broadly corresponding to coring transects, by Minerex Environmental Ltd., providing high resolution peat depth data across the entire relocation area and its immediate surroundings.

Following the collection of peat samples, the following analyses were carried out by Southern Scientific Services Ltd.:

- Dry matter analysis was carried out on the 1505 samples collected from Moneybeg Clareisland SAC. This has allowed the creation of 54 organic matter borehole profiles.
- 156 of the samples were also analysed for loss on ignition (LOI).

RESULTS

A 2D model has been produced to predict subsidence due to cutting, by combining principles of conservation of organic matter with peat thickness data. The relationship of intact organic matter profiles to those impacted by subsidence was combined with thicknesses of uncut peat to quantify subsidence at Moneybeg. This in turn has been used to predict changes in topography, linked to further cutting, by application of an equivalent trend in organic matter content over the full peat thickness, extending into uncut peat from the proposed cutting face. Sample organic matter profiles are displayed in Figure 2. The model was used to simulate 30m of cutting into Moneybeg Bog along the transect shown in Figure 3, the predicted subsided topographic profile output is shown in Figure 4. When the model is calibrated to the conditions present at Clara Bog Co. Offaly it can successfully predict the presence of subsidence hollows indicated at the site by large areas of standing water which have been expanding in recent years, Figure 5.

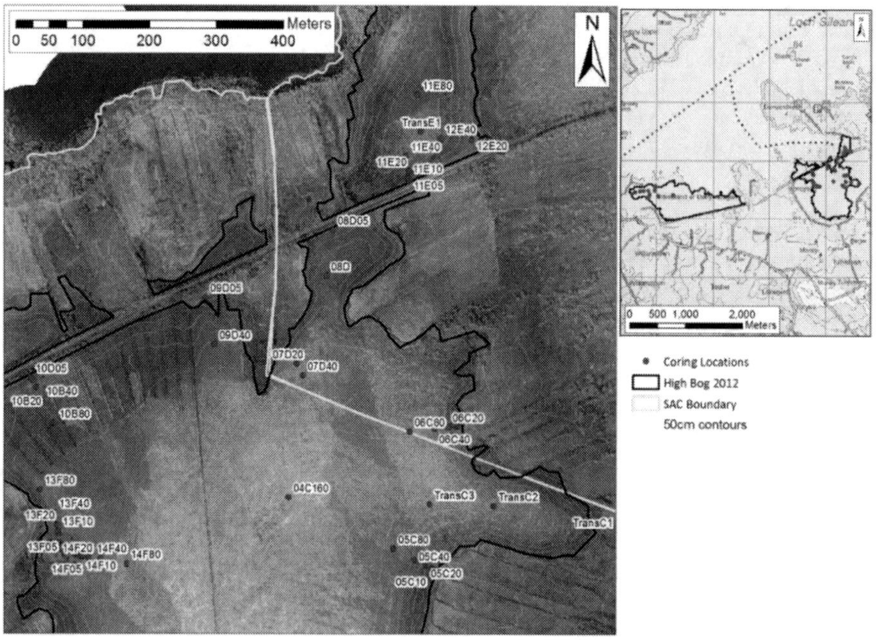

Figure 1: Map of Moneybeg Bog showing locations cored.

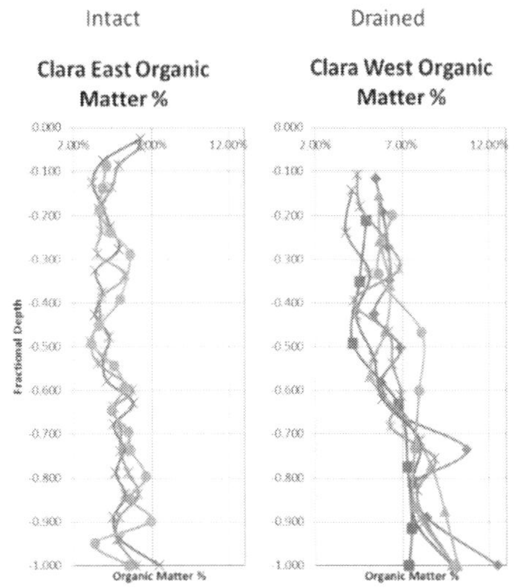

Figure 2: Organic matter profiles for intact and subsided bog.

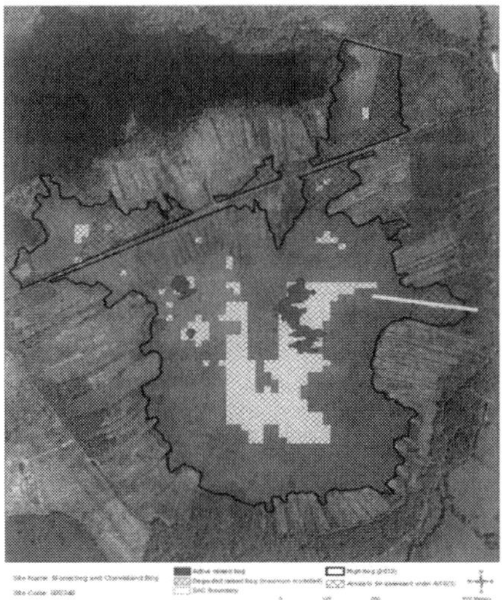

Figure 3: Moneybeg Bog, showing Annexed Habitats (Green), Article 6(3) areas (Red) and Transect modelled for 30m of cutting (Yellow).

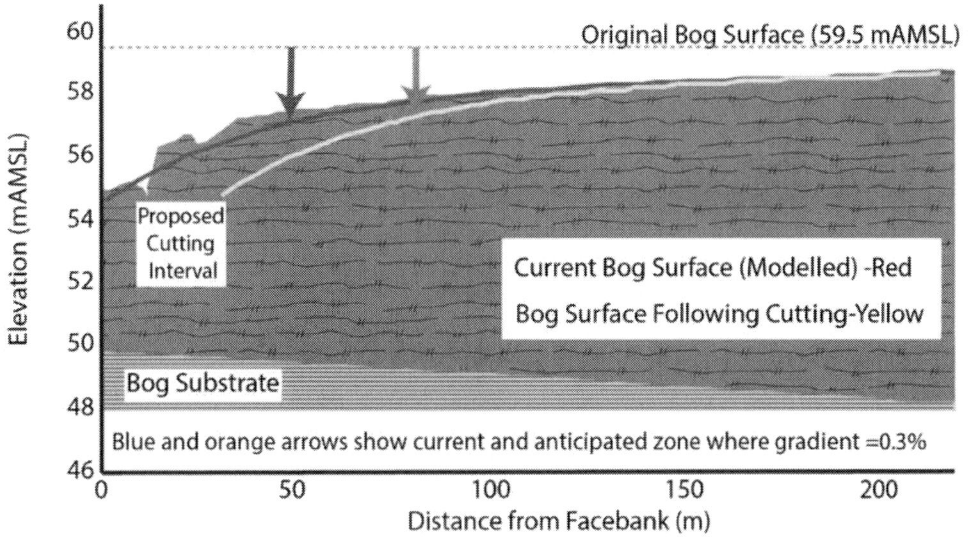

Figure 4: Model output showing predicted subsidence profile following simulated 30m of cutting into Moneybeg Bog along the transect shown in Figure 3.

Figure 5: A subsidence hollow on Clara Bog, Co. Offaly

DISCUSSION

Using the principal of Conservation of Organic Matter a 2D mathematical model has been generated to quantify peat subsidence caused by marginal cutting and hence predict the impact on the conservation status of the bog.

Survey data including Organic Matter % profiles and peat depths taken at Moneybeg has been used to predict changes in topography, potentially caused if further cutting takes place. Calibration of the subsidence model to known features at Clara Bog, Co. Offaly, has permitted simulation of changes in bog topography, including the recent development of areas of standing water, while also generating changes in peat properties arising from turf cutting and marginal drainage. Successful application has the potential to identify suitable sites for continued cutting and help address needs of local stakeholders, while also meeting Habitats Directive requirements.

Currently the model is limited in its applications since it can only predict the final subsided profile of a bog and cannot give a timeframe for its occurrence.

Further development of the current model will create a 3D tool capable of predicting subsidence due to alterations in drainage of the bog. This will be achieved through;

- Adapting the model to accommodate variability in peat properties & structure,
- Development of a discretised model for higher resolution outputs,
- Refinement of empirical approach accounting for recharge in the system and flow rates through the peat,
- Introduction of permeable / semi-permeable substrates,
- Incorporating the effects of drains at varying depths, including increased under drainage from the bog, and
- Development of a time domain feature within the model to predict levels of subsidence at a given time after cutting.

REFERENCES

1. Habitats Directive (1992) 92/43/EEC the conservation of natural habitats and of wild fauna and flora, OJ L 206, 22.7.1992, p. 7–50
2. Joosten, H., & Clarke, D. (2002). *Wise use of mires and peatlands*. International mire conservation group.
3. Kool D. M. et al (2006). *Oxidation and compaction of a collapsed peat dome in Central Kalimantan*. Geoderma 137 (2006) 217–225
4. Mackin F. et al (2015). *The Role of Hydrology in Restoring Ireland's Raised Bogs: A Review of a Nationwide Study. National Hydrology Conference 2015*
5. National Raised Bog SAC Management Plan (2014) Management plan draft for consultation, Department of the Arts, Heritage and the Gaeltacht.
6. Ryan J (2007) Raised Bog Restoration in Ireland, National Parks and Wildlife Service Department of Environment, Heritage and Local Government
7. Schouten, M.G.C., Ryan, J.B., Streefkerk, J.C. (2002). *Introduction, pp 6-9. In: M.G.C. Schouten (ed.). Conservation and Restoration of Raised Bogs. Geological, hydrological and ecological studies. Dublin. Dúchas – The Heritage Service of the Department of the Environment and Local Government, Ireland; Staatsbosbeheer, The Netherlands; Geological Survey of Ireland.*
8. Van der Schaaf, S., (2002). *Bog Hydrology, pp 54-109. In: M.G.C. Schouten (ed.). Conservation and Restoration of Raised Bogs. Geological, hydrological and ecological studies. Dublin. Dúchas – The Heritage Service of the Department of the Environment and Local Government, Ireland; Staatsbosbeheer, The Netherlands; Geological Survey of Ireland.*

Abstract No: A-291

MONITORING THE EFFECTS OF PEATLAND RESTORATION IN INDONESIA USING INSAR TIME SERIES ANALYSIS

Zhiwei Zhou[1,2], Zhenhong Li[3], Susan Waldron[2*] and Akiko Tanaka[4]

[1]*GNSS Research Center, Wuhan University, Wuhan, 430079, China*
[2]*School of Geographical and Earth Sciences, University of Glasgow, Glasgow G12 8QQ, United Kingdom*
[3]*COMET, School of Civil Engineering and Geosciences, Newcastle University, Newcastle Upon Tyne, NE1 7RU, United Kingdom*
[4]*Geological Survey of Japan, AIST, Tsukuba, Japan*

**Corresponding author: Susan.Waldron@glasgow.ac.uk*

In this study, satellite radar observations are employed to reveal spatiotemporal changes in surface height of peatlands that have, and have not, undergone restoration in Central Kalimantan, Indonesia. Our time series analysis with 26 scenes of L-band ALOS PALSAR images acquired between 2006 and 2010, suggests that peatland restoration was affected by the construction time of dams – the earlier the dam was constructed, the more significant the restoration appears; the closer spaced the dams were, the more positive the outcome of restoration. The results also show that the dams resulted in an increase of ground water, which in turn stopped peat losing height. For peatland areas without restoration, the peatland continuously lost peat height by up to 7.7 cm yr^{-1}. InSAR-derived peat height changes allow the investigation of restoration effects over a wide area, and can also be used to indirectly assess the relative magnitude and spatial pattern of peatland damage caused by drainage and fires. Such as assessment can provide key information for guiding future restoration activities.

***Keywords*:-**

Abstract No: A-386

PEATLANDS AFTER-USE IN THE POLISH CARPATHIAN MOUNTAINS – GEOMORPHOLOGICAL AND HYDROGRAPHIC SYMPTOMS OF THEIR RESTORATION

Adam Łajczak

Pedagogical University, Institute of Geography, Poland

**Corresponding author: alajczak@o2.pl*

SUMMARY

Investigation of current changes in the relief and water content of raised bogs after-use is omitted in relation to wider knowledge of human impact on environmental changes of peatlands. Level of knowledge on restoration of peat bogs in mountainous regions in Poland may be considered advanced (peatlands in the Carpathians and the Sudetes). The purpose of this paper is to explain current changes in peat bogs morphology and water retention in peat deposit in the largest peatlands in the Polish Carpathians. The paper is based on an analysis of maps produced over the 20th century, on aerial photographs taken since 1965 and on the newest data (LiDAR). Fieldwork included the geomorphological and hydrographic mapping of specified landforms within peat bogs using GPS methods as well as collecting peat samples in places of various stages of peat bog restoration (depths: 50-60, 90-100, 140-150, 190-200 cm). The maximum capillary water capacity of peat at various depths was assessed in laboratory, and finally the maximum potential water storage capacity was computed for the studied peatlands. Partial peat extraction taking place in the domes has produced major changes in peat bog relief and has substantially reduced peat bog water content (10-95% in individual peat domes) during 200 years economical use of the peat bogs. The increased density of drainage ditches in the area surrounding the remnants of peat domes has led to further drying of the peat bogs. The current stage of peat bogs development is their restoration which started in the 1950's-1990's when peat extraction had been halted in most peat bogs and drainage ditch maintenance had been abandoned. Now, stable and very shallow water level (0-40 cm) in acrotelm is the dominant feature of the peat bogs studied.

***Keywords**: raised bog, post-peat areas, peat bog after-use, peatland restoration*

INTRODUCTION

Knowledge of current changes in relief and water content of raised bogs after-use as a result of peat deposit extraction and drying is less advanced in relation to wider information concerning the human impact on environmental changes of peatlands. Publications on the human impact on peat bogs pay a lot of attention to peat erosion, peat burning and changes in the physical and chemical properties of peat deposits that indicate pollution in the environment (e.g. Cooper, McCann, 1995; Bindler 2006; Coggins *et al.*, 2006). Compared to other areas of the world, there is a good knowledge on anthropogenic changes in the relief and water content of peat bogs in some areas of Poland. This applies not only to peat bogs in lowland Poland but also in mountains in southern Poland, where peat bogs in the Carpathian Mountains and the Sudetes Mountains are also found. Level of knowledge on restoration of peat bogs in the Polish Carpathian Mountains may also be considered advanced (peatlands in the Orawa - Nowy Targ Basin and in some valley floors in the Bieszczady Mountains) (Łajczak, 2007, 2011, 2016).

The purpose of this presentation is to explain current changes in peat bogs morphology and water retention in peat deposit in the largest peatlands in the Polish Carpathian Mountains. The study on raised bog restoration is the most advanced in the Orawa - Nowy Targ peatland and in valley floors in the Bieszczady Mountains. The study which started a few years ago is focused on changes in relief and water content in anthropogenically degraded fragments of peat domes (Łajczak, 2011, 2013).

METHODS

The presentation is based on an analysis of maps produced over the last 230 years (years: 1780, 1855, 1879, 1900, 1934, 1965, 1978, 1996) as well as on aerial photographs taken in 1965, 1988 and 2006, and the newest LiDAR data. Fieldwork included the geomorphological and hydrographic mapping of specified landforms and water phenomena within peat bogs and surroundings using GPS methods and morphometric terrain data from the last 15 years. Information obtained from local water management authorities and other institutions as well as information gathered by interviewing individuals involved in peat extraction for many years were also included in this research. Peat samples were collected in places of various stages of peat bog restoration (depths: 50-60, 90-100, 140-150, 190-200 cm). The maximum capillary water capacity of peat at various depths was assessed in laboratory, and finally the maximum potential water storage capacity was computed for the studied peatlands.

RESULTS

The dominant landscape element of post-peat areas is scarps, which are created where peat extraction takes place. Scarps are initially vertical or step-type, often forming zigzag-shaped sequences. Another important landscape element is numerous hollows filled with water. Older post-peat areas, deprived of peat cover, are used for agriculture. Younger post-peat areas are more frequently drained by manmade drainage systems than older post-peat areas. Active peat extraction fields that are being intensively dried possess the most diverse and dynamic morphology. Once peat extraction ends and drying of the remaining peat deposits is discontinued, the landscape of a post-extraction peat bog is changed and the thickness of the remaining peat deposits is greatly reduced. This is how peat bogs become post-peat areas. The raised bogs of the Polish Carpathians, located in the Orawa - Nowy Targ Basin and in valley floors in the Bieszczady Mountains, were selected for detailed analysis. The direction and rate of change of landforms typical of younger post-peat areas, such as peat extraction scarps, post-extraction hollows, drainage systems including ditches and regulated stream channels, were analyzed. A special emphasis was placed on the period of time when the restoration of such areas has taken place.

The decline in the total area of peat domes in the study areas began as early as the 13th-17th centuries when settlers arrived in the region. The peat dome range decreased at the highest rate in the 19th century and the first half of the 20th century. Partial peat extraction taking place in the domes has produced major changes in peat bog relief and has substantially reduced peat bog water content (10-95% in individual peat domes) during 200 years economical use of the peat bogs. The increased density of drainage ditches in the area surrounding the remnants of peat domes has led to further drying of the peat bogs. In recent years, the peat dome range has begun to stabilize due to reduced interest in peat deposit extraction and reduced water management efforts. This has led to clearly visible revitalization of post-peat areas. At this time, remnants of peat domes occupy 37% of their original area in the Orawa – Nowy Targ Peatland. In addition, the same area is occupied by younger post-peat areas. Today the total area of peat domes in the Polish part of the Bieszczady Mountains is 27 times smaller than in the Orawa – Nowy Targ Basin. The Bieszczady peat dome range is currently 84% of its original size. The younger post-peat areas that surround them cover only 9 ha.

Peat bog reserves were established in the Bieszczady Mountains. Finally, most peat bogs were included into the Bieszczady National Park and the process of their restoration began. The peat bogs in the Orawa – Nowy Targ Basin, except only one peat dome, are not protected as nature reserves and they are not the subject of economic interest.

The most characteristic element of relief in peat bogs affected by human activity is scarps separating fragments of untouched peat domes from extraction areas and younger post-peat areas. Peat bog scarps are more readily visible in the Orawsko-Nowotarska Basin. Scarps also form in the fringe zones of water management areas, where they separate lower areas of dried peat from those saturated with water. This may also explain the origin of peat bogs scarps in the Bieszczady Mountains. In most cases, the remnants of a peat dome are encircled by one wall-type or step-type scarp. In some cases, two or more scarps can be found. Since peat extraction has been halted in the Orawsko-Nowotarska Basin, rapid changes in peat bog scarp relief can be observed. Old photographs show vertical peat walls up to 6 m high that later evolved into different types of scarps and gently sloping dome sides. The drying of peat within scarp walls leads to the formation of fractures parallel to the scarp edge, with a depth of up to 2 m. The sliding of peat packets leads to scarp recession. In addition, rainfall in the early spring causes peat packets to turn to mud and fill peat hollows at the base of the scarp. Peat hangs over an ever smaller scarp and may fall down over time. As long as a scarp remains partially free of vegetation, it continues to flatten. An old scarp that is completely covered by vegetation assumes a convex-concave shape with a gentle slope. The scarp profile becomes even gentler over time as a result of the filling of hollows in post-peat areas and an increase in the amount of base material.

Changes in relief in post-peat areas include the flattening of scarps as well as peat hollows and drainage ditches that become shallow or disappear altogether. Hollows in post-peat areas are the result of uneven peat extraction, which leads to a residual peat layer of varying thickness. In the process of peat extraction, landowners fill peat hollows with residual vegetation removed from the peat dome. In the Orawsko-Nowotarska Basin, peat hollows at the base of the scarp are quickly filled with peat mud. Drainage ditches become shallow in an analogous way at the base of scarps, upstream felled trees and beaver dams and manmade dams halting water flow away from peat bogs. Drainage ditches in peat bogs in the Bieszczady Mountains today are entirely covered by vegetation and had started to become shallow starting in the late 1980s. In the Orawsko-Nowotarska Basin, drainage ditches in the external younger post-peat zone and in older post-peat zones have not been dredged in almost 20 years. This is why they are so shallow at a number of locations and have been overgrown with vegetation.

Many streams found close to peat bogs in the two study areas as well as their tributaries draining post-peat areas have been regulated, which was designed to partially dry wetlands being used for agricultural purposes. Another reason for the stream regulation was the desire to dry peat extraction areas. In the Bieszczady Mountains the goal was to dry peat bogs completely and to turn them into pastures. More than half the length of the streams in peat bogs and adjacent areas was regulated by straightening out channels and widening them. In the Bieszczady National Park, several dozen small earth dams were recently built on streams flowing around peat bogs and in the general vicinity of six peat bogs. The resulting reservoirs play an important ecological role in addition to their traditional role as storage pools (Łajczak 2011, 2016). The reservoirs continue to function; however, they are slowly being filled by silt.

In the past the increased density of drainage ditches in the area surrounding the remnants of peat domes has led to further drying of the peat bogs. Unintended consequences of stream regulation are shallower and wider channels that evolve into braided channels with a local tendency to aggradate material. The current stage of peat bogs development is their restoration which started in the 1950`s-1990`s, when peat extraction had been halted in most peat bogs and drainage ditch maintenance had been abandoned.

CONCLUSIONS

Now, stable and very shallow water level (0-40 cm) in acrotelm is the dominant feature of the peat bogs studied. Currently, most of ditches are overgrown with vegetation and are effectively retarding the flow of water. This helps create wetlands in younger post-peat areas, which are now becoming a secondary edge zone. Peat moss takes about three years to colonize fresh peat pits filled with water. The increasing sinuosity of stream channels regulated in the past helps to make secondary edge zones wetter. Beaver dams built near peat bogs provide another means of retaining water in post-peat areas. Small manmade dams perform the same function. The increasingly wet secondary edge zone and the increasingly flat post-extraction scarp help make peat dome remnants more wet, which prevents the drying of peat and facilitates the growth of peat moss.

REFERENCES

1. Bindler R., 2006. Mires in the past – looking for the future: Geochemistry of peat and the analysis of past environmental changes, *Global and Planetary Changes* 53: 209-221.

2. Coggins A.M., Jennings S.G., Ebinghaus R., 2006. Accumulation rates of heavy metals: lead, mercury and cadmium in ombrothrophic peatlands in the west of Ireland, *Atmospheric environment* 40: 260-278.

3. Cooper A., McCann T., 1995. Machine Peat Cutting and Land Use Change on Blanket Bog in Northern Ireland, *Journal of Environmental Management* 43: 153-170.

4. Łajczak A., 2007. *Natura 2000 in Poland, Area PLH120016 The Orawa – Nowy Targ Peatland.* Publ. of Inst. of Botany, P.A.Sci., Kraków, 139 pp.

5. Łajczak A., 2011. Contemporary changes in the relief of raised bogs on the example of the Polish Carpathians, *Geographia Polonica* 84: 5-22.

6. Łajczak A., 2013 . Changes in Raised Bog Relief During the Holocene. Case Study: Polish Carpathian Mountains. [In:] M.C. Hernandez Soriano (Ed.) *Soil Processes and Current Trends in Quality Assessment*. Publ. INTECH, Rijeka, Croatia, p. 337-363.

7. Łajczak A., 2016. Peat bogs – morphology and water conditions. [In:] A. Górecki, B. Zemanek (Eds). *The Monograph of the Bieszczady National Park (Eastern Polish Carpathians)*, p. 79-90. , p. 79-90. (in print).

Abstract No: A-137

PEATLANDS ON PERMAFROST: OPTIONS FOR MANAGEMENT AND RESTORATION FROM ARCTIC TO STEPPE

Tatiana Minayeva[1,2], Andrey Sirin[1], Marcel Silvius[2], Jozef Bednar[2], Jan Peters[3], Hans Joosten[4], Irina Kamennova[5], Gennady Suvorov[1], Aleksandr Maslov[1], Maria Medvedeva[1], Anastasiya Markina[1], Dmitry Makarov[1], Natalya Valyaeva[1], Olga Tsyganova[1], Tamara Glukhova[1], Anna Vozbrannaya[1,6], John Couwenberg[4], Arina Schrier[2], Inga Gummert[4], Vladimir Panov[7], Igor Semenov[8] and Elena Lobanova[9]

[1]Institute of Forest Science Russian Academy of Sciences, Russian Federation
[2]Wetlands International, The Netherlands
[3]Michael Succow Foundation, Germany
[4]Greifswald University and Greifswald Mire Centre, Germany
[5]Wetlands International Russian Programme, Russian Federation
[6]Meschera National Park, Russian Federation
[7]Tver State Technical University, Russian Federation
[8]EthnoExpert, Latvia
[9]Agencyof System Development, Russian Federation

**Corresponding author: Tatiana.minaeva@wetlands.org*

Considerable areas of peatlands worldwide are represented by mire types whose origin and existence depend on permafrost. Currently the size of their area is underestimated. Mire ecosystems in some regions depend on permafrost as a source of water. On the other hand – the peat cover is protecting permafrost from thawing. These types of peatlands can be found in the tundra, the forest tundra and in northern taiga zones of Eurasia, in North America as well as in many highlands worldwide including semiarid and arid areas. Climate change and anthropogenic impact are equally responsible for permafrost thaw in most of the cases, accompanied by carbon loss and GHG emissions, both from degraded peat and permafrost itself. The paper presents cases from the Russian Arctic (Nenets Autonomous okrug) and Mongolia (Solongate Davaa and Orkhon valey) of dramatic changes in permafrost depth, followed by changes in mire vegetation, carbon losses and GHG emissions. Management and restoration options tested in the field or planned for implementation are described. A system of indicating the status of permafrost, organic matter content and prediction of emission factors by vascular plant species composition is developed for Arctic habitats. Also plant successions following the changes are described for the Mongolian sites mentioned above. The study is aimed to develop clear recommendations for planning, implementation, monitoring and assessment for management and restoration practices in peatlands on permafrost.

Keywords: *restoration, integrated approach, rewetting, mitigation, GHGs, boreal zone*

Abstract No: A-376

RESPONSE TO FIRE OF PLANT COMMUNITIES IN A RESTORED OMBROTOPHIC PEATLAND

Ariane Blier-Langdeau* and Line Rochefort

[1]*Université Laval, Canada*
[2]*Peatland Ecology Research Group (PERG), Canada*

**Corresponding author : ariane.blier-langdeau.1@ulaval.ca; Line.Rochefort@fsaa.ulaval.ca*

SUMMARY

Sphagnum-dominated peatland restoration aims for the return of a functioning carbon accumulating system. One aspect of the carbon dynamics in natural bogs is the passage of fires. Natural bogs are most of the time resilient to fire. The rare current assessments of the return of C sequestration function of restored peatlands show positive organic matter accumulation, it is a different story for restored bog resilience to fire. Indeed, bog restoration requires time and financial resources and a fire post-restoration might be undesirable. Accidently, a fire that occurred in a restored bog in eastern Canada proved to be an opportunity to test the resilience of the restored ecosystem. Two objectives will be presented in this presentation: 1) to determine if the aboveground biomass production and the plant cover is similar between the burned and unburned restored plant communities after one growing season post-fire and 2) to verify if vegetation recovery trajectories of the burned and unburned portions of the restored sector are similar. The first objective was answered with a biomass sampling and a vegetation survey at the beginning and the end of the first growing season following the fire. A plant community approach was used to see how each plant communities react to fire. For the second objective, vegetation surveys in burned and unburned permanent plots used for the monitoring of the restoration were done before and after the fire passage. Preliminary observations suggest that communities dominated by *Sphagnum* mosses of the subgenus *Cuspidata* lost more biomass than other communities and it appears that sections of the peat fields with a higher *Sphagnum* cover in the form of thicker cushion (thus mostly dominated by Sphagna from the *Acutifolia* subgenus) were more protected from the fire. This project is a rare chance to monitor the fire response of a restored bog after one growing season and can be regarded as a starting point for a more complex study on fire resilience of restored bogs.

Keywords: *Bog; revegetation trajectory*

INTRODUCTION

In North America, bog are restored using a Moss Layer Transfer Technique which comprises field preparation, plant reintroduction by spreading plant material coming from a donor site, applying straw mulch and fertilisation (Rochefort *et al.*, 2003). Generally, ecosystem restoration aims for the return of the ecological functions and the main characteristics of reference ecosystems. For bog restoration, general characteristics include the return of a carbon accumulating system, the return of diplotelmic hydrological layers that characterise intact peatlands and a vegetation cover dominated by *Sphagnum* and typical bog species (Rochefort, 2000). The outcomes of bog restoration for those characteristics have been assessed in term of vegetation change (Rochefort and Lode, 2006; Poulin *et al.*, 2012; Rochefort el al., 2013; Gonzalez *et al.*, 2013, 2014; Gonzalez and Rochefort, 2014); of hydrology (McCarter and Price, 2013); of Carbon accumulation and fluxes (Strack and Zuback, 2013; Andersen *et al.*, 2013b; Strack *et al.*, 2014, 2015); and of nutriments cycling (Andersen *et al.*, 2013a). Resilience to fire is also characteristic of bog ecosystems (Jasieniuk and Johnson, 1982; Kuhry, 1994; Clarkson, 1997; Benscoter, 2006; Clark *et al.*, 2015) and thus bog restoration should also aim at restoring plant communities able to return to their former pre-fire restoration trajectory after a fire. Bog restoration requires time and financial resources and a fire post-restoration might be undesirable. In the fall 2014, a fire occurred in a restored bog near Rivière-du-Loup providing a unique chance to monitoring the response to fire of the vegetation of a restored peatland. The main objective of this project is to assess the impact of fire on the vegetation of a restored bog after one growing season as the first step for a more complex study of fire resilience of a restored bog. To reach this objective, two sub objectives have been identified: the first one is to determine if the aboveground phytobiomass production and plant cover are similar between the burned and unburned plant communities after one growing season and the second one to verify if vegetation recovery trajectories of the burned and unburned portions of the restored sector are similar.

METHODS

Study site

The study site is located near the Saint-Lawrence River in South-Eastern Canada (N 47° 50' 24", W 69° 26' 42"). The study area is composed of two restored sections (14 ha) located in a large peatland complex where most of the surface area is currently under peat extraction. The two sections were restored in 2005 and 2006 with the moss layer transfer technique and monitoring performed 2, 3, 5 and 7 years after restoration showed that both sectors were similar in terms of vegetation cover and composition. In August 2014, an accidental fire occurred in the peatland complex. The fire passed through the section that was restored in 2005 yet, many patches of vegetation were left intact. The sector restored in 2006 was not burned and thus can serve as a comparison to assess the effect of fire on restored vegetation as there is very little difference in plant succession at the stage of 9 and 10 years post-restoration.

Above-ground phytobiomass and plant survey

To determine if the aboveground biomass production and vegetation cover are similar between the burned and unburned portions of the restored sectors, a plant community approach was chosen. At the beginning of the 2015 growing season, when the evidences of fire were still clearly visible by the structure of the charred vegetation, a map of the portions affected by the fire was drawn. At the same time, the location of the different plant communities (characterised by their moss and vascular plant cover) present on the field was also recorded. Five plant communities, including burned and unburned portions, were considered for this study. For each plant community, 25 sampling points were randomly located in their burned and in the unburned portions, for a total of 50 sampling points by community. At each of those sampling locations, biomass (all vegetation that have grown as a result of restoration activities down to the remnant peat) was collected in two $1m^2$ quadrats: one in the beginning of the 2015 growing season and the other one at the end of the same growing season. At each sampling point, a plant survey was also performed at the beginning and at the end of the growing season in a 65 cm diameter circular quadrat. Vegetation cover was visually estimated by plant strata and for all plant species. The end of season quadrat was positioned at the same place as the one used at the beginning of the growing season. For this presentation, these five plants communities were regrouped in two major communities presented in table 2.

Table 1: Plant cover description of the two major plant communities

Community name	Vascular Plant Cover Description	Mosses Cover Description
Cuspidata	Vascular strata: dominated by *Scirpus sps.* and *Carex sps.*	Dominated by *Cuspidata* (*Sphagnum*) sps. with presence of *Acutifolia* (*Sphagnum*)
Acutifolia	Dominated by *Eriophorum Vaginatum*	Moss layer dominated by *acutifolia* (*Sphagnum*) sps and *Polytrichum strictum*

Revegetation trajectories

To verify if vegetation recovery trajectories of the burned and unburned portions of the restored sector are similar, a temporal approach was favoured. Monitoring of the development of vegetation in the 2005 restored sector was performed 2, 3, 5 and 7 years after restoration in 5 permanent plots (25 m^2). For each plots, plant surveys were done by strata and by species in 4 quadrats of $1m^2$ for vascular plants and in 12 quadrats of 25 cm^2 for mosses. During the 2014 fire, 3 permanent plots were burned while 2 plots were spared. A plant survey was done at the beginning and the end of the 2015 growing season on the burned plots and one time at the end of the growing season for the unburned plots. That allows observation of the vegetation recovery trajectories of the plots, before and after the fire and comparison of the trajectories between the burned and the unburned plots.

Statistical analysis

The biomass and plant survey data will be analysed with a two-way ANOVA. The vegetation trajectories will be compared using regression curves. The data will be analysed using SAS Software.

PRELIMARY RESULT

Aboveground biomass and plant survey

The fire affected more the *Cuspidata* community than the *Acutifolia* community. First, the *Cuspidata* community lost more biomass (g per m^2) than the *Acutifolia* community (respectively, differences of 44% *vs* 20% between the burned and the unburned sectors as assessed by biomass measures at the beginning of the growing season) (figure 1).

Second, we can observe that the phytomass production (g per m^2 per year) of the burned portion in the first growing season after the fire is much lower in the *Cuspidata* (21g of dry mass) than in the *Acutifolia* (496g of dry mass) community. Indeed, in the Acutifolia community, the biomass collected at the end of the growing season in the burned portion is equivalent to the biomass collected at the beginning of the season in the unburned portion (figure 1). This is not the case for the *Cuspidata* communitiy. However, for the unburned parts, the annual plant production after one growing season (difference between beginning and end of the growing season) was very low for the *Cuspidata* community compare to the *Acutifolia* community (figure1). The biomass increase between the beginning and the end of the growing season for the *Acutifolia* community was of 38% and 45% for the burned and unburned portions, respectively.

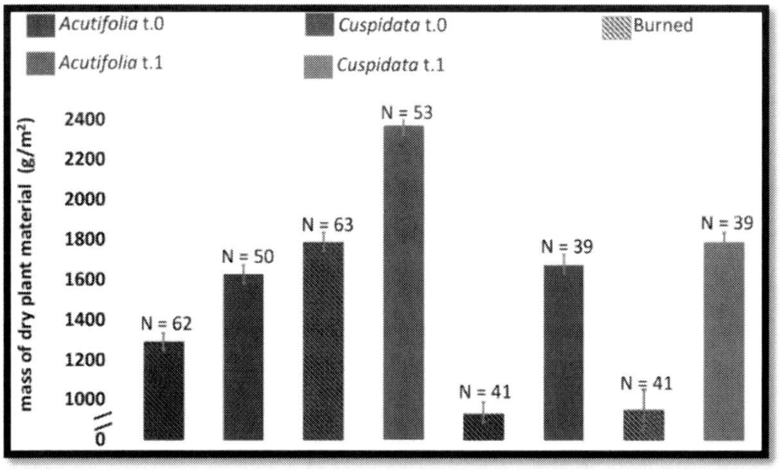

Figure 1: Burned and unburned biomass (g. ± SE of dry plant material) sorted by *Sphagnum* communities and time of collect (beginning of the growing season t.0 and end of growing season t.1).

Revegetation trajectories

The two unburned permanent plots exhibited higher *Sphagnum* cover prior to fire than the one that were burned (Figure2). It also appeared that both burned and unburned plots were affected by the 2014 fire (Figure 2).

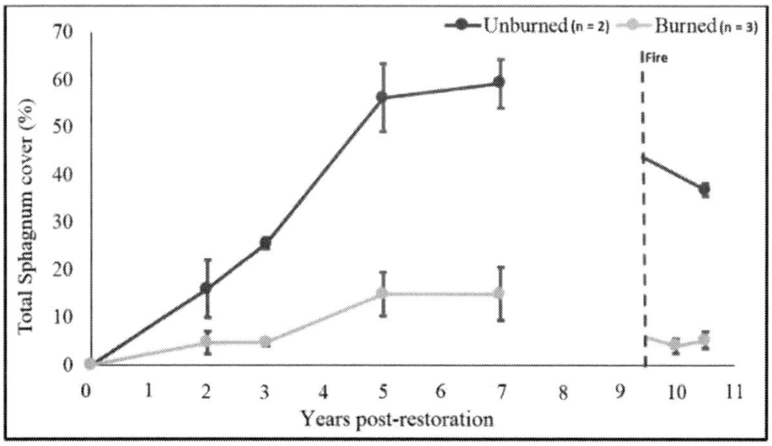

Figure 2: Total *Sphagnum* cover (% ± SE) in burned and unburned permanent plots. The red line represents the fire occurrence.

DISCUSSION

Aboveground biomass

The fire affected more seriously the *Cuspidata* community. *Cuspidata* species are usually found in biotopes composed of wet lawns, depressions and hollows whereas *Acutifolia* peat mosses are found in dryer biotopes of lawns or hummocks. *Sphagnum* hollow species are susceptible to water loss because of their loosely arranged populations (Rydin, 1993) thus they are burning more easily than hummocks species (Benscoter *et al.*, 2011) which form dense population and retain water more efficiently (Rydin, 1993). Previous studies showed that bulk density and fuel moisture influence the combustion (Frandsen 1987, 1991; Hartford1989; Van Wagner 1972; Frandsen 1997; Lawson *et al.*, 1997; Miyanishi and Johnson 2002; Reardon *et al.*, 2007) and the thermodynamics of downward combustion propagation (Benscoter *et al.*, 2011). Since *Cuspidata* species form loosely populations, they probably have a lower bulk density than *Acutifolia* species, making them less resistant to fire in period of drought when fires are most likely to occur. Moreover, Clark *et al.* (2015) present a study in which burned sites with more intact *Sphagnum* patches present a quicker vegetation recovery than the more severely burned site with few intact patches. That could explain the slower biomass recovery of the *Cuspidata* community which burned more severely and have few intact *Sphagnum* population in opposition to the *Acutifolia* community. It is possible that the vascular plants also influence the resistance to fire. *Eriophorum vaginatum* is the vascular plant dominating the *Acutifolia* community. This species forms tight tussocks giving a protection to the inner core of the plant even if the external parts of the tussocks burn.

Revegetation trajectories

All the permanent plots were installed in the same plant community (*Acutifolia* community) so the differences between the burned and the unburned plots couldn't be explained by a difference in plant communities. The total *Sphagnum* cover is more likely an influencing factor. As mentioned above, the plots with a higher *Sphagnum* cover were the ones spared by the fire. This could be explained by the soil humidity and the characteristics of the *Sphagnum* carpet which affect the fire combustion (Jonhson 1992) and propagation (Van Wagner, 1972). Further investigation is required. As for the *Sphagnum* cover drop in the unburned plots, it is hard to explain because it is impossible to know if the drop began before the fire or because of the fire, since the last plant survey was done in 2012. The fire possibly changed the soil and underground water chemical characteristics.

CONCLUSION

Production rate recovery indicates a good recovery of the burned vegetation. The moss strata was not completely nor irremediably lost and even showed promising signs of recovery during the first growing season after the fire. Moreover, the biomass production of the burned portion of the *Acutifolia* community is not so far from the one observed in the unburned portion. Even if we'll have to wait for a few more years to assess the whole vegetation response to this fire, that bodes well for the future of this restoration. With the preliminary results, it is reasonable to suggest that the resistance to fire of restored *Sphagnum* dominated communities depends on its characteristics (cover and species composition). This project is a rare chance to monitor the fire response of a restored bog after the first growing season and can be seen as a starting point for a more complex study on resilience to fire of restored bogs.

AKNOWLEDGEMENTS

Financial support was provided by the Natural Sciences and Engineering Research Council of Canada, the Canadian Sphagnum Peat Moss Association and its members. Special thanks to Premier Tech Horticulture and Les Tourbières Berger ltée for their support. Also thanks to my assistants: Marie Durand, Sébastien Meilleur and Anaël Mayeur for their great work.

REFERENCES

1. Andersen, R., Wells, C., Macrae, M., Price, J. S. 2013a. Nutrient mineralisation and microbial functional diversity in a restored bog approach natural conditions 10 years post restoration. *Soil Biology & Biochemistry* 64: 37-47
2. Andersen, R., Pouliot, R., Rochefort, L. 2013b. Above-ground net primary production from vascular plants shifts the balance towards organic matter accumulation in restored Sphagnum bogs. *Wetlands* 33: 811-821
3. Benscoter, B.W. 2006. Post-fire bryophyte establishment in a continental bog. *Journal of Vegetation Science* 17:647-652.
4. Benscoter, B. W., Thompson, D. K., Waddington, J. M., Flannigan, M. D., Wotton B. M., de Groot, W. J. and Turetsky, M. R. 2011. Interactive effects of vegetation, soil moisture and bulk density on depth of burning of thick organic soils. International Journal of Wildland Fire 20:418-429.

5. Clarke, P. J., Keith, D. A., Vincent, B. E. and Letten, A. D. 2015. Post-grazing and post-fire vegetation dynamics: long-term changes in mountain bogs reveal community resilience. *Journal of Vegetation Science* 26:278-290.
6. Clarkson, B. R. 1997. Vegetation recovery following fire in two Waikato peatlands at Whangamarino and Moanatuatua, New Zealand. *New Zealand Journal of Botany* 35:167-179.
7. Frandsen, W. 1987. The influence of moisture and mineral soil on the combustion limits of smoldering forest duff. *Canadian Journal of Forest Research* 17, 1540–1544.
8. Frandsen, W. 1991. Burning rate of smoldering peat. *Northwest Science* 65, 166–172.
9. Frandsen, W. 1997. Ignition probabilities of organic soils. *Canadian Journal of Forest Research* 27, 1471–1477
10. González, E., Rochefort, L., Boudreau, S., Hugron, S., Poulin, M. 2013. Can indicator species predict restoration outcomes early in the monitoring process? A case study with peatlands. *Ecological Indicators* 32: 232-238.
11. González, E., Rochefort, L., Boudreau, S., Poulin, M. 2014. Combining indicator species and key environmental and management factors to predict restoration success. *Ecological Indicators* 46: 156-166
12. González, E. and Rochefort, L. 2014. Drivers of success in 53 cutover bogs restored by a moss layer transfer technique. *Ecological Engineering* 68: 279-290
13. Hartford, R. 1989. Smoldering combustion limits in peat as influenced by moisture, mineral content, and organic bulk density. In '*Proceedings of the 10th Conference on Fire and Forest Meteorology*', 17–21 April 1989, Ottawa, ON. (Eds D MacIver, H Auld, R Whitewood) pp. 282–286. (Forestry Canada, Petawawa National Forestry Institute, Chalk River, ON)
14. Jasieniuk, M. A. and Johnson E. A. 1982. Peatland vegetation organization and dynamics in the western subarctic, Northwest Territories, Canada. *Canadian Journal of Botany-Revue Canadienne De Botanique*. 60: 2581-2593.
15. Johnson, E. 1992. Fire and Vegetation Dynamics: Studies from the North American Boreal Forest. Cambridge University Press: Cambridge, UK.
16. Lawson, B.D., Frandsen, W., Hawkes, B. and Dairymple, G. 1997. Probability of sustained smoldering ignition for some boreal forest duff types. Natural Resource Canada, Canadian Forest Service, Northern Forestry Centre, Forest Management Note 63. (Edmonton, AB)
17. McCarter, C. P. R., Price, J. S. 2013. The hydrology of the Bois-des-Bel bog peatland restoration: 10 years post-restoration. *Ecological Engineering* 55: 73-81
18. Miyanishi, K., Johnson, E.A. 2002. Process and patterns of duff consumption in the mixedwood boreal forest. *Canadian Journal of Forest Research* 32, 1285–1295.
19. Poulin, M., Andersen, R., Rochefort, L. 2012. A new approach for tracking vegetation change after restoration: A case study with peatlands. *Restoration Ecology*
20. Reardon, J., Hungerford, R., Ryan, K. 2007. Factors affecting sustained smouldering in organic soils from pocosin and pond pine woodland wetlands. *International Journal of Wildland Fire* 16, 107–118.
21. Rochefort, L. 2000. *Sphagnum*-A keystone genus in habitat restoration. *The Bryologist* 103:503-508.
22. Rochefort, L., Quinty, F., Campeau, S., Johnson, K. and Malterer, T. 2003. North American approach to the restoration of *Sphagnum* dominated peatlands. *Wetlands Ecology and Management* 11:3-20.
23. Rochefort, L. and Lode, E. 2006. Restoration of degraded boreal peatlands. . P. 381-423 In *Boreal peatland ecosystems*. R.K. Wieder & D.H. Vitt (ed.). *Ecological Studies*, vol. 188. Springer-Verlag, Berlin, Germany.
24. Rochefort, L., Isselin-Nondedeu, F., Boudreau, S., Poulin, M. 2013. Comparing survey methods for monitoring vegetation change through time in a restored peatland. *Wetlands Ecology and Management* 21: 71-85
25. Rydin, H. 1993. Mechanisms of interactions among *Sphagnum* species along water-level gradients. *Advances in Bryology* 5:153-185.
26. Strack, M. and Zuback, Y. 2013. Annual carbon balance of a peatland 10 yr following restoration. *Biogeosciences*, 10: 2885-2896
27. Strack, M. and Keith, A.M. 2014. Growing season carbon dioxide and methane exchange at a restored peatland on the Western Boreal Plain. *Ecological Engineering* 64: 231-239
28. Strack, M., Zuback, Y., McCarter, C. P. R., Price, J. S. 2015. Changes in dissolved organic carbon quality in soils and discharge 10 years after peatland restoration. *Journal of Hydrology* 527: 345-354.
29. Van Wagner, C.E. 1972. Duff consumption by fire in eastern pine stands. *Canadian Journal of Forest Research* 2, 34–39.

Abstract No: A-268

RESTORATION OF HIGH ALTITUDE PEATLANDS IN RUOERGAI PLATEAU, CHINA

Faizal Parish, [1*], K.L. Chen[2] and X. Zhang[2]

[1]*Global Environment Centre, 2nd Floor, Wisma Hing, No. 78, Jalan SS2/72, 47300 Petaling Jaya, Malaysia*
[2] *Wetlands International China Programme, Beijing, China*

**Corresponding author: fparish@gec.org.my*

The peatlands of the Ruoergai Plateau in Sichuan and Gansu Provinces in China cover about 350,000 ha and are the largest remaining high altitude peatlands in China. They are of critical importance for endangered species such as Black-necked Crane (*Grus nigricollis*) as well as regulating the water flow in the upper yellow River. Large-scale drainage for pasture improvement combined with overgrazing since the 1950s has degraded the ecosystem. Approximately 920 km of artificial ditches excavated from the 1960s to 1990s have degraded more than 65,000 ha. Pilot restoration measures were initiated by Wetlands International and Global Environment Centre in 2005 by blocking drainage channels to raise the landscape water levels. Levels in drains increased up to 50 cm which led to an overflow of water and rewetting of the adjacent peatlands. Drainage from a peat-mining site was also blocked to raise water levels. Pioneer vegetation including Horsetail (*Equisetum heleocharis*) and Halerpestes (*Halerpestes tricuspis*) colonised the restored sites. This initial work was scaled-up with support from Central and local governments in 2007. An increase in 20,000 ha of improved peatlands was recorded after the rewetting in 2009. The paper will report on the findings of repeat surveys of all the restoration sites to be undertaken in June 2016.

***Keywords*:-**

Abstract No: A-325

RESTORATION OF PEATLAND ECOSYSTEMS AND BIODIVERSITY IN U MINH REGION OF MEKONG DELTA, VIETNAM

Le Phat Quoi[1], Nguyen Tan Truyen[2] and Tran Van Thang[3]

[1]*Institute for Environment and Natural Resources, National University at HCM City, Vietnam.*
[2]*U Minh Ha National Park, Vietnam*

* *Corresponding author: quoilp@gmail.com*

SUMMARY

Remaining petlands distributed mainly in U Minh region of Lower Mekong Delta and they have protected as national parks: U Minh Ha and U Minh Thuong National Parks. Since 2010, an appropriate management of fires and water has applied resulted in no forest fires and ecosystems restored significantly. Some previously species of fauna and flora, which disappeared due to forest fires and inappropriate management from 2002 to 2009, were recorded their back presence in 2014. The inventory showed total 14 species of animal and 17 species of plants, which are in IUCN and Vietnam Red Books, were restored in peatland habitats. Some waterfowls (Leptoptilos javanicus, Pelecaniformes, Plegadis falcinellus) have begun choosing peatland forest and grassland habitats as breeding sites. Peatland ecosystems showed the higher density of peatland Melaleuca forests, the lower the number of plant species and vice versa, which resulted in various plant biodiversity index (H') and species evenness (J'). Average H' value of very spare to spare Melaleuca forests varied from 0.78 - 1.70, and species evenness J' = 0.49 - 0.77, while seasonally inundated grasslands ecosystems increased significantly after applying appropriate management (H'= 0.43 up to 1.93 and J' from 0.42 up to 1.0). Restoration of Peatland Melaleuca forest plays an important role in carbon storage and absorbance of carbon dioxides from the atmosphere. The corresponding estimated carbon storage and Co_2-e in Melaleuca forests are of 27.80 tons/ha and Co_2-e is of 102.04 tons.ha^{-1}. Then the total amount of carbon storage and Co_2-e of melaleuca forest estimated are 318,949.949 tons and 1,170,546.312 tons in both national parks. An appropriate management of water and fires is one of the activities has resulted in the successful restoration of ecosystems and biodiversity in peatlands of U Minh region, and UMTNP recognized as ASEAN Heritage Park (2013) and RAMSAR site in 2015.

Keywords: *Peatland, carbon dioxide, ecosystems, biodiversity, Melaleuca*

INTRODUCTION

Tropical peatlands are widely distributed throughout Indonesia, Malaysia and several other countries in South East Asia. Peat swamp forests are unique habitats for flora and fauna, containing a high proportion of endemic species (Page *et al.,* 1999). Peat swamp forests are ombrotrophic wetland ecosystems that sequester carbon into vegetation and, especially, into peat below the forest floor. The woody peat formed in these ecosystems is rich in C (about 56 % on a dry mass basis) and the peat deposits can be several meters thick over vast areas, making tropical peatlands globally important C-stores (Page *et al.,* 2011). In addition, peatlands represent globally significant stores of soil carbon that have been accumulating for millennia and currently, peatlands globally represent a major store of soil carbon sink for carbon dioxide and source of atmospheric methane (Maria S., 2008).

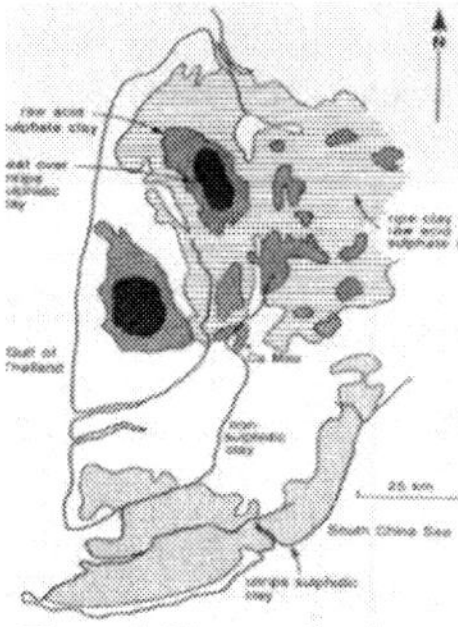

Figure 1: Two peatland areas remained in U Minh region, Lower Mekong Delta

A comparatively small area of peatlands in Vietnam compared to its regional neighbors. They were found in many parts, however mainly located in U Minh region (Fig.1) where was designed as two national parks: U Minh Ha National Park (UMHNP) and U Minh Thuong National Park (UMTNP). Inappropriate management resulted in large-scale peatland loss during past decades, estimated that more than 64,000 hectares of 1962 (VHP, 1974) down to 11,744.19 hectares of 2013 (Quoi, 2014), and ecosystems degradation of peatlands with major environmental and social impacts in U Minh region located in Ca Mau and Kien Giang Provinces.

Most of the peatlands in U Minh region were covered by Melaleuca and mixed forests, which are important natural ecosystems with high value for biodiversity conservation, climate regulation, and water supplies to communities in the dry season. The peatland complex ecosystems play a special role in maintaining biodiversity as a result of habitat isolation in U Minh region.

This paper, used data collected from APFP (2013), SEAPeat Project (2014) and SNV (2015), focuses on restoration of ecosystems and biodiversity resulted from reasonable hydrological management in peatland U Minh region, including UMHNP and UMTNP. Estimation of capable carbon storage and carbon dioxide equivalent (CO_2) absorbed from the atmosphere by forest also is discussed within.

METHODOLOGY

The multi-satellite imagery of SPOT 5 and Landsat TM7 (2006, 2009, 2010, and 2013) was used to identify the ecosystems and plant communities. The observation was conducted on a total area of 61,314.20 ha in peatland U Minh region, however, there were total 643 observed sites were done in two parks.

At each observation site, different size quadrats, of which 1 x 1m^2 and 10 x 20m^2 random quadrats for grasslands and forestlands respectively, were used to observe species occurrences, species dominant, parameters of forest trees (stem density, basal area) used to estimate the amount of carbon dioxide (CO_2) sequestration in Melaleuca forest.

Evenness of species by Peilon Method is applied, which given by J' = H/logS.

Species diversity in plant communities is calculated by biodiversity index (H') of Shannon - Weiner (1949).

$$H' = -\sum_{i=1}^{S} p_i \ln p_i$$

Dominant species is applied by Simpson's dominance index λ, which is given by

$$\lambda = \sum_{i=1}^{n} \left(\frac{ni}{n} \right)^2$$

To estimate carbon content and carbon dioxide equivalents (CO_2-e) absorption by forest, calculation was applied with following steps: average biomass, the amount of carbon stored in plant biomass per area, amount of CO_2 absorbed from the atmosphere by forest trees. The method of NIRI (Norman, 2015 after NIKI, 2001) was used to estimate carbon stored in the tree and CO_2 absorption from the atmosphere by forest.

RESULTS AND DISCUSSION

A large area of peatland was considered for satellite interpretation and the survey to record the presence of peatlands in U Minh region. Base on the result of satellite interpretation and on the ground surveys, once there was a wide distribution of peatland in U Minh region (61,314.20 ha), however, a large area of peatland was destroyed by human activities and natural factors, hence, there is the only small area of peatlands, with 9,174.37 ha, being present mainly in U Minh Ha region and UMTNP (Tab. 1). Except peatlands remained in the national parks, there is still a considerable area of peatlands in the buffer zone of UMHNP, with 2,296.57 ha, while only several small patches of peat soils were identified in that of UMTNP.

Table 1: The peatland areas in U Minh region, Lower Mekong Delta of Vietnam.

Peatland Sites	Previous peatland area (ha)	Remaining Peatland (ha)
U Minh Ha region (Ca Mau province)	35,654.20	5,943.04
U Minh Thuong NP (Kien Giang province)	25,660.00	3,231.33
Total	61,314.20	9,174.37

Ecosystems and biodiversity

From 2000 to 2002, the water level dropped more than 85 cm from soil surface in the dry season was main causes of forest fires resulted in damages of the large-scale area of peatlands that was about a quarter and two-third of peatlands in UMHNP and UMTNP respectively, which caused a forest ecosystems degradation and a significant decline of biodiversity (UMTNP, 2005, UMHNP, 2004).

Since the end of 2003 to 2006, in order to control the forest fires, the water level was kept high throughout the year has caused degradation of ecosystems and biodiversity, especially that of Melaleuca forest habitat in UMTNP. Under the advice of environmentalists and the consent of local authorities, an integrated management of water and fire has been applied in peatlands resulted in effectively restoring the ecosystem and biodiversity since 2010. Area of forest restored in both parks up to 13,564.03 ha, which was however not uniform in density. In UMTNP, Melaleuca forest restored up to 5,504.78 ha, and seasonally inundated grasslands, which disappeared after forest fires in 2002 and then affected by a prolonging high water level, restored significantly up to 765.32 ha (Tab. 2).

Table 2: Changes of ecosystems in UMTNP (Kien Giang Province) from 2006 to 2014

Ecosystems	The year of 2006	The year of 2009	The year of 2011	The year of 2014
	Area (ha)	Area (ha)	Area (ha)	Area (ha)
Melaleuca forests	3,904.16	4,440.87	4,460.78	5,504.78
Grasslands	2,772.50	0.00	1,447.69	765.32
Aquatic swamps	1,126.74	3,393.37	1,912.80	1,551.17
Tall grass - shrubs	141.80	142.55	142.55	142.55
Total area (ha)	7,945.20	7,976.79	7,963.82	7,963.82

Peatland ecosystems are restored simultaneously with the abundance of plant species recorded with 176 plant species (belonging to 62 families) in UMHNP and 254 species (belonging to 64 families) in UMTNP (APFP, 2013 and SNV, 2014). Some waterfowl *(Leptoptilos javanicus, Pelecaniformes, Plegadis falcinellus*) have begun choosing peatland forest and grassland habitats as breeding sites. The fragmentation of forests is a general consequence of forest fires and inappropriate management which has occurred in peatland forests, which were restored by planting, mainly Melaleuca, and natural regeneration resulted in the forest covered in various tree densities (Fig 2, Fig. 3, and Fig. 4).

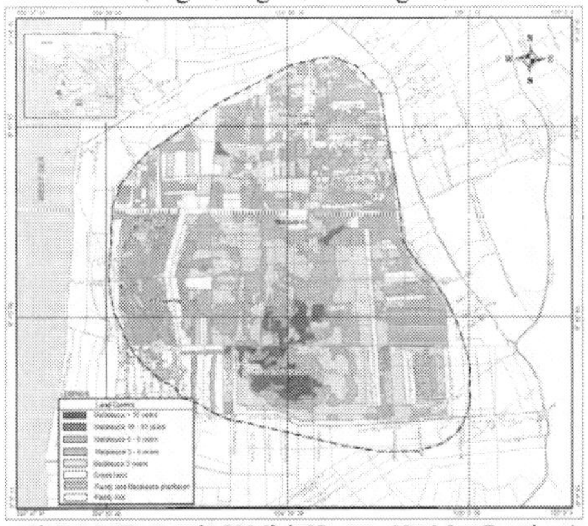

Figure 2: Forests in U Minh Ha area (Ca Mau Province)

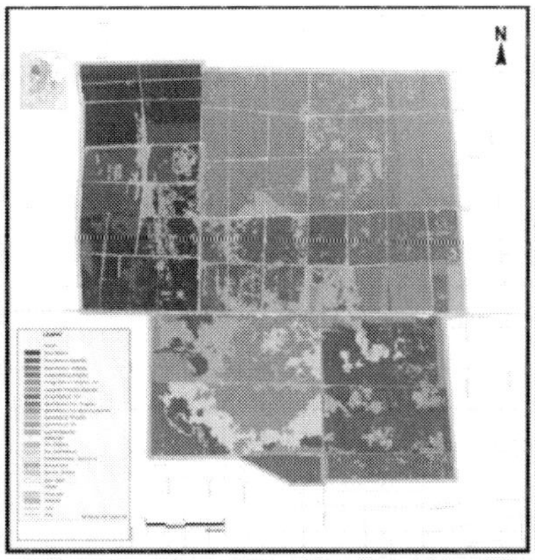

Figure 3: Peatland forests in UMHNP (Ca Mau)

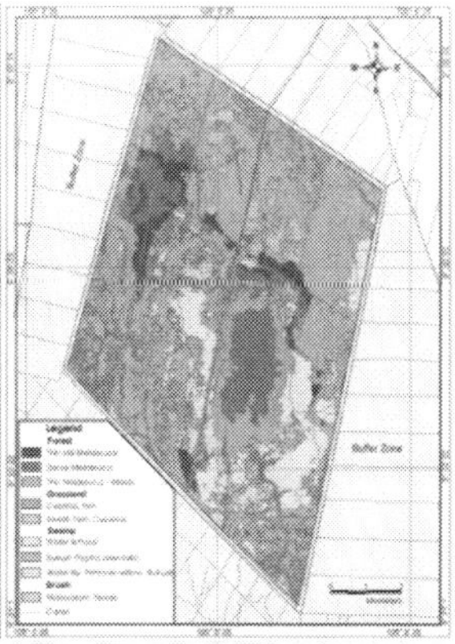

Figure 4: Peatland forests in UMTNP (Kien Giang)

The direct comparison of biodiversity among various forest densities that are from partial clearance to dense forests has received much attention. The high density of Melaleuca forest caused inadequate space and light indispensable for photosynthesis for other plants species developed. Therefore, the densities of Melaleuca forest affected to the number of plant species within it.

Numerical classification revealed a highly diverse pattern of variability in the forest examined. Most of forest plantation is single species forest by Melaleuca, while mixed forests in peat domes dominant by diversity of indigenous species of trees; therefore, value of biodiversity index (H') of mixed forests (H'= 0.85-1.27) in peat dome is higher than that of single Melaleuca forest (average H'= 0.53) (Tab. 3). Biodiversity index is quite low in dense Melaleuca plantation (H'= 0.17- 0.95) (Tab) while this value is high in dense natural Melaleuca forests in UMTNP (H' value is up to 1.75) (Tab. 4). The result showed the forests restored may deliver conserve levels of biodiversity but it rarely matches the composition and structure of the original forest cover in U Minh peatlands where the forest was fired completely from 2000 to 2002.

The analyzed data showed the number of plant species started increasing as the plant density below 4,600 trees.ha^{-1}. As forest tree density decreased simultaneously with the increase in a number of plant species, this resulted in the biodiversity index (H') in sparse to average density forests were higher than that in dense forest (Fig. 5, Fig. 6, Fig. 7, and Fig.8). The higher density of peatland Melaleuca forests, the lower the number of plant species and vice versa (see Fig. 5 and Fig.7). However, the highest number of plant species recorded was not more than 13 species at each observed plot in spare forest. The structural features of peatland forests are a greater abundance and diversity of lianas that could be caused by the competition of dominant lianas and herbaceous species of *Stenochloena palustris, Blechnum serrulatum, Cayratia trifolia* that thrived and then overrode other species.

Table 3: Ecosystems and Biodiversity Index in U Minh Ha National Park (Ca Mau Province)

Ecosystems	**No of sites**	**S**	**N**	**d=S/√N**	**H'**	**λ**	**J**
Dense forest	15	3 - 11	130 - 240	0.23- 0.86	0.17 - 0.95	0.00 - 0.06	0.10 - 0.52
Average forest	96	2 - 8	73 - 156	0.19 - 0.68	0.18 - 1.17	0.00 - 0.21	0.13 - 0.57
Spare forest	72	3 - 10	92 - 142	0.31 - 0,98	0.39 - 1.27	0.03 - 0.25	0.36 - 0.65
Very spare forest	278	3 - 13	11 - 112	0.34 - 1.44	0.08 - 2.20	0.13 - 0.97	0.08 - 0.92
Grassland	66	3 - 12	4 - 105	0.29 - 2.27	0.17 - 2.13	0.10 - 0.92	0.15 - 1.03

Table 4: Ecosystems and Biodiversity Index in U Minh Thuong National Park (Kien Giang Province)

Ecosystems	No of sites	S	N	d=S/√N	H'	λ	J
Dense forest	21	2 - 7	37 - 137	0.23 - 0.81	0.12 - 1.75	0.20 - 0.95	0.18 - 0.96
Average forest	22	3 - 8	48 - 140	0.34 - 0.85	0.81 - 1.81	0.18 - 0.38	0.51 - 0.96
Spare forest	14	4 - 7	66 - 122	0.41 - 0.74	0.57 - 1.63	0.23 - 0.56	0.92 - 0.41
Grasslands	35	2 - 8	11 - 64	0.26 - 1.05	0.91 - 1.58	0.24 - 0.94	0.21 - 0.98
Aquatic swamp	24	1 - 7	30 - 71	0.13 - 0.98	0.00 - 1.75	0.21 - 1.00	0.00 - 0.95

The transition from Melaleuca forest community to grassland community is very sharp due to the environmental condition. Some species of *Stenochloena palustris, Blechnum serrulatum* and *Phragmitex karka* were dominant in the grassland communities and *Stenochloena palustris* which had covered up to 75% of the grasslands. Due to grasslands recently restored and being competitive the dominant species of fern, therefore, biodiversity index varied from 0.17 – 2.20, and evenness of species was among species (J= 0.15 - 1.03). The high values of biodiversity index recorded in some areas of grasslands, where dominant by species of Cyperaceae (H' = 1.67 - 1.91). Swamps occupied by aquatic vegetation communities in various species. Some areas covered by very high density of species of *Typha angustifolia* or *Pistia stratiotes* (95% to 100%) that have very low biodiversity index (H'= 0.00 - 0.03), while the other aquatic communities have high diversity index (H' = 0.18 -1.75) and evenness (J = 0.21 – 0.95).

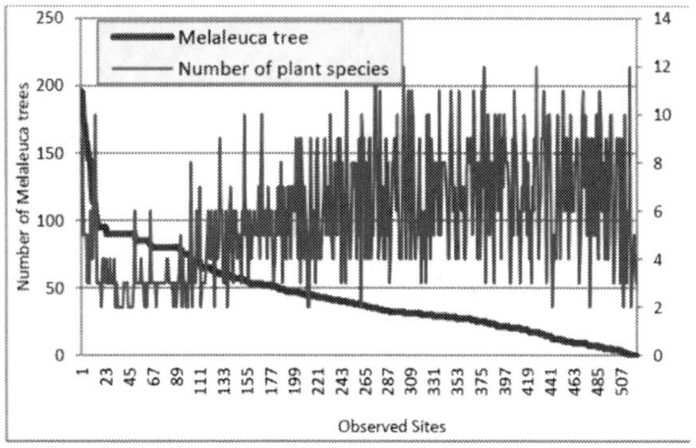

Figure 5: Densities of Melaleuca trees and a number of the plant species in peatland forests in UMHNP. (Ca Mau)

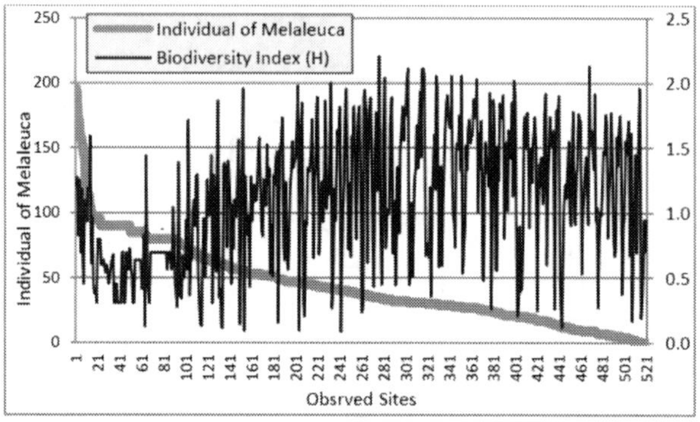

Figure 6: The density of Melaleuca forest and Biodiversity Index (H') in peatland forests in UMHNP.

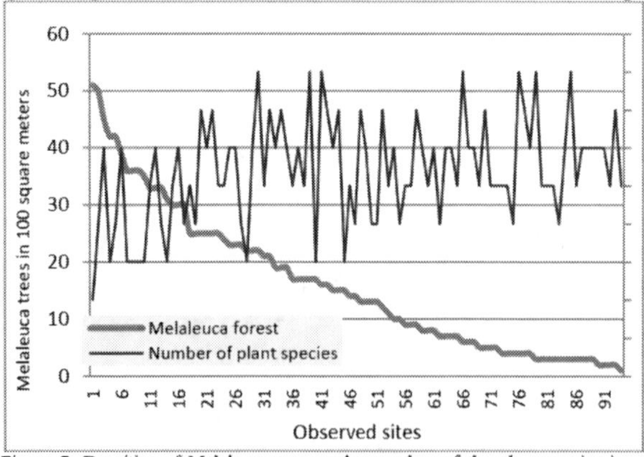

Figure 7: Densities of Melaleuca trees and a number of the plant species in peatland forests in UMTNP (Kien Giang province)

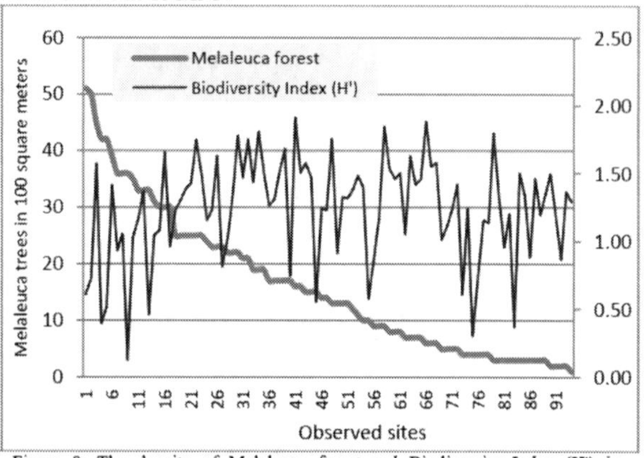

Figure 8: The density of Melaleuca forest and Biodiversity Index (H') in peatland forests in UMTNP (Kien Giang Province)

Carbon storage and carbon dioxide sequestration in peatland forests

Melaleuca forest and plantation dominated in both parks are generally dense and highly productive, and density-dependent mortality is to be expected by the park managers. Amongst other tropical forests, Melaleuca forest is carbon stores, and it is considered as carbon dioxide sinks when it has increased in the area. The Melaleuca forest density, which increased in middle age but decreased in mature age of trees, varied from 5,250 trees.ha^{-1} in dense forests and reduced gradually to 360 trees.ha^{-1} in the very spare forest, in which the different forest densities resulted in the various amount of forest biomass estimated (Tab. 4 & Tab. 5).

Total biomass estimated of Melaleuca forest and plantation, including above-ground biomass, roots, and the forest floor, is of 655,657.939 tons, in which total amount of carbon estimated is of 318,949.949 tons stored in tree tissues and equivalent to 1,170,546.312 tons of CO_2-e sequestration in Melaleuca forests (Table 4, Annex 4 and 5). Due to forest areas has been restored in UMTNP since 2010, the total low biomass, which resulted in the lower amount of carbon and carbon dioxide than those in UMHNP. In UMHNP forest, the average carbon content stored is of 27.80 tons.ha-1 and equivalent to 102.04 tons.ha^{-1} CO_2-e in sequestration. Similarly, a study on carbon adsorption capacity of Melaleuca forests in UMHNP by Vinh (2013) showed average carbon content stored is of 26.90 tons.ha^{-1}.

Table 4: Carbon stored and carbon dioxide equivalent in sequestration in the forest for two parks.

Parameters	UMHNP	UMTNP	Total
Forest area (ha)	8,059.25	5,504.78	13,564.03
Total biomass (tons.$area^{-1}$)	448,147.65	207,510.289	655,657.939
Carbon content (t.C.ha^{-1})	27.803	18.848	-
Carbon dioxides equivalent (tCO_2-e.ha^{-1})	102.038	69.173	-
Carbon content (tons.$area^{-1}$)	218,929.320	100,020.629	318,949.949
Carbon dioxide equivalent (CO_2-e)(tons.$area^{-1}$)	803,470.604	367,075.708	1,170,546.312

In the buffer zone, a land cover map showed Melaleuca covered in a large area; therefore estimates of 277,044.107 tons of carbon (equivalent to 1,016,751.872 tons of CO_2-e) were stored in the standing stock of plantation (Quoi, 2010). However, provincial forest report of 2010 showed a significant decrease of forest land that has been converted to agricultural land; therefore, this has resulted in decrease a large area of forest resulted in the decrease of the amount of C stock and CO_2-e sequestration in the buffer zone.

CONCLUSION

The peatlands remained only a relatively small area in the U Minh region, the Lower Mekong Delta. A significant area of peatlands was known as national parks aiming to conserve ecosystem and biodiversity of peatlands. Unsuitable water management, however, caused to peatland degradation resulted in serious damage to ecosystems and biodiversity. The water management in UMHNP peatlands has not been as expected. The water level dropped down deeper 85 cm from the surface in the dry season, which made it easier for forest fires and oxidation of peat materials.

Melaleuca forest covered predominantly in peatlands in both national parks, however, Melaleuca plantation dominated in the buffer zone of the UMHNP. High biomass estimated of Peatland Melaleuca forest resulted in a considerable amount of carbon and carbon dioxide equivalent sequestration. Thus, if the forest fire, there will be a large amount of carbon content loss and CO_2 equivalent released into the atmosphere.

The application of integrated management of water and fires in peatlands has restored ecosystems and biodiversity, and forest fire risks limited. The success of peatland management in UMTNP has been recognized as an ASEAN Heritage Park (AHP) in 2013 and Ramsar Site in 2015.

REFERENCES

1. APFP-Vietnam. 2013. Final report of APFP-Vietnam activities from 2010 to 2013.
2. Joseph Holder. 2005. Peatland hydrology and carbon release: Why small-scale process matters. Philosophical Transactions of the Royal Society A. 2005. 363. 2891-2913.
3. Maria Strack. 2008. Peatlands and Climate Change. International Peat Society, Vapaudenkatu 12, 40100 Jyväskylä, Finland. ISBN 978-952-99401-1-0.
4. Norman C. Duke , Damien Burrows and Jock Mackenzie. 2015. Mangrove and Freshwater Wetland Habitat Status of the Torres Strait Islands Biodiversity, Biomass, Changing Condition of Wetlands. the Australian Government's National Environmental Research Program (NERP) Tropical Ecosystems. 2015.
5. Page SE, Rieley JO, Shotyk OW, Weiss D. 1999. Interdependence of peat and vegetation in a tropical peat swamp forest. Philosophical Transactions of the Royal Society Lond B 354:1885 – 1897.
6. Page, S.E., Rieley, J.O. & Banks, C.J. (2011) Global and regional importance of the tropical peatland carbon pool. Global Change Biology, 17, 798–818.
7. Quoi, LP. 2010. Inventory of Peatlands in U Minh Ha Region, Ca Mau Province, Vietnam. SNV- Netherlands Development Organization REDD+ Programme. August 2010. www.snvredd.com.

8. Quoi, LP. 2014. Peatland and vegetation biodiversity assessment in U Minh Ha National Park, Ca Mau Province, Vietnam. SNV Netherlands Development Organization, German Bunderstag. December 2014.
9. UMHNP (2004) and UMTNP (2005). Report of forest fires in UMH and UMTNP.
10. VHP. 1974. Land Resources Map in Lower Mekong Basin. Vietnam - Holland Project. 1974. CT University.
11. Vinh T. V. and N. T. Truyen. 2013. Study on capacity of Carbon dioxides in Peatlands Melaleuca Forest of U Minh Ha National Park, Ca Mau Province. Technical Report of UAF, HCM City. 2013.

Abstract No: A-398

SHADE CLOTH TRIALS IN SOUTH-EASTERN AUSTRALIA AS A METHOD OF RESTORING PEATLANDS DAMAGED BY FIRE

Geoffrey Hope[1*], Roger Good[1] Jennie Whinam[2, 1] and Genevieve Wright[3]

[1] *College Asia Pacific, Australian National University Canberra, Australia*
[2] *Discipline of Geography and Spatial Sciences, University of Tasmania, Hobart Australia*
[3] *Office of Environment and Heritage, NSW Government, Queanbeyan, Australia*

Corresponding author: Geoffrey.Hope@anu.edu.au

***Keywords**: fire, shade, peatland recovery, transplants*

In January 2003 wild fires burnt approximately 2.1 million hectares in the mountains of southeastern Australia with a high proportion of the subalpine peatlands being affected. Alpine and subalpine peatlands dominated by shrubs and restiads but including the hummock moss *Sphagnum cristatum* are common in the highlands of southeastern Australia and total 9710 ha (Hope and Nanson 2015). The peatlands in national parks in New South Wales (NSW) and the Australian Capital Territory (ACT) had been recovering gradually from the effects of cattle and sheep grazing which ended more than 50 years ago but the 2003 fires reversed some of these gains. Post-fire, field inspection showed that while the vegetation in many of the peatlands had been severely burnt, most underlying peat surfaces were scorched but remained intact. Although peatlands had been drought affected, residual moisture prevented burning of the peat except where sites had been drained (Hope *et al.*, 2012).

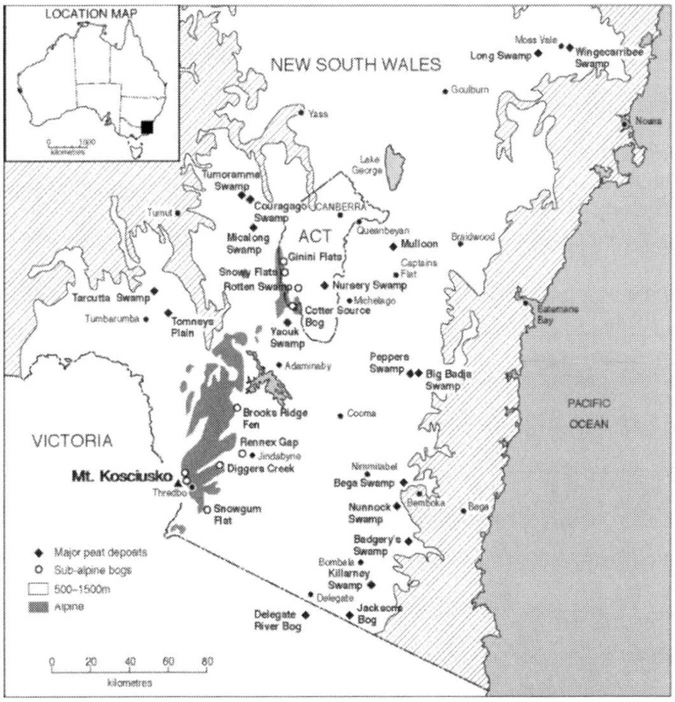

Figure 1 Upland areas of southern New South Wales and the ACT where peatlands are prominent.

The *Sphagnum* mires of the Australian Alps are climatically limited by evapotranspiration in the hottest month (Whinam *et al.*, 2003). Dry conditions result in bleaching of the hummocks and UV may also contribute to this (Good et al 2010). Up to 70% natural shading by other plants has been shown to favour *Sphagnum* moss growth (Whinam and Buxton 1997). The fires removed the shrub and graminoid cover, undermining any prospect for rapid recovery by *Sphagnum*. This prompted a program to trial artificial shading to enhance recovery at selected bogs in Kosciuszko National Park and Namadgi National Park. The aim is to restore and rehabilitate the hydrological functioning of these disturbed peatlands (Hope *et al.*, 2005, Good *et al.*, 2010). A preliminary description of the trials was provided by Hope *et al.* (2005) and the results after four years of monitoring of vegetation have been presented by Whinam *et al.* (2010). Further measurements have been made at 6 years (2009) and 10 years post fire. The results of these trials may help guide future peatland restoration techniques for montane peatlands in the region.

METHODS

At Pengillys Bog three shading treatments were established in 5 burnt and partially burnt peat areas, using 70% beige-coloured shade cloth material and loosely spread straw. Each plot included a 20 m long and 1.6 m high 70% shade cloth fence aligned east-west. Four quadrats were placed on each side of the vertical shade fence and solar radiation levels on northern and southern sides recorded over the 2004 summer. The effect of shading was compared with a second treatment, in which 15 m lengths of 2m wide shade cloth were pegged down horizontally, to lie loosely over the bog surface. Ropes were used to prevent the shadecloth from blowing away. A third shade treatment was established using sterilised grass straw spread at a rate equivalent to 2 tonnes per hectare (70% cover equivalent). Other sites (Rotten Swamp, Ginini Bog, Cotter Source Bog) were treated for varying periods with horizontal shade cloth strips up to 20m in length.

Quadrats were established underneath the shade and in adjacent plots and re-measured up to twice a year for five years between 2003-2009 and biannually thereafter for plant cover, floristic diversity, peat accumulation / depth and pH values. Shade cloth was removed from most areas in 2007 but relaid in two locations over a previously treated area until 2013 to see if longer term treatment can produce additional benefits.

Figure 2: Three shade treatments (vertical, horizontal and straw mulch in 2004.

These plots were assessed in 2016 (year 13).

RESULTS

Spectacular shrub, restiad and *Sphagnum* growth under shade cloth compared to controls was evident on first removing the shade in 2007. Straw mulch was effectively lost by the third year after treatment but caused positive growth in sedges. Any beneficial effects of straw mulch on badly burnt areas were short-lived. There were only slight differences between quadrats adjacent to the vertical shade fences. The sample size of the experiment (a total of 20 quadrats on each side of the shade fences) was probably too small, given the variability in site characteristics and damage class, to establish any effect of vertical shade. Additionally the vertical shade fences may have had the effect of sheltering both shaded and unshaded plots.

Figure 3: Shaded plots at Rotten Swamp, ACT, 1 year after re-exposure, 6 years after the 2003 fire

Horizontal shade cloth had significant impact on the vegetation. When shade cloth was removed, the vegetation was taller, more luxuriant and greener in colour than the surrounds. Shrubs had started to grow through the cloth and in some cases it had to be lifted to accommodate the increased volume of bog vegetation that had developed. Horizontal shade cloth alone provided for the greatest increase in the vegetation cover of *Empodisma minus* and *Baloskion australe*. There was good recruitment of species and patches of *Sphagnum* had expanded to form large mats. Transplants of *Sphagnum* 20x20cm in size showed significantly better survival and subsequent expansion under shade cloth compared to plots with no treatment.

When compared to unshaded plots there was significant difference in recovery of all native plant species (percentage vegetation cover) treated with horizontal shade cloth over time ($p=0.001$), although forbs were the only lifeform that showed significant increases in cover over time ($p=0.005$). After twelve years many control plots showed similar vegetation growth to the plots that had been shaded for four years. Three years after shade had been removed, the plots shaded for longest were easily differentiated in the field from sites subject to shade for a shorter time and control sites, although there were small areas of death in some shrubs and restiads. Comparisons of quadrat results were not dramatic but the longer-term shade plots tended to be dominated by larger shrubs, graminoids or moss with reduced diversity. This resembles more mature bog vegetation structures.

DISCUSSION

The shade cloth technique shows promise in rehabilitating sensitive areas of peatland in regions with strong sunlight and high summer temperatures. As well as providing shade, it retains humidity and protects plants from wind and ice damage. Additionally it may moderate frost effects and limit grazing by marsupials. It is particularly valuable in helping moss transplants to establish and develop. Since recovery of unshaded peatlands did eventually occur (as predicted by Walsh and McDougall 2004) shade is principally a way of accelerating the initial recovery to a mature shrub-bog structure. It is thus feasible to establish a grid of shade plots to establish nuclei of vegetation regrowth that would subsequently spread into the surrounding peatland.

From a practical perspective shade cloth is relatively cheap and showed no deterioration after four years. It is readily transported into remote areas by helicopter but must be removed. It is vulnerable to further fires and is very visible so may be unsuitable in some settings.

ACKNOWLEDGEMENTS

The authors are grateful to ACT and NSW Parks authorities for funding the post-fire trials. We were helped with set up and maintenance by Trish Macdonald, Ken Green, Dave Whitfield, and Colin de Pageter.

REFERENCES

1. Good R 2004. Rehabilitating fire-damaged wetlands in the Snowy Mountains. *Australasian Plant Conservation* 12(4): 3-4.
2. Good, R., Wright, G., Hope, G.S. and Whinam, J. 2010. The impacts of increasing solar ultraviolet light on the wetland mires of the mainland Australian Alps. *Australian Plant Conservation* 8(4), 3-4.
3. Good, R., Wright, G., Whinam, J. and Hope, G.S. 2010. Restoration of mires of the Australian Alps following the 2003 wildfires. In S. Haberle, J. Stevenson and M Prebble eds. Altered Ecologies Fire, climate and human influence on terrestrial landscapes. *Terra Australis* 32, 353-362.
4. Hope, G. and Nanson, R. 2015. Peatland carbon stores and fluxes in the Snowy Mountains, New South Wales, Australia. *Mires and Peat* 15 (11), 1-23.
5. Hope, G.S., Nanson, R. and Jones, P. 2012. Peat-forming bogs and fens of the Snowy Mountains of New South Wales. Technical Report. Office Environment and Heritage, Sydney. Pp. 87.
6. Hope, G., Whinam, J. and Good, R. 2005. Methods and preliminary results of post-fire experimental trials of restoration techniques in the peatlands of Namadgi (ACT) and Kosciuszko National Parks(NSW). *Ecological Management and Restoration* 6, 215-218.
7. Walsh N.G. and McDougall K.L. 2004. Progress in the recovery of the flora of treeless subalpine vegetation in Kosciuszko National Park after the 2003 fires. *Cunninghamia* **8**, 439–452.
8. Whinam J. and Chilcott N. 2002. Floristic description and environmental relationships of *Sphagnum* communities in NSW and the ACT and their conservation management. *Cunninghamia* **7**, 463-500.
9. Whinam J., Hope G. S., Adam P., Clarkson B.R., Alspach P.A. and Buxton R.P. 2003. *Sphagnum* peatlands of Australasia: the resource, its utilisation and management. *Wetlands Ecology and Management* **11**, 37-49.
10. Whinam, J., Hope, G.S., Good, R. and Wright, G. 2010. Five years of post-fire monitoring of the recovery of *Sphagnum* shrub bogs in the ACT and NSW, Australia. In S. Haberle, J. Stevenson and M Prebble eds. Altered Ecologies Fire, climate and human influence on terrestrial landscapes. *Terra Australis* 32, 363-379.

Abstract No: A-447

THE ROLE OF INSTITUTIONS TO PREVENT FOREST FIRE AND MANAGE PEATLANDS IN INDONESIA

Parlindungan Purba

Chairman of Committee II, House of Regional Representative of Republic of Indonesia, Chairman of Special Committee of Indonesia's Forest Fires

* *Corresponding author: parlin_senat@yahoo.co.id*

The recent forest fire crisis has caused massive damage in Indonesia and neighbouring countries in the region, socially and economically. Socially, forest fires cause deterioration in the health and wellbeing of people in the affected region. Economically, fires cost twice as much as a tsunami clean-up. Therefore, preventing forest fire becomes a crucial issue to discuss. In that context, management of peatlands is a very important topic because more than half of these fires have occurred on peatland areas. By putting peatland management onto the agenda, we can prevent forest fires in the future. This paper tries to explore the role of institutions to prevent forest fires. Furthermore, the focus lies on how institutional settings in Indonesia could be arranged to manage peatlands and prevent peatlands from burning. Institutions can serve as players in national legislation, institutional set-ups and inter-institutional coordination, monitoring mechanisms and law enforcement to create constraints and incentives for human behaviour that will lead to fewer forest fires. Most of the studies that have been done focus on technical issues and studies that emphasize the role of institutions are relatively few. Therefore, discussing issues of forest fires and peatlands management from the institutional perspective will advance, both theoretically and empirically, the knowledge of forest fire issues in the region.

***Keywords**: forest fires, institution, peatlands*

3.2: REWETTING & RE-VEGETATION TECHNIQUES

Abstract No: A-148

IDENTIFYING THE AVAILABLE REVITALISATION POTENTIAL OF DRAINED BOGS

Karin Keßler*, Andreas Wahren and Ingo Dittrich

Dr. Dittrich & Partner Hydro-Consult GmbH, Dresden, Germany

**Corresponding author: karin_keszler@web.de*

SUMMARY

Since each drained bog has its own individual structure, the available potential of rewetting differs from one bog to the other. We use the physically-based hydromorphological analysis (EDOM *et al.*, 2007) to calculate the current potential for rewetting bogs affected by drainage, peat extraction or fires like in Indonesia or elsewhere. Only based on a digital elevation model and the annual runoff, future vegetation patterns for the entire bog can be predicted, and different rewetting scenarios can be generated at a moment's notice. With these calculations we distinguish between bogs with a high or low potential for rewetting. Rewetting measures are especially successful in areas with a high potential. In areas with low revitalisation potential, land-use options adapted to low water tables can be considered. We recommend a step-by-step approach, first calculating the potential of rewetting. Afterwards, it is possible to set priorities for the following action planning. This approach focuses on areas where it is possible to revitalise bogs within a reasonable period of time. Being firmly based on the laws of physics, this method can be used for the prioritisation of rewetting areas, action planning, monitoring and evaluation. The hydromorphological analysis is a valuable tool for conservationists, project engineers and politicians to support them in the decision-making process. It will help to allocate resources in a clear and targeted manner, and to avoid unrealistic expectations.

Keywords: *Revitalisation planning, prioritisation, water supply.*

INTRODUCTION

Mutual interactions appear within bogs between water, vegetation and surface relief. For growth, peat-forming species need high water tables close to the surface. Organic plant residues (including dead roots) form peat under anaerobic water-logged conditions. Over thousands of years, this process accumulated thick peat layers of up to 20 m and more. The surface relief of a bog alters slowly over time. Hydraulic properties of the peat depend on the peat-forming plant species. Both the hydraulic properties of the peat and the relief influence the water flow paths and, hence, the distribution of water within the bog.

In pristine bogs, self-regulation processes level off changing environmental conditions like periods of water shortage in contrast to periods of water surplus. During water shortage water loss needs to be minimised, while water surplus must be drained in a gentle way without causing erosion. This regulation takes place in the uppermost layer of the bog (the so-called 'acrotelm'), and in some surface relief structures like rills and ponds. In the boreal zone, the acrotelm consists mainly of sphagnum-mosses and some small vascular plants. In the tropical zone where precipitation is much higher, trees with buttress roots increase surface roughness. The retention of runoff in the depressions between the trees causes prolonged water availability during dry spells (DOMMAIN *et al.*, 2016).

During the last centuries, many bogs and mires were drained by human activities. This included trenching, peat cutting, logging and conversion to agricultural land. After drainage, the spongy peat slumped down. The former anaerobic upper peat layer was air-ventilated, which lead to a mineralisation of the peat. The peat surface dropped, especially near ditches and peat cutting edges, due to the change of hydraulic properties. In some places peat mineralisation and peatland fires changed the relief and - at the same time - the distribution of water. For successful revitalisation the water table needs to be re-established near the surface. Therefore, the individual structure of the drained bog with its current relief needs to be considered for action planning.

The revitalisation of drained bogs is a challenging task in respect of the long time needed. Furthermore, human, financial and technical resources are sometimes limited. Therefore, it is necessary to focus on those bogs with the best potential for rewetting. This applies both for bogs in Europe, and elsewhere.

METHODS

To calculate the potential for rewetting we use the hydromorphological analysis. EDOM *et al.* (2007, 2010) give detailed mathematical descriptions of this method. Requirements are rather simple; only a digital elevation model (DEM) with a high resolution and the mean annual runoff are required. Mostly we use the LIDAR-DEM, which is generated by airborne laser-scanning of the earth´s surface, with a grid-resolution of 5 metres.

In a natural bog, the water table is close to the surface; so the surface roughly represents the water table. Furthermore, we assume all ditches to be refilled with peat; hence, the calculations represent the potential water flow after optimal rewetting measures. Water flow follows the hydraulic gradient from areas with high water level to areas with low water level, and is directed perpendicular to the contour lines of the surface elevation (water table). We calculate the water accumulation along the flow paths using the relief analysis tools from GIS-software (geographic information system, e.g. ARC-GIS).

RESULTS

As a result we generate a map of the spatial distribution of the potential profile flow. We show one example from the bog "Kleiner Kranichsee" in the mountain range "Erzgebirge" (Ore Mountains, 50°25'3" N and 12°40'25" E) in SO Germany in Fig. 1. In general, profile flow is low on ridges and hilltops (places where accumulation starts), and high in rills and valley-like depressions. Profile flow values higher than 50 l/(s·km) characterise natural or natural-like brooks in this region. Since the wetness of an area depends on both the profile flow and the slope, we need to divide the profile flow by the slope. As a result we get a map of potential transmissivity (Fig. 2). Potential transmissivity is strongly related to the vegetation in bogs. High transmissivity values occur either due to high profile flows, or very low slopes. They identify wet vegetation types. It is possible to translate transmissivity into vegetation types on a regional scale. In the Erzgebirge, transmissivity values of more than 3 cm^2/s characterise areas with an open bog vegetation (Fig. 3). Trees are rare and shrub-shaped. Transmissivities less than 3 cm^2/s characterise wooded bogs.

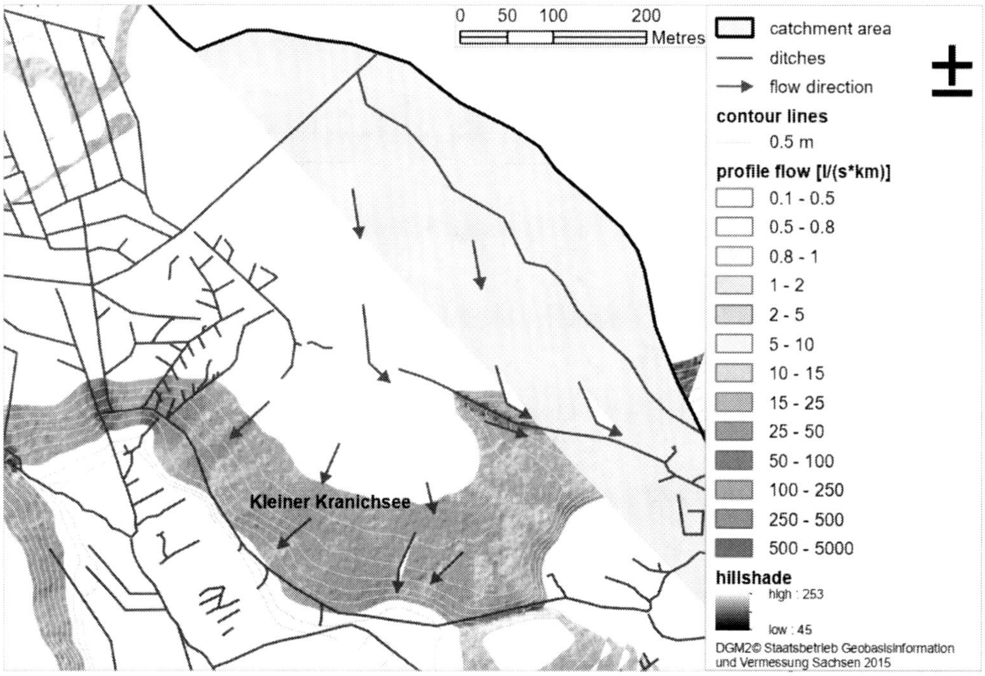

Figure 1: Map of potential profile flow for the bog "Kleiner Kranichsee" in the mountain range "Erzgebirge" (Germany).

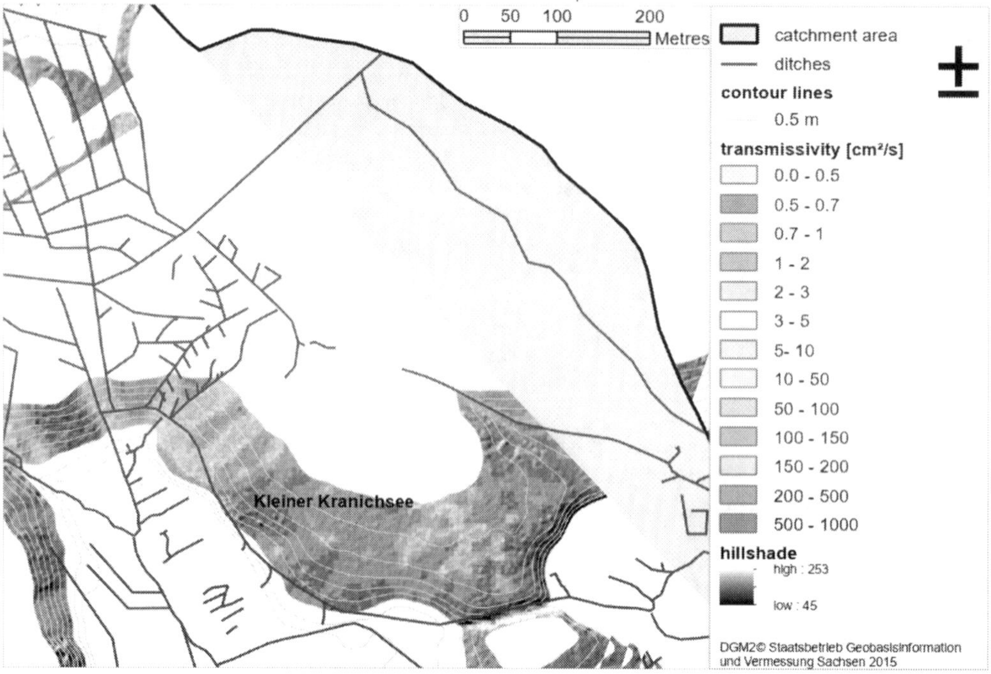

Figure.2: Map of potential transmissivity for the bog "Kleiner Kranichsee" in the mountain range "Erzgebirge" (Germany).

Fig. 3: Hummock-hollow-structure in an area with high transmissivity (> 3 cm²/s) in the bog "Kleiner Kranichsee" in the mountain range "Erzgebirge" (Germany). Foto: K. Keßler, 2014.

In our example, the bog is influenced by mining activities from the 16th-century, peat cutting, and some ditches. Water from the catchment area in the north is drained to the east. The main peat body is relatively dry; only small parts of the former widespread open bog vegetation is preserved, meaning that there are only few areas with transmissivity values higher than 3 cm²/s. Interventions in the water balance of the bog were made a long time ago and there are only a few ditches in the peat body itself. Therefore, the calculations correspond to the current vegetation quite well. In deeply-drained bogs the difference between current and calculated vegetation identifies the direction of succession development after rewetting measures or natural regeneration.

Some more examples will be given in the presentation.

DISCUSSION

In general, we calculate a pattern of dry and wet vegetation-types after rewetting. Because each drained bog has its own individual structure, the available potential for rewetting differs from one bog to the other. Whether or not it is possible to re-establish the former vegetation types depends on the dimension and location of the human impact on the water balance, the current surface relief and the nutrient supply. Sometimes, secondary vegetation types or early succession stages will develop more likely than the original ones. In some bogs, or some parts of them, rewetting is not possible at all, or huge efforts are required. Rewetting measures are especially successful in bogs with a high potential for rewetting, meaning larger areas with high transmissivities. In areas with low revitalisation potential land-use options adapted to low water tables can be considered.

We recommend a step-by-step approach; first calculating the potential of rewetting for several bogs. Then it is possible to set priorities for the following action planning. This approach focuses on bogs where revitalisation is possible within a reasonable period of time.

The calculations of the hydromorphological analysis can also be used for action planning and scenario analysis. The maps contain information about structures and water flow paths within the bog. Artificial drainage ditches should be blocked while natural flow paths and brooks, which can be identified by the profile flow, should be revitalised. In the tropical zone, areas with low transmissivity and low profile flow are preferable places for reforestation with buttressed and mound-forming trees to increase surface roughness and depression storage (DOMMAIN *et al.*, 2016).

It is also possible to calculate the consequences of some measures like removing (or building) barriers for water flow like dams, relief manipulation, or external water supply.

CONCLUSION

Our hydromorphological analysis is a unique tool for conservationists, project engineers and politicians to support their decision-making process before rewetting disturbed bogs. It will help to allocate resources in a clear and targeted manner, and avoid unrealistic expectations about the future of the considered bogs.

The calculations help to understand the effects of hydraulic disturbances on vegetation zones and succession directions. Therefore, they are also a valuable basis for revitalisation planning, scenario analysis, targeted monitoring concepts and the assessment of the resulting development.

REFERENCES

1. DOMMAIN, R., DITTRICH, I., GIESEN, W., JOOSTEN, H., RAIS, D. S., SILVIUS, M. & WIBISONO, I. T. C. (2016): Ecosystem services, degradation and restoration of peat swamps in the South East Asian tropics. In: BONN, A., ALLOTT, T., EVANS, M., JOOSTEN, H. & STONEMAN, R. (2016): *Peatland Restoration and Ecosystem Services. Science, Policy and Practice*. Cambridge University Press, pp. 255-290, in press.
2. EDOM, F., GOLUBCOV, A.A., DITTRICH, I., ZINKE, P. & SOLBRIG, B. (2007): Using IVANOVs hydromorphological theory in mire-ecology – an introduction. In: *Proceedings of the international conference W3M "Wetlands: Monitoring, Modeling, Management"*. Wierzba, 22.-25.9.2005, Poland. Taylor & Francis / Balkema Publishers, Leiden, pp. 239–247.
3. EDOM, F., MÜNCH, A., DITTRICH, I., KEßLER, K. & PETERS, R. (2010): Hydromorphological analysis and water balance modeling of ombro- and mesotrophic peatlands. *Advances in Geosciences* 27, pp.131–137.

Abstract No: A-228

NUTRIENTS IN DRAINED AND RE-WETTED PEATLANDS IN NE POLAND

Barbara Kalisz* and Andrzej Łachacz

Department of Soil Science and Land Reclamation, Faculty of Environmental Management and Agriculture, University of Warmia and Mazury in Olsztyn, Oczapowskiego 2, Olsztyn 10-719, Poland

**Corresponding author: barbara.kalisz@uwm.edu.pl*

Peat soils after drainage undergo the process of transformation of organic matter (moorsh-forming process) and due to mineralization of organic compounds, the content of macro- and microelements increases. Nutrients occur in various forms and proportions. The aim of the research was to evaluate the content of plant-available and total amounts of nutrients in drained and re-wetted peat soils. The total (in *aqua regia*) and plant-available (extracted with hydrochloric acid) content of Ca, Mg, K, Na, P, N, C, Fe, Mn, B, Zn, M and Cu was analysed using ICP technique and CN analysers. Studied drained soils contained less carbon in surface layers due to oxidation in the moorsh-forming process. In studied soils, among other analysed elements, iron and calcium prevailed. In surface layers of drained peatlands, an accumulation of calcium was recorded. Drained peat soils contained more nutrients than re-wetted ones. In peat soils which were located in river valleys or in the vicinity of hills, the nutrient content varied. It resulted from alluvial and deluvial processes that affected the studied peatlands. High amounts of iron in drained peat soils is a result of intensive oxidation of the organic matter of peat and capillary rise of groundwater and may be one of the factors suggesting the degree of moorsh-forming process.

Keywords: *microelements, macro elements, organic soil*

Abstract No: A-164

SPHAGNUM FARMING IN GERMANY: HOW TO MAXIMIZE PEATMOSS YIELDS

Greta Gaudig*, Matthias Krebs and Susanne Abel

University of Greifswald, partner in the Greifswald Mire Centre

**Corresponding author: gaudig@uni-greifswald.de*

Most promising areas for *Sphagnum* farming in Germany are degraded bogs in the northwest (Lower Saxony), like cut-over bogs or bog grasslands to produce *Sphagnum* biomass for growing media. Since 2004 we investigate in greenhouse and field experiments which site conditions stimulate *Sphagnum* growth and how they can be transferred to large-scale application. All experiments show the high and stable water table as the decisive factor for good *Sphagnum* growth, whereas fertilization is not necessary under nutrient rich conditions like in Lower Saxony. Thus, an automatic water management for *Sphagnum* farming sites is indispensable: irrigation during summer and discharge of surplus water to prevent flooding in particular during winter. As vascular plants may impede the growth of the peatmosses and may impair the quality of the raw material for horticultural substrates, their cover could be kept low by regular mowing. In addition to the site conditions *Sphagnum* growth can be accelerated by a rapid establishment of the peatmoss lawn. It depends on sufficient cover density and the size of initially peatmoss fragments when installing the culture. These preconditions at a field experiment on former bog grassland enabled the establishment of a thick, dense and productive peatmoss lawn 1.5 years after field preparation with annual *Sphagnum* growth rates up to 8.7 t dry mass per hectare.

***Keywords**: -*

Abstract No: A-255

REINTRODUCTION OF FEN PLANT COMMUNITIES ON MINEROTROPHIC REMNANT SURFACES AFTER PEAT EXTRACTION

Marie-Claire LeBlanc, Line Rochefort and Sandrine Hugron

Peatland Ecology Research Group (PERG), Université Laval, Canada.

**Corresponding author: marie-claire.leblanc@fsaa.ulaval.ca*

SUMMARY

The Moss Layer Transfer Technique (MLTT) has been developed to restore industrially peat-extracted bogs. It has been applied successfully to several peatlands across Canada over the last 20 years. Recently, the need has emerged for a similar technique focusing on sites that have been harvested down to their sedge peat layers, where richer and less acidic conditions prevail. In 2009, a peatland presenting these conditions was restored after 50 years of peat extraction. The site was rewetted and three restoration techniques inspired by the MLTT were applied. Five years after the restoration, vegetation surveys have been conducted to assess the efficiency of technique at restoring fen plant covers. The results were compared to similar surveys conducted in an undisturbed area of the donor site as well as in a natural fen adjacent to the restored site. Surprisingly, none of the restoration techniques were efficient at establishing plant covers similar to the reference sites, especially for bryophyte species. In sites where fen species already colonized the surface spontaneously, rewetting could be sufficient to support the recovery of typical vascular plants communities. When profiling the surface is necessary, our results showed that reintroducing donor material is an essential step toward the return of fen species.

Keywords: *moderate-rich fen, peatland restoration, diaspore transfer, rewetting.*

INTRODUCTION

Following industrial activities of peat extraction for horticultural substrates production, the highly disturbed remnant surfaces are hardly recolonized by typical peatland communities and active restoration efforts have to be deployed to ensure their recovery (Lavoie *et al.*, 2003, Rochefort *et al.*, 2003, Poulin *et al.*, 2005). In the last 20 years, the Moss Layer Transfer Method (MLTT) has been developed to address the need for an efficient large-scale restoration method for bogs (Quinty and Rochefort 2003, Rochefort *et al*,. 2003). The MLTT consists of six major steps: 1) site preparation: the surface of the extracted bog is profiled to remove any spontaneously established vegetation, to flatten dome-shaped peat fields and to expose fresh peat; 2) diaspore collection: donor material is harvested in a natural fen; 3) diaspore introduction: a thin layer of donor material is spread mechanically on the site; 4) diaspore protection: straw mulch is spread over the donor material; 5) fertilization: slow-release phosphorus fertilizer is applied; 6) rewetting: drainage ditches are blocked or filled to retain water and raise water table level on the site. The MLTT has nowadays been applied in more than 60 restoration projects across Canada (L. Rochefort - unpublished data) and has proven to be an efficient method to enhance bog vegetation recovery (González and Rochefort 2014).

For industrial reasons or because of site characteristics (e.g. shallower peat deposits, nature of the underlying mineral substrate, water circulation patterns), the peat surface left after the cessation of extraction activities can sometimes present richer and less acidic conditions than the former bog conditions. In these cases, restoration toward a fen ecosystem is often more appropriate (Wind-Mulder *et al.*, 1996, Wind-Mulder and Vitt 2000, Triisberg *et al.*, 2014). It is however unknown which restoration method should be applied. Numerous fen restoration projects have been conducted in Europe, but their overall objectives differ from the ones pursued in North America. While European restoration usually aims at repairing fens drained for agriculture by restoring their biodiversity, North American restoration projects usually take place on post-extraction sites devoid of vegetation and focus on the return of the ecosystem functions (Rasran *et al.* 2007, Graf and Rochefort 2008a, Lamers *et al.*, 2015). The restoration methods applied are therefore not directly transferable. In USA and Canada, successful trials of small-scale fen restoration trials have been conducted using sedge plantations and rewetting (Cooper and MacDonald 2000) as well as donor material introduction (Cobbaert *et al.*, 2004, Graf and Rochefort 2008a, 2008b). These results suggest that restoration methods based on some of the steps of the MLTT could be efficient at restoring fens on a larger scale. In this context, distinct restoration methods should be tested and developed for North American fen restoration projects. This project presents the results of the first fen restoration project at the ecosystem-scale following horticultural peat extraction activities in North America. For the purpose of this extended abstract, only partial results are presented and discussed as a scientific manuscript has been submitted for publication in Botany. Please consult and refer to the published article *Reintroduction of fen plant communities on a degraded minerotrophic peatland* for complete results.

METHODS

The Bic-St-Fabien research station is located in Eastern Canada (province of Québec). The 15 ha site is a former bog used for industrial horticultural peat extraction for 50 years before the activities ceased in 2000. In 2009, the site was partly covered with *Schoenoplectus tabernaemontani* (C.C. Gmelin) Palla, *Alnus rugosa* (DuRoi) Sprengel, *Salix sp.* and *Typha latifolia* (Linnaeus) (L. Rochefort – unpublished data). The pore water averaged over the site presented moderately minerotrophic conditions: pH: 6.1 ± 0.3, mean ± sd, n=80 and corrected electric conductivity: 334 ± 158 $\mu S\ cm^{-1}$, mean ± SD; n=80 (L. Rochefort - unpublished data; according to values presented in Vitt *et al.*, 1995). Restoration work towards a fen ecosystem was realised from winter 2009 to spring 2010. Donor material was collected mechanically in a nearby natural fen margin dominated by brown mosses (total cover: 55%). Rewetting was performed by backfilling and blocking former drainage ditches with decomposed peat. No fertilizer was applied. Because of site characteristics, three restoration techniques were tested on the site: **1) Mechanical technique** (2.18 ha): peatland surface was profiled, donor material was introduced and protected by straw mulch, both spread mechanically; **2) Profiling technique** (3.55 ha): surface was profiled but without plant introduction; **3) Rewetting technique** (4.85 ha): ditches were blocked, with no modification to the surface to preserve the spontaneously established vegetation in place.

In order to compare the establishment of fen plants communities in each restored sector, vegetation surveys were conducted 5 years after the restoration. Sampling units were installed in each restored. Within each unit, all vascular plants species were identified in four systematically located 1 m x 1 m quadrats. The ground surface covered by each species was estimated, as well as the total surface covered by all vascular plant strata. Similar surveys were also conducted in two natural fen portions at the margin of the restored site and in an undisturbed sector of the donor site to allow comparisons with nearby natural fen ecosystems that could act as propagule sources. The bryophytes were surveyed using a similar method, in 12 quadrats (25 cm x 25 cm). Plant recovery for each restoration technique was compared using descriptive statistics (mean and standard error of different vegetation classes at the plot level).

RESULTS

Five growing seasons post-restoration, vegetation covers were considerably lower in all restored sectors than in the reference ecosystem (Fig. 1). Vascular plant covers were relatively high in the sectors restored by the Rewetting technique, but the proportions of covers associated to species found in the Reference ecosystem were the lowest. At the opposite, the low vascular plant covers observed in the Profiling and Mechanical techniques showed the highest proportions of species associated to the reference ecosystem (55 and 80 % respectively). The plant communities, however, differed greatly between these two sectors: the Mechanical technique was dominated by *Myrica gale* Linnaeus, *Trichophorum alpinum* (Linnaeus) Persoon and *Sanguisorba canadensis* Linnaeus, which are all found in the reference ecosystem, while the Profiling technique was mainly covered by *Carex aquatilis* Wahlenberg and *Eriophorum vaginatum* Linnaeus, the latter being absent from the reference ecosystem.

While bryophytes formed a major component of the reference ecosystem (mean cover from 37% to 71%), their covers were lower in all restored sectors. Brown mosses were virtually absent from all sectors except the Rewetting technique, where it was very variable.

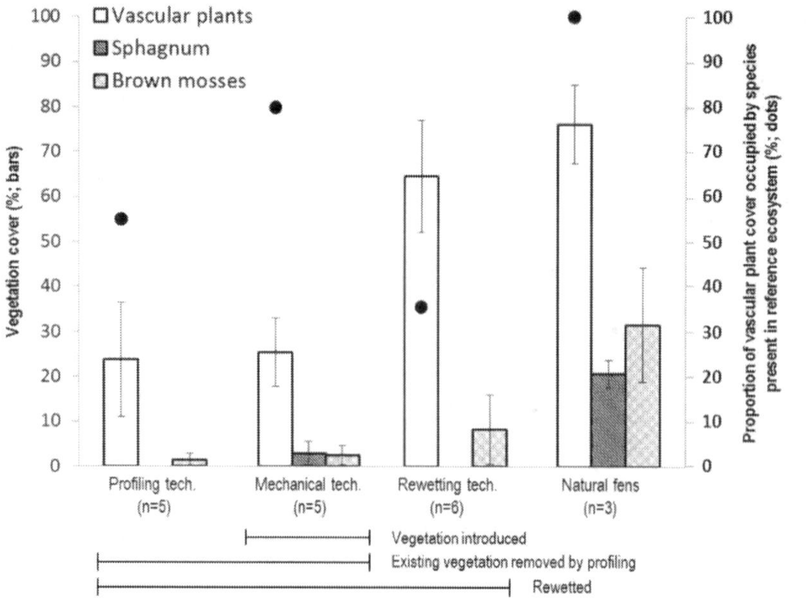

Figure 1: Plant cover (% ± SE) by plant groups in restored sectors (bars) and the proportion of vascular plant cover occupied by species also found in the reference ecosystem (dots). The number of plots (n) by sector is proportional to its size, except for the reference ecosystem where vegetation surveys were performed in three nearby natural fens.

DISCUSSION

Five growing seasons after restoration, none of the techniques applied to restore the Bic-St-Fabien peatland allowed the establishment of vegetation covers similar to the ones observed in the natural fens used as reference ecosystems. The bryophyte communities, which usually form a major part of fen vegetation (Rydin and Jeglum 2013), only established very scarcely. In the sectors where donor material was introduced, the covers obtained suggest that *Sphagnum* and brown mosses might be recalcitrant to mechanical manipulations (including during diaspore collection and spreading steps). This idea is reinforced by the observation that manual introduction of similar donor material elsewhere on site evolved into well-established bryophyte carpets. The Rewetting technique, in which no donor material was introduced, supported the higher brown mosses cover. This could be explained by the presence of bryophytes on this sector prior to restoration work, as well as the creation of conditions (water availability, protective sedge cover) favorable to their establishment and expansion.

The vascular plant communities established in each sector were different in terms of plant composition and covers, the most vegetated being the Rewetting technique. However, the absolute cover associated with the species also found in the natural fens were similar in all sectors regardless of the restoration technique applied, ranging from 15 to 23%. During the restoration, rewetting was performed at the site level and led to a significant rise of the water table (Malloy and Price 2014) in all sectors. In the Rewetted technique, the vegetation that was present before the restoration was preserved and still dominated five years later. As with the brown mosses, spontaneously established vascular plants probably benefited the favorable conditions provided by the rise of the water level. The Rewetting technique could therefore be considered in restoration projects in areas where fen-type vegetation is already in place.

When the site to restore has to be profiled to flatten or reorganise the surface, the conjunction of bare peat areas and high water levels might lead to erosion or frost heaving. In the sector where the Profiling technique was applied, both phenomena, combined with the absence of diaspores to initiate revegetation, resulted in very low plant covers. This technique is therefore not suggested for fen restoration. Donor material could not only promote the establishment of species from the reference ecosystem, but also speed up the colonization process which could facilitate surface stabilization and enhance fen-type communities' growth. However, the vascular plant covers installed following the Mechanical spreading of material were also very low. These disappointing results could be explained by various reasons, including the effect of surface instability the choice of the donor site based on the bryophytes communities. The mechanical manipulation of the bryophytes also appears to impede their recovery and improvement of these steps is essential for large-scale restoration. The effect of donor material timing and collection method should also be further investigated.

CONCLUSION

The restoration of the Bic-St-Fabien peatland is the first ecosystem-scale fen restoration project following horticultural peat extraction in North America. Contrary to our assumptions, the three techniques tested did not lead to identifying a restoration method that could be prescribed to the site level to ensure fen-type vegetation establishment. On the contrary, it highlights the need to consider local site conditions and combining restoration techniques. In areas where fen vegetation established spontaneously, the Rewetting technique could lead to the expansion of the communities already in place by providing favorable conditions. When profiling the surface is needed to ensure better water circulation, to expose fresh peat or to construct erosion control features, diaspore introduction is necessary to launch the establishment of fen vascular plants and bryophytes species, but more research have to be carried out about efficient mechanical reintroduction of material.

ACKNOWLEDGEMENTS

Financial support was provided by the Ministère des Transports du Québec, the Natural Sciences and Engineering Research Council of Canada, the Canadian Sphagnum Peat Moss Association and its members. The authors would like to thank Claire Boismenu and Rémy Pouliot for their revisions of the document, as well as Vicky Bérubé and Stéphanie Boudreau for their participation to the restoration and experimental set-up of the Bic-Saint-Fabien site. We thank the numerous field assistants that contributed to the site restoration and the data survey, as well as all members of the Peatland Ecology Research Group. Special thanks go to landowners that granted us access to their lands.

REFERENCES

1. Cobbaert, D., Rochefort, L., and Price, J.S. 2004. Experimental restoration of a fen plant community after peat mining. *Applied Vegetation Science*. 7: 209–220.
2. Cooper, J. D., and MacDonald L. H. 2000. Restoring the vegetation of mined peatlands in the southern Rocky Mountains of Colorado, U.S.A. *Restoration Ecology*. 8(2): 103–111.
3. González, E., and Rochefort, L. 2014. Drivers of success in 53 cutover bogs restored by a moss layer transfer technique. *Ecological Engineering*. 68: 279–290.
4. Graf, M.D., and Rochefort, L. 2008a. Techniques for restoring fen vegetation on cut-away peatlands in North America. *Applied Vegetation Science*. 11: 521–528.
5. Graf, M.D., and Rochefort, L. 2008b. Moss regeneration for fen restoration: field and greenhouse experiments. *Restoration Ecology*. 18(1): 121–130.
6. Lamers, L.P.M., Vile, M.A., Grootjans, A.P., Acreman, M.C., van Diggelen, R., Evans, M.G., Richardson, C.J., Rochefort, L., Kooijman, A.M., Roelofs, J.G.M., and Smolders, A.J.P. 2015. Ecological restoration of rich fens in Europe and North America: from trial and error to an evidence-based approach. *Biological Reviews*. 90: 182–203.
7. Lavoie, C., Grosvernier, P., Girard, M., and Marcoux, K. 2003. Spontaneous revegetation of mined peatlands: an useful restoration tool?. *Wetlands Ecology and Management*. 11: 97–107.
8. Malloy, S., and Price, J.S. 2014. Fen restoration on a bog harvested down to sedge peat: A hydrological assessment. *Ecological Engineering*. 64: 151–160.
9. Poulin, M., Rochefort, L., Quinty, F., and Lavoie, C. 2005. Spontaneous revegetation of mined peatlands in eastern Canada. *Canadian Journal of Botany*. 83: 539–557.
10. Quinty, F., and Rochefort, L. 2003. Peatland restoration guide, 2nd ed. Canadian Sphagnum Peat Moss Association and New Brunswick Department of Natural Resources and Energy. Québec. 106 pp.
11. Rasran L., Vogt K., and Jensen, K. 2007. Effects of topsoil removal, seed transfer with plant material and moderate grazing on restoration of riparian fen grasslands. *Applied Vegetation Science*. 10(3): 451–460.
12. Rochefort, L., Quinty, F., Campeau, S, Johnson, K. W., and Malterer, T. J. 2003. North American approach to the restoration of Sphagnum dominated peatlands. *Wetlands Ecology and Management*. 11(1-2): 3–20.
13. Rydin, H., and Jeglum., J.K. 2013. The biology of peatlands. Second edition. Oxford University Press, New York (New York). 382 pp.
14. Triisberg, T., Karofeld, E., Liira, J., Orru, M., Ramst, R., and Paal, J. 2014. Microtopography and the Properties of Residual Peat Are Convenient Indicators for Restoration Planning of Abandoned Extracted Peatlands. *Restoration Ecology*. 22(1): 31-39.
15. Vitt, D.H., Bayley, S.E., and Jin, T.L. 1995. Seasonal variation in water chemistry over a bog-rich fen gradient in Continental Western Canada. *Canadian Journal of Fisheries and Aquatic Sciences*. 52(3): 587–606.

16. Wind-Mulder, H.L., Rochefort, L., and Vitt, D.H. 1996. Water and peat chemistry comparisons of natural and post-harvested peatlands across Canada and their relevance to peatland restoration. *Ecological Engineering*. 7(3): 161–181.
17. Wind-Mulder, H.L., and Vitt, D.H. 2000. Comparison of water and peat chemistries of a post-harvested and undisturbed peatland with relevance to restoration. *Wetlands*. 20: 616–628.

Abstract No: A-065

REWETTING OF DEGRADED TROPICAL PEATLAND BY CANAL BLOCKING TECHNIQUE IN SEBANGAU NATIONAL PARK, CENTRAL KALIMANTAN, INDONESIA

Rosenda Chandra Kasih, Okta Simon, Ma'mun Ansori, Muhammad Porkab Pratama and Fenky Wirada*

WWF Indonesia-Central Kalimantan, Indonesia

**Corresponding author: fenkywirada@gmail.com*

SUMMARY

Sebangau National Park is a tropical peat swamp forest previously used for logging activities (illegal and legal) between the 1970s until 2006. Logging activities created the canal networks used for transportation of logs and led to over-drainage in peatland. Two-hundred and seventy three canals were recorded over a total length of 673.486 km in nine locations at the Sebangau National Park. Restoration of degraded peatland area started by rewetting peatland using canal blocking technique in which the dam increases the water table level. This technique was implemented in the Bulan River, Katingan Catchment, southwest of Sebangau National Park. The location of canal blocking were determined using canal elevation, estimated every 25 cm by combining field survey and imagery data from digital terrain model. Final decision on canal blocking was reached through compromised discussions with the villagers in order for them to understand the aims of canal blocking and to come to an agreement with the beneficiaries of non-timber forest products and fisheries around the affected area. The canal blocking have resulted in 645 dams being built along the 92 canals with total length measuring 226 km. Measurement impacts of canal blocking were monitored by monthly data of surface water level (swl) in 16 locations and groundwater level (gwl) in 112 pipes for the period from June 2013 to July 2015. The analysis shows that canal blocking effect is significantly positively correlated with water level controlled by rainfall ($p < 0.05$). The positive impact after the canal blocking is on the increase of swl (mean of swl: before = -33.966 cm, after = -26.099 cm; rainfall = 191.0398 mm) and gwl (mean of gwl: before = -19.442 cm, after = -11.925 cm; rainfall = 191.0398 mm). Other efforts that should be done to promote restoration include peat fire prevention, reforestation and community involvement.

***Keywords**: tropical peatland, canal blocking, rewetting*

INTRODUCTION

The Sebangau National Park area was designated by Ministry of Forestry decree number 423/Menhut-II/2004 on October 19, 2004 with an area 568.700 ha. Of tropical peatland in Sebangau National Park located between Katingan and Sebangau River in Central Kalimantan-Indonesia. Peat accumulation in Central Kalimantan began more than 10,000 years ago (Rieley *et al.*, 1992; Page *et al.*, 2009). The peat swamp is important for biodiversity preservation and water regulatory (Wösten *et al.*, 2008). The peat swamps of Sebangau National Park are also an important habitat for endangered Borneo orang-utan: it is estimated that about 5,400 orangutans are still found in Sebangau National Park (Panda *et al.*, 2010). The peat thickness varies from 1 m – 10.5 m with seven forest type (riverine forest, riverine-mixed swamp forest, mixed swamp forest, mixed swamp – low pole forest, low pole forest, tall interior forest, very low canopy forest) in Sebangau area (Page *et al.*, 1999).

Before Sebangau area become a National Park, it was production forest managed under 13 logging concession from 1970 – 1995. After the logging concession era, an era of rampant and uncontrolled illegal logging activities followed between until 2006. In this era, canals network created in to the peat surface that were used for floating the logs out of the peatland area into the two large rivers. After it was designated to be a national park, two years (2006) were needed to completely eliminate ilegal logging activities in the Park (WWF, 2014). Based on Land Cover Map of Ministry of Forestry (2013), land cover of Sebangau National Park dominated by secondary swamp forest (82%) and other land use and land cover (18%) of total area (Figure 1).

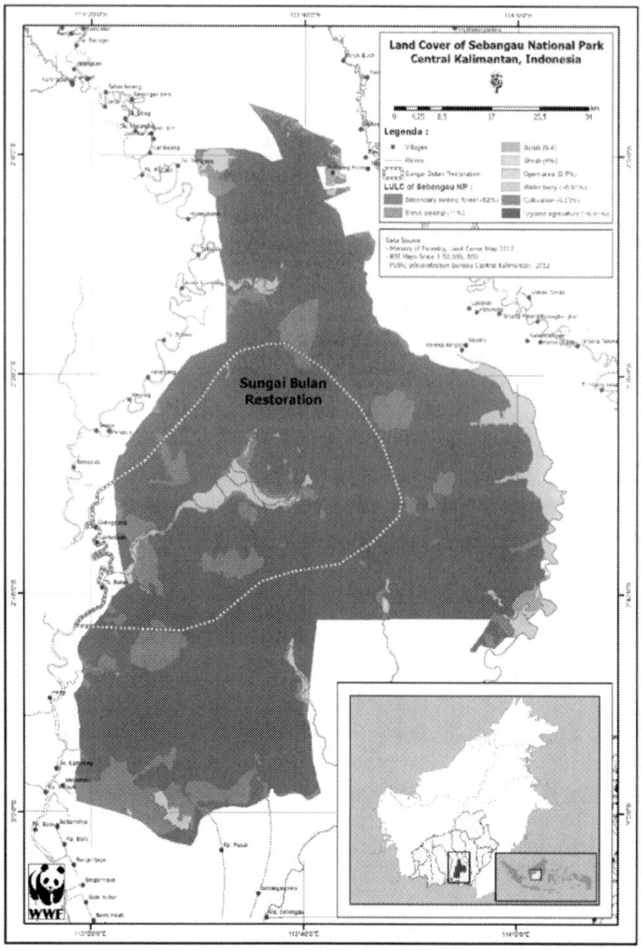

Figure 1: Land cover Map of Sebangau National Park, Central Kalimantan, Indonesia

Based on teresterial survey, 273 canals were recorded, amounting to 673.486 km in 9 locations at the Sebangau National Park. The canals network is having impact on the hydrology of the peat swamp forest, peatland drainage results in peat oxidation and subsidence of the peat surface (Page *et al.*, 2009; Wösten *et al.*, 2008) and also increase the risk of fire. Rewetting the peat is an important key to vegetation restoration and protection of remaining peat carbon stocks (Page *et al.*, 2009). Rewetting in Sebangau National Park is done using canal blocking technique whereby dams are established in drainage canals. The goal of rewetting is to reducing drainage and maintain the groundwater level in degraded peatland in order to restore hydrological and ecological functions. As a result, significant emissions of CO_2 from peatland in that area will be prevented.

The objective of this study is to assess the impact of canal blocking on water table level. Impacts of rewetting was directly measured from ground water and surface water levels data by comparing conditions before and after canal blocking at the project area of Bulan River, Sebangau National Park.

MATERIALS AND METHODS

Site Location

The specific hydrological restoration project sites were chosen in Bulan River, Katingan Catchment, Sebangau National Park. Methods to determine the location of canal blocking were based on canal elevation in each 25 cm by combining field survey and imagery data from digital terrain model. Final decision on canal blocking was reached through compromised discussions with the villagers in order for them to understand the aims of canal blocking and to come to an agreement with the beneficiaries of non-timber forest products and fisheries around the affected area who utilize the canals. In the canals that are used by community members for fishing or to access NTFPs, the dams were built with a spilway that allow access for the types of boats used in his area. In total, 645 dams were built along the 92 canals (226 km) at Bulan River area, Sebangau National Park. The locations of dams are shown in Figure 2.

Hydrological Monitoring

Ground water level (gwl) and surface water level (swl) were monitored to evaluate the effect of canal blocking on rewetting of degraded peatlands. Measurement of surface water level was done using permanent measuring stick which were installed on canals. Measurement of ground water level were carried out using simple tubewells constructed from PVC tubes covered with nylon mesh and with the bottom fitted with a wood block. Sampling points were then established at regular intervals perpendicular to the canal. Transect of tubewell determined by analysis of gradient of slope conditions each canals sample. Two transects were installed in 4 canals sample, each side of canals consisting 7 tubewell with regular interval 50 m for tubewells. Water level are monitored by monthly data of surface water level (swl) in 16 locations and groundwater level (gwl) in 112 pipes. Water level are monitored at the end of the month. Period of monitoring before canal blocking from June to August 2014, and after canal blocking from December 2014 to July 2015. Monthly rainfall data for Sebangau area collected by SSI and Punggu Alas Field Station. Locations of tubewell are shown in figure 2.

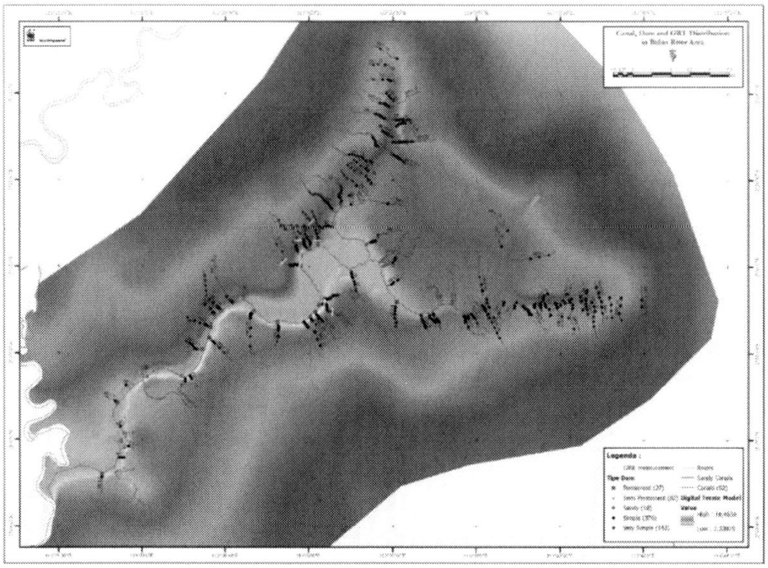

Figure 2: Canals, dams, and tubewells distribution on Bulan River Project area

RESULTS AND DISCUSSION

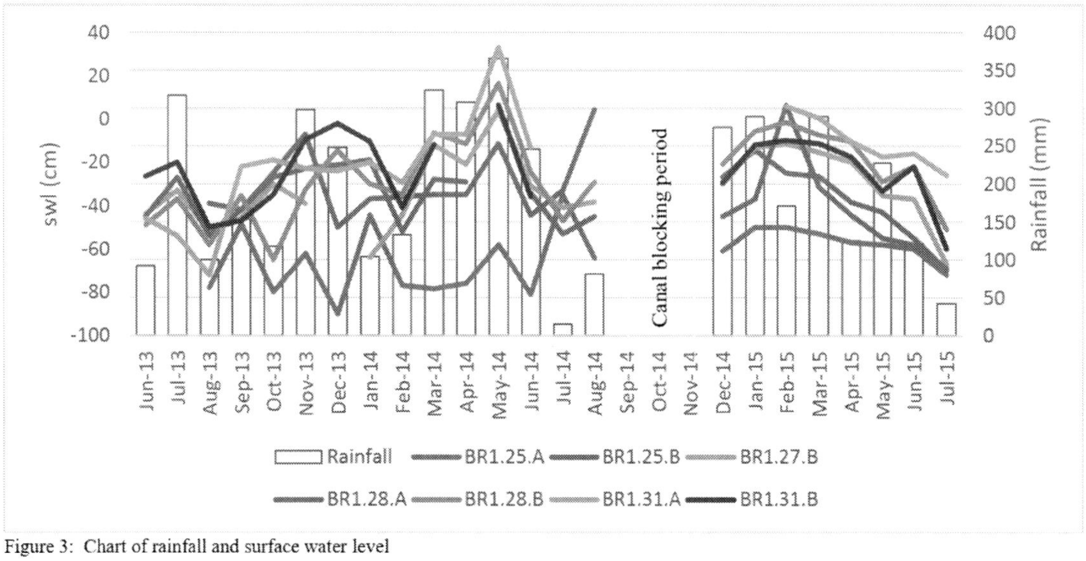

Figure 3: Chart of rainfall and surface water level

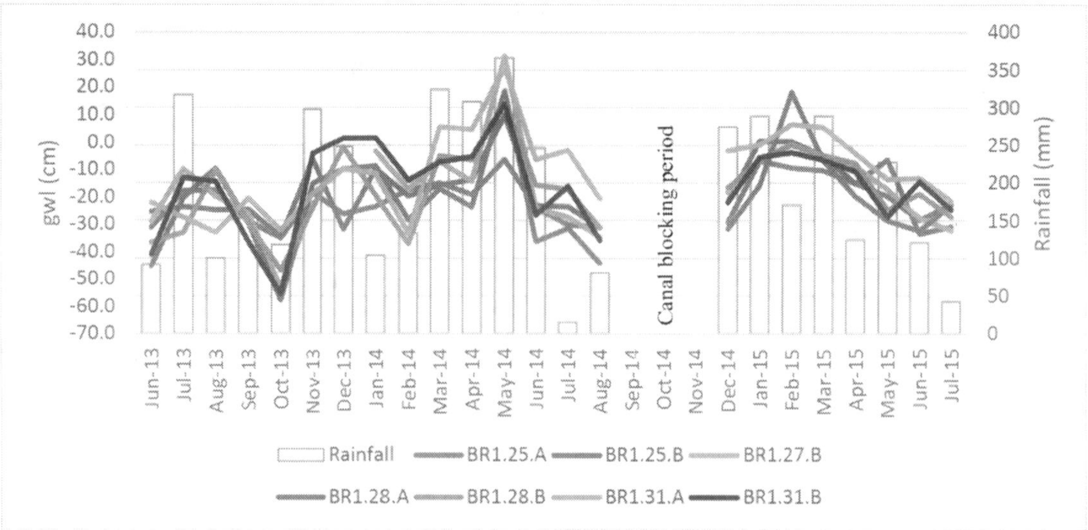

Figure 4: Chart of rainfall and ground water level

The effect of dam constructions on raising water levels in the peatland area measured in the field and compared the situation before and after canals blocking. Before canals blocking period when dry seasons, conditions of surface water level in canals almost -60 cm to -70 cm and ground water level almost -50 cm to -60 cm below soil surface. Rainfall is not distributed evenly over the year, range of rainfall between 10 mm to 300 mm per month in Sebangau area (Fig 4). The existing of the canals cause drainage besides limited rainfall source on dry seasons. Degraded peatland conditions is a major factor to reducing the capacity of peatland to store water during the dry season. Based on water balance condition on tropical peatland (Ritzema, 2008), rainfall is the main factor that determines other hydrologycal factors such as water levels dynamics.

Results of univariate analysis of variance shows the water level is significanly positively correlated with canal blocking treatment controlled by rainfall ($p < 0.05$). The positive impact after the canal blocking is on the increase of surface water level and ground water level. Generally water levels are closer to soil surface after canals blocking. Average water level conditions before and after constructions canal blocking are shown in Table 1.

Table 1: Water level before and after canal blocking period 2013-2015 (WWF Indonesia)

Water Level	Mean	95% Confidence Interval	
		Lower Bound	Upper Bound
gwl before canal blocking	-19.4 ± 1.26	-21.9	-16.9
gwl after canal blocking	-11.9 ± 1.69	-15.3	-8.6
swl before canal blocking	-33.9 ± 2.30	-38.5	-29.4
swl before canal blocking	-26.1 ± 3.08	-32.2	-20.0

a. Covariates are evaluated at the following values: rainfall = 191.

Canals blocking with multiple dams can hold water and decrease rapid drainage during the dry season. Dams can act as barriers restricting water outflow during the dry season and thus decrease depth and duration of the lowest water level conditions (Jauhiainen, 2008). The ultimate goal of rewetting is to restore the hydrological functions of the peat swamp forest. Increase of water levels as the effects after canals blocking is the first and primary way to restore degraded peatland. Deceleration of water discharge after canals blocking also decrease water drainage in canals. Naturally this conditions will be followed by the accumulation of litter and organic materials on several canals that will accelerate process of canals closing.

CONCLUSIONS

This study shows the implementation of management on degraded tropical peatlands through hydrological restoration. Rewetting with canals blocking technique positively correlated to increase the surface and ground water level in peatland. Rewetting degraded peatland as main way to restore the nature ecosystem of tropical peatland. Other efforts such as peat fire prevention, reforestation and community involvement can also contribute to promoting peatland restoration.

ACKNOWLEDGEMENTS

Thanks to Sebangau National Park – The Ministry of Environment and Forestry – Indonesia, Krombacher for financial support on this project. Special thanks to the WWF Germany for cooperation and support on peat restoration programme, WWF Indonesia field team for collecting data. This paper could not have been written without the data and support provided by Project of Restoration Sungai Bulan.

REFERENCES

1. Jauhiainen, J., Limin, S., Silvennoinen, H., Vasander, H. 2008. *Carbon Dioxide And Methane Fluxes In Drainage Affected Tropical Peat Before And After Hydrological Restoration*. Ecology 89, 3503–3514.
2. Jaenicke, J.,Wösten, H., Budiman, A., Siegert, F. 2010. *Planning Hydrological Restoration Of Peatlands In Indonesia To Mitigate Carbon Dioxide Emissions*. Mitig. Adapt. Strateg. Glob. Chang. DOI 10.1007/s11027-010-9214-5.
3. Page SE, Hoscilo A, Wösten JHM, Jauhiainen J, Silvius M, Rieley JO, Ritzema H, Tansey K, Graham L, Vasander H, Limin S. 2008. *Restoration Ecology Of Lowland Tropical Peatlands In Southeast Asia: Current Knowledge And Future Research Directions*. Ecosystems. doi:10.1007/s10021-008-9216-2.
4. Page SE, Wüst RA, Weiss D, Rieley JO, Shotyk W, Limin SH. 2004. *A Record Of Late Pleistocene And Holocene Carbon Accumulation And Climate Change From An Equatorial Peat Bog (Kalimantan, Indonesia): Implications For Past, Present And Future Carbon Dynamics*. J Quaternary Sci 19:625–635.
5. Page SE, Rieley JO, Shotyk W, Weiss D. 1999. *Interdependence Of Peat And Vegetation In A Tropical Peat Swamp Forest*. Phil Trans R Soc Lond B 354:1885–1897.
6. Page, S., Hoscilo, A., Wösten, J.H.M., Jauhiainen, J., Silvius, M., Rieley, J., Ritzema, H.P., Tansey, K., Graham, L., Vasander, H., Limin, S. 2009. *Restoration Ecology Of Lowland Tropical Peatlands In Southeast Asia — Current Knowledge And Future Research Directions*. Ecosystems 12, 888–905.
7. Panda A, Pamungkas B, Ancrenaz M. 2010. *The Population Status Of Bornean Orang-Utans (Pongo Pygmaeus Wurmbii) In Sebangau National Park Central Kalimantan Indonesia*. Paper Presented on International Workshop on Orangutan Conservation, Bali 15-16 July 2010.
8. Rieley JO, SieVermann RG, Page SE. 1992. *The Origin, Development, Present Status And Importance Of The Lowland Peat Swamp Forests Of Borneo*. Suo 43:241–244.
9. Ritzema, H.P. 2008. *The Role of Drainage in the Wise Use of Tropical Peatlands*. Alterra-ILRI, Wageningen University and Research Centre. Netherlands.
10. Suryadiputra, I.N.N., Dohong A, Roh SB, Waspodo, Muslihat L, Lubis IR, Hasudungan F, Wibisono ITC. 2005. *A Guide To The Blocking Of Canals And Ditches In Conjunction With The Community*. Climate change, forests and peatlands in Indonesia project. Wetlands International—Indonesia Programme and Wildlife Habitat Canada, Bogor, Indonesia.
11. Wösten JHM, Clymans E, Page SE, Rieley JO, Limin SH. 2008. *Peat—Water Interrelationships In A Tropical Peatland Ecosystem In Southeast Asia*. Catena 73:212–224.
12. Wösten, J.H.M., Rieley, J.O. and Page, S.E. 2008. *Restoration Of Tropical Peatlands*. Alterra - Wageningen University and Research Centre, and the EU INCO – RESTORPEAT Partnership. 252 pp. ISBN: 978-90-327-0361-5.
13. World Wide Fund for Nature – Indonesia. 2014. *Rewetting Of Tropical Peat Swamp Forest In Sebangau National Park, Central Kalimantan, Indonesia*. Project Design Document V 04. Central Kalimantan, Indonesia: World Wide Fund

THEME 4
PEAT USE, PEATLANDS TECHNOLOGY & AGRO-TECHNOLOGY

4.1: PEAT USE, PEATLANDS TECHNOLOGY & AGRO-TECHNOLOGY

Abstract No: A-354

CHARACTERIZATION AND CLASSIFICATION OF PEAT SOILS IN MALAYSIA

As'ari Hassan[1], Frederick Haili Teck[2], Ngab Dollah Salam[2], Elizabeth Malangkig[3], Roslan Mahali[3], Noranizam Mohd Sahil[1], Wan Mohd Rusydan Wan Ibrahim[1] and COMSSSEM[4]

[1] *Department of Agriculture Peninsular Malaysia*
[2] *Department of Agriculture Sarawak*
[3] *Department of Agriculture Sabah*
[4] *Committee for the Standardization of Soil Survey and Evaluation in Malaysia*

Corresponding author: asari@doa.gov.my

SUMMARY

Peatland in Malaysia covers approximately 2.76 million hectares of which 796,782 hectares are in Peninsular Malaysia (Law and Selvadurai, 1968), 200,600 hectares in Sabah (Acres et al, 1975) and 1,765,547 hectares in Sarawak (Melling, 1999). Tropical peat differs from temperate peat due to differences in climate and the plant species that decomposed to form the peat layer. Temperate peats are mainly derived from remains of low growing plants such as *Sphagnum* spp., Gramineae and Cyperaceae while tropical peats are formed from tropical forest species (Paramananthan, 2016). The types of organic soil material (OSM) in Malaysia are mostly fibric and hemic. The thickness of OSM may reach to over 20.7 m as found in Loagan Bunut National Park (Melling *et al.*, 2006).

The three regions of Malaysia i.e. Peninsular Malaysia, Sabah and Sarawak established their own peat classification system during the reconnaissance soil survey by the teams who surveyed each region. Effort to unify the peat classification system for the three regions was initiated in the early 1980's with the formation of the Committee for the Standardization of Soil Survey and Evaluation in Malaysia (COMSSSEM) by the Department of Agriculture, Malaysia (Paramanathan et al, 1984, 1992). With more knowledge on the peat characteristics and field experienced of the soil surveyors, together with advancement in Soil Taxonomy (Soil Survey Staff, 1975, 1999) a more defined classification system was developed. Peat or organic soil definition in Malaysia adopts the criteria by Soil Taxonomy with modification, especially in the depth criterion. Few approaches in defining the taxa have been adopted by the committee and the consultants doing soil mapping in the three regions (Paramanathan *et al*, 1998; Lah *et al*, 2010). However, the Malaysian Soil Taxonomy (Paramananthan, 2000) is currently considered a reliable system and first approximation to unify the three classification systems in Malaysia. At the highest hierarchy, the organic soils (Histosols) must have a minimum cumulative thickness of 50 cm of organic soil material within 100 cm, or more than half of lithic/ paralithic or terric layer. This is then followed by other parameters - drainage class (either poor or well), thickness of organic layer (shallow 50-150 cm, moderately deep 150-300 cm and deep >300 cm), dominant material in the subsurface tier (at 50-100 cm either sapric, hemic or fibric), nature of stratum, presence of wood and mode of origin.

In its original state, peat soil is considered to have very low capability for agriculture development (Wong, 1986) due to its physical and chemical properties. These include high water table, drainability of the area, presence of woods in the profile and above the ground, type of organic soil material and nature of substratum. With proper soil and water management, various economic crops such as oil palm and pineapple can produce good and economical yields.

Keywords: *Malaysia, peatland, characterization, soil classification, agricultural capability*

References

1. Acres, B. D., Bower, R.P., Burroughs, P.A., Folland, C.J., Kalsi, M.S., Thomas, P. and Wright, P.S.,1975. The Soils of Sabah. Vol 1-5. Land Resource Study 20. Land Resource Division. Min. Overseas Development, England
2. Law, W. M. and Selvadurai, K., 1968. The 1968 Reconnaissance Soil Map of Peninsular Malaysia. 3rd Malaysian Soils Conference, Kuching, Sarawak, Department of Agriculture Sarawak.

3. Lah, J.U., Ngab, D.S., Choo, S.B., As'ari, H., Elizabeth, M. and Roslan, M., COMSSSEM, 2010. Paper Presented in Soil Science Conference (SOILS 2010) in Kuantan
4. Melling, L., 1999. Sustainable Agriculture Development on Peatland. Paper presented at the Workshop on 'Working towards Integrated Peatland Management for Sustainable Development'. 17-18 August 1999, Kuching, Malaysia.
5. Melling, L., Lau, J.U., Goh, K.J., Hartano, R., and Osaki, M., 2006. Soils of Loagan Bunut National Park, Sarawak, Malaysia. Final Report. Peat Swamp Forest Project UNDP/GEF Funded.
6. Paramananthan, S., Zauyah, S., Lim, C.P., Chan, Y.K., Boaklan, D., 1984. Proposals for a Unified Classification of Organic Soils in Malaysia. Proc. Workshop on Classification and Management of Peat in Malaysia. Mal. Soc. Soil Sci., March 1984.
7. Paramananthan, S., Tie, Y.L., Teng, C.S., Lim, J.S., Chan, Y.K., Lim, C.P., Mahinder, S.K., Boaklan, D., Sahibi, M., Choo, S.B., Nor Zailan, A.J., Koonvai, L.,1992. Unified Classification of Organic Soils in Malaysia, Document 7, A discussion Paper for 2nd COMSSSEM Meeting held in Kuching, Sarawak 3 June 1992.
8. Paramananthan, S., 1998. Malaysian Soil Taxonomy - Second Approximation. Mal. Soc. Soil Science and Param Agriculture Soil Surveys (M) Sdn. Bhd., Serdang, Selangor.
9. Paramananthan, S., 2010. Malaysian Soil Taxonomy — Second Edition. Param Agriculture Soil Surveys (in press).
10. Soil Survey Staff, 1975. Soil Taxonomy - Second Edition. Natural Resources Conservation Service, United States Department of Agriculture. Agric. Handbook 436, Washington D.C.
11. Soil Survey Staff, 1998. Soil Taxonomy - Eighth Edition. Natural Resources Conservation Service, United States Department of Agriculture. Agric., Washington D.C.
12. Teng, C.S., 1996. Keys to Soil Classification in Sarawak. Soils Division, Department of Agriculture, Sarawak.
13. Tie, Y.L., 1982. Soil Classification in Sarawak. Technical Paper No. 6, Department of Agriculture, Sarawak.
14. Wong, I.F.T., 1986. Soil-Crop Suitability Classification for Peninsular Malaysia (Revised), Soil and Analytical Services. Bull. No. 1. Ministry of Agriculture, Kuala Lumpur

Abstract No: A-331

CONSOLIDATION OF INFORMATION – A MYTH FOR PEATLAND DATABASE SYSTEM?

Frederick Haili Teck [1*], Ngab Dollah Salam[1], Thomas Chai Ching Siong [2], Richard Kho Shu Yuan[2], Sim Hui Chin[2] and Alexander Chu Kah Choi [3]

[1] *Department of Agriculture Sarawak*
[2] *Sarawak Information Systems Sdn. Bhd.*
[3] *Chief Minister Department Sarawak*

* *Corresponding author: fhteck@gmail.com*

SUMMARY

Peatland covers 1.64 million hectares or 13% of Sarawak's total land area. It has become a subject of interest for stakeholders within and outside the state due to its environmental, economic and social importance. Conflicts of interest and perception on peatland utilization have arisen in the state. Currently, different agencies govern their own databases on peat. Hence, it is crucial that a consolidated peatland database system be developed for use by various stakeholders. The Department of Agriculture Sarawak initiated a peat database project in collaboration with Sarawak Information Systems Sdn Bhd in 2011 to counter these issues. The database is accessible through the Sarawak Government Portal website and currently has entered its third phase. The project includes the compilation of databases on peat soil chemical and physical properties, substratum, peat depth, topography, climatic data, hydrology, height markers, natural drainage patterns, original forests distribution patterns, infrastructure, land use and land cover. Currently, most of the data layers are at 1:50,000 scale. Data sharing is complicated as the governing agencies' policies restrict mutual use due to the sensitivity of the information. Furthermore, rapid land use changes on peatland cause the land use information to become rapidly outdated. The updating process for land use is very tedious due to inaccessibility and the huge areas involved while outdated satellite imagery also poses a problem. In addition, soil information is still updated using conventional methods (ground surveys). With the establishment of the database, peatland development stakeholders will be able to access a centralized data repository for decision making, planning and implementation purposes.

Keywords: *peatland, database system, Sarawak*

INTRODUCTION

Data sources pertaining to peat land exist at various locations, are poorly maintained and in some instances are duplicated and most of the data are neither catalogued nor shared. Consequently, the Department of Agriculture Sarawak (DOA) finds utilisation of this information very unsatisfactory and most state agencies also face similar problems. In order to address these concerns the Sarawak State Government has made many efforts to embark upon setting up a centralised State Geospatial Data Repository (SHARES) to include the development, implementation and management of geospatial information and data sharing through policy frameworks, procedures and guidelines.

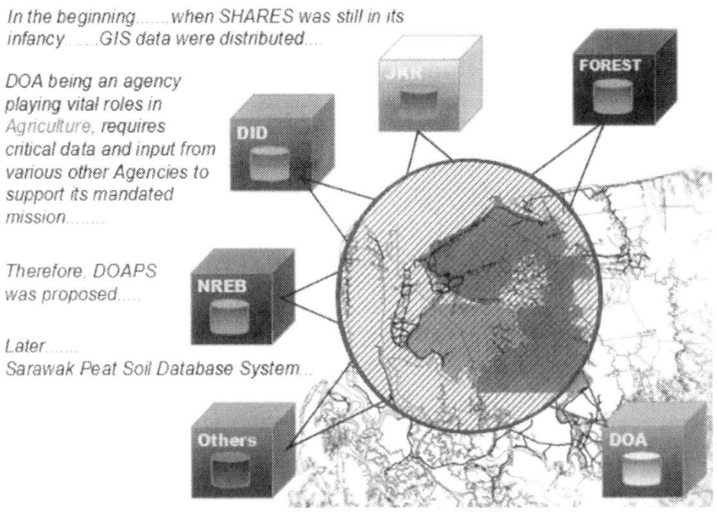

METHODOLOGY

DOA, galvanised by the need for a consolidated database for peat, took the initiative to spearhead the implementation of a centrally hosted peat land database system. In 2011 DOA introduced a peat database project in collaboration with Sarawak Information Systems Sdn. Bhd. (SAINS). The objective was to identify the information technology requirements needed to bridge the information gap in the data most sought out by stakeholders in the sustainability of peat land and related activities.

The peat land database system makes use of the proposed SHARES architecture and framework for its large number of geospatial datasets and application integration. An interface to utilise the SHARES geospatial data infrastructure platform has been developed to further expand the potential of peat land research and development in the State. A series of planned activities, as depicted above, were then implemented to effectuate the inter-agency cooperation needed to support the Sarawak Peat Database System development and implementation strategy.

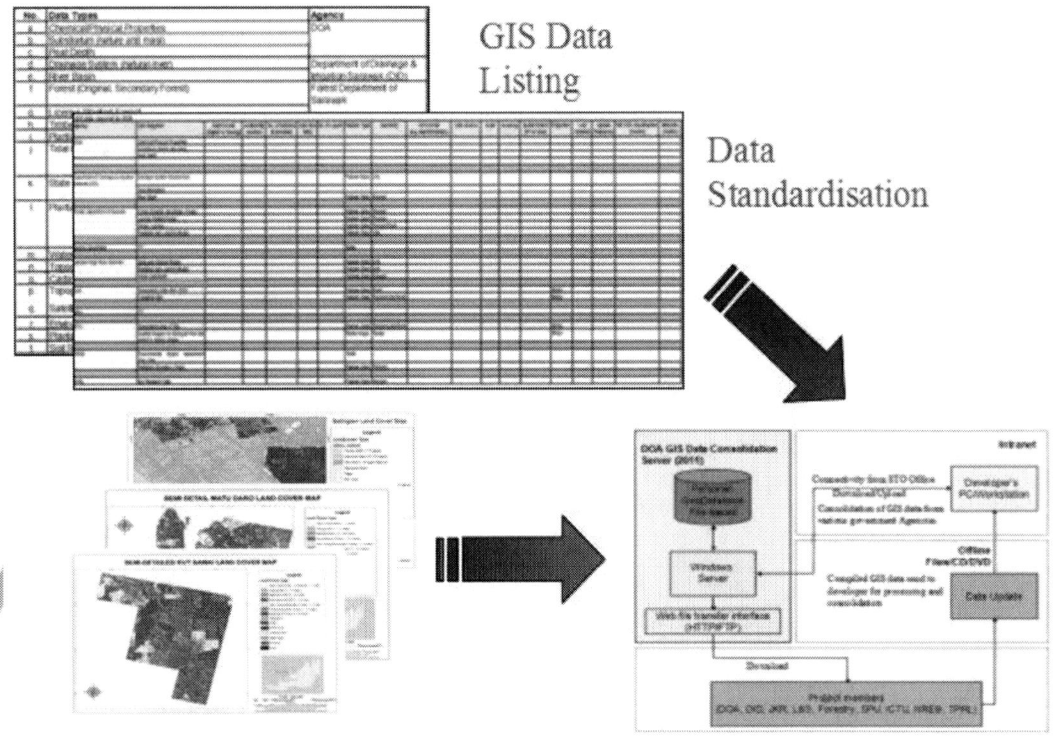

The strategy emphases two major aspects; data consolidation/collection, and data sharing. The data consolidation/collection comprises activities to join forces with various state agencies in the compilation of the geospatial data required for the management and dissemination of peat land information. A task force team led by DOA with members from state agencies, was formed to define the scope of work in developing and implementing the Sarawak Peat Database System. SAINS was tasked to devise an integrated ICT solution to include the appropriate settings for the hardware and software environment, the life-cycle plan of data consolidation/collection, the design and commissioning of GIS application interfaces and to detail the outputs (e.g. digital geospatial datasets and maps) which are to be made available to the stakeholders.

RESULTS AND DISCUSSION

The Sarawak Peat Database System endeavour spanned the years of the 10th Malaysian Plan (2011-2015), with encouraging results the data consolidation/collection endeavour has:

d) resulted in the establishment of an organised and standardised Geodatabase format
e) resulted in the utilisation of the Geodatabase by DOA and state agencies
f) assisted DOA and state agencies to improve their services to the public
g) enabled the sharing and exchange of information/data
h) helped agencies to become open to the sharing concept

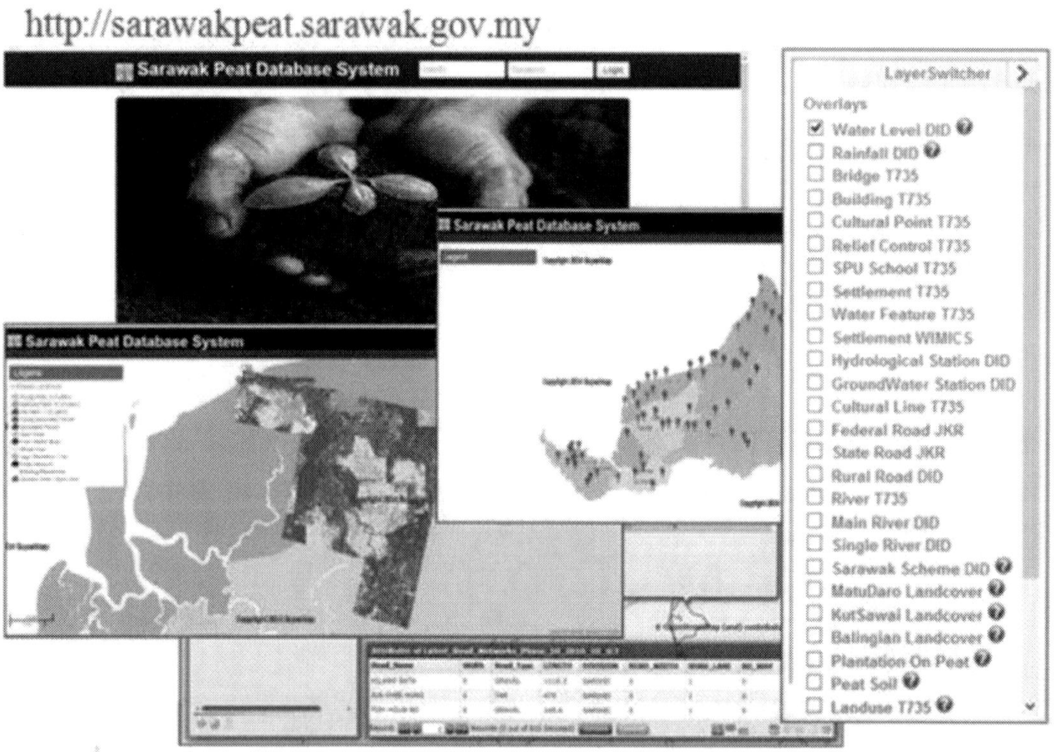

All in all, most of the stakeholders' expectations for the efficient provision of comprehensive peat land data and related information have been met. The project implementation has also promoted data sharing among the stakeholders and will be a catalyst for future data sharing and consolidating exercises. With the implementation of Sarawak Peat Database System, DOA is now leveraging on the information made available from the central repository with much ease and enhanced productivity. The lengthy process of data acquisition has now been simplified such that all consolidated data can be obtained and referenced from a single source. This in turn expedites soil mapping of peat land areas while giving a purview to a good many other potential peat land actors.

CONCLUSION

While the Sarawak Peat Database System has been successfully introduced much work is still needed to fine-tune the system in line with the concepts of data sharing advocated by the Sarawak State Government through SHARES. The stakeholders' experiences with the system suggest that in order to move forward the following challenges must be thoughtfully considered:

i. Management decisions are needed to allow sharing of spatial information
ii. More data to be in digital format
iii. How to utilise SHARES as a framework for DaaS/PaaS/SaaS
iv. How to leverage on current Web/Mobile technology

Abstract No: A-163

INITIATING A GLOBAL DATABASE FOR PEATLAND DEPOSITS

Vera Luthardt[1], Hans Joosten[2], Corinna Schulz[1*] and Jorinna Prinz[1]

[1]*Eberswalde University for Sustainable Development (HNEE), Germany*
[2]*Ernst Moritz Arndt University of Greifswald, Germany*

**Corresponding author: corinna.schulz@hnee.de*

SUMMARY

The sequence of different peat types and often also gyttja types delivers important information on the original hydrological and ecological formation conditions of a peatland, which is a basic prerequisite for successful restoration. Therefore, the authors aim at enhancing the knowledge of the existence, characteristics and distribution of different peatland deposits by initiating a global database for peatland deposits. As first step, a data sheet with instructions for the standardized recording of relevant information and production of significant photographs has been designed and will be implemented and evaluated in some countries. Parallel to this, scientists worldwide are invited to contribute to the global database by mapping peatland deposits in their countries, promoting the constant expansion of the collection over the coming years.

Keywords: *peat, gyttja, macrofossil*

INTRODUCTION

A basic prerequisite to ensure a successful peatland restoration is the knowledge of the peatland's stratigraphy. The sequence of different peat types and often also gyttja types delivers information on the original hydrological and ecological formation conditions. Admittedly, the precise determination of different peat and gyttja deposits is mainly reserved to experts. To facilitate and enhance the investigations of peatland's stratigraphy, the Eberswalde University of Sustainable Development (HNEE) has issued a catalogue with portraits of the 24 most common peatland deposits in Germany including detailed descriptions and meaningful photographs in German language (Meier-Uhlherr *et al.*, 2013). In a second step, the classification systems and distribution of different peatland deposits in the Central European countries are investigated, aiming at a proposal for a generalized deposit classification for this geographic region and an extended catalogue with the most common peat and gyttja types.
Parallel to this, the authors aim at enhancing the knowledge of the global situation of peatland deposits. The World Reference Base for Soil Resources 2014 (IUSS Working Group WRB, 2015) describes global soils by means of diagnostic horizons, properties and materials but does not differentiate botanical peat types, which is a common approach when classifying peatland deposits (*e.g.* Ad-hoc-AG Boden, 2005, Tolpa *et al.,* 1967). Nevertheless, national classification systems, of course, differ or are inexistent, which impedes the comparability between different countries or regions.

APPROACH

In order to enhance the knowledge of the global situation of peatland deposits, a database for peatland deposits is initiated. As first approach, a data sheet with instructions for the standardized recording of relevant information and production of significant photographs has been designed. Besides general information such as precise localization of a sample or general characteristics of the peatland, the data collection focuses on detailed description of the deposit characteristics as macroscopic habitus of macrofossils, particular features of the peat/ gyttja type as well as important physical and chemical parameters, such as dry bulk density and pH-value. The draft of the complete data sheet, exemplarily filled in for a sample of Phragmites peat in Germany, is illustrated in figure 1. Examples for standardized photographs are given in figure 2.

INTENDED AIMS

Scientists worldwide are invited to contribute to the global database by mapping peatland deposits in their countries, hoping to constantly expand the collection over the coming years. The data sheets are intended to be published as portraits of the different peat and gyttja types, reviewed by a group of international experts. An accompanying aim is the attempt of creating a hierarchic systematization of global peatland deposits to facilitate the comparability between different countries and regions. The success of this conception, of course, greatly depends on the possibilities and willingness of scientists worldwide to contribute to the global database. Additionally, a major challenge will be the different state of knowledge as well as different or inexistent classification systems for peatland deposits in the various countries.

If the portrayed project progresses, it will considerably contribute to enhance the state of knowledge regarding the existence, characteristics and distribution of peatland deposits.

Prof. Dr. Vera Luthardt
Eberswalde University for Sustainable Development (HNEE)
Schicklerstraße 5, 16225 Eberswalde, Germany
e-mail: vera.luthardt@hnee.de

Data sheet for recording peatland deposits contributing to the „Data base of global peatland deposits“

Data sheet number (filled in by HNEE):

Annotations:

- The "Data base of global peatland deposits" aims at collecting data and photos of peatland substrates all over the world in order to generate an overview of global peat and gyttja types as it has already been done for Germany and is planned for Central Europe (see: www.mire-substrates.com). Furthermore, the data base aims at facilitating and enhancing the correct determination of peatland deposits and enabling comparisons between different regions of the earth. The classification system for peats is based on the dominant plant group which formed the peat. The classification system for gyttjas is based on the substantial material which formed the gyttja.
- The "Eberswalde University for Sustainable Development" coordinates and collects the data sets. Any data and photos will only be published with explicit permission of contributors and precise reference to the contributors.
- Please use one data sheet for each different deposit type and fill in your data in the grey lines. Complete datasets are most valuable but if you cannot give all information just leave correspondent lines blank. Numbers 1, 2a, 2c, 2d, 2e, 3a, 3b, 3c, 3f, 4a, 4b, 4c, 6a, 6b, 6d, 6e (underlined) are essential to be filled in.
- A deposit sample as well as a sample of the part of the living plant, which forms the peat, would be very valuable for further analysis, too. In this context, please be aware of restrictions by CITES.
- Please send the digitally completed data sheets to vera.luthardt@hnee. If available, please attach a complete stratigraphy of the peatland, the deposit was found in.
- A guideline in order to achieve a collection of standardized photos is given in appendix 3 with examples. Please send any photos on CD-ROM to the postal address given in the header.

Data sheet:

Type of peat/gyttja: *Phragmites* peat

1. Contributor: (full name, institution, postal address, e-mail address)
Corinna Schulz, Eberswalde University of Sustainable Development, Schicklerstraße 5, 16225 Eberswalde, Germany, corinna.schulz@hnee.de
2. Date and location of survey of deposit sample: (multiple nominations possible)
2a. Date
09.09.2010
2b. State:
Germany
2c. Landscape type peatland is located in (e.g. lowland, river valley, high-altitude mountain)
lowland
2d. Coordinates of sample (or peatland) and geodetic reference system:
33U418572, 5876661, UTM (WGS84)
2e. Depth of sample within peatland [m]:
0,8-1,4
3. Deposit characteristics - peat
3a. Main botanical component of peat (either species, e.g. *Cladium mariscus* or genus, e.g. *Pinus* or non-systematic plant group, e.g. brown mosses, dwarf shrubs or amorphous peat):
Phragmites australis (Cav.) Trin. ex Steud.
3b. Detailed verbal description of macroscopic features of peat (color, structure, fraction of amorphous matter or matrix, fraction of macrofossils of main botanical component etc.):
- fraction of macrofossils of Phragmites australis in peat about 70% (partly stolons, partly roots) - stolons embedded in light greyish-brown and soft matrix as mixture of very fine roots and amorphous matter

Figure 1: Standardized data sheet, exemplarily filled in for a sample of *Phragmites* peat in Germany

3c. Detailed verbal description of macroscopic habitus of macrofossil(s) of main botanical component (plant part, e.g. root, stolon, size [cm or mm], color, surface structure etc.):
- plant remains well preserved, clearly recocnisable and present abundantly - stolons: vibrantly shiny, yellowish or bright grey to olive coloured, mostly about 1 - 3 cm wide, sleek or wavy, mostly splitable into two parchment-like layers, nodes 6 - 10 cm apart and glabrous - roots: very fine, mostly smaller than 1 mm thick, pale yellowish, occasionally tangled
3d. Botanical constituents from other plants than the main botanical component:
few stolons of sedges (Carex)
3e. Plant community that presumably formed the peat:
reed bed (Phragmitetum australis Schmale 1939)
3f. Degree of humification according to Von Post (see appendix 1):
H 4
3g. Physical and chemical parameters:
3g1. Dry bulk density [g cm^{-3}] (if more than 1 sample: range and number of samples; additionally drying temperature):
0,12
3g2. Total C [% of dry mass] (if more than 1 sample: range and number of samples; additionally method of derivation, e.g. elemental analyser):
42,1 (elemental analyser)
3g3. Organic C [% of dry mass] (if more than 1 sample: range and number of samples; additionally method of derivation, e.g. elemental analyser):
42,1 (elemental analyser and Scheibler gadgetry)
3g4. Total N [% of dry mass] (if more than 1 sample: range and number of samples; additionally method of derivation, e.g. elemental analyser):
42,1 (elemental analyser)
3g4. Total P [% of dry mass] (if more than 1 sample: range and number of samples; additionally method of derivation, e.g. elemental analyser):
3g5. pH-value (if more than 1 sample: range and number of samples; additionally method of derivation, e.g. field measurement or laboratory, measurement in water or KCl etc.):
5,5 (in KCl)
4. Deposit characteristics - gyttja
4a. Detailed verbal description of macroscopic features of gyttja (color, structure etc.):
4b. Degree of gyttja consistency (see appendix 2) :
4c. Composition:
4b1. Fraction of organic matter [% of dry mass] (if more than 1 sample: range and number of samples; additionally method of derivation, e.g. laboratory measurement or field estimation):
4c2. Fraction of lime ($CaCO_3$) [% of dry mass] (if more than 1 sample: range and number of samples; additionally method of derivation, e.g. laboratory measurement or field estimation):
4c3. Fraction of silicate [% of dry mass] and main silicate component (sand, silt or clay) (if more than 1 sample: range and number of samples; additionally method of derivation, e.g. laboratory measurement or field estimation):
4d. Organic macrofossils incorporated in gyttja (term and description):
5. Deposit classification:
5a. Classification according to national classification system including hierarchic levels (if existing):
botanical peat type unit: herbaceous peats → botanical peat type subunit: reed peats → botanical peat type: Phragmites peat (common reed peat)
5b. References relating to national classification system:
Ad-hoc-AG Boden (2005): Bodenkundliche Kartieranleitung. 5. Aufl., Schweizerbart'sche Verlagsbuchhandlung, Hannover

Figure 1: Continuance

6. Peatland characteristics:

6a. Recent condition of peatland (pristine, near-natural, drained, degraded, under agricultural or silvicultural use etc.):

drained, degraded, under agricultural use (meadow)

6b. For pristine or near-natural peatlands: recent dominating plant species (or communities):

6c. For drained, degraded and /or used peatlands: assumed dominating plant communities under natural conditions:

reed bed (Phragmitetum australis Schmale 1939)

6d. For pristine or near-natural peatlands: ecological mire type (trophic conditions and acidity) as given in Joosten & Clarke, 2002, pp. 25-27* (free download: http://www.peatsociety.org/sites/default/files/files/WUMP_Wise_Use_of_Mires_and_Peatlands_book.pdf):

6e. Hydrogenetic mire type according to Joosten & Clarke, 2002, pp. 26-31 (free download: http://www.peatsociety.org/sites/default/files/files/WUMP_Wise_Use_of_Mires_and_Peatlands_book.pdf):

immersion mire

7. Further annotations: (e.g. further hints facilitating the determination of deposit type, possible confusion with other deposit types or other known areas of occurrence)

- further hints facilitating the determination of substrate type:
  - Phragmites peat often with smell of hydrogen sulphide
  - Phragmites peat often in mixture with Magnocarex peat, occasionally with Bryales peat and Alnus peat
- possible confusion with other substrate types:
  - Magnocarex peat: radicels of Phragmites usually yellower than radicels of Carex, stolons of Carex considerably less wider than stolons of Phragmites

8. National or international references already describing the deposit type:

national references already describing the substrate type (selection):
- Ad-hoc-AG Boden (2005): Bodenkundliche Kartieranleitung. 5. Aufl., Schweizerbart'sche Verlagsbuchhandlung, Hannover
- Göttlich, K. (1990): Moor- und Torfkunde. 3., neubearbeitete Aufl., E. Schweizerbart'sche Verlagsbuchhandlung, Stuttgart
- Grosse-Brauckmann, G. (1962): Torfe und torfbildende Pflanzengesellschaften. Zeitschrift für Kulturtechnik 3: 205-225
- von Bülow, K. (1929): Handbuch der Moorkunde Band I: Allgemeine Moorgeologie. Gebrüder Borntraeger, Berlin
- Grosse-Brauckmann, G. (1972): Über pflanzliche Makrofossilien mitteleuropäischer Torfe. I. Gewebereste krautiger Pflanzen und ihre Merkmale. Telma 2: 19-55
- Grosse-Brauckmann, G. (1994): Zur Gliederung und Ansprache mitteleuropäischer Torfarten (Vorschläge für die 4. Auflage der Bodenkundlichen Kartieranleitung). Telma 24: 19-30
- Overbeck, F. (1975): Botanisch-geologische Moorkunde. Karl Wachholtz Verlag, Neumünster
- Succow, M. (1988): Landschaftsökologische Moorkunde. 1. Aufl., VEB Gustav Fischer Verlag, Jena
- Succow, M. & Jeschke, L. (1986): Moore in der Landschaft. Urania Verlag, Leipzig, Jena, Berlin
- TGL 24300/04 (1985): Aufnahme landwirtschaftlich genutzter Standorte. Moorstandorte. Verlag für Standardisierung, Leipzig
- Tolpa, S., Jasnowski, M. & Palczynski, A. (1967): System der genetischen Klassifizierung der Torfe Mitteleuropas. Zeszyty problemowe postepew nauk Rolniczych 76: 9-99

Figure 1: Continuance

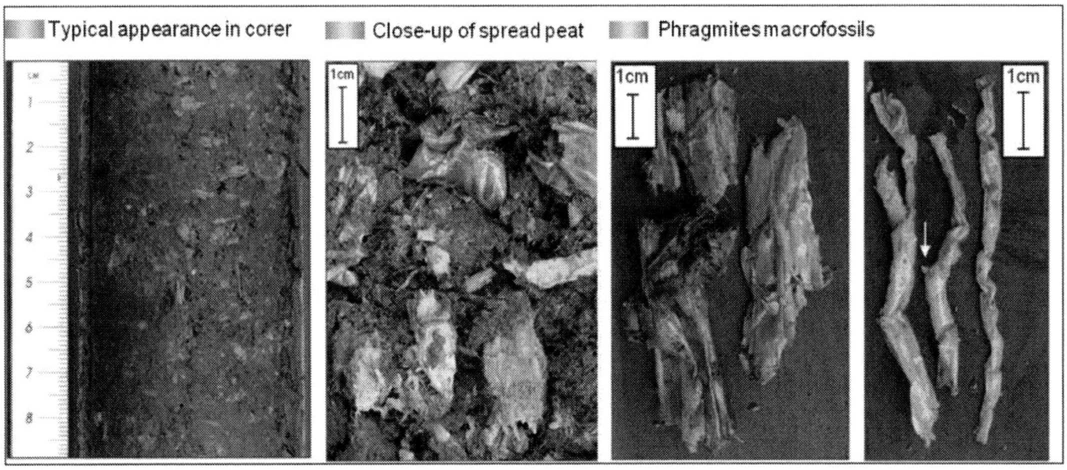

Figure 2: Examples for standardized photographs according to guidelines of the data sheet for a sample of *Phragmites* peat in Germany

REFERENCES

1. Joosten, H. & Clarke, D. (2002): *Wise use of mires and peatlands – background and principles including a framework for decision-making*. International Mire Conservation Group and International Peat Society. Saarijärvi, 253 pp.
2. Meier-Uhlherr, R., Schulz, C. & Luthardt, V. (2013): Steckbriefe Moorsubstrate. 2nd ed. HNE Eberswalde, Berlin
3. IUSS Working Group WRB (2015): *World Reference Base for Soil Resources 2014, update 2015. International soil classification system for naming soils and creating legends for soil maps.* World Soil Resources Reports No. 106., Rome, 192 pp.
4. Ad-hoc-AG Boden (2005): *Bodenkundliche Kartieranleitung*. 5th ed., Hannover , 439 pp.
5. Tolpa, S., Jasnowski, M. & Palczynski, A. (1967): System der genetischen Klassifizierung der Torfe Mitteleuropas. *Zeszyty problemowe postepew nauk Rolniczych 76*: 9-99
6. von Post, L. (1924): Das genetische System der organogenen Bildungen Schwedens. *Mémoires sur la Nomenclature et la Classification des Sols*: 287–304

Abstract No: A-082

MAPPING THE DEPTH OF PEATLANDS USING NEURAL NETWORKS SPATIAL MODELS

Rudiyanto[1*], Budi Indra Setiawan[1], Chusnul Arif[1], Satyanto Krido Saptomo[1], Yudi Chadirin[1] and Budiman Minasny[2]

[1] Department of Civil and Environmental Engineering, Bogor Agricultural University, Bogor, Indonesia
[2]Department of Environmental Sciences, Faculty of Agriculture and Environment, C81 Biomedical building, The University of Sydney, New South Wales 2006, Australia

**Corresponding author: lupusae@yahoo.com*

Peatland is known as a huge carbon pool which plays an important role in the global carbon cycle. One of the crucial properties of peatland is peat depth which can be used to estimate below ground carbon stocks and to develop policy for suitable peatland management. Because of lack of a clear methodology, only a few peat depth maps have been published. Meanwhile digital soil mapping techniques have been developed and successfully applied in mapping soil properties in many areas of the world. Thus, in this study we used a digital soil mapping methodology that used Artificial Neural Networks as a spatial model for estimating peat depth in two regions in Ogan Komering Ilir, South Sumatra and Kubu Raya, West Kalimantan, Indonesia. Peatlands were delineated based on the hydrological peatland unit. Environmental variables derived from SRTM such as elevation, wetness index, slope, aspect and river distance were used as covariates in the model. The model was trained based on peat depth data collected from peat drilling in the field. The neural network model produced peat depth maps with a great accuracy, explaining 90% of the data variation. We proposed this digital soil mapping methodology to be used for efficient mapping of peat depth.

***Keywords**: digital soil mapping, artificial neural networks, peat depth map*

Abstract No: A-329

UTILIZING REMOTE SENSING TECHNOLOGY FOR LAND COVER MAPPING IN PEATLAND AREAS

Frederick Haili Teck[1*], Ngap Dollah Salam[1], Richard Kho Shu Yuan[2], Lim Chun Wee[2], Sim Hui Chin[2] and Alexander Chu Kah Choi[3]

[1]*Department of Agriculture, Sarawak*
[2]*Sarawak Information Systems Sdn. Bhd.*
[3]*Chief Minister's Department Sarawak*

* *Corresponding author: fhteck@gmail.com*

SUMMARY

Sarawak peatland covers 1.64 million hectares (ha). Up-to-date land cover information for peat areas is urgently needed to better monitor and understand the changes and developments in such areas. The Department of Agriculture Sarawak, in collaboration with Sarawak Information Systems Sdn. Bhd., have taken the initiative to produce semi-detailed land cover maps using satellite imagery. The tasks involved in this exercise included the collection of ground control points, geo referencing to the local coordinate system, ground sampling, image segmentation, image classification and random result assessments on the ground. A total area of 530,000 ha of land cover information has been updated and 14 categories of semi-detailed land cover maps with a confidence level of 79% were produced under this initiative. This timely and up-to-date information will help management and decision makers better understand the current situation on the ground and will therefore enable better and more accurate decision making in the planning and monitoring of peatland activities.

Keywords: *remote sensing, land cover, Sarawak*

INTRODUCTION

Sarawak peatland covers 1.64 million hectares (ha). The currently available land cover information for such areas, based on conventional methods such as aerial photography or ground surveys, is mostly outdated. The most up-to-date land cover information for peat areas is obtained through satellite remote sensing. Conventional methods to update the land cover information cannot compare with remote sensing satellite imagery either in terms of time taken to update or cost effectiveness. As such, satellite imagery is crucial to better monitor and understand the changes and developments in peatland areas. A collaborative initiative between Sarawak Information Systems Sdn. Bhd. and the Department of Agriculture Sarawak to produce semi-detailed land cover maps using satellite imagery was carried out from 2010-2014. The objectives of the initiative were to determine the accuracy of using Spot 5 Satellite data and spatial distribution of land cover in selected peatland areas in Sarawak, Malaysia.

SITES

The project areas were located in Balingian, Matu and Daro and Kut Sawai peatland areas and covered a total of 530,000 ha.

METHODOLOGY

Spot 5 Satellite data at 2.5m resolution were used to carry out the land cover classification at the project areas. The methodology used in the processing of the imagery is as listed below:

1) Image dereferencing

A number of Ground Control Points (GCPs) were collected to rectify and geocode the imageries into the local coordinate system (BRSO).An RMMS error of 1.5 pixels (4.0m on the ground) was achieved during this process.

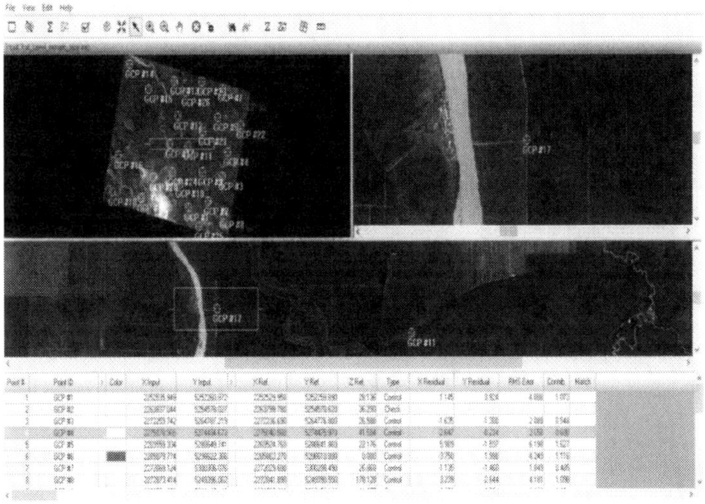

2) Masking process

Areas covered by cloud shadow and the river network were masked in order to avoid confusion and error during the image classification process.

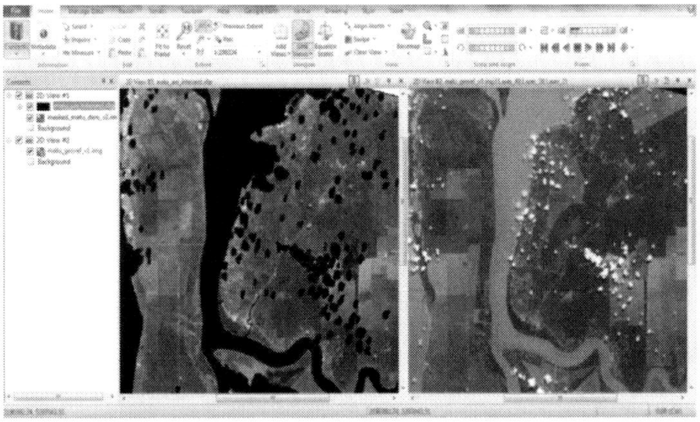

3) Image segmentation

Each image was segmented into areas of 20 km^2 as shown below in order to help improve the accuracy of the final output of the classification result by having a more localized result.

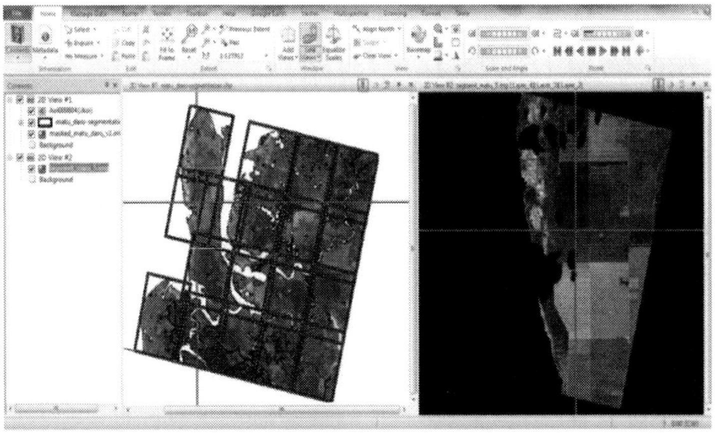

4) Image enhancement process

The Image enhancement process helps enhance the visualisation of the edges of ground objects and thus avoids the collection of incorrect object signatures.

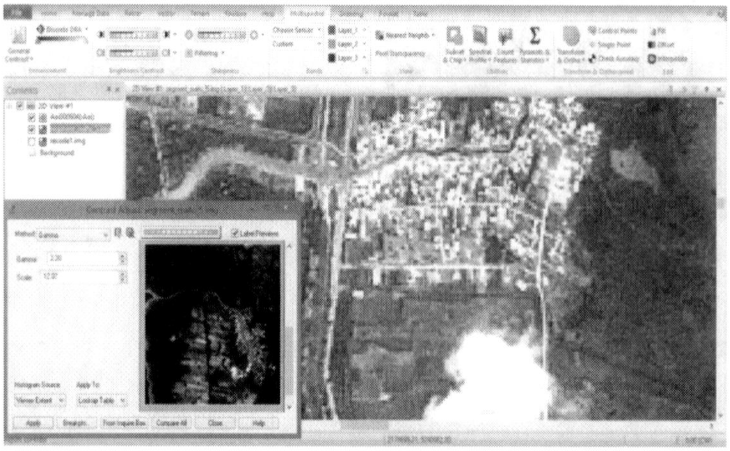

5) Ground sampling data collection

Ground sampling data collection was carried out to understand the land cover types represented on the imagery. Other ancillary information such as topographic maps and old land use maps were used to understand the ground objects before the actual ground sampling collection was carried out.

6) Signature collection

The collected ground sampling points were overlaid with the satellite imagery. Difference image enhancement was applied intermittently during the process of signature collection.

7) Signature evaluation

Collected signatures were evaluated to avoid mistakes in the classification process.

8) Classification process

The Supervised Classification method was chosen to perform the classification process. After the classification process was completed the data were generalized or simplified through the recoding process.

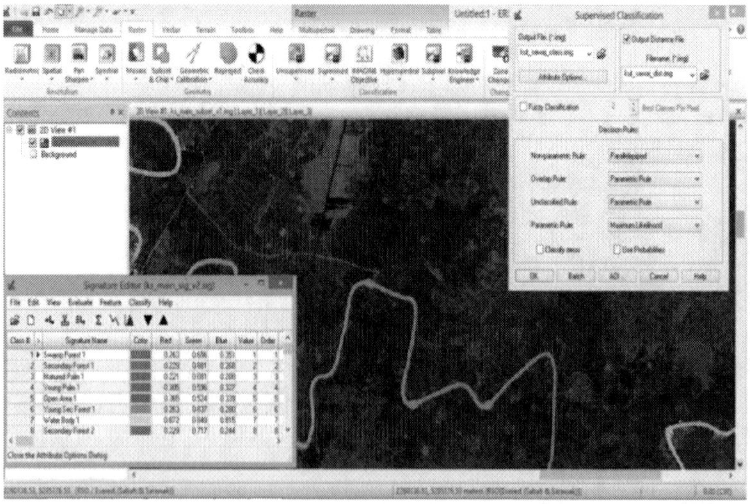

Image mosaic

After all the segments of the imagery were classified all the thematic maps were stitched together into an overall image.

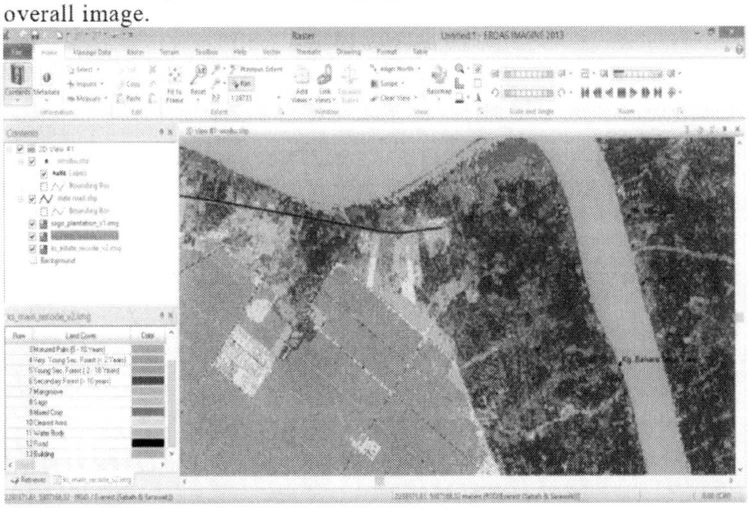

9) Verification process

The classified data were uploaded into the GPS handheld devices to enable them to be verified on site. The on-site verification was carried out by the SAINS Team together with DOA Soil Branch personnel. Verification was performed at randomly selected locations in the project area.

RESULTS

The final output is a semi detailed land cover map with the 14 classes mentioned below.

(i) Very Young oil Palm – Transplant (< 1 year)
(ii) Young oil Palm (1 - 5 years)
(iii) Matured oil Palm (5 -10 years)
(iv) Old Palm (> 10 Years)
(v) Very Young Secondary Forest (< 2 Years)
(vi) Young Secondary Forest (2 – 10 Years)
(vii) Secondary Forest (> 10 Years)
(viii) Mangrove
(ix) Sago
(x) Mixed Crop (Pineapple, Coconut, Rubber, Paddy, Orchard)
(xi) Cleared Area
(xii) Water Body
(xiii) Road
(xiv) Building

The results show that 79% of the classified land cover information match the actual land cover information.

DISCUSSION

Constraints and difficulties faced during this project that affected the accuracy of the final output included:

a) The use of archived satellite data resulted in many changes (environmental, atmospheric and in terms of moisture content) occurred between the time the project started and the time the image was captured.

b) Limitations both in the nature and in the medium resolution of the satellite imagery prevented the production of high accuracy output.

SUGGESTIONS AND RECOMMENDATIONS

a) Satellite imagery less than two months old should be used to ensure that rapid changes on the ground have not altered the classification by the time the inspection is being carried out. DOVES NANOSAT can be considered for this.

b) Higher resolution imagery should be used in order to allow the differentiation of various types of land cover on the imagery and at the same time enable more detailed classification to be performed.

CONCLUSION

The SAINS Geomatics Team in collaboration with officers from the Department of Agriculture, Sarawak successfully conducted the land cover classification. The timely and up-to-date information produced will help management and decision makers better understand the current ground situation. It will therefore enable better and more accurate decision making in the planning and monitoring of peatland activities.

THEME 5
RESPONSIBLE UTILIZATION & MANAGEMENT OF PEATLANDS

5.1: AGRICULTURE & FOREST PLANTATIONS ON PEATLAND

Abstract No: A-115

CHANGES IN THE PHYSICOCHEMICAL PROPERTIES OF TROPICAL PEAT DURING ITS EARLY DECOMPOSITION UNDER OIL PALM PLANTATION ENVIRONMENTS

Masahiro Maeda[1], Nagamitsu Maie[1], Lulie Melling[2], Hajime Tanji[1], Zulhilmy Abdullah Mohd[2] and Akira Watanabe[3]

[1]*School of Veterinary Medicine, Kitasato University, Aomori, Japan*
[2]*Tropical Peat Research Laboratory Unit, Chief Minister's Department, Sarawak, Malaysia*
[3]*Graduate School of Bioagricultural Sciences, Nagoya University, Nagoya, Japan*

**Corresponding author: maie@vmas.kitasato-u.ac.jp*

SUMMARY

Peatland environment, such as groundwater level and nutrient status, determines the vegetation type of tropical peat swamp forest (TPSF). As such, tropical peat (TP) with different vegetation may have different physico-chemical properties and thus exhibit different vulnerability to environmental changes. In Sarawak, oil palm plantation (OPP) has extended into tropical peatlands, due to limited acreage of arable dry field. Therefore, it is crucial to understand the changes in the biogeochemical processes of tropical peatland under OPP environments for the sustainable management. In this study, we aim to evaluate the diversity in the decomposition rate and process of TP under OPP environments. To achieve that purpose, a mesocosm incubation experiment was conducted. Peat samples were collected from three major types of TPSF in Sarawak, namely, mixed peat swamp (*MPS*), *Alan Batu* (*A. Batu*), and *Alan Bunga* (*A. Bunga*) forests. Peat samples were packed in a PVC column (10cm ID x 80 cm L), and buried in an OPP. The mesocosms were recovered after 1-year of incubation, and changes in the mass and the physicochemical properties of TP were investigated for particle size distribution (wet sieving) and C composition (^{13}C CPMAS NMR). Physico-chemical analyses of intact TP (before incubation) revealed that *MPS* had undergone microbial decomposition to a greater extent than *A. Batu* and *A. Bunga*. C composition of TP was relatively similar among different particle size fractions for each forest type. After 1-year incubation, total C (TC) decreased by 14±4% for *A. Batu* but significant decrease was not observed for other two types. TC of <63 μm size fraction increased and/or > 4 mm size fraction decreased significantly for all forest types, suggesting a rapid downsizing of TP at an early stage of decomposition under OPP environments.

Keywords: *decomposition process, physicochemical properties, Tropical peat, vegetation*

INTRODUCTION

Tropical peatland area is estimated to contribute to 11% (44.1x10^4 km^2) of global peatland area, of which 56% is located in Southeast Asia (Page *et al.*, 2011). A large amount of wood peat is accumulated under tropical peat swamp forest (TPSF). Carbon stock of tropical peatland in Southeast Asia is estimated to be 68.5 PgC, of which Indonesia and Malaysia account for 65% and 10% respectively (Page *et al.*, 2011).

Since 1960s, countries such as Indonesia and Malaysia in Southeast Asia, began to develop tropical peatland to OPP due to limited acreage of arable dry field. Once tropical peatland is developed to OPP, the environment changes considerably and may accelerate the decomposition of peat. Therefore, it is important to better understand the changes in the physico-chemical properties of peat accompanied by the changes in peat environment or land utilization to contribute to the sustainable development of TP.

Groundwater level and nutrient status are reported to change with the distance from river. For examples, total phosphorous, total nitrogen, and total potassium decrease as the distance from the river increases (Sjogersten *et al.*, 2011). As such, zones of different vegetation develop along with the distance from the river. Specifically, major species of TPSF successes from *MPS*, *A. Batu*, *A. Bunga*, and *Padan Alan* from the margin to the center of peat dome in Borneo, Malaysia (Melling *et al.*, 2007). Since groundwater level, microbial activity, and the quantity and quality of organic matter supplied are different among different vegetation, physico-chemical properties and vulnerability of peat may also vary between them. As such, it will be desirable to develop tropical peatland considering the variety of the decomposition characteristics. However, little is known on the variation in the decomposition rate and process of TP.

Therefore, we aim to evaluate the variation in the decomposition rate and process of TP converted to OPP environments. To achieve that purpose, we conducted a mesocosm incubation experiment. Peat samples were

Figure 1: A picture of mesocosm incubation experiment conducted in Naman OPP. A mesocosm was 80cm long and 10cm in diameter. A 20 cm extension pipe and a fringe was attached to measure greenhouse gas emission rate (Faustina *et al.*). Each mesocosm contains either *MPS*, *A. Batu*, or *A. Bunga* peat. Incubation experiment was conducted in 4 replicates.

collected from 3 types of primary forests (namely, *MPS*, *A. Batu*, and *A. Bunga*) in Maludam National Park, Sarawak, Malaysia, and incubated in an OPP by using mesocosm (Figure 1). After 1-year incubation, mesocosms were recovered, and changes in the physical and chemical properties of peat were investigated by size fractionation and ^{13}C CPMAS NMR-based C composition.

METHODS

Sample Collection

Peat samples were collected between 20 and 40 cm from *MPS* (1.2 km from Batang Lupar River), *A. Batu* (5.0 km), and *A. Bunga* forests (5.9km) at Maludam National Park, Sarawak, Malaysia.

Preparation of mesocosm

Peat samples were transported to Naman OPP, Sibu, Sarawak, where incubation experiment was conducted. TP samples were mixed thoroughly by hand and large plant debris were removed. TP sample amounting to ca. 800 g was packed into a PVC pipe (9 cm ID X 20 cm L), to which a piece of polyester air filter (1 cm thickness) was inserted beforehand. A mesocosm was prepared by connecting 4 pipes in series using couplers and the bottom was covered with polyethylene net with 7 mm mesh. The mesocosms were buried into peat so that the top surfaces of the peat in the mesocosm and OPP were leveled (Fig. 1). The experiment was conducted in 4 replicates in an OPP.

Particle size fractionation

TP was sieved in wet condition successively into 8 different size fractions of 2mm, 1mm, 0.5mm, 0.25mm, 0.125mm, and 0.063mm. Fractionated samples were freeze-dried and weighed. The <0.063mm size fraction was collected by the combination of centrifugation and filtration.

Chemical Analyses

Total C and N contents were measured using a NC analyzer (Sumigraph NC-22). Solid state ^{13}C NMR spectra were measured at a ^{13}C resonance frequency of 100.7 MHz on a Jeol ECX-400 NMR spectrometer equipped with a commercial 4-mm CPMAS probe using a standard RAMP-CP pulse sequence. Analytical conditions used were as follow; i) rotation frequency of 10.0 kHz; ii) recycle delay0.7-1s; iii) Gaussian line broadening, 50-100Hz.

RESULTS AND DISCUSSION

Variety in the physicochemical properties of TP under different vegetation

A. Batu and *A. Bunga* peats contained large percentages of the finest (< 63 μm) and coarsest (>4.0 mm) size fractions (Fig. 2). *MPS* contained a lower percentage of finest size fraction than other two peats. However, C composition analysis revealed that *MPS* contained higher percentage of alkyl C than *A. Batu* and *A. Bunga* peats, suggesting higher degree of microbial decomposition for the former (Fig. 3). These apparent discrepancies can be explained the types of peat fragmentation processes. One is physical fragmentation by external forces such as root growth, and the other is microbial decomposition accompanied by fragmentation. Changes in the amount of respective size fraction is determined by a balance between supply and consumption. For *MPS* peat, consumption rate of the finest size fraction was probably faster than the supply rate. On the other hand, physical fragmentation was probably more dominant than microbial decomposition for *A. Bunga* peat. Lower percentage of O-alkyl C for *MPS* peat further suggests that *MPS* peat contains less amount of easily decomposable organic matter than other two types.

Decomposition rate and decomposition process

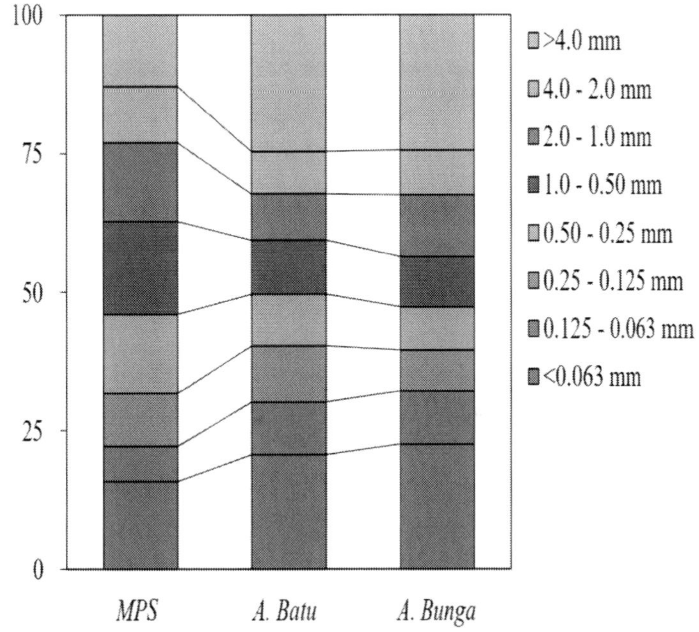

Figure 2: Particle size distribution patterns of tropical peat before incubation.

After 1-year incubation, C amount did not decrease significantly for *MPS* (residual C after incubation; 102±3%) and *A. Batu* (101±3%) peat. However, a significant decrease was observed for *A. Bunga* peat (86±4%; Student's-T test, $p < 0.05$). Faustina *et al.*, (unpublished data) found that mineralization rates of *MPS*, *A. Batu*, and *A. Bunga* peats during 1-year were 2.7%, 3.8%, and 6.6%, respectively. Therefore, a few percentages of mineralization did not seem to be detectable from the mass decrease of mesocosm. However, since mass decrease of *A. Bunga* was about two times of the mineralization rate, leaching of dissolved organic matter (DOM) from mesocosm is considered to be also an important decomposition process for *A. Bunga* peat. Particle size distribution (PSD) showed an increase of the finest particle size fraction (<63 μm) for *MPS* and *A. Batu* peats, and a decrease of the coarsest (> 4 mm) particle size fraction for *A. Bunga* peat, both of which suggested a rapid decrease of particle size of peat during 1-year of incubation.

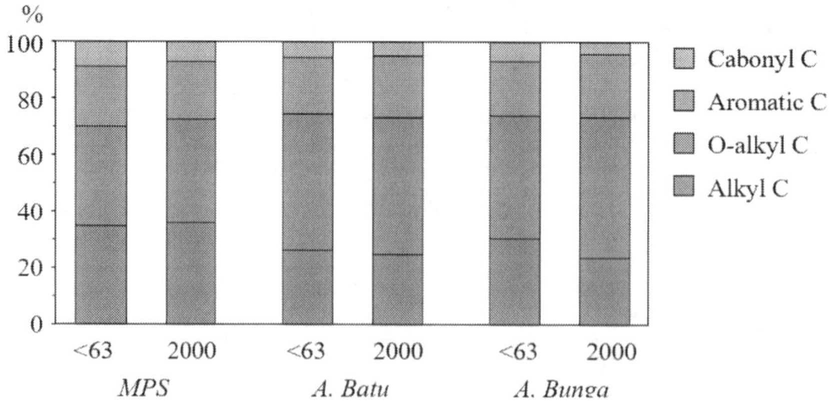

Figure. 3: Carbon composition of peat with different particle size and different vegetation (before incubation). <63 and 2000 refer to <63μm and 1.0-2.0 mm fraction, respectively.

The percentage of O-alkyl C decreased while alkyl-C increased in the finest size fraction for *MPS* and *A. Batu*. Considering the increase of the finest size fraction, selective decomposition probably proceeded accompanied by the decrease of particle size. For *A. Bunga* peat, percentage of alkyl C of the finest size fraction lowered, but O-alkyl C increased. This could be due to a rapid non-selective decomposition of *A. Bunga* peat. This is supported by a resemblance of C composition between the finest size fraction and 2.0-1.0 mm size fraction for *A. Bunga* peat.

The results in this study suggested that decomposition rate can be different among TP with different vegetation. Specifically, *A. Bunga* peat decomposed faster than *A. Batu* and *MPS* peats. Particle size of peat will decrease during a relatively short time (during 1 year) after development to OPP, which can be accompanied by the changes in C composition.

CONCLUSION

Vegetation of tropical peat successes along with the distance from the river, reflecting a gradient in the groundwater level and nutrient status. Peat accumulated under *A. Bunga*, or in the center of peat dome, where low level of nutrients are available, is less decomposed by microorganisms and thus contains more labile organic matter. As such, *A. Bunga* peat will be more vulnerable to development than *MPS* peat. Thus, it is important to consider the variability in the vulnerability when develop TPSF for sustainable use, for which vegetation can be a useful index. Decrease in the particle size of peat changes the physical properties of peat, which may affect air and water status of peat. This change might affect positively or negatively to the decomposition rate, which remains a problem yet to be solved.

ACKNOWLEDGEMENTS

This work was supported by JSPS KAKENHI Grant Number 24405029. We thank to the staff members of tropical peat research laboratory unit (TPRL), Sarawak, for their dedicated cooperation in conducing this research.

REFERENCES

1. Page, S.E., Rieley, J.O., and Banks, C.T.J. 2011. Global and regional importance of the tropical peatland carbon pool. *Global Change Biology* 17, 798–818.
2. Sjögersten, S., Cheesman, A.W., Lopez, O., Turner, B.L. 2011. Biogeochemical processes along a nutrient gradient in a tropical ombrotrophic peatland. *Biogeochemistry* 104, 147–163.
3. Melling, L., Goh, K.J., Uyo, L.J., Sayok, A., Hatano, R.. 2007. Biophysical characteristics of tropical peatland. In: Proceedings of the Soil Science Conference of Malaysia, (Ed. By J. Hamdan et al.), pp. 110-119, Malaysian Society of Soil Science, Serdang, Selangor.

Abstract No: A-104

EFFECTIVE WATER MANAGEMENT FOR OIL PALM IN PEATLAND: FOR PEAT CONSERVATION AND YIELD OPTIMIZATION

Eko Noviandi Ginting, Nuzul Hijri Darlan and Winarna

Indonesian Oil Palm Research Institute (IOPRI), Indonesia

**Corresponding author: nuzulhijri@gmail.com*

SUMMARY

Oil palm developments in peat land need to emphasize an effective water management in order to have optimum and sustainable oil palm productivity and also peat conservation. The effective water management was conducted by drainage through canals to reduce water level and provide appropriate space for palm roots. The aims of the effective water management were to: 1) maintain an optimum and suitable water level for oil palm growth and productivity; 2) drain the excess water and avoid longer flood periods; 3) minimize peat subsidence; 4) restrict CO_2 emissions; 5) avoid peat drought at upper layer; and 6) avoid the risk of peat burnt. The study was carried out to assess the effect of ground water level on soil moisture variability, CO_2 emission and oil palm growth in an oil palm agro-ecosystem. This study was designed with three treatments of ground water level management, namely: 1) GWL-1 (by setting ground water level at 40-60 cm); 2) GWL-2 (by setting ground water level at 60-70 cm); and 3) GWL-3 (without ground water level control). The research showed that the best water level management was around 40-60 cm from peat surface (measurement with piezometer). This water level will result higher oil palm productivity (about 15%), restricted CO_2 emissions up to 18%, and also maintain the moisture of the upper peat layer. Inappropriate water management usually leads to problems such as dry symptom on lower oil palm fronds, caused by too low ground water levels. The application of an effective water management will prevent drought problems at oil palm fronds, especially in dry seasons.

Keywords: *effective water management, peat land, ground water level, oil palm.*

INTRODUCTION

Total oil palm area in Indonesia by 2015 covered approximately 11.4 million hectares (Mha) (Reference). Due to limited availability of suitable land for oil palm cultivation, the development of oil palm focuses nowadays on marginal lands such as peat. However, the management of oil palm on peat is faced with various problems, mainly in terms of both physical and chemical properties such as: (1) a low level of peat fertility; (2) difficulties in measuring the ground water level between rainy and dry seasons; and (3) high flammability when it is dry (References).

The total tropical peat land of Southeast Asia has been estimated as large as 247,778 km^2 or about 24.8 Mha (Page *et al.*, 2011). Within Southeast Asia, Indonesia has a best estimate of 149,056 km^2 (about 14.9 Mha) of peat land (Ritung *et al.*, 2011).

Under natural conditions, tropical peat land are invariably water-logged with high water tables at or near the surface. Meanwhile, to use tropical peat land for oil palm cultivation, a good water management system is required. This system must be able to remove excess water either at the surface or sub-surface immediately during the rainy season and also must be able to hold water at the predetermined level range as long as possible during dry season. It is important, because excess water can inhibit the development of oil palm roots, while the lack of water will cause the damage of peat land. The aims of an effective water management are to: 1) maintain an optimum and suitable water level to oil palm growth and productivity; 2) drain the excess water and avoid longer flood periods; 3) minimize peat subsidence; 4) restrict CO_2 emissions; 5) avoid peat drought at the upper layer; and 6) avoid the risk of peat burnt. (References missing for this part)

Based on the background, a study was conducted to assess the impact of effective water management to achieve optimum and sustainable oil palm productivity and also peat conservation.

MATERIAL AND METHODS

The study was carried out in Panai Jaya (PAJ) Oil Palm Plantation at district Labuhan Batu, province of North Sumatera-Indonesia. The oil palm block chosen as research plot was 6 years old oil palm (planting year was

2008). The Panai Jaya Estate is cultivated on peat land area with a thickness of peat ranging between 344-503 cm and hemic-sapric maturity degree (Yulianti, 2009; Winarna and Sutarta, 2010).

Plots were treated with three variations of ground water level (GWL), namely: 1) GWL-1 (by setting ground water level at 40-60cm; measured using piezometer); 2) GWL-2 (by setting ground water level at 50-70cm; measured using piezometer); and 3) GWL-3 (without ground water level control). Ground water level management was carried out by setting weirs (water level control structures) at the collection drains, equipped with an over-flow facility. Soil bags were used to construct the weirs. The water level at each plots was observed using piezometer to measure the water level fluctuation during the research. The research observation consists actual soil water content (direct measurement in the field), CO_2 emission, oil palm growth and production.

RESULTS AND DISCUSSION

Peat Characteristics

Physical and chemical characteristics of the peat are presented in Table 1. The soil thickness ranged from 343.65 to 502.92 cm, with sapric maturity level in the upper layer (0 to 10/20 cm) and hemic in the lower layer (10/20 to 50 cm). The fibre content of 44% on upper layer and 68% on lower layer. The peat soil acidity was classified very acid and the bulk density of sapric (at the upper layer) was higher than hemic.

Table 1: Peat soil characteristics of research sites

Peat Properties	Peat Maturity	
	Sapric	Hemic
pH (H_2O)	3.68	3.50
C-organic (%)	55.08	55.26
Ash content (%)	5.05	4.73
Fibre content (%)	44	68
Bulk density (g cm^{-3})	0.18	0.17
Porosity (%)	88.00	90.67
Water content pF2.54 (%, w w^{-1})	354.21	375.93
Water content pF4.2 (%, w w^{-1})	171.48	179.10

Variability of Actual Soil Water Content

The differences in depth of the ground water level at the three treatment plots significantly affected the reduction of soil moisture in the layer of 0 – 10 cm. Soil moisture level at the layers of 0-10 cm in the treatment of GWL-1 showed the highest value compared to GWL-2 and GWL-3. However, the effect of a decrease in ground water level was no longer significantly influential on soil moisture at the layer deeper than 10 cm.

Based on the observations of the soil water content during the wet seasons (rainfall > 100 mm), variability of soil moisture on the all GWL was relatively small. This is because the ground water level of all GWL is relatively shallow and has quite similar fluctuations. While in the dry months, all GWL treatments decreased the ground water level. The largest decrease occurred in the GWL-3, i.e., deeper than 70 cm.

There was a considerably great variability of soil moisture content in the field, mainly in the upper layer of peat due to ground water fluctuation. The relatively large decrease of soil moisture occured during the dry seasons and the ground water level became deeper. When the condition of ground water level was too deep (>70 cm from soil surface), the soil layer of 0 – 10 cm were very vulnerable to hydrophobicity.

Carbon Dioxide (CO_2) Emission

CO_2 emissions were 49.99; 37.67; and 25.64 tons ha^{-1} $year^{-1}$ from GWL-1, GWL-2, and GWL-3, respectively. The GWL up to >70 cm from soil surface significantly increased the CO_2 emissions. Figure 1 shows that the CO_2 emission on GWL-3 is higher than GWL-2 and GWL-1, respectively by 49.99; 37.67; and 25.64 tons ha^{-1} $year^{-1}$.

Figure 2 showed the relationship between CO_2 fluxes with ground water level. The figure shows that any reduction in the depth of ground water as deep as 10 cm will increase the flux CO_2 of 30.6 mg m^{-2} $hour^{-1}$ or the CO_2 emissions of 2.7 tons ha^{-1} $year^{-1}$. Setyanto *et al.* (2010) stated that there will be an increase about 5.73 tons of CO_2 ha^{-1} $year^{-1}$ on each 10 cm decrease in the depth of ground water level.

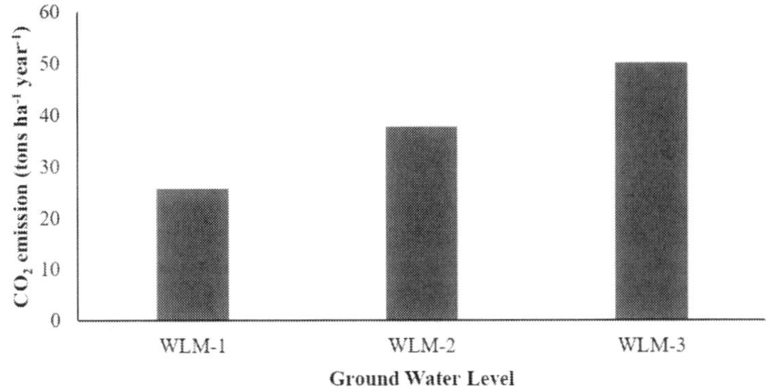

Figure 1: CO_2 emission at three different water level treatments (GWL)

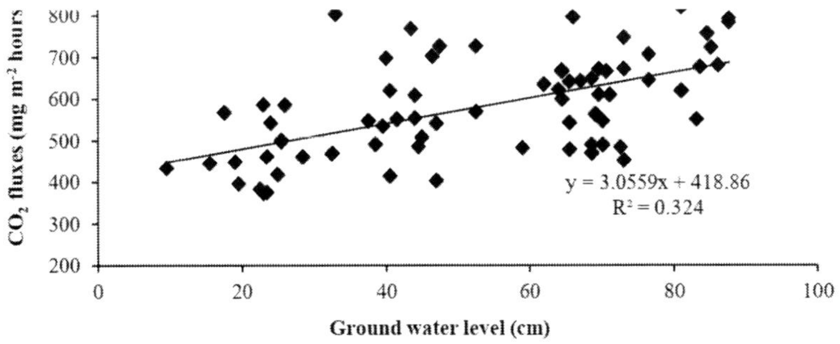

Figure 2: The relationship between CO_2 fluxes with ground water level (GWL-1; GWL-2 and GWL-3)

Oil Palm Growth and Productivity

Oil palm growth parameters observed were petiole cross-section (PCS), leaves dry biomass at 17th frond, and leaf area index (LAI). The GWL-1and GWL-2 treatments significantly increased PCS, leaves dry biomass and LAI compared to GWL-3, whereas comparisons between GWL-1 and GWL-2 showed no significant effect on oil palm growth (Table 2).

The ground water level (GWL) treatment significantly affected fresh fruit bunches (FFB) production (6 years old). The FFB production was in the following order: GWL-1 > GWL-2 > GWL-3. The decrease of GWL deeper than 70 cm significantly reduced the production of FFB up to 11% toward the treatment of GWL in the range of 30-70 cm. The implication of this research was that the application of good water management on the peat soil in the oil palm plantations by regulating the ground water level in the range of 30-70 cm that was adequate of keeping the soil moist until the top layer of peat soil could prevent hydrophobicity, reduce CO_2 emissions, and improve the growth and production of oil palm.

Table 2: Growth and productivity of oil palm in three ground water level

Ground Water Level	PCS (m^2)	Dry Leaves Biomass (kg)	LAI	Ton FFB ha^{-1} $year^{-1}$	Bunch $tree^{-1}$	kg $bunch^{-1}$
GWL-1	20.45 ^{a}	1.98 ^{a}	3.83 ^{a}	20.40^a	17.12^a	7.12^b
GWL-2	18.82 ^{a}	2.13 ^{a}	3.88 ^{a}	19.82^a	16.91^{ab}	7.41^a
GWL-3	15.55 ^{b}	1.80 ^{b}	3.23 ^{b}	18.44^b	15.19^b	6.82^c

Note: different letters denoted the significant differences (α = 0.05)

DISCUSSION

Bulk density at the upper layer (sapric) was higher than the deeper layer (hemic). Increased bulk density occurred in the higher decomposition degree (Andriesse, 1988; Verry *et al.*, 2001), besides the presence of compacted soil at the upper layer as the result of cultivation. Decomposition degree and compaction of soil also affected the water retention capacity of peat. Based on the percentage of water content at pF 2.54 (strongly retained-water), sapric showed higher retention capacity than hemic. Peat characteristics such as bulk density, hydraulic conductivity, and total porosity are closely related to the water retention capability of peat.

Water level in peat fluctuated rapidly during rain or dry seasons. Decrease in ground water levels affect the distribution of soil moisture to the entire peat soil profile in upper layer (Kurnain *et al.,* 2006). Changes of ground water level resulted in the release of a number of volumes of soil water from the upper layer. The soil water content has a considerable influence on the actual hydrophobicity of peat in the field. The peat hydrophobicity can occur if the soil moisture is lower than the critical water content. A critical water content value is issued to determine the actual hydrophobicity of the studied peat soil, which compares the actual water content with critical water content in the corresponding layers. The actual water content above the transition zone which a peat is wettable and below which a peat is hydrophobicity. Soil sample can be either wettable or hydrophobic within the transition zone (Dekker *et al.,* 2001). Differences in critical soil water content at each layer of peat in the field is mainly influenced by the peat properties.

There are significant differences of CO_2 emission rates between GWL-1, GWL-2, and GWL-3 treatments. The results showed that the GWL-1 and GWL-2 treatments the CO_2 emissions are lower than GWL-3. From these result it appears that there is a linear correlation between the depth of ground water level to the rates of CO_2 emission, meaning the CO_2 emission increased as ground water level decreased. This study also showed that at ground water level less than 70 cm (GWL-1 and GWL-2), the CO_2 emission are still lower than the minimum emission constants defined by the Intergovernmental Panel on Climate Change (IPCC) at 40 tonnes of CO_2 ha^{-1} $year^{-1}$. This means that with management of ground water level at about 30-70cm, the requirements of IPCC can be met.

Management of ground water level in peat land for oil palm cultivation should increase water retention and keep it as long as possible until the peat surface, especially during dry seasons (Melling and Hatano, 2010). During rainy seasons, the ground water should be controlled at a lower level to reduce excessive water, whereas in the dry season, the ground water level should be controlled at a higher level for the preservation of peat (Ambak and Melling, 2000; Wosten *et al.,* 2008; Lim *et al.,* 2012).

At the GWL-3 treatment, when the ground water level was set deeper than 70cm, this lead the upper layer of peat to become dry and this caused the plant growth to be disrupted. The analysis of actual water content results showed that the actual water content has decreased by 255% (w w-1) at the GWL-3 treatment. The soil water content on permanent wilting point conditions (pF 4.2) ranged from 231-248%, which means the available water that can be absorbed by plants is only about 7-24%. Since oil palm needs water in adequate volumes to maintain the continuity of physiological functions, this will certainly give a negative impact on oil palm growth.

CONCLUSION

The maintenance of water levels in the range of 40-70 cm significantly increased the ability of the peat soil to retain water at the layer of 0-10 cm. Excessive soil drainage (depth of ground water level > 70 cm) causes soil hydrophobicity (irreversible drying) at the upper layer, especially in dry season. Although drainage is important for oil palm cultivated on peat land, over-drainage should be strongly avoided. For implementation on the ground, it is important to manage ground water levels at 40-60 cm from peat surface by installing water barriers (stop-log) and other water control structures. Since ground water levels in peat can fluctuate rapidly during rainy or dry seasons, it is important to control ground water levels regularly. The implication of this research was that the application of effective water management on the peat soil in the oil palm plantations by regulating the ground water level in the range of 40-60 cm proved an adequate approach to keep the soil moist until the top layer, prevent hydrophobicity, reduce CO_2 emissions, and improve the growth and production of oil palm.

REFERENCES

1. Ambak K, Melling L. 2000. Management Practices for Sustainable Cultivation of Crop Plants on Tropical Peatlands. Proc. Of The International Symposium on Tropical Peatlands 22-23 November 1999. Bogor-Indonesia. hal 119.
2. Andriesse. 1988. Nature and Management of Tropical Peat Soils. FAO Soils Bulletin 59. Food and Agriculture Organisation of the United Nations. Rome.
3. Dekker, L. W., S. H. Doerr, K. Oostindie, A. K. Ziogas, C. J. Ritsema. 2001. Water repellency and critical soil water content in a dune sand. Soil Sci. Soc. Am. J. 65:1667–1674.
4. Kurnain, A. 2008. Availabel water potential of trapical peat soil for crop requirements. Kalimantan Scientiae (in Indonesian). 71 (April): 39-46.
5. Lim, K.H., S.S. Lim, F. Parish and R. Suharto. 2012. RSPO manual on Best Management Practices (BMPs) for existing oil palm cultivation on peat. Roundtable on Sustainable Palm Oil (RSPO), Kuala Lumpur, Malaysia.

6. Melling L and Hatano R. 2010. Sustainable utilization of tropical peatland for oil palm plantation. Proceedings of Palangkaraya International Symposium and Workshop on Tropical Peatland Management, Palangkaraya, Indonesia, 10-11 Juni 2010 "The Proper Use of Tropical Peatland".
7. Page, S. E., R. Morrison, C. Mallins et al. (2011). Review of peat surface greenhouse gas emissions from oil palm plantations in Southeast Asia (ICCT White Paper 15). International Council on Clean Transportation, Washington, DC.
8. Ritung, S., Wahyunto, K. Nugroho, Sukarman, Hikmatullah, Suparto, and C. Tafakresnanto. 2011. Peat land map of Indonesia, Scale 1:250.000. Indonesian Center for Agroclimate Res and Dev. Indonesian Agency for Agr. Res. and Dev., Ministry of Agr., Jakarta, Indonesia.Yulianti N. 2009. Carbon storage of peatland from oil palm plantation agro-ecosystem (Ajamu Estate, PTPN IV), District Labuhan Batu, North Sumatera. Master Thesis, Bogor Agricultural University, Bogor, Indonesia.
9. Setyanto P, Susilawati HL, Rahutomo S, Erningpraja L. 2010. CO_2 emission from peat under oil palm plantation. Proceeding of International Oil Palm Conference, 1-3 June 2010. Yogyakarta. Indonesia.
10. Verry ES, Boelter DH, Päivänen J, Nichols DS, Malterer T, Gafni A. 2011. Physical Properties of Organic Soils, *In* Peatland Biogeochemistry and Watershed Hydrology. Taylor and Francis Group. p135-176.
11. Winarna, Sutarta ES. 2010. Determining peatland properties that affect oil palm productivity: case study in Labuhan Batu Distric, North Sumatra. Proceeding of International Oil Palm Conference, 1-3 June 2010. Yogyakarta. Indonesia.
12. Wosten, J.H.M., E. Claymans, S.E. Page, J.O. Rieley and S.H. Limin. 2008. Peat-water Interrealtionships in a tropical peatland ecosystem in Southeast Asia. Catena, 73:212-224.

Abstract No: A-316

GROUND WATER LEVEL, RAINFALL AND SUBSIDENCE: KEY FACTORS ANALYSIS AFFECTING PEATLAND MANAGEMENT SYSTEM FOR OIL PALM PLANTATIONS IN INDONESIA

Rovy Roland*, Hardy Mulia, Faisal Firmansyah and Bandung Sahari

Indonesian Palm Oil Association

* *Corresponding author: bandung_27@yahoo.com*

Peatland has been cultivated for various agricultural crops for many years in Indonesia However, in recent times, land fires are frequently associated with peatland over-drained due to inappropriate management systems. Here, we present the results of four years' research on key factors analysis affecting the peatland management system i.e. groundwater level (GWL), rainfall, and subsidence. Ecological samplings were conducted in Jambi in oil palm plantations in an area of mature peat of about 5,077 hectares. Peat depth at the study sites varies from 1 m to 7 m. Zonation systems were set up based on topographical information. In total, there were four zones with every single zone covering an elevation from 1.5 m to 2 m and consisting of a canal system, water gate, and overflow. GWL were observed by monitoring 540 piezometers installed in 108 blocks (one block is about 30 ha). Groundwater table was recorded once a week. Rainfall information recorded every day was pooled as one month's observation. Subsidence poles were set up in 20 blocks and peat surface levels were recorded once a month. The results indicate that GWL was strongly affected by rainfall. In the rainy season, GWL reached 14 cm under the soil surface level which flooded the plantation, in contrast during the dry season GWL reached up to 117 cm. By operating water gates and overflows, GWL can be well maintained at around 45 cm and 60 cm to keep the soil wet and not flooded or over-drained. The peat surface level fluctuated following rainfall and subsidence was recorded as very low. The lowest rainfall (30.3 mm month^{-1}) was followed by lowering of the peat surface (-0.5 cm), in contrast at the highest rainfall (474 mm month^{-1}) the peat surface returned to zero. Oil palm yield at the study site was recorded as 24.2 ton year^{-1} on average. In conclusion, the peat management system applied in the study area can ensure high yields and at the same time maintain water expected levels.

Keywords: *peatland, management, groundwater level, subsidence, zonation*

Abstract No: A-415

INCREASED CO_2 EMISSIONS DUE TO REWETTING OF DEGRADED TROPICAL PEATLANDS UNDER OIL PALM PLANTATIONS

Shailendra Mishra[1, 2, 3, *], Romy Chakraborty[4], Jyrki Jauhiainen[5], Hanna Silvennoinen[6], Umashankar Shivshankar[1,3], Peter I Benke[1, 2], Aswandi Idris[7] and Sanjay Swarup[1, 2, 3]

[1]*Metabolites Biology Laboratory, Department of Biological Sciences, National University of Singapore (NUS), Singapore*
[2] *NUS Environmental Research Institute, Singapore*
[3]*Singapore Centre on Environmental Life Sciences Engineering (SCELSE), Nanyang Technological University, Singapore*
[4]*Ecology Department, Earth Sciences Division Lawrence Berkeley National Lab, USA*
[5]*Department of Forest Sciences, POB 27 (Latokartanonkaari 7) University of Helsinki, Finland*
[6]*Bioforsk - Norwegian Institute for Agricultural and Environmental Research, Norway*
[7]*Faculty of Agriculture, University of Jambi, Jambi, Indonesia*

**Corresponding author: smishra@nus.edu.sg*

SUMMARY

Peatlands occupy 44.1 Mha worldwide, of which nearly 15% have been drained and deforested mainly for commercial agriculture. This degradation has resulted in emissions of 1.3 Gt CO_2 yr^{-1}, which excludes the considerable source of emissions arising from peat fires. From the global area under degraded peatlands, nearly 3.1 Mha is present in Southeast Asia, mainly drained and deforested for commercial plantations of oil palm and *Acacia*. The current rate of carbon emissions from these peatlands under commercial plantations is estimated at 230-310 Mt CO_{2e} yr^{-1}. This degradation has led to physical loss of peat resulting in its subsidence, which is a proxy for CO_2 emissions. As drainage of these peatlands has been associated with significant increase in greenhouse gas (GHG) emissions, hydrological restoration by rewetting to bring back the water table levels near to the peat surfaces, is increasingly being considered as an option to reduce peat degradation and GHG emissions. In this study, we have aimed to understand the mechanistic basis of CO_2 emissions in the tropical peatlands, and the effect of rewetting on these processes. We have conducted laboratory-based microcosm studies and have shown that large CO_2 emissions results due to direct CO_2 emissions from different oxic and anoxic state of peat associated with water saturations, and not linked to methane oxidation to CO_2. We also report here metabolic pathways from directly measured metabolites involved in carbon mineralization that are associated with CO_2 emissions and their changes resulting from controlled rewetting. Our findings from the microcosm study corroborate with our field-based monitoring study of peat subsidence that undergo drying-rewetting and subsiding at a rate of 4.4 cm/yr. Finally, we provide field-based GHG emission from different oxic and anoxic state of peat associated with water saturation that corroborates with our microcosm study.

Keywords: *Greenhouse gas emissions, peat oxidation, microcosm study, metabolomics, peat subsidence*

INTRODUCTION

Peatlands are formed by the accumulation of partially decayed vegetation matter in low-lying areas under water-logged conditions. Peatlands occupy 44.1 Mha worldwide, of which nearly 15% have been drained and deforested mainly for commercial agriculture (Page *et al.*, 2011). This degradation is resulting in emissions of 1.3 Gt CO_2 yr^{-1}, which excludes the considerable source of emissions arising from peat fires (Joosten *et al.*, 2010). The current rate of carbon emissions from these peatlands under commercial plantations is estimated at 230-310 Mt CO_{2e} yr^{-1}.This degradation leads to physical loss of peat resulting in subsidence of its surface, which is a proxy for CO_2 emissions (Couwenberg and Hooijer, 2013; Hooijer *et al.*, 2012).

Hydrological restoration by rewetting is increasingly being considered as an option to reduce peat degradation and GHG emissions. The effectiveness of rewetting in reducing emissions has been evaluated mainly by two approaches: (i) direct hydrological interventions in the field and mesocosms and (ii) extrapolation of correlations of water table depth with GHG emissions. In a recent study from temperate peatlands, methane emissions were higher, where peat surface was rewetted till the top when compared to those, which were rewetted till 20 cm below peat surface. However, CO_2 levels were only marginally affected compared to CH_4 levels (Karki *et al.*, 2015). In case of tropical peatlands, hydrological restoration did not reduce emissions from the degraded sites upon rewetting (Jauhiainen *et al.*, 2008). In contrast to field- and mesocosm-based studies, extrapolations based on correlations of water table and GHG emissions have shown that rewetting is associated with reduction in CO_2 emissions. Sites that have relatively low water table have marginally high subsidence, when compared to sites that have relatively high water table (Couwenberg and Hooijer, 2013). Similarly, a trend of low CO_2 emissions has been reported from sites in tropical peatlands with high water table, when compared to low water table sites (Jauhiainen *et al.*, 2005, 2012). Based on these studies, it has been predicted that rewetting in SE Asian peatlands can lead to substantial reductions of net greenhouse gas emissions (Couwenberg *et al.*, 2010). Hence, based on the different reports on the outcomes of the effects of hydrological interventions on GHG emissions using experimental approaches and from modelling studies, it still remains to be established whether rewetting indeed can reduce GHG emissions.

Relationships between water table and GHG emissions can be explained, if the basis of microbial oxidation of peat biomass can be better understood. We have previously shown that fluctuations in water table in low water table sites is linked with changes in bacterial community structure through oxygen and nutrient availability on the one hand and selection of bacteria that can withstand drying–wetting cycles on the other hand (Mishra *et al.*, 2014). The mechanism of large amounts of CO_2 emission and how rewetting affects peat oxidation in the hot tropics leading to these emissions, needs to be better understood. In order to understand the mechanistic basis of CO_2 emissions in the tropics, and the effect of rewetting on these processes, we have conducted microcosm studies and corroborated our findings with the field studies.

MATERIALS AND METHODS

Study site description and sample collection

The study area is located in peatlands of the eastern part of Jambi province, Sumatra, Indonesia (Site map is described in Mishra *et al.*, 2014). The land-use type from where samples were collected was oil palm plantation, having mostly low water table (82±3 cm below peat surface). Peat samples were collected from three depths, (i) 20-30 cm below peat surface- referred as *oxic zone*; (ii) 20-30 cm above water table- referred as *partial oxic zone* and (iii) 20-30 cm below water table- referred as *anoxic zone* (based on dissolved oxygen data). Peat water samples were collected in sterile falcon tubes to conduct rewetting perturbation. These samples were then shipped to Lawrence Berkeley National Laboratory (LBNL), USA, where part of this study (microcosm set-up, measurements of CO_2 and CH_4 emissions using respirometer) was performed.

Microcosm set-up, sampling design and monitoring

In order to understand the microbial physiological responses leading to gas emissions (CO_2 and CH_4) before and after rewetting, a microcosm experimental set-up was designed and samples for microbial and metabolic changes were collected before and after rewetting. Three replicates of sample from respective zone (1. Oxic, 2. Partial oxic, 3. Anoxic) were bottled-up in serum bottles and were then installed in Micro-Oxymax respirometer (Columbus Instruments). A perturbation of rewetting was generated in the middle of the experimental period.

Peat microbial metabolomics and environmental traits

In order to understand the microbial metabolic profiling and predictive functional potential before and after rewetting, samples from each time points were run through in-house developed metabolomics workflow, described in (Benke *et al.*, 2015). In order to monitor the hydrological parameters and subsidence rates, same methodology was adopted as described in Couwenberg and Hooijer, (2013). Physicochemical analysis for anions and cations was also performed based on the methodology described in Mishra *et al.*, (2014).

RESULTS

Effect of oxygen availability and rewetting on microbial CO_2 emissions (Microcosm study)

CO_2 emissions were significantly higher than CH_4 emissions in all the measured zones at all different time–points measured (Figure1). CO_2 emissions were at baseline levels in the autoclaved samples (controls) compared to high levels of emissions in the non-autoclaved samples (Figure 1, Left panel). Thus, establishing that CO_2 emissions are due to microbial respirations only. CO_2 emissions were similar for the first 6 days from the start of microcosm study, indicating an adaptation time of approximately 144 hrs (6 days) for the microbial communities to adapt to the set up. The rates of CO_2 emitted were highest in the anoxic zones (increased 65% after 6 days), followed by –oxic and then partial –oxic zones (35% and 30% after 6 days, respectively), indicating anaerobic CO_2 production dominates such emissions from tropical peatlands. These rates were further increased in the anoxic zones. In the –oxic and partial –oxic zones, the rates at which CO_2 was released increased by 22% and 25%, respectively, upon rewetting. Methane emissions, on the other hand, did not have a clear trend for the emissions patterns from the –oxic, partial –oxic or the anoxic zones (Figure 1, Right panel).

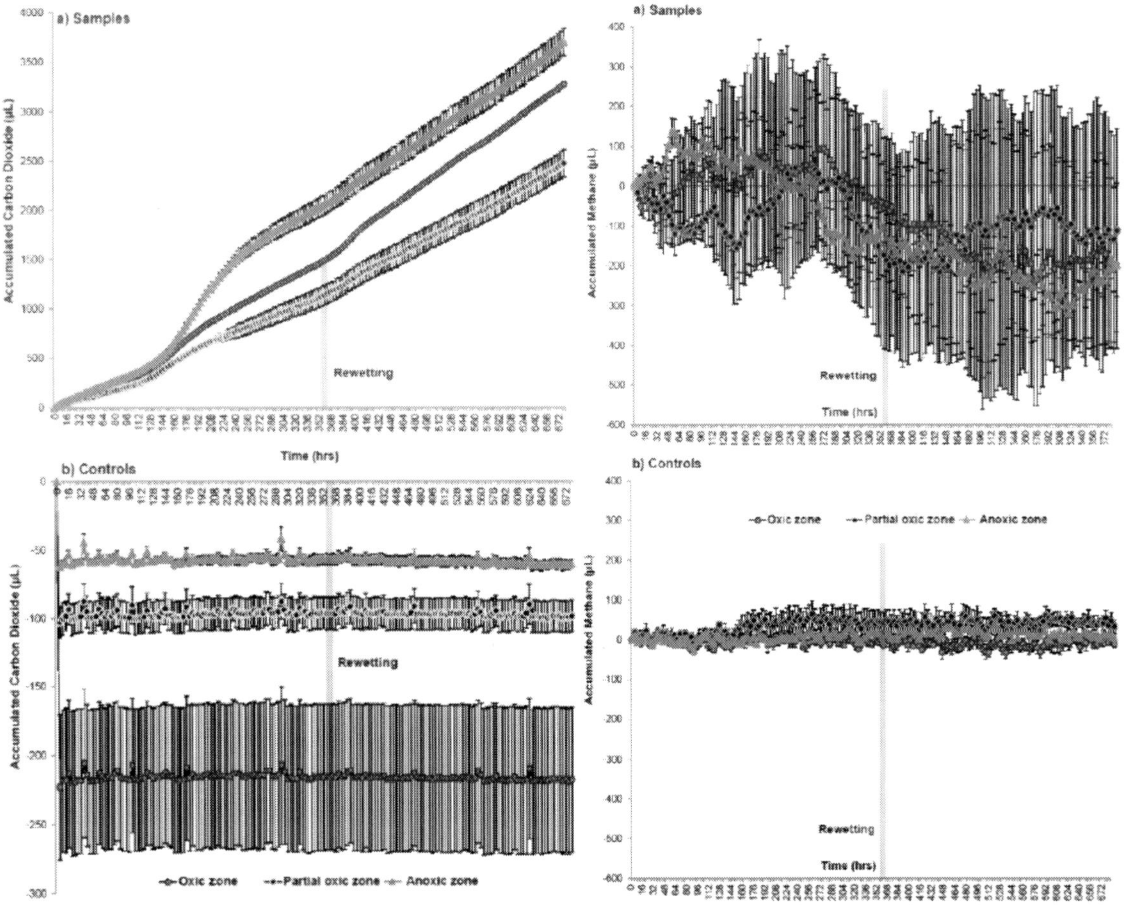

Figure 1: Left Panel- Accumulated carbon dioxide from -oxic, partial-oxic and anoxic zones of peatlands under oil palm plantations, over time before and after rewetting for samples (a) and controls (b). **Right Panel:** Accumulated Methane from -oxic, partial-oxic and anoxic zones of peatlands under oil palm plantations over time before and after rewetting for samples (a) and controls (b).

Effect of rewetting (rainfall inundation and hydrological management) and oxygen availability on subsidence rates (proxy for carbon emissions) and GHG emissions, respectively (Field studies)

Following similar trend as of CO_2 emissions in the microcosm study, its proxy trait *(i.e.)* subsidence from same sites showed that peat oxidation did not slowed down upon inundation due to rainfall. The average annual subsidence rate based on data monitored for 3.5 years was 4.4 cm/yr. During low water table times, peat oxidized at the subsidence rate of 5.7 cm/yr and did not stop during high water table times (continued subsidence rate: 5.4 cm/yr). Based on this field data, it is clearly evident that during rewetting due to rainfall inundation and hydrological management, peat oxidation do not stop. This is similar to findings reported in Couwenberg and Hooijer (2013).

Similarly, peat mean GHG concentrations were lower at depths that were close to the peat surface. On the other hand, GHG concentrations was generally highest from peat profiles at the depth of 100 cm and 150 cm depth, i.e. in water logged conditions (anaerobic conditions). This corroborates to our findings obtained in microcosm study, where anaerobic CO_2 dominates the gas emissions from degraded tropical peatlands under oil palm plantations.

Metabolic functions of the microbial communities

OPLS–DA analysis showed that the metabolic profiles between field conditions and rewetting were slightly different at variation of 17% (Figure 2, Left panel). Selected pathways, which got annotated in KEGG and had highest number of metabolites being shifted are shown in Figure 2 (Right panel). The changes during rewetting when compared to field conditions, shows that more than 3-fold of predicted metabolites (1321 of 6661 peaks – negative mode *vs* 473 of 2459 peaks – positive mode) was identified in negative mode when compared to positive (Figure 2, Right panel). Most of these pathways belonged to secondary metabolism.

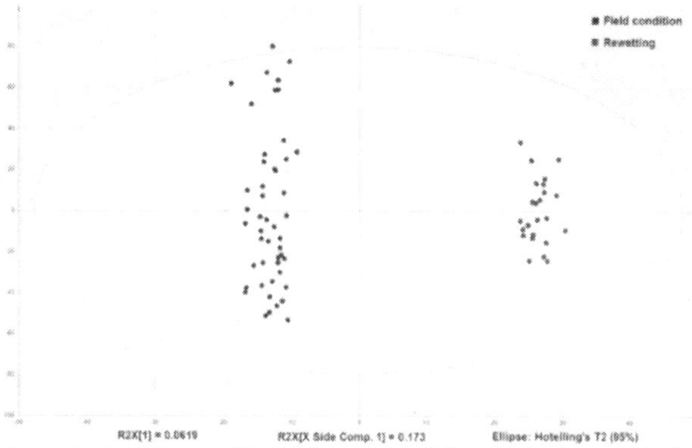

Rewetting vs Field conditions (i.e.) (*Base condition: Field conditions; Experimental condition: Rewetting*)			
KEGG pathways	*Number of metabolites matched at 10 ppm cut-off*	*Number of metabolites changed/affected*	
Negative mode (1321 of 6661 peaks matched potential metabolites)		Oxic zone	Partial oxic zone
Arachidonic acid metabolism	69 out of 74	58	34
Tyrosine metabolism	36 out of 74	20	25
Phenylalanine metabolism	28 out of 64	15	20
Benzoate degradation	23 out of 66	11	12
Phenylpropanoid biosynthesis	20 out of 51	11	15
1,4-Dichlorobenzene degradation	31 out of 74	9	13
Methane metabolism	13 out of 58	5	5
Positive mode (473 of 2459 peaks matched potential metabolites)		Oxic zone	Partial oxic zone
Steroid hormone biosynthesis	27 out of 99	21	16
Indole alkaloid biosynthesis	13 out of 47	12	10
Brassinosteroid biosynthesis	21 out of 27	10	14
1,4-Dichlorobenzene degradation	19 out of 74	8	3
Galactose metabolism	15 out of 41	7	2
Fructose and mannose metabolism	15 out of 43	6	7
Carotenoid biosynthesis	24 out of 91	4	12

Figure 2: Left Panel- OPLS-DA analysis of the microbial metabolic features excluding blanks to estimate the variations between metabolic changes during field conditions (blue) and after rewetting (red). Variation in X-and Y- axis are 17.3% and 6.2%, respectively. **Right Panel:** Functional metabolic potential of microbial communities between field and rewetting conditions based on annotation using KEGG pathways. The second columns show the number of metabolites present in our data that were matched in respective pathways showing potential metabolites. The third and fourth column depicts the number of metabolites that got affected due to rewetting.

DISCUSSION

Microorganisms have a variety of evolutionary adaptations and physiological acclimation mechanisms that allow them to survive and remain active in the face of environmental stress. The stress in our study could be rewetting. Microbes acclimatize to immediate stress by altering their allocation of resources from growth to survival pathways. These microbes may use the material to support growth and survival [1. Cryptic growth (Chapman and Gray 1986)], to enable attack on recalcitrant soil organic matter [2. Priming (Fontaine *et al.*, 2004; Battin *et al.*, 2008)], or to fuel processes such as 3. Denitrification (Sharma *et al.*, 2006) under stress conditions. During rewetting, microbes generally dispose osmolytes rapidly, either by respiring, polymerizing, or transporting them across the cell membrane (Wood *et al.*, 2001). The consequence of disposing of osmolytes could lead to enhanced production of CO_2, DOC, and nutrients released on rewetting (Schimel *et al.*, 2007), as found in this study.

The top 5 metabolic pathways that are affected by rewetting, as identified from microcosm study (Figure 2, right panel), are also highly abundant in the field-based peat metagenome analysis (data not shown). The metabolic changes associated with aromatic aminoacid, xenobiotics and carbohydrate metabolism after rewetting were affected in our study. In the study about rewetting in organic soils, it is demonstrated that aromatic ring compound, amino-acids, glucose, and acetate metabolism decreased after rewetting (Tate, 1979) with aromatic ring compound metabolism to be highly affected upon rewetting. Upon rewetting, compounds, such as, arachidonic acid, linoleic acid and other lipid metabolism were found to be affected in the current microcosm study. The changes in metabolite concentration in phenylalanine metabolism upon rewetting are linked with adaption of tropical peat microbial communities to degrade recalcitrant lignocellulosic materials.

Drying-wetting mainly occur owing to low water table depths and high rainfall patterns, such as, in tropical peatlands. In our microcosm study which demonstrated that there was no effect on CO_2 emissions upon rewetting, shows linkage of fluctuations of water table with peat oxidation. In a study from farmed organic soils in temperate region, it is shown that CO_2 emission rates increased up to 5-fold following wetting (Prieme and Christensen, 2001). In a field study from Kalimantan, it is reported that there was CO_2 emission were not lowered pre- and post-hydrological restoration (Jauhiainen *et al.*, 2008). From our data both on laboratory-based microcosm and field-based study, shows that it is the direct anaerobic and aerobic CO_2 that dominates the large CO_2 production from this part of the world, rather than methane oxidation to CO_2. Hence, a combined approach of hydrological and microbial-based solution is needed to lower the peat oxidation in this region.

CONCLUSION

From this study, we conclude that elevated carbon dioxide emissions and negligible amount of methane emissions are attributed to low water table depths. At such low depth, there would be higher frequency of rewetting during rainfall events. We also show here that large amount of CO_2 emissions from this region is attributed to high amount CO2 production from both aerobic and anaerobic zones of peat, rather than CH_4 oxidation to CO_2. Lastly, it can be concluded that metabolic functions, such as, metabolism of aromatic compounds, amino acids, xenobiotics and carbohydrate metabolism that are distributed among diverse taxa are likely to govern the changes (non-reduced CO_2 emissions) upon rewetting.

ACKNOWLEDGEMENTS

We thank NUS Environmental Research Institute (NERI), Department of Biological Sciences, NUS and CCSERI program under TMSI (NUS) for their funding and infrastructure support. We thank Choon Nam Ong for his insightful comments and kind support throughout the program. Lastly, we thank Sugino, research staff from University of Jambi, for his assistance during the field work. The research presented in this work was supported by funding from the National Research Foundation and the Economic Development Board (SPORE, COY-15-EWI-RCFSA/N197-1), CCSERI (R-347-000-153-133) and NERI (WBS: R706-000-006-133).

REFERENCES

1. Battin, T. J., Kaplan, L. A., Findlay, S., Hopkinson, C. S., Marti, E., Packman, A. I., Newbold, J. D., and Sabater, F.: Biophysical controls on organic carbon fluxes in fluvial networks, *Nature Geoscience*, 1, 95 – 100, 2008.
2. Benke, P. I., Vinay Kumar, M. C. S., Pan, D., and Swarup, S.: A mass spectrometry-based unique fragment approach for the identification of microcystins, *The Analyst*, 140, 1198-206, 2015.
3. Chapman, S. J. and Gray, T. R. G.: Importance of cryptic growth, yield factors and maintenance energy in models of microbial growth in soil, *Soil Biology and Biochemistry*, 18(1), 1–4, 1986.
4. Couwenberg, J. and Hooijer, A.: Towards robust subsidence-based soil carbon emission factors for peat soils in south-east Asia, with special reference to oil palm plantations, *Mires and Peat*, 12, 1–13, 2013.
5. Couwenberg, J., Dommain, R., and Joosten, H.: Greenhouse gas fluxes from tropical peatlands in south-east Asia, *Global Change Biology*, 16, 1715–1732, 2010.
6. Fontaine, S., Bardoux, G., Abbadie, L. and Mariotti, A.: Carbon input to soil may decrease soil carbon content: Carbon input in soil carbon sequestration, *Ecology Letters*, 7(4), 314–320, 2004.
7. Hooijer, A., Page, S. E., Jauhiainen, J., Lee, W. A., Lu, X. X., Idris, A., and Anshari, G.: Subsidence and carbon loss in drained tropical peatlands, *Biogeosciences*, 9, 1053–1071, 2012.
8. Jauhiainen, J., Hooijer, A., and Page, S. E.: Carbon dioxide emissions from an Acacia plantation on peatland in Sumatra, Indonesia, *Biogeosciences*, 9, 617-630, 2012.
9. Jauhiainen, J., Limin, S., Silvennoinen, H. and Vasander, H.: Carbon dioxide and methane fluxes in drained tropical peat before and after hydrological restoration, *Ecology*, 89(12), 3503–3514, 2008.
10. Jauhiainen, J., Takahashi, H., Heikkinen, J. E. P., Martikainen, P. J., and Vasander, H.: Carbon fluxes from a tropical peat swamp forest floor, *Global Change Biology*, 11, 1788–1797, 2005.
11. Joosten H.: The Global Peatland CO_2 Picture: Peatland status and drainage related emissions in all countries of the world, *Wetlands International Ede*, August 2010.
12. Karki, S., Elsgaard, L., and Lærke, P. E.: Effect of reed canary grass cultivation on greenhouse gas emission from peat soil at controlled rewetting, *Biogeosciences*, 12, 595–606, 2015
13. Mishra, S., Lee, W. A., Hooijer, A., Reuben, S., Sudiana, I. M., Idris, A., and Swarup, S: Microbial and metabolic profiling reveal strong influence of water table and land-use patterns on classification of degraded tropical peatlands, *Biogeosciences*, 11, 1727-1741, 2014.
14. Page, S. E., Rieley, J. O., and Banks, C. J.: Global and regional importance of the tropical peatland carbon pool, *Global Change Biology*, 17, 798–818, 2011.
15. Prieme, A., and Christensen, S.: Natural perturbations, drying-wetting and freezing-thawing cycles, and the emission of nitrous oxide, carbon dioxide and methane from farmed organic soils, *Soil Biology & Biochemistry*, 33, 2083-2091, 2001
16. Schimel, J., Balser, T. C. and Wallenstein, M.: Microbial stress-response physiology and its implications for ecosystem function, *Ecology*, 88(6), 1386–1394, 2007.
17. Sharma, S., Szele, Z., Schilling, R., Munch, J. C. and Schloter, M.: Influence of Freeze-Thaw Stress on the Structure and Function of Microbial Communities and Denitrifying Populations in Soil, *Applied and Environmental Microbiology*, 72(3), 2148–2154, 2006.
18. Tate, R. L.: Effect of flooding on microbial activities in organic soils: Carbon metabolism, *Soil Science*, 128, 267 – 273, 1979.
19. Wood, J. M., Bremer, E., Csonka, L. N., Kraemer, R., Poolman, B., Heide, T., and Smith, L. T.: Osmosensing and osmoregulatory compatible solute accumulation by bacteria, *Comparative Biochemistry and Physiology Part A*, 130, 437-460, 2001.

Abstract No: A-201

INTRODUCING A REVISED APPROACH TO PEATLAND DEVELOPMENT ON A LARGE SCALE MULTI-STAKEHOLDER LANDSCAPE, RIAU PROVINCE, SUMATRA, INDONESIA

Anthony Greer*, Yogi Suardiwerianto, Nardi, John Bathgate and Muhammed Fikky Hidayat

Asia Pacific Resources International Limited (APRIL), Indonesia

**Corresponding author: anthony_greer@aprilasia.com*

INTRODUCTION

The east coast of Sumatra is characterised by a complex of low-lying riverine plains. Historically these wetland environments have been difficult to settle and develop, and until recently have been left largely unoccupied. However, within the last three decades, some of the development challenges have been overcome. In response to social and economic development needs, the Government of Indonesia issued large scale licenses for development in these areas. This took place before the linkage between climate change and peat land deforestation was fully understood. For peatland areas, licenses generally took the form of either: (i) production forest management regimes; or (ii), permission for conversion of forested land to agriculture. The large scale planning processes and capital intensive requirements for wetland development meant that larger companies necessarily spearheaded development. Subsequent to the opening up of these lands, a wave of medium scale entrepreneurs and smallholders followed, with the influx of settlers continuing until today. However, as the linkage between tropical peatland use and climate change impacts has become more fully realised, all formal development on forested peatlands has been halted – and indeed there is a now a call for restoration of existing developments. It would appear that the 'normal' forest frontier development process is at an *impasse*. A complete halt to production agriculture, forestry and smallholder gardens on peat would probably result in as many problems as might be solved and would not be practical. Best ways forward must be rationally considered against what can be done and by when. Some form of balanced approach is proposed, the framework of one possible approach is outlined in this paper. Wider applicability of such a model is desirable in the short to medium term.

***Keywords**: peatlands, Sumatra, subsidence, GIS scenarios, management, conservation, production*

APPROACH

Commencing 2002 Asia Pacific Resources International Limited (APRIL) initiated a peat subsidence monitoring programme across its concessions in Riau, Indonesia. Today the programme extends to over 320 points distributed across the landscape, most of which are monitored quarterly. With a focus on the Kampar Peninsula in Riau Province, Sumatra, the results of the monitoring programme are presented here for discussion alongside potential management responses. Simple Geographic Information System (GIS) analysis and modeling predictions extrapolated from this data are also presented.

The 'Management Period' and the 'Management Unit' are key concepts here, with the Management Period being largely determined by the options available at that particular point in time alongside the desired management outcomes and the resources available to achieve them. In this instance - the overall desired outcome will largely center on the reduction of Green House Gas emissions and the various ways of doing so. If for instance the desired outcome is to rehabilitate a production area back to near natural state, the timing and costs of doing so need to be understood, as structural adjustments will be required by state and corporate investments. It must be recognized that at least at a local or regional level, production areas are required to finance restoration and conservation initiatives at the time scale necessary to secure the sites i.e. 10 to 100 years or more. Bilateral assistance and funding schemes seldom extend beyond three to five years. All protected area management options for this point in time require a presence on the ground. The Management Unit is defined by land use over the peat dome area.

The overall findings of the paper provide the basis for discussion around an alternative to prevailing predictions and scenarios. The GIS modeling scenarios indicate that a landscape can be managed for production - and protected for conservation i.e. balancing the carbon books - for interim holding periods i.e. 'Management Period' of up to 100 years or so. Key sections of the paper are outlined below:

1. The case study focuses on the Kampar Peninsula, on the east coast of Sumatra, Indonesia. The area is characterized by an extensive elevated peat dome some 80 x 60 kilometers in extent. The internal morphology of the dome contains bog plains, lakes and rivers interspersed with smaller domes. While most of the actual 'peat dome proper' is afforded some form of protected status, a broader landscape view of the entire Peninsula shows that some 48% per cent of the land-use is currently protected. The core area comprises of the main peat dome and this is surrounded by a production fringe, largely comprising of industrial tree plantations which make up another 27% of the land use. Presented here are the peat subsidence results from the core areas and surrounding development fringe. Production licenses within the fringe zones also have areas zoned for conservation, most of which were previously disturbed by selective logging and are not pristine. Most of these forests are regenerating today.
2. As with mineral soil erosion rates, across peat lands there is considerable variation in subsidence linked to time and space, with the position on the landscape, topography, climate, peat type, water table regime, land-use and land management all playing a role. A single rate for subsidence for the entire landscapes is not applicable although averages do provide a good indication of landscape response and adjustment.
3. It is assumed that the core is not accumulating new peat (carbon) at this point in time although this assumption remains to be verified. This is a key data gap and an area that requires additional monitoring. The severity of recent droughts has probably resulted in the cessation or much reduced peat formation in the remaining undisturbed peat domes of Sumatra.
4. Simple GIS generated scenarios factoring in the land-use specific subsidence rates across the landscape combined with sea level rise estimates are used to visualize the overall landscape impact of both over time. The results to date show that in the medium term i.e. 100 years - the Management Period, operational fringe areas are impacted but not to the extent that the increased drainage gradients would lead to distal drainage impacts and the collapse of the dome in the manner that is frequently projected. The scenarios also show that subsidence and sea level rise will not result in the widespread loss of current production areas. Rather there is a gradual inundation of riparian reserves and other alluvial plains and channels. Some of the natural slopes occurring within the dome complex exceed those of the production fringe.

DISCUSSION

5. What of the continued contribution of GHG emissions during the planning period? While not insignificant, the model shows that subsidence rates are managed - to the extent that it is possible. The management objective is for subsidence to be monitored against a baseline and continuously reduced. More *ad-hoc* management options which would almost certainly see the loss or severe impact of the forested conservation areas. The continued emissions from the production area need to be considered alongside the economic benefits of the production fringe in conserving the production core zone. Thus contributing towards its overall conservation and the suite of benefits associated with its protection i.e. protection from fire, protection of biodiversity, minimizing subsidence and therefore greenhouse gas emissions.
6. The Management Unit, as demonstrated through this example, often comprises of a range of land use license holders. This will depend on the size of the peat deposit. Government land use planning is critical here.
7. The Management Period is the amount of time required to achieve a management outcome (desired state). For example, adjustments to the Planning Unit may require adjustments to legal licenses which may run from 30 years or more up to 100 years. If, for example, the desired outcome is to convert the land to a totally protected area, the capacity to fund and support this function needs to be in place.
8. The formal protected area networked of Indonesia is currently overwhelmed and under-resourced and lacks the capacity to face all of the development challenges of today. Alternative approached to medium term protected area management are required for the interim period.

PRELIMINARY CONCLUSIONS – THE KAMPAR CASE STUDY

Peat domes managed at the landscape level have the potential to result in better conservation benefits and reduced emissions compared to other development scenarios. While this paper does not advocate the further opening up of undisturbed peat domes by this system it does support the use of this approach for existing areas under production – at this point of development time.

Abstract No: A-408

SUSTAINABLE OIL PALM PLANTING ON PEAT SOILS IN SARAWAK

Galau Melayong and Sylvester Fong

Sarawak Oil Palm Plantation Owners Association (SOPPOA), Sarawak

**Corresponding author: galau.melayong@sop.com.my; sylvesterfong@ymail.com*

SUMMARY

To produce high oil palm yields growers have to observe the practices that can ensure the crop is sustainable, namely careful water management, the optimum fertiliser programme and good weed control and logistics.

INTRODUCTION

Peatland is extensive in Sarawak's coastal lowlands, covering approximately 1.6 million hectares (MHA) or 13% of the state's total land area. The single largest usage of peatland in Sarawak is for agriculture (plantations) with a much less significant area converted for housing/township development (particularly in and around Kuching and Sibu) or left under forest. In Sarawak extensive peatland conversion, especially for oil palm plantations, has occurred only since the early 2000s. Probably about one MHA of peatlands still remain to be planted in the state. The main objective of this paper is to highlight the main agro-management practices for sustainable cultivation of oil palm on peat soils.

Map 1: Distribution of peat swamps in Sarawak

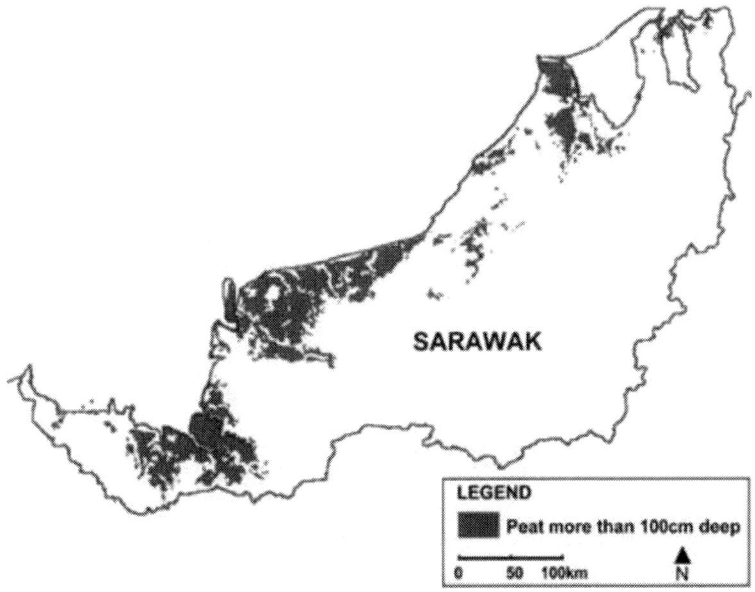

Source: Tie and Kueh 1979

The Sarawak Agriculture Perspective Plan Study 1992 (xxxx 1992) identified the state's coastal peatlands as an important resource for agriculture and other land uses in the state. Realising the enormous potential of the coastal land and looking at peatland as the "most strategic alternative fast track resource (gold mine)" (ref) the Sarawak State Government's approach was to open up such areas for plantation development. The State Government targets the end of 2005 for the completion of a new coastal highway in order to facilitate access into these areas (Abdullah, 1999). Drahman (1999) reported that Sarawak's target for agricultural plantation development (mainly oil palm) in terms of actual planted area by 2020 is one million ha on state land and land under Native Customary Rights (NCR).

UTILIZATION OF PEATLAND

Around 20% of all oil palm plantations in Southeast Asia are on peat. Sumatra has the largest absolute extent of oil palm plantations on peat (1.4 MHA or 29%), followed by Sarawak (476,000 ha or 46%), Kalimantan (307,515 ha or 11%), and Peninsular Malaysia (215,984 ha or 8%) (ref.). The highest rates of oil palm development on peat are in Sarawak: the rate of change of swamp forest in Sarawak in the last temporal period was approximately 7% annually (59,620 ha) and nearly all the conversion of peat swamp forest can be directly attributed to the establishment of new oil palm plantations.

The area of peat under cultivation in the state of Sarawak is 554,775 ha (Ambak and Melling 1999). The most important crop at present is oil palm. Sarawak's climate is ideal for this crop, which establishes well as a plantation crop on peat and has been profitable. Sago (*Metroxylon sagu*) traditionally a staple food crop for some of Sarawak's coastal population, is another crop being planted on a large scale. Coconut, padi, pineapple and mixed horticultural crops also planted on peat in Sarawak.

OIL PALM DEVELOPMENT IN SARAWAK, MALAYSIA

Up until 2008 Sarawak's oil palm plantation area was smaller area than that of either Johor or Pahang, the two top 'performing' states in terms of oil palm hectarage in Peninsular Malaysia, even though these states' total land area is only 16% and 29% respectively, of that of Sarawak. In 2008 Sarawak experienced its largest increase in oil palm plantation areas so far, which grew by 12.8% against the national figure of only 4.5% (MPOB 2010). This brought Sarawak's total hectarage of oil palm to 744,372 hectares (ha) (MPOB 2008), surpassing that of both Johor and Pahang and putting Sarawak well on the way to achieving its target of one million hectares of oil palm plantations by 2010.

A state-wide independent peat basin (IPB) study conducted in 1992 identified 109 IPBs covering 825,156 ha and classified 91 of these IBPs (or one-third of the total hectarage) as having potential for agricultural development (Sime Darby Services 1999, Kamaruddin *et al.*,1999). Sarawak tapped this potential almost immediately: between 1997 and 2001 oil palm plantations doubled in area, reaching 374,827 ha by 2005 (more than 46% of the agricultural land in use and constituting the largest area of commercial crops) (Department of Statistics Sarawak 2005). Sarawak's success in developing oil palm plantations has been helped by the Malaysian government's infrastructure development and economic stimulus initiatives. Road development in Sarawak's coastal plains was enhanced in the late 1990s. This enabled exploitation of the peat swamp forests that dominated these plains as a fast-track approach for large-scale oil palm expansion (Sahamat 1999). SCORE (Sarawak Corridor of Renewable Energy) Sarawak's long-term development strategy for the central region, launched in 2006 to propel the state into the ranks of Malaysia's most developed states by 2020, reaffirmed the state's commitment to further expansion of oil palm plantation, which it identified as a key growth industry in three peat swamp forest dominated centres: Tanjung Manis, Mukah and Similajau.

THE BENEFITS OF OIL PALM TO SARAWAK AND THE WORLD

Sarawak's palm oil had an export value of RM1.38 billion in 2003, making oil palm the commodity with the highest export value among the state's principal agricultural products (Department of Statistics Sarawak 2005). With more than 500,000 ha of peat in Sarawak already planted, palm oil can reach and meet the needs for edible oil of about 80 million people annually. Sarawak will continue to increase its palm products supply to the world edible oil market as the palms planted on peat over the last few years mature and production increases. Previously unproductive and uninhabitable areas with wet soils have been transformed into oil palm plantations with residences, roads and economic activities. Oil palm planted on peat can provide work for 50,000 people (at a rate of one person per ten ha). Other jobs are also created, in oil palm mills, refineries, transportation, shipping, marketing and research, as well as support and management.

ENSURING OIL PALM CULTIVATION ON PEATLAND IS SUSTAINABLE

Sustainability depends on four interconnected factors: legal compliance and social, environmental and economic factors. Each of these carries a risk of undermining the sustainability of oil palm plantations on peat.

Legal compliance

Social factors

Environmental factors

Not all peat soils are the same. Soils have differing maturity levels and some contain big tree roots that would stunt the growth of palms. Thus, there are challenges.

Water management

Fertiliser application on peat areas is different from that on mineral soils. 'Little and often' is the rule so that the palms have a constant supply of food. Some trace elements, possibly zinc, copper and boron, may have to be given following field observations and leaf analysis.

Palms on peat soils have special pest problems such as infestations of termites and *Tirathaba* (coconut spike moth). United Plantations Berhad was among the earliest companies to plant oil palm on peat soil and the company's then head of research, Dr Gurmit Singh, noted, "Considerable progress has been made in United Plantations Berhad since the 1980s in overcoming most of these problems and today yields comparable to [those on] good mineral soils are obtainable on deep peat" (Gurmit 1999). Much has been said, researched and reported on the properties of peat soils all over the world. The

Economic factors

Oil palm cultivation on peatland requires extra effort and costs when compared to cultivation on mineral soils. Additional land preparation work, road maintenance and water management will result in increased operational costs.

Sustainable practices in oil palm operations can only be achieved if oil palm development on peatland is understood and correctly managed. In order to reduce the impact, oil palm cultivation in peatland requires expertise, planning and best management practices. To be effective, supervision and documentation in peatland management are important, in addition to regular monitoring and quantification of the outcomes of best management practices implementation.

CONCLUSION

With better understanding of the peat characteristics, improved peat planting technologies and best agro-management practices, oil palm planting on peat can be carried out sustainably on properly selected peat areas. Continuous training at the estate level on management is important to avoid making costly mistakes. More research is still needed to optimize yield and maximize sustainability of oil palm plantings on deep tropical peat.

ACKNOWLEDGEMENTS

The authors wish to thank their respective organizations for support, and all those who have helped towards the completion of this paper and generously contributed much useful information.

REFERENCES

1. Abdullah 1999
2. http://www.rspo.org/news-and-events/news
3. Amback and Melling 1999
4. Basiron, Y. (2007) Palm oil production through sustainable plantations. Eur. J. Lipid, Sci. Technol. 109: 289-295.
5. Gurmit, S. (1999) Agronomic management of peat soil for sustainable oil palm production. Paper presented at the Seminar on Various Aspects of Large Scale Oil Palm Cultivation on Peat Soil. 23 October 1999, ISP-Central Sarawak Branch, Sarawak, Malaysia: Preprint.

6. Department of Statistics Sarawak. 2005.
7. Drahman 1999
8. Kamaruddin et al. 1999.
9. Lim, K.H. (2007) Effects of peat subsidence on oil palm cultivation and some ameliorating measure. In: Jol, H. *et. al.*(ed) Proc. Soil Science Conference 2007-
10. Peat and other soil factors in crop production. MSSS, DOA Sarawak and ISP, 17-19 April 2007, Mukah, Sarawak: 194-201
11. Lim, K.H. (2005a). Soil, water and fertilizer management for oil palm cultivation on peat soils. In: Proc. PIPOC 2005 International Palm Oil Congress, Biotechnology and Sustainability Conf. 26-28 Sept. 2005. Malaysian Palm Oil Board, Kuala Lumpur: 433-455.
12. Melling, L., Ambak K., Osman, L. and Ahmad H. (1999) Water management for the sustainable utilization of peat soils for agriculture. Paper presented at the International Conference & Workshop on Tropical Peat Swamps, 27 – 29 July 1999. Penang, Malaysia: Preprint.
13. Melling, L. and Hatano, R. (2003) Characteristics of tropical peatland and its implication to agricultural development. Paper presented at 2nd International Conference on Advances in Soft Soil Engineering and Technology. Putra Jaya, Malaysia. 2-4 July 2003: Preprint
14. Malaysian Palm Oil Board (MPOB). 2008. Malaysian oil palm statistics 2007. 27th Edition. Malaysian Palm Oil Board, Kuala Lumpur: 189 pp.
15. Malaysian Palm Oil Board (MPOB). 2010.
16. Sahamat 1999
17. Sime Derby Services. 1999.
18. Tie and Kueh 1979
19. Jason Hon 2011-04-12

Abstract No: A-355

THE EFFECT OF NITROGEN FERTILISER ON NITROUS OXIDE EMISSION IN OIL PALM PLANTATION

Norliyana Zin Zawawi[1, 2*], Yit Arn Teh[1], Kho Lip Khoon[2], Timothy Hill[3], Zulkifli Hashim[2] and Mohd Haniff Harun[2]

[1]*Institute of Biological and Environmental Sciences, University of Aberdeen, UK*
[2]*Biological Research Division, Malaysian Palm Oil Board, Selangor, Malaysia*
[3]*University of Exeter, UK*

* *Corresponding author: norliyanazinz@gmail.com*

SUMMARY

Oil palm is the largest agricultural crop in the tropics, accounting for 13% of all tropical land cover. When it is cultivated on marginal or nutrient-poor land, external inputs of N fertiliser are required to achieve high levels of productivity and yield. However, excess N fertiliser use may lead to negative impacts on the environment, including generation of reactive N-gases (e.g. nitric oxide –NO, nitrous oxide –N_2O), tropospheric ozone (O_3) and nitrate (NO_3^-); all of which may lead to atmospheric pollution and contamination of surface waters. This study investigates spatial and temporal patterns of N_2O fluxes in peatland oil palm plantations associated with existing fertiliser regimes in Sarawak, Malaysian Borneo. Overall N_2O fluxes from plantations on peat were low relative to fluxes reported elsewhere in the literature. This suggests that N inputs were not greatly in excess of plant demand. N_2O fluxes in these plantations was spatially stratified, and influenced by the presence of herbaceous plants, organic residue (excised palm fronds) management and soil moisture availability. N_2O fluxes were enhanced in areas where herbaceous plants or organic residues were present, presumably because the presence of herbaceous plants or excised palm fronds supplies labile C and N for nitrification and denitrification. N_2O fluxes were also enhanced in areas of high moisture content (e.g. near drainage ditches), perhaps because greater soil moisture favoured denitrification.

Key words: *oil palm, fertiliser, nitrous oxide, peatland*

INTRODUCTION

Atmospheric concentrations of nitrous oxide (N_2O) have risen by about 49-50% since the pre-industrial era as results of human activity (Hirsch *et al.*, 2006). Agriculture is the major source of the N_2O, mainly from the soils and N inputs to crops and soil systems. In soils, N_2O is produced mainly through microbial activity through nitrification, denitrification and dissimilatory nitrate reduction (Cayuela *et al.*, 2014).

N_2O is a potent GHG and the third most important climate forcing agent after carbon dioxide (CO_2) and methane (CH_4) (Snyder *et al.*, 2009). N_2O has a global warming potential (GWP) of 298 times larger than an equal mass of CO_2 over a 100-year period (IPCC, 2007), and also catalyses the destruction of ozone in the stratosphere (Hergoualc'h *et al.*, 2009) due its long lifespan (approximately 120 years). N_2O fluxes from soil generally increase with rising N fertiliser application, agricultural intensification, and poor fertiliser management practices (Allen *et al.*, 2010; Kahrl *et al.*, 2010; Mosier *et al.*, 2004).

Oil palm ecosystems are globally significant environments as they take up approximately 16.4 million hectares of agricultural land worldwide (FAO, 2013). As the availability of suitable mineral soil sites have declined in recent years, the oil palm industry has expanded cultivation into peat lands, especially in Southeast Asia. While the aboveground biomass in tropical forests store large amounts of carbon, the peat soils can contain 18 to 28 times more than the aboveground biomass (Page *et al.*, 2011). Mineralisation of peat C stores arising from disturbance or land-use change can lead to large, regionally significant increases in CO_2 emissions. Furthermore, when oil palm is developed on drained peat soils, N_2O emissions may also increase due to accelerated rates of peat decomposition and N mineralisation (Stichnothe and Schuchardt, 2011) as well as nitrogen fertiliser consumption, which vary depending on soil moisture and land-use (Schrier-Uijl *et al.*, 2013). Melling *et al.*, (2007) estimated the N_2O source in the Malaysian oil palm plantation were 566 kg CO_2-eq ha^{-1} yr^{-1}, however, uncertainties were large and data were too limited either to distinguish background emissions from event-based emissions linked to fertiliser application. There has also been a lack of studies that focus on long-term rates and relationship between the emission of N_2O and their driving variables in the oil palm on peatlands ecosystems.

METHODOLOGY

The study was conducted in oil palm plantation located in Bintulu, Sarawak, Malaysia Borneo (3° 12.691' N, 113° 30.008' E). Sampling was conducted within one hectare plot of oil palm planted in 2007 on peat soil and replicated three times. The age of the palms was eight year old (mature palms) at the commencement of the study. Urea was used as the N input at the rate of 106.125 kg ha^{-1} yr^{-1} and was applied by broadcasting method.

In this study, N_2O fluxes from soil were measured using chamber-based methodology (Parkin and Venterea, 2010). Soil collars were installed at least 5 cm into the ground and extend no more than 5 cm above the surface at five different sampling point surrounding the palm. Sampling points were categories into five types; namely, field drain, frond pile, harvest path, inter row and vegetation path. Any vegetation was cut and removed before the collars were pushed into the soil though root growth inside the collars where possible. Gas chamber with dimension of 10.1 cm in diameter and 16 cm high were placed directly on the soil collars.

N_2O fluxes were quantified using an INNOVA portable photo-acoustic spectrophotometer (INNOVA 1412; INNOVA Air Tech Instruments, Denmark). Fluxes were measured from each chamber for approximately two minutes, with a five concentration measurements collected over the enclosure period.

The volumetric soil water content (Θ_v) was measured by portable moisture meter (HH2 Moisture Meter, Delta T Devices, Cambridge) and sampled close to the chamber (within 1-5 cm). Soil temperature, for the top 12 cm, and air temperature were measured using a MultiThermo digital thermometer.

The correlation coefficient, Pearson's *r*, was chosen to illustrate the relationship between N_2O emissions and environment factors, such as soil moisture (v/v), soil temperature (°C) and air temperature (°C).

In this study, log10 transformed data was used to conduct all statistical analysis including one way ANOVA to compare the variability of scores between treatments. All statistical analysis was performed using SPSS 23 software (SPSS Inc., United States), with a probability of 5% to test the significance of treatments effects.

RESULTS AND DISCUSSION

Overall, the mean for N_2O flux was 2.85 kg N_2O ha^{-1} yr^{-1}. N_2O flux was measured from five different sampling points to see the effect of spatial heterogeneity of N_2O flux from the study site as shown in Figure 1. The highest emission of N_2O was from the vegetation path area with the mean (SD) of 1.01 (0.98) mg N_2O m^{-2} d^{-1}, followed by the emission from the harvest path, inter row and the field drain area at 0.99 (0.65) mg N_2O m^{-2} d^{-1}, 0.86 (0.74) mg N_2O m^{-2} d^{-1} and 0.56 (0.4) mg N_2O m^{-2} d^{-1} respectively. The lowest mean emission was recorded from the frond pile area at 0.48 (0.17) mg N_2O m^{-2} d^{-1}. The study showed high N_2O emission from the harvest path area, as it is the most disturbed area due to the heavy managerial task performed on the site such as fertiliser and pesticides application and weeding. In addition, the N_2O emission from the vegetation path area comes from the additional soil organic matter from the vegetation.

A one-way ANOVA was conducted to compare the mean among the sampling points, however, the observed differences in fluxes from different sampling points were not statistically significant.

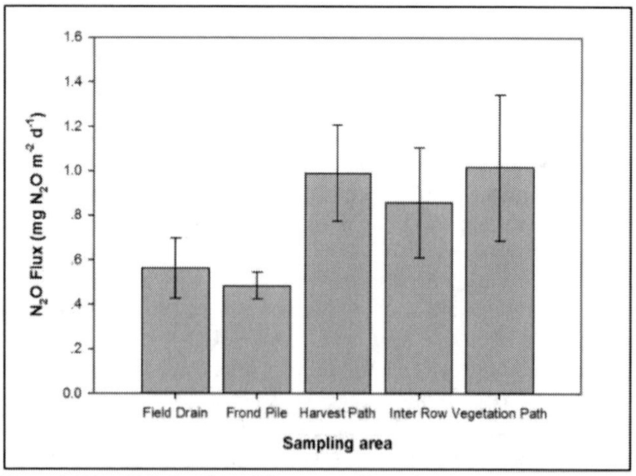

Figure 1: Mean N_2O flux from different sampling points (Bar represents standard error of the mean)

A scatterplot and Pearson's *r* analysis was conducted to summaries the correlation between the N_2O emission and the environmental variables (Figure 2) namely soil moisture, soil temperature and air temperature.

Based on Pearson's *r*, the highest correlation obtained between N_2O flux and environmental variables was soil moisture (r = -0.44, n = 45, p = 0.003) followed by air temperature (r = -0.26, n = 45, p = 0.09) and soil temperature ($r = -0.25$, $n = 45$, $p = 0.098$). However, based on the Pearson's r analysis, only soil moisture shows a significant correlation with the N_2O emission. N_2O fluxes were also enhanced in areas of high moisture content, perhaps because greater soil moisture favoured denitrification.

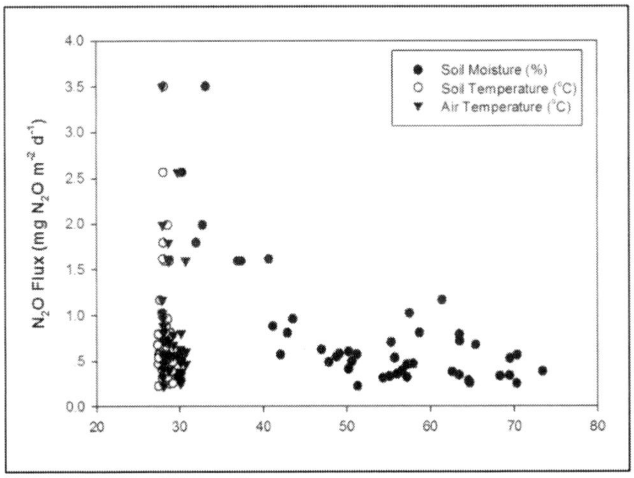

Figure 2: Scatterplot of N_2O flux and environmental variables (soil moisture, soil temperature, air temperature)

CONCLUSION

N_2O fluxes in this plantations was spatially stratified, and influenced by the disturbance and the presence of herbaceous plants, other than the soil moisture availability. Relatively the N_2O emission in this plantation is low compared to the fluxes reported elsewhere in the literature.

ACKNOWLEDGEMENTS

We would like to thank the Malaysian Palm Oil Board (MPOB) for the sponsorship through the MPOB Education Scholarship and also the fieldwork support by MPOB Tropical Peat Research Institute (TROPI)

REFERENCES

1. ALLEN, D. E., KINGSTON, G., RENNEBERG, H., DALAL, R. C. and SCHMIDT, S. 2010. Effect of nitrogen fertilizer management and waterlogging on nitrous oxide emission from subtropical sugarcane soils. *Agriculture, Ecosystems and Environment*, 136, 209-217.
2. CAYUELA, M. L., VAN ZWIETEN, L., SINGH, B. P., JEFFERY, S., ROIG, A., SÀNCHEZ-MONEDERO, M.A. 2014. Biochar's role in mitigating soil nitrous oxide emissions: A review and meta-analysis. *Agriculture, Ecosystems and Environment*, 191, 5-16.
3. HERGOUALC'H, K., HARMAND, J. M., CANNAVO, P., SKIBA, U., OLIVER, R., and HÉNAULT, C. 2009. The utility of process-based models for simulating N_2O emissions from soils: A case study based on Costa Rican coffee plantations. *Soil Biology & Biochemistry*, 41, 2343-2355.
4. HIRSCH, A. I., MICHALAK, A. M, BRUHWILER, L. M., PETERS, W., DLUGOKENCKY, E. J., TANS, P.P. 2006. Inverse modelling estimates of global nitrous oxide surface flux from 1998-2001. *Global Biogeochem Cycles*. 20, GB1008.
5. KAHRL, F., LI, Y., TENNIGKEIT, T., WILKES, A and XU, J. 2010. Greenhouse gas emissions from nitrogen fertilizer use in China. *Environmental Science & Policy*, 13 (8), 688-694.
6. MELLING, L., HATANO, R. and GOH, K. J. 2007. Nitrous Oxide Emissions from Three Ecosystems in Tropical Peatland of Sarawak, Malaysia. *Soil Science and Plant Nutrition*, 53, 792-805.
7. MOSIER, A., WASSMAN, R., VERCHOT, L., KING, J. and PALM, C. 2004. Methane and nitrogen oxide fluxes in tropical agricultural soils: sources, sinks and mechanisms. *Environment, Development and Sustainability*, 6, 11-49.
8. PAGE, S. E., RIELEY, J. O., and BANKS, C. J. 2011. Global and regional importance of the tropical peatland carbon pool. *Global Change Biology*, 17 (2), 798-818.
9. PARKIN, T. B. and VENTEREA, R. T. 2010. Sampling Protocols. Chapter 3. Chamber-Based Trace Gas Flux

Measurements in Sampling Protocols, 1-39.

10. SCHRIER A-UIJL, P., SILVIUS, M., PARISH, F., LIM, K. H., ROSEDIANA, S., and ANSHARI, G. 2013. Environmental and social impacts of oil palm cultivation on tropical peat - a scientific review, reports from the Technical Panels of the 2nd Greenhouse Gas Working Group of Roundtable on Sustainable Palm Oil (RSPO).
11. SNYDER, C. S., BRUULSEMA, T. W., JENSEN, T. L., and FIXEN, P. E. 2009. Review of greenhouse gas emissions from crop production systems and fertilizer management effects. *Agriculture, Ecosystems and Environment*, 133, 247-266.
12. STICHNOTHE, H and SCHUCHARDT, F. 2011. Life cycle assessment of two palm oil production systems. *Biomass and Bioenergy*, 35, 3976-3984.

Abstract No: A-210

THE EFFECT OF NITROGEN FERTILIZATION ON SOIL N_2O EMISSIONS FROM OIL PALM CULTIVATION ON DEEP PEAT

Satria Oktarita*, Kristell Hergoualc'h and Louis V. Verchot

Center for International Forestry Research, Indonesia

**Corresponding author: s.oktarita@cgiar.org*

The addition of nitrogen (N) fertilizer in Histosols is suspected to increase soil organic matter oxidation and nitrous oxide (N_2O) emissions. The objectives of this study were to investigate the impact of N fertilization rate on soil N_2O emissions and to evaluate how key environmental variables such as the soil water-filled pore space (WFPS) and N availability, may affect the emissions. The study was conducted in an oil palm plantation fertilizer trial on peat in Sumatra which included 3 N application rates: 0 kg N ha^{-1} y^{-1} (N0), 153 kg N ha^{-1} y^{-1} (N1) and 306 kg N ha^{-1} y^{-1} (N2). Soil N_2O fluxes were measured using the static chamber method from October 2012 until September 2013. Intensive sampling was carried out for 30 days following two fertilization events in October 2012 and April 2013. The site presented a high spatial variation in emissions with persistent hotspots emitting at rates > 100 g N ha^{-1} even outside of fertilization periods. The magnitude of the fluxes was high with annual emission rates in the N0, N1 and N2 treatments of 22.0 ± 2.8, 12.5 ± 1.3 and 26.6 ± 5.7kg N-N_2O ha^{-1} yr^{-1}, respectively. Fertilizer application exacerbated the emissions especially in the N2 treatment and following the April fertilization. Cumulated emissions over the thirty days following fertilizer application amounted to 0.3% of the N applied. The N_2O fluxes displayed significant positive relationships with soil NH_4^+ content, NO_3^- content and net nitrification rate (R^2 =0.9; R^2 =0.3; R^2=0.5 respectively) but did not appear to depend much upon soil moisture. Indeed no significant effect in water table variation was detected and the relationship between the N_2O fluxes and the WFPS was very weak (R^2 = 0.05).

Keywords: -

Abstract No: A-368

WATER MANAGEMENT APPROACHES IN PEATLANDS BASED ON COMPREHENSIVE FIELD SURVEYS AND ANALYSIS IN WEST KALIMANTAN

Asep Andi Yusup[1], Tsuyoshi Kato[1*], Bong Suhandi[1], Nana Suparna[1] and Michael Allen Brady[2]

[1]*PT. Wana Subur Lestari, Indonesia*
[2]*International Finance Corporation*

* *Corresponding author: tk@wanasl.com*

Poorly planned and controlled drainage has often substantially lowered groundwater levels as well as soil moisture content in Indonesian coastal peatlands, particularly during the dry season. During prolonged dry periods the drained peat becomes a fuel hazard, which when burned, will often lead to uncontrolled fires and associated smoke haze. Plantation companies have introduced some management approaches for peatlands after much trial and error, but their effectiveness has seldom been verified from a scientific perspective. A water management approach should include: 1) planning based on available peat information and site-specific field survey data; 2) operations of well-planned drainage and control systems, 3) intensive monitoring of groundwater and soil moisture levels, and 4) analysis for continuous improvements. A key tool for sound water management is topographic maps at a scale of detail to support hydrological understanding and canal system layout. Such detailed maps unfortunately have not been prepared and used. Prior to starting forest plantation operations in the PT Wana Subur Lestari (WSL) concession in Kubu Raya District of West Kalimantan, we conducted topographical surveys with a total length of 1,600 km to generate a contour map with elevation intervals of 0.5 m. Based on the contour map, we delineated several management water zones enabling groundwater levels to be kept constant across the landscape. We also delineated water conservation areas which supply water during dry periods and remain independent of canals. In principle, there are main and secondary canals. The main canals are aligned across contours, while secondary canals are aligned along contours. Control structures such as dams with spillways have been built between water zones to minimize excessive drainage but allow release of excess water caused by heavy rains. As a result of the detailed surveys and careful placement and management of water control drains and structures, monitoring data during the recent dry period (June to October 2015) showed that groundwater levels remained constant and even exceeded the water levels measured in undeveloped forested peat areas. We present our water management approach and results from monitoring data.

Keywords: *groundwater, topography, water management, forest plantation, West Kalimantan*

5.2: PEATLAND FORESTRY

Abstract No: A-185

ASH FERTILIZATION IN OLD DRAINED SWEDISH PEATLAND FORESTS

Tord Magnusson and Björn Hånell*

Dept. Forest Ecology and Management, Swedish University of Agricultural Sciences, Sweden

**Corresponding author: bjorn.hanell@slu.se*

SUMMARY

Most earlier Swedish and Finnish experiences of the effects of wood ash on soil productivity on peatlands, are strongly positive. Investigations of the environmental effects, for example water quality and net effects on climate forcing gases, have so far not indicated reasons to refrain from this silvicultural measure. There is, however, still a need for further confirmation of these conclusions. Here, we report the effects of ash fertilization on the groundwater and on the nutrient status of pine (Pinus Silvestris (L.)) needles, three years after ash treatment, on five old-drained and forested peatlands in Northern Sweden. The series of trial areas comprises five sites, spread from lat. 62o N to 64.5o N. All sites have moderately deep peat (minimum 0.5 m to ca 1.5 m). The treatments, 0 (control), 5 and 10 tonnes of granulated wood ash per hectare, are repeated 2 – 6 times on each site. The ash treatment had only weak general effects on ground water quality after three years. The concentrations of potassium and sulphate increased, compared to control, whereas ammonium nitrogen showed decreased concentrations on most of the sites. The ash treatment did not affect pH or calculated alkalinity. Likewise, it did not affect leaching of nitrate, phosphate, or the total concentration of organic carbon (TOC) in the water. The groundwater concentration of methyl mercury appeared not to be affected. The ash treatment improved tree nutrition. Needle concentrations of phosphorus, potassium, sulphur, boron and silicon increased. The contents of magnesium decreased somewhat. Calcium and nitrogen, and some other minor elements, were not affected. Our results confirm that the main features of earlier findings are valid for large parts of Sweden and for old-drained peatland forests. Additionally, in the specific study of possible ash effects on methyl mercury in the groundwater, no significant effects were found.

Keywords: -

INTRODUCTION

Plant growth on boreal organic soils is often restricted by the availability of some mineral nutrients and the harvest of plant biomass from drained peatlands can result in severe deficiency symptoms and decreased production. This was made clear by agricultural experience in Northern Europe more than a century ago. Experiments with wood ash amendments of peatlands, to compensate for the element deficiencies and improve forest growth conditions, were established in Sweden and Finland (Malmström, 1935; Lukkala, 1955; Silfverberg and Huikari, 1985). Despite good results in terms of significantly increased growth and yield, ash fertilization of peat soils did not become a common silvicultural measure for most of the 20th century. Instead, wood ash additions to *mineral* forest soils have been recommended by forest authorities since the 1980´s. The purpose of that treatment, however, is different. It is intended to (1) compensate for the increased mineral nutrient export coupled to more intensive biomass harvesting and (2) counteracting ongoing soil and water acidification. Future ash fertilization of forested peat soils in Sweden, if implemented, will concern only areas of long time drained and forested peatlands, which are presently managed for forestry. The main motive for such ash fertilization would be to maintain or even enhance soil fertility, after the inevitable export of mineral nutrients with the harvested biomass. Investigations of the environmental effects, for example water quality and net effects on climate forcing gases, have so far not indicated reasons to refrain from wood ash fertilization of peatland forests (Ernfors *et al.,* 2010; Klemedtsson *et al.,* 2010; Ring *et al.,* 2011; Rütting *et al.,* 2014; Sikström *et al.,* 2012). There is, however, still a need for further confirmation of these conclusions. This study reports on effects of ash fertilization on groundwater quality and on the nutrient status of Scots pine needles, three years after ash treatment of five old-drained and forested peatland sites in Northern Sweden.

MATERIAL AND METHODS

The selection of experimental sites was designed both for this study and a subsequent survey of the tree production. The series of trial areas comprises five sites, spread from lat. 62° N (site S1) to 64.5° N (site S5). All sites had moderately deep peat (ca 0.5 - 1.5 m). The tree stands were pure or mixed medium aged Scots pine (*Pinus sylvestris* L.) and Norway spruce (*Picea abies* (L.) H. Karst.). Silver birch (*Betula pendula* Roth) and downy birch (*Betula pubescens* Ehrh.) occurred as complementary species. The treatments included 0 (control), 5 and 10 tons of granulated wood ash per hectare, represented by sample plots sized 30 x 30 m (net plot 20 x 20 m), or 30 x 40 m (net plot 20 x 30 m). Each treatment was repeated 2 – 6 times on each site. The ash used was a drum granulated fly ash from wood biomass with a mixed in peat proportion of 30% (Table 1). The ash was spread by helicopter in November 2011.

Water sampling

Ground water samples were collected from all experimental sites during September 1-12, 2014. Temporary ground water wells were made with a soil auger (diameter 7.5 cm). The depth of the well was decided by the current groundwater level, in order to collect the most recently formed (uppermost) ground water. On plots with slightly sloping ground surface the well was dug at a downslope position (often close to a drainage ditch). On plots without discernible slope, lacking a bordering ditch, the well was dug at the plot centre. The average well depth was 0.7 m. The wells were left until the next day, when the water samples were collected through PTFE tubing by means of a hand-held evacuation pump connected to a sampling bottle. Water samples for methyl mercury analyses were collected in separate (glass) bottles.

Table 1: Chemical characteristics of the applied wood ash

General			
Loss on ignition (Org C), % of DM: 12.1			
pH (H_2O):	12,34		
Lime effect, % of CaO:	22		
Main elements, % of DM		***Trace elements, mg/kg DM***	
Al	2.9	As	14
Ca	17	B	130
Fe	2.5	Pb	67
K	3.3	Cd	8,3
Mg	1.9	Co	14
Mn	0.77	Cu	85
Na	1.5	Hg	0,2
P	0.97	Mo	6,9
S	1.4	Ni	53
Si	15	Zn	1640

Needle sampling

Needle samples were collected in October 2014. Only Scots pine trees were sampled since this species was found on all plots. Annual shoots from the upper part of the canopy, within the sector SW – SE, were cut with pruning shears, extendable up to 14 m. A sample of 10-15 needle pairs was collected from each of ten randomly selected pines at each net plot.

Water analyses

The following variables were determined in ground water: pH, TOC (organic carbon), elemental Na^+, K^+, Mg^{2+}, Ca^{2+}, Al^{n+}, N-NH_4^+, N-NO_3^-, P-PO_4^{3-}, F^-, Cl^-, S-SO_4^{2-}, and methyl mercury (MeHg). pH was determined in a Mettler-Toledo instrument with a Mettler-Toledo Inlab combination electrode. TOC was determined in a Shimadzu TOC-V instrument. An Omniprocess Autoanalyzer AA3 Spectrofotometer was used to determine NH_4^+, NO_3^- and PO_4^{3-}. For the other anions a Dionex ICS90 instrument with a AS-DV auto sampler and a AS22 Dionex column was used. MeHg in groundwater was determined on a GC-ICP-MS instrument, after isotope dilution, extraction and ethylation. ANC (Acid Neutralizing Capacity) was calculated as the difference between sum of charges for non-acid cations (Ca + Mg + K + Na) and sum of charges for conservative anions, except fluoride (Cl + NO_3 + SO_4).

The detection limits for analysed variables were as follows:
TOC = ca. 0,5 mg L^{-1}; N-NH_4, N-NO_3 and P-PO_4 = <10 ng L^{-1}; Na = 0,01 mg L^{-1}; K = 0,02 mg L^{-1}; Mg = 0,001 mg L^{-1}; Ca = 0,02 mg L^{-1}; Al = 0,001 mg L^{-1}; F = 0,2 mg L^{-1}; Cl = 0,2 mg L^{-1};S-SO_4 = 0,1 mg L^{-1}; ; MeHg = 0,03 ng L^{-1}.

Needle analyses

After drying of needles (70° C, 3 days), 100 randomly selected needle pairs were weighed and the 100-needle weight for the plot was registered. The whole sample was then ground in a ball mill. The needles were analysed for total content of macronutrients N, K, Ca, Mg and S, micronutrients B, Fe, Cu, Mn, Na, Si and Zn, and the content of Al. N and P were determined after Kjeldahl digestion in 8% sulphuric acid with an Omniprocess Autoanalyzer AA3 Spectrofotometer, whereas the determination of other elements was made after digestion in concentrated HNO_3 with a Spectro Ciros Vision ICP-OES instrument.

Statistical analyses

Differences between ash fertilizing treatments 0, 5 and 10 t ha^{-1}, regarding both groundwater and needle analyses, were tested with linear analysis of variance (ANOVA). In addition to treatment (TREAT) also experimental site location (SITE) and block No. (BLOCK) were included in the model used to explain the variation of the effect variable Y:

$$Y= constant + TREAT + SITE + SITE \times TREAT + SITE(BLOCK)$$

The interaction factor SITE x TREAT was included to explain the variation relating to the fact that the effect of a certain treatment may differ between sites. As well, a certain treatment may have different effects in different parts of an experimental site. Therefore, also the factor SITE(BLOCK) was used in the model. The collected data were compiled in EXCEL 2010 and the statistical analyses were made with the SYSTAT 13.1 software.

RESULTS

Ground water analyses

The wood ash fertilization effects on groundwater, 3 years after the amendment, were very weak (Table 2). The only significant effects showed in the contents of ammonium (NH_4), sulphate (SO_4) and potassium (K) (Figure 1). The ammonium concentrations on plots treated with 5 or 10 tons ash per hectare were significantly lower than on control plots ($p = 0.039$ and 0.025, respectively). The sulphate concentration increased with increasing ash dose (10 t > 0 t; $p = 0.042$). Similar to ammonium, the variation between sites was large and the statistical support for higher sulphate concentration with increased ash dose did not exist for all sites. Also the potassium concentration in groundwater was higher on plots that received the highest ash dose compared to control plots ($p = 0.048$). Total organic carbon, pH and calculated ANC did not show any effect of ash treatment (Table 2). The main cause of variation within these variables, similar to most other variables in Table 2, was the variation between sites (not shown).

The mean concentrations of methyl mercury ranged between 0.05 and 0.20 ng L^{-1}, varying mainly between sites. There were no systematic differences between ash treatments.

Table 2: Mean (m) and mean error (m. e.) for analyzed groundwater variables 3 years after ash treatments of 0, 5 or 10 tons ha^{-1}.
"ANC" denotes the calculated Acid Neutralizing Capacity. (N = 12-13).

	0 t ha^{-1}		**5 t ha^{-1}**		**10 t ha^{-1}**	
	m	*m.e.*	m	*m.e.*	m	*m.e.*
TOC, mg L^{-1}	66,71	*11,74*	54,19	*8,73*	62,49	*11,70*
pH	4,86	*0,23*	4,93	*0,22*	4,81	*0,23*
ANC, µmol L^{-1}	265	*54*	257	*36*	236	*21*
Al^{n+}, mg L^{-1}	1,24	*0,27*	1,16	*0,20*	1,29	*0,22*
Ca^{2+}, mg L^{-1}	3,52	*0,63*	3,14	*0,41*	2,73	*0,30*
K^+, mg L^{-1}	0,46	*0,13*	0,78	*0,30*	1,17	*0,17*
Mg^{2+}, mg L^{-1}	0,91	*0,18*	0,81	*0,12*	0,72	*0,09*
Na^+, mg L^{-1}	1,14	*0,31*	1,35	*0,18*	1,55	*0,15*
N-NH_4^+, mg L^{-1}	0,67	*0,17*	0,49	*0,15*	0,36	*0,16*
N-NO_3^-, µg L^{-1}	21,79	*3,29*	29,54	*11,03*	25,15	*3,98*
P-PO_4^{3-}, µg L^{-1}	11,08	*4,42*	18,35	*11,99*	6,39	*0,86*
S-SO_4^{2-}, mg L^{-1}	0,38	*0,21*	0,45	*0,22*	0,80	*0,32*
MeHg, ng L^{-1}	0,09	*0,02*	0,09	*0,02*	0,11	*0,02*

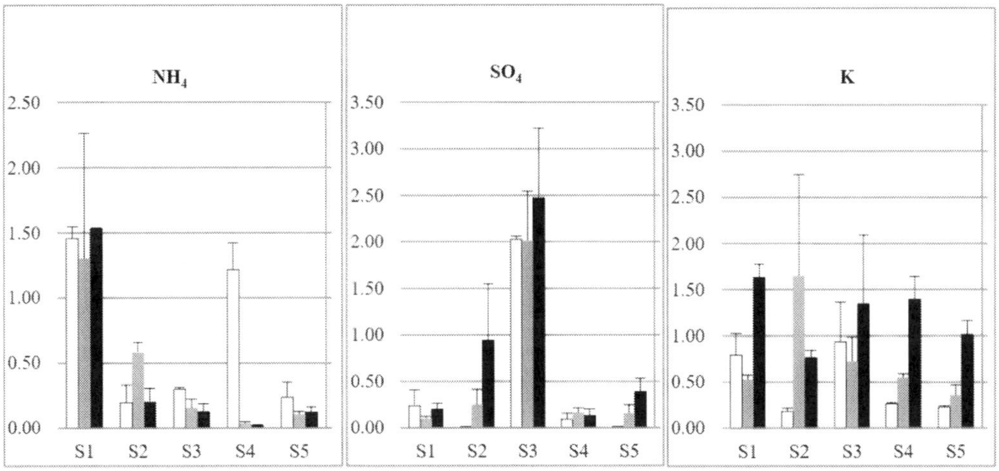

Figure 1: The concentrations (mg L^{-1}) of potassium (K), sulphate (SO_4) and ammonium (NH_4), in groundwater from sites S1 – S5, 3 years after amendments of 0, 5 or 10 t ha^{-1} (white, grey and black bars, respectively). Error bars indicate the error of the mean. (N = 2-3).

Needle analyses

The current-year needles of some trees on ash treated plots had a darker green colour compared to needles from trees on control plots, but differences between treatments were not consistent. Similarly, the 100-needle weight for some of the sites showed a nearly significant increase with ash dose, but the overall treatment means were not significantly different (Figure 2). The treatment mean 100-needle weight and mean error on control plots and on plots treated with 5 and 10 t ash ha^{-1} were 2.67 (0.12), 2.72 (0.16) and 3.06 (0.19), respectively.

The needle concentration of the macronutrients phosphorus, potassium and sulphur increased after the ash amendments of 5 and 10 t ha^{-1} (P: $p_{5t} = 0.001$, $p_{10t} < 0.000$: K: $p_{5t} < 0.000$, $p_{10t} < 0.000$: S: $p_{10t} = 0.018$), whereas the concentration of magnesium became lower (Mg: $p_{10t} = 0.014$) (Fig. 4). Nitrogen and calcium were not affected by the ash fertilization. Among the micronutrients, boron concentration was ca. 50% higher on plots that received 5 or 10 tons of ash per ha (B: $p_{5t} < 0.000$, $p_{10t} < 0.000$), and an increase also showed for silicon (Si: $p_{5t} = 0.010$, $p_{10t} = 0.002$) (Fig. 4).

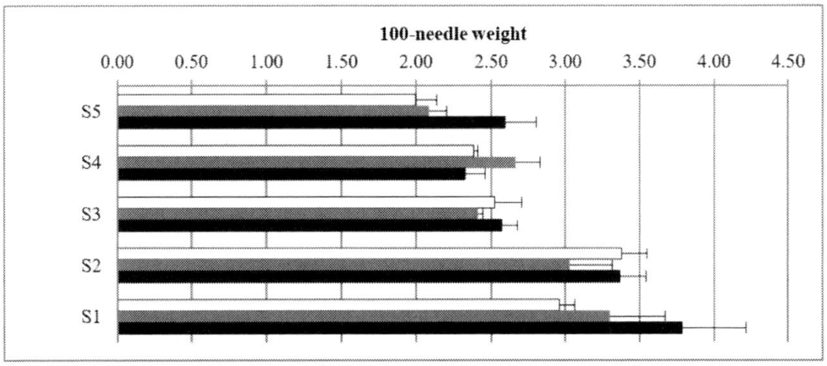

Figure 2: Mean and mean error for the dry weight (g) of 100 pine needle-pairs, by site and treatment, 3 years after ash treatments of 0, 5 or 10 tons/ha. (N = 2-6).

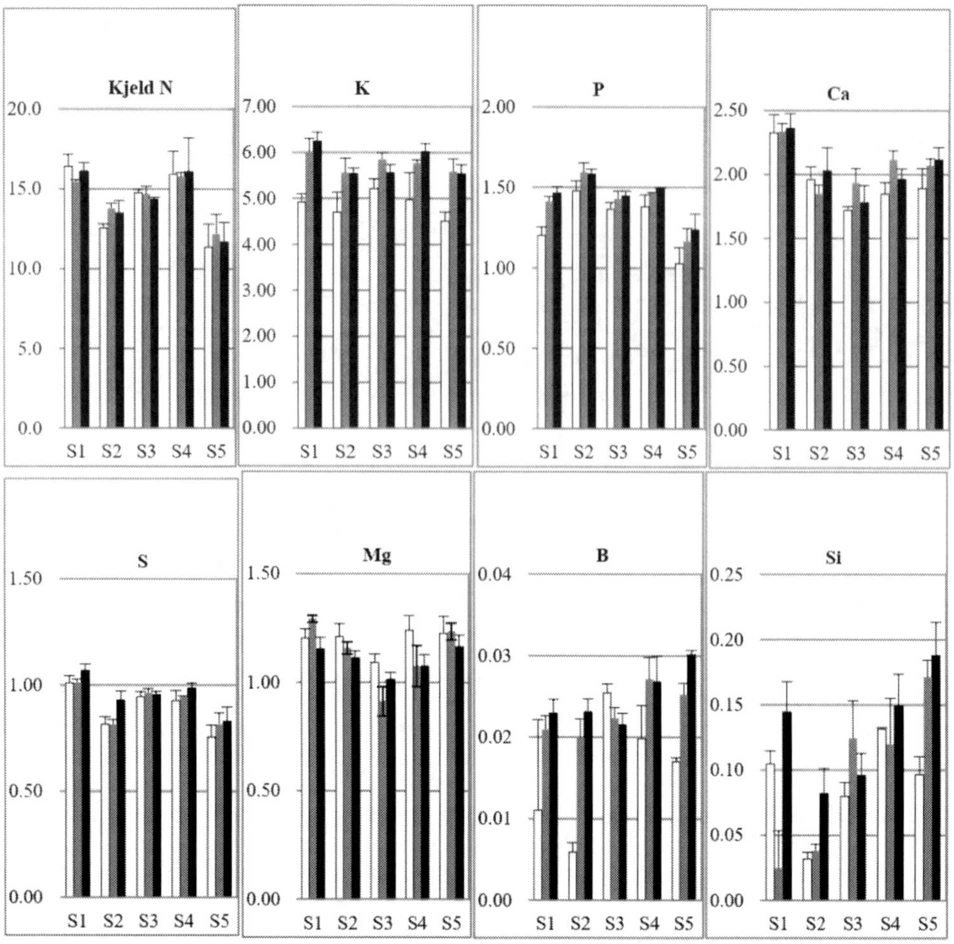

Figure 3: Total concentration (mg g^{-1}) of nitrogen (Kjeldahl), potassium, phosphorus, calcium, sulphur, magnesium, boron and silicon in pine needles, 3 years after ash treatments of 0, 5 or 10 tons/ha. Error bars indicate the error of the mean. (N = 2-6).

DISCUSSION

The wood ash amendment did not increase pH or the Acid Neutralizing Capacity (ANC) in the peat groundwater. Analyses of pH and ANC in runoff water from drains have often shown increases, but not always (Piiranen *et al.,* 2013). The fact that groundwater - not water from drains - was sampled in this study, may be an important difference. The cation exchange capacity of the unsaturated peat layer above the groundwater level is several times greater than the liming effect of 10 tons of ash ha $^{-1}$. The groundwater concentration of K and S increased significantly after an ash dose of 10 t per ha. Neither the eutrophying substances NO_3 and PO_4, nor the organic matter content (TOC), showed increases. These results are, in brief, similar to earlier reports by e.g. Nieminen *et al.* (2005), Piiranen *et al.* (2013) and Ring *et al.* (2011). At several sites, the NH_4 concentration in groundwater was lower on ash treated plots than on control plots. This could possibly be related to improved nutrient status, growth and thus increased assimilation of ammonium from the soil. Another reason may be enhanced nitrification that would intensify competition for mineralised ammonium.

According to diagnostic limit values for mineral nutrient content in pine needles published by Braekke (1994), the concentrations on control plots were within the class "Optimal" for all elements, except N, K, P and Fe (Classes: Optimal, Sub-optimal, Deficient, Strongly deficient). The status for N, P and K were classified as "Deficient", whereas Fe was "Sub-optimal". After ash amendments, the macronutrients K, P, and S, and the micronutrients B and Si, all increased. The increase of K and B agrees with most of earlier reports on ash fertilization effects on needle nutrient status, e.g. Ferm *et al.* (1992) and Moilanen *et al.* (2005). These nutrients are commonly sub-optimal or deficient in peatlands and plant uptake is facilitated by the fact that K and B are mainly bound to easily soluble compounds in the ash. Phosphorus, besides K, is the most critical element limiting plant growth on peatlands. The P compounds in the ash are however poorly soluble, which may retard the increase of the needle P content. Still, in our study a significant increase of P in needles showed after three years. This agrees well with the earlier reports from Ferm *et al.* (1992) and Moilanen *et al.* (2005). The nitrogen content in needles was not affected by the ash amendments. This is in accordance with earlier experiences, which varies between increased, indifferent and somewhat lowered N content after ash fertilization (Silfverberg and Huikari,

1985, Moilanen *et al.*, 2002, Huotari *et al.*, 2015). The ash does not add any N at all. Therefore, increased N content in needles following ash amendments is an indirect effect, caused by gradually enhanced microbial turnover of the existing (organically fixed) nitrogen in the peat substrate.

REFERENCES

1. Braekke F H, 1994. Diagnostiske grenseverdier for naeringselementer i gran- og furunåler. NISK. Aktuellt fra Skogforsk Nr 15 -94, 11 pp.
2. Ernfors M, Sikström U, Nilsson M & Klemedtsson L, 2010. Effects of wood ash fertilization on forest floor greenhouse gas emissions and tree growth in nutrient poor peatland forests. Science of the total environment 408, pp. 4580-4590.
3. Ferm, A, Hokkanen, T, Moilanen, M & Issakainen, J, 1992. Effects of wood bark ash on the growth and nutrition of a Scots pine afforestation in central Finland. Plant Soil 147, pp. 305–316.
4. Huotari N, Tillman-Sutela E, Moilanen M & Laiho R, 2015. Recycling of ash – For the good of the environment? Forest Ecology and Management 348, pp. 226-240.
5. Klemedtsson L, Ernfors M, Björk R G, Weslien P & Rütting T, 2010. Reduction of greenhouse gas emissions by wood ash application to a Picea abies (L.) Karst. forest on a drained organic soil. European Journal of Soil Science 61, pp. 734-744.
6. Lukkala, O J, 1955. Maanparannusaineet ja väkilannoitteet metsäojituksen tukena II (Soil amelioration agents and fertilizers in the peatland forestry). Metsätaloudellinen Aikakauslehti 6–8, 273–276.
7. Malmström C, 1935. Om näringsförhållandenas betydelse för torvmarkers skogsproduktiva förmåga. Meddelanden från Statens skogsförsöksanstalt häfte 28 N:r 6, pp. 571-650.
8. Moilanen M, Silfverberg K, Hokkanen T J, 2002. Effects of wood-ash on the growth, vegetation and substrate quality of a drained mire: a case study. Forest Ecology and Management 171, 321–338.
9. Moilanen M, Silfverberg K, Hökkä H & Issakainen J, 2005. Wood ash as a fertilizer on drained mires growth and foliar nutrients of Scots pine. Canadian Journal of Forest Research. 35, pp. 2734–2742.
10. Nieminen M, Piirainen S & Moilanen M, 2005. Release of mineral nutrients and heavy metals from wood and peat ash fertilizers: field studies in Finnish forest soils. Scandinavian Journal of Forest Research. 20, pp. 146–153.
11. Piirainen S, Domisch T, Moilanen M & Nieminen M, 2013. Long-term effects of ash fertilization on runoff water quality from drained peatland forests. Forest Ecology and Management 287, pp.53-66.
12. Ring E, von Brömssen C, Losjö K & Sikström U, 2011. Water chemistry following wood-ash application to a Scots pine stand on a drained peatland in Sweden. Institute of Forestry and Rural Engineering, Estonian Agricultural University, Tartu, Estonia, Forestry Studies / Metsanduslikud Uurimused, 2011, 54, pp 54-70.
13. Rütting T, Björk R G, Meyer A, Klemedtsson L, Sikström U, 2014. Reduced global warming potential after wood ash application in drained Northern peatland forests. Forest Ecology and Management 328, pp. 159-166.
14. Sikström U, Björk R G & Klemedtsson L, 2012. Wood ash application reduced global warming potential over the five years after application in two drained peatland forests in Sweden. Proceedings of The International Peat Congress, Stockholm, Sweden, 3-8 June 2012.
15. Silfverberg K & Huikari O, 1985. Wood-ash fertilization on drained peatlands. Folia Forestalia 633. 25 pp.

Abstract No: A-215

DEVELOPMENT OF FINNISH PEATLAND AREA AND CARBON STORAGE 1950 – 2015: REVIEW AND UPDATE

Jukka Turunen[1]* and Samu Valpola[2]

[1] *Geological Survey of Finland, Kuopio Unit, P.O. Box 1237, 70211 Kuopio, Finland*
[2] *Geological Survey of Finland, Vaasantie 6, 67100 Kokkola, Finland*

**Corresponding author: jukka.turunen@gtk.fi*

Over 2/3 of the carbon (C) reservoir of ecosystems in Finland is in peat. In 1950, almost 90% of the Finnish peatlands were in a natural state. The use of peatlands for forestry drainage, agriculture and peat harvesting has changed the nature of Finnish peatlands and has had large impacts on their overall role in the national C balance. The present peatland area is estimated at 8.9 million ha, 4.8 million ha of which has been drained for forestry. In the 2008 study, the knowledge of mire area change since 1950 was considered relatively reliable, whereas the net changes in the actual C sequestration and the actual C storage change were much less certain. Since 2008, there have been several new gas balance and C storage change studies of forestry drained peatlands. The results of these studies indicate that a crucial update is needed to evaluate the impact of forestry drainage on C storage changes since 1950. In the 2008 study, the total C storage of Finnish peatland ecosystems was estimated at 5960 Tg. The actual C storage in peat had decreased by 73 Tg since 1950. However, the total C storage of Finnish peatlands, which includes both peat and living plant biomass, was estimated to have increased by 52 Tg because the intensive peatland drainage has significantly increased the total C storage of vegetation. In the present study, the most critical update considers the greenhouse gas emissions of forestry drained peatlands. The newest studies indicate that the drained peatlands can be either large C sinks or large C sources depending on their nutrient status, forest coverage and geographical location. A large synthesis is needed to develop a more reliable picture of the development of peatland area and C storage from 1950.

Keywords: *Finland, peatlands, peat, vegetation, carbon storage*

Abstract No: A-412

PEATLAND SIMULATOR CONNECTING DRAINAGE, NUTRIENT CYCLING, FOREST GROWTH, ECONOMY AND GHG EFFLUX IN BOREAL AND TROPICAL PEATLANDS

Ari Laurén[1*], Hannu Hökkä[2], Samuli Launiainen[3], Marjo Palviainen[4], Aleksi Lehtonen[3] and Anssi Ahtikoski[5]

[1]*Natural Resources Institute Finland (Luke), Yliopistokatu 6, Joensuu, Finland*
[2]*Natural Resources Institute Finland (Luke), Eteläranta 55, Rovaniemi, Finland*
[3]*Natural Resources Institute Finland (Luke), Jokiniemenkuja 1, Vantaa, Finland*
[4]*University of Helsinki, Department of Forest Sciences, Finland*
[5]*Natural Resources Institute Finland (Luke), University of Oulu, Finland*

**Corresponding author : ari.lauren@luke.fi*

SUMMARY

We built and applied peatland simulator Susi that allows simultaneous assessment of economic benefits and adverse environmental effects of peatland forest drainage. The process based simulator was constructed on the following theoretical framework: Forest growth in peatlands is nutrient limited; principal source of nutrients is the decomposition of organic matter. Excess water decreases O_2 diffusion and slows down the nutrient release. Drainage increases O_2 diffusion and consequently organic matter decomposition, CO_2 efflux, and nutrient supply, and enhances the growth of forest. Profitability of the drainage operation depends on costs, gained extra yield and its allocation into timber assortments, and the rate of interest. The performance of hydrology and forest growth part of the simulator was tested against independent datasets. The results showed a clear relation between the stand growth, nutrient availability, and CO_2 efflux. In the test data, potassium was the main limiting factor for the forest growth. In examples we demonstrate the computation of growth response, profitability and environmental effects of ditch cleaning. The simulator and its holistic approach has been successfully implemented in both tropical pulpwood plantations in Sumatra, Indonesia and in Finnish boreal forests.

Keywords: *drainage, hydrology, mathematical modeling, nutrition, peatland forests*

INTRODUCTION

Different criteria have been presented all over the world to evaluate the need of forest drainage, criteria being connected to water table depth (DWT), air-filled porosity (ea) or water potential (h) in the root zone (e.g. Wesseling and van Wijk 1957, Vompersky & Sirin 1997). While these criteria have their practical value in drainage design, they are difficult to generalize outside the experiment areas and the link between the criteria and the forest production remains weak. The problem of these static criteria is that they do not account for the numerous biotic and abiotic factors that affect the onset of oxygen stress (Bartholomeus *et al.*, 2008), such as consumption of oxygen (O_2), peat and stand characteristics, and weather and climate conditions. It is clear that there is no universally applicable critical DWT, ea, or h values, but the adequacy of drainage has to be evaluated dynamically in larger theoretical framework. Furthermore, an evaluation of the need of drainage requires computation of economic feasibility, because drainage is above all, an investment. Feasibility of drainage is decreased by adverse environmental effects such as increased CO_2 emissions, and export of suspended solids and nutrient into watercourses.

The results of numerous studies describing the effects of drainage on forest growth become more understandable if, instead of removing O_2 stress, we assume an indirect effect through nutrition. In peatlands the principal source of nutrients is the decomposition of organic matter. Excess water decreases O_2 diffusion and slows down the nutrient release. Drainage increases O_2 diffusion and consequently organic matter decomposition, CO_2 efflux, and nutrient supply, and enhances the growth of forest. Profitability of the drainage operation depends on costs, gained extra yield and its allocation into timber assortments, and the rate of interest.

Mathematical models are required for systematic and quantitative description of this complex of processes. We constructed Peatland simulator Susi that involves both process based and empirical components for computing above and below ground hydrology, gas diffusion in soil, decomposition of organic matter, nutrient release, forest growth response, CO_2 emissions, suspended solids and phosphorus exports, and economy. The aim of this study was to test the simulator against independent dataset and to apply it for assessing benefits and adverse effects of the main drainage issue in Finland, which is ditch cleaning. Benefits and limitations of the computational approach are discussed in the paper.

METHODS

Simulator description and use. Susi simulator computes daily water fluxes and storages in two dimensions for a peatland forest strip located between drainage ditches. Above ground hydrology is computed using a 'semi-physical' zero-dimensional vegetation model that provides a simplified description of water cycle in a scale of a single forest stand. Soil water storage, DWT, and vertical water content profile is calculated following a simple assumption of equilibrium water content in soil (Skaggs 1980). Soil water potential profile follows instantly the DWT and the soil water content along the vertical profile is calculated using the van Genuchten water retention characteristics. Lateral water movement to open drain takes place below the DWT and is computed explicitly using the Darcy law. Daily O_2 diffusion to soil is quantified using steady-state scheme presented by Glinski and Stepniewski (1985). Soil O_2consumption is computed from daily CO_2 flux model as a function of peat temperature and bulk density (Ojanen *et al.*, 2010). The CO_2 flux is scaled down so that the diffusion is adequate to satisfy the O_2demand of decomposition activity. Nitrogen (N), phosphorus (P) and potassium (K) release is computed from the peat nutrient content and the actual decomposition. Future expected growth of the stand is derived using Schumacher growth curve, stand volume and age. Nutrient demand (N, P, K) is calculated from the expected growth using nutrient accumulation models by Laiho (1997). Export of suspended solids is quantified using simulated runoff, soil type in the ditch bottom, and reported mean concentrations without or with ditch cleaning (Joensuu *et al.*, 1999). The required input for the simulation includes daily meteorological variables, peat type and bulk density, tree species, stand volume, ditch depth, and strip width.

Feasibility of the drainage is assessed by comparing scenarios (length of simulation 1…5 yrs) without and with ditch cleaning. Changes in the environmental variables (CO_2 flux, export of P and suspended solids) are directly gained as difference between the scenarios. The economic benefit is computed as follows: First, the difference in the nutrient release is computed, and growth response is deduced according to the increase in the supply of the growth limiting nutrient and the nutrient accumulation model. The computed extra growth represents the maximum growth response and is extrapolated to the following 20 yrs by using an empirical scheme: the growth response increases from zero to maximum between 0…8 yrs, remains at maximum between 8…10 yrs and thereafter decreases linearly to zero between 10…20 yrs. The integrated growth response over the 20 yrs represents the total extra growth. Then, the gained extra growth is divided into timber assortments (pulp wood and sawn timber), which have distinctly different price. Drainage cost, and pulpwood and timber price, time series of the gained extra pulpwood and timber, and the rate of interest are used to compute the net present value of the drainage investment. Finally, the economic benefits and environmental effects are assessed simultaneously.

Field data and comparison. Susi-simulator performance was validated against independent dataset of 69 Scots pine (*Pinus sylvestris*, L.) dominated peatland sample plots located in Central Finland, measured in 1985 and reported by Hökkä *et al.* (2008). Stand dominant height (H), volume (V, 3m^3 ha^{-1}…303 m^3 ha^{-1}), and mean annual volume growth from 1980 to 1984 (0.1 m^3 ha^{-1}…11.7 m^3 ha^{-1}) were measured, and ditch depth (32cm…108cm), ditch spacing (23m… 111m), peat bulk density (53 kg m^{-3}…192 kg m^{-3}) and peat type of topmost 20 cm peat layer were determined. DWTwas monitored through growing season 1984 in ground water tubes. The measured volume growth was converted to stand net uptake of N, P and K using equations from Laiho (1997). Susi simulator was parameterized with the measured stand data and peat characteristics, and run using daily weather data from November 1, 1979 until October 31, 1984. The computed median DWT for growing season 1984 was compared to field measurements; and the computed nutrient release was related to stand net uptake of N, P and K (Fig. 1).

Scenarios. Economic benefit and adverse environmental effects of ditch cleaning were assessed by comparing scenarios without (ditch depth 35 cm) and with ditch cleaning (ditch depth 90 cm) in different regions (southern and northern Finland) for rainy and dry years, for different initial stand volume (40, 90, 150 m^3 ha^{-1}), and for different peat types occurring in high and medium fertility sites (bulk density 145, 100 kg m^{-3}). Ditch cleaning cost was 205.5 € ha^{-1}, stumpage price timber was 55.5 € m^{-3} and 16 € m^{-3} for pulp wood.

RESULTS

Simulated DWT showed a reasonable fit to the measured DTW in the field, taking into account the limited parameterization data available (Fig.1). Comparison of the net uptake of N, P and K to the simulated nutrient release clearly shows that K was the growth limiting nutrient in the field sites (Fig.1). If the decomposition releases 100 g K ha^{-1} yr^{-1} more, it will be followed by 76 g increase in K assimilation, which can support extra growth of 0.2 m^3 ha^{-1} yr^{-1} at 50 m^3ha^{-1} stand.

The simulation set highlights that the drainage growth response is a result of complicated interactions between weather conditions, stand dimensions and stand development phase, peat characteristics and the drain depth before and after ditch cleaning; and that the economic feasibility mainly depends on the allocation of the gained extra growth into timber and pulpwood assortments. In the simulated ditch cleaning scenarios, the growth response ranged from 2.2 to 15 m^3 ha^{-1} in 20 yrs. The highest growth response occurred in rainy years and in northern Finland; the response was better in the high than medium fertility sites. Absolute value of heterotrophic CO_2 efflux was higher in south, whereas the increase in the CO_2 efflux due to ditch cleaning was greater in north. The export of suspended solids was higher in the north. The economic feasibility of ditch cleaning was better in north.

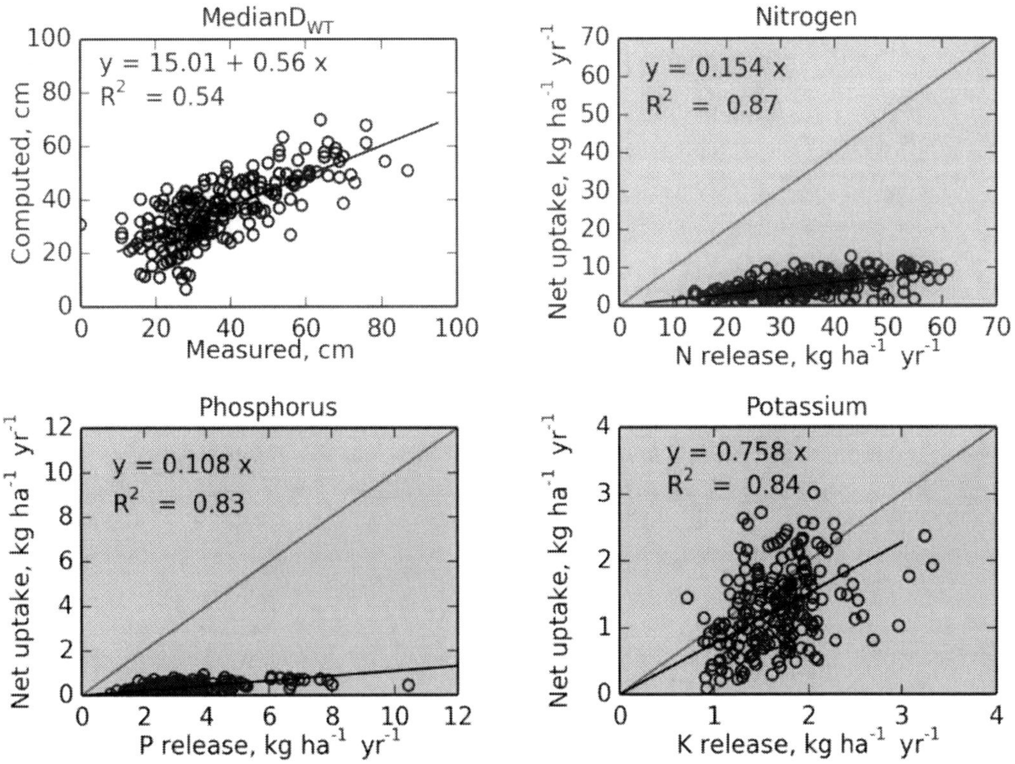

Figure 1: Field data and Susi simulator results. Measured and modelled median depth to water table; and the simulated release of nitrogen, phosphorus and potassium against the stand net uptake derived from the observed stand growth and nutrient accumulation equations (Laiho 1997).

DISCUSSION

Susi peatland simulator is based on extensive theoretical framework and describes the chain of dependencies from the drainage control, via soil biogeochemistry to forest growth, and finally to economy. It allows evaluating the drainage as an investment with distinctive costs and returns; and a simultaneous evaluation of benefit and adverse environmental effects of the drainage. It allows approaching drainage as a multi-target optimization task. The most relevant uncertainties in the in the simulation are connected to parameterization soil hydraulic properties and soil chemical composition. This inevitably causes deviation in the results, but accepting a slight uncertainty allows us to use parameter values reported in literature for each site type, which expands the applicability of the simulation approach.

The simulation set reproduced a general phenomenon that has been earlier shown in field experiments: the growth response was higher in the north than in south. This is due to the fact that the climate in the north is more humid and excess water tends to decrease nutrient release, and in this situation the drainage of the excess water enhances the growth. The calculated range (2…15 m^3 ha^{-1}) of the growth response corresponds to the range in the observed growth responses in field conditions (6…17 m^3 ha^{-1}, Ahtikoski *et al.*, 2008).

Susi simulator is based on process modeling, therefore it is widely applicable in boreal, temperate and tropical conditions provided that the stand growth and decomposition models are parameterized according local conditions, and the model is run using local weather data. The simulator and its holistic approach have been successfully implemented in both tropical pulpwood plantations in Sumatra.

CONCLUSION

The study clearly shows why mathematical simulation models are necessary in the decision making concerning drainage. The occurrence of the growth response, economic feasibility and the environmental effects are a result of complicated interactions between weather, vegetation, soil biogeochemistry, drain depth and spacing, and economics. Due to this complicity, widely applicable general guidelines for drainage are of limited use only, and instead of static guidelines we should pursue towards computerized planning and decision support systems. These systems apply the existing stand, soil, weather and GIS data, and mathematical models that process the data into quantitative estimates of benefits and adverse effects of the drainage, silviculture and other management.

REFERENCES

1. Ahtikoski, A., Kojola, S. Hökkä, H., Penttilä T. 2008. Ditch network maintenance in peatland forest as a private investment: short- and long-term effects on financial performance at stand level. *Mires and Peat* 3: 1-11.
2. Bartholomeus, R.P. Witte, J.-P. M. van Bodegom, P.M. van Dam, J.C. and Aerts, R. 2008. Critical soil conditions for oxygen stress to plant roots: Substituting the Feddes-function by a process-based model. *Journal of Hydrology*, 360: 147– 165.
3. Glinski, J. & Stepniewski, W. 1985. *Soil Aeration and its Role for Plants*. CRC Press, Boca Raton, FL, USA. 229 pp.
4. Hökkä, H., Repola, J. & Laine, J. Quantifying the interrelationship between tree stand growth rate and water table level in drained peatland sites within Central Finland. *Canadian Journal of Forest Research* 38: 1775–1783.
5. Joensuu, S., Ahti, E. & Vuollekoski, M. 1999. The effects of peatland forest ditch maintenance on suspended solids in runoff. *Boreal Environment Research* 4: 343–355.
6. Laiho, R. 1997. Plant biomass dynamics in drained pine mires in southern Finland. Implication for carbon and nutrient balance. *The Finnish Forest Research Institute, Research Papers* 631.
7. Ojanen, P., Minkkinen, K., Alm, J., Penttilä, T. 2010. Soil–atmosphere CO_2, CH4 and N2O fluxes in boreal forestry-drained peatlands. *Forest Ecology and Management* 260:411-421
8. Skaggs, R.W., 1980. *A Water Management Model for Artificially Drained Soils*. North Carolina Agricultural Research Service, Raleigh, 54
9. Vompersky S., Sirin, A. (1997). Hydrology of drained forested wetlands. In: Trettin, C.C., Jurgensen, M.F., Grigal, D.F., Gale, M.R., and Jeglum, J.K. *Nothern forested Wetlands. Ecology and Management*. CRC Press, Lewis Publishers 189–211.
10. Wesseling, J., van Wijk, W.R., 1957. Soil physical conditions in relation to drain depth. In: Luthin, J.N. (Ed.), *Drainage of Agricultural Lands*. American Society of Agronomy, Madison, Wisconson, pp. 461–504.

Abstract No: A-279

SUFFICIENCY OF POTASSIUM (K) FOR WOOD PRODUCTION – LONG-TERM EFFECTS OF FOREST MANAGEMENT ON THE K-BALANCE OF DRAINED BOREAL PEATLANDS

Sakari Sarkkola[1*], Raija Laiho[1], Liisa Ukonmaanaho[1], Tiina Nieminen[1], Ari Laurén[2], Leena Finér[2], Timo Penttilä[1] and Mika Nieminen[1]

[1]*Natural Resources Institute Finland (LUKE), Jokiniemenkuja 1, Vantaa, Finland*
[2]*Natural Resources Institute Finland (LUKE), Yliopistonkatu 6, Joensuu, Finland*

[*]*Corresponding author: sakari.sarkkola@luke.fi*

SUMMARY

Potassium (K) is often a minimum growth-limiting nutrient in boreal peatland forests, mostly on thick-peated sites, and its deficiency may decrease the vitality and growth of trees. Timber harvestings, particularly clear fellings by whole-tree harvesting (WTH), may result in significant K losses by removing not only the K in the stems as in stem-only harvesting (SOH), but also the K in branches, twigs, and needles. Furthermore, the forest harvestings as well as ditch network maintenance (DNM) treatments enhance the off-site hydrological leaching losses of K. Increased interest in bioenergy harvesting in peatland forests has created an urgent need to clarify, if forest management results in severe depletion of site K stores in peatland forests. Based on previous data and the results of our recent field experiments, we quantified the total K balance of drained *Pinus sylvestris* and *Picea abies* dominated peatland forests over the 80-year rotation period under the conditions typical for drained peatlands in Finland. The results showed that the loss of K induced by biomass removal in WTH plus stump harvesting was 2–5 times larger (75–97 kg/ha) than in SOH (15–30 kg/ha), even though –as typical in mechanized WTH with harvesters and forwarders- about 30% of the harvest residues were left on-site. In WTH without stump harvesting, the K-losses induced by biomass removal were about 50–65 kg/ha. About two thirds of the K removed along with biomass removal in WTH plus stump harvesting was in the needle and branch biomass and about 1one-third was in the stumps and roots. When adding to these removals the additional hydrological K-losses induced by harvesting (poor sites: 9 kg ha^{-1}, fertile sites: 28 kg/ha) and two DNM treatments (8.3 kg/ha/treatment), the background hydrological K losses (1–2 kg/ha/year), as well as considering the K input by deposition (ca. 1 kg/ha/yr.), the net total off-site K-loss in SOH was 30–40 kg/ha in poor sites and 135–155 kg/ha in fertile sites during the 80-year rotation period. Respectively, for WTH they were 50–75 kg/ha in poor sites and 160–210 kg/ha in fertile sites. When comparing these losses with the typical K-store in thick-peated soils (<100 kg/ha in the 50 cm-thick surface peat), it appears that, without significant additional K input through fertilization, the K stores are not sufficient to ensure satisfactory stand K nutrition during the development of the next stand generation. Avoiding WTH, i.e. the removal of harvesting residues, decreases the off-site K losses, but may not completely eliminate the risk for K depletion, particularly in fertile thick-peated peatland sites. If repeated K-fertilizations are needed to sustain forestry on these sites, their economic feasibility should be clarified.

***Keywords**: K-loss, forestry, whole-tree harvesting, leaching*

INTRODUCTION

For plants, potassium (K) is an important macronutrient participating in nutrient transport, function of the stomas in leaf cells, as well as syntheses of protein, starch and energy compounds in cells (Mengel & Kirkby 2001). Thus, it has considerable effects on tree growth and vitality. In mineral soil sites, K is rarely a minimum nutrient, because of mostly large availability of K from stores in the mineral soil and bedrock such as clay minerals. However, in boreal peatlands, particularly on thick-peated sites, it is often a minimum growth-limiting nutrient and its deficiency may widely decrease the vitality and growth of trees (Finér 1989, Laiho & Laine 1995, Hoosbeek *et al.*, 2002, Westman & Laiho 2003).

Growth losses caused by K-deficiencies may be particularly significant for forestry on drained peatlands reclaimed for timber production. It has been estimated that in Finland, on about 1 M hectare of drained forested peatlands, i.e., ca 20% of the total drained area, tree stands are suffering from K-deficiency (Moilanen *et al.*, 2010). This is because the K stores in the rooting zone of peat, especially in sites that were originally very wet and sparsely forested, are generally small (Kaunisto & Tukeva 1984, Saarinen 1997, Laiho *et al.*, 1998), and the relatively high supply of nitrogen (N) in peat increases the demand of potassium and other nutrients so that the available K-stores are insufficient (Tripler *et al.*, 2006). Most of the sites with K-deficiency are dominated by Scots pine (*Pinus sylvestris*) growing on ombrotrophic and poor minerotrophic sites, whereas risk of K-deficiency may also occur on more fertile sites, where the dominant tree species is usually Norway spruce (*Picea abies*) with varying mixture of downy birch (*Betula pubescens*).

On thick-peated sites, most of the K-stores in the ecosystem are bound in the tree biomass, and forest harvestings, particularly clear fellings by whole-tree harvesting (WTH), may result in significant K-losses. In this method not only the potassium in the stems as in stem-only harvesting (SOH), but also that bound in branches, twigs, and needles are removed. Furthermore, the forest harvestings as well as ditch network maintenance (DNM) treatments enhance the off-site hydrological K-losses (Joensuu *et al.*, 2002). Atmospheric deposition does not necessarily provide a sufficient input of potassium to compensate for the losses caused by forestry treatments. Other natural K-supplies are also small in thick-peated sites.

Interest in the use of wood-based fuels for bioenergy is drastically increasing and the increased demand may lead to intensified harvesting also in in this kind of peatland sites. This has created an urgent need to clarify, if forest management results in severe depletion of site K-stores in peatland forests

Our study aim was to quantify the total K-balance of drained nutrient poor Scots pine and fertile Norway spruce dominated forest stands over the 80-year stand rotation period in drained peatlands in Finland. For balance calculations and simulations, the input data of the potassium amounts in the stand biomass, surface vegetation, peat and harvest induced K losses were obtained from the previous data and the results of our recent field experiments. The premises for the calculations were that the stands were harvested by clear fellings (stem-only harvesting vs. whole tree harvesting + stump removal) and ditch network maintenance was carried out twice during the stand rotation.

MATERIALS AND METHODS

We quantified the K-balance components of average Scots pine and Norway spruce dominated stands on ombrotrophic and minerotrophic drained peatland sites using the input data from the following studies:

For spruce peatlands, the total potassium bound in the biomass and the removal of potassium in harvested biomass in WTH and SOH harvesting treatments were estimated by using biomass estimates by Nieminen *et al.* (2016) and for pine peatlands, the respective estimates were done by applying equations of biomass and nutrient contents presented by Laiho (1997). Nieminen *et al.* (2016) presents biomass measurements and nutrient stores in an experimental Norway spruce stand located in southern Finland. The have estimated the biomass and nutrient removals in clear-cuttings by conventional stem-only harvesting (SOH), where only the stems down to a diameter limit of 7 cm were removed and in whole-tree harvesting (WTH), where the harvest residues (needles, branches, twigs) were collected following SOH. Additionally, in the most intensive WTH treatment, both the cutting residues as well as the stumps (stump + coarse roots) were harvested.

In the study of Laiho (1997), stand-level biomass and nutrient content regression equations were presented for above-ground tree components in Scots pine dominated drained peatland stands. The equations were based on detailed biomass sampling of 80 sample trees from six sample stands located in southern Finland, and generalization of the allometric relationships to stand level based on diameter, height, and crown height measured for all trees.

The additional leaching of potassium caused by forestry treatments was estimated for ditch network maintenance (DNM) and regeneration harvesting (clear felling) treatments: For DNM, the K-export estimates presented by Joensuu *et al.* (2002) were used. The estimates are based on the long-term monitoring of element exports from 40 drainage areas throughout in Finland.

For regeneration harvestings, the K-losses were quantified for SOH and WTH treatments from 17 experimental catchments in southern and central Finland (Sarkkola *et al.* unpublished). The ditch-outflow K-concentration and water-borne K-export data were analysed by using calibration-period control area method and regression modelling. The K-concentrations and runoff were monitored for 1–2 years before and 3-4 years after treatment and the duration of the harvest impact on K export were estimated by utilizing data from one pair of managed and non-managed catchment. Furthermore, the background K-export (off-site export without the treatment impact) was also quantified.

Finally, the airborne annual deposition of potassium i.e. the external K-input to ecosystem was determined according to the estimates presented by Ruoho-Airola (2003). Other possible K-inputs such as fertilizations, mineralization and moving from surrounding mineral soil sites were neglected from the calculations. Particularly in thick-peated sites, on which we were concentrated in these calculations, the source of potassium from mineral soils can be considered extremely small.

The simulations of the annual changes in the stand K-contents were calculated to the rotation period of 80 years and it was started from stand regeneration treatment with eight year post-harvest period, when the treatment has significant impact on the K-exports. DNM treatment was carried out two times during the rotation period, which is following the widely used forestry practice in Finland. Otherwise, the annual K-losses were expected to be at the given background level with constant K- input of the atmospheric deposition.

RESULTS AND DISCUSSION

The loss of potassium induced by biomass removal in WTH plus stump harvesting was 2-5 times larger (75–97 kg/ha) than in SOH (15–30 kg/ha). This was evident even though – as is typical in mechanized WTH with harvesters and forwarders - about 30% of the harvest residues were left on-site (Nurmi 2007, Hytönen and Moilanen 2014). In WTH without stump harvesting, the K-losses induced by biomass removal were about 50-65 kg/ha. About two thirds of the potassium removed along with biomass removal in WTH plus stump harvesting was in the needle and branch biomass and about one third was in the stumps and roots. For the patterns of temporal changes in K-stores in poor and fertile sites, see Fig. 1.

When adding to these removals the hydrological K-losses induced by harvesting (poor sites: 9 kg ha^{-1}, fertile sites: 28 kg/ha) and two DNM treatments (8.3 kg/ha/treatment), the background hydrological K losses (1–2 kg/ha/year), as well as considering the K input by deposition (ca. 1 kg/ha/yr.), the net total off-site K-loss in SOH was 30–40 kg/ha in poor sites and 135–155 kg/ha in fertile sites during the 80-year rotation period. Respectively, for WTH they were 50–75 kg/ha in poor sites and 160–210 kg/ha in fertile sites. When comparing these losses with the typical K-store in peat in thick-peated soils (<100 kg/ha in the 50 cm-thick surface peat), it appears that without significant additional K-input through e.g. fertilization, the K-stores are not sufficient to ensure satisfactory potassium status in trees during the development of the next stand generation.

It has been widely known that the originally wet and treeless or sparsely forested nitrogen-rich minerotrophic sites are potential K-deficiency risk areas due to their very low K-contents in peat (Kaunisto and Paavilainen 1988). However our calculations showed that even in sites earlier considered to have high applicability for whole-tree harvestings such as thick-peated fertile spruce peatlands (Päivänen & Hånell 2012), the K-stores in site may decrease too much for undisturbed stand growth, if the harvesting residues are removed together with stem wood. Avoiding WTH decreases the off-site K-losses, but may not completely eliminate the risk for K depletion, however. The risk of severe K-depletion caused by WTH may even be larger in fertile thick-peated sites than in poor ones even though the K-stores in peat are generally larger (Figure 1). This is because in spruce stands, proportionally larger amount of potassium is bound in the tree biomass than in pine stands, and the annual background K-loss exceeds the simultaneous input of deposition to the ecosystem.

CONCLUSIONS

Our data showed that the thick-peated sites may have large potential for sever K-depletion irrespective of their fertility. It is evident that in such sites, where the K-stores in peat are larger than the net removal, the K-stores are sufficient to ensure productive forestry also if stands were managed by intensive WTH-treatments. Thus, it would be important to develop tools to recognize better the potential risk areas of anticipated K-deficiency in the field. Respectively, if repeated K-fertilizations are needed to sustain forestry on these sites, their economic feasibility should be clarified before initiation of regeneration activities in drained peatland forests on a large scale.

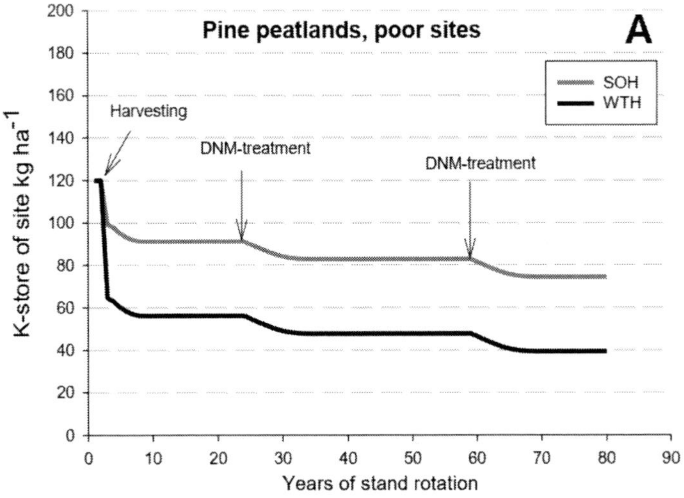

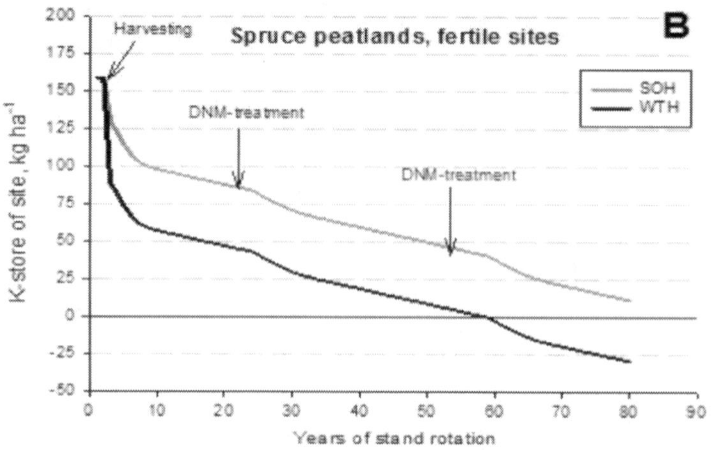

Figure 1: The simulated effects of forest management treatments on the K-balance on poor Scots pine dominated forest sites (A) and on fertile Norway spruce dominated sites (B) on drained peatlands in Finland during the 80-year stand rotation period. For poor sites (A), the initial K-contents were set to be: Peat (0-20 cm): K 50 kg/ha, surface vegetation 20 kg/ha and the K-content of tree stand: 48 kg/ha. For fertile sites (B), the respective K-contents used as initial values were 80 kg/ha, 20 kg/ha and 60 kg/ha. The off-site K-leaching induced by cuttings and ditch network maintenance as well as background K leaching and atmospheric deposition were also taken into considerations as described in the text. SOH=stem-only harvesting; WTH=whole-tree harvesting.

4. REFERENCES

1. Finér, L. 1989. *Biomass and nutrient cycle in fertilized and unfertilized pine, mixed birch and pine, and spruce stands on a drained mire.* Acta Forestalia Fennica 208: 1-63.
2. Hoosbeek, M.R., van Breemen, N., Vasander, H., Buttler, A., Berendse, F. 2002: *Potassium limits potential growth of bog vegetation under elevated atmospheric CO2 and N deposition.* Global Change Biology 8: 1130–1138.
3. Hytönen, J. & Moilanen, M. 2014. *Effect of harvesting method on the amount of logging residues in thinning of Scots pine stands.* Biomass & Bioenergy 67: 347-353.
4. Joensuu, S., Ahti, E. & Vuollekoski, M. 2002. *Effects of ditch network maintenance on the chemistry of run-off water from peatland forests.* Scandinavian Journal of Forest Research 17: 238-247.
5. Kaunisto, S., Paavilainen, E. 1988. *Nutrient stores in old drainage areas and growth of stands.* Communicationes Instituti Forestalis Fenniae 145. 39 pp.
6. Kaunisto, S., Tukeva, J. 1984. *Kalilannoituksen tarve avosoille perustetuissa riukuvaiheen männiköissä.* (Summary: *Need for potassium fertilization in pole stage pine stands established on bogs*). Folia Forestalia 585. 40 s.
7. Laiho, R. 1997. *Plant biomass dynamics in drained pine mires in southern Finland. Implications for carbon and nutrient balance* (Academic dissertation). The Finnish Forest Research Institute, Research Papers 631. 53 pp.
8. Laiho, R., Laine, J. 1995 *Changes in mineral element concentrations in peat soils drained for forestry in Finland.* Scandinavian Journal of Forest Research 10: 218–224.
9. Laiho, R., Sallantaus, T., Laine, J. 1999. *The effect of forestry drainage on vertical distributions of major plant nutrients in peat soils.* Plant and Soil 207: 169–181.
10. Mengel, K., Kirkby, E.A. 2001. Principles of plant nutrition, 5th edition. Kluwer Academic Publishers, London. 849 pp.
11. Moilanen, M., Saarinen, M., Silfverberg, K. 2010. *Foliar nitrogen, phosphorus and potassium concentrations of Scots pine in drained mires in Finland.* Silva Fennica 44: 583-601.
12. Nieminen, M., Laiho, R., Sarkkola, S. & Penttilä, T. 2016. *Whole-tree, stem-only and stump harvesting*

impacts on site nutrient capital of a Norway spruce dominated peatland forest. European Journal of Forest Research (DOI 10.1007/s10342-016-0951-1) (Published online: 24 March 2016)

13. Nurmi, J. 2007. *Recovery of logging residues for energy from spruce (*Picea abies*) dominated stands.* Biomass and Bioenergy 31(6): 375–380.
14. Päivänen, J. & Hånell, B. 2012. *Peatland ecology and forestry - a sound approach.* University of Helsinki, Department of Forest Sciences Publications 3. 267 pp.
15. Ruoho-Airola, T., Alaviippola, B., Salminen, K., Varjoranta, R. 2003. *An investigation of base cation deposition in Finland.* Boreal Environmental Research 8: 83–95.
16. Saarinen, M. 1997. *Kasvupaikkatekijöiden vaikutus vanhojen ojitusalueiden taimettumiseen. Kirjallisuuteen perustuva tarkastelu.* (Summary: *Effect of site factors on restocking of old drainage areas. A literature review*). SUO – Mires and Peat 48(3): 61–70.
17. Sarkkola, S., Ukonmaanaho, L., Nieminen, T., Laiho, R., Laurén, A., Finér, L. & Nieminen, M. *Should harvest residues be left on site in peatland forests to decrease the risk of potassium depletion?* (manuscript submitted to Forest Ecology and Management)
18. Tripler, C. E., Kaushal, S. S., Likens G. E., Walter, M. T. 2006. *Patterns in potassium dynamics in forest ecosystems.* Ecological Letters 9: 451–466.
19. Westman, C. J., Laiho, R. 2003. *Nutrient dynamics of drained peatland forests.* Biogeochemistry 63: 269-298.

5.3: PEATLAND MANAGEMENT: LEGISLATIONS, REGULATIONS & POLICY

Abstract No: A-083

CHALLENGES FOR SOUTHEAST ASIAN TROPICAL PEAT SWAMPS: A REVIEW OF EXISTING MANAGEMENT AND POLICY

Stephanie Evers[1*], Catherine Yule[2], Rory Padfield[3], Patrick O'Reilly[4] and Helena Varkkey[5]

[1] *University of Nottingham Malaysia Campus, Jalan Broga, 43500 Semenyih, Selangor, Malaysia*
[2] *Monash University Malaysia, Jalan Lagoon Selatan, Bandar Sunway, 47500 Subang Jaya, Selangor, Malaysia*
[3] *Malaysia-Japan International Institute of Technology, Universiti Teknologi Malaysia, Jalan Semerak, 54100, Malaysia*
[4] *Crops for the Future, Jalan Broga, 43500 Semenyih, Selangor, Malaysia*
[5] *Asia-Europe Institute, University of Malaya, Jalan Universiti, 50603 Kuala Lumpur, Wilayah Persekutuan Kuala Lumpur, Malaysia*

**Corresponding author: Stephanie.Evers@nottingham.edu.my*

Pristine tropical peat swamp forests represent a unique ecosystem characterized by high water tables, specialist flora and fauna adapted to anaerobic, acidic and waterlogged conditions, and globally significant stores of soil carbon. With over 50% of tropical peatlands occurring in Southeast Asia, they provide significant local regional and global ecosystem services. However, these ecosystems are under considerable anthropogenic pressure due to the rapid development occurring throughout this region. This is having considerable impacts on the ecosystem functionality and carbon emissions as well as being closely linked to the increasing trans-boundary haze pollution of the region. With this in mind, we will review the extent and efficacy of current peatland policies with a focus on Indonesia and Malaysia as well as key policies initiated by non-state actors. In doing so, we will review current policies, guidelines and emerging processes related to land management decisions and consider their implications in relation to the preservation of PSFs and sustainable management of those under altered land-use.

***Keywords**:-*

Abstract No: A-389

DRIVING SUSTAINABILITY OBJECTIVES ON NATIONAL LEVEL

Rosediana Suharto

Responsible Palm Oil Initiatives Indonesia (RPOI), Indonesia

**Corresponding author: indonesian.sustainable@therpoi.com*

SUMMARY

The implementation of sustainability principles should reach its objectives which include better environment, improve economy of the country and fair treatment of labour and fair trade. Although many countries member of UNEP that committed to sustainability since RIO.2 and WSSD , many countries do not implement this principles yet .For countries like Indonesia and Malaysia implementation of sustainability in palm oil has set up in the form of rule and regulations because the national rules and regulation is use to protect national interest , Indonesia has implement sustainability principles also in other commodities such as cacao ,coffee and while tea and rubber still in the process. The implementation of these principles must also protect the national interest which includes country sovereignty, the policy of each country to use the natural resources including biodiversity a, peatland and protect their environment must be respected, the law and regulations in each country must also be respected. The country programme in reducing poverty must be support when implementing sustainability criteria, mean many framers or smallholders shall also to be supported by the government or international organizations to implement sustainability. This is to secure that sustainable commodities is supported by all members in the supply chain. Investors must follow the regulation no intervention by the outsiders, the government must control these local or foreign investor, do not destroy environment and must treat labour, indigenous people in a fair way. The government must also treat the investors according to laws and regulations, open and transparent. Sustainability implementation must be supported by fair trade no discrimination between import and local products and no hidden technical barrier the consumer demand I form of trade must not become barrier to trade which can cause trade injury.

***Keywords**: sustainability principles, national interest, environment, rules and regulations, fair trade*

INTRODUCTION

Indonesia is one of the countries which sustainability requirements of palm oil are made based on the existing rule and regulations, which is why that the implementation of sustainable palm oil, is mandatory. The idea of making these requirements placed on the national interest, which protected the use of land, environment, social economy must be put as priority. Indonesia support fair trade, but cannot agree on impediments in form of non – tariff barrier, under name of sustainability.

Indonesia implement sustainability criteria on palm oil at all level, from palm oil fruit produced to also all palm oil mills, with or without oil palm plantation and also supports smallholders that include in plasma and KKPA program and also non-supported smallholders namely independent smallholders.

DRIVING SUSTAINABILITY OBJECTIVES

The commodity of palm oil is placed at number 5 in the Indonesia export earnings. Indonesia at the beginning invited local and foreign investment with the objectives to open job opportunity, reduce poverty, tax collection and to fulfil the local demand for palm oil and also export earnings. The fast growing of palm oil leads to the increasing amount of local and international demand. However, the impact of these fast growing palm oil plantations, concluded in many of Indonesian forest was destroyed, the decreasing quality of environment around oil palm plantation, and the surrounding biodiversity are disturbed.

From the beginning every investor who are interested to use land for plantation, will be given the necessities to understand that their activity should involve the surrounding people by offering them job to increase their income. The government release forest for plantation with consideration that the piece of land given is in no protected area, protect the riparian and the edge of natural water source, and also avoid eroded land. If there are animal that live near to the plantation their corridor shall be made for those animals.

Government forest are not allowed to be planted, encroachment to government forest will face sanction. This is to protect the destruction of the forest including protected area for examples national park, cultural park and biodiversity inside the forest, etc. This is to follow Agrarian Basic Law No.5/1960 and Forest Law No.41/1999 and Law No. 18/2013 on the prevention and eradication of Forest Destruction.

By implementing government requirement/standard Indonesian Sustainable Palm Oil (ISPO), Plantation Management including land clearance, seeding, planting, water used, plant protection, plant maintenance, harvesting and production all of these activities must follow Law No.12/1992 about Plant Cultivation System. These activities must always consider and protect the environment. The regulation on planting on peat is available separately with full consideration on avoiding environmental damage.

On the environment and Environment Impact Assessment (EIA) should be conducted before the land clearing follow by UKL and UPL this to make sure that the Environment is implemented and monitored. Independent smallholders must make a responsible statement that they are understand the implication of any activities they carry out in their plantation that effect the environment have to be reduce an avoided. This is to follow the law No. 32/2014 about Protection and Management of the Environment.

Base on Law No. 13/2009 about Labour and Law No.31 about Labour Safety guarantee that many plantations should pay their labour at least at their minimum wages, and plantation company must implement occupational health and safety. Plantation company shall strive to improve the welfare and capacities of the workers pursuant the statutory laws, they shall also to facilitate the formation of labour union in order to fight for their rights of workers.

Plantation Companies shall contribute to the welfare of customary law communities/ indigenous people.

The law and regulations in Indonesia related to sustainable criteria shall be implemented by the companies and smallholders consequently so can produced sustainable palm oil.

Abstract No: A-240

IMPLEMENTATION OF INTEGRATED MANAGEMENT PLAN FOR NORTH SELANGOR PEAT SWAMP FOREST 2014-2023 (IMP-NSPSF 2014-2023)

Mohd Puat Dahalan,[1] Mohd Basri Abdul Manaf[1], Badrol Hisam Abdul Rahman[1], Syed Mohd Adzha Syed Khalid[1], Azuan Mohd Sukri[1], Mangsor Mohd Yusoff[1], Yusoff Muda[2], Hamdan Napiah [2], Azid Adam [2], Faizal Parish[1], Nagarajan Rengasamy[1], Lew, S.Y. [1] and Julia Lo[1]

[1] *Jabatan Perhutanan Negeri Selangor, Malaysia*
[2] *Jabatan Perhutanan Semenanjung Malaysia, Malaysia*
[3]*Global Environment Centre, Malaysia*

**Corresponding author: syed.adha@yahoo.com*

SUMMARY

Peat swamp forests cover more than a third of the total permanent forest reserves in Selangor. These forests are vital to the balance of our ecosystem. However, rapid development and booming population have significantly put peatlands in Selangor under threat. Since peat swamp forests have complex ecosystem, there is a need for an integrated landscape approach to deal with this matter. North Selangor Peat Swamp Forest comprises of Raja Musa Forest Reserve, Sungai Karang Forest Reserve, Sungai Dusun Forest/Wildlife Reserve and part of Bukit Belata Forest Reserve Extension and adjacent areas of stateland forest. It covers an area of 81,304 hectares and is the second largest contiguous peat swamp forest in Peninsular Malaysia. Over the years, NSPSF had faced with many challenges (i.e. recurring fires and forest degradation) both from inside and outside the forest reserves. In 2014, an IMP-NSPSF 2014-2023 (Vol. 1 and 2) was developed by the Forestry Department Peninsular Malaysia, Selangor State Forestry Department with support from Global Environment Centre and International Fund for Agricultural Development - Global Environment Facility (IFAD-GEF), funded by ASEAN Peatland Forest Project and European Union supported SEApeat Project which is implementing under the framework of the ASEAN Peatland Management Strategy 2006-2020 (APMS). It was adopted in December 2014 by the Selangor State Government. The paper will highlight the implementation progress made on IMP-NSPSF 2014-2023 in North Selangor with the support and collaboration of NGO and public.

***Keywords**: complex ecosystem, integrated landscape approach, many challenges, collaboration of NGO and public*

INTRODUCTION

Selangor is endowed with a diversity of forest types such as Inland Forest, Peat Swamp Forest and Mangrove Forest. The total area of peatlands is limited to 177, 947 ha (22.4%) (Faculty of Forestry, UPM, 2014) of the total 793,020 hectares of state land (Federal /TUP, 2009). The total area of Peat Swamp Forest Reserves in Selangor is 91,080 hectares. It is located in the North Selangor Peat Swamp Forest (81,304 hectares) and South Selangor Peat Swamp Forest (9,776 acres) (Selangor Forest Management Plan 2011-2020 [Mid-term review, 2015]).

The North Selangor Peat Swamp Forest (NSPSF) is situated on the west coast of Peninsular Malaysia about 50km Northwest of Kuala Lumpur. The North Selangor Peat Swamp Forest (NSPSF) is located on a flat coastal plain in the north western part of the State of Selangor and approximately covers an area of 81,304 hectares. Before being constituted as forest reserve in 1990, the forests were state lands and have been selectively logged on a rotational basis. The first logging operation started about 65 years ago. In the previous Integrated Management Plan NSPSF (2001-2010), NSPSF was described as including only two forest reserves - namely Raja Musa Forest Reserve & Sungai Karang Forest Reserve. Based on the assessment for the revision of the IMP as well as stakeholder discussions it is proposed that Bukit Belata (extension) Forest Reserve and Sungai Dusun Forest Reserve/Wildlife Reserve (Hulu Selangor District) have to be included as part of NSPSF. With this, the strategies are developed will be applied on both the forest reserves to manage and protect the forests and biodiversity from further threats. Tables 1 give details of the NSPSF which is made up of four Forest Reserves.

North Selangor Peat Swamp Forest comprises of Raja Musa Forest Reserve (35,656 ha) , Sungai Karang Forest Reserve (37,417 ha), Sungai Dusun Forest/Wildlife Reserv (5,091 ha) e and part of Bukit Belata Forest Reserve Extension (4,342 ha) and adjacent areas of stateland forest. It covers an area of 81,304 hectares and is the second largest contiguous peat swamp forest in Peninsular Malaysia. Over the years, NSPSF had faced with many challenges (i.e. recurring fires and forest degradation) both from inside and outside the forest reserves.

In 2014, an IMP-NSPSF 2014-2023 (Vol. 1 and 2) was developed by the Selangor State Forestry Department and Forestry Department of Peninsular Malaysia with support from Global Environment Centre and International Fund for Agricultural Development - Global Environment Facility (IFAD-GEF), funded by ASEAN Peatland Forests Project and European Union supported SEApeat Project which is implemented under the framework of the ASEAN Peatland Management Strategy 2006-2020 (APMS). It was adopted in December 2014 by the Selangor State Government.

This Plan significantly updates an earlier Integrated Management Plan (IMP) previously prepared with support from DANCED in 1999. The current plan will cover the next 10 years from 2014 – 2023 and incorporates the findings from a number of studies and activities undertaken through the Smart Partnership programme of the APFP Malaysia (involving the Forestry Department of Peninsular Malaysia and other partners including Forestry Department Selangor, Department of Agriculture, Department of Irrigation and Drainage, Malaysian Meteorology Department, Forest Research Institute of Malaysia, University Putra Malaysia, Malaysian Nature Society, Sahabat Hutan Gambut Selangor Utara and the Global Environment Centre) between 2011 – 2014.

The overall management objective for the ten-year planning period is *"To maintain the geographical extent and integrity of the North Selangor Peatland Forest to sustain and rehabilitate the functions of the ecosystem as provider of goods and services for the benefit of the local and global communities."* Meanwhile, we have set some of specific Management Plan Objectives as follows 1) Re-establish the hydrological functions and the natural water balance of the NSPSF. 2) Prevent all fire occurrence and associated haze in and adjacent to NSPSF. 3) restore the forest ecosystem of NSPSF by encouraging natural forest regeneration and where necessary supplement with planting in severely degraded sites. 4) Establish a buffer zone of at least 500m width along the entire outer boundaries of the NSPSF to minimize impacts of activities in adjacent areas. 5) Develop and promote sustainable use of NSPSF including eco-tourism, harvesting of NTFP, recreation and environmental awareness, education and research. 6) Promote conservation of peatland biodiversity and ecosystem functions. 7) Maintain and enhance carbon stock, minimize GHG emission and develop options for carbon financing. 8) Promote multi- stakeholder participation in the implementation of the IMP.

METHODS

Purpose

The updating of the NSPSF Integrated Management Plan (IMP) has been made necessary due to several factors. One is the end of the timeframe for the existing document; and the other is changes that have happened over the years, creating a need for an updated management plan. For example, an indefinite moratorium was put into place in 2010 to stop all logging activities in Selangor State.

In addition the prevalence of forest fires within and adjacent to NSPSF has increased linked to increasing pressure for development of adjacent lands. Significant experience has also been gained over the past 10 years on the options for rehabilitation of degraded portions of the forest. Furthermore, the cooperation with several governmental agencies and local communities had been strengthened, which should be incorporated into the management plan. The definition of North Selangor Peat Swamp Forest area has also been expanded in this IMP to include Bukit Belata extension and Sg Dusun Forest Reserve so as to create a complete and more effective management unit.

The 2nd National Physical Plan (NPP-2) adopted in 2005 and the Selangor State Structure Plan 2025 (SSSP 2025) adopted in 2007 have both specified the need for a 1km wide buffer zone around the NSPSF where development activities are restricted. This important requirement needs to be incorporated in to the management plan.

Approach

The IMP was prepared using a participatory approach. The plan preparation was guided by the Selangor State Forestry Department and Forestry Department of Peninsular Malaysia with specific inputs from a number of agencies working under the APFP Smart Partnership Programme. Five stakeholder consultations were organized at state and district level between November 2013 and June 2014 to enable inputs to be provided by a broad range of state and local stakeholders. Stakeholder participating tin the meetings included Respective District Offices and District Township Councils (Kuala Selangor, Hulu Selangor and Sabak Bernam), Department of Wildlife and National Park, Malaysia, Economic Planning Unit , Federal Department of Town and Country Panning Peninsular Malaysia,, Fire and Rescue Department, Minerals and Geoscience Department, Malaysian Palm Oil Board, Public Work Department, Department of Environment, Department of Veterinary and Services, Selangor Agriculture Development Corporation, FELDA, LUAS, IADA, Kumpulan Darul Ehsan Bhd, Kumpulan Semesta Sdn Bhd., Sime Darby Plantation and Peers Consult (M) Sdn Bhd.

The scope of the review was as follows:

1. Review and update the Integrated Management Plan for North Selangor Peat Swamp Forest (2001-2010) as a guide for the preparation of the Integrated Management Plan for North Selangor Peat Swamp Forest (2014-2023);
2. Evaluation of fire prone areas and propose preventive and remedial measures. Identify fire-prone areas to confirm the signs of fire and identify new hotspots;
3. Preparing a rehabilitation plan for North Selangor Peat Swamp Forest, including buffer zones, especially for degraded areas (encroached and fire prone areas);and
4. Gather relevant secondary data from 2011 to 2013 for the preparation of the Integrated Management Plan for North Selangor Peat Swamp Forest (2014-2023).

RESULTS

Identified the buffer zone activities or current land use

NSPSF is surrounded by state land and private land that is largely cultivated for agricultural purposes (see Fig. 1). The main land-uses adjoining the forest reserve are Tanjung Karang Rice Irrigation Scheme to the Southwest and West, sand and clay mining in the South, in the oil palm plantations in the south east and north. The forest is separated from the irrigation scheme to the Southwest by the Main Irrigation Canal whereas the Bernam River forms the Northern boundary. Sungai Tengi acts as the natural divider between Sg Karang Forest Reserve and Raja Musa Forest Reserve. NSPSF is under the jurisdiction of three civil districts in Selangor State, namely Kuala Selangor District, Sabak Bernam District & Hulu Selangor District.

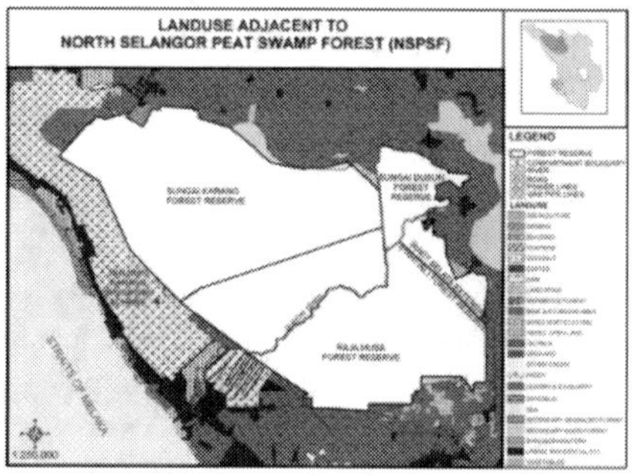

Figure 1: Landuse Adjacent to North Selangor Peat Swamp Forest (NSPSF)

Identified the Management Zones in NSPSF

The studies and inventories conducted during the project showed that some parts of the forest are particularly suitable for pursuing certain objectives such as bio-diversity conservation. A total of 7 categories of zones that have been identified as in need of specific management as follows i) Biodiversity Conservation (25,027ha), ii) Water Catchment Forest (22,594ha), iii) Rehabilitation Zone (18,547ha), iv) Recreation, Eco-tourism and Education (8,299ha), v) Sg. Dusun Wildlife Reserve (5,091ha) vi) Agro-Forestry Zone (1,521ha), and vii) Community Forestry (226ha).

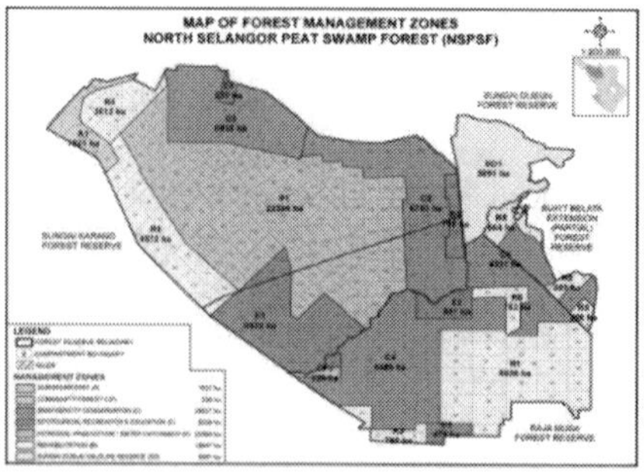

Figure 2: Map of Forest Management Zones in North Selangor Peat Swamp Forest

Identified Fire Risk Area in NSPSF

Several areas within the NSPSF are heavily drained by either canals or the surrounding mining activities creating pockets of the forest to be dryer in the dry season and more susceptible to fire starts. This has proven to be true as past fire incidents often occurred in these areas. A fire risk map has been prepared as part of this plan to detail areas of high, medium and low fire risk which will prioritise activities and works needed to further prevent fires. The area have been identified as fire risk area requires immediate attention and placing of forest guards to prevent illegal clearing, burning and crop growing.

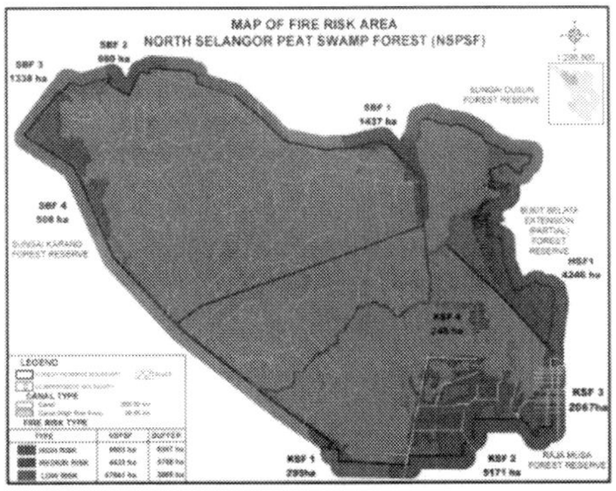

Figure 3: Fire Risk Map of NSPSF

Identified the potential rehabilitation area with appropriate actions

Over the last 30 years, large portions of NSPSF had been degraded due to a few factors including: widespread commercial logging, illegal land clearing, drainage and fires. The combination of these factors has resulted in large areas of NSPSF- close to 20,000 hectares being degraded, although degree of degradation varies greatly from site to site. At the southern portion of NSPSF, most areas had been burned repeatedly that the area had been severely degraded, it is largely void of trees and only covered in grass/ lalang(*Imperata cylindrica*). There were three important steps had been identified in rehabilitation of the degraded area namely hydrology restoration, fire prevention and re-vegetation. These 3 aspects are inter-linked closely and omitting any would not achieve the desired outcome. Therefore, priority has been given to rehabilitate the severely degraded areas in NSPSF. Fig.2 (Map of Forest Managemnet Zones in North Selangor Peat Swamp Forest) has shown the potential rehabilitation area in NSPSF.

DISCUSSION AND CONCLUSION

The IMP-NSPSF 2014-2023 provides a key framework for the management of the largest peatland landscape in North Selangor. This plan will enhance the efforts in preserving the pristine of North Selangor Peat Swamp Forest as they have high potential in payment for ecosystem services (PES), ecotourism and to safeguard the human well-being. The prioritised activities include blocking many abandoned logging canals, preventing fire and rehabilitating degraded forest, and enhancing the engagement of local community and other stakeholders. Combined these measures will significantly reduce GHG emissions and help control further climate change.

This plan includes three key supporting documents which form the backbone of Integrated Management Plan as listed below:-

d) The Cooperative Fire Management Plan provides guidance for multiple stakeholders to work together to prevent, prepare for, respond to and recover after fires
e) The Rehabilitation Plan focusses on facilitating natural regeneration of forests by restoring the hydrology and ecology
f) The Buffer Zone Plan covers an area of 15,000ha in a strip 1km wide around the forest reserves. The buffer zone plan aims to reduce and mitigate the negative influences of the activities taking place adjacent to the Forest Reserve

REFERENCES

1. Selangor State Forestry Department 2014, Integrated Management Plan for North Selangor Peat Swamp Forest 2014-2023.
2. Selangor State Forestry Department 2011, Selangor State Forest Management Plan 2011-2020.

Abstract No: A-360

NOT WASTELANDS, LET'S MANAGE OUR PEAT SWAMPS PROPERLY THROUGH A SYSTEMATIC CONSERVATION PLANNING APPROACH

Jason Hon[1*], Jayasilan Mohd-Azlan[2], Stephanie Alau Apui[1] and Belinda Lip[1]

[1]*WWF-Malaysia, MALAYSIA*
[2]*Department of Zoology, Faculty of Resource Science and Technology, Universiti Malaysia Sarawak, MALAYSIA*

* *Corresponding author: hjason@wwf.org.my*

SUMMARY

The peat swamp forests of Sarawak is largely misconstrued as 'mosquito-infested wasteland', with less than 5% located inside protected areas. The loss of peat swamp forests is mainly associated with large scale agriculture development, notably for oil palm plantations, whereby Sarawak is regarded as the last frontier for expansion in Malaysia. The peat swamp forests in Sarawak are home to some of Borneo's rarest and unique flora and fauna, and play very important roles in ecosystem processes. In this paper, we present the conservation values of peat swamp forests by identifying their areas of conservation importance. Oil palm plantations contributed to a total 25.8% of peat swamp forest cover loss for the period of 2000 to 2014. Five conservation clusters containing peat swamp forest are identified, namely: Marudi-Loagan Bunut; Sebauh; Rajang Delta; Maludam-Sedilu-Sebuyau complex; and Simunjan. Systematic conservation planning approach, strengthened by sound policy decisions, can be used to guide proper land use planning for sustainable development and conservation.

Keyword: *planning, conservation, Sarawak, sustainable development*

INTRODUCTION

Globally, peatlands (areas with peat substance) cover an estimated 400 million hectares or three per cent of the earth's land surface (Strack, 2008). About 11% of tropical peatlands are found in Malaysia, which is second to Indonesia that had until the recent past, 80 per cent coverage of tropical peatlands (Rieley et al., 1996; Page et al., 2006). Sarawak has the largest peat swamp forest coverage in Malaysia, accounting for about 64 per cent of the total 2.6 million hectares in Malaysia (Hon, 2011). However, much of these areas are already opened up for agriculture developments and other uses, putting extensive pressure to the remaining peat swamp forests.

The peat swamp forests of Sarawak contain some of the most unique and rare fauna species, such as the red-banded langur (*Presbytis melalophos cruciger*), which is now restricted to the forests of Maludam National Park (Hon and Gumal, 2004; 2005), and significant populations of the Bornean endemic proboscis monkey (*Nasalis larvatus*). The largest colonies of flying foxes (*Pteropus vampyrus*) are restricted to the peat swamp forests of Loagan Bunut National Park (Gumal et al., 2008) and Sedilu National Park. The orang-utans (*Pongo pygmaeus*) are also found within the peat swamp forests of Sedilu National Park and Ulu Sebuyau National Park, and in the lowland hill dipterocarp forests of Lanjak Entimau Wildlife Sanctuary, Batang Ai National Park and Ulu Menyang Conservation Area. The only sightings of Storm's stork (*Cicornia stormi*) and masked finfoot (*Heliopais personata*) were in peat swamp forest (Hon, 2011) and the only known breeding colonies of Oriental darter (*Anhinga melanogaster*) and little cormorant (*Phalacrocorax niger*) were in Loagan Bunut (United Nations Development Programme & Global Environmental Facility, 1999).

Peat swamp forests perform crucial functions in flood prevention, nutrient storage and carbon sink. During heavy rainfall events, peat swamps absorb most of the excess water, thereby reducing flood peaks and helps in mitigating floods. Absorbed water is released slowly during drier periods, thereby mitigating droughts in adjacent areas and maintains crucial supply of water for many of Sarawak's coastal areas during droughts (Sawal, 2004).

Sadly, the peat swamp forests in Sarawak are imperiled, their loss driven by economic demands to open land for agricultural expansion and other activities. Timber extraction began in the peat swamp forests in the 1950s and continued until the early 1970s, with species such as *Shorea albida* which was found in abundance in former times, mainly targeted for harvesting. Once logged, degraded peat swamp forests are frequently invaded by pioneer species such as *Colocasia* sp., *Macaranga* sp., *Melicope* sp. and *Melastoma* sp., of which most of them are non-merchantable timber species and rarely harvested or utilized by the local communities.

Sarawak, with a land mass of about 12.5 million hectares, has a land use policy of allocating six million hectares as permanent forest estates, one million hectares as totally protected areas and another two million hectares for oil palm plantations. In more recent years, logged-over peat swamp forests in the coastal areas were and continue to be excised from state land and permanent forest estates to make way mainly for oil palm and forest plantations, including other agricultural and land development projects. Oil palm planting intensified in Sarawak in the late 1990s. Despite starting off later than other states, Sarawak experienced the highest rate of oil palm plantations development in Malaysia largely at the expense of peat swamp forests situated in the low lying coastal plains (Hon and Shibata, 2013). In 2015, a total of 1.44 million hectares in Sarawak have already been planted with oil palms.

METHODS

We analysed the extend of peat swamp forest cover in Sarawak based on forest cover map from various sources (see Langner et al., 2007; Miettinen et al., 2010; *WWF internal data*). We identified a suit of species and habitat for both terrestrial and freshwater ecosystems that are important for conservation, which are termed as our conservation features. Based on systematic conservation planning approach, we used the programme MARXAN (Ball et al., 2009) to select a configuration of planning units, with conditions that are best for conservation and meet our specified goals for the conservation features. The results from MARXAN analyses identifies the planning units that are best for conservation. We used ArcGIS to plot planning units that are regarded as our priority conservation area.

In the MARXAN inputs, we set oil palm and industrial tree plantations together with other features such as mines, infrastructures, settlements and forest cover changes since 2010 according to their respective levels of severity rankings as costs layers. This will generate a layer that identifies areas that are costly for conservation and best to be avoided. In the conservation target setting, alongside more than 50 other features, we used different conservation goals for vegetation types. For peat swamp forests, we set the conservation goal of 45% of their current extent. The boundary length modifier was set at 0.2 to improve connectivity of conservation areas. We then inspect where the areas of conservation importance are from the MARXAN output, and by overlaying with current extant of peat swamp forests and oil palm plantations with the map output, we are able to identify areas of conservation concerns where proper land use planning and management interventions are required.

RESULTS

Our MARXAN analysis identified 155,624 hectares of peat swamps forests within the areas of conservation importance. Forest cover loss data from 2000-2012 (Hansen et al. 2013) with updated data for 2014 (earthenginepartners.appspot.com) is largely consistent with areas that have been licensed out for oil palm plantations. Oil palm licensed area when overlaid with forest cover loss areas between 2000-2014 represent 650,117 hectares or 30.7%, of which 545,974 hectares are on peat (Table 1).

Table 1: Coverage of areas of conservation priority, association with forest cover loss and oil palm expansion on peat in Sarawak

	Hectares
Areas of conservation importance in Sarawak*	4,254,500
Peat swamp forests captured inside areas of conservation importance	155,624
Forest cover loss (2000-2014)#	2,116,047
Forest cover loss associated with oil palm plantation	650,117
Forest cover loss associated with oil palm plantation on peat	545,974

**Results from MARXAN analyses*
 # Source: Hansen et al. 2013

Remaining peat swamp forests, adjacent to large scale agricultural activities such as oil palm plantations are identified as clusters at: Marudi-Loagan Bunut; Sebauh; Rajang Delta; Maludam-Sedilu-Sebuyau complex; and Simunjan (Figure 1).

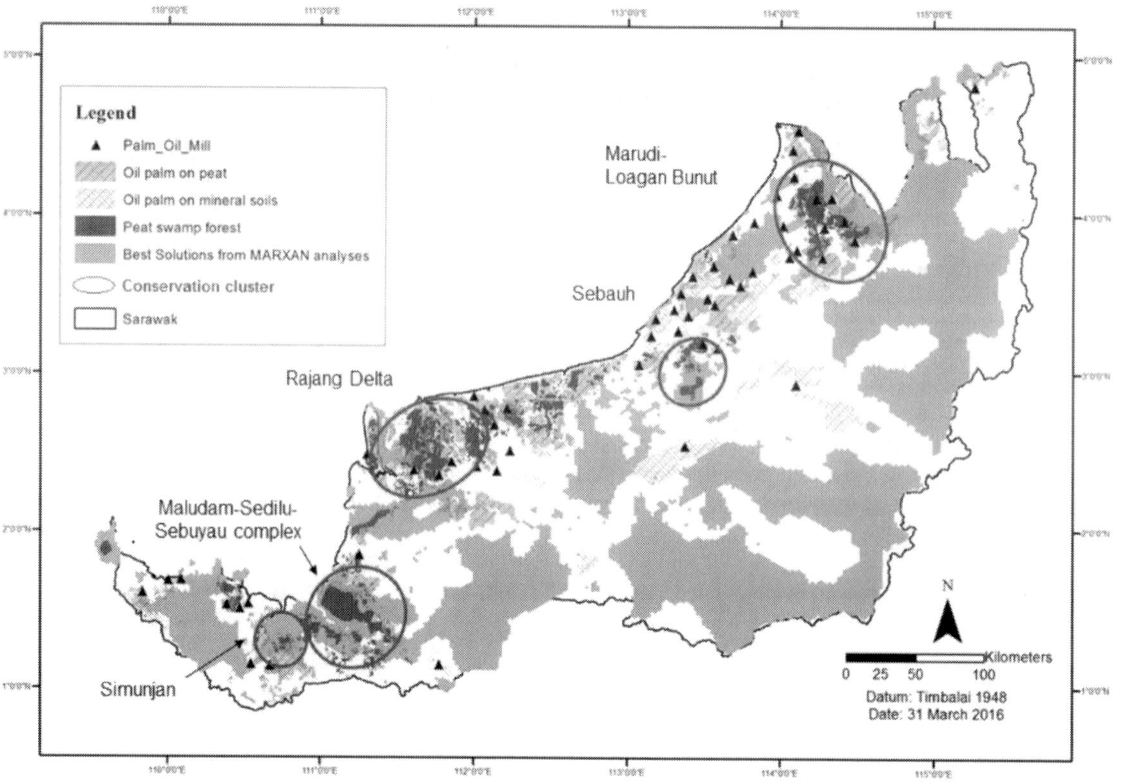

Figure1: Areas of conservation importance (as identified from best solutions score from MARXAN analyses) with five of the conservation clusters where oil palm plantations are established on peat and adjacent to peat swamp forests

Table 2: Conservation features inside conservation areas adjacent to oil palm plantations on peat

Conservation areas cluster	Conservation features present
Marudi-Loagan Bunut	Ramin; legumes-lianas association; flying fox (*Pteropus vampyrus*); false gharial (*Tomistoma schlegelii*); tapah (*Wallago* spp.); mud volcano; peat swamp forests; tagang river system; oxbow lakes.
Sebauh	Peat swamp forests; arowana (*Scleropages formosus*); false gharial (*Tomistoma schlegelii*); tapah (*Wallago* spp.).
Rajang Delta	Ramin (*Gonystylus bancanus*); mangroves; peat swamp forests; tagang river system; terubok (*Tenualosa toli*).
Maludam-Sedilu-Sebuyau complex	Orang utan (*Pongo pygmaeus*); proboscis monkey (*Nasalis larvatus*); red banded langur (*Presbytis chrysomelas cruciger*); terubok (*Tenualosa toli*); dolphins; false gharial (*Tomistoma schlegelii*); tapah (*Wallago* spp.); ramin (*Gonystylus bancanus*); *Dipterocarpus coriaceus*; mangroves; peat swamp forests.
Simunjan	Flying fox (*Pteropus vampyrus*); false gharial (*Tomistoma schlegelii*); tapah (*Wallago* spp.); peat swamp forests; ramin (*Gonystylus bancanus*); *Dipterocarpus coriaceus*.

DISCUSSION

The systematic conservation planning approach when used in combination with government's land use policy is able to come up with the best land use strategy for conservation and development. It is used as a decision support tool to assist in the conservation of biodiversity and ecosystems at a landscape scale, using best available data to identify priority areas for conservation actions. This approach that helps to identify areas of priority conservation importance should be adopted as part of the government policy to aid in decision making for land development in Sarawak, especially in granting greater protection to the remaining peat swamp forests. Where areas of conservation importance lie adjacent to existing agriculture areas such as oil palm plantations, among the measures that could be taken include: management interventions by oil palm plantations through the adoption of best management practices; and government prioritizing areas for conservation that focuses on intact large peat swamp forests. Nevertheless, it must be noted that the output from our analyses is not final and should never be construed as the only and final configurations for the identification of areas of conservation importance. The process should be an ongoing one whenever new data or land use policies are made available. As it is now, the identified peat swamp forests within our areas of conservation importance may actually represent the only remaining areas that urgently require conservation attention.

One of the steps that could be taken by the government in protecting our peat swamp forests now is to relook at the current agriculture policy, by discouraging large scale conversion of remaining intact peat swamp forests into other land uses such as oil palm plantations. The conservation goals of 45% adopted by our analyses is a conservatively low figure and can be adjusted higher to prioritize the conservation of peat swamp forests in Sarawak.

There is an urgent need to protect more peat swamp forests in Sarawak, and to leave them in their natural state. Under our environmental protection ordinance, Article 3 of the Natural Resources and Environment (Prescribed Activities) Order 1997 mentions that development of an oil palm plantation or forest harvesting exceeding 500 hectares falls within the order's prescribed activities, thereby warranting an environmental impact assessment approval before commencement of project implementation (Sawal, 2004).

Sufficient areas of peat swamps forests, pristine and otherwise, must be set aside to ensure that the ecosystem, species and genetic diversity are preserved. Therefore, resources and attention should be focused on conserving peat swamp forest patches that are left, with similar effort expanded on rehabilitation of degraded or logged over forests. In the end, it is envisioned that more pet swamp forests can be legally protected inside our totally protected area network.

CONCLUSION

The remaining peat swamp forests in Sarawak is still important for conservation. Despite being under threats from conversion into other land uses, efforts could be intensified to identify where the remaining peat swamps forests can be accorded better protection. Systematic conservation planning approach can be used as a tool to help in decision making for the conservation of peat swamp forests in Sarawak, and to guide development planning. While we report specifically on the conservation of peat swamp forests, our systematic conservation planning approach has also include a whole suite of other conservation attributes including other forest types that occur in Sarawak. Therefore, it is a holistic and encompassing approach. If used properly, conservation efforts can be optimized to focus on priority areas, which must include the unique, yet important peat swamp ecosystems of Sarawak as one of the conservation targets that warrant our utmost attention now.

REFERENCES

1. Ball, I.R., H.P. Possingham, and M. Watts. 2009. Marxan and relatives: Software for spatial conservation prioritisation. Chapter 14: Pages 185-195 in *Spatial conservation prioritisation: Quantitative methods and computational tools*. Eds Moilanen, A., K.A. Wilson, and H.P. Possingham. Oxford University Press, Oxford, UK.
2. Gumal, M., Hon, J. & Kong, D. (2008) *Birds and bats of Loagan Bunut National Park, Sarawak, Malaysia.* UNDP/GEF Funded Peat Swamp Forest Project, Sarawak, Malaysia & Wildlife Conservation Society. 105 pp.
3. Hansen, M. C., P. V. Potapov, R. Moore, M. Hancher, S. A. Turubanova, A. Tyukavina, D. Thau, S. V. Stehman, S. J. Goetz, T. R. Loveland, A. Kommareddy, A. Egorov, L. Chini, C. O. Justice, and J. R. G. Townshend. 2013. "High-Resolution Global Maps of 21st-Century Forest Cover Change." *Science* 342 (15 November): 850–53. Data available on-line from:http://earthenginepartners.appspot.com/science-2013-global-forest.
4. Hon, J. (2011) SOS: Save our swamps for peat's sake. *SANSAI: An Environmental Journal for the Global Community* (5):51–65.
5. Hon, J. & Gumal, M.T. (2004) Monitoring and conserving primates in Maludam National Park: Final Report. Paper presented at the Joint Working Group Malaysia-Netherlands Maludam-Ramin Projects Workshop: Wise Use of Peat Swamp Forests in Malaysia.

6. Hon, J. & Gumal, M.T. (2005) Monitoring and conserving primates. In: *Maludam Technical Report*. pp: 203–241. Jaafar K.M., Grinang, J. & Sabki, M.S. (Eds.). Wageningen: Alterra and Kuching: Sarawak Forest Department and Sarawak Forestry Corporation.
7. Hon, J. & Shibata, S. (2013) A review on land use in the Malaysian State of Sarawak, Borneo and recommendations for wildlife conservation inside production forest environment. *Borneo Journal of Resource Science and Technology* 3(2), 22–35.
8. Langner, A., Miettinenz, J., & Siegert, F. (2007). Land cover change 2002–2005 in Borneo and the role of fire derived from MODIS imagery. *Global Change Biology* 13: 2329–2340.
9. Miettinen, J., Shi, C. & Liew, S.C. (2011) Deforestation rates in insular Southeast Asia between 2000 and 2010. *Global Change Biology* 17: 2261-2270
10. Page, S.E., Rieley, J.O. & Wüst, R. (2006) Lowland tropical peatlands of Southeast Asia. In: *Peatlands: Evolution and Records of Environmental and Climate Changes*. pp:145–172. Martini, I.P., Martínez Cortizas A. & Chesworth, W. (Eds.). Amsterdam and Oxford: Elsevier.
11. Rieley, J.O., Ahmad-Shah, A.A. & Brady, M.A. (1996) The extent and nature of tropical peat swamps. In: *Tropical Lowland Peatlands of Southeast Asia: Proceedings of a Workshop on Integrated Planning and Management of Tropical Lowland Peatlands*. Cisarua, Indonesia, 3–8 July 1992. pp:17–53. Maltby, E., Immirzi, C.P. & Safford, R.J. (Eds.). Gland: IUCN.
12. Sawal, P. (2004) Threats to peat swamp forest of Sarawak. Joint Working Group Malaysia-The Netherlands Sustainable Management of Peat Swamp Forests of Sarawak with Special Reference to Ramin. Wageningen: Alterra and Kuching: Sarawak Forest Department and Sarawak Forestry Corporation. 54 pp.
13. Strack, M. (Eds.) (2008) Peatlands and Climate Change. *Vapaudenkatu: International Peat Society*. 223 pp.
14. United Nations Development Programme & Global Environmental Facility (1999) Project Document Malaysia: Conservation and Sustainable Use Of Tropical Peat Swamp Forests and Associated Wetland Ecosystems. UNDP-GEF. 133 pp.

THEME 6
CULTURAL, EDUCATIONAL, MEDICINAL & SOCIO-ECONOMIC ASPECTS OF PEATLANDS, PEAT & SAPROPEL

6.1: CULTURAL & SOCIO-ECONOMIC ASPECTS OF PEATLAND

Abstract No: A-156

ANTHROPOGENIC DISTURBANCES AND RESILIENCE: A MESSAGE FROM THE PAST

Kartika Anggi Hapsari[1*], Siria Biagioni[1], Tim Jennerjahn[2], Peter Reimer[3], Asmadi Saad[4], Supiandi Sabiham[5] and Hermann Behling[1]

[1] *Department of Palynology and Climate Dynamics, Albrecht-von-Haller Institute for Plant Sciences, Georg-August-University of Goettingen, Germany*
[2] *Department of Biogeochemistry and Geology, Leibniz Center for Tropical Marine Ecology (ZMT) Bremen, German*
[3] *Department of Biological Science, Goshen College, Indiana, USA*
[4] *Department of Soil Science, University of Jambi, Indonesia*
[5] *Department of Soil Science and Land Resource, Bogor Agriculture University (IPB), Indonesia*

[*] *Corresponding author: kartika.hapsari@biologie.uni-goettingen.de*

SUMMARY

Despite of the number of studies that have been conducted, knowledge of past human activities on peatlands in Southeast (SE) Asia remains fragmented. Hence, anthropogenic activities on peatlands are considered to be recent. In order to see whether and how human conducted activities on peatland in the past, a palaeoecological study on peatland located close to archaeological site of Malayu Empire was undertaken. The results revealed that human activities on tropical peatland began over a millennium ago. By conducting logging, grazing and wild harvesting activities, human changed the vegetation composition and diminished the ecosystem ability to accumulate peat and carbon. Shortly after the abandonment of the site, the vegetation regenerated and the accumulation rate of carbon recovered.

Keywords: *peatland, long-term data, disturbance, human impact, resilience*

INTRODUCTION

Pressures on peatland in SE Asia due to land use and conversion escalate in the past few decades, following the increase in population demand for food, settlements and resources. In order to prevent loss and to maintain the important functions of this ecosystem, management strategies are urgently required. To create effective management strategies on peatland, it is important to include a historical perspective that can provide valuable knowledge on ecosystem response to disturbance and their resilience (Birks, 2012).

Unfortunately, knowledge on past disturbance of peatland in SE Asia remains a large gap, particularly of human disturbance. The evidences of human activities on peatland are only reported by very limited number of studies (Anshari *et al.*, 2001, Yulianto *et al.*, 2005, Cole et *al.*, 2015). The lack of evidence as well as the requirement for tools and technology to utilize peatland compel the extensive human disturbance is considered to be novel (Cole *et al.*, 2015). Therefore, the information how past human interventions controlling vegetation composition and C accumulation in peatlands remains scarce and the understanding the peatland resilience to human-induced disturbance prevail to be missing.

The information of past environment condition is often kept in the natural archive. Peatland is one the natural archives that preserves the palaeo-proxies such as pollen, spores and charcoal. Using palaeoecology, the information from the past therefore can be translated and understood. In order to see whether human

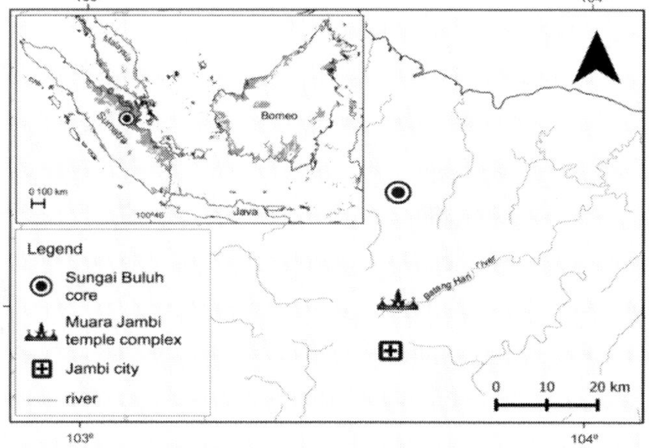

Map of the study site

conducted activities on peatland in the past, the natural archive form Sungai Buluh peatland is chosen, as it is located close to Muara Jambi temple complex, the archeological remains of Malayu Empire.

Malayu Empire is one of the largest Empire in Indonesian history located in Jambi, Central Sumatra. The establishment of the Empire is reported as earlier than the 7th century, however the Muara Jambi temple was built later in the 9th century. The Empire demised in the 14th century by the conquest from Javanese kingdom, Majapahit (Witrianto, 2014). Based on the archaeological study, the Muara Jambi temple complex was the capital of the Empire (Witrianto, 2014).

This study was undertaken in order to see (i) whether or not the inhabitant of Malayu Empire conducted any activities on the peatland. If so, (ii) what kind of activities they conducted, (iii) how the activities affected the peatland, and (iv) how the peatland responded.

METHODS

In 2013, a 3.5 m SB-B core was taken from the area of Sungai Buluh peatland and spanning about 23000 years (Hapsari *et al.*, submitted). In order to see the condition of Sungai Buluh peatland on pre-, during and post- Malayu Empire times, this study was conducted using the same core and focused on around the depth covering the existence period of the Empire in Muara Jambi (1100 to 500 years ago; 120-60 cm). In order to assess the changes in past vegetation of Sungai Buluh peatland, 25 sub-samples from the first 2 m of SB-B core covering from 9000 cal yr BP to present were analyzed for pollen and spore using the standard method from Faegri and Iversen (1989). The pollen and spores are counted, identified to the finest taxonomical possible using the reference collection of Department of Palynology and Climate Dynamics and other available literatures e.g. (Anderson and Muller, 1975; Jones and Pearce, 2015). The identified taxa are subsequently grouped according to the function and common ecology of the source plants e.g. (Sosef *et al.*, 1998; Cole *et al.*, 2015). The results are subsequently combined in the age-depth model of SB-B core constrained from five AMS radiocarbon dates and compared to the peat accumulation rate, carbon accumulation rate and past fire regime that are performed by Hapsari *et al.* (submitted).

RESULTS

The pollen data is presented in pollen diagram prepared using C2 program (Juggins, 2007). The pollen diagram displays the selected pollen and spore taxa and is divided into four zones based on visual inspection. In zone SB I (200-113 cm; 9000-1000 cal yr BP), the pollen is dominated by peat swamp and mixed-riverine forest taxa, while taxa indicating disturbances are presented in low values (average >5%). Zone SB II (113-60 cm; 1000-400 cal yr BP) is characterized by the decrease of the total average value of peat swamp and mixed-riverine forest taxa from 92 to 73%, accompanied by the increase of disturbance indicator taxa from 5 to 24%. In this zone, Piperaceae, Poaceae, Ardisia and Grewioideae increase significantly. Pollen percentage of Poaceae and Grewioideae reach their highest value in the end of this zone. In zone SB III (60-20 cm; 400-100 cal yr BP), the average value of disturbance indicator taxa decrease to 8% followed by the increase of peat swamp and mixed-riverine forest taxa (average 90%). The last zone, SB IV (20-0 cm; 100 cal yr BP to present), is indicated by the increase of disturbance indicator taxa, Piperaceae and *Ficus*, with the average value of 15%. The total average of peat swamp and mixed riverine forest taxa also decrease into 84% in this zone.

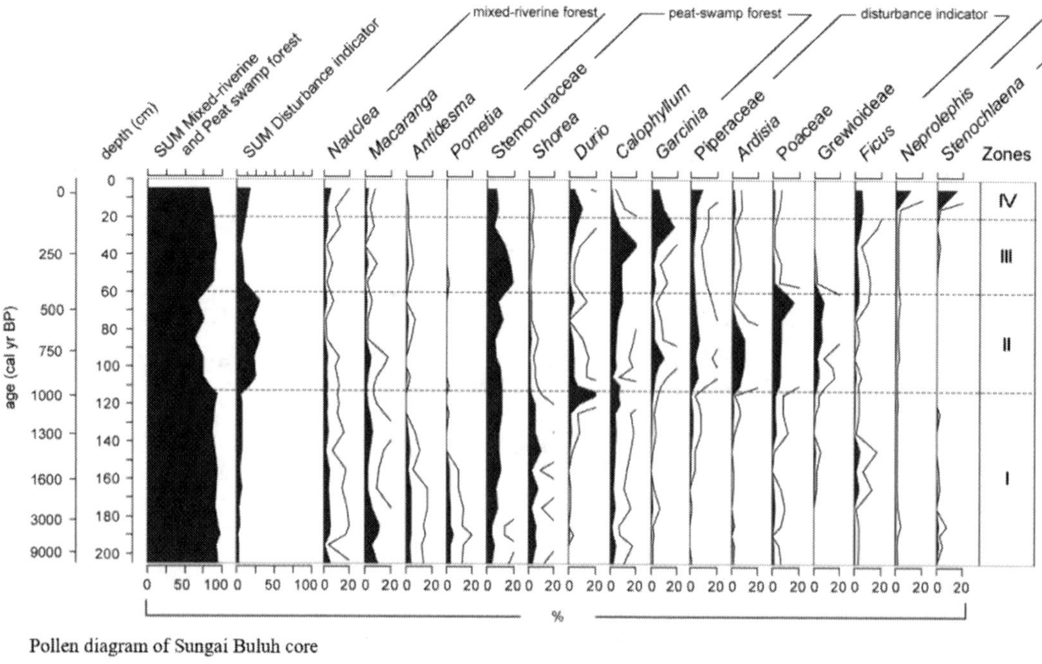

Pollen diagram of Sungai Buluh core

From the depth of 200 to 160 cm (9000 to 1600 cal yr BP), the average value of C accumulation is low (9 g C/m^2 yr). It increases to 91 g C/m^2 yr between the depth of 160 and 145 cm (1600-1300 cal yr BP) and subsequently decreases between the depth of 140 and 70 cm (1300-500 cal yr BP; 65 g C/m^2 yr). The C accumulation rate re-increases in the depth of 70 to the top of the core (500 cal yr BP-modern) with the average value of 102 g C/m^2 yr.
In 9000 to 3000 cal yr BP, the charcoal analysis suggests the period of low fire frequency in the record with average 1 fire episode/1000 year. The fire frequency then increases between 3000 and 1200 cal yr BP with average 4 fire episodes/1000 year. From 1200 to 500 cal yr BP, the fire frequency decreases to average 2 fire episodes/1000 year and subsequently increases to average 3 fire episodes/1000 year from 500 cal yr BP to present.

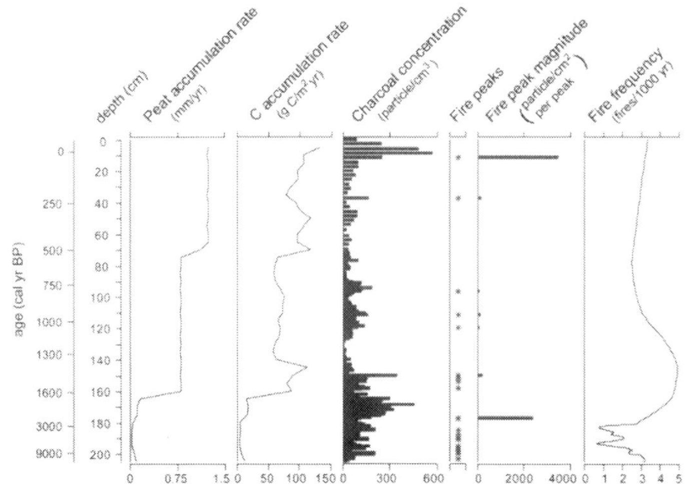

Diagram of peat accumulation rate, C accumulation rate, C_{org} and charcoal analysis results (Hapsari et al., submitted)

DISCUSSION

Based on the result, the vegetation in Sungai Buluh peatland was dominated by both peat swamp and mixed-riverine forest for over thousands of years throughout the record. Before the establishment of Muara Jambi temple or pre-1000 cal yr BP, the level of disturbance was minor. The disturbance indicator taxa such as Poaceae and *Ficus* intermittently present in low values.
After the establishment of Muara Jambi temple, or around 1000 cal yr BP, the peat-swamp taxa such as *Shorea*, *Durio*, and *Calophyllum* decreased. This was accompanied by the increase of Piperaceae, Poaceae and Grewioidea and followed by the decrease of Stemoniraceae and *Garcinia*, indicates the opening in the vegetation. Piperaceeae is a shade intolerant plant that usually grows in disturbed forest (Padmanaba and Sheil, 2014), Poaceae is commonly found as a result of forest clearance (Cole *et al.*, 2014) and Grewioideae is pioneer vegetation in open and dry forest (Chung, 2005). The opening in forest vegetation was feasibly resulted from logging and timber harvesting. *Shorea, Durio* and *Calophyllum* trees are well-known timber plants and commonly used for constructions, boats and furniture (Soerianegara and Lemmens, 1994; Lemmens *et al.*, 1995). Stemonuraceae and *Garcinia* trees are also used as timber. However, due to their lower quality, they are often considered as alternative timbers for tools and charcoal wood (Sosef *et al.*, 1998).
The abundance of *Ardisia*, which grow rapidly on the grazing ground (Hoogerwerf, 1970) indicates that the inhabitant of Malayu Empire is also conducting grazing activities on peatland. The abundance of Piperaceae during the period of forest opening might provide benefit for the Malayu Empire. According to the historical record, Malayu Empire was a renowned pepper (*Piper* sp.) production center in Sumatra (Witrianto, 2014). This suggests that the population has also conducted wild-harvesting activities. The low fire frequency during Malayu Empire time suggests that the population did not use fire extensively for ground clearance or slash-and-burn. Moreover, lack of cultivation Poaceae in the pollen record also supports the argument that the inhabitant of Malayu Empire did not utilize the peatland for agricultural use. During the Malayu Empire time, the C accumulation rate was decreasing around 30%. The decrease of C accumulation might be related to the change in vegetation composition. As the forest cover decreased, the ecosystem received less lignin organic material. This accelerated the decomposition process and released carbon.
In the 14th century, after the conquest of Majapahit, Malayu Empire was ruled by an official court of Majapahit namely Adityawarman. The Empire became a vassal from Majapahit until Adityawarman declared his independence then moved the kingdom to Saruaso, a hinterland area in West Sumatra (Witrianto, 2014). After the abandonment of the site, the pollen evidence showed that the forest started to recover. The ability of forest to regenerate indicates that the ecological threshold has not yet been crossed by the level of disturbance. The regeneration process started with the increase of Poaceae and Grewioideae (Chung, 2005; Sutomo *et al.*, 2011) and followed by Stemonuraceae, *Calophyllum, Garcinia*, and later *Durio,* while *Shorea* seems not to be able to reach the pre-disturbance condition. Following the recovery of the forest, the value of C accumulation rate also recovered. As the intake of lignin organic material also increased and the decomposition rate was impeded, the carbon release through the decomposition process can be hindered. The forest regeneration process took around 100 years before the total proportion of both peat-swamp and mixed-riverine forest reached the pre-disturbance condition. This condition lasted for around 200 years before the level of disturbance re-increased around 100 yr cal BP.

The increase of *Ficus* was feasibly related to the rubber tree planting by local people as an obligation from the colonial governance. Local rubber plant, *Ficus elastica*, was commonly planted before *Hevea brasiliensis* was introduced in the 20th century. The increase of Piperaceae might also be related to the growth of pepper plantation under the colonial state (Karmela, 2014). Pepper was one of the important commodities of Jambi since the era of Jambi sultanate in 17th century. The increase of fire peak magnitude around 30 cal yr BP followed by abrupt increase of *Nephrolepis* and *Stenochlaena* around 10 cal yr BP was feasibly related to the intensive fire use for land clearance under colonial state. Around that time, the local people simultaneously convert their *ladang* into permanent rubber plantation. *Ladang* is a kind of field or farm that is commonly used for planting cassava, corn or different kinds of vegetables. Following the growth of the vehicle industry, the demand for rubber was increasing (Feintrenie and Levang, 2009). This condition escalated the rubber price in the market and encouraged the local farmers to switch from swidden to plant rubber and led to double rubber boom in 1920s and 1930s (Feintrenie and Levang, 2009).

CONCLUSION

Some important information could be asserted from the palaeo study of the natural archive of Sungai Buluh peatland. Albeit the lack of instrument and technology, excessive anthropogenic activities on tropical peatland began already over a million years ago. This result suggests that human impact on peatland is not a recent phenomenon. However, compared to modern land use, the human activities on peatland in the past might restricted to logging, grazing and wild harvesting, without involving extensive fire use and cultivation. Such activities changed the vegetation composition and decreased the ecosystem ability to accumulate carbon. Even without conducting large-scale peatland burning or conversion, human still can affect the ecological function of peatland. Nonetheless, this study shows that peatland can be resilient to excessive human disturbance. The vegetation and C accumulation rate of Sungai Buluh peatland have recovered, taking around 100 years after the cessation of disturbance following the site abandonment. This provides an overview of what kind of disturbances that could be reversed. The past socioeconomic condition during the period of the colonial state are also recorded in the Sungai Buluh archives. The trading commodities, industrial needs and population's wealth are captured by the natural archives. It shows that beside the direct anthropogenic activities, socioeconomic condition is also an important indirect driver of peatland disturbance. This information could define the past disturbances and its impact on the peatland. Furthermore, this also enhanced the understanding of the recovery process as well as the required time of the process. Therefore, in order to maintain the function and sustainability of peatlands, it is important to involve different perspectives throughout consideration regarding decision for peatland management, including palaeoecology that delivers the message from the past.

ACKNOWLEDGEMENTS

We thank Dorothee Dashbach (Chemilabor, ZMT Bremen) for supporting the carbon content measurements. The research is conducted using samples collected under Research Permit No. 1095/FRP/SM/V/2013 recommended by the Indonesian Institute of Science (LIPI) issued by the Ministry of Forestry (PHKA). The financial supports are provided by the DFG Sonderforschungsbereich in CRC 990 (EFForTS) subproject A01 and Erasmus Mundus Lotus Program. We acknowledge also the financial support from Göttingen International for attending the conference.

REFERENCES

1. Anderson, J.A.R., Muller, J., 1975. Palynological study of a holocene peat and a miocene coal deposit from NW Borneo. Review of Palaeobotany and Palynology 19, 291–351.
2. Anshari, G., Kershaw, A.P., van der Kaars, S., 2001. A Late Pleistocene and Holocene pollen and charcoal record from peat swamp forest, Lake Sentarum wildlife reserve, West Kalimantan, Indonesia. Palaeogeography, Palaeoclimatology, Palaeoecology 171, 213–228.
3. Birks, H.J.B., 2012. Ecological palaeoecology and conservation biology : controversies, challenges, and compromises. International Journal of Biodiversity Science, Ecosystem Services & Management 8, 292–304.
4. Chung, R.C.K., 2006. Revision of Grewia (Malvaceae–Grewioideae) in Peninsular Malaysia and Borneo. Edinburgh Journal of Botany 62, 1.
5. Cole, L.E.S., Bhagwat, S.A., Willis, K.J., 2014. Recovery and resilience of tropical forest after disturbance. Nature Communication 5, 3906.
6. Cole, L.E.S., Bhagwat, S.A., Willis, K.J., 2015. Long-term disturbance dynamics and resilience of tropical peat swamp forests. Journal of Ecology 103, 16-30.

7. Faegri, K., Iversen, J., 1989. In: Textbook of Pollen Analysis, revised by Faegri, K., Kaland, P.E., Krzywinski, K. John Wiley, New York.
8. Feintrenie, L., Levang, P., 2009. Sumatra's rubber agroforests: Advent, rise and fall of a sustainable cropping system. Small-scale Forestry 8, 323–335.
9. Hapsari, KA., Biagioni, S., Jennerjahn, T., Reimer, P.M., Saad, A., Sabiham, S., Behling, H., submitted manuscript.
10. Hoogerwerf, A., 1970. Udjung Kulon: The Land of the Last Javan Rhinoceros. E.J. Brill, Leiden.
11. Jones, S.E., Pearce, K.G., 2015. A pollen morphology study from the Kelabit Highlands of Sarawak, Malaysian Borneo. Palynology 39, 150–204.
12. Juggins, S., 2007. C2 user guide: Software for ecological and palaeoecological data analysis and visualization. University of Newcastle, UK.
13. Karmela, S.H., 2014. Kehidupan ekonomi penduduk dalam setiap periodisasi sejarah Jambi. Jurnal Ilmiah Dikdaya 4, 1.
14. Lemmens, R.H.M.J., Soerianegara, I., Wong, W.C., 1995. Plant Resources of South-East Asia No. 5(2). Timber trees: Minor commercial timbers. Prosea Foundation, Bogor, Indonesia
15. Padmanaba, M., Sheil, D., 2014. Spread of the invasive alien species *Piper aduncum* via logging roads in Borneo. Tropical Conservation Science 7, 35-44.
16. Soerianegara, I., Lemmens, R.H.M.J., 1994. Plant Resources of South-East Asia No. 5(1). Timber trees: Major commercial timbers. Prosea Foundation, Bogor, Indonesia.
17. Sosef, M.S.M, Hong, L.T., Prawirohatmodjo, S.,1998. Plant Resources of South-East Asia No. 5(3). Timber trees: Lesser-known timbers. Prosea Foundation, Bogor, Indonesia.
18. Sutomo, S., Fardila, D., Putri, L.S.., 2011. Species composition and interspecific association of plants in primary succession of Mount Merapi, Indonesia. Biodiversitas, Journal of Biological Diversity 12, 212–217.
19. Witrianto, 2014. Potensi sejarah dan purbakala DAS Batanghari. Analisis Sejarah 5, 68–79.
20. Yulianto, E., Hirakawa, K., 2006. Vegetation and environmental change in the early - Middle holocene at a tropical peat swamp forest, Central Kalimantan, Indonesia. Tropics 15, 65-73.

Abstract No: A-292

ECONOMIC VALUES OF PEATFOREST TO LOCAL COMMUNITIES IN MUKAH, SARAWAK

Sulaiman Hj Husaini[1*], Ahmad Shuib[2], Sridar Ramachandran[2], Syamsul Herman Mohd Afandi[3], Shazali Johari[3] and Mohamad Ibrani Shahrimin Bin Adam Assim[4]

[1]*Sarawak Land Custody and Development Authority, Malaysia*
[2]*Institute of Agricultural and Food Policy Studies, University Putra Malaysia, Malaysia*
[3]*Faculty of Forestry, University Putra Malaysia, Malaysia*
[4]*Faculty of Human Ecology, University Putra Malaysia, Malaysia*

**Corresponding author: sulaimh@gmail.com*

SUMMARY

Peat soil forest (as used in this study are the natural forest (peat swamp forest)) serves important ecological and environmental functions and provides perpetual benefits, if properly conserved. The peat swamp forest in the Mukah district represents the most significant protected peat soil area in the state. Communities living in the proximity of this forest are dependent directly or indirectly on it for their livelihood. The main objective of the study was to determine the economic value of the peat swamp forest to the local communities in Mukah. A sample survey of the villagers living along the fringes of the forest was undertaken to determine the types of benefits accrued to the local communities. The results of the study are significant at both the local and state level. At the local level, the peat swamp forest plays an important role because it contributes to the communities' income through the production of fish, wildlife products and wild sago as well as being a source of domestic water. At the international level, an important benefit derived from the peat swamp forest which accrues to the global community is carbon sequestration. Conservation of the peat swamp forest will, in the long run, safeguard the sustainability of the resources to support the livelihood and welfare of the local communities in Mukah.

***Keywords**: natural resources, local communities, non-forest products, income, sustainability, Mukah*

INTRODUCTION

In the coastal areas of many Southeast Asian countries peat soil areas cover approximately 12% of the land area, equalling more than 27 million hectares (MHA). The swampy peat land areas are not suitable for agricultural use and difficult to access and thus have low population densities. Peatlands are still important to millions of people for the production of crops such as sago (*Metroxylon sagu*), rattan, and for fisheries, hunting and forestry.

Very few relatively intact peat swamp forests remain: less than 10% of the original areas of such forests. But even these remnants, including the less than 5% of the South East Asian peat swamp forest that are officially protected, are affected by illegal logging and encroachment. Close to 45% of the remaining peat swamp forests have been severely affected by large-scale development, drainage, deforestation and (often illegal) logging. Another 45% have been destroyed by selective logging and drainage. Many millions of hectares have been consumed by fires (Wetland Organization 2005). "The consequence of millions of hectares of peatlands becoming unproductive will likely increase fire risks in these areas during dry periods for many decades to come. By then it will be too late to restore them" (Silvius, 2015).

The peat swamp forests in Mukah District, Sarawak, are being converted to other uses such as industrial, agricultural and housing , to cater for the needs of the district's increasing population . However, some members of the population depend on the peat swamp forest resources for their livelihood; they will be affected if the forests are not protected. The swampy peat land areas under natural conditions are not suitable for most agricultural uses and are often referred to as marginal lands suitable for marginal crops like sago. In Mukah peat lands are still important to the local communities for the production of sago and rattan crops as well as for fisheries, hunting of wild game and as a source of domestic water. Other important functions include providing flood control, acting as natural water filters, recreation etc.

The purpose of this study was to determine the communities' willingness to pay for peat swamp forest resources as an indicator of the values to them of the peat swamp forests. The value to non-timber forest products collected from peat swamp forests was determined using the market price.

METHODS

The Mukah-Socioculturally-Appropriate Multi-Facet Inventory (MSAMFI) is an instrument that is part of a trial web-based application system developed purposely based on a model partially adapted from the Malaysian Career Facet Inventory (as initially proposed via the Development of the Career Factor Inventory CFI: Chartrand, Robbins, Morrill and Boggs 1990). It was designed to assist Universiti Putra Malaysia's eco-tourism and socio-economics researchers to gather local economic credentials and imperative community development information parameters for Mukah, Sarawak. The instrument aims to gauge and identify pertinent informed economic choices and feasible sago-plantation based factors for economic enhancement opportunities, which will be scrutinized under the lenses of Item Response Theory Model and Knowledge, Attitude and Practice Rating Scale (Ahmad Hariza *et al.*, 2008).

Two categories of entries were constructed within the system: Mukah's socio-economic background and its vital demographic pertinent parameters, which were gathered via multi-tiered platforms of a single-online network, performed with an adaptable infrastructure (hardware) of a customizable-computerized algorithm (software programs). An initial closed-ended and partially open-ended questionnaire was integrated within the systems to be fully constructed as the test-bed for the Mukah-Socioculturally-Appropriate Multi-Facet Inventory (MSAMFI). The current study proposes to replicate Choi *et al.*'s (2010) analyses of a new stopping rule that attempts to address the efficiency and measurement precision problems associated with commonly used stopping rules. Precision measurements of MSAMFI's items were tested as per the aspirations for the instrument's development. According to Choi *et al.*'s (2010) study, the predicted standard error reduction (PSER) stopping rule seeks to balance the dual concerns of measurement precision and testing efficiency by considering the predicted change in measurement precision that would result from the administration of additional items in test system delivery and the complexities of the psychometrics involved in developing the initial version of the Mukah-Socioculturally-Appropriate Multi-Facet Inventory (MSAMFI). Data were extracted and imported to a .csv format to be synchronized with the application of a series of statistical data analytical tools.

RESULTS

Types and values of fish caught

The highly acidic and low oxygen conditions of the peat swamp forest water do not support many fish species. The river water is brown indicating a high tannin levels. Most of the fish are air-breathers such as snakeheads and catfish.

The common species of fresh water fish recorded in the survey are keli (*Clarias batrachus*), seluang (*Puntius* sp.), baung (*Mystus baramensis*), puyu (*Anabas testudinesis*) and sepat (*Trichogaster pectoralis*) (Table 1). The main commercial fish species are the catfish, gobies and snakeheads. During the data collection period of about 12 weeks, about 126kg of fish were caught by one selected respondent who used the "bubu", a traditional apparatus, to catch the fish.

The rivers are used for the transportation of sago logs and this sometimes affected the villagers' normal fishing activities.

Table 1: Types and prices of fish recorded

Type of fish	Price range (RM kg^{-1})
Keli	10 –18
Toman	18
Baung	10 -12
Lajong	10
Tapah	15 –20
Udang	10 –30
Bawang	15
Bureh	18
Haruan	20 –30
Puyu	7 –10
Sepatsiam	10
Ma'en	15
Padek	25
Dak	18

Wildlife conservation benefits

The peat swamp forest has been an important habitat for several game and endangered species. The mammalian population at the study site comprises mainly small mammals such as treeshrews, squirrels, rats, bats, otters and pangolins. The survey indicated that larger animals such as wild boar, deer, mousedeer and barking deer were still occasionally hunted for their meat. The encroachment of human beings into the forests for hunting and logging had caused the larger animals to become scarce. Under these circumstances, hunting of larger animals was no longer a significant activity of the local natives.Table 2 shows the price of game per kg.

Table 2: Types and prices of wild game

Types of game	Price range (RM kg^{-1} or per animal
Tenggiling	12
Wild boar	15 –30
Deer	18 –25
Mousedeer	25 / animal

Carbon stocks of sago forests

Peatlands store approximately 550 Gigatonnes of carbon worldwide, twice the amount stored in the world's forests. Peatlands also absorb atmospheric carbon in their soil and thus help to reduce greenhouse gas emissions which contribute to global climate change (Joosten, 2010).

Willingness to pay for conservation

Given that almost all (98.7%) the respondents either live close to the area and / or own land plots in Mukah peat swamp forest, and 90.6% benefit from the collection of peat swamp products, it could be concluded that the majority of them have made direct use of, and are aware of Mukah peat swamp forest. This indicates that the respondents are the users and receive benefits from the peatland. Therefore it could be expected that they possess sufficient knowledge from the use and benefits received to form a value for the Mukah peat swamp forest. The results from the perception questions (Table 3) demonstrate that the respondents agree on the importance of conserving the Mukah peat swamp forest.

Table 3: Perceptions on importance of Peat land forest

Statement on Importance of Peat swamp forest (PSF)	Mean score
a. PSF helps maintain health of Mukah town	4.75
b. Peat swamp forest provides opportunities for recreational fishing, bird watching, hunting and pleasant scenery	4.73
c. Peat swamp forest helps to clean the water and trap sediments and so improve water	4.73
d. Preserving Peat swamp forests will allow future generations of people to also enjoy them	4.74
e. It is important that the Peat swamp forest has continuously growing stands of Peat palm	4.75
f. It is important that owners of Peat swamp forest have the possibility of earning an income from the Peat swamp forest	4.74
Mean for perception on Importance of PSF	4.74

Scale: 1 Strongly disagree; 2 Disagree; 3 Neutral; 4 Agree; 5 Strongly agree

On a different note, most respondents chose as top priorities for conserving peat swamp forest matters that concerned their immediate livelihood. The results (Table 4) show that the communities have higher preferences for healthy living and better education over the conservation of the peat swamp forests. This is also consistent with their preference for protecting the rivers from pollution since they are dependent on the river systems.

Table 4: Priorities of conserving PSF as a national asset

Statement on priorities for conservation of PSF	Mean score
a. Replanting sago palms that have been cut down	3.15
b. Restoring sago forest on land previously drained	3.28
c. Conserving areas of wildlife	3.19
d. Protecting rivers and streams from pollution	3.85
e. Health services and facilities	3.82
f. Peat forest conservation	3.27
g. Education	3.39
h. Tourism	2.59

Priority Rank: 1 least; 2 low; 3 high; 4 highest

Willingness-to-pay for all cases

The communities' recognition of the significance of the peat swamp forest to their livelihood is reflected in the positive willingness-to-pay bids whereby more than 60% of the respondents are WTP. The changes in the district's environment as economic development takes place have enhanced the communities' awareness of the importance of the peat land forest to sustain their livelihoods. Consistently, the communities place protection of water quality above other values (Table 5).

Table 5: Willingness to pay (WTP) for conservation of PLF per person once in a life time

Items	Conservation of PLF	Wildlife	Water quality	Fish
Percent WTP above RM10	61.8	58.2	62.9	81.5
Percent unWTP above RM10	30.2	41.8	37.1	18.5
Percent WTP below RM10	10.9	11.4	8.1	15.1
Percent unWTP below RM10	89.1	88.6	91.9	85.0
Percent WTP	65.9	63.0	65.9	84.3
Percent unWTP	34.1	37.0	34.1	15.7
Mean WTP above RM10	RM14.43	RM13.72	RM14.74	RM10.91
Mean WTP below RM10	RM2.77	RM2.21	RM1.93	RM2.43
Mean Total WTP	RM13.69	RM12.85	RM14.16	RM10.63

Mean WTPs for conservation of wildlife were RM1.88, for water quality RM3.51 and for fish stocks RM1.84 (Sulaiman, 2005)

CONCLUSION

Conservation of peat swamp forest is an important task since the peat swamp forest has many functions. The secondary benefits derived from conserving the forest must be taken into account and cannot be ignored when deciding on alternative uses for this forest. Serious consideration should be given to the roles the secondary products play in the livelihood of communities living at the periphery of such forests. The social benefits from the peat swamp forest include availability of domestic water, fish and wildlife. The private benefits which belong directly to the land owner (established sago forest) contributing to his income may be derived solely from sago cultivation. The local population not involved directly in sago cultivation benefits from the conservation of the peat swamp forest as it forms a 'green lung' for Mukah new township and acts a buffer between the town and oil palm plantations.

The global benefits derived from peat swamp forest which accrue to the world community include maintenance of or additions to the carbon stock: degradation of peatlands on a global scale leads to an increase in CO_2 emissions, which causes global climate change.

Peat swamp forest should be viewed as wetland in terms of its economic value. This would enhance its use values and result in it being better understood.. If peat swamp forest is regarded as marginal land then it loses its value, being considered of lesser value than mineral land. Discussions of peat swamp forest must be in the context of environment and the total benefits. Society's perceptions have to change in order to make the peat swamp forest a heritage.

The Mukah peat swamp forest will undoubtedly continue to mature and evolve, continuing to be a haven for flora and fauna. And with so much of the state's natural peat swamp forest having been lost to development, it comes as a relief that this peat swamp forest, a living, breathing ecosystem, is able to demonstrate its capacity to buffer the effects of environmental degradation following the developments facing Mukah town and the surrounding areas.

REFERENCES

1. Ahmad Hariza Hashim, Mohd Ibrani Shahrimin Adam Assim, Ma'rof Redzuan and Eddy Azuan. 2008. *Classified Report on Year 1-Year 3 Primary School Children: Knowledge, attitude and practice among Malaysian children in road safety education.* Ministry of Transport, Malaysia.
2. Chartrand, J. M., Robbins, S. B., Morrill, W. H., and Boggs, K. 1990. Development and validation of the Career Factors Inventory. *Journal of Counseling Psychology,* **37:** 491-501.
3. Choi, S. W., Grady, M. W. and Dodd, B. G. 2010. A New Stopping Rule for Computerized Adaptive Testing. *Educational and Psychological Measurement,* 71: 37.
4. Joosten, H. 2010. The Global Peatland CO2 Picture Peatland status and drainage related emissions in all countries of the world. Greifswald University Wetlands International, Ede, August 2010 www.wetlands.org
5. Silvius, M. 2015. UNFCCC CoP21 in Paris.Head of Climate-smart Land-use of Wetlands International
6. Sulaiman, H.H. 2005. *An environmental and economic valuation of sago forest harvesting regimes.* PhD thesis (unpublished) submitted to the Graduate Studies Office, Universiti Putra Malaysia, Serdang, Malaysia.
7. Wetland Organization. 2005. Retrieved from www.wetland .org/what we do/saving peatland

Abstract No: A-294

ECO-TOURISM POTENTIALS OF PEAT SOIL FOREST IN MUKAH, SARAWAK

Sridar Ramachandran[1], Ahmad Shuib[2], Sulaiman Hj Husaini[3], Shazali Johari[4], and Syamsul Herman Mohd Afandi[5]

[1&2]*Institute of Agriculture and Food Policy Studies, UPM*
[3]*Land Custody and Development Authority, Sarawak*
[4&5]*Faculty of Forestry, UPM*

**Corresponding author:*

SUMMARY

Mukah as the administrative centre for the Distrct of Mukah, Sarawak is well known for its sago production. The dependency on peat soil for sago production by the local community as the economic activity has been practiced for decades. However, Mukah is also blessed with long beach, serene rivers system, and the uniqueness of Melanau ethnic community, which offer potentials for a related income generating socio economic activity in the ecotourism sector. Peat soil forest serves important ecological and environmental functions, if managed in a sustainable manner could provide potential eco-tourism benefits to the local communities. The main objective of the study is to determine the agro-forestry benefits derived in the peat soil forest land in Mukah. A sample survey of the villagers living along the fringes of the peat soil forest was undertaken to determine the perception of the communities on the types of potential eco-tourism resources that could be derived and accrued to the local communities. Observational and outdoor recreational inventory surveys were carried out as supplementary data collection.The results of the study are significant at both local and state levels. At the local level, the peat soil forest plays an important role because it could contribute to the communities' income through the development of ecotourism activities relating to natural resources like fishing, wildlife observation, and outdoor endeavors in the natural forest settings. The river systems within the peat soil forest are used for domestic consumption but also provide opportunities for development of water related recreational activities. The communities themselves serve as potential eco-tourism products with respect to their traditional cultural system and lifestyles.

Keywords: *recreational, local communities, resource inventory, satisfaction*

INTRODUCTION

Local residents can gain competitiveness economically in terms of household income by using the rural resources as an asset (Hjalager, 2004). The primary industry in the rural area is often related to agriculture. In Mukah, Sarawak the primary industry is agroforestry based. Many researchers who focus on the eco-tourism will conclude that the current situation of eco-tourism is currently going through a unique change period (Ilbery, 1998; Walford, Everitt and Napton, 1999). The fast growth in eco-tourism destination poses a challenge to decision makers in the development and implementation of rural resource policies. Thus, based on the difficulty of the situation and the views of environmental critics such as Marsden (1998) and Garrod *et al.* (2006), a rural resource framework has been developed to replicate the segregated changes in the rural sites. According to Butler *et al.* (1997) this complexity and connectivity of the theories could possibly cause conflicts in the stakeholder decision-making process on the rural resources. Progress in turning rural resources into tourism capital has been a challenge especially in the context of environment, society and economy. This is due to the fact that rural setting requires the initiative of stakeholders involvement and in the decision making process. Hence, establishing guidelines to encourage a perception that draws an appropriate balance between the stakeholders' different needs and requirement of a sound ecotourism policy is established.

For example, suggestions pointed at refining the economic position of a particular rural area are often conflicting on environmental grounds, as they are believed to threaten rural ways of life. Nevertheless, the challenges facing the rural tourism destination can be more efficiently handled by employing innovative ways of thinking and doing based on the principles of sustainable development (Sharpley, 2000). One of the challenges in Mukah is to identify resources that can be tourism assets. The perception that any rural resource can be a tourism capital has been proved otherwise. It is therefore critical to identify the right resources that meet these criteria. The findings of this study is hoped to eventually assist the community to not only identify the correct rural resource but to turn it into a tourism capital to their benefit in term of income that will eventually increase their standard of living. The purposes of this study are (i) to identify the rural resources and tourism capital; (ii) to demonstrate the linkages between rural resources and tourism capital. From this study, the resources that actually match the tourism capital can be clearly established.

Study Site

Mukah as the administrative centre for the District of Mukah, Sarawak is well known for its sago production. The dependency on peat soil for sago production by the local community as the economic activity has been practiced for decades. However, Mukah is also blessed with long beach, serene rivers system, and the uniqueness of Melanau ethnic community, which offer potentials for a related income generating socio economic activity in the ecotourism sector. Peat soil forest serves important ecological and environmental functions, if managed in a sustainable manner could provide potential eco-tourism benefits to the local communities. The results of the study are significant at both local and state levels. At the local level, the peat soil forest plays an important role because it could contribute to the communities' income through the development of ecotourism activities relating to natural resources like fishing, wildlife observation, and outdoor endeavors in the natural forest settings. The river systems within the peat soil forest are used for domestic consumption but also provide opportunities for development of water related recreational activities. The communities themselves serve as potential eco-tourism products with respect to their traditional cultural system and lifestyles.
This study further identifies that Mukah houses several species of mammals, birds, reptiles and riparian plants. Table 13.1 is an adaptation from (Garrod *et al.*, 2006) which is used in the context of Mukah Sarawak gives a detailed illustration of the elements of which classifies components of rural tourism capital that might be drawn upon by the rural tourism industry at numerous steps of the rural tourism value chain. This can range from the establishment of rural images used to support a rural tourism destination by offering rustic tourists with activities to do and attractions to visit, to the contribution made by natives in making a tourist's holiday unforgettable.

Table 1: Mukah's elements of countryside capital

Elements	Mukah Sarawak
Landscape, including seascape	riparian forests lining the riverbanks, freshwater swamps, peat swamps, mangroves, brackish water lagoon with vegetated sand islands, seagrass beds and beaches
Wildlife, both fauna and flora **Biodiversity**	sharks, wild boar, deer, mouse deer, birds wetlands, mangroves
Geology and soils	peat soils
Rural settlements, from isolated dwellings to market towns	fisherman villages, local wet market
Woods, forests and plantations **Distinctive local customs, languages, costumes, foods, crafts, festivals**	sago farms, Melanau cultures, educational hub, tabaloi, local fruits
Agricultural buildings	local dwelling

Source: Adaptation from (Garrod *et al.*, 2006)

METHODS

This paper looks into the application of the linkages between rural resources and eco-tourism capital. The application of Mukah to the framework is used to understand the relationship between the capital, industry and the end user. The framework is crucial as it looks at the interdependence of rural resources and ecotourism capital.
Eco-tourism is a more widespread terminology used to describe rural resource as a tourism capital. Rural resources that qualify as eco-tourism capital typically come from farm related activities also known as farm tourism and wilderness tourism such as national park, reserve forest (Luloff *et al.*, 1994). They can be found in non-urban territory where the primary economic activity is agriculture. The presence of human is somehow mandatory in these places. As can be seen in these studies, rural resource and tourism capital is a widely studied phenomenon although the exact terminologies where absent in the writing. A clear example is seen in eco-tourism demand drivers such as state and national parks, outdoor recreation, festival and events, agriculture tourism, environmental wonders, scenery and small town atmosphere. All these drivers can be undoubtedly placed into the natural, social and physical atmosphere of eco-tourism capital. Rural resources will remain as a rural resource if its potential is not shifted towards a eco-tourism capital. The aim of this paper is to understand that while rural tourism has long been

seen as an important catalyst towards rural tourism, the understanding of the linkages and dependence of the assets and capital within these vicinities are still lacking.
The main objective of the study is to determine the eco-tourism benefits derived in the peat soil forest land in Mukah. A sample survey of the villagers living along the fringes of the peat soil forest was undertaken to determine the perception of the communities on the types of potential eco-tourism resources that could be derived and accrued to the local communities. Observational and outdoor recreational inventory surveys were carried out as supplementary data collection.

RESULTS

The potential ecotourism activities (Table 2) of Mukah has been identified namely for its eco-tourism and agro-tourism planning. Key potential areas within Mukah need to be addressed for tourism and recreation. Activities related to eco-tourism and agro-tourism includes river cruise, recreation and home stay. The eco-tourism plan can include targeting psychographics of prospective visitors which includes the following:

1. Domestic and daily visitors
2. Visitors with special interest towards flora and fauna biodiversity
3. Visitors with special interest towards seafood and community traditions
4. Educators, researchers and students with special interest towards fisheries and agriculture
5. Visitors with special interest towards heritage and communities

Table 2: Potential Ecotourism activities for the local communities in Mukah

Role	Responsibility
Boatmen	River cruise to watch the fireflies, river cruises, sea cruises and recreational fishing
Tour Guides	Eco-tour guides for forest trekking, wild fauna and flora observation.
Catering business and food stalls	Ample opportunities for locals to be employed in the food industry and the preparation of local delights (food and fruit)
Resort workers	Resort operators, transport and general operations
Cultural village	Cultural dance and music groups
Handicraft village	Promotion of local handicraft and souvenirs by using the local products.

With this, the plan has also suggested several examples of tourism packages and destinations (Table 3) that could be implemented towards boosting eco-tourism capital. Eco-tourism can generate alternative incomes for local communities, who at present depend almost entirely on the agriculture sector for their livelihood. For ecotourism to be successful and sustainable, local community awareness and commitment is vital.

Table 3: Potential Eco-Tourism Packages suggested for Mukah

Example of Package	Targeted Visitors	Destination of Visit
Fishing	International and local visitors	1. Mukah Aquaculture Village 2. Mukah Deep sea fishing 3. Mukah Recreational fishing
Nature Lovers expedition	International and local visitors,	4. Peat land forest adventure
Farming and agriculture	International and local visitors, Educators, researchers and students with special interest towards fisheries and agriculture	5. Sago farm and factory tour 6. Tabaloi and traditional cake makers 7. Kaul festival 8. Special recreational events
"Balik Kampung" or *homecoming*	International and local visitors, Visitors with special interest towards heritage and communities and visitors with families	9. Homestay village 10. Historical village 11. Cultural village
River-Cruise, 9 natural wonders	International and local visitors	12. Wetlands Park 13. Mukah River Systems

CONCLUSION

It is clear that rural resource is an important catalyst for eco-tourism capital. However, there is a lack of understanding on the linkages and dependencies of assets within these areas. Rural resource is a fundamental resource as the stakeholders are able to utilise and understand the relationship between rural resource and eco-tourism. Through the understanding of rural resource as an eco-tourism capital, the importance of a comprehensive approach in managing rural resource will be appreciated by stakeholders. Hence, an urgent need of establishing and promoting best practice policies among stakeholders of the eco-tourism capital. If left unattended, the risk imposed is bound to lead to a decline in the quality of the tourists' experience .This is important as the growth of eco-tourism destinations in Mukah depends heavily on its unique interconnected ecosystems. Therefore, using the resources available, this eco-tourism destination will be able to leverage on the elements of destination imaging in order to create an unambiguous and robust image destination.

REFERENCES

1. Butler, R., Hall, C.M., & Jenkins, J. (1997). Tourism and recreation in rural areas. John Wiley & Sons Ltd.
2. Garrod, B., Wornell, R., & Youell, R. (2006). Re-conceptualising rural resources as countryside capital: The case of rural tourism. *Journal of Rural Studies*, 22(1), 117-128. doi: http://dx.doi.org/10.1016/j.jrurstud.2005.08.001
3. Hjalager, A.M. (2004). Sustainable leisure life modes and rural welfare economy. The case of the Randers Fjord area, Denmark. *International Journal of Tourism Research*, 6(3), 177-188.
4. Husain, M.L., Yaakob, R., & Saad, S. (1995). Beach Erosion Variabiltiy during a Northeast Monsoon: The Kuala Setiu Coastline, Terengganu, Malaysia. Pertanika *Journal of Science & Technology*, 3(2), 337-348.
5. Ilbery, B. (1998). *The geography of rural change*: Addison Wesley Longman Ltd.
6. Luloff, A.E., Bridger, J.C., Graefe, A.R., Saylor, M., Martin, K., & Gitelson, R. (1994). Assessing rural tourism efforts in the United States. *Annals of Tourism Research*, 21(1), 46-64.
7. Marsden, T. (1998). New rural territories: regulating the differentiated rural spaces. *Journal of Rural Studies*, 14(1), 107-117

Abstract No: A-350

REHABILITATION OF DEGRADED PEAT SWAMP ECOSYSTEM SERVICES AND CONSTRUCTION OF IMPLEMENTATION SYSTEM ON REDD+ SAFEGUARD

Shigeo Kobayashi

Center for Southeast Asian Studies, Kyoto University, Japan

Corresponding author: skobayas@cseas.kyoto-u.ac.jp

INTRODUCTION

The Ramseur treaty on wetland conservation was concluded in 1971. Wetland forests in the tropics have, however, been experiencing drastic land-use change for easy access and utilization, which, together with tropical forest decline, has also been a focal point of global environmental issues. Rehabilitation of degraded wetlands has, nevertheless, hardly been attempted. LULUCF (Land-Use, Land-Use Change and Forestry) has been discussed as an agenda of IPCC since 2001. It is, therefore, urgently necessary to conduct research on land resource management option and local society empowerment for global-warming prevention in Southeast Asian wetlands. COP15 of Copenhagen Agreement proposed REDD+ (Reducing Emissions from Deforestation and Forest Degradation in Developing Countries (2009) and COP16 of Cancun proposed REDD+ with Safeguard (2010). Southeast Asia has the widest area of wetlands consisting of mangrove, peat swamp and freshwater swamp forests, with a distribution of 28.3 million hectares compared with 3.5 million ha in Africa and 5.2 million ha in Latin America (Page *et al.* 2010). Indonesia is ranked as the fifth country for highest emission of GHG including peat fire according to President Yudoyono. Therefore, this paper will be discussing on the REDD+ safeguard related to PES (Payment for Ecosystem Services). The Cancun Agreement reached a resolution on December 11 in Cancun, Mexico, during the 2010 United Nations Climate Change Conference putting emphasis on the way forward towards greenhouse gas emissions reduction and to help developing nations in protecting themselves from climate impacts and build their own sustainable future. When undertaking activities with reference to paragraph 70 of this decision, safeguards should be promoted and supported. Action has to complement or are consistent with the objectives of national forest programs and relevant international conventions and agreements. Therefore, this paper will discuss on the safeguards as follows; (1) Transparent and effective national forest governance structure, taking into account national legislation and sovereignty. (2) Respect for the knowledge and rights of indigenous peoples and members of local communities, by taking into account relevant international obligations, national circumstances and laws, and noting that the United Nations General Assembly has adopted the United Nations Declaration on the Rights of Indigenous Peoples. (3) The full and effective participation of relevant stakeholders, in particular, indigenous peoples and local communities, in actions with reference to paragraph 70 and 72 of this decision. (4) Actions are consistent with the conservation of natural forests and biological diversity, ensuring that actions with reference to paragraph 70 of this decision are not used for the conversion of natural forests, but are instead used to incentivize the protection and conservation of natural forests and their ecosystem services, and enhance other social and environmental benefits (5) Actions to address the risks of reversals.

Actions to reduce displacement of emissions

Tropical peat swamp forest ecosystems are the most important target areas in these international arguments. Those areas are appropriate as subject of research for REDD+ particularly because they tend to disintegrate as tropical swamps, accumulate the largest amount of carbon in comparison with other forest ecosystems, and have been subject to recent rapid development. It is thus required to conduct research on REDD+ and safeguards on which little research has yet been made in particular. Therefore, there is a pressing need to conduct research on the assessment of REDD+ and PES for reducing warming in the Indonesian peat swamp forest ecosystem, safeguards as prevention measures against the negative impact of their implementation, and optimal options for peat resource management (Fig.1).

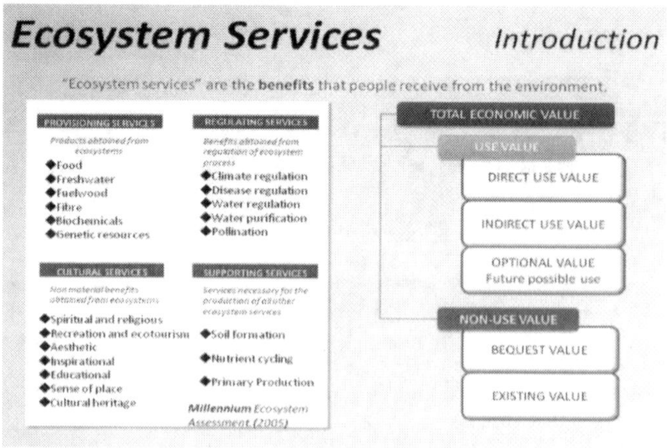

Fig.1 Forest Ecosystem Services (Millennium Ecosystem Assessment 2005)

CASE STUDIES AND RESULTS

Purpose

The local community incentives for the utilization of the forest ecological resources are essential for REDD+, which has been proposed during COP13. Therefore, clarification of these local community incentives to REDD+ by understanding the present utilization of forest ecological resources at logged-over forests, secondary forests, and fallows. It is also crucial to emphasize that NTFP will be planted during the processes of fallow, logged-over and secondary forests successions and evaluate the carbon credit by local community participation. The local community receives incentives from the semi-domestication of forest ecological resources that will allow REDD+ to function effectively and contribute to global environmental policy. In this case, we must pay attention to implementation of "Safeguard System" for the local community.

SITE, METHODS AND RESULTS

1. *Giam Siak Kecil Bukit Batu, Riau, Indonesia*

(1) Site: Logged-over forest, (2) Treatment: Gap planting, (3) NTFP's + 5 commercial species: especially *Dyera lowii* (Julton Paya), (4) Result in Indonesia (Haris, Kobayashi 2016)

Treatments to be taken for gap planting: Gap size will be 10 m x 10 m. Two gap densities (e.g. 9 gaps ha-1) will be tested and tree species suitable for the site condition will be selected. Wildings may be applied (Figure 2). The plantation results are still under continuous observation (Fig.3).

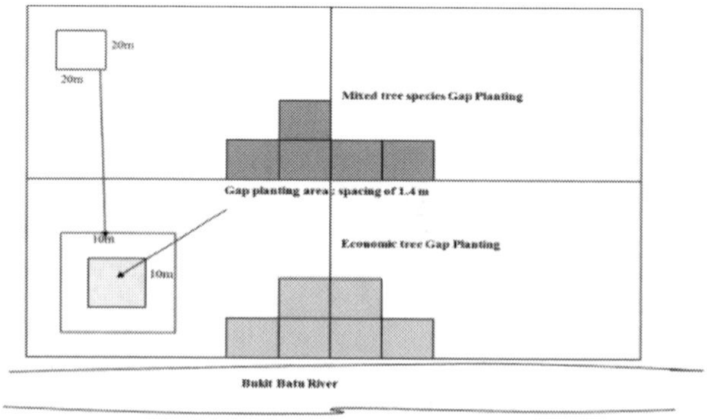

Figure 2. Trial design of land scale level

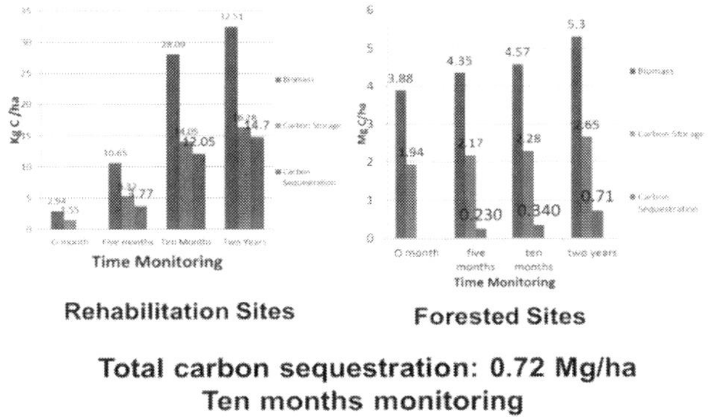

Fig.3 Results of rehabilitation activities

2. *Tha Se, Luang Nam Tha, Laos*

(1) Site: Four years old fallow, (2) Treatment: Forest under plantation with understory clearing, (3) NTFP's: Cardamon (*Amomum spp.*), Alpinia (*Alpinia spp.*), Sapan (*Soehmeria malabarica*) using wildings, (4) Treatments: Size of experimental plots will be more than 200 m x 200 m. Two plots of 1 ha (100 m x 100 m) each will be treated to have two levels of light intensities (e.g. 15% and 30%) on the forest floor by removing the substorey and understorey vegetation;(a)Small quadrats (2 m x 2 m) will be set up to monitor seedling growth; and (b)Upperstorey will be harvested when the seedlings reach 3-4 m.
(5) Result
Evaluation of carbon storage (Kiyono *et al*., 2007)
Forest biomass = 4.71(BA) + 19.4 ------①
Litter = 0.2415 [In(Y)] + 2.6091 ------②
Dead tree = 0.6471(Y) + 2.3165 ------③
Carbon (①+②+③) = 15.378[In(Y)] + 11.815 (0.128Mg/ha/yr)-----④
Data : 2011.1.20: H(6.9m), GBH(23.1cm), Litter(1500g)
2011.6.15: H(6.9m), GBH(24.1cm), Litter(1500g)
Carbon storage at 5 years old fallow by NTFPs semi-domestication

The site gained carbon of 89.2/Mg/ha after 22 months. Then, an estimated 48.74/Mg/ha/yr of carbon which is affected by semi-domestication of NTFPRS. NTFPs will be continued to be planted under the fallow forest and the fallow forest will be maintained for 7 years instead of the current 4 years in Luang Namtha province. It will be an occurrence of carbon credit as 48.74/Mg/ha/yr X 3years= 146.2/Mg/ha /3yrs. In the case of Luang Namtha province (a secondary forest area assumed to be with a certain degree of disintegration), the estimated total carbon storage of about 136,000,000/Mg/3yrs (45,000,000/Mg/yr). If the area is to be expanded, the carbon credit of about 3,993,000,000/Mg/yr for the semi-domestication of NTFPS will be achieved. The approach is effective, however not much changes on the local community's livelihoods will be observed. Cost-Benefit by semi-domestication of non-timber forest products are as follows; (a)Price : Cardamon (10,000-15,000 kip/kg), Alpina (3,000 kip/kg), Sappan (800-1,000 kip/kg)(b) Seedling (wildings) cost = 100 kip X 2,500 : 250,000/kip (c) Labor cost: 10,000 kip/hr (d) Total working time: 25hr/ha(e) Planting cost = 10,000 X 25 :250,000 kip (f) Estimated income from Cardamon = 10,000 X 0.1 (estimated) X 2,500(2,500,000 kip/3yrs).

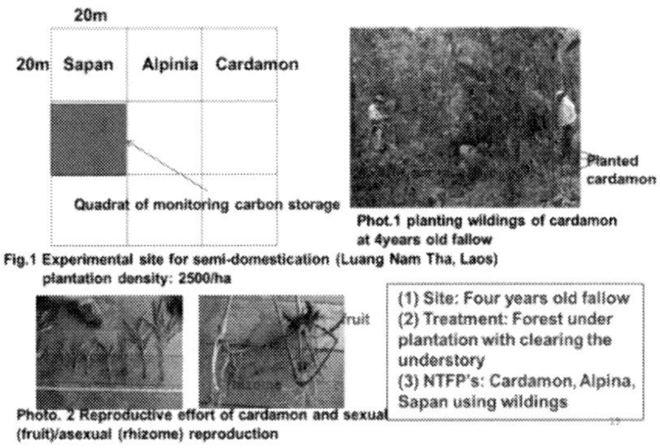

Fig.4 Semi-domestication in Ta Se, Luang Nam Tha, Lao

DISCUSSION

1. *Land Utilization related to REDD+*

Local community engages in Para rubber plantation instead of paddy. Local community is given the incentive of capital intensive land use instead of laborer intensive paddy agriculture. Finally, it is concluded that the local community takes into account the two main factors, economically stable land use and human resources in implementation of any government program for mitigation of global warming.

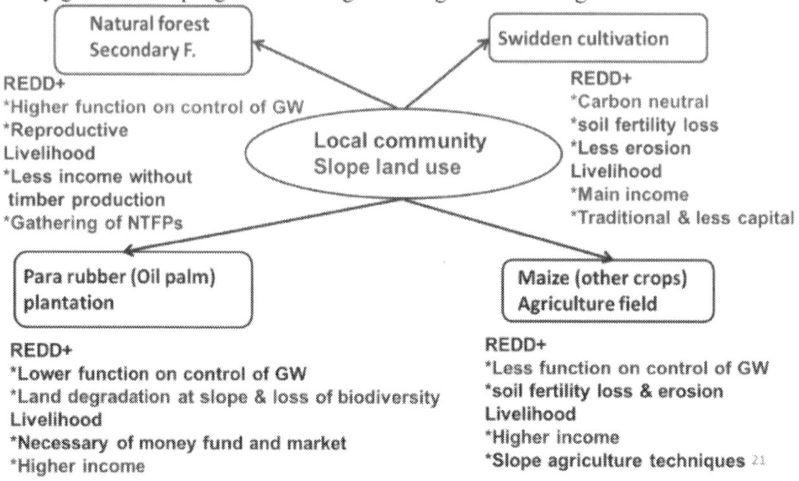

Fig.5 Land use pattern

2. *How to implement the REDD+safeguard?*

The current agriculture practices of the indigenous (Village A) and the migrant (Village B) communities in Tesso Nirro, Sumatra. Households in the Village A has derived only a small part of their income (13%) from agriculture practices related to shifting cultivation. Households in Village B has derived the most of their income (75%) from smallholder oil palm plantations set up by the Nucleus Estate and Smallholder (NES) program (Fig5).

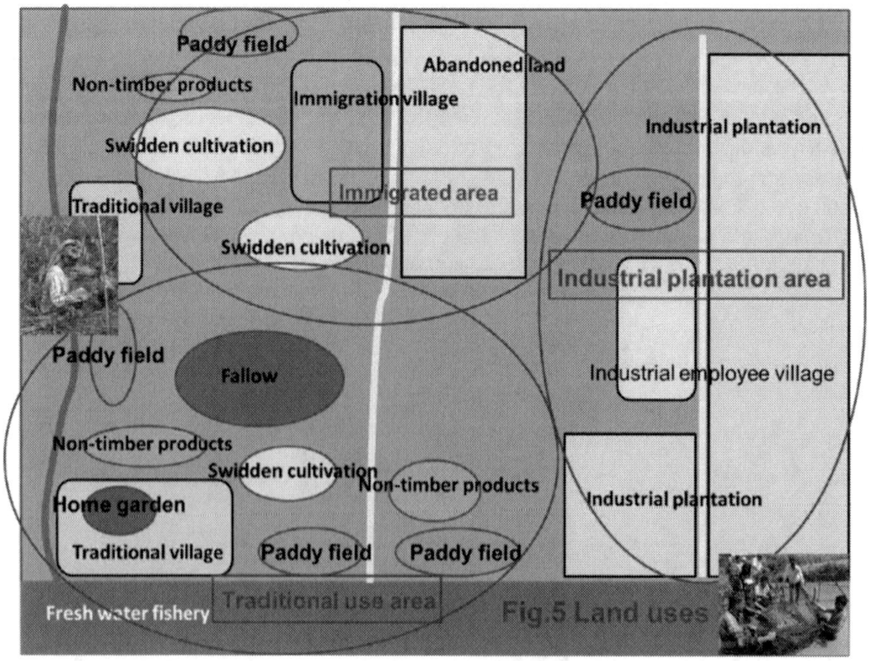

Fig.6 The villages have different the history and livelihoods.

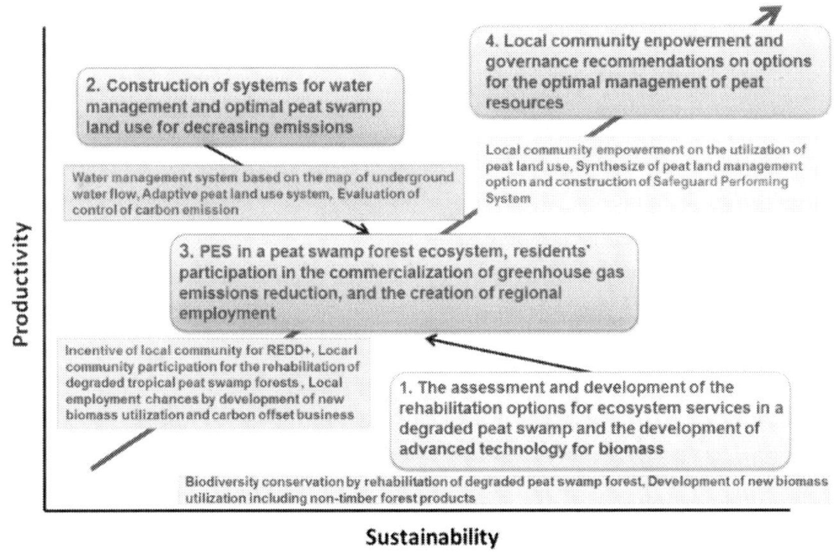

Fig. 6 Safeguard Performing System on REDD+ at Peat Swamp Forest Ecosystem

CONCLUSION

As preventive measures against the negative impact of REDD+ implementation, these safeguards reinforces the purpose of national forest programs and complement or are consistent with relevant conventions and agreements. It is also to construct transparent and effective national forest governance structures, to take into account the semi-domestication of NTFPs andto respect the knowledge and rights of indigenous peoples and membersof local communities. They promote the full and effective local community participation of relevant stakeholders. Semi-domestication has been carried out by local community based on their traditional knowledge to avoid the conversion of land use in natural forests and promote the conservation of ecosystem services, local community keeps their sweddin cultivation area without expanding, to contribute to the conservation of natural forests and biological diversity, that incentivize enhancing other social and environmental benefits to members, of local communities, they avoid over-gathering of NTFPs and conserve biological diversity to take into account actions to address the risks of reversals and incorporate actions to reduce displacement of emissions.

REFERENCES

1. J.O. Rieley & Page, S.E. Eds. 1997. Biodiversity and Sustainability of Tropical Peatlands. Pp.369. SamaraPubliching. UK.
2. M.Osaki & N. Tsuji, Eds. 2016. Tropical Peatland Ecosystems. Pp.651, Springer, Tokyo.
3. K. Mizuno, M. Fujita, S. Kawai Eds. 2016. Catastrophe & Regeneration in Indonesian's Peatland: Ecology, Economy & Society. Kyoto CSEAS Series on Asian Studies 15, NUS PRESS, Singapore.
4. Kiyono et al. Predicting chronosequential changes in carbon stocks of pachymorph bamboo communities in slash-and-burn agricultural fallow, northern Lao People's Democratic Republic. J. For. Res. 2007, 12, 171-183

Abstract No: A-311

SOCIO-CULTURAL-ECONOMIC IMPACTS OF PEAT SOIL ECOSYSTEM IN MUKAH, SARAWAK

Shazali Johari[1*], Mohd Ibrani Shahriman[2], Sulaiman Hj Husaini[3], Ahmad Shuib[4], Sridar Ramachandran[4], Puvaneswaran Kunasekaran[4] and Poh Yee Thoo[1]

[1]*Faculty of Forestry, University Putra Malaysia, Malaysia*
[2]*Faculty of Human Ecology, University Putra Malaysia, Malaysia*
[3]*Sarawak Land Custody and Rehabilitation Authority, Malaysia*
[4]*Institute of Agricultural and Food Policy Studies, University Putra Malaysia, Malaysia*

**Corresponding author: zali_johari@upm.edu.my*

SUMMARY

Peat soil ecosystem serves important ecological, environmental and socio-cultural functions and could provide benefits to the local communities in perpetuity, if proper conservation practices are undertaken. The dependency of the local communities on the peat soil land affects their livelihood either directly or indirectly. The main objective of the study is to determine the socio-cultural-economic benefits derived in the peatland ecosystem in Mukah. A sample survey of the villagers living along the fringes of the peat forest ecosystem was undertaken to determine the types of socio-cultural-economic resources accrued to the local communities. The results of the study are significant at both local and state levels. At the local level, the peat land eco-system provides sources of income to the communities via the production of fishes, wildlife products, non-forest products and as a source of domestic water supply. Among the local Melanau communities who are involved directly in the cultivation of the sago in the peat land, it is found that their involvement helps to maintain their traditional and cultural practices in the form of the production of sago based products and traditional cuisines. The communities are proud to show the cultural and traditional qualities through various events and engagement. The peat land ecosystem also forms a buffer zone between the oil palm plantation and the community settlement of Mukah.

Keywords: *community welfare, peat land eco-system, income, traditional, cultural, cuisines*

INTRODUCTION

Peat swamp plays an important role of water catchment and reservoir, conservation of biodiversity, genetic resources and as carbon sinks. Development of peat land for agricultural purposes must take into account the ecological make-up of the forest and maintenance of the peatland. Sago palm (Metroxylon spp.) grows naturally wild or semi-wild in mixed swampy land forest in Malaysia, Indonesia, Papua New Guinea, Philippines and the Pacific Islands. Sago palm forest has both marketed and unmarketed values.

Cultural resources usually drive the whole tourism business in rural areas which would contribute to positive socio-economic development (Butler and Hall, 1998). One of the most established definitions of cultural resources can be seen in the work of Pedford (1996). According to the scholar, the cultural resources are any living historical attributes such as rural customs and folklore, local and family traditions, values, beliefs, and common heritage. Arguably, culture is the main resource that indigenous people possess. Their unique customs and traditions are developed as attractions to lure tourists to the rural areas (Cohen, 2007; Liu, 2009 and Brown and Cave, 2010). Thus, it can be said that cultural resource is a must for any community as an identity to show their uniqueness to the outsiders.

The cultural uniqueness which is also regarded as the 'cultural otherness' is considered as an important selling point when it comes to tourism business (Hitchcock and King, 2003). From the tourists' perspective, Urry (1990) argued that tourists' motivation to travel is strongly encouraged by their 'gaze' to leave home and see something different compared to their daily life. The statement that indigenous tourism relies fully on the community uniqueness is also not supported. Indigenous tourism has strong relationship with environmental tourism, nature-based tourism, arts and heritage and adventure tourism (Harron and Weiler, 1992). Indigenous communities in many countries had settled in their traditional area since beginning times, before the habitation of other places in the nation. According to Ma'rof and Taufiq (2008) their cultures have blended, mixed and are restricted to the soil; and their world view depends on it.

Cultural aspect has been a popular research area highlighting the indigenous people and their unique and authentic lifestyle. In this area, commercialization of culture has brought tourism attractions to be targeted especially on cultural celebrations. The culture of each community represents their identity. According to Butler (2007), the development of tourism strongly depends on their ethnicity, heritage and festivals. Butler and Hinch (1996) also mentioned that culture has emerged as a powerful attraction not only for tourists but also for entrepreneurs, government agencies and academic researchers.

Many scholars agree that the cultural product has proven to be a medium in boosting tourism development (1993; Liu, 2009; and Brown and Cave, 2010). Besemenji *et al.* (2011) said that tourism emerged as a good way of preserving the customs and culture, but only if the right people are involved and if tourism does not become a business for some individuals. Tourism can also help in the promotion and presentation of Indian customs and cultures. This is the way to introduce their culture to the world and thus contribute to its preservation. However many author argued that commoditization is the only way to sell the community's culture to tourists (*i.e.;* Thompson, 2007 and O'Gorman, 2007). From the cultural tourism perspectives, Commoditization can enhance local economic growth and develop traditions by reducing poverty levels and increasing the inherent value (UNWTO, 2004). However, cultural commoditization has been criticized by several scholars. Cohen (1988) said that using indigenous culture as a mass tourism product can ultimately cause the loss of authenticity, inherent cultural value and significance. The Naxi indigenous community of China went through cultural commoditization and presented their uniqueness to outsiders with the help of the government but they are still in the belief that their culture is well preserved and not faded (Brown and Luo, 2012).

In Mongolia, the cultural festival is the main attraction for international tourists which is represented by local Mongolians (Thompson, 2007). Besides that, the Mongolians reveal their traditional semi-nomadic lifestyle on the mountains in comparison to the people who live in cities such as the capital, Ulaanbaatar (O'Gorman, 2007). In addition, Mongolia is also already well known for its remoteness and wilderness which provide an authentic tourism image. The environmental assets are also utilized by the community to portray an indigenous tourism product that creates a nomadic, exotic and mystic mood for tourists. The cultural strength of the community is also highlighted by organizing national indigenous festivals that symbolize historical traditions (Yu and Goulden, 2006). These efforts show that the indigenous community's culture is exposed to the outsiders as a one- off mega tourism event which can draw massive crowds.

On the other hand, tourism is also popular in northern Europe for its cultural development especially in Sweden and Finland (Petterson, 2007). For both these countries, the municipal is controlled by the Sami constitution system (Viken, 2007). The Sami is a well-known indigenous group in northern Europe where other surrounding cultures determine the language and distinctive traits. As a community who is dominant with their culturistic indigenous product in northern Europe, the Sami are active in cultural tourism with a variety of tourism products such as Sami museum, cultural events, cultural sites and souvenirs. In terms of tourist attraction, indigenous tourism can provide a culturistic environment for international and domestic tourists. As a result, the focus of tourism will rely on culture to illustrate the people, lifestyle, food, language, custom and heritage. The main purpose of the study is to identify the socio-cultural-economic resources of the village communities living along the fringes of the peat land ecosystem in Mukah. The types of socio-cultural-economic impacts accrued to the local communities .

METHODS

Mukah is a coastal town which serves as the administrative center of the Mukah District (2,536 square kilometres) in, Sarawak. It is located by the South China Sea, about 2 hours by road from the major city of Sibu. Mukah is also accessible by air from Kuching and Miri through MasWing Airlines. The duration of air travel is about one hour. There are also speed boats connecting the town of Dalat (about 30 kilometres from Mukah) to Sibu. Sago palms in Sarawak are grown in peat swamp of the coastal areas which can be easily found in Mukah.

Mukah-Socioculturally-Appropriate Multi-Facet Inventory (MSAMFI) is part of a trial web-based application system developed purposively based on a model partially adapted from Malaysian Career Facet Inventory (as initially proposed via the Development of the Career Factor Inventory CFI: Chartrand, Robbins, Morrill and Boggs, 1990). It was designed to assist Universiti Putra Malaysia's eco-tourism and socioeconomic researchers to gather Mukah, Sarawak's local economic credentials and imperative community development information parameters. The objective of the instrument aims to gauge and identify pertinent informed economic choices and feasible sago-plantation based factors for economic enhancement opportunities, in which will be scrutinized under the lenses of Item Response Theory model and Knowledge, Attitude & Practice Rating Scale (Ahmad Hariza, *et al.*, 2008)

Within the system, three categories of entries were constructed which consist of Mukah's socioeconomic background and its vital demographic pertinent parameters, in which were gathered via a multi-tiered platforms of a single-online network, performed with an adaptable infrastructure (hardware) of a customizable-computerized algorithm (software programs). An initial close-ended and partially open-ended questionnaire was integrated within the systems to be fully constructed as the test-bed for the Mukah-Socioculturally-Appropriate Multi-Facet Inventory (MSAMFI). The current study proposes to replicate Choi, Grady, & Dodd's (2010) analyses of a new stopping rule that attempts to address the efficiency and measurement precision problems associated with commonly used stopping rules. As per aspired via the development of MSAMFI, precision measurement of its items were tested accordingly. According to the Choi et al.'s (2010) study, the predicted standard error reduction (PSER) stopping rule seeks to balance the dual concerns of measurement precision and testing efficiency by considering the predicted change in measurement precision that would result from the administration of additional items test system delivery and the complexities of the psychometrics involved in developing the initial version the Mukah-Socioculturally-Appropriate Multi-Facet Inventory (MSAMFI). Data were extracted and imported to a .csv format to be synchronized with the application of a series of statistical data analytical tools.

RESULTS

To understand the perception of the community on the cultural attributes that they have, several questions within the domain of cultural resource were asked. Both tangible and intangible cultural resources that the community has were captured. The data was analyzed by interpreting the mean values of each item.

Table 1: Descriptive Statistics of Cultural Resources

Statements on Cultural Resources	Mean
1. 'Lamin Dala' (traditional house) is a unique cultural products that can be used as a tourism attraction of the Melanau community	4.63
2. Delicacies made of Sago such as 'Tebaloi' and 'Kuih Sepit' are important cultural attractions of the Melanau community	4.71
3. 'Tibou', a traditional giant swing is an important cultural attraction of the Melanau community.	4.69
4. 'Alu Alu' dance is a pride of the community that can be used as a cultural attraction.	4.77
5. 'Baban' and 'Terendak' attires are important cultural attraction of the Melanau community	4.70

Table 1 above reveals the findings of the analysis using descriptive statistics of five community resource items. Cultural resources have been the most important asset of the Melanau community to run tourism successfully. Traditional house, local delicacies, Melanau dance and attires are considered as treasures that determine the identity of the community. For this dimension, highest mean value of 4.77 reveals that 'Alu Alu' dance is a pride of the community that can be used as a cultural attraction. A mean value of 4.71 also explains that local delicacies made of Sago such as 'Tebaloi' and 'Kuih Sepit' are important cultural attractions of the Melanau community. Apart from that, the respondents were strongly agreeable that 'Baban' and 'Terendak' attires are important cultural attraction of the Melanau community. 'Tibou', a traditional giant swing is also considered as an important cultural attraction of the Melanau community with the mean value of 4.69. Lastly, 'Lamin Dala' (traditional house) is a unique cultural product that can be used as a tourism attraction of the Melanau community evident by the high mean value of 4.63. The higher mean values of all the items reveal that the community was also willing to defend and maintain their culture for tourism development. O'Gormon and Thompson (2007) also agreed that culture is the primary attraction of the indigenous community but the key challenge of the community is to protect their unique culture. Kaul is a traditional festival celebrated by the Melanau community living along the coast area in Sarawak. In the past, Kaul was held as a religious ceremony to appease the spirits of the sea, land, forest and farm making it the most important festival in the Melanau traditional calender.

The festival is a ritual of purification and thanksgiving as well as one of the propitiation for good fortune. Today, it is more of keeping a heritage alive. Its marks the beginning of the Melanau calender which begins at the end of the Northeast monsoon. Kaul takes place in third week of the month of April every year.The festival site is on the right bank of the Mukah river estuary. During the week-long festival, activities include stalls selling traditional foods, entertainment programs, and traditional games. The highlight will be the 'Serahang' (decorated flat round basket made from sago leaf which raise on a bamboo pole) procession lead by local Melanau community elders.Some of the activities not to be missed include playing the giant swing (Tibow) and enjoying Melanau traditional food served on the log (Keman Baw Bateng also known as 'Makan Beradat' in Malay)

CONCLUSIONS

In a nutshell, the Melanau communities in Mukah believe that cultural resources that they possess are unique and can be portrayed to the outsiders for tourism business purpose. Culture is seen as a tool not only to create economic benefit, but also to sustain local traditions, beliefs, practices and rituals. Thus, it is important for the local authorities to include preservation culture in any economic and local community development programs. By doing this, the local community will not only enjoy the economic benefit but also the non-economic benefit of cultural sustainability.

REFERENCES

3. Aref, F. Ma'rof Redzuan, & Gill, S. S. (2009). Dimensions of Community Capacity Building: A Review of its Implications in Tourism Development. *Journal of American Science*, 5(8), 74-82.
4. Aref, F., & Gill, S. S. (2009). Rural tourism development through rural cooperatives. *Nature and Science*, 7(10), 68-73.
5. Besermenji, S., Milić, N., & Mulec, I. (2011). Indians culture in the tourism of Ontario. Zbornik radova Geografskog instituta" Jovan Cvijić". *SANU*, 61(3), 119-136.
6. Butler, R., & Hinch, T. (2007). Tourism and indigenous people: issues and implications (2nd edition). *Life Science Journal*, 10(3), 42-56.
7. Brown, K., & Luo, T. (2012). Authenticity versus Commoditization: The Chinese Experience in the UNESCO Heritage Site of Lijiang. *International Cultural Tourism Conference: New Possibilities*, 13 (1), 123-141.
8. Cohen, E. (1998). Authenticity and commoditization in tourism. *Annals of Tourism Research*, 15(3), 371-386.
9. Cooper, D. R., & Schindler, P. S. (1998). *Business Research Methods*. Singapore: McGraw-Hill.
10. Hall, C., & Weler, C. (1992). *Special Interest Tourism*. London: Belhaven.
11. Harron, S., & Weiler, B. (1992). *'Review. Ethnic tourism', in Weiler, B. and Hall, M. (eds), Special Interest Tourism*. London: Belhaven Press.
12. Hjalager, A. M. (1997). Agriculture Diversification into Tourism. *Tourism Management*, 17(2), 103-111.
13. Jabatan Hal-Ehwal Orang Asli (JHEOA). *Data Maklumat Asas Jabatan Hal Ehwal Orang Asli Malaysia*. Kuala Lumpur: Bahagian Penyelidikan dan Perancangan, 2004.
14. Jabatan Kemajuan Orang Asli (JAKOA). *Jabatan Hal Ehwal Orang Asli Report of 2010*. Kuala Lumpur: Jabatan Kemajuan Orang Asli, 2010.
15. King. V.T. (1993). *Tourism and Culture in Malaysia*. In Hitchcock, M., King. V.T. and Parnwell, M.J.G. (Eds.) Tourism in Southeast Asia. London: Routledge.
16. Liu, O. P. (2008). *Packaging Myths for Tourism: The Rungus of Kudat*. Bangi: Universiti Kebangsaan Malaysia Press.
17. Minichiello, V., Aroni, R., Timewell, E. & Alexander, L. (1991). *In-depth Interviewing; Researching People*. Cheshire, Melbourne: Longman.
18. Ministry of Tourism Malaysia. *Downloads - Statistics - MOTOUR*. [online] Retrieved from: http://www.motour.gov.my/en/download/viewcat egory/49-statistik.html [Accessed: 19 July 2012].
19. Musa, G. (2000). *Tourism in Malaysia*. In C.M. Hall and S. Page (Eds.) Tourism in South and Southeast Asia: Issues and Cases Oxford: ButterworthHeinemann.
20. Nikkhah, H. A., Redzuan, M. R., & Abu-Samah, A. (2010). The Effect of Women's Sociodemographic Variables on their Empowerment. *Journal of American Science*, 6(11), 426-434.
21. Nowak, S. (1987). *Marriage and Household: Btsisi' Response to a Changing World*. PhD dissertation. State University of New York at Buffalo.
22. O'Gorman, K. D., & Thompson, K. (2007). Tourism and culture in Mongolia: the case of Ulaanbaatar Naadam. *Tourism and indigenous peoples: Issues and implications*, 161-175.
23. Suet Ching, C. (2010). *Mah Meri on Stage: Negotiating National Policies, Tourism and Modernization in Kampung Sungai Bumbun, Carey Island*. PhD theses. University of Hawai, 14-17.
24. Thompson, K. A. (2007). *An Eye for the Tropics: Tourism, Photography, and Framing the Caribbean Picturesque*. Duke University Press Books, 23-56.
25. Tourism Malaysia Board. *Tourism Malaysia: A bit of culture*. [online] Retrieved from: http://www.tourism.gov.my/en/master/webpage/experiences [Accessed: 2 September 2012].
26. UNWTO (2004). *Sustainable Tourism Development*. [online] (Retreived on 20 September 2012) Available at: http://sdt.unwto.org/en.
27. Zhang, G., & Lew, A. (2003). *Tourism in China*. New York: Haworth Hospitality Press.

6.2: PEATLAND & LOCAL PEOPLE

Abstract No: A-096

LOCAL PEOPLES' APPRECIATION ON AND CONTRIBUTION TO CONSERVATION OF PEATLAND SWAMP FORESTS: EXPERIENCE FROM PENINSULAR MALAYSIA

Tapan Kumar Nath[1], Mohd Puat Bin Dahalan[2] Faizal Parish[3] and Nagarajan Rengasamy[3]

[1]School of Biosciences, University of Nottingham Malaysia Campus
[2]Selangor State Forestry Department, Malaysia
[3]Global Environment Centre, Malaysia

**Corresponding author: Tapan.Nath@nottingham.edu.my; puat@forestry.gov.my; fparish@gec.org.my; nagarajan@gec.org.my*

SUMMARY

Over recent years, industrial plantation development on peatland and / or peat swamp forests (PSF) areas has created intense debate due to its potentially adverse social and environmental effects. In this paper we examined local peoples' appreciation on the values of PSF and how they can contribute to its conservation and protection. The study was carried out by interviewing 100 respondents and holding two focus group discussions in some degraded PSF areas in Perak and North Selangor Peat Swamp Forest. The study adopted participatory rural appraisal and contingent valuation methods. The respondents appreciated PSF for direct values including timber (6% respondents), vegetables (20%) source of fish (28%) and water for agriculture (32%). More than 80% respondents reported environmental values of PSF that includes flood prevention, biodiversity conservation, fresh air, soil fertility, perennial water source, and reduction of storm damages. They also reported several health and cultural benefits including sources of medicinal plants (62%), fresh food (50%), pure environment (92%), and tourism (84%). Even though they mentioned about demerits of PSF conversion such as deforestation (90%), biodiversity loss (90%), flooding (88%), and water scarcity (86%), they also claimed that PSF conversion provides them land for agriculture (50%), housing (24%) and for oil palm (60%). The respondents felt that the government agencies, large and small-scale oil palm companies are equally responsible for PSF degradation. They propose government should enact ban (80%) on PSF conversion and build community-forestry department-NGO partnership (90%) for PSF management. They sincerely want to contribute to PSF conservation through protection (75%), tree planting (82%), donation in cash (60%) and supplying seedlings, and joining in awareness creation programme (85%). The intrinsic values and peoples' enthusiasm for PSF conservation suggest for a community-based approach for sustainable PSF management. A pioneer project on community-based PSF management being implemented in North Selangor Peat Swamp Forest is discussed in this paper.

***Keywords**: direct benefits, indirect values, peoples' contribution, community participation*

INTRODUCTION

Peatland swamp forests (PSFs) serve many functions to both humanity and the balance of the world's ecosystems. A pristine peat swamp forest may be home to many of the rarest endemic species due to the unique environmental conditions it provides (Posa et al., 2011). These forests serve essential ecological functions including flood mitigation, water storage, carbon sequestration and storage, river base flow control and sediment removal (Ritzema *et al.*, 2006; UNDP 2006; Miettinen & Liew 2010; Wetlands International 2010; Posa *et al.*, 2011; Miettinen *et al.*, 2012; Schrier-Uijl *et al.*, 2013). However, these forests are being destroyed drastically through unsustainable logging, conversion to other land uses and indiscriminate fires. The conversion of PSFs causes deforestation, subsidence, long-term inundation, the loss of environmental services, carbon loss and increase greenhouse gas emission (Schrier-Uijl *et al.* 2013). There is growing public concern regarding the harmful environmental and social impacts of large scale conversion of PSFs into industrial plantations, mainly of oil palm (Nagiah and Azmi, 2012). There are serious concerns but yet to be studied about the impacts of oil palm expansion on forest dependent communities and the social and ecological consequences of large scale conversion of peatlands (Schrier-Uijl *et al.*, 2013).

Research on PSFs mostly focuses on carbon emission (Miettinen & Liew, 2010; Posa *et al.*, 2011; Page *et al.*, 2011; Miettinen *et al.*, 2012; Schrier-Uijl *et al.* 2013), and biodiversity (Wetlands International, 2010; Posa *et al.*, 2011; Miettinen *et al.*, 2012). Even though forests provide many benefits to local community but values of PSFs to local people is still poorly understood. In the context of PSFs these values may explain or emphasize social, cultural and environmental values of non-human natural objects (Palmer, 2003). The values of individuals highly affect how they perceive about the existing PSFs and as a result affect the actions taken by individuals in a society towards its existence. The aim of this study was to find out about local peoples' appreciation on the values of PSFs in their life, their understanding on causes of PSFs degradation, and their willingness to contribute to the conservation and protection of peatland swamp forests. We could not find any research contribution particularly on these aspects of PSFs.

METHODS

The study was conducted in several villages inhabiting surrounding the Pondok Tanjung forest reserve (PTFR), Perak and Raja Musa forest reserve (RMFR), Kuala Selangor of Peninsular Malaysia. The PTFR covers an area of about 6718 ha and is probably the largest remaining swamp forest in northern peninsular Malaysia surrounded by oil palm and rubber plantations (Bird Life International, 2016). It is a permanent forest reserve gazetted in 1913 and is classified as a production forest where logging was performed from 1939 to 1989 (Ibid.). The RMFR is a peat swamp forest (about 35,656 ha) subjected to intensive logging since 1950s before its gazettement in 1990 as a forest reserve (GEC, 2013). Intensive logging followed by draining of peat water, encroachment of logged-over land and unsustainable agricultural practices had caused serious forest degradation. In 2008, the Selangor State Forestry Department had recovered about 1000 ha of degraded PSF and took a rehabilitation programme in partnership with Global Environment Centre, a non-government organization and local community people (GEC, 2013). Since then they have been replanting the degraded RMFR sites.

Data for this study was collected through a participatory rural appraisal method by administering a semi-structured questionnaire and holding two group discussions with villagers. We also conducted key-informants interviews with GEC staff members and carried out another group discussion with the members of Friends of North Selangor Peat Swamp Forest (FNSPSF). We interviewed 100 randomly selected households, 50 in each site, living in around the peat swamp forests. We collected data on their basic socio-economy, direct benefits or products obtain from PSF, environmental, health, and cultural benefits, merits and demerits of PSF conversion, actors responsible for conversion and their opinion on conservation or prevention of PSF conversion. By following contingent valuation method (Mitchell and Carson, 1989) we explored local peoples' willingness to contribution to the conservation of PSF. The group discussions also considered the above issues in addition to their willingness to participate in REDD+ programme if government would like to invite them. In order to assess peoples' participation and effectiveness of peatland rehabilitation project on restoration of degraded PSF in RMFR we hold a group discussion with six members of FNSPSF and talked to GEC staff members. A check-list was used to facilitate the discussion. We also asked a few questions to villagers on project activities during household survey. The collected data are compiled and frequency and percentages are calculated. The findings are presented mostly qualitatively with some quantitative inferences.

RESULTS

In this section we first give a brief description of respondents' profile followed by values of PSF to local people, their willingness to contribute towards PSF conservation and peoples' participation in the restoration of peat forests in RMFR.

Respondents' profile

Both male (69%) and female (31%) respondents took part in interviews and their mean age was 37.5 years indicating that they were matured enough to understand the survey questions and responded accordingly. Most of them (63%) obtained secondary education and majority (37%) were farmers. About 67% respondents lived within 1-2 km from the peat swamp forests. The respondents' mean household income level range was RM1500 to RM2500 mainly from agriculture, business and service.

Values of PSF to local people

Like other types of forests PSF also have great importance for local people. Even though the villagers are not heavily dependent on PSF for their living, they obtain several products from these forest resources. They valued PSF for both direct and indirect benefits. The direct benefits they reported included timber (6% respondents), medicinal plants (6%), vegetables (20%), source of fish (28%) and water for agriculture (32%). Some respondents said that they got land for agriculture (4%) and oil palm plantations (25%). In both sites the respondents commented that they get fresh water fishes from canals and use canal water for paddy field irrigation round the year. Based on their responses we estimated that they catch about 46 kg of various types of fishes every month mostly for their own consumption. In group discussion the participants at RMFR reported that PSF is an important source of income for some of the villagers who collect *Palas* leave (*Daun Palas*) from the forests to make handicraft and wrapping of transitional food (i.e kutupat and nasi lemak). They also use the shoots of *Tenggek Burung* (*Euodia redlevi*) as a salad in their meals.

Apart from direct benefits, the respondents profoundly reported the environmental values of PSF. More than 80% respondents reported environmental values of PSF that includes flood prevention, biodiversity conservation, fresh air, soil fertility, perennial water source, and reduction of storm damages. They said the PSF is not only a source of water but also act as water reservoir to protect villages from flood. The PSF provide suitable habitat for wildlife. They also reported several health and cultural benefits including sources of medicinal plants (62%), fresh food (50%), pure environment (92%), place for relaxation (76%) and tourism in S. Selangor (84%). The tourism activities they mentioned include river cruising, fishing, bird and wildlife watching. In K. Selangor villagers with support from GEC have developed homestay agro-tourism and it serves as a substantial income source. They mentioned that due to existence of PSF they could establish agro-tourism destination in their locality. The respondents also reported that students from various institutions visit PSF for education and research purposes and they feel proud of being a part of these novel activities.

Conversion of PSF

Keeping in mind of PSF degradation for other uses we asked respondents about merits and demerits of conversion and who are responsible for that. Even though they mentioned about demerits of PSF conversion such as deforestation (90%), biodiversity loss (90%), flooding (88%), destroy wildlife habitat (85%), reduction of income sources (58%), water scarcity (86%) and non-availability non-timber forest products (72%), they also claimed that PSF conversion provides them land for agriculture (50%), housing (24%) and for oil palm (60%). The respondents felt that the government agencies, large and small-scale oil palm companies are equally responsible for PSF degradation. They also mentioned that villagers themselves clear PSF for growing rice, vegetable, fruits, and oil palm as well as for house building.

PSF conservation and willingness to contribution

The respondents propose government should enact ban (80%) on PSF conversion for oil palm plantation, rice cultivation, housing development and horticulture practices. They emphasized on building community based forestry management-NGO partnership (90%) for PSF management. Further, respondents stress on creating awareness among community people on the importance of and conservation of PSF through education. They sincerely want to contribute to PSF conservation through participation in community-based management (74%), patrolling and fire protection (75%), tree planting (82%), donation in cash (60%) and supplying seedlings, and joining in awareness creation programme (85%). When explained the concept of REDD+ and its importance to forests conservation and local economy, the respondents showed positive attitude to join in any REDD+ programme if initiated by the government. They commented that such a programme would be a worthy way to build community engagement and partnership in protecting the PSF. The intrinsic values and peoples' enthusiasm for PSF conservation suggest for a community-based approach for sustainable PSF management.

PSF rehabilitation project

The PSF rehabilitation project is a pioneer project on community-based PSF management being implemented in North Selangor Peat Swamp Forest. Since 2008 the GEC in collaboration with Selangor state forestry department and local community has been implementing this project. The main activities include monthly tree planting, patrolling, fire monitoring and prevention, awareness creation among villagers and community development through small scale nursery (small medium scale business) and agro-ecotourism promotion. The GEC in collaboration with Selangor State Forestry Department (SSFD) initiated an innovative way of reforestation through inviting corporate agencies, academic institutions, NGOs and other concerned stakeholders to participate in monthly tree planting programme. It circulates invitation through its social media forum and interested agencies confirm their participation by registration. Participation is first-come first-serve basis and 100 participants can register in an event for planting 400-600 seedlings in one hectare of degraded PSF land. The planting cost including seedlings and land preparation is usually arranged through sponsors such as international funders and local corporate agencies.

The GEC staff members reported that till 2014 it established about 310 ha of degraded area was replanted through monthly planting programme. They also said that in 2011 when the planted seedlings in compartment 99 attained at 5-6 m in height all of them (250 ha) were burnt. The GEC suspects small scale palm oil farmers in the buffer zone areas for burning of 250 ha rehabilitated area. The farmers set fire in palm oil areas to prepare the land for planting and the fire might spread out in the compartment 99. The prolonged dry summer season was also expediting the spread of fire. In compartment 73, the Selangor State Forestry Department and GEC established "Centre of Excellence for PSF" where they only manage the watershed to maintain the water level in peatland by blocking the canals to raise water level and facilitating natural regeneration along with reforestation. The areas seem regenerating with diversified tree species and the optimum water level surrounding the areas. In a few planting sites established in 2012 through 2014 we found a survival rate of 85% with a spacing of 3m x 5m and mean height of seedlings 1.6m. The planted species are mahang (*Macaranga pruinosa*) and tenggek burung (*Euodia redlevi*) and these are common pioneer species usually planted in degraded peatland area.

In 2011 the GEC in collaboration with Selangor State Forestry Department established a community based organization called "Friends of North Selangor Peat Swamp Forests" with 40 members, 10 from each of the four villages and currently has 90 members. The organisation was registered in 2012 so that it can work without any legal barriers. The main purpose of the organisation is to create awareness among villagers about the importance of peatland swamp forests. It collaborates with the SSFD and the GEC, works on reforestation, fire control and daily patrolling. Due to awareness creation and motivation there was no incidence of fire in year 2015. The organisation also works on community development through homestay agro-tourism. With the rehabilitation project four farmers were trained on tree nursery and with that knowledge they established nurseries at their homesteads. They collect wildings from palm oil plantations and raised them in polybags. All raised saplings used for monthly planting programs and they reported to have an annual income of RM 30,000.00 by selling saplings. The FNSPSF in collaboration with the GEC established Junior Peatland Forest Ranger Programme at school level to create awareness among school students about the importance of PSF and thereby protection of these forests. Initiated in 2014, this programme has so far been extended in 12 primary schools in North Selangor. It introduces environmental knowledge in school programme, involves students in various outreach events (e.g. planting event) and creates awareness of the responsibility and the role of local youth for environmental protection and conservation for the future generation.

DISCUSSION AND CONCLUSION

The findings of this study show that the interviewed villagers appreciate that they have been benefited directly (resources support) and indirectly (services) by the peatland swamp forest. Even though the direct benefits including timber, medicinal plants, fish are not so great but the indirect benefits that include source of water, flash flood mitigation, biodiversity, environmental protection are of great importance to the local people. The villagers are mostly dependent on PSF's water for their agricultural practices and domestic usages. They are well aware about the possible negative impact of PSF conversion on their life and hence they have been collaborating with GEC and forestry department for the conservation and rehabilitation of degraded PSF. Researchers suggested that understanding peoples' perceptions of the services provided by natural systems can provide insights into the interplay of the innate linkages between humans and their environment which in turn can contribute towards identifying ways to reduce future impacts on society from environmental change (Abram *et al.*, 2014). In order to sustain the inter-linkages of society and environment participation of local community in environmental management is essential. Community participation in natural resource management is nowadays an essential element of natural resource administration. In case of forest management community participation has been proved as a drive tools for sustainable management. The involvement of local community in the rehabilitation of degraded RMRF is a successful pioneer initiative in Malaysia. The local community without any significant economic incentives has been profoundly engaged with forest conservation and protection. The commitment of the GEC and forestry department towards successful collaboration, creation of awareness about the importance of PSF, motivation and formation of social capital between local community and external agencies facilitated the effective community participation in the programme. The formation of the FNSPSF was a milestone for capacity building of the community people for creating environmental awareness among younger generation in the society. Apart from organizing important environmental events, this organization initiated several income generating activities including homestead nursery, agro-ecotourism and handicraft industry in the locality.

In conclusion, the societal and environmental values of PSF warrant that these forests should be conserved for the welfare of society and for other natural beings and that the participation of local community in the conservation and rehabilitation is very crucial. This kind of collaboration among community people, non-government organizations and state agencies can be promoted in the management country's natural resources where relationships between community and natural environment are interconnected.

REFERENCES

1. Abram, N. K., Meijaard, E., Ancrenaz, M., Runting, R. K., Wells, J. A, Gaveau, D., Pellier A-S, and Mengersen, K. (2014). Spatially explicit perceptions of ecosystem services and land cover change in forested regions of Borneo. *Ecosystem Services* 7:116–127
2. BirdLife International. (2016). Important bird and biodiversity area factsheet: Pondok Tanjung Forest Reserve. Downloaded from http://www.birdlife.org on 14/02/2016
3. GEC (Global Environment Centre). (2013). Conservation and rehabilitation of Raja Musa Forest Reserve. 2011-12 project report.

4. Miettinen, J. And Liew, C. S. (2010). Degradation and development of peatlands in Peninsular Malaysia and the islands of Sumatra and Borneo since 1990. *Land Degradation and Development*, 2:285-296
5. Miettinen, J., Hooijer, A., Shi, C., Tollenaar. D., Vernimmen, R., Chin, L. S., Malins, C. And Page, S. (2012). Extent of industrial plantations on Southeast Asian peatlands in 2010 with analysis of historical expansion and future projections. *GCB Bioenergy*, 4:908–918
6. Mitchell, R. C. and Carson, R. T. (1989). *Using surveys to value public goods: The contingent valuation method.* Resources for the future; Washington.
7. Nagiah, C. and Azmi, R. 2012. A review of smallholder oil palm production: Challenges and opportunities for enhancing sustainability – A Malaysian perspective. *Journal of Oil Palm & The Environment,* 3:114-120.
8. Page S. E, Morrison R, Malins C, Hooijer A, Rieley J. O., and Jauhiainen, J. (2011). Review of peat surface greenhouse gas emissions from oil palm plantations in Southeast Asia (ICCT white paper 15). Washington: International Council on Clean Transportation.
9. Palmer, C. A. (2003).An overview of environmental ethics. In: A Light & H Rolston (eds), *Environmental ethics: an anthology.* Blackwell philosophy anthologies, Blackwell, Oxford, p15-37.
10. Posa, M. R. C., Wijedasa, L. S. And Corlett, R. T. (2011) Biodiversity and conservation of tropical peat swamp forests. *Bioscience*, 61(1):49-57
11. Ritzema, H., Mohamed, M., Page. S., Limin, S. and Wösten, H. (2006) Capacity building for sustainable management of peatlands in the humid tropics: From research to application. Workshop proceedings on monitoring and evaluation of capacity development strategies in agricultural water management. IPTRID, Rome pp: 73-86, Kuala Lumpur, Malaysia.
12. Schrier-Uijl, A.P., Silvius, M., Parish, F., Lim, K.H., Rosediana, S. and Anshari, G. (2013). Environmental and social impacts of oil palm cultivation on tropical peat – a scientific review. Roundtable on Sustainable Palm Oil (RSPO).
13. United Nations Development Programme (UNDP) (2006). Malaysia's peat swamp forests: Conservation and sustainable use. UNDP, Kuala Lumpur, Malaysia
14. Wetlands International. (2010). A quick scan of peatlands in Malaysia. Wetlands International Malaysia: Petaling Jaya, Malaysia.

Abstract No: A-097

PARTICIPATORY APPROACH IN THE PEAT SWAMP FOREST MANAGEMENT OF TWO DIFFERENT FOREST STATUSES IN CENTRAL KALIMANTAN, INDONESIA

Hesti Lestari Tata* and Agustinus P. Tampubolon

Forest Research and Development Centre, Indonesia

**Corresponding author: hl.tata@gmail.com*

SUMMARY

Sustainable forest management needs active participation from communities who live in the surroundings forest area. We assessed community participation in two different forest status areas in Central Kalimantan, e.g. Sebangau National Park (SNP) and Kalawa Village Forest. The participatory approaches of the peat swamp forest management in the two sites were assessed based on semi-structured interview to random respondents and in-depth interview to some selected key-respondents. The data were analysed by using descriptive analysis and SWOT analysis. The forest area status determines approach of community participatory management. A national park is designated based on unique characteristics and importance of the ecosystem. A village forest is determined based on a proposal of the local community who has awareness on the forest ecosystem to get access on forest utilization. Forest status has implication on decision making process. Sebangau national park has a top down approach, e.g. a framework driven by government (a high level hierarchy), while Kalawa village forest has a bottom up approach, e.g. local communities' engagement in management of the village forest. Under the management of the SNP, there are three institutional participatory peat swamp forest managements, such as Community Forum (*Forum Masyarakat, Formas*), Group of Fire Fighting (*Regu Pemadam Kebakaran, RPK*), and Public Safety Forces (*Pasukan Pengamanan Masyarakat, Pam Swakarsa*). The three institutions have been developed well; however, the community who lives in the surroundings the SNP has low participation due to lack of awareness. Community participation in the area of the SNP is characterised as consultation participatory type. On the other hand, the Kalawa village forest is characterised as functional participatory type. SWOT analysis showed that the SNP has four internal and external factors, while Kalawa village forest has five internal and external factors, which can be used to develop and improve a strategy on peat swamp forest management in both sites.

***Keywords**: SWOT analysis, village forest, Sebangau national park*

INTRODUCTION

Nowadays, paradigm of forest management has been transformed into community participatory, where community is actively involved in forest landscape management. Sustainable forest management which involved people participatory in the development process aimed to end poverty, as one target of The Sustainable Development Goals (United Nations, 2015). Community participatory in forest management is one program of the Government of Indonesia (GoI) in forestry sector, which is called social forestry. Social forestry is defined as management and protection of forests and afforested of barren land with the purpose of assisting environment, social and rural development (Negi, 1986). In Indonesia, there are four types of social forestry, viz. village forest, community forest, people forest plantation and customary forest. The social forestry programme was initiated to support the success of peat swamp forest management, which needs active participation of community who live in surroundings the forest areas.

We studied participatory approach in the management of peat swamp forests in two different statuses of forest areas in Central Kalimantan province, e.g. a village forest and a national park, by looking at the top-down and bottom-up paradigm (Bell & Morse, 2001; Reed *et al*., 2006; and level of participation. The two forest areas have different characteristics of forest management. The village forest which is a state forest which managed by a custodian of the village, while a national park is a protected area, where central government takes an important role as custodian and in managing the forest area.

METHODS

1. Study Site

The study was conducted in a village forest of Kalawa, in Pulang Pisau District, and in the Sebangau National Park (thereafter the SNP), both in Central Kalimantan Province. Three villages in surroundings SNP, namely Kereng Bangkirai of Palangkaraya, and Baun Bango and Tumbang Runen villages in Katingan District, were selected purposively as study areas of the SNP.

The SNP (total area of 569,700 ha) is located at E 113° 20' – 114° 03' and S 01° 54' – 03° 08'; it was established in 2004. SNP is a peat swamp forest ecosystem which is laid between two rivers of Sebangau and Kahayan. Previously, it was a forest concessionaire area of a production forest and the permit was end in 1990. Some channels have been established during that period to transfer logs. After its status changed into conservation forest, the canals have been blocked to reduce water drainage.

The Sebangau National Park is surrounded by 7 sub-Districts of three Districts, with total inhabitants of 72,859 people (BPS Kabupaten Katingan, 2013; BPS Kota Palangkaraya, 2013).

The Kalawa forest is a peat swamp forest which is located along Kahayan river, in Pulang Pisau District, Central Kalimantan Province. The Kalawa forest is managed by four villages, namely Buntoi, Gohong, Mentaren II and Kalawa, in a total area of 16,245 ha. The forest area that was designated under management of Kalawa village is about 4,230 ha. The community of Kalawa village is dominated by Dayaknese Ngaju, consisted of 1,316 inhabitants (BPS Kabupaten Pulang Pisau, 2013).

2. *Data Collection and Analysis*

Combination of descriptive – explorative – participative approach was used in this study. Descriptive approach is used to identify problems and current evidence. Primary data were collected by using a semi-structure interview and in-depth interview to some key persons. Participative method was used to invite people actively take parts in find out solutions into the current problems. Explorative method is used through field observation and can be used in analysis and synthesis (Dipokusumo, 2011).

The respondents were selected purposively depending on the objectives of interview. Respondents include a village leader, a customary leader, and villagers. Experts include forest service at provincial and district level, management of the national park, environmental agency, and management unit of watershed.

Geography and demography data were based on secondary data of the Statistics Bureau of the district. Survey data were then analyzed by descriptive analysis. Level of participation was identified according to Preety *et al.* (1995). The strengths, weaknesses, opportunities and threats (SWOT) analysis were used to identify and map participatory management of both sites.

RESULTS AND DISCUSSION

1. *Income Sources of the Community*

The inhabitants are dominated by Dayaknese (65%) and some migrants from Banjar and Java and others, who usually live in Kereng Bangkirai, Palangkaraya city. Tumbang Runen and Baun Bango villages were dominated by Dayaknese. Sources of income of the community in three villages in surroundings the SNP were agriculture (annual and mostly perennial crops, such as rubber and oil palm smallholder), fisheries, formal sectors (civil servant, groceries sellers and workers of plantation) and collecting non-timber forest products, such as latex, gemor bark, birds and others.

The inhabitants of Kalawa village are dominated by Dayaknese (85%), Banjar and Javanese. Income sources of Kalawa's people were agriculture, fisheries, collecting forest products and other informal sources.

2. *Participatory Approach in the Forest Management*

a. The Sebangau National Park (SNP)

The management of the SNP has three institutions on participatory forest managements, namely, Community Forum, Group of Fire Fighting, and Public Safety Forces. The three institutions are promoted by management of the national park in order to improve awareness of the importance of forest conservation, to introduce the community in the management of natural resources in a sustainable manner, and to engage with people whom are dependent on the natural resources as their livelihood. Community Forum is established as a discussion forum of villagers with different occupations, such as farmers, fishermen, collectors of forest products, etc. Through this forum, villagers who are member of the group may submit proposal of activities to improve their capacity. The management of national park would provide training and knowledge transfer to the community. Some activities, such as bird breeding, pond fisheries, fish processing and mushroom cultivation, were introduced to the communities to generate income of the communities. The management also would facilitate access to market to sell the products. Benefit of capacity building is to improve motivation of villagers on livelihood and reduce dependency on forest resources. However, such capacity building program were not applied at all villages in surroundings the park, due to limited resources.

Group of fire fighting is established to improve awareness of people on forest fire and to protect forest area from fire. The activity is a voluntary based activity. Tools and simple equipments for fire fighting were provided by the management of national park. In an emergency of fire, they work together with fire brigade of 'Manggala Agni'.

The Public Safety Forces institution was established in 2007 and 2008, to give opportunities to the community to protect the national park in collaboration with management of the national park. Regular patrol is conducted and under coordination with Forest Rangers. The constraint of this activity is little participation from the community, as it is not well informed to the villagers and it does not give financial benefit for them.

As the national park, where the management is controlled by central government, e.g. the Ministry of Environment and Forestry, most programmes on capacity building are approved. Improving awareness and livelihood of people surrounding forest is a major concern of management of the park management.

A problem in the participatory management of the SNP is no clear boundary of utilization zone of the national park. Although the forest area has been gazetted, however, the community is still claiming for the boundary. The biggest threat of management of the SNP is expansion of oil palm estate.

b. The Kalawa Village Forest

Management of the village forest, on the other hand, is a responsibility of the village institution. The right of village forest management is awarded by the authorities. Licence of a village forest management is given to the village institution in a period of 35 years. The area remains as a state-owned forest. Village forest management aims to preserve forest functions and improve welfare of the community. The management of a village forest is based on a business plan. A forest inventory has to be done prior to implementation of the business plan. As mandated in a regulation of the Minister of Environment and Forestry number P.101 year 2014, Forest Service at province and district level plays important roles. In the implementation, however, the Forest Service has not been taken serious action to carry on their mandates. The Kalawa communities were complaining for lack of facilitation. Limited human resources and financial capital hinder the implementation of Kalawa village forest (Tata, 2016).

3. Approach and Level of Participation

Participatory forest management links with strategic planning either top-down or bottom up approach. Top down approach is a strategic planning of central government to the lower level of management. On the contrary, bottom up approach is focused on implementation on the ground level (Bell & Morse, 2001; Reed *et al.*, 2006; Dewi, 2012). The management of the SNP is an example of top down approach. A top down approach affects positively to the collaborative-participative activities. Implementation of a work plan would achieve goals of the organization. The more active the participants, the more benefits they may get.

According to Preety *et al.* (1995), participation is classified into 7 levels, from manipulative participation up to independent movement. Participation analysis showed that level of community participation in the management of the SNP consultation participation, e.g. all programs should be under consultation between the two parties, (i.e. the national park and the communities). One party (financially) depends on another party in the program implementation.

The Kalawa village forest has a bottom up approach, where all processes are based on the community level. Stage of participation was functional participation, where all member work together in developing a business plan and its implementation. Kalawa village forest would shift to be more independent if they get capacity building to alleviate poverty. Such training and transfer practise knowledge that have been applied by the management of the SNP needs to be introduced and applied in the Kalawa village forest. The forest service and a civil society organization (CSO) should facilitate operational of the village forest.

The SWOT analysis showed that the two forest statuses have different management characteristics. Some internal and external factors of participatory management of Kalawa village forest and the SNP are listed in Table 1.

Table 1: Characteristics of participatory management of Sebangau National Park and Kalawa village forest

Internal		External	
Strengths	Weaknesses	Opportunities	Threats
Sebangau National Park (SNP):			
Three institutions, e.g. Community Forum, Group of Fire Fighting, and Public Safety Forces, are supported by the management of the national park	Manipulative participation. People have lack of responsibility	Improving capacity from training and demo-plots	Land use change to oil palm
Participation is developed according to preference of the community (or group of livelihood)	Villagers have low income	Business development and investor	Floods
Species richness and high genetic germ plasm	Lack of knowledge on tree cultivation and human resources	Demand on animals, such as birds and pangolin, and Non-timber forest products, such as gemor (*Alseodaphne* sp.) are considerably high	Limited rules and regulations on marketing non-timber products from cultivation and breeding activity that can support fair price and market
Sufficient human resources of the SNP management	False perception of the communities on the management of national park	People need to get well informed	Land conflict in the utilization zone.
Kalawa village forest:			
High motivation of villagers to protect the forest	False perception of some villagers on the management of village forest	Support and companion of the local government to implement the program	Canal establishment to the village forest
High species diversity	Lack of knowledge on tree cultivation and human resources	Demand on animals, such as birds and pangolin, and non-timber forest products, such as gemor (*Notaphoebe* spp.) are considerably high	Limited support rules and regulations on marketing non-timber products from cultivation and breeding activity
Social ethic is still appreciated	Lack of facility to implement business plan	Eco-tourism shall be developed and community needs to be well informed	Illegal logging, illegal poaching
High motivation on planting fast growing timber tree, such as *Albizzia*, in burnt land to get cash income	Low income and limited resources	Open access to wood market and other forest tree product	Forest fire

To summarize, internal and external characteristics of both forest management can be used as inputs on the development and management strategy of the SNP and Kalawa village forest. Kalawa village forest needs support and facilitation from the local government in order to establish their business plan. It is as a reward mechanism for villagers who actively participate in the management of village forest. The SNP is suggested to improve their management, by doing human resources development, ensuring forest gazette management, and enhancing community collaborative and participative mechanism.

REFERENCES

1. United Nations. 2015. Draft *outcome document of the United Nations summit for the adoption of the post-2015 development agenda*. United Nations. General Assembly. 35 p. [http://www.un.org/ga/search/view_doc.asp?symbol=A/69/L.85&Lang=E.].
2. Negi SS. 1986. *A handbook of social forestry*. International Book Distributor. Dehradun, India. 178p.
3. Bell S & Morse S. 2001. Breaking through the glass ceiling: who really cares about sustainability indicators? *Local Environment*. 6(3):291-309.
4. Reed MS, Fraser EDG, Dougill AJ. 2006. An adaptive learning process for developing and sustainability indicators with local communities. *Ecological Economics*. 59:406-418.
5. BPS (Badan Pusat Statistik) Kabupaten Katingan. 2013. *Kabupaten Katingan Dalam Angka 2013*. BPS Kabupaten Katingan. Kasongan. 36p. [http://katingankab.bps.go.id/]
6. BPS (Badan Pusat Statistik) Kota Palangkaraya. 2013. *Kota Palangkaraya Dalam Angka 2013*. BPS Kota Palangkaraya. Palangkaraya. 324p. [https://bappeda.palangkaraya.go.id/kota-palangka-raya-dalam-angka-tahun-2013/]
7. BPS (Badan Pusat Statistik) Kabupaten Pulang Pisau. 2013. *Kabupaten Pulang Pisau Dalam Angka 2013*. BPS Kabupaten Pulang Pisau. Pulang Pisau. 238p. [http://pulpiskab.bps.go.id/]
8. Dipokusumo B. 2011. *Model Partisipatif Perhutanan Sosial Menuju Pengelolaan Hutan Berkelanjutan (Kasus Pembangungan Hutan Kemasyarakatan pada Kawasan Hutan Lindung di Pulau Lombok*). Sekolah Pasca Sarjana. Institut Pertanian Bogor. Bogor. Dissertation. 285 p. (unpublished dissertation).
9. Dewi U. 2012. *Pendekatan top down versus bottom up: Implementasi dan evaluasi kebijakan publik.* Bahan presentasi IAN-UNY. Universitas Negeri Yogyakarta. Yogyakarta. [http://staff.uny.ac.id/sites/default/files/pendidikan/Utami%20Dewi,%20M.PP/].
10. Pretty JN, Guijt I, Thompson J, Scooner I. 1995. *Participatory learning and actions: a trainer's guide.* IIED Participatory Methodology Series, International Institute for Environment and Development. London. 270p.
11. Tata HL. 2016. Peat swamp forest management through community based participation: a case study of Kalawa village forest. In: Siregar C. *et al.* (eds). *Proceedings of the International Conference of Indonesia Forestry Researchers III*. Bogor 21-22 October 2015. Pp:65-72. Forestry Research and Development Agency. The Ministry of Environments and Forestry. Bogor. *In press*.

Abstract No: A-173

STRATEGY TO CONTROL FOREST AND PEATLAND FIRES AFTER CENTRAL KALIMANTAN FIRE IN 2015

Cakra Birawa, Adi Jaya*, Nina Yulianti, Fengky F. Adji, Yanarita, Yohanna Rotinsulu and Nyahu Rumbang

Faculty of Agriculture, University of Palangka Raya, Indonesia

**Corresponding author: adijaya@agr.upr.ac.id*

SUMMARY

Forest and tropical peatlands fires provide a wide impact on various aspects of life including health, economy and environment. Massive forest and peatland fires in Central Kalimantan began in 1997 and likely to recur in every dry season, including severe drought occurred in the year 2105 in conjunction with the strong influence of El Nino. Impact on health issues, the economy and the environment especially in Central Kalimantan showed the seriousness of the impact caused by land and forest fires. The positive thing that emerges from forest fires and land in 2015 is the presence of a sizable public awareness related impacts. Fire control measures in 2015 proved to be very difficult and costly, since it is necessary to take control of scarce land and forest fires which emphasizes the prevention aspect. Focus group discussions were conducted with various stakeholders and produce a strategy which includes control of peat hydrology, restoration and community-based firefighting must be done, by also promoting the economic development of local communities. The role of each main stakeholder, allocation of resources, should be a concern. Mentoring and coaching that begins with mapping the problems in each region should be absolutely made.

Keywords: *fire, peat, control, community*

INTRODUCTION

Peat swamp forest and peatland area in Central Kalimantan covering approximately two million hectares, which is scattered in several regencies in the southern part of Borneo Indonesia (Wetland, 2004). However, for the last twenty years, these peatlands have experienced the annual wildfire disaster due to the impact of the high nature destruction particularly on the disturbation of its hydrological function. As the results, the worst air pollution due to haze from fires in the history of Southeast Asia happened during the strongest El Niño in 1997-98, which is the worst recorded incident before 2011, dense haze that caused the air pollution was recorded mostly from forest fires and peatland in Indonesia (Heil *et al.*, 2006). Page *et al.* (2002) estimated that 810 - 2,570Mt carbon was emitted during the high fire incidence in 1997. Furthermore, analysis results by Yulianti *et al.* (2012) using MODIS hotspot data for the 2002-2011 clearly showed the highest hotspot density areas in Indonesia located in Kalimantan and Sumatra Islands. The area with the most fires in south Kalimantan is located at the Mega Rice Project (MRP), Central Kalimantan had a mean 2,223 hotspots/yr and hotspot density, 0.188 hotspots/km^2/year. This number remains Indonesia as one of the top carbon emitters, after China and US during latest decade.

In 2015, Indonesia came back into the world's spotlight related to fires and transboundary haze crisis. The fire in the southern MRP, Central Kalimantan mostly occurred in new plantation area, small plot-agriculture, and unclear drained peatland prior to 2015 as mentioned in Atwood *et al.* (2016). During the peak fire season (Late October-Early November), the major trace gases that were mixed in with the dense smoke were carbon dioxide, carbon monoxide, methane, hydrogen cyanide, acetic acid and ammonia (Stockwell *et al.*, 2016). These gases are considered harmful to all living things. Other indicator is the concentration of particulate matter (PM10) in Palangka Raya (Central Kalimantan) showed concentrations >2.500 ug/m^3 (Meteorological Station Tjilik Riwut's document) higher than in 2002 and 2006 severe fires (<2,000 ug/m^3, Hayasaka *et al.*, 2015). According to the technical guidelines for the Air Pollution Standard Index information, the safe limit for human health PM 10 is <400 ug/m^3. If the index threshold is passed, air is in very unhealthy conditions and will increase the sensitivity of patients with asthma and bronhitis diseases. Assuming that condition continues year by year, it will affect not only the climate and biodiversity but also the younger generation in the future. Therefore, the Faculty of Agriculture University of Palangka Raya responds to the problem by conducting a meeting and group discussion with members of the faculty, students, and relevant the Local Government Agencies. This work aims to gather and share information, opinions and solutions to control Central Kalimantan fire after 2015.

METHODS

This forum was held on 20th November 2015 at the hall of the Faculty of Agriculture, University of Palangka Raya. The number of participants was 150 peoples from the Local Government Agencies, professional associations, faculty members and students. The data used are primary data from the Focus Group Discussion (FGD) and interviews (Q and A session). FGD were held to discuss sustainable peat management recommendations that primarily address the repeated incidence of forest fires and peatland in Central Kalimantan. FGD focus on three topics are water management and sustainable use of peatlands, restoration of peat swamp forests and its socio-economic value, and a strategic of carbon emission reduction and fire prevention in Central Kalimantan. Information of FGD relied on information from various stakeholders. Furthermore, the interview (Q and A session) was conducted to explore more detailed information from the key resources, namely Prof. Mitsuru Osaki from Hokkaido University and Chairman of the Association of Japanese Peat, Dr. Adijaya as an expert in Central Kalimantan's peat hydrology and Dr. Yanaritha as an expert in social forestry (community-based knowledge).

RESULTS AND DISCUSSION

Water management and sustainable use of peatlands

There is expected the pilot villages "zero burning" with sustainable management between University of Palangka Raya and University partners. Respondents in this forum recommended rewetting of peatlands and setting the level of the water as a way to restore natural conditions. Rewetting can be done by (i) establishing canal blocking a WWF initiative in Sebangau National Park, (ii) constructing deep well for fire extinction such practiced by CIMTROP and community forests "Jumpun Pambelum", and (iii) digging *Beje* (small ponds) near to the river or canal such as found in Desa Taruna with new construction that can avoid fast drying up during the dry season. Cultivated and drained areas are advised for groundwater levels to be monitored on a regular basis. One of the technologies tested in Central Kalimantan is SESAMEs system. This method is one of the results of long-term cooperation between Hokkaido University and the University of Palangka Raya.

Restoration of peat swamp forests and its socio-economic value

Restoration should involve a unified villages as integrated target for example Tumbang Nusa, Taruna, and Sakakajang in Jabiren regency. So far, an agroforestry system is a great option for peatland near Palangka Raya. To facilitate the restoration activities, there should be an established local tree nursery managed by the University of Palangka Raya in cooperation with Forestry UPTs such as the Central Management of Kahayan Watershed (BPDAS). In addition to increasing the economic value of peatland, it would require the empowerment of local communities on a small scale. Actually, communities in Central Kalimantan of mainly Dayak do understand the natural conditions and its management but only lack in financial support. The future program of pilot village is planned to be related to the potential of the village, to reduce culture shock in the community. Alternative cultivation of food crops that are resistant to high water level management (flooded) is one of the choices for peatlands. Sago palm is one of the suitable plant for this condition. Starch and residual biomass from sago can be used as a food, cattle fodder and a source of energy (bioethanol), which provides economic value to local communities.

Strategic of carbon emission reduction and fire prevention

Fires are a main source of greenhouse gas emissions (GHGs) in Central Kalimantan. Those incidents are man-made and it is possible to predict when and where the occurrences. Recently, a monitoring system has been developed involving NASA satellite data, NOAA and unmanned aircraft (drone). A study developed by researchers Palangka Raya University Faculty of Agriculture, use the integrated early warning technology of satellite-based monitoring with Information Communication Technology (ICT), which involve lower cost in the form of web applications and smartphones (link www.kaltengpeatlandfire.org). On the other hand, there is necessity to propose cooperation between researchers from the University of the Regional Disaster Management Agency both provincial and district level to apply research results to reduce the number of fires in peatlands. The decline in fire occurrences will reduce emissions carbon dioxide. Rewetting and restoration method that described above is also a solution for reducing emissions from decomposition and fires. Moreover, vegetation planting on the sides' of blocking canal should also be done to reduce methane emissions from the reduction process. Hokkaido University and the University of Palangka Raya also have emission measurement tower and chamber for regular monitoring of GHGs from peatland area.

CONCLUSION

Severe fires in 2015 occurred due to the accumulation impact of the lack of sustainable management of peatland in Central Kalimantan during the last decades. This stakeholder's forum have recommended the pilot village in the former Mega Rice Project (MRP), which encourages zero fire use by promoting water management and restoration based on a combination of local knowledge and recent technology in Central Kalimantan. The method can be implemented to reduce the fire with proper early warning system, adaptive plants for high ground water level, empowerment of local communities, and hydrology management.

ACKNOWLEDGEMENTS

This was conducted as a part of 2015 Dies Natalis of Faculty of Agriculture, University of Palangka Raya. We thanked Indonesia Ministry of Research, Technology and Higher Education" for partially support on project works with the tittle *"Development of Integrated Fire Early Warning Systems for Sustainable Palm Oil Agro-ecosistem in Peatlands"*.

REFERENCES

1. Atwood EC, Englhart, S., Lorenz, E., Halle, W., Wiedemann, W., Siegert, F. 2016. Detection and characterization of lLow temperature peat fires during the 2015 fire catastriphe in Indonesia using a new high-sensetivity fire monitoring satellite sensor (FireBird). PloS ONE, 11, 8, p.1-24.
2. Hayasaka H., Noguchi, I.,Putra, E.I., Yulianti, N., Vadrevu, N. 2015. Peat-fire-related air polution in Central Kalimantan. Environmental Pollution, 195, p. 257-266
3. Heil, A., Langmann,B., Aldrian, E. 2006. Indonesian peat and vegetation fire emissions: study on factors influencing large-scale smoke haze pollution using a regional atmospheric chemistry model. Mitigation and Adaptation Strategies for Global Change, 12, p.113-133.
4. Page,S.E., Siegert, F., Rieley, J. O., Boehm,H.D. V., Jaya,A., Limin,S. 2002. The amount of carbon release from peat and forest fires in Indonesia during 1997. Nature, 420, p.61-65.
5. Stockwell, C. E., Jayarathne, T., Cochrane, M. A., Ryan, K. C., Putra, E. I., Saharjo, B. H., Nurhayati, A. D., Albar, I., Blake, D. R., Simpson, I. J., Stone, E. A., Yokelson, R. J. 2016. Field measurements of trave gases and aerosols emitted by peat fires in Central Kalimantan, Indonesia during the 2015 El Nino. Atmos.Chem.Phys.Discuss. doi: 10.5194/acp-2016-411 (*in review*).
6. Wetlands. Maps of Area of Peatlands Distribution and Carbon Content in Kalimantan. 2004. Wetlands International- Indonesia Programme, Bogor.
7. Yulianti, N. Hayasaka H., Usup A. 2012. Recent forest and peat fire trends in Indonesia, the latest decade by MODIS hotspot data. Global Environmental Research 16, 1, p. 105-116.

Abstract No: A-241

USING PEAT SHRUB FOR AGRICULTURE LIKELY REDUCES CO_2 EMISSIONS AND IMPROVES LOCAL LIVELIHOOD

Fahmuddin Agus*, Neneng Laela Nurida, Maswar, Wahyunto, I. GM Subiksa, Husnain, and Dedi Nursyamsi

Indonesian Soil Research Institute, Agency for Agricultural Research and Development
Jl. Tentara Pelajar No. 12, Cimanggu, Bogor, 16114, Indonesia

**Corresponding author: F_agus@litbang.pertanian.go.id*

SUMMARY

Indonesia has around 4 Mha of degraded peat shrub from a total of about 15 Mha peatland nationally. These lands emit CO_2 and are fire prone. Using them for productive uses may not only reduce both problems, but also promises livelihood to local communities. We evaluated the net present values, CO_2 emissions and opportunity costs (OpCosts) of different land uses on peatland in Riau, Jambi, West Kalimantan, Central Kalimantan and Papua Provinces, Indonesia from September 2012 to August 2013. In general the benefits from utilizing peatland for agriculture were so high, especially for rubber and oil palm which create high pressures to use peatland. The net present value (NPV) under oil palm plantation ranged from USD 827 to 2515 ha^{-1} yr^{-1} and under rubber plantation in Central Kalimantan was around USD 4081 ha^{-1} yr^{-1}. The OpCost of not using peat shrub to rubber was USD 132 $(Mg\ CO_2)^{-1}$; a value unaffordable for compensation by any carbon market mechanisms. At the Papua site, converting peat shrub into sago plantation resulted in negative OpCosts, meaning that it reduced CO_2 emissions, as well as generated income. By utilization of peat shrub or productive uses, coupled with a strict control of conserving natural peat forest, the country's chance of success in protecting peat forest and hence reducing emissions from peat forest conversion will likely increase.

Keywords: *degraded peatland, opportunity cost, CO_2 emissions, rubber, peat shrub, oil palm*

INTRODUCTION

Indonesia has about 15 million ha of peatland (Ritung *et al.*, 2011) which is the largest among tropical countries. It is under high pressures for various uses, most of which require drained condition. At the same time its conservation as natural undrained forest is also vital for conserving carbon and maintaining environmental quality. When the peat forest is cleared and drained, its function will change from storage to a source of carbon (Jauhiainen *et al.*, 2012; *Drösler et al.*, 2013). Drained peatlands are also subjected to subsidence and are proned to fire (Stephens and Stewart 1969; Hooijer *et al.*, 2012; Aich *et al.*, 2013; Wösten *et al.*, 2008). However, not all of the drained peatland are productive. Roughly 4 million ha is degraded and being idle. They are covered by shrub, grasses or ferns (Gunarso *et al.*, 2013; Agus *et al.*, 2014). Some of the idle land is in transition for some kind of agriculture, while some others are idle because of insecure status or are within forest jurisdiction. This research was aimed at evaluating the economic and environmental tradeoffs of using peatland, especially the degraded ones, for agriculture.

MATERIALS AND METHODS

The evaluation of land cover of Indonesian peatland was adapted from Agus *et al.*, (2014). These data were generated from 2011 Landsat TM interpretation. Field research was conducted at five sites, each in Riau, Jambi, West Kalimantan, Central Kalimantan, and Papua Provinces. The Riau site represented very deep (4-6 m deep) peat and was used for smallholder oil palm plantation. The Jambi site represented moderately deep (1.5-4.5 m deep) peat and also used for smallholder oil palm plantation. The Central Kalimantan site represented very deep peat (4-6 m) and was used for smallholder rubber plantation. The West Kalimantan site was moderately deep (3-4 m deep) peat and was used for annual food and horticultural crops, while the Papua site was shallow (2-3 m deep) peat and was used for sago forest. Treatments in the former four sites were various kinds of ameliorants including barnyard manure, dolomite, "peat fertilizer" (steel sludge enriched with phosphate rock), Trichoderma and a control. They were arranged in a completely randomized block design with four to five replications. Treatments and the number of replications slightly varied across sites.

For the calculation of net CO_2 emissions as caused by land use and land use changes, two sources of emissions were taken into account; peat decomposition and biomass loss. Peat fire is an important source of CO_2

emission, especially from peat shrub, but was not included in this calculation. For the Riau and West Kalimantan sites, CO_2 emission from peat decomposition was measured using 25 cm diameter by 22 cm tall closed chambers and the gas concentration was measured monthly using an Infrared CO_2 Gas Analyzer (IRGA) as explained by Marwanto and Agus (2014), Dariah *et al.* (2014), and Husnain *et al.* (2014). For the other sites CO_2 peat emissions were based on the IPCC default values (Drösler *et al.* 2014). Emission from biomass loss due to land use change was assessed using the biomass carbon stock difference using default values (Agus *et al.* 2014 & 2013; IPCC 2006).

For the calculation of the Net Present Values (NPV), three kinds of data were used: crop yield, costs associated with land clearing and soil and crop management (including costs for harvest), and revenue at farm level. For oil palm plantation, the first four year fresh fruit bunch (FFB) yield was based on the actual field data and for the life-cycle yield, an *ex-ante* estimation was conducted using the curve of Sutarta and Rahutomo (2013). The lowest case FFB yield scenario of this curve ($Y = -0.1403\ x^2 + 4.164\ x - 1.664$; $R^2 = 0.8494$) was used since we classify peatland as sub-optimal land with low productivity.

Data of the farm inputs were a combination of farmer interview and direct recording of costs associated with treatments. Oil palm revenue was based on the actual (2014 to early 2015) FFB prices. The opportunity costs (OpCosts) of emission reduction was defined as the forgone benefits of not using the land for agriculture divided by the difference in the amount of CO_2 emissions associated with peat oxidation and carbon stock changes.

RESULTS AND DISCUSSION

From the 15 Mha Indonesian peatland around 8.3 Mha is covered by forest. About 1.5 Mha has been used for plantations (including oil palm plantation) and about 0.7 Mha is used for annual food and horticultural crops. Degraded peatland comprised about 4 Mha which are mainly covered by shrub, imperata grass, and ferns. These degraded lands have a good potential for agricultural developments for enhancing livelihood and minimizing environmental impacts, instead of using natural forests for agriculture.

1. Crop Yield

Table 1 shows different responses on crop yield of different amelioration and fertilization treatments. In Jambi, oil palm FFB yield increased with the application of manure indicating insufficiency and/or incompleteness of macro and micro nutrients in the soil since only N, P and K fertilizers were provided under the control treatment. Likewise, the use of "peat fertilizer" and oil palm empty fruit bunch (EFB) increased FFB yield more than 50%. In the Riau location, treatments did not affect crop yield, and this seems to be due the addition of not only N, P, and K, but also magnesium (Mg), copper (Cu) and boron (B) in the control treatments, such that the addition of either manure or EFB did not contribute to the improvement of crop yield. For rubber in Central Kalimantan, only N, P, K was used as the Control treatment and amelioration treatments did not affect crop yield, indicating a high tolerance of this crop to low fertility. For the West Kalimantan site, the non-significant response to amelioration appears to be related to the high fertilizer residue of past cropping. Another observation from Table 1 is that the levels of crop yield on the peat were comparable to those of mineral soils.

Table 1. Mean crop yield under different treatments and different sites.

Treatment	FFB in Jambi (6 yr old oil palm)	FFB in Jambi (6 yr old oil palm)	5 yr old rubber latex in C. Kalimantan	Corn grain yield in W. Kalimantan
	$Mg\ ha^{-1}\ yr^{-1}$			$Mg\ ha^{-1}\ season^{-1}$
Top dressing (Control 1)[1)]	11.4 a	18.5 a	3.8 a	2.7 a
Peat fertilizer	17.4 ab	19.3 a	4.6 a	3.8 a
Manure	18.8 b	19.6 a	4.3 a	3.0 a
EFB/Mineral soil	17.7 ab	20.1 a[2)]	2.9 a[3)]	
Dolomite				3.5 a
Control 2[4)]				3.4 a

[1)]Control 1 = top dressing fertilizer in accordance with the local recommendation; [2)]EFB = empty fruit bunch; [3)]Mineral soil; [4)]Control 2 = combination of dolomite and Trichoderma

2. Net Greenhouse gas emissions from land use change

Table 2 shows net emissions from both biomass loss and peat decomposition, mean NPV from different agricultural uses, and opportunity costs (OpCosts) associated with refraining from using either peat shrub, secondary peat forest, or primary peat forest for agricultural uses. When shrub is converted to sago plantation the estimated net CO_2 emissions was -15.4 $Mg\ ha^{-1}\ yr^{-1}$ because the biomass C of sago plantation was comparable to that of shrub, while CO_2 emission from sago plantation (5.5 t CO_2 ha^{-1} yr^{-1}) was lower than that of shrub (19.5 t CO_2 ha^{-1} yr^{-1}) (Drösler et al. 2014). This means that converting peat shrub to sago plantation reduces CO_2 emissions. For the Riau, Jambi and Central Kalimantan sites, our calculation shows a net positive emissions when peat shrub is converted to agriculture, implying that maintaining the shrub as is would reduce emissions, but practically no profits can be generated from the latter. When either primary or secondary peat forests were converted to agriculture, it very consistently resulted in net CO_2 emissions. Therefore, from the view point of emission reduction (and other environmental consideration), the forest covers should be protected from convertion to agricultural uses.

Table 2. Net present value (NPV) under agricultural uses; net CO_2 emissions from biomass losses or gains and peat decomposition related to land use and land use changes from either shrub, secondary forest, or primary forest to agricultural land; and opportunity costs

Treatment	Jambi (6 year old OP)	Riau (6 year old OP)	Central Kalimantan (5 year old rubber)	West Kalimantan (corn)	Papua, sago forest
NPV (USD ha^{-1} yr^{-1}) at 10% discount factor					
	827	2,515	4,081	291	441
Net emissions from biomass and peat decomposition (Mg CO_2 ha^{-1} yr^{-1})					
Peat shrub	19.6	22.8	30.8	10.6	-15.4
Secondary peat forest	37.9	62.5	49.1	62.8	3.0
Primary peat forest	63.3	87.9	74.5	88.2	28.4
Opportunity costs [USD (Mg CO_2)$^{-1}$]					
	42.19	110.32	132.49	27.43	-28.62
	21.82	40.25	83.11	4.63	146.92
	13.06	28.62	54.78	3.30	15.52

USD 1 = IDR 13,000

3. Net present value and opportunity costs

Despite the emissions, the local landholders as well as the district governments regard peatland as a source of revenue and livelihood. The more intensive management of oil palm plantation in Riau gave a relatively high NPV compared to the one in Jambi with a less intensive management. Rubber in Central Kalimantan site gave the highest NPV of over USD 4000 ha^{-1} yr^{-1} and this seems related to the adaptability of rubber to produce under a low input system.

The trade-off of the emission level and the financial aspect is reflected by the OpCost (Table 2). In all cases conserving peat primary or secondary forests from conversion to agriculture entails high OpCosts. The high opportunity costs were generated from high NPVs, albeit a relatively high carbon saving if the forests were conserved. Low OpCosts (USD 4.63-3.30 (Mg CO_2)$^{-1}$) were associated with conserving peat forests from conversion to corn cultivation for the case of West Kalimantan. This was caused by a low NPV from corn and high net CO_2 emissions. Nevertheless, these levels of OpCosts are still relatively high for compensation by carbon market mechanisms. For peat shrub, the high opportunity costs of oil palm and rubber plantations translate to very small carbon saving amid the high NPVs. The negative OpCost of sago means that conversion of the peat shrub to sago plantation not only reduce CO_2 emissions, but also results in financial benefits. Thus, such conversion should be encouraged.

CONCLUSION

Satellite images shows around 4 Mha of Indonesian peatland, part of which could potentially be converted to agricultural uses without significantly exacerbating the environment relative to converting peat forests. Allowing the use of peat shrub and strictly banning the use of peat forests likely result in an overall win-win solution for the local livelihood and emission reduction.

REFERENCES

1. Agus, F., Santosa, I., Dewi, S., Setyanto, P., Thamrin, S., Wulan, Y. C., Suryaningrum, F. (eds.). 2013. Pedoman Teknis Penghitungan Baseline Emisi dan Serapan Gas Rumah Kaca Sektor Berbasis Lahan: Buku I Landasan Ilmiah. Badan Perencanaan Pembangunan Nasional, Republik Indonesia, Jakarta.

2. Agus, F., Gunarso, P., Sahardjo, B.H., Harris, N., van Noordwijk, M., and Killeen, T.J. 2013. Historical CO_2 emissions from land use and land use change from the oil palm industry in Indonesia, malaysia and Papua New Guinea. *In* Reports from the Technical Panels of RSPOs 2nd Greenhouse Gas Working Group. T. J. Killeen and J. Goon (eds.). Roundtable on Sustainable Palm Oil, Kuala Lumpur, Malaysia.pp. 65–88.
3. Aich, S., McVoy, C.W., Dreschel, T.W. and Santamaria, F. 2013. Estimating soil subsidence and carbon loss in the Everglades agricultural area, Florida using geospatial techniques. Agriculture, Ecosystems & Environment, 171: 124–133. doi:10.1016/j.agee.2013.03.017.
4. Dariah A., Marwanto, S., & Agus F. 2014. Root- and peat-based CO2 emissions from oil palm plantations. Mitig. Adapt. Strateg. Glob. Change, 19:831–843. DOI 10.1007/s11027-013-9515-6.
5. Drösler, M., Verchot, L.V., Freibauer, A., Pan, G., Wang, C., Evans, C.D., Bourbonniere, R.A., Alm, J.P., Page, S., Agus, F., Hergoualc'h, K., Couwenberg, J.. Jauhiainen, J., Sabiham, S. 2013. "CHAPTER 2: Drained Inland Organic Soils." In *2013 Supplement to the 2006 IPCC Guidelines for National Greenhouse Gas Inventories: Wetlands*, IPCC, Geneva.
6. Gunarso, P., Hartoyo, M.E., Agus, F., and Killeen, T.J. 2013. Oil palm and land use change in Indonesia, Malaysia and Papua New Guinea. *In*Reports from the Technical Panels of RSPOs 2nd Greenhouse Gas Working Group, T.J. Killeen and J. Goon. Roundtable on Sustainable Palm Oil, Kuala Lumpur, Malaysia. pp. 29–64.
7. Hooijer, A., Page, S., Jauhiainen, J., Lee, W.A., Lu, X.X., Idris, A. and Anshari, G. 2012. Subsidence and carbon loss in drained tropical peatlands. Biogeosciences 9 (3): 1053–1071. doi:10.5194/bg-9-1053-2012.
8. Husnain, H., Wigena, I.G.P., Dariah, A., Marwanto, S., Setyanto, P., and Agus, F. 2014. CO_2 emissions from tropical drained peat in Sumatra, Indonesia. Mitigation and Adaptation Strategies for Global Change 19 (6): 845–862. doi:10.1007/s11027-014-9550-y.
9. Jauhiainen, J., Hooijer, A., and Page, S.E. 2012. Carbon Dioxide emissions from an *Acacia* plantation on peatland in Sumatra, Indonesia. Biogeosciences 9(2): 617–630. doi:10.5194/bg-9-617-2012.
10. Marwanto, S. and Agus, F. 2014. Is CO2 flux from oil palm plantations on peatland controlled by soil moisture and/or soil and air temperatures? Mitig. Adapt. Strateg. Glob. Change, 19:809–819, DOI 10.1007/s11027-013-9518-3.
11. Ritung, S.. Wahyunto, Nugroho, K., Sukarman, Hikmatullah, Suparto, Tafakresnanto, C. 2011. Peta lahan gambut Indonesia skala 1:250.000. Kementerian Pertanian, Jakarta.
12. Stephens, J.C., and Stewart, E.H. 1969. Effect of climate on organic soil subsidence.. Agricultural Research Service, U.S.D.A. Ft. Lauderdale, Florida, USA, 647–56.
13. Sutarta, F. S. and Rahutomo, S. New standart for FFB yield of IOPRI's planting material based on land suitability. Indonesian Oil Palm Research Institute. Medan. (unpublished)
14. Wösten, J.H.M., Clymans, E., Page, S.E., Rieley, J.O. and Limin, S.H. 2008. Peat–water interrelationships in a Tropical peatland ecosystem in Southeast Asia. Catena 73 (2): 212–224. doi:10.1016/j.catena.2007.07.010.

THEME 7

SPECIAL SESSION

SPECIAL SESSION 1: SOFT SOIL ENGINEERING

Abstract No: A-111

CASE STUDIES ON DESIGN AND CONSTRUCTION OF DEEP FOUNDATIONS IN SARAWAK SOFT SOIL

Frydolin Siahaan[1*] and Junaidi Sahadan[2]

[1]*Bridges and Wharves Branch, Public Works Department, Sarawak, Malaysia*
[2]*Quality Management Sector, Public Works Department, Sarawak, Malaysia*

**Corresponding author: frydolis@sarawak.gov.my*

SUMMARY

Eight (8) structures using deep foundation are selected and discussed in this paper. The eight (8) structures located in difficult ground of Sarawak are namely the Sg. Rimbas Bridge in Pusa, Sg. Sawit Bridge, Sg. Palasan Bridge, and Pusa Ferry Ramp in Pusa; all in Betong Division, Batang Samariang Bridge in Kuching Division, Batang Samarahan Bridge and Batang Sadong Bridge; both in Samarahan Division and Batang Baram Bridge in Miri Division. During the design stage, several important engineering decisions were made in order to meet both the design code and statutory requirements. The design was not to compromise the difficult condition of the ground. The ground at all eight (8) locations were reported to be having low bearing capacity with Standard Penetration Test (SPT) N values between 0 and 5 found at depths from 0 to 20m and (SPT) N values less than 10 found at depths between 20m and 80m. Very soft to soft soil that is of recent sedimentary deposit was found at all locations. This paper emphasizes on decisions made in the design of the bridge foundation and ferry fender foundation. Background and localities of the projects, geological and geotechnical findings, design and types of foundation used, method of constructing the foundation and preliminary test pile results obtained are presented in this paper.

Keywords: *soft clay, deep foundation, Standard Penetration Test (SPT), Sarawak*

INTRODUCTION

Deep foundation design and construction in difficult ground condition involve many considerations to be made on suitable types of deep foundation and construction method. The type of foundation chosen will affect the overall cost of the structure. The selected construction method must be practical. In line with the infrastructure planning to support the economic development of the state of Sarawak in Malaysia, the construction of coastal roads including bridges to link all towns and population centres located in the coastal area is part of the strategy. Besides the many small rivers, a few major rivers need bridge crossings to be constructed. With the completion of the coastal roads network, the economic activities in these coastal regions will be enhanced.

Constructing structures at unfavorable locations on marginally stable river banks requires in depth assessment of the local soil conditions in order to achieve a sound decision. The Sg. Rimbas Bridge in Pusa, Sg. Sawit Bridge, Sg. Palasan Bridge, and Pusa Ferry Ramp in Pusa; all in Betong Division, Batang Samariang Bridge in Kuching Division; Batang Samarahan Bridge and Batang Sadong Bridge both in Samarahan Division and Batang Baram Bridge in Miri Division are the eight (8) bridges located in difficult ground condition (in terms of soil parameters) to be discussed in this paper.

BACKGROUND AND LOCALITY

Sungai Rimbas Bridge is located in Pusa town, Betong Division. It is a tributary to Batang Saribas. When completed, the bridge will link Pusa town and Kampung Pusa. This bridge will link the existing coastal roads network. Pusa Ferry Ramp is also located in Pusa which is used to cross the Sungai Saribas. Additional fendering system at Pusa Ferry Ramp was completed in 2012. The design is done in-house by Jabatan Kerja Raya (JKR) Sarawak. Sg. Palasan Bridge that links Pusa town and Sebuyau was completed in 2006 to replace the collapsed bridge structure. Sg.Sawit Bridge along Jalan Tanjung Assam/ Hilir Saribas/ Beladin is located in Betong. Fig.1 shows locations of all four (4) bridges.

Batang Samariang bridge is located in Kuching, Kuching Division as shown in Fig.1, linking Kuching city to Matang, Telaga Air, and the Lundu/ Sempadi coastal road. The 300m bridge was completed in 2014 and is presented in this paper to show the different soil properties compared with other locations.

Batang Samarahan and Batang Sadong bridges are both located in Samarahan Division, linking Kota Samarahan with other population centres in Sarawak. The construction of Batang Samarahan Bridge commenced in

2015. Load test has been carried out for this bridge. Batang Sadong bridge is under construction and is scheduled to be completed in 2016. A statnamic test has been carried out for this project.

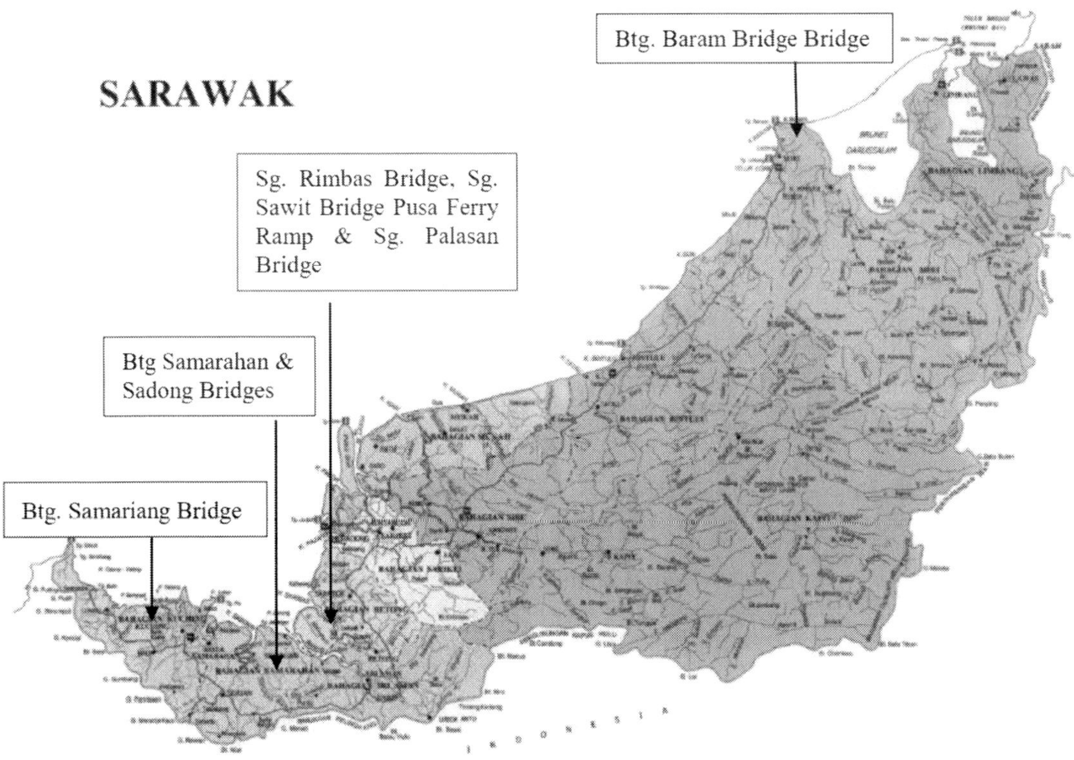

Fig. 1 Locality map of eight (8) bridges

The Batang Baram Bridge (also known as the ASEAN Bridge) is located along the Miri-Baram trunk road, linking Sarawak with Brunei, as shown in Fig.1. The bridge was completed in August 2003. The bridge is included in this paper for comparison with other similar soil condition for other projects.

SITE INVESTIGATION

For the Sg. Rimbas Bridge project six (6) boreholes were drilled; three (3) boreholes overwater and three (3) borehole on land. Typical borehole measurements of SPT are presented in Fig. 2(a). From depths of 0 to 20m SPT value is zero which indicates very soft soil and with top layer is generally of peat. From the depths of 20 to 50m the SPT N values were less than 10 which is classified as soft soil. The soil layers from top to bottom can be classified as very soft to soft clay, firm to stiff silty clay and hard silty clay. With the information derived from SPT the riverbank stability needs to be checked or analyzed prior to choosing the suitable type of deep foundation and treatment of the riverbank. SPT measurements from one borehole for Sg. Sawit Bridge are shown in Fig. 2(b). From depths of 0 to 20m, the SPT N value equals to 0 and from 20 to 40m, the SPT N values were less than 10. This borehole shows that the riverbank is marginally stable. SPT measurements from one of two (2) boreholes available for Sg. Palasan Bridge are presented in Fig. 2(c). The SPT N value equals to 0 from depths of 0 to 15m and greater than 10 from depths of 15m to 72m. The soil consists of mainly very soft to firm clay. The typical borehole of Pusa Ferry Ramp is shown in Fig. 2(d). There are eight (8) boreholes carried out for this project. Typical soils are very soft to soft clay, clayey silt and dense sand. Based on Borehole 4, the condition of soil indicates challenges in the construction of the fendering system. The SPT N value is less than 10 until the depth of 45m and the maximum SPT N value is 32 at depth of 80m. For this project, design requires the steel pipe pile be driven to a depth of at least 80 in order to provide adequate lateral resistance against the lateral force due to Ferry's impact. The above four projects share some similarities on the soil properties, particularly the top 15m to 20m in which the SPT value is equals to zero.

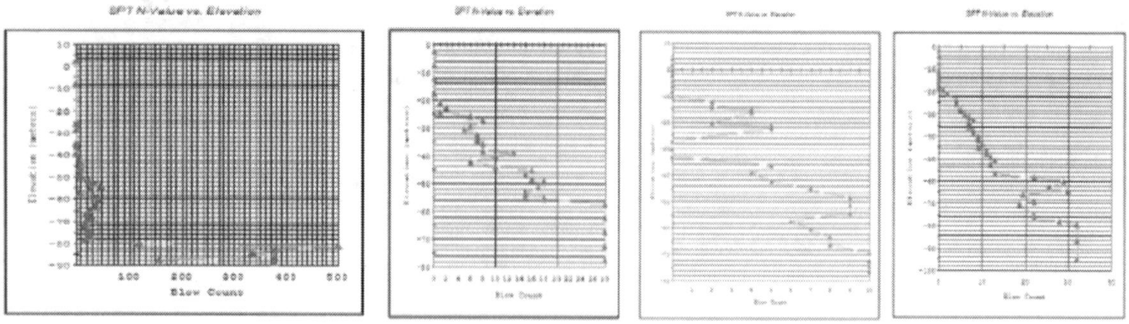

(a) (b) (c) (d)

Fig. 2 (a) SPT for Sg. Rimbas Bridge, (b) SPT for Sg. Sawit Bridge, (c) SPT for Sg. Palasan Bridge, (d) SPT for Pusa Ferry Ramp

Batang Samariang Bridge is located in Kuching Division. It is included in this paper for comparison purpose. The soil condition is better but top soil need to be considered in design, particularly the slope stability analysis of the riverbank where the abutments are located and the type of pile to be used. The top 8 m is very soft soil. The soil could be described as very soft clay to soft clay, firm silt and weathered rock. Typical borehole is shown in Fig. 3(a).

At Batang Samarahan Bridge, twelve (12) boreholes were drilled. The SPT N values are presented in Fig. 3(b). SPT N values were recorded to a depth of 45m. It was also recorded that the SPT N values were zero until a depth of 5 m, indicating very soft clay with layers of peat. The soils could be described as very soft to soft clay, soft to firm clay, hard clayey silt and very poor mudstone. For the Btg. Sadong Bridge project, boreholes were drilled, with two at abutments and nine at the nine piers. The soil layers from top to bottom of the borehole are reported to be very soft to soft clay, firm clay, dense sand, highly fractured and weathered granite. It was also reported that SPT N value is equal to zero until depth of 18m. Fig. 3c shows typical borehole at Btg. Sadong bridge.

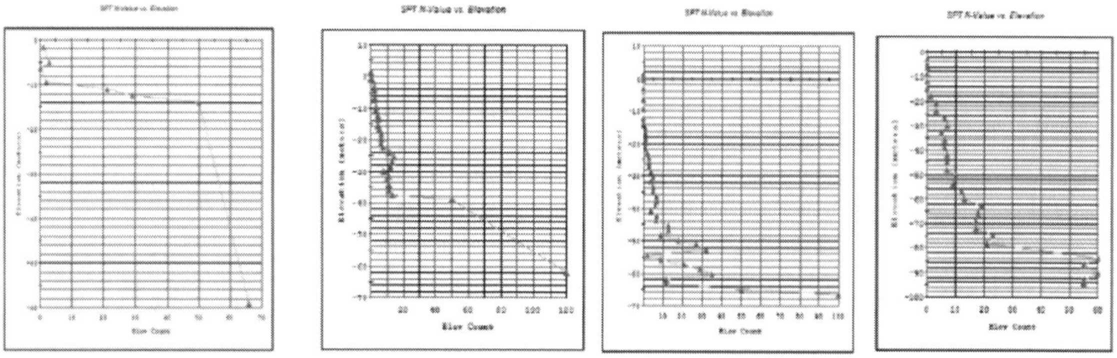

(a) (b) (c) (d)

Fig.3 (a) SPT for Btg. Samariang Bridge, (b) SPT for Btg. Samarahan Bridge, (c) SPT for Btg. Sadong Bridge, (d) SPT for Btg Baram Bridge.

For the Btg. Baram Bridge thirteen (13) boreholes were drilled and a typical borehole is presented in Fig. 3(d). It was reported that SPT N values were recorded until depth of 93m. It was also recorded that soil layers from top to bottom of BH-101 are very soft to soft clay, firm clay, stiff to very stiff, hard clay (with SPT N value greater than 50).

DESIGN, CONSTRUCTION AND TESTING

The Sg. Rimbas Bridge is an 8-span bridge with a total length of 327.2m. The design of substructure for this bridge took into account the slope stability of both riverbanks in view of very soft soil. The recorded SPT N values showed values of 0 up to a depth of 40m. Slope stability analysis carried out for both riverbanks shows that the riverbanks need to be treated in order to increase the factor of safety from 1.06 to at least 1.4. 117 micropiles of 300mm diameter have been drilled and grouted with Grade 30 concrete to a depth of at least 36m between Pier 1 and Pier 2 at Pusa side and 99 micropiles of 300mm diameter between Pier 6 and Pier 7 drilled and grouted to a depth of at least 45m in order to increase factor of safety to about 1.4. It was decided 1000mm diameter steel pipe piles of thickness 19mm for land piers be utilized to support loadings from bridge superstructure and to improve riverbank stability. Some empirical formulas have been used to predict the allowable bearing capacity of 1000mm diameter steel pipe pile with reinforced concrete infill [2, 5]. Meyerhof method (1976) was used to predict the bearing capacity and the allowable bearing capacity obtained is 459 tonnes, with 2.5 factor of safety. With a combination of Alpha method and Meyerhof method the allowable bearing capacity obtained is 380 tonnes in which Alpha method is used for the skin friction resistance and Meyerhof method for tip resistance. Finally the safe working load of 350 tonnes and min length of 60 m was decided upon. This was confirmed by both static load test and PDA test. Vibro hammer was used to install 1000mm diameter steel pipe piles and 20 tons hammer was used to drive the pile to set. Vibro hammer was selected to avoid any damage to nearby building structures. All piles were installed to a depth of around 62m. The strength of the foundation system was mainly derived from its frictional properties. This bridge is expected to be completed in 2016. Fig. 4 shows long section of the bridge and riverbank's treatment with micropiles.

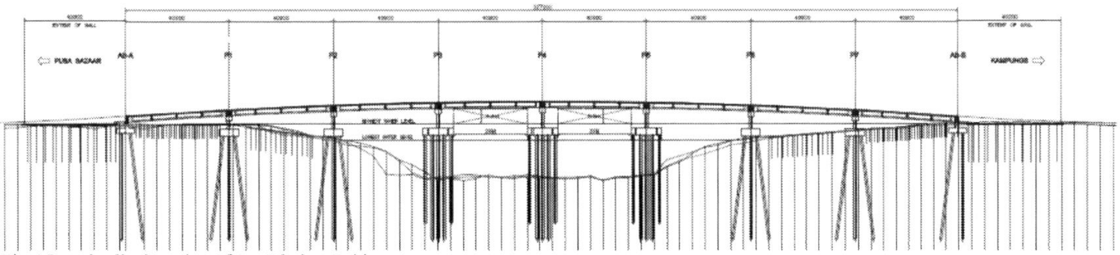

Fig.4 Longitudinal section of Sg. Rimbas Bridge

The second bridge in Betong Division is the Sg. Sawit Bridge, a 3-span prestressed beams bridge with a total length of 90m as shown in Fig. 5. After detailed analysis, it was decided to use 600mm prestressed spun pile for both abutments and piers. The safe working load is 80 tons. For this project 16 numbers of piles were used for each pier and 26 numbers of pile for each abutment. The strength of the foundation system was mainly based on skin resistance of very soft to soft soil. From the slope stability analysis of riverbank it was decided the foundation system for the abutments and piled slab behind each abutment should also be able to improve the riverbank's stability. A minimum factor of safety of 1.2 is required to be able to support embankment for the approach road. Meyerhof's method was used to predict the skin resistance which is approximately 28 kPa. It was decided that 600mm diameter piles with a minimum 60m length were to be driven using a hydraulic hammer of 5 tonnes weight. Static load test and PDA test are to be carried out to confirm the predicted bearing capacity of the pile. This bridge is under construction.

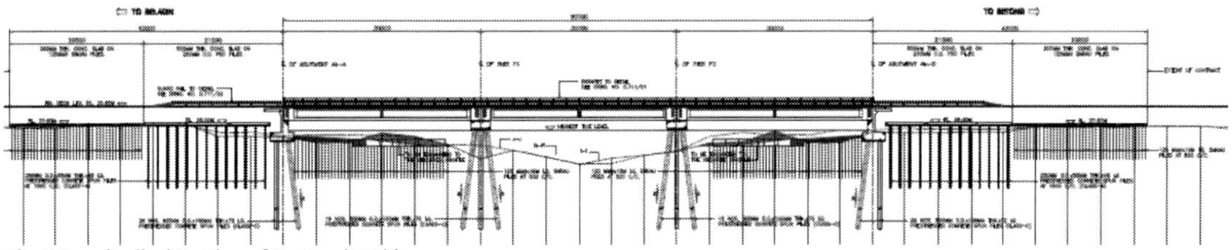

Fig. 5 Longitudinal Section of Sg. Sawit Bridge

The Sg. Palasan Bridge project has three (3) spans with a total length of 58m and the foundation system uses steel H-pile of 305x305x97 kg/m. The pile length was decided to be approximately 75m which is required to mobilize skin resistance. Site investigation report shows that the SPT N values were less than 10 until a depth of 75m and equals to 10 from a depth of 75 to 80m. The steel H-Pile was selected to replace the 450mm diameter prestressed spun piles earlier used for the collapsed bridge structure. The riverbank is marginally stable with a factor of safety around 1 and need to be improved by driving more steel H-piles at each abutment and pier. It was recorded that 24 numbers and 32 numbers were driven respectively for each of the pier and abutment.

For the fendering system in Pusa, it was decided to use 900mm steel pipe piles of thickness 16mm with reinforced concrete infill. Siahaan *et al* [3] has reported the design of this project. A 20 tons hammer was used to drive steel pipe piles through very soft to soft soil and penetrate through an average SPT N value of 26 from a depth of 55 to 80m. The driving was terminated when it reached SPT N values greater than 26. Four numbers of additional fender systems were designed not only to support the vertical loads but also to resist the specified ship impact loads sustained from ferries carrying 32 numbers of cars which have a total load of approximately 212 tonnes. All piles were driven to around 96m. The capacity of pile was mainly mobilized by skin friction.

The Batang Samariang Bridge has a soil condition better than the other bridges. Soil layers were classified as very soft to soft soil and were found from ground surface to a depth of about 8m. Weathered rock was found starting from a depth of 8m. The riverbank needs to be analyzed before deciding the type of deep foundation. A 1200mm diameter bored pile was decided for all piers. The piles were socketed around 8m into weathered rock. The embedment of the pile into rock will provide some amount of lateral restraint at the pile tip [1, 4]. The predicted settlement based on Vesic method (1977) is 6 mm under ultimate load 18,000 kN compared to measured settlement of 10.78mm from static load test.

For Batang Samarahan Bridge 1500 mm diameter steel pipe piles were used. Fig. 6 shows a 771m long Batang Samarahan bridge which has two piers on the river. Each pile was driven into weathered rock identified as highly fracture mudstone. Reese method was used to predict settlement in which the settlement was 5mm under working load 12,000 kN. Each pile needed to be socketed into weathered rock around 8m to handle lateral load due to ship impact. The load test on the instrumented test pile showed that under working load the measured settlement was 8.5mm compared to predicted settlement of 5mm. The difference was mainly due to the driving process that affects the mobilized skin resistance. The number of piles at the river piers was designed to support not only the loads from the bridge superstructure but also to handle the loads from barge impact load of around 2000 DWT.

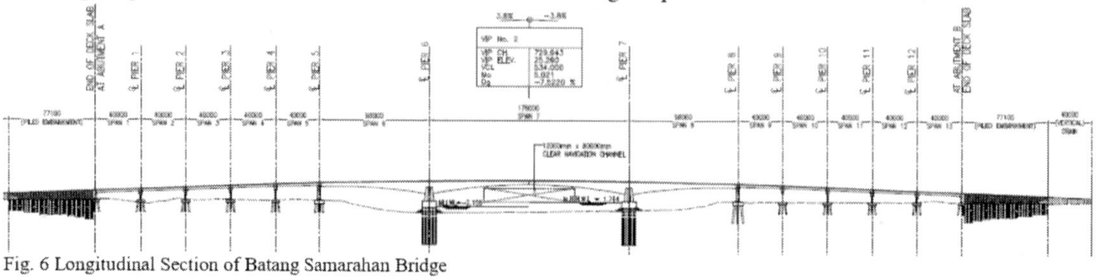

Fig. 6 Longitudinal Section of Batang Samarahan Bridge

The Batang Sadong Bridge which is included in this paper shows the similarities in the soil properties with Batang Samarahan Bridge. A statnamic test was carried out on the preliminary test pile. A 54.15 m long instrumented test pile of 1500mm diameter (hollow section) was performed on 6th December 2012 to confirm the bearing capacity of pile and the required socket length. Based on Reese method the predicted settlement was 7.1mm and 21mm respectively under working load of 9,000 kN and twice working load of 18,000 kN compared to measured settlements of 9.56mm and 23.68mm respectively. Fig 7 shows a longitudinal section of Batang Sadong Bridge in which 33 piles were driven at Piers 4, 5 and 6 on the river.

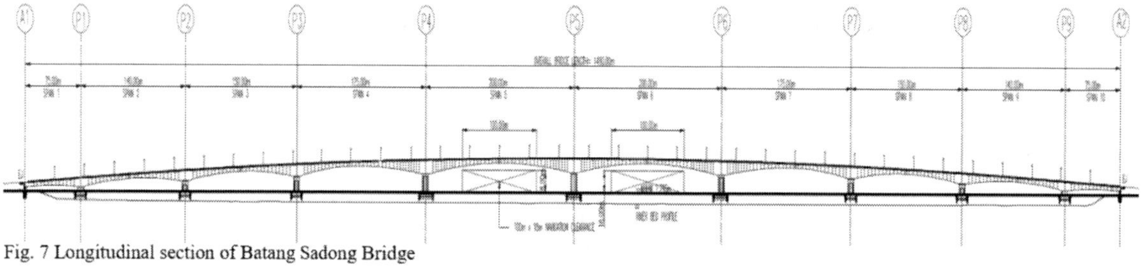

Fig. 7 Longitudinal section of Batang Sadong Bridge

Fig. 8 shows a 19 span Batang Baram Bridge with a total length of 1040m. 33 steel pipe piles of 1500mm diameter with reinforced concrete infill were driven for each river pier. For Batang Baram Bridge, the preliminary test pile of 600 mm prestressed spun pile was driven to 82m through very soft to soft clay and stiff clay. The predicted settlement was 17.5mm compared to measured settlement of 14.2mm from static load test. The pile capacity was mobilized primarily by skin resistance. The static load test was carried out from 9 to 12th December 2000. It was included in this paper because of the similarities of the soil properties with Sg. Rimbas Bridge. Steel pipe piles with concrete infill were used for all abutments and piers which were driven to around 82m.

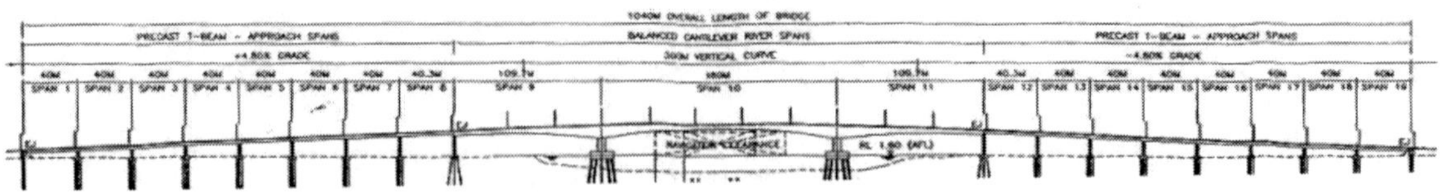

Fig.8 Longitudinal section of Batang Baram Bridge

CONCLUSION

- For deep foundation on very soft to soft clay, longer and larger piles are required to mobilize adequate skin resistance. Large steel pipe piles with concrete infill were utilized in almost all of the projects.
- The piles driven or bored into weathered rock required adequate socket length to mobilize skin resistance and to provide lateral restraint against ship impact load.
- The structures on very soft to soft soils require careful assessment of the stability of the riverbank and the treatment required before selecting the foundation system for the structure.

ACKNOWLEDGEMENTS

The authors and JKR Sarawak, wish to extend their gratitude to all parties who were involved either directly or indirectly throughout the course of these projects which led to their successful implementation.

REFERENCES

1. FHWA (2006) Pile Foundation Design Example and Design Step.
2. Rajapakse, Ruwan (2008), Pile Design and Construction Rules of Thumb, Elsevier Inc
3. Siahaan, Fridolin., and Sahadan, Junaidi. (2003) A Case Study on the Prediction and Measurement of the Bearing Capacity and Settlement of Piles at Batang Baram Bridge and Batang Rajang Bridge, Sarawak, Malaysia, Conference on Recent Advances in Soft Soil Engineering and Technogy, 2-4 July, 2003, Sibu, Sarawak, Malaysia.
4. Siahaan, F., Sahadan, J., and Taib, S.N.L. (2013) Case Histories on Design and Construction of Deep Foundation for Riverine Structures in Sarawak, Malaysia, International Journal of Integrated Engineering, Vol. No. (2013) p.
5. Yamin, Mohammad (2016), Problem Solving in Foundation Engineering Using Foundation Pro Software, Department of Civil Engineering & Construction, Bradley University, Peoria, IL, USA.

Abstract No: A-364

EFFECTS OF COMPRESSIBILITY AND PERMEABILITY OF PEATY SOILS ON THE DESIGN AND CONSTRUCTION OF INFRASTRUCTURE

Dominic E. L. Ong[1]

[1]Swinburne Sarawak Research Centre for Sustainable Technologies
Swinburne University of Technology Sarawak Campus
Jalan Simpang Tiga, 93350 Kuching, Sarawak, Malaysia

Corresponding author: elong@swinburne.edu.my

SUMMARY

In practice, it is near impossible to obtain undisturbed samples of fibrous peat for laboratory testing in order to derive engineering design parameters, as its water and organic contents can be high as 1,200% and 60%, respectively. This forms the challenge that civil and geotechnical engineers have to face in the design of infrastructure on peaty soils. 2 case studies on the design and construction challenges in Sarawak peaty soils are presented. Through these case studies, it is hoped that the effects of construction on challenging peaty soils can be duly recognised so that care and due diligence are taken during both design and construction stages of any infrastructure project so as to minimise potential failures.

***Keywords**: peaty soils, prefabricated vertical drain, hydraulic sand-fill, shaft construction, anisotropy*

CASE STUDY 1: DEEP PEAT REPLACEMENT & PVD ON THICK, SOFT CLAY

INTRODUCTION TO GEOLOGY OF SITE

A 13.5km single-carriageway road was to be constructed in Sibu. The geology of Sibu is characterized by the Quaternary sediments, which consist mainly of clay, silt, sand and peat (Lam, 1998). Peat is a type of fibrous material which contains high organic content, usually in excess of 35%. Peat soils are mostly found on the coastal lowland area and poorly drained valleys. Water content of peat may be as high as 2000% (expressed as percentage of dry weight) (Chen et al., 1989) with high compressibility once drained, thus presenting a challenging engineering problem in Sarawak. If water is drained from the peat swamp, some 75% to 90% reduction of its volume may occur. This will result in excessive settlement when a road embankment is constructed on it.

SITE INVESTIGATION WORKS

Figure 1 shows the anticipated sub-surface soil profiles. It is observed that peat up to 10m deep with underlying soft soil of maximum thickness of 30m can be found at the later road chainages.

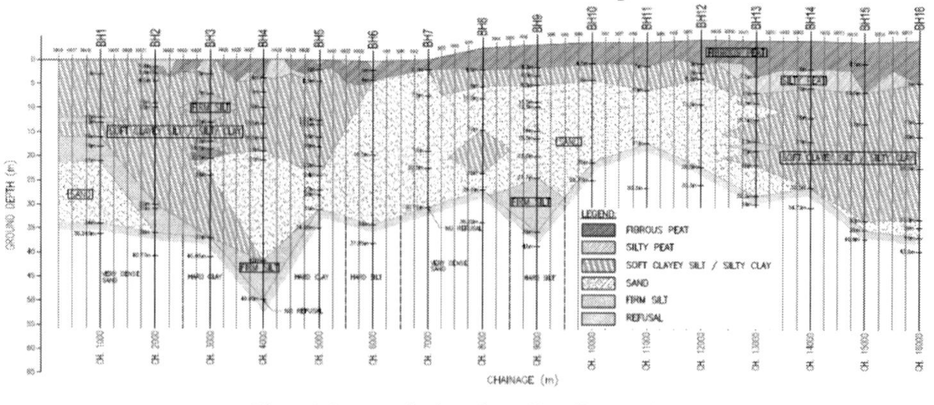

Figure 1: Interpreted sub-surface soil profiles at project site.

SOIL CHARACTERISATION

Figure 2(a) shows that generally, most boreholes show the presence of soft soil layers with low SPT N blow counts for the first 8m depth, except for BHs 6 and 7 where sand is encountered at a depth of 4m and 2m, respectively. BHs 2, 3, 14 and 16 show soft clay layers of up to 30m depth. Figure 2(b) generally confirms that fibrous peat with natural moisture content in excess of 300% can be found as top layers in most. The A-line plot as shown in Figure 2(c) shows that the soft soils (excluding peat samples) are generally more silty with a wide range of consistency.

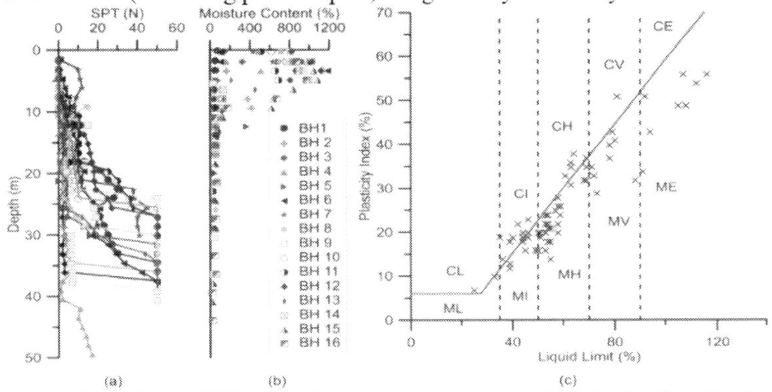

Figure 2: (a) Distribution of SPT N values, (b) moisture content and (c) plasticity chart for soft soil samples tested.

DESIGN CRITERIA AND ESTIMATED SETTLEMENTS

The design criteria states that total settlement of the road embankment should be less than 300mm in 3 years while differential settlement of less than 200mm is desired over 25m in 3 years. Such criteria could not be readily satisfied due to the estimated large post-construction consolidation settlement of the deep clays. As such, some form of ground improvement techniques are required to treat the peat and soft clays.

PROPOSED GROUND IMPROVEMENT SCHEME

It was proposed that underlying peat be replaced with sand-fill as the maximum depth of 10m was not widespread. The main advantage of peat replacement is to reduce the detrimental differential post-construction settlement and to allow the installation of pre-fabricated vertical drains (PVD) to treat the underlying thick soft soil layers whose untreated post-construction consolidation settlement is estimated to be in excess of 1m at certain locations.

CONSTRUCTION OF ROAD EMBANKMENT USING HYDRAULIC SAND-FILLING METHOD

Peat excavation & hydraulic sand-filling works

Firstly, peat excavation was performed using long-arm excavators as shown in Figure 3(a). The excavation started from the centre of the proposed road alignment moving backwards towards the edge of the embankment, in the transverse direction. The excavated peat was subsequently used for the construction of side bunds and the excess materials were spread over the remaining of the road reserve area. A 610-mm diameter mild steel pipeline transporting hydraulic sand-fill was laid from Batang Igan to the project site as shown in Figure 3(b).

Figure 3. (a) (left) Fibrous peat excavation using long-arm excavators and (b) (right) Hydraulic sand-filling works in progress.

Construction cases

For areas to be installed with PVD, two stages of sand-filling works were proposed. In the first stage, the excavated pit was filled up to the existing ground level and PVD installed. The second stage of works involved filling the ground to the required Finished Road Level (FRL) plus a minimum 0.5m high surcharge. The surcharge was subsequently removed and road embankment trimmed to the required formation level after 6 months of treatment. For areas where no surcharge and PVDs were required, the sand-filling works was carried out to the required formation level in one single stage.

Slope stability analyses

Slope stability analyses were carried out on embankments seated on the hydraulic sand-fill. The estimated factors of safety (FOS) provided by the design are all within allowable limits of 1.3 and 1.2 for short-term undrained and long-term drained analyses, respectively.

Ground improvement and field monitoring work

For field monitoring, Asoaka method was implemented to estimate the performance of PVD in treating the soft soils. Table 1 shows the comparison of calculated settlements with the representative measured settlements for various settlement plates.

Table 1: Selected results used for comparison of calculated and measured settlements.

Borehole	Settlement details			
	Calc 90% settlement	Settlement Plate	Measured settlement (mm)	Asoaka 90% settlement (mm)
BH2 (CH2000)	1425.7	S6@ch2150	954@623days	899.0
		S7@ch2360	1249@665days	1165.0
BH3 (CH3000)	837.3	S8@ch2800	545@561days	532.0
		S9@ch3140	1073@576days	990.0

Completion of works

Figure 4 shows the tar-sealed road pavement successfully completed after 1.5 years.

Figure 4: (a) (left) Just completed road and (b) (right) successful turfing of road shoulders.

CASE STUDY 2: EFFECT ON DEEP SHAFT EXCAVATION IN ORGANIC SOILS

INTRODUCTION

The Kuching Wastewater Management System (KWMS) Phase 1 was implemented to channel household grey and black water via a full-gravity underground network of sewer pipelines to a centralised wastewater treatment plant. Therefore, deep primary shafts with depths of between 10m and 25m were constructed to enable the launch and reception of micro-tunnelling boring machines (MTBM). The construction of shafts in the Tuang Formation posed great challenges especially in sandy and organic soils as appreciable ground water drawdown could be resulted, followed by the detrimental effects of ground settlements.

GEOLOGY OF AREA

The geology of the area is characterised by Quaternary deltaic deposits consisting layers of peat, clay, silt and sand overlying the older Tuang Formation of Kuching. At low-lying areas such as where the current project site was located, sediments were deposited due to receding sea level in the ancient times. The sediments remained trapped at foothills and plant matters started to accumulate to form horizontal beds of clays or silts with organic matters. Over long periods of time, the surface organic deposits rose and finally remained above the flood level. The underlying Tuang Formation rock has been described as 'erratic' by Ong & Choo (2011, 2012) in view of its highly sheared and weathered rock mass.

DETAILS OF DEEP SHAFT

Figure 5(a) shows the details of the proposed 7 m diameter, 16 m deep shaft. Advancing cast in-situ circular concrete caisson rings (each measuring 1.3 m in height, with 100 mm overlap) were then installed to provide structural support to the surrounding soils so that excavation inside the shaft could be carried out. The steel reinforcement used was nominal since the hoop stresses were designed to be taken entirely by the concrete.

EFFECT OF LEAKAGE AT UNDERLYING FRACTURED ROCK

At one of the many challenging excavation sites, when the shaft that was being excavated reached the moderately to highly weathered sandstone at depth of about 13.3 m, major leakages occurred and hence, the deep excavation works had to be suspended. Consequently and inevitably, ground water drawdown of about 5 m occurred, triggering settlement of 125 mm to nearby infrastructure as shown in Figure 5(b), mainly due to the relatively high permeability of the 8.5 m upper soft, peaty soils with SPT N = 0.

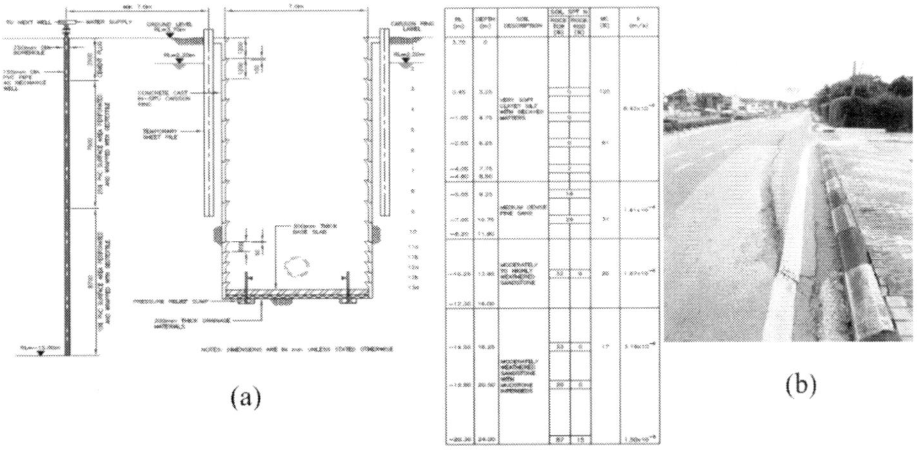

Figure 5: (a) Typical deep shaft construction with recharge well and (b) settlement caused by water drawdown.

GROUND WATER RESPONSES

The quantity and rate of the ground water that seeped into the leaking shaft could be estimated on site by simply calculating upwards from the base of the shaft the number of caisson rings flooded in the shaft after it was successfully pumped dry.

Table 2: Calculated seepage rates based on site measurements.

Elapsed days	No. of hours without pumping (hr)	No. of caisson rings filled with water		Total volume of water (m^3)	Seepage rate (m^3/hr)
		Full ring	Half ring		
Day 404	12	4	0	184.8	15.4
Day 405	11.5	3	0	138.6	12.0
Day 406	11	2.5	1	138.6	12.6
Day 407	9.5	2	2	138.6	14.6
Day 408	9	2.5	3	184.8	20.5
Day 409	20.5	4	3	254.0	12.4
Day 410	14.5	4	3	254.0	17.5
Day 413	15.5	1.5	3	138.6	8.9
Day 414	16.5	1.5	3	138.6	8.4
				Average seepage rate =	13.6

The amount of water that rose in the shaft overnight (no pumping activity) would then give a reliable estimate of seepage rate into the shaft. Table 2 shows the seepage rates measured over 9 occasions. The average measured seepage was 13.6 m^3/hr, which was comparable to the estimated ground water seepage rate of 17.4 m^3/hr based on the finite element seepage analyses conducted during the design stage (see Figure 6).

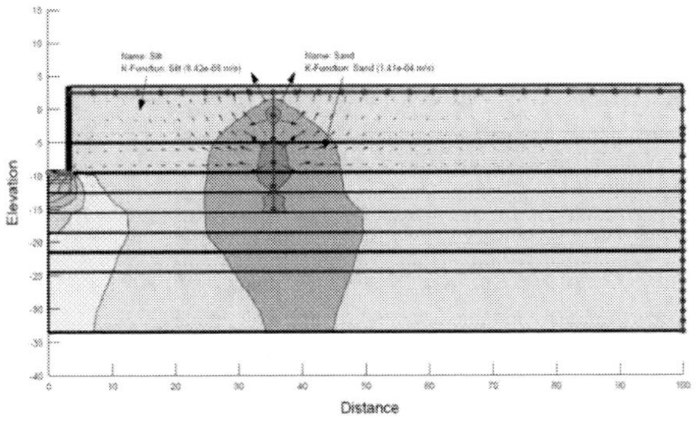

Figure 6: Typical transient seepage analysis showing total pressure head contours

GROUND TREATMENT WORKS

155mm diameter recharging wells were installed to try to recharge the depressed ground water table at site. Field monitoring showed that ground settlements of less than 7.5 mm were observed when the excavation works resumed when the recharging was carried out simultaneously. It took a further 17 days to complete the remaining excavation works, which consisted merely a further excavation of 1.8 m and casting of the base slab to complete the works.

GROUND RESPONSES

Finite element analysis was modelled using 2D transient analysis. Figure 7 shows the predicted and measured ground surface settlement profiles at various stages of the excavation. It is found that the ground settlement magnitudes and profiles are sensitive towards the ratio of k_h:k_v of the top peaty soil layer, where k_h is the horizontal soil permeability and k_v the horizontal. In general, the predicted and measured values show good agreement. Based on Figure 7, the predicted ground surface settlement profile using k_h:k_v ratios of 1, 3 , 5 and 10 consistently fall within the range of measured settlement values in both magnitudes and profiles. Similar range of anisotropy magnitudes in organic soil permeability had also been reported by Mesri et al. (1997), Younger et al. (1997) and Sobhan et al. (2007). This could be due to the greater effect of horizontal permeability than vertical within the soft silt layer with organic materials. Therefore, this implies that for any deep excavation works carried out in such soil condition, water seepage can be considerable in the horizontal direction.

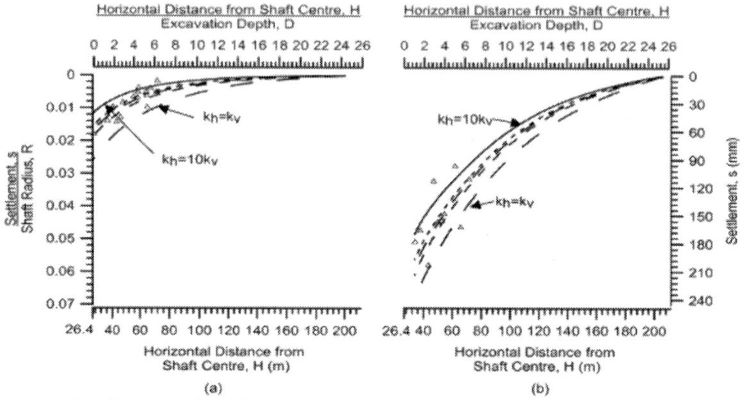

Figure 7: Predicted and measured settlement profiles when excavation depths approach (a) 9.7 m and (b) 13.3 m.

CONCLUSION

Two cases studies on the effects of compressibility and permeability of peaty soils on the design and construction of infrastructure have been discussed. The geotechnical challenges highlighted in this paper are not exhaustive. As Sarawak is located on the third largest island in the world, Borneo, with its generous coastline bordering the South China Sea as well as having the longest river in Malaysia, its geology is comparatively much younger than its Peninsular counterpart due to the presence of trapped peaty soils at foothills and river basins as well as thick, soft sediments found along its long coastlines, wide floodplains and thick deltas. In the field of geotechnical engineering, developing fundamental understanding of soil properties and behaviour based on field observational method via instrumentation and monitoring program is also part of the learning process, alongside good engineering designs and practical construction methodologies.

REFERENCES

1. Chen, S.P., Lam, S.K., Tan, Y.K. (1989). *Engineering characteristics of soft clay deposits in West Sarawak and associated problems.* Eco. & Soc. Comm. for Asia & Pacific, Kuching, Malaysia.
2. Lam, S.K. *Quaternary geology of the Sibu Town area, Sarawak.* Geological Survey Department, Malaysia, Map Report 10, 1998.
3. Mesri, G., Stark, T.D., Ajlouni, M.A. and Chen, C.S. (1997). *Secondary compression of peat with or without surcharging.* J. Geotech. and Geoenviron. Eng., ASCE, 123, pp. 411-421.
4. Ong, D.E.L., Choo, C.S. (2011). *Sustainable bored pile construction in erratic phyllite.* ASEAN-Australian Engineering Congress, Kuching.
5. Ong, D.E.L., Choo, C.S. (2012). *Bored pile socket in erratic phyllite of Tuang Formation.* GEOMATE 2012, 2nd Int. Conf. on Geotechnique, Construction Materials and Environment, KL, pp. 167-171.
6. Sobhan, K., Ali, H., Riedy, K. and Huynh, H. (2007). *Field and laboratory compressibility characteristics of soft organic soils in Florida.* Geo-Denver, ASCE, New Peaks in Geotechnics: Advances in Measurement and Modeling of Soil Behaviour.
7. Younger, J.S., Barry, A.J., Harianti S. and Hardy, R.P. (1997). *Construction of roads over soft and peaty ground.* Conf. on Recent Advances in Soft Soil Eng., Kuching, Sarawak, Malaysia.

Abstract No: A-327

MICROSTRUCTURE OF SOLIDIFIED PEAT AT DIFFERENT DECOMPOSITION LEVELS

Junita Abd Rahman[1*], Radin Maya Saphira Radin Mohamed[1] and Chan Chee Ming[2]

[1]*Faculty of Civil and Environmental Engineering, Universiti Tun Hussein Onn Malaysia, Johor, Malaysia*
[2]*Faculty of Engineering Technology, Universiti Tun Hussein Onn Malaysia, Johor, Malaysia*

**Corresponding author: junita.abdrahman@gmail.com*

SUMMARY

Peat is well known for their inherent high moisture content, porosity and compressibility. This soil type requires pre-treatment, such as solidification, to improve the engineering properties before loads from infrastructure above ground can be applied. There are three decomposition levels for the peat soil, namely fabric, hemic and sapric peat. In the present study, the soil samples were treated using ordinary Portland cement and coal ashes etrieved from the coal power plant. The peat soil was mixed with bottom ash and fly ash using four formulations. The microstructure of the soil was observed before and after solidification by using a Field Emission Spectroscopy Electron Microscope (FESEM). The analysis of FESEM showed needle -like objects known as ettringite which effectively enveloped the treated soil matrix in a progressive manner. The amount of ettringite was increased with the increasing of curing period, resulting in greater coverage of the voids in the soil. The ettringite, which are C-S-H and C-A-H, bound the soil particles and coal ashes, and consequently improves the soil strength and stiffness. However, the amount of ettringite presence in the mixed samples was found parellel with the Unconfined Compressive Stress (UCS) value recorded. The formation of ettringite depends on the proportion of cement and coal ashes, as well as the decomposition level of the organic matter in the soil. The decomposition level of the peat soil affects the environment for solidification and the physical presence of solid matter in the soil for binding with the admixtures (e.g. remaining organic debris). In general, mixtures with high UCS value produced more extensive ettringite development. Prolonged curing was also found to further improve the ettringite formation, leading to more significant strength and stiffness improvement.

Keywords: *decomposition level of peat, solidified peat, FESEM, ettringite, microstructure.*

INTRODUCTION

Peat is known with its challenging properties among geotechnical engineer. Hundreds hectare of peat which were previously agricultural land are being developed as housing and commercial lands (Ling *et al.*, 2014). Mass stabilization is one of the techniques to improve the initial strength of peat before any construction above ground can be built up. Several binders and fillers were studied for centuries and proven the workability of mass stabilization theory (Kalantari 2010 and Kolay *et al.*, 2011). Peat is derived from decomposed plant materials. Its physical characteristics very much depended on the plant origin and the humification degree. The less decomposed peat, known as fibric peat has larger particles and have lots of void in between it. These made fibric peat is able to retain more water compared to the moderately decomposed peat (hemic peat) and most decomposed peat (sapric peat). The difference in decomposition level also affect to the strength improvement after solidification. The organic content in peat make is shows significant different in most peat study. Studies by Axelsson *et al.* (2002) and Alwi (2007) shows that fibric peat can be improve its strength from 12kPa to 300 kPa. Although the additives and technique used in peat solidification study differ among the researchers, they concluded that sapric peat is the most difficult to be solidified. The strongest solidified sapric peat recorded so far was 37.5 kPa where Ordinary Portland Cement (OPC), sand and Ground Granulated Blast Furnace Slag were used as additives in the study (Wong *et al.*, 2009).

The microstructure of peat has been studied by Huat *et al.* (2011) as shown in Figure 1. The cellulose normally can be seen in fibric peat. The particle size is decreasing in increasing peat's decomposition levels. In most studies, the microscopic images shown a tighter particles in solidified peat compared to the loosely arrange particles for fresh peat. Table 1 compares SEM images of other researchers finding before and after solidification at D28. Different techniques and mixing portions were use in the respective studies. SEM images are suggested to be discussed along with its chemical precipitation using Electron Disperse X-Ray (EDX), X-Ray Diffraction (XRD) or X-Ray Fluorescence (XRF) (Ismail *et al.*, 2014).

In soil improvement study, cement has been widely used to improve the strength of soils. Horpibulsuk (2012) explained hydration process which produced ettringite (C-S-H and C-A-H gel); object that bind the soil particles thus improve the soil strength. Etrringite can be observed as needle-like-object in microscopic images. In the present study, the soil samples were treated using ordinary Portland cement and coal ashes. The microstructure of the raw material and solidified peat will be the focus of this paper.

(a) (b) (c)

Figure 1 SEM images of peats: (a) fibrous, (b) sapric and (c) hemic (Huat *et al.*, 2011)

Table 1 SEM images and q_u of solidified peat at D28 with different mixing portion and techniques

Reference	Mixing portion & techniques	Before solidification	After solidification
Islam and Hashim (2010)	100% cement, $CaCl_2$ (4 % of binder) and 25% of sand by volume of soil in-situ peat column q_u of solidified peat = 3000 kPa	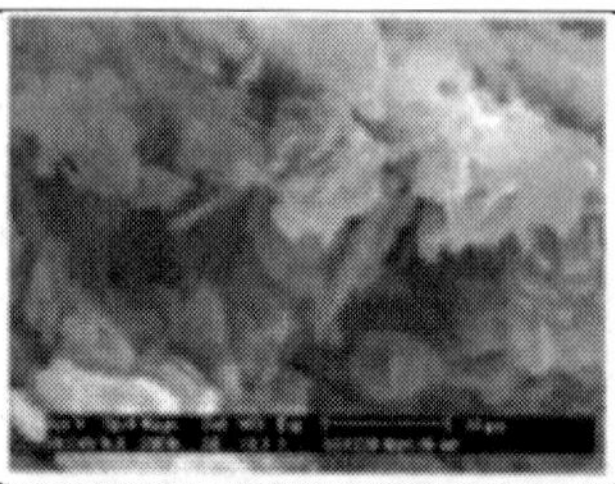	
Wong *et al.* (2013)	90% Portland Composite Cement: 10% Kaolin (4% Calcium Carbonate) Curing in water q_u of solidified peat =574 kPa	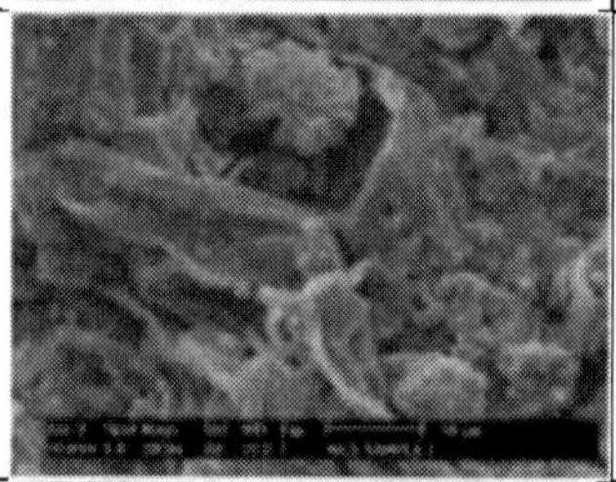	
Leong and Eriktius (2014)	38% municipal solid waste fly ash by dry weight Curing 28 days q_u of solidified peat = 100 kPa	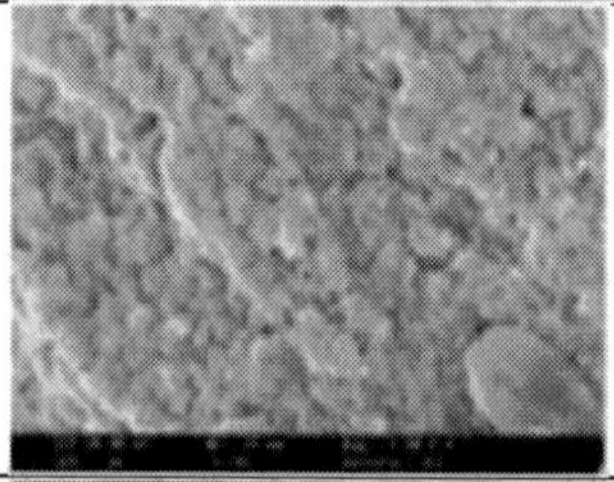	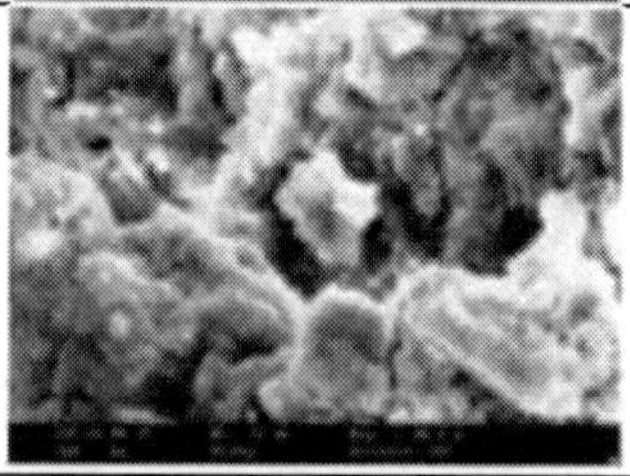
Moayedi *et al.* (2014)	CaO 6% Electrokinetic treatment q_u of solidified peat = 64 kPa		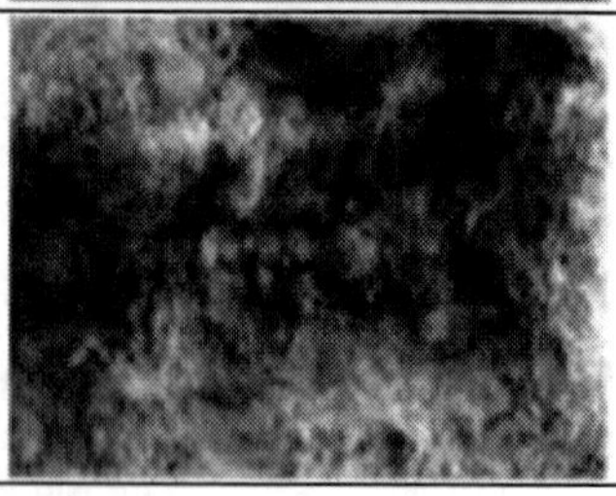

METHODS

Sample Preparation

Peat samples were obtained from Kg Medan Sari, Pontian, Johor, Malaysia. Samples were kept in container, covered with few layer of plastic bags and seal. The samples were placed in a controlled room with temperature of 25 °C to maintain the moisture. Additives used in this study were obtained from Tanjung Bin Power

Plant at Pontian, Johor. The coal ashes; bottom ash (BA) and fly ash (FA) were oven dried at 50 °C to make sure it moist free before mixing process is done. All peat types were mixed using 4 formulation; 100% OPC, 50%OPC + 50%BA; 50%OPC + 25%BA + 25%FA and 25%OPC + 50%BA + 25%FA with two water/binder ratio; 1 and 3. All mixed samples were cured and undergo unconfined compressive stress (UCS) test and imaging test at day 7, 14, 28 and 56.

RESULTS AND DISCUSSION

The UCS test was carried out at four curing days for all mixed samples. Figure 2 shows that there are two patterns of peat solidification for all types of peat. The first pattern shows that the strength of solidified peat increase with increasing of curing days. The second pattern shows decrease of strength after curing 28 and 56 days.

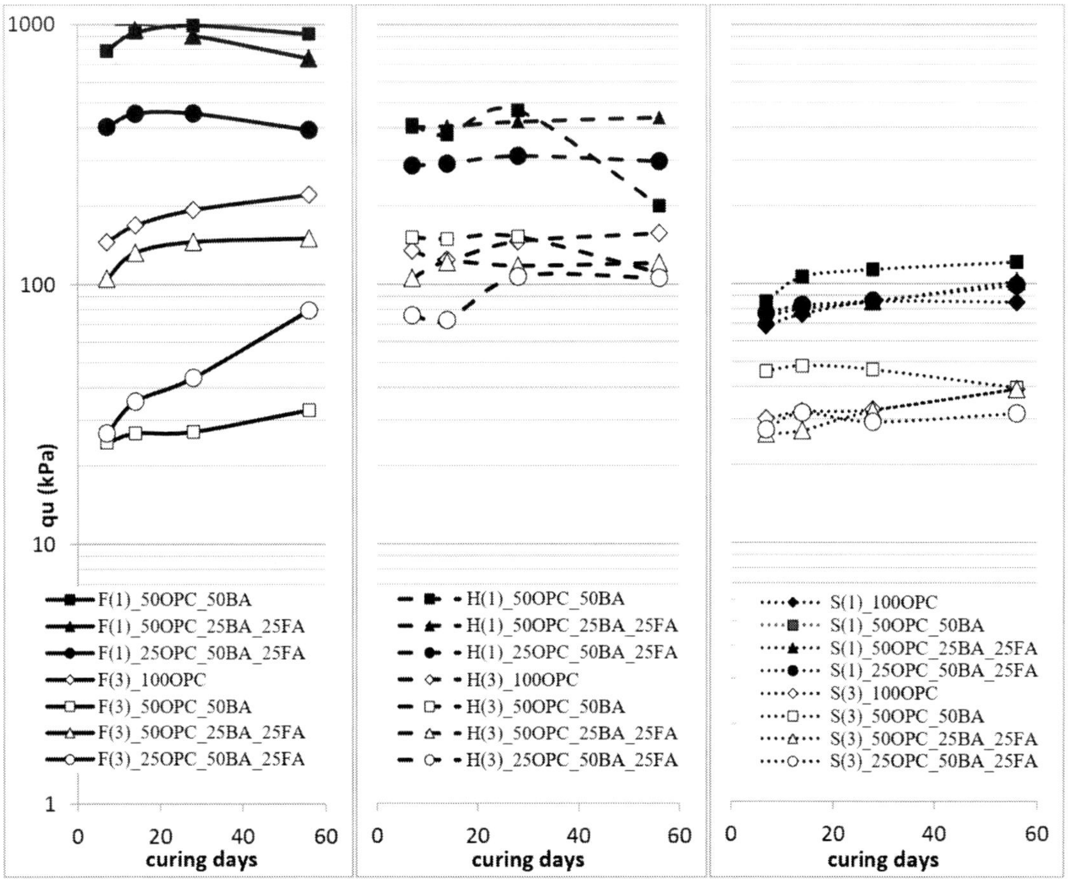

a) Fabric peat b) Hemic peat c) Sapric peat

Figure 2 q_u versus curing days

MICROSCOPIC IMAGE

The microscope imaging was done on all samples before and after solidification. The physical shape, morphological view and size of particles in a sample could be obtained from this method. Figure 3 shows the variety of shapes and sizes of peat, binders and filler. The main components in the respective materials were also labelled in the figure. Physically, the FA, ettringite, humic acid and cement paste were found filling the porous spaces in peat. The variety of sizes of FA and ettringite, fit nicely to these porous spaces.

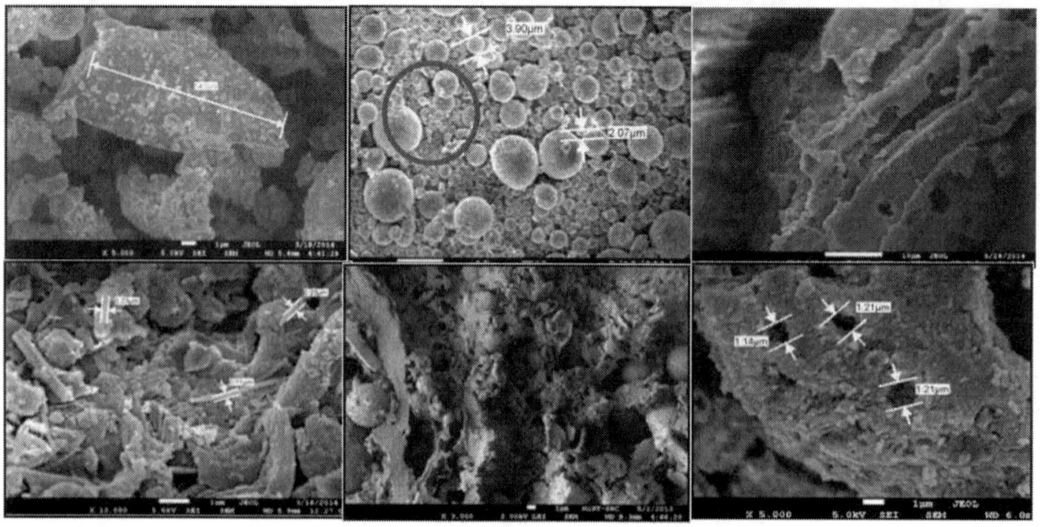

a) Calcium carbonat in OPC b) Fly ash c) Humic acid
d) Ettringite (CSH and CAH gel) e) Void due to arrangement of fiber f) Void in BA

Figure 3 Particles and its sizes in the peat-binder-filler mixture

As discussed in earlier section, there are two patterns recorded for peat solidification. The first pattern (A) shows increasing q_u is parallel with curing days. The second pattern (B) shows that q_u increase at D7 and D14 followed by decrease it q_u on D28 or D56. The differences in the FESEM images of these two samples are compared. Mixture of H(1)50OPC_25BA_25FA (Figure 4) is selected to represent pattern A while mixture of H(1)_100OPC (Figure 5) is selected for pattern B. The patterns are summarized in Table 2.

Table 2 Summary of patterns in solidified peat

Pattern	Description	Sample
A	q_u increase in parallel with curing days	Mixture of H(1)50OPC_25BA_25FA
B	q_u increase at D7 and D14 followed by decrease q_u on D28 or D56	Mixture of H(3)_50OPC_50BA

The images of solidified peat with improving strength show that the hydration products growing from the cement grains connecting the fly ash particles and peat - cement clusters together. Some of the surfaces of fly ash particles were coated with hydration products. At D7, the ettringite was not obvious if compared to D14. It shows that the formation of ettringite increases over time. Image of D28 shows that amount of ettringite increase rapidly and can be captured easily. The ettringite is present in large quantity. Different phenomenons captured at D56 where the ettringite seem to be connected with one another thus interlock with the soil particles. The thickness of the ettringite was also found increasing with the increase of curing days.

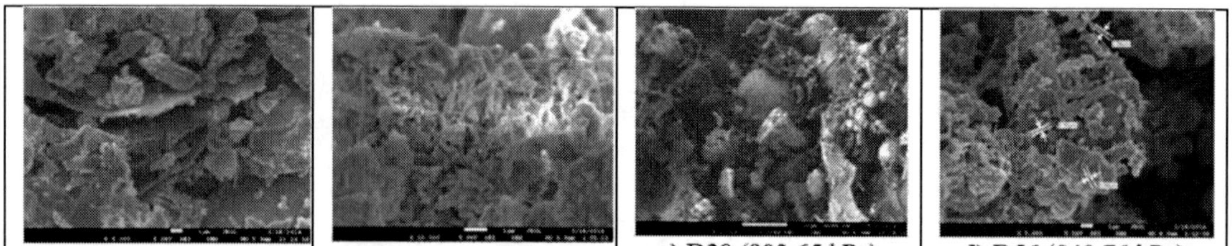

a) D7 (737.38 kPa) **b)** D14 (792.20 kPa) **c)** D28 (903.65 kPa) **d)** D56 (949.76 kPa)

Figure 4 Sample labelled as H(1)50OPC_25BA_25FA

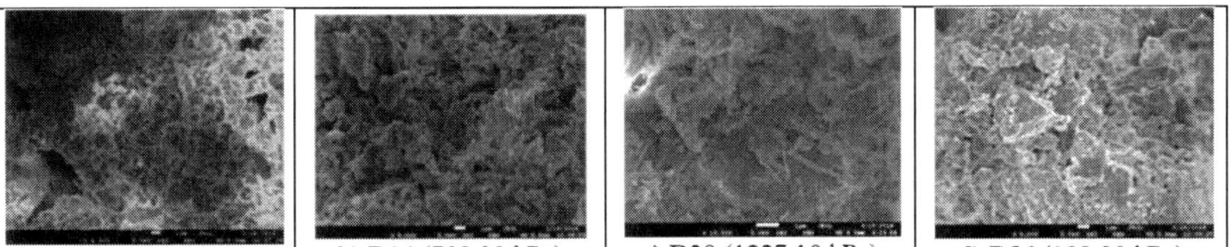

a) D7 (764.00 kPa)	b) D14 (793.30 kPa)	c) D28 (1227.10 kPa)	d) D56 (199.80 kPa)

Figure 5 Sample labelled as H(3)_50OPC_50BA

H (1)_100OPC was found decreasing in strength on D56. The FA, an element of OPC can be easily captured in D7 and D14 samples. Ettringite was also observed at D7 and D14 samples. At D28, ettringite was found fixated to the sample. The ettringite amount has lessened and merely found at D56. The sample was rather uniform. The FA also merely found in D56 sample.

The humic acid may be re-activated after the hydration process has ended, or maybe accumulated due to the decomposition of the peat (microbial activity) was back to active. Theoretically, microorganisms still active in cement mixture (Ismail *et al.*, 1993 and Cwalina, 2008). The same findings were found to all samples that experiencing decrease in strength at D28 and D56.

The findings by Horpibulsuk *et al.* (2012) were similar with current work findings. Horpibulsuk *et al.* (2012), found that after 4 hours of curing (Figure 6(a)), the soil clusters and the pores were covered and filled by the cement gel (hydrated cement). Over time (Figure 6(b)), the hydration products in the pores were clearly observed and the soil–cement clusters tend to be larger because of the growth of cementitious products over time.

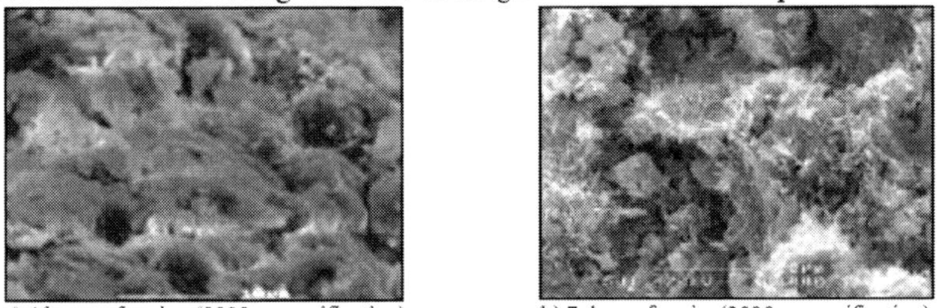

a) 4 hours of curing (3000x magnification) b) 7 days of curing(3000x magnification)

Figure 6 SEM photos of 10 % OPC at different curing time (Horpibulsuk, 2012)

CONCLUSION

Ettringite can be said a dominant factor that increase the peat strength. The amount and size of the ettringite increase with the increase of UCS value and vice versa. The loss of the ettringite could be caused by re-activation of microbe in the non-optimum mixture of solidified peat. Study on the effect and impact of optimum mixture may open a new dimension in peat solidification.

ACKNOWLEDGEMENT

The authors wish to acknowledge the financial support from Fundamental Research Grant Scheme (FRGS) (Vot 1453) , Universiti Tun Hussein Onn Malaysia.

REFERENCES

1. Alwi, A. (2008). *Ground improvement of Malaysian peat soils using stabilized peat column techniques*. PhD thesis, University of Malaya, Kuala Lumpur, Malaysia.
2. Axelsson, K., Johansson, Sven-Erick. and Anderson, R. (2002). *Stabilization of organic soils by cement and pozzolanic reaction-feasability study*. Swedish Deep Stabilization Research Centre, Report 3, 1–51.
3. Horpibulsuk, S. (2012). Strength and Microstructure of Cement Stabilized Clay, Scanning Electron Microscopy. ISBN: 978-953-51-0092-8, InTech.
4. Huat, B.B.K., Kazemian, S., Prasad, A. and Barghchi, M. (2011). State of an art review of peat: General perspective. *International Journal of the Physical Sciences Vol. 6(8)*, 1988-1996.
5. Islam, M. S. and Hashim, R. (2010). Behaviour of stabilised peat: A field study. *Scientific Research and Essays* Vol. 5(17), 2366-2374.

6. Ismail, N., Mohd. Saman, H., Kamaruddin, K. and Md. Jaafar, M. F. (2014). *The Cement Hydration, Chemical Phases and Its Microstructural Examination of Microbed Cement Based Material*. IEEE Colloquium on Humanities, Science and Engineering (CHUSER 2014). Penang, Malaysia. 164- 169.
7. Kalantari, B. (2010). *Stabilization of tropical fibrous peat using ordinary portland cement and additives*. PhD thesis. Universiti Putra Malaysia.
8. Kolay, P.K, Sii, H. Y. and Taib, S.N.L.(2011).Tropical Peat Soil Stabilization using Class F Pond Ash from Coal Fired Power Plant *International Journal of Civil and Environmental Engineering* 3:2. 79-83.
9. Leong, E. C. and Eriktius, D. T. (2013). Improvement of peaty soils with municipal solid waste fly ash. *Environmental Geotechnics* Volume 1 Issue EG4.200–209.
10. Ling, F. N. L., A. Kassim, K., A. Karim, A. T., Tan, C. K. and Tiong, K. P. C. (2014). Geotechnical Properties of Malaysian Organic Soils: Case Study in Batu Pahat, Johor. *International Journal of Integrated Engineering*, Vol. 6 No. 2. 52-59.
11. Moayedi, H., Nazir, R., Kazemian, S. and Huat, B. K. (2014). Microstructure analysis of electrokinetically stabilized peat. *Measurement* 48. 187–194.
12. Wong, L. S., Hashim, R. and Ali, F. (2013). Improved strength and reduced permeability of stabilized peat: Focus on application of kaolin as a pozzolanic additive. *Journal of Construction and Building Materials 40*. 783–792.
13. Wong, L. S., Hashim, R. and Ali, F. (2009). Unconfined Compressive Strength of Cemented Peat. *Australian Journal of Basic and Applied Sciences,* 3(4): 3850-3856.

Abstract No: A-306

PEAT AND ORGANIC SOILS CHALLENGES IN ROAD CONSTRUCTION IN SARAWAK: JKR SARAWAK EXPERIENCE

Vincent Tang Chok Khing

Public Works Department Sarawak

*Corresponding author: vincetck@sarawak.gov.my

SUMMARY

Road construction on peat/organic soils has always posed challenges to Engineers, Contractors and policy-makers, be it a technical, contractual obligation, or cost implication. The success of road construction on soft soils relies on various important factors such as proper planning, analysis, design, construction, control and supervision. For Engineers, the primary boundary conditions are the stability and allowable settlement in terms of serviceability limits both as a function of time. Our current observation reveals that many of the road embankments and culvert foundation failures are associated with geotechnical factors. Majority of these failures are still repeating and quite identical / similar in nature that they are caused by failure to comply with one or a combination of the above factors. This paper presents some of the case histories of the road embankment construction closely related to the geotechnical factors investigated by the Author. Lastly, some simple guidelines on Method of Treatment, Cost and Design Principle to prevent future embankment failures related to geotechnical factors on soft ground are presented.

INTRODUCTION

Sarawak has approximately 1.7 million ha of tropical peat that covers 13% of the total land area (12.4 million ha.). It is the largest area of peatland in Malaysia. It constitutes nearly 63% of the total peatland of the country. More than 80% of the peats are more than 2.5 m depth.

Peat is identified as soils with more than 35% organic matter content. Peatlands present a challenge for road construction in tropical terrain like the lowlands of Sarawak. The lowlands in Sarawak constitute the largest peat areas in Malaysia with 1,657,600 sq. km which make up 13% of the State (Singh *et al.*, 1997). The aerial extent of peat swamp forests in Sarawak is shown in Figure 1.

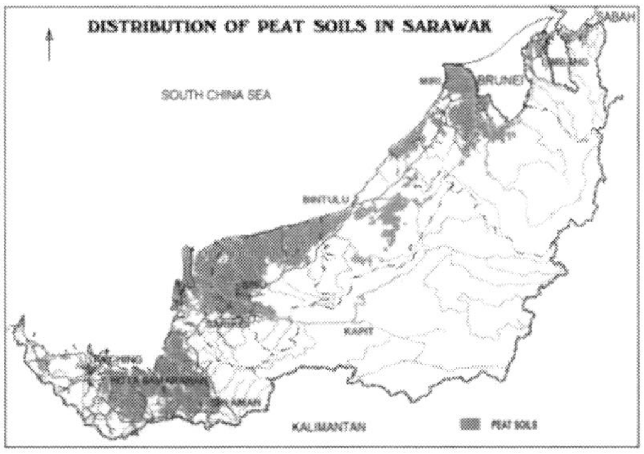

Fig. 1: Distribution of Peat in Sarawak. (Source: Jabatan Pertanian Sarawak 2001)

It is seen that peat is aerially distributed over many parts of the State and the area in different administrative divisions (Singh *et al.*, 1997) is shown in Table 1.

Sibu Town is located at the confluence of the Batang Rajang and Batang Igan. Sibu Town and its surroundings are overlain with substantial formations of peat soils, almost unrivalled when compared to other parts of Malaysia. The peat formations in some parts of Sibu Town are well over 10 metres in depth. Land subsidence is a serious problem in Sibu Town with frequent refilling and repairing being carried out to reinstate structures, platforms and infrastructure.

The problems in designing and construction of embankment over very soft compressible peat and organic soils in Sibu Division arise due to the high compressibility (Cc=1.045-1.64), low shear strength (Cu=<10kPa), high natural Moisture Content and high ground water level (near to ground surface).

The engineering term "soft soils" tends to be used very loosely to refer "peat/organic soils" and "soft clay" which cannot support fill of reasonable height above the existing ground level. The reasonable height could mean 1 metre for some people but 3 or 4 metres for the others. Thus, such a way of defining "soft soils" is subjective and could result in confusion and disputes in some instances. From soil mechanics approach, we shall define "soft soils" with an undrained shear strength less than 40 kN/m^2 based on scale of strength given in B.S.5930:1981.

Table 1: Areas under peat in the various administrative divisions in Sarawak (Singh *et al.*, 1997)

Division	**Area (sq. km)**
Kuching Administration Division	23,059
Samarahan Administration Division	192,775
Sri Aman Administration Division	283,076
Sibu Administration Division	540,800
Sarikei Administration Division	169,900
Bintulu Administration Division	146,121
Miri Administration Division	276,579
Limbang Administration Division	25,300
Total	1,657,600

METHODOLOGIES OF INFRASTRUCTURE CONSTRUCTION OVER PEAT & ORGANIC SOILS

A wide variety of techniques for engineering construction over soft clays have been adopted by engineers. These range from pure structural options (e.g. Viaducts, bridges, pile embankments) to soil mechanics alternatives (e.g. surcharge, preloading, etc). In the soil mechanics approach, sophisticated variants, such as the use of vertical drains and vacuum preloading are commonly applied solutions. The following are some of the conventional displacement construction methods and current soil mechanics construction methodologies of infrastructure development on peat /organic soils adopted by the relevant government agencies and developers in Sibu Division.

CONVENTIONAL DISPLACEMENT APPROACH OF INFRASTRUCTURE DEVELOPMENTS

The New Sibu Airport Road and Salim/New Airport By Pass which was constructed in the 1990s provided a faster linkage of the town center with the New Sibu Hospital and the New Sibu Airport. Most sections of the proposed dual carriageway passed through a very soft peaty terrain. Due to fund and time constraints, the roads were constructed by JKR in-house design team adopting the conventional methods of 'cut and fill' or displacement method by dumping of fill materials using Bulldozer, progressively onto the soft ground. No proper soil investigation works were carried out to determine the thickness of the soft soil and ground water conditions. No geotechnical parameter inputs were incorporated in the design for ground treatment. The road embankment went into severe instability problem coupled with differential settlement during the construction stage. It has been observed that the compensating fills for some of the deep peat areas (approximately 10 meters) are very large or "not sustainable"; meaning that stabilization of the filled ground at the desired platform level cannot be achieved (as shown on photographs in Fig. 2.1a to 2.1c taken during the construction stage)

Fig. 2.1a & 2.1b : "Displacement Method" of Road Construction on Peat & Organic Soils along New Sibu Airport Road.

Fig. 2.1c : "Displacement Method" of Road Construction on Peat & Organic Soils along Salim/New Airport By Pass

Fig. 2.1d : Highlight on the defects of Conventional Method of Road Construction on Peat & Organic Soils

This "displacement method" of road embankment construction was time consuming as the fill materials take time to sink down to the firm bearing stratum due to buoyancy force (high water table level). The rate of filling was not controlled with the help of geotechnical instrumentation and many sections of road embankment experienced rotational base failure during construction. The worst experiences are the long term settlement of road embankment and pavement deformations which contribute to unsafe, poor riding quality and high road maintenance costs (as shown in Fig. 2.1d) JKR were spending about RM 1.5 to 2 million annually for the topping up (approximately 300mm) and resurfacing works for these sections of road to improve the vertical alignment and the pavement deformation. Differential settlement of road embankment problems still persists today. Moreover, the service life of the roads constructed under Conventional Method "Displacement Method" is short and road maintenance costs are exorbitantly high and financially unsustainable.

SUSTAINABLE APPROACHES OF INFRASTRUCTURE DEVELOPMENT

The recent case history of the following infrastructure projects highlights the concepts of sustainable construction on the peat and organic soils in Sibu Town.

The Jalan Nang Sang/Teku Link was constructed with new methodology of *"Partial Replacement of Peat Soils with preloading"*. The very soft compressible peat soils are excavated out and replaced with sand fill materials that provide a stronger and less compressible foundation. The experience on this road indicates that the excavation and replacement depth up to a maximum of 5 m is viable in terms of cost and practicality. The excavation was extended to the toe of the embankment to increase the stability of the embankment. Due to anticipation of high post-construction-settlement of the varying peat depth along the roadway, 1.5 meters surcharge was introduced with rest period of 9 months for the whole stretch. Upon completion of pre-consolidation of road formation, surcharge was removed based on *"ASOKA Method of 90% primary consolidation Analysis"* and subsequently the road pavement works were completed with premix sealing. The geotechnical instrumentation works were adopted to monitor excess pore water pressure and consolidation settlement during and after construction. To date, this stretch of road has minimal pavement deformation recorded at the bridge and culverts approach due to secondary consolidation settlement of the embankment. The average post construction differential settlement is not more than 150mm for duration of two (2) years. It is proven to be viable and sustainable to construct road with ground improvement techniques.

Fig. 2.2a.

Fig. 2.2b.

Fig. 2.2c.
Fig. 2.2e.

Fig. 2.2d.
Fig. 2.2f.

Fig. 2.2a. to 2.2f. Stages of construction

• Settlement Calculations based on Surface Investigation & laboratory testing datas

Borehole	Total Settlement (mm)	Total Settlement for 1 year (mm)	Total Settlement for 2 years (mm)
BH1	347.1	44.5	62.5
BH2	1425.7	132.6	185.1
BH3	837.3	206.0	291.3
BH4	797.0	146.1	206.2
BH5	675.2	122.9	173.5
BH8	241.1	106.6	149.5
BH9	44.1	43.3	-
BH10	49.6	46.3	-
BH11	105.3	76.5	95.7
BH12	87.3	82.9	-
BH13	1020.3	419.1	589.7

Remarks: GROUND TREATMENT REQUIRED DUE TO EXCESSIVE SETTLEMENT

Table 2 : Settlement Criteria and Calculations

In conclusion, this method sums up the essential requirements for a successful embankment construction over very soft compressible soils as follow:

1. Appreciation of the project requirements in terms of serviceability criteria (deformation tolerances, bearing capacity, etc), cost implications (construction and maintenance costs), and time (construction time, service life).
2. Thorough knowledge of the site geology through proper desk study, collection of geological information; effective planning and supervision of subsurface investigation works and laboratory testing for the acquisition of necessary reliable parameters for geotechnical designs.
3. Proper geotechnical design practices to address both stability of the embankment and control of deformation.
4. Full time proper supervision of the construction works by dedicated qualified QAQC personnel/Engineers.
5. Careful and proper monitoring of the geotechnical instrumentation on the performance of the embankment during and after construction.

CASE HISTORIES OF GEOTECHNICAL DISTRESS ON PEAT/ORGANIC & SOFT SOILS

Case History No. 1

The project is the Upgrading of Kuching/Sibu federal trunk road from Julau Junction to New Sibu Airport. The road embankment along Ch. Km 8 + 450 to Km 8 +700 was constructed with Ground Treatment Type 3-BambooMattress/Geotextile design(Peat Areas) as shown in Fig. 3 below but failed to sustain with even 1m height of fill above the existing ground.

Subsequent soil investigation carried out revealed that the peat depth of the site is about 14m underlying with a 3m deep of soft clay and stiff shale formation beneath. The natural moisture content of peat is over 1000% with organic content exceeding 75%. The SPT N-value was recorded "Zero value per 300mm penetration of SPT Hammer" from 0 m to 14 m for the soft organic soils layer.

The construction of the whole embankment was based on stage construction with 15m wide counterberms and instrumentation works installed to monitor the excess pore water pressure and rate of settlement. The entire section of road sealing works was delayed for more than 12 months. To date, the road embankment still undergoes excessive settlement exceeding the serviceability limit of JKR requirement.

The lesson learned on this case study is the inappropriate design approach based on soil mechanics method. The structural design method (pile-supported embankment) should have been adopted to arrest the deep-seated soft organic soil stability problem in the long run and reduce the construction time. A simple bearing capacity equation (q_{allow}=(Su *N_c/FOS) check on the embankment stability should have been adopted as the undrained shear strength of the soft organic soils is in the range of 5 to 10kPa only. The post construction settlement over a duration of 3 years has exceeded 350mm. This is another proof of unsatisfactory design of road construction methodology on soft organic soils.

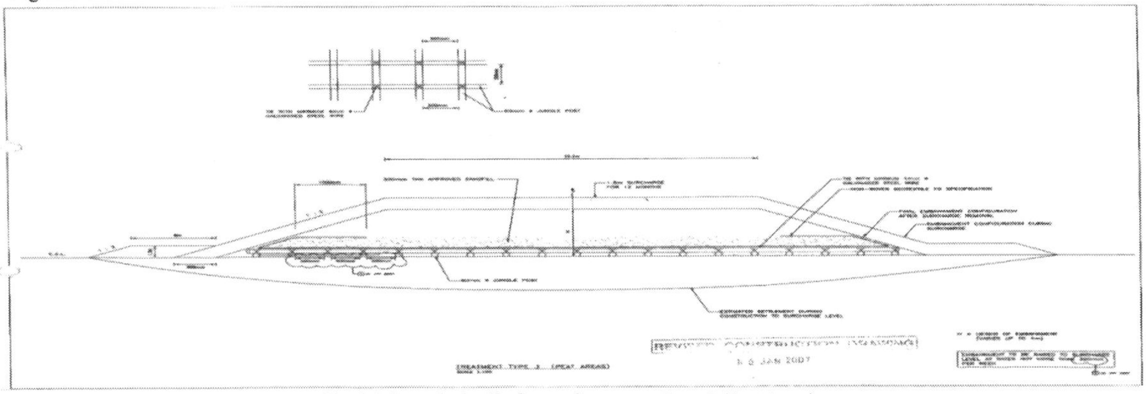

Fig. 3 Schematic detail of ground treatment Type 3 (Peat Areas)

Case History No. 2

The project is the Sg. Bidut access road constructed by hydraulic sandfill based on Total Replacement and Surcharging approach. The overall serviceability limit of the road based on function and performance criteria on settlement seem to be satisfactory based on our 36 months post construction observational studies. However, one section of the road embankment along Km 12 + 100 to Km 12 + 400 recently undergoes severe lateral movement and collapse of road embankment at the R. C. Culvert due to the over draining of ground water from the surrounding oil palm plantation development. (as shown on photographs in Fig. 3.2a to 3.2b)

The lesson learned is the avoidance of using peat soils as the retention bund material for retaining the hydraulic sandfill (fine-grained sands) embankment due to the high permeability of the fibrous peat soils and could not serve as "clay liner" to prevent seepage problem in the event of "Critical Hydraulic Gradient" resultant from blockage or inadequate discharge capacity of balancing culvert. The lowering of future ground water regime and differential level should be incorporated in the design of long term embankment stability of sandfill embankment.

However, another lesson learned is the serviceability limit of the road which is well design within the design criteria. The 36-month maximum post construction settlement data along the whole longitudinal profile of the road is less than 289mm.The maximum change of grade over 25m chainage is less than 1.5%.These data indicate good riding quality of the road based on sustainable road construction methodology on peat/organic & soft ground.

Fig. 3.2a.

Fig. 3.2b.

PROJECT: JALAN SG. BIDUT SIBU DIVISION SARAWAK.

GEOTECHNICAL ANALYSIS ON CONSOLIDATION SETTLEMENT OF ROAD EMBANKMENT DURING & POST CONSTRUCTION

Borehole	Chainage	Calculated 90% Settlement(mm)	Settlement Plate	Measured Settlement(mm)	Asaoka 90% Settlement(mm)	Post construction Settlement(mm)@-36months	Methods of Construction
BH 1	1000(Area 'A') 1450	347.1 347.1	S2 @ Ch.0270 S3 @ Ch.0800 S4 @ Ch.1150	301 @ 350 days 188 @ 554 days 288 @ 584 days	272 176 274	163 @ Ch.1000 284 @ Ch.1450	0.5 m Top Soil excavation
BH 2	2000(Area 'B')	1425.7	S5 @ Ch.1600 S6 @ Ch.2150 S7 @ Ch.2300	532 @ 623 days 964 @ 623 days 1249 @ 665 days	556 [illegible] 1100	131 @ Ch.2150 141 @ Ch.2300	Full depth excavation of peat layer + PVD + 0.5m surcharge
BH 3	3000(Area 'B')	637.3	S8 @ Ch.2800 S9 @ Ch.3140	545 @ 591 days 1073 @ 576 days	532 900	51 @ Ch.2825 117 @ Ch.2875 156 @ Ch.3050	
BH4	4000(Area 'B')	757.8	S10 @ Ch.3556 S11 @ Ch.4145 S12 @ Ch.4425	1041 @ 540 days 771 @ 268 days 589 @ 512 days	964 N.A. 540	170 @ Ch.4550	Full depth excavation of peat layer + PVD + 0.5m surcharge
BH5	5000(Area 'B')	875.2	S13 @ Ch.4825 S14 @ Ch.5135	405 @ 268 days 679 @ 511 days	N.A. 632		Full depth excavation of peat layer + PVD + 0.5m surcharge
BH6	6000 (Area 'B')		S15 @ Ch.5600 S16 @ Ch.6110	77 @ 183 days 94 @ 183 days	73 100	207 @ Ch.5950 200@Ch.6110	Full depth excavation of peat layer + PVD + 0.5m surcharge
BH7	7000(Area 'C')		S17 @ Ch.6600	129 @ 182 days	133	33 @ Ch.6800 117 @ Ch.7675 186 @ Ch.8000	Full depth excavation of peat layer

Table 3: Geotechnical Analysis on Construction Settlement of Road Embankment During and Post Construction.

CONCLUSION

In conclusion, this paper sums up the case histories of geotechnical distress of road construction and lessons learned on the essential requirements for a successful embankment construction over soft compressible peat or soft organic soils.

Therefore, under all the 5 phases of road construction spanning from the Concept Phase, Design Phase, Implementation Phase, Completion Phase up to Maintenance Phase, the following criteria should be taken into consideration in order to ensure that road construction over peat/organic & soft soil is feasible and sustainable throughout the designed service life.

- Appreciation of the project requirements in terms of serviceability criteria (deformation tolerances, bearing capacity, etc.), cost implications (construction and maintenance costs), and time (construction time, service life).
- Thorough knowledge of the site geology through proper desk study, collection of geological information; effective planning and supervision of subsurface investigation works and laboratory testings for the acquisition of necessary reliable parameters of geotechnical designs.
- Proper geotechnical design practices to address both stability of the embankment and control of deformation.
- Full time proper supervision of the construction works by dedicated qualified QAQC personnel/Engineers.
- Proper monitoring, evaluation and interpretation of the geotechnical instrumentation datas on the performance of the embankment during and after construction.
- Review of the current techniques of road design and construction on deep-seated soft soils (peat/organic soils).
- Database collections and observational studies on the recent new techniques of proven infrastructure design and construction.
- Formulate specific guidelines for infrastructure planning, design and construction practices on soft soils (peat/organic soils and soft clay).
- Change of stakeholder's mindset to consider sustainable methods of construction for better long term sustainability of infrastructure developments.
- The relevant government agencies should recognize the escalating cost of maintenance on unsustainable construction methodology and provide "incentive package" for the ratepayers of sustainable infrastructure development.
- Fund allocation for research studies on sustainable methodology of infrastructure design (serviceability limit) on various types of soft soils foundation.

References

1. Map Report 10 – Quaternary Geology of the Sibu Town Area, Sarawak 1998 by Lam Sia Keng of the Geological Survey Department Malaysia.
2. Sarawak Geology by Singh et al, 1997
3. Peat Formations in Sibu Town and related Engineering Issues by Tai Lee Yoon, Director, Jurutera Jasa (Sarawak) Sdn. Bhd.
4. Public Works Department Sarawak.
5. Urban Drainage Masterplan Report for Sibu Town 1988 prepared for DID by Jurutera Jasa (Sarawak) Sdn. Bhd.
6. Compilation of Results from the S.I. Reports lodged with the Geological Department of Sarawak by Lee Kuok Wei.

Abstract No: A-403

PEATLAND FLOOD PROTECTION ENGINEERING – APRIL EXPERIENCE IN COASTAL RIAU

J. Bathgate and T. Nainggolan

APRIL Group, PO Box 1080 Pekanbaru – Riau Sumatra, Indonesia 28000

**Corresponding author: john_bathgate@aprilasia.com*

SUMMARY

APRIL manages extensive peat soil concessions that include natural forest and plantation. Area for fiber plantations is limited and includes the margins of seasonal floodplains in a climate having 500 mm of rain in wettest months. It is highly desirable, now that no more concession land is forthcoming, to fully utilize all marginal land including floodplains. APRIL could find little previous experience of tropical peat engineering to draw on and so developed its own. A peaty-silt soil dike dating to 2007 has kept most floods out of 800 ha of floodplain plantation; it is now being rebuilt to larger dimensions. A first all-peat dike was completed in 2014. It has withstood floods to date enabling fiber production on 1,000 ha of floodplain, previously problematic, to be on track to full production. *Acacia crassicarpa*, the tree crop, tolerates wet soils but not prolonged flooding. These protection works aim to limit flood duration and hasten post flood drainage. Where possible the flood waters are diverted to flow along riparian corridors of natural peat swamp forest and away from plantation. Planning requires hydro data to determine the flood return period, duration and levels, the dike gradient as well as catchment spatial data. Reclamation economy of scale is always a challenge. Dikes are constructed from peat soil taken from a canal dug immediately on each side. Long arm hydraulic bucket excavators are the standard tool for construction. Depending on the in-situ bulk density of peat, each cubic measure of raised compacted dike requires two units of dug material. Design aims to hold a head of 1.5 m flood water, plus a minimum of 1 m freeboard. If needed flood water will be released into the plantation canal before the safe head is exceeded. A dike cross section of around 40 square meters has proven adequate for sites having minimal flow energy of flood water. Geo-felt folded between layers of compacted peat, and sand filled bags, have been used to reinforce critical points. Work is normally done in the drier season when river flows are lowest. Weathering loss of the dike material must be replaced every few years, and material must eventually be brought in. The dike crest can be surfaced with mineral material to serve as a light vehicle road, and grass or bamboo established to assist stability.

***Keywords**: floodplain, catchment plan, hydro data, flood return period, peat dike, flood diversion corridor, acacia plantation, flood duration tolerance, geo-fabric*

INTRODUCTION TO FLOOD PROTECTION

Now that APRIL development of concession lands is completed with more land unlikely in the current policy setting, attention has turned to intensifying fiber output from the most challenging bits of concessions. For example, seasonal flood plains of shallow peat and silt soil, long since cleared of natural cover that had conservation value, have been brought into production. This sort of land tends to be interspersed with marginal small holdings; a patchwork of fragmented ownership (Bathgate *et al.*, 2011) that rule out the landscape scale flood diversion scheme as an option. In the case of one APRIL plantation on seasonal floodplain (Figure 1), much of the upstream catchment has been cleared for agriculture without regard to watershed function. Floods now occur on average 100 days a year (Figure 2); for lower parts of this plantation the options are to build high dikes or restore to flood-tolerant natural forest.

In another location a dike barrier has been built to deflect waters away from plantation and into riparian corridor of recovering peat swamp forest, with aim to keep it hydrated, less prone to fire (Prat *et al.*, 2013) and reduce the seasonal non-flooded period when agricultural squatters could move in. Flood diversion is complemented with drainage systems within the plantations to reduce the duration of flooding. A broad approach is to carry out marginal improvement work each rotation, aimed at reducing the incidence and duration of flooding in the critical period when a newly replanted crop of trees is establishing. Crop vulnerability to short periods of flooding diminishes with stand height; 2 m height by 6 months age is standard for *Acacia crassicarpa*.

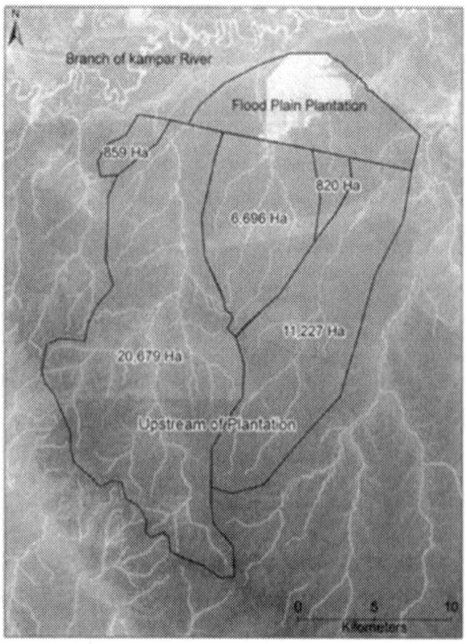

Figure 1: Example of catchment situation of plantation on seasonal floodplain; to the south 40,000 ha of agricultural catchments bring flash runoff, to the north a meandering Kampar R. is fed by a large catchment to the west. Based on Nov 2011 radar image, the light area in plantation is flood water – see Figure 2.

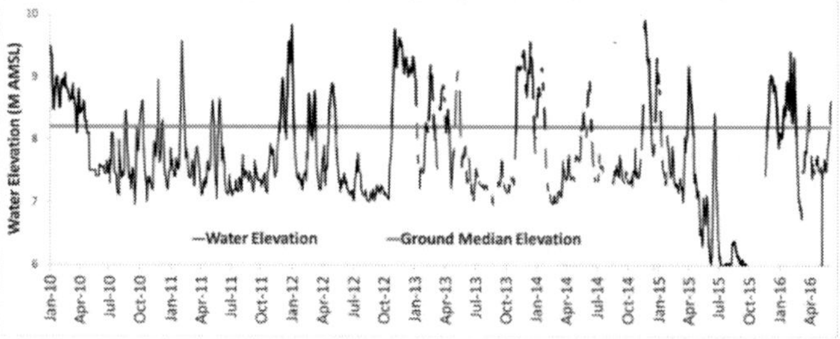

Figure 2: Six-year hydrograph constructed from logged data for central location in plantation depicted in Figure 1

PLANNING

Incompletely developed land in coastal Riau attracts would be agricultural settlers who practice opportunistic burning repeatedly as dry spells allow (Bathgate *et al.,* 2012). APRIL flood protection work to support fiber development involves a sequence of providing access, occupying the land, combating informal settlement and fire, and providing local people with formal livelihoods. In that context the embankment raised against flood often serves a key role as a light road for patrol and fire suppression. Peatland plantations are typically served by a grid of small roads in tandem with roadside drains, or small canals, for transport. The aim of flood protection is to reduce the incidence and severity of floods, particularly while the fiber crop is being established. Submersion of plantations by a ten year return period flood may be acceptable. Canals provide an option, before dikes get overtopped, of channeling flood water through the plantation landscape and beyond with minimal impact. *Acacia crassicarpa* while intolerant of prolonged flooding (Orwa *et al.,* 2009), when mature can survive several months flooded, as in Figure 4 provided water flows, not stagnates (person observation, lead author).

Flood protection works need thorough planning. Whole catchments need to be considered; this has recently become a legal requirement for operating on peatland (Ministry of Environment and Forestry, 2016). Protection work requires hydrological data on the flood return period. An example of a catchment plan requiring flood diversion work is given in Figure 1. Where up-catchment runoff via a major river affects plantations and infrastructure, ten years of rainfall and flood level data is a minimum required to plan. Shorter period detail of flow gradients and responses within the project area can be correlated with the long record to build up the picture. To provide data, water poles are installed first on major rivers at access points. Figure 2 is an example of such a hydrology record. Flood return estimates have a major bearing on the design, cost and expected benefit from flood protection work. There are no design codes. Initially APRIL found little practical experience at dike construction with tropical peat to draw on and so developed its own techniques and standards.

DIKE CONSTRUCTION

Over the past decade a number of low dikes have been erected on APRIL concessions to protect fiber estates and road infrastructure from seasonal flooding. Peat dikes can be a practical solution where flood water turbulence and energy are minimal. In the flat coastal landscape this is usually the case. An embankment of local soil is erected as a flood barrier, ideally combined with a flood diversion channel along the outer side. Soil is commonly peat, silt or a mix of these. Large woody debris that is embedded in the peat deposit adds structural reinforcement. A pair of canals dug 20 m plus apart is dug to borrow local material for a dike. The outer canal directs floods away from plantation and inner canal drains excess rainfall from plantation. Guideline for maximum safe hydraulic head is 1.5 m. Earthworks are seldom reinforced, dike strength depends on mass. A 40 m^2 section is usually adequate mass, built in stepped profile to 1:2 gradient to provide access for excavator to reach and to compact by rolling (Figure 3). Where there are bends in the dike the spacing between side canals is increased for strength and the profile of the dike widened on one side to provide a counterweight to flow pressure.

The long section gradient of a dike is designed and marked to accommodate the gradient of the flood water and to provide a minimum freeboard for the dike crest of 1 m for mineral soil, 1.5 m for compacted peat. A safe width of dike crest is 6 m where it is used as a light road; a minimum crest width is 4 m. Peat material will settle and requires topping up before the first flood season. Be prepared to release water, e.g. over a tarpaulin spillway, to the inner canal to reduce hydraulic head before a dike is damaged by rising water. The plantation canal system inside a dike provides an option to channel spill water through the plantations and out; the optimum water table depth below ground surface for *Acacia* growth can be compromised for a period. Plan to complete earthworks in the drier season.

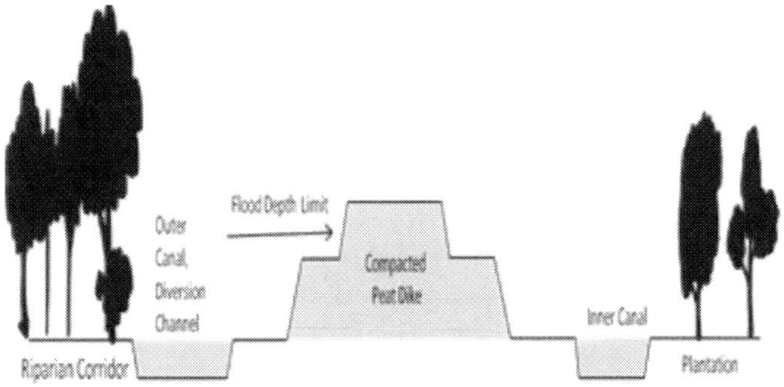

Figure 3:Schematic profile of typical peat dike built to protect plantation

Figure 4: Mature Acacia plantation under flood, Dec 2014; the flood water is between 1 and 2 m deep (refer to Figure 2)

DIKE MATERIALS

In the interest of cost the bulk of structural earthwork is built with on-site materials including peat. This is shifted a minimum distance to raise the dike. Peat is compacted approximately double; 2 m^3 of dug peat to build 1 m^3 of dike compacted in situ. The approach is to use on-site material in sufficient quantity for strength; reinforce only at critical points. Ideal options, like digging out the peat deposit down to mineral substrate, are too costly. Pre-existing canals in the dike path that need to be closed with peat may need strengthening to resist liquid soil being forced up in the inner canal by hydraulic pressure. Driven piling from local wood has too short service life before rotting at the waterline. Geo-fabric mat folded in deep loops to enclose compacted peat can be built into the outer faces of a dike, if dry season canal levels permit equipment operation. Another option is large fabric bags filled with soil and laid on felt matting for load bearing in critical points. A potential weakness of synthetic fabric is it can burn, e.g. fishermen's small fires and even cigarette burns, and may be best covered with soil.

The long arm excavator, or semi long arm, is the standard earthwork tool. Construction scheduling and costing is based on an average number of swings of the excavator arm to cut soil and move it to final position in the dike, e.g. 10 swings (peat is compressed at 2:1) at a fixed rate per swing. Logistic considerations include fuel and support barges, security for equipment and fuel; with logistic support for excavators the earthworks can proceed in parallel at multiple locations.

MAINTENANCE

A light vehicle patrol road along a dike crest serves to patrol for illegal activity and fire, and also compact peat earth works. In time dike crests are surfaced with mineral soil as running surface. A road gives significant benefit for forest maintenance activities during the rotation, including fire and pest surveillance, security, forest measurement and inspection. The peat dike can be constructed to heavy traffic standard but at much higher cost; the haul road needs a much wider base well-spaced from the flanking canals, and also needs layers of heavy grid material to separate the road from underlying peat embankment. Without this, under heavy traffic the peat soil tends to squish into the flanking canals, raising requirement for canal cleaning and embankment maintenance. Peat material is eroded by rain and wind, and needs periodic replacement. Eventually peat soil may need to be long hauled in on the dike crest; taking material from the flanking canals tends to undercut the dike base and hasten its erosion.

CONCLUDING DISCUSSION

The aim of the peat based flood protection works is to minimize flood duration and impacts. Unlike civil work a dike is seldom designed to debit flood waters within a few days or to never fail. A sufficient performance objective for fiber plantation flood protection may be to halve the duration and extent of annual flooding, and safety considerations may be less rigorous than for civil works. Woody peat and silt soils have proven adequate to construct the durable multi-purpose dikes, roads and other flood protection works that serve forest management operations in the flood prone landscape. To date some 30 km of low (1.5 m head) dikes are successfully protecting plantations. As a next step forward, design of peat-based dikes that involve flood gates and pumping are being considered.

ACKNOWLEDGEMENTS

The success of flood protection engineering within APRIL forestry has very much depended on the effort and skill of field supervisors who have developed practical solutions to new challenges in construction – to get it done on time and within budget, and learn by doing. Particular thanks are due to the Project team of Ardi Putra and Tigor Nainggolan, and Lowland team Rosef Putra, Ucin Muksin and others.

References

1. Bathgate, J., Greer, G., Rachmady, R. 2012. Carbon, conservation and agricultural development - the coastal peatlands of Sumatra, Indonesia. World Agriculture, vol.2 No.2, UK
2. Bathgate, J., Iqbal, I. 2011. Development context of coastal Riau peatland, Sumatra, Indonesia. Peatlands in Balance, the 14th International Peat Congress, Stockholm
3. Ministry of Environment and Forestry, Indonesia, 2016. Peat ecosystem damage control assessment criteria. Web document based on Regulation No.32, 2009. Environmental Protection and Management, Jakarta
4. Orwa, C., Mutua, A., kindt, R., Jamnadass, R., Anthony, S. 2009. Agroforestry database: a tree reference and selection guide, version 4.0
5. Prat, N., Hadden, R., Rein, G., Belcher, C., Yearsley, J. 2013. Effect of peat moisture on smoldering fire propagation. Proceedings of 4th fire behavior and fuels conference, Raleigh, US

Abstract No: A-326

RECOMMENDATION OF PRE-SOLIDIFICATION PROCEDURE FOR HIGHLY ORGANIC SOILS AT VARIOUS DECOMPOSITION LEVELS

Junita Abd Rahman[1*], Chan Chee Ming[2] and Radin Maya Saphira Radin Mohamed[1]

[1] *Faculty of Civil and Environmental Engineering, Universiti Tun Hussein Onn Malaysia, Parit Raja, 86400, Batu Pahat, Johor, Malaysia*
[2] *Faculty of Engineering Technology, Universiti Tun Hussein Onn Malaysia, Parit Raja, 86400, Batu Pahat, Johor, Malaysia*

**Coressponding author: junita.abdrahman@gmail.com, chan@uthm.edu.my*

SUMMARY

The peat, also known as soft soils in geotechnics, is highly compressible and soft. The solidification of peat has been studied for years by researchers all over the world. The solidification of peat is one option to sustain the population in peat area. Peat area is not a preferred inhabitants place due to limitation of the road network and infrastructure because of high possibility of settlement issue. The study on peat solidification needs the researcher to handle the peat sample carefully. The pre-solidification procedure is to ensure that the peat sample is prepared to the best condition before begin the mixing process. The preliminary test conducted prior the mixing process based on BS1377:1990. Basically, shear strength test using laboratory vane shear and moisture content test were used in the study. The moisture content and fiber content of peat at various decomposition levels were found to be the important parameter to be controlled during pre-solidification stage. These two parameters affect to the formation of unconfined compressive strength test sample which is the reliable test to measure the strength improvement after solidification. This paper recommends the procedure for pre-solidification process as a guideline for new researcher in this field.

***Keywords**: peat, decomposition level, moisture content, shear strength, solidification*

INTRODUCTION

Peat is an important ecosystem that provides a significant contribution to the global climate stability (Adon *et al.*, 2012). Peat is known as soft soils in geotechnics. The treatment to solidify peat is commonly studied by researchers in this field (Wong *et al.*, 2008 and Ali *et al.*, 2010). High moisture content, acidic, porous and less minerals are the contribution factors that affect the peat solidifications. Different stabilizers or binders have been studied by Kalantari (2010), Kolay *et al.* (2011), and Wong *et al.* (2013), successfully improved the strength of peat from 4 kPa to 300 kPa thus proved that peat, at any decomposition levels are possible to be solidified. The concern of this study is to provide the useful solutions to new researcher in this field on how to work towards solidification and counter measures should be taken at this stage. The solidification process should start with understanding insight the nature of peat and all related parameters before mixing could be done.

UNDERSTANDING NATURE OF PEAT

Peat is formed by accumulation of decomposed materials. The decomposition process depends on the plant origin, climate and the microbial activity (Wong *et al.*, 2008). There are three groups of peat, according to its decomposition level. The less decomposed peat is known as fabric peat. The amount of fiber in fabric peat is high which is more than 67 % (USDA, 1999). The less decomposed material in fabric peat normally has large pore size and void in and between the fibers (Mesri and Ajlouni, 2007). The voids in the peat play the important role in holding water (Ali *et al.*, 2010,). It contributes to the high moisture content in peat. The fiber itself, as not fully decomposed, has tendency is to crush when certain force is applied. It makes the peat highly compressible and soft. When tested using vane shear, the fiber in fabric peat is tend to entangle on the vane blade thus lead to the failure of the test.

The moderately decomposed peat is known as hemic peat. The amount of fiber is between 33 - 67 % (USDA, 1999). The hemic peat has smaller void ratio compared to fabric peat. The fiber size is also smaller. This make the hemic peat, at the same sampling location should have retain less water than the fabric peat. The most decomposed peat, namely sapric peat normally has the least moisture content compared to fabric and hemic peat. As the fiber size is decreasing with increasing of the decomposition level, the tendency of the peat sample to be entangled during vane shear test is lower.

The structure of peat, together with the high moisture content; may up to 2000 % must be given serious consideration when doing mixing for solidification purpose. These two properties are the main concern and essential for the effectiveness of peat solidification.

The peat is naturally acidic with pH ranging 3-4 for most tropical area (Abd Rahman and Chan, 2013, Zainorabidin and Bakar, 2003 and Hashim and Islam, 2008). This can be considered as indicator when selecting binder for solidification purpose. The decompose process involves microbial activity. The microbe is understood to live in acidic environment. Therefore, the solidification should change the environment into alkaline state to freeze the decompose process and hinder the microbe from being active. Ordinary portland cement (OPC) is the popular binder that works well in solidification process (Kalantari and Huat, 2008). OPC is alkaline with pH 10-11. The OPC react with water to form ettringite through hydration process (Horpibulsuk, 2012). This ettringite bind the soil particles thus strengthen the peat.

The nature of peat is very important to be understood well by the researcher. The restrictions due to natural condition of the peat should be given rigorous consideration in order to ensure the mixing process went smoothly. In most solidification study, the improvements of strength of the solidified samples are tested using unconfined compressive strength (UCS) test (Wong *et al.*, 2008 and Kalantari, 2010). Therefore, the peat should be prepared to the best condition to ensure the UCS samples could be made.

METHODOLOGY

The pre-solidification is a crucial stage that often miss looked by new researcher. At this stage, the peat is prepared for a mixing. Mixing is the primary process in solidification work. The step-by-step of the process is shown in Figure 1.

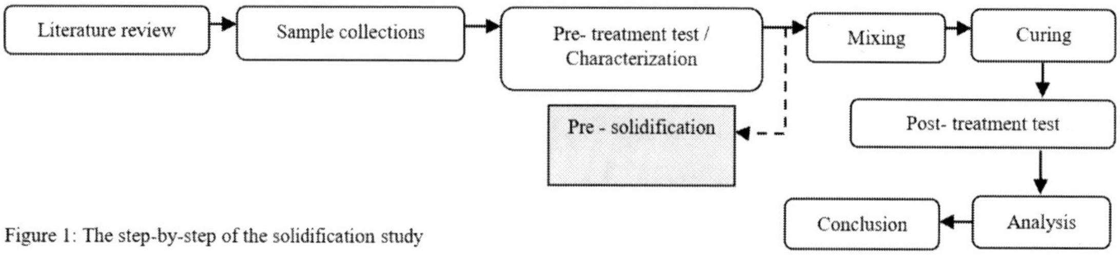

Figure 1: The step-by-step of the solidification study

EXPERIMENTAL TESTS

SHEAR STRENGTH TEST - LABORATORY VANE SHEAR (BS1377 PART 2 :1990)

Laboratory vane shear test was used to determine the strength of the pre-determined mixture as it requires only small amount of sample and can measure small strength. According to ASTM D4648, laboratory vane shear can be used to examine undrained shear strength of below 100 kPa (Figure 2).

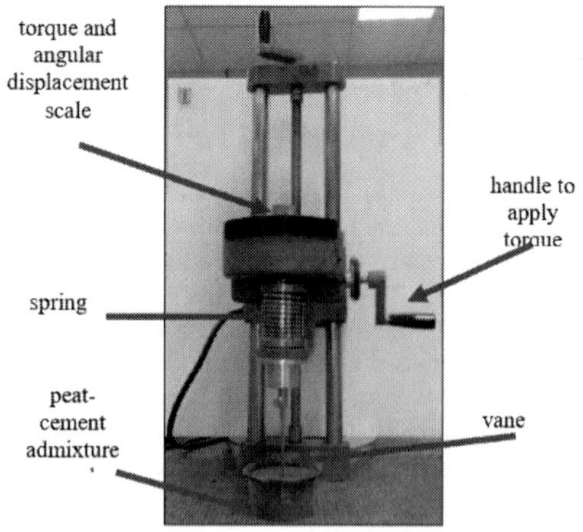

Figure 2: Laboratory vane shear

The strength value, C_u is calculated using formula;

$$C_u = \frac{T}{\pi d^2}\left(\frac{h}{2} + \frac{d}{6}\right) \quad (1)$$

where;

T = Torque, kθf (Nmm)

h = vane height (mm), = 12.67 mm

d = vane diameter (mm), = 12.67 mm

MOISTURE CONTENT (BS1377 PART 2:1990)

The standard method for determining moisture content of soils is the oven drying method. A drying temperature of 105-110°C is specified in the standard procedure. Moisture content test was carried out to each pre-treatment and post-treatment sample.

DISCUSSION

The pre-solidification stage is prepared to ensure that the peat is fit enough for mixing process. This procedure started from sampling, storing, sorting and controlling the peat condition.

SAMPLING

The solidification work is a rough process. The peat sample can be taken as disturbed with minimal control on the way of handling on site. During sampling, the sampling area should be cleared at considerable area. The top layer of peat does not represent the actual peat condition at the respective area. Therefore, the first 30 cm of the soil layer should be removed from the area. The peat could be taken either manually excavate or using an excavator machine at required depth. Normally, the decomposition level of peat is higher at deeper location. The sample should be covered with a few layers of plastic bags to conserve the moisture content (Figure 3). A proper storage will kept the peat at its best original condition for about 1 year.

In this study, the peat was obtained from Pontian, Johor. The peat collected was observed as greyish dark brown and odourless. The labelling of the peat samples was made in accordance to the physical appearance as stated by Von Post Scale (1926). Table-1 describes the sample profile in detail. All bins of samples were placed in sample room with ambiance temperature.

a) The site area was enclosed by rope

b) Sample was covered with few layers of plastic bags

Figure 3: Sample collection

Table 1: Peat profile at Pontian site

	Fibrous	Hemic	Sapric
Picture		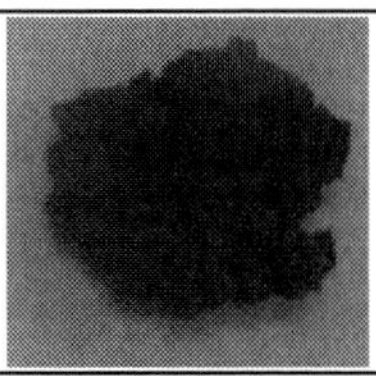	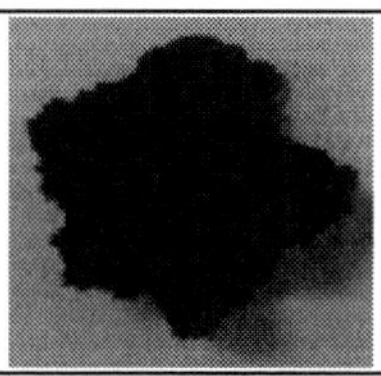
Van Post scale	H3	H5	H8
Physical description	Very much wood, very much amount of brownish water	Half decomposed. Dark brownish water. Some peat leave brown traces at palm when squeeze	Very fine. Little amount of water. Felt-like clay when hold with hand.
Colour	Brown	Dark brown	Brown to red
Odor	Acceptable smell	Odorless	Odorless
Water retention	Very much	Moderate	Little

PREPARING THE PEAT

Any fiber larger than 1 cm should be removed from the container containing peat. Wet peat at controlled moisture content then sieved passed through 2 mm sieve size. The purpose of sieving the wet peat was to remove coarse materials such as roots, stones and large fibers greater than 2 mm size. The peat then mixed thoroughly by hand for about 3 minutes. This is to ensure that only homogenous wet peat is used for mixing.

The peat sample then mixed using food mixer at low speed for 1 minute followed by medium speed for another 4 minutes. The mixer is stopped and the material is scraped off the paddle and sides of the bowl before resuming mixing for another 3 minutes. This process is completed within 8 minutes duration. EuroSoilStab (2002) suggest 10 minutes of blending to achieve sufficiently uniform dispersion mixture. 30 g of peat is then taken for moisture content test. The peat is ready for mixing process.

CONTROL OF PEAT MOISTURE CONTENT

Compilation of previous study in Table 2 shows that no specific range found that relates moisture content with decomposition level of peat. Preliminary mix design with original water content of peat, gives a very weak sample that deformed when moulded into UCS specimen. However, the fresh hemic peat, which has moisture content of 417 %, can stand firmly when moulded into UCS sample.

According to Kosmatka and Farny (1997), a minimum ratio of water needed for hydration of OPC is 0.4. It means the water needed in a mixture is almost half of the amount of OPC. Due to high water content that lead to the deformation of UCS specimen, the fact that only certain amount of water needed for hydration and the water content in all peat types are varies, therefore it is possible to control the water content in the peat before proceed to mixing process.

Table 2: Physical and chemical properties of peat

Peat type	Natural water content (w,%)	Bulk density (Mg/m^3)	Specific gravity (Gs)	Acidity (pH)	Reference
Fabric	1168	-	1.44	5.3	O'Kelly and Pichan (2013)
Fabric	598.5		1.21	3.75	Kolay *et al.*(2011)
Fibric	605-1290	0.87-1.04	1.41-1.7	-	Moayedi *et al.* (2011)
Fibric	850	0.95-1.03	1.1-1.8	-	Asadi *et al.*, (2009, 2010)
Fabric	700-850	1.59	1.343	4.6	Deboucha and Hashim (2009)
Fabric	668	-	1.4	3.51	Wong *et al.* (2008)
Hemic	230-500	-	1.48-1.80	-	Zainorabidin and Ismail (2003)
Fabric and hemic	1090-1210	-	-	-	Jelisic and Leppänen (2000)
Peat (Netherlands)	669	0.97	1.52	-	Termatt and Topolnicki (1994)
Fibric	660-1590	-	1.53-1.68	-	Lefebvre *et al.* (1984)
Peat portage	600	0.96	1.72	7.3	Edil and Mochtar (1984)
Fibric peat (Middleton)	510	0.91	1.41	7	
Coarse Fibric	202-1159	1.05	1.5	4.17	Berry (1983)
Fine Fibric	660	1.05	1.58	6.9	NG and Eischen (1983)
Fine Fibric	418	1.05	1.73	6.9	
Hemic granular	336	1.05	1.72	7.3	
Hemic peat	200-875	1.04-1.23	-	-	
Hemic to Fibric	850	-	1.5	-	Keene and Zawodniak (1968)
Hemic and Fibric	355-425	-	1.73	6.7	Adams (1965)
	500-1500	0.88-1.22	1.5-1.6	-	Lea and Browner (1963)

The original water content for Pontian peat was 860 % for fabric, 447 % for hemic and 602 % for sapric types. Figure 4 shows, to achieve a c_u of 12 kPa at the peat's natural water content, the amount of OPC needed for fabric peat is 1250 %. This amount is somehow not practical.

Kalantari (2010) suggested microwave heating to evaporate the moisture from peat. Despite losing its moisture, heating a peat will shrink the fiber sizes thus damage the original condition of peat. Drying of organic coarse particles causes shrinkage of thin-walled tissues and collapse of cell structure, thereby decreases particle porosity and water holding capacity (Tremblay *et al.*, 2002 and Terzaghi *et al.*, 1996). The drying techniques at 100 °C for 4 hour successfully removed the water but it shrunk the peat and turned it into a very hard solid. The dry peat, when mixed again with water, failed to absorb the water and unable to form into its original condition. Peat will shrink extensively when dried. The shrinkage could reach 50% of the initial volume, but the dried peat will not swell up upon re-saturation because dried peat cannot absorb water as much as initial condition; only 33% to 55% of the water can be reabsorbed (Mokhtar, 1998).

There is different with air dry technique, where the peat can still maintain the original condition with less water content. Therefore, the air drying technique is chosen. The sample is mixed thoroughly by hand for 2 minutes and left uncovered indoor at ambient temperature. The mixing process repeated 3 times a day. Moisture content of the mixed peat is recorded daily.

The process is repeated till the desired moisture content is achieved. Figure 5 shows the moisture content versus time taken for controlling the water content of peat using this technique.

Overall, one week is needed to reduce the moisture content of about 100 kg of sample. When the desired moisture content is achieved, the sample then covered with a few layer of plastic bags to maintain the moisture content and ready for mixing process.

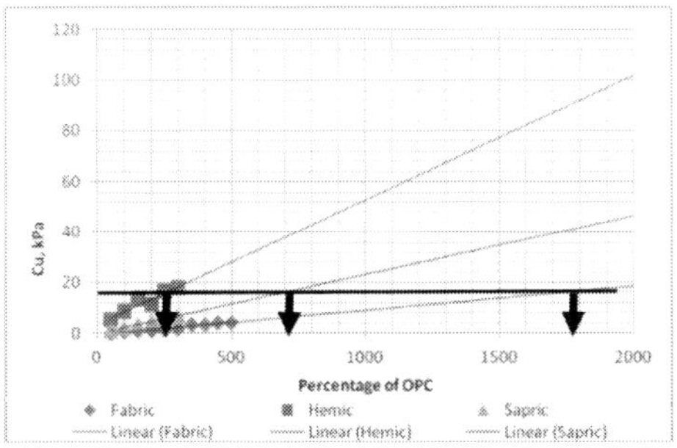

Figure 4: Projection of undrained shear stress versus percentage of OPC

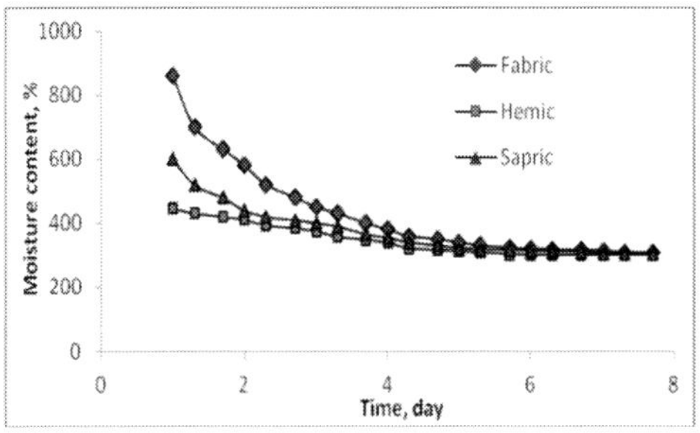

Figure 5: Moisture content versus time taken for controlling the water content of peat using air drying technique

CONCLUSION

The pre-solidification procedure for peat samples at various decomposition levels should be;
1) Sampling - chose the right peat sample for respective study and kept the peat at its original condition.
2) Preparing the peat - Ensure the peat samples to be less than 2 mm. Too much of coarse element will affect the formation of UCS sample.
3) Control the moisture content - for the formation of UCS sample

ACKNOWLEDGEMENTS

The authors wish to acknowledge the financial support from Fundamental Research Grant Scheme (FRGS) (Vot 1453) , and Post Graduate Center, Universiti Tun Hussein Onn Malaysia.

REFERENCES

1. Adams, J. I. (1965). The Engineering Behaviour of a Canadian Muskeg, Proceeding of the 7th Muskeg Research Conference, Ottawa, ON, Canada, April 1961. National Research Council of Canada, Montreal, Canada. 36-54.
2. Adon, R., Bakar, I. Wijeyesekera, D. C. and Zainorabidin, A. (2012). *Overview of the Sustainable Uses of Peat Soil in Malaysia with Some Relevant Geotechnical Assessments*. International Journal of Integrated Engineering – Special Issue on ICONCEES Vol. 4 No. 3. 8-46.

3. Abd Rahman, J. and Chan, C.M. (2013). *Influence of Temperature on the Mass Losses of Tropical Peat at Different Decomposition Level.* Soft soil Engineering International Confrence 2013. Sarawak.
4. Asadi, A., Huat, B. B., Hanafi, M. M., Mohamed, T. A., & Shariatmadari, N. (2009). Role of organic matter on electroosmotic properties and ionic modification of organic soils. *Geosciences journal, 13*(2), 175-181.
5. Asadi, A., Huat, B. B. K., Hanafi, M. M. and Mohamed, T. A. (2010). Physicochemical sensitivities of tropical peat to electrokinetic environment. *Geosciences Journal* Volume 14. 67-75.
6. Ali, F., Wong, L. S. and Hashim, R. (2010). Engineering properties of improved fibrous peat. *Scientific Research and Essay* Vol. 5 (2). 154-169.
7. Berry PL (1983). Application of consolidation theory for peat to the design of a reclamation scheme by preloading. *Q. J. Eng. Geol.*, London, 16(9): 103-112.
8. Deboucha, S. and Hashim, R. (2009). Durability and swelling of tropical stabilized peat soils. *Journal of Applied Sciences* 9 (13). 2480-2484.
9. Edil, T.B. and Mochtar, N.E. (1984). Prediction of peat settlement. Proc. Sediment. *Consolidation Models Symp. Prediction Validation,* ASCE, San Fransisco, California, 411-424.
10. EuroSoilStab. (2002). *Development of design and construction methods to stabilize soft organic soils (design guide soft soil stabilisation).* European Comission, Industrial and Material Technologies programme (Brite-EuRam III), Brussels.
11. Gofar, N. and Sutejo, Y. (2007). Long term compression behaviour of fibrous peat. *Malaysian Journal of Civil Engineering* 19(2) :104-116.
12. Hashim, R. and Islam S. (2008). A Model Study to Determine Engineering Properties of Peat Soil and Effect on Strength after Stabilization. *European J. Scientific Res.*, 2, 205–215.
13. Horpibulsuk, S. (2012). Strength and Microstructure of Cement Stabilized Clay, Scanning Electron Microscopy. ISBN: 978-953-51-0092-8, InTech.
14. Huat, B.B.K., Kazemian, S., Prasad, A. and Barghchi, M. (2011). State of an art review of peat: General perspective. *International Journal of the Physical Sciences Vol. 6(8)*, 1988-1996.
15. Jelisic, N. and Leppanen, M. (2000), *Mass Stabilisation of Peat in Road and railway construction*, Proceedings of the Fourth International Conference on Ground Improvement Geosystems. 81 - 88.
16. Kalantari B., Huat B.B. K. (2008). *Peat Soil Stabilization, using Ordinary Portland Cement, Polypropylene Fibers, and Air Curing Technique.*, University of Putra Malaysia.
17. Kalantari, B. (2010). *Stabilization of tropical fibrous peat using ordinary portland cement and additives.* PHD thesis. Universiti Putra Malaysia.
18. Keene, P. and Zawodniak, C.D. (1968). *Embankment construction on peat utilizing hydraulic fill.* Proceedings of the 3 rd Int Peat Conference, National Research Council of Canada, Ottawa. 45-50.
19. Kolay, P.K, Sii, H. Y. and Taib, S.N.L.(2011).Tropical Peat Soil Stabilization using Class F Pond Ash from Coal Fired Power Plant *International Journal of Civil and Environmental Engineering* 3:2. 79-83.
20. Kosmatka, S. and Farny, J. (1997). *Concrete Technology Today.* Illinois ,USA. Portland Cement Association.
21. Lea N, Brawner CO (1963). Highway design and construction over peat deposits in the lower British Colombia. Highw. Res. Rec., 7: 1–32.
22. Lefebvre G, Langlois P, Lupien C, Lavallee JG (1984). Laboratory testing and in situ behavior of peat as embankment foundation, *Can. Geotech. J.*, 21: 322-337.
23. NG, S.Y. and Eischens, G.R. (1983). Repeated short-term consolidation of peats. Testing of Peat and Organic Soils, ASTM STP 820: 192-206.
24. Mesri, G. and Ajlouni, M. (2007). Engineering Properties of Fibrous Peats. *Journal of Geotechnical and Geoenvironmental Engineering* 133:850-866.
25. Moayedi, H., Asadi, A., Moayedi, F., & Huat, B. B. (2011). Zeta potential of tropical soil in presence of polyvinyl alcohol. *Int. J. Electrochem. Sci, 6*(5), 1294-1306.
26. O'Kelly, B.C. and Pichan, S. P. (2013). Effects of decomposition on the compressibility of fibrous peat — a review. *Geomechanics and Geoengineering: An International Journal* 8(4). 286–296.
27. Soil Survey Staff. (1999).Soil Taxonomy, A Basic System of Soil Classification for Making and Interpreting Soil Surveys, United States Department of Agriculture (USDA). Natural Resources Conservation Service, Number 436, Second Edition. U.S. Government Printing Office, Washington, DC.
28. Termatt R, Topolnicki M (1994). *Biaxial tests with natural and artificial peat.* Proceedings of the International Workshop on Advances in Understanding and Modeling the Mechanical Behavior of Peat, Delft, Netherlands. 241-251.
29. Terzaghi, K., R.B. Peck and G. Mesri (1996). *Soil mechanics in engineering practice.* 3rd ed., John Wiley and Sons, New York. ISBN Number: 978-0-471-08658-1.
30. Tremblay, H ., J. Duchesne, J. Locat and S. Leroueil (2002). Influence of the nature of organic compounds on fine soil stabilization with cement. *Canadian Geotech. Journal*, 39(3). 535-546.
31. Von Post, L. and Granlund, E. (1926). *Södra Sveiges torvtillgangångar I. Peat resources in southern Sweden.* Sveriges geoliska undersökning.

32. Wong, L. S., Hashim, R. and Ali, F. (2013). Improved strength and reduced permeability of stabilized peat: Focus on application of kaolin as a pozzolanic additive. *Journal of Construction and Building Materials 40*. 783–792.
33. Wong, L. S., Hashim, R. and Ali, F. (2008). Behavior of Stabilized Peat Soils in Unconfined Compression Tests. *American Journal of Engineering and Applied Sciences* 1 (4): 274-279.
34. Zainorabidin, A. and Bakar, I. (2003). *Engineering properties of in-situ and modified hemic peat soil in Western Johor*. In Proceedings of 2nd International Conference on Advances in Soft Soil Engineering and Technology, Malaysia. 173-182.

Abstract No: A-203

SARAWAK HEMIC PEAT CONSOLIDATION SETTLEMENT AND SHEAR STRENGTH BEHAVIOUR

N. M.Sa'don, A. R. Abdul Karim, Z. Ahamad and A. Mariappan

Universiti Malaysia Sarawak, Sarawak, MALAYSIA

**Corresponding author: msazzlin@unimas.my*

SUMMARY

Peat layer in Sarawak alone represents 13 percent or about 1.66 million hectares of Sarawak's total land area. They are mostly in low-lying areas; with in some areas, peat exceeding 10 m in depth. During past few decades, the demands of urbanisation resulted in the expansion of land development into swamp and deep peat areas. Thus, proper understanding, management and construction practices should be emphasized on peat to overcome consequential occurrence of ground subsidence problems. The objectives of this study are to investigate the consolidation settlement parameters and shear strength behaviour of hemic peat in Sarawak. The samples were taken from Matang, Batu Kawa, and Kota Samarahan, Sarawak. The initial characteristic tests consist of the degree of humidification, loss on ignition, Atterberg limit, particle density; moisture content and pH value. The results recorded high moisture content and organic content for Sarawak hemic peat. The value of Compression Index, C_c, determined from the oedometer test for hemic peat is in the range of 1.13 to 3.20 and compression ratio, $Cc/1+e_0$ is classified as very compressible (> 0.20) for all three locations; Matang, Batu Kawa and Kota Samarahan,. From the direct shear box test, the cohesion, c' values are in the range of 8.0-18.0 kPa and angle of internal friction φ' in the range of 24°- 37°.

***Keywords**: Sarawak hemic peat, peat consolidation, degree of humidification, loss of ignition.*

INTRODUCTION

Peat is defined as highly organic soil with the heterogeneous mixture of partially decomposed plant remains, with some contents of sand, silt and clay under damp and anaerobic condition at low temperature. The content of organic remains in peat is sufficiently fresh and undisturbed to permit identification of plant remains whose structure ranges from more or less decomposed plant remains to a fine amorphic mass. Approximately 1.7 million ha (13%) of the total land area of the Malaysian state of Sarawak State's total land area, are covered with tropical peat land (refer Figure 1) and about 90 percent is classified as deep peat with depth of more than 1.5 meter (Melling, *et al.*, 2002). The depth of peat layer increases from the coast towards the inlands. According to Huat et al., (1997), field investigation conducted in Western Sarawak has proven that there are three significant layers differentiated by its level of humidification based on the Von Post classification system, where each layer overlays the subsequent layer. The top thin layer of 0.5 m to 1.5 m thick is recognized as sapric (H7-H10) peat with fiber content of less than 33 percent. The second layer of peat, overlain by sapric peat, is recognized as hemic peat (H4-H6) with fiber content ranging from 33 to 66 percent. The near beneath of peat soil layer, overlain by hemic peat, is recognized as fibric peat (H1-H3) with fiber content of greater than 66 percent. A layer of grey mangrove clay may be seen under the fibric layers. The content of peat differs from location to location such as origin fiber, temperature and humidity (Huat *et al.*, 2009).

Peat has poor engineering properties, such as high compressibility and low in shear strength, due to high void ratios which results in higher values of compression index, Cc and secondary compression, Cα, when compared with other soil types. A study by Mesri *et al.* (1997) showed that the secondary compression is prominent in peat deposits because it exists at a high void ratio, which exhibit high values of Cc and displays a high ratio of Cα/Cc. Table 1 presents the summary of the natural moisture content with the relevant Cα/Cc values for different peat deposits (Mesri *et al.*, 1997). Landva (1980) reported the in-situ vane shear tests on peat with void ratio of 6.1 – 11.5 displayed shear strength levels ranging from 5-35 kPa. However, Lea and Brawner, (1963) observed that the low strength will increase when fibers, and the particles of the peat come together under compression. Such a considerable gain in strength is attributed to the exceptionally high values of the effective angle of shearing resistance ϕ', which has been observed in various laboratory testings on peat (Karunawardena, 2007). This paper presents the findings on geotechnical characteristics, consolidation settlement parameters and shear strength of hemic peat. The tests have been performed in Geotechnical Laboratory, UNIMAS and all the experimental investigations were performed in accordance to BS 1377: Part 2 (1990) unless stated otherwise.

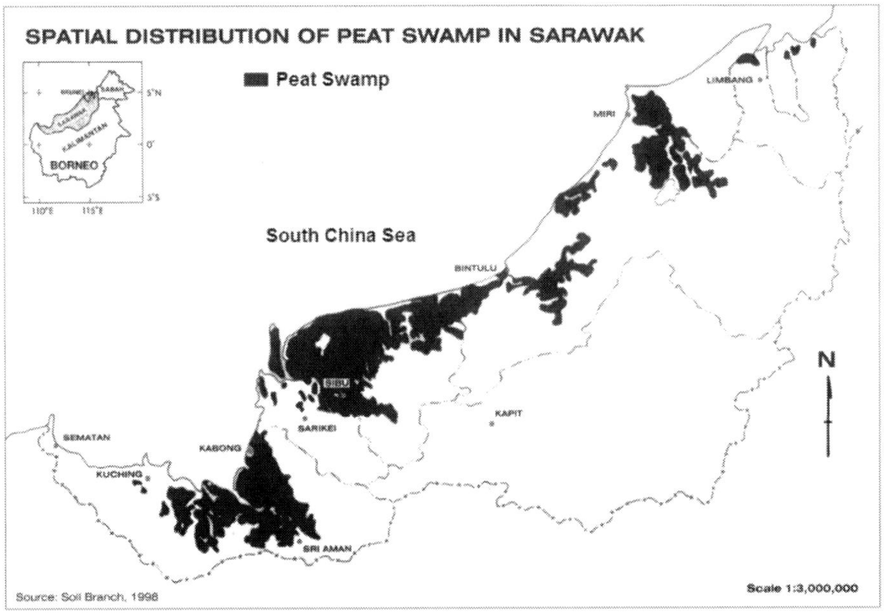

Figure 1 Sarawak peat swamp distribution (Melling et al, 2002)

Table 1 Summary of natural moisture content and Cα/Cc for peat deposits (Mesri *et al*,. 1997)

Peat	Natural Moisture Content	Cα/Cc	Reference
Fibrous peat	850	0.060-0.100	Hanrahan (1954)
Peat	520	0.061-0.078	Lewis (1956)
Armorphous and fibrous peat	500 -1500	0.035-0.083	Lea and Brawner (1963)
Canadian muskeg	200-600	0.090-0.100	Adam (1965)
Amorphous to fibrous peat	705	0.073-0.091	Keene and Zawodniak (1968)
Peat	400-700	0.075-0.085	Weber (1969)
Fibrous peat	605-1290	0.052-0.072	Samson and LaRochell (1972)
Fibrous peat	613-886	0.060-0.085	Berry and Vickers (1975)
Amorphous to fibrous peat	600	0.042-0.083	Edil and Dhowian (1981)
Fibrous peat	660-1590	0.060	Lefebvre et al. (1984)
Dutch peat	370	0.060	Den Haan (1994)
Fibrous peat	610-850	0.052	Karunawardena (2007)

PROPERTIES OF SARAWAK HEMIC PEAT

Table 2 presents the geotechnical properties of Sarawak hemic peat taken from three different locations; Matang, Batu Kawa and Kota Samarahan by using the UNIMAS peat sampler. The samples (Figure 2) were categorized into the hemic group, ranging from H4 to H5 assessed through to the Von Post classification system on a 10-point scale. The description suited the classification made as the samples were slightly decomposed and a very small amount of granular peat with muddy dark water escaped between the fingers upon squeezing. Organic content in Sarawak hemic peat is best determined by performing loss on ignition test. From the test, it can be seen that the organic content for Sarawak hemic peat is very high, which varies from 89% to 95%. Higher percentage of organic matter produced relatively high moisture content in Sarawak hemic peat. Based on the published work, it has been proven reasonable that the voids between organic particles have a high capacity of entrapping moisture content, which resulted in high moisture content of peat. It is clearly shown that, the organic content does affect the moisture content of Sarawak hemic peat. Batu Kawa and Matang samples have shown relatively high organic content, which also resulted in high moisture content records. The pH value for Sarawak peat falls in the range of 3 to 4, to which are classified as acidic and reduced of organic content.

Figure 2 Sarawak hemic peat – Kota Samarahan sample

Table 2 Geotechnical properties of Sarawak hemic peat

Properties	Matang	Batu Kawa	Kota Samarahan
Von Post Classification	H4 - H5	H5	H4
Moisture Content (w_N) (%)	594 - 856	607 - 926	426 - 817
Liquid Limit, LL (%)	234 - 245	252 - 261	192 - 200
Organic Content, OC (%)	95	95	89
Fiber Content, FC (%)	45.6	50.3	23.2
Specific Gravity (G_s)	1.08 - 1.35	1.11 - 1.34	1.25 - 1.67
pH Value	3.2 – 3.8	3.3 - 3.9	3.4 – 4.3
Initial Void Ratio, e_o	2.720-3.104	2.830	3.318

Table 3 Compression parameters of Sarawak hemic peat

Location	Compression Index Cc	Compression Ratio Cr=Cc/(1+e_o)	Coefficient of Secondary Compression Cα	Law of Compressibility Cα/Cc
Matang	3.185	0.790	0.1110	0.035
Batu Kawa	1.130	0.295	0.0395	0.035
Kota Samarahan	1.220	0.282	0.0427	0.035

TEST RESULTS AND DISCUSSION ON SARAWAK HEMIC PEAT

Consolidation Settlement Parameters of Sarawak Hemic Peat

In this section the results of consolidation parameters using the Oedometer test are presented. The study focused on two consolidation parameters, which are Compression Index, Cc and Coefficient of Secondary Compression, Cα. About sixteen (16) oedometer tests with different loading schedules in the range of 10-100 kPa have been performed. The load ranges were chosen to replicate the most common cases in the construction practice. All procedures of the Oedometer test were in accordance to BS 1377: Part 5: 1990. The compression index, Cc values obtained for hemic peat were in the range of 1.13 to 3.20, which were smaller than published work for Cc values of peat reported as 5 to 10 in previous study. This may be due to the samples collected from this tropical region which possesses high compressibility when subjected to higher loading over the time period (Huat, 2007).

The coefficient of secondary compression, Cα, value were determined from the correlation of Cα = 0.035Cc developed by Mesri *et al.* (1997). The Cα value calculated is in the range of 0.0395 to 0.111 for Sarawak hemic peat. According to Mesri (1973), soil with Cα values of more than 0.064 is classified as soil with extremely high compressibility.

The compression ratio, Cr = Cc/1+e_o, for the Sawarak hemic peat is classified as very compressible with greater than 0.20 for all three locations; Matang, Batu Kawa and Kota Samarahan based on the study by O'Loughlin and Lehane (2003). The study presented that the compression ratio of peat ranges from 0.01 to 0.05 is categorized as very slightly compressible; 0.05 to 0.10 is moderately compressible, and between 0.20 to 0.35 is very compressible.

Table 3 tabulated the value for Law of Compressibility; Cα/Cc is 0.035 of Sarawak hemic peat. The value obtained corresponds well with the range, Cα/Cc = 0.020 to 0.100, as reported by Mesri and Castro (1987) for a wide range of soils including sands, inorganic and organic clays and peat. Also, the finding is in agreement with

Duraisamy et al. (2007), where the samples of peat were taken from the West Coast of Peninsular Malaysia. However, further laboratory testing especially involving long-term oedometer test and field investigation of peat throughout Sarawak are still required in order to perform comprehensive parametric studies on Sarawak peat.

Shear Strength of Sarawak Hemic Peat

The shear strengths of Sarawak hemic peat were determined in the laboratory using the shear box. The samples taken from Matang, Batu Kawa and Kota Samarahan are placed in a shear box which has two stacked rings to hold the sample. A confining stress is applied vertically to the sample, and the upper ring is pulled laterally until the sample fails. The load applied and the strain induced is recorded to determine a stress–strain curve for each confining stress. The results from the shear box tests obtained are tabulated in Table 4 and showed that the Sarawak hemic peat has very low cohesion, c' ranging from 8.0 kPa to 18.0 kPa. The hemic peat exhibits a high angle of internal friction ϕ', which ranges from 24° to 37° and these findings have an agreement with Kazemian *et al.*, (2011). The high internal angle of friction is attributed to the existence of fibre content in peat, which acts as a reinforcement, thus modify the strength of the peat.

Table 4 Shear box test results of Sarawak hemic peat

Location	Cohesion c' (kPa)	Angle of internal friction, ϕ'(deg)
Matang 1	17.0	25
	12.0	27
	8.0	30
Matang 2	18.0	25
	16.0	24
	10.0	28
Batu Kawa	12.0	32
	8.0	34
	8.0	37
Kota Samarahan	14.0	33
	12.0	36
	13.0	30

CONCLUSIONS

This paper briefly described the geotechnical characteristics, consolidation settlement parameters and shear strength of hemic peat. Based on the results, the following conclusions were obtained:

- The results from the laboratory show high moisture content and organic content of Sarawak hemic peat.
- The value of Compression Index, Cc for hemic peat is in the range of 1.13 to 3.20 and compression ratio, $Cc/1+e_o$ is classified as very compressible (> 0.20).
- The value for Law of Compressibility, $C\alpha/Cc$ is 0.035 for Sarawak hemic peat, which is lower from the values reported by Mesri and Castro (1987) but in agreement with Duraisamy et al. (2007).
- The cohesion, c' values are in the range of 8.0-18.0 kPa and angle of internal friction φ' in the range of 24°-37° determined from direct shear box test.

ACKNOWLEDGMENT

The first author would like to thank the technical staff for helping in collecting the peat samples. The Faculty of Engineering and Geotechnical Laboratory, Universiti Malaysia Sarawak (UNIMAS) for the resources provided, and also for the scholarship granted by Malaysia government to the third and fourth authors. Finally, to those who are contributed directly and indirectly towards the preliminary study of Sarawak hemic peat.

REFERENCES

1. Adams, J.I. (1965). The engineering behavior of a Canadian Muskeg, In *Proceedings of 6th International Conference on Soil Mechanics and Foundation Engineering*, Montreal, 1, 3-7.

2. British Standard 1377: Part 2 (1990). Classification Tests. *Soils for Civil Engineering Purposes.*
3. Bujang B.K.Huat and Bahia, H.M. (editors) (1997). *Proceedings of International Conference on Recent Advances in Soft Soil Engineering.* pp.510.
4. Duraisamy, Y., Huat, B.K., Aziz, A.A. (2007). Engineering properties and compressibility of Tropical Peat Soil, American Journal of Applied Sciences, 4(10), 768-773.
5. Edil, T.B. and Dhowian, A.W. (1981). At-rest lateral pressure of peat soils, *Journal of Geotechnical Engineering*, ASCE, 107(2), 201- 217.
6. Huat, B.K., Asadi, A. and Kazemian, S. (2009). Experimental investigation on geomechanical properties of tropical organic soils and peat. *American Journal of Engineering and Applied Sciences*. 2(1); pp. 184-188.
7. Karunawardena, W.A. (2007). Consolidation analysis of Sri Lankan peaty clay using elastoviscoplastic theory, *PhD Thesis*, Kyoto University, Japan.
8. Kazemian, S., Prasad, A., Huat, B. B., & Barghchi, M. (2011). A state of art review of peat: Geotechnical engineering perspective. *International Journal of Physical Sciences*, *6*(8), 1974-1981.
9. Landva, A.O. (1980). Vane testing of peat, *Canadian Geotechnical Journal*, 17(1) 1-19.
10. Lea, N.D. and Brawner, C.O. (1963). Highway design and construction over peat deposits in Lower British Colombia, *Highway Research Board*, Research Record 7, 1–33.
11. Melling, L., Ryusuke, H. and Mitsuru, O. (2002). Sustainable agriculture development on tropical peatland. *17th WCSS*, 14-21 August, Thailand.
12. Mesri, G. (1973). Coefficient of secondary compression, *Journal of Soil Mechanics and Foundation Division*, ASCE, 99(1), 123-137.
13. Mesri, G., and Castro, A. (1987). The Cα/Cc concept and K_0 during secondary compression, *Journal of Geotechnical Engineering*, ASCE, 112(3), 230-247.
14. Mesri, G., Stark, T.D., Ajlouni, M.A. & Chen, C.S. (1997). Secondary compression of peat with or without surcharging, *Journal of Geotechnical Engineering*, ASCE, 123(5), 411- 421.
15. O'Loughlin, C.D. and Lehane, B.M. (2003). A study of the link between composition and compressibility of peat and organic soils, *In Proceedings 2nd International Conference on Advances in Soft Soil Engineering and Technology*, Putrajaya, Malaysia 2-4 July.
16. Samson, L. and La Rochelle, P. (1972). Design and performance of an expressway constructed over peat by preloading, *Canadian Geotechnical Journal*, 9, 447-467.

SPECIAL SESSION 2: PEAT FOR HORTICULTURE & ENERGY

Abstract No: A-158

DPPP – A WORLDWIDE SEARCH FOR PALUDICULTURE PLANTS AND THEIR POTENTIAL TO STOP PEAT DEGRADATION

Susanne Abel*, Christian Schröder and Hans Joosten

Institute of Botany and Landscape Ecology, Ernst-Moritz-Arndt University Greifswald, partner in the Greifswald Mire Centre, Soldmannstraße 15, 17487 Greifswald, Germany

**Corresponding author: abels@uni-greifswald.de*

SUMMARY

Paludiculture ('palus' lat. for swamp) is the productive use of wet and rewetted peatlands in a way that the peat body and essential ecosystem services of mires such as carbon store, water regulation and biodiversity conservation are preserved. Next to the few well-established paludiculture plants, a wealth of wetland species is promising for paludiculture. The identification and description of such crops is essential for the wide implementation of paludiculture. The Database of Potential Paludiculture Plants (DPPP) was established to gather information on the variety of useful wetland plants and to present the first global overview of potential paludiculture plants. Paludiculture is a new and diverse land-use concept with fundamental differences in design and management depending on the species cultivated and the crops produced. Paludiculture plants vary from trees, to grasses, mosses, herbs or berry producing shrubs. In order to assess their different potential for peatland sustainability we developed easy accessible criteria for their potential for paludiculture. To date the database contains information on 1128 plant species, of which 735 species grow in the tropical Ecozone (FAO) and 463 in the subtropics. For 469 plant species the current potential for paludiculture is considered to be good because a market exists for products made of their aboveground parts. A large group of Database entries (40%) are assessed as "not defined", which means that the market demand could not be defined. More research and a better data gathering especially in the tropics can precise these unknown number of more potential paludiculture species.

***Keywords**: paludiculture, wetland plants, peatland utilisation, rewetting, peat conservation*

INTRODUCTION

Conventional peatland utilisation for agriculture, forestry or peat extraction requires drainage which results in enormous emissions of greenhouse gases and nutrients. In total an area of c. 460,000 km² of degrading peatlands exists worldwide (Barthelmes 2016). 25 % of worldwide carbon dioxide (CO_2) emissions within the sector land use, land use change and forestry (LULUCF) is caused by drained peatland (Joosten *et al.*, 2012). Rewetting drained peatland is required to avoid further peat degradation and mitigate greenhouse gas emissions.

In many regions worldwide, the pressure of land utilisation continuously increases by a growing population along with their need for shelter, infrastructure, raw materials and not least food. In recent time the losses of usable land occurred due to overexploitation, climate change and new land claims, among other things due to the intensified use of bioenergy and raw materials, which are additional strong drivers of the growing demand for land (Wichtmann *et al.*, 2016). The current focus of extending drainage and thus also degradation of peatlands is on Southeast-Asia (Miettinen *et al.* 2012, Joosten *et al.* 2012), where the amelioration measures lead to accelerated degradation processes for climatic reasons and therefore have often a more severe impact on the environment, economy and living conditions (e.g. Yule 2010)

Paludiculture ('palus'– latin for 'swamp'), the productive use of wet peatlands, may combine the provision of essential ecosystem services of mires such as carbon storage, water regulation and biodiversity conservation with the production of useful biomass (Wichtmann et al. 2016). The precondition for paludiculture is that the peatland is so wet that the peat soil is conserved and that new peat may even accumulate. Paludicultures are currently concentrated in the temperate climate zone but everywhere in the world the same necessities, challenges and possibilities exist in relation to a sustainable peatland use. Specific literature about paludiculture plants is rare and scattered between disciplines (e.g. Haslam 2010, FAO Case studies 2015, Giesen 2013, Oehmke & Abel 2016), meta studies searching for transferable information on wetland plants for paludiculture are more or less not existent.

To facilitate land use change towards paludiculture we developed the Database of potential paludiculture plants (DPPP) for the identification of new peatland crops (Abel *et al.* 2013). Plants suitable for paludiculture must grow under wet conditions, produce biomass in sufficient quantity and quality and their cultivation should conserve the peat soil (Wichtmann & Joosten 2007). But which concrete criteria define whether a wetland species will be suitable for paludiculture?

Here we present the current state of the DPPP and the theoretical considerations to assess the paludiculture potential of wetland plants with special attention to peat conservation and market demand. Furthermore, we want to stress the necessity for the improvement of the tropical plant entries within the DPPP.

METHODS

The DPPP - Database of Potential Paludiculture Plants was constructed using Microsoft Office Access 2010. For every species the DPPP create a 'plant portrait' that contains information on plant characteristics and morphology, distribution and natural habitat, modes of cultivation and propagation as well as utilisation options, if available (Fig. 1). In Europe and North America the availability of data was much easier than in the tropics or Asia. Several online databases provide information about useful plants in English. The accessibility of data in the tropics and in Asia was difficult due to language barriers and lack of online publications.

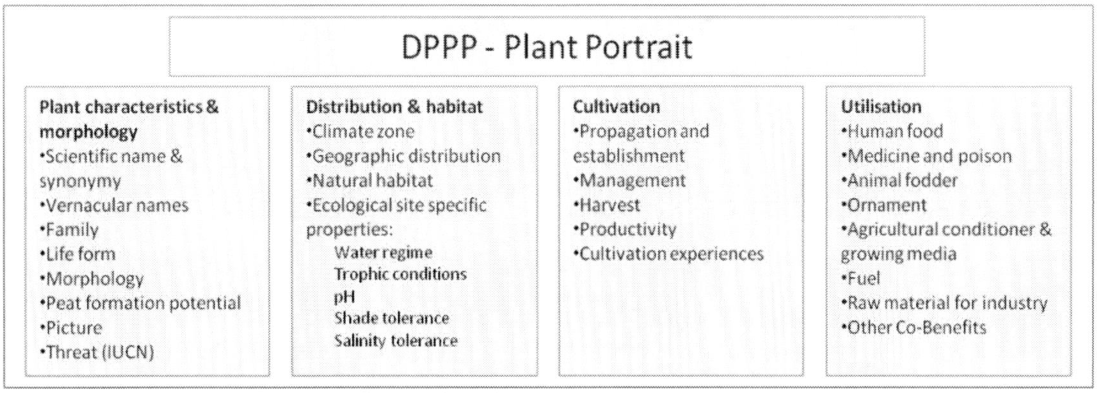

Figure 1: Structure and content of the DPPP 'Plant portrait' entries.

Since not every useful wetland plant will be suitable for paludiculture we developed a decision tree (Fig. 2) to analyse the paludiculture potential in four levels of suitability (promising, good, limited and very low potential). The tree uses as a first step information on the persistency (annual vs. perennial plant) and the used plant parts (above- vs. belowground biomass) to assess the peat conservation potential, followed by questions related to market demand (yes or most likely in future vs. unlikely) and if the plant is already cultivated in paludiculture (yes vs. no).

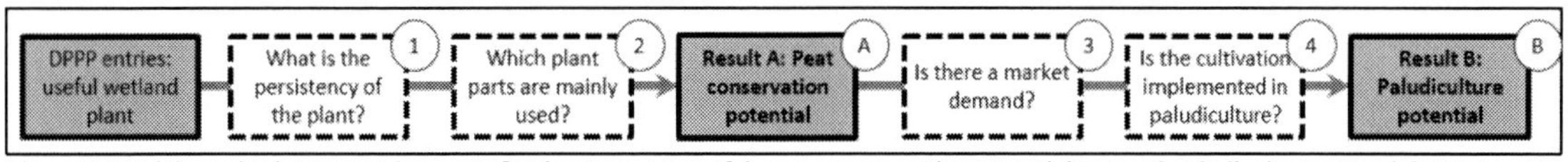

Figure 2: Decision criteria (1-4) and process for the assessment of the peat conservation potential (A) and paludiculture potential (B).

RESULTS AND DISCUSSION

The DPPP - Database of Potential Paludiculture Plants registers currently 1131 plant species (Fig. 3). 469 species listed in the DPPP have a promising or good potential, 272 have only limited or very low potential for paludiculture. The potential of 485 plants could not be assessed because of unknown market demand or missing knowledge about the used plant parts. Here, more and better data gathering especially in the tropics can precise the unknown number of potential paludiculture species. Since the data gathering was done mostly from Germany, a regional analysis would achieve much better results.

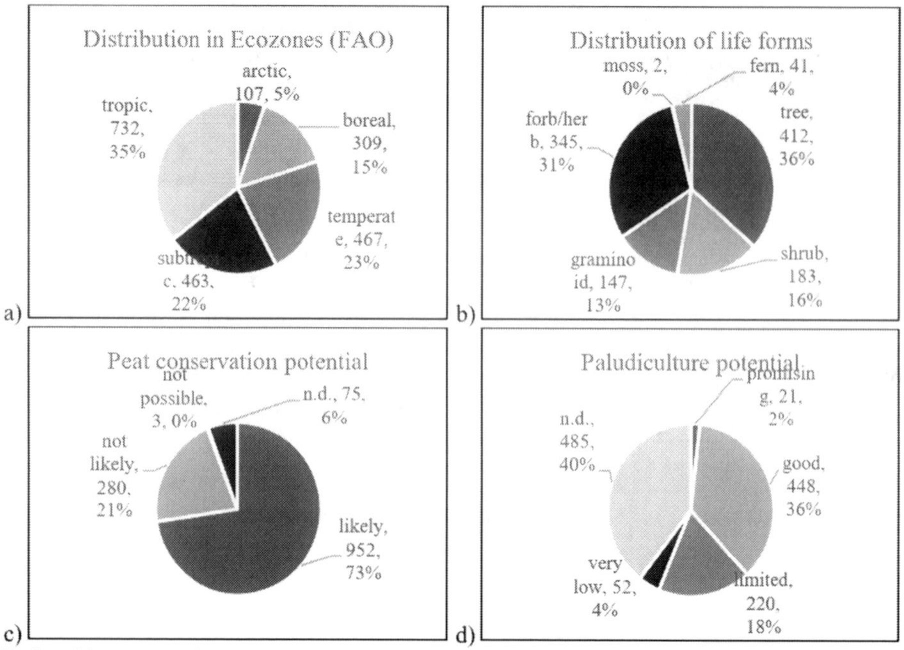

Figure 3: Distribution of the DPPP entries pertaining to a) the FAO Ecozones, b) life forms, c) peat conservation potential and d) paludiculture potential. Multiple selections possible for the ecozone assignment.

The peat conservation potential of a specific paludiculture is likely for 952 entries, 280 plant species show a ‘not likely” potential and only of 3 species the potential to conserve peat under paludiculture is assessed as not possible. 75 species could not be assessed because of a lack of data.

Peat conservation is less likely when annual or short living plants are cultivated in paludiculture. Annual or short living plants usually need a regular mechanical preparation of the topsoil to prepare the seed bed or the planting site for the next crop rotation. Additionally, regular tillage is needed for weed control. These measures increase the decomposition rate by mobilizing nutrients as well as oxygen. The peat conservation potential of perennial plants is usually more likely. Due to the longer life span, the frequency of required soil preparation is usually lower.

We assume that the removal of that part of the biomass that is not necessary for peat accumulation won’t have a negative impact on the peat conservation in paludiculture, neglecting the influence of management practice and harvest devices. The belowground biomass seem to be the main input for peat formation in peatlands that are dominated by vascular plants (e.g. Aerts et al. 1992, Barthelmes 2010, Bernard et al. 1988, Coleman 1976, Hartmann 1999, Hoyos-Santillan et al. 2015), in which the roots and rhizomes are growing into the already accumulated peat and form a so called 'displacement peat'. Harvesting the belowground plant compartments will disturb the soil stratigraphy and conflict with the goal of peat conservation. Harvesting the aboveground biomass, preferably without disturbing the peat soil and in a non-destructive way to sustain the plant cover for a rotational harvest will most likely be peat conserving. There is hardly any literature about the harvest influence on paludiculture (e.g. Kotowsky et al. 2013), further research is necessary to understand and adapt the management to conserve the peat in paludiculture.

Additionally, the installation of more demonstration areas is required to test and optimize cultivation techniques; study selection and propagation of suitable eco-types, development of site adapted machinery, and long-term environmental effects (peat hydraulics, peat formation, emissions, biodiversity). The growing demand for sustainable land use options can be expected to boost innovations in these fields.

The need for land use change on peatland is widely recognized (Joosten et al. 2012), but the cultivation of new crops can be counterproductive if the peculiarities of peat soils are insufficiently respected. Avoidance of peat degradation, greenhouse gas emissions and nutrient discharge requires permanent water saturation, minimal soil disturbance and careful nutrient management. Assessment of the paludiculture potential will help to avoid these counterproductive effects. Cultivation of plants with a promising and good potential will likely contribute to peat conservation and simultaneously sustain the provision of marketable biomass. Species with a limited potential may be suitable as well, but may first require the development of suitable peat conserving crop management techniques or the promotion of a market demand.

A book on potential paludiculture plants of the Holarctic (North America, Europe and Northern Asia) presenting a selection of 90 plant species of the Holarctic, is currently under preparation. This will be a synthesis of the data of the DPPP and further meta-analysis of literature concerning their potential cultivation in wet peatlands.

CONCLUSION

The DPPP provides valuable information on useful wetland plants worldwide. An improved data gathering in the tropical and subtropical zones is necessary to fill the gaps and complete the potential analysis of the entries. The potential for paludiculture is determined by the peat conservation potential and the market demand for products of the respective species. Promotion of species with a promising and good potential for paludiculture will likely contribute to peat conservation. Supporting measures for their promotion bear hardly any risk of being counterproductive as the practice will in any case not be worse than current drainage based land use. Nevertheless, the effects of management practices on carbon and nutrient emissions have to be addressed by further research whereas good practice guidelines must be developed from best practice examples and pilot projects.

ACKNOWLEDGEMENTS

The literature study and the establishment of the DPPP was done in the framework of the project 'VIP-Vorpommern Initiative für Paludikultur'. The VIP Project was promoted by the German Ministry of Education and Research (BMBF) within the program "Sustainable Land Management".

REFERENCES

1. Abel, S., Couwenberg, J., Dahms, T. & Joosten, H. 2013. The Database of Potential Paludiculture Plants (DPPP) and results for Western Pomerania. Plant Diversity and Evolution 130: 219–228.
2. Aerts, R., De Caluwe, H. and Konings, H. 1992. Seasonal allocation of biomass and nitrogen in four Carex species from mesotrophic and eutrophic fens as affected by nitrogen supply. – J. Ecol. 80: 653–664.
3. Barthelmes, A. 2010. Vegetation dynamics and carbon sequestration of Holocene alder (Alnus glutinosa) carrs of NE Germany. Dissertation, Greifswald, 240 p
4. Barthelmes, A. 2016. The global potential of paludiculture. In: Wichtmann, W., Schröder, C. & Joosten, H. (Eds.): Paludiculture – productive use of wet peatlands, Schweizerbart Science Publishers, ~285 S.
5. Bernard, J. M., Solander, D. and Kvet, J. 1988. Production and nutrient dynamics in Carex wetlands. – Aquatic Botany 30: 125–147.
6. Coleman, D. C. 1976. A review of root production processes and their influence on soil biota in terrestrial ecosystems. – In: Anderson, J. M. and Macfadyen, A. (eds), The role of terrestrial and aquatic organisms in decomposition processes. Blackwell Scientific, Oxford, pp. 417–434.
7. FAO Case studies: Peatland management practices 2015. Prepared by different authors for Mitigation of Climate Change in Agriculture (MICCA) Programme. Online at: http://www.fao.org/climatechange/micca/89910/en/
8. Giesen, W. 2013. Paludiculture: sustainable alternatives on degraded peat land in Indonesia. QANS Activity 3.3: Quick Assessment and Nationwide Screening of Peat and Lowland Resources and Action Planning for the Implementation of a National Lowland Strategy. Euroconsult Mott MacDonald, for the Netherlands Partners for Water Programme, Bappenas and the Ministry of Public Works, Indonesia.
9. Hartmann, M. 1999. To the roots of peat formation - production and decomposition processes in a fen. Dissertation University of Greifswald.
10. Haslam, S.M. 2010. A book of reed: Phragmites australis (Cav.) Trin. Ex Steudel, formerly Phragmites communis Trin., Forrest Text.
11. Hoyos-Santillan, J., Lomax, B.H., Large, D., Turner, B.L., Boom, A., Lopez, O.R. & Sjögersten, S. 2015. Getting to the root of the problem: litter decomposition and peat formation in lowland Neotropical peatlands. Biogeochemistry 126: 115-129.
12. Joosten, H., Tapio-Biström, M.-L. & Tol, S. (eds.) 2012. Peatlands - Guidance for Climate Change Mitigation Through Conservation, Rehabilitation and Sustainable Use. Food and Agriculture Organization of the United Nations, Rome, 100 pp. Online at: http://www.fao.org/docrep/ 015/an762e/an762e.pdf
13. Kotowski, W., Jabłońska, E. &Bartoszuk, H. 2013. Conservation management in fens: Do large tracked mowers impact functional plant diversity? Biological Conservation 167: 292–297.
14. Miettinen, J., Hooijer, A., Shi, C., Tollenaar, D., Vernimmen, R., Liew, S.C., Malins, C. & Page, S.E. 2012. Extent of industrial plantations on Southeast Asian peatlands in 2010 with analysis of historical expansion and future projections. Global Change Biology Bioenergy 4: 908–918.

15. Oehmke, C. & Abel, S. 2016. Selected plants for paludiculture. In: Wichtmann, W., Schröder, C. & Joosten, H. (Eds.): Paludiculture – productive use of wet peatlands, Schweizerbart Science Publishers, ~285 S.
16. Wichtmann, W. & Joosten, H. 2007. Paludiculture: peat formation and renewable resources from rewetted peatlands. IMCG Newsletter, 2007-3: 24–28. Online at: http://paludiculture.botanik.uni-greifswald.de/documents/paludiculture_peat_ formation_and_renewable_resources_from_rewetted_peatlands.pdf.
17. Wichtmann, W., Schröder, C. & Joosten, H. 2016. Paludiculture – productive use of wet peatlands, Schweizerbart Science Publishers, Stuttgart.
18. Yule, C.M. 2010. Loss of biodiversity and ecosystem functioning in Indo-Malayan peat swamp forests. Biodiversity Conservation 19: 393–409.

Abstract No: A-183

A CARBON FOOTPRINT FOR THE PEAT AND SUBSTRATE INDUSTRY

Moritz Böcking

Klasmann-Deilmann Gmbh, Germany

**Corresponding author: moritz.boecking@klasmann-deilmann.com*

ABSTRACT

The peat and substrate industry is under fire for its alleged impact on nature and the climate. In view of this, Klasmann-Deilmann GmbH is taking advantage of the opportunities that result from a sustainability strategy aligned with international standards in order to disclose its own performance to the public under ecological, economic and social criteria. A key element here is the publication of an annual Sustainability Report, of which a climate footprint now forms an integral part. This is the first time that a company in the peat and substrate sector has calculated its emissions from peat extraction and from the production and sale of growing media. For example, in 2014, the so called "company carbon footprint" increased by 0.69 % compared to 2013. At the same time the carbon footprint per m³ of substrate decreased by 2.26 % compared to the previous year. The proposed article gives an insight to the calculation of the carbon footprint which leads to a range of projects to reduce or compensate for the emissions generated. They are part of a CO_2 reduction strategy.

Keywords: -

INTRODUCTION

The call for ever-increasing sustainability has long since been heard by industry. A company will no longer be judged solely in terms of profits and job security. Rather, it will increasingly be viewed in terms of its societal role, assessed by the extent to which it is committed to addressing the ecological and social aspects of its own actions, keeping future generations in mind. In 2011, Klasmann-Deilmann began publishing Sustainability Reports. Those for 2013 and 2014 comply with criteria under the fourth generation of the GRI guidelines (published in 2013), which have a distinct focus on the 'materiality of reported issues'.

CLIMATE FOOTPRINT

One focus of international efforts to enhance sustainability is on climate protection. In the light of ongoing climate change, it is necessary to reduce greenhouse gases such as carbon dioxide (CO_2) and methane (CH_4), which are the worst culprits in global warming. In order to be able to demonstrably achieve progress in this regard, more and more businesses are having their own climate footprint calculated, which discloses the greenhouse gases caused in a year and their sources. Annual updates enable a company to find out whether it is succeeding in reducing emissions of these gases. For this purpose, the various gases are usually converted into 'CO_2 equivalents'.

The biggest challenge in drawing up a climate footprint for Klasmann-Deilmann involved calculating emissions from peat, peat extraction and substrate production, since no other business had determined or published such data. The services of Cologne-based firm MEO Carbon Solutions GmbH were enlisted, which developed a 'greenhouse gas calculator' tailored to the company's requirements. SGS United Kingdom Ltd. (Cheshire, UK), contracted to independently assess the results, verified the climate footprint with reference to ISO 14064-1.

This calculator's structure was based on the study commissioned by EPAGMA on the life cycle assessments (LCAs) of key substrate constituents (QUANTIS, EPAGMA 2012). The outcome was a modular structure that served as the basis for carbon footprinting both for the company as a whole and at individual product level. It also adopted other significant parameters, such as standard values for raw peat in terms of storage density, carbon/nitrogen content and degradation rate, as well as pre- and after-use scenarios.

With regard to ongoing and future measures to reduce emissions, the calculator can be employed to assess the positive impact of carbon-offsetting and/or avoidance measures. This calculates, at corporate level, the extent to which the use of fossil fuels is avoided or offset by using – for example – short-rotation forestry (SRF) plantations, forests and managed woodland, photovoltaic plants or woodchip heating systems. Alternative substrate constituents such as wood fibre, compost and coco pith offer further savings potential for the product-based carbon footprint. The choice of production location can also have a positive effect on the carbon footprint of a growing medium.

CARBON FOOTPRINT 2014

On the basis of corporate data for the 2013 financial year, a corporate carbon footprint (CCF) and a product carbon footprint (PCF) were disclosed for the first time in July 2014. The company published its carbon footprint for the 2014 financial year in the autumn of 2015.

Taking into account all climate-related factors along the value chain 'from raw-material extraction to the factory gate, including transport', the corporate carbon footprint for 2014 reveals emissions of 274,271 t CO_2 equivalent (previous year: 272,390 t). At an annual turnover of EUR 165.0 million, this yields a figure for the year under review of 1.66 kg of CO_2 equivalent per euro of turnover. With the total volume of growing media and raw materials sold standing at 3.32 million m^3, this translates into an average carbon footprint – expressed per cubic metre of substrate, per annum – of 82.52 kg of CO_2 equiv.m^{-3}.

Table 1: Carbon footprint of Klasmann-Deilmann GmbH (2014/13)

Emission source	**2014 in t CO_2 eq**	**% of total footprint**	**2013 in t CO_2 eq**	**Change 2013/14 as a %**
Extraction areas: Reference scenarios	- 134,961	- 49.21	- 148,560	- 9.15
Extraction areas: Peat extraction, interim storage	192,618	70.23	210,972	- 8.70
Extraction areas: After-use scenarios	52,177	19.02	54,424	- 4.13
Extraction areas: End use 1/100	7,767	2.83	8,346	- 6.94
Extraction areas: Subtotal for emissions	**= 117,601**	**42.87**	**= 125,182**	**- 6.06**
Energy consumption: Extraction areas	20,575	7.50	19,657	+ 4.67
Energy consumption: Other sites	1,832	0.67	1,414	+ 29.56
Transport: Raw materials, internal	6,518	2.38	5,751	+ 13.34
Transport: Raw materials and substrates to the customer	62,421	22.76	59,690	+ 4.58
External suppliers: Peat inclusive of transport	37,613	13.71	38,021	- 1.07
External suppliers: Packaging materials	4,575	1.67	4,657	- 1.76
Alternative substrate constituents and additives inclusive of transport	22,408	8.17	17,650	+ 26.96
Other areas of activity (SRF, other forestry, photovoltaic installations, woodchip heating)	728	0.27	368	+ 97.83
Carbon footprint of company as a whole	**274,271**	**100.00 %**	**272,390**	**+ 0.69**
Total quantity of substrates and raw materials incl. retail (m^3)	3,323,670 m^3		3,226,356 m^3	
Carbon footprint per m^3 of substrate	82.52 kg CO_2 equiv.		84.43 kg CO_2 equiv.	- 2.26

EXPLANATORY NOTES ON THE CARBON FOOTPRINT FOR 2014/2013

1. Extraction sites: The disclosed decrease in emissions compared with the verified 'base year' (2013) results chiefly from the return of land following cessation of extraction and from below-target extraction quantities owing to unfavourable weather conditions.
2. Reference scenarios: The fundamental idea behind the reference scenario is the fact that bogs and peat extraction areas already emitted trace gases that affect the climate in the form of CO_2, N_2O or CH_4 before they became the company's property and consequently its responsibility in terms of climate change. Even without peat extraction, the sites would have continued to emit these gases into the atmosphere. By this line of reasoning, the emissions pertaining to this time-based reference scenario have been credited to the firm or deducted from its carbon footprint.
3. Peat extraction, interim storage: To date, relatively little is known about the long-term effects of CO_2 emissions from peat products. It is still largely unclear what quantities of greenhouse gases are released in the various stages of the value chain (e.g. actively worked peat extraction sites, storage of peat in stacks, peat in growing media) over a given time. Although the available data (also used in our calculations) are based on scientific findings, they nevertheless contain some uncertain factors – especially because most of the measuring campaigns and studies do not relate to the active phase of peat extraction. With regard to emission factors for peat extraction areas, the calculation is based on the approach adopted by the German Federal Ministry of Education and Research (BMBF) report 'Klimaschutz durch Moorschutz' ('Combating Climate Change by Protecting Peatlands'; source: Drösler 2011). The figures stated in this report are based on the then most up-to-date information obtained from direct greenhouse gas measurements on German bog sites. According to this study, the level of emissions from the different use categories – agriculture, afforestation, drained raised bogs, natural raised bogs and re-wetting – depends on the water table depth in a given case (Drösler 2011, p. 7-9). For the peat extraction phase that was not taken into account in the BMBF report, Klasmann-Deilmann applied a general water depth of –30cm. At the same time, however, a 50% lower emission rate was assumed in order to reflect the reduced respiration processes (no autotrophic respiration, potentially reduced heterotrophic respiration). On this basis, applying the above-mentioned model, an average emissions level of 10.73 t CO_2 equivalent per hectare, per year was calculated, forming the starting point for all further calculations derived from peat and substrates. Most recently, HÖPER referred to measurement results that are below these estimates (see HÖPER 2015, p.142, dry raised bog (NI), p.145, Westermoor 1 and 2).
4. After-use scenarios: These are the emissions that arise after peat harvesting ceases (in relation to peatland restoration, for instance), before the area begins to sequester greenhouse gases once more.

1. End use 1/100: Emissions disclosed here result from degradation of raw peat. Peat used as a raw material or substrate progressively releases stored carbon – by means of respiratory processes as it reacts with atmospheric oxygen – into the environment in the form of CO_2. The assessment of peat's climatic impact is based not on how much carbon remains in the growing medium, but on the proportion emitted in the form of CO_2. In this connection, Klasmann-Deilmann converts emission totals into CO_2 equivalents with a global-warming potential for the next 100 years (GWP100). In the corporate carbon footprint, an aggregate mean value for the year under review is adopted, derived from the overall GWP100 score (1% of the GWP100). In extending the 'cradle to gate' system boundary, emissions from transport are also included. Emissions arising during the end use of products are, however, excluded. A distinction is therefore made between the emissions attributed to the company and those attributed to subsequent users, such as horticultural businesses or consumers. This last point, in particular, prompted extensive discussions, as a considerable proportion of greenhouse gases was not included in the climate footprint. The rationale behind this decision was that, in the same way that an oil producer is not responsible for a car driver's petrol consumption, a substrate producer cannot be held to account for the way a product is used by a customer.
2. Subtotal for emissions in 2014: This line gives the sum total of all emissions resulting from the extraction areas.
3. Energy consumption: The year-on-year increase in emissions is due chiefly to higher diesel consumption in raw-materials extraction owing to unfavourable weather conditions. Additionally, all energy consumed by

our sales companies is also included for the first time although this, totalling 260 t CO_2 equivalent, is fairly negligible.

4. Extraction sites: This line refers to the emissions of the lead company and subsidiaries that own peat extraction operations, and primarily includes diesel, power and natural-gas consumption.
5. Other sites: This gives the total emissions from the production and sales companies which, particularly in administrative buildings, result from electricity and natural-gas consumption.
6. Transport: Substrates and raw peat are relatively bulky and heavy. To an increasing extent, they are shipped abroad from our production facilities – often to destinations overseas. This results in high costs and causes environmental impact. In order to identify the emissions resulting from transport, we have recorded the data for all in-house transport, transport by additive suppliers, transport by other external suppliers of raw peat materials and transport of finished growing media 'ex works' for each individual location and each substrate component, inclusive of the annual supply quantities for the Group. These detailed figures – based on the transport distance between the factory gate and a destination in the centre of the country in question, modes of transport (road, rail and water), and the number of transport units (e.g. containers) involved – are related to appropriate emission factors.
7. Because production quantities were up year-on-year, emissions (disclosed in the climate footprint) from internal transport of raw materials and from the logistics services of external transport providers also rose.
8. Raw materials, internal: This line states the emissions resulting from the transport of raw materials within the Klasmann-Deilmann Group.
9. Raw materials and substrates to customers: These emissions are those originating from transport to the customer worldwide. A detailed breakdown was provided for transport by road, container, water and rail.
10. Not included here are internal and customer-related empty runs, as the hauliers and transport providers whose services are enlisted are (in accordance with relevant joint agreements) responsible for providing onward and return transport.
11. External suppliers: Emissions attributable to the company that arise from the purchase and transport of substrate constituents, as well as from packaging film and pallets, remained roughly unchanged year-on-year.
12. Peat inclusive of transport: The emissions disclosed here are those from the extraction and transport of peat that the company does not extract itself but buys in from outside.
13. Packaging material: This line gives the total emissions resulting from the use of packaging film, paper, cardboard and pallets.
14. Further sources of emissions: Against a background of increasing production quantities of green compost, wood fibre and corporate-owned SRF plantations, and the greater need for additives owing to increased manufacture of growing media, emissions from the following activities rose.
15. Alternative substrate constituents and additives including transport: Emissions stated in this line result chiefly from the production of our own alternative growing-media constituents, 'TerrAktiv' (green compost) and 'Klasmann GreenFibre' (wood fibre). It also includes those emissions generated by suppliers through the manufacture and transport of additives such as fertiliser and lime. As Klasmann-Deilmann uses these products, emissions here are attributed to the company.
16. Other areas of activity: Emissions disclosed here are those resulting from establishment and maintenance of SRF plantations, forestry, woodchip heating systems and photovoltaic installations.

'POSITIVE FOOTPRINT'

17. The Renewable Energy and Resources business unit is to be considerably expanded in the coming years. It will also contribute to emissions avoidance but, under the requirements of the ISO 14064 standard, is disclosed separately from the climate footprint. The chief reason for this is that the bulk of the energy generated in this way will not be consumed by Klasmann-Deilmann itself, but fed into the grid and sold. In addition to the carbon footprint for 2014, a 'positive' carbon footprint has therefore also been drawn up (i.e. one that includes only carbon-positive measures). It discloses how many emissions from fossil energy sources such as coal, oil and natural gas are avoided by the use of renewable energy, and captured by forest resources.

Table 2: Emissions avoidance (2014/13)

Emissions avoidance	2014 in t CO_2 eq	2013 in t CO_2 eq	Change 2013/14 as a %
Use and generation of renewable energy and of forest resources	- 11,209	- 10,467	7.09%

18. The greenhouse gas calculator classifies emissions into three groups known as scopes, in conformity with ISO 14064 and the requirements of the Kyoto Protocol. Scope 1 includes all emissions directly generated from combustion processes within in-house facilities. Scope 2 covers emissions relating to purchased energy, such as electricity or heat. Scope 3 refers to emissions from third-party services and purchased preliminary services.

CO_2 REDUCTION STRATEGY

19. Based on our carbon footprint, measures are identified to reduce or offset the emissions caused by the company, and a CO_2 reduction strategy is developed including the following areas of activity:
20. Of the scenarios for reducing or offsetting emissions, those that are realistic involve measures to either avoid the use of fossil fuels or enable direct carbon capture. These include afforestation, management of woodland and SRF plantations, and production of heat energy from corporate-owned SRF sites. The greater part of the energy generated in this way would not be consumed by the company itself, but fed into the grid and sold. It has therefore been decided not to include the positive effects in the greenhouse gas footprint, but to publish these separately in a footprint including only carbon-positive measures.
21. Internal transport, as well as that bought in from transport providers, is a crucial factor within the carbon footprint and harbours fundamental potential for additional emissions avoidance. One approach relates to the weight of raw materials and growing media: the lighter these are, the greater the volumes that can be carried in each transport unit. A number of internal projects have already been launched, aimed at reducing the weight of raw materials and products.
22. Furthermore, the use of peat-substitute bulking constituents in our growing media has a positive impact on our carbon footprint at both product and corporate level. The target is to increase the proportion of alternative constituents by 2020 to 15% by volume of the annual production total.
23. Since 2015, all Klasmann-Deilmann Group companies based in Germany have obtained their electricity from hydropower with a guarantee of origin.
24. A large part of the emissions originate from extraction sites. The firm is, therefore, discussing ways of putting its methods of extracting peat on a more sustainable footing. However, particular caution needs to be exercised here, as being reliably supplied with raw materials constitutes the backbone of its core business.
25. Moreover, data drawn from the literature – which form the underlying basis for emissions disclosures from the extraction areas – will be reviewed in accordance with scientific criteria. The company is currently, on a trial basis, conducting a measuring campaign on German and Lithuanian peatland sites, the plan being to continue this project if it yields reliable results. In consequence, the actual measured levels arising from peat extraction may lead to revision of the climate footprint. It is also conceivable that the measured values will be lower than expected, allowing emissions to be revised downwards. A 'reduction' of this kind would, then, be a measured, computational effect, not one resulting from emission-reducing measures. In order that acceptance of this project and its outcome is as widespread as possible, dialogue is being sought with interested environmental and climate organisations.

Abstract No: A-025

FEN PEAT PROPERTIES AND METAL ACCUMULATION IN IT

Janis Krumins, Maris Klavins* and Valdis Seglins

University of Latvia, Raina Blvd. 19, LV 1586, Riga, Latvia

**Corresponding author: maris.klavins@lu.lv*

SUMMARRY

There are a few publications about fen peat composition and properties, thus it is important to develop studies on fen peat to find out and to expand the application possibilities of this type of peat. Fen peat is formed from decomposed plant remains - development of these plants mostly was based on nutrient supply from mineral-rich groundwater. In general fen peat is built up from sedges, reeds, grasses, shrubs or wood under waterlogged conditions. The developed surface area and large number of acidic functional groups common to peat, determine the ability to bind trace elements including remains of living organic matter, either both as sedimentary, deposited, particulate matter or as sorbed or complexed metal ions. The main goal of this study was to explore and analyze the distribution and accumulation patterns of major and trace elements in fen peat under differing environmental conditions in Latvia. In this study we found that concentrations of some major elements significantly change depending on their location in the peat profile. In general, there were concentrations of the thirteen chemical elements, Ca, Mg, Fe, Mn, Zn, Cu, Na, K, Cd, Co, Cr, Ni and Pb; however in several peat profiles, for instance, in the *Svētupes* peat profile, concentrations of some elements (i.e. Cd and Co) were below the detection limit and could not be determined

***Keywords**: trace elements; fen peat, accumulation*

INTRODUCTION

Chemical composition of peat changes according to its position in the vertical and horizontal level, water table and peat forming plant composition and their decomposition characteristics (Damman, 1978). The increase of anthropogenic impact causes changes in the natural accumulation pattern, for instance - drainage and peat use in agriculture or forestry significantly affect metallic element cycles. Fen plants are fed predominantly by groundwater and that is why fen peat is rich with lithogenic metallic elements. Weathering of sedimentary rocks and mineral deposits are another important source of metal ions that migrate upward into peat by diffusion, especially in fen ecosystems (Shotyk and Steinmann, 1994). Due to the weathering metal ions are released into groundwater and supplied to peat. Metal ion supply, either by diffusion or by groundwater, as well as the intensity of both these processes depends on basal deposits and mires that are formed on calcareous sedimentary rocks are chemically more affected by ion uptake diffusion than those formed on metamorphic rocks (Givelet *et al.*, 2004).

The developed surface area and large number of acidic functional groups common to peat determine the ability to bind metallic elements included in remains of the plant organic matter, either as sedimentary, deposited, particulate matter, or as sorbed or complexed metal ions (Brown *et al.*, 2000). The ability of peat to accumulate metallic elements depends not only on the element capacity to bind with functional groups, but also on the pH reaction, on the presence of low molecular weight compounds (carboxylic acids, polyphenols) and other dissociating compounds, for instance, sulphate or hydrogen carbonate ions (Tipping *et al.*, 2003). Source of metallic elements in peat mass can be attributed to atmospheric precipitation, to metallic elements present in peat-forming plants, as well as to supply with groundwater and surface runoff. Another important source of metallic elements in peat are sedimentary rocks in the base of mire, as due to the weathering metal ions migrate upward by diffusion into the peat layer (Shotyk and Steinmann, 1994).

All studied metallic elements in peat were divided into groups with similar chemical characteristics, respectively, - alkaline earth metals (Ca and Mg), alkali metals (K and Na), transition metals (Cd, Co, Cr, Cu, Fe, Mn, Ni, and Zn) and post-transition metals (Pb). Many studies (Coggins *et al.*, 2006; Ukonmaanaho *et al.*, 2004; Shotyk *et al.*, 2002; Martinez-Cortizas *et al.*, 2002; Shotyk *et al.*, 2001) have shown a gradual increase of heavy metals in peat mass during the last hundred years as a result of anthropogenic pollution.

The goal of this study was to explore and analyze distribution and accumulation pattern of major and trace elements in fen peat under differing environmental conditions in Latvia.

MATERIALS AND METHODS

To characterize the influence of peat composition on metallic element accumulation, four fens in the territory of Latvia were chosen, those were Elku and Vīķu mire. These fens were chosen as the study subject due to their similar origin, but with significant differences in peat botanical composition and variable Quaternary deposit character in mire catchment area. Field studies were carried out during the period from 2009 to 2015.

Fen peat was studied using standardized methods (Tan, 2005). Peat profiles from each study site were separated into 5 cm thick layers and the metallic element content was determined by acid digestion using atomic absorption spectroscopy (Krachler *et al.*, 2003). Acid digestion was carried out using 25 ml 50% HNO_3 and 5 ml 30% H_2O_2 on 1 g of oven-dried peat sample. Each sample was mixed with the acid solution and left for 24 h; mixtures were then boiled at 150°C until half of the liquid evaporated and then another 25 ml of 50% HNO_3 were added and the mixture boiled until vibrating started. Digested samples were filtered and diluted with Millipore water up to 50 ml of the total volume and transferred into tubes and further used in atomic absorption spectroscopy. Metallic element concentration was normalized against Ti content in peat samples. Sample dating was performed using the conventional liquid scintillation counting technique, but as the scintillation solvent benzene was used. Botanical composition and decomposition degree. The analysis of peat decomposition degree was followed by the centrifugation method according to the ГОСТ 10650-72 standard, and peat decomposition degree was expressed as percentage of the total peat sample mass (Malterer *et al.*, 1992). Peat botanical composition was determined using a binocular microscope at 56 to 140 x magnification according to the ГОСТ 28245-89 standard. The content of organic matter, carbonate matter and mineral matter was determined and values calculated using the Loss on Ignition method (Heiri *et al.*, 2001). Samples were dried in an oven at 105°C for 24 h, heated in a muffle furnace at 550°C for 4 h and at 950°C for 2 h. Elemental composition (C, H, N and S) was determined using a Carlo Erba Elemental Analyzer EA-1108 with PC based data system. All values were normalized against the ash content. The oxygen content was measured as the residual (100% minus the content of C, H, N and S). T

RESULTS AND DISCUSSION

Study sites are of similar origin, but of varied botanical composition, which points on different conditions of mire development. However, in general, the studied mires were formed in similar conditions and characterize environmental conditions in Latvian fens. This situation was assumed as one of the main criteria for selection of particular study area. Relatively simple environmental conditions, similar origin, but differences in further development suggest also a variability in peat properties.

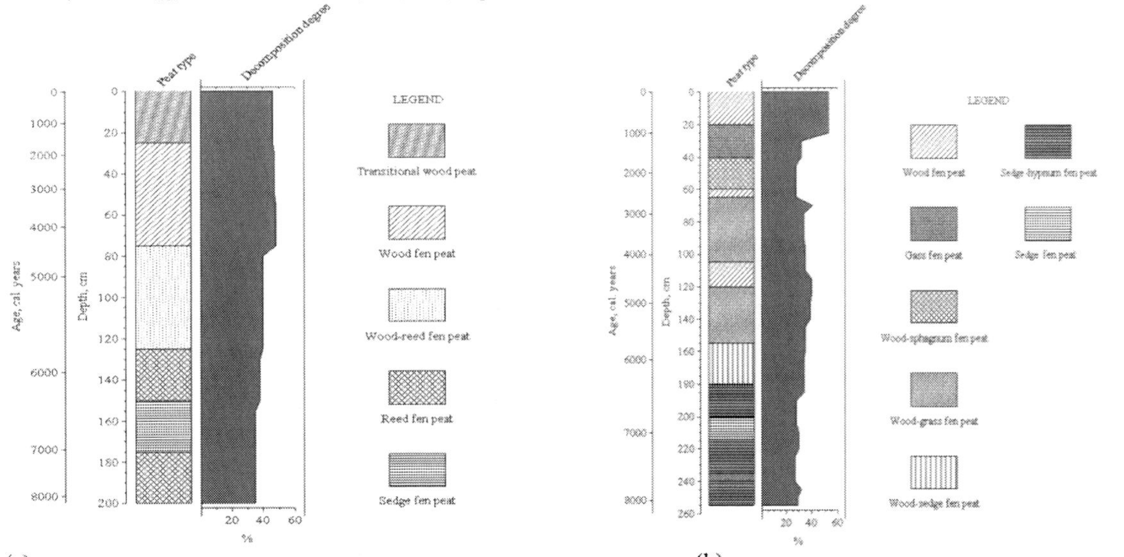

(a) (b)

Figure 1: The botanical composition and decomposition degree of Elku Mire (a) and Vīķu Mire (b) peat

Elku Mire: Nowadays Elku Mire is considered to be transitional mire and is covered by a 0.25 m thick layer of transitional wood peat. The studied Elku Mire peat profile consists of 5 different peat layers with a total depth of 2

m (Fig. 1); the age of the mire is 8000 years. The superficial peat layer (0.00-0.25 m) is composed of transitional wood peat, but the rest of the mire profile consists of various fen peat types (wood, wood-reed, reed and sedge peat). Peat decomposition degree is in the range between 35 and 48% and can be considered as high. Peat botanical composition studies show that Elku Mire has been formed due to a lake overgrow and this fact can also be confirmed by the findings of thick and continuous sapropel layer below mire deposits.

Vīķu Mire: The superficial peat layer in Vīķu Mire is similar to that of Elku Mire.and consists of wood peat. However,lthough - this mire is still in the stage of fen and it's peat is more affected by anthropogenic activity than the fen peat in Elku Mire. Vīķu Mire peat profile (Fig. 1) consists of 7 peat types (wood, grass, wood-*sphagnum*, wood-grass, wood-sedge, sedge-*hypnum* and sedge peat) with a total peat layer of 2.5 m in depth; the age of the mire is 8000 years. Peat decomposition degree in the studied section varies from 27 to 41%.

Five base elements in fen peat elemental composition are C, H, N, O and S. The most part of peat elemental composition is built up of C, being the base element in the organic world, second in line is O, then H and finally N. The content of all elements was normalized against the ash content in peat.

The concentration of C in the studied peat is in range of 27.6 to 48.9%, but the exact value depends on the peat botanical composition, thus this element has no particular accumulation pattern. C content in Elku Mire peat is in the range of 41.2 to 48.9% and it seems to gradually increase with depth, although, C content is practically stable within the peat profile.

In order to obtain the most complete picture of the metallic element accumulation character, it is necessary to analyse thefull peat profile and not particularly selected parts, because the location of specific peat layers can significantly affect data interpretation. Metallic elements were grouped in 4 general classes: 1) alkaline earth metals (Ca, Mg); 2) alkali metals (Na, K); 3) transition metals (Fe, Mn, Zn, Cu, Co, Cd, Cr, and Ni); 4) post-transition metals (Pb).

Alkaline earth metals: Ca and Mg are biophile elements and are closely related to mire vegetation growing conditions. Both metallic elements are main plant nutrients and belong to the most important metallic elements that are involved in fen development. Alkaline earth metals in fen peat are supplied by groundwater, but their source of supply can be both natural and anthropogenic. Amongst natural sources are sediments in mire catchment areas – these can be sapropel, sand, silt, till and others. Quaternary deposits with high carbonate mineral content. Agricultural land use may cause anthropogenic alkaline earth metal supply form mire catchment area – for instance, soil liming can lead to high Ca concentrations in upper peat layers. The highest Ca concentration in Elku Mire is located in the wood-reed fen peat layer, in the middle part of peat profile (Fig. 2), where peak concentration exceeds 40 g/kg. It can be explained by groundwater supply. At the same time, the lowest Ca content is in the bottom part of peat profile, where peat contains 16.8 g/kg Ca. The distribution of Mg is similar (with slight differences) to the Ca accumulation pattern (Fig. 2) and it can be explained by common source of supply – dolomite minerals in Quaternary deposits of mire catchment area. However, Mg concentration is significantly lower than Ca content. Peak concentration is 1.5 g/kg, but minimum amount of Mg in Elku Mire peat profile is 0.5 g/kg. The concentration of both metallic elements is decreasing by the depth, although there is also a relation to the peat botanical composition and decomposition degree.

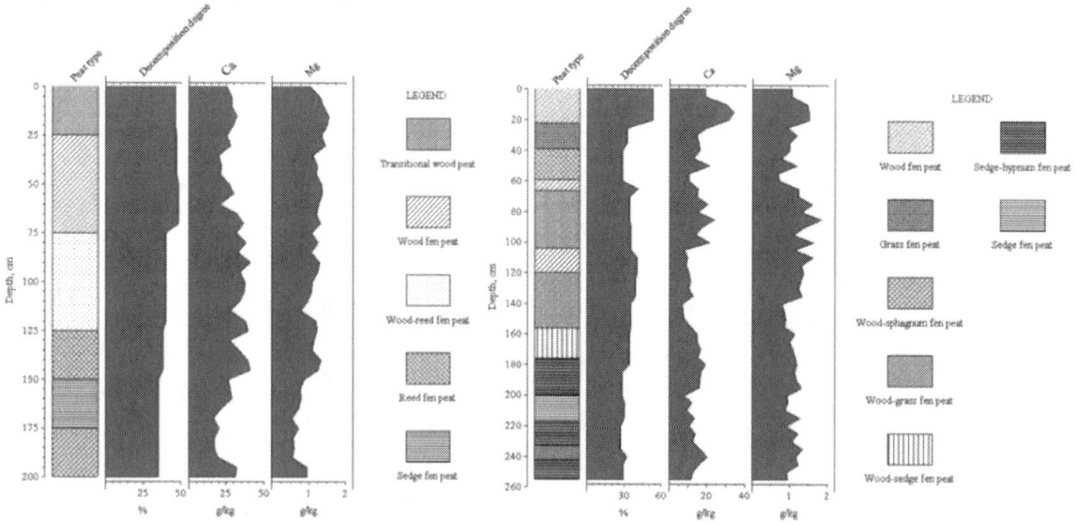

(a) (b)

Figure 2: The accumulation pattern of alkaline earth metals in Elku (a) and Vīķu (b) Mire peat profile

Alkali metals: K is a biophile element and closely related to the growing conditions of mire vegetation, while Na content can also be associated with atmospheric deposition. Alkali metals in fen peat are supplied by groundwater from deposits in mire catchment area, but their supply source can be also of anthropogenic origin. Amongst natural sources is till, which contains K and Na feldspar minerals, but one of the most significant anthropogenic sources might be fertilizers used in agriculture.

The highest K concentration in Elku Mire is located in transitional wood peat, in the upper part of the peat profile (Fig. 3), where peat contains 269 mg/kg K. The location of the mire and the K content in the upper peat layer allows the assumption that K has a natural supply source. The lowest K content is in reed fen peat, in the middle part of the peat profile, where peat contains 1.6 mg/kg K. The highest Na concentration in Elku Mire is located in the transitional wood peat layer (177 mg/kg), where also the least Na content was identified (39 mg/kg). While K concentration seems to be variable throughout the peat profile, because of K high mobility, Na content is rather stable; this can be explained by different sources of supply.

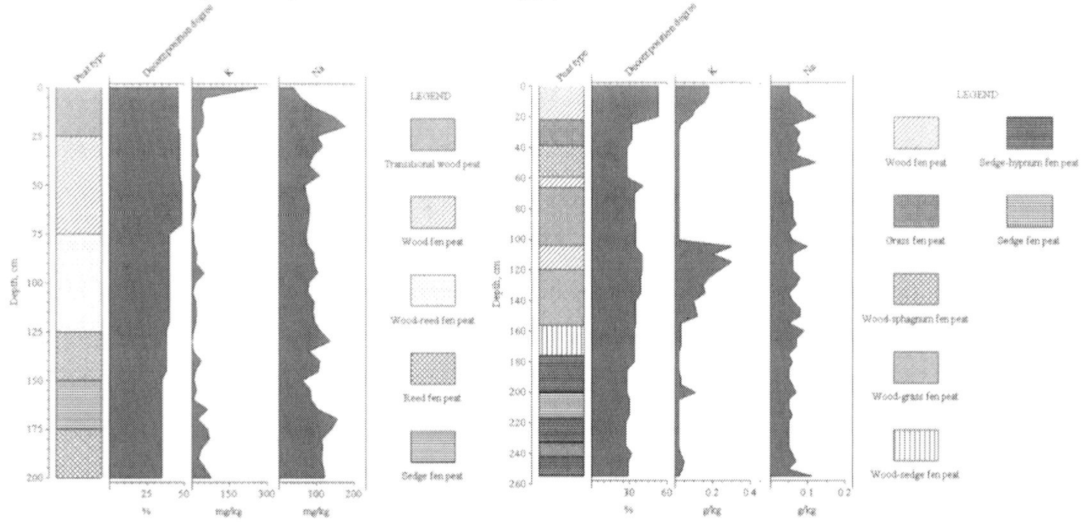

(a) (b)

Figure 3: The accumulation pattern of alkali metals in Elku (a) and Vīķu (b) Mire peat profile

Transition metals: Transition metal accumulation in peat can be explained by both natural and anthropogenic causes. Metallic elements can be supplied with groundwater from deposits in mire catchment areas and with atmospheric precipitation, but agricultural land use can also be of possible consideration. All transition metals in reasonable amounts are essential plant micronutrients, however if their concentration in soil is high, they must be seen as heavy metals and a potential threat. Fe, Mn, Ni and Co are siderophile elements and have no affinity for oxygen (except Fe and Mn), thus they tend to migrate down the peat profile. Moreover, all siderophile elements form strong chemical bonds with carbon and sulphur. Zn, Cu and Cd are chalcophile elements and generally remain in the upper part of peat profile, where they form chemical compounds which do not tend to migrate downwards.

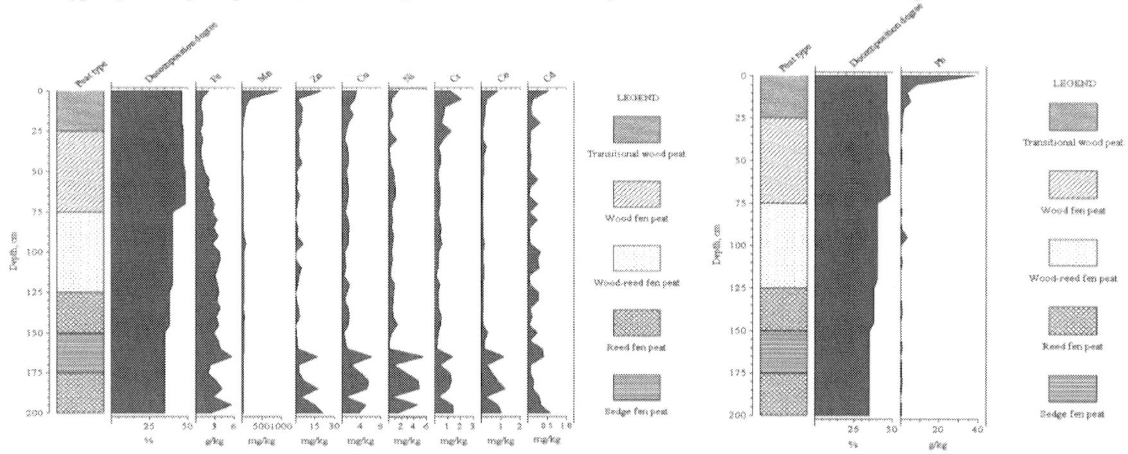

Figure 4: The accumulation pattern of transition metals and lead in Elku Mire peat profile

According to the results (Fig. 4) Zn, Cu, Cr, Ni, Co and Cd have similar accumulation characteristics – these metallic elements have high concentrations in the upper and bottom peat layers, while in the middle layers their content is low and rather stable. This can be explained by groundwater level changes that caused transition metal migration in the bottom part of peat profile, while metallic element content in upper part of peat profile is affected by atmospheric precipitation.

The highest Fe concentration in Vīķu Mire is located in wood fen peat, in the upper part of peat profile (Fig. 4), where peat contains 4.7 g/kg Fe. The lowest Fe content is in wood-*sphagnum* peat, in the middle part of the peat profile where peat contains 216 mg/kg Fe. The highest Mn concentration in Vīķu Mire is located in wood fen peat, in the upper part of peat profile, where peat contains 63 mg/kg Mn. The lowest Mn content is in wood-*Sphagnum* peat, in the middle part of peat profile, where peat contains 1.9 mg/kg Mn. The highest Ni concentration in Vīķu Mire is located in wood fen peat, in the upper part of peat profile (Fig. 4), where peat contains 3.2 mg/kg Ni. The highest Co concentration in Vīķu Mire is located in wood fen peat, in the upper part of peat profile (Fig. 4), where peat contains 2 mg/kg Co. The highest Zn concentration in Vīķu Mire is located in wood fen peat, in the upper part of peat profile (Fig. 4), where peat contains 12.4 mg/kg Zn. The lowest Zn content is in the middle part of peat profile, where peat contains 2.3 mg/kg Zn. The highest Cu concentration in Vīķu Mire is located in wood fen peat, in the upper part of peat profile, where peat contains 6.9 mg/kg Cu. Pb has no known biological functions and can be considered as heavy metal. Pb is chalcophile element, has low affinity for oxygen and under anaerobic conditions forms distinct sulphide phases. Moreover, at its highest concentration, Pb remains close to the surface. Pb solubility in water is pH function and depends on water hardness, salinity and the presence of humic substances. Pb is the most soluble in soft, acidic water; it means that weak acidic fen peat environment limits Pb solubility. The highest Pb concentration in Elku Mire is located in transitional wood peat, in the upper part of peat profile (Fig. 4), where peat contains 38 mg/kg and it can be considered as Pb pollution. The lowest Pb content is below 0.5 mg/kg and the concentration remains low throughout the full peat profile. The highest Pb concentration in Vīķu Mire is located in wood fen peat, in the upper part of peat profile, where peat contains 23.5 mg/kg Pb, but in the rest of the peat profile Pb content remains low (below 0.5 mg/kg).

CONCLUSIONS

Elevated Pb concentration in upper peat layer is related to environmental pollution due to anthropogenic activities. Pb has no tendency to migrate downwards, thus in bottom peat layers its content remains low. Overall, Pb content in studied peat is negligible and does not demonstrate any relations with peat characteristics. However, high Pb concentration in upper peat layers has negative impact on mire vegetation and thus on peat accumulation. Elevated transition metal concentration in upper peat layers is related to their accumulation with precipitation and can be related to atmospheric pollution and modern anthropogenic activities itself. However, it can be also associated with natural processes such as - biomass production and supply from mire catchment areas. An elevated metallic element concentration in bottom layers can be explained by significant groundwater level changes that cause migration of a particular metallic element.

ACKNOWLEDGEMENT

Financial support from Latvia National Research Programme ResProd is acknowledged.

REFERENCES

1. Brown, P.A., Gill, S.A., Allen, S.J. 2000. Metal removal from wastewater using peat. Water Resources 34, 3907-3916.
2. Coggins, A.M., Jennings, S.G., Ebinghaus, R. 2006. Accumulation rates of the heavy metals lead, mercury and cadmium in ombrotrophic peatlands in the west of Ireland. Atmospheric Environment 40, 260-278.
3. Damman, A.W.H. 1978. Distribution and movement of elements in ombrotrophic peat bogs. Oikos 30, 480-495.
4. Givelet, N., Le Roux, G., Cheburkin, A., Chen, B., Frank, J., Goodsite, M., Kempter, H., Krachler M., Noernberg, T., Rausch, N., Rheinberger, S., Roos-Barraclough, F., Sapkota, A., Scholz, C., Shotyk, W. 2004. Suggested protocol for collecting, handling and preparing peat cores and peat samples for physical, chemical, mineralogical and isotopic analyses. Journal of Environmental Monitoring 6, 481-492.
5. Heiri, O., Lotter, A.F., Lemcke, G. 2001. Loss on ignition as a method for estimating organic and carbonate content in deposits: reproducibility and comparability of results. Journal of Paleolimnology 25, 101-110.

6. Krachler, M., Mohl, C., Emons, H., Shotyk, W. 2003. Two thousand years of atmospheric rare elements (REE) deposition as revealed by ombrotrophic peat bog profile, Jura mountains, Switzerland. Journal of Environmental Monitoring 5, 111-121.
7. Malterer, T.J., Verry, E.S., Erjaves, J. 1992. Fiber content and degree of decomposition in peats: review of natural methods. Soil Science Society of America Journal 56, 1200-1211.
8. Shotyk, W. 1996. Natural and anthropogenic enrichments of As, Cu, Pb, Sb and Zn in ombrotrophic versus minerotrophic peat bog profiles, Jura Mountains, Switzerland. Water, Air and Soil Pollution 90, 375-405.
9. Shotyk, W., Steinmann, P. 1994. Porewater indicators of rainwater-dominated versus groundwater-dominated peat bog profiles (Jura Mountains, Switzerland). Chemical Geology 116(1-2), 137-146.
10. Tan, K.H. 2005. Soil sampling, preparation and analysis. 2nd ed. Taylor & Francis Group.
11. Tipping, E., Smith, E.J., Lawlor, A.J., Hughes, S., Stevens, P.A. 2003. Predicting the release of metals from ombrotrophic peat due to drought-induced acidification. Evironmental Pollution 123, 239-253.
12. Ukonmaanaho, L., Nieminen, T.M., Rausch, N., Shotyk, W. 2004. Heavy metal and arsenic profiles in ombrogenous peat cores from four differently loaded areas in Finland. Water, Air and Soil Pollution 158, 277-294.

Abstract No: A-407

FROM CONVERSION OF WASTE TO PRODUCTION OF GROWING MEDIA CONSTITUENTS; CHANGE OF FOCUS

Hein Boon

Foundation RHP, The Netherlands

Corresponding author: boon@rhp.nl

SUMMARY

Peat is by far the most important constituent for growing media. Nowadays (organic) residues from various sources, are offered as potential constituent for growing media. These flows are often derived from processes of waste collection and conversion. Often these products -as such- are not suitable as constituent for growing media, because they do not meet basic requirements with respect to, for example, phytohygienic and nutritional aspects.In order to enhance future prospects of these potential constituents, the production processes need to be converted from waste treatment into the production of a suitable and safe constituent for the production of growing media. A risk assessment is an important precondition and tool to organise and improve production processes with focus especially on phytosanitary safety and quality-guarantees.

Keywords: *growing media, risk-assessment, phytosanitary safety*

INTRODUCTION

Over the past decades the use of growing media has gradually developed. In Europe the annual use of growing media is around 35 million m3. Peat is by far the most important constituent. Nearly 75% of the constituents for growing media consist of sphagnum-peat. Over the years the growing media industry as well as growers, have experienced the favourable properties of peat.

A quarter of the constituents for growing media consists of materials other than peat, it concerns mostly organic materials. The origin of these materials is diverse and mostly consists of organic residues. The properties of these materials often differ considerably from the properties of peat-products. In order to know the properties, it is essential to consistently analyse and assess results. Any undesirable properties must –if possible- already be excluded in the production phase of the raw material, with the objective of obtaining a reliable constituent with consistent properties. Often profound risks cannot be seen in the end-product so must be tackled in the first stages of the production.

ILLUSTRATION BY THREE CASES

Examples of successful new constituents for the production of growing media are coir-pith, bark and green-wasteompost. For these constituents specific problems were recognised during their development.

Example 1: Coir Pith

Coir pith was offered as growing medium in the nineties as being the replacement for peat. Previously it was a waste material from the coir fibre industry. Large waste piles could be found everywhere in Sri Lanka. Compressing coir in briquettes in combination with low fares for container transport from Colombo (due to its function as a major transhipment point in container shipping) made it economically feasible to use coir pith as constituent for growing media. However shortly after introduction many problems appeared. One of the main problems was the abundant availability of waste piles containing undefined quality. The material could be very young or very old, infested with weeds and pathogens for plants and humans. Also the nutritional status and physical structure was of such kind that it was often not suitable for use in growing media.

The occurrence of plant and human pathogens, as well as the occurrence of weeds in the material did lead to severe problems in horticultural corps. The unbalanced nutrition and heterogeneous physical structure resulted in cultural problems when coir was applied in higher percentages in mixtures. Cultural problems often resulted in high financial losses.

For coir the whole chain, from the coconut-tree to the final growing media was assessed on risks. Based on this, requirements were set to prevent the indentified risks. By setting requirements for handling, storage, transport and treatment of coir a reliable growing media constituent was developed.

Example 2: Bark
In the last decade the culture of Phalaenopsis-potplants has grown enormously. Nowadays it is one of the main floricultural crops in the Netherlands. Phalaenopsis is grown mainly on bark based growing media, of which the barks origin is *Pinus pinaster*. In the first years this bark mainly came from France, out of a region around Bordeaux. When demand did increase bark also was imported from Portugal which also has large areas of *Pinus pinaster*. However part of the Portuguese forest area was infested with *bursaphelenchus xylophilus*. Even though this nematode is not dangerous for Phalaenopsis, it is a known quarantine organism which blocked the export of the bark out of Portugal. Nowadays all Portuguese bark is sanitised by steam-sterilisation to guarantee that the bark is free from *B. xylophilus* and to allow export to other EU countries.

Example 3: Green-waste-compost (GWC)
GWC is often considered to become one of the main constituents for growing media production. However GWC in general showed major risks and down-sides. Risk of plant and human pathogens, as well as excessive salt content are the major ones. To get grip on pathogens a strict inspection of the incoming stream of green waste appeared to be necessary. On production locations routing of machinery and flow of product must be considered to obtain a phytosanitary clean product and to prevent (re)contamination In production a high level of sanitation must be met. By choosing a certain mix of input material, the desired quality with respect to low salt contents can be achieved. Total control of the entire process of composting proved to be a necessity. A proper conduct of processes is monitored by means sampling, analysis and review.

The three examples do show clear risks which did appear after the introduction of the products mentioned. To overcome these kinds of situations with newly developed constituents, it is strongly advised to perform a risk-assessment timely. Risks identified in an early phase of development should be followed by measures with the objective to produce a safe product and required properties.

A proper risk assessment should be carried out by experts with knowledge of growing media production, agricultural and horticultural crops. At least the following main principles should be followed in a risk-assessment;

When should risk assessment take place?

- As first step in designing a production process to convert a (waste) input stream to a constituent for growing media.
- Subsequently it must be repeated frequently to check for 'new' or 'not foreseen' risks.

Where should risk assessment take place?

1. The assessment must start as early as possible in the chain. The majority of waste materials are from agriculture. Assessment should start at point where the agricultural product is actually harvested.
2. The assessment should cover all stages of the production process. Everywhere any handling takes place risks must be assessed. This includes in-between-storage and transport.

What procedure should be followed?

1. Determine the Critical Control Points (CCP's).
2. Analyse the risks or hazards
3. Determine (control)measurements to prevent risks or to decrease them
4. Implement the measures

Monitor or watch over the situation and determine whether the measures have the desired effect

Abstract No: A-242

OPPORTUNITIES AND CHALLENGES OF FARMING SPHAGNUM AS A GROWING MEDIA CONSTITUENT IN GERMANY

Gerald Schmilewski* and Jan Felix Köbbing

Klasmann-Deilmann GmbH, Germany

**Corresponding author: gerald.schmilewski@klasmann-deilmann.com*

SUMMARY

Its outstanding physical, chemical and biological properties make peat the most important growing-media constituent for commercial growers and amateur gardeners alike. At the same time, pressure is mounting on the peat and growing-media industry not to carry out peat extraction and thus to reduce emissions of harmful greenhouse gases from production sites. Alternative materials such as green compost, wood fibre, composted bark and coco pith are not sufficiently available; additionally, they also have less beneficial characteristics. One potential alternative to peat is peat moss (*Sphagnum* spp.), the main peat-forming plant in ombrotrophic peatlands. A project launched in 2015 with 10 ha of trials is being funded chiefly by Klasmann-Deilmann GmbH itself and by the federal state of Lower Saxony; it involves different *Sphagnum* species being assessed as to their productivity and suitability. The impact on biodiversity and greenhouse gas emissions is being investigated in cooperation with specialised institutes. A particular challenge is optimizing the hydro management of peat moss cultivation areas. An unusual aspect is that this project, unlike previous trials, is taking place on sites where the residual peat layer following depletion consists of black peat. Such areas are (due to their low water conductivity) less suitable, but in Germany – owing to the scarcity of sites where the residual layer is white peat – are the only realistic option. In general, both in Germany and throughout Europe, considerations need to be made concerning the provision of sufficient land. Further obstacles include the procurement of inoculation material, and colonisation with weeds. This project's overall aim is to assess the industrial feasibility of peat moss cultivation on the basis of a profitability analysis.

Keywords: *Sphagnum, growing media, peat replacement, paludiculture*

INTRODUCTION

A considerable majority of Germany's raised bogs is located in the federal state of Lower Saxony, as is the geographical focus of the country's peat and substrate industry. This article, therefore, refers chiefly to the situation in Lower Saxony.

For decades now, the substitution of peat in growing media has been receiving a lot of attention in public debate. This is evident chiefly in Germany, the United Kingdom, Austria, Switzerland and the Netherlands, but also in other countries. In the past, the reasons for this were rooted primarily in the loss of natural habitat (pristine peatland) and its specific biodiversity, caused by state-driven peatland drainage measures and the creation of cultivated agricultural land and space for settlement. Today, the discussion is centred on greenhouse gas emissions. Moreover, the peat and growing media sector is confronted with a massive decline in available peat extraction sites in western and central Europe.

Efforts to develop alternative growing media constituents go back a long way. The market significance of green compost, wood fibre, coir pith and bark products has now increased. Since early in the last decade, the question of peat moss cultivation has also been increasingly debated. *Sphagnum* farming is a form of paludiculture (Latin: palus = marsh, swamp) and involves the agricultural use of wet areas of raised bog (Wichtmann *et al.*, 2010). Paludiculture on fenland sites is focused primarily on the growing of reed, cattail, willow and alder (Wichtmann & Wichmann 2011). Cultivation of peat moss has been explored for a number of years in Germany, Canada and elsewhere (Gaudig *et al.*, 2014; Pouliot *et al.*, 2014). Caspers (2015) notes that, to date, not a single private landowner in Germany has practised paludiculture. Neither, to our knowledge, has there been any commercial horticultural exploitation of peat moss grown as an outdoor crop.

Cultivated peat moss grows more successfully on white peat (weakly decomposed peat; H1-H5 on the Von Post scale) sites than on black peat (strongly decomposed peat; H6-H10 on the Von Post scale) sites, as the former is a better conductor of water. Virtually all areas of white peat in Lower Saxony are used as private agricultural pastureland. Because of high land prices, strong potential for weed growth and nutrient contamination in these sites, the scope for *Sphagnum* farming is negligible. Moreover, agricultural acceptance and political support for this form of wet land-use is lacking. On peat-depleted areas, however, peat is extracted to the depth of the lower peat horizon, with a 50 cm thick layer of residual peat remaining. Instead of using such sites almost solely for re-wetting, they could alternatively be made available for farming peat moss.

PROJECT PLANNING AND IMPLEMENTATION

Although much of value has already been learned from earlier projects on peat moss cultivation (Gaudig *et al.*, 2014), Klasmann-Deilmann's current project (title: 'Extensive cultivation of peat moss in Lower Saxony as a land use subsequent to black peat extraction and its potential for sustainable production of a growing media constituent as a peat substitute') chiefly involves calculating and assessing the profitability of *Sphagnum* farming on former peat production sites with a residual layer of black peat. The impact on biodiversity and climate is being investigated by the University of Hannover and the Thünen Institute in Braunschweig.

Unfortunately, no former peat extraction areas with residual white-peat layers were available for this project – in Germany, peat is always extracted until the degree of decomposition designated H7-H8 on the Von Post scale is reached, which has hydrological disadvantages compared with sites where the residual layers consist of white peat. Furthermore, a previous attempt persuaded us that *Sphagnum* farming should be started as far away as possible from utilized agricultural land, grassland or woodland, as this means the risk of weed seeds and nutrients entering the site is lower. Other prerequisites are scope for creating access routes and a means of irrigation. As the strict protection status of pristine peatland in Germany means procurement of inoculation material (peat moss) in Germany is a major obstacle, it was decided that the company would create its own *Sphagnum* bank on a special site and actually grow the peat moss for growing media production in a second, separate area.

This *Sphagnum* bank site is located in a nature reserve for which regulations permit paludiculture for trial purposes; it has been in the re-wetting phase for six years. The site is around 5 ha in size, with an additional irrigation polder covering 3 ha. This area will provide *Sphagnum* inoculation material in the future. Owing to the site's protected status, large-scale soil preparation was not carried out; a few open channels were created for irrigation and drainage, but that is all. After the peat moss was manually spread with the aid of wooden walkways, it was covered (alternately) with straw and mesh fabric. Irrigation is augmented by open ditches and by means of pipes laid above ground.

The second site is an area of bogland that was prepared for inoculation with peat moss as soon as peat extraction had ceased. A nearby fire pond provides the water necessary for irrigation. Peat moss was distributed by hand over a total of seven polders, and also alternately covered with mesh fabric and straw. For irrigation purposes, open channels alternating with drainage pipes laid just below the site surface were used.

Peat moss (from peat hummocks) required for inoculation was, with official approval, removed from a landscape conservation area in the autumn of 2015. Unwanted vascular plants covering the peat moss were mown, subsequently removed and the upper centimeters of the peat moss then cut off. This *Sphagnum* inoculation material was collected and taken away from the donor site using temporary wooden walkways. With hummock moss accounting for about 25 % of the donor site, the area was sufficiently fit for purpose.

EXPLORING OPPORTUNITES

Our own horticultural growth trials in the 1990s showed that peat moss is, in principle, suitable as a growing media constituent for various different uses (unpublished data). This has been confirmed many times over by other investigators. For all growing media constituents the characteristics described by Schmilewski (2015) need to be evaluated to prove their suitability or non-suitability for use in horticulture. Overarching criteria in this context are horticultural properties as well as ecological, economic and social aspects.

Large-scale *Sphagnum* farming covering many thousands of ha may contribute to sustainable regional development and:

1. provide another growing media constituent;
2. deliver a long-term perspective for the growing media industry;
3. safeguard jobs in economically weaker regions;
4. optimise the colonisation of former peat extraction areas with *Sphagnum*;
5. initiate enhancement of the ecological value of agricultural land;
6. mitigate greenhouse gas emissions.

Greenhouse gas emissions: Greenhouse gas measurements taken by Beyer & Höper (2014) show that, owing to their constant water level a few centimetres below the surface, sites cultivated with *Sphagnum* have a negative global-warming potential (GWP). Water levels in re-wetted production sites are high in some cases, leading to high methane emissions which may in turn result in a positive GWP. Figure 1 shows yearly greenhouse gas emissions from different types of land use. In the project presented here greenhouse gas emissions will be measured over the entire production chain, including irrigation polders, extraction areas, growing sites and control sites.

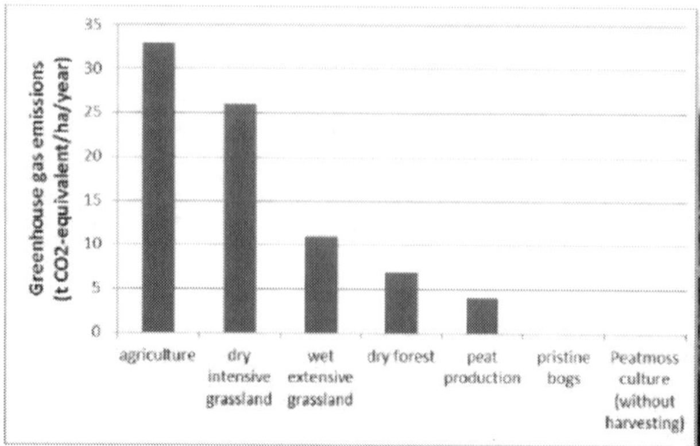

Figure 1: Greenhouse gas emissions for different types of raised-bog use (Lower Saxony Ministry of Environment, Energy and Climate Protection 2015). Figure 2: Distribution of peat moss on the former peat extraction site.

Biodiversity: In Germany, only a very small proportion of the total area of raised bog can be designated as pristine. Even after several decades, many typical plant species, especially peat mosses, struggle to recolonise peatland sites restored through re-wetting. *Sphagnum* farming accelerates peatland regeneration and creates habitat for highly at-risk flora and fauna. As *Sphagnum* is harvested only at intervals of several years, refuge areas for animal and plant species are ensured. Specific aims of our project include assessment of which peat moss species yield the highest biomass productivity on black peat, how their growth is affected by weeds, and which animal and plant species colonise the site.

EXPLORING CHALLENGES

Shortage of sites: In Germany, the only sites suitable are land previously used for agriculture (degraded peatland areas) that have a residual white-peat layer, or former peat extraction sites with the usual thickness of residual black peat, i.e. 50 cm. Because of the poor water conductivity of in situ strongly decomposed (black) peat, it is far more difficult to grow peat moss in these areas than on sites where the residual layer is weakly decomposed (white) peat. Gaudig *et al,*. (2014) assume that 145,000 ha of grassland on peat soil in Lower Saxony (almost all of it privately owned by farmers) may be available for farming peat moss. However, this assumption is only theoretical and is, from the perspective of the farmers who own this land and wish to use it for conventional agriculture, practicable only to an extremely limited degree. *Sphagnum* farming on former peat production areas is possible only where agricultural after-use is envisaged on the land concerned. As almost all such peatland is intended for rewetting/restoration following peat extraction, however, current legislation dictates that these sites cannot be used for peat moss farming.

Hydro management: To create ideal conditions for peat moss growth, an ebb and flow system using local rainwater is recommended (Kamermann & Blankenburg, 2008). This ensures low nutrient availability and a low pH value, which are requirements for *Sphagnum* growth. Overhead irrigation (*e.g.* a sprinkler system) with water from adjacent peatland areas exposes peat mosses to high levels of humic substances, leading to reduced growth (Rochefort & Bastien, 1998). Well water, ditchwater or groundwater are not viable options because of their high nutrient levels and high pH value. The high levels of evapotranspiration from peatland sites necessitate the use of an irrigation system. This loss of water is greatest in the low-rainfall summer months. Irrigation reserves must therefore be set aside for these areas. Different irrigation systems will be trialed in our project: open trenches, drainage pipes laid on the site surface, and surface irrigation pipes.

Inoculation material (peat moss): Procurement of inoculation material from peat moss donor sites is a major challenge. All wild-growing peat moss species are protected in Germany under section 1, sentence 1 of the Country's Federal Regulation on the Protection of Species (BArtSchV 2007). Under section 44 of the Federal Nature Conservation Act, it is forbidden to take these mosses from the wild or to possess, process or market them. However, these prohibitions do not apply to domesticated forms, bred or artificially propagated *Sphagnum* (BNatSchG 2015). Furthermore, the competent authority under federal-state law is entitled – under sections 6 and

17 of the Federal Regulation on the Protection of Species (BArtSchV 2007) – to grant exceptions if this is not in conflict with species protection requirements. Just such an exception was approved for our project. Another potential option is the distribution of inoculation material propagated in vitro, as provided by Micropropagation Services Ltd. (2014).

Selection of *Sphagnum* species: Peats associated with different *Sphagnum* species differ in their horticultural properties. The same applies to the peat mosses from which these peats are formed. In peat moss cultivation, the aim is to establish and grow the most productive moss species. Horticultural aspects are also important, however. For example, Emmel (2007) concluded that, as tested using a range of cultivated plants, *S. fallax* is wholly unsuitable in terms of its propagation, and the proportion of peat moss biomass in growing media for propagation should not generally exceed 50 % (v/v). Depending on the species of *Sphagnum*, biomass production in optimum conditions is between 2 and 16 t/ha/annum of dry mass (Gaudig, 2001). It may be that peat mosses from hollows have greater biomass productivity. However, the intention will be to establish mosses extracted from peat hummocks, as this enables subsequent harvesting to be easier and carried out mechanically. Furthermore, the latter types of moss have better physical and horticultural properties. Gaudig (2001) also points out that mosses from peat hummocks degrade more slowly than those extracted from hollows. Conditions for growth and harvesting are favourable only when the cultivated peat moss has formed an extensive closed carpet of peat moss, *i.e.* when it grows as in a raised bog.

Weeds: The presence of weeds in growing media constituents is not tolerable. Various plant species can present a problem for *Sphagnum* farming on outdoor sites, as experience has shown that associated living plants which are undesirable (or viable plant propagules), such as cross-leaved heath (*Erica tetralix*), ling heather (*Calluna vulgaris*), purple moor-grass (*Molinia caerulea*), grasses or non-peat moss species invade cultivation areas via the inoculation material. It can also be expected that seeds or spores carried on the wind and in irrigation water will enter the site. Moreover, areas previously used for agriculture or sites with increased input of nutrients (e.g. from adjacent farmland) have potential for weed infestation. For example, rushes (*Juncus* spp.) frequently dominate on grassland on peat soils. Some vascular plants may promote the growth of peat mosses by serving as support or improving the microclimate; however, if they progressively spread they will compete strongly with the mosses. They also make harvesting more difficult and considerably affect the quality of the growing medium. As the use of herbicides on peatland is prohibited, the only weed control currently possible is that by mechanical means, which is very costly. The Dutch foundation for quality assurance of growing media, R.H.P. requires the hygienization of any species of *Sphagnum* by means of gamma radiation or steam treatment, the aim being to prove compliance with the zero-tolerance policy for weed infestation.

Sphagnicolous fungi and other fungi: It is fungi, of which more than 600 species are reported to occur in peatlands, that are chiefly responsible for the breakdown of organic matter in peatlands; many of these have also been found on peat mosses (Markus N. Thormann, pers. comm. 2016). Tsuneda *et al.* (2001) note that some of these *Sphagnum*-colonising fungi are pathogenic. *Sphagnurus paluster* is a sphagnicolous fungus that is not uncommon in both natural peatland and in cultivated peat moss sites in spring, and which is dependent on peat moss as its host. Fungi of this kind can lead to spot-like or carpet-like chlorosis, necrosis and ultimately to the death of the peat moss. Although it is unlikely that sphagnicolous fungi lead to symptoms in horticultural crops, it is indisputable that they have an adverse effect on peat moss farming.

Profitability: All costs incurred by the project are recorded on an ongoing basis and included in a profitability analysis. Although the project is still in the early stages, it is already evident that the biggest cost factors are site preparation, the extraction and distribution of the peat moss, and irrigation. However, a number of potential improvements can be made in this respect. If it is to be a realistic after-use alternative, the cultivation of peat moss – like all forms of paludiculture – must be recognised as a form of agriculture and funded accordingly.

CONCLUSION

As early as 1999, Joosten & Timmermann posed questions that make it clear why *Sphagnum* farming to produce a growing media constituent has still not yet caught on to this day. "Paludiculture raises issues concerning the selection of suitable *Sphagnum* species, methods of establishing and harvesting them on peatlands, optimising yields and quality of growing media, the size of site required, financial viability, and positive and negative side-effects." In various projects both in Germany and elsewhere, work has been done on answering these and other questions; however, only partial answers have been obtained. In Germany, obtaining sites for peat moss cultivation remains problematic due to a lack of incentives for the agricultural sector. Furthermore, there are serious misgivings in the peat industry regarding the feasibility and profitability of *Sphagnum* farming. The aim of the project presented here is to help to assess the profitability of growing peat mosses on a large scale following peat extraction, and to create a decision-making basis/tool to help our company consider how to proceed further. Amidst all the euphoria surrounding the potential of *Sphagnum* cultivation, it must be borne in mind that other peat substitutes of different natures and origins are being investigated and have indeed been established on the international growing media market for some years. Whether farmed *Sphagnum* can compete with these remains to be seen.

Abstract No: A-396

PLANNING FOR THE END OF ENERGY PEAT PRODUCTION IN BORD NA MONA

Cathal Byrne

Bord na Mona, Boora, Leabeg, Tullamore, Co. Offaly, Ireland

Corresponding author: cathal.byrne@bnm.ie

SUMMARY

Bord na Mona has announced that it will cease to produce energy peat by 2030. The peatland, currently tied up in the production of energy peat will be released for other uses. With a commitment not to develop any new bogs for production, the defined and declining peat resource must be managed to meet ongoing power generation requirements. This paper looks at the planning and optimisation of energy peat production to closure in 2030, how outlying bogs will quickly become surplus to requirements as co-firing with biomass grows and how some of these bogs will later return into production as the peat resource adjacent to the power stations continues to decline. It presents a picture of what the overall peat resource will look like when production ceases: how the depth of peat remaining will be different in each bog, how the post-production drainage conditions will vary between bogs and how the potential exists for energy in the form of renewables to continue to be produced on the peatlands.

Keywords: *peat, energy, planning*

THE CHALLENGE

The peat-fired power stations in Ireland were originally solely supplied from the surrounding bogs connected by Bord na Mona's extensive narrow gauge railway network. In effect a constant and level demand for energy was met with a declining, and ultimately finite, fuel resource.

As bogs became cutaway and fell out of production, and as the generating capacity of the stations were increased, bogs were developed in the outer hinterland at a longer radius from the stations. Over time the replacement bogs that were available for development were too distant to be connected into the rail network and haulage by road became a necessity. This has resulted in a transport mix of supply by rail and by road.

The decision by Bord na Mona not to develop any new bogs for production has made the management of a level demand for energy with a declining resource more difficult than in the past when new production areas could be developed as needed to replace cutaway bogs.

Bord na Mona has established the peat resource remaining by surveying its bogs using LIDAR and GPR and modelling the results using GIS software. The removal of peat and reduction of peat depths in line with potential production is modelled, offering a window into the future. The categorisation of peat as suitable for horticultural applications or energy production is also required.

Projections of bog production capability to the end of 2030 show a continuing gradual decline in the capability to supply peat over the rail network. The requirements for supply by road should therefore continue to grow. However for the ESB[15] owned peat-fired power stations to maintain their base-load (constant running) status beyond 2019 will require co-firing with biomass to reduce carbon emissions to the levels of the reference thermal plant deemed to be displaced. These biomass volumes will grow and displace peat to the extent that the need for peat to be hauled by road will be completely eliminated, before this need returns as production areas linked by rail to the stations continue to become cutaway over time.

A number of the bogs rendered surplus when peak co-firing is reached will be retained to cover peat production areas which will later become cutaway between 2020 and 2029. This will require a new approach to production and bog maintenance to ensure these bogs are available to replace cutaway bogs as this deferred need arises. This results in a complex supply demand mix which must be modelled to cater for, in particular, the uncertainty around production achieved in any year due to the variability of Irish summer weather and also some uncertainty around demand.

[15] Electricity Supply Board

THE SUPPLY-DEMAND MODEL

Premium Solver Platform[16] linear programming software is used for supply-demand modelling and optimisation. The model seeks to maximise the production and sales each year from the individual bog areas linked by rail to the stations, while minimising road haulage, within the constraints of the chosen stockholding policy (stock: sales ratio). The model provides for rapid optimisation of a range of scenarios, catering in particular for the risk and impact of adverse weather and poor production seasons as well as possible changes to the demand scenario. See Fig.1 below.

The risk associated with poor production seasons is managed by the maintenance of high stock levels. Current contracts require a multiple of 1.5 times next year's sales to be held in stock each year at the end of March. These are high stock levels but in the past, following a succession of poor summers, have proved vital in maintaining supply to the stations, and this stock to sales ratio is used for forward planning to 2030.
The supply of peat for power generation will cease in 2030 and, given our planned stocking strategy, the last year of planned full production will be 2028 with minimal production in 2029 and no production planned for 2030. The supply-demand optimisation model, utilising the GIS resource data, identifies the individual production areas which will become cutaway or surplus to requirements and when this will occur. Bogs will be categorised as surplus based on relative production and transport costs or specific issues such as the likelihood of floods with consequent loss of stock occurring. A further output of the model is the level of road haulage that should be provided for in future planning permission (permit) applications with due consideration given to the risk of poor production seasons.

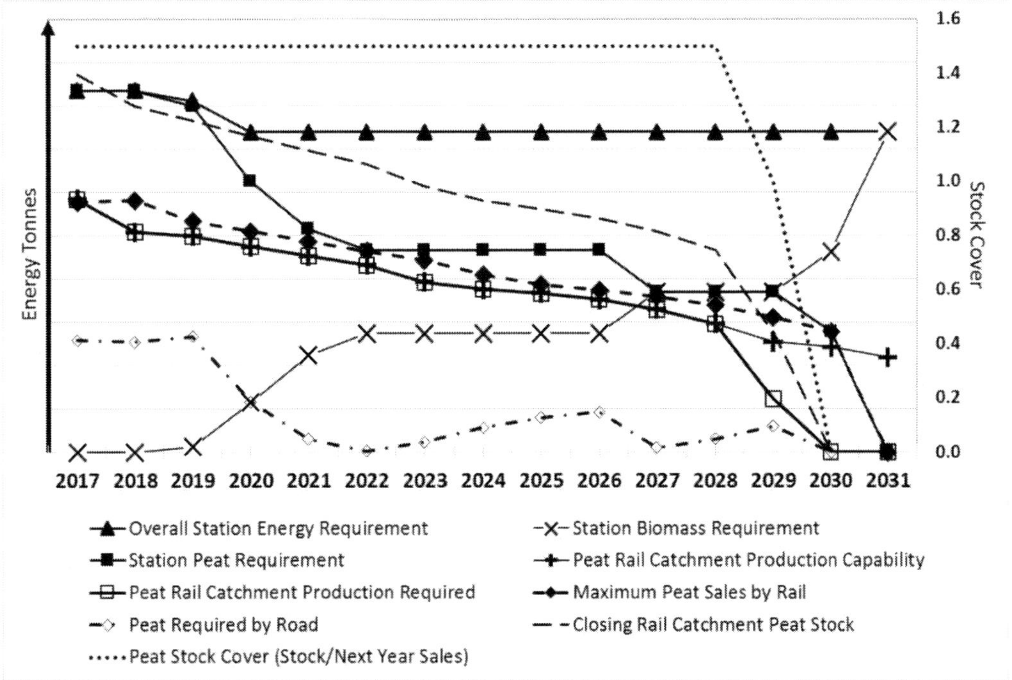

Fig.1 A forecast power station supply-demand scenario

Knowing the extent to which production areas will become surplus to requirements allows the critical examination of all production bogs and, for example, to further extend buffer zones around areas of environmental interest. Manpower and machinery requirements associated with optimising the various chosen scenarios can be identified together with costings.

OPPORTUNITIES

As peat is displaced by biomass the active peat production footprint will be reduced. Between 2017 and 2021 alone over 5,000 ha will be released from peat production with the potential for other uses including continuing energy production in the form of renewables and peatland rehabilitation. See Fig.2 below.
Because cutaway emerges in an incremental and fragmented way, the release of bog areas is complex and requires detailed consideration.

[16] Frontline Systems Inc.

After production ceases, bogs will be cut away to varying degrees and varying depths of peat will remain. The peat depths remaining in 2030, can be projected today and considered at an early stage in future land-use and rehabilitation planning. The post-production drainage conditions can be forecast, and for example, areas with high potential for natural wetlands can be identified.

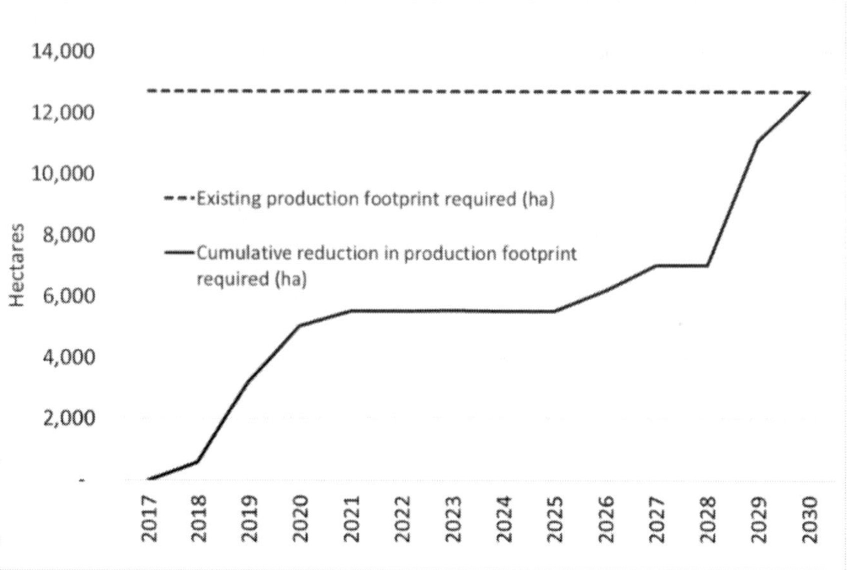

Fig.2 Cumulative reduction in required active peat production footprint (ha) for ESB owned peat-fired power stations to 2030

CONCLUSIONS

The management of the supply of energy peat from now to ultimate closure will be more complex than heretofore. The application of optimisation software in supply demand modelling will identify the minimum cost production and supply configuration and will facilitate a long term view today of when in the future individual bogs will be retired from energy peat production and what they will look like when they are retired.

SPECIAL SESSION 3: PUBLICALLY MANAGED PEATLAND CARBON STORAGE, ECOSYSTEM SERVICES, AND MANAGEMENT

SPECIAL SESSION 3: PUBLICALLY MANAGED PEATLAND CARBON STORAGE, ECOSYSTEM SERVICES, AND MANAGEMENT

Abstract No: A-167

CARBON STORAGE AND ECOSYSTEM SERVICES BY PUBLICALLY MANAGED WETLANDS

Zhiliang Zhu[1] and Chris Lowie[2]

[1]*U.S. Geological Survey, USA*
[2]*U.S. Fish and Wildlife Service, USA*

**Corresponding author: zzhu@usgs.gov*

In a recently completed national assessment of ecosystem carbon sequestration, wetlands (including both freshwater and tidal water, woody and emergent) in the continental United States (CONUS) were found to account for about 4 percent of the total land area, but 8.8 percent of the terrestrial carbon stock and 9.3 percent of the total terrestrial carbon sink. On average, the CONUS wetlands contain 14 Kg of carbon per square meter, and sequester 0.126 Kg of carbon per square meter per year. Using the social cost of carbon discounted to year 2015 at a rate of 3 percent as a simple indication of the value of the ecosystem service provided by wetlands in the CONUS, the total annual avoided carbon dioxide emissions by wetlands in the CONUS would value 5.17 billion USD. Over time, the wetland area in the CONUS is expected to remain stable and the carbon sink strength is projected to increase to an average of 13.3 percent of the overall terrestrial sink, on the basis of a set of scenarios for both the climate change and land use change, including effective public land management. In this presentation, we describe a conceptual approach for assessing carbon sequestration among multiple ecosystem services by publically protected wetlands.

Keywords: -

Abstract No: A-231

FORESTED PEATLAND MANAGEMENT IN SOUTHEAST VIRGINIA AND NORTHEAST NORTH CAROLINA, USA

Frederic C. Wurster[1], Sara Ward[2], and Christine Pickens[3]

[1] *U.S. Fish and Wildlife Service, Great Dismal Swamp National Wildlife Refuge, Suffolk, VA, USA*
[2] *U.S. Fish and Wildlife Service, Raleigh Field Office, Raleigh, NC, USA*
[3] *The Nature Conservancy, Kill Devil Hills, NC, USA*

**Corresponding author: fred_wurster@fws.gov*

SUMMARY

The U.S. Fish and Wildlife Service manage 130,000 ha of forested peatlands in southeast Virginia and northeast North Carolina, U.S.A. at three national wildlife refuges: Pocosin Lakes, Alligator River, and Great Dismal Swamp. The refuges contain extensive networks of roads and drainage canals; the legacy of past logging and farming activities. Canals have contributed to peat subsidence and facilitated the conversion of wetland forest communities to upland forest communities. During drought periods, drained peat is prone to wildfires that can burn for several months and pose health risks to neighboring communities. Refuge managers are working to restore historic forest communities and stop peat loss through hydrologic restoration, forest management, and fire management. Following four separate severe peat fires on refuges in 2008 and 2011, emphasis has been placed on improving water control capability to support habitat restoration and fire suppression activities.

Keywords: *Pocosin, forested peatland, peatland restoration, controlled drainage, national wildlife refuge*

INTRODUCTION

The South Atlantic Coastal plain of the United States is home to extensive forested wetlands on peat soils known as pocosins (Richardson, 1991). Also described as evergreen (or southeastern) shrub bogs, the pocosin vegetation community consists of an open-pine canopy underlain by a dense shrub layer. Pocosins cover hundreds of square kilometers on the Coastal Plain from Virginia to Florida with the highest concentration in coastal North Carolina (Richardson 1991). They are found on peatlands that have formed on interfluves with low topographic relief, near the edge of estuarine wetlands, or in depressions with poor drainage (Brinson, 1991). Maximum peat depths approach 5 meters and peat accretion has been occurring for 8,000 – 10,000 years (Richardson, 1982, Brinson, 1991). Pocosin peatlands are typically ombrotrophic with no inflowing surface water or groundwater supplies (Daniel III, 1981). The peat is typically saturated to land surface during the cool season (November – April) but the water table may drop 60 – 90 cm below land surface during the warm season (May-October) (Richardson, 1982).

The United States Fish and Wildlife Service (USFWS or Service) is the principal federal agency responsible for conserving, protecting, and enhancing fish, wildlife, plants, and their habitats in the United States. The Service protects 130,000 ha of pocosin peatlands at Great Dismal Swamp (45,300 ha), Pocosin Lakes (24,000 ha), and Alligator River (61,200 ha) National Wildlife Refuges (NWR) (Figure 1). The refuges were established between 1974 and 1990 on land previously used for commercial activities like forestry, agriculture and peat mining. There are hundreds of kilometers of drainage canals on each refuge constructed to support previous land use activities. Historic land use and the associated canal construction are implicated in reducing the species diversity of the forest communities, increasing the frequency and severity of peat fires, and significantly altering the peatlands' hydrology (USFWS, 2006; USFWS, 2007; USFWS, 2008).

The primary goal of each refuge is to preserve and protect the unique forested wetlands for the benefit of the species that depend on them. Restoration to mimic the pre-disturbance hydrology of the peatlands is viewed as one of the best management tools for achieving that goal. This paper presents the refuges' approach to hydrologic restoration and describes the application of this approach to address specific management concerns associated with water management, saltwater intrusion, and peat fires.

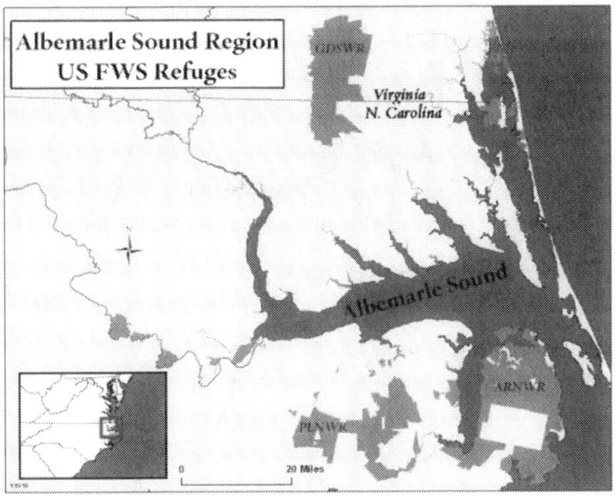

Figure 1: Location of Great Dismal Swamp (GDSWR), Pocosin Lakes (PLNWR), and Alligator River (ARNWR) National Wildlife Refuges in southeast Virginia / northeast North Carolina, USA. Map courtesy of The Nature Conservancy (TNC).

METHODS

Water Control Structure Installation

The Service's strategy for hydrologic restoration follows controlled drainage practices used on agricultural land and managed forests on the Virginia and North Carolina Coastal Plain. Engineered structures (referred to here as water control structures) are installed in canals to slow drainage and set canal water levels (Dukes *et al.*, 2003, Evans *et al.*, 2007). Canal flow rates and water levels are controlled by manually adding or removing 15-cm wide boards, or stop-logs.

Depending on the alignment of the canal with the contours of the peat surface, a single control structure can influence water levels in several kilometers of a canal. Canal blocking strategies developed for Pocosin Lakes NWR, recommend placing water control structures in canals at each 30 cm change in elevation (SCS 1994). The approach is similar to those described in other peatlands (Lunt *et al.*, 2010, Jaenicke *et al.*, 2010, Landry and Rochefort 2012). In practice, water control structures are placed less frequently due to funding limitations or the configuration of the canal network.

The most common structure installed in refuge canals are made locally from corrugated aluminum culvert material (Figure 2). Culvert diameters are typically 1.5 – 2.0 m with 2 – 3 m wide riser sections. Two or three structures may be installed at a site to provide enough capacity for expected flow rates. Structures are usually placed in canals at road crossings using heavy excavating equipment. Headwalls of aluminum, stone, and wood are often added on the upstream and downstream faces of the structures to reduce erosion (Figure 3). After the structure is in place, 15 cm boards are added to the riser section to control the elevation of the water surface in the canal.

Figure 2: Pre-fabricated aluminum water control structure ready for transportation to installation site. Culvert diameter: 1.2 m. Culvert length: 14 m. Riser height: 2.1 m.

Figure 3: Recently installed water control structure at Great Dismal Swamp NWR.

The goal of installing these structures is to give managers the capability to control canal drainage. The refuges monitor hydrologic conditions, soil respiration, peat subsidence, and forest health to evaluate if water control structures are meeting management objectives.

RESULTS / DISCUSSION

Accommodating Variation in Canal Flow Rates

Canals change peatland hydrology by capturing sheetflow and concentrating runoff. Peak flows tend to be higher in drained peatlands than undrained peatlands (Daniel III 1981). Water control structures designed to raise canal water levels can be compromised if they are unable to pass peak flows (Ritzema *et al.*, 2014). At Great Dismal Swamp NWR, canal discharge measurements over 5 years range from 0 m^3/s during dry periods to more than 2 m^3/s following large, intense precipitation events (>200 mm in 48 hours). The refuges prefer water control structure designs that can be adjusted to different flow conditions. Structures that are not adjustable, like canal plugs and fixed weirs, are used infrequently due to concerns they will be compromised by peak flows. In addition to corrugated aluminum structures (Figure 2 and 3), Great Dismal Swamp NWR is installing adjustable weirs to control drainage in some locations (Figure 4).

Figure 4: Example of an adjustable weir type water control structure. Weir width approximately 4.5 m. Great Dismal Swamp NWR. Photo courtesy David Byrd, USFWS.

Limiting Saltwater Intrusion

The unique challenge of hydrologic restoration at Alligator River NWR is the refuge's proximity to the Albemarle and Pamlico Sounds (Figure 1). Canals draining to the sounds act as conduits for salt water, particularly during wind tide events. Saltwater intrusion via canals accelerates the conversion of forested wetlands to saltwater marsh (Bryant et al 2012). Water control structures at Alligator River are fitted with flex check valves (Figure 5) to allow freshwater to exit the canal but prevent the landward migration of saltwater from the Pamlico Sound.

Alligator River NWR is also experimenting with canal plugs to prevent salt water intrusion on smaller canals (< 3 m). Plugs are constructed using vinyl sheetpile surrounded by earthen fill and placed near shoreline outlets. Freshwater flow is insignificant on these canals and no accommodation is made for freshwater outflows.

Figure 5: Water control structures at Alligator River NWR ready for installation. Tide-check flex valves installed on the outlet end to prevent saltwater intrusion upstream of water control structures. Photo courtesy of TNC.

Facilitating Fire Suppression

Fire is considered one of the most important controls on vegetation distribution in pocosins peatlands (Christensen 1981, Frost 1989). Although fire is common enough for pocosins to be considered fire-dependent ecosystems, fire return intervals are sufficiently long in undrained pocosins to allow for peat accretion and forest stand development (Frost 1989, Richardson 1991). Drainage tends to increase the frequency and severity of ground fires in peatlands (Turetsky et al 2010) and large ground fires have been a common occurrence in drained pocosins (Frost 1989). Between 2008 and 2011, approximately 36,000 hectares burned on the three refuges in four separate fires.

Fire suppression techniques developed for pocosin peatlands focus on attempting to douse ground fire by flooding the burning area. Water is transported to the fire using pumps powered by the Power Take-Off (PTO) drives on farm tractors and the existing canal network. Water is pumped from low elevation sources to fires on higher elevation peat. Pumping operations move water against the natural slope of canals using PTO pumps positioned at multiple dams (Figure 6). PTO pumps can move large volumes (18,000 liters/minute) but are limited to low head applications. To maximize efficiency, pump stations are placed every 1-2 km and/or every 30 cm change in elevation. In addition, water must be kept on the land 2 – 3 weeks to extinguish the burning peat. During the most recent fires in 2011, the existing water control structure network at Alligator River and Great Dismal Swamp was insufficient to meet these criteria. Temporary dams were coupled with the existing network of water control structures to transport water to the burning areas.

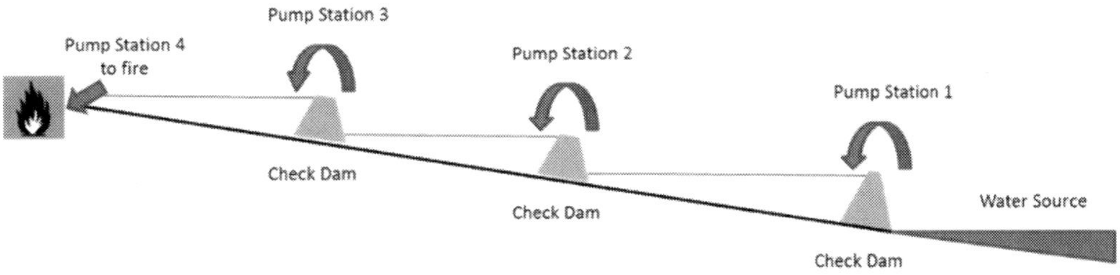

Figure 6: Schematic of pumping stations and temporary dams used to transport water against the slope of a refuge canal.

SUMMARY

Despite the history of disturbance in pocosin peatlands, relatively large tracts of these unique wetlands are protected by the USFWS and other conservations organizations in southeast Virginia and northeast North Carolina. In most cases the protected areas were established after earlier land-use activities such as logging, farming, or peat mining had failed. At each refuge the USFWS has inherited hundreds of kilometers of canals that continue to negatively impact the peatlands' hydrology. Installing water control structures to block canals, slow drainage, and re-wet peat has been a management focus at the refuges since their establishment. The basic concepts guiding canal blocking are similar to those being applied on other peatlands (Lunt et al. 2010, Jaenicke et al 2010, Landry and Rochefort 2012) although the materials and installation techniques follow local practices used on nearby agricultural land. In addition to raising dry season water levels, water control structures are used to facilitate pumping operations during fires and slow saltwater intrusion in freshwater wetlands.

ACKNOWLEDGEMENTS

Preserving and protecting pocosin peatlands is a team effort involving many individuals at multiple agencies and partner organizations. All the individuals cannot be named here but include representatives from the following organizations: U.S. Fish and Wildlife Service, U.S. Geological Survey, U.S. Department of Agriculture Natural Resource Conservation Service, U.S. Army Corps of Engineers, Duke University, North Carolina State University, Christopher Newport University, Virginia Polytechnic Institute and State University, The Nature Conservancy, Albemarle-Pamlico National Estuary Program, Duke Energy, The Conservation Fund, TerraCarbon, North Carolina Department of Environmental Quality, North Carolina State Parks, North Carolina Forest Service, and Virginia Department of Game and Inland Fisheries.

REFERENCES

1. Brinson MM (1991) Landscape properties of pocosins and associated wetlands. Wetlands 11:441-465.
2. Bryant M, Cheater M, Hinds L, and N Matson (2012) National wildlife refuges and sea-level rise, lessons from the frontlines. Defenders of Wildlife Report. 13 p.
3. Daniel III CC (1981) Hydrology, geology and soils of pocosins: a comparison of natural and altered systems. p. 69-108. In Richardson CJ (ed.) Pocosin Wetlands Hutchinson Ross Publishing Company. Stroudsburg, Pennsylvania, USA.
4. Dukes MD, Evans RO, Gilliam JW, and S.H. Kunickis (2003) Interactive effects of controlled drainage and riparian buffers on shallow groundwater quality. Journal of Irrigation and Drainage Engineering 129(2): 82-92.
5. Christensen NL, Burchell RB, Liggett A, and EL Simms (1981) The structure and development of pocosin vegetation. p. 43-61. In Richardson CJ (ed.) Pocosin Wetlands Hutchinson Ross Publishing Company. Stroudsburg, Pennsylvania, USA.
6. Evans RO, Bass KL, Burchell MR, Hinson RD, R Johnson and M Doxey (2007) Management alternatives to enhance water quality and ecological function of channelized streams and drainage canals. Journal of Soil and Water Conservation 62(4): 308-320.
7. Frost CC (1989) History and status of remnant pocosin, canebrake, and white cedar wetlands in Virginia. Report to the Virginia Natural Heritage Program. 35 p.
8. Jaenicke J, Wosten H, Budiman A, and F Siegert (2010) Planning hydrological restoration of peatlands in Indonesia to mitigate carbon dioxide emissions. Mitigation and Adaptation Strategies for Global Change 15: 223-239.
9. Landry J and L Rochefort (2012) The drainage of peatlands: impacts and rewetting techniques. University of Laval, Quebec. 52 p.
10. Lunt P, Allott T, Anderson P, Buckler M, Coupar A, Jones P, Labadz J, and P Worrall (2010) Peatland Restoration. Scientific Review. IUCN UK Peatlands Programme Commission of Inquiry on Peatlands. 45 p.
11. Richardson CJ (1982) An ecological analysis of pocosin wetlands development with management recommendations. Wetlands 2: 231-248.
12. Richardson CJ (1991) Pocosins: an ecological perspective. Wetlands 11: 335-354.
13. Ritzema H, Limin S, Kusin K, Jauhiainen J, and H. Wosten (2014) Canal blocking strategies for hydrological restoration of degraded tropical peatlands in Central Kalimantan, Indonesia. Catena, 114 (2014) 11-20.
14. Turetsky MR, Donahue WF, and Benscoter BW (2011) Experimental drying intensifies burning and carbon loss in a northern peatland. Nature Communications 2(514): 1-5.
15. U.S. Department of Agriculture Soil Conservation Service (SCS) (1994) Pocosin Lakes National Wildlife Refuge Hydraulics and Hydrologic Study and Water Management Plan. 70 p.
16. U.S. Fish and Wildlife Service (USFWS) (2006) Great Dismal Swamp National Wildlife Refuge and Nansemond National Wildlife Refuge Final Comprehensive Conservation Plan. 258 p.
17. U.S. Fish and Wildlife Service (USFWS) (2007) Pocosin Lakes National Wildlife Refuge Draft Comprehensive Conservation Plan. 289 p.
18. U.S. Fish and Wildlife Service (USFWS) (2008) Alligator National Wildlife Refuge Final Comprehensive Conservation Plan and Environmental Assessment. 248 p.

Abstract No: A-254

MANAGEMENT IMPLICATIONS ASSOCIATED WITH CONSIDERATION OF CARBON STORAGE AND ECOSYSTEM SERVICES IN PEATLAND AND BLUE CARBON ECOSYSTEMS OF NATIONAL WILDLIFE REFUGES (USA)

Kurt A Johnson* and John Schmerfeld

US Fish and Wildlife Service, 5275 Leesburg Pike, Falls Church, Virginia 22041-3803, United States

**Corresponding author: kurt_johnson@fws.gov*

National wildlife refuge managers in the United States are faced with the dilemma of maximizing benefits of habitat management with limited resources (the National Wildlife Refuge System (NWRS) is administered by the US Fish and Wildlife Service (FWS), Department of the Interior). Trade-offs must be made. Data on carbon storage and ecosystem services benefits of associated peatland and blue carbon ecosystems help refuge managers make better-informed decisions about the implications of habitat management, including restoration, in these ecosystem types. Scientists have been studying carbon storage in peatland and blue carbon ecosystems in refuges for more than two decades. While much of the research has focused on documenting and monitoring carbon stocks and fluxes, more recent research has focused on: 1) impacts of management actions, especially restoration, on carbon sequestration; and 2) ecosystem services associated with management of blue carbon and peatland ecosystems. Over the past four years, FWS has worked collaboratively with the US Geological Survey (USGS) to institute pilot projects evaluating carbon sequestration and ecosystem services in key wetland ecosystems in refuges around the USA. Pilot projects are now underway in pocosin peatlands in the south-eastern USA (Great Dismal Swamp and Pocosin Lakes NWRs), mangroves along the Gulf Coast of Florida (J.N. "Ding" Darling and Ten Thousand Islands NWRs), recently-restored tidal marshes in Puget Sound of Washington (Nisqually NWR), and freshwater boreal forest wetlands of east-central Alaska (Yukon Flats NWR). Each project is designed to answer basic scientific questions regarding carbon sequestration, while also providing data relevant for managers' conservation decision-making. Most projects are evaluating ecosystem services associated with carbon sequestration and ecosystem recovery, and some are developing carbon accounting methods. This presentation will highlight the collaborative FWS-USGS projects and explain the utility of resultant data and methods for conservation decision-making in peat and blue carbon ecosystems.

Keywords: -

Abstract No: A-155

MODELING, ASSESSING AND VALUING PEATLAND ECOSYSTEM SERVICES

Dianna Hogan[1*], Emily Pindilli[2], Rachel Sleeter[3], Bryan Parthum[2] and Brianna Williams[4]

[1]U.S. Geological Survey Eastern Geographic Science Center, Reston, VA, USA
[2]U.S. Geological Survey Science and Decisions Center, Reston, VA, USA
[3]U.S. Geological Survey Eastern Geographic Science Center, Gig Harbor, WA, USA
[4]U.S. Geological Survey Eastern Geographic Science Center, Lawrenceville, NJ, USA

*Corresponding author: dhogan@usgs.gov

SUMMARY

Accounting for the ecologic, economic, and social benefits provided by peatland ecosystems, and explicitly incorporating the goods and services they provide into land use and land management decision making, can be an effective approach for balancing diverse and often competing objectives at multiple scales. Highlighting a project in the Great Dismal Swamp in southeastern Virginia and northern North Carolina (USA), this paper discusses ecosystem service modeling, assessment, and valuation in support of peatland management decision making. A primary goal of this study is to increase understanding of how targeted peatland management can be used to maximize the regulating service of carbon (C) storage and sequestration, while assessing potential tradeoffs with other services. Local and regional stakeholders identified the following ecosystem services as the most important to consider in addition to C sequestration: wildlife viewing, hazard mitigation (e.g., peat fire), flood protection, and nutrient cycling. Working within an integrated fine-scale spatial modeling framework, service tradeoffs are identified and evaluated given alternative peatland management actions. These ecosystem service modeling, quantification, and valuation methods address the growing demand for more sophisticated analysis of the integrated environmental, economic, and social consequences of biophysical peatland management decisions.

Keywords: *Great Dismal Swamp, ecosystem services, carbon (C) sequestration, modeling, economic valuation*

INTRODUCTION

Ecosystem services are the benefits provided by the natural environment that are of value to humans such as provisioning services (e.g., production of food and clean water), regulating services (e.g., climate and flood protection), cultural services (e.g., cultural and recreational benefits), and supporting services (e.g., nutrient cycling) (MEA 2005). The ability of the natural environment to provide ecosystem services is compromised by factors including development, pollution, fragmentation, resource overuse, and climate change. By modeling, quantifying, assessing, and valuing ecosystem services, this work addresses how the services of C sequestration, recreation (e.g., wildlife viewing), hazard mitigation (e.g., peat fire), flood protection, and nutrient cycling may be impacted through peatland hydrologic and restoration management options. The focus of our study is on providing information that may be used to enhance the service of C sequestration while quantifying ecosystem service tradeoffs to inform land management decision making.

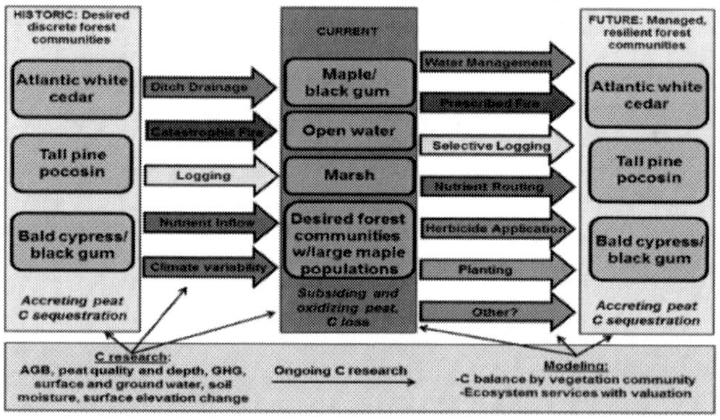

Figure 1: The Great Dismal Swamp Carbon Project Study Design. The C model, ecosystem services assessment, and C field research are organized around historic desired forest communities that, along with proper hydrology,

Study context and objectives

The work reported in this paper is part of a larger project being conducted in the Great Dismal Swamp National Wildlife Refuge (NWR) and the Dismal Swamp State Park (herein collectively referred to as GDS; Figures 1 and 2). That larger project, *The Great Dismal Swamp Carbon Project* (http://www.usgs.gov/climate_landuse/lcs/great_dismal_swamp/default.asp), is designed to (1) characterize potential C sequestration in representative vegetation communities via gaseous and water-based C fluxes and C storage in biomass and soil pools; (2) estimate the effects of refuge management and restoration on C sequestration, fire management, and establishing desirable types of vegetation communities; (3) develop a landscape vegetation-based C model to integrate the C research and support research analyses; and (4) provide an assessment and valuation of ecosystem services. This article describes the development of the vegetation-based C model and the ecosystem services assessment and valuation used to consider the tradeoffs for C sequestration and other ecosystem services associated with select management actions.

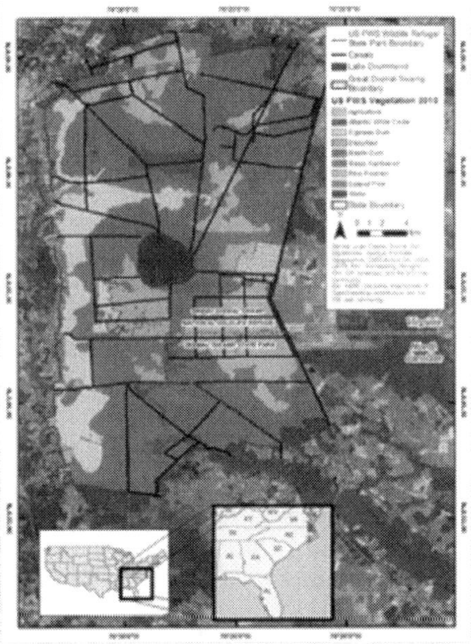

Figure 2: The Great Dismal Swamp National Wildlife Refuge and the Dismal Swamp State Park.

METHODS

The C modeling and ecosystem service assessment and valuation rely on values derived from *The Great Dismal Swamp Carbon Project* (Figure 1) and on published literature values. Because the C research is still ongoing (field research began in June 2014), the current C model and ecosystem service assessment are done primarily using literature values and will be updated as the results of the C research become available.

Study area

The GDS is composed of approximately 53,433 ha of forested peatlands located on the coastal plain in southeastern Virginia and northeastern North Carolina (USA) (Figure 2). The area was formerly privately-owned forest that was logged and ditched beginning in the 1700s. The extensive ditch networks have altered the natural water flow and led to drier, disturbed conditions (Lichtler and Walker, 1974; Ferrell *et al.*, 2007). These conditions have led to the replacement of desirable, peat-forming, historic vegetation communities, specifically Atlantic white cedar (*Chamaecyparis thyoides*), and tall pond pine pocosin (*Pinus serotina*), with a more drought tolerant, less desirable community of mixed red maple (*Acer rubrum*)/blackgum (*Nyssa sylvatica*) that currently covers more than 60% of the refuge. This project focuses on these three vegetation communities to represent a spectrum from natural to highly disturbed vegetation types within the refuge. The GDS NWR is undergoing management actions including hydrologic modifications, selective tree logging and planting, herbicide application, and prescribed fires with the goals of increasing soil saturation, reestablishing desired vegetation communities, and promoting ecological integrity to improve the provision of ecosystem services (USFWS, 2006).

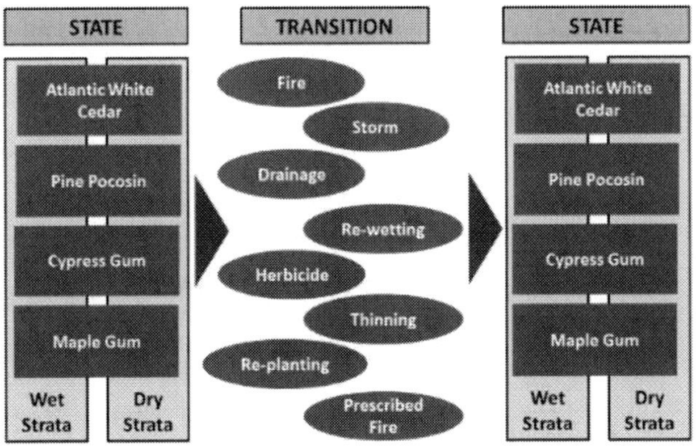

Figure 3: C model concept.

Ecosystem C Model Development

The Land Use and Carbon Scenario Simulator (LUCAS) uses the ST-Sim software package (www. apexrms.com) to integrate a state and transition simulation model with a stock flow model to characterize the effects of land use, land management, and disturbance on terrestrial C dynamics and other ecosystem services (Daniels and Frid, 2011; Sleeter *et al.*, 2015). The model framework spatially organizes the landscape into a grid of simulation cells that represent current conditions as a combination of dominant vegetation community, age, and moisture zone (Figure 3). Transitions between vegetation types reflect the complex spatial relationships between states associated with disturbances due to wildfire, hurricanes, drainage, and drought. Management or restoration actions include re-wetting, herbicide application, re-planting, and prescribed burn.

To evaluate C balance as a function of land management, biomass field measurements paired with existing literature values are used. Model parameterization includes C biomass and flux rates; fire history and probabilities; nominal ('wet' vs 'dry') soil moisture; vegetation response to disturbance, restoration, or management; probabilities of transitions between states; and the age and time since transition for every simulation cell as factors such as climate change can have different probabilities at different ages (Figure 3; Sleeter *et al.*, in prep). The landscape is then simulated through time using Monte Carlo methods.

Ecosystem Service Assessment

The ecosystem service assessment is an integrated ecologic-socioeconomic analysis of baseline (current) and potential future quantity, quality, and value of selected ecosystem services in the GDS (Figure 4). The assessment includes modeled biophysical endpoints, identification of beneficiaries, and valuation of the services. Alternative management scenarios are developed to estimate the impact of specific management actions or disturbance on priority ecosystem services incorporating decision maker input on scenario details (Figure 5). Substantial stakeholder input was obtained for the prioritization of selected services and on the development of alternative management scenarios through stakeholder meetings held in Chesapeake, VA in June 2014 and September 2015.

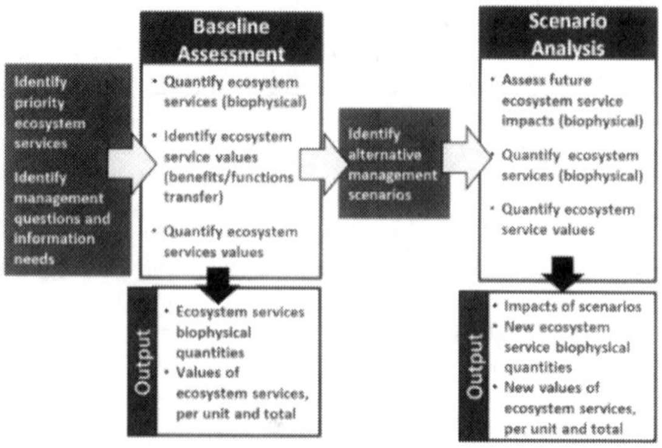

Figure 4: Ecosystem Service Assessment Approach. Red boxes signify key stakeholder participation activity.

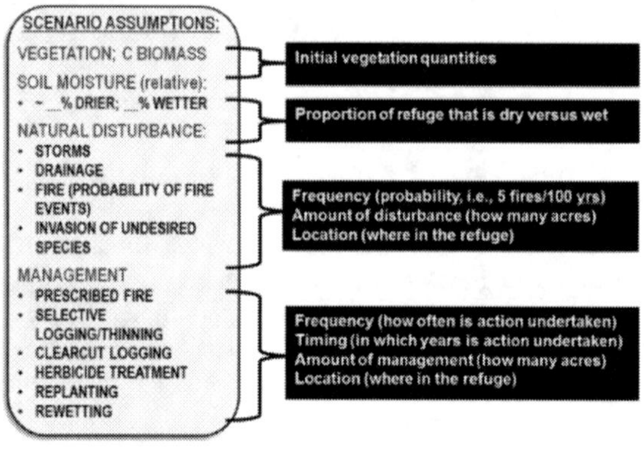

Figure 5: Stakeholder input to the model for development of alternative management scenarios for analysis.

The assessment of baseline ecosystem services incorporates in-situ ecologic (e.g., bird populations), social (e.g., visitor information), and economic (e.g., travel-costs) information. The relationships between the baseline services and parameters in the LUCAS model (e.g., wetness) are considered to assess the impacts on services under select management scenarios. Valuation relies on a hybrid methodology considering damages avoided (as in the case of fire mitigation or flood protection) assessed at the local scale, the application of standardized values (e.g., the Social Cost of Carbon), and benefits transfer from relevant and applicable research sites (e.g., the travel-costs associated with recreation) with the use of as much primary data as are available (e.g., refuge visitation numbers). The overall approach provides GDS specific quantities and values while also providing a framework with which to evaluate the services provided by similar peatland ecosystems.

RESULTS

The spatial, vegetation-based ecosystem model supports evaluation of management actions and disturbances in the GDS to identify ecosystem service tradeoffs and evaluate alternative peatland management actions. Priority ecosystem services as identified by local and regional GDS stakeholders are shown in Table 1.

Table 1: Priority GDS ecosystem services with a summary of the ecologic and economic assessment details.

Ecosystem Service	Ecologic	Economic
Carbon Sequestration	1. C storage and sequestration as a function of vegetation community using biomass, soil gas flux data, water flux data, and literature values	2. Climate change mitigation 3. Valuation via Social Cost of Carbon (SCC) (IWG SCC, 2013; US EPA 2015)
Wildlife Viewing	4. Provision of natural habitat for representative species as a function of management actions 5. Assuming all "non-consumptive" visitation	6. Non-consumptive visitation rates (GDS NWR, 2014; FWS, 2009) 7. Valuation via consumer surplus or "willingness to pay" above actual costs
Fire Mitigation	8. Annual probability, magnitude and/or effects of catastrophic fire 9. Mitigation via hydrologic balance and other management actions	10. Valuation via a. Air quality/human health impacts based on quantified cost of illness b. C emissions (SCC) c. Recreation; tourism lost due to closures
Nutrient Cycling	11. Water quality; impacts under consideration	12. May reduce need to decrease nutrients from urban or agricultural sources; methods under development
Flood Protection	13. Flow control / flood probability (magnitude and/or frequency) as a function of hydrologic management	14. Valuation via reduction in property flood damage

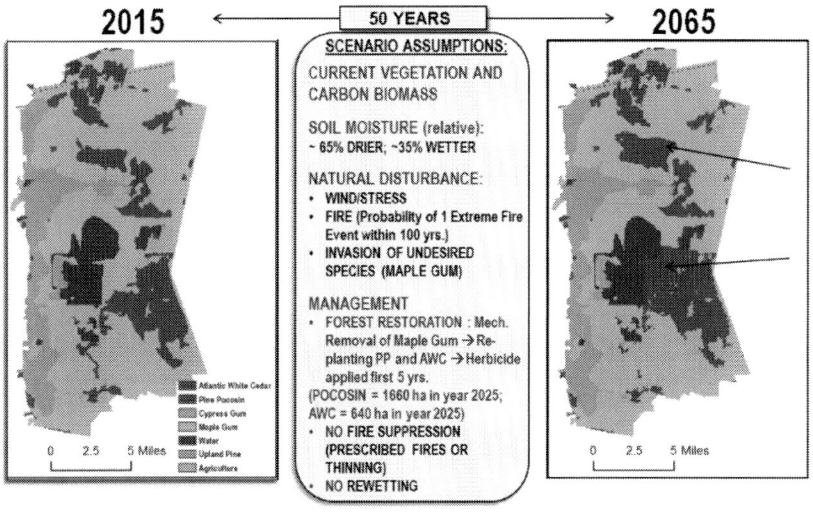

Figure 6: Forest restoration (Atlantic white cedar and pine pocosin) management scenario. Study area shown is the extent of the GDS.

Figure 6 outlines one management decision scenario, temporally modeled to estimate effects on vegetation, hydrology, and habitat, and examine potential future changes in ecosystem service provision given the specified management actions. This scenario simulates forested wetland restoration for Atlantic white cedar and pine pocosin imposed in specified locations, and assessed at baseline (current) and after 50 years. The management assumes the removal of undesirable maple/gum communities through management logging, and the subsequent planting of pine pocosin in one area, and Atlantic white cedar in another area. An assumption was made that herbicide was used within the first 5 years of new growth to prevent hardwood invasion. Using relationships among vegetation communities, condition, and other model parameters with the provision of ecosystem services, the output of the model estimates future (year 2065) ecosystem services that can be compared to initial (2015) services (Table 1). Scenario modeling such as this can provide a range of alternative outcomes given different assumptions, map products of landscape change, and the ability to analyze ecosystem service tradeoffs.

DISCUSSION AND CONCLUSION

The Great Dismal Swamp Carbon Project quantifies C sequestration in representative vegetation communities via gaseous and water-based C fluxes and C storage in biomass and soil pools. These data, along with literature values, are being used to develop a landscape vegetation-based C model and provide an ecosystem service assessment with valuation for the GDS to support land management decision making. This work will contribute to the understanding of current ecosystem services, the economic and qualitative values of those services, and the impacts of management decisions and disturbances on net benefits (or tradeoffs) for peatland ecosystems.

The ecosystem service assessment reported in this paper includes the direct use of the in-situ ecologic studies, and the LUCAS model to provide more accurate data for ecosystem service tradeoff analyses and decision support. The valuation work utilizes methods that incorporate both primary socio-economic information of beneficiaries and leverages previous work on valuation. The ecosystem service valuation is conducted at a fine scale, evaluating benefits at a detailed and site-specific level while also incorporating a suite of services. There are examples of national-level studies that evaluate ecosystem services using primarily meta-analysis and benefits transfer such as the noteworthy study conducted by Patton *et al.* (2012) that provided an ecosystem service valuation model applied to Fish and Wildlife Service (FWS) NWRs (Arrowwood, Blackwater, Okefenokee, and Sevilleta & Bosque del Apache). There are also detailed analyses related to peatlands that focus on single services and may or may not provide socio-economic values of outcomes (e.g., health impacts of catastrophic fires by Rappold *et al.*, 2011). The current work seeks to capture the benefits of both scales and add to the state of knowledge on the values of ecosystem services provided by peatlands.

Although the explicit use of ecosystem service concepts is relatively new, it is increasingly being used to guide land use and land management decision making. The ecosystem services approach focuses on the benefits provided by the natural environment that are of value to humans and provides a useful framework for directly integrating ecologic, economic, and social information. This supports the consideration of how ecological resources can be strategically and sustainably managed to meet the ecosystem service needs of the growing global human population.

ACKNOWLEDGEMENTS

This work is funded by USGS LandCarbon, and is part of a multi-partner project with the U.S. Fish and Wildlife Service, The Nature Conservancy, the U.S. Geological Survey, and George Mason, Clemson, East Carolina, and Southern Methodist Universities. The authors thank the Coordination Team (Adam Carver, Joy Greenwood, Chris Lowie, Chuck Peoples, Howard Phillips, Christine Pickens, Brad Reed, John Schmerfeld, Brian van Eerden, Sara Ward, Fred Wurster, Zhiliang Zhu), and the Research Teams (Kim Angeli, Karen Balentine, Nicole Cormier, Judy Drexler, Jamie Duberstein, Gary Fisher, Chris Fuller, Laurel Gutenberg, Todd Hawbaker, Ken Krauss, Tim Larson, Courtney Lee, Zhong Lu, Rebecca Moss, Christina Musser, Jim Orlando, John Qu, Marek Salanski, Josh Salter, Gary Speiran, Craig Stricker, Chris Wright).

Any use of trade, firm, or product names is for descriptive purposes only and does not imply endorsement by the U.S. Government.

REFERENCES

1. Daniels C.J., and L. Frid, 2011, Predicting landscape vegetation dynamics using state-and-transition simulation models, In *Proceedings of the First Landscape State-and-Transition Simulation Modeling Conference*, Portland, OR, USA, 14-16 June 2011; Kerns, B.K., Shlisky, A.J., Daniel, C.J., Eds.; U.S. Department of Agriculture, Forest Service, Pacific Northwest Research Station: Portland, OR, USA, pp.5-22. http://www.fs.fed.us/pnw/pubs/pnw_gtr869/pnw_gtr869_002.pdf
2. Ferrell, G.M., Strickland, A.G., and T.B. Spruill, 2007, Effects of Canals and Roads on Hydrologic Conditions and Health of Atlantic White Cedar at Emily and Richardson Preyer Buckridge Coastal Reserve, North Carolina, 2003–2006. *USGS Scientific Investigations Report* 2007–5163. http://pubs.er.usgs.gov/publication/sir20075163
3. GDS NWR, 2014, Visitation Rates of the Great Dismal Swamp National Wildlife Refuge (GDS NWR) in 2014, personal communication.
4. IWG SCC (Interagency Working Group on Social Cost of Carbon), US Government, 2013, Technical Update of the Social Cost of Carbon for Regulatory Impact Analysis Under Executive Order 12866. https://www.whitehouse.gov/sites/default/files/omb/inforeg/social_cost_of_carbon_for_ria_2013_update.pdf
5. Lichtler, W.F., and P.N. Walker, 1974, Hydrology of the Dismal Swamp, Virginia – North Carolina, *USGS OFR* 74-39. http://pubs.er.usgs.gov/publication/ofr7439
6. Millennium Ecosystem Assessment (MEA), 2005, Ecosystems and human well-being: Synthesis. Island Press, Washington. 155pp. http://www.millenniumassessment.org/documents/document.356.aspx.pdf
7. Patton, D., Bergstrom, J., Covich, A., and Moore, R., 2012, National Wildlife Refuge Wetland Ecosystem Service Valuation Model, Phase 1 Report: An Assessment of Ecosystem Services Associated with National Wildlife Refuges, University of Georgia, 107 pgs

http://www.fws.gov/economics/Discussion%20Papers/USFWS_Ecosystem%20Services_Phase%20I%20Report_04-25-2012.pdf

8. Rappold, A., Stone, S., Cascio, W., Neas, L., Kilaru, V., Carraway, M., Szykman, J., Ising, A., Cleve, W., Meredith, J., Vaughan-Batten, H., Deyneka, L., and Devlin, R., 2011, Peat bog wildfire smoke exposure in rural North Carolina is associated with cardiopulmonary emergency department visits assessed through syndromic surveillance, *Environmental Health Perspectives* 119:1415-1420. doi: 10.1289/ehp.1003206.
9. Sleeter, B.M., Liu, J., Daniel, C., Frid, L., and Z. Zhu, 2015, An integrated approach to modeling changes in land use, land cover, and disturbance and their impact on ecosystem carbon dynamics: a case study in the Sierra Nevada Mountains of California. *AIMS Environmental Science* 2(3): 577-606. doi:10.3934/environsci.2015.3.577
10. Sleeter, R., Williams, B., Hogan, D., *in prep*, Carbon Balance Model for the Great Dismal Swamp, *USGS Techniques and Methods Report*, 31 pages.
11. US EPA (United States Environmental Protection Agency), 2015, The Social Cost of Carbon. http://www.epa.gov/climatechange/EPAactivities/economics/scc.html.
12. US FWS (United States Fish and Wildlife Service), 2006, Great Dismal Swamp National Wildlife Refuge and Nansemond National Wildlife Refuge Final Comprehensive Conservation Plan. 272 pages. http://www.fws.gov/refuge/Great_Dismal_Swamp/what_we_do/conservation.html
13. US FWS (United States Fish and Wildlife Service), 2009, Net Economic Values of Wildlife-Related Recreation in 2006: Addendum to the 2006 National Survey of Fishing, Hunting, and Wildlife-Associated Recreation, Report 2006-5.
http://nctc.fws.gov/resources/knowledge-resources/pubs/nat_survey2006_economicvalues.pdf

Abstract No: A-169

QUANTIFYING ABOVE AND BELOWGROUND CARBON LOSS FOLLOWING WILDFIRE IN PEATLANDS USING REPEATED LIDAR MEASUREMENTS

Todd J. Hawbaker[1*], Ashwan D. Reddy[2], Zhiliang Zhu[3], Fredric C. Wurster[4], and Jamie A. Duberstein[5]

[1]*U.S. Geological Survey, Denver, CO, USA;*
[2]*University of Maryland, College Park, MD, USA;*
[3]*U.S. Geological Survey, Reston, VA, USA;*
[4]*U.S. Fish and Wildlife Service, Suffolk, VA, USA;*
[5]*Clemson University, Clemson, SC, USA*

**Corresponding author: tjhawbaker@usgs.gov*

SUMMARY

Natural disturbances like fires are often unavoidable and their negative effects in peatlands can be amplified by concomitant human-driven changes such as artificial drainage. This study used pre- and post-fire airborne lidar to estimate aboveground and belowground carbon loss as a result of the South One and Lateral West Fires which burned 24 and 25 km^2 in 2008 and 2011, respectively in the Great Dismal Swamp National Wildlife Refuge, Virginia and North Carolina, USA. Total carbon lost from the 2 fires was 0.60 and 1.23 Tg C, respectively. Our results demonstrate the value of sustained lidar data collection efforts to quantify the impacts of ecosystem disturbances on carbon cycling. Our findings document that fires in drained peatlands can result in substantial amounts of belowground carbon loss that could potentially be avoided by restoring drained and protecting existing peatlands.

Keywords: *lidar, fire, carbon, biomass consumption*

INTRODUCTION

Globally, peatlands hold between 16 and 33% of global soil carbon stocks even though they account for just 3% of the land surface (Bridgham *et al.*, 2006). Peatlands can contribute methane (CH_4) to the atmosphere as a result of methanogenesis in the anaerobic conditions present in saturated soils. Over extended time periods, however, peatlands sequester carbon from the atmosphere and develop large belowground carbon (C) stocks as vegetation falls to the ground and decomposes at relatively slow rates that are influenced by soil saturation and litter quality (Bridgham *et al.*, 2006; Day, 1982). Because their potential to sequester carbon from the atmosphere is offset by CH_4 emissions, peatlands are valued for the large C stocks they hold and not necessarily their sequestration rates (Bridgham *et al.*, 2006); preventing the loss of those C stocks is a pressing concern for agencies managing peatlands.

Human-driven changes in land use and management are a primary threat to the C stored in peatlands. These changes include drainage through canal construction, forest harvest, peat harvesting, and conversion to agriculture. Threats to peatlands are especially evident in the southeastern United States where legacies of land use have altered the hydrology, disturbance regimes, and vegetation dynamics of peatlands, and made vulnerable the large stocks of C stored within them (Batzer and Baldwin, 2012). Specifically, past efforts to drain peatlands have altered the hydrology and disrupted historic carbon cycling patterns. The effects of these changes on C include direct oxidation of peat, decreased peat accretion rates, and increased severity of fires resulting in loss of both above and belowground biomass. Consequently, peatlands in the southeastern U.S. are the focus of many management efforts to mitigate and reduce the negative impacts of past land use.

Consistent monitoring of C stocks and changes in C stocks is essential to understanding how land management and natural disturbances influence the ability of peatlands and other ecosystems to sequester carbon dioxide from the atmosphere and offset anthropogenic greenhouse gas emissions. Light-detection and ranging (lidar) is one technology that can be utilized to monitor changes in above and belowground C stocks because of its ability to characterize surface elevations and vegetation heights. In contrast to traditional field surveys, lidar can provide continuous coverage over large areas (Lefsky *et al.*, 2002; Ballhorn *et al.*, 2009). However, challenges remain in quantifying change with lidar data because there is no concerted effort to repeatedly collect lidar in the U.S. and most data collection efforts are designed for constructing digital elevation models with pulse densities lower than ideal for monitoring vegetation. The lidar data that do exist were collected under varying vegetation conditions and have differences in pulse densities and pulse footprints of the lidar collections. Most lidar-based biomass mapping efforts have relied on relating forest inventory data to lidar collected during coincident time periods; methods to relate forest inventory data collected at one time period to lidar collections from multiple time periods have not been as well developed, but would be valuable to facilitate consistent, cost-effective monitoring of biomass, C stocks, and disturbances.

To better understand how disturbances affect carbon stocks in peatlands and identify ways to overcome the challenges of using repeated lidar measurements, we conducted this study with two goals: (1) to determine how well repeated lidar measurements can be used to monitor changes in above and belowground C stocks in forested peatlands in the southeastern U.S., and (2) to estimate the amount of aboveground and belowground C lost following two recent fires in the Great Dismal Swamp.

METHODS

Study Area

Our study was conducted within the 450 km^2 Great Dismal Swamp National Wildlife Refuge and Dismal Swamp State Natural Area located in the southeastern U.S. (referred to as Great Dismal Swamp or GDS). Prior to becoming a refuge, the land was owned by several timber companies that built a 158-mile network of roads and canals to drain the wetland and facilitate timber harvesting. Most of the canals in the GDS were constructed between 1954 and 1968 (USGS, 1954, 1968) and are thought to have created drier conditions throughout the swamp, contributing to peat subsidence, decreased C stocks and sequestration rates, changes in vegetation communities, and increased fire severity (USFWS, 2006).

Present-day vegetation in GDS is dominated by several forest types, often with very dense shrub understories. These forest types include (1) bald cypress (*Taxodium distichum*)/black gum (*Nyssa sylvatica*) mix, (2) Atlantic white cedar (*Chamaecyparis thyoides*), (3) red maple (*Acer rubrum*)/blackgum mix, and (4) tall pond pine (*Pinus serotina*) pocosins. The type of forest present at any location is a result of disturbance and management and hydrologic conditions, especially duration of soil saturation (Dabel and Day, 1977; Carter *et al.*, 1994).

On August 4, 2011, lightning ignited the 'Lateral West' fire within the refuge that burned 25 km^2 over 126 days. That fire overlapped with the areas burned in the 2008 'South One' fire (24 km^2) and the 2006 'West Drummond' fire (2.3 km^2). Few trees were left standing in areas affected by these three fires and soil loss of more than 1 meter was observed in some areas.

Field Data Collection and Analysis

To estimate aboveground biomass, tree data were collected at 76 plots located in unburned areas throughout the GDS during the summer of 2014. At each location, we established a 5.6 m fixed-radius plot (100 m^2) and recorded the species, status (*e.g.*, live or dead), and measured the diameter of all trees with diameter at breast height ≥ 2.54 cm. For a subset of trees, selected using a prism with a basal area factor of 2 m^2/ha, we also measured total tree height using a Haglöf Vertex Laser Hypsometer. Biomass of each tree was calculated using allometric equations (Jenkins et al., 2003), and summed to generate plot-level totals of live tree aboveground biomass (referred to as biomass from here on). The location of each plot was recorded with a Trimble ProXH global positioning system (GPS) and post-processed to differentially correct the locations. Horizontal accuracy of the post-processed GPS locations ranged between 0.1 and 0.9 m and averaged 0.4 m.

Soil bulk density and carbon content analysis were calculated for 23 samples collected at unburned locations in areas near the Lateral West fire in August 2013 and 3 samples from a previous 1999 study (NRCS Soil Survey Lab in Lincoln, NE, USA). Bulk density ranged from 0.09 to 0.24 g/cm^3 and had a mean of 0.16 g/cm^3. Carbon content was between 46 and 64% of total soil matter, with a mean of 59%. Consistent with the characteristics of peatland soils, organic matter averaged 95% among all samples. Mean values for bulk density and carbon content were used to convert elevation change to carbon loss.

Lidar Data Collection and Analysis

Lidar flights were made in 2006, 2010, 2012, and 2014, parts of which were overlapping. These collections were made with similar flight and sensor characteristics, but during different times of year (Table 1). We selected lidar pulse returns within 5.6 m radius of our 2014 field plot centers from each collection. We derived the surface elevations and canopy height data from each lidar collection to build a series of regression models at the plot level for predicting biomass at the landscape level. To generate landscape-level results, all lidar pulses were assigned to 10 x 10 m grid cells, to match the area of the field plots (100 m_2).

Table 1. Characteristics of lidar collections overlapping the Great Dismal Swamp.

Collection	Year	Month	Pulse density (#/m^2)
Chesapeake County	2006	Sep.	1 pulse / m2
Great Dismal Swamp (GDS)	2010	Mar.	2 pulses / m2
Lateral West Burned Area	2012	Aug.	2 pulses / m2
North Carolina	2014	Mar. & Apr.	4 pulses / m2

We estimated plot-level elevation for each lidar collection using the mean of the lowest three elevation values per plot or grid-cell. When compared to the 2010 GDS-wide elevation models, the 2006 elevation model had significantly higher surface elevations in vegetated areas (0.62 m difference; t-test p-value=0.0002). This was likely a result of the lower pulse density in the 2006 data. Therefore, we related 2010 and 2006 elevations to each other using a simple linear regression, and then applied the regression to adjust the 2006 elevations (intercept=1.0; slope=0.72; R^2=0.71; RMSE=0.41). A second t-test of the adjusted 2006 elevations confirmed that they were not significantly different from the 2010 elevations (0.02 m difference; p-value=0.86). T-tests comparing the 2012 and 2014 elevations to the 2010 elevations were not significant (difference=0.02 m; p-value=0.93 for 2012 vs. 2010; difference=0.16 m; p-value=0.14 for 2014 vs. 2010). The differences in elevation models across collections were minimal, especially after adjusting the 2006 data, providing confidence that lidar-derived vegetation heights would be consistent across the collections.

Potential predictor variables for biomass were generated for both the plot-level and landscape-level data by calculating the mean and standard deviation of lidar pulse heights, and mean of the highest five pulses heights. We fit a series of regressions using the individual predictors and all combinations of two predictors to determine which of the 2014 lidar canopy metrics were most strongly related to biomass measured in 2014 at the plot locations. All variables were natural-log + 1 transformed prior to analysis. The fit regressions were used to predict biomass for all plots and all lidar collections. We calculated the average of plot-level standard deviation in biomass over time as an instability metric to further evaluate the models; larger values indicate that the predictions are less consistent (i.e. less stable) across the different lidar collections. We selected the most stable regression to make landscape-level predictions of biomass for the four different lidar collections.

To scale up our results to the entire GDS, we applied the methods used for the plot-level lidar analysis to each lidar collection, calculating and adjusting elevation and vegetation heights, and predicting biomass within 10 x 10 m^2 grid cells. Changes in surface elevations and belowground C stocks within the South One and Lateral West fire perimeters were estimated by differencing elevation data from either the 2010 and 2006 or 2012 and 2010 lidar collections, calculating total volume of change, and then multiplying that volume by bulk density and carbon content values, following methods outlined in Reddy *et al.* (2014). Elevation change and belowground C loss were calculated for the portion of the South One fire that was also covered by the 2006 lidar collection. Similarly, changes in biomass within the South One and Lateral West fire perimeters were estimated by differencing biomass data from either the 2010 and 2006 or 2012 and 2010 collections (depending on the fire) and then multiplying the biomass values by 0.5 to convert to C (Jenkins *et al.*, 2003).

RESULTS

Of the six models fit for this study, significant relationships (slope coefficient p-values < 0.05) between biomass and the predictors were only identified for the univariate models. Error rates and R^2 values were similar across the three univariate models (Table 2). The regression predicting biomass using the mean of the highest five pulse returns (H.max) had the greatest stability in biomass predictions (instability = 6.5 kg/m^2); all other models had greater instability measures (7.3 or larger). Thus, landscape-level predictions of biomass were made with the regression using mean of the highest five pulse heights (H.max) as a predictor.

Table 2. Regressions of live tree aboveground biomass vs. lidar height summaries; H.max = mean of highest five lidar pulses; H.mean = mean of lidar pulse heights; H.sd = standard deviation of lidar pulse heights; ln = natural log. Significant level of regression coefficients: ' 0.1; * 0.05; ** 0.01; *** 0.001.

Model form	RMSE	R^2	Instability
ln(biomass+1) = -4.41* + 2.31 × ln(H.max+1)***	0.65	0.30	6.48
ln(biomass+1) = -2.24* + 1.96 × ln(H.mean+1)***	0.63	0.33	8.73
ln(biomass+1) = -0.53 + 1.82 × ln(H.sd+1)***	0.64	0.31	7.34
ln(biomass+1) = -2.43 + 1.04 × ln(H.max+1) + 1.08 × ln(H.sd+1)	0.65	0.30	7.10
ln(biomass+1) = -1.97' + 1.22 × ln(H.mean+1)' + 0.89 × ln(H.sd+1)	0.63	0.34	8.15
ln(biomass+1) = -3.77* + 1.28 × ln(H.max+1)' + 1.05 × ln(H.sd+1)	0.63	0.34	8.30

For the South One fire, average elevation decrease was 0.17 m and belowground C loss was 16.0 kg/m^2 (Figure 1). With these C loss rates, total belowground C loss from the entire South One fire was 0.38 Tg C. There is a large degree of uncertainty around this estimate as there are visible patterns in the 2006 to 2010 elevation change maps outside the fire perimeter that are likely artifacts of the different lidar collections and not true elevation change. The Lateral West fire occurred 3 years after the South One fire and burned almost the exact same area, resulting in an additional decrease in elevation of 0.46 m (mean within the perimeter). This resulted in a loss of 43.4 kg C/m^2 or a total of 1.09 Tg C. These estimates are nearly identical to those made in our previous study using slightly different methods (Reddy *et al.*, 2014).

Patterns of aboveground biomass change were more pronounced than elevation change in both the South One and Lateral West perimeters (Figure 2). Average aboveground C loss within the portion of the South One perimeter covered by the 2006 lidar collection was 4.5 kg C/m^2, resulting in a total loss of 0.13 Tg C. Within the entire South One perimeter, total aboveground C loss was 0.22 Tg C. Aboveground C lost in the Lateral West fire was less than in the South One fire, averaging 2.8 kg C/m^2 and totaling 0.14 Tg C.

Figure 1. Lidar-derived elevation for 2010 (A), and elevation change between 2006 and 2010 (B), 2010 and 2012 (C), and 2010 and 2014 (D) for the Great Dismal Swamp National Wildlife Refuge (GDS NWR) and Dismal Swamp State Natural Area (DS SNA). The area over which changes were calculated was limited by the extent of the 2006, 2012, and 2014 lidar collections. Landsat 8 bands 7-4-2 from Feb. 28, 2014, in background.

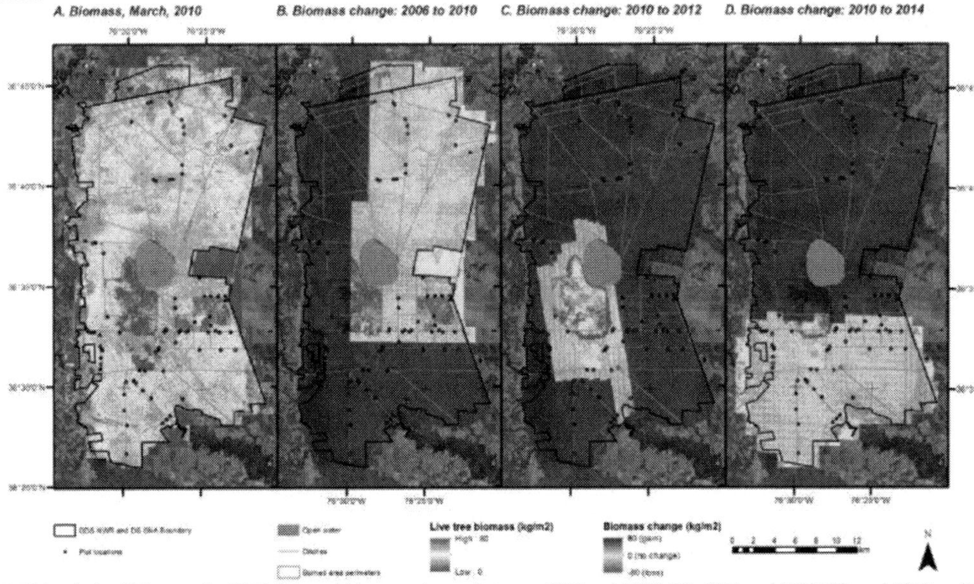

Figure 2. Lidar-derived biomass for 2010 (A), and biomass change between 2006 and 2010 (B), 2010 and 2012 (C), and 2010 and 2014 (D) for the Great Dismal Swamp National Wildlife Refuge (GDS NWR) and Dismal Swamp State Natural Area (DS SNA). Landsat 8 bands 7- 4-2 from Feb. 28, 2014, in background. The area over which changes were calculated was limited by the extent of the 2006, 2012, and 2014 lidar collections.

DISCUSSION

Between 2008 and 2011, two large fires burned 5.6% of the area of the Great Dismal Swamp. Using repeated lidar height measurements, we assessed the impacts of those fires on above and belowground C. The South One fire in 2008 consumed a total of 0.60 Tg C and 63% of that was belowground. The loss of canopy cover and exposure of previously buried peat deposits after the South One fire created conditions that amplified the severity of the later Lateral West fire in 2011, which consumed 1.23 Tg C, 88% of which was belowground. An accurate peat-depth map does not exist for the GDS so it was not possible to estimate total belowground C stocks in the GDS and the proportion that was lost in the two fires. However, the impacts of the fires on belowground C will be long lasting. Average peat accumulation rates are 0.07 cm/year in the conterminous U.S. (Bridgham *et al.*, 2006), and at this rate, recovery of peat in the burned areas would take nearly 900 years.

A complete aboveground biomass dataset for the GDS was based on the 2010 lidar flight data (Figure 2). Total biomass in the GDS in 2010 after the 2006 South One fire and other disturbances (e.g. harvest shown in Figure 2) was 4.50 Tg C. The 2011 Lateral West fire consumed 3% of that. Normally, we would expect aboveground biomass to recover over a period of several decades. However, following the fire, much of the burned area filled with water, creating a lake, which will impede revegetation of this area. Given that the burned area now holds standing water, it is difficult to predict when the aboveground C lost in the South One and Lateral West fires will be recovered.

Fire is a natural and historically frequently occurring process that plays an important role driving vegetation succession in the forest types present in the GDS (Frost, 1993). Extensive drainage of the GDS through canal construction has altered hydrologic conditions, leaving GDS much drier than it was historically. Consequently, fires substantially change C storage and in some cases result in a state change from forested swamps to open water. These changes could potentially be mitigated by managing the hydrology of GDS for wetter soil conditions so that when fires do occur, primarily aboveground C stocks are consumed and belowground C stocks are left intact.

CONCLUSION

Making use of repeated lidar collections for monitoring forest biomass has been challenging because of differences in flight and sensor configurations and vegetation conditions. The methods used in this study demonstrate an approach that may be promising to overcome those challenges. Using an approach along these lines may help to extend the amount of lidar information that is usable to monitor changes in forest vegetation and biomass when temporally coincident forest inventories are not available.

REFERENCES

1. Ballhorn U., F. Siegert, M. Mason, S. Limin. 2009. Derivation of burn scar depths and estimation of carbon emissions with LIDAR in Indonesian peatlands. Proceedings of the National Academy of Sciences, 106:21213-21218
2. Batzer, D.P. and A.H. Baldwin (editors). 2012. Wetland Habitats of North America; Ecology and Conservation Concerns. University of California Press, Berkeley, CA, USA, 389 p.
3. Bridgham, S.D., J.P. Megonigal, J.K. Keller, N.B. Bliss, and C. Trettin. 2006. The Carbon Balance of North American Wetlands. Wetlands, 26:889-916
4. Dabel, C.V. and F.P. Day. 1977. Structural comparisons of four plant communities in the Great Dismal Swamp, Virginia. Bulletin of the Torrey Botanical Club, 104:352-360
5. Day, F.P. 1982. Litter decomposition rates in the seasonally flooded Great Dismal Swamp. Ecology, 63:670-678 Carter, V., P.T. Gammon and M.K. Garrett. 1994. Ecotone dynamics and boundary determination in the Great Dismal Swamp. Ecological Applications, 4:189–203
6. Frost, C.C. Presettlement fire regimes in southeastern marshes, peatlands, and swamps. Pages 39-60 in Proceedings of the 19th Tall Timbers Fire Ecology Conference, Nov. 3-6, 1993, Tallahassee, FL
7. Jenkins, J.C., D.C. Chojnacky, L.S. Heath, and R.A. Birdsey. 2003. National-scale biomass estimators for United States tree species. Forest Science, 49:12-35
8. Lefsky, M.A., W.B. Cohen, D.J. Harding, G.G. Parker, S.A. Ackerand S.T. Gower. 2002. LiDAR remote sensing of aboveground biomass in three biomes. Global Ecology and Biogeography, 11:393–399
9. Reddy, A.D., T.J. Hawbaker, F. Wurster, Z. Zhu, S. Ward, D. Newcomb, and R. Murray. 2015. Quantifying soil carbon loss and uncertainty from a peatland wildfire using multi-temporal lidar, Remote Sensing of Environment 170:306-316
10. U.S. Fish and Wildlife Service (USFWS). 2006. *Great Dismal Swamp National Wildlife Refuge and Nansemond National Wildlife Refuge Final Comprehensive Conservation Plan*. 258 p.
11. U.S. Geological Survey (USGS). 1954. Topographic maps (*variously named*) 1:7,500, 1 sheet each.
12. U.S. Geological Survey (USGS). 1968. Topographic maps (*variously named*) 1:7,500, 1 sheet each

Abstract No: A-205

QUANTIFYING ABOVEGROUND BIOMASS AND ITS RATE OF CHANGE IN GREAT DISMAL SWAMP, VIRGINIA, USA

Jamie A Duberstein[1], Todd J Hawbaker[2], Gary K. Speiran[3], Zhilang Zhu[4], Nicole Cormier[5] and Frederic C Wurster[6]

[1] *Baruch Institute of Coastal Ecology and Forest Science, Clemson University, Georgetown, SC, USA*
[2] *U.S. Geological Survey, Geosciences and Environmental Change Science Center, Denver, CO, USA*
[3] *U.S. Geological Survey, Virginia Water Science Center, Richmond, VA, USA*
[4] *U.S. Geological Survey, National Center, Reston, VA, USA*
[5] *U.S. Geological Survey, Wetland and Aquatic Research Center, Lafayette, LA, USA*
[6] *U.S. Fish and Wildlife Service, Great Dismal Swamp National Wildlife Refuge, Suffolk, VA, USA*

**Corresponding email: JamieDuberstein@gmail.com*

SUMMARY

To better understand differences in carbon budgets among peatland forest types, we surveyed trees, saplings, and shrubs at three replicate field plots across three different forest types (n = 9 field plots) in the Great Dismal Swamp, a 450 km^2 forested peatland in Virginia and North Carolina, USA. Our goal was to estimate standing carbon stocks via biomass calculations, and measure growth rates of co-dominant trees. Forest types included healthy, mature Atlantic white cedar (*Chamaecyparis thyoides*); healthy, mature tall pond pine (*Pinus serotina*) pocosin; and a mix of red maple (*Acer rubrum*) and blackgum (*Nyssa sylvatica*), which are associated with degraded conditions and not desired by managers of this ecosystem. Total carbon stocks were greatest in the Atlantic white cedar forest type (14.1 kg C m^{-2}) compared to red maple/blackgum (8.1 kg C m^{-2}) and tall pine pocosin (13.1 kg C m^{-2}). The Atlantic white cedar forest type also had the greatest tree growth rates (8.6 cm^2 tree^{-1}) compared to red maple/blackgum (7.3 cm^2 tree^{-1}) and tall pine pocosin (3.8 cm^2 tree^{-1}). Our results indicate that Atlantic white cedar may have potential to play a role in restoration efforts to meet the management goal of protecting and expanding this native forest ecosystem, while also providing an added benefit of sequestering and storing carbon to help offset greenhouse gas emissions from fossil fuel combustion.

***Keywords**: Chamaecyparis thyoides, Pocosin, carbon sequestration, tree growth, dendrometer*

INTRODUCTION

In global efforts to ameliorate the impacts of greenhouse gases, it has become increasingly important to quantify changes in standing stocks of aboveground woody biomass and associated carbon sequestration rates. Peatlands are especially important ecosystems with regard to global carbon dynamics because they accumulate large above and belowground carbon stocks over time (Mitsch and Gosselink, 2000).

In 2014, a multifaceted study (the Great Dismal Swamp Carbon Project) was initiated by the U.S. Fish and Wildlife Service and the U.S. Geological Survey to quantify different components of the carbon budget and inform the development of management plans for the swamp. In the current study, we estimated the standing carbon stocks and changes in aboveground biomass in three dominant forest types (Cedar, Maple, and Pocosin) of interest to refuge managers planning long-term strategies to restore and/or manage tree communities. We used surveys of trees and shrubs to develop biomass estimates that yielded relative amounts of in situ aboveground carbon storage within the forest types studied (Jenkins *et al.*, 2003; Woodall *et al.*, 2011). We are also monitoring (sub-) surface water levels and growth rates of co-dominant trees. Relating tree growth to water levels may facilitate the management goal of determining the impact that water levels have on aboveground biomass.

The Great Dismal Swamp (GDS) is a large forested peatland that once covered more than 600,000 ha (Shaler, 1890). Since colonial times, the swamp was owned by numerous forest products companies and others. A network of canals and adjacent levees (spoil piles) were constructed to drain the swamp to facilitate harvesting timber and agriculture (Shaler, 1890), though most canals were constructed between 1954 and 1968 (USGS, 1954, 1968). A portion of the original GDS was preserved as the Great Dismal Swamp National Wildlife Refuge (North Carolina and Virginia, USA) and Dismal Swamp State Park (North Carolina, USA) in 1974 (Figure 1). These preserves now comprise the current GDS, and are managed to protect and restore the ecological integrity of the area, enhance wildlife observation, and maintain sound working relationships with adjoining, neighboring, and other key stakeholders (USFWS, 2006). The primary challenge facing GDS is to manage water levels in canals using an extensive network of adjustable-height dams to reduce the hydrologic changes the canals have created and mitigate the impacts on ecosystems in the GDS.

The pre-development forest communities that existed in GDS included extensive tracts of the cypress-gum forest type, composed largely of bald cypress [*Taxodium distichum* (L.) Rich.] and water tupelo (*Nyssa aquatic* L.) (Shaler,1890; Kearney,1901). Additional forest types included: maple-gum (hereafter, "Maple"), dominated by red maple (*Acer rubrum* L.) and blackgum (*Nyssa sylvatica* Marshall); tall pine pocosin (hereafter, "Pocosin"), dominated by pond pine (*Pinus serotina* Michx.); and peatland Atlantic white cedar (hereafter "Cedar"), composed largely of Atlantic white cedar [*Chamaecyparis thyoides* (L.) B.S.P.]. The canal and levee system caused hydrologic changes within GDS, which had an impact on tree regeneration following timber extraction. Because of the combined impacts of timber harvest, associated wetland draining, and wildfires, relatively few tracts of the Cedar forest type currently exist in GDS. And while Cedar and cypress-gum were originally the dominant forest types with the Maple forest type as a minor constituent, the Maple forest type now covers more than 60 percent of the swamp (Carter, 1976; USFWS, 2006). A current management goal is to increase the coverage of the Cedar forest type and decrease the dominance of the red maple.

METHODS

Three replicate 20 x 25 m (500 m^2) field plots were established in representative stands of each of the three forest types of interest (Cedar, Maple, Pocosin) for a total of nine total field plots (Figure 1). Two of the cedar plots were located in close proximity (40 m) to each other because few mature stands of the Cedar forest type exist in the swamp today. Smaller subplots were established within each 500 m^2 plot for purposes of quantifying saplings and shrubs (Figure 2). All trees, defined as ≥12.7 cm diameter at breast height (DBH, taken at 1.4 m from ground level), within the 500 m^2 plots were identified to species with the exception of ash which was identified to the genus level (*i.e., Fraxinus* spp.). Trees were measured for DBH and height, and estimated for cull (nearest 1%) if the individual tree was missing major branches or had areas of obvious decay; snags (*i.e.*, dead trees) were also inventoried, but assigned a decay class so that biomass reduction factors could later be applied (Domke *et al.*, 2011). Saplings (2.5 ≤ DBH (cm) ≤ 12.7) within nested 100 m^2 subplots (Figure 2) were identified to species and measured for DBH; sapling snags were also inventoried and assigned a decay class. Shrubs (DBH < 2.5 cm) within 5.5 m^2 subsections (Figure 2) were identified and measured for diameter at the root collar (DRC); dead shrubs were not inventoried.

Ten co-dominant trees in each field plot were selected for growth measurements. These trees spanned the 12 to 60 cm DBH range of the dominant trees in each field plot, though DBHs were not necessarily uniform between field plots. When adequate trees were not available inside the field plots, trees immediately adjacent to field plots were selected for growth measures. During the winter of 2014, a section of the bark of selected trees was smoothed with a mini file and equipped with dendrometer bands that were immediately scribed with a reference line adjacent to the band collar (Bormann and Kozlowski 1962; Keeland and Sharitz 1993). Atlantic white cedar and pond pine trees were selected to represent the Cedar and Pocosin forest types, respectively, while trees banded in the Maple forest type were half red maple and half blackgum (*i.e.*, five of each per field plot). Growth measurements, measured as increase in circumference (mm) of the main tree bole, began in March 2015, and continued every three months through 2015 (*i.e.*, quarterly) with the exception of one field plot (Pocosin 2) that could not be accessed for the December 2015 measurement.

Aboveground biomass was computed for all non-vine woody plants measured in the field plots (Figure 2) and scaled to represent biomass as kilograms of carbon per square meter (kg C m^{-2}). Biomass of trees and saplings were calculated using the component ratio method, which utilizes species-specific algorithms to sum individual components (*e.g.*, bole, bark, stump, branches, foliage) based on DBH, height, percent cull, and decay class for snags (Jenkins *et al.*, 2003; Woodall *et al.*, 2011). Tree-level biomass error from these equations can be as high as 20 to 35%, but the errors are assumed to be random and cancel out when aggregated at the plot-level (Jenkins *et al.*, 2003). Biomass of shrubs was calculated as the sum of individual stem and foliage components using DRC measurements and parameters for hardwoods (Day and Monk, 1974). We assumed that biomass was 50 percent carbon (Woodall *et al.*, 2011).

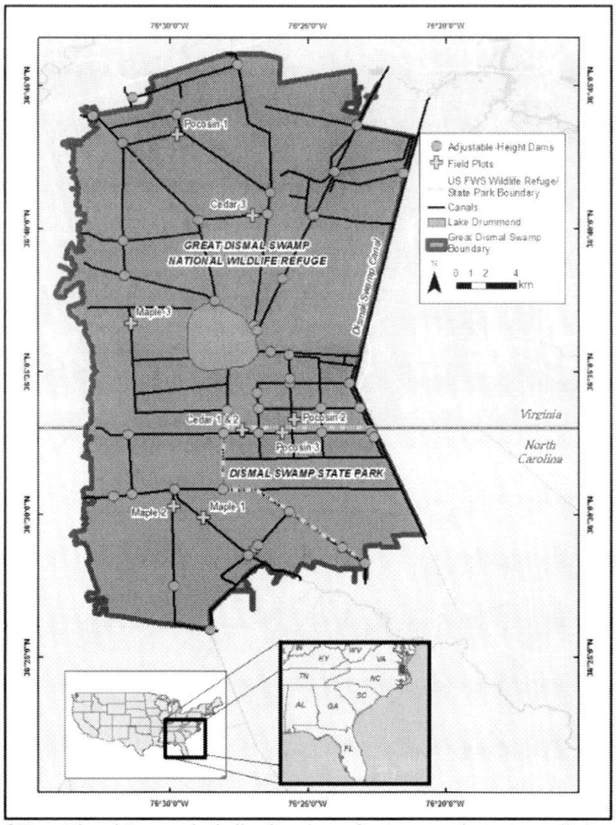

Figure 1: Map of Great Dismal Swamp, including locations of water control structures, ditches, and field plots.

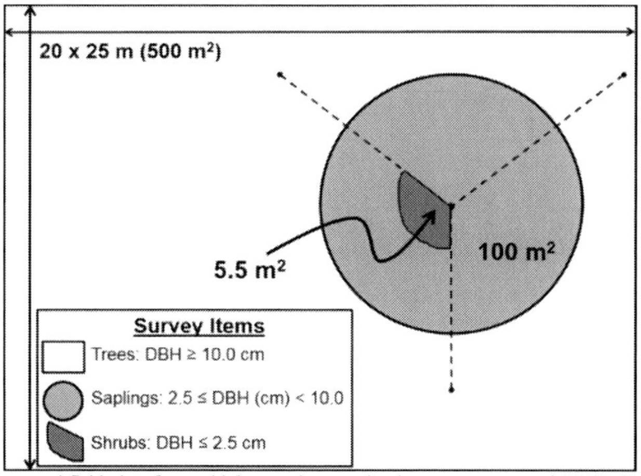

Figure 2: Layout of the nested field plots from which non-vine woody plants were surveyed. DBH, diameter at breast height.

Tree growth was calculated for individual trees outfitted with dendrometer bands. Quarterly measurements of dendrometer band expansion were used to calculate the new individual tree DBH and basal area, which was used to calculate the amount of basal area growth (increment) relative to either the previous measurement (*i.e.*, quarterly) or initial DBH (for annual growth computations). Basal area increments were averaged across trees within each field plot, and across trees within the same forest type, on a quarterly and annual basis; values reported are average basal area increment per tree (cm^2 $tree^{-1}$) for the specified time period. Dendrometer measurements (mm) were not used in calculations of basal area increment until after the first positive dendrometer measurement had been previously obtained. This protocol protected against underestimates of quarterly growth, as the first positive dendrometer measurement may have been smaller due to dendrometer band settling. Because of this calculation protocol there were no qualified measurements to calculate first quarter growth (December – March). Some dendrometer bands were damaged by wildlife, in which cases the trees were re-banded and subject to the same calculation protocol.

RESULTS

The mature Cedar forest type had the largest total amount of total biomass (14.1 kg C m^{-2}) compared to the other forest types. The Pocosin forest type had a moderate amount of total biomass (13.1 kg C m^{-2}), and the degraded Maple forest type had the least (8.1 kg C m^{-2}). Even though there was some overlap in the distribution of total biomass values, they were significantly different (2-tailed t-test p-values were 0.04 for Cedar vs. Maple and $<$ 0.01 for Pocosin vs. Maple). The distribution of aboveground non-vine woody biomass was similar for the Cedar and Maple forest types, with trees as the major constituent, averaging roughly 94% of total biomass for both forest types (Table 1). Shrubs were the smallest constituent to total biomass for the Cedar and Maple forest types, averaging 4% or less. However, while total biomass in the Pocosin forest type was also dominated by trees (94.3% on average), shrubs (5.5%) were a larger constituent than saplings (<1%).

Average basal area increment of trees (Table 2) in the Cedar forest type was greatest of all forest types for all calendar quarters and the duration of the 2015 growing season (8.6 cm^2 tree^{-1}). Trees in the Maple forest type had an average basal area increment that was similar (7.3 cm^2 tree^{-1}) to the Cedar trees, while the pond pine trees in the Pocosin forest type averaged much less (3.8 cm^2 tree^{-1}). There was substantial overlap in the range of basal area increments, and the differences between the Cedar and Maple, and Pocosin and Maple forest types were not significant (2-tailed t-test p-values $>$ 0.05).

Table 1. Carbon storage (kg C ha^{-1}) of trees, saplings, and shrubs in three replicate Great Dismal Swamp field plots of three forest types (Cedar, Maple, Pocosin), and averaged within forest type (□). Surveys of trees (DBH $\geq$ 12.7 cm) utilized 500 m^2 areas, saplings (2.5 $\leq$ DBH (cm) $\leq$ 12.7) 100 m^2 areas, and shrubs (DBH $<$ 2.5 cm) 5.5 m^2 areas (see also Figure 2). DBH, diameter at breast height.

Field Plot	Shrubs	%	Saplings	%	Trees	%	Total
Cedar 1	0.4	2.3%	0.1	0.4%	15.1	97.3%	15.5
Cedar 2	0.2	1.5%	0.5	5.1%	9.6	93.5%	10.3
Cedar 3	1.4	8.4%	0.1	0.8%	15.2	90.8%	16.7
x̄:	**0.6**	**4.0%**	**0.2**	**2.1%**	**13.3**	**93.9%**	**14.1**
Maple 1	0.1	0.7%	0.4	5.0%	7.4	94.3%	7.8
Maple 2	0.1	1.8%	0.4	5.6%	6.9	92.6%	7.4
Maple 3	0.1	1.5%	0.3	3.2%	8.5	95.3%	8.9
x̄:	**0.1**	**1.3%**	**0.4**	**4.6%**	**7.6**	**94.1%**	**8.1**
Pocosin 1	0.4	2.8%	0.0	0.1%	13.2	97.1%	13.6
Pocosin 2	0.9	7.3%	0.0	0.3%	11.3	92.4%	12.2
Pocosin 3	0.9	6.3%	0.0	0.2%	12.6	93.5%	13.4
x̄:	**0.7**	**5.5%**	**0.0**	**0.2%**	**12.4**	**94.3%**	**13.1**

Table 2. Year 2015 basal area increase (BAI: cm^2 tree^{-1}) of trees in the Great Dismal Swamp, VA and NC, USA. BAIs are averaged over trees in replicate field plots (*e.g.*, Cedar 1), and within forest type (□). Numbers of individual trees (n) vary due to dendrometer settling time and occasional wildlife interference.

	Mar - Jun		Jun - Sep		Sep - Dec		2015 Growing Season	
Field Plot	BAI	(n)	BAI	(n)	BAI	(n)	BAI	(n)
Cedar 1	6.3	(8)	3.2	(8)	1.0	(10)	11.5	(8)
Cedar 2	1.9	(2)	1.4	(7)	0.8	(10)	5.8	(7)
Cedar 3	4.7	(7)	3.0	(10)	1.1	(10)	8.2	(8)
x̄ (total n):	**5.1**	**(17)**	**2.4**	**(25)**	**1.0**	**(30)**	**8.6**	**(23)**
Maple 1	3.0	(4)	2.1	(10)	0.9	(10)	6.1	(6)
Maple 2	6.8	(6)	3.2	(10)	0.4	(10)	9.9	(10)
Maple 3	2.5	(7)	1.6	(10)	0.4	(11)	5.5	(10)
x̄ (total n):	**4.1**	**(17)**	**2.3**	**(30)**	**0.6**	**(31)**	**7.3**	**(26)**
Pocosin 1	1.0	(1)	0.9	(10)	0.6	(10)	4.0	(8)
Pocosin 2	N/A[a]	(0)	2.6	(4)	N/A[b]	0	N/A[b]	(0)
Pocosin 3	1.4	(1)	2.4	(6)	1.0	(8)	3.7	(9)
x̄ (total n):	**1.2**	**(2)**	**1.7**	**(20)**	**0.8**	**(18)**	**3.8**	**(17)**

[a]: No dendrometer bands in this field plot had previously measured positive growth.
[b]: Pocosin 2 field plot could not be accessed in December 2015.

DISCUSSION

The Cedar and Pocosin field plots were in healthy, mature stands of large DBH trees with few individuals that qualified as saplings (2.5 $\leq$ DBH (cm) $\leq$ 12.7). The notable exception was Cedar 2 that contained several large (>10 cm DBH) saplings, though this field plot was still considered "healthy and mature." The Cedar and Pocosin forest types also averaged a higher percentage of total biomass as shrubs compared to saplings, while the inverse was true of the Maple forest type (Table 1). The fact that Maple field plots had more biomass in saplings than shrubs may be due to their degraded nature that resulted from the altered hydrology; many trees appear to have been established prior to loss of nearly 1 m of peat. The relatively large contribution to total biomass by shrubs in the Pocosin forest type is due to the abundance of *Clethra alnifolia* (L.). Cedar 1 and Cedar 2 also had numerous *C. alnifolia*, but the survey of Cedar 3 (shrubs contributing 8.4% to total biomass) did not include *C. alnifolia* but rather numerous *Ilex coriacea* [(Pursh) Chapm.] and *Lyonia lucida* [(Lam.) K. Koch]. This may be attributed to the fact that Cedar 3 was in a presumably wetter part of the refuge (Figure 1); hydrologic monitoring may confirm this supposition. Shrubs in Maple field plots were dominated by *C. alnifolia*, but densities were lower.

Tree growth in the Pocosin field plots was markedly lower than those in Cedar and Maple field plots, especially for the March-June growing period (Table 2). Indeed, the low number of dendrometer readings used in computations for Pocosin field plots was more a product of slow growth that led to extended time for dendrometer band settling (n = 22 trees), as opposed to damage by wildlife (n = 9 trees). Further monitoring in 2016 will clarify these trends and future work will relate the differences in biomass among the forests types to their unique hydrologic regimes.

CONCLUSION

Aboveground biomass was significantly greater in the Cedar forest type as compared to Pocosin forest type and the less desirable Maple forest type. Tree growth rates were also greatest in the Cedar forest type, but not significantly greater than the Pocosin and Maple forest types. Our findings to date confirm previous results from Dabel and Day (1977) and indicate that Atlantic white cedar restoration will help meet the management goal of protecting and expanding this periled forest type while concurrently protecting large carbon stocks and enhancing carbon sequestration to help offset greenhouse gas emissions from fossil fuel combustion.

REFERENCES

1. Bormann FH, Kozlowski TT (1962) Measurements of tree growth with dial gage dendrometers and vernier tree ring bands. *Ecology* 43: 289-294.
2. Carter V, Garrett MK, Shima L, Gammon P (1977) The Great Dismal Swamp: Management of a hydrologic resource with the aid of remote sensing. *Water Resources Bulletin* 13:1-12.
3. Dabel CV, Day FP (1977) Structural comparisons of four plant communities the Great Dismal Swamp, Virginia. *Bulletin of the Torrey Botanical Club 104*: 352-360.
4. Day FP, Monk CD (1974) Vegetation patterns on a southern Appalachian watershed. *Ecology* 55: 1064-1074.
5. Domke GM, Woodall CW, Smith JE (2011) Accounting for density reduction and structural loss in standing dead trees: Implications for forest biomass and carbon stock estimates in the united states. *Carbon Balance and Management* 6: 14.
6. Jenkins JC, Chojnacky DC, Heath LS, Birdsey RA (2003) National-scale biomass estimators for United States tree species. *Forest Science* 49: 12-35.
7. Kearney TH (1901) Report on a botanical survey of the Dismal Swamp region. *Contribution from the U.S. National Herbarium* 5: 321-550.
8. Keeland BD, Sharitz RR (1993) Accuracy of tree growth measurements using dendrometer bands. *Canadian Journal of Forest Research* 23: 2454-2457.
9. Mitsch WJ, Gosselink JG (2000) *Wetlands*, Third Edition. John Wiley & Sons, Inc. New York, NY, USA. 920 p.
10. Shaler NS (1890) General account of fresh-water morasses of the United States with a description of the Dismal Swamp district of Virginia and North Carolina. *U.S. Geological Survey Annual Report* 10: 255-339.
11. U.S. Fish and Wildlife Service (USFWS) (2006) *Great Dismal Swamp National Wildlife Refuge and Nansemond National Wildlife Refuge Final Comprehensive Conservation Plan*. 258 p.
12. U.S. Geological Survey (USGS) (1954) Topographic maps (*variously named*) 1:7,500, 1 sheet each.
13. U.S. Geological Survey (USGS) (1968) Topographic maps (*variously named*) 1:7,500, 1 sheet each.
14. Woodall CW, Heath LS, Domke GM, Nichols MC (2011) Methods and equations for estimating aboveground volume, biomass, and carbon for trees in the U.S. Forest inventory, 2010. *General Technical Report* NRS-88. U.S. Department of Agriculture, Forest Service, Northern Research Station. Newtown Square, PA, USA. 30 p.

Abstract No: A-150

SPATIAL DIFFERENCES IN HYDROLOGIC AND GEOCHEMICAL CHARACTERISTICS ACROSS A TEMPERATE COASTAL PLAIN PEATLAND: THE GREAT DISMAL SWAMP, USA

Gary Kenneth. Speiran[1], Frederic C. Wurster[2] and Jack Eggleston[3]

[1]*U.S. Geological Survey, 1730 E. Parham Rd., Henrico, VA, USA 23228-2202, 804-261-2642*
[2]*U.S. Fish and Wildlife Service, 3100 Desert Road Suffolk, VA, USA 23434*
[3]*U.S. Geological Survey, 10 Bearfoot Road, Northboro, MA USA 01532,*

**Corresponding author: gspeiran@usgs.gov*

INTRODUCTION

Spatial differences in hydrologic and geochemical characteristics across forested peatlands can control the distribution of wetland species and affects their resiliency to natural and anthropogenic disturbances. Knowledge of these characteristics can be critical to (1) the effective management of the peatlands, (2) the selection of research sites to achieve specific research objectives, and (3) the interpretation of research results. The Great Dismal Swamp (the swamp) is a peatland that originally covered about 600,000 hectares (ha) in the Atlantic Coastal Plain of southeastern Virginia and northeastern North Carolina, USA (fig. 1). Draining the swamp for timber harvesting and agriculture has reduced the size of the swamp to the 45,325 ha managed by the U.S. Fish and Wildlife Service (the Service) as a national wildlife refuge and 6,475 ha managed by the State of North Carolina as a park (U.S. Fish and Wildlife Service, 2006). The existing distribution of forest species across the swamp is a remnant of the original communities altered by timber harvesting, hydrologic alteration by canals and adjacent spoil piles, and fire. Water levels in the canals are controlled by use of adjustable-height dams on the canals to manage the wetland-species composition and resiliency, increase carbon storage to mitigate the effects of climate change, and other purposes.

Since 2009, research into the hydrologic and geochemical characteristics of the swamp by the U.S. Geological Survey (USGS) in cooperation with the Service has expanded knowledge of groundwater and canal-water levels and flow paths, water chemistry, hydrologic response to precipitation events, peat characteristics, and relations between water and vegetation. Much of this research has been funded by the Service. The USGS Great Dismal Swamp Carbon project also funds an evaluation of the carbon budget and ecosystem services of the swamp. This paper describes a conceptual model of sources of water to the peat near land surface and hydrologic flow paths and describes selected geochemical characteristics across the swamp. It also discusses how these hydrologic and geochemical characteristics can affect (1) the management of swamp as resilient wetland habitats and for sequestering carbon to mitigate the effects of climate change, (2) the selection of research sites to achieve specific research objectives, and (3) the interpretation of research results.

Keywords: *Hydrology, geochemistry, nutrients, peatland, wetlands*

STUDY AREA

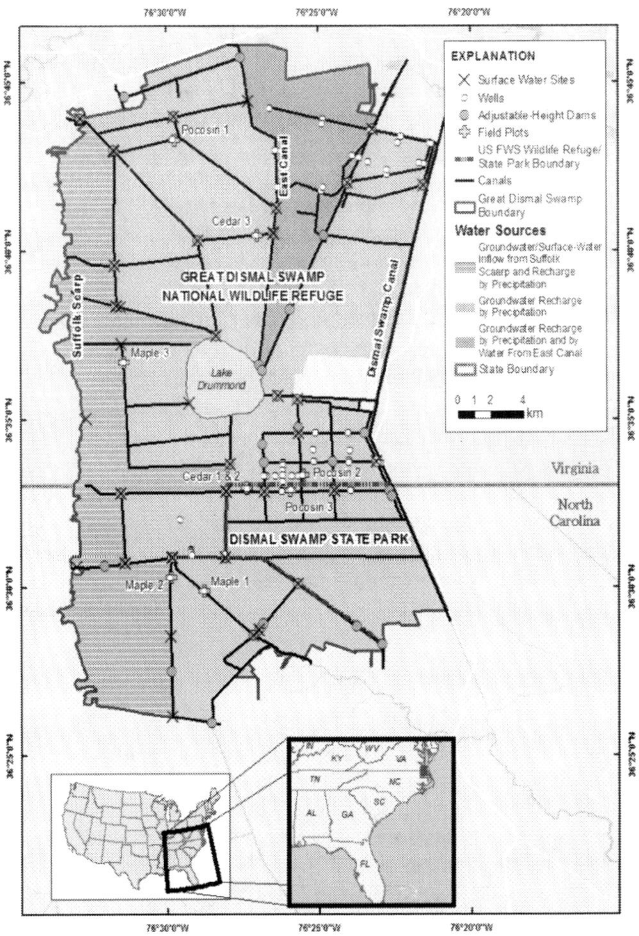

Figure 14. Conceptual model of sources of water to the peat near the land surface, data-collection sites, and other feature, the Great Dismal Swamp, Virginia and North Carolina, USA

The swamp is bounded to the west by the Suffolk Scarp, to the north by the urbanizing Hampton Roads area of southeastern Virginia, to the east by the Dismal Swamp Canal, and to the south by agricultural areas of northeastern North Carolina (fig. 1). Hydrology has been altered by a 235 kilometer network of canals and adjacent spoil piles constructed to drain the swamp for timber harvesting and agriculture. The first canals were constructed in the 1760's; the Dismal Swamp Canal (the largest canal) was constructed in the early 1800's to provide an inland route for commerce between Chesapeake Bay to the north and Albemarle Sound to the south (not shown). Shaler (1890) indicates that the spoil pile on the western side of the Dismal Swamp Canal formed a dam to the natural flow of water from the west and created up to 1 meter (m) of standing water during wet periods. Standing water persisted across much of the swamp during the dry parts of the growing season of most years. Although several canals were present in 1890 (Shaler, 1890) and a few additional canals were constructed by 1940, most of the canals were constructed between 1954 and 1977 based on a comparison of Shaler's map (Shaler, 1890) and topographic maps of the area (U.S. Geological Survey, 1940; 1954; 1977).. The expanded extent of the canal network and associated breaches in the spoil pile west of the Dismal Swamp Canal drained large parts of the swamp. Although ditches drain parts of the swamp directly adjacent to the ditches, spoil piles on the other sides of the canals impede the flow of water and locally retain standing water in parts of the swamp. Drier conditions have altered tree growth as reflected in tree-ring analyses (Phipps *et. al.,* 1978.) The ditch network creates a pattern of variously sized and shaped blocks across the swamp (fig. 1).

Land-surface-altitude characteristics change abruptly across the Suffolk Scarp. On the plain just west of the scarp land-surface altitude is 17 to 20 m above National Geodetic Vertical Datum of 1929 (NGVD 1929) with the altitude of stream valleys 8 to 9 m above NGVD 1929. Topography across the swamp east of the scarp, however, is flat, decreasing only about 3 m from about 8 m to about 5 m above NGVD 1929 across the 14 to 20 kilometers (km) between the toe of the scarp and the Dismal Swamp Canal. Shaler (1890) describes how critical differences in wetness of the peat over short distances that resulted from changes in land-surface altitude of less than 1 m that "the eye fails to detect" caused differences in the forest species. Locally, hummocks and hollows create relief of 0.5 to 1 m. Drainage of groundwater from the peat by the canals has altered this wetness regime and caused subsidence of the peat surface from the loss of physical support by groundwater and decomposition of the drained peat. Subsidence of up to 1 m is indicated by exposure of tree roots, particularly those of red maple (Acer rubrum), and differences in LiDAR altitudes across canals caused by the damming of water on one side and draining of water on the other.

Current forest communities appear to be the matured surviving remnants from the harvesting that include individuals of the harvested species that were considered too small to harvest and species not considered of sufficient value for harvesting, particularly red maple. The original wetland forests primarily consisted of two types: the bald cypress (Taxodium distichum)/black gum or tupelo (Nyssa aquatic L.) communities present in the wettest areas and the Atlantic white cedar (Chamaecyparis thyoides) communities found on slightly drier low ridges (Shaler, 1890; Kearney, 1901). Harvesting apparently focused on the cypress and cedar because of their resistance to rot. By the late 1800's, the cypress had been harvested extensively although red maple remained short and a minor part of the forest community (Shaler, 1890). Today, maple/gum is the dominant forest community, occupying over 62 percent of the swamp (U.S. Fish and Wildlife Service, 2006). Pine-forest communities identified by Shaler (1890) on slightly higher ground likely were pocosins, a pine and shrub wetland, which also covers an appreciable part of the present-day swamp. Pollen analysis of peat cores indicates that pocosins began to replace parts of the cedar communities with the arrival of colonists and increased fire frequency (Stevens and Patterson, 1998). Current forest communities thrive, in part, because of the drier conditions. Even where mature individuals of wetland species are present, it is not certain if these species can regenerate and compete against non-wetland species to establish and maintain resilient, wetland, forest communities.

The organic peat soil is a key characteristic exerting a major control on the hydrology of the swamp. The thickness of the peat ranges from near zero to 5 m across the swamp (Oaks and Coch, 1973). Kearney (1901) identifies two types of peat based on their forest cover: juniper (cedar) peat is a reddish-brown fibric peat and black gum peat is a dark, decomposed muck. Although more recent descriptions of the peat typically describe it as a decomposed muck throughout its depth (Henry, 1971; Oaks and Coch, 1973), the peat has a distinctly coarser upper zone to a depth of about 0.5 m overlying a dense, mucky lower peat. Main (1971) differentiates these zones as colloidal (upper peat) and non-colloidal (lower peat.) Hydrologically, although not by the degree of decomposition, these layers are similar to the acrotelm and catotelm, respectively, common in many peatlands (Ingram, 1978).

The upper peat forms a surficial aquifer that can store large amounts of water and transmit it rapidly to the canals. The peat is underlain by interlayered sand, silt, and clay that extend throughout nearby parts of the Coastal Plain including those wests of the Suffolk Scarp, forming the surficial and the Yorktown/Eastover aquifers (McFarland and Bruce, 2006). Although these aquifers can be important sources of water west of the Suffolk Scarp, the flow of water through these sand aquifers likely is limited beneath the swamp because the sand has a substantially lower permeability than the upper peat (based on water yield when each is pumped separately) and the low hydraulic gradient caused by the low topographic gradient across the swamp would limit flow based on Darcy's Law (Freeze and Cherry, 1979). The lower peat impedes the flow of groundwater between the sand and the upper peat.

METHODS

A map depicting a conceptual model of the sources of water to the peat surface across the swamp was developed. Delineation and descriptions of the areas are based on knowledge of (1) the interconnections of the peat with canals, and other surface waters, (2) data collected during previous and ongoing monitoring and research, and (3) general field observations of seasonal and other patterns in water levels and flow directions. Knowledge of the system also was derived from basic hydrologic principles such as Darcy's Law (Freeze and Cherry, 1979).

A discussion of general water chemistry is based on results from analysis of water samples from selected well and canal sites (Fig. 1). A large part of the groundwater samples were from the Great Dismal Swamp carbon project (Land Carbon) with one well sampled every other month at each of nine field plots (fig. 1). Field plots included three plots in each of three forest habitats: cedar, pocosin, and maple/gum. Canal and other groundwater samples also were collected as a part of other past studies. Some of the canal sites are located in areas known to have differing contributions of flow from streams crossing the Suffolk Scarp. Samples were analyzed for pH, specific conductance, dissolved-oxygen concentrations, and concentrations of major ions, nutrients, dissolved organic carbon (DOC), and dissolved gasses. Water-level and water-quality data are available on the USGS Nation Water Information System web interface (NWIS web: http://waterdata.usgs.gov/nwis).

RESULTS

Although groundwater and surface water collectively interact to control the hydrologic characteristics of the swamp, groundwater is the dominant water volume stored and transmitted throughout the swamp and has a dominant control on the hydrology of the swamp. Surface water consists of water in the canals, in Lake Drummond, and standing on the peat surface. Water in the canals is derived from five streams flowing across the Suffolk Scarp and into the swamp, groundwater that flows from west of the scarp through the surficial and Yorktown/Eastover aquifers and discharges to the canals, precipitation falling directly on the canals, and groundwater discharge from the peat. Water in Lake Drummond is derived primarily from groundwater discharged from the peat, direct precipitation, and canal inflows. Standing water typically is present from winter into early spring in low areas and areas where water is dammed by the spoil piles, Standing water reflects the shallow water table in many areas. Standing water also is derived from water in the canals near the scarp when high inflows inundate that part of the swamp. Surface runoff generally is limited to locations having a water table at land surface or standing water because of the highly permeable upper peat. Only when water levels rise enough to interconnect these low areas does water flow across the peat. Such flow is widespread only after selected, extremely large precipitation events. At the end of a dry period in 2011, even a couple days producing more than 30 centimeters of precipitation did not produce widespread evidence of surface runoff.

Groundwater is derived from one main source and two lesser sources. Recharge by precipitation that falls directly on the peat and percolates to the water table is the dominant source of groundwater across the entire swamp (fig. 1) and nearly the only source of water across much of the swamp (fig. 1, green area). Groundwater also is derived from flow from the west, beneath the scarp through the surficial and Yorktown/Eastover aquifers that discharges into the peat between the toe of the scarp and the first canals east of and parallel to the scarp (fig. 1, blue area). An even more limited source of groundwater is the lateral flow from East Canal that recharges the upper peat in the block to the east (fig. 1, violet wedge to the north). This source likely is greatest in the mid-section of the canal where a flow divide occurs and water levels tend to remain high because of inflows from ditches from the west. Across the swamp, groundwater rapidly discharges from the upper, high-permeability peat to the ditches and to the vegetation as evapotranspiration.

Concentrations of dissolved organic carbon ranged from 73 to 156 milligrams per liter (mg/L) and generally increased with increased pH (R^2=0.53) (fig. 2a). All groundwater and most canal-water samples were acidic; pH typically was less than 5.0 and less than 4.0 for many samples (fig 2b). The specific conductance of samples generally increased as the pH decreased (fig. 2a). This relation was stronger for the Land-Carbon wells (R^2=0.69) than other wells (R^2=0.52), and least for the ditches (R^2=0.12).

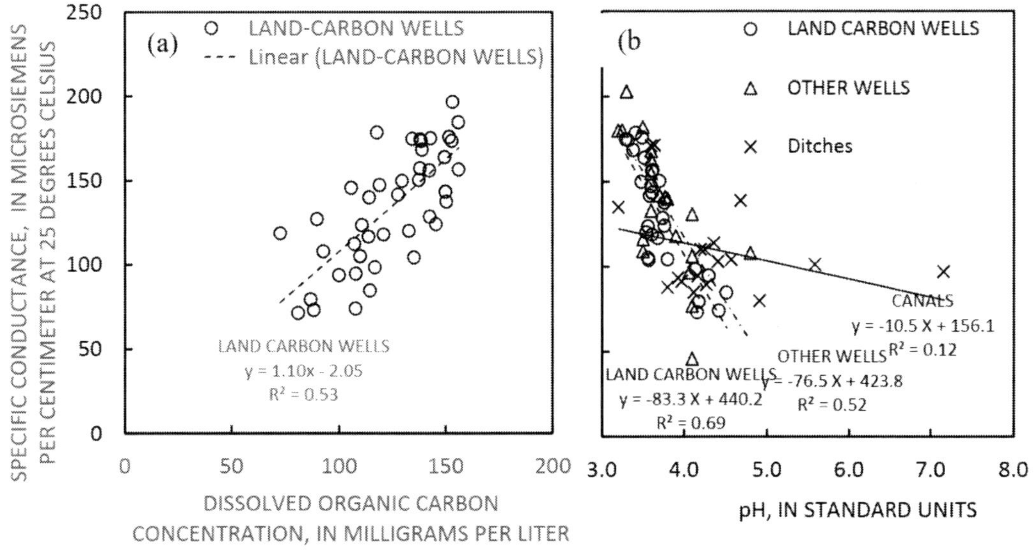

Figure 2. Relations of pH to specific conductance (a) and dissolved organic carbon concentration to specific conductance (b) of well and canal (ditch) water samples, the Great Dismal Swamp, Virginia and North Carolina, USA.

DISCUSSION

The hydrologic conceptual models of sources of water to the peat near land surface are important considerations for water-management decisions, research-site selection, and data interpretation. Because precipitation-recharge amounts likely are similar across the swamp, more water will be stored in and discharged from areas that also receive water from other sources (west of the Suffolk Scarp or canals). Areas receiving surface and groundwater from west of the scarp typically have wetter conditions during high precipitation periods because they also receive abundant water from west of the scarp. These areas continue to receive groundwater inputs from west of the scarp even after precipitation stops and stream inflows decrease. The wetter conditions created by the additional sources Although East Canal is an additional source of water to the block to its east, low water levels in canals north, east, and south of this block could help create the lateral gradient to promote such recharge. As more dams are constructed and operated, retaining high level in these other canals could limit such discharge and help retain water. Dams on selected canals could promote similar recharge from canals into the peat elsewhere.

The high yield and hydraulic conductivity of the upper peat and the effective hydraulic connection between the upper peat and canals make controlling water levels in the canals critical. Controlling the height of the adjustable-height dams can be critical to managing water and keeping the upper peat saturated to a desired depths throughout the swamp will support resilient wetland forest communities and promote carbon storage. The high DOC in the groundwater that discharges from the peat to the canals indicates a loss of carbon from the swamp through groundwater discharge to the canals that migh

The water chemistry is heavily influenced by the chemistry of the organic peat soil as indicated by the relations between dissolved organic carbon concentrations and specific conductance and pH and specific conductance of water samples (fig. 2). The 73 to 156 mg/L of DOC is high for the 30 to 40 mg/L average but within the 3 to 400 mg/L range reported for swamps (Thurman, 1985). The low pH results from the organic acids that make part of the DOC.

The chemistry appears to have limited influence from the mineral soil except for selected canal samples. The seven canal samples having the highest pH (4.36 to 7.16) are from canals flowing east from the Suffolk Scarp. Four of those samples are along Corapeake Canal and generally decrease from 7.16 nearest the scarp to and lower specific conductance tend to be more affected by the stream inflows across the scarp based on their locations. The general trend is for the specific conductance to increase as the pH decreases; hydrogen is the dominant cation in most of the samples. For wells at the carbon-project field plots, the pH of two of the three maple/gum filed plots was greater than 4.0; pH of all pocosin and cedar plots and the remaining maple/gum plot was below 4.0.

The low pH likely results from the abundance of organic acids from decomposition of the peat as also supported by concentrations of dissolved organic carbon (DOC) that ranged from 71 to 156 milligrams per liter (mg/L)(fig. 2b). These concentrations are high in comparison to the highest DOC concentration of 20 mg/L observed in a coastal plain black-water stream in Virginia (Speiran, 2000). Such streams typically are considered to be high in DOC.

Although the spatial distribution in the water chemistry has not be evaluated to the extent of the hydrology, differences in sources of water also could affect the chemistry of the water as indicated by differences in the chemistry among ditch samples. Inflows from west of the scarp can be affected by the mineral content of the aquifers and agricultural and other activities west of the scarp. Differences in water chemistry also can result from such factors as differences in the current forest communities or differences in peat as affected by historic forest communities as indicated y Kearney (1901). Differences in water sources and chemistry can be critical in selecting research sites to limit variable and in interpreting results from these sites.

ACKNOWLEDGEMENTS

This effort has been supported by staff and funding from the U.S. Fish and Wildlife Service Great Dismal Swamp National Wildlife Refuge and staff and funding from the USGS Land-Carbon project.

REFERENCES

1. Charles T. Main, Inc., 1971, Dismal Swamp Study 1659-25: Charlotte, NC, variously paginated.
2. Freeze RA, Cherry JA, 1979, Groundwater: Prentice Hall, Englewood Cliffs, NJ, 582 p.
3. Henry, E.F., 1970, Soils of the Dismal Swamp of Virginia: The Virginia Journal of Science, v. 21, n. 2, p. 41-46.
4. Ingram, H.A.P., 1978, Soil layers in mires: function and terminology: Journal of Soil Science v. 29, p. 224-227.
5. Kearney, T.H., 1901, Report on a botanical survey of the Dismal Swamp region: Contributions from the U.S. National Herbarium, VI: 6, Washington, D.C., 263 p.McFarland, E.R., Bruce, T.S., 2006, The Virginia Coastal Plain hydrogeologic framework: U.S. Geological Survey Professional Paper 1731, 118 p., 25 plates.
6. Oaks, R.Q., Jr, Coch, N.K., 1973, Post-Miocene stratigraphy and morphology, southeastern Virginia: Virginia Department of Conservation and Recreation, Division of Mineral Resources, Bulletin 82.
7. Phipps, R.L., Ireley, D.L., Baker, C.P., 1978, Tree rings as indicators of hydrologic change in the Great Dismal Swamp, Virginia and North Carolina: U.S. Geological Survey Water-Resources Investigations Report 78-136, 26 p.
8. Shaler, N.S., 1890, General account of fresh-water morasses of the United States with a description of the Dismal Swamp district of Virginia and North Carolina: U.S. Geological Survey, Annual Report 10, n 1, p. 255-339.
9. Stevens, A., and Patterson, W.A. III, 1998, Millennium-long fire and vegetation histories of pocosins of southeastern Virginia: Virginia Department of Conservation and Recreation, Natural Heritage Technical Report 98-1735, 35 p.
10. Thurmond, E.M. 1985, Organic geochemistry of natural waters: Martinus Nijhoff/Dr. W. Junk Publishers, Boston, MA, 497 p.
11. U.S. Fish and Wildlife Service, 2006, Great Dismal Swamp National Wildlife Refuge and Nansemond National Wildlife Refuge Final Comprehensive Conservation Plan.
12. U.S. Geological Survey, 1940, Topographic maps (variously named) 1:15,000, 1 sheet each.
13. U.S. Geological Survey, 1954, Topographic maps (variously named) 1:7,500, 1 sheet each.
14. U.S. Geological Survey, 1968, Topographic maps (variously named) 1:7,500, 1 sheet each.

Abstract No: A-252

THE CARBON SEQUESTRATION AND CLIMATE ADAPTATION BENEFITS OF REWETTING POCOSIN PEATLANDS IN POCOSIN LAKES NATIONAL WILDLIFE REFUGE, NORTH CAROLINA, USA

Sara Ward[1], Jamie Eaton[2], Christine Pickens[3], Scott Settelmyer[4], and John Schmerfeld[5]

[1] *U.S. Fish and Wildlife Service, Raleigh Field Office, P.O. Box 33726, Raleigh, NC 27636-3726, USA*
[2] *Terra Carbon, 700 Harris Street, #201B, Charlottesville, VA 22903, USA*
[3] *The Nature Conservancy, North Carolina Chapter Outer Banks Office, 701 West Ocean Acres Drive, Kill Devil Hills, NC 27948, USA*
[4] *Terra Carbon, 5901 N. Sheridan Road, Peoria, Illinois 61614, USA*
[5] *U.S. Fish and Wildlife Service, 5275 Leesburg Pike, Falls Church VA 22041, USA*

**Corresponding author: kurt_johnson@fws.gov*

Keywords: *pocosin, peatland, rewetting, carbon sequestration, restoration*

"Pocosins" are unique wetlands, also known as southeastern shrub bogs, which occur from southern Virginia to northern Florida along the southeastern USA Coastal Plain. Pocosins are characterized by a unique mixture of dense, broadleaf evergreen shrubs, cedars, and pond pines, as well as poorly-drained organic soils that stay saturated from fall to spring. Belowground, pocosins have low-nutrient, poorly-drained organic soils that stay seasonally saturated from fall to spring and release very few greenhouse gases (carbon dioxide and methane) into the atmosphere (Sharitz and Gibbons 1982; Bridgham and Richardson 1992). These conditions allow for the accretion of biomass and sequestration of carbon in the form of peat, making pocosins a carbon and nutrient sink when in a natural, un-drained state. The peat soils that underlie pocosins take thousands of years to develop. Soil cores from northeast North Carolina suggest that the deep, organic soil has been developing since the last Ice Age, 8,000-10,000 years before present (Daniel 1981). For example, recent site-specific measurements confirm soils at Pocosin Lakes National Wildlife Refuge (NWR) are over 8,000 years old (Richardson pers. com). At Pocosin Lakes NWR the underlying peat depth typically exceeds 4-feet and exceeds 8-feet over large acreages (Daniel 1980, Environmental Sciences and Engineering, Inc. 1982; USFWS, 1990). Since it takes thousands of years to develop the peat soils and complimentary pocosin vegetative community, the only way to preserve these environs are to protect and/or restore the existing peat soil regions and pocosin habitat.

Millions of hectares of former peatlands in the U.S. have been drained and converted to agriculture and forestry. North Carolina's Albemarle-Pamlico peninsula is the site of the greatest pocosin acreage in the U.S. (Richardson et al. 1981); however, 70% of pocosin habitat in North Carolina alone has been lost since the 1960s (Richardson 1991). In northeastern North Carolina, the pocosins that became Pocosin Lakes NWR were significantly ditched and drained in the 1970's for now defunct farming and peat mining operations (Heath 1975; Sharitz and Gibbons 1982; Ash *et al.* 1983; McDonald *et al.* 1983), resulting in the releases of significant amounts of carbon dioxide to the atmosphere and dissolved and particulate organic carbon to adjacent waters. When these lands became part of Pocosin Lakes NWR in 1990, managers began to restore the hydrology conditions in these important peat wetlands. Pocosin Lakes NWR protects over 60,000 acres (ac) (24,000 hectares, ha) of predominantly pocosin wetlands that were altered by prior human land use, particularly ditching and drainage. Drained pocosin peatlands are a source of carbon emissions and are particularly vulnerable to catastrophic wildfires that emit large amounts of carbon and negatively impact wildlife habitat and air quality. Peatlands, like those at the Pocosin Lakes NWR, are one ecosystem where the U.S. Fish and Wildlife Service (USFWS) are collaborating with an array of stakeholders to increase resiliency to climate change through restoring the hydrology of these carbon-rich wetlands. Partnerships among the USFWS, The Nature Conservancy (TNC), and the State of North Carolina have restored over 20,000 ac (8,000 ha) of the most severely altered pocosin habitats on the refuge to date.

Drainage has rendered the peatlands of the U.S. Atlantic Coastal Plain more vulnerable to climate change-related threats including changes in precipitation, increased drought, wildfire occurrence, and sea-level rise. When pocosins are ditched, the rain necessary for saturating soils drains off of the surface too quickly. When the soils dry out, the carbon stored in the ground is released via oxidation to the atmosphere either slowly through time or rapidly during a wildfire. In fact, water table depth and soil temperature are primary drivers of carbon dioxide release into the atmosphere from pocosin soils (Bridgham and Richardson 1992; Miao *et al.*, 2013). In North America, climate models predict that precipitation is expected to increase, especially with more heavy/extreme weather events; however, droughts may also increase, summer precipitation is expected to decline, and warmer temperatures may reduce soil moisture (Dore 2005). In the U.S. Southeast, days above 95°F will increase and water availability will decrease in the coming years (Carter *et al.*, 2014). As temperatures increase and precipitation patterns become more variable, it will be even more imperative to capture rainfall necessary to maintain saturated soil conditions thus reduce CO_2 emissions. Pocosins that are in a drained state now are vulnerable to these expected climate change impacts and to wildfire. Soil loss and subsidence due to the aforementioned ditching and drainage is readily apparent. There are descriptions of subsidence exceeding 3-feet as a consequence of drainage and agriculture (Ruffin 1861, Dolman and Buol 1967, Lilly 1981, Whitehead and Oaks 1979). Drainage of organic soils can result in the loss of at least a third of peat thickness (Farnham and Finney 1965), and sometimes more (Dolman and Buol 1967, Lilly 1981). Some of the initial loss in volume is due to mechanical shrinkage (Dolman and Buol 1967, Skaggs *et al.*, 1980). Much of the coastal pocosins are at sea level where soil loss due to subsidence, oxidation, and fire result in lower land surface elevation and accelerated habitat loss due to sea level rise. Therefore, a restoration strategy of re-establishing seasonally saturating conditions is expected to prevent carbon loss, in addition to conserving pocosin for wildlife.

In addition to the carbon benefits realized through peatland restoration, restoring hydrology conditions provides other important benefits to terrestrial and aquatic ecosystems, and human communities. Restoring the hydrology is a fundamental climate change adaptation strategy as it allows the soil to re-accumulate by preventing incremental (via oxidation) and catastrophic (via burning) soil loss, limits saltwater intrusion, maintains necessary soil moisture and promotes carbon sequestration benefits, and helps mitigate impacts of flooding and storm events.

Drainage canals artificially lower the groundwater table and enhance off-site transport of soil constituents that, when delivered in excess to downstream fresh water streams and estuaries, become contaminants (Daniel 1980, 1981, Gale and Adams 1984, Gregory *et al.*, 1984). The wetland hydrology that allowed for peat accumulation also provided the conditions for accumulation of atmospheric mercury and nutrients over geologic time (Zillioux *et al.*, 1993). There is well-documented concern that drainage-enhanced oxidation of soils re-mobilizes mercury (Lodenius *et al.* 1987) and nutrients (Brinson 1991). Artificial drainage also contributes to off-site water quality impacts by speeding the pace of run-off and increasing discharge peaks (Kirby-Smith and Barber 1979, Daniel 1980, Gregory *et al.*, 1984).

Extensive drainage also leaves refuge and surrounding private lands vulnerable to catastrophic fires. A warming climate is also expected to result in an increase in wildfire potential and longer fire season in the U.S. Southeast due to lower soil moisture (Liu *et al.*, 2013). Healthy pocosins require periodic fire, but lowered water tables render peatlands vulnerable to more frequent and severe fires. Soil moisture is a major factor contributing to the likelihood that the peat soils of pocosin will smolder when ignited during a fire; lower soil moisture results in higher chances for soil smoldering (Reardon *et al.*, 2007). Following even a low intensity peat fire, up to 90% of soil mass can be lost after one hour (Rein *et al.*, 2008). A 1985 wildfire covering 38,000 hectares resulted in the loss of as much as a meter of peat soils at what is now Pocosin Lakes NWR (USFWS 1990). Four catastrophic wildfires have occurred on refuges in northeast North Carolina and southeast Virginia between 2008 and 2011.Notably, two of these recent fires occurred within the footprint of prior catastrophic burns exacerbating peat depletion. The wildfires cost millions of dollars to contain, each fire lasted several months, and resulted in losses of up to five feet of peat deposits (releasing approximately 20 million tons of carbon, Mickler and Welch 2011, Mickler 2012). These wildfires also had a negative effect on human health and safety. During the Evans Road Fire, emergency room visits for cardiopulmonary complications increased significantly in counties exposed to the smoke (Rappold *et al.*, 2011). These fires are considered catastrophic compared to the historic fire regime associated with pocosin forests (Bailey *et al.*, 2007). If the pocosins are restored through the re-establishment of soil saturation, soil moisture will increase, lessening the chances for very damaging wildfires that burn into the ground. Pocosins with restored hydrology may also then be considered for application of appropriate aboveground fire management.

Another climate change related threat to pocosins of the southeastern US Coastal Plain is sea-level rise. In low elevation peatlands, the extensive network of ditches also allow the wind-tide-driven systems to jet brackish water much further into the interior resulting in accelerated shoreline erosion and peat decay. Sea level rise can impact carbon storage in peat soils and aboveground biomass through erosion, vegetative die-off with storm surge, and peat collapse due to increased decomposition (Henman and Poulter 2008). A Sea-Level Rise Affecting Marshes Model (SLAMM) analysis was performed at a nearby pocosin dominated ste, Alligator River NWR. Predictions given 1.5 m of sea-level rise resulted in a projected loss of 98% of forested wetlands at Alligator River NWR by 2100 (Clough 2008). For these reasons, restoring pocosin at Pocosin Lakes NWR, which is upslope is a long-term approach to ensure this habitat will be available for wildlife and flora in the future.

There is a tremendous opportunity to reduce GHG emissions, restore natural hydrological processes, reduce fire frequency and intensity, and improve ecosystem resilience to climate change by rewetting peatlands in the US, including on USFWS lands (USFWS 2010), and globally. The development of carbon market incentives to re-wet peatlands could provide significant funding and attract new partners to undertake peatland restoration activities. However, funding to undertake these activities at scale will require strong carbon market incentives. Project development is presently limited by the lack of approved methodologies for quantifying the GHG benefits of peatland restoration. To date, there is only one approved peatland re-wetting methodologies which has been developed in the voluntary carbon market under the Verified Carbon Standard (Winrock International 2012), but it is applicable only to projects in Southeast Asia. There is another methodology under development (Silvestrum, 2011) that is globally applicable and can be applied using local or regionally appropriate research data on GHG emission relationships with proxy variables such as water levels or vegetation. While this methodology lays out a practical and robust approach to measuring GHG emissions, there is no experience with applying it to "proof of concept" demonstration projects (e.g., no projects have been advanced to date). These projects are critical to demonstrating the technical feasibility of peatland re-wetting methodologies to regulatory agencies such as the California Air Resources Board (ARB), the regulatory body with oversight of the only compliance carbon market in the U.S. The State of California's cap and trade program was established in 2012 and compliance with the program became enforceable in 2013. Voluntary offset programs such as the American Carbon Registry, Climate Action Reserve, Verified Carbon Standard, and others may submit protocols to ARB for their review and potential approval.

Proof of concept projects using voluntary carbon market standards are intended to demonstrate to regulators (who could in turn could approve peatland carbon offsets for use in California's GHG cap-and-trade program) that the GHG benefits of peatland re-wetting can be credibly quantified, undertaken at scale on federal lands with appropriate legal and policy tools to satisfy regulatory eligibility requirements, and meaningfully contribute to achieving GHG emission reduction targets. Currently, the USFWS is partnering with the US Geological Survey, TNC and TerraCarbon to implement a 1,325-ac (536-ha) peatland rewetting demonstration project at Pocosin Lakes NWR to test a first-of-its-kind draft accounting methodology specific to pocosin habitats to quantify the carbon sequestration benefits of peatland restoration. The draft methodology was submitted to the ACR for consideration in 2015. For this particular location, the previous impediment to hydrologic restoration was that adjacent landowners would incur flooding on their property. For the proposed work, this is being addressed through the addition of a berm. Construction of the berm with installation of water control structures will result in increasing the water levels of the project area. Saturation of the soil will increase soil moisture to reduce wildfire vulnerability, reduce and potentially reverse the patterns of soil subsidence and carbon loss associated with drainage, and provide the conditions necessary to support the vegetation and wildlife communities that inhabit pocosin ecosystems. Specific project goals are to: (1) restore pocosins that were previously ditched and drained by constructing water control structures and a berm that will allow water levels to rise and restore the site to conditions that mimic seasonal saturation typical of pocosins; and (2) assess the carbon sequestration and ecosystem service benefits resulting there from. The Pocosin Lakes NWR project serves as a demonstration effort for which the results should be applicable to similarly-impacted peatlands in the USA and elsewhere.

Monitoring of this demonstration project is underway and includes pre-installation water level monitoring. Post restoration, water level monitoring will occur at the water control structures and throughout the project area using groundwater wells outfitted with water level logging devices. Groundwater levels will also be monitored in a control drained site adjacent to the restoration project area for comparison. In addition to the work described, we will be working with researchers from the U. S. Geological Survey and East Carolina University to measure greenhouse gas emissions from soil and from changes in biomass at the project location and at the controlled drained site. This research effort is related to the U. S. Geological Survey's Land Carbon project and will complement extensive research at Great Dismal Swamp National Wildlife Refuge. This presentation will discuss the Pocosin Lakes NWR project as a case study and applicability of the results to similarly-impacted peatlands in the USA and elsewhere.

REFERENCES

1. Sharitz, R.R. and J.W. Gibbons. 1982. The ecology of southeastern shrub bogs (pocosins) and Carolina bays: A community profile. FWS/OBS-82-04. U.S. Fish and Wildlife Service, Washington, DC. 99 pp.
2. Bridgham, S. D. and C.J. Richardson. 1992. Hydrology and nutrient gradients in North Carolina peatlands. *Wetlands* 13: 207-218.
3. Daniel, C. C., III. 1981. Hydrology, geology and soils of pocosins: a comparison of natural and altered systems. Pages 69-108 In: C.J. Richardson (ed). *Pocosin Wetlands: An Integrated Analysis of Coastal Plain Freshwater Bogs in North Carolina*. Hutchinson Ross Publishing Co. Stroudsburg, PA.
4. Daniel, C.C., III. 1980. *Hydrology, geology and soils of pocosins: a comparison of natural and altered systems*. U.S. Geological Survey, Raleigh, NC. 49 p.
5. Environmental Sciences and Engineering, Inc. 1982. *Hydrology, biology, and water quality studies for the Pungo River area of North Carolina*. Preliminary assessment prepared for Peat Methanol Associates, Methanol Plant, Creswell, North Carolina. Environmental Sciences and Engineering, Inc., Gainesville, FL.
6. USFWS. 1990. Environmental assessment for the proposed Pocosin Lakes National Wildlife Refuge. U.S. Fish and Wildlife Service, Atlanta, GA.

7. Richardson, C.J., R. Evans and D. Carr. 1981. Pocosins: an ecosystem in transition. Pages 3-19 In : C. J. Richardson (ed). *Pocosin wetlands: an integrated analysis of coastal plain freshwater bogs in North Carolina*. Hutchinson Ross Publishing Co., Stroudsburg, PA.
8. Richardson, C. J. 1991. Pocosins: An ecological perspective. *Wetlands* 11:335-354.
9. Miao, G., A. Noormets, J. Domec, C. C. Trettin, S. G. McNulty, G. Sun, and J. S. King. 2013. The effect of water table fluctuation on soil respiration in a lower coastal plain forested wetland in the southeastern U. S. Journal of Geophysical Research: *Biogeosciences* 118:1-15.
10. Dore, M. H. I. 2005. Climate change and changes in global precipitation patterns: What do we know? *Environment International* 31:1167-1181.
11. Carter, L. M., J. W. Jones, L. Berry, V. Burkett, J. F. Murley, J. Obeysekera, P. J. Schramm, and D. Wear. 2014. Chapter 17: Southeast and the Caribbean. In Melillo, J. M, R. Richmond, and G. W. Yohe, eds. *Climate Change Impacts in the United States: The Third National Climate Assessment*. U. S. Global Change Research Program, 396-417.
12. Ruffin, E. 1861. The origin and manner of geological formation of the great swamps of the Atlantic Coast. Pages 155-249 In: *Agricultural, geological and descriptive sketches of lower North Carolina and the similar adjacent lands*. NC Agric. and Geol. Survey, Raleigh.
13. Dolman, J.D. and S.W. Buol. 1967. *A Study of Organic Soils (Histosols) in the Tidewater Region of North Carolina*. North Carolina Agricultural Research Service Technical Bulletin 181, 52 p.
14. Lilly, J. P. 1981. A history of swamp land development in North Carolina. Pages 20-39 In: C. J. Richardson (ed.). *Pocosin wetlands: an integrated analysis of Coastal Plain freshwater bogs in North Carolina*. Hutchinson Ross. Stroudsburg, PA.
15. Whitehead, D. R. and R. Q. Oaks, Jr. 1979. Developmental history of the Dismal Swamp. Pages 25-43 In: P. W. Kirk (ed). *The Great Dismal Swamp*. University Press of Virginia, Charlottesville.
16. Farnham, R. S. and H. R. Finney. 1965. Classification and properties of organic soils. *Advances in Agornomics* 17:115-162
17. Skaggs, R. W., J. Gilliam, T. Sheets and J. Barnes. 1980. Effect of agricultural land development on drainage water in the North Carolina tidewater region. Water Resources Research Institute Report No. 159, Raleigh, NC. 164 p.
18. Gale, J.A. and D.A. Adams (eds.). 1984. Cumulative impacts of peat mining project, final project report. CEIP Report No. 40. Office of Coastal Management, Raleigh, NC.
19. Gregory, J.D., R.W. Skaggs, R.G. Broadhead, R.H. Culbreath, J.R. Bailey and T.L. Foutz. 1984. Hydrologic and water quality impacts of peat mining in North Carolina. Water Resources Research Institute Report No. 214, Raleigh, NC. 215 p.
20. Zillioux, E.J., D.B. Porcella and J.M. Benoit. 1993. Mercury cycling and effects in freshwater wetland ecosystems. *Environmental Toxicology and Chemistry* 12: 2245 2264.
21. Lodenius, M., A. Seppanen and S. Autio. 1987. Leaching of mercury from peat soil. *Chemosphere* 16: 1215 1220.
22. Brinson, M.M. 1991. Landscape properties of pocosins and associated wetlands. *Wetlands* 11: 441-465.
23. Kirby-Smith, W.W. and R.T. Barber. 1979. The water quality ramifications in estuaries of converting forest to intensive agriculture. Water Resources Research Research Institute of the University of North Carolina Report No. 148, Raleigh, NC. 70 p.
24. Liu, Y., S. L. Goodrick, and J. A. Stanturf. 2013. Future U.S. wildfire potential trends projected using a dynamically downscaled climate change scenario. *Forest Ecology and Management* 294:120-135.
25. Reardon, J., R. Hungerford, and K. Ryan. 2007. Factors affecting sustained smouldering in organic soils from pocosin and pond pine woodland wetlands. *International Journal of Wildland Fire* 16:107-118.
26. Rein, G., N. Cleaver, C. Ashton, P. Pironi, and J. L. Torero. 2008. The severity of smouldering peat fires and damage to the forest soil. *Catena* 74:304-309.
27. Mickler, B and D. Welch. 2011. GIS Mapping for Atlantic White Cedar. Final Report to U.S. Fish and Wildlife Service, 45 p.
28. Mickler, B. 2012. Post-Burn Vegetation and Organic Soil Assessment For FWS Lands on the Pains Bay Fire. Final Project Report to U.S. Fish and Wildlife Service. 58 p.
29. Rappold, A. G., S. L. Stone, W. E. Cascio, L. M. Neas, V. J. Kilaru, M. S. Carraway, J. J. Szykman, A. Ising, W. E. Cleve, J. T. Meredith, H. Vaughan-Batten, L. Deyneka, and R. B. Devlin. Peat bog wildfire smoke exposure in rural North Carolina is associated with cardiopulmonary emergency department visits assessed through syndromic surveillance. *Environmental Health Perspectives* 14:1415-1420.
30. Bailey, A. D., R. Mickler, and C. Frost. 2007. Presettlement fire regime and vegetation mapping in southeastern Coastal Plain forest ecosystems. In Butler, B. W. and W. Cook, comps. 2007. The fire environment—innovations, management, and policy; conference proceedings. 26-30 March 2007; Destin, FL. Proceedings RMRS-P-46CD. Fort Collins, CO: U.S. Department of Agriculture, Forest Service, Rocky Mountain Research Station. 662 pp.

31. Henman, J. and B. Poulter. 2008. Inundation of freshwater peatlands by sea level rise: Uncertainty and potential carbon cycle feedbacks. *Journal of Geophysical Research* 113: G01011, doi:10.1029/2006JG000395
32. Clough, J. 2008. Application of the Sea-Level Affecting Marshes Model (SLAMM 5.0) to Alligator River National Wildlife Refuge. Final Report, U. S. Fish and Wildlife Service, National Wildlife Refuge System, Division of Natural Resources and Conservation Planning, Conservation Biology Program, Arlington, VA. 58 pp.
33. Winrock International, Remote Sensing Solutions GmbH, Alterra Wageningen, UR, TerraCarbon LLC, and WWF Indonesia. 2011. Rewetting of Drained Tropical Peatlands in Southeast Asia.
34. Silvestrum, and Greifswald University. 2012. Baseline and Monitoring Methodology for the Rewetting of Drained Peatlands used for Peat Extraction, Forestry or Agriculture.

Abstract No: A-253

THE UNITED STATES' NATIONAL WILDLIFE REFUGE SYSTEM: A NATURAL LABORATORY FOR STUDYING PEATLAND CARBON STORAGE, ECOSYSTEM SERVICES, AND IMPACTS OF MANAGEMENT

Kurt A. Johnson* and John Schmerfeld

U.S. Fish and Wildlife Service, 5275 Leesburg Pike, Falls Church, Virginia 22041 USA

**Corresponding author: kurt_johnson@fws.gov*

INTRODUCTION

The National Wildlife Refuge System (NWRS), administered by the U.S. Fish and Wildlife Service (FWS; an agency of the U.S. Department of the Interior), consists of over 560 national wildlife refuges (refuge or NWR) and 38 wetland management districts (WMDs) throughout the United States of America (USA) and its territories. Refuges and WMDs protect a wide variety of wetland habitats that are peat-forming, from pocosin wetlands in North Carolina to extensive peat bog systems in Alaska. In addition, the NWRS has over 180 coastal refuges, many of which sequester carbon underground in "blue-carbon" ecosystems—mangroves, seagrass beds and salt marshes. A large number of refuges occur on lands that were extensively modified in the past (e.g., drained and ditched), or that are intensively managed today (e.g., managed wetlands where water levels are manipulated).

The NWRS is a natural laboratory for studying peatland carbon storage, ecosystem services, and impacts of management and climate change. Indeed, peatland carbon research has been occurring on NWRS lands and waters for more than two decades, with studies in such ecosystems as tidal salt marshes in the northeast and along Chesapeake Bay, northern Michigan peatlands, coastal wetlands in north Florida, and Alaska peatlands. In recent years, FWS has undertaken collaborative pilot projects with the U.S. Geological Survey (USGS) to evaluate carbon sequestration and ecosystem services in key wetland ecosystem types in refuges around the USA.

This presentation summarizes carbon research in peatlands and blue carbon ecosystems managed by the NWRS. Lessons learned and their applicability to management of these ecosystem types are discussed. Specific refuges mentioned in the text are shown in Figure 1.

***Keywords**: National Wildlife Refuge; carbon; peat; peatlands; blue carbon*

RESULTS

Peatlands

American peatlands occur in a varied array of wetland ecosystem types: freshwater marshes of many types; forested and shrub swamps; bogs; and freshwater fens. All of these peatland types occur on refuges and most have been studied to a greater or lesser degree to document basic ecology; peat paleohistory; carbon sequestration; and ecosystem services. Following is a regional overview of important peatland research on refuges. For each refuge, a brief summary of peatland type and research projects/results are given.

- Southeastern United States

- **Okefenokee NWR** is a 402,000-acre refuge in southeastern Georgia. Peat deposits in Okefenokee have been studied extensively by Arthur Cohen and associates, who have mapped deposits and studied their petrology/petrography and palynology. The swamp has a more or less continuous layer of peat varying from 1 to 4.5 meters in thickness (Cohen *et al.* 1984). Extensive fires in 2007 affected peat thickness, petrography and chemistry (Cohen 2009). Preliminary results showed reductions in peat thickness of as much as two feet in some intensely burned areas, and evidence that severe deflation of domed peat surfaces occurred during the droughts prior to burning (Cohen 2009).
- **Pocosin Lakes NWR** in northeast North Carolina protects over 60,000 acres (ac) (24,000 hectares, ha) of predominantly pocosin wetlands. Much of this landscape has been altered by past human land use, primarily ditching and drainage. Effects of fires and drought on peat have been investigated at the refuge. Wang *et al.* (2015) linked field and microcosm experiments to show how previously unrecognized mechanisms regulate the build-up of phenolics, which protect stored carbon directly during short-term drought and, indirectly after long-term moderate drought. Poulter *et al.* (2006) estimated carbon emissions from a peatland fire in the refuge

using remote sensing to reconstruct burn severity and topographic lidar to constrain peat burn depths. Total carbon emissions for the fire ranged from 1 to 3.8 Tg. *FWS is working with partners including USGS to implement a 1,325-acre peatland rewetting demonstration project at Pocosin Lakes. Carbon sequestration will be monitored—this project is discussed in another presentation in the special session.*

- **Alligator River NWR**, located on the Albemarle-Pamlico peninsula of North Carolina, inludes approximately 152,260 acres. The refuge has undertaken considerable habitat restoration work to restore hydrology and increase coastal resiliency to climate change and sea level rise. A detailed study of ecosystem carbon storage pools and transfers (fluxes) was begun in 2009 by King and associates of North Carolina State University, to characterize mechanisms controlling the rate of soil and ecosystem carbon sequestration and loss. To date, at least one research paper has resulted from this work. Miao *et al.* (2013) measured soil carbon dioxide efflux (Rs) continuously from 2009 to 2010 in a forested wetland in the refuge. The study indicated that Rs is highly linked to hydroperiod and microtopography in these forested wetlands and droughts will accelerate soil carbon loss therein.
- **Great Dismal Swamp NWR** occupies 111,203 acres in southeastern Virginia. The Great Dismal Swamp has a long history of human impact, primarily the construction of large canals to drain the swamp and convert it to farmland. In recent years, the refuge has endeavored to restore the natural hydrology of the refuge by constructing a series of water control structures. The refuge burned extensively in 2011. Reddy *et al.* (2015) used multi-temporal lidar to obtain pre- and post-fire elevations and estimate soil carbon loss caused by this 2011 fire, called the Lateral West fire. *This project is discussed in another presentation in the special session.* FWS and USGS are collaborating on the Great Dismal Swamp Study, an application of USGS LandCarbon research results and protocols. The project is designed to produce local-scale carbon estimates (including fluxes, ecosystem balance, and long-term sequestration rate) to include in an ecosystem service assessment in support of refuge management activities. *This project is discussed in another presentation in the special session.*

- Appalachians and Northeast
  a) **Canaan Valley NWR**, West Virginia encompasses the majority of West Virginia's largest wetland complex, including five mapped peatlands totaling 460 acres, the most voluminous central Appalachian peat deposits south of the glacial limit. Schaney (2015) conducted radiocarbon dating of histosols in refuge peatlands.
  b) **Sunkhaze Meadows NWR**, Maine includes a large portion of the Sunkhaze peatland which encompass an area of approximately 3,301 acres. During 1983-84, numerous multilevel ground water monitoring wells and piezometers were drilled, stream discharge was measured, and precipitation and evaporation rates were monitored in order to characterize hydrogeologic conditions.
  c) A multi-scale approach was used to reconstruct the landscape history in the **Great Swamp NWR,** a 7,800-acre refuge in New Jersey. The Great Swamp is the remnant of a lake bottom of a once-mighty glacial lake called Glacial Lake Passaic that about 15,000 to 11,000 years ago.

- Upper Midwest
  - **Seney NWR**, Michigan includes approximately 95,000 acres of wetland and forest habitats. Approximately 2/3 of the refuge is covered with peat often exceeding 1 m in depth. In the late 1800s, the greater Seney area was heavily logged, burned, ditched, and drained. Researchers have investigated the effect of long-term water table changes (approximately 80 years) on gaseous carbon fluxes in a peatland experiencing levee induced long-term water table drawdown and impoundment in relation to an unaltered site (Ballantyne *et al.* 2014).
  - **Necedah NWR** in Wisconsin and **Agassiz NWR** in Minnesota also have peat deposits that have been studied to a degree.

- Alaska
  - **Kenai NWR** is a nearly 2-million acre refuge on the Kenai Peninsula of south-central Alaska. Berg *et al.* (2009) investigated recent woody invasion of lowland wetlands in the refuge and determined through peat cores that these peatlands originated as wet Sphagnum–sedge fens with very little woody vegetation. Results suggest that wet Sphagnum–sedge fens began to dry in the 1850s and that this drying has greatly accelerated since the 1970s.
  - **Koyukuk NWR** is a 3.5-million-acre refuge in central Alaska, just north of the Yukon River. USGS researchers studied the effects of permafrost thaw on soil hydrologic, thermal, and carbon dynamics in collapse-scar bog chronosequence in the refuge (O'Donnell *et al.* 2012). They observed dramatic changes in the distribution of soil water associated with thawing of ice-rich frozen peat. The impoundment of warm water in collapse-scar bogs initiated talik formation and the lateral expansion of bogs over time. Their findings suggested that permafrost thaw and the subsequent release of organic carbon from thawed peat will likely reduce the strength of northern permafrost-affected peatlands as a carbon dioxide sink.

- **Innoko NWR** consists of two units in west-central Alaska, a northern unit of 750,000 acres and a larger southern unit of 3.85 million acres. To examine the effects of lowland permafrost thaw over millennial timescales, Johnston *et al.* (2014) measured carbon dioxide and methane exchange along sites that constitute a ~1000 yr thaw chronosequence of thermokarst collapse bogs and adjacent fen locations in the refuge. Their results provide evidence that methane emissions following lowland permafrost thaw are enhanced over decadal time scales, but limited over millennia.
- **Yukon Flats NWR** encompasses approximately 8.6-million acres of federal lands and 2.5-million acres of other lands in east-central, Alaska. Researchers examined charcoal records from 14 lakes in the Yukon Flats to infer causes and consequences of fire regime change over the past 10,000 years (Kelly *et al.*, 2013). They found that "the apparent limit to MCA burning has been surpassed by the regional fire regime of recent decades, which is characterized by exceptionally high fire frequency and biomass burning." USGS is collaborating with the refuge to develop a modeling framework that will help us improve our understanding of the impact of thermokarst disturbance on ecosystem structure and functions at the regional scale. The project is just getting underway.

Blue Carbon (Mangroves, Seagrasses, Saltmarshes)

The NWRS has over 180 coastal refuges, many of which sequester carbon underground in "blue-carbon" ecosystems—mangroves, seagrass beds and salt marshes. Blue carbon systems have the capacity to store tremendous amounts of carbon. Following is a regional overview of important peatland research on refuges. For each refuge, a brief summary of peatland type and research projects will be given.

- Mangroves

1. Coastal NWRs in Florida (**J.N. "Ding" Darling, Ten Thousand Islands, Merritt Island, Pelican Island NWRs**) have a variety of blue carbon systems, including mangroves, seagrasses and salt marshes. USGS and FWS have initiated a multi-component project in these four refuges to assess the vulnerability of mangroves, their carbon stocks, and key ecosystem service to climate change, sea level rise, and other stressors. Specific components of the project are: (1) mangrove remote-sense mapping and monitoring; (2) Surface Elevation Table (SET) network establishment; (3) carbon stock assessment; and (4) ecosystem services assessment. By assessing these components at the same time, researchers can assess changes in mangrove distribution and abundance due to climate change and concomitant sea level rise, and determine the impact on carbon storage and key ecosystem services.

- Seagrasses

2. **Izembek NWR**, located on the Alaska Peninsula, surrounds the Izembek Lagoon which is recognized as the largest contiguous eelgrass bed in the world. The Lagoon itself is a State of Alaska Game Refuge. Approximately 13,690 ha of Izembek Lagoon's 34,662 ha are covered with eelgrass. Tippery (2013) compared recent (2008) stable isotope (C and N) values and benthic community metrics to results from a similar study from the mid-1970's to gauge temporal food web and community structure differences. "An increase in reliance on seagrass carbon was detected in organisms involved in detrital and sediment processing. An increase in abundance of certain benthic organisms and a decrease in overall community evenness were also seen."

- Salt marshes (Eastern USA)

3. **St. Marks NWR** is located in the so-called panhandle of Florida on the Gulf of Mexico. Researchers studied the dynamics of carbon sequestration in St. Marks wetlands using radiocarbon measurements (Choi and Wang 2004).
4. **Sabine NWR** encompasses 126,000 acres of southwest Louisiana near the Gulf of Mexico. Researchers estimated vertical accretion of impounded salt marsh and adjacent natural salt marsh over three decades at four sites in southwestern Louisiana in 1994 by determining the depth of a stratum containing Cs137 deposited in 1963 (Bryant and Chabreck 1998).
5. **Cedar Island NWR** is a 14,500-acre refuge in east-central North Carolina on Pamlico Sound. Researchers measured soil carbon accumulation rates in salt marsh habitats (Chmura *et al.*, 2003).
6. **Blackwater NWR** is a 28,000-acre refuge on the eastern shore of Chesapeake Bay in Maryland.. Blackwater has a long history of carbon sequestration related research by scientists from regional universities and USGS. One key investigation sought to understand carbon sequestration and methane emissions in restored and natural tidal marshes at the refuge. In order to test and develop restoration methods using dredged material, a tidal marsh restoration project was undertaken in 2003. Collaborating scientists have been monitoring sites in these restored marshes as well as natural marshes for elevation changes and vegetation status to assess carbon sequestration and methane emissions (Wills *et al.*, 2008; Poffenbarger *et al.*, 2011). Kirwan and colleagues

have conducted several studies on the refuge (Kirwan *et al.*, 2013, Kirwan *et al.*, 2014, Kirwan and Guntenspergen 2015).

7. Four northeastern NWRs (**Forsythe (New Jersey); Wertheim (New York); Parker River (Massachusetts); Rachel Carson (Maine)**) occur along the Atlantic coast in the northeast USA. All four have natural and managed salt marsh systems. Researchers examined soil properties and carbon sequestration at one marsh managed with open marsh water management and one natural marsh in each of these four refuges (Drake *et al.*, 2015). They found that soil properties exhibited no consistent differences among managed and non-managed marshes. Soil organic carbon pools also did not differ.

- Salt marshes (Western USA)
  1. California NWRs (**Tijuana Slough, San Pablo and Don Edwards**) have been sampled for carbon accumulation in salt marsh sediments.
  2. **Billy Frank Jr Nisqually NWR** is a 2,900-acre refuge at the southern end of Puget Sound, Washington in the Nisqually River delta. In the past decade the refuge and the Nisqually Indian Tribe (Tribe) completed the largest wetland restoration project to date in the Pacific Northwest, removing an extensive dike system to restore tidal flow in a large portion of the estuary. USGS and FWS have undertaken the Nisqually River Delta Carbon project to document the carbon co-benefits of a restoring marsh compared to a natural marsh. Specific goals are to: (1) identify the relative importance of different carbon sources essential to support juvenile Chinook salmon prey resources and to contribute to current and historic peat accretion; (2) determine the net ecosystem carbon balance in a reference and restored marsh; and (3) model the sustainability of restored and reference marshes under projected sea-level rise and analyze historical vegetation change.

- Economic valuation of carbon in NWRs
  1. Patton et al. (2015) attempted to quantify the economic value of carbon stored in wetlands ecosystems found in four NWRs: **Blackwater NWR (Maryland), Sevilleta and Bosque del Apache NWRs (New Mexico), Arrowwood NWR (North Dakota), Okefenokee NWR (Georgia)**. Results suggest that wetlands in NWRs provide substantial carbon storage benefits to the U.S. and world. For example, based on U.S. social costs of atmospheric carbon researchers "estimated the present value of carbon storage services supported by Okefenokee wetlands at approximately US $960 per hectare and US $146,000,000 in aggregate."

DISCUSSION

National Wildlife Refuges have provided a natural laboratory for studying the effects of fire and drought on peatland ecosystems. New methods have been tested for assessing peat loss through remote sensing (lidar). NWRs are also laboratories for assessing the impacts of peatland restoration activities on carbon storage and ecosystem services. Refuges have provided laboratories for evaluation of the impacts of wetland water management on carbon storage and carbon dynamics. Managed freshwater and salt marshes have been compared to their natural counterparts to assess differences and similarities and address causal mechanisms. Alaskan refuges are facing severe threats from global warming and have become natural laboratories for assessing the impact of warming on thawing permafrost, thermokarst development, and boreal forests. Refuges have provided a test case for the economic valuation of carbon in peatlands and other wetland systems and demonstrated the incredible value of carbon storage services in peatland systems

REFERENCES

1. Ballantyne, D.M., J.A. Hribljan, T.G. Pypker, and R.A. Chimner. 2014. Long-term water table manipulations alter peatland gaseous carbon fluxes in Northern Michigan. Wetlands Ecol. Manage. 22:35–47.
2. Berg, E.F., K. McDonnell Hillman, R. Dia and A. DeRuwe. 2009. Recent woody invasion of wetlands on the Kenai Peninsula Lowlands, south-central Alaska: a major regime shift after 18 000 years of wet Sphagnum–sedge peat recruitment. Canadian Journal of Forest Research 39(11): 2033-2046.
3. Bryant J.C. and R.H. Chabreck. 1998. Effects of impoundment on vertical accretion of coastal marsh. Estuaries 21:416–422
4. Choi, Y. and Y. Wang. 2004. Dynamics of carbon sequestration in a coastal wetland using radiocarbon measurements. Global Biogeochemical Cycles 18: GB4016.
5. Chmura, G.L., S.C. Anisfeld, D.R. Cahoon and J. C. Lynch. 2003. Global carbon sequestration in tidal, saline wetland soils. Global Biogeochemical. Cycles 17(4): 1111
6. Cohen, A.D. 2009. Comparisons of pre-fire and post-fire peat thicknesses, petrography, and chemistry in the Okefenokee Swamp of Georgia following the fires of 2007. Paper Presentation to Southeastern Section GSA - 58th Annual Meeting.

7. Cohen, A.D., M.J. Andreiko, W. Spackman and D. Corvinus. 1984. Peat deposits of the Okefenokee Swamp. Pp. 493-524 in A.D. Cohen et al. (eds.), Okefenokee Swamp: Nat. Hist. Geol. & Geochem., Wetland Surveys, Los Alamos, N. Mexico.
8. Drake, K., H. Halifax, S.C. Adamowicz and C. Craft. 2015. Carbon sequestration in tidal salt marshes of the Northeast United States. Environmental Management DOI 10.1007/s00267-015-0568-z
9. Johnston, C.E., S.A. Ewing, J.W. Harden, R.K. Varner, K.P. Wickland, J.C. Koch, C.C. Fuller, K. Manies and M T. Jorgenson. 2014. Effect of permafrost thaw on CO2 and CH4 exchange in a western Alaska peatland chronosequence. Environmental Research Letters 9(8).
10. Kelly, R., M.L. Chipman, P.E. Higuera, I. Stefanova, L.B. Brubaker, and F.S.Hu. Recent burning of boreal forests exceeds fire regime limits of the past 10,000 years. Proceedings national Academy of Science 110(32): 13055–13060.
11. Kirwan, M.L. and Guntenspergen, G.R., 2015. Response of plant productivity to experimental flooding in a stable and a submerging marsh. Ecosystems 18, 903-913.
12. Kirwan, M.L., Guntenspergen, G.R., and Langley, J.A., 2014. Temperature sensitivity of organic-matter decay in tidal marshes. Biogeosciences 11, 4801-4808.
13. Kirwan, M.L., Langley, J.A., Guntenspergen, G.R., and Megonigal, J.P., 2013. The impact of sea-level rise on organic matter decay rates in Chesapeake Bay brackish tidal marshes. Biogeosciences 10, 1869-1876.
14. Miao, G., A. Noormets, J.-C. Domec, C.C. Trettin, S.G. McNulty, G. Sun, and J.S. King. 2013. The effect of water table fluctuation on soil respiration in a lower coastal plain forested wetland in the southeastern U.S., J. Geophys. Res. Biogeosci., 118, 1748–1762.
15. O'Donnell J.A., M.T. Jorgenson, J.W. Harden, A.D. McGuire, M.Z. Kanevskiy and K.P. Wickland. 2012. The effects of permafrost thaw on soil hydrologic, thermal, and carbon dynamics in an Alaskan peatland. Ecosystems 15: 213–29.
16. Patton, D., J.C Bergstrom, R. Moore, and A.P. Covich. 2015. Economic value of carbon storage in U.S. National Wildlife Refuge wetland ecosystems. Ecosystem Service 16: 94-104.
17. Poffenbarger H.B., B. Needleman and P.J. Megonigal. 2011. Salinity influence on methane emissions from tidal marshes. Wetlands 31:831–842.
18. Poulter, B., N.L. Christensen and P.N. Halpin. 2006. Carbon emissions from a temperate peat fire and its relevance to interannual variability of trace atmospheric greenhouse gases. Journal of Geophysical Research: Atmospheres, 111 (D6) (2006), Article D06301.
19. Pypker, T.G., P.A. Moore, J.M. Waddington , J.A. Hribljan and R. C. Chimner. 2013. Shifting environmental controls on CH4 fluxes in a sub-boreal peatland. Biogeosciences, 10, 7971–7981.
20. Reddy, A.D., T..J. Hawbaker, F. Wurster, Z. Zhu, S. Ward, D. Newcomb, R. Murray. 2015. Quantifying soil carbon loss and uncertainty from a peatland wildfire using multi-temporal LiDAR Remote Sensing of Environment 170 (2015) 306–316.
21. Schaney. M.L. 2015. Radiocarbon dating histosols in the peatlands of Canaan Valley National Wildlife Refuge, West Virginia. 2015 GSA Annual Meeting in Baltimore, Maryland, USA.
22. Wang, H., C.J. Richardson and M. Ho. 2015. Dual controls on carbon loss during drought
23. in peatlands. Nature Climate Change (5), DOI: 10.1038/NCLIMATE2643
24. Wills, S.A., B.A. Needelman and RR. Weil. 2008. Carbon distribution in restored and reference marshes at Blackwater National Wildlife Refuge. Archives of Agronomy and Soil Science 54(3): 239-248

Abstract No: A-196

THE USE OF LONG-TERM AND INTERDISCIPLINARY DATA TO PLAN THE SUSTAINABLE USE OF PEATLANDS

Anne Tolvanen[1,2*] and Miia Parviainen[1]

[1]*Natural Resources Institute Finland, Oulu, Finland*
[2]*Department of Ecology, University of Oulu, Finland*

**Corresponding author: anne.tolvanen@luke.fi*

The sharing and utilization of long-term monitoring data and scientific information in land use planning is still at its early phase. Plenty of challenges constrain the use: long-term databases are distributed in different organizations, their use is regulated or restricted by different policies, they are built using different platforms, and the data have usually been measured using different methods, spatial and temporal scales, and using different response variables. Consequently, planning is based on the most easily accessible data, the quality of which is variable. Furthermore, ecological, economic and socio-cultural information are generally produced separately, and the integration of complicated interdisciplinary data is done outside the expert group, e.g. by politicians and land managers. The ecological and socioeconomic sustainability of peatland use planning can be improved by a wider and simultaneous use and integration of data. At the present, the approach needs deep expert knowledge, but in the long run the data and models can be used to produce operations models and tools to be used also by non-experts. I present our research, in which we use long-term ecological monitoring data 1) to estimate and predict the impact of peatland uses (including ecological restoration) on ecosystem services, 2) to numerically optimize cost efficient land uses so that benefits from ecosystem services are safeguarded, 3) to provide socio-ecological values for habitats in order to locate and prevent conflicts from competing land uses, and 4) to provide tools that support decision making.

Keywords: -

Abstract No: A-122

VALUING AND MAPPING ECOSYSTEM SERVICES HOTSPOT AND TRADE-OFFS TO SUPPORT SUSTAINABLE PEATLAND MANAGEMENT

Uda, Saritha Kittie[1] and Pristiwati, Garika[2]

[1]*Environmental Systems Analysis Group, Wageningen University / University of Palangka Raya, Central Kalimantan, Indonesia*
[2]*Ministry of Agrarian and Spatial Planning, Republic Indonesia*

**Corresponding author: saritha.uda@wur.nl*

SUMMARY

Indonesian tropical peatlands are rapidly degrading. Peatlands provide multiple services and therefore peatland conversion will affect society locally, regionally, nationally and internationally. Ecological and societal processes determine the impacts of such conversion and the medium-term and long-term effectiveness of different management options. The current drainage-based peatland uses in Indonesia have resulted in high peat soil subsidence rates (Wösten *et al.*, 2008;Hooijer *et al.*, 2010). In the future, this peat soil subsidence will lead to extensive flooding on Indonesian lowland peatland areas as the soil levels are lower than river or sea water levels (Hooijer *et al.*, 2012).

Indonesian tropical peatlands, mainly distributed in Sumatera (42%), Kalimantan (32%) and Papua (23%), cover about 10% of Indonesia's land area (Rintung *et al.*, 2011). Historically, all Indonesian peatlands were forested and have sequestered and stored carbon for thousands of years. Within the last decade, many Indonesian natural peatland areas have been continually converted for economic purposes into agricultural land, settlements, timber and pulp plantations, and oil palm plantations (Murdiyaso *et al.*, 2010; Law *et al.*, 2015). Some of those areas have been abandoned. These conditions will affect peat dynamics. The peat dynamics are complex and are influenced by a range of ecological mechanisms such non-linear interactions and feedbacks. For instance, conversion of peatland ecosystems involves reduced forest cover and drainage which lead to dryer top soils and enhanced fire risks. This causes further degradation. Spatial relations in peatlands are also important, since drainage in one part of a peat dome will also affect the others parts (Wösten *et al.*, 2008;Hooijer *et al.*, 2010). However, the good and services provided by ecosystem will be affected due to land use change (Sumarga and Hein, 2014). It means that peatland conversion and degradation will influence peatland ecosystem good and services supplies.

In the extensive domain of ecosystem assessment and land use planning, integrating the science of ecosystems and landscape functions and services to identify optimal allocation and management of land use options remains challenging (De Groot *et al.*, 2010). It is important to understand trend of ecosystem services and trade-off between different services when considering peatland uses and maintenance in order to support sustainable peatland management. This study focuses on the peatland area in Indonesia with specific case study on Riau province. This particular area is one of extensively forested peatlands, with a deforestation rate that has attracted global attention due to the high greenhouse emissions released in the process (Miettinen *et al.*, 2011). This research had aimed to measure and assign values to selected ecosystem services in peatland area through biophysical and monetary approaches in order to spatially map the distribution and "hotspot" ecosystem services. This research had analysed the synergy and conflict across ecosystem services with different land uses on peatland in order to explore policy options for sustainable land use planning and management.

The selected ecosystem services were assessed i.e. timber production, oil palm production, paddy production, carbon storage and carbon sequestration, and endangered species habitat. The research methodology adopted three main steps: (i) the analysing trends on peatland uses/cover change; (ii) the quantification and mapping of ecosystem services by assigning biophysical and monetary values; and (iii) the analysis of synergy and conflict that are present across ecosystem services on peatland areas. The case study will focus on Indonesian tropical peatland area, particularly inside the legalized forest area in Riau Province, Indonesia with a total coverage 32,579 km^2. The lookup table approach is applied for valuing and mapping of the seven selected ecosystem services (adopted from Sumarga *et al.*, 2014).

Our study shows; (i) Trends on peatland uses/cover change in study area show several significant land cover changes from 1990 – 2013. For example, the identified estate crop area was recorded at 6% in 1990, increasing to 17% in 2013; there were no area detected containing plantation forest in 1990, yet it showed to be covered at 16% in 2013; secondary swamp forest in this area decreased from 70% in 1990 to 29% in 2013. From 1990 – 2013, the estate crop was increasing over time as well as the wet shrubland area. Most notably, the plantation area increased drastically in 2013. Meanwhile, primary and secondary swamp forests shrank over time significantly. (ii) Biophysical quantification and monetary valuation of ecosystem services show that timber production area dominates the study area while oil palm and paddy rice productions are found in the area adjacent to the (legally) non-forest area. In terms of the habitat for Sumatran tiger habitat, almost half of the study area was detected as Sumatran tiger habitat. The carbon sequestration has the highest positive monetary value (€ 528 million) calculated taken from six land cover types out of 20 land cover classes. This trend is followed by pulpwood production (€ 455 million) from more than 1 million hectares of production forest with land cover of secondary swamp forest, open swamp, and plantation forest. The oil palm production covers more than 500 thousands hectares of area, and this is half the value of pulpwood production (€ 216 million). Meanwhile, the paddy rice production in the area was only worth € 33 million, as taken from more than 100 thousands hectares, and the non-pulpwood production contributed € 2 million from more than 40 thousands hectares. On the other hand, the carbon emissions caused a very high cost equal to more than € 2 billion, from nine land cover types out of two land cover classes for which the value is hardly comparable to the values from provisioning productions and carbon sequestration. (iii) Synergy between non-pulpwood timber production and carbon sequestration is possible in secondary dryland forests and primary swamp forests. This synergy is possible because non-pulpwood timber studied in this context is timber with a 35-year production cycle. In these types of land cover, maintaining carbon sequestration services while executing selective logging is possible. Not only is there synergy between non-pulpwood timber production and carbon sequestration, but these types of land cover can also support the Sumatran tiger habitat. In secondary swamp forests, a synergy between pulpwood production, carbon sequestration, and Sumatran tiger habitat are also found. The monetary value gained from the pulpwood production is less compared to that of plantation forests. However, this land cover is more favourable to maintaining carbon sequestration since the peatland is not massively drained. Other synergies are found between carbon sequestration services and Sumatran tiger habitats in secondary mangrove forests and open swamps. Conflicts or trade-offs between ecosystem services are present in several land covers. Among others, there are plantation forests, estate crops, settlement areas, agriculture activity, and mining areas. In plantation forests, conflict or trade-off are found between pulpwood production and carbon sequestration, as well as potential tiger-human conflict caused by frequent cultivation activities by humans. In the estate crop areas, the condition is similar to plantation forests, which are conflict or trade-off between oil palm production and carbon sequestration as well as potential tiger-human conflict. In settlement areas, there is no conflict between carbon sequestration and other types of ecosystem services because neither carbon sequestration nor emission is detected. The conflict has potentially arisen between human and the tiger since both are occupying the same area. In any type of agricultural area, most trade-offs occur between agriculture production and carbon sequestration. In addition to this, some potential tiger-human conflict are present in those areas also inhabited by Sumatran tigers. This kind of potential conflict is likewise possible in the mining areas. As a result, the other types of land use/cover do not show any synergy or conflict; instead, a neutral state is present. However, a favourable or unfavourable land use/cover for carbon sequestration could be found. The result of this analysis is therefore applied in providing a discussion space on the implications of spatial planning.

Based on the results of this study, there are several implications for spatial planning and decision making in order to conserve the Sumatran tiger habitat. If the extinction of Sumatran tiger takes place, the spatial planning should be part of the decision to support the current conservation effort to save Sumatran tigers by preventing their habitat landscapes from further damage. By restricting oil palm plantation and massive timber production on peatland areas, efforts to conserve the Sumatran tiger habitat can be complemented through less deforestation and forest fragmentation. Even though it will be difficult within the planning process if the governments still focus largely on economic development, ecosystem-based spatial planning still needs to be introduced objectively (Wibisono and Pusparini, 2010). The World Bank/Global Tiger Initiative has launched an approach of smart and green infrastructure as a main contributor to the vast and growing deforestation and fragmentation of the natural tiger habitat (Wibisono and Pusparini, 2010), a prominent example in how an integrated policy approach can maintain the ecosystem services as discussed in this study. Where synergy and conflict has not been evident, the policy approach should consider the likeliness of future potential benefits or costs according to the ecosystem services valuation based on trends of the land use changes.

This study combines three different dimensions of ecosystem services: biophysical, economic, and spatial, followed by a simple trade-off analysis to see the synergy and conflict across ecosystem services to explain the implication on the spatial planning processes. This study only focuses on the valuation of selected ecosystem services in the study area. The hydrological function of peatland areas were not carried out in this study due to its complexity and it should be done in a separate research. The hydrological function is part of the important ecosystem services on peatland in relation to soil subsidence and flooding risks due to peat drainage for cultivation purpose. Beside that fact, some other limitations and uncertainties of the study are present.

Future research on how ecosystem services supply in response to different future land use projections or scenarios is recommended using trade-off analyses for spatial planning purposes. The study should incorporate scenarios and further spatial mapping that likewise involves multi-layer analysis, stakeholder analysis, and future social demand analysis, among others. As such, these studies can help formulate the most appropriate land use strategies, management instruments, and financing mechanisms.

REFFERENCES

1. Groot, R. S. d., J. R. M. Alkemade, L. Braat, L. G. Hein, and L. L. J. M. Willemen. (2010). Challenges in integrating the concept of ecosystem services and values in landscape planning, management and decision making. *Ecological Complexity* 7 (3): 260-272. doi:10.1016/j.ecocom.2009.10.006
2. Hooijer, A., S. Page, J. G. Canadell, M. Silvius, J. Kwadijk, H. Wösten, and J. Jauhiainen. (2010). Current and future CO2 emissions from drained peatlands in Southeast Asia. *Biogeosciences* 7 (5): 1505-1514. doi:10.5194/bg-7-1505-2010.
3. Hooijer, A., S. Page, J. Jauhiainen, W. A. Lee, X. X. Lu, A. Idris, and G. Anshari. (2012). Subsidence and carbon loss in drained tropical peatlands. *Biogeosciences* 9 (3): 1053-1071. doi:10.5194/bg-9-1053-2012
4. Law, E.A., Bryan, B.A., Meijaard, E., Mallawaarachchi, T., Struebig, M., and Wilson, K.A. (2015). Ecosystem services from a degraded peatland of Central Kalimantan: implications for policy, planning, and management. *Ecological Applications* 25 (1): 70-87. doi: 10.1890/13-2014.1
5. Miettinen, J., Shi, C., & Liew, S. C. (2011). Two decades of destruction in Southeast Asia's peat swamp forests. *Frontiers in Ecology and the Environment*, 10(3), 124-128. doi: 10.1890/100236
6. Murdiyarso, D., K. Hergoualc'h, and L. V. Verchot. (2010). Opportunities for reducing greenhouse gas emissions in tropical peatlands. *Proceedings of the National Academy of Sciences* 107 (46): 19655-19660. doi: 10.1073/pnas.0911966107
7. Ritung S., Wahyunto, Nugroho K., Sukarman, Hikmatullah, Suparto, C. T. (2011). *Peta lahan gambut Indonesia Skala 1:250.000* (p. 11). Kementerian Pertanian, Jakarta.
8. Sumarga, E. and Hein, L. (2014). Mapping ecosystem services for land use planning, the case of Central Kalimantan. *Environmental Management* 54: 84-97. doi:10.1007/s00267-014-0282-2.
9. Wibisono, H.T. and Pusparini, W. (2010). Sumatran tiger (Panthera tigris sumatrae): A review of conservation status. *Integrative Zoology* 5: 313-323. doi: 10.1111/j.1749-4877.2010.00219.x.
10. Wösten, J. H. M., E. Clymans, S. E. Page, J. O. Rieley, and S. H. Limin. (2008). Peat–water interrelationships in a tropical peatland ecosystem in Southeast Asia. *Catena* 73 (2): 212-224. doi:10.1016/j.catena.2007.07.010

Table 1: Synergy and conflict of selected Ecosystem services provided by Indonesian peatlands (Riau case study)

Land cover	Provisioning service				Regulating service	Sumatran tiger habitat	Synergy (↑↑); Conflict (↑↓); Neutral (→)
	Timber production (€/ha/year)		Oil palm production (€/ha/year)	Paddy production (€/ha/year)	Carbon sequestration (€/ha/year)	Tiger is present (+); Tiger is absent (-)	
	Non-pulpwood	Pulpwood					
Secondary dryland forest	66				421	+	↑↑ : Synergy between non-pulpwood production, carbon sequestration, and Sumatran tiger habitat
Primary mangrove forest					813	-	→ : No synergy or conflict exists, but favourable for carbon sequestration
Primary swamp forest	48				507	+	↑↑ : Synergy between non-pulpwood production, carbon sequestration, and Sumatran tiger habitat
Plantation forest		483			-1,913	+	↑↓ : Conflict between pulpwood production and carbon sequestration as well as potential tiger-human conflict
Dry shrubland					-392	+	→ : No synergy or conflict between carbon sequestration and Sumatran tiger habitat, but unfavourable for carbon sequestration
Estate crop			701		-2,219	+	↑↓ : Conflict between oil palm production, carbon sequestration, and Sumatran tiger habitat
Settlement area					0	+	↑↓ : Potential tiger-human conflict
Bare ground					-469	+	→ : No synergy or conflict between carbon sequestration and Sumatran tiger habitat, but unfavourable for carbon sequestration
Savanna and grasses					-469	-	→ : No synergy or conflict between carbon sequestration and Sumatran tiger habitat, but unfavourable for carbon sequestration
Open water					0	+	→ : No synergy or conflict between carbon sequestration and Sumatran tiger habitat
Secondary mangrove forest					813	+	↑↑ : Synergy between carbon sequestration and Sumatran tiger habitat
Secondary swamp forest		256			497	+	↑↑ : Synergy between pulpwood production, carbon sequestration, and Sumatran tiger habitat
Wet shrubland					0	+	→ : No synergy or conflict between carbon sequestration and Sumatran tiger habitat
Pure dryland agriculture				286	-899	-	↑↓ : Conflict between paddy production and carbon sequestration
Mixed dryland agriculture					-1,243	+	↑↓ : Potential tiger-human conflict
Paddy field				286	-899	+	↑↓ : Conflict between paddy production and carbon sequestration as well as potential tiger-human conflict
Fish pond/aquaculture					0	-	→ : No synergy or conflict exists
Port/harbour					0	-	→ : No synergy or conflict exists
Mining area					-469	+	↑↓ : Conflict between carbon sequestration and Sumatran tiger habitat as well as potential tiger-human conflict
Open swamp					497	+	↑↑ : Synergy between carbon sequestration and Sumatran tiger habitat

SPECIAL SESSION 4: TROPICAL PEATLAND BIODIVERSITY & CONSERVATION IN SOUTHEAST ASIA

Abstract No: A-213

BIODIVERSITY OF TROPICAL PEATLAND IN SOUTHEAST ASIA

J. O. Rieley [1, 2]

[1]The University of Nottingham
[2]International Peatland Society

*Corresponding author: jack.rieley@btinternet.com

SUMMARY

Natural lowland peat swamps of Southeast Asia support forest vegetation forming a catena of types from their perimeter to centre, a change that is reflected in variations in canopy height, peat thickness, waterlogging and nutrient availability. Recognition of the biological, environmental and economic importance of tropical peatlands has been a slow process. The earliest interest in the peat swamp forests of Southeast Asia was in the 1930s by British foresters working in the former British Protectorates of Malaya, Sarawak and Brunei and Dutch scientists in Kalimantan and Sumatra. The ecological and taxonomic studies of peat swamp forests of northern Borneo by J.A.R. Anderson became a benchmark for all subsequent research on tropical peatland. Many plant species are restricted to this stressful habitat and some are endemic to it. Several historical accounts of the fauna of tropical peat swamp forests suggested that animal diversity was low but more recent ones, for example in the upper Sg. Sabangau catchment of Central Kalimantan, show the opposite that they are vital habitats for many rare and endangered species of animals and plants including orang utan (*Pongo pygmaeus*). By the end of the 1980s, extensive areas of peatland in Indonesia, Malaysia and Thailand had been drained and converted to agriculture for a large range of crops including rice and vegetables and plantations of oil palm and paper pulp trees. Associated problems of peat shrinkage, subsidence, nutrient deficiency, toxicity and low plant productivity are also documented. Deforestation, drainage and conversion of tropical peatland to other land uses has continued apace since then over increasingly larger areas with consequent problems of fire, flooding, greenhouse gas emissions and poverty all of which have had negative impacts on biodiversity. These are now regional and global problems some of which will be the subject of other presentations at this congress.

Keywords: *biodiversity, peat swamp forest, deforestation, plantations*

HISTORICAL PERSPECTIVE

The presence of extensive areas of peatland in Southeast Asia, especially the islands of Borneo and Sumatra and Peninsular Malaysia has been known for over 300 years (Rieley & Page, 1997). These were mostly casual references made by explorers in their pursuit of land exploration and discovery without detailed scientific survey. Even the area of these peatlands was subject to confusion and doubt with early estimates of around one million hectares in Borneo and Sumatra combined. It was not until the 1930s that specific studies were made of these lowland tropical peatland ecosystems over a period of 20 years. These were the basis for later development of some of these peatlands for agriculture and human settlement.

A detailed survey of peatland in Peninsular Malaya, carried out in the 1950s, estimated that there were about 800,000 hectares (approximately 6 per cent of the total area) mostly in poorly draining coastal areas in the centre and south of the country. Most of this peat was classified as 'oligotrophic', which is low in mineral nutrients, especially calcium, and high in acidity. The vegetation of Malayan peat swamp forests was described in detail by Wyatt-Smith (1959). This work was followed by studies carried out in Sarawak and Brunei, including the first ecological appraisal of this ecosystem (Anderson, 1983). Anderson carried out extensive field surveys of peat thickness, surface levels and tree species composition and described a catena of vegetation types on pristine peat swamps that is related to differences in ecological conditions and environmental factors across very extensive peat domes.

Little emphasis was placed upon the study of peatlands during the first quarter century of the Republic of Indonesia but, in the early 1970s, interest accelerated because the need to increase domestic food production was highlighted in a five year development plan (REPELLITA) that promoted increased rice production in coastal areas. As a result, multidisciplinary studies of soils, ecology, agronomy, engineering and social economy were carried out in the coastal peat areas of Riau and Central and West Kalimantan, jointly by Dutch and Indonesian scientists, which identified the principal problems of reclamation of tropical peatlands (Soepraptohardjo and Driessen, 1976).

BIODIVERSITY

Whilst the diversity associated with ombrotrophic peatlands, especially in boreal and temperate parts of the world is usually lower than adjacent dryland ecosystems, many peatland species are specialists, which are not found in other habitats. The inaccessibility of peatlands has also drawn in species that, although not confined to these habitats, are dependent upon the shelter and food peatlands provide. Until fairly recently little was known of the biodiversity of tropical peatlands anywhere in the world and, as a result, it was largely ignored (Rieley & Page, 2007). Early accounts of this ecosystem refer to uninteresting plant and animal communities and their general lack of species. However, as more information on the biodiversity of tropical peat swamp forest accumulated it became clear that this ecosystem had been undervalued for its vast biodiversity and as a habitat for rare and threatened species.

South-east Asia's tropical peat-swamp forests are important for biodiversity conservation, being home to at least 1,524 plants, 123 mammals, 268 birds, 219 fresh-water fish species and an unknown, but very high number of invertebrates not to mention a vast range of bryophytes, ferns and fungi. They also support many threatened species, including the Bornean orang utan, southern Bornean gibbon, Sumatran tiger and Sumatran elephant.

Flora

The vegetation of the peat swamp forests of Southeast Asia has been investigated in more detail than the associated animal communities (Rieley & Page, 1997). The tree species diversity of these forests is lower than in most other types of lowland rain forest in the region, but some are restricted to this ecosystem and make an important contribution to regional. The species composition and vegetation types of peat swamp forest are not uniform across Southeast Asia and there is significant local and regional variation, although there is presently insufficient information available to establish definite phytogeographical trends (Rieley & Ahmad-Shah, 1996).

Within a tropical peatland catchment, there may be a catena of between four and seven different forest types, reflecting differences in peat thickness, hydrology and nutrient availability. These range from a mixed swamp community with up to 240 tree species per hectare to a less diverse, low canopy, small pole forest, usually associated with the wettest, deepest peat in which tree species number declines to 30–55 species per hectare. Local differences in peatland hydrology and nutrient availability probably exert strong influences on forest composition and structure (Brady, 1997; Page *et al.*, 1999). In overall terms, tall peat swamp forest sub-types, which have the greatest tree species diversity and canopy stratification, support the greatest faunal. The lower canopy sub-types are less species diverse.

Fauna

The faunal diversity of tropical peat swamp forests is of great interest but base-line information is very limited and has not been related to the different vegetation types (Page *et al.*, 1997). A few studies have highlighted the role that peat swamp forests play in providing habitats for a number of endangered and rare species, especially birds, fish, mammals and reptiles.

Mammals

Several recent studies have highlighted the role that tropical peat swamp forests play in providing habitats for many species of mammals (Page *et al.*, 1997). Of particular conservation importance is the relatively large population of orang utan (*Pongo pygmaeus pygmaeus*) associated with peat swamp forest in Borneo and Aceh in Sumatra (Morrogh-Bernard *et al.*, 2003), which provide some of the most important remaining habitats for this endangered primate. A study carried out in the upper Sg. Sebangau catchment (Page *et al.*, 1997) revealed 35 species of mammal, the majority of which are arboreal. Twenty nine species were observed in the field whilst six were captured in traps as part of small mammal surveys. Observations at sunrise and sunset ensured that some nocturnal animals (e.g. civets) were recorded; other nocturnal groups, however, notably lorises and bats, were under-represented. The largest number of animals was identified in the mixed swamp forest (26), nearest to the river, followed by tall interior forest on the watershed (20). Only 8 species were encountered in low pole forest from which most arboreal species were absent. Several species are regarded as endangered, threatened or vulnerable by the Convention on Trade in Endangered Species (CITES) and the International Union for the Conservation of Nature (IUCN) (Table 1).

Birds

The avian species diversity of peat swamp forest is considerable and the importance of this habitat as a refuge for a number of rare and threatened species has been demonstrated (Page *et al.*, 1997). It is now evident that peat swamp forest is important for many bird species and some have specific preferences for this habitat, which acts as one of their last refuges. Preliminary observations suggest that the majority of bird species (80%) can survive in selectively logged forest. Whilst a number of birds may utilise regenerating peat swamp forest for feeding, this habitat may be unsuitable at other stages of the avian life cycle. Loss of nesting sites and nesting materials, for example, may reduce breeding potential of some species and alterations in the forest microclimate may also exclude species.

Studies over several years in peat swamp forest in the upper catchment of Sg. Sebangau in Central Kalimantan revealed more than 150 bird species. These were dominated by insectivores, the main guild being foliage gleaning species. The largest number was recorded in mixed swamp forest (106) followed by tall interior forest (77), while the smallest number of species was recorded in low pole forest (27). In addition, 32 species were observed in deforested, riverine sedge swamp. Six of the bird species recorded is Red Data Book species constituting 50% (six out of 13) of the listed bird species for the island of Borneo (Table 2). Several bird species within the Southeast Asian region are considered to be peat swamp specialists, i.e. they are not associated with any other wetland or forest habitat. This group includes white-winged duck (*Cairina scutulata*), Storm's stork (*Ciconia stormi*) and grey-breasted babbler (*Malacopteran albogulare*).

Table 1: Checklist of rare, endangered and vulnerable mammal species recorded in peat swamp forest in the upper Sg. Sebangau catchment (status according to CITES & IUCN)
(MSF: mixed swamp forest, 1-5 km from river; LPF: low pole forest, 5-12 km from river; TIF: tall interior forest, 12-25 km from river)

Common name	Scientific name	Status	Habitat		
			MSF	LPF	TIF
Agile gibbon	*Hylobates agilis*	Endangered	*		*
Orang utan	*Pongo pygmaeus pygmaeus*	Endangered	*	*	*
Pig-tailed macaque	*Macaca nemestrina*	Endangered	*	*	*
Red leaf monkey	*Presbytis rubicunda*	Endemic to Borneo	*		*
Sun bear	*Helarctos malayanus*	Endangered	*	*	*
Clouded leopard	*Neofelis nebulosa*	Threatened	*		
Leopard cat	*Felis bengalensis*	Threatened	*		
Marbled cat	*Felis marmorata*	Threatened	*		*
Flat-headed cat	*Felis planiceps*	Rare	*		
Binturong (bear cat)	*Arctitis binturong*	Vulnerable			
Small-toothed palm civet	*Arctogalidia trivirgata*	Status indeterminate	*		*
Plain pygmy squirrel	*Exilisciurus exilis*	Endemic to Borneo	*		*
Painted tree shrew	*Tupaia picta*	Endemic to Borneo	*		*

Fish

The rivers and drainage streams of the Southeast Asian peat swamp forests have long been considered to have low fish biomass, productivity and species diversity owing to low pH, low oxygen concentrations, toxicity from plant-derived chemicals, lack of transparency and hence primary productivity, and depauperate invertebrate communities owing to the lack of minerals such as calcium. In the last twenty years, however, efforts have been made to reassess the fish communities of these habitats. For example, several new species were found associated in a peat swamp habitat in North Selangor, Malaysia (Ng *et al.*, 1994). In addition, 44 species from 17 families, including 10 new species or subspecies, have been identified from blackwater rivers and pools in the upper Sg. Sebangau catchment, Central Kalimantan (Page *et al.*, 1997) demonstrating that the peatland rivers of Southeast Asia have a higher degree of localised endemism of fish species than alluvial rivers in the region.

Invertebrates

There has been little systematic collection of or research on the invertebrates of peat swamp forest. In the Sebangau catchment in Central Kalimantan, preliminary investigations of several invertebrate groups have highlighted the presence of many noteworthy species.

DISCUSSION

Lowland tropical peat swamp forest in Southeast Asia is undoubtedly one of the highest biodiversity ecosystems on this planet. Although a large number of animals and plants has been identified this information has been gathered from relatively few locations and most areas of peat swamp forest have not been investigated. Owing to the high rate of deforestation and conversion to other land uses large numbers of species are likely becoming extinct before they are discovered and described. In addition, it is not possible to extrapolate species existence and numbers from the current restricted database because there are major biogeographical species and population differences across the Southeast Asian region. For example, *Shorea albida,* also known as alan batu or light red meranti, is endemic to the north west of the island of Borneo. It does not occur on either Sumatra or in Central and East Kalimantan where its ecological niche is occupied by other tree species. There are also major species differences between peat swamp forests located near to the coast where they are exposed to off-shore winds and receive sea-spray containing additional nutrients and those forests further inland.

Table 2: Checklist of notable bird species recorded in peat swamp forest, upper Sg. Sebangau catchment (records from 1993, 1994 and 1995)

Common name	Scientific name	Status	Habitat			
			RSS	MSF	LPF	TIF
Storm's stork	*Ciconia stormi*	Red Data Book Peat swamp forest specialist		*		
Lesser adjutant stork	*Leptopilus javanicus*	Red Data Book	*			
Wrinkled hornbill	*Aceros corrugatos*	Red Data Book		*		*
Helmeted hornbill	*Buceros vigil*	Red Data Book				*
Short-toed coucal	*Centropus rectunguis*	Red Data Book		*		*
Wallace's hawk eagle	*Spizaetus nanus*	Red Data Book		*	*	*
Grey-breasted babbler	*Malacopteran albogulare*	Uncommon species of wetlands & swamp forests				*
Hook-billed bulbul	*Setornis criniger*	- as above -		*		*
Great-billed heron	*Ardea sumatrana*	- as above -	*			
Black bittern	*Dupetor flavicollis*	- as above -	*			
Cinnamon-headed green pigeon	*Treron fulvicollis*	- as above -		*		
Striped wren babbler	*Kenopia striata*	- as above -		*		*
Malaysian blue flycatcher	*Cyornis turcosus*	- as above -				*
Crestless fireback pheasant	*Lophura erythrophthalma*	Uncommon species of lowland forests				*
Greater coucal	*Centropus sinensis*	- as above -		*		
Brown wood owl	*Strix leptogrammica*	- as above -				*
Red-naped trogon	*Harpactes kasumba*	- as above -		*		*
Rufous-backed kingfisher	*Ceyx rufidorsa*	- as above -		*		*
Rufous-collared kingfisher	*Actenoides concretus*	- as above -		*		
Asian black hornbill	*Anthracoceros malayanus*	- as above -		*		*
White-bellied woodpecker	*Dryocopus javensis*	- as above -		*		
Lesser cuckoo-shrike	*Coracina fimbriata*	- as above -	*	*		
Grey-bellied bulbul	*Pycnonotus cyaniventris*	- as above -				*
Rufous-tailed shama	*Trichixos pyrropygus*	- as above -		*		*

There is still much that is unknown about these peat swamp forests but, unfortunately, will never be known. Until 1990 the lowland tropical peatlands of Southeast Asia were still relatively undisturbed and in near pristine condition (Hooijer *et al*, 2006). In 1990 the area of industrial plantation on tropical peatland in Peninsular Malaysia, Borneo and Sumatra was only 4% (120,000 hectares) of today's area of 3.1 Mha. Since then the rate of peatland conversion has been extremely high (10% per year) with 70% occurring between 2000 and 2010 (Miettinen *et al.*, 2012). By 2020 it is estimated that 6-9 Mha of peatland in this region will be converted to plantations. Much of what remains will not be in pristine condition but degraded as a result of timber extraction, water table drawdown because of adjacent plantation water management (drainage) activities and fire and with much reduced biodiversity.

The following speakers will add much more to this introduction to the session on 'Tropical Peatland Biodiversity and Conservation in Borneo and Sumatra'.

Wim Giesen will explain that the plants of Southeast Asian peat swamps are mostly not endemic to that ecosystem but most also occur in other habitats including freshwater swamps, heath forests, montane forests and other dryland forest.

Sara Thornton and colleagues will describe the high degree of endemism of the fish that inhabit tropical peat swamp forests and the blackwater flowing from them. Increasing deforestation and pollution are a matter of concern with implications for biodiversity and livelihoods of local people.

Marcel Silvius will highlight that the biodiversity of tropical peat swamp forests is poorly understood and undervalued with little regard given to its conservation. Even protected peatlands are at risk from illegal logging and drainage promoted by timber extraction canals and adjacent plantations.

Susan Cheyne and colleagues will describe the first comprehensive survey of gibbons across Indonesian Borneo to determine population densities and relate these to vegetation characteristics.

Mark Harrison and colleagues present evidence of the impact of recent fires on peat swamp biodiversity in Indonesian Borneo. These fires have had major impact on animal populations through loss of habitat, overcrowding in remaining habitats, toxic haze inhalation and reduction in food sources and water availability.

Doug Cress and colleagues will talk about protection and restoration of tropical peatland in Sumatra for orang utans. The rapid expansion of the palm oil industry is a major driver of loss of peatland and orang utan habitat.

REFERENCES

1. Anderson, J.A.R. (1983) The tropical peat swamps of western Malesia. In: Gore, A.J.P. (Ed.), *Ecosystems of the World: Mires: Swamp, Bog, Fen and Moor. 4B, Regional Studies*. Elsevier, New York, pp. 181-199.
2. Brady, M.A. (1997) Organic matter dynamics of coastal peat deposits in Sumatra, Ph.D. Thesis, Faculty of Graduate Studies, Department of Forestry, University of British Columbia, Vancouver, Canada
3. Hooijer A, Silvius M, Wösten H, Page S (2006) PEAT-CO2, Assessment of CO2 emissions from drained peatlands in SE Asia. Delft Hydraulics Report Q3943, Delft, The Netherlands.
4. Miettinen, J., Hooijer, A., Chenghua, S., Tollenaar, D., Vernimmen, R., Soo, C.L. and Page, S.E. (2012) Extent of industrial plantations on Southeast Asian peatlands in 2010 with analysis of historical expansion and future projections. Global Change Biology Bioenergy, 4: 908-918.
5. Morrogh-Bernard, H., Husson, S., Page, S.E. and Rieley, J.O. (2003) Population status of the Bornean orang-utan *(Pongo pygmaeus)* in the Sebangau peat swamp forest, Central Kalimantan, Indonesia. *Biological Conservation,* 110: 141-152.
6. Ng, P.K.L., Tay, J.B. and Lim, K.K.P. (1994) Diversity and conservation of blackwater fishes in Peninsular Malaysia, particularly in the North Selangor peat swamp forest. *Hydrobiologia,* **285**: 203-218.
7. Page, S.E., Rieley, J.O., Shotyk, W. and Weiss, D. (1999) Interdependence of peat and vegetation in a tropical peat swamp forest, Philosophical Transactions of the Royal Society London, Series B, 354: 1885-1897.
8. Rieley, J.O. and Ahmad-Shah, A. (1996) The vegetation of tropical peat swamp forests. In: E. Maltby, C.P. Immirzi & R.J. Safford (eds.) *Tropical Lowland Peatlands of Southeast Asia.* International Union for Conservation of Nature and Natural Resources, Gland, Switzerland. pp. 55-74.
9. Rieley, J.O. and S.E. Page. (1997) *Biodiversity and Sustainability of Tropical Peatlands. Proceedings of the International Symposium on Biodiversity, Environmental Importance and Sustainability of Tropical peat and Peatlands, Palangka Raya, Central Kalimantan, 4-8 September 1995.* Samara Publishing Limited, Cardigan. UK.
10. Soepraptohardjo, M. and Driessen, P.M (1976). The lowland peats of Indonesia, a challenge for the future. *Soil Research Institute, Bogor Bulletin* **3:** 11-19
11. Wyatt-Smith, J. (1959) Peat swamp forests in Malaya. *Malayan Forester,* **22:** 5-23.

Figure 1 :
Pristine peat swamp forest in Central Kalimantan

Figure 2:
Deforested, burned peatland in Central Kalimantan

Abstract No: A-349

DIVERSITY AND CHARACTERISTICS OF *CRYPTOCORYNE* (ARACEAE) SPECIES OF PEAT SWAMP ECOSYSTEM IN BORNEO

I.B. Ipor*, C.S. Tawan, C, S. Wongso, N. Jacobsen., J.D. Bastmeijer, and H. Budianto

Department of Plant Science and Environmental Ecology, Faculty of Resource Science and Technology, Universiti Malaysia Sarawak, 94300, Kota Samarahan, Sarawak

**Corresponding author: ibipor@frst.unimas.my*

Cryptocoryne (Araceae) is a genus of submerged aquatic plants commonly known as water trumpet. *Cryptocoryne* spp. have been increasingly popular and used in the aquarium industry worldwide. They are found in rivers, streams or swampy areas mostly in fresh water and peat swamps while a few species are able to grow in mangroves. Some *Cryptocoryne* species are rare and grow within their native habitats and are considered localised in their distribution and endemic to certain areas. This study was carried out in Borneo focusing on areas within Sarawak, Malaysia and Kalimantan, Indonesia. Our surveys recorded about 14 *Cryptocoryne* species in Sarawak. The species that inhabit the peat swamp ecosystem of Sarawak are *C. ferruginea* Engler, C. *fusca* de Wit, *C. longicauda* Engler, *C. striolata* Engler, *C. pallidinervia* Engler, and *C. yujii* Bastmeijer. The most common species, is *C. ciliata* (Roxburgh.) Schott., is the only species that thrives in mangrove and brackish water habitats. Two varieties of *C. cordata* Griff., namely *C. cordata* var. *zonata* and *C. cordata* var. *grabowskii,* have also been recorded. The common species that occur in peat swamp areas in Kalimantan are *C. edithiae* de Wit, *C. fusca*, *C. longicauda*, *C. pallidinervia* and three varieties of *C. cordata* namely *C. cordata* var. *grabowskii*, *C. cordata* var. *griffithii* and *C. cordata* var. *zonata* while *C. purpurea* Ridl. has one variety known as *C. purpurea* var. *borneoensis*. Our field observations of *Cryptocoryne* populations in natural habitat indicated that they are often in a stage of high disturbance due to human activities for land conversion and also overharvesting to cater for the commercial demand for aquarium culture. Hence *ex situ* conservation of *Cryptocoryne* species in suitable totally protected areas, especially in Sarawak, should be considered to avoid species extinction in the future.

Keywords: *Cryptocoryne, peat swamp ecosystem, Borneo, conservation*

Abstract No: A-040

IMPACTS OF THE 2015 FIRE SEASON ON PEAT-SWAMP FOREST BIODIVERSITY IN INDONESIAN BORNEO

Mark E. Harrison[1, 2, 3], Bernat Ripoll Capilla[2], Sara A. Thornton[1, 2], Megan E. Cattau[2, 4] and Susan E. Page[1]

[1]*Department of Geography, University of Leicester, Leicester, UK*
[2]*Orangutan Tropical Peatland Project, Borneo Nature Foundation, Palangka Raya, Central Kalimantan, Indonesia*
[3]*Department of Ecology, Evolution, and Environmental Biology, Columbia University, New York, USA*

Corresponding author: m.harrison@borneonature.org

SUMMARY

Southeast Asia's tropical peat-swamp forests (PSFs) are important for biodiversity conservation, but decades of peat mis-management, illegal logging and largely unrestricted agricultural development in Kalimantan has led to peat drainage in most areas and consequent fire vulnerability. This was highlighted in 2015, when a strong El Niño event led to extensive peatland fires, which reached their peak during August to October 2015. Thousands of square kilometres of peatland were burned, including fires in/around such important PSFs as Sabangau, Mawas, Katingan and Tanjung Puting. We consider the potential impacts of these fires on Kalimantan's biodiversity. The huge majority of PSF fauna species will have been negatively impacted, owing to (1) forest area/habitat loss, including destruction of entire smaller forest fragments; (2) toxic haze inhalation; (3) impacts of drought and low sunlight on forest trees; and (4) increased river acidity. Less mobile, longer-lived and slower-breeding species, such as the endangered Bornean orangutan and southern Bornean gibbon, are expected to be among the worst affected. Negative impacts will persist and worsen in future, if Kalimantan's mis-managed and drained peatland area continues to increase, and strict burning bans are not enforced.

Keywords: *peat-swamp forest, biodiversity, fire, Indonesia, orangutan.*

INTRODUCTION

Peatland fires in Indonesia, and Kalimantan in particular, are now an annual dry season occurrence that are most severe during drier conditions associated with El Niño events (Spessa *et al.*, 2015). Fire prevalence has increased over time, owing to a combination of peat mis-management and drainage, which in many cases has occurred over decades, coupled with fire use by both industrial plantations and local communities, particularly in degraded areas (Page *et al.*, 2009). Prior to 2015, the most severe fire season on record in Kalimantan occurred during the strong 1997-98 El Niño event. Comparisons of the Oceanic Niño Index and other indicators suggest that the 2015-2016 El Niño event is of near identical strength to that of 1997-98 (NOAA, 2016),. During the peak Kalimantan fire season from August-October 2015, a total 49,615 hotspots were detected by NASA MODIS satellites, with 54% in peat areas (http://www.globalforestwatch.org/).

Fire damaged millions of hectares of peatland in Indonesia and released 810-2,570 Mt of carbon into the atmosphere during the 1997-98 El Niño; an amount equivalent to 13-40% of annual fossil fuel emissions at that time (Page *et al.*, 2002). Reports from this period indicate that 20 million people suffered from respiratory problems due to toxic haze inhalation for prolonged periods, with 19,800-48,100 premature mortalities (Heil, 2007), and national economic losses totalled USD 20 billion (Varma, 2003). While the impacts of these fires on carbon emissions, public health and the economy are becoming better understood, our knowledge of their impacts on biodiversity is limited. Here, we provide a preliminary and non-exhaustive overview of some potential biodiversity impacts of the 2015 fires, which we will build on over the coming months through further publications.

METHODS

Fire hotspot data were sourced from the Global Forest Watch portal and NASA FIRMS Earth Data server provider; peat distribution data from (WI, 2004) via Global Forest Watch; and orangutan distribution data from the IUCN (Ancrenaz *et al.*, 2008). Land cover change in Block C of the ex-Mega Rice Project (MRP) in 2015 was assessed by conducting supervised classifications on Landsat data from 8th August 2006 (pre-fire), and composites of data from 14th October and 23rd November 2015 (post-fire) (cf. Cattau *et al.*, 2015). We conducted a preliminary estimate of burned area in Block C during the 2015 fire season by establishing a 3-2-1 band combination and using a QGIS Semi-automatic Classification Plugin to obtain the shape-file, establishing 7 as Range radius for Region of Interest creation and performing a spectral angle mapping algorithm (3.0 thresholds). Pollution data (PM 10) were obtained from the Indonesian Meteorology, Climatology and Geophysics Agency (BMKG). Data on forest litterfall were collected from 16 traps (1 m^2) on a monthly basis in the Natural Laboratory of Peat-Swamp Forest (NLPSF), Sabangau since 2005, using methods described in Harrison *et al.* (2007). Data on fish populations from 20 wire fish traps and water pH at sampling locations along a 7.6 km stretch of the Sabangau River were collected for pre- and post-fire as part of a larger study involving monthly fish and water surveys in the river (see Thornton *et al.*, 2016 for methods). No litterfall, fish or water sampling were conducted during the height of the fires in October 2015, when field conditions were unsafe, but these data were collected before, during the initial stages of, and after the 2015 fire period.

RESULTS

The precise amount of peatland and forest area burned, and overlap with up-to-date fauna species' ranges (based on Struebig *et al.*, 2015), will be the topic of future publications. However, comparison of NASA FIRMS fire hotspot data between August and December 2015 and WI peatland distribution indicates that 24.1% of hotspots in Central Kalimantan occurred in areas with a peat depth > 2 m (Figure 1a). Further, comparison of hotspot and IUCN orangutan distribution data indicate that 29.9% of hotspots occurred within the orangutan's distribution range (Figure 1b). This included fires in/around the Sabangau (home to 6,900 orangutans), Tanjung Puting National Park (6,000 orangutans), Mawas (3,500 orangutans) and Katingan Forests (3,000 orangutans) (population sizes from Wich *et al.*, 2008).

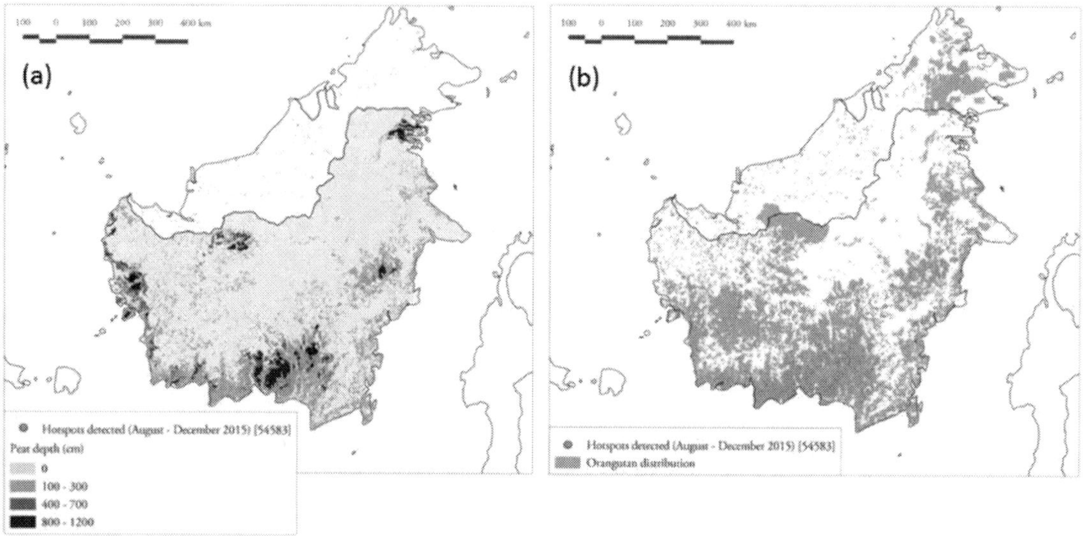

Figure 1. Overlap between NASA FIRMS fire hotspots from August-December 2015, with (a) WI peat distribution and depth data, and (b) IUCN Bornean orangutan distribution data. *See text for descriptions of data sources.*

Analysis of forest loss in individual PSF areas further illustrates this. For example, in the 55,000 ha Sabangau NLPSF, we estimate that two particularly large fires at both the forest edge and in the interior burned a combined 5,665 ha of forest in 2015 (10% of the total area). On-the-ground observations and drone photo-compositions of the burn scar suggest almost complete tree mortality in much of this area (M. E. Harrison and B. Ripoll Capilla, pers. obs.). This occurred despite the presence and extraordinary fire-fighting efforts of the CIMTROP Community Patrol Team protecting this long-term research site. Forest was also burned around the Tuanan research area in Mawas, where a Borneo Orangutan Survival Foundation (BOSF) fire-fighting team operates (Ela, 2015).

In more heavily drained and degraded PSF, such as Block C of the ex-MRP, even larger areas have suffered fire damage. From our preliminary analysis, we estimate that total forest cover reduced by 40.1% from 106,554 ha in August 2008 to 63,848 ha in October/November 2015 (Figure 2). This estimate is likely conservative, because fires continued to burn for more than 15 days after 14th October 2015. Comparison with August 2015 satellite images indicates this owes mostly to the 2015 fires, though some is also due to previous agricultural expansion and fires. Within this burned area, entire individual smaller PSF patches have been burned (Figure 2). This suggests a high probability of local faunal extinctions in some areas, in particular for less mobile species (i.e., those with limited dispersal capabilities and/or showing very strong territoriality). This is supported by observations of starving orangutans, feeding on ferns and nesting on the ground in burned PSF areas (L. Sugiarti, pers. comm.).

Further ecological impacts of the 2015 fires beyond direct forest loss are also evident, including:

1. Large increases in total litterfall in the Sabangau Forest during each of the three El Niño/major haze events within our 2005-2015 dataset (mean 1,079.2 ± 707.9 kg/ha/mo from August-November during the 2006, 2009 and 2015 El Niño/fire seasons; vs. 697.0 ± 697.0 kg/ha/mo during the same months in non- El Niño/major years; Mann-Whitney, $p < 0.001$).
2. Prolonged high levels of airborne pollutants. In Palangka Raya, PM10 levels reached 12 times "hazardous" levels on some days (e.g., 3,761 $\mu g/m^3$ on 20st October 2015; is 300 $\mu g/m^3$ considered hazardous), with a mean daily value of 1,120 ≥ $\mu g/m^3$ in October 2015 (BMKG, unpublished data). This level of pollution is known to have serious health consequences for humans (see Introduction), and similar health impacts should be expected across wildlife species. In particular, colleagues from the Borneo Orangutan Survival Foundation's Central Kalimantan Orangutan Rescue Project at Nyaru Menteng reported acute respiratory and other ailments related to smoke inhalation, particularly among young orangutans at the centre (Harvey, 2015); gibbon territorial singing is compromised (Cheyne, 2007); and the thick haze, which on occasion reduces visibility to < 10 m, is almost certain to impact animals such as birds and fruit bats, which are dependent on sight to find food and mates.
3. An almost five-fold increase in acidity of the Sabangau River post-fires and consequent impacts on fish: river pH dropped from a pre-fire mean of 3.88 to 3.20 immediately after the fires. This corresponded with a decline in fish captures per unit effort from 18.21 to 4.02, respectively.

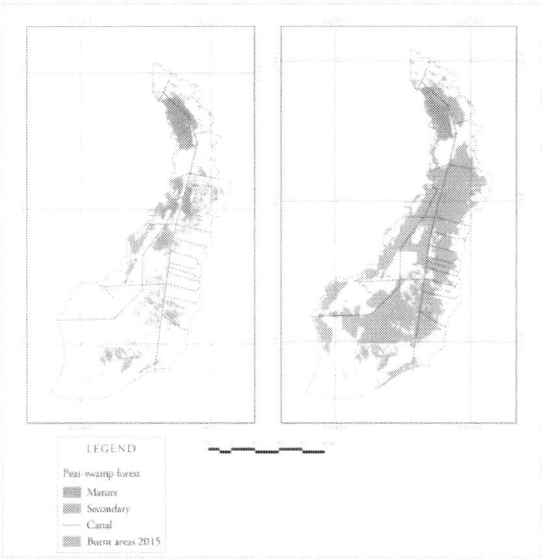

Figure 2. Peat-swamp forest cover in Block C of the ex-Mega Rice Project in August 2008 (left) and November 2015 (right – also shows areas burned during the 2015 fire season). *See text for descriptions of data sources.*

DISCUSSION

Although preliminary, our analysis indicates overall strong negative impacts of the 2015 peat and forest fires in Kalimantan on biodiversity. Firstly, fire hotspot distribution in 2015 showed strong overlap with both peatlands (54%) and the range of the (soon to be) Critically Endangered Bornean orangutan (30%). Further analyses will refine these figures, by incorporating accurate estimates of burned peat area (Hooijer *et al.*, unpublished data) and more up-to-date distribution data (Struebig *et al.*, 2015). The loss of habitat includes the apparently complete burning of entire smaller forest fragments in some areas, such as Block C of the ex-MRP. Reports of large numbers of orangutans rescued from fire-struck peatland areas confirm this (e.g., Mawas, (Hermanu, 2016). We can therefore state with some confidence that this loss of habitat alone will have had severe negative impacts on this already highly threatened and slow-breeding ape species.

A total 123 mammal, 268 bird, 75 reptile, 27 amphibian and 219 freshwater fish species have been recorded from South-east Asian peat-swamp forests (Posa *et al.*, 2011). The distribution of many of these species bears strong similarities to that illustrated above for the Bornean orangutan; i.e. a preference among many mammal and bird species for lowland and peat-swamp forests (Payne and Francis, 1985; Phillipps and Phillipps, 2009; Struebig *et al.*, 2015). PSF fires are known to cause extremely high tree mortality, plus decreases in tree species richness and non-tree flora abundance (Yeager *et al.*, 2003). Despite the fact that very few fauna species appear restricted to PSFs (Posa *et al.*, 2011), the huge areas of peatland and lowland forest burned suggest that habitat loss resulting from the 2015 fires will have had negative impacts on most species found in peat-swamp forests, and strong negative impacts on many, including local extinctions of selected species in some areas.

Similarly, given the known human health impacts of prolonged exposure to haze from peat fires, the observations quoted above on rescued orangutans (Harvey, 2015) and wild gibbon singing (Cheyne, 2007), and the thickness of the haze during the peak of the 2015 fire season, it is inconceivable that the region's wildlife did not experience negative health impacts, even in unburned forest areas. As in humans (who can to some extent mitigate health impacts through wearing face masks), this will include chest and breathing ailments, lethargy and reduced physical performance, which should be expected to have negative impacts on both fitness and mortality. Such impacts may be particularly severe in sight-reliant species, which likely suffer from additional nutritional stresses owing to compromised ability to find food. Impacts may also be more severe in longer-lived animals that experience multiple haze events during their lifetime and in slower-breeding species, for which the impacts of any reductions in breeding fitness or increases in mortality may be more long lasting.

Further, it is likely that many non-sight-dependent species will have suffered additional nutritional stress, through either reduced drinking water availability and/or reduced fruit/flower availability in forests. Although this latter relationship has yet to be confirmed (this will form the subject of a future analysis by the authors), the dramatic increases in forest litter-fall observed during haze periods (Harrison *et al.*, 2007; this study) coupled with reduced photosynthesis by forest trees during haze periods (Davies and Unam, 1999) suggests that trees are likely to need to divert resources to replacing shed leaves following severe haze events, which we hypothesise will lead to decreased resource investment in reproduction; i.e. reduced availability of fruit and flower foods for forest fauna.

Finally, evidence from our fish and river surveys indicates that the impacts of these fires are not limited to terrestrial ecosystems and species. The recorded decrease in pH of Sabangau River water is likely to cause changes in fish behaviour and potentially survival (Thornton *et al.*, 2016). A decrease in water pH can disrupt the ion balance in fish by inhibiting active salt uptake, which can impact gill function and structure (Gonzalez *et al.*, 1998). Decreasing river pH is therefore likely to cause a decrease in local fish catches, as documented in our fish surveys, which in turn is expected to have negative implications for the income and livelihoods of local communities, given high levels of local fish consumption.

CONCLUSION

Our preliminary and non-exhaustive assessment highlights a number of negative impacts of the 2015 peat and forest fires on biodiversity in Kalimantan. This is due to forest loss, including reduced size of large forest patches and complete loss of some smaller forest patches, health impacts of prolonged haze inhalation, potentially compromised availability of and/or ability to find food by forest animals, plus increasing river acidity and reduced local fish catches. We suggest that these impacts affect a very large number of species, and are likely felt most strongly in species that are forest dependent, long-living, slow breeding, flying, sight dependent and/or that live in typically stagnant or slow-flowing waterways. Among the species that possess these characteristics are many that are already threatened, including flagship species such as the highly endangered Bornean orangutan and southern Bornean gibbon, for which the impacts of the 2015 fires raise particular conservation concern. While on-the-ground fire-fighting efforts will remain essential during dry periods to reduce fire spread and prevalence, and thus reduce forest loss and haze, in the long term the fire problem can only be effectively addressed by improved legislation, law enforcement, public awareness and ultimately peat management. Such developments must become a national and international priority if the devastating biodiversity (and human) impacts of the 2015 fire season are not to be repeated during the next strong El Niño event.

ACKNOWLEDGEMENTS

We thank the CIMTROP, the University of Palangka Raya and RISTEK for research permissions. Palangka Raya PM10 data were provided by Alphon Sepriando/the Indonesian Meteorology, Climatology and Geophysics Agency (BMKG); permission to use hotspot data was provided by NASA FIRMS and for orangutan distribution data by the IUCN. Funding was provided by the Arcus Foundation, US Fish and Wildlife Service Great Ape Conservation Fund, The Orangutan Project, StOLT Foundation, Orangutan Appeal UK, Orangutan Outreach, Ocean Parks Conservation Foundation Hong Kong, Orangutan Conservancy, Rufford Foundation and International Peat Society. We thank all our team members for assistance in numerous ways, in particular Simon Husson, Karen Jeffers and Joana Aragay Soler; plus Matthew Struebig for stimulating discussions.

REFERENCES

1. Ancrenaz, M., A. Marshall, B. Goossens, C. van Schaik, J. Sugardjito, M. Gumal and S. Wich. (2008). "*Pongo pygmaeus*. The IUCN Red List of Threatened Species 2008: e.T17975A7640635."
2. Cattau, M. E., S. Husson and S. M. Cheyne (2015). Population status of the Bornean orang-utan *Pongo pygmaeus* in a vanishing forest in Indonesia: the former Mega Rice Project. *Oryx* **49**(3): 473-480.
3. Cheyne, S. M. (2007). Effects of meteorology, astronomical variables, location and human disturbance on the singing apes: *Hylobates albibarbis*. *American Journal of Primatology* **70**(4): 386-392.
4. Davies, S. J. and L. Unam (1999). Smoke-haze from the 1997 Indonesian forest fires: effects on pollution levels, local climate, atmospheric CO2 concentrations, and tree photosynthesis. *Forest Ecology and Management* **124**: 137-144.
5. Ela, P. L. (2015). "Fires Spread to Wild Orangutan Habitat." Borneo Orangutan Survival Foundation, 22 October 2015. http://orangutan.or.id/fires-spread-to-wild-orangutan-habitat/.

6. Gonzalez, R. J., C. M. Wood, R. W. Wilson, M. L. Patrick, H. L. Bergman, A. Narahara and A. L. Val (1998). Effects of Water pH and Calcium Concentration on Ion Balance in Fish of the Rio Negro, Amazon. *Physiological Zoology* **71**(1): 15-22.
7. Harrison, M. E., S. M. Cheyne, Y. Sulistiyanto and J. O. Rieley (2007). Biological effects of smoke from dry-season fires in non-burnt areas of the Sabangau peat-swamp forest, Central Kalimantan, Indonesia. In: J. O. Rieley, C. J. Banks and B. Radjagukguk (Eds). *Carbon-Climate-Human Interaction on Tropical Peatland. Proceedings of The International Symposium and Workshop on Tropical Peatland, Yogyakarta, 27-29 August 2007, EU CARBOPEAT and RESTORPEAT Partnership, Gadjah Mada University, Indonesia and University of Leicester, United Kingdom*.
8. Harvey, A. (2015). Borneo's orangutans forced out of habitat by haze from Indonesian peat blaze. ABC News, 2 November 2015. http://www.abc.net.au/news/2015-11-02/orangutans-forced-out-of-habitat-by-indonesian-peat-blaze/6906156.
9. Heil, A. (2007). *Indonesian Forest and Peat Fires: Emissions, Air Quality, and Human Health* PhD thesis, Max Planck Institure for Meteorology, Hamburg, Germany.
10. Hermanu, N. (2016). "Post Fires the BOS Foundation Launched a Large-scale Orangutan Rescue Mission in Kapuas." Borneo Orangutan Survival Foundation, 17 December 2015. http://orangutan.or.id/press-release-the-bos-foundation-launched-orangutan-rescue-mission-in-kapuas/.
11. NOAA (2016). "February 2016 El Niño update: Q & A...and some Thursday-morning quarterbacking." National Oceanic and Atmospheric Administration. https://www.climate.gov/news-features/blogs/enso/february-2016-el-ni%C3%B1o-update-q-a%E2%80%A6and-some-thursday-morning-quarterbacking.
12. Page, S. E., A. Hoscilo, A. Langner, K. J. Tansey, F. Siegert, S. H. Limin and J. O. Rieley (2009). Tropical peatland fires in Southeast Asia. In: M. A. Cochrane (Ed). *Tropical Fire Ecology: Climate Change, Land Use and Ecosystem Dynamics*. Springer-Praxis, Heidelberg, Germany, 263-287.
13. Page, S. E., F. Siegert, H. D. V. Boehm, A. Jaya and S. Limin (2002). The amount of carbon released from peat and forest fires in Indonesia during 1997. *Nature* **420**: 61-65.
14. Payne, J. and C. M. Francis (1985). *A Field Guide to the Mammals of Borneo*. Sabah Society, Malaysia.
15. Phillipps, Q. and K. Phillipps (2009). *Phillipps' Field Guide to the Birds of Borneo: Sabah, Sarawak, Brunei and Kalimantan*. John Beaufoy Books, Oxford.
16. Posa, M. R. C., L. S. Wijedasa and R. T. Corlett (2011). Biodiversity and conservation of tropical peat swamp forests. *BioScience* **61**(1): 49-57.
17. Spessa, A. C., R. D. Field, F. Pappenberger, A. Langner, S. Englhart, U. Weber, T. Stockdale, F. Siegert, J. W. Kaiser and J. Moore (2015). Seasonal forecasting of fire over Kalimantan, Indonesia. *Natural Hazards and Earth System Sciences* **15**: 429-442.
18. Struebig, M. J., A. Wilting, D. Gaveau, E. Meijaard, R. J. Smith, The Borneo Mammal Consortium, M. Fischer, K. Metcalfe and S. Kramer-Schadt (2015). Targeted conservation to safeguard a biodiversity hotspot from climate and land-cover change. *Current Biology* **25**(3): 372-378.
19. Thornton, S. A., Dudin, S. H. Limin, S. E. Page, C. Upton and M. E. Harrison (2016). Peatland fish of Sabangau, Borneo: Ecology and implications for future monitoring and conservation. In: (Eds). *Peatlands in Harmony - Agriculture, Industry & Nature. Proceedings of the 15th International Peat Congress, 15-19 August 2016, Sarawak, Malaysia*. International Peat Society.
20. Varma, A. (2003). The economics of slash and burn: A case study of the 1997/1998 Indonesian forest fires. *Ecological Economics* **46**: 159-171.
21. WI (2004). *Peta Sebaran Lahan Gambut, Luas dan Kandungan Karbon di Kalimantan 2000-2002 [Map of Peatland Distribution Area and Carbon Content in Kalimantan 2000-2002]*. Wetlands International - Indonesia Programme, Bogor, Indonesia.
22. Wich, S. A., E. Meijaard, A. J. Marshall, S. Husson, M. Ancrenaz, R. C. Lacy, C. P. van Schaik, J. Sugardjito, T. Simorangkir, K. Traylor-Holzer, M. Doughty, J. Supriatna, R. Dennis, M. Gumal, C. D. Knott and I. Singleton (2008). Distribution and conservation status of the orangutan (*Pongo* spp.) on Borneo and Sumatra: how many remain? *Oryx* **42**(3): 329-339.
23. Yeager, C. P., A. J. Marshall, C. M. Stickler and C. A. Chapman (2003). Effects of fires on peat swamp and lowland dipterocarp forests in Kalimantan, Indonesia. *Tropical Biodiversity* **8**(1): 121-138.

Abstract No: A-226

MANGROVE PEAT OF BOTUM SAKOR IN CAMBODIA

Julia Lo[1*], Le Phat Quoi[2] and Sun Visal[3]

[1]*Global Environment Centre, 2nd Floor, Wisma Hing, No. 78, Jalan SS2/72, 47300 Petaling Jaya*
[2]*Institude of Environmental and Natural Resources, Vietnam National University, Ho Chi Minh City, Vietnam*
[3]*Ministry of Environment, Cambodia*

**Corresponding author: azura@gec.org.my*

SUMMARY

Peatland areas in Cambodia is relatively unknown until recently, therefore, it came as pleasant surprise that the first ever peatlands discovered in Cambodia would be located within a mangrove ecosystem. Mangrove peat was first discovered in 2012 and later confirmed in 2014 in the Koh Kong Province of Cambodia. Survey carried out in 2014 saw 4,976 hectares of mangrove peat being confirmed in Peam Krasop Wildlife Sanctuary. In 2015, another survey conducted in the same Province, but different location - at Botum Sakor National Park resulted in additional 4,768 hectares of mangrove peat are being confirmed. This survey focused on coastal area as well as riverine mangrove, moved further along the rivers.

Overall, peat located within this mangrove area is not very deep, with only one location recorded at 135cm. About half of the measurements were in the range of 50cm – 100cm. About 22 mangrove species are recorded during the survey. It should be noted that *Melalueca leucodendron* was also found here. The species is often located immediately behind the mangrove species, sometime, seen together with *Brugueira sexangula*. However, usually forming a pure stands of its' own.

***Keywords**: Peatlands, Mangrove peat, peat depth*

INTRODUCTION

Mangrove can be found in on tops of different subtractes i.e. clay, sand or peat. Although peat can form in various geological setting all over the world, mangrove peat can only form in salt and brackish mangroves along tropical and subtropical coastlines and islands (Cameron and Palmer, 1995).
Peat forming mangrove are widely reported (Joosten, 2010). In fact mangrove peat is common in other part of the world; it has been extensively studied in Belize (Cameron and Palmer, 1995, Mckee & Faulkner, 2000, Macintyre *et al*, 2004, Middleton & McKee, 2010), Puerto Rico (Medina *et al.*, 2010), Honduras & Panama (McKee *et al.*, 2007) and Florida (Giesen *et al.*, 2006).

However, mangrove peat in not common in Southeast Asia; only two areas has been reported to have mangrove peat- one in Lariang-Lumu area in South Sulawesi (where Rhizophora- Bruguiera thrived on 3m deep peat, and another one in Thousand Islands group, off Jakarta Bay (Giesen *et al.*, 2006, Rusila Noor *et al.*, 2006).
That is why the recent discovery of mangrove peat in coastal area of Cambodia had generated much excitement within the peatlands circle as peatlands in peatlands in Cambodia is relatively unknown prior to the discovery of mangrove peat in Peam Krasop Wildlife Sanctuary in Koh Kong Province.

METHODOLOGY

The survey was carried out using the combining of remote sensing in the beginning to identified potential peatlands and later was confirmed by ground- thruthing. Where able possible, a few peat depth measurements were taken moving from the bank towards further inland in order to see where the deepest peat is located and where the peat end. The farthest from river bank is about 180m. Vegetation of the survey locations was also recorded.

STUDY SITE

Botum Sakor National Park, with 183,408 hectares is located at the southwest border of Cambodia and covering three districts of Koh Kong, Kiri Sakor and Botum Sakor in the Koh Kong Province. The majority of Botum Sakor's area comprises gently sloping lowland and flood plains. This area consists of lowland evergreen forest, Melaleuca woodland, grassland, mangrove forest and swamp forest with patches of *Oncosperma* palm. The climate is characterised by tropical monsoons and the area has two high tides per day, with a range of approximately 1.5 m. (Frontier Cambodia, 2010).

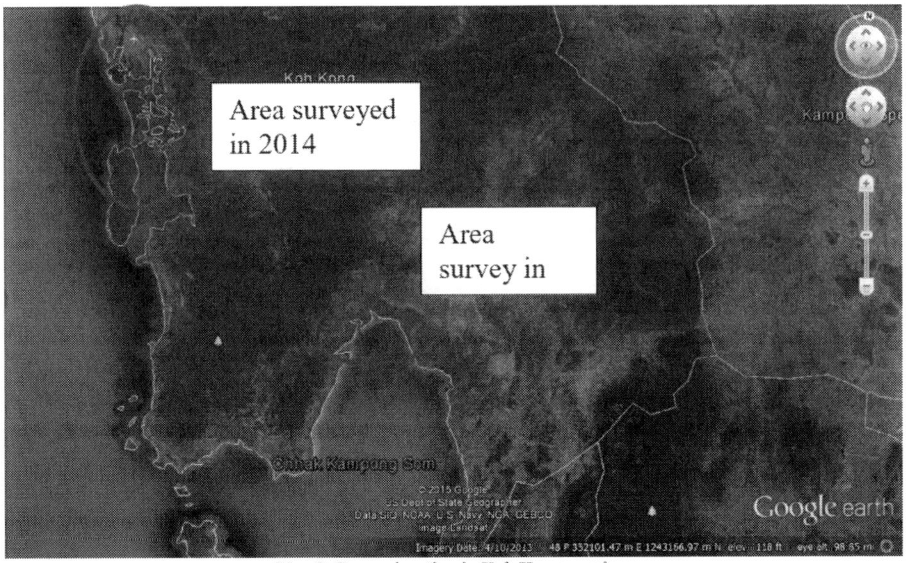

Map 2: Survey location in Koh Kong province

RESULT AND DISCUSSION

Based on the field survey and combining with remote sensing, it is estimated that 4,768 hectares of mangrove peat are being confirmed in Botum Sakor National Park. The confirmed location is mostly located in the western part – coastal and riverine mangrove area (see Map 2).

PEAT DEPTH

Along 4 of the riverine mangrove, a total of 23 locations were surveyed with 49 peat depth measurements were carried out. Of the 49 measurements for peat depth, all areas recorded peat layer except 1 site, even though the peat depth recorded is not uniform and varied from location to locations. The range of peat layer recorded is from 20cm to 135cm, where low figure mostly found at the edge.

The peat depth recorded in Botum Sakor is comparable to peat depth (0.2-1.65m) recorded in Pelican Cays, Belize (McKee at Faulkner, 2000) and peat depth recorded (0.44- 2m) at Peam Krasop Wildlife Sanctuary (Lo *et al.*, 2016). This is however considered shallow if compared with 9m thick peat deposits at Twin Cays (Macintyre *et al.*, 2004).

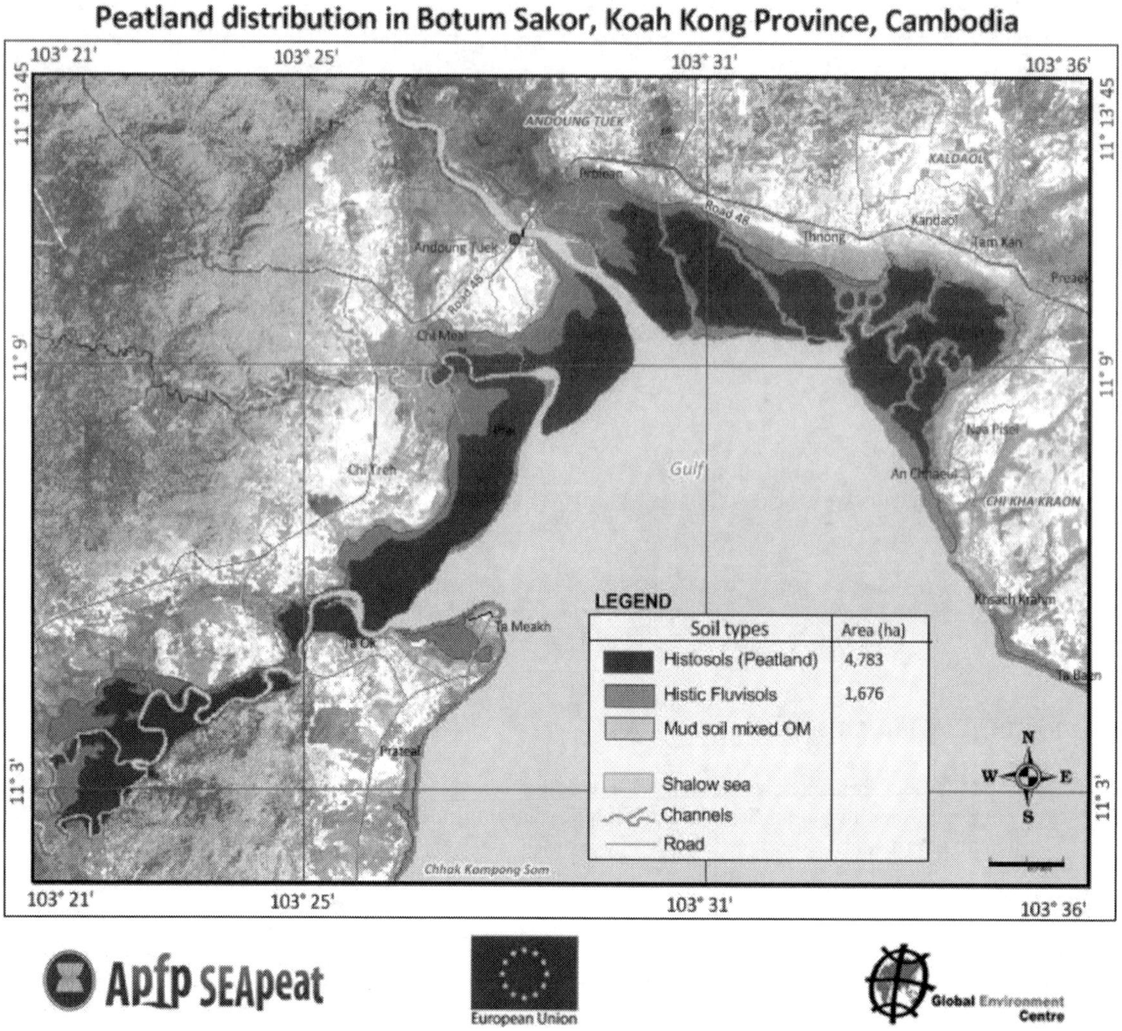

Map 3: Peatlands (mangrove peat) in Botum Sakor

VEGETATION TYPES

Generally, survey in Botum Sakor mangrove area shows both similar and different result compare to survey result from Peam Krasop Wildlife Sanctuary. For example, both site showed that vegetation near the edge is different from vegetation further inland. However, the outer layer in PKWS is almost entirely dominated by single species which is *Rhizophora apiculata*, whereas in Botum Sakor mangrove area, *Rhizophora apiculata* dominate in river bank with sedimentation/mudflats, while mixture species such as *Xylocarpus granatum, Bruguiera gymnorrhiza, Heritiera littoralis, Nypa fruiticans and Pheonix paludosa*, dominate in river banks which faces erosion. Most common species are *Rhizophora apiculata*, *Bruguiera gymnorrhiza*, *Xylocarpus granatum* and *Bruguiera sexangula*.

In general, most of the vegetation encountered during this fieldtrip can be categorized as *Rhizophora* zone and *Lumnitzera-Xylocarpus-Brugueira* zone. However, other species zonation also noted; for example area where only *Rhizophora- Lumnitzera, Bruguiera-Melaleuca, Lumnitzera only and also one single location where Bruguiera* is mixing with normal lowland species i.*e. Syzygium sp.* Incidentally, this site registered the deepest peat measurement . In addition to that, other type of vegetation also been observed; *Melaleuca- Bruguiera* zone and *Melaleuca* stands. It should be noted that peat depth in *Melaleuca* stands is not very deep.

Species zonation is Botum Sakor mangrove area is not as cleared cut as shown in PKWS (Lo *et al.*, 2016), only 2 areas shown similar stunted species such as *Rhizophora apiculata* further inland. In a study on mangrove peat in Puerto Rico (Medina *et al.*, 2010), dwarf version of *Rhizophora mangle* was observed further inland, and the study concluded that the combination of phosphorus limitation and seasonal water stress most likely caused the stunted growth of *Rhizophora mangle*. The stunted *Rhizophora apiculata* may be due to the sharp rise in the land where it was mainly above flood water (FAO, 2007).

In term of flora biodiversity, flora in Botum Sakor mangrove area more diverse (24 species) compared to mangrove species in PKWS (15 species). The forest floors in Botum Sakor also over-grown with undergrowth such as ferns and *Acanthus sp.*, which make accessibility a problem. It should be noted that in PKWS, the areas survey is along the coastal with many waterways/ creeks, whereas in Botum Sakor, most of the area surveyed is along river estuary. This may explain the differences between these 2 areas.

CONCLUSION

The occurrence mangrove peat in the coastal/ riverine mangrove of Cambodia indicate that it is more similar to the mangrove located in the Pacific islands i.e. Belize, Puerto Rico as compared to mangroves areas found along the coast of mainland or peninsular in Southeast Asia. It is believe that there could be more mangrove peat in other coastal area of Cambodia, and further assessment should be made to inventory these areas.
It is hope that with the finding of mangrove peat in Cambodia, it importance and role in carbon sequestration should be highlighted in the future Cambodia national strategy and action plan.

ACKNOWLEDGEMENT

Field surveys were financed by the Sustainable Management of Peatland Forests in Southeast Asia (SEApeat) project, funded by the European Union and implemented through Global Environment Centre. We thank the Cambodian Ministry of Environment for their full commitment to this effort especially the representatives Mr. Sun Visal, Mr. Hong Lork, Mr. Pech Moran, Mr. Sotha Tann and Mrs. Phon Nalin with the assistance of local officer: Mr. Eoung Vunny (Deputy director of Butom Sakor National Park), Mr. Eoung Vunny & Mr. Yourn Tra (Ranger of Butom Sakor National Park), Mr. Chun Sopheak (Ta Ouk Village chief), Mr. Chun Sopheak (Ta Ouk Community leader), Mr. Prav Peuk (Commune council), Mr. Sriv Senghy (Andoung Teuk Community leader) and Mr. Phong Sam-Ong (Andoung Teuk village chief). 2 students from Pahnasastra University of Cambodia- Eang Phallis and Taing PorChhay also joined the assessment.

REFERENCES

1. Cameron, C. C & Palmer, C.A. 1995. The Mangrove Peat of the Tabacco Ranger Islands, Belize Barrier Reef, Central America. Atoll Research Bulletin No. 431: 1-32.
2. Frontier Cambodia. 2010. Royan, A., Lyon, M., Irwin, R., Ward, E., Belle, E.M.S. & Fanning E. Fauna and flora diversity studies in Botum Sakor National Park, Cambodia: April 2005 - September 2009. Frontier Cambodia Environmental Research Report 4. The Society for Environmental Exploration UK and DNCP.
3. Giesen, W., Wulffraat, S., Zieren, M. & Scholten, L. 2007. Mangrove Guidebook of Southeast Asia. FAO and Wetland International, RAP PUBLICATION 2006/07..
4. Joosten, H. 2010. The Global Peatland CO2 Picture Peatland Status and Emissions in All Countries of the World. Greifswald University. Wetlands International, Ede. The Netherlands.
5. Lo, J. Parish, F & Quoi, L. P. 2016. (In Press). Mangrove Peat Found In Koh Kong Province, Cambodia. Malaysian Forester Volume 79 (No. 1 and 2)
6. Macintyre, I. G., Marguerite, A. T, Lithty, R..G. & Bond, G. B. 2004. Holocene History Of The Mangrove Island Of Twin Cays Belize. Atoll Research Bulletin No. 510.
7. Mckee, K.L. & Faulkner, P. L. 2000. Mangrove Peat Analysis and Reconstruction of Vegetation History at the Pelican Cays, Belize. Atoll Research Bulletin No. 468: 47-58.
8. Medina, E., Cuevas, E. & Lugo, A. E. 2010. Nutrient Relations of Dwarf Rhizophora mangle L. Mangroves on Peat in Eeastern Puerto Rico. Plant Ecology 207:13–24.
9. Middleton, B. A. & Mckee, K. L. 2010. Degradation of Mangrove Tissues and Impications for Peat Formation in Belizen Island Forests. Journal of Ecology 89: 818-828
10. Rusila Noor, Y., Khazali., M., & Suryadiputra, I. N.N. 2006. Panduan Pengenalan Mangrove di Indonesia. PHKA/WI-IP, Bogor.

Abstract No: A-348

PEAT SWAMP FLORA AND CONSERVATION OF MALUDAM NATIONAL PARK, SARAWAK

C.S. Tawan*, A.M. Nadia, I.B. Ipor and K. Meekiong

Department of Plant Science and Environmental Ecology, Faculty of Resource Science and Technology, Universiti Malaysia Sarawak, Kota Samarahan, Sarawak, Malaysia

**Corresponding author: cheksum@frst.unimas.my*

Peat swamp forest (PSF) of Sarawak is a unique and interesting ecosystem. The original total of peatland area of Sarawak is estimated at about 1,657,600 hectares, representing 13% of the whole land area of Sarawak. The natural PSFs have a rich a floral diversity with several endemic species distributed within the six distinct communities classified by Anderson in 1963. These PSFs are considered very important natural resources and are of economic importance. The flora inventory involved sampling 25 subplots measuring 20 x 20 m at Maludam National Park (NP) in Sarawak. All individual trees of ≥ 5 cm at diameter breast height (dbh) were measured and their height was estimated using a Haga meter. A total of 1,121 individual trees belonging to 76 species in 33 families were recorded. Among the most common tree species identified were *Vatica mangachapoi* Blanco. (Resak), *Madhuca motleyana* J.F. Macbr. (Ketiau paya), *Dactylocladus stenostachys* Oliv. (Jongkong), and *Baccaurea bracteata* Müll.=Arg. (Tampoi). Important peat swamp species of the Dipterocarpaceae family, namely *Shorea albida* Symington (Alan bunga), *Sh. inaequilateralis* Symington (Semayur) and *Sh. teysmanniana* Dyer ex Brandis (Meranti paya) were also recorded but were few in numbers. *Gonystylus bancanus* (Miq.) Kurz (Ramin) used to be dominant in peat swamp forest but only two individuals trees were recorded in the sampling area. The remaining floral diversity in Sarawak's PSFs is very important and should be fully conserved. Biomass accumulation from the PSF plays an environmentally important role in carbon storage and sequestration. It is crucial that this should be researched be conducted to gain information needed for ecological conservation and to discover its economic potential so that it could be utilized sustainably within the remaining PSFs in Sarawak.

***Keywords**: Sarawak, peat swamp forest, tree flora, conservation.*

Abstract No: A-055

PEATLAND FISH OF SABANGAU, BORNEO: ECOLOGY AND IMPLICATIONS FOR FUTURE MONITORING AND CONSERVATION

Sara A. Thornton[1,2], Dudin[2], Suwido H. Limin[3], Susan E. Page[1,2], Caroline Upton[1] and Mark E. Harrison[1,2]

[1]*Department of Geography, University of Leicester, UK*
[2]*The Orangutan Tropical Peatland Project (OuTrop), UK*
[3]*Center for International Cooperation in Sustainable Management of Tropical Peatland (CIMTROP), University of Palangka Raya, Indonesia*

**Corresponding author: -*

SUMMARY

Fishing is one of the main sources of livelihood and dietary protein in villages in tropical peatland areas, yet peatland rivers remain at high risk from human disturbance, making assessments of fish biodiversity and monitoring of water quality a high priority. This project has completed some of the first in-depth assessments of local fish biodiversity of both tropical peat-swamp forest (TPSF) standing water and blackwater river habitats in the Sabangau catchment in Central Kalimantan, Borneo. Monthly environmental and fish data were collected over a 13-month period. These form the baseline for future monitoring projects and also allow an evaluation of locally initiated sustainable livelihood projects (such as the use of fish ponds) which have been piloted in this location. In the long-term this information will be vital to improved understanding of these wetland habitats, their importance for community livelihoods, and ultimately to finding ways of promoting ecosystem conservation alongside community development.

Keywords: *fish, peat, Borneo, monitoring, livelihoods*

INTRODUCTION

Due to the unique characteristics of the tropical peat swamp forest (TPSF) habitat, including their acidic waters, Indonesia's peatland rivers are important fish habitats that often have a higher degree of endemism than other rivers (Ng *et al.*, 1994; Noor *et al.*, 2005). Fishing is one of the main sources of livelihood for the communities living along the rivers and forests in Central Kalimantan (Lyons, 2003). However, with ever-increasing human populations, alarming deforestation rates throughout Indonesia, and ongoing pollution and habitat degradation, the prognosis for water habitats throughout Asia is a matter of growing concern (Dudgeon, 2000). There have been few studies of fish in this region, but one by Giam *et al.* (2012) found that if TPSF deforestation continues, 77% of fish species are likely to become extinct in Sundaland, with Central Kalimantan being most heavily impacted. This would have severe implications for the wetland ecosystems as well as the local communities depending on the forest and water habitats for their livelihoods. It is therefore vital to understand these wetland habitats, their importance for community livelihoods and cultures, and ultimately to find ways of promoting conservation alongside community development.

The results presented in this paper are part of a larger interdisciplinary project that is evaluating broader values related to fishing and the importance of fish for local communities. The ecological element of this project reported here was focused on sampling the local fish to add to our understanding of TPSF fish ecology and biodiversity in this region. Therefore, this project involved monthly fish and water quality surveys in the Sabangau Forest and River, including measurements of water pH, turbidity, oxygen saturation, nutrient levels and other environmental variables. The research methodology was also designed to identify appropriate approaches for fish population sampling to form the basis of future monitoring and sampling strategies.

The results of 13 months of fish and water surveys in the Sabangau river and 5 months of surveys in the forest are presented followed by discussion of the implications of the results for future fish and river water quality monitoring.

METHODS

The Sabangau River was sampled from September 2014 to September 2015, and the Sabangau Forest from January 2015 to August 2015. A shorter sample period was used in the forest due to insufficient water to set traps (a minimum of 10cm water depth is needed) during the other months. Traditional wire traps, *tampirai*, were used to sample fish, with a mesh size of 0.6 cm and dimensions of approximately 89 x 38 x 38 cm (length x width x height). The bait used was a mixture of *tempeh* and *terasi* (fermented soya bean with fermented shrimp paste). This bait is commonly used by local fishermen and was recommended for use in this project by them.

Every month, a total of 5 sampling days were completed. Traps were set up on alternating sides of the river over a 7km stretch. Kereng Bangkirai, the nearest village, is located in the middle of this sampling area. Twenty traps were used, with a distance of 400 m between each trap. In the forest, the traps were placed in standing water pools and small canals (max width 2.5m). Two canals were used where seven traps were placed in each canal, 50m away from each other. The further 6 traps were placed in standing water pools.
Traps were set the day before the first sampling day. Each trap was then checked and emptied daily, with all fish caught identified and their standard length (SL) measured to the nearest mm. If a large number of fish was caught (over 100 individuals), a sample of 20 individuals of each species were measured with the rest counted. Mortality was noted. Environmental measurements were taken at each site, including: weather conditions, pH, surface water temperature, dissolved oxygen content of the surface water (% and mg/L) and Secchi depth (as a proxy for turbidity). On the final sampling day, samples were taken of the surface water and brought to the University of Palangka Raya laboratory to be tested for NH_3, NO_2 and NO_3.

The river and forest surveys had some variations in terms of the environmental data that were gathered. In the river, the water depths (from middle of the river as well as trap locations) were measured. In the forest, Secchi depth data were not obtained due to the pools and canals in the forest being too shallow. Lastly, flow measurements were not taken in the river, but were taken in the forest where surface water flow in the canals was measured using a stopwatch and a floating ping-pong ball.
Fish catch per unit effort (CPUE) was calculated using the following formula (Merilä, 2015):

$$CPUE = N_{catch}/(N_{traps}*N_{nights})$$

where N_{catch} = Number of fish trapped, N_{traps} = Number of traps set, N_{nights} = Number of nights set

RESULTS

In the river, a total of 55,147 fish were trapped and counted from September 2014 to September 2015 over 1,300 trap nights, with 22,917 fish measured. In the forest, a total of 3,938 fish were trapped and counted from February to July 2016 over 600 trap nights, with 3,905 fish measured. In the river 39 different species were trapped, and in the forest 27 species were trapped. *Rasbora kalbarensis* was added to the list following observations in the river. This species is too small to be trapped using the methods used. This addition leads to a final count of 47 different species from 15 different families (Table 1).

Table 1: Fish species found in the Sabangau River and Forest between September 2015 and September 2016

Family	Latin Name
Osphronemidae	*Betta anabatoides, Betta foerschi, Luciocephalus pulcher, Luciocephalus aura, Belontia hasselti, Sphaerichtys osphromenoides, Sphaerichtys acrostoma, Trichopodus pectoralis*
Cyprinidae	*Cyclocheilichthys janthochir, Osteochilus spilurus, Desmopuntius foerschi, D. hexazona, D. rhoboocellatus, D. johorensis, Eirmotus sp., Rasbora kalochroma, R. cephalotaenia, R. dorciocellata, R. kalbarensis, Osteochilus melanopleura, Trigonopoma gracile, Striuntius lineatus*
Channidae	*Channa pleurophthalmus, C. micropeltes, C. lucius, C. bankanensis, C. sp.*
Siluridae	*Silurichtys hasseltii, Kryptopterus macrocephalus, Ompok leiacanthus, Wallago leeri*
Helostomatidae	*Helostoma temminickii*
Hemiramphidae	*Hemirhamphodon chrysopunctatus*
Mastacembelidae	*Macrognathus maculatus, M. aculeatus*
Clariidae	*Clarias sp., Clarias sp., Enchelochlarias tapeinopterus*
Bagridae	*Mystus olyroides, Leiocassis micropogon, Leiocassis sp.*
Pristolepididae	*Pristolepsis grooti*

Anabantidae	*Anabas testudineus*
Nandidae	*Nandus nebulosus*
Horabagridae	*Pseudeutropius moolenburghae*
Chacidae	*Chaca bankanensis*
Synbranchidae	*Monopterus sp.*

Table 2 illustrates the species richness, total number of fish trapped, Catch Per Unit Effort (CPUE) and the inverse of Simpson's diversity index.

Table 2: Species richness, number of fish trapped and calculated inverse Simpson's diversity for each habitat

Habitat	Species richness	Number of fish trapped	Average CPUE	Simpsons 1-D
River	39	55145	42.21	0.82
Forest	27	3938	1.22	0.70

Figure 1: Monthly CPUE in the river and forest

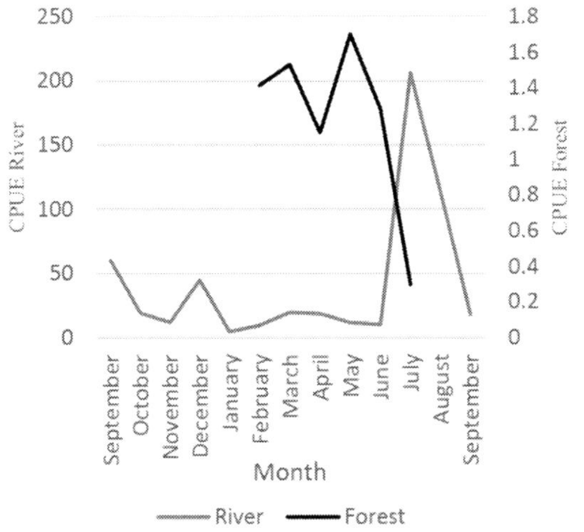

Figure 2: Average rainfall (mm) per month and river and forest water depth (m) from September 2014 to September 2015

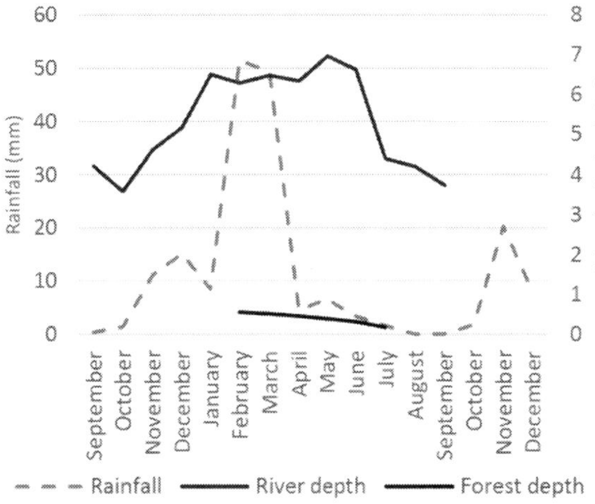

Figure 1 illustrates the calculated CPUE for each month from September 2014 to September 2015 in the Sabangau River and from February to July 2016 in the forest. In the river, the two increases in CPUE in December and July are related to the changing seasons from dry season to wet season (December) and wet season to dry season (July). During these months, large changes in environmental conditions occurred in, for example, rainfall and water depth (Figure 2). These months also coincide with the main fishing seasons in the area, when increased numbers of local villagers are seen fishing on the river.

Percent mortality was calculated for each month of trapping and Figure 3 illustrates the mortality rates of the river surveys. In October 2014 we had the maximum level of fish mortality in our traps, reaching 50%. This then dropped to less than 10% for the majority of the wet season when dissolved oxygen levels were also higher. We see an increasing trend of mortality rates after July (with the onset of the dry season) where there is also a corresponding decrease in dissolved oxygen levels.

Figure 3: Monthly mortality rate (%) and dissolved oxygen levels (mg/L) in the Sabangau river

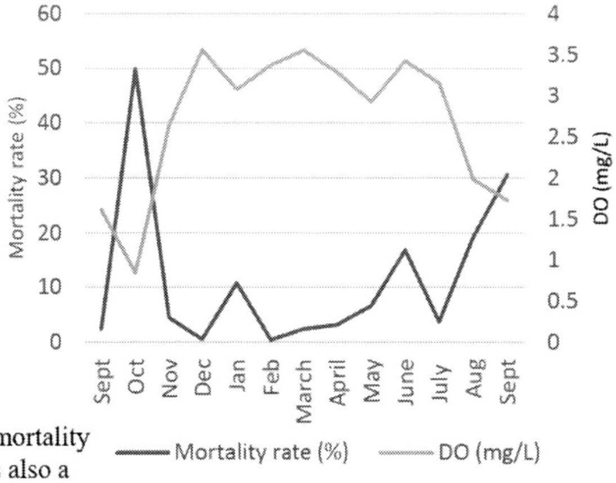

DISCUSSION

The sampling programme produced a species list comprising 47 fish species across both the Sabangau river and forest habitats. Giam *et al.* (2012) found 45 different species in Central Kalimantan TPSF habitats which our results support and add to. As with any fauna trapping methods, our fish traps have limitations including being selective against certain fish sizes, being dependent on fish behaviour and potentially being selective against certain species. With the use of a wider range of sampling methods this species list could be added to in the future. On the other hand, sampling was carried out over a much longer period than in most other surveys in this region. The species total is comparable to and at times higher than those from other surveys in peat-swamp environments. In Batang Kerang in Balai Ringin, Sarawak, 12 species were found in the black water habitat (Rahim *et al.*, 2009). In the North Selangor PSF 48 different species were recorded (Ng *et al.*, 1992, 1994) and in Raja Musa PSF 22 species were recorded (Norhisyam *et al.*, 2012). Sabangau is therefore a notable area for peat-swamp forest fish diversity.

A greater total number and diversity of fish were caught in the river than in the forest, thus the river has a higher diversity index than the forest. While the forest was sampled for fewer months and further sampling might encounter more species, this difference in diversity is also likely due to the river providing a greater range of habitats than the forest in terms of, for example, greater range of water depths and vegetation densities and types.

In order to continue to build a complete fish species list for the area, the use of additional fishing methods, including nets and rod fishing, would be necessary. When designing future sampling programmes, it is also recommended to take into consideration the perspectives of the local community members and fishers: fishing methods with high mortality rates should not only be avoided to limit fish deaths while sampling, but also to avoid fishers perceiving the researcher as fishing for consumption and taking fish from the river. This could potentially have negative implications for local perceptions of fish research and, thus, for conservation efforts.

Due to the limitations of the trapping method and its selectivity in terms of fish capture, it is not possible to produce absolute population estimates for the various species that were identified during the study. However, the same traps used in this research could be used in the future to monitor catch trends and population dynamics e.g. decreasing catch trends are a likely sign of decreasing fish populations in the area.

In addition to dissolved oxygen, this project is also investigating the other environmental variables that may contribute to fish mortality. A drop in dissolved oxygen levels in the river during October could have played a significant role in the increase in mortality seen in that month, but other factors may also have an influence. Based on correlations between environmental data and fish mortality, the project aims to provide guidelines for future monitoring of the river, by recommending time periods and environmental conditions that minimise mortality and are therefore most appropriate for fish surveys to be undertaken.

CONCLUSION

This project identified 47 fish species in the Sabangau peatland, with 39 species found in the Sabangau river and 27 in the peat swamp forest. Local trapping methods (*tampirai*) were used, with trapping in the river undertaken on a monthly basis over the period of 13 months, while the forest habitat was sampled over a 5-month period. Environmental variables including dissolved oxygen, water temperature, pH, turbidity and nutrient levels were also measured in both locations monthly. Fish mortality data were obtained which along with the environmental data will be used to inform appropriate sampling strategies for future monitoring in order to minimise fish mortality. The traps employed in this study were shown to be an effective sampling tool since they trapped fish according to a consistent and reasonably well understood bias, were available locally and required little expertise in deployment. These were important considerations for a baseline study that is anticipated to be continued by local staff in future years. In addition, the data from sampling in both the forest and river will be compared to data from traditional fish ponds that have been built as a sustainable livelihood initiative at the forest edge in order to better understand the potential of these artificial fish habitats for local livelihood support.

Continued monitoring in the sample locations is highly recommended in order to collect longer-term data on fish catch, and hence population, trends and water quality to facilitate on-going evaluation of river health. Fishing is an important source of protein and income locally and therefore surveys of fish populations and river health are vital not only to understand the TPSF environment but also the implications of environmental changes on local human communities. These data also provide essential information by which to evaluate local sustainable livelihood projects such as the use of fish ponds. While fish may not be the most charismatic of peat swamp forest species, like great-apes or felids, they provide one of the clearest faunal links between people, livelihoods and their natural environment. In areas with high dependence on fish for livelihoods, fish research and conservation projects could be a great opportunity to increase the relevance of environmental research to local communities and to potentially increase local support for conservation projects, as well as providing improved knowledge and understanding of livelihood strategies.

ACKNOWLEDGEMENTS

Many thanks to the research assistants who have supported this research in the field; Iwan, Amat, Krisyoyo, Karno and Unyil. Thanks are given to CIMTROP, the local counterpart who supported the project, as well as OuTrop and their staff and volunteers for their helped with logistics and fieldwork. Finally, thanks to the Rufford Foundation and the International Peat Society for their vital funding.

REFERENCES

1. Dudgeon D, Choowaew S, Ho SC. (2000). *River conservation in Southeast Asia: Conflicts, constraints and compromise.* Pages 279–308 in Boon PJ, Davies BR, Petts GE, eds. Global Perspectives on River Conservation: Science, Policy and Practice. Chichester (UK): John Wiley & Sons.
2. Giam, H., Koh, L.P., Tan, H.H., Miettinen, J., Tan, H.T.W. and Ng, P.K.L. (2012) *Global extinctions of freshwater fishes follow peatland converstion in Sundaland.* Frontiers in Ecology and the Environment, 10:465-470.
3. Merilä, J. (2015). *Baiting improves CPUE in nine-spined stickleback (Pungitius pungitius) minnow trap fishery.* Ecology and evolution, 5(17):3737-42.
4. Ng, P. K. L., J. B. Tay, K. K. P. Lim & Yang, C.M. (1992) *The conservation of the fish and other aquatic fauna of the North Selangor Peat Swamp Forest and adjacent areas.* AWB Publication No. 81, Kuala Lumpur, Malaysia, pp. I-iv, 1-90, figs. 1-110.
5. Ng, P. K. L., J. B. Tay & Lim, K. K. P. (1994) *Diversity and conservation of blackwater fishes in Peninsular Malaysia, particularly in the North Selangor peat swamp forest.* Hydrobiologia, 285, 203-218.
6. Noor, Y. R., Heyde, J., & Suryadiputra, I. N. (2005). *Community-based approach to peatland adaptation and management in Central Kalimantan, Jambi, South Sumatra, Indonesia.* In D. Murdiyarso & H.
7. Norhisyam, M.S., Roshani, O., Zuhairi, A.N.M., Akmal, S.N., Mohd M.Z., Syahril, Ainil Hawa, S., Wahidah, M.N., Harmin, S.A. (2012) *Water Quality, Diversity and Distribution of Blackwater Fishes in Selected Locations of Raja Musa Peat Swamp Forest Reserve.* Malaysian Sciences and Technology Congress 2012.

Abstract No: A-441

PROTECTION AND RESTORATION OF PEAT AREAS FOR ORANGUTANS

Doug Cress[1*], Johannes Refisch[1], Julien Simery[1] and Serge Wich[2]

[1]*Great Apes Survival Partnership (GRASP)*
[2]*Liverpool John Moores University, United Kingdom*

* *Corresponding author: douglas.cress@unep.org*

Large areas of peat swamps in Southeast Asia have been converted through agro-industrial development to palm or pulp plantations over the last 25 years, and today only about 34% of the original peatlands remain under natural forest cover. Lowland humid tropical peat swamp forests are important habitat for Orangutan – which are found only on the islands of Borneo and Sumatra - and other endangered species. Recently, vast forest areas have been affected by fires and the Great Apes Survival Partnership (GRASP) estimates that 28.4% of those fires in Borneo occurred within Orangutan habitat. As critical habitat for Orangutan, the peat forests in Indonesia and Malaysia represent biodiversity hotspots of global importance. Over 80% of the Orangutan's remaining habitat in Borneo could be lost by the year 2080 if the island's current land use policies remain intact, according to the report, *The Future of the Bornean Orangutan: Impacts of Change in Land Cover and Climate* (UNEP-GRASP, 2015), leaving fragmented forests and isolated Orangutan populations that could effectively render the species extinct. GRASP also partnered with UN-Reducing Emissions from Deforestation and Degradation (REDD) and the Max Planck Institute for Evolutionary Anthropology to create an on-line tool that overlays maps containing information on carbon stocks with information on great ape distribution. Special emphasis was given to potential corridor areas that a) could link fragmented and endangered great ape populations and b) have the potential for reforestation. The maps are valuable resources that help decision-makers in great ape range states, the "climate community" and conservation NGOs access data and link the carbon and great ape layers with other context data. The rapid expansion of the palm oil industry is a major driver of deforestation and peatlands destruction, but industry leaders recognize that that business model is short-sighted and ultimately doomed. GRASP is working closely with the Roundtable on Sustainable Oil Palm (RSPO) to drive market demand for sustainably produced palm oil, and is also taking lessons learned and best practices from Asia to Africa, as the Congo Basin contains huge and largely undisturbed peat swamps. Production pressure on forests is increasing in the region, threatening Africa's great apes, but GRASP is committed to understanding and avoiding policies that increase forest destruction, exploring options for fines and incentive payments for sustainable practices, and generating consumer demand for certified sustainable products in order to avoid the environmental crises currently plaguing Southeast Asia.

Keywords: -

Abstract N: A-061

SOUTHEAST ASIAN PEAT SWAMP FOREST BIODIVERSITY LOST BEFORE EVEN BEING RECOGNIZED

Marcel Silvius

Programme Head, Climate-smart Land-use, Wetlands International

**Corresponding author: marcel.silvius@wetlands.org*

As peat swamp forest biodiversity has received relatively little scientific attention the value of this particular wetland habitat for biodiversity conservation is poorly understood. Some comparisons with biodiversity values of other tropical forest habitats lacked reference to special wetland species groups such as freshwater fish and dragonflies. Other studies have noted that that lack of sampling in peat swamp forests may have contributed to a skewed picture. They also noted that peat swamp forests support a substantial number of rare, specialised and threatened species. Peatlands of Southeast Asia harbour a high biodiversity. Surveys in Central Kalimantan, Indonesia, found a total of 54 species of Odonata (dragonflies and damselflies) in June-July 2012. Of the species found, 13 had not been recorded in Central Kalimantan previously, and of these at least five are completely new to science. Six species, originally described from Central Kalimantan and not recorded anywhere since 1953, were rediscovered. At least 16 of the species found during the survey are considered to be of conservation concern. The discovery of at least five new species to science in a relatively short survey indicates a high probability that many more species await discovery in this habitat, and that many undiscovered species may be lost or highly threatened by the rapid demise of peat swamp forest. Our survey was carried out entirely in the lowlands and concentrated on peat swamp areas, including many areas where logging and conversion to agriculture and plantations was on-going and remains a severe threat. Most of the remaining peat swamp forests, including those in protected areas, are affected by drainage from illegal logging channels which contribute to a high fire risk. In 2015 major fires raged through the peatlands of Central Kalimantan and other peatlands in Indonesia, and only larger protected areas appeared to be spared. Some of the peatland endemics and new species that we discovered were found only in small remaining forest patches that seemed very vulnerable to fire. It seems therefore likely that some of these may have already become extinct due to the fires in 2015, even before they could be described and receive a name.

***Keywords**: tropical peat swamp forest, Odonata, Central Kalimantan, peat fires*

Abstract No: A-199

UNIQUE SOUTHEAST ASIAN PEAT SWAMP HABITATS HAVE RELATIVELY FEW DISTINCT PLANT SPECIES

Wim Giesen[1] and Susan Page[2]

[1]*Euroconsult Mott MacDonald, Amsterdamseweg 15, 6814 CM Arnhem, The Netherlands.*
[2]*Department of Geography, University of Leicester, University Road, Leicester, UK.*

**Corresponding author: wim.giesen@mottmac.nl; sep5@le.ac.uk*

SUMMARY

Peat swamp forests of Southeast Asia are often described as having a unique biodiversity. While these watery and nutrient-poor habitats are indeed unique and include a distinct fauna (esp. fish), the peat swamp flora is much less distinct and shares a surprising number of species with other habitats. Out of 1,436 higher plant species found in Southeast Asian swamps (from Thailand to Papua), 1,332 are found in the lowlands (<300m asl). Of the latter, 212 (16.2%) mainly occur in lowland swamps, while 75 species (5.7%) are shared with freshwater swamps on mineral soils and riparian habitats, 49 species (3.7%) are shared with heath forests, 7 species (0.5%) are shared with montane ecosystems, and 86 species (6.5%) are shared with a range of lowland habitats. 116 (8.9%) species occur in lowland swamps only, including freshwater swamps on mineral soils, and 41 of these species (3.1%) are restricted to lowland peat swamps. More than 80% of the peat swamp forest flora is therefore common to a wide range of habitats, while 166 species (12.4%) are opportunistic pioneer or secondary forest species. The largest percentage of the 200+ most common lowland peat swamp species in Southeast Asia occurs on Borneo (97%), followed by Peninsular Malaysia (87%), Sumatra (82%) and Thailand (56%). Due to sea level rise since the last glacial maximum (10-13,000 years BP) the present location of coastal peat swamps is probably at the highest elevation it has been for millennia. This 'landward retreat' of the peat swamp habitat has probably contributed to the relative paucity of unique plant species and an abundance of opportunistic species. Comparison with tropical peatland systems in South America reveals a similar lack of endemic species.

Keywords: *peat swamp flora, unique & opportunistic species*

INTRODUCTION

Peat swamp forests (PSFs) of Southeast Asia are often described as having a unique biodiversity, including endemic tree species and rare and endangered animals (e.g. van der Meer *et al.*, 2008; Yule 2010). These watery and nutrient-poor habitats are indeed unique and include a distinct fauna (esp. fish, Ng *et al.*, 1994, Kottelat & Widjanarti 2005, Kottelat *et al.*, 2006) and the largest remaining populations of species such as false gavial *Tomistoma schlegelii*, Storm's stork *Ciconia stormi*, white-winged wood duck *Asarcornis (Cairina) scutulata*, and Bornean orangutan *Pongo pygmaeus* (Hussen *et al.*, 2009, Yule 2010, Wetlands International 2010). However, botanists have observed that the peat swamp flora is less distinct and appears to share a surprising number of species with other habitats (Anderson 1963, Whitmore 1984). The aim of this study was to assess the degree of floristic distinction of peat swamp forests, and relationships with other habitat types.

METHODS

Over the past five years a simple (Microsoft Excel) database of PSF plant species has been compiled by the author based on species habitat records in key taxonomic references (Flora Malesiana, Tree Flora of Malaya, Flora of Java), scientific papers and grey literature/reports on peat swamp forests (140+ references in all, available from the first author upon request). Where doubtful, for example due to uncertainty regarding taxonomy or locality, species were excluded. Taxonomy follows the Plant List (2010) Version 1.0 (www.theplantlist.org/). It was assessed if a species occurred in lowland peat swamp habitat by referring to the habitat listed in the key taxonomic references mentioned above, and consulting herbarium records made accessible via the Global Biodiversity Information Facility Version 1.2.6 (http://data.gbif.org/), in which all major herbaria with Southeast Asia collections collaborate. Some leniency was required here, and some records list 'swamp' as habitat type, although strictly speaking this could mean freshwater swamps on mineral soils. In such cases the information was not used to add a species to the list, but not used to strike a species from the list. Information on geographic distribution and habitats other than peat swamps in which a species occurs was also obtained from the aforementioned flora and data sheets of the herbarium collections. Few species are fully confined to one habitat, so a single or a just a few examples of occurrence outside the PSF habitat was regarded as probably too rigorous for excluding a species from the restricted PSF list, and these were therefore retained. Information about whether species were pioneer species or common to secondary forest was obtained from Kostermans (1958), Kessler *et al.* (1995), Kessler (2000), van Eijk *et al.* (2009), Giesen *et al.* (2009), Palangkaraya University (2012) and Giesen (2013). Species most often recorded (i.e. 4 times or more) in peat swamp forest species lists were regarded as 'common'; many species are only seldom recorded in peat swamp forests, and a cut-off of four records or more was used to identify common species.

RESULTS

The peat swamp database includes 1,436 plant species found in Southeast Asian swamps, from Thailand and Vietnam to Papua. Of these, 1,332 are lowland swamp species (i.e. <300m asl) and 1,309 are lowland swamp angiosperms, of which 214 (16.2%) mainly occur in lowland swamps (Table 1). Of these 212 species, 116 (8.9%) are found in lowland swamps only including freshwater swamps on mineral soils (75/5.7%) or are restricted to lowland peat swamps (41/3.1%; Table 2); the remainder (96/7.3%) are mainly found in lowland swamps. By far the largest percentage (>80%) of species is found both in peat swamps and a variety of other habitats including many dryland habitats. 405 species are shared with dry lowlands and hill/ridge habitats (300-800m asl), 331 species are shared with a variety of lowland habitats, while 305 species are shared with a range of habitats from dry lowlands to montane habitats (>800m asl). Further, 49 species (3.7%) are shared with heath forests (*kerangas*) only and 7 species (0.5%) are shared with montane/highland ecosystems (i.e. >800m asl) only. [Note that many more species are shared by both peat swamp forests and *kerangas,* and by peat swamp forests and montane habitats, but these are not exclusive to these habitats and are shared among a range of habitats.] A total of 166 lowland swamp species (12.4%) are pioneer species or are characteristic of secondary habitats. The largest percentage of the 200+ most common lowland peat swamp species in Southeast Asia occurs on Borneo (97%), followed by Peninsular Malaysia (87%), Sumatra (82%) and Thailand (56%).

The 41 species restricted to peat swamp forests (Table 2) are generally found on Peninsular Malaysia, Borneo and Sumatra, and 31 species are found in both Indonesia and Malaysia. None of the restricted species are found in Vietnam while only 2 are found in Thailand's PSFs.

Table 1: Swamp species in Southeast Asia: overlap with other habitats

	Habitat	Number of plant species	% of total
1	All Southeast Asian swamps	1436	
2	Variety of habitats including lowland swamps	1332	
	Of which angiosperms*	1309	100
3	Swamps, plus lowlands (>300m asl) to hills/ridges (300-800m asl)	405	30.9
4	Swamps, plus variety of lowland habitats	331	25.3
5	Swamps, plus variety of lowland to montane habitats	305	23.3
6	Lowland swamps & montane habitat	7	0.5
7	Lowland swamps & heath forest (*kerangas*)	49	3.7
8	Predominantly in lowland swamps	212	16.2
	8.a. Only in lowland swamps	116	8.9
	8.a.i: Lowland peat swamps & riparian/mineral soil swamps	75	5.7
	8.a.ii: Restricted to lowland peat swamps	41	3.1
	8.b Mainly in lowland swamps	96	7.3

* Sum of 3-8 = 1309 species

Table 2: Species restricted to peat swamp forests

#	Scientific name	Family	Status	Brunei	Indonesia	Malaysia	Singapore	Thailand	vietnam
1	*Baijiania borneensis* var. *paludicola* Duyfjes	Cucurbitaceae	U			+			
2	*Calophyllum hosei* Ridl. *(C. fragrans)*	Calophyllaceae	C		+				
3	*Calophyllum lowei* Planch. & Triana	Calophyllaceae	R		+				
4	*Calophyllum sundaicum* P.F. Stevens	Calophyllaceae	R		+				
5	*Croton macrocarpus* Ridl.	Euphorbiaceae	R			+			
6	*Crudia venenosa* de Wit	Caesalpiniaceae	R			+			
7	*Cryptocarya enervis* Hook.f.	Lauraceae	R	+	+	+			
8	*Dactylocladus stenostachys* Oliv.	Penaeaceae	C	+	+	+			
9	*Dichilanthe borneensis* Baill.	Rubiaceae	R		+				
10	*Diospyros pseudomalabarica* Bakh.	Ebenaceae	R		+				
11	*Diospyros siamang* Bakh.	Ebenaceae	C	+	+	+	+		
12	*Dyera polyphylla* (Miq.) Steenis *(D. lowii)*	Apocynaceae	C	+	+	+			
13	*Garcinia apetala* Pierre	Clusiaceae	R		+				
14	*Ixora pyrantha* Bremek.	Rubiaceae	R			+			
15	*Knema mamillata* W.J. De Wilde	Myristicaceae	R		+				
16	*Korthalsia paucijuga* Beccari	Arecaceae	U	+	+	+			
17	*Lepidaria oviceps* Danser	Loranthaceae	R	+	+	+			
18	*Lithocarpus andersonii* Soepadmo	Fagaceae	U	+	+	+			
19	*Litsea crassifolia* (Blume) Boerl.	Lauraceae	R		+	+			
20	*Litsea grandis* var. *paludosa* (Kosterm.) Ng	Lauraceae	R		+				
21	*Lophopetalum sessilifolium* Ridl.	Celastraceae	R		+	+			
22	*Mesua congestiflora* P.F. Stevens	Calophyllaceae	R		+				
23	*Palaquium burckii* H.J. Lam	Sapotaceae	C		+	+			
24	*Palaquium cochleariifolium* P. Royen	Sapotaceae	C		+				
25	*Pandanus vinaceus* B.C. Stone	Pandanaceae	R			+			
26	*Parastemon urophyllus (Wall. ex A.DC.) A.DC.*	Chrysobalanaceae	C	+	+	+	+		
27	*Prunus turfosa* Kalkman	Rosaceae	C		+	+			
28	*Sandoricum beccarianum* Baill.	Meliaceae	C		+	+		+	
29	*Shorea hemsleyana* (King) King ex Foxw . ssp. *hemsleyana*	Dipterocarpaceae	C	+	+	+		+	
30	*Shorea inaequilateralis* Symington	Dipterocarpaceae	C	+		+			
31	*Shorea pachyphylla* Ridl.	Dipterocarpaceae	C	+	+	+			
32	*Shorea platycarpa* Heim.	Dipterocarpaceae	C	+	+	+			
33	*Shorea teysmanniana* Dyer ex Brandis	Dipterocarpaceae	C	+	+	+			
34	*Shorea uliginosa* Foxw.	Dipterocarpaceae	C	+	+	+			
35	*Stemonurus scorpioides* Beccari	Stemonuraceae	C	+	+	+	+		
36	*Tarenna adpressa* (King) Merr.	Rubiaceae	U			+	+		
37	*Ternstroemia hosei* Ridl.	Pentaphyllaceae	R			+			
38	*Tristaniopsis beccarii* (Ridl.) Peter G.Wilson & J.T.Waterh.	Myrtaceae	R			+			
39	*Willughbeia grandiflora* Dyer ex Hook.f.	Apocynaceae	R	+	+	+			
40	*Xanthophyllum ramiflorum* Meijden	Polygalaceae	U			+			
41	*Xylopia coriifolia* Ridl.	Annonaceae	C		+	+			
	Status: c=common (17); u=uncommon (5); r=rare (19)	**Totals**		**16**	**31**	**31**	**4**	**2**	**0**

DISCUSSION

Only a relatively small number (41 or 3.1%) of species found in peat swamp forests are found to be restricted to this habitat. This contrasts with findings by Posa *et al* (2011) who report 172 plant species (11% of their total) restricted to peat swamps. Given that total numbers of peat swamp species are similar (1332 in this report versus 1524 for Posa *et al.*, 2011) this difference can only be explained by a different definition of 'restricted'. In the present study, if habitat records were unclear, herbarium records were consulted as these often include habitat descriptions. Regularly, species that are described as 'typical for peat swamps' (e.g. *Campnosperma coriaceum, Combretocarpus rotundatus, Cratoxylum arborescens, Eleiodoxa conferta, Gonystylus bancanus, Ilex cymosa, Lophopetalum multinervium, Madhuca malayana, Syzygium zeylanicum, Tetramerista glabra*; Whitmore 1984) were also found to regularly occur in other habitats and are therefore not exclusive to peat swamp forests. However, a total of about 200+ species (a number similar to Posa *et al.*'s restricted species) are typically found in peat swamp forests and are less commonly found in other habitats – these can be therefore be considered (non-exclusive) peat swamp species. The 17 species restricted to PSFs that are common are either found on Borneo (8 spp.) or on Borneo, Sumatra and Peninsular Malaysia (9 spp.).

Peat swamp forests are rapidly declining and by 2010 only 2.1%% and 4.6% was respectively left in a pristine condition in Kalimantan and Sumatra (Miettinen *et al.*, 2010), while a dramatic 70% decline has occurred in key peat swamp forests in Sarawak during 2000-2014 alone (Deltares 2015). Wetlands International (2010) conclude that 'No example of a hydrologically intact peat dome remains anywhere in Malaysia.' Given the rate and extent of change, it is to be expected that uncommon (5 spp.) and rare (19 spp.) peat swamp forests plant species restricted to this habitat may be under threat. Three of these rare species are known from 1-2 locations/collections and these are either endangered (*Crudia venenosa*, known from type collection in Sabah only), or are possibly extinct (*Croton macrocarpus* from the now fully converted Telok peat swamp forest in Selangor, Peninsular Malaysia; *Knema mamillata* known from peat swamp forest in South Kalimantan only, where this habitat is fully converted). A number of rare species known only from Sarawak and Peninsular Malaysia can be considered endangered given the state of this habitat, and these include *Garcinia apetala, Ixora pyrantha, Litsea crassifolia, Pandanus vinaceus, Tarenna adpressa, Ternstroemia hosei* and *Tristaniopsis beccarii. Lophopetalum sessilifolium*, which is known from Sarawak and the now disappeared peat swamp forests of Sungai Landak in West Kalimantan further completes the list of endangered species.

Near coastal peat swamps in Southeast Asia are only 5-15,000(-25,000) years old and therefore relatively young (Page *et al.*, 2010; Dommain *et al.*, 2011), but the habitat itself is older as peat formations at 75 m BPL (dating from 13,000 years BP) have been found in the South China Sea off the east coast of Peninsular Malaysia (Voris 2000). Peat swamps of Borneo, Sumatra and Peninsular Malaysia may have remained (relatively) inter-connected until about 8-10,000 years BP, when the Sunda shelf was still exposed (Voris, 2000). Due to sea level rise since the last glacial maximum (10-13,000 years BP) the present location of coastal peat swamps is probably at the highest elevation it has been for millennia. According to Hanebuth *et al.* (2011), the development of peat swamps would be especially affected by rates of coastal migration, and the rate of sea level rise would have influenced their degree of development and duration at any specific location. It is hypothesized that this relatively rapid 'landward retreat' of the peat swamp habitat may have contributed to the relative paucity of unique plant species and an abundance of opportunistic species able to adapt. 166 lowland peat swamp species (12.4%) are pioneer species or are characteristic of secondary habitats, which compares to 4% for lowland rain forest in Peninsular Malaysia (Putz & Appanah 1987) and 8.7% for similar habitat in eastern Borneo (Slik & Eichhorn 2003).

Interestingly, a recent study of the floristic composition of lowland tropical peatlands in northern Peru shows that these comparable ecosystems, albeit in a very different geographical setting, likely have no endemic tree species (Draper 2016). Instead, the peatlands provide a habitat for many generalist tree species, as well as some specialists from adjacent white sand and floodplain forests. Draper (2016) attributes the paucity of endemics to the dynamic geomorphological setting of these peatlands, although environmental filtering and dispersal limitations may also play a role. As more information becomes available about the vegetation of peatlands across the tropical zone, it will be interesting to make further comparisons and to establish whether any commonalities can be identified in terms of the processes that determine the assembly of peatland plant communities.

CONCLUSION

Of the 1332 angiosperm plant species found in Southeast Asian peat swamps, only 41 are exclusive to the habitat while about 200+ species are commonly found in this habitat. The vast majority (>80%) of species found in peat swamps are generalists and include a large number (166) of pioneer species and species common in secondary forests.

REFERENCES

1. Anderson, J.A.R. (1963) The Flora of the Peat Swamp Forests of Sarawak and Brunei, including a catalogue of all recorded species of flowering plants, ferns. Gardens Bulletin (Singapore), 20:131-228.
2. Deltares (2015) Flooding projections from elevation and subsidence models for oil palm plantations in the Rajang Delta peatlands, Sarawak, Malaysia. Deltares Report 1207384, commissioned by Wetlands International under the project: Sustainable Peatlands for People and Climate funded by Norad. 76 pp.
3. Draper, F.C.H. (2016) Carbon storage and floristic dynamics in Peruvian peatland ecosystems. Unpublished PhD thesis, University of Leeds, UK. 193 pp.
4. Giesen, W. (2013) Paludiculture: sustainable alternatives on degraded peat land in Indonesia (revised draft). Quick Assessment and Nationwide Screening (QANS) of Peat and Lowland Resources and Action Planning for the Implementation of a National Lowland Strategy. PVW3A10002. Agentschap NL 6201068 QANS

Lowland Development. Euroconsult Mott MacDonald & Deltares. For: Bappenas & Ditjen Sumber Daya Air, PU, Government of Indonesia. Jakarta, 71 pp.

5. Giesen, W., S. Page & L. Graham (2009) Natural Succession in Peat Swamp Forests of Central Kalimantan. Master Plan for the Rehabilitation and Revitalisation of the Ex-Mega Rice Project Area in Central Kalimantan, Technical Review No. 2, 32 pp. Euroconsult Mott MacDonald and Deltares | Delft Hydraulics in association with DHV, Wageningen UR, Witteveen+Bos, PT MLD and PT INDEC. For Government of Indonesia & Royal Netherlands Embassy, Jakarta.
6. Hanebuth, T.J.J., H.K. Voris, Y. Yokoyama, Y. Saito and J. Okuno (2011) Formation and fate of sedimentary depocentres on Southeast Asia's Sunda Shelf over the past sea-level cycle and biogeographic implications. Earth-Science Reviews 104 (2011) 92–110.
7. Hussen, S., S.A. Wich, A.J. Marshall, R.D. Dennis, M. Ancrenaz, R. Brassey, M. Gumal, A.J. Hearn, E. Meijaard, T. Simorangkir and I. Singleton (2009) Orangutan distribution, density, abundance and impacts of disturbance. In: S.E. Wich, S.S.U. Atmoko, T.M. Setia and K. Van Schaik (editors) Orangutans: Geographic variation in Behavioral Ecology and Conservation. Oxford University Press, Chapter 6: 77-96.
8. Kessler, P.J.A., K. Sidiyasa, Ambriansyah and A. Zainal (1995) Checklist of Secondary Forest trees in East and South Kalimantan, Indonesia. The Tropenbos Foundation, Wageningen, The Netherlands. 84pp.
9. Kessler, P.J.A. (editor) (2000) Secondary Forest Trees of Kalimantan, Indonesia. A Manual to 300 selected species. MOFEC & Tropenbos Kalimantan Project, Jakarta & Leiden, 404 pp.
10. Kostermans, A.J.G.H. (1958) Secondary growth on areas of former peat-swamp forest. Proceedings of the Symposium on Humid Tropics Vegetation. Tjiawi, Indonesia, December 1958, p: 155-169.
11. Kottelat, M. and E. Widjanarti (2005) – The Fishes of Danau Sentarum National Park and the Kapuas Lakes area, Kalimantan Barat, Indonesia. The Raffles Bulletin of Zoology, Supplement 13:139-173.
12. Kottelat, M., R. Brit, T.H. Hui and K.E. Witte (2006) *Paedocypris,* a new genus of Southeast Asian cyprinid fish with a remarkable sexual dimorphism, comprises the world's smallest vertebrate. Proceedings Royal Society. B (2006) 273, 895–899. doi:10.1098/rspb.2005.3419
13. Miettinen, J. and S.C. Liew (2010) Status of Peatland Degradation and Development in Sumatra and Kalimantan. Ambio, 39:394–401. DOI 10.1007/s13280-010-0051-2.
14. Ng PKL, Tay JB, Lim KKP. 1994. Diversity and conservation of blackwater fishes in peninsular Malaysia, particularly in the north Selangor peat swamp forest. Hydrobiologia 285: 203–218.
15. Page, S., R. Wüst and C. Banks (2010) Past and present carbon accumulation and loss in Southeast Asian peatlands. PAGES News, 18 (1), 25-26.
16. Palangkaraya University (2012) Silviculture Research & Monitoring- Final Report. Research collaboration between Forestry Department Faculty of Agriculture, Palangkaraya University & the Kalimantan Forest and Climate Partnership (KFCP). Palangkaraya, Central Kalimantan, June 2012, 36 pp.
17. Posa, M.R.C., L.S. Wijedasa and R.T. Corlett (2011) Biodiversity and Conservation of Tropical Peat Swamp Forests. BioScience, 61(1):49-57.
18. Putz, F.E. and S. Appanah (1987) Buried seeds, newly dispersed seeds, and the dynamics of a lowland forest in Southeast Asia. Biotropica 19(4): 326-333.
19. Slik, J.W.F. and K.A.O. Eichhorn (2003) Fire survival of lowland tropical rain forest trees in relation to stem diameter and topographic position. Oecologia (2003) 137:446–455.
20. Van der Meer, P., Beintema, A., Hilligers, P. (2008) Tropical Peat Swamp Forests of Sarawak – Sustainable Use and biodiversity conservation in a changing environment. Alterra Wageningen University and Research Centre, The Netherlands. 35 pp.
21. Van Eijk, P., P. Leenman, I.T.C. Wibisono & W. Giesen (2009) Regeneration and restoration of degraded peat swamp forest in Berbak NP, Jambi, Sumatra, Indonesia. Malayan Nature Journal 2009, 61(3), 223 - 241.
22. Voris, H.K. (2000) Maps of Pleistocene sea levels in Southeast Asia: shorelines, river systems and time durations. Journal of Biogeography, 27: 1153–1167.
23. Wetlands International (2010) A quick scan of peatlands in Malaysia. Wetlands International-Malaysia: Petaling Jaya, Malaysia. 74 pp.
24. Whitmore, T.C. 1984. Tropical rain forests of the Far East. (2nd edition). Oxford University Press, Oxford. 352 + xvi pages. ISBN 0-19-854136-8.

Special Session 5: PEATLAND RESTORATION: THE WAY FORWARD

Abstract No: A-460

RESTORING INDONESIA'S DEGRADED AND POST-FIRE PEATLANDS: POLICY FRAMEWORK, STRATEGIC ACTIONS AND TECHNIQUES

Alue Dohong

Peatland Restoration Agency, Republic of Indonesia

Correspondence: aluedohong@gmail.com

President Republic of Indonesia has enacted the Presidential Regulation No. 1 of 2016 concerning the establishment Indonesia's Peatland Restoration Agency. This new special government agency has been tasked to coordinate and facilitate the restoration activities in 7 provinces covering a total area of 2 million hectares degraded and post-fires peatlands during the period of 2016-2020. In order to achieve this target, therefore, several strategies and actions have been currently implemented among others are the establishment of national and provincial institutions; mapping and zoning of restoration target areas; development of master and technical action plans; preparing restoration guidelines for peatland rewetting and revegetation; communication and awareness activities; and the implementation of restoration interventions on the ground. In the meantime, several restoration techniques have been introduced for restoring degraded and post-fire peatlands in Indonesia covering the construction of peatland rewetting infrastructures, revegetation of bare peatland and sustainable livelihoods interventions. This paper aims to present the current policy, strategic actions and techniques that have been and will be applied for peatland restoration in Indonesia.

Keywords: *degraded peatland, restoration, rewetting, revegetation*

Abstract No: A-461

RESTORING PEAT SWAMP ECOSYSTEM IN THE VILLAGE AREAS

Haris Gunawan

Peatland Restoration Agency, Republic of Indonesia

Correspondence: haris1901@gmail.com

The degradation of peat swamp ecosystem for the development of dry land crops on a massive scale has disturbed the functions of peat swamp as hydrology buffering zone of the surrounding area leading to vulnerability to fires. Based on the restoration experiment that has been carried out since 2010, a better attempt has been made to restore the hydrological conditions as well as natural characteristic of peat swamps through water management improvements. This has been achieved by constructing canal blockings, to increase water level of the canal that allow lands at both side of the canal to get sufficient water for planting of suitable plants. Community support was essential to ensure that intervention was running well. A solution has been implemented on a small-scale known as the 3 RE model entailing: revitalizing water management, replanting local species, and remobilizing community. Implementation of the 3 RE model has been carried out in some villages as targeted restoration areas. In Tanjung Leban Village, six years after experiment showed that survival rate of *(Dyera lowii* (Miq.) Steenis) 87%, bintangor (*Callophylum lowii.*) 69%, geronggang (*Cratoxylon arborescens* (Vahl.) Blume is at 51%, meranti batu (*Shorea uliginosa* Miq.) 40% and 35% of *Mezettia parviflora* Becc with total biomass recovery of 5247.153 kg/ha or 5.247 ton/ha. In Sei Tohor Village, local communities planted traditionally sago palm (*Cratoxylon sago*) in wet peatland with mix planting techniques. Sei Tohor Village system is one of the promising modal for establishment of sustainable community based restoration..

Keywords: *Community based restoration model, restoring peat swamp ecosystem, 3 RE Model*

Gap in pagination due to unavailable paper.

Page 738

SPECIAL SESSION 6: ASIA FLUX

SPECIAL SESSION 6: ASIA FLUX

Abstract No: A-420

ADVANCED ESTIMATION OF TROPICAL PEATLAND/WETLAND ECOSYSTEMS USING INNOVATIVE TECHNOLOGIES

Prof. Mitsuru Osaki, Dr.[1*], Dr. Kazuyo Hirose[2], Dr. Hidenori Takahashi[3], Dr. Nobuyuki Tsuji[4], and Dr. Bambang Setiadi[5]

[1]Research Faculty of Agriculture, Hokkaido University, Japan
[2]Agency for the Assessment and Application of Technology,
[3]Hokkaido Institute of Hydro-climate, Japan,
[4]University of Malaysia Sabah, Malaysia
[5]National Research Council of Indonesia, Indonesia

**Corresponding author: mosaki@chem.agr.hokudai.ac.jp*

SUMMARY

High Carbon Reservoir (HCR) Ecosystems is most important Ecosystem for Carbon Flux affecting strongly Climate Change and Human Impact, where are as Peatland/Wetland (by CO_2 and CH_4), Costal Ecosystem including Mangrove and Coral Reef (by CO_2), and Permafrost (by CH_4). The HCR Ecosystems is very important not only for storage and conservation of carbon, but also the conservation of water stock and biodiversity. To establish the HCR Ecosystems, a MRV system that is coupled with two components – satellite sensing and grand truth data - is urgently required. For this purpose, several satellite data were integrated with ground truth data in our JST-JICA (SATREPS) Project on "Wild Fire and Carbon Management in Peat-Forest in Indonesia", then it is successes to make carbon content mapping and water table mapping in peatland, using model and remote sensing data, which were first success in the world. These mappings are excellent innovated technology, however as these mapping must integrate many data of satellite sensing and grand truth, resolution of mapping is low and it is not real time. As Hyper-sensor of HISUI as next generation sensor have high performance of Ecological Sensing on The HCR Ecosystems including Plant Phenology Changing, which make a possibility to take under ground information, such as nutrients condition, water table in Peatland/Wetlands, carbon accumulation in Peatland/Wetland, Permafrost melting level, so on. Thus, Hyper-sensor function in UAV and Airborne is introduced and discussed on innovation of ecological research, not only The HCR Ecosystems.

Keywords: *MRV, SESAME, Hypersensor, Carbon emission, Groundwater level*

INTRODUCTION

Recent anthropogenic disturbances have had significant impacts to tropical peatland ecosystem. Particularly drainage system constructed in Pearland makes ground water level lower drastically. As a result, huge amount of carbon dioxide (CO_2) is released due to decomposition of soil carbon and peatland fire. It is thought that CO_2 emission will keep on increasing if no appropriate monitoring system is introduced into peatland monitoring.

Thus, the introduction of a carbon credit mechanism such as REDD (Reducing Emissions from Deforestation and Forest Degradation in Developing Countries) and JCM (Joint Credit Mechanism) to protect and rehabilitate tropical peatlands is an urgent issue. COP15 in Copenhagen, **MRV** (Measurement, Reporting and Verification) focused on establishing reference emission levels, national monitoring systems, use of IPCC guidelines, and parameters to be MRV-ed. Therefore, the most reliable methodologies for the "Reference Emission Level (REL)" and "Measuring, Reporting and Verification (MRV) "should be developed based on a precise carbon estimation system using advanced sensors. An effective MRV system must include new integration of data truly necessary, data analysis, modeling and simulation.

MATERIALS AND METHODS

(1) Research field of tropical peatland

Hokkaido University has been studying on Various Topics in tropical peatland; GHG Flux (CO_2, CH_4, N_2O) measuring, Fire Detection and Protection, Water Table Monitoring and Management, Peatland Ecology, Soluble Carbon Monitoring, Peatland Subsidence Monitoring, which is almost 20 years in Central Kalimantan, Indoneshia after Mega Rice Project (Fig. 1). Hokkaido University has been studying on Various Topics in tropical peatland; GHG Flux (CO_2, CH_4, N_2O) measuring, Fire Detection and Protection, Water Table Monitoring and Management, Peatland Ecology, Soluble Carbon Monitoring, Peatland Subsidence Monitoring, which is almost 20 years in Central Kalimantan, Indonesia after Mega Rice Project.

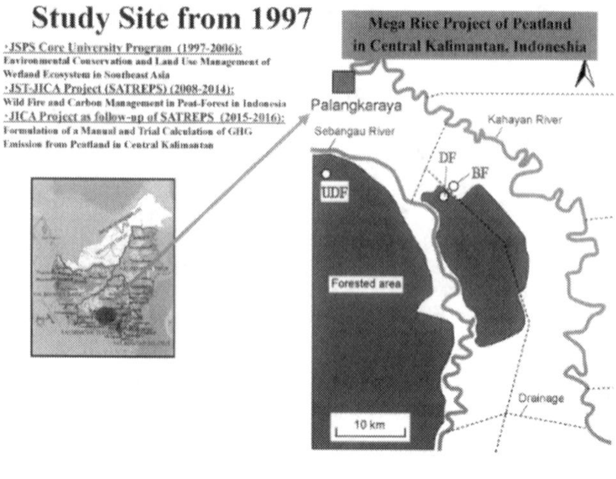

Fig. 1 Map of study site in Central Kalimantan, Indonesia

(2) Estimation of carbon stock and emission from peatland

Peatland monitoring can be conducted at three levels of altitude: from ground, airborne, and space borne. Hokkaido University and collaborative research group with Indonesian experts concluded that eight key elements are essential for reliable and comprehensive monitoring based on over ten-year long-term ground observation data in the peatland of Central Kalimantan, Indonesia. Proposed monitoring system is shown in Figure 2 and the eight key elements are as follows; 1) CO_2 flux and concentration, 2) Hotspots detection, 3) Forest degradation and species mapping, 4) Deforestation, forest biomass changes, 5) Water level and soil moisture, 6) Peat dome detection and peat thickness, 7) Peat-subsidence, and 8)Water soluble organic carbon.

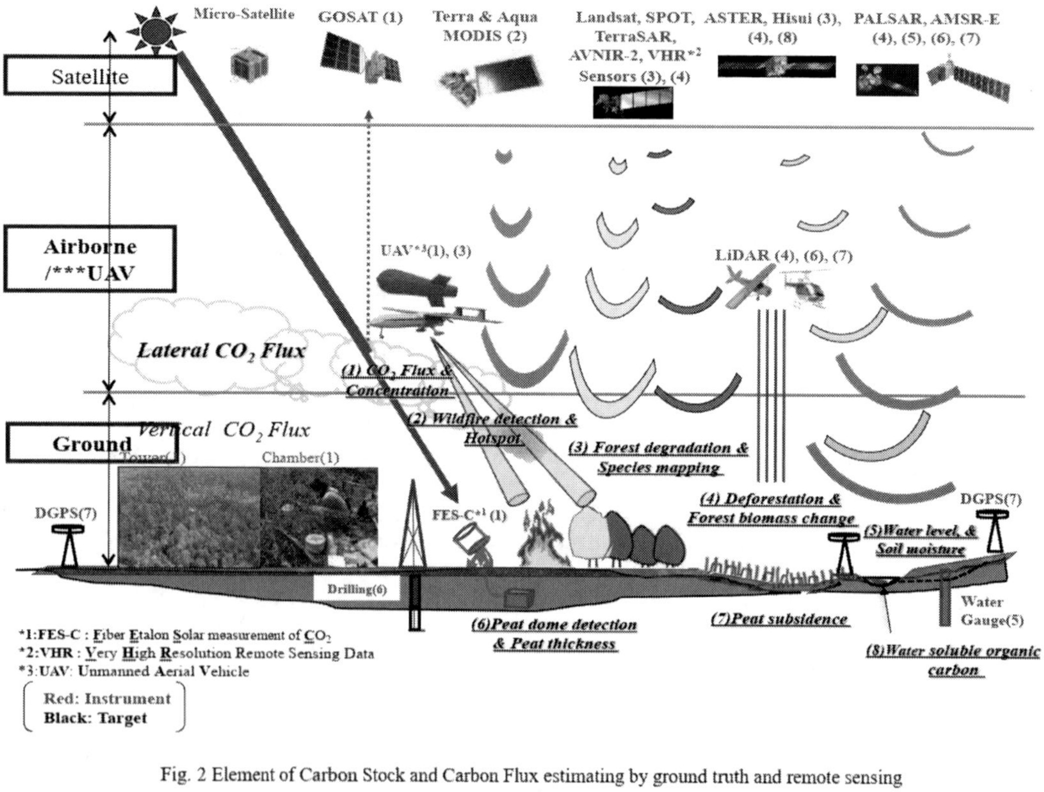

Fig. 2 Element of Carbon Stock and Carbon Flux estimating by ground truth and remote sensing

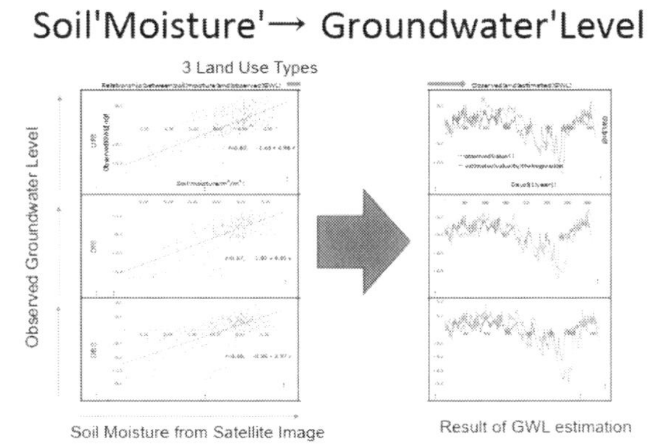

Fig. 3 Groundwater level estimation

RESULTS AND DISCUSSION

(1) Groundwater level mapping

Water level data obtained under different land types were coupled with soil moisture grid data served by the European Centre for Medium-Range Weather Forecasts in order to estimate water level distribution in Central Kalimantan peatland (Fig. 3). Annual CO_2 emission from ecosystem respiration was then estimated by applying the relationship between the water level and net ecosystem CO_2 exchange, which was obtained by eddy covariance in previous studies (Fig. 4). Annual carbon emission from peat fire was estimated based on the relationship between water level observed at a monitoring well and annual peat carbon loss by fire, also established in a previous study.

(2) Guidebook on MRV on Carbon Budget

"GUIDEBOOK FOR ESTIMATING CARBON EMISSIONS FROM TROPICAL PEATLANDS IN INDONESIA" (2016) was published for estimation on annual carbon emission by fire and microorganisms activity in peatland degradation. What is this guidebook about? This guidebook provides step-by-step procedures to: 1) Collect spatial information from remote sensing data sources, 2) Collect field sampling data of GWL and other parameters, 3) Estimate GWL distribution based on the field samples and remote sensing data , 4) Establish a linear relationship (model) between carbon emissions and GWLs, and 5)Predict GWLs several days into the future based on field sampling data.

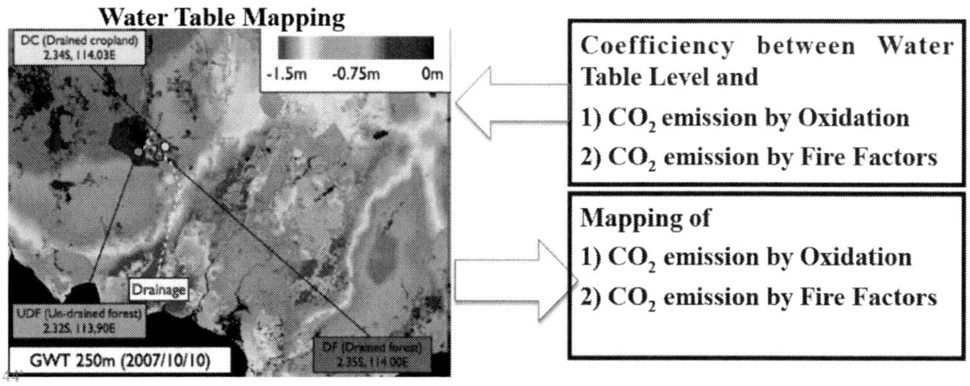

By Wataru Takeuchi, University of Tokyo, Japan

Fig. 4 Water table Mapping and Mapping on CO_2 emission by Fire and Oxidation

CONCLUSION

In non-forest (peat land and agriculture land) REDD+, peat carbon (storage and flux) MRV is one of most important missions. If the MRV system for non-forest REDD+ is established, it will be easier to apply this MRV system to forest REDD/REDD+. To achieve a non-forest REDD+, *"Integrated Monitoring/Sensing System (IMSS)"* on Carbon Flux and Biodiversity in Tropical Peat and Forest is proposed here, which is composed of an "MRV Unit" and a "Capacity Building Unit". As an institution for maintaining the *"Integrated Monitoring/Sensing System (IMSS) with the* "MRV Unit" and the "Capacity Building Unit", we propose a Peat Carbon Initiative. The Peat Carbon Initiative has two functions: 1) the sensing monitoring and capacity building for REDD+ in Indonesia, which is the most advanced country for REDD+ activity, and 2) the establishing of an international network to develop collaboration research for the MRV, especially Verification.

ACKNOWLEDGEMENT

The authors express great thanks for foundation by JSPS Core University Program between Hokkaido University, Japan and Research Center for Biology (LIPI), Indonesia on " Environmental Conservation and Land Use Management of Wetland Ecosystem in Southeast Asia" from 1997 to 2006, and by JST-JICA program on "Wild fire and Carbon Management in Peat-Forest in Indonesia" from 2008 to 2014, for which more than 200 scientists and also 200 students have been jointing. Also this study was conducted as a part of Indonesia-Japan Project for Development of REDD+ Implementation Mechanism (IJ-REDD+) supported by Japan International Cooperation Agency (JICA) and Indonesian Ministry of Environment and Forestry (Kementerian Lingkungan Hidup dan Kehutanan, KLHK).

REFERENCES

1. Gibbs, K. H., Brown, B., Niles, O. J. and Foley, A. J. (2007) Monitoring and estimating tropical forest carbon stocks: making REDD a reality. Environ. Res. Lett: 2 045023: 13.
2. Jaenicke, J., Rieley, J.O., Mott, C., Kimman, P. and F. Siegert (2008) Determination of the amount of carbon stored in Indonesian peatlands. Geoderma: 147: 151–158.
3. Maria Strack ed.(2008) Peatland and Climate Change, International Peat Society, 223.
4. Rieley, J.O., Wüst, R.A.J., Jauhiainen, J., Page, S.E., Wösten, H., Hooijer, A., Siegert, F., Limin, S. H., Vasander H. and Stahlhut, M. (2008) Chapter 6: Tropical peatlands: carbon stress, carbon gas emissions and contribution to climate change process, Maria Strack ed. "Peatlands and climate change" International Peat Society, Finland :148-181
5. Page, S. E., Rieley, J.O. and Banks C.J., 2011, Global and regional importance of the tropical peatland carbon pool, Global Change Biology 17: 798 – 818.
6. Yohei Hamada・Nobuyuki Tsuji・Yasuhito Kojima・Muhammad Abdul Qirom ・Albertus Sulaiman Firmanto ・Yusurum Jagau・Dedy Irawan ・Rumi Naito・Eli Nur Nirmala Sari : GUIDEBOOK FOR ESTIMATING CARBON EMISSIONS FROM TROPICAL PEATLANDS IN INDONESIA (2016), Indonesia-Japan Project for Development of REDD+ Implementation Mechanism, Technical cooperation project between Ministry of Environment and Forestry Indonesia and Japan International Cooperation Agency, Manggala Wanabakti Building, Block VII 6th Floor, Jl. Jenderal Gatot Subroto, Jakarta 10270, Indonesia, March 15, 2016

Abstract No: A-293

CARBON DIOXIDE BALANCE OF A SECONDARY TROPICAL PEAT SWAMP FOREST IN SARAWAK, MALAYSIA

Frankie Kiew[1, 2*], Ryuichi Hirata[2], Takashi Hirano[1], Wong Guan Xhuan[1, 2], Edward Baran Aries[2], Kevin Kemudang[2], Joseph Wenceslaus[2] and Lulie Melling[2]

[1]*Laboratory of Environmental Informatics, Graduate School of Agriculture, Hokkaido University, Sapporo, 060-8589, Japan.*

[2]*Tropical Peat Research Laboratory Unit, Chief Minister's Department of Sarawak, 94300 Kota Samarahan, Sarawak, Malaysia.*

[3]*National Institute for Environmental Studies, Tsukuba 305-8506, Japan*

**Corresponding author: kiew.frankie@gmail.com*

Tropical peatlands are important reservoirs of terrestrial carbon. Therefore, net ecosystem exchange (NEE) of carbon dioxide (CO_2) from this ecosystem is potentially important to the global carbon cycle. We conducted an eddy covariance observation over a secondary tropical PSF in Betong division in Sarawak, Malaysia (01°24'N, 111°23'E). The objectives of our study were: 1) to investigate the environmental controls on CO_2 fluxes of ecosystem photosynthesis (GPP) and ecosystem respiration (RE), 2) to investigate seasonality in CO_2 fluxes and 3) to assess annual NEE and discuss its inter-annual variation. CO_2 and energy fluxes were measured at the height of 41 m from October 2010 using a sonic anemometer/thermometer (CSAT3, CSI) and an open-path CO_2/H_2O analyser (LI7500A, LICOR). CO_2 profile was also measured at six heights for CO_2 storage change estimation. NEE was calculated as the sum of eddy CO_2 flux and CO_2 storage change every 30 minutes and partitioned into RE and GPP using a conventional method. Meteorological data were also measured along with ground water level (GWL) and volumetric soil water content. Annual values for NEE, RE and GPP from 2011 to 2014 were 198 ± 198, 4012 ± 377 and 3815 ± 265 g C m^{-2} yr^{-1} (Mean ± 1 SD) respectively. Annual NEE was most negative in 2011, when annual precipitation was the largest (2,965 mm yr^{-1}). Annual RE decreased with the increase in precipitation except in 2014, with lowest precipitation. Night-time NEE, corresponding to RE, showed a negative linear relationship with both GWL and soil water content ($p<0.05$). Annual GPP increased from 2011 to 2013 but decreased in 2014. Maximum GPP obtained from light-response curve fitting also showed a pattern of increase over time. In general, GPP was slightly lower in the rainy season from December to February because of relatively lower solar radiation.

Keywords:-

Abstract No: A-410

COMPARISON OF SEVERAL STUDIES ON GREENHOUSE GAS (GHG) EMISSIONS FROM PEAT SOIL

Helena Lina Susilawati[1,2*], Yuichiro Furukawa[3], Abdul Hadi[4], Hironori Arai[1], Rosnaeni Sakata[1] and Kazuyuki Inubushi[1]

[1]*Graduate School of Horticulture, Chiba University, Matsudo 648, Matsudo-shi 271-8510 Japan*
[2]*Indonesian Agricultural Environment Research Institute, Central Java, 59182, Indonesia*
[3]*Niigata Agricultural Research Institute Niigata 940-0826, Japan*
[4]*Division of Soil Science, Faculty of Agriculture, Lambung Mangkurat University, Jl. A. Yani Km 36, P.O. Box 1028, Banjarbaru 70714, Indonesia*

* *Corresponding author: inubushi@faculty.chiba-u.jp*

SUMMARY

Peatlands are the most important ecosystems in the global carbon cycle as they store significant amounts of carbon and are important sources of greenhouse gas (GHG) emissions. Recently, large areas of tropical peatlands have been converted to support agroforestry and paddy rice ecosystems in Southeast Asia. Land use change of tropical peatlands is usually accompanied by draining excess water. The drainage of peat soils produces increased carbon dioxide (CO_2), methane (CH_4) and nitrous oxide (N_2O) emissions. In this study, we compare CO_2, CH_4 and N_2O emissions from different land use, drainage and organic-inorganic fertilizer applications from a peatland in Indonesia. The results showed that water table in the different land use categories varied. The CO_2, CH_4 and N_2O emissions were affected by water table, land use and organic/inorganic fertilizer. Water table was negatively related to CO_2 emissions. Lowering of the water table increased CO_2 emissions by approximately 65%. There was a negative relationship between CH_4 fluxes and water table because there was response with water filled pore space (WFPS) and population of methanotrophs. The highest N_2O fluxes were detected at intermediate water depths and were possibly caused by nitrification and denitrification. GHG emissions from the different land use categories varied and were affected by vegetation, precipitation, temperature, quality and supply of organic material, soil moisture, and water field pore space.

***Keywords**: tropical peat soil, drainage, land-use change, GHG emissions*

INTRODUCTION

The main factor in global warming is the increasing concentrations of greenhouse gases (GHG) carbon dioxide (CO_2), nitrous oxide (N_2O), and methane (CH_4) in the atmosphere (IPCC 2007). Carbon dioxide, CH_4, and N_2O contribute approximately 60%, 15% and 5%, respectively, to global emissions (Watson *et al.* 1996). Peatlands play important roles in the global cycling of carbon (C) as they are net sinks of atmospheric CO_2 and under natural decomposition release by-products, such as N_2O, CH_4 and CO_2 (Gorham 1991). Recently, one of the main contributors of GHG emissions from the agricultural sector has been the land use change of peat forest for agriculture development. It has been estimated that peat and forest degradation contribute to about 45% of total GHG emissions from Indonesia (Ridlo 1997). Land use change in tropical peat soils rapidly increases GHG emissions as organic matter decomposition is enhanced.

Globally, peat soils cover more than 420 million ha (Clymo, 1987), which is around 3% of the earth's surface (Immirzi *et al.* 1992; Maltby and Proctor 1996). Approximately 14.9 million ha of peatlands are found in Indonesia, which are estimated to account for 47% of the total tropical peatland area (Ritung *et al.* 2011; Page *et al.* 2011). Peat soils are fragile ecosystems with important biological and hydrological functions. Peat soils have specific properties that are different to mineral soils. Peatlands are now being used for agricultural activities. These conditions resulted the water adjustment and soil improvement that suitable for agriculture or for other land use due to excess water, low nutrient content and high acidity. Land use, the hydrological condition and organic-inorganic fertilizer application strongly affect GHG emissions from tropical peatlands (Hadi *et al.* 2000, 2001). Drainage leads to a number of effects including increased soil decomposition, dissolved organic carbon (DOC) losses, and CO_2 emissions. In addition, land use management in peat soils give impact to large amount of organic nitrogen (N) and C undergo aerobic and anaerobic decomposition by heterotrophic microorganism tend to increase GHG emission (Ismunadji and Soepardi, 1984). Therefore, this paper summarizes data on GHG emissions from several studies representing different land uses, water levels and organic-inorganic fertilizer applications in order to estimate GHG emissions from peatlands in Indonesia.

MATERIALS AND METHODS

Data sources

The data were collected from published papers that reported GHG emissions in a tropical peat area in Kalimantan, Sumatera Indonesia, and from Malaysia as a comparison. Detailed information is provided in Table 1.

RESULTS AND DISCUSSION

Figure 1 shows that there was relationship between CO_2 fluxes and water level the both studies ($p < 0.001$ and $p > 0.01$). This result is similar to the finding reported by Funk *et al.* (1994); Moore and Knowles (1988) and Moore and Dalva (1993), i.e., that CO_2 emission from peat soil are related to water depth. In the study of Furukawa *et al.* (2005), a water level drawdown from the soil surface of 10 cm resulted in a 50% increase in CO_2 emissions. While in Susilawati *et al.* 2015, CO_2 emissions at lower water levels (35 and 55 cm) were approximately 56 and 62% higher, respectively, than the 15 cm water depth. This likely occurred because oxygen diffusion into the soil increases when the water depth is lowered; promoting aerobic decomposition (Silvola *et al.* 1996; Nykanen *et al.* 1998). Consequently, CO_2 emissions from soils increase under aerobic conditions (Moore and Dalva 1993).

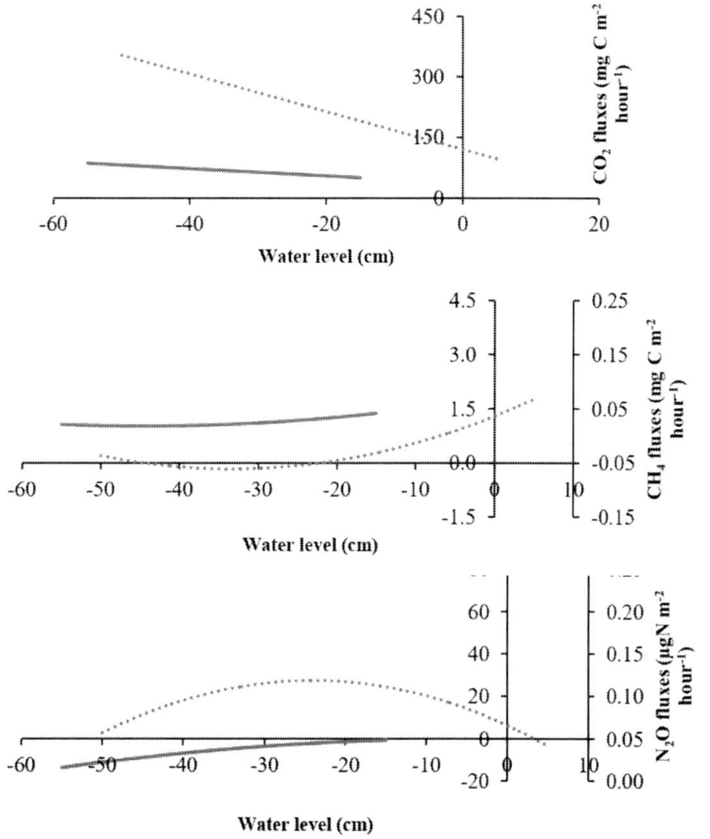

Figure 1: Effect of different water levels on CO_2, CH_4 and N_2O fluxes: Susilawati *et al.* (2015), Furukawa *et al.* (2005)

Water levels were positively related to CH_4 fluxes in both studies ($p < 0.01$ and $p > 0.05$). Furukawa et al. (2005) showed that a lowering of the WT by 10 cm from soil the surface decreased CH_4 emissions by 25%. The CH_4 emissions measured at the 35 cm and 55 cm water depths were 32 and 12% lower, respectively, than those measured at the 15 cm water depth (Susilawati *et al.* 2015). Roulet *et al.* (1992) and Nykanen *et al.* (1998) show that the critical water depth for high CH_4 emissions is approximately 10–20 cm. The reduction in CH_4 emissions due to the lowering of the water depth is probably related to the soil redox potential.

Table 1: Carbon dioxide (CO_2), methane (CH_4) and nitrous oxide (N_2O0 emissions from different land uses in Indonesia

Location	Land-use	Range (min-max) of CO_2 mg C m^{-2} $hour^{-1}$	CH_4 mg C m^{-2} $hour^{-1}$	N_2O µg N m^{-2} $hour^{-1}$	References
South Kalimantan, Kalimantan	Abandoned upland crops field, abandoned paddy fields, secondary forest	113 to 176	0.07 to 0.22	-12.56 to -0.42	Inubushi *et al.* 2003
Jambi, Sumatera	Drained forest, cassava field, upland paddy field, lowland paddy field	30 to 266	0.10 to 4.24	3.77 to 62.21	Furukawa *et al.* 2005
South Kalimantan, Kalimantan	Secondary forest, paddy field, upland crops field, abandoned paddy field, abandoned upland, rice-soybean rotation field	30 to 804	-0.08 to 8.01	-30 to 1040	Hadi *et al.* 2005
Riau, Sumatera (1°30'N, 103°40'E)	Sago palm	24 to 150	-0.04 to 0.99	nd	Watanabe *et al.* 2009
Central Kalimantan, Kalimantan (02°21'S, 114°02E and 2°19'S, 114°01E)	Natural forest, regenerated forest, burned forest, grassland cropland	nd	nd	5 to 2.957	Takakai *et al.* 2010
Central Kalimantan, Kalimantan (2°20'27.74"S, 114°2'16.48"E)	Ferns, sedges, pulp wood	10 to 455	0 to 158.63	-1.05 to 292.29	Jauhiainen and Silvennoinen 2012
South Kalimantan, Kalimantan	Paddy, oil palm, vegetable	-0.38 to 1.30	0.02 to 0.19	-7.78 to 52.34	Hadi *et al.* 2012
Kalampangan, Kalimantan (2°17'-2°21'S, 113°54-114°01'E)	Undrained natural forest, drained forest, burned forest, cropland	80 to 349	-0.02 to 0.36	0.01 to 13.13	Arai *et al.* 2014a, 2014b
Central Kalimantan, Kalimantan (02°12'26"S, 55'00"E)	Flooded forest, drained forest, flooded burnt site, drained burnt site	108 to 340	0.01 to 5.75	-2.40 to 8.10	Adji *et al.* 2014
Tatau, Malaysia (02°57.924N, 112°45.851'E)	Oil palm	90 to 223	nd	131 to 523	Sakata *et al.* 2015
Sarawak, Malaysia (2°49'N, 111°51E; 2°47'N, 111°50E and 2°49'N, 111°56'E)	Sago, oil palm, forest	46 to 533	nd	-3.4 to 176.3	Melling *et al.* 2005, 2007

nd: no data

The trend line between water level and N_2O fluxes in both studies was almost similar but in the Furukawa *et al.* (2005) study no relationship was found. However, Susilawati *et al.* (2015) found nonlinear relationship between water level and N_2O fluxes ($p > 0.01$). Jungkunst *et al.* (2008) also observed a quadratic function between water depths and N_2O fluxes. This indicates that the N_2O emitted during both nitrification and denitrification depends on the soil water content. Both studies found that the highest N_2O emissions are found at intermediate water depths (i.e. xxcm), where it which allows for both aerobic and anaerobic conditions (Davidson *et al.* 2000). Denitrification rates in soil generally depend on the oxygen concentration, the nitrate concentration and the availability of easily metabolizable organic matter (Stepniewski and Stepniewska 1998). Lowering the water table generally increases the N_2O emission rate; however, this relationship is rather complex (Regina *et al.* 1996).
Differences in land-use management affected GHG emissions in the field (Table 1). Differences in emissions between studies were influenced by many factors, primarily water level. Land-use management and water level affect GHG emissions and both of them were not independent factors and influence each other (Furukawa *et al.* 2005). Other factors that affect GHG emissions from peat soil are vegetation; micro-climate, precipitation, temperature, soil physicochemical and biological properties, *e.g.*, quality and supply of organic material, soil moisture and water field pore space (Hadi *et al.* 2001; Furukawa *et al.* 2005, Arai *et al.* 2014b)

CONCLUSIONS

It could be concluded that the contribution of agricultural land use management in tropical peat soil varied on controlling GHG emission.

REFERENCES

1. Adji FF, Hamada Y, Darung U, Limin SH, Hatano R 2014: Effect of plant-mediated oxygen supply and drainage on greenhouse gas emission from a tropical peatland in Central Kalimantan. *Soil Science and Plant Nutrition*, **60**, 216–230.
2. Arai H, Hadi A, Darung U, Limin SH, Hatano R, Inubushi K 2014b: A methanotrophic community in a tropical peatland is unaffected by drainage and forest fires in a tropical peatlands. *Soil Science and Plant Nutrition,* **60**, 577–585.
3. Arai H, Hadi A, Darung U, Limin SH, Takahashi H, Hatano R, Inubushi K 2014a: Land use change affects microbial biomass and fluxes of carbon dioxide and nitrous oxide in tropical peatlands. *Soil Science and Plant Nutrition*, **60**, 423–434.
4. Davidson EA, Keller M, Erickson HE, Verchot LV, Veldkamp E 2000: Testing a conceptual model of soil emissions of nitrous and nitric oxides. *Bioscience*, **50**, 667–680.
5. Funk DW, Pullman ER, Peterson KM, Grill PM, Billings WD 1994: Influence of water table on carbon dioxide, carbon monoxide, and methane fluxes from taiga bog microcosms. *Global Biogeochemical. Cycles*, **8**, 271–278.
6. Furukawa Y, Inubushi K, Ali M, Itang AM, Tsuruta H 2005: Effect of changing groundwater levels caused by land-use changes on greenhouse gas fluxes from tropical peat lands. *Nutrient Cycling in Agroecosystem,* **71**, 81–91.
7. Gorham E 1991: Northern peatlands: role in the carbon cycle and probable responses to climatic warming. *Ecological Application*, **1**, 182–195.
8. Hadi A, Fatah L, Syaifuddin, Abdullah, Affandi DN, Bakar RA and Inubushi K 2012: Greenhouse Gas Emissions from Peat Soils Cultivated to Rice Field, Oil Palm and Vegetable. *Journal of Tropical Soils,* **17**, 105-114
9. Hadi A, Haridi M, Inubushi K, Purnomo E, Razie F, Tsuruta H 2001: Effect of land-use change in tropical peat soil on the microbial population and emission of greenhouse gases. *Microbes and Environment*, 16, 79–86.
10. Hadi A, Inubushi K, Furukawa Y, PurnomoE, Rasmadi M, Tsuruta H 2005: Greenhouse gas emissions from tropical peatlands of Kalimantan, Indonesia. *Nutrient. Cycling in Agroecosystem*, **71**: 73–80.
11. Hadi A, Inubushi K, Purnomo E, Razie F, Yamakawa K, Tsuruta H 2000: Effect of land-use changes on nitrous oxide (NO) emission from tropical peatlands. *Global Change Science*, **2**, 347–358.
12. Immirzi CP, Maltby E, Clymo RS 1992: The global status of peatlands and their role in carbon cycling. A report for the Friends of the Earth by the Wetlands Ecosystems Research Group, Department of Geography, University of Exeter. Friends of the Earth, London.
13. Inubushi K, Furukawa Y, Hadi A, Purnomo E, Tsuruta H 2003: Seasonal changes of CO_2, CH_4, and N_2O fluxes in relation to land-use change in tropical peatlands located in coastal area of South Kalimantan. *Chemosphere*, **52**, 603–608.
14. IPCC 2007: Climate Change 2007: the Physical Science Basis – Summary for Policymakers. http://www.ipcc.ch/SPM2feb07.pdf

15. Ismunadji, Soepardi D 1984: Peat soil: problems and crop production. In. IRRI (ed.), Organic matter and Rice . IRRI, Los Banos, Philippines. Pp. 489-502.
16. Jauhiainen J, Silvennoinen H 2012: Diffusion GHG fluxes at tropical peatland drainage canal water surfaces. *Suoseura*, **63**, 93–105
17. Jungkunst HF, Flessa H, Scherber C, Fiedler S 2008: Groundwater level controls CO_2, N_2O and CH_4 fluxes of three different hydromorphic soil types of a temperate forest ecosystem. *Soil Biology Biochemistry*, **40**, 2047–2054.
18. Maltby E, Proctor MCF 1996: Peatlands: their nature and role in the biosphere. *In*: Lappalainen E. (ed), Global Peat Resources. International Peat Society and Geological Survey of Finland, Jyska Finland.
19. Melling L, Hatano R, Goh KJ 2005: Nitrous oxide emissions from three ecosystems in tropical peatland of Sarawak, Malaysia. *Soil Science and Plant Nutrition*, **53**, 792–805.
20. Melling L, Hatano R, Goh KJ 2005: Soil CO_2 flux from three ecosystems in tropical peatland of Sarawak, Malaysia. *Tellus, 57B*, 1–11.
21. Moore TR, Dalva M 1993: The influence of temperature and water-table position on carbon dioxide and methane emissions from laboratory columns of peatland soils. *Journal of Soil Science*, **44**, 651–664.
22. Moore TR, Knowles R 1988: The influence of water table levels on methane and carbon dioxide emissions from peatland soils. *Canadian Journal of Soil Science*, **69**, 33–38.
23. Nykanen H, Alm J, Silvola J, Tolonen K, Martikainen PJ 1998: Methane fluxes on boreal peatlands of different fertility and the effect of long-term experimental lowering of the water table on flux rates. *Global Biogeochemistry Cycles*, **12**, 53–69.
24. Page SE, Rieley JO, Banks CJ 2011: Global and regional importance of the tropical peatland carbon pool. *Global Change Biology*, **17**, 798–818.
25. Regina K, Nykanen H, Silvola J, Martikainen PJ 1996: Fluxes of nitrous oxide from boreal peatlands as affected by peatland type, water table level and nitrification capacity. *Biogeochemistry*, **35**, 401–418.
26. Ridlo R. 1997. CO_2 emissions at peat reclamation for mega rice project in Central Kalimantan. *Journal Alami.*, **2**, 57-58 (in Bahasa Indonesia).
27. Ritung S, Wahyunto, Sukarman 2011: Peat land map of Indonesia, scale 1:250.000. Indonesian Center for Agro-climate Research and Development, Indonesian Agency for Agriculture Research and Development, Ministry of Agriculture, Jakarta, Indonesia.
28. Rosnaeni Sakata, Shimada S, Arai H, Yoshioka N, Yoshioka R, Kimoto N, Sakamoto A, Melling L, Inubushi K 2015: Effect of soil types and nitrogen fertilizer on nitrous oxide and carbon dioxide emissions in oil palm plantations. *Soil Science and Plant Nutrition*, 61, 48-60.
29. Roulet N, Moore TR, Bubier J, Lafleur P 1992: Northern fens: methane flux and climatic change. *Tellus* (B), **44**, 100–105.
30. Silvola J, Alm J, Ahlholm U, Nykanen H, Martikainen PJ 1996: CO_2 fluxes from peat in boreal mires under varying temperature and moisture conditions. *Journal of Ecology*, **84**, 219–228.
31. Stepniewski W, Stepniewska Z 1998: Oxygenology as a new discipline in the environmental sciences. *International Agrophysics*, **12**, 53–55.
32. Susilawati HL, Setyanto P, Ariani M, Hervani A, Inubushi K 2015: Influence of water depths and soil ameliorations on greenhouse gas emissions from columns of peat soil. *Soil Science and Plant Nutrition*. http://dx.doi.org/10.1080/00380768.2015.1107459.
33. Takakai F, Morishita T, Hashidoko Y, Darung U, Kuramochi K, Dohong S, Limin SH, Hatano R 2006: Effects of agricultural land-use change and forest fire on N_2O emission from tropical peatlands, Central Kalimantan, Indonesia. *Soil Science and Plant Nutrition*, **52**, 662–674.
34. Watanabe A, Purwanto BH, Ando H, Kakuda K, Jong F 2009: Methane and CO_2 fluxes from an Indonesian peatland used for sago palm (*Metroxylon sagu* Rottb.) cultivation: Effects of fertilizer and groundwater level management. *Agriculture, Ecosystem and Environment*, **134**, 14–18.
35. Watson RT, Zinyowera MC, Moss RH, Dokken DJ 1996: Climate Change 1995, impacts, adaptations and mitigation of climate change: Scientific-technical analyses, Intergovernmental Panel on Climate Change. Cambridge University Press, USA. 879p.

Abstract No: A-369

CONTINUOUS MEASUREMENTS OF SOIL CO_2 AND CH_4 FLUXES IN TWO TROPICAL PEAT FORESTS WITH HIGH AND LOW GROUND WATER LEVEL IN SARAWAK, MALAYSIA, BY USING AN AUTOMATED MULTI-CHAMBER SYSTEMS

Ryuichi Hirata[1*], Yosuke Okimoto[2], Takashi Hirano[2], Frankie Kiew[1,3] and Lulie Melling[3]

[1]*National Institute for Environmental Studies, Tsukuba, Japan*
[2]*Research Faculty of Agriculture, Hokkaido University, Sapporo, Japan*
[3]*Tropical Peat Research Laboratory Unit, Sarawak, Malaysia*

* *Corresponding author: hirata.ryuichi@nies.go.jp*

We will present new observations on soil carbon dioxide (CO_2) and methane (CH_4) fluxes, which were started in September 2015 in two tropical peat forests in Sarawak, Malaysia. The sites were one tropical swamp forest with a high groundwater level and one with a low groundwater level. At each site we installed an automated multi-chamber system consisting of 16 chambers of opaque PVD cylinders (40 cm high and 25 cm in internal diameter). The chambers were closed for 225 s sequentially and it took one hour for one rotation. The air from the closed chamber was pumped into a gas analyser (Ultraportable Greenhouse Gas Analyser, Los Gatos Research). In each site, soil and trenching plots were established to divide soil respiration into root respiration and microbial respiration. CO_2 and CH_4 fluxes were found to be strongly affected by groundwater levels, so comparison of tropical peat forests with different groundwater levels is useful for understanding the mechanisms of soil CO_2 and CH_4 fluxes. Degradation of peatlands and less precipitation cause lowering groundwater level. Therefore, we will know how soil greenhouse gases change by land use change and climate change through comparison between tropical swamp forests. Comparison of CO_2 and CH_4 fluxes between these two sites will provide useful information about water management for reducing greenhouse gases.

***Keywords**: -*

Abstract No: A-047

EVALUATION OF CARBON EMISSION FROM TROPICAL PEATLAND IN CENTRAL KALIMANTAN, INDONESIA AND TECHNOLOGY TRANSFER OF THE EVALUATION METHOD

Yohei Hamada[1]*, Nobuyuki Tsuji[1], Hidenori Takahashi[2], Yukihisa Shigenaga[3], Eli Nur Nirmala Sari[4], Rumi Naito[4], Gun Gun Hidayat[5], Hiroshi Kobayashi[6], Shigeru Takahara[7], Nina Yulianti[8], Yusurum Jagau[8] and Mitsuru Osaki[1]

[1] *Hokkaido University, Sapporo, Japan*
[2] *Hokkaido Institute of Hydro-climate, Sapporo, Japan*
[3] *Midori Engineering Laboratory, Sapporo, Japan*
[4] *Starling Resources, Bali, Indonesia*
[5] *Ministry of Environment and Forestry, Jakarta, Indonesia*
[6] *Japan International Cooperation Agency, Jakarta, Indonesia*
[7] *Nippon Chisan Chisui Kyokai, Tokyo, Japan*
[8] *University of Palangka Raya, Palangka Raya, Indonesia*

**corresponding author: yham@chem.agr.hokudai.ac.jp*

SUMMARY

As a part of a technical cooperation for REDD+ in Indonesia, the authors organized existing methodologies into a set of estimation models that can be utilized by Indonesian authorities for estimating carbon emission from tropical peatland. Annual carbon emissions from peat decomposition and peat burning were estimated by groundwater levels, whose spatial distribution had been estimated from soil moisture data. Twice five-day-long on-site training courses were held to transfer these methodologies to Indonesian authorities. In addition, five members who are capable of operations on GIS and satellite imagery were selected from the trainees and dispatched to Japan to deeply learn the model calculation. The advantage of the models applied in this study is their dependency on groundwater level, the most important regulation factor in a wetland ecosystem. Although the applied methodologies were rather simplified and their precision was still rough, estimating carbon emission by the local authorities themselves is a big step toward their enhanced consciousness of the peatland management and expansion of monitoring systems for carbon emission and groundwater level.

Keywords: *carbon emission, groundwater level, REDD+, technology transfer, and tropical peatland*

INTRODUCTION

Indonesia ranks the third in the world for its greenhouse gas (GHG) emissions after US and China, if land-use change is included (World Bank, 2007). In recent decades, a lot of peatland areas have been developed for agricultural use and caused ecosystem degradation, aerobic decomposition of peat carbon, and a huge scale peatland fire. Thus, action plans to prevent deforestation and development of peatland are an urgent issue in tackling climate change problems. Because tropical peatlands have large storage of carbon and also larger impact they get from water level change, the uncertainty in estimating total GHGs emission may become fairly large.
Recently, in the international discussion on climate change, Reducing Emissions from Deforestation and Forest Degradation (REDD) including the role of conservation, sustainable management of forests and enhancement of forest carbon stocks (REDD+) has become highly important. An effective implementation of REDD+ mechanism is essential for the conservation of tropical peatland in Indonesia. For the purpose of enhancing Measurement, Reporting, and Verification (MRV) system in a provincial level, the authors developed and formulated a series of methodologies for evaluating carbon emissions and related parameters, and transferred the related techniques to Indonesian stakeholders.

MATERIALS AND METHODS

1. Development of estimation models

In the study area, previous studies have already found relationships between the lowest value of monthly-averaged groundwater level (GWL) and annual net ecosystem exchange (NEE; Hirano *et al.*, 2016) and annual peat carbon loss by peat burning (Takahashi *et al.*, 2013). Based on these existing information, the monthly lowest GWLs were used to estimate carbon emissions from the peatland. Spatial distribution of GWL was estimated from soil moisture data provided by European Centre for Medium-Range Weather Forecast (ECMWF). Boundaries of peatland and mineral soils were identified based on a peatland map provided by Wetlands International (Wahyunto and Suryadiputra, 2008). Three different peatland types were identified by the analysis of satellite imageries.

2. Technology transfer

On-site trainings were held twice. In the first training course held in August 2015, the trainees conducted fieldwork and laboratory work including installation of GWL monitoring apparatus. In the second training course in December 2015, the trainees conducted PC exercises on the estimation of carbon emissions from peat decomposition and peat burning. To make the technology transfer more effective and efficient, five trainees were selected as core-members and invited to Japan to learn the PC exercises before the second training. The core-members were also involved in the processes of formulating the methodologies of carbon emissions estimation as a guidebook and translating it to Indonesian language.

RESULTS AND DISCUSSION

(1) Estimation of carbon emission from peatland

Actual monitored GWLs in the three peatland types were investigated to observe the linear correlations with the ECMWF soil moisture data. All of them showed good correlations (r = 0.59 – 0.67). A regression analysis was conducted between annual NEE presented by Hirano *et al.* (2016) and GWLs estimated for each peatland type. These regression equations were applied to convert estimated GWLs to annual NEE. The total amount of annual CO_2 emission was 5.37 MtC/year.
A regression analysis was also conducted between the estimated GWLs and annual carbon emission from peat burning from the ex-Mega Rice Project (MRP) area, which was reported by Putra and Hayasaka (2009). Very good correlation was obtained (r = 0.90). The estimated lowest monthly average GWL in 2012 was 0.2856 m below the ground surface, so the carbon emission from peat burning in 2012 in the ex-MRP area was 0.0421 Gt C.

(2) Technology transfer

The core-team members played a great role not only as the teaching assistants in the Advanced Training Course, but also the formulation and translation of the guidebook. In addition, the core-team members presented the contents in the guidebook and the training courses by themselves. From the viewpoint of technology transfer, on how to involve local participants is quite important. In any international cooperative program, however, insufficient communication between Japanese lecturers and the trainees from developing countries is likely to occur. Selection of core-team members would be one of the promising methods for this purpose.

CONCLUSIONS

So many computer-based numerical ecological models applicable for carbon and water balance estimation have been presented. Although many of the models reveal their calculation procedures in academic papers, these procedures are too difficult and complex to understand and utilize at an administrative level. The GWL-based linear regression approach adopted in this study may be very simple relative to the other approaches; however, all the trainees in the second training courses actually succeeded to trace all the steps of calculation and estimate carbon emissions by themselves. This must be a big step toward the utilization of the model at the administrative levels and the improvement of the model in the future.

ACKNOWLEDGEMENT

This study was conducted as a part of Indonesia-Japan Project for Development of REDD+ Implementation Mechanism (IJ-REDD+) supported by Japan International Cooperation Agency (JICA) and Indonesian Ministry of Environment and Forestry (Kementerian Lingkungan Hidup dan Kehutanan, KLHK). The authors greatly thank Muhammad Abdul Qirom, Albertus Sulaiman, Firmanto, and Dedy Irawan for their reading roles in the formulation of the guidebook and in the training courses.

REFERENCES

1. Hirano, T., Sundari, S., and Yamada, H. (2016): CO_2 balance of tropical peatland ecosystems. In: Osaki, M. and Tsuji, N. (eds.) *Tropical Peatland Ecosystems*, 329-337, Springer, Tokyo, Japan.
2. Putra, E.I. and Hayasaka, H. (2009): Carbon emission from severe peat fires in Mega Rice Project area, Indonesia. *Proceedings of Japan Association for Fire Science and Engineering (JAFSE) Annual Symposium*, 226-227, Tokyo, Japan.
3. Takahashi H., Jaya, A., and Limin, S.H. (2013): The scenario of carbon management by water management, firefighting and forest recovery in tropical peatland. *Proceedings of International Symposium on Wild Fire and Carbon Management in Peat-Forest in Indonesia*, 43-49, Palangka Raya, Indonesia.
4. Wahyunto and Suryadiputra, N. (2008): Peatland Distribution in Sumatra and Kalimantan: Explanation of its data sets including source of information, accuracy, data constraints and gaps. *Wetlands International – Indonesia Programme*, Xiii + 52, Bogor, Indonesia.
5. World Bank (2007): *Executive Summary: Indonesia and Climate Change*. Working Paper on Current Status and Policies, 9 p.

Abstract No: A-298

FACTORS CONTROLLING THE CONTRIBUTION OF NET CARBON LOSS AND TOTAL SUBSIDENCE IN A WATER-MANAGED TROPICAL PEATLAND

Kiwamu Ishikura[1], John Bathgate[2] and Ryusuke Hatano[1, 3]

[1]*Graduate School of Agriculture, Hokkaido University*
[2]*APRIL Group, Indonesia*
[3]*Research Faculty of Agriculture, Hokkaido University*

**Corresponding author: ishikura.kiwamu@gmail.com*

SUMMARY

Acacia plantation on tropical peatland has the issue of subsidence and water management is important to avoid serious subsidence. However, subsidence in the well-managed tropical peatland is seldom reported. Objective of this study is to explore the factors controlling net carbon loss (NCL) and total subsidence (S) and the proportion of NCL in S (P_{ncl}) in a water-managed tropical peatland. Our study site had three major land uses: *Acacia* plantation (sites A1 and A2), buffer zone (site B) and natural forest (site N). Small abandoned canals from a previous era exist throughout the natural forest. New canals were constructed only in *Acacia* plantation, following the contour of the peat dome, with aim to avoid water flow from the high to low elevation. CO_2 flux (peat decomposition), groundwater level (GWL), soil temperature (T_s), relative humidity (RH), and total subsidence (S) were measured from once a month to twice a week at each site. Bulk density (BD) and total organic carbon (TOC) in 30 cm depth of topsoil were measured, and amount of litter fall was measured. GCR was defined as the rising rate of GWL, NCL = CO_2 emission − litter fall, $S_{ncl} = 0.1\times\text{NCL} / BD / TOC$, and $P_{ncl} = S_{ncl} / S \times 100$. BD (g cm^{-3}) was 0.14 at A1 and A2, 0.11 at B and 0.10 at N, and TOC was 58% for all land uses. Annual cumulative S (cm yr^{-1}) was 6.3 (A1), 8.0 (A2), 3.3 (B) and 2.5 (N). The S significantly correlated with GWL at B and N, but not at A1 and A2, which suggested irreversible subsidence in *Acacia* plantation. NCL (kg C m^{-2} yr^{-1}) was significantly larger at B (1.06 ± 0.18), followed by A1 (0.52 ± 0.38), A2 (−1.14 ± 1.19) and N (−1.63 ± 0.17) ($p < 0.01$), and significantly correlated with T_s ($p < 0.001$, $R^2 = 0.66$). Annual cumulative S_{ncl} (cm yr^{-1}) was almost linear to the P_{ncl} (%), and both were significantly larger at B (1.6 ± 0.5 and 49.0 ± 16.1, respectively), followed by A1 (0.7 ± 0.6 and 11.9 ± 10.1), A2 (−1.8 ± 2.0 and −22.2 ± 25.4) and N (−2.5 ± 0.6 and −98.1 ± 25.3) ($p < 0.01$ and $p < 0.001$, respectively). The P_{ncl} significantly correlated with T_s ($R^2 = 0.90$, $p < 0.001$). In conclusion, water management in our study site could mitigate CO_2 emission, S and P_{ncl} compared with the other reports in *Acacia* plantation on tropical peatland.

***Keywords**: subsidence, net carbon loss, CO_2 flux, water management, tropical peatland*

INTRODUCTION

Acacia plantation for pulp production is one of the agricultural uses in tropical peatland (Miettinen and Liew, 2010), and Indonesia produced 7 million tons of pulp and 10.5 million tons of paper in 2010 (Obidzinski and Dermawan, 2012).

Acacia plantation on tropical peatland has the issue of subsidence (Hooijer *et al.*, 2012). Subsidence is composed of physical processes (shrinkage and consolidation) and chemical processes (net carbon loss (NCL) from peat materials) (Schothorst, 1977), and it is reported that water management is important to prevent serious peat subsidence (Couwenberg *et al.*, 2010, Hooijer *et al.*, 2012). However, subsidence of water-managed tropical peatland has not been thoroughly reported. Objective of this study is to investigate the controlling factors of NCL and total subsidence (S) and the proportion of NCL in S (P_{ncl}) in a water-managed tropical peatland.

METHODS

We studied at a peat dome in Kampar River basin, Riau, Indonesia. The site was opened in 2010 giving in 2012-13 three major land uses: *Acacia* plantation in 2 and 3 year old (A1 and A2, respectively), buffer zone with 2-3 year old *Melaleuca* sp. trees in which had not yet closed canopy (B) and conserved natural forest (N). The canals were constructed only in *Acacia* plantation, following the contour.

Peat samples were taken from top 25 cm soil by peat sampler to measure bulk density (BD, g cm^{-3}) and total organic carbon content (TOC, g C g^{-1}). CO_2 flux (peat decomposition, mg C m^{-2} h^{-1}) was measured by trench method using closed chamber method with three replications from once a month to twice a week in each site. Soil temperature at 4-cm depth (T_s, °C), atmospheric relative humidity (RH, %), total subsidence (S, cm yr^{-1}) and groundwater level (GWL, m) were also measured. Litter was trapped with three replications in each site, and the carbon content of litter was analyzed. Rate of GWL change (GCR, m day^{-1}), NCL (kg C m^{-2} yr^{-1}), subsidence induced by NCL (S_{ncl}, cm yr^{-1}) and proportion of NCL in total subsidence (P_{ncl}, %) were calculated by the following equations:

$GCR = (GWL(i) - GWL(i-1)) / (\text{date}(i) - \text{date}(i-1))$ (Eq. 1)
$NCL = CO_2$ emission − Litter fall (Eq. 2)
$S_{ncl} = 0.1 \times NCL / BD / TOC$ (Eq. 3)
$P_{ncl} = S_{ncl} / S \times 100$ (Eq. 4)

RESULTS

BD was the largest at A1 and A2, followed by B and N (Table 1). TOC contents were 0.58 g C g^{-1} for all land uses. Annual cumulative CO_2 emission was the largest at A1, followed by A2, N and B ($p < 0.001$, Table 1). GWL (m) was the deepest at A2, followed by A1, B and N ($p < 0.001$, Table 1). T_s was the highest at B, followed by A1, A2 and N ($p < 0.001$, Table 1). RH was the lowest at B, followed by A1, A2 and N ($p < 0.001$, Table 1). According to the results of step-wise multiple regression for log-transformed CO_2 flux using GWL, GCR, T_s, RH, CO_2 flux was higher for the deeper GWL, the higher GCR (faster rise in GWL), higher T_s, and lower RH, respectively (Table 2).

Annual cumulative NCL was significantly larger at B, followed by A1, A2 and lastly N ($p < 0.01$, Table 3). Especially, NCL at A2 and N were negative, which showed the net carbon increase in these sites. Annual cumulative S was the largest at A2, followed by A1, B and N (Table 2). S was significantly correlated with GWL at B ($p < 0.001$) and N ($p < 0.001$), but not at A1 and A2 (Fig. 2). Annual cumulative S was larger in the deeper average GWL (Table 3). Annual cumulative S_{ncl} (cm yr^{-1}) and P_{ncl} (%) were almost parallel to NCL (Table 3), and both were the significantly largest at B, followed by A1, A2 and N ($p < 0.01$ and $p < 0.001$, respectively, Table 3). The P_{ncl} significantly correlated with the average T_s ($R^2 = 0.90$, $p < 0.001$, Fig. 3).

Table 7 Annual cumulative CO_2 emission, litter fall, bulk density (BD), groundwater level (GWL), soil temperature (T_s) and relative humidity (RH). All the values represent average ± standard deviation.

Plot	CO_2 emission	Litter fall	BD	GWL	T_s	RH
	kg C m^{-2} yr^{-1}		g cm^{-3}	m	°C	%
A1	3.7 ± 0.4 ^{a}	3.2	0.14	−0.58 ± 0.12 ^{b}	27.9 ± 1.3 ^{ab}	65.8 ± 9.6 ^{b}
A2	1.7 ± 0.6 $_b$			−0.93 ± 0.15 ^{c}	27.0 ± 1.3 ^{bc}	69.1 ± 8.4 ^{b}
B	1.1 ± 0.2 ^{b}	0.0	0.11	−0.33 ± 0.16 ^{a}	29.1 ± 2.4 ^{a}	57.2 ± 11.5 ^{c}
N	1.3 ± 0.2 ^{b}	2.9	0.10	−0.28 ± 0.12 ^{a}	25.9 ± 0.8 ^{c}	78.1 ± 4.9 ^{a}

Table 8 Results of stepwise multiple generalized linear model for log CO_2 flux using GWL, GCR, T_s and RH.

Plot	Equation	P	R^2
A1	$-0.56 + 0.15\times T_s - 3.88\times GWL + 1.18\times GCR$	< 0.01	0.49
A2	$-1.70 + 0.27\times T_s - 2.77\times GWL + 3.73\times GCR - 0.04\times RH$	< 0.01	0.73
B	$5.52 - 1.92\times GWL - 0.02\times RH$	< 0.05	0.30
N	Not significant		

The annual cumulative CO_2 emission, S and P_{ncl} in A1 and A2 were smaller than the previously reported results in *Acacia* plantation on tropical peatland in the short drainage periods (Table 4). On the other hand, the average *GWL* in A1 and A2 were not different from the previous results, but the standard deviation of *GWL* decreased in A1 and A2 (Table 4).

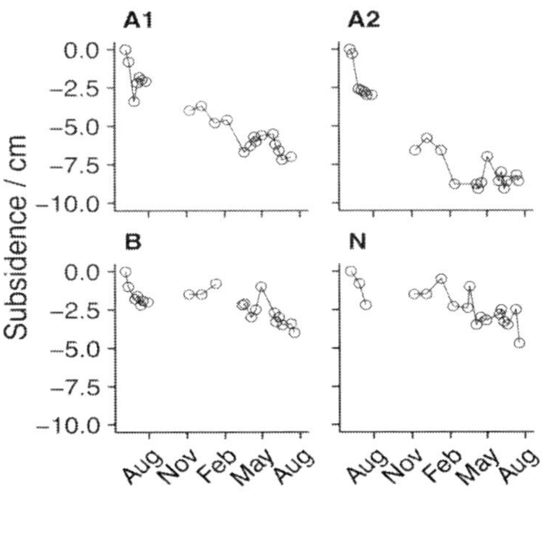

Fig. 1: Time-series of subsidence in *Acacia* plantation (A1 and A2), buffer zone (B) and natural forest (N)

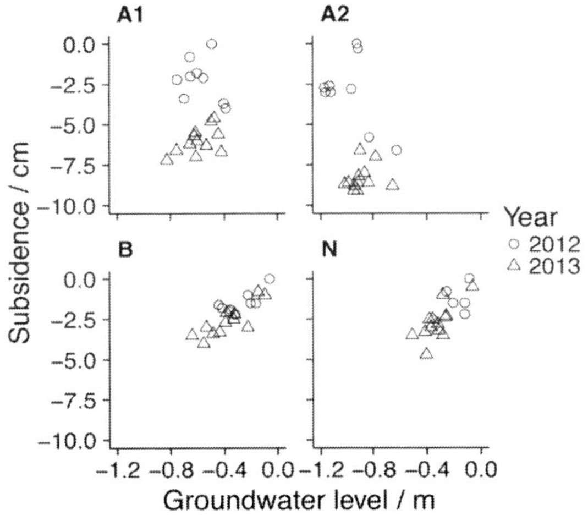

Fig. 2: Relationship between subsidence and groundwater level in *Acacia* plantation (A1 and A2), buffer zone (B) and natural forest (N.

DISCUSSION

CO_2 flux was larger in deeper *GWL* and lower *RH* (Table 1, 2), suggesting that the aerobic condition promoted peat decomposition. Also, CO_2 flux was larger in the higher *GCR* (faster rise of *GWL*, Table 2), indicating that the "soil-drying effect" (Birch, 1958). CO_2 emissions in A1 and A2 were smaller than previous results (Table 4). The average water table depth in our study was similar to previously reported, but with decreased standard deviation of *GWL* (Table 4). This might result in the smaller CO_2 emission in our study due to the decrease of fluctuation of *GWL*.

The S at B and N was significantly correlated with *GWL*, but not at A1 and A2 (Fig. 2). This result indicates the subsidence at B and N was reversible subsidence, while the subsidence in *Acacia* plantation was irreversible subsidence. Also, the annual cumulative S was larger in the deeper average *GWL* within our study site (Table 3), suggesting that higher *GWL* mitigates the annual cumulative S. Note that total subsidence at each land use in our study was very much higher than subsidence in extensive long-term records collected by APRIL.

The P_{ncl} in A1 and A2 were smaller than the previous results (Table 4), resulting from the smaller CO_2 emission. . The largest P_{ncl} was obtained at B, which had the least dense vegetation cover (Table 3). This may be because of following three reasons: 1) small litter fall, 2) high temperature and 3) small *BD* (Table 1). Decrease of *BD* increases P_{ncl} (Eq. 3). Consequently, the difference of *BD* between A1 and B (0.14 and 0.11 g cm^{-3}, respectively) explains 27.2% of the difference of P_{ncl} between them.

Table 9: Annual cumulative net carbon loss (NCL), subsidence induced by NCL (S_{ncl}), total subsidence (S), and proportion of NCL in total subsidence (P_{ncl}). All the values represent average ± standard deviation

Plot	*GWL* m	NCL kg C m^{-2} yr^{-1}	S_{ncl} cm yr^{-1}	S	P_{ncl} %
A1	-0.58 ± 0.12^{b}	0.52 ± 0.38^{a}	0.7 ± 0.6^{a}	6.3	11.9 ± 10.1^{ab}
A2	-0.93 ± 0.15^{c}	-1.14 ± 1.19^{b}	-1.8 ± 2.0^{b}	8.0	-22.2 ± 25.4^{b}
B	-0.33 ± 0.16^{a}	1.06 ± 0.18^{a}	1.6 ± 0.5^{a}	3.3	49.0 ± 16.1^{a}
N	-0.28 ± 0.12^{a}	-1.63 ± 0.17^{b}	-2.5 ± 0.6^{b}	2.5	-98.1 ± 25.3^{c}

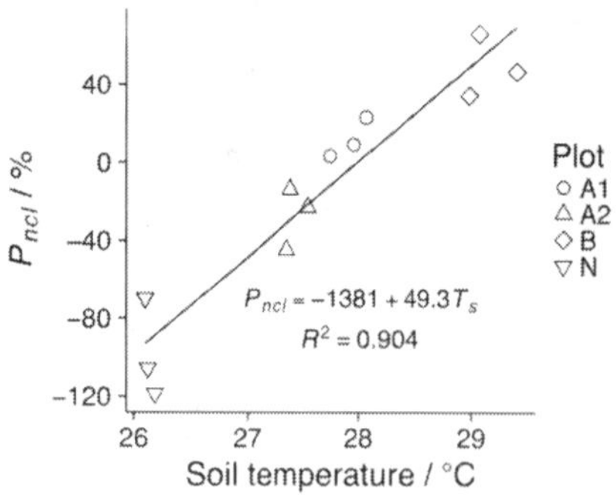

Fig. 3: Relationship between the proportion of net carbon loss in total subsidence (P_{ncl}) and the average soil temperature (T_s)

Table 10: Comparison of drainage year, groundwater level (*GWL*), CO_2 emission, total subsidence (*S*) and proportion of NCL to total subsidence (P_{ncl}) with the published references in *Acacia* plantation on tropical peatland. The values show average ± standard deviation or range.

Reference	Drainage	*GWL*	*S*	CO_2 emission	P_{ncl}
	years	m	cm yr^{-1}	kg C m^{-2} yr^{-1}	%
A1 (this study)	3 to 4	−0.58 ± 0.12	6.3	3.7 ± 0.4	11.9 ± 10.1
A2 (this study)	3 to 4	−0.93 ± 0.15	8.0	1.7 ± 0.6	−22.2 ± 25.4
Hooijer *et al.* (2012)	2 to 5	−0.70 ± 0.20	16.8	17.8	75
Jauhiainen *et al.*(2012)	0 to 5	−0.8		9.4	

CONCLUSION

Water management in our study site could mitigate CO_2 emission, *S* and P_{ncl} compared with the other reports in *Acacia* plantation on tropical peatland. The largest NCL, S_{ncl} and P_{ncl} were obtained in B, but the closed canopy may be able to improve the NCL, S_{ncl} and P_{ncl} by the increase in litter fall and by decrease in soil temperature in the water-managed tropical peatland.

ACKNOWLEDGEMENTS

This study was financially supported by the study and research achievement for short visit program in fiscal year of 2013 in "Re-Inventing Japan Project" of The Japan Society for the Promotion of Science (JSPS). The authors thank Rosef Putra, Sahat Marpaung, Rony L. Silaen and Asep Suwargana (APRIL Group), and Haiki Yupi Maret (Hokkaido University) for supporting our field observations. The authors also thank Dr. Basuki Sumawinata and Dr. Suwardi (Bogor Agricultural University) for giving us helpful suggestions.

REFERENCES

11. Birch H 1958: The effect of soil drying on humus decomposition and nitrogen availability. Plant and Soil, 10, 9–31.
12. Grønlund A, Hauge A, Hovde A, Rasse DP 2008: Carbon loss estimates from cultivated peat soils in Norway: a comparison of three methods. Nutrient Cycling in Agroecosystems, 81, 157–167.
13. Hooijer A, Page S, Jauhiainen J, Lee WA, Lu XX, Idris A, Anshari G 2012: Subsidence and carbon loss in drained tropical peatlands. Biogeosciences, 9, 1053–1071.
14. Jauhiainen J, Hooijer A, Page SE 2010: Carbon dioxide emissions from an Acacia plantation on peatland in Sumatra, Indonesia. Biogeosciences, 9, 617–630.
15. Kool DM, Buurman P, Hoekman DH 2006: Oxidation and compaction of a collapsed peat dome in Central Kalimantan. Geoderma, 137, 217–225.
16. Leifield J, Müller M, Fuhrer J 2011: Peatland subsidence and carbon loss from drained temperate fens. Soil Use and Management, 27, 170–176.
17. Miettinen J, Liew S 2010: Degradation and development of peatlands in Peninsular Malaysia and in the islands of Sumatra and Borneo since 1990. Land Degradation & Development, 21, 285–296.
18. Murayama S, Bakar ZA 1996: Decomposition of tropical peat soils. 2. Estimation of in situ decomposition by measurement of CO2 flux. Japan Agricultural Research Quarterly, 30, 153–158.
19. Obidzinski K, Dermawan K 2012: Pulp industry and environment in Indonesia: is there sustainable future? Regional Environmental Change, 12, 961–966.
20. Schipper LA, McLeod M 2002: Subsidence rates and carbon loss in peat soils following conversion to pasture in the Waikato Region, New Zealand. Soil Use and Management, 18, 91–93.
21. Schothorst C 1977: Subsidence of low moor peat soils in the western Netherlands. Geoderma, 17, 265–291.

Abstract No: A-043

GREENHOUSE GAS (GHG) EMISSIONS IN RELATION TO WATER TABLE AND SOIL AMELIORATION FROM TROPICAL PEAT SOILS

H. L. Susilawati[1, 2*], P. Setyanto[1], A. Miranti[1] and K. Inubushi[2]
[1]*Indonesian Agricultural Environment Research Institute, Jl. Jakenan-Jaken km 05 Pati, Central Java, 59182, Indonesia*
[2]*Graduate School of Horticulture, Chiba University, Matsudo 648, Matsudo-shi 271-8510 Japan*

**Corresponding author: helenalina_s@yahoo.com*

SUMMARY

Tropical peatlands could be a source of greenhouse gases (GHG) as they contain large amounts of soil carbon (C). In order to be suitable for cultivation, peatlands must be drained, limed and fertilised due to the excess water, acidic soil properties and low soil fertility. On the other hand, drainage and soil amelioration may influence GHG emissions. This study was conducted with the aim to understand the effect of water table depth and soil amelioration on GHG emissions on tropical peat soils. Peat soil columns from Central Kalimantan, Indonesia were used to estimate GHG emissions under different water tables and soil amelioration treatments. Twenty seven peat columns were arranged using a randomized block design with two factors; water table position at 15 cm, 35 cm and 55 cm from the soil surface, and secondly 3 different ameliorants: without ameliorant/control, biochar (2.5 tonnes ha^{-1}) + compost (2.5 t ha^{-1}); steel slag (2.5 t ha^{-1}) + compost (2.5 t ha^{-1}). Each of the treatments was replicated three times. Carbon dioxide (CO_2), methane (CH_4) and nitrous oxide (N_2O) emissions from the peat soil columns were measured at weekly intervals for 92 days and analysed using gas chromatography in the Indonesian Agricultural Environment Research Institute (IAERI). Results showed that soil ameliorations influenced CO_2 and N_2O emissions from the peat soil. As application of soil ameliorants tended to stimulate GHG emissions, amelioration of peat soils to enhance soil fertility should be more wisely considered due to the effect on GHG emissions. Estimated GHG emissions from the treatments were between 0.12-0.32 kg CO_2-C $column^{-1}$ 92 $days^{-1}$. Water tables affected the C-stock and net CO_2-C exchange in peat soil columns.

***Keywords**: biochar, columns, compost, steel slag, water table depths*

INTRODUCTION

Tropical peatlands in Indonesia are mostly distributed in Sumatra, Kalimantan and Papua and cover an estimated 14.9 million ha and account for about 47% of the total tropical peatland area which contain an estimated 33-55 Gt of carbon (C) (Wahyunto *et al.*, 2004 and 2005; Ritung *et al.*, 2011; Page *et al.*, 2011). However, tropical forest peatlands are susceptible to large-scale C losses, due to their large C store and rapid rates of deforestation (Langner *et al.*, 2007). Large areas of tropical forest peatland in Indonesia have been converted into agricultural and non-agricultural sectors because of human population growth and economic development. In the agricultural sector, the C-stock in soil is affected by changes in land-use or management practices

Both natural and converted tropical peat soils are important contributors to the global C cycle as they could be a source of carbon dioxide (CO_2), methane (CH_4) and nitrous oxide (N_2O) (Inubushi *et al.*, 2003). Natural peatlands that are used for agricultural activities need to be drained, limed and fertilized due to excess water, low nutrient content and high soil acidity. Drainage and soil management of peat soils influence greenhouse gas (GHG) emissions. Lowering the water table increases C mineralization and CO_2 and N_2O emissions but decreases CH_4 emissions (Moore and Dalva 1993; Regina *et al.*, 1996; Berglund and Berglund 2011). Soil ameliorants are applied not only to enhance the nutrient status of the soil and to improve crop yield but also to reduce GHG emissions (ICCTF 2011; Susilawati *et al.*, 2016). Most studies on soil ameliorations/amendments have been conducted in mineral soils; however, a few publications on the effects of soil amelioration in peat soil have also been reported (Subiksa *et al.*, 2009)

Most GHG studies in tropical peatlands are based on remote sensing data as direct measurements of gas fluxes are expensive, complicated and have technical constraints (Jaenicke *et al.*, 2008; Page *et al.*, 2011). While in the field, daily GHG emissions can vary depending on the climate and hydrologic regime. Therefore, we conducted this study to investigate the influence of water table depth and soil amelioration treatment on peat soil columns adjusted to the same conditions.

MATERIALS AND METHODS

The soil sampling site was located at Jabiren, Pulang Pisau district, in Central Kalimantan province, Indonesia (02°30′52.5′′S, 114°10′11.6′′E). Polyvinyl chloride (PVC) pipes, with length of 100 cm and diameter of 21 cm were used to collect the peat soil.

A randomized block design with two factors was used to establish 3 different water tables depths (15 cm, 35 cm and 55 cm from the soil surface) and 3 different ameliorants (without ameliorant/control, biochar (2.5 tonnes ha^{-1}) + compost (2.5 t ha^{-1}); steel slag (2.5 t ha^{-1}) + compost (2.5 t ha^{-1})). There were three soil columns replicates for each treatment and a total of 27 soil columns were manipulated. Each soil column was placed into a large bucket in the greenhouse and the water table of each bucket was checked using a transparent tube (diameter 10 mm) that was installed on the outside wall of each the bucket. The water tables were checked daily to ensure they remained at a constant level. Rain water was used to set the water depths.

Gas samples for CO_2, CH_4 and N_2O from the soil columns were measured simultaneously once a week for 92 days. Gas samples were measured with the closed chamber method (Sapkota *et al.*, 2014). Gas samples from the chamber were taken once a week using 10-cm^3 syringes and the sampling was repeated 5 times during chamber closure (at 5, 10, 15, 20 and 25 minutes). Gas sampling commenced at 06:00 in the morning on each sampling day. Gas samples were determined by a gas chromatograph (GC) which was equipped with a thermal conductivity detector (TCD) for CO_2 analysis, a flame ionization detector (FID) for CH_4 analysis and an electron capture detector (ECD) for N_2O analysis.

According IPCC (2007), GHG emissions was calculated as $CO_2 + (25 \times CH_4) + (298 \times N_2O)$. Soil carbon stocks (per unit area) was estimated as the product of C concentration (%C), bulk density (g cm^{-3}), and soil volume (m^{-3}) (Warren *et al.*, 2012).

A two-way analysis of variance (water tables and ameliorations) followed the Least Significant Difference (LSD) test were used to compare the mean values of GHG emissions, soil C-stock and net CO_2-C exchange. Soil C-stock changes were measured using C content of the peat soil after treatments. Statistical analyses were conducted using SAS University Edition.

RESULTS AND DISCUSSION

There was no interaction between water tables and ameliorations on GHG emissions (Figure 1). There was no significant effect of water tables on GHG emissions, however, there was a significantly ($P < 0.01$) effect of amelioration on GHG emissions from the peat soil columns. The GHG emissions from all treatments ranged from 0.12-0.32 kg CO_2-C $columns^{-1}$ 92 $days^{-1}$. The GHG emissions from the control treatment were approximately 0.14 kg CO_2-C $columns^{-1}$ 92 $days^{-1}$ and those from the biochar+compost and steel slag+compost treatments were approximately 0.29 and 0.20 kg CO_2-C $columns^{-1}$ 92 $days^{-1}$, respectively. The application of biochar+compost and slag+compost to the peat soil columns significantly increased GHG emissions compared to the control treatment by approximately 51% and 29%, respectively.

The high GHG emissions from the biochar+compost treatment are likely due to the increased availability of the microbial substrates following biochar+compost application and subsequent increased microbial decomposition and mineralization of the organic matter (Smith *et al.* 2010; Jones *et al.* 2011).The application of compost in this treatment increased the availability of the nitrogenous substrates and the easily degradable organic matter for denitrification (Linn and Doran 1984; Dobbie *et al.*, 1999). GHG emissions from the soil amended with biochar depend on the characteristics of the biochar, the addition of exogenous nitrogen and soil properties (Zhang *et al.*, 2010).

The application of steel slag+compost most likely stimulated GHG emissions as the electron acceptor activity associated with steel slag was not sufficient to accept all of the electrons released from the reduction process due to the high organic matter content (Lee *et al.*, 2012). Compost and peat soils have high soil organic matter (SOM) contents and that the application of steel slag+compost caused lower GHG emissions compared to the biochar+compost treatment. In this study, both soil ameliorants increased soil pH. According to Ali *et al.* (2009), the alkaline pH of steel slag contributes to an increase in soil pH. In addition, soil pH increases in tropical acid soils supplied with composts derived from organic products (van der Watt *et al.*, 1991). Although the mechanism of increasing soil pH through the application of organic matter is not fully understood it likely occurs because of the specific adsorption of organic anions and the corresponding release of hydroxyl ions (Hue, 1992). This study showed that the biochar+compost and steel slag+compost treatments increased GHG emissions as both soil ameliorants increased the soil pH.

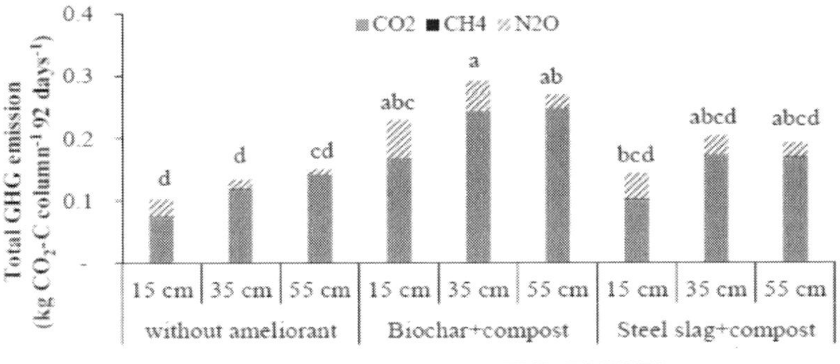

Figure 1: GHG emissions from the different water table depths (15, 35 and 55cm) and soil amelioration treatments in the peat soil columns.

There was no interaction between water table and soil amelioration on the C-stock in the peat soil columns. This study indicates that the water table depth had a major impact on the C-stock, while soil ameliorant was relatively unimportant (Figure 2). The C-stock ranged from approximately 0.96-1.41 kg C column^{-1}. In the different water table treatments, the highest C stock (1.39 kg C column^{-1}) was found when the water table was -35 cm below the soil surface followed by -15 cm (1.30 kg C column^{-1}) and -55 cm (1.00 kg C column^{-1}).
The carbon stock in agricultural soils is an important indication of CO_2 sequestration from the atmosphere (Paustian *et al.* 1998). According to Mazzoleni *et al.* (2012), C-stock in agro-ecosystems depends on C-inputs as well as on its outflows, as regulated by the organic matter decay rates. The C losses in the peat soil columns recorded over the short term may be a transient phenomenon. Therefore, longer-term experiments should be developed to monitor changes that occur over time in response to amelioration at various water table depths. In this study, CO_2 emissions contributed the highest emissions compared to CH_4 and N_2O emissions. The contribution of CO_2 emissions was approximately 81%, followed by N_2O (17.6%) and CH_4 (1.33%) emissions (Figure 1). Deeper water tables tend to lead to more intensified oxidation rates, faster soil decomposition and lower C-stocks in peat soil column (Moore *et al.* 1993).

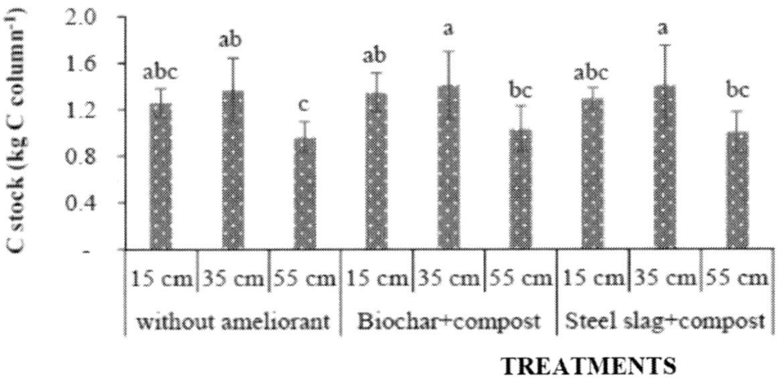

Figure 2: Carbon (C) stock under different water tables depths (15, 35 and 55cm) and soil ameliorations in peat soil columns.

The CO_2-C exchange between the atmosphere and terrestrial systems represents the balance between C inputs by autotrophic fixation and outputs by autotrophic respiration and heterotrophic oxidation of organic material. In this study, net CO_2-C exchange was determined from changes in the topsoil organic C and total CO_2-C fluxes. The net CO_2-C exchange between the atmosphere and terrestrial were approximately 0.75-1.22 kg CO_2-C column^{-1} 92 days^{-1} (Figure 3). There was no interaction between the treatments but there was a significant effect of water table on net CO_2-C exchange in the soil. The lowest values were found at 55 cm below the soil surface. According to Hirano *et al.* (2009) hydrology is one of the most important abiotic factors influencing the net CO_2-C exchange in tropical peatlands. Drawdown of the water table increases oxygen content in the soil, thereby stimulating aerobic decomposition

In this study there was a linear correlation between CO_2 emission and water table. This likely occurred because oxygen diffusion into the soil increases when the water table is lowered; therefore the soil becomes aerated stimulating aerobic decomposition (Silvola *et al.* 1996; Nykanen *et al.* 1998).

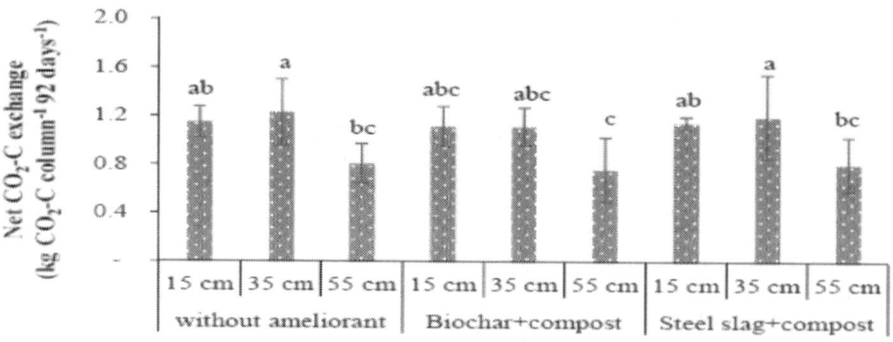

Figure 3: Net carbon dioxide (CO_2-C) exchange under different water tables depths (15, 35 and 55cm) and soil ameliorations in peat soil columns.

CONCLUSIONS

The biochar+compost and steel slag+compost treatments increased GHG emissions from the peat soil columns. Water table drawdown resulted in lower C-stocks and net CO_2-C exchange. Long-term experiments should be developed to monitor changes that occur over time in response to amelioration at various water tables.

ACKNOWLEDGEMENTS

This study was financially supported by Indonesian Agency for Agricultural Research and Development, Ministry of Agriculture.

REFERENCES

36. Aerts R, Ludwig F 1997: Water-table changes and nutritional status affect trace gas emissions from laboratory columns of peatland soils. *Soil Biology and Biochemistry*, **29**, 1691–1698.
37. Ali MA, Lee CH, Lee YB, Kim PJ 2009: Silicate fertilization in no-tillage rice farming for mitigation of methane emission and increasing rice productivity. *Agriculture, Ecosystems and Environment*, **132**, 16–22
38. Berglund Ö, Berglund K 2011: Influence of water table level and soil properties on emissions of greenhouse gases from cultivated peat soil. *Soil Biology and Biochemistry,* **43**, 923–931.
39. Dobbie KE, Mc Taggart IP, Smith KA 1999: Nitrous oxide emissions from intensive agricultural systems: Variations between crops and seasons, key driving variables, and mean emission factors. *Journal of Geophysical Research*, **104**, 26, 891–26,899.
40. Hirano T, Jauhiainen J, Inoue T, Takahashi H 2009: Controls on the carbon balance of tropical peatlands. Ecosystems, **12**, 873–887
41. Hue NV 1992. Correcting soil acidity of a highly weathered Ultisol with chicken manure and sewage sludge. *Communications in Soil Science and Plant Analysis,* **23**, 241–264.
42. IAEA-International Atomic Energy Agency 1992: Manual on measurement of methane and nitrous oxide emission from agricultural. pp. 91. IAEA-TECDOC-674 Vienna: IAEA.
43. Inubushi K, Furukawa Y, Hadi A, Purnomo E, Tsuruta H 2003: Seasonal changes of CO_2, CH_4, and N_2O fluxes in relation to land-use change in tropical peatlands located in coastal area of South Kalimantan. *Chemosphere*, **52**, 603–608.
44. ICCTF (Indonesia Climate Change Trust Fund) 2011: Final report of research and development on peatland management technology for increasing carbon sequestration and mitigating GHG emission. Indonesian Center for Agricultural Land and
45. Jaenicke J, Rieley JO, Mott C, Kimman P, Siegert F 2008: Determination of the amount of carbon stored in Indonesian peatlands. *Geoderma*, **147**, 151–158.
46. Jones DL, Murphy DV, Khalid M, Ahmad W, Edwards-Jones G, DeLuca TH 2011: Short-term biochar-induced increase in soil CO_2 release is both biotically and abiotically mediated. *Soil Biology and Biochemistry*, **43**, 1723–1731.
47. Langner A, Miettinen J, Siegert F 2007: Land cover change 2002–2005 in Borneo and the role of fire derived from MODIS imagery. *Global Change Biology*,**13**, 2329–2340.
48. Lee CH, Kim SY, Villamil MB, Pramanik P, Hong CO, Kim PJ 2012: Different response of silicate fertilizer having electron acceptors on methane emission in rice paddy soil under green manuring. *Biology and Fertility of Soils,* **48**, 435–442.

49. Linn DM, Doran JW 1984: Effect of water-filled pore space on carbon dioxide and nitrous oxide production in tilled and non-tilled soils. *Soil Science Society of America Journal*, **48**, 1267–1272.
50. Mazzoleni S, Bonanomi G, Incerti G, Piermatteo D 2012: New modelling approach to describe and predict carbon sequestration dynamics in agricultural soils. In. Piccolo A. (ed.), Carbon Sequestration in Agricultural Soil. Spinger, London, New York. Pp 291-307.
51. Moore TR, Dalva M 1993: The influence of temperature and water-table position on carbon dioxide and methane emissions from laboratory columns of peatland soils. *Journal of Soil Science*, **44**, 651–664.
52. Nykanen H, Alm J, Silvola J, Tolonen K, Martikainen PJ 1998: Methane fluxes on boreal peatlands of different fertility and the effect of long-term experimental lowering of the water table on flux rates. *Global Biogeochem. Cycles*, **12**, 53–69.
53. Page SE, Rieley JO, Banks CJ 2011: Global and regional importance of the tropical peatland carbon pool. *Global Change Biology*, **17**, 798–818.
54. PaustianK, Andren O, Janzen HH, LaL R, Smith P, Tian G, Tiessen H, Van Noordwijk M, Woorner PL 1997: Agricultural soils as a sink to mitigate CO_2 emissions. Soil Use and Management, 13,230-244
55. Regina K, Nykanen H, Silvola J, Martikainen PJ 1996: Fluxes of nitrous oxide from boreal peatlands as affected by peatland type, water table level and nitrification capacity. *Biogeochemistry*, **35**, 401–418.
56. Ritung S, Wahyunto, Sukarman 2011: Peat land map of Indonesia, scale 1:250.000. Indonesian Center for Agro-climate Research and Development, Indonesian Agency for Agriculture Research and Development, Ministry of Agriculture, Jakarta, Indonesia.
57. Sapkota TB, Rai M, Singh LK, Gathala MK, Jat ML, Sutaliya JM, Bijarniya D, Jat MK, Jat RK, Parihar CM, Kapoor P, Jat HS, Dadarwal RS, Sharma PC, Sharma DK 2014: Greenhouse gas measurement from smallholder production systems: guidelines for static chamber method. International maize and wheat improvement center (CIMMYT) and India Council of Agricultural Research (ICAR), New Delhi, India. p.18
58. SAS Institute 2003: *System for Windows Release 9.1.* SAS Institute, Carry, NC.
59. Silvola J, Alm J, Ahlholm U, Nykanen H, Martikainen PJ 1996: CO_2 fluxes from peat in boreal mires under varying temperature and moisture conditions. *J. Ecology*, **84**, 219–228.
60. Smith JL, Collins HP, Bailey VL 2010: The effect of young biochar on soil respiration. *Soil Biology and Biochemistry*, **42**, 2345–2347.
61. Subiksa IGM, Suganda H, Purnomo J 2009: research development of fertilizer to improve soil nutrient and mitigate greenhouse gas emission in peatland. Report of research collaboration between Indonesian Soil Research Institute and ministry of education. (In Bahasa)
62. Susilawati HL, Setyanto P, Miranti A, Hervani A and Inubushi K 2016: Influence of water depth and soil amelioration on greenhouse gas emissions from peat soil columns. Accepted for publication in Soil Science and Plant Nutrition October 9, 2015.
63. Van der Watt H, Barnard RO, Cronje IJ, Dekker J, Croft GJB, Van der Walt MM 1991: Amelioration of subsoil acidity by application of a coal-derived calcium fulvate to the soil surface. *Nature*, **350**, 146–148.
64. Wahyunto, Ritung S, Suparto and Subagjo H 2005: Peat land distribution and carbon content in Sumatra and Kalimantan. Wetland International- Indonesia Program and Wildlife Habitat Canada (WHC). Bogor – Indonesia.
65. Wahyunto, Ritung S, Suparto, Subagjo H 2004: Map of peatland distribution area and carbon content in Kalimantan. Wetland International- Indonesia Program and Wildlife Habitat Canada (WHC). Bogor – Indonesia.
66. Warren MW, Kauffman JB, Murdiyarso D, Anshari G, Hergoualc'h K, Kurnianto S, Purbopuspito J, Gusmayanti E, Afifudin M, Rahajoe J, Alhamd L, Limin S, Iswandi A 2012: A cost-efficient method to assess carbon stocks in tropical peat soil. *Biogeosciences*, **9**, 4477–4485
67. Zhang A, Cui L, Pan G, Li L, Hussain Q, Zhang X, Zheng J, Crowley D 2010: Effect of biochar amendment on yield and methane and nitrous oxide emissions from a rice paddy from Tai Lake plain, China. *Agriculture Ecosystem and Environment*, **139**, 469–475.

Abstract No: A-402

GREENHOUSE GAS FLUXES AT BOREAL AND ARCTIC WETLAND IN ALASKA

Masahito Ueyama[1*], Hiroki Iwata[2], Hirohiko Nagano[3], Kazuhito Ichii[4] and Yoshinobu Harazono[1]

[1]*Graduate School Of Life And Environmental Sciences, Osaka Prefecture University, Japan*
[2] *Department Of Environmental Sciences, Faculty Of Science, Shinshu University, Matsumoto, Japan*
[3]*Graduate School Of Horticulture, Chiba University, Japan*
[4]*Japan Agency For Marine-Earth Science And Technology, Japan*

**Corresponding author: miyabi-flux@muh.biglobe.ne.jp*

SUMMARY

For evaluating long-term greenhouse gas budget, we have continuously measured CO_2 and CH_4 fluxes by the eddy covariance and gradient methods at boreal and Arctic wetlands in Alaska. In this study, we review our recent activities of the field measurements and synthesis based on multi-site eddy covariance measurements with satellite remote sensing. Based on a decade of measurements, an autumn warming shifted the annual CO_2 balance at a peatland forest on permafrost from sink to source. CH_4 fluxes at the forest played a minor role on the greenhouse gas budget. In contrast, CH_4 fluxes played a major role on greenhouse gas budget at Arctic wet sedge tundra. Synthesizing CO_2 fluxes from 21 eddy covariance towers in Alaska, most of ecosystems acted as growing-season CO_2 sink, and its spatial variability was explained by growing-degree days, satellite derived LAI, and growing-season length. Applying satellite data with a machine learning technique, upscaled CO_2 fluxes showed that GPP and RE were 369 ± 22 and 362 ± 12 Tg C yr^{-1} for Alaska, respectively, indicating an approximately neutral CO_2 budget from 2000 to 2011. Network of long-term eddy covariance measurements can be particularly useful for evaluating greenhouse gas fluxes at high-latitude ecosystems.

Keywords: *alaska, eddy covariance, greenhouse gas flux, synthesis*

INTRODUCTION

Northern high-latitudes contains substantial extent of wetland, most of which are on peat soils with permafrost. The high-latitude soils contained substantial amount of carbon (Ping *et al.*, 2008). These regions currently suffer rapid environmental change, including air and soil warming, permafrost thawing, and hydrological cycle (Chapin *et al.*, 2005; Hinzman *et al.*, 2005). Greenhouse gases (GHGs) budget of high latitude ecosystems are highly vulnerable to the current and predicted future changes associated with stimulated carbon, water, and nutrient cycles.

The eddy covariance method is a strong tool to evaluate GHG fluxes at terrestrial ecosystems (Baldocchi 2014). Currently, a number of eddy covariance sites were established in order to understand carbon and water budgets (Euskirchen *et al.*, 2012; Harazono *et al.*, 2003; Nakai *et al.*, 2013; Kwon *et al.*, 2006; Oechel *et al.*, 2000; Vourlitis *et al.*, 2000; Ueyama *et al.*, 2006, 2014b), role of understory vegetation (Ikawa *et al.*, 2015), methane dynamics (Euskirchen *et al.*, 2014; Harazono *et al.*, 2006; Iwata *et al.*, 2015; Sturtevant and Oechel, 2013), disturbance effects (Iwata *et al.*, 2011; Randerson *et al.*, 2006; Rocha and Shaver, 2011; Welp *et al.*, 2007), and effect of vegetation shift (Beringer *et al.*, 2005; McFadden *et al.*, 2003) in Alaska. Integrating those data and knowledge could provide insight into the current status and possible future state of high-latitude GHGs flux on different spatial and temporal scales.

Key restriction for understanding the high-latitude GHG balance is the limited availability of long-term data, especially of methane (CH_4) flux, and lack of appropriate methodology of spatio-temporal scaling GHG fluxes. Consequently, we have conducted long-term observations at ecosystems in the Arctic (*e.g.*, Harazono *et al.*, 2003, 2006) and boreal (*e.g.*, Iwata *et al.*, 2015; Ueyama *et al.*, 2014b) peat-dominated wetlands in Alaska, obtaining decade of GHG fluxes data. Then, we compared our flux data with those observed in Alaska by other groups (Ueyama *et al.*, 2013b); finally empirically upscaled the GHG fluxes using satellite remote sensing with a machine learning method (Ueyama *et al.*, 2013a, 2014a). In this study, we review our recent activities of the field measurements and synthesis based on multi-site eddy covariance measurements.

METHODS

6. Flux measurements

We have conducted micrometeorological flux measurements at a boreal peat-dominated forest and Arctic wet sedge tundra in Alaska, USA. The tower sites were located at an open black spruce forest at interior Alaska (FAI site; 62.87°N, 147.86°W, Iwata *et al.*, 2012; Ueyama *et al.*, 2006, 2009, 2014b) and a wet sedge tundra in the Arctic Coastal Plain (CMS site; 71.31°N, 156.62°W; Harazono *et al.*, 2003). Both sites were on peat soil over permafrost. Heat, water vapor, and CO_2 fluxes were measured by the eddy covariance method since October 2002 at FAI and from 1999 to 2005 at CMS. CH_4 flux was measured by the eddy covariance method at FAI (Iwata *et al.*, 2015), and by the gradient method (Harazono *et al.*, 2006).

7. Inter-site comparison

Growing-season CO_2 fluxes measured at various landscapes, including Arctic tundra, boreal forests, and fire scars, in Alaska, were synthesized in order to understand spatial and temporal dynamics of CO_2 exchange (Ueyama *et al.*, 2013b). We used flux data from 13 eddy covariance towers (Beringer *et al.*, 2005; Euskirchen *et al.*, 2012; Harazono et al., 2003; Ikawa *et al.*, 2015; Nakai *et al.*, 2013; Kwon *et al.*, 2006; Randerson *et al.*, 2006; Rocha and Shaver, 2011; Ueyama *et al.*, 2014b; Welp *et al.*, 2007), and compared NEE, GPP and RE among the sites. Consistent data processing, including gap-filling and flux partitioning, were applied based on a method proposed by Ueyama *et al.* (2012).

8. Upscaling CO_2 fluxes using satellite remote sensing

Regional CO_2 budget of Alaska was estimated based on upscaling eddy-covariance CO_2 fluxes from the 21 sites using satellite remote sensing and machine-learning techniques (Ueyama *et al.*, 2013a). Eight-day mean GPP and RE were upscaled by inputting green ratio (Harazono *et al.*, 2009) and land surface temperature from MODIS, solar radiation by JRA25 (Onogi *et al.*, 2007), landcover classification, and fire-scar information by Alaska Fire Service into support vector regression model (SVR; Yang *et al.*, 2006; Ichii *et al.*, 2009). Regional NEE was calculated at eight-day interval based on balance between upscaled GPP and RE, and then compared with those by a top-down approach (CarbonTracker; Peters *et al.*, 2007).

RESULTS AND DISCUSSION

9. CO_2 and CH_4 Fluxes at two selected wetlands

Based on the decade of the measurements at FAI, an autumn warming shifted annual CO_2 balance at the peatland forest (FAI) from sink to source (Fig. 1; after Ueyama *et al.*, 2014b). During the same period, GPP and RE increased significantly, indicating that the measured shift of annual CO_2 balance was mainly due to increase in RE. Separating contributions of spring, summer, and autumn months, the positive trends in CO_2 fluxes were mostly contributed by increases in autumn fluxes. This autumn fluxes was highly explained by autumn warming. During the study period from 2003 to 2014, the autumn warming (0.10 °C yr^{-1}; $p = 0.13$) was six times greater than the long-term warming trend between 1905 and 2014 (0.015 °C yr^{-1}; $p < 0.01$) due to decadal climate oscillation. This indicates that most of the shifts in observed CO_2 fluxes could be due to the decadal climate variability.

Both wetlands acted as net CH_4 source throughout the growing season (Fig. 2). The greater emission was observed in early growing season at the Arctic tundra (CMS; Harazono *et al.*, 2006), whereas in late growing season at FAI (Iwata *et al.*, 2015). CH_4 fluxes at CMS were approximately an order of magnitude higher than those by FAI. This could be due to larger oxidation in unsaturated surface soil at FAI than CMS. Consequently, CH_4 fluxes at the peatland forest played a minor role on the GHGs budget; however, CH_4 fluxes played a major role on GHGs budget in the Arctic tundra.

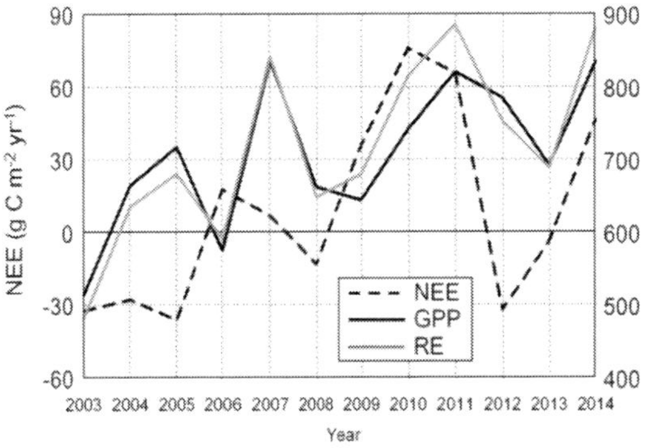

Fig.1 Annual NEE, GPP, and RE from 2003 to 2014 at the peatland forest in Fairbanks (After, Ueyama *et al.*, 2014b).

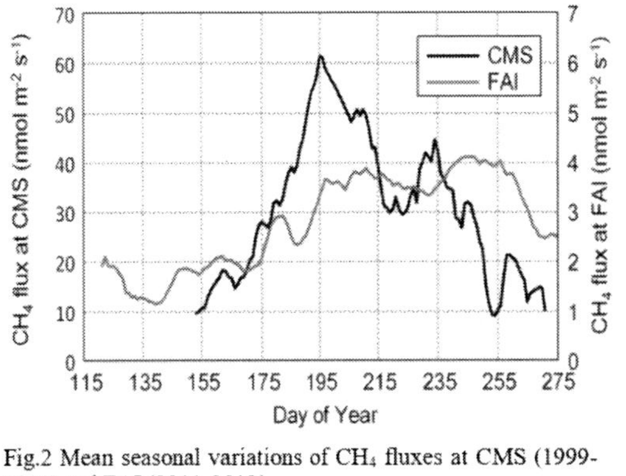

Fig.2 Mean seasonal variations of CH_4 fluxes at CMS (1999-2000) and FAI (2011-2013).

10. Inter-site comparison

Spatial variations of growing-season GPP, RE, and NEE among 13 sites in Alaska were explained by multiple linear regressions using growing degree days, growing season length, and leaf area index by MODIS (Fig. 3; Ueyama *et al.*, 2013b). The regression models were not different among wetland and upland ecosystems, indicating scaling CO_2 fluxes of both wetland and upland was possible using same environmental variables. Except one burned forest and one Arctic tundra, terrestrial ecosystems in Alaska acted as net growing-season CO_2 sink (Fig. 3b).

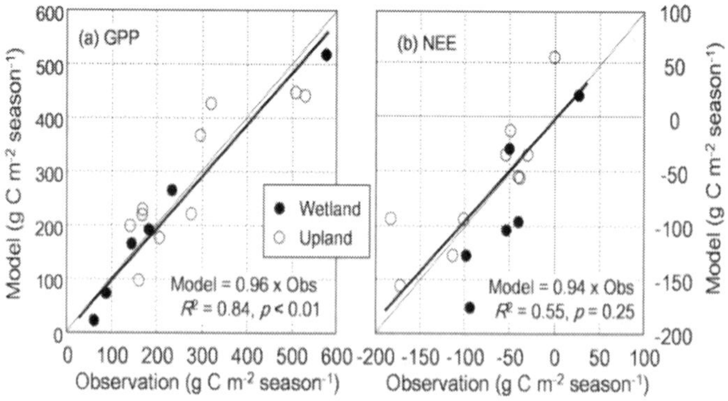

Fig.3 Comparison of growing season GPP (a) and NEE (b) among observations and a multiple liner regression model based on growing degree days, growing season length,

11. Regional fluxes based on upscaling

Applying satellite data with the SVR method, upscaled CO_2 fluxes showed that GPP and RE were 369 ± 22 and 362 ± 12 Tg C yr^{-1} for Alaska (Ueyama et al., 2013a), respectively, indicating an approximately neutral CO_2 budget for the decade. Upscaled fluxes suggested that boreal regions acted as a net annual CO_2 sink, but the arctic tundra acted as a source (Fig. 4). Magnitude and interannual variations in growing-season regional NEE were highly consistent with those estimated by the top-down approach, CarbonTracker. Interannual variability in the regional fluxes positively correlated with air temperature from June to August, indicating Alaska acted as a greater CO_2 sink in warmer years.

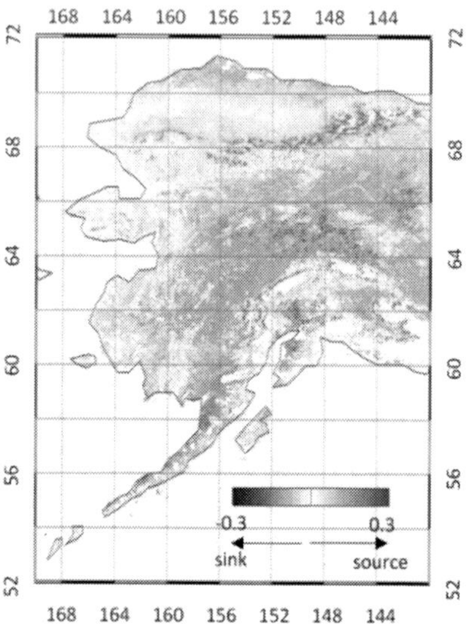

Fig.4 Spatial distribution of upscaled NEE for 2004 (g C m^{-2} yr^{-1}).

FUTURE DIRECTIONS

Based on the decade of the studies, seasonal, inter-annual, decadal, and spatial variabilities in CO_2 fluxes and physical controlling factors are beginning to be clarified; however, biological, ecological and physiological processes behind and further long-term changes are yet to be studies. Decade of the CO_2 fluxes indicate that carbon balance of the high-latitude wetland is highly vulnerable to ongoing warming; thus, continuous monitoring are particularly important at high-latitude wetland. Model-data synthesis could improve our understanding and expand our knowledge into further long and wide spatiotemporal scales (Ueyama *et al.*, 2013a, 2014b, 2016). Continuous monitoring CH_4 fluxes started in recent years at various landscapes in Alaska (Euskirchen *et al.*, 2014; Iwata *et al.*, 2015; Sturtevant and Oechel, 2013). Such measurements will clarify detailed picture of interannual and decadal variations of CH_4 flux at various landscapes. Linking and modelling CH_4 fluxes from towers with other dataset, such as satellite remote sensing, are challenge to estimate regional CH_4 fluxes in future. From 2015, Arctic Challenge for Sustainability (ArCS) project are initiated in Japan, and will facilitate challenging these issues.

ACKNOWLEGEMENTS

Our synthesis activities using eddy covariance towers were conducted based on a collaboration with E. S. Euskirchen of University of Alaska Fairbanks, D. Zona of University of Sheffield, A. V. Rocha of University of Notre Dame, T. Nakai of Nagoya University, and W. C. Oechel of San Diego State University. The study of continuous observations at Fairbanks was supported by IARC/NSF of the US National Science Foundation, IJIS (IARC/JAXA information Systems), and JSPS KAKENHI Grant Number 23310009 and 23248023. The study for upscaling fluxes was supported partly by the Environment Research and Technology Development Fund (RFa-1201) of the Ministry of the Environment, Japan. The study is currently supported by Arctic Challenge for Sustainability.

REFERENCES

1. Baldocchi, D. (2014). Measuring fluxes of trace gases and energy between ecosystems and the atmosphere – the state and future of the eddy covariance method. *Global Change Biology*, **20**, 3600-3609.
2. Chapin, F. S. III., Sturm, M., Serreze, M.C., McFadden, J. P., Key, J. R., Lloyd, A. H., McGuire, A. D., Rupp, T. S., Lynch, A. H., Schimel, J. P., Beringer, J., Chapman, W. L., Epstein, H. E., Euskirchen, E. S., Hinzman, L. D., Jia, G., Ping, C. –L, Tape, K. D., Thompson, C. D. C., Walker, D. A., Welker, J. M. (2005). Role of land-surface changes in arctic summer warming. *Science*, **310**, 657-660.
3. Euskirchen, E. S., Bret-Harte, M. S., Scott, G. J., Edgar, C., Shaver, G. R. (2012). Seasonal patterns of carbon and water fluxes in three representative tundra ecosystems in northern Alaska. *Ecosphere*, **3**, 1–19.
4. Euskirchen, E. S., Edgar, C. W., Turetsky, M. R., Waldrop, M. P., Harden, J. W. (2014). Differential response of carbon fluxes to climate in three peatland ecosystems that vary in the presence and stability of permafrost. *Journal of Geophysical Research Biogeosciences*, **119**, 1576-1595.
5. Harazono, Y., Chikamoto, K., Kikkawa, S., Iwata, T., Nishida, N., Ueyama, M., Kitaya, Y., Mano, M., Miyata, A. (2009). Applications of MODIS-visible bands index, greenery ratio to estimate CO_2 budget of a rice paddy in Japan. *Journal of Agricultural Meteorology*, **65**, 365-374.
6. Harazono, Y., Mano, M., Miyata, A., Yoshimoto, M., Zulueta, R. C., Vourlitis, G. L., Kwon, H., Oechel, W. C. (2006). Temporal and spatial differences of methane flux at arctic tundra in Alaska, *Memories of National Institute of Polar Research, Special Issue*, **53**, 79-95.
7. Harazono, Y., Mano, M., Miyata, A., Zulueta, R. C., Oechel, W. C. (2003). Inter-annual carbon dioxide uptake of a wet sedge tundra ecosystem in the Arctic. *Tellus*, **55B**, 215-231.
8. Hinzman, L. D., Bettez, N. D., Bolton, W. R., Chapin, F. S., Dyurgerov, M. B., Fastie, C. L., Griffith, B., Hollister, R. D., Hope, A., Huntington, H. P., Jensen, A. M., Jia, G. J., Jorgenson, T., Kane, D. L., Klein, D. R., Kofinas, G., Lynch, A. H., Lloyd, A. H., McGuire, A. D., Nelson, F. E., Oechel, W. C., Osterkamp, T. E., Racine, C. H., Romanovsky, V. E., Stone, R. S., Stow, D. A., Sturm, M., Tweedie, C. E., Vourlitis, G., Walker, M. D., Walker, D. A., Webber, P. J., Welker, J. M., Winker, K. S., Yoshikawa, K. (2005) Evidence and implications of recent climate change in northern Alaska and other arctic regions. *Climatic Change*, **72**, 251–298.
9. Ichii, K., Wang, W., Hashimoto, H., Yang, F., Votava, P., Michaelis, A. R., Nemani, R. R. (2009). Refinement of rooting depths using satellite-based evapotranspiration seasonality for ecosystem modeling in California. *Agricultural and Forest Meteorology*, **149**, 1907–1918.
10. Ikawa, H., Nakai, T., Busey, R. C., Kim, Y., Kobayashi, H., Nagai, S., Ueyama, M., Saito, K., Nagano, H., Suzuki, R., Hinzman, L. (2015). Understory CO_2, sensible heat, and latent heat fluxes in a black spruce forest in interior Alaska. *Agricultural and Forest Meteorology*, **214-215**, 80-90.
11. Iwata, H., Harazono, Y., Ueyama, M. (2012). The role of permafrost on water exchange of a black spruce forest in Interior Alaska. *Agricultural and Forest Meteorology*, **161**, 107-115.
12. Iwata, H., Harazono, Y., Ueyama, M., Sakabe, A., Nagano, H., Kosugi, Y., Takahashi, K., Kim, Y. (2015). Methane exchange in a poorly-drained black spruce forest over permafrost observed using the eddy covariance technique. *Agricultural and Forest Meteorology*, **214-215**, 157-168.
13. Iwata, H., Ueyama, M., Harazono, Y., Tsuyuzaki, S., Kondo, M., Uchida, M. (2011). Quick recovery of carbon dioxide exchanges in a burned black spruce forest in interior Alaska. *SOLA*, **7**, 105-108.
14. Kwon, H.-J., Oechel, W. C., Zulueta, R. C., Hastings, S. J. (2006). Effects of climate variability on carbon sequestration among adjacent wet sedge tundra and moist tussock tundra ecosystems. *Journal of Geophysical Research*, **111**, doi:10.1029/2005JG000036.
15. Nakai, T., Kim, Y., Busey, R. C., Suzuki, R., Nagai, S., Kobayashi, H., Park, H., Sugiura, K., Ito, A. (2013). Characteristics of evapotranspiration from a permafrost black spruce forest in interior Alaska. *Polar Science*, **7**, 136-148.
16. Oechel, W. C., Vourlitis, G. L., Hastings, S. J., Zulueta, R. C., Hinzman, L., Kane, D. (2000). Acclimation of ecosystem CO_2 exchange in the Alaskan Arctic in response to decadal climate warming. *Nature*, **406**, 978-981.
17. Onogi, K., Tsutsui, J., Koide, H., Sakamoto, M., Kobayashi, S., Hatsushika, H., Matsumoto, T., Yamazaki, N., Kamahori, H., Takahashi, K., Kodokura, S., Wada, K., Kato, K., Oyama, R., Ose, T., Mannoji, N., Taira, R. (2007). The JRA-25 reanalysis. *Journal of the Meteorological Society of Japan*, **85**, 369–432.
18. Peters,W., Jacobson, A. R., Sweeney, C., Andrews, A. E., Conway, T. J., Masarie, K., Miller, J. B., Bruhwiler, L. M. P., Pétron, G., Hirsch, A. I., Worthy, D. E. J., var der Werf, G. R., Randerson, J. T., Wennberg, P. O., Krol, M. C., Tans, P. P. (2007). An atmospheric perspective on North American carbon dioxide exchange: CarbonTracker. *Proceedings of the National Academy of Sciences*, **104**, 18,925–18,930.
19. Ping, C.-L., Michaelson, G. J., Jorgenson, M. T., Kimbale, J. M., Epstein, H., Romanovsky, V. E., Walker, D. A. (2008). High stocks of soil organic carbon in the North American Arctic region. *Nature Geoscience*, **1**, 615-619.

20. Randerson, J. T., Liu, H., Flanner, M. G., Chambers, S. D., Jin, Y., Hess, P. G., Pfister, G., Mack, M. C., Treseder, K. K., Welp, L. R., Chapin, F. S., Harden, J. W., Goulden, M. L., Lyons, E., Neff, J. C., Schuur, E. A. G., Zender, C. S. (2006). The impact of boreal forest fire on climate warming. *Science*, **314**, 1130-1132.
21. Rocha, A. V., Shaver, G. R. (2011). Burn severity influences postfire CO_2 exchange in arctic tundra. *Ecological Applications*, **21**, 477-489.
22. Sturtevant, C., Oechel, W. C. (2013). Spatial variation in landscape-level CO_2 and CH_4 fluxes from arctic coastal tundra: influence from vegetation, wetness, and the thaw lake cycle. *Global Change Biology*, **19**, 2853-2866.
23. Ueyama, M., Harazono, Y., Kim, Y., Tanaka, N. (2009). Response of the carbon cycle in sub-arctic black spruce forests to climate change: Reduction of a carbon sink related to the sensitivity of heterotrophic respiration. *Agricultural and Forest Meteorology*, **149**, 582-602.
24. Ueyama, M., Harazono, Y., Okada, R., Nojiri, A., Ohataki, E., Miyata, A. (2006). Controlling factors on the inter-annual CO_2 budget at a sub-arctic black spruce forest in interior Alaska. *Tellus*, **58B**, 491-501.
25. Ueyama, M., Hirata, R., Mano, M., Hamotani, K., Harazono, Y., Hirano, T., Miyata, A., Takagi, K., Takahashi, Y. (2012). Influences of various calculation options on heat, water and carbon fluxes determined by open- and closed-path eddy covariance methods. *Tellus*, **64B**, 19048.
26. Ueyama, M., Ichii, K., Iwata, H., Euskirchen, E. S., Zona, D., Rocha, A. V., Harazono, Y., Iwama, C., Nakai, T. and Oechel, W. C. (2013a). Upscaling terrestrial carbon dioxide fluxes in Alaska with satellite remote sensing and support vector regression. *Journal of Geophysical Research Biogeosciences*, **118**, 1266-1281.
27. Ueyama, M., Ichii, K., Iwata, H., Euskirchen, E. S., Zona, D., Rocha, A. V., Harazono, Y., Iwama, C., Nakai, T. and Oechel, W. C. (2014a). Change in surface energy balance in Alaska due to fire and spring warming, based on upscaling eddy covariance measurements. *Journal of Geophysical Research Biogeosciences*, **119**, 1947-1969.
28. Ueyama, M., Iwata, H., Harazono, Y. (2014b). Autumn warming reduces the CO_2 sink of a black spruce forest in interior Alaska based on a nine-year eddy covariance measurement. *Global Change Biology*, **20**, 1161-1173.
29. Ueyama, M., Iwata, H., Harazono, Y., Euskirchen, E. S., Oechel, W. C., Zona, D. (2013b). Growing season and spatial variations of carbon fluxes of arctic and boreal ecosystems in Alaska. *Ecological Applications*, **28**, 1798-1816.
30. Ueyama, M., Tahara, N., Iwata, H., Euskirchen, E. S., Ikawa, H., Kobayashi, H., Nagano, H., Nakai, T., Harazono, Y. (2016). Optimization of a biochemical model with eddy covariance measurements in black spruce forests of Alaska for estimating CO_2 fertilization effects. *Agricultural and Forest Meteorology*, **222**, 98-111.
31. Vourlitis, G. L., Harazono, Y., Oechel, W. C., Yoshimoto, M., Mano, M. (2000). Spatial and temporal variations in hectare-scale net CO_2 flux, respiration and gross primary production of Arctic tundra ecosystems. *Functional Ecology*, **14**, 203-214.
32. Welp, L. R., Randerson, J. T., Liu, H. P. (2007). The sensitivity of carbon fluxes to spring warming and summer drought depends on plant functional type in boreal forest ecosystems. *Agricultural and Forest Meteorology*, **147**, 172-185.
33. Yang, F., White, M. A., Michaelis, A. R., Ichii, K., Hashimoto, H., Votava, P., Zhu, A.-X., Nemani, R. R. (2006). Prediction of continental-scale evapotranspiration by combining MODIS and AmeriFlux data through support vector machine. *IEEE Transactions Geoscience and Remote Sensing*, **44**, 3452–3461.

Abstract No: A-233

SOIL GREENHOUSE GAS EMISSIONS IN TROPICAL PEAT SWAMP FORESTS AND OIL PALM PLANTATIONS IN CENTRAL KALIMANTAN, INDONESIA

Nisa Novita*, Dede Hendry Tryanto, Kristell Hergoualc'h and J. Boone Kauffman

Center for International Forestry Research, 2950 NW Tyler Ave, Apt 305, Corvallis 97330, United States

**Corresponding author: novitan@onid.oregonstate.edu*

Conversion of tropical peat swamp forests to oil palm plantations disrupts the carbon (C) and nitrogen (N) cycles, and contributes substantially to greenhouse gas emissions into the atmosphere. Despite the importance of tropical peat swamp forests and the impacts of their conversion on global C and N cycles, only a small number of published studies directly compare GHG emissions in undisturbed forest and oil palm plantation ecosystems. To fill this knowledge gap, we conducted a series of monthly soil CO_2, CH_4 and N_2O emissions measurements using the dynamic (CO_2) and static (CH_4 and N_2O) chamber methods in three forest plots and three oil palm plantations over 1.5 year. Soil respiration was in addition partitioned into root-based and peat-based respiration by trenching. Annual soil respiration rates amounted to 14.9 ± 0.4 and 12.1 ± 0.2 Mg C ha^{-1} yr^{-1} in the forests and oil palm plantations, respectively, and peat respiration represented 57% of total emissions in the forest and 72-89% in the plantations depending on their age. Annual CH_4 emission rates were 52.4 ± 7.4 and 0.4 ± 1.2 kg C ha^{-1} yr^{-1} and annual N_2O emissions rates 0.5 ± 0.1 and 5.5 ± 0.6 kg N ha^{-1} yr^{-1} in the forests and oil palm plantations, respectively. The temporal variation of the fluxes did not show any significant pattern between dry and wet months. The water table depth, water-filled pore space and peat temperature were the main factors controlling CO_2, CH_4 and N_2O emissions, respectively. Our results indicate that peat swamp forest conversion to oil palm plantation promoted peat soil organic matter decomposition, decreased substantially CH_4 emissions and exacerbated N_2O emissions, mainly as a result of nitrogen fertilization in the plantations.

Keywords: -

Abstract No: A-078

SPATIAL DISTRIBUTION OF N_2O FLUX FROM AGRICULTURAL FIELD ON TROPICAL PEATLAND, KALIMANTAN, INDONESIA

Yo Toma[1], Fumiaki Takakai[2], Kiwamu Ishikura[3], Untung Darung[4], Kanta Kuramochi[3], Suwido H. Limin[4], Ryusuke Hatano[3]

[1]*Faculty of Agriculture, Ehime University, Japan;*
[2]*Faculty of Bioresource Sciences, Akita Prefectural University, Japan*
[3]*Graduate School of Agriculture, Hokkaido University, Japan*
[4]*Faculty of Agriculture, University of Palangka Raya, Indonesia*

**Corresponding author: toma@agr.ehime-u.ac.jp*

SUMMARY

Nitrous oxide (N_2O) is one of major greenhouse gases emitted from agricultural field. In drained tropical peatland, significant amount of N_2O emission (maximum 698 kg N ha^{-1} y^{-1}) has been reported from an agricultural field in Palangka Raya, Kalimantan, Indonesia. Due to high organic matter and mineral nitrogen supply by peat decomposition, N_2O was mainly produced by denitrification process in rainy season and not mainly from applied nitrogen fertilizer. However, it is unknown whether large amount of N_2O emission can be observed from other agricultural fields on drained tropical peatland in the region. In this study, N_2O fluxes from 10 agricultural fields located in the same village and analyzed controlling factor of N_2O flux were investigated. In rainy (February, 2006) and dry (September, 2006) seasons, N_2O fluxes were measured at 10 fields, in which vegetables were cultivated, soil physical- and chemical-properties were measured. N_2O flux in rainy season (0.008-3.46 mg N m^{-2} h^{-1}) was significantly ($P < 0.01$) higher than in dry season (0.008-0.205 mg N m^{-2} h^{-1}). Positive relationships were observed between N_2O and CO_2 fluxes ($R^2 = 0.56$, $P < 0.01$) and soil nitrate concentration ($R^2 = 0.30$, $P < 0.10$) in rainy season indicated that N_2O production was influenced by peat decomposition and denitrification. Significant positive correlation between N_2O flux and soil sulfate concentration was also observed in rainy season ($R^2 = 0.86$, $P < 0.001$). Land drainage status might not influence N_2O production, because spatial distribution of N_2O flux was not related to canal location and water filled pore space. Soil C and N concentrations and C:N ratio did not influenced N_2O flux in rainy season. Field management practice such as multiple cultivation, plowing, and soil improving material application as well as nitrogen fertilizer application might influence peat decomposition cause large N_2O emission.

***Keyword**: Nitrous oxide, peat soil, agricultural field, soil characteristics, organic matter decomposition*

INTRODUCTION

Table 1. Landuse type, duration of cultivation, and cultivars in rainy and dry seasons in the study field.

Site	Landuse	Cultivation Period (yr)	Cultivars: Rainy season	Dry season
A	Upland	26	*Solanum melongena*	*Spinacia oleracea*
B	Upland	26	*Pennisetum purpureum*	*Pennisetum purpureum*
C	Upland	Not detected	*Spinacia oleracea*	*Spinacia oleracea*
D	Upland	10	*Arachis hypogaea*	*Spinacia oleracea*
E	Upland	26	*Zea mays*	*Zea mays*
F	Upland	19	*Manihot esculenta*	*Zea mays*
G	Upland	16	Fallow	*Solanum melongena*
H	Upland	24	*Cucumis sativus*	*Solanum lycopersicum*
I	Upland	26	*Manihot esculenta*	*Cucurbita moschata*
GL	Meadow pasture	26	Not detected	Not detected

Site A~C and GL were the same fields as CL-A, CL-B, CL-C, and GL studied in Toma *et al.* (2011).

Peat soil is widely distributed in Southeast Asia. Especially in Indonesia, tropical peatland contributes approximately 47% (206950 ha) to that in Southeast Asia (Page *et al.* 2011). However, tropical peatland in Indonesia has been disturbed due to land development and annual burning, and part of them have been cultivated for food production. In the recent study conducted in tropical peatland in Indonesia, large amount of nitrous oxide (N_2O) has been emitted from upland field. Toma *et al.* (2011) reported that annual soil N_2O emission reached to 698 kg N ha^{-1} yr^{-1}, which is currently the highest value reported not only in tropical peatland but all around the world. In the upland field, soil N_2O flux increased especially in rainy season and positively correlated with soil nitrate (NO_3^-) concentration (Takakai *et al.* 2006). In addition, nitrogen (N) fertilizer application did not influence on N_2O production, while N_2O was mainly produced in surface soil layer (0-15 cm depth) (Toma *et al.* 2011). Hashidoko *et al.* (2008) isolated denitrifying bacteria, *Janthinobacterim* sp., which was acid-tolerant and had high potential of N_2O production under the existence of organic matter. Those study were based on long-term field monitoring in four experimental fields, then, we still do not know there are other upland fields in which large amount of N_2O was emitted from tropical peat soil. Production and emission of N_2O from soil are strongly influenced by the environmental factors (eg.topography and soil characteristics) and land management practice. Therefore, to find out the main factors affecting soil N_2O emission are necessary to quantify soil N_2O emission and develop strategies for reducing soil N_2O emission from upland field in tropical peatland. In this study, spatial distribution of soil N_2O flux in rainy and dry seasons and analyzed the relationship between soil N_2O flux and environmental factors were investigated.

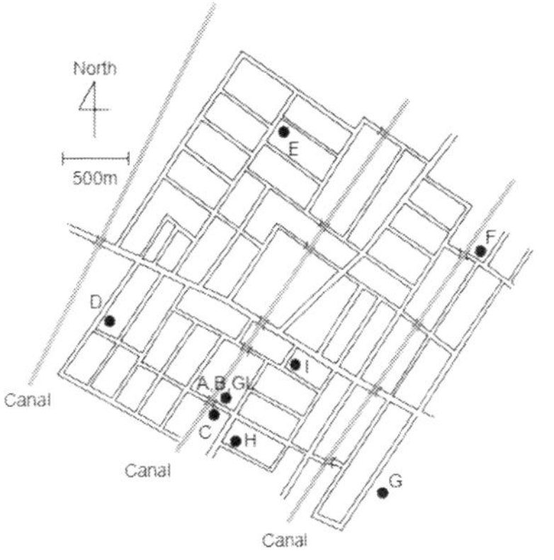

Fig. 1: Location of the study site in Kalampangan village, central Kalimantan, Indonesia.

METHODS

This study was conducted in Kalampangan Village (2°17'S, 114°1'E) near Palangka Raya City in central Kalimantan, Indonesia. Soil type is classified as *Typic Tropofibrists*, and detail chemical characteristics were provided in Takakai *et al.* (2006). Nine upland fields and one meadow pasture were selected (Fig. 1; Table 1). Site A~C and GL were the same fields as CL-A, CL-B, CL-C, and GL described in Toma *et al.* (2011). Soil greenhouse gas (N_2O, CH_4 and CO_2) fluxes were measured in both rainy (February 2006) and dry (September 2006) seasons using closed chamber methods at three replications. Details of the method for gas measurement were provided in Toma *et al.* (2011). After the measurement of soil greenhouse gas fluxes, undisturbed soil samples (0-5 cm depth) were collected using stainless steel core (φ5 cm and 5.1 cm height) from each point where chambers were installed. We measured soil pH, ammonium (NH_4^+) concentration, nitrate (NO_3^-), sulfate (SO_4^{2-}) and water soluble organic C (WSOC) concentrations, total carbon (C) and N concentrations, soil C:N ratio, and water filled pore space (WFPS). Easily oxidizable sulfur (EOS) in soil collected during rainy season were estimated by measuring difference in sulfate concentration before and after the hydrogen peroxide application under heating condition. Duration of cultivation and history of land management were obtained from farmers. Amount of applied N fertilizer was unknown in the study fields. We used "R" software for statistical analysis.

RESULTS

Soil N_2O fluxes were higher in rainy season than dry season, except for site I (Fig. 2). Highest soil N_2O flux was observed in C, and mean soil N_2O flux in rainy season was 1.06 mg N m^{-2} hr^{-1} (0.0084−3.46 mg N m^{-2} hr^{-1}), which was similar range of soil N_2O flux (0.00-9.27 mg N m^{-2} hr^{-1}) observed in Toma *et al.* (2011). In dry season, mean soil N_2O flux was 0.070 mg N m^{-2} hr^{-1} (0.0081−0.20 mg N m^{-2} hr^{-1}). Soil N_2O flux in rainy season was approximately 23 times higher than dry season ($P < 0.01$). Canal location, duration of cultivation, and cultivar did not clearly influence soil N_2O flux in both seasons. In rainy season, soil CO_2 flux, soil NO_3^- and SO_4^{2-} concentrations were positively correlated with soil N_2O fluxes (Fig. 3). Tradeoff relationship between soil N_2O and CH_4 fluxes was observed in rainy season (Fig. 3d). Other environmental factors were not correlated with soil N_2O fluxes in both season. Difference in soil N_2O flux between in rainy and dry seasons (ΔN_2O flux) was positively correlated with difference in soil SO_4^{2-} concentration (ΔSO_4^{2-} concentration), except for site F which had higher concentration of SO_4^{2-} in dry season compared to other sites (Fig. 4). On the other hand, EOS did not influence soil N_2O flux in rainy season (Fig. 5).

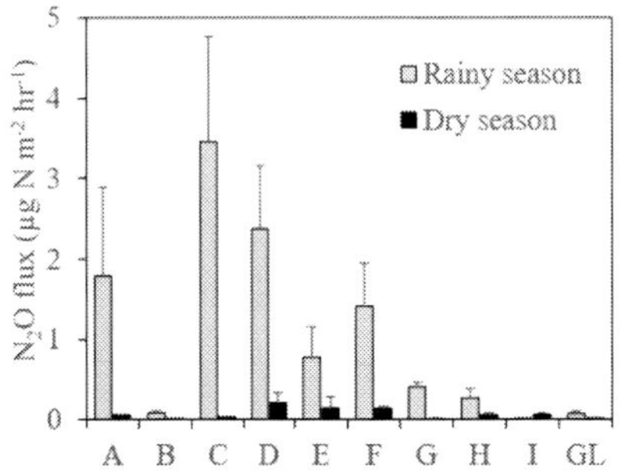

Fig. 2: Soil N_2O fluxes in rainy and dry seasons. Error bars represent standard deviations.

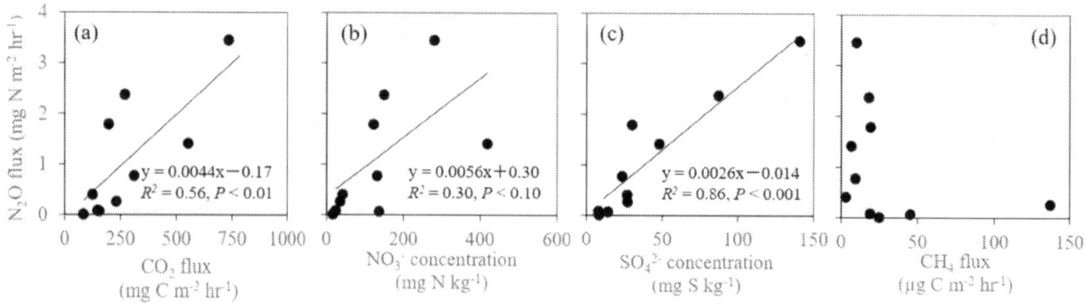

Fig. 3: Relationships between soil N_2O flux and CO_2 flux (a), NO_3^- (b), SO_4^{2-} (c) concentrations, and CH_4 flux in rainy season.

DISCUSSION

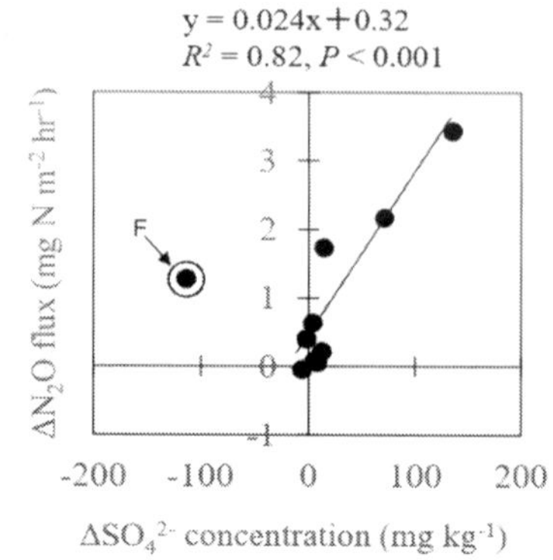

Fig. 4: Relationship between ΔN_2O flux and ΔSO_4^{2-} concentration (rainy−dry).

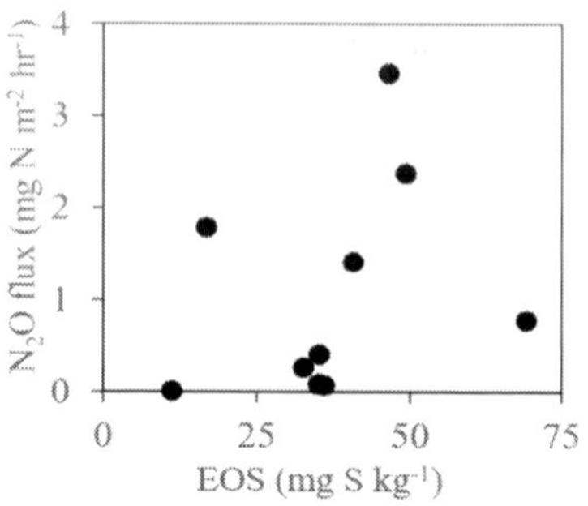

Fig. 5: Relationship between easily oxidizable sulfur (EOS) and soil N_2O flux in rainy season.

Variation of soil N_2O flux is generally influenced by land management, such as fertilization and plowing, and timing of rainfall. Soil N_2O flux from upland field measured in tropical peatland in Indonesia depended on the dry and rainy seasons rather than other factors of management practice (Takakai *et al.* 2006; Toma *et al.* 2011). In this study, higher soil N_2O flux in rainy season than in dry season showed that the investigation of spatial variation of soil N_2O flux in rainy season can determine the location that has higher or lower potential of soil N_2O emission, leading to more understanding of absolute controlling factors for N_2O production and emission from upland field on tropical peatland. In addition, no effect of canal location and WFPS to spatial variation of soil N_2O flux indicated that topography may not be main factors affecting spatial variation of soil N_2O flux.

Existence of crop or vegetables on study field and these species did not influence soil N_2O flux in our study. Klemedtsson *et al.* (2005) showed that soil N_2O emission from boreal peat soil increased with decreasing of peat C:N ratio of below 25. Higher peat C:N ratio in our study sites ranging from 34.4 to 57.5 may not be useful as an indicator for explaining spatial distribution of soil N_2O flux. Positive correlation between soil N_2O and CO_2 fluxes suggested N_2O production was significantly influenced by CO_2 production induced by peat decomposition (Fig. 3a), though soil CO_2 flux included root respiration. Fertilizer N did not significantly affect soil N_2O emission in this study which agreed with Toma *et al.* (2011). A significant positive correlation between soil N_2O flux and soil NO_3^- concentration was found in this study, indicating that soil N_2O emission from upland soil in tropical peatland was probably resulted from mineral N release by peat decomposition followed by nitrification and denitrification in rainy season. However, no correlation between soil N_2O flux and soil NH_4^+ concentration was observed showing that nitrification was not the main process of N_2O production. Large soil N_2O emission might be due to field management practices, which influence peat decomposition.

Increasing in soil N_2O flux with decreasing soil CH_4 flux showed N_2O could be reduced to nitrogen (N_2) under the reduced condition in which CH_4 was produced. As N_2O has higher potential for global warming than CH_4, to establish environmental condition suitable for CH_4 production rather than N_2O production may be one of the strategies for reducing impact of global warming in upland field on tropical peatland. This strategy might be also effective for reducing C release by aerobic decomposition of peat.

On the sulfur-denitrification process, autotrophic sulfur-denitrification bacteria uses elemental sulfur and NO_3^- as an electron donor and accepter, respectively, without requirement of organic matter as C source (Sahinkaya and Kilic 2014). Under the sulfur-denitrification process, therefore, SO_4^{2-} is produced by oxidation of elemental sulfur. Significant positive correlation between soil N_2O flux and soil SO_4^{2-} concentration in our study can indicate N_2O production by the process of sulfur-denitrification. Furthermore, significant positive relationship between ΔN_2O flux and ΔSO_4^{2-} concentration possibly showed that higher potential of sulfur oxidation closely linked to higher N_2O production potential in rainy season, though type of fertilizer applied to the study field should be determined. However, no correlation between N_2O flux in rainy season and EOS showed more specific type of sulfur, such as SO_4^{2-} bounded to ionized metals, might be origin of sulfate in peat soil, since EOS measured in this study included sulfur in hydrogen peroxide decomposable organic matter in peat. Hasegawa and Hanaki (2001) showed that soil NO_3^- concentration and the ratio of soil NO_3^- concentration reduction and N_2O production rates were decreased by addition of S^0 or FeS to soil by column experiment. This indicates that sulfur application enhanced both denitrification and N_2O reduction. Hasegawa and Hanaki (2001) also showed that sulfide produced under the reduced condition possibly inhibited N_2O reduction, showing that N_2O can be greatly produced under the sulfide rich condition in soil due to the acceleration of denitrification process and inhibition of N_2O reduction on that process. Therefore, investigation on the relationship between soil N_2O flux and soil sulfide concentration and existence of sulfur-denitrifies in our study sites are needed to verify above hypothesis. Source of the sulfide should also need to be determined in the future study. If there is significant correlation between soil N_2O flux and soil sulfide concentration in rainy season, source of the sulfide should also be determined in the future study.

CONCLUSION

Spatial variation of soil N_2O flux did not depend on topography, while soil N_2O flux potentially influenced by season, quality of peat and land management practice which influence the peat decomposition. In our study site, sulfur-denitrification may potentially contribute to large amount of N_2O emission. Understanding on these mechanisms can help to establish good strategy for mitigating N_2O emission from upland field established on tropical peatland.

REFERENCES

1. Hasegawa Kiyo, Hanaki Keisuke (2001) *Nitrous oxide and nitric oxide emissions during sulfur denitrification in soil-water system*, in "Advances in Water and Wastewater Treatment Technology - Molecular Technology, Nutrient Removal, Sludge Reduction, and Environmental Health", T. Matsuo, K. Hanaki, S. Takizawa and H. Satoh (eds.), Elsevier, The Netherlands, pp185－196.
2. Hashidoko Yasuyuki, Takakai Fumiaki, Toma Yo, Darung Untung, Melling Lulie, Tahara Satoshi, Hatano Ryusuke (2008) Emergence and behaviours of acid-tolerant *Janthinobacterium* sp. that evolves N_2O from deforested tropical peatland. Soil Biology & Biochemistry, 40, 116－125.
3. Klemedtsson Leif, Von Arnold Karin, Weslien Per, Gundersen Per (2005) Soil NC ratio as a scalar parameter to predict nitrous oxide emissions. Global Change Biology, 11, 1142－1147.
4. Page E. Susan, Pieley O. John, Banks J. Christopher (2011) Global and regional importance of the tropical peatland carbon pool. Global Change Biology, 17, 798－818.
5. Sahinkaya Erkan, Kilic Adem (2014) Heterotrophic and elemental-sulfur-based autotrophic denitrification processes for simultaneous nitrate and Cr (Ⅳ) reduction. Water Research, 50, 278－286.
6. Takakai Fumiaki, Morishita Tomoaki, Hashidoko Yasuyuki, Darung Untung, Kuramochi Kanta, Dohong Salampak, Limin H. Suwido, Hatano Ryusuke (2006) Effects of agricultural land-use change and forest fire on N_2O emission from tropical peatlands, Central Kalimantan, Indonesia. Soil Science and Plant Nutrition, 52, 662－674.
7. Toma Yo, Takakai Fumiaki, Darung Untung, Kuramochi Kanta, Limin H. Suwido, Dohong Salampad, Hatano Ryusuke (2011) Nitrous oxide emission derived from soil organic matter decomposition from tropical agricultural peat soil in central Kalimantan, Indonesia. Soil Science and Plant Nutrition, 57, 436－451.

AUTHOR INDEX

AUTHOR INDEX

AUTHOR INDEX

AUTHOR INDEX

AUTHOR INDEX

AUTHOR INDEX

AUTHOR INDEX

International Peatland Society (IPS)
Vapaudenkatu 12
40100 Jyvaskyla Finland

ISBN 978-1-5108-6213-5

CURRAN ASSOCIATES INC.
proceedings.com

15th International PEAT Congress (IPC 2016)

Peatlands in Harmony

Poster Presentations

Kuching, Malaysia
15-19 August 2016

Volume 2 of 2

International Peatland Society

15th International PEAT Congress (IPC 2016)

Peatlands in Harmony

Poster Presentations

Kuching, Malaysia
15-19 August 2016

Volume 2 of 2

ISBN: 978-1-5108-6213-5

Printed from e-media with permission by:

Curran Associates, Inc.
57 Morehouse Lane
Red Hook, NY 12571

Printed by Curran Associates, Inc. (2018)

International Peatland Society (IPS)
Vapaudenkatu 12
40100 Jyvaskyla Finland

Phone: 358 14 3385 440
Fax: 358 14 3385 410

ips@peatlands.org

Additional copies of this publication are available from:

Curran Associates, Inc.
57 Morehouse Lane
Red Hook, NY 12571 USA
Phone: 845-758-0400
Fax: 845-758-2633
Email: curran@proceedings.com
Web: www.proceedings.com

TABLE OF CONTENTS

TABLE OF CONTENTS

1.1: PEAT CHARACTERISTICS

1.1: PEAT CHARACTERISTICS

1.2: GEOCHEMISTRY, HYDROCHEMISTRY & HYDROLOGY

1.3: PEATLAND REMOTE SENSING, AERIAL & SATELLITE IMAGERY

1.4: PEATLAND CONSERVATION AND MANAGEMENT

1.5: PEATLAND BIODIVERSITY

1.5: PEATLAND BIODIVERSITY

1.6: CONSERVATION OF PEATLAND FOREST & WILDLIFE

2.1: PEATLAND CARBON BALANCE, STOCKS, STORAGE & LOSSES

2.2: GHG EMISSION FROM NATURAL & MANAGED PEATLANDS

2.2: GHG EMISSION FROM NATURAL & MANAGED PEATLANDS

2.3: PEAT FOREST-WILDFIRE-IMPACT ON ENVIRONMENT & SOCIETY

3.1: RESTORATION OF BOREAL, TEMPERATE & TROPICAL PEATLANDS

4.1: PEAT USE, PEATLANDS TECHNOLOGY & AGRO-TECHNOLOGY

5.1: AGRICULTURE & FOREST PLANTATIONS ON PEATLANDS

5.1: AGRICULTURE & FOREST PLANTATIONS ON PEATLANDS

6.1: CULTURAL & SOCIO-ECONOMIC ASPECTS OF PEATLAND

6.2: PEATLAND & LOCAL PEOPLE

SPECIAL SESSION 2: PEAT FOR HORTICULTURE & ENERGY

SPECIAL SESSION 4: TROPICAL PEATLAND BIODIVERSITY & CONSERVATION IN SOUTHEAST ASIA

Proceedings

15th International PEAT Congress 2016

Peatlands in Harmony

-Agriculture, Industry and Nature-

POSTER PRESENTATIONS

15th - 19th August 2016

Kuching, Sarawak, Malaysia

Organized by:

MPS

MALAYSIAN PEAT SOCIETY

In partnership with:

IPS

International Peatland Society

GREEN
SUSTAINABILITY
Through planting trees and stringent forest resource management, we establish a sustainable resource base for producing quality and price competitive products that are eco-friendly so as to deliver exceptional value to our customers and stakeholders.
CERTIFICATIONS
PEFC Certified Eco- Products
HSBC Forest Policy
SGS TLTV (Timber Legality & Traceability Verification) & Chain of Custody (CoC) standard for Ta Ann Plywood Sdn Bhd & Lik Shen Sawmill Sdn Bhd
SGS TLTV (Timber Legality & Traceability Verification) – VO (Verification of Origin) standard for Tanjong Manis Holdings Sdn Bhd, Raplex Sdn Bhd & Pasin Sdn Bhd
TA ANN HOLDINGS BERHAD (419232-K)
Ta Ann Building, No. 6, Jalan Rawang, P.O. Box 1489, 96008 Sibu, Sarawak, Malaysia.
Tel: +6 084 320200 Fax: +6 084 313328 Email: tahb@taann.com.my

15th International PEAT Congress 2016

Peatlands in Harmony

"Agriculture, Industry and Nature"

15th - 19th August 2016

Kuching, Sarawak Malaysia

Supported by:

Sarawak Government

Malaysian Palm Oil Council

International Union of Soil Sciences

International Union of Forest Research Organizations

With Thanks to Our Valued Sponsors

Lead Partner :

Ta Ann Holdings Berhad

Rimbunan Hijau Group of Companies

WTK AGRIBUSINESS

Titanium :

PELITA

SAMLING

PEATMAX

Platinum :

SARAWAK OIL PALMS

Diamond :

WEIDA

PT SMART TBK
Agribusiness and Food

Gold :

sarawak energy

PALMHEAD GROUP

HGI

MPOC
Malaysian Palm Oil Council

Silver :

K 1913
we make it grow
Klasmann Deilmann

SARAWAK TIMBER ASSOCIATION

TURFTECH INTERNATIONAL

Foreword

The theme of the 15th International Peat Congress 2016, 'Peatlands in Harmony' was chosen to highlight the closely linked relationship of the environment, industry and socio-economic factors in relation to peat. It serves as a reminder for all to find balance in social and economic progress with the conservation of the ecosystem and biodiversity of peatlands towards ensuring the development of peatland is in harmony with the environment and ecosystem. The congress has striven and driven hard at stringing together industry players, government agencies and policy makers, who are hungry for information as well as enthusiastic researchers and academicians, who are passionate in proving that science is the key to unlocking potentials, solving problems and creating opportunities for the next generation. With the balance of these people, the congress aims at bringing to reality its theme 'Peatlands in Harmony'.

The Scientific Secretariat accepted 332 contributions for oral and poster presentations under six main themes with a major input from Theme 1: Inventory, Biodiversity, Conservation and Functions of Peatlands and Theme 2: Peatlands and Ecosystem Management. A special whole day session on Peat Forest-Wildfire – Impacts on Environment & Society was dedicated under Theme 2 to gather papers related to peat fire that comes at an important time in addressing the haze issue in the region. It has successfully attracted a total of 179 papers from both Malaysia and Indonesia, a huge leap in number for the very first time in the history of the congress. The congress also opened up six other special sessions with two unconventional topics; Soft soil engineering and Asia flux. Soft soil engineering addresses the challenging engineering problems from construction on peat and soft soils whereas Asia flux brings forward a discussion on the potential changes and sustainability/resilience of peatland ecosystems, especially those of tropical peatlands, in terms of terrestrial biosphere-atmosphere exchanges.

Overall, the congress had received an overwhelming request for papers to be included in the oral sessions. However, with the limited number of available rooms and slots, the Scientific Secretariat had had to select the best representative papers. Without the extended members of the Scientific Secretariat, it would have been havoc in the selection and arrangement of all the papers. With this, the congress wishes to thank the extended members of the Scientific Secretariat for giving so much of their time and expertise in making this congress a success.

The Scientific Secretariat
August 11, 2016

Organizing Committee

Patron

YAB Datuk Patinggi Tan Sri (Dr) Haji Adenan Bin Haji Satem,
Chief Minister of Sarawak

Congress Chairman

YB Tan Sri Datuk Amar Haji Mohamad Morshidi Bin Abdul Ghani
State Secretary of Sarawak

Congress General

Dr Lulie Melling
Tropical Peat Research Laboratory (TPRL)

Secretariat

Nur Azima Busman *(TPRL)*
Priscilla Esther Mikin *(TPRL)*
Immas Janggok *(TPRL)*
Jicqueline Ratai *(TPRL)*
Davina Halpi *(TPRL)*
Jared Jimbau Chabu *(TPRL)*

Treasurer

George Chong Chook Voon *(TPRL)*
Alexson Gura *(TPRL)*
Candy Robun *(TPRL)*

Sponsorship

Dr Lulie Melling *(TPRL)*
Datu Dr Hj. Sulaiman Bin Haji Husaini
(Land Custody and Development Authority)

Scientific Programme

Dr Wan Rashidah Bt Wan A.Khadir
(Forest Research Institut, Malaysia)
Dr Sharon Lau Yu Ling *(TPRL)*
Auldry Chaddy Petrus Rudut *(TPRL)*
Nur Azima Busman *(TPRL)*

Congress Venue

Priscilla Esther Mikin *(TPRL)*
Lo Mei Lieng *(TPRL)*

Excursion

Frederick Haili Teck
(Department of Agriculture)
Mohd Zulhilmy Abdullah *(TPRL)*
Donny Sudid *(TPRL)*

Opening / Closing Ceremony

Dr Sharon Lau Yu Ling *(TPRL)*
Bobbie Yamoh *(TPRL)*
Auldry Chaddy Petrus Rudut *(TPRL)*
Lo Mei Lieng *(TPRL)*
Jared Jimbau Chabu *(TPRL)*

Gala Dinner

Auldry Chaddy Petrus Rudut *(TPRL)*
Bobbie Yamoh *(TPRL)*
George Chong Chook Voon *(TPRL)*

Ice-Breaking

Frazer Midot *(TPRL)*
Chesles Merikan *(TPRL)*

Organizing Committee

Cultural

Auldry Chaddy Petrus Rudut *(TPRL)*
Sydney Augustine Assom *(Institute of Teachers Education Tun Abdul Razak Campus)*

Exhibition & Poster

Priscilla Esther Mikin *(TPRL)*
Alexson Gura *(TPRL)*
Dr Sharon Lau Yu Ling *(TPRL)*
Auldry Chaddy Petrus Rudut *(TPRL)*

Technical

William Nyigor
(Information and Communication Technology Unit)
Michael Meling *(TPRL)*
Edward Baran Aeries *(TPRL)*
Joseph Wenceslaus *(TPRL)*

Design & Printing

Tiffany Sam *(TPRL)*
Jicqueline Ratai *(TPRL)*
Su Li Yang *(TPRL)*

Protocol

Dato Haji Khir Bin Haji Busrah
(State Protocol and Public Relation Unit)
Bobbie Yamoh *(TPRL)*

Decoration

Donny Sudid *(TPRL)*
Joshua Rengga *(TPRL)*
Aicher Joseph Toyat *(TPRL)*
George Dinggat David Among *(TPRL)*
Su Li Yang *(TPRL)*

Accommodation & Logistics

Lo Kim San *(TPRL)*
Sim Siew Yen *(TPRL)*
Simon Peter *(TPRL)*

Scientific Secretariat

Chairman

Dr Wan Rashidah Wan Abdul Khadir
Forest Research Institute, MALAYSIA

Deputy Chairman

Dr Sharon Lau Yu Ling
Tropical Peat Research Laboratory Unit, MALAYSIA

Members

Prof Lars Lundin
Swedish University of Agricultural Sciences, SWEDEN

Prof Gerald Schmilewski
Klasmann-Deilmann GmbH, GERMANY

Dr Barbara Kalisz
University of Warmia and Mazury in Olsztyn, POLAND

Prof Jürgen Schoenherr
Zittau University of Applied Sciences, GERMANY

Prof Maris Klavins
University of Latvia, LATVIA

Dr Catherine Farrell
Bord na Móna Energy Limited, IRELAND

Dr Roxanne Andersen
University of the Highlands and Islands, UNITED KINGDOM

Dr Leena Larva
Aino Klinikat, FINLAND

Dr Sakari Sarkkola
Natural Resources Institute, FINLAND

Dr Sylvain Jutras
Université Laval, CANADA

Dr Michiel Gerding
Assen, The NETHERLANDS

Prof Jack Rieley
Nottingham University, UNITED KINGDOM

Dr David Wilson
Earthy Matters Environmental Consultants, IRELAND

Prof Son Radu
University of Putra Malaysia, MALAYSIA

Dr Irnayuli R. Sitepu
Indonesia International Institute for Life Sciences, INDONESIA

Dr Nagamitsu Maie
Kitasato University, JAPAN

Dr Tasren N Mahamooth
Advanced Agriecological Research Sdn. Bhd, MALAYSIA

Dr Goh You Keng
Advanced Agriecological Research Sdn. Bhd, MALAYSIA

Dr Dave Siak-Wei Ow
Bioprocessing Technology Institute, SINGAPORE

Prof Che Fauziah Ishak
University of Putra Malaysia, MALAYSIA

Dr Jeyanny A/P Vijayanathan
Forest Research Institute Malaysia, MALAYSIA

Dr Margaret Abat
Department of Agriculture Sarawak, MALAYSIA

Dr Helena Varkkey
University of Malaya, MALAYSIA

Prof Monique Leclerc
The University of Georgia, USA

Dr Pozi Milow
University of Malaya, MALAYSIA

Prof Ryusuke Hatano
Hokkaido University, JAPAN

Prof Takashi Hirano
Hokkaido University, JAPAN

Dr Suwardi
Bogor Agricultural University, INDONESIA

Assoc Prof Dominic Ong
Swinburne University of Technology, MALAYSIA

Dr Ian Singleton
Sumatran Orangutan Conservation Programme, INDONESIA

Dr Kho Lip Khoon
Malaysian Palm Oil Board, MALAYSIA

Assoc Prof Catherine Yule
Monash University, MALAYSIA

Prof Mats Nilsson
Swedish University of Agricultural Sciences, SWEDEN

Prof Dr Andre-Michael Beer
Klinik Blankenstein, GERMANY

Dr Annette Freibauer
Institute of Agricultural Climate, GERMANY

Prof Dr Budi Indra Setiawan
Bogor Agricultural University, INDONESIA

Dr Basuki Sumawinata
Bogor Agricultural University, INDONESIA

Dr Bandung Sahari
Indonesian Palm Oil Association, INDONESIA

Dr Choo Chung Siung
Swinburne University of Technology, MALAYSIA

Prof Harri Vasander
University of Helsinki, FINLAND

Dr Hendrik Segah
University of Palangka Raya, INDONESIA

Dr Hwang Siaw San
Swinburne University of Technology, MALAYSIA

Dr. Irine R Ginjom
Swinburne University of Technology, MALAYSIA

Dr Lydia Eve Spencer Cole
University of Oxford, UNITED KINGDOM

Dr Moritz Müller
Swinburne University of Technology, MALAYSIA

Dr Tan Lee Tung
Swinburne University of Technology, MALAYSIA

Dr Wong Wei Chee
Advanced Agriecological Research Sdn. Bhd, MALAYSIA

Auldry Chaddy Petrus Rudut
Tropical Peat Research Laboratory, MALAYSIA

Jaithish John
Minerals and Geoscience Department, MALAYSIA

Gwendelynne Bulan Tanil
Genting Plantations Berhad, MALAYSIA

Katharine Georgina Pearce
Freelance

John Ko Wai Seng
Freelance

An ordinary housefly, if placed within a hollow clear glass globe having a single hole for an outlet, generally escapes tather promptly. But a bee, under like circumstances, seldoms escapes. This ... does not indicate superior wisdom on the part of the fly - quite the countrary. For the fly, dashing hither and thither in planless flight, continues to try to force its way through what must seem to it to be queerly resistant atmosphere.

From the preface to Colloid Chemistry, Vol. III, J. Alexander, 1931

Wonderful are the ways of God
In creation, and the love with which
He guides His creatures' destinies,
Gives them the means by which to strive
For maturity by ordered steps, and reach
The end most fitted for their natures,
His Law is just and easy, and His grace
Is ever ready to help: let us look
To the Eternal Goal, with hearts and souls
Of purity and glorify His name:
For in this changing, fleeting world,
His word is always true, and will remain,
Through all the ages, ever the same.

SURAH 87 - AL A' LA

WTK Group
Harnessing Ingenuity
for Sustainable Growth
Loytape
Principal Business Activities
■ Palm Oil
■ Timber
■ Hotel
■ Insurance
■ Property Development
■ Trading
■ Aluminium Foil & Adhesive Tapes Manufacturing
BANGUNAN HUNG ANN
Bangunan Hung Ann, No. 1, Jalan Bujang Suntong
P. O. Box 256, 96007 Sibu, Sarawak, Malaysia
Phone: +60 84 326155 Fax: +60 84 316160
Website: www.wtk.com.my
Email: info@wtk.com.my

TABLE OF CONTENTS

TABLE OF CONTENTS

THEME 1
INVENTORY, BIODIVERSITY, CONSERVATION & FUNCTIONS OF PEATLANDS

1.1: PEAT CHARACTERISTICS

1.1: PEAT CHARACTERISTICS

Abstract No: A-107

ACCUMULATION RATE OF TROPICAL PEAT SOILS UNDER DIFFERENT TYPES OF FOREST

Faustina E. Sangok[1, 2], Yuki Sugiura[1], Nagamitsu Maie[3], Lulie Melling[2], and Akira Watanabe[1]

[1]Graduate School of Bioagricultural Sciences, Nagoya University, Chikusa, Nagoya, Japan
[2]Tropical Peat Research Laboratory Unit, Chief Minister's Department, Sarawak, Malaysia
[3]School of Veterinary Medicine, Kitasato University, Aomori, Japan

**Corresponding author: faustina270187@gmail.com*

SUMMARY

In recent years, conversion of peatland to oil palm plantation has increased in Malaysia due to the higher demand on palm oil. Although it is considered that the land use change from primary forest to agricultural land accelerates the rate of peat decomposition, the strength of impact may vary among the different types of forests. The difference in the rate of peat accumulation may also be related to the decomposability of peat. The objective of the present study is to compare the rate of peat accumulation among the representative types of forests in the Maludam National Park, Sarawak, Malaysia. Soil samples were collected from three forests of Mixed Peat Swamp (MPS), Alan Batu (ABt), and Alan Bunga (ABg), which are located at the edge, middle, and centre parts of peatland in the dome shape. ^{14}C age, infrared and ^{13}C nuclear magnetic resonance spectra, and physico-chemical properties were analysed for 5–6 samples from each soil profile, between 100–450 cm depth (MPS), 200–700 cm depth (ABt), and 200–800 cm depth (ABg), respectively. The bottom layer was older in the order of MPS, ABt, and ABg, while the rate of peat soil accumulation based on ^{14}C age was estimated to be faster in the order of ABg, ABt, and MPS. Spectroscopic analysis suggested the difference in the transition of chemical structure of soil organic matter among the three forest soils, e.g., alkyl components were stored preferentially in the ABg soil while it was reduced with time in the MPS soil.

Keywords: *accumulation, ^{14}C dating, tropical peat, vegetation*

INTRODUCTION

Recent studies on the global carbon (C) cycle and climate change have identified the importance of peatland as the sink for the atmospheric CO_2. Peatland ecosystem has accumulated C because of the slower rate of decomposition compared to net primary production (Frolking *et al.*, 2001). Boreal and tropical peatlands have been estimated to accumulate 455 and 50–70 Pg of C, respectively (Gorham, 1991; Yu *et al.*, 2010). However, the estimation cannot be made with greater precision because of insufficient information on the rate of accumulation of peat deposits (Page *et al.*, 2004). The difference in accumulation rate may also be related to the stability of soil organic matter (SOM), which could be reflected in the rate of peat loss after land-use change for agricultural use. The objective of the present study is to investigate the rate of tropical peat soil accumulation under different types of primary forests.

MATERIALS AND METHODS

Soil samples were collected from three forests of Mixed Peat Swamp (MPS), Alan Batu (ABt), and Alan Bunga (ABg) in the Maludam National Park, Sarawak, Malaysia in April 2013 (Figure 1). The soil cores were collected by using a peat auger (Eijkelkamp, The Netherlands), with connecting 1-m extensions to the auger head, until reaching mineral substratum (4.5, 7, and 8 m deep in the MPS, ABt, and ABg, respectively). Soil samples with a thickness of 10 cm were collected at intervals of 1.0 or 0.5 m, and those from several cores were combined (100–150 g). Soil samples were covered doubly with aluminum foil and stored immediately in the plastic bags, brought back to the laboratory, and freeze-dried. pH, ash content, and total C and total nitrogen (N) contents were measured using a pH meter (Metrohm 827, Metrohm, Herisau, Switzerland), a thermal gravimetric analyzer (TGA 701, Leco, St. Joseph, MI, USA), and a NC analyzer (TruMac CN, Leco, St. Joseph, MI, USA), respectively. Fourier transform infrared (FT–IR) spectra of the soil samples from upper and lower peat layers of each profile were recorded on a FT-IR spectrometer (FT/IR-4100, JASCO, Tokyo, Japan) using the pellet made from the mixture of soil sample and potassium bromide. The ramp cross polarization/magic angle spinning (CPMAS) ^{13}C nuclear magnetic resonance

(NMR) spectra of the soil samples were recorded at a ^{13}C frequency of 176 MHz on an NMR spectrometer (ECA-700, JEOL, Tokyo).

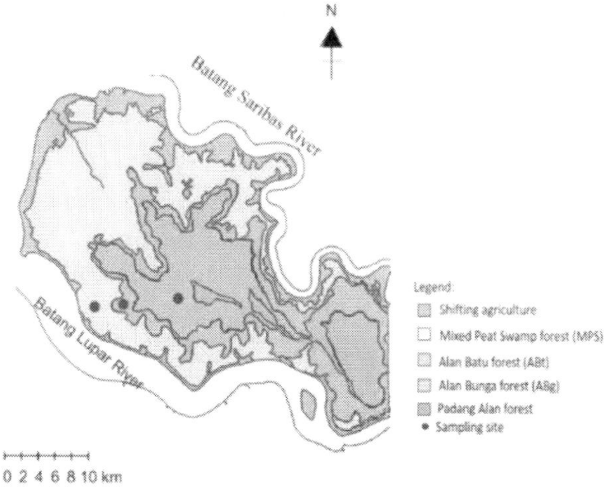

Figure 1: Location of sampling site in Maludam National Park, Sarawak, Malaysia. One red circle covers two sampling sites.

For ^{14}C dating, the <100 or <200 cm depth layer soils were not used to avoid contamination from living roots. After removal of large plant debris manually, the acid-alkali-acid (AAA) treatment was applied to the soil samples to remove colloidal organic matter contamination from the different layers as follows: The samples soaked in 1 M hydrochloric acid were boiled for 1 hour, and the supernatant was discarded by decantation after it got cold. Similar procedures were repeated using 1 M sodium hydroxide until the supernatant became almost colorless, followed by using 1 M HCl once. The residues were washed with ultrapure water repeatedly and dried up at 80°C in an oven dryer. A sample containing 3 mg of C and 800 mg of CuO were packed in a 9 mm outer diameter quartz tube, evacuated, and sealed at a length of 300 mm. The tube was heated at 850°C for 3–4 h to produce CO_2. The CO_2 generated was purified in a vacuum glass line system and reduced to graphite by reaction with reduced Fe and H_2 in a vacuum quartz tube at 650°C for 6 h. The $^{14}C/^{12}C$ and $^{13}C/^{12}C$ ratios of the graphite targets were measured using a Tandetron accelerator mass spectrometer (Model 4130-AMS, High Voltage Engineering Europa B.V., Amersfoort, the Netherlands). The HOx-II standard (National Institute of Standards and Technology new oxalic acid standard, SRM-4990C) and commercial dehydrated oxalic acid containing no ^{14}C (Wako, Tokyo, Japan) were used as a reference for the C isotope ratios and for ^{14}C blank subtraction in the data analysis, respectively. The one standard deviation of the ^{14}C age of the sample was <±50 years. The rate of peat accumulation was estimated by linear regression of ^{14}C age data and soil depth.

RESULTS

Throughout this abstract, we show results from one of two profiles for each forest. The pH and ash content of peat soil samples increased at the bottom layers, due to inputs from the below mineral soil layers. Total C content, total N content, and C/N ratio were in the range of 437–592 g kg^{-1}, 7–17 g kg^{-1}, and 33–65, respectively (Table 1). Although total C and total N contents in the MPS soils tended to decrease as the soil depth increased, the C/N ratio at 400 and 450 cm depth, 59, was similar to that at 100 cm depth, 60.

The ^{14}C age was in the range of 2920–5162 years before present (yBP; 0 yBP = AD1950), 1420–4020 yBP, and 928–3277 yBP at the MPS, ABt, and ABg forests respectively. The rate of peat soil accumulation was estimated to be larger in ABg (0.20 cm $year^{-1}$) and ABt (0.17 cm $year^{-1}$) profiles than in MPS (0.07 cm $year^{-1}$).

The IR spectra of the soil samples from an upper (100 or 200 cm depth) and lower (450, 600, or 700 cm depth) layers are shown in Figure 3. Spectral pattern was similar among the samples and major absorptions were observed at around 3410 (O-H), 2850 and 2920 (aliphatic CH_2 and CH_3), 1710 (carboxylic C=O), 1620 (aromatic ring C=C/quinone C=O), 1450–1420 (C-H), and 1030–1066 (alcoholic C-O) cm^{-1}, respectively. The absorptions at 2850 and 2920 cm^{-1} were greater at the upper layer than the lower layer in the MPS soil, while those absorptions were greater in the lower layer soil than in the lower layer soil in the ABg soil profile. The opposite trend was observed in the absorption at 1030–1066 cm^{-1} in the MPS and ABg soil profiles, respectively.

Table 1: Physico-chemical properties of soil samples used

Study site	GPS point	Sample depth (cm)	pH	Ash (%)	Total C (g kg^{-1})	Total N (g kg^{-1})	C/N ratio
Mixed Peat Swamp	1° 25' 53" N	100	3.5	0.7	578	10	60
(MPS)	111° 7' 59" E	200	3.8	0.4	560	12	45
		300	3.9	0.9	573	11	54
		350	3.9	1.6	566	10	58
		400	4.1	5.7	542	9	59
		450	4.2	24	437	7	59
Alan Batu	1° 27' 16" N	200	3.6	0.9	579	11	51
(ABt)	111° 9' 4" E	300	3.5	0.4	565	14	40
		400	3.6	0.5	575	12	50
		500	3.7	0.7	577	11	53
		600	4.1	1.1	582	10	57
		700	4.5	2.0	570	12	47
Alan Bunga	1° 27' 36" N	200	3.8	0.5	577	15	40
(ABg)	111° 9' 27" E	300	3.8	0.4	584	14	43
		400	3.9	0.8	585	13	44
		500	4.2	1.3	584	12	47
		600	4.4	1.4	592	11	54
		800	4.3	1.4	583	12	50

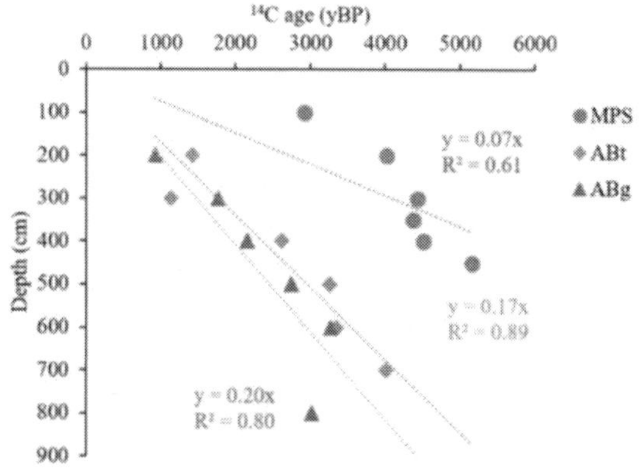

Figure 2: Relationships between soil depth and ^{14}C age of Mixed Peat Swamp (MPS), Alan Batu (ABt), and Alan Bunga (ABg) forests

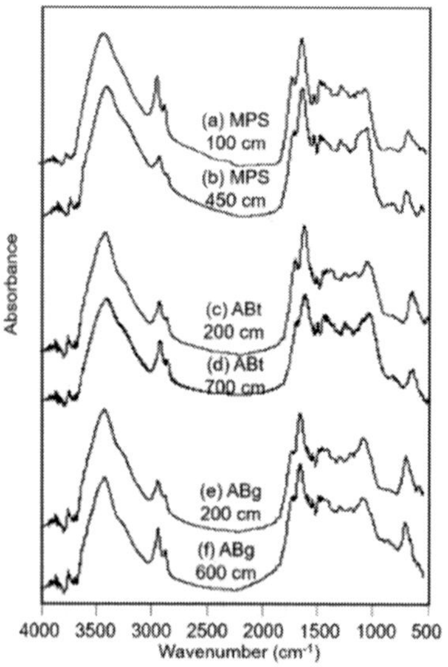

Figure 3: FT-IR spectra of Maludam peat soils from different types of forests. The depth indicates the upper (100 and 200 cm) and lower (450, 600, and 700 cm) layers of each soil profile

DISCUSSION

The ^{14}C ages of the bottom layers indicated that the peat accumulation started earlier in the MPS > ABt > ABg, while the thickness of the peat soil was the opposite. These results confirmed that peat accumulation started from the outside of the present peat dome. As the basal dates reported for the lowland peat domes in Sarawak, Malaysia ranged from 1140–6400 yBP (Tie and Kueh, 1979; Staub and Esterle, 1994; Dommain *et al.*, 2011), the history of the Maludam peatland is within this range. Smaller accumulation rate at the MPS site suggests the progression of decomposition/humification. Because the groundwater table was lower in the MPS site, -15 cm, than the ABt (-8 cm) and ABg (-4 cm) sites, more aerobic conditions when each layer was at the surface may have accelerated the SOM decomposition. As the increase in ^{14}C age with increasing soil depth in the MPS profile was further smaller below 200 cm, when (older than 4,000 yBP) the peat accumulation had not started at the ABt and ABg sites yet, it is contemplated that SOM decomposition was more active or still continue. The rate of peat soil accumulation at the ABg site was closer to that reported for a peatland under continuous saturated condition, 0.25 cm year^{-1} (Dommain *et al.*, 2011). In the dome-shape peatland, the inner area is generally more oligotrophic (Funakawa *et al.*, 1996). Such conditions may have accelerated the peat accumulation the ABg forest.

The smaller absorption peaks of aliphatic CH_2 and CH_3 in the IR spectrum of the lower layer than those of upper layer in the MPS soil profile (Figure 3a and b) suggested the loss of lipids and/or other alkyl components with the passage of time. As lipids are less decomposable under anaerobic conditions, this observation agreed to the slower accumulation rate of bulk peat soil in the MPS forest compared to the other forests. Similarity in the IR spectra between the upper and lower layers from the ABt soil profiles is also not contradictory to their almost constant accumulation rates (Figure 2). ^{13}C NMR results supported these observations.

CONCLUSION

The ^{14}C age of the oldest peat soils in the three forest sites indicated the peat dome formation from the edge toward the center of Maludam National Park. The rate of peat soil accumulation was larger in the order of ABg > ABt > MPS. Spectroscopic analysis of the peat soil samples suggested that the transition in the chemical structure with depth or time varies among the three forests, possibly associated with the variation in the accumulation rate.

ACKNOWLEDGEMENTS

This research was supported by a Grant-in-Aid for Scientific Research from the Japan Society for the Promotion of Science (No. 24405029). The authors wish to thank staff members of Tropical Peat Research Laboratory Unit for their technical assistance and support in the field work.

REFERENCES

1. Dommain R, Couwenberg J, Joosten H. Development and carbon sequestration of tropical peat domes in south-east Asia: links to post-glacial sea-level changes and Holocene climate variability. Quaternary Science Reviews 2011; 30: 999–1010.
2. Frolking S, Roulet NT, Moore TR, Richard PJH, Lavoie M, Muller SD. Modelling northern peatland decomposition and peat accumulation. Ecosystems 2001; 4: 479–498.
3. Funakawa S, Yonebayashi K, Jong SH, Chai EOK. Nutritional environment of tropical peat soils in Sarawak, Malaysia based on soil solution composition. Soil Science and Plant Nutrition 1996; 42 (4): 833–843.
4. Gorham E. Northern peatlands: role in the carbon cycle and probable responses to climatic warning. Ecological Applications 1991;1: 182–195.
5. Page SE, Wüst RAJ, Weiss D, Rieley JO, Shotyk W, Limin SH. A record of Late Pleistocene and Holocene carbon accumulation and climate change from an equatorial peat bog (Kalimantan, Indonesia): implications for past, present and future carbon dynamics Journal of Quarternary Science 2004;19 (7), 625–635.
6. Staub JR, Esterle JS. Peat-accumulating depositional systems of Sarawak, East Malaysia. Sedimentary Geology 1994;84: 91–106
7. Tie YL, Kueh HS A Review of Lowland Organic Soils of Sarawak. Techinical Paper No. 4, Department of Agriculture, Sarawak (Malaysia); 1979. p. 1–34.
8. Yu Z, Loisel J, Brosseau DP, Beilman DW. Global peatland dynamics since the Last Glacial Maximum. Geophysical Research Letters 2010;37: L13402, doi:10.1029/2010GL043584.

Abstract No: A-100

CELLULOSE OXYGEN ISOTOPES OF PEAT AS A TOOL OF PALEOCLIMATE RECONSTRUCTION; APPLICATIONS IN RISHIRI AND BORNEO PEATS

Masanobu Yamamoto[1], Osamu Seki[1], Takafumi Kikuchi[1], Ryoma Hayashi[2], Abdullah Sulaiman[3], Hasrizal Shaari[4] and Lulie Melling[5]

[1]*Faculty of Environmental Earth Science, Hokkaido University, Japan*
[2]*Lake Biwa Museum, Japan*
[3]*Jabatan Mineral Dan Geosains Malaysia, Malaysia*
[4]*Universiti Malaysia Terengganu, Malaysia*
[5]*Tropical Peat Research Center, Malaysia*

**Corresponding author: myama@ees.hokudai.ac.jp*

SUMMARY

Technique of cellulose oxygen isotope analysis was applied to the peats from the Rishiri Island, Japan, in the Sea of Japan. Sphagnum remains were carefully separated and their cellulose was purified by lipid extraction and subsequent lignin decomposition processes. The purified cellulose was analyzed by pyrolysis isotope ratio monitoring mass spectrometry to measure its $\delta^{18}O$. The 4000-year record of $\delta^{18}O$ showed millennial scale variation with maxima around 2,500 years ago and the last several centuries. The periods showing heavier $\delta^{18}O$ corresponded to those of the intensified Tsushima Warm Current in the Japan Sea (Koizumi *et al.*, 2006), suggesting that changes in the vapor source affected the oxygen isotopes of precipitated water in the Rishiri Island.

Keywords: *peat, cellulose, oxygen isotopes, paleoclimate, Rishiri Island, Japan*

INTRODUCTION

The oxygen isotope composition of precipitation is sensitive to the atmospheric dynamics. The tree-ring cellulose $\delta^{18}O$ is thus increasingly used for paleoclimate reconstruction of the recent centuries (e.g., Anderson *et al.*, 1998; Roden *et al.*, 1999; Nakatsuka *et al.*, 2004; Sternberg, 2009). Peat contains sphagnum and plant remains, and their $\delta^{18}O$ values are potentially used for long-term climate reconstruction (e.g., Hong *et al.*, 2000). Because the cellulose $\delta^{18}O$ is discriminated in different tissues in a single plant, and the value is also different among different species in a same location, the cellulose $\delta^{18}O$ of a bulk peat sample has a mixed signal of environmental, physiological, biochemical, and ecological conditions, resulting in a complex interpretation on the paleoclimate.

In this study, the difference of $\delta^{18}O$ in different remains in peat samples and reconstructed paleoclimate records from sphagnum and plant tissue cellulose $\delta^{18}O$ in the peats from the Rishiri Island, Japan, in the Sea of Japan were examined.

SAMPLES AND METHODS

Cores MHWL-1 (4.6 m long) and MHWL-3 (4.0 m long) were taken from the Minamihama Swamp developed in a volcanic crater, south of Rishiri Island in the Sea of Japan by a Russian peat sampler on June 2013.

Sphagnum remains and other plant remains were carefully separated by hand picking. Their cellulose was purified by lipid extraction and subsequent lignin decomposition processes (Nakatsuka *et al.*, 2004). The purified cellulose was analyzed using a Finnigan DELTAplus pyrolysis isotope ratio monitoring mass spectrometry to measure its $\delta^{18}O$.

RESULTS

In MHWL-1 core, six different stems, four different roots, and sphagnum moss were separated for 37 samples. In MHWL-3 core, five different stems, four different roots, and sphagnum were separated for 38 samples. Plant tissue remains, i.e., stems and roots, and sphagnum remains show different $\delta^{18}O$ variations. The $\delta^{18}O$ values of plant tissues were generally higher than those of sphagnum. The amplitude of variation was larger in sphagnum (12 permil) than in plant tissues (5 permil). Depth variation of sphagnum $\delta^{18}O$ showed higher values in top 1 m and at around 2.5 m. According to a preliminary age model (Takada *et al.*, 2005; Igarashi, 2006), the former interval corresponded to the last several centuries, while the latter interval corresponded to around 2,500 years ago.

DISCUSSION

The higher $\delta^{18}O$ in plant tissues than in sphagnum is attributed to the condensation of isotopically heavier water molecules in plant body by transpiration via stromata. The transpiration of sphagnum might be limited when the surface of sphagnum is covered by water, resulting in smaller fractionation. Thus, the $\delta^{18}O$ of sphagnum reflects more directly that of precipitated water.

The $\delta^{18}O$ of precipitated water in Rishiri Island was ~2 permil heavier in summer than in winter (Yuta Tsuzuki, unpublished data), but this seasonal variation was not sufficient to explain the changes in sphagnum $\delta^{18}O$. The periods showing heavier $\delta^{18}O$ of sphagnum corresponded to those of the intensified Tsushima Warm Current in the Japan Sea indicated by diatom records (Koizumi *et al.*, 2006). This suggests that changes in the vapor source affected the oxygen isotopes of precipitated water in the Rishiri Island. The intensified Tsushima Warm Current carried warm water to the area of Rishiri Island and may have enhanced evaporation. The shorter transportation of water vapor may have decreased the degree of fractionation of $\delta^{18}O$ in residual water vapor, resulting in higher $\delta^{18}O$ of precipitated water.

The difference of $\delta^{18}O$ between plant tissues and sphagnum indicates the degree of transpiration of plants, which depends on relative humidity. Large difference implies a dry condition. Its difference was larger when the Tsushima Warm Current was weaker. This correspondence suggests that the intrusion of Tsushima Warm Current is a key factor determining precipitation amount and resultant relative humidity in Rishiri Island.

CONCLUSIONS

Our results suggest that sphagnum cellulose $\delta^{18}O$ is useful to understand the $\delta^{18}O$ of precipitated water, while the difference of $\delta^{18}O$ between plant tissues and sphagnum can be used to understand relative humidity. This technique was applied to the reconstruction of hydrological history of Rishiri Island, showing a linkage between the intensity of the Tsushima Warm Current and the precipitation in Rishiri Island. We try to apply this method to Borneo peats. We retrieved peat cores from Marudi and Timbarap areas. We plan to generate paleoclimate records from Borneo peatlands.

REFERENCES

1. Anderson, W.T., Bernasconi, S.N., McKenzie, J.A., 1998. Oxygen and carbon isotopic record of climatic variability in tree ring cellulose (*Picea abies*): An example from central Switzerland (1913-1995). Journal of Geophysical Research 103, 31625-31636.
2. Hong, Y.T., Jiang, H.B., Liu, T.S., Zhou, L.P., Beer, J., Li, H.D., Leng, X.T., Hong, B., Qin, X.G., 2000. Response of climate to solar forcing recorded in a 6000-year d18O time-series of Chinese peat cellulose. The Holocene 10, 1-7.
3. Igarashi, Y., 2006. Late Holocene vegetation history in Minamihama wetland and Numaura wetland, Rishiri Island, Hokkaido. Rhishiri Kenkyu 25, 71-82 (in Japanese).
4. Koizumi, I., Tada, R., Narita, H., Irino, T., Aramaki, T., Oba, T., Yamamoto, H., 2006. Paleoceanographic history around the Tsugaru Strait between the Japan Sea and the Northwest Pacific Ocean since 30 cal kyr BP. Palaeogeography, Palaeoclimatology, Palaeoecology 232, 36–52.
5. Nakatsuka, T., Ohnishi, K., Hara, T., Sumida, A., Mitsuishi, D., Kurita, N., Uemura, S., 2004. Oxygen and carbon isotopic ratios of tree-ring cellulose in a conifer-hardwood mixed forest in northern Japan. Geochemical Journal 38, 77-88.
6. Roden, J.S., Lin, G., Ehleringer, R., 1999. A mechanistic medel for interpretation of hydrogen and oxygen isotope ratios in tree-ring cellulose. Geochimica et Cosmochimica Acta 64, 21-35.
7. Sternberg, L.S.L.O, 2009. Oxygen stable isotope ratios of tree-ring cellulose: the next phase of understanding. New Phytologist 181, 553–562.
8. Takada, M., Kosugi, K., Nogawa, H., Sato, M., 2005. Peat stratigraphy of Minamihama mire and Tanetomi Mire, Rishiri Island, Hokkaido. Rishiri Kenkyu, 24, 49-64 (in Japanese).

Abstract No: A-166

CHANGE OF PHYSICAL AND CHEMICAL PROPERTIES OF PEAT AFTER FIRE IN DRAINED TROPICAL PEAT SWAMP FOREST

Y.Sulistiyanto*, O. Umar, Jaya A. Lendraand R. Umbing

Faculty of Agriculture University of Palangka Raya, Palangka Raya, Indonesia

**Corresponding author: sulistiyanto_y@yahoo.co.uk*

A study on the change of physical and chemical properties of peat after fire in tropical peat swamp forest in the University of Palangka Raya area of Central Kalimantan, Indonesia was carried out on two plots from October to December 2014. One plot was examined two weeks after it was burned while the other plot was not burned. In each plot, replicate samples were taken from different peat depths (0-10, 10-20, 20-30, 30-40, and 40-50 cm)at three locations for analysis of physical and chemical properties. Physical analysis of peat bulk density (BD) and water content were determined for each depth. Chemical analyses of pH, K, Ca, and Mg were also carried out on each sample. Results show that water content in the non-burned area is higher than in the burned area, while bulk density in the burned area is higher than in the non-burned area. In general, pH, K, Ca and Mg in the burned area are higher than in the non-burned area.

***Keywords**: bulk density, drained tropical peat swamp forest, fire, physical properties, chemical properties*

Abstract No: A-106

CHARACTERIZATION OF ORGANIC CARBON COMPOUNDS OF TROPICAL PEAT FROM VARIOUS LAND MANAGEMENT TYPES

Könönen Mari [1], Jauhiainen Jyrki[1], Laiho Raija[2], Spetz Peter[3], Kusin Kitso[4], Limin Suwido[4] and Vasander Harri[1]

[1]*University of Helsinki, Department of Forest Sciences, Finland*
[2]*Natural Resources Institute Finland, Finland*
[3]*Natural Resources Institute Finland, Finland*
[4]*Center for International Cooperation in Sustainable Management of Tropical Peatland (CIMTROP), University of Palangka Raya, Indonesia*

**Corresponding author: mari.parkkari@luke.fi*

SUMMARY

The carbon chemistry largely determines the decomposability of organic substrate. The advanced knowledge of tropical peat organic carbon chemistry (OCC) improves understanding of carbon dynamics, which is needed for sustainable management of these ecosystems. Yet, tropical peat OCC is a highly understudied subject. To study tropical peat OCC we gathered samples from undrained peat swamp forest and three other land uses altered 20–30 years prior to the study, which together form a continuum of increasing land-use intensity. From studied peats collected from in Central-Kalimantan, Indonesia, the OCC, i.e. the hemicellulosic carbohydrate and uronic acid compositions and concentrations of extractives, cellulose, acid-soluble lignin and acid-insoluble residue were determined. With this study we aim to answer the following questions: (i) Does land-use change affect tropical peat OCC? (ii) How does land-use change affect OCC? (iii) What kind of implications could changes in OCC cause to carbon dynamics at various land use types?

***Keywords**: tropical peat, land-use, decomposability, carbohydrates, polymers*

INTRODUCTION

Decomposability of organic substrate largely depends on its carbon chemistry (Berg, 2000; Zhang *et al.*, 2008; Sanaullah *et al.*, 2010; Strakova *et al.*, 2011). This relationship particularly holds true for tropical peatlands, which are formed of deep organic matter depositions. Large-scale land reclamation including drainage and deforestation has taken place in Southeast Asia with accelerating extent (Murdiarso *et al.*, 2010; Miettinen *et al.*, 2016). Land reclamation influences peat formation and decomposition processes by lowering litter input rates and water table level (Laiho *et al.*, 2006). This has likely led to changes in peat organic carbon chemistry (OCC). To achieve sustainable utilization of reclaimed peatlands, increased understanding on OCC at various land management types is needed in order to improve land management towards increased sustainability. With this study we aim to answer following questions: (i) Does land-use change affect tropical peat OCC? (ii) How does land-use change affect OCC? (iii) What kind of implications could changes in OCC cause to carbon dynamics at various land-use types?

MATERIALS AND METHODS

To study tropical peat OCC we collected soil samples from an undrained peat swamp forest and three sites altered 20–30 years prior to the study. The included land uses form a continuum of increasing land-use intensity (undrained forest; drainage-affected forest; drained, deforested degraded open site; drained, deforested, site under cultivation) in Central-Kalimantan, Indonesia. Information of central peat properties from the sites are presented in Table 1 (Könönen *et al.*, 2015). Sampling depths below the peat surface covered mostly oxic (-10 cm), frequently waterlogged (-45 cm for undrained forest; -45 cm and -80 cm for altered sites) and permanently waterlogged, anoxic conditions (-80 cm for undrained forest, -110 cm for altered sites). To study peat OCC, we analyzed the total concentrations of hemicellulose, of extractives, cellulose, acid-soluble lignin (ASL) and acid-insoluble residue (AIR) in peat. The total hemicellulose concentration included non-cellulosic polysaccharides formed of combination of concentrations of neutral sugars (arabinose, rhamnose, xylose, mannose, galactose, glucose) and uronic acid (glucuronic, galacturonic and 4-O-Me-glucuronic acids). The composition of hemicelluloses and uronic acids were analyzed with method described in Sundberg *et al.* (1996) and composition of celluloses with method described in Sundberg *et al.* (2003). The concentration of extractives was analyzed using acetone:water solution (v:v, 9:1). The concentration of AIR was analyzed with a standard procedure (TAPPI Test Method T 222-om-88, 2000), and the solution for analyzing ASL concentration was formed as by-product in AIR analyses and analyzed using UV spectroscopy at an absorbance of 203 nm (Brunow *et al.*, 1999).

Table 1: The average dry bulk density (BD g cm^{-3}), proportion of different sized fractions in peat (presented as percentage from BD), total C and N concentration, and C/N-ratio for peat from the study sites. Data published in Könönen *et al.* (2015).

Site	BD, g cm^{-3}	<0.15 mm, %	0.15-1.5 mm, %	>1.5 mm, %	C, %	N, %	C/N-ratio
Undrained forest	0.140	51.15	36.90	11.58	58.11	1.35	47.62
Drained forest	0.164	45.29	44.22	9.30	59.72	1.09	62.97
Degraded, open site	0.153	57.97	34.74	9.56	58.48	0.78	75.92
Agricultural, open site	0.152	60.73	27.10	8.53	58.69	0.80	74.92

RESULTS

In forest sites the average total hemicellulose, extractives, and ASL concentrations were higher (646.7%, 37.8% and 56.1%, respectively) and total cellulose and AIR concentrations were lower (3.6% and 11.3%, respectively) than at the open sites (Figure 1). The greatest difference in OCC between the two forest sites occurred at 40-45 cm depth, where peat from drained forest had less hemicellulosic carbohydrates and more extractives, and it started to have increasingly similar characteristics with the peat in open sites (Figure 1 and Figure 2). The hemicellulose concentration was higher in the forest than in the open sites, but the non-cellulosic polysaccharides were present in following order: glucose > xylane > mannose > galactan > galacturonic acid >arabinose > rhamnose > glucuronic acid > 4-O-Me-glucuronic acid (Figure 2). The peat hemicellulosic concentration decreased with depth at the forest sites, but the concentrations was low and rather constant at the open sites' peat profiles.

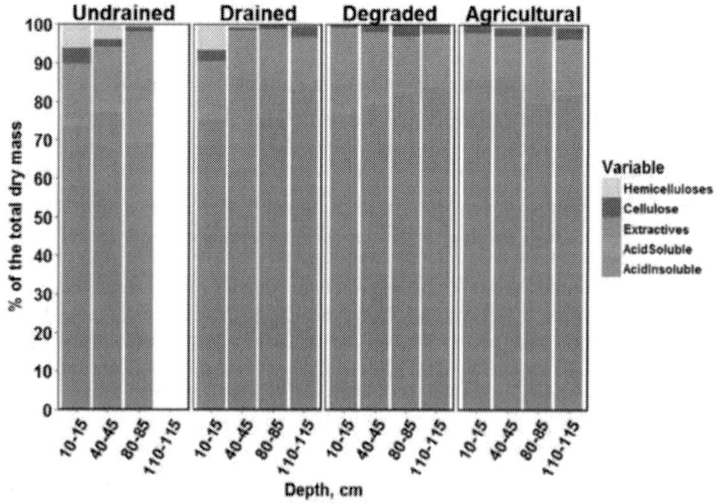

Figure 1: Cumulative proportional (%) concentration of hemicelluloses, cellulose, extractives, acid soluble lignin and acid insoluble residue in peat from various land management types and depths.

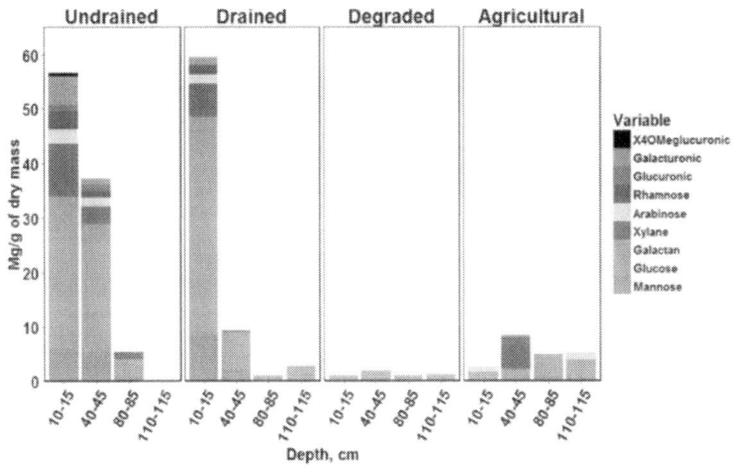

Figure 2: Cumulative concentration (mg g^{-1} in dry peat) of uronic acids (glucuronic, galacturonic and 4-O-Me-glucuronic acids) and neutral sugars (arabinose, rhamnose, xylose, mannose, galactose, glucose) in peat from various land management types and depths.

DISCUSSION

Our results show that land-use change leads to enrichment of recalcitrant OCC in peat, and the effects are greater when both water table level is permanently lower level and the original forest vegetation is removed. The peat AIR concentration was generally higher in comparison to boreal *Sphagnum* peats (Andriesse, 1988), and it is consistent with woody characteristics of organic matter forming peat (Yule & Comez, 2009; Mehta *et al.*, 2013). In the forest sites the main litter (i.e. roots, leafs and branches) deposition occurs close to peat surface (Page *et al.*, 1999; Sulistiyanto 2004; Wüst *et al.*, 2008), and as a consequence of progressive decomposition the concentration of labile carbohydrates decrease and recalcitrant polymers increase with increase in distance from peat surface at the forest sites.

Deforestation leads to permanently reduced vegetation biomass and litter deposition rates, which together with improved conditions for aerobic decomposition due to water-level drawdown. This management driven condition has led to the detected increase of recalcitrant compounds in the topmost surface peat. At the open sites, also recurrent fires modify peat structure and composition (see Könönen *et al.*, 2015). At the study sites at open areas it has been estimated that c. 50 cm of surface peat has disappeared due to fires (Hoscilo *et al.*, 2011). Fires have exposed and resurfaced aged and thus more decomposed peat, but also modified surface peat properties. Especially at the agricultural site the AIR concentration at the depth of -10 cm was high, which is likely due to management fires and soil tilling that mix the surface peat layer and transport this most decomposed top peat deeper in the profile.

The peat properties altered in land reclamation change decomposability properties in the substrate. Due to progressive enrichment of recalcitrant compounds in peat, the gaseous C emissions have been noticed to decrease in with time after land reclamation. This can be explained by decreased availability of labile carbohydrates, which are providing easier energy source for the peat decomposition resulting microbes. Yet, reintroducing labile C and N substrates (i.e. fertilization) may induce decomposition process at the open sites with more recalcitrant peat (see Jauhiainen *et al.* this volume).

CONCLUSION

Land-use change leads to enrichment of recalcitrant carbon compounds over time, especially when both deforestation and drainage are included. Due to maintained continuous litter input, in forest covered peatlands the total hemicellulosic concentration at surface peat can remain high despite the drainage. In reclaimed sites, fires and lack of litter input leads to progressive enrichment of recalcitrant compounds at the surface peat.

ACKNOLEDGEMENTS

We acknowledge the Centre for International Cooperation in Sustainable Management of Tropical Peatland (CIMTROP) for providing facilities and assistance during field sampling. This research was supported by the Academy of Finland -funded 'Restoration Impact on Tropical Peat Carbon and Nitrogen Dynamics' -project (RETROPEAT), University of Helsinki prize money for Peatlanders and the Jenny and Antti Wihuri foundation.

REFERENCES

1. Andriesse JP (1988) Nature and management of tropical peatsoils. FAO Soils Bulletin 59. Food and agriculture organization of the United Nations, Rome. pp 179
2. Berg B (2000) Litter decomposition and organic matter turnover in northern forest soils. Forest Ecology and Management 133:13–22
3. Blackham G, Webb E, Corlett R (2014) Natural regeneration in a degraded tropical peatland, Central Kalimantan, Indonesia: Implications for forest restoration. Forest Ecology and Management 324:8–15
4. Brunow G, Lundquist K, Gellerstedt G, (1999) Lignin. In: Sjöström E, Alén R (ed) Analytical Methods in Wood Chemistry, Pulping, and Papermaking. Springer, Berlin/Heidelberg/New York, pp 77–125
5. Hoscilo A, Page S, Tansey K, Rieley J (2011) Effect of repeated fires on land-cover change on peatland in southern Central Kalimantan, Indonesia, from 1973 to 2005. International Journal of Wildland Fire 20:578–588
6. IPCC (2014) 2013 Supplement to the 2006 IPCC Guidelines for National Greenhouse Gas Inventories: Wetlands. Hiraishi T, Krug T, Tanabe K, Srivastava N, Baasansuren J, Fukuda M, Troxler TG (ed). IPCC, Switzerland, pp 353
7. Könönen M, Jauhiainen J, Laiho R, Kusin K, Vasander H (2015). Physical and chemical properties of tropical peat under stabilised land uses. Mires and Peat 16(8): 1-13
8. Laiho R (2006) Decomposition in peatlands: Reconciling seemingly contrasting results on the impacts of lowered water levels. Soil Biology & Biochemistry 38:2011–2024
9. Mehta N, Dinakaran J, Patel S, Laskar A, Yadava M, Ramesh Y, Krishnayya N (2013) Changes in litter decomposition and soil organic carbon in a reforested tropical deciduous cover (India). Ecological Research 28: 239-248
10. Miettinen J, Shi C, Liew SC (2016) Land cover distribution in the peatlands of Peninsular Malaysia, Sumatra and Borneo in 2015 with changes since 1990. Global Ecology and Conservation 6: 67-78
11. Murdiyarso D, Hergoualc'h K, Verchot V (2010) Opportunities for reducing greenhouse gas emissions in tropical peatlands. Proceedings of the National Academy of Sciences USA 107(46):19655–19660
12. Page S, Rieley JO, Shotyk Ø, Weiss D (1999) Interdependence of peat and vegetation in a tropical peat swamp forest. Philosophical Transactions of the Royal Society B 354(1391):1885–1897
13. Sanaullah M, Chabbi A, Lemaire G, Charrier X, Rumpel C (2010) How does plant leaf senescence of grassland species influence decomposition kinetics and litter compounds dynamics? Nutrient Cycling in Agroecosystems 88:159–171
14. Straková P, Niemi R, Freeman C, Peltoniemi K, Toberman H, Heiskanen I, Fritze H, Laiho R (2011) Litter type affects the activity of aerobic decomposers in a boreal peatland more than site nutrient and water table regimes. Biogeosciences 8:2741–2755
15. Sulistiyanto Y (2004) Nutrient dynamics in different sub-types of peat swamp forest in central Kalimantan, Indonesia. PhD thesis, University of Nottingham, UK. pp 388
16. Sundberg A, Sundberg K, Lillandt C, Holmbom B, (1996) Determination of hemicelluloses and pectins in wood and pulp fibres by acid methanolysis and gas chromatography. Nordic Pulp & Paper Research Journal. 11:216–219
17. Sundberg A, Pranovich AV, Holmbom B (2003) Chemical characterization of various types of mechanical pulp fines. Journal of Pulp and Paper Science 29:173–178
18. Wüst R, Jacobsen G, van der Gaast H, Smith A (2008) Comparison of radiocarbon ages from different organic fractions in tropical peat cores: Insights from Kalimantan, Indonesia. Radiocarbon 50(3):359–372
19. Yule C, Gomez L (2009) Leaf litter decomposition in a tropical peat swamp forest in Peninsular Malaysia. Wetlands Ecology and Management 17: 231-241
20. Zhang D, Hui D, Luo Y, Zhou G (2008) Rates of litter decomposition in terrestrial ecosystems: global patterns and controlling factors. Journal of Plant Ecology 1(2):85–93

Abstract No: A-116

DIVERSITY IN THE PHYSICOCHEMICAL PROPERTIES OF TROPICAL PEAT IN SARAWAK, MALAYSIA

Norika Kato[1], Nagamitsu Maie[2], Lulie Melling[3], Sonoko D. Bellingrath-Kimura[4], Haruo Tanaka[1], Masahiro Maeda[2], Zulhilmy Abdullah Mohd[3] and Akira Watanabe[5]

[1]*Graduate School of Agriculture, Tokyo University of Agriculture and Technology, Japan*
[2]*School of Veterinary Medicine, Kitasato University, Japan*
[3]*Tropical Peat Research Laboratory Unit, Chief Minister's Department, Malaysia*
[4]*Leibniz Center for Agricultural Landscape Research, Germany*
[5]*Graduate School of Bioagricultural Sciences, Nagoya University, Japan*

**Corresponding author: maie@vmas.kitasato-u.ac.jp*

SUMMARY

Tropical peat swamp forests (TPSFs) in Sarawak, Malaysia, consist of three major types of vegetation, namely *mixed peat swamp* (*MPS*), *Alan Batu* (*A. Batu*), and *Alan Bunga* (*A. Bunga*) forests, reflecting the variance in the groundwater-level and nutrient concentrations. Tropical peats developed under different vegetation are expected to have different physicochemical properties, which may lead to the different vulnerability to environmental change. However, TPSFs have been developed for oil palm plantation (OPP) irrespective of vegetation types. Sustainable management of OPP depends on the understanding of the variability in the physicochemical properties (or decomposition processes) of TP. Therefore, a variety of peat samples was collected from sapric, hemic, and fibric layers at *MPS*, *A. Batu*, and *A. Bunga* forests in Maludam National Park in Sarawak, and their physicochemical properties were investigated in terms of particle size distribution (PSD) (wet sieving), C composition (^{13}C CPMAS NMR), and humus composition (alkaline extraction). PSD patterns were different among different layers and different forest types with finest PS (< 63μm) fraction was dominant for all the samples. The percentage increased from fibric to hemic layers for *MPS*, but the changes were subtle for the other two types. Both *Alkyl C/O-alkyl C* ratio and the amount of alkaline-extractable humic acids as indicator of decomposition were higher for sapric layer than other layers and for *MPS* and *A. Batu* than *A. Bunga*. These results suggested *MPS* peat had undergone a higher extent of microbial decomposition than other types. In conclusion, the physicochemical properties of TP under different vegetation can vary, reflecting different microbial activities and decomposition processes which are important in determining the best approaches on development and management of peat swamps for oil palm production.

Keywords: *diversity, physicochemical properties, tropical peat, vegetation*

INTRODUCTION

Tropical peatland area, of which 77% is found in coastal region of Southeast Asia, is estimated to cover 11% of global peatland area (Page *et al.*, 2011). Tropical peatland is usually ombrotrophic, and the pH is low (2.9-4.5) due to organic acids formed during decomposition process. Different from many temporal and boreal peatlands of which major vegetation is bryophytes, herbaceous plants, and shrubs, whereas tropical peatlands is covered with trees (tropical peat swamp forests).

Groundwater level and nutrient concentrations of tropical peatland show gradient with the distance from the river: For examples, contents of total phosphorous, total nitrogen, and total potassium decrease as the distance from the river increases (Sjogersten *et al.*, 2011). As such, zones of different forest type are formed with the distance from the river. TPSF in Sarawak successes from mixed peat swamp forest (MPS), *Alan Batu* forest (*A. Batu*), and *Alan Bunga* forest (*A. Bunga*) from the margin to the center of a peat dome. Physicochemical characteristics of peat may vary among these forest types, reflecting the differences in groundwater and nutrient environments, and thus microbial activities. Therefore, it is important to understand the characteristics of tropical peat, considering the forest types.

However, there is still little knowledge on the physicochemical characteristics of tropical peat considering its variety. Therefore, our purpose in this research is to unveil the variability in the physicochemical characteristics of TP under major vegetation of TPSF in Sarawak. Physical properties of peat is investigated in terms of particle size distribution pattern (wet sieving), and chemical properties were investigated by humus composition (alkaline extraction), and carbon composition (^{13}C CPMAS NMR) of TP.

METHODS

Sample Collection

Soil samples were collected from sapric, hemic, and fibric layers at MPS, *A. Batu*, and *A. Bunga* forests in Maludam National Park, Sarawak, Malaysia (Figs. 1 and 2). *A. Batu* and *A. Bunga* belong to Dipterocarpaceae, and have the identical scientific name, *Shorea albida,* but they are different in phenotype. Seasonal variation of groundwater level at three sampling sites is shown in Figure 3. The groundwater level was low in the order of *MPS, A. Batu*, and *A. Bunga*, which corresponded to the distance to the river.

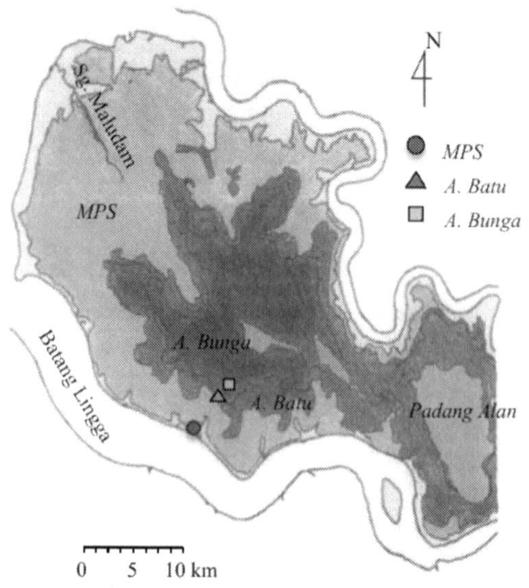

Figure 1: Vegetation map of Maludam National Park and sampling sites. Map is provided from Tropical peat research laboratory, Sarawak (TPRL).

Size fractionation

TP was wet-sieved successively into 8 different size fractions using sieves with openings of 2 mm, 1 mm, 0.5 mm, 0.25 mm, 0.125 mm, and 0.063 mm. Fractionated samples were freeze-dried and weighed. The <0.063 mm size fraction was collected by centrifugation and filtration.

Chemical Analyses

Total C and N contents were measured on a NC analyzer (Sumigraph NC-22). C composition of the <63μm, 125-250, 500-1000 μm fractions were measured by solid state ^{13}C NMR spectra at a ^{13}C resonance frequency of 100.7 MHz on a Jeol ECX-400 NMR spectrometer equipped with a commercial 4-mm CPMAS probe using a standard RAMP-CP pulse sequence. Analytical conditions were as follows; rotation frequency, 10.0 kHz; recycle delay, 0.7-1s; Gaussian line broadening, 50-100Hz. Humus composition was analyzed by alkaline extraction method described as follows. Humus was extracted from peat with 0.1 M NaOH for 24h on an oscillating shaker. Alkaline extractable humus was recovered by centrifugation, and it was acidified to separate into fulvic acid (FA, supernatant) and humic acid (HA, precipitate) fractions. HA and FA contents were determined by a wet-digestion method using $K_2Cr_2O_7$ as an oxidant.

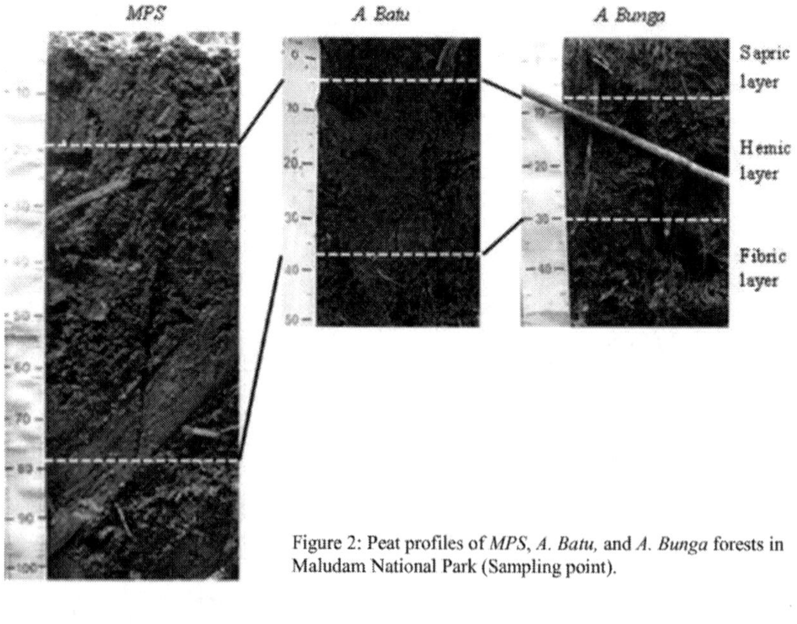

Figure 2: Peat profiles of *MPS, A. Batu,* and *A. Bunga* forests in Maludam National Park (Sampling point).

RESULTS

Particle size distribution

The <63μm fraction was dominant for all types of peat and contributed to 30-60%. Sapric layer, which is considered to have undergone highest degree of decomposition, did not necessary contained high proportion of <63μm fraction compared with other layers. Fragmentation proceeded apparently from fibric to hemic layer for *MPS* and *A. Bunga* forests, while such a trend was not observed for *A. Batu* forest.

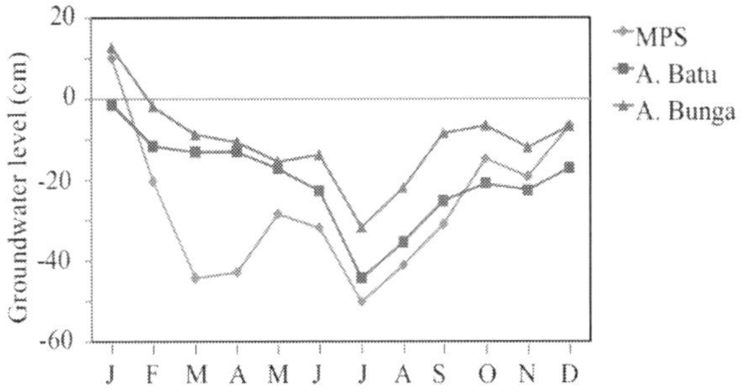

Figure 3: Temporal variations in the groundwater level at *MPS*, *A. Batu*, and *A. Bunga* sites in 2014. Provided from TPRL

Humus composition

Percentages of humic acids (%HAs) extracted from sapric and hemic layers were higher for *MPS* (28-29%, and 33-40%, respectively) than other two types (17-21% and 10-24%, respectively). It is interesting to note that %HAs did not appreciably different among different particulate size fractions for sapric layers, but increased with decrease of particle size for hemic and fibric layers.

C composition

% *O*-alkyl C in the <63μm fraction was higher in the order of *A. Bunga* > *A. Batu* > *MPS*. On the other hand, % alkyl C increased as the particle size decreases, showing the highest variations. Alkyl C/O-alkyl C ratio, which is often used as an index of decomposition of plant residue (Baldock *et al.*, 1992, 1997), was higher for *MPS* and *A. Batu* forests than *A. Bunga* forest. In accordance with humus composition, this value increased as the size decreased for hemic and fibric layers.

DISCUSSION

Physicochemical characteristics of tropical peat are different among different forest types, which were formed in a band-shape reflecting a distance to a river. *MPS*, which forms the nearest to the river, is more microbially decomposed than others. Content of humic acids, which was formed by oxidative decomposition of plant residue, and alkyl C/O-alkyl C values were both high for *MPS* compared with other two types. Furthermore, particle size distribution pattern of MPS in sapric and hemic layers were finer than other two types. The reason may include a lower groundwater level and higher nutrient concentration of *MPS* than other types, which enhanced microbial activity. The *A. Bunga* peat, which is dominated near the center of peat dome was considered to have experienced less extent of microbial decomposition. This was obvious from generally low humic acid content and Alkyl C/O-alkyl C ratio for *A. Bunga* peat. *Alan Batu* showed an intermediate characteristics between *MPS* and *A. Bunga*.

Chemical characteristics of "<63μm" fraction between three types of forests were significantly different. The reason may be explained as follows: different fragmentation processes were proceeded between *MPS* and *A. Bunga*, i.e. microbial decomposition was the dominant process for *MPS* while physical fragmentation by external force associated with root growth was dominant for *A. Bunga*.

CONCLUSION

Vegetation of tropical peat successes with the distance from the river, reflecting the gradation of groundwater level and nutrient concentrations. Physicochemical properties of tropical peat under different vegetation is also different, which is, if not all, partly attributable to the difference in the microbial activity. *A. Bunga* peat is considered to have undergone less microbial decomposition than *MPS* peat. However, *A. Bunga* peat still contains a higher amount of easily decomposable organic matter than *MPS* peat. Therefore, it is possible that *A. Bunga* peat is more vulnerable to development, and as such it would be better to avoid development of *A. Bunga* forest.

ACKNOWLEDGEMENTS

This work was supported by JSPS KAKENHI Grant Number 24405029. We thank to the staff members of tropical peat research laboratory unit (TPRL), Sarawak, for their dedicated cooperation in conducting this research.

REFERENCES

1. Baldock, J.A., Oades, J.M., Nelson, P.N., Skene, T.M., Golchin, A., Clarke, P. 1997. Assessing the extent of decomposition of natural organic materials using solid-state ^{13}C NMR spectroscopy. Australian Journal of Soil Research 35, 1061-1083.
2. Baldock, J.A., Oades, J.M., Waters, A.G., Peng, X., Vassallo, A.M., Wilson, M.A., 1992. Aspects of the chemical structure of soil organic materials as revealed by solid-state ^{13}C NMR spectroscopy. Biogeochemistry 16, 1-42.
3. Page, S.E., Rieley, J.O., Shotyk, O.W., Weiss, D. 1999. Interdependence of peat and vegetation in a tropical peat swamp forest. Philosophical transactions B 354, 1885-1897.
4. Page, S.E., Rieley, J., Banks, C.J. 2011. Global and regional importance of the tropical peatland carbon pool. Global Change Biology 17, 798-818.
5. Sjogersten, S., Cheesman, A.W., Lopez, O., Turner B.L. 2010. Biogeochemical process along a nutrient gradient in a tropical ombrotrophic peatland. Biochemistry 104, 127-163.

Abstract No: A-381

GAUGING DIFFERENCES BETWEEN BLANKET AND RAISED BOGS USING LEGACY DATA

Stephen James Chapman

The James Hutton Institute, UK

**Corresponding author: steve.chapman@hutton.ac.uk*

SUMMARY

The oceanic climate of Scotland leads to the formation of both blanket and raised bogs, with some intermediate types also evident. Apart from their location and mode of formation, superficially the vegetation and underlying peat can look much the same. Using legacy data from the Scottish Peat Surveys, mainly carried out in the 1950s, subtle differences in peat properties and vegetation at that time have been teased out. Raised bogs tended to be deeper than blanket bog but have a lower bulk density. Regardless of type, there was an inverse relationship between the mean bulk density and the depth of a bog. Bulk density changed little with depth to 5 m (blanket) or 6 m (raised) but then decreased in both types. The vegetation pattern varied between both types but was also influenced by latitude and drainage. Raised bogs had more *Eriophorum vaginatum* and *Calluna vulgaris* whereas blanket bog had more *Trichophorum caespitosum, Eriophorum angustifolium, Molinia caerulea, Sphagnum* spp., *Erica tetralix* and *Myrica gale*.

Keywords: *blanket bog, raised bog, peat depth, bulk density, vegetation*

INTRODUCTION

Wherever they are found, peatlands constitute a significant store of carbon. Assessing this store requires knowledge of the peatland area, depth, bulk density and carbon content. Often, information on bulk density and peat depth is lacking. Scotland's peatlands fall into two major types: blanket bog (aka hill peat) and raised bogs (aka valley peat). While the latter are similar to the raised bogs of more continental climates and form in natural basins, blanket bog can develop on sloping terrain due to the very cool and wet oceanic climate, typical of Scotland's upland areas. Once considerable blanket bog has formed, it can confine itself and take on more of a raised bog structure; hence there are also intermediate types (aka semi-confined peatlands).

In the search for more information on bulk density and peat depth, legacy data from the Scottish Peat Surveys, was utilized (e.g. Department of Agriculture and Fisheries for Scotland, 1964). These surveys were mainly carried out on major peatland deposits across Scotland in the 1950s. While peat depth was recorded, bulk density as such was not recorded. However, peat moisture content was measured, together with peat ash content. Assuming a value for peat specific gravity, it is possible to estimate the peat dry bulk density for saturated peat using these values. For peat above the water table, this method gives slightly inflated bulk density values. Nevertheless, it is a useful method for the majority of the peat body lying below the water table.

METHODS

Data which formed part of the Scottish Peat Surveys and was only found as figures within the original reports was digitised and analysed. Additional information as to whether it was a blanket or raised bog, as well as any details on dominant vegetation and any drainage features, was also collated. Drainage was not recorded quantitatively during the surveys but described as part of the surface features. We made a semi-quantitative index, scored as follows: '-' (No mention of drainage or only natural drainage); '+' (Little drainage or only sheep drains (shallow 20 inches deep), now overgrown (inoperative, unsatisfactory, not maintained); '++' (Has been drained in past with more frequent/deeper drains (one metre or more), but now not working); '+++' (Drained and still effective (this would be case for cut-over areas or areas recently prepared for harvesting or forestry)). Vegetation was recorded as a list of species present within the area; in some cases this was semi-quantified by descriptors such as 'frequent', 'abundant' and 'dominant'. Hence the vegetation was scored on a scale of 1–3 (present–dominant) accordingly.

RESULTS

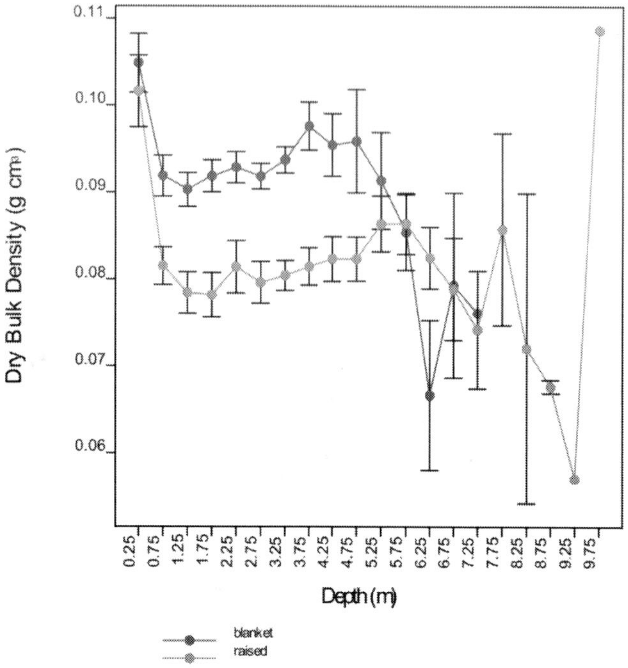

Figure 1: Bulk density over depth as determined using a pedotransfer function and using data from the Scottish Peat Surveys. Bars show standard deviation

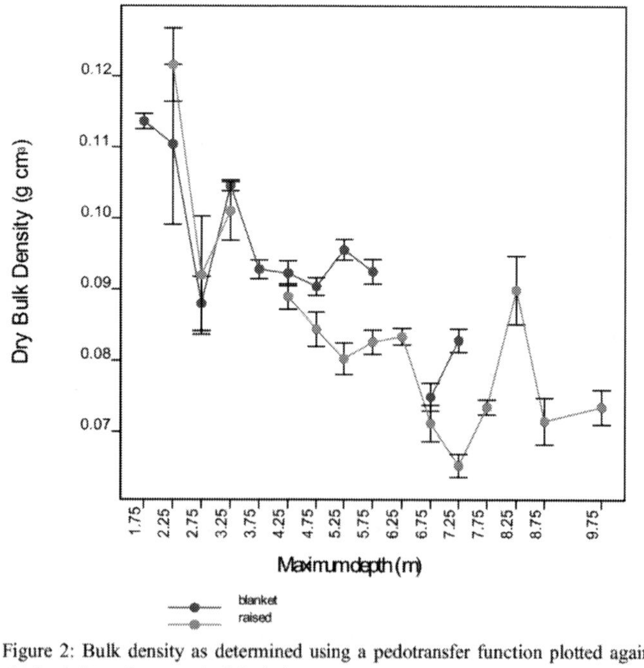

Figure 2: Bulk density as determined using a pedotransfer function plotted against the maximum depth of the bog from which the data was obtained. Bars show standard deviation

Figure 1 shows mean bulk density over depth for both blanket and basin peats. The apparent increase at the very surface is an artefact of the pedotransfer function which over-estimates bulk density where the soil is not saturated. Hence, essentially there is little evidence of much change with depth until about 5 m where there is some decrease in bulk density (for those peats that are that deep). Also the standard deviations increase around this point as there are fewer examples of bogs with these depths. It is also clear that blanket peats have a slightly higher bulk density than basin peats. Replotting the data against the maximum depth of each particular peat bog (Figure 2) reveals that the deeper the particular bog, the lower the mean bulk density. Also, there is not a lot of difference in this plot between blanket bogs and raised bogs, suggesting that the reason basin peats have a lower bulk density than blanket peats is not so much an intrinsic difference in the peat per se but that basin peats tend to be deeper than blanket peats.

The vegetation pattern varied between both types but was also influenced by latitude, drainage and maximum peat depth. Raised bogs had more *Eriophorum vaginatum* and *Calluna vulgaris* whereas blanket bog had more *Trichophorum caespitosum, Eriophorum angustifolium, Molinia caerulea, Sphagnum* spp., *Erica tetralix* and *Myrica gale*. There was no relationship between either vegetation or drainage and bulk density (restricting this to the surface, 0–50 cm, values). However, the '++' drainage category had the greatest bulk density (there were only two values in the '+++' category) but this was not statistically significant. Multivariate analysis of the vegetation patterns showed no relationship with bulk density.

DISCUSSION

In previous estimations of peatland carbon stock within Scotland (Chapman *et al.*, 2009) it was assumed that bulk density did not vary with depth, based upon a preliminary analysis of the Scottish Peat Survey data (Smith *et al.*, 2009). Here it is indicating that bulk density can vary between blanket and raised bogs but that this is partly due to the latter being typically deeper than the former. There is evidence that bulk density is in fact little changed to about 5 m but then decreases slightly in those bogs deeper than 5 m. It is also apparent that the carbon stock of deeper bogs may be offset to some extent by the lesser values of bulk density. There were also significant differences in vegetation pattern between blanket and raised bogs at the time of the surveys. However, these were surveyed over 60 years ago so it is not known if this would still hold true today. Also, the bogs were selected based on the assumed size of the peatland deposit and hence were a biased sample; they may not completely reflect all bogs, particularly those which are shallower and smaller in area. Nevertheless, these findings will potentially aid the prediction of bulk density and hence of carbon stock across areas where bulk density determinations are rare or missing.

REFERENCES

1. Chapman,S.J., Bell,J., Donnelly,D., Lilly,A., 2009. Carbon stocks in Scottish peatlands. *Soil Use and Management* 25, 105-112.

2. Department of Agriculture and Fisheries for Scotland, 1964. *Scottish Peat Surveys Volume 1 - South West Scotland.* HMSO, Edinburgh, 1-234pp.

3. Smith,J.U., Chapman,S.J., Bell,J.S., Bellarby,J., Gottschalk,P., Hudson,G., Lilly,A., Smith,P., Towers,W.. *Developing a methodology to improve soil C stock estimates for Scotland and use of initial results from a resampling of the National Soil Inventory of Scotland to improve the ECOSSE model: Final Report.* 2009. Edinburgh, Rural and Environment Research and Analysis Directorate of the Scottish Government, Science Policy and Co-ordination Division.

Abstract No: A-032

LONG-TERM DISTURBANCE DYNAMICS AND RESILIENCE OF TROPICAL PEAT SWAMP FORESTS

Lydia E.S. Cole1,4, Shonil A. Bhagwat2,4 and Katherine J. Willis1,3,4,5

[1]*Oxford Long-term Ecology Laboratory, Department of Zoology, University of Oxford, United Kingdom*
[2]*Department of Geography, Faculty of Social Sciences, The Open University, United Kingdom*
[3]*Department of Biology, University of Bergen, Norway*
[4]*Biodiversity Institute, Oxford Martin School, Department of Zoology, University of Oxford, United Kingdom*
[5]*Royal Botanical Gardens, United Kingdom*

**Corresponding author: lydcole@googlemail.com*

SUMMARY

The coastal peat swamp forests of Southeast Asia are rapidly undergoing logging and conversion into oil palm plantations. These ecosystems are assumed to have experienced little significant natural or anthropogenic disturbance in the past, persisting under a single ecologically-stable regime. However, their long-term disturbance history has been poorly assessed, and little is known of their resilience to internal and external stresses. Have peat swamp forests been disturbed in the past? What were the drivers? How did the vegetation respond? In order to answer these questions, three peat cores were extracted from coastal peatlands in Sarawak, Malaysian Borneo. Fossil pollen grains and charcoal particles were surveyed at regular depths in all cores, and inferred past vegetation change plotted. Results suggest that the peat swamp forest community has been the dominant vegetation type in these ecosystems throughout the last 4000 years, demonstrating resilience to episodes of burning and climatic change, such as short-term ENSO events. Only within the last 200 years, coincident with increasing indicators of human presence and elevated burning, does the peat swamp forest vegetation show a decline. Thus, it appears that recent anthropogenic disturbances are challenging the resilience of these ecosystems. This research highlights the ecological functioning and requirements of this unique ecosystem, and provides information on what levels of disturbance they can tolerate.

***Keywords**: peat swamp forest, long-term ecology, resilience, disturbance, burning*

FULL ARTICLE

For more information on this study and research findings, please refer to: Cole, L.E.S., S.A. Bhagwat. and Willis, K.J. (2015) Long-term disturbance dynamics and resilience of tropical peat swamp forests. Journal of Ecology – Special Issue on Forest Resilience. DOI: 10.1111/1365-2745.12329. (Open Access.)

Abstract No: A-244

MINERAL VARIATION ACROSS AN ESTURINE RAISED BOG IN WALES

Fred M. Slater

School of Biosciences, Cardiff University, Bridgehill, Newbridge on Wye, Llandrindod WellsLD1 6LY, United Kingdom

**Corresponding author: slaterfm@cf.ac.uk*

Cors Fochno or Borth Bog is a raised bog on the southern side of the Dyfi estuary on the west coast of Wales, United Kingdom. It forms part of the Dyfi Biosphere Reserve, is a Ramsar listed wetland, a National Nature Reserve and a Special Area of Conservation (SAC). The JNCC say of this site "Although a substantial part of the former peatland complex has been taken for agriculture, the surviving core area supports the largest expanse of primary near-natural raised bog in an estuarine context within the UK". Indeed of the 2,400ha of Cors Fochno listed in the land enclosures of the nineteenth century some 700ha still remain with an active raised dome of some 200ha. Current local sources of pollution onto the site are mainly limited to occasional drift of lime dust from agricultural sources, smoke from the now rare surface vegetation fires, the occasional marginal ingress of seawater in times of flood and the almost constant input of marine minerals in the inland drift of sea spray. Historically some parts of the bog margins were contaminated by lead mining activity which can still be detected in analyses of overlying peats. This paper examines the mineral content of peat and plants from across the bog in relation to these external inputs and speculates on their ecological significance.

Keywords: -

Abstract No: A-026

PROPERTIES OF PEAT HUMIC SUBSTANCES

Maris Klavins

Department of Environmental Science, University of Latvia, Latvia

**Corresponding author: maris.klavins@lu.lv*

SUMMARRY

The acidity, elemental, functional and spectral characteristics of humic substances isolated from peat of different origin is described to evaluate the character of processes during humification. The elemental, functional, mass-molecular and spectral characterization of peat humic substances stresses the impact of their origin on the properties of humic substances. Substantial dependence of properties of humic substances on the humification conditions is found. Chemical processes influencing the formation of HA's can be evaluated by the van Krevelen diagram. Since the most important processes influencing the structure of HS can be described as demethylation (removal of - CH_3 group), dehydration and decarboxylation (removal of - COOH group). The same diagram can be used to study the humification process. Demethylation, dehydration and decarboxylation processes result in increased aromaticity and increased humification degree. Demethylation and dehydration processes dominate in the generation of humic acids. Highest is the aromaticity of peat HA and HA from hydromorphic soils. Lowest among humic acids is the humification degree for HA's from anthrosols and sod-calcareous soils.

***Keywords**: humic substances, peat, humification*

INTRODUCTION

Humic substances (HS) are the most widely found organic substances on Earth. Humic substances are a general category of naturally occurring, biogenic, heterogeneous organic substances that can generally be characterised as being yellow to black in colour, of high molecular weight and refractory. Humic substances can be divided in three fractions: a) humin is the fraction of humic substances that is not soluble in water at any pH; b) humic acid (HA) is the fraction of humic substances that is not soluble in water under acidic conditions (below pH 2), but becomes soluble at greater pH; c) fulvic acid (FA) is the fraction of humic substances that is soluble under all pH conditions. Humic substances form most of the organic component of soil, peat and natural waters, they influence the process of formation of fossil fuels, and play a major role in the global carbon geochemical cycle (Stevenson, 1994).

In the studies of humic substances a still prevailing question is that of the dependence of their properties in relation to their origin. It has been shown, that the structure and properties of humic substances differ for humic acids of different origin (Klavins, 1998), but at the same time, considering the great variability in natural organic matter properties, the actual relationship is far from being explained. Another open question can be related to the genesis of peat and fossil carbon deposits and development of peat. Character of transformation of living organic matter is a very complex object of study, considering the high variability of the environmental conditions under which the living organic matter is decaying, slow pace of the humification reactions and the large number and structural differences in organic molecules composing living organic matter. It can be supposed that the humification conditions may have impact on structure and properties of refractory intermediate transformation products of living organic matter - humic substances. From this perspective it is important to study humification processes under the conditions where the transformation of living organic matter could be studied in a relatively homogeneous and stable environment - in the bogs.

The interest in peat properties is growing as far as peat as a substance supports and influences bog and wetland ecosystems, but peat profiles can serve as an archive indicating conditions in past environments (Zaccone *et al.*, 2007). In form of peat significant amounts of organic carbon are stored. Thus peat reserves play a major role in the carbon biogeochemical cycle and they play a significant role considering the ongoing climate change process (Yeloff and Mauquoy, 2008). Industrial and agricultural uses of peat are growing and significant amounts of peat are extracted industrially. Considering this, there is an increasing interest into the study of peat properties diagenesis of their properties. Peat humification occurs under very much differing conditions both at spatial scale and under temporally changing conditions (historically peat development can last for many thousand years). During peat development and even at one specific site major changes in vegetation, temperature, amount of precipitation and correspondingly of the bog hydrological conditions, land use changes in the basin of wetland can take place

(Caseldine *et al.*, 2000), thus it might be expected to find corresponding changes in the properties of peat humic substances, identifying molecular descriptors of organic matter diagenesis processes. However, relations between peat properties (especially in full peat profiles) and properties of peat humic substances have been an object of very few studies (Barančikova *et al.*, 1998, Cocozza *et al.*, 2003, Zaccone *et al.*, 2007).

The aim of this study is to characterize humic acids from raised bog peat samples through appropriate chemical and spectroscopic techniques to evaluate the homogeneity of humic acids isolated from the bog bodies and study peat humification impact on properties and structure of humic acids.

MATERIALS AND METHODS

Materials: Analytical quality reagents (Merck Co., Sigma – Aldrich Co., Fluka Chemie AG) were used without purification. For preparation of solutions, high purity water Millipore Elix 3 (Millipore Co.) 10 – 15 MΩcm was used throughout the study.

Peat sampling and characterization: Peat profiles were obtained from well-characterized, typical raised bogs – Eipurs, Dižpurvs and Dzelve. Studied bogs are located in lowlands, they are of similar origin (they have developed due to ground paludification), although their lithology is largely differing. Full peat profiles were obtained and cut into layers (Table 1). Peat samples were dried at 105°C, and then homogenized and sieved through a 1-mm sieve. The analysis of botanical composition was performed microscopically, using a Carl-Zeiss binocular microscope and decomposition degree was determined (Lishtvan and Korol, 1975)[9]. Humic and fulvic acid ratio (HA/FA) was determined as suggested by Tan (2005), but humification degree by Borgmark (2005). The ^{14}C dating of peat samples was done at the Institute of Geology of the Tallinn Technical University (Estonia). Carbon, hydrogen, nitrogen and sulphur concentrations in the peat and humic acid samples were determined by combustion-gas chromatography technique, using an Elemental Analyzer Model EA-1108 (Carlo Erba Instruments). Ash content was measured after heating 50 mg of each peat sample at 750 ^{0}C for 8 h. Elemental composition was corrected considering the ash content, and the oxygen amount was calculated as a difference.

Isolation of humic acids: Humic acids were extracted from peat and purified as suggested previously (Tan, 2005). Characterization of humic acids: Elemental composition: Carbon, hydrogen, nitrogen and sulphur concentrations in the peat and humic acid samples (elemental analysis of C, H, N, S) were determined by combustion-gas chromatography technique, using an Elemental Analyzer Model EA-1108. Ash content was measured after heating 50 mg of each peat sample at 750 ^{0}C for 8 h. Elemental composition was corrected considering the ash content, and the oxygen amount was calculated as a difference. The Van Krevelen graphical-statistical method was applied as used for the study of the structure on the basis of elemental analysis data (Orlov, 2005).

Carboxylic groups and total acidity: An automatic titrator TitroLine easy was used for measuring carboxylic and phenolic acidity of each HA. The known Ca-acetate method, based on the formation of acetic acid, was used for determining the total number of carboxylic groups. HAs (20 mg) were weighed into a 100 ml Erlenmeyer flask and under N_2 10 ml of the 0.2 N calcium acetate solution were added. Samples were potentiometrically titrated to pH 9.0 with 0.1 N NaOH.

Colloidal stability test: In coagulation tests (Tombácz, 1999), 0.2 g/l of HA were used, increasing the amounts of coagulation electrolyte (NaCl, up to 1 mol/l) at constant pH 3. Samples were left for 3 days. The coagulation intensity was determined with a HACH DR/2000 spectrophotometer, measuring turbidity at 450 nm. The coagulation ratio was calculated using the equation:

$T = \frac{T_{0.0001} - T_1}{T_{0.01} - T_1}$, where T stands for turbidity and the concentration of coagulation electrolyte is 0.0001 – 1 mol/l.

Hydrophobicity of humic substances: Hydrophobicity of humic substances was characterized by their distribution between the water and polyethyleneglycol phases (Zavarzina *et al.*, 2002) (PEG 20000) as the distribution coefficient $K_{PEG/W}$ (analogous to the octanol/water distribution coefficient K_{ow}).

UV-Vis spectral ratios: UV-Vis spectra were recorded on a Helios γ UV spectrophotometer in a 1-cm quartz cuvette. The UV-Vis spectral ratios E_2/E_3 and E_4/E_6, i.e. the ratio of absorbance at 280 and 360, and 465 and 665 nm respectively, was determined for 10 mg of humic acid solutions in 1000 ml of 0.05 M NaOH.

RESULTS AND DISCUSSION

For the isolation of humic acids peats from 3 representative bogs were studied, covering major lithological classes of raised bog peat (Table 1). Upper peat layers are common for raised bog, but lower layers of peat profiles represent fen peat. Peat decomposition degree changes from 10 % till 60 %, but the age of the studied layers from < 100 ^{14}C years till ~ 9000 ^{14}C years. If in upper peat layers humification degree is lower and correspondingly HA/FA ratio is < 10, then in more decomposed peat this ration is >30, respectively peat humic matter is dominated by humic acids, later selected as a major object of studies.

Basic peat properties can be analysed using peat elemental (C, H, N, O, S) composition. The ash content in the studied bogs ranges between 1.11 % until >6 %. The C concentration ranges from ~40 to 55 % and H from 5.4 to 6.2 %, N from 0.5 to >2 %, S from 0.3 to 1.2 %. The elemental composition of peat in the Eipurs Bog is comparatively variable and reflects the changes in the peat decomposition degree and peat type. C concentration in the peat is increasing starting from the upper layers up to a level of 53 %. Changes of N concentrations (increased in the upper and lower horizons of the bog, but also demonstrating increased values coinciding with the changes in the peat composition and formation conditions) could be associated with changes in the peat botanical composition and decomposition degree. S concentrations are significantly lower just in the upper layer of the peat bog, but comparatively stable along the peat column. At the same time the elemental composition of Dzelves Bog is very much different and largely reflects the peat column composition: the C content in the upper layers is much lower (~ 45 %) and comparatively uniform up to depth of 3.25 m, but then rapidly increases reaching 55 % for highly decomposed peat. The same trends of changes reflect elemental ratios (O/C, H/C, N/C).

Table 1: Properties of peat used for extraction of humic acids

Bog	Peat location depth from surface, cm	Peat decomposition degree, %	Peat age, ^{14}C years	Peat botanical composition	Peatland type	Humification degree	HA/FA
Eipurs	0-25	10	70	*Sphagnum fuscum*	Raised	0.49	5.95
	135-170	30	1300	Cotton grass-Sphagnum	Raised	0.84	25.53
	230-240	23	2660	*Sphagnum fuscum*	Raised	0.67	16.01
	320-358	41	6830	Pine, wood	Raised - transitional	1.29	33.49
	410-456	27	8800	*Hypnum*, sedge	Fen	1.27	38.52
Dzelve	30-40	12	75	*Sphagnum fuscum*	Raised	0.48	10.27
	190-200	10	1940	*Sphagnum fuscum*	Raised	0.38	6.80
	310-320	12	2230	*Sphagnum fuscum*	Raised	0.74	8.13
	340-350	> 60	4810	Cotton grass	Raised	2.99	71.76
Dižpurvs	0-20	13	50	Sphagnum – Cotton grass	Raised	0.45	6.75
	240-260	37	2300	Sedge - pinus	Fen	0.65	8.43
	400-430	40	5740	Sedge - hypnum	Fen	1.32	24.55

There was significant variation in elemental composition of HAs within the peat profiles (Table 2). Depending on the bog and the intervals of changes, the elemental composition of the studied peat has been highly variable: C was 49–57%; H was 4.6–5.7%, N was 1.6–2.8%, S was 0.5–1.5% and ash was 0.1–1.2%. The O content, with range 32–42%, was determined by mass balance. In general, C and H concentrations increased with depth. N concentrations decreased with depth, but S concentration was very variable down the profile. The elemental composition of HAs from peat in Latvia is of similar magnitude to those for peat has from other regions of the world. The peat HAs were analyzed using van Krevelen graphs as frequently applied for studies of HA and the C biogeochemical cycle. According to Orlov (1990), the index of atomic ratios O/C, H/C and N/C is useful in identification of structural changes and the degree of maturity of HSs obtained from different environments. The relation between H/C atomic ratio and O/C atomic ratio of HAs of differing decomposition degree – beginning with bog plants up to brown coal, lignite and coal – reveals changes in the associated elemental composition (Figure 1). Figure 1 could be considered a graphical representation of the humification process, indicating the degree of maturity and intensity of degradation processes such as dehydrogenation (reduction of H/C ratio), decarboxylation (reduction of O/C ratio), demethylation occurring during the decay of peat-forming plants, and peat humus maturation continuing up to coal. These changes are especially evident if atomic ratios of peat-forming plants (Sector 3 in Figure 1) are compared to the atomic ratio of organic matter of a high decomposition degree (low moor peat, coal) (Sector 3 in Figure 1). From the point of view of chemistry, peat HAs have an intermediate position (Sector 5 in Figure 1) between the living organic matter and coal organic matter and their structure is formed in a process in which more labile structures (carbohydrates, amino acids, etc.) are destroyed, but thermodynamically more stable aromatic and polyaromatic structures emerge. Comparatively, the studied peat has are at the start of the transformation process of living organic matter.

The dominant functional groups in the structure of peat humic acids are carboxyl and phenolic hydroxyl groups. In humic substances from peat, concentrations of carboxyl groups and phenolic hydroxyl groups are lower (Table 1) than in humic substances from other sources (waters, soils, sediments). Concentrations of carboxyl and phenolic hydroxyl groups change depending on the depth of peat from which humic acids have been isolated: in upper layers the concentration of carboxyl groups is lower for all three studied bogs and total acidity is determined by presence of phenolic hydroxyl groups. The pattern of changes of concentration of carboxyl groups demonstrates that carboxylic acidity increases with the depth of the peat location and the humification degree. In general, the concentrations of carboxyl groups correlate to the O/C ratio, thus indicating that the dominant portion of the oxygen in humic molecules is in form of carboxyl groups. An important characteristic of humic acids is their ability to coagulate in acidic environment or due to changes of ionic strength. We have studied the changes in the ability of humic acids to coagulate in the presence of increasing concentrations of dissolved salt (coagulation test), and have found that peat humic acid coagulation ability increases with depth of humic acid within a peat profile (Table 3).

Table 2: Elemental composition of peat humic acids

Humic acid	C, %	H, %	N, %	S, %	O/C	H/C	N/C
Eipurs HA 0.0 - 0.25	52.40	5.39	2.43	1.50	0.55	1.23	0.04
Eipurs HA 1.35 - 1.70	53.20	4.80	2.13	1.05	0.55	1.07	0.03
Eipurs HA 2.30 - 2.40	54.70	5.04	1.87	0.87	0.51	1.10	0.03
Eipurs HA 3.20 - 3.58	52.70	4.34	2.25	0.83	0.57	0.98	0.04
Eipurs HA 4.10 - 4.56	55.30	4.49	2.48	1.01	0.49	0.97	0.04
Dzelve HA 0.30 - 0.40	52.25	4.51	2.59	0.77	0.57	1.03	0.04
Dzelve HA 1.90 - 2.00	56.17	5.11	2.29	0.84	0.47	1.08	0.03
Dzelve HA 3.10 - 3.20	57.05	5.16	2.66	0.80	0.45	1.08	0.04
Dzelve HA 3.40 - 3.50	59.49	3.98	2.02	0.68	0.43	0.80	0.03
Dižpurvs HA 0.0 - 0.20	56.54	5.71	3.24	0.88	0.45	1.20	0.05
Dižpurvs HA 2.40 - 2.60	56.05	4.35	2.14	0.89	0.49	0.93	0.03
Dižpurvs HA 4.00 - 4.30	58.11	4.78	3.10	0.90	0.43	0.98	0.05

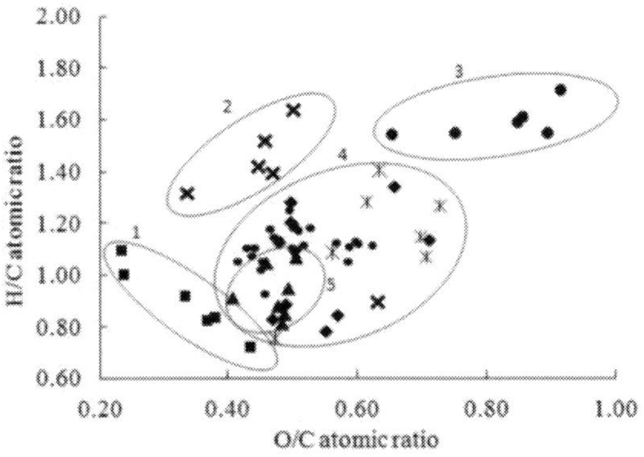

Figure 1: Van Krevelen (H/C *vs*. O/C atomic ratio) graph of bog plants (●); has isolated from peat samples from bogs in Latvia (•); reference peat HA and peat HA (✳); soil HA (◆); HA from different coals and lignite (■), sedimentary HA (✕) and aquatic HA (▲).

Table 3: Functional properties of peat humic acids

Humic acid	-COOH, mmol g^{-1}	Total acidity, mEq g^{-1}	ArOH, mmol g^{-1}	$K_{PEG/W}$	E_4/E_6	E_2/E_3	Coagulation ratio T
Eipurs HA 0.0 - 0.25	2.70	8.50	5.80	1.66	5.00	3.4	0.968
Eipurs HA 1.35 - 1.70	4.70	7.71	3.01	11.80	6.23	2.84	1.035
Eipurs HA 2.30 - 2.40	4.60	6.13	1.53	10.82	6.40	2.92	1.010
Eipurs HA 3.20 - 3.58	6.20	6.40	0.20	8.19	8.00	3.09	1.019
Eipurs HA 4.10 - 4.56	4.70	7.60	2.90	9.86	6.55	3.08	1.023
Dzelve HA 0.30 - 0.40	4.60	8.16	3.56	8.63	10.00	3.39	0.972
Dzelve HA 1.90 - 2.00	4.20	9.31	5.11	10.60	9.00	3.31	1.000
Dzelve HA 3.10 - 3.20	4.40	8.41	4.01	17.60	3.43	2.94	1.016

Humic acid	-COOH, mmol g^{-1}	Total acidity, mEq g^{-1}	ArOH, mmol g^{-1}	$K_{PEG/W}$	E_4/E_6	E_2/E_3	Coagulation ratio T
Dzelve HA 3.40 - 3.50	5.40	6.70	1.30	6.70	5.75	2.97	1.037
Dižpurvs HA 0.0 - 0.20	3.60	7.00	3.40	6.18	3.00	3.26	0.940
Dižpurvs HA 2.40 - 2.60	5.20	8.10	2.90	16.10	3.25	2.63	0.950
Dižpurvs HA 4.00 - 4.30	5.00	7.50	2.50	8.06	3.12	2.77	1.147

Important information about basic structural differences of humic substances can provide their UV spectra. The UV-Vis spectra of peat HA examined are featureless, and they monotonically decrease with increasing wavelength. The ultraviolet spectra of humic acids from different peat layers are similar, differing only slightly in optical density. The slope of the adsorption curves as measured by the ratios of UV absorbancy (Table 3) at 280 and 360 (E_2/E_3) and 465 and 665 nm, (E_4/E_6) have been suggested to be related to the condensation of aromatic groups (aromaticity), and also to particle size and molecular weight. Higher E_4/E_6 ratios measured for humic acids from deeper bog layers accordingly to data in the literature suggest a lower degree of condensed aromatic systems and smaller particle sizes or molecular weights.

CONCLUSIONS

Peat humic acids (HA) have an intermediate position between the living organic matter and coal organic matter and their structure is formed in a process in which more labile structures (carbohydrates, amino acids, etc.) are destroyed, but thermodynamically more stable aromatic and polyaromatic structures emerge. Comparatively, the studied peat has are at the start of the transformation process of living organic matter. Concentrations of carboxyl and phenolic hydroxyl groups changes depending on the depth of peat from which Has have been isolated: and carboxylic acidity is increasing with depth of peat location and the humification degree.

ACKNOWLEDGEMENT

Financial support from Latvia National Research Programme ResProd is acknowledged.

REFERENCES

1. Barančikova G., Senesi N. and Brunetti G., Chemical and spectroscopic characterization of humic acids isolated from different Slovak soil types, *Geoderma*, 78, 251 – 266 (1997)
2. Borgmark A., The colour of climate: changes in peat decomposition as a proxy for climate change – a study of raised bogs in South-central Sweden, PhD thesis, Stockholm University, Stockholm (2005)
3. Cocozza C., D'Orazio V., Miano T. M. and Shotyk W., Characterization of solid and aqueous phases of a peat bog profile using molecular fluorescence spectroscopy, ESR and FT-IR, and comparison with physical properties, *Organic Geochemistry*, 34, 49–60 (2003)
4. Klavins M., Aquatic humic substances, University of Latvia, Riga, 234 (1998)
5. Lishtvan I. I. and Korol N. T., Basic Properties of Peat and Methods for Their Determination, In: Nauka I Teknika, Minsk (1975) (in Russian)
6. Stevenson F.J., Humus chemistry: Genesis, composition, reactions, 2nd ed., Wiley, New York, 496 (1994)
7. Tan K. H., Soil Sampling, Preparation, and Analysis, Second Edition, Taylor & Francis group, New York (2005)
8. Tombácz E., Colloidal properties of humic acids and spontaneous changes of their colloidal state under variable solution conditions, *Soil Science*, 164(11), 814-824 (1999)
9. Zavarzina A. G., Demin V. V., Nifanteva T. I., Shkinev V. M., Danilova T. V. and Spivakov B. Y., Extraction of humic acids and their fractions in poly(ethylene glycol)-based aqueous biphasic systems, *Analytica Chimica Acta*, 452, 95-103 (2002)
10. Zaccone C., Miano T. M. and Shotyk W., Qualitative comparison between raw peat and related humic acids in an ombrotrophic bog profile, *Organic Geochemistry*, 38, 151-160 (2007)
11. Yeloff D. and Mauquoy D., The influence of vegetation composition on peat humification: implications for paleoclimatic studies, *Boreas*, 35, 662-673 (2006)

Abstract No: A-426

RESPONSES OF PEAT CARBON AT DIFFERENT DEPTHS TO SIMULATED WARMING AND OXIDIZATION

Liangfeng Liu[1, 2, 3] and Huai Chen[1, 2, 3*]

[1]*Chengdu Institute of Biology, Chinese Academy of Sciences, China*
[2] *College of Forestry, Northwest A&F University, China*
[3]*Zoige Peatland and Global Change Research Station, Chinese Academy of Sciences, China*

[*]*Corresponding author: chenhuai@cib.ac.cn*

SUMMARY

Warming and water table drawdown greatly reshapes carbon cycle in peatlands, especially when the old carbon stored under the peatland subsurface is considered. However, little is known about the effects of warming, oxidization or their combination on carbon decomposition at different peat depths (0-100 cm). In this research, soil from different depths from the Zoige Plateau, China was incubated under four scenarios to detect the exported carbon. Our result showed that with enhanced temperature and oxygen, total carbon dioxide (CO_2) fluxes increased by 40.7-176.5%, and average dissolved organic carbon (DOC) concentration increased by 44-159.4%. Soil respiration (Rs) rates and variability under warming and oxidization differed significantly with depth, probably caused by the differences of soil substrate distribution at the various depths. By classifying the source of Rs as young soil (YS: 0-20 cm) and old soil (OS: 21-100 cm), this research found that the OS accounted for a large proportion of total Rs under 8°C-anaerobic conditions (CO_2: 74.2%; DOC: 60.7%). The relative contribution of OS to total Rs did not show an obvious change with warming or oxidization. Although YS and OS responded equally to warming and oxidization, OS was responsible for a larger proportion of total increase in Rs. Compared with other studies, we conclude that the peat samples at our site are less sensitive to warming and oxidization than peatlands at higher latitudes, but that the OS at this site may be more critical in predicting the regional carbon cycle.

Keywords: *Zoige plateau, peatlands, incubaiton, aerobic environment, anaerobic environment*

INTRODUCTION

With 15-30% of total global soil carbon, peatlands, mainly distributed in the northern high latitude areas, are an important carbon sink (Gorham, 1991). The large quantities of carbon deposited in peatlands have resulted from water saturated conditions and the consequent anaerobic environment accompanied with low temperature (Griffis *et al.*, 2000). In a changing environment, the fate of carbon in peatlands will depend on the response of the soil substrate to changes of water regime, oxygen (O_2) abundance and temperature (Chen *et al.*, 2014). Global warming has increased mean global air temperatures by 0.88°C from 1988 to 2012, and temperatures are predicted to increase even more by the end of the 21st century (IPCC, 2013). Climate warming and hydrologic redistribution have changed the global carbon cycle (Hicks Pries & Schuur, 2013) and have the potential to shift natural peatlands from a carbon sink to a carbon source (Schuur *et al.*, 2009; Yan *et al.*, 2014). High altitude areas are experiencing a much larger than average increases in temperature (Peng *et al.*, 2014). In recent decades, water table drawdown has resulted in degradation of peatlands on the Zoige Plateau (Chen *et al.*, 2010). Water table drawdown has exposed the preserved carbon to aerobic (AE) environment (Oechel *et al.*, 1998), resulting in a shift in the soil respiration (Rs) pathway from anaerobic (AN) respiration to AE respiration, which responds to climate change differently (Schuur *et al.*, 2008; Yang *et al.*, 2014). Studies have shown that the stored older carbon in the deep soil of degraded peatlands participates in the contemporary carbon cycle (Schuur *et al.*, 2009). However, the responses of peat to the changing environment at different depths remains poorly understood. The main objective of this study was to detect the response of peat at different depths to warming and oxidization. The specific objectives were to: 1) determine the changes of peat Rs under warming and oxidizing conditions; 2) quantify the Rs increase increment of each layer with warming and oxidization, the contribution of young soil (YS: 0-20 cm) and old soil (OS: 21-100 cm) to total Rs and their contribution to increased Rs under warming and oxidization conditions.

METHODS

Samples (0-100 cm, at 10 cm intervals) were collected randomly from the Zoige peatland and the Global Change Research Station, Chinese Academy of Sciences (33°06′25″ N, 102°38′33″ E) in October 2013. Soil at each depth was divided into two parts; one for incubation and the other for DOC analysis. Soils of each depth were incubated under four scenarios: (1) anaerobic at 8°C (8°C-AN); (2) aerobic at 8°C (8°C-AE); (3) anaerobic at 18°C (18°C-AN); (4) aerobic at 18°C (18°C-AE). The Rs rates at each depth and under each scenario were monitored during a 35-day incubation. The presumption was that warming and oxidization function in a gradual pattern on the soil from the surface to a depth (Figure 1). We recorded total Rs (the sum of Rs at all ten depths) and the source of Rs was classified as YS and OS. We detected the proportion of YS and OS to total Rs under each scenario, and the relative contribution of OS to the total Rs increment in response to warming and oxidization. DOC concentration was detected before and after incubation and the concentration differences as exported DOC during incubation. One way analysis of variance (ANOVA), linear regression analytical methods and SPSS 20.0 for Windows (SPSS Inc., Chicago, IL, USA) were used in statistical analysis. All data were checked and confirmed to be normally distributed before ANOVA analysis (K-S test).

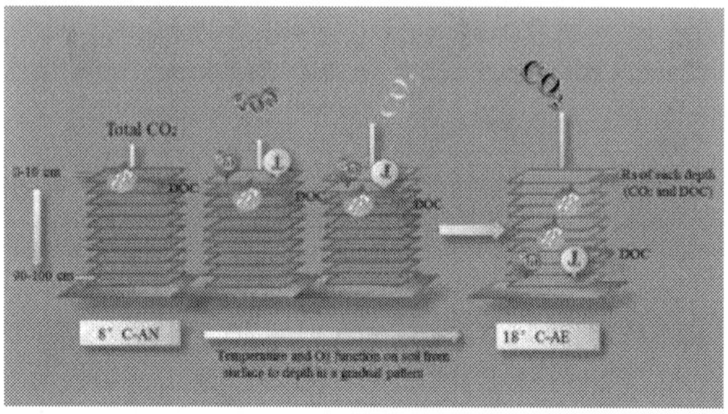

Figure 1: Gradual pattern of warming and oxidization functions on soil from surface to depth of 100 cm (10 cm as a depth).

RESULTS

The CO_2 and DOC exported rates were significantly related to temperature and O_2 concentration ($P < 0.01$ for both).Total CO_2 emissions integrated over the whole depth was 2400.2 ± 57.7 mg m^{-2} d^{-1} under the 8°C-AN scenario, and it increased by 40.7%, 73.6% and 176.5% under the 8°C-AE, 18°C-AN and 18°C-AE scenarios, respectively. The highest DOC concentration was 194.3 ± 11.9 mg kg^{-1} at 18°C-AE and the lowest was 74.9 ± 8.1 mg kg^{-1} at 8°C-AN, an increase of 44% and 53.5% in response to a 10°C warming and aerobic conditions. CO_2 and DOC export showed significant variations among all depths under the four scenarios ($P < 0.01$ for all). Both CO_2 emission and DOC concentrations at 0-20 cm depth was higher than those of the deeper layers, but the variation pattern at deeper depths was different among the four scenarios. For example, CO_2 emissions at 8°C-AN were similar among depths, although a considerable difference was observed under the other three scenarios. By classifying the peat into YS and OS, we found that OS was the major carbon contributor to total Rs under all four scenarios (CO_2: 65.9-74.2%; DOC: 60.7-70.6%). Rs and DOC showed a substantial increase under the 8°C-AE, 18°C-AN and 18°C-AE scenarios, but at different degrees at each depth. Over the whole depth profile, OS was responsible for 59.6-67.5% and 71.7-76.9% of the total increase in CO_2 and DOC.

DISCUSSION

The effect of temperature on Rs has been illustrated in a wide range of studies (Eliasson *et al.*, 2005; Tucker *et al.*, 2013). Biasi *et al.* (2005) reported that temperature could influence the utilization of carbon source by microbes or microbial metabolism leading to changes in Rs rates. Treat *et al.* (2014) found that a warmer and drier climate could result in a substantial increase in carbon loss (Biasi *et al.*, 2005; Treat *et al.*, 2014). DOC also was driven by rising temperature (Freeman *et al.*, 2001b). Water table drawdown in peatlands could supply more soil porosity for gas diffusion, permitting O_2 to increase Rs by being the terminal electron acceptor during Rs (Kane *et al.*, 2013). The increased CO_2 and DOC export rate in this study under the warming and oxidization scenario was lower than in other incubation studies, demonstrating that our soil from mid- and high altitudes had a lower sensitivity to warming and oxidization, which can be explained by the difference of climate and vegetation between sites.

Rs differed significantly throughout the whole peat profile demonstrating the high variation in the response of the different peat depths to warming and oxidization. Higher CO_2 and DOC export rates at the 0-20 cm depth was consistent with other studies (Biasi *et al.*, 2014) and in agreement with the idea that older carbon in deeper layers is more "recalcitrant" than younger carbon at the surface (Bosatta & Agren, 1999; Knorr *et al.*, 2005). CO_2 emissions from deeper depths (21-100 cm) were stable under the 8°C-AN scenario but had unequal increases under warming/oxidization conditions. This was probably because in a restricted environment, environment factors restricted Rs; but in a looser environment with higher temperature and more O_2, soil substrate character was the main factor controlling Rs. The unequal increases also reflected the variation of soil substrate among all profiles (Treat *et al.*, 2014).

By classifying the source of Rs into YS and OS, we found OS was a major contributor to total Rs and responsible for a large part of the total increase in Rs. With climate warming and increased oxidization, most peatland carbon pools may become destabilized, releasing their stored carbon (Freeman *et al.*, 2001a; Freeman *et al.*, 2004). Aged carbon exporting DOC to rivers is receiving increasing attention (Butman *et al.*, 2015). The contribution of OS to total Rs was much higher in our study than that in other studies (6-18% in Hicks Pries & Schuur, 2013; 7-41% in Schuur, 2009) and this difference may be due to wide differences in peat type, climate and carbon cycle patterns among the studied peatlands.

CONCLUSION

This study showed that enhanced temperature and O_2 levels substantially increased Rs, at different rates among all layers of our study site, suggesting that soil substrate characteristics vary among the whole profile of peat. By dividing the source of Rs into YS and OS, we found that OS was responsible for a large proportion of the total increase in Rs. Compared with other peatlands studies, this research observed lower rates of Rs with 10°C warming or oxidization, but higher contribution of OS to total Rs. We can conclude that the soil in our study site is less sensitive to warming and oxidization than other peatlands and that OS in this peatlands is more critical in predicting regional peatland carbon cycle. Our results could be very useful for modeling scientists to calibrate their models.

ACKNOWLEDGEMENTS

This study was supported by the 100 Talents Program of Chinese Academy of Sciences, the External Cooperation Program of BIC, Chinese Academy of Sciences (No.151751KYSB20130027), 1000 Talents Program of Sichuan Province of China, National Natural Science Foundation of China (No.31570480 and 41201205) and the Open Project from Key Laboratory of Physical Geography and Environment Process of Qinghai Province, Qinghai Normal University. The authors give special thanks to Ms. Wan Xiong for her editing and valuable comments on the manuscript.

REFERENCES

1. Biasi, C., Jokinen, S., Marushchak, M.E., Hämäläinen, K., Trubnikova, T., Oinonen, M. & Martikainen, P.J. (2014) Microbial Respiration in Arctic Upland and Peat Soils as a Source of Atmospheric Carbon Dioxide. *Ecosystems*, **17**, 112-126.
2. Biasi, C., Rusalimova, O., Meyer, H., Kaiser, C., Wanek, W., Barsukov, P., Junger, H. & Richter, A. (2005) Temperature-dependent shift from labile to recalcitrant carbon sources of arctic heterotrophs. *Rapid Communications in Mass Spectrometry*, **19**, 1401-1408.
3. Bosatta, E. & Agren, G.I. (1999) Soil organic matter quality interpreted thermodynamically. *Soil Biology & Biochemistry*, **31**, 1889-1891.
4. Butman, D.E., Wilson, H.F., Barnes, R.T., Xenopoulos, M.A. & Raymond, P.A. (2015) Increased mobilization of aged carbon to rivers by human disturbance. *Nature Geoscience*, **8**, 112-116.
5. Chen, H., Wu, N., Wang, Y., Gao, Y. & Peng, C. (2010) Methane Fluxes from Alpine Wetlands of Zoige Plateau in Relation to Water Regime and Vegetation under Two Scales. *Water, Air, & Soil Pollution*, **217**, 173-183.
6. Chen, H., Yang, G., Peng, C., Zhang, Y., Zhu, D., Zhu, Q., Hu, J., Wang, M., Zhan, W., Zhu, E., Bai, Z., Li, W., Wu, N., Wang, Y., Gao, Y., Tian, J., Kang, X., Zhao, X. & Wu, J. (2014) The carbon stock of alpine peatlands on the Qinghai–Tibetan Plateau during the Holocene and their future fate. *Quaternary Science Reviews*, **95**, 151-158.
7. Eliasson, P.E., McMurtrie, R.E., Pepper, D.A., Stromgren, M., Linder, S. & Agren, G.I. (2005) The response of heterotrophic CO_2 flux to soil warming. *Global Change Biology*, **11**, 167-181.
8. Freeman, C., Evans, C. & Monteith, D.T. (2001a) An enzymic 'latch' on a global carbon store-a shortage of oxygen lacks up carbon in peatlands by restraining a singe enzyme. *Nature*, **409**, 149-150.
9. Freeman, C., Evans, C. & Monteith, D.T. (2001b) Export of organic carbon from peat soils. *Nature*, **421**, 785-786.
10. Freeman, C., Fenner, N., Ostle, N.J., Kang, H., Dowrick, D.J., Reynolds, B., Lock, M.A., Sleep, D., Hughes, S.

& Hudson, J. (2004) Export of dissolved organic carbon from peatlands under elevated carbon dioxide levels. *Nature*, **430**, 195-198.
11. Gorham, E. (1991) Northern Peatlands: Role in the Carbon Cycle and Probable Responses to Climatic Warming. *Ecological Applications*, **2**, 182-195.
12. Griffis, T.J., Rouse, W.R. & Waddington, J.M. (2000) Interannual variability of net ecosystem CO_2 exchange at a subarctic fen. *Global Biogeochemical Cycles*, **14**, 1109-1121.
13. Hicks Pries, C.E. & Schuur, E.A.G. (2013) Thawing permafrost increases old soil and autotrophic respiration in tundra: Partitioning ecosystem respiration using $\delta^{13}C$ and ^{14}C. *Global change biology*, **19**, 649-661.
14. IPCC (2013) Climate Change 2013: the Physical Science Basis. Cambridge University Press,Cambridge.
15. Kane, E.S., Chivers, M.R., Turetsky, M.R., Treat, C.C., Petersen, D.G., Waldrop, M., Harden, J.W. & McGuire, A.D. (2013) Response of anaerobic carbon cycling to water table manipulation in an Alaskan rich fen. *Soil Biology & Biochemistry*, **58**, 50-60.
16. Knorr, W., Prentice, C., House, J.I. & Holland, E.A. (2005) Long-term sensitivity of soil carbon turnover to warming. *Nature*, **433**, 298-301.
17. Oechel, W.C., Vourlitis, G.L. & Hastngs, S.J. (1998) The effects of water tale manipulation and elevated temperature on the net CO_2 flux of wet sedge tundra ecosystem. *Global Change Biology*, **4**, 77-90.
18. Peng, F., Xue, X., You, Q., Zhou, X. & Wang, T. (2014) Warming effects on carbon release in a permafrost area of Qinghai-Tibet Plateau. *Environmental Earth Sciences*, DOI 10.1007/s12665-014-3394-3.
19. Schuur, E.A., Vogel, J.G., Crummer, K.G., Lee, H., Sickman, J.O. & Osterkamp, T.E. (2009) The effect of permafrost thaw on old carbon release and net carbon exchange from tundra. *Nature*, **459**, 556-559.
20. Schuur, E.A.G., Bockheim, J. & Canadell, J.G. (2008) Vulnerability of Permafrost Carbon to Climate Change:Implications for the Global Carbon Cycle. *BioScience*, **58**, 701-714.
21. Treat, C.C., Wollheim, W.M., Varner, R.K., Grandy, A.S., Talbot, J. & Frolking, S. (2014) Temperature and peat type control CO_2 and CH_4 production in Alaskan permafrost peats. *Global Change Biology*, **20**, 2674-2686.
22. Tucker, C.L., Bell, J., Pendall, E. & Ogle, K. (2013) Does declining carbon-use efficiency explain thermal acclimation of soil respiration with warming ? *Global Change Biology*, **19**, 252-263.
23. Yan, J., Zhang, W., Wang, K., Qin, F., Wang, W., Dai, H. & Li, P. (2014) Responses of CO_2, N_2O and CH_4 fluxes between atmosphere and forest soil to changes in multiple environmental conditions. *Global Change Biology*, **20**, 300-312.
24. Yang, G., Chen, H., Wu, N., Tian, J., Peng, C., Zhu, Q., Zhu, D., He, Y., Zheng, Q. & Zhang, C. (2014) Effects of soil warming, rainfall reduction and water table level on CH_4 emissions from the Zoige peatland in China. *Soil Biology & Biochemistry*, **78**, 83-89.

Abstract No: A-211

SOIL PHYSICAL PROPERTIES OF TROPICAL PEATLAND AT THREE DIFFERENT TYPES OF LAND USE IN KUBU RAYA DISTRICT OF WEST KALIMANTAN, INDONESIA

Mateus Aba [1], Urai Edi Suryadi[2] and Sutarman Gafur[2*]

[1]*Department of Agronomy, Faculty of Agriculture, Tanjungpura University, Indonesia*
[2]*Department of Soil Science, Faculty of Agriculture, Tanjungpura University, Indonesia*

**Corresponding author: sutarman.g@faperta.untan.ac.id*

SUMMARY

Tropical peatland in West Kalimantan, Indonesia, has become more intensively used not only for agricultural land, but also for other uses. This study is aimed to observe changes in soil physical properties of peatland having been used as secondary forest, temporarily open land, and as oil-palm plantation. Soil samples were collected from study sites in Kubu Raya District of West Kalimantan. Parameters include water table in each site and in secondary canal, field capacity water content, bulk and particle density, porosity, hydraulic conductivity, and soil maturity levels. The results showed that water table was deeper in temporarily open land (66.35 cm) and in oil palm plantation (64.0cm), and shallow in secondary forest (54.26cm). Percentage of field water capacity was highest in secondary forest (79.65%), lower in temporarily open land (77.62%), and lowest in oil palm plantation (75.41%). Water table at secondary canal was also deeper in temporary open land (109cm), higher in oil palm plantation (100.5cm), and highest in secondary forest (99.25cm). Furthermore, bulk density was highest in oil palm plantation (0.46g/cm^3), lower in secondary forest (0.29g/cm^3), and lowest in temporarily open land (0.23g/cm^3). Particle density was also highest in oil palm plantation (1.59g/cm^3), lower in temporarily open land (1.34 g/cm^3), and lowest in secondary forest (1.26g/cm^3). Meanwhile, porosity was lowest in oil palm plantation (70.92%), higher in temporarily open land (78.9%), and highest in secondary forest (81.80%). Hydraulic conductivity was also highest in oil palm plantation (10.61cm/h), lower in temporarily open land (7.88 cm/h), and lowest in secondary forest (5.23cm/h). Finally, there were vary in peat soil maturity levels, namely hemic and fibric in secondary forest, hemic, fibric, and sapric in temporarily open land, and only sapric in oil palm plantation. Conclusion, different management types had caused changes in soil physical properties of tropical peatland in District of Kubu Raya, West Kalimantan, Indonesia.

***Keywords**: soil physical properties, tropical peatland, land use*

INTRODUCTION

Tropical peatland in West Kalimantan, Indonesia, has become more intensively used not only for agricultural land, but also for other uses. The shift to other uses, especially for oil palm plantation and for industrial plant forest, has become more concern because it might have caused a destructive impacts to both local and regional environment. Destruction of tropical peatland ecosystem will impact both its in-situ and ex-situ environmental conditions (Noor, 2013). Data from previous study showed that land use change from tropical peat forests into cleared and drained peats used for intensive timber harvesting, oil palm and industrial plantations has greatly degraded major ecological function of tropical peats as carbon storage (Anshari *et.al.*, 2010).

Recently, as newly developed district in West Kalimantan, government of District of Kubu Raya has been actively promoting their tropical peatland to be developed either for agricultural land, oil palm plantation, industrial timber plantation, or other uses. In Rasau Jaya District, in the last few year, oil palm plantation areas has increased about 4.38% per year. In 2011, there was only about 172 ha of oil palm plantation. Then, in the year of 2012 and 2013 oil palm plantation areas increased to 534 and 609 ha, respectively (BPS, 2014). This type of development has greatly increased public concern, especially because it might have a great impact on tropical peatland degradation in Kubu Raya District. This study is aimed to observe changes in soil physical properties of tropical peatland having been used as secondary forest, temporary open land, and as oil-palm plantation. This study only focus on the parameters representing peat soil physical properties as they are too fragile to field management activities. Thus, this paper discuss the impacts of three different types of land use on soil physical properties of tropical peatland.

METHODS

The three study sites are located in the Village of Rasau Jaya 3 and in the Village of Rasau Jaya Umum, Kubu Raya District of West Kalimantan. They represent three types of land use; secondary forest, temporarily open land, and oil palm plantation. The secondary forest is belong to local people. This secondary forest is the natural forest that previously had been logged by local peoples. At the moment, the forest now is left uncultivated for its natural resources stocks. Temporarily open land is a site belong to PT. Mitsubishi that formerly prepared for industrial timber plantation. It was mechanically opened in 2006, however, up to now it is not yet planted and left opened. Some part of it is naturally inhabitated by acasia trees and shrubs. Oil palm plantation site is belong to PT. Sumatera Unggul Makmur. It was mechanically opened and drained in 2010, and planted in 2011. The planting density was 160 palms per hectar. Total planted areas is about 196 ha.

Soil samples were collected using ring sample to collect undisturbed soil samples from each site. Undisturbed soil samples were used for its physical properties analyses, while disturbed samples were used for its chemical properties analyses. Soil samples were analysed in both Soil physical Lab, and Soil Chemistry and Fertility Laboratories of Faculty of Agriculture, Tanjungpura University. Parameters observed include water table depth in each site and in secondary canal, bulk density, particle density, porosity, hydraulic conductivity, field water capacity, and soil maturity levels.

RESULTS

Water Table Depth

Data on water table depth presented in figure 1 shows that average data in each observation site is higher in temporarily open land (66.35 cm) and lower in oil palm plantation (64.0cm), and lowest in secondary forest (54.26cm). Similar trend is also showed for average water table data in secondary canal.

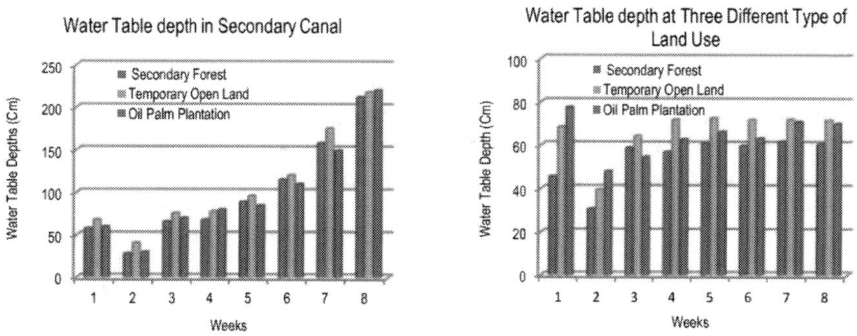

Figure 1: Water Table in Secondary Canal (left) and Water Table Depth of Tropical Peatland at Three Different Types of Land Use (right).

During eight weeks observation, water table at secondary canal was also higher in temporary open land (109cm), slightly lower in oil palm plantation (100.5cm), and lowest in secondary forest (99.25cm). Week 8 of observation was the peak of dry season of this year. This data shows that secondary forest dominated by young trees has more capacity to retain water compared to that of either in temporary open land and in oil palm plantation.

Soil Bulk and Soil Particle Density, Hydraulic Conductivity, and Porosity

Data on soil bulk density is highest in oil palm plantation (0.46g/cm^3), lower in secondary forest (0.29g/cm^3), and lowest in temporarily open land (0.23g/cm^3) (Figure2). Similar trend for data on soil particle density which is also highest in oil palm plantation (1.59g/cm^3), lower in temporarily open land (1.34 g/cm^3), and lowest in secondary forest (1.26g/cm^3). This trend is also occured for data on hydraulic conductivity, it is highest in oil palm plantation (10.61cm/h), lower in temporarily open land (7.88 cm/h), and lowest in secondary forest (5.23cm/h). On the other hand, data for porosity was lowest in oil palm plantation (70.92%), higher in temporarily open land (78.9%), and highest in secondary forest (81.80%).

Field Water Capacity and Soil Maturity

Field water capacity is the amount of water remaining in a soil after the free water has been allowed to drain away after it is saturated. Findings data show that field water capacity percentage was highest in secondary forest (79.65%), lower in temporary open land (77.62%), and lowest in oil palm plantation (75.41%) (**Figure** 3).

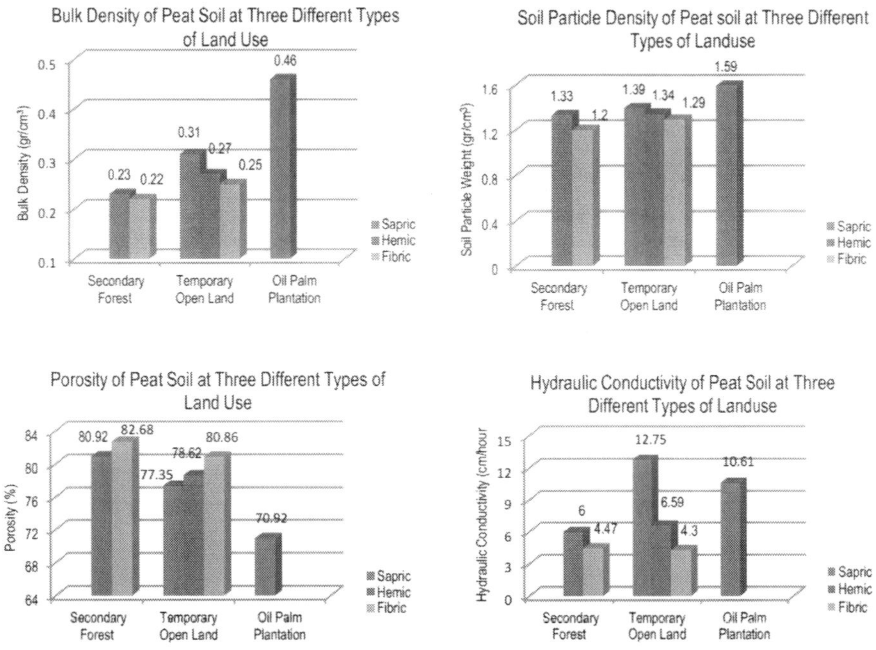

Figure 2: Soil Bulk Density, Particle Density, Porosity, and Hydraulic Conductivity of Peat Soil at Different Types of Land Use.

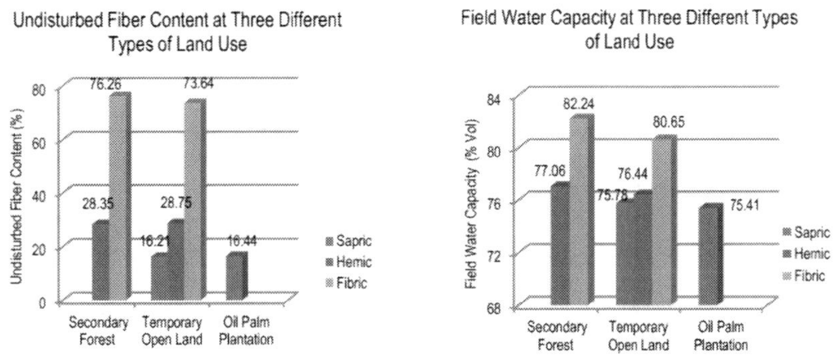

Figure 3: Percentage of Undisturbed Fiber Content (left) and Field Water Capacity (Right) in Peat Soil at Different Types of Land Use.

To study peat maturity levels we observed it through its undisturbed fiber content as proposed by Mc Kenzie (19.). Beside that we also used quick field method of Von Post. Both methods showed relatively similiar results that there were vary in soil maturity levels among observation sites, namely hemic and fibric in secondary forest, hemic, fibric, and sapric in temporarily open land, and only sapric in oil palm plantation (Figure 3). Method of Mc Kenzi resulted the data for average undisturbed fiber content as presented in Figure 3 (left). The higest percentage for average undisturbed fiber content was found in secondary forest (52.30%), followed by percentage in temporary open land 39.53%), and the lowest is found in oil palm plantation site (16.44%).

C-Organic and C/N Ratio

Soil organic matter is a complex and varied mixtured of organic substance. The results on avergae C-organic content and C/N ratios presented in Figure 4 below showing that the highest C-organic percentage is found in secondary forest (57.09%), followed by in temporary open land (55.0%), and lowest in oil palm plantation (32,09%). Similar trend occured for average data of C/N ratios, the highest also found in secondary forest (24.09), followed by in temporary open land (19.27), and lowest in oil palm plantation (17.73).

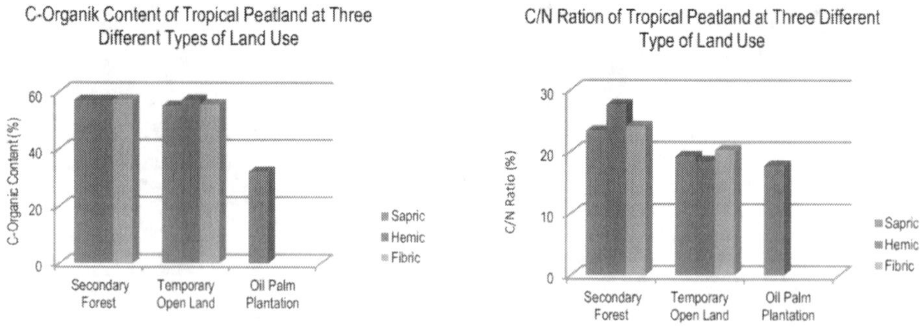

Figure 4: C-Organic content (left) and C/N Ratio (Right) of Tropical Peatland at Different Types of Land Use.

DISCUSSION

Water Table Depth

This study found that the type of land use has affected water table dept in each observation site. The average data for water table depth in each observation site is higher in temporarily open land and lower in oil palm plantation, and lowest in secondary forest. Similar trend is also showed for average water table data in secondary canal (Figure1). Since there are different in management strategy and also in dominating vegetation species within each site, it was predictable that water table will be higher in temporarily open land and lower in oil palm plantation. These data on water table depth have similar trend to that of Soewandita (2008) where in reclaimed plantation water table was higher than that of in forest. A significant decrease of water table, either in secondary canal or in each study site (Figure1), during eight weeks observation is mainly due to climate condition. During measurement period, from July to September 2015, it was a long dry season accompanied with heavy smoke covered most part of West Kalimantan Province. The fluctuation in water table depth is parallel with seasonal change, it increases during rainy season and decreases regularly when dry season (Asdak, 1995).

Bulk and Particle Density, and Hydraulic Conductivity,

Average data of bulk density, particle density, and hydraulic conductivity have similar trend, highest in oil palm plantation and lower in temporary open land and secondary forest. Bulk density which is higher in oil palm plantation than that of in secondary forest was similar to the data found by Melling et.al. (2005). Bulk and particle densities represent the soil characteristics of the mass per unit volume (Miller and Donahue, 1990). Therefore, the higher the values mean the denser the soil. Furthermore, hydraulic conductivity shows the readiness with which a liquid, such as water, flow through a solid, such as soil, in response to given potential gradient (Brady and Weil, 2008). Therefore, denser soil may result in higher soil hydraulic conductivity, as it is the proportionality factor in Darcy's Law (Miller and Donahue, 1990). These findings show that different type of land use has resulted different effects on bulk and particle densities so that its hydraulic conductivity.

Porosity and Field Water Capcity

As mentioned above that data for percentage of porosity was lowest in oil palm plantation, higher in temporarily open land and highest in secondary forest. It was in contrast to that of data either on soil bulk and particle densities, or data on hydraulic conductivity. It shows that the denser the soil the lower its soil porosity, as it shows the percentage volume of the total soil bulk not occupied by soil particles (Brady and Weil, 2008). It is clearly explain that pore space is greatly affected by both bulk and particle densities. Similar trend is also found in data on percentage of volume field water capacity (Figure3). The relationship between these porosity and field water capacity data is clear since field water capcity is expressing the amount of water remaining in a soil after the free water has been allowed to drain away after it is saturated (Miller and Donahue, 1990). The more porous the soil, the higher its field water capacity as it is presented in Figure4. In the case of peat soil, it is not unusual when peat soil may hold a mass of water equal to 200 to 400% of its dry weight (Brady and Weil, 2008). However, water content of peatsoil is greatly affected by its maturity level, (Barchia, 2006). Less mature the peat soil (fibric and hemic), the higher its field water capacity (see Figure4).

C-organic, Undisturbed fiber content, C/N Ratios, and Peat Soil Maturity Levels,

Findings on the characters explained above are greatly supported by data on the C-organic content at which the highest C-organic percentage is found in secondary forest, lower in temporary open land, and lowest in oil palm plantation (Figure4). For average data of C/N ratios, the highest is also found in secondary forest, lower in temporary open land, and lowest in oil palm plantation. This ratios is likely showing its rate of decomposition

(Anshari *et.al.*, 2010). This data is also parallel with the data on undisturbed fiber content that is usually used to expres its maturity level (Figure3). Therefore, data for C-organic, C/N ratios, and undisturbed fiber content will be higher in less mature site such as in secondary forest and temporary open land than that of in more mature site such as in oil palm plantation. Figure 3 shows that there is only one maturity level (sapric) in oil palm plantation, two levels (fibric and hemic) in secondary forest, and three maturity levels (fibric, hemic, and sapric) in temporary open land. Bulk and particle density also become higher (denser) in oil palm plantation (sapric material), because they have decreased in pore space, lost their carbon and fiber content due to decomposition process. Porosity, C-organik, undisturbed fiber all are decreased in mature peat soil (Figures. 2, 3 and 4). The cultivation tend to lower pore space compare to that uncultivated soil, and this reduction usually is associated with a decrease in organic mater content (Brady and Weil, 2008). The decomposition process might have been fastened when the land use is changed from peat forest into cleared and drained management (Anshari *et al.*, 2010). On the other hand, average data for bulk density and particle density are lower in both temporary open land and secondary forest sites because they still have higher undisturb fiber and C-organic content (see Figure3 and Figure4). Therefore, in these both temporary open land and secondary forest sites vary in their maturity levels.

CONCLUSION

It is found that different management types had caused changes in soil physical properties of tropical peatland in Kubu Raya District, West Kalimantan, Indonesia. Industrial timber plantation, oil palm plantation and all their field management activities might have greatly fastened peat soil maturity, increased not only its soil bulk density but also its particle density and its hydraulic conductivity. As the results other characteristics such as soil porosity, field water capacity, and water table in oil palm plantation site are lowest compare to that of in secondary forest and that of in temporary open sites. It is recommended to use proper management strategies and choose less destructive impact technologies when using tropical peatland either as agricultural land, industrial timber plantation, oil palm plantation, or another cleared and drained field management practices.

ACKNOWLEDGEMENTS

We thank the Rector of Tanjungpura University for supporting Mateus Aba with full scholarship *Bidik Misi* scheme both for tuition and research.

REFERENCES

1. Adriesse, J. P. 1988. *Nature and Management of Tropical Peat Soil.* Soil Resources, Management and Conservation Service, FAO Land and Water Development Division. FAO. Rome. Pp. 50-52.
2. Anshari, G. Z., M. Afifudin, M. Nuriman, E. Gusmayanti, L. Ariani, R. Susana, R.W. Nusantara, J. Sugardjito, and A. Rafiastanto. 2010. *Drainage and Land Use Impacts on Changes in Selected Peat Properties and Peat Degradation in West Kalimantan Province, Indonesia.* Biogeosciences, 7, 3403-3419.
3. Asdak, C. 1995. *Hidrologi dan Pengelolaan Daerah Aliran Sungai.* Gadjah Mada University Press. Yogyakarta.
4. Badan Pusat Statistik, 2013. *Kecamatan Rasau Jaya Dalam Angka.* Badan Pusat Statistik Kabupaten Kubu Raya.
5. Barchia, M. F. 2006. *Gambut Agroekosistem dan Transformasi Karbon.* Gadjah Mada University Press. Yogyakarta.
6. Brady, N.C., and Ray R. Weil. 2008. *The Nature and Properties of Soils.* Revised Fourteenth Edition. Pearson Prentice Hall, New Jersey 07458, USA. 975pages.
7. Klute, A. 1986. *Water Retention*: Laboratory Methods of Soil Analysis Part 1. Madison, Wisconsin, USA.
8. Melling, L., Ryusuke Hatano, and Kah Joo Goh. 2005. Soil CO2 Flux from Three Ecosystem in Tropical Peatland of Sarawak, Malaysia. Tellus; 57B:1-11.
9. Miller, R.W. and Roy L. Donahue. 1990. *Soils. An Introduction to Soils and Plant Growth.* Sixth Edition. Prentice-Hall, Inc. Englewood Cliffs, New Jersey, 07632. 768pages.
10. Soewandita, H. 2008. *Studi Muka Air Tanah Gambut dan Implikasinya Terhadap Degradasi Lahan Pada Beberapa Kubah Gambut di Kabupaten Siak.* Pusat Teknologi Sumberdaya Lahan Wilayah dan Mitigasi Bencana-Badan Penelitian dan Pengembangan Teknologi.

Abstract No: A-232

SUBSIDENCE RATE OF DRAINED PEAT IN SUMATRA AND KALIMANTAN ISLANDS, INDONESIA

Maswar* and F. Agus

Indonesian Agency for Agriculture Research and Development (IAARD), Balai Penelitian Tanah (Indonesian Soil Research Institute). Jln Tentara Pelajar No 12 Cimanggu, Bogor 16114, Indonesia

**Corresponding author: maswar_bhr@yahoo.com*

With land scarcity, more and more peatland areas have been drained and converted to agricultural and other development uses. However, the drainage of peatlands leads to accelerated CO_2 emissions and subsidence which are related to global and local problems. A series of observations of peat subsidence rate was made in the year 2013 to 2015 using permanent, vertical subsidence poles made of 6cm diameter steel poles on peatland that had been used for about five years for agriculture. Each subsidence pole was hammered vertically into the peat profile until it penetrated about one m into the underlying mineral soil layer and about one m of its top appeared above ground. Twenty three subsidence poles were installed at the research sites, i.e. 5; 6; 5; and 7 poles, in West Kalimantan, Central Kalimantan, Riau, and Jambi Provinces, respectively. The changes in carbon content and bulk density were monitored annually for a later estimation of carbon loss. The mean thickness of the peat were 224±27 cm; 379 cm±18; 576±46 cm; and 647±28 cm at the Jambi, West Kalimantan, Riau and Central Kalimantan sites, respectively. The study found that the mean subsidence rate were 3.0±0.4 cm yr^{-1}, 3.7±0.8 cm yr^{-1}, 3.8±1.0 cm yr^{-1}, and 6.4±1.9 cm yr^{-1}, for the locations at Jambi, Riau, West Kalimantan and Central Kalimantan provinces respectively. The results indicate that the subsidence rate was influenced by the distance from the observation points to the drainage canal, and the peat thickness. The closer the observation point to the drainage canal, the deeper the mean water table and the higher the rate of subsidence. The thicker peat tended to subsides more rapidly.

Keywords: *subsidence, peat thickness, environmental problems*

Abstract No: A-433

TEMPORAL CHANGES OF SELECTED PHYSICO-CHEMICAL PROPERTIES OF TROPICAL PEAT UNDER MANAGED OIL PALM PLANTATION

Zulhilmy Abdullah*, Nur Azima and Lulie Melling

Tropical Peat Research Laboratory Unit (Chief Minister's Department)

**Corresponding author: mdzoolhillmy@gmail.com.*

SUMMARY

Tropical peatland has been developed widely in Southeast Asia for agricultural plantation especially for oil palm. This is to meet the food and energy sources demand as world population is increasing over time. However, development of peatland with emphasis on monocultures has led to changes in physico-chemical properties of peat soil and less attention has been paid to the changes of peat matrix especially on nutrient cycling. Therefore, the objective of this study was to evaluate the temporal changes of physico-chemical properties of peat soil after oil palm plantation has been established over seven years and is in a more stabilised condition. The peat soil was collected from matured oil palm plot with the palms age of about 7 years old at the commencement of this study, for four consecutive years. PCA was used to generate statistical correlation among the variables and subsequently by linear regression model to observe changes to selected physico-chemical properties. The pH of peat soil decreased with temporal changes (-0.047 units year^{-1}, $p < 0.05$) and this could be due to the accumulation of organic matter or from N fertilizer input. Other properties such as nutrient level (total C, N, P, K, NH_4^+, CEC, base saturation and ash contents) also showed decreased pattern with time except for nitrate content. The negative slopes showed that fertilization is likely to be a necessity for maintaining land production capacity (Kononen *et. al*, 2015). The physical properties of peat soil particularly bulk density was observed to be constant in value with the practice of mechanical compaction before planting that leads to better water retention. The enhanced water retention with time was indicated by the positive slope of water-filled pore space (WFPS) at the rate of 1.531% year^{-1}.However, the decreasing pattern in the soil chemical properties over time can either be from palm uptake to maintain its productivity or from unidentified factors that contribute to the nutrient depletion in peat soil. Further investigation must be conducted to quantify the factors contributing to the nutrient depletion in peat soil.

Keywords: *tropical peatland, oil palm plantation, temporal changes, physicochemical properties*

INTRODUCTION

Global agriculture sector in the 21st century faces rising challenges to meet the food and fibre demands in feeding a growing population and producing more feedstocks for potentially huge bioenergy market. In Southeast Asia, tropical peatland occupies an area about 30 Mha (Miyamoto, 2013) and is one of the major potential land resources to produce foods and energy. Therefore, tropical peatland has been developed widely for agricultural purposes especially for oil palm plantation. In 2010, industrial plantations on peatlands in Malaysia and Indonesia covered around 3.1 Mha and could be doubled by 2020 (Miettinen *et al.*, 2012). This large-scale land use change has great impacts on the converted areas. One of the possible effects of conversion to oil palm plantation is the temporal changes and variation of the physico-chemical properties of peat soil.

There are many reports and scientific publications on the physico-chemical properties of converted peatland to oil palm plantation but the variation may differ from area to area as the oil palm plantation management practices are also known to be additional factors affecting changes in the physico-chemical properties over time. For instance, carbon cycling in peat is driven by four key factors; environmental condition (temperature, water table), substrate quality (recalcitrant peat), nutrients (N requirement for palm growth) and microbial community (microbe types for substrate utilization) (Savage *et.al.*, 2010). Among the four drivers listed, substrate quality is seen as the most significant and is highly dependent on vegetation type. The distribution of woody materials contributes to the variation of decomposition rate and nutrient cycling in peat soil.

Therefore, the aim of this paper is to investigate the variation of temporal changes of physico-chemical properties of peat soil from a properly-managed and stabilised oil palm plantation. The selected physical and chemical properties of peat soil were investigated and this includes bulk density, water filled-pore space, pH, carbon, nitrogen, C:N ratio,, organic matter, ammonium, nitrate, phosphorus, potassium, cation exchange capacity

(CEC) and base saturation. The environmental variables were also taken into consideration because of its influence on the physical and chemical properties of peat soil. By evaluating the properties will enable us to discern the major temporal changes in peat physico-chemical properties in an oil palm plantation.

MATERIALS AND METHOD

Study Site

The peat soils use in this experiment was collected from oil palm plantation located in Sibu, Sarawak (N 02° 11' E 111° 50'). Two plots within the oil palm plantation were selected for peat soil collection. The peat soil sampling started when the oil palm age was 7 years old (matured oil palm trees) and the soil sampling was done on a monthly basis throughout the four years. The peat soil samples were collected at the depth of 0-25 cm (top soil) and 25 – 50 cm (sub soil). The samples were brought to the laboratory and immediately stored in refrigerator at 4 °C. The fresh peat soil were dried using microwave dryer to speed up the drying process as peat soils are very moist and wet.

Soil Variables

The physical properties of peat soil were determined by measuring bulk density and WFPS. Core samples were collected concurrently during peat soil collection using 100 cm^3 core-rings. The undisturbed core samples were analysed by using digital soil volume meter (DIK-1150, Daiki, Japan) and the data were used for WFPS calculation. The core samples were then analysed gravimetrically by drying the samples in 105 °C oven for 48 hours (Melling *et al.*, 2005). The pH of peat soil was extracted with distilled water with the ratio 1:2.5. The peat slurry was measured using pH meter (Metrohm 827, USA). Carbon and Nitrogen content was analysed using Trumac CN analyser (Leco, USA). The organic matter content was measured gravimetrically by heating the samples using Thermogravimetric Analyzer 701 (Leco, USA) at 800 °C for an hour. Total phosphorus and potassium were analysed by using the ashing and subsequently acid digestion method. The samples were digested by using concentrated hydrochloric acid (HCl) and determined using ICP-OES (Perkin Elmer, USA). Exchangeable cation was determined by leaching the samples in the glass column with 1.0 M ammonium acetate and the distillate was measured for its concentration using ICP-OES. Then the same samples were washed using 70% ethanol and continued with the leaching step using 0.05 M potassium sulphate for Cation Exchange Capacity (CEC) determination. CEC was done by collecting the leachate and distilled the samples using Buchii distillation unit. The distillate was then titrated using 0.1 M HCl. Base saturation was calculated based on the ratio between sums of EC and divided by CEC value. Environmental variables for relative humidity and air temperature were measured using Humidity/Temperature digital meter (Testo 632, Germany), soil moisture meter (Daiki 311E, Japan) was used for monitoring soil moisture and soil temperature was determined using soil meter probe (Hannah, Malaysia) at the depths of 5 cm and 10 cm. Water table was determined by measuring perforated pipe that has been previously installed at the experimental site.

Data Analysis

Principle Component Analysis (PCA) was used to group the physical and chemical properties and show the percentage of variation for each group. Then the data were statistically analysed for correlation among the parameter and lastly regression was decided to be used when data shows significant correlation between the parameters and time. Each parameter was determined on their linear relationship against time and significant interaction shows the temporal changing rate (slope) of physical and chemical properties of peat soil during four year measurement. We performed all analysis with SPSS software (SPSS, Version 2.1).

RESULT AND DISCUSSION

The result of the PCA for the physical, chemical and environmental variables are shown in Table 1. From the result, variance was distributed into seven components with total cumulative of 75%.

Table 1: Variance of physicochemical properties and environmental variables in oil palm plantation

Component	Eigenvalue	% of variance	cumulative %
1	4.349	21.744	21.744
2	3.827	19.134	40.878
3	1.814	9.071	49.949
4	1.552	7.758	57.707
5	1.343	6.717	64.423
6	1.121	5.603	70.026
7	1.078	5.388	75.414

The first principal component (PC1) accounted for 21.7% of the total variance, and was highly correlated with the WFPS, soil moisture and NO_3^- content as shown in Table 2 ($r > 0.6$) , characterizing the distribution of air and water in peat soil influence the availability of NO_3^- content. PC2 accounted for 19.1% of the total variance with strong correlation with peat soil pH, organic matter and base saturation ($r >0.6$), characterizing the distribution of mineral and organic matter which influence pH value of peat soil. PC3 accounted for 9.1% of total variance correlated with NH_4^+ content, air temperature and relative humidity ($r > 0.6$), characterizing that mineralization was affected by air temperature and relative humidity of the surrounding environment. PC4, PC5, PC6 and PC7 show no differences in their total variance with 7.8%, 6.7%, 5.6% and 5.4% respectively ($r >0.6$), characterizing nutrient contents and bulk density of peat soil. The bulk density was categorized solely in PC7 showing that the compaction and water management in the oil palm plantation supported nutrient availability for the palms. The experiment area also does not display fluctuation in bulk density and this shows that the area is stabilised over time with proper management. Table 2 shows the correlation matrix of physico-chemical and environment variables.

Table 2: Correlation matrix of the PCA for the physicochemical and environmental variables

Variables	PC1	PC2	PC3	PC4	PC5	PC6	PC7
$NO3^-$	**-0.770**	0.612	0.328	0.060	-0.141	0.132	-0.095
WFPS	**0.904**	-0.223	-0.320	0.084	0.080	0.084	0.195
Soil Moisture	**0.744**	0.063	-0.005	-0.095	-0.119	-0.003	0.093
pH	0.245	**0.702**	-0.274	-0.101	0.166	-0.439	0.196
Organic Matter	0.373	**-0.750**	0.320	-0.273	-0.108	-0.144	-0.025
Base Saturation	-0.190	**0.822**	-0.083	0.214	0.078	-0.343	0.145
NH_4^+	0.064	0.474	**0.664**	0.438	-0.394	-0.266	-0.126
Relative Humidity	0.543	-0.287	**0.742**	0.386	-0.119	0.104	-0.147
Air Temperature	-0.817	0.282	**-0.834**	-0.377	0.222	0.003	0.248
Total Nitrogen	0.193	-0.483	0.119	**0.866**	-0.079	-0.077	0.009
CN Ratio	-0.050	0.649	0.244	**-0.868**	0.476	-0.084	0.074
Total Carbon	0.297	0.031	0.640	-0.052	**0.865**	-0.296	0.014
Total Phosphorus	-0.122	0.470	0.358	-0.198	**0.656**	0.196	-0.253
CEC	0.068	0.465	0.23	-0.114	-0.075	**0.642**	0.207
Total Potassium	-0.093	0.307	0.268	0.187	0.066	**0.782**	0.555
Bulk Density	-0.055	0.098	-0.513	0.059	0.382	0.197	**0.836**

The temporal changes of physico-chemical properties of peat soil were determined by linear regression model. The interaction between physico-chemical properties against time were shown in Table 3 below. The homogeneity test of regression slopes showed 13 parameters with significant difference against time while 2 parameters were not significant.

Table 3: Comparison of the significant, non-significant changing rates and other related parameters derived from the linear regression model

Variables	Changes Rate Slope	Mean	Standard Deviation	F Value	Significance $P < 0.05$
Significant homogeneous slopes					
pH (Unit $Year^{-1}$)	-0.047	3.430	0.129	19.063	0.000
NH_4^+ (mg kg^{-1} $year^{-1}$)	-11.081	54.671	29.091	21.089	0.000
Total Nitrogen (g kg^{-1} $Year^{-1}$)	-0.057	18.680	0.119	38.219	0.000
Total Carbon (g kg^{-1} $Year^{-1}$)	-0.562	550.230	2.310	7.602	0.007
CN Ratio (g kg^{-1} $Year^{-1}$)	0.605	29.49	2.579	7.012	0.009
Organic Matter (% $Year^{-1}$)	0.169	97.608	0.508	15.330	0.000
Cation Exchange Capacity (cmol kg^{-1} $Year^{-1}$)	-2.018	32.27	5.036	23.897	0.000
Base Saturation (cmol kg^{-1} $Year^{-1}$)	-1.157	8.187	2.927	23.108	0.000
Total Phosphorus (mg kg^{-1} $year^{-1}$)	-130.208	332.578	259.021	44.073	0.000
Total Potassium (mg kg-1 $Year^{-1}$)	-78.142	293.19	281.049	10.172	0.002
WFPS (% $Year^{-1}$)	1.531	78.709	6.121	8.069	0.006
Non-Significant homogenous slopes					
$NO3^-$ (mg.kg^{-1} $year^{-1}$)	0.707	86.443	64.878	0.014	0.906
Bulk Density (g.cm^{-3} $Year^{-1}$)	0.001	0.228	0.016	0.191	0.663

The linear regression slopes showed an increase or decrease of physicochemical properties value with time. The pH shows a negative slope with the rate of -0.047 units $year^{-1}$. It shows that the hydrogen ions, H^+ or cation contributed by organic acid are increasing or possible depletion of anion in peat soil. One of the possible factors that cause soil acidification is accumulation of organic matter (Ritchie and Dolling, 1985) faster than decomposition rate of peat soil. Based on the temporal changes of organic matter, the result shows increasing rates of organic matter in peat soil with 0.169 %. $year^{-1}$. However, the accumulation of organic matter is not the only mechanism that can lead to soil acidification in cultivated soils (Ritchie and Dolling, 1985). Ammonium-based fertilizers are one of the factors in lowering of the pH of soil when it is leached rather than taken up by plants. Based on the results above, nitrate content does not give significant temporal changes but the slopes show positive slope which means the tendency for nitrate to accumulate in peat soil after nitrification process. Hydrogen ions can be released and neutralised or possibility to have extra charge of hydrogen ions which lead to lower pH during nitrification process.

Ammonium, NH_4^+ marked temporal decrease; -11.081 mg.kg^{-1}. $year^{-1}$ in peat soil and this could be due to slow mineralization rate, faster nitrification of NH_4^+ ion in peat soil or taken up by plant as a as a nutrient source. Total nitrogen and carbon also show the temporal decrease with at the rate of -0.057 g kg^{-1} $year^{-1}$ and -0.562 g kg^{-1} $year^{-1}$ respectively. However the CN ratio marked positive temporal rates with 0.605 g kg^{-1} $year^{-1}$. This explained the accumulation of nitrogen in soil, which is higher than carbon or it could be contributed by nitrogen fertilization to the soils. The cation exchange capacity and base saturation was observed to have temporal changes in decreasing manner. Other nutrients that show the same pattern is phosphorus and potassium. The depletion of nutrients could be due to the increase in uptake of the oil palm trees for their growth. Therefore fertilization of cultivated area must be done in order to supply sufficient nutrients to the crops.

The physical properties of WFPS were observed to have temporal increase with 1.531% $year^{-1}$ while the bulk density was statistically not significant in their temporal changes but the rate shows an increasing pattern. This is because the experiment sites in the plantation area were very consistent in their compaction that leads to increase of WFPS. This can also be caused by mineralization of organic matter into small particles and reduce porosity of air percentage in the peat soil. The physical properties showed that oil palm plantation was properly managed.

CONCLUSION

The physico-chemical results observed do not show erratic changes in their properties because the oil palm plantation has been properly managed and stabilised over time. However, certain chemical properties such as total phosphorus and potassium show a very large variation and fluctuation which could be affected by surface soil which is generally believed to be the most active layer in terms of fertility-related parameters (Wang *et. al.*, 2013). The depletion of nutrients in oil palm plantation need to be further investigated to minimise the losses. With the improvement in physical properties such as compaction level with consistent bulk density result, reduce air porosity and increase water capillary-rise, these will enhance the efficiency of nutrient uptake by crops for their growth. Therefore, it is very important to continuously manage oil palm plantation sustainably in peat area.

REFERENCES

1. Kononen, M., Jauhiainen, J., Laiho., R., Kusin., K. and Vasander., H. (2015). Physical and chemical properties of tropical peat under stabilised land uses. Mires and Peat. 16 (8), 1-13.
2. Miettinen, J., Hooijer, A., Shi, C., Tolenaar, D., Vernimmen, R., Liew, S.C., Malins, C. and Page, S.E., (2012). Extent of industrial plantations on Southeast Asian peatlands in 2020 with analysis of historical expansion and future projections. Global Change Biology Bioenergy, 4(6), 908-918.
3. Melling, L., Hatano, R. and Goh, K.J. (2005). Soil CO2 flux from three ecosystems in tropical peatland of Sarawak, Malaysia. Tellus, 57B, 1-11.
4. Miyamoto, E., Ando, H., Kakuda, K., Jong, F.S. and Watanabe, A. (2013). Fate of microelements applied to a tropical peat soil: column experiment. Communications in soil science and plant analysis, 44(17), 2524-2534.
5. Savage, A., Holden, J. and Wainwright, J. (2010). Assessing the impact of land management on organic matter composition in peat soils. Geophysical research abstract. 12.
6. Wang, H.M., Wang, W.J., Chen, H., Zhang, Z., Mao, Z. and Zu, Y.G. (2014). Temporal changes of soil physic-chemical properties at different soil depths during larch afforestation by multivariate analysis of covariance. Ecology and Evolution, 4(7), 1039-1048.
7. Ritchie, G.S.P. and Dolling, P.J., (1985). The role of organic matter in soil acidification. Australia Journal Soil Resources, (23), 569-76.

Abstract No: A-283

THE ROLE OF PEAT LAYER ON NUTRIENTS AND METAL CONCENTRATION ON PEATLAND WITH A SUBSTRATUM OF SULPHIDIC MATERIALS

Arifin Fahmi[*] and Siti Nurzakiah

Indonesian Swampland Agriculture Research Institute (ISARI), South Kalimantan, Indonesia

**Corresponding author: Fahmi.nbl@gmail.com*

SUMMARY

Peat soil in tropical area is characterized as marginal or infertile soil. In Indoneia, the majority of them have sulphidic materials as substratum. The disappearance or depletion of peat layer may lead to the changes in environmental condition and quality due to increasing of peat material oxidation, moreover sulfidic material as subtratum mineral of peatlands may oxidized when contact with oxygen. This paper aims at reviewing the contribute of peat layer on contentration of phosphate (P), nitrogen (N), iron (Fe) and aluminium (Al) in the peatland with sulphidic material as substratum. Peat layer might act as the main source nutrients and had an important role on the solubility of Fe and Al in peatland with sulphidic material substratum. The Depletion or disappearance of peat layer decreased P concentration and total N but increased Al and Fe^{2+} concentration in soil solution. Disappearance of peat layer mean loss of a natural sources of N and P for peatland with sulphidic material as substratum, therefore peat layer must be kept in order to maintain of peatlands.

***Keywords**: nutrients, metal, peat layer, sulphidic materials*

INTRODUCTION

In the tropical area, peat material are formed on anaerobic condition. Peat layer is organic material that relative resistant on decomposition processes. Duly, peat material may contain nutrient even though in low amount. However, peat soil in tropical area is characterized as marginal or infertile soil. Most of the peatlands in Indonesia have sulphidic material as substratum layer, the soil layer contain metal element in large concentration, especially iron and aluminium. Considering the present of peatland with sulphidic material as substratum layer in tropical area that in the fact has important role on environmental function. This paper aims at reviewing the contribute of peat layer on contentration of phosphate (P), nitrogen (N), iron (Fe) and aluminium (Al) in the peatland with sulphidic material as substratum.

PHOSPHORUS AND NITROGEN CONCENTRATION

Phosphorus and nitrogen in peat layer was higher than sulphidic material layer, the concentration pattern was gradually decrease with increasing soil depth (Figure 1). These fact indicated role of peat layer as the main source of P and N in peatland with sulphidic material substratum. According to Xing *et al.* (2011) peat matter is N reserves in peatland. The presence of P and N in surface layer mainly supplied through mineralization process of peat. Organic matter that highly humified or poorly decomposable provides a small but constant source of nutrients which may favour the formation of organic P (Malik *et al.*, 2012) and Geurts *et al.* (2010) also have reported that peat mineralization process enhance P concentration in the soil surface of peatland. According to Yonebayashi *et al.* (1997) P tend to accumulated in the upper layer due to the relatively rapid decomposition processes in forest soil ecosystems. Stone and Plante (2014) concluded that low P concentration in subsurface of mineral soil corelated with microbial communities and substrate concentrations.

Plant and organism residue indirectly may be a source of renewal of peat material, peat layer and organic material that continues to be added from the plant and organism residue is the main source of P and N in the peatland with sulphidic material substratum. The majority of P residue in plant litter that lies aboveground has the potential to be delivered to soil in a form readily available to plants and soil microorganisms (Noack *et al.*, 2012). Weedon *et al.* (2014) demonstrated the important role of substrate input from organic material on nutrient cycling on the peatland.

Higher N and P concentration in upper layer of the peatland is indication that peat layer act as source of soil nutrients. The depletion or disappearance of peat layer may decreased N and P concentration in soil solution, this mean loss of a natural sources of P for peatland with sulphidic material as substratum, therefore peat layer must be kept in order to maintain of peatlands.

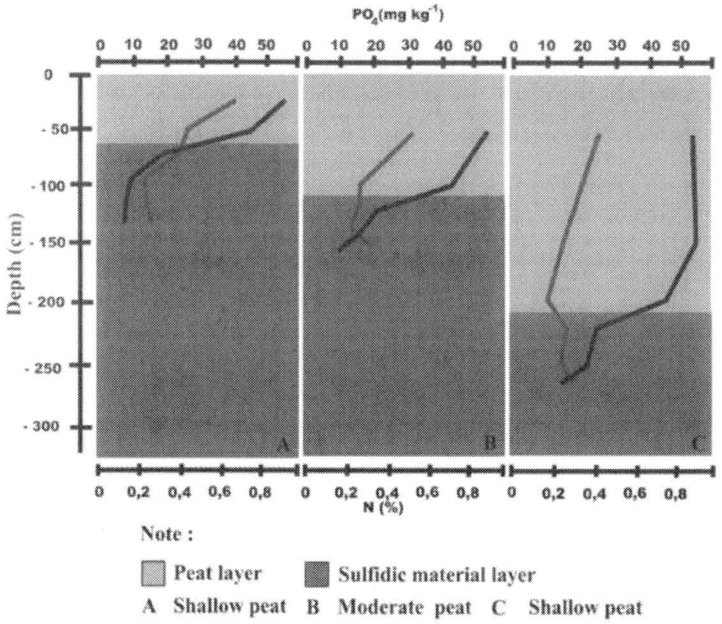

Figure 1: Phosphate concentration (red line) and total nitrogen (blue line) in shallow, moderate and deep peat (Fahmi *et al*., 2013; Fahmi *et al* ., 2014).

ALUMINIUM AND IRON CONCENTRATION

The presence of peat layer above on sulfidic material decreased Fe concentration and exchangeable Al concentration (Figure 2). In addition, Fe concentration and exchangeable Al concentration in the shallow peat are higher than moderate peat. This condition shows the influence of the peat thickness on the dynamics and movement of Al and Fe in the peat layers. Aluminium and Fe tend to be more easily dissolved in a peatland with thinner peat layer, although peat has a large fixation ability on metal ion but low affinity of the peat for Al compared to Fe (Saragih, 1996). This condition may cause the high content of exchangeable Al in the shallow peat. This result is similar to an experiment conducted by Kolii *et al.* (2010), they reported that Al concentration in the peaty soil was higher than in peat soil. High content of organic compound in peat leads to higher of Al in the peat layer chelated by these compound. This condition is reflected by low exchangeable Al concentration in peat layer. Depletion in peat layer leads to increased in exchangeable Al concentration. These facts indicated the roles of peat thicknesss and peat material such as humic substances in complexation of Fe and Al, especially by humic matter (Karlsson dan Persson, 2010).

Large of exchangeable Al concentration in shallow peat shows that 50 cm of the peat thickness (shallow peat) was critical for peat to reduce the Al solubility in the peatland. The thinner peat will decrease the retention power for the metal ions. This condition leads to the increasing concentration of dissolved Al and Fe in the peat layer. Aluminium and Fe in peat soil may originated from sulphidic material layers. Concentration is very high in sulphidic material layer but low in peat layer due to chelation by humic substances contained in peat. The depletion in peat layer will potentially release of Al and Fe to surrounding environment. For this reason, the existency of peat layer must be conserved.

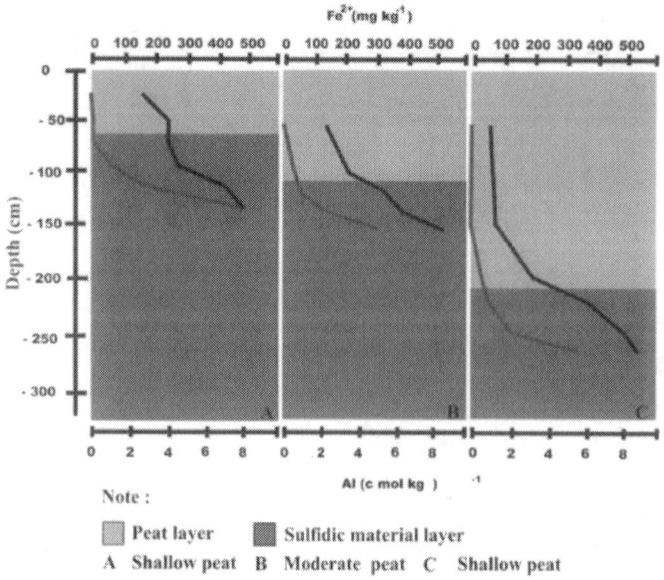

Figure 2: Exchangable aluminium (dot line) and Ferro concentration (red line) in shallow, moderate and deep peat (Fahmi *et al.*, 2010; Fahmi *et al.*, 2012).

REFFERENCES

1. Fahmi, A., B. Radjagukguk, B.H. Purwanto and E. Hanudin. 2010. The role of peat layers on iron dynamics in peatlands. *J Trop Soils*. 15 (3): 197-202.
2. Fahmi, A., B. Radjagukguk, B.H. Purwanto dan E. Hanudin. 2012. The influence of peat layer on hidrogen and aluminium concentration originating from the sulfidic material substratum. *J Trop Soils,* 17 (3): 197-202.
3. Fahmi, A. dan B. Radjagukguk. 2013. Peran gambut bagi kandungan nitrogen total tanah di lahan rawa. *J Berita Biologi,* 12 (2): 223-229.
4. Fahmi, A., B. Radjagukguk, and. B.H. Purwanto 2014. Interaction of peat soil and sulphidic material substratum: role ofpeat layer and groundwater level fluctuations on phosphorus concentration. *J Trop Soils, 19,(3); 161-169.*
5. Geurts JJM, AJP Smolders, AM Banach, JPM Van de Graaf, JGM Roelofs and LPM Lamers. 2010. The interaction between decomposition, net N and P mineralization and their mobilization to the surface water in fens. *Water Res* 44; 3487–3495.
6. Karlsson T and P Persson. 2010. Coordination chemistry and hydrolysis of Fe(III) in a peat humic acid studied by X-ray absorption spectroscopy. *Geochim Cosmochim Acta* 74; 30–40.
7. Kolii R, E Asi, V Apuhtin, K Kauer and LW Szajdak. 2010. Chemical properties of surface peat on forest land in Estonia. *Mires and Peat* 6:1–12.
8. Malik MA, P Marschner, and KS Khan. 2012. Addition of organic and inorganic P sources to soil – Effects on P pools and microorganisms. *Soil Biol Biochem* 49; 106-113.
9. Noack SR, MJ McLaughlin, RJ Smernik, TM McBeath and RD Armstrong. 2012. Crop residue phosphorus: speciation and potential bio-availability. *Plant Soil* 359; 375–385.
10. Saragih ES. 1996. Pengendalian Asam–Asam Organik Meracun dengan Penambahan Fe (III) pada Tanah Gambut dari Jambi, Sumatra. *A Tesis.* IPB, Bogor. 172 p. (*In Indonesian*).
11. Stone MM and AF Plante. 2014. Changes in phosphatase kinetics with soil depth across a variable tropical landscape. *Soil Biol Biochem* 71; 61–67.
12. Weedon JT, R Aerts, GA Kowalchuk, R Van Logtestijn, D Andringa, and PM Van Bodegom. 2014. Temperature sensitivity of peatland C and N cycling: Does substrate supply play a role? *Soil Biol Biochem* 61; 109-120.
13. Xing Y, J Bubier, T Moore, M Murphy, N Basiliko, S Wendel and C Blodau. 2011. The fate of ^{15}N–nitrate in a northern peatland impacted by long term experimental nitrogen, phosphorus and potassium fertilization. *Biogeochemistry* **103**, 281–296.
14. Yonebayashi K, M Okazaki, N Kaneko, and S Funakawa. 1997. Tropical peatland soil ecosystems in Southeast Asia: Their characterisation and sustainable utilization. In : JO Rieley and SE Page, (Eds). *Biodiversity and Sustainability of Tropical Peatlands.* Samara Publ. Ltd., Cardigan. pp. 103-111.

1.2: GEOCHEMISTRY, HYDROCHEMISTRY & HYDROLOGY

Abstract No: A-312

COMPARISON OF CHEMICAL CHARACTERISTICS OF DISSOLVED ORGANIC MATTER IN RIVER WATER FLOWING THROUGH PEATLANDS IN SARAWAK, MALAYSIA AND EASTERN HOKKAIDO, JAPAN

Kiyoshi Tsutsuki[1*], Emi Yoshida[2], Akira Watanabe[2], Nagamitsu Maie[3] and Lulie Melling[4]

[1]*Obihiro University of Agriculture and Veterinary Medicine, Japan*
[2]*Graduate School of Bioagricultural Sciences, Nagoya University, Japan*
[3]*School of Veterinary Medicine, Kitasato University, Japan*
[4]*Tropical Peat Research Laboratory Unit, Sarawak, Malaysia*

* *Corresponding author: tsutsuki@obihiro.ac.jp*

SUMMARY

Composition and structural characteristics of dissolved organic matter in river water were compared between tropical (Sarawak, Malaysia) and cool temperate (eastern Hokkaido, Japan) climates. DOM samples were concentrated and purified by using a tangential flow filtration system, Millipore Pellicon Mini2 modules. Molecular size distribution, elementary composition, sugar composition, and fluorescence characteristics were compared between the samples. According to the size exclusion chromatography, the average molecular weight was larger and the molecular weight distribution was narrower in the Sarawak samples than those in Hokkaido samples. Protein like and sugar components were more depleted in Sarawak samples. Fluorescence characteristics suggested the larger contribution of peat humic substance in Sarawak samples than in Hokkaido samples.

Keywords: *dissolved organic matter, Sarawak, Hokkaido, size exclusion chromatography, PARAFAC analysis*

INTRODUCTION

Dissolved organic matter (DOM) in river water has diverse functions related to the dissolution and transportation of trace elements by complex formation, the supply of nutrients to aquatic biota and microbes, and the transportation and storage media in the carbon cycle and contributes to the biogeochemical processes in the local ecosystem. However, these functions of DOM differ significantly according to its composition and structure, which vary according to the natural environment where it is formed. Therefore, it is important to investigate the DOM formed under different environments. In this study, we aimed at the comparison of DOM formed in the tropic wetland and in the cool temperate wetland, selecting Sarawak in Malaysia and the eastern estuarial area, Hokkaido, Japan. This is a part of a series of studies aimed to clarify the dynamics of DOM in wetlands from different climates (Watanabe *et al.*, 2012).

MATERIALS AND METHODS

Sites of sample collection

Tropical river samples were collected at two sites along Mukah river in Sarawak, Malaysia. One site is a branch river Lebang (N2° 51.118', E112° 09.990') flowing through a relatively unaffected wetland swamp forest. Another site was a branch river Bakong (N2° 46.200', E112° 08.139') which was flowing through a newly cleared wetland swamp forest. We visited these places two times, December in 2007 and August in 2008, and collected the winter and summer samples. River water samples under cool temperate climate were collected at three wetland sites in eastern Hokkaido, Japan. These wetlands were Kiritappu (N43° 05.092', E145° 03.565') in Hamanaka town, Chiraikaribetsu (N43° 06.458', E144° 53.526') in Akkeshi town, and Kimontou (N42° 37.173', E143° 28.698') in Taiki town. These sites were visited several times in 2007 – 2009 and samples were collected in different seasons.

Method of DOM sample preparation

River water samples were passed through a 0.4 μm glass-fiber filter (Advantec GB-140), then the fraction with particle size < 0.22 μm and molecular weight > 1 kD was concentrated using a tangential flow filtration system, Millipore Pellicon Mini2 modules. DOM sample was purified by mixing with ultrapure water and treating with > 1 kD module. The concentrated sample was passed through a 0.2 μm Millipore membrane filter and freeze-dried.

Elementary composition

Elementary compositions (C, H, N, O, S) of the DOM samples were determined by dry combustion method at the element analysis laboratory of Hokkaido University.

Sugar composition

Sugar composition of the DOM samples were determined by capillary gas chromatography following the alditol-acetate method.

Size exclusion chromatography

DOM sample (10 mg) was solubilized into 10 mL of 0.033 M borate buffer (pH 9.2, ionic strength 0.1). This solution was passed through a short column of Chelex 100 resin (Bio-Rad). One mL of the eluate was loaded on Toyopearl HW65S (i.d. 10 mm x 450 mm length) or Toyopearl HW50F column (i.d. 10 mm x 480 mm length), and eluted with the 0.033 M borate buffer. The eluate was collected in 5 mL fractions using a fraction collector. The absorbance of the eluate was also detected continuously at 250 nm using a flow cell UV detector unit (Amersham Biosciences UV-1). Calibration of molecular weight was done with SIGMA MW-GF-70 kit composed of blue dextran (> MW 2.0×10^6), albumin (MW 66,000), carbonic anhydrase (MW 29,000), cytochrome (MW 12,400), and vitamin B12 (MW 1,355). Folic acid (MW 441) and tryptophan (MW 204) were also analyzed to cover the low molecular weight range.

Analysis of the eluted solution

Various constituents in the eluates fractionated by the fraction collector were determined by colorimetry. Carbon contents: after dichromate oxidation, sugars: with phenol sulfuric acid method and anthron method, phenol: with Folin-Ciocarteu's reagent. Protein like compounds were determined by Bio-Rad protein assay (Bradford method), and the absorbance at 250, 280 and 400 nm were determined in a quartz cell using a UV-Vis spectrophotometer (Shimadzu UV1240).

EEM-PARAFAC analysis

Excitation-emission matrix (EEM) fluorescence spectra of the DOM samples and their SEC fractions were determined using a spectrophotometer (FluoroMax-3, Horiba Jobin Yvon) according to Maie *et al.* (2014). Data of fluorescence spectra were statistically analyzed further using parallel factor analysis (PARAFAC) to obtain five representative components from the spectra as shown by Maie *et al.* (2014).

RESULTS AND DISCUSSION

Elementary composition

River water DOM samples collected at two sites in Mukah, Sarawak, compared with those from the three wetland areas in north-eastern Hokkaido, Japan, showed lower H, N, S %, lower H/C, and higher C/N and N/S ratios, which suggested that tropical DOM was in more oxidized state and depleted of protein-like components.

Sugar composition

Sugar contents in DOM as well as Xylose/Mannose ratio were lower in Sarawak samples than in Hokkaido samples, which suggested that sugar components derived from plants were more decomposed in tropical DOM samples. The Xyl/Man, Ara/Glc, Gal/Glc and Fuc/Glc ratios tended to be high in early summer in Hokkaido samples, which may reflect the vigorous plant growth in summer in Hokkaido. In the Mukah river DOM samples, little change was observed in sugar composition between wet season (December, 2007) and dry season (August, 2008) samples.

Molecular size distribution by GPC

According to the size exclusion chromatography, the average molecular weight was larger and the molecular weight distribution was narrower in the Sarawak samples than those in Hokkaido samples. Mukah river DOM samples had maximum peaks at MW 26,400– 27,900, while DOM samples from eastern Hokkaido at MW 14,900- 19,100 when eluted on Toyopearl HW-50F column. Mukah DOM samples showed no excluded fraction on Toyopearl HW-50F column which cover the MW to 80,000, while Hokkaido samples showed large excluded fraction. On Toyopearl HW-50S column which cover the MW to 5000,000, excluded fractions did not appear even for most of Hokkaido samples.

Characterization of size fractions by various colorimetric methods

Fractions eluted from the Toyopearl HW-50F column were subjected to various colorimetric methods for the ratio of absorbance at 400 nm and 250 nm (degree of humification), phenolic substance, protein-like substance, and saccharides.

Ratio of the absorbance at 400 and 250 nm (OD 400/250) increases when dark brown color of the DOM becomes stronger, suggesting the larger contribution of longer conjugated double bond system. OD 400/250 of Mukah samples were larger than Hokkaido samples in the whole range of molecular size distribution, reflecting the darker color of the river water in Mukah samples. Both in Mukah and Hokkaido samples, OD 400/250 was highest in the largest MW fractions, but decreased when MW became smaller and attained to the lowest value at the MW lower than the peak MW. After attaining to the lowest value, OD 400/250 increased again with decrease in molecular weight. From this result, it is suggested that the fraction with high degree of humification are contained in the very large and very small size fractions and not in the dominant fraction.

Phenolic substance determined by Folin-Ciocarteu's reagent showed the same peak as the elution curve by the absorbance at 250 nm. Concentration of phenolic substance was higher in the Mukah samples than in Hokkaido samples. When the elution curves by 250 nm and phenolic substances were compared, phenolic substance had larger contribution in the permeated fraction than in the excluded fraction, suggesting that phenolic substance contributed to the smaller MW fractions of DOM.

Protein-like substance showed a broad molecular size distribution and a relatively larger contribution in the macro size components of the DOM. The peak of the elution curve was shifted to larger molecular size compared with that by 250 nm absorbance. The shapes of the elution curve for protein-like substance were more complex than those by 250 nm absorbance or by phenolic substance, and it showed also shoulders and small peaks in the elution curves. This suggests that protein-like substances are contained in various components with different MW sizes in the DOM. Mukah river DOM samples showed a single peak mode and stronger response to protein-like substance compared with those of Hokkaido DOM samples.

As Bradford reagent for protein is also reactive to phenolic substances, its interpretation should be made carefully and we expressed it as "protein like substance". However, the shapes of the elution curves for protein-like substance and phenolic substance were very different, and we may affirm the larger contribution of protein in the color reaction by the Bradford reagent.

Sugars were determined by phenol sulfuric acid method and anthron method, where phenol sulfuric acid method showed stronger response in the DOM. Molecular size of sugars was shifted to larger MW compared with those by 250 nm absorbance or by phenolic substances. Sometimes, the intensity in the excluded fraction was much larger than that in the permeated fraction for Hokkaido DOM samples. The Mukah river DOM samples showed a single peak molecular size distribution, with larger molecular size compared with the permeated fraction of the Hokkaido samples. Significant seasonal change in the molecular size distribution was observed both in Mukah and Hokkaido samples.

PARAFAC analysis

Based on the PARAFAC analysis of three dimensional fluorescence spectra, five components (fulvic acid like, humic acid like, microbial origin, photo-degradation products, and protein like) were characterized."Humic acid like" component was higher in Sarawak samples, while "fulvic acid like", "microbial origin", "photo-degradation products" and "protein like" components were higher in Hokkaido samples. Fluorescence Index, the ratio of emission intensity (470 nm/ 520 nm) at 370 nm excitation, was lower in Mukah river DOM samples than in Hokkaido samples. This index decreases with the contribution of organic matter derived from soil or peat, while increases with the contribution of organic matter from microbial origin. Due to high temperature, microbial intermediate products are decomposed faster and the contribution of organic matter from peat is larger in the tropical river DOM samples and the opposite tendency may be applied to the DOM formed under cool temperate climate.

Comparison of the river DOM in wetlands under tropical and cool temperate climates

Compared with cool temperate river DOM, tropical river DOM was characterized by more oxidized state from the elementary composition, and depleted of protein-like and sugar components. The average molecular weight was larger and the molecular weight distribution was narrower. It was richer in humic components and not susceptible to seasonal change in the tropical river DOM.

ACKNOWLEDGEMENTS

This research was supported by a Grant-in-Aid for Scientific Research from the Japan Society for the Promotion of Science (No. 19405021)

REFERENCES

1. Watanabe, A., Moroi, K., Sato, H., Tsutsuki, K., Maie, N., Melling, L. and Jaffe, R., 2012. Contribution of humic substances to the dissolved organic carbon pool in wetlands from different climates. Chemosphere, 88, 1265-1268
2. Maie, N., Sekiguchi, S., Watanabe, A., Tsutsuki, K., Yamashita, Y., Melling, L., Cawley, K.M., Shima, E., and Jaffe, R., 2014. Dissolved organic matter dynamics in the oligo/meso-haline zone of wetland-influenced coastal rivers. J. Sea. Res., 91, 58-69

Abstract No: A-382

DISSOLVED ORGANIC CARBON (DOC) IN PEAT WATER SUGGESTS LIMIT TO DECOMPOSITION

Muhammad Nuriman[1], Gunawan Djajakirana[2], Darmawan[2] and Gusti Z Anshari[1, 3]

[1]Soil Science Department, Faculty of Agriculture, Tanjungpura University, Indonesia
[2]Soil Science Department, Bogor Agriculture University, Bogor, Indonesia
[3]Magister of Environment, Tanjungpura University, Indonesia

**Corresponding Author: nuriman.wetlander@gmail.com: nuriman@untan.ac.id*

SUMMARY

The majority of Carbon studies on peats focus on soil carbon. It is rare to examine the amounts of carbon in peat water. As a wetland, peat water contains lots of Dissolved Organic Carbon (DOC). This study aims to portray contents of DOC in peat water from agriculture, shrubs and secondary forests. The research site is Rasau Jaya peat dome, which was firstly opened in 1972 for agricultural development. This peat dome is massively drained and disturbed by human activities. A total of 60 peat water samples were analysed. We used Total Organic Carbon (TOC) Analyser. This study showed that DOC concentrations in peat water ranged from 21.18 to 89.78 mg/L. DOC mostly concentrates in the upper part of peat water profile. Further, DOC concentration in agriculture is significantly lower than concentration in secondary forest. This seems to indicate that rates of peat decomposition tend to decrease in most disturbed peats. In other words, limit the peat decomposition.

***Keywords**: peat water, dissolved organic carbon, limit to decomposition*

INTRODUCTION

Dissolved Organic Carbon (DOC) is an important component in the carbon cycle of drained peats (Moore *et al.*, 2013; Nuriman, 2015). Drained peats act as DOC discharge, and escalate DOC production as a result of peat decomposition. Deforestation of peatlands usually makes drainage firstly (Hooijer *et al.*, 2006). It will influence DOC concentration in peat pore water, Gandois et al. (2013) result show DOC concentration in the pore water was significantly greater in the deforested site (79.9 ±5.5 mg/l) than the pristine site (62.2 ± 2.2 mg/l).
Only a few DOC studies were conducted in Indonesia. These mostly focus on DOC studies in selected rivers in Sumatra and Central Kalimantan (Ishikawa *et al.*, 2006; Baum *et al.*, 2007; Alkhatib *et al.*, 2007; Moore *et al.*, 2011; Moore et al. 2013), but on the peat pore water in Indonesia not yet. This study aims to find a portray contents of DOC in peat water following different land uses.

METHODS

This study was conducted at the peatland region of Rasau Jaya i.e around the Sub-watershed Kapuas Hilir, West Kalimantan. The location of this research has 53,129 ha of peatland (Anshari *et al.*, 2013). Peat depth in this area ranged from 140 to 525 cm. Sampling locations and GPS coordinates as well as soil taxonomy according to USDA, 2010 are presented in Table 1. Peat pore water samples were collected from secondary forest, open area, bush, agriculture, young rubber plantation and oil palm. A total of 60 pore water samples were collected, using a hand pump, at three depth intervals (See Figures 1). These samples were collected in both rainy and dry seasons of 2013.

Table 1: Coordinate, land use, soil taxonomy and peat dept on peat pore water sampling.

No	Code	Coordinate (UTM 49M) X	Coordinate (UTM 49M) Y	Land Use	Soil Taxonomy (USDA 2010)	Peat Dept (cm)
1	AT1	332460	9964326	Secondary Forest	Fibric Haplohemists	360
2	AT2	330269	9965149	Secondary Forest	Hemic Haplosaprists	240
3	AT3	330667	9968380	Open	Hemic Haplosaprists	287
4	AT4	324243	9966844	Open	Hemic Haplofibrists	375
5	AT5	324809	9972593	Bush	Hemic Haplofibrists	184
6	AT6	321387	9977190	Agriculture	Typic Haplofibrists	525
7	AT7	312578	9972549	Young Rubber	Typic Haplofibrists	224
8	AT8	308643	9972775	Oil Palm	Typic Haplofibrists	210
9	AT9	306833	9973601	Oil Palm	Sapric Haplohemists	140
10	AT10	305618	9974373	Oil Palm	Sapric Haplohemists	177

Source: Field inventory, 2013

Peat pore water was carried out using the modified pore water sampling tools which plugged into the peat soil at a depth of 0.2 (surface); 0.5 (middle) and 0.8 (bottom) of peat depth below the water table. At this depth, the water inside of peat soil (pore water) was sucked using the manual hand pump (mityvac) which had been connected by the hose in pore water sampling.

The determination formulation of the depth of the peat soil pores water sampling were as follows:
Surface: 0.2 (PD-WT) + WT
Middle: 0.5 (PD-WT) + WT
Bottom: 0.8 (PD-WT) + WT; where:
PD: Peat Depth (cm)
WT: Water Table (cm)

A B

Figure 1: Peat pore water sampling using modified pore water sampling. A: Peat pore water sampling. B: The depth of the peat pores water sampling.

We used TOC-VCPH (SHIMADZU) to measure DOC concentration. All pore water samples were filtered with pre-combusted Glass Microfiber Filters Whatman GF/G 47 mm Ø with pore size of 0.7 µm. We also measured rubbed fiber contents (Andriesse, 1988). We used T-test and oneway ANOVA to analyze differences of DOC concentration according to corresponding land uses. Correlation of fiber content to DOC was analyzed by simple linear regression.

RESULTS AND DISCUSSION

Average DOC concentrations in dry and rainy seasons were 58.4±15.65 mg/l, and 54.63±14.77 mg/l. T-test result shows indifferent between DOC concentrations in dry and rainy seasons (See Figure 2).

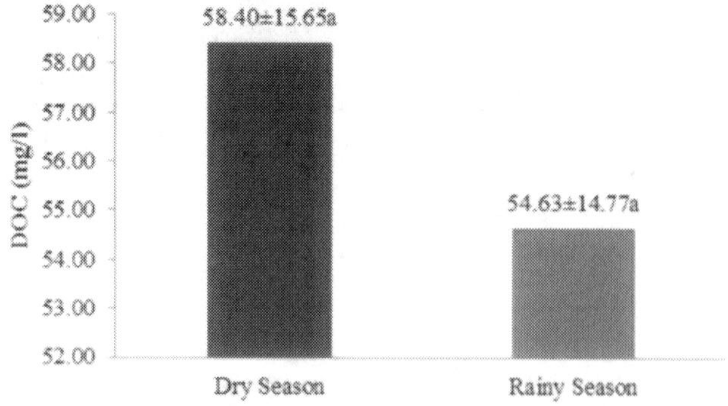

Figure 2: A record of average DOC concentrations.

Profiles of DOC concentrations in dry and rainy seasons showed a descending pattern from surface to bottom layers. These were 66.62 mg/l, 56.69 mg/l, and 51.89 mg/l in dry season, and these were 61.58 mg/l, 53.27 mg/l, and 49.04 mg/l in rainy season (See Figure 3). Result of Anova on these DOC profiles was not significantly different. A decline of DOC in bottom layer suggests different rates of peat decomposition from surface to bottom. Decomposition is more active in the surface than in the bottom.

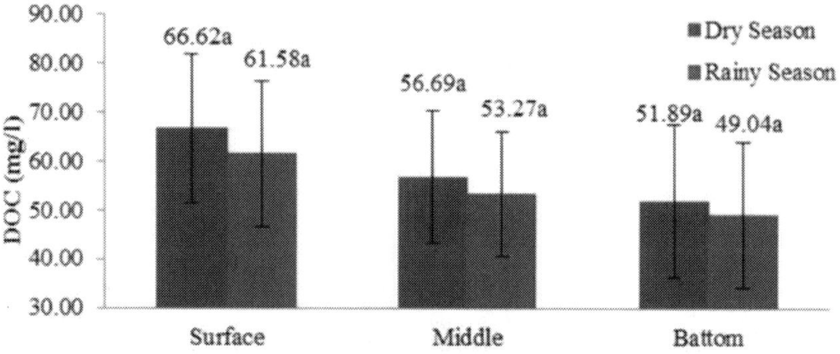

Figure 3: Profiles of DOC concentration.

Figure 4 presents total DOC concentrations of dry and rainy seasons on land uses. Higher DOC values were recorded at young rubber plantation and secondary forest than at other sites, but palm oil is quite as well. This suggests that DOC concentrations tend to decrease due to intensive land cultivation (Kalbitz *et al.*, 2000). Young rubber plantation is freshly disturbed peat, so releases the most DOC from the peat solid due to oxic conditions and microbial activity.

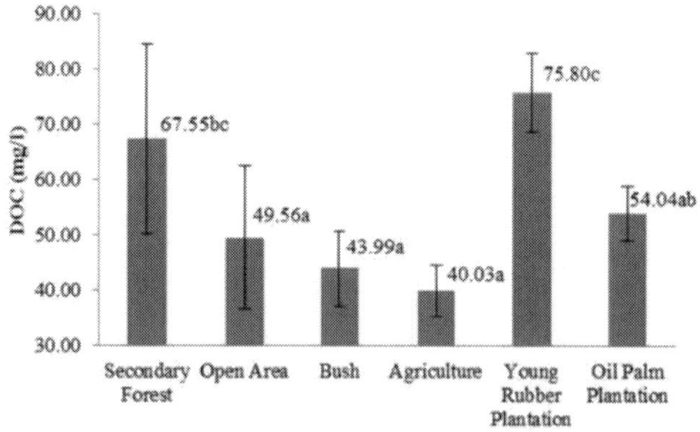

Figure 4: The Average DOC concentrations depending on land use.

Ranges of DOC concentration and fiber content on this research were 24.10-87.74 mg/l and 15.28-85.71 %. Average of DOC concentration was 56.51 mg/l and average of fiber content was 48.64 %. The fiber content is illustration from degree of peat decomposition (Andriesse, 1988), and the degree of peat decomposition is a genetic differentiation of Histosols or peat soil (Soil Survey Staff, 2010). Pearson correlation between DOC concentration and rubbed fibers is negatively significant, with an correlatiion value -0.49 or $R^2 = 0.236$. A simple linear regression suggests that high rubbed fibers produce low DOC, and vice versa (See Figure 5). Gandois et al. (2012) also reported DOC production is correlated with degrees of peat decomposition.

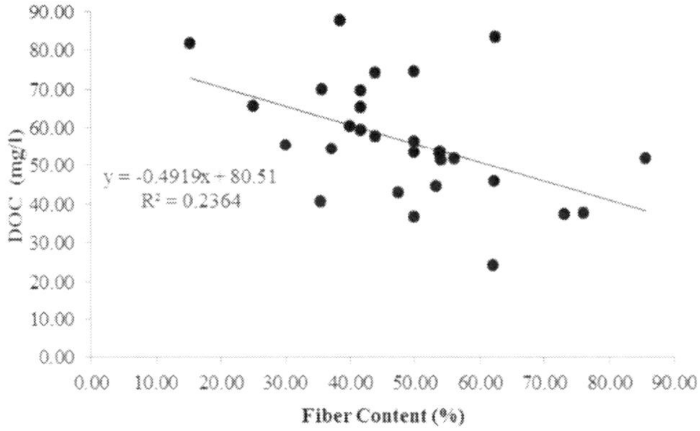

Figure 5: A simple linear regression between rubbed fiber content and DOC concentration.

CONCLUSIONS

This research shows that DOC production has a moderately negative correlation with rates of peat decomposition. Degrees of peat decomposition, however, are very complex because of limit to peat growths. Therefore, DOC is more produced in recently disturbed peats than old disturbed peats. This also implies that peat decomposition is constrained by internal factors of peats, as organic compounds in peats have different degrees of resistance to disturbances.

ACKNOWLEDGEMENTS

This study was supported by Partnerships For Enhanced Engagement In Research (PEER) United States, NSF Grant No: 1114161. Further information is available at http://sites.nationalacademies.org/pga/ peer/index.htm. My special thanks also went to Tya for inspiration and to Armen, Tita, Randi and Putri for assistance in the field and laboratory during this research.

REFERENCES

1. Andriesse, J.P. 1998. *Nature and Management of Tropical Peat Soils*. FAO, Rome.
2. Alkhatib M, Jennerjahn TC, Samiaji J. 2007. *Biogeochemistry of the Dumai River estuary, Sumatra, Indonesia, a tropical black-water river*. Limnol Oceanogr. 52(6): 2410–2417
3. Anshari G, Afifudin M, Gusmayanti G. 2013. Assessing Degradation of Tropical Peat Domes and Dissolved Organic Carbon (DOC) Export from the Belait, Mempawah and Lower Kapuas Kecil Rivers in Borneo. Pontianak (ID): PEER Science Project.
4. Baum A, Rixen T, Samiaji J. 2007. *Relevance of peat draining rivers in central Sumatra for the riverine input of dissolved organic carbon into the ocean*. Estuari, Coast and Shelf Sci. 73 (3): 563-570.
5. Gandois L, Cobb AR, Chieng-Hei I, Lim LBL, Salim KA and Harvey CF. 2012. *Impact of deforestation on solid and dissolved organic matter characteristics of tropical peat forests: implications for carbon release*. Biogeochemistry. DOI 10.1007/s10533-012-9799-8.
6. Ishikawa T, Trisliana, Yurenfrie, Ardianor, Gumiri S. 2006. *Dissolved organic carbon concentration of a natural water body relationship to water color in Central Kalimantan, Indonesia*. Limnology. 7: 143-146.
7. Moore S, Gauci V, Evans CD, Page SE. 2011. *Fluvial organic carbon losses from a Bornean black water river*. Biogeosciences. 8:901-909.
8. Moore, S., Evans, C.D., Page, S.E., Garnett, M.G., Jones, T.G., Freeman, C., Hooijer A., Wiltshire, A. Limin, S. Gauci, V. 2013. *Deep instability of deforested tropical peatlands revealed by fluvial organic carbon fluxes*. Nature. 493: 660-664.
9. Nuriman M. 2015. *Karbon Organik Terlarut dan Partikulat pada Air Saluran dan Air Tanah Gambut Rasau Jaya, Kalimantan Barat*. Tesis. Institut Pertanian Bogor. Indonesia. http://repository.ipb.ac.id/handle/123456789/75629.
10. Soil Survey Staff. 2010. *Keys to Soil Taxonomy*. Eleventh Edition. Washington (US): USDA, NRCS.

Abstract No: A-263

DYNAMICS AND DISTRIBUTION OF PEAT WATER MACRO NUTRIENTS (N, P, K, Ca, Mg AND S) IN OIL PALM PLANTATION BASED ON SEASON, PEAT THICKNESS, CHANEL DISTANCE AND PLANT AGE

Heru Bagus Pulunggono*, Syaiful Anwar, Budi Mulyanto, and Supiandi Sabiham

Department of Soil Science and Land Resource, Bogor Agricultural University (IPB), Indonesia

**Corresponding author: heruipb@yahoo.co.id*

SUMMARY

Peatland that has been converted to other land uses such as oil palm plantation has to be well managed. Fertility of peatland will influence oil palm productivity. Macro nutrients such as nitrogen, phosphorus, potasium, magnesium and sulfur is required by oil palm for optimal growth and production. Naturally, oil palm requirement of the nutrients could not be supplied sufficiently from the soil so that fertilization is needed. Fertilizing has to be well carried out in order to increase nutrient absorbtion efficiency. The objective of the research is to study peat water macro nutrients (N, P, K, Ca, Mg and S) distribution in oil palm plantation based on season, peat thickness, channel distance and plant age. Result of the research showed that content of dissolved P, K, Ca, Mg and S were higher in dry season whereas N was higher in rainy season. In shallow peat, content of dissolved N, P, K, Ca and Mg were higher than that in deep peat however S was lower. Dissolved N, P, K, Ca Mg and S tendedto increase by distance from channel. Dissolved N, P, K, Ca, Mg and S were higher in more than 15 years old oil palm than that in 6-15 years old oil palm.

Keywords: *peatland, peat water macro nutrients, distribution, oil palm*

INTRODUCTION

The utilization of peatland for oil palm plantations has been increasingly widespread due to the limited availability of mineral land. Peatland area in Indonesia is about 14.93 million ha and about 15.1% in the form of peat that has been cultivated as farmland (annual crops, plantations and industrial plants) (Wahyunto, 2013). Approximately 1.54 million hectares or 20% of the total area of oil palm plantations in Indonesia are on peatlands (Ritung *et al.*, 2012). Utilization of peatlands for oil palm plantations become a major challenge not only related to the amount of input that should be given, but also related to specific management of peatlands in order to avoid land degradation.

Utilization of peatland for oil palm plantations will not only be challenged by problems of oil palm production, but also by efforts for preserving the environmental balance. Peatland management into productive land must comply to the principles of sustainability by utilizing environmentally friendly and low emission technologies. These technologies are including water management, setting up drainage network, amelioration, and fertilization (Las *et al.*, 2012).

Peatland that has been converted to other land uses such as oil palm plantation has to be well managed. Fertility of peatland will influence oil palm productivity. Tropical peatland usually has low fertility. Macro nutrients such as nitrogen, phosphorus, potasium, magnesium and sulfur is required by oil palm for optimal growth and production. Naturally, oil palm requirement of the nutrients could not be supplied sufficiently from the soil so that fertilization is needed. In oil palm plantation, fertilization is given regularly in the form of macro nutrients and micronutrients fertilizer. Fertilizer is given higher in older oil palm than younger oil palm. Nutrients from fertilizer are easily diluted and leached to the ground water due to high porosity of peat. Fertilizing has to be well carried out in order to increase nutrient absorbtion efficiency.

Objective of the research is to study peat water macro nutrients (N, P, K, Ca, Mg and S) distribution in oil palm plantation based on season, peat thickness, channel distance and plant age.

METHODS

The study was carried out at Kimia Tirta Utama Oil Palm Plantation Company at Siak Regency, Riau Province, Indonesia (0^0 43' 33" - 0^0 46' 9" N and 101^0 44' 24" - 101^0 46' 22" E). The study was conducted in rainy season (March) and dry season (August) of 2015 in peatland. The peatland used in this study was shallow (thickness less than 3 meters) and deep (thickness more than 3 meters) peat, with hemic level of decomposition stage (rate of 33 – 66 %) and clay substratum. The oil palm plantation used in this study were in two ages, ie 6 – 15 and more than 15 years old plantation. Fertilizer is given about 57 kg N, 7 kg P, 40 kg K, 15 kg Ca kg, 15 kg Mg , 0 S kg/ha/year and about 115 kg N, 41 kg P, 105 kg K, 17 kg Ca kg, 15 kg Mg , 6 S kg/ha/year for 6-15 and more than yers old plantation respectively. The observations were done in varies distances from chanel, those are 10, 25, 50, 75, 100, 150 meters by installing piezometer (Figure 1).

Peat water samples in piezometers were collected at 1 meter deph from surface. Peat water samples were analized to determine peat water macro nutrients (N, P, K, Ca, Mg and S). N was determined by micro Kjeldahl. P was extracted by Bray 1 and determined using UV Vis. K was determined using flame fotometer. Ca, Mg were determined using atomic absorption spectrophotometer and S was determined using UV Vis. The data were analyzed by descrptive analysis to understand distribution trend of the data.

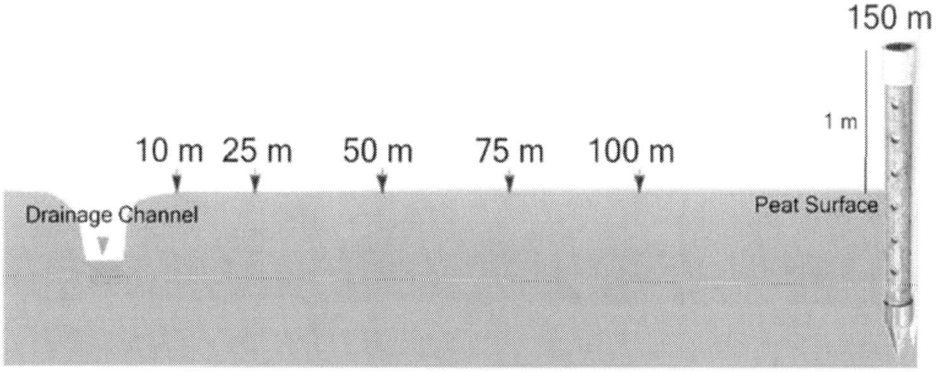

Figure 1: Peat water colection from piezometers installed based on distance from chanel.

RESULTS AND DISCUSSION

Results of the research showed that content of dissolved P, K, Ca, Mg and S were lower in dry rainy season compare to that in dry season (Table 1). Contrary to these results dissolved N was higher in rainy season (Table 1). Oil palm plantation was fertilized with almost complete nutrients, especially those that contain N, P, and K. These results suggested that N fertilizer in peatland was easily subject to leaching such that dilution of nutrients in rainy season was not causing lower N concentration in peat soil water. On the other hand, other studied nutrients in particular P and K were subject to dilution in rainy season as indicated by their low concentration in rainy season compare to that in dry season.

Table 1: Peat water macro nutrient of oil palm plantation in dry and rainy seasons.

Season	N (ppm)	P	K	Ca	Mg	S	(n)
Rainy	23.40 (13.45-53.82)	0.68 (0.08-2.29)	2.80 (0.37-9.38)	5.46 (2.01-12.04)	1.16 (0.44-4.80)	1.92 (0.35-5.26)	24
Dry	21.95 (13.45-53.82)	1.64 (0.1-5.87)	4.14 (0.25-17.41)	9.15 (1.54-12.04)	1.91 (0.43-16.02)	2.03 (0.42-4.42)	24

In shallow peat, content of dissolved N, P, K, Ca and Mg were higher, except dissolved S that was lower compare to that in deep peat (Table 2). There are two reasons that might explain these results. Firstly, shallow peat has shallow mineral soil substratum such that some parts of the nutrients supplied by this mineral substratum. Secondly, water and water movement in deep peat are expected to be in higher amount and more dynamic compare to that in shallow peat such that dilution effect was higher in deep peat which in turn resulted in lower concentration of nutrients in the water of the deep peat. Sulfur is an exception probably due to the amount of S fertilization was lower compare to fertilization of other nutrients.

Table 2: Peat water macro nutrient of oil palm plantation in deep and shallow peat.

Peat Thickness	N (ppm)	P	K	Ca	Mg	S	(n)
Shallow	24.08 (13.45-53.82)	1.49 (0.08-5.87)	3.67 (0.25-17.41)	5.52 (1.61-12.04)	1.93 (0.44-16.92)	1.92 (0.35-7.30)	24
Deep	21.64 (13.45-53.82)	0.88 (0.1-5.10)	3.29 (0.37-11.73)	4.58 (1.54-12.04)	1.14 (0.43-16.02)	2.02 (0.42-4.42)	24

Dissolved N, P, K, Ca Mg and S are in general tended to increase by distance from channel (Table 3). The data, however, very fluctuated. The channel networks in oil palm plantation on peatland functioned more as a controlled and limited drainage of excess water in the land. Sites that is closer to the channel was expected to experienced higher leaching that accompany the drainage process to the channel, in particular in rainy season. This higher tendency of losing nutrient content in the site closer to the channel has resulted in the tendency of lower nutrient concentration of peat water closer to the channel.

Table 3: Peat water macro nutrient of oil palm plantation based on distance from channel.

Distance from Channel (m)	N (ppm)	P	K	Ca	Mg	S	(n)
0	17.94 (13.45-40.36)	0.13 (0.08-0.23)	2.41 (0.25-7.04)	2.51 (1.54-3.77)	0.64 (0.43-0.95)	1.78 (0.56-3.72)	8
10	21.14 (13.45-40.36)	1.69 0.13-5.87()	5.06 (0.86-10)	6.02 (3.55-17.04)	1.96 (0.71-11.67)	1.55 (0.35-4.07)	8
25	23.54 (13.45-53.82)	2.13 (0.13-5.10)	4.89 (0.75-11.73)	5.89 (1.88-7.26)	1.28 (0.55-16.02)	1.55 (0.63-4.91)	8
50	26.91 (13.45-40.36)	0.57 (0.13-1.50)	2.36 (0.37-6.03)	5.54 (2.21-12.44)	0.84 (0.58-1.88)	2.37 (0.84-5.26)	8
75	23.06 (13.45-53.82)	0.81 (0.12-2.29)	3.24 (0.37-8.27)	4.88 (3.05-7.72)	1.50 (0.51-5.21)	2.26 (0.77-4.91)	8
100	23.06 (13.45-40.36)	0.64 (0.17-1.88)	2.67 (1.74-6.67)	4.36 (2.93-7.06)	1.77 (0.44-4.80)	2.23 (0.42-4.21)	8
150	17.94 (13.45-40.36)	0.81 (0.21-1.90)	1.91 (0.62-3.82)	7.45 (2.01-9.07)	1.67 (0.54-5.94)	1.94 (1.05-4.42)	8

Dissolved N, P, K, Ca, Mg and S were higher in more than 15 years old oil palm than that in 6-15 years old oil palm (Table 4). Fertilization of nutrient on oil palm plantation of > 16 years old oil palm was higher than fertilization on oil palm plantation of 6 – 15 years old. This is the cause of higher dissolved nutrients in peat water of the > 16 years old oil palm plantation.

Table 4: Peat water macro nutrient of oil palm plantation in 6-15 years old and more than 15 years old.

Oil Palm Age (year)	N (ppm)	P	K	Ca	Mg	S	(n)
6-15	18.35 (13.45-40.36)	0.88 (0.1-4.71)	2.46 (0.37-9.38)	4.47 (1.54-8.36)	1.47 (1.45-6.79)	1.35 (0.35-2.53)	24
>16	27.58 (13.45-53.82)	1.49 (0.08-5.87)	4.72 (0.62-17.41)	5.54 (1.22-12.44)	1.51 (1.44-16.92)	2.72 (0.7-4.91)	24

CONCLUSION

Dissolved P, K, Ca, Mg and S were higher in dry season whereas N was higher in rainy season. In shallow peat content of dissolved N, P, K, Ca and Mg were higher than that in deep peat however S was lower. Dissolved N, P, K, Ca Mg and S tended to increase by distance from channel. Dissolved N, P, K, Ca, Mg and S were higher in more than 15 years old oil palm than that in 6-15 years old oil palm.

REFERENCES

1. Las. I, M. Sarwani, A. Mulyani and M. F. Saragih. 2012. Dilema dan rasionalisasi kebijakan pemanfaatan lahan gambut untuk areal pertania (in Indonesian). Prosiding Seminar Nasional. Pengelolaan Lahan Gambut Berkelanjutan.
2. Bogor, 4 Mei 2012. Badan Penelitian dan Pengembangan Pertanian Kementrian Pertanian.
3. Ritung. S, Wahyunto and K. Nugroho. 2012. Karateristik dan sebaran lahan gambut di Sumatera, Kalimantan dan Papua(in Indonesian). Prosiding Seminar Nasional. Pengelolaan Lahan Gambut Berkelanjutan.
4. Bogor, 4 Mei 2012. Badan Penelitian dan Pengembangan Pertanian Kementrian Pertanian.
5. Wahyunto, Ai Dariah, D.Pitono and M. Sarwani. 2013. Prospek pemanfaatan lahan gambut untuk perkebunan kelapa sawit di Indonesia(in Indonesian). Perspektif Vol 12 No. 1Juni 2013. Hlm 11-22 ISSN: 1412-8004

Abstract NO: A-399

HYDROLOGICAL CHANGES OF FENS SITES IN THE COURSE OF SOIL DEVELOPMENT

Uwe Schindler*, Lothar Müller, Frank Eulenstein and Axel Behrendt

Leibniz Centre for Agricultural Landscape Research (ZALF), Germany

**Corresponding author: uschind@zalf.de*

SUMMARY

This study deals with the change and evaluation of soil hydrological properties of peat soils (FAO: Terric Histosols) in the course of soil development. For 84 fen sites in 19 fen regions in North-East Germany, besides ash content, unit water content and dry bulk density, the unsaturated hydraulic conductivity, the water retention function and the wetting properties were measured. The porosity decrease. Opposed to that, the macro pore space and the capillary rise increased. With the start of consolidation processes and the development of segregation structure, first of all a noticeable reduction of the macro pores and the unsaturated hydraulic conductivity began. In the course of further soil development and decreasing aggregate size, these processes reversed. Both parameters increased starting from segregation structure horizon, to earthyfied fen and weak moorshyfied fen horizon until finally partly exceeding the starting values of the pedogenetic almost unchanged fen in the strongly moorshyfied stadium. Differences in wetting properties could not be explained by changes of peat properties as a result of soil development. Additionally, field measurements at 84 fen sites of 19 fen regions in North- East Germany were carried out to study the hydraulic performance directly under field conditions Capillary water supply of all soil development stages was not limited up to 70 cm ground water level depth. Worsening plant water supply could be the result of sapric horizons (mud) in the capillary fringe, ground water levels deeper than 70 cm below soil surface, low hydraulic conductivity in the ground water zone and hysteresis effects, affected by high ground water level dynamics in the course of the day.

Keywords: *fen, soil development, soil hydrological properties, capillary rise, pore space distribution*

INTRODUCTION

Oxidative as well as biochemical processes led to the reduction of peat thickness up to the total loss of fens. Fens seam to loss there biological and hydrological function in the course of intensive soil development (Klimkowsk *et al.*, 2010). Kechavarzi *et al.*, (2010) reported about significant changes of physical and hydraulic properties as the result of peat decomposition. Less decomposed peat had higher saturated hydraulic conductivity values, a lower air entry pressure and drained faster than degraded peats. They conclude that decomposition and pedogenic alterations lead to the loss of structural pores. According to Sauerbrey and Zeitz (1999), degradation is seen as a reduction in suitability for plant production and as a difficulty for soil workability. Schultz-Sternberg *et al.*, (2000) conclude in their report on the status and future development of fens in Brandenburg, that they have been destroyed by amelioration measures during the 1960 s and 70 s and have therefore lost their main function within nature and water balance. Soil hydrological laboratory and field investigations were performed to clarify to what extent the soil water balance and the plant water supply of fens in Northeast Germany have been changed due to soil development.

MATERIAL AND METHODS

SITES

Soil hydraulic properties were measured from 84 sites of 19 fens regions in North and North-East Germany. The sites included mire types- paludification and percolation mires, as well as deep and shallow mud underlain ancient lake mires- with the soil types earthyfied fen (Erdfen), weak moorshyfied fen (Fenmulm) and moorsh (Mulm). The choice of the site was an attempt to consider a wide range of existing fen types, soil development stages and land use systems within these investigations. Different pedogenetic changed soil types of deep and shallow fens, with and without sapric horizons (mud) in the profile were considered. The land use varied between fallow, pasture, low input and intensive meadow, arable land and forest. The investigations of this study consider the soil types earthyfied fen (Erdfen), weak moorshyfied fen (Fenmulm) and moorsh (Mulm) with the horizons following Succow and Joosten, 2001. Moreover, half fen soils (AMO) with organic matter content lower than 30 % as well as sand covered fens were included.

nH: Pedogenetic almost unchanged peat below the water table.
nHa: Peat subsoil horizon with segregation structure in consequence of swelling and shrinkage.
nHv: Earthyfied peat topsoil horizon, crumbles and small-polyhedric aggregates.
nHvm: Weak moorshyfied topsoil horizon, intermediate stage between nHv and nHm
nHm: Moorsh topsoil horizon, small aggregates, under dry conditions powder-like, under wet conditions smeary

The climate of the study region is characterized by an annual precipitation of 500 to 650 mm, an avarage annual air temperature of 8.1 – 8.5 °C and a potential evapotranspiration of 550 – 650 mm/yr.

LABORATORY MEASUREMENTS

Disturbed samples were taken to measure the ash and lime content, the water penetration time as measure for the rewetting properties (Schindler *et al.*, 2015) and the unit water content w1 (Ohde, 1950, modified by Schmidt 1989). From the undisturbed cylinder cores, the actual water content, the water retention curve and unsaturated hydraulic conductivity function were measured using the evaporation method (Schindler *et al.* 2015).

Short description of the evaporation method:

The measurements can be performed either at undisturbed or disturbed soil samples. The samples are taken in 250 cm^3 stainless steel cylinders. The soil cores are slowly saturated by placing them in a pan of water. The tensiometers are inserted and the core is sealed at the bottom. The assembly with the core is placed on weighing scales and the soil surface is exposed to free evaporation. Tension (Ψ) and sample mass (m) are recorded at consecutive times. The hydraulic gradient is calculated on the basis of the tension recorded during the time interval. The water flux is derived from the associated soil water volume difference. Single points of the water retention curve are calculated on the basis of the water loss per volume of the sample at time t_i and are related to the mean tension in the sample at this time. The unsaturated hydraulic conductivity (K) is calculated according to the Darcy-Buckingham law (Equation 1).

$$K(\Psi_{mean}) = \frac{\Delta m}{aA\rho_{H2O}\,\Delta t\, i_m} \qquad (1)$$

where: Ψ_{mean} is the mean tension over the upper tensiometer at position z_1 (3.75 cm above the bottom of the sample) and the lower tensiometer at position z_2 (1.25 cm above the bottom), geometrically averaged over a time interval of □$t_J = t_{i+1} - t_i$, with $i = 1...n$, $j = 1...n-1$; □m is the sample mass difference in the time interval (assumed to be equal to the total evaporated water volume □V_{H2O} of the whole sample in the interval); □$_{H2O}$ is the density of water and is assumed to be 1 g cm^{-3}; a is the flux factor (in the case of rigid soils a = 2); A is the cross sectional area of the sample and i_m is the hydraulic gradient averaged over the time interval.

Data points of the water retention curve are pairs of mean tension at time t_i and t_{i+1} for $i = 1...n$ and the corresponding volumetric water content. Generally, the soil is assumed to be rigid. A data set of a single sample consists of plenty user-defined water retention and hydraulic conductivity data pairs. At the end of the measurement cycle, the residual amount of storage water is derived from the water loss upon oven drying (105 °C), and the initial water content is calculated. The dry bulk density is derived from the dry soil mass.

FIELD MEASUREMENTS

The soil type classification was carried out on the basis of structure evaluation according to Succow and Joosten (2001). Organic matter content was used in order to decide whether the soil was fen or already half fen soil. Accordingly, the organic matter content of 30 cm topsoil must exceed 30 % (AG Boden, 2005). Otherwise, in case of organic matter content ranging between 15 and 30 % fen soil is not classified as fen but rather as half fen soil. Soil types, as well as stratification of horizons were characterized by the soil pit and auger holes in the field (Tab. 1). The kind of land use was apparent at the site. The fen depth was measured by means of a penetration probe. Generally, ground water level, tension and water content were measured at the soil depths of 10, 30 and 50 cm. In order to evaluate the capillary function of the sites, tension measurements were mainly carried out on sunny and rainless days with high transpiration demand and dry past weather conditions.

Table 1: List of measurements and methods used in the field

Parameter	Method/ Equipment
Tension at depth of 10, 30, 50 cm	Mobile field tensiometer
Water content at depth of 10, 30, 50 cm	TDR, Easy Test
Ground water level	Ground water table in the auger hole
Saturated hydraulic conductivity	Time of ground water rise in the auger hole
Fen depth	Penetration probe
Soil type	Succow and Joosten, 2001
Soil structure	Succow and Joosten, 2001
Kind of land use and intensity	Visual and information from farmers

Tension and hydraulic gradient above ground water table are good indicators when characterizing the capillary properties of the system (Fig. 1), provided that measurements are carried out in dry periods. In the sites influenced by ground water, the tension distribution is determined by the ground water level. At equilibrium state ($v = 0$, $i = 0$), the absolute value of tension is an equivalent to the gravitational potential. The tension distribution in the soil profile allows the identification and the assessment of water flow direction as well as the soil hydrological properties. Upward hydraulic gradients ($i > 0$) resulting in ground water flow under pressure in the ground water zone and capillary rise above the ground water table. Hydraulic gradients $i < 0$ resulting in downward water movement. Capillary rise is sufficient, if the hydraulic gradient in the capillary fringe only differs slightly ($0 < i < 2$) from the equilibrium state. Reversing, the case of high tensions in the profile can be indicated by capillary defects or deep ground water levels. Opposed to that, perched water at the soil surface at deep ground water levels are indications of reduced infiltration.

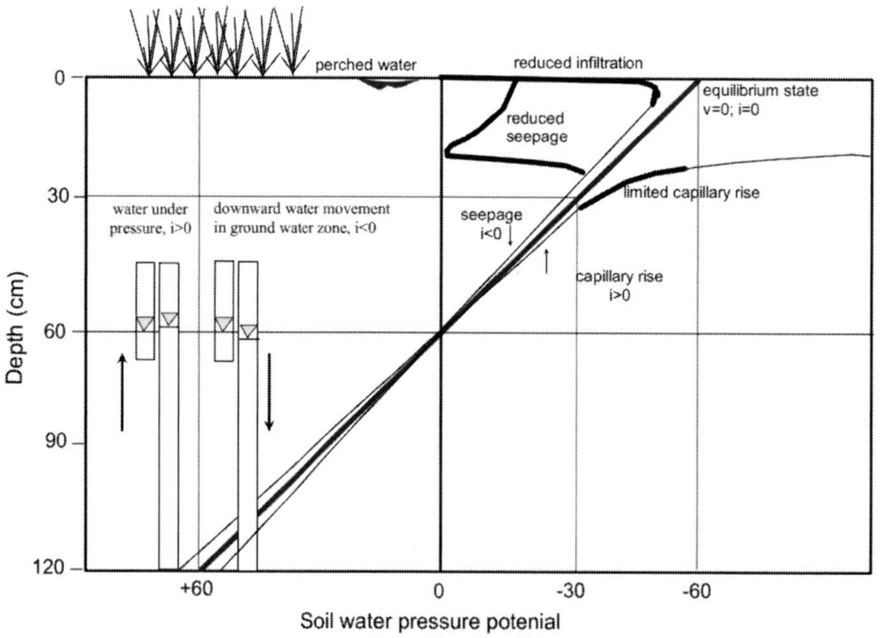

Figure 1: Soil water potentials as indication of flow direction and soil hydrological function at ground water influenced sites- positive below and negative above a free-water table.

RESULTS AND DISCUSSION

Pore Size Distribution And Capillarity

The porosity (GPV) decreased and the dry bulk density (DBD) increased with increasing soil development (Fig. 2). The wide macro pores MP1 (> 50 □m) are very important for the capillary plant water supply at ground water sites. As the cause of segregation structure, MP1 decreased in the first stage of soil development from nH (9.9 % by vol.) to nHa (7.3 % by vol.). Afterwards with further increases of soil development the soil aggregates become finer. As the result of this, the wide macro pores increased again and reached its maximum (10.8 % by vol.) at the final stage of moorshyfication (nHm). However, the differences between the horizons were not significant. The small macro pore space MP2 (10-50 □m) was significantly lower in all soil development stages than in the original peat. The largest differences were measured between the nH (21.9 % by vol.) and the nHa horizon (9.9 % by vol.). The capillary rise was calculated based on the single measurements of the unsaturated hydraulic conductivity. Strongly diminished capillarity due to soil development (Tab. 2) could not be observed. The height of capillarity rise was estimated for a steady state capillary flux of 5 mm*d^{-1}. Pedogenetic not or onlyweakly developed fens (nH) showed best capillarity (Table 2). However, the capillary rise of the pedogenetic heavily changed soils was also high and differed only a little and not significantly from the unchanged fens. On the contrary, the fen horizons with segregation structure (nHa) as well as the half fen soil (AMO) showed reduced values of the heights of capillary rise. In these soils, however, a capillary height of about 60 cm was also achieved.

The measured wetting time varied between a few seconds and several hours. The differences between the soil types were small and not significant. The lowest wetting time was almost always measured at full saturation. With decreasing moisture, the wetting properties of the soils changed very differently. There was no systematic and no statistical correlation between soil development and wetting properties.

GROUND WATER LEVEL AND CAPILLARY PLANT WATER SUPPLY

The tension conditions of the earthyfied and the weak moorshyfied fen as well as the sand covered fen sites differed only negligibly from the equilibrium state. Compared with the other soil types, the hydraulic gradients showed clearly diverging conditions at the moorsh and, though only faintly, also at the half fen soil. The tension values were significantly higher in moorsh than in earthyfied fen. However, it is to be noted that the ground water levels were also significantly deeper at moorsh and half fen sites (71 cm, SD 23 cm and 75 cm, SD 22 cm) compared to the earthyfied and weak moorshyfied fen sites (47 cm, SD 17,7 cm and 59 cm, SD 16,7 cm). Due to this ground water level differences, a direct comparability of hydraulic properties of soil types was therefore not possible.

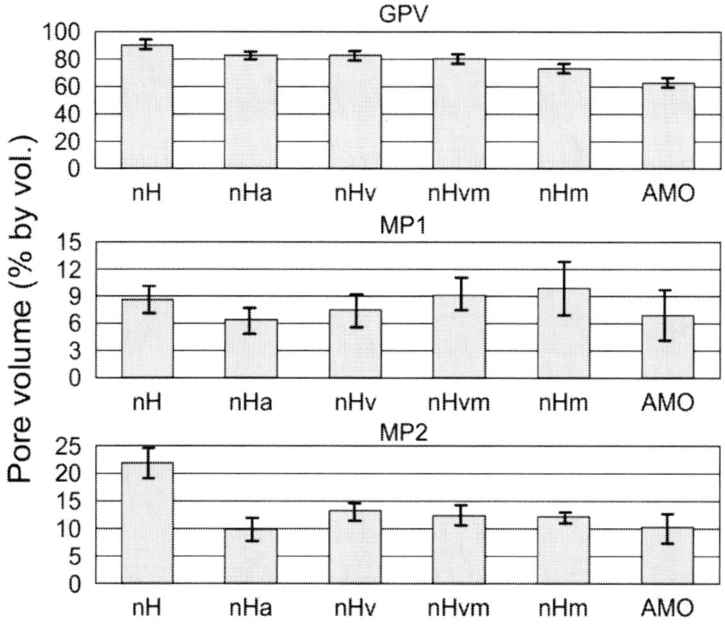

Figure 2: Porosity (GPV) and macro pore space MP1 (>50 □m) and MP2 (10-50 □m) of fen horizons (ash content 0 < x < 70 %) and AMO soils (70% < x < 85 %) with the range of significance.

Table 2: Height of capillary rise in peat horizons for a capillary flux of 5 mm * d^{-1}.

Horizont	n	x %	z cm	SD cm
nH	39	6 - 54	87	37
nHa	33	6 - 56	58	41
nHv	36	7 - 62	68	43
nHvm	22	9 - 63	73	31
nHm	30	9 - 59	77	32
AMO	21	71 - 85	61	43

n: number of samples; x: ash content; z: height of capillary rise; SD: standard deviation

With increasing ground water level, the capillary rise decreased and the tensions in the top layers of the soil strongly increased. Figure 3 presents this relationship for fen soils without sapric horizons (mud) in the capillary fringe. Ground water levels up to 70 cm were sufficient for capillary water supply for all considered soil types. The hydraulic gradients were small and differed only marginally from the equilibrium state. With increasing ground water level, the tension at 10 cm soil depth increased exponentially. During the field measurements it became clear, that the hydraulic conditions in the field were strongly influenced by the occurrence of sapric horizons (mud) and its location depth in the profile (Fig. 4). Mud in the capillary fringe zones partly reduced the capillarity and sometimes led to very high tensions in the topsoil layer even when mud thickness was low. At other sites however, effect of mud on the capillary rise was rather low. Consequently the coefficient of determination of the relation between tension and ground water level showed to be significant but the correlation was weak ($r^2 = 0.42$).

CONCLUSIONS

Shallow ground water levels should be aspired for reduction of peat loss and for protection of fens as landscape features, assumed the planned land use is ensured. Capillary water supply of all soil development stages was not limited up to 70 cm ground water level at the investigated fen sites in Brandenburg and Mecklenburg-Vorpommern. Most critical for capillary plant water supply and peat protection are the formation of segregation structure (nHa horizon) and mud in the capillary fringe. However, important are not only the existence of mud but rather its consistency and structure. The soil stratification, the existence, the consistency and the structure of mud as well as the hydraulic conductivity of the underground have to be more strongly considered for the specification of controlling ground water levels at fens sites in future.

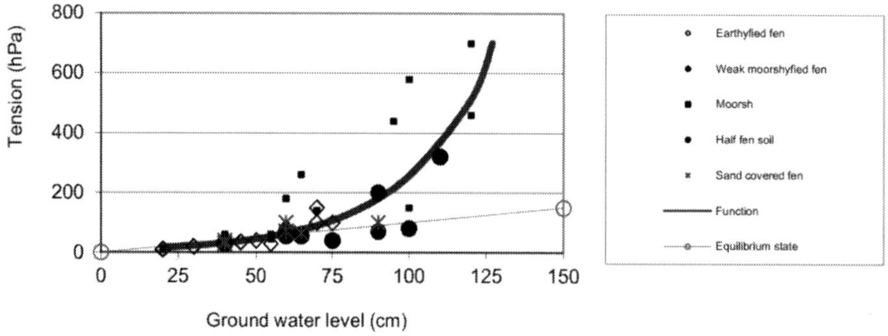

Figure 3: Tension at 10 cm soil depth (h10) at varying ground water levels (GWF) for soil types without mud in the capillary fringe zone, ($h10 = \exp(-0.034738 * GWF + 2.071349)$; $r^2 = 0.73$; n=48).

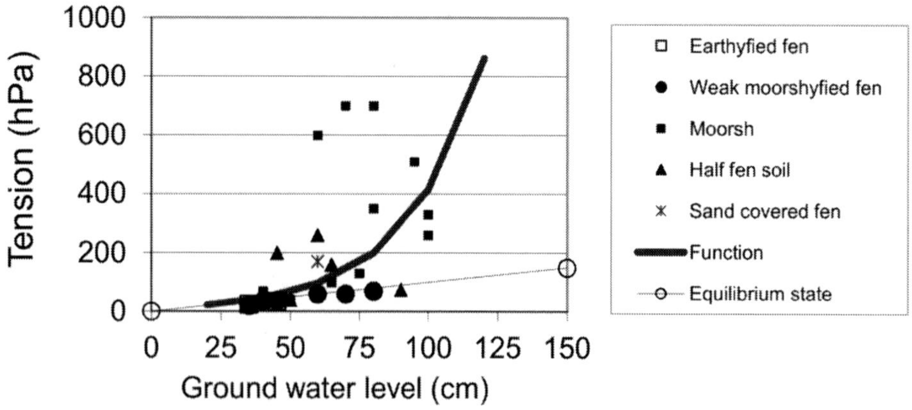

Figure 4: Tension at 10 cm soil depth (h10) at different ground water levels (GWF) for soil types with mud in the capillary fringe, ($h10 = \exp(-0.036633 * GWF + 2.362686)$; $r^2 = 0.42$; n=36).

REFERENCES

1. Bodenkundliche Kartieranleitung, KA5. (2005). *E. Schweizerbart'sche Verlagsbuchhandlung, Stuttgart, 438 p.*
2. Kechavarzi, C., Dawson, Q. Leeds-Harrison, P.B., 2010. Physical properties of low-lying agricultural peat soils in England. *Geoderma, Volume 154, Issues 3–4, 196-202.*
3. Klimkowska A., Van Diggelen, R., Grootjans, P., Kotowski, W., 2010. Prospects for fen meadow restoration on severely degraded fens. Perspectives in Plant Ecology, *Evolution and Systematics, Volume 12, Issue 3, 20, 245-255.*
4. Ohde (1950) in Schultze, E. and H. Muhs (1967): Bodenuntersuchungen für Ingenieurbauten. *Springer Verlag. Zweite Auflage. 722 pp.*
5. Sauerbrey, R. and J. Zeitz (1999): In: Handbuch der Bodenkunde. Landsberg: ecomed, Hrsg. Hans-Peter Blume. Kap. 3.3.3.7., Moore,. 1-24.
6. Schindler, U., Müller, L., Eulenstein, F. (2015) Measurement and evaluation of the hydraulic properties of horticultural substrates. Archives of Agronomy and Soil Science.Schultz-Sternberg, R., Zeitz, J., Landgraf, L., Hoffmann, E., Lehrkamp, H., Luthardt, V. und D. Kühn (2000): Niedermoore Brandenburgs. *TELMA. (30), 139-172.*
7. Schmidt, W. (1989): Untersuchungen zur Bestimmung des Verformungsverhaltens von Torfen und Mudden und der dafür maßgeblichen Bodenkennwerte. *Habil-Schrift Humboldt Univ. Berlin. 265 pp.*
8. Succow, M. and L. Jeschke (2001): Landschaftsökologische Moorkunde. *E. Schweizerbart'sche Verlagsbuchhandlung. pp. 622.*

Abstract No: A-465

HYDROLOGICAL MONITORING AT PEAT SWAMP FOREST, AYER HITAM FOREST RESERVE, JOHOR, MALAYSIA FOR FOREST CONSERVATION

Siti Aisah Shamsuddin*, Ibharim Hasim, Mohd Muflif Mohd Rodzi and Hafizi Mohd Jaafar

Forest Research Institute Malaysia, Malaysia

**Corresponding author: sitiaisah@frim.gov.my*

SUMMARY

The quick hydrological assessment was carried at peat swamp area of Ayer Hitam Forest Reserve (N), Johor. This preliminary study at the site is part of the component that will be included in the management and conservation of the forest area as this is the only peat swamp forest left in this state. The observation was carried out in June 2015 for water quality and water level at 2 m below the surface. Basically the longer term monitoring is necessary to determine the fluctuation in water level in accordance to the monsoon seasons. The conservation of this peat area is important as its functions in flood control in case if there is an extreme rainfall event occurred. This area also conducive to the forest fire and appropriate action should be taken as an alternative to face the problem. This project will be continuing in the second phase for details study in hydrology and method selected to help forestry department in the management of the forest.

***Keywords**: water quality, ground water, water level, water pumping test*

INTRODUCTION

The Ayer Hitam Forest Reserve (AHFR) is located in Muar district, state of Johor with the total area of 3,797 hectares (ha.). This is the largest and the last remaining peat swamp forest in the state of Johor (Figure 1). This forest reserve is surrounded by oil palm estates, cash crops and also settlement areas, thus there are canals established at the edge of the forest area in the management of agriculture and plantation. Hence, there is a possibility that water resource in this peat swamp forest is affected by the canals system. The dark yellowish water from the forest will be drained into the canals and these canals also protected the oil palm trees from submersion during wetted season. Besides that, this forest reserve is threatened by fire.

Basically there are no river systems that flow in this forest area but a small stream was found at point Wq 14, which is located at the forest border between AHFR and oil palm plantation. This is not a stream originated from peat swamp area as identified from the colour of the water and the soil properties. Hence, there are no inflow to and outflow from the areas so that water flows slowly or it seems not moving at most of the locations. Naturally, water bodies in the area of peat swamp are depending on rainfall for replenishment.

There was an ex-mining water body located inside the AHFR that is at the southeastern part of the area and canals were constructed along the access road to the site. A canal at one side of the road is bigger than the other side. Water in the big canal will remain and the water level slightly dropped only during drought period.

The objectives of the study are to determine the status of water quality and water availability below the surface by measuring the water levels which can be represented the values for peat swamp area of AHFR.

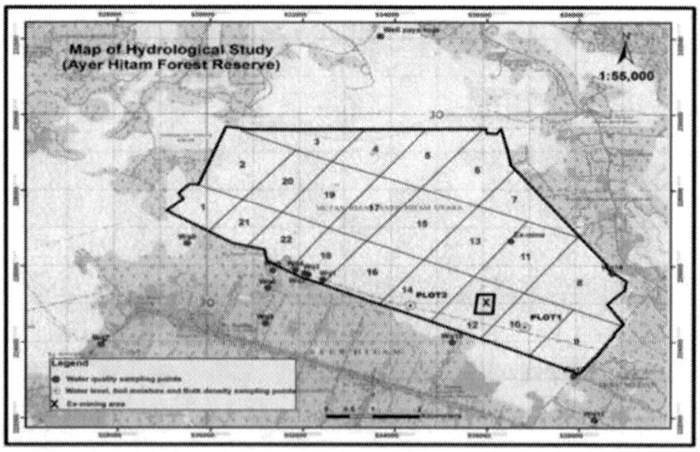

Figure 1: Map of hydrological study at AHFR

METHODS

Water quality monitoring was carried out inside AHFR where water bodies can be found and most of the points of observations were outside the AHFR which many of the canals were established.

The water quality were measured at 15 locations (Figure 1) which 6 points inside the forest (Wq 1, Wq 2, Wq 3, Wq 4, Wq 14 and at ex-mining area), 9 points outside the AHFR area (Wq 5, Wq 6, Wq 7, Wq 8, Wq 9, Wq 10, Wq 11, Wq 12, Wq 13) which are located in oil palm plantation areas. Points Wq 1-4 are surface water body retention in the canal that has been covered with sediment. YSI Profesional Series Pro Plus (S.N: 14B101084) Multiparameter was used in the measurement.

Water quality sample from pumping test was also measured and another reading was taken from the canal located at Paya Kopi, AHFR Tambahan. The water quality parameters measured were pH, dissolved oxygen (DO), Conductivity (Cond), total dissolved solids (TDS) and turbidity. The observations were carried out from 9 to 11 June and 23 to 25 June 2015.

Figure 2: Observation on water body inside the forest reserve.

Figure 2: Observation on the canal outside the forest reserve.

The water levels were measured at two locations (plots 1 and 2) as shown in figure 1. Cera Diver was used to measure the water level while mini diver is a barometer to measure the pressure (Figure 2). The pvc with 5.0 cm in diameter and 2.5 m length was inserted into the borehole at 2.0 m depth below the surface (Figure 3). The divers were carefully installed into the borehole casing and all the measurements needed were determined as shown in Figure 4. The monitoring was started on 27 May 2015 on hourly basis at plots 1 and 2. Figures 5 and 6 show the process of water pumping and it was carried out continuously after one event to the next event in order to get the consistent rates of recovery period.

Figure 2: Mini diver (above) and Cera Diver (below) used in the water quantity study.

Figure 3: Cera diver was placed in the pvc tube.

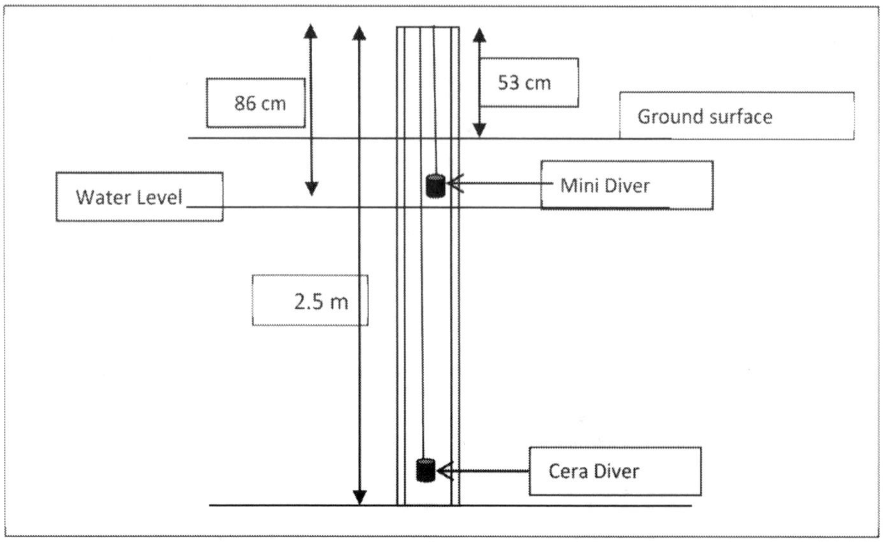

Figure 4: Schematic diagram of instrumental set-up for water level measurement.

Figure 5: Inserting the water pump instrument into borehole casing.

Figure 6 Water yield from the pumped well.

RESULTS

Tables 3 to 6 show the results for water quality observation at the study site and also surrounding areas.

Table 3: Water quality observation near the border and inside the AHFR

Date (June)	Location	Time	Temp. °C	DO %	DO mg/l	Cond. uS/cm	TDS mg/l	pH	Turb. NTU
9	Wq 1	11:10	30.9	71.0	5.22	58.5	34.45	4.2	72.50
	Wq 2	11:22	31.8	59.8	4.44	77.2	44.20	3.9	46.10
	Wq 3	11:31	28.5	29.7	2.32	67.5	40.95	3.8	2.59
	Wq 4	11:40	32.1	80.6	6.03	24.8	14.30	5.0	25.80
11	Wq 14	9:50	26.3	51.1	4.16	112.0	70.85	6.3	82.10
25	Ex-mining	10:10	27.0	14.0	1.1	99.4	62.4	3.2	2.2

(Note: Wq 14 is not water body from the peat swamp forest)

Table 4: Water quality observation at oil palm plantations

Date (June)	Location	Time	Temp. °C	DO %	DO mg/l	Cond. uS/cm	TDS mg/l	pH	Turb. NTU
9	Wq 5	11:50	29.9	26.8	2.13	61.2	36.40	5.5	43.50
	Wq 6 (1)	12:00	28.0	32.1	2.58	102.6	63.05	3.6	42.00
	Wq 6 (2)	12:00	28.0	32.4	2.58	102.9	63.05	3.4	20.10
	Wq 6 (3)	12:00	28.1	30.0	2.37	103.0	63.05	3.5	44.20
10	Wq 7	9:00	27.7	46.2	3.68	102.3	63.05	4.9	5.89
	Wq 8	9:36	26.9	33.0	2.72	58.0	36.40	5.4	13.70
	Wq 9	10:16	28.1	35.6	2.90	56.0	34.46	4.6	8.69
	Wq 10	10:38	27.8	43.1	3.44	95.7	59.15	3.6	1.62
	Wq 11	10:56	27.7	44.7	3.58	140.2	86.45	3.4	2.29
	Wq 12	11:08	27.3	49.0	3.97	131.4	81.90	3.4	1.20
	Wq 13	11:36	28.8	32.0	2.47	645.0	390.00	3.3	55.20

(*Note: Canal maintenance work had just carried at point Wq 13 when observation was carried out*)

Table 5: Water quality of water sample from pumping tests and at Paya Kopi.

Date (June)	Location	Time	Temp. °C	DO %	DO mg/l	Cond. uS/cm	TDS mg/l	pH	Turb. NTU
23	Plot 1	11:19	26.9	15.2	1.21	74.8	46.8	5.9	18.8
24		10:40	27.0	21.5	1.80	73.5	45.8	5.0	14.4
25	Paya Kopi	11:04	27.7	18.4	1.5	83.8	51.8	3.9	5.3

The acidity of surface water at peat swamp forest is high which the value can be as low as pH 3.2 (ex-mining area) and it was found that water pH from pumping test (2 m below surface) was less acidic than surface water. The pH values obtained from pumping test were 5.0 and 5.9. Basically, most of the pH values ranging from 3.2 to 3.9. These values are consistent with the pH values obtained at Sungai Bebar peat swamp forest at Pekan Forest Reserve, Pahang which ranged from 3.3 to 4.2 (Suhaimi & Lim, 2005).

The water turbidity was low when there is no influence of sedimentation such as at points Wq 10-12 which ranged from 1.2 to 1.62 NTU. Conductivity was quite high ranges from 56 to 103 uS/cm while, DO was low ranges from 1.1 to 3.9 mg/l. The TDS is also high which ranged from 34.5 to 86.4 mg/l.

Table 7: The water volume obtained from the pumping test was 3.09 L The parameters involved and volume of water determined from the pumping test about 2 m below the surface.

1.	Length of pump inserted in the pvc tube.	2.23 m
2.	Distance between pvc tube pump and soil moisture sensor point.	4.67 m
3.	Water level from the surface before water pumping.	33 cm
4.	Drawdown period of time.	23 s
5.	Saturated level at the soil moisture sensor measured after water was pumped.	38 cm
6.	Volume of water.	0.00309 m^3 /23s (3.09 L)

DISCUSSION

The hydrological study conducted at the peat swamp forest has given basic information on the availability of water through pumping below the surface and also the status of water quality found at the study site and also from the surrounding area.

The canals were also established in the preparation of the construction of high voltage power along the border line of the southern part of the forest. The canals were at both sides of the road but through time already covered by sedimentation. The existence of the roads had effected the water level under the surface and resulted in subsidence occurred slowly through time and this can be evidenced by the exposure of the power line's pole.

The most important thing when conducting the water pumping test is the interval of water level recorded by the water level sensor. The small interval will give more accurate time of recovery phase. In this study the interval will be changed from one hour to 1 second for the next water pumping test. This result will provide us with the frequency of water that could be pumped from the tube well. Another aspect that is also need to be determined is the zone around the point of pvc tube well that will be affected by the drawdown of water.

The water level measured at AHFR was about 33 cm below the surface. The study reported at Pekan Forest Reserve that water level seldom fall below 40 cm (Danida, 2004) and the same condition was also reported at north Selangor peat swamp forest (DANCED, 2000). The water resource from the peat swamp forest is not obtained from the 2 m level below the surface but should be at the depth of the aquifer level. The mineral level at the study site was found between 7–9 m below the surface.

This area is very sensitive to forest fire every year as it is near to the agricultural site which is involved in forest burning prior to planting during the dry season especially from January to Mac. The forest reserve was affected by the worst forest fire event in year 2013. The government has taken action under the Ministry of Natural Resources to construct a check dam and ground water tube well as an effort to mitigate the problem. Both infrastructures were established at peat swamp of Paya Kopi, Pagoh which ground water tube well was provided by the Mineral and Geoscience Department (JMG), Johor while, the check dam was provided by Drainage and Irrigation Department (DID), Johor. The ground water tube well is planned to establish at another two sites.

CONCLUSION

The AHFR area is not similar with other peat area in Peninsular Malaysia as there is no streamflow into and out of the area. The quick assessment on water quality indicated the acidic condition of water at the surface (as low as pH 3.2) but the water quality pumped from 2 m below the surface is less acidic (up to pH 5.6). The water volume obtained was little (~ 3 L) with long recovery period of 12 hours.

ACKNOWLEDGEMENT

The author would like to thank the Yayasan Kemanusiaan Muslim Aid Malaysia and Coca-Cola Foundation for providing the fund through grant No. 51310904003 and support to this project.

REFERENCES

1. DANCED. 2000. Malaysia-DANCED Project on Sustainable Management of Peat Swamp Forest. Integrated Management Plan for the North Selangor Peat Swamp Forest (2004-2010).
2. DANIDA. 2004. Management for Conservation and Sustainable use of Peat Swamp Forest and Associated Water Regimes in Malaysia-Hydrology Assessment of the Pekan Forest Reserve, Pahang.
3. Suhaimi, M.O. and Lim, E.C. 2005. Biodiversity Expedition Sungai Bebar, Pahang. Summary Findings. Peat Swamp Forest Project, UNDP/GEF Funded, in collaboration with the Pahang Forestry Department and Universiti Kebangsaan Malaysia, 169 pp.

Abstract No: A-229

HYDROPHOBICITY OF DISSOLVED ORGANIC CARBON IN FEN PEATLANDS

Barbara Kalisz* and Andrzej Łachacz

Department of Soil Science and Land Reclamation, Faculty of Environmental Management and Agriculture, University of Warmia and Mazury in Olsztyn, Poland,

**Corresponding author: barbara.kalisz@uwm.edu.pl; andrzej.lachacz@uwm.edu.pl*

SUMMARY

Peatlands contain various organic carbon fractions; among which dissolved and labile carbon are the most important, especially in drained peatlands, which are the source of CO_2 emissions. The research was carried out in fen (lowland) peatlands drained and used as grasslands, in NE Poland. Hydrophobicity is a very important parameter in peatlands protection, as it suggests the possibilities of water retention. Potential soil hydrophobicity can be measured using the Water Drop Penetration Time test. In this test the time of retention of drops of distilled water is measured. The aim of the study was to assess: (i) the hydrophobicity of a soil, and (ii) its content of hydrophobic/hydrophilic compounds, i.e. hot water-extractable carbon and cold water-extractable carbon fractions, using the solid phase extraction (SPE) technique. Hot water-extractable carbon and cold water-extractable carbon were divided into hydrophobic and hydrophilic fractions. The study revealed that both studied peatlands are hydrophobic. However, the peatland influenced by alluvial and deluvial processes had lower hydrophobicity. The extracts of HWC and CWC contained more hydrophilic fraction than hydrophobic one (the ratio of hydrophilic to hydrophobic fraction amounted to 4.032 in HWC extracts and 2.173 in CWC extracts) additionally, the extracts of HWC had diversified retention times (1.802-1.831 min.) in chromatographic analysis, whereas in case of CWC the retention times were similar (1.801-1.815 min.).

Keywords: *organic soil, water repellency, polarity*

INTRODUCTION

Globally, soil organic carbon plays an important role in carbon (C) cycling. It can be divided into labile and refractory carbon forms (Lützow *et al.*, 2007). Labile organic carbon compounds may oxidize easily and are degradable. The labile organic carbon fraction of organic soils can be extracted using for example hot and cold water and SPE technique. These two fractions respond to changes in C supply in organic soils very quickly (Zhang *et al.*, 2006) and may indicate changes occurring in land use. The hot water-extractable fraction corresponds with microbial biomass and is a good indicator of peatland transformations.

After drainage peatlands decrease their ability to retain water and become hydrophobic. In hydrophobic soils, absorption of water decreases and the filtration of water occur mainly through "preferential paths", made by cracks and holes (Łachacz and Kalisz, 2006). High hydrophobicity often occurs in drained peats (Szatyłowicz *et al.*, 2006). Hydrophobicity is also dependent on the activity of microorganisms and soil physical and chemical properties. The amount and type of soil organic matter (quantity of labile and refractory carbon fractions) may influence soil hydrophobic / hydrophilic properties (Bisdom *et al.*, 1993; Maryganova, Szajdak, 2006). The quality of organic matter fractions (content of polar / non-polar groups of compounds; labile or refractory forms; content of fulvic acids, humic acids and humins) and their influence on soil hydrophobicity is of great importance. We decided to examine labile fraction of organic matter (dissolved organic carbon) and find out whether it influenced the hydrophobicity of drained peat soils used as grassland and influenced by alluvial and deluvial processes.

The aim of the study was to assess

- the potential hydrophobicity of studied soil
- amounts of dissolved organic carbon
- relations between hydrophobic and hydrophilic compounds which are present in cold and hot water extracts of drained peat soils.

METHODS

The study area was located in north-eastern Poland, which was shaped during the period of the Vistulian Glaciation. The studied peat soils were drained in 20th century. Peat samples were taken from surface horizons (0-30cm) from two drained peatlands used as grasslands (A) and two peatlands modified by alluvial and deluvial processes (B). Organic matter (OM) content was calculated on the basis of loss-on-ignition after dry ashing of soil samples for 6 hours at a temperature of 550°C. The hydrophobicity of the samples was determined at 20°C using the Water Drop Penetration Time (WDPT) test (Doerr, 1998). This test was carried out on air-dried soil samples therefore the results reflect potential hydrophobicity and are regarded as a proxy for soil hydrophobicity. Based on the time taken for the water drop to infiltrate the soil sample, the studied peat soils were classified according to the following classes:

Class 1 – hydrophilic (WDPT < 5s);
Class 2 – slightly hydrophobic ($5 < \text{WDPT} \leq 60$s);
Class 3 – strongly hydrophobic ($60 < \text{WDPT} \leq 600$s);
Class 4 – very strongly hydrophobic ($600 < \text{WDPT} \leq 3600$s);
Class 5 – extremely hydrophobic (WDPT > 3600s).

Two types of dissolved organic carbon were determined: hot water-extractable carbon (HWC) and cold water-extractable carbon (CWC). The hot-water extractable C was determined in air-dried soil samples according to the method described by Sparling *et al.* (1998) with the incubation of soil samples at 70 °C for 18 h. Cold water extractable carbon was determined in air-dried soil samples according to Landgraf *et al.* (2006). The HWC and CWC quantities were measured using a TOC (total organic carbon) analyzer (Multi NC 3100 Analityk Jena). All measurements were carried out in triplicate.
In the study, the method of extraction of organic matter dissolved in hot and cold water to solid phase using modified polymeric sorbents was applied. It is not commonly used in the soil science but is frequently used in the studies of surface waters. Hydrophilic (with higher polarity) and hydrophobic fractions were separated from HWC extracts using SPE (Solid Phase Extraction) technique and STRATA-X Phenomenex 30 mg 30 μm columns. The obtained fractions were studied chromatographically.

RESULTS

The studied peat horizons contained 53-80% of organic matter on average (Table 1). The hydrophobicity of studied peat horizons was high (3344.48-11788.69s on average) and was related to organic matter content. Extreme hydrophobicity and a WDPT exceeding 1 hour (Class 5 of WDPT) was recorded in peatlands used as grasslands (A). Various classes of hydrophobicity (Class 2-5 of WDPT) were stated in peat horizons influenced by alluvial and deluvial processes (B) (Table 1).

Studied surface horizons of peatlands contained more carbon extracted with hot water than with cold water. Peatlands used as grasslands contained more HWC than the peatlands modified by alluvial and deluvial processes but in the case of CWC, the tendency was the reverse (Table 1).

Table 1: Amounts of hot water-extractable and cold water-extractable fractions.

	WDPT	OM	HWC	CWC	WDPT	OM	HWC	CWC
	s	g kg^{-1}			s	g kg^{-1}		
	A (Grasslands)				B (Alluvial and deluvial influence)			
mean	11788.69	806.98	5.00	0.74	3344.48	535.77	3.54	0.85
min	4157.55	690.74	4.00	0.46	155.60	304.88	2.12	0.20
max	24098.00	892.45	6.07	0.94	6578.00	776.33	5.31	1.19
SD	6376.46	66.42	0.60	0.17	2674.16	158.81	1.10	0.31

The extracts of HWC and CWC contained more hydrophilic fraction than hydrophobic one (the ratio of hydrophilic to hydrophobic fraction amounted to 4.032 in HWC extracts and 2.173 in CWC extracts) additionally, the extracts of HWC had diversified retention times (1.802-1.831 min.) in chromatographic analysis, whereas in case of CWC the retention times were similar (1.801-1.815 min.).

DISCUSSION

Generally, hydrophobicity occurs in the soils containing more than 20% of organic matter. Apart from the amount of organic matter, the activity of microorganisms also influences the repellency of a soil (Doerr *et al.*, 2000). Deluvial and alluvial admixtures stabilize organic matter (Orzechowski *et al.*, 2013) and decrease hydrophobicity. The study revealed that both studied peatlands are hydrophobic. However, the peatland influenced by alluvial and deluvial processes had lower hydrophobicity. The study revealed that there is a correlation between hydrophobicity and amount of organic matter but the relation between hydrophobicity and hot water-extractable carbon, which corresponds to microbial biomass, is insignificant (Figure 1).

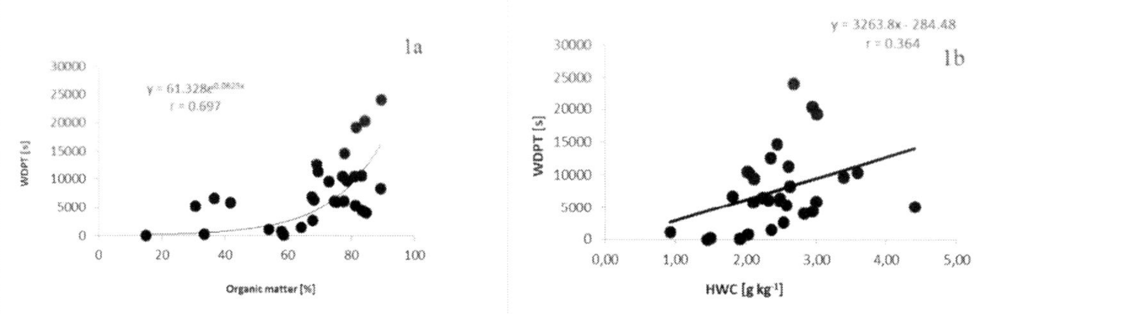

Figure 1: Relationship between the water absorption time in WDPT test (in seconds) and the content of organic matter (1a) and hot water-extractable fraction (in g kg^{-1}) (1b).

The chromatographic analysis of HWC extracts revealed that the polarity of hydrophilic and hydrophobic fractions are similar, as are the retention times. The retention time depends on the polarity of organic fraction and the mass of the molecules. The higher the polarity of the fraction and higher the mass of the molecule, the longer the retention time. The relationship between the hydrophobic fraction of HWC expressed as the peak on the chromatogram and organic matter content or hydrophobicity was weak and insignificant (Figure 2). Similar relations were stated for hydrophilic fraction of HWC. However, the chromatographic analyses revealed the relationship between the retention time of hydrophobic or hydrophilic fractions of HWC and the hydrophobicity but the correlation was negative (Figure 3). The peatland influenced by alluvial and deluvial processes had varied retention time and lower hydrophobicity whereas peatland used as grassland had varied hydrophobicity with more similar retention times (Table 1, Figure 3). This suggests that less hydrophobic peats had longer retention times, i.e. HWC extracts of those peats had higher polarity and mass of molecules in a chemical sense. To conclude, composition of dissolved organic carbon fraction does not reveal direct relation to the potential hydrophobicity of a peatland.

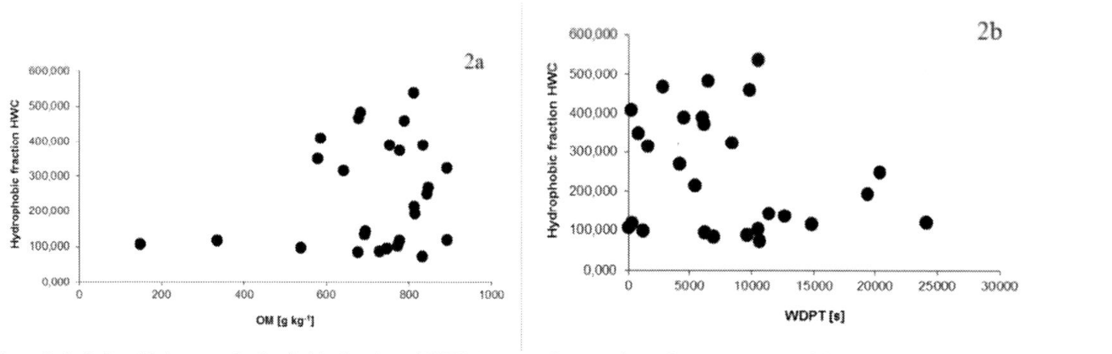

Figure 2: Relationship between hydrophobic fraction of HWC (expressed as a peak on chromatogram) and the amount of organic matter (2a) and hydrophobicity (WDPT) (2b).

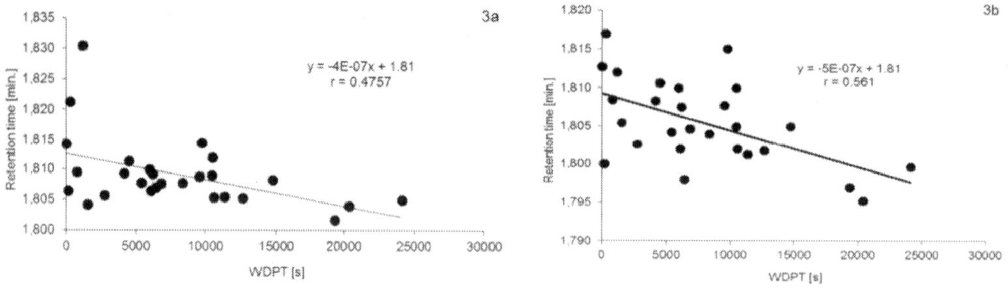

Figure 3: Relationship between the retention time of hydrophobic (3a) and hydrophilic (3b) fraction and the hydrophobicity (WDPT).

REFERENCES

1. Bisdom E.B.A., Dekker L.W., and Schoute J.F.T. 1993. Water repellency of sieve fractions from sandy soils and relationships with organic material and soil structure. *Geoderma* 56: 105-118.
2. Doerr S.H., Shakesby R.A., and Walsh R.P.D. 2000. Soil water repellency, its characteristics, causes and hydro-geomorphological consequences. *Earth-Science Reviews* 55: 33-65.
3. Doerr S.H. 1998. On standardizing the 'Water Drop Penetration Time' and the 'Molarity of an Ethanol Droplet' techniques to classify soil hydrophobicity: a case study using medium textured soils. *Earth Surface Processes and Landforms* 23: 663–668.
4. Łachacz A., and Kalisz B. 2006. Hydrofobowość powierzchniowych utworów gleb o zróżnicowanej zawartości materii organicznej. In: *Physical and Chemical Properties of Organic Soils*. T. Brandyk, L. Szajdak, J. Szatyłowicz (eds.), Wyd. SGGW Warszawa: 95-103. (in Polish)
5. Landgraf D., Leinweber P., Makeschin F. 2006. Cold and hot water-extractable organic matter as indicators of litter decomposition in forest soils. *Journal of Plant Nutrition and Soil Science* 169: 76-82.
6. Lützow M.V., Kögel-Knabner I., Ekschmitt K,. Flessa H., Guggenberger G., Matzner E., Marschner B. 2007. SOM fractionation methods: Relevance to functional pools and to stabilization mechanisms. *Soil Biology and Biochemistry* 39: 2183-2207.
7. Maryganova V., Szajdak L. 2006. Właściwości hydrofilne i hydrofobowe związków humusowych gleb organicznych. In: *Physical and Chemical Properties of Organic Soils*. T. Brandyk, L. Szajdak, J. Szatyłowicz (eds.), Wyd. SGGW Warszawa: 77-84. (in Polish).
8. Orzechowski M., Smólczyński S., Sowiński P., Rybińska B. 2013. Water repellency of soils with various content of organic matter in north-eastern Poland. *Soil Science Annales* 64: 30-33.
9. Sparling G., Vojvodic-Vukovic M., Schipper L.A. 1998. Hot-water-soluble C as a simple measure of labile soil organic matter: The relationship with microbial biomass C. *Soil Biology and Biochemistry* 30:1469-1472.
10. Szatyłowicz J., Oleszczuk R., Gnatowski T., Mączyńska E. 2006. Ocena zwilżalności utworów torfowych i murszowych na podstawie pomiarów kąta zwilżania pomiędzy fazą stałą gleby a wodą. In: *Physical and Chemical Properties of Organic Soils*. T. Brandyk, L. Szajdak, J. Szatyłowicz (eds.), Wyd. SGGW Warszawa: 84-94. (in Polish).
11. Zhang J., Changchun S., Wenyan Y. 2006. Land use effects on the distribution of labile organic carbon fractions through soil profiles. *Soil Science Society of America Journal* 70: 660-667.

Abstract No: A-117

SEASONAL AND INTERANNUAL VARIATIONS OF DISSOLVED ORGANIC MATTER COMPOSITION IN THE GROUNDWATER OF TROPICAL PEAT UNDER OIL PALM PLANTATION MANAGEMENT

Nagamitsu Maie[1], Lulie Melling[2], Sonoko D. Bellingrath-Kimura[3], Kosuke Ikeya[4], Eikichi Shima[1], Hajime Tanji[1], Zulhilmy Abdullah Mohd[2] and Akira Watanabe[4]

[1]School of Veterinary Medicine, Kitasato University, Aomori, Japan
[2]Tropical Peat Research Laboratory Unit, Chief Minister's Department, Sarawak, Malaysia
[3]Leibniz Centre for Agricultural Landscape Research, Müncheberg, Germany
[4]Graduate School of Bioagricultural Sciences, Nagoya University, Nagoya, Japan

**Corresponding author: maie@vmas.kitasato-u.ac.jp*

SUMMARY

Dissolved organic matter (DOM) is the most reactive fraction of natural organic matter, of which composition reflects its source and biogeochemical processes. As such, compositional information of DOM can serve as a useful clue to better understand its surrounding environments. In this study, a long-term monitoring of DOM composition in groundwater of tropical peat (TP) under oil palm plantation (OPP) was conducted to better understand the environmental change of. Monitoring sites are located in an OPP in Sarawak, Malaysia. Twelve sampling wells were installed across the OPP and groundwater samples were collected once a month over 5 years. Dissolved organic carbon (DOC) concentrations and UV-visible spectra were measured to calculate specific UV absorption (SUVA) values (absorbance at 254 nm per unit C; a proxy for aromaticity of DOM). Fluorescence properties of DOM were measured by excitation-emission fluorescence matrices (EEMs) combined with parallel factor (PARAFAC) analysis. The average DOC concentration was approximately 48 mg C L^{-1} and increased during wet-season, while SUVA value did not change during the monitoring period. EEM was decomposed into 7 PARAFAC components with different behavior. Fluorescent component composition showed intra- and inter-annual variation. Principal component analysis of PARAFAC component compositions successfully extracted two factors responsible for the temporal changes in fluorescence compositions. One is development of reductive conditions over time, and the other is seasonal variation of the percentage of humic acid-type humic-like fluorescence associated with the seasonal variation of groundwater level.

Keywords: *dissolved organic matter composition, EEM-PARAFAC, long term monitoring, oil palm plantation, tropical peat*

INTRODUCTION

Tropical peatland area is estimated to contribute to 11% (44.1×10^4 km^2) of global peatland area, of which 56% is located in Southeast Asia (Page *et al.*, 2011). A large amount of wood peat is accumulated under tropical peat swamp forest (TPSF). Carbon stock of Tropical peat (TP) in Southeast Asia is estimated to be 68.5 PgC, and Indonesia and Malaysia account for its 65% and 10%, respectively.

Since 1960s, countries in Southeast Asia, as typified by Indonesia and Malaysia, began to develop TP to oil palm plantation (OPP) due to limited acreage of arable dry field. Once TP is developed to OPP, peat environment changes considerably, which may accelerate peat decomposition. Therefore, it is important to better understand the changes in the biogeochemical processes of peat accompanied by the changes in peat environment or land utilization to contribute to the sustainable management of tropical peat.

Dissolved organic matter (DOM) is the most reactive fraction of peat organic matter, of which composition reflects sensitively its source and biogeochemical processes. As such, compositional information of DOM can provide useful information to better understand its surrounding environments. In recent years, the analysis of optical properties as a means of characterizing DOM quality has received increasing attention. In particular, the combination of excitation emission matrix (EEM) fluorescence and parallel factor analysis (PARAFAC) modeling has enabled biogeochemists to draw out the full information contained in the fluorescence signature of DOM (e.g. Yamashita 2010).

In this study, we aim to better understand the changes in the TP environment under OPP, focusing on the quality of DOM in the groundwater. For that purpose, DOM composition in the groundwater of TP at OPP was monitored monthly for 5 years by using EEM-PARAFAC.

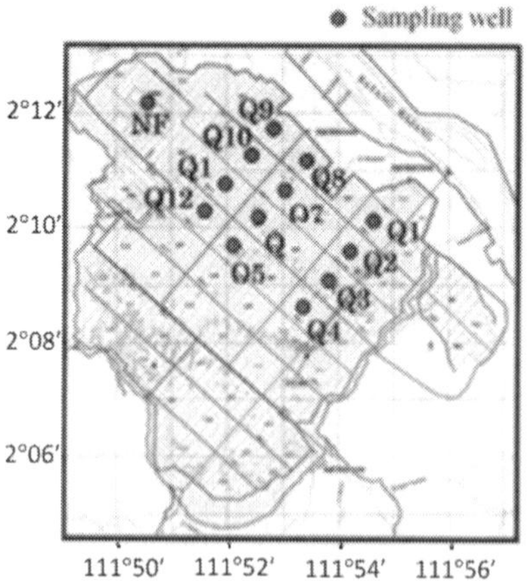

Figure 1: Map of Naman oil palm plantation and location of sampling wells. Q1 to Q12 are the monitoring wells established in OPP. NF is monitoring well established in secondary forest preserved in OPP.

METHODS

Study area and water sampling

A long term monitoring of groundwater quality was conducted at Naman OPP, which is located in the southwest region of Sarawak, Malaysia (2° 9'N, 111° 53'E) (Figure 1). Sarawak belongs to tropical rainforest climate, with an average temperature of 26-35°C and annual precipitation of 2000-4000 mm with unclear wet (Nov-Feb) and dry season (Mar-Oct). The elevation of the OPP is 1-17 m asl, and the peat depth ranges from 0-16m. Oil palm trees in the study site were transplanted in 2000 at Q1-Q4, in 2001-2002 at Q5-Q8, and in 2003-2004 at Q9-Q12 (Q5 was excluded in this paper since the hydrology of Q5 was very different from other sites). a total of 12 monitoring sites Groundwater monitoring wells were established in 2008 (Figure 1). Water samples were collected at monthly interval from the wells from October 2008 to June 2013. Water samples were transported under refrigerated condition to the laboratory of water environment in Kitasato University, Japan.

Chemical Analyses

The water samples were filtered through pre-combusted at 450°C for 4h through glass fiber filters (nominal pore size 0.4μm; GB-140, ADVANTEC, JAPAN). The dissolved organic C concentrations were measured using a high-temperature catalytic oxidation (TOC-V_{CNH}, Shimadzu, Japan).

Spectroscopic analysis

The excitation-emission matrices (EEMs) of water samples were measured using a spectrofluorometer (FluoroMax-4, Horiba Scientific, Japan) equipped with a 150 W xenon lamp as the light source (Abe *et al.*, 2011). EEM was measured with an excitation wavelength from 240 to 550 nm at an increment of 5 nm and the emission signal was scanned in the range of 260 to 600 nm at an increment of 2 nm. The inner filter effect was corrected by measuring the UV-Vis absorption spectra of the sample (McKnight *et al.*, 2001; Maie *et al.*, 2006) on a UV-Vis spectrophotometer (UV-1800, Shimadzu, Japan). The obtained EEMs were further statistically analyzed using parallel factor analysis (PARAFAC) modeling with DOMFluor toolbox (Stedmon and Bro, 2008) using MATLAB software ver. 7.7 (MathWorks, Inc.) to decompose EEMs into distinct fluorescence components (Stedmon *et al.*, 2003; Stedmon and Bro, 2008). The validity of the model was confirmed based on split half analysis and Tucker's congruence coefficient (Stedmon and Bro 2008).

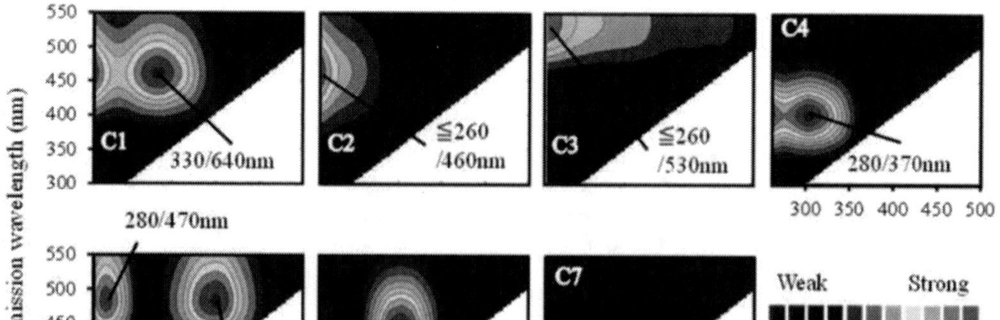

Figure 2: Contour graph of 7 fluorescence components decomposed by PARAFAC analysis. C1, C2, & C6, terrestrial fulvic acid-type humic like peak; C3, terrestrial humic acid-type humic like peak; C4, Microbial fulvic acid-type humic like peak; C5, Ubiquitous fulvic-type humic like peak; C7, protein-like peak.

RESULTS AND DISCUSSION

Average DOC concentration was 48±8 mgC $L^{-1}$and showed seasonal variation. DOC generally increased during wet season (Nov. – Feb) when groundwater level became high. Specific UV absorbance (SUVA) value, which is a proxy for aromaticity of DOM, did not change appreciably during the monitoring period.
DOM in the groundwater of OPP contained different amount of these 7 PARAFAC components (Figure 2). To extract factors which induce variations in the PARAFAC component composition, principal component analysis (PCA) was conducted.. The PC1 scores increased from Oct. 2008 to Aug. 2010 and generally continued to be flat without seasonal variation (Figure 3). Factor loading plots (Figure 4) indicated that the increase of PC1 score was associated with either the increase of C1, C4, and C7, or the decrease of C2 and C6. When groundwater was incubated with nutrients (N & P) under anoxic conditions, %C1 increased. However, when groundwater was oxidized with laccase, %C2 and %C6 increased. Therefore, the variation in PC1 score can be attributed to the lowering of redox potential from Oct. 2008 to Aug. 2010, which may be caused by the increase of microbial activity in groundwater due to long term fertilizer application. The PC2 score showed seasonal cycle, which generally increased during wet season and decreased toward the end of dry season. Variations in the PC2 score shows the changes in the relative proportion of humic-like (C3) and fulvic-like humic substances (C4) (Figure 4). The reason of this variation may be explained as follows. Water soluble organic matter (WSOM), which is rich in humic acid-like fluorescence, is formed in peat at above groundwater level during dry season. The WSOM is dissolved into groundwater in wet season when groundwater level rises. During dry season, DOM, rich in humic acid-like fluorescence, runs off and decreases its contribution.

CONCLUSION

Quality of DOM provides useful information on peat environment and formation process of DOM. Microbial activity in groundwater might increase under oil palm plantation, leading to the development of reductive conditions of groundwater. DOM composition in groundwater changes seasonally, which might indicate that the fluctuation of groundwater level accelerates runoff of peat organic matter from OPP in dissolved form.

ACKNOWLEDGEMENTS

This work was supported by JSPS KAKENHI Grant Numbers 19405021 and 24405029. We thank to the staff members of tropical peat research laboratory unit (TPRL), Sarawak, for their dedicated cooperation in conducing this research.

REFERENCES

1. Abe, Y., Maie, N. and Shima, E. (2011). Influence of Irrigated Paddy Fields on the Fluorescence Properties of Fluvial Dissolved Organic Matter. *Journal of Environmental Quality* **40**, 1266-1272.
2. Maie, N., Parish, K.J., Watanabe, A., Knicker, H., Benner, R., Abe, T., Kaiser, K., and Jaffé, R. (2006). Chemical characteristics of dissolved organic nitrogen in an oligotrophic subtropical coastal ecosystem. *Geochimica et Cosmochemica Acta* **70**, 4491-4506.
3. McKnight, D.M., Boyer, E.W., Westerhoff, P.K., Doran, P.T., Kulbe, T. and Andersen, D.T. (2001). Spectrofluorometric characterization of dissolved organic matter for indication of precursor organic material and aromaticity. *Limnology and Oceanography* **46**, 38 – 48.
4. Page, S.E., Rieley, J., Banks, C.J. 2011. Global and regional importance of the tropical peatland carbon pool. Global Change Biology 17, 798-818.
5. Stedmon, C.A., Markager, S. and Bro. R. (2003). Tracing dissolved organic matter in aquatic environments using a new approach to fluorescence spectroscopy. *Marine Chemistry* **82**, 239-254.
6. Stedmon, C. A. and Bro, R., 2008. Characterizing dissolved organic matter fluorescence with parallel factor analysis: a tutorial. *Limnology and Oceanography: Methods* **6**, 572-579.
7. Yamashita, Y., Scinto, L.J., Maie, N. and Jaffé, R. 2010. Dissolved organic matter characteristics across a subtropical wetland's landscape: application of optical properties in the assessment of environmental dynamics. *Ecosystems*, 13, 1006-1019.

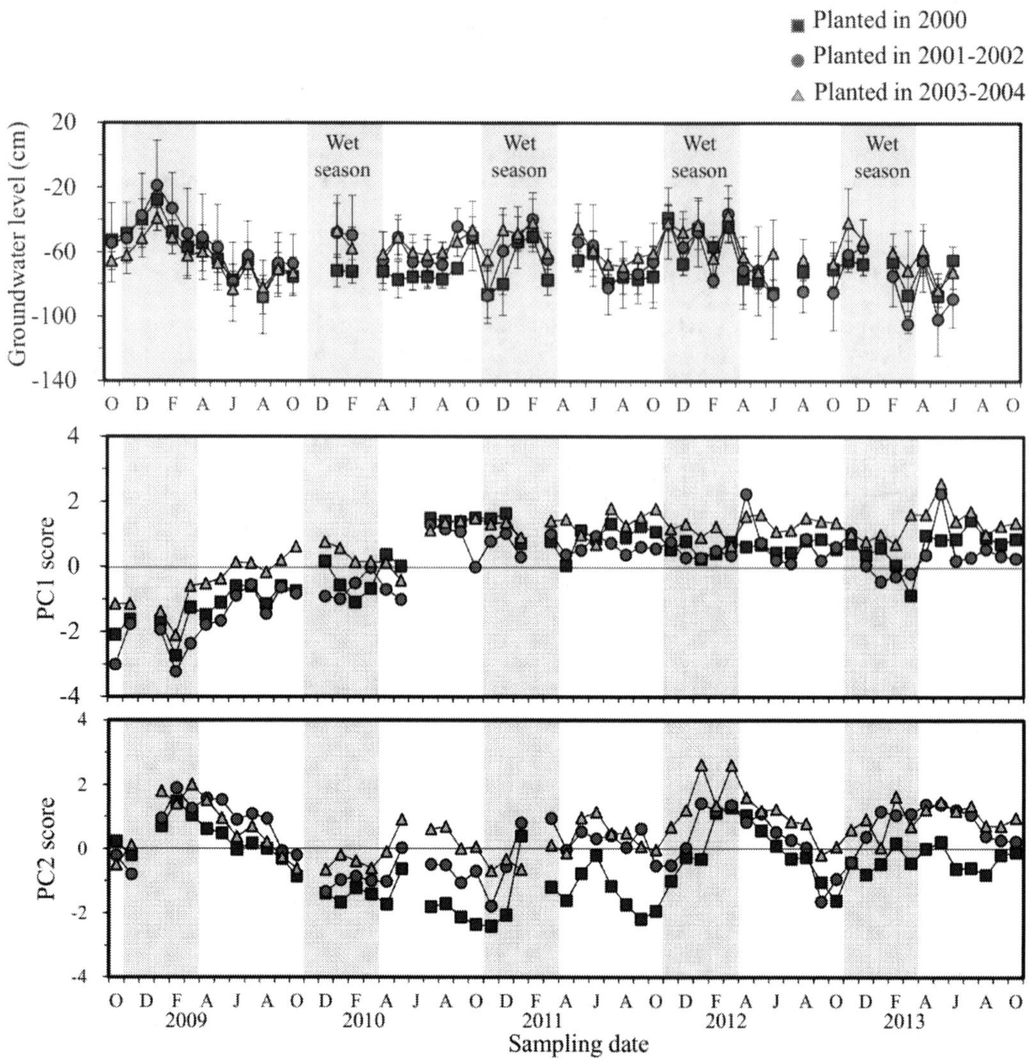

Figure 3: Temporal variations of groundwater level (upper panel), and PC1 (upper panel) and PC2 (lower panel) score plots.

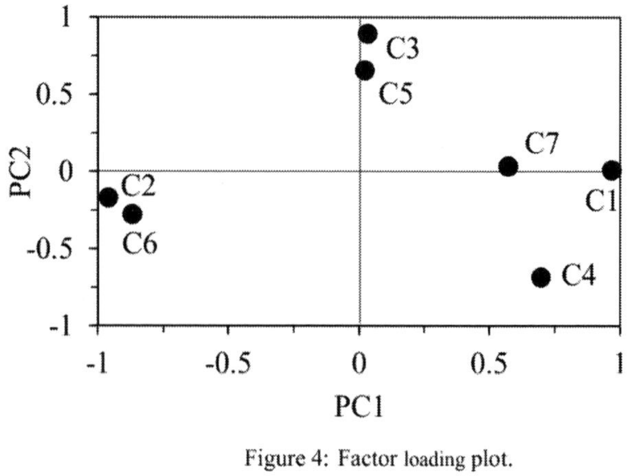

Figure 4: Factor loading plot.

Abstract No: A-290

THE EXPORT OF OLD DOC FUELS EFFLUX OF OLD CARBON DIOXIDE FROM DISTURBED TROPICAL PEAT DRAINAGE SYSTEMS IN MALAYSIA

Susan Waldron[1*], Leena Vihermaa[1], Stephanie Evers[2], Mark Garnett[3], Jason Newton[4] and Rory Padfield[5]

[1] *School of Geographical and Earth Sciences, University of Glasgow, Glasgow, G12 8QQ, Scotland*
[2] *University of Nottingham Malaysia Campus, Kuala Lumpur, Malaysia,*
[3]*NERC Radiocarbon Laboratory, Scottish Enterprise Technology Park, East Kilbride, G75 0QF, Scotland*
[4]*Scottish Universities Environmental Research Centre, Scottish Enterprise Technology Park, East Kilbride, G75 0QF, Scotland*
[5]*Malaysia Japan International Institute of Technology (MJIIT), University of Technology Malaysia, Kuala Lumpur, 54100, Malaysia*

**Corresponding author: Susan.Waldron@glasgow.ac.uk*

Tropical peatlands constitute ~11% of global peatland area and ~12% of the global peat C pool. Malaysia alone contains 10% of tropical peats. Due to rising global demands for food and biofuels, increasing amounts of drainage, fire, and conversion to plantation have threatened the existence of the Southeast Asian peat swamp forest ecosystem, and changed the greenhouse gas (GHG) emission balance. With this realization, in many areas logged peats have been left to regenerate to minimize these losses. The consequence of this is that unpicking the legacy of multiple land uses on GHG emissions is challenging but required to support land management decisions. Here, we present the results of a field campaign (in July 2013) to a peat swamp forest reserve and a peat-based oil palm plantation in peninsular Malaysia to primarily assess if peat drainage and land use change have resulted in the loss of sequestered carbon to the atmosphere. We found that gas effluxed ranged in age from 500 yr BP at the most disturbed sites, to having a 'modern age' at the most pristine site. The ^{14}C age of the DOM was generally very similar to the effluxed CO_2 and thus old CO_2 flux from organic matter respiration and uv-oxidation of the DOM pool is fuelling old CO_2 efflux. This is the first evidence that old DOM export results in atmospheric CO_2 efflux of old CO_2 and confirms that anthropogenic land use is causing loss of C that has accumulated over millennia: the older, slower carbon cycles are becoming shorter and faster. This finding allows the refinement of C payback calculators in informing land management decisions.

***Keywords**:-*

Abstract No: A-385

THE ROLE OF LOCAL WATER CONDITIONS IN DISTRIBUTION OF RAISED BOGS IN MOUNTAINOUS AREAS: CASE STUDY OF THE POLISH CARPATHIAN MOUNTAINS

Adam Łajczak

Pedagogical University, Institute of Geography, Poland

**Corresponding author: alajczak@o2.pl*

SUMMARY

It has been often argued that the formation of peat bogs, especially of the raised type, is predominantly influenced by a humid climate (precipitation greatly exceeds evaporation during the vegetation growth season). In many areas, even in mountains, where precipitation during vegetation growth season is greater than evaporation, raised bogs do not cover all gently sloping areas and valley bottoms and often develop within certain landforms with specific hydrological conditions. In the flysch Carpathian Mountains local water conditions determined by land relief and bedrock structure are the most crucial factor in the development of peat bogs. This study covers bogs in selected areas in the Polish Carpathians: intra-mountain basins, floors of river valleys and mountain ridges (slopes, passes). The paper is based on an analysis of maps produced over the 20th century, on aerial photographs taken since 1965 and on the newest data (LiDAR). Fieldwork included the geomorphological and hydrographic mapping of specified landforms with peat bogs studied using GPS methods as well as the field measurement of water infiltration. Peat bogs of the Polish Carpathians demonstrate that bogs, irrespective of altitude and total precipitation, develop most frequently in concave landforms, where outcrops of poorly permeable rocks offer numerous low-capacity but stable outflows of groundwater that continuously humidifies the slopes lying below thus supporting the formation of habitats for hydrophilic plants. Thus, the common belief that raised bogs with well-grown domes in the areas of the Polish Carpathians under study are fed exclusively by rainwater must be questioned, as throughout the development of such bogs, an integral part, i.e. the fringe zone, is largely fed also by groundwater outflows.

***Keywords**: raised bogs, peat substratum, low-capacity groundwater outflows, Polish Carpathians*

INTRODUCTION

It has been often argued that the formation of peat bogs, especially of the raised type, is predominantly influenced by a humid climate (precipitation exceeds evaporation during the vegetation growth season). By many authors for a bog to develop specific geological, geomorphological, hydrographic and hydrogeological conditions must also be met (e.g. Cooper, McCann, 1995, Ilnicki, 2002). In mountain areas where precipitation greatly exceeds evaporation during this season, vast blanket bogs develop, covering ridges, slopes and the feet of the slopes (e.g. Shaw *et al.*, 1997, Bragg, Tallis, 2001). In many areas, even in mountains, however, where precipitation during vegetation growth season is greater than evaporation, bogs (especially of the raised type) do not cover all gently sloping areas and valley bottoms and often develop within certain landforms with specific hydrogeological conditions and stream network. In the Carpathian Mountains local water conditions determined by land relief and structure are the most crucial factor in the development of peat bogs (Łajczak, 2014).

The goal of the presentation is to discuss the impact of water conditions on distribution of raised bogs in different geomorphological locations in Polish part of the Carpathian Mountains.

METHODS

This study is based on an analysis of maps produced over the 18th-20th centuries, on aerial photographs taken since 1965 and on the newest LiDAR data. Fieldwork included the geomorphological and hydrographic mapping of specified landforms with peat bogs studied using GPS methods as well as the field measurement of water infiltration and discharge of groundwater outflows.

RESULTS

In the Polish part of the Carpathian Mountains bogs (including the raised bogs with well-developed domes) are concentrated in two areas named as The Carpathian Peatlands: The Orawa - Nowy Targ Basin (intramountain basin) and the Bieszczady Mountains (floors of two deep valleys). In that areas eight geomorphological situations were distinguished in which expanding raised bogs changed the land relief on a local scale. The locations featuring the groups of bogs that have been distinguished are discussed in order from those lying on the highest ground to those lowest bogs lying in valley and basin bottoms. The following situations are distinguished in terms of the pattern of bog development: (1) watershed bogs, (2) bogs in spring niches of shallow erosion-induced incisions, in the bottom of these incisions and on their slopes, (3) bogs in palaeochannels, (4) bogs on high various-age Quaternary terraces near the base of a higher terrace, (5) bogs on evenly inclined fragments of the terrace formed during the last glaciation in spots with numerous groundwater outflows, (6) bogs fully developed on an alluvial fans, (7) bogs on the edges of single or neighbouring alluvial fans, (8) bogs on the post-glacial terrace between an inactive levee and undercut flysch slope, locally at former oxbows. The development of bogs in situations (1), (5) and (6) leads to a gradual local increase in the terrain height difference. In the other situations, as the low bog develops, the terrain levels out, and then, as the peat dome builds up, local height differences increase. Thus, hollow forms in the mineral substratum of the bogs are replaced by convex forms made of peat. The most significant changes in the relief occur in situation (3), where an extensive peat dome may even grow on top of several fossilised channels of former neighbouring watercourses. In such a situation, local watersheds shift.

The Orawa - Nowy Targ Basin with the largest Carpathian peatland has an area of 600 km^2. The Basin lies between the high-mountain massif of the Tatra Mts and the Beskidy Mts and is inclined northwards. Thirty raised bogs in the Basin developed on glaciofluvial fans, on river terraces and on small alluvial fans at altitudes of 590-770 m a.s.l., lying from 5 to 40 m above river channels. The bogs cover a poorly permeable 2-metre thick layer of clay, sitting on strongly hydrated Quaternary gravels. The formation of bogs in the Basin is enhanced by its cool and humid climate (precipitation of approx. 1000 mm). Despite the substantial shrinkage of peatland in the last 500 years, as a result of peat extraction and drying, the peat-covered area in the Basin can nevertheless be compared with some of the largest peat-covered areas in other massifs in Europe. The bottoms of river valleys in the Polish part of the Bieszczady Mts feature remnants of 17 raised bogs. The bogs in that mountain are much smaller and surrounded by narrower post-peat areas. Bogs are at an altitude of 550-700 m a.s.l. and extend over post-glacial terraces and alluvial fans, lying from 5 to 8 m above river channels. The bog substratum is formed by a layer of silt atop gravel. The precipitation in the area is 1000-1200 mm. Most bogs located at the feet of flysch slopes are recharged by groundwater seepage.

In the Polish Carpathian Mountains many small bogs, including raised bogs, are located in the Tatra Mountains with typical glacial morphology and in numerous places in the flysh Beskidy Mountains. Bogs in the Tatra Mountains are developed in U-shaped valleys on substratum overlain by moraines. Most frequently, they are present between the ridges of lateral moraines and the valley slopes and between the ridges of recessional moraines. Many of these places previously functioned as a small post-glacial lakes. Thus the parent material of these bogs is formed by poorly permeable (fine grained) lake material deposited on moraine debris. Peat bogs on slopes occur above moraine ridges and in depressions formed by the melting of dead ice. In the Beskidy Mountains, peat bogs are found on slopes in the following situations: on flat areas and in landslide niches, in depressions surrounding springs, at mountain ridge passes and on cryoplanation terraces – mostly at the base of steep slopes. The substratum of bogs on slopes is formed by locally deposited fine-grain eluvium, which, in the Flysch Carpathians, is located on shale rock outcrops. The above morphological situations always involve outflows of groundwater, even minute ones, which hydrate the area surrounding the peat bogs and the nearby hydrophilic vegetation habitats not yet undergoing the peat-bog forming process.

Peat bogs of the Polish Carpathian Mountains demonstrate that bogs, irrespective of altitude, develop most frequently in concave landforms, where outcrops of poorly permeable rocks offer numerous low-capacity but stable outflows of groundwater that continuously humidifies the slopes lying below thus supporting the formation of habitats for hydrophilic plants.

Locally, the number of bogs in the study area is large enough for their location to be analysed on the basis of the lithological, geomorphologic and, especially, hydrogeological properties of the substratum. Most bogs in the Polish Carpathians have an area of less than 1 ha, with only a few being larger than 100 ha. In intramountain basin they occur from hilltops to the old-Holocene terraces, in valley floors on alluvial fans especially. The bogs developed on mountain ridges are located on slopes, passes and locally at the tops. The bogs located on ridges with very varied relative altitude are for the most part ombrogenous in nature; while the more numerous slope bogs are soligenous (hanging bogs). The lowest located bogs are topogenous and fluviogenous and also limnogenous. The above types of bogs are transformed into ombrogenous ones.

By analysing the relief of raised bogs in the Polish Carpathians some of the characteristics of bogs were examined which had not been previously addressed. Considering the geomorphological criteria for their occurrence, all the bigger bogs examined are of the valley type, although they developed within different mesoforms. Raised bogs in the areas under investigation do not solely occur, as claimed by other authors, on clearly visible watersheds, but mainly in locations that are topographically lower than these. Raised bogs with an extensive dome may develop across the range of altitudes of the areas under study, yet hollow landforms, such as spring niches, palaeochannels, scarp bases of higher terraces and alluvial fan edges are favored in this respect. Stable outflows of shallow groundwater, which are the most intensive in such places, guarantee the development of low bogs, and then, as raised bogs expand, they keep the fringe area highly humidified.

The formation of raised bogs, not only in the initial phase of their growth, but also during the growth of the dome, is largely determined by the system of watercourses, which transform with time into fringe watercourses (Łajczak, 2007). High levels of dampness of the soil in the vicinity of such watercourses fed by the nearby outflows of groundwater guarantee the continuation of the peat-forming process in the fringe zone, and in the marginal zone of the peat domes, which is a prerequisite for their further expansion. Examples of a dense system of fringe watercourses in the vicinity of the largest peat domes in the Orawa – Nowy Targ Basin before the initiation of the drainage activity are shown by the maps produced at the turn of the 18th and 19th centuries.

CONCLUSION

The common belief that raised bogs with well-grown domes in the peatland areas of the Polish Carpathians under study are fed exclusively by rainwater must be questioned, as throughout the development of such bogs, an integral part, i.e. the fringe zone, is largely fed also by groundwater outflows (Łajczak, 2007, 2009).

REFERENCES

1. Bragg O.M., Tallis J.H., 2001. The sensitivity of peat-covered upland landscapes, *Catena* 42: 345-360.
2. Cooper A., McCann T., 1995. Machine Peat Cutting and Land Use Change on Blanket Bog in Northern Ireland, *J. of Environ. Management* 43: 153-170.
3. Ilnicki P., 2002. *Hoohmors and peat*. Poznań, 606 pp.
4. Łajczak A., 2007. *Natura 2000 in Poland, Area PLH120016 The Orawa – Nowy Targ Peatland*. Publ. of Inst. of Botany, P.A.Sci., Kraków, 139 pp.
5. Łajczak A., 2009. Development conditions and distribution of peat bogs in the Orawa – Nowy Targ Basin, Western Carpathian Mountains. *Przegląd Geologiczny* 57(8): 694-702.
6. Łajczak A., 2014. The role of mineral substratum in development of peat bogs in the Polish Carpathuians. *Studia Limnologica et Telmatologica* 8(1): 19-36.
7. Shaw S., Wheeler B., Backshall J., 1997. Review of effects of burning and grazing of blanket bogs – conservation issues and conflicts. [In:] J.H. Tallis, R. Meade, P.D. Hulme (eds) *Blanket Mire Degradation: Causes, Consequences and Challenges*. Macaulay Land Use Research Institute, Aberdeen, pp. 174-182.

1.3: PEATLAND REMOTE SENSING, AERIAL & SATELLITE IMAGERY

Abstract No: A-392

ASSESSMENT OF TROPICAL PEATLAND MAP IN WEST KALIMANTAN, INDONESIA

Kazuyo Hirose[1*], Tomomi Takeda[1], Gusti Anshari[2], Muhammad Nuriman[2], Tesuo Tanimoto[3], Ronny Christianto[4], Shigeru Takahara[5], Hiroshi Kobayashi[4] and Gun Gun Hidayat[4]

[1] *Japan Space Systems, Japan*
[2] *Center for Wetlands People and Biodiversity, Tanjungpura University, Indonesia*
[3] *Ministry of Agriculture, Forestry and Fisheries*
4 IJ-REDD+ Project, Ministry of Environment and Forestry, Indonesia
[5] *Japan Soil and Water Conservation Association, Japan*

* *Corresponding author: Hirose-Kazuyo@jspacesystems.or.jp*

SUMMARY

Tropical peatland preserves huge amount of carbon with rich biodiversity. However, recent anthropogenic disturbance has affected significant impacts to the ecosystem, carbon balance including release of carbon dioxide into atomosphere. In 2009, Government of Indonesia made a commitment to reduce greenhouse gas (GHG) emissions by 26% to Business as Usual (BAU) baseline. As potential GHG reduction from forest and peat sector has been estimated to 88%, assessment of peatland in Indonesia is crucial. Wetlands International prepared a revised peatland distribution maps for Sumatera, Kalimantan and Papua during 2003-2006 and they have been widely used in Indonesia. Experts of Ministry of Agriculture have developed the latest peatland distribution map of Indonesia (Ritung *et al.,* 2011) using all available data collected during 1989-2011. It was authorized by Indonesian government as a national peatland map of Indonesia in 2014. Those two peatland maps by WI (2004) and Ritung et al. (2011) reported different figures of total peatland area in Indonesia, 20.7 million hectares and 14.9 million hectares, respectively. In West Kalimantan, the difference of peatland area is about 50, 000 hectares. As there are large uncertainties in those two peatland maps, it is important to review the maps and recheck with ground truth data. Assessment of those peatland maps was carried out at four districts (Pontianak, Kubu Raya, Kayong Utara and Ketapang) and Pontianak City in West Kalimantan. An improved peatland map was prepared based on by peat thickness measurements at 324 field plots with careful interpretation of various data sets such as satellite images (Landsat, ASTER, PALSAR and DEM), geological maps, land cover maps and others. The result of the assessment showed that the the peatland area derived from WI (2004) was about 52,000 hectares smaller compared to the area determined from the improved peatland map. The peatland map by Ritung et al. (2011) showed a greater peatland area, about 32,000 hectares larger than improved peatland map.

Keyword: *tropical peatland, West Kalimantan, Landsat, ASTER, PALSAR*

INTRODUCTION

Tropical peatland is one of the important carbon pools and it forms unique ecosystem. However, recent intensive developments for industrial plantation and agricultural land have caused significant carbon loss. As a result, huge amount of carbon dioxide is released into atomosphere from the dried peat which is formed by constructing canals and decreasing ground water table. Thus peatland development has great impact to the global warming issue. Although amount of carbon dioxide from peatland is estimated based on the area of peatland map, there is an uncertainty of accuracy of peatland map because of the insufficient information and difficulty of the access to the peatland. Since 1970s, Ministry of Agriculture, Ministry of Public Works, Universities and many institues have developed peatland maps at national and local level, but different extents of peatland have been reported ranging from 13.5 to 26.5 million hectares (Fig. 1).

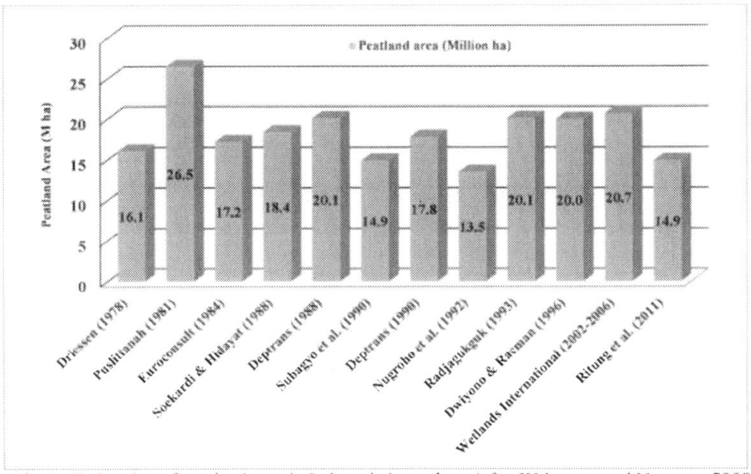

Fig. 1: Estimation of peatland area in Indonesia by authors (after Wahyunto and Nyoman, 2008)

In 2004, Wetlands International compiled a peatland distribution map for Kalimantan (hereinafter referred as "WI (2004)"), and it has been widely used in Indonesia. In 2011, Ministry of Agriculture has released the latest peatland distribution map of Indonesia (herein after reffered as "Ritung *et al.*, 2011") and it was authorized by Indonesian government as a national peatland map of Indonesia in 2014. However, those two peatland maps showed different figures of peatland area as 20.7 million hectares by WI (2004) and as 14.9 million hectares by Ritung *et al.* (2011). In West Kalimantan Province, the difference of peatland area is about 85,000 hectares for four districts (Pontianak, Kubu Raya, Kayong Utara and Ketapang) and Pontianak City. Thus there are large uncertainties in those two peatland maps and it is necessary for reviewing and rechecking.

The purpose of this study is to improve the accuracy of two peatland maps (WI, 2004 and Ritung *et al.*, 2011) which are often used in Indonesia. Improved peatland map is expected to contribute to local spatial plan, REDD+ project, environmental management plan, and national/provincial greenhouse gas reduction plans (RAN/RAD-GRK) in Indonesia.

METHODS

Definition of peat was appleied based on the definitions of US Soil Taxsonomy (Soil Survey Staff, 1990) and Purunomo *et al.*, (2014) as follows;

[Peat Definition]

- Thickness of peat : more than 50 cm thickness of organic matter
- Carbon content: more than 12% organic carbon (Soil Survey Staff, 1990)

The peatland boundary was determined by using two peatland maps produced by WI (2004) and Ritung et al. (2011) shown as Fig. 2. Landsat-MSS/TM images from before 1990 were used to identify potential peatland area. As intensive peatland development and canal construction were made from 1990s, the characteristics of peatland forests could only be recognized on the satellite images from before the 1990s. ASTER, PALSAR, Digital Elevation Model (DEM) of Shuttle Radar Topographic Mission (SRTM), geological map, tipographic map and land cover map were also used to determine the peatland area. The following procedure was used for improving peatland area (Fig. 3)

1. Comparison between peataland boundary on WI(2004) and Ritung *et al.* (2011)
2. Comparison of geologic map, LANDSAT images (1970~1980s) and SRTM/DEM
3. Distribution of oil palm, industrial plantation with drainage => high possibility of peat forest
4. Distribution of large-scale drainage => high possibility of peat forest
5. Distribution of large-scale agricultural land=> high possibility of peat forest development by immigrants
6. Interpretation for land use type and land cover type using Landsat-7/8, ASTER and PALSAR.

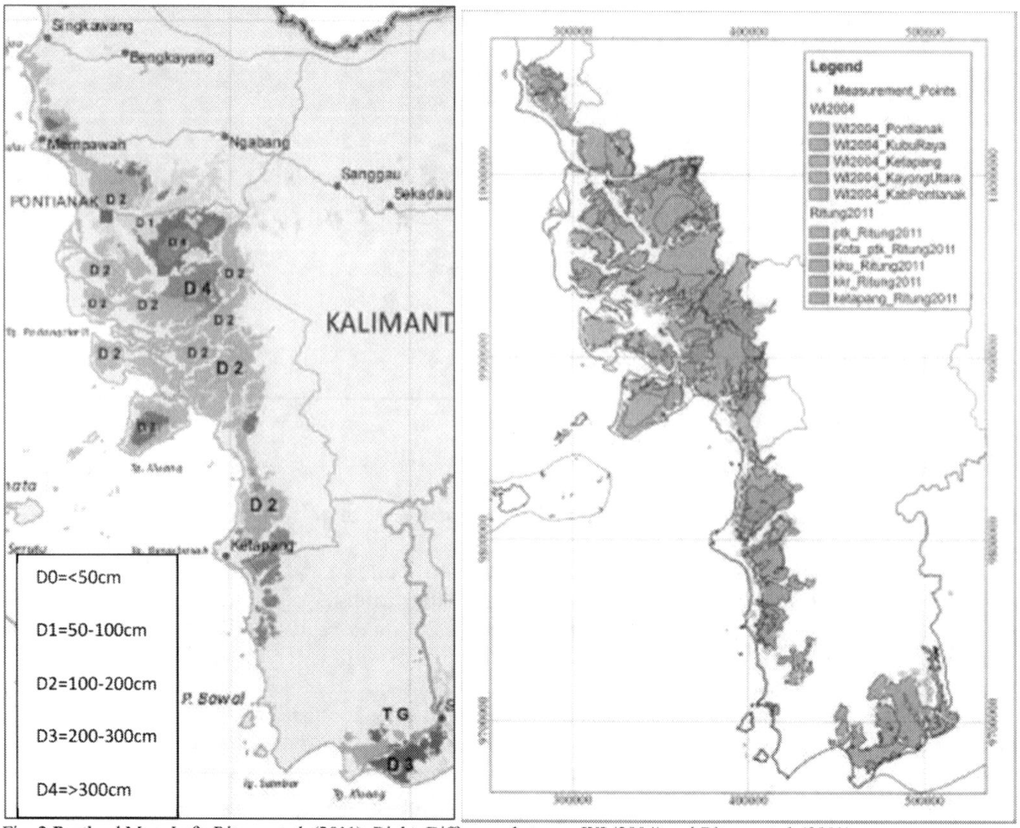

Fig. 2 Peatland Map, Left: Ritung et al. (2011), Right: Difference between WI (2004) and Ritung *et al.* (2011)

After determining the peatland boundary by using various of the above mentioned data sets, field measurements of the peat thickness was carried out at 324 sampling points by using a peat sampler auger (Eijkelkamp) from August to November 2014. The purpose of the field survey was to confirm the existance of the peat soil type, its thickness and thus determine the peat boundaries. The physical and chemical properties of 265 peat samples were analysed. The analyses included Bulk density, Loss of Ignition (LOI), Total Organic Carbon (TOC), and Total Nitrogen Content.

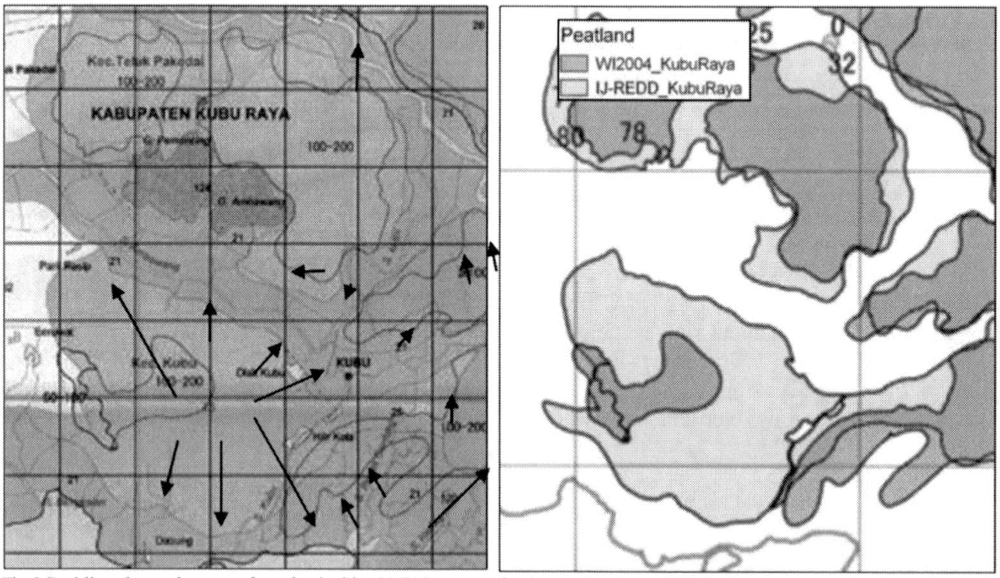

Fig.3 Red line shows the area of peatland with 100-200cm peat depth suggested by WI (2004). Ocher color is peatland area suggested by Hidayat *et al.* (2010)

RESULTS AND DISCUSSIONS

The peatland map for four districts and Pontianak City was improved by using the results of 324 peat thickness measurements, interpretation of satellite images and various geospatial data. Comparisons with the earlier work by WI (2004),and Ritung *et al.* (2011) were made (Table 3, Fig. 4).

Fig.4-(1) shows that peatland area by WI (2004) is about 52,000 hectares smaller than the area resulting from the peatland map of our work, from here referred to as "IJ-REDD+ (2015)". Areas where WI (2004) are larger compared to the IJ-REDD+(2015) figure are recognized with blue color at the southern part of Ketapang District. The Ritung *et al.* (2011) peatland area is 32,000 hectares greater than the IJ-REDD+ (2015) area. This is shown at central parts of Kubu Raya District, Kayong Utara District and Ketapang District with green color (Fig. 4-(2)).

Table 1 Comparison of peatland area for four distrcts (Pontianak, Kubu Raya, Kayong Utara and Ketapang) and Pontianak City among WI (2004), Ritung et al., (2011) and IJ-REDD+ (2015)

Peatland Area (ha)	(1) WI (2004)	(2) Ritung (2011)	(3) IJ-REDD+ (2015)
KayongUtara	163,303	214,054	193,930
Ketapang	337,552	255,873	259,283
KubuRaya	410,241	519,885	503,990
Pontianak	70,889	74,755	74,441
KotaPontianak	398	2,280	2,801
Total	982,383	1,066,847	1,034,445

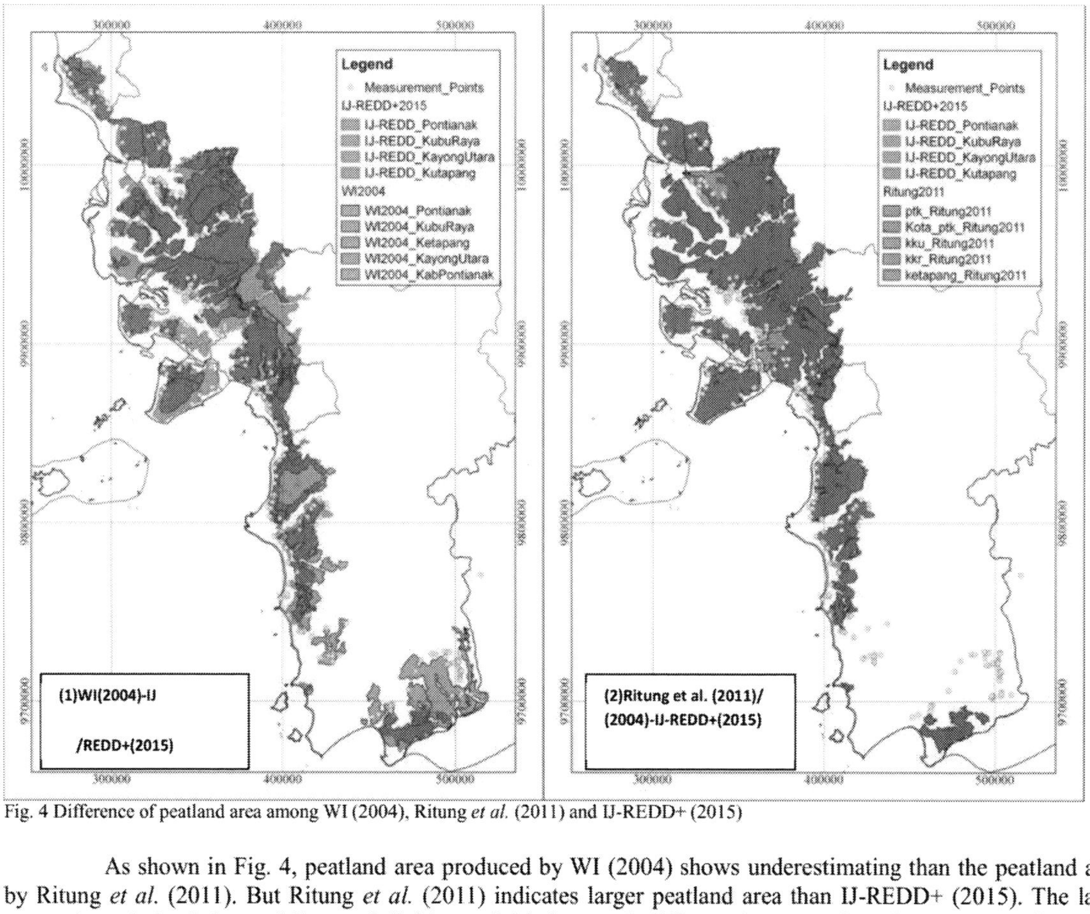

Fig. 4 Difference of peatland area among WI (2004), Ritung *et al.* (2011) and IJ-REDD+ (2015)

As shown in Fig. 4, peatland area produced by WI (2004) shows underestimating than the peatland area by Ritung *et al.* (2011). But Ritung *et al.* (2011) indicates larger peatland area than IJ-REDD+ (2015). The large uncertainty derived from different definitions, field data and different interpretations by experts still exists. Therefore, further field survey and interpretation are necessary for delineating the peatland distribution area more precisely. Intensive artificial drainage has caused degradation of peatland and it accelerates the decrease of peatlands. In 2013 the Ministry of Agriculture published an Indonesian peatland degradation map (Wahyunto *et al.*, 2013) showing the peatland distribution area in seven degradation classes. The most severe degradation class accounts for 4.3 % (72,330 ha) in West Kalimantan where the most vulnerable peatland area is located. For the future improvement of the peatland map also the degradation of peatlands caused by forest fires should be monitored by using satellite images.

CONCLUSION

An assessment of the two existing peatland maps was carried out for four districts (Pontianak, Kubu Raya, Kayong Utara and Ketapang) in West Kalimantan. An improved peatland map was prepared to check those two peatland maps by 324 ground truth data with careful interpretation with various data sets such as satellite images (Landsat, ASTER, PALSAR and DEM), geological maps, land cover maps and others. The result of assessment showed that peatland map by WI (2004) was an underestimating of about 52,000 hectares than the improved peatland map by IJ-REDD+ (2015). Peatland map by Ritung *et al.* (2011) was about 32,000 hectares larger than IJ-REDD+ (2015).

Although a Presidential Moratorium was issued in 2011 on the conversion of primary and natural forests and peat lands, peatland has been developed and disappeared. Thus further field survey and improvement of peatland map is necessary to contribute to various strategies on climate change issues such as national GHG emissions reduction plan.

ACKNOWLEDGEMENTS

This work was conducted as part of JICA project "Indonesia-Japan Project for Development of REDD+plus Implementation Mechanism (REDD+plus Planning Study)". We are thankful to JICA for sharing data with the opportunity to present this paper. We also sincerely thank Dr. Kusmo, Dr. Wahuynto of Ministry of Agriculture of Indonesia and Mr. Nyoman of Wetlands International Indonesia for their invaluable advice.

REFERENCES

1. Hidayat A., Hikmatullah and Suparto, 2010, Peta Sumberdaya Tanah Tingkat Tinjau, Provinsi Kalimantan Barat, Indonesia, Skala 1:250, 000, Balai Besar Penelitian dan Pengembangan Sumberdaya Lahan Pertanian.
2. Purnomo A, Sukadri D, Helmy F, Osaki M, Hirose K and Mackie C (2012): "Policy Memo: Peatland Definition from Uncertainty to Certainty", Indonesia Climate Change Center, p36.
3. RePPProT, 1986-1990. A National Overview from the Regional Physical Planning Programme for Transmigration. UK Overseas Development Administration and Directorate Bina Program, Ministry of Transmigration, Jakarta.
4. Ritung S, Wahyunto, Nugroho K, Sukarman, Hikmatullah, Suparto, Tafakresnanto C, 2011. Peta alahan gambut Indonesia. Skala 1:250.000. Balai Besar Penelitian dan Pengembangan Sumberdaya Lahan Pertanian.
5. Soil Survey Staff, 1990. US Soil Taxonomy. Keys to soil taxonomy. Soil Management Support Services Technical Monograph No. 19. Virginia Polytechnic Institute and State University, Blacksburg, VA.
6. Wahyunto and Nyoman N., 2008, Peatland Distribution in Sumatra and Kalimantan: Explanation of its data sets including source of information, data constraints and gaps, p51.
7. Wahyunto, Ritung S., Nugroho N., Sulaeman Y., Hikmatullah, Tafakresnanto C., Suparto and Sukarman, 2013, Atlas Lahan Gambut Terdegradasi Pulau Kalimantan dan Papua, Skala 1:250,000, Indonesia Climate Change Trust Fund, Badan Penelitian dan Pengembangan Pertanian.

Abstract No: A-159

GIS - PEATLAND MAPPING BASED ON DISCONTINUOUS DATA - THE EXAMPLE OF NORTHERN JUTLAND (DENMARK)

Cosima Tegetmeyer[1], Alexandra Barthelmes[1*], Mette Risager[2] and Hans Joosten[1]

[1] *Greifswald University, Department for Botany and Landscape Ecology, Soldmannstraße 23, 17487 Greifswald, Germany*
[2] *Risager Consult, Gl. Viborgvej 418, Ålum 8920 Randers NV, Denmark*

**Corresponding author: abarthelmes@gmx.de*

The Greenhouse gas (GHG) emissions from drained peatland, especially in peatland-rich countries (e.g. Iceland, Finland, the Baltics, Indonesia and Mongolia) can amount to a substantial proportion of the total annual emissions reported to the UNFCCC. Thus, the elaboration of area data that is in line with IPCC requirements is key. For this, it is necessary to include all peatlands and organic soils that have been drained (for any reason), regardless of whether the active land use has already ceased. The following need to be known: 1) the total peatland or organic soil area, 2) the extent of drainage (any ditches), 3) the extent of land use categories Forest Land, Cropland, Grassland and Peat Extraction. We use the example of Northern Jutland (Denmark) to illustrate redundant shortcomings that hamper the assessment of appropriate area data according to IPCC: a lack of comprehensive peatland or organic soil data on national scale, the use of inappropriate datasets instead (e.g. EU subsidy schemes) or the exclusion of still drained (and emitting) peatlands and organic soils that have been turned, for example, into nature protection sites. This sometimes fragmentary and land use biased national data need to be evaluated based on ancillary data bases (e.g. from geology), expert knowledge and remote sensing data (digital elevation model and satellite images). Through implementation of this mapping approach we developed a new organic soil map for Northern Jutland that is stratified according to the necessary land use categories for emission reporting under UNFCCC. This assessment was complicated due to the fact that Danish peatlands and organic soils are highly affected by drainage, degradation and subsidence resulting from centuries of intensive drainage and use.

***Keywords**: Denmark, GIS-peatland mapping, ancillary data, data synthesis, UNFCCC*

Abstract No: A-143

GLOBAL PEATLAND DATABASE @ GREIFSWALD MIRE CENTRE - INTEGRATION, EVALUATION AND GENERATION OF GEOSPATIAL DATA

Alexandra Barthelmes, Cosima Tegetmeyer, Franziska Tanneberger, Reni Barthelmes, Stephan Busse and Hans Joosten

Greifswald University, Institute of Botany and Landscape Ecology, Germany

*Corresponding author: alex.barthelmes@greifswaldmoor.de

SUMMARY

The importance of the huge amounts of greenhouse gases emitted by drained peatlands has recently been recognised by e.g. UNFCCC, IPCC, FAO and the European Union. Also ecosystem services delivered by undrained natural and restored peatlands, like biodiversity, conservation, water retention and -regulation, nutrient retention or provision of facilities for tourism gain increasing interest. However, the development of adequate restoration strategies requires the availability of comprehensive and exact geospatial data on the drainage status of peatlands and organic soils worldwide.

The Global Peatland Database (GPD) hosted at the Greifswald Mire Centre (http://tiny.cc/globalpeat) holds estimates on the location, extent and drainage status of peatlands and organic soils for 268 countries and regions of the World. Because of the large diversity of definitions and terms, the GPD follows a broad definition and includes all soils with a minimum soil organic carbon threshold of 12% and any depth of the organic layer larger than 10 cm (cf. Hiraishi *et al.*, 2014).

The GPD collects available GIS datasets, analyses the terms and concepts used, and evaluates their completeness and accuracy. Currently, the GPD contains geospatial data on peatlands and organic soils for all countries of Europe, for other important areas of the northern hemisphere (e.g. Canada and Siberia), as well as for SE Asia and Tierra del Fuego. For countries without adequate geospatial data, new organic soil maps are generated. The recent focus of GIS mapping is on East Africa with organic soil maps at scale 1:25,000 completed for Burundi, Kenya, Rwanda, Tanzania, Uganda and Zambia. The GPD aims at completing the global inventory of distribution and status of peatland and organic soil until 2020.

Keywords: *Global Peatland Database (GPD), peatland, location, distribution, drainage status, GIS*

INTRODUCTION

Peatlands cover only 3% of the global land surface. Some 15% of these peatlands have been drained for agriculture, forestry and grazing, and peat extraction. Drained peatlands are - even when emissions from peat fires are excluded - responsible for 5% of the global anthropogenic greenhouse gas emissions, which is almost double the amount of CO_2 emissions from aviation (Wetlands International 2015). Rewetting drained peatlands has therefore a large mitigation potential. Undrained, intact peatlands provide many important ecosystem services, including water regulation, nutrient retention, as well as provision of habitats for nationally and internationally threatened wildlife (Joosten & Clarke, 2002; Parish *et al.*, 2008; Bonn *et al.*, 2016). Overall, an urgent need exists to identify the location of peatlands and organic soils, to protect them against any drainage, and to rewet already drained areas in order to decrease greenhouse gas emissions and to prevent hazardous peat fires. Comprehensive and exact geospatial data are needed to evaluate the drainage status of peatlands and organic soils and to develop effective restoration strategies.

Unfortunately, adequate geospatial data on location, extent and land use of peatlands and organic soils are rare, even in northern Europe (Barthelmes *et al.*, 2015). Moreover, the concepts, definitions and terms used differ strongly, whereas data are often spread across national authorities and scientific institutions and difficultly accessible. Also the rapidly developing remote sensing technologies do not manage to fill this gap, because the large diversity of peatlands worldwide and the multitude of land use types prevent the extrapolation of local results to the global scale. Therefore, global peatland mapping continues to depend on the aggregation of local and national data (Montanarella, 2014).

For more than 20 years, information has been collated in the Global Peatland Database (GPD), which is hosted at the Greifswald Mire Centre (http://tiny.cc/globalpeat). Currently, the GPD provides estimates on location, extent and drainage status of peatlands and organic soils for 268 countries and regions of the World. The database predominantly contains digital data, but also printed information stored in the 'Peatland and Nature Conservation International Library'(PeNCIL), also hosted at the Greifswald Mire Centre. Furthermore, thousands of digital photos from peatlands across the globe are connected with the GPD. Since 2012 the peatland/organic soil information of countries without spatially explicit data is being transferred into vector geographic information systems (GIS; scale 1:25,000) and raster GIS (0.01 x 0.01 degree grid). Additionally, GIS data on peatlands, organic soils and useful proxies are continuously collated, evaluated and integrated in the Global Peatland Database.

METHODS

To accommodate for the large diversity of definitions and terms for peatlands and organic soils, the GPD includes all soils with a minimum soil organic carbon threshold of 12% and a depth of the organic layer larger than 10 cm (cf. Hiraishi 2014).

A - Bundling and evaluation of available GIS data

A prime focus of the Global Peatland Database is the identification and collation of geospatial data on peatlands, organic soils and useful proxies (e.g. hydromorphic soils, wetlands, wetland vegetation, Holocene sediments). The analysis of these datasets includes the comprehension of underlying concepts, definitions and terms, the evaluation of their completeness and accuracy, and the detection of inherent weaknesses or failures. These assessments result in the estimation of the completeness, accuracy, and information content of the collated GIS datasets (Table 1).

Table 1: Criteria for the evaluation of completeness, accuracy, and information content of GIS datasets.

cate	**completeness**				**accuracy**			
crite rion 1	*obvious/known gaps in GIS data* [1]				*type of data*			
	yes		no		point		polygon	
crite rion 2	*accordance with best available non-GIS-data*				*accuracy of location*		*accuracy of borders*	
	l	hig	lo	h	l	high	low	h
pred	**l**	me	me	**h**	**l**	medi	medi	**h**

category	**information content**			
criterion 1	*type of data*			
	point		polygon	
criterion 2	*additional information* [2]			
	no	yes	no	yes
predicate	**low**	medium	medium	**high**

1) Expert knowledge and judgement; comparison with satellite and aerial imagery.

2) Additional information of e.g. peatland type, drainage status, applied land use types.

B - High resolution mapping of peatlands and organic soils

We developed a mapping approach that links various science networks, methodologies and databases, including those of peatland/landscape ecology for understanding where and how peatlands may occur, those of remote sensing (RS) for identifying possible locations and those of pedology (legacy soil maps) and (palaeo-)ecology for ground truthing. Such integration of field data, specialized knowledge and modern RS and GIS techniques enables acquiring a comprehensive, detailed and rather reliable overview. A crucial element in this mapping process is the weighting of conflicting information (Figure 1).

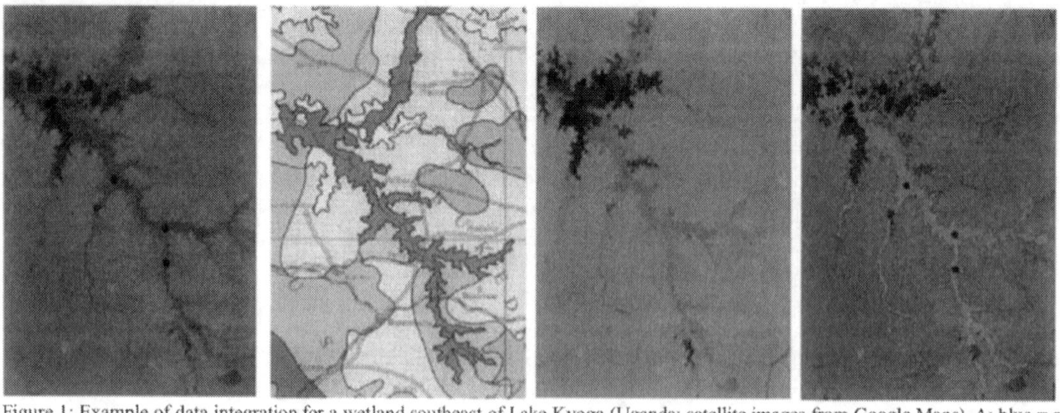

Figure 1: Example of data integration for a wetland southeast of Lake Kyoga (Uganda; satellite images from Google Maps). A: blue = peat point data (National Survey for Energy Peat 2004); B: blue = Fluvisols and Gleysols on available legacy soil maps; C: Topographical Wetness Index (TWI from AfSIS): high TWI in red, darker green and darker blue (in depressions and valleys); D: orange = deduced probable peatland area in final GPD map.

Main sources of spatially explicit information on (organic) soil and proxy data (e.g. digital maps of bedrock, relief, landforms, wetlands, vegetation, land use) have been open access online archives including those of ISRIC (World Soil Information), JRC (Joint Research Centre), FAO Corporated Document Repository, SPHAERA (Base de données Sphaera du service Cartographie), WOSSAC (World Soil Survey Archive and Catalogue) and the Perry Castanea Library of Austin University.

Soil degradation intensity (using the classes 'no, 'slight' and 'heavy degradation', Barthelmes et al. in prep.) is determined for each mapped polygon using satellite and aerial imagery by assessing the density of the drainage channel network, its connection to main outlets and soil surface disturbance by trampling and peat cutting.

RESULTS

A - Bundling and evaluation of available GIS data

An assessment of the available datasets of all European countries shows that satisfactory datasets on the location of peatlands and organic soils are only available for Estonia, Germany, Greece, Lithuania, Sweden, Switzerland, The Netherlands and Cyprus. All other countries possess datasets with different shortcomings, e.g. an incomplete coverage of peatlands and organic soils, or inaccuracies regarding the location and borders of polygons. Beside Austria and France, several countries of southern and eastern Europe have solely or predominantly point data for the location of peatlands and organic soils in place, e.g. Bulgaria, Croatia, Georgia, Italy, Portugal, Slovakia, Spain, and Turkey.

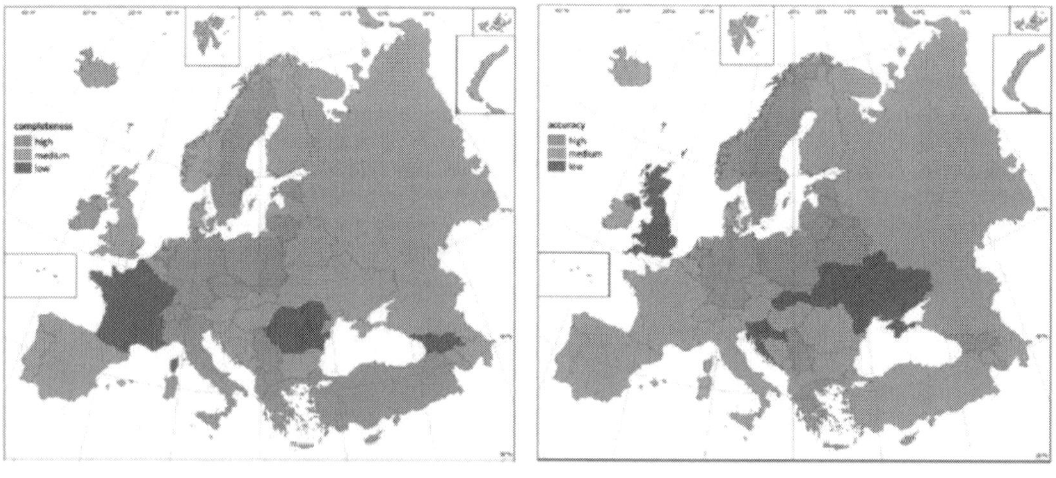

Figure 2: Assessment of the completeness (left) and accuracy (right) of available GIS datasets of European countries.

B - High resolution mapping of peatlands and organic soils

Organic soil maps (incl. peatlands) at a scale of 1:25,000 have been prepared for Burundi, Kenya, Rwanda, Tanzania, Uganda and Zambia. The mapping revealed a total organic soil area for Zambia of 16,663.5 km², of which about 1,500 km² are slightly drained for subsistence agriculture. In contrast, 900 km² of the 960 km² of organic soils in Burundi are intensively drained and heavily degrading. For Rwanda 1,201 km² of organic soils have been mapped, of which 649 km² are still undisturbed ('no degradation'), 115 km² slightly drained ('slight degradation') and 437 km² heavily drained ('heavy degradation'). Figure 3 shows the derived raster maps illustrating the degradation of organic soils in Rwanda (1 km² grid cells).

DISCUSSION

Drained peatlands and organic soils are hotspots of greenhouse gas emissions (incl. hazardous peat fires), whereas in natural condition they provide manifold ecosystem services. The effective prevention of new drainage of peatlands and organic soils, especially in developing and emerging economies, requires that their location is known. Detailed geospatial data showing the location, extent and degradation (drainage) status of peatlands and organic soils are, however, rare, and available datasets are highly variable in concepts, definitions and terms, but also in completeness and accuracy. Shortcomings, failures and gaps need to be urgently assessed by peatland experts.

For more than 20 years the Global Peatland Database has been collating peatland related information and since 2012 these data are transferred into GIS datasets. The GPD approach enables a rather fast, comprehensive, detailed and reliable mapping. Background data and key references, as well as ground truthing results, are kept for each mapped polygon. The country data in the GPD are continuously updated, refined and filled with additional information such as peat depth, carbon content, vegetation or peatland type.

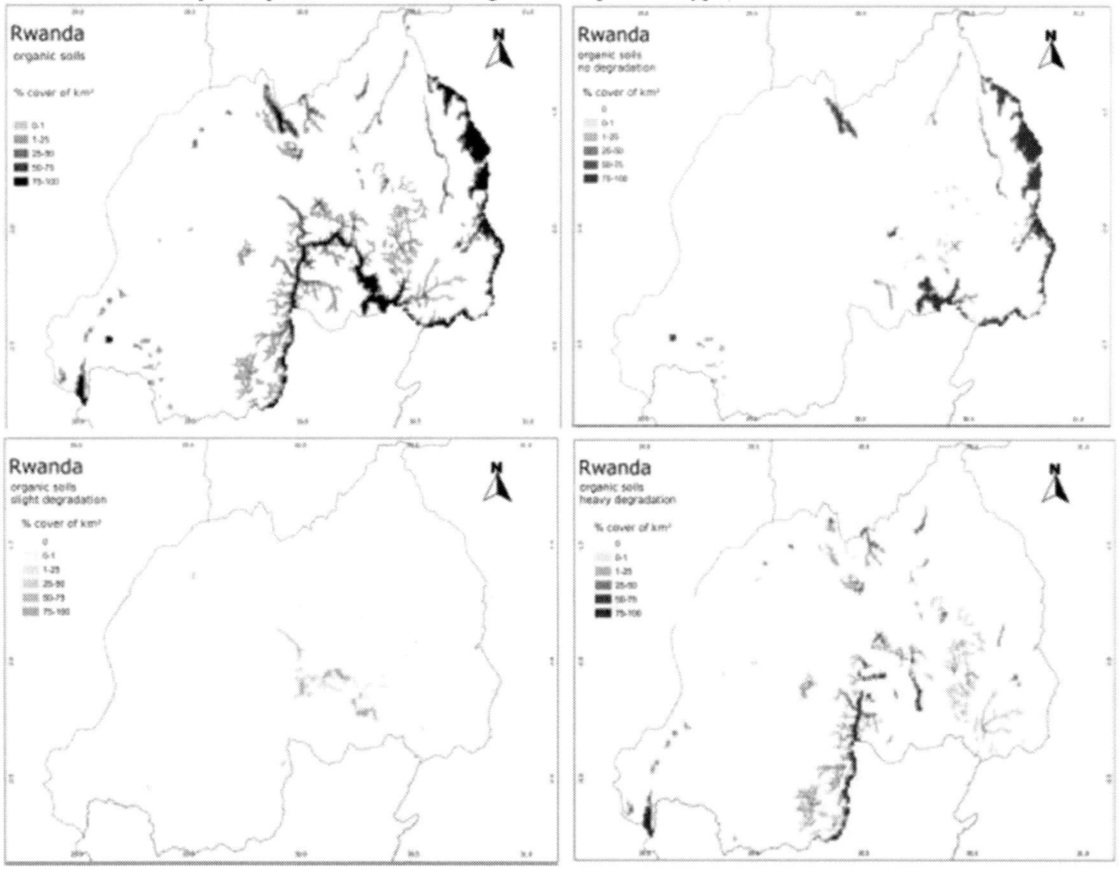

Figure 3: Raster maps of drainage induced degradation of organic soils in Rwanda (% degrading organic soils per 1 km²).

Currently, the GPD contains geospatial data on peatlands and organic soils for all European countries and other important areas of the northern hemisphere (e.g. Canada and Siberia), as well as for SE Asia, East Africa, and Patagonia. The GPD aims at completing collection and mapping of the location, extent and drainage status of peatlands and organic soils for 268 countries and regions of the World until 2020.

CONCLUSION

Greenhouse gas emissions from drained peatlands and organic soils have a disproportionally large impact on the climate. To develop effective strategies for rewetting drained and protecting wet peatlands, it is urgently necessary to know their location. Remote sensing is still no adequate option because the diversity of peatlands and land use types prevents the extrapolation of local studies to the global scale.

Several existing, national vector GIS data for location and extent of peatlands and organic soils for European countries are incomplete in coverage or inaccurate regarding the location and borders of polygons. Furthermore, several European countries solely or predominantly possess point data indicating the location of peatlands and organic soils. The profound evaluation of existing national GIS data is necessary and done in the framework of the GPD by peatland experts of the Greifswald Mire Centre in cooperation with foreign partners.

The Global Peatland Database has developed a rather simple, fast, but spatially highly resolved method to map peatlands and organic soils by linking methodologies of landscape and peatland ecology, remote sensing, pedology and (palaeo-)ecology.

REFERENCES

1. Barthelmes A, Couwenberg J, Risager M, Tegetmeyer C & H. Joosten 2015. Peatlands and climate in a Ramsar context - A Nordic-Baltic perspective.Nordic Council of Ministers, Rosendahls-Schultz Grafisk, Copenhagen, Denmark, 81 p. + Annexes.
2. Barthelmes A, Barthelmes R, Dommain R & H Joosten in prep. Extent and status of peatlands and organic soils in Central East Africa.
3. Bonn A, Allott T, Evans M, Joosten H & R Stoneman R 2016. Peatland restoration for ecosystem services. Cambridge University Press, Cambridge.
4. Hiraishi T, Krug T, Tanabe K, Srivastava N, Baasansuren J, Fukuda M. & Troxler TG (eds) 2014. 2013 Supplement to the 2006 IPCC guidelines for national greenhouse gas inventories: Wetlands. IPCC, Switzerland.
5. Joosten H & D Clarke D 2002. Wise use of mires and peatlands – Background and principles including a framework for decision-making. International Mire Conservation Group / International Peat Society. Saarijarven Offset Oy, Saarijarvi, Finland.
6. Montanarella L 2014. State of the art of peatlands mapping. In: Biancalani R. &A Avagyan (eds.), Towards climate-responsible peatlands management. Mitigation of climate change in agriculture Series 9, FAO, Rome (Italy).
7. Parish F, Sirin A, Charman D, Joosten H, Minayeva T, Silvius M & L Stringer (eds.) 2008. Assessment on peatlands, biodiversity and climate change: Main Report. Global Environment Centre, Kuala Lumpur and Wetlands International, Wageningen, 179 p.
8. Wetlands International 2015. Briefing paper: accelerating action to Save Peat for Less Heat! Available at: http://www.wetlands.org/WatchRead/Currentpublications/tabid/56/mod/1570/articleType/ArticleView/articleId/3763/Default.aspx

Abstract No: A-318

HISTORICAL DEVELOPMENT OF INDUSTRIAL SCALE OIL PALM PLANTATION OVER PEATLAND IN RIAU AND WEST KALIMANTAN PROVINCES, INDONESIA

Syaiful Anwar[1*], Syed Aziz Ur Rehman[2], Untung Sudadi[1], Bandung Sahari[3] and Supiandi Sabiham[1]

[1]*Faculty of Agriculture, Bogor Agricultural University, Indonesia*
[2]*Former graduate student, Faculty of Agriculture, Bogor Agricultural University, Indonesia*
[3]*Indonesian Palm Oil Association, Indonesia*

* *Corresponding author: syaianwar@yahoo.com*

SUMMARY

Over the past three decades oil palm plantation (OPP) in Indonesia has been developed on peatland. Expansion of OPP is a large scale land use change and is having dynamics to the environments. In the perspective of national-level resource management and policy development regarding peatlands, understanding the historical expansion of OPP over peatland and explores the dynamics of above-ground biomass (AGB) during the land use changes is much needed. The study area consisted of two provinces in Indonesia, namely Riau and West Kalimantan. This study highlights the conversion of peat swamp forests (PSF) based on the status of primary or secondary forests. The study also reported on the transitions occurred in AGB in the peatlands that have been developed for OPP by distinguishing classes of peat thickness. Landsat imagerywas used to visually interpret OPP followed by intersection with peat thickness and swamp forest maps to create province-wide maps; spanning three temporal periods spanning from 1990 to 2000 to 2010 to 2013. The AGB estimates reported in the scientific literature were used to assess the AGB loss associated with each land use change. The results show that in 1990, the two provinces collectively had approximately 0.31 Mha of OPP, which expanded to 3.04 Mha by 2013. The OPP grew at an approximately constant rate (11% yr–1). Only 0.94% (29,137 ha) of the OPP had been derived directly from primary peat swamp forest (PPSF), and 21.55% (0.67 Mha) of the OPP had been established on land previously covered with secondary peat swamp forest (SPSF) within the past 23 years (1990-2013) in Riau and West Kalimantan. Higher portion of SPSF converted to wet shrublands (WSL) leading to the greatest loss of AGB (85.5 M tons). Lower loss of AGB resulted by conversion from SPSF to OPP (47.5 M tons). Similarly, the loss of AGB from the conversion of PPSF to OPP (estimated to be only 4.39 M tons) was higher than for conversions from PPSF to WSL (3.44 M tons).

Keywords: *land use change, oil palm, peat swamp forest, plantation, above-ground biomass*

INTRODUCTION

During the mid-1980s, Indonesian government implemented policies to promote diversification of products outside the oil and gas sector focused on development of tree crop plantations. Original proposed development was Industrial Tree Crop Estate (*Hutan Tanaman Industri* or HTI) as a model to be established on degraded land, supposedly to reduce the demanding of natural timber. At almost the same time, there has been booming in development of oil palm plantation (OPP) from about 0.5 ha in 1984, increased to over 1.0 Mha by 1990, to approximately 2.4 Mha in 1997, and to nearly 3.0 Mha in 2000 (Pagiola, 2000). Expansion of OPP in previously swampy areas including peatlands involved the drainage of land during preparation; therefore, since the 1980s, there has been an increase in the distortion of landscapes and a loss of small segments of land held by poor landholders in the logged peatlands (Page *et al.*, 2009). The drainage of land during preparation involves civil engineering work such as the development of road networks and waterways, ultimately leads to lowering the ground water level, creating aerobic conditions within the peat that accelerate oxidation, nitrogen mineralization and microbial activities (Hirano *et al.*, 2007). Such logging activity causes the humid tropical forests to be highly prone to forest fires and desiccation because of wood loss and the opened canopy (Siegert *et al.*, 2001).

Therefore, from the perspective of national-level resource management and policy development regarding peatlands, understanding the historical expansion of OPP in Indonesia allegedly drivers of deforestation and the mechanisms involved is much needed. The current study is aimed to observe the historical expansion of OPP and explores the dynamics of above-ground biomass (AGB) during land use changes in peatland ecosystems.

MATERIALS AND METHODS

The study was conducted in Riau and West Kalimantan Indonesia. . Landsat imagery (4, 5, 7 and 8) of the study area were downloaded from the US Geological Survey website: http://glovis.usgs.gov/. Province-wide scale (1:250,000) peatland distribution maps were prepared by Wetland Internationals (WI) in 2003/2004, followed by the Indonesian Centre for Agricultural Land Resources Research and Development (ICALRRD) in 2011. Peatland distribution data and peat thickness were obtained from ICALRRD (2011), which was used to obtain details related to peat thickness. The land use data for forest lands were acquired from the Indonesian Ministry of Forestry and used to locate swamp forests. Primary peat swamp forest (PPSF) and secondary peat swamp forest (SPSF) polygons were intersected with peat thickness polygons to obtain the locations of PSF.

Landsat imagery (4, 5, 7 and 8) was processed using ArcGIS® 9.3 software by performing on-screen analysis to locate OPP. During on-screen interpretation, multistage visual technique images were displayed as false color composites of various Landsat bands. The OPP were then identified and delineated, intersected with spatial extent and thickness of peat soils. The peat-layer thickness information was used to determine the extent of OPP above two groups of peat soil with thickness identified as being either more or less than 3 m. Similarly, the peat soil polygons were intersected with OPP and swamp forests data to circumscribe the PSF and to further distinguish between the peatlands and PSF. To extract PSF and differentiate it from swamp forests above mineral soils, the land use change data for forests was overlaid with peatland maps across each time periods of 1990-2000, 2000-2010, and 2010-2013. The primary outputs of the data analysis were land cover change matrices. The results were then compared with land cover maps and published statistics from other studies. To estimate the changes in AGB across selected land uses, the reported estimates of AGB from the scientific literature were used. The decline in biomass was estimated by multiplying the spatial change (ha) in AGB during each land use transition based on the difference of biomass.

The average time for carbon storage in standing oil palm tree excluded harvested and cut palm frond is 25 years during the rotation period. Applying the differences in the AGB carbon stocks, the C lost during each land use transition was estimated by multiplying the difference factor with the areal increase in each time period, following the time-averaged biomass stocks from this study and applied C fraction (CF = 0.50) [ton C (ton dm) 1] from IPCC (2006) for the selected land uses. The results thus show similar trends to that of biomass losses, i.e. the greatest C loss in AGB was estimated to occur in areas converted from SPSF to WSL, i.e. 42.8 M tons. This is followed by conversion from SPSF to OPP, i.e. 23.8 M tons. Whilst C loss in AGB from the conversion of PPSF to OPP was estimated to be only 2.19 M tons, and this is higher than C loss in AGB from the conversion of PPSF to WSL i.e. 1.72 M tons.

RESULTS AND DISCUSSION

Current and Historical Oil Palm Plantations in Peatlands

Peatlands distribution was processed from raw data obtained from ICALRRD, and the results show that the total peatland area based on peat thickness in Riau and West Kalimantan was 3.83 Mha (2.24 Mha < 3 m; 1,59 Mha > 3 m), and 1.69 Mha (1.44 Mha < 3 m; 0.25 Mha > 3 m), respectively. Table 1 summarized the OPP that have been developed over peatland in Riau and West Kalimantan since 1990 based on the peat thickness classes. Riau and West Kalimantan had 1,552,165 ha (91.60%) and 359,879 ha (80.00%) of peatland, respectively, that has been converted to OPP with legally permitted thickness (< 3 m). The results show that much of the peatlands with legally permitted thickness that are available for further development and plantations from 2013 onwards in both provinces are now greatly limited. Riau has 0.32 Mha and West Kalimantan has 0.79 Mha of remaining peatland that can be developed. Similarly, the spatial extent of peat soils supporting OPP increased from 22,992 ha (7% of total oil palm area) in 1990 to 1.3 Mha (43%) by 2013 in both provinces, of which 1.04 Mha (30%) occurs in Riau, compared with 0.26 Mha (29%) in West Kalimantan. The use of peatlands for OPP in areas with peat thickness > than 3 m (legally not permitted) increased in both provinces, from 26 ha and 0 ha (0.11% and 0%) in 1990 to 0.31 Mha and 24,796 ha (30% and 9%) in 2013 in Riau and West Kalimantan, respectively. The analysis revealed that the OPP expanded almost linearly in both provinces with a more drastic rise in Riau from 1990 to 2000, and from 2010 onwards.

The Conversion of Peat Swamp Forest to Oil Palm Plantations

Table 1. Oil palm plantations in peatlands based on peat thickness in West Kalimantan and Riau, Indonesia

Year	Land Use	Mineral soil (ha)	Oil Palm over Peat (ha)				
			D1	D2	D3	D4	Grand Total
West Kalimantan							
1990	Oil Palm	43,518	140	--------	--------	--------	43,658
2000	Oil Palm	181,498	3,193	7,035	2,490	--------	194,216
2010	Oil Palm	359,960	57,571	39,877	9,288	12,558	479,253
2013	Oil Palm	641,799	81,449	131,287	27,549	24,796	906,880
Riau							
1990	Oil Palm	246,402	4,855	42,37	13,734	26	269,255
2000	Oil Palm	845,340	59,415	147,643	130,425	25,718	1,208,541
2010	Oil Palm	972,696	61,116	212,804	187,477	52,791	1,486,884
2013	Oil Palm	1,087,486	66,364	268,721	395,374	310,755	2,128,700

Peat thickness classes: D1, 50–100 cm; D2, 100–200 cm; D3, 200–300 cm; D4, > 300 cm

The results show that a very minute fraction of OPP has been derived from primary peat swamp forests (PPSF); most of the OPP has been established on land previously inhabited by secondary peat swamp forests (SPSF). Our results supported the finding (Figure 1) that in both provinces the expansion took place initially using SPSF and then in the later stages (from 2010 to 2013) some portion of PPSF has also been used. This study revealed that the exploitation of PSF for OPP is indirect and that PSF is not only being converted to OPP but also to other land uses. After analyzing all regions and temporal periods in both provinces, only 0.94% (29,137 ha) of the OPP had been derived directly from PPSF; 21.55% (0.67 Mha) had been established on land previously covered with SPSF. In particular, Riau had the overall highest observed magnitude of SPSF conversion from 1990–2000, while in West Kalimantan more expansion took place from 2000–2010. An overall comparison shows that Riau had the highest spatial extent of OPP that had replaced both primary and secondary PSF, i.e. 26,424 ha and 499,782 ha compared to 2,749 ha and 171,865 ha in West Kalimantan, respectively. The research results are both similar to and distinct from study of Miettinen *et al.* (2012). Some researchers believe that the expansion of OPP in Indonesia is one of several drivers of deforestation. However, it is a misconception to allege that all OPP originate from PPSF, as described by Pagiola (2000).

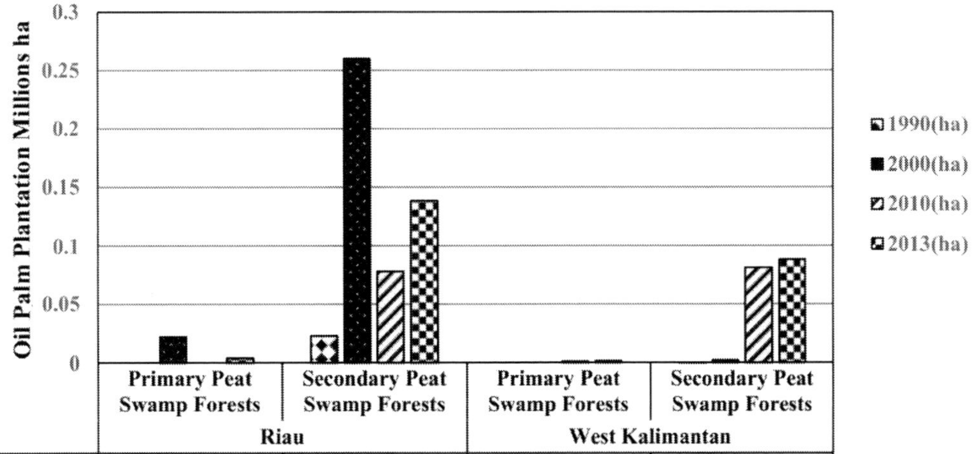

	Riau Primary Peat Swamp Forests	Riau Secondary Peat Swamp Forests	West Kalimantan Primary Peat Swamp Forests	West Kalimantan Secondary Peat Swamp Forests
1990(ha)	0	22852	0	140
2000(ha)	22136	260202	0	2142
2010(ha)	0	78026	1065	81255
2013(ha)	4288	138701	1684	88329

Figure 1. Temporal expansion of oil palm plantations and conversion of primary and secondary peat swamp forest in Riau and West Kalimantan, Indonesia

Loss of Above-Ground Biomass Because of Land Use Changes

The change in AGB is an obvious outcome in various land use changes. These changes involve a change from systems such as forests with high levels of biomass stock to less densely vegetated ecosystems such as shrublands or monocultures such as OPP. The biomass lost from 1990 to 2013 during all time periods was estimated (Table 2 and Figure 2) for each land use change category using the difference of biomass in each land use type per hectare. By totaling the AGB lost during all time periods and in both provinces, the highest amount of AGB loss was found to be a result of the conversion of SPSF to WSL (85.5 M tons); this was followed by 47.5 M tons from the conversion of SPSF to OPP. Similarly, the AGB loss from the conversion of PPSF to OPP was estimated to be only 4.39 M tons, which is higher than the 3.44 M tons lost by the conversion from PPSF to WSL. During the three periods analyzed, the greatest loss of AGB was estimated in areas converted from SPSF to WSL i.e. 19.30 M tons, 58.66 M tons and 7.59 M tons; this was followed by areas with a conversion from SPSF to OPP i.e. 19.21 M tons, 11.66 M tons and 16.62 M tons, respectively. During the same time periods, the estimated loss of AGB from conversion of PPSF to OPP was 3.32 M tons, 0.16 M tons and 0.89 M tons, which is higher than the loss of AGB from conversions of PPSF to WSL, which were 2.17 M tons, 1.13 M tons and 0.13 M tons, respectively.

Table 2. Loss of above ground biomass from primary and secondary PSF conversion to oil palm plantation and other land uses in Riau and West Kalimantan

Time Period	**Loss of above-ground biomass due to land use change (tons)**				
	PPSF to SPSF	**PPSF to OPP**	**PPSF to WSL**	**SPSF to OPP**	**SPSF to WSL**
West Kalimantan					
1990 to 2000	----	Nil	1,774,679	156,889	6,757,022
2000 to 2010	----	160,115	14,881	5,951,580	9,700,927
2010 to 2013	----	253,295	----	6,469,717	1,436,183
Riau					
1990 to 2000	13,010	3,328,848	397,608	19,058,732	12,550,926
2000 to 2010	4,046,240	----	1,120,022	5,715,127	48,967,606
2010 to 2013	264,224	644,759	132,374	10,159,292	6,162,210

PPSF: Primary peat swamp forest; SPSF: Secondary peat swamp forest; OPP: Oil palm plantations; WSL: Wet Shrubland

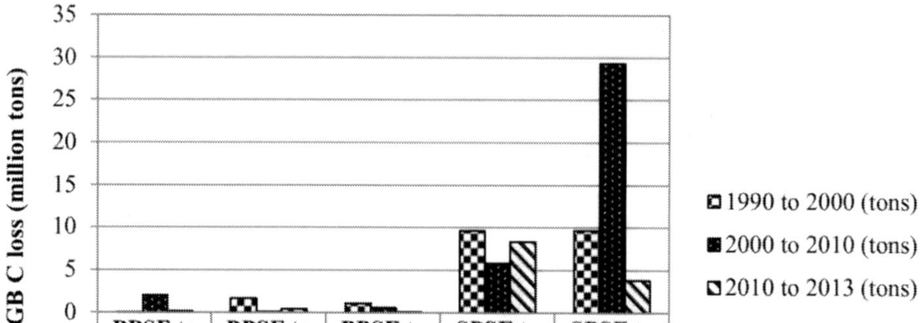

	PPSF to SPSF	**PPSF to OPP**	**PPSF to WSL**	**SPSF to OPP**	**SPSF to WSL**
1990 to 2000 (tons)	**6505**	**1664424**	**1086144**	**9607810**	**9653974**
2000 to 2010 (tons)	**2023120**	**80058**	**567452**	**5833353**	**29334266**
2010 to 2013 (tons)	**132112**	**449027**	**66187**	**8314504**	**3799196**

PPSF: Primary peat swamp forest; SPSF: Secondary peat swamp forest; OPP: Oil palm plantations; WSL: Wet shrubland; AGB: Above-ground biomass; LUs: Land uses

Figure 2. Overall loss of AGB carbon from primary and secondary PSF conversion to OPP and other land uses

CONCLUSION AND RECOMMENDATIONS

It is obvious that oil palm plantation (OPP) in Indonesia have developed extensively over time. This research revealed that OPP replaced secondary peat swamp forest (SPSF) to the extent that secondary in terms of areas. OPP that directly converted primary peat swamp forest (PPSF), in fact, only minor, less than 1% of the total OPP expansion during 1990 to 2013 in Riau and West Kalimantan. Similarly, higher area of SPSF was converted to wet shrubland (WS), leading to the greatest loss of above-ground biomass (AGB) when compared with all other types of land use change. This study does not cover the social and economic aspects of the trajectory of land use change; therefore, we recommend further studies should analyze shorter time periods and use advance remote-sensing technologies other than visual interpretation to identify the economic and social factors that drive the land use change. Special consideration should be given to exploring the causes of major and spontaneous land use changes, *e.g.* conversion of SPSF to WSL, using field surveys and the knowledge of local indigenous peoples.

ACKNOWLEDGEMENTS

The authors acknowledge the research team of the Indonesian Palm Oil Association (GAPKI) who financed this study in collaboration with Peat Society of Indonesia (HGI). We are also grateful to the Indonesian Agency for Agricultural Research and Development of the Ministry of Agriculture for helping us obtain secondary data and technical support.

REFERENCES

a) ICALRRD (Indonesian Centre for Agricultural Land Resources Research and Development). 2011. *Peta Lahan Gambut Indonesia Skala 1:250.000 (Indonesian peatland map at the scale 1:250,000). Indonesian Agency for Agricultural Research and Development, Ministry of Agriculture, Republic of Indonesia.* Bogor, Indonesia. 30pp.

b) IPCC (Intergovernmental Panel on Climate Change). 2006. IPCC *Guidelines for National Greenhouse Gas Inventories, Prepared by the National Greenhouse Gas Inventories Programme*, H.S. Eggleston, L. Buendia, K. Miwa, T. Ngara, and K. Tanabe (eds). Published: IGES, Japan.

c) Hirano, T., H. Segah, T. Harada, S.H. Limin, T. June, R. Hirata, and M. Osaki. 2007. *Carbon dioxide balance of a tropical peat swamp forest in Kalimantan, Indonesia.* Global Change Biology. 13(2): 412-425.

d) Miettinen, J., A. Hooijer, D. Tollenaar, S. Page, C. Malins, R. Vernimmen, and S.C. Liew. 2012. *Historical analysis and projection of oil palm plantation expansion on peatland in Southeast Asia.* International Council on Clean Transportation. 22pp.

e) Page, S.E., A. Hoscilo, H. Wösten, J. Jauhiainen, M. Silvius, J. Rieley, H. Ritzema, K. Tansey, L. Graham, H. Vasander, and S.H. Limin. 2009. *Restoration ecology of lowland tropical peatlands in Southeast Asia: current knowledge and future research directions.* Ecosystems. 12(6): 888-905.

f) Pagiola, S. 2000. *Land use change in Indonesia.* Washington, DC: World Bank Environment Department. 29pp.

g) Siegert, F., G. Ruecker, A. Hinrichs, and A.A. Hofmann. 2001. *Increased damage from fires in logged forests during droughts caused by El Nino.* Nature. 414(6862): 437-440.

Abstract No: A-146

IDENTIFICATION OF TROPICAL PEAT FOREST VEGETATION USING SPECTRORADIOMETER AND HYPERSPECTRAL IMAGERY IN CENTRAL KALIMANTAN, INDONESIA

Hendrik Segah[1,*], Freddy Wijaya[2], Laju Gandharum[3] and Hiroshi Tani[4]

[1] *Department Of Forestry, Faculty Of Agriculture, University Of Palangka Raya, Indonesia*
[2] *Magister Program Of Natural Resources Management, University Of Palangka Raya, Indonesia*
[3] *Badan Pengkajian Dan Penerapan Teknologi (BPPT), Indonesia*
[4] *Graduate School Of Agriculture, Hokkaido University, Japan*

**Corresponding author: segah@for.upr.ac.id; hsegah@gmail.com*

SUMMARY

This paper reports about the compilation of the spectral library of dominant trees in peat-forest in Central Kalimantan, Indonesia performed by the ASD FieldSpec-3 Spectroradiometer with a spectral range of 350-2500 nm (a rapid data collection time of 0.1 second per spectrum) and combined with images of Hyperspectral Mapper (HYMAP) sensor which was mounted at an aircraft (type CESSNA 402-B). Spectral libraries are commonly established as a means to archive representative signatures of natural materials. Such signatures can then be used to train feature extraction and classification algorithms applied to remote sensing data imagery. This study uses Spectral Angle Mapper (SAM) to compare the spectra of individual pictures for spectrum or spectral library. We found, each vegetation type has unique spectral signature or characteristics. The shapes of reflectance spectra can be used for identification of vegetation types combine with remote sensing data. With threshold set to 0.2 radians, the SAM results showed that the Bangka species dominated 56 % of the study site, followed by *Garcinia* sp. (29%) and the rest are for Balau/Alau (*Dacridium* sp.), Gerunggang (*Cratoxylon* sp.), Meranti (*Shorea* sp.) and unclassified class over study area of peat-forest in Central Kalimantan, Indonesia.

Keywords: *hyperspectral, peat-forest, spectroradiometer, Spectral Angle Mapper and Spectral library/signature.*

INTRODUCTION

Remote sensing applications in precision identification of agriculture and forest vegetation have been steadily increasing in recent years due to improvements in spatial and spectral resolutions of remotely sensed imagery. There is a rapidly growing interest in methods for automatic plant identification, especially in agricultural and forestry researches. Innovations in sensors are permitting the connection of remote sensing with methods of laboratory spectroscopy (Raymond *et al.*, 2003; Andres Kuusk *et al.*, 2004). The Spectral library is "a set of class or end member spectrum to be referred during feature extraction process from hyperspectral data". It can be further explained as a collection of spectral plots which is being compiled so that it can be used as a reference in information extraction from hyperspectral data. The reflection of radiation from the forest understorey and ground vegetation, in particular, plays a significant role in the forming of total forest reflectance (Satterwhite and Henley 1990; Danson and Curran, 1993).

Field campaign is the most common and easiest way to collect object spectra of different land cover types or vegetations, and this method produces results which can be easily compiled into spectral library (Andres Kuusk *et al.*, 2004; Alvin Lau and Mazlan Hashim, 2007). To carry out a field campaign, a spectroradiometer is needed to record the spectra received from the objects found especially tropical forest vegetation (tree species) in the study area.

METHODS

The study was conducted at educational forest of University of Palangka Raya (UPR) in Hampangen, approximately 60 km from Palangka Raya, the capital city of Central Kalimantan Province, Indonesia (*Figure 1*) with the elevation between 15-20 m above sea level (Shimada *et al.*, 2001; Weiss *et al.*, 2002). Peat swamps cover extensive areas of lowland Kalimantan, with estimates varying between 8% and 11% (McKinnon *et al.*, 1996). Area of Central Kalimantan is 153,564 km2, comprising mostly jungle (ca. 126,200 km2, 82.18%), swamps (11.80%), rivers and lakes (2.97%), and agricultural land (3.05%). Central Kalimantan contains about three million hectares of peatland which is one of the largest unbroken peatland in the world and located between 0° 45' N and 3° 3' S, between 111° and 116° E. Ground surveys and field investigations were carried out in the study area in 2011-2014.

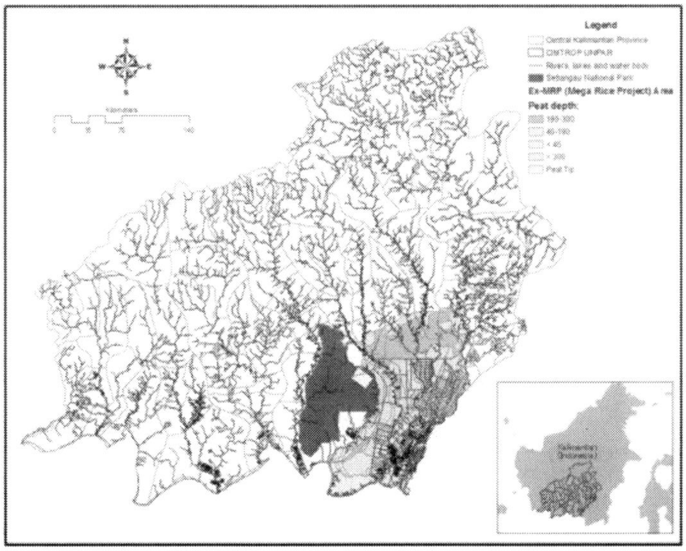

Figure 1: Map of study area in Central Kalimantan Province, Indonesia.

In the 2011-2014 field experiment, two types of ground truth were measured: ground spectral reflectance and location data for the measured trees. The measurements of the reflectance spectra of ground vegetation were performed by the ASD FieldSpec-3 Spectroradiometer with a spectral range of 350-2500 nm and a rapid data collection time of 0.1 second per spectrum. The main purpose of this study is to develop the spectral library of individual tree of peat-forest using a ground-based FieldSpec Spectroradiometer. The instrument uses three detectors spanning the visible and near infrared (VNIR) and shortwave infrared (SWIR1 and SWIR2). The FieldSpec spectroradiometer (FieldSpec 3 FR) is specifically designed for field environment remote sensing to acquire visible near-infrared (VNIR) and short-wave infrared (SWIR) spectra. A white reference panel was used for calibration.

Figure 2: Spectral library data collection activities (field survey and sample measurements).

A contact probe fore optic was used to minimise BRDF effects from shiny surfaces. Measurements were made with a standard laboratory setup using the high intensity contact probe at 30° of nadir. The ASD contact probe used is equipped with an internal light source (a halogen bulb light source 6.5 W, with colour temperature 2901 ± 10% K). Spot size of the Contact Probe has the diameter of 22 mm as shown in *Figure* 2. The contact probe is an alternative method for collection of laboratory spectra because SWIR spectra collected are found to exhibit improved signal to noise (S:N) ratios, lower standard deviation and less intrinsic uncertainty than spectra collected using more traditional laboratory techniques. The spectrometer and contact probe were warmed prior to use for 90 minutes and 30 minutes, respectively. A white reference measurement was undertaken prior to each material (tree leaves) being sampled. Spectral measurements were made using 30 averages.

Hyperspectral Mapper (HYMAP) sensor which was mounted at an aircraft (type CESSNA 402-B). HYMAP is an airborne hyperspectral imaging sensor that has 128 spectral bands spanning the wavelength interval 0.45–2.5 μm. The HYMAP data for the study site was taken on July 16th, 2011.Spectral Angle Mapper (SAM) is a method for comparing image spectra to individual spectra or to a spectral library.

The SAM, as a spectral matching method, has been widely used in lithological type identification and mapping using hyperspectral data. The SAM quantifies the spectral similarity between an image pixel spectrum and a reference spectrum with known components. The algorithm determines the similarity between two spectra by calculating the spectral angle between them, treating them as vectors in *n*-D space, where *n* is the number of bands. Smaller angles represent closer matches to the reference spectrum and pixels further away than the specified maximum angle threshold in radians are not classified.

RESULTS

The samples of the library spectra measurements from 10 dominant trees species in peat-forest in Central Kalimantan are shown in *Figure 3* from the total of 33 species during field survey and measurements in full-range wavelength (*350 – 2500 nm*). The definition of dominant trees are trees (or shrubs) with crowns receiving full light from above and partly from the side; usually larger than the average trees or shrubs in the stand, with crowns that extend above the general level of the canopy and that are well developed but possibly somewhat crowded on the sides. A dominant tree is one which generally stands head and shoulders above all other trees in its vicinity. However, there may be a young, vigorous tree nearby, but not overtopped by a dominant tree. This smaller tree may be considerably shorter than the dominant, but still be receiving full light from above and partly from the sides. In its own immediate environment, it is dominant and should be recorded as such. Only understory trees immediately adjacent to the overstory tree will be assigned subordinate crown classes (Hirose *et al*., 2016; Miles *et al*., 2003).

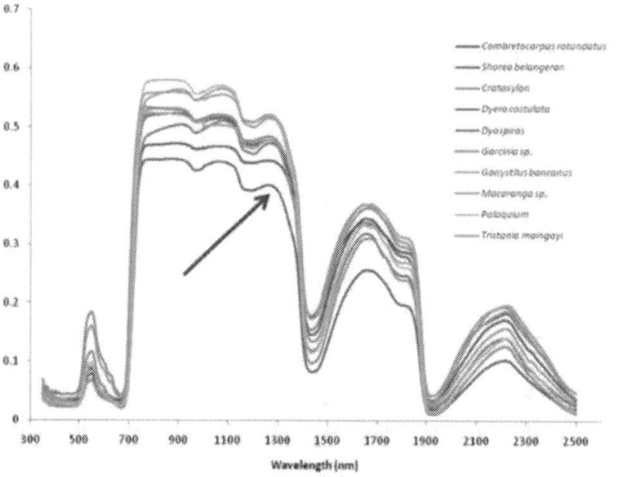

Figure 3: Spectral reflectance's from 10 species of peat-forest in full-range wavelength (350 – 2500 nm).

Figure 3 also presents examples of spectral reflectance's from 10 dominant tree species of peat-forest in SWIR wavelength (1000-1800 nm) with special characteristic of Tumeh (*Combretocarpus rotundatus*) which was always in lowest reflectance values than other tree species such as Belangeran (*Shorea belangeran*), Gerunggang (*Cratoxylon* sp.), Jelutung (*Dyera costulata*), Kayu Hitam (*Dyospiros* sp.), Manggis Hutan (*Garcinia* sp.), Ramin (*Gonystilus bancanus*), Mahang (*Macaranga* sp.), Nyatoh (*Palaquium* sp.), and Kayu Pelawan (*Tristania maingayi*).

As shown in *Figure 4*, we found that each type of vegetation (species) has unique spectral signature or characteristics. The shapes of reflectance spectra can be used for identification of vegetation types combine with remote sensing data (HYMAP). With threshold set to 0.2 radians, the SAM results showed that the Bangka species dominated 56 % of the study site, followed by *Garcinia* sp. (29%) and the rest are for Balau/Alau (*Dacridium* sp.), Gerunggang (*Cratoxylon* sp.), Meranti (*Shorea* sp.) and unclassified class over study area of peat-forest in Central Kalimantan, Indonesia. So that, the choice of spectral library was vital to the result of SAM classification. To build the spectral library needed in SAM algorithm, instead of using the average of all the training set, pure pixels were found using vertex component analysis (VCA).

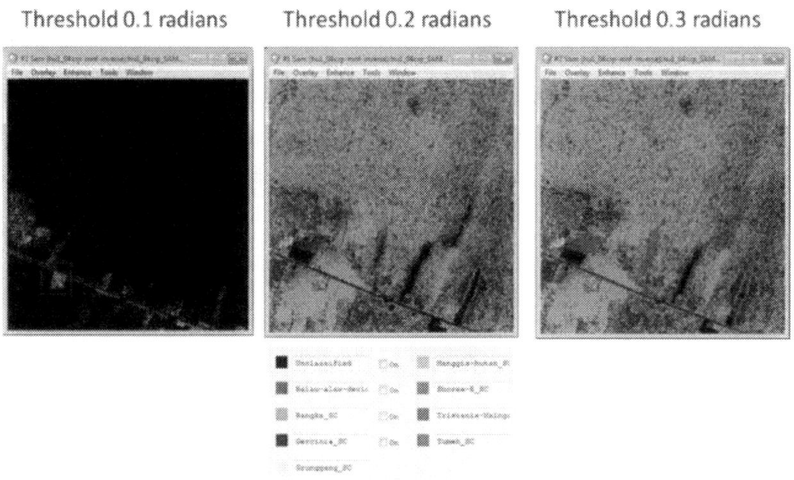

Figure 4: Results of tree classification by SAM results comparison (Source: Laju Gandharum, 2013).

DISCUSSION/CONCLUSION

Spectral analysis and measurements were performed during the field campaign to 33 vegetation species spectra and found that the vegetation spectra are very sensitive to environmental parameters such as leaf condition, vigorous and other physiological and biochemical parameters. Spectral libraries are data archives that consist of spectral signatures measured on selected natural and/or man-made materials. These libraries should also include the corresponding meta-information on the records. There are in principle two potential purposes: the use of the data in remote sensing as in-situ radiance/reflectance measurements for the calibration and/or end-members selection for further data processing (Selige *et al.*, 2006). Our results highlight the potential of hyperspectral remote sensing data as well as object-based classification approach for mapping heterogeneous land use/cover in a peat forest ecosystem such as in peatland areas in Central Kalimantan.

The knowledge gained from laboratory and field studies of vegetation spectra and laboratory spectral analysis methods are directly applicable to remote sensing data. This analysis highlights the possible integration of in-situ hyperspectral measurements with airborne/space-borne hyperspectral remote sensing data for automatic identification and discrimination of various species/vegetation on the study areas.

The continually updated of spectral library in peatland forest provides initial collections of spectra covering the wavelength range 350–2500 nm that allows for the modeling of basic vegetation and land-cover properties by statistical inference. This study has produced the first preliminary spectral library of the dominant forest tree species of the peat-forest in Central Kalimantan (Indonesia) taking into account the range of spectral variability expected for the species measured under natural illumination conditions.

Meanwhile, spectral libraries from ground measurements and hyperspectral sensors can collect continuous spectral reflectance data with narrow that enable classification of peat-forest types, discrimination of plant/tree species (through biophysical parameters), forest degradation, soil types and so on could support the integrated Measurement, Reporting and Verification (MRV) of Reducing Emissions from Deforestation and Forest Degradation (REDD) programs in Indonesia. Monitoring systems that allow for credible measurement, reporting and verification of REDD+ activities are among the most critical elements for the successful implementation of any REDD+ mechanism.

Furthermore, hyperspectral sensors have more capacity by observing terrain objects with very high spectral resolutions, the following five elements are potentially assessed among the eight key elements on tropical peatland ecosystem monitoring, such as: (i) Forest degradation and species mapping; (ii) Deforestation, forest biomass changes; (iii) Water level and soil moisture; (iv) Peat dome detection and peat thickness; and (v) Water soluble organic carbon (Hirose *et al.*, 2016)

ACKNOWLEDGEMENTS

This research was supported by Hokkaido University, JST-JICA SATREPS Project "*Wild Fire and Carbon Management in Peat-Forest in Indonesia*" collaborate with University of Palangka Raya (UNPAR) and Indonesia Agency for the Assessment and Application of Technology (BPPT). The authors would like to thank to Dr. Suwido H. Limin, Mr. Ici P. Kulu, Mr. Kitso Kusin and the staffs from the Centre for International Management of Tropical Peatland (CIMTROP) University of Palangka Raya, Central Kalimantan, Indonesia for their field support and assistance during the field campaign.

REFERENCES

1. Alvin Lau and Mazlan Hashim (2007). The Design and Building of Spectral Library of Tropical Rain Forest in Malaysia. Proceedings of the 28th Asian Conference on Remote Sensing, Kuala Lumpur, Malaysia, 12-16 November 2007. Asian Association of Remote Sensing (AARS).
2. Andres Kuusk, Mait Lang and Tiit Nilson (2004). Simulation of the reflectance of ground vegetation in sub-boreal forests. *Agricultural and Forest Meteorology* 126, 33–46.
3. Danson, F.M., and Curran, P.J. (1993). Factors affecting the remotely sensed response of coniferous forest plantations. *Remote Sensing of Environment* 43 (1), 55–65.
4. Frederic Raulier, Marie-Claude Lambert, David Pothier and Chhun-Huor Ung (2003). Impact of dominant tree dynamics on site index curves. *Forest Ecology and Management* 184, 65–78.
5. Hirose, Kazuyo, Mitsuru Osaki, Tomomi Takeda, Osamu Kashimura, Takashi Ohki, Hendrik Segah, Yan Gao, and Muhammad Evri. "Contribution of Hyperspectral Applications to Tropical Peatland Ecosystem Monitoring." In *Tropical Peatland Ecosystems*, pp. 421-431. Springer Japan, 2016.
6. MacKinnon, K., Hatta, G., Halim, H. and Mangalik, A. (1996). *The Ecology of Kalimantan*, pp. 802. Oxford University Press UK.
7. Miles R. Silman, John W. Terborgh, and Richard A. Kiltie (2003). Population regulation of a dominant rain forest tree by a major seed predator. *Ecology* 84 (2), 431–438.
8. Raymond F. Kokaly, Don G. Despain, Roger N. Clark and Eric Livo (2003). Mapping vegetation in Yellowstone National Park using spectral feature analysis of AVIRIS data. *Remote Sensing of Environment* 84, 437–456.
9. Selige, T., Bohner, J. and Schmidhalter, U. (2006). High resolution topsoil mapping using hyperspectral image and field data in multivariate regression modeling procedures. *Geoderma* 136, 235–244.
10. Shimada, S., Takahashi, H., Haraguchi, A. and Kaneko, M. (2001). The carbon content characteristics of tropical peats in Central Kalimantan, Indonesia; Estimating their spatial variability in density. *Biogeochemistry*, 53, 249–267.
11. Weiss, D., Shotyk, W., Rieley, J., Page, S., Gloor, M., Reese, S. and Martinez-Cortizas, A. (2002). The geochemistry of major and selected trace elements in a forested peat bog, Kalimantan, SE Asia, and its implications for past atmospheric dust deposition. *Geochimica et Cosmochimica Acta*, 66, 2307–2323.

Abstract No: A-413

REMOTE SENSING IMAGERY IN TROPICAL PEATLAND MAPPING: A REVIEW

Chloe Brown[1*], Doreen Boyd[1], Sofie Sjögersten[1] and Paul Aplin[2]

[1] *University of Nottingham, United Kingdom*
[2] *Edge Hill University, United Kingdom*

* *Corresponding author: c.z.z.brown93@gmail.com*

SUMMARY

Remote sensing has been recognised as a powerful tool in the study of the Earth's surface, providing a wealth of information on peatland ecology at spatial scales ranging from leaf-level chemistry to regional mapping of carbon fluxes. Various sources of remotely sensed imagery are known for their differences in spectral, spatial, radioactive and temporal characteristics and thus their suitability for different peatland applications. This research presents a review on the use of remote sensing imagery in the mapping and monitoring of tropical peatlands, specifically focusing on sensor technology applied to: peat depth, estimating above ground biomass, and disturbance and land use change.

INTRODUCTION

Covering an estimated 439,238 km^2 (~11% of global peatland area) (Page *et al.*, 2011), tropical peatlands have been increasingly recognised for their global importance as a terrestrial carbon sink and store, both in their above-ground biomass and underlying rich peat soils. Furthermore, tropical peatlands provide a wealth of valuable ecosystem services, including biodiversity, water supply, flood mitigation, and climate regulation (Padfield *et al.*, 2014). With minimal disturbance, tropical peatlands are generally stable environments (Law *et al.*, 2015. However, a shift in land use dynamics in many tropical regions has seen the large scale drainage and deforestation of tropical peat swamps, threating this vulnerable environment's ability to maintain ecosystem function. The need to be able to identify and predict changes in tropical peat environments for effective management and restoration programs has never been greater. Ecologists and conservation biologists have long been challenged by the spatially heterogeneous nature and complexity of tropical peatlands. Remote sensing has been recognised as a powerful tool in the study of the Earth's surface, providing a wealth of information on peatland ecology at spatial scales ranging from leaf-level chemistry (Detto *et al.*, 2015) to regional mapping of carbon fluxes (Lawson *et al.*, 2014). The continued development in sensor technology, processing and analysis procedures has greatly advanced our knowledge and understanding of tropical peatlands structure and function. This review aims to capture the wide variety of remote sensing technologies successfully applied in tropical peatland studies, encouraging their use as vital data sources in peatland conservation and management practices for these vulnerable ecosystems.

Keywords: -

REMOTE SENSING IN TROPICAL PEATLANDS

Due to the capacity for large coverage, easy access and low cost, optical imagery from medium spatial resolution satellite sensors has become the most widely applied remotely sensed datasets in tropical peatland research. An optical satellite sensor records the electromagnetic radiation emitted by the sun and reflected back to the sensor by the Earth's surface. Spectral and textual features derived from satellite imagery have been used to assess land use dynamics (Miettinen and Liew 2010; Wijedasa *et al.*, 2012), forest biomass (Li *et al.*, 2010), and species identification (Laheenoja and Page 2011). The major limitation of optical sensor technology is that they cannot record below the forest canopy level, therefore the data obtained cannot observe vegetation structure or peat surface below the dense canopy. Advances in high-resolution commercial satellite imagery (1-4m spatial resolution (Mather and Knoch, 2011)) have facilitated a higher level of detail obtained for peatland mapping and monitoring. High-resolution satellite sensors - such as GeoEye-1, IKONOS, QuickBird, RapidEye and WorldView 3 – offer a spatial resolution fine enough to detect forest structure at the scale of individual trees over large areas (Chambers *et al.*, 2007), providing highly detailed data sets with great potential for fine scale vegetation and disturbance monitoring (Franke *et al.*, 2012).

Active sensors, radar and LiDAR (Light Detection And Ranging), can penetrate through the canopy layers, giving the key advantage of recording forest structure and patterns unobserved by passive remote sensing. An active sensor maps the environment by recording the signal that is emitted by the sensor and reflected back to the sensor by the Earth's surface. Radars unique ability to produce distinctive radar signals (at different wavelengths) from interactions with standing water and vegetation (Hess *et al.*, 2003; Hoekman and Vissers 2007) has enhanced the level of detail and information we can derive from remote sensed imagery (Betbeder *et al.*, 2014; ; Schlund et al., 2014; Collins and Mitchard 2015). Additionally, radar sensors are unimpeded by cloud cover, lending themselves perfectly for tropical peatland studies over the humid tropics. LiDAR, both airborne and orbital sensors, has revolutionised the way we record and detect vegetation in forestry application, as a result LiDAR data has been increasingly adopted in remote tropical peatlands studies including in the assessment of forest regeneration (Boehm *etal.*, 2013), distinguishing between different species (Thapa *et al.*, 2015) and above ground biomass (AGB) (Jubanski et al., 2013; Hayashi *et al.*, 2015). LiDAR data additionally provides terrain surface elevation information, airborne sensors in particular generate highly detailed data points with a geometric accuracy in the range of decimetres – centimetres (*Konecny et al.*, 2016), this has produced a wealth of data for topographic peat dome and landscape studies (Ballhorn *et al.*, 2011; Wedeux and Coomes 2015).

Sensor fusion allows us to overcome the limitations of individual sensors and maximise the information derived from the different types of sensor technology, active and optical sensors have been integrated in several tropical peatland studies (Collins and Mitchard 2015; Saatchi *et al.*, 2011; Jaenicke *et al.*, 2009; Beteber *et al.*, 2014). Combining optical imagery with radar and/or LiDAR utilises both the spectral information recorded by optical sensors and the 3-D structural information derived from active sensors, producing a more accurate and detailed characterisation of a tropical peatland environment.

PEAT DEPTH

Tropical peatland's ability to sequester and contain large stores of carbon is under great threat from persistent human induced disturbance (Law *et al.*, 2015; Reddington *et al.*, 2016). The global importance of these carbon rich reserves is an active area of research, thus there is a real need for a robust scientific measure on the volume of tropical peat, and hence store of carbon, to inform national and international polices on the preservation of tropical peatlands (Padfield *et al.*, 2014). Several examples of remote sensing technology have been applied in tropical environments to derive peat thickness. Hashim et al., (2002) found a strong correlation between soil moisture and radar backscatter (L band) in drained peatlands; Jaenicke *at al.*, (2008) subsequently built upon these findings, applying a 3D peatland development model, built from multiple remote sensing data sources, to determine peat volumes and estimate carbon storage for a selection of Indonesia's peatlands. The study integrated Landsat Enhanced Thematic Mapper (ETM+), Shuttle Radar Topography Mission (SRTM) data, and a network of 750 field measurements of peat thickness to successfully map the extent and topography of the peat dome shaped surfaces, with a strong correlation found between the convex peat dome surface and the underlying mineral soil. Some have questioned this approach in assessing tropical peat landscapes, as they believe that the success of the study was too dependent on the specific properties (the uniform shape and thick peat deposits) associated with the peat domes selected in the study site (Lawson *et al.*, 2014). Ballhorn *et al.*, (2011) additional criticised the use of the SRTM data in determining vegetation height growing on peat domes, as the C-band sensor on-board cannot penetrate tall dense forest cover directly to the soil surface.

Several studies have found peat thickness to correlate with properties which are more readily derived from remotely sensed imagery. For example, Ballhorn *et al.*, (2011) used ICESat/GLAS (orbital LiDAR system) data to measure peatland topography as a proxy for peat volume for Central Kalimantan, Indonesia. A strong correlation between in situ peat measurements found that ICESat/GLAS was an effective data source to measure peat topography and assess peat volume for remote and inaccessible tropical peatlands. Wedeux and Coomes (2015) applied airborne laser scanning (ALS) data to measure the peat swamp forest canopy across a peat dome to determine if canopy structural metrics can be used as a proxy for peat depth. The study did find a strong relationship between canopy structure and peat depth, however, this relationship began to breakdown in areas where selective logging had taken place. Further research into the use and relationship of topographic and vegetation proxies for inferring peat thickness must be made to assess whether these properties are purely influenced by peat depth or if they are more influenced by other natural or anthropogenic controls.

ESTIMATING ABOVE GROUND BIOMASS

Tropical peatlands store carbon both in their dense forest vegetation and in the peat soil, however 89% of carbon losses in peat swamps is due to loss of AGB (Houghton, 2005). As a result, a great effort has been focused on estimating and mapping AGB, providing data not only for assessing carbon stores but also in peatland biomass productivity, diversity, and other key vegetation parameters (Hayashi *et al.*, 2015). The assessment of AGB in tropical regions by remote sensing can be challenging due to the complexity of the dense overlapping canopy structure and high cloud cover in the tropic. Passive optical remote sensing, for example from medium spatial resolution satellites (Landsat, SPOT and MODIS), has been used as an affordable source of data (Li *et al.*, 2010) however this approach has several disadvantages. Optical data is limited in that it can only record the canopy in two dimensions; additionally the signal can become saturated when recording high biomass forests, leading to underestimates of AGB (Hayashi *et al.*, 2015).

Avoiding the limitations posed by passive remote sensing, LiDAR (Ballhorn *et al.*, 2011; Thapa *et al.*, 2015 ; Hayashi *et al.*, 2015) and radar (L-band) (Collins and Mitchard 2015; Morel *et al.*, 2011) are considered the most appropriate data source used to estimate AGB and have been widely applied in tropical peatland environment. The size of the study area and the subsequent quality of the remotely sensed data has a major influence on the accuracy of the AGB estimate product. Saatchi *et al.*, (2011) for example, investigated largescale regional patterns of AGB for over 2.5billion hectares of tropical peat forest over three continents. The study combined data from multiple satellite LiDAR datasets and over 4,000 in situ inventory field plots. The projects estimation of AGB gave uncertainties at the pixel level (100 ha) ranging from ±6% to ±53%, however at a national scale (>1,000,000 ha) uncertainties were greatly reduced to ca. ±1%, successfully producing an AGB map illustrating regional patterns and carbon stock at a national scale.

DISTURBANCE AND LAND USE CHANGE

Land use planning and management is a controversial topic in tropical peatland environments, balancing growing demands to increase land under agricultural production with global calls for conservation (Padfield *et al.*, 2014). Anthropogenic land use change in the tropics - through deforestation, drainage, and fires for logging activities and conversion to plantation - has severally degraded these valuable ecosystems. Improved estimates for current and past land cover change are essential to aid in climate change mitigation and conservation schemes, for example the UNREDD (Reducing Emissions from Deforestation and forest Degradation) programme. The direction and extent of land use change over time has been extensively studied using medium resolution satellite imagery (Wijedasa *et al.*, 2012; Langner *et al.*, 2007), high resolution satellite imagery (Franke *et al.*, 2012), and radar satellite data (Collins and Mitchard 2015; Schlund *et al.*, 2014). Several of the studies adopt a post classification comparison approach, comparing land cover maps derived from a multi-temporal series of images. As a result, the overall accuracy of the final assessment is determined by the product of the individual land cover map accuracies, this approach is limited in that any errors on an individual image basis could transmit through to the final analysis of change (Phau *et al.*, 2007). Miettinen and Liew (2010) investigated the extent of peatland degradation in Southeast Asia over a two decade period of change. The study used satellite imagery from Landsat (30m) and SPOT (10–20m) to produce land cover maps for 1990 and 2008. Analysis of the land cover change between 1990-2008 revealed that in less than 20 year 5.1 Mha of the total 15.5 Mha of peatland had been deforested, with the majority of remaining intact forest having already been selective logging.

Small scale fires, often started to clear vegetation for land conversion into plantation, can ignite peat soil, quickly developing into long lasting smouldering fires, causing a severe deterioration in air quality (Reddington *et al.*, 2016), as well as the release of large stores of carbon into the atmosphere (Ballhorn *et al.*, 2009; Page *et al.*, 2011). Remote sensing fire disturbance studies often adopt a similar approach to land use change detection, comparing pre and post disturbance land cover maps or land surface spectral differences (Phua *et al.*, 2007). Ballhorn *et al.*, (2009) determined depth of peat burnt using LiDAR data acquired for the years 2006 and 2007, a period of severe El Nino induced peatland fires in Central Kalimantan, Indonesia. The study measured the elevation difference at the border between burned and unburned peatland, finding on average a burn scar depth of 0.33 ± 0.18 m. Konecny *et al.*, (2016) used LiDAR data to develop a pre fire event surface model methodology, which allowed repeated analysis of burnt areas over multiple fire events. Observations showed a strong interdependence between burned area depth, fire frequency and distance to drainage canals.

Groundwater level is a major control on carbon emissions from peatlands. When peat is drained it oxidises due to microbial activity, releasing previously stored carbon into the atmosphere. Extensive canals and ditches, built to control and lower groundwater level for plantations and as access points for the extraction of timber logs, have severely degraded tropical peat swamps (Hoekman and Vissers 2007). Long radar wavelengths (L-band) have been extensively used in topical peatlands to map standing water extent (Hess *et al.*, 2003; Bwangoy *et al.*, 2010) and in monitoring periods of drought and flooding (Hoekman and Vissers 2007; Beteber *et al.*, 2014). These studies are vital in providing timely information needed to support protection and restoration efforts. Jaenicke *et al.*, (2011) investigation into restoring tropical peatlands explored the use of multi temporal radar remote sensing imagery for monitoring the hydrological effects of rewetting the peat through the blocking of drainage canals. The study successfully highlighted the advantages of radar as a tool in soil moisture detections, showing an increase in peat soil moisture after dam construction

CONCLUSION

Peatland research has traditionally focused on temperate or boreal peat environments, however growing international recognition on the importance of tropical peatlands as an active terrestrial carbon store under threat has advanced this area of research greatly. The studies reviewed confirm that remote sensing is a valuable tool in the assessment of tropical environments, yielding accurate results in the mapping and quantifying of tropical peatlands. However, limitations still remain in tropical remote sensing research, most notably the frequent high cloud cover, vegetation structural complexity, canopy and soil moisture levels and landscape heterogeneity (Li *et al.*, 2010). A fusion of active and optical sensor imagery, in combination with field measurements, has been shown to provide the optimal balance for acquiring reliable and accurate datasets for tropical zones (Xu *et al.*, 2015). The continued development of sensor technology and data analysis in tropical environments is essential for improving current climate carbon models and in supporting management initiatives and policy making for carbon accounting and climate change mitigation.

REFERENCES

1. Ballhorn, U., Jubanski, J. and Siegert, F. (2011) ICESat/GLAS data as a measurement tool for peatland topography and peat swamp forest biomass in Kalimantan, Indonesia. *Remote Sensing*, 3(9), pp.1957-1982.
2. [Ballhorn, U., Siegert, F., Mason, M. and Limin, S. (2009) Derivation of burn scar depths and estimation of carbon emissions with LIDAR in Indonesian peatlands. *Proceedings of the National Academy of Sciences*, 106(50), pp.21213-21218.
3. Betbeder, J., Gond, V., Frappart, F., Baghdadi, N.N., Briant, G. and Bartholomé, E. (2014) Mapping of Central Africa forested wetlands using remote sensing. *Selected Topics in Applied Earth Observations and Remote Sensing, IEEE Journal*, 7(2), pp.531-542.
4. Boehm, H.D., Liesenberg, V. and Limin, S.H. (2013) Multi-temporal airborne LiDAR-survey and field measurements of tropical peat swamp forest to monitor changes. *Selected Topics in Applied Earth Observations and Remote Sensing, IEEE Journal*, 6(3), pp.1524-1530.
5. Chambers, J.Q., Asner, G.P., Morton, D.C., Anderson, L.O., Saatchi, S.S., Espírito-Santo, F.D., Palace, M. and Souza, C. (2007) Regional ecosystem structure and function: ecological insights from remote sensing of tropical forests. *Trends in Ecology & Evolution*, 22(8), pp.414-423.
6. Collins, M. and Mitchard, E.T.A. (2015) Integrated radar and lidar analysis reveals extensive loss of remaining intact forest on Sumatra 2007–2010. *Biogeosciences Discussions*, 12(22), pp.6637-6653.
7. Detto, M., Asner, G.P., Muller-Landau, H.C. and Sonnentag, O. (2015) Spatial variability in tropical forest leaf area density from multireturn lidar and modeling. *Journal of Geophysical Research: Biogeosciences*, 120(2), pp.294-309.
8. Franke, J., Navratil, P., Keuck, V., Peterson, K. and Siegert, F. (2012) Monitoring fire and selective logging activities in tropical peat swamp forests. *Selected Topics in Applied Earth Observations and Remote Sensing, IEEE Journal*, 5(6), pp.1811-1820.
9. Hashim, M., Busu, I., Sim, P. H. S., Jong, T. K., Kadir, W., Hazli, W., and Ngap, D. S. (2002) Soil moisture, depth of water table and peat decomposition in Sadong Simunjan river basin, Sarawak using AIRSAR/TOPSAR data. Third Malaysian Remote Sensing & GIS Conference and Exhibition. pp. 17.
10. Hayashi, M., Saigusa, N., Yamagata, Y. and Hirano, T. (2015) Regional forest biomass estimation using ICESat/GLAS spaceborne LiDAR over Borneo. *Carbon Management*, 6(1-2), pp.19-33.
11. Hess, L.L., Melack, J.M., Novo, E.M., Barbosa, C.C. and Gastil, M. (2003) Dual-season mapping of wetland inundation and vegetation for the central Amazon basin. *Remote Sensing of Environment*, 87(4), pp.404-428.
12. Hoekman, D. and Vissers, M. (2007) ALOS PALSAR radar observation of tropical peat swamp forest as a monitoring tool for environmental protection and restoration. In Geoscience and Remote Sensing Symposium, 2007. IGARSS 2007. IEEE International (pp. 3710-3714). IEEE.
13. [13] Houghton, R.A. (2005) Aboveground forest biomass and the global carbon balance. *Global Change Biology* 11, 945–958.
14. Jaenicke, J., Englhart, S. and Siegert, F. (2011) Monitoring the effect of restoration measures in Indonesian peatlands by radar satellite imagery.*Journal of Environmental Management*, 92(3), pp.630-638
15. Jaenicke, J., Rieley, J.O., Mott, C., Kimman, P. and Siegert, F. (2008) Determination of the amount of carbon stored in Indonesian peatlands. *Geoderma*, 147(3), pp.151-158.
16. Jubanski, J., Ballhorn, U., Kronseder, K., Franke, J. and Siegert, F. (2013) Detection of large above-ground biomass variability in lowland forest ecosystems by airborne LiDAR. *Biogeosciences*, 10(6), pp.3917-3930.
17. Konecny, K., Ballhorn, U., Navratil, P., Jubanski, J., Page, S.E., Tansey, K., Hooijer, A., Vernimmen, R. and Siegert, F. (2016) Variable carbon losses from recurrent fires in drained tropical peatlands. *Global change biology*. 22 (4), pp.1469–1480.
18. Lähteenoja, O. and Page, S. (2011) High diversity of tropical peatland ecosystem types in the Pastaza-Marañón basin, Peruvian Amazonia. Journal of Geophysical Research: *Biogeosciences*, 116(G2).
19. Langner, A., Miettinen, J. and Siegert, F. (2007) Land cover change 2002–2005 in Borneo and the role of fire derived from MODIS imagery. *Global Change Biology*, 13(11), pp.2329-2340.
20. Law, E.A., Bryan, B.A., Meijaard, E., Mallawaarachchi, T., Struebig, M. and Wilson, K.A. (2015)

Ecosystem services from a degraded peatland of Central Kalimantan: implications for policy, planning, and management. *Ecological Applications*, 25(1), pp.70-87.

21. Lawson, I.T., Kelly, T.J., Aplin, P., Boom, A., Dargie, G., Draper, F.C.H., Hassan, P.N.Z.B.P., Hoyos-Santillan, J., Kaduk, J., Large, D. and Murphy, W. (2015) Improving estimates of tropical peatland area, carbon storage, and greenhouse gas fluxes. *Wetlands Ecology and Management*, 23(3), pp.327-346.
22. Li, H., Mausel, P., Brondizio, E. and Deardorff, D. (2010) A framework for creating and validating a non-linear spectrum-biomass model to estimate the secondary succession biomass in moist tropical forests. *ISPRS Journal of Photogrammetry and Remote Sensing*, 65(2), pp.241-254.
23. Mather, P.M., and Koch, M. (2011) *Computer processing of remotely-sensed images: An Introduction*. 4th ed. Wiley
24. Miettinen, J. and Liew, S.C. (2010) Degradation and development of peatlands in Peninsular Malaysia and in the islands of Sumatra and Borneo since 1990. *Land degradation & development*, 21(3), pp.285-296.
25. Morel, A.C., Saatchi, S.S., Malhi, Y., Berry, N.J., Banin, L., Burslem, D., Nilus, R. and Ong, R.C. (2011) Estimating aboveground biomass in forest and oil palm plantation in Sabah, Malaysian Borneo using ALOS PALSAR data. *Forest Ecology and Management*, 262(9), pp.1786-1798.
26. Padfield, R., Waldron, S., Drew, S., Papargyropoulou, E., Kumaran, S., Page, S., Gilvear, D., Armstrong, A., Evers, S., Williams, P. and Zakaria, Z. (2015) Research agendas for the sustainable management of tropical peatland in Malaysia. *Environmental Conservation*, 42(01), pp.73-83.
27. Page, S.E., Rieley, J.O. and Banks, C.J. (2011) Global and regional importance of the tropical peatland carbon pool. *Global Change Biology*,17(2), pp.798-818.
28. Phua, M.H., Tsuyuki, S., Lee, J.S. and Sasakawa, H. (2007) Detection of burned peat swamp forest in a heterogeneous tropical landscape: A case study of the Klias Peninsula, Sabah, Malaysia. *Landscape and urban planning*, 82(3), pp.103-116.
29. Reddington, C.L., Spracklen, D.V., Artaxo, P., Ridley, D., Rizzo, L.V. and Arana, A. (2016) Analysis of particulate emissions from tropical biomass burning using a global aerosol model and long-term surface observations. *Atmos. Chem. Phys. Discuss*., doi:10.5194/acp-2015-967.
30. Saatchi, S.S., Harris, N.L., Brown, S., Lefsky, M., Mitchard, E.T., Salas, W., Zutta, B.R., Buermann, W., Lewis, S.L., Hagen, S. and Petrova, S. (2011) Benchmark map of forest carbon stocks in tropical regions across three continents. *Proceedings of the National Academy of Sciences*, 108(24), pp.9899-9904.
31. Schlund, M., von Poncet, F., Hoekman, D.H., Kuntz, S. and Schmullius, C. (2014) Importance of bistatic SAR features from TanDEM-X for forest mapping and monitoring. *Remote Sensing of Environment*, pp.16-26.
32. Thapa, R.B., Watanabe, M., Motohka, T., Shiraishi, T. and Shimada, M. (2015) Calibration of aboveground forest carbon stock models for major tropical forests in central Sumatra using airborne LiDAR and field measurement data. *Selected Topics in Applied Earth Observations and Remote Sensing, IEEE Journal*, 8(2), pp.661-673.
33. Wedeux, B.M.M. and Coomes, D.A. (2015) Landscape-scale changes in forest canopy structure across a partially logged tropical peat swamp. *Biogeoscience*, 12, pp.6707-6719.
34. Wijedasa, L.S., Sloan, S., Michelakis, D.G. and Clements, G.R. (2012) Overcoming limitations with Landsat imagery for mapping of peat swamp forests in Sundaland. *Remote Sensing*, 4(9), pp.2595-2618.
35. Xu, C., Morgenroth, J. and Manley, B. (2015) Integrating data from discrete return airborne LiDAR and optical sensors to enhance the accuracy of forest description: a review. *Current Forestry Reports*, pp.206-219.

Abstract No: A-444

TROPICAL PEATLANDS CHARACTERIZATION USING TEMPORAL PALSAR/PALSAR-2 MOSAIC DATA: A CASE STUDY IN SIAK REGENCY, RIAU, INDONESIA

Dandy Aditya Novresiandi[1,3]; Ryota Nagasawa[2]

[1]*United Graduate School of Agricultural Sciences, Tottori University, Japan, dandyaditya@gmail.com*
[2]*Faculty of Agriculture, Tottori University, Japan, nagasawa@muses.tottori-u.ac.jp*
[3]*Center for Remote Sensing Institut Teknologi Bandung (CRS-ITB), Indonesia*

SUMMARY

Tropical peatlands monitoring activity has become essential towards the sustainable management of tropical peatlands. Synthetic Aperture Radar (SAR) offers cloud-free observation to monitor the vast area of tropical peatlands by remote sensing application. This study was carried out to obtain characteristics of tropical peatlands using temporal PALSAR/PALSAR-2 mosaic data. Three temporal mosaic data—2007 (PALSAR), 2010 (PALSAR), and 2015 (PALSAR-2)—were used in this study. Five parameters that represent the channels of polarization and theirs combinations were derived from each data; i.e. HH (Horizontal-Horizontal), HV (Horizontal-Vertical), HH/HV, HV/HH, and HH-HV. These parameters were evaluated for their capability to examine characteristics of tropical peatlands from the viewpoint of L-band dual-polarimetric SAR. Overall, relationships have been found that HV was consistently produced the highest mean value for the very-deep peat class in all dataset, while HH-HV was consistently yielded the lowest mean value for the same class. Moreover, the HV and HH-HV were useful to distinguish the combined-peat and non-peat classes. However, both PALSAR and PALSAR-2 mosaics could not discriminate the shallow, medium and deep peat classes due to the highly overlapping parameter values between those classes. There was a slight shift between parameter values in 2007-2010 data which most likely due to the LULC changes between the observation times. The bigger shifts in the parameter values were found in 2007-2015 and 2010-2015 data. These bigger shifts could be due to the rapid LULC changes and the different sensor sensitivity between PALSAR and PALSAR-2.

***Keywords**: tropical peatlands, L-band dual-polarimetric SAR, Gamma naught*

INTRODUCTION

Tropical peatlands act as one of the largest terrestrial carbon stores, and have a great contribution to the global carbon balance (Jauhiainen *et al.*, 2005; Page *et al.*, 2011). However, tropical peatlands are being subjected to rapid economic development, which has led to massive carbon emission (Rieley *et al.*, 2008). Thus, tropical peatlands monitoring activity has become essential towards the sustainable management of tropical peatlands (Page *et al.*, 2002; Jaenicke *et al.*, 2008; Wahyunto *et al.*, 2012). Synthetic Aperture Radar (SAR) offers cloud-free observation to monitor the vast area of tropical peatlands by remote sensing application (Hoekman *et al.*, 2007). To date, the availability of SAR dataset is increasing along with the growing interest of SAR remote sensing applications. The Global 25m Resolution PALSAR/PALSAR-2 Mosaic open dataset provided by Japan Aerospace Exploration Agency (JAXA), is a particular concern, as it freely available and covers global coverage.

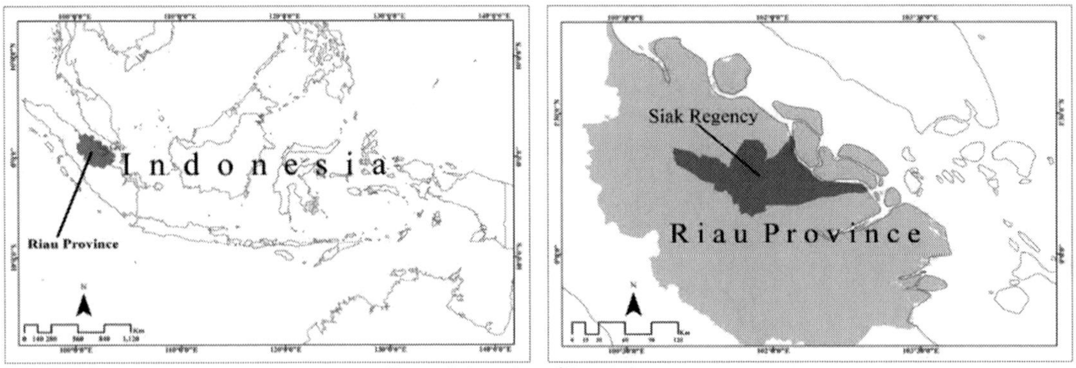

Figure 1: Location of the study area.

This data was generated by mosaicking, applying ortho-rectification and slope correction to the L-band dual-polarimetric SAR images in backscatter coefficient as measured by PALSAR/PALSAR-2 (JAXA 2016). The present study was carried out to obtain characteristics of tropical peatlands using temporal PALSAR/PALSAR-2 mosaic data. In addition, a temporal analysis was done to examine temporal variability of tropical peatlands from the viewpoint of L-band dual-polarimetric SAR.

MATERIALS AND METHODS

The study area was located in Siak Regency, Riau Province, Indonesia (Figure 1). Based on the existing distribution map published by the Indonesian Agency for Agricultural Research and Development (IAARD), tropical peatlands is estimated to cover more than 50% of the Siak Regency land area. In this study, three temporal mosaic data were used as the primary data; i.e. 2007 (generated by PALSAR), 2010 (generated by PALSAR), and 2015 (generated by PALSAR-2). Data was converted to the ortho-rectified and slope corrected backscatter coefficient (γ^o) values in decibel unit (dB) prior to data analysis (JAXA 2016). Existing peat map and land use/cover (LULC) map published by the IAARD were used as secondary data. Additionally, an existing topographic map of Siak Regency published by the *Badan Informasi Geospasial* (BIG) was used as the reference map. Five parameters that represent the channels of polarization and theirs combinations were derived from each data; i.e. HH (Horizontal-Horizontal), HV (Horizontal-Vertical), HH/HV, HV/HH, and HH-HV (Figure 2).

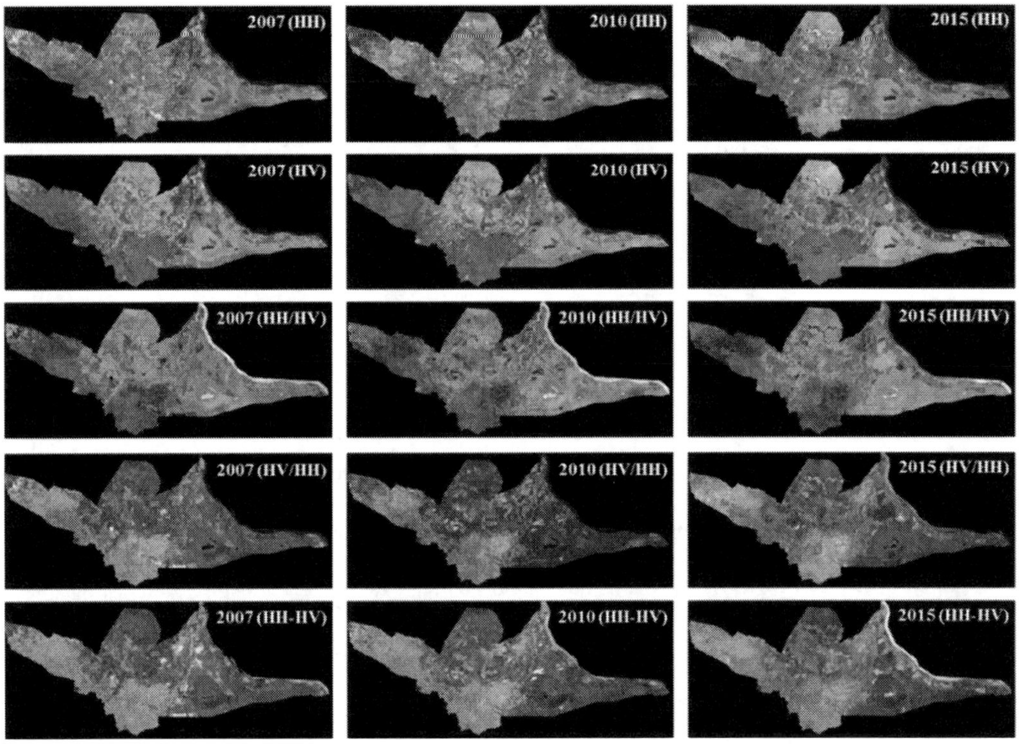

Figure 2: Preview of five parameters derived from each mosaic data (left row: 2007, middle row: 2010, and right row: 2015).

These parameters were evaluated for their capability to examine characteristics of tropical peatlands from the viewpoint of L-band dual-polarimetric SAR. Concurrently, six classes—shallow peat (d1), medium peat (d2), deep peat (d3), very-deep peat (d4), combined peat (p), and non-peat (np)—were derived from the existing peat map and LULC maps. These classes refer to the extent and depth of tropical peatlands as classified by the IAARD. The d1 refers to the peatland with less than 100 cm of depth. The d2 refers to the peatland with 100 to 200 cm of depth. The d3 refers to the peatland with 200 to 400 cm of depth. The d4 refer to the peatland with more than 400 cm of depth. The p refers to the peatland area as represents by the combination d1, d2, d3, and d4 classes. Meanwhile, the np refers to the area that did not classified as peatland area. A total of 32.419 observation points were generated on the reference map, with each point situated within a 500 x 500 meter mesh. These observation points represent the six classes of peat distribution over the study area, i.e. 353 points for d1, 4023 points for d2, 3244 points for d3, 11.939 points for d4, 19.559 points for p (sum of the d1, d2, d3, and d4 points), and 12.860 points for np. Subsequently, mean and standard deviation (sd) values of each peat class on each parameter were generated by superimpose the observation points onto parameter images. These values were then analyzed to obtain the characteristic of tropical peatlands, and for the temporal analysis purposes.

Table 2:Absolute differences of mean value for PALSAR/PALSAR-2 mosaic data.

Year	Parameter	d(mean)					
		d1	d2	d3	d4	p	np
2007-2015	HH	0.5	0.9	0.9	0.8	0.8	0.5
	HV	1.3	1.9	1.6	1.4	1.5	1.3
	HH/HV	0.0	0.0	0.0	0.0	0.0	0.0
	HV/HH	0.1	0.0	0.0	0.0	0.0	0.1
	HH-HV	0.8	1.0	0.7	0.6	0.7	0.8
2007-2010	HH	0.2	0.1	0.2	0.0	0.0	0.3
	HV	0.1	0.0	0.3	0.0	0.1	0.3
	HH/HV	0.0	0.0	0.0	0.0	0.0	0.0
	HV/HH	0.1	0.0	0.0	0.0	0.0	0.1
	HH-HV	0.2	0.1	0.1	0.1	0.1	0.1
2010-2015	HH	0.7	1.0	0.6	0.8	0.8	0.8
	HV	1.4	1.9	1.3	1.3	1.4	1.6
	HH/HV	0.0	0.0	0.0	0.0	0.0	0.0
	HV/HH	0.0	0.0	0.0	0.0	0.0	0.0
	HH-HV	0.7	0.8	0.6	0.5	0.6	0.8

RESULTS

Overall, relationships have been found that HV was consistently produced the highest mean value for the d4 class in all dataset, while HH-HV was consistently yielded the lowest mean value for the same class (Table 1). Moreover, the HV and HH-HV were useful to distinguish the p and np classes as they show a larger discrepancy of mean value compared to other parameters. In addition, both PALSAR and PALSAR-2 mosaic data could not discriminate d1, d2, and d3 classes due to the highly overlapping parameter values between those classes. These highly overlapping parameter values were clearly seen in mean and sd values in all parameters for d1, d2 and d3 classes. As for the temporal analysis, there was a slight shift found between parameter values in 2007-2010 data. The bigger shifts in the parameter values were observed in 2007-2015 and 2010-2015 data. These conditions were observed in HH, HV, and HH-HV (Table 2).

DISCUSSION

Each parameter derived from temporal PALSAR/PALSAR-2 mosaic data has particular characteristic to the tropical peatlands classes. HV and HH-HV parameters were consistently produced the highest and lowest mean value for the d4 class in all dataset, respectively.

Table 2 Mean and standard deviation (sd) values of the ortho-rectified and slope corrected backscatter coefficient (γ^o) of tropical peatlands classes for each parameter.

Year	Parameter	d1		d2		d3		d4		p		np	
		Mean	Sd	Mean	Sd	Mean	Sd	Mean	Sd	Mean	Sd	Mean	Sd
2007	HH	-7.3	1.0	-7.6	1.1	-7.4	1.0	-7.3	0.8	-7.4	0.9	-7.5	1.3
	HV	-13.6	1.6	-13.4	1.8	-13.6	1.7	-12.6	1.4	-13.0	1.6	-14.0	1.7
	HH/HV	0.5	0.1	0.6	0.1	0.5	0.1	0.6	0.0	0.6	0.1	0.5	0.1
	HV/HH	1.9	0.2	1.8	0.4	1.9	0.2	1.7	0.2	1.8	0.2	1.9	0.2
	HH-HV	6.2	1.1	5.8	1.2	6.2	1.4	5.3	1.0	5.6	1.2	6.5	1.2
2010	HH	-7.1	1.1	-7.4	1.1	-7.7	0.9	-7.3	0.8	-7.4	0.9	-7.2	1.2
	HV	-13.5	1.5	-13.4	1.6	-13.9	1.6	-12.7	1.3	-13.0	1.5	-13.8	1.6
	HH/HV	0.5	0.1	0.6	0.1	0.6	0.1	0.6	0.1	0.6	0.1	0.5	0.1
	HV/HH	1.9	0.2	1.8	0.2	1.8	0.2	1.8	0.2	1.8	0.2	1.9	0.3
	HH-HV	6.4	1.1	5.9	1.2	6.3	1.3	5.4	1.0	5.7	1.2	6.6	1.1
2015	HH	-7.8	1.0	-8.5	1.3	-8.3	1.1	-8.1	1.2	-8.2	1.2	-8.0	1.4
	HV	-14.9	1.4	-15.2	2.0	-15.2	1.7	-14.0	2.1	-14.4	2.1	-15.4	1.7
	HH/HV	0.5	0.1	0.6	0.1	0.5	0.1	0.6	0.1	0.6	0.1	0.5	0.1
	HV/HH	1.9	0.2	1.8	0.2	1.9	0.3	1.7	0.2	1.8	0.2	1.9	0.3
	HH-HV	7.0	1.2	6.8	1.3	6.9	1.6	5.9	1.4	6.3	1.5	7.3	1.3

The combinations of a different transmit and receive channel that presented in HV as well as the subtraction between HH and HV show a higher sensitivity to the existence of tropical peatlands, especially for the very deep (more than 400 cm of depth) tropical peatlands. Moreover, both HV and HH-HV could also be used to discriminate the p and np classes as they show a larger discrepancy of mean value compared to other parameters. Therefore, these parameters could identify the existence of tropical peatlands, especially for the purpose of classification. However, for d1, d2 and d3 classes, both PALSAR and PALSAR-2 mosaics were unable to discriminate these shallow, medium and deep tropical peatlands due to the highly overlapping parameter values between those classes. These classes showed similar characteristic as observed in all parameters derived from the dataset. The temporal analysis shows that there was a slight shift between parameter values in 2007-2010 data. This slight shift might be occurs due to the LULC changes between observation time. However, there were bigger shifts found in 2007-2015 and 2010-2015 data. These bigger shifts might be occurs due to the rapid LULC changes and the different sensor sensitivity between PALSAR and PALSAR-2. As a concern, these shifts were clearly seen in HH, HV, and HH-HV.

CONCLUSION

In conclusion, the study shows that HV and HH-HV were prominent to characterize tropical peatlands using time series PALSAR and PALSAR-2 mosaics data. Additionally, the temporal analysis shows that there was a considerable shift on the produced mean value of the ortho-rectified and slope corrected backscatter coefficient (γ^o) generated by PALSAR and PALSAR-2, particularly in the context of tropical peatlands monitoring. Finally, this study should aid to improve the state of knowledge about tropical peatlands monitoring, especially involving the use of L-band dual-polarimetric SAR. In terms of future research, findings obtained from this study ought to be used as considerations for further analysis and developing methodology to classify tropical peatlands using remote sensing application.

ACKNOWLEDGEMENTS

The authors would like to thank the *Badan Informasi Geospasial* (BIG) of Republic of Indonesia for providing the topographic maps, the Indonesian Agency for Agricultural Research and Development (IAARD) for providing the peat map and land use/cover maps, and the Japan Aerospace Exploration Agency (JAXA) for providing the temporal PALSAR/PALSAR-2 mosaic data.

REFERENCES

1. Hoekman, D., and Vissers, M., 2007, *ALOS PALSAR radar observation of tropical peat swamp forest as a monitoring tool for environmental protection and restoration*. In International Geoscience and Remote Sensing Symposium, Barcelona, IEEE International, pp. 3710-3714.
2. Jaenicke, J., Rieley, J. O., Mott, C., Kimman, P., and Siegert, F., 2008, *Determination of the amount of carbon stored in Indonesian peatlands*. Geoderma, Vol. 147, pp. 151-158.
3. Jauhiainen, J., Hidenori, T., Juha, E. P. H., Pertti, J. M., and Harri, V., 2005, *Carbon fluxes from a tropical peatswamp forest floor*. Global Change Biology, Vol. 11, pp. 1788-1797.

4. JAXA, 2016, *Global 25m resolution PALSAR-2/PALSAR mosaic and forest/non-forest map (FNF) dataset description*.
5. Page, S. E., Siegert, F., Rieley, J. O., Boehm, H. V., Jaya, A., and Limin, S., 2002, *The amount of carbon released from peat and forest fires in Indonesia during 1997*. Nature, Vol. 420, pp. 61-65.
6. Page, S. E., Rieley, J. O., and Banks, C. J., 2011, *Global and regional importance of tropical peatland carbon pool*. Global Change Biology, Vol.17, No. 2, pp. 798-818.
7. Rieley, J. O., Wüst, R. A. J., Jauhiainen J., Page, S. E., Wösten, H., Hooijer, A., Siegert, F., Limin, S. H., Vasander, H., and Stahlhut, M., 2008, *Tropical peatlands: carbon stores, carbon gas emission and contribution to climate change processes*. In Peatlands and Climate Changes edited by M. Strack, International Peat Society, pp. 148-181.
8. Wahyunto, Supriatna, W. & Agus, F., 2012. *ALOS satellite data to explore areal extent of peatland. Case study: Kubu Raya District, West Kalimantan Province*. In Report and proceedings of ALOS application and verification project in Indonesia, LAPAN and JAXA pp. 26-31.

1.4: PEATLAND CONSERVATION AND MANAGEMENT

Abstract No: A-272

25 YEARS OF TROPICAL PEATLAND RESEARCH: A REVIEW

J. O. Rieley[1,2]

[1]*The University of Nottingham, UK*
[2]*International Peatland Society, Finland*

**Corresponding author: jack.rieley@btinternet.com*

SUMMARY

The presence of peat in Riau, Sumatra was noted as long ago as 1794. It was referred to by several explorers in the 19th Century who described vast areas of lowland peatland in Kalimantan and Sumatra. However, it wasn't until the 1930s that scientific studies were carried out on them by Polak who investigated their genesis, botanical diversity and agricultural potential over a period of 20 years. There seems to have been little interest in peatlands in Malaysia until the 1950s when Coulter carried out a detailed survey of their agricultural potential, estimating there were some 800,000 hectares of peatland in Peninsular Malaya. This was followed by other researchers on peatland in Malaysia, especially Anderson who carried out detailed ecological studies in Sarawak and Brunei. Little emphasis was placed upon study of peatlands in Indonesia during the first quarter century of the Republic but interest accelerated in the 1970s because of the need to increase domestic food production for its rapidly increasing population. In spite of the lack of nutrients, poor physical properties and remoteness of most peatland in Indonesia large areas were developed for agriculture and settlement over the ensuing 25 years. The next major period of interest in tropical peatlands research started around 1991 at the *International Symposium on Tropical Peatlands* that was held here in Kuching. This led to me combining with Susan Page of the UK, Gaston Sieffermann of France and Bambang Setiadi and Suwido Limin of Indonesia to commence field studies of the ecology, biodiversity and chemical and physical properties of peatland and peat in the upper catchment of Sg. Sabangau in Central Kalimantan. From small beginnings this led to major inter- and multidisciplinary projects funded by the European Union spanning more than 10 years and involving more than 100 scientists, researchers, students and assistants.

Keywords: -

INTRODUCTION

My journey on tropical peatland began 30 years ago almost by accident. I was on study leave in 1986/7 visiting a former Ph.D. student at the University of Malaya, Kuala Lumpur when I decided to attend a conference in Yogyakarta on 'Tropical Peat and Peatlands for Development'. After the conference I went on a field excursion to Kalimantan, first to Palangkaraya in Central Kalimantan and then to Pontianak in West Kalimantan, to view tropical peat and peatland for the very first time. This was an 'eye-opener' for me since before this visit I hadn't known that tropical peat existed. Unfortunately we only visited peat research stations and areas where peatland was being used for small farmer agriculture or evaluated for larger scale projects such as the potential of using peat for energy generation and I never saw the peat swamp forest ecosystem at close range. The excursion, however, made me determined to find a way to get closer and assess the prospects for carrying out field research on it. In this respect it was fortunate I made the acquaintance during the excursion of Gaston Sieffermann a soil scientist who worked for the French overseas aid agency (ORSTOM) and who had spent much of his life investigating tropical soils in Amazonia and Indonesia.

Back in Kuala Lumpur I realised that there was little interest or scope for research into tropical peatland Peninsular Malaysia where much had already been converted to rice padi, oil palm, pinapple and rubber plantations while the remainder was impacted severely as a result of excessive logging and drainage. Most of what was left was near to the coast in the states of Selangor, Perak, Pahang and Johor while the largest area remaining in Malaysia, some 2.5 million hectares, was located in Sarawak where I did not have any contacts. I decided to focus my tropical peatland ambitions on Indonesia but realised this could take several years to bring to fruition. What was I to do in the meantime so I could return to the region to promote my ambitions? The answer was provided by British Council but for a completely different project!

URBAN GREENING IN KUALA LUMPUR

A major focus of my research in the United Kingdom had been urban ecology, including the importance of urban green spaces, especially informal ones, as reservoirs of biodiversity and potential areas for nature conservation, education, and amenity and leisure activities. I had carried out green space surveys of several cities and their conurbations in England, including Nottingham, Norwich and Tyne and Wear and built up a network of British and international contacts, some of whom I would meet during my study leave. This led me to consider if there might also be opportunities in the tropics for similar studies since nothing like this had been attempted there. I was pleasantly surprised therefore, to find several researchers at the University of Malaya (UM) who were interested in my previous work, in particular Professor Lim Teck Ghee, socio-economist and Richard Dorrall, remote senser and GIS expert of the Institute of Applied Studies and Teh Tiong Sa of the Department of Geography who were keen to apply my methods to the entire 273 square kilometres of the Federal Territory of Kuala Lumpur. We obtained funding from British Council to establish a Higher Education Link (HEL) between the University of Nottingham and the University of Malaya. The objectives were to carry out a detailed survey of the location, size and nature of green spaces, of minimum area one hectare, within the Federal Territory. These would be achieved by using a combination of aerial photographs, remote sensing, detailed maps and ground checking to assess their potential for biodiversity and wildlife conservation. The information would be transferred to a Geographical Information System and the results presented to the Mayor and Principal Planning Officers of Kuala Lumpur with recommendations for action to promote integration of green space planning and urban wildlife conservation into the Federal Territory Government planning process. The University of Malaya provided co-funding for some sraff to undertake the mapping and I was joined by Susan Page of the University of Leicester and Peter Shepherd of the University of Nottingham for the field checking and evaluation of urban green spaces.

The Urban Greens HEL link operated for three years ending with a Malaysia National Symposium on Urban Green Space but, because the issue turned out to be politically sensitive and was regarded as a possible constraint to the development of the Federal Territory that was taking place at a rapid rate, we were unable to convince the Mayor and City Council of Kuala Lumpur that they should take on board our recommendations.

TRANSFER OF INTEREST TO TROPICAL PEATLAND

Since the urban greens project in KL seemed to have no immediate future, and with DFID withdrawing its funding for CICHE, I decided to concentrate my efforts on tropical peatlands. I had advanced my ambition of researching tropical peat swamp forest when I attended the 8th International Peat Congress in Leningrad in August 1988 where I met Gaston Sieffermann once more. He had described to me the lowland tropical peat swamps of Indonesia and the wonderful rain forest that grew there and had formed the peat over thousands of years. I accepted his offer to meet him in Yogyakarta to discuss the possibility of visiting peat swamp forest in Central Kalimantan in 1989.

1989 was a significant year in another respect because Hidenori Takahashi, whom I had visited in Hokkaido, Japan during my study leave peatland tour in 1987, came to the University of Nottingham to commence 10 months of study leave collaboration with me on ecology, microclimatology and conservation of Chartley Moss National Nature Reserve, Staffordshire. This close relationship gave us the opportunity to discuss and formulate plans for joint work on peatland in Central Kalimantan, Indonesia. Our plans advanced further when I visited him in Hokkaido in August 1990 and on a subsequent visit in 1992. This reinforced my relationship with Dr. Takahashi who became a committed member of the research team working on tropical peatland in Central Kalimantan.

Through my activities in Peninsular Malaysia and my interest in peatland there I was invited to speak at the 'International Symposium on Tropical Peat' that was held here in Kuching at the beginning of May 1991, organised by the Malaysian Agricultural Research and Development Institute (MARDI) and Department of Agriculture, Sarawak. This was an honour for me but I was somewhat apprehensive because the topic I was asked to deliver on was tropical peatland and so far I had not carried out any of my own work on it. Not to be put off, I delivered my presentation on 'The Ecology of Tropical Peat Swamp Forest – a Southeast Asian Perspective' based on literature, the 1987 Conference and my visits to Central Kalimantan peatlands in the company of Gaston Sieffermann. It is published in the proceedings of the Kuching Symposium that also contains numerous other presentation of greater importance to tropical peatland and peat than mine.

The Kuching meeting was important in other ways to the future of my research intentions on tropical peatland. In preparing my presentation I had drawn heavily for background on the publications and work of Robb Anderson who had carried out benchmark studies of peat swamp forest in Sarawak and Brunei in the 1950s and 60s and he was a guest at this symposium. He was rather frail because of being ill with leishmaniasis but his presence was a great encouragement to us younger peatland scientists. Robb was become of great assistance to me later in identifying many of the peat swamp trees.

It was also at this Kuching Symposium in 1991 that I met another person who was to have a major influence on the course of my research on tropical peatland, Bambang Setiadi. Bambang was a young researcher who worked for the Indonesian Agency for the Assessment and Implementation of Technology (BPPT) of the Ministry of Technology. He was undertaking a Ph.D. on peatland agronomy at Gadjah Mada University in Yogyakarta. He was impressed by my presentation and we spent time discussing my plans and problems and he offered to help. We became good friends and have worked together for the last 25 years. Without him I would have been unable to understand and work through the beaurocracy of the Indonesian Government procedures and systems. In addition, he introduced me to Suwido Limin, lecturer at the University of Palangka Raya (UNPAR), Central Kalimantan, who would be the person who would make everything in the field possible from finding the study location, establishing its base camp, allocating Indonesian students to help and providing all of the logistics to make the venture possible and sustainable. The four most important people to me who through their belief and support made it possible to carry out a very large programme of research on tropical peatland in Central Kalimantan linked to education and postgraduate training of numerous staff of UNPAR are Gaston Sieffermann, Bambang Setiadi, Suwido Limin and my wife Susan Page. Susan provided the moral and academic support that kept me going even when times were hard and things looked impossible.

SETIA ALAM JAYA

I visited Central Kalimantan in again in 1992 with Gaston Siefferman to find a suitable base from which to carry out ecological research on natural peat swamp forest. Whilst in Indonesia, I contacted the British Council office in Jakarta to discuss my intentions and find out if there was an opportunity for funding. I was well-received and came away with the first of several travel grants to visit the University of Palangka Raya in Central Kalimantan with which I forged a formal partnership that was funded subsequently through two successive HEL Link projects. As a result, I decided to commence research in mid-July of 1993 and the pressure to find a suitable field base mounted.

I visited several logging concessions in peat swamp forest in the company of Gaston Sieffermann and, after several abortive attempts, finally settled on that of Pt. Setia Alam Jaya in the upper catchment of the River (Sungai) Sabangau as the most suitable place to commence field surveys. The timber extraction railway at this concession ran almost at right angles to the river, extending onto the peat dome about 20 km away and provided a near perfect transect line along which to carry out field investigations of the forest. An agreement was negotiated with the concession contractor for the use of facilities in the logging base camp near to Sg. Sabangau and the railway to move researchers to and from study sites along it. This was formalised by the Provincial Government authorities in Palangka Raya. We started field work in July 1993 and although we were in business and British Council provided us with a couple of travel grants to consolidate collaboration with UNPAR, there was no money to fund either the base camp or field data collection activities. This problem was overcome in the first year by combining with Earthwatch UK to enable volunteers from around the world, mostly the USA, to participate in the field research. This provided a small income with which to build accommodation in the field and purchase basic survey equipment for the enumeration of forest trees and keys for identification of animals and plants. We also obtained a small grant from the Conservation Foundation UK that enabled us to pay for some Indonesian students to collaborate. After the first year we operated very effectively with groups of students, mainly from the universities of Nottingham and Leicester, UK who organised their own travel arrangements and worked continuously in the field for one to two months at a time in company with students from the University of Palangka Raya.

For the first few years research focussed on basic aspects of peat swamp forest ecology including, biodiversity, tree enumeration and structure, biomass and peat and water chemistry. In addition, we surveyed the peat surface levels every 500 metres from the river to the peat dome watershed, a distance of 25 km and determined the thickness of the peat over the same distance. We produced the first detailed inventory of tropical peat swamp forest ecological characteristics, and formulated plans for biodiversity and wildlife conservation, that have become the benchmark with which all subsequent studies of this ecosystem are compared. The field research activities were extended in 1994 and 1995, culminating in an international symposium on tropical peatland that was held in Palangka Raya in September 1995. The proceedings of this meeting were published as a book entitled "Biodiversity and Sustainability of Tropical Peatlands" containing 42 papers and statements on many aspects of tropical peatland.

DISAPPOINTMENTS AND SUCCESSES

By the end of 1995 we had achieved all of our initial research and training objectives, especially quality field research involving more than 20 international peatland scientists and over 100 volunteers. In addition, we had held an international symposium accumulated a large data base of primary information and made numerous presentations at scientific meetings in the UK, Indonesia, Malaysia and Japan and some scientific papers were published. Several things were happening, however, over which we had no control and were to have profound implications for the future direction of our work. The first, and most serious, was cessation of the logging concession, which was due to take place by the end in 1996, in common with most other timber operations in peat swamp forest in Kalimantan when their 20 year licences expired. This threatened our entire research programme because we could lose access into the peat swamp forest. We managed to obtain a postponement of this closure until the end of 1997 but, for two years, we had to work against the clock as the company lifted its rail tracks. Secondly, we learned of the Mega Rice Project, promoted by President Suharto, to convert a million hectares of wetland, mostly peatland, in Central Kalimantan to rice cultivation. This ill-conceived development project was supposed to replace one million hectares of prime rice padi that had been lost to commercial and industrial development in Java, with consequential loss of Indonesia's self-sufficiency in this staple food since the mid-1980s when Suharto has been awarded a medal by the FAO. Thirdly, but more promising, were applications I was making for core funding for tropical peatland research to the UK Darwin Initiative and the EU.

The loss of base camp facilities and access to the peat swamp forest was the most serious immediate threat to the entire research programme because maintaining a bridgehead near to Sg. Sabangau and creating and maintaining access routes into the jungle were difficult logistically, time consuming and expensive. We had little money for our research never mind the large sums needed to provide and safeguard infrastructure. The first step we took was to establish the official status of this important field research facility and, in 1998, we persuaded Nasution, then Indonesian Minister of Forestry, to transfer, by Decree, management of a 500 square kilometre section of peat swamp forest in the Sabangau catchment to the BPPT Division of the Ministry of Research and Technology, under the direction of Dr. Bambang Setiadi and designate it the "Natural Laboratory for Sustainable Management of Tropical Peat Swamp Forest" (NAMTROP). This was the first research station for tropical peat swamp forest and its day to day management was vested in the "Centre for International Cooperation in Management of Tropical Peatland" (CIMTROP) of the University of Palangka Raya, under the directorship of Suwido Limin.

Initially, commencement of the Mega Rice Project (MRP) was a major setback to our long term ambitions for sustainable management of peat swamp forest in Central Kalimantan. We had believed, perhaps naively, that our studies would reinforce the case for conservation of a large area of this important ecosystem. This disastrous project would destroy one million hectares of wetland, mostly peatland in one go! We felt let down and helpless when the magnitude of the proposal became clear but, in those days, under the rule of President Suharto it was not possible to voice dissent or express contrary opinions. The MRP did not include the Sg. Sabangau peatland area where we carried out most of our field research but it came right up to it along the east bank of the river and there would be major knock on effects over time because of drainage and increased access by people. Our disappointment did not last long, however, because it was realised that the MRP presented a new opportunity for research by using our data to monitor the impact of this huge development project on tropical peatland and include this information in funding applications. This became even more important when the deforested, drained and degraded MRP landscape went on fire in 1997 as it has done almost every year since then releasing large amounts of carbon to the atmosphere and contributing to climate change processes.

A NEW DAWN - FUNDING GALORE!

Perhaps it was fate, or maybe our research had 'come of age', or more likely we happened to be in the right place at the right time because our proposals to both the Darwin Initiative and the EU (EUTROP) were successful. The former was entitled "Impacts of Land Use Change and Fire on Peatland in Central Kalimantan" and the latter "Natural Resource Functions, Biodiversity and Sustainable Management of Tropical Peatland". The background information for both proposals was derived from the four years of field research (1993-1997), towards which British Council had contributed funding at a critical time, and through the HEL link that brought together key scientists from the UK and Indonesia and enabled them to collaborate.

From 1998 we entered into a new era of field-based research and capacity development. The Darwin Project lasted for three and a half years until March 2002. It contained, obviously, a large element of field based data collection following on from our preliminary studies but now this was carried out mostly by UNPAR staff, four of whom were being trained at the University of Nottingham to obtained masters' degrees funded from the Darwin budget. The EUTROP Project lasted four years until the end of September 2002 and it included study of the impact of the failed MRP and fire on tropical peatland and the implications of these for sustainable management of these vast landscapes. This budget also allowed for the training, at the University of Nottingham, of two doctoral and one master's candidates from UNPAR.

As a result of this greatly increased funding and the large number of scientists participating, the surveys of biodiversity and ecological functions of peat swamp forest were extended and comparisons made between pristine, logged, degraded and developed tropical peatland. The extent of, and damage caused by the 1997 El Niño fires were determined and assessment made of the impact of this catastrophic event on the biodiversity and sustainability of this ecosystem and the implications for the global environment. In addition, the resource capacity of UNPAR was increased considerably in terms of both staff and support infrastructure. CIMTROP was placed on a more stable financial footing; the Natural Laboratory base camp and service facilities were repaired and upgraded; the Darwin Herbarium was created in which specimens of all plants found in the peatland areas were identified and stored; and staff were trained in aspects of environmental science and management. British Council contributed in many different ways to these developments through the HEL link.

By the end of the Darwin and first EU Project (EUTROP) in 2002 the stage was set for the future. We had accumulated sufficient information to understand the ecology and functioning of the tropical peatland ecosystem and evaluate the impacts upon it of land use change and fire. We also knew to what extent peat swamp forests underpinned the livelihoods of local people and what they did in response to its degradation or loss. UNPAR now had a large body of young researchers trained in this knowledge and capable of making sound use of it, largely as a result of the catalytic effect of the first Nottingham/UNPAR HEL link. Unfortunately, the Indonesian Local and National Government authorities did not have our knowledge and understanding and seemed to be unwilling to embrace this new scientific information and put our recommendations into practice.

The success of the Darwin and EUTROP projects led to subsequent applications to the EU for additional funding and these were successful. STRAPEAT (Strategies for Implementing Sustainable Management of Tropical Peatland) operated from 2001 to 2004; RESTORPEAT (Restoration of Tropical Peatland for the Sustainable Management of Renewable Natural Resources) commenced in 2004 and will terminate at the end of 2007; CARBOPEAT (Carbon-Climate-Human Interactions in Tropical Peatland) commenced in January 2007 and will run until December 2008. With each of these projects the scientific partnership has grown from three in the Darwin Initiative to 14 in RESTORPEAT and so has the size of successive budgets from £120,000 to 1.45 million Euros!

The EU projects enabled us to train a much larger number of young researchers than before and every partner had obligations in this respect. We were now able to train a few of the most capable and promising researchers to obtain Ph.D. degrees as well as many more for masters' degrees. UNPAR staff, for example, studied at the universities of Nottingham, Gadjah Mada and Sriwijaya whilst Universiti Sains Malaysia, Penang and Universiti Malaysia Sarawak trained some of their own researchers. Other postgraduate degrees were obtained by European candidates in the Universities of Leicester, Nottingham, Helsinki, Munich and Wageningen. Our overall efforts intensified and the impact of our activities increased considerably from 1998 to the present day.

As a result of our research and training activities UNPAR, through CIMTROP, became a major focus for scientific and socio-economic research on tropical peatland while capacity building of staff and resources proceeded apace. Another consequence of our work on tropical peatland was that, following recommendations of a National Seminar on Tropical Peatland held in Jakarta in 1999, President Habibie formally closed down the Mega Rice Project and issued directives for the future development of this peatland landscape. We held our second international symposium on tropical peatland in Jakarta in 2001 entitled *"Peatlands for People: Natural Resource Functions and Sustainable Management"*. This was another benchmark meeting and once again British Council was one of the sponsors. The proceedings, published in 2002, contains 37 oral papers and 7 posters covering a wide range of topics related to tropical peatland, including ecological and natural resource functions, hydrology, peat soils and their properties, impact of fire and land use change, role of tropical peatlands as carbon stores and sinks and their importance in climate change processes, socio-economic importance of tropical peatlands and their value to local communities and wise use and sustainable development.

As our work continued it became apparent that fire control was the greatest obstacle to sustainable development in Central Kalimantan, not only in the peatland areas, and that poverty was increasing and was much higher than the national average. On reflection, as I reach the twilight of my academic and research career I am satisfied with what I have done. If I had the opportunity to live the last 20 years over again I would not wish to do anything differently.

ACKNOWLEDGEMENTS

The people who have been involved or helped at the various stages of my research activities in Southeast Asia are far too numerous to mention but I acknowledge sincerely all of their contributions to my success. In particular, however, I thank the following British Council Staff for their assistance, kindness and understanding: Andrew Norris of British Council Kuala Lumpur; Richard Phillips and Neil Kemp and Muriel Dunbar, successive Directors of British Council, Jakarta and their colleagues Alan Rogerson, Nick Mawdsley and Maggie Dewiyani. I have always had tremendous assistance from the British Embassy in Jakarta, especially Richard Gozney who provided his residence for a critical meeting, and also Charles Humfrey the present incumbent. I have experienced four UNPAR Rektors and many Vice Rektors during my association with that university and I mention in particular Professor Idris Makmur, Professor Ali Hasymi (the late), Professor Napa Awat and Professor Henry Singarasa. I also wish to express my sincere thanks to the many Indonesian and Malaysian colleagues who believed in me and helped promote research and capacity building in those two countries, especially Bambang Setiadi (Deputy Minister of Research and Technology, Government of Indonesia), Suwido Limin (Director of the Centre for International Co-operation in Sustainable Management of Tropical Peatland (CIMTROP), University of Palangka Raya, Indonesia, Dr. Abdul-Aziz Ahmad Shah (the late), Professor Lim Tech Ghee and Teh Tiong Sa of the University of Malaya and Professor Mashhor Mansor, Universiti Sains Malaysia, Penang. A special mention must be made of my wife Dr. Susan Page, University of Leicester who contributed to and shared in most of what is described in this chapter. Last, but certainly not least I pay the strongest tribute to Gaston Sieffermann who introduced me to tropical peat swamp forest and started it all. I salute you! (GS passed away in 2001 but supported this work to the end.)

Abstract No: A-411

A FIELD STUDY OF THE TRIPA PEAT SWAMPS

G. Usher, M.G. Nowak and I. Singleton

Sumatran Orangutan Conservation Programme (PanEco-YEL), Indonesia

**Corresponding author: kimabajo1@gmail.com*

SUMMARY

In 2012, amidst the backdrop of devastating environmental management in Tripa, Aceh, Sumatra, Indonesia, non-governmental organization the Yayasan Ekosistem Lestari (YEL) undertook a conservation programme in the peat swamps of the region. This combined three interrelated aspects, socio-economic development, field research/surveys, and peatland rehabilitation. Despite the fact that Tripa was previously mapped and surveyed by other stakeholders, a detailed understanding of its peat swamps was until then hampered by the broad scale utilized, small sample sizes, non-random sampling, and ineffective post-collection analyses/calculations. This presentation thus reports the results of our regional field survey conducted from June 2013 – March 2014. This represents an in-depth analysis of the Tripa swamps, including: 1) a delineation of the remaining peatland area; 2) an estimate of peat depths; 3) an analysis of soil characteristics across various land cover types, and relative to various forest disturbance levels; and 4) an estimate of below-ground carbon stocks. As such, we provide a much improved understanding of this peatland, its local, national, and global value, and insight into current and future conservation and rehabilitation processes for Tripa and other peatlands across the world.

Keywords: *Tripa, tropical peatland, below-ground carbon stock*

INTRODUCTION

Peatlands are known to be a vital component to global carbon stocks, the degradation of which can lead to the emission of greenhouse gases into the atmosphere, and as such, peatlands are intimately linked to global climate/environmental change processes (Rieley & Page, 2005). While the majority of peatlands can be found in boreal and temperate areas, tropical peatlands represent an important contribution to global carbon storage (Page *et al.*, 2011). Indonesia, which is currently estimated to have a below-ground peatland carbon pool of ~27 Gt, has the largest known tropical peatland carbon stock in the world (Agus *et al.*, 2013). Unfortunately, Indonesia has also been documented as having an unprecedented amount of forest loss in recent years (Hansen *et al.*, 2013), with a considerable amount of this forest loss occurring on peatland areas (Koh *et al.*, 2011). On Sumatra alone, for example, it was estimated that between 1985-2007 that a total of 39% of all swamp forests were cleared, with a total of 51% of all peat swamp forests being deforested during the same period of time (Laumonier *et al.*, 2010). Given that the Indonesian Government has promised to reduce CO2 emissions by 26-41% (amounting to 0.67-1.04 Gt CO2e) by 2020 in the forestry and peatland sectors (Presidential Regulation No. 61/2011), the conservation of even the smallest extents of Indonesia's peatland must be considered a high priority.

The Tripa peat swamps are located on the west coast of the Province of Aceh, Indonesia, where they overlap two local districts, Aceh Barat Daya and Nagan Raya. Up until 1990, the Tripa peat swamps were covered by nearly 61,000 ha of primary forest and were tremendously biodiverse, including the currently Critically Endangered Sumatran orangutan (*Pongo abelii*) and Sumatran tiger (*Panthera tigris sumatrae*). During the 1990's, the Tripa peat swamps fell victim to the expansion of oil palm concessions and small-scale agricultural, with nearly 35,000 ha of primary forest being converted during this time. It wasn't until 1998-1999 that deforestation and land clearing was gradually reduced by the escalating violence of the Aceh civil conflict. Nevertheless, following the 2004 Aceh tsunami and subsequent 2005 Helsinki Peace Accord, deforestation (both 'illegal' and 'legal') would again plague the Tripa peat swamps. As of 2013, it was estimated that only 9,500 ha of primary forest remain, which amounts to roughly an 84% loss of forested area during the years 1990-2013. Enigmatically, prior to much of this deforestation, Tripa was firmly established as part of the Leuser Ecosystem which became a National Strategic Area (NSA) for its Environmental Function under national spatial planning law in 2007 (National Law No. 26/2007) and 2008 (Government Regulation No. 26/2008).

In May 2011, President Susilo Bambang Yudhoyono signed a moratorium preventing new concessions in primary forests and on peatlands. This moratorium was ultimately the result of a USD 1 billion pledge by the Government of Norway, as a way to help Indonesia reduce the carbon emissions related to deforestation and forest degradation. Shortly after, in August 2011, Aceh's then Governor, Irwandi Yusuf approved a new concession permit in Tripa for the palm oil company PT Kallista Alam, on land clearly off limits under Indonesia's moratorium, and also within the Leuser Ecosystem NSA. This decision was challenged in Aceh's courts by local NGO WALHI Aceh. The case was subsequently won after appeal to the higher court in Medan and Aceh's new Governor (Zaini Abdullah) cancelled the permit accordingly.

In addition, as a result of massive national and international interest in the case, Indonesia's National Government took interest and investigative teams were sent to the field on several occasions, investigating not only the legality and activities of PT Kallista Alam, but also those of the other major companies still operating in Tripa. Namely PT Surya Panen Subur 2, PT Cemerlang Abadi, PT Gelora Sawita Makmur, and PT Dua Perkasa Lestari. These investigations led to several more legal cases being filed against all the major companies, including several civil cases filed by the Ministry of Environment, and criminal cases brought by the state, mostly based on illegal use of fire to clear forests on deep peatland.

Some of these cases have already been decided, but a number are still under appeal. The civil case against PT Kallista Alam found the company guilty and ordered them to pay approximately USD 11 million compensation to the state and to spend USD 23 million to restore the forest in the concession to its former condition. The courts also found the company's Director and Field Manager guilty of illegal practices, sentencing them to 8 months and 3 years in prison, respectively.

In December 2013, the current Government of Aceh ratified a new spatial plan (Qanun RTRWA) that contravenes a number of national laws and completely ignores the existence of the Leuser Ecosystem NSA. If that wasn't bad enough, on 12th February 2014, the Governor of Aceh signed a new Regulation, Governor's Regulation No 5, 2014, outlining "Procedures and guidelines for OBTAINING NEW PERMITS within the Leuser Ecosystem in Aceh".

In 2012, amidst the backdrop of Tripa's devastating past, the Yayasan Ekosistem Lestari (YEL) undertook a large conservation project in the Tripa peat swamps. The overall project combines three interrelated aspects, including local socio-economy, field research/survey, and peatland rewetting/rehabilitation. This report presents the results of a large field survey that was conducted by YEL during June 2013 – March 2014 in the Tripa peat swamps. Despite the fact that Tripa has previously been mapped and surveyed (e.g., H Darul Sukma WP *et al.*, 1990; Wahyunto *et al.*, 2003; Agus & Wahdini 2008; Van Belle & Hennin 2008; Sufardi *et al.*, 2013), a detailed understanding of the Tripa peat swamps is still hampered by the broad scale utilized during the majority of these surveys, small sample sizes, non-random sample locations, and ineffective post-collection analyses/calculations. The results of these studies, which inaccurately portray Tripa as being currently devoid of rich peatlands, have facilitated the expansion of exploitive activities in the area. In contrast to previous studies, the current study represents an in depth analysis of the Tripa peat swamps, which seeks to prove that the Tripa peat swamps maintain an expansive peatland area and are thus of conservation value. The main focuses of the study include: 1) a delineation of the remaining peatland area; 2) an estimate of peat depths; 3) an analysis of soil characteristics across various land cover types and relative to various forest disturbance levels; and 4) an estimate of below-ground carbon stocks. As such, this study promises to not only provide a more detailed understating of Tripa's peatland areas and their local, national, and global value, but will also aid current and future conservation and rehabilitation processes.

MATERIALS & METHODS

Field Survey

We conducted a field survey between June 2013 – March 2014 in the Tripa peat swamps, located in the Aceh Barat Daya and Nagan Raya Districts of Aceh Province. During the field season, a total of 81 locations were sampled. All locations were randomly chosen by creating a 1 km x 1 km grid atop our 'area of interest' and then randomly generating sample locations. We initially sampled 54 locations; however, following this initial survey, it became clear that the underlying peat substratum is highly complex, and we therefore surveyed an additional 27 random locations to facilitate the delineation of the underlying peat.

For all of the initial 54 sample locations, peat was sampled in 50 cm sections (i.e., the length of the peat auger), and coupled with an inner area of 10 cm^2, produced a total soil sample of 500 cm^3 per each 50 cm sample. Each sample was photographed and then the sample was divided into two portions, an upper 10 cm sample and a lower 40 cm sample, so that laboratory analyses could be conducted. The wet weights for each sample portion were recorded once samples were brought back from the field. At the 27 additional sample locations, only total peat depth was sampled, and as such, no soil samples were taken. For all sample locations, the pH of topsoil was assessed whenever possible.

Laboratory Analysis of Peat Samples

The smaller 100 cm3 portion of a sample was air dried over a series of days and then was ground into a fine powder. These samples were packaged and labeled and then were sent to Tadulako University (Palu, Sulawesi) so that the organic carbon content (%), nitrogen content (%), and the C:N ratio could be calculated for each sample. All analyses were conducted using a CN elemental analyzer.

The larger 400 cm3 portion of a sample was sent to the Indonesian Center for Agricultural Land Resources Research and Development (Bogor, Jawa). These were utilized to calculate the bulk density (t/m3), ash content (%), and organic matter content (%) of a given sample.

Statistical Analysis of Peat Samples

For purposes of comparative analyses, the 54 full core samples were divided by land use type (forest, transitional [non-forested & non-agricultural areas], and agricultural) and then also by time since forest disturbance (i.e., forested, <5 years deforested, >5 years deforested). To test for differences in the calculated chemical and physical soil properties among these two classifications, we compared groupings at specific depth below surface (DBS) levels using Kruskal-Wallis tests with Mann-Whitney post-hoc tests. To correct for multiple comparisons, we employed the Holm stepwise Bonferroni procedure. Due to small sample sizes at DBS levels >300 cm, samples >300 cm DBS were pooled for each land use type and time since forest disturbance level, and then these pooled samples were statistically tested.

Kriging Analysis

Using a combined peat depth sample distribution of 255 useable sample points, including data from Leuser Ecosystem Management Authority (BPKEL) and Floresta 2011 (n=49), World Agroforestry Centre (ICRAF) 2007 (n=12), Universitas Syiah Kuala (UNSYIAH) 2013 (n=98), Yayasan Ekosistem Lestari (YEL) and partners 2007 and 2012 (n=14), and YEL 2013-2014 (n=82), we conducted a kriging analysis to estimate the extent of peatland and to delineate the total area of specific DBS levels in our Tripa peat swamp 'area of interest'. An additional 295 sample points were added to the kriging analysis, and these were placed every 1 km along major rivers (i.e., Batee, Seumanyam, Seuneam, and Tripa Rivers), the ocean's southern coast, and Tripa's northeastern mountain border. These 'non-peat dummy points' were given a zero value and were deemed necessary for the interpolation process of the kriging analysis, due to the complex topography of the area. Nevertheless, given that all 'non-peat dummy points' represent a zero peat value, we feel that the results of the kriging analysis are likely a conservative underrepresentation of Tripa's peatland area.

Using the total 550 sample points, we first fit a variogram and then used the best-fit model to interpolate the remaining unknown peatland area within a 50 m x 50 m prediction grid of our 'area of interest'. We limited the output of our kriging analysis to 11 depth categories, including <25 cm, 26-50 cm, 51-100 cm, 101-200 cm, 201-300 cm, 301-400 cm, 401-500 cm, 501-600 cm, 601-700 cm, 701-800 cm, and >800 cm.

Calculation of Carbon Stock

Using the results of the laboratory and kriging analyses, were able to estimate the total carbon stock in our defined 'area of interest'. In particular, an area for each peat DBS level was calculated and then these values were multiplied by the carbon density value that corresponded to a respective depth level. The total carbon stock in our 'area of interest' is simply the total sum of these values.

RESULTS & DISCUSSION

-The chemical and physical properties of high organic soil samples (i.e., >65% organic matter in upper 50 cm DBS) are highly comparable to the same values from other studies of tropical peat/peat soils. Thus, despite a long history of site disturbance, a large majority of Tripa's peatlands still maintain their organic integrity.

-The primary differences comparing high organic soil samples (i.e., >65% organic matter in upper 50 cm DBS) to non-high organic samples (i.e., <65% organic matter in upper 50 cm DBS) are the generally higher bulk density, greater % ash content, lower % organic carbon content, and lower % nitrogen content in non-high organic samples. However, the differences are not as marked as differences between organic and non-organic soils (Rieley & Page, 2005; Page et al. 2006, 2011), which indicates that the majority of the non-high organic soil samples are still in transition from highly organic soils to that of non-organic/mineral soils.

-When sample data were grouped by land use type, the primary statistically significant differences were in pH content and slope of the depth x carbon content RMA regression. For pH of topsoil, agricultural lands displayed higher values than forested lands, with transitional land use samples displaying an intermediate position. This indicates a more neutral pH value in agricultural lands, likely related to ongoing agricultural practices. Conversely, the depth x carbon content slope of agricultural lands was found to be larger than either forested or transitional land use types. This interesting result is likely related to ongoing soil subsidence/compaction in agricultural lands.

-When data were grouped by time since forest loss, the primary statistically significant differences were in peat depth, organic matter content (<50 cm DBS), and ash content (<50 cm). For all comparisons, the distinctions were between the <5 year forest loss group and the >5 year forest loss group, with forested areas maintaining an intermediate position. This is a highly interesting result and indicates that the lands that are currently being converted are 'high quality' peatlands. This is likely related to a current lack of 'low quality' peatlands in the area.

-The chemical and physical properties of the soil samples that are discussed within this report display a considerable amount of variation within depth below surface levels, land use types, and time since forest loss groupings. This reflects a long complex history of modification, including but not limited to, flooding episodes, drainage, deforestation, forest regrowth, and agricultural development. This large amount of variation may also account for the limited number of statistically significant differences between different land use types and time since forest loss groupings. More specifically, the lack of numerous statistically significant differences from the two aforementioned grouping schemes suggests that current and past land degradation throughout the 'area of interest' is impacting peatlands in the remaining and otherwise pristine forest covered peatland areas. Thus, current anthropogenic disturbances are essentially in the process of homogenizing the peatland area.

-The maximum peat depth found was 850 cm, with an overall peatland average of 346 cm.

-We estimate that there is roughly 53,114 ha (71% of the total 'area of interest') of peatland >50 cm DBS and 20,791 ha of peatland >300 cm DBS (28%% of the total 'area of interest') in our 'area of interest'. Again, we stress that 50 cm is consistently highlighted as a requirement for classifying organic soils as 'peat' (e.g., Rieley & Page, 2005 - and references within). Furthermore, there is little scientific basis for conserving only peatlands >300 cm (e.g., Stahlhut & Rieley, 2007), a commonly cited value from Indonesian Presidential Decree No. 32/1990 that states peatlands >300 cm should be maintained as conservation areas. Here, deferring to scientific study (Rieley & Page, 2005), we recognize all peatland areas >50 cm DBS as areas with 'high conservation value'.

-There is a significant linear relationship between depth below surface and total carbon stock. This has allowed us to more accurately estimate the below-ground carbon stock of our 'area of interest'. We estimate the total below-ground carbon stock within Tripa to be 69,186,242 Mg. For peatland areas >50 cm DBS, the estimated below-ground carbon stock is 66,703,359 Mg (96.4% of the total carbon stock in our 'area of interest').

-When comparing peatland area and below-ground carbon stock to Indonesia and Sumatra, Tripa makes up roughly 0.35% of Indonesia's 15 Mha of peatland and 0.25% of Indonesia's estimated 27,000,000,000 Mg below-ground peat carbon stock. Conversely, Tripa makes up roughly 0.83% of Sumatra's 6.4 Mha of peatland and 0.56% of Sumatra's estimated 12,000,000,000 Mg below-ground peat carbon stock (Agus et al. 2013).

-We estimate that in the period leading up to Indonesia's 2011 moratorium on deforestation that between 35,310,534 – 51,849,534 Mg CO2 were released from Tripa into the atmosphere. CO2 emissions are predicted to continue to increase, provided that deforestation continues at its average rate.

CONCLUSION

In view of the massive damage that has already been inflicted on the Tripa peat swamp forests, many doubt whether the area has any future conservation value. However, field visits in 2005 to some of the inactive oil palm plantations showed that if left undisturbed, the drainage canals close up and self-regeneration of natural vegetation can occur quite quickly. Furthermore, our results highlight that forest loss does not immediately equate with peat loss, that Tripa still harbors a relatively large carbon stock, and that further degradation of the area would lead to a significant amount of carbon emissions. Thus, there is still hope for the Tripa peat swamp forests, but only if the remaining forest areas can be protected, the draining of the swamps stopped, and plantations found breaching the law be evicted.

ACKNOWLEDGEMENTS

This report would not have been possible without field and manuscript contributions from the following individuals: Adji Darsoyo (YEL), Anto Indrianto (YEL), Diana Kosmanto (YEL), Fahmuddin Agus (Indonesian Agency for Agricultural Research), Gunung Gea (YEL), Hermansyah (YEL), Mistar Kamsi (YEL), Nuzuar (YEL), Riswan Zein (YEL), Sugesti (YEL), and Suratman (YEL). We are indebted to Floresta, the Leuser Ecosystem Management Authority (BPKEL), Universitas Syiah Kuala (UNSYIAH), and the World Agroforestry Centre (ICRAF) for sharing their peat depth data, in addition to all who participated in early surveys of the Tripa peat swamps. This report was prepared with financial support from KEHATI's Tropical Forest Conservation Action

(TFCA)-Sumatra; however, we note that the content of this report does not necessarily reflect the opinion of KEHATI TFCA-Sumatra.

REFERENCES

1. Agus F, Wahdini W. 2008. Assessment of carbon stock of peatland at Tripa, Nagan Raya District, Nanggroe Aceh Darussalam Province of Indonesia. Unpublished field report.
2. Agus F, Henson IE, Sahardjo BH, Harris N, van Noordwijk M, Killeen TJ. 2013. Review of emission factors for assessment of CO2 emission from land use change to oil palm in Southeast Asia. Reports from the Technical Panels of the 2nd Greenhouse Gas Working Group of the Roundtable on Sustainable Palm Oil. 28 pp.
3. Hansen MC, Potapov PV, Moore R, Hancher M, Turubanova SA, Tyukavina A, Thau D, Stehman SV, Goetz SJ, Loveland TR, Kommareddy A, Egorov A, Chini L, Justice CO, Townshend JRG. 2013. High-resolution global maps of 21st-century forest cover change. Science 342: 850-853.
4. Koh LP, Miettinen J, Liew SC, Ghazoul J. 2011. Remotely sensed evidence of tropical peatland conversion to oil palm. Proc Natl Acad Sci 108:5127-5132.
5. Laumonier Y, Uryu Y, Stüwe M, Budiman A, Setiabudi B, Hadian O. 2010. Eco-floristic sectors and deforestation threats in Sumatra: identifying new conservation area network priorities for ecosystem-based land use planning. Biodivers Conserv 19:1153-1174.
6. Page SE, Rieley JO, Wüst R. 2006. Lowland tropical peatlands of Southeast Asia. In: Martini IP, Martinez Cortizas, Chesworth W, eds. Peatlands: Evolution and records of environmental and climate changes. Oxford: Elsevier. p 145-172.
7. Page SE, Rieley JO, Banks CJ. 2011. Global and regional importance of the tropical peatland carbon pool. Global Change Biology. 17:798-818.
8. Rieley JO, Page SE (eds.). 2005. Wise use of tropical peatlands: Focus on Southeast Asia. The EU INCO – STRAPEAT and RESTORPEAT. Alterra: Netherlands. 209 pp.
9. Stahlhut M, Rieley JO. 2007. Uncertainties in mapping the area of peatland and estimating the depth and volume of peat in Central Kalimantan, Indonesia. Paper Presented at the Proceedings of the International Symposium and Workshop of Tropical Peatland, Yogyakarta, 27-29 August 2007, EU Carbopeat and Restorpeat Partnership, Gadjah Mada University, Indonesia and University of Leicester, United Kingdom.
10. Sufardi , Thomy Z, Basri H, Anhar A, Fajri, Halim A. 2013. Scientific studies for the rehabilitation and management of the Tripa peat swamp forest. Unpublished field report.
11. Van Belle JF, Hennin T. 2008. Above ground carbon assessment: Coastal peat swamp rain forest of Tripa Nanggroe Aceh Darussalam Province, Indonesia. Unpublished field report.
12. Wahyunto, Suryadiputra INN. 2008. Peatland distribution in Sumatra and Kalimantan-explanation of its data sets including source of information, accuracy, data constraints, and gaps. Wetlands International, Indonesian Programme. Bogor. Xiii + 52 pp.

Abstract No: A-141

LOCATION, EXTENT AND DRAINAGE STATUS OF PEATLANDS AND ORGANIC SOILS IN EAST AFRICA

Reni Barthelmes[1], Alexandra Barthelmes[1], René Dommain[2] and Hans Joosten[1]

[1]Institute of Botany and Landscape Ecology, Ernst-Moritz-Arndt University of Greifswald, Germany
[2]Smithsonian Institution, USA

**Corresponding author: karen-d.barthelmes@web.de*

SUMMARY

In discussions on peatlands and organic soils in the tropics, SE Asia prevails in public and scientific perception, whereas Africa remains largely out of focus. However, evaluation of legacy soil maps and scientific literature reveals that also East Africa contains large areas of organic soils. They basically occur in the high altitudes of the uplifted flanks of the East African Rift System, isolated volcanoes and the Ethiopian highlands, in the floodplains of the Zambezi (Zambia), and in coastal environments (Mozambique and Madagascar). We developed a mapping approach that links various science networks, methodologies and databases, including those of peatland/landscape ecology for understanding where and how peatlands may occur, those of remote sensing for identifying possible locations, and those of pedology (legacy soil maps) and (palaeo-)ecology for ground truthing. Such integration of old field data, specialized knowledge, and modern RS and GIS techniques enables acquiring a comprehensive, detailed and rather reliable overview. Due to the large diversity of definitions and terms for peatlands and organic soils, the mapping approach follows the broad definition of organic soils of IPCC, i.e. a minimum soil organic carbon threshold of 12% and any depth of the organic layer larger than 10 cm. In the framework of the Global Peatland Database (GPD), organic soil maps (incl. peatlands) at a scale of 1:25,000 have been prepared for Burundi, Kenya, Rwanda, Tanzania, Uganda and Zambia. The mapping exercise revealed, for example, for Zambia a total organic soil area of 16,663.5 km^2, of which about 1,500 km^2 are slightly drained for subsistence agriculture. In contrast, 522 km^2 of the in total 657 km^2 of organic soils of Burundi are intensively drained and heavily degrading.

***Keywords**: peatland mapping, human impact, GIS, East Africa, legacy soil maps*

INTRODUCTION

Scientific studies of tropical peatlands and organic soils have hitherto mainly concentrated on SE Asia (Hooijer *et al.*, 2010, Dommain *et al.*, 2014, Comas et al. 2015, Osaki & Tsuji 2016), whereas Africa has largely remained out of focus. East African organic soils occur in the high altitudes of the uplifted flanks of the East African Rift System, isolated volcanoes and the Ethiopian highlands, in the floodplains of the Zambezi (Zambia), and in coastal environments (Mozambique and Madagascar). Their coverage in recent soil maps or GIS databases is very poor, although they play a crucial role for water supply and regulation, water and nutrient retention, food security, and for overall livelihoods (Schuyt 2005, Finlayson 2007, McCartney 2010). Furthermore, peatlands and organic soils store huge amounts of carbon (Joosten *et al.*, 2010, Barthelmes *et al.*, 2015b), which is mobilized by drainage and consequent microbial oxidation and catastrophic fires, especially in the Tropics. As population growth, economic development and expanding agriculture is increasing pressure on land, especially in emerging economies and developing countries, knowing the location and drainage status of tropical peatlands must have high priority for land use planning and management (Barthelmes *et al.*, 2015a).

In spite of rapid developing remote sensing methods, peatland mapping from space still has to struggle with the complexity of peatlands and their use (Montanarella, 2014). Across the globe a vast diversity of natural peatlands exist with certain intrinsic signatures for remote sensing, which hampers the successful extrapolation of these signatures to other regions. Furthermore, drained and used organic soils loose many of their key features like the even vegetation and high soil moisture. Accordingly, our mapping approach concentrates on the merging of already existing, often national geospatial soil and proxy information and the use of recent satellite and aerial imagery (Barthelmes *et al.*, 2015a). Furthermore, we assess the drainage and degradation intensity of each organic soil polygon.

METHODS

Our mapping uses a broad definition of organic soils as soils having a minimum organic carbon threshold of 12% and any depth of the organic layer larger than 10 cm.

We developed a mapping approach that links various science networks, methodologies and data bases, including those of peatland/landscape ecology for understanding where and how peatlands may occur, those of remote sensing for identifying possible locations, and those of pedology (legacy soil maps) and (paleo-)ecology for ground truthing. Spatially explicit information on soil and proxy data (e.g. bedrock, relief, landforms, wetlands, vegetation, land use) has been assessed from open access online archives including ISRIC (World Soil Information), JRC (Joint Research Centre), FAO Corporated Document Repository, SPHAERA (Base de données Sphaera du service Cartographie, WOSSAC (World Soil Survey Archive and Catalogue) and the Perry Castanea Library of Austin University.

In order to avoid high costs our approach for wall-to-wall organic soil mapping across vast areas basically uses freely available GIS, satellite and aerial imagery. Furthermore, we applied the Topographical Wetness Index from the African Soil Information Service.The mapping has been carried out manually in high resolution (1:25,000). The resulting GIS database includes for every organic soil polygon information on key references, the reliability of the integrated information (3 classes: confirmed, probable and possible occurrence of organic soil following a detailed decision key) and information on drainage and degradation intensity (3 classes: no, slight and heavy degradation). The methodological background will be in detail published in Barthelmes et al. (in prep.).

RESULTS

Our mapping resulted in the identification of 10,985 km^2 of organic soils in the Lake Victoria neighbouring countries. Burundi contains 657 km^2 of organic soils (= 2.4% of the country area), Kenya 455 km^2 (0.1 %), Rwanda 1,202 km^2 (4.6%), Tanzania 4,221 km^2 (0.4 %) and Uganda 4,111km^2 (1.7 %). For Zambia we could elaborate a total organic soil area of 16,664 km^2 (2.2 % of the country area). The distribution centres of organic soils in East Africa are the uplifted flanks of the Rift Valley System, the upper Congo River Basin and the Zambesi plains. Zambia host vast wetlands that are are regularly rich in organic soils, with the largest areas at Lake Bangweulu and Lake Mweru, in the Lukanga swamp, and in the Barotse floodplain of the Zambesi River. The highest density of organic soils was found in the Lake Victoria region for Burundi, Rwanda .

Many organic soil areas are still unaffected by human activity (24,024 km^2 = 87.9 % of total; Table 1). Zambia, Tanzania and Uganda hold most of these undisturbed organic soils with 15,165 km^2, 3,999 km^2, and 3,907 km^2, respectively. The largest areas are located in extensive valleys that end in Lake Kyoga, and around Lake Victoria in Uganda, in northeast Tanzania close to Lake Victoria, and in Lake Bangweulu and the Lukanga Swamp in Zambia. Of the mapped organic soils, 1,945 km^2 (7.1%) show 'slight degradation', as inferred from satellite and aerial imagery by e.g. the occurrence of few drainage ditches or superficial irregular drainage ditches not connected with a main runoff ditch (Barthelmes *et al.*, in prep.). These areas are generally used for subsistence agriculture without enhanced drainage. Heavily degrading organic soils with intensive agriculture and a dense drainage network connected to a main runoff ditch were found to cover 1,339 km^2 (5 %).

Table1: Extent of organic soils according to their degradation status (for details see Barthelmes et al. in prep). Included are only the reliability classes 'confirmed organic soil' and 'probable organic soil'.

Degradation	Burundi		Rwanda		Uganda		Tanzania		Kenya		Zambia	
Status	km^2	%	km^2	%	km^2	%	km^2	%	km^2	%	km^2	%
1- no	57	9	649	54	3,907	95	3,999	95	247	55	15,165	91
2- slight	78	11	115	10	126	3	149	3	96	21	1,382	8
3- heavy	522	80	437	36	78	2	73	2	111	24	117	1
total	657	100	1,201	100	4,111	100	4,221	100	454	100	16,664	100

The degradation hotspots are situated in the highest areas of the African rift system in Burundi, where slight and heavily drained and degrading organic soils cover 600 km^2 (91% of the total organic soil area), and only 57 km^2 (9%) have remained untouched (Table 1). In Rwanda and Kenya approximately half of the organic soils are drained and degrading, including 552 km^2 (46% of the total) in Rwanda, and 207 km^2 (46%) in Kenya. Only 5% of the organic soils in Uganda and Tanzania are slightly or heavily degraded (Table 1).

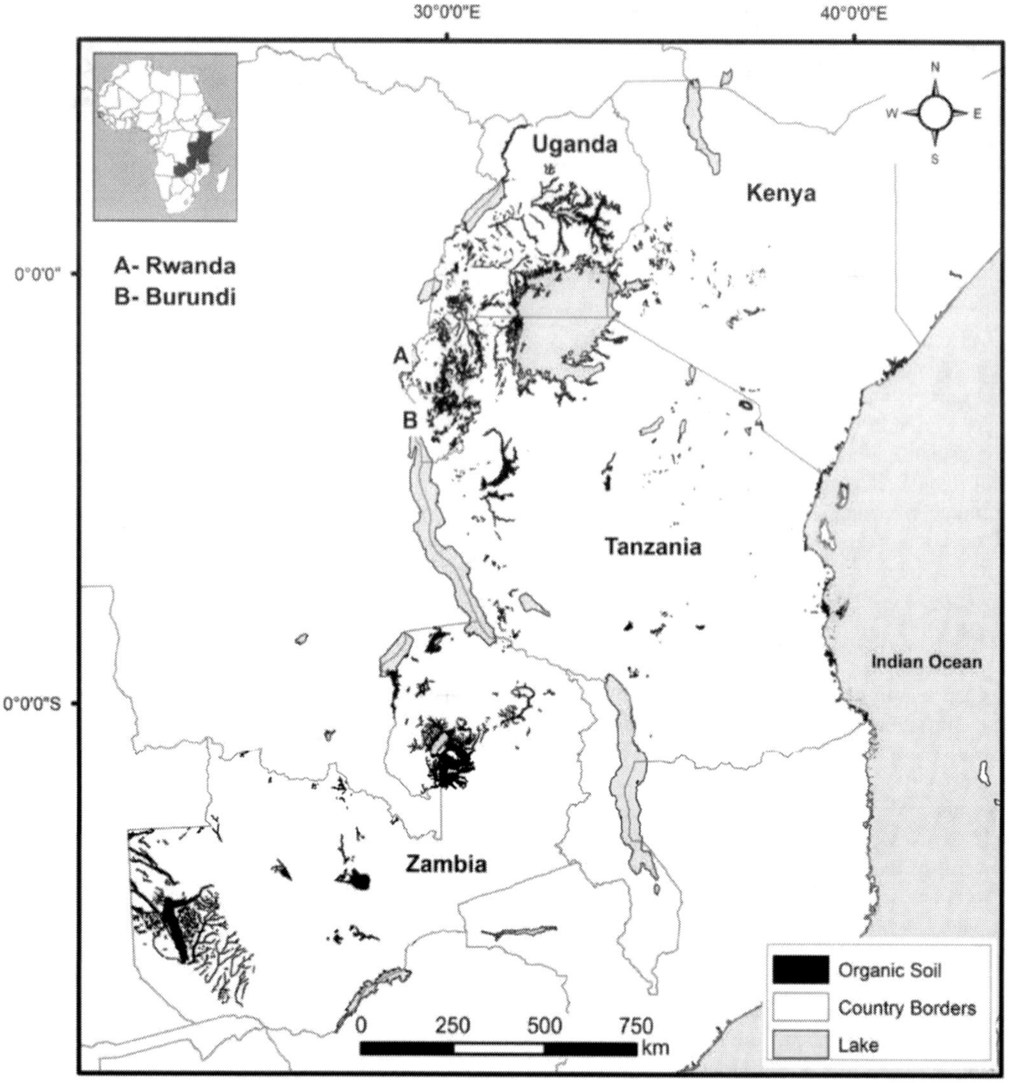

Figure 1: Organic soil map of Burundi, Kenya, Rwanda, Tanzania, Uganda and Zambia (original scale 1:25,000). Shown is the coverage of 'confirmed organic soils', 'probable organic soils' and 'possible organic soils'. Furthermore, also aggregated soil units are displayed that include different proportions of organic soil.

DISCUSSION

Undrained wetlands (incl. peatlands) provide manifold and unique ecosystem services with - especially in Africa - major impact on water supply, food security and socioeconomic welfare (McCartney, 2010; Grundling 2014). Drained peatlands loose these ecosystem services. Furthermore, catastrophic burning (Gaveau *et al.*, 2014) and the growing risk of flooding due to subsidence (Couwenberg & Hooijer, 2013) show the urgency of protecting tropical peatlands against any use that implies drainage. To implement effective policies it is essential to know where peatlands and organic soils are located. However, the current state of their remote sensing based mapping is not satisfying (Montanarella, 2014), whereas the recent 'AfSIS Soil organic carbon map for Africa' (resolution 250 m; Hengl et al. 2015) seem not to have adequate coverage on organic soils, as the modelled carbon values hardly reach 10% in the known wetlands and peatlands of Africa.

Our mapping approach integrates legacy maps, field and ancillary data, specialized knowledge on landscape and peatland ecology and remote sensing derived tools (e.g. Digital Elevation Models and Topographical Soil Index). The approach enables acquiring a fast, comprehensive, detailed and rather reliable overview by manual mapping. The rough assessment of drainage and degradation status has been feasible using freely available satellite and aerial imagery. Key references are stored kept in the 'Global Peatland Database' (Greifswald Mire Centre, University Greifswald) and are available for further review.

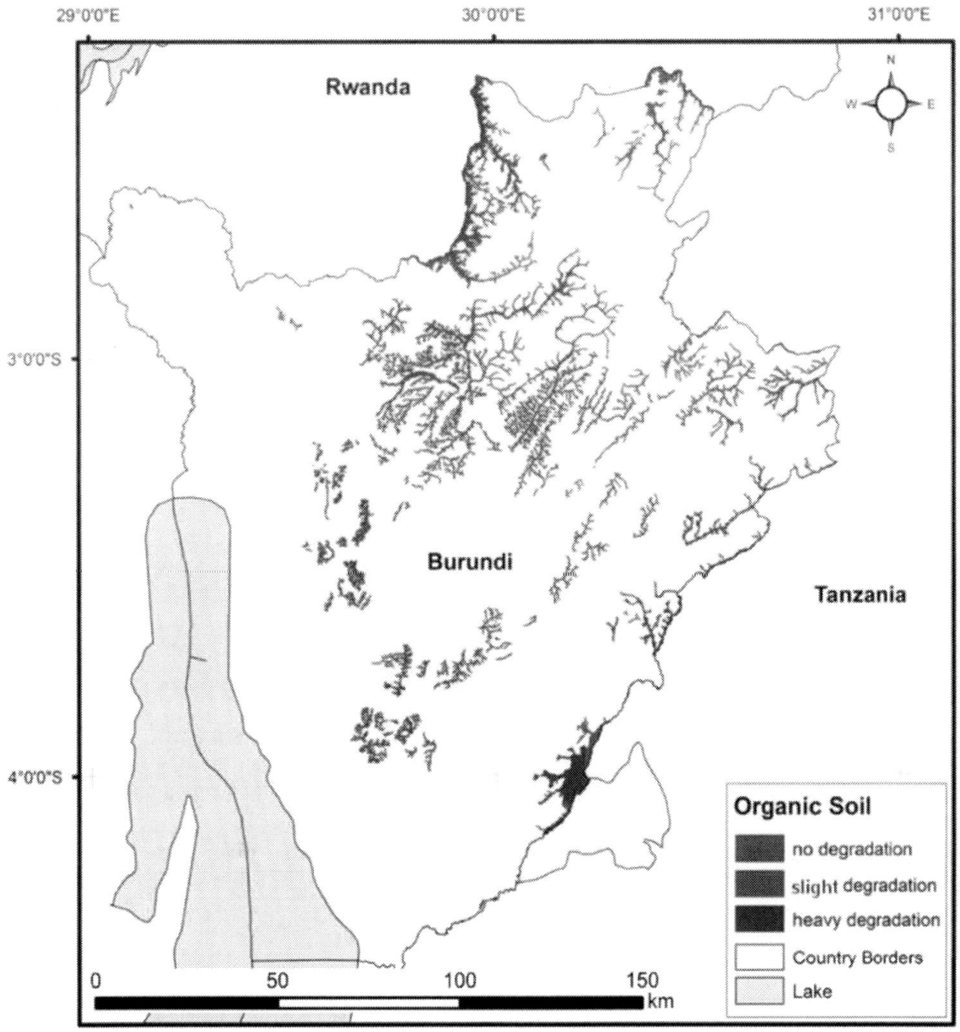

Figure 2: Inferred drainage and degradation status for organic soil areas in Burundi. Shown is the coverage of 'confirmed organic soils', 'probable organic soils' and 'possible organic soils'.

To avoid overestimation of the extent of organic soils, we excluded all areas that have been classified as 'possible organic soil' from the area assessment in Table 1, meaning that another 6,773 km^2 of predominantly wetland areas in East Africa might also include organic soils. Most of these occur in Tanzania (2,919 km^2), followed by Uganda (2,041 km^2), and Kenya (1,582 km^2).

CONCLUSION

Tropical organic soils of Africa provide crucial ecosystem services and are vital for socioeconomic welfare. They need to be protected against drainage, but the knowledge on their location and extent is very poor. We developed a mapping approach that enables a rather fast, comprehensive, detailed and rather reliable mapping of organic soils. We found a total extent of 27,309 km^2 of organic soils for Burundi, Kenya, Rwanda, Uganda, Tanzania and Zambia. Furthermore, we assessed the drainage and degradation status of each organic soil area by evaluating freely available satellite and aerial imagery, which revealed that most organic soils are still hardly touched by humans (24,024 km^2). Degrading organic soils cover 3,284 km^2 with a pronounced degradation hotspot occurring in Burundi (91 % of the total organic soil area).

ACKNOWLEDGMENT

This study was supported by PBL - The Netherlands Environmental Assessment Agency and the Federal Ministry of Education and Research of Germany.

REFERENCES

1. Barthelmes A, Ballhorn U, Couwenberg J & H. Joosten 2015a.Consulting Study 5: Practical guidance on locating and delineatingpeatlands and other organic soils in the Tropics.The High Carbon Stock Science Study 2015, available at: http://www.carbonstockstudy.com/resource-centre/reports.
2. Barthelmes A, Couwenberg J, Risager M, Tegetmeyer C &H. Joosten 2015b.Peatlands and Climate in a Ramsar context - A Nordic-Baltic perspective.Nordic Council of Ministers, Rosendahls-Schultz Grafisk, Copenhagen, Denmark, 81 p. + Annexes.
3. Barthelmes A, Barthelmes R, Dommain R & H Joosten (in prep.), Extent and status of peatlands and organic soils in Central East Africa.
4. Comas X, Terry N, Slater L, Warren M, Kolka R, Kristiyono A, Sudiana N, Nurjaman D &T Darusman 2015. Imaging tropical peatlands in Indonesia using ground-penetrating radar (GPR) and electrical resistivity imaging (ERI): implications for carbon stock estimates and peat soil characterization. Biogeosciences 12: 2995-3007.
5. Couwenberg J &Hooijer A 2013.Towards robust subsidence-based soil carbon emission factors for peat soilsin south-east Asia, with special reference to oil palm plantations. Mires & Peat 12: 1-13.
6. Dommain R, Couwenberg J, Glaser PH, Joosten H. & INN Suryadiputra 2014. Carbon storage and release in Indonesian peatlands since the last deglaciation. Quaternary Science Reviews 97: 1-32.
7. Finlayson CM 2007. Managing wetland ecosystems - balancing the water needs of ecosystems with those for people and agriculture. In: King C, Ramkissoon J, Clusener-Godt M & Z Adeel (eds), Water and Ecosystems: Managing Water in Diverse Ecosystems to Ensure Human Well-being, UNU-INWEH, Hamilton, Canada. pp. 24-38.
8. Gaveau DLA, Salim MA, Hergoualc'h K, Locatelli B, Sloan S,Wooster M, Marlier ME, Molidena E, Yaen H, DeFries R, Verchot L,Murdiyarso D, Nasil R, Holmgren P &S Douglas. 2014. Major atmospheric emissions from peatfires in Southeast Asia duringnon-drought years: evidence from the2013 Sumatran fires. Scientific Reports 4: 6112. doi:10.1038/srep06112
9. Grundling P-L 2014. Genesis and hydrological function of an African mire: understanding the role of peatlands in providing ecosystem services in semi-arid climates. PhD thesis at University of Waterloo, Ontario (Canada); available at: https://uwspace.uwaterloo.ca/handle/10012/9037
10. Hengl T, HeuvelinkGBM, Kempen B, LeenaarsJGB,Walsh MG &KD Shepherd 2015. Mapping SoilProperties of Africa at 250 m Resolution: RandomForests Significantly Improve Current Predictions.PLoS ONE 10: e0125814.
11. Hooijer A, Page SE, Canadell JG, Silvius M, Kwadijk J, Wösten H &J Jauhiainen 2010. Current and future CO_2 emissions from drained peatlands in Southeast Asia. Biogeosciences 7: 1505-1514.
12. McCartney M, Rebelo L-M, SenaratnaSellamuttu S &S. de Silva 2010.Wetlands, agriculture and poverty reduction. Colombo, Sri Lanka: International Water Management Institute,IWMI Research Report 137, 39p. doi: 10.5337/2010.230
13. Montanarella L. 2014. State of the art of peatlands mapping. In: Biancalani R. &A Avagyan (eds.), Towards climate-responsible peatlands management. Mitigation of climate change in agriculture Series 9, FAO, Rome (Italy).
14. Osaki M & N Tsuji (eds.) 2016. Tropical peatland ecosystems. Springer, Tokyo.
15. Schuyt KD, 2005. Economic consequences of wetland degradation for local populations in Africa. Ecological Economics 53: 177-190.

Abstract No: A-464

FOREST MANAGEMENT IN THE PEAT SWAMP FORESTS OF SARAWAK

Abdul Rani Jaili

Forest management and Planning Division
Forest Department Sarawak

SUMMARY

Sarawak has the largest peatland in Malaysia approximately 1.2 million hectares which 353,067 hectares or 29 % comprised of peat swamp forests. 283,018 hectares of peat swamp forest of Sarawak has been allocated for sustainable timber production where a stringent terms and conditions had been imposed on the operators. This include diameter limit 40 cm dbh and above for Ramin and 50 cm dbh for other species. For areas of High Conservation Value Forest in terms of biodiversity and its wildlife, Sarawak has conserved and protected Loagan Bunut National Park, Maludam National Park, Sebuyau National Park, Sedilu National Park and Gunung Lesong National Park as National Parks with a total area of 78,761 hectares. Maludam is home to the unique red banded langurs where the only viable population of it exists in the world. Sebuyau National Park, Sedilu National Park and Gunung Lesong National Park still has the wild population of orang utans.

Keywords: *peat swamp forest, forest management, harvesting, conservation*

INTRODUCTION

Sarawak, is second to Peninsular Malaysia in term of a landmass and is located on the third largest island in the world – Borneo. Known as the land of the Hornbills, Sarawak has a comprehensive landuse plan. It has 12.38 million hectares of land area or 37.6% of Malaysia's 32.83 million hectares landmass. About 8.03 million hectares or 64.9% of its land is still covered with forests. As of 31 December 2014, 4.35 million hectares has been designated as Permanent Forest Estate (PFE) for Sustainable Forest Management (SFM) practices, 0.56 million hectares for Totally Protected Area and the remaining areas of 3.12 million hectares falls under the category of stateland forest (Forest Department Sarawak 2014).

Although five types of natural forest are recognized in Sarawak, only three main types predominate and are considered as major forest types. These are Hill Mixed Dipterocarp Forest, Peat Swamp Forest and Mangrove Forest with cover 78.2%, 4.5% and 0.7% of Sarawak's land area under forest cover respectively. The other two types, the Kerangas and Montane Forests are minimal in size and of less economic importance (Forest Department Sarawak, 2014).

Administratively, the forests are managed by four Regional Forest Office – Kuching, Sibu, Bintulu and Miri, spread over the twelve State Administrative Divisions, namely Kuching, Samarahan, Sri Aman, Sarikei, Sibu, Kapit, Bintulu, Miri, Limbang, Betong, Mukah and Serian. The forest industry sector are important to the State and has played a significant role in contributing to the state government's earning with an average of RM700 million anually or one third of the state revenue. It provides direct employment to about 100,000 persons and also has one of the highest multiplier effects of any sector.

The tropical rain forest in Sarawak has been recognized as one of the mega-biodiversity spot in the world. Hence the forest has to be managed properly with a systematic and sustainable manner to ensure that it continues to contribute significantly to the development of social, economic and environmental sectors of Sarawak.

WHAT IS PEAT SWAMP FOREST?

Peat swamp forest is a type of wetland, waterlogged forest growing on a layer of dead leaves and plant material up to 20 metres thick. It is characterized by evergreen forest, a type of tropical rainforest. The forest is comprise an ancient and unique ecosystem characterized by waterlogging, with low nutrients and dissolved oxygen levels in acidic water regimes. Its continued survival depends on a naturally high water level that prevents the soil from drying out to expose combustible peat matter. This harsh waterlogged environment has led to the evolution of many species of flora uniquely adapted to these conditions.

Peat swamp forest are an important component of the world's wetlands – the dynamic link between land and water, a transition zone where the flow of water, the cycling of nutrients and the energy of the sun combine to produce a unique ecosystem of hydrology, soils and vegetation. These swamp forest provide a variety of goods and services, both directly and indirectly, in the form of forestry and fisheries products, energy, flood mitigation, water supply and groundwater recharge.

IMPORTANCE OF PEAT SWAMP FOREST

Peat swamp forests are unique habitats for fauna and flora, commonly with a high proportion of endemic species that give these areas worldwide significance not only for unusual species but as a gene bank with untapped and even undiscovered resources for medicinal and other important human uses. They play an important part in stabilizing the ecosystem, particularly in the control of drainage, microclimate, water purification and soil formation. Coastal peat swamps act as a buffer between marine and freshwater systems, preventing excessive saline intrusion into coastal land and groundwater.

Peat swamps often serve as a natural gene bank, preserving potentially useful varieties of plant species. At a global scale the peat swamp forests contribute to the storage of atmospheric carbon that is an agent of global warming, helping to slow down that process. Peat swamp forest areas can also be very productive through the managed extraction of fish, timber and other forest products.

PEAT SWAMP FORESTS IN SARAWAK

In Sarawak, the domain of the peat swamp forest is low lying coastal plains with a high water table reaching inland along the lower reaches of major river systems. Peat swamp forests are less diversified than Mixed Hill Dipterocarp Forests and can be divided into 5 different sub-categories i.e Mixed Swamp Forest, Alan Batu Forest, Alan Bunga Forest, Padang Batu Forest and Padang Paya Forests.

FOREST MANAGEMENT

Sarawak sustainable management of forest resources has had a head start, from the beginning of the century, and it has been carried out systematically. The sound management practice and conservation of forests in terms of both ecology and the environment have been developed over the years to ensure forest renewal and sustainable results.

Of the five peat swamp forest types classified by the Forest Department Sarawak (FDS), mixed swamp forest is the most extensive and has the greatest commercial value. Within the Permanent Forest Estate (PFE), the mixed swamp forests are managed to optimize forest resource utilization, regulate harvest on a sustainable yield basis, extract timber with minimal damage and regenerate, rehabilitate and improve the yield of logged-over forests by application of silvicultural treatments (Lee and Chai 1995). Beginning in the fifties the mixed swamp forest was selectively logged following a felling-girth limit. Silvicultural treatment has been applied to the logged-over mixed swamp forests since 1961.

Forest Harvesting

Since the 1950s, a selective and systematic harvesting of the Peat Swamp Forest with the aim of providing a sustainable supply of timber in perpetuity has been successfully practised. This system of harvesting unlike large-scale felling, imitate the phenomenon of natural gap formation. Only mature trees are felled while the lower layers of forest are left untouched. This allows seedlings, saplings to grow into another generation of timber trees and at the same time protects soil from erosion while controlling river siltation and water pollution.

Forest harvesting in the PSF within the PFE is limited to forest management units which are managed according to what is known as a Forest Management Plan (FMP). The FMP is a legal document and forms the Second Schedule of the Forest Timber Licence contains in general a description of the concession area, the objectives of management or prescriptions on how the harvesting may be carried out, the species to be removed, the minimum cutting diameter limits, the annual allowable harvest, penalties of harvesting damage, infrastructure to be set up for the FDS staff, etc. It also states the responsibilities and duties of the concession holder and the FDS with respect to the implementation of the prescriptions of the Plan.

In the PFE, the Selective Felling System is adopted in the harvesting of PSF with the objective of removing selectively in a single felling operation the mature and overmature trees, while at the same time, leaving behind a residual stand with sufficient number of trees in the intermediate diameter classes to form the next crop.

Because of the multi-layered structure of the forest stands, the system has been designed to safeguard the environment and at the same time, takes advantage of the timber market demands. Thus, in harvesting the mature and over-mature trees, sustainability of the forests is assured. After all, trees that are mature and over-mature are, in an economic sense, idle capital because they are well past their prime in value accretion and increasingly subject to death. So the sooner they can be harvested the more likely is the realisation of their value.

The control and monitoring of harvesting activities and yield of harvest on an annual basis is carried out using the annual coupe system with specific sequence of operations commonly known as Permit to Enter Coupe (PEC).

Log extraction in the swamp forests is carried out exclusively by manpower using wooden-runnered sleds, known locally as "Kuda-Kuda" and further transportation is carried out by using narrow-gauge rail cars. Although the method of log extraction and transportation is very labour-intensive, it contributes less negative impacts on the environment. The management system differs for the mixed swamp forest and the Alan Forest.

Typical old-growth stands of Alan Forests are composed entirely of Alan (Shorea albida) trees of uniform size. These stands are usually harvested by clear felling and therefore there is no diameter limit imposed on Alan trees. The distribution of the natural regeneration after harvesting is irregular, some parts are well stocked, others have little or the distribution is patchy, causing problems of management.

The cutting cycle of Alan forest is estimated to be around 60-70 years and the annual average diameter increment is around 0.32 cm per year. The yield after a 60 years rotation was estimated by FAO/UNDP to be around 183 m^3 per ha (FAO/UNDP 1974c).

In the Mixed Swamp Forest, the selective felling system is applied, and the yield is controlled by area and volume. Based on the results of the pre-harvest inventory (100% enumeration) the annual allowable cuts are fixed. Yield control is subsequently by volume in which the total merchantable volume of obligatory species (obligatory species are species which have to be harvested if they are beyond a certain diameter limit) determined by the FDS, within the licence area is divided by the harvesting cycle. Any excess or deficit of volume yield from the prescribed annual coupe is adjusted in the following year.

Exploitation of all obligatory species is carried out based on diameter limits which are 40 cm for Ramin and 50 cm for others. The calculated cutting cycle is 45 years. The average annual increment is estimated around 2.3 m^3 per ha (FAO/UNDP 1974c). In 1990, ITTO evaluated that the management system of the peat swamp forest in terms of total timber production was sustainable.

Forest Conservation

The conservation of biodiversity and environmental protection can only be effectively executed if forested lands are designated as Totally Protected Area where certain human activities are strictly regulated by law. Therefore, the classification of forested lands as National Parks, Wildlife Sanctuaries and Nature Reserves within the designated Totally Protected Area system under the provisions of the National Parks and Nature Reserve Ordinance 1998 and Wild Life Protection Ordinance 1998 has put Sarawak in the forefront in biodiversity conservation.

In Sarawak's peat swamp forests 224 genera and 389 species of flowering plants, 24 genera and 32 species of ferns and fern allies, and over 250 tree species have been identified. Among the trees, ramin (*Gonystylus bancanus*) is considered a peat swamp forest endemic which is now listed under the Convention on International Trade in Endangered Species (CITES). Peat swamp forest is not only the source of commercial timber but on the other hand it also provides important ecological services to the local communities as sociated with the habitat while the peat itself is an important carbon sink.

Sarawak has set aside an area of 1 million hectares as Totally Protected Areas comprising National Parks, Wildlife Sanctuaries and Nature Reserves. These totally protected areas include 78,761 hectares still covered by peat swamp forest, namely the Loagan Bunut National Park, Maludam National Park, Ulu Sebuyau National Park, Sedilu National Park and Gunung Lesong National Park. In addition to that, some 25% of the peat swamp forests are also conserve as Forest Reserves in the PFE. This illustrates Sarawak's commitment to conserve and protect the peat swamp forests and its biodiversity.

Loagan Bunut National Park

Loagan Bunut National Park was gazetted in 1990 and located between Batang Tinjar and Sungai Teru in the upper reaches of the Baram River basin in northern Sarawak. This Park serves to conserve about 7,000 hectares of peat swamp forest which is highly significant as an ecosystem that buffers excess water from the upper Sungai Teru catchment. The peat swamp forest in the Park more or less marks the inland limits of forest on organic peat in the Baram River basin and currently represents the only protected swamp forest in the lower Baram basin.

The Integrated Management Plan has been developed to manage the Park with the objective of ensuring biodiversity conservation, maintenance of local fishing activities and sustainable tourism while keeping the area's ecological integrity and hydrological functions intact. It also addresses issues of local community settlements in the Park and surrounding land development activities.

Maludam National Park

Maludam National Park, located in the Maludam Peninsula, in Betong Sub-District of the Sri Aman Division, was gazetted in 2000 primarily for the protection of its peat swamp ecosystem and its associated flora and fauna. One of its most important roles is to conserve the last known potentially viable population in the world of the Red Banded langur, one of the most endangered primates in Asia. The overall conservation and management goal of the Park are to protect the Maludam peat dome and its associated peat swamp forest, in order to maintain the hydrological characteristics of the Maludam Peninsula for the cultural and socioeconomic benefits of the local populations, to manage the natural habitats of flora and fauna, and to promote eco-tourism.

A comprehensive management plan for the conservation, protection and management of peat swamp forest in Maludam National Park has been developed in 2005 through a joint project between the Governments of Malaysia and the Netherlands. The management plan outlines strategies to address the direct and indirect threats to the Park such as enforcement, establishing management presence on the ground, Special Park Committee, protecting the Maludam dome (activities involve monitoring the hydrological system, redefining park boundaries, establishment of buffer zones, prevention of forest fire, and establishment of coordinating committee), marking and securing park boundaries, eco-tourism structures, research priorities, strengthening management capacity and awareness campaign.

A monitoring plan also formulated to evaluate success in conservation strategies in achieving the following targets: monitoring changes in forest structure and floral diversity, monitoring land use at the fringes, monitoring the Maludam River, monitoring wildlife populations (especially the keystone species), monitoring utilization of non-timber-resource, monitoring eco-tourism activities, and monitoring research activities.

ISSUES AND CHALLENGES

The main issues and challenges to conservation and sustainable use of peat swamp forest are largely due to uncontrolled human intervention. These threats usually occur simultaneously as an area is drained to facilitate land conversion and timber extraction. These activities have direct negative physical impacts on peat swamp ecosystems and its associated biodiversity. These impacts also have associated effects on remaining peat swamp forests due to drainage, such as peat subsidence, fire and loss of vital ecological services.

Land conversion

The major threats to the peat swamp forest ecosystem are the large scale land conversion schemes into agriculture, infrastructure and urbanization projects. The agricultural practices that have been managed in an unsustainable manner has threaten the integrity of peat swamp ecosystems and have resulted in significant loss of ecological support services such as flood mitigation, prevention of saline water intrusion, sediment and toxic removal, groundwater recharge and micro-climate regulation. Many agricultural and plantation projects for oil palm and various other crops on peatlands have failed due to unsuitable conditions and the application of inappropriate methods.

Unsustainable timber harvesting

Unregulated and unsustainable timber harvesting contributes to loss of biodiversity and soil compaction, radically changing the habitat and the natural processes of regeneration. Although there are strict guidelines for forest harvesting in the peat swamp forest within the PFE, clear felling is practised in stateland forests. This caused a major threat to the overall integrity of the ecosystem, destroying natural habitats, degrading the peat substrate and altering the peat swamp hydrology.

Forest fire

Peat swamp forest fires are often associated with periodic drought occurrences and closely-linked with forest clearance and drainage activities by the agricultural and plantation sectors. When peat swamp forests are drained for such purposes the peat swamps tend to become highly susceptible to combustion and peat fires are a recurrent problem. The El Nino cycles also play a significant role in peat swamp forest fire incidents. Adverse impacts associated with peatland fires are the negative effects on the socio- economy of local communities that depend on peatland resources, environmental pollution and a significant reduction or loss of important floral and faunal populations.

CONCLUSION

Forests are a source of natural treasures that have been inherited from previous generations and our responsibility to nurture it so that it can be passed down to future generations. Sustainability in forest management is a dynamic and evolving concept, reflecting changing social values and changes in the scientific understanding of the effects of human activities on the functioning of forest ecosystems. Roadmap for sustainable resource management is like a journey. Therefore, efforts will continue to be implemented to improve the conservation and sustainable management of peat swamp forests while promoting closer cooperation among stakeholders in addressing environmental issues.

REFERENCES

1. Abang Arabi Abang Aimran et al. 2007. Loagan Bunut National Park Management Plan. Sarawak Sarawak State Government and Peat Swamp Forest Project, UNDP/GEF Funded, in collaboration with Forest Department Sarawak and Sarawak Forestry Corporation. 122 pp.
2. Chai P.P.K. 2005. Management Plan for Maludam National Park Betong Division Sarawak. Forest Department Sarawak.
3. FAO/UNDP 1974c. The peat swamps of Sarawak and their potential for development. Malaysia. FO: DP/MAL/72/009 Technical Report No.3. Rome.
4. FD Sarawak. 2014. Forest areas by forest types in Sarawak as of 31 December 2014.
5. ITTO, 1990a. The promotion of sustainable forest management. A case study in Sarawak Malaysia. International Tropical Timber Organisation, Yokohama, Japan. 208 pp.
6. United Nations Development Programme (UNDP). 2006. Malaysia's Peat Swamp Forests: Conservation and Sustainable Use. United Nations Development Programme (UNDP), Kuala Lumpur, Malaysia. ISBN: 983-40995-5-X. 40 pp.
7. Van der Meer, P.J., Demies, M.A., Shabudin, M.S., Verwer, C., Beintema, A., Hilligers, P.J.M., Teo, S.P. 2013. Tropical peat swamp forests of Sarawak. Sustainable Use and biodiversity conservation in a changing environment. Alterra, Wageningen UR, The Netherlands.

Abstract No: A-436

MONTANE PEATLAND CONSERVATION: AN INSIGHT ON NUTRIENT CHARACTERISTICS AND CARBON DATING

Jeyanny Vijayanathan[1*], Wan Rasidah Wan Abdul Kadir[1], Ahmad Husni, Mohd. Hanif[2] and Suhaimi Wan Chik[1]

[1]*Forest Research Institute of Malaysia, Malaysia*
[2]*Universiti Putra Malaysia, Malaysia*

**Corresponding author: jeyanny@frim.gov.my*

SUMMARY

In tropical montane forests (TMF), low temperatures and accumulation of peat allow a temporary carbon (C) reservoir at high altitudes, acting as an important C pool. It consists of hemic and sapric materials which are lesser known compared to lowland peatlands. The study was initiated to determine the chemical characteristics of montane peat and the age of its carbon. Sapric and hemic peat samples were removed separately from the Sungai Kial Forest Reserve, Cameron Highlands, Malaysia. Samples were sent to the laboratory for chemical analysis (C, N. S, K, P, K, Mn, lignin and cellulose) and for C dating. Carbon and lignin concentrations were 55% lower in the sapric samples compared to the hemic samples. The peat materials were 60 years of age. Hemic had higher nutrient (C, N, S, P) and lignin concentrations as it was less decomposed. Both materials were able to reside close to 60 years thereby affirming that permanence of C (stocks) in montane forests.

Keywords: *highland peat, chemical characteristics, carbon age*

INTRODUCTION

Tropical montane forests are mainly concentrated on higher elevations (> 1,000 masl) with low mean annual temperatures of 10-18°C. They boast thick organic soils and contain rich montane biodiversity. Usually beneath the forest floor (i.e. leaf litter), a humic layer is formed which is a partially decomposed litter or hemic peat (Oe). The Oa horizon consists of dark, well decomposed organic soil material of unrecognizable origin (sapric materials) above the mineral soil (Soil Survey Staff, 1993). These organic layers are montane 'peat', a lesser known material compared to the highly studied lowland peat. Montane peat /organic soils consist of elevated levels of carbon (C) and may play a pivotal role in climate change mitigation (Brunjinzeel and Veneklass, 1998). Global warming and deforestation may impede the biological role of tropical montane forest as an ecosystem which needs to be conserved for soil and climate security. Our objective was to determine the nutrient characteristics of the montane peat and date the material to provide an overview on C storage.

MATERIALS AND METHODS

The samples were collected from the Sungai Kial FR, Cameron Highlands, Malaysia (4°31'17" N, 101°25'55" E) in October 2012. Some of the basic characteristics of the study site are given in Table 1. Monthly average air temperature for Sungai Kial Forest Reserve for the past 4 years (2009 –2012) was 18.0°C and the mean annual rainfall for that period was 2,918 mm year^{-1}. The most common tree families in Sungai Kial FR are derived from Myrtaceae, Lauraceae and Polygalaceae. The maximum and minimum diameter at breast height (dbh) encountered in the Sungai Kial FR was 41.5 and 5.0 cm, respectively. A 25 x 25 cm frame was first placed on the litter layer and litter depth was measured to the nearest 1-2 mm. Litter was collected and stored in plastic bags. The peat layer is a combination of sapric and hemic layers of decomposing organic material. The sapric and hemic materials beneath the litter layer were cut and removed using a secateur or a machete. The hemic and sapric samples were dried and then, further ground in a Wiley mill, passed through a 1 mm sieve and sent for analysis of the C, nitrogen (N), sulphur (S), phosphorus (P), potassium (K), manganese (Mn), lignin and cellulose concentrations.

Table 1: Basic information on environmental conditions at the study site.

Site	Elevation (masl)	Slope (°)	pH (H_2O)	Soil	Air
				Temperature (°)	
Sungai Kial	1,405-1,644	22-41	4.5-5.7	17.0-18.8	16.1-20.2

C, N and S concentrations were determined using a LECO- TruMac CNS analyzer (Michigan, United States). Total P, K, and Mn were determined using the dry ashing and nitric acid digestion method followed by determination of element concentration using inductively coupled plasma (ICP) spectrometer. The Van Soest (1963) method was used to determine substrate quality such as lignin and cellulose. The results are given in Table 2.

Hemic and sapric material from the site were sent for C dating analysis in Beta Analytic Inc, Miami, Florida, United States. The samples were pre-treated first using hydrochloric acid (HCl) and sodium hydroxide (NaOH) alkali washing. The radiocarbon age was determined using the Accelerated Mass Spectrometry (AMS) instrument (Beta Analytic, 2013). The age was expressed in percent modern carbon (pmC) as the samples had more ^{14}C than the modern AD 1950 reference standard (Table 3).

RESULTS AND DISCUSSION

The amount of C and lignin was 55% lower in the sapric samples compared to the hemic (Table 2). Similarly, N levels decreased in a similar manner in the summit forest floor material. Sulfur and P were 2 and 4-fold higher in the hemic samples. Potassium content ranged from 0.1- 0.2%, and Mn was minimal in both the hemic and sapric. Cellulose was stable at 33-38%.

Table 2: Initial nutrient concentration of litter, hemic and sapric n=3

Peat fragments	C	N	S	P	K	Mn	Proximate cellulose	Proximate lignin
			%			mg/g	%	
Hemic	31.19 (5.16)	1.55 (0.29)	0.12 (0.03)	0.15 (0.10)	0.10 (0.02)	0.04 (0)	37.80 (6.28)	27.07 (7.78)
Sapric	13.84 (3.04)	1 (0.12)	0.07 (0)	0.03 (0)	0.12 (0.04)	0.03 (0)	36.05 (4.03)	12.40 (3.57)

Values in parentheses represents standard error

Continuous decomposition by microbes altered the C, lignin and N contents. Low levels of Mn found in peat also suggests that lignin decomposition is not highly active in these materials compared to litter due to its role in the lignin degrading enzyme (Perez and Jeffries, 1992). However favourable levels of P in the hemic component suggest decomposition is positively stimulated to facilitate P release (Baggio *et al.*, 2004). C and lignin are modified during humification processes, where it goes through condensation reactions and microbial degradation (Berg and McClaugherty, 2008) creating materials (hemic and sapric) rich in lignin and C that are protected by lignin and humic acid compounds (Table 2).

Table 3: Carbon dating results of hemic and sapric, Sungai Kial FR

Sample	Material	Radiocarbon age (pMC)	Conventional radiocarbon age (pMC)	Proximate year AD	Calibrated age AD
Hemic	peat	111.7 ± 0.3	112.7± 0.3	1955-56 / 1991-1998	670-680; 790-810
Sapric	peat	111.0 ± 0.3	111.9± 0.3	1955-56 /1994-1999	850-850

Montane peat was able to reside and accumulate for approximately 60 years due to little pedoturbation (Table 3). Our results recorded longer durations compared to Schiffman and Johnson (1989), who studied the accumulation of humus in forest floors over time in Scots pine *(Pinus sylvestris)* and Loblolly pine (*Pinus taeda*) and discovered that humus resided between 47 and 55 years. Previous activities in this site before 1955 are unknown but based on the agricultural activities in the surrounding areas, it is assumed that some fragments of peat moss would have been removed for agricultural purposes. In the absence of disturbance, peat has the tendency to accumulate over millennia (Paul, 1984). Although the results gave an approximate age, it may not be conclusive due to i) contamination of fragments of recent plant tissues from the soil surface and ii) the contamination of carbon dioxide (CO_2) produced from the depleted ^{14}C by the naturally decomposing older plant tissues from the underlying layers (Goslar *et al.*, 2005). The determination of the mean residence time (MRT) of peat however were pertinent in this study as they may explain new insights on soil properties; clay content and mineralogy, soil aggregation and humification of soil organic carbon.

CONCLUSION

Montane peatlands of hemic materials had relatively higher nutrient concentrations (C, N, S, P, and lignin) compared to sapric. Both materials were able to reside close to 60 years affirming that the permanence of C (stocks) in montane forests is crucial and needs to be considered for conservation purposes.

ACKNOWLEDGEMENTS

This study was financially supported by the Ministry of Agriculture via the E- Science Fund (Project No. 05-03-10-SF1029). Thanks are due to the staff of Forest Research Institute Malaysia and Universiti Putra Malaysia for field and technical assistance. Gratitude is also extended to Dr. S. Paramananthan for reviewing this abstract.

REFERENCES

1. Baggie, I., Rowell, D., Robinson, J., and Warren, G., 2005. Decomposition and phosphorus release from organic residues as affected by residue quality and added inorganic phosphorus. *Agroforestry systems* 63(2): 125-131.
2. Berg, B., and McClaugherty, C., 2008. *Plant litter: Decomposition, humus formation, carbon sequestration.* Berlin: Springer Verlag
3. Beta Analytic Inc., 2013. Introduction to Radiocarbon Determination by the Accelerator Mass Spectrometry Method. Retrieved 20 February 2013 from http://www.radiocarbon.com/PDF/Beta-AMS-Methodology.pdf
4. Bruijnzeel, L. A. & Veneklaas, E. J., 1998. Conditions and tropical montane forest productivity: The fog has not lifted yet. *Ecology:* 3–9.
5. Goslar, T., Van der Knaap, W., Hicks, S., Andric, M., Czernik, J., Goslar, E., Rasanen, S., and Hyotyla, H., 2005. Radiocarbon dating of modern peat profiles: pre-and post-bomb 14C variations in the construction of age-depth models. *Radiocarbon* 47(1): 115-134.
6. Paul, E., 1984. Dynamics of organic matter in soils. *Plant Soil* 76: 75-285.
7. Perez, J. and Jeffries, T.W., 1992. Roles of manganese and organic acid chelators in regulating lignin degradation and biosynthesis of peroxidases by *Phanerochaete chrysosporium. Applied and Environmental Microbiology* 58(8): 2402-2409.
8. Soil Survey Staff, 1993. *Soil survey manual.* USDA Agricultural Handbook No. 18. Washington: U.S. Government Printing Office.
9. Schiffman, P.M., Johnson W.C., 1989. Phytomass and detrital carbon storage during forest regrowth in the southeastern United States Piedmont. *Canadian Journal of Forest Research* 19:67–78.
10. Van Soest, P.J., 1963. Use of detergents in analysis of fibrous feeds: a rapid method for the determination of fiber and lignin. *J. Assoc. Off. Agric. Chem,* 46: 829-835.

Abstract No: A-195

QUANTIFICATION AND VALUATION OF ECOSYSTEM SERVICES TO OPTIMIZE SUSTAINABLE RE-USE FOR LOW-PRODUCTIVE DRAINED PEATLANDS

Anne Tolvanen[1, 2] and Miia Parviainen[1]

[1] *Natural Resources Institute FinlandFINLAND.*
[2] *Department of Ecology, University of Oulu, FINLAND*

**Corresponding author: anne.tolvanen@luke.fi*

SUMMARY

Almost one-third of European peatland resource is situated in Finland, where more than half of the original peatlands have been drained to increase tree growth. However, 20% of the drained peatland area does not produce enough timber to fulfil commercial purposes. At the same time, their biodiversity is degraded, they may continue environmental loading to watercourses and act as greenhouse gas (GHG) sources. A key question concerning the use of peatlands is what to do with these low-productive drained peatlands that have been left aside from active forestry. There are needs to use the low-productive peatlands in the production of bioenergy, timber and peat. Simultaneously, there are needs to restore the most valuable drained peatland habitats, which might recover towards their original state. The problem is that the impacts of the different options on biodiversity, environment and economy are not yet fully understood and thus it is hard to give proposals for re-use actions for specific areas. The challenge is to develop mechanisms that can balance the conflicting demands on the use of the drained peatlands and to ensure their sustainable use. Our 5-year EU funded LIFE+ project LIFEPeatLandUse (LIFE12 ENV/FI/000150, 2013-2018) consolidates and increases the knowledge on the impacts of peatland re-use on ecosystem services. The aim is to find cost-efficient re-use options to low-productive drained peatlands, which help to prevent or stop decline of biodiversity and environmental loading to watercourses, and improve capacity of peatlands to store greenhouse gases. There are seven different peatland re-use options under investigation, representing the economic activity as well as measures related to the protection. The purpose is to evaluate and predict their potential impacts on the peatland landscapes, if they were applied in practice.

***Keywords**: peatlands, biodiversity, greenhouse gases, hydrology, optimization*

INTRODUCTION

Ecosystem service concept and the valuation efforts of ecosystem services are changing the discussion concerning land use policy and natural resource management (Costanza *et al.*, 1997, de Groot *et al.*, 2010). Increasing knowledge on the importance of healthy ecosystems for human wellbeing is leading to situations, where multi-functional and ecologically sustainable land use is seen as an option to simultaneously generate ecological, economic and social benefits. EU has recognized the importance of peatlands in maintaining biodiversity, in modifying environmental loading, and in contributing to the global GHG balance, and has set various Directives and Conventions to protect these values.

In many countries, peatlands have been drained and utilized for forestry, agriculture and peat harvesting for centuries. Peat has ceased to accumulate in Europe within over 50 % of the former mire area, and almost 20 % of original peatland area no longer exists as peatland (Joosten & Clarke, 2002). Almost one-third of European peatland resource is situated in Finland, where the use of peatlands has been intensive during the past decades. Large-scale drainage, the consequent overgrowing of open mires and the isolation of pristine mires are the main causes of the deterioration in the natural state of mires in Finland. Large-scale drainage has also increased significantly the environmental loading i.e. leaching of nutrients, suspended solids and organic matter from peatlands to downstream watercourses and widely weakened the state of these water bodies. It has also recently become clear that the degradation of peatlands is contributing significantly to global emissions of greenhouse gases (GHG). For instance, drainage of peatlands results in increased emissions of CO_2 and nitrous oxide (N_2O). Appropriate peatland use can protect the carbon store, and suitable re-use options can decrease the GHG emissions and create conditions for carbon sequestration and peat formation in drained and degraded peatlands. Thus, to mitigate the human-induced GHG emissions as defined in the Kyoto Protocol, there is a need to find solutions for the management of peatlands to minimize the emissions of GHG.

The main objective of the EU funded LIFEPeatLandUse (LIFE12 ENV/FI/000150) project is to quantify and valuate ecosystem services to assist land use planners and policymakers in making ecologically, economically and socio-culturally sustainable land use decisions. This is done by developing and demonstrating a decision support system, where ecological and economical information is aggregated to numerically optimize cost efficient land use options so that benefits from ecosystem services are safeguarded. The monetary value of the land use options is maximized under given constraints set to the biodiversity, environmental loading, and GHG emissions, to fulfill the constraints set in the regional, national, and EU level policies. The system is tested and demonstrated to optimize the re-use for low-productive drained peatlands, which is the key issue concerning peatland use in Finland. These peatlands, where timber production is not commercially productive without specific maintenance options, cover 20% (ca. 0.8. million ha) of the drained peatland area in Finland. The decision support system provides an innovative, quantitative approach to increase the sustainability and reduce conflicts concerning peatland use, and it is applicable to any land use planning, where ecological, economic and socio-cultural values may be in trade-off.

METHODS

1) The decision support system consists of i) data compilation and modelling to quantify and predict the present and future states of ecosystem services in terms of biodiversity, environmental loading, GHG balance, and monetary value, ii) numeric optimization, which maximizes the monetary value of the land use option by using results from the ecosystem service predictions and from the requirements and constraints set to these services in national and international policies, iii) a participatory decision support tool, which analyses trade-offs and stakeholder preferences towards the predicted land use impacts on ecosystem services and increases the socio-cultural sustainability of land use, and iv) GIS based maps to demonstrate the predicted impacts of peatland re-use options on ecosystem services. The project outline is presented in Figure 1.

2) The present state of ecosystem services are evaluated based on existing data and new data monitored in this project. Future scenarios on the impacts and cost efficiency of seven re-use options; 1) no measures, 2) tree biomass harvesting, 3) intensive forestry, 4) restoration, 5) peat harvesting, 6)peat harvesting and reforestation, 7) peat harvesting and rewetting, on ecosystem services are predicted up to 100 years by using state of the art modelling techniques.

3) Project results are disseminated in domestic and international events and networks. Information is available for professionals, general public, and for domestic and international actors working with land use. Stakeholders participate in a regional planning process to promote co-operation and create better opportunities for consensus on sustainable peatland use decisions.

4) Scattered data from long-term databases, publications, and new established monitoring are compiled to model the present and future states of ecosystem services and to promote ecologically, economically and socio-culturally sustainable land use.

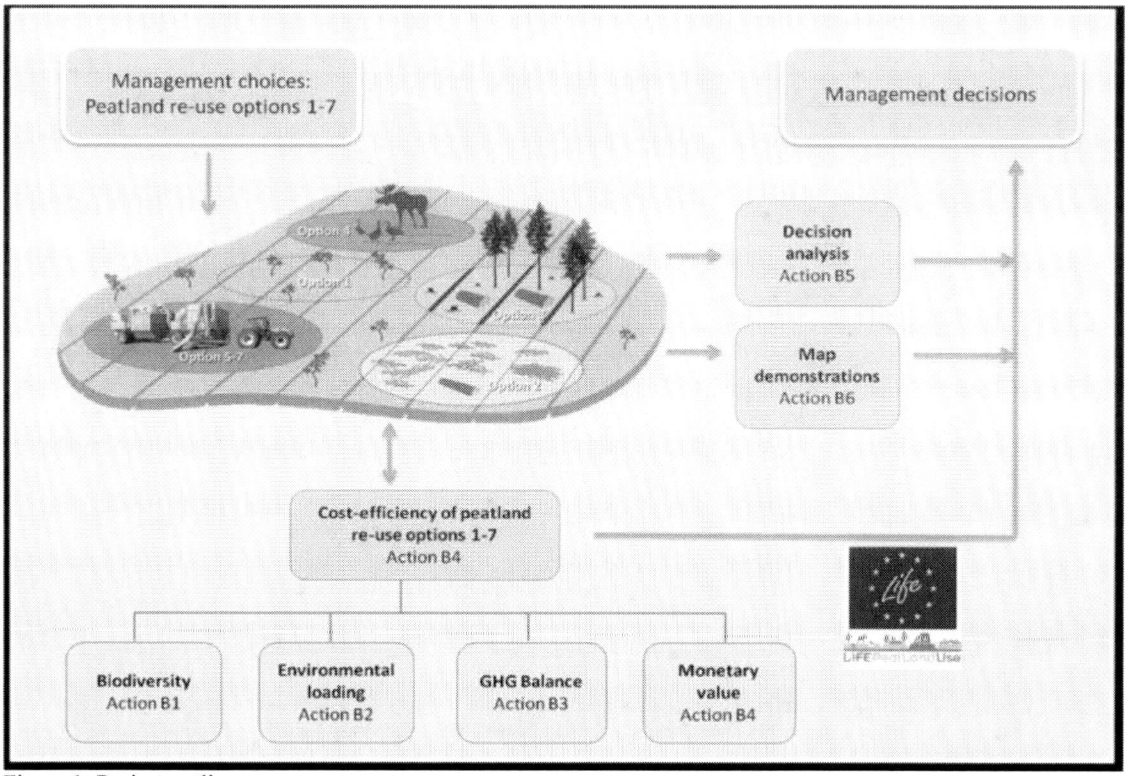

Figure 1: Project outline.

RESULTS

The expected results of the project are:

1) New innovative decision support system that quantifies, values and predicts the state of selected ecosystem services and optimizes their levels to fulfil requirements and constraints set at the regional, national and EU levels, has been produced. The system is a procedure of goal setting, data compilation, assessment of current conditions, predictive modelling, optimization of alternative options, stakeholder participation, analysis of results, and map demonstrations. Due to the quantification and valuation of the ecosystem services, the system assists land use planners and policymakers in making more objective and sustainable decisions. Demonstration of the system will be done through web based maps to reach all interested parties.

2) Knowledge has been increased concerning the impacts of peatland use on the biodiversity, environmental loading, GHG balance and monetary value of low-productive drained peatlands. These ecosystem services have been quantified for the peatland landscapes selected during the project, the two project subareas and for the whole project area, and their states have been predicted up to 100years.

3) General awareness and understanding concerning the sustainable use of peatlands have been increased for example by a public website, and by disseminating project results in several domestic and international events. A participatory decision support tool has been tailored and tested by at least 20 stakeholders in a planning process, where 20 peat harvesting sites have been allocated. The tool has provided better opportunities for consensus among stakeholders.

4) Data from long-term monitoring, publications and newly established monitoring have been aggregated into a database, which can be used to model, predict and optimize the impacts of sustainable peatland use. Project has acted as an example of the sharing of data between research organizations.

DISCUSSION

In the present situation of land use planning, ecological, economic and socio-cultural impacts are generally evaluated, but in separate surveys (Tolvanen *et al.*, 2013). The integration of complicated interdisciplinary results is done outside the expert group, e.g. by politicians and land managers. A separate consideration of the constraints set for example in the Habitats Directive, EU Water Framework, Kyoto protocol, and Rural Development Policy, may each lead to a different decision depending on which of the policies is emphasized. The decisions may also depend on the quality and amount of ecological and economic information related to these policies.

The decision support system developed in this project considers simultaneously the most relevant peatland re-use options in Finland, based on the national needs and guidelines. The system results into an integrated evaluation of different re-use options that are evaluated amongst each other using modern state of the art modelling techniques. Using the modelling, not only local or regional impacts are evaluated, but impacts are predicted for larger area, covering most of Finland. National, EU and international policies and standards are considered in the modelling through requirements and constraints concerning the state of ecosystem services, which are set to the numeric optimization process. Constraints have an impact on the outcome of the optimization.

The project provides an integrated view and future predictions on peatland ecosystem services up to 100 years. The project structure supports this so that each Action brings information on a separate ecosystem service, and the data are further elaborated to produce cost-efficiency predictions, to be evaluated in a participatory planning process, and to be demonstrated as GIS-based maps in the internet. Although long term predictions should be considered with caution due to uncertainties in model assumptions, they provide a useful tool to coarsely evaluate long-term consequences of land use decisions. Long-term predictions give an insight on where the present policies are leading to and what should be done in order to reach the aims set in the policies.

CONCLUSION

Land-use planning is a sensitive process, which can cause conflicts between stakeholders due to different opinions on ecological and economic values of natural resources, and due to different impacts on the decisions on people's well-being. Although full consensus can rarely be achieved, increased information on potential ecological and economic impacts of decisions creates a potential for objective and open evaluation of the impacts. LIFEPeatLandUse project demonstrates, how ecological and economic data can be modelled and integrated in order to quantify and valuate ecosystem services, and to predict their future states. In practice, high quality information and data on ecosystem services, state of the art modelling techniques, and high level of expertise are needed for the predictions and for the simultaneous examination of ecosystem services after different land use options. The project approach is therefore also a demonstration on how planning can be done in an optimal situation. The predictions demonstrate, where the present peatland management is leading to considering biodiversity, environmental loading, GHG balance and monetary value of peatlands, where the alternative re-use options are leading to, and what should be done in order to reach the aims set in national, EU and international policies.

ACKNOWLEDGEMENTS

The project is funded by EU (LIFE12 ENV/FI/000150), Natural Resources Institute Finland (Luke), Finnish Environment Centre (SYKE), Metsähallitus, University of Helsinki, University of Oulu, Vapo oy, Ministry of the Environment and Turveruukki oy.

REFERENCES

1. Costanza R, d'Argr R, et al. (1997) The value of the world's ecosystem services and natural capital. Nature 387: 253–260.
2. De Groot R (2006) Function-analysis and valuation as a tool to assess land use conflicts in planning for sustainable, multi-functional landscapes. Landscape and Urban Planning 75:175–186.
3. Joosten H & Clarke D (2002) Wise use of mires and peatlands – background and principles including a framework for decision-making. International Mire Conservation Group and International Peat Society.
4. Tolvanen, A., Juutinen, A. & Svento, R. 2013. Preferences of local people for the use of peatlands: The case of peatland-richest region in Finland. Ecology & Society, 18(4): 12 p.

Abstract No: A-224

REGIONAL APPROACH TO PEATLAND CONSERVATION IN SOUTHEAST ASIA

Faizal Parish, S.Y. Lew and Noor Azura A.

Global Environment Centre, 2nd Floor, Wisma Hing, No. 78, Jalan SS2/72, 47300 Petaling Jaya

* *Corresponding author: azura@gec.org.my*

SUMMARY

Southeast Asia hosts more than 60% (approximately 25 million hectares) of the total tropical peatlands in the world. However, not all countries are able to fully understand and protect these precious land areas. To bridge this, the ASEAN Peatland Forests Project (APFP) and SEApeat project were designed to share resources and join forces in protecting peatlands in the region. From 2010 to 2015, these two projects played key roles in peatland conservation and rehabilitation in the region through information and knowledge sharing, joint training, workshops and peer learning programmes to engage the relevant stakeholders including government institutions, private sector and local communities. Activities included joint peat surveys between local community and local authority, regional peer-to-peer learning programmes on good management practices on peatlands, training/capacity building to enhance knowledge on peatland management, policy development to minimise further peatland degradation, rehabilitation efforts with public-private partnership with multi stakeholder, and many others. This paper showcases how regional efforts helped protect peatlands in Southeast Asia through multi-stakeholder activities which saw government departments working hand in hand with line agencies, private sector, research institutions, NGOs and local communities to build capacity and achieve desired results.

Keywords: *peatlands, Southeast Asia, conservation, community involvement*

İNTRODUCTION

Southeast Asia hosts more than 60% (approximately 25 million hectares) of the total tropical peatlands in the world. However, not all countries are able to fully understand and protect these precious land areas. To bridge this, the ASEAN Peatland Forests Project (APFP) and SEApeat project were designed to share resources and join forces in protecting peatlands in the region. From 2010 to 2015, these two projects played key roles in peatland conservation and rehabilitation in the region through information and knowledge sharing, joint training, workshops and peer learning programmes to engage the relevant stakeholders including government institutions, private sector and local communities.

Activities included joint peat surveys between local community and local authority, regional peer-to-peer learning programmes on good management practices on peatlands, training/capacity building to enhance knowledge on peatland management, policy development to minimise further peatland degradation, rehabilitation efforts with public-private partnership with multi stakeholder, and many others. Regional efforts helped protect peatlands in Southeast Asia through multi-stakeholder activities which saw government departments working hand in hand with line agencies, private sector, research institutions, NGOs and local communities to build capacity and achieve desired results.

METHODS

The key players in this initiative include ASEAN Secretariat, ASEAN member states (AMS), Global Environment Centre was the Regional Project Executive Agency (RPEA). The project objectives were in line with those of the ASEAN Peatland Management Strategy (APMS) which is centred on controlling peat fire, climate change and haze issues. Activities were held in all ASEAN member states, with funding given to all except Brunei Darussalam and Singapore. The efforts are guided by the projects' objectives and planned outputs.

Firstly, in countries which have unconfirmed peat areas, especially Cambodia, Lao PDR, Myanmar and the Philippines; funds and technical assistance was provided for surveys. This resulted in 20,000 ha new peatland areas confirmed in the Philippines, and several new areas confirmed in the Mekong countries. It also confirmed the presence of mangrove peat in Cambodia, and rare spring mound peat in Myanmar.

To ensure good governance of peatland areas, all AMSs developed a National Action Plan for Peatlands for their respective countries. This formed the foundation for land use policies, Integrated Management Plans and Best Management Practices on the ground.

Next, to educate and create awareness, several training courses and peer learning workshops were held over the 5 years. Participants learned from each other, visited peatland sites and were exposed to different methods of dealing with challenges that came with living on peatlands. Through these sessions, several techniques such as Surjan Farming was transferred between countries.

The projects enabled expeditions to update ground information and review publications such as the ASEAN Peatland Management Strategy. Community engagement was very much part of the project, from local communities in Riau and Kalimantan; U Minh Thuong and U Minh Ha regions; Caimpugan and Visayas; as well as the North Selangor Peat Swamp Forests in Indonesia, Vietnam, Philippines and Malaysia respectively. Through the projects, they learnt to manage their lands more sustainably and explore new ways to protect the lands from fire.

Fire and haze is one of the major issues, and to tackle this problem, the capabilities of the Fire Danger Rating System, hotspot monitoring and community firefighting were enhanced. A smartphone app was also developed to alert land managers of fires on their lands via satellite monitoring.

Publications and awareness materials were developed and disseminated, also made available online at www.aseanpeat.net.

FINDINGS AND ARGUMENT

Progress can be seen, especially in places where the presence of peatlands was not confirmed before. The regional approach is especially beneficial in terms of learning from each other and saving on consultancy costs.

Sharing helps capitalise on local resources who are expert in the field of tropical peatland ecology, hydrology and restoration. For example, Dr Le Phat Quoi from Vietnam. He not only refined the use of GIS in detecting possible peatland areas, he is also able to lead surveys to confirm the presence of peatlands.

Compared to the single country approach, which often benefits only a few communities and issues at a time, the regional approach is able to magnify and combine efforts to achieve greater results. Countries learn from each other across borders and share project templates. It saves time and effort to organise and replicate activities across the region. Even research and publications can be combined and replicated. Some materials such as the Training Module on Peatland Assessment and Management were translated into several languages, saving time and effort in redeveloping the same material across borders.

When countries share their progress during meetings, other countries sometimes adopt and replicate efforts which are applicable. This creates a synergy between countries and information flows more freely as everyone is basically working on the same platform. It also eases the way for cross border information transfer and advisory.

CONCLUSION

The projects have successfully improved the management of peatland forests in the region through multi-directional approaches and multi-stakeholder efforts. Both the European Union and IFAD/GEF were satisfied with the achievements gained in the region.

RECOMMENDATIONS

Following the completion of both the APFP and SEApeat projects by 2015, a scaled-up programme which builds on the success of the current projects is required to continue the long journey towards sustainable peatland management in Southeast Asia.

This was pursued based on the positive recommendations from APFP Mid Term Review in 2012 and Terminal Evaluation Review in 2014, as well as the SEApeat Results Oriented Monitoring Missions in 2012-2013. Hence, ASEAN explored options for scaling up activities.

The Ministerial Level COP on AATHP in September 2013 endorsed the development of a new programme towards sustainable peatland management and control of transboundary haze. Through meetings in September and December 2013, April and August 2014, an ASEAN Programme on Sustainable Management for Peatland Ecosystems (2014 – 2020, APSMPE) was formed. The AMS identified prioritized proposed projects of approximately USD$240 million for the Programme. Further discussions were held in November 2014, March and June 2015 to fine-tune and further prioritise the projects.

The aims of the APSMPE are

i. To realize fully the ultimate goals of the APMS 2006-2020, i.e. to promote sustainable management of peatlands in the ASEAN region;
ii. Through enhanced stakeholder collaboration to support and sustain local livelihoods;
iii. Reduce the risk of fire and associated haze; and
iv. Contribute to global environmental management.

APSMPE Six Targets by 2020

Below are the proposed targets for the ASEAN Programme on Sustainable Management of Peatland Ecosystems which was approved by ASEAN Environment Ministers in October 2013.
1. All peatland areas identified and inventorised;
2. Zero-burning uniformly practiced to prevent any uncontrolled wildfires on peatlands, and eliminate any widespread smoke haze;
3. Fire prone sites rehabilitated by focusing on root causes of fire,
4. Peatlands sustainably managed, sustainable livelihoods enhanced, and
sustainable economic use mainstreamed;
5. Peatlands conserved to contribute to significantly reduced emissions of greenhouse gases and increased peatland biodiversity in the region; and
6. APMS and NAPPs implemented; national and regional capacity enhanced.

Work is under way to secure funds and start the next phase of activities for peatland conservation in Southeast Asia.

REFERENCES:

1. ASEAN 2013, ASEAN Peatland Management Strategy 2006-2020.
2. Lim, K.H. , Lim, S.S, Parish. F. and Suharto, R. (eds) 2012. RSPO Manual on Best Management Practices (BMPs) for Existing Oil Palm Cultivation on Peat. RSPO, Kuala Lumpur.
3. MacMillan, D. C. 2013. Development of Financing and Incentive Options for Sustainable Management of Peatland Forests in Southeast Asia. APFP and SEApeat projects. ASEAN Secretariat and Global Environment Centre
4. Schumann, M. & Joosten, H. (2008). Global Peatland Restoration Manual. Greifswald University, Germany.
5. Selangor State Forestry Department 2014, Integrated Management Plan for North Selangor Peat
a. Swamp Forest 2014-2023.
6. Suryadiputra, N. (2007). Options for rehabilitation of degraded peatland. Wetlands International (Powerpoint)

Abstract No: A-285

SUSTAINABLE WETLANDS ADAPTATION AND MITIGATION PROGRAM (SWAMP)

R.K. Kolka[1*] and D. Murdiyarso[2]

[1]*USDA Forest Service Northern Research Station, United States*
[2]*Center for International Forestry Research*

**Corresponding author: rkolka@fs.fed.us*

Carbon-rich tropical wetlands (mangroves and peatlands) are important in climate change adaptation and mitigation strategies and provide numerous ecosystem services such as storm protection, nursery areas for fish, habitat for rare species, long-term storage of carbon, and food, fiber, and fuel for humans. Because of their importance we developed the Sustainable Wetlands Adaptation and Mitigation Program (SWAMP) to assist countries with their accounting and conservation of tropical wetlands. SWAMP is a collaborative effort between the Center for International Forestry Research, USDA Forest Service, and Oregon State University through support from the US Agency for International Development. The goal of SWAMP is to provide policy makers and natural resource professionals with credible information and training to make sound decisions regarding the role of tropical wetlands in climate change adaptation and mitigation. The SWAMP objectives are to: (1) Quantify greenhouse gas emissions from intact and disturbed wetlands; (2) Quantify carbon stocks of representative tropical wetlands; (3) Develop carbon modeling tools and scaling approaches using remote sensing; (4) Define roles for tropical wetlands in climate change adaptation strategies; and (5) Promote capacity building and outreach as integral parts of all activities. Here we discuss the accomplishments of SWAMP, current activities and the future.

***Keywords**:-*

Abstract No: A-064

TROPHIC STATUS OF THE MIRES IN CHANGBAI MOUNTAINS, NORTHEAST CHINA

Na Xu, Yanmin Dong, Hongyan Zhao*, Shasha Liu, Hongkai Li, Ming Wang, Yiwen Cao, Shengzhong Wang and Xianmin Meng

Institute for Peat and Mire Research, Northeast Normal University, China

**corresponding auther: hyzhao@nenu.edu.cn*

SUMMARY

Trophic status of mires is a significant indicator of the processes and trends of mires development, which help guide rational use of peat resources and reconstruct the past environmental changes during the formation of mires. Changbai Mountains in Northeast China is one of areas in which mires are widely distributed. However, little attention has been paid to the trophic status of the mires in it. We investigated 130 plant quadrats of 75 mires in Changbai Mountains in 2014, and collected the peat samples from the depth of 15cm beneath each plant quadrat. Total organic carbon (TOC), total nitrogen (TN) and pH (KCl) were measured for all peat samples. The types of plants are mainly the herbs (*Carex* spp, reed, sedge) and the shrubs (*Salix* spp, *Betula* spp, *Spiraea* spp, *Ledum palustre* and *Vaccinium uliginosum*). In addition, *Sphagnum* spp and *Polytrichum* spp have been found in some peatlands. TOC/TN ratio is 9.8-50.0, and pH (KCl) is 3.53-5.54. Hence, we conclude the majority of the mires are still in eutrophic condition although they originated at least 2000 years ago. Some mires developed at the early-middle Holocene at the foot of Changbai Mountains and some ones developed at the late Holocene in the ridge appear to be in a transition from the eutrophic status to the mesotrophic one. The trophic status of the mires in Changbai Mountains may be attributed to abundant nutrition sources, especially atmospheric deposition derived from the East Asia monsoon.

***Keywords**: mires; Changbai Mountains; trophic status; TOC/TN*

INTRODUCTION

Mire ecologists have recognized the importance of trophic status of mires (Olchev *et al.*, 2013). Trophic status of mires is usually considered when peat resource is developed and utilized or vegetation and climate history are reconstructed in palaeoecology (Minaeva *et al.*, 2008). The ecological basis of the poor-rich gradients in mires is principally the level of inflow of mineral water (Comeau and Bellamy, 1986; Proctor et al, 2009). However, several studies have questioned whether the poor-rich gradients coincide with a trophic gradient in mires. The plant community compositions are frequently used as the indication of trophic status in mires (Malmer *et al.*, 1994). But there are some studies about the extreme difference of trophic status with the same dominant species in mires (Charman, 2002). Succow and Joosten (2001) provided a comprehensive study of trophic status of mires, using plant community composition, pH and carbon-nitrogen ratio in peat soils. The results showed that a majority of mires were in poor condition in central Europe.

The objective of this paper was to investigate the trophic conditions of mires in China – a case study in Changbai Mountains. Although it is one of the areas in which mires are widely distributed in Northeast China, only a small number of studies on the trophic status in the mires have been reported (Jia *et al.*, 2006). Our work has been devoted to present data on trophic status of the mires in Changbai Mountains and to provide the theoretical basis for the future integrative development and protection of the mires.

MATERAILS AND METHODS

Study sites

The investigated sites are situated at the east of Weihu Ridge - Longgang Mountains (41°41'21.17" N - 44°31'10.13" N, 125°18'39.32" E - 128°12'50" E) composed of lava plateau with elevation ranging between 200 and 1800 m above sea level (a.s.l.). The area has a temperate continental monsoon climate characterized by zonal distribution laws with increasing altitudes. The mean annual temperature is 2 - 6 °C, and annual rainfall is 650 - 894 mm. The maximum precipitation falls from June to August, which accounts for over 60% of annual rainfall. The zonal vegetation in this region is Korean pine - dominated mixed coniferous and broad leaved forest.

Experimental Methods and Measurements

The 130 plant quadrats from 75 mires in Changbai Mountains were investigated for the types of plant community in July 2014. The size of quadrats was 1m×1m for the herbs, 4 m × 4 m for the shrubs and 10m×10m for the arbors. At the same time, peat samples were taken out using a stainless knife from the peatland surface (0 - 15 cm) beneath each plant quadrat, sealed in polythene bags and brought back to laboratory. These peat soils were air dried naturally, and sieved through a 2mm nylon mesh, then analyzed for total organic carbon, total nitrogen and pH.

Total organic carbon (TOC) was measured by the K2Cr2O7-H2SO4 oxidation method, total soil nitrogen (TN) was measured using the Kjeldahl digestion procedure, and pH was measured by pH meter (1mol/L KCl). The distribution map of the plant communities was drawn using ArcGIS10.0 software package. The statistical analysis of soil pH and TOC/TN ratio were conducted with Spss version 21.0.

RESULTS

The types of the plant communities

Seven kinds of plant communities were found in this area, including *Betula ovalifolia* Rupr - *Oxyeoceus quadripetalus* Gilib. - *Sphagnum* spp, *Vaccinium uliginosum* L. - *Hododendron patvifolium* Adams. - *Sphagnum* spp, *Latix* spp - *Ledum palustre var. angustum* E. Busch. - *Sphagnum* spp, *Latix* spp - *vaccinium uliginosum* L. - *Sphagnum* spp, *Latix* spp - *Betula* spp-Carex spp, *Phragmites australis* Trin., *Carex* spp and *Latix* spp – *Eriophclrum* spa. Three vegetation types consisting of seven plant communities display apparent features along different altitudes (Fig.1). The community structure in an altitudinal zone below 500 m a.s.l. is distinctly simple compared with other altitudinal zones. The plant communities are mainly represented by *Betula* spp - *Carex schmidtii* Meinsh. and *spiraea salicifolia* L. – *C. schmidtii* Meinsh. below 500m a.s.l. for swamps; and *C. schmidtii* Meinsh., *Phragmites australis* Trin. - *C. schmidtii* Meinsh. and *Eriophclrum* spp - *C. schmidtii* Meinsh for fens. However, bogs emerge in the altitudinal zone above 800 m a.s.l., where the mosses play a crucial role in communities. The dominant species included *Sphagnum* spp, *Polytriehum eontortum* Lesq. and so on for bogs. In addition, significant variations in the community types are observed among different altitudinal zones, for example, *Larix* spp - *Betula* spp - *C. schmidtii* Meinsh. is typical for swamps above 500 m a.s.l., but this community type is rare below 500 m a.s.l.

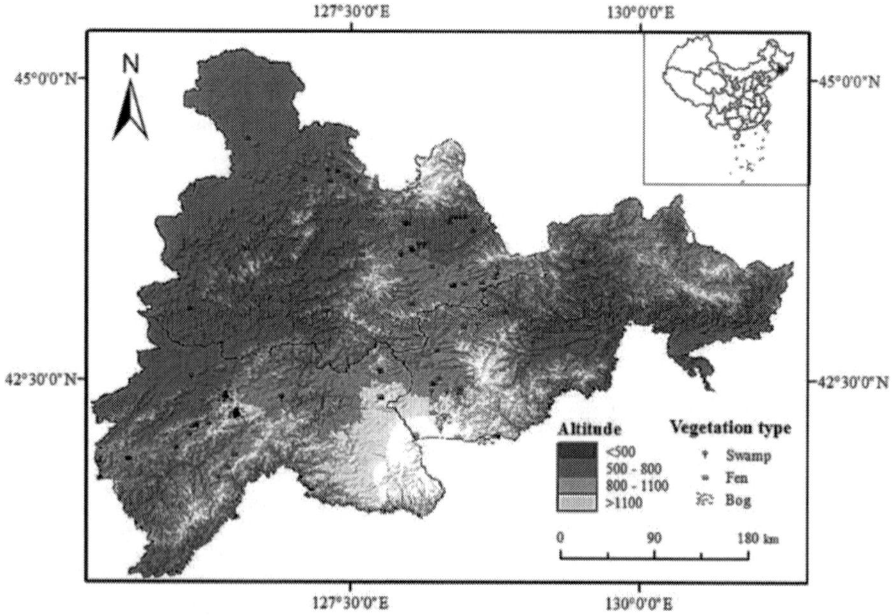

Fig.1: The vegetation type of the mires from Changbai Mountain.

The pH values

The average pH of all peat samples is 4.6, ranging from 3.53 to 5.54. The soil pH exhibits a notably declining trend along the increasing altitudes (Fig.2-1). To illustrate the pH variance among different altitudinal zones, the one-way ANOVA analysis was performed. Our results show that the soil pH from the altitudinal zones below 1100 m a.s.l. is similar to each other, while it is significantly different from other zones in the altitudinal zones above 1100 m a.s.l. ($p<0.05$) (Fig.2-2).

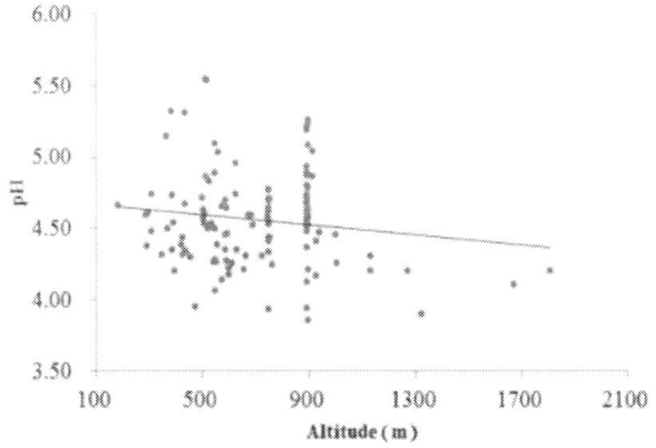

Fig. 2.1: pH in surface soil at different altitudes.

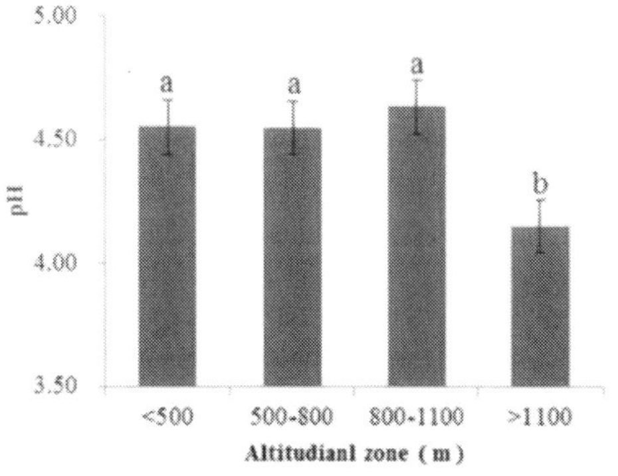

Fig. 2.2: pH in surface soil among different altitudinal zones ($p<0.05$).

The ratio of TOC/TN

The average TOC/N is 21.4, ranging from 9.8 to 50. In comparison to soil pH, TOC/TN shows an obviously opposite trend along the altitudes (Fig.3-1). The ratio from altitudinal zones above 500m a.s.l. has a statistically significant difference from each other ($p<0.05$). No significant variance in TOC/TN ratio is detected between the altitudinal zones below 500m a.s.l. and 500-800m a.s.l., while notable difference between the altitudinal zones below 500m a.s.l. and above 800m a.s.l. ($p<0.05$) (Fig.3-2).

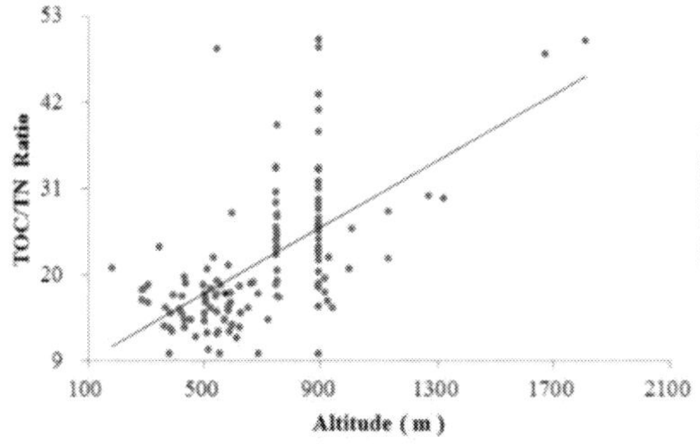

Fig. 3.1: TOC/TN at different altitudes.

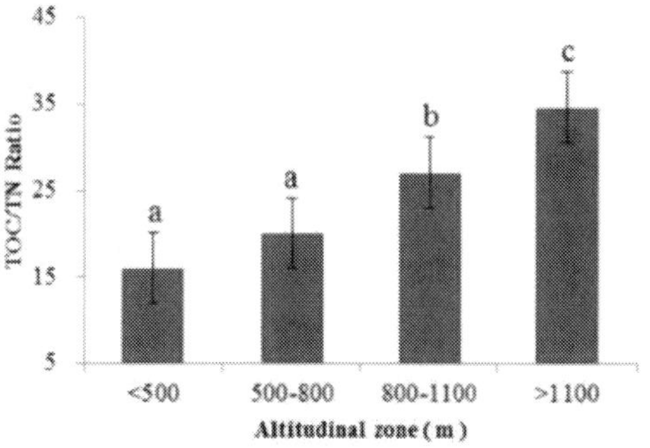

Fig.3.2: TOC/TN variance among different altitudinal zones ($p<0.05$).

DISCUSSION

Characteristics of trophic status of the mires in Changbai Mountains

Based on plant community composition, pH and carbon-nitrogen ratio in peat soils, 53.8% of the mires investigated was the entrophic status, 33.8% was mesotrophic, and 12.4% was oligotrophic status (Fig.4). The distribution of trophic status of the mires is characterized by vertical zoning along altitudinal gradient. The eutrophic mires are mainly in the zones below 500 m a.s.l.; a small number of mires are in mesotrophic condition in the zones of 500-800 m a.s.l.. The number of mires in oligotrophic state rises up in proportion when the altitudes are beyond 800 m a.s.l.. The transitional mires, from the eutrophic to the mesotrophic or from the mesotrophic to oligotrophic, have also been found in high altitude zones.

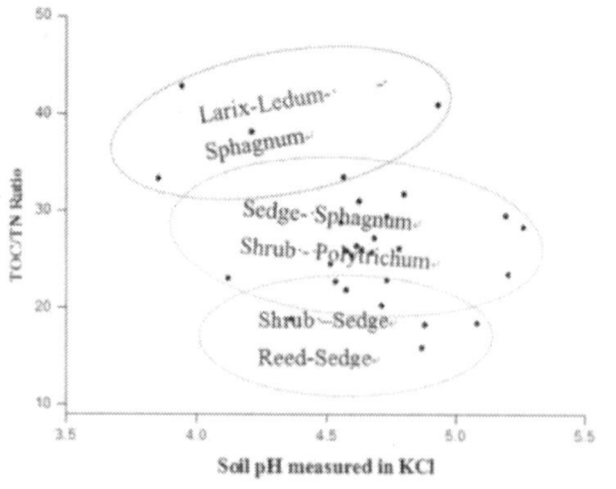

Fig. 4: The pH, TOC/TN and plant community types in Hani mire.

The variance of mire types is significant among mires in different altitudinal zones. Besides, the plant communities from different habitats within a mire were found to be in different trophic status. For example, plant communities in Hani mire located in west Changbai Mountains shows a character of zonation. The plant communities are represented by *Larix* spp - *Betula ovalifolia* Ruprecht - *Sphagnum* spp; *Phragmites australis* Trin. - *Carex schmidtii* Meinsh. and relatively pure *Carex* spp communities from the periphery to the center of the mire. The TOC/TN (10.1-50.0) increases and pH values (3.8-5.3) decrease along altitude (Fig.4). These suggested the trophic status also changed from oligotrophic to mesotrophic condition, or was a transition from mesotrophication to eutrophication.

The developmental mechanism of trophic status of the mires

Precipitations at higher altitudes are higher than that at lower altitudes while mean annual air temperature decreased with increasing altitude in Changbai Mountians. Given the strong relations between the decomposition rates of organic matter and climatic variables (Liski et al, 2003), it is to be expected that changes in rainfall and temperature along altitudes will lead to the decrease of decomposition rates of organic matter and thus a lower nutrient level in mires. Moreover, precipitations are the main nutrition source for mires at higher altitude. Hence the proportions of the mires in mesotrophic or oligotroghic status will increase with altitudes.

However, a part of mires originated from Early Holocene were still in eutrophic condition at higher altitude. They are different from that in European mires developed in the same period. For example, Hani mire located at over 900m a.s.l., was chiefly in eutrophic-mesotrophic stage at present although it was formed at least 8780$\pm$95 years ago (Li et al, 2001). This would be attributed to atmospheric deposition derived from the East Asia monsoon, especially airborne components (mineral dust and particles et al) could bring abundant nutrients in winter for half year into Hani mire.

CONCLUSION

Our study showed that trophic status of the mires in Changbai Mountains in Northeast China was characterized by vertical zoning along altitudinal gradient although the majority of the mires were still in eutrophic condition. The mires located in high-altitude sites are different from that in Europe and North America in trophic status although they were developing at the similar periods. It is supposed that the eutrophic status or transitions from euthophic to mesotrophic status of the mires from Changbai Mountains may be closely related to atmospheric deposition derived from the East Asia monsoon.

REFERENCES

1. Charman D, 2002. Peatlands and environmental change. Chichester: John Wiley & Sons Inc, 3 - 23pp.
2. Clymo RS, Hayward PM, 1982. *The Ecology of Sphagnum*. In: Smith AJE eds. Bryophyte ecology. London: Chapman and Hall, 229 - 290pp.
3. Comeau PL, Bellamy DJ, 1986.An ecological interpretation of the chemistry of mire waters from selected sites in eastern Canada. *Canadian Journal of Botany*, 64: 2576 - 2581.
4. Gore AJP, 1983. Ecosystems of the world: mires - swamp, bog, fen and moor - regional studies. *Ecosystems of*

the World, 4b.
5. Jia L, Wang GP, Liu JS, 2006 Distribution and implication of major and trace elements in peat profiles of Yuanchi, Changbai Mountains. *Journal of Mountain Science*, 24(6): 662 - 666.
6. Li JD, Wu BH, Sheng LX, 2001. *Jinlin Vegetation*. Changchun: Jilin Science and Technology Press, 230pp.
7. Liski, J, Nissinen, A, Erhard, M, 2003.Climatic effects on litter decomposition from arctic tundra to tropical rainforest. *Global Change Biology*, 9: 575 - 584.
8. MalmerN, Svensson BM, Wallen B, 1994.Interactions between Sphagnum mosses and field layer vascular plants in the development of peat-forming systems. *Folia Geobotanicaet Phytotaxonomica*, 29: 483 - 496.
9. Minaeva TY, Trofimov SY, Chichagova OA, et al, 2008. Carbon accumulation in soils of forest and bog ecosystems of southern Valdai in the Holocene. *Biology and Bulletin*. 35(5): 524 - 532
10. Michaels AF, Karl DM, Capone DG, 2001.Element stoichiometry, new production and nitrogen fixation. *Oceanography*, 14(4): 68 - 77.
11. OlchevA et al, 2013.Growing season variability of netecosystem CO2 exchange andevapotranspiration of a sphagnummire in the broad-leaved forest zone of European Russia. Environmental Research Letters, 8(3): 1 - 7.
12. Proctor MCF, McHaffie HS, Legg CJ, Amphlett A, 2009. Evidence from water chemistry as a criterion of ombrotrophy in the mire complexes of Abernethy Forest, Scotland. *Journal of Vegetation Science*, 120: 160 - 169.
13. Succow, M, Joosten, H, 2001. *Landschaftsökologische Moorkunde*. E. Schweizerbart'sche Verlagsbuchh.

1.5: PEATLAND BIODIVERSITY

1.5: PEATLAND BIODIVERSITY

Abstract No: A-189

ASSESSING THE DIVERSITY OF VIRUSES IN SOILS OBTAINED FROM LIMESTONE CAVES

Hasina Mohammed Mkwata, Lee Tung Tan, and Peter Morin Nissom*

Swinburne University of Technology Sarawak Campus, Malaysia

**Corresponding author: pmorin@swinburne.edu.my*

SUMMARY

Viruses influence bacterial abundance and community composition through lysis and alter bacterial genetic diversity through transduction and lysogenic conversion. Bacteriophages are DNA containing viruses that infect their bacteria hosts. This project investigates the biodiversity of bacteriophages in soil samples obtained from limestone cave environment in Sarawak. Phage lysates were obtained and spot tested on six representative pathogenic bacteria (*Escherichia coli, Staphylococcus aureus, Pseudomonas aeruginosa, Streptococcus pneumoniae, Klebsiella pneumoniae* and *Vibrio parahaemolyticus*) so as to determine their lysis spectrum. We show successful isolation of bacteriophages and some members exhibited multiple host ranges.

***Keywords**: biogeochemical cycles, host range, lysis, transduction*

INTRODUCTION

Viruses are the most abundant and diverse nucleic acid-based entities on earth (Aziz *et al.*, 2015). There are approximately 10 times as many viruses as the combined number of all cellular organisms, most of which are bacteriophages (Edwards and Rohwer 2005). Bacteriophages (phages) are bacterio-specific viruses which infects and lyse their respective hosts (Sulakvelidze *et al.*, 2001). Phages are by far the most abundant viruses in the ocean with numbers estimated at 10^{27} phage particles where as the entire viriosphere is estimated to contain 10^{31} phage particles (Wilhelm and Suttle, 1999; Suttle 2005). Due to their widespread in the environment, phages can be isolated from any material that supports bacteria proliferation. Majority of work derived from marine ecosystem have reported environmental viruses to be the largest reservoir of genetic diversity on the planet; they mould microbial communities, cause lysis of a large portion of the ocean biomass on a daily basis, transfer genetic material among host organisms and shunt nutrients between particulate and dissolved phases (Hambly and Suttle, 2005; Suttle 2005). In recent years, the use of bacteriophages as antimicrobial agents has rekindled due to the emergence and increased incidence of multidrug resistance in bacteria. For example, carbapenemase-producing gram-negative bacteria such as extensively drug resistant *Actinobacter spp* and enterobacteriaceae producing New Delhi metallo-protease 1 (NDM-1), *Klebsiella pneumoniae* carbapenemase (KPC) or oxallinase 48 (OXA-48), and most recently, the plasmid-mediated colistin resistance mechanism in animals and humans (Yong *et al.*, 2009, Kumarasamy *et al.* 2010, Huttner *et al.*, 2013, Liu *et al.*, 2016).

The ubiquitous presence of bacteriophages in nature and the reported diversity of their genomes have also renewed interest in phage research (McAuliffe *et al.*, 2007). Different studies have revealed that phages are incredibly diverse in their properties, from host range, genetic content, regulatory mechanisms and physiological effects. For instance, most of the genes identified on the genome sequencing of cultured phages and metagenomic analysis of uncultured phages show no similarity to anything in the current available databases (McAuliffe *et al.*, 2007).This explains that diversity do exist in the types of phages that infect individual or interrelated bacterial species and also among genomically related phages that do not share the same bacterial hosts. Caves are considered to be extreme environments to life as a result of lack of organic carbon input from photosynthesis and absence of light and various physicochemical micro-gradients (Northup and Lavoie, 2001). However, studies have reported on the presence of vast microbial communities with unexpected biodiversity (Tomczyk-Żak and U., 2015). This current study aimed at investigating the biodiversity of bacteriophages from soil samples collected at Fairy caves, a limestone outcrop in Sarawak, Malaysia. Host range assay was performed on successful phage candidates to assess their ability to infect other bacterial species.

METHODS

Soil sample collection and phage screening

Soil samples used in this study were collected at a depth of 0-25cm from Fairy caves, in Sarawak, Malaysia. Bacteria host strains *E.coli, Ps.aeruginosa, S.aureus, K.pneumoniae* (K48), *S.pneumoniae* and *V.parahaemolyticus* (DSM10027) used during phage screening and host range assay were purchased from American Type Culture Collection (ATCC) Manassas, VA, USA. Pour-plate technique was employed for initial phage screening from soil samples. Briefly, 1 g of each soil sample was inoculated separately into 100 mL of sterile Brain-heart infusion (BHI) broth supplemented with 4 mL of sterile 10mM $CaCl_2$ solution and the contents incubated for 1 hr at 37°C. Five millilitres (5 mL) of host bacteria culture (*S. aureus, S.pneumoniae, K.pneumoniae, Ps.aeruginosa, E.coli* or *V.parahaemolyticus*) at its early exponential phase was then inoculated into the soil sample broth and contents incubated overnight at 37°C and 150 rpm. Next morning, 1 mL of 1% TTC (2,3,5-Triphenyltetrazolium chloride) and 1.2 mL sterile 10mM $CaCl_2$ solutions were added into a Schott bottle containing 100 mL of liquefied nutrient agar. About 5 mL of host bacterial culture at its mid log phage was then inoculated into the Schott bottle and the contents slowly mixed and poured out into petri dishes avoiding formation of any bubbles. The plates were allowed to air dry in the laminar flow biosafety cabinet (BSC) and then incubated without inversion for up to 24 hours at 37 °C. 1% TTC (2,3,5-Triphenyltetrazolium chloride) solution was incorporated into the phage screening media so as to enhance the resolution of plaques.

Phage isolation, amplification and lysate preparation

Plates were examined carefully and plaques identified. A sterile straw was used to core/dig out the agar part containing the plaque from each petri plate and then dropped into a universal bottle containing 4mL BHI broth supplemented with 100µl of 10 mM $CaCl_2$ solution. Immediately, 1mL of respective bacteria host culture grown to its mid log phage was inoculated and the bottle incubated for 24 hours with shaking at 37°C and 150 rpm. After bacteria lysis was observed, each solution was centrifuged at 8000g for five minutes and the supernatant containing phage particles was filtered through a 0.22µm syringe filter. A drop of chloroform (~ 50µl) was added into each of the recovered phage lysates and the tubes stored temporarily in the fridge at 4°C.

Host range assay

Bacteria strains used for host range determination were grown to an OD 600 of 1.0 in BHI broth. About 0.3mL of host bacteria culture was inoculated into 3mL of sterile Top agar supplemented with 100µl of 10mM $CaCl_2$ solution prepared in a culture tube (molten at 45°C). The contents were inverted gently and quickly poured onto a pre-warmed BHI agar plate and left to air dry in the laminar flow biosafety cabinet for about 15min. Phage host range was determined by spotting 10µl of phage lysate preparation (~10^{10} pfu/ml) three times onto different host plates. The plates were then incubated at 37°C for up to 36 hrs. A successful phage infection was scored based on plaque formation on a susceptible bacterial lawn.

RESULTS

A total of 25 bacteriophages were isolated from soil samples based on their ability to propagate and form plaques on their respective bacteria lawns. Figure 1 shows plaque formation from bacteriophages capable of infecting bacteria strain *S.pneumoniae*. The ability of each phage to lyse each bacteria strain was performed to give an indication of the breadth of host specificity of each phage. Table 1, summarises the lytic pattern measured for each bacteriophage. Generally, most phages showed broad host specificity with each one able to infect bacteria strain *Ps. aeruginosa*. Bacteriophages designated as VPSS3-2, VPSS4-1 and VPSS4-2 which are *V.parahamemolyticus* infecting phages showed the broadest host specificity with each of them able to lyse bacteria strains *S. aureus, Ps.aeruginosa and E.coli*. However, none of these phages were able to infect bacteria strains *S.pneumoniae* and *K.pneumoniae*.

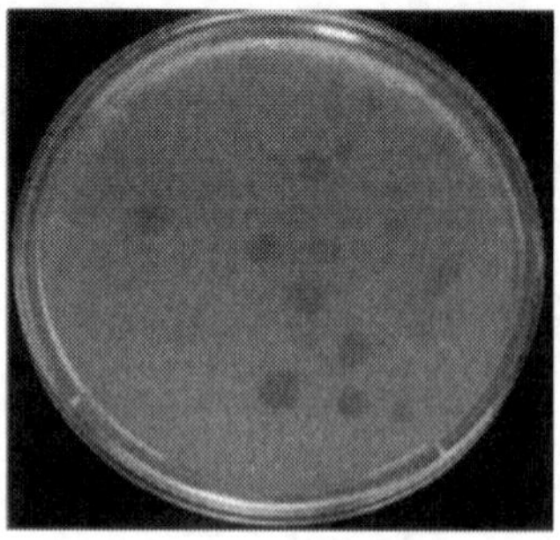

Figure 1: Plaque appearance of bacteriophages infecting *S. pneumoniae* after incubation for 24 hours at 37°C.

Table 1: Host range analysis of phage isolates. Lysis pattern was measured qualitatively as (++) for full lysis, (+) for partial lysis and (-) for no lysis

Phage isolates	Bacterial host					
	V.parahaemolyticus	*S.aureus*	*Ps.aeruginosa*	*S.pneumoniae*	*K.pneumoniae*	*E. coli*
VPSS3-1	+	++	++	-	-	-
VPSS3-2	++	++	+	-	-	++
VPSS4-1	++	++	++	-	-	++
VPSS4-2	++	++	++	-	-	++
VPLND-1	++	-	++	-	-	-
VPLND-2	++	-	++	-	-	++
SA1	-	++	++	-	-	++
SA2	-	++	++	-	-	-
SA3	-	-	++	-	-	-
SA4	-	-	++	-	-	+
SASSI-1	-	++	++	-	-	++
SASS2-2	-	++	++	-	-	++
PASS1-1	-	++	+	-	-	-
PASS4-1	-	++	++	-	-	++
PASS4-2	-	++	+	-	-	++
SP1	-	-	++	++	-	++
SP2	-	-	++	++	-	++
SPSS1-1	-	-	++	++	-	++
SPSS2-1	-	-	++	-	-	-
SPSS2-2	-	+	++	-	-	-
KP1	-	-	++	-	-	-
KP2	-	-	++	-	-	++
EC1	-	-	++	-	-	++
EC2	-	-	++	-	-	++
ECSS3-1	-	-	++	-	-	++

DISCUSSION

This study reports successful isolation of lytic bacteriophages from soils collected at Fairy caves in Sarawak, Malaysia. The isolated phages exhibited distinctive features such as mixed plaque morphologies suggesting presence of different phage traits infecting the same bacterial host (Gallet *et al.*, 2011). Bacteriophage host-range analysis is a crucial factor in assessing phage diversity in the environment (Malki *et al.* 2015). Table 1 summarises the results obtained from bacteriophage host-range testing. As indicated, *V. parahaemolyticus* infecting bacteriophages designated as VPSS3-2, VPSS4-1 and VPSS4-2 obtained from Fairy cave soils exhibited the broadest host specificity with each member able to lyse bacteria strains *S. aureus, Ps. aeruginosa* and *E. coli.* Interestingly, this broad lysis spectrum extended beyond a single bacteria phylum. This was observed by the ability of these phage isolates to infect *S. aureus* bacteria which belongs to a completely different phylum i.e. Eubacteria. Previous studies have assigned classification as a "generalist" when a phage demonstrates capacity to infect more than one species of a bacterial genus, while some restricting the definition further to include strains of a particular species (Bono *et al.*, 2013, Czajkowski *et al.*, 2014, Merabishvili *et al.*, 2014). Similar findings have been reported by Malki *et al.* (2015) where bacteriophages isolated from lake Michigan were capable of infecting several bacteria phyla and it was proposed that such a broad host-range was likely related to the oligotrophic nature of the lake and the competitive benefit this characteristic may have contributed to phages in nature. These findings suggest that bacteriophage host-range is not always genera-restricted and the oligotrophic environment of Fairy cave might have in one way or another contributed to the broad lytic spectrum exhibited by *V. parahaemolyticus* infecting phage isolates.

The host range assay results also revealed that a significant number of these phage isolates failed to infect some bacteria strains such as *V.parahaemolyticus*, *S.pneumoniae* and *K.pneumoniae*. This could have been due to alteration of bacteriophage surface receptors that reduces or eliminates phage adsorption to the host cell. This phenomenon appears to be the most common mechanism of phage resistance (Bohannan and Lenski 2000). Moreover, some of the phage isolates such as KP1, SA3 and SPSS2-1 which are *K. pneumoniae, S. aureus* and *S. pneumoniae* infecting phages respectively as indicated in Table 1, failed to lyse their original hosts from which they were first isolated during host range analysis experiments. The possibility that these bacteriophages could not re-infect the host bacteria might be due to spontaneous single mutation in the host bacteria which caused it to gain resistance to the phage (Khan *et al.* 2002). Nevertheless, despite the broad lysis spectrum showed by the isolated phages, none was able to infect bacteria strain *K. pneumoniae* during host-range analysis and this could have been due to variation of its receptor molecules or its restriction modification system (O'Flynn *et al.* 2004).

CONCLUSION

Bacteriophages capable of infecting bacterial strains *V.parahaemolyticus*, *S.aureus*, *Ps.aeruginosa*, *S.pneumoniae*, *K.pneumoniae* and *E.coli* were successfully isolated from a limestone cave (Fairy caves) in Sarawak. Some of these phage isolates displayed broad lysis spectrum with a few members able to infect bacteria belonging to a completely different phylum. We propose that, due to high lytic nature and broad host spectrum exhibited by the isolated phages, they show potentials to be employed in biocontrol of animal and foodborne pathogens.

ACKNOWLEDGEMENTS

The authors express their sincere gratitude to Swinburne University of Technology, Sarawak campus, Malaysia for providing financial support (SSRG 25502) and facilities used to complete this short study. We also thank Sarawak Biodiversity Centre (SBC) and Sarawak Forestry Department (SFD) for their permission to collect soil samples from Fairy cave and Lundu Palm Oil Plantation.

REFERENCES

1. Aziz, R. K., Dwivedi, B., Akhter, S., Breitbart, M. and Edwards, R. A. (2015) 'Multidimensional metrics for estimating phage abundance, distribution, gene density, and sequence coverage in metagenomes', *Front Microbiol*, 6, 381-394.
2. Bohannan, B. J. M. and Lenski, R. E. (2000) 'Linking genetic change to community evolution: insights from studies of bacteria and bacteriophage', *Ecology Letters*, 3, 362-377.
3. Bono, L. M., Gensel, C. L., Pfennig, D. W. and Burch, C. L. (2013) 'Competition and the origins of novelty: experimental evolution of niche-width expansion in a virus', *Biol Lett*, 9(1), 2012-2016.
4. Czajkowski, R., Ozymko, Z., Zwirowski, S. and Lojkowska, E. (2014) 'Complete genome sequence of a broad-host-range lytic Dickeya spp. bacteriophage varphiD5', *Arch Virol*, 159(11), 3153-3155.
5. Edwards, R. A. and Rohwer, F. (2005) 'Viral metagenomics', *Nat Rev Microbiol*, 3(6), 504-10.
6. Gallet, R., Kannoly, S. and Wang, I. N. (2011) 'Effects of bacteriophage traits on plaque formation', *BMC Microbiol*, 11(1), 1-16.
7. Hambly, E. and Suttle, C. A. (2005) 'The viriosphere, diversity, and genetic exchange within phage communities', *Current opinion in Microbiology*, 8, 444-450.
8. Huttner, A., Harbarth, S., Carlet, J., Cosgrove, S., Goossens, H., Holmes, A., Jarlier, V., Voss, A. and Pittet, D. (2013) 'Antimicrobial resistance: a global view from the 2013 World Healthcare-Associated Infections Forum', *Antimicrob Resist Infect Control*, 2, 1-31.
9. Khan, M. A., Satoh, H., Katayama, H., Kurisu, F. and Mino, T. (2002) 'Bacteriophages isolated from activated sludge processes and their polyvalency', *Water research*, 36(13), 3364-3370.
10. Kumarasamy, K. K., Toleman, M. A., Walsh, T. R., Bagaria, J., Butt, F., Balakrishnan, R., Chaudhary, U., Doumith, M., Giske, C. G., Irfan, S., Krishnan, P., Kumar, A. V., Maharjan, S., Mushtaq, S., Noorie, T., Paterson, D. L., Pearson, A., Perry, C., Pike, R., Rao, B., Ray, U., Sarma, J. B., Sharma, M., Sheridan, E., Thirunarayan, M. A., Turton, J., Upadhyay, S., Warner, M., Welfare, W., Livermore, D. M. and Woodford, N.

(2010) 'Emergence of a new antibiotic resistance mechanism in India, Pakistan, and the UK: a molecular, biological, and epidemiological study', *Lancet Infect Dis*, 10(9), 597-602.

11. Liu, Y. Y., Wang, Y., Walsh, T. R., Yi, L. X., Zhang, R., Spencer, J., Doi, Y., Tian, G., Dong, B., Huang, X., Yu, L. F., Gu, D., Ren, H., Chen, X., Lv, L., He, D., Zhou, H., Liang, Z., Liu, J. H. and Shen, J. (2016) 'Emergence of plasmid-mediated colistin resistance mechanism MCR-1 in animals and human beings in China: a microbiological and molecular biological study', *Lancet Infect Dis*, 16(2), 161-168.
12. Malki, K., Kula, A., Bruder, K., Sible, E., Hatzopoulos, T., Steidel, S., Watkins, S. C. and Putonti, C. (2015) 'Bacteriophages isolated from Lake Michigan demonstrate broad host-range across several bacterial phyla', *Virol J*, 12(1), 1-5.
13. McAuliffe, O., Ross, R. P. and Fitzgerald, G. F. (2007) *The new phage biology: from genomics to applications*, Norfolk: Caister Academic Press.
14. Merabishvili, M., Vandenheuvel, D., Kropinski, A. M., Mast, J., De Vos, D., Verbeken, G., Noben, J. P., Lavigne, R., Vaneechoutte, M. and Pirnay, J. P. (2014) 'Characterization of newly isolated lytic bacteriophages active against Acinetobacter baumannii', *PLoS One*, 9(8), 1-11.
15. Northup, D. E. and Lavoie, K. H. (2001) 'Geomicrobiology of caves:a review', *Geomicrobiology Journal*, 18, 199-222.
16. O'Flynn, G., Ross, R. P., Fitzgerald, G. F. and Coffey, A. (2004) 'Evaluation of a cocktail of three bacteriophages for biocontrol of Escherichia coli O157:H7', *Appl Environ Microbiol*, 70(6), 3417-3424.
17. Sulakvelidze, A., Alavidze, Z. and Morris, J. G., Jr. (2001) 'Bacteriophage therapy', *Antimicrob Agents Chemother*, 45(3), 649-659.
18. Suttle, C. A. (2005) 'Viruses in the sea', *Nature*, 437(7057), 356-361.
19. Tomczyk-Żak, K. and U., Z. (2015) 'Microbial Diversity in Caves', *Review of Geomicrobiology*, 1-19.
20. Wilhelm, S. W. and Suttle, C. A. (1999) 'Viruses and Nutrient Cycles in the Sea', *BioScience*, 49(10), 781-788.
21. Yong, D., Toleman, M. A., Giske, C. G., Cho, H. S., Sundman, K., Lee, K. and Walsh, T. R. (2009) 'Characterization of a new metallo-beta-lactamase gene, bla(NDM-1), and a novel erythromycin esterase gene carried on a unique genetic structure in Klebsiella pneumoniae sequence type 14 from India', *Antimicrob Agents Chemother*, 53(12), 5046-5054.

Abstract No: A-346

ASSESSMENT OF MICROBIAL DIVERSITY IN AN UNDISTURBED TROPICAL PEAT-DRAINING RIVER USING 16S rRNA PYROSEQUENCING, WITH A PARTICULAR FOCUS ON METHANOTROPHS AND METHANOGENS

N. Denis[1*], D. Müller[2], T. Warneke[2], A. Mujahid[3], D. Tan[1] and M. Müller[1]

[1]*Swinburne University of Technology Sarawak Campus, Faculty of Engineering, Computing and Science, Jalan Simpang Tiga, 93350 Kuching Sarawak, Malaysia*
[2]*Institute of Environmental Physics, University of Bremen, Otto-Hah-Allee 1, 28359 Bremen, Germany*
[3]*Department of Aquatic Science, Faculty of Resource Science and Technology, University Malaysia Sarawak, 94300 Kota Samarahan, Sarawak, Malaysia*

**Corresponding author: nasdenis82@gmail.com*

Surprisingly, despite the important role of peatlands in the global carbon cycle, microbial communities in these environments remain severely understudied. In previous studies we were able to show that the undisturbed peat-draining river in the Maludam National Park contains some of the highest dissolved organic carbon concentrations ever recorded worldwide, but interestingly the release of carbon dioxide was relatively low. While both chemical and physical reasons exist for the moderate CO_2 fluxes, microbiology is likely one of the key reasons as to why so little outgassing was observed and our study aimed at assessing the microbial diversity in the river sediments. Surface sediment samples were collected along a transect in Sungai Maludam (from source to coast), DNA extracted and analysed on a MiSeq (250bp PE) using universal primers that amplify for both Bacteria and Archaea. Results revealed a high abundance of *Acidobacteria, Firmicutes* and *Proteobacteria* which is similar with past studies but with exception of *Firmicutes* noted to be outstandingly high. Occurrence of methanotrophs was highest in stations upriver implying low CH4 release from the river and offering a potential explanation as to why so little outgassing of greenhouse gases (GHG) was observed in Maludam.

Keywords: -

Abstract No: A-431

BIOCONTROL ASSESSMENT OF ACTINOBACTERIA FROM TROPICAL PEATLAND AGAINST *GANODERMA* SPP.

Frazer Midot*, Sharon Yu Ling Lau and Lulie Melling

Tropical Peat Research Laboratory Unit, Chief Minister's Department, Sarawak, Malaysia

**corresponding author: frazer.m@sarawak.gov.my*

SUMMARY

Ganoderma spp. are major phytopathogens of oil palm which cause basal stem rot and upper stem rot disease in Southeast Asia. In Malaysia, it was estimated that by 2020, approximately 400,000 hectares (ha) of oil palm plantation would be affected with yield reductions of 0.04 to 4.34 tonnes ha^{-1} based on *Ganoderma* incidence rates in 10 to 22 years of planting record (Roslan and Idris, 2012). Cumulative economic losses due to *Ganoderma* spp. were also reported to be in the range of RM 225 million to RM 1.5 billion a year (Arif *et al.*, 2011). Consequently, there is an urgent need to carry out R&D to explore effective *Ganoderma* control measures. The practice of using fungicides such as hexaconazole is promising but can be costly and environmentally unfriendly. Biocontrol offers an alternative control measure if phytopathogens develop resistance towards chemical control, as biocontrol agents are capable of co-evolving with the phytopathogens. Actinobacteria, especially those in the order Actinomycetales, are known to produce a variety of secondary metabolites that can potentially be used as biocontrol agents. Quantitatively and qualitatively, Actinobacteria are vital to a plant's rhizosphere as they can colonize the plant's root system. Actinobacteria such as *Streptomyces* spp. are known to produce antifungal and extracellular enzymes that could potentially inhibit *Ganoderma* growth. The exact mechanism of control however is not fully understood. As Actinobacteria produce a variety of active compounds, the antagonism could be due to synergic interaction between excreted bioactive metabolites. Screening of Actinobacteria for potential antifungal metabolites in tropical peatland could contribute to the discovery of novel active compounds as they survive in harsher conditions than those of other terrestrial ecosystems. In this study, culturable Actinobacteria from Sarawak tropical peatland were collected to study their antagonism against *Ganoderma* spp. wild strains. Screening of Actinobacteria was performed with dual culture plate assay and poison agar assay. From 234 Actinobacteria isolates tested, 74 isolates showed potential antagonistic activity. Molecular identification based on 16S rDNA analysis revealed that 72 isolates belong to the genus *Streptomyces* and two to the genus *Kitasatospora.* Preliminary results indicate that isolates of *Streptomyces flavogriseus, S. aburaviensis, S. tsukiyonensis, S. sampsoni, S. coeruleofuscus, S. citricolor* and *S. lacticiproducens* in this study exhibit potential antagonistic activity against *Ganoderma*.

Keywords: *Actinobacteria; Ganoderma spp.; phytopathogen; biocontrol*

INTRODUCTION

Oil palm is an economically important crop in Malaysia. Unfortunately, it faces the threat of infection by *Ganoderma* spp. a major disease-causing agent of oil palm in Malaysia (Naher *et al.*, 2015). According to Roslan and Idris (2012), approximately 400,000 ha of oil palm plantation will be affected by *Ganoderma* by year 2020. It was also estimated that losses cause by *Ganoderma* disease can be up to RM 1.5 billion per year (Arif *et al.*, 2011). *Ganoderma* spp. especially *G. boninense*, causes both basal stem rot (BSR) and upper stem rot (USR) and still remains Southeast Asia's most devastating oil palm disease (Hushiarian *et al.*, 2013). To date, there is no method to effectively control this phytopathogen. Difficulties in controlling disease development arise from insufficient information about *Ganoderma* spp. needed for the development of an early detection system (Rolph *et al.*, 2000). *Ganoderma boninense*, *G. zonatum* and *G. miniatocinctum* have been identified as the cause of BSR and USR in Malaysia (Naher *et al.*, 2015; Rakib *et al.*, 2014). It is realistically impossible to be able to manage a crop field to be pathogen free; however, disease reduction can be achieved *via* proper management. Practices such soil mounding prolongs oil palm economic life and trench digging prevents root contact between infected and healthy palms (Naher *et al.*, 2015). Usage of chemical treatment such as hexaconazole, although promising, does not cure an infected plant (Chung, 2011) and is harmful to the environment. As an alternative, biological control has potential in plant disease management. Fungi such as *Trichoderma* spp. have attracted attention due to their antagonistic effect on *Ganoderma* (Soepena *et al.*, 2000). Disease incidence was shown to be lower in a field treated with *T. harzianum* (Susanto *et al.*, 2005). *Trichoderma,* however, produced toxic secondary metabolites and that raises concerns if used as a biocontrol agent (Paterson, 2006).

Actinobacteria, particularly Actinomycetes, have gathered attention in screening as effective biocontrol agents for *Ganoderma* spp. (Pithakkit *et al.*, 2015; Sharifah-Muzaimah *et al.*, 2015). Actinomycetes are known to produce a diverse array of bioactive metabolites and may possess effects antagonistic to *G. boninense* (Tan *et al.*, 2002). As the frequency of novel bioactive metabolites discovered from terrestrial Actinobacteria decreases with time, more attention has been focused on diverse environments (Thenmozhi and Krishnan, 2011; Cheah *et al.*, 2015). Less studied and rare Actinobacteria from unique ecosystems are targeted to increase the discovery of new metabolites (Ng *et al.*, 2013). As tropical peat microbes live in a different environment from those of other soil types, it is reasonable to expect that their metabolites will differ considerably. The objective of this study was, therefore, to isolate, screen and identify Actinobacteria from tropical peatland for antagonistic activity against *Ganoderma* spp. and screen for isolates, especially Actinomycetes, with potential inhibition activity that do not required high inocula to exhibit antagonistic effects.

MATERIALS AND METHODS

i) Actinobacteria strains

Actinobacteria were isolated from tropical peat soil samples from oil palm plantation in Sibu, peat swamp forest in Maludam National Park, Sri Aman and peat secondary forest in Betong, all in Sarawak, Malaysia. All strains were preserved in glycerol suspension (20% v/v) at -80°C prior to analysis.

ii) Selective isolation of *Ganoderma* spp.

Ganoderma spp. wild strains were isolated from oil palm plantation in Miri and Asajaya, Sarawak, Malaysia. The internal tissues were cultured on *Ganoderma* Selective Medium (GSM) as described in Ariffin and Idris (1992). Pure cultures were maintained on Potato Dextrose Agar (PDA).

iii) Dual Culture Plate Assay (DCPA)

Actinobacteria were screened for antifungal activity using DCPA. *Ganoderma* plugs (6 mm in diameter) were plated and allowed to grow for two days on PDA. Actinobacteria were then inoculated 10 mm from the margin of the *Ganoderma* mycelia. Incubation was carried out at 30°C for up to 21 days. Control plates were cultures of *Ganoderma* without Actinobacteria. Potential antifungal activity was determined based on Percentage Inhibition of Radial Growth (PIRG):

$$\text{PIRG (\%)} = ((A - B)/A) \times 100\%$$

with A as the average width of the *Ganoderma* radial growth and B the average width of *Ganoderma* radial growth facing the direction of biocontrol agent.

iv) Poison Agar Assay (PAA)

Preliminary evaluation of extracellular antifungal compounds was determined using PAA (Azadeh *et al.*, 2010; Sinha *et al.*, 2014). Five plugs (6 mm) from four-day-old selected Actinobacteria were inoculated in 1% (w/v) glucose and 2 % (w/v) peptone broth (pH 7.2) for four days at 30°C in a rotary shaker (180 rpm). Controls were without Actinobacteria inoculation. Cell-free crude extract was obtained by centrifugation at 8,000 rpm for 15 minutes at 4°C and filtering the supernatant through a sterile 0.2 μm pore size membrane (Acrodisc Supor Membrane, PALL Life Sciences). Poison agar plates are made by adding 10 ml of crude extract to 10 ml of molten double-strength PDA. Seven-day-old *Ganoderma* plugs (6 mm) were inoculated at the centre of solidified poison plates and incubated at 30°C for seven days. *Ganoderma* growth inhibition was calculated using PIRG similar to DCPA.

v) Molecular identification of Actinobacteria

Genomic DNA extracted from selected Actinobacteria isolates were subjected to amplification using polymerase chain reaction (PCR) using universal primers targeting their 16S rDNA region. Sequences obtained were identified by comparing sequences in the National Centre for Biotechnology Information (NCBI) GenBank database using the Basic Local Alignment Search Tool (*blast*).

RESULTS

A total of 234 isolates of Actinobacteria with different morphology was screened for antagonistic activity against *Ganoderma*. In DCPA, interactions between tested Actinobacteria and *Ganoderma* spp. resulted in the production of a clear distance between them or inhibition zone, contact inhibition or no inhibition, indicated by *Ganoderma* overgrowth. A total of 74 potential isolates that produced an inhibition zone with a PIRG ranging from 14-100% were identified and selected for further screening with PAA. Control plates containing only *Ganoderma* spp. plugs without Actinobacteria inoculation showed normal growth with the appearance of white cottony mycelia. A total of72 isolates were identified as belonging to the genus *Streptomyces* and only two isolates to the genus

Kitasatospora. The highest PIRG based on DCPA was achieved by *S. sampsonii* MA1 (T) A7 isolated from primary peat swamp forest, with a value of 100% as shown in Figure 1a and Table 1. Inoculated *Ganoderma* plugs were not able to grow in the presence of this isolate. Reculturing the *Ganoderma* plugs on fresh PDA plates did not produce any mycelial growth, indicating possible fungicidal capability. Screening with cell-free culture filtrate from *S. sampsonii* using PAA, as shown in Figure 1b, was only capable of producing a PIRG of 30.93 %. Only isolate *S. flavogriseus* NA12 (T) A7 produced a PIRG above 80% on DCPA and PAA, as shown in Table 1 as well as Figure 1c and Figure 1d, respectively. Assessment of the effectiveness of the PAA was re-evaluated with non-inhibitor *Streptomyces* isolate towards *Ganoderma* as a negative control and as expected no inhibition was expressed in PAA. Based on the preliminary results of DCPA and PAA in Table 1, it was determined that isolates of *S. flavogriseus, S. aburaviensis, S. tsukiyonensis, S. sampsoni, S. coeruleofuscus, S. citricolor* and *S. lacticiproducens* in this study exhibit potential antagonistic activity against *Ganoderma*.

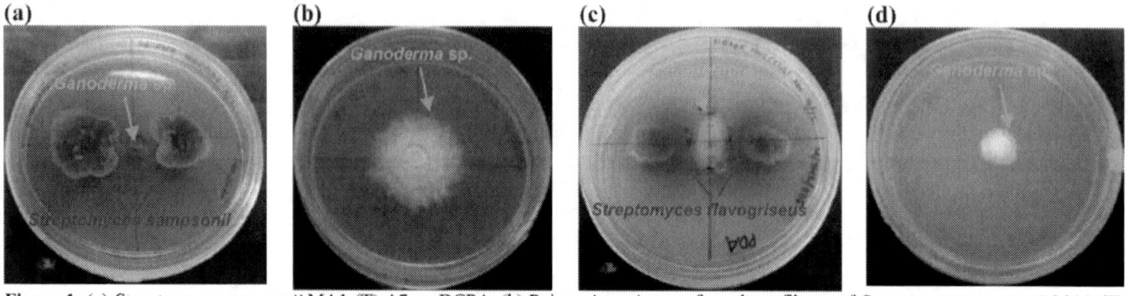

Figure 1. (a) *Streptomyces sampsonii* MA1 (T) A7 on DCPA. (b) Poison Agar Assay of a culture filtrate of *Streptomyces sampsonii* MA1 (T) A7. (c) *Streptomyces flavogriseus* NA12 (T) A1 on DCPA. (d) Poison Agar Assay of a culture filtrate of *Streptomyces flavogriseus* NA12 (T) A1.

Table 1: Actinobacteria isolates' antagonistic effect on *Ganoderma* mycelia growth using DCPA and PAA. The following are isolates with a PIRG above 80% using DCPA or PAA

No.	Actinobacteria	DCPA (PIRG, %)	PAA (PIRG, %)
1.	*Streptomyces sampsonii* MA1 (T) A7	100.00	30.93
2.	*Streptomyces lacticiproducens* MA1 (B) A12	86.32	48.04
3.	*Streptomyces flavogriseus* NA13 (T) A4	85.47	43.38
4.	*Streptomyces flavogriseus* NA12 (T) A1	83.76	85.39
5.	*Streptomyces coeruleofuscus* CB1 (T) A3	79.49	89.95
6.	*Streptomyces citricolor* NE1 (B) A10	52.56	100.00
7.	*Streptomyces aburaviensis* subsp. *tuftformis* ND1 (B) A16	45.46	100.00
8.	*Streptomyces aburaviensis* subsp. *tuftformis* MA1 (T) A15	38.36	100.00
9.	*Streptomyces citricolor* ND1 (T) A13	36.62	100.00
10.	*Streptomyces aburaviensis* subsp. *tuftformis* NC11 (T) A10	28.21	100.00
11.	*Streptomyces tsukiyonensis* NE1 (B) A2	28.75	96.80
12.	*Streptomyces aburaviensis* subsp. *tuftformis* NC11 (T) A8	16.92	93.85
13.	*Streptomyces aburaviensis* subsp. *tuftformis* CB1 (B) A5	37.68	93.30
14.	*Streptomyces aburaviensis* subsp. *tuftformis* NC12 (T) A5	57.32	91.35
15.	*Streptomyces flavogriseus* CA1 (T) A2	30.00	91.35
16.	*Streptomyces aburaviensis* NE1 (T) A10	24.00	90.48
17.	*Streptomyces citricolor* CB1 (T) A11	42.31	86.09
18.	*Streptomyces aburaviensis* subsp. *tuftformis* CA1 (T) A10	60.53	81.01

DISCUSSION

Temporal frame of antagonist colonization would be beneficial for the establishment of competitiveness for space and substrate against phytopathogens (Adebola and Amadi, 2010); this however, might not be practical for field application if the disease has established itself first. In this study, the direction taken was that *Ganoderma* was allowed to grow first and the antagonists were inoculated later. Results obtained demonstrated the competitiveness of Actinobacteria isolated from peatland against tested *Ganoderma* isolates. Viability tests on the affected *Ganoderma* hyphae in inhibition zones should also be conducted by transferring the hyphae onto fresh medium. If the *Ganoderma* does not recover, this may reflect a non-culturability of hyphae caused by antifungal substances produced by the biocontrol agent (Yuan and Crawford, 1995). This will indicate that the tested isolates are producing extracellular diffusible bioactive metabolites that affect the growth of *Ganoderma* mycelia as observed with the presence of an inhibition zone. Another possibility for potential antifungal activity is contact inhibition which is characterized by lysis of hyphae walls that are in contact with biocontrol colony (Bacon and Hinton, 2002). However, in this study only isolates with an inhibition zone were further tested due to difficulties in measuring the extent and effectiveness of contact inhibition. *Ganoderma* mycelia not in contact with a biocontrol agent can still be a viable source of *Ganoderma* inoculum. Actinobacteria, and most importantly the genus *Streptomyces*, have been shown to produce antagonistic capability against *Ganoderma* (Pithakkit *et al.*, 2015; Tan *et al.*, 2002). In this study, an isolate of *S. sampsonii* was capable of expressing fungicidal properties against tested *Ganoderma*. A strain of *S. sampsonii* has also been reported to possess antagonistic activity against *Candida albicans, Aspergillus niger* and *Microsporum gypseum* (Jain and Jain, 2007). These antagonistic effects may be due to the production of bioactive metabolites such as antibiotics, enzymes and antifungal substances (Crawford *et al.*, 1993; Prapagdee *et al.*, 2008). Identification of these bioactive metabolites may discover novel metabolites which could also be used in other fields of application. In terms of biotechnological potential, Actinobacteria can be a promising source for antimicrobial substances, pigments, plant growth promoting agents, enzymes, biosulfactants, pesticides, herbicides, probiotics and nanoparticle synthesis (Anandan *et al.*, 2016).

Cultural conditions such as pH, temperature, incubation period, carbon sources, nitrogen sources and addition of minerals can affect biomass production and bioactive metabolites expression (Bundale *et al.*, 2015). Islam *et al.*, (2009) determined that carbon source, such as maltose and sucrose, increased the production of *S. albidoflavus* antifungal compounds. Islam *et al.* (2009) and Bundale *et al.* (2015) found that compared to inorganic nitrogen sources, organic nitrogen sources increased the production of bioactive metabolites. It is acknowledged that Actinobacteria isolates will behave differently under different cultural conditions and may need specific conditions for optimum growth and production of bioactive metabolites. Apart from cultural conditions, competition for space and substrate can also influence the production of bioactive metabolites which may explain the variation in results observed for both DCPA and PAA (Table 1). Laboratory experiments with microbes have revealed various active mechanisms which enable them to kill or stop the growth of other microbes (Hibbing *et al.*, 2010). In this study, when Actinobacteria were co-cultured in a plate which contained an established *Ganoderma* culture, the Actinobacteria's competitive potential enabled them to produce antifungal compounds that impaired the growth of the *Ganoderma*. This may explain why DCPA of *S. sampsonii* produced the highest PIRG but the culture filtrate that was produced without a competitor for the PAA showed a low PIRG (30.93%). The fermentation broth used may also not support bioactive metabolites production for this isolate. Nonetheless, other Actinobacteria which produced less than 80% PIRG on DCPA were able to increase their PIRG when assayed on PAA (Table 1). The increment in the production of bioactive metabolites in submerged fermentation might be attributed to the type of carbon and nitrogen sources used. Glucose was reported to increase bioactive metabolites concentration for *Pseudonocardia* sp. (Kiranmayi *et al.*, 2011). Organic nitrogen source such as peptone were also reported to increase bioactive metabolites production (Reddy *et al.*, 2011; Bundale *et al.*, 2015).

Volatile organic compounds may be another potential antifungal compounds that affect the growth of *Ganoderma* (in addition to extracellular diffusible bioactive metabolites). The possible production of antifungal volatile organic compounds by Actinobacteria in this study was observed in terms of the growth reduction of *Ganoderma* mycelia facing away from the tested isolate, as shown in Figures 1a and 1c. Volatile organic compounds produced from *Streptomyces* spp. have been reported to possess antifungal activities to phytopathogens such as *Aspergillus flavus*, *Sclerotinia sclerotiorum* and *Fusarium oxysporum* (Wang *et al.*, 2013; Wu *et al.*, 2015). Generally, however, laboratory findings may not translate into natural settings as most tested microbe interactions are not mutually exclusive (Hibbing *et al.*, 2010; Cray *et al.*, 2015). Thus, further study is needed on the impact of biocontrol agents on soil microbial communities to assess the dynamics of soil microbial diversity prior to promoting the usage of selected biocontrol agents. Incorporation of biocontrol agents has also been reported to improve the microbial diversity of an oil palm plantation (Alexander and Chong, 2014).

CONCLUSION

This study demonstrated Actinobacteria (mainly *Streptomyces* spp.) with the potential to control *Ganoderma* growth. Dual Culture Plate Assay was carried out to determine the capability of the isolates to inhibit *Ganoderma* growth. No mycelial growth was observed in the direction facing the Actinobacteria isolates with antifungal capability. Mycelial growth was also observed to be affected, with sparse growth of *Ganoderma* mycelia in the direction away from the isolates, suggesting volatile antifungal compound production. Future screening for biocontrol capabilities should also include assessment of selected strains for production of volatile organic compounds active against *Ganoderma*. Selected Actinobacteria also produced extracellular bioactive metabolites with antifungal properties as shown by testing of cell-free crude extract. The potential of Actinobacteria in the management of plant diseases is still being actively explored despite the genus being well documented as a producer of bioactive metabolites. In the present study, specific metabolites responsible for the inhibition of *Ganoderma* mycelial growth have not yet been identified.

REFERENCE

1. Adebola, M. and J.E. Amadi. 2010. Antagonistic activities of *Paecilomyces* and *Rhizopus* species against the cocoa black pod pathogen (*Phytophthora palmivora*). *African Scientist* **11 (4)**: 467-470.
2. Alexander, A. and K.P. Chong. 2014. The impact of biological control agents on soil microbial communities in oil palm plantation soils. *American-Eurasian Journal of Sustainable Agriculture* **8 (7)**: 8-17.
3. Anandan, R., D. Dharumadurai and G.P. Manogaran. 2016. An introduction to actinobacteria. In D. Dhanasekaran, and Y. Jiang, (eds.) *Basic and Biotechnological Applications*. InTech.
4. Arif, M.S., A. Roslan and A.S. Idris. 2011. Economics of oil palm pests and *Ganoderma* disease and yield losses. In: *Proceedings of the Third MPOB-IOPRI International Seminar: Integrated Oil Palm Pests and Diseases Management*. Kuala Lumpur Convention Centre.
5. Ariffin, D. and A.S. Idris. 1992. The *Ganoderma* selective medium (GSM). PORIM Information Series. ISSN 0128-5726.
6. Azadeh, B.F., M. Sariah and M.Y. Wong. 2010. Characterization of *Burkholderia cepacia* genomovar I as potential biocontrol agent of *Ganoderma boninense* in oil palm. *African Journal of Biotechnology* **9 (24)**: 3542-3548.
7. Bacon, C.W. and D.M. Hinton. 2002. Endophytic and biological control potential of *Bacilus mojavensis* and related species. *Biological Control* **23**: 274-284.
8. Bundale, S., D. Begde, N. Nashikkar, T. Kadam and A. Upadhyay. 2015. Optimization of culture conditions for production of bioactive metabolites by *Streptomyces* spp. isolated from soil. *Advances in Microbiology* **5**: 441-451.
9. Cheah, Y.K., L.H. Lee, C.C.Y. Chieng and, C.M.V.L. Wong. 2015. Isolation, identification and screening of actinobacteria in volcanic soil of Deception Island (the Antarctic) for antimicrobial metabolites. *Polish Polar Research* **36 (1)**: 67-78.
10. Chung, G.F. 2011. Management of *Ganoderma* diseases in oil palm plantations. *Planter* **87 (1022)**: 325–339.
11. Crawford, L.D., J.M. Lynch, J.M. Whipps and M.M. Ousley. 1993. Isolation and characterization of actinomycete antagonists of a fungal root pathogen. *Applied and Environmental Microbiology* **59 (11):** 3899-3905.
12. Cray, J. A., J.D.R. Houghton, L.R. Cooke and J.E. Hallsworth. 2015. A simple inhibition coefficient for quantifying potency of biocontrol agents against plant-pathogenic fungi. *Biological Control* **81**: 93-100.
13. Hibbing, M.E., C. Fuqua, M.R. Parsek and S.B. Peterson. 2010. Bacterial competition: surviving and thriving in microbial jungle. *Nature Reviews. Microbiology* **8 (1)**: 15-25.
14. Hushiarian, R., N.A. Yusof and S.W. Dutse. 2013. Detection and control of *Ganoderma boninense*: strategies and perspectives. *Springer Plus* **2**: 555.
15. Islam, M.R., Y.T. Jeong, Y.J. Ryu, C.H. Song and Y.S. Lee. 2009. Isolation, identification and optimal culture conditions of *Streptomyces albidoflavus* C247 producing antifungal agents against *Rhizoctonia solani* AG2-2. *Mycobiology* **37 (2)**: 114-120.
16. Jain, P.K. and P.C. Jain. 2007. Isolation, characterization and antifungal activity of *Streptomyces sampsonii* GS1322. *Indian Journal of Experimental Biology* **45**: 203-206.
17. Kiranmayi, M.U., P. Sudhakar, K. Sreenivasulu and M. Vijayalakshmi. 2011. Optimization of culturing conditions for improved production of bioactive metabolites by *Pseudonocardia* sp. VUK-10. *Mycobiology* **39 (3)**: 174-181.
18. Naher, L., S. Siddiquee, U.K. Yusuf and M.M.A. Mondal. 2015. Issues of *Ganoderma* spp. and basal stem rot disease management in oil palm. *American Journal of Agricultural Science* **2 (3)**: 103-107.
19. Ng, Y.H., J.Y. Ting and T.C. Yeo. 2013. Antimicrobial activity of actinomycetes isolated from Paya Maga, Sarawak. *Jurnal Teknologi* **62 (2)**: 17-19.
20. Paterson, R.R.M. 2006. Fungi and fungal toxins as weapons. *Mycological Research* **110 (9)**: 1003-1010.
21. Pithakkit, S., V. Petcharat, S. Chuenchit, C. Pornsuriya and A. Sunpapao. 2015. Isolation of antagonistic actinomycetes species from rhizosphere as effective biocontrol against oil palm fungal diseases. *Walailak Journal of Science and Technology* **12 (5):** 481-490.
22. Prapagdee, B., C. Kuekulvong and S. Mongkolsuk. 2008. Antifungal potential of extracellular metabolites produced by *Streptomyces hygroscopicus* against phytopathogenic fungi. *International Journal of Biological Science* **4 (5):** 330-337.
23. Rakib, M.R.M., J.C.F. Bong, A. Khairulmazmi and A.S. Idris. 2014. Genetic and morphological diversity of *Ganoderma* species isolated from infected oil palms (*Elaeis guineensis*). *International Journal of Agriculture and Biology* **16**: 691-699.
24. Reddy, N.G., D.P.N. Ramakrishna and S.V. Rajagopal. 2011. Optimization of culture conditions of *Streptomyces rochei* (MTCC 10109) for the production of antimicrobial metabolites. *Egyptian Journal of Biology* **13**: 21-29.

25. Rolph, H., R. Wijesekara, R. Lardner, F. Abdullah, P.M. Kirk and M. Holderness. 2000. Molecular variation in *Ganoderma* from oil palm, coconut and betel nut. Pp. 205–221 in: J. Flood, P.D. Bridge and M. Holderness (eds.). *Ganoderma diseases of perennial crops*. P. D. Wallingford, U.K.: CABI Publishing.
26. Roslan, A., and A.S. Idris. 2012. Economic impact of *Ganoderma* incidence on Malaysian Oil Palm Plantation – A case study in Johor. *Oil Palm Industry Economic Journal* **12 (1)**: 24-30.
27. Sharifah-Muzaimah, S.A., A.S. Idris, A.Z. Madihah, O. Dzolkhifli, S. Kamaruzzaman and P.C.H. Cheong. 2015.Isolation of actinomycetes from rhizosphere of oil palm (*Elaeis guineensis* Jacq.) for antagonism against *Ganoderma boninense*. *Journal of Oil Palm Research* **27 (1)**: 19-29.
28. Sinha, K., R. Hegde and A. Kush. 2014. Exploration on native actinomycetes strains and their potential against fungal plant pathogens. *International Journal of Current Microbiology and Applied Sciences* **3 (11)**: 37-45.
29. Soepena, H., R.Y. Purba and S. Pawirosukarto. 2000. A control strategy for basal stem rot (*Ganoderma*) on oil palm. Pp. 83-88 in: J. Flood, P.D. Bridge and M. Holderness. (eds.) *Ganoderma diseases of perennial crops*. Wallingford, U. K.: CABI Publishing,.
30. Susanto, A., P.S. Sudharto, and R.Y. Purba. 2005. Enhancing biological control of basal stem rot disease (*Ganoderma boninense*) in oil palm plantations. *Mycopathologia* **159 (1)**: 153-157.
31. Tan, C.J., K.C. How, P.P. Loh-Mia, A. Ismet, K. Getha, T. Seki, and S. Vikineswary, 2002. Bioactivity of selected actinomycetes against *Ganoderma boninense*. *Asia Pacific Journal of Molecular Biology and Biotechnology* **10:** 119–125.
32. Thenmozhi, M. and K. Krishnan. 2011. Anti-Aspergillus activity of *Streptomyces* sp. VITSTK7 isolated from Bay of Bengal coast of Puducherry. *Indian Journal Natural Environmental Science* **2 (2)**: 1-8.
33. Wang, C., Z. Wang, X. Qiao, Z. Li,F. Li and M. Chen. 2013. Antifungal activity of volatile organic compounds from *Streptomyces alboflavus* TD-1. *FEMS Microbiology Letters* **341**: 45-51.
34. Wu, Y., J. Yuan, Y. E, W. Raza, Q. Shen and Q. Huang. 2015. Effect of volatile organic compounds from *Streptomyces albulus* NJZJSA2 on growth of two fungal pathogens. *Journal of Basic Microbiology* **55**: 1104-1117.
35. Yuan, W.M. and D. L. Crawford, 1995. Characterization of *Streptomyces lydicus* WYEC108 as a potential biocontrol agent against fungal root and seed rots. *Applied and Environmental Microbiology* **61 (8)**: 3119-3128.

Abstract No: A-437

CARABID BEETLE AND ANT ASSEMBLAGES IN THE WESTERN BALKANS PEAT BOG

Andreja Brigić[1*], Jelena Bujan[2], Antun Alegro[3], Ivančica Ternjej[1] and Mladen Kerovec[1]

[1] *Division of Zoology, Department of Biology, Faculty of Science, University of Zagreb, Croatia*
[2] *Department of Biology and Graduate Program in Ecology and Evolutionary Biology, University of Oklahoma, Oklahoma, USA*
[3] *Division of Botany, Department of Biology, Faculty of Science, University of Zagreb, Croatia*

**Corresponding author:andreja.brigic@biol.pmf.hr*

SUMMARY

Peat bogs in the Western Balkans are scarce, small in size, fragmented and critically endangered. Carabid beetles and ants were studied in the largest and oldest Croatian peat bog and at its edges. Altogether, 811 carabid beetles representing 37 species and 11,450 ants representing 23 species were collected by pitfall trapping. Carabid beetle and ant assemblages showed asymmetric responses in terms of species richness and activity density, e.g. ant assemblages in the peat bog were significantly different from those at the edge, with 2 times lower species richness, while species richness did not differ for carabid beetles. Additionally, activity density of carabid beetles was significantly higher in the edge, and did not differ for ants. Assemblages of both taxa were strongly affected by specific conditions in the peat bog – high soil moisture and *Sphagnum* moss dominance. The edge was more favourable habitat for both taxa due to more suitable microclimatic conditions. Moreover, our findings indicate that the peat bog is colonised from its edges. Additionally, tyrphophilous carabid beetles and globally endangered, *Carabus variolosus nodulosus*, are associated with edge habitats in the Western Balkans peat bog. Occurrence of tyrphophilous and rare stenotopic species highlights the great conservation value of this peat bog. However, successional changes caused by the invasion of grassy and woody vegetation, in particular *Molinia caerulea* grass, are changing hydrological conditions of this peat bog. Here we suggest active conservation measures to preserve these unique soil invertebrate zoocoenoses.

***Keywords**: peatlands, Tyrphophilous, environmental indicators, succession*

INTRODUCTION

In the Western Balkans, peat bogs represent small habitat islands embedded in a matrix of different land cover types (e.g. wet meadows, wetlands, forests). They were formed during, or after the last glaciation period, when temperatures were low and precipitation was high (Horvat, 1950). Such climatic conditions were favourable for the development of peat bogs in this region. Peat deposits found beneath current agricultural lands show that peat bogs were more widespread in the past than they are today (Topić & Stančić, 2006). Nowadays, these habitats patches are critically endangered mainly due to the abandonment of traditional land management practices, climate change and drainages (Hršak ,1996; Topić & Stančić, 2006).

All these processes resulted in progressive vegetation succession, which is evident in a spreading of woody and grassy vegetation from adjacent matrix habitats towards peat bogs. Successional changes alter peat bog vegetation composition and structure, as well as soil properties (Topić & Stančić, 2006; Alegro & Šegota, 2008). Ultimately, they have a profound impact on peat bog soil arthropod assemblages, particularly carabid beetles and ants (Galle et al. 1998; Buchholz *et al.*, 2009). Both taxa were successfully used as environmental indicators of changes in North European peat bogs (Vepsäläinen *et al.*, 2000; Mossakowski *et al.*, 2003). Moreover, the composition and structure of their assemblages reflects quality of peat bog habitats (Mossakowski *et al.*, 2003; Buchholz *et al.*, 2009), since both taxa are highly sensitive to changes in environmental factors (Lovei & Sunderland, 1996; Maes *et al.*, 2003).

The objectives of our study were to: (1) compare carabid beetle and ant assemblages from two focal habitat types: peat bog and the edge and (2) determine the impact of vegetation and environmental variables that affect spatial distribution of carabid beetles and ants in the Western Balkans peat bog.

METHODS

Study area

Đon močvar peat bog is located in the continental region of Croatia (N 45°, E 15°), at 130 m a.s.l.. It is the oldest and largest peat bog in Croatia, covering an area of 10 ha (Alegro & Šegota, 2008). The region is characterised by the temperate humid climate with warm summers, with an average annual temperature of 10.5°C and an average annual precipitation of 1,050 mm (Zaninović *et al.*, 2008). The peat bog area reduced from 40 ha to 10 ha since the beginning of the 20th century, due to drainage and abandonment of traditional land management practices. Consequently, it resulted in changes in vegetation composition and structure of the peat bog, by the spread of woody and grass vegetation (Alegro & Šegota 2008). Nowadays, the peat bog and its adjacent area are protected as a Botanical Reserve and included in the NATURA 2000 network.

Đon močvar peat bog is a complex ecosystem, represented by a mosaic of different habitats such as open woodless *Sphagnum* spp. sites, deep hollows and small ponds. Majority of vegetation belongs to *Drosero-Caricetum echinatae* Horvat (1950) 1962 association. Swampier areas are characterised by *Rhynchosporetum albae* W. Koch 1926 association and *Phragmites australis* stands. Shrub layer is highly dominated by *Molinia caerulea* grass, which is overgrowing *Sphagnum* mosses. Tree layer is composed of scattered trees of *Betula pendula* Roth. and *Alnus glutinosa* (L.) Gaertner.

The peat bog edge is mainly overgrown with flooded forest of *Frangulo-Alnetum glutinosae* Rauš 1968 association. These edges are a source of woody vegetation which spreads into the peat bog. The *Sphagnum* mosses are sporadically found at the edge. The forests surrounding the slopes around the peat bog belong to *Epimedio-Carpinetum betuli* (Ht. 1938) Borh. 1963 association.

Soil arthropods sampling

Carabid beetles and ants were sampled by pitfall traps at two main habitats – peat bog and peat bog's edge. Within each habitat 6 sites were selected, each sampled with 5 pitfall traps (5 m apart), placed in a linear transect. The traps (8.5 cm wide and 12.0 cm deep polythene cups) were partially filled with saturated sodium chloride solution. Neutral-smelling detergent was added to reduce the surface tension. A Styrofoam roof was placed 10 cm above each trap to protect it from the leaf litter and rain. The samples were collected monthly, from May to November of 2010.

Vegetation analysis and soil properties

Vegetation was sampled using phytosociological relevés according to standard Central European methodology (Braun-Blanquet, 1964) using an expanded cover-abundance scale (Barkman *et al.*, 1964). The total abundance of each vegetation layer was analysed separately. It was expressed as pooled abundances of each plant species in the layer. Soil moisture was measured from the core samples taken at each site and their water content was determined using the gravimetric method (**Reynolds, 1970**).

Data analyses

To compare the differences among environmental variables and vegetation between the habitats, t-tests or Mann Whitney U tests were used. The selection of parametric or non-parametric tests depended on the data distributions, which were tested with the Shapiro Wilk W normality test. The same tests were used to detect differences in species richness and abundance of both taxa between studied habitats. These tests were performed using the Statistica 12.0 software package (StatSoft Inc., 2013). The relationships between carabid beetle and ant assemblages and environmental variables were tested using Canonical Correspondence Analysis (CCA) in the CANOCO version 5.04 package (ter Braak & Smilauer 2012). Carabid beetles represented by less than 0.5% of the total catch, and ants recorded as singletons or doubletons, were omitted from the ordination analyses. Prior to analyses, carabid beetle activity densities were square root transformed, while for ants binary data were used. A Monte Carlo test using 499 permutations ($p < 0.05$) was performed to test the significance of the correlations between species occurrence and environmental variables.

RESULTS

Species composition of carabid beetle assemblages

In total 37 species and 811 carabid beetles were recorded at the peat bog and its edge. In the peat bog 22 species and 134 carabid beetles were collected, while at the edge 33 species and 677 carabid beetles were recorded.

Species richness did not differ significantly between studied habitats (mean ± SE, peat bog: 7 ± 1.69 *vs.* edge: 13 ± 2.48; U = 8.00, p > 0.05). Activity density of carabid beetles was 5 times higher at the edge (112.83 ± 43.88; U = 5.00, p < 0.05) compared to the peat bog (22.33 ± 8.28).

In total 23 species and 11,450 ants were collected in both habitats. In the peat bog 16 ant species and 3,486 individuals were recorded and 20 species and 7,964 individuals were caught at the edge. Ant species richness was significantly higher at the edge (11.67 ± 1.20) compared to the peat bog (7.33 ± 1.09; U = 4.50, p < 0.05). There was a non-significant trend (U = 13.00, p > 0.05) of higher ant abundance at the edge (1,327.33 ± 408.19) compared to the peat bog (581 ± 128.12).

Effects of environmental variables on insect assemblages

In the CCA analysis, four environmental variables explained 51.9% of the total variation of the carabid beetle assemblages. The first two axes explained 42.1% of the variance in carabid beetle occurrence and 81.0% of the variance in the relationship between environmental variables and carabid beetles. The eigenvalues of first two axes were 0.368 and 0.186, respectively. A Monte Carlo randomization test showed that the ordination was statistically significant (F = 2.7, p = 0.04). The second ordination axis indicated a strong separation between the peat bog and the edge sites (Fig. 1a). Peat bog sites (positioned above the first axis) are mainly associated with high soil moisture and *M. caerulea* abundance, while edge sites (positioned mainly below the first axis) are linked with the abundance of tree and shrub layers. Thus, the spatial distribution of carabid beetles is governed by soil moisture and density of vegetation cover. Tyrphophilous species (*Platynus livens* and *Pterostichus rhaeticus*) and stenotopic hygrophilous species (e.g. *Carabus variolosus nodulosus*), are closely associated with edge habitats. Moreover, most of other carabid beetles show a similar pattern and occur at a shaded and drier environment and thus are positioned below or on the first axis.

The environmental variables considered in the CCA analysis explained 50.4% of the total variation in ant assemblages. The first two axes of species-environmental variables explained 37.7% variance in ant occurrence and 74.8% of the variance in the relationship between ants and environmental variables. The axes had eigenvalues of 0.223 and 0.155, and the ordination was statistically significant (Monte Carlo randomization test: F = 2.0, p = 0.038). The first axis indicated clear separation between peat bog sites - all positioned on the right side of the ordination (Fig. 1b) - and most of the edge sites positioned on the left side of the ordination. Peat bog ant assemblages are closely associated with high soil moisture and *M. caerulea* abundance, while ant edge assemblages are associated with tree and shrub layer abundance. Tyrphophilous species (*M. scabrinodis*), together with other hygrophilous ant species (e.g. *Lasius platythorax*, *Myrmica rubra* and *M. ruginodis*) are positioned on the right side of the ordination, but closer to the centre than the peat bog sites. Other species were mainly associated with edge sites that were shadowed by the trees and shrubs.

Soil and vegetation analyses

Abundance of *Sphagnum* spp. mosses was significantly higher at the peat bog (18.17 ± 2.56) than at the edge (3.50 ± 1.82; U = 0.00, p < 0.01). *M. caerulea* abundance was 6 times higher at the peat bog (6.50 ± 1.00) than at its edges (1.00 ± 1.00, U = 0.00, p < 0.01). Edges are more shaded than the peat bog due to a higher abundance of trees (11.83 ± 3.05 *vs.* 3.83 ± 0.75) and shrubs (11.33 ± 1.63 *vs.* 6.67 ± 2.23). Tree abundance was significantly higher at the edge (U = 5.50, p < 0.05), while shrub abundance did not differ between the two habitats (U = 8.00, p > 0.05). The soil moisture of the peat bog was extremely high, over 90% throughout the year, and the peat bog was always more moist than its edges (93.13 ± 0.66 *vs.* 49.04 ± 6.41; U = 0.00, p < 0.001). Soil pH was low both in the peat bog (4.72 ±0.14) and at its edge (4.64 ± 0.12), and did not differ between the two (t-test, (46) = 0.656, p > 0.05).

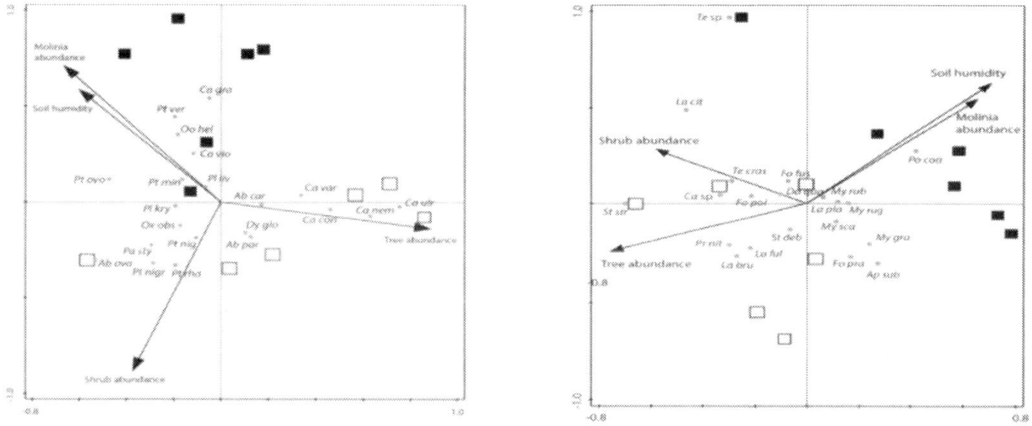

Figure 1: CCA ordination of carabid beetles/ants and environmental variables. Species are marked with grey circles and environmental variables with arrows. Peat bog habitats are indicated by black squares and edge habitats by white squares. Arrow lengths show the relative importance of the explanatory variables and their directions indicate positive or negative correlations. Species abbreviations: a) Carabid beetles: *Ab car - Abax carinatus, Ab ova - A. ovalis, Ab par - A. parallelus, Ca con - Carabus convexus, Ca gra - C. granulatus, Ca nem - C. nemoralis, Ca ulr - C. ulrichii, Ca var - C. variolosus nodulosus, Ca vio - C. violaceus, Dy glo - Dyschirius globosus, Oo hel - Oodes helopioides, Ox obs - Oxypselaphus obscurus, Pa sty - Patrobus styriacus, Pl kry - Platynus krynickii, Pl liv - P. livens, Pt min - Pterostichus minor, Pt nig - P. niger, Pt nigr - P. nigrita, Pt ovo - P. ovoideus, Pt rha - P. rhaeticus, Pt ver - P. vernalis.* B) Ants: *Ca* sp - *Camponotus* sp., *Do qua - Dolichoderus quadripunctatus, Fo fus - Formica fusca, Fo pol - F. polyctena, Fo pra - F. pratensis, La bru - L. brunneus, La cit - L. citrinus, La ful - L. fuliginosus, La pla - L. platythorax, My gra - Myrmecina graminicola, My rub - Myrmica rubra, My rug - M. ruginodis, My sca - M. scabrinodis, Po coa - Ponera coarctata, Pr nit - Prenolepis nitens, St deb - Stenamma debile, Te cra- Temnothorax crassispinus; Te sp. -T.* sp.

DISCUSSION

This study shows that the peat bog is characterised by specific environmental conditions: high soil moisture, dense *Sphagnum* moss cover and high acidity of the substrate, corresponding to the conditions typical for peatland habitats (Rydin & Jeglum, 2006). Key environmental variables which affect carabid beetle and ant distributions – soil moisture and vegetation composition and structure – differed considerably between the peat bog and its edges. Some peat bog microhabitats are rarely used by carabid beetles and ants, particularly sites dominated by *Rhynchospora alba*. These sites have permanent semiaquatic conditions, resulting in extremely low activity densities of both taxa, which is in accordance with other studies (Främbs, 1994; Ratchford *et al.*, 2005). However, sites that are characterised by more dry *Sphagnum* hummocks and overgrown with scattered shrubs, were suitable microhabitats for carabid beetles and nesting patches for ants, consequently having higher activity density of both taxa.

In contrast to the peat bog, the edge is a more favourable habitat for both taxa, containing a higher ant species richness and carabid beetle activity density. The recorded patterns could be a consequence of edge effects, since edges are habitats of enhanced diversity and productivity compared to adjacent matrix habitats (c.f. Farina, 2006). Similar patterns are documented for other peat bogs and their adjacent habitats (e.g., for carabid beetles (Máthé *et al.*, 2005) and ants (Bujan, 2010). Additionally, our findings indicate that edges act as filters (Forman & Moore 1992) by enhancing the movement of insects and enabling colonization of the peat bog from its edges (Främbs *et al.*, 2002). The peat bog is colonised via walking, by pes pedes colonizers, e.g. large carabid beetles of the genus *Carabus*, and via flight by small-sized macropterous carabid beetles that have good flight and dispersal abilities. These edges are thus important for maintaining peat bog insect biodiversity, and management plans should be designed accordingly.

CONCLUSION

The occurrence of tyrphophilous carabid beetle and ant species, as well as the globally endangered *Carabus variolosus nodulosus*, highlights the great conservation value of this habitat. These species are associated with edge habitats, implying that both habitats are important for the conservation of these species. At the same time edges represent a source of woody vegetation which spreads into the peat bog, causing deleterious changes in vegetation and soil properties (Alegro & Šegota, 2008). Hydrological properties of the studied peat bog need to be preserved and enhanced by mowing *M. caerulea* grass and cutting down woody vegetation. However, woody vegetation should not be cut from edge habitats, to preserve tyrphophilous and endangered carabid beetle species. Additionally, several "woody islands" should be left in the peat bog and they could serve as stepping stones between edge habitats. In that way, we can ensure favourable habitat conditions for soil invertebrates, which require moist shaded habitats. Using a holistic approach to the conservation, we could preserve both plant and *Sphagnum* moss diversity, together with soil invertebrate diversity.

REFERENCES

1. Alegro A, Šegota V. 2008. Florističke i vegetacijske značajke botaničkog rezervata „Đon močvar" u Blatuši. General technical report. State Institute for Nature Protection, Zagreb, Croatia.
2. Barkman JJ, Doing H, Segal S. 1964. Kritische Bemerkungen und Vorschläge zur quantitativen Vegetationsanalyse. *Acta Botanica Neerlandica* 13: 394-419.
3. Braun-Blanquet J. 1964. *Pflanzensoziologie: Grundzüge der Vegetationskunde*. Verlag Eugen Ulmer, New York, 865 pp.
4. Buchholz S, Hannig K, Schirmel J. 2009. Ground beetle assemblages of peat bog remnants in Northwest Germany. *Entomologia generalis* 32: 127-144.
5. Bujan J. 2010. Ant fauna (Hymenoptera: Formicidae) in Croatian peat bogs. Graduation Thesis.
6. Farina A. 2006. *Principles and methods in landscape ecology. Towards a science of the landscape*. Springer, Dordrecht, 412 pp.
7. Forman RTT, Moore PN. 1992. *Theoretical foundations for understanding boundaries in landscape mosaics*. Pages 236-258 in Hansen AJ, di Castri F, editors. Landscape boundaries: consequences for biotic diversity and ecological flows. Springer, New York.
8. Främbs H. 1994. The importance of habitat structure and food supply for carabid beetles (Coleoptera, Carabidae) in peat bogs. *Memoirs of the Entomological Society of Canada* 169:145-159.
9. Främbs H, Dormann W, Mossakowski D. 2002. Spatial distribution of carabid beetles on Zehlau bog. *Baltic Journal of Coleopterology* 2: 7-13.
10. Horvat I. 1950. Flornogenetski odnosi cretova u Hrvatskoj. *Periodicum biologorum* 2: 13-21.
11. Hršak V. 1996. Vegetation succession at acidic fen near Dubravica in the Hrvatsko zagorje region. *Natura Croatica* 5: 1-10.
12. Lövei GL, Sunderland KD. 1996. Ecology and behavior of ground beetles (Coleoptera: Carabidae). *Annual Review of Entomology* 41: 231-256.
13. Maes D, Van Dyck H, Vanreusel W, Cortens J. 2003. Ant communities (Hymenoptera: Formicidae) of Flemish (north Belgium) wet heatlands, a declining habitat in Europe. *European Journal of Entomology* 100: 545-555.
14. Máthé I, Urák I, Balog A, Balázs E. 2005. The community structure of the ground dwelling carabid beetles (Coleoptera: Carabidae) and spiders (Arachnida: Araneae) in peat bog "Mohos" (Transylvania, Romania). *Entomologica Romanica* 10: 37-42.
15. Mossakowski D, Främbs H, Lakomy W. 2003. The Carabid and Staphilinid fauna of raised bogs. A comparison of Northwest Germany and the Baltic region. Baltic *Journal of Coleopterology* 3: 137-144.
16. Ratchford JS, Wittman SE, Jules ES, Ellison, AM, Gotelli NJ, Sanders NJ. 2005. The effects of fire, local environment and time on ant assemblages in fens and forests. *Diversity and Distributions* 11: 487-497.
17. **Reynolds SG. 1970. The gravimetric method of soil moisture determination I. *Journal of Hydrology* 11: 258-273.**
18. Rydin H, Jeglum J. 2006. *The Biology of Peatlands*. Oxford University Press, New York, 343 pp.
19. Statistica (Date Analysis Software System), Version 12. http://www.statsoft.com/
20. ter Braak CJF, Smilauer P. 2012. Canoco reference manual and user's guide: software for ordination, version 5.0.
21. Topić J, Stančić Z. 2006. Extinction of fen and bog plants and their habitats in Croatia. *Biodiversity and Conservation* 15: 3371-3381.
22. Vepsäläinen K, Savolainen R, Tiainen J, Vilén J. 2000. Successional changes of ant assemblages: from virgin and ditched bogs to forests. *Annales Zoologici Fennici* 37: 135-149.
23. Zaninović K, et al. 2008. *Klimatski atlas Hrvatske*: 1961.-1990., 1971.-2000. Državni hidrometeorološki zavod, Zagreb.

Abstract No: 430

CHARACTERIZATION OF NITROUS OXIDE (N_2O) EMITTERS FROM TROPICAL PEATLANDS OF SARAWAK

Sharon Yu Ling Lau*[1], Frazer Midot[1], Yasuyuki Hashidoko[2] and Lulie Melling[1]

[1]*Tropical Peat Research Laboratory Unit, Chief Minister's Department, Sarawak, Malaysia*
[2]*Research Faculty of Agriculture, Hokkaido University, Sapporo, Japan*

**corresponding author: lauyuling@gmail.com*

SUMMARY

Microbial studies in relation to nitrous oxide (N_2O) in tropical peatlands are limited in number. Among the few reports on microbial N_2O emissions are Hashidoko *et al.* (2008), who successfully isolated potent N_2O emitting bacteria, *Janthinobacterium* sp. and *Burkholderia* sp., from reclaimed tropical peatland and Yanai *et al.* (2007), who described fungal N_2O production from tropical peatland. Nitrous oxide production from other groups of microbes such as Archaea, Actinobacteria and yeast still remains uncertain. Consequently, by adapting the method of N_2O emission assay using Modified Winogradsky's (MW) medium, bacterial, yeast, fungal and Actinobacterial isolates from tropical peatlands in Sarawak were screened for their N_2O-emitting ability. The N_2O level in the vial headspace was measured by ECD-GC analysis. Bacteria and Actinobacteria isolates were detected to produce N_2O and were identified mainly from *Bacillus* spp., *Paenibacillus* spp. and *Streptomyces* spp. *Wiiliopsis saturnus* was identified to be a N_2O-emitter yeast isolate. Conversely, most fungi exhibited the tendency to emit N_2O. This study aims to screen microbes of different groups isolated from tropical peatlands of Sarawak for nitrous oxide-emitting abilities and simultaneously identify key N_2O producers from the tropical peatlands of Sarawak.

Keywords: Nitrous oxide emission assay, tropical peat, N_2O emitters

INTRODUCTION

Greenhouse gases (GHGs) are atmospheric contaminants responsible for global warming and the on-going climate change. Nitrous oxide (N_2O) is one of the major GHGs, of which the current trace level in the atmosphere is recorded at 324 parts per billion (ppb) by volume (Ussiri and Lal, 2013). N_2O is considered as globally important due to its dual impacts on the environment: firstly, its ability to absorb infrared radiation 300 times more powerfully than does carbon dioxide (CO_2), contributing significantly (7%) to the global greenhouse effect that causes climate change and secondly, its activity as an ozone-depleting agent when it reaches the stratosphere (IPCC, 2007; Ravishankara *et al.*, 2009).

The largest N_2O source is agriculture, from the use of more than 80 million tons of nitrogen (N) annually in the form of chemical-synthetic nitrogen fertilizer or manure, as well as biological nitrogen fixation (Mosier *et al.*, 1998; IPCC, 2007). Therefore, rises in the rate of N_2O emission are significantly associated with the increasing rates of N fertilisation. Production of N_2O in soil is predominantly biological, with microbial N_2O production being widely reported for bacteria and fungi (Bollag and Tung, 1972; Bleakley and Tiedje, 1982; Kurakov *et al.*, 1997; Yanai *et al.*, 2007; Lavrent'ev *et al.*, 2008; Prendergast-Miller *et al.*, 2011; Chen *et al.*, 2014). However, Stieglmeier *et al.* (2014) properly measured the N_2O production by the first pure culture of ammonia-oxidizing Archaea (AOA) from soil, *Nitrososphaera viennensis*, as most Archaea were known to be extremely difficult to culture (Butterbach-Bahl *et al.*, 2013).

Microbial studies in relation to N_2O, specifically in tropical peatlands, are limited in number. To date, research has solely been based on the culture-dependent method of pure and enrichment cultures of soil microbes, in which N_2O production ability can be readily measured. Hashidoko *et al.* (2008) successfully isolated potent N_2O emitting bacteria, *Janthinobacterium* sp. and *Burkholderia* sp., from reclaimed tropical peatland. Fungal N_2O production from tropical peatland, on the other hand, was described by Yanai *et al.* (2007). N_2O production from other groups such as Archaea, Actinobacteria and yeasts still remains uncertain (Baggs and Philippot, 2010). Therefore, this study aims to screen for nitrous oxide-emitting abilities of the different groups of microbes isolated from tropical peatlands of Sarawak and simultaneously identify key producers of nitrous oxide from the tropical peatlands of Sarawak.

MATERIALS AND METHODS

Soil sampling

Peat samples were collected from sites in three ecosystems: an oil palm plantation in Sibu and secondary and primary peat swamp forest at Maludam National Park in Betong, Sarawak. at each site, soil samples at 0-25cm and 25-50cm were taken with a peat auger sampler (Eijelkamp, The Netherlands). Using a sterile spatula, approximately 50g of the peat soil samples were placed in polyethylene zipper bags, which then had the air eliminated and were immediately placed in a cooler packed with ice for transport back to the laboratory, where they were stored at 4 C.

Isolation and identification of microbes

The enumeration of microorganisms comprised of bacteria, fungi, yeasts and Actinobacteria was carried out using conventional culturing techniques on nutrient agar (NA), potato dextrose agar (PDA), yeast extract peptone dextrose agar (YEPD) and actinomycete isolation agar (AIA) respectively. Bacteria and Actinobacteria were identified based on the 16S rRNA gene sequences subjected to homology search on DNA databases (DDBJ and NCBI). The 16S rRNA gene sequences were obtained using primer pair 27F (5' AGA GTT TGA TCC TGG CTC AG 3') and 1525R (5' GGA GGT GAT CCA GC 3'). Yeasts and fungi were identified based on the internal transcribed spacer (ITS) region in the nuclear ribosomal repeat unit using primer pair ITS1 (5' TCC GTA GGT GAA CCT GCG G 3') and ITS4 (5' TCC TCC GCT TAT TGA TAT GC 3').

Culture-based N_2O emission assay

The medium for the culture-based N_2O emission assay contained 0.5% sucrose and 0.05% yeast extract as substrate for N_2O production. Winogradsky's mineral mixture served as the medium for the N_2O emission assay (Hashidoko *et al.,* 2008). The medium was autoclaved, adjusted to pH 5.0 with 2 M sulphuric acid (H_2SO_4) and then solidified to a soft gel with 0.3% gellan gum (Sigma Aldrich, USA). After cooling, 10 mL aliquots of medium were poured into 30 mL gas chromatography vials equipped with butyl-rubber plugs (Nichiden-Rika Glass Co., Japan).

A 100 µL aliquot of each broth culture was inoculated onto the soft gel medium contained in a gas chromatograph vial, leaving a 22.5 mL headspace volume. The vials were vortexed thoroughly and incubated at 30°C in the dark for 5-14 days. Headspace gas (1 mL) was sampled from each vial using a Hamilton gas-tight syringe and injected into a gas chromatograph (model 7890A, Agilent Technologies Inc., USA). Production of N_2O is expressed as parts per million by volume (ppmv) in the headspace gas relative to the atmospheric trace level at about 324 parts per billion by volume (ppbv).

RESULTS AND DISCUSSIONS

A total of 507 microbe species, comprising 190 bacteria, 181 Actinobacteria, 120 fungi and 16 yeasts, were isolated from the three sites (oil palm plantation, secondary forest and primary peat swamp forest). Approximately 30% of the isolates from this study, mainly those from oil palm plantation, showed N_2O production. This is considered primarily due to the application of N fertilizer to oil palm in plantations, which provides an environment where substrates for the production of N_2O by microbes are more readily available. There is evidence that the relationship between N_2O release and fertilizer input is linear (Bouwman, 1990). The two major groups of microbes producing nitrous oxide were observed to be Actinobacteria (**Table 1**) and fungi (**Figure 1B**). The highest N_2O productions were from three Actinobacterial isolates identified as *Streptomyces nodosus* (45.8 – 58.1 ppmv) and a fungal isolate, *Diarporthe longicolla*, (50.3 ppmv), all of which were isolated from the oil palm plantation.

Bacteria

Bacterial isolates were screened for their nitrous oxide emitting ability and seven (7) were observed to be emitters. The most active N_2O-emitter was identified as *Paenibacillus* sp., producing 6.8 ppmv in the headspace gas at five (5) days' incubation. The other active N_2O-emitters were identified as *Lysinibacillus* sp., *Bacillus subtilis* and *Pantoeastewartii* sp. Bacterial N_2O production is the best reported and occurs via various pathways, namely nitrification, denitrification (Firestone and Davidson, 1989), nitrifier denitrification (Wrage *et al.*, 2001) and nitrate ammonification/dissimilatory nitrate reduction to ammonium (DNRA) (Burgin and Hamilton, 2007). Bacterial N_2O emitters have also been reported as isolated from various recognized N_2O hotspots from different peatland ecosystems; *Burkholderia phenazinium* and *Pseudomonas* sp. from boreal peatlands (Nie et al., 2015) and *Burkholderia* spp. and *Janthinobacterium* sp. from tropical peatland in Riau, Indonesia (Hashidoko *et al.*, 2008).

Actinobacteria

Of the 181 Actinobacteria isolates that were screened, 24 showed active N_2O production. Shoun *et al.* (1998) first reported that denitrification is commonly distributed among Actinomycetes. Actinomycetes were found to be incomplete denitrifiers in that they cannot reduce N_2O to dinitrogen and thus produce N_2O as the end-product. As *Streptomyces* spp. is are the dominant members of the soil microflora it is reasonable to postulate that a major percentage of soil N_2O would originate from this group. In this study, *Streptomyces nodosus* was isolated from various plots at all three sites and was observed to produce N_2O in the range of 6.8 to 58.1 ppmv. However, the highest reading (58.1 ppmv) was from *S. nodosus* isolated from the oil palm plantation in comparison to *S. nodosus* isolated from the forest (**Table 1**). The other active N_2O emitters were observed to be *Streptomyces aburaviensis, S. anandii, S. flavogriseus* and *Kitasatospora setae.*

Fungi

A total of 120 fungal isolates was screened and most of them showed N_2O production in the range of 2.3 to 4.3 ppmv. All fungal isolates exhibited the tendency to produce N_2O, as shown in **Figure 1(B)**. However, the four isolates that showed the highest N_2O emitting potentials were identified as *Diaporthe longicolla* (50.3 ppmv), *Penicillium aculeatum* (13.8 ppmv) and *Trichoderma* sp. (5.7 ppmv), isolated from oil palm plantation and *Trichoderma harzianum* (5.3 ppmv) isolated from primary peat swamp forest (**Table 1**). Fungi were reported to produce N_2O since as long as 20 years ago, with cases of N_2O production observed in *Trichoderma harzianum, Fusarium oxysporum* and *Aspergillus nidulans* (Shoun *et al.*, 1992; Tanimoto *et al.*, 1992). Previous studies have reported that fungi could contribute up to 18% of potential denitrification and be significant N_2O producers in some terrestrial systems (Laughlin *et al.*, 2009). Maeda *et al.* (2014) reported that N_2O production is a common and widespread trait in fungi. However, nitrite instead of nitrate was the substrate preferred by fungi and N_2O was always the end-product of denitrification as N_2O was unable to be converted to dinitrogen. This underlines the importance of quantifying the fungal contribution to terrestrial N_2O emissions (Maeda *et al.*, 2014).

Yeasts

Of the 16 yeast isolates that were screened for N_2O production, only *Wiiliopsis saturnus* var. *mrakii*, isolated from the oil palm plantation, was observed to produce N_2O (9.0 ppmv) in the headspace gas of the vial after five (5) days' incubation at 30 C (**Table 1**). Tsuruta *et al.* (1998) screened yeasts of various genera for denitrifying activity and *Trichosporon cutaneum, Fellomyces fuzhouensis* and *Candida* sp. were found to convert nitrite to nitrous oxide. This was the first report that showed that denitrification was distributed among yeasts, although their systems are incomplete, therefore N_2O is produced as the denitrification product.

CONCLUSION

In conclusion, N_2O production from bacteria is mainly from nitrification, denitrification, nitrifier denitrification and nitrate ammonification/dissimilatory nitrate reduction to ammonium processes. Conversely, the more recently reported systems of N_2O production in Actinobacteria, fungi and yeasts, were solely incomplete denitrifying systems, i.e. these organisms cannot reduce N_2O and thus emit it. However, the source of N_2O evolution is not completely understood. It seems possible that these incomplete denitrifying systems play an important role in the global N_2O budget. Therefore, further studies are warranted to elucidate more information on the key N_2O producers of the tropical peatlands of Sarawak.

Table 1: Isolation and identification of N_2O-emitting microorganisms from peat soil

Isolates		Origin	Nearest relative	Homology (%)	N_2O production (ppmv)
Bacteria					
T17	MA1(B)B2	Primary peat swamp forest	-	-	1.5
T30	MA2(T)B2		*Lysinibacillus* sp.	-	2.5
T34	MB1(B)B3		*Klebsiella pneumoniae*	94	1.9
T42	MB1(T)B9		*Paenibacillus* sp.	93	6.8
T50	MC1(B)B5		*Bacillus subtilis*	99	1.5
T55	MC1(T)B4		*Bacillus subtilis*	100	1.2
T93	NA31(T)B1	Oil palm plantation	*Pantoeastewartii* subsp. *stewartii*	99	1.7
Actinobacteria					
A5	NA12(B)A1	Oil palm plantation	*Streptomyces rhizophilus*	99	1.2
A19	NC11(T)A2		*Kitasatospora kepongensis*	99	2.5
A20	NC11(T)A3		*Kitasatospora setae*	99	3.6
A21	NC11(T)A4		*Streptomyces lannensis*	98	7.3
A32	NC13(B)A1		*Streptomyces aburaviensis*	99	11.9
A58	NC12(B)A1		*Streptomyces nodosus*	99	10.5
A61	NC14(T)A1		*Streptomyces nodosus*	99	49.9
A69	NC14(B)A4		*Streptomyces anandii*	99	16.4
A81	NA14(B)A4		*Streptomyces tsukiyonensis*	99	5.1
A83	NA14(T)A7		*Streptomyces nodosus*	99	58.1
A89	NC14(T)A8		*Streptomyces flavogriseus*	99	11.8
A90	NE1(T)A5		*Streptomyces aureofaciens*	99	5.5
A95	NB12(B)A5		*Micrococcus luteus*	98	5.3
A97	ND1(B)A13		*Streptomyces nodosus*	100	6.8
A106	ND1(B)A18		*Streptomyces nodosus*	99	26.1
A130	NC11(B)A3		*Streptomyces nodosus*	99	45.8
A143	NA14(B)A3		*Streptomyces tsukiyonensis*	99	3.9
A146	ND1(B)A5		*Streptomyces aburaviensis*	99	8.3
A151	NC12(T)A4		*Streptomyces nodosus*	99	6.8
A156	NC11(T)A8		*Kitasatospora setae*	99	17.8
A45	CA1(B)A1	Secondary forest	*Streptomyces nodosus*	100	7.2
A75	CA1(B)A7		*Streptomyces griseus*	98	3.1
A110	CA1(T)A11		*Streptomyces nodosus*	99	28.4
A167	MA1(B)A14	Primary peat swamp forest	*Streptomyces nodosus*	99	10.4
Fungi					
F12	NA12(B)F1	Oil palm plantation	*Penicillium aculeatum*	100	13.8
F81	NE1(T)F2		*Trichoderma* sp.	98	5.7
F84	NE1(B)F2		*Diaporthe longicolla*	97	50.3
F116	MB1(T)F2	Primary forest	*Trichoderma harzianum*	99	5.3
Yeast					
A30	NC13(T)A3	Oil palm plantation	*Wiiliopsis saturnus* var. *mrakii*	81	9.0

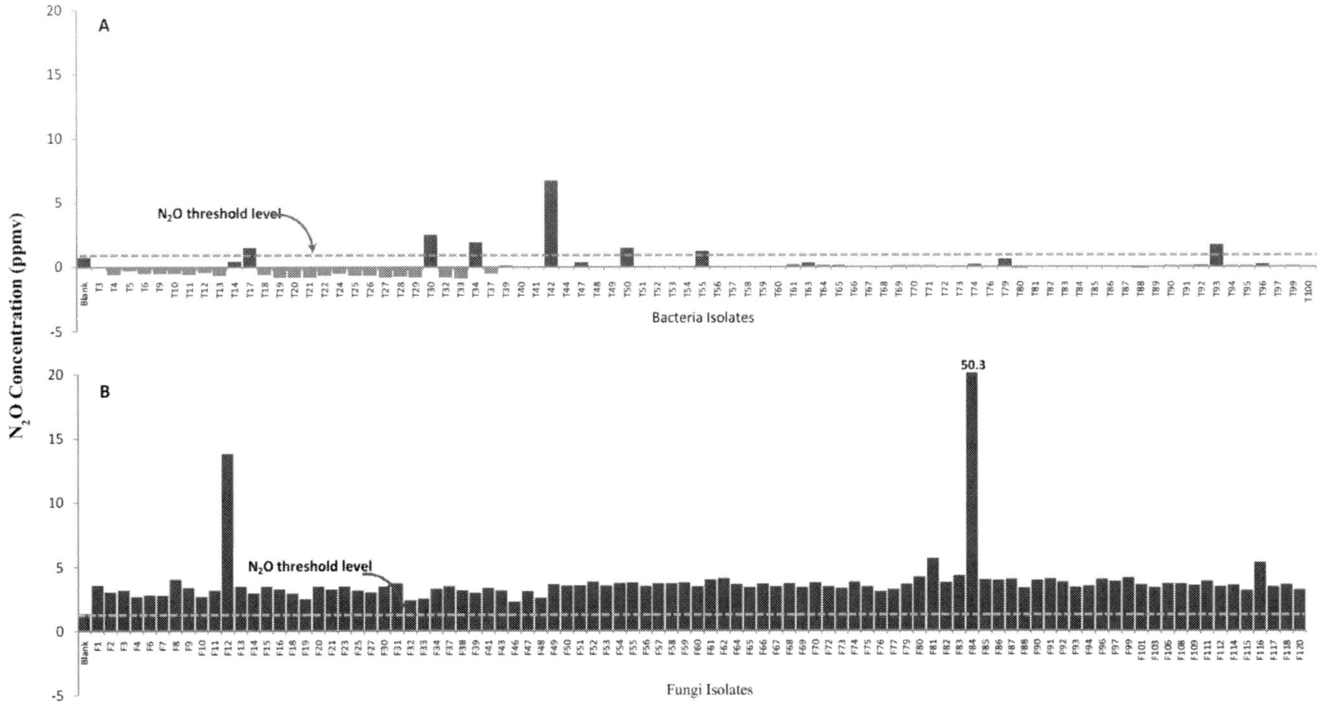

Figure 1: Bacterial and fungi N_2O emitter screening using the Modified Winogradsky's (MW) media assay system

Nitrous oxide measurement was conducted using ECD-GC after (A) 5-days' incubation of vials inoculated with individual bacteria isolates and (B) 14-days' incubation of vials inoculated with individual fungi isolates respectively at 30 C. Classification of N_2O emitters is based on the ability of isolates to produce N_2O concentration exceeding the threshold level, set based on blank reading of vials without inoculation.

REFERENCES:

1. Baggs, E.M. and L. Philippot. 2010. Microbial terrestrial pathways to N_2O. Pp 4-35 in K.A. Smith (ed.), Nitrous Oxide and Climate Change, Earthscan, London.
2. Bleakley, B.H. and J.M. Tiedje. 1982. Nitrous oxide production by organisms other than nitrifiers or denitrifiers. *Appl. Environ. Microbiol.* **44(6)**:1342-1348.
3. Bollag, J.M. and G. Tung. 1972. Nitrous oxide release by soil fungi. Soil. Biol. Biochem. **4(3)**:271-276.
4. Bouwman, A.F. 1990. Exchange of greenhouse gases between terrestrial ecosystems and the atmosphere. Pp. 61–127 in A.F. Bouwman, (ed.) *Soils and the Greenhouse Effect.* Wiley, Chichester.
5. Burgin, A.J. and S.K. Hamilton. 2007. Have we overemphasized the role of denitrification in aquatic ecosystems? A review of nitrate removal pathways. *Front. Ecol. Environ.* **5(2)**:89-96.
6. Butterbach-Bahl, K., E. M. Bagg, M. Dannenmann, R. Kiese and S. Zechmeister-Boltenstern. 2013. Nitrous oxide emissions from soils: How well do we understand the processes and their controls? *Phil. Trans. R. Soc. B.* **368**:20130122.
7. Chen, H., N.V. Mothapo and W. Shi. 2014. The significant contribution of fungi to soil N_2O production across diverse ecosystems. *Appl. Soil Ecol.* **73(1)**:70-77.
8. Firestone M.K. and E.A. Davidson. 1989. Microbiological basis of NO and N_2O production and consumption in soil. Pp. 7-21 in M.O. Andreae and D.S. Schimel (eds.), Exchange of trace gases between terrestrial ecosystems and the atmosphere. John Wiley, New York.
9. Hashidoko, Y.F. Takakai, Y. Toma, U. Darung, L. Melling, S. Tahara and R. Hatano. 2008. Emergence and behaviors of acid-tolerant *Janthinobacterium* sp. that evolves N_2O from deforested tropical peatland. *Soil Biol. Biochem.* **40(1)**:116-125.
10. IPCC. 2007. Mitigation of climate change. Pp. 27-93 in B. Metz, O. Davidson, P. Bosch, R. Dave and L. Meyer (eds.), Climate change 2007. Working group III contribution to the fourth assessment report of the intergovernmental panel on climate change, Cambridge University Press, Cambridge.
11. Kurakov, A.V., O.V. Pakhnenko, N.V. Kostina and M.M. Umarov. 1997. Microscopic fungi producing nitrous oxide in nutrient media and in sterile soil. *Eurasian Soil Sci.* **30(12)**:1344-1349.
12. Laughlin, R.J., T. Rutting, C. Muller, C.J. Watson and R.J. Stevens. 2009. Effect of acetate on soil respiration, N_2O emissions and gross N transformations related to fungi and bacteria in a grassland soil. *Appl. Soil Ecol.* **42**:25-30
13. Lavrent'ev, R., S. Zaitsev, I. Sudnitsyn and A. Kurakov. 2008. Nitrous oxide production by fungi in soils under different moisture levels. *Mosc. Univ. Soil Sci. Bull.* **63(4)**:178-183.
14. Maeda, K., A. Spor, V. Edel-Hermann, C. Heraud, M. Breuil, F. Bizouard, S. Toyoda, N. Yoshida, C. Steinberg and L. Philippot 2015. N_2O production, a widespread trait in fungi. *Scientific Reports* **5**:9697.
15. Mosier, A., C. Kroeze, C. Nevison, O. Oenema, S. Seitzinger and O. van Cleemput. 1998. Closing the global N_2O budget: nitrous oxide emissions through the agricultural nitrogen cycle. *Nutr. Cycl. Agroecosys.* **52(2)**:225-248.
16. Nie, Y., L. Li, M. Wang, T. Tahvanainen and Y. Hashidoko. 2015. Nitrous oxide emission potentials of *Burkholderia* species isolated from the leaves of a boreal peat moss *Sphagnum fuscum. Bioscience, Biotechnology and Biochemistry* **79**:2086–2095.
17. Prendergast-Miller, M.T., E.M. Baggs and D. Johnson. 2011. Nitrous oxide production by the ectomycorrhizal fungi *Paxillus involutus* and *Tylospora fibrillosa*. *FEMS Microbiol. Lett.* **316(1)**:31-35.
18. Ravishankara, A.R., J.S. Daniel and R.W. Portmann. 2009. Nitrous oxide (N_2O): the dominant ozone-depleting substance emitted in the 21st century. *Science* **326(5949)**:123-125.
19. Shoun, H., D.H. Kim, H. Uchiyama and J. Sugiyama. 1992. Denitrification by fungi. *FEMS Microbiol. Lett.* **94**:277–281. (doi:10.1111/j.1574-6968.1992.tb05331.x).
20. Shoun, H., M. Kano, I. Baba, N. Takaya and M. Matsuo. 1998. Denitrification by Actinomycetes and purification of dissimilatory nitrite reductase and azurin from *Streptomyces thioluteus*. *Journal of Bacteriology* **180(17)**:4413-4415.
21. Stieglmeier, M., M. Mooshammer, B. Kitzler, W. Wanek, S. Zechmeister-Boltenstern, A. Richter and C. Schleper. 2014. Aerobic nitrous oxide production through N-nitrosating hybrid formation in ammonia-oxidizing archaea. *ISME J.* **8(5)**:1135-1146.
22. Tanimoto, T., K. Hatano, D.H. Kim, H. Uchiyama and H. Shoun. 1992. Co-denitrification by the denitrifying system of the fungus *Fusarium oxysporum*. FEMS *Microbiol. Lett.* **93**:177–118. (doi:10.1111/j.1574-6968.1992.tb05086.x)

23. Tsuruta, S., N. Takaya, L. Zhang, H. Shoun, K. Kimura, M. Hamamoto and T. Nakase.1998. Denitrification by yeasts and occurrence of cytochrome P450nor in *Trichosporon cutaneum*. *FEMS Microbiol. Let.* **168(1)**:105–110.
24. Ussiri, D. and R. Lal. 2013. The role of nitrous oxide on climate change. Pp. 1-28 in D. Ussiri and R. Lal (eds.), Soil emission of nitrous oxide and its mitigation. Springer, Dordrecht, The Netherlands.
25. Wrage, N., G.L. Velthof, M.L. van Beusichem and O. Oenema. 2001. Role of nitrifier denitrification in the production of nitrous oxide. *Soil Biol. Biochem.* **33(12-13)**:1723-1732.
26. Yanai, Y., K. Toyota, T. Morishita, F. Takakai, R. Hatano, S.H. Limin, U. Darung and S Dohong. 2007. Fungal N_2O production in an arable peat soil in Central Kalimantan, Indonesia. *Soil. Sci. Plant. Nutr.* **53(6)**:806-811.

Abstract No: A-323

COMBINED ASSESSMENT OF ARCHAEAL AND BACTERIAL COMMUNITIES IN SOIL SAMPLES FROM HORNSUND, SPITSBERGEN USING ILLUMINA MI-SEQ

Sia, Edwin[1*], Denis, Nastassia[1], Mujahid, Aazani[2], Zhang, Jing[3], Alias, Siti Aisyah[4,5], Ali, Siti Hafizah[4,5], Samah, Azizan Abu [5] and Mueller, Moritz[1]

[1] *Faculty of Engineering, Computing and Science, Swinburne University of Technology, Sarawak Campus*
[2] *Department of Aquatic Science, Faculty of Resource Science and Technology, University Malaysia Sarawak*
[3] *State Key Laboratory of Estuarine and Coastal Research, East China Normal University*
[4] *Institute of Biological Science, Faculty of Science, University Malaya, 50603 Kuala Lumpur, Malaysia;*
[5] *National Antarctic Research Centre, IPS Building, University Malaya*

* *Corresponding author: edwinsia92@gmail.com*

Hornsund is a fjord which lies on the southern-most tip of Spitsbergen Island with limited studies of its prokaryotic community. The bacterial and archaeal communities from nine habitats of peat origin were assessed on a MiSeq (250PE) using a universal bacterial and archaeal primer primers to assess the diversity of the prokaryotic communities. 16s rDNA was analyzed using Mothur as well as MEGAN5 (MetaGenome ANalyzer) for more detailed analyses. From the analyses, total assigned reads were normalized using sub-sample counts and the relative abundance was compared and analyzed for probable function based on the community composition. The Taxonomy Cluster Analyses revealed that ornithogenic influence showed the highest degree of dissimilarity. The dominance shown by Acidobacteria, Proteobacteria, Actinobacteria, Bacteroidetes, and Verrumicrobia in the shared biome is in agreement with other literature on Arctic soils, with the exception of Bacteroidetes in which Gemmatimonadetes was found to be the most prominent in other literature. Moreover, Acidobacteria was the most predominant in the ornithogenic tundra whereby only this soil contains bacteria from the phylum Nitrospirae, indicating their role in the cycling of nitrogen from feces of ornithogenic origin. Six out of nine samples contained bacteria from the Chloroflexi phyla, even though the highest percentage in a sample was only 7.14%, indicating potential photosynthesis for nitrogen-fixation during the Arctic summer in the oligotrophic environment. Lastly, archaeal reads from the phylum Crenarchaeota were found only in moist moss tundra from Hyttevika (2.67%). The results from this study show that the distinct habitats in the Hornsund region exhibit varying degrees of variability in terms of their prokaryotic community composition. To our knowledge, this is the first comparison of prokaryotic communities within this region, thus providing a platform for further work involving temporal and diurnal studies.

Keywords: -

Abstract No: A-302

EUKARYOTIC BIODIVERSITY UNDER OIL PALM ON PEAT AT SARAWAK DETERMINED USING 454 NEXT GENERATION SEQUENCING

Siti Ramlah Ahmad Ali[1]*, Mohd Noor Mat Isa[2], Mohd Shawal Thakib Maidin[1], Sakinah Safari[1], Nur Aziemah Abu Ghani[3], Sharifah Azura Syed Ibrahim[1], and Norman Kamarudin[1]

[1]*Biology Research Division, Malaysian Palm Oil Board, 6 Persiaran Institusi, Bandar Baru Bangi, 43000 Kajang, Selangor, Malaysia.*
[2]*Malaysian Genomic Institute of Malaysia.*
[3] *Faculty of Medicine, University of Malaya, Jalan Universiti, 50603, Kuala Lumpur, Malaysia.*

**Corresponding author:* ramlah@mpob.gov.my

SUMMARY

Information on the eukaryotic biodiversity in different peat ecosystems in Sarawak remained lamentably low. The eukaryotic community in seven tropical peat ecosystems in Sarawak was examined using 454-next-generation sequencing technology. The operational taxonomic units (OTU) were 1103, 924, 718 for Pelitanah Alan Bunga logged over forest(PF), Pelitanah planted with young oil palm (PT) and Pelitanah Alan Bunga logged over clean cleared unplanted area (UP), respectively. In the mixed forest peat at Sri Aman the OTU for eukaryotic community were 986, 1853, 1677, 865 for primary forest at Muladam National Park (MD), logged over forest Cermat Ceria (CC), 7 years oil palm plantation at Durafarm (DF) developed from degraded logged over mixed peat, Sri Aman Sarawak and 11 years oil palm at Naman (NM) developed from degraded logged over Alan Bunga peat, Sibu Sarawak, respectively. The α-diversity of eukaryotic community for PF indicated average species per sample ID of 280 species as compared to 230 and 50 species per sample ID for in PT and UP, Sibu Sarawak. While, the α-diversity of eukaryotic community indicated average species per sample ID were 70, 500, 300, 150 species for MD, CC, DF at Sri Aman Sarawak and NM, Sibu Sarawak, respectively. The 3D Bi-Plot and taxonomic composition of eukaryotic community indicated that the eukaryotic population at MD, CC, PF and PT comprised mainly of fungi and other unclassified Eukaryota. Whilst, the eukaryotic community in peat at UP and under the matured oil palm plantations on peat (DF, NM) comprised of mainly fungi. For all sites, the most dominant phylum of fungi was Ascomycota followed by Basidiomycota, Chytridiomycota and Fungi incertae sedis. The third dominant phylotype after unclassified Eukaryota for all sites was Aveolata mainly the Ciliphora and Apicomplexa.

***Keywords**: Eukaryotes, biodiversity, 454-next generation sequencing, peat ecosystems, Sarawak.*

INTRODUCTION

Tropical peat ecosystems respiration consists of heterotrophic and autotrophic respiration. The former is a process assisted by degrading microbes in the peat while autotrophic respiration is a process of respiration from plants and roots (Page *et al.*, 2010). Tropical peat forests remained relatively unexploited and acting as a carbon sink for several decades. Accumulating almost one-third of the global terrestrial carbon pool, peat contains considerable reservoirs of carbon and nitrogen (Turunen *et al.*, 1999). This contributed to the beta diversity with their groups of specialized and unique plants and animals and in global climate regulation from methane (CH4) emission in which the methane–oxidizing bacteria are involved (Couwenberg and Fritz, 2012). Generally, nutrient mineralization and uptake by the microbes can be beneficial to the plant productivity and overall ecosystem functioning (Van Der Heijden *et al.*, 2008). Fungal diversity, community structure and spatial patterns is one of the main issues in soil microbial diversity. As a decomposers and plant symbionts, fungi play an important role in the soil. They played prerequisite roles in many factor of ecosystem development, function and stability. In contrast, fungi are considered to be the important decomposers in peat soil and have received the most attention based on previous findings (Myers *et al.*, 2012). However, current study has suggested that bacteria could be more active in aerobic decomposition compared to fungi due to the case of anoxic upper layers in different types of peatland (Winsborough and Basiliko, 2010). Forest management (e.g. drainage) can also change the physical and chemical properties of peat soil as well as the vegetation communities, which, in turn, alters the microbial environment in peat soil (Laine *et al.,* 1995). In addition, the diverse litter input probably also has a great impact on the microbial community structure in forest (Straková *et al.,* 2012) and soil types.

Alveolata are single-celled eukaryotes with extremely diverse modes of nutrition, such as predation, photoautotrophy and intracellular parasitism. The Alveolata forms two major clades of photosynthetic eukaryotes, namely the Stramenopiles and clade consisting of Haptophytes and Cryptophytes. The photosynthetic lineages, such as Chromera and Dinoflagellates, and non-photosynthetic lineages, such as ciliates, Colpodellids, Apicomplexans and Perkinsids. Ciliates are complex freshwater or saltwater protozoans which are unicellular heterotrophs. Free-living ciliates are found almost anywhere there is liquid water, but different forms predominate in different habitats. Ciliates in soils tend to be small forms and can form resistant cysts in order to survive long periods of drying. Apicomplexa is a single celled eukaryotic organisms, known to parasitise vertebrates including humans and invertebrate hosts. About 0.1% out of 1.2 to 10 million Apicomplexan species have been named and described (Adl *et al.,* 2007). Apicomplexans reasonably host specific, inhabiting a wide array of terrestrial and marine environments depending on their host niche environments. Rhizaria comprises of several very large and diverse groups of amoebae, flagellates and amoeboflagellates, ubiquitous in nature and important predators in many environments (Cavalier-Smith and Chao, 2003). Rhizaria is the most recently recognized supergroup, identified exclusively from molecular phylogenetic reconstruction.

Identification of fungi in peat soil was done using the plate culture, phospholipid and fatty acid analysis, fingerprinting techniques, other DNA-based techniques such as restriction analysis and Sanger sequencing, and denaturing gradient gel electrophoresis (DGGE) (Peng *et al.* 2014). As the majority of microbial population in the environments are unculturable, it is best studied using the molecular methods. Nevertheless, these tools usually underestimate the overall diversity of a microbial community and are unable to detect rare species in complicated environmental samples. Next generations sequencing through pyrosequencing has gained increasing attention as a novel tool for studying microbial diversity and allow us to better understand the microbial community structure (Yuanyuan *et al.* 2014). In this study, the 454-pyrosequencing of the 18S rRNA gene was used to analyse the diversity and community of eukaryota in different tropical peat ecosystems.

MATERIALS AND METHODS

Peat sampling – Peat samples was taken in April 2012 from three peat ecosystems in Sri Aman, Sarawak namely at tropical primary peat with mixed forest Maludam National Park (MD) and secondary drained logged-over peat forest at Cermat Ceria (CC) and mature oil palm aged 7 planted from logged over forest at Durafarm (DF) and four peat ecosystems in Sibu Sarawak namely the young oil palm aged 4 years (PT), drained degraded logged over Alan Bunga peat forest (PF) and drained clean-cleared logged over Alan Bunga at Pelitanah and 11 years oil palm planted on logged over Alan Bunga at Naman plantation (NM) (*Figure 1).* For each peat ecosystem, 10 different GPS points were determined for samplings which was undertaken twice a year. The mean central point for the ten sampling points for MD, CC, DF and NM are with latitude 1° 37' 45.4116" N and longitude 111° 2' 23.5644" E, latitude 1° 23' 56.4" N and longitude 111° 24' 21.6" E, latitude 1° 23' 50.3808" N and longitude 111° 24' 49.6476" E, and latitude 1° 37' 45.4116" N and longitude 111° 2' 23.5644" E, respectively. While the mean central point for PT and UP at Pelitanah in Sibu Sarawak are latitude 2° 33' 38.7108" N and longitude 111° 59' 10.104" E, and latitude 2° 33' 46.836" N and longitude 111° 58' 4.6632" E, respectively.

The peat sites situated at Block 3E, MPOB plot, Ladang Pelitanah 2, Sibu, Sarawak, with parent material organic deposit of very deep Naman Series. Elevation 10 meter, slope 2%, very poor artificially drained. The peat classification was *Sapric Ombrogambist* (Paramananthan, 2010). For Muladam, Cermat Ceria and Durafaram ten sampling points were taken at the Kenyana soil series, the peat was dark brown to black sapric organic soil material with undecomposed wood. The soil is poorly drained with underlying marine clay at 300 cm depth. *Naman* study area consists of sedimentary rocks of the Kapit Member (P2Kt) and organic deposits with parent material organic deposit of very deep Naman Series. The oil palm plantation has level, undulating, rolling and hilly terrain slopes (0-38% or 0-20°). The rolling and hilly areas are well drained while the organic deposits are artificially drained with the water-table maintained around 50-60 cm. Naman has an annual rainfall of between 2,012 to 3,189 mm per annum with an occasional dry month (<100 mm).

Experiment Overview - Metagenomics DNA peat samples were PCR amplified using specific 18S rRNA phylogenetic markers for eukaryotic diversity analysis. Amplified products were purified, quantified and quality checked prior to 454 Amplicon Library Preparation procedures. The amplicons were then sequenced using 454 FLX machine at the Malaysia Genome Institute using the 454 GS-FLX Titanium protocol (454 Life Sciences/Roche Diagnostics, CT, USA) (Roche, 2013), which yields reads length of ~400bp. The sequence data were analysed using QIIME (Quantitative Insights into Microbial Ecology) pipeline.

DNA extraction, PCR amplification & purification - GeneMATRIX Soil DNA Purification Kit (Eurx Ltd, Gdansk, Poland) was used for total DNA extraction from peat samples. The amount and quality of DNA measured using a Nanophotometer™ P360, must meet minimum concentration and purity of 10ng/μL and $OD_{260/280}$ of 1.8, respectively. Twenty five microliters of PCR reaction mixture was prepared using FastStart high fidelity PCR System (Roche). The Multiplex Identifier (MID) fusion primer pair, EF4 (GGAAGGGRTGTATTTATTAG) and fung5 (GGCCTTGGTCCTGAAAATG) amplifies a 550 bp fragment. The PCR reaction with denaturation at 95 °C for 5 min, followed by 25 cycles of template denaturation at 95 °C for 1 min, primer annealing at 63 °C for 1 min, extension at 72 °C for 1 min with final extension performed at 72 °C for 5 min. A reaction without template DNA was conducted under the same conditions as control.

Post Run Analysis using QIIME pipelines - DNA sequence reads were filtered for quality and assign multiplexed reads to starting samples by nucleotide barcode. Operational Taxonomic Units (OTUs) were picked based on sequence similarity within the reads, and pick a representative sequence from each OTU. The OTUs were assigned to a taxonomic identity using reference databases (SILVA release 108). The OTU sequences were aligned and phylogenetic trees were constructed. The diversity metrics for each sample were calculated and the types of communities were compared using the taxonomic and phylogenetic assignments. The UPGMA, PCoA bootstrapped trees and 3D bi-plots were generated to visually depict the differences between the samples.

Nutrients Analysis - Nutrients analysis was done using ICP-MS (ELAN DRC-e) and C and N was conducted using CNS Analyser (SKALAR SPrimac SNC Analyzer).

RESULTS AND DISCUSSION

Analysis of 454 pyrosequencing data. A total of 176,228, 369,693, 288,005, 369,693, 371,513, 315,069 and 371,513 16SrRNA sequencing reads were obtained for 10 samples subjected to 454 pyrosequencing for peat ecosystem (MD), (CC), (DF), (NM), (PF), (UP) and (PT), respectively. The average read length was 428 bp, 429 bp, 426 bp and 430 bp, 426 bp, 430 bp and 427 bp for MD, CC, DF, NM, PF, UP and PT respectively. While, the average number sequences passing quality filters (HQ) was 394, 395, 392, 396, 392, 396, and 393 for MD, CC, DF, NM, PF, UP and PT, respectively. All chimeras and singletons were removed before further analysis. For the 10 samples, the total number sequences passing quality filters (HQ) or remained after quality control and chimera detection was 65,627 reads (37 % of all reads), 152,266 (41% of all reads), 252,971 (88 % of all reads), 75,364 (47% of all reads) 150,282 (40% of all reads), 49,577 (15% of all reads) and 371,513 (44% of all reads) for MD, CC, DF, NM, PF, UP and PT, respectively. The moisture content and pH for the different peat ecosystems MD, CC, DF, NM, PF, UP and PT in the dry period, April 2012 are as seen in *Table 1*. During this dry month the moisture content and the total operational taxanomic units (OTUs) was lowest for MD. The total OTUs for MD, CC, DF, NM, PF, UP and PT was 986, 1853, 1677, 865, 1103, 718 and 924, respectively (*Table 1*).

Alpha and Beta diversity – It is clearly revealed peat ecosystems which had the greatest α–diversity contained the highest numbers of exclusive species. The simplest measure of biodiversity is species richness, which measure the number of species found in a given area, niche or habitat. The α-diversity of eukaryotic communities for peat ecosystems PF, UP, PT, MD, CC, DF and NM indicated average species per sample ID ranged 200-450, 43-60, 150-460, 40-80, 300-600, 200-800, 100-550, respectively. Beta-biodiversity as seen in the bootstrapped trees with internal nodes coloured red shows 75-100% similarity, yellow for 50-75%, green for 25-50%, and blue for < 25%. DF, MN, CC, NM, UP, PT and PF had 7, 6, 6, 6, 6, 5 and 2 samples ID with 75-100%. For PF eight samples ID have less than 25% similarity.

Generate 3D bi-plots and taxanomic composition – The 3D biplots show coordinates of a given taxon are plotted as a weighted average of the coordinates of all samples, where the weights are the relative abundances of the taxon in the samples. The size of the spheres representing a taxon is proportional to the mean relative abundance of the taxon across all samples. The generated 3D biplots displaying the five most abundant taxon were Fungi Others, Fungi Dikarya, Fungi Chitridiomycota, Alveolata Cilliphora, Unidentified Eukaryota for CC, DF, NM, PT, UP and PT but in the primary forest, MD Fungi Chitridiomycota was absent and Alveolata Apicomplexa was present (*Figure 2*). The mean taxanomic composition showed that fungi is the most abundant eukaryotic phylotype for the seven peat ecosystems, amount to 88.66 %, 79.1%, 73.23%, 59.77%, 55.93%, 46.39% and 45.12% in

NM,UP, DF, PT, CC, PF and MD, respectively. The second most abundant taxon was the unclassified Eukaryota followed by Alveolata (*Figure 3*). Statistically, Duncan test indicated that the population of fungi in the NM, UP and DF ecosystems were significantly higher than CC and PT. For ecosystems MD and PF were significantly lower than the rest of the peat ecosystems at $p = 0.05$ (*Figure 4*). The Alveolata in MD was significantly higher as compared to the other six peat ecosystems at $p = 0.05$. Minor phylotypes present at <4% were Amoeboza, Choanoflagellida, Nucleariidae and Fonticula group, Rhizaria, Stramenopiles, Metazoa, Viridiplantae, Haptophyceae, Ichthyosporea, Apusozoa and Cryptophyta. Rhizaria and Stramenopiles were significantly higher in MD and CC as compared to other peat ecosystem at $p = 0.05$.

Major nutrients in the peat ecosystems, N was between 1-1.5% (highest in MD), P 180-340 mg/L (lowest in PF and UP), K between 80 to 760 mg/L (high in PT, NM and DF), C >50% (54% in MD, CC, DF, NM and PT). While minor nutrients, Bo was between 10 to 17 mg/L (low in PF and UP), Fe between 200 to 3000 mg/L (highest in MD), Mg between 240 to 100 mg/L (highest in PT and lowest in DF and NM), Mn between 7 to 17 mg/L (high in CC and MD) and Mo < 0.06 mg/L for all peat ecosystems. Amount of heavy metals such as Ld, Cd, Ni and Cr ranged from 0.8 to 2 mg/L (high in UP and PT), 0.04 to 1.8 mg/L (highest in MD), Ni 0.2 to 1.7 mg/L (highest in MD) and 1.2 to 3.2 mg/L (high in PT and MD), respectively.

CONCLUSION

Poorly drained peat habours less fungi but higher protista. In contrast cultivated drained peat allow the establishment of fungi in the aerobic condition and abundance of woody and litters. In the dry period, the moisture content in the primary peat forest was lowest compared to cultivated peat which are artificially drained with the water-table maintained 50-60 cm. The low moisture in primary forest resulted in low diversity of eukaryota particularly the fungi and low P, K and Mg but high Fe, Mn and heavy metal such as Cd, Ni and Cr.

ACKNOWLEDGEMENTS

The authors thank the Director General of MPOB and Deputy Director General of Research, for their permission to present this paper and the Board members of MPOB for the special board funding for the project.

REFERENCES

1. Adl, S.M., Leander, B.S., Simpson, A.G.B., Archibald, J.M., Anderson, O.R., Bass, D., Bowser, S.S., Brugerolle, G., Farmer, M.A., Karpov, S., Kolisko, M., Lane, C.E., Lodge, D.J., Mann, D.G., Meisterfeld, R., Mendoza, L., Moestrup, O., Mozley-Standridge, S. E., Smirnov, A.V. and Spiegel, F. 2007. Diversity, nomenclature, and taxonomy of protista. *Systematic Biology, 56*, 684-689.
2. Cavalier-Smith, T. and Chao, E.E. 2003. Phylogeny and classification of phylum Cercozoa (Protozoa). *Protist*, 154, 341-358.
3. Couwenberg, J. and Fritz C.2012. Towards developing IPCC methane emission factors for peatland organic soils. *Mires Peat10*, 1-17
4. Myers, B., Webster, K.L., Mcaughlin, J.W. and Basiliko, N.2012. Microbial activity across a boreal peatland nutrient gradient: the role of fungi and bacteria. *Wetlands Ecology Management. 20*, 77–88.
5. Page Sue, Wust C. and Bank, C.2010. Past and present carbon accumulation and loss in Southeast Asian peatlands; Science Highlights: Peatlands Vol 18.
6. ROCHE, 2013. 454 Sequencing: emPCR Amplication manual – Lib-L LV.
7. Strakova, P., Penttila, T., LAINE, J. and Laiho, R. 2012. Disentangling direct and indirect effects of water table draw down on above- and belowground plant litter decomposition: consequences for accumulation of organic matter in boreal peatlands. *Global Change Biology. 18(1)*, 322–335.
8. Turunen, J., Tolonen, K., Tolvanen, S., Remes, M., Ronkainen, J. and Jungner, H. 1999. Carbon accumulation in the mineral subsoil of boreal mires. *Global Biogeochemistry Cycles.13*:71–79.
9. Winsborough, C. and Basiliko, N. 2010. Fungal and bacterial activity in northern peatlands. *Journal Geomicrobiology. 27*, 315–320.
10. Yuanyuan Li, Longqian Chen, Hongyu Wen, Tianjian Zhou, Ting Zhang and Xiali Gao, 2014; 454 Pyrosequencing analysis of bacterial diversity revealed by a comparative study of soils from mining subsidence and reclamation areas; *Journal of Microbial Biotechnology. (2014), 24(3)*, 313-323.

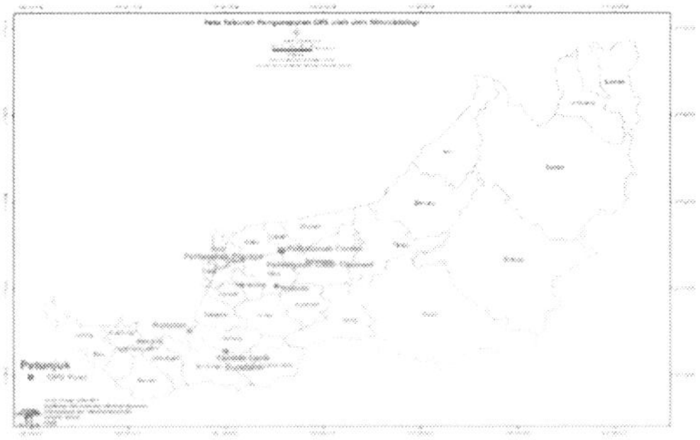

Figure 1: Map showing the sites of sampling for peat in Sarawak.

Table 1: Moisture content, pH and total operational taxanomic units for different peat ecosystems (April 2012).

Sites	Moisture content (%)	pH	Total OTUs
MD	42.30±8.23	3.58±0.12	986
CC	204.20±48.28	3.68±0.08	1853
DF	181.10±35.54	3.37±0.05	1677
NM	139.38±40.58	3.25±0.06	865
PF	159.85±27.12	3.48±0.08	1103
UP	208.91±64.82	3.13±0.03	718
PT	223.55±33.29	3.34±0.07	924

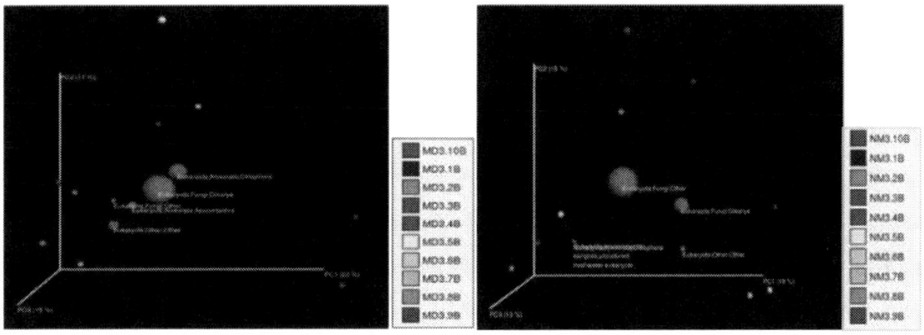

Figure 2: Generate 3D Bi-Plot for peat ecosystems at (MD) primary mixed peat forest at Sri Aman and (NM) 11 years oil palm planted on logged over clean-cleared Alan Bunga Naman, Sibu Sarawak.

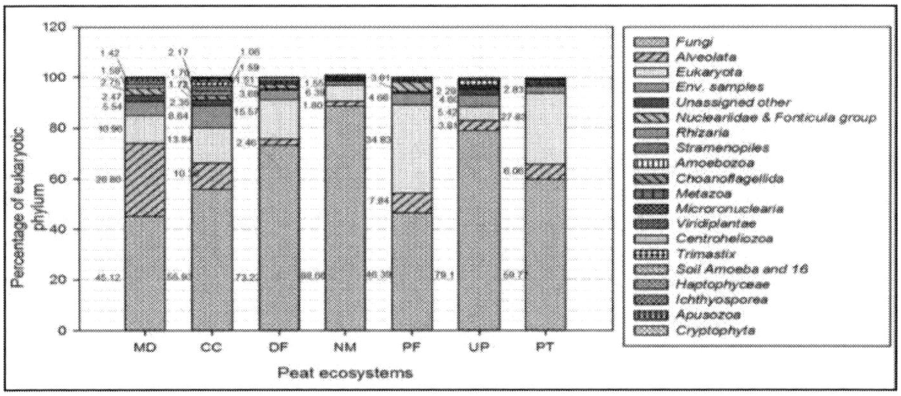

Figure 3: Average taxonomic composition of eukaryotic community for different peat ecosystems at Sri Aman

Sarawak and Sibu Sarawak. (MD) Muladam National Park, (CC) drained logged over peat forest at Cermat Ceria, (DF) under 7 years oil palms and (NM) under 11 year oil palms at Naman, (PT) 4 years oil palm planted on drained degraded logged over Alan Bunga peat, (UP) unplanted drained cleaned cleared area and (PF) secondary logged over Alan Bunga peat. Values are mean for 10 samples.

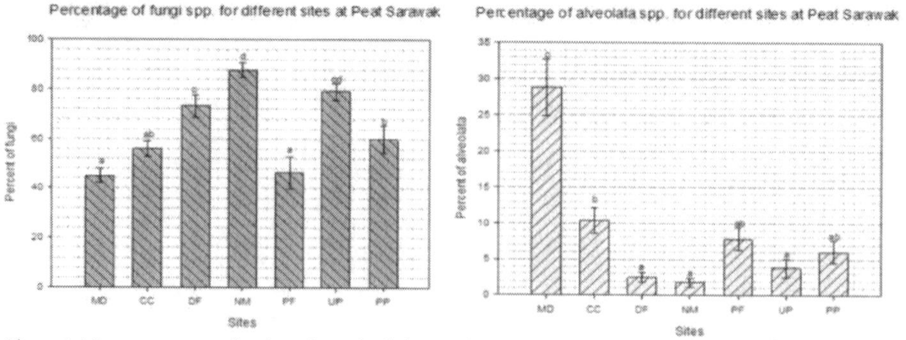

Figure 4: Mean percentage of major eukaryotic phylotypes in seven peat ecosystems. (MD) is Maludam National Park, (CC) is drained logged over peat forest at Cermat Ceria, (DF) under 7 years oil palms developed from drained degraded logged over mixed forest peat at Sri Aman Sarawak and (NM) under 11 year oil palms at Naman, (PF) secondary logged over peat Pelitanah Forest (UP) unplanted drained cleaned cleared area and (PT) 4 years oil palm planted on peat, at Sibu Sarawak.

Abstract No: A-091

FUNGI OF INTEREST ISOLATED FROM LOAGAN BUNUT NATIONAL PARK, MIRI, SARAWAK

Jamilah Hassan, Elaine Remi, Chia Hwa Chuan and Noreha Mahidi

Sarawak Biodiversity Centre, Malaysia

Corresponding author email: milah@sbc.org.my

SUMMARY

Loagan Bunut, near Miri, with its predominant cover of peat swamp forest, is one of Sarawak's unique national parks. The acidic soils, rich in organic matter, provide an excellent habitat for the proliferation of a wide assortment of microorganisms, including fungi that are adapted to this environment. The aim of this study is to identify fungi that possess the ability to inhibit the growth of Gram-negative bacteria. There is currently an interest in the discovery of new antibiotics, particularly those effective against Gram-negative bacteria, in view of the increasing prevalence of multidrug-resistance among this group of bacteria. A total of 616 fungal strains were isolated from Loagan Bunut soil, and screening of antimicrobial activity against Gram-negative bacteria was carried out using the agar plug method. Preliminary screening results showed that 28 fungal strains were active against *Escherichia coli* (NBRC 3301), a Gram-negative species. Secondary screening was carried out on the active fungal extracts using the microtitre plate assay. Three extracts exhibited strong antibacterial activity with more than 90% of growth inhibition against *E. coli*. Microscopy studies and molecular techniques identified the three fungal strains as *Penicillium* sp. The results of this study suggest that the fungi from the peat soil of Loagan Bunut could be a useful resource for the isolation of fungi that are effective in controlling Gram-negative bacteria.

***Keywords**: peat swamp forest, gram-negative bacteria, antibacterial activity, fungi, Sarawak*

INTRODUCTION

Peat swamp forest is considered as one of a unique ecosystem of flora and fauna. They play an important role in stabilizing the ecosystem. The ecosystem is defined as organic soil with mineral contents not exceeding 35% and is formed from the product of degraded organic matter or partially degraded for over a long period in waterlogged or formerly waterlogged areas [4].

The Loagan Bunut National Park, Sarawak is located about 120 km southeast of Miri between the Tinjar and Teru rivers, in the upper reaches of the Baram River basin in Sarawak. The peatland is predominantly covered by peat swamp forest with a complex mosaic of wetland habitats, including a 650 ha scenic natural lake, at the centre. Tropical peat swamp forests are unique dual ecosystems, characterized by rainforest and peatland, and highly influenced by the characteristics and nature of the peatland [2].

MATERIALS AND METHODS

Soil sampling

Soil samples were collected from eleven different points in the vicinity of the lake (dry areas) in Loagan Bunut National Park, Miri, Sarawak. The soil samples, collected at 5-10cm depth, were acidic, with pH ranging from 3.75 to 4.52.

Isolation of culturable fungi

Culturable fungi were isolated using four isolation methods (two pre-treatment method and two dilution methods), and subsequently transferred to six growth media (Czapek-dox, leaf extract agar, modified potato dextrose agar, sodium acetate agar, soil extract agar and water agar). The isolation plates were incubated at 28^{0}C for 7 days, and were observed daily from the third day onwards. Cultured fungi were picked using a sterile needle and transferred on to fresh plates of potato dextrose agar.

Preliminary screening of pure fungi isolates

Selection of fungi were based on their morphological characteristics. The isolates were tested for their antimicrobial activities using the agar plug method against four test strains of microorganism, a Gram-negative bacteria, *Escherichia coli* (NBRC 3301), a Gram-positive bacteria, *Bacillus subtilis* (NBRC 3134), a fungus, *Aspergillus niger* (NBRC 31125), and lastly a yeast, *Saccharomyces cerevisae* (ATCC 9763). In this method, agar plugs bearing the fungal isolates were tested directly against the test cultures, and the appearance of a clearer zone around the plugs denoted sensitivity to the isolate. In this study, fungal isolates exhibiting anti-microbial activity against *E. coli* will be discussed.

Anti-bacterial extracts of fungal isolates

Fungal isolates that showed activity against Gram-negative bacteria during the preliminary screening were selected and fermented in potato dextrose broth for 7 days at 28^0C. Crude extracts extracted from fungal cultures with 1-butanol (100% 20ml/20ml). The collected crude extract was screened by using Microtitreplate (MTP) assay. Briefly, 200µl of crude extract were aliquoted into a well in a 96-well plate and dried in a fume hood. The dried extract was dissolved with DMSO and *E. coli* strain was placed into the well containing extracts including negative control, growth control and positive control. The final optical density (OD) was read at 600nm wavelength using the software, Softmax 5.4.5. Percentage inhibition was calculated using the formula: % inhibition = [1- (differential OD/ growth control)] * 100

Fungal DNA extraction

Small amount of fungal mycelium was transferred into a 96-well plate containing 100µl 1xTE (Tris-EDTA) buffer. The plate went through freezing (keep at -80^0C for at least 3 hrs) and thawing method. The frozen cells were immediately put in a water bath at 60^0C for 10 sec. followed by shaking in a horizontal shaker.

Fungal DNA Amplification

The DNA was amplified by the polymerase chain reaction (PCR) using the universal reverse primer ITS 4 and forward primer ITS 5. The 30µl reaction mixture contained 23.2µl sterile water, 3µl PCR buffer, 0.3µl Pfu DNA polymerase, 0.3µl dNTP mix, 20uM ITS4, 20uM ITS5 and 2µl DNA template.

DNA Purification and Sequence Analysis

The PCR product was subjected to agarose gel electrophoresis at 80V for 45 minutes. The DNA was purified using a Gel Purification kit (GE Healthcare) and the purified PCR product was sent out to 1st Base Sdn. Bhd. for DNA sequencing analysis. The sequences were aligned and taxonomically identified via the Blast algorithm via the National Center for Biotechnology Information (NCBI) Genbank online database to identify the nearest relatives sequenced genes.

Identification by Microscopy

Sterile PDA plug were transferred onto clean slides using sterile small drinking straw. Spores were picked using a sterile picking needle and placed on the plug.Coverslip was used to cover the agar plug and the slide was placed inside a sterile petri dish. The growth of fungi at the plug edges was observed and were viewed under a compound microscope.

RESULTS AND DISCUSSION

Preliminary screening of pure fungi isolates

A total of 616 fungi were isolated from the Loagan Bunut soil samples. Based on the taxonomic identification, 318 strains were classified into 22 known fungal families belonging to 43 fungal genera. The remaining 298 fungal isolates are in process of being taxonomically identified. The most common fungal genera found in Loagan Bunut soils were *Penicillium* (25%), *Talaromyces* (9%), *Chaetosphaeria* (3%), and *Gongronella* (2%).

Table 1: Abundance of culturable fungal genera identified from Loagan Bunut soils

No.	Fungus genera	No. of isolates
1.	*Penicillium*	155
2.	*Talaromyces*	56
3.	*Chaetosphaeria*	21
4.	*Gongronella*	15
5.	*Trichoderma*	8
6.	*Pseudallescheria*	6
7.	*Chaunopycnis*	5
8.	*Mortierella*	5
9.	*Pestalotiopsis*	4
10.	*Viridispora*	4
11.	*Aspergillus*	3
12.	*Cladosporium*	3
13.	*Coniochaeta*	3
14.	*Purpureocillium*	3
15.	*Staphylotrichum*	3
16.	*Eupenicillium*	2
17.	*Ganoderma*	2
18.	*Metarhizium*	2
19.	*Rhodoveronaea*	2
20.	*Tolypocladium*	2
21.	*Trichosporon*	2
22.	*Xylomelasma*	2
23.	*Zasmidium*	2
24.	*Blastobotrys*	1
25.	*Calonectria*	1
26.	*Calonectria*	1
27.	*Chaetomium*	1
28.	*Cordana*	1
29.	*Exophiala*	1
30.	*Fusarium,*	1
31.	*Hypomyces*	1
32.	*Letendraea*	1
33.	*Massariosphaeria*	1
34.	*Microsphaeropsis*	1
35.	*Ophiocordyceps*	1
36.	*Phialemonium*	1
37.	*Prosthecium*	1
38.	*Pseudocercosporella*	1
40.	*Scedosporium*	1
41.	*Scolecobasidium*	1
42	*Sporothrix*	1
43.	*Xenocylindrocladium*	1

From the first preliminary screen, a total of 10 fungal strains showed formation of inhibition zones in media containing *E.coli (Table 2).* Screening against *E.coli* using the agar plug method was repeated twice to reconfirm inhibitory activities obtained. From the first screening assay againsy *E. coli*, 10 strains (LB52, LB128, LB281, LB328, LB428, LB455, LB531, LB533, LB574 and LB575) produced an inhibition zones. LB574 produced the largest zone of inhibition against *E.coli,* followed by LB575 and LB428.

Table 2: Inhibition zone of *E.coli on fungal* agar plug culture on Luria bertani agar containing *E.coli* inoculum in 3 replicates.

No.	Strain No.	Zone of Inhibition, mm (Average ± standard deviation)
1	LB52	18.33±2.89
2	LB128	10±8.66
3	LB130	0
4	LB276	0
5	LB281	14.33±0.58
6	LB328	13.67±0.58
7	LB400	0
8	LB428	25.67±0.58
9	LB455	15.33±0.58
10	LB531	15.33±1.15
11	LB533	14.33±0.58
12	LB574	28.00±1.00
13	LB575	27.67±2.08
14	-ve control (PDA)	0

Additionally, screening on fungal extracts were carried out using the MTP assay. The screening results of 12 extracts from selected fungal strains obtained by the MTP assay are summarised in Table 3. Three fungal strains shows strong antibacterial activity with more than 90% of *E.coli* growth inhibited. LB128 shows the highest percentage of inhibition with an average inhibtion of 99.14%, followed by LB455 (98.63%) and LB531 (97.79%).

Table 3: OD reading of fungal crude extracts against *E. coli* growth inhibition.

No.	Strain No.	OD reading of 3 replicates Average (%) ± Standard deviation
1	LB52	0
2	LB128	99.14±0.67
3	LB281	0
4	LB328	0
5	LB428	1.01±1.76
6	LB455	98.63±0.75
7	LB531	97.79±0.09
8	LB533	0
9	LB574	19.23±2.74
10	LB575	24.02±2.61
11	-ve control (PDB)	-11.83

Both methods used in this study produced different inhibitory effects which we have attributed it to the difference in experimental conditions. With the agar plug method, inhibitory activity was assayed on solid medium comprising metabolic active fungal cultures living cultures while the MTP assay relied on crude fungal extracts to screen for inhibitory activity. This implies that inhibitory compounds (proteins or metabolites).

Based on the MTP assay result, three strains were selected for microscopic and molecular taxonomic identification. The morphological characteristics of mycelium and spores on PDA plates were similar and that all three strains belong to the genus *Penicillium*. The microscopic photographs in Figure: 1 shows that both LB128 and LB455 are *Penicillium sp.* The conidiophores of LB128 however is 40% smaller compared to LB531. Phylogeny tree in Figure: 2 shows that LB455 and *Penicillium rolfii,* NBRC7735T map to the same phylogenetic clade. Similar to LB128, the branch showed that fungus could be a strain of *Penicillium rolfii.*

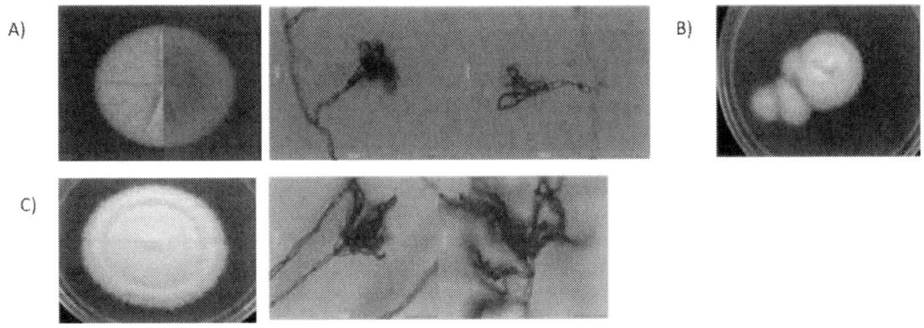

Fig. 1: Morphology on PDA plates for strains A) LB128, B) LB455 and C) LB531 and microscopic photographs (magnification x50).

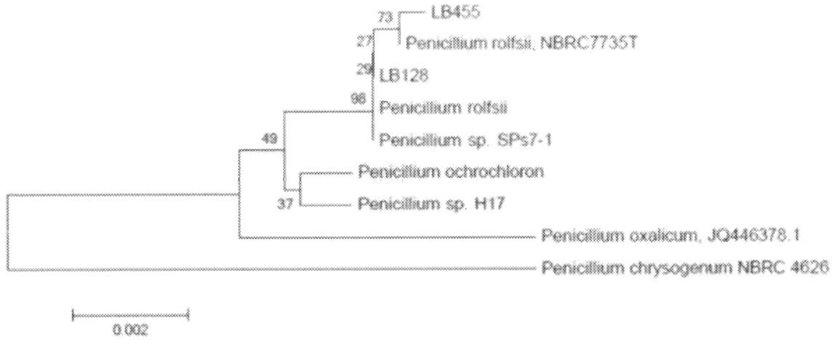

DISCUSSION

From this study, a total of 616 fungi was isolated from tropical peat soil showed that the habitat offers a wide range of soil fungi that may exhibit antimicrobial activities or othet beneficial traits. Based on the molecular taxonomic identification, a few common fungi found in Loagan Bunut soil samples are *Penicillium, Talaromyces, Chaetosphaeria,* and *Gongronella.* Further research needs to be performed especially in the field of diversity and their occurrence in peat soils. This study also exemplifies that peat soils harbours a wide diversity range of microbes that remains unexplored and also a good source for the discovery of potent microorganisms for various biotechnological applications.

ACKNOWLEDGEMENTS

The authors would like to thank Mrs. Harny Chapi and Ms. Arzie Ramlie for their support and assistance in this project. We would like also to extend our gratitude to Mr. Kenny for their assistance with the antimicrobial screening experiments.

REFERENCES

1. Berdy, J. (2005). Bioactive microbial metabolites. *The Journal of antibiotics*, *58*(1), 1-26.
2. Sayok, A. K., Nik, A. R., Melling, L., Samad, R. A., & Efransjah, E. (2007, August). Some characteristics of peat in Loagan Bunut National Park, Sarawak, Malaysia. In *Carbon-climate-human interactions on tropical peatland: carbon pools, fire, mitigation, restoration and wise use, edited by: Rieley, JO, Banks,CJ, and Ragjagukguk, B., Proceedings of the International Symposium and Workshop on Tropical Peatland, Yogyakarta* (pp. 27-29).
3. Lihan, S., Choon, Y. K., Hua, N. K., & Wasli, M. E. (2014). Screening For Antimicrobial Activity Of Fungi In Soil Samples Collected From Kubah National Park. *International Journal of Technology Enhancements nd Emerging Engineering Research*, *3*(2), 1-9.
4. Soil Survey Staff: *Keys to Soil Taxonomy*, 11th ed. USDA-Natural Resources Conservation Service, Washington, DC. (2010).
5. Cavalcanti, M.A., Oliveira, L.G., Fernandes, M.J., Lima, D.M., 2006. Filamentous fungi isolated from soil in districts of the Xingó region, Braz. Acta Bot. Bras. 20 (4), 831–837.

Abstract No: A-458

MICROSATELLITE MARKER INFERRED GENETIC DIVERSITY OF GANODERMA BONINENSE IN TROPICAL PEATLAND, SARAWAK

Wei Chee Wong[1*], Hung Jiat Tung[1], Kah King Tan[1], Mei Lieng Lo[2] and Sharon Yu Ling Lau[2]

[1]*Advanced Agriecological Research Sdn. Bhd. (AARSB), AAR-UNMC Biotechnology Research Centre, Malaysia.*
[2]*Tropical Peat Research Laboratory Unit (TPRL), Chief Minister's Department, Sarawak, Malaysia*

**Corresponding author: wongwc@aarsb.com.my*

SUMMARY

Ganoderma boninense is the main causal pathogen of Basal Stem Rot (BSR) disease in oil palm (*Elaeis guineesis* Jacq.). The ever-increasing fast spreading of BSR disease in Southeast Asia has become an issue of great concern particularly to Indonesia and Malaysia oil palm industry as they are the first and second largest palm oil exporters, respectively. After several decades of research, there is still no effective control to prevent *G. boninense* infection in oil palm because the disease cycle and epidemiology of this fungal pathogen is still poorly understood. Microsatellite markers (cDNA-SSR) developed using transcriptome sequences of axenic *G. boninense* have been effectively applied in a genetic diversity and population study of *G. boninense* (AARSB, unpublished data). We report here a total of 13 polymorphic cDNA-SSR markers that were used to determine the genetic variation of 30 *G. boninense* isolates collected from oil palm plantations in tropical peat areas in Sarawak. This topic is relatively unexplored in Sarawak where BSR disease rarely occurs on oil palm planted on tropical peatland. The UPGMA cluster analysis based on Nei & Li's distance matrix showed that the majority of isolates from Miri (Northern Sarawak) and Kuching (Southern Sarawak) were highly conserved with 90.9-100.0% similarity. No subpopulation of *G. boninense* was detected. The calculated fixation index (F) is close to zero, suggesting that *G. boninense* undergoes random mating within the sampled region. The mean of unbiased heterozygosity (or genetic diversity) was measured based on the genetic profiles of 48 alleles amplified across 13 loci for all the *G. boninense* isolates. The genetic diversity was 54.4% for the 21 isolates from Miri and 50.0% for the 9 isolates from Kuching. A Principal Coordinates Analysis (PCoA) was performed but it did not reveal any distinct pattern of genetic differentiation. It is currently not known whether the cDNA-SSR markers described here fulfill the characteristics of ideal markers for population genetic studies of *G. boninense*. Larger sample sizes are probably necessary to improve the estimation of genetic diversity, and discernible infection aggressiveness compared among the isolates will allow more precise elucidation of the population biology of *G. boninense* in future studies.

Keywords: *Ganoderma boninense, oil palm, tropical peatland, genetic diversity*

INTRODUCTION

In Malaysia, the area of peatland developed for agriculture can be divided into three regions which are Peninsular Malaysia (313,600 ha), Sarawak (554,775 ha) and Sabah (38,457 ha) (Abdul Jamil *et al.*, 1989; Melling, 1999; Wetlands International, 2010). According to Wahid et al. (2010), the total peatlands counted for oil palm planting is 666,038 ha in Malaysia and the mainstream of oil palm cultivation, 37.45%, is under the peatlands in Sarawak. *G boninense,* a basidiomycete pathogen was identified as the causal agent for Basal Stem Rot (BSR) disease in oil palm since five decades ago. It is now widely distributed in Southeast Asia where oil palm trees are grown. However, the BSR disease in oil palm rarely occurs in Sarawak peatlands, instead higher incident of Upper Stem Rot disease (USR) was reported, which thought to be infected by the same *Ganoderma* spp., have yet to be systematically investigated with respect to the pathogen genetic diversity and population structures. To understand the *G. boninense* invasion and disease spread pattern (or pathogen movement), we initiated the molecular epidemiological analyses for *G. boninense* isolates collected from BSR and USR oil palm trees found in Sarawak peatlands. Additionally, we would also like to examine the genetic differences of *G. boninense* isolates attributed to BSR and USR in oil palm. It is envisaged the outcomes of this study will provide new knowledge of how *G. boninense* can survive, invade and interact with the oil palm, as well as host habitat, tropical peat area.

MATERIALS AND METHODS

Transcriptome sequences of the *G. boninense* were used to developed cDNA-SSR markers (AARSB, unpublished data) to study the genetic variation of *G. boninense* isolates collected from Lambir, Sungai Balim, Taniku Estates located in Miri and Asajaya Estate in Kuching. Fruiting bodies of *G. boninense* were sampled and pure cultures were isolated using *Ganoderma* selective media (GSM) as described by Ariffin and Seman (1991). The genomic DNA of *G. boninense* was extracted according to the modified protocol described by Orozco-Castillo *et al.* (1994) and Hayati *et al.* (2011). The identity of *G. boninense* was confirmed using 18S rRNA (Borneman and Hartin, 2000) direct PCR-sequencing approach. Microsatellite genotyping of 30 *G. boninense* isolates (Table 1) was performed on NEN 4300 DNA Analyzer (Li-COR Biosciences, USA) using 13 *G. boninense* cDNA-SSR markers i.e. P3_005, P3_016, P4_001, P4_024, P4_062, P4_064, P5_013, P6_011, P6_021, F1_61, F44_93, F67_43 and F74_18 (Wong *et al.*, 2015; Tung *et al*, in preparation). UPGMA clustering, allele frequency and Principal Coordinates Analysis (PCoA) to deduce the genetic diversity and population structure of *G. boninense* isolates were analysed using the multivariate statistical package MVSP (Kovach Computing Services, Anglesey, Wales). The mean number of effective alleles, unbiased heterozygosity and fixation index over *G. boninense* populations were calculated using frequency based statistical procedures in GenAlEx 6.5 (Peakall and Smouse, 2012).

RESULTS AND DISCUSSION

A set of 30 *G. boninense* isolates (26 BSR and 4 USR) was used to assess the polymorphism of candidate cDNA-SSR markers. This set of *G. boninense* comprised 21 isolates collected from Miri i.e. Lambir, Sungai Balim, Taniku Estates and 9 isolates from Asajaya Estate in Kuching. Majority of the isolates were collected from BSR diseased oil palm trees, only 4 USR isolates from Sungai Balim Estate (Table 1). In this study, we investigated the movement of the *G. boninense* isolates on an ecological timescale by directly observing the present-time movement of individuals. Population structure is defined as the distribution of genetic variation within and among populations, which a population is denoted as a group of individuals of the same species that occupy the same area at the same time (Milgroom, 2015).

Microsatellite genotyping of all the *G. boninense* isolates that showed 13 out of 35 screened cDNA-SSR markers were informative and suitable to use for assessing the genetic diversity of the fungal pathogen. The result of marker polymorphism analysis by population was summarized in Table 2. The unweighted pair-group method with arithmetic mean (UPGMA) dendogram of 30 isolates constructed using 48 alleles amplified across the 13 loci for the Miri and Kuching population suggested that majority of the isolates from Lambir, Sungai Balim, Taniku and Asajaya Estate formed a distinct clade (Figure 1). All of the four USR isolates from Sungai Balim showed no distinction of genetic composition in comparison with BSR isolates that were placed under the same clade. Based on Figure 1, one isolate K/FA/005 from Asajaya Estate was diverged foremost from the main clade at 0.909 similarity coefficient, and two isolates K/FA/016 and M/SB/32 were placed under another outgroup at 0.928 similarity coefficient based on Nei and Li's distance. The degree of pathogenicity of these isolates have not yet been tested at this stage of research.

There was no subpopulation (distinct group) of *G. boninense* observed at each region (Fig. 1 and 2). This observation corresponded to the calculated fixation index (F) with value close to zero (Table 2 and 3) suggesting that *G. boninense* isolates undergoes random mating (panmixia). Furthermore, non-restricted dispersal of spores could encourage outcrossing among the *G. boninense* isolates that making the population becomes genetically homogenous because of frequent mixing of alleles and resulting in a single panmictic population.

The genetic diversity between all isolates collected from Miri and Kuching was calculated based on Nei's distance. The genetic diversity was 54.4% for the 21 isolates from Miri and 50.0% for the 9 isolates from Kuching (Table 3). A Principal Coordinates Analysis (PCoA) was performed but it did not reveal any distinct pattern of genetic differentiation, regardless BSR or USR isolates. The degree of genetic differentiation is important to deduce the interactions of evolutionary processes with pathogen migration. Understanding of pathogen genetic structure and processes influence the genetic differentiation would be highly relevant to disease management.

CONCLUSIONS

This is the first report of utilising *Ganoderma* cDNA-SSR marker for systematically revealing the genetic diversity of *G. boninense* collected from oil palm trees planted on tropical peat areas. Our result is suggesting that high heterozygosity within and between the two populations of *G. boninense* from Miri and Kuching was present as expected due to the outcrossing is preferred. Majority of the isolates were collected from considerably far geographical distance,but highly conserved genetic constitution was still observed. Result of genetic difference between BSR and USR isolates was not conclusive for the current study because of the practical limitations during time in conducting routine BSR and USR diseased palm census, field sampling and sample processing. Perhaps, larger sample sizes could be sought to improve the estimation of genetic diversity and population structure.

Additionally, the information of pathogenicity and infection aggressiveness compared among the isolates collected from different host habitat and regions will be advantageous for more accurate elucidation of the population biology of *G. boninense* in future studies.

ACKNOWLEDGEMENTS

The authors thank Dr Lulie Melling (Director of TPRL, Sarawak), Mr Chua Kian Hong (Plantation Controller, Sarawak Oil Palms Berhad), Mr Lo Kim San and Mr Frazer Midot (Research Officer, TPRL) who assisted us in our exhaustive sampling at Miri and Kuching sites. We acknowledge Ms Christina Christy and Beatrice Aren (TPRL Molecular Microbiology Laboratory) who provided assistances for samples processing, pure culture isolation and maintenance. We are grateful to Mr Goh Kah Joo (Director of Research, AARSB) and Dr Goh You Keng (Head of P&D Section, AARSB) for their valuable comments on the drafts. We would also like to thank AARSB Principals, Boustead Plantations Berhad and Kuala Lumpur Kepong Berhad, for their permission to publish and financial support given to the research activities that generated the data presented in this article.

REFERENCES

1. Abdul Jamil M.A., Chow W.T., Chan Y.K., & Siew K.Y. (1989). Land use of peat in Peninsula Malaysia. *Bengkel Kebangsaan Penyelidikan dan Pembangunan Tanah Gambut*. 21-22 Febuary, 1989. Bangi, Selangor: MARDI.
2. Ariffin D., Seman I.A. (1991). A selective medium for isolation of Ganoderma from diseased tissues. Pages 517-519 in: Proceedings of the 1991 international palm oil conference, progress, prospects and challenges towards the 21st century. Malaysian Palm Oil Board, Selangor, Malaysia.
3. Borneman J., Hartin R.J. (2000). PCR primers that amplify fungal rRNA genes from environmental samples. Applied Environmental Microbiology, 66(10): 4356–4360.
4. Hayati M., Dyah Lingga N.P., Darmono T.W., & Elis N.H. (2011) Analisis keragaman genetic Ganoderma spp. yang berasosiasi dengan tanaman kakao dan tanaman pelindungnya menggunakan random amplified polymorphic DNA (RAPD), Menara Perkebunan, 79 (1): 6-14
5. Melling L. (1999). Sustainable agriculture development on peatland. Paper presented at the Workshop on "Working Towards Integrated Peatland Management for Sustainable Development", 17-18 August 1999, Kuching, Malaysia.
6. Milgroom M.G. (2015). Population biology pf plant pathogen: Genetics, ecology, and evolution. U.S.A.: APS Press.
7. Orozco-Castillo C, Chalmers KJ, Waugh R, Powell W. (1994) Detection of genetic diversity and selective gene in coffea using RAPD markers, Theoretical Applied Genetics, 87: 332-339.
8. Peakall R., Smouse P.E. (2012). GenAlEx 6.5: genetic analysis in Excel. Population genetic software for teaching and research – an update. Bioinformatics. 28: 2537-2539.
9. Wetlands International (2010). A Quick Scan of Peatlands in Malaysia. Petaling Jaya, Wetlands International-Malaysia.
10. Wong W.C., Teo C.J., Wong C.K., Mayes S., Singh R., Soh A.C. (2015). Development of an effective SSR-based fingerprinting system for commercial planting materials and breeding applications in oil palm. Journal of Oil Palm Research, 27 (1): 113-127.

Table 1: Geographic regions where thirty *G. boninense* isolates were collected.

Estate	Region	No. BSR isolate	No. USR isolate
Lambir	Miri	9	0
Sungai Balim	Miri	6	4
Taniku	Miri	2	0
Asajaya	Kuching	9	0

Table 2: Informativeness of 13 cDNA-SSR markers and their polymorphism by population. *N*: Sample Size, *Na*: No. Alleles, *Ne*: No. Effective Alleles, *I*: Shannon's Information Index, *Ho*: Observed Heterozygosity, *He*: Expected and *uHe*: Unbiased Expected Heterozygosity, and *F*: Fixation Index.

Population	Locus	N	Na	Ne	I	Ho	He	uHe	F
Miri	**P3_005**	21	3.000	1.276	0.445	0.238	0.217	0.222	-0.099
	P3_016	21	2.000	1.569	0.549	0.190	0.363	0.372	0.475
	P4_001	19	6.000	4.349	1.616	0.158	0.770	0.791	0.795
	P4_024	21	4.000	3.852	1.367	0.429	0.740	0.758	0.421
	P4_062	20	4.000	3.670	1.341	0.400	0.728	0.746	0.450
	P4_064	20	6.000	4.124	1.568	0.600	0.758	0.777	0.208
	P5_013	21	5.000	3.528	1.372	0.381	0.717	0.734	0.468
	P6_011	20	3.000	2.524	1.004	0.300	0.604	0.619	0.503
	P6_021	20	3.000	2.360	0.954	0.400	0.576	0.591	0.306
	F1_061	20	4.000	2.025	0.974	0.250	0.506	0.519	0.506
	F44_093	21	3.000	1.556	0.656	0.333	0.357	0.366	0.067
	F67_043	21	2.000	1.208	0.314	0.095	0.172	0.177	0.447
	F74_018	21	2.000	1.630	0.575	0.238	0.387	0.396	0.384
Kuching	**P3_005**	9	1.000	1.000	0.000	0.000	0.000	0.000	N/A
	P3_016	9	3.000	1.573	0.655	0.444	0.364	0.386	-0.220
	P4_001	8	5.000	3.048	1.321	0.625	0.672	0.717	0.070
	P4_024	9	3.000	2.656	1.037	0.667	0.623	0.660	-0.069
	P4_062	9	4.000	3.057	1.211	0.556	0.673	0.712	0.174
	P4_064	9	4.000	3.857	1.369	0.444	0.741	0.784	0.400
	P5_013	9	5.000	4.378	1.542	0.444	0.772	0.817	0.424
	P6_011	7	2.000	1.324	0.410	0.286	0.245	0.264	-0.167
	P6_021	8	3.000	1.855	0.777	0.375	0.461	0.492	0.186
	F1_061	8	4.000	2.560	1.070	0.375	0.609	0.650	0.385
	F44_093	9	2.000	1.385	0.451	0.111	0.278	0.294	0.600
	F67_043	9	2.000	1.385	0.451	0.111	0.278	0.294	0.600
	F74_018	9	2.000	1.670	0.591	0.111	0.401	0.425	0.723

Table 3: Mean allele frequency over 13 loci for population in Miri and Kuching. *N*: Sample Size, *Na*: No. Alleles, *Ne*: No. Effective Alleles, *I*: Shannon's Information Index, *Ho*: Observed Heterozygosity, *He*: Expected and *uHe*: Unbiased Expected Heterozygosity, and *F*: Fixation Index.

Population		N	Na	Ne	I	Ho	He	uHe	F
Miri	Mean (±SE)	20.462 (±0.183)	3.615 (±0.385)	2.590 (±0.322)	0.980 (±0.123)	0.309 (±0.037)	0.530 (±0.059)	0.544 (±0.060)	0.379 (±0.062)
Kuching	Mean (±SE)	8.615 (±0.180)	3.077 (±0.348)	2.288 (±0.294)	0.837 (±0.127)	0.350 (±0.059)	0.471 (±0.065)	0.500 (±0.068)	0.259 (±0.087)
Combined Total	Mean (±SE)	14.538 (±1.191)	3.346 (±0.260)	2.439 (±0.216)	0.908 (±0.088)	0.329 (±0.034)	0.500 (±0.043)	0.522 (±0.045)	0.321 (±0.053)

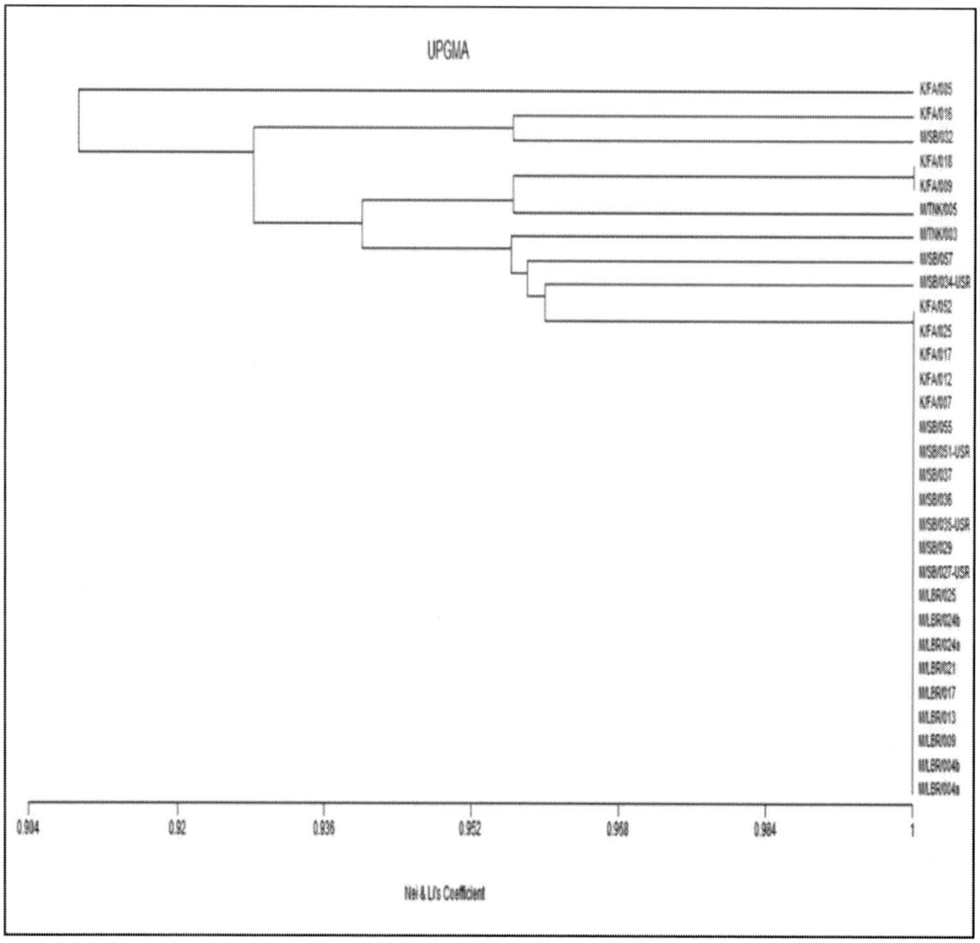

Figure 1: A dendogram based on UPGMA clustering of 30 *G. boninense* isolates using 13 polymorphic cDNA-SSRs (Table 2). *K*: Kuching, *M*: Miri, *FA*: Asajaya, *TNK*: Taniku, *SB*: Sungai Balim, *LBR*: Lambir, *USR*: Upper Stem Rot, *a,b*: isolates from the same palm.

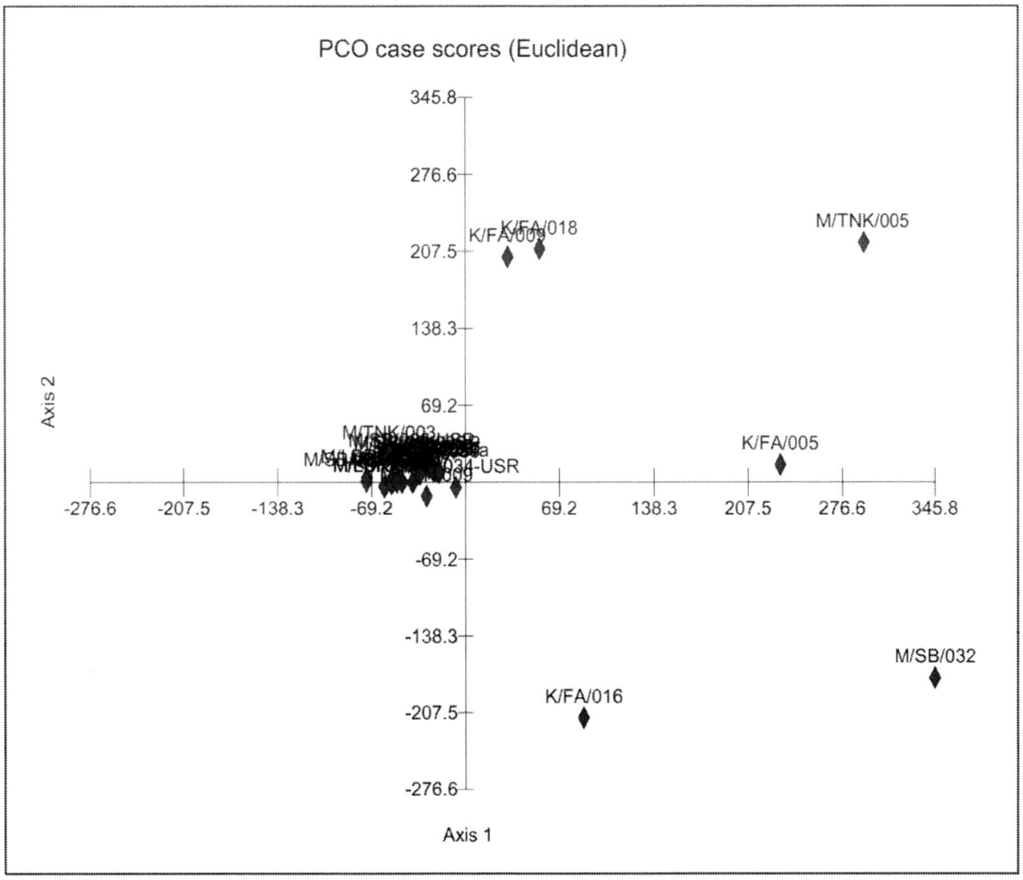

Figure 2: The PCoA presented the relationship of the 30 *G. boninense* isolates collected from Miri and Kuching. The genetic variation was explained by the first two principal coordinates (Axis 1: 38.279%, Axis 2: 25.519%). PCoA suggested close genetic distance of the majority of *G. boninense* isolates regardless of the isolates origin i.e. BRS or USR diseased oil palm.

Abstract No: A-300

MOLECULAR ASSESSMENT OF CULTURABLE BACTERIA IN SARAWAK'S DEEP FOREST CONVERTED TO OIL PALM PLANTATION

Mohd Shawal Thakib Maidin[1], Sakinah Safari[1], Halimatun Saadiah Hafid[2], Zahidah Ayob[1], Sharifah Azura Syed Ibrahim[1], Shamsilawani Ahamed Bakeri[1] and Siti Ramlah Ahmad Ali[1]*

[1]*Applied Entomology and Microbiology Unit, Biology Research Division, Malaysian Palm Oil Board, 6 Persiaran Institusi, Bandar Baru Bangi, 43000.*
[2]*Faculty of Biotechnology and Biomolecular Sciences, University Putra Malaysia, Serdang, 43400.*

**Corresponding author: ramlah@mpob.gov.my*

SUMMARY

Sarawak has the largest peat areas in Malaysia covering more than one million ha. The soil fertility is crucial for the oil palm plantations which, depends on the microbial population inhabiting the areas. Therefore, it is important to examine the microbial population in detail through culturing in the laboratory which can contribute to disease related microbes discovery and development of beneficial microbes for agriculture. For this purposes, the preliminary trials have been done in order to gain more information on the culturable microbial population in the matured oil palm at Durafarm plantation aged 7 years old, primary deep peat mix forest at Maludam National Park and degraded drained logged-over forest at Cermat Ceria, Sri Aman, Sarawak. Prokaryotic DNA was extracted from bacteria isolated from peat sampled in April 2012. The bacteria was identified via 16S rDNA amplification by using 341/907 primer, sequenced and blasted using NCBI databases. Results showed that Firmicutes are the most abundant culturable bacterial phyla in deep peat. The total number of Firmicutes species found in Durafarm oil palm plantation aged 7 years old was (17 species) as compared to Cermat Ceria (15 species) and Maludam National Park Forest (13 species). Methane consuming and plant growth promoter, Bacillus methylotrophicus was detected at the primary forest where release of methane is highest compared to the other two sites. While, the methane consuming and plant growth promoting bacteria for the drained logged over forest at Cermat Ceria and oil palm plantation at Durafarm was Methylobaterium radiotolerans from the phylum α-Proteobacteria. Bacteria that are involved in degradation of biomass, the β-Proteobacteria and γ-Proteobacteria were more frequently detected in Cermat Ceria where there was abundance of biomass as compared to Maludam National Park Forest and Durafarm oil palm plantation. In addition to this, Cermat Ceria has got an additional bacteria, Flavobacterium sp. which was not detected in other two sites. Several of these culturable bacteria can be exploited and developed as agro-products.

***Keywords**: culturable bacteria, soil microbial diversity, deep peat, primary forest, secondary forest, oil palm plantation, 16S rDNA.*

INTRODUCTION

Oil palm cultivation on peatlands represents about 20% of oil palm in Southeast Asia (Lim *et al.*, 2012). Therefore, it is crucial to apply a good land management practice to sustain the peatland function and fertility. Peatlands are considered suitable for oil palm development due to homogeneous soil features, constant availability of water and flatness. The organic peat soils also play important roles in global climate via the long term net sequestration of carbon dioxide. The reservoir of carbon and nitrogen in peat accumulates up to one third of global terrestrial carbon (Sun *et al.*, 2014).

The most abundant group of microorganisms on peatland is bacteria. They can easily colonize dead wood and facilitate uptake of simple nutrients. On the other hand, the microorganisms that received the most attention as decomposers in peatland are fungi (Thormann, 2011; Myers *et al.*, 2012). Nonetheless, Winsborough and Basiliko (2010) stated that bacteria play a more active role as decomposer across various peatland types.

In order to improve the knowledge of the bacterial community in peatlands, molecular biology technologies such as polymerase chain reaction (PCR) of 16S rDNA and phylogenic tree are required in this study (Saman *et al.*, 2010). These technologies have assisted in the identification and classification of bacteria through direct DNA extraction from culture samples then sequencing the isolated DNA (Saman *et al.*, 2010). The soil bacterial biodiversity analysis was conducted in three different peat ecosystems (deep peat at Maludam, National Park, Cermat Ceria secondary logged-over forest and Durafarm oil palm plantation) in Sri Aman, Sarawak using

16S rDNA PCR. Therefore, the aim of the study is to investigate the bacterial diversity in peat forest soils as a whole and to provide baseline to understand the relative contribution of each groups of bacteria in an environment.

METHODOLOGY

Isolation of prokaryotes. Nutrient agar, Soil Enriched medium, Nitrogen Deficient medium, Pikovskaya medium, Aleksandrov medium, Anaerobic medium and Actinomycetes medium were used for isolating the prokaryotes using spread plate method. The cultures were incubated at 30°C for 2 to 3 days.

PCR amplification of 16s rDNA from plate cultures. The colonies from plate cultures were collected and inserted into 100 µl of sterile distilled water (dH_2O) and boiled for 10 minutes at 100°C to lyse the cells. Subsequently, the cells were amplified using PCR. The primers, 341F(5'-cct-acg-gga-ggc-agc-ag-3') and 907R (5'-ccc-cgt-caa-ttc-att-tga-gtt-t-3') were used to generate 16S rDNA gene fragments (Muyzer *et al*, 1997).

Purification of DNA from Agarose. The gel-bands were excised and purified using QIA quick gel extraction kits (QIAGEN, Inc., Valencia, CA) as described by manufacturer's protocol.

Sequencing and blast. The sequencing was conducted by First Base Laboratories Sdn Bhd. The DNA sequences were subjected to basic logic alignment search tool (BLASTn) at NCBI.

Phylogenetic analysis. The aligned sequences were used in construction of phylogenetic tree using MEGA version 5.2 software. Phylogenetic analysis was constructed using Neighbor-joining method via Kimura two-parameter.

RESULTS AND DISCUSSION

The presence of prokaryotic phyla in primary deep peat mix forest at Maludam National Park, degraded drained logged-over forest at Cermat Ceria and matured oil palm at Durafarm plantation aged 7 years old in Sri Aman, Sarawak (*Figure 1*). Firmicutes were the main culturable bacterial phyla identified in the three ecosystems with the occurrence of 77%, 38% and 46% at Maludam National Park, Cermat Ceria and Durafarm oil palm plantation, respectively. This showed that Firmicutes population were dominant within area occupied with plants as Maludam is a primary forest. Forest clearing showed increased population percentage of unclassified Bacteria in Cermat Ceria (*Figure 1b*) with 38%; while, Durafarm plantation (*Figure 1c*) showed increased population of Firmicutes with 46%. The Firmicutes population increase in Durafarm showed that the soil is recovering from forest clearing as the sites were planted with young oil palm tree aged 7 years old. Morikawa, (2006) stated that Firmicutes play a vital role in replenishing soil nutrients for terrestrial carbon cycle and nitrogen fixing via degradation of polymers such as protein, starch and pectin.This is consistent with previous findings that reported a large number of Firmicutes in the acidic grassland (Kuramae *et al*., 2010). Firmicutes are spore formers which ensure its survival through period of environmental stresses such as the changes in plant species ecosystem and forest logging activity. The high numbers of Firmicutes were recorded in Durafarm ecosystem could be due to the ability to improve plant health through antagonism of pest and pathogens, promotion of host nutrition and growth and stimulation of plant host defences. The example of bacterial species in firmicutes, *Bacillus methylotrophicus* was reported as the methane consuming and plant growth promoter. This bacteria was highest detected at the primary forest where the release of methane was suggested to be highest as compared to the other ecosystems (Madhaiyan *et al*., 2010).

The other dominant phyla were distributed in the ecosystem i.e unclassified bacteria, β-Proteobacteria, α-Proteobacteria, γ-Proteobacteria and Actinobacteria. The distribution of β-Proteobacteria was 6%, 17% and 5% at Maludam National Park, Cermat Ceria and Durafarm oil palm plantation, respectively. The phylum β-Proteobacteria in Maludam comprised mainly of *Alcaligenes feacalis*, *Alcaligenes spp.* and *Burkholderia spp.* compared to *Alcaligenes spp.* and *Ralstonia spp.* for logged over forest at Cermat Ceria. The β-Proteobacteria consists of heterotrophs, autotrophs and methanotrophs. Burkholderia and Alicaligenes are the best known heterotrophs in soil. Burkholderia species play a major function in carbon turnover which is metabolically diverse by using simple amino acids, sugars and recalcitrant aromatic and phenolic compounds as carbon substrates (de Boer *et. al*., 2004). It plays an important role in nitrogen fixation in various types of plants, oxidizing ammonium to produce nitrites for plant function. These microbial community compositions have been identified among deep peat with different vegetation characteristics (Andersen *et al*., 2010). In contrast, the population of α-Proteobacteria was highest at Durafarm planted area with 26% occurrence compared to 2% and 1% in Maludam and Cermat Ceria, respectively. In this phylum, *Sphingomonas spp.* was found to be the most abundance genus with 34 isolates. This genus is considered as a soil indigenous and plant-associated bacterium with the role as nitrogen-fixing bacteria (Lee *et al*., 2012) which explained the higher number of this genus in oil palm planted area. In addition, *Methylobaterium radiotolerans* which is the methane consuming and plant growth promoting bacteria (Kwak *et al*., 2014) was also identified in Cermat Ceria and Durafarm.

The phylum Bacteroidetes and Unclassified Bacteria were only found in Cermat Ceria based on the phylogenetic trees in *Figure 2, 3* and *Figure 4*. Species occurring in these phylums are *Flavobacterium sp.* and

Compost bacterium in Bacteroidetes and Unclassified Bacteria group, respectively. This is due to the ability of both bacterial species to degrade dead plant material and cellulose in the clean cleared logged-over forest (Mayrberger, 2011, Fathallh *et al.*, 2012).

Other phyla present in the three ecosystems were γ-Proteobacterium and Actinobacteria. Both phyla were less abundance compared to Firmicutes, Unclassified Bacteria, β-Proteobacteria and α-Proteobacteria. However, the important of these bacterial phyla cannot be neglected. *Pseudomonas aeruginosa* from the phylum γ-Proteobacterium involves in chemical secretion during root-microbial interaction of the root system, as well as, assisting in the release of free nitrogen or nitrous oxide into the atmosphere (Bhattacharyya and Jha, 2012). *Micrococcus* in Actinobacteria group are responsible in humus formation and decomposition of plant material in Maludam and Cermat Ceria, respectively.

CONCLUSION

The three peat ecosystems at deep peat forest; Maludam National Park, Cermat Ceria secondary logged over forest and Durafarm oil palm plantation, showed that the dominant phylum was Firmicutes followed by unclassified Bacteria groups and β-Proteobacteria despite differences in geographic location, nutrient status, and plant community composition. However, there were differences in the percentage and species within the phyla, with Bacteroidete*s* occurring in Durafarm and Cermat Ceria.

REFERENCES

1. Bhattacharyya, P.N. and Jha, D.K. (2012). Plant growth-promoting rhizobacteria (PGPR): emergence in agriculture. *World Journal of Microbiology and Biotechnology*, 28(4), pp.1327-1350.
2. Fathallh Eida, M., Nagaoka, T., Wasaki, J. and Kouno, K. (2012). Isolation and characterization of cellulose-decomposing bacteria inhabiting sawdust and coffee residue composts. *Microbes and Environments*, 27(3), pp.226-233.
3. Kuramae, E.E., Gamper, H.A., Yergeau, E., Piceno, Y.M., Brodie, E.L., Desantis, T.Z., Andersen, G.L., Van Veen, J.A. and Kowalchuk, G.A. (2010). Microbial secondary succession in a chronosequence of chalk grasslands. *The ISME journal*, *4*(5), pp.711-715.
4. Kwak, M.J., Jeong, H., Madhaiyan, M., Lee, Y., Sa, T.M., Oh, T.K. and Kim, J.F. (2014). Genome information of Methylobacterium oryzae, a plant-probiotic methylotroph in the phyllosphere. *PloS One*, 9(9), p.e106704.
5. Lee, J., Shin, S.C., Kim, S.J., Kim, B.K., Hong, S.G., Kim, E.H., Park, H. and Lee, H. (2012). Draft genome sequence of a Sphingomonas sp., an endosymbiotic bacterium isolated from an arctic lichen Umbilicaria sp. *Journal of Bacteriology*, 194(11), pp.3010-3011.
6. Lim K.H, Lim S.S, Parish F, Andsuharto, R. (2012). RSPO Manual On Best Management Practices (Bmps) For Existing Oil Palm Cultivation On Peat. RSPO, Kuala Lumpur.
7. Madhaiyan, M., Poonguzhali, S., Kwon, S.W. and Sa, T.M. (2010). Bacillus methylotrophicus sp. nov., a methanol-utilizing, plant-growth-promoting bacterium isolated from rice rhizosphere soil. *International Journal of Systematic and Evolutionary Microbiology*, 60(10), pp.2490-2495.
8. Mayrberger, J.M. (2011). Studies of genera cytophaga-flavobacterium in context of the soil carbon cycle. *Dissertation Abstracts International*, 73(01).
9. Morikawa, M. (2006). Beneficial biofilm formation by industrial bacteria Bacillus subtilis and related species. *Journal of Biosciences and Bioengineering*. Vol.101, No.1, 1-8.
10. Muyzer, G, Waal, E.C.D and Uitterlinden, A.G (1997). Profiling of complex microbial populations by denaturing gradient gel electrophoresis analysis of polymerase chain reaction-amplified genes coding for 16S rRNA. *Applied and Environmental Microbiology*, 59, 695 – 700.
11. Myers, B, Webster, K.l, Mclaughlin, J.W and Basiliko, N, (2012). Microbial activity across a boreal peatland nutrient gradient:the role offungi and bacteria.*Wetlands Ecology and Management, 20*, 77–88.
12. Preston, M, Smemo, K, Mclaughlin, J and Basiliko, N. (2012). Peatland microbial communities and decomposition processes in the James Bay Lowlands, Canada. *Front Microbiology*, 3, 70.
13. Saman, S., Slattery, P and Saman, S. (2010) Microbial biodiversity investigation techniques. Current Research, Technology and Education Topics in Applied Microbiology and Microbial Biotechnology. *A. Mendez-Vilas* (Ed.) p. 1546 – 1550.
14. Sun, H, Terhonen, E, Koskinen, K, Paulin, L, Kasanen, R, and Asiegbu, F.O. (2014). Bacterial diversity and community structure along different peat soils in boreal forest. *Applied Soil Ecology*, 74, 37–45
15. Thormann, M (2011). In vitro decomposition of Sphagnum-derived acrotelm and mesotelm peat by indigenous and alien basidiomycetous fungi. *Mires Peat*, 8, 3.
16. Winsborough, C and Basiliko, N. (2010). Fungal and bacterial activity in northern peatlands. *Geomicrobiology Journal*. 27, 315–320.

17. Yule, C.M. (2010) Loss of biodiversity and ecosystem functioning in Indo-Malayan peat swamp forests. Biodiversity and Convertion, Volume 19, 2:393-409.

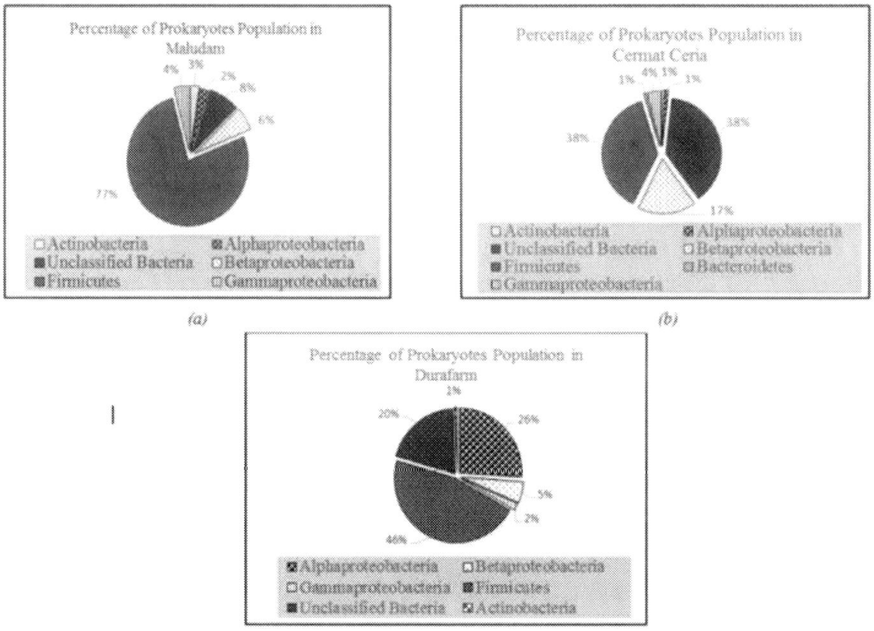

Figure 1: The Percentage of prokaryotes population in (a) Maludam National Park (b), Cermat Ceria secondary logged over forest and (c) Durafarm Oil Palm Plantation.

Figure 2: Phylogenetic tree based on similar nucleotide sequences detected by BLASTn, obtained from total microbes isolated from deep peat, Maludam National Park April 2012

Figure 3: Phylogenetic tree based on similar nucleotide sequences detected by BLASTn, obtained from total microbes isolated biodiversity of deep peat, Cermat Ceria secondary logged over forest, April 2012.

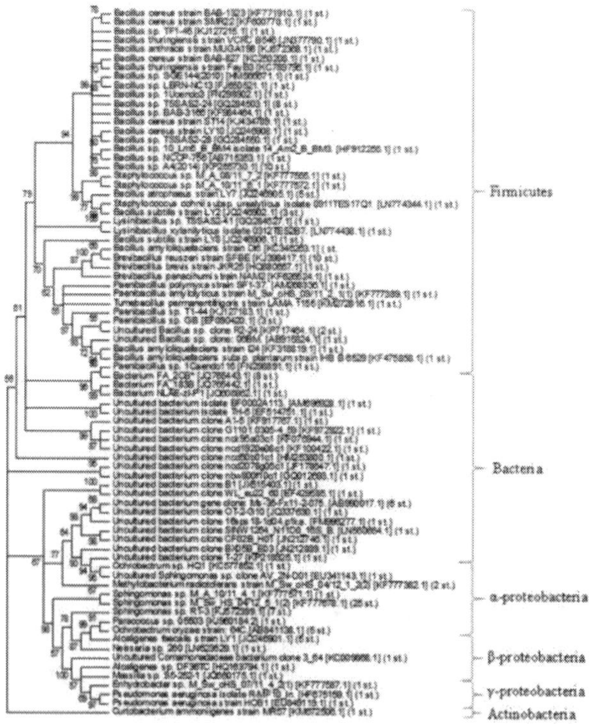

Figure 4: Phylogenetic tree based on similar nucleotide sequences detected by BLASTn, obtained from total microbes isolated from deep peat, Durafarm April 2012.

Abstract No: A-299

PROKARYOTIC DIVERSITY STUDY IN DIFFERENT OIL PALM DEVELOPMENT SITES USING PCR-DGGE ASSESSMENT IN SARAWAK

Mohd Shawal Thakib Maidin[1], Nur Aziemah Ab Ghani[2], Sakinah Safari[1], Shamsilawani Ahamed Bakeri[1] and Siti Ramlah Ahmad Ali[1*]

[1]*Biology Research Division, Malaysian Palm Oil Board, 6 Persiaran Institusi, Bandar Baru Bangi, 43000 Kajang, Selangor, Malaysia.*
[2]*Faculty of Medicine, University of Malaya, Kuala Lumpur, Malaysia.*

**Corresponding author: ramlah@mpob.gov.my*

SUMMARY

Soil microbes play an important role in conserving soil productivity and are sensitive to the changes in its natural environment. Therefore, microbial biodiversity analysis can be utilized for examination of soil quality, which is crucial for agricultural purposes. Hence, the prokaryotic population differences between the young oil palm aged four years old, drained clean-cleared Alan Bunga logged-over peat forest and drained Alan Bunga peat forest at Pelitanah, Sibu, Sarawak was analyzed. The PCR coupled with denaturing gradient gel electrophoresis (PCR-DGGE) has been conducted to visualize the DNA bands representing dominant bacterial group or species. Cluster analysis of DGGE profiles grouped the entire bacterial DNA from drained Alan Bunga peat forest, clean cleared logged-over Alan Bunga forest and young oil palm planted area into 3 major clusters and 1 minor cluster. The populations of bacteria in the three sites are different since majority of the Alan Bunga forest bacteria DGGE profiles falls in the major cluster II. While, the DGGE profiles for samples taken at the oil palm planted areas falls in the major cluster I and minor cluster IV and the profiles for samples taken at the drained clean-cleared Alan Bunga area falls in the major cluster III. This showed that the population is divided in four different clusters. Total mean bands with standard error,which represent the number of bacterial groups or species was highest at young palm planted area at 14 $\pm$4.15 followed by clean cleared at 11.75 $\pm$ 2.86 and forest at 9.65 $\pm$ 5.03, respectively. According to Fischer LSD all pairwise multiple comparisons, the microbial population in the four years old oil palm plantation was significantly higher as compared to Alan Bunga forest but was not significantly different with clean cleared Alan Bunga logged-over forest. This showed that the young oil palm planted area has the highest prokaryotic diversity followed by clean clearedand forest areas in Pelitanah.
Keywords: *microbes, 16S rDNA, microbial diversity, PCR-DGGE, oil palm*

INTRODUCTION

Interestingly, the most diverse natural environment on earth is located in the soil (Lauber *et al.*, 2013). Microbial community living in the soil is an important organism that affects the healthiness of the ecosystem. The community contains variety of different microbial species that make up the whole ecological unit (Delmont *et al.*, 2011). Therefore, soil structure changes can result in the damage of the population dynamic in that environment.Thus, lead to the microbial changes and affect the nutrients mobilizationthat is crucial in maintaining the soil fertility.

The nutrient recycling, organic matter dynamics and decomposition processes that occur in the soil are highly influence by the microbial community (Schimel and Schaeffer, 2015). These features determine the availability of the peatland as a growing media, biota habitat, biodiversity and hydrotopography. However, the microbial diversity in peatland can be influenced by the anthropogenic activities that modified the natural habitats of the bacterial population. Thus, good management practice can effectively control the microbial ecosystem in the agricultural soil. Conversely, the structure of the below grown ecosystems can be badly deteriorated due to the lessening of the soil carbon and biodiversity loss if the inappropriate handling were performed (Lauber *et al.*, 2013). Hence, deep understanding on the ecosystem processes is in need to characterize the genetic and functional diversity of soil bacterial communities for agricultural purposes.

Soil microbial diversity plays an important role in conserving soil productivity and it is susceptible to the changes in soil. This study was conducted to investigate the prokaryotic population in Pelitanah area, which involved in different peat ecosystems, which consisted of drained Alan Bunga peat forest, clean cleared logged-over Alan Bunga forest, and young oil palm planted area. Application of DNA fingerprinting methods enables the detection of diverse members of soil bacterial community, including the unculturable microbes. The PCR coupled with denaturing gradient gel electrophoresis (PCR-DGGE) has been used widely as culture-independent methods to determine species richness and structure of microbial communities for this study. Amplicons of the same length but with different nucleotide compositions are separated in a denaturing gradient gel of polyacrylamide, based on their differential denaturation profile(Duerte *et al.*, 2012).

METHODOLOGY

Peat Soil Sampling.

The soil microbial biodiversity study was performed at selected deep peatland forest and conversion of oil palm plantations in Sibu, Sarawak. Sampling of soil at four different level of peat was taken twice a year at Pelitanah Forest, Unplanted/clean cleared, Planted.

Dna Extraction.

Total DNA was extracted from peat soil samples using Gene MATRIX Soil DNA Purification Kit (Eurx Ltd, Gdansk, Poland). The amount and quality of DNA were measured using a Nanophotometer^{TM} P360 (Implen GmbH, Schatzbogen, Germany). The extracted DNA was stored at -20°C freezer until further procedures.

PCR-DGGE Analysis

PCR amplifications of the V3-V5 region (550bp) of the 16S rRNA gene of bacteria were performed with universal bacterial primers 341F-GC clamp and 907R using the PCR program. The PCR products were subjected to DGGE analysis. The gradient of denaturants and running conditions were optimized. PCR products were visualized, bands excised, and purified for sequencing with a QIAquick PCR purification kit (QIAGEN, US).

Similarity Analysis of PCR-DGGE Profiles

PCR-DGGE patterns were analyzed using Phoretix 1D Gel Analysis software (Total Lab Quant Ltd, United Kingdom), with which hierarchical cluster comparisons were carried out to group similar profiles and to generate band classes. All the images were normalized using the internal control samples described above and the comparison among whole profiles was performed using the Dice similarity coefficient (D_{sc}). The dendrogram was generated using the method of unweighted pair group with mathematical averages (UPGMA) at 1% position tolerance.

RESULTS AND DISCUSSION

The DGGE profiles were subjected to Phoretix 1D software for the analysis of DGGE fingerprints by using dice coefficient and UPGMA in *Figure* 1. Dendrogram was constructed with the 16S rDNA bacterial community fingerprint for the three Alan Bunga peat ecosystems at Pelitanah area. This cluster analysis enables the differentiation of the bacterial communities between the ecosystems (Cleary *et al.*, 2012). Furthermore, variations in community structure from the forest, logged-over forest and young palm planted ecosystems can be easily detected.The differences between profiles are indicated by the percentage of similarity. The major cluster II showed 35% genetic similarity with themajority of the drained Alan Bunga peat forest bacteria DGGE profiles. This followed by the major cluster I and III, which was also by 35% genetic similarity which, consists of young palm planted area and clean cleared Alan Bunga logged over peat forest. Minor cluster IV showed the indistinguishable profile with the lowest genetic similarity at less than 15%.

The mean of bands on DGGE gels is shown in Table 1 and *Figure* 2. The mean value for young palm planted ecosystem, clean cleared Alan Bunga logged-over forest and Alan Bunga forest were 14 ± 4.155, 11.75 ± 2.863 and 9.65 ± 5.029, respectively. The mean value also showed that the prokaryotic sample in young palm planted ecosystem was higher compared to clean cleared Alan Bunga logged-over forest and Alan Bunga forest. On the other hand, Alan Bunga forest showed the lowest number of microbial group among the three ecosystems. The distribution of microbes was not only related to environmental factors but also can vary in relation to spatial distance (Martiny *et al.*, 2011). The consideration is important because logging and cultivation may have different effects on local scale richness (α-diversity) and on the turnover of species between sites (β-diversity).For example, studies on plants show that while α-diversity increases or remains the same in disturbed habitats, there is a decrease in β-diversity (Smart *et al.*, 2006), which suggests that there is a homogenization of communities across space and the loss of species from the broader-scale community (γ-diversity).

The Fischer LSD all pairwise multiple comparison statistical analysis in Table 2 showed P-values < 0.05, for young palm planted ecosystem and drained Alan Bunga peat forest, which is significantly difference between the groups. There were no significant different between young palm planted ecosystemversus clean cleared Alan Bunga logged-over forest and clean cleared Alan Bunga logged-over forest versus drained Alan Bunga peat forest.

This showed that the bacterial composition was not largely differed between the ecosystems except between forest and oil palm planted areas. The oil palm plantation results in the increment of the bacterial community to the soil. The cultivation activities such as tillage and crops residues are some of the factors that promote the richness of the bacterial community (Shange*et al.*, 2012).

CONCLUSION

In conclusion, the averageof DNA bands or microbial group/ species and statistical analysis using pairwise multiple comparisons showed that young palm planted ecosystem had the most diverse prokaryotic population. Conversion of logged-over Alan Bunga forest to oil palm seems to improve the microbial biodiversity. This could be accelerated by successive biomass under ground cover with proper drainage system.However, further study on the dominant microbes present in these peat ecosystems has to be carried out in order to provide deeper insight in microbial biodiversity. Prominent DGGE bands need to be excised and sequenced to gain the identities of bacterial populations.

ACKNOWLEDGEMENT

We would like to thank the Director General of MPOB and the Director of Biological Research Division of MPOB for allowing this manuscript to be published in the 15th International Peat Congress 2016. We also would like to express our gratitude to the MPOB Peat Manuscript Review Committee for reviewing this manuscript. This research is supported by the MPOB Research Fund: R009711000.

REFERENCES

1. Cleary, D.F., Smalla, K., Mendonça-Hagler, L.C., and Gomes, N.C. (2012).Assessment of variation in bacterial composition among microhabitats in a mangrove environment using DGGE fingerprints and barcoded pyrosequencing. *PloS One*, *7*: e29380.
2. Delmont, T.O., Prestat, E., Keegan, K.P., Faubladier, M., Robe, P., Clark, I.M., Pelletier, E., Hirsch, P.R., Meyer, F., Gilbert, J.A. and Le Paslier, D. (2011). Accessing the soil metagenome for studies of microbial diversity. *Applied and Environmental Microbiology*. 77: 1315–1324.
3. Duarte, S., Pascoal, C. and Cassio, F.(2012). Denaturing gradient gel electrophoresis (DGGE) in microbial ecology-insights from freshwaters.*INTECH Open Access Publisher*.
4. Lauber, C.L., Ramirez, K.S., Aanderud, Z., Lennon, J., Fierer, N. (2013). Temporal variability in soil microbial communities across land-use types.*International Society for Microbial Ecology Journal*. 7: 1641–1650.
5. Martiny, J.B.H; Eisen, J.A; Penn, K; Allison, S.D and Horner-Devine, C. (2011). Drivers of bacterial-diversity depend on spatial scale. *Proceedings of the National Academy of Sciences*. 108: 7850 –7854.
6. Schimel, J.P., and Schaeffer, S.M. (2015).Microbial control over carbon cycling in soil.*The causes and consequences of microbial community structure*. 155.
7. Shange R.S, Ankumah R.O, Ibekwe A.M, Zabawa R, Dowd S.E. (2012).Distinct soil bacterial communities revealed under a diversely managedagroecosystem.*PLoSOne* 7:e40338.doi:10.1371.
8. Smart, S.M; Thompson, K; Marrs, R.H; Le Duc, M.G; Maskell, L.C and Firbank, L.G. (2006). Biotic homogenization and changes in species diversity across human-modified ecosystems. *Proceedings of the Royal Society of London B: Biological Sciences*. 273: 2659 –2665.

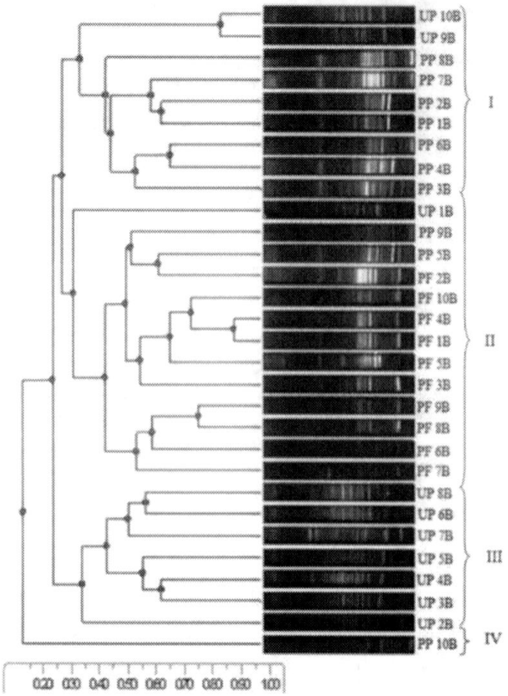

Figure 1: Dendrogram constructed with the 16S rDNA bacterial community fingerprint in three peat ecosystems. Alan Bunga forest (PF), clean cleared Alan Bunga logged over forest (UP) and young oil palm planted area (PP) developed from UP. The differences between profiles are indicated by percentage of similarity. The dendrogram was based on Dice Coefficent index and cluster analysis by the unweighted pair group method using arithmetic averages (UPGMA). Note: B – Peat level at above water table. (Phoretix 1D).

Table 1: Mean of bands on DGGE gels.

Sites	Mean	Std error
Pelitanah Planted	14.00	4.154896
Pelitanah Forest	9.65	5.029126
Pelitanah Clean Cleared	11.75	2.863105

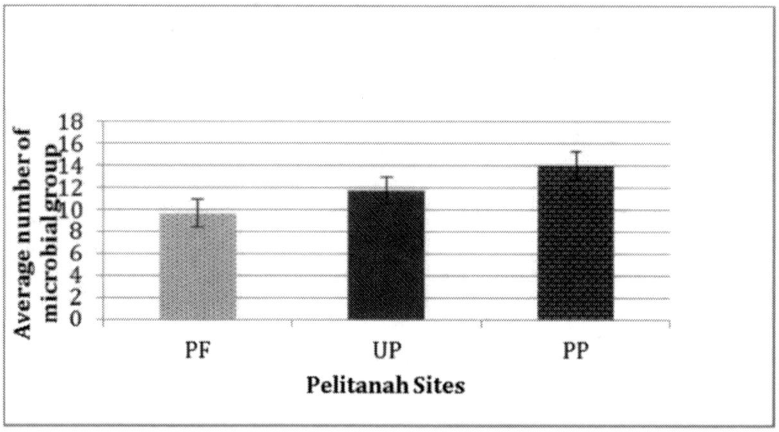

Figure 2: Mean value of microbial group in Alan Bunga forest (PF), clean cleared Alan Bunga logged over forest (UP) and young oil palm planted area (PP) developed from UP.

Table 2: All Pairwise Multiple Comparison (Fisher LSD Method).

Comparisons for factor:				
Comparison	Diff of Means	t	P	P<0.050
P.Planted(c) vs. P.Forest (a)	8.700	5.541	0.003	Yes
P.Planted (c) vs. P.Clean Cleared (b)	4.500	5.541	0.107	No

Abstract No: A-424

SOIL MICROBIAL COMMUNITIES AND ASSOCIATED GHG EMISSIONS AT DIFFERENT LAND USE TYPES IN MALAYSIAN PEATLANDS: AN IMPLICATION FOR CLIMATE CHANGE

Selvakumar Dhandapani[1,2*], Sofie Sjogersten[1], Stephanie Evers[2] and Karl Ritz[1]

[1]Agriculture and Environmental Science Division, University of Nottingham, UK.
[2]School of Biosciences, University of Nottingham, Malaysia.

Corresponding author: sccalva@gmail.com ; stxsd14@nottingham.ac.uk

SUMMARY

The tropical peatlands are complex and globally important ecosystems for its distinctive biodiversity and high carbon storage because of its unique acidic, nutrient poor and waterlogged conditions. About 68% of the carbon-rich tropical peatlands are present in South East Asia (SEA) with highest cover in Indonesia and Malaysia. The SEA peatlands store about 70 Gt of carbon, and absorb at least 2.6 tonnes of CO_2 per hectare per year. The carbon has been gradually amassed in these peatlands since the last ice age for last 10,000 years, when the peatlands have played a major role in maintaining the carbon balance of the earth. This carbon accumulation is a result of delicate balance among different environmental and biological conditions. This delicate balance is disturbed by anthropogenic disturbances that are turning the peatlands from carbon sinks to sources of three major greenhouse gases. The microbes in peatlands play an important role not only in the formation of peat itself, but also directly influence ecosystem carbon turnover and nutrient mineralization for high primary production, effecting overall ecosystem function and maintaining the balance. Despite the importance of microbes in maintaining the peatland functions and their importance on climate change, there is minimal research done on the microbes in different land use types within the tropical peatlands. There is an increasing need to know the changes in microbial communities with land use change and understand the relationship between soil microbial communities and biogeochemical cycling in the peatlands. This research aims to quantify the carbon loss and the changes in microbial community structure along the different disturbance gradients in the tropical peatlands of North Selangor. The emissions of CO_2 and CH_4 are measured using Los Gatos greenhouse gas analyser. The microbial community structure is determined using PLFA (phospholipid Fatty Acids) and PLEL (Phospholipid Ether Lipids) analysis. The outcome is expected to help understand the relationship between soil communities and biogeochemical cycling, and observe the pattern of change along the disturbance gradient. The results would also help estimate the impact of land use change in tropical peatlands on global climate change.

***Keywords**: tropical peatlands, oil palm plantations, greenhouse gas emissions, microbial community structure, PLFA*

INTRODUCTION AND PROBLEM STATEMENT

The peatlands are complex and globally important ecosystems for its distinctive biodiversity and high carbon storage because of its unique acidic, nutrient poor and waterlogged conditions (Parish *et al.*, 2008; Miettinen *et al.*, 2012). The peatlands cover about 3% of total land area of the earth, distributed all around the world (Strack, 2008; Hooijer *et al.*, 2006). Though most of the peatlands are located in the Northern hemisphere, , there remains a considerable area of tropical peatlands present in south America, southern Africa and South East Asia, covering 0.25% of global land surface and accounting 3% of global soil carbon (Strack, 2008; Hergoualc'h & Verchot, 2011; Hergoualc'h & Verchot. 2014). About 68% of these carbon-rich tropical peatlands are present in South East Asia, located mostlyin Indonesia and Malaysia (Lo and Parish, 2013; Hergoualc'h & Verchot, 2011; Hergoualc'h & Verchot, 2014). Other than serving as a home and refuge for unique biodiversity and ecosystem services, the South East Asian peatlands store about 70 Gt of carbon (Miettinen and Liew, 2010; Page *et al.*, 2011), and absorb at least 2.6 tonnes of CO_2 per hectare per year (Norwana *et al.*, 2011)The carbon has been gradually amassed in these peatlands since the last ice age and has since played a major role in maintaining the carbon balance of the earth (Lo and Parish, 2013). This carbon accumulation is a result of delicate balance among different environmental and biological conditions, including hydrology, ecology, topography and landscape morphology (Page *et al.*, 1999; Miettinen *et al.*, 2012). This delicate balance is disturbed by anthropogenic disturbances that are turning the peatlands from carbon sinks to carbon sources (Lo and Parish, 2013).

Even though natural peatlands emit large amounts of methane, they store huge amounts of carbon and have a net cooling effect on the environment (Parish *et al.,* 2008). The sequestration of carbon in peatlands is mainly due to high primary productivity and low decomposition activity by microbes, due to anaerobic conditions (Andersen *et al.,* 2013). The degradation of peatlands would not only emit large amount of carbon that is stored over the last thousands of years, but also still emit large amounts of methane through drainage ditches (Parish *et al.,* 2008). The conversion of peatlands to agriculture landscapes and use of fertilizers would also become a source of nitrous oxide (Parish *et al.,* 2008). Thus, the degradation of carbon rich tropical peatlands would potentially fasten climate change, with emissions of three important greenhouse gases.

The oil palm is considered as one of the fastest expanding equatorial crops (Koh and Wilcove, 2008). The expansion of oil palm plantations is the biggest threat to peatlands in south East Asia (Miettinen *et al.,* 2012; Hooijer *et al.,* 2006; Koh and Wilcove, 2008). 8.4% of oil palm plantations in Malaysia are in peatlands (Rashid *et al.,* 2013). As available mineral soils become scarce for oil palm plantations, the plantations are expected to increase in peatlands (Miettinen *et al.,* 2012). Hoojer *et al* (2006) observed that one quarter of oil palm concessions in Indonesia are in peatlands. A major portion of planned oil palm expansions in Indonesia are expected to encroach on peatlands as well (Sheil *et al.,* 2009). The peatlands are usually scarcely populated, making it easy to claim and gain ownership for the oil palm industries, without any social conflict (Casson *et al.,* 2007).

The oil palm can directly affect forest by clearing forest meant for its expansion into degraded, or burnt peat, or combined economic enterprise of paper and oil palm industry to cut costs of oil palm establishment and indirectly affect peat forests by construction of roadways to the oil palm plantations and industries or moving other crops to peatlands (Fitzherbert *et al.,* 2009; Hirano *et al.,* 2007; Miettinen *et al.,* 2012). There was about 3 Million ha of industrial oil palm plantation in peatlands in South East Asia by 2010 (Miettinen *et al.,* 2012), which is expected to increase to 4 Million ha by 2020 (Hooijer *et al.,* 2006).

The forest land should be completely cleared of vegetation to establish a palm oil plantation (Bruhl and Eltz, 2010). The clearing and draining of peatlands leave dead wood and debris that are easily susceptible to fire (Bruhl and Eltz, 2010). The forest fires in South East Asia are often associated with land clearing for oil palm plantations (Chazdon, 1998; Cao, 2000; Dennis et al., 2005). The ground is terraced after clearing the forest in preparation for establishing the oil palm plantations causing further damage to the topsoil (Bruhl and Eltz, 2010),.

The microbes in peatlands play an important role not only in the formation of peat itself, but also directly influence ecosystem carbon turnover and nutrient mineralization for high primary production, affecting overall ecosystem functions and maintaining their balance. Despite the importance of microbes in maintaining the peatland functions and their importance on climate change, there is minimal research carried out on microbial diversity and activities in different land uses such as oil palm cultivation within the tropical peatlands. There is an increasing need to know the changes in microbial communities with land use changes and understanding the relationship between soil microbial communities and biogeochemical cycling in the peatlands.

AIMS AND OBJECTIVES

The research aims to quantify the carbon losses and the changes in microbial community structure along different disturbance gradients in tropical peatlands, and understanding/establishing patterns of changes in microbial communities and associated GHG emissions along the disturbance gradients.

The main objectives are;

- To examine how land use change and agricultural expansion have altered soil microbial communities and the microhabitat of the soil fauna
- To quantify the carbon loss associated with land use change by measuring total carbon and soil respiration in different land uses
- To examine the consequence of changes in microbial communities on biogeochemical cycling
- To establish an understanding of the relation between soil microbial communities and geochemical cycles in different land uses and their impact on climate change

METHODS AND FIELD WORKS

DURATION: 6 Months (3 months wet season and 3 months dry season)

LOCATION: North Selangor Peatlands (pristine forest, degraded forest, oil palm -2 years, oil Palm – 15 to 20 years, small scale agriculture – paddy, oil palm and cassava intercropping, oil palm and pineapple intercropping)

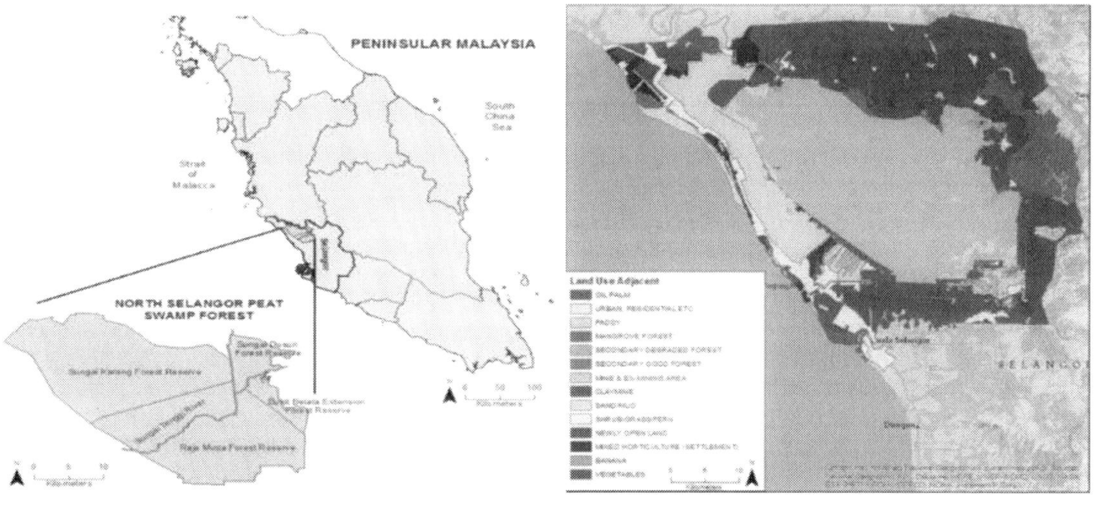

Fig. 1: North selangor peat swamp forests and the surrounding site classifications.

MEASUREMENTS: soil pH, moisture, temperature, organic content (LOI), nutrient content, total carbon and nitrogen, carbon and methane emissions (using Los-Gatos GHG analyser), ground water table height, and microbial community structure (using phospholipid fatty acid analysis- PLFA and phospholipid ether lipids- PLEL analysis).

DETAILS

1) The samples are collected from 20 points per site following stratified random sampling. The emissions are measured from 20 random points per site, stratified by 5 points each near both crops in intercropping system or 10 points that are near dominant trees in forest habitat and 10 points in inter rows in intercropping systems or 10 points that are away from trees in forest habitats
2) The surface soil parameters (pH, moisture, temperature, organic content), water table height and GHG emissions are measured twice every month for six months, including three months of dry period and three months of wet period
3) The surface soil samples were collected for PLFA and PLEL once every month during the sampling period, to understand the changes between wet and dry season
4) The surface soil samples collected for PLFA and PLEL analysis were also used to measure the nutrient content, to observe the relationship between nutrient contents and microbial communities between seasons.
5) The total carbon and nitrogen are measured once during the sampling period to quantify the carbon loss with different land uses

SUMMARY

IMPACT:

The tropical peatlands are increasingly degraded and vigorously converted to industrial and agricultural plantations, affecting above and below ground diversity, with potential increase in GHG emissions influencing climate change.

OUTPUTS:

The effect of land use change on soil properties and microbial communities are known

The GHG emissions from different peatland ecosystems are known

The total carbon loss with the conversion of natural peatlands to other land use are quantified

The seasonal changes of emissions, microbial communities and nutrient availability are recognised for different land use types in tropical peatlands

OUTCOMES:

A detailed understanding of the patterns of change in soil microbial communities and GHG emissions in different land use types in tropical peatlands and the establishment of understanding the relationship between soil communities and biogeochemical cycling.

An estimation of the impact of land use change in tropical peatlands on climate change.

REFERENCES

1. Andersen, R., Chapman, S. J. and Artz, R. R. E. (2013) *'Microbial communities in natural and disturbed peatlands: A review'*, Soil Biology & Biochemistry, 57, pp. 979-994.
2. Bruhl, C. A. and Eltz, T. (2010) *'Fuelling the biodiversity crisis: species loss of ground-dwelling forest ants in oil palm plantations in Sabah, Malaysia (Borneo)'*, Biodiversity Conservation, 19(2), pp. 519-529.
3. Cao, K. F. (2000) *'Water relations and gas exchange of tropical saplings during a prolonged drought in a Bornean heath forest, with reference to root architecture'*, Journal of Tropical Ecology, 16, pp. 101-116.
4. Casson, A., Tacconi, L. and Deddy, K. (2007) *Strategies to reduce carbon emissions from the oil palm sector in Indonesia.*
5. Chazdon, R. L. (1998) 'Ecology - Tropical forests - *Log 'em or leave 'em?'*, Science, 281(5381), pp. 1295-1296.
6. Dennis, R. A., Mayer, J., Applegate, G., Chokkalingam, U., Colfer, C. J. P., Kurniawan, I., Lachowski, H., Maus, P., Permana, R. P., Ruchiat, Y., Stolle, F., Suyanto and Tomich, T. P. (2005) *'Fire, people and pixels: Linking social science and remote sensing to understand underlying causes and impacts of fires in Indonesia'*, Human Ecology, 33(4), pp. 465-504.
7. Hergoualc'h, K. and Verchot, L. V. (2011) *'Stocks and fluxes of carbon associated with land use change in Southeast Asian tropical peatlands: A review'*, Global Biogeochemical Cycles, 25, pp. 13.
8. Hergoualc'h, K. and Verchot, L. V. (2014) *'Greenhouse gas emission factors for land use and land-use change in Southeast Asian peatlands'*, Mitigation and Adaptation Strategies for Global Change, 19(6), pp. 789-807.
9. Hirano, T., Segah, H., Harada, T., Limin, S., June, T., Hirata, R. and Osaki, M. (2007) *'Carbon dioxide balance of a tropical peat swamp forest in Kalimantan, Indonesia'*, Global Change Biology, 13(2), pp. 412-425.
10. Hooijer, A., Silvius, M., Wosten, H. and Page, S. (2006) *PEAT CO2 Assessment of Co_2 emissions from drained peatlands in SE Asia*: Delft Hydraulics.
11. Koh, L. P. and Wilcove, D. S. (2008) *'Is oil palm agriculture really destroying tropical biodiversity?'*, Conservation Letters,, 1(2), pp. 60-64.
12. Lo, J. and Parish, F. (2013) *Peatlands and Climate Change in Southeast Asia, Selangor, Malaysia*: Global Environment Centre.
13. Miettinen, J., Hooijer, A., Tollenaar, D., Malins, C., Vernimmen, R., Shi, C. and Liew, S. C. (2012) *Historical Analysis and Projection of Oil Palm Plantation Expansion on Peatland in Southeast Asia*, Washington DC: International Council on Clean Transportation.
14. Miettinen, J. and Liew, S. C. (2010) *'Degradation and development of peatlands in peninsular malaysia and in the islands of sumatra and borneo since 1990', Land Degradation & Development*, 21(3), pp. 285-296.
15. Norwana, A. A. B. D., Kunjappan, R., Chin, M., Schoneveld, G., Potter, L. and Andriani, R. (2011) *The local impacts of oil palm expansion in Malaysia; An assessment based on a case study in Sabah state*, Bogor, Indonesia: CIFOR.
16. Page, S. E., Rieley, J. O. and Banks, C. J. (2011) *'Global and regional importance of the tropical peatland carbon pool'*, Global Change Biology, 17(2), pp. 798-818.
17. Page, S. E., Rieley, J. O., Shotyk, O. W. and Weiss, D. (1999) *'Interdependence of peat and vegetation in a tropical peat swamp forest'*, Philosophical Transactions of the Royal Society of London Series B-Biological Sciences, 354(1391), pp. 1885-1897.
18. Parish, F., Sirin, A., Charman, D., Joosten, H., MInayeva, T., Silvius, M. and Stringer, L. (2008) *Assessment on peatlands, biodiversity and climate change*, Selangor, Malaysia and Wageningen, The Netherlands: Global Environment Centre and Wetlands International.
19. Rashid, A. H. A. M., Hamzah, K. A. and Joseph, K. T. 2013. *Land use change in Malaysia. Reports from the technical panels of the 2nd green house gas.* Roundtable on Sustainable palm oil.
20. Sheil, D., Casson, A., Meijaard, E., Van Noordwijk, M., Gaskell, J., Sunderland-Groves, J., Wertz, K. and Kanninen, M. (2009) *The impacts and opportunities of oil palm in Southeast Asia; What do we know? what do we need to know?* , Indonesia: CIFOR.
21. Strack, M. (2008) *Peatlands and Climate Change.* Saarijarvi, Finland: International Peat Society.

Abstract No: A-337

STUDY OF FUNCTIONAL MICROBES POPULATION IN PEAT SOIL TREATED WITH TWO PESTICIDES

Syaiful Anwar, Maipa Dia Pati*, Rahayu Widyastuti and Dadang

Faculty of Agriculture, Bogor Agricultural University, West Java, Indonesia.

* *Corresponding author: maipadiapati.misdjan@gmail.com*

SUMMARY

Necessity in agricultural land expansion for food security in Indonesia has been faced by the fact in utilizing marginal land such as shallow peat soil in Central Kalimantan. Among problems encountered in such marginal land is incidence of pests and diseases. Common practice of farmers in dealing with this problem is the application of chemical pesticides in order to ensure production. Unintended chemical pesticides that fall on/into the soil might have an adverse effect to soil microbes activity. This research was aimed to assess the effect of pesticides on population of functional soil microbes in peat soil. The research was in the form of incubation of peat soil in pots in completely randomized factorial design with two factors. First factor was 7 combinations of pesticide types (paraquat, and buthylphenylmethyl carbamate = BPMC) and doses (50, 100, and 200% of recommended dosage). Second factor was 4 incubation times (1, 7, 14, and 28 days). After the each of incubation times, the soil samples were treated and analyzed for population of phosphate solubilizing microbes (bacteria and fungi), cellulolytic microbes (bacteria and fungi), and N_2-fixing bacteria (Azotobacter and Azospirillum). The results in general show fluctuation of microbes population with doses of pesticides and incubation. Of the six microbes studied, pesticides only significantly affecting population of Azospirillum, Azotobacter and phosphate solubilizing fungi, whilst incubation times significantly affecting all microbes population. Adverse effects to microbes population occurred on phosphate solubilizing bacteria by both pesticides, on Azotobacter and Azospirillum by paraquat, and on phosphate solubilizing fungi by BPMC, although all microbes population recovered after 7 days of incubation times. Cellulolytic microbes are the most un-affected by the two pesticides. Although there is adverse effect at the beginning of incubation time by paraquat, significantly increased population, however, found on Azospirillum by the two pesticides.

Keywords: *peat soil, pesticides, paraquate, BPMC, functional microbes*

INTRODUCTION

Agricultural activities in peatland is faced with several problems, such as the low soil fertility and the high of pests incidents (Noor, 2001). Incidences of pests to agricltural plants, among others, are caused by the change of land function from peat forest with high varieties of plants to agricultural land with low varieties of crops. One common efforts to control pests and almost always practiced by farmers in intensive agriculture is the application of agrochemical pesticides Handayanto and Hairiah, 2007) in order to ensure production. Controlling pests chemically as also practiced by farmers on peat soil in Central Kalimantan is considered as the easiest and the most practical in their applications, and faster responses of pests. On the other hand, however, chemical pesticides that fall on/ into the soil is feared would have adverse effects towards population of soil functional microbes. Only about 20% of the pesticides will arrive at targets, while the rest will fall on/ into soils then move spatially and leach to surface or ground waters (Sa'id, 1994). The present of soil functional microbes in agricultural soil is very important in supporting plant growth and production. These soil microbes have different roles in the agricultural ecosystem which related energy flow and nutrients cycles caused by main activities of the microbes (growth and development).

Adverse effects of pesticides on functional microbes population in mineral soil has been widely reported. For example, Busse et al. (2001) suggested that the herbicides glyphosate toxic to bacteria and fungi isolated from soil Ponderosa Pine Plantations, and the total population of heterotrophic bacteria decreased after application glyphosate. On peat soils that information is still lacking. Zimdhal (1993) stated that the soil contains clay and organic matter adsorbs pesticides greater than sandy soils. Since peat soil is almost entirely organic matter, the adverse effect of pesticides on the functional microbes activity in peat soil would not as drastic as it did in the mineral soil. This research was aimed to assess the effect of pesticides application on the functional microbes population in peat soil.

METHODS

This research was conducted from August 2014 to May 2015, at the Laboratory of the Department of Soil Science and Land Resource, Faculty of Agriculture, Bogor Agricultural University. This research used completely randomized factorial design with two factors. First factor was 7 combinations of types (paraquat and buthylphenylmethyl carbamate = BPMC) and doses (50, 100, and 200% of recommended dosage) of pesticides; second factor was 4 incubation times (1, 7, 14, and 28 days) with three replications. The 100% doses of pesticides were equal to 80% that will fall on/ into soils, that equal to active compound of 2208 μg kg^{-1} for paraquat, and 970 μg kg^{-1} for BPMC.

The treated soils were stored and incubated in open chamber in dark room at room temperature. After the each of incubation times, aliquot of the soil samples were treated and analyzed for population of phosphate solubilizing microbes (bacteria and fungi), cellulolytic microbes (bacteria and fungi), and N_2 fixing bacteria. Analysis of microbial populations were using two methods; they were total plate count (TPC) method for phosphate solubilizing microbes, cellulolytic microbes, and Azotobacter, and most probable number (MPN) method for Azospirillum.

RESULT

In general, the results showed that functional microbes population fluctuated at various doses of pesticides and incubation times. Results of ANOVA showed that the pesticide treatment does not affect the population of phosphate solubilizing bacteria (PSB), cellulolytic bacteria, and cellulolytic fungi (Table 1). On the contrary, the pesticide treatment affects the population of Azotobacter, Azospirillum and phosphate solubilizing fungi (PSF). 100% paraquat, 200% paraquat, 100% BPMC, and 200% BPMC treatments have Azospirillum population significantly higher than that of Control. Different response shown by PSF, in which 50% and 100% BPMC treatments indicates that the population PSF significantly lower than that of Control and all treatments of paraquat. Significant different is also demonstrated by Azotobacter but with a fluctuating population. Paraquat treatment tends to reduce the population of Azotobacter. Treatment of 50% BPMC is significantly higher in Azotobacter than that of the treatments of 50% and 100% paraquat, though not significantly different with that of the Control.

Table 1: Effects of pesticide treatment on average population of soil functional microbes.

Pesticide treatment	Population of functional microbes							
	PSB	Cellulolytic bacteria	Azotobacter		Azospirillum		PSF		Cellulolytic fungi
	..........................($x10^5$ CFU g^{-1} soil)...........................						....($x10^4$ CFU g^{-1} soil)...		
Control	8.80	1.22	27.10	abc	2.84	c	4.57	a	19.26
50% Paraquat	8.48	1.67	19.56	bc	5.40	bc	4.81	a	14.45
100% Paraquat	5.80	1.18	14.93	c	6.45	ab	3.16	a	12.64
200% Paraquat	5.57	1.06	20.21	abc	7.24	ab	5.39	a	19.53
50% BPMC	11.51	1.52	36.06	a	6.10	bc	1.03	b	12.39
100% BPMC	6.62	0.95	34.88	ab	8.89	a	1.65	b	11.98
200% BPMC	12.11	1.02	21.06	abc	7.49	a	5.56	a	22.38

Note: CFU = colony forming unit; PSB = phosphate solubilizing bacteria; PSF = phosphate solubilizing fungi; Different letter in the same column indicates significant different according to Duncan test at 5% level; Doses of 50, 100 dan 200% mean a half, equal to, twice of recommended dose, respectively.

Table 2 show that the incubation time real effect on the population of PSB, PSF, cellulolytic bacteria, fungi cellulolytic, Azotobacter and Azospirillum, although fluctuating but an increase in population with increasing incubation time, except PSB 7th day, Azospirillum day 14 , Azotobacter day 7, and day-to-7 PSF. At the end of the incubation period of functional microbial population groups studied significantly higher than the day-to-1. Except, the population of cellulolytic bacteria and Azospirillum which shows the effect didn't differ significantly when compared with the day 1.

Tabel 2: Effects of incubation time's on average population of soil functional microbes.

Incubation time's (Day)	Population of functional microbes											
	PSB		Cellulolytic bacteria		Azotobacter		Azospirillum		PSF		Cellulolytic fungi	
	........................(x10^5 CFU g^{-1} soil)........................								.........(x10^4 CFU g^{-1} soil)......			
1	3.37	c	0.89	b	5.71	ab	22.85	b	1.23	b	9.72	b
7	2.42	d	1.44	a	6.17	ab	16.11	b	1.05	b	12.41	b
14	21.01	a	1.62	a	4.55	b	27.27	b	7.18	a	18.57	a
28	6.85	b	0.97	ab	8.30	a	33.08	a	5.49	a	23.67	a

Note: CFU = colony forming unit; PSB = phosphate solubilizing bacteria; PSF = phosphate solubilizing fungi; Different letter in the same column indicates significant different according to Duncan test at 5% level.

The study also showed the presence of interactions between pesticide treatment with incubation time against the group Azospirillum, Azotobacter and PSB. However, after a further test Azospirillum population (Table 3) show the influences that are not real. Instead, the group PSF (Table 4) and Azotobacter (Table 5) shows the real effect is different. Table 4 shows that the negative effects due to the application of pesticides most influential groups of the PSB. The population of PSB decreased in all treatment pesticides, except for treatment of paraquat 200% on day 1. Day 7 also shows a decrease in the population of PSB on pesticide treatment, unless the treatment Paraquat BPMC 200% and 50%. on the 14th day of the downward trend seen in the treatment population Paraquat PSB 100%, 200% Paraquat, and BPMC 100%. Meanwhile, on the 28th day is not a decline in the population of PSB. this shows that the negative effects of pesticide application is shown mainly on day 1 and day 7, although it later occurred subsequent recovery in the incubation time.

Tabel 3: Effects interaction of pesticide treatment and incubation time's on average population of Azospirillum.

Pesticide treatment	Population of Azospirillum bacteria (x10^5 CFU g^{-1} soil)			
	Day-1	Day-7	Day-14	Day-28
Control	0.17	0.17	1.51	4.08
Paraquat 50%	0.00	0.00	5.17	7.05
Paraquat 100%	0.00	0.00	7.87	6.90
Paraquat 200%	6.91	6.91	2.84	8.20
BPMC 50%	8.43	8.43	3.97	11.83
BPMC 100%	12.24	12.24	6.43	12.23
BPMC 200%	12.24	12.24	4.08	12.23

Note: CFU = colony forming unit; PSB = phosphate solubilizing bacteria; PSF = phosphate solubilizing fungi; Different letter in the same column indicates significant different according to Duncan test at 5% level; Doses of 50, 100 dan 200% mean a half, equal to, twice of recommended dose, respectively.

Tabel 4: Effects interaction of pesticide treatment and incubation time's on average population of phosphate solubilizing bacteria.

Pesticide treatment	Population of phosphate solubilizing bacteria (x10^5 CFU g^{-1} soil)							
	Day-1		Day-7		Day-14		Day-28	
Control	7.46	ab	2.54	abc	22.95	a	2.25	abc
Paraquat 50%	4.50	ab	0.29	de	24.66	a	4.46	ab
Paraquat 100%	4.10	ab	0.42	cd	14.65	ab	4.06	ab
Paraquat 200%	7.56	ab	6.80	ab	4.84	ab	3.07	ab
BPMC 50%	0.00	e	2.94	ab	27.46	a	15.66	ab
BPMC 100%	0.00	e	2.10	abc	13.90	ab	10.48	ab
BPMC 200%	0.00	e	1.84	bc	38.63	a	7.96	ab

Note: CFU = colony forming unit; PSB = phosphate solubilizing bacteria; PSF = phosphate solubilizing fungi; Different letter in the same column indicates significant different according to Duncan test at 5% level; Doses of 50, 100 dan 200% mean a half, equal to, twice of recommended dose, respectively.

Table 5 below shows that there is a trend of population decline Azotobacter treatment with Paraquat 50% on day 1, Paraquat treatment 200% and BPMC 200% at day 7, all treatments of pesticides on day 14 and day 28 except BPMC treatment on day 28.

Tabel 5: Effects interaction of pesticide treatment and incubation time's on average population of Azotobacter.

Pesticide treatment	Population of Azotobacter bacteria ($x10^5$ CFU g^{-1} soil)							
	Day-1		Day-7		Day-14		Day-28	
Control	4.72	ab	13.49	ab	49.39	a	40.80	a
Paraquat 50%	5.50	ab	26.18	ab	20.15	ab	26.40	ab
Paraquat 100%	1.41	b	16.64	ab	23.09	ab	18.58	ab
Paraquat 200%	8.03	ab	9.52	ab	33.87	a	29.41	a
BPMC 50%	41.13	a	16.59	ab	45.78	a	40.75	a
BPMC 100%	65.10	a	19.60	ab	5.71	ab	49.11	a
BPMC 200%	34.07	a	10.78	ab	12.88	ab	26.52	ab

Note: CFU = colony forming unit; PSB = phosphate solubilizing bacteria; PSF = phosphate solubilizing fungi; Different letter in the same column indicates significant different according to Duncan test at 5% level; Doses of 50, 100 dan 200% mean a half, equal to, twice of recommended dose, respectively.

DISCUSSION

The results showed that microbial functional have different responses to the use of agrochemical in this case there are two types of pesticides (active ingredient herbicide paraquat and the insecticide active ingredient BPMC). Pesticides or pesticide dose levels can decrease or increase the population of certain microbial groups. The tendency population of Azospirillum higher pesticide treatment (Table 1), possibly due to the pesticides applied an organic pesticide. BPMC insecticide containing carbon, while the herbicide paraquat group containing carbon and nitrogen. Azospirillum bacterium groups allegedly capable of using carbon or nitrogen (nutrients) contained in pesticides to support cell metabolism. The different results expressed by Cycon and Seget, (2007) reported that the application of herbicide and insecticide diazinon linuron at high doses, reduce the population of bacteria-free N2 fastening by 40% compared to controls. Nevertheless, in the study also stated that the use of three types of selective pesticides (herbicides, insecticides and fungicides) significantly stimulates an increase in population of heterotrophic bacteria. In addition, some studies suggest that pesticides can be used as a carbon source, an energy source and a source of nutrients by some groups of soil microbes, but toxic for other microbial groups (Bhuyan *et al.*, 1993; Johansen, 2001). Instead, PSF group showed lower populations with insecticide treatments BPMC. This is presumably because the insecticide BPMC not compatible with PSF group, insecticides BPMC act as inhibitors and inhibit mycelial growth and spore germination by inhibiting the synthesis of amino acids through the path "shikimic acid". Cycon and Seget, (2007) also noted that the application of insecticides diazinon lower the total population of fungi day after application. Application of pesticides may inhibit / kill a particular microbial groups but increases the number of other microbial groups by exempting them from the competition (Hussain et al., 2009). More Akbar et al. (2012) states that all insecticides used in these studies, significantly inhibits mycelial growth and germination of conidia of entomopathogenic fungi. The incubation period (Table 2) showed that the application of pesticides generally degrade the functional microbial population at the beginning of treatment. During the incubation period of functional bacterial groups studied showed a fluctuating population, except cellulolytic fungi. However, the overall functional microbial population at the end of the incubation period is higher than the beginning of the incubation period. This, presumably because of pesticides applied a foreign substance and is toxic to some soil microbial nutrients or there is competition. Application of pesticides would hamper soil microbial populations that are not sensitive to pesticides for a while, so that the microbes will adapt first. Over time incubation, the microbial groups utilize the nutrients released from microbes that have died for growth, and or a process of degradation of the compounds of pesticides in soil within 30 days of incubation. At the beginning of the application of pesticides, some microbial populations will be affected so that the population declined, but after a period of adaptation of microbial populations is slowly returning to normal even higher (Fliessbach and Mader, 2004; Niewiadomska, 2004). Cellulolytic fungus thought to potentially solve complex carbon chain of pesticides (for their enzyme cellulase), so that the cellulolytic fungus capable of utilizing pesticides as a carbon source which then led to population increases continuously. Cellulolytic fungus is also often used as an agent for biodegradation of pesticides. Subowo (2013) states that the Aspergillus niger besides having cellulase activity can also degrade pesticides deltamethrin at 500 ppm. Maloney (2001) also states that the Aspergillus, Penicillium, Fusarium and Paecillomyces Spp. able to degrade pentachlorophenol (PCP), which is a follow-up material and are toxic pesticides. The high content of organic matter in peat, is thought to be one factor that plays an important role to support the process of functional microbial adaptation. In addition to the availability of organic material needed for the functional microbial growth and metabolism are met. Organic material also adsorbs pesticides applied, so that the negative effects of the application of pesticides on microbial functional groups can be minimized. In addition, the high content of organic material on peat soil will also increase the rate of degradation of pesticides biotic or abiotic (Roger *et al.*, 1994). Rache and Coats, (1998) in his study suggests that increased soil bacterial populations associated with biodegradation time of pesticide used. This indicates a change in microbial catabolism capabilities that allow microbes have the ability to degrade pesticides and or changes in the microbial groups (Hussain *et al.*, 2009) on peat soil after application of pesticides. The interaction between the pesticide treatment with incubation time indicates that the negative effects of pesticides seen in bacteria Azospirillum and PSB at the beginning of the incubation period (day 1 and day 7), whereas the negative effects of pesticides Azotobacter bacteria seen at the end of the incubation period (day ke- 14 and day 28). The absence of colonies PSB on day 1 after the application of insecticides BPMC, allegedly due to dilution rate used is still high, (10-4 and 10-3), there is a possibility if used lower dilutions (10-1 or 10-2) will be found the population of PSB. In addition, it is also believed to be related to the adaptability of the PSB is lower than other functional microbe against pesticide application. BPMC insecticide applications, encouraging PSB to dormancy early in the application of pesticides as a form of adaptation to environmental conditions that are less supportive of growth, and then on the 7th day when environmental conditions are more favorable, phosphate solvent bacterial colonies grow back. This could be due, pesticides applied have undergone a process of degradation on the 7th day.

Pesticides applied to soil may be used as a substrate by a specific group of microbial soil and then to degradation (Rao, 1994), in this case a group of bacteria-free N2 fastening allegedly able to utilize the pesticide as a source of nutrition for the population is not disturbed at the beginning of the application of pesticides. Rahayuningsih (2009) states that microbes play a role in the decomposition of pesticides in the soil, and pesticides used or can be used by microbes as a source of carbon to support activities / cell metabolism. Several groups of soil microbial functional besides being able to provide nutrients, it is also able to produce plant growth regulators, and act as agents of biodegradation of chemical compounds.

In this study, the negative effects of pesticides are used more demonstrated by a group of bacteria phosphate solvent (PSB), the opposite of pesticides stimulates an increase in population groups of bacteria Azotobacter and Azospirillum. In general, higher functional microbial populations present in BPMC insecticide application of the herbicide paraquat.

CONCLUSIONS

Based on the results of research that has been done, it is concluded that there are fluctuations in functional microbial populations at different doses of pesticides and incubation time. Of the six groups studied microbes, pesticides significantly affect populations of Azospirillum, Azotobacter and fungi significantly phosphate solvent, but does not affect the population of PSB, cellulolytic bacteria and fungi cellulolitic. The incubation time significantly affect all functional microbial populations studied. Both pesticides are used only negatively affects bacterial populations phosphate solvent, paraquat negative effect on the population of Azotobacter and Azospirillum, and BPMC only negatively affect the fungi populations phosphate solvent. However, the negative effect is especially true on day 1 and day 7, then some degree of recovery in the incubation period is longer. Cellulolytic microbe is a microbe groups most affected by the pesticides used. Although there are negative effects of paraquat early in the incubation period, the two pesticides significantly increase Azospirillum population.

REFERENCES

1. Busse MD, Ratcliff AW, Shestak CJ, Power RF. 2001. Glyphosate toxicity and effect of long-term vegetation control on soil microbial communities. *Soil Biol. Biochem.* 33: 1777-1789.
2. Bhuyan S, Sreedharan B, Adhya TK, Sethunathan N. 1993. Enhanced biodegradation of γ-hexachlorocyclohexane (γ- HCH) in HCH (commercial) acclimatized flooded soil: factors affecting its development and persistence. *Pest. Sci.* 38: 49–55.
3. Cycon M, Seget ZP. 2007. Effect of selected pesticide on soil microflora involved in organic matter and nitrogen transformation: pot experiment. *Pol. J. Ecol.* : 207.
4. Fliessbach A, Mader P. 2004. Short and long-term effects on soil microorganisms of two potato pesticide spraying sequences with either glufosinate as defoliants. *Biol. Fertil. Soils* 40:268–276.
5. Handayanto E, Hairiah K. 2007. Biologi tanah: Landasan Pengelolaan Tanah Sehat. Malang: Pustaka Adipura.
6. Hussain S, Tariq S, Muhammad S, Muhammad A, Azeem K. 2009. Impact of pesticides on soil microbial diversity, enzymes, and biochemical reactions. *Elsivier* 102: 163.
7. Johansen K, Jacobsen CS, Torsvik V. 2001. Pesticide effect on bacterial diversity in agricultural soil. *Biol. Ferti. Soil.* 33: 443-453.
8. Niewiadomska A. 2004. Effect of carbendazim,imazeta pirand thiramon nitrogenase activity, the number of microorganisms in soil and yield of red clover (*Trifolium pretense* L). *Pol. J. Environ* 13, 403–410.
9. Noor M. 2001. Pertanian Lahan Gambut: Potensi dan Kendala. Jakarta (ID): Penerbit Kanisius.
10. Rache KD, Coats J. 1998. Comparative biodegradation of organophosphorus insecticides in soil. Specificity of enhanced microbial biodegradation. *J. Agric. Food Chem.* 36: 193–199.

11. Rahayuningsih E. 2009. Analisis Kuantiatif Perilaku Pestisida di Tanah. Yogyakarta: Universitas Gadjah Mada.
12. Rao S. 1994. Mikroorganisme Tanah dan Pertumbuhan Tanaman. Jakarta (ID): UI-Press.
13. Roger PA, Simpson I, Oficial R, Ardales S, Jimenez R. 1994. Effect of pesticides on soil and water microflora and mesofauna in wetland ricefields: a summary of current knowledge and extrapolation to temperate environments. *Australian J. Of Experimental Agric*. 34: 1057-1068.
14. Zimdhal RL. 1993. Fundamental of Weed Science. Sandiego (NY): Academia Press.

Abstract No: A-088

STUDY OF PEAT SOIL MICROBIAL COMMUNITIES OF LOAGAN BUNUT NATIONAL PARK

Barbara Ngikoh*, Hii Mei Mei, Ng Lee Tze

Sarawak Biodiversity Centre, Malaysia

Corresponding author email address: nbarbara@sbc.org.my

SUMMARY

Loagan Bunut National Park (LBNP) features a unique ecosystem which is covered by variety of forests including peat swamp forest. Tropical peat swamp forest is an important ecosystem for its role in carbon cycle but increasingly has become an endangered ecosystem. The study on diversity of tropical microbial in this ecosystem is limited, and none has reported on population of microbial communities in LBNP. In this study, metagenomic approach was used to study the microbial communities in the peat soil samples collected from LBNP. DNA from peat soil was extracted and 16S and 18S rRNA regions were amplified and cloned to produce a library of 100 colonies for each region. 16S sequences results showed that bacterial clone library consisted of a wide diversity of bacteria with *Prosthecobacter* species as major group (14%). *Prosthecobacter* has been known to be involved in carbohydrate degradation. As for the fungi community, 18S sequences result showed that 64.4% of the clones represented various uncultured fungi species, suggesting that there is a potential to discover new fungal species. A total of 15 fungal species with various biological roles has been identified. This study provides an insight to biodiversity of microbial communities and their possible roles in tropical peat soil of LBNP.

***Keywords**: soil microbial community, ribosomal RNA gene, peat soil*

INTRODUCTION

Tropical peat swamp forests, found mostly in Southeast Asia, are created from prolonged accumulation of plant organic matter (Kanokratana *et al.*, 2011). Tropical peat soils have a low level of nutrients and receive an input of rainwater, dust, and marine aerosol (Yule, 2010). The peat soils are characterized by high content of tannins, low oxygen and pH levels (Anderson 1983). Degradation of plant biomass in peat swamp is slow as the acidity of the soil and anaerobic condition of peat soils lowering the microbial activity (Kamal & Varma, 2008, Kanokratana *et al.*, 2010).

As one of the largest carbon reservoirs in the region, peat swamp forests play a major part in carbon cycle. Nevertheless, the size of the forests has shrunk over the years as a result of logging, fire, drainage, and conversion to agricultural land (Rose *et al.*, 2011). Further changes to peat swamp forests will affect indigenous microbial composition, reflecting the changes on nutrient cycling (Yule, 2008). A few studies have been published on the microbial diversity in tropical peat soil (Jackson *et al.*, 2009, Kanokratana *et al.*, 2011, Voglmayr & Yule 2006). However, there has yet to be a study on microbial diversity in Loagan Bunut National Park (LBNP), a tropical peat swamp forest in Sarawak. LBNP features a unique ecosystem that encompasses a variety of forests, including pristine peat swamp forests, and is thus ideally suited for this study.

A culture-independent or metagenomic approaches have been used to study microbial community structure and functions of microbial assemblages in a defined ecosystem (Harnpicharnchai *et al.*, 2007). A metagenome is defined as a collection of genomes combined for all community members in a defined environment (Rajendhran & Gunasekaran, 2008). In this study, microbial community from peat soils were analysed using a metagenomic approach via 16S and 18S rRNA gene clone libraries. The information from this LBNP metagenomic study can be used to identify microbial communities, and to relate their roles in tropical peat soils. This study would also be useful to the rehabilitation process of disturbed peat swamp forest.

METHODS

Sample collection and processing

Soil samples were collected from the top-soil forest floor during the rainy season (May 2014). Four replicate samples of peat soil were sampled, and the soil was eventually mixed together to form one homogenous sample. Vegetative debris were removed manually. The soil was stored in a zip lock bags and kept in an ice box for shipping.

Metagenome extraction

Metagenome DNA was extracted from peat soil samples as described by Griffiths et al. (2000). The concentration and quality of the DNA were determined using a NanoVue UV/Visible Spectrophotometer (GE Healthcare). The extracted DNA was used as the template for the polymerase chain reaction (PCR) amplification of partial rRNA genes.

DNA amplification

Amplification of rRNA genes was performed on the 16s rRNA region for bacteria and the 18S rRNA region for fungi. A serial dilution was performed on the metagenome template to accommodate amplification of samples diluted 10 to 100 times. The primers for amplification are listed in Table 1. PCR reactions were performed for 30 cycles where annealing temperature was set at 52°C. Amplicons were analysed from the agarose gel (1% w/v).

Table 1: PCR primers for amplification

Region of Amplification	Primer	Sequence
16s region	SRR181 (Forward)	5'-GTTTGATCCTGGCTCAGGAC
	SRR182 (Reverse)	5'- CAGATATCDKGAGGAACACC
18S region	ITS 4 (Forward)	5'-TCCTCCGCTTATTGATATG
	ITS 5 (Reverse)	5'-GGAAGTAAAAGTCGTAACAAGG

16S and 18S library construction

The amplicon for each rDNA was excised from the agarose gels and purified using the GFX PCR DNA and Gel Band Purification Kit (GE Healthcare, UK). The purified amplicon was ligated to a cloning vector TOPO® (Invitrogen, USA) and propagated in *Escherichia coli* DH10B. The *E. coli* transformants were screened on Luria-Bertani agar supplemented with Ampicillin. The transformant colonies were later screened for rDNA inserts by PCR using universal M13 primers. A total of 100 positive clones, each for the16S and 18S rDNA regions, were randomly selected to generate the 16S and 18S library, respectively.

Library sequencing

The insert of each clone was sequenced using M13 primers. BLAST search was performed on sequences obtained from the 16S library against the 16S ribosomal RNA sequence database while sequences obtained from the 18S library were searched against NCBI nucleotide collection database (GenBank BLAST) to identify closest related species.

RESULTS

The topmost surface layer was previously reported to be the most microbial populated sediment, and active in biomass degradation (Jackson *et al.* 2008). Soil was collected during wet season and at the time of sampling, its pH value was measured at pH3.4-pH4.8.

Metagenome DNA extraction

Metagenomic DNA was successfully isolated (Figure 1) although the purity obtained was low. The concentration of extracted metagenome DNA averaged at 90.3 ng/µL. The A_{260}/A_{280} ratio averaged at 1.22 while the A_{260}/A_{230} ratio averaged at 0.72. The low A_{260}/A_{280} ratio implies the presence of proteins while the low A_{260}/A_{230} ratio suggested contamination with humic acids, a known PCR inhibitor. Hence, a range of template DNA dilutions was required for PCR (Wang *et al.* 2012).

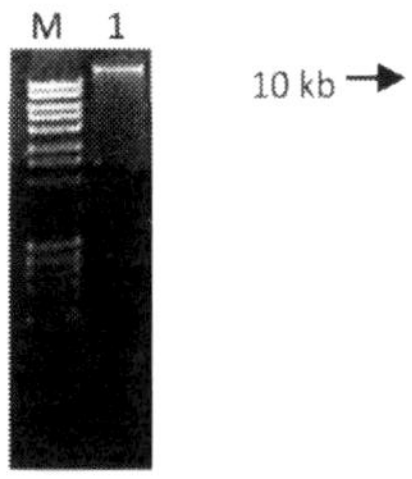

Figure 1: Agarose gel 1% (w/v) electrophoresis profile of extracted metagenome. M: MassRuler High Range DNA ladder. 1: Profile of extracted metagenome.

PCR amplification

PCR amplification yielded amplicons of the expected sizes; 700-800 bp for amplification of the 16S region (Figure 2A) and 500-600 bp for amplification of 18S region (Figure 2B). The PCR result demonstrates the necessity to dilute DNA templates in order to obtain successful amplification.

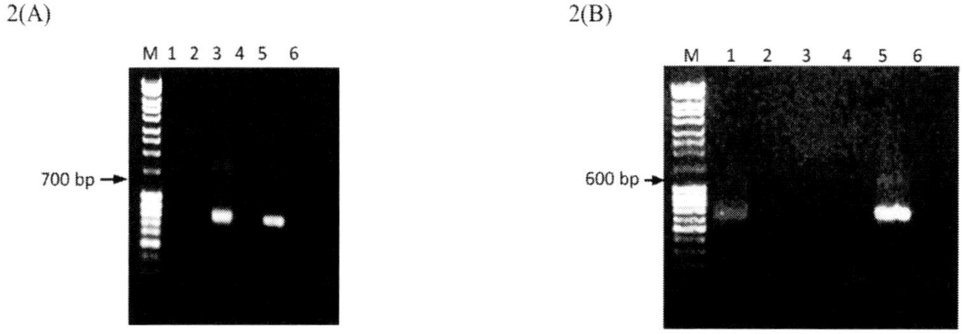

Figure 2: Agarose gel 1% (w/v) electrophoresis profile of partial rDNA amplification. (A) Amplification of 16S rDNA region. (B) Amplification of 18S rDNA region. The profiles show the amplification results using diluted metagenomic DNA 1: 10x diluted template, 2: 25x diluted template, 3: 50x diluted template, 4: 100x diluted template, 5: positive control, 6: negative control. M: MassRuler High Range DNA ladder.

Cloned library analysis

Bacterial diversity was determined from a total of 100 partial 16S sequences. The library was represented by 35 bacteria genera with representatives of *Prosthecobacter* spp. accounting for the majority of the library (14%). *Prosthecobacter,* which falls under the *Verrucomicrobia* phylum, is a freshwater micro-organism known for its involvement in carbohydrate degradation (Cardman *et al.* 2014). Further analysis revealed that the bacterial community comprised 4 bacterial lineages, *viz. Actinobacteria* (33.3%), *Proteobacteria* (33.3%), *Firmicutes* (21.4%) and *Verrucomicrobia* (11.9%). *Actinobacteria* particularly are generally known as soil inhabiting bacteria. In the library, *Proteobacteria* was dominated by *Geobacter* spp., a known anaerobe capable of Fe(III) reduction (Lipson *et al.* 2013).

With the 18S fungal clonal library, sequences were taxonomically assigned to 3 phyla groups, namely *Ascomycota* (41.67%), *Basidiomycota* (41.67%) and *Chytridiomycota* (16.67%), although 64.4% of the clones were represented by various uncultured and uncharacterized fungi species. From the identified clones, 15 species of fungi representing 12 genera with known functions such as cellulolytic fungi (*Trichoderma*), lignolytic fungi (*Phanerochate*), and plant pathogens (*Calonectria* and *Rhyzophydium*) were discovered. Some of the fungal species are also known as ectomycorrhizal fungi such as *Russula* sp. and *Scleroderma* sp.

DISCUSSION

Yule (2008) states that the bacteria community plays a vital role in the tropical peat ecosystem as it supports the aquatic food web *via* the recycling of dissolved organic carbon leached from the leaves. In turn, the composition and quantity of dissolved organic matter plays a major role in determining microbial communities (Mishra *et al.*, 2014). Additionally, microbial composition in peat land is largely affected by peat characteristics such as oxygen availability, land-use pattern, age of drainage, and peat thickness (Mishra *et al.*, 2014).

Two of the largest bacterial lineages from the library, Proteobacteria and *Actinobacteria* are important in denitrification (Palmer & Horn, 2012) and as nitrate reducers (Palmer *et al.*, 2012), respectively. As peat soils contains up to 30% nitrogen, nitrification and denitrification processes occur through utilisation of carbon as the energy source and nitrate as an electron receptor by bacteria which may contribute to nitrogen loss from soils (Koops *et al.*, 1997, Kamal & Varma 2008). Apart from acting as nitrate reducers, *Actinobacteria* are known to produce many biologically active secondary metabolites such as antibiotics, parasiticides, herbicides and pharmacologically active substances (Ohnishi *et al.*, 2008). Members of *Firmicutes* and *Verrucomicrobia* which appear to be ubiquitous in soil may play an important role in plant biomass degradation (Aislabie & Deslippe, 2013, Cardman *et al.*, 2014). Studies by Kanokratana *et al.*, (2011) and Jackson et al. (2009) show that *Acidobacteria* account for the majority of bacterial phyla found on tropical peat swamp soils because they are highly adaptable and metabolically flexible in acidic and low nutrient environments and fluctuating conditions of the soil. Interestingly, no member of the *Acidobacteria* phylum was represented in the present study. A possible explanation for this is that the 16S sequences that correspond to *Acidobacteria* were not numerically dominant or failed to amplify during PCR amplification. Apart from the latter observation, our findings are consistent with those of other published studies (Jackson *et al.*, 2009, Kanokratana *et al.*, 2011).

Many fungi isolated from peat soil are reported to exhibit broad enzymatic profiles, enabling them to degrade a myriad of structural or storage polymers of peat (Thormann, 2006). There are also fungi identified in this study that act as decomposer such as *Trichoderma* (polymer-degraders) and *Basidiomycota* (involved in degradation of complex polymers). *Chytridiomycota* are saprophytic fungi that can decompose complex plant and animal compounds such as chitin (Aislabie & Deslippe, 2013). Despite hosting a diverse collection of decomposer micro-flora, decomposition of organic matter and nutrient cycling processes in tropical peat soil occurs at a slow rate (Jackson *et al.* 2009). Fungi also play a major role in maintaining the peat ecosystem through symbiotic interaction with host plants (Aislabie & Deslippe, 2013). A few of the fungi identified from this study are ectomycorrhizal fungi which usually form an association with living plants and are involved in nutrient assimilation from the soil for the benefit of the host as well as protecting it against soil pathogens. More than half of the 18S library consisted of various uncultured fungi, suggesting a potential to discover new fungal species. Future studies could be done to tie their biological functions with peat soil ecosystem processes via molecular approaches.

CONCLUSION

Tropical peatland soil is an important and unique ecosystem as it not only plays a major role in nutrient cycling of carbon, nitrogen, and other chemical elements, but it also harbours a diversity of fungi and bacterial species. These microbes, as demonstrated by their functions, evidently contribute towards maintaining the ecology of tropical peat soils.

ACKNOWLEDGEMENTS

We would like to thank Sarawak Biodiversity Centre for their assistance in this project and Sarawak State Government for financing the project.

REFERENCES

1. Aislabie, J. & Deslippe, J.R. 2013. Soil microbes and their contribution to soil services. In Dymond, J.R. (ed) *Ecosystem services in New Zealand – conditions and trends*. Manaaki Whenua Press, Lincoln, New Zealand. 143-161.
2. Anderson JAR, 1983. The tropical peat swamps of western Malesia. In: Gore AJP (ed), *Ecosystems of the World 4B*, Mires: Swamp, Bog, Fen and Moore. Regional Studies. Elsevier, Amsterdam, pp. 181–199.
3. Cardman, Z., Arnosti, C., Ziervogel, K., Cox, C., Steen, A.D. & Teske, A. 2014. *Verrucomicrobia* are candidates for polysaccharide-degrading bacterioplankton in an arctic fjord of Svalbard. *Applied Environmental Microbiology*. 80(12): 3749-3756.
4. Griffiths, R., Whitely, A.S., O'Donnell, A.G. & Bailey, M.J. 2000. Rapid method for coextraction of DNA and RNA from natural environments for analysis of ribosomal DNA- and RNA-based microbial community composition. Applied and Environmental Microbiology 66(12):5488-5491.

5. Harnpicharnchai, P., Thongaram, Sriprang, R., Champreda, V., Tanapongpipat, S. & Eurwilaichitr. 2007. An efficient purification and fractionation of genomic DNA from soil by modified troughing method. *Letters in Applied Microbiology*. 45: 387-391.
6. Jackson, C.R., Liew, K.C. & Yule, C.M. 2008. Structural and functional changes with depth in microbial communities in a tropical Malaysian peat swamp forest. *Microbial Ecology* 57:402-412.
7. Jacobs M, 1988. The Tropical Rain Forest: a First Encounter. Springer, Berlin.
8. Kamal, S. & Varma, A. 2008. Peat Microbiology in Microbiology of Extreme Soils in Dion, P. & Nautiyal, C.S. (ed). *Soils Biology*. Springer-Verlag Berlin Heidelberg. 13:177-203.
9. Kanokratana, P., Uengwetwanit, T., Rattanachomsri, U., Bunterngsook, B., Nimchua, T., Tangphatsornruang, S., Plengvidhya, V., Champreda, V. & Eurwilaichir, L. 2011. Insights into the phylogeny and metabolic potential of a primary tropical peat swamp forest microbial community by metagenomic analysis. *Microbial Ecology*. 61:518-528.
10. Koops, J.G., van Beusichem, M.L. & Oenema, O. 1997. Nitrogen loss from grassland on peat soils through nitrous oxide production. *Plant Soil* 188:119-130.
11. Lipson, D.A., Haggerty, J.M., Srivinas, A., Raab, T.K., Sathe, S. & Dinsdale, E.A. 2013. Metagenomic insights into anaerobic metabolism along an arctic peat soil profile. *Metagenomic Analysis of Arctic Peat Soil*. 8(5).
12. Mishra, S., Lee, W.A., Hooijer, A., Reuben, S., Sudiana, I.M., Idris, A. & Swarup, S. 2014. Microbial and metabolic profiling reveal strong influence of water table and land-use patterns on classification of degraded tropical peatlands. *Biogeosciences* 11:1727-1741.
13. Palmer, K., Biasi, C. & Horn, M.A. 2012. Contrasting denitrifier communities relate to contrasting N2O emission patterns from acidic peat soils in arctic tundra. *International Society for Microbial Ecology*. 6:1058-1077.
14. Palmer, K. & Horn, M.A. 2012. Actinobacterial nitrate reducers and proteobacterial denitrifiers are abundant in N2O-metabolizing palsa peat. *Applied Environmental Microbiology*. 78(16): 5584-5596.
15. Posa, M.R.C., Wijedasa, L.S. & Corlett, R.T. 2011. Biodiversity and conservation of tropical peat swamp forests. *BioScience* 61(1):49-57.
16. Rajendhran, J. & Gunasekaran, P. 2008. Strategies for accessing soil metagenome for desired applications. *Biotechnology Advances* 26:576-590.
17. Thormann, M.N. 2006. Diversity and function of fungi in peatlands: a carbon cycling perspective. Canadian *Journal of Soil Science*. 86: 281-293.
18. Voglmayr, H. & Yule, C.M. 2006. *Polyancora globosa* gen. sp. Nov., an aeroaquatic fungus from Malaysian peat swamp forests. *Mycological Research* 110: 1142-1252.
19. Wang, Y., Hayatsu, M. & Fujii, T. 2012. Extraction of bacterial RNA from soil: challenges and solutions. *Microbes and Environments*. 27(2):111-121.
20. Yule, C.M. 2010. Loss of biodiversity and ecosystem functioning in Indo-Malayan peat swamp forests. *Biodiversity and Conservation*. 19:393-409.

1.6: CONSERVATION OF PEATLAND FOREST & WILDLIFE

Abstract No: A-214

ALLOMETRIC RELATIONS OF THE TREES IN THE TROPICAL PEAT SWAMP FORESTS OF SARAWAK: INFLUENCE OF HOLLOW STEMS ON TREE BIOMASS

Yukako Monda[1], Yoshiyuki Kiyono[2], Lulie Melling[3], Christopher Damian[3] and Auldry Chaddy[3]

[1]*Graduate school of Agriculture, Kyoto University, Japan*
[2]*Forestry and Forest Products Research Institute, Japan*
[3]*Tropical Peat Research Laboratory Unit. Sarawak, Malaysia*

**Corresponding author: monda.tungalag@gmail.com*

SUMMARY

To accurately estimate forest biomass, it is preferable to develop allometric equations specific to each forest type. As predictions outside the range of tree sizes used to develop the allometries may be inaccurate it is important to cover the whole tree size class of a target forest when developing allometric equations. *Shorea albida* is dominant or co-dominant in the peat swamp forests of Sarawak, Malaysia. Most large *S. albida* have hollows in their stems. In our previous study, destructive sampling was done to determine both aboveground biomass (AGB) and belowground biomass (BGB) and the sizes of these hollows for trees in a logged peat swamp forest in Sarawak, and we developed allometric equations considering the influence of hollow trees. To assess the importance of allometric equations specific to the tropical peat swamp forests in Sarawak, we compared biomass based on our allometric relations with biomass based on allometries for lowland dipterocarp forests in East Kalimantan and Pasoh, which did not account for hollow trees. In comparison with the estimated tree height (*H*) on lowland dipterocarp forests, Sarawak peat swamp forest trees with diameter at breast height (*DBH*) > 100 cm attained 91%. When we compared the *DBH*–biomass relationships, both AGB and BGB using the Sarawak allometries were significantly lower than those obtained using the lowland dipterocarp allometries. We therefore recommend using the Sarawak allometric equations for biomass estimates in tropical peat swamp forests.

Keywords: *Aboveground biomass, below ground biomass, Allometric equations, Biomass estimation*

INTRODUCTION

To accurately estimate forest biomass, it is preferable to develop allometric equations specific to each forest type. *Shorea albida* is a dominant or co-dominant species in the peat swamp forests of Sarawak (Anderson 1961, Whitmore 1975). Most large *S. albida* have hollows in their stems (Anderson 1961, 1972) that contain no biomass. Therefore, biomass is overestimated when the hollows are not taken into account.

Several sets of allometric equations have been developed to estimate aboveground biomass (AGB) and belowground biomass (BGB) in tropical lowland dipterocarp forests (e.g., AGB, Yamakura *et al.*, 1986; BGB, Niiyama *et al.*, 2010). However, in these previous studies, hollow trees were not considered in model development. In our previous study, we performed destructive sampling for both AGB and BGB and determined the sizes of the hollow regions in trees in a logged over peat swamp forest in Sarawak, and we developed allometric equations that accounted for the influence of the hollows (Monda *et al.*, 2015). To assess the importance of developing allometric equations specific to the tropical peat swamp forests in Sarawak, we compared allometric relationships between Sarawak peat swamp forest and lowland dipterocarp forests from East Kalimantan and Pasoh.

METHODS

Information on the tree form was obtained from the tree size dataset of Monda *et al.* (2015). This study was conducted in Maludam National Park, in a logged over peat swamp forest in the Betong division of Sarawak, Malaysia (01° 25.846′ N, 111° 07.754′ E). This dataset includes data on the diameter at breast height (*DBH*), tree height (*H*), stem biomass, branch biomass, leaf biomass, and BGB in the logged over forest. Tree size data (DBH and H; $n = 81$) from Maludam National Park and the logged over forest were also used for tree size analysis.

The tree sizes in this study were compared with those in two previously published tree size datasets: the data of Yamakura *et al.* (1986) and Niiyama *et al.* (2010) for tropical lowland dipterocarp forests growing on mineral soil. The dataset of Yamakura *et al.* (1986) contained *DBH*, *H*, stem biomass, branch biomass, and leaf biomass values and was obtained from a tropical lowland dipterocarp forest in East Kalimantan, Indonesia (LDF_{Kal}).

The dataset of Niiyama *et al.* (2010) contained *DBH*, *H*, BGB values and was obtained from a tropical lowland dipterocarp forest in the Pasoh Forest Reserve (LDF_{Pasoh}: Malay Peninsula, Malaysia). Neither dataset contained data for hollow trees. We retained only data for trees with DBH > 5 cm in our analysis.

Tree height was compared between measured data in the peat swamp forest and estimates using the LDF_{Kal} and LDF_{Pasoh} models. For this comparison, the Sarawak *H* data was used in the calculation, as described below. We defined *DBH* classes at 5-cm intervals to a maximum of 29 cm in *DBH*, then at 10-cm intervals thereafter. We defined the maximum tree height (H_{max}) in each DBH class as the average *H* of the three tallest trees in each *DBH* class. We defined the H_{max} ratio for each *DBH* class as the ratio of the tropical peat swamp forest's H_{max} to that estimated based on the *H* data from the tropical lowland dipterocarp forests for trees in the same *DBH* class.

Allometric analysis was also used to describe the differences in the *DBH*–biomass relationships for each forest. Logarithmically transformed values (to obtain a normal distribution) of stem biomass, branch biomass, and leaf biomass were regressed against *DBH*. The effects of forest type on tree size and biomass were analyzed using analysis of covariance (ANCOVA), with *DBH* as the covariate. All data was analyzed using version 3.0.2 of the R software for Windows (available at http://cran.r-project.org/bin/windows/base/old/3.0.2/)

RESULTS

In comparison with the H estimated by LDF_{Kal} and LDF_{Pasoh} models, the H_{max} ratio for the peat swamp forest averaged 99 ± 33% across all *DBH* classes (Figure 1). The mean H_{max} ratio for trees with *DBH* > 100 cm was 91 ± 16% (LDF_{Kal}, 82 ± 12%; LDF_{Pasoh}, 100 ± 15%). At smaller tree sizes (*DBH* 20 to 30 cm) in the tropical peat swamp forest, the mean H_{max} ratio was higher than lowland dipterocarp forests. However, the mean H_{max} ratio for trees with *DBH* > 40 cm was 84 ± 15% (LDF_{Kal}, 76 ± 11%; LDF_{Pasoh}, 92 ± 14%).

DBH–biomass relationships differed significantly between the tropical peat swamp forest and the lowland dipterocarp forests (Figure 2). For stem and branch biomass, the slopes of these relationships differed significantly between the two forest types, indicating that large trees in the tropical peat swamp forest had smaller biomass than trees of comparable size in LDF_{Kal} (Figure 2a,b; $p<0.001$ for stems, $p<0.05$ for branches). For leaf biomass, the intercept differed significantly between the two forest types, with a larger value for tropical peat swamp forest than for LDF_{Kal} (Figure 2c, $p<0.01$). For BGB, the intercept differed significantly between the forest types, with a smaller value for the tropical peat swamp forest than for LDF_{Pasoh} (Figure 2d, $p<0.01$).

DISCUSSION

The trees in the peat swamp forests attained nearly the same size as trees in the lowland dipterocarp forests that grew on mineral soil (Figure 1). The wood density of *S. albida*, which dominates the canopy layer in the Sarawak peat swamp forest, was close to 0.6 based on the air-dry specific gravity at a 15% water content (Tropical Agriculture Research Center 1977) and Suzuki's (1999) equation. These facts lead to misunderstanding that these trees would have high biomass in their woody parts. However, these woody parts in the peat swamp forest had significantly lower biomass than trees of an equivalent size in the lowland dipterocarp forest, especially for the largest trees (Figure 2 a,b,d). The decreased biomass in the largest trees was caused by frequent and large hollow in the stems (Monda *et al.*, 2015). Branch biomass in the peat swamp forest may also have been affected by wind damage to the crowns (Anderson 1961, 1972; Whitmore 1975). BGB may have been affected both by hollow in the stump and by the shallow root system that develops in a peat soil. These factors suggest that the allometric relations for all tree parts differed significantly between peat swamp forest and the lowland dipterocarp forests, and that using the models developed for lowland dipterocarp forests to predict biomass in the peat swamps would create significant errors.

CONCLUSION

Because of the large differences between the allometries for the two forest types, we recommend that researchers and managers who work in peat swamp forests use the allometric equations developed specifically for the tropical peat swamp forests in Sarawak. Our dataset of measured biomasses and sizes of the hollow regions obtained through destructive sampling will provide valuable data for future studies of trees in tropical peat swamps.

ACKNOWLEDGEMENTS

We wish to thank Mr. Johnny Kon and Mr. Leong Fad Weng of the Sarawak Timber Association (STA) for species identification, Mr. Frankie Tieh for incisive comments and useful advice, and Mr. Mathew Parie and Mr. Lo Kim San and the people in Sarawak who had cooperated with us in the field. This research was conducted as part of the research project (Emergency Project to Develop the Structure of Promoting REDD Action) funded by the Forestry Agency, Japan, and the research program (A-0802) supported by the Global Environment Fund of the

Ministry of the Environment, Japan.

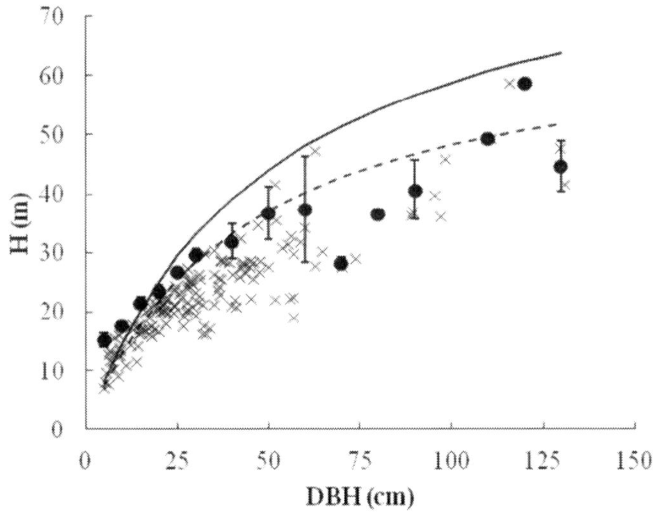

Figure 1: Comparison between trees in the Sarawak tropical peat swamp forest and trees in the lowland dipterocarp forests for the DBH–H relationship. Circles and vertical lines represent the maximum tree height (H_{max}) and SD in each DBH class in the tropical peat swamp forests of Sarawak; crosses represent trees from the Sarawak dataset. Solid and broken lines represent estimates of H based on the East Kalimantan and Pasoh models, respectively.

REFERENCES

1. Anderson JAR. 1961. The ecological and forest types of the peat swamp forests of Sarawak and Brunei in relation to their silviculture. PhD Dissertation, Edinburgh University.
2. Anderson JAR. 1972. Trees of peat swamp forests of Sarawak. Forest Department, Sarawak, Malaysia.
3. Monda, Y., Kiyono, Y., Melling, L., Damian, C. & Chaddy, A. (2015) Allometric equations considering the influence of hollow trees: A case study for tropical peat swamp forest in Sarawak. *Tropics*, 24(1), 11-22.
4. Niiyama K, Kajimoto T, Matsuura Y, Yamashita T, Matsuo N, Yashiro Y, Ripin A, Kassim AR, Noor NS. 2010. Estimation of root biomass based on excavation of individual root systems in a primary dipterocarp forest in Pasoh Forest Reserve, Peninsular Malaysia. *Journal of Tropical Ecology* 26: 271–284.
5. Suzuki E. 1999. Diversity in specific gravity and water content of wood among Bornean tropical rainforest trees. *Ecological Research* 14: 211–224.
6. Tropical Agriculture Research Center 1977. Tropical timber trees [Nettai no yūyō jyushu]. The Tropical Forestry Association of Japan. Japan, Tokyo. (in Japanese)
7. Whitmore TC. 1975. Tropical rain forests of the Far East. Oxford University Press, London, UK.
8. Yamakura T, Hagiwara A, Sukardjo S, Ogawa H. 1986. Aboveground biomass of tropical rain forest stands in Indonesian Borneo. *Vegetatio* 68: 71–82.

Figure 2: Comparison between trees in the Sarawak tropical peat swamp forest and those in the lowland dipterocarp forests based on allometric relationships between *DBH* and the biomass of (a) stems, (b) branches, (c) leaves, and (d) belowground biomass (BGB). Data sources: Circles, peat swamp forests in Sarawak; squares, lowland dipterocarp forest in East Kalimantan; triangles, lowland dipterocarp forest in Pasoh. Solid and broken lines indicate relationships for peat swamp and lowland dipterocarp forests, respectively; *p* indicates the significant parameter based on ANCOVA.

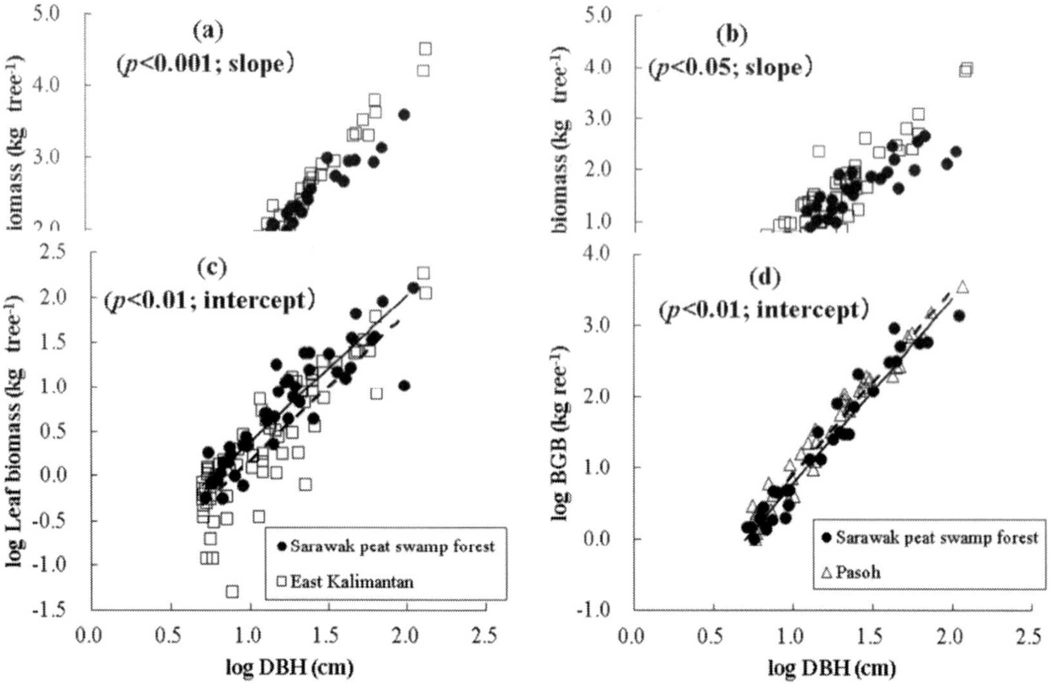

Abstract No: A-340

BIODIVERSITY AND ITS DISTRIBUTION, KAMPAR PENINSULAR, RIAU PROVINCE INDONESIA

Petrus Gunarso* and Anthony Greer

[1] *APRIL Group*

* *Corresponding author: petrus_gunarso@aprilasia.com*

Kampar Peninsular is a unique ecosystem with a unique biodiversity distribution. Although the peninsular was categorized as production forest in the eighties, the core Kampar Peninsular is considered the least degraded in the region. The role of industrial forest plantations in the peninsula and the peat depth that characterized the peat dome areas discouraged massive logging operations in the area. Although extensive canals have been developed for small scale illegal logging operation, the remoteness and intensive efforts to stop illegal practices has shown positive results. Under the moratorium status of the area, a large tract of peat dome in the peninsular is now designated as ecosystem restoration concession. Biodiversity assessment has been conducted in collaboration with our partner Fauna and Flora International and included the installation of extensive camera traps across the landscape. Biodiversity richness in this lightly degraded area is significant, and its potential for finding new species remains high. So far, five species of native cat are found in this landscape. Large mammal species such as tiger, Sun Bear, and bearded pigs are found in the area. Given this mammal distribution and the presence of the region's top predator, biodiversity distribution in the whole Kampar Peninsular appears to be potentially normal and its conservation status most likely more significant than the neighbouring designated conservation areas.

Keywords: -

Abstract No: A-186

BIRDS IN PEAT SWAMP FOREST OF THE MALUDAM NATIONAL PARK, SARAWAK

Bettycopa Amit[1*], Andrew Alek Tuen[2], Khalid Haron[1] and Mohd Haniff Harun[1]

[1]*Malaysian Palm Oil Board, Selangor, Malaysia*
[2]*University of Malaysia, Sarawak, Malaysia*

**Corresponding author: bettycopa@mpob.gov.my*

SUMMARY

The birds of tropical peat swamp forest have not been well documented in Sarawak, Malaysia. This study presents the list of birds at the Maludam National Park tropical peat swamp forest, based on observation and mist-netting methods. The surveys recorded a total of 121 bird species belong to 36 families. Although the peat swamp forest (PSF) was more depauperate than dipterocarp forest, it is still an important habitat associated with nutrient-poor forest species such as Hook-billed Bulbul (*Setornis criniger*) and Grey-breasted Babbler (*Malacopteron albogulare*). This study also recorded a high-profile of endangered species such as Great Slaty Woodpecker (*Mulleripicus pulverlentus*), Large Green Pigeon (*Treron capellei*) and Lesser Adjutant (*Leptoptilos javanicus*). Evidently, there was a diverse species of birds including some protected bird species at the Maludam National Park tropical peat swamp forest. The presence of these diverse bird species shows the importance of protection and conservation of tropical peat swamp forest for future generation.

Keywords: *Maludam National Park, Sarawak, Borneo, protected bird species, tropical peat swamp forest*

INTRODUCTION

The tropical peat swamp forests in Sarawak, Malaysia are important habitats for endemic and protected species of flora and fauna (Phillips, 1998; Page *et al.*, 1999; Yule, 2010). Peat land is characterized as water-logged, with low nutrients and dissolved oxygen levels in acidic water. It is therefore a unique habitat for fauna and flora. Even though species diversity is lower than that of the lowland dipterocarp forest (Gaither, 1994; Myers, 2009), it can still have a high number of endemic species. Tropical peat swamp forest differ from north temperate and boreal peat lands which is dominated by *Sphagum* spp. grasses, shrubs and sedges, while tropical peat swamp forests have trees that can grow up to over 70 m and a spongy layer of peat substrate that can accumulate up to 20 m deep or more (Yule, 2010).

Birds make up an integral component of the fauna diversity in the tropical peat swamp forests. They perform various important ecological functions, such as pollination, seed dispersal and pest control as part of their food chain (Şekercioğlu *et al.*, 2004). The top bird predators and some rare endemic bird species are protected by law. Out of 673 species of birds recorded in Borneo, a total of 59 are endemic to the island (Phillipps and Phillipps, 2004. Many of these bird species cannot adapt to any disturbances to their habitats, especially by anthropogenic activities such as logging or agriculture. Conserving the tropical peat swamp forests is vital for the survival of these bird species. Forest birds have been suggested as indicator species because they are particularly sensitive to changes in their habitat conditions. They are entirely dependent on the forest and highly sensitive to habitat disturbance that may affect their survival (Zakaria *et al.*, 2005).

The largest protected peat swamp forest in Sarawak was Maludam National Park with 43, 147 ha. This park is one of the parks in Sarawak that is made up of entirely peat swamps. A study on bird by Beintema and Sim (2004) showed that 166 species of birds were found in Maludam National Park, adding to an earlier report by Bennett (1994) of 22 species. Hence, the objective of this paper is to document the bird species at the Maludam National Park tropical peat swamp forest.

METHODS

The study site is at Maludam National Park tropical peat swamp forest that is situated on the Maludam Peninsula, southeastern of Sarawak, Malaysia. The survey of birds was conducted from August 2010 until November 2014. A transect line of about 500 meters is walked for bird observational survey using binoculars and vocalization. All the birds seen or heard along the transect line are recorded and field guides are then used to aid in

identifying the birds (Smythies, 1999; MacKinnon and Phillipps, 1993; Myers, 2009).
A mist-netting method using fifteen mist-nets (9 m x 2.5 m, 36 mm mesh-size with three shelves) is used to sample the birds. These nets were set up at least 0.5 – 3 m above the ground to catch ground and understory dwellers. The nets are operated for 12 hours and checked regularly at two-hour intervals for three days. Captured birds are gently removed and place separately in cloth bags. The captured birds are identified to species level according to Phillipps and Phillipps (2014) at the camp site and processed immediately to reduce stress before their released.

RESULTS

A total of 121 bird species belonging to 36 families from the surveys (mist-netting method: 585 birds from 51 species; observation method: 1,125 birds from 114 species) were recorded at Maludam National Park tropical peat swamp forest. This represents approximately 18% of the total birds known in Borneo. Some bird species of particular interest recorded in this study, include four globally endangered birds, 25 near threatened species as well as two peat swamp forest specialist [i.e. Hook-billed Bulbul (*Setornis criniger*) and Grey-breasted Babbler (*Malacopteron albogulare*)] and three Bornean endemics [*i.e.* Dusky Munia (*Lonchura fuscans*), Golden-naped Barbet (*Megalaima pulcherrim*), and Bornean Blue Flycatcher (*Cyornis superbus*)].
The family Timaliidae (babblers) was the most diversed at Maludam National Park with 12 species followed by Nectariniidae (Sunbirds and Spiderhunters) and Pycnonotidae (bulbuls) with 10 species each. The most dominant species was Hook-billed Bulbul (*Setornis criniger*) (5.96%) followed by Chestnut-rumped Babbler (*Stachyris maculate*) (5.26%) and Green Imperial Pigeon (*Treron capellei*) (3.21%). Anhingids is poorly represented with only a single species recorded.

DISCUSSION

This study recorded 121 species of Borneo's 398 resident bird species at the Maludam National Park tropical peat swamp forest, including three of the 59 Bornean endemics. This clearly shows that species richness was lower compared to other lowland sites (Cleary *et al.*, 2007; Edwards *et al.*, 2011). Rahman (2004) reported a total of 192 bird species at Maludam National Park by using data from surveys conducted by Bennett (1994) and, Beintema and Sim (2004). Good representation from the family Timaliidae (babblers) in peat swamp forest was similar to the finding by Posa and Marques (2012) and, Rahman and Tuen (2006). According to Zakaria *et al.* (2005) babbler species is well represented in primary forest rather than logged forest. Sporadic mist-netting study carried out by Rahman and Tuen (2006) in PSF adjacent to University of Malaysia Sarawak recorded a total of 68 species of birds where 15 species were protected species listed under Sarawak Wildlife Protection Ordinance (1998). Another study conducted in Logan Bunut National Park, Sarawak by Laman *et al.* (2006) captured 18 species of birds at the peat swamp habitat. Periodic bird surveys by Sheldon *et al.* (2014) in Klias Forest Reserve from 1998 to 2004 reported a total of 114 species of bird. The most dominant bird in Klias Forest Reserve was Yellow-vented Bulbul (*Pycnonotus goiavier*).

CONCLUSION

This study shows that PSFs hold a unique and high conservation value bird species, even though they were previously reported to have lower bird species diversity as compared to other forest types. It is an important habitat for the conservation of a number of globally endangered bird species to PSF and Bornean endemic birds. The current status of these bird species need to be monitored since they might be affected by anthropogenic activities. Further studies are still needed on factors or habitat requirements that could influence the existence of bird species in PSF and their trend over time.

ACKNOWLEDGEMENTS

The authors would like to thank the Director General of MPOB for permission to present this paper. Comments from the MPOB Peat Manuscript Review Committee were very much appreciated. Besides that, authors would like to thank UNIMAS for their invaluable assistance.

REFERENCES

1. Beintema A, Sim LK (2004) Bird list of August 2004, Maludam National Park. Unpublished report
2. Bennett EL (1994) Report on the survey of primates in the Maludam Area. Wildlife Conservation Society.
3. Cleary DFR, Boyle TJB, Setyawati T, Anggraeni CD, Van Loon EE, Menken SBJ (2007). *Birds species traits associated with logged and unlogged forest in Borneo*. Ecology Applied 17:1184-1197.
4. Edwards DP, Larsen TH, Docherty, TDS, Ansell FA, Hsu WW, Derhé MA, Hamer KC, Wilcove DS (2011)

Degraded lands worth protecting: the biological importance of Southeast Asia's repeatedly logged forests. Proceeding Royal Society Bulletin 278(1702:82-90.

5. Gaither JC (1994) *Undestorey avifauna of Bornean peat swamp forest: Is it depauperate?* Wilson Bulletin 106(2):381-390.
6. Laman, CJ, Gawin, DFA, Rahman, MA (2006) Quantifying the diversity of avifauna at Loagan Bunut National Park. In: Scientific Journey Through Borneo: Loagan Bunut. A.A. Tuen, A.K. Sayok, A.N. Toh and G.T. Noweg (Eds). Peat Swamp Forest Project, UNDP/GEF (MAL/99/G31), Sarawak Forest Department and Institute of Biodiversity and Environmental Conservation, Universiti Malaysia Sarawak. pp. 163-174.
7. MacKinnon J, Phillipps K. (1993) A *Field Guide to the Birds of Borneo Sumatra, Jawa and Bali.* Oxford University Press, Oxford.
8. Myers, S. (2009) *A field guide to the birds of Borneo.* Talisman Publishing Pte Ltd. Singapore.
9. Page SE, Rieley JO, Shotyk OW, Weiss D (1999) *Interdependence of peat and vegetation in a tropical peat swamp forest.* Philosophical Transactions of the Royal Society Biological Science 354:1885-1897.
10. Phillips VD (1998) *Peatswamp ecology and sustainable development in Borneo.* Biodiversity Conservation 7:651-671.
11. Posa MRC, Marques DA (2012) Peat *swamp forest birds of the Tuanan research station Central Kalimantan, Indonesia, with notes on habitat specialists.* Forktail 28:29-37.
12. Rahman, M.A. (2004). A study on fauna of Maludam National Park Betong Division Sarawak. Joint working group Malaysia-The Nertherlands: Development and Management of Maludam National Park Report.
13. Rahman, MA Tuen, AA (2006) The avifauna. In: F. Abang and I. Das (Eds.), The biodiversity of a peat swamp forest in Sarawak (pp. 129-136). Institute of Biodiversity and Environmental Conservation, Universiti Malaysia Sarawak, Kota Samarahan.
14. Sheldon, FH, Geoffrey D, Anna W, Moyle RG (2014) *Birds in peatswamp at Klias Forest Reseve and Environs, Sabah, Malaysian Borneo.* Paper of the Museum of Natural Science. Louisiana State University.
15. Şekercioğlu, ÇH, Daily, GC, Ehrlich, PR (2004) *Ecosystem consequences of bird declines.* www.Pnas.org/cgl/dol/10.1073/pnas.0408049101.
16. Smythies BE (1999) *The Birds of Borneo.* Fourth Edition (Revised by Davision GWH) The Sabah Society, Kota Kinabalu and Malayan Natural Society, Kuala Lumpur.
17. Yule C (2010) *Loss of biodiversity and ecosystem functioning in Indo-Malayan peat swamp forests.* Biodiversity Conservation 19:393-409.
18. Zakaria M, Puan CL, Yusuf ME (2005) *Comparison of species composition in three forest types: towards using bird as indicator of forest ecosystem health.* Journal of Biological Science 5(6):734-73.

Abstract No: A-439

EFFORTS TO CONSERVE *GONYSTYLUS BANCANUS* (RAMIN) IN THE PEAT SWAMP FORESTS OF GUNUNG MULU NATIONAL PARK

Aurelia Dulce Chung*, Mohizah Mohamad and Runi Sylvester Pungga

Research Development & Innovation Division,Forest Department Sarawak, Malaysia

**Corresponding author: aurelidc@sarawak.gov.my*

SUMMARY

The peat swamp forests (PSF) of Sarawak are part of a complex and unique forest ecosystem, both physically and in terms of their ecological relationships (with flora and fauna). The ability of the peat domes to store water and moderate water flow is important in stabilising local water levels (Lee, 2004). Peat domes also act as buffers between sea water and waters inland. Peat is made up of large quantities of organic matter and so plays an important role in global carbon balance. Environmentally, the PSF plays a very significant role in carbon storage, and it has been estimated that 25% of global carbon is stored in peat areas (Peter, 2003). PSF is not as diverse as the Mixed Dipterocarp Forest (Tan, 2004) but it also acts as an important reservoir of biodiversity, containing a large number of endemic tree species and several endangered animals. Ramin or scientifically known as *Gonystylus bancanus* (Miq.)Kurz, is a threatened species found in PSF and is listed as a protected plant in The Wild Life Protection Ordinance, 1998 and also in Appendix II CITES. A comprehensive study on Sustainable Management of Peat Swamp Forest with special reference to Ramin has been carried out in 2000-2003 following the formation of the Malaysian-The Netherlands Joint Working Group. Moving forward, we continue the effort to conserve Ramin in the PSF. A study on distribution and population of Ramin has been carried out in Gunung Mulu National Park. It is found to be growing on shallow and deep peats. The estimated population density of Ramin in this area was about 6 individuals (dbh> 10.0cm) per hectare. The purpose of this paper is to establish a basic data for population viability monitoring in the future and also to determine important information on the microhabitat characteristics. Besides conserving Ramin in its natural habitat, an effort to plant Ramin elsewhere has also been carried out. Seedlings of Ramin has been collected and planted for ex-situ conservation in Bukit Lima Nature Reserve.

***Keyword**: Peat Swamp Forest, Gonystylus bancanus, ramin, conservation*

INTRODUCTION

The introduction of this paper will concentrate on the general overview of Sarawak's peat swamp forest. The overview will cover on description of PSF, its function and the current challenges that this ecosystem is facing. Another aspect to cover inside the paper's introduction would be on the biodiversity of PSF and examples of endemic flora and fauna. Emphasize will be given to *Gonystylus bancanus* or locally known as ramin. "It is a species commonly found in PSF and is under threat due to habitat loss and timber over exploitation. Currently this species is listed as a protected plant in The Wild Life Protection Ordinance, 1998 and also in Appendix II CITES." The realisation of the importance of peat swamp forest as an important ecosystem (biological or economic) which need to be conserved by the locals and also governing bodies. For the freshwater swamp found in Medalam, Ulu Mentawai it is protected within the Gunung Mulu National Park and is seen to be pristine. It is also the preferred habitat for particular species of Ramin which is *Gonystylus bancanus*. (Miq) Kurz. The paper will discuss further more on the importance of ramin and challenges faced by ramin's and PSF in Sarawak. The paper also discuss on the previous research studies which has been done in Maludam National Park better known as "Sustainable Management of Peat Swamp Forest with special reference to Ramin has been carried out in 2000-2003 following the formation of the Malaysian-The Netherlands Joint Working Group."

To support previous works on conservation of ramin, a thorough study was previously done in2014 and 2015 to collect data information on ramin in Medalam which are used as baseline information and collection of ramin seedlings after fruiting season for ex-xitu conservation activities such as transplanting. The overall objective of this study is to improve *Gonystylus bancanus* (Ramin) resources through conservation.

METHODOLOGY

Locality

The baseline study was conducted at a small area located at Medalam of Ulu Mentawai situated within Gunung Mulu National Park. The area consists of about 3 types of forest which are riverine, heath (kerangas) and swamp forest. The freshwater swamp area is estimated to be about 100-150 ha.

Choosing a suitable site for *ex-situ* conservation of *G. bancanus* (ramin) plays an important role in ensuring the success of transplanting of this species outside its natural habitat. Ramin is a site specific species therefore the main criteria for the site for replanting that it must be a peat swamp forest. Generally, most PSF in Sarawak are either converted to agriculture land or logged over and are already in degraded form. Ex-situ conservation is best to be carried out in a protected area for example Bukit Lima Nature Reserve in Sibu.

Study Procedure

Frequent fieldworks were conducted at targeted area during 2014 and 2015 with the purpose of gathering data on the ground in terms of detailing the *Gonystylus bancanus* population and distribution characteristics within the Medalam, Ulu Mentawai freshwater swamp. Data was collected through research plot establishments. Study on *G. bancanus* phenology was also observed and recorded between period of 2 years and collection of its seedlings in the wild for future conservation purposes.

Trial planting is an experimental research to determine the adaptation of a tree species of site specificity to a different area with different environmental condition. This experiment will observe the growth and regeneration of the species a on a small piece of land outside of its original habitat. The area where trial planting applied are called plot. The trial therefore consists of several plots that together form the trial area. The established plots will also functions as a research plot for long-term study and observation.

Plot

Baselinewas established on the north-south orientation across the selected area within Bukit Lima as a reference point and starting point. The plot was established within the area of equal sizes as the soil fertility gradient of the area is not known. The size of the plot is 1 hectare with the shape of equal square sizes 100 m x 100 m where the fertility gradient is the same at both directions.

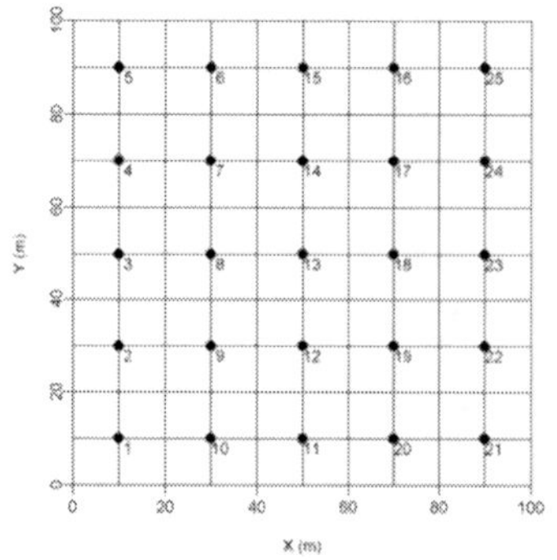

Figure 1: Layout of the ramin trial plot

Planting

Planting lines are to be aligned in east-west direction to allow planted ramin seedlings to obtain maximum exposure to sunlight. Seedlings will be planted at 5 m x 5 m intervals. At intervals of 5 by 5 along baseline temporary pegs marked the planting lines to be planted.

Recording of Information

Information on the ramin seedlings was collected to ensure effective propagation and rate of growth success for future reference, the following information should be collected during trail planting sampling (Adapted and modified from " A Manual of Enrichment Planting From Logged Over Forest In Peninsular Malaysia, 2006).

Maintenance and Monitoring

The frequency of maintenance and monitoring should be carried out about 4 (four) times a year during the first two years of planting. Followed by twice (2) a year for the next three (3) years of planting until the trees are five (5) years old. The activities included in maintenance are weeding and applying fertilisers. Monitoring and documenting the mortality and growth of the seedlings until becoming trees will be conducted in a yearly manner according to the standards of a research plot. The data will be recorded inside a field data sheets.

RESULT AND DISCUSSION

Documentation on the number of *G. bancanus* individuals are conducted through assessment of the species within each research plot established within the swamp. Successfully established total of 6 research plot each with the size of 1 hectare which was set up randomly within Medalam and ramin individuals with the diameter of ≥ 10 cm are enumerated and to date successfully recorded a total number of 39 trees. The largest ramin individual measures at 75 cm diameter at breast height (dbh) which was found at about 1600 m from the baseline.

Table 1: Diameter Size Class of ramin in Medalam

Size class	Plot 1	Plot 2	Plot 3	Plot 4	Plot 5	Plot 6	Total
10 cm ≤ dbh 30 cm	0	2	3	4	0	1	10
30 cm ≤ dbh 50 cm	2	4	6	8	0	0	20
≥ 50 cm	3	0	0	5	1	0	9
Subtotal							39

The fertility of the swamp is observed to be richer in nutrients on the outer rim of the swamp beginning from the 100 m until 200 m of the transect line and beginning to decrease in the middle. This can be observed with the number of ramin individuals on different distance as the species is commonly found on the rim of peat swamp forest and number of individuals decrease or absent in the middle.

A temporary nursery was set up at Mentawai Ranger Post for propagation and storage of ramin seeds and seedlings. During our phenology study, ramin mother tree seen flowering in March and April of 2016 and fruiting in July-August 2014. In October, plenty ramin seedlings were seen sprouting at Medalam swamp forest floor and were then collected sustainably in the wild and transported back to the Ranger Post to be propagated inside the nursery. We successfully transferred to and propagated 4500 m from Medalam freshwater swamp.

To ensure the long term longevity of *G. bancanus*, improvement of the population can be done with long term action plan through conservation activities. An example of this action plan is done through promotion of ex situ conservation. Ex situ is conservation of biological diversity outside of its natural habitat. Ex situ of this species can be achieved through trial planting.

Bukit Lima Nature Reserve, Sibu was chosen as a conservation area for *G. bancanus* mainly because the area matches the habitat specificity and is in need of rehabilitation due to previous degradation by forest fires in 2013. A one (1) hectare plot with the layout of 100 m × 100 m was established. Every quadrate of 5 m × 5 m is marked with a pole and at every point of the quadrate ramin seedlings are planted. There are a total of 400 ramin seedlings planted within the established plot in Bukit Lima. The planted ramin seedlings are tagged with individual numbers and recorded in field data sheet for growth and regeneration studies. Currently, the trial planting of this is still at preliminary level and the success rate still cannot be tabulated as the study was only carried out in November 2015.

The success of this conservation effort will only be long term with continuous monitoring and maintenance of the ramin seedlings within the area which include weeding and adding fertilizers during the first few months of its planting. Monitoring and maintenance should be done about four (4) times in a year during the first 2 years of planting followed by twice (2) a year during the 3rd to 5th year.

CONCLUSION

This project enables fragile species of *Gonystylus bancanus* (ramin) to be preserved with ex-situ conservation activities through trial planting in Bukit Lima Nature Reserve, Sibu. Conservation in this manner will allow advantages in longevity of this species for example a long term establishment of *G. bancanus* research/yield plots for future studies and references, ensuring a long term, sustainability and longevity of this species outside of its natural habitat and potentially serve as a source of future ramin seed bank that will able to provide viable germplasm for future use.

ACKNOWLEDGEMENT

We would like to express our gratitude and gratefulness for the funding provided by the Sarawak State Government through the State Development Fund Project P17 on the project "Conservation of Endangered Species: Ramin and Gaharu" since 2014 until 2015. We acknowledge the support of Sarawak Forest Department, Research Development and Innovation Division (RDID), District Forest Office Limbang and also contribution provided by

Heart of Borneo (HOB) Sarawaktowards this project. We express our gratitude to the community leader and local communities from Melaban Longhouse for their hospitality and services as field guides throughout our project. We are indebted to our Assistant Director of RDID, Section Head of Biodiversity Flora and the commitment and hard work of our research team from Botany and Ecology program.

REFERENCES

1. Chen, H.K. (2007). Implementing ramin's CITES listing. *ITTO Tropical Forest Update*. pp. 3
2. Hansen, P.K. (1997). *Field Trial Manual*: Principles, Planning and Implementation of Agricultural Field Trials: http://lad.nafri.org.la/fulltext/441-0.pdf
3. Hazebroek, H.P. &Abang Khasim, A.M., 2002. A Guide to Gunung Mulu National Park: A World Heritage Site in Sarawak, Malaysian Borneo. Natural History Publications (Borneo), pp. 75.
4. Khalil, A.H. *et al.* (2010). *Gonystylus bancanus*: Jewel of the peat swamp forest. Forest Research Institute Malaysia.pp 10http://www.itto.int/files/user/cites/malaysia/Gonystylus%20bancanus%20-%20jewel%20of%20the%20peat%20swamp%20forest.pdf
5. Sheikh Ibrahim, S.A. (2006). A Manual of Enrichment Planting In Logged Over Forests In Peninsular Malaysia, Malaysia-International Tropical Timber Organisation Joint Project PD 185/91 Rev.2 (F) – Phase II: Forestry Department Peninsular Malaysia, pp. 26-28
6. Sia, P. C. (2004). Growth and Yield of Logged-Over Peat Swamp Forests of Sarawak: Lee Ming Press Sdn Bhd, pp. 12.
7. Soepadmo, E., Saw, L. G., & Chung, R. C. K. (eds) (2004). *Tree flora of Sabah and Sarawak, Vol. 5.* Malaysia: Ampang Press Sdn Bhd, pp. 442-455.

Abstract No: A-450

GROUND-DWELLING MAMMALS AND BIRDS IN A PEAT SWAMP FOREST IN SUMATRA AND THE IMPACT OF INDUSTRIAL TREE PLANTATION

Hiromitsu Samejima[1, 2*], Motoko S. Fujita[2], Ahmad Muhammad[3], Jason Hon[4] and Gono Semiadi[5]

[1]*Institute for Global Environmental Strategies, Japan*
[2]*Center for Southeast Asian Studies, Kyoto University, Japan*
[3] *Riau University, Indonesia*
[4] *WWF Malaysia, Kuching, Sarawak, Malaysia*
[5]*Research Center for Biology, Indonesian Institute of Science, Cibinong, Indonesia*

**Corresponding author: samejima@iges.or.jp*

Peat swamp forests of Southeast Asia are considered one of the unique ecosystems in the region. They form a huge carbon stock and also are a refuge of rich biodiversity. To understand the faunal composition and the effect of land use changes, we investigated ground-dwelling mammals and birds using camera traps in a natural peat swamp forest and a planted *Acacia* forest in the Giam Siak Kecil–Bukit Batu Biosphere Reserve, Sumatra. We obtained a total of 1,856 images, comprising 23 species, including 11 vulnerable or endangered species. The species composition of faunal communities in the natural peat swamp forest was different from that of lowland/hill forests of Sumatra and Borneo. Just three species, namely wild boar (*Sus* sp.), lesser mouse-deer (*Tragulus* sp.), and southern pig-tailed macaque (*Macaca nemestrina*), dominated 75%–93% of all camera-trap images, indicating a predominance of species with diet preferences for fruit resources with lower edible herbaceous resources in the peat swamp forest. Faunal diversity was low in the planted *Acacia* forest. The range of mean trapping rates of all animals and species richness in each plot ranged from 9.68–49.68 (mean: 22.16) and 9–11 (10.29) respectively in the natural peat swamp forest, but only 2.14–6.49 (3.98) and 4–6 (5.33) in the planted *Acacia* forest. These results indicate that the remnant natural peat swamp forests should be carefully protected and the landscape design of industrial tree plantations could be improved to retain the original rich biodiversity of the peat swamp forests.

Keywords: *mammals, camera-trapping, Sumatra, peat swamp forest, Acacia plantation*

Abstract No: A-343

MyCITES: A DATABASE FOR *GONYSTYSLUS BANCANUS*

Siti Yasmin Yaakub*, Mohd Azahari Faidi, Abd Rahman Kassim and Muhamad Afizzul Misman

Forest Research Institute of Malaysia (FRIM), Malaysia

**Corresponding author: sitiyasmin@frim.gov.my*

SUMMARY

MyCITES (www.mycites.frim.gov.my) is a final output from project titled "Development of An Information Database for The Conservation and Sustainable Use of *Gonystylus bancanus* (Ramin) and *Aquilaria malaccensis* (Karas) in Malaysia. As the name of website "MyCITES", this website developed to compile the information related to Malaysian species that listed in Appendix I, II and III of Convention of International Trade on Endangered Species of Wild Flora and Fauna (CITES) as endangered and protected species from over-exploitation. Currently MyCITES includes database for two species, *Gonystylus bancanus* (peat swamp species) which listed in Appendix II by CITES and *Aquilaria malaccensis* (non-peat swamp species). In future, we are expecting the need by other researchers to include another Malaysian CITES tree species database into MyCITES. Therefore, we designed the web to cater the expansion when database for another Malaysia CITES species to insert in future. For *Gonystylus bancanus* database, there are five component included in MyCITES; namely (i) non-spatial information such as habitat, ecology and phenology of *Gonystylus bancanus*; (ii) distributions map of *Gonystylus bancanus* at forest reserve level for whole Malaysia; (iii) list of research and development (R&D) made in Malaysia about *Gonystylus bancanus*; (iv) list of publications by local researchers and students including journals, proceedings, reports, review, bulletins, books and thesis; (v) Trade statistic and production of *Gonystylus bancanus* in Malaysia; and (vi) Malaysia's policy and management practices of *Gonystylus bancanus*. The MyCITES is intended for user that comes from various field such as students, researchers, stake holders and planters that work on the species contained in MyCITES which will provide the latest information and details on CITES species for the purpose of learning, monitoring, conservation planning and other related activities in Malaysia.

Keywords: *Gonystylus bancanus, Ramin, Aquilaria malaccensis, Karas, database*

INTRODUCTION

Gonystylus is a genus comprised of 33 species (species discovered to date). However, only 29 species can be found in Malaysia with *Gonystyls bancanus (Miq.) Kurz* is often the most dominant species in mixed peat swamp forest and the most heavily exploited in this country. *Gonystylus bancanu*s only can be found in tropical lowland peat swamp forest (PSF) are distributed widely in Southeast Asia including Malaysia, Indonesia (Kalimantan and Sumatra), and Brunei. PSF are waterlogged forest that made up to 20 meters thick layer of dead leaves and plant materials. Generally the PSF water is acidic with pH less than 4.5. Other than producing timbers, PSF also serve as barrier for preventing the mixing between saline water and freshwater, fresh water and carbon storage, reduce water flows velocity during flood and etc.

In the last four years, Malaysia had successfully conducted and completed eight research Activities from 2008 to 2010 under Phase 1 of the ITTO-CITES Program entitled "Ensuring International Trade in CITES-listed Timber Species is Consistent with their Sustainable Management and Conservation". There were four implementing agencies in Malaysia entrusted to carry out all those Activities, namely, the Forest Research Institute Malaysia (FRIM); the Forestry Department Peninsular Malaysia (FDPM); the Forest Department of Sarawak (FD Sarawak); the Sarawak Forestry Corporation (SFC); and the Malaysian Timber Industry Board (MTIB). All the Activities covered various aspects of *Gonystylus bancanus* (Ramin) and to a certain extent also *Aquilaria malaccensis* (Karas).

As a continuation from the research Activities, MyCITES has been developed as a web-based database and information system that becomes a one-stop centre for dissemination of information on these threatened tree species in Malaysia. MyCITES has been developed under Activity funded by ITTO Work Program for 2013 on Support to ITTO-CITES Implementation for Tree Species and Trade/Market Transparency (TMT), entitled "Development of an Information Database for the Conservation and Sustainable Use of *Gonystylus bancanus* (Ramin) and *Aquilaria malaccensis* (Karas) in Malaysia".

MyCITES comprise a full and complete set of information on *Gonystylus bancanus*, including the current status of their population, research and development, import and export, publication, production and trade of their product. It will also be very useful to all relevant stakeholders with regard to access of information on current sustainable management and conservation efforts taken on these species. Relevant government agencies in Malaysia, particularly the forestry departments have better understanding on these species in the natural forest and can contribute to better management of this species in the future.

At the completion of this project, the comprehensive web-based database information system *of Gonystylus bancanus* in Malaysia has been developed, the outputs could influence the research and development activity, policies and management programme in the Ministry of Natural Resources and Environment Malaysia, particularly with regards to the following, i) Methods of gathering information in an organized manner for endangered species, and ii) Information storage procedures , such as reports and publications in a more efficient information system database. This information system database are necessary to support and enhance Sustainable Forest Management (SFM) and conservation of Ramin in Malaysia.

The successful development of the web-based database information system of *Gonystylus bancanus* will contribute towards the best practices in managing and monitoring these endangered species in Malaysia. As a one-stop centre of Malaysian CITES-listed tree species, the information database that will be known as the MyCITES will comprise a full and complete set of information on *Gonystylus bancanus*, including the current status of their population, production, trade and management practices in Malaysia.

The MyCITES will be used as a platform to disseminate information on *Gonystylus bancanus*, including the outcomes and findings of previous ITTO-CITES Activities implemented in Malaysia. The development of the MyCITES could also provide a guide for developing integrated information systems for other endangered tree species not only in Malaysia, but also in other countries. Indirectly, it could assist ITTO and CITES in monitoring the management activities of threatened tree species. The outcomes of this project could also be used as an input to generate relevant information required for the preparation of non-detrimental findings (NDF), as required for species listing under CITES in Malaysia.

METHODS

Figure 1 shows the methodology used in this research. The information with regard to *Gonystylus bancanus* such as its habitat, ecology, phenology, distribution map by forest reserve, products, import, export, research, development, publications, management policy and practice in Malaysia are collected and compiled in standard data format and served as database for MyCITES. Once completed, this database will be inserted into MyCITES and finally the user can access the information by browsing www.mycites.frim.gov.my.

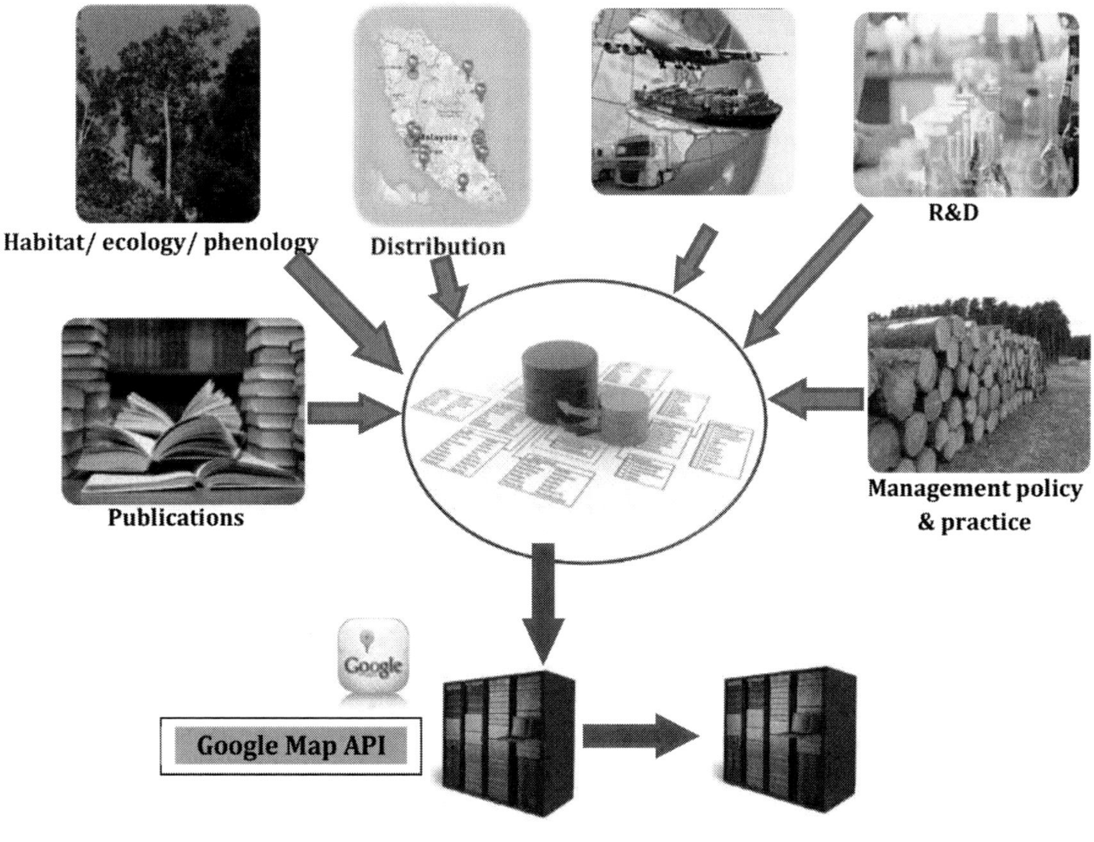

Figure 1: Methodology for MyCITES development

RESULTS

The operating system used in MyCITES are Window Server, PHP programming language, Microsoft SQL database platform and Internet Information Services (ISS) web server.

MyCITES has two types of page; static page and dynamic page. Static page refer to unchanged or constant page, while dynamic page means changing or lively page. Static web pages contains the same prebuilt content each time the page is loaded, while the content of dynamic web page can be generated on-the-fly.

In MyCITES, static page is the page which contains the information that remain as a guide and general information for visitors, including the Homepage, Guidelines, About Us and Contact Us where all this information located at Homepage.

Meanwhile, the structure of the dynamic page can vary depending on the content of information stored. The capacity of dynamic page will increase if new information are entered into MyCITES database. In MyCITES, the *Gonystylus bancanus* species page is a dynamic page. The content for dynamic *Gonystylus bancanus* species page are shown in Table 1 below.

Table 1: Contents in *Gonystylus bancanus* species page

No.	Database Input	Contents	Summary of Content
1	Overview	Taxonomy & nomenclature	Introduction of the species, the taxonomic hierarchy and the vernacular name used to refer *G. bancanus* from over the world
		Habitat	List of distribution location of *Gonystylus spp.* all over the world, percentage of peat swamp area in Malaysia and types of PSF in Sabah and Sarawak
		Ecology & phenology	Contains the ecological information of *G. bancanus* including the characteristic of *G. bancanus* in peat swamp forest, population density, annual increment, etc. Meanwhile, some information on phenological study such as flowering, fruiting, pollinators, predators, seed dispersal and seedlings regeneration also included.
		Distribution map by forest reserve level	The mapping of *Gonystylus bancanus* was restricted only to forest reserve level due to the security factor. Detailed mapping on individual standing tree population were not exposed to public as this will give an accurate information on population of *G. bancanus*.
2	Research and development R&D	Research Projects	List of projects conducted in Malaysia by researchers from local government agencies, research institutional, lecturers and students of higher education institutional. The other information included in this part are name of project leader, summary or objectives of the project, the start date, duration , funding source, amount of fund (if available and the implement agency. The duration of the listed projects varies from 6 months up to 4 years with the source of financial support coming either from local funding such as TPIKM fund, Levy Funding Grant under Ministry of Plantation Industries & Commodities or international funding (ITTO-CITES Program)

No.	Database Input	Contents	Summary of Content
		Publications	Contains the list of publications with the study scope around Malaysia. At each publication, the information included such as the author's name, abstract, year of publication, types of publication and the status of publication (either free or require to purchase for access of the publications). There are eight types of publications including journals, proceedings, review, report, books, bulletin, poster and thesis (undergraduates, Masters and PhD)
		Technologies and Inventions	The new technologies and invention disclosure from research findings by research and higher education institutions. For example, the technologies of chain of custody and forensic DNA for Ramin profiling
3	Trade	Statistic	The collection of import and export statistic data started from year 2013 onwards. For 2012 and below, there is no complete record on the import and export of Ramin products and derivatives parts, so this data are excluded. The import and export statistic data were specified according to the importers and exporters countries. From the 2013 statistic, the major importers of Ramin's product are Germany and Japan (both 36%), meanwhile Taiwan contribute to 8%. The major product exported are sawn timber (80%), moulding (14%) and louvers door (2%). The other Ramin's product exported in small amount such as dress timber, picture frame, dowel and flooring
		Production	About 104 products from Ramin were identified and listed. The products sold in the market varies from raw, semi-finished and to fully finished. The raw product which is Ramin logs are bought by industries to be processed in factory as semi-finished and fully finished products. Some of semi furnished products such as sawn timber, dressed timber, dowel, flooring, plywood, louver doors, etc. Meanwhile, various fully finished products can be found in the market for example furniture, baby coat, barrels, rulers, hanger, shoe tree, ornaments and toothpicks as well.
4	Policy	Contains the explanation of six policy-related topics including i) CITES and Malaysia, ii) Appendix, iii) Act 686, iv) CITES Management Authority, v) CITES Malaysia Authorities Directory, vi) Export Quota and Permit Application	
5	Management	Contains the explanation of three management-related topics including: i) PSF Management System, ii) Harvesting Method, iii) Ramin Transportation Methods	

All the content in this dynamic page can be added or remove when required. Among the crucial contents that require regular update are research projects and publications where the information increase from time to time. Meanwhile, statistical data will be updated on an annual basis. Some contents that also required for updates, but infrequent such as production (under trade), policy, and management. Whereas, the other contents almost unchanged.

DISCUSSION AND RECOMMENDATIONS

Apart from Gonystylus bancanus species page, MyCITES is also intended for other Malaysian CITES species database, therefore Homepage www.mycites.frim.gov.my contains the list of available species's database and the search tool. The search tool in Homepage is designed for user to find and directed to the desired species database. Currently, this search tool is not too useful as only two databases are included which is *Gonystylyus bancanus* and *Aquilaria malaccensis*. In future, when the number of database increase, the search tool would be important to enable the MyCITES user to find their desired species information in a short time.

As the threat landscape for web application changes on a very dynamic basis, attackers need to stay ahead the curve in order to get in. Therefore, the security test of MyCITES has been carried out using Acunetix Web Application Security software. Acunetix application provides a comprehensive web applications before it can be published online. Result from this testing is being used to identify weakness and vulnerabilities, while at the same it can help to improve the structure and design of MyCITES web and database.

Once the development of MyCITES is completed, the main concern is to maintain the web and also updating the information. However, the costings would be a hindering factor as there are no budget allocated for this purposes. To deal with this problem, the team (FRIM researcher) will undertake maintenance and update of MyCITES website and database based on existing human and financial resources in FRIM; where the task was previously managed by the web developer hired to develop MyCITES. On the other hands, the financial contribution either from the Government of Malaysia or The International Tropical Timber Organization (ITTO) is most welcome when it involves the hardware and software upgrade in the future, if necessary.

The maintenance activity including updating information on new publications, new R&D, next coming annual statistic on production, import and export of Gonystylus bancanus's products, and new policy implemented regarding this species. The developed database and website will be regularly updated with current information.

The information shared in MyCITES can be used by the relevant government agencies in Malaysia, particularly the forestry departments to have better understanding on these species in the natural forest and can contribute to better management of this species in the future.

CONCLUSION

The successful development of the web-based database information system of *Gonystylus bancanus* will contribute towards the best practices in managing and monitoring this endangered species in Malaysia. As a one-stop centre of Malaysian CITES-listed tree species, MyCITES will comprise a full and complete set of information on *Gonystylus bancanus*, including the current status of their population, production, trade and management practices in Malaysia.

MyCITES will be used as a platform to disseminate information on *Gonystylus bancanus*, including the outcomes and findings of previous ITTO-CITES Activities implemented in Malaysia. The development of the MyCITES could also provide a guide for developing integrated information systems for other endangered tree species not only in Malaysia, but also in other countries. Indirectly, it could assist ITTO and CITES in monitoring the management activities of threatened tree species.

The outcomes of this project could also be used as an input to generate relevant information required for the preparation of non-detrimental findings (NDF), as required for species listing under CITES in Malaysia.

ACKNOWLEDGEMENT

The authors would like to acknowledge to the contributors for MyCITES database; researchers from Research Institute of Malaysia, Malaysian Timber Industry Board (MTIB and all staff in Geoinformation Programme, Department of Forestry and Environment, Forest Research Institute of Malaysia (FRIM) for helping the team during the field inventory.

Abstract No: A-035

POPULATION MAPPING OF GIBBONS IN KALIMANTAN, INDONESIA: CORRELATES OF GIBBON DENSITY AND VEGETATION ACROSS THE SPECIES RANGE

Susan M. Cheyne[1, 2, 3, 4, 5], Bernat Ripoll Capilla[1] and Mark E. Harrison[1, 6]

[1] *Orangutan Tropical Peatland Project, Indonesia.*
2 BRINCC Expedition C/O Flat 2, UK
[3] *Wildlife Conservation Research Unit (WildCRU), Department of Zoology, Oxford University, UK.*
[4] *Faculty of Humanities, School of Social Sciences and Law, Oxford Brookes University, UK*
[5] *School of Anthropology and Conservation, University of Kent*
[6] *Department of Geography, University of Leicester, University Road, UK*

Corresponding author: scheyne@outrop.com

SUMMARY

The first comprehensive survey of gibbons across peatlands in Indonesian Borneo was carried out over three years to 1) determine population density in the survey areas and threats to these areas; and 2) determine if densities of gibbon species correlate with vegetation characteristics and, if so, whether the same characteristics are correlated with density across all forest types. To achieve this, a total of five forest blocks were surveyed, involving 31 independent survey locations and repeat surveys in three forest blocks. Our data show that gibbons are ubiquitous where there is forest but forest quality affects population density, especially in peat-swamp forests. Forest block size affects longevity of populations and populations are susceptible to the 'compression effect' i.e. population overcrowding at unsustainable densities, especially in areas where there are contiguous habitat sub-types with variable characteristics. We show the effects of forest disturbance (logging, fragmentation, drainage and fire) on gibbon distribution and density. We discuss the importance of remaining peat-swamp forests as refuges for viable populations of gibbons and highlight issues for long-term conservation in this habitat. The use of minimum cross-sectional area, density of figs and fallback foods, habitat variables and presence of top foods are considered as determinants of population density to identify population thresholds below which gibbons cannot persist.

Keywords: *gibbons, survey methods, triangulation, conservation, habitat, density*

INTRODUCTION

Studies around the world have found that primate densities are influenced by the quality of their habitat. Wildfires and logging have been found to negatively affect the abundance of primates (Felton *et al.*, 2003, Michalski & Peres 2005), and to have resulted in lower densities of gibbons, principally because of a decrease in food availability (Johns 1985, 1987, 1988, O'Brien *et al.*, 2003, 2004). Findings suggest, however, that gibbons are able to persist in disturbed forests thanks to their dietary flexibility (Harrison *et al.*, 2007, Cheyne 2010), but their reproductive potential is lowered by this shift towards folivory (O'Brien *et al.*, 2004). Furthermore, primates have been found to be less abundant near forest edges (Lehman *et al.*, 2003). To date, a lack of systematic gibbon population surveys in forest blocks across Kalimantan have prevented assessment of the impact of these variables on gibbon populations in the region's tropical peat-swamp forest (TPSF), which therefore forms the focus of this paper.

With this project we sought to address the following research questions:

1) Do densities of the *Hylobates albibarbis* correlate with vegetation characteristics in different field sites across peat-swamp forest?
2) What are the estimated populations in the survey areas, the threats to these areas and the status of these forests?

It is hoped that the answers to these research questions will help inform Indonesia's management of peat-swamp forest areas in order to mitigate threats to gibbons and their habitat, as well as identify key habitat characteristics that are important to the survival of the gibbon populations within and outside the protected area network.

Study sites

The surveys were carried out at five sites across Central and East Kalimantan and involved 93 listening posts and 31 separate locations. Habitat sizes were obtained from GIS surveys carried out by the authors and/or from protected area maps. The study sites varied across habitat types and climate. Additional analyses focusing on both peat and non-peat areas are presented elsewhere (Cheyne *et al.*).

METHODS

Analysis of density data

Gibbon density was estimated using fixed-point counts, as described by (Brockelman & Ali 1987) and following the protocol described in (Buckley *et al.*, 2006, Cheyne *et al.*, 2007, Hamard *et al.*, 2010). This method has been recommended for the survey of gibbons because the gibbons' inconspicuous behaviour and preference for high canopy makes the use of line transects for surveying unsuccessful (Brockelman & Ali 1987, Brockelman & Srikosamatara 1993, Nijman & Menken B.J. 2005). Data collection took place between 04:30 hr and 08:00 hr each morning for four consecutive days at each survey site, excluding rainy mornings and mornings for which rain had stopped less than two hours before the planned start of data collection, as rain has been found to influence negatively the gibbons' singing behaviour (Brockelman & Ali 1987, Brockelman & Srikosamatara 1993).

Habitat assessment

Habitat characteristics were measured in plots of 10 m x 10 m situated along transects around the listening posts, in the same time frame as the auditory sampling. In each plot the following data were recorded: 1) canopy cover at 20 m, at each corner and in the middle of the plot, using visual estimation by the same observer throughout the survey; 2) diameter at breast height (DBH) of all trees exceeding 10 cm DBH; 3) height of all trees exceeding 10cm DBH, placing each tree into classes from 0–5 m to 35 m by visual estimation by trained researchers; 4) local name of the species of all measured trees; 5) total number of trees in the plot. DBH was then converted into cross-sectional area using the formula cross-sectional area $(DBH/2)^2 \times \pi$ and used as an indicator of tree biomass (Hamard *et al.*, 2010).

RESULTS

Gibbon population density

Bawan Forest has an estimated density of 7.04 groups/km^2 yet a low population size (based on available forest for each area which is almost double the next closest value (2.49 groups/km^2 in Sabangau). We suspect this is due to a compression effect in Bawan where the gibbons are being compressed into a small area of suitable forest thereby creating an unusually high density. The forest has been affected by logging and fire as well as some of the unaffected forest being unsuitable for supporting gibbons. The long-term sustainability of this density is unknown. The average density of *H. albibarbis* across all PSF sites was 2.5 group/km^2 and the total number of individuals across all the sites estimated to be 115,000.

Habitat Variables and Density

All vegetation variables had a normal distribution, as did gibbon density ($Z=0.69$, $P=0.774$ for gibbon density). The most degraded forest (ex-MRP) exhibited low tree species richness and diversity with relatively even distribution. A MANOVA with general contrasts was performed on gibbon density and habitat type with survey effort as a covariate (based on the number of independent survey locations). There were no significant difference between gibbon densities across habitat types (χ (15) = 31.76, $p > 0.05$). When data were analysed by habitat type and specific density, the gibbon density was also found to be correlated to all the measured vegetation variables, except the cross-sectional area of all tree classes (Table 1)

Table 1: Analysis of habitat variables

Variable	Pearson correlation	Sig. (2-tailed)
Mean canopy cover at 20 m (%)	0.802	0.003
Median tree height (m)	0.648	0.002
Mean DBH (cm)	0.584	0.002
CSA all trees (cm^2)	0.248	NS

DISCUSSION

Populations and density

Overall, densities of gibbons in TPSF range from 1-4 groups/km², well within the values of 0.06-9 groups/km² reported for all gibbons (based on a survey of 67 published studies of which only 29 reported density information). Thus, TPSF should be considered an important habitat for all the region's gibbons, in particular *H. albibarbis*, which has the highest proportion of its population in TPSF. These figures are only based on data from this study and should be considered in the wider context of all gibbon populations across Kalimantan.

Habitat

Previous work in TPSF has highlighted that the availability of most consumed gibbon foods was not a predictor of gibbon density (Hamard *et al.*, 2010). Here, gibbon density was found to be highly correlated to vegetation parameters, in particular canopy cover and tree height. We do not have tree species identified at all sites nor gibbon feeding ecology data. Data from Sabangau suggest that in peat-swamp forests figs are not a fallback food (Cheyne 2008, 2010) as has been suggested in dryer forests (Mather 1992, Marshall & Leighton 2006). Given these differences and the lack of detailed information on gibbon diet in many forests, more work is needed into the effects of tree species richness, evenness and diversity on gibbon population density.

Thresholds for sustaining gibbon

From this work we have a tentative estimate of lower and upper densities which are sustainable. We recognize that without further modelling e.g. through Vortex, these values are estimates only. We agree with (Brockelman & Srikosamatara 1993) and propose that habitats with a density <2 groups/km² bear further research and increased monitoring. Equally the Bawan population density of 7.04 groups/km² is above the typical range for high density (5-6 groups/km²) and also warrants further study, particularly for creating corridors to allow the gibbons to disperse into other forest. Thus the ideal range for these species appears to be 2-5 groups/km², but we recognize that a low density in a degraded but recovering habitat could mean a healthy population that may increase in the long term as habitat quality recovers.

Conclusion and Relevance for Conservation

This study represents the first ever survey of *H. albibarbis* population densities across Kalimantan. We estimate there are 115,000 individuals of *H. albibarbis* living in Kalimantan. There is a severe lack of data on gibbons in non-protected areas or small forest areas which may also contain viable populations. Current data suggest the population of *H. albibarbis* is between 75,000-130,000 individuals throughout its range of which at least 50% are found in TPSF. In the absence of a full Population and Habitat Viability Analysis (PHVA) all survey data are vitally important to obtain accurate population estimates of this gibbon species. Gibbons are able to maintain a good density across habitat types and over time even in unprotected areas. Our population estimates are based on known forest sizes, predominantly forest with some level of legal protection. The numbers of gibbon living in non-protected TPSF is a cause for concern as it is almost impossible to extrapolate current population numbers to these areas. It is crucial to remember that while these numbers indicate that gibbon populations are thriving, the habitat loss, wildlife trade and presence of so many populations in non-protected TPSF areas means that all gibbons in Kalimantan are still endangered.

REFERENCES

1. Brockelman WY, Ali R (1987) Methods of surveying and sampling forest primate populations. In: Mittermeier RA, Marsh RW (eds) Primate Conservation in the tropical rainforest. Alan Liss, New York, p 23–62
2. Brockelman WY, Srikosamatara S (1993) Estimation of Density of Gibbon Groups by Use of Loud Songs. Am J Primatol 29:93–108
3. Buckley C, Nekaris KAI, Husson SJ (2006) Survey of Hylobates agilis albibarbis in a Logged Peat Swamp Forest: Sabangau catchment, Central Kalimantan. Primates Online fir
4. Cheyne SM (2008) Feeding ecology, food choice and diet characteristics of gibbons in a disturbed peat-swamp forest, Indonesia. In: Lee PC, Honess P, Buchanan-Smith H, MacLarnon A, Sellers WI (eds) 22nd Congress of the International Primatological Society (IPS). Top Copy, Bristol, Edinburgh, UK, p 342
5. Cheyne SM (2010) Behavioural ecology and socio-biology of gibbons (Hylobates albibarbis) in a degraded peat-swamp forest. In: Supriatna J, Gursky SL (eds) Indonesian Primates. Springer, New York, p 121–156
6. Cheyne SM, Gilhooly LJ, Hamard MC, Höing A, Houlihan PJ, Kursani, Limin SH, Loken B, Phillips A, Rayadin Y, Capilla BR, Rowland D, Sastramidjaja WJ, Spehar S, Thompson CJH, Zrust M Population mapping of gibbons in Kalimantan, Indonesia: Correlates of Gibbon Density and Vegetation across the species range. Endanger Species Res

7. Cheyne SM, Thompson CJH, Phillips AC, Hill RMC, Limin SH (2007) Density and Population Estimate of Gibbons (Hylobates albibarbis) in the Sabangau Catchment, Central Kalimantan, Indonesia. Primates 49:50–56
8. Felton AM, Engstrom LM, Felton A, Knott CD (2003) Orangutan population density, forest structure and fruit availability in hand-logged and unlogged peat swamp forests in West Kalimantan, Indonesia. Biol Conserv 114:91–101
9. Hamard MCL, Cheyne SM, Nijman V (2010) Vegetation correlates of gibbon density in the peat-swamp forest of the Sabangau catchment, Central Kalimantan, Indonesia. Am J Primatol 72:607–616
10. Harrison ME, Cheyne SM, Morrogh-Bernard H, Husson SJ (2005) What can apes tell us about the health of their environment? A Preliminary Analysis of the use of orang-utans and gibbons as biological indicators of changes in habitat quality in tropical peat swamp forests. . In: Reiley JO (ed) Proceedings of the International Symposium and Workshop on "Restoration and Wise Use of Tropical Peatland." CIMTROP, Palangka Raya, Indonesia, p 104–109
11. Johns AD (1985) Selective logging and wildlife conservation in tropical rainforest: problems and recommendations. Biol Conserv 31:355–375
12. Johns AD (1987) The use of primary and selectivly logged rainforest by Malaysian hornbills (Bucerotidae and implications for their conversion. Biol Conserv 40:179–190
13. Johns AD (1988) Effects of "selective" timber extraction on rain forest structure and composition and some consequences for frugivores and folivores. Biotropica 20:31–37
14. Lehman SM, Sussman RW, Phillips-Conroy J, Prince W (2003) Ecological biogeography of primates in Guyana: The effects of natural and anthropogenic disturbances. In: Twenty-Sixth Annual Meeting of the American Society of Primatologists July 29-August 02. 2003 Calgary, p 139
15. Marshall AJ, Leighton M (2006) How does food availability limit the population density of white-bearded gibbons? In: Hohmann G, Robbins MM, Boesch C (eds) Feeding Ecology in Apes and Other Primates. Ecological, Physical and Behavioral Aspects. Cambridge University Press, Cambridge, p 311–333
16. Mather R (1992) A field study of hybrid gibbons in Central Kalimantan, Indonesia. University of Cambridge.
17. Michalski F, Peres CA (2005) Anthropogenic determinants of primate and carnivore local extinctions in a fragmented forest landscape of southern Amazonia. Biol Conserv 124:383–396
18. Nijman V, Menken B.J. S (2005) Assessment of census techniques for estimating density and biomass of gibbons (Primates: Hylobatidae). Raffles Bull Zool 53:169–179
19. O'Brien TG, Kinnaird ME, Nurcahyo A, Iqbal M, Rusmanto M (2004) Abundance and distribution of sympatric gibbons in a threatened Sumatran rain forest. Int J Primatol 25:267–284
20. O'Brien TG, Kinnaird MF, Wibisono HT (2003) Crouching tigers, hidden prey: Sumatran tiger and prey populations in a tropical forest landscape. Anim Conserv 6:131–139

Abstract No: A-042

TREES COMPOSITION OF ULU SEBUYAU NATIONAL PARK, SARAWAK

Malcom Demies*, Jacqualine Henry, Ling Chea Yiing, Sundai Silang and Julaihi Abdullah

Sarawak Forestry Corporation, Sarawak

**Corresponding author: malcom@sarawakforestry.com*

SUMMARY

Ulu Sebuyau National Park is located in Sri Aman Divisions, in the Lupar River basin in the Southern Sarawak. The study site is concentrated in the eastern side of the park and it is a logged-over peat swamp forest. This study was conducted to determine the diversity and species composition of trees in the park. All trees with diameter at breast height (dbh) ≥ 10 cm in eight sampled of 50 m x 50 m plots were enumerated. A total of 1,290 individual trees were recorded; 87 species, 57 genera from 31 families. The area is dominated by the family of Fagaceae with 429 individuals. *Lithocarpus dasystachya* is the highest total number of individuals which recorded 232 trees. Most of the tree species and individual trees enumerated were from the lower storey.

***Keywords**:Floristic composition, tree species, sample plots, enumeration, Ulu Sebuyau, Sarawak*

INTRODUCTION

The Ulu Sebuyau National Park (USNP) was officially gazetted in 25 March 2010 covering an area of 18,287 ha. The area is covered by logged over peat swamp forest (PSF) and has been logged over at least once. Pockets of clear or open area can be found in the Park which covered mainly by climbers, fern and pioneer species. Logging activities in the past has created forests with a clear zonation pattern. This has affected the structure and biodiversity of PSF in the area.

Sarawak's peat swamp forests (PSFs) have been subjected to various degrees of intervention since the mid-1900s including USNP. Wong (2002) indicates that in 1995/1996 *c.* 12,264,830 ha of Sarawak's land was still covered by forests. Of this, *c.* 1,140,744 ha (about 9 %) were in peat swamp areas. However, it is estimated that approximately 98.5% of PSF areas have been opened up over the years, leaving various degrees of canopy cover (Lee 2004).

Due to their accessibility and the occurrence of stands of highly valuable *ramin*, Mixed Swamp Forest (MSF) has been logged since the 1950s. From 1972 onwards, as the timber market expanded, other peat swamp forest species like *alan*, and *Alan* Swamp and *Alan Bunga*forests were increasingly logged. Lately, with advancements in peat management techniques, there is growing interest in utilizing even deeper peatland for agricultural development (particularly oil palm). Due to this recent development PSF areas have declined from *c.* 700,000 ha in the 1960s and 1970s to only *c.* 612,400 ha (Chai 1999).

No comprehensive inventory or resource accounting has been carried out in the state so it is very difficult to qualify and quantify the status of PSF in Sarawak. Floristic analyses are very useful for identifying spatial patterns in plant diversity and composition, and when combined with environmental, geological and historical variables, can provide important information on the processes that maintain the high levels of tree species diversity in tropical forests. For that reason floristic analyses have recently received considerable attention in the Neotropics (Hedl *et al.* 2009, Suratman*et al.* 2010, Duivenvoorden, 1996; Terborgh & Andresen, 1998; Pyke *et al.*, 2001). In Borneo, these kind of studies are still rare, and have been limited to parts of northern Borneo (Ashton, 1976; Proctor *et al.*, 1983; Baille *et al.*, 1987; Newbery, 1991; Potts *et al.*, 2002). The USNP is an additional to PSF areas that have been gazetted as TPAs, namely LoaganBunut N.P. (10,736 ha), Maludam N.P. (43,401 ha) and Sedilu N. P. (6,311 ha).

MATERIALS AND METHODS

Study Area

The study was carried out at USNP. It is located in Samarahan and Sri Aman Division, in the Lupar River basin in southern Sarawak, at 1° 21'–1° 29' N and 110°54' – 111°9' E. The area occur in low-lying areas where slow-flowing streams drain shallow *valley*. In such habitats, saturated substrates with high, subterranean water tables are often prone to flooding and persistent water retention. The study site is logged over PSF, surrounded by oil palm plantation. Anderson, 1963 reported that there are six zones of phase for vegetation in PSF. However only mixed swamp forest (MSF) zone encountered during this study. The forest is diverse and mixed in species, found toward the Sg. Sebuyau.

Selection of Sample Plots

There are three transects line established and eight (8) sample plots were established within the transect lines. The sample plots were established randomly and scattered throughout thetransect line. The location and GPS coordinate for the plots are shown in Table 1.

Table 1: Attributes for the sample plots at each locality

Plot No.	Transect No.	Distance from base line	Coordinate	Area	Plot description
Plot 1	3	300 m	N 01° 23' 29.1" E 110° 54'.55.5"	50m x 50m	Logged-over forest
Plot 2	2	3400 m	N 01° 22' 07.2" E 110° 56'.36.8"	50m x 50m	Mixed swamp forest (near river)
Plot 3	1	1200 m	N 01° 24' 08.2" E 110° 55' 30.0"	50m x 50m	Logged-over forest
Plot 4	1	700 m	N 01° 24' 08.7" E 110° 55'.13.6"	50m x 50m	New generation of Padang Empili
Plot 5	2	2050 m	N 01° 23' 35.3" E 110° 55'.57.4"	50m x 50m	New generation of Padang Empili
Plot 6	2	1050 m	N 01° 23' 36.1" E 110° 54'.24.0"	50m x 50m	Old Locomotive Trail
Plot 7	3	1100 m	N 01° 23' 28.3" E 110° 55'18.6"	50m x 50m	Logged-over forest
Plot 8	3	50 m	N 01° 23' 31.7" E 110° 54'.49.9"	50m x 50m	Old Locomotive Trail

Establishment of Sample Plots

Each sample plot measured 50m x 50m, containing 25 square quadrats measuring 10m x 10m each. The quadrats were numbered consecutively from 001 to 025, as shown in Figure 1. The compass bearing was located to indicate the direction of the ranging pole in setting up the plot boundary.

Enumeration and Data Collection

A tree stem with diameter breast height (DBH) of 10.0 cm or more ($\geq$ 10.0cm) is enumerated. The trees species were identified in the field. Leaf samples were collected for further identification and confirmation in the Sarawak Herbarium. The leaf samples collected were labelled accordingly. The sampling intensity for the tree species is 100%.

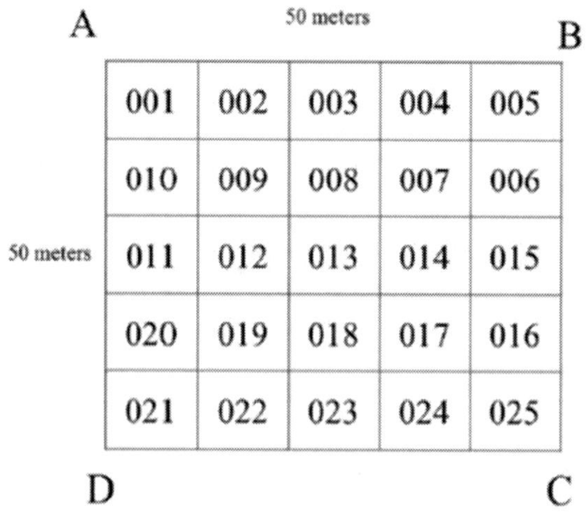

RESULTS AND DISCUSSION

The total sampling area for the eight plots were 2.0 ha. A total of 1,290 individual trees were recorded from 8 plots. This includes a total of 87 species, 57 genera from 31 families. Thea area was dominated by the family of Fagaceae with 429 individuals the genera *Lithocarpus* (e.g. *L. andersonii, L. dasystachya*and *L. pseudo-kunstleri*). *Lithocarpusdasystachya*was the highest total number of individual recorded a total 232 of trees. This was followed by *Lithocarpusandersonii* (184 trees), *Nepheliummaingayi* (87 trees), *Syzygiumhavilandii* (86 trees), *Litseagracillipes*(82 trees) and others range from 1 to 75 individual trees.

The distribution of trees varies in each plot. The forest lack of emergent canopy which larger trees either singly or in small clusters. A total of 5% of the individuals were the emergent trees, mostly *Diospyrosevena*. These trees reached height of 20 to 25 m and dbh of 23.2 to 48.8 cm. The lack of big trees is evidence of past disturbance and damage, at a scale that could only be caused by the harvesting of commercial timber.

The trees at lower storey are denser with heights of 10 m to below 20 m. A total of 18.1% and 54.8% of trees were within the range of 15.0 m-19.9 m and 10.0 m-14.9 m height respectively. The lower storey canopy with height of 15.0 m-19.9 m was dominated by *Lithocarpusandersonii* with 46 trees, *Shoreauliginosa* (26), *Syzygiumhavilandii* (24) *Nepheliummaingayi* (17) and *Madhucabarbata* (11). The DBH of trees are in the range of 10.5 cm – 42.8 cm. Trees at the height of 10.0 m-14.9 m creates most dense canopy at the lower stratum. The species found here were mainly saplings of the above strata and at some quadrats the forest gap was present. Forest gaps promote regeneration and thus create a different species composition. The common species found here are *Lithocarpusdastachya* with 163 trees, *L. andersonii*(98),*Litseagracillipes*(50),*Nepheliummaingayi*(49) and*Syzygiumhavilandii*(46). The trees dbh are within the range of 10 cm – 33.7 cm. 22% of tree within the plots are below 10 m with dbh of 10 cm-31.2 cm. The dominant species found here are *Lithocarpusdasystachya*with 66 trees, *L. andersononii*(44),*Litseagracillipes*(24),*Nepheliummaingayi*(11) and*Dilleniapulchella*(11). Some trees here having big dbh but short due to broken top.

The ground flora consisted of saplings, seedlings and other non-woody plant species especially Arecaceae (e.g. rattan) which were below 3 m height. The distribution of saplings and seedlings were variable for each quadrat. Quadrats that had less number of trees and dominated mainly by pioneer species had more ground vegetation. Ground flora was not common in this plot. Climbers were abundant and attached to the trees. It is interesting to note the presence of *Gonystylusbancanus* with two individual recorded. Many individuals measured fell below the size of 10 cm dbh, indicating that this species may be regenerating with some success if not disturbed. The high population of *Nephelummaingayi*and*Syzygiumhavilandii* also indicate that the forest have plenty of fruit trees for the wild animals.

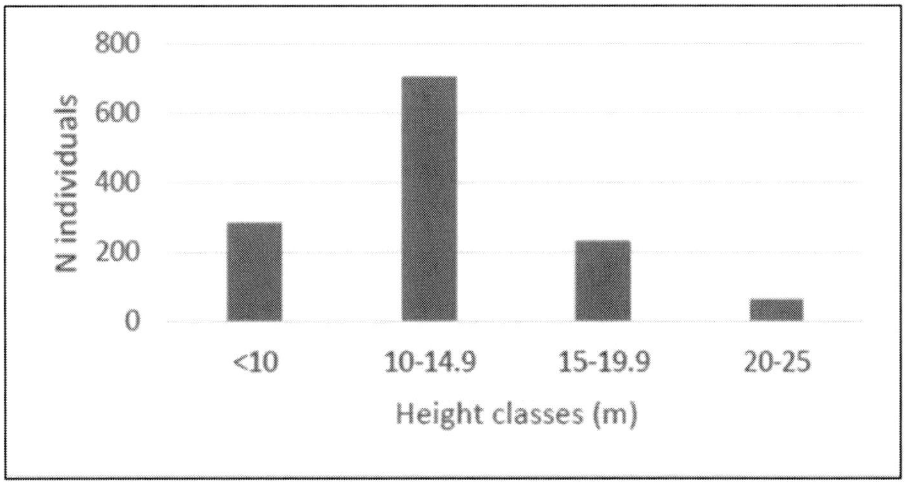

Figure 1: Distribution of height classes

The most abundant class is 10-14.9 m comprises about half of all individual (Figure 1). Taller trees are rare as it had been heavily affected by past logging activities.

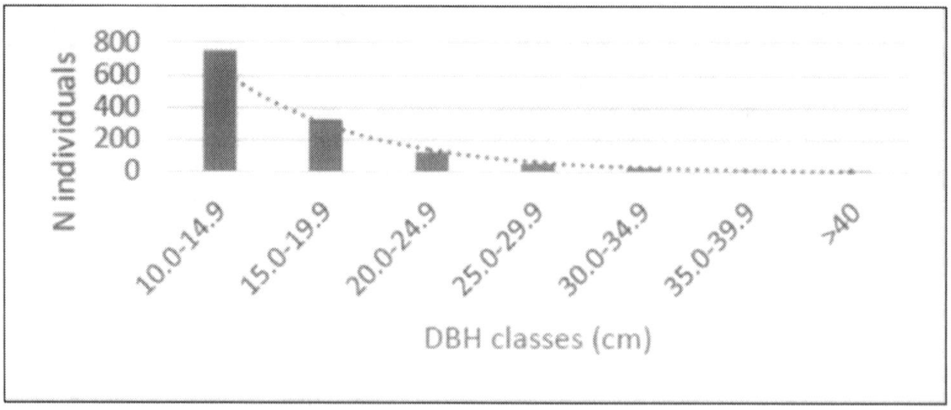

Figure 2: Distribution of DBH classes

The entire plots showed that the diameter classes' distribution is in reversed J-curve (Figure 2). It showed that the distribution of tree diameter is similar to that natural forest. It also showed that the forest consisted of uneven-aged stands. The most abundant class is 10.0 cm-14.9 cm and this distribution showed that the forest is in regenerate stages after disturbance.

Different patterns of vegetation were observed in Plot 5 which had the highest total number of trees with 204 individuals and also the most species diverse with 41 species (Figure 3). Plot 5 and Plot 6 are the most diverse in term of family with 22 family. Plot 6 also the second highest in term of species richness with 35 species. However number of trees for Plot 6 is the lowest with 94 individuals mainly with secondary species. Forest at plots 6 and 8 were established at the old locomotive trail and have the lowest species composition. The past logging activities had affected the species composition here and tend to have more undergrowth and seedlings compared to the less or undisturbed plots. The *Lithocarpusandersonii*and *L. daystachyus* found in every plots except at plot 2 and are dominant at Plot 1, 3, 4 & 8. The two species are secondary species that have successfully colonised logged-over PSF, taking advantage of the abundant light provided by the opening of the forest canopy. Openings of canopy enhanced the germination of seeds that stay dormant in the soil. The forest gaps increased the diversity of forest regeneration and raised the opportunities for shade-intolerant species to rejuvenate. Light gaps maintain and promote the diversity of shade-intolerant trees in tropical forests by creating spatial and micro-environmental heterogeneity.

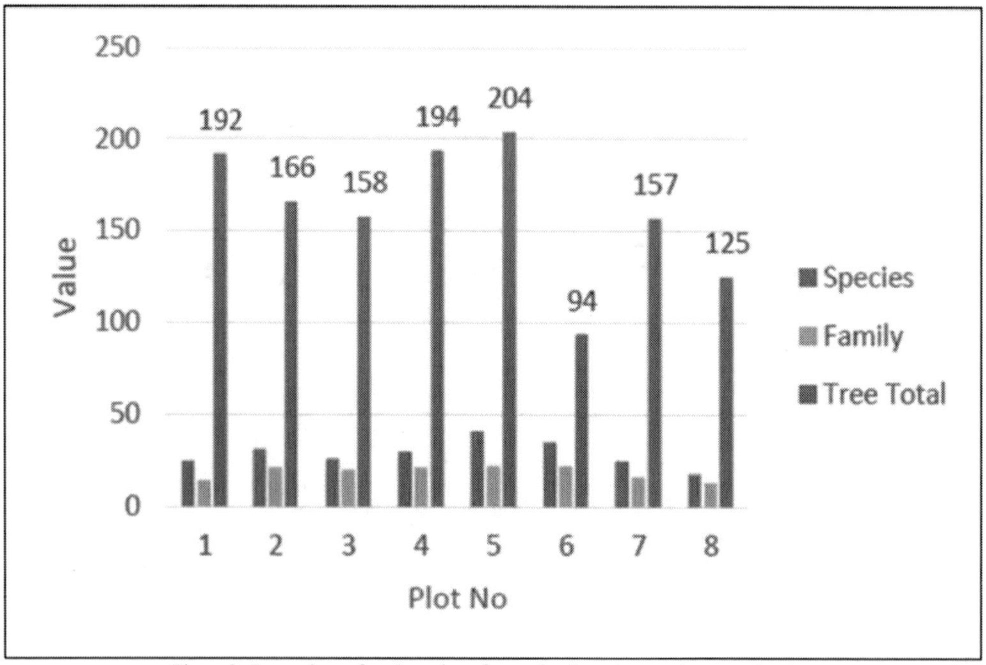

Figure 3: Comparison of total number of trees, family and genera between the plots

CONCLUSION

Eight sample plots of 50 m x 50 m (2 ha) were established and enumerated. A total number of 893 trees from at least 74 genera comprising 23 families were recorded. Results of this study showed that the vegetation, distribution and the species composition were variable among the plots. Based on our observation in the sample plots, there was good regeneration of seedlings. Enumeration of saplings and seedlings should also be conducted to determine the degree of regeneration and mortality occurring in the area.

Numerous studies and assessment records very clearly show that unregulated exploitation of PSF resources will cause considerable environmental stress. Effects include irreversible land subsidence, loss of biodiversity, alteration of ecology, degradation of air and water quality and many other environmental issues. With the rapid development taking place in the state, where vast PSF areas have been identified as potential development areas, there is an urgent need to formulate a holistic, integrated and comprehensive multi-sectoral plan for PSF management and conservation. In particular, greater attention should now be focused on conserving some of what is left, for, *inter alia*, biodiversity, water resources, recreation, climate regulation and hydrological regimes. This will ensure that PSF is utilized wisely to generate economic benefits for the state and at the same time to ease resource use conflicts.

ACKNOWLEDGEMENT

The authors gratefully acknowledge MPOC for funding this project. Thanks are also due to CEO of SFC Wong Ting Chung andDGM of PABC Oswald BrakenTissen for guidance and support. We would like to thank, SFC staff who involved in the project. We were ably assisted in the field by Khairul Ariffin B. Abdullah and Francis Tiam.

REFERENCES

1. Anderson, J.A.R. 1963. Flora of Peat Swamp Forests. *Garden Bulletin Singapore*, vol XX, Part II.
2. Ashton, P.S. 1976. Mixed dipterocarp forest and its variation with habitat in the Malaysian lowlands: A re-evaluation at Pasoh. *Malaysian Forester* 39: 56-72.
3. Baillie, I. C., Ashton, P. S., Court, M. N., Anderson, J. A. R., Fitzpartick, E. A. &Tinsley,J. 1987. Site characteristics and the distribution of tree species in mixed dipterocarp forest on tertiary sediments in central Sarawak, Malaysia. *Journal of Tropical Ecology* 3: 201-220.
4. Bennett, E.L. and Z. Shebli. 1999. *Sarawak's system of Totally Protected Areas: will it protect Sarawak's biodiversity*? Proceeding, 3rd Workshop on Sarawak's National Parks and Wildlife, Dec. 1999, Hornbill 3: 38-45, Forest Department, Sarawak.
5. Chai, F.Y.C. 1999. *Forestry and peatland development in Sarawak*. Paper presented at a Workshop on Working Towards Integrated Peatland Management for Sustainable Development, 17-18, August 1999, Kuching, Sarawak.
6. Duivenvoorden, J. F. 1996. Patterns of tree species richness in rain forests of middle Caqueta area, Colombia, NW Amazon. *Biotropica*28: 142-158.
7. Gumal, M.T. 1999. Are flying foxes really pests? Some considerations from case studies of durian (*Duriozibethinus*), pedada (*Sonneratiaalba*) and rambutan (*Nepheliumlappaceum*). Proceeding, 3rd Workshop on Sarawak's National Parks and Wildlife, 23-26 November 1999, Hornbill 3: 126-148, Forest Department, Sarawak.
8. Hedl. R, Svatek M, Danc M., Rodzay A.W., Salleh M.A.B, Kamariah A.S. 2009. A new technique for inventory of permanent plots in tropical forests: a case study from lowland dipterocarp forest in Kuala Belalong, Brunei Darussalam. *Blumea*54: 124–130
9. Lee, H.S. 2004. *Improving Biodiversity and Sustainability of Peat Swamp Forests of Sarawak*. Report JWG/RAM/12. Joint Working Group Malaysia – The Netherlands. Forest Department Sarawak, Kuching, Malaysia/Alterra, Wageningen, The Netherlands.
10. Newbery, D. M. 1991. Floristic variation within kerangas (heath) forest: re-evaluation of data from Sarawak and Brunei. *Vegetatio*96: 43-86.
11. Potts, M. D., Ashton, P. S., Kaufman, L. S. &Plotkinj. B. 2002. Habitat patterns in tropical rain forests: A comparison of 105 plots in northwest Borneo. *Ecology* 83.
12. Proctor, J., Anderson, J.M., Chai, P. &Vallack, H.W. 1983 Ecological studies in four contrasting rain forests in GunungMulu National Park, Sarawak. *J. Ecol.* 71: 237–260.
13. Pyke, C.R., Condit, R., Aguilar, S. & Lao, S. 2001 Floristic composition across a climatic gradient in a neotropical lowland forest. *J. Veg. Sci.* 12: 553–566.

14. Sebastian, A.C. 2000. The status and conservation of globally significant birds in Sarawak. Proc. 4th Workshop on Sarawak's National Parks and Wildlife, 6-9 November 2000, Hornbill4: 140-167, Forest Department, Sarawak.
15. Suratman M.N, M. Kusin, S.A.K. Yamani, K. Saleh, M. Ahmad and S.A. Bahari. 2010. *Stand structure and species diversity of Keniam Forest, Pahang National Park.* 2010. International Conference on Science and Social Research, 772-777.
16. Terborgh, J. & Andresen, E. 1998. The composition of Amazonian forests: patterns at local andregional scale. *Journal of Tropical Ecology* 14:645-664.
17. Wong, J. 2002. Report on status of peat swamp forest in Sarawak for the sustainable management of peat swamp forests of Sarawak with special reference to ramin (*Gonystylusbancanus*), Forest Department, Sarawak.

THEME 2
PEATLANDS & ECOSYSTEM MANAGEMENT

2.1: PEATLAND CARBON BALANCE, STOCKS, STORAGE & LOSSES

Abstract No: A-070

A PRELIMINARY ASSESSMENT OF CARBON STORAGE AND PRODUCTIVITY OF PEAT SWAMP FOREST IN KATINGAN, CENTRAL KALIMANTAN, INDONESIA

Meli Fitriani Saragi[1, 2*], Daniel Murdiyarso[1, 2] and Sigit Deni Sasmito[2, 3]

[1]*Department of Geophysics and Meteorology, Bogor Agricultural University, Indonesia*
[2]*Center for International Forestry Research, Indonesia*
[3]*Research Institute for the Environment and Livelihoods (RIEL), Charles Darwin University, Australia*

**Corresponding author: M.Saragi@cgiar.org*

SUMMARY

Tropical peat swamp forests (PSFs) have been known globally as one of the carbon-rich wetland ecosystems. However, scientific literatures on these ecosystem carbon (C) stocks and net productivity rates are still lacking. This study presents ecosystem C-stocks and litter fall productivity based on field assessments in restored secondary peat swamp forests (PSF) at Katingan, Central Kalimantan. We established four (20 x20 m^2) permanent plots for regular biophysical field parameters, such as peat depths, tree diameter, species diversity and litter fall. We find that these PSFs store approximately 1253 ± 129 Mg C ha^{-1}, of which, 80% was stored in belowground peat soils. The tree density varied from 1200 to 1825 trees per hectare across plots, whereas the mean of stand basal area was 32.86 ± 4.72 m^2 ha^{-1}. We also find that aboveground litter production was 6.4 ± 1.1 Mg C ha^{-1} y^{-1}, which was considerably higher than global summary review of canopy net primary productivity or litter fall production of 4.8 ± 0.3 Mg C ha^{-1} y^{-1} reported by Malhi *et al.* (2011). This suggests that restoring these C-rich ecosystems like PSF that improve net primary production is key for national and global climate change mitigation strategies.

Keywords: *ecosystem carbon stocks, litter production, net primary production, tropic, climate change mitigation*

INTRODUCTION

Peatland ecosystems cover only 3% of land surface of the planet with 65% of them are located in Indonesia. However, these ecosystems store significant terrestrial carbon (C) with up to 88.6 Pg of globally (Page *et al.*, 2002), and equal with 15 – 30% of the total worlds soil C (Limpens *et al.*, 2008). In addition, forested peatlands such as tropical peat swamp forests (PSFs) could store about 220 Mg C ha^{-1} within phytomass (Hergoualc'h & Verchot 2013) and 670 Mg C ha^{-1} per meter depth of peat (Warren *et al.*, 2012). Although PSFs have significant C stocks, there are still limited number of studies on the understanding these ecosystems carbon budget.

The aim of this study is to quantify ecosystem C stocks and aboveground litter fall production in tropical restored peat swamp forests. The preliminary findings of this study provide insight on the significant contribution of PSF ecosystems C storage and aboveground litter fall production to tropical forests carbon cycle.

METHODS

Study sites

This study is located in Katingan PSF restoration project in Central Kalimantan (-2.924°S, 113.144°E), administered by PT. Rimba Makmur Utama (RMU), which one of the Indonesia companies who has ecosystem restoration concession (ERC). This PSF ecosystem restoration area was 203,750 ha, where mainly covered by secondary dense forest and small area of open forest or shrublands. This restoration area is located in between two main river outlets of Mentaya in the west and Katingan in the east. Consequently, the water balance condition is relatively maintained from rainfall and high tidal inputs through those two rivers. Annual rainfall in study area is 2064 mm and categorized as equatorial rainfall pattern. The average air temperature is 27°C with minimum and maximum temperatures of 20°C and 37°C, respectively.

Carbon stocks assessments

We assessed above ground and below ground biomass, and organic peat soil carbon pools in four permanent plots of 20 x 20 m^2. Above and belowground biomass carbon were estimated through collected tree diameter dataset. All standing tree diameter were measured consistently at breast height (DBH) or about 130 cm above forest floor. Local and scientific tree species names were also identified and recorded. We converted DBH data into aboveground biomass (kg) by using a special allometric equation for peat swamp forests introduced by Manuri *et al.* (2014). In addition, belowground biomass was estimated by using general allometric equation for root in tropical forests developed by Cairns *et al.* (1997). Biomass C stocks (Mg C ha^{-1}) were obtained by multiplying biomass (kg) with commonly used C concentration of 50% in per sampled area (ha^{-1}) (Murdiyarso *et al.* 2009).

Belowground peat soil carbon stock was determined through peat soil samples collection. We collected peat soil samples by using special peat auger (76 cm^{-3}) from consistent depth intervals as follow: 0–15, 15–30, 30–50, 50–100, 100–200, 200–300, and 300–400 cm. Peat soil samples were dried until constant weight, homogenized and sieved prior C concentration analysis. C stocks were the product of C contents (%) x bulk density (gr cm^{-3}) x peat layer (cm). We employed LECO CNS analyzer for direct C content analysis in Laboratory of Soil Biotechnology at Bogor Agricultural University (IPB).

Aboveground litter fall production

We assessed aboveground litter fall production through regular litter fall sampling within four replicated 20 x 20 m^2 permanent plots. Four replicates of 50 x50 cm^2 litter trap were established in each permanent plot. Litter traps were placed 100 cm above forest floor. We collected litter fall every 15 days over one year cycle from September 2014 until August 2015. This long-term regular sampling resulted litter fall production rates and its variation throughout time of observation.

RESULTS AND DISCUSSION

Forest structure

We found wide range variation of tree density, species richness and basal area across sampled plot in secondary forests. The number of trees in all (20 x 20 m^2) plots was varied from 1,200 to 1,825 trees per hectare. The average of all >5cm measured individual tree diameter entire plots was 13.97 cm. As a result, the basal area varies between 20.01 to 42.09 m^2 ha^{-1}. We encountered about 19 tree species diversity in average throughout four different plots where dominated by *Macaranga pruinosa*, *Melaleuca* sp., *Chaetocarpus castanocarpus*, *Diospyros siamang*, *Shoreamecis topteryx*, and *Camnosperma coriaceum*.

Ecosystem carbon stocks

The mean of total ecosystem C stocks including biomass and belowground peat soil was 1253 ± 129 Mg C ha^{-1}. This amount is similar with previous study (mean: 894 ± 192 Mg C ha^{-1}) from Tanjung Puting National Park, Central Kalimantan which was located around 150 km from our study site (Murdiyarso *et al.*, 2009). The aboveground biomass carbon was 124 ± 45 MgC ha^{-1}. Soil carbon constituted major amount C with the proportion of 88%, while the rest proportion was biomass carbon. The high soil carbon allocation was mainly due to the substantial of organic rich peat layer of 3.5 m depth in average, and carbon concentration of 49.55 ± 0.19%.

Aboveground litter fall production

We observed litter fall production rates in secondary forest site over a year period from September 2014 to August 2015. While the overall litter fall accumulation production mean was only 1.1 ton DW ha^{-1} $month^{-1}$, we discovered major or more than doubly rates occurred in October 2014 with 3.83 Mg DW ha^{-1} $month^{-1}$. We analyzed that 90% of total litter fall biomass is mainly contributed from dead leaves, whereas 8% and 2% are from felled branches and flowers (and fruits) respectively. In general, litter fall accumulation rates of secondary PSF in this study was calculated as equal with 0.53 Mg C ha^{-1} $month^{-1}$ or 12.8 Mg DW ha^{-1} $year^{-1}$. This amount is considerably higher than global summary review of canopy net primary productivity or litter fall production of 4.8 ± 0.3 Mg C ha^{-1} y^{-1} reported by Malhi *et al.* (2011).

CONCLUSION

The study quantifies ecosystem C stocks and aboveground litter fall production in secondary PSF. The findings imply that PSF store significant organic C, which was supported by high aboveground litter fall production as canopy net primary production. Belowground peat soils contain major allocation of C stocks, while dead leaves contributed 90% of total litter fall biomass production. This study suggests that restoring remained PSF ecosystems could provide significant benefits for atmospheric C sequestration in order to mitigate climate change.

ACKNOWLEDGMENTS

All authors owe their gratitude to CIFOR–Indonesian Peatland Network (IPN) for funding supports. We would also thank PT. Rimba Makmur Utama and Kesbangpol, Ministry of Internal Affairs, Republic of Indonesia for research permits.

REFERENCES

1. Cairns, Michael A., *et al.* "Root biomass allocation in the world's upland forests." Oecologia 111.1 1997: 1-11.
2. Hergoualc'h, K. & Verchot, L. V., 2013. Greenhouse gas emission factors for land use and land-use change in Southeast Asian peatlands. *Mitigation and Adaptation Strategies for Global Change*, 19(6), pp.789–807. Available at: http://link.springer.com/10.1007/s11027-013-9511-x [Accessed February 16, 2015].
3. Limpens, J. *et al.* 2008. Peatlands and the carbon cycle : from local processes to global implications – a synthesis. , pp.1475–1491.
4. Malhi, Y., Doughty, C. & Galbraith, D., 2011. The allocation of ecosystem net primary productivity in tropical forests. *Philosophical transactions of the Royal Society of London. Series B, Biological sciences*, 366(1582), pp.3225–45. Available at: http://www.pubmedcentral.nih.gov/articlerender.fcgi?artid=3179639&tool=pmcentrez&rendertype=abstract [Accessed November 25, 2014].
5. Manuri, S. *et al.* 2014. Tree biomass equations for tropical peat swamp forest ecosystems in Indonesia. *Forest Ecology and Management*, 334, pp.241–253. Available at: http://linkinghub.elsevier.com/retrieve/pii/S0378112714005209 [Accessed December 5, 2014].
6. Murdiyarso, D., Donato, D., Kauffman, J. B., Kurnianto, S., Stidham, M., & Kanninen, M. (2010). Carbon storage in mangrove and peatland ecosystems: a preliminary account from plots in Indonesia (No. CIFOR Working Paper no. 48, p. 35p). Center for International Forestry Research (CIFOR), Bogor, Indonesia.
7. Page, S.E. *et al.* 2002. The amount of carbon released from peat and forest fires in Indonesia during 1997. *Nature*, 420, pp.61–65.
8. Warren, M.W. *et al.* 2012. A cost-efficient method to assess carbon stocks in tropical peat soil. *Biogeosciences*, 9, pp.4477–4485.

Abstract No: A-023

AGE AND CARBON ACCUMULATION RATE IN SELECTED PEATLANDS AND MARSH OF ANCIENT ICE CAPS ALONG A MOUNTAIN RANGE ON THE EASTERN TIBETAN PLATEAU

Dan Zhu [1, 2, 3*], Huai Chen [1, 2] and Ning Wu [1, 3]

[1]*Chengdu Institute of Biology, Chinese Academy of Sciences, China*
[2]*Zoige Peatland and Global Change Research Station, Chinese Academy of Sciences, China*
[3]*International Centre for Integrated Mountain Development, Nepal*

**Corresponding author: nakata1982617@163.com*

SUMMARY

Despite a high coverage of peatlands on the Tibetan Plateau, little has been documented in term of their origin, content and carbon (C) accumulation rates. The Shaluli Mountain Range Region (SMRR), which runs in a north-south direction, extends for 500 km, with elevations between 4000-6000 m a.s.l. It is with a high incidence of peatlands and marshes, particularly around the ancient ice caps that were generated during the last glacial maximum. In the summer of 2015, we chose five typical sites that ranged along a transect from north to south in SMRR (a distance of 250 km, with elevations between 4200 and 4500 m a.s.l.). The organic soil layer of the sampled sites ranged from 40 to 140 cm in depth. Among the five sites, four were identified as peatlands, whereas the one located in the central area was a marsh. In the peatland sites, the basal age of the C ranged from 1160 to 4540 BP, with accumulation rates of peat and C from 0.14 to 2.35 mm yr^{-1} (mean 0.61 mm yr^{-1}) and 10 to 67 g m^{-2} yr^{-1} (mean 28 g m^{-2} yr^{-1}), respectively. In the marsh site, the basal age of the C ranged from 720 to 1180 BP, with C accumulation rates from 14 to 106 g m^{-2} yr^{-1} (mean 60 g m^{-2} yr^{-1}). In general, the initiation of peat was much earlier in the northern sites than in the other two sites. Both peat and C accumulation rates showed a decreasing trend from deep to the top peat layer in both the northern and southern sites, while a contrary trend was found in the central site, indicating the diverse interactions between peat development and on-site climate across the SMRR. Furthermore, relative higher rates of peat or organic soil accumulation were found in the shallow soil layer (also younger sites), which implies the promising development of peatlands in those areas in the future.

***Keywords**: High altitude peatland, The Tibetan Plateau, Carbon accumulation, Peat development Climate*

INTRODUCTION

The Tibetan Plateau, which is the largest plateau in the world with a vast area of 2.5 x 10^6 km^2, has a high cover of peatlands and therefore a considerable carbon (C) stock (Chen *et al.*, 2014). Since the 1960s, much research has focused on the area and on the deposits of those peatlands (Cai and Jin, 1963; Song *et al.*, 1985; Wang, 1987), however, insight into the peatland formation and development process on the plateau have only emerged in the most recent decades at a limited number of sites (e.g. Sun *et al.*, 1998 and 2001; Gao *et al.*, 2010; Guo *et al.*, 2013). The latest evaluation shows that the initiation of peatlands in this region started at 14000 BP, with relatively higher accumulation rates during the mid-Holocene (Chen *et al.*, 2014).

In the high mountain areas of the plateau, peatland development was inhibited by glaciation even during the early Holocene because of the persistence of glaciers until the mid-Holocene (Sun *et al.*, 1998). Currently, in such areas with mesa (flattop), combined landscapes of glacial erosion lakes, glaciated valleys, drumlins and lateral moraine are often found, and as they are actually postglacial relics, geologists have named this geomorphological type as "ancient ice caps" (Zheng and Ma, 1997). Based on the literature, the Shaluli Mountain Range (SMRR), which runs in a north-south direction, extends some 500 km long with elevations between 4000-6000 m a.s.l., is thought to be the central area of ancient ice cap on the Tibetan Plateau (Shi *et al.*, 1995). Previous surveys have reported the distribution of peatlands in these ancient ice caps, with sporadic records on their depth and basal age (Sun *et al.*, 1998). However, those peatlands have not been well documented in terms of their initiation and development process. Therefore, we aim to study 1) the depth of peatland in SMRR; 2) the initiation age of peatland in SMRR; 3) the peat and C accumulation rates of peatland in SMRR.

MATERIALS AND METHODS

Study area

The SMRR is the largest mountain range in the eastern part of the Tibetan Plateau. It located between 27 ° and 32° N, and is the watershed for the upper reaches of the Yangtze River and its longest tributary Yalong River. There are two well-known ancient ice caps, i.e. the Xinlong ancient ice cap in the north with an approximate area of 2000 km^2 and the Daocheng ancient ice cap in the south with an approximate area of 3000 km^2. The elevations of the two ancient ice caps are between 4,200 to 4,500 m a.s.l. This region belongs to the cold Qinghai-Tibetan climatic zone.

Field site selection

We selected five typical sites along a transect in a north-south direction in SMRR, which represent different geographical types. The Yinduo site and the Heni site are mountain valleys, the Youyi site and Qudeng site are alluvial plains, and the Dengbo is a mesa site.

Peat/soil sampling

For each site we established a sampling transect along a straight line from the edge to the center of the site. The length of these transects were about 80 m. One study point was set every 10 m along each transect, so that 9 study points were determined for each transect. Peat depth was determined with a peat sampler (8 cm in diameter, 80 cm in length) at each of the study points. At each study point, we collected peat samples from one core. The peat samples were taken at 20 cm intervals until sand and mud appeared visually in the core. Then the peat samples were sealed in polyethylene ziplock bags for later analyses.

Sample analyses

The collected samples were transported to the laboratory and air-dried on brown paper. Soil samples for C analysis were passed through a 75 micron mesh sieve. Then approximately 0.1 g was taken to measure the C content with a CN Analyzer (Multi N/C 2100S, Jena, Germany). The dry bulk density was defined as dry weight (g)/field volume (cm^3).

The samples for radiocarbon dating were collected from the central part of the peat core, since the outer layer of the core might be contaminated when the sampler was drawn out. Root remains were removed from the samples in the laboratory before drying, and double checked before dating. Those samples were dated using the AMS radiocarbon dating method in the Beta Analytic Radiocarbon Dating Laboratory at Florida, USA. The final data was reported as a calendar-calibrated date. Beta Analytic Radiocarbon Dating Laboratory using the INTCAL09 database calibrate radiocarbon age to calendar years (radiocarbon years before present, "present"=AD 1950). By international conventions, the modern reference standard was 95% the ^{14}C activity of the National Institute of Standards and Technology (NIST) oxalic acid (SRM 4900C) and calculated using the Libby ^{14}C half e life (5668 years). [Beta Analytic Radiocarbon Dating Laboratory: http://radiocarbon.com/index.htm (Talma and Vogel, 1993)].

Accumulation rates calculation

Peat accumulation rates (mm yr^{-1}) were calculated for peat layers between the dated depths of the profiles, and C accumulation rates were obtained from the following equation (Lähteenoja *et al.*, 2012).

$$CA=r/1000*n *c$$

Where CA is C accumulation rate (g m^{-2} yr^{-1}); r is the peat accumulation rate (mm yr^{-1}); n is dry bulk density (g m^{-3}); c is C content (g C g^{-1} dry weight).

RESULTS

The organic soil layer of the sampled sites ranged from 40 to 140 cm in depth (mean 70 cm). Based on the C content (Joosten *et al.*, 2012), four sites were identified as peatlands, whereas the one located in the central area was a marsh (Table 1).

Table 1: Core depth and characteristics of the study sites

Study site	Location	Elevation, m	No of cores	Mean core depth, cm	Range of core depth, cm	Mean water table, cm	Mean bulk density, g cm^{-3}	Range of the bulk density, g cm^{-3}	Mean C content, %	Range of the C content, %	C content per cm^3, g cm^{-3}
Yinduo	31°24'37"N 99°51'08"E	4244m	9	99	90-130	-60	0.40	0.16-0.76	25.44	9.60-41.93	0.102
Youyi	30°51'54"N 99°49'17"E	4205m	9	63	50-90	-22	0.33	0.19-0.54	16.41	1.73-32.35	0.054
Dengbo	29°24'39"N 99°58'43"E	4524m	9	57	50-70	-18	0.15	0.07-0.36	30.68	5.29-44.45	0.046
Heni	30°15'04"N 99°51'19"E	4322m	9	79	30-70	-63	0.69	0.13-1.37	11.85	2.20-31.06	0.082
Qudeng	30°17'10"N 99°50'59"E	4535m	9	48	50-110	-67	0.68	0.43-0.93	6.77	4.29-11.13	0.046

In the peatland sites, the basal age of the C ranged from 1160 to 4540 BP, and peat and C accumulation rates ranged from 0.14 to 2.35 mm yr^{-1} (mean 0.61 mm yr^{-1}) and 10 to 67 g m^{-2} yr^{-1} (mean 28 g m^{-2} yr^{-1}), respectively. In the marsh site, the basal age of C ranged from 720 to 1180 BP, with C accumulation rates from 14 to 106 g m^{-2} yr^{-1} (mean 60 g m^{-2} yr^{-1}). In general, the initiation of the peatland was much earlier in the northern sites (Youyi and Yinduo) than those in the other two sites (Heni and Dengbo). Both peat and C accumulation rates showed a decreasing trend from deep to the top peat layer in both the northern (Youyi and Yinduo) and southern sites (Dengbo), while a contrary trend was found in the central site (Heni) (Table 2).

Table 2: Radiocarbon ages and peat and Carbon accumulation rates of the dated profile

Study site	Core code	Sample depth, cm	^{14}C dates, year BP	Calibrated age, cal year BP/Mean, Range	Interval, cm	C content, %	Bulk density, g cm^{-3}	Peat/soil accumulation rate, mm yr^{-1}	C accumulation rate, g m^{-2} yr^{-1}
Yinduo	1-2	40-60	2850 +/- 30	3060-2875, 2968	0-50	31.2	0.278	0.18	15
	1-2	80-100	3890 +/- 30	4420- 4235, 4328	50-90	27.7	0.494	0.38	40
Youyi	2-1	40-60	3500 +/- 30	3850-3695, 3773	0-50	21.4	0.341	0.14	9
	2-1	80-100	4540 +/- 30	5315-5055, 5194	50-90	14.7	0.459	0.38	19
Dengbo	3-1	20-40	990 +/- 30	955- 800, 859	0-30	22.1	0.151	0.35	12
	3-1	60-80	1160 +/- 30	1175-980, 1078	30-70	17.7	0.162	2.35	52
Heni	4-9	40-60	630 +/- 30	665-550, 608	0-50	21.0	0.320	0.79	55
	4-9	100-120	2560 +/- 30	2750-2545, 2635	50-110	12.9	0.565	0.31	22
Qudeng	5-4	20-40	980 +/- 30	935-800, 876	0-30	7.3	0.575	0.31	14
	5-4	60-80	1180 +/- 30	1180-1005, 1065	30-70	5.7	0.879	2	106

DISCUSSION

Previous study showed that peatland depths in SMRR were between 0.5 to 1 m, and limited data showed a basal age of 3240 BP in southern part of SMRR (Sun *et al.*, 1998). Although the peat cores sampled in our study were in a similar range to the previous study, we found an earlier peat initiation date in the northern part of SMRR. The peat deposit in SMRR was much shallower than that in the Zoige Peatland (another peatland complex on the Tibetan Plateau), and the basal age of peat in SMRR was much younger (Chen *et al.*, 2014). As a relative elevated region of the eastern part of the Tibetan Plateau, the SMRR was thought to be covered by a huge glacial area until the mid-Holocene, i.e. Holocene Thermal Maximum (Zheng and Ma, 1995). After about 1,000 years the glacier retreated and the peat might have started to accumulate in certain areas (Sun *et al.*, 1998). This could be an explanation for the relative shallow and young peat deposits in this region.

Our study found higher peat accumulation rates in SMRR (0.61 mm yr^{-1}) than the previous study (0.40 mm yr^{-1}) (Sun *et al.*, 1998). When compared to other peatlands on the Tibetan Plateau, the peat accumulation rate is comparatively high. One notable result is the increasing trend of both peat and C accumulation rates in the central site (Heni), which showed very high rates during the period 0-630 BP (0.79 mm yr^{-1}, 53 g m^{-2} yr^{-1}). At the marsh site (Qudeng), relative high C accumulation rates (60 g m^{-2} yr^{-1}) were recorded across the 80 cm vertical soil profile (0 to 1180 BP), though the soil there could not be defined as peat because of the low C content. Therefore, it could be inferred that recent climate (0 to 4540 BP) in SMRR, at least at specific sites, has favored peatland development more than other regions on the Tibetan Plateau.

CONCLUSION

We found young (1160 to 4540 BP) and shallow (40-140 cm) peatlands distributed in ancient ice caps on the eastern Tibetan Plateau, however, the mean accumulation rates of both peat and C were comparatively higher than other peatlands on the Tibetan Plateau. Various patterns of peat and C accumulation were found across the study sites. The relative higher rates of C accumulation in the upper layers of the central site indicated a favorable climate for peatland development.

ACCKNOWLEDGEMENT

This study is financially supported by National Natural Science Foundation of China (31200371, 41571220).

REFERENCES

1. Chen, H., Yang, G., Peng, C.H., Zhang, Y., Zhu, D., Zhu, Q.A., Hu, J., Wang, M., Zhan, W., Zhu, E.X., *et al.* (2014). The carbon stock of alpine peatlands on the Qinghai-Tibetan Plateau during the Holocene and their future fate. Quaternary Science Reviews 95, 151-158.
2. Cai, X., Jin, S., 1963. Mire types and their development on the Zoige Plateau. Acta Geographica Sinica 29, 219-240 (in Chinese with a Russian abstract).
3. Gao, J., Ouyang, H., Wang, G., Xu, X., 2010a. Recent peat accumulation rates in Zoige peatlands, Eastern Tibet, inferred by 210Pb and 137Cs radiometric techniques. Procedia Environmental Sciences 2, 1927-1933.
4. Guo, C., Luo, F., Ding, X., Luo, Q., Luo, C., Cai, Y., Zhao, J., Feng, S., Yang, Z., and Zhang, J. (2013). Palaeoclimate reconstruction based on pollen records from the Tangke and Riganqiao peat sections in the Zoige Plateau, China. Quaternary International 286, 19-28.
5. Joosten, H., Tapio-Biström, M. L., and Tol, S. 2012. Peatlands-guidance for climate change mitigation by conservation, rehabilitation and sustainable use. Food and Agriculture Organization of United Nations (FAO). Rome.
6. Lähteenoja, O., Reátegui, Y.R., Räsänen, M., Torres, D.D.C., Oinonen, M., and Page, S. (2012). The large Amazonian peatland carbon sink in the subsiding Pastaza-Marañón foreland basin, Peru. Global Change Biology 18, 164-178.
7. Shi, Y., Zheng, B., Li, S., Ye, B. 1995. Studies on altitude and climatic environment in the middle and east parts of Tibetan Plateau during Quaternary Maximum Glaciation. Journal of Glaciology and Geocryology 17: 97-112.
8. Song, H., Wang, D., Zhao, K., 1985. Formation and evolution of peatlands in Xizang(-Tibet) Plateau. Science Geographica. Sinica. 5, 173-178 (in Chinese with an English abstract).
9. Sun, G., Zhang, W., Zhang, J., 1998. The Mire and Peatland of the Hengduan Mountains Region. Science Press, Beijing.
10. Sun, G., Luo, X., Turner, R.E., 2001. A study on peat deposition chronogy of Holocene of Zoige Plateau in the northeatern Qinghai-Tibetan Plateau. Acta Sedimentologica Sinica 19, 177-181 (in Chinese with an English abstract).
11. Talma, A., Vogel, J.C., 1993. A simplified approach to calibrating $\Delta\,^{14}C$ dates. Radiocarbon 35.
12. Wang, M., 1987. The spore-pollen groups of peatland on Ruoergai Plateau, paleobatany and paleoclimate. Acta Geographica Sinica 7, 147e155 (in Chinese with an English abstract).
13. Zheng, B., Ma, Q., 1995. A study on the geomorphological characteristics and glaciations in Paleo-Daocheng Ice Cap, Western Sichaun. Journal of Glaciology and Geocryology 17: 23-32 (in Chinese with an English abstract).

Abstract No: A-443

COLLECTING ORIGINAL DATA ON ATMOSPHERIC CARBON BALANCE FROM A FORESTED LANDSCAPE – RIAU, INDONESIA

Chandrashekhar Deshmukh*, Anthony Greer, John Bathgate

Asia Pacific Resources International Limited (APRIL)

* *Corresponding author: chandra_deshmukh@aprilasia.com*

The identification and accurate quantification of sinks or sources of atmospheric carbon has become a key challenge for scientists and policy-makers groups working on climate change or global warming mitigation. Tropical peatlands, which are predominantly located in Southeast Asia, have accumulated significant global carbon over millennia. The sensitive peat accumulation process is jointly governed by hydrology, ecology and landscape morphology of the ecosystem. In the last few decades, tropical peatlands have been intensively modified via widespread activities (e.g. drainage, wildfire, and logging). Reliable measurement of carbon exchange at landscape scale are needed to help countries such as Indonesia to measure, report and verify (MRV) their greenhouse gas emissions from land use and land use change within the framework of climate mitigation programmes. Unfortunately, very few scientifically sound, indisputable and detailed "Tier 3" greenhouse gas flux measurements are currently available from tropical peatlands. Hence, there is a great need for long term monitoring, with more measurements, integrating a wider range of managed and unmanaged tropical peatlands, and using more rigorous techniques to provide comprehensive information on the temporal and spatial variability. High frequency and long term measurements are useful to investigate the link between carbon exchanges and their drivers. This could increase our understanding of the underlying processes regulating carbon exchanges on different time scales. In this project, we attempt to quantify the carbon exchange at landscape scale in Riau, Indonesia. The study area is heterogeneous, consisting of managed and unmanaged forests, i.e. intact peat swamp forest, degraded forest (logged, drained and affected by fire), and *Acacia crassicarpa* plantations, representative of the South-eastern tropical peatlands. The project establishes long-term direct carbon exchange monitoring using eddy covariance technique combined with automated soil CO_2 chamber and aims to explore: 1) the carbon sequestration potential; 2) the CH_4 exchange with the atmosphere; and 3) the carbon export through the drainage networks. Further, we also aim to investigate the factors controlling the spatial and the temporal variability that will assist the extrapolation of carbon exchange on the regional/national/global scale. Our sampling strategy also allows quantifying the net impact of the land use change by comparing carbon exchange in managed land use to those in intact peatlands. This project will provide comprehensive information about the carbon balance at the landscape scale in tropical peatlands and integrate knowledge to deliver enhanced resolution and accuracy in estimates of GHG exchanges at regional, national and global GHG inventories under the UNFCCC framework.

Keywords: *carbon balance, net ecosystem exchange, methane, eddy covariance, forest, peatlands, Sumatra*

Abstract No: A-418

EFFECTS OF EXPERIMENTAL CLIMATE WARMING ON C SINK FUNCTION IN A TEMPERATE PEATLAND

F. Laggoun-Defarge[1*], A. Buttler[2, 5], F. Delarue[1], D. Epron[3], A.J. Francez[4], D. Gilbert[5], V.E. J. Jassey[5], L. Grasset[6], C. Guimbaud[7], A. Huguet[8] and E.A.D. Mitchell[9]

[1] Univ. Orleans, CNRS-INSU, BRGM, UMR 7327, ISTO, Orleans, France
[2] EPFL/WSL, Lausanne, ECOS, 1015 Lausanne, Switzerland
[3] Univ. Nancy, INRA UMR 1137, EEF, Nancy, France
[4] Univ. Rennes, CNRS, UMR 6553, ECOBIO, Rennes, France
[5] Univ. Franche Comté, UMR 6249, Chrono-Environnement Besançon, France
[6] Univ. Poitiers, CNRS UMR 6514, SRSN, Poitiers, France
[7] Univ. Orléans, CNRS UMR 6115, LPC2E, Orléans, France
[8] UPMC, CNRS/ UMR 7618, BioEMCo, Paris, France
[9] Univ. Neuchâtel, Neuchâtel, Switzerland

** Corresponding author: Fatima.Laggoun-Defarge@univ-orleans.fr*

Global warming induces complex interactions which could have a positive or a negative feedback on C storage in soils. Peatlands have stored one-third of the global C stock of soils because of low rates of plant residue decomposition due to oxygen limitation resulting from flooding which inhibits microbial activities. Given the multiple possible responses of peatlands to global warming, it is presently impossible to predict their future contribution to the global C cycle. Several approaches have attempted to assess the effect of warming on peatlands: mesocosms, latitudinal transects, and *in situ* field experimental warming. Most of these studies only assessed the warming impact on vegetation and surface gas emissions, and so far, no study to date has addressed the entire range of biodiversity, community structure and ecosystem function responses to increased temperature, particularly in temperate peatlands. Within the PEATWARM project (ANR-07-VUL-010), we investigated the response of a *Sphagnum* peatland in the Jura Mountains (France) to climate change using an experimental system (Open Top Chambers – OTC's) to simulate *in situ* an increase in average temperature. We examined the effects of temperature increase along a narrow fen-bog gradient on the vegetation, above- and below-ground gas fluxes (CO_2 and CH_4), microbial diversity and activity in *Sphagnum* mosses and in peat, CNS interactions between macro- and micro-organisms in the peat biota, and the dynamics of labile and recalcitrant peat organic matter. We showed that warming modifies the C and nutrient cycling of the peatland via changes in above- and below-ground interactions. Furthermore, the contrasted responses to warming between the fen and the bog sites suggest that the spatial variability of moisture and hydrochemistry is critical for understanding the impact of global warming on the fate of organic matter and the C cycle in peatlands.

***Keywords**:-*

Abstract No: A-234

ESTIMATION OF ORGANIC CARBON FLUX FROM TWO STREAMS IN TROPICAL PEAT SWAMP FOREST OF RIAU PROVINCE, SUMATRA, INDONESIA

Haiki Mart Yupi[1*], Takashi Inoue[2], John Bathgate[3] and Rosef Putra[3]

[1]Graduate School of Agriculture, Hokkaido University, Japan
[2]Research Faculty of Agriculture, Hokkaido University, Japan
[3]PT. Riau Andalan Pulp and Paper, Indonesia

**Corresponding author: haiki.yupi@yahoo.com*

SUMMARY

Organic carbon (C) fluxes (i.e. organic C load and C yields) were estimated in two stream of tropical peat swamp forest (TPSF) within a peatland area of Riau Province, Sumatra, Indonesia. One stream, Meranti Ditch (MD) is an artificial ditch with a small catchment (4.8 km^2) in semi-intact condition. Another stream, Turip River (TR) is a large catchment (458 km^2) covered with TPSF that is largely intact. Due to large content of carbon store in TPSF, it is necessary to know how much organic C fluxes in the stream are released from this type of landscape. By combining the concentration of total organic carbon (TOC) with continuous discharge, organic C load (Gg C yr^{-1}) in TPSF stream water was estimated. Organic C yields (g C m^{-2} yr^{-1}) were obtained from C load divided by catchment area. Stream dissolved organic carbon (DOC) constituted the greatest portion (95.0 to 99.8% in concentration) of TOC, with stream TOC concentration in MD range from 85 to 94 mg C l^{-1} which was higher compared to the TR range from 50 to 58 mg C l^{-1}. The high concentration in MD is expected as this catchment has been disturbed from several rounds of logging including intensive pattern of ditch dug a decade ago. TOC load of stream water in MD and TR were 0.23 and 14.0 Gg C yr^{-1} respectively. TOC yields or fluxes through the fluvial system ranged from 26.2 g C m^{-2} yr^{-1} in TR to 55.5 g C m^{-2} yr^{-1} in MD.

***Keywords**: TOC; DOC; carbon leaching; tropical peatland*

INTRODUCTION

Southeast Asia's peat deposits contain an estimate of 68.5 Gt C (77% of the total tropical Peat C, 88.6 Gt). This amount is equivalent to 11 to 14% of global peat C. The largest tropical peat C accumulation is in Indonesia (57.4 Gt, i.e. 65% of the total C in tropical peat) and followed by Malaysia (9.1 Gt, 10%) (Page *et al.*, 2011). The TPSF within a peatland area has the potential to release large amounts of organic C into the environment through air (gaseous) and water (fluvial) by anthropogenic activities (IPCC 2000).

Despite increased interest regarding C released through TPSF river systems, limited studies have been conducted. To improve accuracy and to identify the influences of discharge variability on organic C load in TPSF, it is necessary to have continuous measurement of water discharge because the flow rates are affected by the occurrence of both rain events and discharge response. Organic C released through stream and river system within TPSF may have influences on C loss in peat. The purpose of this study is to quantify C flux (C load and C yield) from TPSF of Sumatra using continuous flow rate combined with organic C concentration in the stream. Furthermore, the differences in periodic and continuous measurement of organic C load would be defined.

MATERIALS AND METHODS

Study site descriptions

The study area is located in the southwest portion of Kampar Peninsular, in Pelelawan District of Riau Province, Sumatra, Indonesia. It lies approximately 130 km east-southeast from Pekanbaru, the capital city of Riau Province. Two sites were selected for hydrological measurement. One is a small stream named Meranti Ditch (MD) and the other is a river named Turip River (TR). Water sampling and flow rate measurement were conducted in the downstream end of both MD and TR catchments (0° 15' 0.1" N, 102° 34' 29.6" E and 0° 17' 26.3" N, 102° 37' 50.4" E, respectively).

MD and TR catchments are formed entirely of recent peat deposits (Brady, 1997). A high content of humic acids is found in the stream runoff water as indicated by dark orange-black color of the water. Peat depth of MD and TR were 6 m and 7 m respectively as measured using peat samplers. Vegetation of the study area is tropical peat swamp forest (TPSF). MD is a small catchment with semi-intact TPSF, and terminates in the regenerating forest buffer between conserved TPSF and *Acacia* plantation. Whereas TR is a natural river system having no artificial river control and has a large catchment. TR study catchment is almost entirely covered in TPSF. The condition is estimated from remote images to be 75% intact and 25% degraded.

Continuous data of stream flow rate, groundwater depth and rainfall

Hydrological measurement was conducted from May 24, 2012 to December 12, 2013 for MD, and from May 25, 2012 to February 8, 2013 for TR. In both study sites, the stream water level (SWL) was measured continuously by using water level data logger. At the same time, in both catchment areas, groundwater depth (GWD) was measured. The measured points were located at 0° 15' 12.5" N, 102° 34' 34.0" E for MD, and 0° 17' 37.8" N, 102° 37' 58.7" E for TR. The location of GWD measurement sites was only about 300 to 400 m apart from the stream. Flow rate was measured using an electromagnetic velocity meter at the same location of stream water level measurement with stable stream cross section in MD and TR. Data was gathered 12 times at both sites during the observation period. For each site, discharge rating curves were created from the relationship between each flow rate and SWL, to get continuous flow rate data. Amount of rainfall was recorded at the open area near the MD stream measurement site by using a 0.5-mm tipping-bucket type rain gauge, equipped with a data logger.

Estimation of catchment area

In this study, catchment area of MD and TR sites was estimated using two approaches. First, the water balance approach in which runoff depth (q) was calculated by subtracting the assumed evapotranspiration (ET) value from the rainfall (P). Then the catchment area (A) was determined from dividing the total discharge (Q) by runoff depth (q). The ET value was determined using data obtained from the studies conducted by Kumagai *et al.* (2005) and Hirano *et al.* (2014) in tropical peatland of Borneo, and also the study by Baum *et al.* (2007) in Sumatra. Under this approach, it was assumed that the groundwater inflow and outflow did not change the stored water volume in each catchment. The second approach to estimate catchment area used spatial analyst of SRTM-DSM (Shuttle Radar Topography Mission–Digital Surface Model).

Water sampling, analytical procedures and quantifying TOC, DOC, POC fluxes (load and yield)

Stream water sampling was carried out at the same time and locations as flow rate measurement, at weekly intervals from May 24, 2012 to July 30, 2012, then once a month from November 2012 to March 2013. In the field, stream water samples were obtained using 250 ml plastic bottles from *ca.* 30 cm depth below the stream surface without filtering.

Stream water samples were stored at low temperature (*ca.* 5^0C) in the dark until laboratory analysis. In laboratory, TOC and DOC concentration of water samples were analyzed using a TOC analyzer. The amount of POC concentration was not measured, but it was determined from the difference of TOC and DOC concentrations.

TOC and DOC loads were obtained by multiplying the values of instantaneous concentration of TOC or DOC with flow rate at the time of sampling. Then the relationship between organic C load ($L_{(TOC)}$ or $L_{(DOC)}$) and the flow rate (Q) at MD and TR, i.e., the L-Q formula was determined. To quantify the continuous organic C load during the observation period, this L-Q formula was applied to the continuous flow rate data. The total POC load was obtained by subtracting DOC load from TOC load. The organic C yield was then obtained by dividing organic C load by the catchment area.

RESULTS AND DISCUSSION

Catchment area

For estimation of catchment area using the water balance approach, the percentage of water loss by evapotranspiration was assumed to be 60, 65, and 70% of the total rainfall recorded at MD. The values of rainfall and stream discharge used in this estimation would be described in the later part of this section. Consequently, the estimated catchment area of MD ranged from 4.2 to 5.6 km^2, while that of TR ranged from 401 to 535 km^2 (Table 1). Using the spatial analyst of SRTM-DSM, the catchment area was 3.6 km^2 for MD and 420 km^2 for TR (Table 1). To test the accuracy of catchment areas obtained from SRTM-DSM data, water balance was back calculated. Catchment area estimation using spatial analyst of SRTM-DSM approach gave no significant difference with the estimation using water balance approach. Indicated value of total rainfall loss through ET in MD is 53% and TR is 62%.

Rainfall, stream water level, and groundwater depth

The seasonal variation in rainfall during the rainy and dry seasons was distinguished clearly. The amount of annual rainfall (from September 2012 to August 2013) for MD was 1,836 mm.

SWL and GWD at both sites are shown in Figure 1. SWL and GWD rapidly rose up after rain events and then gradually decreased due to drainage and ET. At MD, the rise of SWL against rainfall was direct, whereas at TR site, the rise of SWL was rather smooth. This is attributed to the difference between MD and TR catchment areas.

The pattern of fluctuations in SWL and GWD was closely resembled at each catchment suggest that there are no significant deep groundwater contribution to stream flow. During the monitoring period, the GWL in MD was always below the ground surface even in the rainy season. Considering that the peat ground surface consists of hummock and hollow micro topography, the shallow groundwater in MD had more contact time with peat in the form of shallow subsurface flow state (Figure 1).

The GWD in TR became much higher than the ground surface during a certain period of the year (until June 2012, November 2012 to January 2013, and after November 2013) (Figure 1). During these high water periods, water level fluctuations in stream water and the groundwater in TR were very similar and the response to rain event was not apparent. The range and the pattern of water level fluctuation in this period were exactly the same (Figure 1), indicating that during high water season the stream water flooded and inundated the adjacent peatland area. On the other hand, fluctuation of stream water as well as groundwater levels in the low water period was different from the high water period. Response of the GWD to a rain event was much more sharp and direct compared to the SWL, showing only a slight response at most. The general trend of both water level fluctuations was quite similar. It appeared that the GWD in the peatland fluctuated directly due to rainfall, discharge, and ET, but the base of GWD movement seems to be controlled by the SWL.

Stream discharge

Based on Q (discharge) and h (stream water level) relationship discharge rating curves equation have obtained, for MD was $Q = 0.21\ h^{6.09}$ ($R^2 = 0.86$) and TR was $Q = 13.9\ h - 69.8$ ($R^2 = 0.63$). By using these discharge rating curve equations, continuous discharge was calculated from continuously recorded SWL, shown in Figure 2. The continuous discharge data for TR was shorter than the period of measurement for MD, due to the loss of the logger.

In MD, the average discharge was 0.10 $m^3\ s^{-1}$ while in TR it was 9.27 $m^3\ s^{-1}$. Maximum and minimum discharge in MD was 0.32 $m^3\ s^{-1}$ and 0.003 $m^3\ s^{-1}$ respectively, while in TR it was 18.55 $m^3\ s^{-1}$ and 2.20 $m^3\ s^{-1}$. The coefficient of stream regime (maximum/minimum discharge ratio) for the period of 259 days was 107 in MD and 8 in TR, indicating that the difference of discharge in dry season and rainy season is not high in TR. TR had a larger discharge and more stable river regime compared to MD, presumably due to TR's larger catchment area.

TOC, DOC, and POC concentrations

TOC concentrations of stream water ranged from 85 to 94 mg C l^{-1} at MD and from 50 to 58 mg C l^{-1} at TR. For both streams, greatest portion of TOC was in the form of DOC with a range of 82 to 90 mg C l^{-1} for the MD and of 49 to 57 mg C l^{-1} for the TR. Only a small portion of TOC was in the form of POC (0.2% through 5%, or around 0.2 mg C l^{-1} through 4.5 mg C l^{-1}). The TOC concentration at the MD was higher compared to TR. The likely reason is because the catchment has been highly disturbed by several rounds of logging including intensive pattern of ditch dug a decade ago, with associated of changes in peatland gradients topography as the influence of subsidence after ditch digging; enhanced surface and subsurface water flow may readily flush the peat C to the stream. Whereas TR is large catchment where 75% of the area is intact TPSF including large peat plain headwater that is untouched by logging hence the smaller contribution for organic C into stream water.

TOC, DOC, and POC fluxes (yield and load)

As the results of the difference in catchment area estimation as shown in Table 1, the TOC yield values were 55.5 g C $m^{-2}\ yr^{-1}$ and 34.9 g C $m^{-2}\ yr^{-1}$ as upper estimated values, and 41.6 g C $m^{-2}\ yr^{-1}$ and 26.2 g C $m^{-2}\ yr^{-1}$ for lower estimated values for MD and TR, respectively (Table 2). DOC yield values were 54.8 g C $m^{-2}\ yr^{-1}$ and 34.7 g C $m^{-2}\ yr^{-1}$ as upper estimated values, and 41.1 g C $m^{-2}\ yr^{-1}$ and 26.0 g C $m^{-2}\ yr^{-1}$ for lower estimated values for MD and TR, respectively The POC yields were very small and it was only 0.6 to 1.3% of the TOC yield. The organic C yield (TOC, DOC, and POC) was higher in MD than in TR. This is a reflection of higher organic C concentration in MD compared to TR.

Compared to estimates of the total amount of C released to the atmosphere from TPSF e.g., 974.0 to 1,035.3 g C $m^{-2}\ yr^{-1}$ (Hirano *et al.*, 2009), released organic C per unit area through MD and TR stream water ranged from 2.7 to 5.4%. These estimations of small amounts of C released through stream water are useful for better estimation of the TPSF C budget and for better understanding of C supply from TPSF to the hydrosphere.

The TOC load released from TPSF to MD was calculated as 0.23 Gg C yr^{-1} whereas the TOC load for TR was estimated as 14.0 Gg C yr^{-1} (Table 2). This value is based on 1-yr hydrological continuous observation data that has shown in Figure 2. In Table 2, significant differences between estimated value of organic C load based on continuous and periodic data are also shown. In MD, TOC load estimation using the periodic data show higher value compared to the estimation by the continuous load (difference of 27%), whereas in TR, periodic data gave lower estimation than estimation calculated by the continuous data (difference of 8.8%). This was due to influences of discharges variability during the monitoring period that could not be detected by the periodic data.

CONCLUSIONS

The greatest portion of TPSF stream water TOC was in the form of DOC and only a small portion was in the form of POC (0.2 to 5.0 % of TOC). TOC load transported from the TPSF catchment to the stream during the study period was estimated as 0.23 Gg C yr^{-1} for MD and 14.0 Gg C yr^{-1} for TR. There were significant differences of organic C load estimation between continuous and periodic data.

From DOC load per unit area, or DOC yield values, summarized from the previous studies for different catchment types and different regions, it is obvious that the DOC yield from TPSF is higher compared to other catchment types in boreal and temperate regions. TOC yields ranged from 41.6 to 55.5 g C m^{-2} yr^{-1} in MD and from 26.2 to 34.9 g C m^{-2} yr^{-1} in TR. In small catchment of MD (4.8 km^2) having higher organic C yields than in larger catchment of TR (458 km^2). This result is appropriate with the result of Dawson *et al.* 2004, which have reported that smaller catchment in C-rich landscapes typically having higher C yields or fluxes than the similar but larger catchment. Relative to total C released from TPSF to the atmosphere according to some estimates, e.g., 974.0 to 1,035.3 g C m^{-2} yr^{-1} (Hirano *et al.*, 2009), the released organic C yields through MD and TR stream water were very small (ranged from 2.7 to 5.4%).

ACKNOWLEDGMENTS

This research was supported by the JST-JICA Project entitled "Wild Fire and Carbon Management in Peat Forest in Indonesia", and Integrated Field Environment Science - Global Centre of Excellence (IFES-GCOE) program of the Government of Japan. The authors thank Dr. Anthony Greer and people of PT. Riau Andalan Pulp and Paper in Meranti sub-district for their support during this study. Further thanks go to the students of Laboratory of Land Improvement and Management, Graduate School of Agriculture, Hokkaido University for their support. Finally, the authors appreciate the support received from Dr. Ryusuke Hatano and Mr. Kiwamu Ishikura.

REFERENCES

1. Baum, A., Rixen, T. & Samiaji, J. (2007) Relevance of peat draining rivers in central Sumatra for the riverine input of dissolved organic carbon into the ocean. *Estuarine, Coastal and Shelf Science,* 73, 563–570.

2. Brady, M.A. (1997) *Organic matter dynamics of coastal peat deposits in Sumatra, Indonesia*. Doctor's thesis report, The University of British Columbia, Canada, 258 pp

3. Dawson, J.J.C., Billett, M.F., Hope.D., Palmer, S.M., Deacon, C.M. (2004) Sources and sinks of aquatic carbon in peat land stream continuum. *Biogeochemistry*, 70, 71–92.

4. Hirano, T., Jauhiainen, J., Inoue, T. & Takahashi, H. (2009) Controls on the Carbon Balance of Tropical Peatlands. *Ecosystems,* 12, 873–887.

5. Hirano, T., Kusin, K., Limin, S. & Osaki, M. (2014) Evapotranspiration of tropical peat swamp forests. *Global Change Biology,* doi: 10.1111/gcb.12653

6. Intergovernmental Panel on Climate Change (IPCC). (2000) *IPCC Special Report. Land use, land-use change and forestry. Summary for Policymakers,* 24 pp.

7. Kumagai, T., Saitoh, T.M., Sato, Y., Takahashi, H., Manfroi, O.J., Morooka, T., Kuraji, K., Suzuki, M., Yasunari, T. & Komatsu, H. (2005) Annual water balance and seasonality of evapotranspiration in a Bornean tropical rainforest. *Agricultural and Forest Meteorology,* 128, 81–92.

8. Moore, S., Evans, C.D., Page, S.E., Garnet, M.H., Jones, T.G., Freeman, C., Hooijer, A., Wiltshire, A.J., Limin, S. & Gauci, V. (2013) Deep instability of deforested tropical peatlands revealed by fluvial organic carbon fluxes. *Nature,* 493, 660–663.

9. Page, S.E., Rieley, J.O. & Banks, C.J. (2011) Global and regional importance of the tropical peatland carbon pool. *Global Change Biology,* 17, 798–818.

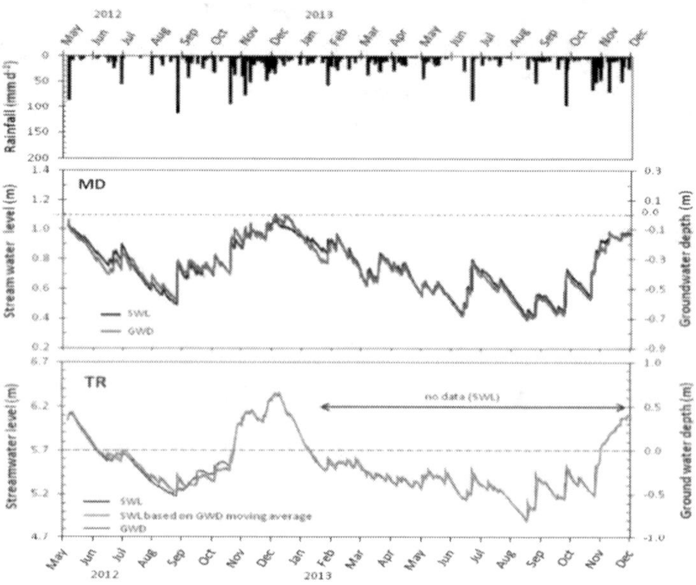

Figure 1: Rainfall, stream water level and groundwater depth in Meranti Ditch (MD) and Turip River (TR)

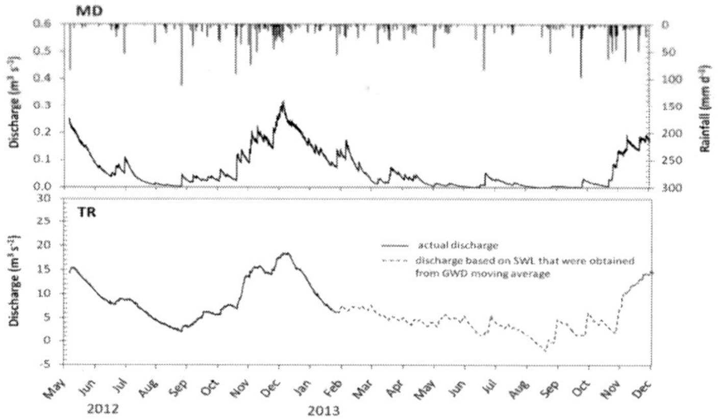

Figure 2: Discharge from Meranti Ditch (MD) and Turip River (TR)

Table 1: Estimation of catchment areas

Study site (period of measurement)	Total observed rainfall	Estimated evapotranspiration (ET)		Runoff depth (q)	Total observed stream discharge	Estimation of catcment area (1 = water balance basis)	Estimation of catcment area (2 = spatial analyst SRTM-DSM basis)
	(mm)	(%)	(mm)	(mm)	(m^3)	(km^2)	(km^2)
	i	ii	iii = (i*ii)/100	iv = i - iii	v	vi = (v/iv*10^3)/10^6	vii
MD (2012.5.25-2013.2.8/259 days)	1,291	60	775	516	2.17E+06	4.2	3.6
		65	839	452		4.8	
		70	904	387		5.6	
TR (2012.5.25-2013.2.8/259 days)	1,291	60	775	516	2.07E+08	400.9	420.0
		65	839	452		458.1	
		70	904	387		534.5	

Table 2: Annual organic C (TOC, DOC, POC) yields and load of Meranti Ditch (MD) and Turip River (TR) obtained by continuous and periodic data.

Site		TOC	DOC	POC
MD	yield (g C m^{-2} yr^{-1}) continuous estimation	55.5 *	54.8 *	0.7 *
		41.6 **	41.1 **	0.5 **
	load (Gg C yr^{-1}) continuous estimation	0.233	0.230	0.003
	load (Gg C yr^{-1}) periodic estimation	0.296 127% ***	0.287 125% ***	0.009 200% ***
TR	yield (g C m^{-2} yr^{-1}) continuous estimation	34.9 *	34.7 *	0.2 *
		26.2 **	26.0 **	0.2 **
	load (Gg C yr^{-1}) continuous estimation	14.0	13.9	0.1
	load (Gg C yr^{-1}) periodic estimation	12.8 91.2% ***	12.7 91.5% ***	0.1 58% ***

Note: * = upper estimate
** = lower estimate
*** = % against continuously estimated load
yield = load / catchment area

Abstract No: A-397

POTENTIAL CARBON STORES IN NEW GUINEA PEATLANDS

Geoffrey Hope

Australian National University Canberra, Australia

**Corresponding author: Geoffrey.Hope@anu.edu.au*

SUMMARY

Peatlands in the large (0.8 M km^2) equatorial island of New Guinea are very extensive but poorly understood. The lowland and montane peatlands include grass-sedge swamps and swamp forests. Large peat domes, similar to those in Kalimantan, may be present but they have not been measured. Near Popondetta an 80,000 ha area of peatland has a maximum altitude of 27m falling over 8 km to rivers at about 17m (Figure 2). This peatland is described by Hantjens (1964) as lacking dipterocarps but having other Malesian swamp forest genera such as *Campnospermum, Terminalia, Myristica, Bischofia, Pouteria, Planchonella, Neoscortechinia, Garcinia*, and *Gardenia.* There are also extensive mangrove areas and riverine floodplain sedgelands ( ) and grasslands and seasonally flooded swamps underlain by organic-rich silts and clays as well as peat. The mountain peatlands (850-4700 m) include grass and sedge valley-fill deposits and swamp forests (Hope 2015). In the cool wet subalpine above 2800 m, there is a greater diversity of grass, herb, fern and shrub covered peat-forming communities and blanket bog is extensive. The total area of these subalpine peatlands is probably around 1 M ha

***Keywords**: Tropical peat, New Guinea, carbon stocks*

PEATLAND EXTENT

The peat soils of Papua New Guinea (the eastern half of New Guinea) have been mapped in PNGRIS, a Resource Information System prepared by the CSIRO (Australia) that compiles soil and land use categories (Hanson *et al.*, 2001). The data on wetland soils (mainly histosols such as tropohemist and tropofibrists) was compiled for sixteen provinces, generating 4849 regional mapping units (RMU). In Papua province of Indonesia (the western part of New Guinea) satellite and aerial mapping of peatland vegetation onto 31 map sheets has been supported by limited stratigraphic investigations (Wahyunto *et al.*, 2006). The author has collected limited stratigraphic data for peatlands in New Guinea, largely from the montane and subalpine zone (eg Haberle 1998, Hope 2014, Walker and Flenley 1979).

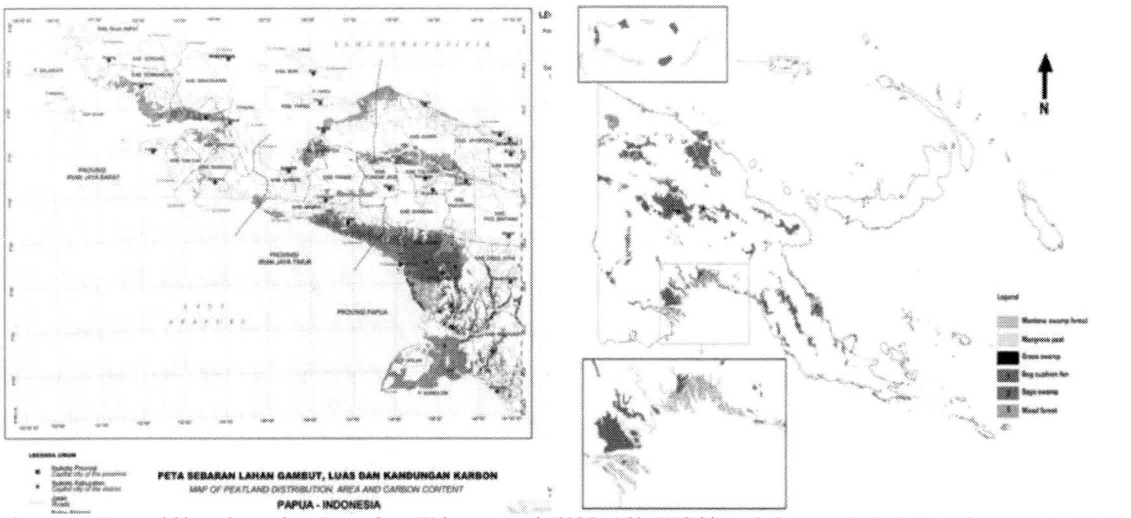

Figure 1(a): Peat and histosol mapping- Papua from Wahyunto *et al.* (2006); 1(b): PNG histosols from PNGRIS. Colours from Papua relate to estimated depth classes, with green >100cm and blue >200cm.

In the lowlands (altitude <850m) estimates of peatland area range from 4.1-13.6 M ha while the uplands (>850 m) may contain 1.5 M ha or more of peat covered landscapes. However most of the montane peats are not mapped on the Papuan map (Fig 1 a) and it also omits very large apparent peat domes in the Mamberamo basin. On the PNG map several large areas of lowland peats, for example near Vanimo, have not been included. Peat depths are poorly known – based on limited coring, estimated mean depths are shown in Table 1.

Major peat-forming wetland areas in New Guinea

Dominant vegetation	Peat types	altitude range m	Peat thickness m	Area PNG MHa	Area Papua MHa	Area All NG MHa
Lowland forest and swamp	Hemic-Sapric	0-300	0.5-3	5.6	8.0	13.6
Montane swamp forest	Fibrous wood peat	300-3000	1.5-8.5	0.14	0.2	0.3
Tall and short sedge-grass swamp	Fibrous peat, humic clays	500-2900	2.0-9.0	0.08	0.1	0.2
Subalpine moorlands and fens and: blanket bog,	Humic and fibrous peats	2900-4500	0.4-3.0	0.4	0.7	1.0
All fen and bog				6.2	8.9	15

Table 1: Summary of peat area and estimates of mean depths

CARBON STOCKS

Using these area and depth values and average values for carbon content, a preliminary estimate for carbon stocks is that 7.1 M ha of peatlands in Papua contain 3.6 Tg of carbon while 5.1 M ha of peatlands in PNG contain about 5-6 Tg of carbon. The total carbon store of 9-10 Tg is about 14% of estimated carbon stocks in Southeast Asian lowland peats (Page *et al.*, 2011).

DISCUSSION

This estimate of carbon stock is clearly an underestimate given the suspected areas of un-mapped peat and conservative mean depth estimates.

For example peat depths exceeding 20 m have been found during drilling in the southern Sepik River basin. There are also extensive fossil peat deposits known, buried by tephra or slope deposits. These include a 20m peat section buried by a lahar around 50,000 years ago.

Figure 2: Peatland with apparent doming, north of Popondetta, PNG. This area has experienced frequent tephra falls over the past 80,000 years.

Stratigraphic work (eg Haberle 2009, Hope 2009) demonstrates that some of the montane peatlands span more than 30-50 ka BP although most form at the end of the last glaciation. A lowland peatland at 65m altitude near Vanimo, PNG has an age of 7000 yr BP at 7 m but the total depth is unknown. The peatlands and lake systems on the extensive floodplains are likely to reflect post-glacial sea level rise, eg Ono *et al.* 2015.

RESEARCH QUESTIONS

The obvious need is to improve the mapping and

particularly the stratigraphic knowledge of the peatland systems across the island. The carbon density of the peat is also poorly understood as bulk density data are generally absent. Particularly in the lowlands the age structure of peat can provide an approximation to carbon sequestration and changing peat accumulation rates through time and under different land covers, as shown in Kalimantan by Dommain *et al.* (2011).

There is a gradient in tephra content from east to west, with peatlands in Papua lacking the tephra layers found in PNG. This may affect different preservation processes as the weathering of dacitic ash in PNG seems to help preserve old organic deposits. It may also influence peat accumulation rates through nutritional inputs to highly oligotrophic settings.

A possible model is provided by the accumulation of organic lake sediments in shallow post-glacial tarns. One site on the border area of PNG and Papua has built up about 2.5m compared to 8-10 m in a tephra prone area to the east.

A major research question is whether lowland peat forests in New Guinea share the characteristics of the biogeographically distinct western Indonesian domed peatlands. In the SE Asian lowland tropics, ombrotrophic peat formation under forest cover may depend on mycorrhizal activity that maintains dramatically low pH with consequent inhibition of other decay processes. The presence of such fungi has still to be established in New Guinea although low pH litter with mycorrhiza are known in the Pacific.

ACKNOWLEDGEMENTS

I am grateful to Rachel Nanson and Bryant Allen for mapping histosol extent in PNG. I am grateful to Simon Haberle, Allen Allison, Ken Aplin, Richard Corlett, Jan Finn, Mike Prentice and Donald Walker for unpublished data on New Guinean peatlands. The research has been supported by the Australian National University, LIPI and the PNG Research Institute. Access to the peatlands has always depended on the knowledge and enthusiasm of New Guinean people.

REFERENCES

1. Dommain, R., Couwenberg, J. and Joosten, H., 2011. Development and carbon sequestration of tropical peat domes in south-east Asia: links to post-glacial sea-level changes and Holocene climate variability. *Quaternary Science Reviews* 30(7), 999-1010.
2. Haantjens, H. A. 1964. General Report on Lands of the Buna-Kokoda Area, Territory of Papua and New Guinea. Melbourne: Commonwealth Scientific and Industrial Research Organization; 113 pp. Land Research Series; v. 10.
3. Haberle, S. G. 1998. Late Quaternary vegetation change in the Tari Basin, Papua New Guinea. *Palaeogeography, Palaeoclimatology, Palaeoecology* 137, 1-24.
4. Haberle, S. 2007. Prehistoric human impact on rainforest biodiversity in highland New Guinea. *Philosophical Transactions of the Royal Society of London Series B* 362, 219–228.
5. Hanson, L.W., Allen, B.J., Bourke, R.M. & McCarthy, T.J. 2001. *Papua New Guinea Rural Development Handbook*. Land Management Group, Australian National University, Canberra, 326 pp.
6. Hope, G.S. 2009. Environmental change and fire in the Owen Stanley Ranges, Papua New Guinea. *Quaternary Science Reviews* 28, 2261–2276.
7. Hope, G.S. 2014. The sensitivity of the high mountain ecosystems of New Guinea to climatic change and anthropogenic impact. *Arctic, Antarctic and Alpine Research* 46(4), 777-786.
8. Hope, G.S. 2015. Peat in the mountains of New Guinea. *Mires and Peat* 15: Art. 13, 1-21.
9. Ono, E., Umemura, M., Ishida, T. and Takenaka, C., 2015. Preliminary investigation of the formation age and chemical characterization of the tropical peat in the middle Sepik Plain, northern Papua New Guinea. *Geoscience Letters 2*(1), 1-6.
10. Page, S.E., Rieley, J.O. and Banks, C.J. 2011. Global and regional importance of the tropical peatland carbon pool. *Global Change Biology* 17(2), 798-818.
11. Paijmans, K. 1990. Wooded swamps in New Guinea. In A.E. Lugo, M. Brinson & S. Brown(eds), Forested wetlands 335 - 355., Ecosystems of the World 15, Elsevier, Amsterdam.
12. Radjagukguk, B., 1997. Peat soils of Indonesia: location, classification and problems for sustainability. Pp. 45-54 in J.O. Rieley and, S.E. Page (eds), *Biodiversity and Sustainability of Tropical Peatlands*. Samara Publishing, Cardigan.
13. Wahyunto, Heryanto, B., Bekti, H. and Widiastuti, F. 2006. Peta-Peta Sebaran Lahan Gambut, Luas dan Kandungan Karbon di Papua / *Maps of Peatland Distribution, Area and Carbon Content in Papua, 2000 - 2001. Wetlands International – Indonesia Programme* & Wildlife Habitat Canada (WHC), pp 52.

Abstract No: A-209

SOIL CARBON DYNAMICS AS THE IMPACT OF CHANGE IN TROPICAL PEATLAND USES IN WEST KALIMANTAN, INDONESIA

Rossie Wiedya Nusantara[1], Sudarmadji[2], Tjut S. Djohan[3] and Eko Haryono[2]

[1]*Faculty of Agriculture, Tanjungpura University, Indonesia*
[2]*Faculty of Geography, Gadjah Mada University, Indonesia*
[3]*Faculty of Biology, Gadjah Mada University, Indonesia*

**Corresponding author: rwiedyanusantara@gmail.com*

SUMMARY

Peatland in Indonesia is a major natural sink of organic carbon (C). Changing of tropical peat forest to another land uses, especially for oil palm plantation, might have destroyed peat characteristics and released large amounts of C to the atmosphere. C isotopic ratio ($^{13}C/^{12}C$) of organic C have been used to study environmental changes, especially in changing of peatland-use. This research aimed to analyze the soil C and C isotope ($\delta^{13}C$) of peatland based on its maturity level on several types of peatland use. The study area is based on the type of use of peatlands in West Kalimantan, include primary peat forest, secondary peat forest, shrubs, oil palm plantation, and corn field. The research site areas were determined based on five types of commonly peatland used in West Kalimantan, namely: primary peat forest, secondary peat forest, shrubs, oil palm plantation, and corn field. Soil samples were collected based on peat maturity levels (fibric, hemic, sapric). The sample is analyzed for its soil organic C and $\delta^{13}C$. The samples were analyzed for its soil organic C and $\delta^{13}C$. The results showed that soil organic C in fibric peatland is higher than that of in hemic and sapric. Meanwhile, based on the types of land-use, soil organic C was 57.9% on primary peat forest, followed by secondary peat forest (57.1%), shrubs (57.0%), oil palm plantation (56.4%) and corn field (56.0%) soil organic C was the highest on primary peat forest, followed by secondary peat forest, oil palm plantation, corn field, and on the shrubs shrubss, respectively. Based on peat maturity levels, $\delta^{13}C$ value shows its various patterns with a tendency that of fibric was higher than that of hemic and that of sapric. Meanwhile, with respect to the types of land-use, $\delta^{13}C$ value varies with the tendency pattern that of the secondary peat forest was the highest, followed by that of primary peat forest, oil palm plantation, corn field, and shrubs, respectively. Conversion of tropical peat forest to other land uses will decrease its soil C content and $\delta^{13}C$ value. It is might be due the changing in its environmental conditions from anaerob to aerob condition. As a result, peat organic matter will be intensively decomposed.

Keywords: *Tropical peat forest, land-use change, aerobic-anaerobic condition, soil C, stable carbon isotope ($\delta^{13}C$)*

INTRODUCTION

Tropical peatlands cover approximately 27 million ha in Southeast Asia, distributed in Malaysia and Indonesian lowlands, particulary in Kalimantan, Sumatera, West Papua and Malaysia Peninsula (Page and Banks, 2007; Hooijer *et al.*, 2010; Rieley *et al.*, 1996). Tropical peats store subtantial stocks of soil carbon (C), due to the anaerobic soil conditions restricting decomposition of organic matter (Page *et al.*, 2011; Farmer *et al.*, 2013).

The existence of peat swamp forest in Indonesia is the most endangered due to the pressure from various human activitie (Page and Rieley, 2008; Harrison, 2013). The conversion of forest into agricultural land, plantation and production forest may threaten the existence of natural peat swamp forest. Changes in land use activities include the establishment of drainage channels, land clearing in the form of deforestation, logging and shrubs cutting, burning to land clearance, and land preparation such as planting line compaction and *surjan-guludan* practices (Radjagukguk 2000; Andriesse 1988; Limpens *et al.*, 2008; Rieley and Page 2008; Page *et al.*, 2009; Ojanen *et al.*, 2012; Farmer *et al.*, 2011; Wösten *et al.*, 2008; Hooijer *et al.*, 2010). The impact of peat swamp forest destruction significantly contributes to the environment a result of the massive losses of soil C and large number of C released to the atmosphere during such destruction (Hooijer *et al.*, 2010).

The conversion has the potential to change the dynamics of soil organic matter. Stable C isotope ($\delta^{13}C$) can be used to study of environmental change during land-use change or to investigate the degradation processes of peatlands (Bernoux *et al.*, 1998; Balesdent *et al.*, 1998; Lane *et al.*, 2004). Depth profiles of stable carbon isotopes generally reflect organic matter dynamics in soils with an decrease of $\delta^{13}C$ values (high minus values) during aerobic decomposition and stable or increase $\delta^{13}C$ values (low minus values) with depth during anaerobic decomposition (Krüger *et al.*, 2014; Alewell *et al.*, 2011).

Detail studies on the dynamics of C in tropical peat land, particularly based on the peat maturity (sapric, hemic, fibric) in Indonesia are very limited. Most of the studies were conducted on mineral land and some on temperate peat lands. Therefore, this study presents the peat soil C dynamics and $\delta^{13}C$ of peat land as the result of peatland conversion, from primary forest into secondary forest, shrubs, oil palm plantation and corn plantation. The purpose of this research was to analyze the dynamics of soil C and $\delta^{13}C$ based on the peat maturity within several types of peatland.

MATERIALS AND METHODS

The study areas were The study areas were five peatland types, namely: (1) primary forest (HP), (2) secondary forest (HS), (3) shrubs (SB), (4) oil palm plantation (KS) and (5) corn plantation (KJ). Map, coordinates and description of the study area (Figure 1 and Table 1). Soil samples were collected by through stratified random by considering peat maturity or development (fibric, hemic, sapric), then samples were randomly take from each stratum, repeated for five times. The maturity level of the drilled pear was identified by using von Post scale (Notohadiprawiro 1985). Sapric, hemic, fibric identify decomposed peat, half-mature and immature, respectively.

Soil C-organic (%) and ash was determined based on loss on ignition (LoI) (Agus *et al.*, 2011) in the laboratory of Indonesian Soil Research Institute in Bogor, Indonesia. Stable isotope abundances wereaare expreessed, using the δ notation in per mil (‰), as the deviation of isotopic ratio of the sample from that of an arbitrary standard, where $\delta^{13}C$ = [(R sample - R standard/ R standard] x 1000, R sample = $^{13}C/^{12}C$ of the sample and R standard = $^{13}C/^{12}C$ of the PDB standard (R_{PDB} = 0.0112372) (Bernoux *et al.*, 1998). $\delta^{13}C$ was obtained by using SIRA-9 mass spectrometer in the laboratory of Center of Isotope and Radiation Technology Applications, Jakarta-Indonesia.

The correlation between two factors (land use and peat maturity) and variables (soil C and $\delta^{13}C$) was identified by using ANOVA and Tukey's HSD (P = 0.05), if there was a positive effect between one and another within variables. All analyses were performed with SPSS version 21 (SPSS Inc).

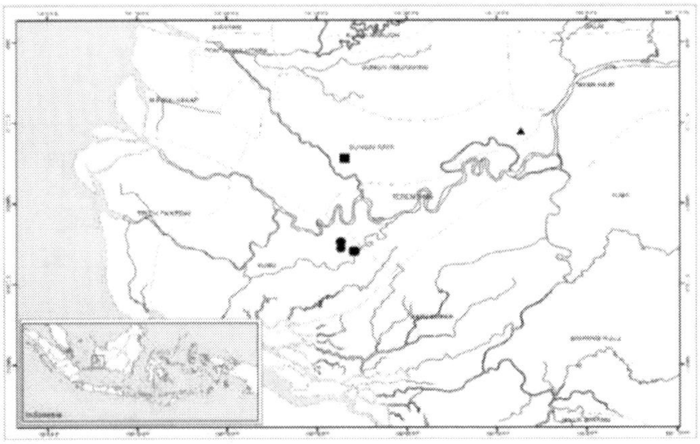

Figure 1: Sampling sites on the study area of primary forest (HP), secondary forest (HS), shrubs (SB), oil palm plantation (KS) and corn plantation (KJ)

RESULT

Soil Organic C

Soil organic C based on the land use and peat maturity in the study ranged from 54.8% to 58.0% (Figure 2). Such data indicated a tendency that organic C in fibric was higher (57.2%) than hemic (57%) and sapric (56.4%). Meanwhile, based on the type of land use, it indicated a tendency that organic C in HP was higher (57.9%) than HS (57.1%), SB (57%), KS (56.4%) and KJ (56%) respectively.

Stable ^{13}C isotope ($\delta^{13}C$)

The $\delta^{13}C$ based on the peat maturity in the study area ranged from -29.81‰ to -18.94 ‰ (Figure 3). The $\delta^{13}C$ based on the peat maturity indicated various patterns with a tendency of fibric $\delta^{13}C$ was higher than hemic and sapric, with their average value of -19.744‰, -25.688‰, -27.403‰ respectively. Meanwhile, based on the types of land use, $\delta^{13}C$ was varied in which the tendency pattern of HS (-23.2‰), HP (-23.48‰) were higher than KS (-23.65‰), KJ (-24.56‰), SB (-26.5‰) respectively. Test between the type of land with soil organic C there is a difference, but for peat maturity showed no difference. C-organic arable land (KJ and KS) significantly different with forest areas (HP and HS) but not different with shrub land (SB). Test between the maturity of peat with peat δ13C there is a difference, but for the type of land did not show a difference. δ13C in sapric significantly different with fibric or hemic.

Table 1: Description of the study area

Land-use	Location	Description
Primary forest (HP)	Sungai Raya Subdistrict, Kubu Raya Regency – 16.649 m^2 S = $00^{0}11.287$ until 355 E = $109^{0}49.456$ until 618	In this location, there were road and drainage channel crossing Protected Peat Forest. Road and drainage construction was a part of the National Program for Community Empowerment (PNPM) activities conducted in the middle of 2011. The road was 5 km long and 400 cm wide, while the drainage channel is 350 cm wide and water level of 100 cm. While surveying the location in February 2011, the condition of HP was in natural condition with muddy peat land surface and water level of approximately 1-2 cm. The dominant vegetation in the location included Ubah (*Syzygium* spp.), Tanjan (*Dialium* spp.), Mahang (*Macaranga pruinosa*), Rengas (*Drmycarpus* spp.), Kayu malam (*Diospyros borneensis*), Kempas (*Koompasia mala*), Resak (*Cotylelobium* spp). Water-table depth = 45.1 cm
Secondary Forest (HS)	Kubu Subdistrict- Kubu Raya Regency – 16.333 m^2 S = $00^{0}21.697$ until 814 E = $109^{0}21.813$ until 928	In this location there was a drainage channel (as the border of protected forest) with 180 cm wide and water level of 70 cm. The dominant vegetation in this location included Tanjan (*Dialium* spp.), Rengas (*Drmycarpus* spp.), Resak (*Cotylelobium* spp.), Bintagor (*Calophyllum* spp.), Ilas (*Nephelium cuspidatum*), Tanang (*Calophyllum* spp.). Water-table depth = 32 cm
Shrubs (SB)	Kubu Subdistrict- Kubu Raya Regency – 27.414 m^2 S = $00^{0}21.418$ until 549 E = $109^{0}21.514$ until 596	In this location, the condition was varied; tree trunks of the logged over and burnt spread out in sampling 3 and 4 points. Another sampling point was in the form of shrubs. The dominant vegetation in the location included pakis (*Diplazium esculentum*), pandan hutan (*Pandanus tectorius*) and cengkodok (*Melastoma malabathricum*) and wood from burned trees. Water-table depth = 43.1 cm
Oil palm plantation (KS)	Kubu Subdistrict- Kubu Raya Regency – 26.299 m^2 S = $00^{0}23.874$ until 962 E = $109^{0}22.648$ until 718	In this location, there was a drainage channel circling around the block. Main drainage channel was 280 cm wide and water level of 40 cm; channel of the right block was 100 cm wide and water level of 77 cm; channel of the left block was 250 cm wide and water level of 30 cm. There were also ferns as cover crop. Water-table depth = 52.6 cm
Corn Plantation (KJ)	Rasau Jaya Subdistrict- Kubu Raya Regency – 26.680 m^2 S = $00^{0}12.759$ until 897 E = $109^{0}23.552$ until 719	In this location, there was a drainage channel, that the primary channel was 380 cm wide and had water level of 40 cm, tertiary channel was 50 cm wide and had water level of 20 cm. Water-table depth = 55.1 cm

DISCUSSION

At the study areas, peat forest had higher of soil C than any other shrubs and cultivated land (SB, KS and KJ). In Similar result found by Monde *et al.* (2008) suggested that the forest area had total C absorption higher than and significantly different from the land use for maize, peanut, agroforestry and cocoa, decreasing from 91.2% until 99.4%. Tomich *et al.* (1998) reported that the natural forest can storage C higher than any other land-use, that its decrease take place after being converted into agroforestry of vanilla and cocoa, totally 44.5% and 41.0%, respectively. According to Sarkhot *et al.* (2007), intensively processed land may reduce content of soil C totally 23.0 %.

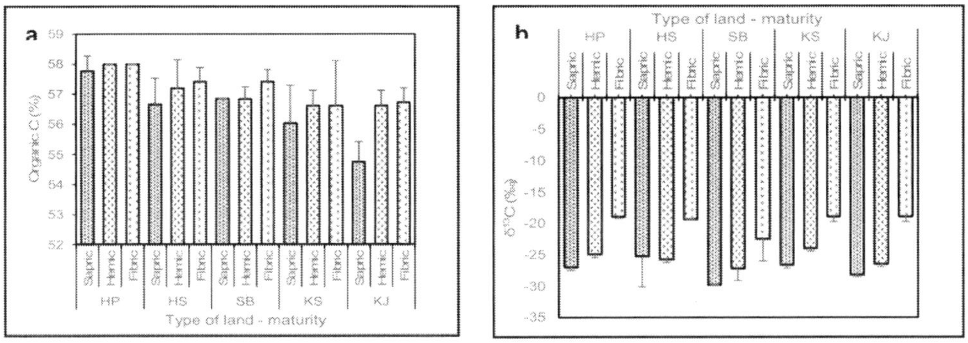

Figure 2: Organic C (a) and $\delta^{13}C$ (b) on the types of peat land use of primary forest (HP), secondary forest (HS), shrubs (SB), oil palm plantation (KS) and corn plantation (KJ)

The change of long-term land use results in the difference in quantity and composition of soil organic materials or soil C content, and soil fertility (Prentice and Webb, 2010; Tan and Lal, 2005). Similar to the result by Del Galdo *et al.* (2003), they reported that the use of common agricultural decreases soil organic C totally 48.0% of 10 cm from the op and only 3.0% from the deeper profile of the soil. Meanwhile, Qiming *et al.* (2003); Firdaus and Gandaseca (2010); Satrio *et al.* (2009) suggested that soil organic matter in the that SOM in forestland was higher than farmland, decreasing totally by 87.0%, and 4.7%, respectively. Several possible explanations could be proposed in the present case : (1) inorganic fertilizers may enhance microbial activity and nutrient availability but reducing the stabilized organic matter; (2) physical protection of SOM within stable aggregates may be affected by soil tillage (Qiming *et al.*, 2003); (3) greater soil aeration during and after the opening of peat swamp forest might have caused breakdown of organic residues and hence encouraged decomposition of organic matter by microbes (Brady and Weil, 2007).

The above mention explanations describe that the change in the land use of primary peat swamp forestry accompanied with the making of drainage and intensive processing land will change its natural ecosystem, becoming aerobic condition. Such a condition may change the characteristics of land such as the height of water table and physical and chemical characteristics of peat -soil. A previous study by Nusantara, *et al.* (2013) showed that change of land use in water-table depth in the forest area was shallower than the water-table depth of the SB, KS, and KJ (Table 1). Well-drained and aerated peat land increased the decomposition rate of peat materials, resulting in the physical characteristics of land such as ; low BD and soil porosity, high soil compaction (Nusantara *et al.*, 2013); chemical characteristics such as: low organic C content while ash content increases (Fig 1 and Table 2). Also, according to Usuga, *et al.* (2010), the increase of ash content in the top layer of drained peat land comes from the peat materials whose organic materials had disappear due to decomposition process. The increase of ash content indicates the loss of C, particularly because of decomposition process of organic materials.

Based on the peat maturity, sapric had $\delta^{13}C$ lower than the deeper layers, such as hemic and fibric. The $\delta^{13}C$ enrichment of them was 1.73‰ and 7.66‰, respectively.The same opinion was suggested by Billings dan Richter (2006) that $\delta^{13}C$ increased totally 1.1‰, 1.3‰ and 2.3‰ from upper (0-7.5 cm) to deeper layers (7.5-15 cm) in 1962, 1977, 1997, respectively. $\delta^{13}C$ of upper layers of native forest (0-7.5 cm) increased totally 2‰ while of deeper layers (30-100 cm) increased totally 3‰ (Rhoades *et al.*, 2000). In the tropic, the $\delta^{13}C$ enrichment increased until 2-4‰ (Bernoux *et al.*, 1998). Other studies , for example, in primary peat forest in Jambi Province, was known increasing $\delta^{13}C$ amounting to 1.6 ‰ and 2‰ at 10-20 cm and 20-30 cm depth of peat soil upper layers, respectively (Ueda *et al.*, 2005). Upland soils in Maya Lowland, Guetemala, showed $\delta^{13}C$ enrichment until 8.56‰ (Beach *et al.*, 2011). On the contrary, decreased of $\delta^{13}C$ of the peat bog in Japan was 4.1‰ at the depth of 0.5-4.5 m (Akagi *et al.*, 2004).

Based on type of land, forest area (HP-HS) had $\delta^{13}C$ higher than KS, KJ and SB. It increased totally 3.3‰ and 3.02‰ of SB against HS and HP. This condition was opposite from clay soil in which $\delta^{13}C$ decreased amounting 1‰ and 3.4‰ after 7 and 35 years, respectively, of maize cultivation compared with forest (Balesdent *et al.*, 1998). The same condition was suggested by Rhoades *et al.* (2000) in which $\delta^{13}C$ decreased totally 4.6‰ and 3.9‰ of sugar cane and mixed-species pasture, respectively compared with old-growth forest.

Table 2: Ash on the land use of primary forest (HP), secondary forest (HS), shrubs (SB), oil palm plantation (KS) and corn plantation (KJ)

Land use	Maturity	Ash (%)
Primary forest (HP)	Sapric	0.4
	Hemic	0.0
	Fibric	0.0
Secondary forest (HS)	Sapric	2.3
	Hemic	1.4
	Fibric	1.0
Shrubs (SB)	Sapric	2.0
	Hemic	2.0
	Fibric	1.0
Oli palm (KS)	Sapric	3.6
	Hemic	2.4
	Fibric	1.4
Corn plantation (KJ)	Sapric	5.6
	Hemic	2.4
	Fibric	2.2

CONCLUSION

The impact of changing in tropical peat forest to another land use tends to decrease the soil C and $\delta^{13}C$. It is might be due the changing in its environmental conditions from anaerobic to aerobic condition.There are similar trends between the soil C and $\delta^{13}C$, based on the peat maturity and land type. On the peat soil upper layers, sapric has C content and $\delta^{13}C$ lower than fibric on the deeper layers. On land use, the HS has a C content and $\delta^{13}C$, otherwise on SB has a C content and $\delta^{13}C$ low. Changing of tropical peat forest to another land uses, especially agricultural tend to lower C $\delta^{13}C$ soil and peat soil. C dynamics of soil due to land conversion is affected by changes in anaerobic to aerobic conditions on peat soil. This condition causes the acceleration of the rate of decomposition and mineralization of organic matter soils. The opposite situation occurs in forest areas that have deposits of soil and $\delta^{13}C$ C higher; and maturity fibric have deposits C soil greater than sapric and hemic.

ACKNOWLEDGEMENT

I would like to express my gratitude to staff of Soil Conservation and Physics Laboratory of Tanjungpura University, Pontianak-Indonesia and Prof. Dr. Gusti Z. Anshari, MESS, for providing peat drilling the other tools for this research; Ir. Warganda, MMA helps to data analysis.

REFERENCES

1. Agus, F., Hairiah, K., Mulyani, A., 2011. Measuring carbon stock in peat soils. World Agro-forestry Centre (ICRAF) Southeast Asia Regional Program and Indonesian Centre for Agricultural Land Resources and Development.
2. Akagi, T., Minomo, K., Kasuya, N., Nakamura, T., 2004. Variation in carbon isotopes of bog peat in the Ozegahara peatland, Japan. *Geochemical Journal* 38, 299-306.
3. Alewell, C., Giesler, R., Klaminder, J., Leifeld, J., Rollog, M., 2011. Stable carbon isotopes
4. as indicators for environmental change in palsa peats. Biogeosciences 8(7), 1769-1778.
5. Andriesse, J. P., 1988. *Nature and management tropical peat soils*. FAO-Food and Agriculture United Nations. Rome.
6. Balasdent, J., Besnard, E., Arrouays, D., Chenu, C., 1998. The dynamics of carbon in particle-size fractions of soil in a forest-cultivation sequence. Plant and Soil 201, 49-57.
7. Beach, T., Luzzadder-Beach, S., Terry, R., Dunning, N., Houston, B., Garrison, T., 2011. Carbon isotopic ratios of wetland and terrace soil sequences in the Maya Lowlands of Belize and Guatemala. Catena 85, 109-118.
8. Bernoux, M., Cerri, C.C., Neill, C., de Morales, J.F.L., 1998. The use of stable carbon isotopes for estimating soil organic matter turnover rates. Geoderma 82, 43-58.
9. Billings, S.A., Richter, D.D., 2006. Changes in stable isotopic signatures of soil nitrogen and carbon during 40 years of forest development. Oecologia 148, 325-333.
10. Brady, N.C., Weil, R.R., 2007. The nature and propeties of soils. 14th Edn. , Prentice Hall, USA, ISBN:10:0873718615, pp:980.

11. Del Galdo, I., Six, J., Peressottis, A., Cotrufo, M. F., 2003. Assessing the impact of land-use change on soil C sequestration in agricultural soils by mean of organic matter fractionation and stable C isotopes. Global Change Biology 9, 1204-1213.
12. Farmer, J., Matthews, R., Smith, P., Langan, C., Hergoualc'h, K., Verchot, L., Smith, J.U., 2013. Comparasion of methods for quantifying soil carbon in tropical peats. *Geoderma*, xxx: xxx-xxx (Articles in Press). http://dx.doi.org/10.1016/j.geoderma.2013.09.013
13. Firdaus, M.F., Gandaseca, S., 2010. Effect of converting secondary tropical peat swamp forest into oli palm plantation on selected peat soil physical properties. American Journal of Environmental Sciences 6(4), 402-405.
14. Harrison, M.E. 2013. Using conceptual models to understand ecosystem function and impacts of human activities in tropical peat-swamp forest. Weland, DOI 10.1007/s13157-013-0378-0
15. Hooijer, A., Page, S., Canadell, J.G., Kwadijk, J., Wösten, H., Jauihianen, J., 2010. Current and future CO_2 emissions from drained peatland in Southeast Asia. Biogeosciences 7, 1505-1514.
16. Krüger, J.P., Leifeld, J., Alewell, C., 2014. Degradation changes stable carbon isotope depth profiles in palsa peatlands. Biogeosciences 11(12), 3369-3380.
17. Lane, C.S., Horn, S.P., Mora, C.I., 2004. Stable carbon isotope ratio in lake and swamp sediments as a proxy for prehistoric forest clearance and crop cultivation in the Neotropics. Journal of Paleolimnology 32, 375-381.
18. Limpens, J., Berendse, F., Blaodau, C., Canadell, J.G., Freeman, C., Holden, J., Roulet, N., Rydin, H., Schaepman-Strub, G., 2008. Peatlands and the carbon cycle: from local processes to global implications-a synthesis. Biogeosciences 5, 1475-1491.
19. Nusantara, R.W., Sudarmadji, Djohan, T.S., Haryono, E., 2013. Physical characteristic of peat land use change of peat swamp forest. Proceeding seminar on national and annual meeting dean of the field of the sciences agricultural BKS-PTN the western conference 2013. Pontianak, 19-20 March 2013.
20. Ojanen, P., Minkkinen, K., Lohila, A., Badorek, T., Penttila, T., 2012. Chamber measured soil respiration: A useful tool for estimating the carbon balance of peatland forest soil? Forest Ecology and Management 277, 132-140.
21. Page, S., Banks, C., 2007. Tropical peatlands : distribution, extent and carbon storage-uncertainties and knowledge gaps. Peatl Int 2, 26-27.
22. Page, S., and J. Rieley. 2008. Overview of the need for restoration and rehabilitation of tropical peatland and review of the contents of this book. In Wösten, H., Rieley, J., Page, S. (Eds.), Restoration of Tropical Peatlands, pp 13-18.
23. Page, S., Hoscilo, A., Wösten, H., Jauhiainen, J., Silvius, M., Rieley, J., Ritzema, H., Tansey, K., Graham, L., Vasander, H., Limin, S., 2009. Restoration ecology of lowland tropical peatlands in Southeast Asia: Current knowledge and future research directions. Ecosystems 12, 888-905.
24. Page, S., Rieley, J., Banks, C., 2011. Global and regional importance of the tropical peatland carbon pool. Global Change Biology 17, 798-819.
25. Prentice, A., Webb, E., 2010. A comparison of extraction techniques on the stable carbon-isotope composition of soil humic subtances. Geoderma 155, 1-9.
26. Qiming, L., Shijie, W., Hechun, P., Ziyuan, Q., 2003. The variation of soil organic matter in a forest-cultivation sequence traced by stable carbon isotopes. *Chinese Journal of Geochemistry* 22, 83-87.
27. Radjagukguk, B., 2000. Physic and chemical characteristics change of peat soil as result of peat land reclamation to agricultural. In Enviroment and Soil Journal 2(1), 1-15.
28. Rieley, J.O., Ahmad-Shah, A.A., Brady, M.A., 1996. The extent and nature of tropical peat swamps. In: E. Maltby, C.P. Immirzi and R.J. Safford (eds) Tropical Lowland Peatlands of Southeast Asia. IUCN, Gland. pp.17-53.
29. Rieley, J.O., Page, S., 2008. Carbon budget under different land uses on tropical peatland. In Rieley JO, Banks CJ, Page SE (Eds) Future of Tropical peatlands in Southeast Asia as Carbon pools and sinks.
30. Rhoades, C.C., Eckert, G.E., Coleman, D.C., 2000. Soil carbon differences among forest, agriculture, and secondary vegetation in lower Montane Ecuador. Ecological Applications 2, 497-505.
31. Sarkhot, D.V., Comerford, N.B., Jokela, E.J., 2007. Effects of forest management intensity on carbon and nitrogen content in different soil size fractions of a North Florida Spodosol. Plant Soil 294, 291-303.
32. Satrio, A.E., Gandaseca, S., Ahmed, O.H., Majid, N.M.A., 2009. Effect of logging operation on soil carbon storage of a tropical peat swamp forest. American Journal of Environmental Sciences 5(6), 748-752.
33. Tan, Z., Lal, R., 2005. Carbon sequestration potential estimates with changes in land use and tillage practice in Ohio, USA. Agriculture, Ecocyctems and Enviroment 111, 140-152.
34. Ueda, S., Go, C.S.U., Ishizuka, S., Tsuruta, H., Iswandi, A., Murdiyarso, D., 2005. Isotopic assessment of CO2 production through soil oganic matter decomposition in the tropics. Nutrient Cycling in Agroecosystems 71, 109-116.
35. Wösten, J.H.M., Clyman, S.E., Page, S., Rieley, J.O., Limin, S.H., 2008. Peat-water interralation in tropical peatland ecosystem in Southeast Asia. Catena 73, 201-217.

Abstract No: A-282

SOIL CARBON STOCK AND PEAT ORGANIC PROPERTIES IN FRESH WATER SWAMPLAND

Siti Nurzakiah[1*], Nur Wakhid[1] and Haris Syahbuddin[2]

[1]Indonesian Swampland Agriculture Research Institute, South Kalimantan, Indonesia
[2]Indonesian Research Institute for Agro-climate and Hydrolog, Bogor Indonesian Agency for Agricultural Research and Development (IAARD), Indonesia

**Corresponding author: zakiah_balittra@yahoo.co.id*

SUMMARY

Peat soils have varying characteristics with the variability the result of differences in climate, groundwater level fluctuations, the quality and the quantity of inorganic material deposited during the process of accumulation of peat. The process will produce peat with various stratification (i.e. peat layers), which are all from peat substance or mineral substance insertions in the midst of peat substance. These conditions are often found in peat soils in fresh water swampland. The existence of minerals in the peat will affect the amount of carbon (C) stocks and the organic properties of the peat. Several studies have concluded that soil C stocks are strongly influenced by ash content and bulk density whereas the organic characteristics of peat (chemical bond structures) can be distinguished based on the degree of maturity of the peat. Functional groups are dominant in fibric peat, namely OH groups and bond NH (3400 cm^{-1}) and a series combination of CO and OH (1033 cm^{-1}), which is a carrier of hydrophilic properties. Sorption peaks around 2924 cm^{-1} and 2854 cm^{-1} (absorption bands 3000-2800 cm^{-1}) is a series of aliphatic group CH, $C\text{-}H_2$, and carboxylate ions that indicate the presence of fats, waxes and lipids are abundant in sapric peat. The knowledge of peat characteristic is required for sustainable peatland management. Peatland use change for agriculture should be considered the peat physical-chemical characteristic that associated with peat stability. Measuring and monitoring of C stocks is required as a basis for impact assessment of land management technology applications.

Keywords: *Fresh water swampland, peat maturity, peat organic properties, soil carbon stock*

INTRODUCTION

The carbon (C) stored in peat soils is enormous and is emitted as carbon dioxide (CO_2) when land is cleared or drained. The amount of C stored in tropical peatlands has been reported by several researchers. Page *et al.* (2011) reported that the total amount of C in tropical peat amounted to 89 Gt, or about 15-19% of the total C stored globally in peatlands (550 Gt), while the total C stored in peatlands in Southeast Asia is estimated at 42000 Mt (Hooijer *et al.* 2010). Peat decomposition leads to a loss of peat structure and a change in the main chemical composition of peat. This process was affected by the peat main component formations such as mineral material, organic matter, moisture and air. A change in one components results in changes in the characteristics of the peat. Therefore, necessary prudence is required in the management of peat soils.

Peat soils are composed of layers derived from organic matter substances or mineral substance insertions in the midst of peat substance. The presence of mineral substance in the peat will affect soils properties, such as C content, ash content, bulk density and degree of decomposition. The degree of decomposition affects the concentration of humic and fulvic acids. Generally, humic acid in sapric peat is greater than in fibric peat. The main functional groups in humic acid are the carboxylic acids, alcohols, phenols, carbonyl, phosphates, sulfates, amides and sulphides (Stevenson, 1994). One way to determine the functional groups in the peat is with Fourier Transform Infra-Red (FTIR) Spectra, which can be used as an indicator of quantitative composition and the degree of decomposition of organic matter by spectroscopy as indicators of the presence of carbohydrates, lignin, cellulose, lipid and protein compounds, through the structural characteristics of chemical bonds (Artz *et al.*, 2008 Haberhauer *et al*, 2000; Hsu, JH and SL Lo, 1999).

Knowledge of peat characteristics is required in sustainable peatland management. Measuring and monitoring of C stocks is required as the basis for impact assessment of land management technology applications. This research was conducted to study soil C stocks and peat organic properties based on peat maturity in fresh water swampland.

METHODS

The study was conducted by a survey method, and then field sampling. The study was carried out in Pulau Damar Village, Hulu sungai Utara District, South Kalimantan Province, Indonesia (2^0 26' 32.93''S, 15^0 22' 24.89'' E) on rubber and rice paddy fields. Soil sampling was conducted along a transect at nine (land use rubber) and fifteen observation points (land use rice paddy fields) assuming a variation in peat thickness and other soil properties. Soil sampling with a peat auger (Eijkelkamp model) was conducted until the substratum was encountered. At each observation point, soil sampling with a peat auger were performed twice in the points adjacent to each other. One point of soil sampling for C stock determination, and the other point for peat organic properties analysis.

Parameters to determine the C stock were; bulk density ($t.m^{-3}$, gravimetric method), C content (wt %, dry ash method) and thickness of peat (observed directly in the field using the peat auger) (Agus, 2009). Soil organic matter content (OM) was calculated based on % of the soil dry weight, namely: OM (wt%) = (DW-AW)/DW * 100%, where AW was ash weight determined with the ash method in a furnace at 550 °C for 6 hours while DW was soil dry weight. Degrees of soil organic C (Org-C % by weight) was calculated based on the conversion of organic matter to the constant 1.724 [Org-C: wt%) = OM/1.724] and Org-C (% vol) was weight of C per unit soil volume ($t.m^{-3}$), namely: [Org-C (% vol) = Org-C (% by weight) * BD-ash]. Carbon stocks in the soil were weight of C in a unit volume of soil, namely: C-stock = Org-C (% vol) * A * L, where L was the peat soil area (m^2) and A was thickness of the peat (m). Soil C stock using estimated with published data (Nurzakiah *et al.*, 2013; 2014). Peat organic properties (chemical bond structures) were investigated with FTIR spectra. The data processing was carried out using the MS Excel program and drawn with SigmaPlot program by Systat Software Inc.

RESULTS

The thickness of peat at the rubber and rice paddy fields ranged from 310-465 cm and 32-500 cm, respectively. The maturity of peat was fibric, and in the middle of peat profile was found the mineral substance insertions. In the rubber fields, the C stock of peat including mineral substance insertions was 2251.68 ± 152.40 Mg C ha^{-1} (the thickness of the mineral substance is 3-24 cm). However, when the inserted mineral substance was omitted from the analyses, the C stock was decrease become 2025.21 ± 132.77 Mg C ha^{-1} (Nurzakiah *et al.*, 2014). In the rice paddy fields, the C stocks (including the mineral layer in the peat) was 967.93 ± 202.08 Mg C ha^{-1}, and 907 557 ± 188.39 Mg C ha^{-1} when the mineral layer was omitted from the analyses (Nurzakiah *et al.*, 2013) (Figure 1). There was a positive correlation between soil C stock and peat thickness (Figure 2).

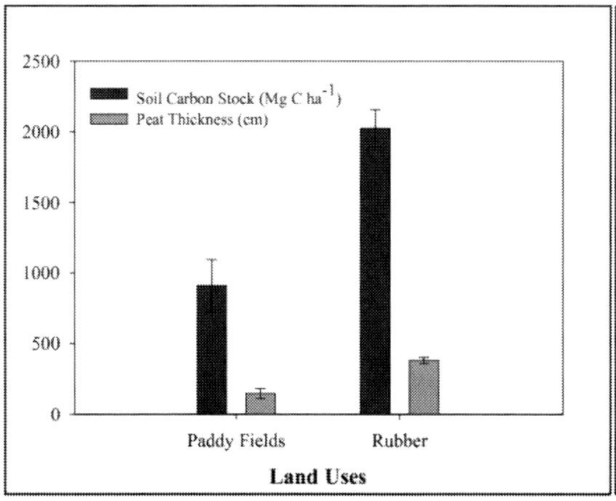

Figure 1: Variations of soil carbon stocks and peat thickness

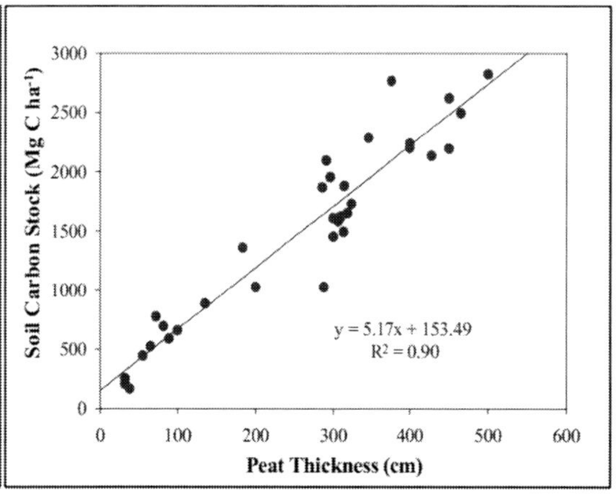

Figure 2: Regression of soil carbon stock and peat thickness

Spectrum pattern on the FTIR spectrograph of the peat (Figure 3) was almost identical at all degree of peat maturity, the differential was the wide of absoption area. In this study the infrared spectrum from the sapric, hemic and fibric peat indicates the sorption peaks, at around 3400 cm^{-1}, 2924 cm^{-1}, 2854 cm^{-1}, 1627 cm^{-1}, 1512 cm^{-1}, and 1033 cm^{-1}.

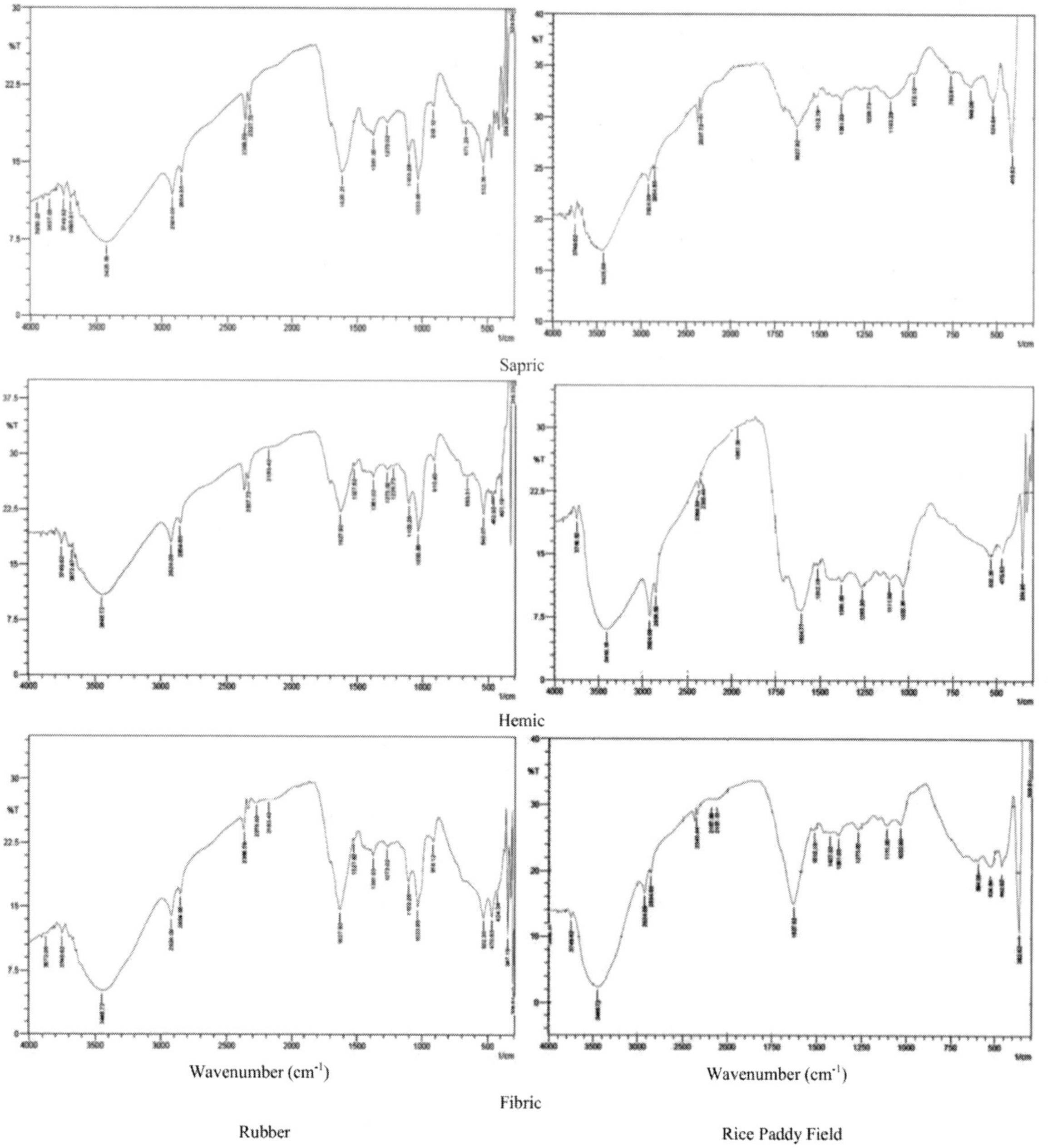

Figure 3: Fourier Transform Infra-Red (FTIR) spectrograph of peat land uses

DISCUSSION

Peat soils in fresh water swampland located in hollows is influenced by the river water during periodic flooding that normally occurs during the rainy season, so that mineralized material is frequently inserted between the layers of peat. The peat layers with mineral substance insertions will affect the amount of C stored in the ecosystem. This is due to increased levels of ash. For instance, fibric peat has an ash content of 5.03-27.28%. The great value of peat ash content causes by the peat position in above of substratum or between mineral substance insertions. Therefore, in the calculation of C stocks, the inserted mineral substance was neglected. Variation in soil C stocks at each layer of peat soil was due to differences in peat maturity. Sapric peat has a higher carbon store than hemic and fibric peat with a ratio of 2.0: 1.5: 1.0 (rubber fields) and 2.1: 1.3: 1.0 respectively (rice paddy fields).

Peat organic properties play an important role in determining the characteristic of a soil. Humic acid and fulvic acid generated from the decomposition of organic matter, contribute to the negative charge, and have a function as organic colloid. Humic acid is the main organic element abundant in peat soils and this role is affected by the degree of peat decomposition. The content of humic acid was higher in sapric peat than that of hemic and fibric peats. In this study, the organic properties the peat were analyzed by the presence of functional groups with

FTIR spectrophotometer and its interpretation by Artz *et al.* (2008). Functional groups can be identified based on the different of infrared absorption intensity on the specific wavenumber (cm^{-1}). Krumins *et al.* (2012) states that each functional group absorbs the infrared light at specific frequency. The functional groups intensity determine by peak area calculation from each functional groups curve. The percentage of each functional group calculated based on the total area of spectra curve.

The functional groups that found were hydroxyl group (O-H) and bond NH (absorption bands 3750-3300 cm^{-1}), methyl and/or methylene group (C-H; absorption bands 3000-2800 cm^{-1}) with two distinct peaks at 2924 and 2854 cm^{-1}, alkenyl group (C=C; absorption bands 1627-1512 cm^{-1}) and ester group (C-O; absorption bands 1045-1035 cm^{-1}. The functional group of hydroxyl (O-H) and bond NH was cellulose indicators that easily decompose while C-H group indicate the fats, waxes and lipids that mostly found in sapric peat. Sorption peaks around at 2924 cm^{-1} dan 2854 cm^{-1} (C-H group) were carrier of hydrophobicity, even though at the peak of 2854 cm^{-1} there is an aliphatic group is a carrier of hydrophilic, but non-polar ethyl and methyl group have difficulties to bind the water (valat *et al.*, 1991 Utami *et al*, 2009). The hydrophobicity also seen at sorption peak of 1627 cm^{-1} and 1512 cm^{-1} showed the presence of double bonds C=C derived from lignin and other aromatic groups.

In the rice paddy field, fibric peat in the absorption bands at 3750-3300 cm^{-1} has a wide area sorption of 41.54% greater than sapric peat i.e 22.93%. The existence of O-H group decreases in line with the increasing of maturity of peat which is associated with the decrease of soil water content. Conversely, the increasing of C-H group in sapric peat due to the increasing of concentration of the aliphatic group and methyl and/or methylene (Krumis *et al.*, 2012). In this study, the total wide area of the sorption peak at 2942 and 2854 cm^{-1} (C-H group) of sapric peat was higher than fibric peat that was 23.71% and 16.87%, respectively. In the sapric peat, there was no ester group (C-O) identified as polysaccharide (1033 cm^{-1}).

In the rubber field, hydroxyl group (O-H) and bond NH, C-H group, C=C group and C-O group were discovered at all degree of maturity peat. Hydroxyl group (O-H) and bond NH and C-O group (absorption bands 3750-3300 and 1033 cm^{-1}) were abundant in fibric peat, while a series of C-H group aliphatic, C-H2 and carboxylate ion (2924 and 2854 cm^{-1}) were a lot of sapric peat by 21.18%.

Based on previous description, it could be concluded that the maturity degree of peat determining the amount of soil C stock and the peat organic properties or the percentage of functional groups found in peat soil that will determine the peat character. This is crucial for sustainable peatland management due to the activities on peatland will give impact of changing of peat properties such as changes in functional groups, humic compounds and decrease of carbon stock. However, peatland still could be cultivated for agriculture as long as the activities keep considering the characteristic of the physical-chemical of peat related to peat stability.

CONCLUSION

1. Soil C stock in sapric peat is higher than in hemic and fibric peat with ratio of 2.0: 1.5: 1.0 (rubber) and 2.1: 1.3: 1.0 respectively (rice paddy fields).
2. Functional groups are dominant in fibric peat, namely OH groups, bond NH (3400 cm^{-1}) and a series combination of CO and OH (1033 cm^{-1}), which is a carrier of hydrophilic properties. Sorption peaks around 2942 cm^{-1} and 2854 cm^{-1} (absorption bands 3000-2800 cm^{-1}) is a series of aliphatic group CH, C-H2, and carboxylate ions which indicate the presence of fats, waxes and lipids are abundant in sapric.

REFERENCES

1. Agus, F. 2009. Guide Method of Measuring Carbon Stock in Peatland. Indonesian Center for Agricultural Land Resources Research and Development. World Agroforestry Centre, SEA, Bogor, Indonesia (In Indonesian).
2. Artz, R.R.E., S. J. Chapman, A.H. J. Robertson, J.M. Potts, F. Laggoun-Défarge, S. Gogo, L. Comont, J.R. Disnar, and A.J. Francez. 2008. FTIR spectroscopy can predict organic matter quality in regenerating cutover peatlands. *Soil Biology and Biochemistry*, 40 ; 515-527.
3. Haberhaur, G., B. Feigl, M.H. Gerbazek, and C. Cerri. 2000. FTIR spectroscopy of organic matter in tropical soils: changes induced through deforestation. *Applied Spectroscopy*. 54; 221-224.
4. Hooijer, A., S. Page, J.G. Canadell, M. Silvius, J. Kwadijk, H. Wosten, and J. Jauhiainen. 2010. Current and future CO_2 emissions from drained peatlands in Southeast Asia. *Biogeosciences*, 7: 1505–1514. Doi: 10.5194/bg-7-1505-2010.
5. Hsu, J.H., and S.L. Lo. 1999. Chemical and spectroscopic analysis of organic matter transformations during composting of pig manure. *Environmental Pollution* 104; 189-196Krumins, J., M. Klavins, V. Seglin, and E. Kaup. 2012. Comparative study of peat composition by using FT-IR spectroscopy. *Material Science and Applied Chemistry* 26: 106-114.

6. Nurzakiah, S., M. Noor, and D. Nursyamsi. 2014. Carbon stock stratification of peat soils in South Kalimantan, Indonesia. *Journal of Wetland Environmental Management* Vol. 2, No. 2, August 2014. ISSN 2354-5844.
7. Nurzakiah, S., Nur wakhid, D. Nursyamsi, and H. Syahbuddin. 2013. Carbon stock stratification of swampy peatland. Proceedings of 11th International Conference The East and Southeast Asia Federation of Soil Science Societies. Land for Sustaining Food and Energy Security. Bogor. 21 -24 Oktober 2013. ISBN 978-979-19904-1-7
8. Page, S.E., J.O. Rieley, and C.J. Banks. 2011. Global and regional importance of the tropical peatland carbon pool. Global Change Biology, 17: 798-818.
9. Stevenson, F. J. 1994. Humus Chemistry: Genesis, composition and reaction. Sec. Edition. JohnWilley & Sons Inc.NewYork. 496 p.
10. Utami, S.N.H., A. Maas, B. Radjagukguk, and B.H. Purwanto. 2009. The physical, chemical and FTIR spectrophotometry of hydrophobic peat in Central Kalimantan. *Journal of Tropical Soils* 14 (2); 159-166 (In Indonesian).
11. Valat, B., C. Jouany, and L.M. Riviere. 1991. Characterization of the wetting properties of air-dried peats and composts. *Soil Sci.* 152 (2); 100 - 107.

2.2: GHG EMISSION FROM NATURAL & MANAGED PEATLANDS

2.2: GHG EMISSION FROM NATURAL & MANAGED PEATLANDS

Abstract No: A-089

BIOCHAR AMENDMENT TO IMPROVE SOIL FERTILITY AND REDUCE CO_2 EMISSIONS IN TROPICAL PEATSOIL

Eni Maftu'ah[1*], Herman Subagio[1] and Dedi Nursyamsi[2]

[1]Indonesian Swampland Agriculture Research Institute (ISARI), Indonesia
[2]Indonesian Center for Agricultural Land Resources Research and Development (ICALRRD), Indonesia

**Corresponding author: eni_balittra@yahoo.com*

SUMMARY

The effect of biochar amendments on CO_2 emissions in tropical peatlands has not been widely studied. Biochar is able to improve the soil characteristics, due to it ability to increase soil pH, water and nutrient retention, and improve soil biological activity also reduce pollution. Biochar has chemical and physical structure that is very complex, and the surface of biochar able to absorb several gases including CO_2. Greenhouse research was conducted in June-October 2014 at ISARI, Banjarbaru, South Kalimantan. Sapric peatsoil was taken from Kalampangan village, municipality Palangkaraya, Central Kalimantan. The experimental design was factorial randomized block design with three replications. The first factor was the type of biochar, there were biochar from rice husks, coconut shells, Galam stalks and midrib of palm oil. The second factor was the dose of biochar, there were 0, 2, 4, 8 and 16 t ha^{-1}. The results showed that biochar amendment was able to reduce CO_2 emissions. Biochar from coconut shell at a dose of 2-4 t ha^{-1} able to improve the soil pH and K-available and reduce CO_2 emissions up to 60%.

***Keywords**: biochar, peatsoil fertility, reduce, CO_2 emissions*

INTRODUCTION

Indonesian tropical peat swamp forest is a unique wetland ecosystem and an important natural resource with considerable environmental and economic value (Rieley and Page, 1995). Peatland in Indonesia have an area of about 14.09 million ha (Ritung *et al.*, 2011). The utilization of peatland for agricultural purposes faces problems involving both chemical and physical soil properties. Sustainable peatland management should include some kinds of soil amelioration in addition of water table management. Ameliorant was a material added to the marginal soil to improve soil fertility to support plant growth (Attiken *et al.*, 1998).

Amelioration that used biochar in peatlands has not been done. Biochar is a charcoal from pyrolysis that containing high carbon. Biochar was able improve the quality land through its ability to increase the pH, water retention, nutrient retention, and improve biological activity in the soil and reduce pollution (Laird *et al.*, 2008). However biochar did not able to provide nutrients directly, but indirectly able to reduce the loss of nutrients from leaching, thus fertilizing efficiency can be improved. Biochar could improve the nature of the chemical, physical and biological soil. N losses from fertilization can be reduced by the addition of biochar (Steiner, 2007). Biochar is an alternative material to improve soil fertility, sustainable peat land management and environmentally friendly.

The main role of biochar not only as the contributor of nutrients for soil, but also as material for soil amelioration. Biochar is able to provide a combination of air and water that is good for the growth of microbes that play a role in soil. Additionally, biochar could also be used as an effective carrier for microbes that play an important role in the soil, so that it could play a role in the manufacture of biological fertilizers (Santi and Goenadi, 2010). Fungi could sporulate in the micro pores in the biochar pores because the competition with other saprofit was quite low (Saito and Marumoto, 2002).

Giving biochar able to increase the availability of P, soil pH, K and Ca-dd (Masulili *et al.*, 2010). Biochar able to increase nutrient availability for plants and plant productivity (Glaser *et al.*, 2002). Biochar can improve crop productivity directly or indirectly. The direct influence of biochar on crop productivity through donations nutrients are released, whereas indirectly through improved soil buffering capacity to hold nutrients, increase soil pH and increase CEC, improvement of soil physical properties and its effect on the function and the microbial (Graber *et al.*, 2010).

The influence of biochar on emissions depend on the type of biochar. As presented by Mukherjee and Lal (2013), emissions from biochar additions depending on the type of biochar, pyrolysis conditions (temperature and time), type of soil, climatic conditions and physical properties of soil. Further explained that biochar could increase or decrease the CO_2 emissions. Biochar has a chemical and physical structure is very complex. Surface of biochars was able to absorb various gases (LeLeuch and Bandosz, 2007), and these gases can interact with water or cations inside or on the surface of the biochar. Some compounds in biochar had the potential to react with N_2O so could be reducing N_2O emissions (Milne *et al.*, 1998). The research aims to study the influence of biochar and doses to improve soil fertility and reduce CO_2 emissions.

METHODOLOGY

The pot experiment was conducted at a greenhouse, of the Indonesian Swampland Agriculture Research Institute (ISARI), Banjarbaru, South Kalimantan from Juni – September 2014. Soil samples were taken from peatlands in the village Kalampangan, District Sebangau, municipality of Palangkaraya, Central Kalimantan. Biochar materials that used came from material that was abundantly in wetlands among others, rice husks, coconut shells, palm midrib and galam stems. Biochar made by a pyrolysis method that using Pirolisator (retort) at a temperature of 400°C. The study design used factorial randomized block design with the first factor was type of biochar (biochar from rice husk, coconut shell, galam stem, and palm midrib), the second factor was the dose of biochar, that consisting of 0, 2, 4, 8 and 16 t ha^{-1}. All combination treatment was repeated three times.

Research using 7.5 kg of peat soil in natural conditions on the water content of about 120%, then the peat entered in a polybag that the bottom of the hollow. The chemical characteristics of the soil before being treated was H_2O pH 3.59, pH KCl 2.95, EC 0234 mS dt^{-1}, 51.83% organic C, total N 0.81%, P available 170 mg kg^{-1}, K-exc 2.38 $cmol^{(+)}$ kg^{-1}, Ca-exe 3.00 $cmol^{(+)}$ kg^{-1}, 2.31 Mg-exe $cmol^{(+)}$ kg^{-1}, H-exe 3.54 $cmol^{(+)}$ kg^{-1}. Biochar was given at 2 weeks before planting. NPK compound at a rate of (300 kg ha^{-1}) was applied at planting corn seed. Supplementary urea fertilizer of 200 kg ha^{-1} was applied at two week after planting (WAP) and 4 WAP. Nutrient contents of the NPK compound fertilizer was 9% N; 13.5% P_2O_5; and 10.9% K_2O. Soil moisture in the experiment was maintained at field capacity conditions.

The analysis prior to application of biochar was pH, total concentration of P, K, Ca, Mg, Fe, SiO_2, ash, and CEC. The observations on the vegetatif stage was high of plant, soil properties include pH, EC, total N, P dan K available, CEC and CO_2 emissions.

Gas sampling is done by injecting a volume of 10 ml. Gas samples taken in the morning (6:00 to 8:00) using the chamber closed. The time interval used in sampling is the 5th minute, 10, 15, 20, 25 and 30. The gas samples were analyzed using a gas chromatograph GHG models Varian 450. In this study, piezometers installed to measure ground water levels at the time of the study. Measurement of pH using a pH meter, whereas Eh meter used to measurement potential redoxs. The rate of production of CO_2 calculated using the equations used by Khalil *et al.* (1991).

RESULT AND DISCUSSION

Characteristics of biochar

Biochar that used has the characteristics of different chemicals, as presented in Table 1. All biochar is used has a water content below 10%. C/N ratio depends on the type of biochar and positively associated with C/N material of biochar (Balittra, 2014). The water content of the resulting biochar also vary depending on the type of biochar. The water content of biochar is more related to the cellulose content than the lignin content (Balittra, 2014). The ash content of biochar also vary depending on the type of biochar. The ash content was positively related to lignin content of biochar materials (Balittra, 2014).

Table 1: Characteristics of biochar that used in the study

Type of material	C/N	pH	CEC	SiO_2	ash content	N	P	K	Ca	Mg	Fe	Water content
			$Cmol^{(+)}$ kg^{-1}	%								
Rice husk	43,92	8,99	37,38	34,83	44,35	0,73	0,48	0,54	0,21	0,18	0,26	5,10
palm midrib	39,64	9,74	9,74	6,30	31,17	1,01	0,39	1,53	0,53	0,96	0,15	9,19
Coconut shell	23,20	9,61	9,61	4,04	48,96	1,28	0,52	2,96	0,29	4,43	0,29	5,87
Galam stem	83,46	9,04	9,04	2,13	23,15	0,54	0,42	1,14	0,43	0,05	0,14	5,56

All biochar that used has water content below 10%. C/N ratio depends on the type of biochar and positively correlated with C/N materials (Balittra, 2014). The water content of biochar also vary depending on the type of biochar. The water content of biochar is more related to the cellulose content than the lignin content of material biochar (Balittra, 2014). The ash content of biochar also vary depending on the type of biochar. The ash content was positively related to lignin content of biochar material (Balittra, 2014). The composition of the ash fraction of biochar is largely dependent on the mineral raw materials, due largely inorganic elements do not evaporate at a pyrolysis temperature (Brewer, 2012). Raw materials and the pyrolysis process determine the number and distribution of minerals on biochar (Amonette and Joseph, 2009).

Material derived from wood generally has a low ash content (<1 percent by weight), while grass, hay and grain (husk) has a high silica content to 24% (Raveendran *et al.,* 1995). Most of the mineral content of the raw materials will be available in the biochar and partially lost (C, H and O) during pyrolysis. Biochar of organic fertilizers and waste usually has very high ash content. Biochar from chicken manure have 45% ash of the raw material (Koutcheiko *et al.,* 2007), and biochar from bone have mineral content reaches 84% of the raw materials (Purevsuren *et al.,* 2004).

CEC biochar studied varied, the highest CEC indicated by biochar from rice husk. The content of N, P, K and Ca on biochar that was highest on coconut shell. Characteristics of biochar not only determined by the raw materials, but also the process of pyrolysis. Temperature, the partial pressure of O_2, and carbon dioxide (CO_2) determine the amount of mineral ash of biochar (Bridgwater and Boocock, 2006). During thermal degradation, highly mobile ion as K and Cl would begin to vaporize at relatively low temperatures (Yu *et al.,* 2005). Ca and Si released during the degradation at temperatures higher than K and Cl (Bourke, 2006). Magnesium (Mg) both ionic and covalently bound to organic molecules and only evaporate at high temperatures. Phosphorus (P) and sulfur (S) associated with the complex organic compounds in cells and is relatively stable at low temperatures. Nitrogen is associated with a number of different organic molecules and can be removed at relatively low temperatures (Schnitzer *et al.,* 2007). Other elements such as Fe and Mn largely retained during the formation of biochar (Amonette and Joseph, 2009).

Plant height

Plant height at the maximum vegetative phase indicated by the treatment of biochar from coconut shell on a dose of 4 t ha^{-1}. The optimum dose of each type of biochar was diverse. Effect of dose as presented in the quadratic equation according to the equation in Figure 1. The optimum dose biochar coconut shell based on the equation $y=-1,\ 214x^2 + 8,\ 885x + 180,\ 3$ ($R^2=0{,}930$) was 3, 64 t ha^{-1}. $y=-2{,}464x^2 + 15{,}28x + 174{,}2$ was 3,1 t ha^{-1}, whereas biochar from stem Galam by the equation $y=-1{,}375x^2 + 9{,}475x + 181{,}5$ was 3,45 t ha^{-1}, biochar from palm midribs by the equation $y=-1{,}214x^2 + 8{,}785x + 182{,}5$ was 3,62 t ha^{-1}.

Based on the results of characterization showed that biochar from coconut shell has a functional group which more complete than the others (Balittra, 2013), CEC of biochar from coconut shells was low, so it suitable for peat soils that have a CEC high, ash content at biochar coconut shell was very high (48.96%) so that the availability of bases mainly Ca, Mg and K were also higher than the others. In addition, based on the pore, biochar from coconut shell have many pores of macro and micro, thus corresponding to the habitat of microorganisms (Balittra, 2014).

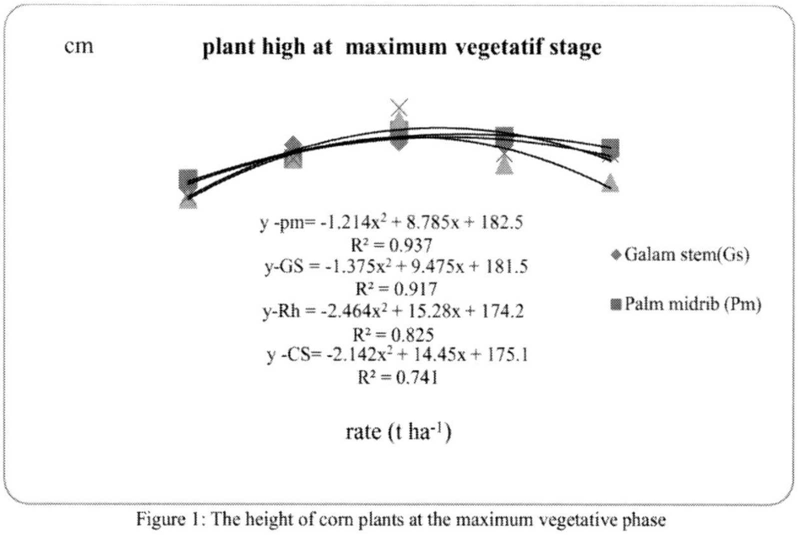

Figure 1: The height of corn plants at the maximum vegetative phase

Soil characteristics

Soil characteristics at the maximum vegetative phase was presented in Figure 2. Soil pH showed improvement at a dose of 2 t ha^{-1}, however for biochar from oilpalm midrib and Galam stems decreased in a dose of 4 t ha^{-1}.

Organic C contents varies depending on the type of biochar that given, whereas total N in the maximum vegetative phase ranged 0.9 to 1.2%.

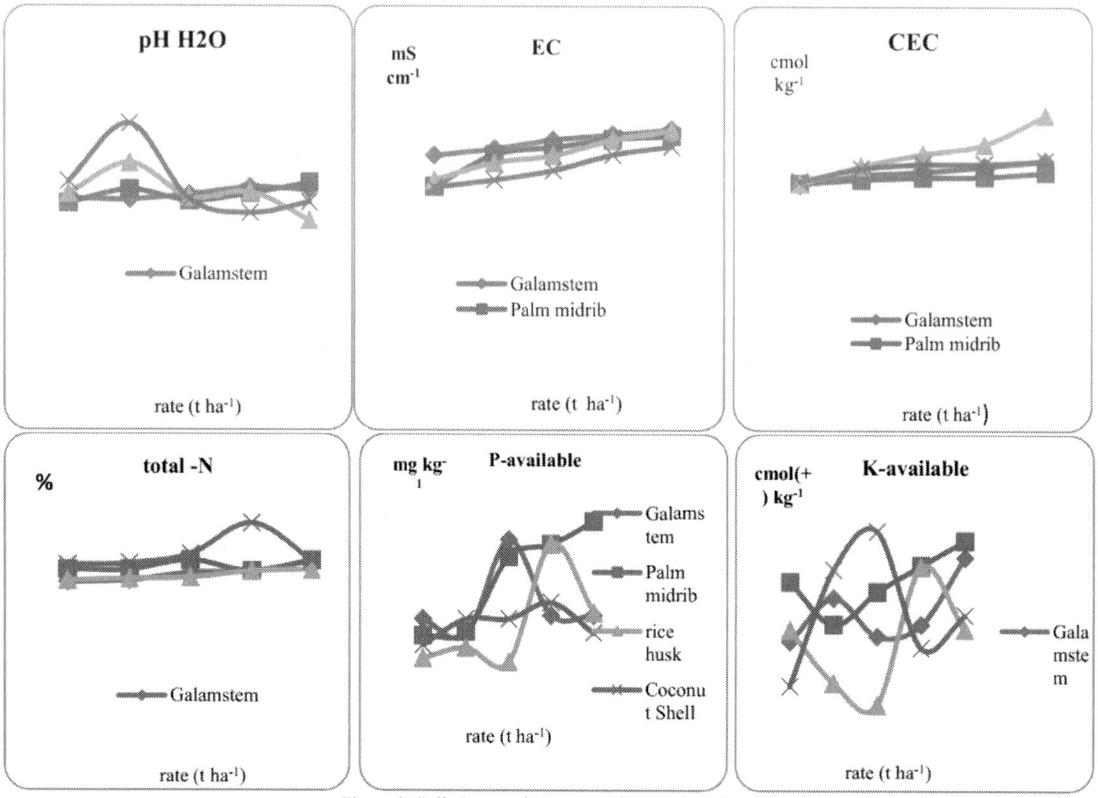

Figure 2: Soil characteristics at maximum vegetative phase

Increasing doses of biochar tend to increase total soil N content. The influence of biochar on EC was the similar relatively with total N, EC value increased with increasing doses of biochar. Biochar improves concentration P provided primarily on biochar from palm midribs dose of 4 -16 t ha^{-1}, whereas at coconut shell biochar increased concentration of P is not as big as at palm midribs biochar. The concentration of K available varies between the type and dose of biochar. The highest concentration of K available indicated by coconut shell biochar dose of 4 t ha^{-1}.

CO_2 emissions

Influence the type and dose of biochar to the emission of CO_2 measured at planting time and the maximum vegetative phase (Figure 3).

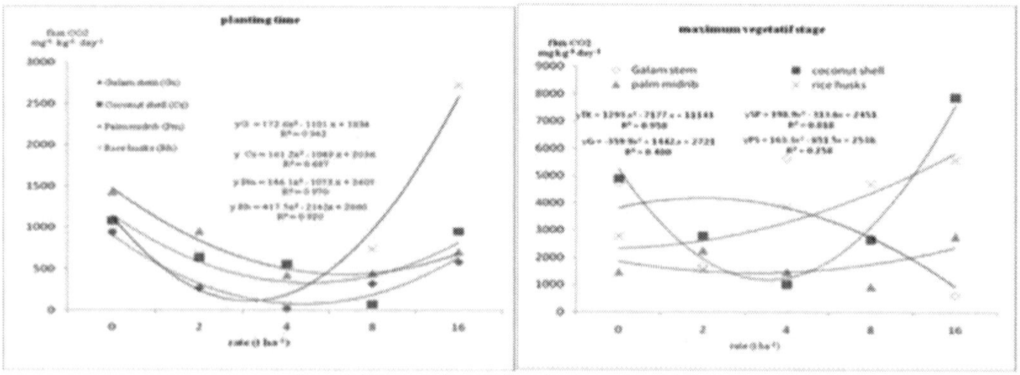

Figure 3: CO_2 emissions during planting and vegetative phase maximum

At planting time (biochar application was two weeks before planting), that treatment type and dose biochar showed different responses. However overall the addition of biochar was able to reduce emissions to a dose of 4 ha-1, increasing doses would increase of CO_2 emissions, especially for rice husk biochar. Increasing doses of biochar could increase the decomposition of peat due to increasing CO_2 emissions. Based on the regression equation that presented in Figure 3a, the optimum dose of biochar at rice husk to reduce CO_2 emissions was 2.56 t ha^{-1}, whereas palm midribs biochar was 3.67 t ha^{-1}, biochar Galam was 3.19 t ha^{-1} and a biochar coconut shell was 3.25 t ha^{-1}. Biochar rice husk dose of 2 t ha^{-1} considered effective in reducing CO_2 emissions at the beginning phase.

CO_2 emissions at maximum vegetative phase as presented in Figure 3b. Biochar from coconut shell at dose of 2 - 4 t ha^{-1} was able to reduce CO_2 emissions compared with the control, and an increase in the dose to be 16 tons would increase CO_2 emissions. Biochar rice husk at dose of 2 t ha^{-1} was also able to reduce emissions compared to the control, but increase the dose to 8 t ha^{-1} would likely increase emissions. The optimum dose of coconut shell biochar to reduce CO_2 emissions by the equation $y = 1293x^2 - 7177x + 11\ 141$ was 2.8 t ha^{-1}.

Biochar has a chemical and physical structure is very complex. Biochar surfaces could be absorb various gases (LeLeuch and Bandosz, 2007), and these gases could interact with water or cations on the surface of the biochar. Mukherjee and Lal (2013), biochar could increase or decrease the CO_2 emissions. Application biochar initially could increase the CO_2 emissions because: (i) decompotition by microbial that used fraction C labile of biochar (Smith *et al.*, 2010), (ii) the release of C inorganic (Zimmerman *et al.*, 2010) and (iii) 'priming effect 'due to the decomposition of C in addition of biochar (Wardle *et al.*, 2008). Emissions of carbon dioxide could be used as an index of microbial activity in the soil (Murayama and Zahari, 1996). Microbial heterotrophic initially utilizing C organic in a simple chain and biochar has little a simple chain. All of biochar in soil peat effectively reduce CO_2 and CH_4, thought to be caused by retention of C labile with pores biochar (Santi and Goenadi, 2012). Furthermore, biochar would inhibit microbial activity in producing CO_2. Utilization of rice husk biochar could be a promising technology for reducing CO_2 emissions of peat land (Agus *et al.*, 2008).

CONCLUSION

The influence of biochar on soil fertility and emissions in peatlands vary, depending on the type and dose of biochar. Increasing doses of biochar from 8 t ha^{-1} to 16 t ha^{-1} tends to increase CO_2 emissions during planting. Biochar from coconut shell at a dose of 2-4 t ha^{-1} able to improve the soil pH and K-available and reduce emissions of CO_2 up to 60% compared to control.

REFERENCES

1. Agus, F. dan I.G.M. Subiksa, 2008. Lahan Gambut: Potensi untuk Pertanian dan Aspek Lingkungan. Balai Penelitian Tanah. Badan Litbang Pertanian. Bogor.
2. Amonette and Joseph. 2009. Characteristics of biochar microchemical properties,In: J. Lehman and S. Joseph (eds).Biochar for Environmental Management Science and Technology.Eartscan. UK.
3. Attiken, W.P., P.W. Moody and T.Dickson, 1998. Field amelioration of acid soil in south – east Queenland. I. Effect of amendements on soil properties *Australian. J. Agric. Res.* 49 (4);627– 638.
4. Balittra, 2013. Laporan Hasil Penelitian. Badan Litbang Pertanian. Banjarbaru.
5. Balittra, 2014. Laporan Hasil Penelitian. Badan Litbang Pertanian. Banjarbaru
6. Brewer, C.E. and Brown, 2012. Biochar. In Sayigh, A. (Ed) Comprehensive Renewably Energy. Elsevier. Oxford. Pp357-384.
7. Bridgwater, A. and Boocock, D. G. B. 2006. Science in Thermal and Chemical Biomass Conversion. CPL Press, Newbury, UK
8. Bourke, J., Manley-Harris, M., Fushimi, C., Dowaki, K., Nunoura,T. and Antal, M. J. Jr. 2007. 'Do all carbonized charcoals have the same chemical structure? 2. A model of the chemical structure of carbonized charcoal',Industrial and Engineering Chemistry Research.
9. Glaser, B., Lehmann, J., Zech, W. 2002. Ameliorating physical and chemical properties of highly weathered soils in the tropics with charcoal – a review. Biology and Fertility of Soils 35:4
10. Graber E.R., Harel Y.M., Kolton M., Cytryn E., Silber A., David D.R., Tscehansky L., Borenshtein M. and Elad T. 2010. Biochar impact on development and productivity of pepper and tomato grown in fertigated soilless media. Plant Soil. 337:481-496.
11. Laird, D.A., Chappell, M.A., Marteus, D.A., Wershaw, R.L. and Thompson, M. 2008. Distinguishing black carbon from biogenic humic substances in soil clay fraction. Geoderma, vol 143, pp 115-122.
12. Le Leuch, L.M. and Bandosz, T.J. 2007. The role of water and surface acidity on the reactive adsorption of ammonia on modified activate carbons. Carbon, vol 45:568-578
13. Koutcheiko, S., Monreal, C.M., Kodama, H., McCracken,T. and Kotlyar, L. (2007) 'Preparation and characterization of activated carbon derived from the thermochemical conversion of chicken manure', Bioresource Technology ,vol 98, pp2459–2462.

14. Masulili, A. W. H. Utomo, dan Syechfani, 2010. Rice husk biochar for rice based cropping system in acid soil 1. The characteristics of rice husk biochar and its influences on the properties of acid sulfate soils and rice growth in west Kalimantan, Indonesia. Journal of Agricultural Science. Vol. 2, No.1.
15. Milne, T.A., Evans, R.J. and Abatzoglou, N. 1998. Biomass Gasifier Tars: Their Nature, Formation, and Conversion, Report No NREL/TP-570-25357pdf, National Renewable Energy Laboratory, Colorado, www.nrel.gov/docs/fy99osti/25357.pdf, accessed July 2008.
16. Mukherjee A. and Lal R. 2013. Biochar impact on soil physical properties and green house gas emissions. Agronomy 3:313-339.
17. Murayama, S. and Zahari, A.B. 1996. Decomposition of tropical peat soils: 1. Decomposition kinetics of organic matter of peat soils. JARQ 30: 145-151.
18. Purevsuren, B., Avida, B., Gerelmaa, T., Davoajava, Y., Morgan T.J., Herod, A.A. and Kandiyati, R. 2004. The characterization of tar from the pyrolysis of animal bones. Fuel. Vol 83. pp799-805.
19. Raveendran, K., Ganesh, A. and Khilart, K.C. (1995). Influence of mineral matter on biomass pyrolysis characteristics. Fuel, vol 74; pp1812-1822.
20. Rieley, J.O and S.E. Page (2005) Wise use of tropical peatlands:Focus on Southeast Asia. Nottingham. UK. 168
21. Ritung, S., Wahyunto, K. Nugroho, Sukarman, Hikmatullah, Suparto & C. Tafakresnanto, C. 2011. Peta Lahan Gambut Indonesia Skala 1:250.000. Balai Besar Penelitian dan Pengembangan Sumberdaya Lahan Pertanian, Bogor.
22. Santi S.L.P. and D.H. Gunadi, 2010. The use of biochar as a microbial carrier for aggregate stabilizer of Ultisol in Taman Bogo Lampung. Biotechnology Research Institute for Estate Crops. Bogor.
23. Steiner, C.,Teixeira,W. G., Lehmann, J., Nehls,T., Macedo, J. L.V., Blum,W. E. H. and Zech,W. (2007) 'Long term effects of manure, charcoal and mineral fertilization on crop production and fertility on a highly weathered Central Amazonian upland soil', Plant and Soil, Vol 291, pp275–290
24. Saito M and T. Marumoto, 2002. Inoculation with arbuscular mycorrhizal fungi: The status quo in Japan and the future prospect. Plant and Soil 244; 273-279
25. Schnitzer, M. I., Monreal, C. M., Jandl, G. and Leinweber, P. (2007b) 'The conversion of chicken manure to biooil by fast pyrolysis II. Analysis of chicken manure, biooils, and char by curie-point pyrolysis-gas chromatography/ mass spectrometry (Cp Py-GC/MS)', Journal of Environmental Science and Health B vol 42, pp79–95
26. Yu, C.,Tang.Y., Fang, M., Luo, Z. and Cen, K. (2005) 'Experimental study on alkali emission during rice straw pyrolysis', Journal of Zhejiang University (Engineering Science) vol 39, pp1435–1444.
27. Zimmerman, A., 2010. Abiotic and microbial oxidatioin of Laboratory-produced black carbon (biochar). Environmental Science and Technology 44. 1295-1301.
28. Wardle, D.A., Nilsson, M. C. and Zackrisson, O. 2008. Fire-derived charcoal causes loss of forest humus. *Science* 320:269

Abstract No: A-052

CARBON DIOXIDE EMISSIONS FROM CULTIVATED PEAT SOIL CROPPED WITH BIO-ENERGY CROPS, A RECARE PROJECT

Kerstin Berglund and Örjan Berglund*
Swedish University of Agricultural Sciences, Sweden
**Corresponding author: orjan.berglund@slu.se*

SUMMARY

Peatlands store a major share of the world's soil organic carbon and are widespread in Northern and Central European countries. Drainage is a precondition for traditional agricultural production on organic soils. Drainage fosters peat mineralization and changes the physical and chemical soil quality. Only a few decades after initial drainage, agricultural systems on drained organic soils start experiencing a high risk of crop failure. Decreased hydraulic conductivities lead to decreased infiltration, ponding, and finally to abandonment as drainage will not be effective anymore. The Broddbo case study site is located in the Bälinge Mossar peatland area on a typical Swedish fen peat soil and cropped with reed canary grass, tall fescue and timothy to investigate the yield and greenhouse gas emissions from the different crops. The yield in 2015 was about 2 t d.m. ha^{-1} for Timothy and Reed canary grass and 1 t d.m ha^{-1} for Tall fescue. The CO_2 emission was 26.5 t CO_2 ha^{-1} and was influenced by crop growth, ground water level and temperature.

Keywords: *Peat, CO_2, Reed canary grass, Tall fescue, Timothy, RECARE*

INTRODUCTION

Peatlands store a major share of the world's soil organic carbon and are widespread in Northern and Central European countries (Görres *et al.*, 2014). Drainage is a precondition for traditional agricultural production on organic soils (Berglund 1996) and can also foster peat mineralization and changes to the physical and chemical soil properties and it can affect the CO_2 emission (Berglund *et al.*, 2011a). Only a few decades after initial drainage, agricultural systems on drained organic soils start experiencing a high risk of crop failure. Decreased hydraulic conductivities lead to decreased infiltration, ponding, and finally to abandonment as drainage will not be effective anymore.

The degradation of drained peat soils in agricultural use is often an underestimated source of loss of organic matter due to oxidation and wind erosion. The oxidation can cause a loss of organic matter of 11 – 22 t ha^{-1} y^{-1} equivalent to CO_2 emission of 20 – 40 t ha^{-1} y^{-1}.

Flooding agricultural peat soils to decrease the emissions is in many cases not possible without high costs, high GHG emissions and severe water pollution (Reddy *et al.*, 1983). Moreover sometimes cultural and historical landscapes and meadow birds' areas are lost. In areas where the possibility to regulate the water table is limited the mitigation options are either to increase biomass production that can be used as bioenergy to substitute some fossil fuel, try to slow down the break-down of the peat by different amendments that inhibit microbial activity, or permanent flooding.

The aim in this project is to investigate the yield and CO_2 emission from a peat soil cropped with timothy (T), reed canary grass (RCG) and tall fescue (TF) to see if the choice of crop is of importance on cultivated peat fields with periods of very high ground water level.

METHODS

In the Swedish part of the EU-funded RECARE project, a field experiment (randomized block design,4x3) was set up at a former cultivated, but now abandoned, fen peat (Euic Typic Haplosaprist H8-10, pH 5.3-5.8, LOI 82-87%) located at Bälinge Mossar (60.02821N, 17.43008E). The plots were sown with RCG, T and TF (Figure 2) in the autumn 2014 and re-sown in the spring 2015 (RCG and TF). Meteorological parameters were measured at the site and logged every half hour.

Figure 2: Reed canary grass, Thimoty and Tall fescue at Broddbo field trial

CO_2 emission was measured every second hour with automatic chambers from ADC Bioscientific (Herts, England) using the dark chamber method (Martikainen *et al.*, 1995). The crop in the chamber frame was cut regularly since the CO_2 contribution from the roots can be high (Berglund *et al.*, 2011b). T was harvested two times (in June and in September) and the RCG and TF only once, in September.

RESULTS

The summer of 2015 was very wet and the ground water level was very high during the summer (Figure 3).

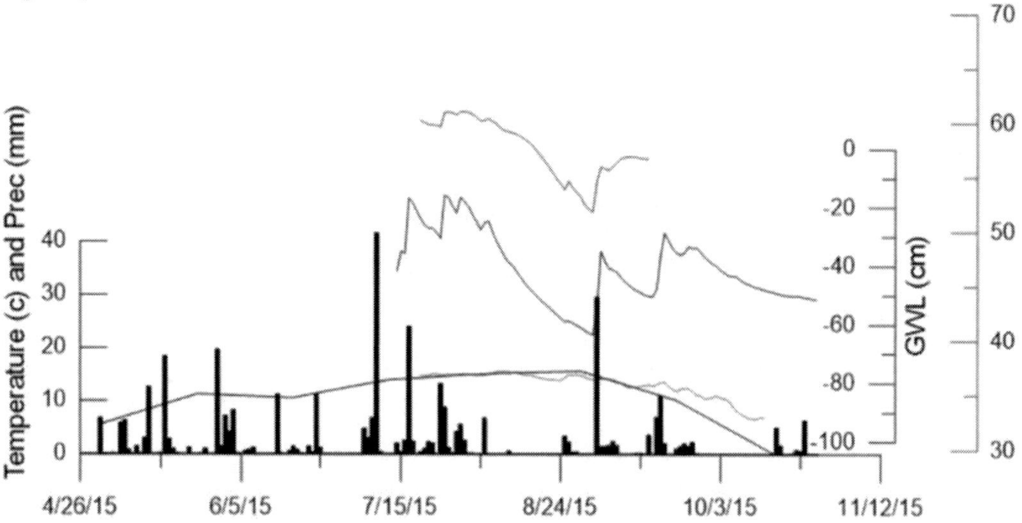

Figure 3: Precipitation, Air and Soil Temperature, Groundwater level and soil moisture 2015 at Broddbo Field Site

The total yield of T was 1.92 t d.m./ha and 0.52 t d.m./ha in the first cut . RCG yielded 2.02 t d.m./ha and TF 1.19 t d.m./ha.

In the early part of the summer, it was only T that was established and the root respiration contributed to the CO_2 emission which is shown in Figure 4. RCG and TF was re-sown in the beginning of the summer and at this time these plots could be considered to be bare soil. In the middle of the summer the ground water level was very high and the CO_2 emission low. Later in the summer RCG and TF started to grow quite well and the CO_2 emission from these plots increased. The average CO_2 emission during this period was 26.5 t CO_2/ha.

DISCUSSION

It was an obvious effect of root respiration on the CO_2 emission and since RCG and TF were re-sown in the beginning of the summer, these plots were almost like bare soil plots. The emission from the T plots was almost twice

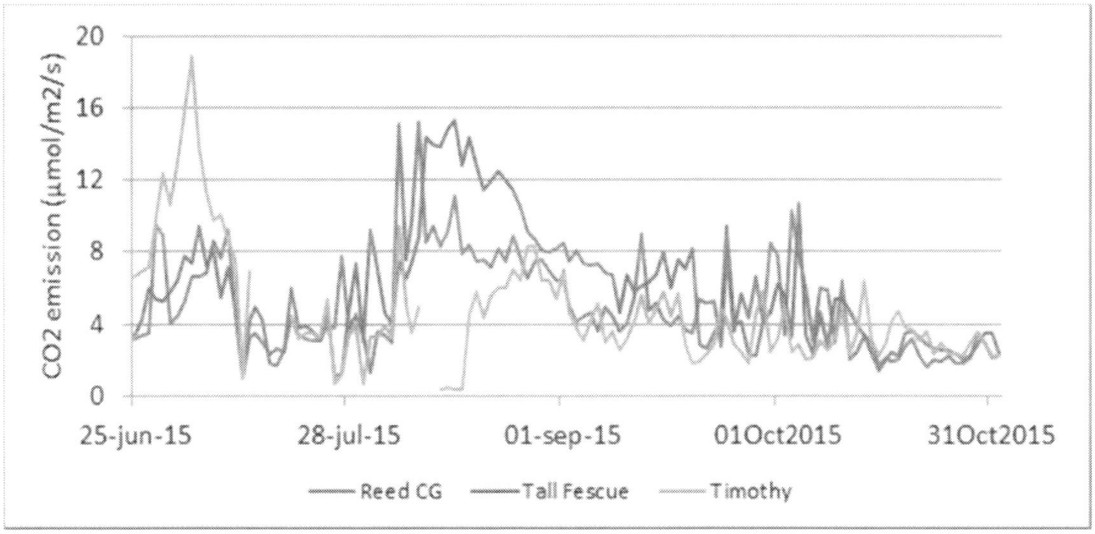

Figure 4: CO_2 emission from plots with 0, 2.5 and 5 cm of foundry sand added.

as high as from the bare soil plots, which is similar to results shown in Berglund and Berglund (2011b). After the T was cut in June, the emission dropped to the same level as the other crops. The high groundwater level in July seems to have lowered the CO_2 emission due to low oxygen content in the soil (Karki *et al.*, 2014). Later in the autumn when the temperature dropped, also the CO_2 emission is lower, similar to data shown in Berglund *et al.* (2010).

CONCLUSION

The CO_2 emission from plots with different crops showed no significant difference. Bare soil emitted less CO_2 than plots with a crop. The high groundwater level during the summer hampered the CO_2 emission as well as the low temperature during late autumn.

ACKNOWLEDGMENTS

This project has received funding from the European Union's Seventh Framework Programme for research, technological development and demonstration under grant agreement no 603498.

REFERENCES

1. Berglund, K. (1996). Cultivated Organic Soils in Sweden: Properties and Amelioration. Department of Soil Sciences. Uppsala, Swedish University of Agricultural Sciences. **Reports and Dissertations:** 39.
2. Berglund, Ö. and K. Berglund (2011a). "Influence of water table level and soil properties on emissions of greenhouse gases from cultivated peat soil." Soil Biology and Biochemistry **43**(5): 923-931.
3. Berglund, Ö., K. Berglund, *et al.* (2010). "A lysimeter study on the effect of temperature on CO2 emission from cultivated peat soils." Geoderma **154**(3-4): 211-218.
4. Berglund, Ö., K. Berglund, *et al.* (2011b). "Plant-derived CO_2 flux from cultivated peat soils." Acta Agriculturae Scandinavica, Section B - Plant Soil Science **61**(6): 508-513.
5. Görres, C. M., L. Kutzbach, *et al.* (2014). "Comparative modeling of annual CO2 flux of temperate peat soils under permanent grassland management." Agriculture, Ecosystems & Environment **186**(0): 64-76.
6. Karki, S., L. Elsgaard, *et al.* (2014). "Mitigation of greenhouse gas emissions from reed canary grass in paludiculture: effect of groundwater level." Plant and Soil **383**(1-2): 217-230.
7. Martikainen, P. J., H. Nykanen, *et al.* (1995). "Change in Fluxes of Carbon-Dioxide, Methane and Nitrous-Oxide Due to Forest Drainage of Mire Sites of Different Trophy." Plant and Soil **169**: 571-577.
8. Reddy, K. R. and P. S. C. Rao (1983). "Nitrogen and Phosphorus Fluxes from a Flooded Organic Soil." Soil Science **136**(5): 300-307.

Abstract No: A-038

CO_2 EMISSIONS FROM CULTIVATED PEAT SOIL WITH SAND ADDITION, A CAOS PROJECT

Örjan Berglund and Kerstin Berglund

Swedish University of Agricultural Sciences, Sweden

**Corresponding author: orjan.berglund@slu.se*

SUMMARY

Peatlands store a major share of the world's soil organic carbon and are widespread in Northern and Central European countries. Drainage is a precondition for traditional agricultural production on organic soils. Drainage fosters peat mineralization and changes the physical and chemical soil quality. Only few decades after initial drainage, agricultural systems on drained organic soils start experiencing a high risk of crop failure. Decreased hydraulic conductivities lead to decreased infiltration, ponding, and finally to abandonment as drainage will not be effective anymore. Another problem is the low trafficability. The aim in this experiment is to investigate if the addition of foundry sand to the top soil will improve the trafficability without increasing the CO_2 emission. In the Swedish part of the EU-funded CAOS project, a field experiment (randomized block design, 3x3) was set up at a former cultivated, but now abandoned, fen peat located at Bälinge Mossar (60.02821N, 17.43008E). We will compare trafficability, yield and CO_2 emission from plots sown with Phleum pretense and treated with 0 cm, 2.5 cm or 5 cm foundry sand. The sand was applied in the autumn of 2015 and mixed in the top 10 cm of the soil. Penetration resistance, yield and CO_2 emissions will be compared during three years. The first preliminary results (15/9-1/11) show that the CO_2 emissions are highest from the plots without sand addition (3.4 $\mu mol\ m^{-2}\ s^{-1}$) and lowest from the plots where 5 cm sand was added (1.4 $\mu mol\ m^{-2}\ s^{-1}$). The emission from the 2.5 cm treatment was 1.8 $\mu mol\ m^{-2}\ s^{-1}$. Yield and trafficability have not been measured yet, but initial emission results are promising with no increase of CO_2 emissions with sand application.

***Keywords**: Peat, CO_2, sand, CAOS*

INTRODUCTION

Peatlands store a major share of the world's soil organic carbon and are widespread in Northern and Central European countries (Görres *et al.*, 2014). Drainage is a precondition for traditional agricultural production on organic soils (Berglund 1996). Drainage fosters peat mineralization and changes the physical and chemical soil quality and it can affect the CO_2 emission (Berglund *et al.*, 2011). Only few decades after initial drainage, agricultural systems on drained organic soils start experiencing a high risk of crop failure. Decreased hydraulic conductivities lead to decreased infiltration, ponding, and finally to abandonment as drainage will not be effective anymore. Another problem is the low trafficability connected to the high water table level (Myllys 1999).

In this article we describe a field trial where we added foundry sand to a cultivated peat soil to investigate how it effect the bearing capacity, trafficability and CO_2 emission.

METHODS

In the Swedish part of the EU-funded CAOS project, a field experiment (randomized block design, 3x3) was set up at a former cultivated, but now abandoned, fen peat located at Bälinge Mossar (60.02821N, 17.43008E). The plots was sown with Phelum pretense and treated with 0 cm, 2.5 cm or 5 cm foundry sand (Figure 1). The sand was applied in the autumn of 2015 and mixed into the top 10 cm of the soil.

Figure 1: Foundry sand spread on Broddbo field trial.

Penetration resistance was measured 10 times per plot down to a depth of 50 cm with a penetrometer from Eijkelkamp. CO_2 emission from the soil was measured every second hour with automatic chambers from ADC Bioscientific (Herts, England) using the dark chamber method (Martikainen *et al.*, 1995).Yield and trafficability have not been measured yet.

RESULTS

The summer of 2015 was very wet (Figure 2) and it was not until September that the groundwater level was low enough for traffic and we could spread the foundry sand.

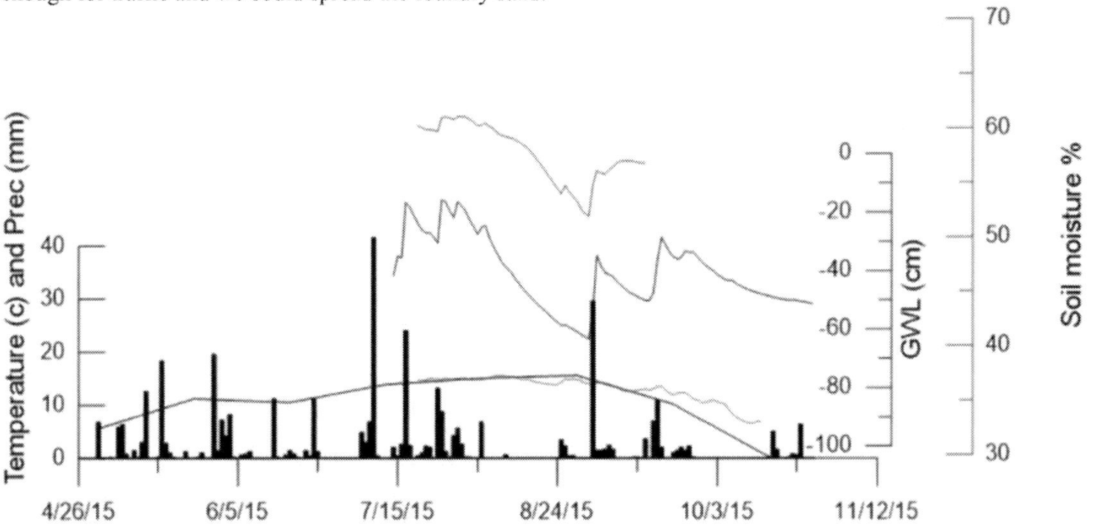

Figure 2: Precipitation, Air (black line) and Soil Temperature (brown line), Groundwater level (blue line) and soil moisture (red line) 2015 at Broddbo Field Site.

Penetration resistance was measured after the sand was mixed into the top 10 cm. Since the soil was not re-packed, it was very loose and the penetration resistance very low and no significant differences were found (Figure 3).

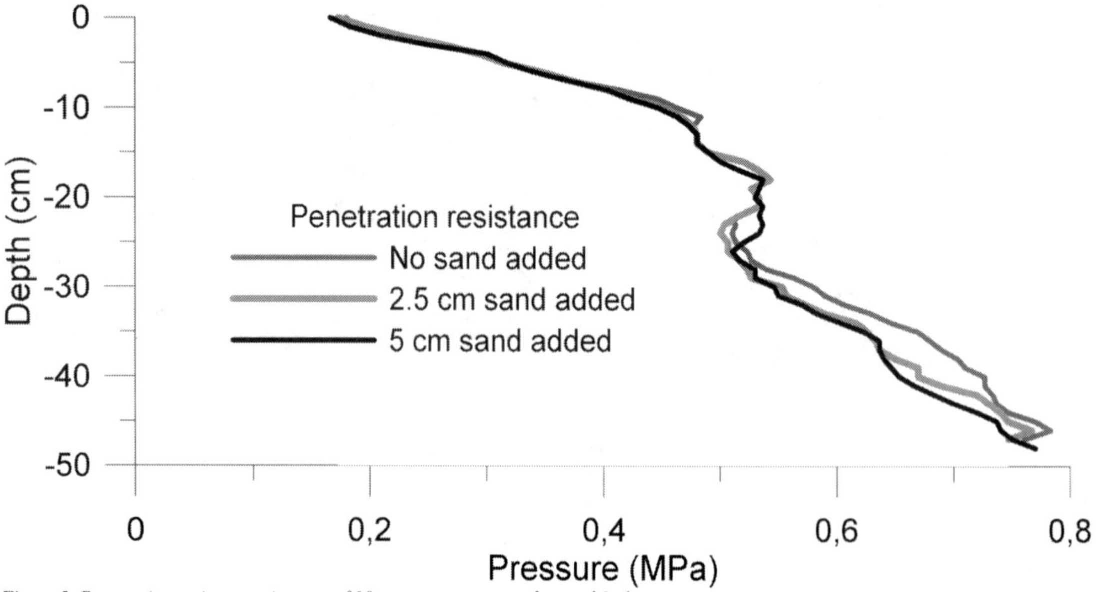

Figure 5: Penetration resistance. Average of 10 measurements per plots and 3 plots per treatment.

Since the foundry sand was added so late in the season, also the CO_2 measurements started quite late and stopped in the beginning of November. There was a consistent trend that CO_2 emission was largest from the plots were no sand was added, and lowest from the plots where we added most sand (Figure 4). The CO_2 emissions are highest from the plots without sand addition (3.4 µmol m^{-2} s^{-1}) and lowest from the plots where 5 cm sand was added (1.4 µmol m^{-2} s^{-1}). The emission from the 2.5 cm treatment was 1.8 µmol m^{-2} s^{-1}.

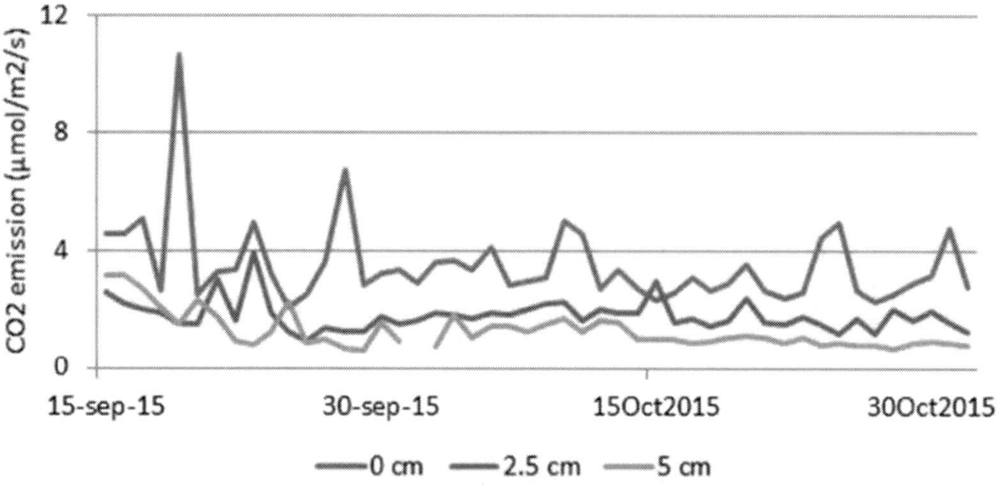

Figure 6: CO_2 emission from plots with 0, 2.5 and 5 cm of foundry sand added.

DISCUSSION

This is the first season of measurements with-in this project and a very short period with CO_2 measurements. Still it is interesting that it seems that the addition of foundry sand might have lowered the CO_2 emission rate. How and if it affects the penetration resistance and trafficability will be interesting to investigate after the winter when the soil will have consolidated. Sand has been used to improve soils in general (Lindsay *et al.*, 2005) and in peat soils in particular (Osvald 1937) where the yield and trafficability was improved by adding sand or clay to peat soils.

CONCLUSION

During the autumn CO_2 emission rates were lowest from the treatment where 5 cm of foundry sand was added and highest from the reference-plots. No difference in penetration resistance could be shown directly after mixing in the sand into the soil.

ACKNOWLEDGMENTS

This project has received funding from the European Union's Seventh Framework Programme for research, technological development and demonstration under grant agreement no 618105.

REFERENCES

1. Berglund, K. (1996). Cultivated Organic Soils in Sweden: Properties and Amelioration. Department of Soil Sciences. Uppsala, Swedish University of Agricultural Sciences. Reports and Dissertations: 39.
2. Berglund, Ö. and K. Berglund (2011). "Influence of water table level and soil properties on emissions of greenhouse gases from cultivated peat soil." Soil Biology and Biochemistry 43(5): 923-931.
3. Görres, C. M., L. Kutzbach, *et al.* (2014). "Comparative modeling of annual CO2 flux of temperate peat soils under permanent grassland management." Agriculture, Ecosystems & Environment 186(0): 64-76.
4. Lindsay, B. J. and T. J. Logan (2005). "Agricultural reuse of foundry sand." J. Resid. Sci. Technol 2: 3-12.
5. Martikainen, P. J., H. Nykanen, *et al.* (1995). "Change in Fluxes of Carbon-Dioxide, Methane and Nitrous-Oxide Due to Forest Drainage of Mire Sites of Different Trophy." Plant and Soil 169: 571-577.
6. Myllys, M. (1999). The effect of soil water content on the trafficability of cultivated peat soils. Chemical, Physical and Biological Processes in Peat soils, Jokioinen, Finland, International Peat Society.
7. Osvald, H. (1937). Myrar och myrodling. Stockholm, Kooperativa förbundets bokförlag.

Abstract No: A-090

CO_2 EMISSIONS FROM GROUND SURFACE OF OIL PALM PLANTATION IN SARAWAK, MALAYSIA

Yosuke Okimoto[1], Takashi Hirano[1], Ryuichi Hirata[2], Lulie Melling[3], Yoshiyuki Ishii[4], Frankie Kiew[1,3] and Wong Guan Xhuan[1,3]

[1]*Research Faculty of Agriculture, Hokkaido University, Sapporo, Japan*
[2]*National Institute for Environmental Studies, Tsukuba, Japan*
[3]*Tropical Peat Research Laboratory Unit, Chief Minister's Department, Sarawak, Malaysia*
[4]*Institute of Low Temperature Science, Hokkaido University, Sapporo, Japan*

**Corresponding author: okimoto@env.agr.hokudai.ac.jp*

SUMMARY

Drainage, mechanical compaction and water management are important land preparation and management practices in any agricultural development on tropical peatland. Drainage is prerequisite to create aerobic zone for better root growth for the crop. Mechanical compaction is essential to consolidate the peat, and which increase soil bulk density and moisture content. Drainage has been claimed to accelerate soil CO_2 emission due to oxidative peat decomposition (OPD), contributing to peat subsidence. However, subsidence in tropical peatland for oil palm plantation is also due to mechanical compaction and consolidation more than carbon loss via peat oxidation (Melling *et. al*, 2008). Therefore, sole reliance on subsidence data for carbon emission alone is not correctly represented. Hence, more accurate data shall be obtained through direct measurement of the CO_2 emissions through OPD and root respiration in order to better understand the net carbon emission of the tropical peatlands. This study is located in an oil palm (*Elaeis guineensis*) plantation of the 6-10 year-old palms on tropical peat in Sibu, Sarawak, Malaysia (2.11°S, 114.50°E). Groundwater level was controlled at 0.65 ± 0.09 m (mean ± 1 SD). The CO_2 efflux was measured continuously using an automated chamber system, consisting of 16 opaque chambers (40 cm high with a 25-cm internal diameter) and an infrared CO_2 analyzer (LI820, Licor). Eight chambers were installed outside and inside the trench for each in May 2014 for the measurements of total soil respiration (TR) and OPD, respectively. The soil subsidence was measured using a tube, which was inserted vertically into the peat layer and anchored firmly in the underlying mineral substrate. This study provides the first estimate of annual carbon loss of 842 ± 465 and 724 ± 513 g C m^{-2} yr^{-1} from the oil palm plantation based on continuous field data of TR and OPD obtained throughout a year, respectively.

INTRODUCTION

Peat swamp forest is significant carbon stores and sinks, which store soil carbon up to 88.6 Pg (15-19% of the global peat carbon pool) (Page *et al.*, 2011). When the peatlands were converted to agricultural land that entails drainage and burning or both, carbon accumulated over centuries or millennia is being released to the atmosphere contributing to the greenhouse effect and climate change. The current total peatland carbon dioxide (CO_2) emissions from drainage in South-east Asia are estimated at an average of 635 Mt yr^{-1} (over 90% originating from Indonesia) (Wetland International, 2010).

With higher global demand for the palm oil, oil palm plantations have to extend into marginal lands, which include peatland. Drainage, mechanical compaction and water management are important land preparation and management practices in any agricultural development on tropical peatland. The drainage is prerequisite to create aerobic zone for better root growth for the crop and the mechanical compaction is essential to consolidate the peat, which increase soil bulk density and moisture content. However, it has been claimed that drainage contributes to soil CO_2 emission via oxidative peat decomposition (OPD), resulting in peat subsidence. Hooijer *et al.* (2006) estimated that the production of one tonne of palm oil on well-drained peatland can result in CO_2 emissions of 10-30 tonnes due to peat oxidation. There is a supposition that the projected increased demand for oil palm (including as biofuel) will generate further conversion and subsequently drainage and exposure of intact peatland areas (Wetland International, 2010).

As a consequence, the peat swamp ecosystem was reported could switch from a net carbon sink to a net carbon source (i.e. peat accumulation is replaced by peat degradation), with large carbon losses arising particularly from enhanced aerobic peat decomposition and the loss of any future carbon sequestration by the native peat swamp forest vegetation (Page *et al.*, 2011). According to the Wetland Supplement (IPCC, 2013), the default values of CO_2

emission from the tropical peatlands, i.e. Emission Factor (EF), were determined based on limited numbers less than fifty of the peer-reviewed papers but there are a wide-range from 150 to 2000 g C m^{-2} s^{-1}. Especially for the oil palm plantation, the reported 12 papers based on the data obtained from the 10 sites were applied to determine the EF of 11 tonC ha^{-1} yr^{-1} (i.e. 1100 g C m^{-2} yr^{-1}).

In the oil palm plantation, subsidence is due to mechanical compaction and consolidation more than carbon loss via OPD (Melling *et. al*, 2008). Therefore, sole reliance on subsidence data for carbon emission alone is not correctly represented. Direct chamber measurement is conducted to obtain accurate data of carbon loss from the tropical peatland (e.g. Hooijer *et al.*, 2010, 2012; Jauhiainen *et al.*, 2012; Couwenberg and Hooijer, 2013). However, very few reports showed heterotrophic respiration (HR) of OPD (Jauhiainen *et al.*, 2012; Hirano *et al*, 2014), separately from total peat soil respiration (TR), involving litter decomposition and root respiration (RR). Total soil respiration measurements are inadequate for determining the net CO2 fluxes as the RR may varies erratically. (Couwenbeg *et al.*, 2010). Thus, it is crucial to quantify oxidative peat decomposition for estimation of CO_2 emission. Limited number of studies have reported on direct measurement of OPD using the chamber technique in the tropical peatlands. The only available studies that included these measurements are reported in an Acacia plantation (Jauhiainen *et al.*, 2012), oil palm plantation (Husnain *et al.*, 2014; Dariah *et al.*, 2014), agricultural land and drained land (Astiani *et al.*, 2015; Jauhiainen *et al.*, 2012) and drained burnt area (Hirano *et al.*, 2014).

Hence, more accurate data shall be obtained through direct measurement of the CO_2 emissions through OPD and root respiration in order to better understand the net carbon emission of the oil palm plantation. We therefore measure OPD and TR and investigate the relationship between OPD, TR and environmental factors. Based on the obtained data, annual CO_2 emission and carbon loss was quantified.

MATERIAL AND METHOD

This study was carried out in an oil palm (*Elaeis guineensis*) plantation of the 6-10 year-old palms with a mean canopy height of around 10 m on tropical peat in Sibu, Sarawak, Malaysia (2.11°S, 114.50°E) (Fig. 1). The water-table was maintained between 50 to70 cm from the peat surface.

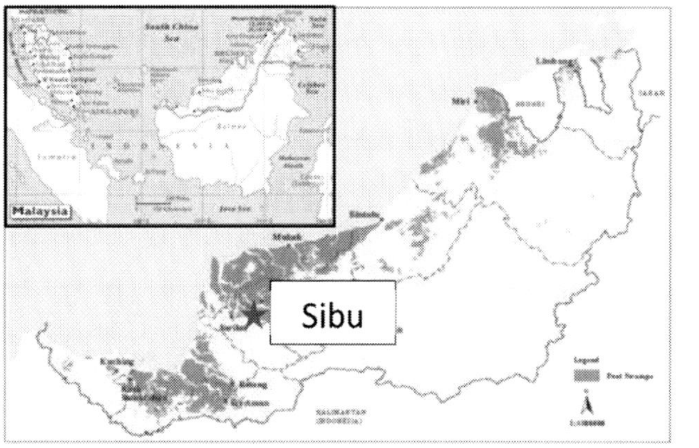

Fig. 1: Location of study site in Sibu. Sarawak, Malaysisa.

The CO_2 efflux was measured continuously using automated close/open chamber system, consisting of sixteen (16) opaque chambers (40 cm high with a 25-cm internal diameter) and an infrared CO_2 analyzer (LI820, Licor Biosciences, Lincoln, NE, USA). Eight (8) trenches (80 cm x 60 cm; two chambers for each) were installed between the oil palm trees around a flux tower within 20 m on May 7th 2014. The trenches were established by making 100 cm vertically deep cuts along the boundaries below the ground surface using a chainsaw to sever all roots. Plant detritus was removed and no plants existed inside the chamber throughout the measurement period. Eight (8) chambers were installed between the trees outside and inside the trench for each in May 2014 for the measurements of total soil respiration (TR) and OPD, respectively. Each chamber was closed for 225 sec sequentially. It took 60 min to complete a round of sixteen (16) chambers. Soil CO_2 flux was calculated from an increase in the rate of CO_2 concentration in the chamber headspace for the last 3 min of each closing. CO_2 concentration was measured every 5 s, and its increasing rate was calculated by linear fitting using the least squares method. Using a data logger (CR1000, Campbell Scientific, USA), the CO_2 data at 5-sec intervals was stored. Simultaneously, temperatures both of air and soil inside and outside the chamber measured at four (4) points with Type T (copper-constantan) thermocouples, soil water content measured by time-domain-reflectometry (TDR) probes (CS616, Campbell Scientific Inc., UK) at 30-min intervals were stored. Soil subsidence was measured using a steel pole, which was inserted vertically into the peat layer and anchored firmly in the underlying mineral substratum.

RESULTS AND DISCUSSION

Environmental factors of groundwater level (GWL), soil water content (SWC) and soil temperature were concurrently measured with CO_2 efflux (Fig. 1). Except some missing data due to technical issue in June and August 2015, GWL varied from -0.81 to -0.32 m and the annual mean value was -0.63 m. This study site of oil palm plantation is controlled SWC varied from 0.46 to 0.59 m^3 m^{-3} and the mean value was 0.51 m^3 m^{-3}. Soil temperature varied from 24.6 to 30.4 °C and the mean value was 26.7 °C.

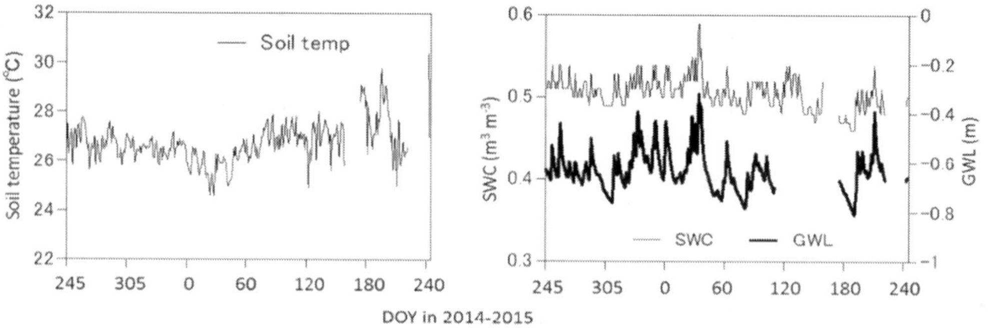

Fig. 1. Seasonal variations of soil temperature, soil water content (SWC) and ground water level (GWL) from September 2014 to August 2015. Some data is lacking due to trouble of the power supply system in the field.

CO_2 efflux from the ground surface was obtained except those in January and June 2015. Seasonal variations of the monthly mean values (± 1 SD) for total respiration (TR) and oxidative peat decomposition (PD) were ranged from 1.59±1.01 to 3.13±1.66 μmol m^{-2} s^{-1} and from 1.37±1.03 to 2.58±1.67 μmol m^{-2} s^{-1}, respectively Fig. 2). The annual mean values of TR and OPD were 2.38±1.43 μmol m^{-2} s^{-1} and 2.03±1.51 μmol m^{-2} s^{-1}, and a ratio of OPD to TR was 85.4%.

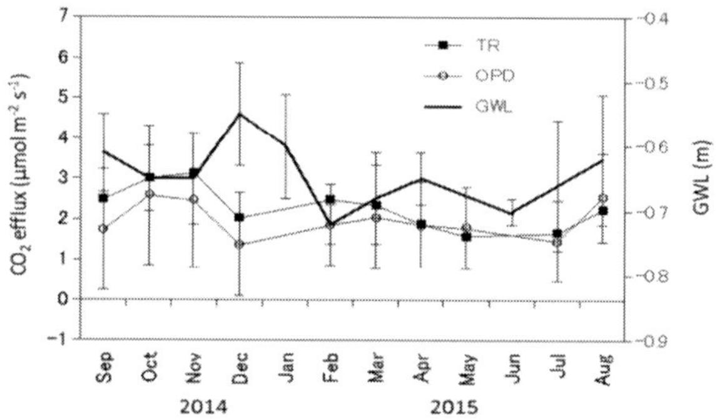

Fig. 2. Seasonal variations in the mean values of CO_2 efflux of total soil respiration (TR) and oxidative peat decomposition (OPD) measured by the automated chamber system in an oilpalm plantation in Sibu, Sawarak, Malaysia. Bars denote a standard deviation.

A trend was found that CO_2 effluxes decreased as GWLs were lowered, but there was no significant relationship between the CO_2 efflux and GWL ($p > 0.05$) (Fig. 3). Nevertheless the GWL varied seasonally, the SWC showed few changes (Fig. 1). It is considered that this stability of the water condition is owed to mechanical compaction of the plantation ground, leading to water uptake by capillary rise in the compacted soil particles. This condition contributes to consistent retention of soil water condition, although the GWL varied by precipitation and drainages besides water management of the plantation.

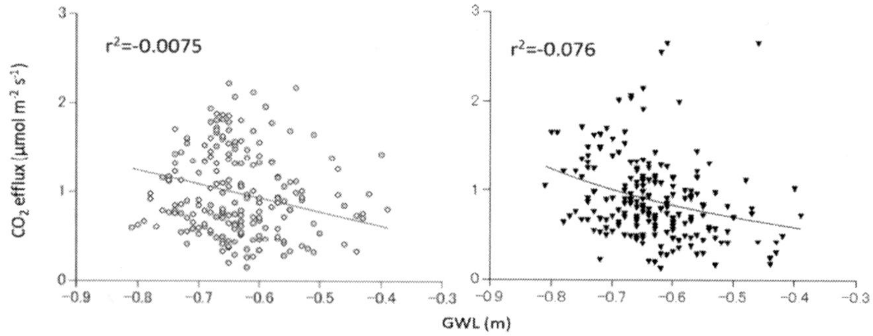

Fig. 3. Correlation between CO_2 efflux of total soil respiration (TR; left) and oxidative peat decomposition (OPD; right) and groundwater level (GWL) obtained from September 2014 and August 2015, respectively.

Based on the measured TR and OPD values (mean ± 1 SD) of each month, estimated value of annual carbon loss was 842 ± 465and 724 ± 513 g C m^{-2} yr^{-1}, respectively. These are similar to those reported for 4 year-old oil palm plantations (693 ± 95 g C m^{-2} yr^{-1}; Melling *et al.*, 2013) and 6 and 15 year-old plantations in Sumatra (1042 ± 259 and 930 ± 434 g C m^{-2} yr^{-1}, respectively; Dariah *et al.*, 2014). Meanwhile, some larger estimation on the oil palm plantation (1800 ± 682 g C m^{-2} yr^{-1}; Husnain *et al.*, 2014, 1590 to 1760 g C m^{-2} yr^{-1}; Couwenberg and Hooijer, 2013) was reported.

This study is the first report of annual carbon loss of the oil palm plantation in the tropical peatland, which was estimated on a basis of a continuous field measurement of oxidative peat decomposition throughout a year.

ACKNOWLEDGEMENT

This work was supported by JSPS KAKENHI (No. 25257401), the Asahi Glass Foundation and the Environment Research and Technology Development Fund (2-1504) of the Ministry of the Environment, Japan.

REFERENCES

1. Astiani D., Mujiman, Muhammad Hatta, Hanisah, Firda Fifian. 2015. Soil CO_2 Respiration Along Annual Crops or Land-Cover Type Gradients on West Kalimantan Degraded Peatland Forest. Procedia Environmental Sciences, 28: 132–141.
2. Couwenbeg J, Dommain R and Joosten. 2010. Greenhouse gas fluxes from tropical peatlands in South-east Asia. Global Change Biology, 16: 1715–1732.
3. Couwenberg J and Hooijer A. 2013. Towards Robust Subsidence-Based Soil Carbon Emission Factors For Peat Soils In South-East Asia, With Special Reference To Oil Palm Plantations. Mires and Peat, 12: 1–13.
4. Dariah A, Marwanto S and Agus F. 2013. Root- and Peat-Based CO_2 Emissions From Oil Palm Plantations. Mitigation and Adaptation Strategies for Global Change, 19(6): 831–843.
5. Hirano T, Jauhiainen J, Inoue T, Takahashi H .2009. Controls on the Carbon Balance of Tropical Peatlands. Ecosystems, 12: 873–887.
6. Hirano T , Kusin K, Limin S, Osaki M. 2014. Carbon Dioxide Emissions through Oxidative Peat Decomposition on a Burnt Tropical Peatland. Global Change Biology, 20: 555–565.
7. Hooijer A., Silvius M., Wösten H and Page S. 2006. PEAT-CO_2, Assessment of CO_2 emissions from drained peatlands in SE Asia. Delft Hydraulics report Q3943: Delft, Netherlands. Maas, E.F., Tie Yiu Liong and Lim Chin Pang 1986. Sarawak Land capability classification and evaluation for agricultural crops. Technical Paper No. 5 (2nd Edition), Soils Division, Dept. of Agriculture, Sarawak. 69pp.
8. Hooijer A, Page S, Canadell JG, Silvius M, Kwadijk J, Wösten H and Jauhiainen J. 2010. Current and future CO_2 emissions from drained peatlands in Southeast Asia. Biogeosciences, 7(5): 1505–1514.
9. Hooijer A, Page S, Jauhiainen J, Lee WA, Lu XX, Idris A and Anshari, G. 2012. Subsidence and Carbon Loss in Drained Tropical Peatlands. Biogeosciences, 9(3): 1053–1071.
10. Husnain H, Wigena IGP, Dariah A, Marwanto S, Setyanto P and Agus F. 2014. CO_2 Emissions from Tropical Drained Peat in Sumatra, Indonesia. Mitig. Adapt. Strategy Glob. Change, 19: 845–862.
11. IPCC. 2014. 2013 Supplement to the 2006 IPCC Guidelines for National Greenhouse Gas Inventories: Wetlands, Hiraishi, T., Krug, T., Tanabe, K., Srivastava, N., Baasansuren, J., Fukuda, M. and Troxler, T.G. (eds). Published: IPCC, Switzerland.
12. Jauhiainen J, Hooijer A and Page SE. 2012. Carbon Dioxide Emissions From an Acacia Plantation on Peatland in Sumatra, Indonesia. Biogeosciences, 9(2): 617–630.
13. Melling L, Goh KJ, Beauvais C and Hatano R. 2008. Carbon flow and budget in a young mature oil palm agroecosystem on deep tropical peat. The Planter, 84 (982), 21.
14. Melling L, Tan CSY, Goh KJ and Hatano R. 2013. Soil microbial and root respirations from three ecosystems in tropical peatland of Sarawak, Malaysia. J Oil Palm Res, 25(1), 44-57.
15. Page SE, Morrison R, Malins C, Hooijer A, Rieley JO and Jauhiainen J. 2011. Review of peat surface greenhouse gas emissions from oil palm plantations in Southeast Asia (ICCT White Paper 15). Washington: International Council on Clean Transportation.
16. Wetlands International. 2010. A quick scan of peatlands in Malaysia. Wetlands International Malaysia: Petaling Jaya, Malaysia. 50 pp.

Abstract No: A-218

CO_2 FLUXES FROM SECONDARY FOREST, OIL PALMS, ALOE VERA, AND SHRUB PEATLAND ON DRAINED TROPICAL PEAT

Randi Adi Candra[1], Evi Gusmayanti[1, 2*] and Gusti Anshari[2, 3]

[1]*Department of Agrotechnology, Faculty of Agriculture, Tanjungpura University, Indonesia*
[2]*Magister of Environment, Tanjungpura University, Indonesia*
[3]*Department of Soil Science, Faculty of Agriculture, Tanjungpura University, Indonesia*

Corresponding author: evi.gusmayanti@faperta.untan.ac.id

SUMMARY

Drained tropical peats are widely used for agriculture, and become a major source of CO_2 emissions. However, measurements of CO_2 fluxes from these peats are rarely carried out and reported. We investigate CO_2 fluxes from different land uses, i.e., secondary forest (SF), young oil palm (OP), aloe vera (AV), shrub peatland (SL), on drained peats of Rasau Jaya in West Kalimantan Province, Indonesia. The site of smallholder oil palm plantation (OP) is adjacent to secondary forest (SF). Shrub and aloe vera sites are about 1 and 2 km far from the secondary forest. All sites are located on the same peat complex. We have conducted this research since July 2015, and will continue this research for several years. We used an EGM-4, an infrared gas analyzer, to measure CO_2 fluxes from six plots at each land use. We employed Analysis of Variance, and contrast tests to detect mean differences among land uses. Average values of CO_2 fluxes in SF, OP, AV, and SL are 0.292 ± 0.122; 0.467 ± 0.217; 0.674 ± 0.302; and 0.467 ± 0.185 g CO_2 m^{-2} hr^{-1}. Results of ANOVA show that CO_2 fluxes are significantly different from one land use to another land use. CO_2 fluxes from SF and SL sites are significantly different from OP and AV sites, and SF from SL sites. Low water contents in Aloe vera plantation and shrub lands imply more water loss than in secondary forest and oil palm plantation. In conclusion, we confirm that one of important factors determining CO_2 flux is type of crops. We show that crops with open canopy as in case of Aloe vera enhance more CO_2 emissions than other closed canopy tree crop.

***Keywords**: Land Uses; Drained Tropical Peats; CO_2 Fluxes*

INTRODUCTION

Peatland has been used for agriculture uses in Indonesia for many decades. Cultivation on peatland is usually preceeded by draining peat to lower water table and provide favourable aerob layer for root respiration of marketable crops. This condition has changed a role of peatlands as a sink into source of carbon emissions. However, the measurement of CO_2 flux from these peatlands are rarely carried out and reported.

In this study, we investigated CO_2 flux from four different land uses. These are natural land uses, i.e., secondary forest and shrubland, and cultivated peatlands, i.e., oil palm and aloe vera.

MATERIALS AND METHODS

We carried out this study in Rasau Jaya Peat Dome, West Kalimantan, Indonesia. There were four different land uses (Table 1). The oil palm is about three years old and cultivated with minimal input and located adjacent to the secondary forest. The shrub land is about 1 km apart and dominated by fern. Aloe vera plantation is about 2 km away from the other sites. The age of aloe vera in this site is more than ten years and experienced to frequently application of woody debris ash to improve the soil acidity.

The flux of CO_2 is measured with, a closed chamber equipped with an infra-red gas analyzer (EGM-4). There were six plots in every land use measured twice a month, starting from July 2015 until February 2016. We adjusted the measured CO_2 Flux (Un-normalized) with quotient temperature (Q10) to calculate normalized CO_2 flux as done by Hatfield and Parkin 2012. In addition to the CO2 flux, we also measure environmental variables i.e. gravimetric water content, Oxidation Reduction Potential (ORP), soil pH, soil temperature and air temperature. Rain and relative humidity data were also collected from the nearest weather station.

Table 3: Description of four landuses for CO2 Flux measurement

No	Landuse	Coordinate (UTM)	Decomposition Degree	Peat Depth (cm)
1	Secondary Forest (SF)	X: 0323614 Y: 9977700	Hemic	660
2	Oil Palm (OP)	X: 0323643 Y: 9978140	Hemic	648
3	Aloe Vera (AV)	X: 0322267 Y: 9980802	Hemic	264
4	Shrub Peatland (SL)	X: 0322196 Y: 9977883	Hemic	764

Note: SF site is mainly covered by saplings of pioneer species, e.g., Pandanus and Macaranga spp; OP site is not well maintained, and very much covered by ferns; AV site is well maintained and cleaned from ferns and other herbs; and SL site is mainly covered by ferns, and prone to annual fire.

An analysis of Variance (ANOVA) is employed to analyze the data. Variables except soil pH and ORP were analyzed with Brown Forsythe ANOVA after having the significant results of Levene's homogeneity test. Contrast test is applied to detect the difference of CO_2 flux and environmental variables between land uses. There are five contrasts, i.e. C1 (SF + SL vs. OP + AV), C2 (SF vs. SL), C3 (OP vs. AV) and C4 (SF + SL vs OP). Contrast 1 – 3 is to compare the natural and agricultural land uses, while contrast 4 is to compare oil palm plantation with natural land uses.

RESULT AND DISCUSSION

Variabilty of flux from each land use is presented in Figure 1. According to the results of Brown Forsythe ANOVA, land use type significantly affected the fluxes (40.57**and 32.67**, respectively for un-normalized and normalized flux). The average of CO_2 flux in all land uses is 0.475 ± 0.254 g CO_2 m^{-2} $hour^{-1}$ and 0.336 ± 0.169 g CO_2 m^{-2} $hour^{-1}$ respectively for un-normalized and normalized flux.

The average value of fluxes from agricultural lands (oil palm and aloe vera) was 0.38 and 0.57 g CO_2 m^{-2} $hour^{-1}$ for normalized and un normalized flux. These values are higher than values obtained in Palangkaraya, which was 0.29 g CO_2 m^{-2} $hour^{-1}$ (Hatano *et al.*, 2010). The flux from oil palm plantation is 0.47 ± 0.22 g CO_2 m^{-2} $hour^{-1}$, which is higher but still in the range of fluxes measured in oil palm plantation in Sarawak Malaysia, which was 0.05 – 0.34 (Melling, Hatano, and Goh 2005; Melling *et al.*, 2008).

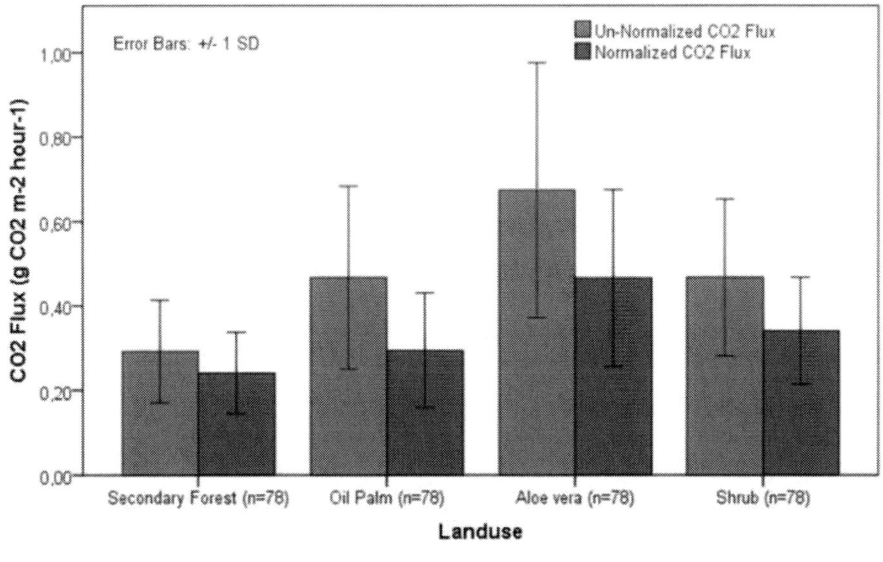

Figure 7: The average of CO_2 flux (error bars indicate standar deviation) on different landuses

Table 4: Contrast resuts of CO_2 flux from different landuses (SF: Secondary forest, SL: Shrub peatland, OP: Oil palm, AV: *Aloe vera*)

CO2 Flux	Contrast Statistics (contrast value; sig. 2-tailed)			
	SF + SL vs OP + AV	SF vs SL	OP vs AV	SF + SL vs OP
Un-Normalized	-0.381; <0.01	-0.175; <0.01	-0.207; <0.01	-0.1741; <0.01
Normalized	-0.178; <0.01	-0.100; <0.01	-0.171; <0.01	-0.0071; 0.844

Contrast results are presented in Table 2. According to the table, fluxes from agricultural peatlands differ from non-agricultural peatland. The differences are also detected at C2 (SF vs SL) and C3 (OP vs AV). It indicates there is a significant difference between each landuses. And, C4 (SF+SL vs OP) shows that oil palm (OP) emits similar amount of normalized CO_2 flux to combination of secondary forest and shrubland (SF+SL, See Table 2).

Table 5: Average and standard deviation of environmental variables during CO2 flux measurement in four different land uses

Variables (n = number of samples; N = total samples)	Mean ± SD				
	Secondary Forest (SF)	Oil Palm (OP)	*Aloe vera* (AV)	Shrub peatland (SL)	Total
Gravimetric Water Content (%) (n=78, N=312)	450 ± 91	325 ± 127	113 ± 77	240 ± 91	282 ± 157
Soil pH (n=54, N=216)	3.42 ± 0.30	3.57 ± 0.26	4.53 ± 0.31	3.62 ± 0.23	3.78 ± 0.52
ORP (mV) (n=54, N=216)	463 ± 55	468 ± 49	424 ± 60	442 ± 56	449 ± 57
Soil Temperature (°C) (n=72, N=288)	27.03 ± 0.99	30.25 ± 1.80	30.88 ± 2.38	28.98 ± 1.18	29.28 ± 2.23
Air Temperature (°C) (n=78, N=312)	28.43± 1.34	33.10 ± 2.24	29.73 ± 3.39	29.97 ± 2.33	30.31 ± 2.97

The different of fluxes from each land uses is a result of various environmental variables. Table 3 provides average values of selected variables observed during flux measurement. The gravimetric water content in *Aloe vera* is the lowest among the land use types. Canopy characteristics of *Aloe vera*, which allows soil to have direct solar radiation exposure, and cause to increase evaporation rates, and high soil temperature. As shown in Table 3, soil temperature in *Aloe vera* is the highest despite of the highest air temperature observed in oil palm. Increasing soil temperature leads to increasing in CO_2 flux (Berglund, Berglund, and Klemedtsson 2010). Furthermore, soil pH in *Aloe vera* is also the highest among the other land uses resulted from intensive farming practices, in particular the use of woody ash for improving fertility. The present degree of soil pH in *Aloe vera* land use creates a favourable environment for microorganisms to decompose peats. In contrast, low pH in other three land uses is not favorable for peat breakdown.

The fluctuation of CO_2 fluxes every month is presented in Figure 2. The fluxes tend to increase in November 2015. It may be related to rainfall starting to increase in November after drought periods in the previous months (See Figure 3). It leads to the increase of water content and temporarily enhanced soil respiration. Land uses have significant influence on temporal CO_2 flux dynamics. In response to water availability, soil respiration in *Aloe vera* seems largely to escalate.

Records of the 2015 monthly rainfall in this area are 328 mm in June; 187 mm in July; 76 mm in August; 53 mm in September; 220 mm in October; 416 mm in November; and 281 mm in December. So, July 2015 was considered as a slightly dry month. The 2015 dry months were August and September, and the 2015 wet months were October, November and December (See Figure 3).

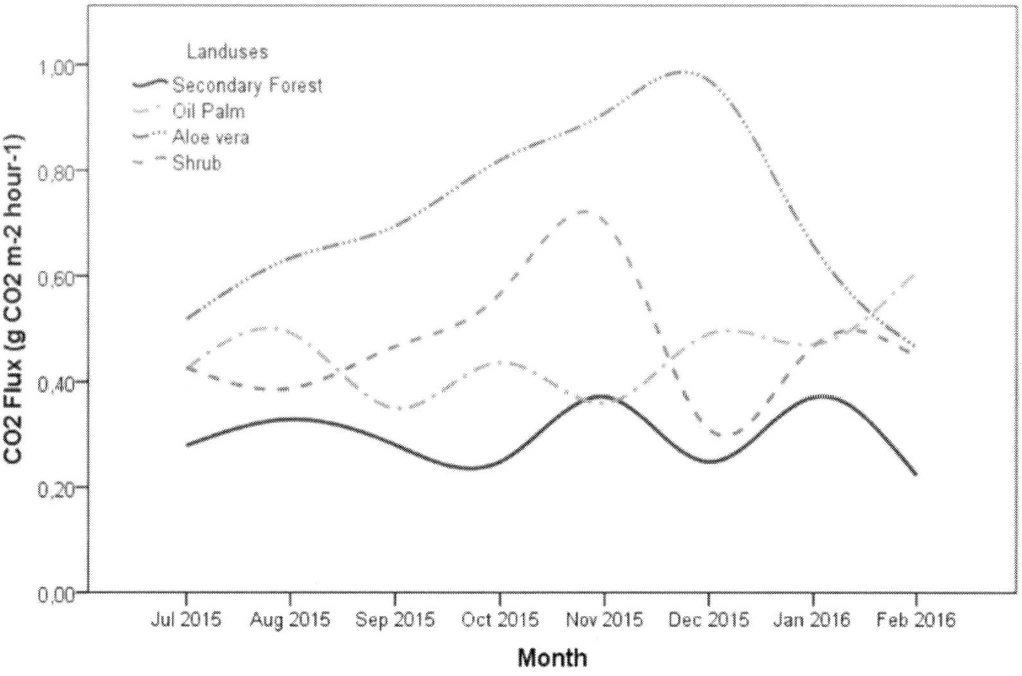

Figure 2: Fluctuation of CO_2 flux every month at different land use

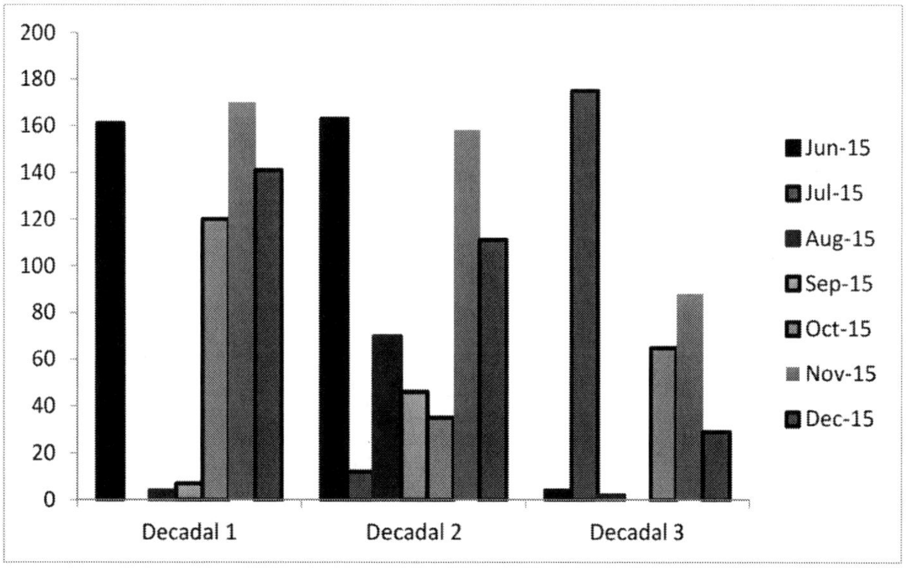

Figure 8: Monthly Rainfall record in research site, showing a period of ten days (decadal)

CONCLUSION

The CO_2 flux is affected by type of land uses. Different land uses create specific microclimates such as air temperature, soil temperature and water content. These factors influence soil respiration rates and hence affect CO_2 flux rates from disturbed and drained peatlands. In this study, CO_2 fluxes from July 2015 to February 2016 from secondary forest were substantially low, while the fluxes from *Aloe vera* were largely high, and more dynamics. And, the temporer fluxes from oil palm were indifferent from shrubland and secondary forest.

AKNOWLEDGEMENTS

This study was supported by Partnerships for Enhanced Engagement in Research (PEER) United States, NSF Grant No: 1114161. Further information is available at http://sites.nationalacademies.org/pga/ peer/index.htm

REFERENCE

1. Berglund, Ö, K. Berglund, and L. Klemedtsson. 2010. "A Lysimeter Study on the Effect of Temperature on CO2 Emission from Cultivated Peat Soils." *Geoderma* 154 (3-4). Elsevier B.V.: 211–18. doi:10.1016/j.geoderma.2008.09.007.
2. Hatano, R, T Inoue, U Darung, Suwido H. Limin, Tomoaki Morishita, Fumiaki Takaki, Yo Toma, and Hiroyuki Yamada. 2010. "Carbon Dioxide and Nitrous Oxide Emissions Associated with Tropical Peatland Degradation." In *Proceedings of the 19th World Congress of Soil Science, Soil Solutions for a Changing World*, 13–16. Brisbane. http://www.ldd.go.th/swcst/Report/soil/.\symposium/.\pdf/0064.pdf.
3. Hatfield, Jerry L, and Timothy B Parkin. 2012. "Spatial Variation of Carbon Dioxide Fluxes in Corn and Soybean Fields." *Agricultural Sciences* 3 (8): 986–95.
4. Melling, Lulie, Kah Joo Goh, Constance Beauvais, and Ryusuke Hatano. 2008. "Carbon Flow and Budget in Young Mature Oil Palm Agroecosystem on Deep Tropical Peat." *Planter* 84 (2005): 21.
5. Melling, Lulie, Ryusuke Hatano, and Kah Joo Goh. 2005. "Soil CO2 Flux from Three Ecosystems in Tropical Peatland of Sarawak, Malaysia." *Tellus, Series B: Chemical and Physical Meteorology* 57: 1–11. doi:10.1111/j.1600-0889.2005.00129.x.

Abstract No: A-208

EFFECT OF ACID MINE DRAINAGE ON GREENHOUSE GAS EMISSIONS FROM PEAT SOILS IN SOUTH KALIMANTAN

Abdul Hadi[1*] and Bahtiar Rifai[2]

[1]*Faculty of Agriculture, University of Lambung Mangkurat, Banjarbaru, Indonesia*
[2]*Legal Division, PT. Gawi Makmur Kalimantan Corp., Banjarmasin, Indonesia;*

**Corresponding author: atakhadi@gmail.com*

SUMMARY

Acid mine drainage (AMD) is liquid discharge with low pH derived mainly from coal mining areas. The AMD contains also high concentrations of polyvalent ions like Fe, Al and Mn. The polyvalent ions in AMD may eliminate C transformations in peat soils, which are considered as a main source of carbon emissions. Laboratory incubation experiments were carried out to elucidate the effects of AMD on C emissions from peat soils and the mechanism(s) involved. Peat soils were air-dried and sieved using a 2 mm sieve. Sixteen peat sub-samples each weighing 250 g were then placed in sixteen vessels. Four vessels were filled with 5 mL of AMD, each of other four vessels were filled with 10 mL and 15 mL AMD, respectively. The rest of the vessels were kept without AMD and placed as a control group. The soils were then adjusted to 70% of its water holding capacity by adding distilled water. The experimental units were incubated following a completely randomized design. The CO_2 concentrations in the vessels containers headspace were determined by titrimetric method at 1, 2, 4, 7, 14, 17, 30, 45 and 60 days after incubation. The results showed that the AMD limited the C emissions from the peat soils. The C emissions were reduced with the increase in dosage of AMD being applied. The mechanism of reduction was presumed to occur through the chelating in peat soils by polyvalent ions present in the AMD. Effects of AMD and other soil ameliorants on methane (CH_4) and nitrous oxide (N_2O) from peat soils cultivated for oil palm are also discussed.

INTRODUCTION

Wetlands only cover 3% wide of terrestrial in a whole world, but store 550 Giga ton off carbon or equal with 30% of land carbon, 75% from all of the atmosphere carbon, equal with all of carbon that contained in terrestrial biomass and equal with twice of carbon storage from the whole forest in the world (Joosten, 2007 in Agus and Subiksa, 2008). The carbon in wetlands is potentially to be released to the atmosphere as soon as the organic matter in of wetland is decomposing by microorganism (Agus and Subiksa, 2008). The process of decomposition in wetland environment is caused by the condition of organic material, environmental factors such as weather and rain. The highest carbon evolution occurs in peat soils with fibric materials (Murayama, *et al.*, 1989).

The decomposition process in the wetland will produce greenhouse gases, mainly carbon dioxide (CO_2), nitrous oxide (N_2O) and methane (CH_4) (Hadi *et al.*, 2005). Currently there are about one million hectares of peat land planted with oil palm. Hadi *et al.* (2010) reported a peat land planted with oil palm has a global warming potential higher than peat land planted with rice and vegetables, mainly due to higher emissions of nitrous oxide (N_2O).

Various attempts can be made to reduce the peat evolution. One such experiment was conducted by Sabiham *et al.* (2000), which examined the effect of Fe^{3+} cations (in the form of $FeCl_3.6H_2O$) at a dose of 25 to 75 g / kg of peat. Under this treatment, the release of carbon could be reduced by 10-27%. This is because peat contains many organic compounds capable of forming complex compounds with the polyvalent Fe^{3+} (Tan 1995).

In South Kalimantan (Indonesia), coal mining usually releases acid mine drainage (AMD) as a waste. AMD contain iron (Fe) in high concentrations (Reference). This study aims to determine (1) the effect of AMD on CO_2 emissions from peat soil under laboratory conditions and (2) effects of AMD and other soil ameliorants on methane (CH_4) and nitrous oxide (N_2O) from peat soils cultivated for oil palm.

MATERIALS AND METHODS

This study was a laboratory experiment with a completely randomized design single factor. Treatment of these experiments was the provision of acid mine drainage (AMD), which consisted of four doses of 0 (control), 5 mL (T1), 10 mL (T2) and 15 mL (T3). Peat soils were incubated for 60 days and measured the evolution of carbon to CO_2 on days 1, 2, 4, 7, 14, 17, 30, 45 and 60. This experiment used five replications, so there were 20 experimental units.

Peat soil samples were taken in the District Barambai, Barito Kuala District. Acid mine drainage samples were taken in the coal mining area of PT Pamapersada Corporation at Sungai Pinang village, Banjar District. Peat soil samples (disturbed soil samples) were taken from three points at a distance of every point of about 5 meters, then mixed.

Acid mine drainage samples were taken from the three points, namely in the mining pits, drains, and acid mine water treatment plant. Each sample taken was approximately 5L pH and Al-dissolution was measured. Soluble Fe content of the three samples was measured and samples with the highest concentration used in subsequent experiments.

Disturbed soil samples were immediately dried for ± 3 days or until the peat was able to pass the sieve (2 mm sieve). Sixteen peat sub-samples each weighing 250 g were then placed in sixteen vessels. Four vessels were filled with 5 mL of AMD selected from previous step, 10 mL and 15 mL AMD, respectively. The rest of the vessels were kept without AMD and placed as a control group. The soils were then adjusted to 70% of its water holding capacity by adding distilled water. The experimental units were incubated following a completely randomized design. Containers that have been prepared were weighed and recorded, then container inserted into a glass jar. Vials were filled with 0.5 N NaOH solutions of 10 mL, then put in a glass jar right next to the container and tightly closed. There were three jars without soil (empty containers) containing only 0.5 N NaOH 10 mL (in vials) as a blank for the measurement of the evolution of carbon to CO_2 during the incubation period.

Glass jars were placed in the dark and at room temperature. Incubation was carried out for 60 days. Evolution of carbon to CO_2 was measured on days 1, 2, 4, 7, 14, 17, 30, 45 and 60. The evolution of carbon to CO_2 was measured by opening a jar lid and removing the NaOH, which was then titrated with a solution of HCl-standard. After the evolution of carbon to CO_2 measurement was completed, distilled water was added to the container containing the soil until it weighs the same as before the experiment. Suggest adding reference for this method. After incubation, peat soils were removed from the container and analyzed for Fe-chelate, Mn-chelate, soil pH and water content using methods described by Page *et al.* (1982).

Palm plantation in south Kalimantan was subjected to study the effect of AMD on the emission of greenhouse gases *in-situ*. Plant density of the plantation was 149 trees per ha and 24 oil palm trees with similar age and growth were selected in peat soils for this study. Acidic mine drainage, iron slag, chicken manure, river sediment and rice husk charcoal were applied to the soils of four selected trees with the rate of two tons per ha. No ameliorants including AMD was applied to four trees. An open-top-mica chamber was constructed with a dimension of 50 x 50 x 50 cm and its bottom edge inserted 5 cm below soil surface. Canopies of trees with treatments were covered by the chamber for the gas sampling. Gas sampling was carried out using a capillary plastic tube with rubber septum. A small electric fan was set in a box to homogenize the air within the box prior to the gas sampling. The gas sampling was carried out in order to determine the concentration of CH_4, N_2O and CO_2 from sampled trees. Gas chromatograph was used for the measurement by the same method mentioned by Hadi *et al.* (2010). Samples were taken in each three weeks starting from 11 October until 13 December, 2011. At each sampling, samples were taken after 2, 7 and 12 minutes when the chamber was closed.

The effect of acid mine drainage on gas emissions from peat soil was done by analysis of variance using the F test at 95% confidence level. If there is a difference in treatment continued with different test value (LSD) at 95% confidence level.

RESULTS AND DISCUSSION

Evolution of carbon to CO_2 in the peat soil, measured on days 1, 2, 4, 7, 14, 17, 30, 45 and 60 are shown in Figure 1. Results of analysis of variance by F test showed that administration of AMD significantly affected the evolution of carbon to CO_2 on peat soil. Provision of AMD was able to suppress the evolution of carbon to CO_2 on the 2nd day until the 60th day except on day 1 that actually increased the evolution of carbon into CO_2. The cumulative evolution of carbon to CO_2 on peat soil up to the 60th day can be reduced 7-17% after administration of acid mine water, the more the provision of acid mine drainage, the lower the evolution of carbon.

The mechanism of reduction was presumed to occur through the chelating in peat soils by polyvalent ions present in the AMD. It was observed by measuring the concentration of Fe-Mn-chelate chelate and improved after being given AMD (data not shown). Evolution of carbon to CO_2 negatively correlated with the concentration of Fe-chelate (Figure 2). The lower the evolution of carbon to CO_2, the higher the concentration of Fe-chelate. Evolution of carbon and Fe-chelate has a regression equation $y = -1{,}4056x + 15058$, with the evolution of carbon y and x is Fe-chelate.

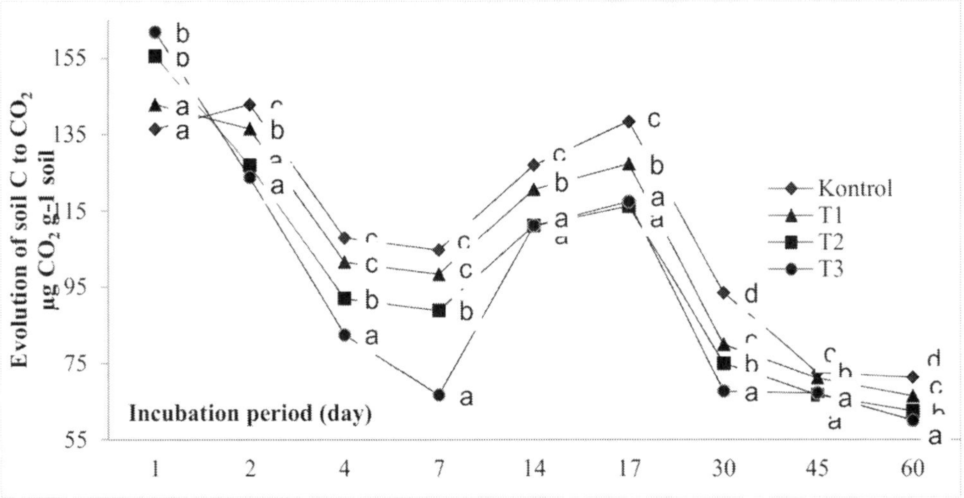

Figure 1: Evolution of carbon to CO_2 in the peat soil after being treated. Averages followed by the same letter are not significantly different shows based on LSD at the level of 95%. T1=AMD 5 mL, T2=AMD 10 mL, T3=AMD 15 mL.

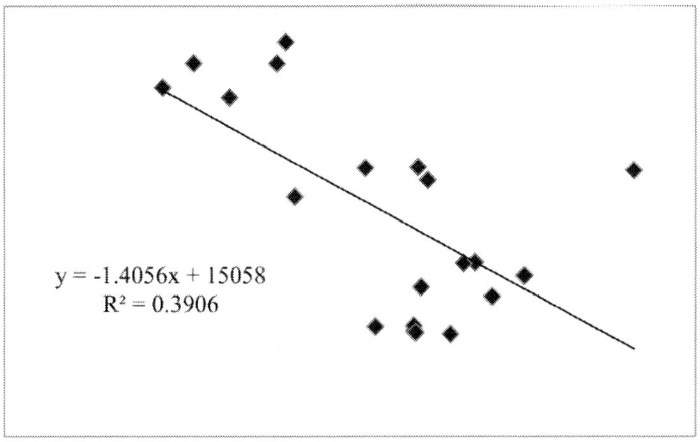

Figure 2: Regression between cumulative evolutions of CO_2 on day 60 with Fe-chelate.

CONCLUSIONS

From this study it can be concluded that:

1. Provision of acid mine drainage on the peat soil at 70% Water Holding Capacity reduced the evolution of carbon to CO_2 on peat soil up to 17%.
2. The more acid mine water is given the lower the CO_2 evolution on peat soil.
3. Chelating reaction between Fe and Mn with the organic acids in peat soil suspected as the cause of decrease in the evolution of carbon to CO_2.

REFERENCES

1. Agus, F. dan I. G. M. Subiksa. 2008. Lahan Gambut: *Potensi untuk Pertanian dan Aspek Lingkungan*. Balai Penelitian Tanah dan World Agroforestry Centre (ICRAF). Bogor. Indonesia.
2. Hadi A., K. Inubushi, Y. Furukawa, E. Purnomo, M. Rasmadi, & H. Tsurata. 2005. Greenhouse Gas Emission from Tropical Peatlands of Kalimantan. *Nutrient Cycling in Agroecosystems*. ***71***: 73-80.
3. Hadi, A., Fatah, L., Syaifuddin, Abdullah, Affandi, DN., Bakar, RA. And Inubushi, K. 2010. Greenhouse Gas Emissions from Peat Soil Cultivated to Paddy Field, Oil Palm and Vegetable. J. Tropical Soil, 17: 105-114.
4. Tan, Kim H. 1995. Dasar-Dasar Kimia Tanah. Diterjemahkan oleh Goenadi, D.H. Gadjah Mada Univ. Press. Yogyakarta.

5. Murayama, S., Asakawa, Y. and Ohno, Y. 1990. Chemical Properties of Subsurface Peats and Their Decomposition Kinetics under Field Conditions. Soil Sci Plant Nutr. 36: 129-140.
6. Page, A.L., Miller, R.H., Keeny, D.R. 1982. Methods of Soil Analysis. Amer. Agronomy Inc., Wisconsin, USA.
7. Sabiham, S. 1997. Penggunaan Kation Terpilih untuk Menurunkan Asam-Asam Fenolat Toksik dalam Tanah Gambut dari Jambi. J.I.I. Indon. 7(1): 19-27.

Abstract No: A-086

ESTIMATING GREENHOUSE GAS EMISSIONS FROM PEATLAND IN INDONESIA: AN ANNUAL TIME SERIES ANALYSIS USING INCAS FRAMEWORK

Haruni Krisnawati[1,2*], Rinaldi Imanuddin[1,2], Wahyu Catur Adinugroho[1,2] and Silver Hutabarat[2]

[1]*Research, Development and Innovation Agency – Indonesian Ministry of Environment and Forestry, Indonesia*
[2]*INCAS (Indonesian National Carbon Accounting System) Team, Indonesia*

**Corresponding author: h.krisnawati@yahoo.co.id*

SUMMARY

Forest and land use sectors have been considered as a significant contributor to global greenhouse gas (GHG) emissions. However, estimates of their total contribution have always been uncertain. The Indonesian National Carbon Accounting System (INCAS) has been developed to better account for these net emissions, including GHG emissions from peatland fire and biological oxidation. This paper reported the estimated annual GHG emissions resulting from both biological oxidation and peat fires in Indonesia for the period 2001 to 2012 and its contribution to the total net GHG emissions from forests and peatland in Indonesia during the analysis period. The GHG emissions from Indonesia's peatlands were estimated using a Tier 2 methodology, incorporating spatial and non-spatial data inputs. Annual changes in the area of drained peatland were estimated using the Land Cover Change Analysis outputs and land management information. Annual areas of peatland burnt and the frequency of fires were estimated using MODIS hotspot data, corrected by Landsat and LiDAR burn scar data. Total annual GHG emissions for 2001–2012 were estimated by multiplying the area affected by drainage and fires by activity specific emission factors derived from the IPCC 2013 Wetlands Update, supplemented by peat fire data from studies in Indonesia. Results indicated that significant annual variations in GHG emissions from peat fires occurred across Indonesia throughout 2001–2012. High emissions from peat fires in 2002 and 2006 contributed significantly to the elevated emissions from peatlands in those years. A greenhouse gas emission from the biological oxidation of peatlands was the largest single source of emissions. This reflects the large areas of peatlands cleared and subsequently drained in the years prior to the analysis period.

Keywords: *INCAS, peatland, greenhouse gas emission, fire*

INTRODUCTION

Forest and land use sectors, including peatlands, have been considered as a significant contributor to global greenhouse gas (GHG) emissions. This sector has been reported to be the most dominant source of GHG emissions in Indonesia (Indonesia's Second National Communication), contributing to more than 60% of the total GHG emissions (State Ministry of Environment, 2010). This might be a function of Indonesia having one of the largest areas of forests with huge amount of carbon, coupled with high rates of deforestation, forest degradation and large areas of degraded peatlands.

The area of peatlands in Indonesia are estimated to be around 14.9 million ha (Ritung *et al.*, 2011), spreading across large islands of Sumatra (40%), Kalimantan (34%) and Papua (26%). This ecosystem has been decreasing rapidly over the past few decades (Miettinen *et al.*, 2012). The condition of this peatlands remains degraded for a period of time before reverting to forest or being converted to plantations or cropland. Most of this degraded peatland is drained, although the degree may not be the same as plantations or croplands at the same landscape (Hooijer *et al.*, 2014). Study by Hooijer *et al.* (2010) has shown that the degraded peatland and drainage cause the GHG emissions with the emission rates vary depending on management conditions, including the depth of peat water table. Over the last two decades, the peatland use change due to clearing or conversion to plantation or cropland, and the drainage which leads to biological oxidation, has contributed to degradation and loss of this ecosystem, which resulted in increased GHG emissions (Page *et al.*, 2002). This condition becomes worse with the incidence of fires on peatland.

There are an increasing number of studies that provide information on carbon loss estimates on peatland, whether from biological oxidation or fire (e.g. Page *et al.*, 2002; Hooijer *et al.*, 2010; Konecny *et al.*, 2016). However, the estimates of resulted emissions and their contribution to the total GHG emissions have always been uncertain. Understanding the source and size of historical emissions is critical to planning efficient and effective emissions mitigation intervention, as well as assessing the potential impact of alternative land management options on future emissions. The Indonesian National Carbon Accounting System (INCAS) has been developed to better account for these emissions. The system has been designed to help meet the future measurement, reporting and verification (MRV) requirements for the land-based sectors, including peatland.

The objective of this study was to estimate the annual GHG emissions from Indonesia's peatlands resulting from biological oxidation and peat fires for the period 2001 to 2012 based on the approach developed under INCAS framework. The contribution of GHG emissions from peatland to the total net GHG emissions from forests and peatland in Indonesia during the analysis period is also discussed.

MATERIALS AND METHODS

Analysis conducted here showing a national level account of annual GHG emissions from peatland in Indonesia from the period 2001 to 2012. The emissions from peat biological oxidation and peat fires across Indonesia's peatlands were estimated using a Tier 2 methodology of the INCAS framework, incorporating spatial and non-spatial data inputs (Figure 1). The spatial data were collated from existing sources available across government agencies, e.g. land cover map (Ministry of Environment and Forestry), peat map (Ministry of Agriculture), annual land cover change (LAPAN), with the exception of the burnt area map that was produced under INCAS.

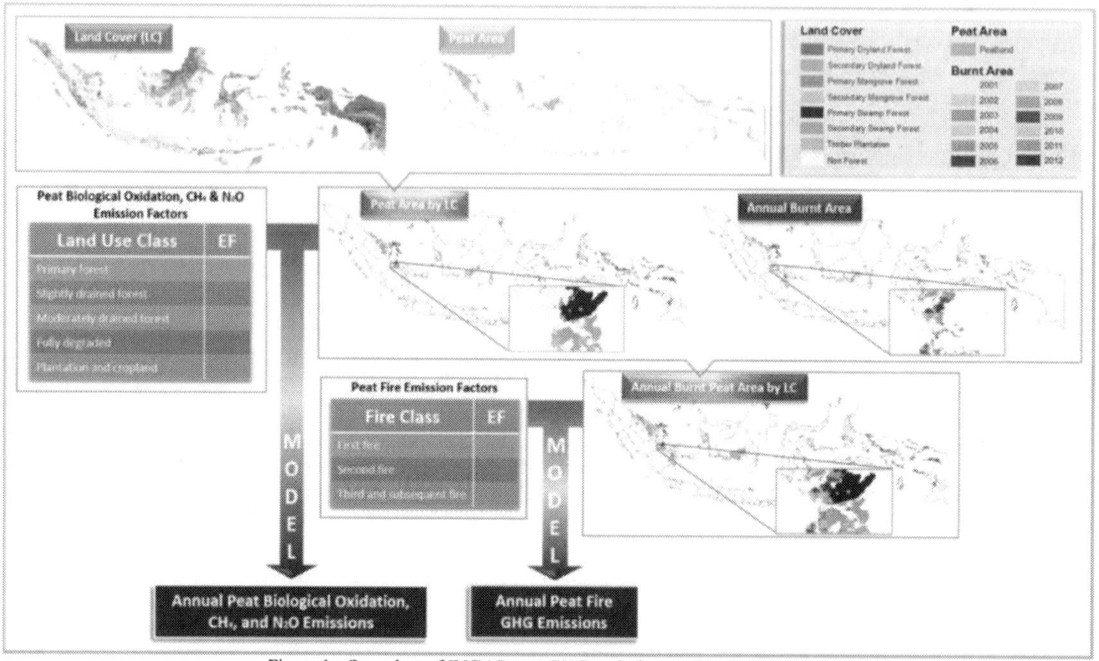

Figure 1: Overview of INCAS peat GHG emissions estimation approach

Annual areas of peatland burnt during the period 2001 to 2012 were estimated based on annual burnt area estimates using MODIS hotspot data, corrected using Landsat and LiDAR burn scar data following the method of Ballhorn *et al.* (2014). The annual corrected burned area estimates were then used to derive fire frequency and the area extent of each fire frequency (1 to 10) for the period between 2000 and 2012. The procedures are described in Krisnawati *et al.* (2015a) as follows: (i) First fires were assumed to occur in the year of forest clearing where clearing and fire were observed on the same area; (ii) Second and third/subsequent fires were defined from the same dataset by tracking the annual burnt area throughout the analysis period on non-forest land. It was assumed that fire within forest that remained as forest would not have ignited peat soils.

Annual changes in the area of drained peatland were estimated using the Land Cover Change Analysis outputs (LAPAN, 2014) and land management information. The annual area of natural forest cleared on peat land during the period of analysis was determined based on the deforestation areas occurring on peat soil. Areas where no change in the broad type of land management occurred during the period were assigned a constant area for all years. These included areas of peatland deforested prior to 2000 and areas of secondary natural forest on peatland that were assumed to be drained (Krisnawati *et al.*, 2015a). The allocation area subject to peat biological oxidation represents the cumulative peat land area affected by biological oxidation in each year which includes the area of peat lands disturbed in the period when the disturbance event occurs plus the areas of peat land disturbed in the previous years which continue to contribute to ongoing emissions.

Total annual GHG emissions were estimated by multiplying the area affected by drainage and fire by an activity specific emission factor (EF). In addition, direct emissions from drained organic soils were also accounted for to cover all relevant gases. Separate EFs were used for peat biological oxidation, direct N_2O and CH_4 emissions from drained organic soils, and peat fires. EFs from peat biological oxidation, N_2O and CH_4 were derived from the

2013 Supplement to the 2006 IPCC Guidelines for National GHG Inventory on Wetlands (IPCC, 2014), for which most of the figures were generated from studies in Indonesia. EFs from peat fires were adopted from the studies in Indonesia reported by Page *et al.* (2014) which used the information on depth of burn for the first and subsequent fires, peat bulk density and carbon content values, but adapted to meet international reporting requirements following the approach described in Equation 2.8 IPCC (2014) (Table 1). These emission factors have been considered to be more representative of normal fire conditions than the emission factors presented in the IPCC 2013 (Hooijer *et al.*, 2014; Konecny *et al.*, 2016).

Equation 2.8 (IPCC, 2014)

Annual CO_2-C and Non-CO_2 Emission from Organic Soil Fire

$$L_{fire} = A \times M_B \times C_f \times G_{ef} \times 10^{-3}$$

Where :

L_{fire} = amount of CO_2 or non- CO_2 emissions, e.g. CH_4 from fire, tonnes

A = total area burnt annually, ha

M_B = mass of fuel available for combustion, t ha^{-1}

C_f = combustion factor, dimensionless

G_{ef} = emission factor for each gas, g kg^{-1} dry matter burnt

Mass of fuel available for combustion = area (m^2) * burn depth (m) * bulk density (t m^{-3})

Table 1: Input parameters and CO_2-C, CO and CH_4 emissions per ha for organic soil fire.

Peat fire EF calculation	**First fire**	**Second fire**	**Third/subsequent fires**
Burn depth (cm)	18	11	4
Area (ha)	1	1	1
Bulk density (g cm^{-3})	0.121	0.121	0.121
Combustion factor	1	1	1
EF CO_2-C (g kg^{-1})	464	464	464
EF CO (g kg^{-1})	210	210	210
EF CH_4 (g kg^{-1})	21	21	21
Mass of fuel available for combustion (t dm ha^{-1})	217.8	133.1	48.4
CO emissions (t CO ha^{-1})	45.7	28.0	10.2
CH_4 emissions (t CH_4 ha^{-1})	4.6	2.8	1.0
CO_2-C emissions (t C ha^{-1})	101.1	61.8	22.5
CO-C emissions (t C ha^{-1})	19.6	12.0	4.4
CH_4-C emissions (t C ha^{-1})	3.4	2.1	0.8
Total C emissions (t C ha^{-1})	**124.1**	**75.8**	**27.6**

Source of CO_2-C, CO and CH_4 emission factors: Table 2.7 (IPCC, 2014)
Source of burn depth, bulk density and combustion factor: Page *et al.* (2014)

RESULTS

Figure 2 presents peat burn areas and fire frequency generated for the entire country, differentiated into areas with single frequency of fire, and areas with repeated fires. The annual estimates of GHG emissions resulted from peat fires in Indonesia for the period 2001 to 2012 is presented in Figure 3, which includes CO_2 emissions and non-CO_2 emissions (CH_4).

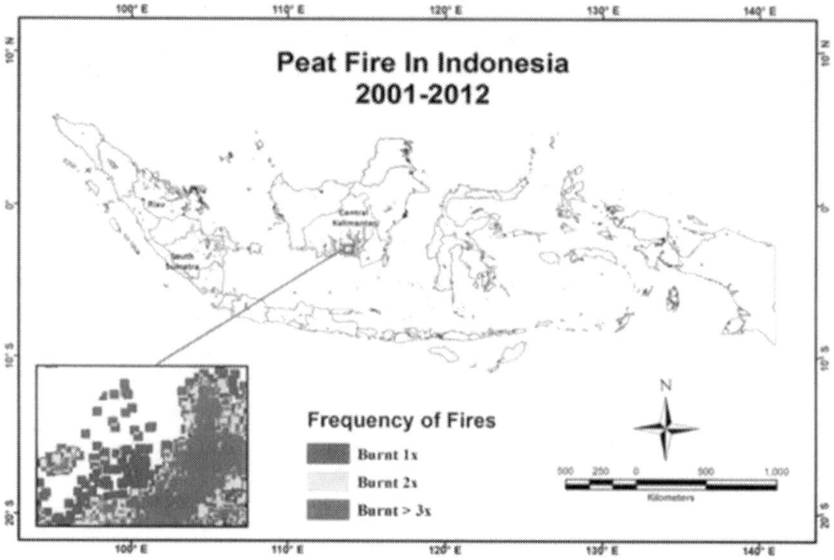

Figure 2: Peat fires In Indonesia during the period 2001-2012

Annual GHG emissions from peat fires varied substantially during the period 2001 to 2012. Riau, Central Kalimantan and South Sumatra are the three provinces in Indonesia with highest incidence of peat fires throughout the analysis period (Figure 2).

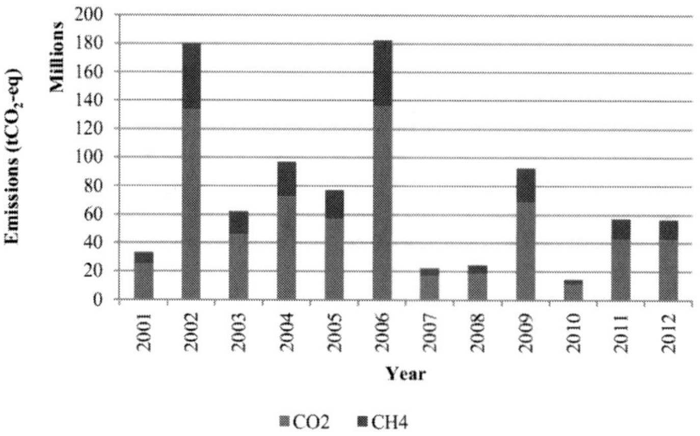

Figure 3: Annual estimates of GHG emissions from peat fires in Indonesia for the period 2001 to 2012

Figure 4 presents the annual estimates of GHG emissions from peat biological oxidation in Indonesia for the period 2001 to 2012. This figure also includes direct N_2O, dissolved organic carbon (DOC) and CH_4 emissions from disturbed peatland.

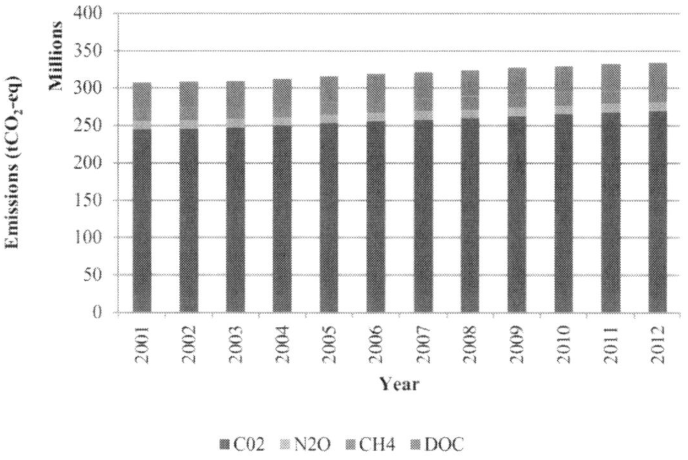

Figure 4: Annual estimates of GHG emissions from peat biological oxidation in Indonesia for the period 2001 to 2012

DISCUSSION

Annual emissions from peatlands in Indonesia (estimated from peat biological oxidation and fires) were 395 Mt CO_2-e on average during the analysis period (2001-2012), peaking in year 2006 with 502 Mt CO_2-e. Greenhouse gas emissions from disturbed peatland gradually increase from about 307 Mt CO_2-e in 2001 to about 335 Mt CO_2-e in 2012. The high peatland GHG emissions were resulted from the large areas of peatlands that were cleared and subsequently drained in the years prior to the analysis period, hence making these areas highly susceptible to oxidation. The drained peatland also creates fire-prone condition during the dry season which increases high GHG emissions.

Annual GHG emissions from peat fires in Indonesia varied substantially during the period 2001 to 2012. The highest occurrence of peat fires was found in 2002 and 2006 that account for 180 Mt CO_2-e and 183 Mt CO_2-e, respectively; while the lowest occurrence was found in 2010 that accounts for 15 Mt CO_2-e. High emissions from peat fires in 2002 and 2006 contributed significantly to the elevated emissions from peatlands in those years. Riau, Central Kalimantan and South Sumatra are three provinces in Indonesia with high incidence of peat fires throughout the years, which contributed to more than 70% of the total GHG emissions from peat fires in Indonesia.

Greenhouse gas emissions from the biological oxidation of peatlands were generally the largest source of emissions (Krisnawati *et al.*, 2015b). This reflects the large areas of peatlands cleared and subsequently drained in the years prior to the analysis period. The high peatland GHG emissions contributed to more than one third of the total net GHG emissions from forests and peatland estimated in Indonesia during the analysis period.

CONCLUSION

Results of analysis presented in this paper showing a national level account of annual GHG emissions from peatland in Indonesia from the period 2001 to 2012. This peatland GHG emissions estimation will be improved in the future using a higher Tier method similar to the current forest component that has been applied under INCAS framework. Additional analysis should be undertaken to improve the spatial accuracy of data about historical fire areas and fire intensity. Similarly, data on management activities on peatland throughout Indonesia and their impacts on peat carbon stocks need to be improved. These can be used to update input data and the estimates of GHG emissions. The capability built into the INCAS framework allows for dynamic input of data, enabling GHG emissions estimates generated with greater certainty.

ACKNOWLEDGEMENT

This study was part of the Indonesian National Carbon Accounting System (INCAS) within the Ministry of Environment and Forestry, under phase one of the INCAS program. Support for the program was provided by Australian Government through a partnership with the Center for International Forestry Research (CIFOR) and previoulsy through Indonesia–Australia Forest Carbon Partnership (IAFCP).

REFERENCES

1. Ballhorn, U., Navratil, P. and Siegert. F. 2014. Generation of spatial burned area data of the Central Kalimantan Province for the Indonesian National Carbon Accounting System (INCAS), Final Report, prepared for the Indonesia-Australia Forest Carbon Partnership. IAFCP, Jakarta. 31p.
2. Hooijer, A., Page, S., Canadell, J.G., Silvius, M., Kwadijk, J., Wösten, H. and Jauhiainen, J. 2010. Current and future CO_2 emissions from drained peatlands in Southeast Asia. *Biogeosciences*, 7, 1505–1514.
3. Hooijer, A., Page, S., Navratil, P., Vernimmen, R., van der Vat, M., Tansey, K., Konecny, K., Siegert, F., Ballhorn, U. and Mawdsley, N. 2014. Carbon emissions from drained and degraded peat land in Indonesia and emission factors for measurement, reporting and verification (MRV) of peat land greenhouse gas emissions - summary of KFCP research results for practitioners. IAFCP, Jakarta. 53p.
4. [IPCC] Intergovernmental Panel on Climate Change. 2014. 2013 Supplement to the 2006 IPPC Guidelines for National Greenhouse Gas Inventories: Wetlands. Hiraishi, T., Krug, T., Tanabe, K., Srivastava, N., Baasansuren, J., Fukuda, M. and Troxler, T.G. (eds). IPCC, Switzerland. 354p.
5. Konecny, K., Ballhorn, U., Navratil, P., Jubanski, J., Page, S., Tansey, K., Hooijer, A., Vernimmen, R. and Siegert, F. 2016. Variable carbon losses from recurrent fires in drained tropical peatlands. *Global Change Biology*, 22(4), 1469–1480.
6. Krisnawati, H., Imanuddin, R., Adinugroho, W.C. and Hutabarat, S. 2015a. Standard Methods for Estimating Greenhouse Gas Emissions from Forests and Peatlands in Indonesia (version 2). Research, Development and Innovation Agency of the Ministry of Environment and Forestry, Bogor. 101p.
7. Krisnawati, H., Imanuddin, R., Adinugroho, W.C. and Hutabarat, S. 2015b. National Inventory of Greenhouse Gas Emissions and Removals on Indonesia's Forests and Peatlands. Research, Development and Innovation Agency of the Ministry of Environment and Forestry, Bogor. 66p.
8. [LAPAN] Lembaga Penerbangan dan Antariksa Nasional. 2014. The Remote Sensing Monitoring Program of Indonesia's National Carbon Accounting System: Methodology and Products, Version 1. LAPAN–IAFCP, Jakarta.
9. Miettinen, J., Hooijer, A., Shi, C., Tollenaar, D., Vernimmen, R., Liew, S.C., Malins, C. and Page, S.E. 2012. Extent of industrial plantations on Southeast Asian peatlands in 2010 with analysis of historical expansion and future projections. *GCB Bioenergy*, 4(6), 908–918.
10. Page, S.E., Siegert, F., Rieley, J.O., Boehm, H.D.V., Jaya, A. and Limin, S. 2002. The amount of carbon released from peat and forest fires in Indonesia during 1997. *Nature*, 420, 61–65.
11. Page, S., Tansey, K., Navratil, P., Hooijer, A. and Mawdsley, N. 2014. Measuring emissions from peat fire: commentary on a proposed methodology for Indonesia. Draft Report, prepared for the Indonesia-Australia Forest Carbon Partnership. IAFCP, Jakarta.
12. Ritung, S., Wahyunto, Nugroho, K., Sukarman, Hikmatullah and Suparto, C.T. 2011. Peta Lahan Gambut Indonesia skala 1:250.000. Kementerian Pertanian, Jakarta. Pp. 11.
13. State Ministry of Environment. 2010. Indonesia Second National Communication under the United Nations Framework Convention on Climate Change (UNFCCC). State Ministry of Environment, Jakarta. 200p.

Abstract No: A-459

FIELD CHALLENGES OF EDDY COVARIANCE MEASUREMENT IN TROPICAL PEAT SWAMP ECOSYSTEMS IN SARAWAK, MALAYSIA – THE TPRL EXPERIENCE

Edward Baran Aeries[1], Wong Guan Xhuan[1], Joseph Wenceslaus Waili[1], Lo Kim San[1], Ryuichi Hirata[2] and Lulie Melling[1]

[1]*Tropical Peat Research Laboratory Unit, Chief Minister's Department, Sarawak, Malaysia*
[2]*National Institute for Environmental Studies, Tsukuba, Japan*

**Corresponding author: edward.b.aeries@gmail.com*

SUMMARY

Over the past decade considerable attention has been devoted to understanding the role of tropical peatland ecosystems in regulating climate. In 2010 the Tropical Peat Research Laboratory Unit (TPRL) constructed three eddy covariance towers at sites representing three different ecosystems: primary peat swamp forest, secondary forest and oil palm plantation. The purpose was to quantify the magnitude of the greenhouse gas fluxes and identify the environmental factors that regulate the carbon balance in these ecosystems. This paper describes the field challenges TPRL researchers faced in measuring fluxes using the eddy covariance method. Challenges ranged from the logistics of getting to the sites to wildlife issues and power supply disruptions. While some of the challenges were unavoidable others can be prevented with proper planning and preventive maintenance.

Keywords: *Tropical peatlands, eddy covariance*

INTRODUCTION

The majority of tropical peatlands are located in Indonesia and Malaysia (Page *et al.*, 2011). Malaysia's total peatland area is estimated at 2.6 million hectares with 62% of that area located in the state of Sarawak. Over the last decade more and more peatlands have been subjected to land use change, mainly for oil palm cultivation (Schrier-Uijl *et al.*, 2013). Concomitantly there has been an increased interest in the impact of land use change on the carbon-rich tropical peatlands. Consequently, considerable attention has been devoted to understand the role of tropical peatland ecosystems in regulating climate change (Furukawa *et al.*, 2005; Melling *et al.*, 2005; Hirano *et al.*, 2014). Therefore, we have measured carbon dioxide (CO_2), methane (CH_4), and energy fluxes (sensible and latent heat) using the eddy covariance method at sites at three different tropical peatland ecosystems to quantify the magnitude of the fluxes and identify the environmental factors that regulate the carbon balance in these ecosystems. This paper highlights some of the challenges faced in the field during the period of our study since the beginning of 2011.

SITES

Three sites, located in three different tropical peatland ecosystems, were selected: a primary peat swamp forest located in Maludam National Park (MLM; 01°27'55"N, 111°09'20"E), a secondary forest (CMC; 01°24'01.6"N, 111°23'54.0"E) and an oil palm plantation (SBW; 02°11'12"N, 111°50'35.7"E).

METHODOLOGY

CO_2 and energy fluxes were measured starting in 2011 on towers at a height of 21 m in SBW and 41 m in both CMC and MLM using the eddy covariance method with a sonic anemometer-thermometer (CSAT3; Campbell Scientific Inc., Logan, UT, USA) and an open-path CO_2/H_2O analyser (LI7500; Li-Cor Inc., Lincoln, NE, USA). An open-path CH_4 analyser (LI7700; Li-Cor Inc., Lincoln, NE, USA) was added to the existing system in 2013. These instruments record data at a frequency of 10 Hz.

Meteorological data were measured at all sites. A net radiometer (CNR4; Kipp & Zonen) was installed at 41 m to measure downward and upward short-wave and long-wave radiation. Downward and upward photosynthetic photo flux densities (PPFD) were measured at 41 m using quantum sensors (LI-190; Licor). Wind velocity and direction were measured using a wind vane and a three-cup anemometer (03001-5; R.M. Young Co.) at

42 m. Relative humidity and air temperature were measured at 41 and 11 m with a temperature and relative humidity sensor (CS215; Campbell Sci.). Rainfall was measured at 1 m above ground using a tipping-bucket rain gauge (TE525; Campbell Sci.). Soil temperatures were measured at depths of 5 and 10 cm using a thermocouple thermometer while soil moisture was measured at 10 and 30 cm using time-domain-reflectrometry (TDR) sensors (CS616; Campbell Sci.). In addition, water table depth was recorded near each tower at hourly intervals using a water level logger (DL/N; Sensor Technik Sirnach AG). All measuring systems, except the water level logger, were powered by solar energy. These parameters are recorded every 5 minutes.

CHALLENGES

Logistics

The SBW site was the easiest of the three sites to access, being located at an oil palm plantation. However, road conditions were sometimes very bad, especially during the wet season. Only 4WD vehicles were able to access the site. The access road from the plantation adjacent to the CMC site was sometimes flooded. The research team needed to trek 1.2 km from the edge of the plantation to the forest. Researchers each needed to carry an average of 20 kg of equipment for system maintenance. To access the MLM site the research team had to take a 25 minute boat ride across the crocodile infested Batang Lupar River (Fig. 1) where strong winds sometimes caused waves that could be hazardous to those on board. For this reason, researchers were required to wear their life jackets at all time when on board. This was followed by a 4.5 km trek through the jungle, carrying equipment and food supplies for two nights. A 0.3 m wide concrete footpath was constructed from the riverbank to the tower to ease the trekking (Fig. 2) but this could be slippery when moss started to grow on it.

Figure 1: Batang Lupar River

Figure 2: Footpath to the tower in Maludam National Park

Wildlife

Birds nested at all the sites. Nests, normally of species of swallow (*Hirundinidae*) (Fig. 3), were often built on the towers' working platforms located every 10 m up to 40 m. Researchers often had to deal with 'attacks' from birds trying to defend their nests. Bird nests were removed from the working platforms to ensure safe working conditions. There were cases also where hornets built their nests below working platforms. In MLM hornets built a nest below the 20 m platform (Fig. 4). This posed a danger as stings from this hornet, while not necessarily deadly, can be really painful and would put researchers at risk of falling if they were stung while climbing the ladder. The nest has since been removed and researchers are always on the lookout for any new ones. The most extreme wildlife issue encountered so far was at CMC when a mangrove cat snake (*Boiga dendrophila*) was found hiding in the canvas where the gas tanks for calibration were kept (Fig. 5). We suspect it was preying on infant birds or eggs. Spiders such as Tarantulas were sometimes found hiding in the canvas as well. Ants were also found building a nest inside the radiation shield of our CS215. On the ground, cables connecting the equipment were observed to have chew marks possibly made by rats. It is compulsory that first aid kits be available during each visit in case of emergencies. Researchers are always reminded to thoroughly check that all working spaces are free from any potential threat on arrival at each site.

Figure 3: Bird's nest on working platform at SBW site

Figure 4: Hornet's nest on working platform at MLM site

Figure 5: Mangrove Cat Snake hiding in the canvas cover for the calibration gas tanks on a working platform at 40 m at CMC

Power supply disruption

The system at all sites obtains its power supply from solar energy stored in a series of eight deep cycle batteries (Fig. 6) able to output a combined 1 KW of electricity. This output is more than sufficient to keep the system operating continuously throughout the day. However, in May 2015, the battery power output at all three sites attenuated drastically, causing the system to shut down at night when the solar panels were not charging. All the sites were commissioned at the end of 2010 therefore all the batteries had deteriorated almost concurrently. In addition, the commissioning of another ultra-portable gas analyser at each of the sites may have caused the power shortage. This was verified by the voltage that was recorded by the datalogger. The batteries had to be changed as soon as possible to avoid further loss of night-time data. The batteries (each weighing at least 65 kg) were transported by wheel barrow (Fig. 7) which required intense labour. Humidity and loose wire connections at the power control box had also blown the solar charge controller's fuse. Power supply status and battery condition at all sites is now closely monitored for any sign of degradation. In addition, the solar panels are cleaned every six months to ensure optimum battery charging. The fuse is checked and wire connections are tightened during every maintenance trip.

Figure 6: Deep cycle solar batteries weighing about 65 kg each

Figure 7: Wheel barrow used to transport the batteries

CONCLUSION

TPRL researchers started measuring fluxes using the eddy covariance method in 2011. Since then, they have overcome many challenges in performing their field tasks. Such experience is invaluable and much can be learnt from it for future improvements. While some of the challenges were unavoidable, proper planning and preventive maintenance should help to enable safe field work conditions and the collection of continuous good quality scientific.

REFERENCES

1. Furukawa, Y., Inubushi, K., Ali, M., Itang, A.M. and Tsuruta, H. 2005. Effect of changing groundwater levels caused by land-use changes on greenhouse gas emissions from tropical peatlands. *Nutrient Cycling in Agroecosystems* **71:** 81-91.
2. Hirano,T., Kusin, K., Limin, S. and Osaki, M. 2014. Evapotranspiration of tropical peat swamp forests. *Global Change Biology* **20:** 555-565. DOI: 10.1111/gcb.12653.
3. Melling, L., Hatano, R. and Goh, K.J. 2005. Methane fluxes from three ecosystems in tropical peatland of Sarawak, Malaysia. *Soil Biology and Biochemistry* **37:** 1445-1453.
4. Page, S. E., Morrison, R., Malins, C., Hooijer, A., Rieley, J. O. and Jauhiainen, J. 2011. Review of peat surface greenhouse gas emissions from oil palm plantations in Southeast Asia. *International Committee on Clean Transportation (ICCT).*
5. Schrier-Uijl, A.P., Silviu, M., Parish, F., Lim, K.H., Rosediana, S. and Anshari, G. 2013. Environmental and social impacts of oil palm cultivation on tropical peat; a scientific review. Reports from the Technical Panels of the 2nd Greenhouse Gas Working Group of the Roundtable on Sustainable Palm Oil (RSPO).

Abstract No: A-345

MEASURING CO_2 FLUX OVER OIL PALM AGRO-SYSTEM: SPECTRAL ANALYSIS AND CORRECTION APPLICATION

Bram Hadiwijaya*, Bayu Septiwibowo, and Jean-Pierre Caliman

SMART Research Institute, Riau, Indonesia

*Corresponding author: bram.hadiwijaya@gmail.com

SUMMARY

Measuring CO_2 flux using micrometeorology method above tall canopy such as oil palm agro-system is different from measurement on short vegetation or flat uniform terrain. Due to the high roughness of oil palm agro-system, fast response instruments should installed high enough to avoid a height region called roughness sublayer. The trees element, in this case is oil palm canopy, could impose strong influences on the flow characteristics, and difficult to apply the surface layer Monin-Obukhov similarity. A small study has been conducted to analyze the spectra and co-spectra of measurement within the roughness sublayer, above oil palm canopy and applying spectral correction. The result has shown that measurement within roughness sublayer above oil palm canopy has opposite spectral trend compared to measurement at inertial sublayer over flat terrain. Meanwhile co-spectra analysis has shown that the instruments still respond sufficiently on high frequency and the spectra correction did not affect the CO_2 flux result much.

Keywords: *spectra, roughness sublayer, oil palm canopy.*

INTRODUCTION

CO_2 flux measurement is ideally studied from the horizontal homogenous flow where the advection term is very small. This condition can only achieved over a flat terrain where turbulence as determined by g/T_0(g: gravity acceleration, T_0: surface temperature), u (friction velocity), and $q/(c_p\rho)$ where q: kinematic heat flux, c_p: specific heat, and ρ: air density. These parameters become the basic structure of Obukhov length (L). This length is used with height (z) to form dimensionless coefficient z/L in Monin-Obukhov similarity theory (Foken, 2006).

However, the ideal conditions for flux measurement seldom occur in nature. The flux measurement on short vegetation can be the closest condition to the ideal, which could be described by simple mathematical equations (Foken, 2008). In contrast, on the tall vegetation such as on oil palm plantation which has high roughness, flux measurement become more complicated.

Above the tall vegetation canopy within a distance of two times the canopy height, is the layer called roughness sublayer (Raupach *et al.*, 1980). In this layer the trees element, in this case oil palm canopy could impose strong influences on the flow characteristics, and it would be difficult to apply the surface layer Monin-Obukhov similarity theory (Kaimal and Finnigan, 1994).

Nevertheless, it may be almost impossible to make measurements above two canopy heights above very tall vegetation, such as oil palm plantation. Moreover, CO_2 gradients may become extremely small outside the roughness sublayer. The rapid decrease in CO_2 gradients tempts many scientists to measure CO_2 flux within the roughness sublayer, where gradients are large and more easily measured (Kaimal and Finnigan, 1994).

The objective of this study is to analyze the co-spectra from measurement on the roughness sublayer above oil palm canopy. Furthermore, we investigate the effect of spectral correction on the result of CO_2 flux calculation.

METHODS

Measurement site and instruments installation

The dataset for evaluating the characteristics of turbulence co-spectra and spectral correction to the CO_2 flux was collected at a homogenous mature oil palm plantation located on Riau, Indonesia. The mean height of the oil palm (including the upper fronds) was 17.2 m. In order to evaluate the co-spectra above the oil palm canopy, a set of EC system was installed at 25 m high, within the roughness sublayer.

The installed EC system consisted of: (1) a sonic anemometer (CSAT-3, Campbell Sci, USA) for measuring three wind velocity components and virtual temperature, and (2) an open-path infra-red gas analyzer (IRGA) for measuring CO_2 and H_2O (LI-7500 Li-Cor, USA). Data acquisition rate of the EC system was set to the commonly used 10 Hz. In order to minimize the high-frequency flux losses due to distance between IRGA and sonic anemometer, both instruments were only separated 1 cm vertically, whiles the Northward and Eastward separation was 16.5 cm and 1 cm respectively. The IRGA was tilted approximately 30° to minimize accumulation of dust and water on the windows.

Data processing

Time series data sample for this study was collected from 11-20 February 2014. The data was processed using program created using MATLAB R2011b for Windows (MathWorks, USA) based on processing routines from EddyPro ver. 4.1.0 (Li-Cor, USA). In the processing routine, spectral analysis and correction are implemented to 30 minutes average of 10 Hz data by analytical band pass filter correction which consisted of high-pass and low-pass filter correction according to Moore (1986), Moncrieff *et al.* (1997, 2004) and Massman (2000, 2001) as well as co-spectral model in the atmospheric surface layer according to Kaimal *et al.* (1972) which derived from Kansas experiment over a flat terrain.

For this study, we use a simple block average or mean removal in order to keep spectral and co-spectral integration over frequencies equal to directly calculated covariance (Su *et al.*, 2004). The block average actually is not a true filtering operation as it involves subtraction in the time and frequency domain. Therefore the effect on the signal spectra can be approximated by transfer functions under certain conditions. Since block average is used, the transfer function for high pass filter correction is expressed by,

$$\overline{w'c'} = 1 \quad \frac{\sin^2(\pi f T_b)}{(\pi f T_b)^2}$$

where f is frequency and T_b is block average averaging period (Moncrieff *et al.*, 2004).

The high pass filter correction is based on co-spectra model from Kaimal *et al.* (1972) which separated by each stability atmospheric conditions. Based on Eq. 12-16 in Moncrieff *et al.* (1997), for stable conditions:

$$nCo_{wc}(n) = \frac{f_k}{A_{wc} + B_{wc} f^{2.1}}$$

$$A_{wc} = 0.284\left[1 + 6.4\left(\frac{z \quad d}{L}\right)\right]^{0.75}$$

$$B_{wc} = 2.34 A_{wc}^{-1.1}$$

where $z \quad d$ is height above zero-plane displacement.

And for unstable conditions:

$$nCo_{wc}(n) = \frac{12.92 f_k}{[1+26.7 f_k]^{1.375}} \; f_k < 0.54$$

$$nCo_{wc}(n) = \frac{4.378}{[1 + 3.8 f_k]^{2.4}} \; f_k \geq 0.54$$

The low pass filter correction itself containing:

a. Sonic anemometer and IRGA frequency response $T_d(n)$:

$$T_d(n) = \frac{1}{\sqrt{1 + (2\pi n t_r)^2}}$$

b. Sonic anemometer path-averaging $T_w(n)$:

$$T_w(f_p) = \frac{2}{\pi f_p}\left\{1 + \frac{\exp(\;2\pi f_p)}{2} \quad \frac{3[1 \quad \exp(\;2\pi f_p)]}{4\pi f_p}\right\}$$

c. IRGA path-averaging $T_c(n)$:

$$T_c(f_p) = \sqrt{\frac{[3 + \exp(\;2\pi f_p)] \quad \left[\frac{4}{2\pi f_p}\right][1 \quad \exp(\;2\pi f_p)]}{2\pi f_p}}$$

d. Sensor separation loss $T_s(n)$:

$$T_s(f_s) = \exp(\;9.9 f_s^{1.5})$$

where t_r is instrument response time, f_p and f_s is normalized frequency (Moncrieff *et al.*, 1997)

RESULTS

Wind and CO_2 flux measurement

The daily stability stratification cycle is depends on the gradient of potential temperature (Foken, 2008). The dimensionless z/L has been recognized as indicator of stability. The negative sign denote unstable stratification and positive when it is stable (Kaimal and Finnigan, 1994). From the vertical wind and F_c result we found stable stratification during the nighttime and unstable stratification during the daytime (Fig. 1). The stable stratification (nighttime) has less turbulence since it strongly dumped due to negative buoyancy (Foken, 2008).

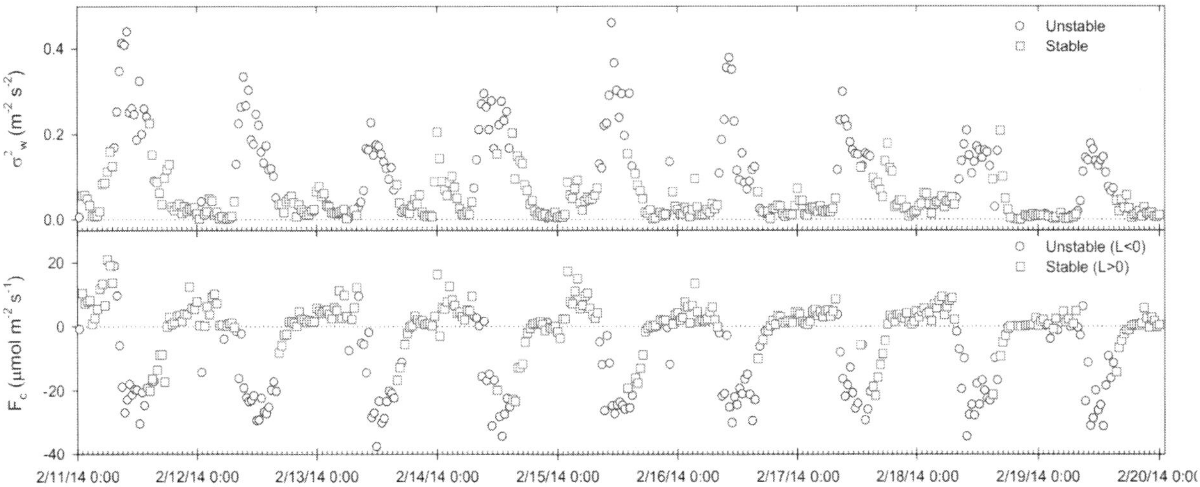

Figure 1: Time series of σ^2_w, and CO_2 flux under stable and unstable stratification.

Spectral analysis

Under unstable condition, the co-spectra vertical wind and CO_2 has smooth and same trend with Kaimal (1972) model which represent inertial sublayer, especially on the low frequency. The co-spectra exhibit a -4/3 slope, which required by the theory (Roth *et al.*, 1989), and roll-off at the highest frequency (Fig. 2a). We also apply analytical co-spectra model by Massman and Clement (2004),

$$fCo(f) = A_0 \frac{f/f_x}{[1 + m(f/f_x)^{2\mu}]^{\frac{1}{2\mu}\left(\frac{m+1}{m}\right)}}$$

where f is frequency (Hz), A_0 is a normalization parameter, m is the slope parameter and μ is the broadness parameter.

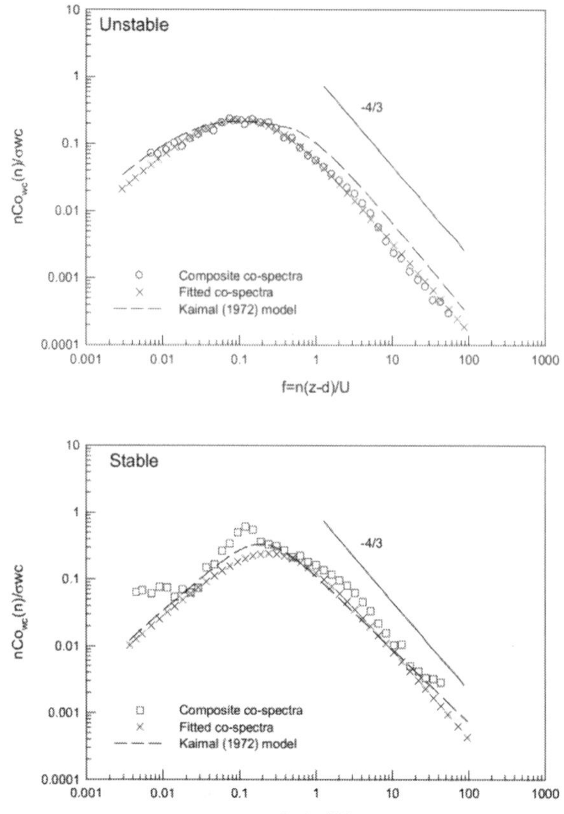

Figure 2: Composite co-spectra, fitted co-spectra after Massman model, and Kaimal *et al.* (1972) model under stable and unstable stratification.

However, the composite co-spectra under stable condition has shown different pattern, especially on the low frequency. There were some peaks and prominent dip at f <1 and some at higher frequency (Fig. 2b). Nevertheless, the instrument seems still respond sufficiently well above a frequency of 1 Hz. The Massman and Clement (2004) analytical model was able to follow the Kaimal *et al.* (1972) model.

Spectral correction

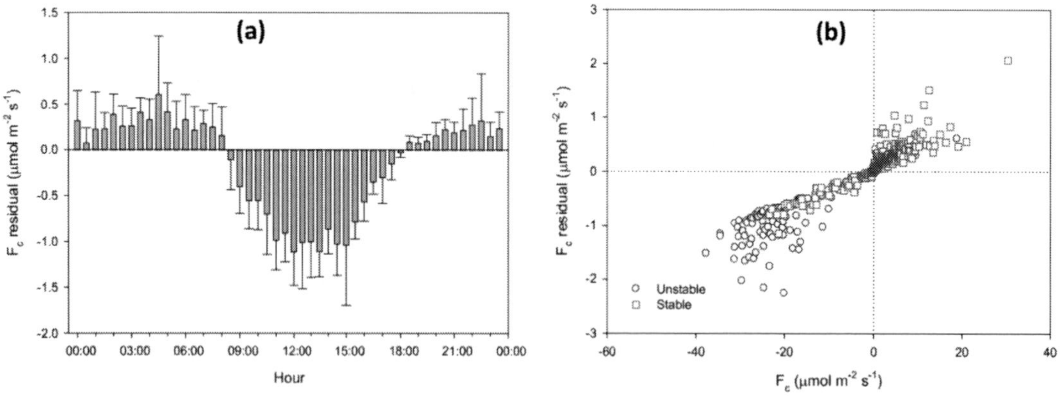

Figure 4: (a) Diurnal variation residual of F_C; (b) Scatter plot of residuals of the corrected F_c vs. the uncorrected F_c.

The band pass filter correction has make modification in the final F_c result. Averagely the F_c residual, the difference between corrected F_c and the uncorrected one, during the CO_2 up taking process was -0.62±0.47 μmol m^{-2} s^{-1}, while during the CO_2 release process was 0.29±0.26 μmol m^{-2} s^{-1} (Fig. 4a). The residual of F_c was linearly correlated with the original F_c value, because in the last step of calculation process the obtained F_c was simply multiplied with the correction factor (Fig. 4b).

CONCLUSIONS

The measurement on the roughness sublayer above oil palm canopy has different co-spectra of vertical wind and CO_2 compared to the measurement on flat terrain. However, based on the co-spectra analysis the instrument still could respond sufficiently well at high frequency. Nevertheless, the spectral correction is required since the measurement was not taken under ideal condition. The correction affected the final F_c result, where there was underestimation on the uncorrected result. Further analysis is needed to confirm the result.

ACKNOWLEDGEMENTS

This study was supported by PT. Smart Tbk., Indonesia and partially funded by CIRAD, France. We acknowledge Hiroki Ikawa (National Institute for Agro-Environmental Sciences, Japan) and John Kochendorfer (National Oceanic and Atmospheric Administration, USA) for fruitful discussion.

REFERENCES

1. Foken, T. (2006) 50 years of the Monin-Obukhov similarity theory. *Boundary-Layer Meteorology*, **119**:431-447.
2. Foken, T. (2008) Micrometeorology. Springer-Verlag, Berlin Heidelberg.
3. Kaimal, J.C., Wyngaard, J.C., and Coté, O.R. (1972) Spectral characteristics of surface-layer turbulence. *Quart. J. Roy. Meteorol. Soc.*, **98**: 563-589.
4. Kaimal, J.C. and Finnigan, J.J. (1994) Atmospheric boundary layer flows: Their structure and measurement. Oxford University Press, New York.
5. Massman, W.J. (2000) A simple method for estimating frequency response corrections for eddy covariance systems. *Agricultural and Forest Meteorology*, **104**: 185-198.
6. Massman, W.J. (2001) Reply to comment by Rannik on "A simple method for estimating frequency response corrections for eddy covariance systems." *Agricultural and Forest Meteorology*, **107**: 247-251.
7. Massman, W.J. and Clement, R. (2004) Uncertainty in eddy covariance flux estimates resulting from spectral attenuation, in Handbook of micrometeorology: A guide for surface flux measurement and analysis, eds. Lee, X., Massman, W., and Law, B. Dordrecht: Kluwer Academic, 67-99.
8. Moncrieff, J.B., Massheder, J.M., de Bruin, H., Ebers, J., Friborg, T., Heusinkveld, B., Kabat, P., Scott, S., Soegaard, H., and Verhoef, A. (1997). A system to measure surface fluxes of momentum, sensible heat, water vapor and carbon dioxide. *Journal of Hydrology*, **189**: 589-611.
9. Moncrieff, J., Clement, R., Finnigan, J., and Meyers, T. (2004) Averaging, detrending, and filtering of eddy covariance time series, in Handbook of micrometeorology: A guide for surface flux measurement and analysis, eds. Lee, X., Massman, W., and Law, B. Dordrecht: Kluwer Academic, 7-31.
10. Moore, C.J. (1986) Frequency response corrections for eddy correlation systems. *Boundary-Layer Meteorology*, **37**: 17-35.
11. Raupach, M.R., Thom, A.S., Edwards, I. (1980) A wind-tunnel study of turbulent flow close to regularly arrayed rough surface. *Boundary-Layer Meteorology*, **18**: 373-379
12. Roth, M., Oke, T.R., and Steyn, D.G. (1989) Velocity and temperature spectra and cospectra in an unstable suburban atmosphere. *Boundary-Layer Meteorology*, **47**:309-320.
13. Su, H.-B., Schmid, H.P., Grimmond, C.S.B., Vogel, C.S., and Oliphant, A.J. (2004) Spectral characteristics and correction of long-term eddy-covariance measurements over two mixed hardwood forests in non-flat terrain. *Boundary-Layer Meteorology*, **110**: 213-253

Abstract No: A-400

MEASURING EMISSIONS OF CO_2 AND CH_4 FROM THE SOIL USING THE LI-COR LI-8100A TOGETHER WITH THE LGR UGGA

Richard L Garcia*, Jason Hupp and Liukang Xu

Li-Cor Biosciences, USA

* *Corresponding author: rick.garcia@licor.com*

SUMMARY

The LI-COR LI-8100A Automated Soil CO_2 Flux System is designed to measure soil CO_2 efflux using automated chambers and a non-steady state measurement protocol. While CO_2 is an important gas in many contexts, it is not the only gas of interest for many research applications. With some simple plumbing modifications, many third party analyzers capable of measuring other trace gases, *e.g.* N_2O, CH_4, or $^{13}CO_2$ *etc.*, can be interfaced with the LI-8100A System, and LI-COR's data processing software (SoilFluxPro™) can be used to compute fluxes for these additional gases. In this paper we describe considerations for selecting an appropriate third party analyser to interface with the system, how to integrate data into the system, and the procedure used to compute fluxes of additional gases in SoilFluxPro™. A case study is presented to demonstrate methane flux measurements using an Ultra-Portable Greenhouse Gas Analyser (Ultra-Portable GGA, model 915-0011), manufactured by Los Gatos Research and integrated into the LI-8100A System. Laboratory and field test results show that the soil CO_2 efflux based on the time series of CO_2 data measured either with the LI-8100A System or with the Ultra-Portable GGA are essentially the same. This suggests that soil GHG fluxes measured with both systems are reliable.

Keywords:-

INTRODUCTION

The LI-COR LI-8100A Automated Soil Gas Flux System measures soil CO2 efflux using an automated protocol with up to 16 chambers. There is considerable interest in measuring fluxes of other trace gases (e.g. CH4, N2O, ^{13}CO2, etc.) in a similar way. Here we show a general method to integrate other trace gas analyzers into the LI-8100A System using the Los Gatos Research Ultra-Portable Greenhouse Gas Analyzer (UGGA, model 915-0011) to measure CO2 and CH4 emissions, as an example. Results were computed using SoilFluxPro™ software (LI-COR Biosciences).

TWO IMPORTANT QUESTIONS WE DESIRED TO ADDRESS

1. Does placing an additional volume in parallel with the LI-8100A analyzer sampling loop alter measured fluxes?
2. Will CO2 flux estimates made by both systems agree when they simultaneously measure the same emission rate?

MATERIAL AND METHODS - CONFIGURATION OF THE INSTRUMENTS

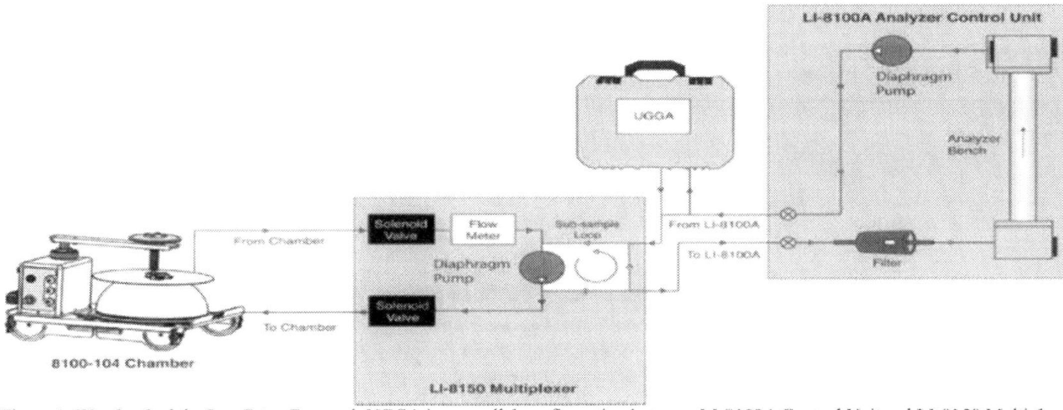

Figure 1: We plumbed the Los Gatos Research UGGA in a parallel configuration between LI-8100A Control Unit and LI-8150 Multiplexer.

For a closed-chamber measurement system, the soil gas flux (F, tmol $m^{-2}s^{-1}$) is given as:

$$F = (1 \;\; w0)\frac{\rho V}{S}\frac{dC'}{dt} \qquad (1)$$

Where, dC'/dt = rate of change of dilution-corrected trace gas mole fraction (tmol $mol^{-1}s^{-1}$), $w0$ is initial water vapor mole fraction (mmol mol^{-1}), V = system volume (m^3), p = air density (mol m^{-3}) (pV = total moles of air in the system) and S = area inside the soil collar (m^2).
Any volume added to the system brings additional air that must be accounted for in the flux calculation. The LGR UGGA optical cell has a physical volume of 325 cm^3 but operates at 18.75 kPa and 300.12°K, which gives an effective volume of 60.6 cm^3 when corrected to system P and T (100 kPa and 298.5°K). So, 60.6 cm^3 was added to the total system volume.

RESULTS

Laboratory and field experiments were conducted to compare simultaneous measurements of soil CO2 fluxes using CO2 readings made with the LI-8100A and LGR UGGA.

Lab-test with known flux

The LGR UGGA was integrated into a LI-8100A/8150 system as shown in Figure 1. A LI-8100A-104 chamber was placed on a collar with a sealed bottom. A constant flow (0.2 SCCM) of pure CO2 was injected into the chamber with a mass flow controller.

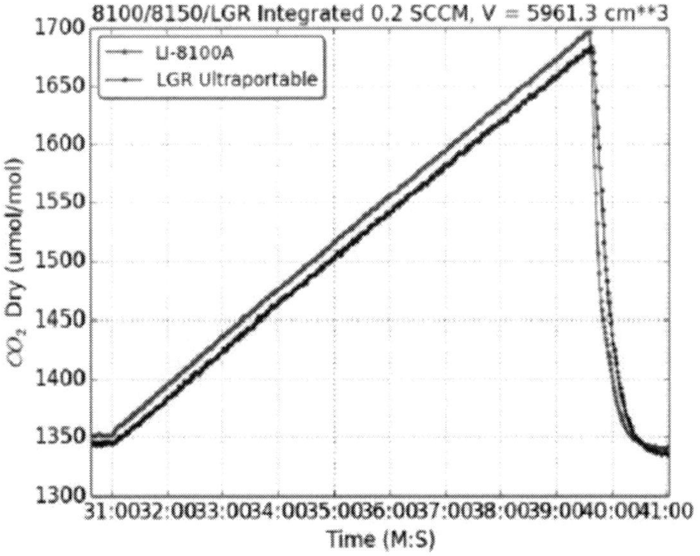

Figure 2: Time series of CO2 concentration measured with LI-8100A and UGGA. Instantaneous flux was computed using the linear slope of the time series from 20-s interval in Figure 2. Known CO2 flux was calculated from the injection rate of pure CO2.

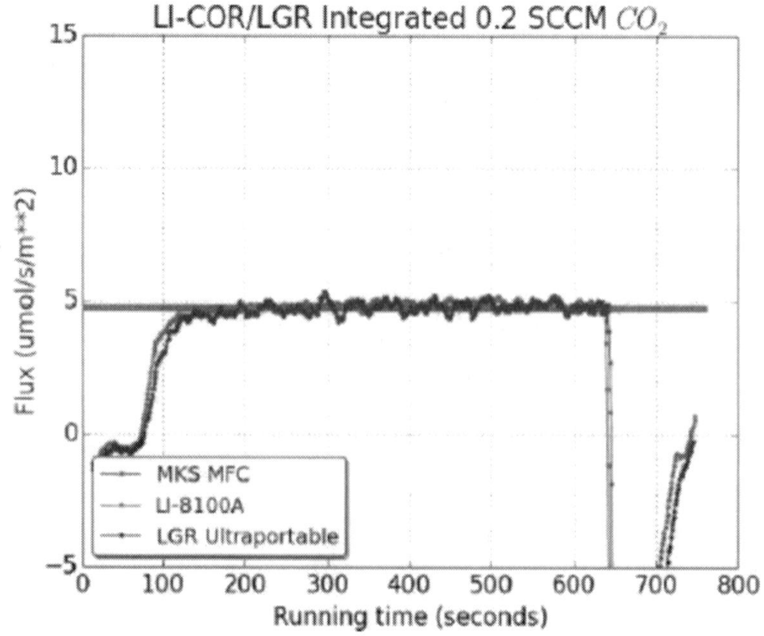

Figure 3: CO2 fluxes calculated from readings made with LI-8100A (red line), LGR UGGA (blue line), and known CO2 injection rate (green line). Fluxes measured with the LI-8100A and LGR UGGA agrees with each other and with the known CO2 injection rate.

Field tests

Field comparisons were made on a mowed lawn and an artificial peat bog in Lincoln, Nebraska USA (Figure 4).

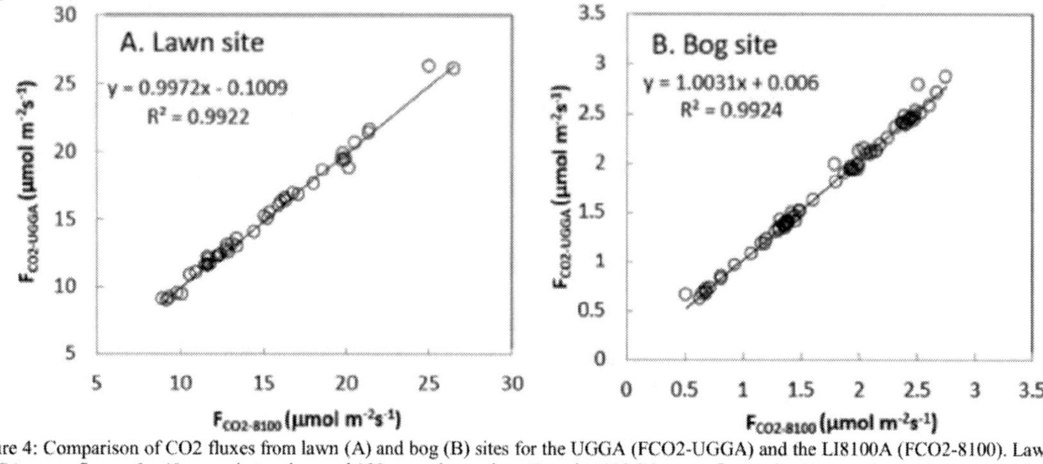

Figure 4: Comparison of CO2 fluxes from lawn (A) and bog (B) sites for the UGGA (FCO2-UGGA) and the LI8100A (FCO2-8100). Lawn site: UGGA curve fits used a 40 second start time and 120 second stop time. Bog site: UGGA curve fits used a 30 second start time and a 120 second stop time. For the LI-8100A, start times were 20 seconds and stop times were 120 seconds at both sites.

Fluxes were quite large at the lawn site, being supported by abundant soil moisture and warm temperatures (Tmean 25.7 °C). Fluxes were low at the artificial bog, possibly due to low gas conductance of the saturated peat and cooler temperatures (Tmean 19.4°C). At each site, CO2 fluxes from the LI-8100A and LGR UGGA showed excellent agreement when appropriate start and stop times were used in the curve fits.

Methane flux

Lawn site: A small negative CH4 flux (downward) was observed (Figure 5A). Over the one-week period, the mean CH4 flux was -0.33 nmol $m^{-2}s^{-1}$, probably due to oxidation occurring at the root zone.

Bog site: Due to its anaerobic condition, a consistent positive flux with a mean of 4.32 nmol $^{m\text{-}2s\text{-}1}$ was observed during the 3-day testing (Figure 5B). We also see a large temporal variation in methane flux. The maximum flux was 182.9 nmol $m^{-2}s^{-1}$.

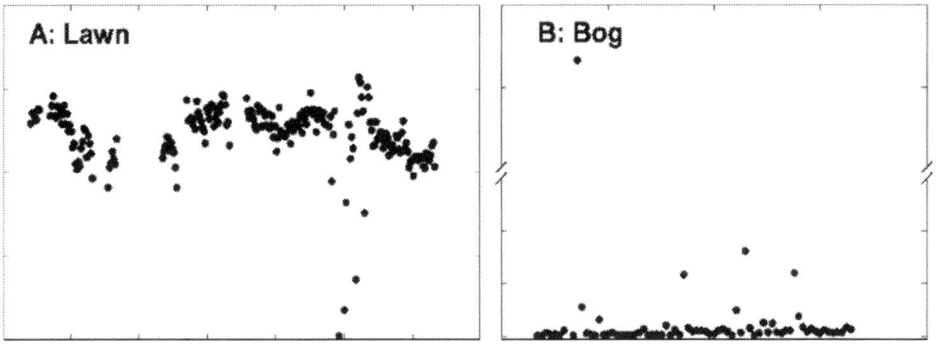

Figure 5: Methane flux (*FCH4*) estimated with UGGA from the lawn site (A) and the bog site (B).

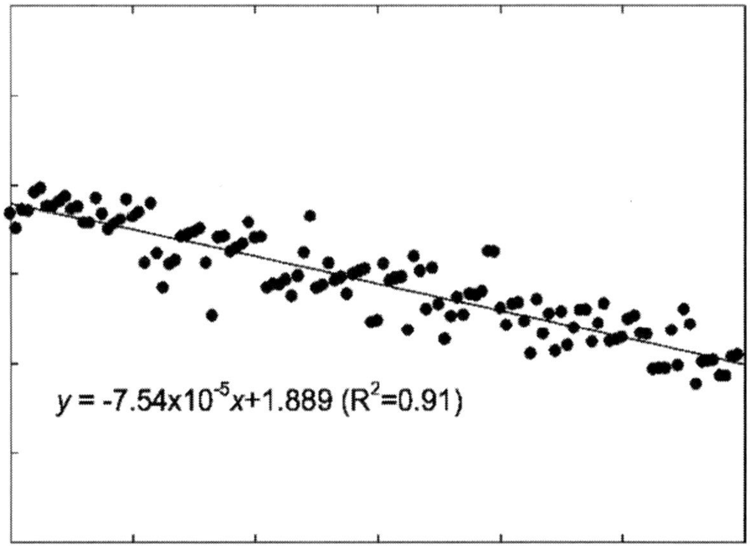

Figure 6: Typical time series of chamber CH4 concentration over one measurement cycle from the lawn site.

CONCLUSIONS

1. Placing an additional volume in parallel with the analyzer sampling loop of the LI-8100A does not alter measured fluxes (Figures 2 & 3).
2. Both in the laboratory and in the field, CO2 flux estimates made by the LI-8100A and LGR UGGA set up in a hybrid configuration were found to agree well when they simultaneously measured the same CO2 emission rates (Figures 3 & 4).
3. The hybrid LI-8100A/LGR UGGA system was able to measure soil methane oxidation with adequate precision (Figures 5A & 5B).

See Application Note (#138) for further information about integrating CO2 and CH4 readings from the LGR UGGA into LI-8100A data files and computing CH4 fluxes using LI-COR's flux processing software, SoilFluxPro™.
$y = -7^5 4$

REFERENCE

1. LI-COR Biosciences, 2015. Capturing and Processing Soil GHG Fluxes Using the LI-8100A. Application Note, 138.

Abstract No: A-110

METHANE EMISSIONS FROM STEM SURFACE OF *MELALEUCA CAJUPUTI* TREES IN PEAT SWAMP AREA IN SOUTHERN THAILAND

Mariko Norisada[1*], Takashi Yamanoshita[1], Pisoot Vijarnsorn[2] and Katsumi Kojima[1]

[1]*Asian Natural Environmental Science Center, The University of Tokyo, Japan*
[2]*Chaipattana Foundation, Thailand*

**Corresponding author: norisada@fr.a.u-tokyo.ac.jp*

SUMMARY

Carbon dioxide emissions from tropical peatlands that had been drained for agricultural productions account for a considerable amount of CO_2 emissions from land surface. A large reduction of CO_2 emission can be expected by reflooding of drained peatlands and planting *Melaleuca cajuputi* for biomass production. To make sure that the to-be-proposed bioresource production under flooded conditions is GHG-negative, methane emissions from peat as well as from the stem surface of planted trees need to be evaluated. Methane emissions from stem surface of *Melaleuca cajuputi* trees was investigated focusing on stem height position effects, diurnal fluctuation, water-level responses and the pathway in the tree body. The study site is located in peat swamp area in Nakhon Si Thammarat, Thailand. The closed-chamber method was used to evaluate the methane emissions from the stem surface. We found that the methane emission is more at the base of the stem than at higher part and it shows diurnal fluctuation. Methane was emitted from the stem surface even under unflooded condition, but it was less than the amount emitted under flooded condition. Debarking treatment revealed that the major pathway of methane in tree body seems to be the bark.

***Keywords:* -**

INTRODUCTION

Large area of tropical peat swamp forest, which had been originally a huge carbon stock, has been drained and developed for agriculture and turned to carbon source because of accelerated microbial peat decompositions under aerobic conditions and more vulnerability to fire. More than half of the CO_2 emission from peatlands is occurring in Southeast Asia (Joosten and Couwenberg 2008). The increase of CO_2 emissions from tropical wetlands have an impact on global warming and thus need to be reduced. We are seeking to establish a sustainable woody biomass production system under flooded condition in tropical peat swamp area, which can replace the ongoing production systems that demand extensive drainage. *Melaleuca cajuputi* Powell is a promising tree species which can be used for biomass production system under flooded condition due to its considerably high flood tolerance (Yamanoshita *et al.*, 2005, Kogawara *et al.*, 2006, 2014). A large reduction of CO_2 emission can be expected by reflooding of drained peatlands and planting *Melaleuca cajuputi* for biomass production. Reflooding may accelerate methane production and emission and thus reduce or even nullify the CO_2 emission reduction effect. Methane produced under anaerobic condition may be emitted from peat/water surface or conveyed by tree bodies and emitted from the stem surface. As for the methane emission from peat/water surface, previous works reported low methane emissions from tropical peatlands, suggesting low probability of its significant negative impact on the CO_2 emission reduction effect by reflooding (Couwenberg *et al.*, 2009, Norisada *et al.*, unpublished). As for methane emission through tree bodies, our preliminary evaluation detected emissions from stem surface that were low enough to confirm its little negative impact on CO_2 emission reduction effect by reflooding. Aerenchyma developed in the stem or root is considered to play a major role in transferring methane through tree bodies (Pangala *et al.*, 2013, Terazawa *et al.*, 2015). The thick, multi-layered bark that *Melaleuca cajuputi* develops could play as a conduit for methane produced in the soil. In the present study, we will report the results of evaluations of methane emission from *Melaleuca cajuputi* stem surface, focusing on height position effects, diurnal fluctuation, water-level response and methane pathway within the stem.

METHODS

Study Site

The study site is located in swamp area in Nakhon Si Thammarat, Thailand. Annual means of daily maximum temperature and daily minimum temperature are 33 °C and 23 °C, respectively, and annual precipitation is more than 2000 mm. Nearly half of the annual rainfall occurs from November to December, when the area, even the sites drained for agricultural development, is prone to flooding. Measurements of methane emissions from stem surface of *Melaleuca cajuputi* trees were carried out on naturally grown trees of 3.5 - 5.1 m in height or planted trees of 14.4 m on average. The site where *Melaleuca cajuputi* trees naturally grow has been once developed for rice production and then abandoned.

Measurement of Methane Emission from Melaleuca Stem Surface

Methane emissions from *Melaleuca cajuputi* stem surface was measured by the close-chamber method. Cylindrical chambers of 20-cm long, which can be split into two parts so as to enclose the stem, with a variety of diameters to fit with the size of the stem were used for the measurement. One part of the chamber has three holes to equip a buffer bag, a sampling tube and a thermocouple sensor, respectively. The joints were sealed with foam and sealant paste. Effective chamber capacity was determined from the chamber inside capacity and the volume of stem enclosed in the chamber. The volume and surface of the enclosed stem part was determined by assuming the enclosed stem part as a circular truncated cone. After chamber was closed, gas samples were taken through the sampling tube by a syringe at a certain interval and stored in vials that were vacuumed beforehand until analysis. Methane concentrations of the gas samples were analyzed using a gas chromatograph at laboratory.

Height Position Effects on Methane Emissions from Stem Surface

Methane emissions from stem surface were measured at two to three heights on the stem to evaluate the height position effects on methane emissions from stem surface.

Diurnal Fluctuation of Methane Emissions from Stem Surface

Methane emissions from stem surface were measured three to several times during daytime to evaluate the diurnal fluctuation of emission.

Water-level Responses of Methane Emissions from Stem Surface

Water-level responses of methane emissions from stem surface was evaluated by measuring the methane emissions under different water level conditions, flooded condition of 20 cm depth of water and drained condition of 35 cm of water level below the soil surface.

Pathway of Methane in the Tree Body

In order to examine the pathway of methane in the tree body, methane emissions from stem surface was measured before and after debarking the stem at the position just below the chamber. CO_2 emissions from stem surface were measured as well. The debarked part was filled and coated with sealant paste to prevent the gas leakage out of the chamber through the cross section of the bark. Methane emissions after debarking can be considered as derived from transfer through the xylem, while the difference of emissions between before and after debarking can be considered as derived from transfer through the bark. As for CO_2 emission, the former can be considered as the sum of the xylem transfer and respiration originated CO_2, while the latter can be, as for the methane emission, as bark transfer originated.

RESULTS

Height Position Effects on Methane Emissions from Stem Surface

Methane emissions from stem surface of *Melaleuca cajuputi* trees varied widely among the trees. When compared among the height positions within a tree, methane emissions near the base were generally higher than those at higher positions.

Diurnal Fluctuation of Methane Emissions from Stem Surface

Methane emissions from stem surface showed diurnal fluctuations, more than two-fold differences within a day. Two of the three examined trees showed less emission before sunset than during midday.

Water-level Responses of Methane Emissions from Stem Surface

Methane emissions from stem surface were measured under flooded condition and drained condition on the same trees. Methane was emitted from the stem surface even under unflooded condition, but it was less than those under flooded condition.

Pathway of Methane in the Tree Body

Most of the examined trees, nine among the twelve, showed less methane emissions after debarking the stem just below the chamber attachment position, suggesting the existence of methane transfer through the bark. CO_2 emissions from the stem surface also showed reductions after debarking. Methane emission originated from the transfer through the bark accounted for a major part, more than 60%, of the emission from the stem surface and contributed its considerably wide variation among the trees. Trees that had considerably high methane emissions originated from bark transfer showed also considerably high emissions originated from xylem transfer. Excluding these extraordinarily high emission trees, the methane emissions originated from bark transfer showed a correlation with CO_2 emissions originated from bark transfer.

DISCUSSION

Methane emissions from stem surface decreased with height, which is in line with the findings by Palanga *et al.* (2013) for seven species in tropical peat forests, indicating that methane produced in soil under anaerobic condition is the major source of the stem-emitted methane.

The debarking experiment revealed that the major source of the methane emission from the stem surface of *Melaleuca cajuputi* trees is the methane transferred through the bark. The bark of *Melaleuca cajuputi* trees has a multi-layer structure of alternation of highly spongy layer and tough and fibrous layer, which has much aerial space within it. An anatomical property of stem is a key factor determining the extent of methane emission form the stem surface. Palanga *et al.* (2013) reported that the variation in methane emissions from stem surface of trees in tropical peat forest showed a strong dependence on the wood specific density. Aerenchyma developed in the plant body is known to play as a conduit of methane produced in the soil to atmosphere. In the case of *Melaleuca cajuputi* trees, the bark with high aerial space seems to play as a conduit of methane produced in the soil.

The result that the trees showing very high methane emissions originated from bark transfer had also very high methane emissions originated from xylem transfer indicates that the wide variation in methane emissions from stem surface among trees reflects the heterogeneity of methane concentrations in the soil. Water-level responses of methane emissions from stem surface also indicated this likelihood. The correlation between methane emissions and CO_2 emissions both originated from bark transfer observed in trees with ordinary level of methane emission indicates that the gas conductivity and leakiness of the bark may affect the methane emission originated from bark transfer.

Diurnal fluctuation of methane emissions from stem surface detected in *Melaleuca cajuputi* trees is in contrast with the findings by Terazawa *et al.* (2015) in *Fraxinus mandshurica* in a cool-temperate floodplain, which showed mostly stable methane emissions throughout the day. When considering that the major pathway of the methane emissions from stem surface of *Melaleuca cajuputi* trees is bark, it may not be likely that the xylem sap plays a role in diurnal fluctuation of methane emissions. Further works is needed to confirm the diurnal fluctuation and reveal its background.

CONCLUSION

The bark of *Melaleuca cajuputi* trees was revealed to be the major pathway of methane that emits from the stem surface. Physical properties of the bark and the heterogeneity of methane concentration in soil seem to affect the extent of methane emissions from stem surface.

ACKNOWLEDGEMENTS

The present study was partly supported by JST, CREST, Japan.

REFERENCES

1. Couwenberg J, Dommain R, Joosten H. (2009) Greenhouse gas fluxes from tropical peatlands in south-east Asia. *Global Change Biology* 16: 1715-1732.
2. Joosten H, Couwenberg J. (2008). Peatlands and carbon. *In* F. Parish *et al.* (eds.), *Assessment on peatlands, biodiversity and climate change: Main report*. pp. 99-117. Global Environment Centre, Kuala Lumpur, and Wetlands International, Wageningen.
3. Kogawara S, Yamanoshita T, Norisada M, Masumori M, Kojima K. (2006) Photosynthesis and photoassimilate transport during root hypoxia in *Melaleuca cajuputi*, a flood-tolerant species, and in *Eucalyptus camaldulensis*, a moderately flood-tolerant species. *Tree Physiology* 26: 1413-1423.
4. Kogawara S, Yamanoshita T, Norisada M, Kojima K. (2014) Steady sucrose degradation is a prerequisite for tolerance to root hypoxia. *Tree Physiology* 34: 229-240.
5. Palanga SR, Moore S, Hornibrook ERC, Gauci V. (2013) Trees are major conduits for methane egress from

tropical forested wetlands. *New Phytologist* 197: 524-531.

6. Terazawa K, Yamada K, Ohno Y, Sakata T, Ishizuka K. (2015) Spatial and temporal variability in methane emissions from tree stems of *Fraxinus mandshurica* in a cool-temperate floodplain forest. *Biogeochemistry* 123: 349-362.
7. Yamanoshita T, Masumori M, Yagi H, Kojima K. (2005) Effects of flooding on downstream processes of glycolysis and fermentation in roots of *Melaleuca cajuputi* seedlings. *Journal of Forest Research* 10: 199-204.

Abstract No: A-020

PARTITIONING CARBON DIOXIDE EMISSIONS AND DISSOLVED ORGANIC CARBON LEACHING OF A TROPICAL PEAT CULTIVATED WITH PINEAPPLE AT SARATOK, MALAYSIA

Liza Nuriati Lim Kim Choo[1*] and Osumanu Haruna Ahmed[2]

[1]*Climate Change, Adaptation, and Mitigation Programme, Agrobiodiversity and Environment Research Centre, MARDI Saratok, Malaysia*
[2]*Department of Crop Science, Faculty of Agriculture and Food Science, Universiti Putra Malaysia, Bintulu Campus, Malaysia*

**Corresponding author: lizanuriatilim@gmail.com*

SUMMARY

Pineapple (*Ananas comosus* (L.) Merr.) cultivation on drained peat soils could affect the release of carbon dioxide (CO_2) into the atmosphere and also leaching of dissolved organic carbon (DOC) due to microbial metabolism. Although attempts have been made to measure CO_2 emissions from cultivated tropical peats, such studies only account for total soil CO_2 emissions, and do not partition soil respiration into root respiration, microbial respiration, and oxidative peat decomposition. With the growing concern about the effects of greenhouse gases on the environmental, coupled with the need to achieve sustainable agriculture, it is essential to partition CO_2 emissions before deciding whether cultivated or degraded soils are net sinks or net sources of atmospheric greenhouse gases. In this study, partitioning CO_2 emission into root respiration, microbial respiration, and oxidative peat decomposition was achieved using a lysimeter experiment with three treatments: peat soil cultivated with pineapple, bare peat soil, and bare peat soil fumigated with chloroform. Drainage water leached from cultivated peat and bare peat soil was also analyzed for DOC. On a annual basis, CO_2 emissions were higher under bare peat (218.8 t CO_2 ha/yr) than under bare peat treated with chloroform (205 t CO_2 ha/yr), and were lowest under cultivated peat. Decreasing CO_2 emissions under pineapple contributed to the positive effects of photosynthesis and soil autotrophic activities. An average 235.7 mg/L loss of DOC under bare peat suggests a rapid decline in peat organic carbon through heterotrophic respiration and peat decomposition. Soil CO_2 emission depended on moderate temperature fluctuations but was not affected by soil moisture.

Keywords: *Greenhouse gases, carbon leaching, land degradation, organic soils management, lysimeter*

INTRODUCTION

Tropical peatlands cover approximately 2.6 million hectares in Malaysia (Ismail and Jamaludin, 2007). The peats are increasingly being cultivated for large-scale agriculture. Although peats store large amounts of organic carbon, drainage for agriculture in particular, accelerate decomposition rates. Rapid decomposition of peats leads to an increase in CO_2 release to the atmosphere (Kløve *et al.*, 2010). Carbon dioxide is emitted from peatlands through microbial respiration, root respiration, physical oxidation, and burning by wildfires (Kuzyakov, 2006; Kasimir-Klemedtsson *et al.,* 1997). Emissions are related to water table depth (Berglund and Berglund, 2010), soil temperature (Jauhiainen et al., 2012), and land use type (Ismail, 2010). In addition, carbon is also lost in the form of DOC through leaching due to microbial metabolism (Fenner *et al.*, 2007).

In Malaysia, approximately 740, 582 hectares of peatland are cultivated with oil palm, pineapple, rubber, sago, coconut, and as rice paddies (Paramananthan, 2008). Presently, there is scarce information on soil CO_2 emissions from pineapple cultivation on peat soils. An understanding of the contribution of pineapple cultivation on peats to greenhouse gas emissions is important as 90% of pineapples are grown on peat soils of Malaysia (Raziah and Alam, 2010). Although attempts have been made to measure CO_2 emissions from cultivated tropical peats, measurements generally only account for total soil CO_2 emissions as they do not partition soil respiration into root respiration, microbial respiration, and oxidative peat decomposition (Hadi *et al.*, 2005; Inubushi *et al.*, 2003). With the growing concern about the effects of greenhouse gases on the environmental coupled with the need to achieve sustainable agriculture, it is essential to partition CO_2 emissions before deciding on whether cultivated soils are net sinks or sources of atmospheric greenhouse gases (Kuzyakov, 2006). Accounting for CO_2 emissions from cultivated peats is needed to evaluate future rates of increase in atmospheric greenhouse gases and their effect on global environmental change processes (Ahmed *et al.*, 2013).

Based on the above rationale, the objective of the study was to partition soil CO_2 emission from pineapple cultivation on tropical peat into root respiration, microbial respiration, and oxidative peat decomposition. The second objective of the study was to estimate DOC with lysimeters in waters drained from peat soils.

MATERIALS AND METHODS

The study was carried out at the Malaysian Agricultural Research and Development Institute (MARDI) Peat Research Station at Saratok, Sarawak, Malaysia. The peat soil is classified as well-decomposed dark brown to almost dark coloured sapric peat (Von Post Scale of H7 to H9) with a strong smell. Partitioning of CO_2 emissions into root respiration, microbial respiration, and oxidative peat decomposition was achieved using a lysimeter experiment with three treatments. Twelve cylindrical field lysimeters (measuring 1.43 m in diameter and 1.58 m in height) made from high-density polyethylene were set up in April 2012 to mimic the natural condition of drained tropical peats. The three treatments involved in this lysimeter experiment were peat soil cultivated with pineapple (A), bare peat soil (B), and bare peat soil treated with chloroform (C). Each treatment had four replications. The treatments were arranged in a completely randomized design. Treatment A represents the total amount of CO_2 emitted from root respiration, microbial respiration, and peat decomposition, whereas treatment B represents CO_2 emitted by microbial respiration and peat decomposition. Treatment C represents CO_2 emitted by oxidative peat decomposition. For this treatment, concentrated chloroform was applied evenly on the peat soil surface to eliminate microbial respiration, and 64.6 litres of concentrated chloroform was used. This volume was based on the water holding capacity of the peat soil. The concentrated chloroform was used to fumigate the peat soil one week before the CO_2 measurements commenced (optimum time interval achieved for the biocidal effect on soil microorganisms). The soil microbial population (bacteria, fungi, and actinomycetes) before and after chloroform application was determined using the culture method (Suhaimi *et al.*, 2007).

Carbon dioxide emissions from the field lysimeters were measured using the closed chamber method (IAEA, 1992). Extracted gas samples from the chamber were analyzed for CO_2 using gas chromatography (Agilent 7890A) equipped with thermal conductivity detector (TCD). The gas flux was calculated from the increase in the chamber concentration over time using the chamber volume and soil area covered (Widen and Lindroth, 2003). Soil CO_2 emissions were measured in the early morning, morning, mid-morning to afternoon, afternoon, evening, and night to obtain a 24-hour CO_2 emission estimate. The flux measurements were carried out in September 2012, November 2012, and January 2013 to represent the concentrations of CO_2 in the wet season whereas April 2013 and July 2013 flux measurements represent the concentrations of CO_2 in the dry season. Dissolved organic carbon from the lysimeters was determined using a total carbon analyzer (Shimadzu TOC-V CPH). Treatment effects were tested using analysis of variance (ANOVA) and means of treatments were compared using Duncan's New Multiple Range Test at $P \leq 0.05$ using Statistical Analysis System (SAS) Version 9.3.

RESULTS AND DISCUSSION

Soil CO_2 emissions under treatments A, B, and C varied throughout the wet and dry seasons (Figure 1). In the wet season, CO_2 emissions under treatment A were significantly lower than under treatments B and C. However, in the dry season, CO_2 emissions under treatment C were significantly lower than under treatments A and B. CO_2 emissions under treatment A was affected by root development and growth of the pineapple plants. Differences in day and night temperatures in the wet and dry season (Table 1) may have also impeded photosynthetic activity of the pineapple plants (Selamat, 1996). Heterotrophic respiration and decomposition of root exudates in the rhizosphere (Kuzyakov, 2006; Mäkiranta *et al.*, 2008) may also have contributed to the CO_2 emissions under treatment A. CO_2 emissions under treatment B is related to the microbial population of the peat soil and the availability of adequate substrate for microbial metabolism, but not to plant root activities (Kechavarzi *et al.*, 2010). CO_2 emissions under treatment B was also regulated by moderate temperature fluctuations (Table 1), which is in agreement with previous studies in peat soils (Berglund *et al.*, 2010; Kechavarzi *et al.*, 2010). CO_2 emissions under treatment C was mainly due to oxidative peat decomposition (shrinkage and consolidation) as the fumigant (chloroform) used inhibited microbial respiration. Bacteria and actinomycetes population before and after fumigation were statistically similar but fungi were not detected. These findings are in agreement with most previous findings, which demonstrate that chloroform can effectively kill microorganisms (Dickens and Anderson, 1999; Hu and Van Bruggen, 1998). The effectiveness of the fumigation is supported by the decrease in the mean microbial biomass carbon (Table 2). In addition, the fact that the subsidence rates of the peat soil in treatments A, B, and C were statistically similar suggests that the chloroform used did not affect CO_2 emissions. The higher CO_2 emissions under treatment C in the wet season was due to the decomposition of dead microorganisms (Jenkinson and Powlson, 1976). In contrast, the decrease in CO_2 emissions under treatment C in the dry season was because of the adaptation of the microorganisms towards the biocidal effect of chloroform.

CO_2 emissions were also affected by time of sampling (Figure 2). In the wet season, CO_2 emissions decreased from morning to mid-morning to afternoon followed by an increase in the evening. In the dry season, CO_2

emissions decreased from the early morning to mid-morning to afternoon followed by an increase in the evening and night. These observations are consistent with the significant negative correlation between soil CO_2 emissions and soil temperature (Table 3). These findings also suggest that CO_2 emissions increased with decreasing temperature. Although CO_2 emissions were negatively correlated with soil temperature, the overall data (wet and dry seasons) showed no correlation between CO_2 emissions and soil temperature (Table 3). This indicates that although soil temperature regulates soil CO_2 emissions, the differences in the CO_2 emissions under treatments A, B, and C across time depended rather on the moderate fluctuation in soil temperature of the tropics. There was no correlation between CO_2 emissions and soil moisture (Table 3) because the water table in the lysimeters was maintained at 50 and 60 cm.

The DOC losses from the bare peat soil (treatment B) (235.7 mg/L) were significantly higher than from bare peat soil cultivated with pineapple (treatment A) (194.6 mg/L) because of the greater decomposition of organic substrate by heterotrophs. The lower DOC values under treatment A is related to the consumption of carbon, nitrogen, and root exudates by microbes at the rhizosphere (Kuzyakov, 2006; Saggar *et al.*, 2013). The DOC values observed under treatment B are in accordance with the results of the field monitoring, as mean annual CO_2 values under treatment B (218.8 t CO_2 ha/yr) were higher than under treatment A (179.6 t CO_2 ha/yr). The DOC was statistically similar irrespective of the monitoring period as the peat water table was controlled to fluctuate between 50 and 60 cm in the lysimeters in order to minimize oxygen availability for carbon decomposition in the aerobic zone. In addition, the higher DOC values observed in this study compared to the initial concentration (63.4 mg/L) suggests that drainage of peat soils accelerates their chemical oxidation. This buttresses the fact that carbon is not only lost as CO_2 but also lost through DOC.

CONCLUSION

Peat soils drained for agriculture released 218.8 t CO_2 ha/yr under bare conditions, followed by bare peat soil treated with chloroform (205 t CO_2 ha/yr), and peat soil cultivated with pineapple (179.6 t CO_2 ha/yr). The lower CO_2 emissions from the peat soil cultivated with pineapple was due to the regulation by pineapple photosynthetic activity, heterotrophic respiration, and decomposition of root exudates at the rhizosphere whereas the CO_2 emission from the bare peat fumigated with chloroform was mainly due to shrinkage and consolidation of the soil. Soil CO_2 emission was neither affected by soil temperature nor by soil moisture but the emission seemed to be controlled by moderate soil temperature fluctuation in the wet and dry seasons. Drainage of peat soils affected leaching of DOC. An average 235.7 mg/L loss of DOC under bare conditions, principally from microbial respiration and oxidative peat decomposition, suggests a rapid decline of peat organic matter through heterotrophic microbial activities.

ACKNOWLDEGEMENTS

The authors acknowledge the financial support of the Ministry of Education Malaysia through Universiti Putra Malaysia. This research was funded through Research University Grant Scheme (RUGS), Project Number 9324300. The facilities provided by the Malaysian Agricultural Research and Development Institute at MARDI Saratok Peat Research Station for this study is appreciated.

REFERENCES

1. Ahmed, O.H., Ahmad Husni, M.H., Anuar, A.B., and Hanafi, M.M. (2013). *Sustainable production of pineapples on tropical peat soils*, Universiti Putra Malaysia Press, pp. 144, Selangor, Malaysia.
2. Berglund, Ö., Berglund, K., and Klemedtsson, L. (2010). *A lysimeter study on the effect of temperature on CO_2 emission from cultivated peat soils. Geoderma* 154 (3-4): 211-218.
3. Dickens, H.E. and Anderson, J.M. (1999). *Manipulation of soil microbial community structure in bog and forest soils using chloroform fumigation. Soil Biology and Biochemistry* 31 (14): 2049-2058.
4. Fenner, N., Ostle, N.J., McNamara, N., Sparks, T., Harmens, H., Reynolds, B., and Freeman, C. (2007). *Elevated CO_2 effects on peatland plant community carbon dynamics and DOC production. Ecosystems* 10 (4): 635-647.
5. Hadi, A., Inubushi, K., Furukawa, Y., Purnomo, E., Rasmadi, M., and Tsuruta, H. (2005). *Greenhouse gas emissions from tropical peatlands of Kalimantan, Indonesia. Nutrient Cycling in Agroecosystems* 71 (1): 73-80.
6. Hu, S. and Van Bruggen, A.H.C. (1998). *Efficiencies of chloroform fumigation in soil: effects of physiological states of bacteria. Soil Biology and Biochemistry* 30 (13): 1841-1844.
7. IAEA (1992). *Sampling techniques and sample handling. In: Manual on measurement of methane and nitrous oxide emissions from agriculture*. IAEA-TECDOC, pp. 45-67, IAEA, Vienna, Austria.

8. Inubushi, K., Furukawa, Y., Hadi, A., Purnomo, E., and Tsuruta, H. (2003). *Seasonal changes of CO_2, CH_4, and N_2O fluxes in relation to land-use change in tropical peatlands located in coastal area of South Kalimantan.* Chemosphere 52 (3): 603-608.
9. Ismail, A.B. and Jamaludin, J. (2007). *Land clearing techniques employed at MARDI Peat Research Station, Sessang, Sarawak, and their immediate impacts. In: A case study at MARDI Peat Research Station Sessang, Sarawak, Malaysia*, A.B. Ismail, H.K. Ong, M.J. Mohamad Hanif, and M.S. Umi Kalsom, eds., pp. 1-8, MARDI, Sarawak, Malaysia.
10. Ismail, A.B. (2010). *Farm management practices for mitigation of carbon dioxide emission in peatland agrosystems.* In: Proceedings of the International Conference on Balanced Nutrient Management for Tropical Agriculture, pp. 72-76, Pahang, Malaysia, August 2010.
11. Jauhiainen, J., Hoojier, A., and Page, S.E. (2012). *Carbon dioxide emissions from an Acacia plantation on peatland in Sumatra, Indonesia. Biogeosciences* 9 (2): 617-630.
12. Jenkinson, D.S. and Powlson, D.S. (1976). *The effects of biocidal treatments on metabolism in soil – I. Fumigation with chloroform. Soil Biology and Biochemistry* 8 (3): 167-177.
13. Kasimir-Klemedtsson, A., Klemedtsson, L., Berglund, K., Martikainen, P., Silvola, J., and Oenema, O. (1997). *Greenhouse gas emissions from farmed organic soils: a review. Soil Use and Management* 13 (4): 245-250.
14. Kechavarzi, C., Dawson, Q., Bartlett, M., and Leeds-Harrison, P.B. (2010). *The role of soil moisture, temperature and nutrient amendment on CO_2 efflux from agricultural peat soil microcosms. Geoderma* 154 (3-4): 203-210.
15. Kløve, B., Sveistrup. T.E., and Hauge, A. (2010). *Leaching of nutrients and emission of greenhouse gases from peatland cultivation at Bodin, Northern Norway. Geoderma* 154 (3): 219-232.
16. Kuzyakov (2006). *Sources of CO_2 efflux from soil and review of partitioning methods. Soil Biology and Biochemistry* 38 (3): 425-448.
17. Mäkiranta, P., Minkkinen, K., Hytönen, J., and Laine, J. (2008). *Factors causing temporal and spatial variation in heterotrophic and rhizospheric components of soil respiration in afforested organic soil croplands in Finland. Soil Biology and Biochemistry* 40 (7): 1592-1600.
18. Paramananthan, S. (2008). *Tropical lowland peats: To conserve or develop them?*. In: International Palm Oil Sustainability Conference (IPOSC) 2008, Kota Kinabalu, Sabah, Malaysia, April 2008.
19. Raziah, M.L. and Alam, A.R. (2010). *Status and impact of pineapple technology on mineral soil. Economic and Technology Management Review* 5: 11-19.
20. Saggar, S., Jha, N., Deslippe, J., Bolan, N.S., Luo, J., Giltrap, D.L., Kim, D.G., Zaman, M., and Tillman, R.W. (2013). *Denitrification and N_2O:N_2 production in temperate grasslands: processes, measurements, modeling and mitigating negative impacts. Science of the Total Environment* 465: 173-195.
21. Selamat, M.M. (1996). *Biologi tanaman dan keperluan persekitaran. In: Penanaman Nanas – Nanas makakn segar dan nanas kaleng*, M.M. Selamat, ed., pp. 7-16, MARDI, Selangor, Malaysia.
22. Suhami, M., Emmyradeziawatim K.R., Umi Kalsom, M.S., Sahilah, A.M., and Ismail, A.B. (2007). *Effect of land-clearing methods on distribution of microbial populations in peat ecosystem. In: A case study at MARDI Peat Research Station Sessang, Sarawak, Malaysia*, A.B. Ismail, H.K. Ong, M.J. Mohamad Hanif, and M.S. Umi Kalsom, eds., pp. 1-8, MARDI, Sarawak, Malaysia.
23. Widén, B. and Lindroth, A. (2003). *A calibration system for soil carbon dioxide-efflux measurement chambers: description and application. Soil Science Society of America Journal* 67 (1): 327-334.

Table 1: Day and night temperatures at the experimental site (Saratok, Malaysia)

Variable	Wet season			Dry season	
	September 2012	November 2012	January 2013	April 2013	July 2013
Mean day time temperature (°C)	26.7	29.2	29.6	26.3	27.0
Mean night time temperature (°C)	23.6	24.9	24.5	24.6	24.7
Mean day and night time temperature differences (°C)	3.1	4.3	5.1	1.7	2.3
	Mean soil temperature (°C)				
Early morning	29.8^{a}	30.0^{bc}	28.2^{bc}	30.1^{a}	28.7^{b}
Morning	30.8^{a}	32.1^{ab}	29.8^{a}	30.5^{a}	29.5^{b}
Mid-morning to afternoon	30.9^{a}	32.8^{a}	30.7^{a}	30.5^{a}	30.6^{b}
Afternoon	29.7^{a}	31.1^{abc}	30.5^{a}	29.3^{ab}	32.6^{a}
Evening	29.5^{a}	30.1^{bc}	29.4^{ab}	28.7^{ab}	29.2^{b}
Night	29.0^{a}	29.2^{c}	27.9^{c}	27.7^{b}	28.7^{b}

Mean values with different letters within the same column are significantly different at $P \leq 0.05$.

Table 2: Effect of fumigating drained peat soil with chloroform on soil microbial biomass carbon

Monitoring cycle	Mean soil microbial biomass carbon (µg C/g soil)
Initial before chloroform application	94.7a
September 2012	29.6f
November 2012	73.4b
January 2013	56.0d
April 2013	67.2c
July 2013	46.0e

Mean values with different letters are significantly different at P ≤ 0.05.

Table 3: The relationship between soil carbon dioxide (CO_2) emissions, soil temperature (°C), and soil moisture in dry and wet seasons

Weather season	Monitoring period	Variable	Soil temperature	Soil moisture
Wet season	September 2012	Soil CO_2 emissions	r = 0.2253 P = 0.1464	r = 0.1955 P = 0.2091
	November 2012		r = -0.5169 P = 0.0001	r = 0.1127 P = 0.4264
	January 2013		r = -0.4829 P = 0.0004	r = 0.2290 P = 0.1135
Dry season	April 2013		r = -0.7431 P = 0.0001	r = -0.0776 P = 0.5558
	July 2013		r = -0.5992 P = 0.0001	r = -0.2299 P = 0.0854
Pooling data throughout the wet and dry seasons			r = -0.1119 P = 0.0710	r = 0.1027 P = 0.0980

Note: top values represent Pearson's correlation coefficient (*r*) while bottom values represent probability level at 0.05 (*n* = 72 for each monitoring period, *n* = 360 for pooling data throughout wet and dry seasons).

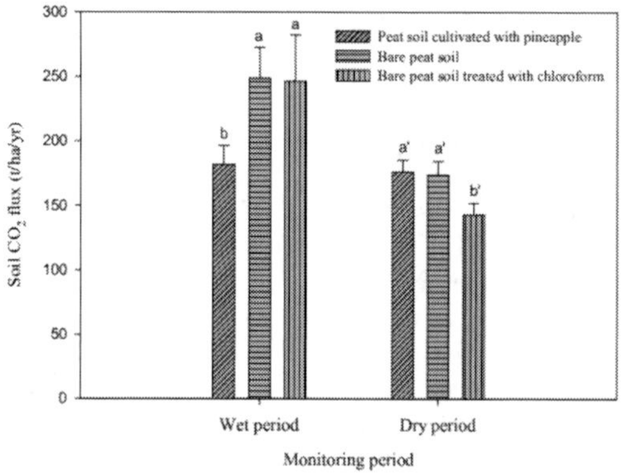

Figure 1: Carbon dioxide emissions (wet and dry seasons) from peat soil cultivated with pineapple, bare peat soil, and chloroform fumigated peat soil (Error bars represent standard error and soil mean fluxes with different letters are significantly different at P ≤ 0.05).

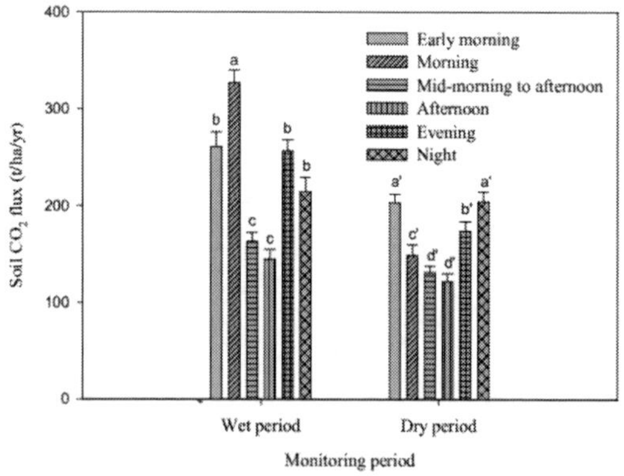

Figure 2: Carbon dioxide emissions (at different times of the day and different seasons) from peat soil cultivated with pineapple (Error bars represent standard error and soil mean fluxes with different letters are significantly different at P ≤ 0.05).

Abstract No: A-188

SPATIAL EVALUATION OF GREENHOUSE GAS BUDGET IN DWARF BAMBOO (*SASA*) INVADED WETLAND ECOSYSTEM IN CENTRAL HOKKAIDO, JAPAN

Fumiaki Takakai[1,2], Akane Kagemoto[1], Osamu Nagata[3,4], Masayuki Takada[5,6] and Ryusuke Hatano[7]

[1]*Graduate School of Agriculture, Hokkaido University, Japan*
[2]*Faculty of Bioresource Sciences, Akita Prefectural University, Japan*
[3]*Hokkaido Agricultural Research Center, National Agriculture and Food Research Organization, Japan*
[4] *Forestry and Fisheries Research Council, Ministry of Agriculture, Forestry and Fisheries of Japan*
[5]*Hokkaido Institute of Environmental Sciences, Japan*
[6]*Faculty of Humanity and Environment, Hosei University, Japan*
[7]*Research Faculty of Agriculture, Hokkaido University, Japan*

**Corresponding author: ftakakai@gmail.com*

SUMMARY

To evaluate the effect of vegetation change on greenhouse gas (GHG) budget from a wetland ecosystem, CO_2, CH_4 and N_2O budgets from whole area (21.5 ha) of the Bibai wetland, where dwarf bamboo (*Sasa*) or *Ilex* has invaded into original *Sphagnum* dominated vegetation, located in Hokkaido, Japan were estimated. Original *Sphagnum* dominated vegetation was changed from a sink to a source of CO_2 by invasion of short-*Sasa* (50 cm > height). While, invasion of tall-*Sasa* (50 cm < height < 150 cm) or *Ilex* increased CO_2 uptake. Annual CH_4 emission was decreased by invasion of *Sasa* or *Ilex*. Annual N_2O emission was slightly increased by invasion of *Ilex* only. The whole wetland area was considered to be a sink for GHG (-113 Mg CO_2-eq y^{-1}) and CO_2 uptake by tall-*Sasa* occupied 71% of the GHG budget in the current status.

***Keywords**: Greenhouse gas, spatial evaluation, vegetation change, wetland ecosystem*

INTRODUCTION

Wetlands, which forms peatlands, account for c.a. 1.5% of global terrestrial area and carbon dioxide (CO_2) uptake because plant photosynthesis exceed organic matter decomposition under wet condition. Consequently, wetlands accumulate large amount of carbon accounting for one third of global soil carbon storage as peat (Clymo 1984). On the other hand, wetlands are the major source of atmospheric methane (CH_4) accounting for c.a. 20% of global CH_4 source. Though N_2O emission is considered to be low in a natural wetland, there is a possibility that a wetland affected by artificial drainage and drying could be a significant source of N_2O (Kasimir-Klemedtsson *et al.*, 1997). Though a scaling-up of greenhouse gas (GHG) flux measured at a plot level to a landscape level is important for evaluating effects of climate change on GHG budget in a wetland ecosystem, the approach is considered to be difficult due to their high temporal and spatial variations.

In Hokkaido, northern part of Japan, drastic decrease in natural wetland area has occurred during the past 150 years due to agricultural reclamation. The remaining wetlands also have been degraded by indirect effects of the reclamation of the surrounding area. For example, a change in wetland vegetation such as invasion of dwarf bamboo (*Sasa*) associated with a progressive drying up of the wetland has been occurring (Kasubuchi *et al.*, 1994). To evaluate the effect of *Sasa* invasion on GHG budget from a wetland ecosystem affected by agricultural reclamation indirectly, spatial evaluation of GHG flux from the wetland was conducted.

METHODS

This study was conducted at the Bibai wetland (43°19′N, 141°48′E), a part of the Ishikari peatland in central Hokkaido, northern part of Japan. The natural wetland (21.5 ha) is surrounded by open ditches constructed for agricultural reclamation of peatland (Figure 1). As a result of the drainage, dwarf bamboo (*Sasa*) or *Ilex* (*I. crenata* var. *paludosa*) has invaded into original Sphagnum moss (*Sphagnum papillosum*) and sedge plants dominated vegetation. Currently, only an area of 2 ha in the center of wetland maintains the original vegetation. The depth of peat soil in the center of wetland is about 4 to 5 m. The annual precipitation is 1156 mm, and the average annual temperature is 7.1 °C in this area.

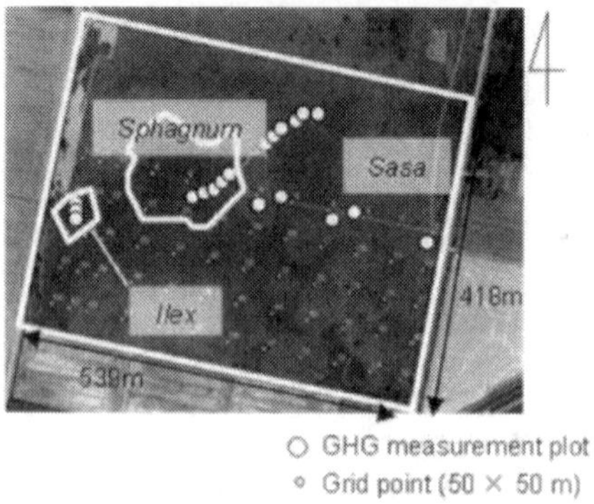

Figure 1: Survey points

GHG flux was measured from January 2004 to November 2006 by a closed chamber method involving vegetation in a transparent acryl chamber. Corresponding to the vegetation change, 3 to 7 monitoring plots were established in the *Sphagnum*, *Sasa* (short-*Sasa*: plant height < 50 cm, tall-*Sasa*: 50 cm < plant height < 150 cm) and *Ilex* sites, respectively (Figure 1). Soil temperature at a depth of 3 cm, water table depth and photosynthetically active radiation (PAR) were measured at the time of gas sampling.

NEE (i.e., CO_2 fluxes from the whole ecosystem [plant and soil]) consisted of CO_2 emission respiration of the whole ecosystem and CO_2 uptake by photosynthesis. Therefore, the relationship is described as equation (1).
$NEE = R_{TOT} - P_G$ (1) where R_{TOT} is the total ecosystem respiration, and P_G is the gross photosynthetic CO_2 uptake. In terms of NEE, CO_2 uptake is a negative value and CO_2 emission to the atmosphere is a positive value. In the equation, both R_{TOT} and P_G are presented by absolute values. R_{TOT} was measured under light shielding condition (100% shading) with opaque cover just after each NEE measurement by a transparent chamber. P_G was estimated by subtracting NEE by R_{TOT} according to equation (1). To calculate cumulative NEE during the growing season, estimation curve of T_{3cm} (soil temperature at a depth of 3 cm)-R_{TOT} and PAR-P_G were established at each measurement plots:
$R_{TOT} = a \times e^{b \times T3cm}$ (2); $P_G = (Q \times PAR) / (K + PAR)$ (3)
where T_{3cm} is the soil temperature at a depth of 3 cm, Q is an asymptote at the maximum P_G, K is the light intensity at which 50% of the maximum P_G is reached and a and b are regression constants. Hourly P_G and R_{TOT} values were calculated from equations (3) and (4) using continuous PAR and soil temperature data, then calculated hourly NEE using Equation (1). To evaluate the net GHG budget, the budget of each GHG was integrated by using the global warming potential (GWP, CO_2:CH_4:N_2O=1:34:298) (IPCC 2013).

Grid points were established at intervals of 50 × 50 m in the southern half-plane of the wetland (Figure 1). Vegetation coverage in a 15-m radius from each grid points were recorded and classified into five vegetation communities (*Sphagnum-Moliniopsis*, *Moliniopsis-Myrica*, *Sasa*, *Sasa-Myrica* and *Ilex*). Environmental factors (height of *Sasa*, water table depth, moisture content of surface peat [0-10 cm depth] and dissolved organic carbon [DOC] concentration in ground water) were also measured at each grid point. All measurements were also conducted at all flux measurement points (total of 20 points). Using satellite image of IKONOS (4m in ground resolution, 4 bands), pixel values of bands were obtained at each grid point. With bands of satellite image as explanatory variables, spatial distribution of vegetation communities and other environmental factors in the whole wetland area were estimated by a discriminant analysis and a multiple regression analysis, respectively. Area of each vegetation site corresponding to GHG flux measurement site was estimated by spatial distributions of vegetation community and height of *Sasa*. Based on distributions of environmental factors and relationship between them and annual GHG budgets, GHG budgets in the whole wetland area were estimated.

RESULTS AND DISCUSSIONS

Seasonal changes in GHG flux were shown in Figure 2. Daytime NEE in the *Sphagnum* and *Ilex* sites showed uptake of CO_2 throughout the growing season, and the uptake increased during the summer. Daytime NEE in the short- and tall-*Sasa* sites showed emission of CO_2 just after the snow melting, thereafter, tended to uptake CO_2 from the beginning of July. Large CO_2 uptake was found just before the snow season in the tall-*Sasa* and *Ilex* sites. CH_4 flux in the *sphagnum* site tended to increase in the summer. Though CH_4 flux in the short- and tall-*Sasa* sites remained at a lower level compared to those in the *Sphagnum* site, sometimes episodic high CH_4 emission was found. CH_4 flux in the *Ilex* site varied between slight net emission and slight net uptake. N_2O fluxes in the *Sphagnum*, short-and tall-*Sasa* sites varied between slight net emission and slight net uptake, except for slightly higher emission from the *Ilex* site.

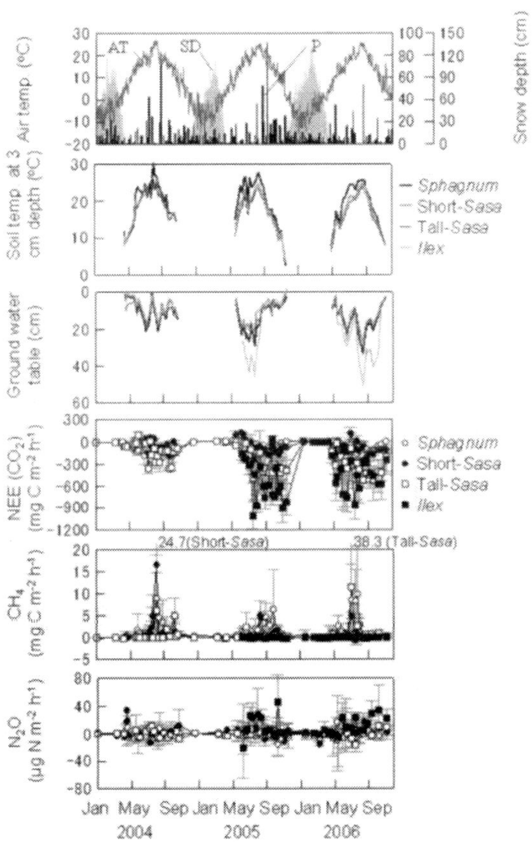

Figure 2: Seasonal changes in environmental factors and GHG fluxes. Error bars indicate minimum and maximum value. Positive fluxes indicate net emissions to the atmosphere and negative fluxes indicate net uptake from the atmosphere.

There were significant exponential correlations between the soil temperature (3 cm) and $R_{TOT,}$ and significant regression expressions with R^2 = 0.67 to 0.94 (P < 0.05) were obtained in all plots (data not shown). Regression expressions for P_G were also established using PAR (data not shown).

Annual budgets of GHGs were shown in Table 1. The *Sphagnum* site was a net sink of CO_2 and the short-*Sasa* site was a net source of CO_2. Carbon dioxide uptake in the tall-*Sasa* and *Ilex* sites were higher than that in the *Sphagnum* site. Annual CH_4 emissions from the tall-*Sasa* and *Ilex* sites were significantly lower than that from the *Sphagnum* site. Annual N_2O emission from the *Ilex* site was significantly higher than those in other sites. Annual net GHG budgets in the tall-*Sasa* and *Ilex* sites were negative, suggesting a sink for GHG.

Table 1: GHG budgets at each vegetation site

Site	*Sphagnum*		Short-*Sasa*		Tall-*Sasa*		*Ilex*	
R_{TOT} (g C m^{-2} y^{-1})	494 ± 38.8	a	594 ± 117	a	815 ± 119	a	1713 ± 127	b
P_G (g C m^{-2} y^{-1})	544 ± 18.3	c	470 ± 76.3	c	1055 ± 178	b	2702 ± 148	a
NEE (g C m^{-2} y^{-1})	-49.7 ± 40.2	bc	124 ± 42.9	c	-240 ± 79.5	b	-990 ± 90.9	a
CH_4 (g C m^{-2} y^{-1})	11.2 ± 1.94	b	6.91 ± 2.52	ab	3.42 ± 1.23	a	0.169 ± 0.166	a
N_2O (mg N m^{-2} y^{-1})	5.05 ± 4.02	a	4.37 ± 3.91	a	-4.54 ± 9.24	a	47.2 ± 9.52	b
Net GHG (g CO_2-eq m^{-2} y^{-1})	326 ± 203	c	771 ± 130	c	-728 ± 302	b	-3599 ± 335	a

NEE: net ecosysytem exchange of CO_2, R_{TOT}: Total ecosystem respiration, P_G: Gross photosynthesis. Both R_{TOT} and P_G are presented by absolute values. For NEE, CH_4 and N_2O, positive values indicate net emissions to the atmosphere and negative values indicate net uptake from the atmosphere. Numbers represent the cumulative value and standard error. Numbers within a line followed by different letters differ significantly among the sites. (P < 0.05, Tukey test).

Annual NEE in the *Sasa* sites were negatively correlated with the height of *Sasa*, suggesting that net CO_2 uptake by ecosystem increases along with an increase in growth of *Sasa* (Figure 3). Annual CH_4 and N_2O emissions across all the sites were negatively correlated with concentrations of DOC in ground water and moisture contents of surface peat, respectively.

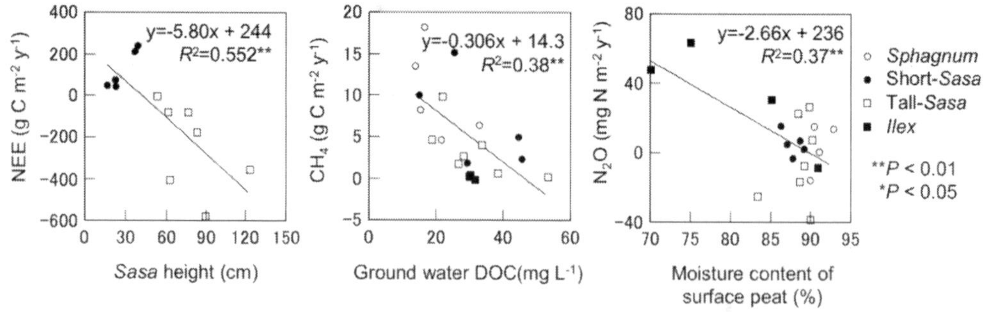

Figure 3: Relationships between environmental factors and annual GHG budgets

From a survey at grid points in the southern half-plane of wetland, significant correlations between water table depth and height of *Sasa* or moisture contents of surface peat were found (Figure 4). There was a slight correlation between ground water table and DOC in ground water ($R = 0.231$, $P = 0.08$). Drawdown of ground water table could make *Sasa* grow larger followed by an increase in CO_2 uptake, and it also could make surface peat aerobic followed by a decrease in CH_4 emission and an increase in N_2O emission.

From satellite images, spatial distributions of vegetation communities and environmental factors were estimated (Figure 5), and then, GHG budgets were estimated based on the results. The whole wetland area (21.5 ha) was considered to be a sink for GHG (-113 Mg CO_2-eq y^{-1}) and CO_2 uptake by tall-*Sasa* occupied 71% of the GHG budget (Table 5), suggesting the importance of accuracy enhancement on estimation for CO_2 balance of *Sasa* dominated vegetation. Before 1960s, most of the wetland had been occupied by *Sphagnum* dominated vegetation (Kasubuchi *et al.*, 1994). Carbon accumulation rate of the whole wetland at the time estimated by carbon exchange ($CO_2 + CH_4$) rate in the *Sphagnum* site in this study was 8.26 Mg C y^{-1}, one-fifth of the current rate (41.7 Mg C y^{-1}).

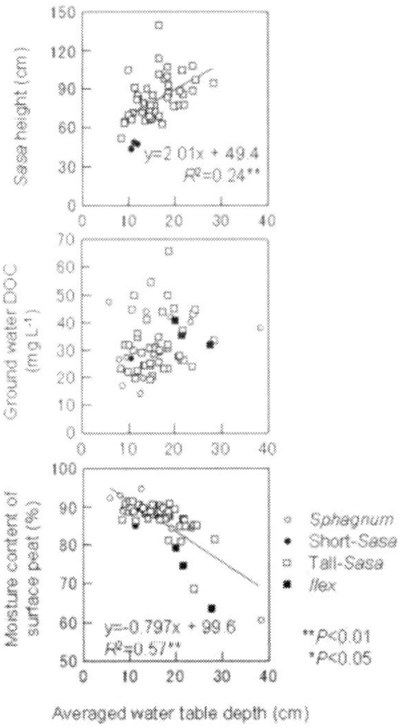

Figure 4: Relationships between averaged water table depth and *Sasa* height, ground water DOC or moisture content of surface peat at grid points.

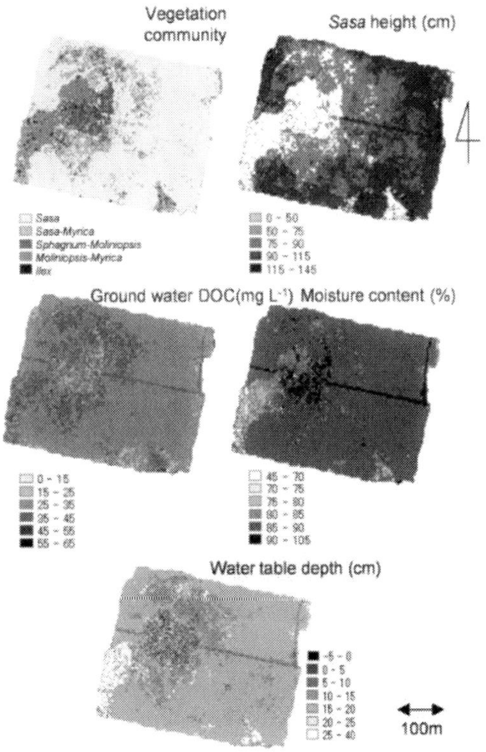

Figure 5: Spatial distributions of vegetation communities and environmental factors in the Bibai wetland.

Table 2: GHG budgets from the Bibai wetland estimated by spatial distributions of environmental factors

Site	*Sphagnum*	Short-*Sasa*	Tall-*Sasa*	*Ilex*	Whole wetland
Area (ha)	3.86	0.122	17.3	0.21	21.5
CO_2 (Mg C y^{-1})	-1.92	0.0561	-38.7	-2.07	-42.6
CH_4 (Mg C y^{-1})	0.167	0.00150	0.756	0.00432	0.929
N_2O (kg N y^{-1})	0.486	0.0141	1.11	0.103	1.72
CO_2 (Mg CO_2-eq y^{-1})	-7.04	0.206	-142	-7.61	-156
CH_4 (Mg CO_2-eq y^{-1})	7.58	0.0680	34.3	0.196	42.1
N_2O (Mg CO_2-eq y^{-1})	0.227	0.00659	0.522	0.0481	0.804
Net GHG (Mg CO_2-eq y^{-1})	0.76	0.280	-107	-7.36	-113

CONCLUSION

Drawdown of water table followed by invasion of *Sasa* and *Ilex* into *sphagnum* dominated wetland increased carbon accumulation to the wetland ecosystem and changed it from a source to a sink for GHG at present.

REFERENCES

1. Clymo RS 1984: The limits of peat bog growth. Philosophical Transactions of the Royal Society of London B, 303, 605-654
2. IPCC 2013: Climate Change 2013: The Physical Science Basis.
3. Kasimir-Klemedtsson A, Klemedtsson L, Berglund K, Martikainen P, Silvola J, Oenema O 1997: Greenhouse gas emissions from farmed organic soils: a review. Soil Use and Management, 13, 245-250
4. Kasubuchi T, Miyaji N, KohyamaK, Yanagiya S 1994: The water conditions of the Bibai wetland and the investigation of its conservation method. Japanese Journal of Soil Science and Plant Nutrition. 65, 326-333 (in Japanese with English summary).

Abstract No: A-265

THE EFFECT OF PESTICIDES APPLICATION ON PHENOLIC ACID CHANGES AND CO_2 AND CH_4 PRODUCTIONS FROM PEAT SOIL

Syaiful Anwar, Dadang and Fuzi Suciati*

Institut Pertanian Bogor, Indonesia

**Corresponding author:fuzi.suciati@gmail.com*

SUMMARY

Peat soil contains organic matters, in which their degradation produces phenolic acids, CO_2 and CH_4. Phenolic acids are known to be toxic to plants. This study was aimed at evaluatingeffects of two pesticides: herbicide paraquat dichloride and insecticide BPMC, on phenolic acids of peat soil. Pesticides that fall into peat soil will react with organic matters and its degradation products. Soil samples were taken from paddy field peat soil at Kanamit Jaya Village, District of Maliku, Pulang Pisau, Central Kalimantan. The pesticide dosages usedwere based on the recommended application dose, *i.e.* 4 liter ha-^{1} for paraquat and 1 liter ha^{-1} for BPMC. Treatments consisted of 3 levels of dosage (half, equal and twice): 1104 μg kg^{-1}, 2208 μg kg^{-1}, 4416 μg kg^{-1} for paraquat and 485 μg kg^{-1}, 970 μg kg^{-1}, 1940 μg kg^{-1} for BPMC with single control. After 1, 7, 14 and 28 days of incubation, soil in each treatment was analyzed for phenolic acids, pesticide residues, function groups, and CO_2 and CH_4 productions.Results showed that pesticide applications reduced total phenolic acids in peat soil. Paraquate and BPMC applications showed similar pattern. BPMC at the rate of 242.5 μg/500 g soil showed 95% residues reduction, higher than other dosages. Meanwhile, all dosages of paraquat provided 100% reduction of residues. Analysis using FTIR did not detect any additional functional groups. However, altered intensity of absorption peaks could be an indication of compositional changes of chemical substances within peat soil during incubation period. Pesticides application did not increase $CO_2$and CH_4 emissions.

Keywords: *Peat soil, paraquat, BPMC, phenolic acid, gas emission*

INTRODUCTION

Peat soil is a suboptimal land for cultivation because it is less fertile, has low pH, high cation exchange, low base saturation, and poor drainage. Peat soils of Jambi and Central Kalimantan contained phenolic acid derivatives such as ferulic, sinapic, coumaric, vanilic, siringic, galic and hydroxybenzoic acids (Mario &Sabiham2002). As a result of population increase and limitation of land,peat soils are cultivated.

Phenolic acids are toxic to plants and reduce plant growth. At a concentration 250 μM, phenolic acids reduced potassium absorption by barley (Hartley &Whitehead 1984). Salisylic and ferulic acids at concentrations 500 – 1000 μM reduce potassium and phosphorus absorptions by wheat and soybean (Tadano *et al.*,1992). Hydroxybenzoic acids at 7 – 70 μM retard the growth of corn, wheat, and nut and at 360 μM retard growth of sugar cane roots (Wang *et al.*, 1967). Because of pests the success of developing peat soil for cultivation heavily relies on pesticides. When applied, only approximately 20% of this pesticide will arrive at targets. The rest will move spatially such as leach to surface or ground waters (Sa'id 1994).

Peat organic matters contain functional groups such as carboxyl, hydroxyl and amine capable of interacting with pesticides (Yong *et al.,* 1992). Non-olar pesticides are able to bond to peat organic matters (Harrad 1996). Pedersen *et al.* (1995) revealed that bonding of pesticides to peat organic matters will influence properties and mobility of pesticides and physiologically causing the pesticides to be inactive and difficult to degrade by soil microbes. In addition, Gerstler(1991) stated that bonding of pesticides and peat organic matters reduce activity of phenolic acids.

Peat soil is carbon emitter when altered from natural forest and could be the biggest contributor of green house gases. This research was aimed at evaluating effects of pesticide addition on interactions and bonding of phenolic acids linked to $CO_2$and CH_4 emisions from peat soil.

METHOD

Cultivated peat soil samples were taken from Kanamit Jaya Village, Maliku District, Pulang Pisau Regency, Central Kalimantan Province. The sampling coordinates were 2^0 55'46" north latitude and 114^0 10'16" east latitude. The sampling techniques followed. Composite samples were taken at depth 0 - 25 cm. Physical and chemical analyses include pH, C-organic content, N-total, fiber content, colorand level of decomposition.

This study included 2 types of pesticide and 3 dose levels (half, equal, and twice dose of application). Pesticide dose refer to recommended application, *i.e.* 4 liter ha^{-1} for paraquat and 1 liter ha^{-1} for BPMC. With peat soil *bulk density* 0.25 g cm^{-3} and soil depth 10 cm then such the dose will equal to active compounds 2208 μg kg^{-1} for paraquat and 970 μg kg^{-1} for BPMC. Treatments were labeled: K/kontrol (peat soil without pesticide addition); A1(soil + paraquat 552 μg); A2 (soil + paraquat 1104 μg); A3 (soil + paraquat 2208 μg); B1 (soil + BPMC 242.5 μg); B2 (soil + BPMC 485 μg) and B3 (soilt + BPMC 970 μg). Analyses were include phenolic acids, pesticide residues, functional groups, CO_2 and CH_4. Effects of phenolic acids and pesticides interaction was studied with 0.00389 mmol paraquat and 0.00482 mmol BPMC and 0.005 mmol pure phenolic acids.

Incubation and sampling

To 500 g soil sample, pesticide was added and incubated at room temperature. Samplings were done at 1, 7, 14 and 28-day based on pesticide *degradation time* (DT_{50}) as referenced from EPA (1998). CO_2 and CH_4 were sampled in dark room at room temperature after incubation for 24 h in closed chamber. Prior to closing the chamber, a bottle contained 5 mL 0.2N KOH was placed in the chamber. To sampling CH_4 gas the bottle lid was modified through addition of capillary hose equipped with a stop cock.

Phenolic acids analysis

Sample of weight 5 gram was added with 25 mL methanol and shaken for 60 minutes. The extract then was centrifuged at 3000 rpm, filtered through millipore of size 0.2 μm. Aliquot was analysed by HPLC equipped with reverse phase column C18 and ultraviolet (UV) detector. Aliquots were read at a wavelength 280 nm. The HPLC system was operated at column temperature 30°C, flow rate 0.7 mL $minute^{-1}$ and mobile phase consisted of TFA 0.1% and metanol mixture (75:25) (Deptan 2003).

Pesticide residues analysis

Peat soil sample of 20 g weight was added with 50 mL of acetone and dichlorometane mixture, shaken for 8 h and then eluted through florisil and sodium sulphate (1:1) column. After evaporation for 15 minutes the aliquot was redissolved in 25 mL metanol for paraquat residues determination by HPLC 20A. The operating temperature was 30°C, mobile phase a mixture of methanol-water (60:40) set at flow rate 0.5 mL $minute^{-1}$, and using UV detector. BPMC residues were determined by using GC operated at temperature 60°C using mobile phase helium gas set at flow rate 1 mL $minute^{-1}$ (Deptan 2003).

$CO_2$and CH_4 measurement

According to Anas (1989), CO_2 concentration can be measured by using acid-base titration method. After the sample was incubated, to the 5 mL KOH solution in an erlenmeyer which was placed in the incubated closed container was added with 2 drops of phenolphtalein indicator (PP) then was titrated with HCl which was already standardized with sodium borate until the color changed from pale red to clear. Then methyl orange indicator was added and back titrated with HCl until the liquid color change from orange-yellow to red. The added volume of HCl was then recorded. The production of $CH_4$was measured using GC operated at column temperature 48°C, injector and *Flame Ionization Detector* (FID) temperature 140°C, with helium carrier gas set at flow rate47 mL $minute^{-1}$.

RESULTS AND DISCUSSION

Physical and chemical properties of peat soil

The soil samples were classified as very acidic soil (Table 1). This in accordance to Salampak (1999) findings where the pH of peat soil of Central Kalimantan wasin the range 3.25–3.75. Acidity of peat soil is correlated to organic acids humic and fulvic. The levels of organic-Cwas 52.07% and total-Nwas 0.94%. Ash and organic matter contents were correlated with maturity of peat soil (Noor 2001). Indonesian peat soil is an ombrogen peat soil consisted of thick soil peat but less nutrients.

Table 1: The main properties of peat soil used in this experiment. Samples were taken from 0-25 cm depth

Parameter	Value
pH	3,50
Organic-C (%)	52,07
Total-N (%)	0,94
C/N ratio	55,39
Ash (%)	10,24
Water (%)	70,87
Fiber volume (%)	46
Munsell color	10 YR 3/1 (very dark grey)
Decomposition level	hemic

Phenolic acids

Phenolic acids prior to treatments demonstrated domination of ferulic and vanilic each at 1.327 and 1.291 mg kg^{-1}. Other phenolic acids such as galic, protocatechuic, hydroxybenzoic, siringic, and fumaric were in the range 0.4 – 0.6mg kg^{-1} (Table 2).

Table 2:Concentrations of various phenolic acids in the soil prior to pesticide application

Phenolic acid	Concentration (mg kg^{-1})
Ferulic	1,32
Vanilic	1,29
Coumaric	0,57
Hydroxybenzoic	0,54
Siringic	0,54
Protocatechuic	0,47
Galic	0,43
Total	5,16

Phenolic acids after treatments

Results of A1 (Figure 1) showed that protocatechuic decreased 46.7% (highest) and ferulic 20.04% (lowest). This indicated that addition of 552 µg paraquat did not influence phenolic acid biodegradation by soil microbes. Ferulic and vanilic consistently demonstrated decreasing concentrations for the whole incubation period. However, other phenolic acids showed increasing concentration at 14-days of incubation. Ferulic and vanilic dominated phenolic acids composition for the whole incubation period. Compared to control, phenolic acids demonstrated decreasing concentrations at 28-days of incubation.

The same pattern was developed by B1. Phenolic acids demonstrated a decreasing tendency in the range 16.4–39.4%.At 242.5 µg,BPMC treatment showed the highest reduction of phenolic acids to protocatechuic meanwhile the lowest was ferulic acid.

For A2, at 28-days of incubation, the phenolic acid concentrations showed increasing pattern except for protocatechuic and galic acids. Significant increment happened to ferulic acid, i.e. 21%. Galic acid decreased significantly at 31%. For 4 weeks incubation, vanilic and ferulic concentrations dominated the composition of phenolic acids. At 14-days incubation phenolic acid concentrations decreased and start to increase while approaching 28-days incubation. It is predicted that at 14-day incubation the 1104 µg paraquat addition induced toxicity to soil microbes producing enzyme for phenolic acids biodegradation. In general results of B2 demonstrated fluctuating concentration changes of phenolic acids for the whole incubation period except ferulic acid that tend to decrease. For B2 the highest reduction was ferulic acid, i.e 15.2%.

Results of A3 showed fluctuating concentration changes during 28-days of incubation. On the other hand,B3 showed decreasing concentrations of phenolic acids. The highest reduction was galic acid at 39.1% and the lowest was siringic at5.9%. Ferulic and vanilic acids dominated the phenolic acids composition for the whole incubation period.

Eventhough decreasing concentrations of phenolic acid derivatives was fluctuating, however, the total concentrations decreased. Paraquat treatment for A1, A2 and A3 were each 21.4%, 20.8% and 13.6%, respectively, and for BPMC were 26.5%, 20.3% and 25.8%, consecutively.

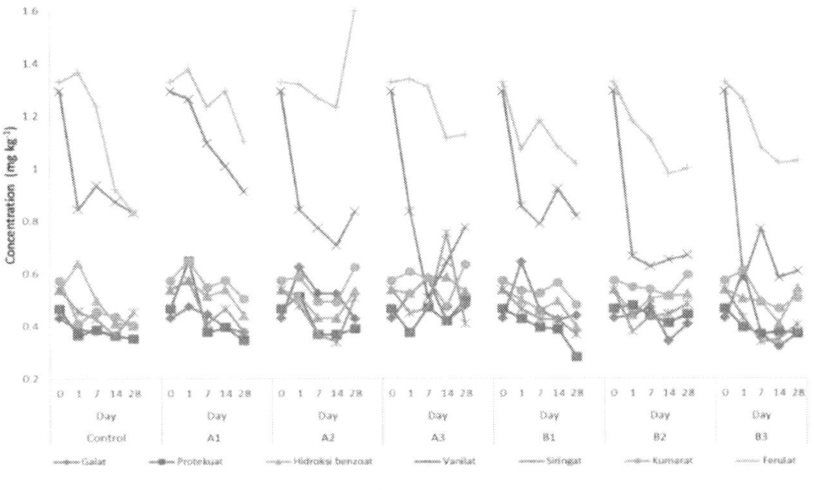

Figure 1: Composition of phenolic acids from various rates of paraquat and BPMC treatments on 1-28 days of incubation period

The decreasing of phenolic acids concentration showed that the interaction between pesticide and phenolic acid occured via covalent bonding, Van der Waals force, ion exchange, hydrogen bonding, ligand exchange, and hydrophobic interaction mechanisms (Khan 1989).According to Bollag (1992) decreasing of phenolic acids concentration might be caused by the coupling reaction between pesticide and phenolic acid. Fluctuation of phenolic acid derivatives might also caused by transformation via C oxidation of the phenolic acid.

Pure phenolic acids

Paraquat treatment on day-1 showed decreasing of phenolic acid concentration in the 19.48–30.55% (Figure 2). The highest reduction occured to ferulic acid and the lowest to protocatechuic acid. On another hand galic acid showed very high concentration rising. Such a significant rise as the result of interfering peak originated from paraquat such that overlapping the peak of galic acid. In that situation galic acid peak appeared within the interfering peak resulting in the reading for galic acids become overestimated. On day-28 coumaric and ferulic acids experienced very high concentration reduction, i.e 75% and 72%, respectively, meanwhile hydroxybenzoic acid showed the lowest reduction.

BPMC treatment on day-1 demonstrated that protocatechuic acid concentration decreased significantly at 62.66% followed by ferulic acid at 36.87%. On day-28 ferulic acid concentration experinced the highest reduction, i.e 75%. Vanilic and siringic concentration increased by 4.27% and 1.78% respectively. Similar to paraquat treatment the presence of interfering peak also happened to BPMC treatment. Splitting of ferulic and coumaric acid peaks happened in paraquat and BPMC treatments on day-14 and 28. It is suspected a new compound has been created as the result phenolic acid and pesticide reation.

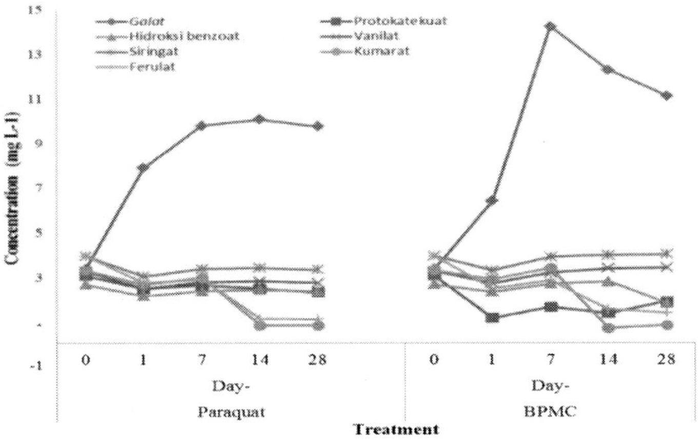

Figure 2: Composition of pure phenolic acids from various rates of paraquat and BPMC treatments on 1-28 days of incubation period

$CO_2$and CH_4 productions

Addition of paraquat and BPMC did not affect the production of $CO_2$and CH_4 (Figure 3). Incubation at day-28 revealed CO_2 emission tend to higher than at day-1, 7, and 14. Soil samples treated at half and twice BPMC dose rates for 28 days of incubation showed the highest CO_2emission. This finding was different from CO_2emisson of soil samples without pesticide addition or paraquat and BPMC additions at all dose rates but at incubation time less than 28 days (day-1, 7 dan 14).

The highest CH_4production occured at day-28 incubation (Figure 4). Compared to others, addition of paraquat at twice dose rate of recommended value and incubated for 28 days demonstrated the highest emission of CH_4. Pesticide addition on peat soils tend to show similar production of CO_2 and CH_4. Although the addition of pesticide showed a similar pattern, however, responded to CO_2 and CH_4 productions seemed lacking. This result contradicted to those of Fitriani (2013) who stated that the adddition of pesticides at recommended dose rates and incubated for 30 days will increase CO_2production. Pesticide addition of peat soil showed a lesser CH_4 prodution compared to control incubated for less than 14 days. Reduction of emission linked to the decreasing mehtanogenic microbes population. Results of study by Cahyaningtyas (2012) showed carbamate insecticide on inceptisol soil enhanced by biochar husk CH_4 emission by 33.2%. Water logged agricultural lands (anaerobic) also produce higher CH_4.

B1 treatment (addition of half BPMC dose) demonstrated higher methane emission compared to control. Such the increasing of CH_4emission compared to control was predicted that at the dose rate application did not induce toxic effects. Kimura *et al.* (1993) reported that beside pesticides, the formation of $CH_4$was strongly inflenced by organic matter, temperature, pH, moisture and Eh of soil.

CONCLUSION

BPMC and paraquat pesticides capable of interacting with phenolic acid via condensation or coupling reactions. As the result of interaction the concentrations of phenolic acids and pesticides in peat soil decerased. The implication of this is the pesticide will have a positive impacts in reducing the negative effects of phenolic acids to plants. Differences in pesticide doses did not show linear correlation to CO_2 and CH_4 productions.

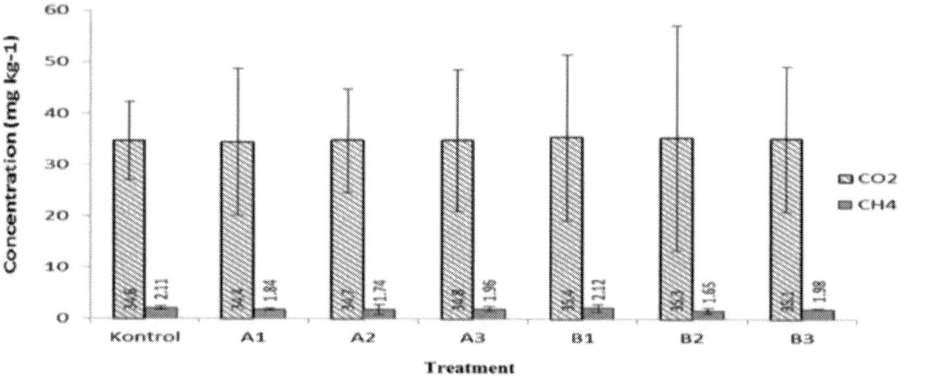

Figure 3: Emission of CO2 and CH4 from various dosages of paraquat and BPMC treatmentson 1-28 days of incubation period

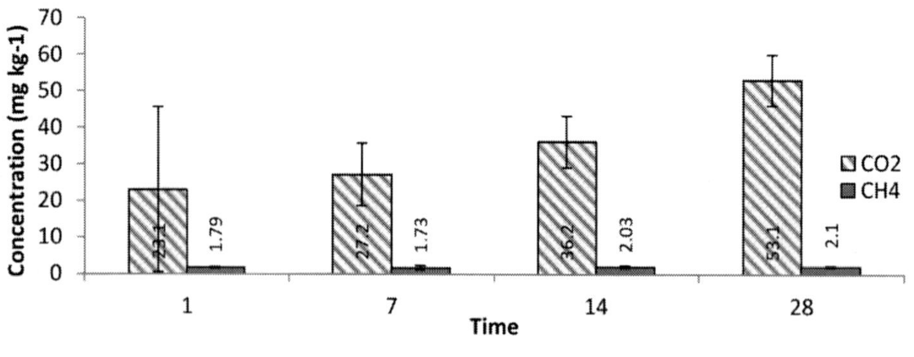

Figure 4: Emission of CO2 and CH4 from various dosages of paraquat and BPMC treatmentson 1-28 days of incubation period

REFERENCES

1. Bollag, J. M, C. J Myers dan R. D Minard. 1992. Biological and chemical interactions of pesticides with soil organic matter. The Science of the Total Environment: 205-217.
2. Cahayaningtyas, W.P., dan I. Sumantri. 2012. Pengaruh penambahan biochar limbah pertanian dan pestisida pada inkubasi tanah inceptisol untuk menekan emisi gas metan (CH_4) sebagai gas rumah kaca. J. Teknologi kimia dan industri 1(1): 521-527.
3. Deptan (Departemen Pertanian). 2005. Metode Pengujian Residu Pestisida dalam Hasil Pertanian. Departemen Petanian. Jakarta.
4. Fitriyani, I.H. 2013. Uji pemberian paraquat, difenolconazole dan buthylphenylmethyl carbamat (BPMC) terhadap emisi CO_2 dan CH_4 serta perubahan konsentrasi asam-asam fenolat di tanah gambut
5. (Thesis). Institut Pertanian Bogor, Bogor
6. Harrad, S.J. 1996. The Environmental Behaviour of Toxic Organic Chemicals. In Harrison R.M, editor. Pollution, Cause, Effects and Control. The Royal Society of Chemistry. Cambridege
7. Hartley, R.D. dan D. C Whitehead. 1984. Phenolic Acids in Soil and Their Influence of Plant Growth and Soil Microbial Processes. In Vaughan D, Malcolm R.E, editor. Soil Organic Matter and Biological Activity. Martinus Nijhoff, DR W. Junk Publisher. Lancaster
8. Mario, M.D. dan S. Sabiham. 2002. Penggunaan tanah mineral yang diperkaya oleh bahan berkadar Fe tinggi sebagai amelioran dalam meningkatkan produksi dan stabilitas gambut.
9. Pedersen, H.J, P. Kudsk, dan A. Helweg. 1995. Adsorption and ED50 values of five soils applied herbicides. Pes Sci. 44: 131-136.
10. Sa'id, E.G. 1994. Dampak negatif pestisida, sebuah catatan bagi kita semua. J Agrotek. 2(1): 71-72.
11. Salampak. 1999. Peningkatan produktivitas tanah gambut yang disawahkan dengan pemberian bahan amelioran tanah mineral berkadar besi tinggi.(Disertasi). Institut Pertanian Bogor. Bogor
12. Yong, R.N., A.M.O Mohamed, and B.P Warkentin. 1992. Principle of Contaminant Transport in Soils. Amsterdam (NL): Elsevier Science Publisher.
13. Wang, T.S.C., T.K Yang, and T.T Chuang. 1967. Soil phenolic acids as plant growth inhibitors. Soil Sci. 103:239 –246.

Abstract No: A-216

THE RELATION BETWEEN WATER CONTENTS AND CO_2 FLUXES FROM DRAINED TROPICAL PEATS

Randi Adi Candra[1], Evi Gusmayanti[1, 2], Gusti Anshari[2, 3]

[1]*Department of Agrotechnology, Faculty of Agriculture, Tanjungpura University, Indonesia*
[2]*Magister of Environment, Tanjungpura University, Indonesia*
[3]*Department of Soil Science, Faculty of Agriculture, Tanjungpura University, Indonesia*

Corresponding author: gzanshari@live.untan.ac.id

SUMMARY

It is commonly assumed that water table directly regulates CO_2 fluxes from drained tropical peats. In facts, many factors govern this CO_2 emission. In a simple model, water table directly influences water content, and peat decomposition causing CO_2 emission depends upon the availability of soil moisture or water content. This research aims to find a relationship of water content to CO_2 fluxes from several land uses on a drained peat dome in West Kalimantan Province, Indonesia. These land uses are secondary forest (SF), oil palm (OP), Aloe vera (AV), and shrub peatland (SL). We have conducted this research since July 2015. The current data was up to February 2016. We manually measured water tables (WT). We calculated gravimetric water content (WC) after drying at 105 °C for 24 hours, and used an infrared gas analyzer to measure CO_2 concentration. We also measured pH, and Eh state of these peats. We used a linear Pearson correlation and simple linear regression approach to determine a relationship of water content to CO_2 fluxes. All peats in these land uses are at oxidative states, as values of Eh are greater than 600 mV. Average pH values are 3.37, 3.57, 4.51, and 3.58 in SF, OP, AL, and SL. Means and standard deviations of water contents in SF, OP, AV, and SL are 446.74 ± 44.68%; 327.27 ± 47.53%; 112.53 ± 56.10%; and 239.36 ± 57.80%. Means and standard deviations of CO_2 fluxes in SF, OP, AV, and SL are 0.24 ± 0.04; 0.28 ± 0.05; 0.49 ± 0.13; and 0.34 ± 0.05 g CO_2 m^{-2} hr^{-1}. The height of ground water table from the surface in SF, OP, AV and SL ranges from 10.25 to 70.50 cm; 46.13 to 78.25 cm; 32.75 to 74.75 cm; and 25.00 to 74.75 cm respectively. The amounts of rainfall and land cover types affect the height of water table, and hence water contents. An overall Pearson correlation of water tables (WT) and water contents (WC) is negatively strong (R=-0.83). Pearson correlations of WT to CO_2 fluxes in every land use are varied. The Pearson correlations of WT to CO_2 fluxes in OP and SL are negatively moderate and weak (R = -0.51 and -0.30), and the correlations of WT to CO_2 fluxes in SF and AV are extremely poor (R = -0.05, and 0.07). Overall, the correlation of WT to CO_2 fluxes is negatively moderate (R=-0.42), with a weak coefficient regression (R-sq= 0.18). This research indicates that WT has strong influences on WC. The correlations of WT and WC to CO_2 fluxes are not always strong. This suggests WT and WC are not the only factors regulating rates of CO_2 emissions from disturbed and drained tropical peats. The use of WT as a single factor to predict CO_2 emissions from tropical peats suffers from a substantial amount of inaccuracy. Therefore, the current practice using water table as a sole indicator of CO_2 flux needs revisited.

Keywords: *CO_2 Emission; Tropical Peats; Water Table; Water Content*

INTRODUCTION

A current model of CO_2 emissions from drained tropical peats is based on water table (Hooijer *et al.*, 2012). This model is widely used, for an example in RSPO. In facts, many factors govern this CO_2 emission. In a simple model, water table directly influences water content, and peat decomposition causing CO_2 emission depends upon the availability of soil moisture or water content. This research aims to find a relationship of water content to CO_2 fluxes from several land uses on a drained peat dome. In contrast to most researchers who pointed out large emissions of Carbon from drained tropical peats (Hooijer *et al.* 2010; Hooijer *et al.*, 2012; Hergoualc'h and Verchot 2011; Page *et al.*, 2011; Carlson *et al.*, 2012), this research presents a complex relationship of water contents to CO_2 flux rates.

METHODS

We have conducted this research since July 2015, and plan to do regular observations for coming year. Data collection is planned at fortnightly interval. We have used an infra-red gas analyzer, EGM-4, to measure CO_2

concentration. Soil samples for gravimetric water contents were collected from ground surface, about 5 cm deep, at a distance of 10 cm from the sample plot collar. We also measured soil and air temperatures, soil acidity (pH) and Oxidation Reduction Potential (ORP). All of these samples were either collected or measured at time of CO_2 measurements.

The research site is located in Rasau Jaya peat dome, West Kalimantan Province. This peat was drained in 1970s for an agriculture development associated with transmigration project. All forests in this peat dome were heavily logged, and the peat is massively drained. Data were collected from secondary forest (SF), oil palm (OP), Aloe vera (AV), and shrub peatland (SL).

We calculated gravimetric water content after drying at 105 °C for 24 hours (Anshari *et al.*, 2010; Agus, Hairiah, and Mulyani 2011). CO_2 flux was linearly estimated (Parkin, T. B., and Venterea 2010). We also measured pH, and Eh state of these peats. We used a linear Pearson correlation and simple linear regression approach to determine a relationship of water content to CO_2 fluxes. Flux estimates are reported as CO_2 fluxes normalized to temperature 25° C (Parkin, Doran, and Franco-Vizcaino 1996)

RESULTS AND DISCUSSIONS

Table 1 presents average values and standard deviations of gravimetric water contents (WC), water tables (WT), and CO_2 fluxes on land uses. The CO_2 fluxes on Aloe vera (AV) and shrub peatland (SL) is temporarily higher than those on secondary forest (SF) and oil palm (OP). The lowest water table was recorded in oil palm, with a moderate value of CO_2 flux.

Table 6: Mean and Standard Deviations of Gravimetric Water Contents (WC), Water Tables (WT) and CO_2 Fluxes on Land Uses

Value	WC (%)	WT (cm)	Normalized Flux (g CO_2 m^{-2} hr^{-1})	Site
Mean	446.74	36.95	0.24	SF
SD	44.68	20.97	0.04	
Mean	327.37	59.66	0.28	OP
SD	47.53	11.91	0.05	
Mean	112.53	52.93	0.49	AV
SD	56.10	13.81	0.13	
Mean	239.36	52.23	0.34	SL
SD	57.80	17.61	0.05	
Grand Mean	281.50	50.44	0.34	
SD	43.13	15.12	0.03	

Figure 1 present scatter plots of gravimetric water contents (WC) to CO_2 fluxes on land uses. Pearson correlations of these variables show a negatively moderate correlation on SF, and positively weak correlation on other land uses. Overall, a linear correlation of WC to CO_2 flux is positively moderate, with a poor linear regression coefficient (See Table 2).

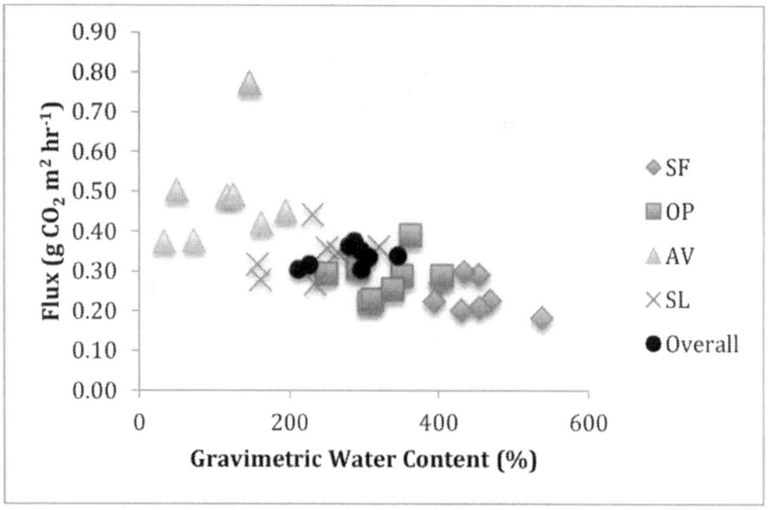

Figure 9: Scatter plots of water contents to CO_2 fluxes on land uses

Table 7: Pearson Correlation and Linear Regression between Water Contents and CO_2 Fluxes on land uses

Land Use	Pearson Corr. (WC and Flux)	Linear Reg
SF	-0.45	Y = -0.0004x + 0.4327, R-sq=0.20
OP	0.25	Y = 0.0003x + 0.1913, R-sq=0.06
AV	0.31	Y = 0.0007x + 0.4058, R-sq=0.10
SL	0.34	Y = 0.0003x + 0.2592, R-sq= 0.12
All	0.42	Y = 0.0003x + 0.2629, R-sq=0.18

Figure 2 presents scatter plots between water tables (WT) and CO_2 fluxes on land uses. These are negatively moderate and weak correlations on OP and SL. Other Pearson correlations are very poor. Overall, a Pearson correlation is negatively strong, and it also results a weak linear regression determinant (See Table 3).

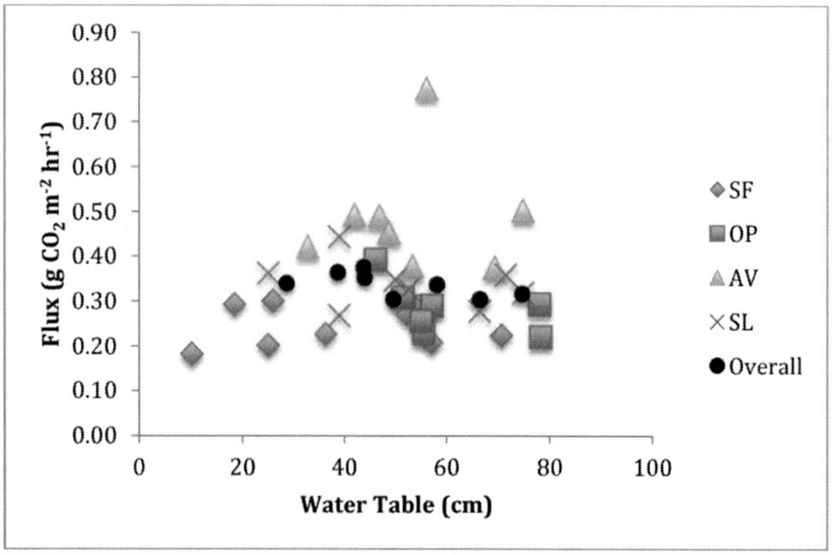

Figure 10: Scatter plots of Water Tables to CO_2 fluxes on land uses

Table 8: Pearson Correlation and Linear Regression between Water Tables and CO_2 Fluxes on land uses

Land Use	Pearson Corr. (WT and Flux)	Linear Reg
SF	-0.05	
OP	-0.51	Y = -0.0023x + 0.4199, R-sq=0.26
AV	0.07	
SL	-0.30	
Overall	-0.60	Y =- 0.001x + 0.3885, R-sq=0.36

This study shows that water table has direct influence on water contents, together with other factors, i.e., land cover, peat types, and rainfall. The influence of water table on CO_2 flux seems to be indirect, as water contents are not singly dependent upon water tables. Variability of water contents is very complex, and strongly associated with degrees of drainage, rainfall, and land uses or land cover. It is interesting to note that CO_2 fluxes in OP and SF are indifferent. In this research, the CO_2 flux on Aloe vera is the highest. This may be a result of land cover similarities of secondary forest to this young oil palm. At present, both peats on secondary forest and oil palm are very much covered by wild ferns and young trees. In contrast, ferns only cover shrub peat, and peat on Aloe vera is substantially open.

CO_2 flux from floor of peat swamp forest in Central Kalimantan was about 0.41 g CO_2 m^{-2} hr^{-1} (Jauhiainen *et al.*, 2005). The estimated CO_2 emission from Acacia plantation on peats in Sumatra was about 0.93 g CO_2 m^{-2} hr^{-1} (Jauhiainen, Hooijer, and Page 2012). Based on subsidence rate of 5 cm per year and water table at 0.7 m, CO_2 emission from oil palm and Acacia plantations was estimated to be 0.85 g CO_2 m^{-2} hr^{-1} (Hooijer *et al.*, 2012). All of these values are largely greater than the result of this study. In contrast, Melling, Hatano, and Goh (2005) and Melling *et al.* (2008) reported that a low CO_2 flux rate from peat forest, sago plantation and oil palm plantation on peats in Sarawak, Malaysia. These are 0.24 g CO_2 m^{-2} hr^{-1} on peat forest, 0.13 g CO_2 m^{-2} hr^{-1} on sago plantation, and 0.18 g CO_2 m^{-2} hr^{-1} on oil palm. In addition, CO_2 fluxes from 4-5 years ex-burnt peat areas used for pineapple farm, shrub covered by ferns, and corn cultivation on Rasau Jaya peat dome was recorded to be 1.5; 1.4; and 1.0 g CO_2 m^{-2} hr^{-1} (Astiani, Hatta, and Fifian 2015). These authors also reported that CO_2 flux from recently burnt peat was about 1.6 g CO_2 m^{-2} hr^{-1} due to favorable condition for aerobically heterotrophic and autotrophic respirations.

CONCLUSION

This research indicates that WT has strong influences on WC. The correlations of WT and WC to CO_2 fluxes are not strong. This suggests WT and WC are not the only factors regulating rates of CO_2 emissions from disturbed and drained tropical peats. The use of WT as a single factor to predict CO_2 emissions from tropical peats suffers from a substantial amount of inaccuracy. Estimates of CO_2 fluxes from drained Rasau Jaya peat dome in West Kalimantan are found to be in between estimated CO_2 flux rates in Sarawak and in Sumatra, and in Central Kalimantan as reported by Melling, Hatano and Goh (2005), Jauhiainen *et al.* (2005), and Hooijer *et al.* (2012). Factors that control rates of CO_2 flux from tropical peats are water tables associated with rainfall and drainage, peat types, and soil moistures associated with land cover and cultural practices. Both low and high water content has substantial influence on decreases of CO_2 flux. However, a range of optimum values that favors CO_2 emission from tropical peats is not known.

ACKNOWLEDGMENTS

This study was supported by Partnerships for Enhanced Engagement in Research (PEER) United States, NSF Grant No: 1114161. Further information is available at http://sites.nationalacademies.org/pga/peer/index.htm

REFERENCE

1. Agus, Fahmuddin, Kurniatun Hairiah, and Anny Mulyani. 2011. *Measuring Carbon Stock in Peat Soils: Practical Guide*. World Agroforestry Center and Indonesian Center for Agricultural Land Resources Research and Development.
2. Anshari, M. Afifudin, M. Nuriman, E. Gusmayanti, L. Arianie, R. Susana, R. W. Nusantara, J. Sugardjito, and A. Rafiastanto. 2010. "Drainage and Land Use Impacts on Changes in Selected Peat Properties and Peat Degradation in West Kalimantan Province, Indonesia." *Biogeosciences* 7 (11): 3403–19. doi:10.5194/bg-7-3403-2010.
3. Astiani, Dwi, Muhammad Hatta, and Firda Fifian. 2015. "ScienceDirect Soil CO 2 Respiration along Annual Crops or Land-Cover Type Gradients on West Kalimantan Degraded Peatland Forest." *Procedia*

Environmental Sciences 28 (SustaiN 2014). Elsevier B.V.: 132–41. doi:10.1016/j.proenv.2015.07.019.

4. Carlson, Kimberly M., Lisa M. Curran, Gregory P. Asner, Alice McDonald Pittman, Simon N. Trigg, and J. Marion Adeney. 2012. "Carbon Emissions from Forest Conversion by Kalimantan Oil Palm Plantations." *Nature Climate Change* 3 (3). Nature Publishing Group: 283–87. doi:10.1038/nclimate1702.
5. Hergoualc'h, Kristell, and Louis V. Verchot. 2011. "Stocks and Fluxes of Carbon Associated with Land Use Change in Southeast Asian Tropical Peatlands: A Review." *Global Biogeochemical Cycles* 25 (2): n/a – n/a. doi:10.1029/2009GB003718.
6. Hooijer, A., S. Page, J. G. Canadell, M. Silvius, J. Kwadijk, H. Wösten, and J. Jauhiainen. 2010. "Current and Future CO_2 Emissions from Drained Peatlands in Southeast Asia." *Biogeosciences* 7 (5): 1505–14. doi:10.5194/bg-7-1505-2010.
7. Hooijer, A., S. Page, J. Jauhiainen, W. A. Lee, X. X. Lu, A. Idris, and G. Anshari. 2012. "Subsidence and Carbon Loss in Drained Tropical Peatlands." *Biogeosciences* 9 (3): 1053–71. doi:10.5194/bg-9-1053-2012.
8. Jauhiainen, J., a. Hooijer, and S. E. Page. 2012. "Carbon Dioxide Emissions from an *Acacia* Plantation on Peatland in Sumatra, Indonesia." *Biogeosciences* 9 (2): 617–30. doi:10.5194/bg-9-617-2012.
9. Jauhiainen, Jyrki, Hidenori Takahashi, Juha E.P. Heikkinen, Pertti J. Martikainen, and Harri Vasander. 2005. "Carbon Fluxes from a Tropical Peat Swamp Forest Floor." *Global Change Biology* 11: 1788–97. doi:10.1111/j.1365-2486.2005.01031.x.
10. Melling, Lulie, Kah Joo Goh, Constance Beauvais, and Ryusuke Hatano. 2008. "Carbon Flow and Budget in Young Mature Oil Palm Agroecosystem on Deep Tropical Peat." *Planter.*
11. Melling, Lulie, Ryusuke Hatano, and Kah Joo Goh. 2005. "Soil CO2 Flux from Three Ecosystems in Tropical Peatland of Sarawak, Malaysia." *Tellus, Series B: Chemical and Physical Meteorology* 57 (1): 1–11. doi:10.1111/j.1600-0889.2005.00129.x.
12. Page, S.E., R Morrison, C Malins, and A Hooijer. 2011. *Review of Peat Surface Greenhouse Gas Emissions from Oil Palm Plantations in Southeast Asia*. Washington D.C. http://www.theicct.org/sites/default/files/publications/ICCT_Peat-Emissions_Sept2011.pdf.
13. Parkin, T. B., and Venterea, R.T. 2010. "Chapter 3. Chamber-Based Trace Gas Flux Measurements." In *Sampling Protocols. R.F. Follet, Editor*, edited by R.F. Follett, 2010:1–39. www.ars.usda.gov/research/GRACEnet.

Abstract No: A-039

TROPICAL PEAT GHG EMISSIONS FROM OIL PALM PLANTATION MICROSITES UNDER COMPRESSION

Marshall Kana Samuel[1, 2*] and Stephanie Evers[1]

[1]*School of Biosciences, The University of Nottingham Malaysia Campus, Malaysia.*
[2]*Climate Change, Adaptation and Mitigation Programme, MARDI Saratok, Malaysia*

Email: m.kanasamuel@gmail.com

SUMMARY

Oil palm plantation on tropical peat could contribute to the heterogeneity of soil properties. This attribute is mainly found in and between palm rows and specifically within microsites; harvesting path (HP), under canopy (UC), frond pile (FP) and far from palm (FF). We measured carbon emissions in conjunction with soil sampling at 20 cm depths from microsites within KLIA, Sepang, Malaysia oil palm plantation. Sample collection was carried out at three land use age classes, namely LU1 (15 years), LU2 (9 years) and LU3 (2 years, 2nd generation) during the rainy season. The relationship between peat properties and carbon emissions was also established. In microsites the variation of soil moisture, bulk density, loss on ignition and pH values was 32%, 24%, 14% and 13%, respectively. These reflected on carbon emissions variation from microsites within land uses, of which 60% and 103% for carbon dioxide (CO_2) and methane (CH_4). We found that CO_2 emission rates were associated with moisture level ($r = -0.345$, $p < 0.05$), peat depth ($r = 0.444$, $p < 0.01$) and pH value ($r = 0.573$, $p < 0.001$) and CH_4 emission or uptake rates were found to be associated with water table level ($r = 0.458$, $p < 0.05$), peat depth ($r = 0.532$, $p < 0.001$) and CO_2 emission ($r = 0.491$, $p < 0.001$). The heterogeneity of peat properties within oil palm microsites could lead to the wide range of CO_2 and CH_4 emissions or uptake. Meanwhile, regeneration of above ground plant pool and decayed frond stacks at FF and FP microsites could increase soil moisture and probably carbon content that subsequently reduce CO_2 and CH_4 emissions during the rainy season. Therefore, consideration of these microsites could provide interim information for emission factors from tropical peatland oil palm plantations.

Keywords: *Land uses, Microsites; Peat properties, Carbon emissions, Emission factor*

INTRODUCTION

Peatlands are vital for global ecological functioning as well as for terrestrial carbon sequestration. These fragile ecosystems can potentially mitigate climate change (Lal, 2004). According to Wetland International, it is estimated the world carbon pool under this ecosystem amounts to 550 Gt, of which approximately 68.5 Gt C or 247,778km^2 is distributed in Southeast Asia (Page *et al.*, 2011). In Malaysia, it is estimated that this constitutes an approximate 9.1Gt carbon pool and accounts for around 60% of the total forest carbon pool (Page *et al.*, 2011). However, peatland areas have been exploited intensively through deforestation, drainage, clearance and burning. One of the main reasons for peatland exploitation in this region is oil palm plantation establishment. The current carbon loss from the conversion of pristine peatlands to oil palm plantation in Malaysia, using modelling integration of mass balance or subsidence with a water table level at 0.7 m based on various references (Comeau *et al.*, 2013; Couwenberg & Hooijer, 2013; Murdiyarso *et al.*, 2010; Page *et al.*, 2011), has been estimated at approximately 13.3 Mt C yr^{-1} (Carlson *et al.*, 2015) from 666,038 hectares (year 2009) of oil palm plantation areas.

During the last decades, the design of oil palm plantation layout has become important in maximising the productivity of Fresh Fruit Bunch (FFB) yields (Mutert *et al.*, 1999). However, while this artificial defragmentation of forest ecosystems does cause landscape-scale reduction of species richness, our understanding of the impacts of within-plantation management heterogeneity is limited. The potential for a certain level of natural regeneration to occur in microsites at lower harvesting or management activity intensities, such as areas of less weeding (Luskin & Potts, 2011) or frond piling (Henson *et al.*, 2012) has yet to be explored. Thus, each microsite has distinct characteristics in accordance to standard planting density and management practices with some facilitating the growth of above ground regeneration of plants (e.g. *Imperata* sp. or other herbaceous plants). As a consequence, these attributes could affect site specific peat properties and peat heterogeneity. Variation in microsites occurs across the timeline of a plantation cycle, not only within the management of the established plantation (e.g. fertiliser and liming application) (Hooijer *et al.*, 2012), harvesting of FFB and frond piling (Yahya *et al.*, 2011), but also in the variation of heavy machinery usage for land opening practices (van Asselen *et al.*, 2009; Wösten *et al.*, 1997).

These involve land clearance and construction of water canals to control the water table level (Hooijer *et al.*, 2012; Ritzema *et al.*, 2014) and land preparation for planting oil palm seedlings (Mutert *et al.*, 1999). As such, there is continuously occurring alterations to artificial microsites throughout an entire palm cycle due to cultural activities. Indirectly, carbon emissions through gas species such as carbon dioxide (CO_2) and methane (CH_4) are also affected by these attributes. The CO_2 and CH_4 emissions or uptake are strongly dependent on micro-topography, hydro-period, biophysical or above ground plant biomass (Jauhiainen *et al.*, 2014; Miao *et al.*, 2013; Moore & Dalva, 1997).

In this study, we determined the rates of CO_2 and CH_4 emission or uptake during the rainy season in November 2015 at the KLIA oil palm plantation, Sepang, Malaysia. These represent specific carbon emissions and uptake from microsites, such as harvesting path (HP), Under canopy (UC), Frond Pile (FP) and Far from Palm (FF). In line with this, we determined the soil physical properties at 20 cm peat depth. In this paper, we have also examined the statistical associations between the wide range of emission and uptake rates from each microsite within microsites and soil properties such as moisture content, temperature, peat soil depth, water table level, bulk density, loss on ignition and pH value.

MATERIALS AND METHODS

The study was conducted on sapric peat at three sites in the KLIA oil palm plantation, Sepang, Selangor that has been established for 15 years (2° 43' 52.1" N, 101° 39' 34.9" E), 9 years (2° 44' 31" N, 101° 39' 11.7" E) and 2 years (of 2nd generation) (2° 46' 6.5" N, 101° 39' 40.6" E). In this paper, all sites were denoted as LU1, LU2 and LU3 respectively. LU3 is a replanted site that was subject to a fire event. The peats thickness was 2.5 m, 1.3 m and 0.9 m at LU1, LU2 and LU3, respectively. Peat samples within the microsites were collected using a Russian corer (Eijkelkamp Agrisearch Equipment, Giesbeek, the Netherlands) at 20cm depths and consisted of a total of 36 samples (3 land uses x 4 microsites x 3 replicates). Fresh peat samples were analysed for bulk density (BD), pH value of 1:2.5 (peat: water) and loss of ignition (LOI) following the standard procedures as prescribed by (Melling *et al.*, 2014). Soil moisture and temperature were measured at 10 cm peat depth during gas sampling using a soil moisture probe (Procheck, Decagon Devices, Inc. Pullman, WA. USA).

Gas sampling was carried out during the rainy season, with an average of rainfall 13.3 mm day^{-1} as measured by KLIA weather station (2° 43' 51" N, 101° 42' 11" E). Apart from the UC microsite, all other microsites and associated chambers were placed > 3.0 m from the palm trunks in accordance with the distance of potential heterotrophic respiration as suggested by Dariah *et al.*, (2014). Gas samples were collected in the morning to mid-afternoon (10.00am – 2.00pm). CO_2 emissions were measured using the static closed chamber method following gas sampling protocols prescribed in the *GRACEnet* project (Parkin and Venterea, 2010). Four square closed chambers with open-ended base and sharp edges were fabricated using clear acrylic material measuring 20 cm (width) x 20 cm (height) x 20 cm (length). They were wrapped with aluminium foil to minimise the effect of temperature difference in the chamber. The top of the chamber was fitted with two sampling ports and were plugged with a rubber septum for gas sampling and thermometer installation. A battery operated fan was also attached inside the chamber to mix the air within the headspace. Before chamber placement, peat soil was cut accordingly to chamber area parameter using sharp knife to minimise possible leakage then leave for approximately 2 hours. The chamber was then inserted vertically into cut lines to the depth of 5.0 cm. A 20 mL gas sample was extracted from the chamber at T_0 to T_5 (1, 3, 6, 9 and 12 minutes) time intervals using a polypropylene syringe equipped with a three-way stopcock. The extracted gas sample was transferred into a 20 mL glass vial that has been pre-evacuated earlier and stored in a refrigerator prior to analysis.

Gas samples were analysed using a gas chromatograph (*Agilent model 7890A*) equipped with thermal conductivity detector (TCD) for CO_2 determination and flame ionization detector (FID) for CH_4 determination. For the GC calibration, standard mixed gases; 1 ppm of CH_4, 350 ppm of CO_2 and 50 ppm of N_2O, were used until reached approximately 90% of sensitivity value. The gas concentration in (ppm) was calculated using the ideal gas law: PV = nRT where: P = Atmospheric pressure (101,325 pa); V = Volume of headspace (m^3); n = Number of moles (mol); R = Universal Gas Constant law (8.314J. $K^{-1}mol^{-1}$) and T = Temperature in kelvin (K) with conversion number of 1 mol of gas to gram, CO_2 = 44.01 g and CH_4 = 16.02 g, respectively. The increase or decrease in the chamber concentration over time (hour, h^{-1}) by chamber volume (cm^3) from soil area covered (m^2) were fitted into linear regression (LR) with at least three sampling points, including T_0. The slope from the LR was considered as the rate of CO_2 emission or CH_4 emission or uptake and presented in mg CO_2 m^{-2} hr^{-1} or µg CH_4 m^{-2} hr^{-1}. Any outlier concentration point observed in the LR graph was omitted from the calculation. Another prerequisite for LR was that the regression line must be greater than R^2=0.60. Treatment differences for carbon emissions were analysed using analysis of variance (ANOVA) and means were compared using Tukey's Studentized Range at the 0.05 probability level. The relationship of peat properties and carbon emissions were tested using Pearson correlation coefficient with two-tailed at the 0.05 probability level. Both statistical analyses were analysed using SAS® University Edition statistical software.

RESULTS AND DISCUSSION

Results indicated that soil properties varied according to microsites within different land uses (Table 1). Water table levels were high and fluctuated between -10.0 cm to -42.0 cm at all microsites. The highest water table levels were found at LU3 and reflect the shallow peat of 0.9 m as the drainage system is controlled by the same water gate. Soil surface moisture at the three sites showed a clear pattern of high moisture levels ranging from 14%-31% and higher in LU1 as compared to LU2 and LU3. This results were also in line with (Luskin & Potts, 2011) as the oil palm plantation was drier in the 8 year old sites as compared to 22 years old oil palm. Our observation assumed that the high soil moisture in the older plantations, especially at the FF microsite was the result of increased above ground plant biomass (e.g. *Dryopteris* sp. and other herbaceous plants), which is also likely to affect the decay rate of oil palm fronds at the FP microsite. The incorporation of above ground and decayed plant biomass as "mulches" retain and preserve soil moisture by 35% as compared to bare land (Chalker-Scott, 2007).
Bulk density at 20 cm peat depth had a range of 0.10 - 0.23 g cm^{-3} for all microsites at difference land uses. The higher value was consistently measured at microsites with higher plant biomass and decayed oil palm fronds such as FF and FP. Higher bulk density was probably from root bulk attributes (Lestariningsih & Hairiah, 2013) or severe peat compression by the horizontal weight of frond stacks (Yahya *et al.*, 2011). Loss on ignition from all sites ranged from 84.8-95.5 %, and was clearly lowest at LU3. This indicated that peat at LU3 was mineralised due to the previous fire event. Furthermore, the pH values within microsites ranged from 3.51 to 4.09. The highest pH value was measured at the oldest oil palm plantation (15 years) and was significantly higher in the UC microsite within this plantation. This could be due to the level of mineralisation by active fertiliser and other agriculture inputs such as lime to enhance the palm plantation (Dariah *et al.*, 2014). In contrast, the soil temperatures had shown no differences regardless on microsites or age classes (29.7°C – 33.3°C).

Table 1: Peat characteristics from our study sites, means ± standard error, significant differences between microsites within land uses are indicated[1].

Land Use	Microsites	Moisture ($m^3.m^3$)	Temperature (°C)	Water Table (-) cm	Bulk Density ($g.cm^3$)	LOI (%)	pH Value
LU1	HP	0.36 ± 0.01^{Acb}	30.1 ± 0.4^{Aa}	40.3 ± 1.5^{Aa}	0.10 ± 0.00^{Bc}	96.32 ± 0.02^{Ba}	3.57 ± 0.08^{Ab}
	UC	0.34 ± 0.02^{Ac}	30.7 ± 0.3^{Aa}	33.3 ± 2.4^{Aa}	0.14 ± 0.00^{Bb}	88.04 ± 0.22^{Bb}	4.71 ± 0.05^{Aa}
	FP	0.63 ± 0.04^{Aa}	31.0 ± 0.1^{Aa}	39.3 ± 1.8^{Aa}	0.22 ± 0.01^{Ba}	86.64 ± 0.33^{Bcb}	3.61 ± 0.05^{Ab}
	FF	0.44 ± 0.00^{Ab}	31.0 ± 0.4^{Aa}	34.0 ± 3.1^{Aa}	0.15 ± 0.00^{Bb}	85.29 ± 1.08^{Bc}	3.74 ± 0.02^{Ab}
LU2	HP	0.46 ± 0.08^{Ba}	32.5 ± 1.3^{Aa}	32.5 ± 1.8^{Aa}	0.13 ± 0.00^{Ac}	96.10 ± 0.78^{Aa}	3.46 ± 0.09^{B}
	UC	0.15 ± 0.02^{Bb}	32.1 ± 1.4^{Aa}	37.3 ± 1.3^{Aa}	0.17 ± 0.00^{Ab}	83.17 ± 0.23^{Ac}	3.57 ± 0.19^{B}
	FP	0.48 ± 0.01^{Ba}	30.3 ± 0.6^{Aa}	36.3 ± 4.5^{Aa}	0.20 ± 0.00^{Aa}	95.86 ± 1.19^{Aa}	3.65 ± 0.02^{B}
	FF	0.42 ± 0.01^{Ba}	30.6 ± 0.9^{Aa}	36.7 ± 4.1^{Aa}	0.19 ± 0.01^{Aba}	90.76 ± 0.51^{Ab}	3.57 ± 0.06^{B}
LU3	HP	0.26 ± 0.02^{Ccb}	31.8 ± 0.2^{Aa}	20.0 ± 10.0^{Ba}	0.15 ± 0.00^{Ca}	87.09 ± 0.24^{Ca}	3.37 ± 0.11^{Bb}
	UC	0.18 ± 0.01^{Cc}	31.8 ± 0.2^{Aa}	23.0 ± 10.5^{Ba}	0.12 ± 0.00^{Cb}	85.5 ± 0.71^{Cba}	3.74 ± 0.12^{Bba}
	FP	0.34 ± 0.02^{Cb}	32.4 ± 0.9^{Aa}	23.3 ± 8.7^{Ba}	0.12 ± 0.00^{Cb}	86.59 ± 1.67^{Cba}	4.07 ± 0.02^{Ba}
	FF	0.44 ± 0.02^{Ca}	31.2 ± 0.5^{Aa}	25.3 ± 6.8^{Ba}	0.13 ± 0.00^{Cb}	82.61 ± 0.20^{Cb}	3.49 ± 0.10^{Bb}

[1]Uppercase (land uses) and lowercase (Microsites) superscript letters indicate significance of differences between peat characteristics (ANOVA $P < 0.05$).

The CO_2 emissions (Figure 1a) and CH_4 emissions and uptake (Figure 1b) in the oil palm plantations varied according to the land uses and microsites. The highest CO_2 and CH_4 emissions were measured from the oldest converted site; LU1 followed by LU2 and LU3, with the rate of emission 1368.6 ± 257.1 mg CO_2 m^{-2} hr^{-1}, 906.8 ± 64.7 mg CO_2 m^{-2} hr^{-1}, 739.6 ± 90.8 mg CO_2 m^{-2} hr^{-1}, and CH_4 emissions of 562.6 ± 70.6 µg CH_4 m^{-2} hr^{-1}, 496.9 ± 116.7 µg CH_4 m^{-2} hr^{-1} and -6.4 ± 13.0 µg CH_4 m^{-2} hr^{-1}, respectively. The negative value indicated CH_4 uptake. In fact, CH_4 emissions were positive correlated with CO_2 emissions by ($r=0.49$, $P = 0.002$). The lower carbon emissions in LU2 and LU3 were found to be influenced by the thickness of peat; 1.3 m and 0.9 m as compared to 2.0 m in LU1.

In addition, carbon emissions varied between microsites. The highest CO_2 emissions at UC were to be expected, being both a combination of microbial and root respiration and corresponding to low soil moisture level. This was confirmed by our results that indicated that the peat surface moisture content was negatively correlated with CO_2 emission ($r = -0.345$, $p=0.04$). Nevertheless, in the case of CH_4 emissions, the high emissions at UC was due to the gas exchange from CO_2, via integration with methanotrophs and methanogenesis activities at rhizosphere level in anaerobic conditions. This is probably caused by CO_2 and CH_4 potential exchange. Moore & Dalva (1997) found a strong positive relationship between aerobic CO_2 emission and anaerobic CH_4 ($r = 0.376$, $p < 0.001$). Thus, at high water table levels during the rainy season, CO_2 emissions subsequently could enhance CH_4 emissions from the anaerobic horizon even under moisture limited conditions.

The remaining microsites showed interesting trends with established understory vegetation and decayed fronds, such as FF and FP which exhibited lower carbon emissions than the HP and UC microsites. However, the reduced C emissions from microsites with established understory requires further investigation to explain the C balance associated with organic matter contribution and moisture content retention.

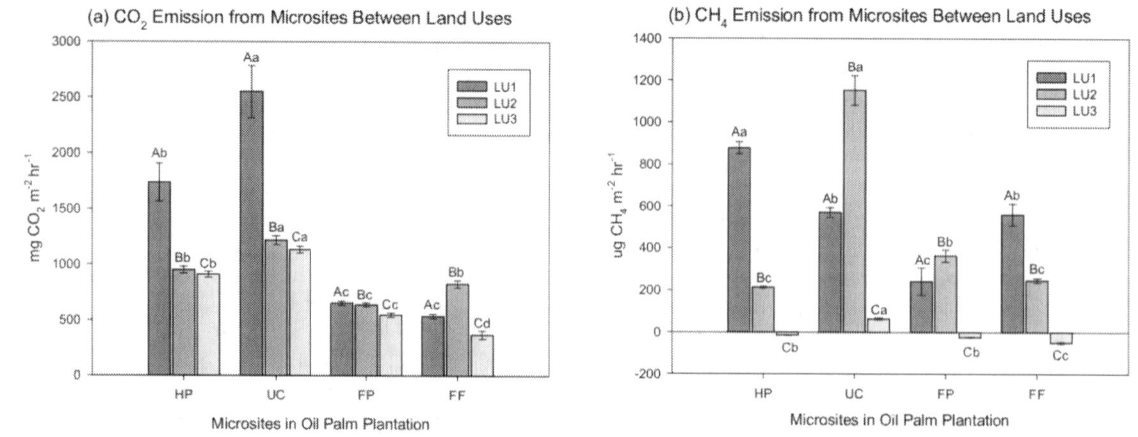

Figure 1(a): The CO_2 emission rates from microsites at various land uses.; (b): The CH_4 emission and uptake (represent by negative value) from microsites at various land uses.

CONCLUSION

The heterogeneity of peat properties within oil palm microsites could lead to a wide range in CO_2 and CH_4 emissions or uptake. CO_2 emission rates were associated with moisture level, peat depth and pH value. Meanwhile, CH_4 emission or uptake rates were associated with water level, peat depth and CO_2 emissions. In line with this, the management practices that lead to regeneration of understory plants or decaying frond stacks at FF and FP microsites could increase soil moisture and probably carbon content that subsequently reduce CO_2 and CH_4 emissions. However, it should be noted that these improvements cannot significantly mitigate the larger-scale extent of C loss associated with drainage-based agriculture on peat.

ACKNOWLEDGEMENTS

We would like to acknowledge the MARDI for funding this PhD studentship. Appreciation to the University of Nottingham Malaysia Campus (UNMC) as the host institution and MAB Agriculture-Horticulture Sdn. Bhd. (MAAH) for providing experimentation sites. Special thanks to Mr. Dzularsyil Aizat Shahrin for assisting during field works.

REFERENCES

1. Carlson, K. M., Goodman, L. K., & May-Tobin, C. C. (2015). Modeling relationships between water table depth and peat soil carbon loss in Southeast Asian plantations. *Environmental Research Letters, 10*(7), 074006. http://doi.org/10.1088/1748-9326/10/7/074006
2. Chalker-Scott, L. (2007). Impact of mulches on landscape plants and the environment-a review. *Journal of Environmental Horticulture, 25*(December), 239–249. Retrieved from http://www.gufc.org/wp-content/uploads/2010/12/Mulch review article (2).pdf
3. Comeau, L., Hergoualc'h, K., Smith, J., & Verchot, L. (2013). Conversion of intact peat swamp forest to oil palm plantation: effects on soil CO $_2$ fluxes in Jambi. Retrieved from http://www.cifor.org/publications/pdf_files/WPapers/WP110Comeau.pdf
4. Couwenberg, J., & Hooijer, A. (2013). Towards robust subsidence-based soil carbon emission factors for peat soils in south-east Asia, with special reference to oil palm plantations. *Mires & Peat, 12*, 1–13. Retrieved from http://pixelrauschen.de/wbmp/media/map12/map_12_01.pdf
5. Dariah, A., Marwanto, S., & Agus, F. (2014). Root- and peat-based CO2 emissions from oil palm plantations. *Mitigation and Adaptation Strategies for Global Change, 19*(6), 831–843. http://doi.org/10.1007/s11027-013-9515-6
6. Henson, I. E., Betitis, T., Tomda, Y., & Chase, L. D. C. (2012). The estimation of frond base biomass (FBB) of oil palm. *Journal of Oil Palm Research, 24*(DECEMBER), 1473–1479.
7. Hooijer, A., Page, S., Jauhiainen, J., Lee, W. A., Lu, X. X., Idris, A., & Anshari, G. (2012). Subsidence and carbon loss in drained tropical peatlands. *Biogeosciences, 9*(3), 1053–1071. http://doi.org/10.5194/bg-9-1053-

2012

8. Jauhiainen, J., Kerojoki, O., Silvennoinen, H., Limin, S., & Vasander, H. (2014). Heterotrophic respiration in drained tropical peat is greatly affected by temperature—a passive ecosystem cooling experiment. http://doi.org/10.1088/1748-9326/9/10/105013
9. Lal, R. (2004). Soil carbon sequestration to mitigate climate change. *Geoderma*, *123*(1-2), 1–22. http://doi.org/10.1016/j.geoderma.2004.01.032
10. Lestariningsih, I. D., & Hairiah, K. (2013). Assessing Soil Compaction with Two Different Methods of Soil Bulk Density Measurement in Oil Palm Plantation Soil. *Procedia Environmental Sciences*, *17*, 172–178. http://doi.org/10.1016/j.proenv.2013.02.026
11. Luskin, M. S., & Potts, M. D. (2011). Microclimate and habitat heterogeneity through the oil palm lifecycle. *Basic and Applied Ecology*, *12*(6), 540–551. http://doi.org/10.1016/j.baae.2011.06.004
12. Melling, L., Goh, K. J., Chaddy, A, & Hatano, R. (2014). Soil CO2 Fluxes from Different Ages of Oil Palm in Tropical Peatland of Sarawak, Malaysia. http://doi.org/10.1007/978-3-319-04084-4
13. Miao, G., Noormets, A., Domec, J. C., Trettin, C. C., McNulty, S. G., Sun, G., & King, J. S. (2013). The effect of water table fluctuation on soil respiration in a lower coastal plain forested wetland in the southeastern U.S. *Journal of Geophysical Research: Biogeosciences*, *118*(4), 1748–1762. http://doi.org/10.1002/2013JG002 354
14. Moore, T. R., & Dalva, M. (1997). Methane and carbon dioxide exchange potentials of peat soils in aerobic and anaerobic laboratory incubations. *Soil Biology and Biochemistry*, *29*(8), 1157–1164.
15. Murdiyarso, D., Hergoualc'h, K., & Verchot, L. V. (2010). Opportunities for reducing greenhouse gas emissions in tropical peatlands. *Proceedings of the National Academy of Sciences of the United States of America*, *107*(46), 19655–19660. http://doi.org/10.1073/pnas.0911966107
16. Mutert, E., Fairhurst, T. H., & von Uexküll, H. R. (1999). Agronomic Management of Oil Palms on Deep Peat. *Better Crops International*, *13*(1), 22–27. Retrieved from http://www.ipni.net/ppiweb/bcropint.nsf/$webindex/3144342CDB40DECD852568F60059A7DC/$file/i99-1p22.pdf
17. Page, S. E., Rieley, J. O., & Banks, C. J. (2011). Global and regional importance of the tropical peatland carbon pool. *Global Change Biology*, *17*(2), 798–818. http://doi.org/10.1111/j.1365-2486.2010.02279.x
18. Parkin T.B. and Venterea, R. T. (2010). Sampling Protocols. Chapter 3. Chamber-Based Trace Gas Flux Measurements. IN Sampling Protocols. R. F. Follet, editor. P. 3-1 to 3-9.
19. Ritzema, H., Limin, S., Kusin, K., Jauhiainen, J., & Wösten, H. (2014). Canal blocking strategies for hydrological restoration of degraded tropical peatlands in Central Kalimantan, Indonesia. *Catena*, *114*, 11–20. http://doi.org/10.1016/j.catena.2013.10.009
20. van Asselen, S., Stouthamer, E., & van Asch, T. W. J. (2009). Effects of peat compaction on delta evolution: A review on processes, responses, measuring and modeling. *Earth-Science Reviews*, *92*(1-2), 35–51. http://doi.org/10.1016/j.earscirev.2008.11.001
21. Wösten, J. H. M., Ismail, a. B., & Van Wijk, a. L. M. (1997). Peat subsidence and its practical implications: A case study in Malaysia. *Geoderma*, *78*(1-2), 25–36. http://doi.org/10.1016/S0016-7061(97)00013-X
22. Yahya, Z., Husin, A., Talib, J., Othman, J., Darus, S. Z., Ahmed, O. H., & Jalloh. (2011). Pores Reconfiguration in Compacted Bernam Series Soil. *American Journal of Applied Sciences*, *8*(3), 212–216. http://doi.org/10.3844/ajassp.2011.212.216

Abstract No: A-267

UTILIZATION OF AMELIORANTS FOR CORN AND THE EFFECT ON GHG EMISSIONS IN TROPICAL PEATLANDS

Eni Maftu'ah[1*], Herman Subagio[1] and Dedi Nursyamsi[2]

[1]*Indonesian Swampland Agriculture Research Institute (ISARI), Indonesia*
[2]*Indonesian Center for Agricultural Land Resources Research and Development (ICALRRD), Indonesia*

**Corresponding author: eni_balittra@yahoo.com*

SUMMARY

Low-emission ameliorant is needed to support sustainable agriculture on peatlands. The purpose of the study was to determine the effect of ameliorant formulation in reducing emissions in peatland. Research was carried in Kalampangan village, Palangkaraya at June – September 2013. The treatments were: (1) F1=80% chicken manure + 20% dolomite; (2) F2=20% chicken manure + 20% local farm weed + 20% purun tikus (*Eleocharis dulcis)* + 20% mineral soil + 20% dolomite; (3) F3=19% chicken manure + 71.5% mineral soil + 9.5% dolomite, and (4) control. The treatments were arranged in a randomized block design with four replications. Ameliorant dose used was 7.5 t ha^{-1}. The parameters were observed periodically in the form of CO_2 and N_2O emissions, ground water levels, soil Eh, as well as plant growth and yield. The results showed that ameliorant was able to reduce 20-31% of emissions of CO_2 and N_2O compared with control. Application of ameliorant could increase the plant growth and yield of maize as well as reduce emissions of CO_2 up to 24-36% and N_2O emission up to 19-31% compared to control. In peatlands, ameliorant from 80% chicken manure + 20% dolomite at dose 7.5 t ha^{-1} would increase the growth and yield of corn and decrease CO_2 emission up to 30% compared to control. However, the lowest N_2O emissions was indicated by the F3 ameliorant (19% chicken manure + 71.5% mineral soil + 9.5% dolomite), it can decrease N_2O emission up to 31% compared to control.

Keywords: *Ameliorant, GHG emissions, peat*

INTRODUCTION

Peatland area in Indonesia is around 14.91 million hectares, about 9-10 million hectares could otherwise be used for agriculture (Ritung, 2012). Agricultural activities in peatland needs attention to environmental aspects in addition to efforts to increase the peatland productivity. Utilization ameliorant absolutely necessary in order to improve the management of peatland productivity (Maftu'ah, 2012). Ameliorant was a material added to soil to improve the soil properties for the growth of plant (Attiken *et al.,* 1998). Soil ameliorant with lime at rates of 5 to 5.2 t ha^{-1} increased pH of saprik peat from 3.34 to 4.5 (Supriyo, 2006), whereas addition of 20 t ha^{-1} chicken manure increased corn yield (Utami, 2010). An ameliorant consisted of 16 t ha^{-1} mineral soil + 1.5 t ha^{-1} calcite + 3 t ha^{-1} dolomite + 80 kg ha^{-1} iron increased soybean yield 1.77 t ha^{-1} (Saragih, 1996). The ameliorant materials that rich with polyvalent cations was very effective for improving land productivity and stability of peat (Agus *et al.*, 2008).

Effectiveness ameliorant material depends on the quality of materials, especially the chemical composition of materials. Increasing the effectiveness of ameliorant can be done through the formulation of some materials ameliorant. Appropriate ameliorants both type and dosage are expected besides being able to improve the quality of peat but also able to reduce GHG emissions in peatlands. Information on the impact of the use of ameliorant to increase land productivity that low carbon emissions and N_2O in peatlands is still very limited. The aim of research to determine the effect of some type ameliorant against GHG emissions in peatlands to corn plants.

METHODS

Research carried on peat in the Kalampangan village, Palangkaraya at June – September 2013. The treatments were: (1) F1=80% chicken manure + 20% dolomite; (2) F2=20% chicken manure + 20% local farm weed + 20% purun tikus (*Eleocharis dulcis)* + 20% mineral soil + 20% dolomite; (3) F3=19% chicken manure + 71.5% mineral soil + 9.5% dolomite, and (4) control. The treatments were arranged in a randomized block design with four replications. Ameliorant dose used were 7.5 t ha^{-1}.

Research was performed using corn crops; whereby planting was done after 2 weeks from the application of ameliorant. Dose of NPK fertilizer used were 300 kg ha^{-1}. Supplementary urea fertilizer at a dose of 300 kg ha^{-1} gradually given on 2, 3 and 4 weeks after planting. Characterization of soil and ameliorant properties were performed before the research was conducted. The observed parameters were observed periodically in the form of CO_2 and N_2O emissions, ground water levels, soil pH and Eh, as well as plant growth and yield. The CO_2 and N_2O, pH and Eh were observed every month for 5 periods.

Gas sampling is done by injecting a volume of 10 ml. Gas samples taken in the morning (6:00 to 8:00) using the chamber closed. The time interval used in sampling is the 5th minute, 10, 15, 20, 25 and 30. The gas samples were analyzed using a gas chromatograph GHG models Varian 450. In this study, piezometers installed to measure ground water levels at the time of the study. Measurement of pH using a pH meter, whereas Eh meter used to measurement potential redoxs .

The rate of production of CO_2 and N_2O are calculated using the equations used by Khalil *et al.* (1991), as follows:

$$E = \frac{dc}{dt} X \frac{Vch}{Ach} X \frac{mW}{mV} X \frac{273{,}2}{(273{,}2+T)}$$

Description :

E	: Emmission CO_2/N_2O (mg/m^2/day)
dc/dt	: the change in CO_2 concentration over the change of time, which is the slope of the linear relationship of concentration and time (ppm/sec)
Vch	: Volume of tube (m^3)
Ach	: surface area of the tube (m^2)
mW	: The molecular weight CO_2/N_2O (g)
mV	: The volume of CO_2 / N_2O at a pressure of 1 bar (22,41 l)
T	: The average temperature during the gas sampling (^{o}C)

RESULT AND DISCUSSIONS

Characteristics of Peat

Peat characteristics that studied presented in Table 1. The results of chemical analysis showed that peat had very high acidity with pH H_2O of 3.49 and pH KCl of 3.33. H-exc concentration was 1.80 cmol$^{(+)}$ kg^{-1} and Al-exe was 2.50 cmol$^{(+)}$) kg^{-1}. This condition indicates that the leaching of base cations happened on the upper layer in high amounts, so that the exchange complex was saturated by acid cation ie H and Al. This condition was supported by pH KCl value about 3.33, which indicates the concentration of H^+ from the dissociation of organic acids were strong. It was estimated that the charge on peat 80 to 95% due to carboxylic and phenolic groups (Rachim, 1995).

Table 1: Characteristics of peat soil in the village Kalampangan, Central Kalimantan, in 2013

Peat	Value
pH H_2O	3.49
pH KCl	3.33
EC (mS cm^{-1})	0.279
Total N (%)	0.448
Organic C (%)	45.89
K-exe (cmol$^{(+)}$ kg^{-1})	0.342
Ca-exe (cmol$^{(+}$ /kg^{-1})	4.784
Mg-exe (cmol$^{(+)}$ kg^{-1})	6.068
CEC (cmol$^{(+)}$ kg^{-1})	70.00
Al-exe (cmol $^{(+)}$ kg^{-1})	2.50
H-exe (cmol$^{(+)}$/kg)	1.80
P_2O_5 (mg 100g^{-1})	0.134
Available P (mg kg^{-1})	15.45
The level of peat decomposition	Sapric

EC value of peat land that studied was low (0.279 mS cm^{-1}). Giving both inorganic fertilizers and ameliorant form of chicken manure on cultivated peatlands could increase the value of EC (Utami, 2010). This condition caused by fertilizers and ameliorant contain nutrients that were easily soluble and mineralized that produce cations and anions.

The content of organic C (45.89%) was relatively high. Peatlands that used research were peatland that has been cultivated intensively for 5 years. Total N content of about 0.448%, there has been a reduction in the total N levels when compared to total N on peatlands that have not been cultivated around 1.05 to 1.08% (Maftuah, 2012). Organic nitrogen in the peat was unusable for plant because the C/N ratio was high (Dohong, 1999). However, the cultivated peat decreased total N levels significantly (approximately 0.6%), so that the C/N ratio was high. This condition indicated that there had been a high nitrogen mineralization of peat material due to the conversion into cultivated land through the addition of materials ameliorant and fertilization (Suhardi, 2005).

Availability K in the studied peat classified as moderate (0.342 cmol$^{(+)}$ kg^{-1}). K levels at study sites were lower compared with the results of research Salampak (1999), which ranges (from 0.29 to 1.13 cmol $^{(+)}$ kg^{-1}). The content of K on peatlands varies depending on the level of decomposition and mineralization of peat. The process of mineralization of peat material may affect the availability of K (Koretsky *et al.*, 2007). According Andriesse, 1997 *in* Purnamayani *et al.* (2004) generally peatland deficiency K.

The Ca-exe concentration at the study site was low, it's related to low of soil pH. According to McLaughlin and Webster (2010) at the time of low pH, the Ca consumption would increase, so the Ca concentration decreased. Sulistiyanto *et al.* (2007) reported differences in the concentration of Ca-exe on peatland due to differences in input that given.

Acidity source of peat soil that studied dominated by H^+, while Al^{3+} usually only found on the top layer. The H ions derived from dissociation of organic acids which were usually dominated by fulvic and humic acid (Rachim, 1995). Organic acids contributed significantly to the low pH of peat (Charman, 2002). Organic materials have undergone decomposition having reactive groups, include carboxylic (-COOH) and phenolics (C_6H_4OH). These reactive groups dominate the exchange complex and could act as an organic acid that strong enough so that it could dissociate and produce H^+ in large quantities. The cause acidity on the top layer was also due to the presence of Al ions. Al concentration in acidic pH would increase, and it would decrease with increasing soil pH, because Al would precipitate formed $Al(OH)_3$ at pH 5 (Tan, 2010).

Ameliorant characteristics

Ameliorant materials used are; chicken manure, agricultural weeds, mineral soil, *purun tikus* grass and dolomite. Ameliorant characteristics of the formulations used are presented in Tables 2. Ameliorant that have the highest pH is a formula from 80% chicken manure+20% dolomite (F1). Similarly for the content of bases and the content of K and N. The highest of organic C found in ameliorant F2 that derived from several types of organic materials combined with dolomite and mineral soil.

Table 2: Characteristics of ameliorant that used

characteristics	**Ameliorant type**		
	F1 (80% chicken manure+20% dolomite)	**F2** (chicken manure, agriculture weed, mineral soil, purun tikus grass, dolomite each 20%)	**F3** (19% chicken manure + 71.5% mineral soil + 9.5% dolomite)
pH	7.23	6.72	6.76
C (%)	28.24	31.33	11.43
N (%)	1.68	0.56	0.27
K (%)	2.132	1.525	0.434
Na (%)	0.419	0.152	0.026
Ca (%)	19.417	16.388	9.694
Mg (%)	3.119	2.107	1.458
Fe (%)	0.667	0.486	0.260
P (%)	2,039	2.331	1.392
Water content (%)	12.20	88.02	21.44

Emissions of CO_2 and N_2O

The results of measurements of CO_2 emissions each month presented in Figure 1. At the first month occured an increase in CO_2 emissions in all treatments of 3526 mg/m^2/day to 4756-7435 mg/m^2/day. In observation of the 2nd month, emissions decline significantly until the end of observation. Giving ameliorant could reduce CO_2 emissions in peatlands. The use of of chicken manure could reduce GHG emissions and increase crop yields (Agus and Subiksa, 2008). The addition of ameliorant Fe^{2+} and rock phosphates that containing Fe cations high could reduce effect of toxin from organic acids, increase peat stability through formation of complex compounds and reduce carbon emission (Nelvia, 2009).

Ameliorant treatment given also able to reduce N_2O emissions. In general, an increase in N_2O emissions in the first month, and a decrease in the 2nd month to the end of the observation. Reduction of emissions at the 2nd month due to increased groundwater levels (Figure 2). As reported by Tauchnitz *et al.* (2008), an increase in N_2O emissions in peatlands due to declining groundwater levels so that conditions are more oxidative. According Maljanen *et al.* (2001), N_2O emissions not related to the age of the plant. In contrast to CO_2 emissions, the increase in CO_2 emissions from the soil due to land management could compensate by the absorption of CO_2 by plants. Increased N_2O emissions could occur due to the addition of urea (Reddy and DeLaune, 2008).

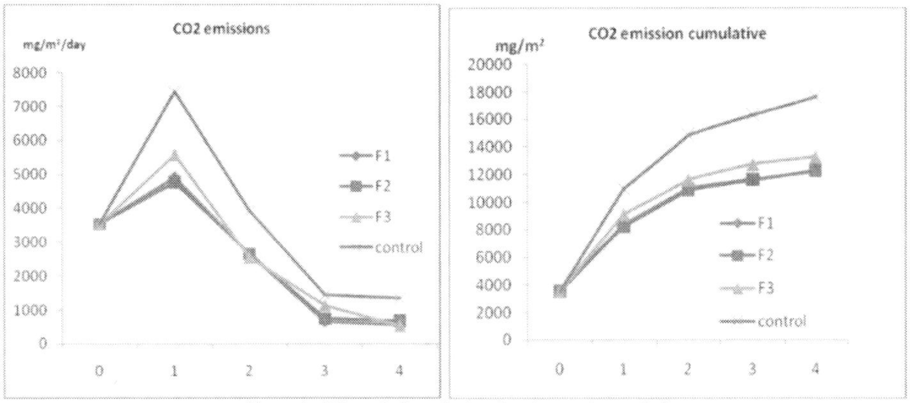

Figure 1: CO_2 emissions during the observation period

N_2O emissions that occur in the study area was relatively low at around 0.33 to 2.20 mg/m^2/day, equivalent to 0.12 to 0.80 g/m^2/year. Based on the measurements Syvasalo *et al.* (2002) in Nykanen (2003), emissions in agricultural land in peat for N_2O between 0,5 - 3,7g/m^2/yr. On peat N_2O emissions are low compared to CO_2 emissions. N_2O emissions of peatlands that have not been managed was low (<4 mg N_2O/m^2/yr), which is due to the availability of low nitrite (Nykanen, 2003)

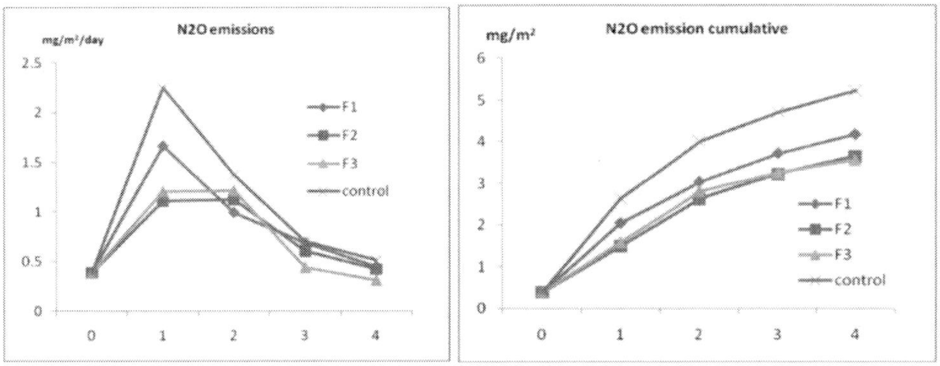

Figure 2: N_2O emissions during the observation period

Groundwater levels in the study site related to the amount of rainfall (Figure 3). Increased rainfall would be increased groundwater levels. The fluctuations of ground water level would affect the transformation and transport of nutrients in the peat. The decreasing water level will caused soil conditions more aerobic so could be increase the rate of decomposition and mineralization (Strakovo *et al.*, 2011). The difference will affect the decomposition and mineralization of CO_2 and N_2O emissions in the period of observation.

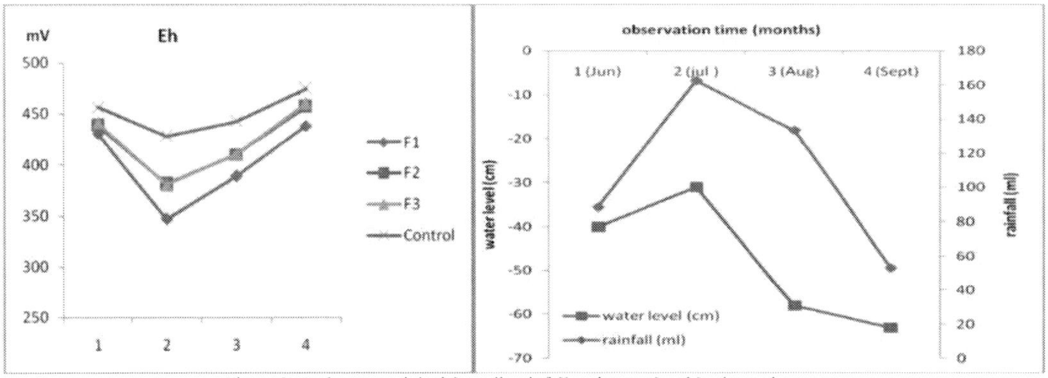

Figure 3: Redox potential of the soil, rainfall and water level in the study area

Soil productivity

Productivity (plant growth and crop yield) was improved by applying ameliorant. Until the 3rd month, ameliorant F1 (80% chicken manure + 20% dolomite) showed the highest plant height (Fig. 3a). Maize yield differs significantly among treatments (Fig. 3b). The highest corn production indicated by ameliorant F1 however not significantly different to F2.

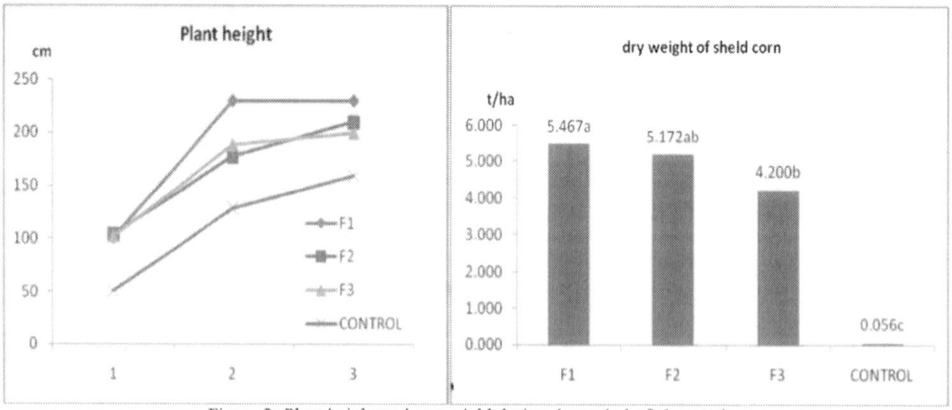

Figure 3: Plant height and corn yield during the period of observation

CONCLUSION

Application of ameliorant could increase the plant growth and yield of maize as well as reduce emissions of CO_2 up to 24-36% and N_2O emission up to 19-31% compared to control. In peatlands, ameliorant from 80% chicken manure + 20% dolomite, increase the growth and yield of corn and decrease CO_2 emission up to 30% compared to control. However, the lowest N_2O emissions indicated by the F3 ameliorant (19% chicken manure + 71.5% mineral soil + 9.5% dolomite), it's can decrease N_2O emission up to 31% compared to control.

REFERENCES

1. Agus, F. dan I.G.M Subiksa, 2008. Lahan Gambut: Potensi untuk Pertanian dan Aspek Lingkungan. Balai Penelitian Tanah. Badan Penelitian dan Pengembangan Pertanian. Bogor.
2. Attiken, W.P., P.W. Moody and T. Dickson, 1998. Field amelioration of acid soil in south – east Queenland. I. Effect of amendements on soil properties. *Australian. J. Agric. Res.* 49 (4);627– 638.
3. Charman, D. 2002. *Peatlands and Environmental Change*. Jhon Wiley & Sons. Ltd. England.
4. Dohong, S. 1999. Peningkatan produktivitas tanah gambut yang disawahkan dengan pemberian bahan amelioran tanah mineral berkadar besi tinggi. *Disertasi*. Institut Pertanian Bogor, Bogor. 171 halaman.
5. Khalil, M.A.K., R.A. Rasmussen, M.X. Wang and L. Ren, 1991. Methane emission from rice fields in China. *Environment Science Technology*. 25: 979-981.
6. Koretsky, C.M., M. Haveman, L. Beuving, A. Cuellar, T. Shattuck and M. Wagner. 2007. Spatial variation of redox and trace metal geochemistry in a minerotrophic fen. *Biogeochemistry*. 86;33-62.
7. Maftu'ah, E. 2012. Ameliorasi lahan gambut terdegradasi dan pengaruhnya terhadap produksi tanaman jagung manis. *Disertasi*. UGM. Yogjakarta.
8. Masganti, 2003. Kajian upaya meningkatkan daya penyediaan fosfat dalam gambut oligotrofik. *Disertasi*. Program Pascasarjana Universitas Gadjah Mada. Yogyakarta. 350 halaman.
9. Maljanen, M., J. Hytonen and P.J. Martikainen, 2001. Fluxes of N_2O, CH_4 and CO_2 on afforested boreal agricultural soils. *Plant and Soil* 231: 113-121.
10. McLauglin, J.W. and K.L. Webster, 2010. Alkalinity and acidity cycling and fluxes in an intermediate fen peatland in Nothern Ontorio. *Biogeochemistry*. 99:143-155.
11. Nelvia, 2009. Kandungan fosfor tanaman padi dan emisi karbon tanah gambut yang diaplikasikan dengan amelioran Fe^{3+} dan fosfat alam pada beberapa tingkat pemberian air. *J.Tanah Trop.*, Vol.14, No 3, 2009: 195-204.
12. Nykanen, H., 2003. Sensitivity of CH_4 and N_2O dynamics in Boral Peat Lands to Antropogenic and global changes. Doctoral Disertation. University of Kuopio. Finland.
13. Purnamayani R., S. Sabiham, Sudarsono dan L.K. Darusman, 2004. Nilai muatan titik nol (MTN) dan hubungannya dengan erapan kalium tanah gambut pantai Jambi dan Kalimantan Tengah. *J.Tanah Lingk.*, 6(2):75-82.
14. Reddy, K.R. & DeLaune R.D. (2008). WETLAND Science and Applications. CRC Press & Francis.774p.
15. Ritung. S., Wahyunto dan K. Nugroho 2012. Karakteristik dan Sebaran Lahan Gambut di Sumatera, Kalimantan dan Papua. *Dalam* Edi Husen, M. Anda, M. Noor, Mamat HS., Maswar, A. Fahmi dan Y. Sulaiman (ed.). *Pengelolaan Lahan Gambut Berkelanjutan*. Bogor: Balai Besar Litbang SDLP.

16. Rachim A. 1995. Penggunaan kation-kation polivalen dalam kaitannya dengan ketersediaan fosfat untuk meningkatkan produksi jagung pada tanah gambut. *Disertasi.* Program Pascasarjana IPB. Bogor. 268 hal.
17. Salampak, 1999. Peningkatan Produktivitas Tanah Gambut yang Disawahkan dengan Pemberian Amelioran Tanah Mineral Berkadar Besi Tinggi. *Disertasi.* Program Pascasarjana, IPB.Bogor.171 p.
18. Saragih E.S. (1996). Pengendalian asam-asam fenolat meracun dengan penambahan Fe(III) pada tanah gambut dari Jambi, Sumatera. *Tesis.* Program Pascasarjana IPB. Bogor. 172 halaman.
19. Suhardi, 2005. Pengaruh penggunaan tanah gambut sebagai lahan pertanian terhadap pola perubahan laju mineralisasi nitrogen. *Jurnal Ilmu-ilmu Pertanian Indonesia.* 7 (2);104-110.
20. Sulistiyanto, Y., H. Vasander, J. Jauhiainen, J.O. Rieley and S.H. Limin, 2007. Mineral nutrient content of water at different depths in peatland in Central Kalimantan, Indonesia. *Dalam*: J.O. Rieley, C.J. Banks and B. Radjagukguk (Eds). *Carbon-Climate-Human Interactions on Tropical Peatland; Carbon pools, fire, mitigation, restoration and wise use.* Proceedings of International Symposium and Workshop on Tropical Peatland. Yogyakarta. Pp77-82.
21. Strakova, P., R.M. Niemi, C. Freeman, K. Peltoniemi, H. Toberman, I. Heiskanen, H. Fritze and R. Laiho, 2011. Litter type affects the activity of aerobic decomposers in a boreal peatland more than site nutrient and water table regimes. *Biogeosciences.* 8; 2741-2755.
22. Supriyo, A. 2006. Dampak Penggenangan, Pengatusan dan Amelioran Terhadap Sifat Kimia dan Hasil Padi Sawah (Studi Kasus Pangkoh, Kalimantan Tengah). *Disertasi.* Program Pascasarjana. UGM. Yogyakarta.
23. Tan, K.H. 2010. Principles of Soil Chemistry. Fourth Edition. CRC Press. Taylor and Francis Group. New York. 362p.
24. Tauchnitz, N., R. Brumme, S. Bernsdorf, and R. Meissner, 2008. Nitrous oxide and methane fluxes of a pristine slope mire in the German National Park Harz Mountains. *Plant Soil* 303:131-138.
25. Utami, S. H. 2010. Pemulihan gambut hidrofobik dengan surfaktan dan amelioran, serta pengaruhnya terhadap serapan P jagung. *Disertasi.* UGM. Yogyakarta.

2.3: PEAT FOREST-WILDFIRE-IMPACT ON ENVIRONMENT & SOCIETY

Abstract No: A-099

DEMONSTRATION OF A COST-EFFECTIVE UAV SYSTEM TO MEASURE DEPTH OF BURN FOR EMISSIONS ESTIMATES FROM PEAT FIRES IN INDONESIA

Jake E. Simpson[1*], Thomas E. L. Smith[1], Mandar Trivedi[2] and Martin Wooster[1]

[1]King's College London Geography, UK
[2]Science and Innovation Directorate, DECC, UK

**Corresponding author: k1457927@kcl.ac.uk*

SUMMARY

Between 20 August and 8 November 2015, more than 51,000 ha of tropical peatlands burned within the Berbak landscape, Jambi, Sumatra. The fire ravaged primary and secondary forests, as well as peatland converted for plantation and industrial agricultural land. Estimating the GHG emissions from peat fires requires information on burned area (from satellites), and in situ data such as depth of burn, bulk density, and combustion completeness. Depth of burn is a critical term, but has so far only been quantified on sites on Borneo either using airborne LiDAR (which is very expensive) or, metal rods (which are much localized). There are also very few *in situ* studies characterizing burn scar characteristics, such as peat bulk density and combustion completeness. We demonstrate the use of unmanned air vehicle (UAV) photography for improving emissions estimates of individual burn scars. Firstly, we model depth of burn from microtopography of peatland burn scars, using "Structure from Motion" algorithms to build high-resolution (0.01m) 3D surface models which compare in accuracy to those from airborne LiDAR, for a fraction of the cost. Vertical and horizontal accuracy is assessed using control points from a GNSS, total station and terrestrial laser scanner. Once the emissions from individual burns have been estimated using this method, they can be extrapolated across the landscape using satellite imagery-derived land use/cover and burn history.

Keywords: *UAV, photogrammetry, peat fire, emissions, REDD+*

INTRODUCTION

The world's leaders met at COP21 in Paris in December 2015 and agreed that in order to avert dangerous global warming, the United Nations mechanism for Reducing Deforestation and forest Degradation (REDD+) through financial incentives should be implemented to halt deforestation and promote the conservation of natural forests, particularly in developing countries. This agreement was signed just a month after Indonesia experienced one of the most destructive wildfire episodes in modern history. Exacerbated by the El Niño event in Pacific, initial estimates suggest that over 4 million hectares of peatland burned in just three months, producing more daily emissions than the entire United States economy [1].

Compared to flaming surface vegetation fires, peat fires smoulder and are very long lived, and can spread deep into the peat layer causing significant subsidence as biomass is combusted [2]. To estimate GHG emissions from these fire events, the amount of peat consumed by the fire can be quantified by measuring the depth of burn, which, when multiplied by the burnt area and pre-fire bulk density, gives total mass of fuel load [3]. Burned area and peat bulk density can be measured using optical satellite data and ground sampling respectively [4–6], however to date depth of burn measurements have most successfully been retrieved using Light Detection And Ranging (LiDAR) equipment [7,8]. However, the costs of these surveys are prohibitive for land managers and scientists working in developing countries such as Indonesia. Furthermore, the most accurate way to measure depth of burn is to compare pre-burn and post-burn topography, therefore coordinating the survey at appropriate times may be difficult.

Unmanned air vehicles (UAVs) are increasingly becoming useful tools for environmental monitoring because they can be deployed quickly and easily (no specialist licensing or qualifications are required for research), they can cover a relatively large area compared to ground-based surveys, and they are considerably cheaper than manned aircraft surveys. Furthermore, image resolution from UAVs can be sub-centimetre [9]. Using overlapping, high resolution aerial photographs taken from different viewing angles, Structure from Motion techniques (SfM) can reconstruct accurate three-dimensional point clouds (similar to LiDAR), which can then be used to produce digital elevation models (DEM). DEM vertical accuracy and precision of other environmental UAV surveys is comparable to that of airborne LiDAR: [10] achieved 0.015 m accuracy (RMS = 0.220m) in a coastal setting by comparing UAV-

and terrestrial laser scanner-derived DEMs, [11] achieved between 0.004-0.04 m accuracy and 0.02-0.07 m precision for a river area and [12] generated DEMs accurate to 0.025 – 0.04 m in a dune environment.

Intergovernmental Panel on Climate Change (IPCC) Tier III guidelines provide carbon accounting methodologies for project-specific forest conservation projects which aim to fund their activities through carbon credit schemes (such as Verified Carbon Standard or American Carbon Registry). Project practitioners can claim carbon credits for avoided emissions from deforestation, forest degradation and fires within intact forests by using reference data from other, previously-impacted sites. The largest uncertainty in emissions estimates from peat fires comes from the depth of burn term [13]. Currently, REDD+ practitioners can use published depth of burn data collected in three studies from Central Kalimantan [2,7,13], but without the funds to hire expensive LiDAR equipment there is no accessible methodology available to conservationists for estimating depth of burn on an *ad hoc* basis.

UAVs can provide this flexibility for a fraction of the price of LiDAR, and here I demonstrate the feasibility of using a cheap drone, camera and ground control system (<$2000) in conjunction with a GNSS or total station for collecting highly accurate topographical data in peat burn scars.

METHODS

Our field site is situated in the Taman Hutan Raya protection forest in Jambi Province, Sumatra (from 104.0481, -1.3650 to 104.0603, -1.3725 WGS84 datum). The site was burned in early September 2015 (according to local reports, and MODIS MCD14ML hotspot data), having previously been densely forested. The site is situated approximately 100 m from a canal. The site was surveyed between 07-16 December 2015.

Ground surveys

We positioned 121 small- and 14 large ground control points (GCPs) in a rough 100 x 400 m grid (20 and 80 m spacing respectively) throughout our survey site. The X, Y, and Z coordinates of each GCP were recorded using a Leica GS10 Global Navigation Satellite System. To assess the relative accuracy of the GNSS points, we measured the local project coordinates of 70 GCPs using a total station. The total station was also used to measure the height profile of the deepest burns which had been submerged by the rising water table. In total we measured 47 transects through water-logged pits, extending approximately 1-2 outside of the submerged area.

We used a Reigl VZ-1000 terrestrial laser scanner (TLS) to create a control point cloud of the study site to assess the accuracy of the UAV point cloud. We took twelve 360° scans which covered approximate 60% of the study area, however the ground coverage was much less owing to its comparatively low scanning height. We positioned reflective targets so that they were scanned from multiple positions, and their X, Y, Z coordinates were recorded with the GNSS for geo-referencing purposes. The 12 point clouds were joined together with a reported accuracy of 0.03m.

UAV measurements

For the aerial survey I used a DJI innovations Phantom 2 because of its price (<$500), readiness to fly (i.e. it is light and transportable, as well as easy to fly), and because it is one of the most popular UAV on the market, spare parts are easy to find. In conjunction with the DJI iPad ground station, up to 16 waypoints, flight altitude, heading and speed can be pre-programmed and uploaded from an Apple iPad via bluetooth and 2.4G wireless data link to the UAV. This functionality makes the Phantom 2 a suitable platform for aerial photogrammetry because the flight path can be planned in advance to ensure that there is adequate photo overlap for the SfM algorithm to capture ground microtopography. Furthermore, the aircraft's position can also be tracked on the iPad's screen in real-time, meaning that for longer and higher flights, the pilot knows where the aircraft is relative to his or her position. Once the flight path is uploaded to the Phantom 2, it automatically takes off and flies the predetermined route.

I strapped a Ricoh GR to the bottom of the Phantom, with a slice of foam 5 cm thick to absorb the vibrations from the propellers. The Ricoh GR was used because it is relatively cheap (<$500), light (245 g with battery), has a wide-angle lens), has a large, high-sensitivity sensor, and can also produce uncompressed 12-bit RAW images in DNG format (so there is no loss of information). The camera is ideally suited to photogrammetry because it can be focussed manually (so that the ground is always in focus even if vegetation is present), produces high-resolution photos with excellent colour rendition, and has an in-built intervalometer, so that photos can be taken automatically at regular intervals. Before each flight, the camera was pointed towards the ground and the aperture, ISO, shutter speed and focus distance were adjusted so that the histogram was normally distributed.

To test how altitude affects point cloud accuracy, I flew 8 UAV surveys at different altitudes over the site. I flew the higher-altitude surveys first to visually assess the UAV clearance above standing trees, and gradually reduced the survey altitude. To assess how camera angle might affect accuracy, I used two foam wedges to mount the camera onto the UAV; one pointing the camera downwards (nadir) and the other pointing the camera forwards 20° (oblique). Using an oblique shooting angle has been shown to reduce systematic point cloud errors [14].

RESULTS

A subset of 57 GCPs were used to register the point clouds, these were evenly distributed across the survey site. The remaining 78 GCPs were used as control points, to assess the registration accuracy. The root mean squared deviation in all axes was 0.05 m, 0.03 m in the XY axes and 0.04 m in the Z axis.

Both the TLS and UAV point clouds were clipped to an area of 1.4 ha in XY plane for control 1 and 2 the area in which the ground was extensively covered by the TLS scans. For control 3, the area was clipped so that only areas close to the scan positions were included. All point clouds were sectioned along the Z axis, 2 m above and below a common central Z point, resulting in scans of equal size in all axes. Over 400 million UAV point cloud data points were compared against each TLS control mesh. The mean distances and standard deviation between UAV reference and TLS control scans were calculated by Gaussian distribution fitting of the differences (Figure 1). An analysis of variance and post-hoc Tukey's Honestly Significant Difference test demonstrate that the mean differences of all clouds against all controls were significantly different.

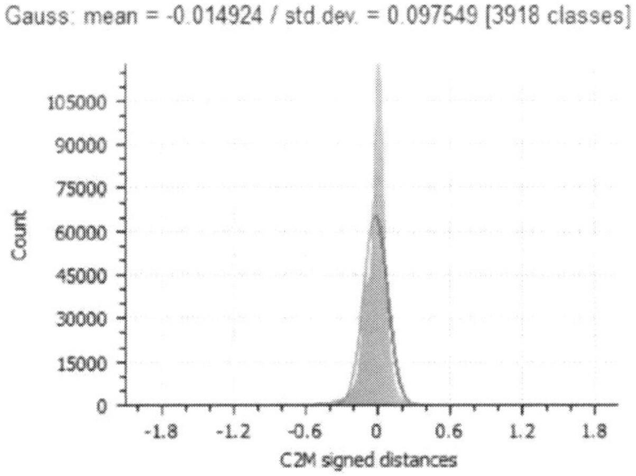

Figure 1: Cloud to mesh signed differences (m) for 60m oblique flight

The errors can be represented on the clouds themselves to highlight where the largest errors occur (Figure 2). The largest errors are found towards the edge of the control area, specifically around the deepest parts of the pits. Furthermore there are large errors (>25cm) in the centre where fallen trees or vegetation has been over estimated by the UAV or underestimated by the TLS. UAV point clouds produce errors in the pits which were scanned by the TLS from one direction, and these are mainly situated around the Southern and Eastern edges of the survey area. These errors are further propagated by the presence of water in the pits, as there are no returns detected by the TLS from water. There is also a widespread area of systematic error for ground returns in the Northern section between the line of scan positions 10-12 and the edge of the survey area. However, most of the points are within 0.1 m of the control layer, (~12% < -0.1 m, ~5% > 0.1 m).

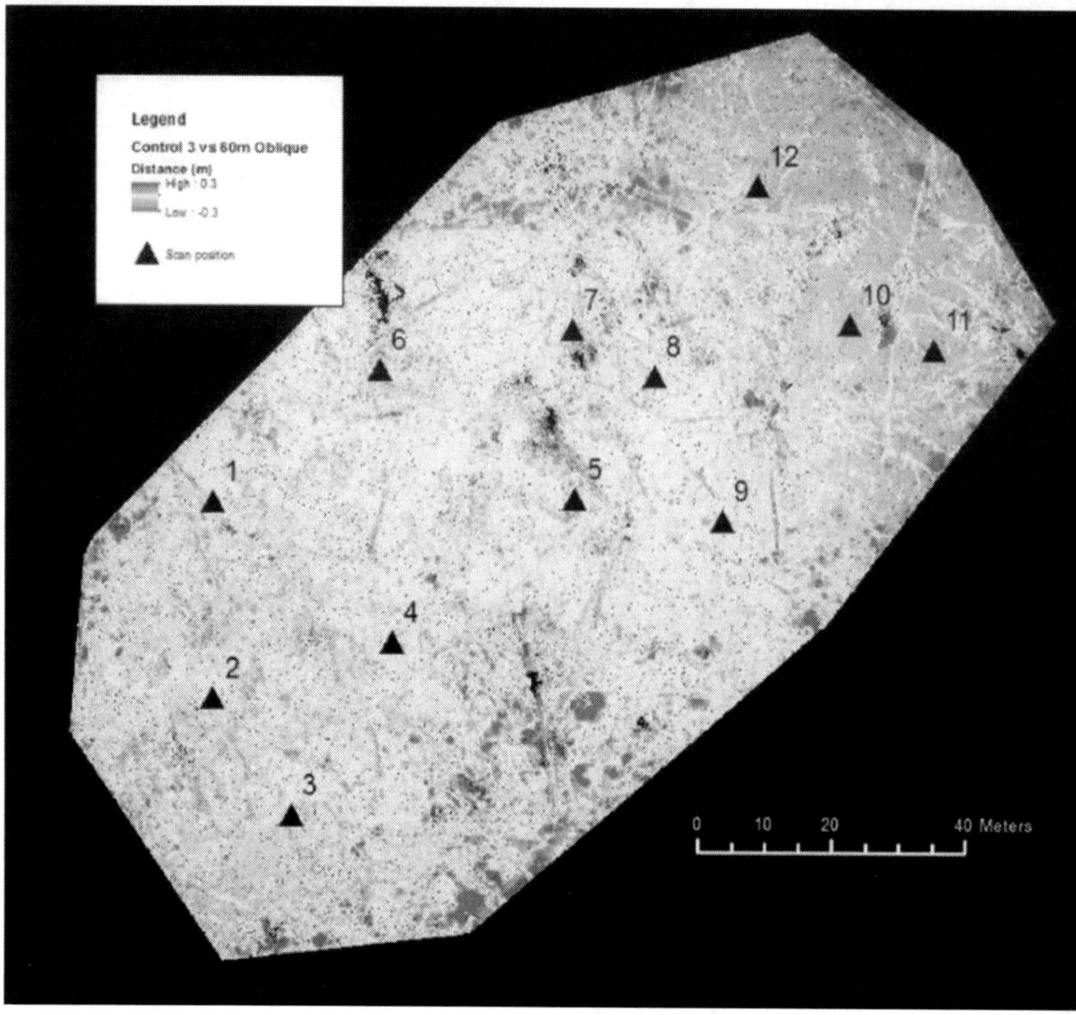

Figure 2: Distribution of errors across the survey site. There are systematic errors around scan positions 10-12, which are most likely a result of poor registration of the laser scanners (as these positions were not recorded using GNSS). High negative errors in some of the pits around the edges (South of scan positions 3-5) are the result of the pits being outside of the coverage area of the TLS.

DISCUSSION

Implications for emissions estimates

From our initial results, we have demonstrated that although each survey flight produced significantly different accuracies, they were all accurate to within 10 cm (including fallen vegetation). In fact the most accurate results came from the highest altitude flight, which demonstrates that firstly, the ground coverage could be scaled up markedly (providing sufficient sideways and forward overlap), secondly, this method can be used safely in forests with intact, tall standing trees. With more time to process the data to exclude fallen vegetation, we anticipate even higher levels of accuracy (because most of the error is caused by the different coverage of TLS and UAV of residual vegetation).

We have assessed the accuracy of the UAV point clouds and have created very accurate high-resolution point clouds and DEMs, especially of the peat surface. To date (17 March 2016), we have not finalized the methodology for estimating emissions. The deepest burns are situated around the roots of trees where the peat combusted completely, whereas much of the site was mostly affected by surface burns or charring (evident from residual vegetation that was not fire-affected, as well as no evidence of ash). Using optical data from two previous field campaigns, we demonstrate that there is large combustion heterogeneity within burn scars, and argue that by using the range between local height minima and maxima to establish depth of burn, it will be possible to estimate emissions from peat fires. We anticipate to have finalized this methodology by the time of the IPC 2016 conference.

Here we compare the practicalities of the UAV and TLS systems for measuring depth of burn in peatlands. It took a total of 18 man hours to set up the GCPs needed for the UAV survey. Subsequent to this, a further 2 man hours was needed to fly the drone for a complete survey. The TLS scans took 4 afternoons with three operators, at a total of 48 man-hours. Furthermore, the UAV weighs 4kg with its carry case and special batteries, compared to over 30kg for the TLS. In terms of out-right costs, the TLS costs >$110,000 compared to ~$2,000 for the UAV and camera and software licenses (however, both the UAV and TLS system require a GNSS for GCP registration, these can be rented from survey companies, or bought second hand for <$7,500). The cost ($) multiplied by man effort (hr) and weight (kg) (user inputs) divided by usable coverage area (outputs) the UAV survey requires 0.01 $kghr m^{-2} compared to the TLS which requires 13.01 $kghr m^{-2}. This shows that the UAV system can provide an efficient, cheap and flexible alternative to terrestrial laser scanning systems and is more suitable to use in rugged, remote and challenging conditions in burned peat swamp forests. While UAV coverage might be much lower than airborne LiDAR, this method might be the only affordable option to conservationists and REDD+ practitioners without large budgets.

ACKNOWLEDGEMENTS

The authors would like to thank Zoological Society of London for their additional funding, in-country support and efforts for helping to develop this project. We also express our deepest gratitude to Universitas Indonesia Research Centre for Climate Change for their sponsorship and support. This project is Natural Environment Research Council funded.

REFERENCES

1. World Resources Institute. Indonesia's Fire Outbreaks Producing More Daily Emissions than Entire US Economy. (2015). Available at: http://www.wri.org/blog/2015/10/indonesia%E2%80%99s-fire-outbreaks-producing-more-daily-emissions-entire-us-economy. (Accessed: 14th January 2016)
2. Usup, A., Hashimoto, Y., Takahashi, H. & HAYASAKA, H. Combustion and thermal characteristics of peat fire in tropical peatland in Central Kalimantan, Indonesia. *Tropics* **14,** 1–19 (2004).
3. Hiraishi, T. *et al.* 2013 Supplement to the 2006 IPCC Guidelines for National Greenhouse Gas Inventories: Wetlands. (2014).
4. Hooijer, A. *et al.* Subsidence and carbon loss in drained tropical peatlands. *Biogeosciences* **9,** 1053–1071 (2012).
5. Mazher, A. Comparative analysis of mapping burned areas from landsat TM images. *J. Phys. Conf. Ser.* **439,** 012038 (2013).
6. Gaveau, D. L. A. *et al.* Major atmospheric emissions from peat fires in Southeast Asia during non-drought years: evidence from the 2013 Sumatran fires. *Sci. Rep.* **4,** 6112 (2014).
7. Ballhorn, U., Siegert, F., Mason, M. & Limin, S. Derivation of burn scar depths and estimation of carbon emissions with LIDAR in Indonesian peatlands. *Proc. Natl. Acad. Sci.* **106,** 21213–21218 (2009).
8. Reddy, A. D. *et al.* Quantifying soil carbon loss and uncertainty from a peatland wildfire using multi-temporal LiDAR. *Remote Sens. Environ.* **170,** 306–316 (2015).
9. Colomina, I. & Molina, P. Unmanned aerial systems for photogrammetry and remote sensing: A review. *ISPRS J. Photogramm. Remote Sens.* **92,** 79–97 (2014).
10. Mancini, F. *et al.* Using Unmanned Aerial Vehicles (UAV) for High-Resolution Reconstruction of Topography: The Structure from Motion Approach on Coastal Environments. *Remote Sens.* **5,** 6880–6898 (2013).
11. Woodget, A. S., Carbonneau, P. E., Visser, F. & Maddock, I. P. Quantifying submerged fluvial topography using hyperspatial resolution UAS imagery and structure from motion photogrammetry: SUBMERGED FLUVIAL TOPOGRAPHY FROM UAS IMAGERY AND SfM. *Earth Surf. Process. Landf.* **40,** 47–64 (2015).
12. Harwin, S. & Lucieer, A. Assessing the Accuracy of Georeferenced Point Clouds Produced via Multi-View Stereopsis from Unmanned Aerial Vehicle (UAV) Imagery. *Remote Sens.* **4,** 1573–1599 (2012).
13. Konecny, K. *et al.* Variable carbon losses from recurrent fires in drained tropical peatlands. *Glob. Change Biol.* **22,** 1469–1480 (2016).
14. James, M. R. & Robson, S. Mitigating systematic error in topographic models derived from UAV and ground-based image networks. *Earth Surf. Process. Landf.* **39,** 1413–1420 (2014).

Abstract No: A-113

ESTIMATION OF FIRE AFFECTED AREAS AND CARBON EMISSIONS ON THE BASIS OF SENTINEL-1

Sandra Englhart[1*], Matthias Staengel[1] and Florian Siegert[1, 2]

[1]Remote Sensing Solutions GmbH, Germany
[2] Biology Department II, GeoBio Center, Ludwig-Maximilians-University, Germany

**Corresponding author: englhart@rssgmbh.de*

SUMMARY

Vast and disastrous forest and peat fires affected Sumatra and Borneo during the dry season in 2015, putting Indonesia on track to be one of the world's largest carbon emitters. The region was experiencing a very strong El Niño climate phenomenon, similar or even stronger compared with the severest ever recorded in 1997/1998. El Niño leads to rainfall anomalies and a more severe dry season in Indonesia, resulting in increased fire occurrence. Peat fires smoulder underground and produce thick haze which hampers detection of burned areas using optical remote sensing sensors. The burn scar assessment by multispectral imagery is not only hampered by haze but also frequent cloud cover during the wet season which directly starts after the fire season. Active SAR (synthetic aperture radar) systems are daylight and weather independent as the signal can penetrate clouds, haze and smoke. Therefore, these sensors are very suitable for delineating burned areas in the tropics. ESA's Sentinel-1 satellite continuously acquires C-band data. These were used to assess the burned areas in a peatland dominated landscape in Central Kalimantan by comparing images before and after the fire season. As changes in vegetation cover strongly affects C-band SAR backscatter, different ratios were calculated based on pre- and post-fire images. The results clearly showed burned areas due to a decrease in backscatter after the removal of vegetation cover by fire. In a next step, the delineated burned areas were intersected with available pre-fire land cover classification maps and peat layers. This allowed the production of integrated carbon emission estimation within our study area using literature or field and airborne-LiDAR derived emission factors.

***Keywords**: GHG emissions, carbon, SAR, Sentinel-1, burned area*

INTRODUCTION

Vast and disastrous forest and peat fires raged across Indonesia in 2015, putting Indonesia on track to be one of the world's largest carbon emitters that year. In particular, peat fires smoulder underground and produce thick haze which can drift into neighbouring countries like Malaysia, Singapore and Thailand. The thick haze causes not only economic damage but also pollution by raising the Pollutant Standards Index (PSI) to record levels exceeding the value 300, which is rated as "hazardous" and thus a great risk for public health. In Central Kalimantan, an alarming PSI value of 1,801 was recorded on 1st October 2015. It is assumed that fires are mostly started deliberately and illegally for developing large-scale plantations for pulpwood and oil palm. Drainage of peatland areas increases susceptibility to fires, which is further enhanced by prolonged El Niño-induced drought periods. In 2015, the region was experiencing a very strong El Niño climate phenomenon similar or even stronger compared to the severest one recorded in 1997/1998. Indonesia's emissions during the record forest and peat fires of 1997 are estimated between 0.81 and 2.57 Gt (Gigatonnes) of carbon, which is equivalent to 13-40% of the entire world's annual fossil fuel emissions (Page *et al.*, 2002). More recent estimates from the Global Emission Fire Database indicate that Indonesia's fire emissions from 1997 released app. 4.27 Gt of carbon dioxide, equivalent to 1.63 Gt of carbon. As of mid-October 2015, Indonesia's fire emissions from 2015 had already exceeded 0.33 Gt of carbon (GFED 2015).

These estimates contain a substantial amount of uncertainty related to a complex fire situation and the fact that they are based on fire detections derived from MODIS. NASA's two MODIS sensors, situated on the Aqua and Terra satellites, provide active fire data every day by applying a fire and thermal anomalies algorithm (Giglio *et al.*, 2003). In this case, thermal anomalies or active fires represent the centre of a 1km pixel containing one or more fires within this area. This is the most basic fire product in which active fires and other thermal anomalies, such as volcanoes, are identified. However, thick haze and clouds prevent the detection of active fires which in turn result in substantial underestimation of fire events. Fires are only detected in areas where the blanket of haze is sufficiently thin.

In an attempt to monitor and contain these fires, ground teams assess the extent and intensity of fire damage. However, their reports describe difficulties in measuring impacts onsite and underline the need for additional

management techniques. In contrast, remote sensing approaches appear to present a viable solution for fire management. Modern European satellites such as Sentinel-1 can penetrate thick haze, for example, and detect damage caused by recent fires on the ground. Similarly, valuable multispectral imagery of regions before and after fires can be acquired by Sentinel-2 and implemented in time series analyses.
The aim of this study is to produce comprehensive burned area maps derived from Sentinel-1 imagery using a robust and highly automated object-based classification approach. Two Sentinel-1 full-coverage, pre- and post-fire acquisitions were used to detect burn scars on the basis of different ratios.

METHODS

In a first step, the fire season of 2015 was analysed on the basis of monthly precipitation and MODIS active fire hotspot data. This indicated the approximate period of the fire season even if not all fires were detected by MODIS hotspot data.

The latest MODIS Collection 5 hotspot data are provided by the University of Maryland's Fire Information for Resource Management System (FIRMS) as point shape files. Each hotspot/ active fire detection represents the centre of a $1km^2$ pixel flagged as containing at least one active fire. The pixel centre, in other words the derived shapefile point location, is not necessarily the real location of the active fire event due to the coarse resolution of the data. Based on this information, two complete Sentinel-1 coverages of Kalimantan (Indonesian Borneo), Sumatra and West Papua, were downloaded: one before May-July and one after the October/November fire catastrophe (app. 150 scenes). Even if MODIS does not capture all active fire events, together with the precipitation data it gives an indication of the duration of the dry season and fire occurrence. It is important to carefully select Sentinel-1 images for classification of burned areas, since the moisture content of the vegetation has a considerable influence on backscatter. Therefore, it is important to select the images shortly before and after the dry season to ensure similar moisture content.

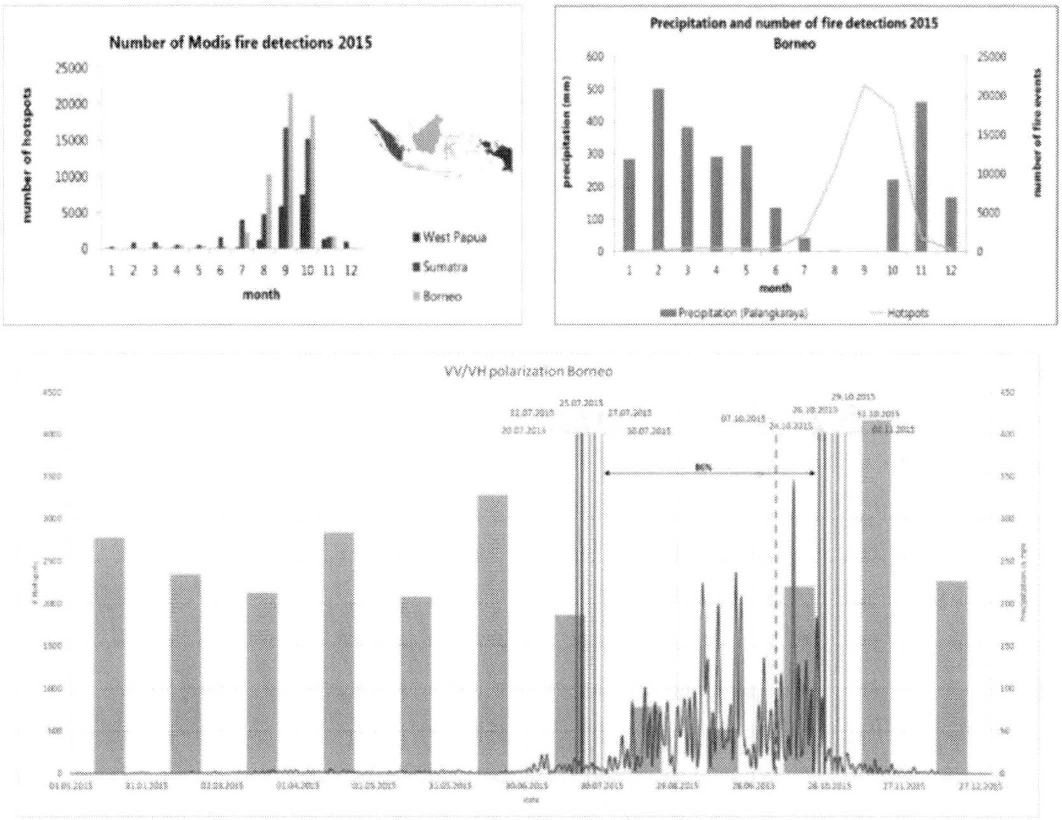

Figure 1: MODIS active fire hotspot data for fire season analysis over the whole study area (upper left) and in combination with monthly precipitation data for Borneo (upper right). The lower graph depicts daily hotspots, monthly precipitation and available Sentinel-1 acquisition dates for the different orbits.

The pre-processing of Sentinel-1 imagery included radiometric calibration (□^{0} backscatter coefficients), geometric correction, co-registration and speckle filtering using the Sentinel-1 Toolbox. To reduce speckle in the SAR scenes, a refined Lee filter with a 7x7 moving window was applied.

A robust, object-based classification approach was developed for a test site in Central Kalimantan using Trimble's eCognition software in order to automatically classify burned areas in the pre- and post-fire acquisitions, excluding regions where slopes exceed 15°. These regions cannot be reliably monitored by Sentinel-1 data due to physical constraints and effects of the SAR methodology, and thus were not assessed. In the light of these constraints, these regions are assumed to be unaffected by fire. This assumption is supported by the low number of hotspots (<1%) in areas with slope >15°. In addition to the backscatter images, different ratios were calculated in order to yield more information and improve classification accuracy.

These inputs (backscatter and ratios) allow a robust classification approach that can be applied to all scenes without any parameter adaptation. It will be applied in a next step to the whole target area (Sumatra, Kalimantan, West Papua), allowing investigation of the full burned area extent.
Related fire emissions are then assessed by intersecting classified burned areas with pre-fire land cover classifications and literature or field and airborne-LiDAR derived emission factors.

RESULTS

In a first step, pre- and post-fire Sentinel-1 images in VH and VV polarisation were compared and visually analysed for burned area assessment (Figure 2). Areas affected by fire are depicted in purple in the Landsat image from 23.11.15. The post-fire Sentinel-1 images from 24.10.15 show that burn scars can be clearly identified in images acquired shortly after the fire event. Areas affected by fire are more explicit in VV polarisation than in VH polarisation. This fact is also obvious in the RGB composite from this date. The ratio image in the upper right highlights changes between both acquisitions and areas affected by fire appear in orange to brown depending on fire intensity.

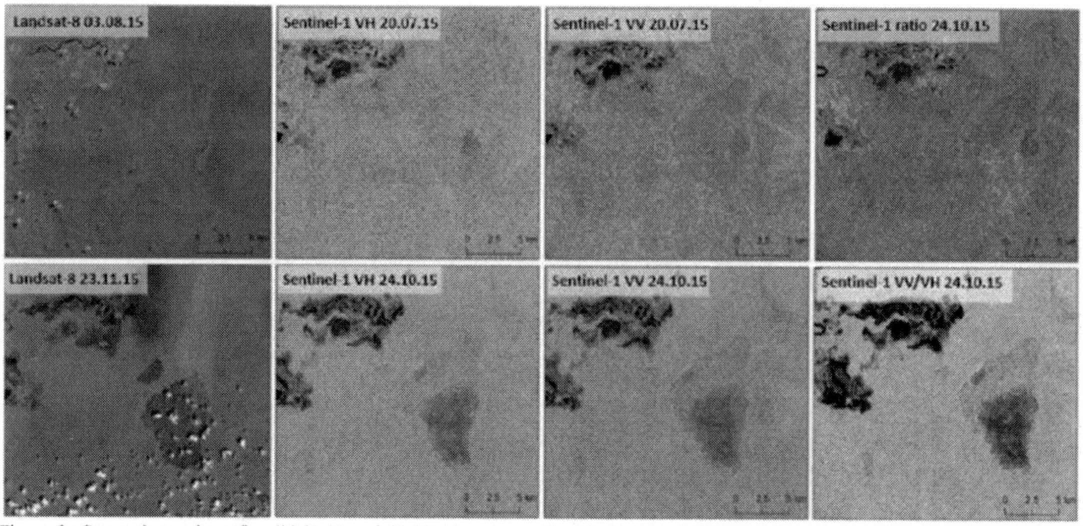

Figure 2: Comparison of pre-fire (20.07.15 and 03.08.15) and post-fire (24.10.15 and 23.11.15) Landsat-8 and Sentinel-1 images and image composites.

Initial burned area assessment results, produced using different ratios based on pre- and post-fire Sentinel-1 VV and VH polarised images, indicate that burned areas can be evaluated based on these image data. Figure 3 depicts a comparison of pre- and post-fire Sentinel-1 images and ratios compared to MODIS hotspots. The images in the upper panel are RGB composites based on VH and VV polarisation. Areas that have burned between image acquisition dates appear very dark in the October image as the change in vegetation cover reduces backscatter. The ratio image calculated on the basis of pre- and post-fire Sentinel-1 images is depicted in the lower left. Blueish areas represent forested and vegetated areas that didn't change between both acquisitions. Burn scars are delineated in light orange to brown depending on fire intensity and oil palm plantations appear are shown in light green.

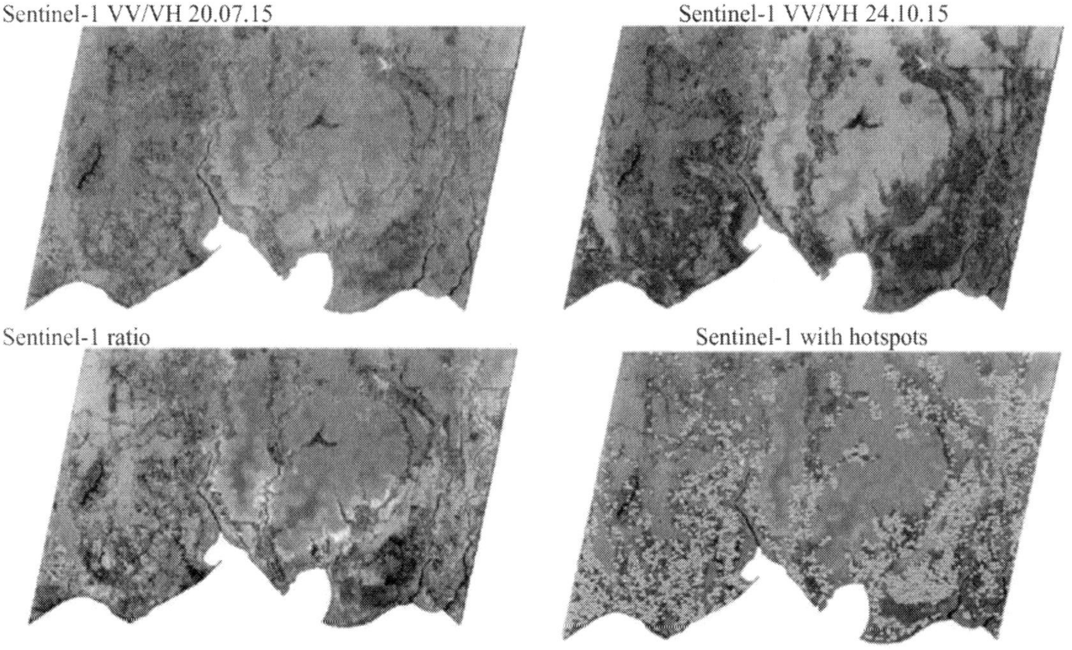

Figure 3: Sentinel-1 pre-(left) and post-fire (right) images (RGB: VV, VH, VV) from 20.07.15 and 24.10.15, respectively (upper panel). The Sentinel-1 ratio image between both acquisition dates also with hotspots in yellow (right) are depicted in the lower panel.

Figure 4 depicts a detail of Figure 3 around an oil palm plantation. The Sentinel-1 ratio image, MODIS hotspots and a preliminary burned area classification compared to a Landsat scene is shown. Fresh burned areas appear in orange in the ratio image and in purple in the Landsat scene. Intersection with an available oil palm plantation concession layer shows that only the area around the plantation and not inside the plantation has been burned. The preliminary classification results indicate that the approach, which is currently under development, is highly suitable for burned area delineation.

Figure 4: Initial burned area classification derived from Sentinel-1 around an oil palm plantation compared to MODIS hotspots and Landsat8 image acquired on 22. October 2015.

DISCUSSION AND CONCLUSIONS

Initial results presented here demonstrate that Sentinel-1 can feasibly detect burned areas. A special advantage of SAR systems is that the detection of burned areas is not hampered by clouds, haze or smoke, all of which often occur in tropical regions during fire events. It is important to note that this approach captures not only burned areas but also other changes that reduce the backscatter signal, such as clear cuts. Currently, Sentinel-1A satellite is operational and the launch of Sentinel-1B is planned for 22 April 2016. Each satellite has an exact repeat period of 12 days which allows timely monitoring of fire impact and burn scar assessment. Sentinel-1C and Sentinel-1D satellites are currently planned and will further improve the revisit cycle.

Furthermore, it is important to select appropriate pre- and post-fire event SAR scenes such that a similar moisture content of the vegetation is ensured. Water has a strong influence on the SAR backscatter signal as it changes the dielectric constant. Therefore, it is crucial to select scenes with similar moisture content for burned area assessment in order to avoid false positives. The presented approach will be applied to the whole project area extent of app. 1,500,000 km^2 (Kalimantan, Sumatra and West Papua) which were extremely affected by fires during the 2015 El Niño event. The intersection with land cover/ land use maps will provide further information on the total damage and related emissions. This work is still ongoing and the results will be presented at the conference.

ACKNOWLEDGEMENTS

Funding was provided by ESA through the Fire_cci project. We kindly acknowledge the use of data from Sentinel-1 imagery operated by ESA, (MODIS) LANCE FIRMS operated by the NASA/GSFC/Earth Science Data and Information System (ESDIS) with funding provided by NASA/HQ, (Landsat) NASA Goddard Space Flight Center and USGS.

REFERENCES

1. GFED. 2015. Global Fire Emission Database.
2. Giglio, Louis, Jacques Descloitres, Christopher O. Justice, and Yoram J. Kaufman. 2003. An Enhanced Contextual Fire Detection Algorithm for MODIS. *Remote Sensing of Environment* 87: 273–282. doi:10.1016/S0034- 4257(03)00184-6.
3. Page, S E, F Siegert, J O Rieley, H D V Boehm, A Jaya, and S Limin. 2002. The amount of carbon released from peat and forest fires in Indonesia during 1997. Nature 420: 61-65.

Abstract No: A-120

FIELD RESEARCH METHODOLOGIES FOR COLLECTING PEAT FIRE DATA TO ENHANCE UNDERSTANDING OF TROPICAL PEAT FIRE EVENTS

Laura Graham[1*], Grahame Applegate[2], Erianto Indra Putra[3, 4], Kevin Ryan[5] and Mark Cochrane[3]

[1]*Borneo Orangutan Survival Foundation, Indonesia,*
[2]*University of the Sunshine Coast, Australia,*
[3]*South Dakota State University, USA,*
[4]*Institut Pertanian Bogor, Indonesia*
[5]*US Forest Service, Missoula Fire Sciences Laboratory (ret), USA*

**Corresponding author: l.l.b.graham.02@cantab.net*

SUMMARY

Each year peat fires burn Indonesia's peatlands resulting in large volumes of greenhouse gas emissions. There is little published field data on peat fire behaviour and related carbon loss. The behaviour of peat fires and their emissions require improved characterisation for Indonesia to participate fully in carbon accountancy, and to manage their peatlands. A joint Indonesian-US Peat Fire Research Project was established to address this research gap, with a particular focus on how and why surface fires transition to smouldering peat fires, and how these events might be recognised and characterised by satellite. An integral component to this project is the field collection of biophysical peat-fire data. We developed new field methods to undertake 1) in-depth fire scene evaluations including assessments of surface fire intensity, fuel availability and consumption, and peat fire characteristics; and 2) the horizontal and vertical spread rates of, volume of peat consumed and linking this information to environmental conditions (peat moisture content at different locations at the face of the peat fire, water table depth, surface fuel loads, peat type and vegetation (available fuel). These research methods have been documented in a practical field manual. Initial data include maps of 2014 and 2015 hotspots, peat volume loss, peat fire rate of spread in relation to prevailing environmental conditions including peat moisture content and depth of water table and fuel loads. In-depth field data from the project will provide updated emissions data, with the possibility to transfer these methods and data implications to other peatland sites.

Keywords: *Tropical peat fires, methodologies, peat volume, rate of spread, fire evaluation, IPCC emissions*

INTRODUCTION

Each year thousands of hectares of peatland burn in Indonesia emitting tonnes of greenhouse gasses, particulates, and aerosols, with current estimates calculating up to 114 t C ha^{-1} released (Page *et al.*, 2002, Ballhorn *et al.*, 2009, Hooijer *et al.*, 2012, Konecny *et al.*, 2016). Emission calculations for tropical peatlands in relation to fire have previously been based upon limited field data, as noted in IPCC, and there remains little published field data on peat fire behaviour and related carbon loss (Konecny *et al.*, 2016, Ballhorn *et al.*, 2009, Drosler *et al.*, 2014). Data on tropical peat fires' behaviour and emissions must be improved for Indonesia to participate fully in carbon accountancy, and to manage their peatlands (Konecny *et al.*, 2016). Robust methodology is necessary for emissions estimation, as it is required to monitor the overall target of emissions reduction through the UNFCC Measurement, Reporting, and Verification (MRV) system, and ultimately to support necessary steps in prevention and control of peat fires. To address this data gap, a joint Indonesian-US project, the South Dakota State University (SDSU) – Institut Pertanian Bogor (IPB) Peat Fire Research Project was established, funded by NASA. The aims of this project were to explore how and why peatland surface fires transition to smouldering peat fires, and how these events might be recognised and characterised by satellite. An integral component to this project is the field-based collection of biophysical (and social, not discussed in this paper) data relating to peat fires. New field methods were developed to undertake in-depth fire scene evaluations and record fire-related peat characteristics, notably rate of peat fire spread and loss of volume of peat after a fire. The aims of this component of the project were to develop appropriate and transferable methods for collecting peat fire data, to facilitate improved emissions calculations that could be used at this focal site and elsewhere. This paper will present these new methods and initial results.

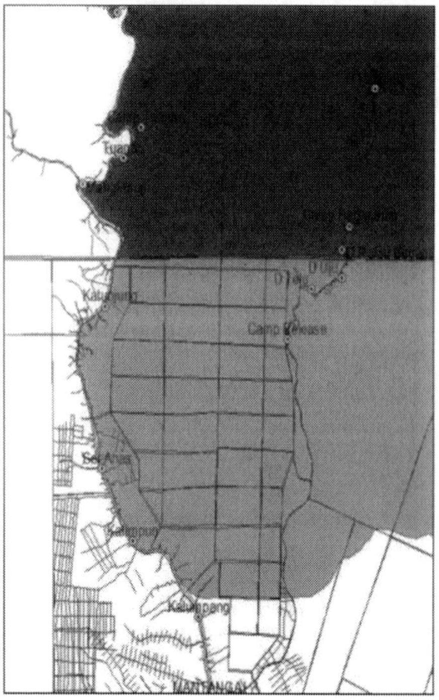

Figure 1: Map of the focus study area; Block A of the BOS-Mawas tropical peat dome

METHODS

Study site

The SDSU-IPB Peat Fire Research Project is partnered with the Borneo Orangutan Survival Foundation, BOS-Mawas Program, who, together with the Provincial Government of Central Kalimantan and the District Government of Kuala Kapuas, Indonesia, help protect and manage an area of 309, 000 ha of tropical peatlands. Towards the north of this location the area remains as relatively intact tropical peat swamp forest, but to the south, the area is heavily degraded by logging, regular fires and the establishment of canals as part of the Ex-Mega Rice Project. This project focused on an approximately 60,000 ha area, which has been heavily degraded (Fig.1), leading to extensive drainage, decomposition, oxidation and burning of the peat, and related forest loss.

Timing and duration

The project began activities in the BOS-Mawas area in June 2014. This paper presents methods and initial data from the 2014 and 2015 fire seasons (August-November). The project will continue to collect field data until the end of the 2016 fire season.

Fire reporting

BOS-Mawas currently uses two fire reporting techniques: 1) daily email updates from NASA's Aqua and Terra satellites, and NOAA, reporting hotspots in the Mawas area. 2) BOS-Mawas has monitoring team that patrols the area regularly to report fires and logging, and also works closely with the local communities that border the area, and have sms and telephone fire reporting systems in place.

Fire scene evaluation

A 65-question fire scene evaluation (FSE) form was developed before and during the 2014 dry season. Once a fire is reported via either of the above methods, the BOS-Mawas Fire Evaluation Field Team departs to the location. If there are multiple fire locations on a given day, the team prioritises a) deep peat locations, b) locations that have recorded three or fewer previous burns and c) locations that represent a range of environmental conditions as compared to previous FSEs, such as burning near forested areas, burning along berms, and burning far from the canal. A FSE field manual has been developed which provides descriptions and explanations of the questions to ensure answers are comparable between sites and fires.

The FSE form consists of two parts. Part I (36 questions) address general environmental and fire data-collection. If a peat fire (as opposed to a surface fire) is occurring, then the team proceeds to Part II of the form, which is more-detailed and includes peat and peat-fire questions (table 1). On the form each question must be given a confidence rating ranging from some confidence/quite confident/confident. Furthermore, many of the form's answers must be accompanied by a photograph, taken by the team, so answers can be cross-checked by fire-experts. In addition to Part II of the FSE form, other methods have been developed and are carried out in the field, if a peat fire is currently occurring. Some of these must be set-up on day one of the evaluation and returned to record data on day two.

Fine, medium and heavy surface fuel load assessment

Following the Line Intersect Method (Van Wagner 1982) and the method developed during the KFCP project (Graham *et al.,* 2014) at an unburned area adjacent to where the peat has burned, the surface fuel is assessed. Heavy fuel (>7.5 cm) is measured using a 90 m long triangle-transect (i.e. each side 30 m) where the diameter of each fuel item (dead trunks, roots, branches, etc.) that intersects the line is measured at the point where it bisects the line. Medium fuel (2.5-7.5 cm) is measured similarly using a 30 m long triangle-transect (i.e. each side 10 m). Fine fuel is measured by placing a 1 x 1 m square onto the peat surface, along each side of the 90 m triangle-transect. All the fine fuel material is cut-away, and placed in a large bag. The contents are then weighed, then dried in a drying oven to a constant dry weight.

The peat moisture content at the peat-fire interface

At the peat fire interface a section of peat is dug away, perpendicular to the interface, approx. 50 x 50 cm in area. Half way down, and parallel to the fire interface, peat samples are cored into the excavated wall, at 5, 10, 15, 25 cm horizontally, and every 10 cm additionally, away from the interface, until the peat is cool to touch. Samples are then similarly taken at 5, 10, 15, 25 cm vertically down, until the peat is again cool (Fig. 2). These peat samples are then bagged in small plastic sample bags. Upon return to the laboratory, the samples are weighed, dried to a constant weight, then weighed again. The percentage moisture content is then calculated.

Water table depth

Two dipwells (plastic pipes, 4.5 cm in diameter, 4 m long, with 0.5 cm diameter holes drilled at 7 cm intervals for the length of the pipes) are inserted 10 m behind and 10 m in-front of the peat-fire interface, 3.7 m into the peat. The water table inside the dipwell is left to stabilise for 24 hours, then site is returned to and the water table depth measured using the blow-straw method (Ichsan *et al.*, 2014).

Table 1: Data collected in the developed Fire Scene Evaluation form

Part	Section	Type of data collected
I	Fire identification	Dates and unique fire code
	Fire control	Authorities involved
	Fire information & location	Maps, access routes, fire reporting, ignition point GPS, source and cause, start/end dates, land tenure, land use
	Weather conditions	Wind speed, direction, relative humidity, temperature
	Surface fire - intensity	Height of burn, scorch height, depth of surface fuel burnt, vegetation type
	Peat fire	Peat burn depth, estimate of area burnt, water table depth, fuel load
	Fire damage info	Area burned, infrastructure, vehicles, houses, animals, crops lost or damaged
	Fire sketch	Detailed sketch of area, fire, land tenure, recoded data points etc.
II	Fire identification	Dates and unique fire code
	Peat fire	Peat ignition – point, source, description, weather, moisture content, depth. Fuel – size, availability, ignition potential
	Fuel	Fine, medium, heavy fuel load triangles, fuel descriptions
	Assessing the burned area	Vegetation type and loss, fuel type and loss, evidence of fuel blackening, charring, scoring, peat decomposition stage, signs of previous burns
	Human action observations	Human nearby land-use, human use of weather or other biophysical features to start, spread or modify the fire

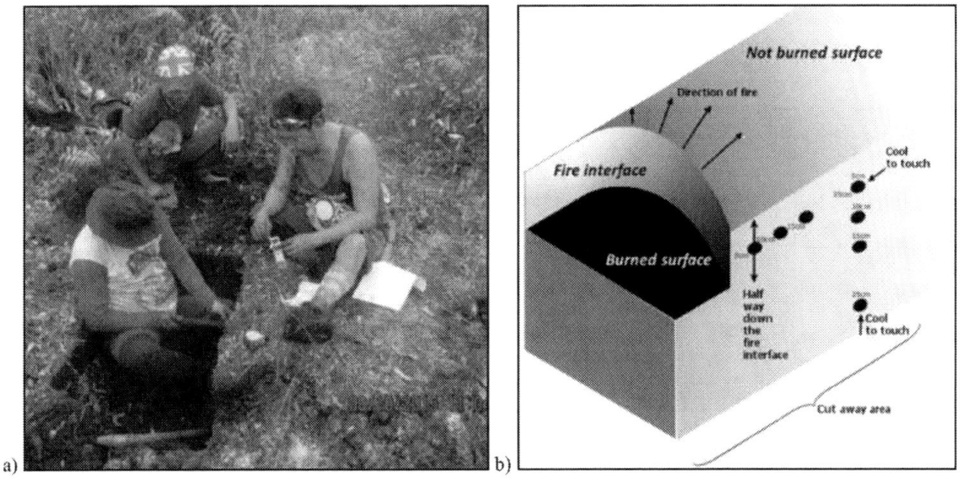

Figure 2: Photo (a) and illustration (b) showing peat core sampling method away from the fire interface, for moisture content analysis.

The rate of peat fire spread

At the point of smouldering peat, fifteen metal rods, 8 mm in diameter, 1.3 m in length are inserted into the burning face of the peat, with each rod given a unique number. Each rod has a line etched into it, at 70 cm from one end. Each rod is inserted into the peat until the etch point is at the height of the peat surface, with approx. 80 cm between each rod. This layout is repeated at three positions around the edge of the peat fire (i.e. 45 rods, 3 replicate points). After 24 hours, the rods are re-measured and the depth of burn and the horizontal distance and direction (compass bearing) to the closest point on the peat-burn face. Additional metal poles can be inserted in a similar layout at the new peat-burn face, and returned again 24 hours later and re-measured (Fig. 3).

The volume of peat lost from the burn

A 160 cm square is made from PVC pipe, with cords strung to form a 20 cm x 20 cm grid to create a square matrix with 81 intercept points. This square is set-up in the field horizontally, 1 m above the general peat surface. The square is set-up in the direction of movement of the fire and just ahead of the peat-fire interface. At every intersection a measuring pole is used to measure the distance to the unburnt peat surface, thus creating an x, y, z measurement (Fig. 4). When the square is removed, four metal rods are inserted into the peat to mark the location of the square, with etches marked on the rods to mark the position of the current peat surface. This is repeated for three locations ahead of the fire interface. Several days later, after the fire has passed through the peat, the squares are re-established and all x, y, z re-measured, taking into account the new peat surface height from the etched mark on the metal rod. Using the x, y, z coordinates collected before and after the fire, a change in peat surface volume can be calculated. A detailed formula has been developed that takes into account the potential uneven surface for each prism volume calculated, and is available upon request.

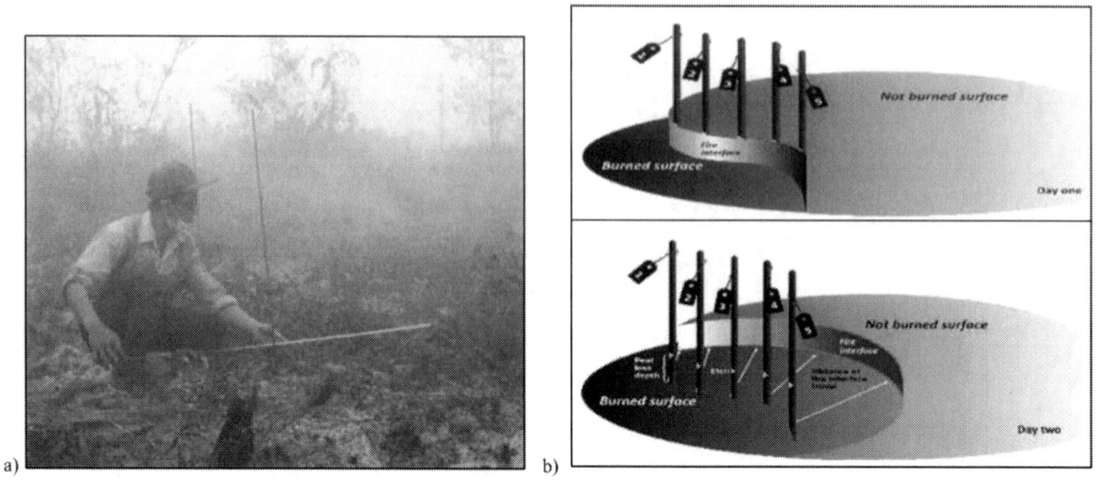

Figure 3: Photo (a) and illustration (b) showing the method for recording rate of peat fire spread.

Figure 4: Photo (a) and illustration (b) of taking the peat volume loss measurements.

Data management

A custom-designed Access database with user-interface and analysis capabilities has been developed for the project, building from the KFCP Vegetation Database. All peat-fire and FSE data is housed within the database (in addition to the vegetation and hydrology data, not discussed in this paper), and references temporally and spatially, facilitating export queries based on all combinations of the environmental data, for both time and space.

RESULTS

During the two years of study 28 FSE were measured across 6 different village districts. Eighteen of these were peat fires, and had the fuel volume measured therein. FSEs have been conducted across a range of forest and degradation types, including land being prepared for palm oil development with fire, rubber forest land, reforested land, land used for hunting and fishing, with some fires becoming out of control and spreading several kilometres and fires that spread into primary forest for the first time. Fires ranged from 4 to 200 ha in size on peat depths ranging from 1 to 8 m.

In 2014 peat fires were primarily restricted to the "berms" along the canals where the depth of peat burned averaged 16 cm with a forward rate of peat-fire spread of 46 cm/day. In 2015 peat fire rate of spread as well as the moisture content of the peat ahead of the fire interface and the volume of peat loss from burning were recorded at five FSE. These data are now currently under analysis.

The methods described have been written into a single SOP, based around a flowchart decision diagram describing which methods to use when. The project, development of the methods and the emerging data have been socialised to the Indonesian government at the national, provincial, district and village-level at twice-yearly workshops, to which other NGOs, academic and other relevant parties are also invited.

DISCUSSION

The SDSU-IPB-BOS-Mawas methods and data improve understanding and calculation of tropical peatland fire behaviour, particularly, with respect to the biophysical conditions associated with surface fire transition into a peat fire and the rate at which fires spread through the peat under a range of biophysical conditions, notably the relevant peat moisture content. The methods also define the actual volume of peat loss during a peat fire. These data can then be coupled to other components of this project, such as, the smoke analysis of burning peat, the generation of emission factors and emissions models for burning peatland landscapes, and to other projects and data-sets, such as providing calibration and verification tools for remotely-sensed peat volume loss techniques.

At the time of writing, the field component of this project has been running for nearly two-years, and for two fire seasons. It will continue to collect fire data through the 2016 dry season. At the start of this period, there were no field methods or SOPs for recording tropical peatland fires, in terms of fire scene evaluation, peat-fire dynamics (fuel loads, rate of spread, peat moisture content) or peat volume loss. In 2014 the FSE form was developed and data collected, and methods for the latter components trialled. In 2015, the peat-fire dynamics, and the peat volume loss methods were finalised, and data collection began. These methods were all developed by peat fire scientists and together with the BOS-Mawas Peat Fire Research Team. The level of complexity and experience needed to complete these data evaluations indicated that a confidence-rating tiered form was helpful, as were photographs to compliment data recorded in the field to support subsequent data analysis.

These methods have been written into a soon-to-be-published comprehensive SOP, which the government partners to the project have been particularly interested in as to meeting their own needs, notably the Provincial Environmental Agency, the District Forest Management Unit, and the University of Palangka Raya. It is hoped these rigorous and replicable field methods will be transferred and implemented to other locations.

CONCLUSION

The science of tropical peat fire analysis is relatively new, and due to the difficulty in collecting direct field data, there remains practically no on-the-ground data for how a smouldering peat-fire is established or behaves. If Indonesia is to better manage their peatlands, and engage in the international carbon market, it is essential to address this research gap. It is hoped that the methods presented in this paper, and the subsequent published findings will have direct application across Indonesia to address this gap.

ACKNOWLEDGEMENTS

The research was funded by NASA. The authors wish to thank the Ministry of Forestry, Indonesia, in close cooperation with the Kapuas District Government and the Central Kalimantan Provincial Government. We also thank the field team from BOSF who have undertaken most of the monitoring activities, and Pavla Graham who developed the Access database, and graphic design for the project.

REFERENCES

1. Ballhorn, U., Siegert, F., Mason, M. and Limin S. Derivation of burn scar depths and estimation of carbon emissions with LIDAR in Indonesian peatlands. PNAS 2009 106: 21213-21218.
2. Drosler, M., Verchott, L. V. Freibauer, A. *et al.* (2014) Chapter 2: Drained inland organic soils. In: 2013 Supplement to the 2006 IPCC Guidelines for National Greenhouse Gas Inventories: Wetlands (eds. Hiraishi, T., Krug, T., Tanabe, K., Srivastava, N., Jamsranjav, B., Fukuda, M., Troxler, T.) pp. 2.1-2.74, IPCC, Switzerland.
3. Graham, Laura L. B., Manjin, S., Juni, E.T., Waldram, M., Massal, F., Ichsan, N., Fatkhurohman and Applegate, G.B. (2014b) KFCP Heavy Fuel Load Assessment: Line Intersect Method and Heavy Fuel Load

Results. Kalimantan Forests and Climate Partnership, Indonesia.
4. Hooijer, A., Page, S., Jauhiainen, J., Lee, W. A., Lu, X. X., Idris, A. and Anshari, G. (2012) Subsidence and carbon loss in drained tropical peatlands. *Biogeosciences* 9: 1053–1071,
5. Ichsan, N., Hooijer, A., Vernimmen, R. Applegate, G.B. (2014) KFCP Hydrology and Peat Monitoring Methodology. Scientific Report, Kalimantan Forests and Climate Partnership, Indonesia.
6. Konecny, K., Ballhorn, U., Navratil, P., Jubanski, J., Page, S. E., Tansey, K., Hooijer, A., Vernimmen, R., Siegert, F. (2016) Variable carbon losses from recurrent fires in drained tropical peatlands. *Global Change Biology* - doi: 10.1111/gcb.13186
7. Page, S.E., Siegert, F., Rieley, J.O., Boehm, H-D.V., Adi Jaya and Suwido Limin (2002) The amount of carbon released from peat and forest fires in Indonesia in 1997. *Nature*, 420, 61-65
8. van Wagner, C.E. 1982. Practical aspects of the line intersect method. Information Report PI-X-12. Petawawa Canadian National Forestry Institute , Forestry Service, Canada, ISSN 0706-1854

Abstract No: A-453

MANAGING PEAT FIRE RISKS IN TANJUNG JABUNG BARAT DISTRICT, JAMBI, INDONESIA

Hesti Lestari Tata*, Niken Sakuntaladewi, Lukas R. Wibowo, Bastoni and Agustinus P. Tampubolon

Agency of Research Development and Innovation, the Ministry of Environment and Forestry, Indonesia

**Corresponding author; email: hl.tata@gmail.com*

SUMMARY

The catastrophe forest fire in Indonesia in 2015 covers large area including peatlands. A study on socio-political of peat fire on peatlands in Tanjung Jabung Barat district, Jambi province, was conducted to provide recommendation on managing peat land without fire. The Forest Service district reported that hotspots in forest area in 2015 were significantly higher than that of in non-forest area. Land tenure issue was a triggered factor of forest and land fire in Jambi. The booming of high profitable commodities, such as oil palm and coffee, lead people to cultivate the tree crops intensively, by opening up the forest with slash and burning technique. Fire is used as tool to open up the land and as a weapon to occupy the peat forest reserve area. Situation is more complex when there was overlap planning among different sectors in managing the peatland in the district. The fire continues to happen in forest area owing to weedy control and weak law enforcement over the reserve peat area. However, on the cultivated land, the community would protect their land and combat fire to prevent their land from fire. We came up with five recommendations which can be applied for the community and the local government. Those are: (i) strengthening the capacity of the Forest Management Unit; (ii) provide incentive and disincentive scheme; (iii) national and local government should make intervention on zero burning policy; (iv) social engineering in strengthening the community; and (v) effort to put refinement on political system and economy.

***Keywords**: fire, peat forest reserve, forest management unit*

INTRODUCTION

The catastrophe of forest fire in Indonesia in 2015 covers 2.6 million ha, including 927,132 ha of peatland. Jambi is one of the most vulnerable provinces to fire in Indonesia. Jambi province has long fire history from 1982 to 1997/1998 (Applegate *et al.*, 2001) and from 2004 to 2015. Fire is caused by several factors, from biophysical characteristics of the land, climate, long drought and El Nino, and social, economy and political situation in the area. It is reported that soil type, such as peat and non-peat soil, has the lowest determine-coefficient to fire (Widodo, 2014). About 18.4 % of total area of Jambi (about 9,208.20 km^2 is the most susceptible to fire.

The Ministry of Environment and Forestry reported that forest and land fire in Jambi in 2015 was 111,391 ha (MOEF, 2015). However, the Forest Service of Jambi province reported that total indicative burnt area of Jambi in 2015 was about 19,528 ha, consisted of 7,221 ha of forest area and 12,307 ha of non-forest area. It seems that different methods would result different result. In this paper, definition of forest refers to institutional forest definition, i.e. an area that has been determined and gazetted as a forest according to the Indonesia's law. Owing to fire and haze in 2015, the governor of Jambi stated that Jambi was in status of "emergency response". Fire and haze negatively effects on deficit economy, reduce human health, reduce environments quality (air, soils and water), and loss of biodiversity (Kompas, 2016).

This study aimed to (i) assess social study of peat fire on peatlands, and (ii) to provide recommendation on managing peat land without fire.

METHODS

The study consisted of two aspects of research, e.g. (i) social political study of peat fire on peatlands, and (ii) silviculture techniques on peatland rehabilitation. The study was located in Tanjung Jabung Barat (hereto Tanjabar) district, Jambi province. The district has an area of 5,010 km^2 (BPS Tanjung Jabung Barat, 2011); 40% of the area composes of peatland (Mulia *et al.*, 2014).

The socio political aspect was assessed using qualitative method and it was analyzed from the perspective of political economy (Lawrence & Wishart, 1957). In-depth interview was conducted to some relevant key informants at different layers, such as provincial, district, and field levels. They consisted of forestry services, District House of Representatives, CSO, local farmers, District Planning Agency, and experts. In addition, the research also organized series of focus group discussion (FGD), at field level and government level. At local level, the FGD aims to gather local understandings and experiences regarding to peatland fires and the effectiveness of forest fire policy in field level. There were 10-20 people participated in each FGD represented the diversity of people in the village: formal or informal leaders, women, youth, etc. The duration of each FGD was around 2-3 hours. Some topics had been discussed during FDG, such as: history of settlement, people's livelihood, and forest dependency. In addition, the studies also used field observation to deepening and grasping the context of the research. At the National or Provincial level, the FGD aims to explore the political obstacles in dealing with peat land fires issues.

The study was completed by collecting secondary data from village annual report and Statistical Bureau, and some literatures. Hotspot data that was captured by using NOAA-18 satellite was collected from the Forest Service of Tanjabar district.

RESULTS AND DISCUSSION

The Fact of Fire in Tanjabar District in 2015

The Forest Service of Tanjabar district reported that number of hotspots in forest area in 2015 was significantly higher than that of in non-forest area. Series hotspots number in Tanjabar district from 2011-2015 is shown in Figure 1. The hotspots were captured by using NOAA-18 satellite with data confidence of >80%. The Forest Service District is also reported their effort on combating fire in forest and non-forest area. Undoubtedly, total area that could control from fire in non-forest area was significantly higher than that of in forest area. This owing to accessibility and effortlessness in managing fire in non-forest area compare with forest area.

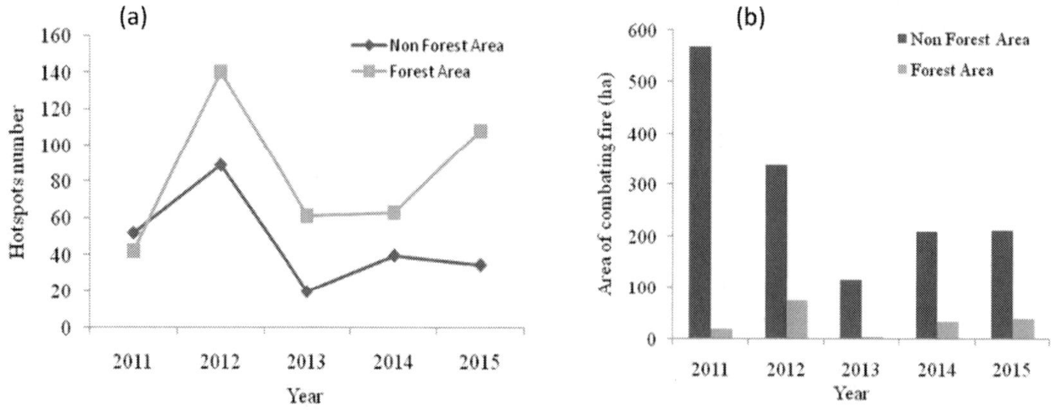

Figure 1: The fact of fire in Tanjabar district in 2011-2015. (a) Hotspots number based on NOAA-18; (b) Area of combating fire.

The Forest Service and The Agency of Disaster Management have duties on fire fighting on forests and lands. Both institutions have brigade units of forest and land fire fighting. They are supported by sufficient equipments and tools for fire fighting. In 2015, they could control and combat fire in the state forest and land up to 251 ha (from 81 hotspots) (Figure 1b). Fire was also occurred in an area of a big forest concession holder, which covers an area of 136 ha. However, this is not significant number compare with actual fire on the field.

Social Aspect of Fire in Tanjung Jabung Barat district

Forest fires, as a phenomenon, have regularity, a yearly circle that logically allows people to plan for disaster management in an ordered way (Xanthopoulos, 2007). A lot of conflicts and peat fires were found in Jambi peat land. WALHI (a national NGO) indicated that there were 300 conflicts between '99 to 2012, of which 27% of them were related to natural resources. These conflicts were related to overlap permits in land uses and the peat fire was related to land preparation in peat land for agricultural purposes and plantation

Based on the Minister of Forestry Decree No. 421 of 1999, the peatland area of ex-one timber concession has been designated as Protected Peat Forest Land (*hutan lindung gambut, HLG*). Although the decree is issued in 1999, but most people had just know it around year 2007. This peatland is known mostly as the 'free' land ex timber concession, so that they feel free to use it. Conflict of land tenure was also reported by Galudra *et al.* (2013). Determination of peat forest land is not running smoothly. This determination has triggered a manifest conflict that reached its peak around 2007. The migrant is rested, particularly the ones who had been there before the licensing regime operated and the establishment of protected forest peat. They claimed the land area of 500 hectares located within the protected peat land as their land. After a long process of mediation carried out by the Parliament, in 2009, the conflict can be eased temporarily. In the mediation process there is agreement that the public is not evicted but were obliged to plant *Dyera polyphylla*. Observations and interviews with some the residents revealed that most of them were still cautious to plant *D. polyhylla* due to the uncertain of forest claim and unclear latex market.

A competition on living space becomes increasingly sharp as the commencement of licensing regimes (forest concession) operated in the territory of Kuala Tungkal (the capital city of the district). Competitions of living space or forest land do not only involve indigenous people and migrants, but also corporations. Around 1970 the Great Betara Timber logging began to operate until 1995. The industrial forest plantation Mekarjaya Wirakarya Way is located about 2 km to 4 km away from the village Muntiala.

It is to be considered that policy-makers depend on technical and scientific information, but the choices made are inherently political ones. For this reason, even if a particular issue is relatively uncomplicated and the design of a solution may be easily understood, policy formulation is often complicated. Substantive objectives, such as fuel hazard reduction, must compete for legislative and administrative attention and resources with other worthwhile objectives and programs. Similarly, other forces can deflect the consideration of substantive objectives and priorities, even when they are supported by scientific and technical information.

Peatland fire is not new in Tanjabar. The community used fire as tool. The community will seriously keep this area from fire for the existence of their family sources of income. It is found that the peatland sensitive to fire is located further away from the road. There is no or limited access to that area, making more difficult to put of the fire when the peat fire occurred. This technology is considered easy to do, relatively cheap (around IDR[1] 300,000 up to IDR 500,000), does not take time (relatively fast to do), great result (clean, as it is required for coffee plantation), and it is believed that the ashes make the soil fertile.

The local communities are aware on the risk of peat fire in applying burning technology in agricultural land preparation. To prevent the peat fire from happening, fire break (2 meter width) is constructed, particularly along the side close to neighbouring plantation. The trash are placed in the side of prepared land and burned either against or following the wind direction. Burning following the wind direction will be faster, but burning against the wind direction will be cleaner. The communities have done their best to prevent the peat fire or to prevent burning their neighbouring plants for penalties applied. However these people often cannot avoid or prevent the 'flying fire'.

The factor of commodities' booming, like palm oil and coffee, significantly give more control or drive mobility of people and capital more intense into area rich with forest resource. The mobility of people and capital are no longer locally but has across administrative boundaries and geographical region. Mobility of people and capital even tangled with various political needs both at local level, sub-national, national, national and global. As a result, primary forest, secondary forest, and peat swamp forest as important areas for water regulation and habitat of various endemic fauna and flora (like *Ramin*), has now been much damaged by forest fire and converted to coffee and palm oil plantations.

Various motives or the modus operandi of people to get into forest, such as to survive, to plant palm oil, or land speculation or profit taking. Many of them also have political interests. They consolidate power and capital base reproduction. Some of them abuse their power for personal benefit and strengthen the administrative power control by providing a Certificate of Land, and take society browser into control areas of jurisdiction.

Fires continue to happen in Tanjabar district due to, among other things, the low control and the weak law enforcement over the protected peat area. Some residents reveal that only few forestry officials control the protected peat area. Illegal logging is still happening there and it is not a secret anymore, but no prosecution efforts. The people believe that apparatus know the illegal activity is happening but they do nothing, as if there was negligence. The phenomenon of illegal logging makes some people feel jealous, so they feel it does not matter if they do encroachment.

The institutional of Protected Forest Management Unit (FMU) that is expected to be a permanent solution to the problems of forestry at the site level appears to be still far from the expected. The FMU institutionalization based on a decree of head of Tanjabar District (No. 18 year 2010), does not run properly. Limited human resources and the authority make the FMU slow in the progress. The FMU as the site level organization could not move significantly to address encroachment, and forest and land fires. Dysfunctional FMU institutional has become one of the causes of fire to continue happening at the protected peat forest area.

The local district government has tried in many ways to make clear on what can/not to do in the peat land to avoid peat fire and save them from being encroached the forest. Banners have been placed in the fields; trainings on fire extinguisher have been conducted targeted to the local communities, and allocation of fire equipments. This program was jointly organized with a big concession holder company, in 2013. Three to four times training and simulation of forest fire were conducted in 2013. This program was attended by representatives of community unit, in particular from areas sensitive to forest fire.

---

[1] 1 US$=13,500 IDR

These efforts have made local communities realized not to do burning in land preparation. In Mekar Jaya village, the communities have used herbicide. Sialang village has equipment for fire distinguished and fire-cared community (*'masyarakat peduli api, MPA'*). Local government, in particular the district forest agency, has had fully equipped division to distinguish faire, and the oil and gas company has helped in putting sign on prohibition to cut trees and the danger of peat forest fire. The efforts to control peat fire have to continue for the communities. Up to October 2014, however, some communities still clear up the peat forest for agricultural purposes. Slash and burning in land preparation is a major threat for peat forest fire.

Institutionally, the central government and local authorities have been put many efforts on fire prevention. For Jambi itself, based on the Governor's Decree (No. 385 year 2006), the Center of Land and Forest Fire Control has been established, but it is still not effective yet in the field due to lack of funds and personnel. To strengthen the control process, the Chief Police officer has established local government communication forum to strengthen field level coordination, although it is still not effective. Fire control approaches undertaken by various institutions at the local government level are still an emergency reaction. Efforts are still in the preventive stage and it is still minimal. Even if it is done, it is not yet well planned. The preventive policy is still project-based and no monitoring and evaluation of the activities undertaken.

Five recommendations to the local government were proposed to reduce fire risk in the district; those are: (i) strengthening the capacity of the FMU; (ii) provide incentive and disincentive scheme; (iii) national and local government should make intervention on zero burning policy; (iv) social engineering in strengthening the community; and (v) effort to put refinement on political system and economy.

ACKNOWLEDGEMENT

This study was financially supported Alternative Slash and Burn (ASB) Partnership for The Tropical Forest Margins, Norwegian Agency for Development (NORAD), and World Agroforestry Centre (ICRAF) Southeast Asia Regional Programme.

REFERENCES

1. Applegate G, Chokkalingam U, Suyanto. 2001. *The underlying causes and impacts of fires in South-East Asia*. CIFOR/ICRAF final report. Bogor. 54p.
2. BPS Tanjung Jabung Barat. 2015. *Tanjung Jabung Barat Dalam Angka*. Kuala Tungkal. 328 p.
3. Galudra G, van Noordwijk M, Agung P, Suyanto S, Pradhan P. 2013. Migrants, land markets and carbon emissions in Jambi, Indonesia: Land tenure change and the prospect of emission reduction. *Mitigation Adaptation Strategy Global Change*. 19(6):715-731. DOI: 10.1007/s11027-013-9512-9
4. Kompas. 2016. *Kabut asap sudah darurat*. http://print.kompas.com/baca/2015/09/05/Kabut-Asap-Sudah-Darurat
5. Lawrence and Wishart. 1957. *Political Economy*. A Textbook issued by the Economics Institute of the Academy of Sciences of the U.S.S.R. A Textbook issued by the Institute of Economics the Academy of Sciences of the U.S.S.R. London. 858p.
6. Mulia R, Widayati A, Suyanto, Agung P, Zulkarnain MT. 2014. Low carbon emission development strategies for Jambi, Indonesia: simulation and trade-off analysis using the FALLOW model. *Mitigation Adaptation Strategy Global Change*. 19(6):773-788. DOI 10.1007/s11027-013-9485-8
7. Ministry of Environment and Forestry (MOEF). 2015. *Sistem pemantauan kebakaran emisi karhutla 2015*. Direktorat Jenderal Planologi Kehutanan dan Tata Lingkungan. Kementerian Lingkungan Hidup dan Kehutanan. Jakarta. 24p.
8. Widodo RB. 2014. Pemodelan spasial resiko kebakaran hutan (Studi kasus Provinsi Jambi, Sumatera). *Jurnal Pembangunan Wilayah & Kota*. 10(2):127-138.
9. Xanthopolous G. 2007. *Forest fire policy scenarios as a key element affecting the occurrence and characteristics of fire disasters*. An abbreviated version of this document was presented at the 4th International Wildland Fire Conference, May 13-17, 2007, Sevilla, Spain. 11p.

Fire on peat soil is more dominated by fire on vegetation on peat surface, both on live vegetation such as sago plants and weed fern as well as dry leaves and woodpiles.

Chemical Characteristics of Soil

Summary of chemical analysis result on soil samples, both from the burned and unburned land presented on Table 1.

Table 1: Summary of chemical analysis of soil samples from the burned and unburned land

Parameter	Layer (cm)	Unburned Land (Blok M-24 and U-10 Block)	Burned Land (K-26, I-28, V-11 Block)
pH	0-20	3.5 - 3.6	3.5 - 3.8
	20-40	3.6	3.5 - 3.7
Organik-C (%)	0-20	31.9 - 43.7	33.0 - 38.6
	20-40	26.1 - 36.4	23.3 - 45.5
Total-N (%)	0-20	1.04 - 2.03	0.96 - 1.26
	20-40	0.92 - 1.12	0.90 - 0.99
Calcium (me/100g)	0-20	6.66 - 19.72	3.05 - 13.92
	20-40	2.87 - 4.60	2.08 - 3.93
Magnesium (me/100g)	0-20	3.01 - 4.63	3.29 - 4.63
	20-40	3.19 - 3.21	3.18 - 4.44

Table 1 shows that various parameters of soil chemical characteristics measured from soil samples from the burned and unburned land do not show significant differences. Soil acidity (pH) is still categorized very acid, C-organic and N-total are relatively very high, Ca is low to high, and Mg is high.

Physical Characteristics of Soil

Summary of physical analysis result on soil samples, both on the burned and unburned land presented on Table 2.

Table 2: Summary of physical analysis of soil samples from the burned and unburned land

Parameter	Layer (cm)	Unburned land (M-24 and U-10 Block)	Burned land (K-26, I-28, V-11 Block)
Bulk density (g/cm^3)	0-20	0.13 - 0.20	0.17 - 0.18
	20-40	0.11 - 0.16	0.14 - 0.15
Porosity (%)	0-20	85.90 - 90.82	87.09 - 88.03
	20-40	88.91 - 91.83	89.59 - 90.15
Available water (%)	0-20	20.89 - 21.38	14.14 - 24.85
	20-40	13.90 - 22.87	21.26 - 23.77

Table 2 shows that bulk density, porosity, and available water of the samples collected from unburned land are not significantly different from the samples collected from burned land.

Biological Characteristics of Soil

Summary of biological analysis result on soil samples, both on the burned and unburned land, is presented on Table 3.

Table 3: Summary of biological analysis of soil samples from the burned and unburned land

Parameter	Layer (cm)	Unburned land (M-24 and U-10 Block)	Burned land (K-26, I-28, V-11 Block)
Amount of soil microbes ($x 10^6$) cfu/g	0-20	0.3 - 5.6	0.1 - 0.6
	20-40	0.2 - 0.4	0.4 - 4.5
Amount of P dissolving bacteria ($x 10^4$) cfu/g	0-20	0	0.3 - 1.4
	20-40	0	0.0 - 0.2
Amount of Fungi ($x 10^5$) cfu/g	0-20	1.2 - 4.3	0.3 - 19.0
	20-40	0.3 - 4.5	4.9 - 6.7
Respiration (mg C-CO_2/kg soil/day)	0-20	12.7 - 15.1	6.7 - 10.3
	20-40	6.3 - 10.8	5.7 - 8.1

Table 3 shows that the amount of microbes in the upper layer and total respiration decrease after the fire, while other parameters such as the amount of P dissolving bacteria and fungi increase. The decrease in the amount of microbes and total respiration is a natural condition as a result of high temperature during the fire. However, this is only temporary and will go back to normal in a short period of time, as shown by the sprout of vegetation on burned peat.

One year after forest fire

Field observation conducted one year after forest fire showed that there is no indication for land degradation over the ex-burned land. Sago palm and weed grow normally. Result of chemical analysis on soil samples collected from the same sites as the sampling in 2014 also showed no significant difference, as shown for example in the pH of about 3.3-4.4 on ex-burned land and about 3.3-3.7 on unburned land.

CONCLUSIONS

1. Based on field observation, the fire on peat soil is more dominated by fire on vegetation on peat surface, both on live vegetation such as sago plants and weed fern as well as dry leaves and woodpiles.
2. Based on laboratory analysis result on peat soil samples collected from the depth of 0-20 cm and 20-40 cm, soil chemical and physical characteristics between the burned and unburned peat are not significantly different.
3. The amount of soil microbes and total respiration decrease after the fire, but expected to happen temporarily and will go back to normal as shown by the sprout of burned sago and weed fern.

REFERENCES

1. Giardina, C.P., R.L. Sanford Jr., and I.C. Døckersmith. 2000. Changes in soil phosphorus and nitrogen during slash-and-burn clearing of a dry tropical forest. Soil Sci. Soc. Am. J. 64:399–405
2. Giardina, C.P., R.L. Sanford Jr., I.C. Døckersmith and V.J. Jaramillo. 2000. The effect of slash burning on ecosystem nutrients during the land preparation phase of shifting cultivation. Plant and Soil 230: 247-260
3. Thomaz, E.L., V. Antoneli and S.H. Doerr. 2014. Effects of fire on the physicochemical properties of soil in a slash-and-burn agriculture. Catena 122:209–215

Abstract No: A-077

SURFACE ELEVATION CHANGES OF TROPICAL PEATLANDS UNDER DIFFERENT LAND COVERS: A PRELIMINARY ACCOUNT FOLLOWING 2015 FIRES IN CENTRAL KALIMANTAN, INDONESIA

Adi Jaya[1], Daniel Murdiyarso[2, 3], Sigit D. Sasmito[2, 4] and Nyahu Rumbang[1]

[1]*Faculty of Agriculture, University of Palangka Raya, Indonesia*
[2]*Center for International Forestry Research (CIFOR), Indonesia*
[3]*Department of Geophysics and Meteorology, Bogor Agricultural University, Indonesia*
[4]*Research Institute for the Environment and Livelihoods (RIEL), Charles Darwin University, Australia*

Corresponding author: adijaya_unpar@yahoo.co.id; s.sasmito@cgiar.org

SUMMARY

Tropical peatlands play important roles in global climate change, as they store large amount of carbon and at the same time facing tremendous pressure from land conversion. Fires have been extensively used in agricultural land development following excessive drainage of water in the landscape. Rod Surface Elevation Table (RSET) technique (Cahoon and Lynch 1997) is used to monitor surface elevation change due to accretion and subsurface subsidence or expansion due to oxidation, compaction, and consolidation. In addition, water table was monitored throughout study period and peat soils were sampled periodically for bulk density analysis. This study aims to propose RSET technique for long-term peat subsidence measurements. We set up a network of 22 RSET-MH benchmark stations in Central Kalimantan, Indonesia to represent gradient of peat degradation ranging from protected to managed and drained Peat Swamp Forests (PSF). These sites were affected by 2015 and some areas were burned more than once. Our preliminary assessments are performed every month regularly in order to provide useful scientific information on the estimation of carbon loss due to peat drainages and fire events.

Keywords: *subsidence, compaction, drainage, peat conversion*

INTRODUCTION

Tropical wetlands such as peat swamp forests (PSF) are globally known as carbon (C)-rich ecosystem. These swamped forests could store organic C up to five times higher compared to other types of tropical forests in mineral soil (Murdiyarso *et al.*, 2009), especially in Indonesia where it is home for 65% of tropical peatlands (Page *et al.*, 2011). However, these ecosystems have been threatened and degraded due to deforestation and land conversions (Koh *et al.*, 2011; Miettinen *et al.*, 2012). Peatlands degradation contributes major consequences of greenhouse gas (GHG) emissions, since peatlands contain high concentration of accumulated organic matters over millennia (Kurnianto *et al.*, 2015). In addition, annual extreme event such as peat fires also emit huge number of atmospheric C and equal with 27% of national land use activities in Indonesia (MoE, 2009; Gaveau *et al.*, 2014). While the roles of tropical PSF in global climate change mitigation are crucially important (Murdiyarso *et al.*, 2013), there is still scientific gaps on the impacts of land use and cover changes to biophysical characteristic of peat soils. For example, there are still few studies on the quantification of carbon losses associated with peat subsidence due to drainage and annual fire events (Hooijer *et al.*, 2012; Couwenberg & Hooijer, 2013).

The objective of this study is to propose a new technique called Rod Surface Elevation Table (RSET) for measuring peat surface elevation changes. RSET has been used widely to measure coastal wetlands surface elevation dynamic and could provide high precision of measuring data (Cahoon *et al.*, 2002; Webb *et al.*, 2013; Sasmito *et al.*, 2015), but none tested in tropical peatlands.

METHODS

Study sites

This study is mainly located several land use of tropical peatlands in Palangkaraya, Central Kalimantan, Indonesia. We set up a network of 22 RSET benchmark stations to represent gradient of peat degradation ranging from protected to managed and drained peatlands. Six RSET benchmarks were installed in protected PSF in order to see the dynamic of belowground peat soils within natural conditions. The remaining

RSET benchmarks were installed in the post Mega Rice Project sites which represent managed or drained peatlands. The field work was carried out on August 2015, and the measurements are being conducted regularly.

Table 1: Geographical location and depth of installed stable RSET benchmarks

Location	Benchmark name	Latitude	Longitude	Land use type	Rod depth (meter)
KHDTK	RSET-1	-2.35	114.09	Protected PSF	9
KHDTK	RSET-2	-2.36	114.09	Protected PSF	9
KHDTK	RSET-3	-2.35	114.09	Protected PSF	9
CIMTROP Sebangau	RSET-4	-2.32	113.91	Protected PSF	7
CIMTROP Sebangau	RSET-5	-2.32	113.91	Protected PSF	6
CIMTROP Sebangau	RSET-6	-2.32	113.91	Protected PSF	7
Tanjung Taruna	RSET-7	-2.32	114.06	Drained peatlands	8
Tanjung Taruna	RSET-8	-2.32	114.06	Drained peatlands	8
Tanjung Taruna	RSET-9	-2.32	114.06	Drained peatlands	8
Tanjung Taruna	RSET-10	-2.32	114.06	Drained peatlands	8
Tanjung Taruna	RSET-11	-2.32	114.06	Drained peatlands	8
Tanjung Taruna	RSET-12	-2.32	114.06	Drained peatlands	8
Kameloh	RSET-13	-2.30	114.03	Drained peatlands	8
Kameloh	RSET-14	-2.30	114.03	Drained peatlands	8
Kameloh	RSET-15	-2.30	114.03	Drained peatlands	8
Kameloh	RSET-16	-2.30	114.03	Drained peatlands	8
Kameloh	RSET-17	-2.30	114.03	Drained peatlands	8
Kameloh	RSET-18	-2.30	114.03	Drained peatlands	8
Kameloh	RSET-19	-2.29	114.03	Drained peatlands	8
Kameloh	RSET-20	-2.29	114.03	Drained peatlands	8
Kameloh	RSET-21	-2.29	114.03	Drained peatlands	7
Kameloh	RSET-22	-2.29	114.03	Drained peatlands	6

Rod Surface Elevation Table (RSET)

RSET technique has been used widely to measure soil surface elevation change and accretion in coastal wetland ecosystems. Figure 1 shows RSET-MH setting and paired with tide gauge to observe coastal vulnerability from accelerated sea level rise (Webb *et al.*, 2013). High precision of RSET design is able to measure long term surface elevation change and accretion processes in millimeter high resolution unit (Cahoon *et al.*, 2002). The detail of RSET size, design and specification has been described clearly by Cahoon *et al.* (2002). Generally, RSET-MH consists of three parts including stable rod benchmark, measuring arm (Figure 2). Rod benchmark has fundamental function to keep it in a steady position from relative sub surface peat movement since it reaches until the mineral or bedrock layer. The measuring arm which has 9 pins attached to it is used to measure surface elevation changes periodically.

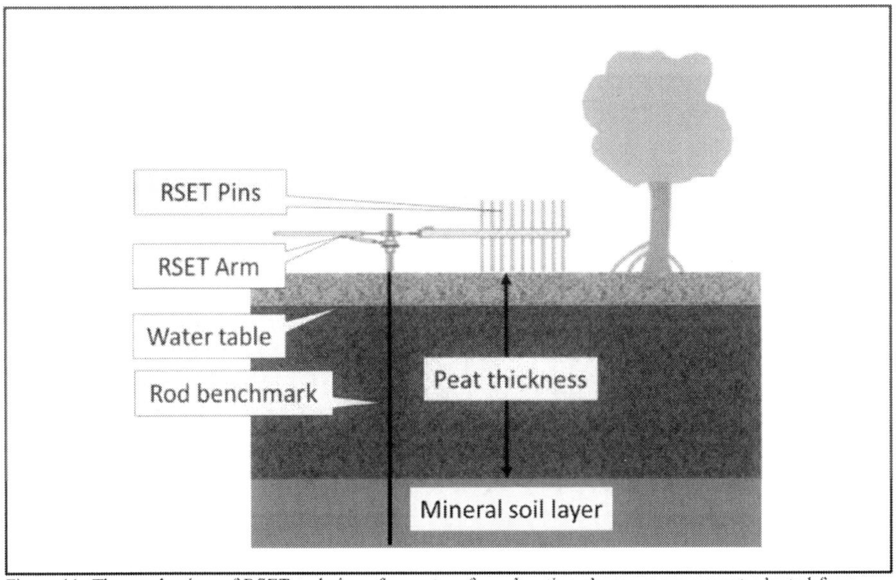

Figure 11: The mechanism of RSET technique for peat surface elevation change measurement adopted from Webb *et al.* (2013) and Cahoon *et al.* (2002)

RESULT AND DISCUSSION

Peat surface elevation dynamic is maintained by several processes, such as aboveground organic matter accumulation, and belowground biological and physical activities (Figure 2). Water table movement is key parameter in determining seasonal stability and dynamic of these belowground processes. As described in (Hooijer *et al.*, 2012), there are at least three processes within belowground peat soils including oxidation, compaction, consolidation, root production and peat surface loss cost by fires. The RSET technique able to measure total peat surface elevation change (SEC) as resulted from those belowground biological and physical processes. Additional data collection of above and below water table bulk density is required in order to quantify the proportion of oxidation, compaction and consolidation. These three processes are mainly caused belowground peat subsidence or collapse.

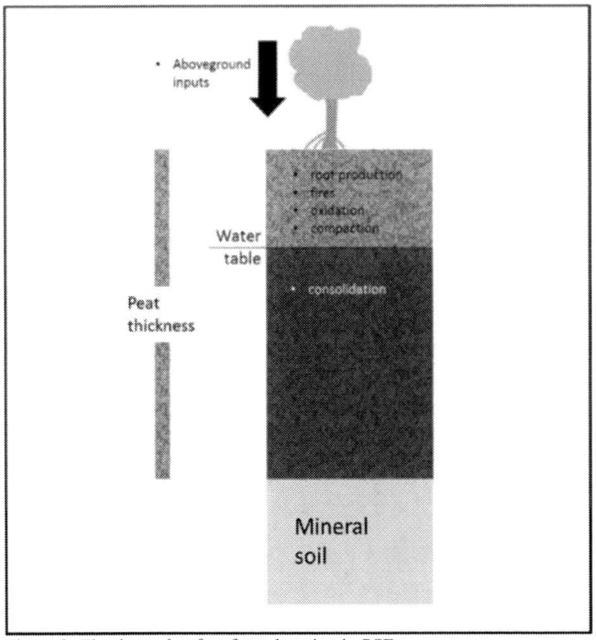

Figure 2: The dynamic of surface elevation in PSFs

The dynamic of peat surface elevation change associated with peat fires and drainage is described in Figure 3. The stable of RSET rod allow us to observe SEC as cost by peat fires as well as drainage. Combined with bulk density and C content analysis, RSET technique could possibly quantify the amounts of C losses both disturbances. RSET provides better spatial data coverage on peat surface elevation dynamic compare to conventional subsidence pole. RSET has nine pins and covers approximately 2 x 2 m^2 of measuring plots.

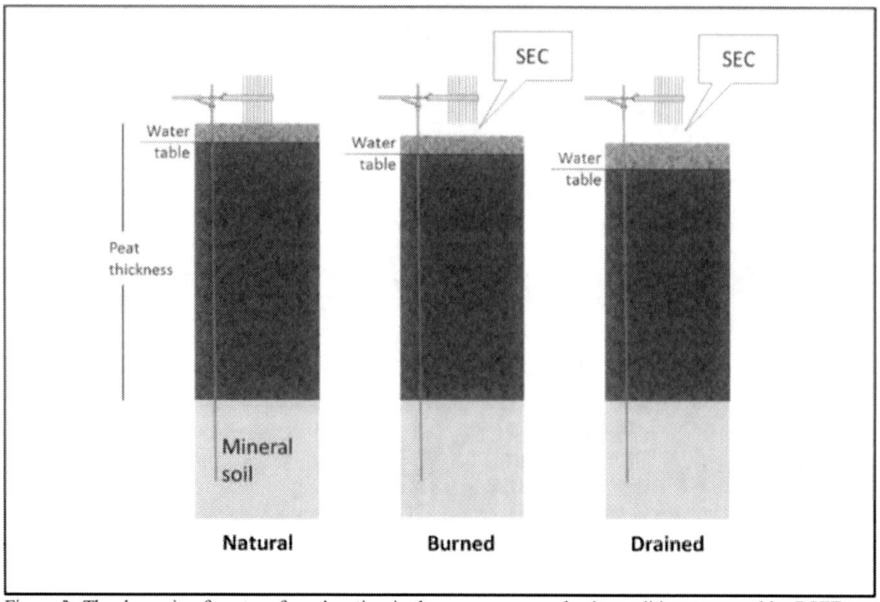

Figure 3: The dynamic of peat surface elevation in three common peatlands condition measured by RSET technique.

CONCLUSION

The study proposes a new technique called Rod Surface Elevation Table (RSET) for measuring peat surface elevation changes. Several measurement stations of RSET have been established and tested in Central Kalimantan. A series of field measurements are currently being conducted. The preliminary results of this study could provide insight on the quantification of C loss associated with peat fires and drainages, in order to develop better peatland conservation strategies.

ACKNOWLEDGEMENTS

All authors thank to CIFOR–Indonesian Peatland Network (IPN) and Sustainable Wetlands Adaptation and Mitigation Program (SWAMP) for funding supports. We would also thank to Kesbangpol, Ministry of Internal Affairs, Republic of Indonesia for research permits.

REFERENCES

1. Cahoon DR, Lynch JC, Perez BC *et al.* (2002) High-Precision Measurements of Wetland Sediment Elevation: II. The Rod Surface Elevation Table. *Journal of Sedimentary Research*, **72**, 734–739.
2. Couwenberg J, Hooijer A (2013) Towards robust subsidence-based soil carbon emission factors for peat soils in south-east Asia, with special reference to oil palm plantations. *Mires & Peat*, **12**, 1–13.
3. Gaveau DL a, Salim M a, Hergoualc'h K *et al.* (2014) Major atmospheric emissions from peat fires in Southeast Asia during non-drought years: evidence from the 2013 Sumatran fires. *Scientific reports*, **4**, 1–7.
4. Hooijer A, Page S, Jauhiainen J, Lee WA, Lu XX, Idris A, Anshari G (2012) Subsidence and carbon loss in drained tropical peatlands. *Biogeosciences*, **9**, 1053–1071.
5. Koh LP, Miettinen J, Liew SC, Ghazoul J (2011) Remotely sensed evidence of tropical peatland conversion to oil palm. *Proceedings of the National Academy of Sciences of the United States of America*, **108**, 5127–32.
6. Kurnianto S, Warren M, Talbot J, Kauffman B, Murdiyarso D, Frolking S (2015) Carbon accumulation of tropical peatlands over millennia: A modeling approach. *Global Change Biology*, **21**, 431–444.
7. Miettinen J, Shi C, Liew SC (2012) Two decades of destruction in Southeast Asia's peat swamp forests. *Frontiers in Ecology and the Environment*, **10**, 124–128.
8. MoE (2009) [MoE] Ministry of Environment (2009) Indonesia Second National Communication under the United Nations Framework Convention on Climate Change (UNFCCC). Ministry of Environment of the Republic of Indonesia, Jakarta. 2009.

9. Murdiyarso D, Donato D, Kauffman JB, Kurnianto S, Stidham M, Kanninen M (2009) *Carbon storage in mangrove and peatland ecosystems. A preliminary account from plots in Indonesia*. Bogor, 33 pp.
10. Murdiyarso D, Kauffman JB, Verchot L V (2013) Climate change mitigation strategies should include tropical wetlands. *Carbon Management*, **4**, 491–499.
11. Page SE, Rieley JO, Banks CJ (2011) Global and regional importance of the tropical peatland carbon pool. *Global Change Biology*, **17**, 798–818.
12. Sasmito SD, Murdiyarso D, Friess DA, Kurnianto S (2015) Can mangroves keep pace with contemporary sea level rise? A global data review. *Wetlands Ecology and Management*.
13. Webb EL, Friess DA, Krauss KW, Cahoon DR, Guntenspergen GR, Phelps J (2013) A global standard for monitoring coastal wetland vulnerability to accelerated sea-level rise. *Nature Climate Change*, **3**, 458–465.

Abstract No: A-227

THE ASEAN FIRE ALERT TOOL, A SMARTPHONE APPLICATION FOR HOTSPOT AND FIRE RISK ALERTS

Faizal Parish[1], S.Y. Lew[1], Mohd Faiz M.P.[1] and Noor Azura A.[1]

Global Environment Centre, Malaysia

**Corresponding author: fparish@gec.org.my*

SUMMARY

Burning peatlands is a serious issue in Southeast Asia, especially when it causes prolonged haze that envelope the region, leading to much damage to public health and economies. One of the challenges is to know the exact location of hotspots. Fires may occur in remote places with very few inhabitants and poor communication coverage. One cannot be everywhere at the same time; and this applies to land owners and managers too. Due to the extent of land that they manage, it may take a long time before a land manager knows that their land is burning. However, satellites are able to detect hotspots and show them on a map. Using satellite data collated by the ASEAN Specialised Meteorological Centre (ASMC) and Malaysian Meteorological Department, combined with online databases and mapping technologies, land managers can be notified of hotspot locations and fire danger risks. A smartphone application – the ASEAN Fire Alert Tool has been developed to send push notifications to alert the land managers when a hotspot occurs on their land and inform the land managers fire risk level of the land. They are then able to verify ground conditions and take necessary action. The application allows users to determine their land boundaries and select Registration Points for monitoring changes in Fire Danger Rating.

Keywords: *Peat Fire, Hotspot Monitoring, FDRS, Technology Application*

INTRODUCTION

Fire activity had occurred every year in this world. Those incidents were considered as one of a large factor in prevalent our world landscape. The unmonitored fire could be caused us to lose thousand hectares of forested land, plantation and homes, in some cases human lives.

Forest and land fires and associated haze are one of the most serious environmental problems in Southeast Asia. The problem gets worse if it is fall during El Nino dry spell. Each year thousands of hectares of forests and peatlands burn – leading to direct losses of forests, plantations and agricultural crops worth millions of dollars. The smoke from peatland fires is responsible for 90% of the transboundary haze in Southeast Asia which impacts the health and welfare of millions of people and disrupts travel, tourism, agriculture and economy. Several key tools have been developed to provide fire managers and land owners with useful information on hotspots and fire danger rating across the region. A smartphone application, ASEAN Fire Alert Tool, simply takes those information sources and puts it in a useful alert system.

The ASEAN Fire Alert Tool uses hotspot information from the ASEAN Specialised Meteorological Centre based in Singapore. The Centre supports ASEAN Member States (AMS) by enhancing regional capacity and strengthening support in provision of meteorological services, which include observation and forecast information related to forest fires and smoke haze. The ASMC monitors hotspots information possibly land and forest fires, disseminates information on occurrence of transboundary smoke haze and conducts seasonal land and climate predictions for the Southeast Asia region.

The Tool uses Fire Weather Index (FWI), one of information from Fire Danger Rating System of Malaysian Meteorological Department (MMD). The FWI values shown on the map are numerical ratings of fire intensity and general fire danger across the landscape that combines Initial Spread Index and Build Up Index. The weather data collected from stations being used are wind speed, temperature, relative humidity and rain. This FWI is often used to indicate the difficulty of fire control based on the head fire intensity and fire-fighting capability. MMD aims to fulfil the needs of people for meteorological, climatological and geophysical services for national security, society wellbeing and sustainable socio-economic development. MMD utilises the weather information gathered at stations through World Meteorological Organisation (WMO) to provide forecast pattern of fire risk up to three days in Malaysia and the region which will then be used by interest groups especially land managers to take precaution measures if there is a risk of extreme weather. As its effort thus far, the MMD has been overlaying a layer of peatland areas in the region onto the FDRS specifically for interest groups working on the peatland related issues.

The ASEAN Fire Alert Tool is created in aiming the smartphone based application which was designed for improvement of the early warning system. The goal is to be the best medium as community network about the tracking of early warning for the high potential area to fire. It is a new smartphone application as its capability is to provide early warning and information from two agencies to sense the hotspot and fire risk for land area. The application is also assist to bridge the technological information between the government and public. The application is linked to a website (http://www.aseanfirealert.org/) for achieve and easy viewing using a computer.

The users who have registered, downloaded and paired-up the application (both the website and the application on smartphone) will receive push notification every evening 7pm Malaysian time (UTC+8) if a hotspot occurs on or adjacent to the specified plotted land. The users can plot up to 20 polygons of land of their interest and place up to 20 Registration Point to receive notifications whenever the system observes a change in FWI. The benefit for the land owner to register as a user is that the land manager will be alerted to a hotspot rather than having to scour websites and determine whether a hotspot is near to the plotted land.

METHODS

After registering on the website, the system will show a mapping screen where land parcels could be plotted out. The users can digitally select parcels of land through pre-determined administrative boundaries or manually plot the interested land areas in monitoring for hotspots and put FDRS Fire Weather Index (FWI) point(s) on the areas of interest. The users can select up to 20 separate parcels of land and up to 20 FWI points then name each of them. A parcel of land can be as large or as small as required. If a hotspot occurs on or adjacent to the specified land, an alert is sent to the phone, another alert on the fire risk level based on the FWI points.

Through this website (http://www.aseanfirealert.org/index.cfm) users have plotted boundaries to their land on a map. The software programme matches these two sources of data and trigger alert messages to registered users through the phone application.

Hotspot data is published daily by the ASEAN Specialised Meteorological Centre (ASMC), each day at a pre-determined time. A software programme designed for the application automatically visits and reads the published pre-formatted hotspot data "as is", displaying them as points on a map. The programme also reads other data sources including NOAA and MODIS. This information forms the daily set of hotspot data. Land parcels are drawn as 'regions' by registered users (accuracy determined by the map zoom levels). The system uses a buffer-zone of an additional 1km surrounding user selected regions in its computations of whether one or more hotspots are found within the 'region'. User can select locations to be Registration Points for monitoring changes in Fire Danger Rating. When any of these coordinate points rises or lowers in Fire Danger Rating (based on Fire Weather Index - FWI), the users will be sent a push notification alerting on the condition.

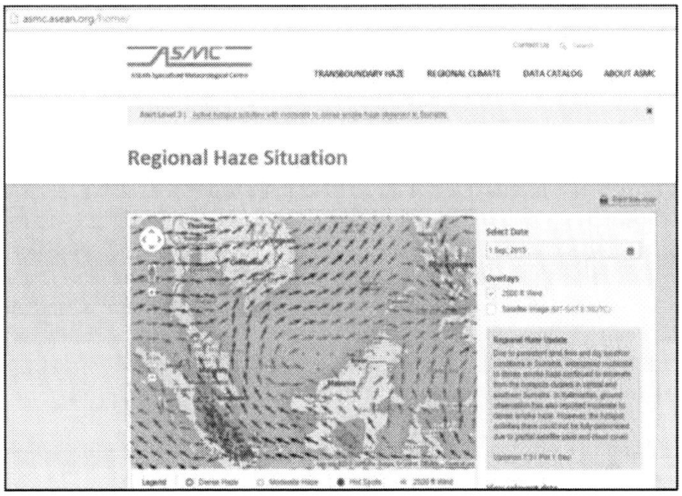

Registration as a "secondary" user will allow you to nominate one or more "primary" user who will all receive joint notifications on their respective individual registered/verified mobile smartphones. These new features are available for both Android and iOS devices (iPhone).

Push notifications are sent to users with installed and verified Phone Apps, once a day shortly after reading satellite hotspot data from ASMC and FWI from MMD. The notification is sent on a best effort basis only and without expressed or implied warranty of any kind (disclaimer).

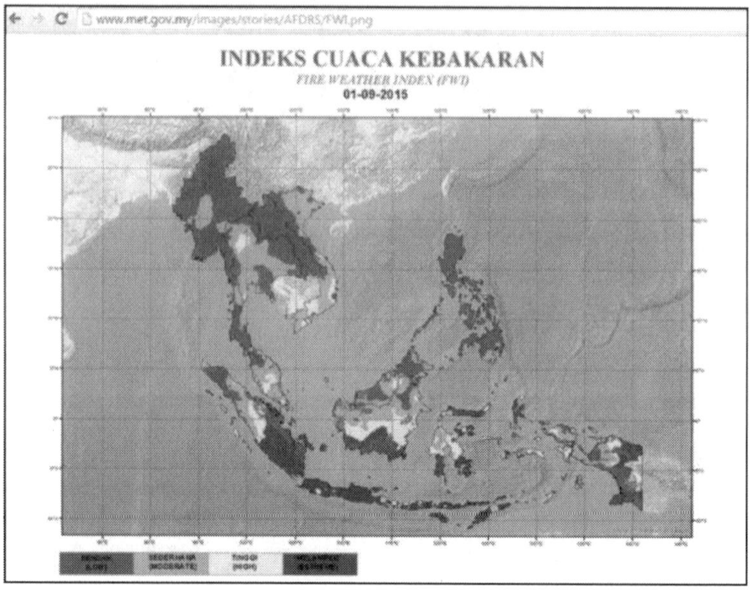

DISCUSSION

Preliminary surveys have come back with positive feedback such as the following:

1. Early warning of wildland fire danger on a global basis will provide international agencies, governments and local communities with an opportunity to mitigate fire damage by assessing threat likelihood and possibility of extreme behaviour enabling implementation of appropriate fire prevention, detection, preparedness, and fire response plans before wildfire problems begin.
2. A globally robust operational early warning framework with an applied system that will provide the foundation with which to build resource-sharing agreements between nations during times of extreme fire danger.
3. Development of local expertise and capacity building in wildland fire management for system sustainability through technology transfer and training.

CONCLUSION

It is highly recommended that land managers should download and use this application to manage fires on their lands. Several key tools such as hotspot and FDRS maps have been developed over the years to provide fire managers and land owners with useful information on hotspots and fire danger rating across the region. The smartphone application simply takes those information sources and puts it in a useful alert system.

There is still a need to verify and enhance the functions of the application, which can study on other similar services available such as Si Pongi website by Government of Indonesia, and Air4ASEAN application by Government of Thailand.

ACKNOWLEDGEMENTS

Much appreciation is recorded to funders – European Union, USAID funded programmes – Lowering Emissions in Asia's Forest (LEAF) and Indonesian Forest and Climate Support (IFACS), and technical service providers Spatial Informatics Group and Cornerstone Content Management System for enabling the development of the Tool. Appreciation also goes to ASMC (Singapore) and MMD (Malaysia) for providing technical content.

REFERENCES

1. Lee J.S.H., Jaafar, Z., Tan, A.K.J., Carrasco, L.R., Ewing, J.J., Bickford, D.P., Webb, E.L. and Koh, L.P. 2015. Toward clearer skies: Challenges in regulating transboundary haze in Southeast Asia. Environmental Science and Policy (www.elsevier.com/locate/envsci)
2. Malaysian Meteorological Department, 2013. Refinement on Fire Danger Rating System (FDRS) to Reduce Peat Fires in Malaysia. ASEAN Technical Workshop on Development of the ASEAN Peatland Fire Prediction and Early Warning System
3. Malaysian Meteorological Department, 2015. Standard Operating Procedure Operational Wave Numerical Forecast Model JMA MRI-III-MMD (NAVGEM)
4. Tacconi, L., Jotzo, F. and Grafton R.Q. 2007. Local causes, regional co-operation and global financing for environmental problems: the case of Southeast Asian Haze Pollution. Int Environ Agreements. Springer Science+Business Media B.V. 2007
5. Websites:
   - http://asmc.asean.org/asmc-about/
   - http://www.asb.cgiar.org/Publications%202015/PBs/ASB_PB51.pdf
   - http://www.aseanfirealert.org/
   - http://www.bmkg.go.id/
   - http://www.channelnewsasia.com/news/asiapacific/malaysia-won-t-protect/2144672.html
   - http://www.met.gov.my/
   - http://www.met.gov.my/web/metmalaysia/publications/meteorologicalnewsletter/document/155211/apc2015.pdf
   - www.aphref.aph.gov.au-house-committee-jfadt-indonesia-subs-subindo6.pdf

Abstract No: A-098

THE REDUCED COMPLEXITY OF THE TERMITE COMMUNITY STRUCTURE IN TROPICAL FIRE-IMPACTED PEATLANDS: A CASE STUDY FROM SUMATRA INDONESIA

Kok-Boon Neoh[1], Masayuki Itoh[2] and Osamu Kozan[2]

[1]*Department of Entomology, National Chung Hsing University, Taiwan*
[2]*Center for Southeast Asian Studies, Kyoto University, Japan*

**Corresponding author: neohkokboon@nchu.edu.tw*

SUMMARY

Termites and earthworms are equally important as ecosystem engineers and detritivores in forest soil. Given that the absence of earthworms in acidic soil conditions, termites are viewed as potentially major players in a variety of ecosystem functions in tropical peatlands. In this study, the termite assemblage in tropical peatlands, Sumatra Indonesia was studied using a standardized 100 m belt transect. Overall, the termite species richness in fire-impacted peats decreased up to 65% of the total species found in peat swamp forests. Our result demonstrated that fire changed termite community structure significantly. Only termites of family Rhinotermitidae (rhinotermitids) survived through fire event; while family Termitidae could have been diminished during the fire events. The implication of the likely ecosystem function change owing to the reduced complexity of termite composition is also discussed.

Keywords: *Peatland, Termite assemblage, Soil engineer, Peat fire*

INTRODUCTION

Both Indonesia and Malaysia comprised of 62% of tropical peatlands worldwide (Page *et al.*, 2006). These peatlands are known as biodiversity hotspot for many endemic species of flora, fauna and microbe habitats (Yule 2010). The co-existence of local communities with the resource-rich forest for living has been establishing for decades. In recent years, hectares of peat swamp forest were exploited for more agro-industrial plantations owing to political policy and agricultural expansion following the global food and fuel consumption demand increase. In the early 2000s, Koh *et al.* (2011) documented that approximately 6% of tropical peatlands in the Indo-Malayan region had been converted to oil-palm plantations. This poses massive biodiversity loss consequence upon land conversion. Earthworms as soil ecosystem engineer are disturbance-sensitive and virtually absent from disturbed peat (Blanchart and Julka 1997). Considering termites are dominant in tropical peatland, they are seen as major soil engineer.

To harness termites' ecosystem services efficiently in restoring the peat soil fertility, the land use in peat should be developed in compliance with coherent scientific knowledge on local termite assemblage and ecosystem functions provided. This would promote human-termites coexistence and sustainable ecosystem management program in the future. As a first step to understand the termite assemblage in tropical disturbed peatlands, termite samplings were carried out in abandoned degraded peatland and peatland cultivated with oil palm in Riau, Sumatra.

METHODS

In this study, we selected an abandoned degraded peatland site and a peatland cultivated with 5-6 years of oil palm. The sites are located in the GiamSiak Kecil–Bukit Batu Biosphere Reserve (0°44'–1°11'N and 0°11'–102°10'E). The study sites were 2 km apart. The canopy cover recorded approximately 38% in oil palm plantation; In contrast, the abandoned degraded peatland is open. In addition, a peat swamp forest was also surveyed and was treated as reference of the biodiversity loss in fire-impacted peatlands.

The termite samplings were carried out using a standardized belt transect (Jones and Eggleton 2000). The belt transect comprised of a survey area of 100 × 2 m and was divided into 20 sections, hence 5 × 2 m. A collector spent an hour on each section to collect the soldiers and worker termites from termite potential habitats such as dead tree branches, tree logs, soil under the log, termite gallery, and nest. The termites sampled were stored in 80% ethanol until identified. The termites were sorted to species level (Thapa 1977, Tho 1992, Gathorne-Hardy 2004).

Termite species richness was estimated using Chao2 and the diversity indices (Shannon and Simpson Indies) were also generated. All the analyses were carried out using Estimate S Version 8.2 (Colwell 2005). The relative abundance of termite was also generated based on the encounter rate in 20-section transect.

RESULTS

For fire-impacted peatlands, a total of six species of termite which comprising of a single family Rhinotermitidae, two subfamilies (i.e., Rhinotermitinae and Coptotermitinae) and three genera (i.e., *Coptotermes*, *Schedorhinotermes* and *Parrhinotermes*) were collected (Table 1). The observed species richness accumulation curve for both study sites reached an obvious asymptote close to estimated species richness curves (i.e., Chao2). In addition, all termite species were consistently encountered throughout the sampling as evidenced from none of the termite species that only found once or twice (Singletons = 0; Doubletons = 0). All termite species found were wood feeders and wood nesting termites. In contrast, for forests, 17 species of termite from four subfamilies were collected. It is worth noting that the additional subfamilies were Nasutitermitinae and Termitinae that were predominantly soil and plant litter feeding termites.

In terms of relative abundance, *Coptotermes kalshoveni* (Kemner), *Parrhinotermes aequalis* (Havilandi) and *Schedorhinotermes medioobscurus* (Holmgren) were predominately distributed in the abandoned degraded peat (Shannon index: 3.34; Simpson index: 3.45), which account for the relative abundances of 23%, 41% and 32%, respectively. In contrast, the termite dominance in oil palm is even (Shannon index: 4.93; Simpson index: 5.50). Each species registered approximately 20% of encounter rate in the transect sampling.

Table 1: Preliminary study of termite assemblage in tropical peat conducting in Riau, Sumatra. The termites were sampled based on Jones and Eggleton (2000).

Termite taxonomic group	Fire-impacted peats	
Natural forest	Unmanaged secondary peatland	Burnt peatland cultivated with oil palm
RHINOTERMITIDAE		
Coptotermitinae		
Coptotermes curvignathus	*Coptotermes gestroi*	*Coptotermes gestroi*
Coptotermes gestroi	*Coptotermes kalshoveni*	*Coptotermes kalshoveni*
Coptotermes kalshoveni		
Rhinotermitinae		
Parrhinotermes aequalis	*Parrhinotermes pygmaues*	*Parrhinotermes pygmaues*
Parrhinotermes pygmaues	*Parrhinotermes aequalis*	*Parrhinotermes aequalis*
Schedorhinotermes medioobscurus	*Parrhinotermes minor*	*Schedorhinotermes malaccensis*
	Schedorhinotermes malaccensis	*Schedorhinotermes medioobscurus*
	Schedorhinotermes medioobscurus	
TERMITIDAE		
Nasutitermitinae		
Bulbitermes sarawakiensis		
Nasutitermes neoparvus		
Nasutitermes proatripennis		
Nasutitermes regularis		
Subulitermes-group		
Termitinae		
Amitermes-group		
Microcerotermes havilandi		
Termes-group		
Pericapritermes nitobei		
Pericapritermes semarangi		
Pericapritermes speciosus		
Procapritermes sp.		
Termes rostratus		

DISCUSSION

The termite assemblage in fire-impacted peatlands contained only a single family of lower termite – Rhinotermitidae (rhinotermitids) which consist of two subfamilies (Coptotermitinae and Rhinotermitinae), three genera and six termite species. Similarly, low termite species richness was found in newly cleared peatland by Vaessen *et al.* (2011). The low termite species richness might result from the land perturbation during the land clearing event or repeated fire causing the collapse of susceptible termite species. Those termites that managed to survive at post-fire are exclusively wood-nesting termites. This indicated that tree bark could have acted as heat insulator and allows termites to survive under high temperature (> 400°C). The phenomenon is new and somewhat contrast with those occurred in savanna system in which those termites that build mound had better survival rate.

In mineral soils, termites are known to make subterranean tunnels to improve soil water infiltration rate, decompose plant litter and mound building via soil translocation and improve soil bulk density (Holt and Lepage 2000). In Indo-Malayan region, the termite assemblage in peat swamp forest mainly comprised of decay wood-feeder and soil-feeder (Table 1). The nest of soil feeders generally contained high level of organic carbon in their nest due to their feeding habits of highly decaying soil-like cellulose materials (Black and Okwakol 1997). In Columbian savanna, a study of soil feeding termites revealed that the group was reportedly more important in soil nutrient enrichment rather than what ants can do (Jiménez *et al.* 2008). Soil studies impacted by *Nasutitermes sp.* revealed that the mounds can act as `sinks' of essential nitrogen source for plants in the nutrient depleted savanna systems (López-Hernández 2001, Jiménez *et al.* 2006).

In the present study, our results demonstrated the drastic reduced complexity of community structure of termite in tropical fire-impacted peatlands. The presence of soil-feeding and plant-litter feeding termites in natural peat swamp forests may reflect the possibility of those termites wiped out during the fire event. This in turn may impede the degraded peat restoration process.

ACKNOWLEDGEMENTS

K.-B.N. was an international researcher fellow of the Japan Society for the Promotion of Science. This study was partly funded by Large-Scale Research Program 'Promoting the Study of Sustainable Humanosphere in Southeast Asia' funded by the Japanese Ministry of Education, Culture, Sports, Science, and Technology (MEXT), 2011-2016, the Institutional Collaboration Feasibility Studies "Toward the Regeneration of Tropical Peat Land Societies: Establishment of an International Research Network and Proposal of its Future", Research Institute for Humanity and Nature (RIHN), and the Ministry of Science and Technology, Taiwan (MOST 105-2313-B-005-004-MY2).

REFERENCES

1. Black, H. I. J., and M. J. N. Okwakol. 1997. Agricultural intensification, soil biodiversity and agroecosystem function in the tropics: The role of termites. Applied Soil Ecology 6: 37-53.
2. Blanchart, E., and J. M. Julka. 1997. Influence of forest disturbance on earthworm (Oligochaeta) communites in the Western Ghats (South India). Soil Biology & Biochemistry 29: 303-306.
3. Colwell, R. K. 2005. EstimateS: Statistical estimation of species richness and shared species from samples Version 8.2. User's Guide and application published at: http://purl.oclc.org/estimates.
4. Gathorne-Hardy, F. J. 2004. The termites of Sundaland: A taxonomic review. The Sarawak Musuem Journal 81: 88-133
5. Holt, J. A., and M. Lepage. 2000. Termites and soil properties, pp. 389-407. *In* T. Abe, D. E. Bignell and M. Higashi [eds.], Termites: Evolution, Sociality, Symbioses, Ecology. Kluwer Academic Publishers, Dordrecht.
6. Jiménez, J. J., T. Decaëns, and P. Lavelle. 2006. Nutrient spatial variability in biogenic structures of Nasutitermes (Termitinae; Isoptera) in a gallery forest of the Colombian 'Llanos'. Soil Biology and Biochemistry 38: 1132-1138.
7. Jiménez, J. J., T. Decaëns, and P. Lavelle. 2008. C and N concentrations in biogenic structures of a soil-feeding termite and a fungus-growing ant in the Colombian savannas. Applied Soil Ecology 40: 120-128.
8. Jones, D. T., and P. Eggleton. 2000. Sampling termite assemblages in tropical forests: testing a rapid biodiversity assessment protocol. Journal of Applied Ecology 37: 191-203.
9. Koh, L. P., J. Miettinen, S. C. Liew, and J. Ghazoul. 2011. Remotely sensed evidence of tropical peatland conversion to oil palm. Proceedings of the National Academy of Sciences 108: 5127-5132.
10. López-Hernández, D. 2001. Nutrient dynamics (C, N and P) in termite mounds of *Nasutitermes ephratae* from savannas of the Orinoco Llanos (Venezuela). Soil Biology and Biochemistry 33: 747-753.
11. Page, S. E., J. O. Rieley, and R. Wüst. 2006. Lowland tropical peatlands of Southeast Asia., pp. 145-172. *In* I. P. Martini, A. Martinez Cortizas and W. Chesworth [eds.], Peatlands: evolution and records of

environmental and climate changes. Elsevier, The Netherlands.
12. Thapa, R. S. 1977. Termites of Sabah. Sabah Forestry Department, Sandakan.
13. Tho, Y. P. 1992. Termites of peninsular Malaysia. Forest Research Institute of Malaysia, Kuala Lumpur.
14. **Vaessen, T., C. Verwer, M. Demies, H. Kaliang, and P. J. van der Meer. 2011.** Comparison of termite assemblages along a landuse gradient on peat areas in Sarawak, Malaysia. Journal of Tropical Forest Science 23: 196-203.
15. **Yule, C. M. 2010.** Loss of biodiversity and ecosystem functioning in Indo-Malayan peat swamp forests. Biodiversity and Conservation 19: 393-409.

Abstract No: A-445

TUBE WELL CONSTRUCTIONS AND PEAT MANAGEMENT TO COMBAT AND PREVENT PEAT FIRES AT KUALA BARAM, MIRI, SARAWAK, MALAYSIA

Roslan Rajali

Jabatan Mineral dan Geosains Malaysia, Sarawak, Malaysia

**Corresponding author: roslanra@jmg.gov.my*

SUMMARY

Groundwater investigation and development was carried out to identify the source of water supply as an assisting tool to combat or prevent peat fire. It covers an area of 76 sq. km. The peat thickness ranges from 1 to 5 m. The reduced resistivity value from geophysical profile analysis of sand body which is 5 to 100 Ωm and the clay layer which is 0 to 5 Ωm is due to saline water. Ten (10) tube wells were constructed with depth ranging from 11 to 147 m and the discharge rate are in the range of 4.0 to 100 m^3/hr. There are two (2) types of aquifer exist namely, top aquifer of less to moderate groundwater potential and the lower aquifer of high groundwater potential. The top aquifer is of the unconfined type whereas; the lower aquifer is of the confined and leaky types. The lower aquifer can sustain long hours of pumping at the recommended discharge rate even pumping occurred during the dry season. The sand lower aquifer is of fine to medium grained, clean and 21 to 58 m thick. Analyses of the investigations at the project area revealed that the sand lower aquifer has a lateral continuity. The groundwater has a moderate to high chloride value in the range of 520 – 12,426 mg/l. The source of groundwater has a high value and extremely needed to be used in combating and preventing peat fire, especially the smouldering effect of the peat. A well-planned peat management system and with proper mitigation measures in place is vital for peat preservation.

Keywords: *Peat fire, tube well, groundwater, smouldering, peat management*

INTRODUCTION

On the 10th June 2002, the Governments of the ten ASEAN Member Countries signed the ASEAN Agreement on Transboundary Haze Pollution in Kuala Lumpur, Malaysia. The ASEAN Agreement on Transboundary Haze Pollution (AATHP), which has been enforced since 2003, attempts to create a frame work that will allow parties to reduce transboundary haze pollution. Most of the haze are caused by the peat fire especially the prolonged haze, which is due to the smouldering effect of the peat. Peat fires are mostly concentrated in south Sumatra, south and central Kalimantan, as well as Papua. The BBC News (2015) in October 19, 2015 quoted the Indonesian health ministry saying, the hardest hit by these peat fires is the city of Palangkaraya in Central Kalimantan whereby, the Pollutant Standard Index has reached more than 2,000 at times.

The surrounding Project area at Kuala Baram, Miri, Sarawak, Malaysia (Figure 1) had faced frequent peat fire during the dry season. Haze caused by this burning had created an unhealthy environment to the people living nearby and also to the neighbouring country, Negara Brunei Darussalam. Due to this haze problem, a task force has been formed under the supervision of Ministry of Environment and Natural Resources (NRE) and the Department of Environment Malaysia (DOE) as a Coordinator. Department of Minerals and Geossience Malaysia, Sarawak (JMG) has been given the task to carry out the study to identify the potential aquifer for groundwater extraction through constructed tube wells, as a source of water supply to combat and prevent peat fire. The Project area lies at approximately 12 km north-north east of Miri city. It is bounded by Baram River to the north. This work, which was carried out since 2010 involved tube well constructions plus its infrastructures. Other departments involved in this project and part of the committee members include Department of Irrigation & Drainage (DID), Fire and Rescue Department of Malaysia (BOMBA), Miri Resident Office, Miri City Council (MCC), Natural Resources & Environment Board Sarawak (NREB), The People's Volunteer Corps (RELA) and Malaysia Civil Defence Department (JPAM). The project area is estimated to be 76 sq. km, covering Kuala Baram, Tudan, Permyjaya and Senadin.

Under DOE as the Coordinator, the whole project is called *Program Pencegahan Kebakaran dan Pengurusan Tanah Gambut Yang Sering Terbakar* (Peat Fire Management and Preventive Programme). JMG at every state in Malaysia which has peat deposits is given the task to carry out this project. Some additions and modifications to the actual task given to the JMG were introduced and carried out by the JMG. These include carrying out geological study, peat study, geophysical survey, well exploration, hydrogeological study, groundwater resource management and peat management.

OBJECTIVE

The objective of this project is to locate and develop groundwater by constructing tube wells as a source of water supply for combating and preventing peat fire and for peat management and preservation through mitigating processes.

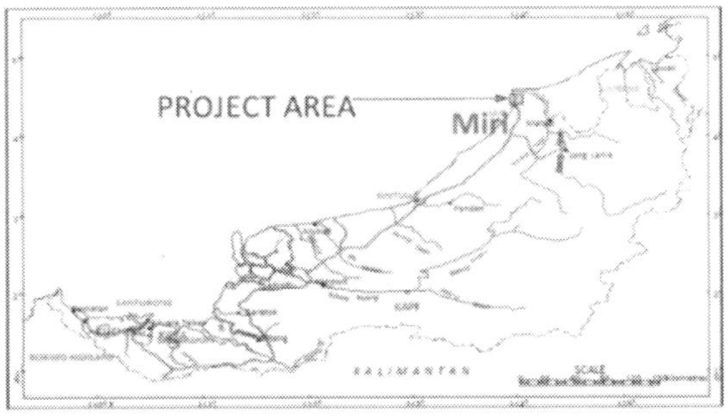

Location of the Project area

Part of the project area, including surrounding SJK(C) Chung Hua Tudan and Permyjaya.

Figure 1: Locality map and image part of the Project area.

REGIONAL GEOLOGY

The regional geologic framework of the Miri area reflects the ancient marine environment which characterised this portion of Sarawak many millions of years ago. Thick marine sandstone, siltstone, limestone and shale formations are evidence that at one time the Miri area was inundated by the ocean (Wilford, 1961). The regional geology surrounding the Miri area is defined by several geologic formations, that is from oldest to youngest as follows:Lambir Formation, Tukau Formation, Miri Formation, Liang Formation, Terrace Deposits and finally Recent Alluvium. The Liang Formation is at the coastal areas from Miri to Brunei Bay, beneath the ocean and from the Lambir Hills to the lower Baram area where it is covered by alluvium. It is comprised of marine and deltaic deposits which reflect the inland transgression of the ancient marine environment. The Liang Formation is overlain by the Quaternary deposits. Quaternary deposits cover most of the undulating and low-lying area in the Miri area. It consists of terrace and alluvial deposit. The alluvial deposits which underlying the study area are composed of clay, sand, gravel and peat. This recent alluvium dominated the coastal area. The alluvial sediment has been carried from the upland areas by local streams and rivers. The sediment has filled the embayment and created deltas which extend into the ocean. Peat deposits have accumulated on the majority of the alluvial flatlands.

PEAT STUDY

Ley (1995) had carried out the peat study. He reported that the area is underlained mainly by fine sand intercalating with soft, sticky clay layers and with the top layer covered with peat of various thickness. The peat deposits are of ombrogeneous and topogeneous types. The ombrogeneous peat consists of leaves, roots, reeds, branches and tree trunks. The plant remains are slightly to moderately decomposed, ranging from H_2 to H_4 on the van Post scale of humification. The topogeneous or clayey peat is generally characterised by its clastic component of mainly silt and clay, contributed by the flood water. Ombrogeneous peat tends to get burns quite easily as compared to topogeneous peat. According to Ley (1995), based on the level surveys undertaken by Anderson (1964), that all the peat swamps in the lower reaches of the Batang Baram area are of raised-bog type, i.e. the elevation at the centre is generally the highest.

An isopach map of peat was generated based on the data available from Ley (1995) study. The eastern part of the study area is covered with deep peat, with depth up to 5 m and with average thickness of 3 m whereas; the western part is covered with shallow peat of 1 to 2 m in thickness.

GEOPHYSICAL SURVEY

The survey was carried out using the 2D resistivity vertical imaging method to locate the groundwater potential area. Based on the 2D resistivity inversion model of the study area, the resistivity value of sand body falls between 5 to 100 Ωm and for clay layer falls between 0 to 5 Ωm. The presence of saline water had reduced the resistivity values of these geological materials and likewise the presence of gas pocket caused the geological material to increase in the resistivity values. The top layer is identified as peat. The underlying sand layer below the peat is of uniform thickness, averaging 7 m thick. Thick clay layer is underlying the sand layer with probable thickness of about 40 m. The clay layer covers the targeted sand body, predicted to be of a good aquifer with average thickness of about 30m thick. Based on the 2D resistivity inversion model, the sand body has a lateral continuity.

SITE GEOLOGY

The study area is covered by peat layer ranging from 2 to 5 m in thickness. Underlying the peat layer is the sand layer. It is of very fine grained and sometime observed as dirty sand. There are abundant fossils, wood and silt in small to significant amounts. The thickness of this sand layer is 7 to 11 m. Thick clay layer is found underneath the sand layer. The clay layer at some locations occurred as silty clay or silt interlayered with the clay itself. The thickness of clay layer in the study area ranges from 28 to 48 m. Underlying this thick clay layer is the sand layer. The thickness of the sand layer ranges from 21 to 58 m. This sand is predominantly fine to medium quartz grained. The sand is mostly clean. There are presence of fossils and wood in small amount. Underlying the sand layer is the clay and silt layers.

DRILLING AND WELL CONSTRUCTIONS

A total of ten (10) tube wells were constructed at the project area. The depth of the tube wells ranges from 11 m to 147 m. The discharge rate ranges from 4.0 to 100 m^3/hr. The size of the tube well ranges from 100 mm (4 inch) to 200 mm (8 inch) in diameter.

HYDROGEOLOGY

There are two (2) types of aquifer exist in the study area. The top aquifer which is of the unconfined type exists at an average top of 11 m, which is underlying the peat deposit. The lower aquifer, which is of the confined and leaky types, occurred at deeper depth below the average 40 m thickness of clay.

The sand of the top aquifer is of very fine grained, clean and sometime dirty. Areas where exploration wells are tapping the dirty sand, it would give low yields. This is the area with low groundwater potential except for area with clean sand, which has a moderate groundwater potential.

The sand layer of the lower aquifer below the thick clay layer which acts as an aquitard has a high groundwater potential and has a lateral continuity. The sand is clean and fine to medium grained. Most of the tube wells were constructed to tap this lower aquifer, which have a very high discharge rate or safe yield of 100 m^3/hr.

WATER QUALITY

The iron content is low to high, ranges from 0.15 to 5.84 mg/l. pH is moderate, ranges from 7.16 to 8.02. The groundwater is of moderate to very high chloride value, ranges from 386 to 6,257 mg/l. The Ca, Mg, Na and K range from 5.35 to 50.37 mg/l, 8.36 to 99.97 mg/l, 124.5 to 1,116 mg/l and 6.19 to 44.86 mg/l respectively. Based on the Piper Diagram, which is based on the classification quoted by Freeze and Cherry (1979), in terms of anions, all the groundwater samples fall under chloride type of water. In terms of cations, most of the samples fall under sodium or potassium type of water except for groundwater samples from the western and northern parts, which fall under magnesium type of water. The groundwater samples fall under Cl+SO4 and Cl+SO4, HCO3 types of water. One sample from the western part falls under Na +K type of water.

PEAT MANAGEMENT

The processes involved in peat management includes works such as geology, peat study, geophysical survey, hydrogeological study, groundwater resource management and finally the construction of the infrastructures. The infrastructures (Figure 2) should be in place in order to manage the peat. These infrasructures include Observation Tower (*Menara Tinjau*, which was constructed by the MCC), Check Dam (constructed by the DID), Fire Breaker (constructed by the DID) and tube wells (constructed by the JMG). A well-planned peat management system is vital for peat preservation. To preserve peat, any scenario which could destroy peat structures need to be solved immediately. The events that could destroy the peat structures are peat fires or the smouldering effects of the peat which cause the haze problem.

To tackle these issues, a proper mitigation measures should be in place.

Tube Wells Construction

The tube wells are needed as a source of water supply. The problem faced at the affected areas is that there are no available source of water supply nearby to combat and prevent peat fire. Solving the water source problem by laying pipeline from the nearest river or water source could be very costly and furthermore, this water source may be unreliable during the dry season.

Peat Study

Peat study provides information such as the thickness and type of peat. Areas with greater thickness of peat should have better infrastructures in place to combat and prevent peat fire. These areas would produce more haze when there is smouldering effect at the dry peat during a drop in water level. Due to its high carbon content, dry peat is extremely susceptible to burning. The water source should be quickly identified to moist the peat in order to prevent this smouldering of peat.

Fire Breaker Construction

The Fire Breaker is a drainage system constructed to prevent fire from spreading or migrating to other area. This drainage system should not be kept dry. The RELA would monitor the surrounding from the Observation Tower (*Menara Tinjau*) and would inform the DOE or Resident Office immediately, whenever they noticed the drain dried up or there is peat fire. The DOE or Resident Office would immediately inform JMG to start pumping. JMG would then mobilise their team to start pumping from the groundwater tube wells to fill up the drainage system and eventually spread out into the peat area, thereby keeping the peat moist all the time. Moist peat would prevent the subsurface from burning during fire broke out on surface and helps prevent smouldering of the peat which produced heavy haze (Figure 3).

Installed High Capacity Submersible Pump and Generator Set

If the affected area (peat fire) is quite large, we need to install high capacity submersible pump and generator set to discharge large amount of groundwater from the tube wells. Bigger yield such as giving discharge of 100 m^3/hr or more for every tube well with a combination of the nearby tube well would help to expedite the filling up of the drainage system and eventually spreading out to the surrounding peat.

Check Dams Construction

The purpose of the Check Dam is to prevent the water from flowing away from the affected area. Any suspected fire prone area would be constructed with a drainage system followed up by Check Dam construction. At the end point of fire prone area, the constructed Check Dam would maximize the volume of water filling up the drain and finally spreading to the surrounding peat, which would then produce moist peat to prevent smouldering effect.

High Level Observation Tower (Menara Tinjau) Construction

The function of the high level Observation Tower (*Menara Tinjau*) is for monitoring the surrounding for any open burning, identifying peat drying up based on observation at the water level inside the drain and also for a place to discuss before any quick or immediate action taken to tackle peat fire.

Weather Forecast

Continuous weather forecast announcement by the Meteorology Department Malaysia plus future prediction would help in early preparation for incoming hazardous condition (peat fire) especially prediction involved any severe drought condition or future incoming dry season and also the presence of El Niño.

Promote Community Involvement

Surrounding people living nearby should be taught or explained on the detrimental effect resulting from open burning that is hazardous in nature as a result of the haze. The community must be involved in any dialogue session and help in preventing peat fire.

Team Work

The technical and management committee members or personnel must work as a group and communicate frequently among themselves for best outcome. The Miri Resident Office, which was appointed as a Committee Team Leader and Chair Person, would advise for any next move after consulting with committee members. Any action by the committee members once being informed, should be very fast in mobilising its personnel and equipment to combat and prevent peat fire.

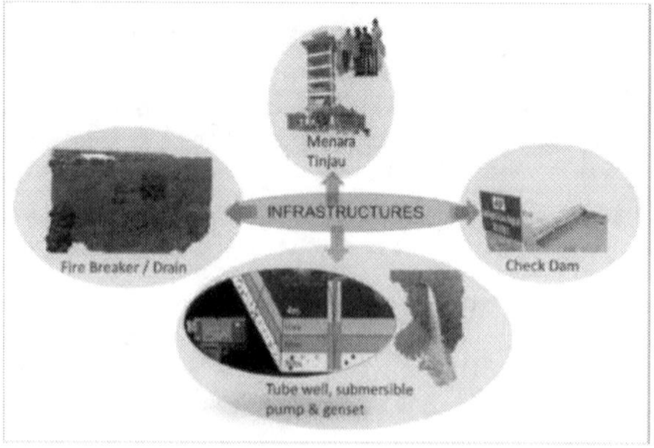

Figure 2: Infrastructures needed to combat and prevent peat fire.

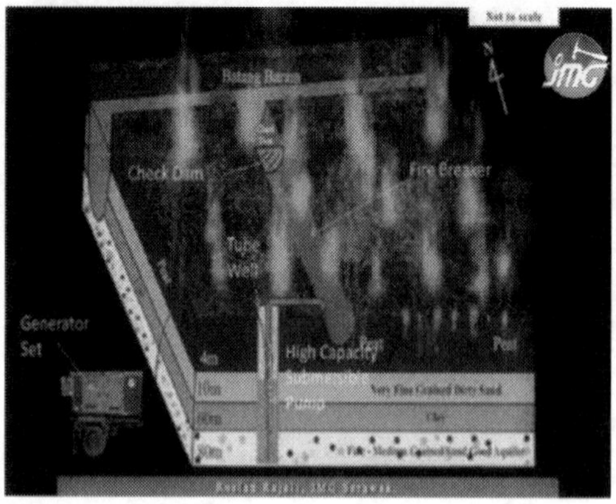

Figure 3: 3D model showing the process involved in combating and preventing peat fire and the smouldering effect of the peat

OUTCOME

The constructed tube wells, which have high discharge rate, would be the source of water supply to assist in combating and preventing peat fires and also in preventing the Transboundary Haze Pollution. Peat fire prevention would result in reducing haze which, if left unchecked would have detrimental effect on the health of the people living nearby and also our neighbour such as Negara Brunei Darussallam. These health effects include sneezing, running nose, eye irritation, dry throat and dry cough. People with medical problems like asthma, chronic lung disease, chronic sinusitis and allergic skin conditions are more likely to be affected. The haze can affect the nation's economy such as shut down in daily works (e.g. industrial production, airline and airport, fishing industry and also tourism). It can also create contention between governments of nations affected and less foreign investors coming in.

CONCLUSIONS

The study area is underlain by two (2) types of aquifer namely, top and lower aquifer. The top aquifer has less to moderate groundwater potential whereas, the lower aquifer has high groundwater potential. The top aquifer is of the unconfined type whereas, the lower aquifer is of the confined to leaky type. The thick sand layer of the lower aquifer consists of a clean and fine to medium grained sand. The constructed tube wells which tapped the lower aquifer have a very high discharge rate or safe yield of 100 m^3/hr. The sand lower aquifer has a lateral continuity and can sustain long hours of pumping at the recommended discharge rate even during the dry season. The presence of the groundwater source managed to combat and prevent peat fires and the smouldering effects of the peat that caused prolonged haze problem and thus preserve the peat for the next generation.

REFERENCES

1. Anderson, J.A.R., 1964. *Observations on climatic damage in peat swamp forest in Sarawak.* Commonwealth Forestry Review Vol. 43: 145-158.
2. BBC News., 2015. *http://www.bbc.com/news/world-asia-34571356.* Accessed on October 23, 2015.
3. Freeze, R.A. and Cherry, J.A., 1979. *Groundwater.*New Jersey: Prentice-Hall, Inc. pp252.
4. Ley, L.N., 1995. *Progress Report: Quaternary geology mapping of Miri area, Sarawak.* Unpubl.
5. Wilford., 1961. *The Geology and mineral resources of Brunei and adjacent parts of Sarawak.* Memoir 10. Geological Survey Department, British Territories in Borneo.

THEME 3
PEATLANDS AFTER-USE, RESTORATION & REHABILITATION OF EX-PRODUCTION PEATLANDS

3.1: RESTORATION OF BOREAL, TEMPERATE & TROPICAL PEATLANDS

Abstract No: A-142

PEATLANDS IN SUB HUMID REGIONS UNDER CHANGING CLIMATE AND HUMAN ACTIVITIES

Andrey Sirin[1], Tatiana Minayeva[1], Danil Ilyasov[1], Gennady Suvorov[1], Vasily Martynenko[2], Yury Fedotov[3], Tamara Glukhova[1], Natalya Valuayeva[1], Olga Tsuganova[1], Aleksandr Maslov[1], Albert Muldashev[2], Pavel Shirokikh[2] and Evgeny Kuznetsov[4]

[1]Institute of Forest Science Russian Academy of Sciences, Moscow Oblast
[2]Ufa Institute of Biology Russian Academy of Sciences, Ufa, Republic of Bashkortostan
[3]Nature State Biosphere Reserve "Bryansk Les", Bryansk Oblast
[4]UNDP Russia, Moscow

**Corresponding author: sirin@proc.ru*

SUMMARY

Peatlands are especially important in sub humid climates like forest-steppe and steppe areas in the European part of Russia. They store carbon, maintain specific flora and fauna, support biodiversity far beyond their borders by regulating adjacent environment and providing temporary habitats. However many of them were lost in last decades due to land use and climate changes. Peatlands in these regions are often disregarded as specific ecosystems, and therefore raising awareness is the key issue to save them for future generations. Wise use of peatlands, protection within Specially Protected Areas SPAs, and restoration of disturbed sites can facilitate adaptation to climate change and mitigate the latter by saving carbon storage in peat and controlling GHG emissions. These activities are discussed by the example of the EC Clima East Pilot Project focused to peatlands in the forest-steppe and steppe regions of the European part of Russia.

Keywords: *Peatlands, forest steppe, carbon loss, protection, restoration*

INTRODUCTION

Peatlands are highly integrated and important natural ecosystems with specific regulation functions, characteristic biodiversity, high value for the environment and welfare. These ecosystems are especially important in sub-humid climates, such as in the forest-steppe and steppe regions. They store carbon and water, maintain specific flora and fauna, support biodiversity far beyond their borders by regulating the adjacent environment and providing temporary habitats. But, many of them were lost during recent decades due to land use and other threats aggravated by climate change. Forest steppe and steppe peatlands are considered the most vulnerable to the climate change (Parish *et al.*, 2008, Minayeva *et al.*, 2009). Unfortunately, peatlands in these regions are often disregarded as specific ecosystems, and therefore raising awareness is the key issue to save them for future generations. Wise use of peatlands, protection within Specially Protected Areas (SPAs), and restoration of disturbed ones can facilitate adaptation to climate change and mitigate the latter by saving carbon storage in peat and controlling GHG emissions. To solve these problems by the example of peatlands in the forest-steppe and steppe regions in European part of Russia, the EC Clima East Pilot Project "Conservation and sustainable management of peatlands in Russia to minimize carbon emissions and help ecosystems to adapt to climate change" has been developed and implemented under the UNDP/GEF project "Improving the coverage and management efficiency of protected areas in the steppe biome of Russia".

The main activities under the project are as follows:

- Inventory and threats analysis for steppe and forest steppe peatlands (distribution, natural values and losses, impacts, threats and ecosystem status);
- Improvement of land use management and planning, expansion and strengthening of the protected areas system in pilot regions to increase ecosystem resilience and improve their adaptive capacity to climate change;
- Peatland ecosystem restoration and maintenance in pilot project regions with a view to reduce carbon emissions.

The project has been implemented in a large number of administrative regions of the Russian Federation that are situated, completely or partially, in the forest steppe zone of the European part of the country (Fig. 1). Distribution, biological diversity, and anthropogenic disturbance were analyzed in all of these regions.

As a result, possible measures aimed to improve protection of intact peatlands, including through the development of a Specially Protected Areas SPA network, and to restore peatlands disturbed by economic activities were proposed. Practical implementation of these activities takes place in the main model region (Bashkortostan Republic) and some others. This paper discusses major issues associated with scientific provision of project solutions and operative implementation results.

PEATLAND DISTRIBUTION IN FOREST STEPPE ZONE OF EUROPEAN RUSSIA

The forest-steppe and steppe zone form a belt 500-700 km wide and 1500 km long in the south-eastern part of European Russia that stretches from Ukraine in the west to the Southern Urals and Kazakhstan in the east. Forest-steppe landscapes were formed under typical continental climate, relatively warm and dry. The overall sum of active (>0 °C) temperatures is 2500-2700°C, with the humidity coefficient < 1. The dry season lasts from April to September. Annual precipitation varies from 400 to 600 mm; evaporation reaches 500 mm. Originally, the area was occupied by expansive ecotone landscapes formed with fragments of broadleaved forests and meadow-like steppes, and some pine forests on sandy grounds. Nowadays, 70-80% of the areas are arable lands. Steppe landscapes have been formed under the continental climate with a pronounced deficit of moisture. The total annual sum of active temperatures reaches 3500°C, while annual precipitation is 300-400 mm (400-500 mm in East European sector). Evaporation could reach 1000 mm, while the humidity coefficient measures 0.8-0.6 in the northern subzone and 0.5-0.3 in the southern subzone.

Figure 1: Distribution of mires and peatlands (black dots) within forest-steppe zone of European Russia.

It is usually considered that forest-steppe and steppe zones of European Russia have no or very few mires and peatlands; they are "white spots" in general descriptions of peatland area in the country (Vompersky *et al.,* 1994, 2005, 2011). However, according to the Land Cadaster, peatlands are present in all administrative regions in the forest-steppe zone and in most of the steppe zone, even though their area does not exceed n × 0.1% (Sirin, Minayeva 2001; Minayeva *et al.,* 2009). Project activities include mapping mires and peatlands in the forest steppe and steppe zones of European Russia for further submission of this information to the GIS "Peatlands of Russia" maintained by the Institute of Forest Science Russian Academy of Sciences (Vompersky *et al.,* 2005, 2011). Mapping approach for mires and peatlands was developed for and tested in other regions of the country (Sirin et al. 2014). It uses an inventory of peat deposits and other sectoral and cartographic data available. This information was georeferenced based on high-resolution remote sensing data. Special attention has been given to ordering and preparation of high-resolution EO data for the model areas. Presently, within forest-steppe zone up to 3000 peatlands with a total area of over 100,000 ha were added to the GIS database. The digital map of peatlands and mires in the forest steppe and steppe zones of European Russia is under development. It should be edited by local experts and developed further.

PEATLANDS DIVERSITY

Climatic conditions of the forest steppe zone do not support peatland development and their formation is related to additional sources of excessive moisture, such as ground, artesian, deluvial, or flood water. This is why most of these peatlands are small in size (usually no more than 50 ha), while larger peatlands (from 100 to over 1000 ha) are very rare and bound to river valleys. Peat deposits usually do not exceed 2-3 m in depth, but there are some peatlands (e.g. karst mires) with peat layer of up to 6-8 m deep. Eutrophic peats prevail here; they consist of sedge, wood-sedge, and wood peats having a medium or, more often, high decomposition degree. They are often enriched by carbonates.

The majority of forest steppe peatlands are located in river valleys. The most common geomorphological mire types are floodplain, oxbow, floodplain terrace, and gully mires. Vegetation cover of the mires is dominated by eutrophic communities: sedge, reed, black alder, and others. Less often, mires are found on watersheds and river terraces. There, they are confined to hollows of various origins. Usually these hollows are shallow and have groundwater levels close to the surface. These mires are groundwater-fed. Vegetation cover is dominated by eutrophic communities, such as grasses and trees. In the course of mire development and peat accumulation, peatlands of this type can become mesotrophic, but in reality they mostly become oligotrophic due to a lack of atmospheric input. Typically, vegetation cover of these mesotrophic mires is dominated by grass-sphagnum and tree-sphagnum communities. Occasional lacustrine quagmires can be found in deep, waterlogged depressions on watersheds. Such mires are usually associated with karst-suffusion holes and depressions and have high water levels. Interestingly, a rare peatland type, the spring mire depending on outcome of carbonate-rich artesian water is often found in downslope locations in river valleys and gullies.

Forest-steppe peatlands in Russia were described in detail in a monograph by N. Piavchenko (1958). Later on, they were mentioned in general reviews on national peatlands and local studies carried out in various parts of the region. Generally, however, forest-steppe peatlands are much less studied than expansive forest-zone peatlands. In the course of the project, local researchers have been collecting actual data on biological diversity and ecological peculiarities of forest-steppe peatlands that later will be analyzed and summarized.

PEATLANDS VALUE

Peatlands are highly complex and important natural ecosystems with specific regulation functions, characteristic biodiversity, and high environmental and welfare values. They store water, regulate hydrological regimes of headwaters, river valleys, and streams, maintain characteristic flora and fauna, and support biodiversity far beyond their borders by regulating the adjacent environment and providing temporary habitats for non-mire species (Minayeva Sirin, 2012). These peatland functions are especially important under sub-humid conditions. Storage of water and carbon, as well as maintenance of specific biodiversity is key ecosystem functions of peatlands in the forest-steppe and steppe zones. Performance of these functions strongly affects human well-being and subsistence. At the same time, forest-zone peatlands have been attractive for people as rare sources of peat (Sirin, Minayeava, 2001, Minayeva Sirin, 2005, Minayeva *et al.*, 2009) and as more productive agricultural lands (e.g. pastures, haylands, croplands), especially in view of climate warming and aridization. As a result, most peatlands in the steppe and forest-steppe zones have been irreversibly lost, which has also affected water regime, lands productivity, and biodiversity status. To prevent further dramatic changes, science-based peatland management should be introduced as soon as possible in this area.

ANTHROPOGENIC AND CLIMATIC THREATS TO PEATLANDS

Peatland uses depend on traditional practices molded in Russia's regions (Minayeva *et al.*, 2009). Peat extraction is rather limited in the forest-steppe and steppe zones, but still provides a direct threat to peatlands. These regions stopped using peat for fuel a long time ago. However, peat has still been extracted there at previously utilized areas, in particular as a soil improver.

Agricultural uses put the greatest impact on peatlands in the region. Most of the peatlands were drained in the 1950-1970s for agriculture. Some of them were partially extracted and then recultivated for agricultural purposes. Later on, all these lands were used as croplands, hayfields and pastures. The latter type of land use affected peatlands to a lesser degree than tilled-crop agriculture. In recent years, however, many peatlands used in agriculture were abandoned, especially after economic changes in the early 1990s. At present, they are overgrown with weeds, and in some places with trees and shrubs. Some floodplain peatlands were destroyed in the establishment of water reservoirs and ponds. Before and especially after the World War II, many rivers were dammed to build small hydropower stations, with their waterlogged floodplains partially flooded. Some mire was also affected by the construction of roads and other infrastructure.

As a result of these impacts, most peatlands in the steppe and forest-steppe zones in European Russia were completely destroyed or deeply transformed by man. When compared with earlier studies (e.g. Pyavchenko 1958), available data on present-day peatland distribution indicate that over half of peatlands in most administrative regions were drained, extracted, deeply transformed or even lost in the last 50 to 60 years.

Human activities increase vulnerability of peatlands to climate change. Wetter lands with relatively fertile peaty soils have higher vegetation productivity. This makes them attractive as pastures, especially as the climate becomes dryer, but they are much less resilient to over pasturing as compared with mineral soils. The climate-driven desertification of mires is aggravated by over-pasturing, which leads to disturbance of plant and soil cover, and consequently, to drying out of the mires, peat degradation, and fires. Fires affect peatlands in almost all natural zones, including the forest-steppe and steppe regions (Sirin *et al.*, 2011, Minayeva *et al.*, 2013). Peatlands with disturbed or lost vegetation cover become vulnerable to water and wind erosion, especially in view of heavy rains and strong winds that are more frequent nowadays.

CARBON STORAGE AND GHG FLUXES

Peatlands are terrestrial ecosystems that have the greatest carbon content (Parish *et al.*, 2008). Peatlands in the forest steppe and steppe zones originated in more favorable climatic conditions of the past and have progressively degraded in many regions in the latest decades. This phenomenon is known for both lowlands and highlands, especially in Northern Eurasia. The process correlates with the overall decreasing trend of peat increment during warm periods within the last 3 millennia (Klimanov, Sirin, 1997, Parish *et al.*, 2008).

It is expected that carbon sequestration rates will further decrease in future climate conditions due to greater decay rates of soil organic matter and limited carbon uptake by plants. Higher temperatures and transpiration rates will make soil much drier, and consequently, more prone to erosion. During droughts, upper peats layers become eroded by wind and then are washed away by water during intense rainfalls, with further release of CO_2 or CH_4 to the atmosphere. Human activities can increase vulnerability of peatlands to climate change. Climate-driven desertification of mires is aggravated by over-pasturing that leads to disturbance of plant and soil cover, and consequently, to drying out of the mires, peat degradation, and fires.

Greenhouse gas flux measurements carried out in summer 2015 at the pilot site Berkazan-Kamush Peatland (N54°15'18.78", E54°41'15.4) covering an area of over 600 ha in the Republic of Bashkortostan (model region of the EC Clima East project) reveal much higher carbon losses from drained and utilized peatlands as compared with available data from boreal regions. But these measurements also showed low carbon dioxide emissions from intact mire fragments preserved within the drained peatlands. This clearly shows positive perspectives for rewetting and restoration activities that have been developed or implemented.

FIELDS OF ACTIVITY

Peatlands in the arid and semi-arid regions of steppe and forest-steppe belt of Eurasia have some specific features. They require a special approach to management and conservation. Wise use of peatlands based on managerial solutions, such as spatial planning, regulated use, peatland protection within specially protected areas (SPAs), and restoration of disturbed peatlands, can help these areas adapt to climate change and mitigate its impacts by maintaining carbon storage in peat and controlling GHG emissions.

To make the wise use approach possible, we need to promote environmental awareness and education, because peatlands have often been disregarded as specific ecosystems in the steppe and forest-steppe regions. The main problems we identified are insufficient knowledge about peatlands distribution, diversity, structural and functional characteristics. Consequences of this insufficient knowledge are underestimation of peatlands as well as poor protection and conservation measures (Action Plan, 2003). Peatlands are usually overlooked and poorly represented in the systems of natural protected areas in forest-steppe and steppe zones. This is true for federal SPAs (strict nature reserves, national parks, and natural monuments) and, to the greatest degree, regional and local protected areas.

When developing the SPA networks, land management plans, and ecosystem restoration projects in the forest-steppe and steppe regions, special measures on peatlands are mostly disregarded. This is another important activity alley under the project that has been implemented in several model regions. In the model Bashkortostan Republic, nearly all peatlands in the forest-steppe zone were surveyed, with their status, threats, and protection needs analyzed. Over 10 sites were proposed for designation as regional protected areas. In the development of these SPAs, special attention was given to land use in areas adjacent to the peatlands. Most lands adjacent to peatlands in the forest-steppe zone are intensively used. Therefore, protection of water basins and ecotone lands from external threats is a key peatland conservation issue.

Climate change significantly aggravates impacts from both direct and indirect peatland uses. Restoration of the peatlands is limited due to a low input of atmospheric water. Isolation of preserved peatland fragments disables a natural exchange of diaspores, and, thus, prevents restoration of plant communities. Assimilative and regenerative capacity of mire ecosystems with limited and isolated distribution is very low. Therefore, special approaches should be developed and proposals on peatland restoration in the steppe and forest-steppe zones elaborated. In most cases, however, drainage was the original reason of peatland degradation. Construction of dams on drainage canals and other discharge-blocking measures can improve water regimes on these peatlands, which, in its turn, will promote restoration of peatland vegetation.

Peatland restoration activities under the project have been carried out at the pilot site of Berkazan-Kamush Peatland in the Republic of Bashkortostan. They are aimed at reduction of water discharge from the drainage network of the peatland. Local inhabitants have already tried to build a dam and thus to restrict water discharge from the drained peatland that was no longer used for cattle grazing or haymaking, and often caught fires in dry years. However, the dam they built was partially destroyed by high water. Nevertheless, it proved effective: fires became less frequent, mire vegetation began to restore, and waterfowl returned. Local population and authorities have kept memories of these advantages, which is the main ground for our dam construction activities, improvement of water regime, and, eventually, restoration of the peatland ecosystem. To find the best engineering solutions, we primarily need understanding and support of all stakeholders. Effective implementation of these activities will become the best argument for extending this experience to other degraded and abandoned peatlands in the forest-steppe zone.

REFERENCES

1. *Action Plan for Peatland Conservation and Use in Russia.* Moscow: Wetlands International Russia Programme. 2003. 24 pp.
2. Parish, F., Sirin, A., Charman, D., Joosten, H., Minayeva, T., Silvius, M., Stringer, L. (Eds.) *Assessment on Peatlands, Biodiversity and Climate Change.* Main Report. Global Environment Centre, Kuala Lumpur and Wetlands International, Wageningen. 2008. 179 pp.
3. Klimanov, V.A., Sirin, A.A. The Dynamics of Peat Accumulation by Mires of Northern Eurasia During the Last Three Thousand Years / Chapter 22. In: Trettin C.C., et al. Editors. *Northern Forested Wetlands: Ecology and Management.* Boca Raton-N.Y.-London-Tokyo: Lewis Publishers / CRC Press. 1997. pp. 313-324.
4. Minayeva, T., Sirin, A. Peatland biodiversity and climate change // *Biology Bulletin Reviews.* 2012. V. 2. N.2. pp. 164-175.
5. Minayeva, T., Sirin, A. Use and Conservation of Mires in Russia. In: *Mires – from Siberia to Tierra del Fuego* (ed. by G.M. Steiner). Linz: Oberösterreichisches Landesmuseum. 2005. pp. 275-292.
6. Minayeva, T., Sirin, A., Bragg, O. *A quick scan of peatlands in Central and Eastern Europe.* Wageningen: Wetlands International. 2009. 132 pp.
7. Minayeva, T., Sirin, A., Stracher, G. The peat fires of Russia. In: *Coal and peat fires: A global perspective* (ed. by G. Stracher). Amsterdam: Elsevier B.V. 2013. pp. 376-394.
8. Piavchenko, N.I. *Peatlands of Russian forest-steppe.* Moscow: USSR Academy of Science Publ. 1958. 190 pp. [In Russian]
9. Sirin, A., Minayeva, T., Vozbrannaya, A., Bartalev, S. How to avoid peat fires? *Science in Russia.* 2011. N 2. pp. 13-21.
10. Sirin, A.A., Maslov, A.A., Valyaeva, N.A, Tsyganova, O.P., Glukhova, T.V. Mapping of Peatlands in the Moscow Oblast Based on High Resolution Remote Sensing Data. *Contemporary Problems of Ecology.* 2014. V. 7. N. 7. pp. 809-815. DOI: 10.1134/S1995425514070117.
11. Sirin, A.A., Minayeva, T.Yu. (Eds.) *Peatlands of Russia: towards the analysis of sectoral information.* Moscow: GEOS Publ. 2001. 190 pp. [In Russian].
12. Vompersky, S.E., Ivanov A.I., Tsyganova O.P., Valyaeva N.A., Glukhova, T.V., Dubinin, A.I., Glukhov, A.I., Markelova, L.G. Bog organic soils and bogs of Russia and the carbon pool of their peat. *Eurasian Soil Science.* 1994. V. 28. pp. 91-105.
13. Vompersky, S.E., Sirin, A.A., Tsyganova, O.P., Valyaeva, N.A., Maikov, D.A. Peatlands and Paludified Shallow-Peat Lands of Russia: Attempts of Analysis of Spatial Distribution and Diversity. *Izvestuya Rossiyskoj Academii Nauk. Seriya Geograficheskaya.* 2005. N. 5. pp. 39-50. [In Russian]
14. Vompersky, S.E., Sirin, A.A., Sal'nikov, A.A., Tsyganova, O.P., Valyaeva, N.A. Estimation of Forest Cover Extent over Peatlands and Paludified Shallow-Peat Lands in Russia. *Contemporary Problems of Ecology.* 2011. V. 4. N.7. pp. 734-741. DOI: 10.1134/S1995425511070058

Abstract No: A-225

PEATLAND REHABILITATION EFFORTS IN NORTH SELANGOR PEAT SWAMP FORESTS

Faizal Parish[1], S.Y. Lew[1], Noor Azura A.[1] and Nagarajan R.[1]

[1]*Global Environment Centre, 2nd Floor, Wisma Hing, No. 78, Jalan SS2/72, 47300 Petaling Jaya*

**Corresponding author: azura@gec.org.my*

SUMMARY

From 1998 to 2008, a portion of the North Selangor Peat Swamp Forest in Central Peninsula Malaysia was encroached and cleared for agriculture, including some parts of the Permanent Reserved Forests. In 2008, the Selangor State Forestry Department took action by evicting the illegal settlers and reclaiming the forest lands. Unfortunately, drainage canals and agricultural activities had dried out the peat soil and removed the natural vegetation from the area. Early efforts to rehabilitate the forest land met with failure due to various reasons. Global Environment Centre joined forces with the Forestry Department in 2008 and helped to figure out ways to rehabilitate the degraded area. The efforts are not without challenges, among which are high mortality rate of planted saplings and rogue fires that destroyed the replanted areas. After several years, the degraded areas are much improved, thanks to the collective effort of government departments, NGOs/GEC, corporate sponsors, volunteers and local community members. The Selangor State Government has approved Integrated Management Plan for NSPSF for 2014-2023 (IMP-NSPSF) in December 2014 at a State Level Meeting. Tripartite Smart Partnership between government, private sector and local community is crucial in implementing the activities proposed in the IMP-NSPSF.

Keywords: *Peatland Rehabilitation, Malaysia, Community involvement*

INTRODUCTION

The North Selangor Peat Swamp Forest (NSPSF) is an area 73000 hectares located to the Northwest of the state of Selangor in Peninsula Malaysia. A large area is gazetted as Reserved Forest, with some areas inhabited, mined and used for agriculture along its edges.

It is divided into a few forest reserves, as listed below.

No.	Forest Reserve	Size (ha)
1.	Raja Musa Forest Reserve	35,656
2.	Sungai Karang Forest Reserve	37,417
3.	Part of Bukit Belata (Extension) Forest Reserve	3,140
4.	Sungai Dusun Wildlife Reserve / Sungai Dusun Forest Reserve	5,091
	Total	81,304

The conservation of NSPSF involves several key organisations, especially the Selangor State Forestry Department, Global Environment Centre, Kuala Selangor Municipal Council and local communities. They are also assisted by the Fire & Rescue Department as well as private land owners like Sime Darby.

No	Organisation	Key responsibilities
1	Selangor State Forestry Department	Management of Reserved Forest, fire control
2	Global Environment Centre	Coordination of rehabilitation of degraded areas and awareness campaigns
3	Fire & Rescue Department	Fire control on public lands
4	Kuala Selangor Municipal Council	Management of grants and land ownership records
5	Sime Darby	Management and sustainable use + fire control on own lands
6	Sahabat Hutan Gambut	Awareness, nurseries, rehabilitation, patrolling, firefighting
7	Peatland Forest Rangers & Junior PFRs	Awareness and education

Location and land use map

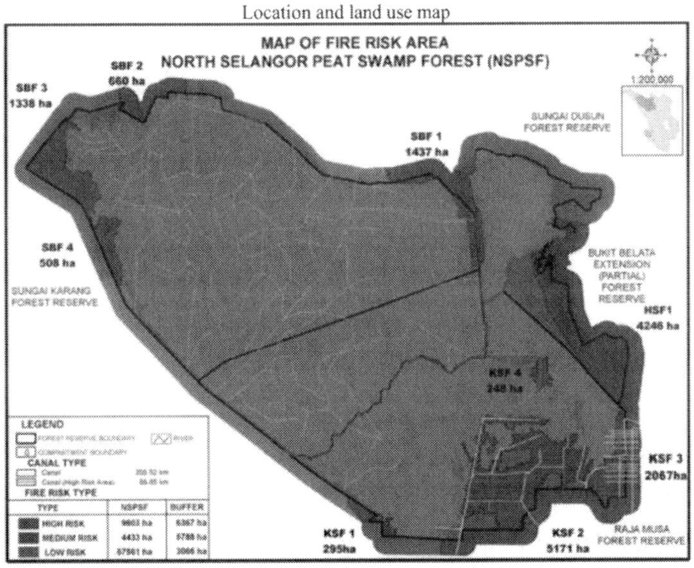

In the 1990s, the area around Compartment 100 of the Raja Musa Forest Reserve was encroached for agriculture. Canals were built to float out timber and drain the land. Oil palm and other crops were planted on the lands. In 1998, the Selangor State Forestry Department took decisive action to the illegal settlers and destroy the crops.

The next step was to rehabilitate the peat swamp forest back to its natural state. This proved challenging due to various factors: 1) the land was drained to a point that the water table was far below where it should be; 2) the degraded areas were covered in bracken, weeds and lalang, which are combustible and very susceptible to fire; 3) the area is at the edge of the forest reserve, surrounded by a clay mine and private land where the public may visit. This made the area highly susceptible to accidental fires which start outside the forest reserve and make their way inside the reserve land.

METHODS

Rehabilitation efforts began in 2008, with funds coming from several corporate sponsors. All activities were held in collaboration with government departments with manpower from volunteers.

The APFP and SEApeat projects began in 2010, enabling more efforts on the ground, such as boundary marking and revision of the existing Integrated Management Plan 2000-2010. Communities living in nearby peatland areas were engaged via several channels especially Sahabat Hutan Gambut, Peatland Forest Rangers and Junior Peatland Forest Rangers. Tree planting was supported by corporate sponsors; including CIMB, HSBC and Bridgestone.

In the beginning, the degraded areas were planted with high value timber trees such as ramin and meranti paya; but mortality rate was very high, up to 85% at times. There is also the threat of fires during the dry season from February to June as the area was badly drained and overgrown with highly combustible weeds; the worst being lalang (*Imperata cyclindrica)* and ferns/bracken.

The number of volunteers then was not restricted. But too many volunteers were found to be counterproductive as there was a higher tendency for mistakes, and more facilitators were required to supervise. Now only up to 100/200 volunteers are allowed per session.

Beginning in 2010/2011, more effort was put in to block the drains. Raising the water level helped reduce the severity and duration of burning if and when it occurred. This also helped with regeneration. Tree species was changed to pioneer species, specifically *Macaranga* sp and *Euodia* sp. as these grew well in exposed and degraded areas. In 2014, a long dry season hampered efforts to douse flames which had entered the forest reserve. In the end, water was pumped from an abandoned mining pond located 1.2 kilometres away, using HDPE pipes. This helped douse the fires, but a lot of replanted areas were destroyed. Efforts to rehabilitate these areas are ongoing. Once the pioneer trees are tall enough, higher value species such as *Meranti paya* are planted in their shade.

The trees used for rehabilitation are not commercial species. Therefore, to supply seedlings for rehabilitation, nurseries were set up in nearby villages, partly supported by the projects. Nursery owners raised wild seedlings collected in oil palm estates until they are at a suitable size for replanting. These are bought from the nursery owners at an agreed price as and when required.

The Fire Danger Rating System (FDRS) is a tool used to calculate the likelihood of fire starting due to weather conditions. The outputs are coded maps which are posted on the Malaysian Meteorological Department website daily. These are used by local communities to check for fire danger. FDRS boards are located around peatland areas to inform the public of the current fire danger rating. A smartphone app was also developed in 2014, which allows land managers to be alerted if their land is on fire.

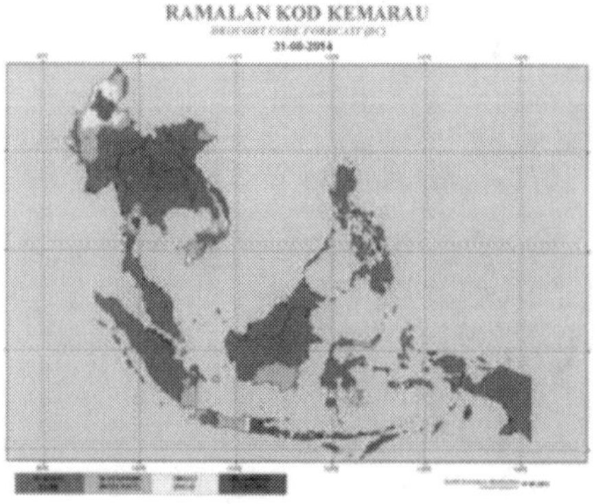

In the event of fires, the Forestry Department is the key coordinator. They are assisted by the Fire & Rescue Department and volunteers. In the dry season, Sahabat Hutan Gambut (SHG) members assist in monitoring the area, updating FDRS boards and spotting fires. They also help to advise anyone who are burning plant waste or making bonfires for camping. The SHG is also furnished with firefighting equipment to help put out small fires and control larger blazes until help arrives.

To ensure sustainable management of the forest area, the Integrated Management Plan for NSPSF which was first developed in 2000 was updated. A scientific expedition was held to update the species checklists and review the numbers. The books are available online via http://www.aseanpeat.net/view_file.cfm?fileid=511 (Vol.I) and http://www.aseanpeat.net/view_file.cfm?fileid=512 (Vol. II). The summary of these is available as a poster (please click to download).

In 2014, work began on a Centre of Excellence, which is a facility in Compartment 73 of the same forest reserve, where visitors can learn about peatlands, their importance, issues and conservation. Areas around the centre, which burned in 2012, are also being rehabilitated with *Euodia* sp. and ramin melawis (*Gonystylus bancanus*) saplings.

The Sahabat Hutan Gambut is exploring opportunities for additional income generation through ecotourism activities, harvesting of non-timber forest products and development of handicrafts using materials collected from the forests.

The PFR and JPFRs are school clubs, focusing on peatland awareness and education. They learn about peatlands, their importance and conservation. Some clubs have their own nursery for seedlings. It is hoped that this will become a new generation of informed citizens who care about the environment, particularly peatlands.

FINDINGS AND ARGUMENT

1. We found that in restoring peatland areas, hydrological management needs to be restored before trees are replanted.
2. Tree species selection is important. If the area is much degraded and far from natural regeneration sources, pioneer species would be better to help recolonise the peatlands.
3. Volunteers must be at manageable numbers
4. Plants must be monitored to improve survival rate.
5. Weeds need to be controlled to reduce the risk of fire.
6. Education and awareness is important to avoid human destruction of existing peatland areas.
7. Alternative income sources are just as important to curb deforestation of peatland areas. It is better if communities can generate income from peatland areas without degrading the forests.

CONCLUSION

Rehabilitation is a multi-stakeholder effort. Various departments and organisations need to come together in order to manage peat areas, put out fires, do patrolling, fund rehabilitation efforts, build canal blocks and plant trees in degraded areas. It is important to take it step by step; to re-assess the situation often and make necessary adjustments. Awareness and education is the key to peatland conservation, as not many members of the public are aware of the issues surrounding peatlands, even people who have been living on peatlands for a long time.

RECOMMENDATIONS

Conservation work needs to be continues, and peat fire control abilities strengthened. The public, local communities should continue to be educated regarding peatland conservation.

REFERENCES

1. Silvius and Diemont, (2007). M. Silvius, H. Diemont. Deforestation and degradation of peatlands, Peatlands Int., 2 (2007), pp. 32–34
2. Shamsudin, I. and Ismail, H. (1991). The impacts of the present landuse on peat swamp forests in Peninsular Malaysia. Malayan Forester 54(1): 15-23.
3. Yule, C. (2010) Loss of biodiversity and ecosystem functioning in Indo-Malayan peat swamp forest. Biodiversity Conservation 19: 393–409

Abstract No: A-463

SOIL MANAGEMENT FOR INDONESIAN PEATLAND RESTORATION

Samantha Grover[1], Budiman Minasny[2] and Ewen Silvester[1]

[1]*School of Life Sciences, La Trobe University, Australia*
[2]*Centre for Carbon, Water and Food, The University of Sydney, Australia*

Correspondence: S.Grover@latrobe.edu.au

Indonesian peatlands comprise a globally significant carbon store and their current degraded condition is causing internationally damaging smoke haze and greenhouse gas emissions. Peatland restoration has been identified by the Indonesian government as a high priority. They have established the Peatland Restoration Agency, which ambitiously aims to restore 2 million hectares of degraded peatland by 2020. Australian scientists could make a valuable contribution to this work. The Australian Centre for International Agricultural Research has commissioned a scoping project to evaluate the multidisciplinary research needed to ensure that peatland restoration is based on a sound scientific understanding of the unique physics and chemistry of peat soils and accurate mapping of peatland distribution. The project will ascertain the current state of scientific knowledge of peatlands in Indonesia. Potential partnership arrangements with the relevant government agencies and research institutions in Indonesia and Australia will be explored in order to identify the most pressing research questions and possible approaches to answer them.

Keywords: *peatland restoration, peatland mapping and distribution*

Abstract No: A-434

THE USE OF NATIVE TREE SPECIES TO REHABILITATE DEGRADED HEATH FORESTS AT LUMUT, BRUNEI DARUSSALAM

Wardah Haji Tuah, Faizah Metali and Rahayu Sukmaria Sukri*

Environmental and Life Sciences Programme, Faculty of Science, Universiti Brunei Darussalam, Brunei Darussalam

**Corresponding author: rahayu.sukri@ubd.edu.bn*

SUMMARY

Heath forests are unique lowland of tropical forests that house high levels of plant diversity and endemism. Brunei Darussalam's heath forests cover an area of 3500 ha and in recent years, these forests face increasing anthropogenic disturbances such as land use changes and fires. These lose greatly decrease native plant diversity, and thus there is an urgent need to implement rehabilitation approaches on degraded heath forests to counteract these loses. We focus on degraded heath forests in Lumut that were completely logged over in 2013 to create a fire corridor. We identified and evaluated native plant species that are naturally regenerating in uncleared and cleared logged areas. Our findings show that after logging, predominant plant species that naturally regenerate in Lumut comprised *Nephlorepsis* sp., *Ischaemum* sp. and *Scleria* sp., with only one record of *Shorea albida* and *Dryobalanops rappa* seedlings in the uncleared area. We then set up a field experiment to observe and monitor growth and survival of native tree saplings planted on cleared logged areas, and utilized saplings of four native tree species (*Dipterocarpus borneensis*, *Dryobalabops rappa*, *Shorea albida* and *Agathis borneensis*) in order to determine which species has the potential to rehabilitate cleared logged areas. Our results to date show that *D. rappa* has the highest potential as a rehabilitation species, in terms of faster seedling growth rates and higher seedling survival in our plots. Our study is expected to provide preliminary information on best practices to improve rehabilitation of degraded heath forests in Brunei Darussalam.

***Keywords**: Kerangas forests – restoration – logged over – potential plant species – saplings transplant*

INTRODUCTION

In Brunei Darussalam, heath forests cover 3500 ha and are unique in its biodiversity and ecosystem features (Brunig, 1974; Wong & Kamariah, 1999). Heath forests are predominantly found along the coastal region of Brunei-Muara and Tutong district, although there are some inland heath forests found within the peatland region of Belait district. There are two types of heath forests: those that are found on higher and drier areas known as *kerangas* and those that are found on permanently waterlogged lower elevation areas known as *kerapah* (Wong et al., 2015). *Kerangas* forests house plant species that are adapted to low nutrients environment such as *Nepenthes* (pitcher plants) that acquire nutrients by trapping insects, *Hydnophytum* and *Myrmecodia* (Rubiaceae) and *Lecanopteris* ferns (Polypodiaceae) which has swollen stems where ants bring debris and thus provide nutrients for the plants (Wong & Kamariah, 1999). These forests are found intermixed within the Belait peat swamp complex in Belait district (Coode *et al.*, 1996).

In 2013, a 20 m wide fire corridor was created by contractors for the Brunei Liquefied Natural Gas Company (BLNG) parallel to the BLNG water pipeline in Lumut, Belait district, in which all trees were logged and vegetation were cleared. The fire corridor was constructed as part of preventive measures to reduce peat fire threats to these existing water pipes. However, it has recently been suggested that the fire corridor has not just resulted in forest degradation, but also elevated fire risks by exposing highly flammable peat (Langner *et al.*, 2007).

Studies on rehabilitation of degraded peat swamp forests have been attempted (see e.g. Ismail, 2001; Wibisono & Gandrung, 2008) but not heath forests. Ismail (2001) focused on planting native peat swamp species on the degraded peat swamp in Raja Musa Forest Reserve in Selangor, Peninsular Malaysia, followed by monitoring of their development for a period of 12 months. The accomplished result showed that open planting technique as a potential planting treatment with 83.3% seedling survival and *Madhuca motleyana* is the highest surviving species with 92.2% survival. A similar study was done in Central Kalimantan, Indonesia by Wetlands International Indonesia (Wibisono & Gandrung, 2008), in which they planted *Shorea balangeran*, *Dyera polyphylla* and *Stemonurus secundiflora* on a heavily degraded peat swamp forest. Their findings indicate that *S. balangeran* has the highest survival rate of 84% in just 8-months period, followed by *D. polyphylla* with 55% and *S. secundiflora* with only less than 1% survival.

The present study aims to conduct a preliminary investigation on rehabilitation of degraded heath (*kerangas* and *kerapah*) forests along Lumut water pipeline in Brunei Darussalam by using native tree species. The objectives of our study are to: (1) identify native tree species that can become good candidates for rehabilitation of degraded *kerangas, kerapah* and peat swamp forests and, (2) document the natural regeneration of vegetation in the logged over forest.

METHODS

The study area was located along the 20 m width fire corridor parallel to the BLNG water pipeline (Figure 1). The area is situated on a sand ridge, which is covered with shallow peat. A total of nine 15 x 50 m plots were set up within the fire corridor and divided into three treatments: Treatment 1 (vegetation left uncleared; T1), Treatment 2 (vegetation cleared but no planting conducted; T2) and Treatment 3 (vegetation cleared with planting; T3). Plots were set up 20 m apart from each other, with three replicates per treatment.

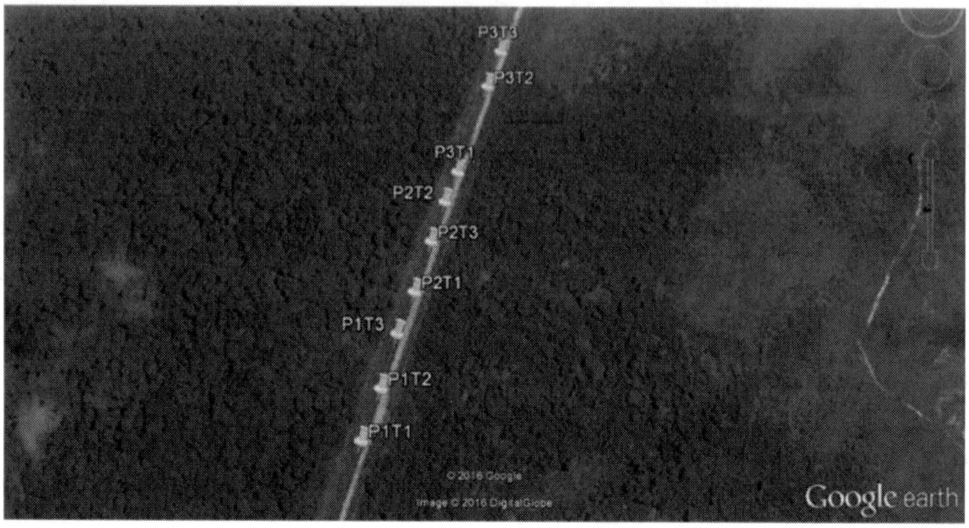

Figure 1: Location of the study plots using Google Earth. It consists of nine 15 m x 50 m plots that were set up parallel to the water pipeline. T1 = vegetation left uncleared (n = 3 replicates), T2 = vegetation cleared but no planting conducted (n = 3 replicates) and T3 = vegetation cleared with planting (n = 3 replicates)

Within T1 and T2 plots, we collected voucher specimens of all plants that naturally regenerated within the plots, and determined the abundance per species. Voucher specimens were identified with the help of botany staff from the Brunei National Herbarium (BRUN) of the Forestry Department, Ministry of Primary Resources and Tourism. For each species, percentage cover (%) was estimated per plot to indicate their abundance within the treatments. Census of T1 plots was only conducted once, in October 2015, to observe species that has naturally regenerated after the initial logging event in 2013. In contrast, census of T2 plots were conducted twice, in November 2015 and May 2016, to observe which plant species have the potential to naturally regenerate after competition from grasses and ferns which covered the plots has been reduced.

Within the T3 plots, the seedlings of four Dipterocarp species namely *Dipterocarpus borneensis* (Keruing), *Dryobalanops rappa* (Kapur paya), *Shorea albida* (Alan) and *Shorea rubra* (Merah Kesumba) were planted after clearing in May 2015. However, since *S. rubra* had high mortality by November 2015, we replaced it with a tropical conifer, *Agathis borneensis* (Tulong) on the following month. Seedlings were supplied by the Forestry Department, and had been grown from seeds collected during mast fruiting events in several forests in the Belait district. Upon transfer of the seedlings from the Forestry Department nurseries to our study sites, all seedlings were acclimatized and fertilized. The seedlings were chosen because of their conservation and economic values, and the availability of seedlings for planting. A total of 16 seedlings per species were planted in each T3 plot, at 3 m x 3 m apart, giving a total of 64 seedlings (16 seedlings x 4 species) planted in each T3 plot and 48 seedlings per species planted in all three T3 plots.

Non-destructive measures of survival and growth of seedlings were determined during initial planting and then monthly over a 12-month period. Seedling measurements include the survival (dead or alive), total height (m) and basal diameter (0.5 m above ground in mm).

RESULTS

There are a total of 68 species and 38 families of plant species in all three plots of T1. As for T2, there are a total of 69 species and 38 families of plant species in all of the three plots. There are 32 species that can be found in both T1 and T2. A number of 36 plant species were only found in T1 but not in T2 including *Dryobalanops rappa* and *Shorea albida* and there are also 36 species that can only be found in T2 as shown in Table 1.

Table 1: List of plant species collected and identified in only T1 and T2. First column represents plant species that can only be found in T1, second column represents plant species that can be found in both T1 and T2 and third column represents plant species that can only be found in T2 (T1 = vegetation left uncleared, T2 = vegetation cleared but no planting conducted, T3 = vegetation cleared with planting)

T1	T1 and T2	T2
Alpinia aquatica	*Adenia cordifolia*	*Clerodendrum umbellatum*
Archidendron cylperia	*Alphitonia philippinensis*	*Fimbristylis pauciflora*
Baccaurea bracteata	*Blechnum indicum*	*Clerodendrum umbellatum*
Barringtonia revoluta	*Chromolaena ordorata*	*Alstonia iwahigensis*
Canthium confertum	*Cissus hastata*	*Pycreus polystachyos*
Chilocarpus obtusifolia	*Connarus semidecandrus*	*Horsfieldia crassifolia*
Cratoxylum arborescens	*Dillenia suffruticosa*	*Timonius mutabilis*
Dialum indum l.var.indum	*Eleocarpus acmocarpus*	*Ageratum conyzoides*
Dicranopteris linearis	*Eleocarpus stipularis*	*Spathulifolia corner var. spathulifolia*
Dillenia pulchella	*Ericaulon longifolium*	*Dacryodes incurvata*
Dracena elliptica	*Hydnophytum formicarium*	*Dillenia pulchella*
Dryobalanops rappa	*Ilex cymosa*	*Santiria apiculata var. apiculata*
Eleocarpus mastersii	*Ischaemum barbatum*	*Cratoxylum arborescens*
Ficus spathulifolia	*Lygodium microphyllum*	*Croton oblungus*
Glochidin lanceisepalum	*Macaranga caladiifolia*	*Dianella ensifolia*
Gynochtithodes motleyi	*Melastoma malabathricum*	*Chilocarpus conspicuous*
Lithocarpus sp. indet	*Mikania micrantha*	*Ampelocissus rubiginosa*
Litsea resinosa	*Nephlorepsis biserrata*	*Barringtonia revoluta*
Macaranga aetheadenia	*Scleria cilliaris*	*Asystasia gangetica*
Nepenthes rafflesiana	*Stenochlaena palustris*	*Nepenthes ampullaria*
Nephelium maingayi	*Syzygium incarnatum*	*Dracaena elliptica*
Nepheliumlappaceum l.var.lappaceum	*Timonius flavescens*	*Scurulla ferrugineae*
Palaqium ridleyi	*Uncaria callophylla*	*Scleria sumatrensis*
Parishia maingayi	*Uncaria gambir*	*Macaranga gigantae*
Shorea albida	*Xanthophyllum ramiflorum*	*Eleocarpus marginatus*
Strychnos ignatii	*Adenanthera sp.1*	*Alseodaphne insignis*
Syzygium accuminatissima	*Callicarpa sp.1*	*Argeratum conyzoides*
Tetractomia tetrandum	*Maranthes sp.*	*Brackenridgea palustris*
Willughbeiae angustifolia	*Paspalum sp.1*	*Blechnum sp.1*
Xanthophyllum amoenum	*Rothmania sp.1*	*Lasianthus sp.*
Zehneria marginata	*Strychnos sp. 1*	*Timonius billitonensis*
Archidendron sp.1	*Uncaria sp.1*	*Adinandra sp.*
Carallia sp.1		*Helicia sp*
Desmodium sp.1		*Blechnum sp.2*
Hedyotis sp.1		*Dioscorea sp.*
Spatholobus sp.1		*Similax sp.*

Current survival of saplings from T3 indicate that three species namely *D. borneensis, S. albida* and *S. rubra* shows decreasing trend over first 5 months of census (Figure 2). *D. rappa,*on the other hand, was found to have sustained its survival rate (100%) over the period. All four species was alive during the first census (i.e after one month) showing survival rate of 100%. In the second census, *S. albida* and *S. rubra* exhibited survival rates of 81.3% and 80%. Survival of *S. albida* decreased in the third census (75%) but remained generally constant in the following censuses. The survival of *D. borneensis* saplings during the third census was similar to the previous census (87.5%) but fell to 75% survival during the fourth and fifth censuses. *S. rubra* recorded the highest mortality rate due to its substantial decrease in survival rate (20%) between second and third censuses. However, there were no changes in survival rates observed for *S. rubra* between the fourth and fifth censuses. *A. borneensis* saplings, which were planted in December 2016 to replace *S. rubra*, maintained its survival rate of 100% during the second census, however, its survival reduced in the third census.

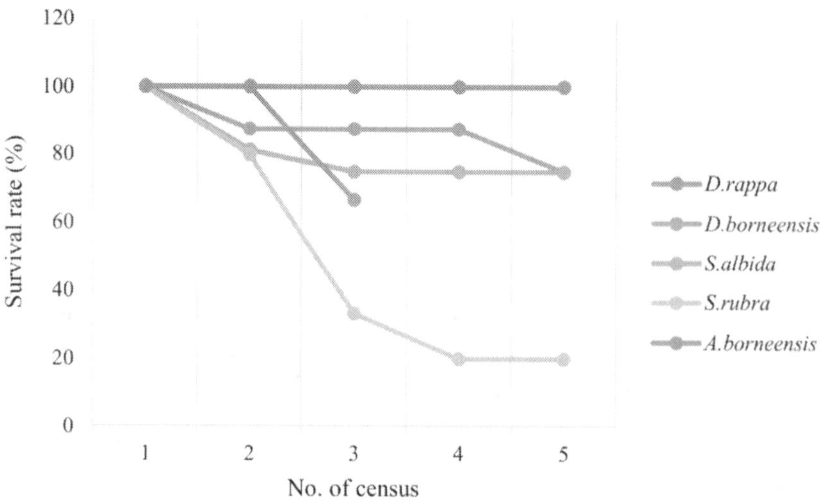

Figure 2: The survival rate (%) of the native tree species (*Dipterocarp borneensis, Dryobalanops rappa, Shorea albida, Shorea rubrea and Agathis borneensis*) that has been planted in T3 (vegetation cleared with planting). The first four Dipterocarp species were planted in May 2015, and *A. borneensis* in December 2016.

DISCUSSION AND CONCLUSION

Our findings for the T1 and T2 plots show that some native tree species do have the potential to regenerate naturally after the logging event, including the high conservation value species, *Shorea albida* and *Dryobalanops rappa*. The presence of these seedlings may have originated from the neighbouring mother trees found at close proximity, *c.* 10 m away from the fire corridor. Although these native species were able to regenerate, intense competition with pioneer species such as *Nephlorepsis biserrata*, extreme exposure to light and wind, waterlogging and other environmental and climatic factors may decrease likelihood for good survival and healthy growth for species found in these treatments (Crawley, 1997; Giesen, 1990; Kobayashi, 2000).

The results for T3 plots indicate that *D. rappa* has the highest survival rates, and likely has the most potential for use in rehabilitation of degraded heath and peat swamp forests. Basirah (2015) has determined that the seedling survival of *D. rappa* was higher than *S. albida* in the understorey of peat swamp forests in Brunei Darussalam. We also determined that *S. rubra* is not a good dipterocarp species to use for rehabilitation of degraded heath and peat swamp forests and this is not surprising as in a study by Daisuke *et al.* (2013) dipterocarp seedlings seem to have low chance of survival and growth due to high light intensity.

ACKNOWLEDGEMENTS

This project was funded by the ASEAN-Korea Environmental Cooperation Project (AKECOP) regional research funding for Brunei Darussalam. We would like to express our sincere gratitude to our project partners: Forestry Department (FD), Brunei Liquefied Natural Gas Sdn Bhd (BLNG) and Wetlands International (WI) for supply of seedlings, logistics support and advice, respectively. We thank our collaborators, Dr Jonathan Davies, Aziah Muhammad and Samhan Nyawa from WI, as well as Noralinda Ibrahim from FD and Joffre Hj Ali Ahmad, Muhd Ariffin Bin Kalat, Liming Daman and Azlan Pandai from BRUN.

REFERENCES

1. Basirah, B. (2015). *Assessment Of Seedling Survival And Growth Of Two Dipterocarp Species In The Understorey Of Peat Swamp Forests.* BSc Dissertation, Universiti Brunei Darussalam.
2. Brunig, E.F. (1974). *Ecological Studies In The Kerangas Forests Of Sarawak And Brunei.* Borneo Literature Bureau For Sarawak Forest Department, Kuching, Sarawak.
3. Coode, M.J.E., Dransfield J., Forman, L.L., Kirkup, D.W. & Said, Idris M. (Eds.) (1996). A Checklist Of The Flowering Plants & Gymnosperms Of Brunei Darussalam. Bandar Seri Begawan, Brunei Darussalam: Ministry of Industry and Primary Resources.
4. Crawley, M.J. (1997). Life History And Environment. In M.J. Crawley (ed.) Plant Ecology, pp. 101-131. Blackwell Scientific Publications, Oxford.
5. Daisuke, H., Tanaka, K., Jawa, K. J., Ikuo, N. & Katsutoshi, S. (2013). *Rehabilitation Of Degraded Tropical Rainforest Using Dipterocarp Trees In Sarawak, Malaysia.* International Journal of Forestry Research:

Hindawi Publishing Corporation.

6. Giesen, W. (1990). *Vegetation Of The Negara River Basin.* Proceedings of Workshop on Integrating Wetland Conservation with Land-use Development, Sungai Negara, Barito Basin, Indonesia, 6-8 March 1989. Banjarbaru, South Kalimantan, p. 1-51.
7. Ismail, P. (2001) *Rehabilitation Of Degraded Peat Swamp Forests In Raja Musa Forest Reserve, Selangor, Malaysia.* MSc Dissertation, Universiti Putra Malaysia, Serdang.
8. Kobayashi, S. (2000). *Initial Phase Of Secondary Succession In The Exploited Peat Swamp Forest (Shorea Albida) At Sungei Damit, Belait In Brunei Darussalam.* In: T. Iwakuma et al. (editors), Proceedings of the International Symposium on Tropical Peatlands, Bogor, Indonesia, 22-23 November 1999. Hokkaido University and Indonesian Institute of Science, Bogor, p. 205-214.
9. Langner A.Miettinen J., Siegert, F. (2007). *Land Cover Change 2002–2005 In Borneo And The Role Of Fire Derived From MODIS Imagery.* Global Change Biology 13(11): 2329-2340.
10. Wibisono, I.T.C. & Gandrung, A.Y. (2008). *Ujicoba Penanaman Beberapa Jenis Tanaman Asli Hutan Rawa Gambut Pada Beberapa Lokasi Di Lahan Gambut Terdegradasi. Laporan Penelitian. Central Kalimantan Peatlands Project.* Result-3 Poverty Reduction-Intensifikasi dan Penelitian Hutan non Kayu (3f2). Wetlands International Indonesia Programme, Central Kalimantan Office, Palangka Raya. Unpublished raw data.
11. Wong, K.M. & Kamariah, A.S. (1999) *Forests And Trees Of Brunei Darussalam.* Brunei Darussalam: Universiti Brunei Darussalam, Forestry Department & Brunei Shell Petroleum Co. Sdn. Bhd.
12. Wong, K., Joffre, A., Low, Y., & Ariffin, A. (2015). *Rainforest Plants And Flowers Of Brunei Darussalam.* Bandar Seri Begawan: Forestry Department, Ministry of Industry and Primary Resources, Brunei Darussalam.

THEME 4
PEAT USE, PEATLANDS TECHNOLOGY & AGRO-TECHNOLOGY

4.1: PEAT USE, PEATLANDS TECHNOLOGY & AGRO-TECHNOLOGY

Abstract No: A-401

A REVIEW OF ADVANCED ANALYTICAL INSTRUMENTS FOR PEAT SOIL CHARACTERIZATION

Sathrugnan Karthikeyan

Thermo Fisher Scientific Pte Ltd, Singapore

**Corresponding author: sathrugnan.karthikeyan@thermofisher.com*

SUMMARY

Characterization of peat soil, water, hazes from peat fires are critical part of ecological assessment. In this presentation, we will give an overview of different analytical techniques that are commonly employed for peatland monitoring and assessment. This includes Inductively Coupled Plasma Optical Emission Spectrometry or Mass Spectrometry (ICP/OES/MS), Elemental Analyzer (C, N and O) and Discrete Analyzer (photometric-Nutrients). The advantage of modern analytical techniques in terms of sensitivity, selectivity and productivity will be discussed for each technique. The sample preparation for trace element analysis and nutrient analysis will be presented and discussed. A literature survey on the use of these instrument techniques for different peatland related projects will be reviewed and key findings will be briefly discussed. In Particular, A research study on investigating Nutritional Environment of Peatland soils in Malaysia will be presented as a case study where the use of ICP for sodium(Na), potassium(K), magnesium(Mg), cadmium(Ca), aluminum(Al), Silicon(Si) and Iron(Fe) and Nutrients (N and P) by Discrete Analyzer will be presented and discussed.

Keywords: *Peat soil, chemistry, Nutrition, Haze, Human health*

INTRODUCTION

Peat Soils play a crucial role in the carbon cycle as they are generally net sinks for atmospheric carbon dioxide and net sources of GHG (Green House Gases) on a long term basis. Southeast Asia has more than 60 % of world tropical peatland resources and store around 45 Gt of carbon in this region. It is of great significance for water resource management and provision of economic development. Despite their importance, peatland forests of Southeast Asia are at risk of over exploitation, clearance, drainage and Fires. In Particular, the clearance through Fire causes severe health, safety and socioeconomic consequences.

It has been considered that natural peat soils and swamp forest ecosystems in the tropics are quite oligotrophic. This concept seems to be related to the low mineral contents in the solid phase of the peat soils. However, some nutritional elements such as K, Mg, Ca, and/or P may be abundant in the soil solution phase and could easily migrate in peat soils. Similarly, Industrial and agricultural uses of peat are growing, and significant amounts of peat are mined industrially (Brown *et al.*, 2000). Considering this, there is an increasing interest in studies of properties and diagenesis of peat. Humification in peat has been taking place in very different conditions both geographically (from tropical regions to the Arctic environment) and temporally (peat development can last for many thousands of years). During peat formation even at one particular site, significant changes could have happened in vegetation, temperature, amount of precipitation and, correspondingly, in the bog hydrological conditions and land use in the basin of the wetland (Zaccone *et al.*, 2007). As a result, not only changes in the properties of peat humic substances should be understood, but also the molecular descriptors of organic matter diagenesis should be identified. For these reasons, the peat soils are most commonly characterized for organic elemental analysis (C, H, N and O).

In this presentation, the analyses of peat soils for major, minor elements and nutrients using Inductively Coupled Plasma Optical Emission Spectrometry or Mass Spectrometry (ICP/OES/MS), Elemental Analyzer (C, N and O) and Discrete Analyzer (photometric-Nutrients) will be described. Further, the importance of such characterization of peat soils from different locations and their role nutritional and organic carbon budgeting are discussed based on various published scientific reports.

Advanced Analytical Techniques:

ICP-OES is popular trace element analytical technique which is widely used for the major and minor elements in different matrices.. ICP-OES employs Argon plasma (a high temperature source) for atomization of trace elements and emitted radiations filtered through a polychromatic grating to collect discrete lines of individual elements. The use of CID detector allows detection of several elements simultaneously. ICP-OES can be used for dynamic range concentration which allows us to analyze major and minor elements in a single analysis. It is useful to detect ppb to ppm ranges.

Organic Elemental Analyzer: It is well known analytical technique to analyze elemental composition in various materials. It is rapid analytical technique and analysis can be done with any sample preparation. This instrument use high temperature source to convert the elemental (C, H, N and O) to corresponding gases which are then separated by in built gas chromatograph and TCD detector.

Discrete Analyzer: It is automated colorimetric analyzer which is used for analysis of nutrients (nitrite, nitrate, phosphate and silica) mainly and also other analysis like pH, conductivity, chloride etc. It is capable of doing multiple analyses simultaneously and use disposable sample cells which avoids cross contamination issues.

General description on sample preparation

The trace elemental concentration of peat soils are analyzed through three stage fractionation. The first one was washable metals which are determined shaking known amount of peat soils with 100 ml of deionized water. The second was acid leachable metals which are determined by shaking known amount of peat soils with 6 M HCl. The total trace elemental concentrations are determined by microwave digestion using acid mixture (HNO_3-H_2O_2 and HF).

For elemental analysis, soils are grounded to fine powder form (< 10 μm) and weighed small amount in aluminum capsules (1-2 mg) and transferred to auto sampler of OEA.

For nutrient analysis, water and acid leachable solutions are directly measured after required pH adjustments. For total nitrogen and phosphorus are determined after persulfate oxidation.

Peat Soil characterization

The use of advanced analytical techniques for peat soil characterization is briefly discussed based on published scientific reports. S. Funakawa *et al.* (1996) studied the peat soil composition in Malaysia (Naman Forest Reserve, Sibu and Talau peat research station, Sarawak). Their studies revealed that the concentration of Al, Si and Fe were higher in shallow peat than the deep peat. Further the concentration of Na, Mg and Cl in soil solution and soil phase reflected the distance from the sea. They concluded their study saying that 'the potential use of reclaimed peat land was considered to be rather limited in view of nutrient dynamics. In another study, De la Rosa *et al.* (2001) employed ICP-OES to study metal binding to three different peat soils which are differed in humic fractions. The results demonstrated that binding affinity was co related to humic acid fractions.

O Purmalis and M Klavins (2012) investigated formation and changes of humic acid properties during humification process where elemental analyzer was used basic peat properties. The results showed that the elemental compositions of peats are variable, reflect changes in peat decomposition degree and types.

W Koerselman *et al.* (1993) studied the release of inorganic nutrients (N, P and K) from peat soils into river water where nutrient analyses are done using discrete type analyzers. The results showed that *Sphagnum* peat released much more 'P' than *Carex* peat.

More details above reports will be presented and discussed in view of the potential use of analytical instrumentation in such investigations.

REFERENCES

1. Brown P. A., Gill S. A., Allen S. J. (2000) Metal removal from wastewater using peat. Water Res., 34, 3907–3916
2. Funakawa S., Yonebayashi, K., Soon J. F., Chai Oi Khun E., (1996) Nutritional Environment of tropical peat soils in Sarawak, Malaysia based soil solution composition, Soil Sci. Plant Nutri. 42, 833-843
3. Koerselman W (1993) Release of Nutrients (N, P and K) from peat soils: Effect of temperature, water chemistry and water level. Biogeochemistry 20, 63-81.
4. Purmalis O and Klavins, M (2012) Formation and changes of humic acid properties during humicification process. Open Journal of Soil Science 2, 100-110
5. Zaccone C., Miano T. M., Shotyk W. (2007) Qualitative comparison between raw peat and related humic acids in an ombrotrophic bog profile. Org. Geochem., 38, 151–160

Abstract No: A-261

FIELD DATA TRANSMISSION SYSTEM, SESAME-II, BY UNIVERSAL MOBILE TELECOMMUNICATION NETWORK

Yukihisa Shigenaga[1], Hideyuki Saito [2], Hidenori Takahashi [3]*, Wisnu Kencana [4], Rony Teguh[5], Adi Jaya [5] and Bambang Setiadi[6]

[1]Midori Engineering Laboratory Co., Ltd, Japan
[2] Hokkaido University, Japan
[3] Hokkaido Institute of Hydro-climate, Japan
[4] Hydrosix, Bandung, Indonesia
[5] University of Palangka Raya, Indonesia
[6] National Research Council of Indonesia, Jakarta, Indonesia

**Corresponding author: nana77hihc@gmail.com*

SUMMARY

The new field data transmission system using universal mobile telecommunication network, SESAME-II system, was developed and applied to monitor the items which is related to global warming in tropical peatlands, Indonesia. The transmission system is mainly composed of the sensor, data logger, data communication module and a battery system. The sensors for water depth, distance, moisture tension and length of circumference were combined with SESAME- II, are used to measure the groundwater and ground surface levels in peatlands, water levels in the river and the dam lake, soil moisture and growing process of trees in a plantation, in Indonesia. The interval of monitoring was 10 minutes, and the data were transmitted successfully to the data server in Japan with 3-6 hours interval. The data in the server was downloaded in Japan and Indonesia through the domestic internet network and analyzed.

Keywords: *M2M system, SIM free, Real time monitoring, Sensors, Internet*

INTRODUCTION

The population of mobile phone user increased remarkably not only in developed countries but also in developing countries in the recent 10 years. It seems the mobile phone communications network is established at a frightful speed all around the world. Especially the data transmission system using a mobile phone communications network can build telemeter system easily and cheaply. Moreover, comparing with the conventional infrastructure, it is pointed out that the restoration is earlier than normal wired telecommunication system at the time of disasters. To conserve and manage tropical peatlands activities, measures must start from the correct understanding of the present conditions. Specifically in the efforts to solve global warming, the importance of carbon management in tropical peatlands has been emphasized (Page *et al.*, 2002). The most important environmental factor for peat management is water in peatland. Groundwater level and peat moisture are closely related to peat/forest fires (Takahashi *et al.*, 2003), and carbon flux on the peatland (Hirano *et al.*, 2012). The hydrological information in the river catchment is also important for regional water management to keep the water condition in the farmland in suitable condition for plant growth. However, the conventional monitoring method of environmental parameters in the field was not convenient in the local area with poor accessibility. Poor accessibility to the sites in the field hinders the emergency use of data. Particularly in case of tropical peatlands, the accessibility is very poor with high groundwater level, muddy and peaty ground surface.

Field data transmission system by using mobile phone network has been developed around 10 years ago. However, the quality and speed of data communication was not enough to send smoothly and quickly the amounts of data from the field to user. But the data communication system by mobile phone network is remarkably developed from the second generation 2G to 2.5G and 3G since recent couple of years ago. The digital data communication system became possible to be used in the network after 2.5G. The data transmission from the field to user became easily available using the mobile phone network after 2.5G.

It is estimated that the prevalent rate of mobile phone users has reached more than 50% of the world population (eMarket, 2013). The area of the mobile phone network is also spreading widely year by year not only in developed countries but also in the developing country. With this opportunity, we developed the new field data transmission system, SESAME- II , using universal mobile telecommunication network.

Data Transmission System

Data transmission systems can be largely classified into P2P (Peer to Peer) and M2M (Machine to Machine) systems. The P2P system uses a communication method in which data is received and transmitted by directly connecting two terminal devices which have an equal relation on a network. This technology was established a long time ago, and is commonly used. However, it has the shortcoming in the system. It takes a long time to complete data transmission if the number of terminals increases. This is because the host has to acquire the data by calling out each terminal. The M2M system uses an advanced data transmission system that enables an autonomous control and operation in the data transmission. This makes it possible for machines to exchange information mutually through a communication network. This enables monitoring and data collection in remote areas, by mounting a sensor, a processing unit, and a communication apparatus into a machine. With this method, a large volume of data can be processed in a very short time. This has become possible because a server can communicate simultaneously with many channels, and it is the technology of the internet that makes the data communication easier. Therefore, for future data communications, the M2M system is advantageous, taking communication expenses and time restrictions into account.

The M2M system-1 shown was used in the SESAME-I, which was the first version of the development of SESAME series. However, if a SIM-free data communication card is used taking advantage of the liberalization of SIM regulations, the communication expenses will be very low. With a modem that enables communication both in the home country and abroad (communication box) as the M2M system-2, we can easily transmit data abroad. The SESAME-II adopted the M2M system-2.

System Development

In the process of system development, it is important to pay attention to the following points: (1) administrative and maintenance expenses are low, (2) equipment costs for the entire system also are low, (3) future maintenance and repair are easy, and (4) it is possible to operate without connecting to a power grid (self-contained solar cell driven). If we develop the system using universally available components and the cloud server which does not require a data management in an office, the maintenance fee of the data transmission system will be kept at low cost.

Most of the present communication modules have a GPS function and can display the information where the instruments are installed using the GPS function. Using this function, the locations of the devices are updated to the server, and it becomes possible to map the data to the existing GIS data. With such a system, it will be possible to monitor observation sites from anywhere by using an internet connection. SESAME-II has been developed following the policy mentioned above.

Sesame System In Indonesia

The field data transmission system, SESAME-II, was applied to monitor the many kind environmental items, such as groundwater and ground surface levels, precipitation, air and soil temperatures, water levels of river and dam lake, soil moisture in crop field and diameter of tree in Indonesia. SESAME-II uses the M2M-2 system with two types of SIMs, Telekomsel and Indosat for internet communication, which are popular in Indonesia. Using the M2M-2 system, SESAME-II can send data periodically to the server with high security. The process of transmitting data to a server in Japan is as follows: firstly, the local SIM is inserted in the modem in SESAME-II, then the communication module connects to the APN (access point name which is specified by a mobile phone company), and finally SESAME-II is connected to the internet using the mobile phone network of GSM/GPRS widely used in Southeast Asia. The observation interval is possible to change from 1 minute to 24 hours in 14 steps. Thedata transmission interval also is possible to be changed from 5 minutes to 24 hours in 11 steps. The transmitter is programmed to send event data when the data exceeds the threshold value. This function is useful for emergency announcement in the case of natural disasters.

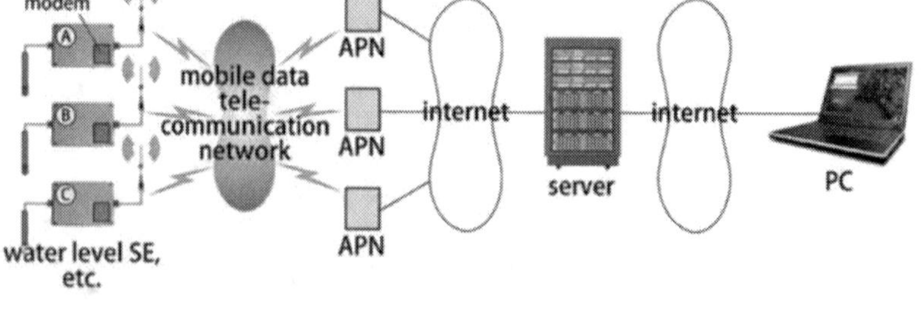

Fig. 1: Diagram of SESAME-II system

CASE STUDIES IN INDONESIA

Groundwater and ground surface level in peatland

A water pressure gauge (ATM.1ST/N, STS, hydrostatic water level sensing type, output: 4-20 mA), a rain gauge (RT-5E, Ikeda Keiki), a laser distance meter (IL-1000, Keyence) and a thermistor sensor were installed in the SESAME-II. The system was set up on a peatland near Palangka Raya city, Central Kalimantan, Indonesia. Measurement of the groundwater level, rainfall and air temperature started on 1st June, 2012 and the

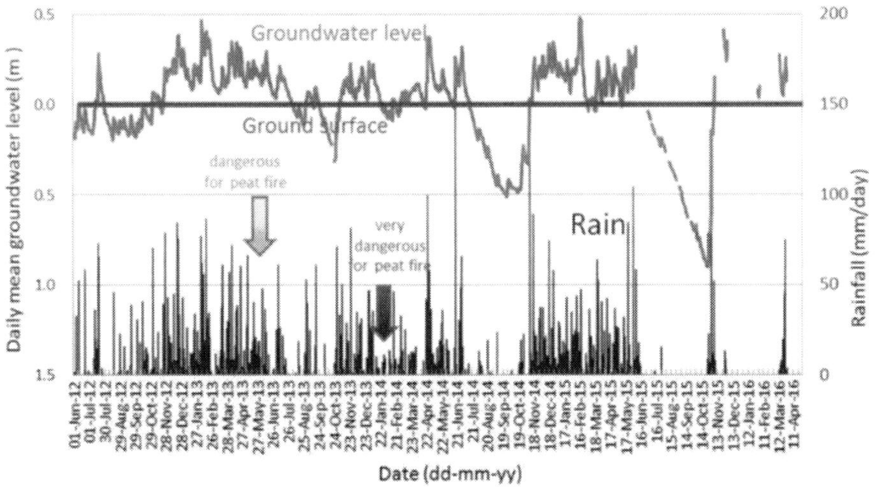

Fig.2: Groundwater level and rainfall monitored by SESAME-II in the tropical peatland, Central Kalimantan, Indonesia.

measurement of the ground surface level started on 13th October, 2013. The daily mean groundwater level and daily total rainfall measured by SESAME-II is shown in Fig. 2. Using the ground water level and the amount of rain in a tropical peatland, the hazardous groundwater level for peat/forest fire is possible for easy estimation (Takahashi and Limin, 2011). The daily changes of ground surface of the peatland were monitored. Ground surface level changed with changing of the ground water level. And the ground surface level during rainy season in the site lowered year by year.

Water level in a river and a dam lake

The observations of water level of a river and the amount of rainfall are the basic of flood control in a watershed. The water level of the Kahayan River, which flows from the middle of a tropical peatland in Central Kalimantan, Indonesia, is monitored since September, 2012 without any trouble and supply of electricity has been consistent. The data from this observation point was downloaded in Japan. The observation point is located at the upstream of the river, where mobile phone is the only communication system and no stable commercial electricity is used. The water level fluctuation of the river was very large and very fast. The water level has sometimes been higher than the river bank. This information is very useful for the early warning of flooding in the middle stream and downstream areas.

The management of water level of a dam lake is very important for flood control, irrigation and electrical power supply. The Jatiluhur Dam is a multi-purpose embankment dam on the Citarum River in West Java, Indonesia. It is located 70 km east of Jakarta and 50 km northwest of Bandung. Water of the dam lake is used for electric power plant, irrigation for rice field, daily life water, and fish culture. The real time monitoring of water level is very important for the governmental office which has a responsibility of water management of the downstream area. The water level of the Jatiluhur Dam, which is monitored with one hour interval.

Soil moisture

The observation of soil moisture is important not only for the management of plant growth but also for understanding and estimation of the activity of microorganisms in the soil. The moisture of surface layer of peatlands is key information for estimating the ignitability of peat and warning the peat/forest fire in tropical peatland (Adi Jaya, *et al.*, 2012). From the view point of plant growth, the water potential in soil is important. The tensiometer, which is consisting of a porous cup and pressure gauge, is popular for measuring water tension in soil. The tensiometer (SS-203A, Rogu Denshi) which has a semiconductor pressure gauge was combined with SESAME-2 and set in the field observatory of the Indonesian Coffee and Cacao Research Institute, Jember, East

Java, Indonesia. Using this system, the soil moisture in the field can be easily monitored from the office not only in the country but also from any foreign country through internet.

Tree growth

The wire dendrometer, which consist of the stainless wire, potentiometer and data logger, is suitable for monitoring of the radial growth of trees (Yamashita *et al.*, 2006). They mentioned that the wire dendrometer detected the start of xylem growth, and a slow growth period. The new wire dendrometer was designed for combining to SESAME-2. The strait potentiometer, effective stroke of 50 mm and accuracy of ±0.5%FS, and the stainless wire having a low linear thermal expansion coefficient, α=1.4×10-6 oK, were used for the new dendrometer. The tree diameter of Shorea balangeran growing in a tropical peatland in Central Kalimantan, Indonesia were measured by this system.

ACKNOWLEDGEMENTS

Results shown in this paper were mainly obtained from SATREPS (Science and Technology Research Partnership for Sustainable Development) project entitled as "Wild fire and carbon management in peat-forest in Indonesia" founded by JST (Japan Science and Technology Agency) and JICA (Japan International Cooperation Agency).

REFERENCES

1. Adi J, Takada M, Hirano T, Mishima Y, Inoue T and Takahashi H (2012) Moisture behavior of surface peat layer in areas of different surface cover and different ground condition during dry season in Central Kalimantan. Proceedings of 3rd International Symposium on Wild Fire and Carbon Management in Peat-Forest in Indonesia, Palangka Raya, Indonesia, 67-73. eMarketer (2013) http://www.emarketer.com/Article/Asia-Pacific-Reaches-Whopping-25-Billion-Mobile-Phone-Users/1010247
2. Hirano T, Segah H, Kusin K, Limin S, Takahashi H and Osaki M (2012) Effect of disturbances on the carbon balance of tropical peat swamp forests, Global Change Biology, 18(11), 3410-3422.
3. Page E. S, Siegert F, Rieley J, Boehm H. D. V, Jaya A and Limin S (2002) The amount of carbon released from peat and forest fires in Indonesia during 1997. Nature, 420(7), 61-64.
4. Shigenaga Y, Takahashi H, Teguh R , Kencana W, Yokoyama S and Adi J (2013) Field data transmission system, SESAME-SATREPS, by using cell-phones digital telecommunication network. Proceedings of International Symposium on Wild Fire and Carbon Management in Peat-Forest in Indonesia, Bogor, Indonesia, 207-212.
5. Takahashi H, Usup A, Hayasaka H and Limin S (2003) Estimation of groundwater level in a peat swamp forest as an index of peat/forest fire. Proceedings of International Symposium on Land Management in Southeast Asia, Bali, 2002, 311-314.
6. Yamashita K, Okada N and Kamo K (2006) Application of the Wire Dendrometer for Monitoring the Radial Growth of Trees, A comparison with the conventional band dendrometer and the pinning method. Journal of Wood Science, 52(1), 8-18 (written in Japanese with English abstract.

Abstract No: A-258

SPECTRAL CHARACTERISTICS OF OIL PALM LEAVES USING SPECTRORADIOMETER IN INDONESIA

Takane Ogino, Sawahiko Shimada, Ayako Sekiyama and Hiromichi Toyoda

Tokyo University of Agriculture, Japan

**Corresponding author: 45515003@nodai.ac.jp*

SUMMARY

The Oil Palm plantation in Indonesia had led the peatlands dry and it is reported to be one of the factors of the peat fire. Therefore grasping of the present plantation development status is necessary. The objective of this study is to clarify the difference in spectral reflectance characteristics between leaf of Peat Swamp Forest (PSF) and leaf of Oil Palm. The possibility of plant classification from the surface spectral information was indicated from NDSI difference maps between PSF and Oil Palm leaves. The difference of NDSI maps between PSF and Oil Palm were shown only with the two year-old Oil Palm.

Keywords: *NDSI, Oil Palm, Remote sensing*

INTRODUCTION

The establishment of Oil Palm plantation has led the peatlands drying and it is reported to be one of the factors of the peat fire. Therefore grasping of the plantation development status is necessary. The objective of this study was to clarify the difference in spectral reflectance characteristic between leaf of Peat Swamp Forest (PSF) and leaf of Oil Palm.

MEASUREMENT TARGET

The study areas were located at the suburb of Pangkalan Bun City for Oil Palm plantation site and the suburb of Palangka Raya City for peat swamp forest site in the southwestern part of Central Kalimantan, Indonesia.

MEASUREMENT SUMMARY

The Oil Palm leaf reflectance of 2 (12 samples), 3 (27 samples), 5 (8 samples), 6 (11 samples), 7 (16 samples) and 8 (11 samples) year-old palms were measured in August, 2014, 2015, and the PSF leaf reflectance samples were measured in August, 2014 and 2015.

In the PSF site, 5 kinds (*Palaquium palaquium cochleariifolium, Cratoxylum cratoxylum glaucum, Randia sp, Xylopia sp*) of tree leaves were selected as dominant plants.

METHODS

NDSI (Normalized Difference Spectral Index) is an index normalized by dividing a difference of the spectral reflectance in 2 wavelength regions by the sum. This index has characteristics of reducing the influence of the error in observation condition or a background effects. In addition, NDSI has the effect that resembled differential calculus processing to be able to express the characteristic of the spectrum reflection from the drop in a few crest of a wave domains (Inoue *et al.* 2008). The expressions are as follows.

$$NDSI = (R_y - R_x)/(R_y + R_x)$$

R: Spectral reflectance

X: Wavelength X (450'-900 nm)

Y: Wavelength Y (450'-900 nm)

In this study, surface reflectance of target plant leaves using spectroradiometer (MS-720, Eiko Seiki) was measured. The measurement wavelength is 450-900 nm (3.3 nm interval) by using mean values NDSI of the sample. Thereafter, we derived NDSI difference map (NDSI difference strength distribution) by calculating difference in NDSI of each age of Oil Palm and PSF. When the NDSI difference exceeds 0.28, in consideration of the standard deviation, we assumed it as spectrally notable difference strength.

We calculated NDSI difference between the following combinations.
(1) Oil Palm leaf age of 2 year-old vs. PSF leaf
(2) Oil Palm leaf age of 3 year-old vs. PSF leaf
(3) Oil Palm leaf age of 5 year-old vs. PSF leaf
(4) Oil Palm leaf age of 6 year-old vs. PSF leaf
(5) Oil Palm leaf age of 7 year-old vs. PSF leaf
(6) Oil Palm leaf age of 8 year-old vs. PSF leaf

RESULTS AND DISCUSSION

In all NDSI difference maps except (1), we confirmed that NDSI difference strength appeared. In this way, we suggested possibility of the extraction of the difference in spectral characteristics Oil Palm leaf and PSF leaf (Fig.1, 2, 3, 4, 5, 6). In addition, it was found that this characteristic appeared after transplanting of oil palm as the oil palms at the study site were seedlings before transplanting.

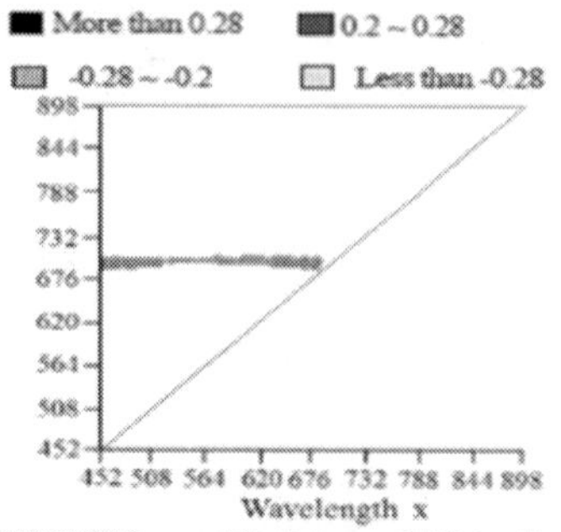

Fig 1 NDSI Difference Map between Oil Palm (2 year-old) and Peat Swamp Forest

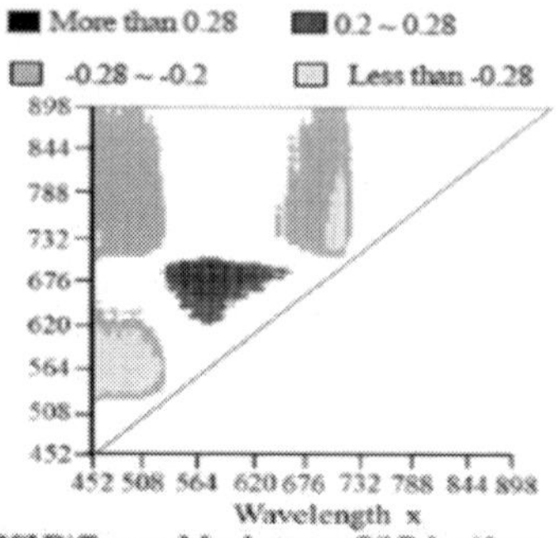

Fig 4 NDSI Difference Map between Oil Palm (6 year-old) and Peat Swamp Forest

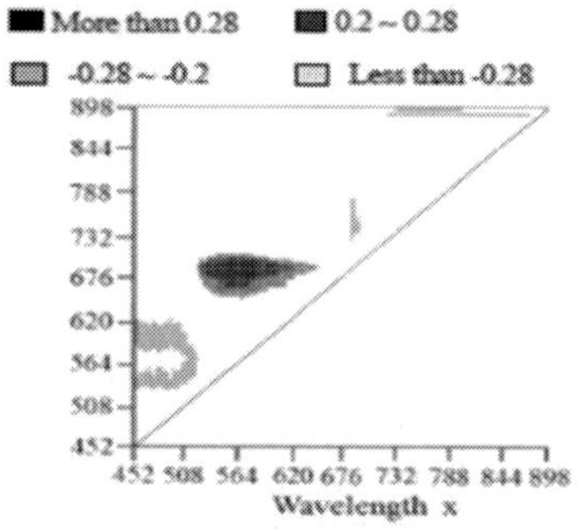

Fig 2 NDSI Difference Nap between Oil Palm (3 year-old) and Peat Swamp Forest

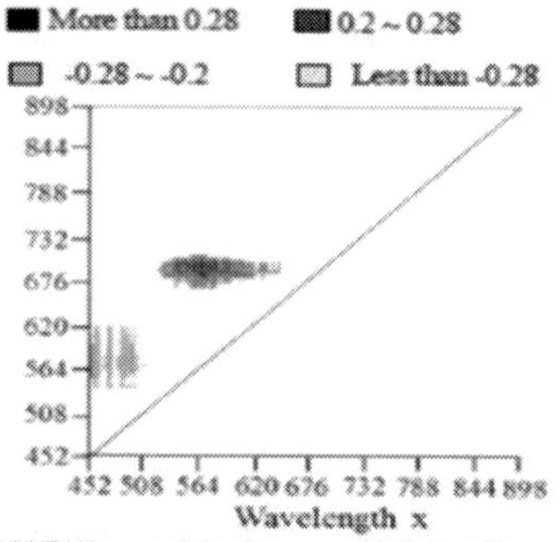

Fig 5 NDSI Difference Map between Oil Palm (7 year-old) and Peat Swamp Forest

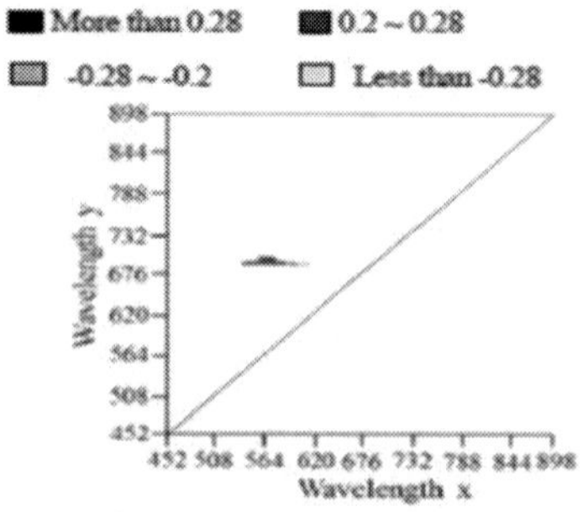

Fig 3 NDSI Difference Map between Oil Palm (5 year-old) and Peat Swamp Forest

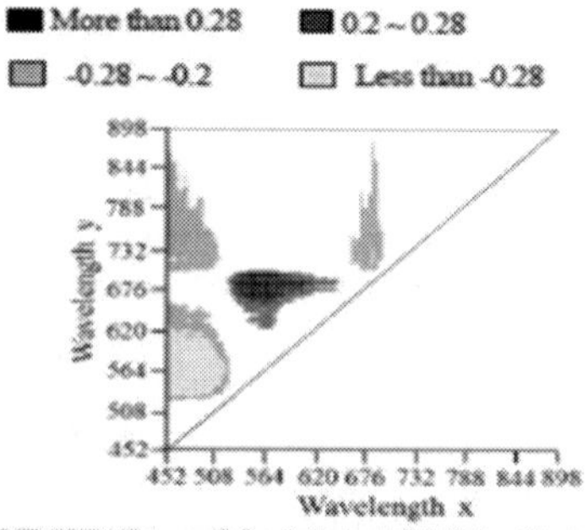

Fig 6 NDSI Difference Map between Oil Palm (8 year-old) and Peat Swamp Forest

Abstract No: A-335

A REVIEW OF THE RESEARCH ON THE ANTI-TUMOR PHARMACOLOGY OF PEAT FULVIC HUMIC ACID

Min Li

Yunnan Yunya Biological Technology Co., Ltd., China

** Corresponding author: wang_jonnie@163.com; 290643773@qq.com*

SUMMARY

In this research, we studied the feasibility of the adjuvant treatment of tumors by using chemical stimulation of mouse torsion test, lymphocyte transformation test, peritoneal macrophages to tumor cell toxicity test, the immune induced by cyclophosphamide and doxorubicin induced rat intestinal mucosal injury model. Research results show that: The clinical dosage of Fulvic acid sodium can be used to resist the pain induced by two kinds of different chemical substances; The preventive medication of peat Fulvic acid sodium can promote lymphocyte transformation and macrophage on tumor cell killing effect; The peat Fulvic acid sodium can prevent low immunity caused by chemical treatment, and can directly promote the lymphocyte proliferation; The peat fulvic sodium can prevent against doxorubicin induced gastrointestinal mucosal injury, and reduce the doxorubicin-induced weight loss in animals. In summary, the peat fulvic sodium has analgesic effects and can prevent the gastrointestinal injury and low immunity caused by the chemotherapy drugs, and can mobilize the immune system to promote immune cell proliferation, which has developed into broad prospects for the development of anti-tumor drugs.

Keywords :-

INTRODUCTION

Fulvic sodium (Sodium Fulvate) is a component of complex natural organic macromolecular compound, mainly composed of carbon, hydrogen, oxygen and other elements. It is a multi-unit structure by a variety of natural and natural macromolecules random polymerized shrink material, and its chemical structure is not fully understood. Currently, the main source of fulvic acids raw materials used in the field of agriculture, industry, medicine are some of the low heat production of coal, including lignite, peat and weathered coal. Since the 1980s, lots of research about the sodium fulvic has been carried out by the China's medical professionals and the following effects of fulvic sodium have been discovered:

(1) anti-inflammatory,
(2) treatment of gastric,
(3) liver protection,
(4) protection of pancreatic B cells, significantly reduce the role of blood sugar in diabetic mice,
(5) reduce pain in cancer patients,
(6) enhance blood circulation, swelling and itching, and promote wound healing,
(7) Dentistry treatment of common diseases, such as oral ulcers, periodontitis and the like.

The fulvic sodium as a tan liquid produced by Yunnan Yunya Biological Technology Co., Ltd is Intended for the adjuvant treatment of cancer patients, mainly for patients with tumors can cause pain, can occur late severe weight loss, fatigue, anemia and systemic failure of the state, often in patients with advanced cancer anorexia, decreased ability to digest. Clinically used dose: oral, 0.24g / day / person, according to the 60kg weight calculated as 0.04 / kg.bw. For the development of fulvic become sodium hospital preparation, design and pharmacology.

Pharmacological Studies

This research is mainly to study the fulvic sodium immunomodulatory for patients with advanced cancer pain analgesic effect to protect the gastrointestinal mucosa and to restore the effectiveness of appetite systematic study. The following pharmacological experiments are for the proposed development progress of fulvic acid:

Analgesic Chemical Stimulation Tests

Pain stimulus generalization method can be divided into physical (heat, electricity, machinery) and chemical. Cancer pain is mainly for the chemical visceral pain, pain properties can have a variety of performance: sharp pain, dull pain, pain, burning pain, and so on. The area is not fixed. So choose chemical excitation method in mice body torsion experiment. Chemical stimulation method available to a variety of stimulus material, this experiment used potassium antimony tartrate (potassium) on behalf of acid-base imbalances, acetate (inflammatory pain) two substances in mice to body torsion experiment. The results showed that sodium fulvic acid had against antimony potassium tartrate, body torsion effect caused by acetic acid, with significant difference as compared with solvent control group the lowest dose of 24 mg/kg.

Mouse Lymphocyte Transformation Test

MTT was used to observe different doses of sodium fulvic lymphocyte proliferation of murine spleen. The results show that with increasing dose of fulvic sodium, mouse spleen lymphocyte proliferation rate is rising, when fulvic concentration of sodium 120mg / ml, the most obvious effect, compared with the negative group difference was statistically significant ($P < 0.05$). Conclusion mouse. Normal mouse spleen lymphocyte proliferation in vitro effect under the experimental conditions, can promote sodium fulvic concanavalin A (Con A) activated: conclusions.

Peritoneal Macrophages to Tumor Cytotoxic Reaction Test

MMT is used to observe the different doses of sodium fulvic acid induced rat PEM phi (peritoneal macrophages, abdominal macrophage) on mice sarcoma S180 cell cytotoxic effect. According to the results: fulvic acid sodium and PEM phi develop together with the increase of dose of fulvic acid sodium and the PEM phi on S180 cell toxicity is obviously enhanced. While sodium fulvic acid is reaching the concentration of 120 mg/ml, the effect is most obvious, statistically significant difference compared with negative group ($P < 0.05$). Conclusion: sodium fulvic acid can be effective in vitro activation of PEM phi resistance of tumor cells.

The Body Immune Adjustment Tests

Cyclophosphamide can depress the immune function of rats with low immune model, made in cyclophosphamide die before given different doses of fulvic acid sodium, contrast model and fulvic acid sodium group rat WBC count and classification, plasma albumin and globulin, serum cytokine IL - 2, INF the role of the fulvic acid sodium. The results showed that sodium fulvic acid 12 mg/kg, 24 mg/kg, mg/kg 48 gastric drug 7 days in advance, and during the period of building and building for irrigation to 7 days after can make SD rats spleen and thymus lymphocyte proliferation, increase serum globulin, the serum levels of IL - 2 and TNF alpha to relieve cyclophosphamide induced immunosuppression.

Gastric Mucosal Protective Effect in the Body

Doxorubicin may induce gastrointestinal mucosal injury model before doxorubicin modeling different doses of fulvic sodium, gastrointestinal mucosa comparison model group and fulvic sodium rats to assess the fulvic effects of sodium. The results showed that gastric fulvic sodium group, more flexible small intestinal mucosal injury doxorubicin group, animal weight gain considerably with the control group. Conclusion: Under the experimental conditions, fulvic sodium can prevent gastrointestinal mucosa against injury induced by doxorubicin and reduce doxorubicin-induced weight loss in animals.

Table 1: Pharmacology Experimental Summary

Analgesic Chemical Stimulation Tests	Mice	Oral Gavage	7d	Fulvic antimony potassium tartrate, sodium and confrontation, mouse acetic acid-induced writhing role
Mouse Lymphocyte Transformation Test	Mice	In Vitro	14d	Fulvic acid can promote normal Con A activation in vitro splenic lymphocyte pr oliferation in mice
Peritoneal Macrophages to Tumor Cytotoxic Reaction Test	Rat	In Vitro	14d	Fulvic acid sodium can be effective activation of PEM in vitro a nti-tumor cells
The Body Immune Adjustment Tests	Rat	Oral Gavage	21d	Fulvic acid sodium can promote the sple en, thymus hyperplasia of lymphoid cell s, promote increased serum IL-2 and TNF-alpha, reduce the immune suppression i nduced by cyclophosphamide
Gastric Mucosal Protective Effect in the Body	Rat	Oral Gavage	21d	Fulvic acid sodium can prevent against doxorubicin-induced gastrointestinal tract mucosa injury in rats

The Comprehensive Analysis and Evaluation

The reason of cancer pain falls into three categories: direct tumor-induced pain, about 88%; pain caused by cancer treatment, accounting for about 11%; tumors indirectly by pain, about 1%. Cancer pain leading to chemical visceral pain, pain can have many manifestations: sharp pain, dull pain, pain, burning pain, and so on. Chemical stimulation of mouse writhing test, is a simple classic Pharmacology, clinical intended dose in this study of fulvic acid sodium may fight pain induced by two different chemical substances, that fulvic acid sodium has analgesic effects, and more appropriate for the reasons are complex, complicated cancer pain.

Lymphocyte transformation test and peritoneal macrophages cytotoxic response experiment 2 experiment on tumor cells can directly reflect yellow rot acid sodium salt of important immune cells (lymphocytes and macrophages) Regulation. According to the clinical situation, yellow rot acid sodium salt on the role of adjuvant therapy, globulin of lymphocyte transformation test with Concanavalin a, activated, and fulvic acid sodium in advance; on tumor cells in peritoneal macrophages of HIV tests first yellow rot acid sodium, and no holes located fulvic acid sodium and tumor cells. Therefore, the results only reflect the yellow rot acid sodium salt in the role of adjuvant therapy, and no direct immunity ability. Tip fulvic acid sodium prophylaxis can lymphocyte transformation and macrophage killing effect on tumor cells.

Rats immunosuppressed by cyclophosphamide model is commonly used immunosuppressive model, this model to reflect the situation of chemical treatment of immunocompromised cancer patients, so the results of this study can be read as yellow rot acid sodium salt chemical treatment can prevent drug-induced immunosuppression. Spleen, thymus hyperplasia of lymphoid cells, serum globulin, serum IL-2 and TNF-α from the cells, proteins, and molecular levels reflect the level of immune function, and initially embody the immune regulation of sodium fulvate possible mechanisms, and showed yellow rot acid sodium salt can promote the proliferation of lymphoid cells.

Cancer patient's gastrointestinal mucosal lesions can be caused by the cancer itself can also be caused by cancer treatment chemotherapy and radiotherapy. Since the 80's, yellow rot acid sodium salt there is plenty of research on protecting gastrointestinal mucosa and pathological study in this research, we can observe the changes of gastric mucosa. Gastrointestinal mucosa of rats with doxorubicin-induced damage model, more consistent with the clinical use of sodium fulvate purposes, results can be read as yellow rot acid sodium salt can prevent against gastrointestinal mucosa of rats with doxorubicin-induced damage, and reduce animal of doxorubicin-induced weight loss.

Research on fulvic acid sodium is not the analgesia mechanism and gastrointestinal mucosal protective mechanisms for further study, the limited research on immunoregulatory function, but can determine the fulvic acid sodium as a cancer treatment drug effects.

In conclusion, fulvic acid sodium has analgesic, can prevent against chemotherapy-induced gastrointestinal damage and immunosuppression, and can stimulate the immune system, immune cells, there are prospects for development as a cancer treatment drug.

REFERENCES

1. Gao Fan, Qian Jialin, Liu Changxi, strict satellite. Cyclophosphamide on Mice Immune-Suppressing Animal Models. The Environment and Occupational Medicine. 2004 (21) 4:314-317.
2. Shou Qi Yang, Hua Zhong, Zhou Weimin, Chen Min Li, Lin Lin. Two Methods of Injecting Cyclophosphamide Induced Leukopenia in Mice Model Comparison. Laboratory Animal and Comparative Medicine. 2008 (28) 4:266-268.
3. Xu Shuyun et al. Methodology of Pharmacological Experiment. Third Edition. Beijing: People's Medical Publishing House, 1982:824-825.
4. Liang Yulong, Wu Zhihong, Liu Xiangdong. Rhubarb Table Adriamycin-induced Rat Intestinal Mucosa Barrier of Protection. Chinese Journal of Surgery. 2010 (25) 5:28-32.
5. Zhu Yaqin, Li Yanmin, Tang Li, etc. Peat Humic Acid Sodium Experimental Study on Anti-inflammatory and Analgesic Action. 2000;2:25-27.
6. Wang Yan, Wang Changzheng. MTT Assay for Detection of Ovalbumin Stimulates Proliferation of Splenic Lymphocytes in Asthmatic Mice Optimum Experimental Conditions Studied. Journal of Toxicology., 2014 (28) 3:170-172.
7. Shi Haiyan, Gu Junyi, Zhang Tianyi, Lin Lin, Zhu Chang. HSPgp96 in Vitro Anti-tumor Cytotoxicity in Peritoneal Macrophages. Journal of Biological Therapy for Tumor in China. 2005;4:272-274.

THEME 5
RESPONSIBLE UTILIZATION & MANAGEMENT OF PEATLANDS

5.1: AGRICULTURE & FOREST PLANTATIONS ON PEATLANDS

5.1: AGRICULTURE & FOREST PLANTATIONS ON PEATLANDS

Abstract No: A-423

ACHIEVING CLIMATE-SMART AGRICULTURE IN DRAINED PEATLANDS THROUGH CANAL BLOCKING AND AGROFORESTRY: A MULTI-AGENT SYSTEMS BASED CASE STUDY IN CENTRAL KALIMANTAN

Yohana Maria Indrawati[1], Hakyoung Kim[2], Takashi Hirano[3] and Joon Kim[1, 2, 4]

[1]*Interdisciplinary Program in Agriculture and Forest Meteorology, Seoul National University, Korea*
[2]*National Center for AgroMeteorology, Korea*
[3]*Research Faculty of Agriculture, Hokkaido University, Japan*
[4]*Department of Landscape Architecture and Rural Systems Engineering/ Institute of Green Bio Science and Technology, Seoul National University, Korea*

* *Corresponding author: yohana.m.indrawati@gmail.com*

SUMMARY

Tropical peat swamp forest conversion to agricultural land so called Mega Rice Project (MRP) in Central Kalimantan resulted in the dramatic increase of carbon emission through excessive draining and frequent fire. Mitigation actions (e.g. canal blocking) have been applied, which promote hydrology restoration as the most effective way to reduce emission from drainages and fire. Agroforestry system that has been developed in order to support the rehabilitation effort in drained peatlands claimed to increase local livelihood. The framework of FAO climate-smart agriculture (CSA) (i.e. increasing productivity, adapting and building resilience, and reducing greenhouse gas emission) can be used as a measure of the effectiveness of hydrological restoration and agroforestry in drained peatlands. Under the framework of CSA, this research aimed to get a better understanding of the interaction among climate change, peatlands restoration and farm-households by examining the decision made by farm household. This study is taking place in the Kalampangan village Central Kalimantan that covers 4625 ha of the block C of former MRP in Central Kalimantan. In this study, we employ the mathematical programming-based multi-agent systems (MPMAS) (Schreinemachers & Berger, 2011) to simulate different scenarios of canal blocking and agroforestry patterns in Kalampangan village. The expected outcome is a better understanding of the interactions among technology diffusion (such as canal blocking and agroforestry), decision-makings of farm households, and policy interventions and land-use strategies in response to climate change.

Keywords: *drained peatlands, hydrological restoration, agroforestry, climate-smart agriculture, MPMAS*

INTRODUCTION

The demand for agricultural ecosystem has been increasing not only to provide food, but also to combat the climate change (Lipper *et al.*, 2014, Smith *et al.*, 2007). The integrity of an agricultural ecosystem is mainly to gain food security without the depletion of natural resources. Such integrity may be examined in the context of climate-smart agriculture (CSA) which pursues: (1) sustainably increasing agricultural productivity and incomes; (2) adapting and building resilience to climate change; and (3) reducing and or/removing greenhouse gases emission, where possible ((Lipper *et al.*, 2014, Palombi & Sessa, 2013). However, in many cases, land-use change to agriculture is a major source of greenhouse gas emission especially in peatland ecosystems.

In the tropic, peatlands have been intensively managed and drained for agriculture. The conversion of tropical peat swamp forests to agricultural lands so called Mega Rice Project (MRP) in Central Kalimantan had been reported to increase carbon emissions from excessive draining and frequent fire (Hooijer *et al.*, 2010, Jauhiainen *et al.*, 2008). The long term CO_2 flux measurements in block C of MRP from July 2004 to July 2008 showed that the CO_2 emission in drained peat swamp forest (328 ± 204 g C m^{-2} y^{-1}) was almost two times higher than that of forest with little drainage (174 ± 203 g C m^{-2} y^{-1}) (Hirano *et al.*, 2012). The mitigation of greenhouse gas (GHG) emissions from peatlands by avoiding new drainage in the existing drained areas can be achieved for example by raising the groundwater table. Hydrological restoration efforts in peatlands (e.g. canal blocking) have been promoted as the most effective way to reduce emission from drainages and fire (Biancalani & Avagyan, 2014). Hydrology controls the carbon balance of peatlands so that drainage to lower ground water level (GWL) enhances oxidative peat decomposition and the resultant CO_2 emission (Hirano *et al.*, 2015, Hirano *et al.*, 2012, Hooijer *et al.*, 2012).

In conjunction with hydrological restoration, agroforestry system has been developed as a responsible management in drained peatlands, which claimed to increase local livelihood (Biancalani & Avagyan, 2014, Harun & Yuwati, 2015). Several studies on the economic values of agroforestry that combine native tree species and seasonal crops showed profitable results (Harun, 2011, Itta *et al.*, 2013, Widyati, 2011). It is important to consider the peat characteristic to implement agroforestry system especially for peat depth > 3 m. Based on government regulation (PP no 71 2014), peatlands for cultivation purpose need to maintain GWL less than 0.4 m and or avoid the exposure of pyrite sediment and quart sand under the peat layer.

The framework of climate-smart agriculture used as the measure of the effectiveness of on-going effort of hydrological restoration and agroforestry system can in the form of biophysical and economic indicators. Biophysical indicators is identified and analyzed using observation data of eddy covariance (EC) systems to capture the emerge changes of carbon, water and energy exchange between peatlands and its environment. Economic indicators derived from farm household activities to optimize the income. Then, interconnection between biophysical and economic indicators is analyzed through multiple scenarios using mathematical programming-based multi-agent systems (MPMAS), simulation model that couple cellular component representing a geographical landscape with an agent based-component representing human decision-making (Parker *et al.*, 2002, Parker *et al.*, 2003). In this study, our objectives are (1) identifying biophysical and economic indicators that affected the diffusion of canal blocking and agroforestry in farm-households, (2) setting the experimental framework of MPMAS study and (3) simulating the diffusion of canal blocking and agroforestry under normal condition (baseline case). The expected outcome is the clear understanding of canal blocking and agroforestry diffusion and the current policy intervention among farm households.

METHODS AND MATERIALS

The Kalampangan village (i.e. Kalampangan) located in Sabangau district, Palangkaraya, Central Kalimantan. Kalampangan covers 4625 ha of the block C of former MRP which ± 3586 ha are farmland and 3300 ha of the farmland is peatlands. There are two catchments (i.e. Sebangau and Kahayan) which connected by primary canal (Kalampangan canal) 10 km in length.

Biophysical indicators are presented from multi-years flux measurement of energy, carbon and water from drained peat swamp forest in the study site. Eddy covariance (EC) measurement is conducted in the 50 meter high tower (2.35°S, 114.14°E) with the canopy height was about 26 m at secondary forest in Block C, MRP (Hirano et al 2012). Annual time scale is defined from DOY 192 to DOY 191 in the following year with dry season between July and October and wet season between November and June (Hirano *et al.*, 2012). Spatial data used for biophysical indicators are peat depth map, river and canal map.

Economic indicators are used to simulate two MP problems (investment, production) with the output include adoption rate and the net household incomes (Schreinemachers et al., 2009). Basic characteristic of economic indicators such as: (1) farm household, (2) farm size, (3) major crops, (4) agroforestry types and (5) percentage of canal blocking activities. Economic data are gathered from statistical office, literature, and field survey. The schematic of MAS analysis presented in figure 1.

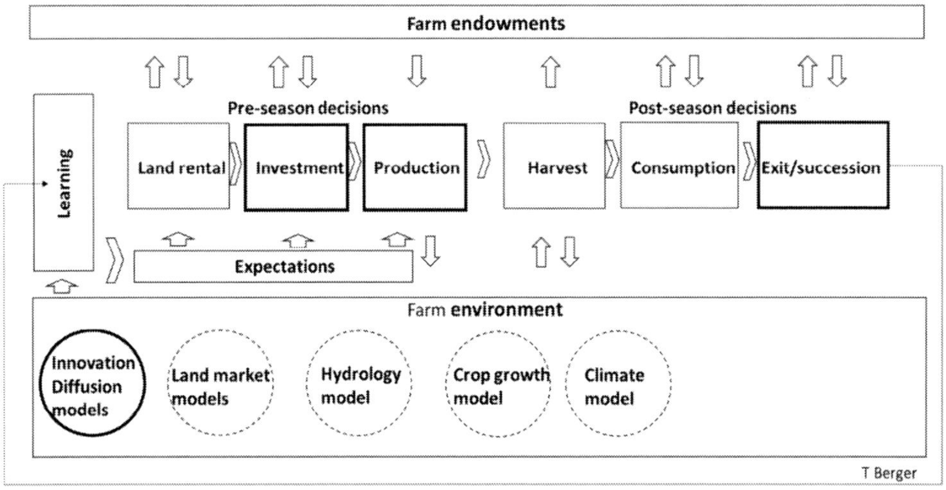

Figure 1: Farm agent module simulation. Linear programming concept of farm household decision making (Berger, 2015)

RESULTS AND DISCUSSION

1. *Biophysical indicators*

Climatological condition

Severe fire occurred during El Nino Southern Oscillation (ENSO)-induced drought in 02-03, 04-05, and 06-07 respectively (Ballhorn *et al.*, 2009). There was small interannual variability in climatological condition which characterized with relatively constant temperature (Ta) and high precipitation (P) (26.13 ± 0.19 °C and 2,352 ± 146 mm, respectively). However, in seasonal time scale, below normal P in dry season observed especially in 2002-2003 and 2006-2007 (166 mm and 70 mm, respectively).

Table 1: Climatological condition

Year	02-03	03-04	04-05	05-06	06-07	07-08	avg	std
Ta (deg C)	26.51	26.09	26.16	25.92	25.99	26.09	26.13	0.19
Rn (M J m-2)	4586	4768	4693	4794	4411	4868	4687	151
P (mm)	2287	2459	2586	2394	2140	2248	2352	146
Daytime VPD (hPa)	12.86	11.54	11.00	10.85	12.17	10.34	11.46	0.85

CO_2 emission

From annual carbon balance, we could see that in general, from 2002 to 2008, peatlands in this area were still acted as a carbon source (i.e. the positive value of net ecosystem exchange, NEE). The peatlands emitted more CO_2 in the ENSO year and then decreased the CO_2 emission in non-ENSO year which also related with fire. However, the amount of carbon released in non-ENSO year showed decreasing trend despite large increase of CO_2 emission in previous year (444, 202, and 107 g C m^{-2} y^{-1} for year 2003-2004, 2005-2006, 2007-2008, respectively).

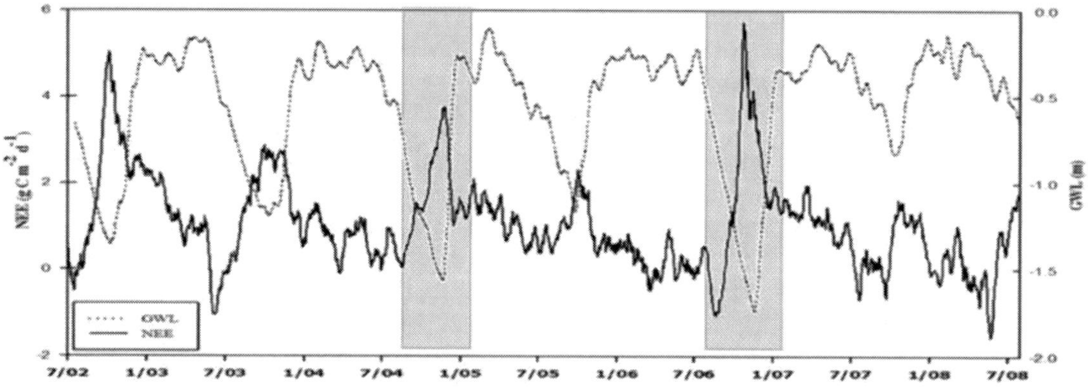

Figure 2. Daily observation data (15 days running means) of NEE and GWL from 2002 to 2008 from PDF site.

Productivity

Productivity is presented as the Gross primary Productivity (GPP) which showed small interannual variability (3215 ± 90 g C m^{-2} y^{-1}) although we could see that GPP was increase in non-ENSO years. More carbon was use for ecosystem respiration (RE) than for growth (lower GPP). The noticeable decrease in RE was observed in 07-08 which also showed lowest carbon release during these period.

Resilience

The elevation of CO_2 emission connected with drought and fire is directly related to hydrological condition. High CO_2 emission happen under ground water level (GWL) condition lower than the threshold value of -0.4 m (Rieley & Page, 2005). Indeed, for most of the time, annual GWL was lower than the threshold value with the exception in 07-08 (-0.4 m). We could see that the dramatic decrease of CO_2 emission observed under GWL was right on its threshold value. Water release to atmosphere through evapotranspiration (ET) was higher in non-ENSO year and showed increasing pattern. Water use efficiency (WUE) was low (2.46 ± 0.07 g C kg H_2O^{-1}) and were similar between ENSO and non ENSO year. WUE showed lowest value in 07-08 when carbon release was decreased.

Table 2. Biophysical indicators

Year	02-03	03-04	04-05	05-06	06-07	07-08	avg	std
GPP (g C m^{-2})	3125	3252	3184	3327	3059	3254	**3215**	**90**
RE (g C m^{-2})	3656	3674	3661	3506	3547	3351	**3548**	**118**
NEE (g C m^{-2})	555	444	496	202	504	107	**351**	**164**
GWL (m)	-0.6	-0.6	-0.7	-0.5	-0.7	-0.4	**-0.56**	**0.09**
ET (mm)	1297	1365	1315	1384	1302	1451	**1352**	**55**
WUE (g C kg H_2O^{-1})	2.51	2.47	2.51	2.51	2.48	2.30	**2.46**	**0.07**

2. *Economic indicators*

Basic characteristics

There are ± 300 farm-households and 23 group of farmers from 1172 households in Kalampangan village (statistical data 2014). From the statistical data of Sabangau district, majority of farm-households product are horticulture (27%) then followed by livestock (20%), fishing (17%), and staple crop (15%). In horticulture sector, production for major horticultural plant in 2014 was increasing especially for water spinach, chili and green mustard. For staple crop, major production is come from cassava, sweet potato and maize (on average 15.6, 5.8, and 2.0 ton ha^{-1} respectively). In term of land size own by farmer, from 2003 to 2013, there is decreasing number of farmer own larger than 0.25 ha land by 40% and small increase of number of farmer own less than 0.25 ha land by 6%.

Agroforestry System

One of agroforestry system in Kalampangan is jelutung agroforestry which combine forestry plant (i.e. jelutung (Dyera polyphylla)) with seasonal crops (e.g. maize, water spinach and spring onion). Several researches had been conducted in order to promote jelutung which is peatlands native species for restoration. Jelutung export from Central Kalimantan for 10 years (2002-2012) was about USD 962118, however it was mostly come from nature. Financial analysis of jelutung both in monoculture and mix cropping type reported to have high Net Present Value (NPV) (USD 2300 per ha and USD 5300 per ha respectively) as a measure of profitability (Harun, 2011).The ratio of benefit and cost for jelutung agroforestry for maize, spring onion, green mustard and chili also reported higher than 1 (i.e. profitable) (Itta *et al.*, 2013).

Table 3: Revenue of each commodity in Jelutung agroforestry (Widyati 2009).

Commodity	production/ha/6 month	price in USD (2008)	Total revenue in USD
maize	500 – 800 kg	0.23	115-185
water spinach	1000 – 1300 kg	0.15	154-200
spring onion	1000 – 1300 kg	0.38	385-500
chili	1.000 – 1100 kg	0.77	769-846
green mustard	1000 – 1200 kg	0.08	77-92
jelutung	100 -140 kg /tree	0.62	62-86

Build up of MPMAS model

Current results showed some indications as follows:

1. There is an indication of ground water table increase and lower CO_2 emission in non-ENSO year.
2. Jelutung agroforestry is observed to give economic benefit for farmers.

Based on those indications, we are going to present the experimental framework to understand the interactions among climate change, hydrological restoration and the farm activities. Then, we will present the simulation results for those interactions in relation with the diffusion of canal blocking strategy and jelutung agroforestry system under normal conditions (baseline case).

ACKNOWLEDGEMENT

This work was funded by the Korea Meteorological Administration Research and Development Program under Grant Weather Information Service Engine (WISE) project, KMIPA-2012-0001-A.

REFERENCES

1. Ballhorn U, Siegert F, Mason M, Limin S (2009) Derivation of burn scar depths and estimation of carbon emissions with LIDAR in Indonesian peatlands. Proceedings of the National Academy of Sciences, **106**, 21213-21218.
2. Berger T (2015) Lecture presentation: MPMAS in practice pp Page.
3. Biancalani R, Avagyan A (2014) Towards climate-responsible peatlands management. Mitigation of Climate Change in Agriculture Series (MICCA).
4. Harun M (2011) Analisis pengembangan jelutung dengan sistem agroforestry untuk memulihkan lahan gambut terdegradasi di Provinsi Kalimantan Tengah. Tesis). Program Studi Pengelolaan Sumberdaya Alam dan Lingkungan, Sekolah Pascasarjana Institut Pertanian Bogor, Bogor.
5. Harun MK, Yuwati TW (2015) Agroforesty System For Rehabilitation of Degraded Peatland in Central Kalimantan. Journal of Wetlands Environmental Management, **3**.
6. Hirano T, Kusin K, Limin S, Osaki M (2015) Evapotranspiration of tropical peat swamp forests. Global Change Biology, **21**, 1914-1927.
7. Hirano T, Segah H, Kusin K, Limin S, Takahashi H, Osaki M (2012) Effects of disturbances on the carbon balance of tropical peat swamp forests. Global Change Biology, **18**, 3410-3422.
8. Hooijer A, Page S, Canadell J, Silvius M, Kwadijk J, Wösten H, Jauhiainen J (2010) Current and future CO [subscript 2] emissions from drained peatlands in Southeast Asia.
9. Hooijer A, Page S, Jauhiainen J, Lee W, Lu X, Idris A, Anshari G (2012) Subsidence and carbon loss in drained tropical peatlands.
10. Itta D, Arifin YF, Abadi AL, Maryunani (2013) Agroforestry Pattern in Peatland of Ex-Transmigration in Kalampangan Village of Sabangau Sub District Palangkaraya Central Kalimantan Province. OSR Journal Of Environmental Science, Toxicology And Food Technology (IOSR-JESTFT), **4**, 4.
11. Jauhiainen J, Limin S, Silvennoinen H, Vasander H (2008) Carbon dioxide and methane fluxes in drained tropical peat before and after hydrological restoration. Ecology, **89**, 3503-3514.
12. Lipper L, Thornton P, Campbell BM *et al.* (2014) Climate-smart agriculture for food security. Nature Climate Change, **4**, 1068-1072.
13. Palombi L, Sessa R (2013) *Climate-smart agriculture: sourcebook*, Food and Agriculture Organization of the United Nations (FAO).
14. Parker DC, Berger T, Manson SM, Use L (2002) *Agent-based models of land-use and land-cover change: report and review of an international workshop, October 4-7, 2001, Irvine, California, USA*, LUCC Focus 1 Office.
15. Parker DC, Manson SM, Janssen MA, Hoffmann MJ, Deadman P (2003) Multi-agent systems for the simulation of land-use and land-cover change: a review. Annals of the association of American Geographers, **93**, 314-337.
16. Rieley J, Page S (2005) Wise use of tropical peatlands: focus on Southeast Asia: synthesis of results and conclusions of the UK Darwin Initiative and the EU INCO EUTROP, STRAPEAT and RESTORPEAT Partnerships together with proposals for implementing wise use of tropical peatlands. Wageningen, The Netherlands: ALTERRA–Wageningen University and Research Centre and the EU INCO–STRAPEAT and RESTORPEAT Partnerships, **266**.
17. Schreinemachers P, Berger T (2011) An agent-based simulation model of human–environment interactions in agricultural systems. Environmental Modelling & Software, **26**, 845-859.
18. Schreinemachers P, Berger T, Sirijinda A, Praneetvatakul S (2009) The Diffusion of Greenhouse Agriculture in Northern Thailand: Combining Econometrics and Agent-Based Modeling. Canadian Journal of Agricultural Economics/Revue canadienne d'agroeconomie, **57**, 513-536.
19. Smith P, Martino D, Cai Z *et al.* (2007) Agriculture. W: Climate Change 2007: Mitigation. Contribution of Working Group III to the Fourth Assessment Report of the Intergovernmental Panel on Climate Change (Metz B., Davidson OR, Bosch PR, Dave R., Meyer LA). pp Page, Cambridge University Press.
20. Widyati E (2011) Kajian optimasi pengelolaan lahan gambut dan isu perubahan iklim. Jurnal Tekno Hutan Tanaman, **4**, 57-58.

Abstract No: A-377

CAN WE SCAN OIL PALM ROOTS IN TROPICAL PEAT SOIL?

Elisa Rumpang[1*], Mizue Ohashi[2], Tomonori Kume[3], Kho Lip Khoon[1] and Mohd Haniff Harun[1]

[1] *Tropical Peat Research Institute, Biological Research Division, Malaysian Palm Oil Board, Malaysia*
[2] *School of Human Science and Environment, University of Hyogo, Japan*
[3] *School of Forestry and Resource Conservation, National Taiwan University, Taiwan*
[4] *Sarawak Oil Palms Berhad, Miri, Sarawak, Malaysia*

* *Corresponding author: lisarumpang@gmail.com*

SUMMARY

Root productivity plays an important role in terrestrial ecosystems. The production and mortality of roots contribute substantially to the carbon dynamics in the soil system. There is limited information available for root processes in oil palm ecosystems. Considerable methods have been used to understand belowground biomass and productivity. Minirhizotron method has been progressively improved to determine root processes of oil palm. However, most advances were conducted for forests on mineral soils. It is still unclear how the growth and mortality of roots are determined in oil palm ecosystem. Moreover, it is challenging to understand belowground carbon dynamics in oil palm, particularly on tropical peat soils due to the complexities of soil properties and condition. In this study, we aimed to develop a new economical technique using an optical scanner for assessing root processes. Scanner method enables us to observe larger images across wider spatial area and at a lower cost. We installed scanner boxes on various management zones of oil palm on peat soil – harvest path, vegetation pile, between palms, and palm base. Using this technique, we were able to follow live and dead root dynamics in the soil clearly with a wider view compared from minirhizotron from one sampling point. This is an ideal, also cheaper method to characterize root processes in peat soil ecosystems as well as other soil types.

Keywords: *root behavior, root dynamics, scanner method*

INTRODUCTION

Roots are the lifeline of a plant, taking up air, water, and nutrients from the soil and moving them up into the leaves. More importantly, root productivity plays an important role in terrestrial ecosystems and as a central component of ecosystem carbon storage and cycling. Roots constitute approximately 33% of terrestrial net primary productivity (Jackson *et al.* 1997). Hence, the production and mortality of roots contribute substantially to the carbon dynamics in the soil system.

There is limited information available for root processes in oil palm ecosystems because special techniques are required to investigate root systems since they are hidden in the soil. Traditionally, destructive techniques like coring, trenching, and excavating have been used to access roots in situ. More recently, non-destructive techniques like minirhizotrons were developed in order to allow direct and repeated observations of the roots life span and turnover (Lauenroth and Gill 2003). These methods have been used to understand belowground biomass and productivity.

The minirhizotron method has been progressively improved to determine root processes of oil palms but common problem of these methods is that they are expensive (Hendrick and Pregitzer, 1992).
However, most advances of minirhizotron method were established for forests on mineral soils. There is limited information available for root processes in oil palm ecosystems. The observed area by minirhizotron method is quite small, so it is unclear whether this method can determine the growth and mortality of root processes spatially in oil palm ecosystem. The carbon dynamics in tropical peat soils is especially difficult due to the complexities of the soil properties and condition.

In this study, we aimed to develop a new economical technique using an optical scanner for assessing root processes of oil palm in a tropical peatland. This scanner method enables us to observe larger images across a wider spatial area and at a lower cost (Dannoura *et al.* 2008). Using this technique, we were able to observe live and dead roots in the soil clearly following a wider scale of view from one sampling point.

METHODS

The study was conducted at Sebungan and Sabaju oil palm estates, Bintulu between Latitudes 3°07.81' N and 3°14.91'N and Longitudes 113°18.72' E and 113°32.19'. The oil palm was planted in 2007 on peat soil. Four transparent scanner boxes installed in each estate of four management zones in the study plot – harvest path, vegetation pile, between palms, and at the palm base. We dug a trench in the soil about the size and length of the scanner box. The scanner box was inserted into the soil and ensured the box was compact and firm. The procedure was conducted carefully to prevent supplementary root damage and losses. The scanner box was protected using half PVC pipe to prevent water leakage and disturbances. The scanner boxes were left in the field approximately 14 days to allow for stability. We scanned images at monthly interval.

Figure 1: The transparent box was installed vertically into the soil

Scanner images were taken using a Charge Coupled Device (CCD) flatbed image scanner with an area of 216mm x 297mm (GT-S630, Epson, Japan). All images were saved in TIFF file. The roots were analyzed using GIMP 2.8 and ImageJ 1.49. The user must trace the grown and dead roots manually by marking roots on a computer screen by moving the mouse along the roots. The size of pencil was defined according to the diameter of each root.

RESULTS

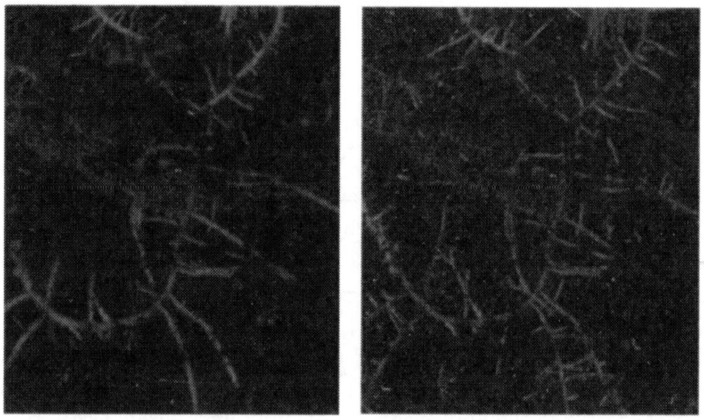

a) 10/10/2015 (b) 04/11/2016

Figure 2: An example of some roots part development (zoom in images) within two month

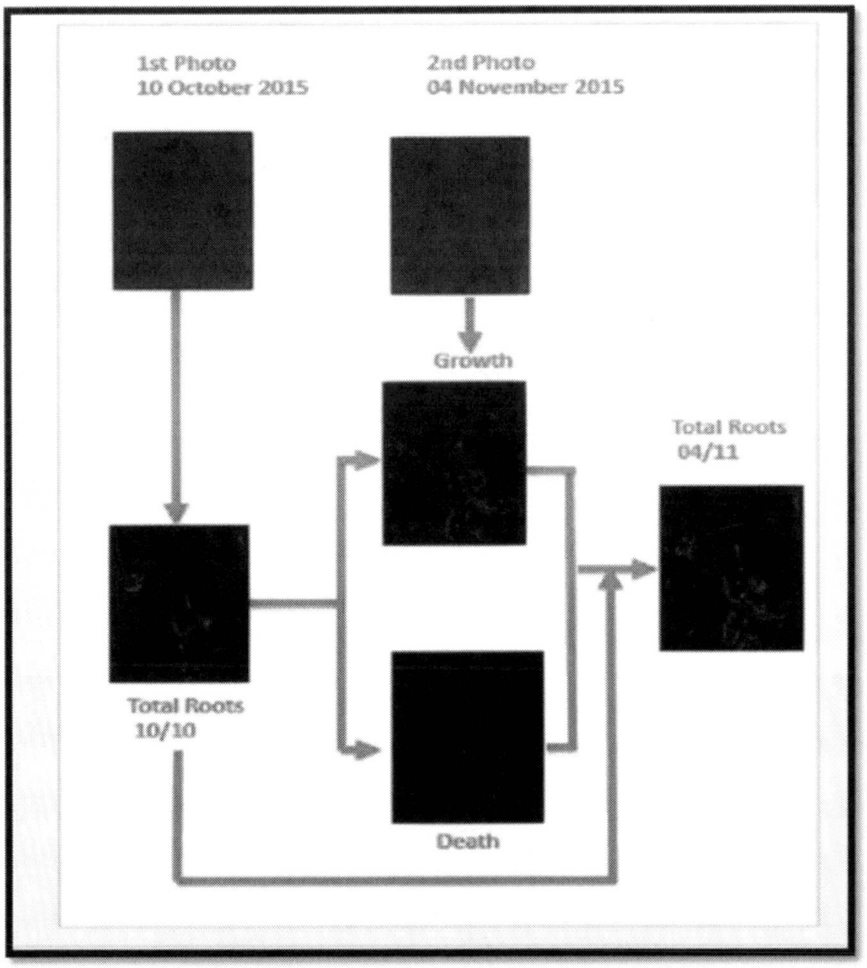

Figure 3: The instructions how to analyses roots presence and absence

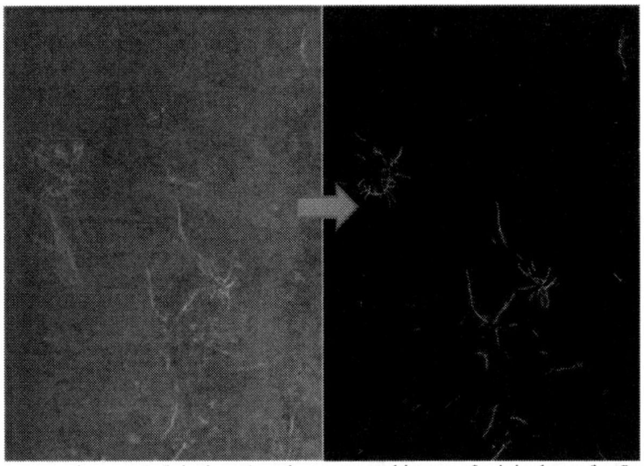

Figure 4: An example of whole scanner images (original root) and an extracted image of original root for October 2015. The white coloured lines are oil palm roots.

Figure 5: Total of growth roots

Figure 6: Total of death roots

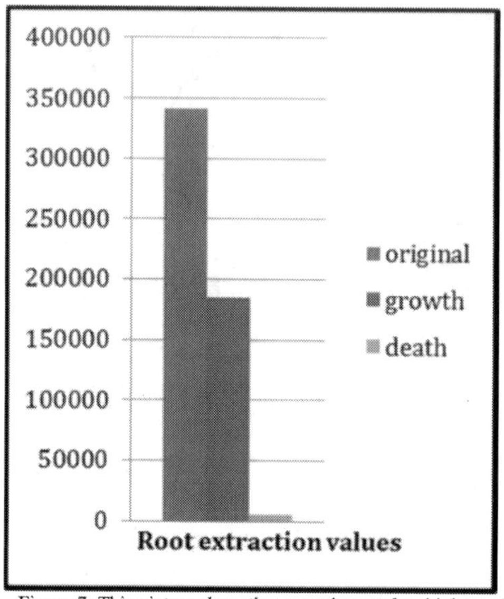

Figure 7: This picture show that growth roots has higher values

The roots development of oil palm can be seen clearly at Figure 2a and 2b. Root tips and hair were clearly growing and increased in the second month (04/11/2015). The analysis process for root production to extract growth and death roots was illustrated in Figure 3. The oil palm root growth and death value was estimated by the difference of current image and previous image. An example of extracted root images from the original scanned image is shown in Figure 4. The dark brown or black coloured tips and hair were determined as dead roots (Figure 5), while those white in colour were regarded as root growth (Figure 6). However, colours may be darker as a result of secondary growth or due to the effect of the soil colour. Hence, it may be difficult to distinguish between roots and organic debris because they can be the same colour, shape and size. In addition, cracks and slits in soil may also look like roots. These are some of the difficulty to determine if roots are alive or dead (Tierney and Fahey, 2002). We solved this challenging by adjusting the brightness of the image. (Figure 7). The study is currently ongoing and methodology is constantly being improved.

DISCUSSION

Based on the preliminary investigation it appears that there were more live roots than dead roots in the second month after the scanner box was installed. The initial results of scanner images from October 2015 and November 2015 are presented (Figure 7). On-going data collection will provide valuable results and trend of root production over time.

CONCLUSION

The scanner method is a technology that is very easy, cheap and quick technique for directly viewing and studying the root dynamics. It can be applied either in peat and mineral soil. This method has helped improve our understanding of root systems because it is a non-destructive method and easier to determine roots behaviour relative to using destructive methods. Further work will be necessary to obtain more images over time to comprehensively understand the applicability of the scanner method in peat soil.

ACKNOWLEDGEMENTS

The financial support for this study was provided by Malaysian Oil Palm Board. The author would like to thank the Sarawak Oil Palms Berhad for the permission to conduct this study in Sebungan and Sabaju Estate. We also thank Ham Jonathan, Steward Emang Saging and Xyxtus Tan for their help in field assistance.

REFERENCES

1. Dannoura M, Kominami Y, Oguma H, Kanazawa Y. The development of an optical scanner method for observation of plant roots dynamics. Plant root 2:14-18. doi: 10.3117/plantroot.2.14
2. Gaudinski, J.B., Trumbore, S.E., Davidson, E.A., Cook, A.C., Markewitz, D., Richter, D.D. 2001. The age of fine-root carbon in three forests of the eastern United States measured by radiocarbon. Oecologica 129: 420-429.
3. Guo, D., Li, H., Mitchell, R.J., Han, W., Hendricks, J.J., Fahey, T.J., Hendrick R.L. 2008. Fine root heterogeneity by branch order: exploring the discrepancy in root turnover estimates between minirhizotron and carbon isotopic methods. New Phytologist 177:443-456.
4. Hendrick, D.L. and K.S. Pregitzer 1992a: Spatial variation in tree root distribution and growth associated with minirhizotrons. Plant and Soil 143, 283–288.
5. Jackson, R. B., Mooney, H. A. & Schulze, E. –D. (1997). A global budget for fine root biomass, surface area and nutrient contents. Proceedings of the National Academy of Sciences, USA 94: 7362-7366.
6. Joslin JD, Wolfe MH, Hanson PJ (2000) Effects of altered water regimes on forest root systems. New Phytol 147:117-129.
7. King JS, Pregitzer KS, Zak DR (1999) Clonal variation in above and below-ground growth responses of Populus tremuloides Michaux: influence of soil warning and nutrient availability. Plant soil 217:119-130.
8. Lauenroth WK, Gill R (2003) Turnover of roots systems. In: de Kroon H,Visser EJW (eds) Ecological studies; root ecology. Springer, Berlin Heidelberg New York, pp 61-89.
9. Pregitzer, K.S. 2002. Fine roots of trees- a new perspective. New Phytologist 154:267-270
10. Tierney, G.L., Fahey, T.J. 2002. Fine root turnover in a northern hardwood forest: a direct comparison of the radiocarbon and minirhizotron methods. Canadian Journal of Forest Research 32: 1692-1697.

Abstract No: A-277

CARBON ISOTOPE DISCRIMINATION AND LEAF GAS EXCHANGE OF OIL PALM PLANTED ON PEAT IN TELUK INTAN, PERAK

A'fifah, A.R[1*], Haniff, M.H[1], Amanina, N.S[1], Maisarah, N.J[1], Hasimah, M[1], Syamsul Kamal, R[2], Izzati, N.M.Z[1] and Saiful, B.B[1]

[1]*Biological Research Division, Malaysian Palm Oil Board, Selangor, Malaysia*
[2]*Advanced Biotechnology and Breeding Centre, Malaysian Palm Oil Board, Selangor, Malaysia*

**Corresponding author: afifah@mpob.gov.my*

SUMMARY

Carbon isotope discrimination ( ) and leaf gas exchange were conducted on five-year old clonal and DxP palms grown on peat in Teluk Intan, Perak. Physiological responses such as photosynthetic rate (P_N) and stomatal conductance (g_s) were generally higher in DxP palms than clonal palms. Higher instantaneous water use efficiency (WUE) was found in clone PL106 palms due to lower transpiration rate (T_r), g_s and intercellular CO_2 concentration (c_i). Clone PL106 palm had a higher leaf carbon isotope discrimination ( ) value that was 5.04% greater compared DxP palm. The in leaf tissues was positively correlated with WUE. Leaf tissue was negatively correlated with transpiration rate (R^2= - 0.63) and stomatal conductance (R^2 = - 0.55). Further study on and WUE from different oil palm ages and seasonal variations are needed to understand the variation in the values and the relationship between WUE and gas exchange.

Keywords: *leaf gas exchange, water use efficiency, carbon isotope discrimination, oil palm*

INTRODUCTION

The oil palm in Malaysia is primarily grown as a rain fed agricultural crop. An adequate supply of water and nutrients are important factors that could affect the oil palm crop yield. Many studies have been done to explore the activity of gas exchange in oil palm. Dufrêne and Saugier (1993) found that stomatal conductance (g_s) of oil palm is very sensitive to the changes in vapour pressure deficit (VPD) and declined linearly with increases in VPD above the critical value of 1.8 kPa. Photosynthetic rate (P_N) will decline with decreasing stomatal conductance when VPD exceeded the critical value. Henson (1995) reported that canopy photosynthesis was halved when the VPD value increased from 0.8 to 2.0 kPa.

Carbon isotope discrimination ( ) is a technique for evaluating water use efficiency (WUE) in C3 plants. It has been used widely on other crops such as alfafa, wheat, tomatoes and cocoa (Moghaddam *et al.*, 2013; Erice *et al.*, 2011; Carelli *et al.*, 1999; Wei *et al.*, 2016). Leaf has been used as an integrated measure of photosynthetic gas exchange to evaluate for changes in environmental conditions (Farquhar *et al.*, 1982; Meinzer *et al.*, 1990; Zimmerman and Ehleringer, 1990). Leaf was found to be strongly correlated with WUE in many crops (Meinzer *et al.*, 1990; Brito *et al.*, 2014).

This study was done to determine relationship between leaf gas exchange parameters, leaf and WUE in different oil palm planting materials grown on peat.

METHODS

The study was conducted at MPOB Peat Research Station in Teluk Intan, Perak. The peat was classified as Penor series with sub-group level as Terric Sulfisaprist in the keys to soil taxanomy and as Sapric Topogambrist in the Malaysian Soil Taxanomy (Paramanathan, 2012). The oil palm planting materials were planted at a density of 160 palm ha^{-1} in December 2007 and measurements were taken when they were about five year old. The planting materials used consist of a commercial DxP and four clonal palms (i.e. PL68, PL104, PL106 and PL127). Meteorological parameters were recorded at hourly intervals by an automated weather station (Campbell Scientific, USA) installed at the plantation (Fig.1).

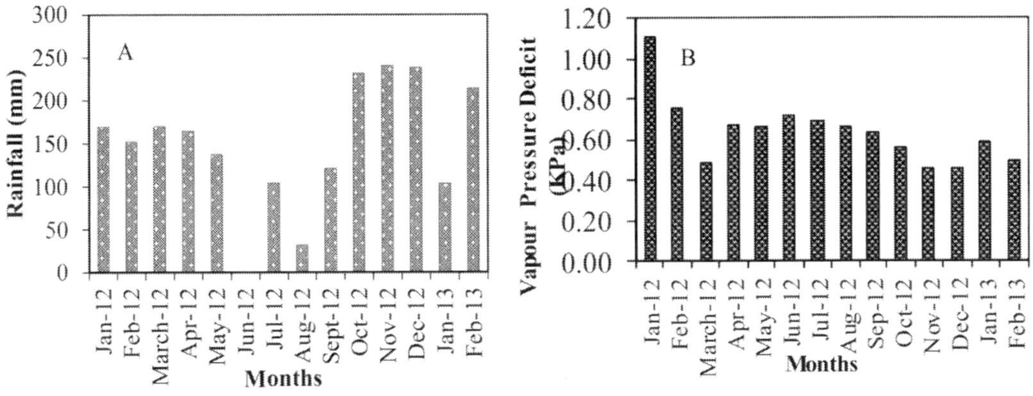

Fig. 1. Monthly rainfall (A) and vapour pressure deficit (B) throughout the measurement time.

Leaf gas exchange parameters were measured on intact leaflets attached to frond 17 with a portable photosynthesis system (Model LI-6400XT, LI-COR, Inc., USA). Conditions inside the leaf cuvette were selected as follows: ambient temperature, ambient humidity, photosynthetically active radiation (PAR) of 1000 µmol photon $m^{-2}s^{-1}$ (red/blue light source), and reference CO_2 of 400 µmol mol^{-1} air. Leaf transpiration (T_r), g_s, and P_N were determined and ambient PAR, temperature, CO_2, and vapour pressure deficit (VPD) were recorded. Leaf temperature was measured with a thermistor, and instantaneous water use efficiency (WUE) was calculated as P_N / T_r. Photosynthetic gas exchange characteristics were determined for the five planting materials and measurements taken at 3-month intervals over a 13 month period.

Carbon isotope ratios ($\delta^{13}C$) were determined from the leaflets taken from frond 17. Leaf samples were oven dried at 70°C for 48h and ground to a fine powder. Carbon isotope composition of the leaf samples was determined using an Isotopic Ratio Mass Spectrometer at the Malaysian Institute of Nuclear Technology.

RESULTS

The P_N was significantly different ($p \leq 0.05$) between planting materials but was not significant in February 2013 (Fig.2A). The DxP palm had the highest P_N in February, August and November 2012 compared to the other planting materials. However, clone PL127 had higher P_N than DxP palm in May 2012. The c_i between planting materials was significantly difference in May 2012 and February 2013 (Fig.2B). Clone PL127 palm had a high c_i (348.66 µmol$m^{-2}s^{-1}$) in May 2012 but was not significant between clone PL68 (343.27 µmol$m^{-2}s^{-1}$), PL106 (324.06 µmol$m^{-2}s^{-1}$) and DxP (335.99 µmol$m^{-2}s^{-1}$) in February 2013. The g_s value was significantly different ($p \leq 0.05$) between planting materials in February, May and August 2012 (Fig.2C). Meanwhile, T_r was significantly influenced by the planting materials throughout the year except in November 2012 (Fig.2D). The g_s and T_r were higher in DxP palms in February and August 2012. In general, seasonal trend in gas exchange of DxP palms was higher than clonal palms throughout the measurement period. Clonal palms had decreasing gas exchange parameters such as P_N, g_s and c_i during months with low rainfall and high VPD (August 2012) than in month with high rainfall and low VPD (November 2012). Water use efficiency between planting materials were significantly difference in February 2013 (Fig.2E). The WUE in PL106 palm was about 22% higher than DxP palm. However, WUE between clones PL106 and PL104 were not statistically different ($p \leq 0.05$).

There were significant differences ($p \leq 0.05$) in WUE and leaf values in February 2013 between the planting materials (Fig.3). Clone PL106 had the highest leaf value (23.15‰) and DxP palm the lowest leaf value (22.04‰). The relationship between WUE and leaf of five oil palm planting materials in February 2013 was a positive quadratic (Fig.4). There was a significant correlation between leaf , transpiration rate (Fig.5) and stomatal conductance (Fig.6). However, relationship between leaf and P_N was not significant ($p \leq 0.05$) (Fig.7).

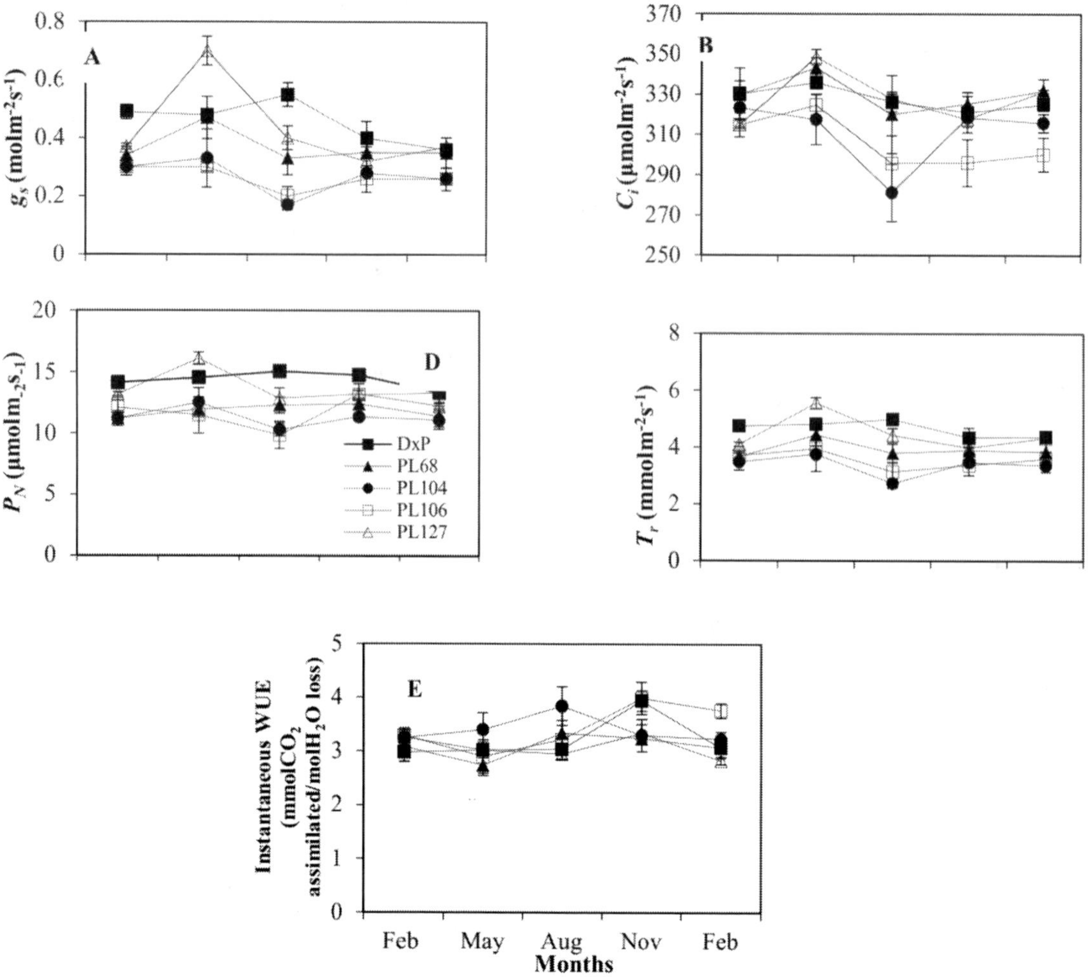

Fig. 2: Gas exchange parameters of different oil palm planting materials throughout the measurement times; Photosynthetic rate, P_N (A), Intercellular CO_2 concentration, c_i (B), Stomatal conductance, g_s (C), Transpiration rate, T_r (D) and Instantaneous water use efficiency, WUE (E). Bar represent the standard error of means (n=3).

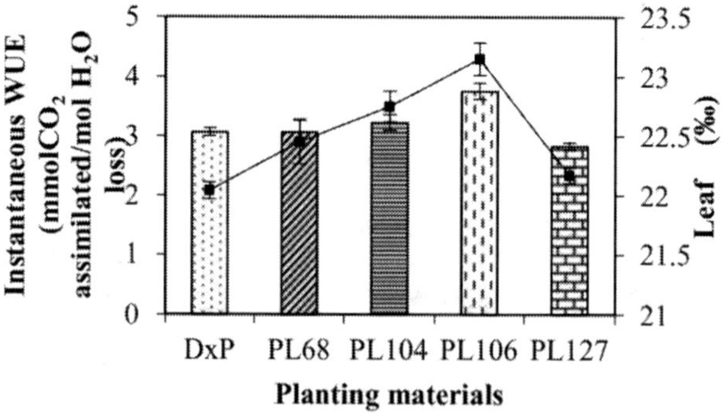

Fig. 3: Instantaneous water use efficiency and leaf carbon isotope discrimination of different oil palm planting materials in February 2013. Bar represent standard error bar (n=3).

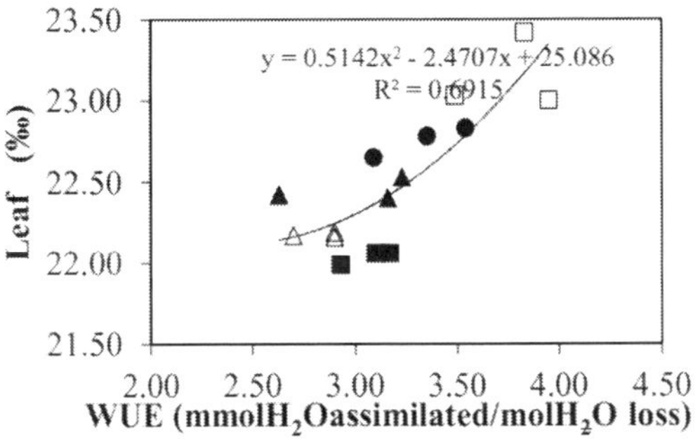

Fig. 4: Instantaneous water use efficiency and leaf carbon isotope discrimination of different oil palm planting materials in February 2013. Symbol ■ represent the DxP palm ,▲represent the PL68 palm, • represent the PL104 palm, □ represent PL106 palm and represent PL127 palm (n=15)

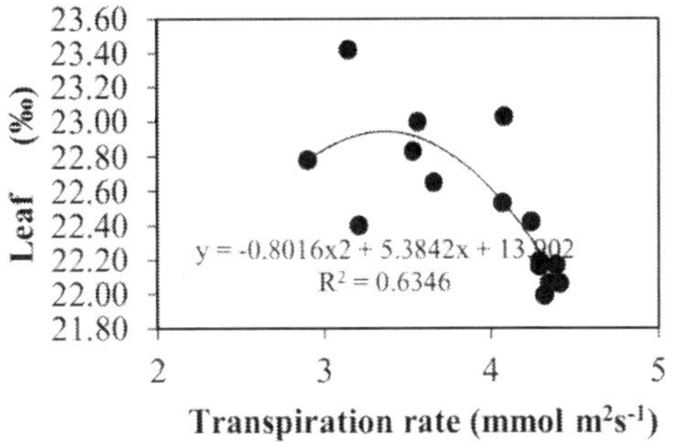

Fig. 5: Relationship between leaf carbon isotope discrimination and transpiration rate in February 2013 (n=15).

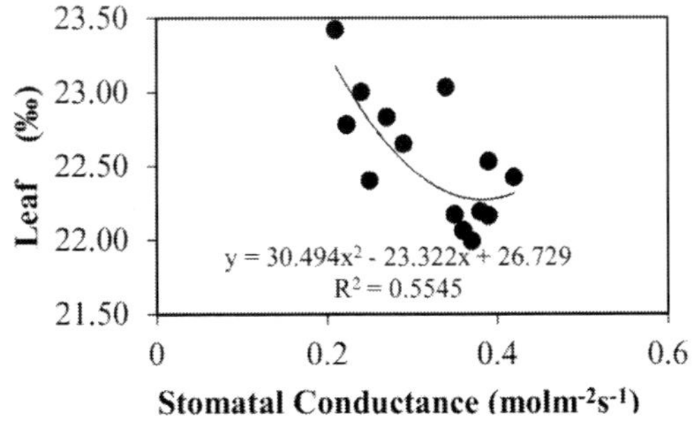

Fig. 6: Relationship between leaf carbon isotope discrimination and stomatal conductance in February 2013 (n=15).

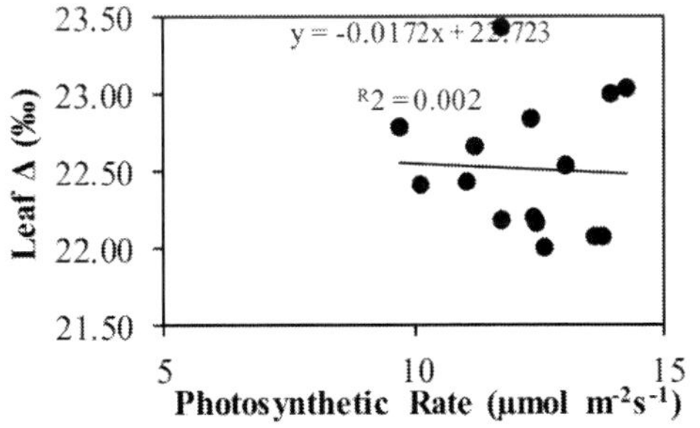

Fig. 7: Relationship between leaf carbon isotope discrimination and photosynthetic rate in February 2013 (n=15).

DISCUSSION

Planting materials had a significant influence on the palm P_N. The higher P_N in DxP palm was related to higher gs. The DxP palms tend to sustain the P_N and g_s during higher and lower rainfall distribution in February (152.1 mm/month) and August 2012 (31mm/month) respectively. In general, P_N, g_s and T_r pattern in all clonal palms throughout the period were lower than DxP palm. The seasonal gas exchange pattern such as P_N, g_s and c_i in all clonal palms were lower in August than in November due to higher evaporative demand and temperature during the dry period. Temperature, humidity, water availability and light intensity and interception influenced the seasonal pattern of carbon fixation (Teskey *et al.*, 1994; Ellsworth, 2000; Gough *et al.*, 2004).

Clone PL106 could be considered as the best water saver because of the highest WUE value. This might be attributed to the lower T_r, g_s and c_i values. Farquhar *et al.* (1989) suggested that WUE was negatively correlated with c_i. A similar study in *Phaseolus vulgaris* had shown that WUE could be improved either through lowering g_s, raising photosynthetic capacity or both (Guo *et al.*, 2006). The relationship between WUE and leaf of different planting materials was positively quadratic. This indicates that palm with higher WUE had greater leaf . Leaf was found to be negatively correlated with transpiration rate and stomatal conductance. The result was inconsistent with findings by Zhang *et al.* (1994) in forest tree. They reported that WUE had a strong negative correlation with leaf . This might arise from several reasons. First, the P_N was measured on a small subsample of leaves over a short period and may not represent the whole palm or the whole growing period. It contradicted with the finding by Farquhar *et al.* (1989) who reported that carbon isotope ratio was more integrative because all the carbon in the leaf was represented. Second, variation in the monthly rainfall throughout the measurement time, since palms studied experienced six months of low rainfall and the ability to photosynthesize more with less amount of water could have a great influence on total carbon fixation than would short-term photosynthetic rates.

CONCLUSION

Carbon isotope discrimination can be a suitable tool for screening oil palm planting materials for WUE. However, further study is needed on the relationship between , leaf gas exchange and WUE at different palm age and seasonal variation.

ACKNOWLEDGEMENTS

The authors would like to thank the Director General of MPOB for permission to present this paper.

REFERENCES

1. Brito, G G., N.D, Suassuna, V.N, Silva, V, Sofiatti, V, Diola, and C.L, Morello, 2014. Leaf-level carbon isotope discrimination and its relationship with yield component as a tool for cotton phenotyping in unfavorable conditions. *Acta Science Agronomy*. 36: 335-345.
2. Carelli, M.L.C., J.I. Fahl, P.C.O. Trivelin, and R.B. Queiroz-Voltan, 1999. Carbon isotope discrimination and gas exchange in coffea species grown under different irradiance regimes. *Revista Brasileira de Fisiologia Vegetal.*, 11: 63-38.
3. Dufrêne, E, and B. Saugier, 1993. Gas exchange of oil palm in relation to light, vapour pressure deficit, temperature and leaf age. *Functional Ecology* 7:97–104.
4. Ellsworth, D.S. 2000. Seasonal CO_2 assimilation and stomatal limitations in a Pinus taeda canopy. *Tree Physiologyl*. 20:435–445.
5. Erice, G., S. Louahlia, J.J. Irigoyen, M. Sanchez-Diaz, I.T. alami, and J.C. Avice, 2011. Water use efficiency, transpiration and net CO_2 exchange of four alfafa genotypes submitted to progressive drought and subsequent recovery. *Environmental and Experimental Botany*. 72: 123-130.
6. Farquhar, G.D., M.C. Ball, S.von Caemmerer, and Z, Roksandic. 1982. Effect of salinity and humidity on $d^{13}C$ value of halophytes - evidence for diffusional isotope fractionation determined by the ratio of intercellular/atmospheric CO_2 under different conditions. *Oecologia*. 52: 121-124.
7. Farquhar, G.D., J.R. Ehleringer, and K.T. Hubick, 1989. Carbon isotope discrimination and photosynthesis. Ann *Rev Plant Physiol Plant Mol Bio*. 40: 503–537.
8. Gough, C.M., J.R. Seiler, K.H. Johnsen and D.A. Sampson. 2004. Seasonal photosynthesis in fertilized and non-fertilized loblolly pine. *For. Sci.* 50:1–9
9. Guo S.W.,Y. Zhou., N. Song and Q.R. Shen, 2006. Some Physiological Processes Related to Water Use Efficiency of Higher Plants. *Agricultural Sciences in China*. 5(6): 403-411.
10. Henson, I.E, 1995. Carbon assimilation, water-use and energy balance of an oil palm plantation assessed using micrometeorological techniques. *In Proceedings 1993 PORIM International Palm Oil Conference – Agriculture,* (Ed.Y. Basiron). Palm Oil Research Institute, Malaysia, Kuala Lumpur, 137–158.
11. Meinzer,F.C., G, Goldstein, and D.A, Grants, 1990. Carbon isotope discrimination in coffee genotypes grown under limited water supply. *Plant Physiology,* 92:130-135.
12. Mohgaddam, A., A. Raza, J. Vollmann, M.R. Ardakani, W. Wanek, G. Gollner, and J.K. Friedel, 2013. Carbon isotope discrimination and water use efficiency relationships of alfafa genotypes under irrigated and rain-fed organic farming. *European Journal Agronomy*, 50: 82-89.
13. Paramanathan, 2012. Soils of the MPOB's Teluk Intan Research Station (Incorporating A Detailed Soil Map) Mukim Hutan Melintang Lower Perak District Perak Darul Ridzuan.pp 1-24.
14. Teskey, R.O., H.L. Gholz and W.P. Cropper Jr. 1994. Influence of climate and fertilization on net photosynthesis of mature slash pine. *Tree Physiology*. 14:1215–1227
15. Wei, Z., T. Du, J. Zhang, S. Xu, P.J. Cambre, and W.J. Davies, 2016. Carbon isotope discrimination shows a higher water use efficiency under alternate partial root-zone irrigation of field-grown tomatoes. *Agricultural Water Management,* 165: 33-43
16. Zhang J.W., L, Fins, and, Marsshall, J.D, 1994. Stable carbon isotope discrimination, photosynthetic gas exchange, and growth differences among western larch families. *Tree Physiology*, 14:53 l-539.
17. Zimmerman, J.K. and J.R, Ehleringer. 1990. Carbon isotope ratios are correlated with irradiance levels in the Panamanian orchid *Catasetum viridiflavum*. *Oecologia*, 83:247-249, 1990.

Abstract No: A-462

EFFECTS OF CONTROLLED RELEASE NITROGEN FERTILIZER ON VEGETATIVE GROWTH AND LEAF NITROGEN OF IMMATURE OIL PALM PLANTED ON TROPICAL PEATLAND

Auldry Chaddy[1], Lulie Melling[1] and Hiroshi Aoki[2]

[1]Tropical Peat Research Laboratory Unit, Sarawak, Malaysia.
[2]JCAM AGRI. Co. LTD., Tokyo, Japan

SUMMARY

The objective of this study was to compare the effects of controlled release urea fertilizer (CRUF) and conventional urea on vegetative growth and leaf nitrogen (N) of oil palm cultivated on tropical peatland. The study was conducted in a young oil palm plantation on tropical peatland in Sarawak for four (4) years. The treatments included without N fertilizer (Control) (T1), 100% conventional urea (T2), 50% CRUF (T3) and 100% CRUF (T4). Vegetative growth parameters such as number of pinnae, pinnae length, pinnaewidth , petiole width and petiole depth , were measured and recorded. Leaf samples were collected from the midsections of themiddle leaflets, oven-dried and ground for total N analysis. No statistically, significant difference in number of pinnae, width of pinnae or leaf N was observed between conventional urea and CRUF, regardless of rate of application of N. However, pinnae length, petiole width and petiole depth were significantly higher in palms treated with 100% urea than those treated with 100% CRUF. This might be due to the lack of adequate release of the substantial N from CRUF to fulfil the requirements of the oil palm, especially during its rapid growth, possibly resulting in the palms absorbing the N from peat mineralization rather than from the fertilizers. Leaf N concentration from fertilized palms (T2, T3 and T4) demonstrated an obvious increasing trend for the first three (3) years after planting and thereafter decreased to a constant phase. A decrease in the leaf N concentration to deficiency level (<2.5%) in the control plot in March 2012 may due to high rainfall during that period, causing more N leaching and dilution in both soil and plant tissue. Long-term measurements are still needed to evaluate the efficiency of CRUF on oil palm growth and productivity on tropical peatland.

Keywords: *urea, oil palm, tropical peatland, vegetative growth, leaf nitrogen*

INTRODUCTION

The oil palm industry has been one of the main generators of the Malaysian economy, driving the country's growth while fulfilling global demand for oils and fats. The need for increased production to meet the global demand has resulted in the widespread expansion of oil palm plantations into tropical peatlands. However, the peatlands' marginal properties, such as high porosity, high acidity and low fertility, pose severe limitations to plant growth. The peat's high porosity coupled with heavy rainfall most of the time, makes nutrients, particularly nitrogen (N), particularly susceptible to loss by leaching (N being one of the primary nutrients essential for plant structural development and physiological processes). Therefore, extensive quantities of N fertilizers are applied as one of the efforts to optimize the growth and productivity of oil palm on peat.

Urea is noted as the most widely used N agricultural fertilizer. However, rapid hydrolysis of urea in soil following surface application can lead to significant ammonia loss (Mohd. Taufik *et al.*, 2009). Accordingly, controlled release N fertilizers, particularly based on urea, have been developed to reduce losses from either leaching or volatilization and at the same time improve nitrogen use efficiency and reduce nitrate pollution (Shaviv and Mikkleson, 1993; Simonne and Hutchinson, 2005). Polymer coating is used to control the rate that the granules dissolve (which depends primarily on soil moisture and temperature). To date, CRUF has been tested on a number of different crops including paddy and barley (Kamekawa *et al.*, 1990; Zhang *et al.*, 2000) but little information is available on the effects of this formulation of urea on the nutrient status and growth performance of oil palm, particularly those planted on tropical peatland. Therefore, this study was conducted to compare the effects of CRUF and conventional urea on vegetative growth and leaf N of oil palm cultivated on tropical peatland.

STUDY SITE

This study was conducted in an oil palm plantation at Sibu, Sarawak (002° 7' 37.4" N, 111°86' 37.9" E). The location has an equatorial climate with temperatures between 30.6 to 33.7° C and annual rainfall of more than 3000 mm. The peat soil was classified as *Typic Tropofibrist* using the USDA soil classification system (Soil Survey Staff, 2010). Drainage had been carried out to lower the water table to between 50 and 70 cm and the soil had been compacted during plantation establishment.. The oil palms at the site were approximately one year old (planted in January 2010) at a density of 153 palms ha $^{-1}$.

MATERIALS AND METHODS

The experiment was started in September 2011 and completed in September 2015. Four treatments were applied: T1: No N fertilizer (Control), T2: 100% conventional Urea, T3: 50% CRUF, and T4: 100% CRUF. The first fertilization was on September 2011. Frond number nine (9) was used as a standard foliar sampling protocol for immature palm (Corley and Tinker, 2003). Vegetative growth parameters, such as pinnae number, pinnae length, pinnae width, petiole width and petiole depth, were measured and recorded. Leaf samples were collected from the midsections of the middle leaflets, oven-dried and ground for total N analysis.

One-way Analysis of variance (ANOVA) was used to test the effect of the treatments on vegetative growth measurements and leaf N concentration while means of the variables were compared using Tukey's Range Test. All statistical analysis was performed using the Statistical Analysis System (SAS) version 9.2.

RESULTS AND DISCUSSION

The effects of treatments on vegetative growth measurements and leaf N are shown in **Table 1**. No significant difference in pinnae number or pinnae width was observed between palms treated with conventional urea and those treated with CRUF, regardless of N application rate. However, pinnae length, petiole width and petiole depth were significantly higher in palms treated with 100% urea than those treated with 100% CRUF. In contrast, a study by Rasid *et al.* (2014) found that CRUF gave better results for oil palm growth than conventional urea. Although not significant, the highest values for pinnae number, pinnae width and leaf N were recorded from palms fertilized with 100% conventional urea. It was suspected that the substantial N from CRUF may not be released adequately to fulfil the oil palm's requirements especially during its rapid growth phase, possibly resulting inthe palms absorbing N from the mineralization of the peat rather than from the fertilizers.

The determination of nutrients concentration in the leaves of palms is the most general and practical way to determine nutrient deficiency in palms (Corley and Tinker, 2003). Leaf N concentration did not differ significantly between palms treated with CRUF and those treated with conventional urea. Purwanto *et al.* (2002) also reported lack of significant differences between leaf N concentrations in sago palms on tropical peatland treated with conventional urea or CRUF. As shown in **Figure 1**, leaf N concentration in fertilized palms (T2, T3 and T4) demonstrated an obvious increasing trend for the first three years after planting and thereafter decreased to a constant level. According to Goh and Hardter (2003), during the second and third years after planting, there is a large increase in the demand for nutrients, particularly N, due to rapid growth. The annual nutrient demand tends to stabilize from years 3 to 5 onwards.The concentration of N in oil palm leaves in all the treatments was at a satisfactory level for young palm (between 2.6 to 2.9 mg kg^{-1} (Foster, 2003). A decrease in leaf N concentration to deficiency level (<2.5%) of the control plot in March 2012 may have been due to higher rainfall during that period, causing more N loss via leaching. Higher rainfall also contributes to the dilution of N in the soil and plant tissue. This suggests that oil palms not fertilized with of fertilizer may possibly not be capable of sustaining adequate N levels in the leaves for optimum growth as N from mineralization in tropical peatland cannot be treated as the key N source as its production is erratic.

Table 1: Vegetative growth measurements and leaf N under different treatments

Treatment	Number of pinnae	Pinnae length	Pinnae width	Petiole width	Petiole depth	Leaf N
		cm	cm	cm	cm	mg kg^{-1}
T1 (Control)	251.07^{b}	78.98^{bc}	4.01^{a}	5.51^{c}	2.98^{c}	2.59^{b}
T2 (100% urea)	262.57^{a}	80.78^{a}	4.08^{a}	5.69^{d}	3.02^{d}	2.71^{ab}
T3 (50% CRUF)	260.60^{a}	80.11^{ab}	3.95^{a}	5.64^{b}	3.02^{b}	2.71^{ab}
T4 (100% CRUF)	256.84^{a}	77.61^{c}	3.87^{a}	5.52^{a}	2.88^{a}	2.76^{a}

Different letters within columns indicate significant differences between means using Tukey's Range Test at $p<0.05$.

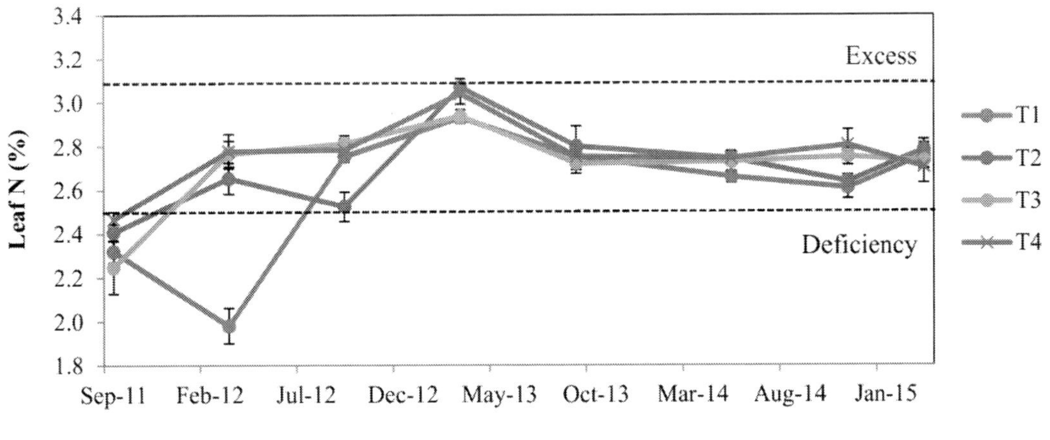

Figure 1 : Effect of different treatments on leaf N concentration of oil palm with time

CONCLUSION

This study indicated no significant difference between the effects of CRUF and of conventional urea on the number of pinnae, pinnae width and leaf N of young oil palm in tropical peat. However, conventional urea was found to be more efficient than CRUF especially during the rapid growth of oil palm. Thus, long-term measurements are still needed to evaluate the efficiency of CRUF on oil palm growth and productivity on tropical peatland.

ACKNOWLEDGEMENTS

We would like to thank the oil palm plantation industry, Chiba University, Japan and JCAM Agri, Japan for their support.

REFERENCES

1. Corley, R.H.V. and P.B. Tinker. (2003). *The Oil Palm* (4th ed.). Blackwell Sciences Ltd., Oxford, United Kingdom.
2. Foster, H. (2003). Assessment of oil palm fertilizer requirements. Pp. 231-257 in: T.H. Fairhurst and R. Hardter (eds.) *Oil Palm: Management for Large and Sustainable Yields*. PPI, Switzerland.
3. Goh, K.J. and R. Hardter. (2003). General oil palm nutrition. Pp. 191-230 in: T.H. Fairhurst and R. Hardter (eds.) *Oil Palm: Management for large and sustainable yields*. PPI, Switzerland,.
4. Kamekawa, K. I., T. Nagai, S.I. Sekiya and T. Yoneyama. (1990). Nitrogen uptake by paddy rice (*Oryza sativa* L.) from 15N labelled coated urea and ammonium sulfate. *Soil Science and Plant Nutrition* 36(2): 333-336.

5. Mohd Taufik, M.Y., O.H. Ahmed and A.M. Nik Muhamad. (2009). Effect of mixing urea with humic acid and acid sulphate soil on ammonia loss, exchangeable ammonium and available nitrate. *American Journal of Environmental Sciences* 5(5): 588-591.
6. Purwanto, B.H., K.I., Kakuda, H. Ando, J.F. Shoon, Y. Yamamoto, A. Watanabe and T. Yoshida. (2002). Nutrient availability and response of sago palm (*Metroxylon sago* Rottb.) to controlled release N fertilizer on coastal lowland peat in the tropics. *Soil science and plant nutrition*, 48(4):529-537.
7. Rasid, M. N. A., T.C. Chek and A.F. Redzuan. (2014). Effectiveness of urea-coated fertilizer on young immature oil palm growth. *Journal of Advanced Agricultural Technologies* 1(1).
8. Shaviv, A. and R. Mikkelson. (1993). Controlled-release fertilizers to increase efficiency of nutrient use and minimize environmental degradation: A review. *Fert. Res.* 35:1–12.
9. Simonne, E.H. and C.M. Hutchinson. (2005). Controlled-release fertilizers for vegetable production in the era of best management practices: Teaching new tricks to an old dog. *HortTechnology* 15:36–46.
10. Zhang, M., M. Nyborg, S.S. Malhi, and E.D. Solberg. (2000). Yield and protein content of barley as affected by release rate of coated urea and rate of nitrogen application. *Journal of plant nutrition* 23(3): 401-412.

Abstract No: A-093

EFFECT OF DIFFERENT COMBINATION OF ORGANIC AND CHEMICAL FERTILIZERS APPLICATION ON GROWTH AND YIELD OF HYBRIMAS SWEET CORN ON PEAT

K. Mohamad Hafis [1*], A. Izham [1] and M. S. Halimi [2]

[1]*Crop Science Department, Faculty of Agriculture, Universiti Putra Malaysia, Malaysia*
[2]*Agriculture Technology Department, Faculty of Agriculture, Universiti Putra Malaysia, Malaysia*

**Corresponding author: Hafisenot89@gmail.com*

The expansion of sweet corn cultivation offers an alternative option to the present planting of pineapple on peat in Malaysia. The major sweet corn growing areas are located in West Johor, Selangor and Sarawak. This experiment was conducted at the Integrated Peat Research Station (IPRS) in January-April 2015. The research objective was to find out which fertilizer types and their combinations are best for growing Hybrimas sweet corn on peat. The experimental design was a randomized complete block (RCBD) with four replications. Chemical fertilizer, poultry manure and *Bacillus sphaericus* (UPMB10) were used and were applied at T1: Control (No fertilizer), T2: Chemical fertilizer (N: 348 kg ha^{-1}, P_2O_5: 70.8 kg ha^{-1} and K_2O: 150 kg ha^{-1}), T3: Poultry Manure (3.56 ton ha^{-1}), T4: *Bacillus sphaericus* (UPMB10) (50L solution per10,000L water), T5: 50% Chemical Fertilizer + 50% Poultry Manure, T6: 50% Poultry Manure + 50% UPMB10, T7: 50% Chemical Fertilizer + 50% UPMB10, and T8: 30% Chemical Fertilizer, 30% Poultry Manure and 40% UPMB10. All the fertilizer treatments were applied at planting. The combination of 50% Poultry Manure and 50% UPMB10 (T6) resulted in the highest plant height at 6, 8 and 10 weeks after planting compared to other treatments. Root volume was largest for Hybrimas sweet corn (6077.5 cm^3) on the same treatment. Root and ear lengths and wet and dry weights ear were highest at T4 (UPMB10) but these parameters were not significantly different from those at T6. The nitrogen and phosphorus content in the leaves for T6 were also found to be high at 2.64% and 0.31% respectively. A combination of 50% Poultry Manure and 50% UPMB10 was shown to be suitable from the growing of Hybrimas sweet corn on peat at Pontian, Johore, Malaysia.

Keywords: *poultry manure, biofertilizer, hybrid sweet corn, chemical fertilizer, peat soils*

Abstract No: A-435

EFFECT OF DRAINAGE IN *ACACIA CRASSICARPA* PLANTATION FOREST TOWARDS THE MATURITY LEVEL OF PEAT SOIL

Yunita Lisnawati and Chairil Anwar Siregar

Forest Research and Development Center
Jl. Gunung Batu No.5 Bogor 16610, Indonesia

* *Correspondence author, email: salvinia nita@yahoo.co.id*

SUMMARY

Utilization of peatlands for *Acacia crassicarpa* plantations begins with drainage channel construction that aims to control the depth of water table so that the availability of oxygen for the roots will increase and the plants can grow well. In general, a decrease in the depth of peat soil's water table will cause decomposition and hence peat soil maturity appears faster. Study on the influence of the drained peatlands on the nature and characteristics of peat soil was conducted in Riau. This study was aimed to determine the dynamics of water table depth and to evaluate the maturity level of the peat either vertically and horizontally. Research plots were placed in a 100 m transects and built perpendicularly to the tertiary canal. Parameters observed were rainfall characteristics, dynamics of water table depth and fiber content value of the peat soil. Test for homogeneity of the rainfall data was conducted to determine whether the inter-annual rainfall data differed significantly or not. A simple regression analysis was conducted to see the relationship between the values of water table depth with rainfall, while the analysis of variance was conducted to evaluate the fiber content of peat soil as affected by water table depth. The results showed that the characteristics of annual rainfall per year were not significantly different and negatively correlated to the water table depth, in which the higher the rainfall the higher the water table depth became (closer to the ground), and vice versa. The effect of drainage/water table depth to the maturity level of peat was significant at up to 2 m peat depth.

Keywords: drainage, water table depth, fiber content, peat maturity

INTRODUCTION

The potential of peatlands in Indonesia is estimated at 20.6 million hectares or around 10.8% of Indonesia's land area (Wahyunto *et al*, 2005). In Indonesia, peatlands utilization has started in 1960s as agricultural land for the transmigration program (Suryadi, 1996; Rahmadi 2009; Saefudin, 2009). Since 1990s, the government developed peatland as Industrial Forest Plantation (IFP) areas, particularly in Sumatra and Kalimantan to produce pulp. The primary species grown in peatlands is *Acacia crassicarpa* with 4.5-6 years of the harvest cycle.

Peatlands in natural conditions are always waterlogged, therefore to utilize this land for growing *A. crassicarpa,* the abundant water has to be drained through establishment of drainage canals to increase the oxygen availability to the roots, thus, the plants can grow and flourish properly (Hooijer *et al.*, 2006). According to Radjagukguk (1991), the regulation and management of drainage systems are considered as very important aspects because they are closely related to the physical properties of peat, one of which is the maturity level of the peat soil. On the drained peatlands condition, brown waste and peat materials are weathered faster due to the much faster decomposition process under aerobic conditions than in anaerobic conditions.

This study aimed to: (1) determine the characteristics of rainfall and the dynamics of water table depth; (2) evaluate the maturity level of peat either vertically (based on the depth of peat) and horizontally (based on the distance from the canal's edge).

RESEARCH METHODS

Time and Location

This research was conducted in the Industrial Plantation Forest area of PT Arara Abadi, Rasau Kuning District, Siak, Riau Province, from July 2012 to June 2013. The research plots were placed on the third rotation *Acacia crassicarpa* stand growing on peatland at 1, 2, and 3 years of age.

Research Methods

Determination of research plots was conducted using purposive sampling method (to determine representative plots). Observation points in each study plot was placed in a 100 m transects and built perpendicularly to the tertiary canal. The first observation point was placed 20 m from the canal's edge, then the next points spaced every 50 m, resulting in three observation points or soil sampling sites in one transect which could represent the distance from the drainage canal. Transect lane was placed at 12 plots of *A. crassicarpa* stands, thus the total observation points were 36. Parameters measured were the maturity level of peat soil by looking at the value of peat soil fiber content using McKinzie method, the dynamics of water table depth using Piezometer, and rainfall data.

Peat Soil Sampling. It was conducted by using *Eidjel Kemp* peat drill on each 50-cm depth interval up to the mineral soil substratum.

Climate Data Collection. Rainfall data time series from 2004-2007 were collected from the Research and Development (R&D) Bunut office stations, while the data from 2008-2013 were collected from Rasau Kuning District office station of PT. Arara Abadi.

Measurement of Water Table Depth. On each observation point at selected locations, piezometers were installed sizing 1-inch diameter and 1.5-m length PVC pipes which have been perforated (thus the soil water from around the hole can flow into the pipes), then the pipes were vertically implanted into the ground, and approximately 0.25 m of the pipes' tops appeared on the ground surface to monitor the water table levels. Piezometers were installed at 27 observation points and measured every month for one year (from July 2012 to June 2013).

RESULTS AND DISCUSSION

Rainfall Characteristics

Distribution of average monthly rainfall in the study area showed peak rainfall (highest rainfall) occurred in March and November, while the minimum rainfall (lowest rainfall) occurred in June. The rainfall trend in the study site is presented in Figure 1.

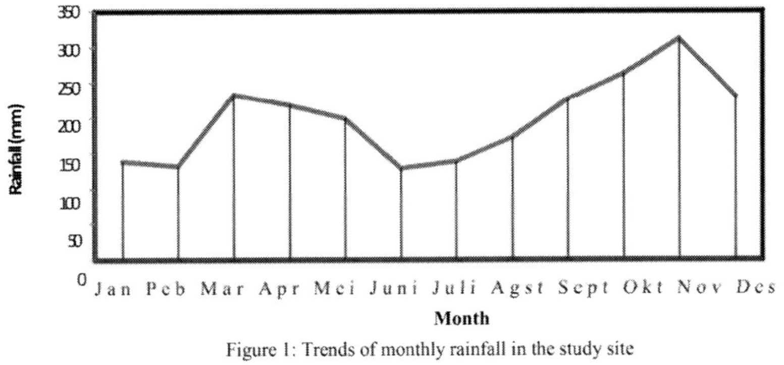

Figure 1: Trends of monthly rainfall in the study site

According to Boerema (1922), the monthly rainfall pattern in the research location was categorized as equatorial type, which generally had an average monthly rainfall pattern with two maximum rainfall peaks, in March and November. Peak rainfall usually occurs when the sun is above the position of the region. Meanwhile, when a 10-year rainfall data time series are tested for their homogeneity, it turns out that each year's rainfall is not significantly different. As a result, it can be assumed that the amount of rainfall throughout the years is the same in terms of influencing the water table depth of peat soils.

Spearman's rank correlation test was conducted based on the rainfall data during 2004-2012 in Rasau Kuning District, and indicated no change in trend, as shown in Figure 2.

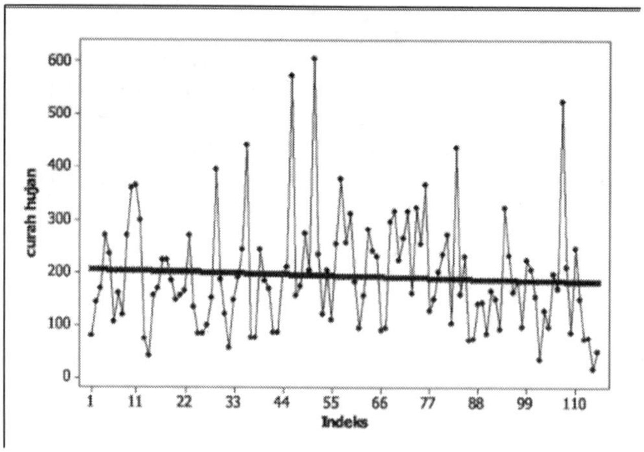

Figure 2: Trends of rainfall during 2004-2012 in the study site

Characteristics of Water Table Depth

The dynamics of water table depth under the third rotation of *A. crassicarpa* stands at 1, 2 and 3 years of age in the study site across all the distance from canal is summarized in Figure 3.

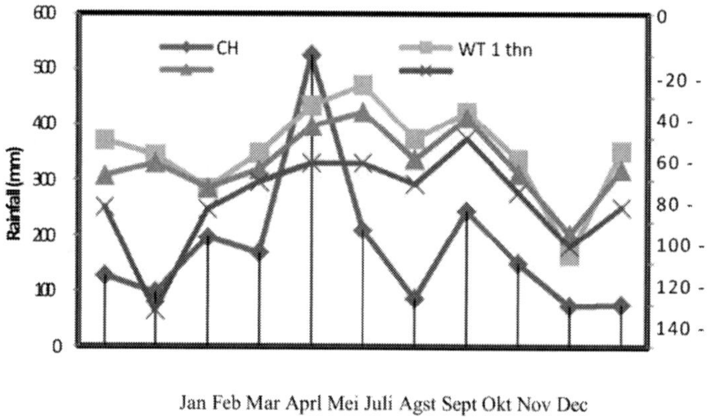

Figure 3: Dynamics of water table depth on research plots

The relationship between water table depths with rainfall in the study site is presented in Figure 4.

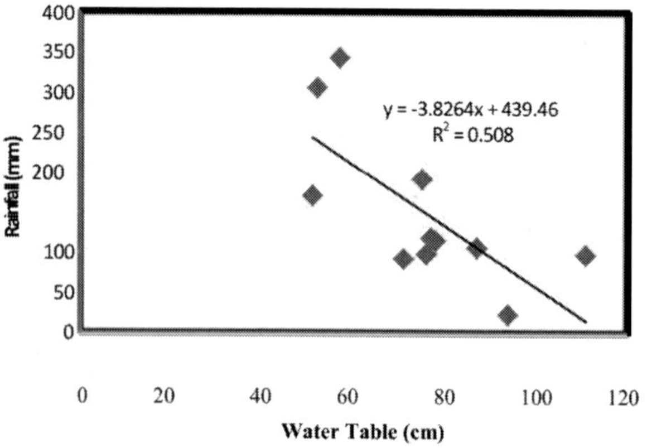

Figure 4: Relationship between water table depths with rainfall at the study site

During the rainy season the water table could reach 10 cm near the ground, whereas in the dry season it was far from the ground reaching 200 cm under the ground level. This is in accordance with those reported by Andrie *et al.* (2010) and Rieley *et al.*, (1997. Water table depth of peat soil may be influenced by the distance from the canal's edge as reported by Andrie *et al.* (2010). This field study, however, showed that the effect of the distance from the canal on the water table depth of peat soil under *A. carsicarpa* stands was not significantly different except in the case of 1 year old plantation.

Maturity Level of Peat Soil in the Study Site

The grouping of peat decomposition rate can be conducted based on the fiber content of the peat as mentioned in the USDA Soil Taxonomy (Soil Survey Staff 2010). The average value of fiber content which indicates the maturity level of peat vertically under the third rotation of *A. crassicarpa* stands at 1, 2, 3, and 4 years of age are presented in Table 2.

Table 2: The average value of fiber content and the decomposition degree of peat based on the peat thickness at different ages of *A. crassicarpa* stands

Peat Depth (cm)	The average value of fiber content (%) and the decomposition rate of peat under *A. crassicarpa* stands				The average value of fiber content (%) and the decomposition rate of peat in the secondary peat swamp forest
	1 year	2 years	3 years	4 years	
0-50	46,92 (Hemik)	53,49 (Hemik)	46,51 (Hemik)	23,16 (Saprik)	56,60 (Hemik)
50-100	58,02 (Hemik)	55,77 (Hemik)	50,07 (Hemik)	26,20 (Saprik)	60,13 (Fibrik)
100-150	59,27 (Hemik)	63,13 (Fibrik)	64,92 (Fibrik)	25,85 (Saprik)	63,60 (Fibrik)
200-250	66,28 (Fibrik)	58,97 (Hemik)	73,51 (Fibrik)	46,55 (Hemik)	57,00 (Hemik)
250-300	64,19 (Fibrik)	53,48 (Hemik)	70,97 (Fibrik)	43,23 (Hemik)	59,20 (Hemik)
300-350	58,76 (Hemik)	54,48 (Hemik)	65,10 (Fibrik)	45,22 (Hemik)	51,73 (Hemik)
350-400	36,34 (Hemik)		67,48 (Fibrik)	47,67 (Hemik)	56,00 (Hemik)

The average value of the peat fiber content based on the distance from the canal's edge on *A. crassicarpa* stands in Rasau Kuning District is presented in Table 3. Although the value of the water table depth affects the maturity level of peat, but according to the significance difference test result of the distance measurement from the canal's edge, all observation points did not significantly affect the maturity level of peat. Analysis of changes in the maturity level of peat was also conducted by Wahyunto *et al.*, (2005), in which the result showed that for 12 years (1990-2002) the maturity level of peat in Sumatra was relatively unchanged. In 2002 the condition of peat maturity level stayed the same as in 1990, i.e. to: (1) Peat-very shallow: Hemist/Saprist, Hemist/Mineral and Saprist/Hemist; (2) Peat-shallow: Fibrist/Saprist, Hemist/Saprist, Hemist/Mineral, Saprist/Hemist and Saprist/Mineral; (3) Peat-deep: Hemist/Saprist, Saprist and Saprist/Hemist; (4) Peat-very deep: Hemist/Saprist and Saprist/Hemist.

Table 3: The average value of the fiber content of peat based on the distance from the canal's edge on *A. crassicarpa* stands in Rasau Kuning District

No.	Distance from The Canal's Edge		
	20 (m) %	70 (m) %	120 (m) %
1 .	45,74	62,66	63,53
2 .	68,74	59,27	52,86
3 .	67,41	54,54	59,75
4 .	52,13	54,00	62,75
5 .	66,53	57,51	28,13
6 .	26,93	30,53	38,00
7 .	38,5	41,87	34,33
8 .	34,74	30,93	38,95
9 .	27,78	32,74	34,19

Peat maturity level is generally correlated with the current land use pattern. In locations that have been cleared as for Industrial Forest Plantation/IFP (*Hutan Tanaman Industri*, HTI), the maturity level in the upper layer is generally hemic/sapric, while in the natural land as in Lake Pulau Besar Game Reserve the maturity level in the upper layer is generally between fibric and hemic.

The maturity level of the bottom layer on the natural land showed lower fiber content values due to the older age of peat bottom layer than the layers above it. Under the natural conditions, the water table depth in the dry season ranged from 15 to 25 cm below the ground, thus this condition allow the peat soils to remain humid and wet. As a result, the decomposition process was slower than the drained peat soils.

CONCLUSION

Drainage pattern in the study site was influenced by the rainfall, in which during November, December and February (high rainfall levels), the average water table depth was shallow (-10 cm), while in June, July and August the water table depth was very deep (-175 cm).

The drainage effect on the maturity level of peat was only affecting the maturity level of peat under 2 m of depth, whereas the 125 m of tertiary canal distance did not significantly affect the maturity level of peat.

REFERENCES

1. Andrie, E. 2010. The dept of ground water table dynamics and characteristic of peatland near drainage canal ex, mega rice project in Central-Kalimantan. Makalah Seminar Ilmiah VI Lingkungan Tropis-Ikatan Ahli Teknik Penyehatan dan Tehnik Lingkungan Indonesia (IATPI). Denpasar. 29 Juli 2010.
2. Boerema, J., 1922. Typen van den regenval in Nederlandsh Indie (Rainfall types in the Netherlands Indies). Verhandelingen 18, Koninklyk Magnetisch en Meteorologisch Observatorium, Verhandelingen no.24, Batavia. 13 maps each.
3. Hooijer, A., Silvius, M., Wosten, H., dan Page, S., 2006. Peat-CO_2. Assessment of CO_2 Emissions From Drained Peatlands in SE Asia. *Delf Hydraulics Report* Q3943.
4. Radjagukguk, B., 1991. Utilization and management of peatlands in Indonesia for agriculture and forestry. *Proceedings of the International Symposium on Tropical Peatland*, 6 -10 May 1991 Kuching, Sarawak, Malaysia.
5. Rahmadi., 2009., Effects of Climate Change and Land Subsidence on Water Management zoning in Tidal Lowlands Case Study TelangI, South Sumatra. MSc Thesis. UNESCO – IHE Delft, the Netherlands.
6. Rieley, J.O., Page, S.E., Limin, S.H., dan Winiarti, S., (1997). The peatland resources of Indonesia and the Kalimantan peat swamp forest research project. *Proceedings International. Symposium Biodiversity, Environmental Importance and Sustainability of Tropical Peat and Peatland.* Samara Publ.
7. Saefudin, A., 2009. North EasLand and Water Evaluation of Lowland Areas Case Study: Lowlands intern Muara Enim Region Indonesia. MSc Thesis. UNESCO – IHE Delft, the Netherlands.
8. Soil Survey Staff., 2010. *Key to soil taxonomy.* 11th United States Department of Agriculture Natural Resources Conservation Service.
9. Suryadi, F.X., 1996. Soil and Water Management Strategies for Tidal Lowlands in Indonesia. PhD Dissertation, Delft University of Technology – IHE Delft, Aa. Balkema, Rotterdam, the Netherlands.
10. Wahyunto., Ritung, S., Suparto., dan Subagjo, H., 2005. *Sebaran Gambut dan Kandungan Karbon di Sumatera dan Kalimantan.* Proyek Climate Change, Forests and Peatlands in Indonesia. Wetlands International – Indonesia Programme dan Wildlife Habitat Canada. Bogor.

Abstract No: A-432

EFFECTS OF ENVIRONMENTAL FACTORS ON SOIL N_2O FLUXES FROM OIL PALM PLANTATION ON TROPICAL PEATLAND

Auldry Chaddy* and Lulie Melling

Tropical Peat Research Laboratory Unit, Chief Minister's Department, Sarawak, Malaysia
**Corresponding author: auldrcpr@sarawak.gov.my*

SUMMARY

The objectives of this study were to quantify soil nitrous oxide (N_2O) fluxes and identify the environmental factors influencing soil N_2O fluxes from three different ages of oil palm plantation on tropical peatland in Sarawak, Malaysia. Monthly soil N_2O fluxes were measured from July 2006 until June 2008 in three different ages of oil palm plantation (1, 5 and 7-year old palm) on tropical peatland using a closed chamber method. Soil N_2O flux from 1-year old palm was significantly higher (383.4±93.6 μg m^{-2} hr^{-1}) than from 5-year old palm (140.7±29.4 μg m^{-2} hr^{-1}) or 7-year old palm (235.0±55.8 μg m^{-2} hr^{-1}). This may be due to the canopy of the younger palms being still open, thus that exposing the soil surface to direct sunlight, resulting in higher soil temperatures which increased the soil N_2O flux. Multiple regression analysis revealed that air temperature, soil temperature at 10 cm, relative humidity and water table depth were significantly correlated with soil N_2O fluxes in 1-year old palm only. However, water table depth was an important factor in controlling the soil N_2O fluxes in oil palm plantation on tropical peatland regardless of palm age. Understanding the processes of N_2O formation and the factors influencing these emissions is fundamental in managing soil N_2O fluxes in cultivated tropical peatland.

Keywords: tropical peatland, oil palm plantation, temperature, water table, N_2O fluxes

INTRODUCTION

Nitrous oxide (N_2O) is one of the most important greenhouse gases and contributes a high global warming potential of 298 CO_2-equivalents (CO_2-Eq) for a 100-year time horizon (IPCC 2007). Nitrous oxide is a by-product of the biological process of nitrification (the conversion of ammonium, NH_4^+, to nitrate, NO_3^-) and an intermediate in denitrification (conversion of NO_3^- to N_2O or N_2) (Smith, 2010). Agricultural soils have generally been identified as the main anthropogenic source of N_2O. Peat soils in tropical peatland are now used for oil palm plantation in response to increasing global demand for palm oil. Tropical peatland has been reported to release greater amounts of N_2O into the atmosphere, most likely linked with drainage and nitrogen (N) fertilizer application (Page *et al.*, 2011).

Intensively drained peat has been reported to emit large volumes of N_2O because drainage increases the aerated layer and enhances the mineralisation of soil organic matter (Hadi *et al.* 2000). Furthermore, when N fertilizer is applied to peat it provides a substrate for N_2O production and denitrification and nitrification rates are expected to increase. Environmental factors such as temperature (Smith *et al.* 1998), water-filled pore space (Ball *et al.* 2008), water table depth (Berglund and Berglund 2011), soil bulk density (Ruser *et al.* 1998), soil pH (Cuhel *et al.* 2010) and soil nitrogen availability (Verchot *et al.* 2006) also regulate the nitrification and denitrification processes. However, N_2O fluxes generally fluctuate and do not correlate well with any single environmental factor so there remains a dearth of information on the key factors affecting soil N_2O emission. Thus, this study was conducted to 1) quantify soil N_2O fluxes and 2) identify the environmental factors influencing soil N_2O fluxes from three different ages of oil palm plantation on tropical peatland.

MATERIALS AND METHODS

Three sites, bearing oil palms of 1, 5 and 7 years old, were selected in an oil palm plantation at Mukah, Sarawak, Malaysia (2° 51'N, 112° 13'E). The sites were drained to lower the water table to between 50 and 70 cm. The characteristics of each site are detailed in **Table 1**.

Measurements of monthly soil N_2O fluxes were conducted using a closed-chamber method from July 2006 until June 2008. Environmental variables such as air temperature, relative humidity (RH) and soil temperature at 5 and 10 cm, depth of water table and rainfall, were measured simultaneously. Soil N_2O concentrations were determined in the laboratory using a gas chromatograph (Agilent 7890A).

Undisturbed core soil samples were taken after gas sampling at each chamber point to determine soil bulk density and percentage water-filled pore space (WFPS). Soil samples were taken using a peat auger at each chamber point at depths of 0-25 cm and 25-50 cm and analysed for selected chemical properties as shown in **Table 1**.

One-way Analysis of Variance (ANOVA) was used to test the effect of different ages of oil palm on soil N_2O fluxes while means of the variables were compared using Duncan's New Multiple Range Test (DNMRT). Multiple regressions were used to determine relationships between environmental variables, soil physical properties and soil N_2O fluxes. All statistical analysis was performed using the Statistical Analysis System (SAS) version 9.2.

RESULTS AND DISCUSSION

Soil N_2O flux from 1-year old palm was significantly higher (383.4±93.6 μg m^{-2} hr^{-1}) than that from 5-year old palm (140.7±29.4 μg m^{-2} hr^{-1}) or 7-year old palm (235.0±55.8 μg m^{-2} hr^{-1}) shown (**Table 2**). The annual soil N_2O flux was highest in the site of 1-year old palm (32.4±5.0 kg N ha^{-1} yr^{-1}) followed by that 7-year old palm (21.5±0.9 kg N ha^{-1} yr^{-1}) and then that 5-year old palm (11.2±1.0 kg N ha^{-1} yr^{-1}). The highest values for soil N_2O fluxes, found in the youngest palm, may be due to exposure of the soil surface to direct sunlight due to the lower canopy density, resulting in higher soil temperatures. **Table 1** shows the highest air temperature was recorded at the 1-year old plantation. Denitrification and nitrification rates that increased with increasing temperature were also observed in another study (Skiba and Smith, 2000). The results of the multiple regressions provided further evidence for this proposition: air temperature, soil temperature at 10 cm and RH were highly significantly ($p<0.001$) related with soil N_2O fluxes in the 1-year old palm only. The open canopy of the younger palm is likely to increase diurnal temperature fluctuations, causing higher sensitivity of the soil N_2O fluxes to temperature compared to older palm. The closed canopy of the more mature palms (>4-year old) resulted in lower and more constant temperatures.

Water table depth is one of the most important factors controlling soil N_2O fluxes in an oil palm plantation on tropical peatland (**Table 3**). Regardless of age of palm a negative relationship between water table depth and soil N_2O fluxes was recorded at all sites, indicating that a higher water table may increase soil N_2O fluxes and vice versa. Jauhiainen *et al.* (2012) observed similar results in which the highest N_2O fluxes tended to be associated with a rise in water table which promotes anoxic conditions, leading to potential predominance of N_2 production in the denitrification process (Takakai *et al.* 2006).

Table 9: Values (mean ± SE) for the main characteristics of oil palm at three different ages

Characteristic	Age of palm		
	1-year old palm	5-year old palm	7-year old palm
Air temperature (°C)	33.8±0.5	31.7±0.5	30.6±0.4
Annual rainfall (mm)	3493	4058	3447
Bulk density (g cm^{-3})	0.23±0.004	0.21±0.002	0.22±0.003
Soil pH	3.6±0.02	3.8±0.04	3.9±0.03
Loss on ignition (%)	94.4±1.0	93.9±1.1	94.2±1.0
Total C (%)	55.62±0.6	55.02±0.8	56.07±0.5
Total N (%)	2.1±0.1	1.9±0.1	1.9±0.1
Ammonium (mg kg^{-1})	89.4±12.3	80.1±7.7	72.0±8.0
Nitrate (mg kg^{-1})	165.5±26.0	117.3±18.8	111.6±13.2
Base saturation (%)	40.7±1.5	60.4±2.4	61.8±3.0

Table 10: Soil N_2O flux and cumulative flux for oil palm plantation

Site	Soil N_2O flux ($\mu g\ N\ m^{-2}\ hr^{-1}$)	Cumulative soil N_2O flux ($kg\ N\ ha^{-1}\ yr^{-1}$)
1-year old palm	383.4 ± 93.6^a	32.4 ± 5.0
5-year old palm	140.7 ± 29.4^c	11.2 ± 1.0
7-year old palm	235.0 ± 55.8^b	21.5 ± 0.9

Superscript letters indicate significant difference between means using Duncan's New Multiple Range Test (DNMRT) at $p<0.05$

Table 11: Multiple regression of soil N_2O flux in different ages of oil palm with soil environmental factors and physical properties

Site	R^2	Corrected R^2	*P*-value
1-year old palm : $N_2O = 7116.9 - 170.9Tempa + 264.7Tempt - 28.2RH - 16.4WT$	0.31	0.22	0.0017
5-year old palm : $N_2O = -5.6WT + 3.0BD$	0.24	0.15	0.0183
7-year old palm : $N_2O = -9.6WT$	0.23	0.13	0.0307

Tempa=air temperature; Tempt=soil temperature at 10 cm; WT=water table; BD = bulk density
Significance at $P<0.05$

CONCLUSION

Soil N_2O fluxes from 1-year old palm were significantly higher than from 5 and 7-old palm. This may be due to higher soil temperatures. One-year old palm had a lower canopy density than older palms where the canopy had closed and this exposed the soil surface and caused higher sensitivity of soil N_2O fluxes to temperature. Regardless of palm age, the water table is one of the most important factors in controlling soil N_2O fluxes in an oil palm plantation on tropical peatland. The controlling factors for soil N_2O flux in cultivated tropical peatland varied erratically and were very site-specific. Understanding the processes of N_2O formation and the factors influencing these emissions is fundamental in managing soil N_2O fluxes in cultivated tropical peatland.

ACKNOWLEDGEMENTS

We thank the Department of Agriculture, Sarawak for their assistance in the laboratory and field. We would also like to thank the oil palm plantation industry for their support. This study was supported by an e-Science grant from the Ministry of Science, Technology and Innovation (MOSTI), Malaysia.

REFERENCES

1. Ball, B. C., Crichton, I., and Horgan, G. W. (2008). Dynamics of upward and downward N_2O and CO fluxes in ploughed or no-tilled soils in relation to water-filled pore space, compaction and crop presence. *Soil and Tillage Research,* **101(1):** 20-30.
2. Berglund, Ö. and Berglund, K. (2011). Influence of water table level and soil properties on emissions of greenhouse gases from cultivated peat soil. *Soil Biology and Biochemistry,* **43(5):** 923-931.
3. Čuhel, J., Šimek, M., Laughlin, R. J., Bru, D., Chèneby, D., Watson, C. J. and Philippot, L. (2010). Insights into the effect of soil pH on N_2O and N_2 emissions and denitrifier community size and activity. *Applied and Environmental Microbiology,* **76(6):** 1870-1878.
4. Hadi, A., Inubushi, K., Purnomo, E., Razie, F., Yamakawa, K. and Tsuruta, H. (2000). Effect of land-use changes on nitrous oxide (N_2O) emission from tropical peatlands. *Chemosphere-Global Change Science* **2(3):** 347-358.

5. Intergovernmental Panel on Climate Change (IPCC). (2007). Contribution of working groups I, II and III to the fourth assessment report of the Intergovernmental Panel on Climate Change. IPCC, Geneva, Switzerland.
6. Jauhiainen, J., Silvennoinen, H., Hämäläinen, R., Kusin, K., Limin, S., Raison, R. J. and Vasander, H. (2012). Nitrous oxide fluxes from tropical peat with different disturbance history and management. *Biogeosciences* **9(4):** 1337-1350.
7. Page, S. E., Morrison, R., Malins, C., Hooijer, A., Rieley, J. O. and Jauhiainen, J. 2011. Review of peat surface greenhouse gas emissions from oil palm plantations in Southeast Asia. International Committee on Clean Transportation (ICCT). In press.
8. Ruser, R., Flessa, H., Schilling, R., Steindl, H. and Beese, F. (1998). Soil compaction and fertilization effects on nitrous oxide and methane fluxes in potato fields. *Soil Science Society of America Journal* **62:** 1587–1595.
9. Skiba, U. and Smith, K. A. (2000). The control of nitrous oxide emissions from agricultural and natural soils. *Chemosphere-Global Change Science* **2(3):** 379-386.
10. Smith, K. A. (2010). Nitrous oxide and climate change. *Earthscan.*
11. Smith, K. A., Thomson, P. E., Clayton, H., McTaggart, I. P. and Conen, F. (1998). Effects of temperature, water content and nitrogen fertilisation on emissions of nitrous oxide by soils. *Atmospheric Environment,* **32(19):** 3301-3309.
12. Takakai, F., Morishita, T., Hashidoko, Y., Darung, U., Kuramochi, K., Dohong, S., Limin, S.H. and Hatano, R. (2006). Effects of agricultural land-use change and forest fire on N_2O emission from tropical peatlands, Central Kalimantan, Indonesia, *Soil Science and Plant Nutrition,* **52(5):** 662-674.
13. Verchot, L. V., Hutabarat, L., Hairiah, K. and Van Noordwijk, M. (2006). Nitrogen availability and soil N_2O emissions following conversion of forests to coffee in southern Sumatra. *Global Biogeochemical Cycles,* **20(4)**

Abstract No: A-041

EFFECT OF SOIL AND FERTILIZER TYPES ON GREENHOUSE GAS EMISSIONS AND PLANT GROWTH IN OIL PALM PLANTATIONS

Hiroshi Aoki[1*], Rosnaeni Sakata[2], Shuzoh Shimada[2], Hironori Arai[2], Naho Yoshioka[2], Ryo Yoshioka[2], Narutoshi Kimoto[1], Atsushi Sakamoto[1], Shew Ngie Wong[3], Lulie Melling[3] and Kazuyuki Inubushi[2]

[1]*JCAM AGRI. Co. LTD., Tokyo, Japan*
[2]*Graduate School of Horticulture, Chiba University, Chiba, Japan*
[3]*Tropical Peat Research Laboratory Unit, Chief Minister's Department, Sarawak, Malaysia*

**Corresponding author: h.aoki@jcam-agri.co.jp*

SUMMARY

Oil palm plantations have been reported to release large quantities of N_2O into the atmosphere, most likely linked to nitrogen fertilizer use. This study aimed to evaluate the effects of soil types in comparison peat soil with others and nitrogen fertilizer on N_2O and CO_2 emissions in oil palm plantations. Field experiments were conducted in sandy loam soil (7 years oil palm), sandy soil (9 years oil palm) and peat soil (5 years oil palm) from 2010 to 2013 treated with coated fertilizer and conventional fertilizer. N_2O and CO_2 fluxes showed high variations with seasons, types of soil and fertilizer treatments. The N application rate of coated fertilizer was about half that of conventional fertilizer and was applied as deep placement. The vegetation and yield were no significant difference among treatments. To get rid of previous dosage of fertilizer, cultivation test of immature trees (2 years oil palm) was done with coated fertilizer and conventional fertilizer in peat soil and sandy loam at the same plantation from 2011 to 2015. The N application rate of coated fertilizer was as same as that of convention fertilizer and half of that. Measurement of actual nitrogen release from coated fertilizer in the field was also evaluated from 2011 to 2013.

***Keywords**: N fertilizer, N_2O fluxes, CO_2 fluxes, sandy, sandy loam, peat soil*

INTRODUCTION and OBJECTIVES

Oil palm production in Indonesia and Malaysia

Oil palm production in Indonesia and Malaysia is currently the focus of debates concerning the potential impact to the greenhouse gas emissions and global warming. Oil palm plantations have been reported to emit large quantities of N_2O into the atmosphere, most likely due to nitrogen fertilizer use[1)].

Application of coated fertilizer to reduce soil N_2O and NO emissions in Japan

Study have shown that N_2O and NO emissions from a field of Chinese cabbage is decreasing by using the coated urea in an Andosol soil in Japan[2)]. This suggests that there is a possibility to reduce N_2O and CO_2 emissions from the oil palm field in Indonesia and Malaysia.

Coated Urea "MEISTER"

Coated urea "MEISTER" is the polyolefin coated urea with 50-70μm layer. There are two releasing patterns. The linear type and the sigmoid type. The release longevity is from 30 days to 360 days at 25°C (**Fig.1**). Releasing rate is based on osmic pressure.

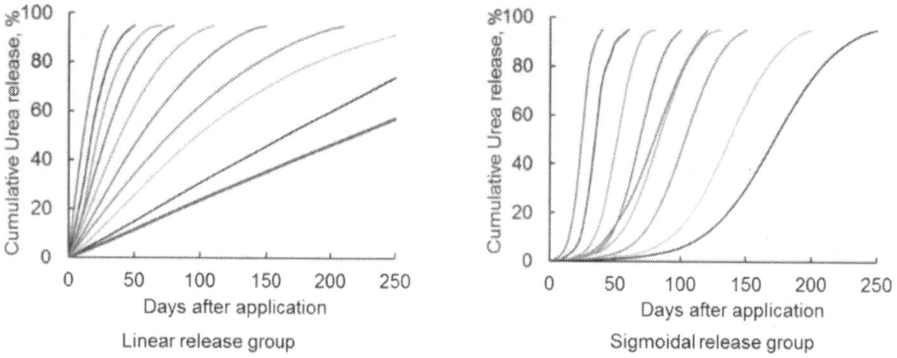

Fig.1 Nitrogen release from "MEISTER" in water at 25°C

The objectives of this study are as follows

1) To study the effect of soil type with nitrogen fertilizer on N_2O and CO_2 emissions.
2) To determine the effectiveness of reducing fertilizer rate of coated fertilizer "MEISTER" on growth and fresh bunch (FFB) production in different soil types.

MATERIALS and METHODS

Study sites

Peat, sandy and loamy sand soil was chosen as study sites. **Fig.2** shows location of study sites. **Table 1** shows site description and soil properties.

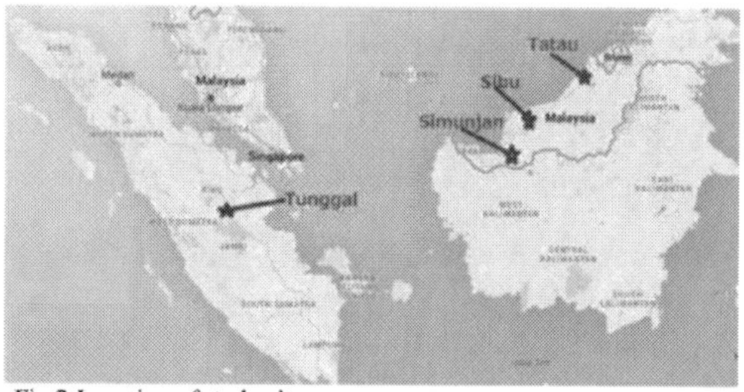

Fig 2 Location of study sites

Table 1 Soil characteristics of study sites

Study sites	Soil Type	Bulk Density (gcm^{-3})	pH	NH_4^+ ($mgNkg^{-1}ds$)	NO_3^- ($mgNkg^{-1}ds$)	T-C ($gkg^{-1}ds$)	T-N ($gkg^{-1}ds$)	Rainfall (mm) in 2011
Tunggal	Sandy Loam	1.1	4.7	32	16	23	2	1,387
Simunjan	Sandy	1.5	4.8	16	1	19	2	4,095
Tatau	Peat	0.2	3.3	123	78	467	17	2,225
Sibu	Loamy Sand	1.2	4.8	17	4	16	1	3,218
	Peat	0.2	4.0	233	115	387	17	

Cultivation experiment at matured oil palm fields

Cultivation experiments were designed as illustrated in **Table 2**. As the oil palm's nitrogen uptake patterns vary depending on the growth stage, study was conducted with 5 years, 7 years and 9 years oil palm. Nitrogen application rate of "MEISTER"(Linear 350 Day Type at 25°C) blended fertilizer was about 50% of conventional fertilizer at each study sites. "MEISTER" blended fertilizer was applied into 4 holes around an oil palm. Conventional fertilizer was applied by top dressing. Each treatment has 3 repetitions.

Table 2 Application rates of study sites

Study sites	Treatments (% of N Application Rate)	Application Rates (KgN·ha-1·Y-1)	(KgP·ha-1·Y-1)	(KgK·ha-1·Y-1)	Experiment Period	Planted Date	Plot Scale Trees/Plot	Repetition
Tunggal	C:Conventional	151	38	236	May. 2011 – Jan. 2013	Oct. 2005	525	3
	M:Meister Blended (50%)	76	35	157				
Simunjan	C	114	86	326	Dec. 2010 – Dec. 2012	May. 2003	50	3
	M(51%)	58	53	141				
Tatau	C	86	34	248	Dec. 2010 – Dec. 2012	Jan. 2007	48	3
	M(44%)	38	13	145				

Measurement of N_2O and CO_2 emissions at mature oil palm fields

Emission rate was measured by chamber method[3]. Briefly, cylindrical chamber base (inner diameter 21.0 cm; height 14.0 cm) was buried at the beginning of this study at three oil palms of each fertilizer treatment. Nitrogen application rate in a chamber was as illustrated in **Table 3**. Application rates of phosphate and potassium were at the same quantity for all treatments.

Table 3 Nitrogen application rate in a chamber

Symbol	Fertilizer Treatment	Nitrogen application rate in a Chamber ($KgN \cdot ha^{-1} \cdot Y^{-1}$) Tunggal	Simunjan	Tatau	Soil Disturbance
B	No Nitrogen	0	0	0	No
C	Conventional	151	107	92	No
M	MEISTER(Linear 350 Day Type)	76	62	46	Do
B2	No Nitrogen	0	0	0	Do

About two weeks interval, each chamber was covered with a lid, then 5 min. later, gas samples were taken with gas-tight syringe from each chamber at 10 min intervals. The concentrations of CO_2 and N_2O were quantified with GC (gas chromatograph; Shimadzu 14B, Japan) equipped with thermal detector and electron capture detector, respectively. Soil temperature and moisture content were recorded with sensors (TR-0306, Water Mark) and data logger (Ondotori, Japan), respectively. Emission rate was measured at each site for more than 1 year. Emission factor (EF) was calculated based on total N_2O emission as percentage of applied N with or without soil disturbance.

Cultivation experiment at young oil palm fields

To prevent the effect of previous dosage of fertilizer, young oil palm trees (2nd year) were chosen at two soil types in Sibu. The nitrogen application rates of "MEISTER" (Linear 350 Day Type at 25°C) were 50% and 100% of conventional. Application rates of phosphate and potassium were at the same quantity for all treatments. Cultivation experiments were designed as illustrated in **Table 4** with 3 repetitions for each treatments.

Table 4 Application rates at Sibu

Soil Type	Treatments (% of N Application Rate)	Application Rates (KgN·ha-1·Y-1)	(KgP·ha-1·Y-1)	(KgK·ha-1·Y-1)	Experiment Period	Planted Date	Plot Scale Trees/Plot	Repetition
Loamy Sand	T1:Conventional	93	61	486	Sep. 2011 – Dec. 2015	Aug. 2009	25	3
	T2:No Nitrogen (0%)	0	61	486				
	T3:Meister (100%)	93	61	486				
	T4:Meister (50%)	47	61	486				
Peat	T1:Conventional	93	61	486	Sep. 2011 – Dec. 2015	Jan. 2010	25	3
	T2:No Nitrogen (0%)	0	61	486				
	T3:Meister (100%)	93	61	486				
	T4:Meister (50%)	47	61	486				

Measurement of Nitrogen release from the "MEISTER" at the cultivation site

The polyethylene bags containing with 2.5g of "MEISTER" (Linear 350 Day Type at 25°C) were buried under the soil with depth of 5 – 10cm at Sibu site (Peat and Sandy loam soil). After 1, 2, 3, 5, 7, 9 and 11 months, three polyethylene bags were retrieved at each time and the residual nitrogen were analyzed by P-dimethylaminobenzaldehyde colorimetry. Nitrogen releasing rate is calculated by the residual nitrogen from "MEISTER" nitrogen.

RESULT AND DISCUSSION

Cultivation experiment at matured oil palm fields

Oil palms at the study site were well mature, so vegetative growth (Trunk Girth) showed no difference among treatments. The Table 5 shows the total FFB weight at each study sites. "MEISTER" treatment performed better than conventional, though nitrogen application rate is only 50% of conventional. But there is no significant difference.

Table 5 Yield at the matured oil palm field

Study sites	Treatments (% of N Application Rate)	Total FFB Weight, kg/Plot	Measuring Period	Planted Date in Field	Plot Scale Trees/plot
Tunggal	C:Conventional	37,995	Nov. 2011 – Jan. 2013	Oct. 2005	525
	M:Coated Urea(50%)	42,808			
Simunjan	C	4,054	Jan. 2011 – Dec. 2012	May. 2003	50
	M(51%)	4,300			
Tatau	C	3,098	Nov. 2011 – Dec. 2012	Feb. 2008	48
	M(44%)	3,266			

N_2O and CO_2 emissions from cultivation sites

Table 6 shows the N_2O flux and the CO_2 flux from experimental sites. **Table 7** shows the emission factor (EF) of N_2O. In Tungal, "MEISTER" reduced N_2O emission by 31% and 48% in wet and dry seasons respectively, as compared to the conventional fertilizer. However, N_2O emissions increased in Simunjan and Tatau during dry season. There was no significant difference between treatments. These results show that N_2O and CO_2 fluxes in the tropical oil palm field were significantly affected by the type of soil, but not always by fertilizer treatments.

Table 6 N_2O and CO_2 fluxes from matured oil palm fields

Study sites	Treatment	N_2O flux ($\mu gNm^{-2}H^{-1}$)		CO_2 flux ($mgNm^{-2}H^{-1}$)	
		Wet Season	Dry Season	Wet	Dry
Tunggal (Sandy Loam)	B	33.7±49.6	6.27±0.44	45.5±0.93	56.4±2.78
	C	89.7±14.1	17.3±1.45	49.0±18.9	95.4±10.9
	M	28.2±36.0	8.30±5.87	56.8±15.3	96.5±15.1
	B2	27.4±20.3	19.1±4.52	50.6±11.3	61.3±6.05
Simunjan (Sandy)	B	3.81±1.42	2.40±4.79	72.1±10.9	104±8.55
	C	1.60±1.57	3.20±2.51	101±14.0	126±10.2
	M	2.18±2.73	5.34±7.03	114±7.93	105±46.5
	B2	0.80±3.65	1.63±1.12	71.1±3.66	134±34.5
Tatau (Peat)	B	131±77.2	66.1±49.9	89.8±43.5	92.7±23.1
	C	249±77.3	185±15.5	158±45.0	153±75.7
	M	272±151	606±421	153±49.9	208±107
	B2	523±441	93.7±80.6	223±93.2	129±31.7

Table 7 Emission factors (EF) of N_2O calculated from matured oil palm fields

Study sites	EF (%)	
	Conventional	"MEISTER"
Tunggal	2.29±0.33	-0.33±0.35
Simunjan	-0.26±0.08	0.49±0.40
Tatau	19.13±2.46	43.8±16.7

Cultivation experiment at young oil palm fields

Figures 3 and 4 are showing the vegetative growth (Frond Length) of oil palm at Peat and Loamy Sand soil. There was no significant difference among treatments. No nitrogen treatment still gave the similar growth as other treatments until Sep. 2015. **Table 8** shows the total FFB weight at both soil types. Conventional and "MEISTER" seem better than no nitrogen at the loamy sand. But there is no significant difference among treatments.

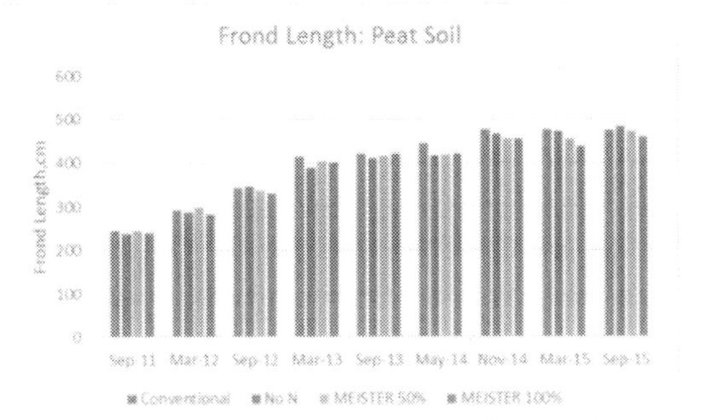

Fig. 3 Frond length of young oil palm at peat soil

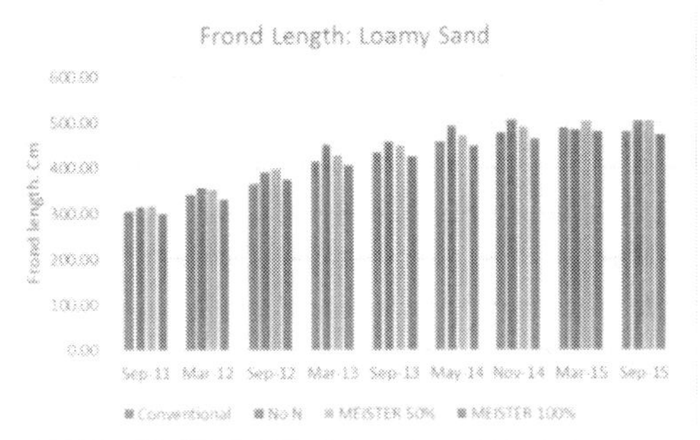

Fig. 4 Frond length of young oil palm at loamy sand

Table 8 Yield at the young oil palm field

Soil Type	Treatments (% of N Application Rate)	Total FFB Weight, kg/Plot	Measuring Period	Planted Date	Plot Scale Trees/Plot
Loamy Sand	T1:Conventional	15,613	Jan. 2012 - Dec. 2015	Aug. 2009	25
	T2:No Nitrogen (0%)	15,974			
	T3:Meister (100%)	15,656			
	T4:Meister (50%)	15,532			
Peat	T1:Conventional	10,490	Apr. 2012 - Dec. 2015	Jan. 2010	25
	T2:No Nitrogen (0%)	9,477			
	T3:Meister (100%)	10,009			
	T4:Meister (50%)	10,258			

Nitrogen release from the "MEISTER" at the cultivation site

Nitrogen releases from the "MEISTER" were as in **Figs 5 and 6**. About 80% of nitrogen was linearly released from the "MEISTER" until 290 days at both of Peat and Sandy loam soil.

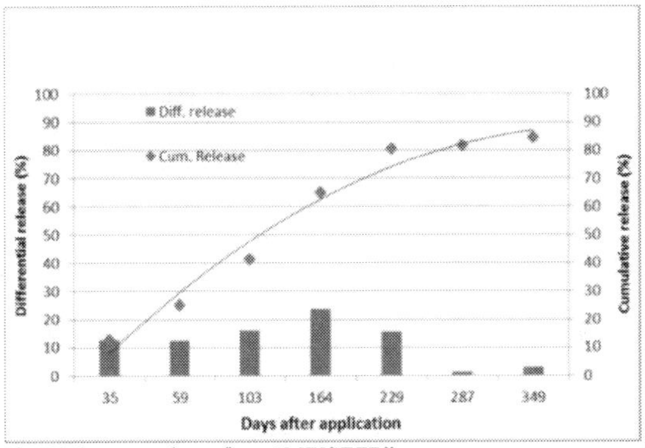

Fig. 5 Nitrogen release from "MEISTER" at peat

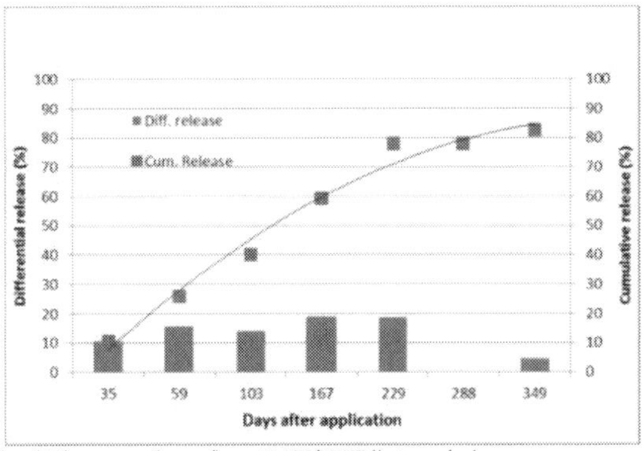

Fig. 6 Nitrogen release from "MEISTER" at sandy loam

The nitrogen release rate from "MEISTER" is mainly governed by soil temperature. So, simulation of nitrogen release is obtained by relating to the soil temperature. Releasing pattern is almost the same between the actual release of nitrogen and the simulation by the computer (**Fig. 7**). This suggests that it is possible to use the computer simulation in choosing the suitable type of "MEISTER" for the oil palm.

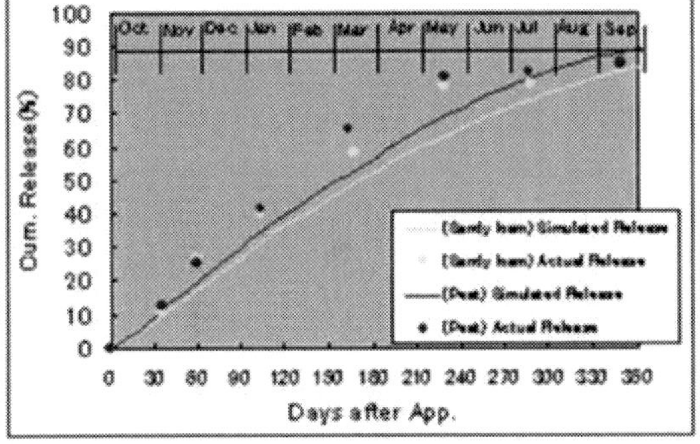

Fig. 7 Comparison between actual nitrogen release and simulation from "MEISTER"

CONCLUSION

N_2O and CO_2 fluxes

The effect of soil types on N_2O and CO_2 fluxes in the studied tropical oil palm plantations was highly significant, but no consistent tendency was observed using different N fertilizers from this study. Applications of fertilizer have to be considered with the suitability of soil type to mitigate the gas emission to the atmosphere. Further detailed study is needed to assess a more accurate interpretation of the mechanism of N_2O and CO_2 fluxes in oil palm plantations.

Vegetation and yield

Summarizing the vegetation and yield of cultivation tests, "MEISTER" can reduce the amount of nitrogen dosage at least 50% with keeping same growth and yield from the conventional. "MEISTER" was applied into 4 holes around an oil palm at this field study. Further study is needed to optimize the dosage points and way by considering the oil palm root for reducing the amount of dosage.

ACKOWLEDGEMENTS

We would like to thank the staff of the oil palm plantations and Tropical Peat Research Laboratory of Sarawak, Malaysia, for their assistance in the field. This study was funded by the Ministry of Economy, Trade and Industry (METI), Japan.

REFERENCES

1. Bouwman AF 1990: Exchange of greenhouse gases between terrestrial ecosystems and the atmosphere. *In* Soils and the Greenhouse Effect, Ed. Bouwen AF, pp. 61-127, Wiley, Chichester.
2. Cheng W, Nakajima Y, Sudo S, Akiyama H, Tsuruta H 2002: N_2O and NO emissions from a field of Chinese cabbage as influenced by band application of urea or controlled-release urea fertilizer. Nutrient Cycling in Agroecosystem, 63, 231-238.
3. Inubushi K, Furukawa Y, Hadi A, Purnomo E, Tsuruta H 2003: Seasonal change of CO_2, CH_4 and N_2O fluxes in relation to land-use change in tropical peatlands located in coastal area of South Kalimantan. Chemosphere, 52, 603-608.

Abstract No: A-179

EFFECT OF WATER TABLE ON GREENHOUSE GAS EMISSIONS FROM A MINERAL SOIL-DRESSED PEATLAND IN CENTRAL HOKKAIDO, JAPAN

Shimizu Mariko*, Ishida Tetsuya and Takeuchi Hideo

Civil Engineering Research Institute for Cold Region, Hokkaido, Japan

*Corresponding author: shimizum23@gmail.com

SUMMARY

Subsurface irrigation-drainage system is recently used to control water table in paddy fields in Japan. We carried out a soil column experiment to clarify the effect of water table on greenhouse gas emissions from a mineral soil-dressed peatland in central Hokkaido. Soil columns (15 cm diameter) were packed with peat soil in 30-45 cm depth at a dry bulk density of 0.2 g cm ^{3} and with mineral soil in 0-30 cm depth at a dry bulk density of 0.94 g cm ^{3}. Distilled water was supplied from the bottom of the columns. The soil columns were incubated for 12 days under water-flooding condition (1st flooding period), and then drained to set up two water table treatments (30 cm and 45 cm depth) for 14 days (non-flooding period). After the 14-day incubation, both treatments were flooded again for 4 days (2nd flooding period). The soil columns were incubated at 25°C. CO_2 emission during the non-flooding period was significantly higher in low water table treatment (125±9.6 g C m ^{2}) than in high water table treatment (97±6.2 g C m ^{2}), and there was no significant difference in CH_4 emission between the treatments (0.21±0.08 and 0.32±0.15 g C m ^{2} in the low and high water table treatments, respectively). The difference in N_2O emission during the non-flooding period between the treatments was not significant, but a significant high peak of N_2O flux was observed in high water table treatment one day after water supply during 2nd flooding period. At the end of the non-flooding period, denitrification potential of top layer (0-15 cm) was greater in high water table treatment because of high water content, and this may contribute to the N_2O flux peak. High water table treatment could decrease CO_2 emission, but increase N_2O emission after reflooding.

Keywords: *subsurface irrigation, greenhouse gas emissions, paddy field*

INTRODUCTION

In Hokkaido, Japan, peat soils are widely distributed. The total area of peat soils amounts to about 241,000 ha, and about 40% of which is used for agriculture (Hashimoto, 2006). Many peat soils were drained, top-dressed with about 30 cm of mineral soil to turn into productive crop fields (Naser *et al.*, 2005).

In Hokkaido, the number of farm households has been decreasing, and large-scale farming is practiced. Subsurface irrigation-drainage system is recently used to control water table in paddy fields. The system is equipped with underdrains and both irrigation and drainage facilities.

The control of water table in peatland will have effect on greenhouse gas (CO_2, CH_4 and N_2O) emissions. High water table could decrease CO_2 and N_2O condition, but increase CH_4 emission (Dinsmore *et al.*, 2009). In this study, we carried out a soil column experiment to clarify the effect of water table on greenhouse gas emissions from a mineral soil-dressed peatland in central Hokkaido.

METHODS

Mineral soil sample was collected from paddy field in central Hokkaido in August, 2013, and the air-dried sample was sieved through a 2 mm. Peat soil sample was collected near the paddy field in July, 2014, and stored at 4°C. Soil columns (15 cm diameter) were packed with fresh peat soil in 30-45 cm depth at a dry bulk density of 0.2 g cm ^{3} and with mineral soil in 0-30 cm depth at a dry bulk density of 0.94 g cm ^{3}. Distilled water was supplied from the bottom of the columns (Fig. 1).

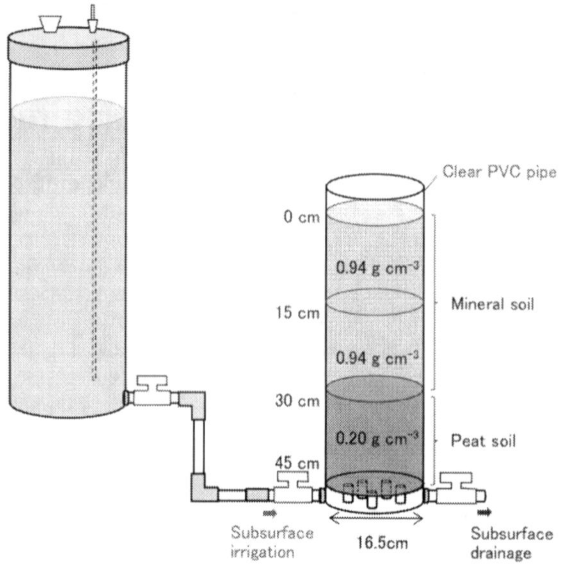

Fig. 1 Schematic diagram of a soil column

The soil columns were incubated for 12 days under water-flooding condition (1st flooding period), and then drained to set up two water table treatments, high water table (HWT; 30 cm) and low water table (LWT; 45 cm), for 14 days (non-flooding period). After the 14-day incubation, both treatments were flooded again for 4 days (2nd flooding period) (Fig. 1). The soil columns were incubated at 25°C with three replications.

Soil solution samples were collected from the center of 0-15, 15-30, and 30-45 cm using the suction-cup method. Subsurface drainage water samples were collected at the end of flooding period. The concentrations of NH^{4+}-N and NO^{3} -N in the soil solution and drainage water were analyzed. The concentrations of dissolved CO_2, CH_4 and N_2O in soil solution and drainage water were measured using the multiple phase equilibration method.

Soil samples at 0-15, 15-30, 30-45 cm depth were collected on day 0, 13, 26 and 31, and soil water content, NH^{4+}-N and NO^{3} -N concentrations were analyzed. Denitrification potential of soil samples were determined by acetylene-block incubations with NO^{3} -N. Soil water content was measured continuously by Amplitude Domain Reflectometry (ADR) method.

CO_2, CH_4 and N_2O fluxes from soil surface were measured by closed chamber method manually.

RESULTS AND DISCUSSIOIN

Soil water content of mineral soil during non-flooding period decreased to 0.36 m^{-3} m^{-3} at 0-15 cm depth and 0.45 m^{-3} m^{-3} at 15-30 cm depth in LWT, but maintained in HWT (0.45 m^{-3} m^{-3} at 0-15 cm depth and 0.51 m^{-3} m^{-3} at 15-30 cm depth) (Fig. 2). In LWT, Soil water content of peat soil during non-flooding period decreased to 0.50 m^{-3} m^{-3}.

NH^{4+}-N concentrations of subsurface drainage water ranged from 0.2 to 0.4 mg N L^{1}, and NO^{3} -N concentrations ranged from 0.03 to 0.06 mg N L^{1}. At the end of 2nd flooding period, there was no significant difference in NH^{4+}-N and NO^{3} -N concentration of subsurface drainage between the treatments.

NH^{4+}-N concentrations of mineral soil were higher than those in peat soil, and increased during the flooding period (Fig. 2). At the end of the non-flooding period, there was no significant difference in the NH^{4+}-N concentrations of mineral soil between the treatments, and the concentration at 0-15 cm depth is significantly higher than at 15-30 cm depth in both treatments ($p < 0.01$). On the other hand, NH^{4+}-N concentration of peat soil is higher in HWT than in LWT (Fig. 2).

NO^{3} -N concentrations of mineral soil and peat soil were lower than NH^{4+}-N concentrations throughout the incubation period. During the non-flooding period, NO^{3} -N concentrations of mineral soil increased only at 0-15 cm depth (Fig. 2). The NO^{3} -N concentration was significantly higher at 0-15 cm depth than at 15-30 cm depth at the end of the non-flooding period, and there was no significant difference between the treatments. NO^{3} -N concentrations of peat soil tended to be higher in LWT than in HWT (Fig. 2). These results indicate that groundwater recharge could increase NH^{4+}-N and decrease NO^{3} -N because of suppression of nitrification in peat soil.

CO_2 emission during the non-flooding period was significantly higher in LWT (125±9.6 g C m^{2}) than in HWT (97±6.2 g C m^{2}) (Fig. 2). The dissolved CO_2 concentration of soil solution decreased during non-flooding period except at a 35-40 cm depth in HWT. The decrement of dissolved CO_2 during the non-flooding period was estimated as 13.7±1.8 and 6.5±1.6 g C m^{-2} in LWT and HWT, respectively. Higher CO_2 emission in LWT would indicates the organic matter decomposition was promoted under aerobic condition.

There was no significant difference in CH_4 emission during the non-flooding period between the treatments (Fig. 2). However, the CH_4 emission in HWT was 0.32±0.15 g C m^{-2} (2.1±0.3 g CO_2-C_{eq} m^{-2}), and higher than in LWT (0.21±0.08 g C m^{-2} (3.0±1.4 g CO_2-C_{eq} m^{-2})). The dissolved CH_4 concentration of soil solution increased up to 64 μg C L^{-1} in HWT during the non-flooding period, while ranged from 1 to 8 μg C L^{-1} in LWT.

N_2O emission during the non-flooding period was 4.6±1.1 mg N m^{-2} (0.6±0.1 g CO_2-C_{eq} m^{-2}) in LWT and 6.9±8.6 mg N m^{-2} in HWT (0.9±1.1 g CO_2-C_{eq} m^{-2}), and there was no significant difference between the treatments (Fig. 2). However, a significant high peak of N_2O flux was observed in HWT one day after water supply during 2nd flooding period. At the end of the non-flooding period, denitrification potential of top layer (0-15 cm) was greater in HWT treatment because of high water content, and this may contribute to the N_2O flux peak.

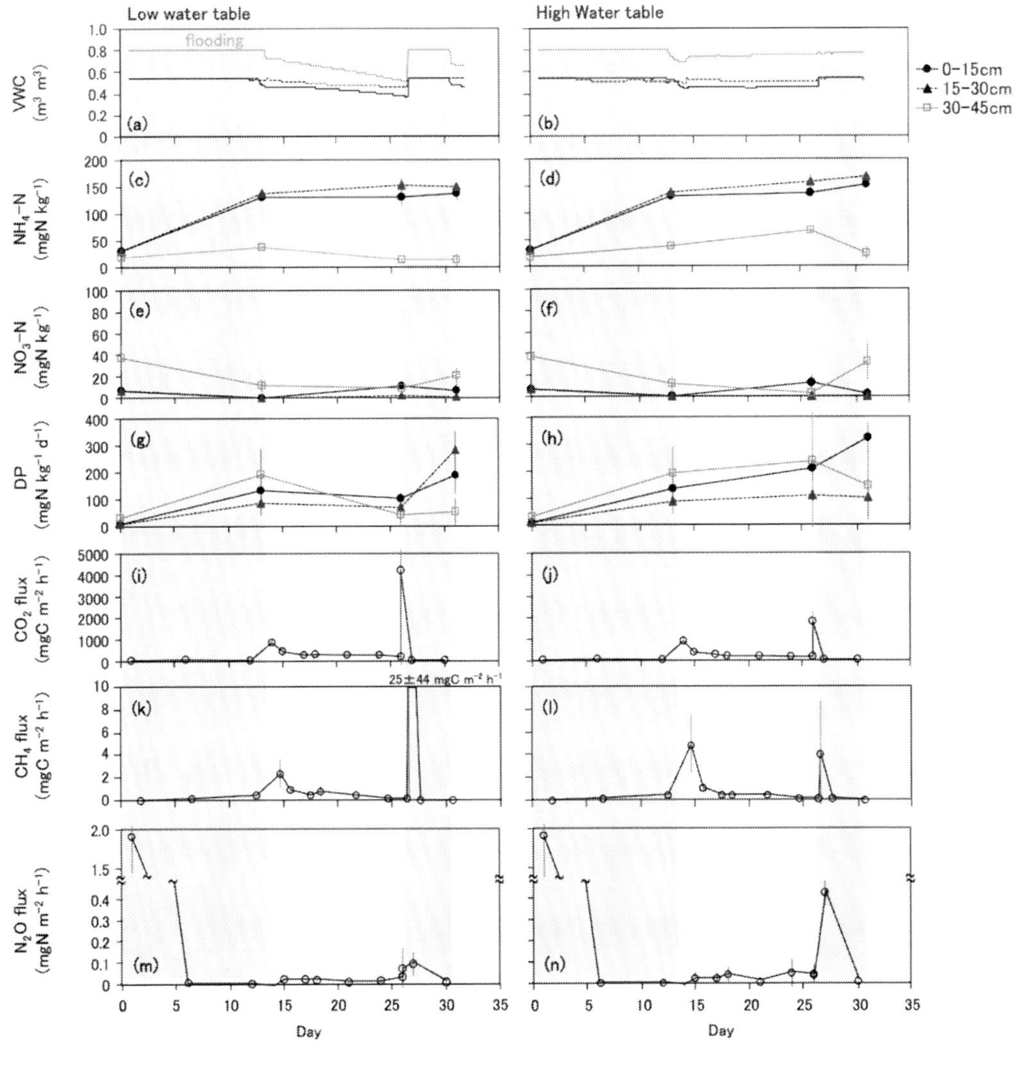

Fig. 2 Volumetric water content (VWC) (a, b), NH^{4+}-N and NO^{3} -N concentration of soil (c, d, e, f), denitrification potential (DP) (g, h), and CO_2, CH_4, N_2O fluxes from soil surface (i, j, k, l, m, n) in the low and high water table treatments.

CONCLUSION

Soil columns were packed with peat soil in 30-45 cm depth and with mineral soil in 0-30 cm depth, and incubated under different water table conditions. High water table treatment could decrease CO_2 emission, but increase N_2O emission after reflooding.

REFERENCES

1. Dinsmore KJ, Skiba UM, Billett MF, Rees RM 2009: Effect of water table on greenhouse gas emissions from peatland mesocosms. *Plant and Soil*, 318, 229-242.
2. Hashimoto H 2006: Actual soil conditions of peaty arableland in Hokkaido. *Journal of Japanese Society of Soil Physics*, 103, 87-94. (In Japanese)
3. Naser HM, Nagata O, Hatano R 2005: Greenhouse gas fluxes and grobal warming potentials in crop fields on soil-dressed peatland in Hokkaido, Japan. *Phyton*, 45, 285-293.

Abstract No: A-073

EFFECTS OF BIOLOGICAL AND CHEMICAL CONTROL ON POPULATION OF BUNCH MOTH, *TIRATHABA RUFIVENA* IN OIL PALM PLANTED ON PEAT IN SARAWAK

Zulkefli Masijan[1], Saharul Abillah Mohamad[1], Ramle Moslim[1], Mohamad Rosman Sulaiman[1], Su Chong Ming[2], Norman Kamarudin[1], Siti Ramlah Ahmad Ali[1] and Siti Nurulhidayah Ahmad[1]

[1]*Applied Entomology and Microbiology Unit, Biology Research Division, Malaysian Palm Oil Board (MPOB), Malaysia*

[2]*Research and Development Department, Sarawak Oil Palms Berhad (SOPB), Malaysia*

**Corresponding author: saharul.abillah@mpob.gov.my*

SUMMARY

Bunch moth, *Tirathaba rufivena* is a serious pest of oil palm planted on peat. Severe infestation in oil palm plantation may reduce the production of yield if no proper control measures were implemented. The pest was commonly controlled by the use of biological control agents and chemical products. In this study, the effectiveness of biological agents and selected chemical insecticides to control the infestation of *T. rufivena* in field was evaluated. The study was conducted from April to May 2015 on 4 years old palm, covering 960 treated palms. The treatments were *Bacillus thuringiensis*, *Metarhizium anisopliae*, *Chlorantraniliprole* and *Cypermethrin* applied by spraying method. The effectiveness of treatment in reducing the larval population was compared to untreated control. The study found that all treatments were effective in reducing the population of *T. rufivena*. As early as seven days after first treatment (DAFT), the number of live larvae in the treated plots started to reduce, and at 21 DAFT the population was significantly lower than control. Afterward it maintained below the economic threshold level of 5 live larvae per sample (LPS). The lowest live larvae per sample were 0.5 LPS, recorded from plots treated with chlorantraniliprole. The low population of bunch moth was continued at 35 DAFT and 49 DAFT. Based on results of this study, all treatments were equally good in controlling the bunch moth. More comprehensive study need to be carried out by incorporating treatment on mass trapping of adults and spraying of larvae in the coastal peat areas. These strategies, coupled with the implementation of sanitation practices perhaps will further reduce the infestation of *T.rufivena* in oil palm planted on peat.

***Keywords**: Oil palm, bunch moth, Tirathaba rufivena, cypermethrin, chlorantraniliprole, Bacillus thuringiensis, Metarhizium anisopliae, peat, pest control*

INTRODUCTION

The oil palm bunch moth, *Tirathaba rufivena* (Family: Pyralidae) is a serious pest of oil palm planted on peat (Lim, 2012). Severe infestation in oil palm plantation may reduce the yield production. If no proper control measures were implemented, the pest infestation may increase from 30% to 50%. Palm with age ranging from three to five years old are the most vulnerable to this pest (Lim, 2012). Larvae are the most destructive stage of this pest, infesting mostly on post-anthesis male inflorescences, female inflorescences and the developing bunches. Severe infestation led fruits to rot and subsequently causing the whole bunch to rot (Alouw *et al.*, 2005). According to Yaakop *et al.*, (2015), the species of *Tirathaba* consists of five larval stages, where each stage is differentiated by size and body length. Agus *et al.*, (2011) reported that besides unharvested ripe bunches, the continuous development of inflorescences was also found one of the factors for population increment, as it act as a food source and breeding sites of the insect. Field control studies of *T.rufivena* had reported inconsistent results. Lim (2012) reported that the application of *B.thuringiensis* was more effective in supressing the population of *T.rufivena* as compared to cypermethrin. However, recent study by Zulkefli *et al.*, (2015) showed that *B.thuringiensis* was gave a satisfactory control only until 21 days after first treatment, before the population increase again. Therefore, this study was aimed to compare the effectiveness of biological control agents and chemical pesticides in controlling the population of *T.rufivena* in oil palm planted on peat.

MATERIALS AND METHODS

Location of the study

The study was conducted on 4 years old palm planted on peat at Block K39, Tinbarap 9 Estate, Bakong, Sarawak. The pre census was conducted a week before treatment in late March 2015.

Treatments

There are 5 treatments, including untreated control, this study. Two biological agents (*Bacillus thuringiensis* and *Metarhizium anisopliae*) and two chemical pesticides (cypermethrin and chlorantraniliprole) were evaluated in the field. Treatments were applied by directly spraying the product solution onto the crown region of palm. No guard palm was used in this study since the possibility of spraying drifts in contact onto the neighbouring palm was considered negligible. The first application of treatment was conducted on 8th April 2015. The experimental design was Randomized Complete Block Design (RCBD), covering twenty experimental sub-plots with 4 replicates for each treatment.

The treatments were compared against untreated control plot. The rates of application for each treatment are showed in Table 1. Spraying of treatments was done by using a 16 litre knapsack sprayer equipped with a 4ft long lance and adjustable cone-shaped nozzle. Prior to application, calibration was done to ensure uniform and accurate application rate. Based on calibration, 1 litre of solution was required to treat each palm, regardless of the sizes of fruit bunches. The treatments were applied and targeted onto all stages of fruit bunches, female inflorescences and male inflorescences in the crown region of the palms. To improve adherence and deposition of droplets, 10ml of sticking agent Nufarm Bond® was added into the solution. Four rounds of treatments were applied with 2 weeks interval between each rounds (days 0, 14, 28 and 42).

Table 1: Types and application rates of treatments applied in this study

No	Active Ingredient	Concentration	Application rate/16L knapsack
1	Control		
2	Cypermethrin	5.5%	15ml
3	Chlorantraniliprole	5.0%	8ml
4	*Bacillus thuringiensis*	17,600 I.U/mg	24ml
5	*Metarhizium anisopliae*	1.1×10^{11} spores/kg	150g

Data Recording

Data was recorded at 7 days after first treatment (DAFT), 21 DAFT, 35 DAFT and 49 DAFT. For both pre and post treatment census, five samples were collected from each study plot, which consisted of one post anthesis male inflorescence, two female inflorescences and two developing fruit bunches. Before the samples were collected, the level of infestation on bunches were recorded based on the presence of reddish brown-coloured, wet and fresh frass. Both samples of female inflorescences and developing fruit bunches were chopped to manageable sizes to facilitate counting on bunch moth population. The spikelets of male inflorescences were also separated individually and carefully inspected for the presence of bunch moth developmental stages' larvae. The numbers of larvae, pupae and adults were counted and recorded. Analysis of variance (ANOVA) was performed to compare the population difference for each treatment.

RESULT AND DISCUSSION

Based on pre-census data, the experimental area was experiencing severe infestation of bunch moth. The level of infestation between treatments was not significantly different ($P > 0.05$) The number of live larvae in plots treated with cypermethrin, chlorantraniliprole, *B. thuringiensis* and *M. anisopliae* was 10.38, 8.88, 15.96 and 9.88 live larvae per sample (LPS) respectively, not significantly different as compared to untreated control of 10.71 LPS (Table 2).

At 7 DAFT, the numbers of live larvae per sample for all experimental plots were reduced, including in the control plot. However, the population of live larvae per sample in the plots treated with all products was significantly lower ($P < 0.05$) than the control. This indicated that the application of treatments have affected the live larvae population of bunch moth.

Table 2: Effects of selected pesticides and biological agents on population of live larvae of bunch moth

Treatment	Mean number of live larvae / sample at day after first treatment (DAFT)				
	0	7	21	35	49
Ctr - Control	10.38 a	6.50 a	7.29 a	9.67 a	19.04 a
T1 - Cypermethrin	8.88 a	0.21 b	1.46 b	0.08 b	0.33 b
T2 - Chlorantriniliprole	15.96 a	0.42 b	0.50 b	0.13 b	1.21 b
T3 - *B. thuringiensis*	9.88 a	3.71 ab	2.33 b	1.79 b	0.17 b
T4 - *M. anisopliae*	10.71 a	1.67 b	2.79 b	3.04 b	2.46 b

Note: Means in columns with the same letters are not significantly different after DMRT at P=0.05.

Starting from 21 DAFT, the numbers of live larvae per sample in all of the treated plots was maintained and significantly lower ($P<0.05$) as compared to the control plot. From this point onward, no significant difference was recorded on the number of live larvae per sample between treatments. The lowest population of 0.5 LPS was recorded in plots treated with chlorantraniliprole. This low trend population in the treated plots continued at 35 DAFT and 49 DAFT, where the treated plots recorded significantly lower number of live larvae per sample as compared to control. At 49 DAFT, all four treatments gave significantly good control on bunch moth as compared to untreated control. Based on this study, it was found that all treatments were equally good in controlling the population of bunch moth. It was also observed that both biological agents, the *B. thuringiensis* and *M. anisopliae* were able to control the population of oil palm bunch moth in the field as good as the chemical pesticides.

Previous study by Zulkefli *et al.*, (2015) found that the *B. thuringiensis* gave good control to bunch moth only up to 21 DAFT, before the bunch moth population increased to above the threshold of 5 LPS. However, in this study, although the treatments were applied at the same interval of 14 days, the application of *B. thuringiensis* seemed to give satisfactory control even up to 49 DAFT.
This study also supported findings of studies by Basri *et al.*, (1991) and Lim (2012), where they reported that the *B. thuringiensis* are as good as chemical pesticides in controlling the bunch moth. The continuous application of *B. thuringiensis* at the rate of 1g per litre for six rounds at the interval of 15 days had reduced the bunch moth infestation from more than 50% to less than 15%.

Based on the findings of this study, it was clearly observed that the use of biological agents or chemicals could reduce the population of oil palm bunch moth to below the threshold level. The use of these elements coupled with other methods such as field sanitation practices could maintain the bunch moth population below the threshold level. Sanitation techniques such as the removal of rotten and seriously infested post anthesis male inflorescences and bunches should be implemented with the continuous application of biological agents. The implementation of sanitation techniques alone was not effective in controlling the population of bunch moth (Basri *et al.*, 1991). Lim (2012) also reported that in order to achieve satisfactory control of bunch moth, the sanitation techniques have to be implemented with the application of biological agents such as the *B. thuringiensis*. This integration technique could reduce the application frequency of biological or chemical control, thus reducing costs.

CONCLUSION

The infestations of *T.rufivena*, especially the early larval stages had occurred mainly on post-anthesis male inflorescences. the late stages of larvae were found more on female inflorescences and developing fruit bunches. This study showed that application of cypermethrin, chlorantraniliprole, *B.thuringiensis* and *M.anisopliae* were equally able to give satisfactory control in reducing the population of *T.rufivena* It was suggested that more comprehensive trials should be conducted by incorporating treatments on mass trapping of adult moths and spraying of larvae especially in the infested palm in coastal peat areas. This two-pronged strategy, along with the implementation of sanitation techniques hopefully will further reduce the infestation of *T. rufivena*.

ACKNOWLEDGEMENTS

The authors would like to extend their gratitude to the Director General of Malaysian Palm Oil Board (MPOB) for permission to publish this paper. We would also like to thank the hardworking staff of the Entomology and Ecological Research Group of the MPOB Research Station Lahad Datu, Sabah and MPOB Sessang, Sarawak. Thanks to the staff of Research and Development (R&D) Department, Sarawak Oil Palms Berhad, the managements of the Tinbarap 9 Estate and the tireless workers assisting this study.

REFERENCES

1. AGUS S, SUDHARTO and PERDANA ROZZIANSHA T A (2011). Penggerek tandan kelapa sawit, *Tirathaba mundella* Walker. Informasi Organisme Pengganggu Tanaman Vol H (0004) - October 2011. Retrieved February 1, 2016, from http://iopri.org/jdownloads/OPT%20Info/Hama/tirathaba_mundella.pdf
2. BASRI M W, MUKESH S and NORMAN K (1991). Field evaluation of insecticides and cultural practice against the bunch moth, *Tirathaba rufivena* (Lepidoptera: Pyralidea) in a mature oil palm plantation. *Elaies* 3(2): 355 -362.
3. ALOUW J C, MORALLO-REJESUS B and OCAMPO V R (2005). Biology of the coconut spike moth, *Tirathaba fructivora* (Meyr.)(Lepidoptera: Pyralidae). *Philippines Entomologist* 19(1): 84-93.
4. LIM K H (2012). Integrated pest management of Tirathaba bunch moth on oil palm planted on peat. *The Planter* 88(1031): 97-104.
5. YAAKOP S and SHAFARIZA M A M (2015). The bunch moth of the Tirathaba species as a hidden pest on the peat soil of oil palm plantations: Implications of biological life cycles, the DNA barcoding approach, and infestation pattern detection. *In proceeding of the 3rd International Conference on Chemical, Agricultural and Medical Sciences (CAMS-2015)*, Singapore. 10-11 December 2015.
6. ZULKEFLI M, ALINDRA G S, SAHARUL A M , NORMAN K, RAMLAH S A A , SIAW T C, RAMLE M, and SITI NURULHIDAYAH A (2015). Evaluation of chemical insecticides and biological agents to control bunch moth, *Tirathaba rufivena* in young oil palm area in Sarawak, Malaysia. *In proceeding of PIPOC 2015, MPOB International Palm Oil Congress and Exhibition: Oil Palm: Powering the World, Sustaining the Future*, Kuala Lumpur, Malaysia. 6-8 October 2015.

Abstract No: A-352

FERTILISER RESPONSE OF OIL PALM IN A LOGGED OVER, DEGRADED AND DRAINED PEAT IN RIAU, INDONESIA

Arif Sugandi[1] and Goh Kah Joo[2]

[1]*PT Applied Agricultural Resources Indonesia, Indonesia*
[2]*Applied Agricultural Resources Sdn. Bhd., Malaysia*

**Corresponding author: aar_indo@aarsb.com.my; aarsb@aarsb.com.my*

SUMMARY

Despite the large areas of oil palm on peat at about 1.4 million ha in Sumatera, Indonesia, fertiliser response studies of oil palm on peat were very limited in the region. Amongst the key agro-management practices for oil palm on peat such as effective drainage and water management, peat compaction and integrated pest and disease management, judicious fertiliser input is probably the costliest and important. This paper discusses the results of 8-year (2005-2013) NPK factorial fertiliser response trial on young mature oil palm (4 to 12 years old palms) planted on deep, dysic, isohyperthermic, Typic Tropohemist in Riau region, Sumatera, Indonesia, which was logged over, degraded and drained before the concession was bought by a plantation company. The primary objectives of the study were to categorize the growth and yield response of oil palm to N, P and K fertilizer, to determine the optimum oil palm yield to fertilizer inputs over time and to establish the Site Yield Potential of oil palm on the peat. Results showed significant responses of bunch weight and mean annual and cumulative fresh fruit bunch (FFB) yield to K input only. K application also increased leaf and rachis K significantly. The optimum K rate was between 4 and 6 kg palm^{-1} year^{-1}. No significant responses of FFB yield and leaf/rachis N and P concentrations to both N and P inputs were obtained. Low fertiliser rates of between 1 and 2 kg Urea palm^{-1} year^{-1} and 0 and 1 kg of rock phosphate (RP) palm^{-1} year^{-1} were sufficient for young immature palms on the peat. Nevertheless, higher N was required to obtain optimum FFB yield in the presence of K and P. On the side trial, no significant response in all yield component of oil palm between application of Urea and Ammonium Sulphate and different rates of N. The average site yield potential of the trial area was about 28.6 ton FFB ha^{-1} year^{-1} during the stable peak yielding period with optimum N, P and K inputs. Thus, with better nutrition management, oil palm planting on peat is economically viable.

***Keywords**: Peat, Oil Palm, Fertilisers, Riau, Indonesia*

INTRODUCTION

To date, it is estimated that about 1.7 million ha of peat have been developed for oil palm cultivation in Indonesia (Agus *et al.*, 2011) with about 80% located in Sumatra alone. These peat areas constituted about 20% of the total oil palm plantings in Indonesia. With new government regulations and greater commitment on environmental issues by responsible plantation companies, oil plantings on peat have slowed down tremendously particularly since 2011/2012.

The existing large peat planting of oil palm in diverse locations warrants further study on fertiliser and nutrient management, especially in Indonesia, where the peat is largely heterogeneous in term of inherent chemical fertility, stage of mineralisation, depth to the underlying mineral soils, type of previous vegetation etc. The current scarce information on fertiliser responses of oil palm on peat (Manjit *et al.*, 2014), fertiliser inputs might be indiscriminate leading to nutrient imbalances and poor yield. Therefore, apart from water management, peat compaction and integrated pest and disease management, judicious fertilizer programme is vital for high productivity of oil palm on peat.

The primary objectives of this paper were to categorize the growth and yield response of oil palm to N, P and K fertilizer, to determine the optimum oil palm yield to fertilizer inputs over time and to establish the Site Yield Potential of oil palm in deep peat.

MATERIALS AND METHODS

Trial 1- Growth and yield responses of oil palm to NPK fertilizers

A $N^3K^3P^3$ confounded factorial trial with 2 replicates and 3 blocks per replicate was laid down in 2005 on four-year-old (2001 planting) DxP oil palm on dysic, isohyperthermic, Typic Tropohemists in Pangkalan Kerinci, Pelalawan district, Riau. The fertilizer types and rates tested are shown in Table 1 below.

Table 1. Nutrient level and the corresponding fertiliser and nutrient rates of Trial 1

Nutrient level			Fertilizer rate (kg p^{-1} yr^{-1})			Nutrient rate (kg p^{-1} yr^{-1})		
N	K	P	Urea	MOP	GRP	N	K_2O	P_2O_5
0	0	0	0	0	0	0	0	0
1*	1*	1	1*	2*	1	0.46*	1.20*	0.28
2	2	2	2	4	2	0.92	2.40	0.56
3	3	3*	3	6	3*	1.38	3.60	0.84*

Remarks: Urea = 46% N; MOP = 60% K_2O; GRP = 28% P_2O_5; * = not included in the factorial combinations

Trial 2 – Different rates and types of N

A randomised complete block design trial to investigate two sources of N fertilizers (i.e. Urea vs. Ammonium Sulphate (AS)) × 3 rates of N + one control N_0 was also set up in the same area. All treatments are replicated 3 times, except N_0 (replicated 2 times only). All the treatments were tested at the predicted optimum level of K and P (Table 2).

Table 2. Nutrient level and the corresponding fertilisers and nutrient rates of Trial 2

Nutrient level			Fertiliser rate (kg p^{-1} yr^{-1})			
N	K	P	Urea/AS		MOP	GRP
0	2	1	0		4	1
1	2	1	1.00	Urea	4	1
2	2	1	2.00	Urea	4	1
3	2	1	3.00	Urea	4	1
1	2	1	2.19	AS	4	1
2	2	1	4.38	AS	4	1
3	2	1	6.57	AS	4	1

Remarks: Urea = 46% N; AS = 21% N; MOP = 60% K_2O; GRP = 28% P_2O_5

The experiments were conducted on first generation oil palm planting on logged over, degraded secondary forest. The planting density was 148 palms ha^{-1} in triangular pattern. Plot size was 28 (7x4) palms with inner 16 (4x4) palms serving as measurement/assessment palms. The plots were guarded by existing field drains at every 4th palm rows and a row of four palms served as guard rows at the other side of plots to avoid possible poaching effect.

Differential fertiliser treatments started in January 2006, after one year of no fertiliser application in 2005 in all treatment plots. N and K fertilisers were applied in two equal split application per year (i.e. in April and August). P fertiliser was applied once per year in April. Other non-treatment fertilisers i.e. Borate, Copper and Zinc Sulphate were all applied at 100 g $palm^{-1}$ $year^{-1}$ in September every year. Mg fertiliser was not applied in all treatment plots during the trial period. All the fertilisers were evenly broadcast in the weeded palm circles. Prior to 2005, during the immature period, all plots received equal fertiliser rates following the commercial estate's manuring programme.

FFB yields were recorded at 10-day intervals. Foliar and rachis samplings (frond 17) were conducted every year and in selected years respectively in January. Vegetative growth measurement was also carried out annually. Field upkeep and maintenance was carried routinely as per the estate practices. A cost benefit analysis was carried out at the end of 2013 (8th year) to determine the optimum and most profitable fertiliser treatments.

RESULTS AND DISCUSSION

Fertiliser Response to Oil Palm Yield Components

The unfertilised plots produced significant lower FFB yield of 153 kg $palm^{-1}$ yr^{-1} compared with fertilised plots probably because of the poor inherent soil fertility of peat (Table 3). The FFB yields of unfertilised plots declined significantly after 3 years of fertilizer withdrawal due to residual effect of fertilisers applied during its immature phase (3 years) and possibly nutrient release by peat mineralisation. It widened the yield gap between control plots and fertiliser plots until the trial closed in 2013.

Trial 1 showed that there was a significant FFB yield response to K fertiliser application mainly through heavier bunch weight. The results conformed with the findings in Indonesia (Manjit *et al.*, 2004) and Malaysia (Gurmit, 1999). The average yield responses to K application ranged from 17 to 20%. The optimum K rate was about 4.0 kg MOP $palm^{-1}$ $year^{-1}$.

On the other hand, there were no significant yield responses to the applications of N and P fertilisers probably due to the rapid mineralization of hemic peat (Gurmit, 1999; Manjit *et al*, 2004) upon cultivation, particularly drainage. Excessive N and P applications when the palms were mature could suppress FFB yield as recorded in some years in this trial (Table 3).

Table 3. Effect of NPK fertiliser application on average (a) FFB production and (b) Bunch weight of oil palm on deep peat in Pangkalan Kerinci, Pelalawan District, Riau, Indonesia

a. FFB Yield

Fertilizer			Average FFB per palm (kg palm^{-1} yr^{-1})									
Type	Level	Rate kg p^{-1} yr^{-1}	2005*	2006	2007	2008	2009	2010	2011	2012	2013	Mean
Nil	$N_0P_0K_0$	0	88.1	145.9	169.7	181.3	152.3	139.1	143.0	148.8	143.9	153.0
Urea	N_0	0	92.1	163.2	182.8	190.1	153.2	150.8	163.0	169.1	165.6	167.2
	N_2	2	90.2	158.8	188.3	187.3	157.2	157.3	158.8	165.9	158.5	166.5
	N_3	3	92.8	161.1	193.1	189.0	153.4	162.5	153.0	168.5	160.5	167.7
MOP	K_0	0	98.1	163.4	184.0	176.8	145.7	140.5	141.6	157.1	149.1	157.3
	K_2	4	87.7	158.5	188.2	190.0	160.2	165.0	166.4	173.7	166.5	171.1
	K_3	6	90.5	157.4	190.8	199.6	157.9	165.1	166.9	172.2	167.3	172.1
RP	P_0	0	89.6	155.4	182.2	188.2	165.0	154.0	154.2	164.1	157.7	165.1
	P_1	1	94.2	162.1	191.3	189.8	149.9	160.0	164.3	169.2	163.2	168.7
	P_2	2	91.3	165.6	190.7	188.5	148.9	156.6	156.3	170.6	163.0	167.5
	LSD (5%)		6.5	10.1	10.0	9.5	14.3	14.7	15.9	28.6	20.2	9.8

*=pre-treatment yield recording (only 8 months); Mean = 8-year average of 2006-2013.

b. Bunch Weight

Fertilizer			Average Bunch Weight (kg)									
Type	Level	Rate kg p^{-1} yr^{-1}	2005*	2006	2007	2008	2009	2010	2011	2012	2013	Mean
Nil	$N_0P_0K_0$	0	7.2	7.9	8.3	10.7	9.9	10.9	10.5	9.6	9.8	9.7
Urea	N_0	0	7.9	8.4	9.0	11.6	11.0	12.5	12.5	10.9	11.2	10.9
	N_2	2	7.8	8.3	9.2	11.7	11.2	12.6	12.3	10.7	10.9	10.8
	N_3	3	7.7	8.2	8.2	9.2	11.5	10.9	12.3	10.5	10.7	10.6
MOP	K_0	0	8.0	8.5	9.1	11.3	10.6	11.5	11.2	10.3	10.4	10.4
	K_2	4	7.8	8.3	9.1	11.7	11.3	12.8	12.4	10.9	11.1	11.0
	K_3	6	7.7	8.1	9.2	11.7	11.2	13.1	12.8	10.9	11.2	11.0
RP	P_0	0	7.7	8.3	9.1	11.6	11.1	12.2	12.0	10.7	10.8	10.7
	P_1	1	7.8	8.3	9.2	11.6	11.1	12.9	12.5	10.8	11.1	10.9
	P_2	2	7.9	8.3	9.1	11.5	10.9	12.3	11.9	10.6	10.7	10.7
	LSD (5%)		0.3	0.4	0.3	0.5	0.5	0.6	0.6	0.6	1.1	0.3

*=pre-treatment yield recording (only 8 months); Mean = 2006-2013.

In Trial 2, on average, there were no significant yield differences between Urea and Ammonium Sulphate treated palms and different rates of N (Table 4). However, 0.46 kg N palm^{-1} year^{-1} of Ammonium Sulphate gave similar yield to 1.38 kg N palm^{-1} year^{-1} of Urea probably due to the high N volatilization losses in the latter treatments. However, higher rates of Ammonium Sulphate resulted in a declining yield trend caused by lower bunch weight and bunch number. The exact cause is still uncertain.

Table 4. Effect of application different types/rates of N fertilisers (at optimum rates of K and P) on mean yield components of oil palm on deep peat in Pangkalan Kerinci, Pelalawan District, Riau, Indonesia

Treatments	Average FFB Yield (kg ha^{-1} year^{-1})	Average Bunch Weight (kg)	Average Bunch Number palm^{-1}
Control	179.2	11.3	17.1
Urea – N_1	166.5	11.3	15.5
Urea - N_2	174.4	11.8	15.5
Urea - N_3	183.0	11.9	16.4
AS - N_1	187.4	12.1	16.7
AS - N_2	177.7	11.6	16.4
AS - N_3	169.1	11.3	15.8
Mean Urea	174.7	11.7	15.8
Mean Ammonium Sulphate	178.1	11.7	16.3

Remarks: Average of 2006-2013

Leaf and rachis nutrient concentrations

Palms in the fertilised plots had significantly better leaf and rachis nutrient concentrations than those in unfertilised plots (Table 5). The improved palm nutritional status of the former treatments probably explained their higher FFB yields. The leaf N concentrations of oil palms in unfertilised plots were sustained at optimum level since trial commencement indicating sufficient soil N probably from continuous peat mineralisation. Leaf P concentration was mainly sufficient at the beginning of the trial but deteriorated with time in the unfertilised plots.

Application of K gave strong response to both leaf and rachis K concentrations with 4 kg MOP palm^{-1} year^{-1} providing the optimum status. Application of N and K gave positive response to both leaf and rachis P concentrations, which indicated improved P uptake.

Table 5. Effect of NPK fertiliser application on (a) leaf macronutrient concentration and (b) rachis nutrient concentration of oil palm on deep peat in Pangkalan Kerinci, Pelalawan District, Riau, Indonesia

(a) Leaf macronutrient concentration

Fertiliser			Average Leaf Nutrient Concentration (% dry matter) – Macronutrient									
Type	Level	Rate kg p^{-1} yr^{-1}	N		P		K		Mg		Ca	
			2005*	2007-13	2005*	2007-13	2005*	2007-13	2005*	2007-13	2005*	2007-13
Nil	$N_0P_0K_0$	0	2.78	2.71	0.175	0.153	0.99	0.88	0.47	0.40	0.44	0.49
Urea	N_0	0	2.77	2.73	0.168	0.166	1.00	0.99	0.47	0.38	0.48	0.53
	N_2	2	2.79	2.83	0.169	0.171	0.97	1.06	0.48	0.35	0.48	0.49
	N_3	3	2.80	2.85	0.170	0.170	0.97	1.08	0.49	0.34	0.46	0.48
MOP	K_0	0	2.81	2.79	0.170	0.171	0.97	0.85	0.47	0.41	0.46	0.53
	K_2	4	2.77	2.81	0.168	0.167	0.98	1.14	0.49	0.32	0.47	0.49
	K_3	6	2.79	2.80	0.169	0.167	0.97	1.12	0.49	0.34	0.45	0.49
RP	P_0	0	2.79	2.78	0.170	0.158	0.97	1.09	0.49	0.35	0.48	0.46
	P_1	1	2.82	2.81	0.168	0.172	0.98	1.01	0.49	0.36	0.46	0.51
	P_2	2	2.76	2.81	0.169	0.175	0.98	1.01	0.47	0.36	0.46	0.54
	LSD (5%)		0.06	0.04	0.005	0.003	0.05	0.04	0.03	0.02	0.04	0.02

*=pre-treatment samples

b. Rachis nutrient concentration

Fertiliser			Average Rachis Nutrient Concentration (% dry matter)		
Type	Level	Rate (kg p^{-1} yr^{-1})	N	P	K
Nil	$N_0P_0K_0$	0	0.39	0.075	1.23
Urea	N_0	0	0.44	0.144	1.74
	N_2	2	0.55	0.153	1.99
	N_3	3	0.56	0.148	2.02
MOP	K_0	0	0.48	0.134	1.14
	K_2	4	0.52	0.149	2.29
	K_3	6	0.53	0.156	2.25
RP	P_0	0	0.48	0.079	1.93
	P_1	1	0.52	0.157	1.83
	P_2	2	0.53	0.203	1.92
	LSD (5%)		0.02	0.014	0.19

Rachis were sampled only in 2008, 2009, 2012, 2013.

Economic analysis of NPK fertilization

The highest yielding treatment was $N_3P_1K_3$ (Optimum 4) but the most profitable treatment was $N_0P_1K_2$ (Optimum 1) (Table 6). At cheaper MOP prices, it would be advisable to increase the rate of MOP above 4 kg palm^{-1} for higher FFB yield. However, higher N will also be required to obtain the optimum FFB yield in the presence of K and P. Application of K without N fertilisers gave lower FFB yield.

Table 6. Optimum fertiliser regimes of oil palm planted on deep peat in Pangkalan Kerinci, Pelalawan District, Riau, Indonesia

Fertiliser Regimes	Treatment	Fertiliser rate (kg palm^{-1} ha^{-1} year^{-1})				Mean FFB Yield (ton ha^{-1}yr^{-1})	Marginal returns (Rp ha^{-1} yr^{-1})
		Urea	RP	MOP	Total		
Control	$N_0P_0K_0$	0	0	0	0	20.8	-
Optimum 1	$N_0P_1K_2$	0	1	4	5	25.4	2,301,000
Optimum 2	$N_2P_1K_1$	2	1	2	5	24.8	1,581,000
Optimum 3	$N_2P_0K_2$	2	0	4	6	25.5	1,200,000
Optimum 4	$N_3P_1K_3$	3	1	6	10	27.6	1,241,000
Optimum 5	$N_0P_0K_2$	0	0	4	4	24.0	880,000

Remarks: at price of Urea = Rp 5,000,- per kg, MOP = Rp 5,000,- per kg, RP = Rp 1,750,- per kg; FFB price level at Rp 1,200,- per kg FFB.

Site Yield Potential of Peat

Oil palm yields varied significantly with various types of peat soil (Ramesh *et al*, 2015). In this trial laid down on dysic, isohyperthemic, Typic Tropohemists in Pangkalan Kerinci, Pelalawan District, Riau, Indonesia, the oil palm achieved the highest FFB yield of 33.4 ton ha^{-1} (at full stand of 148 palm ha^{-1}) at the rapid ascending yield phase. The average site yield potential at the trial site was about 28.6 ton FFB ha^{-1} year^{-1} during the stable peak yielding period (9-11 YAP) with optimum and balance N, P and K inputs and no other limiting nutrients.

Table 7. FFB yield (ton ha^{-1}) of oil palms planted on dysic, isohyperthemic, Typic Tropohemists in Pangkalan Kerinci, Pelalawan District, Riau, Indonesia

FFB Yield (ton/ha)	**Rapid Ascending Yield Phase (3 to 8 YAP)**				**Stable Yield Phase (9 to 18 YAP)**			
	2006 (5 YAP)	2007 (6 YAP)	2008 (7 YAP)	2009 (8 YAP)	2010 (9 YAP)	2011 (10 YAP)	2012 (11 YAP)	2013 (12 YAP)
Control	21.6	25.1	26.8	22.5	20.6	21.2	14.5	14.4
Max	27.5	31.7	33.4	26.6	31.4	28.6	25.9	23.9
Mean	24.0	28.1	28.1	23.0	23.5	23.7	18.5	15.1
Best Treatment	$N_3K_2P_1$	$N_3K_3P_1$	$N_3K_3P_1$	$N_2K_2P_0$	$N_3K_3P_1$	$N_0K_1P_1$	$N_3K_3P_1$	$N_3K_3P_1$

Remarks: YAP = year after planting

CONCLUSION

The oil palm on dysic, isohyperthermic, Typic Tropohemist in logged over, degraded deep peat responded significantly to K input in terms of bunch weight, FFB yield and leaf and rachis K concentration. The optimum K rate was between 4 and 6 kg palm^{-1} year^{-1}. No significant responses N and P inputs were obtained for all parameters measured. Low fertiliser rates between 1 and 2 kg Urea palm^{-1} year^{-1} and 0 and 1 kg of rock phosphate (RP) palm^{-1} year^{-1} were sufficient for oil palms in the experimental site. Ammonium Sulphate had higher N use efficiency compared with urea but excessive rate can depress oil palm yield in deep peat. The average site yield potential of the trial site was about 28.6 ton FFB ha^{-1} year^{-1} during the stable peak yielding period with optimum and balance N, P and K inputs. Thus, with better nutrient management, oil palm planting on peat is economically viable.

ACKNOWLEDGEMENTS

The authors wish to thank Applied Agricultural Resources Sdn. Bhd. and our Principals, Kuala Lumpur Kepong Bhd and Boustead Plantation Bhd for their support and permission to publish this paper. Thanks are also due to Ms. Tan Suet Yee for statistical analysis and to all staff and management at PT AAR Indonesia and PT Adei Plantation and Industry who provided full support to the authors throughout the trial period.

REFERENCES

1. Agus, F., Gunarso, P., Sahardjo, B.H., Joseph, K.T., Rashid, A., Hamzah, K, Harris, N. and Van Noordwijk, M. 2011. Reducing greenhouse gas emissions from land use changes for oil palm development. Presentation to Plenary session, RSPO RT9, November 2011.
2. Manjit S., Zulkasta S and Abdul H. 2004. Yield responses of young mature oil palms to NPK fertiliser application on deep peat in North Sumatera Province, Indonesia. The Planter, Kuala Lumpur, 80 (941): 489-506.
3. Gurmit, S. 1999. Agronomic management of peat soil for sustainable oil palm production. In: Proceeding of Seminar on Various Aspects of Large Scale Oil Palm Cultivation on Peat Soil. Incorporated Society of Planters, Sibu. 37-47.
4. Ramesh, V., Eric van Ranst, Paramananthan, S. 2015. Peat characteristic and its impact on oil palm yield. NJAS – Wageningen Journal of Life Sciences 72-73 (2015), 33-40.

Abstract No: A-131

FRUIT YIELD, FRUIT QUALITY AND SEED YIELD OF FOUR CHILLI VARIETIES GROWN IN OPEN-FIELD AS AFFECTED BY CONVENTIONAL SYSTEM IN PEAT SOIL AREA AND FERTIGATION SYSTEM

Nurul Atilia Shafienaz binti Hanifah[1]*, Mohd Aziz bin Rashid[2] and Amat Jupri bin Ahmat[1]

[1]Genebank and Seed Centre, MARDI Klang, Malaysia
[2]Plant and Soil Science Research Centre, MARDI Headquarters, Malaysia

**Corresponding author: natilias@mardi.gov.my*

SUMMARY

A field experiment was conducted to compare two different cultivation systems, conventional and fertigation on plant growth, fruit yield and physical fruit qualities of two commercial varieties (151 and 461) and two local varieties (MC11 and Kulai) of chili and seed yield among local varieties. In conventional system, plants were grown in peat soil area with two times of fertilizer applications, basal and top dressing following recommended dose (18 g N, 3 g P and 15 g K/plant in total). In fertigation system, fertilizer was supplied with irrigation water. Dependent variables on plant growth were taken at the first harvest meanwhile data on fruit quality and seed yield were taken at the second harvest. Stem height was taken weekly from 1 to 10 weeks after transplant. Results showed that cultivation system does not have significant effect on fruit yield all varieties but type of variety does ($P<0.001$). Type of variety also had significant effect on stem height, number of fruit per kilogram and all fruit physical qualities at $P<0.0001$. Type of cultivation system had significant effect on number of fruit per kilogram at $P<0.0001$ and fruit length at $P<0.001$. Among all varieties tested, variety of 461 abled to produce highest fruit yield and all physical fruit qualities especially when grown conventionally in peat soil. Therefore, it is recommended to use variety of 461 and growing conventionally in peat soil area for high fresh fruit production. Seed yield of MC11 was recorded the highest when grown under conventional system while vice versa for Kulai. Therefore, for high production of MC11 seeds, it is recommended to grow the plants under conventional system, however, fertigation system for Kulai. This study also would like to suggest repeating this study with a modification on fertilizer rate of fertigation system.

Keywords: *Capsicum annum, fertigation system, conventional system, peat soil*

INTRODUCTION

The average self-sufficiency level (SSL) of chili from 2008 until 2012 was recorded at 58.5% meanwhile the SSL of other popular vegetables like tomato, cucumber, eggplant, long bean, okra, mustard and spinach was recorded more than 100% (FAMA, 2014). Therefore, the farm price of chili is always higher ranged from RM4.60 to RM6.45 per kilogram compared to other vegetables (RM0.85 to RM3.75 per kilogram). This is the main reason why many farmers prefer to grow chili than other vegetables. Most common varieties used by the fertigation farmers are imported varieties like 151, 461 and 568. Meanwhile, most common local varieties used in conventional system are Kulai and MC11.

The main activity in the MARDI Klang is the production of vegetable seeds and mainly is seed of local chilli varieties. Soil type in MARDI Klang is peat soil which always having problem with irrigation and permanently waterlog. To overcome these problems, fertigation might be a better cultivation system. However, no study has been done to determine the performance of local varieties grown under fertigation system. In MARDI Klang, there are also many farmers growing imported chili varieties using fertigation system. They might be able to increase their revenue if imported varieties can produce higher yield when grown under lower cost of cultivation system or if local varieties can produce higher yield than imported varieties. However, no study has been done to see the potential of imported varieties grown under conventional system.

Therefore, two very popular commercial varieties (151 and 461) and two very common local varieties (MC11 and Kulai) of chilli were used in this study. The first objective is to determine the fruit yield performance of commercial varieties grown under conventional method and the second objective is to determine the best cultivation system for the high production of seeds of local varieties.

MATERIALS & METHODS

Two commercial varieties (151 & 461) and two local varieties (MC11 & Kulai) were used in this study. All of the four varieties were planted using two types of cultivation system; fertigation and conventional in peat soil area with four replications of 30 plants per replication arranged in complete randomized block design. MC11 is an inbred line developed by Malaysian Agricultural Research & Development Institute (MARDI) and Kulai is a local variety recommended by Department of Agriculture (DOA). Meanwhile, commercial varieties are imported hybrid varieties that often used by the fertigation farmers. Soil type of conventional plot was peat soil while growing media for fertigation plot was 100% cocopeat. Plants grown under conventional system were irrigated daily with surface irrigation method and fertilized two times, basal and top dressing following recommendation by MARDI (18 g N, 3 g P, and 15 g K per plant in total) (MARDI, 1997). Plants grown under fertigation system were irrigated five times a day with total of 500ml water per plant. Fertilizer were injected through irrigation water with electrical conductivity of 1.8 dS m^{-1} when plants 1-3 weeks old then was increased to 2.4 dS m^{-1} when plants 4 weeks old until the season ends following recommendation by MARDI (Yaseer *et al.*, 2014). Other agronomic practices were done equally to both plots. Fruits were harvested once a week.

Dependent variables of total leaf number, leaf area index, and total fresh and dry weight of plant were taken at first harvest (70 days after sowing). Stem height was taken weekly from 1 to 10 weeks after transplanting. Number of fruit and fruit weight were recorded at each harvesting time. Data on fruit quality and seed yield were taken at the second harvest. Statistical procedure was carried out using the SAS software and data were analysed using ANOVA. Treatment means were compared using the Least Significant Difference (LSD) test.

RESULTS & DISCUSSION

Growth parameters

Cultivation system had significant effect on leaf area ratio (LAR) at $P<0.05$ (Table 1). The values of LAR of all the varieties tested were recorded 18% to 40% higher when grown under conventional system. It indicates that plants grown conventionally in peat soil area had higher efficiency of a given leaf area to produce a given plant size than plants grown in fertigation system. A few factors such as high leaf area and high leaf weight ratio also can result to high LAR. In contrast, study done by Maisiri *et al.* (2005) on kale (*Brassica napus*) showed that fertigation system gave better leaf production compared to conventional system.

Type of variety had significant effect on stem height at $P<0.0001$. In both cultivation systems, stem height of local varieties was recorded higher than stem height of commercial varieties (Figure 1). Obviously, variations in stem height among varieties were due to variation in the varietal genetic constituents. The interaction between cultivation system and variety had significant effect on crop growth rate (CGR) at $P<0.05$. CGR of 461 grown under conventional system was recorded the highest (4.88×10^{-4} g cm^{-2} day^{-1}), but the lowest (3.22×10^{-4} g cm^{-2} day^{-1}) when grown under fertigation system, however, vice versa for 151. In conventional system, CGR of MC11 was not significantly different to all other varieties, however CGR of Kulai was significantly different to CGR of 461. In fertigation system, CGR was not significantly different among all varieties. This is might because of plants grown in fertigation system received fertilizer and water equally thus not showing much differences on CGR regardless the type of variety.

Table 1: Growth parameters of chillies at first harvest as affected by cultivation systems

	Leaf area ratio (cm^2/g)	Leaf area index (cm^2_{leaf}/cm^2_{soil})	Crop growth rate (g cm^{-2} day^{-1})	Stem height (cm)
Conventional				
151	87.11a	1.53b	2.66×10^{-4}b	17.08c
461	109.29a	3.75a	4.88×10^{-4}a	20.51c
MC11	83.34a	2.18b	3.78×10^{-4}ab	25.99b
Kulai	80.75a	1.90b	3.33×10^{-4}b	29.85a
Fertigation				
151	57.70a	1.76a	4.40×10^{-4}a	17.14c
461	65.51a	1.56a	3.22×10^{-4}a	21.10b
MC11	64.80a	1.59a	3.55×10^{-4}a	27.18a
Kulai	66.15a	2.01a	4.08×10^{-4}a	27.27a
ANOVA (F values)				
Cultivation system	0.005 (*)	0.079 (ns)	0.691 (ns)	0.788 (ns)
Variety	0.559 (ns)	0.191 (ns)	0.796 (ns)	<.0001 (***)
Cultivation system x Variety	0.622 (ns)	0.062 (ns)	0.027 (*)	0.256 (ns)

Means within each column in the same box with the same letter are not significant different at P<0.05. (ns), not significant at P<0.05; (*), significant at P<0.05; and (***), significant at P<0.0001.

Figure 1: Plants structure of commercial (461 & 151) and local (Kulai & MC11) varieties grown under fertigation and conventional system at 70 days after transplanting (C;Conventional, F; Fertigation).

Fruit yield, physical fruit quality and seed yield

Type of cultivation system does not have significant effect on fruit yield, however type of variety does (Table 2). Fruit yield of 461 was recorded the highest when grown under conventional system (0.95 kg/plant) followed by 151, Kulai and MC11 with 0.66, 0.61 and 0.60 kg/plant, respectively. Under fertigation system, similar order was observed, however fruit yield of 461 was not significantly different to 151. In both cultivation systems, fruit yields of both local varieties were lower than commercial varieties but not significantly different to fruit yield of 151. These results were in contrast with the finding by Maisiri *et al.* (2005) in his study on kale. They found out that yield was significantly affected by cultivation system. Yield of kale was recorded higher when plants were fertilized and irrigated using fertigation system than conventional system and drip system with no fertilizer. This is because fertigation has a better fertilizer application as the fertilizer was injected through water supply directly to the plants which is totally different to the application of granular fertilizer which always done at once off. Study done by Yaseer *et al.* (2013) on *Capsicum frutescence* grown in open area also showed that plants grown under fertigation system have higher yield than plants grown conventionally. Contrast result obtained in this study was might due to the unsuitable fertilizer rate used in the fertigation system. The fertilizer rate was recommended for growing chili under protected structure meanwhile this study was done in an open area where plants were directly exposed to excessive hot and humid conditions. Therefore, a better fertilizer rate for growing chili in open area using fertigation system should be identified. Besides that, type of variety also had high significant effect on number of fruit per kilogram and all physical fruit quality characteristics at P<0.0001. 461 had the lowest number of fruit per kilogram (41.75 and 59.75 fruit/kg in conventional and fertigation system, respectively) but its fruits were recorded heavier, longer, larger and thicker fruit wall than all three other varieties.

Type of cultivation system had significant effect on number of fruit per kilogram at $P<0.0001$ and fruit length at $P<0.001$. All varieties had more number of fruit per kilogram when grown under fertigation system than under conventional system. However, fruits were observed longer when grown under conventional system (Figure 2). Results also showed that there were significant interactions between type of cultivation system and type of variety on fruit weight at $P<0.05$ and seed yield at $P<0.0001$. When plants grown under conventional system, 461 showed the highest fruit weight (27.79 g) followed by 151 (19.84 g), MC11 (11.23 g) and Kulai (11.08 g). Same sequence was observed when plants grown under fertigation system, however, the fruits were observed slightly lighter than fruits weight of plants grown under conventional system. Seed yield of local varieties was recorded significantly different among different type of cultivation. Seed yield of MC11 was observed the highest (47.88 g) when plants grown under conventional system, while seed yield of Kulai was observed the highest (38.33 g) when plants grown under fertigation system. For high production of MC11 seed, it is recommended to use fertigation system for MC11, meanwhile for Kulai, conventional system is recommended.

Table 2: Fruit yield, physical fruit quality & seed yield of chillies as affected by cultivation systems

	Yield (kg/plant)	**No. of fruit/kg**	**Fruit weight (g)**	**Fruit length (cm)**	**Fruit diameter (mm)**	**Fruit wall thickness (mm)**	**Seed yield/kg fruit (g)**
Conventional							
151	0.66b	51.75b	19.84b	14.28b	17.64b	2.36b	32.12c
461	0.95a	41.75c	27.79a	19.01a	19.85a	2.82a	21.51d
MC11	0.60b	89.25a	11.23c	14.77b	16.22c	1.78c	47.88a
Kulai	0.61b	89.00a	11.08c	15.52b	15.70c	1.89c	36.58b
Fertigation							
151	0.61ab	73.25b	18.44b	13.55b	17.92ab	2.44a	29.56c
461	0.79a	59.75b	29.53a	15.43a	19.15a	2.65a	25.82d
MC11	0.51b	101.50a	9.60c	13.72b	16.76bc	2.07b	31.93b
Kulai	0.56b	103.75a	9.36c	14.05b	15.06c	1.79b	38.33a
ANOVA (F values)							
Cultivation system	0.094 (ns)	<.0001 (***)	0.0004 (**)	0.0002 (**)	0.725 (ns)	0.707 (ns)	<.0001 (***)
Variety	0.0009 (**)	<.0001 (***)	<.0001 (***)	<.0001 (***)	<.0001 (***)	<.0001 (***)	<.0001 (***)
Cultivation system X Variety	0.861 (ns)	0.626 (ns)	0.028 (*)	0.063 (ns)	0.560 (ns)	0.051 (ns)	<.0001 (***)

Means within each column in the same box with the same letter are not significant different at $P<0.05$. (ns), not significant at $P<0.05$; (*), significant at $P<0.05$; (**), significant at $P<0.001$; and (***), significant at $P<0.0001$.

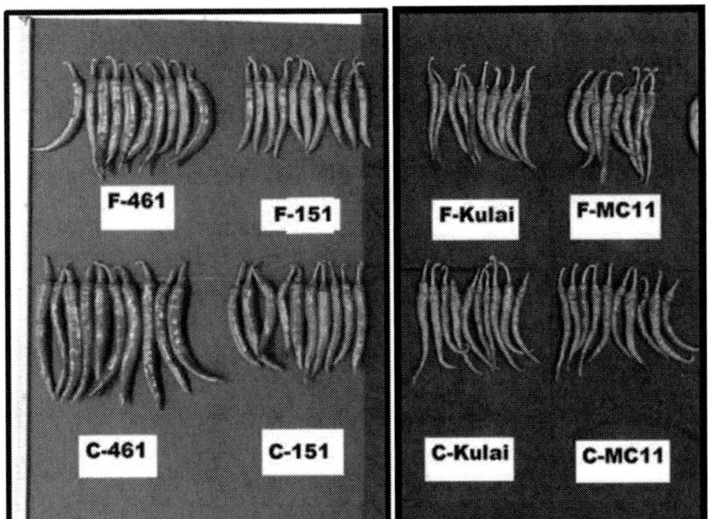

Figure 2: Fruit shape and length of commercial (461 & 151) and local (Kulai & MC11) varieties of chili grown in fertigation and conventional system (C;Conventional, F; Fertigation)

CONCLUSION

From this study, cultivation system does not have significant effect on fruit yield of both local and commercial varieties however variety 461 was observed having highest yield when grown under both cultivation systems. Besides that, it also has the ability to produce the highest physical fruit qualities. For seed production of local varieties, it is recommended to use fertigation system for high production of MC11 seeds, meanwhile for Kulai, conventional system is recommended. However, it is recommended to repeat this experiment at least one more time with a modification on fertilizer rate for fertigation system to see the differences.

ACKNOWLEDGEMENT

I would like to thank to all my staffs especially Mohd Ridzuan bin Ruhaizat and Roy Feroz bin Johan Shah Chan for their commitment to help me to complete the study from the very beginning until the end of this study. Besides that, I would like to thank the Director of Plant and Soil Science Research Centre and the laboratory manager of Seed Quality Control Laboratory of Genebank and Seed Centre, MARDI for their kindness for letting me using their lab equipment. Last but not least, I also would like to thank Mohd Faiz bin Musa for his guidance on fertigation system.

REFERENCES

1. FAMA. 2014. *Statistik Utama Pemasaran FAMA 2014*. Lembaga Pemasaran Pertanian Persekutuan (FAMA), Selangor, Malaysia: 3-63.
2. Maisiri, N., Senzanje A., Rockstrom, J. and Twomlow, S. J. 2005. On farm evaluation of the effect of low cost drip irrigation on water and crop productivity compared to conventional surface irrigation system. *Physics and Chemistry of the Earth* 30: 783-791.
3. MARDI. 1997. *Panduan Pengeluaran Sayur-sayuran*. Institut Penyelidikan dan Kemajuan Pertanian (MARDI), Kuala Lumpur, Malaysia: 32-47.
4. Yaseer, S. M., Mohamad, A. M. and Abu, H. I. 2014. Integration cultivation between chili and leafy vegetables using fertigation system under rain shelter structure. *Buletin Teknologi MARDI* 5: 71-76.
5. Yaseer, S. M., Mohamad, A. M., Omar, T., Abu, H. I. and Omran, H. 2103. Comparative performance of bird's eye chili using open fertigation and conventional planting system. *Buletin Teknologi MARDI* 3: 25-28.

Abstract No: A-442

OIL PALM SUSTAINABILITY STANDARDS IN MALAYSIA AND PEATLAND MANAGEMENT

Sanath Kumaran and Harnarinder Singh

Malaysian Palm Oil Certification Council, Malaysia

**Corresponding author: sanath@mpocc.org.my*

SUMMARY

At present, in the context of the Malaysian palm oil sector, there are two certification schemes under which a management unit or entity can be verified to provide assurance of compliance to agreed sustainability standards. These are the Malaysian Sustainable Palm Oil (MSPO) Certification Scheme using the MSPO Standards and the Roundtable on Sustainable Palm Oil (RSPO) Scheme using the RSPO Principles and Criteria. The Malaysian Palm Oil Certification Council (MPOCC) was incorporated in December 2014 and started its operations in October 2015. MPOCC is now the scheme owner of the MSPO Certification Scheme. MPOCC is an independent organisation tasked with developing and implementing the national palm oil certification scheme for all the three regions of Peninsular, Sabah and Sarawak. The MSPO Standards used under the scheme cover a range of Principles that take into account aspects related to transparency, management responsibilities, compliance to legal requirements, best practices, environmental and social responsibilities, employment conditions, health and safety of workers, and development of new plantings. However, the depth and level of details in the Principles, Criteria, Indicators and requirements that address the topics vary. The Standards also have consideration for plantings by independent and organised smallholders. This paper reviews the background on the development of the MSPO Standards, the institutional set-up of MPOCC and the compliance requirements of the MSPO Standards with specific emphasis on oil palm development and management on peat lands.

Keywords: *MSPO, MPOCC, certification scheme, peat lands*

INTRODUCTION

In the world today, oil palm is the highest yielding source of vegetable oil. Palm oil is an important commodity and a versatile raw material used in many processed foods, and is found in many household names. Increasingly, palm oil is used as a renewable feedstock for electricity and biofuel generation. Driven by global demands, in the past several decades, the world has seen rapid expansion of palm oil production leading to a significant and positive economic impact, promoting rural development by improving the livelihood standards of smallholders. At the same time, degradation of land and quality of water, and adversity of ecological impacts have also risen as a result of the expansion of palm oil production. Therefore, there is an urgent need to expand **sustainable** oil palm areas and production. The expansion is more than just improved management practices, but more of what can be done to support producers to work responsibly towards achieving sustainability certification.

In Malaysia, the benefits of oil palm cultivation have contributed significantly to the national economy. In 2015, the total export revenue from palm oil and palm based products was RM60.17 billion. However, large scale oil palm cultivation on forested lands and peat lands has inadvertently also impacted our nation's biodiversity, and in many instances continue to pose a threat. The expansion of oil palm cultivation also gives rise to negative social impacts, especially in the form of conflicts over land use and ownership rights, and lack of free and prior informed consent (FPIC) of local communities and indigenous peoples.

The core of oil palm sustainability is intertwined by four primary aspects, encompassing legal compliance, environment, social and economy. The development and effective implementation of certification of oil palm management practices is seen as a feasible way for the industry to demonstrate compliance with good practices and continued improvement. In Malaysia, there are two dominant oil palm management certification standards that are relevant to the above scenario. These are the MSPO and RSPO Standards. The MSPO Standards are the national oil palm certification standards that have been developed through a standards development process with inputs from the relevant stakeholders of the palm oil sector. The MSPO Standards are currently voluntary and align the management of palm oil production with existing national laws and regulations to achieve the implementation of sustainable practices of oil palm operations on peat lands. This paper reviews the MSPO Standards on the requirements for compliance with environmental provisions, with specific emphasis on oil palm development and management on peat lands.

BACKGROUND OF MSPO STANDARDS

The MSPO Standards are voluntary and industry driven, aimed at defining the principles and criteria for sustainable palm oil production. In 2011, two committees for the development of MSPO Standards were established; the National Committee and the Technical Working Committee. Both committees had representatives from the oil palm industry, academia, MPOB and MPOC and met regularly during 2012 and 2013 to draft the MSPO Standards. In 2013, the final MSPO Standards were adopted as MS Standards. Following that, in 2014, a number of pilot audits were carried out and under this initiative, several large companies were awarded MSPO certification. During this period, MPOB also conducted training sessions for auditors and held awareness sessions with potential clients on the requirements of the MSPO Standards and auditing procedures in the implementation of the scheme. In January 2015, the Honourable Minister of MPIC had officially announced the start of the MSPO Certification Scheme. By May 2016, a total of 128,160 ha of oil palm plantings by 9 large companies have been MSPO certified, together with 13 palm oil mills. In addition, eight smallholder groups with a total of 5,301 ha have also been certified.

Beginning January 2016, MPOCC has become the scheme owner and is now overall responsible for the development and operation of the MSPO Certification Scheme.

MPOB is a Standards Writing Organisation (SWO) sanctioned by SIRIM Berhad which is the national Standards Development Agency (SDA), and is responsible for the development and review of standards for the palm oil products, oil-based food products, palm kernel products and oil palm-based products. MPOB will continue to be the facilitator for the National Committee for MSPO and the Technical Working Committee for MSPO to further develop and review the MSPO Standards.

INSTITUTIONAL SET-UP OF MPOCC

Incorporated as a company in December 2014, MPOCC is an independent organisation and the owner of the MSPO Certification Scheme. MPOCC has been tasked with the implementation and operation of the national scheme in Peninsular, Sabah and Sarawak. The objects for which MPOCC is established are: (i) to create, maintain and administer a fund to be used for the purposes of establishing and operating a sustainable palm oil certification scheme in Malaysia; (ii) to engage with non-governmental organisations, institutions of higher learning, trade associations, and accreditation and certification bodies in Malaysia; (iii) to establish a mechanism for the certification of premises complying to sustainability requirements of auditable sustainability standards to process applications of certifications, formulating rules with regards to the use and issues of certification, approval of assessors' certification reports, appeals and complaints procedures, and certification costs.

The management of the affairs of MPOCC is governed by a 13-member Board of Trustees, comprising representatives from MPIC, MPOB, academic/research and development institutes, NGOs, oil palm industry associations, smallholders' organisation and civil society. Being overall in charge for the development and operation of the MSPO Certification Scheme, MPOCC is accountable, amongst others, for the development and implementation of the scheme documents, and for providing briefing and training sessions to stakeholders and auditors of the certification bodies (CBs) and Department of Standards Malaysia (DSM), with the aim to facilitate and increase the uptake of MSPO certification.

DEVELOPMENT AND REVIEW OF STANDARDS

The MSPO Standards (MS 2530:2013 series) are national standards, committing the oil palm industry players in the country to voluntarily meet sustainability requirements. It targets the entire industry on board within the shortest possible time and strive for continuous improvement. The MSPO Certification Scheme provides for independent third party auditing of oil palm cultivation and mill management practices to ensure the sustainable management of oil palm as well as to meet the demand for certified palm oil. Independent assessors (Certification Bodies) have to comply with *ISO 17021 – Requirements for bodies providing audit and certification of management systems* to obtain accreditation from DSM, the NAB, in order for the CBs to operate oil palm management certification under the MSPO Certification Scheme. The MSPO Standards address requirements pertaining to the principles and criteria of sustainability based on the 5P's of the sustainable development model (People, Planet, Peace, Partnership and Prosperity), which includes taking into consideration stakeholders processes. As the MSPO Standards have just recently been developed and implemented, it is only natural that they will take some time to gain full and meaningful acceptance by the various stakeholders, and in doing so, gain traction in the market.

The MS 2530:2013 series of MSPO Standards consists of four parts; i.e. Part 1: General principles; Part 2: General principles for independent smallholders; Part 3: General principles for oil palm plantation and organised smallholders; and Part 4: General principles for palm oil mills. This series of MSPO Standards was developed by MPOB as the SWO, under its Technical Committee on Fats and Oils. The entire process was under the purview of DSM which is the National Standards Body, providing confidence to various stakeholders, through credible standardisation and accreditation services for global competitiveness.

The final drafts of the MSPO Standards were submitted to SIRIM Berhad and were put up on the SIRIM website in 2012 and again in 2013 for public comment. The public comments received were collated and incorporated into the final drafts of the MSPO Standards, which were submitted to DSM to be adopted as the Malaysian Standards (MS). The MS Standards were approved by the Honourable Minister of Science, Technology and Innovations on 5 September 2013 and launched by the Honourable Deputy Prime Minister on 19 November during the MPOB International Palm Oil Congress and Exhibition (PIPOC) 2013.

The accreditation system of DSM is in accordance with the international standard, MS *ISO/IEC 17011 Conformity assessment - General requirements for accreditation bodies accrediting conformity assessment bodies*. Conformance to this standard ensures that the accreditation services provided are impartial, non-discriminatory and credible. All certification bodies accredited by DSM receive international recognition through the accreditation granted by the International Accreditation Forum's (IAF) Multilateral Recognition Arrangement (MLA), and the ILAC Mutual Recognition Arrangement (MRA) accreditation body signatories that are recognised worldwide.

SMALLHOLDERS PROVISION

It is a known fact that any kind of sustainability certification for smallholders is challenging. There is a huge set of requirements, both managerial and agronomic capacities, which many smallholders lack at present in order to meet the certification standards. Smallholders face various problems and challenges when it comes to sustainability certification. Most of them are small land holdings, while many of them are unorganised, have low oil palm productivity and lack the knowledge and capacity to embrace new and more effective oil palm technologies.

The MSPO standards apply to all producers, large plantations, estates and smallholders, both organised and independent. In Malaysia, smallholders are an important group of producers in the oil palm sector. The smallholders (independent and schemes such as FELDA, FELCRA, RISDA, SALCRA, SEDC / government agencies) in total account for 40% of the oil palm planted area, while the remaining 60% is owned by private plantation companies and estates. Standards can only be effective from an economic, ecological and social perspective if they apply to this important group of palm oil producers. Hence, the MSPO Standards (MS 2530:2013 series) have been developed to include this important group of palm oil producers. For the independent smallholders who operate independently throughout all the phases of production, the MS 2530-2:2013 is applicable, while for organised smallholders who are tied to large plantations and mills, the MS 2530-3:2013 is applicable.

To assist these smallholders, MPOB has extension workers (TUNAS) spread all over the country, particularly in areas with a high concentration of independent smallholders, to group and organise the smallholders by establishing Sustainable Palm Oil Clusters (SPOCs) (Wahid, *et. al.*, 2012). For this purpose, MPOB being aware of this daunting challenge of certifying smallholdings, is committed to the inclusion of these significant key players and have begun to address the needs of smallholders being certified against the MSPO Standards. MPOB has set aside funding and technical expertise support for the smallholder sector. In August 2015, the Malaysian government announced the allocation of RM53 million to assist the oil palm smallholders in obtaining MSPO certification within the next five years.

Definition of peat

Peat soils are soils with organic soil material which make up more than half the total cumulative thickness of the upper 100 cm. If the depth of the bedrock is less than 100 cm, the total thickness of the organic soil layers taken cumulatively is more than half the depth to bedrock. (Source: MS 2530:2013)

Tropical peat soils (Histosols) are defined as organic soils with 65% or more organic matter and a depth of 50 cm or more. (Source: Lim, et al.,2012)

COMPLIANCE REQUIREMENTS FOR OIL PALM DEVELOPMENT ON PEAT LANDS

Peat or organic soils, are formed by the accumulation of organic soil materials on the soil surface. These materials consist of undecomposed, partially decomposed and highly decomposed plant remains (Paramananthan, 2016). In Malaysia, peat lands have been experiencing rapid land use changes over the past decade which has resulted in alteration on peat land ecology, biodiversity and hydrology to globally significant carbon emissions. Analyses done by various researchers show continued peat land deforestation and conversion into industrial oil palm plantations and smallholder areas in Malaysia. The majority of these conversions on peat lands are for oil palm plantations (99%), while the remaining (1%) are for pulp wood plantations and others.

Table 1 shows that in the last decade, there has been an increase in industrial oil palm plantation areas in the peat lands, with most of the expansion occurring in Sarawak (Omar, *et. al.*, 2010; Miettinen *et.al.*, 2016). With such a trend, it is therefore imperative that for oil palm development on peat lands to be in compliance with the sustainability requirements of the MSPO Standards, the practitioners must adopt good agricultural and management practices and other industry standards.

Table 1. Distribution oil palm planted areas, extent of peat lands, and oil palm, pulp and other plantations on peat lands in Peninsular, Sabah and Sarawak ('000 ha)

Region	Oil palm planted areas (2015)#	Extent of peat lands (2016)*	Oil palm plantations on peat lands (2010)^	Oil palm plantations on peat lands (2016)**	Pulp and other/unknown plantings on peat lands (2016)**	Total (2016)**
Peninsular	2,659.36	796.78	207.46	275.68	3.67	279.35
Sabah	1,544.22	200.60	21.41	66.00	0.20	66.20
Sarawak	1,439.36	1,765.55	437.17	717.83	7.22	725.09
Malaysia	5,642.97	2,762.93	666.04	1,060.00	11.09	1,070.64

Reference: #MPOB, 2015; *Paramanathan, 2016; ^Omar *et al.*, 2010; **Miettinen *et al.*, 2016

It is for this reason, that the oil palm industry is constantly being pressured to implement policies and regulations for sustainable peat land management in improving the existing management practices, while at the same time protecting the remaining peat swamp forests and increasing rehabilitation efforts in deforested and degraded peat lands. It is a known fact that the annual repeated peat land fires contribute to the transboundary haze episodes (Gaveau, *et al.*, 2014), causing significant economic losses as well as inflicting adverse health impacts. Therefore, compliance requirements for good oil palm practices on peat land are clearly embedded in the MSPO sustainability standards which have provisions on peat land plantings and good management practices.

The MSPO Standards clearly explain and define principles, criteria, indicators and requirements for compliance with environmental provisions. For this, the standards rely heavily on national legislation as one of the means of compliance. Even though the MSPO Standards do not outright prohibit oil palm planting on peat lands, there is a common aim amongst industry players and relevant stakeholders to find solutions on the pressing peat land management challenges. The provisions in the MSPO Standards for the development of new plantings that are related to peat land development and management are as described in Table 2.

Table 2. Specific provisions in the MSPO Standards for compliance requirements on planting on marginal and fragile soils, which include peat lands

Principle 7: Development of new plantings	
Criterion	**Indicator**
Criterion 2: Peat land	Indicator 1: New planting and replanting may be developed and implemented on peat land as per MPOB guidelines on peat land development or industry best practice.
Criterion 4: Soil and topographic information	Indicator 1: Information on soil types shall be adequate to establish the long-term suitability of the land for oil palm cultivation. Indicator 2: Topographic information shall be adequate to guide the planning of planting programmes, drainage and irrigation systems, roads and other infrastructure.
Criterion 5: Planting on steep terrain, marginal and fragile soils	Indicator 1: Extensive planting on steep terrain, marginal and fragile soils shall be avoided unless permitted by local, state and national laws. Indicator 2: Where planting on fragile and marginal soils is proposed, plans shall be developed and implemented to protect them and to minimise adverse impacts (e.g. hydrological) or significantly increased risks (e.g. fire risk) in areas outside the plantation. Indicator 3: Marginal and fragile soils, including excessive gradients and peat soils, shall be identified prior to conversion.

It must be noted that the MSPO Standards call for avoidance of planting on these soils unless permitted by the local, state and national laws. As a mitigation measure, where planting on peat lands is proposed, mitigation plans shall be developed and implemented to protect them without incurring adverse impacts. As for the establishment of new plantings and replanting, the MSPO Standards allow for the development of oil palm on peat lands as per the guidelines on peat land development or industry best practices (MPOB, 2011). The guidance includes good water management to minimise peat oxidation and subsidence, fertilizer and nutrient management, management of leaning and fallen palms, minimizing greenhouse gases, fire prevention and control, and cooperation with local communities and indigenous peoples.

Conclusion

The MSPO Standards have an ultimate aim of being credible sustainability standards for the palm oil industry in Malaysia, to bring about positive social, environmental and economic impacts, while minimising negative impacts. Legality requirements are fundamental compliance aspects which are covered in the Principles and Criteria of the sustainability standards.

There is ample evidence to show that certification also improves visibility and inventory management of all suppliers and provides a competitive advantage to access international markets. Certification provides proof of a robust management system which enhances stakeholder confidence while improving compliance to meet all legal, regulatory and sustainability requirements.

The MSPO Standards have their own strengths and shortcomings, depending very much on the aspects in comparison. The Standards address oil palm development on peat lands by adopting best management practices for existing plantations and for new plantings on peat lands. The oil palm industry is indeed very dynamic and certification is seen as an effective tool to demonstrate compliance to good practices and agreed standards. As such, the MSPO Standards will be subject to periodic reviews to ensure that the requirements and thresholds contained in the standards not only meet but exceed stakeholder expectations.

REFERENCES

1. Gaveau, D.L.A., Salim, M.A., Hergoualc'h, K., Locatelli, B., Sloan, S., Wooster, M., Marlier, M.E., Molidena, E., Yaen, H., DeFries, R., Verchot, L., Murdiyarso, D., Nasi, R., Holmgren, P., Sheil, D., 2014. Major atmospheric emissions from peat fires in Southeast Asia during non-drought years: evidence from the 2013 Sumatran fires. Sci. Rep. 4, 6112.
2. Lim, K.H., Lim, S.S., Parish, F. and Suharto, R. (Eds), 2012. RSPO Manual on Best Management Practices (BMPs) for Existing Oil Palm Cultivation on Peat. RSPO, Kuala Lumpur, 220 pp.
3. Miettinen, J., Shi, C and Liew, S.C., 2016. Land cover distribution in the peatlands of Peninsular Malaysia, Sumatra and Borneo in 2015 with changes since 1990. Global Ecology and Conservation 6(2016): 67-78.
4. MPIC, 2014. Statistics on Commodities 2014, Ministry of Plantation Industries and Commodities, 196pp.
5. MPOB, 2011. Guidelines for the Development of a Standard Operating Procedure for Oil Palm Cultivation on Peat.
6. MS2530:2013. Malaysian Sustainable Palm Oil Standards, Department of Standards Malaysia.
7. Omar, W., Abd Aziz, N., Mohammed, A. T., Harun, H. H. and Din, A. K., 2010. Mapping of Oil Palm Cultivation on Peatland in Malaysia. MPOB Information Series. ISSN 1551-7871. MPOB TT No. 473. June 2010.
8. Paramananthan, S., 2016. Organic Soils of Malaysia: Their characteristics, mapping, classification and management for oil palm cultivation. MPOC, 156 pp.
9. Wahid, O, Nazirah, C.J and Nur, H.M., 2012. Smallholder Palm Oil Cluster: Sharing MPOB's Experience. Presentation at RT10, Annual Roundtable Meeting on Sustainable Palm Oil, Singapore.

Abstract No: A-245

PEAT SOIL RECLAMATION FOR MAIZE (Zea mays L.)

F. B. Arief [1], S. W. Atmojo[2], S. Sagiman [3], J. Sutrisno [4] and T. Onishi [5]

[1] *Department of Soil Sciences, Faculty of Agriculture, Tanjungpura University, Indonesia,*
[2] *Department of Soil Sciences, Faculty of Agriculture,Sebelas Maret University, Indonesia*
[3] *Department of Soil Sciences, Faculty of Agriculture, Tanjungpura University, Indonesia,*
[4] *Department of Agribusiness Sciences, Faculty of Agriculture, Sebelas Maret University, Indonesia*
[5] *Department of Applied Bioscience, Gifu University, Japan*

**Corresponding author: feirabarief@untan.ac.id; suntoro_uns@yahoo.co.id; saerisagiman@untan.ac.id; jokotris_uns@yahoo.com; takeon@gifu-u.ac.jp*

SUMMARY

By the pressure of agricultural land outside needs will require expansion of agricultural land in Indonesia to achieve national food needs. Expansion of agricultural land leads to marginal lands that exist such as peat land. Past research has shown that the use of peat for agriculture needs to be reclaimed in advance in order to improve its fertility. The purpose of this study is to examine the use of coastal sediment as an alternative to peat land reclamation material for maize. This study was conducted on two types of peat soil thickness (less than 2 meters and more than 2 meters). Coastal sediment that is used is sourced from the Kijing beach with three dose levels based on the percentage of weight. The result showed that 10% coastal sediment provides more good results for maize production.

***Keywords**: peat soil, reclamation, coastal sediment*

INTRODUCTION

Peat land area in the world is estimated at about 400 million ha. Indonesia is a country with the fourth largest peat swamp in the world, which is about 17.2 million ha as Canada covering 170 million hectares, the Soviet Union of 150 million ha, and the United States covering 40 million hectares (Euroconsult, 1984). However, from the various reports, Indonesia is actually the country the largest tropical peat in the world, which is between 13.5 to 26.5 million ha (average of 20 million ha). If the area of Indonesian peat is 20 million ha, about 50% of the world's tropical peat covers about 40 million ha in Indonesia. Up to now the data peat land area in Indonesia is not standardized, so the data extents that can be used is in the range of 13.5 to 26.5 million ha. The extent of peat and complex functions, shows how peat has a very important meaning for human life . Indonesia is a vast country with the fourth largest peat in the world is about 20 million hectares (ha) after Canada (170 million ha), the USSR (150 million ha) , and the United States (40 million ha). But from the reports turned out to peat land area in Indonesia varied between 13.5 to 26.5 ha (average of 20 million ha). The spread of peat lands is generally found on larger islands, such as Sumatra, Kalimantan and Papua.

According Subiksa *et al* (2009) diversity of tropical peat land physical and chemical properties are large, both spatially and vertically. Characteristics are determined by the thickness of the peat, mineral soil substratum or below the peat, maturity, and presence or absence of enrichment of the surrounding river overflow.

The peat soils are very acidic in nature with a pH of 3.7 (Melling *et al*, 2002). Base on some previous researches, the application of costal sediment can increase pH of peat soil. The improvement of peat soil properties than increased the crops growth such as soybean and maize (Sagiman and Pujianto, 1994; Suyadi, 1995; Sagiman, 2001; Suswati, 2012).

Therefor the aims of this study were to obtain the best number coastal sediment in peat soil reclamation for maize growth in different thicness of peat soil (less than 2 meters and more than 2 meters). A series of stages of the research will be carried out in the laboratory and an experiment was conducted on peat soil at the District of Kubu Raya, West Borneo Province, Indonesia.

METHODS

Time and Stages of Research:

This research was conducted for approximately one growing season of maize (6 months). From preparation, preliminary survey locations peat, soil survey and land evaluation, sampling, laboratory analysis and data analysis. This study was conducted in four stages. The first stage of the study is peat soil evaluation to find the peat soil thickness in research location. The second stage of the study is collecting coastal sediment from several locations and analyzed in the laboratory to determine the physical and chemical characteristics. The third stage of the study is to find out soil properties from coastal sediment, especially chemical properties of coastal sediment that related with the peat soil improvement for plant growth. The last stage is the plant test of maize or corn (*Zea mays* L.) in the research location.

Sites Description:

The first studied site is peat soil at Kuala Dua Village, the District of Kubu Raya, West Borneo Province, Indonesia. This site have peat soil with diferent thichness from 50 cm to more than 5 m (deep peat). Same location have agriculture cultivation with more than three crops, like vegetable, maize or corn (*Zea mays* L.) , and soybean (*Glycine max*).

The second are the location of the source coastal sediment from Kijing beach, the District of Mempawah, approximately 160 kilometers from Pontianak, as a capital provincial of West Borneo and coastal sediment from the District of Kubu Raya coast, West Borneo Province.

Methods:

The site of peat soil in the location be divided two levels of peat thickness (0 to 2 meters as T_1 and more than 2 m as T_2). We use four dose of coastal sediment (four treatment): 1) L0 : 0 % of weigh or without coastal sediment (as control), 2) L1 : 5 % weigh, 3) L2 : 10 % weigh, 4) L3 : 15 % weigh and as the comparison we used lime (D) as a comparison (10% weight).

The study results will be seen from production of maize with corncob and shelled corn. Analysis of the survey results at the Laboratory of Soil Survey and Land Evaluation and analysis of samples in the Laboratory of Soil Physics and Chemistry, Faculty of Agriculture, University of Tanjungpura.

RESULTS

From the first stage of the study (peat soil evaluation to find out peat soil thickness) are two category of land base on field (on two types of peat soil thickness: 1) less than 2 m, and 2) more than 2 m)(Figure 1).

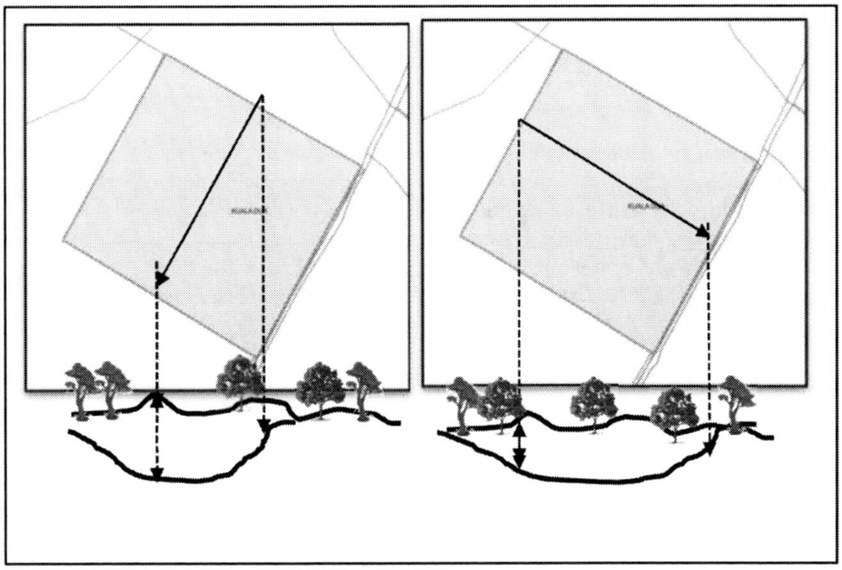

Figure 1. Illustration thickness of the peat in the study site

From the second stage of the study (collecting coastal sediment from several locations and analyzed in the laboratory to determine the physical and chemical characteristics) show coastal sediment from Kijing beach, the District of Mempawah, have good physical (finely textured) and chemical characteristics (high pH)(Table 1).

Table 1. Data Analysis Of Ph And Texture Of Coastal Sediment From Several Location In West Borneo, Indonesia

Number	Coastal Location	Parameters analysis				
		pH		(%)		
		H_2O	KCl	Sand	Silt	Clay
1.	Muara Dabong 1	5,50	5,14	2,53	55,71	41,76
2.	Muara Dabong 2	5,67	5,28	37,04	29,13	33,83
3.	Muara Dabong 3	5,77	5,37	53,79	20,31	25,90
4.	Kijing	8,03	7,73	0,71	51,58	47,71
5.	Muara Kubu	5,80	5,45	2,89	53,37	43,74
6.	Tanjung Radak	4,20	4,07	0,28	53,01	46,71

Note: The results of the analysis of Chemistry and Soil Fertility Laboratory, Faculty of Agriculture, Tanjungpura University

From the last stage (the peat soil improvement for plant growth) in general show that the use of coastal sediment having the same effect in supporting the harves of maize in the peat soil like lime(Table 2).

Table 2. Data Corn Yields With The Use Of Coastal Sediment As A Treatment In Peat Soil Reclamation

Peat Soil thickness	Treatment	Corn cob	Shelled corn	Peat Soil thickness	Treatment	Corn cob	Shelled corn
	D-1	148	88		D-1	160	102
	D-2	150	92		D-2	182	126
	D-3	154	94		D-3	174	114
	L_0-1	140	80		L_0-1	154	94
	L_0-2	172	114		L_0-2	152	92
	L_0-3	174	114		L_0-3	148	88
T_1 (less than 2 m)	L_1-1	136	76	T_2 (more than 2 m)	L_1-1	192	132
	L_1-2	202	160		L_1-2	206	156
	L_1-3	150	90		L_1-3	204	134
	L_2-1	154	94		L_2-1	194	134
	L_2-2	200	144		L_2-2	206	146
	L_2-3	158	98		L_2-3	204	134
	L_3-1	156	96		L_3-1	198	138
	L_3-2	190	132		L_3-2	192	132
	L_3-3	154	94		L_3-3	204	144

Note: L_0 : 0 % of weigh or without coastal sediment (as control), 2) L_1 : 5 % weigh, 3) L_2 : 10 % weigh and 4) L_3 : 15 % weigh and furthermore, as the comparison we used lime (D) as a comparison (10% weigh)

DISCUSSION

Soil survey and land evaluation on the research location show that area have is a stretch of peat-shaped dome from the edge of the river flow toward the middle of the field and back thinning on the other side. Farmers generally prefer to carry out planting food crops on land with shallow peat soil thickness while in ditanamai plantation crops such as rubber and oil palm.

Coastal sediment as treatment for T_1 (peat soil thickness less than 2 m) reclamation with 10%, give the best effect on corn yield. The grafic show that corn yield increasing from lime to 10% coastal sedimen than decrease in 15%. But for T_2 (peat soil thickness more than 2 m) show reclamation with 5% is highes. Chart shows also that for T_2 coastal sedimen or lime must give or essential to support the growth of corn harvest. This can be seen in the treatment without giving coastal sediment (L0) have very low results.

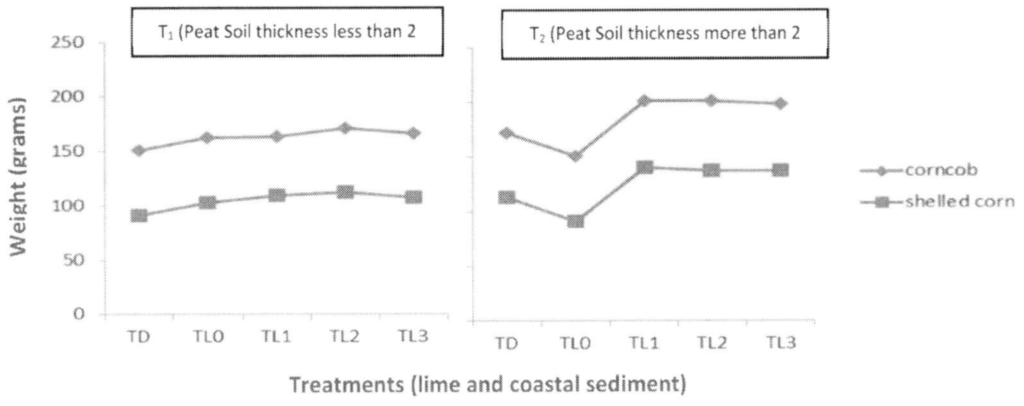

Figure 2. The graphs of the average production of corn cobs and shelled corn from all treatment: 1) TD (lime 10% weight), 2) TL0 (without coastal sediment), 3) TL1 (5% coastal sediment), 4) TL2 (10% coastal sediment) and 5) TL3 (use 15% coastal sediment)

CONCLUSION

1. In general this study indicate that the use of coastal sediment having the same effect in supporting the growth of maize in the peat soil like lime.
2. Award coastal sediment treatment of as much as 10% give the best effect on corn yield in peat soil with thicness less than 2 m and for peat soil with thickness more than 2 m, 5% is highes.
3. The influence of the use of coastal sediment applies to both the peat with a thickness of less than 2 meters and a thickness of more than 2 meters.

ACKNOWLEDGMENTS

1. Ministry of Research Technology and Higher Education was financed in part from the study.
2. Rector of Tanjungpura University and Dean of Agricultur Faculty Tanjungpura University that financed a trip to 15th International Peat Congress 2016 (15th IPC 2016), 15-19 August 2016, Pullman Hotel Kuching, Sarawak, Malaysia.
3. Mr. Adi Yani and staff, who help to pay the registration fee in 15th IPC 2016.
4. Ph. D. Program of Agricultural Sciences, Graduate Program, University Sebelas Maret, Surakarta, who give recommendation to register in 15th IPC 2016 as student from Indonesia.

REFERENCES

1. Euroconsult. 1984. Nation–wide Study Coastal and Near –coastal Swamps Land in Sumatra, Kalimantan and Irian Jaya. Executive Report. Dir. Gen. of Water Res. Development, Min. of Public Work, Jakarta and Euroconsult, Arnhem/BIEC. Bandung.
2. Melling, L., Ryusuke Hatano and Mitsuru Osaki. 2002. Sustainable Agriculture Development on Tropical Peatland. Paper no. 1919 Poster Presentation at 17th WCSS. Thailand. 14-21 August 2002.
3. Sagiman,S. 2001. Peningkatan produksi kelelai di tanah gambut melalui inokulasi *Bradyrhizobium japonicum* asal tanah gambut dan pemanfaatan bahan ameliorant (lumpur dan kapur). Disertasi Doktor Program Pasca Sarjana IPB.
4. Sagiman,S. dan Pujianto. 1994. Lumpur laut sebagai pembenah gambut untuk produksi tanaman kedelai. Seminar Nasional 25 tahun pemanfaatan gambut dan pengembangan kawasan pasang surut. BPPT. Jakarta. 14-15 Desember, 1994.
5. Subiksa, IGM., Ai Dariah dan F. Agus. 2009. Sistem Pengelolaan Lahan Eksisting di Kalimantan Barat serta Implikasinya terhadap Siak Kimia Tanah Gambut dan Emisi GRK. Laporan Penelitian Kerjasama Balai Penelitian tanah dengan Kementrian Ristek.
6. Suswati, D. 2012. Pemanfaatan Bahan Amelioran Dalam Meningkatkan Potensi Kesesuaian Lahan Gambut Untuk pengembangan Jagung Di Rasau Jaya III Kabuparen Kubu Raya. Disertasi Doktor Program Pasca Sarjana Fakultas Pertanian Universitas Gajah Mada Yogyakarta.
7. Suyadi. 1995. Influence of coastal sediment and lime on peat chemical properties in relation to soybean cultivation. Thesis for Master of Science in Agriculture. Institute of Agronomy in the tropics Faculty of Agriculture Georg-August-University-Gotingen, Germany.

Abstract No: A-075

PERFORMANCE OF BIOLOGICAL AGENT AND CHEMICAL TO CONTROL SUBTERRANEAN TERMITE, *COPTOTERMES CURVIGNATHUS* IN OIL PALM PLANTED ON PEAT IN SARAWAK

Saharul Abillah Mohamad[1], Mohamad Rosman Sulaiman[1], Ramle Moslim[1], Zulkefli Masijan[1], Siaw Ting Chuan[2] and Norman Kamarudin[1]

[1]*Applied Entomology and Microbiology Unit, Biology Research Division, Malaysian Palm Oil Board (MPOB), Malaysia*
[2]*Research and Development Department, Ta Ann Plantations Sdn Bhd, Malaysia*

**Corresponding author: saharul.abillah@mpob.gov.my*

SUMMARY

The subterranean termite *Coptotermes curvignathus* is a major insect pest for oil palm planted on peat. The termite infestation can be found on oil palm as early as 12 month after planting and could kill palm up to 5.3%. A field evaluation of two entomopathogenic fungi, *Beauveria bassiana* and *Metarhizium anisopliae* and a chemical pesticide, fipronil, was conducted to control subterranean termite *C. curvignathus*. The experiment was conducted from June 2015 to January 2016 on 10 years old oil palm planted on peat in Sibu, Sarawak. Pre-census data conducted a week prior treatment showed that severity of termite infestation in the experimental site was relatively high at 24.75%. Only infected palms with termite colonies were treated. The treatments were applied by soil injection and spraying of palm trunk. At three months after treatment (MAT), there were no significant differences were recorded between treatments in terms of their effectiveness in controlling the termite population. At this stage the percentage of control by *M. anisopliae* and *B. bassiana* were 51% and 28.66%, respectively. It was also observed that 58.30% of the palms treated with fipronil were free from termite. At 7 MAT, the performance of all three treatments is equally good in controlling the population of termite. It was found that the fungus *M. anisopliae* gave the highest control of 66.54%, followed by *B. bassiana* of 65.07% and fipronil of 58.08%. This experiment provided a positive encouragement towards the ability of biological control agents in providing long term control of termite. Further trials are needed to evaluate the baiting method to reduce especially the termite population in peat planted with oil palm.

Keywords: *Oil palm, subterranean termite, Coptotermes curvignathus, fipronil, Beauveria bassiana, Metarhizium anisopliae and peat*

INTRODUCTION

Termite is one of the major pests that are threatening oil palm planted on peat areas in Sarawak. The most damaging genus to oil palm was *Coptotermes*. They feed on healthy tissues of oil palm, causing the severely infected palms to topple. Basri (2003) reported that termite infestation could cause death to palm up to 5.3%. It was also reported that termite colonies attack oil palm as early as 12 month after field planting (Lim *et al.*, 2001). Management of termite was mostly relying on organophosphate termiticides, best applied by drenching or spraying at the base of the infected palms (Lim *et al.*, 2001 and Zulkefli *et al.*, 2012). Sustainable managements of termite to replace hazardous chemical termiticides were urgently needed. Pik Kheng *et al.*, (2009) and Ramle *et al.*, (2011) reported that the entomopathogenic fungi *Beauveria bassiana* and *Metarhizium anisopliae* have a potential to control termite. Laboratory screening tests showed that these fungi could kill 100% termite when treated with spores solution between 10^7 spores/ml and 10^8 spores/ml. This study aims to evaluate the field performance of both entomopathogenic fungi and the chemical pesticide, fipronil, to control the population of *C. curvignathus* on mature oil palm planted on peat in Sarawak.

MATERIALS AND METHODS

Experimental site and severity of termite infestation

The study commenced on June 2015 in deep peat at Block 306 3A, Naman Estate, Ta Ann Plantations Sdn Bhd in Sibu, Sarawak. The experiment was covering 120 palm rows with 17 planting points in each row, thus accounted a total of 2040 palms. The palm age was 11 years old, mostly planted in 2004 using the DxP planting material of FELDA. A week prior treatment, pre census were conducted to determine the severity of termite infestation in the experimental site. Numbers of infested palms, vacant planting points as palm collapsed due to termite infestation and numbers of newly supply palms were counted for estimation. The pre census data showed that the level of termite infestation was at 24.75%. There are 387 vacant planting points, 25 newly supply palms and 93 infested palms in the experimental plot. Active termite colonies are still visible on most of the rotting stumps of collapsed palms.

Palms with active termite activities indicated by having fresh mud-works on trunks, fronds and bunches were marked for treatment.

Treatments

Three treatments were evaluated in this study. Treatment 1 (T1) was entomopathogenic fungi *Beauveria bassiana*, T2 was *Metarhizium anisopliae* var. *major* and T3 was the chemical insecticide, fipronil.

Both of the entomopathogenic fungi *B.bassiana* and *M.anisopliae* was mass produced on 150gm of autoclaved rice placed inside the head resistant transparent plastic bags. The bags were incubated for two weeks at 28°C then the bags were transferred to the experimental site. The spores were harvested by adding 500 ml of water with 0.02% Tween 80 into the bags, then thoroughly shaken and sieved through 150µm sieve. The concentration of spore suspension was adjusted to 10^7 spores/ml. For preparation of treatment fipronil solution, 1ml of Chalcid 5SC (fipronil 5.5% w/w) was diluted by mixing it with 10ml of water (Table 1).

Table 1: Rate of application of treatments used in this study

Treatment	Application rate
T1 - *B. bassiana*	10^7 spores/ml
T2 - *M. anisopliae*	10^7 spores/ml
T3- *Fipronil*	1ml/10L

Experimental design and application of treatments

The experimental was carried out in a randomized complete block design (RCBD) with three sub-plots for each treatment. As termite infestation was scattered throughout the blocks, the numbers of infected palms used for treatment was varied, ranging from more than 5 to 20 infected palms in each sub-plot. Treatments were applied on palms with termite activities. Application of treatments was done using the following methods:

1. Direct spraying on the palm trunk
2. Soil injection around the palm base

Spraying of palm trunk was targeted onto fresh mud-work on palm trunk using a standard 16L knapsack sprayer. The whole palm trunk was sprayed with 8 litres of product solution until sufficient coverage was achieved. The palm was then further treated by soil injection product solution at 10 holes around the palm base at rate of 1 L per hole. The distance of the holes from the palm base and between holes was approximately one feet. Soil injection was conducted using a motorised soil injector equipped with a nozzle attached to bottom part of 4 feet long stainless rod with handle.

The effectiveness of treatments was assessed based on the presence of termite activities on the treated palms at 3 months after treatment (MAT) and 7 MAT. Palm was successfully controlled from termite attack when termites were not found on the whole palm trunk

RESULT AND DISCUSSION

The performance of treatments to control termite was showed in Table 2. At 3 MAT, palms treated with fipronil have the highest percentage of palms free from termite of 58.30%, followed by palms treated with *M. anisopliae* at 51% and *B.bassiana* at 28.66%. At this stage, the mean was not significantly different (P>0.05) between the treatments. At 7 MAT, the percentage of palms treated with *B.bassiana* and *M. anisopliae* free from termite were increased. Treatments of fungus *B. bassiana* and *M. anisopliae* have successfully controlled 65.07%

and 66.54% palms, respectively. Treatment of fipronil have successfully controlled 58.08% palms from the termite attack. As at 3 MAT, there were no significant difference (P>0.05) between means in all treatments.

Table 2: Percentage of treated mature standings free from active termite colonies

Treatment	Percentage of palms without termite activities over time after treatment (Month)	
	3 MAT	7 MAT
T1 - *B. bassiana*	28.66a	65.07a
T2 - *M. anisopliae*	51.00a	66.54a
T3 - *Fipronil*	58.30a	58.08a

Note. Means in columns with the same letters were not significantly different after DMRT at P=0.05.

Results from this study showed a potential used of both biological control agents in providing long term control on oil palm from termite infestation. This conformed to laboratory test findings of both Pik Kheng *et al.*, (2009) and Ramle *et al.*, (2011) who reported that both fungi were efficient in controlling termite *C. curvignathus*. In this study, both fungi *B.bassiana* and *M.anisopliae* were found equally good as fipronil to control termite infesting palm up to 6 MAT. The performance of these two fungi to control termites was much better as compared to our previous study (Saharul *et al.*, 2015). In our previous study, we found that fungus *B. bassiana* only gave 42% control and *M. anisopliae* gave 20% control at 9 MAT.

All three treatments gave satisfactory control over termite population when applied on matured palm in areas heavily infested by subterranean termite. It was suggested by Saharul *et al* (2015) that early preventive treatment should be practiced by applying entomopathogenic fungi or insecticide on young palms planted on areas with pest termite infestation history.

CONCLUSION

The biological agents, fungus *B. bassiana* and *M. anisopliae* applied by spraying on trunks and soil injection were equally good to control termite infestation on mature oil palm planted on peat. These two fungi was as good as chemical pesticide fipronil to control termites. A long term study on the potential of both fungi in reducing high termite population in peat need to be carried out. A baiting technique with entomopathogenic fungi is being developed and their efficacy in field will be evaluated soon.

ACKNOWLEDGEMENTS

The authors thank the Director General of Malaysian Palm Oil Board (MPOB) for permission to publish this paper. Thank also to staff of the Entomology and Ecological Research Group of the MPOB Research Station in Sessang, Sarawak. Thanks also dedicated to staff of Research and Development (R&D) Department, Ta Ann Plantations Sdn Bhd and workers of Naman Estate who involved in assisting this study.

REFERENCES

1. BASRI, M W., NORMAN, K., IDRIS A S., ARIFFIN D., SHAMALA, RAMLE M., and RAMLAH S A A (2003). Handbook of Pests and Diseases of Oil Palm, MPOB, Bangi.
2. LIM K H and SILEK, B (2001). Termite infestation on oil palm planted on deep peat in Sarawak; Tradewinds experience, Proceeding of the 2001 International Palm Oil Conference, 20-22 August 2001, Kuala Lumpur.
3. PIK KHENG H., CHONG FAH B J., KADIR J and AMARTALINGAM (2009). Evaluation of Metarhizium anisopliae (Deuteromycotina: Hyphomycete) isolated and their effects on subterranean termite *Coptotermes curvignathus* (Isoptera:Rhinotermitidae). American Journal of Agricultural and Biological Science 4(4):287-297
4. RAMLE M., ZULKEFLI M., BASRI M W. (2011). Susceptibility of termite *Coptotermes curvignathus* (Isoptera:Rhinotermitidae) sampled from oil palm tree against the entomopathogenic fungi. In proceeding Fourth IOPRI-MPOB International Seminar: Existing and Emerging Pests and Disease of Oil Palm Advances in Research and Management. 14 November 2011. KLCC.
5. SAHARUL A M.,ZULKEFLI M., RAMLE M., ROSMAN M S., and SIAW T C (2015). Field evaluation of entomopathogenic fungi and chemical to control termite, *Coptotermes curvignathus* on supply seedlings and mature oil palms on peat in Sarawak. In proceeding of 2015 PIPOC International Oil Palm Conference. 6-8 October 2015. Kuala Lumpur Convention Centre, Malaysia.
6. ZULKEFLI M., NORMAN K., BASRI M W., and MASRI M M (2012). Termites of oil palm in Malaysia: Identification and Management. MPOB. pp 3434

Abstract No: A-220

RESPONSES OF ONION TO *ARBUSCULAR MYCORRHIZAL* FUNGI AND TO WATER STRESS IN TROPICAL PEAT SOIL OF WEST KALIMANTAN, INDONESIA

Rini Suryani[1], Sutarman Gafur[2] and Tatang Abdurrahman[3]*

[1]Postgraduate Programme, Faculty of Agriculture, Tanjungpura University, Indonesia
[2]Department of Soil Science, Faculty of Agriculture, Tanjungpura University, Indonesia
[3]Department of Agronomy, Faculty of Agriculture, Tanjungpura University, Indonesia

Corresponding author: Mobile +62853 8600 3880; E-mail: sutarman.g@faperta.untan.ac.id

SUMMARY

Peat soil is one of the soil types in West Kalimantan that is potentially used for onion cultivation. The main concern for onion cultivation in peat soil are its physical characteristics which is easy to store and release water. Onion planted during dry-season will grow well when supplied with enough irrigation. Therefore, the use of arbuscular mycorrhizal fungi (AMF) in onions cultivation during water stress is a potential alternative approach to be studied. This research is designed to study the response of onions to AMF application and to water stress treatments in peat soil of West Kalimantan. The main aim is to find out a specific recommendation for onion cultivation in peat soil with limited water supply. The experiment was conducted in polybags within a plastic-roof building at the Field Experimental Land of Faculty of Agriculture, Tanjungpura University. The research used Split Plot Experimental Design with three replications.. AMF treatments functioned as main-plot consisting of 2 levels. Water stress treatments functioned as sub-plot consisting of 4 levels. There were in total 8 treatment combinations and 32 experimental units. AMF used consisted of the mixture of 3 types of AMF, namely: *Gigaspora margaritha, Glomus manihotis,* and *Acaulospora sp.* Parameters observed for this paper consist of plant height, leaves per clump, tillers per polybag, and total plant dry weight. The results showed that water stress over a period of more than 4 weeks will be a major obstruction in onion cultivation in peat soil. Onion grown in peat soil with limited level water stress condition responded significantly to AMF application. During limited water supply, onion will grow well either at 3 or 5 days watering interval when combined with AMF application.

Keywords: *Onion, arbuscular mycorrhizal fungi, drought stress, peat soil*

INTRODUCTION

Onion has become one of the strategic comodities in Indonesia. It has great economic value due to its increasing demand from year to year. Recently, however, there is a serious problem in onion distrubution system in Indonesia (BPS, 2015) which has translated to a big margin between the prices at producion level and prices at the consumers level, especially in metropolitan cities. The main factor is that planting sites are only found in certain places. Onion production in Indonesia is centered in East, Central, and West Java. There is a need to spread onion cultivation out side of Java, especially in Kalimantan. In West Kalimantan, onion is not yet a special commodity, eventhough peatland is a promising areas for onion cultivation.

Peat soil is one of the soil types in West Kalimantan that is potentially used for onion cultivation. Its total areas is about 1.73 billion hectars. The main concern for onions cultivation in peat soil are its physical characteristics of the peat which is easily to stores but also easily releases water. Onion planted during dry-season will grow well when supplied with enough water through irrigation. However, alternatives solution are nedded for the dry season. AMF hypha enable the plants to absorb water from the soil during dry season, especially when plants are unable to do it anymore (Setiadi, 1989). Previous studies had showed significant role of AMF on plant growth related to water conditions (Auge, 2001), water stress effect on onion yield in mineral soil (Pangaribuan, 2001, Pejic, et.al., 2014, Whalley, et.al., 2001). However, there is lack of studies on water stress and onion growth in peat soil. This research is designed to study the response of onions to AMF application and to water stress treatments in peat soil of West Kalimantan. The main aim is to find out a specific recommendation for onion cultivation in peat soil with limited water supply.

METHODS

The experiment was conducted by planting onions in polybags within the plastic-roof building at Field Experimental Land of Faculty of Agriculture, Tanjungpura University. It was started in January up to April 2016. The research is using Split Plot Experimental Design with three replications. The treatment consists of two factors. AMF treatments function as main-plot consisting of 2 levels (Without and With AMF). While water stress treatments function as sub-plot consisting of 4 levels (watered everyday, 3, 5, and 7 days watering intervals). There are total 8 treatment combinations and 32 experimental units. AMF used consist of the mixture of 3 types of AMF, namely: *Gigaspora margaritha, Glomus manihotis,* and *Acaulospora sp.* Parameters observed consist of plant height, leaves per clump, tillers per polybag, bulbs per polybag, total plant dry weight, bulb fresh weight per polybag, bulb dried weight per polybag, percentage of infected root, and nutrient content of N, P and K in the leaves.

RESULTS

Total leaves per clump

It was not significantly different among the treatment, but total leaves per clump is slighlty higher in AMF treatment than that of in without AMF (Figure 1). It had a similar trend either at 4 or 5 weeks after planting. At without AMF total leaves tended to decrease when the water stress level increased, while at with AMF total leaves increased in medium water stress levels (3 and 5 days watering intervals) then decreased when water stress increased into 7 days watering interval.

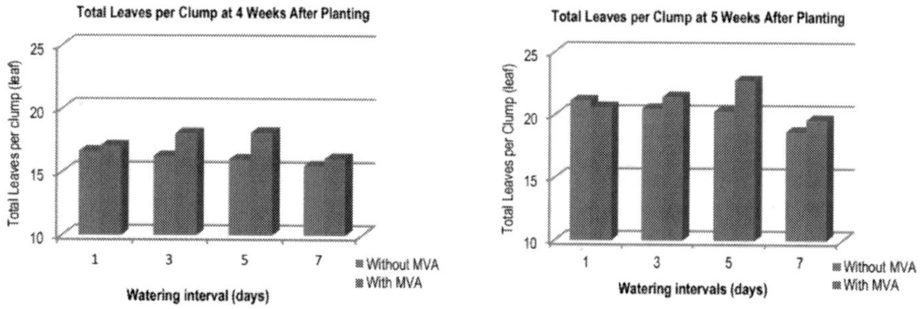

Figure 1. Total Leaves per Clump at 4 and 5 Weeks After Planting.

Total tillers per polybag

In general, total tiller per polybag was not significantly different among treatments (Figure 2). However, total tiller was higher in AMF treatment at higher stress level (5 and 7 days watering intervals). This trend was similar both in 4 and 5 weeks after planting.

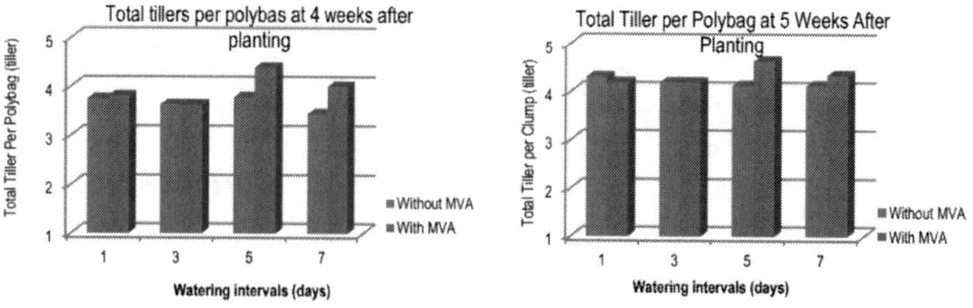

Figure 2. Total Tillers per Polybag at 4 and 5 weeks after Planting.

Plant height

AMF treatment greatly affected plant height (Figure 3), either at 4 or 5 weeks after planting. It has the same trend, plant height increased at medium water stress levels (3 and 5 days watering intervals) then decreased when water stress increased into 7 days interval. At the same time, at without AMF treatment plant height decrease proportionally when water stress gradually increase. The higher water stress level, the lower plant height.

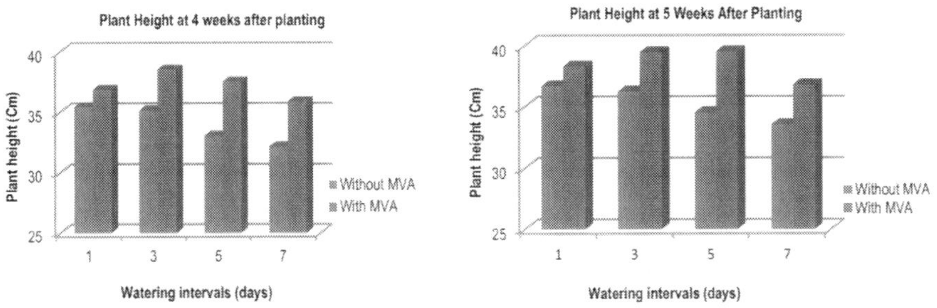

Figure 3. Plant heights at 4 and 5 weeks after planting.

Total Plant Dry Weight

Total plant dry weight (g) in figure 4 is the last parameter mirroring plant growth at this stage of this experiment. The best plant growth for treatment with AMF occured at 5 days watering interval, but at without AMF the best plant growth occured at everyday watering treatment. General trend of growth on without AMF treatment was decreased proportionally with the increase in water stress level. The longer the watering interval the more suffer plant growth.

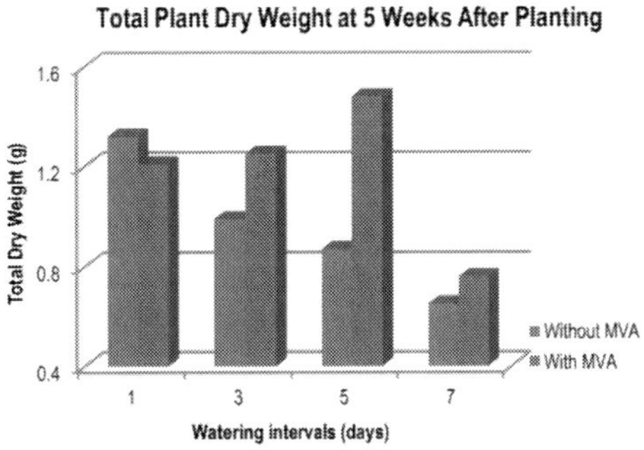

Figure 4. Total plant dry weight at 5 weeks after planting.

DISCUSSION

Plant growth

In this experiment plant growth were monitored by observations of plant height, total leaves per clump, total tiller per polybag, and total dried weight. After two phase observations, data on plant growth parameters were varied. There were no significant different of total leaves either at 4 or 5 weeks after planting. However, AMF showed a significant effect. The effect was proportionally with the increase in water level stress. Total leaves at AMF treatment was significantly higher than that of in without AMF. At 4 weeks after planting, total leaves was highest at combination of AMF and 5 days watering interval, while at without AMF the highest total leaves occured at watering every days treatment. Our data shows that AMF has enabled the plant to grow well under certain water stress level. AMF has likely enabled the plant to absorb nutrients needed for growth. It is known that some nutrients, such as nitrogen, are significantly affected by soil moisture (Harjadi dan Yahya, 1988), so that at stress condition AMF plays a significant role in providing nutrients. As shown in the above data, there was also no significant effect of water stress and AMF treatment on plant height either at 4 or 5 weeks after planting. However, the data does show a proportional decrease of plant height without AMF treatment with the increase of water stress, and thus, the highest plant height occured with AMF treatment. Clearly, a lack of water in peat soil during water stress condition affected growth and development of onion, as water plays a significant role both in physiological and in biochemical processes within the plant cells. Plant growth is known to be very sensitive to water stress condition as it is directly related to the plant turgor. The loss of its turgidity will affect the division and development process of plant cells (Mapegau, 2006), and will result in smaller plant growth. In our experimental units, we observed symptoms that plants suffered at high stress levels occuring 5 weeks after planting.

Statistically, there was no significant diffrent on data of total tiller per polybag either at 4 or 5 weeks after planting. At this stage, there was no significant effect of combination treatment between AMF and water stress levels. The findings showed that water stress condition in this experiment did not affect tiller formation. This result is likely due to its genetics potential playing a dominant factor in tiller formation. It was already understood that nutrients needed for its early growth stage are fulfilled through nutrient stock available within the seedling bulb (Murniati, 2008).

Although there was no significant difference on total dry weight among the treatments (Figure 4) at 5 weeks after planting, total dry weight was higher with AMF treatment. Without AMF, total dry weight decreased proportionally with the increase in water stress levels. This decrease in total plant dry weight is clearly showing the total response of plants under severe water stress condition. On the other hand, AMF showed its important role in supporting the plant facing bad environmental conditions. Up to 4 weeks after planting, plants with AMF fungi treatment increased in total dry weight at 3 and 5 days watering intervals, then it started decreasing at 7 days watering interval. A previous study showed that AMF in water stress condition can increase P nutrient absorption of the plants, so that it was more tolerant to bad environmental conditions (Auge, 2001). Furthermore, plants associated with mycorrhiza absorbed P faster compared to that of non-mycorrhizal plants (Fitter and Hay, 1998). AMF is a promising technology package to be applied when cultivating onions in peat soil. Especially, when it is designed as a part of strategies in anticipating unpredictable or severe drought season in the future.

CONCLUSIONS

It is concluded that water stress condition, occured in a period of more than 4 weeks, is a major obstruction in onion cultivation in peat soil. Onion plants grown in peat soil under certain level water stress condition responded significantly to AMF application. During limited water supply, onion plants grow well either at 3 or 5 days watering interval when combined with AMF application. Therefore, as a part of a preventive strategy in facing unpredictable climate change phenomena, it is recomended to apply AMF when cultivating onions in peatland.

ACKNOWLEDGEMENTS

Special thank to Post Graduate Programme, Department of Agrotechnolgy, Faculty of Agriculture, Tanjungpura University, for supports during my study and research to pursue a master degree in the university. Thank also to both of my supervisors Drs. Sutarman Gafur and Tatang Abdurahman for their kind sharing of ideas and knowledges.

REFERENCES

1. Auge, R.M. 2001. *Water Relations, Drought and Vesicular-Arbuscular Mycorhizal Symbiosis*. Mycorrhiza 11:3-42.
2. Badan Pusat Statistik. 2015. *Distribusi Perdagangan Komoditas Bawang Merah Indonesia 2015*. http://bps.go.id/website/pdf_publikasi/Distribusi Perdagangan-Komoditi-Bawang-Merah di Indonesia-2015.pdf. Diakses 3 November 2015.
3. Fitter, A.H. and Hay, R.K.K. 1998. Fisiologi Lingkungan Tanaman. Universitas Gadjah Mada Press. Yogyakarta. 421pages.
4. Harjadi, S.S. and S. Yahya. 1988. *Fisiologi Stress Tanaman*. Pusat Antar Universitas Bioteknologi, Institut Pertanian Bogor. Bogor. 236 pages.
5. Mapegau, 2006. *Pengaruh Cekaman Air Terhadap Pertumbuhan dan Hasil Tanaman Kedelai (Glycine max L. Merr)*. Jurnal Ilmiah Pertanian KULTURA.
6. Murniati. 2008. *Peningkatan Produksi Bawang Merah dengan Agihan Cendawan Mikoriza*. Fakultas Pertanian Riau. Jurnal Sagu. Maret 2008. Vol.7. Hal:19-25.
7. Pangaribuan, D.H. 2001. *Pengaruh Waktu Cekaman Air Terhadap Produksi Bawang Merah*. J. Penelitian Pengembangan Wilayah Lahan Kering. 23 (2):94-97. Lembaga Penelitian Universitas Lampung.
8. Pejic, B., B. Gajic, Dj. Bosnjak, R. Stricevic, K. Mackic, and B. Kresovic. 2014. *Effects of Water Stress On Water Use and Yield of Onion*. Bulgarian Journal of Agricultural Science, 20:297-302. Agricultural Academy.
9. Setiyadi, Y. 1989. *Pemanfaatan Mikroorganisme Dalam Kehutanan*. Departemen Pendidikan dan Kebudayaan, Direktorat Jenderal Pendidikan Tinggi. Pusat Antar Universitas Bioteknologi, Institut Pertanian Bogor. Bogor.
10. Whalley, W.R., J. Lipiec, W.E. Finch-Savage, R.E. Cope, L.J. Clark, and H.R. Rowse. 2001. *Water Stress Can Induce Quiescence in Newly-Germinated Onion (Allium cepa L.) Seedling*. Journal of Experimental Botany, Vol. 52, No.358, pp, 1129-1133.

Abstract No: A-063

TIRATHABA CONTROL AND TREATMENT MANAGEMENT IN A PLANTATION GROUP: TH PLANTATIONS BERHAD'S EXPERIENCE

Muhammad Pilus Zambri[1], Khairul Ismadi Ismail[3], Rafiyudin Abd Rashid[3] and Mohamad Azim Hazny Abd Hafiz[3]

[1]*TH Plantations Berhad, Kuala Lumpur, Malaysia*
[2]*TH Plantations Berhad, Sarawak Regional Office, Sarawak, Malaysia*
[3]*TH Plantations Berhad, Agronomy & Innovation Sarawak, Malaysia*

**Corresponding author: ismadi@thplantations.com*

SUMMARY

One of the most devastating pests that cause significant losses especially in oil palm planted in peat soil in Sarawak is *Tirathaba rufivena*, commonly known as 'oil palm bunch moth'. Early usage of contact insecticides e.g Cypermethrin, a wide spectrum synthetic pyrethroid, which was generally recommended among all industry players as a treatment control for *Tirathaba*, contributed to severe reduction of weevil population, thus directly affecting the formation and production of bunches in the field. The introduction of bio-insecticides containing the bacteria *Bacillus thuringiensis v. kurstaki* in 2004 was proximately accepted as the substitute for Cypermethrin as it demonstrated no toxicity effect for other non-target organism. Selection of the right treatment, census-based treatment and correct spraying technique, is paramount for maximum effectiveness and negligible side effects.

Keywords: *Oil Palm, Tirathaba, Control, Treatment, Management*

INTRODUCTION

Early work on *Tirathaba* spp in Malaysia is dated back to the 60's whereby few researches attempted to establish the biology and bionomics of the pest and to discover better solutions for its control. It cannot be denied that the peat environment predisposes this pest in oil palms grown on it with biological element (peat forests are natural hosts) and cultural element (poor sanitation of subsequently planted fields) encourages their proliferation.

Tirathaba rufivena is a major pest problem in TH Plantations Berhad's Pusa Complex. *Tirathaba* bunch moth attack was detected in 2010 at Kenyalang Estate and Raja Udang Estate from the 2007 and 2008 plantings. Due to labour shortage at that time, ablation and removal of rotten bunches were not done satisfactorily. It was later established that if the infestation is not well controlled especially during immature stages, it can be a major problem even at the later mature stage. *Tirathaba* bunch moth is attracted by over-ripe and rotten bunches. *Tirathaba* bunch moth attack usually occur if harvesting of over-ripe and rotten bunches were delayed. It is therefore important to carry out ablation from 12-18 months at monthly intervals and remove rotten bunches, to minimise proliferation of the pest (Lim, 2011).

Crop loss is substantial, with smaller fruit bunches, malformed bunches, non-formation of kernel, chewed, thin and damaged mesocarp, which can reduce fresh fruit bunches (FFB) production up to 50% thus resulting in lower production of oil extraction rate (OER). The damage caused is well documented by Yunus and Balasubramaniam in 1981. However in the later years, there were extensive reports on the damage caused by this pest in many technical papers. Initially the larvae attacked the inflorescence just after anthesis and bore holes into the developing fruit, showing fruits with holes. The larvae also damage the fruit by feeding on the pericarp, and the outer layer of the ripening fruit. The presence of fresh or old frass around the fruit bunch is an indication that the larvae are present inside the fruits and around the fruit bunch or at least they had been there. *Tirathaba bunch moth* not only attacks the black bunch, it also penetrate and damage the unopened spathe of female inflorescence before anthesis, during anthesis and post anthesis stages. The male infloresecene is equally affected. This is a significant finding which require bio-insecticide spraying to be targeted to all opened as well as unopened female and male inflorescences. The previous use of Cypermethrin (a wide spectrum synthetic pyrethroid) which exclude spraying of inflorescences also explained why recurrence of fresh damage was observed 2 months after treatment.

The use of *Bacillus thuringiensis* as a biocontrol agent was considered because of the many associated advantages as compared with the use of a chemical insecticide; it is toxic only to target insect and generally harmless to natural enemies, man, fish and livestock (Tyron, 1986). A field trial was done on the effect of *B. thuringiensis* on the bunch moth, *Tirathaba rufivena* in 1988. (Wahid *et al.*, 1991). Besides *B. thuringiensis*, which was applied at a rate of 0.5 kg formulated product per hectare, several chemical insecticides, namely Cyfluthrin,

Diflubenzuron and Endosulfan were also included as treatments. The results of the trial showed that *B. thuringiensis* gave the best performance followed by cyfluthrin and diflubezuron. This was assessed on the basis of larval densities and bunch damage after treatment. Further, the cost of application of *B. thuringiensis* was much cheaper than that of diflubenzuron. The bio-insecticides Dipel ES containing the bacteria *Bacillus thuringiensis* v. *kurstaki.* was used to control *Tirathaba* both in Pusa and Beladin plantation complex. It is a safe product with no demonstrated toxicity for other non-target organism. It preserves other beneficial insects like predatory bugs, wasps, as well as parasitic flies in the plantation. The mode of action of Dipel Es is through stomach poisoning. The larvae will stop feeding and will die within several days after consuming lethal dosage of *Bacillus.*

Weaver ant and earwig are the natural predators for *Tirathaba.* They attack the eggs and larvae. Other reported predators which prey on *Tirathaba* include *Cosmolestes picticeps, Eucanthecona sp. and Cantheconidea sp.* Conservation of these predators is necessary to control the natural balance of *Tirathaba* population. Heavy and continuous spraying of cypermethrin inadvertently killed these beneficial predators. However, further trials may be necessary to enhance the potential and benefits of this new and novel compound as the understanding and activity towards this pest is still at preliminary stage but with very convincing biological activity.

TREATMENT MANAGEMENT

The recommended rate for Dipel ES is as follow:

i. 30ml / 16 liter + 1 ml of Miracle S 240 (Polyether Modified Polysiloxane) water for Conventional Knapsack Sprayer (CKS)
ii. 38 ml / 20 liter water + 1.25 ml of Miracle S 240 (Polyether Modified Polysiloxane) for Motorised Knapsack Sprayer (MKS)

Spraying Equipment

The recommended spraying equipment is Conventional Knapsack Sprayer (CKS) and Motorized Knapsack Sprayer (MKS). Long spraying lance with 0.91 metre, 1.22 metre or 1.52 metre length with only solid cone nozzle and LS4 nozzle to be used. Both nozzle to be elbow fitted with the lance.

Spray to wet all the following plant parts:

i. Unopened inflorescence
ii. Male and Female inflorescence
iii. All black bunches

Spraying of unripe bunches (to be harvested within the next 10-12 days) is not necessary.

Spraying Interval

The spraying interval using Dipel ES will be 14 days. Only 2 rounds per campaign is recommended for Pusa Plantation Complex. The target will be on the larvae damaging stage.

Tirathaba Field Census

i. Census to be carried out at 30 days after second spraying.
ii. Intensity of census is 10% (census all palms on every alternate 10 rows)
iii. To resume spraying if new fresh attack is more than threshold level of 5%
iv. Data from census to be categorised as follows;
    a) Severe = > 10% of fresh attack
    b) Moderate = 5% - 10% of fresh attack
    c) Mild = < 5% of fresh attack (**No spraying to be done)**
v. Census to be done at monthly interval.

Spraying Productivity

The following spraying productivity regime was adopted by the estate in Pusa Complex.

i. Conventional Knapsack Sprayer (CKS): 16-17 palms per 16 litres solution
ii. Motorised Knapsack Sprayer (MKS): 20-22 palms per 20 litres solution

The average coverage per sprayer is estimated at 2.0 to 2.5 hectares per day.

DISCUSSION AND CONCLUSION

Planting oil palms in peat areas involves deep planting. As such bunch formation is not always visible which lead to bunches rotting on the palms and consequently *Tirathaba* infestation. As such, it is recommended to commence timely pruning at 10-12 months after planting (senescence frond pruning) without fail. Another round of pruning is to be carried out not later than 12 months after the first pruning. First round of ablation is to be carried out not later than 14 months after planting followed by a further ablation at 6 weekly intervals for 3 rounds. On mature palm, good sanitation practices is important as an integral part of *Tirathaba* bunch moth control. Before spraying, all rotten aborted bunches and badly infested bunches on the palm which attract the bunch moths, should be harvested and taken out of the field and left on road sides to desiccate.

A general field hygiene, especially within palm circle, need to be well maintained. Excellent accessibility for field inspectionsshould be prepared especially at the back of the block. Water logged condition should be avoided. Crop losses can be as much as 50%. Prevention is better than cure. The key to cost-effective control is to ensure early detection of *Tirathaba* infestation through monthly census, and timely treatment of infested palms. Effective implementation of IPM approach, emphasising on good sanitation and 2-weekly spraying with *Bacillus thuringiensis* (*Bt*) when the population is above the threshold level will greatly reduce the overall cost.

Proper spraying technique is crucial to ensure treatment mixture is delivered thoroughly into the fruit bunch. The spray volume used was sufficient to cover the specific target site of infestation with the right nozzle and spray equipment. The choice of nozzle type also plays a very important role for effective control. It is preferable to use a low-volume nozzle with smaller droplet size of less than 250 micron.

ACKNOWLEDGEMENT

The authors wish to thank all those who have helped towards the completion of this paper and generously contributed much useful information.

REFERENCES

1. BASRI, M W, SHARMA, M, K NORMAN. 1991. Field Evaluation of Insecticides and a Cultural Practice
2. against the Bunch Moth, *Tirathaba rufivena* in a mature oil palm plantation. *Elaeis*, 3 (2) 355-362.
3. CHUNG, G F and SHARMA, M. 1999. Integrated pest and disease management and associated impact of
4. pesticides. In: *Oil Palm and the Enviroment, a Malaysian Perspective* (Gurmit Singh, Lim, K H, Teo
5. Leng & D Lee Kow, eds.). Kuala Lumpur, Malaysian Oil Palm Grower's Council. 83-112.
6. LIM K H 2011. Best management practices for sustainable cultivation of oil palm on peat soils. Presented at the
7. International Conference and Exhibition of Palm Oil, Jakarta, Indonesia, 11-13 May 2011. BIMATAMA INKA, Indonesia (pre-print).
8. LIM, K H. 2002. R&D focus-Oil palm planting on deep peat in Sarawak. MPOA R&D Seminar, 19-20 March
9. 2002, at MPOB, Bangi, Selangor. Organised by Malaysian Palm Oil Association (Preprint).
10. WOOD, BJ. 1971. Developments of integrated control programmes for pest of tropical Perennial crops in
11. Malaysia. 442-457. In: *Biological Control* (C B Huffaker, ed.). New York, Plenum Press.
12. WOOD, B J. 1984. Implementation of integrated pest management in plantation crops. In: *Integrated pest*
13. *Management in Malaysia* (B S Lee, W H Loke and K L Heong, eds.). Malaysian Plant Protection Society, Kuala Lumpur. 295-309.
14. WOOD, B J. 2005 IPM in practice – The oil palm story. *The Planter*, 81 (950): 321-326

Abstract No: A-139

TOWARDS MORE PRODUCTIVE AND SUSTAINABLE USE OF PEATLAND FOR ACACIA PLANTATIONS IN RIAU, INDONESIA

Budi Indra Setiawan[1], Sabar T. Siregar[2], Nawari[2], Agung Nugroho[2] and Mukesh Sharma[2]

[1]*Bogor Agricultural University, Indonesia*
[2]*Riau Andalan Pulp and Paper, Indonesia*

**Corresponding author: budindra@yahoo.com*

SUMMARY

Intensive monitoring of water table, peat subsidence, carbon emission and biomass in peatland managed to produce acacia wood was carried from 2011 to 2014. In general, water table and CO_2 fluxes exhibited dynamic fluctuation, which were highly influenced by rainfall. During dry season, water table dropped but could be brought back within desired optimum range with the onset of rain. Surface level detectibly dropped at 3–4 months after planting but then its change was invisible owing to the stabilization of peat following many rounds of compaction. CO2 flux distributed unevenly with space and time. No significant correlation occurred between CO_2 flux with water table, peat moisture and peat temperature. CO_2 flux tended to increase the deeper the water table, the lower the peat moisture and higher the temperature. CO_2 flux fluctuated abruptly with time ranging 0–1.21 g m^{-2} h^{-1} with its overall weight 0.63 g m^{-2} h^{-1} and in one-planting cycle amounted to 48.3 t C ha^{-2}. Acacia biomass increased with age distributed over 62% stem, 17% roots, 10% branches, 7% bark and 4% leaves. Stem growth levelled off after 3.5 years old. Total biomass accumulated at the end of rotation was 123 ton ha^{-1} equivalent to 58.2 ton C ha^{-1}. It is concluded that this sort of peat management would be potential to absorb CO_2 from rather that emit it to the atmosphere.

BACKGROUND

Acacia crassicarpa is a very important tree species for the production of wood for pulp and paper industries in Indonesia. This species is fast growing, highly adaptive to the moist condition on peat. It has been planted intensively on the islands of Kalimantan and Sumatra. A good and active water management system is the key factor for obtaining high productivity in forest plantations on peat. This report deliberates a part of MRV results conducted by Riau Andalan Pulp and Papers Company between 2009–2014 under the auspices of the Ministry of Environment and Forestry with the main purpose to validate the best practice of peat management proposed by the company. This study was aimed to make clear effects of Acacia Plantation managed by the company in peatland on water table, peat subsidence, carbon emission.

MATERIALS AND METHODS

The research site located in Riau province (**Error! Reference source not found.**) used for Acacia plantation managed by Riau Andalan Pulp and Papers Company (RAPP) started to plant the trees in 2009. The whole concession area is about 30 thousands hectare consists of three types of landuse each for conservation, buffer and cultivation. Intact forest and riparian were the main land cover in the conservation zone; Melaleuca was chosen to be planted in the buffer zone; and in the cultivation zone there was also rubber trees planted in collaboration with the local community (RAPP, 2014).

To monitor water table, peat subsidence and CO_2 fluxes, we prepared 5 transects across each landuse from the lowest to the highest elevation. In this paper, however, we only report monitoring results from transect A and B (**Error! Reference source not found.**) since they have lasted corresponding to a one-cycle of the Acacia trees from 2011 to 2014.

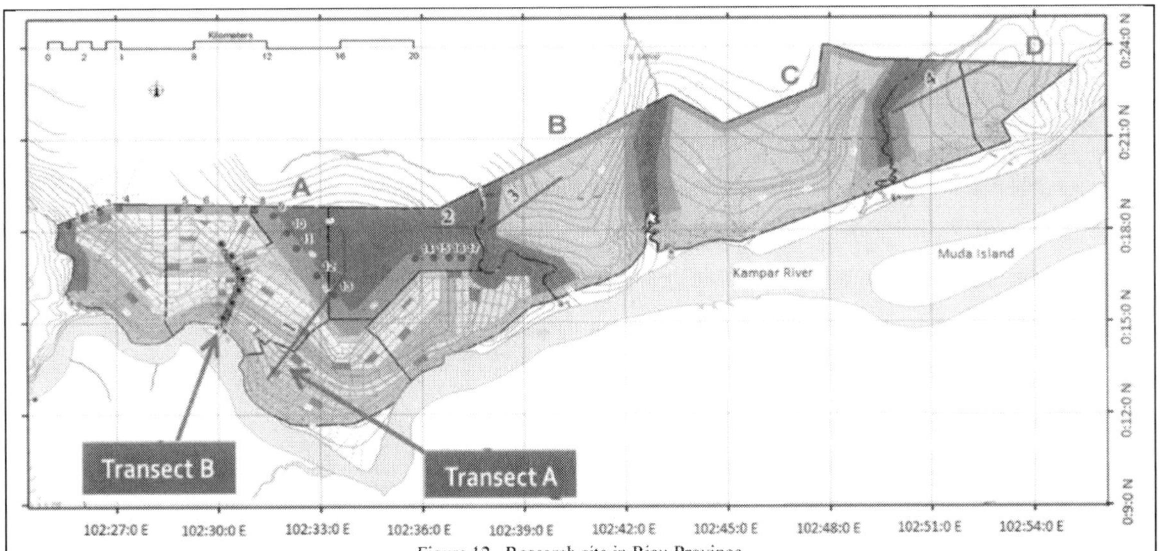

Figure 12. Research site in Riau Province

There were 21 monitoring points in transect A and 9 points in transect B. The interval between each point was about 500 m. Transect A completely covered the areas for rubber, acacia, melaleuca and forest while transect B covered only the areas for acacia and rubber. A dipwell made of 2 inch pipe in diameter stretched up to the bottom of peat and extended about 50 cm above its surface was installed in each monitoring point. The monitoring point was located in the middle of 4 adjacent trees. Water table, peat surface and surface CO2 flux were measured routinely each month but not at the same day and time. CO2 fluxes together with peat moisture and temperature were measured using portable instruments.

Destructive samplings from 1, 2, 3 and 4 years old of acacia were carried out to get its biomass and carbon content. We introduce an allometric equation to interpolate the data and to draw relationships among tree variables. The equation takes a general form as follows.

$$y = y_m\left[1 \quad \left(1+\left(\frac{x}{a}\right)^b\right)^{-c}\right]$$

Where, y is dependent variable, y_m is the maximum value of y, x is the independent variable, and a, b and c are fitted parameters.

RESULTS AND DISCUSSION

Water Table

Error! Reference source not found. shows water table in two dipwells that extremely fluctuated in transect A and B. In general, water table positively but not proportionally fluctuated with rainfall. In transect A, there was a clear gap of water table in forest and acacia which tended to decrease with time. As a matter of fact, in dry season, water table dropped and happened to reach 130 cm but then be close to the peat surface after rain events. The lowest averaged water table was between 7.9–84.1 cm in acacia, 23.7 cm in rubber and 26.3–31.7 cm in forest. These values were still within the preferable water table which is below 90 cm.

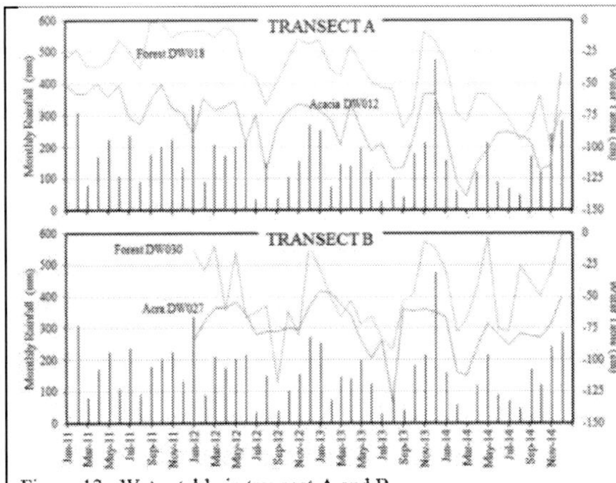

Figure 13. Water table in transect A and B.

Peat Subsidence

Figure 14 shows peat surface level relative to the initial value in two dipwells that extremely in contrast on each other in transect A and B. In general, surface level deviated from the initial value but with a very small value indicating that this peat was already in a stable condition due to prior compactions at the time of land preparation. In most cases, surface level dropped gradually up to 3–4 months after planting but then its change was undetectable and herewith its pattern was well represented by 3rd polynomial equation. Inflated surface level as shown by DW06 and DW022 may be caused by root developments or due to random errors in level reading.

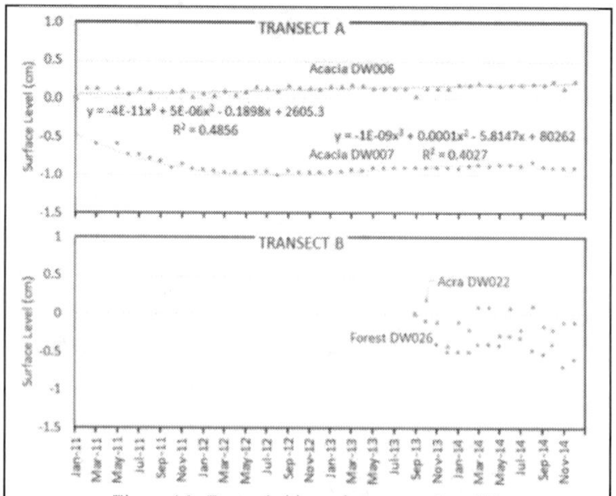

Figure 14. Peat subsidence in transect A and B

CO_2 Fluxes

Figure 15 shows CO_2 fluxes related to water table, peat temperature and peat moisture gathered from all measured points. Though the data are extremely dispersed, CO_2 flux tended to increase as water table deeper, as peat temperature higher and as peat moisture lower. These results suggest that CO_2 flux is not influenced by a single variable such as water table but by a combination of involving variables (Setiawan at al., 2013). Also as obtained in this research, CO_2 flux exhibited different value with different landuse indicating that there is tree influence. In consequence, CO_2 flux distributed unevenly with space and time. It has maximum value 1.21 g m^{-2} h^{-1} with its weight average of incidence was 0.63 g m^{-2} h^{-1} or equal to 13.8 t C ha^{-2} y^{-1}, and was about 48.3 ton C ha^{-2} in 3.5 years.

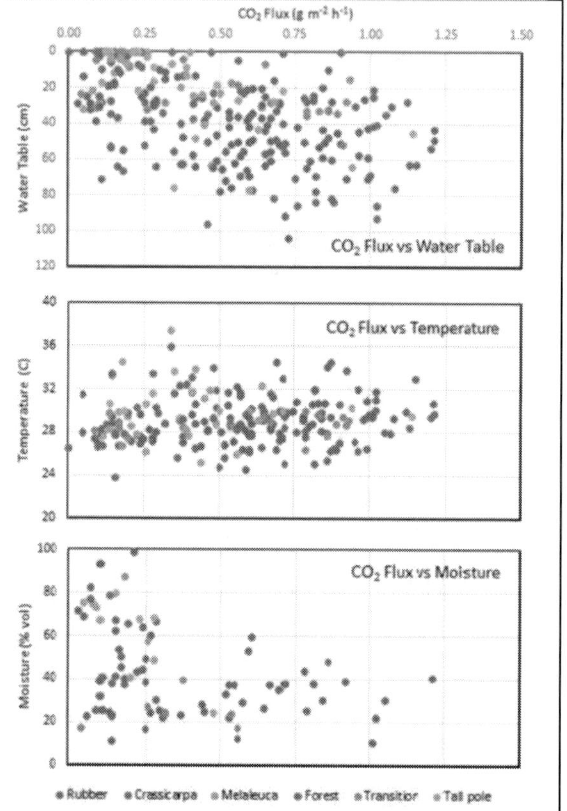

Figure 15. CO_2 fluxes related to water table, peat temperature and peat moisture

Acacia Biomass

Figure 16 shows allometric relationship of acacia expressing tree height as a function of diameter; tree weight as a function of height × diameter; weight of each tree component as a function of age. Those tree height and weight function are well represented by Equation 1 as each coefficient of determination is relatively higher (>0.7). After 4.5 years old, the total weight reached 126 kg dry per tree with a composition of stem 62%, root 17%, branch 10%, bark 7% and leaf 4%. Growth of stem weight increased with time, reached a maximum rate 89 kg y^{-1} at 2.2 years old, levelled off after 3.5 years old, and gained a total weight 73 ton with its mean annual increment 21 ton ha^{-1} y^{-1}. The merchantable stem (60%) was extracted while rest of the components (40%) were left to degrade in the field. The total produced biomass at the end of this rotation amounted to 123 ton ha^{-1} which is equivalent to 58.2 ton C ha^{-1} in 3.5 years.

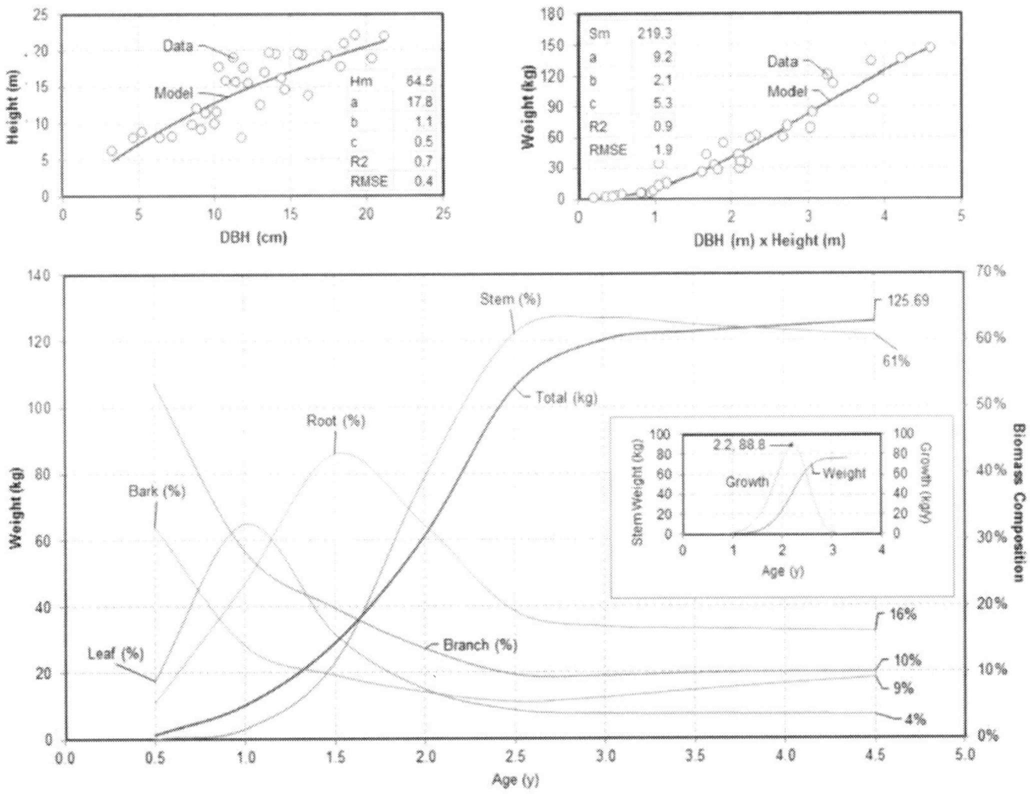

Figure 16. Allometric relationship of acacia tree

CONCLUSIONS

This peatland designed and allocated for conservation and cultivation planted with acacia as the main tree along with rubber tree has shown promising achievements in term of produced stem wood and its accumulated biomass, water level attainments, insignificant peat subsidence within one period of cultivating cycle. CO_2 flux distributed unevenly with space and time with its weight averaged value 13.8 ton C ha^{-2} y^{-1} and in one cycle amounted to 48.3 ton C ha^{-2}. Comparing with accumulated biomass from acacia alone that could produce 58.2 ton C ha^{-1}, it is worth to deliberate that this sort of peat management would be potential to absorb CO_2 from rather that emit it to the atmosphere. However, more thoroughly a long span investigation is absolutely still necessary to verify it.

ACKNOWLEDGEMENTS

Data and information was collected and analyzed from a series of MRV reports produced by Riau Andalan Pulp and Papers Company conducted between 2009–2014 under the auspices of the Ministry of Environment and Forestry with the main purpose to validate the best practice of peat management proposed by the company.

REFERENCES

1. RAPP. 2014. A compilation of MRV annual report of MRV from 2009 to 2014. Riau Andalan Pulp and Papers Company.
2. Setiawan, B.I., S. K. Saptomo, M. Bachtiar, A. Halim, T. Nagano and K. Osawa. 2013. Patterns of CO_2 Flux in a Bared Tropical Peatland. Proceeding of 11th International Conference, the East and Southeast Asia Federation of Soil Science Societies and for Sustaining Food and Energy Security. Bogor, October 21-24, 2013.

Abstract No: A-036

WHICH POLICY INSTRUMENT FOR A MORE SUSTAINABLE MANAGEMENT OF ORGANIC SOILS IN SWITZERLAND? – A COMPUTERIZED FRAMED EXPERIMENT

Marie Ferré[1*], Stefanie Engel[2] and Elisabeth Gsottbauer[3]

[1]*Chair of Environmental Policy and Economics, Institute for Environmental Decisions, ETH Zürich, Switzerland*
[2]*Alexander-von-Humboldt Professorship of Environmental Economics, Institute of Environmental Systems Research, University of Osnabrück, Barbarastrasse Germany*
[3]*Institut für Finanzwissenschaft, Innsbruck University, Austria*

**Corresponding author: marie.ferre@usys.ethz.ch*

SUMMARY

Peat soil degradation substantially contributes to national greenhouse gas emissions in many countries. Their preservation is therefore crucial in the achievement of national climate change mitigation goals. However, peat soil degradation is usually a consequence of productive utilization of these soils (e.g. in agriculture), and preservation is in conflict with such usage. Furthermore, peat soils differ in their nature and state of degradation due to differences in past management and conditions of creation, which translates into heterogeneity among landowners' costs of preserving these soils and their future production potential on them. Using a case study from Switzerland, the paper focuses on the design of economic incentives promoting a more sustainable management of cultivated peat soils. Through a computerized and interactive framed experiment conducted with agricultural students, we compare the effects of homogenous versus differentiated agglomeration payment schemes on the implementation of extensive peat soil use. We also analyze the impact of fairness and social preferences on policy design and effectiveness.

Keywords: *Agglomeration payment, peatland, economic experiment*

INTRODUCTION

Peat soils represent less than 1% of Switzerland's acreage but their role as a pool of carbon is substantial (Reiche, 2008). Agricultural production activities associated with intensive drainage and field operations lead to severe forms of degradation of these soils (Xintu, 2009) which are today at risk of disappearance. Subsidence and mineralization result in the reduction of the peat soil layer over time and contributes to greenhouse gas emissions with accompanying losses of soil fertility and ecosystem services. Besides negative environmental impacts, the loss of the peat soil layer is also a threat for the future of the agricultural activities. Despite farmers' duty to protect their soil (legal Swiss framework) and the fact that peat soil degradation is recognized among policy makers as a fundamental problem, these soils are not the object of specific management regulations. Using Switzerland as a case study, this paper aims at identifying policy instruments effective in promoting a more sustainable management of cultivated peat soils in order to prevent their on-going degradation and to protect the remaining peat layer. Based on interviews with regional experts, the understanding of the issue highlights two core aspects which are crucial in enabling this change. First, given that drainage systems are regulated at the community level, raising the water table and switching to a more extensive land use can only occur if all farmers who depend on the same drainage system agree. Cooperation between farmers is therefore necessary. Second, peat soils are highly variable with respect to both the thickness of the peat layer and the nature and suitability of the underlying mineral soil layer for the current farming activities. This translates into heterogeneity among farmers in their vulnerability to peat soil degradation and thus in their potential future farm profits from peat soils. In consequence, farmers' opportunity costs for switching to a more extensive peat soil use differ. Payments are selected as relevant potential incentives for two main reasons: 1) the issue is politically and ethically sensible (these soils are highly economically profitable) implying that land use restriction options would not be feasible and 2) farmers' heterogeneity in peat soils' states induces that payments may be more prompt to flexibility and adaptation to farming situations than other options. More specifically, under the conditions stated above, agri-environmental agglomeration payments are identified as promising instruments in fostering a collective decision on raising the water table, as necessary for sustainable peatland use. Building up on the "agglomeration bonus" defined by Parkhurst *et al.* (2002), the concept of agglomeration payment was introduced by Drechsler *et al.* (2010) in the context of habitat pattern creation across farm lands. It is used as an incentive for the spatial coordination of conservation areas. An agglomeration payment is based on the joint activities of multiple farmers and is only attributed if farmers commonly undertake a similar activity, while an agglomeration bonus includes a base participation component and a bonus component which the amount depends on the number of farmers undertaking the joint activity. Yet this tool might not be sufficient to cope with the high profitability of these cultivated peat soils and the time-constraint to protect the remaining peat soil layer before it is too late. This study tackles the question of an optimal design of agglomeration payments by comparing the effect of homogeneous versus differentiated agglomeration payment schemes. While homogeneous payments pay the same amount to each farmer, differentiated payments mirror the differences in farmers' opportunity costs. Different payment designs imply different incentives and potentially different fairness perceptions and may lead to different behavioral patterns. This study aims at analyzing the agglomeration payment design which would be most effective in enhancing farmers' cooperation and promoting alternative peat soil use. We also study how fairness and social preferences affect policy design and effectiveness.

CONTRIBUTIONS

This paper contributes to the literature in several ways. First, while previous research on peat soils has concentrated on its degradation aspects and on restoration strategies, the present study tackles peat soil management from an agricultural and economic perspective. Second, in reference to the need for "real-world experience with agglomeration payments" (Parkhurst & Shogren, 2007), this study contributes by testing agglomeration payments in the context of a framed experiment, involving participants from the field, and with a heterogeneous payment scheme design. Third, beyond studying participants' decision making processes under alternative policies, the study links participants' behaviors to their socio-economic preferences. This is especially important in the context of land management as landowners with similar land features may have similar concerns but do not necessarily share the same objectives and vision regarding land management (Rickenbach, 2011). Moreover, the study analyses the details of the cooperation bargaining process (players are placed in groups of two, they can communicate, and they have the possibility to make binding transfer-payments to their group member).

METHOD

An experiment in the form of an interactive computer-game-like representation of farmers' decision situations was developed for this study. It simulates, over time, farmers' decision situations under alternative agri-environmental payment schemes promoting a more extensive peat soil use. This tool builds on the "highly visualized framed lab-in-the-field experiment" approach used by Reutemann *et al.* (2014) in a study about Brazilian cattle rancher's behavior. The core aspects of this experimental concept reside in the framing of the experiment with the actual context-study including the representation of its actual economic data. Contrary to Reutemann *et al.* (2014), this experiment includes interactions between players, a dependency of player's decisions on a group agreement, and a structure which draws on the established literature on game theory and behavioral economics. The experiment was conducted with agricultural students, for whom 87% of the participants are already or intend to become farmers. Five agricultural schools in Switzerland cooperated to take part in this study. Two agglomeration payment designs were tested, each one over a sample of 44 groups (i.e. 88 players). Additionally to these two treatments, the baseline was also run as a treatment (T_B) in order to ensure comparability between baseline and policy treatments. It was tested over a sample of 39 groups (i.e. 78 students).

EXPERIMENTAL DESIGN

The structure of the experiment emerges from a compromise between capturing the essence of the issue and making it comparable to other studies to ensure academic rigor and tractability. The experiment consists of a defined environment with a set of possible actions and constraints, where players are invited to make decisions. Testing a certain payment scheme corresponds to the modification of one condition on which players can act. Three parts compose the experimental session. Part 1 is a computerized Social Value Orientation test (SVO) used to assess players' social preferences (Murphy *et al*, 2011). Part 2 is the baseline phase (no policy intervention) and Part 3 is the treatment phase where one of the two payment schemes is introduced. A socio-economic survey ends the session. Participants received then a compensation payment which depended on their own and others' decisions. The experiment is designed as follows. Players are asked to take the role of vegetable producers and are placed into groups of two players, which represent the community of farmers depending on a joint drainage system. To reflect farmers' asymmetry, each group consists of a Yellow- and a Blue-farmer who differ in the type of the underneath mineral soil layer of their peat soils. The thickness of the peat soil layer degrades and reduces with drainage. Yellow-farmer has an underneath mineral soil layer which is not suitable for vegetable production while Blue-farmer has one which is suitable for vegetable production. This translates into different profit functions for Blue and Yellow, represented in Figure 1 below. Peat soil degradation does not affect Blue-farmer's farm profit: regardless of the number of time-periods Blue-farmer produces vegetables, his farm profit remains constant for this activity. But peat soil degradation negatively affects Yellow-farmer's farm profit which depends on the number of time-periods used previously for farming vegetables.

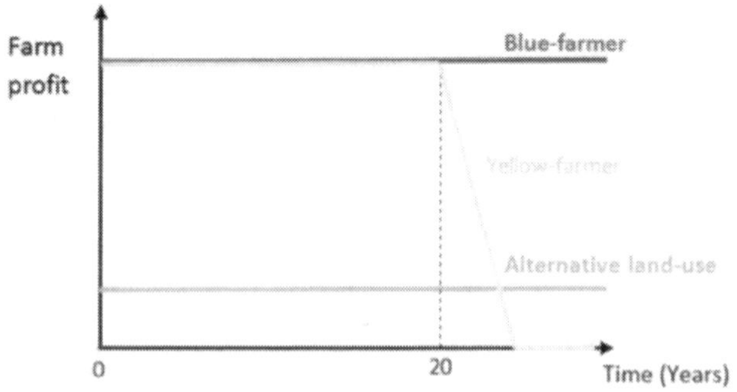

Figure 1: Profit functions of Blue and Yellow farmers over time.

The baseline and the treatment phases consist each of ten time-periods. Each time-period develops as follows. Group members can first anonymously communicate through chat messages. They are then given the option to make a binding transfer-payment offer to the other member. Each member is then invited to vote on increasing the water table for the group, or not. If at least one of the members rejects to increase it, peat soils are not rewetted and farmers continue producing vegetables. Their payoffs for this time-period is as in Figure 2. It stays constant for Blue (800) while, for Yellow, it depends on the number of time-periods used for vegetable farming (it decreases after 3 time-periods and reaches 0 at the 6th one). If both members agree on stopping the drainage, peat soils are rewetted and vegetable farming is no longer possible on these soils. Each farmer needs then to decide between two land use types: A) implementing an extensive land use adapted to high water table (farm profit equal to 40 if no policy, and equal to 40+X if policy intervention), or B) pursuing vegetable farming by draining back the peat soils with the installation of a personal drainage system (farm profit = farm profit of vegetable production minus a costs of 25) (cf. Figure 3). Players can consult their actions' payoffs all along the experiment. Through the option to make transfer-payment offers, they can influence the policy-context by negotiating conditions of cooperation within their group.

		Blue Farmer
		Does not increase the water table: continues farming vegetables on the peat soils
Yellow Farmer	Does not increase the water table: continues farming vegetables on the peat soils	800 800

Figure 2: Players' payoffs with vegetable farming when the group rejects to increase the water table.

		Blue Farmer	
		Adopt another land use on rewetted peat soils (A)	Pursue vegetable production (B)
Yellow Farmer	Adopt another land use on rewetted peat soils (A)	40 + X 40 + X	40 800 – 25 = 775
	Pursue vegetable production (B)	800 – 25 = 775 40	800 – 25 = 775 800 – 25 = 775

Figure 3: Players' payoffs after cooperating, X = agglomeration payment. The matrix does not account for possible transfer-payment offers which are transferred from one player to the other if and only if the latter chooses option A.

The effects of even (homogenous per hectare) versus uneven (differentiated) agglomeration payments are compared. The payment level is determined so that it is slightly higher (2%) than the opportunity costs of the respective farmers. This "surplus" (a payment above the minimum payment) is necessary to induce farmers' cooperation and participation (Ferraro, 2008; Van Soest, 2013). The two treatments tested in this paper are defined as: T_{AC}: constant agri-environmental agglomeration payment, equal between Yellow and Blue farmers regardless of the time-period (equal to 770), and T_{AO}: Agri-environmental agglomeration payment which matches the farmers' opportunity costs from switching land use. It is constant for Blue. For Yellow, it evolves according to the number of time-periods used for vegetable farming: when Yellow's farm profit decreases, the payment that he/she could receive in exchange of switching land use on rewetted peat soils decreases by the same proportion. The introduction of the payment creates a structure which can be referred to as a double coordination game. Cooperating or not is the first step-decision requiring coordination. In case of cooperation, when deciding for one land use option, players face a "coordination game" similar to the one commonly used in the literature, which consists of two equilibria: [both Yellow and Blue switch land use], and [both Yellow and Blue implement a local drainage system]. The former is the equilibrium that the policy instrument aims at achieving and sustaining, in order to protect the remaining peat soil layer.

HYPOTHESES

Based on standard predictions from behavioural economics and game theory, the following hypotheses are developed:

- Hypothesis 1 - Baseline: As long as Yellow's farm profit from vegetable farming is higher than the profit from the alternative land use on rewetted peat soils, players do not cooperate. Once Yellow's farm profit is lower (i.e. equal to zero), cooperation depends on Blue's fairness and social preferences. Blue players characterized as individualists are expected to focus on maximizing their profits and thus prevent cooperation, while Blue players characterized as prosocial are expected to cooperate and, maybe, to make a transfer-payment to Yellow. In case of cooperation, the equilibrium is that Blue defects by implementing a local drainage system on the rewetted peat soils and Yellow adopts an extensive land use.
- Hypothesis 2 - T_{AC}: Both farmers have an incentive to cooperate and to switch land use, in all time-periods. Blue players which do not consider the constant payment as fair with regards to the diminishing opportunity costs of Yellow from switching land use, and risk-averse Blue players (as a coordination game also involves risk) cooperate under the condition of a transfer-payment from Yellow to Blue.
- Hypothesis 3 - T_{AO}: Both farmers have an incentive to cooperate and to switch land use. Given that Yellow's potential payment diminishes with his/her opportunity costs, players tend to cooperate early, i.e. as from the first time-periods. Blue players with strong negotiation power may use Yellow's situation at their advantage and cooperate at the condition of a transfer-payment from Yellow.
- Hypothesis 4: Agglomeration payments following farmers' respective opportunity costs (T_{AO}) are more effective in incentivizing the preservation of the peat soil layer than undifferentiated payments (T_{AC}).

RESULTS

The rate of cooperation of players in the baseline as compared to the treatments (Figure 4 below) provides information on the effect of the policy intervention on farmers' behaviors.

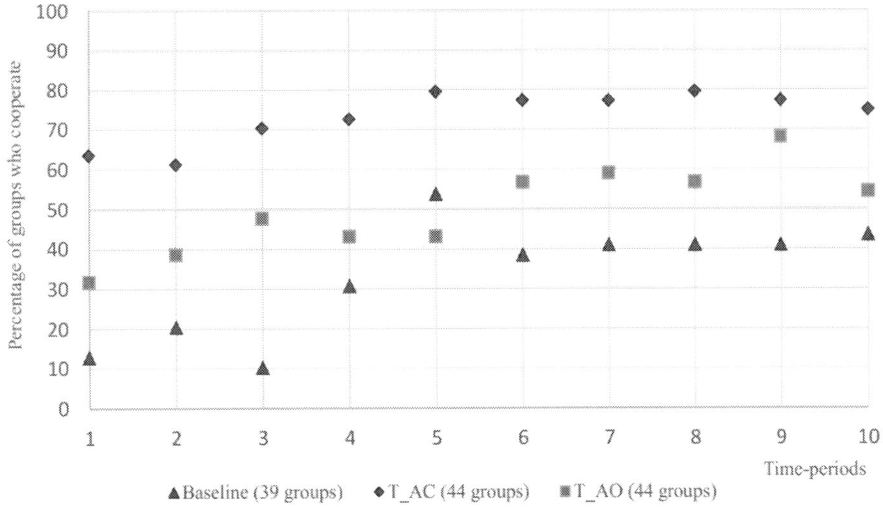

Figure 4: Comparison of the rate of cooperation (both players vote for increasing the water table) in the baseline, versus T_{AC} and T_{AO}

In the baseline, as predicted, cooperation increases as from time-period 4 as Yellow's farm profit from vegetable farming decreases. This concerns about 40% of the groups between time-periods 5 and 10. Among the groups who cooperate, the predicted equilibrium emerges as from time-period 6: about 65% of the Blue players defect and pursue vegetable production and about 85% of the Yellow players adopt another land use on rewetted peat soils. Furthermore, among these same groups, the number of Blue players who make a positive net offer to Yellow players gradually increases along the ten time-periods. The average amount of these net offers increases too, from about 100 to 200. Comparing group patterns with regards to their decisions towards cooperation and correlating players' decision with their socio-economic characteristics will enable to further characterize the groups who cooperate as well as the ones who do not.

Based on proportion tests (Z test at the 5% significance level), in T_{AC}, the rate of cooperation is significantly higher in each time-period than in the baseline: 2 to 3 times higher. However, in comparison with the baseline, the introduction of the differentiated agglomeration payment (T_{AO}) induces a significantly higher rate of cooperation in time-periods 2 and 9 only; cooperation towards rewetting the peat area is not significantly higher in the other time-periods. Comparing both treatments effects, the level of cooperation in T_{AC} is significantly higher than in T_{AO}. However, in both T_{AO} and T_{AC}, 70 to 90% of the players do switch land use on rewetted peat soils after cooperating.

Contrary to the predictions, the heterogeneous payment scheme did not induce early cooperation among players and was less effective than the homogeneous payment scheme in incentivizing a switch of peat soil use. Analyses of the transfer-payments and correlations of those and players' decisions with their social preference profiles will provide information on the reasons underlying this behavioural difference. One potential explanation could reside in the emergence of conflicts of interest in T_{AO} leading to counter-productive effects with regards to the implementation of a more sustainable peat soil management. Indeed, as Yellow's potential payment falls with the use of peat soils for vegetable production, Blue players may tend to wait and use Yellow's situation to their advantage by requesting transfer-payments.

CONCLUSION

This framed computerized experiment enables to gather valuable information on how future farmers would make their decision regarding peat soil management and on the type of agglomeration payment policy which would be most effective in this specific context. The introduction of an agglomeration payment leads to a higher rate of farmers implementing an extensive land use on peat soils. However, the effect is strongly influenced by the design of the payment scheme, and very likely, by farmers' social and fairness preferences. Further analyses will be completed in the next weeks and will enable to disentangle the effects more systematically in order to provide more solid explanations for the observed future farmers' behaviours.

ACKNOWLEDGEMENTS

Acknowledgements go the Swiss National Foundation for Science which funded this project ("Sustainable management of organic soils in Switzerland") as part of a National Research Program (NRP 68). We are very grateful to the agricultural schools which accepted to take part in this study, in particular to the professors who collaborated with us and made students' participation in this experiment possible.

REFERENCES

1. Drechsler *et al.* (2007): "An agglomeration payment for cost-effective biodiversity conservation in spatially structured landscapes", UFZ-Diskussionspapiere, No. 4/2007.
2. Murphy *et al.* (2011): "Measuring Social Value Orientation", *Judgment and Decision Making*, Vol. 6, No. 8, December 2011, pp. 771–781.
3. Ferraro, P.J. (2008): "Asymmetric information and contract designs for payments for environmental services", *Ecological Economics* 65: 810-821.
4. Parkhurst, G.M. *et al.* (2002): "Agglomeration bonus: an incentive mechanism to reunite fragmented habitat for biodiversity conservation", *Ecological Economics* 41: 305-328.
5. Parkhurst, G.M. & Shogren, J.F. (2007): "", *Ecological Economics* 64 (2), 344-355. Spatial incentives to coordinate contiguous habitat
6. Reiche, M. *et al.* (2008): "Effect of peat quality on microbial greenhouse gas formation in an acidic fen", *Biogeosciences*, 7, 187–198, 2010
7. Reutemann, T. & Engel, S. 2014. "Return per hectare or per dollar? Opportunity costs of conservation under capital constraints and intensification potential", Working paper, Professorship of Environmental Policy and Economics, ETH Zurich.
8. Rickenbach, M. *et al.* (2011): "Cross-boundary cooperation: A mechanism for sustaining ecosystem services from private lands", *Journal of Agricultural and Resource Economics* 66 (4).
9. Van Soest, D. *et al.* (2013): "Preference heterogeneity, asymmetric information, and the inevitability of informational rents in environmental subsidy programs", HYPERLINK "http://www.lse.ac.uk/GranthamInstitute/wp-content/uploads/2014/10/grantham_vansoest_2015_01_07.pdf" accessed 08.03.2016.
10. Xintu, L. (2009): "Conditions of peat formation", *Coal, oil shale, natural bitumen, heavy oil and peat*, Vol. 2 (452 pages).

THEME 6
CULTURAL, EDUCATIONAL, MEDICINAL & SOCIO-ECONOMIC ASPECTS OF PEATLANDS, PEAT & SAPROPEL

6.1: CULTURAL & SOCIO-ECONOMIC ASPECTS OF PEATLAND

Abstract No: A-359

FARMING ON UNDRAINED PEATLAND IN RIAU, INDONESIA: IMPLICATION FOR SUSTAINABILITY

Oka Karyanto, Rohman, Teguh Yuwono, Slamet Riyanto, Wahyu Tri Widayanti, Ari Susanti And Satyawan Pudyatmoko

Faculty Of Forestry, Universitas Gadjah Mada, Bulaksumur Yogyakarta Indonesia

**Corresponding author: okka@ugm.ac.id*

SUMMARY

In spite of growing debates on the values of peatforest for global climate & future of human civilization, peatland in the tropics has been seen as a merely producers of economic commodities and recently been exploited for supporting national economic development agenda, especially through extensive farming on drained peatland. Few existing farming on undrained peatland has been available but it has not attracted much attention due to few factors. Those evidences represent the future political economy landscape of peatland management, where more people have depended on drained peatland. We have analyzed different farming systems especially that are undrained both on (large scale and small scale) to explore different options for peatland management which is in line with sustainable development agenda. Our financial and economic analysis showed that small scale farming on undrained or small-scale drained peatland produced economically viable revenue or developmental impacts per Ha. Our study also showed that an outcompeting performance and threat of such less risky farming system is due to its incompatibility (it degrades) when co-managed with those large scales draining under a same peatland hydrological unit landscape. We recommend that understanding on boundary impact of large scale peatland drainage is crucial before promoting different farming systems and also the fact that such undrained farming system could only well perform under very narrow range of peatland landscape, where an intensive management would be still challenging. A new political economy landscape for less risky peatland management should consider both limitations.

BACKGROUND OF PEATLAND USES: PEATFOREST IN INDONESIA ONCE AS PRODUCER FOR WORLD-CLASS AND HIGH-VALUE TIMBER

Exploitation of peatforest in Sumatera dates back to 1870, to satisfy construction timber needs (Anonymous, 1986). Traditional architecture in many Sumatera kingdoms, especially in the coastal areas, was closely related with use of these native timbers. Commercial logging of peatforest started at 1970s and had been rapidly increasing in 1980s, which around 13 million Ha of good peatforest in Central Kalimantan, West Kalimantan, Riau, Jambi and South Sumatera provinces were logged by around 200 large forest concessionaires using silviculture system which was based on selective cutting and non-drainage (Ministry of Forestry, 1983). One of the main commercial timbers are ramin (*Gonystylus bancanus*), a highly-sought of internationally traded timber and also dipterocarp and non-dipterocarp commercial timbers. Before logging, these commercial timber stock were oftenly higher that 150 m^3/Ha. It was estimated that the total ramin timber stock in 1990s was 130 million m^3 (Ministry of Forestry, 1983) but then was rapidly declined down to 14 million in 2006 (Bismark *et al.*, 2006). Most of the peat forest areas of Indonesia were managed under forest concession system (HPH) in the form of production forest (IUPHHK: permit for utilization of wood forest product) (Istomo 2006). Various methods were used, including the Indonesian selective cutting (TPI) (year 1972), and the Indonesian Selective cutting and planting (TPTI) (year1989). However in many cases rules for sustainable forest management were not followed leading to a severe over-exploitation of PSF areas. In the last 20 years ramin timber supply has significantly decreased ~~e.g.~~ (Meer *et al.* 2005). Substantial habitat loss and degradation of existing populations are the major causes for the constant decrease in ramin timber which led to the inclusion of ramin in the CITES list for critically endangered species in 2005. Due to the high abundance of commercial tree species, notably ramin (*Gonystylus bancanus* (Mig.) Kurz and several *Shorea* species, the remaining 50% of the original peat swamp forest have been heavily used for timber extraction. As a result only a small portion of the original peat swamp forest area in SE Asia is undisturbed. By 2010, some 69-72% of Sumatra's peat swamp forest had disappeared, with only 4.6% remaining as 'pristine forest', and on Kalimantan some 50-53% of the peat swamp forest was lost, with only 2.1% remaining in a pristine condition (Miettinen and Liew 2010); (Posa *et al.*, 2011).

Under ever rapid increasing global demand on cpo and pulp and local factor on higher demands on employment, such large scale industrial plantation have shaped peatland utilization landscape. Likewise, such rapid expansion on drained peatland has also occurred through smallholders. Poor land governance has caused extensive malpractice of environmental assessment and spatial planning that has led to rapid encroachment of protected areas and vast policy which promotes inequitable resource access has trigger sporadic tenurial conflicts. The inability to manage the water at both site- and landscape-level has led to the over-draining of peatland. The inavailability of technology and capital has resulted low productivity those supposedly intensive farming practice using introduced exotic species not adapted to natural peatland. These are among the main causes of recurrent peatfire, peatland degradation hence the unstainable farming. In this situation, it is crucial to examine options available or farming on peatland that has lower environmental impacts but at the same time could provide sustainable livelihood. Thus the objectives of this study were to examine different farming systems and their consequences on financial, economic and environmental impact. Riau is one of a province in Sumatra were more or less half of the area lies on (deep) peatland and is subject to a very rapid and extensive draining-although a revised spatial plan has not been endorsed

METHODOLOGY

First we used a proposed spatial plan revision on Riau to examine the scale of utilization of peatland especially for productive (draining) ones. We compared two available farmings of undrained peatland ie : selective logging without disturbing its hydrology (removal of harvested trees using trail track) and smallholder agroforestry on non-drained peatland using mixed sago and local tree species. We used historical analysis (2000-2012) remote sensing (Landsat) to evaluate impact of selective logging without draining on the native peatforest recovery. We also used manual delineation of Landsat imageries to identify distribution and intensity of peatland canal in across Riau and how it relate to the proposed spatial plan. UAV mission was conducted to examine mixture of community sago-local tree species. Financial analysis of those different farmings was conducted and presenting result using how much revenue per Ha per month for each farming. An economic analysis was also conducted using Output multiplier and income multiplier generated by peatland economic activities in Riau. To examine site productivity of non-drained farming especially how the surrounding drained peatland impact, we used a 5 km transect with 200 m interval to examine salt intrusion of non-drained community sago impacted by surrounding peatland draining. At the same transect we also compared monthly ground water level.

RESULTS AND DISCUSSION

There is only one active company in Sumatra that has a concession certified for native forest production on peatland (PT. Anonimous) in one of the peatblock in Riau province. The total area of this concession is about 90.956 ha, managed according to the Indonesian Selective Cutting and Replanting System (TPTI) which has complied with *Indonesian Ecolabeling Institute*) - LEI or Forest Stewardship Council (FSC) and therefore this concession obtained an exception to harvest ramin through a quota setting system. Setting a harvest quota of ramin was carried out annually by "ramin working group" lead by CITES Scientific Authority of Indonesian Institute of Sciences (Partomihardjo, 2006).

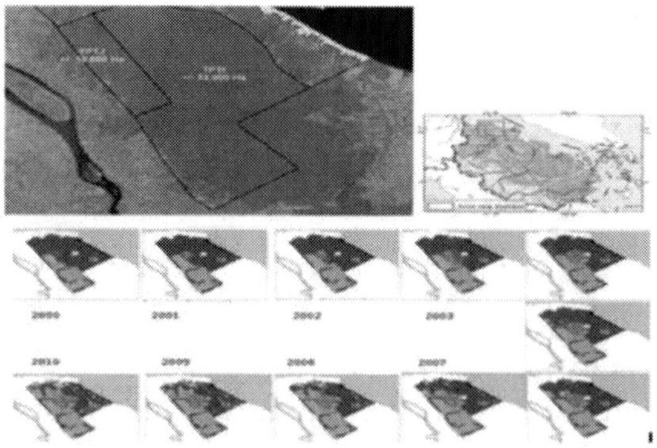

Figure 1: The logging forest that has been managed through non-draining and selective logging and Landsat interpretation of the forest condition 2000-2010, (despite its natural recovery) still showing detectable canopy impact following selective logging

The following principle for selective logging system has been adopted: 1) Only 2/3 of allowable cut (diameter limit 50 cm) are harvested to ensure that the canopy is not heavily disturbed 2) Re-vegetation of the logged over forest using pioneer trees otherwise the open area will be occupied by creeping weeds ie. palas (*Liquala pimula*) and invasive weeds (*Zalacca* sp.) that inhibiting the natural regeneration of commercial timber, 3) No further canopy opening and transporting the seedlings, 4) Adopt reduced impact logging (RIL) and directive felling, 5) Monitoring the stock and forest areas and establishment of permanent sample plot and 6)Comply with annual cut schedule/rotation. To avoid/to minimize peatland destruction, the forest operation has been done using manual, with minimum use of heavy machine. A limited heavy machine called *LogFisher* has been recently introduced to help in log yarding (200-300 m distance). The log is transported using reel system without canal establishment so the hydrological condition is kept intact.

From the timber productivity perspective, there is no distict differences between mineral soil vs. peat-forests. For dipterocarp tress grow on mineral soils, growth rates of 0.30–0.50 cm/yr, and sometimes 1 cm/yr, appear normal (see Sist & Nguyen-Thé 2002). Likewise, based on permanent plot monitoring for several peatforest in Sumatera, productivity of the commercial timber on peatforest at 0,59 cm/y whilst the non-commercial timber 0,35 cm/y were recorded in Riau (Prasetyo & Istomo, 2006); re-analysed by Soraya (2012) 0,35-0,53 cm/y and in Jambi 0,3-0,46 cm/y (Krisnawati & Wahjono, 2010). This shows that managing native peatforest for timber production is possible without peat-drainage.

Forest business account model has been used to calculate profitability of this selective logging forest operation. The forest management includes forest planning, inventory, harvesting and silviculture to ensure that the logged over forest could sustain allowable cut timber in the next rotation. In this study, the profit is calculated at annual basis with assumption of timber price, traded timber volume and the operational cost are constant. It is interesting that manual logging with reel making the production cost of peatforest is cheaper than those non-peatforest (IDR 509,431/m^3 vs. IDR 700,000/m^3). At 52,000 Ha basis, total government revenue (Rehabilitation fund and other tax) is IDR 8,8 billion/year. Based on a constant 40 year time analysis, the company could get IDR 7,3 billion annually, sufficient to sustain long-term business operation.

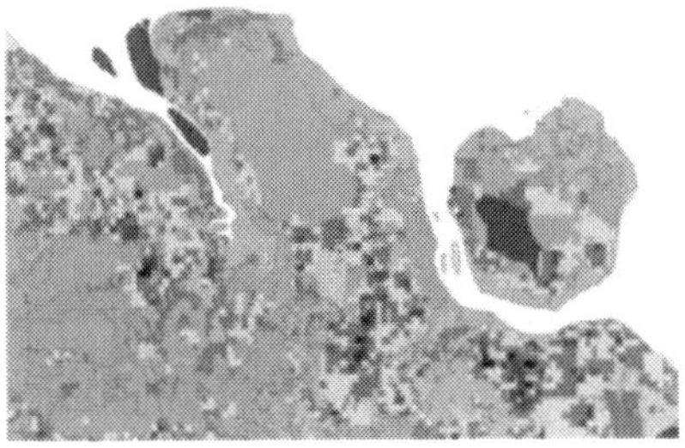

Fig 2: Historical hotspot 2000-2014, indicating that the concession area (light green area) due to undrained peatland have escaped from peat fire. The red and yellow color indicating the recurrent peatfires (red is the more often)

The following are causes of unsutainability of logging concessionaire o undrained peatland : 1) Spatial planning to establish a access district road and draining the concessionaire and pressure to delitigimate the concessionaire from local politics, 2) Timber price is far too low, 3) Pressure from surrounding palm oil expansion and 4) Poor government commitment to encourage sustainability of native forest management

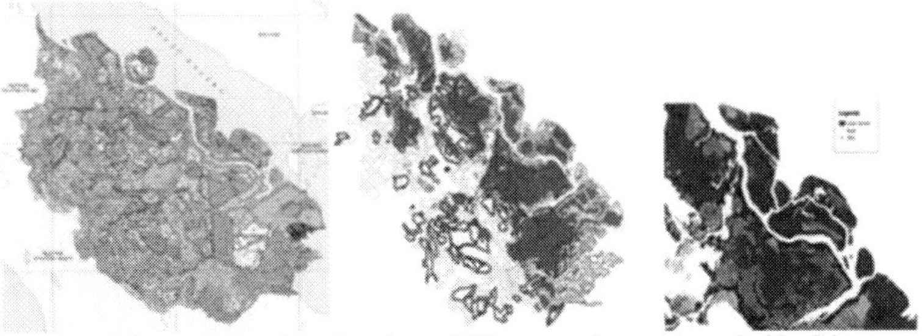

Figure 3: From left-centre-right. (i) Spatial planning of Riau province where half of its terrestrial areas are on peatland (4,1 million Ha) showing that most of the peatland are designated for drained farming systems (the conservation areas are in sky blue color), (ii) Licences granted on peatland for palm oil plantation (yellow line) and for pulp plantation (green-line), areas for peatland (mostly deep peat) are given with purple color (most of the licence have been already drained and planted), the areas of smallholder palm oil plantation not included but it is the most expanding areas on peatland, (iii) and canal infrastructure drainage of peatland for *Acacia crassicarpa* and palm oil pulp plantation digitalized from different satellite imageries.

SMALLHOLDER SAGO PLANTATION ON UNDRAINED PEATLAND (CASE STUDY IN KEPULAUAN MERANTI DISTRICT, RIAU)

Sago accounts for at least 3% of international traded starches, but has potential to upscale this scale since it has been so far still rely on harvesting natural stands. Indonesia has more than 50% of world natural sago areas 1,2 million ha with production status at 8,4-13,6 million ton annually, of which 90% of them resides in Papua. However, so far only ca. 210 000 ha of sago is planted mostly in Indonesia and Malaysia and few others in PNG and Pacific islands. To increase the productivity, there has been intention to intensify natural sago with respect to:

planting intensity, selection of varieties, managing stands, and harvesting, in order to produce larger quantity of starch. This is not the case because most of the sago has been managed traditionally by local people.

In contrast to those large scale sago management, in Riau (Kepulauan Meranti district), sago had been introduced and grown on undrained peatland and provide a candidate for model of Sustainable Peatland Management. Tebingtinggi island is a small peat island has been chosen as a case study, along with other 4 small islands ca. 100,000 Ha (Rupat, Bengkalis, Padang and Rangsang) make unique peatland landscape adjacent to the ocean and lacking upland areas and thus most of the water comes from rain and salt water influence in the edge areas occurs, thus any canalization could cause serious saltwater intrusion and has been documented recently. The farming on those islands are characterized by undrained farming system on peat using high commercial commodity, ie. sago and to less extend mixed sago with high value (timber producing) local tree species for local housing and traditional ship construction such as *Tetramerista glabra* (punak) and *Shorea ulliginosa* (meranti bakau). Sago was introduced 19 century and beside selective timber cutting (especially prior to the logging concession era) has became main local livelihood. Selat Panjang had been a trading centre for Malaka strait with main commercial traded commodity was sago fluor, this happened until establishment of Singapore.

From the biophysical perspective, this sago farming should be sustainable due to following reasons: 1)at peat landscape, sago are planted on peat leeves (shallow) with undrained peatdome areas, 2) High productivity as it grown on shallow mineral rich peatsoil and tidal influenced zone eventhough it never been fertilized, 3) The peatland has never been drained, it frequently flooded (due to rain and tidal influence) and the natural draining is through natural small river. It has never been influenced by peatfire which totally only produce smaller greenhouse gas emission compared to the drianed farming system (ie. it resembles native undrained peatforest) 4) The sago has been introduced by strip planting on the native forests, there is association of native trees which develop a good micro-climate suitable for sago production. It has never been established on cleared land neither by burning and 5) Once it planted it constantly provide sago log. The sago is cut selectively ie. selective logging silviculture system especially once the sago has matured ie. no immature sago log cutting as it produce small quantity of fluor. The non-trunk biomass has been left to retain the nutrients

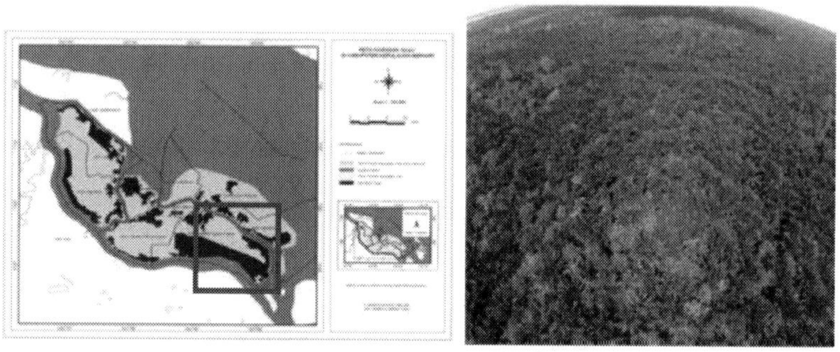

Figure 4: Distribution of sago on peatland in Kepulauan Meranti district, Riau. The red insert is the case study in this report (left). Typical sago farming on undrained peatland in Kepulauan Meranti district where sago once line-planted on logged-over forest and thus we could see associated native tree in the sago farming. Note there is no canal

The proposed model will be aiming to develop : (i) Landscape management for green economy (low carbon development program ie. emission reduction from drained peatland and biodiversity maintenance of natural sago) especially utilization of peatland for non-drained farming activities for supporting food security (starch production) and regional economy, (ii) Strengthening the local participation and livelihoods by establishing a model of an integrated small scale sago management-industry cluster and (iii) Establishment of cluster integrated study on sustainable sago on peatland without drainage as a model for paludiculture (climate smart farming technique) on peatland which has been integrated with off farming sago-based value adding activities.

Tohor river village represents as a model of a 2,650 Ha smallholder sago farming owned by 320 families (average 11,88 Ha per family) grown on (undrained) peatland with production totally ca 60 ton/month wet fluor (worth 1 billion IDR). This sago farming has been since 1900s and known to be the most intensive sago farming in Indonesia. Previously, mature sago tree is cut when the owner needs cash money, this once resemble to those community forest practice in Java. But once sago processing facilities are available, the demand for sago tree increases and now even the supply for sago tree is becoming limited. At village level, there is a total 68,900 standing mature sago trees annually (equivalent to IDR 20,67 billion or IDR 65,4 million peer family ie. price for a single mature sago tree is in average IDR 300,000). The value adding related to processing are: (i) sago log felling and starch extraction IDR 80,000 per tree and (ii) sago fluor collection and packing (IDR 100,000 per ton). Per individual tree, sago could yield in average 8 log cut (tual) that contains each 30 kg wet fluor. Under IDR 2000 per wet fluor, the total wet fluor value is IDR 33 million and additional IDR 12,3 billion due to processing obtained by the sago industry workers.

A number of off farm economic activity are also available to support sustainability of livelihood on peatland. First, a value adding of this peatland farming is supported by 12 small industry scale sago processing facilities owned by the locals, with further sago-based production at home industry: noodle, crackers, snacks and fruit (local jackfruit, mangosteen, durio) and limited extend of government program animal husbandy. Rubber farming on limited drained peatland has also provided important livelihood in addition to self-sustained timber logging for housing. However, most of the income are come from sago. 1,5 Ha sago plantation could support a single family and there is negligible maintenance cost for sago farming. Since 1970s, sago farming has been subjected to intensive studies at International forum (included FAO sponsored initiatives) especially due to its potential to support low input global food security program. Three cultivars of sago have been widely planted in Tohor village namely Bemban, Duri and Sangka (it differs in the number of spine in the petioles). The trees are 10-12 m high, 1-2 cm bark thickness and 38-43 cm diameter size. Leaves are supported by 6,5 m petiole length, with 63-72 leave pairs (150-170 cm leave length and 7-9 cm width) (BPTP Riau, 2011). Duri is the most planted due to good propagation ability and resistance to the pest-disease and tolerance on peat.

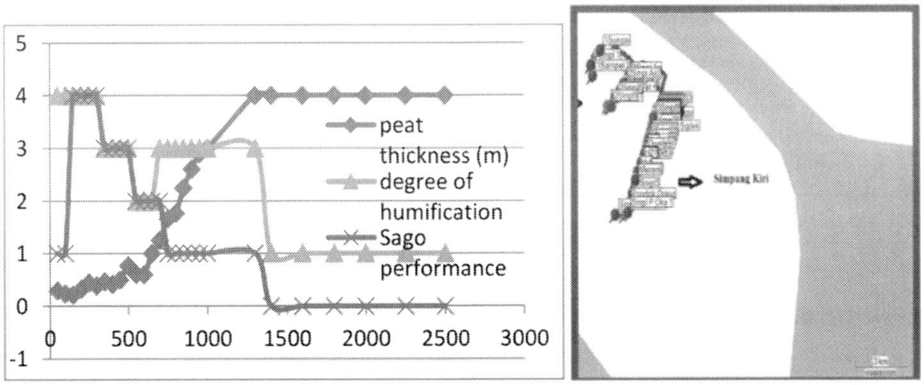

Figure 5: Peatland suitability for sago. As indicated by the transect from coastal to the peatdome (right figure), sago performance are best on shallow peatland with advanced humification stage and then declining when approaching peatdome. The low sago performance in the edge of the river, however, caused by high salinity due to saltwater intrusion (following canal establishment at the edge) (starch producing plant species demands macronutrients esp. K, it easily leached; saltwater macronutrient abundance: Ca>Mg>K).

Sago palm accumulates a large quantity of starch in its trunk (pith) on average 200-500 kg of dry starch per palm depending on species and site condition. The palm is propagated by suckers or off-shoots and it takes 4-6 years to grow to form the trunk. Depending on fertility status, it takes 8-15 years to mature. On average in Tohor village, there are 109 clumps per Ha. Without harvesting, the palm dies after flowering (hapaxanthis) but the clump consisting of various stages of individual continues to grow (Flach, 1983). Sago palm is the only crop which can grow well as an economic crop under constrained soils ie. wetland, acidic, brackish and peatsoil without any soil amelioration. But as shown in this study, best sago only occurs on fertile (shallow) peatland without saltwater intrussion

Tabel 1: Standing stock of sago trunk in Tohor village

Number	Number of shoots	Shoots making trunk	Mature sago trunk year-					
			5	4	3	2	1	Total
/ clump	8,25	5,32	0,17	0,22	0,32	0,30	0,21	1,22
/ Ha	900	580	19	24	34	32	23	133
Total	2,383,965	1,537,202	50,328	64,301	91,100	85,610	59,927	351,267

For each sago clump, there are only 1-2 mature harvestable trunk within 5 years, thus per Ha with average 109 sago clumps would produce 133 mature trunk within 5 years (or 26 trunks per year). The number of shoot availability are abundant ie. 1,5 million shoots and would provide a mature trunk in the second 5 rotation year. We could expect that it would be 750,000 mature trunk in the coming 10 years (assuming 50% of shoot turn to trunk) or 150,000 mature trunk harvestable (this double that the existing standing stock). There are uncertainties on the yield regulation: (i) only 5.32 new shoots could form trunk, (ii) sago trunk has not constantly matured thoughout the year so there will be more/less harvest annually. With total 2650 Ha, total mature sago trunk harvestable annually are 68,900 trunks (or per family they could harvest 215 trunks per year ie. equivalent to IDR 64,5 million per family per year).

The locals have noticed a decline in the sago productivity (shoot and flour concentration) since 2011, which is associated with the negative impact of large scale peatland drainage at the dome areas done by a pulp plantation concessionaire who granted the licence recently. The large scale draining of the peatdome (peatdome is supposed to store the water thus establishing canal on peatdome which has drastically reduced the water storage capacity). The water level dropped at ~~1,5~~ 1.5 m during the recent dry seasons and has not been recorded before. This has triggered fire (in fact it attacked aboveground biomass and a thin layer of peat).

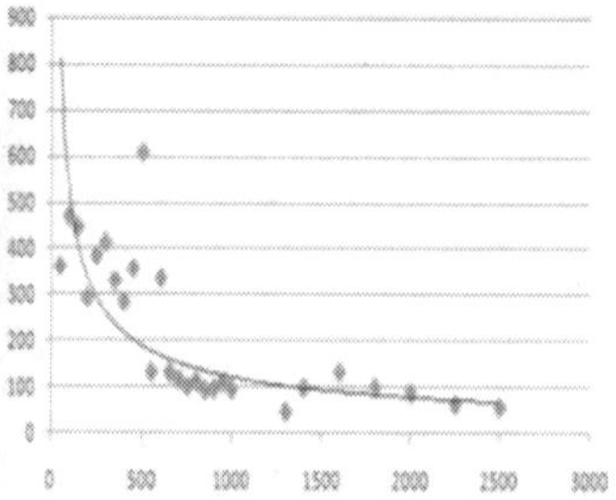

Figure 6: Threat of community sago due to surrounding peatland drainage for pulp plantation in Tohor village which trigger massive forest fire recently (February 2014). This fire has not been recorded during the history of Tohor farming system on undrained peatland. The impact of this draining of the peatdome has threatened sustainability of farming system in Tohor village (above left). Threat of salt intrusion on sago farming due to canalization. The sago performance are worst at the edge of the new canal recently established by the local government. Depending on how fast the salt intrusion will continue, it will threat the sustainability of sago farming on undrained peatlandsalt intrusion from the surrounding coastal drainage for settlement (distance from the edge of canal in metre- (above centre) and recurrent peatfire showing that the Tohor village has been approached by peatfire recently which has not been recorded previously

CONCLUSION

Two farming system on undrained peatland (selective logging native forests without digging canal and mixed community sago plantation with native trees) have provided a potential commercially viable palludiculture practices. Upscale of these farming is not possible due to limited area of fertile shallow peatland. Likewise, their sustainability have been threatened by surrounding peatland draining under different unit management which use exotic monoculture commercial plant/tree species that only could be grown on drained peatland. Those threats could be through salt intrusion and recurrent peatfire.

REFERENCES

1. Anonimous. 1986. History of Forestry in Indonesia (in Indonesian), *volume 2*.Ministry of Forestry, Jakarta
2. Bismark, M., Wibowo, A., Kalima, T. and Sawitri, R. 2006. *Current Growing Stock of Ramin in Indonesia.* Prosiding Workshop Nasional Alternatif Kebijakan dalam Pelestarian dan Pemanfaatan Ramin. Pusat Penelitian dan Pengembangan Hutan Konservasi Alam in collaboration with ITTO. Bogor, 22 Februari 2006
3. Sist, P. & Nguyen-Thé, N. 2002. Logging damage and the subsequent dynamics of a dipterocarp forest in East Kalimantan (1990–1996). *Forest Ecology and Management* **165**: 85–103.
4. Sist P, Fimber R, Sheil D, Nasi R and Chevallier M. 2003. Towards sustainable management of mixed dipterocarp forests of Southeast Asia: moving beyond minimum diameter cutting limits. *Environmental Conservation* 30 (4): 364–374
5. Istomo, Komar TE, Tata MHL, Sumbayak ESS and Rahma A. 2010. Evaluation of silvicultural system of tropical peatswamp forest (in Indonesia). ITTO CITES PROJECT in collaboration with FORDA, MOF.115p.
6. Krisnawati H and Wahjono D. 2010. Stand Diameter Increment of Logged-Over Swamp Natural Forest in Jambi Province)
7. Soraya, E. 2012. A simple empirical individual-tree growth model for Sumatran peat-swamp forests (~~not published~~ unpublished)

Abstract No: A-428

PEATLAND DEVELOPMENT: A VIABLE OPTION TO UPLIFT THE SOCIO-ECONOMIC WELL-BEING OF RURAL COMMUNITIES IN SARAWAK, MALAYSIA

Jiram Sidu

Ministry of Modernisation of Agriculture and Rural Economy Sarawak, Malaysia

**Corresponding author:jirams1@sarawak.gov.my*

SUMMARY

Sarawak is the largest state in Malaysia with a total area of 12.4 million hectares. It has also the biggest reserve of peatland covering about 1.7 million hectares or 13% of the total land area. Based on the state government's policy, 3.0 million hectares will be allocated for agriculture development and these include part of the peatlands. The government emphasizes the development of commercial plantations, which focus on oil palm as the driver to boost the state's agricultural sector. Peatlands were previously considered as wastelands or areas with marginal soils. The present utilization of peatlands for oil palm and other cash crops in Sarawak has proven that peat can be cultivated and converted into economically productive areas. Peatland development is therefore considered one of the best options to accelerate rural development in the state. It is well-recognised that peatland areas play a crucial role in providing ecological services to humanity, but in the case of a developing state like Sarawak, socio-economic considerations are overriding. Since oil palm plantations have proven to be feasible in well-managed peatland areas, the government will continue its efforts to uplift the socio-economic wellbeing of the state's rural population by developing its peat resources. Most importantly, oil palm plantations in the state will be sustainably managed with concern both for the environment and adjacent communities.

Keywords: *commercial oil palm plantations, socio-economic wellbeing, peatland development*

INTRODUCTION

BACKGROUND

Sarawak is the largest state in Malaysia with a total area of 12.4 million hectares (MHA) and a land area of 12.3 MHA. This represents 37.7% of the total land area of Malaysia. However, in terms of its agricultural capability, only about 3.48 MHA (or 28%) of the state's lands are suitable for any kind of agriculture (Teng 1994). The greater part of the land comprising 8.82 MHA (or 72%) is considered unsuitable for agriculture as it comprises mainly dissected hills and mountains in the interior uplands and peat swamps in the coastal areas. Peatlands alone constitute about 1.7 MHA or about 13% of the state's total land area.

Generally, peatlands have been considered as marginal agricultural land due to their inherent waterlogged and highly acidic nature, which result in low fertility and make it difficult to use machinery. However, Sarawak's peatlands are strategically located and form an almost contiguous strip along much of the state's coastal zone, covering almost 50% of this zone (Melling and Teng 2000). Furthermore, Sarawak has experience in peatlands research and development dating back many years and the importance of peatland for agricultural development in the state is well recognized (Tie 1991). This means, there is great potential for their development. In particular, oil palm has been successfully grown and sustainably managed in many peatland areas in Sarawak. Up until 2014 a total of 704,740 hectares (ha) of peatland had been utilized for plantations in Sarawak, of which, 682,812 ha (or 97%) are planted with oil palm, while another 21,928 ha (3%) are under sago plantations (Anon, 2014a). This is not surprising as the country has a history of oil palm production going back as far as 1930s in Peninsular Malaysia, 1959 in Sabah and to the 1970s in Sarawak, where expansion of oil palm plantations has been increasing, particularly, since the 1990s; there was a rapid surge in the area of its plantations. Initially, most of the plantations were on mineral soil. As a result, available mineral soil areas were fast dwindling with suitable agricultural land for plantations becoming increasingly scarce. This leads to the opening up of marginal areas, including degraded forests some of which were on peatlands, and there is, therefore, a real need for the state to explore the vast potential of its peatlands. Further impetus for peatlands utilization comes because they are low-lying close to population centres and are subject to fewer land claims under Native Customary Rights (NCR) than many other areas in the state. Moreover, much of the peatlands are logged over, with degraded forests. Thus, vast areas of peatland, particularly, in the state's coastal belt, provide the best alternative for further development of oil palm plantations in the state.

With this brief background and the growing importance of oil palm plantation to both the state and national economies, the main purposes of this paper are to highlight the state's crucial needs to develop further its vast areas of degraded peatlands for oil palm plantations and show how far plantation development in the state has benefitted its rural communities.

THE SOCIO-ECONOMIC SETTING OF SARAWAK'S RURAL COMMUNITIES

Big disparities in terms of development still exist between Sarawak's urban and rural areas. Yet substantial numbers of the state's population live in rural areas. An estimated 6,439 villages with 212,787 farming families and a population of 1.215 million, or about 47% of the state's population were found in rural areas in 2014 (Table 1). About 40% of such farm families reside in the coastal areas, such as, in Mukah, Samarahan, Sarikei, Betong and Sri Aman Divisions, in widely scattered settlements, and these areas coincide with the peatlands (Map 1). In fact, historically and geographically, most of the state's large population centres were established in coastal areas as the main mode of transportation used to be by rivers.

Table 1: Summary of estimated Villages/Longhouse Profile by Divisions 2014

DIVISIONS	VILLAGE	FARM FAMILIES	FARM POPULATION
KUCHING	390	25,561	220,196
SRI AMAN	604	17,952	61,648
SIBU	1,145	18,636	89,549
MIRI	525	21,089	106,484
LIMBANG	298	8,955	65,560
SARIKEI	834	15,578	78,701
KAPIT	566	15,017	97,334
SAMARAHAN	543	33,183	212,473
BINTULU	512	10,902	62,860
MUKAH	391	15,080	96,123
BETONG	631	30,834	124,598
SARAWAK	**6,439**	**212,787**	**1,215,526**

Source: Agricultural Statistics of Sarawak 2014 (Department of Agriculture, Sarawak)

Map 1 – Distribution of peatlands and settlements in Sarawak

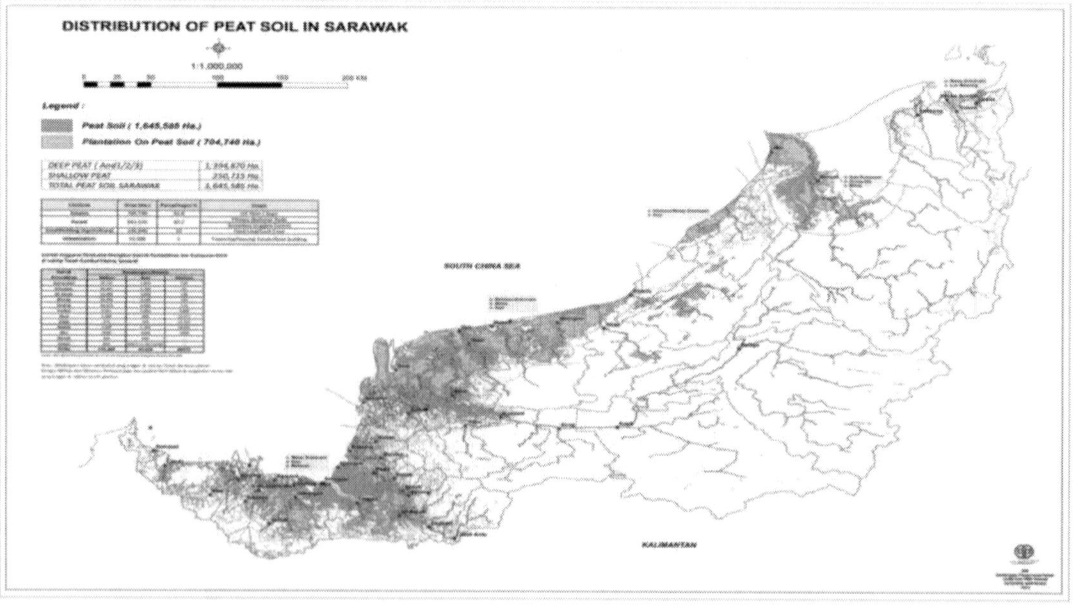

Source: Soil Management Branch, Department of Agriculture, Sarawak, Malaysia (2014)

Currently, many households in farming communities in Sarawak's rural areas earn a monthly income of much less than RM 2,000, and it would be a great challenge for them to attain a monthly income of RM4,000 by 2020 (the target of the Malaysian Vision 2020) (Sarawak Tribune, 2015). It would be difficult, if not impossible, to uplift the socio-economic status of such farming communities from poverty based on their existing traditional farming practices. In view of the prevailing socio-economic situation in the rural areas, rural development and poverty eradication has been, and will continue to be, among the state government's important areas of focus. The State needs to further develop its lands into oil palm plantations in order to generate greater economic activities in the rural areas, not only to accelerate rural development, but more importantly to help the government uplift the rural poor out of poverty. In the long run, greater development in the rural areas will ensure more balanced economic development in the state.

The state's coastal belt represents the best alternative for the state to modernize and boost the agricultural sector beyond the traditional subsistence agriculture of the past, as the terrain in the mountainous interior makes development there difficult. Realizing the great potentials of its coastal belt peatlands, the state government has adopted a regional development approach in constructing road networks into these areas and thus opening up large tracts of the coastal areas for agriculture, including oil palm (the most viable option at the moment). Simultaneously, both federal and state governments, through the relevant agencies, have encouraged rural communities, especially small-holders to be involved in agricultural plantations to raise their farm income. In fact, peatland has been considered *"The Gold Mine" and "is now regarded as the most strategic alternative fast tract resource"* for accelerated economic growth in the state (Sahamat, 1999).

A NEW ECONOMIC MODEL AND RURAL TRANSFORMATION PROGRAM

Under the federal government's Economic Transformation Program, oil palm development has been singled out as one of the National Key Economic Areas, which is expected to increase the Gross National Income (GNI) from RM 52.7 billion (in 2009) to RM 170 billion by 2020. To achieve this ambitious target, the government has set eight (8) Entry Point Projects (EPPs) that various and states need to undertake together. Of particular relevance to this paper is the EPP entitled, "Accelerating the replanting and new planting of oil palm and increasing the income of independent small-holders". Naturally, the respective states, like Sarawak, will need to open up more areas for oil palm plantations. Therefore, in tandem with the federal government's initiatives and transformation programs, Sarawak State Government's land development policy has been to continue developing its lands for oil palm plantations. This can be seen from the total hectarage of oil palm planted in the state, which has been increasing with an average annual growth rate of 10%. From a total area of only 403,738 ha in 2001, the area increased to 1,441,104 ha as of December 2015, with an average growth annually (Anon. 2015).

Overall, oil palm plantations in the state are dominated by the private sector, as by December 2015, a majority of the plantations are owned by private sector, which owns the majority (74.6%) of the plantations, independent small-holders own (12%), Government agencies (including Sarawak Land Consolidation & Rehabilitation Authority (SALCRA), Federal Land Development Authority (FELDA), and Federal Land Consolidation & Rehabilitation Authority (FELCRA)) own (7.7%), while 5.5% are developed on Native Customary Rights (NCR) land. With attractive prices and considered the most suitable crop due to the fact that it can be grown on even marginal soils as compared to other agriculture commodities, there is a growing interest among the state's rural community in planting oil palm, particularly, with the assistance and support of the Malaysian Palm Oil Board (MPOB). Moreover, small-holders can sell their fruits to nearby processing mills. To date, smallholders have planted a total of 175,098 ha, a figure is expected to increase as planting oil palm has directly improved their income and socio-economic status.

In view of oil palm's valuable contributions to both the national and state economy, as well as, to the rural community, the state has targeted to develop about 2 MHA of land for oil palm plantation by 2020. In order to achieve this target, the state will continue its efforts in encouraging small-holders to develop their marginal lands with oil palm. The state government's policy to promote the development of oil palm plantation is based on its overriding objectives towards:

i) Reducing poverty in the state (Poverty Level Income (PLI) for the state is RM 990. per month per household) (Anon. b 2014)
ii) Bringing the rural community into the mainstream of development
iii) Uplifting the socio-economic status of the rural community and
iv) Utilizing idle NCR lands belonging to the native community throughout the state.

With these objectives, the state government, through its Ministry of Modernization of Agriculture and Rural Economy Sarawak (MOARE) and other relevant agencies, is now focusing on and encouraging the development of idle NCR lands through Joint-Venture (JV) projects with NCR land owners. Since the new NCR Land Initiative was launched in October 2010, the Land and Survey Department has surveyed a total of 626,728 ha of NCR land in 426 different areas. Although these areas may have potential for plantation development, a lot of them are within the state's generally rugged and mountainous interior, and thus, the only choice for development seems to be Sarawak's coastal belt.

THE POTENTIAL OF PEATLANDS FOR PLANTATION DEVELOPMENT AND THE SOCIO-ECONOMIC BENEFITS

Agricultural development in peatland has encountered a multitude of problems. However, the prospects for developing peatland for oil palm have been encouraging and commercially viable as indicated by the rapid growth of the area of oil palm plantations throughout state, especially, within its populated coastal zone.

Among oil palm projects that have been successfully implemented in the coastal peatlands for the benefit of the rural communities are the "Ladang Sejahtera" in Seduku, Sri Aman, under the "Agropolitan Project" and the "Ladang Rakyat" under FELCRA's Consolidation and Rehabilitation Program. Both projects are community-based as the participants are pre-determined and selected from nearby villages, particularly, among households, classified as "hard-core poor" and "poor". Being fully funded by the government, and implemented by FELCRA, the projects have really benefitted the participants, who were given a share based on the land allocated to them. The participants of the "Ladang Sejahtera" project have been especially fortunate, as in addition to the expected returns from their share, as well as, employment opportunities offered to their families, they have been resettled in a completely new area with proper housing and basic amenities. In this case, the focus of the plantation development has been the marginal and poor households in the rural areas – it would be difficult to drastically change their socio-economic well-being without the implementation of such projects.

The outcomes and multiplier effects of the development of the oil palm industry in Sarawak give rise to a myriad of socio-economic benefits, some of which are :-

a) State revenue and sales tax

The increase in total areas planted with oil palm has seen a corresponding increase in contributions to the state GDP and GNI due to the export of oil palm products. In terms of value, the total export of oil palm products from Sarawak also increased from RM 4,041 million in 2007 to RM 8,266 million in 2015 (MPOB, 2015). In addition, the industry contributes a direct sales tax to the state government annually, which over the period 2010-2015 amounted to a total of RM1.9 billion (MOARE). All such revenue is channeled to the State Development Fund and used to help improve basic facilities for the rural community, for example, by constructing access roads and providing supplies of treated water and electricity.

b) Poverty reduction and increasing income of smallholders in rural areas

The state government's top priorities to open up new areas for plantations, as well as, to encourage small-holders to utilise their idle NCR land, are aimed to reduce the incidence of poverty in the farming community and increase their cash income. This is in line with the Government Transformation Program, which aims to reduce the great disparity in income and amenities between urban and rural areas. To a great extent, the government has been successful in achieving its goals as apart from receiving regular payment of dividends and bonuses from the plantations, project participants can also earn cash income by working in nearby plantations. Small-holder farmers who plant their own oil palm derive more direct benefits. The MPOB Farmer's Record for Sungai Berkulei, Matu, Sarawak (a peat area) indicates an average yield of Fresh Fruit Bunches (FFB) at 1.85 tonnes per month per hectare, for which a smallholder can receive an average monthly income of RM 616.50 per hectare (MPOB Farmers Record for 2015). Therefore, such opportunities will certainly enable the farming community to increase their household income well above the PLI of RM 920 per month for rural areas (with the planting of a minimum of 2 ha of oil palm (Anon.b, 2014).

c) Employment and generation of business opportunities

The creation of employment and business opportunities for local communities is of the greatest importance. Currently, a total of 103,000 workers is engaged in various categories of work in the oil palm industry in the state. Even then, being labour intensive, plantations are facing labour shortage, especially for the harvesting and collection of fresh fruit bunches. As such, job opportunities are available to members of the local communities if they are interested in this type of work. Local community members can also take advantage of business-related opportunities undertaking various types of contract works (including the daily operation and maintenance of the plantations) and provision of logistical and transportation services. In the long-run, such opportunities will help the more enterprising persons to build their entrepreneurial skills to take on larger tender and contract jobs.

Utilisation of idle land

The utilization of peatlands, including state land and land subject to NCR claims, for oil palm plantation, is the best option to convert idle lands into productive areas. Development of NCR lands "Joint-venture" projects will enable such NCR lands to be legalized with the issuance of land titles to participants.

Corporate social responsibility (CSR)

Most plantations, particularly, those located adjacent to local communities, have regular and wide ranging CSR programs as part of their public relation exercises to establish good rapport with the local communities. CSR programmes include the construction of access roads to villages and farms, charitable works and donations to local schools and other welfare works. In addition, government-linked bodies such as, FELCRA and FELDA, have established cooperatives for their participants that provide their members special loans to undertake some businesses, and also provide some training and skills development. All these measures are meant for community empowerment, which will help the community members improve their socio-economic status and general well-being.

Holistic development of the rural community

The benefits that accrue to the rural community from participation in plantation development depend on the level of their involvement. As the former State Minister of Land Development has rightly stressed, the development of NCR land in Sarawak should not be looked at purely from the angle of "dollars and cents", but in terms of the "holistic" development of the rural community (Borneo Post, 2015). In particular, plantation developments in Sarawak's rural interior have not only improved accessibility for the rural communities, but have opened up markets, where they can easily sell their farm produce and have better access to modern facilities in urban centres.

CONCLUSION

Overall, it can be concluded that remarkable achievement and positive outcomes have been realised from the oil palm plantation development in the state. There is no doubt that the industry has contributed much to the national and state economies. Most importantly, the development of oil palm plantation has fast-tracked development in rural areas with its multiplier and spin-off effects.

REFERENCES

1. Anon. 2014a. Agricultural Statistics of Sarawak. Department of Agriculture Sarawak.
2. Anon. 2014b. Household Income and Basic Amenities Survey Report, Department of Statistics, Malaysia.
3. Anon. 2015. Bi-Annual Statistical Report on palm oil industry in Sarawak as at 30th December 2015. Ministry of Modernisation of Agriculture and Rural Economy Sarawak.
4. Borneo Post, 31st December, 2015.
5. Melling, L. 1999. Sustainable Agriculture Development on Peat land. Paper presented at the Workshop on Working Towards Integrated Peat Land Management for Sustainable Development, Kuching, Sarawak, 17-18 August 1999.
6. Melling, L. 1999. Water management for sustainable utilisation of peatland for oil palm cultivation. Paper presented at the Incorporated Society of Planters Seminar, Sibu, Sarawak, 23 October.
7. MPOB 2015. Data on palm oil industry in Sarawak.
8. Sahamat, A.C. 1999. Development of Peat land: Socio-economic perspective. Paper presented at the Workshop on Working Towards Integrated Peat Land Management for Sustainable Development, Kuching, Sarawak, 17-18 August, 1999.
9. Sarawak Tribune, 24th August 2015.
10. Tie Y.L. & H.S. Kueh. 1979. A review of Lowland Organic Soils of Sarawak. Department of Agriculture Sarawak. Technical Paper No. 4.

Abstract No: A-387

RATIONAL CHOICE OF FARMERS IN THE PEAT LAND CONVERSION THE GAMBUT SUB-DISTRICT, SOUTH KALIMANTAN

Budi Suryadi

Faculty of Social cience and Political Science, Lambung Mangkurat University, Indonesia

**Corresponding author: budisuryadi@unlam.ac.id*

SUMMARY

Peat land existence from day to day has decreased. Peat land deficit is correlated with increasing development activity. From beginning until now peat lands are always faced with the need for development. Peat land fact be one of the land used for the interest of development activities from government and private. Research method used a qualitative approach with a variant of phenomenology. Data collection techniques used a thick description while data analysis a used interactive model with four grooves that is data collection, data reduction, data presentation and conclusion continuously until saturated. Research result show that farmers become actor in conversion process peat lands to other functions. Farmers action to sell peat lands to government and private sector is rational choice at the time. Although selling land, farmers do not lose land because farmers have land a broad through purchase new land from money sales result peat lands previous.

Keywords: *rational choice, farmer, conversion land, and peat land*

INTRODUCTION

Indonesia denote state a four with peat land the widest in the world, with composition distribution as follows Indonesia 20 million ha, Kanada 170 million ha, Rusia 150 million ha and Amerika Serikat 40 million ha (Euroconsult, 1984).

Thereafter distribution of peat land a Indonesia be based interpretation Citra Landsat mention region Sumatera 10.888.199 ha, region Kalimantan 10.385.047 ha, region Papua 10. 682.262 ha, region Sulawesi 89. 446 ha and region Jawa 89.446 ha (Enviroment of Ministry, 2012). Dynamics peat land in map peat land by Wahyunto et.al year 2003-2006 with map peat land by Sofyan Ritung et.al year 2011, estimates from year 2004 until year 2011 (along seven year) peat land region Sumatra diminish 10,7%, region Kalimantan diminish 17,2% and region Papua diminish 28,8% (Wahyunto, 2015).

Special region Kalimantan distribution of peat land be four provinces, is West Kalimantan, middle Kalimantan, east Kalimantan and south Kalimantan. In south Kalimantan existence peat land the widest there at regency Banjar, is Gambut sub-district. The widest peat land this opened since 1920 and into the region centra rice production at to date. But from year to year peat land experience shrinking with switching function a land used for government interest and interest private sector.

METHOD

Research method used a qualitative approach with a variant of phenomenology. Qualitative research phenomenology is research which aim understanding the meaning individual farmers peat lands with digging farmers interpretation in daily.

Technique data collection used three activities is field observation, indepth interview with farmers peat land and documentation secondary data which support research. Research informant used purposive sampling and snowball sampling in select farmers peat land.

Data analysis in research used data analysis qualitative with interactive model Miles and Huberman (1992). This interactive model consist activities data collection, data reduction, data display and conclusion. Analysis conducted continuously until saturated with validity data used triangulation method.

RESULT

Sub-district Gambut have an area around 129,31 km2, partially peat land used for paddy field dan no paddy field, for no paddy field used for plantation, yard, fishery, housing, office complex and industry. Peat land at sub-district Gambut consist four thickness is thickness peat under 1 meter, thickness peat between 1- 2 meter, thickness peat between 2 - 3 meter and thickness peat above 3 meter.

Thickness peat under 1 meter used for development paddy field, thickness peat between 1-2 meter used for food crops, thickness peat between 2-3 meter used for plantation crops and thickness peat above 3 meter used for area water infiltration.

Sub-district Gambut denote one of sub-district mainstay rice producer for Banjar regency at south Kalimantan. Meanwhile sub-district Gambut still domination jobs on farmer sector, which the main job occupant is farmers with land advantage support daile life them.

Farmer peat land used land as paddy field and food crops and plantsalam but for plants galam because plants galam include plants a slow growth so that plants galam quickly exhausted yet for fulfillment than growth. Existence plants galam cannot balance fulfillment interest road construction, housing and office complex so that plants galam more quickly exhausted than paddy field. The sub-district Gambut plants galam not yet exhausted so that peat land a area empty or overgrown small plants.

From year to year peat land experience convertion a land for building houses, although building hause privat sector, office complex government and privat. Data Distanbunak (2014), be treated show peat land with use paddy field experience lowering from the year 2012 until the year 2014 around 121 ha, while housing developers who do activities in the area from year 2012 until year 2014 experience increase round three depelopers so that peak on year 2014 there is ten depelopers who do activities developmen at peat land.

DISCUSSION

At first sub-district Gambut denote sub-district enough with green peat land and livelihoods domination people a farmer. But a long time change become sub-district full of housing, office complex and industrial fasilities. Housing people from cementitious materials and colorfull a denote housing complex or hause building individual or housing privat, which domination a people outside the village.

Meanwhile office complex who built by the government for administration service publik and representative office who built by privat sector for expand business network them. The change convertion land include the change permanently, which land place established house, office complex and fasility industry while cannot change become a peat land for use paddy field although area water infiltration.

However interestingly changes peat land to residential land, office complex and industrial facilities caused by own desire farmers. Farmers become one of from actor conversion land. The farmers are sell his own land to the government and private with voluntary and no because coercion from the government although private sector.
Often farmers as sell land them wait about increase land prices and presence highway and other buildings. Hope increase high price support the who do land sale while when low price them delay land sale. Farmers land sell with the maximum benefit through logical thinking sale with high price then partially from money result sale used for buy new land it is located into from land previously.

Value land price very dependent with located highway, if land near with highway then land price be expensive and if located land so far from higway then land price will cost, moreover land located area no way. Although new peat land that is located far but cheap price. Farmers are calculation of profit for can buy and have extensive land from peat land previously.

Other than that farmers are can atmosphere paddy with is free from household waste and noise track vehicles. Thereafter an habit all money result land sell be devided used. Partially used for is buy new land, and money partially used for buy goods household other, such as television, radio, refrigerator and repair the house them that look nicer.

That possession of goods and new ferformance house denote some are status and prestige family farmers. An family farmers have the goods is responses local community as successful family. Thereafter money resul land sell for need engage worship haji. That farmers society are worship haji engage as duty, such as become social status for a person. An haji is can prestige local villages although an haji no have great wealth. An habit worship haji who do farmers together with family other, such as wife and child.

CONCLUSION

Farmers sub-district Gambut are take rational choice be based motif profits calculation through action sale peat land them to government part and private. Rational choice are do so that result land sell can are buy new land wider and fertile then increase agricultural production. Other farmers are can social status through possession of goods household, repair house them and engage worship haji.

ACKNOWLEDGEMENTS

Article reasearch denote result research the independent from development research our previously when do complete scholar at faculty of social science and political science Lambung Mangkurat University since year 1997 with title policy government Banjar regency in decrease covertion agricultural land. Thereafter advance research independent since year 2007 about rational choice farmers at sub-district Kertak Hanyar South Kalimantan, be delivered on event Simposium Internasinal Journal Antropologi 5 2008, thema Future of Indonesia, Sustainable Development and Lokal Initiatives Pos Kapitalis Era, by collaboration Indonesia University and Lambung Mangkurat University.

REFERENCES

1. Euroconsult, 1984. Nationwide Study of Coastal and Near Coastal Swampland in Sumatra, Kalimantan, and Irian Jaya. Vol I & II. Arhhem
2. Strategi Nasional: Pengelolaan Lahan Gambut Berkelanjutan di Indonesia, Kementerian Lingkungan Hidup 2012.
3. Wahyunto, 2015. Lahan Gambut di Indone

6.2: PEATLAND & LOCAL PEOPLE

Abstract No: A-363

COMMUNICATION, EDUCATION AND PUBLIC AWARENESS AT LOAGAN BUNUT NATIONAL PARK, SARAWAK

Kamal Abdullah*, Anthony Chong, Bistari Mahmood, Abang Arabi B. Abang Aimran, Karen Beverly Seem and Baei Hassan

Sarawak Forestry Corporation, Sarawak

**Corresponding author: kamalk@sarawakforestry.com*

SUMMARY

Loagan Bunut National Park, in northern Sarawak, is mostly situated on Peat Swamp Forest. It is surrounded bythree ethnic communities as well as oil palm plantations and commercial logging concessions. Land clearing for settlements and cultivation and also from commercial logging and plantation activities have negative effects on the park's biodiversity. This paper briefly outlines four interventions taken in the park under the Asean Peatlands Forest Project, namely a field study on best management practices on peatland, a community/stakeholder outreach, a community enhancement programme and the erection of signage.

Keywords: *Peat swamp forest, forest health, stresses, Asean Peatland Forests Project, Loagan Bunut National Park.*

INTRODUCTION

Loagan Bunut National Park (LBNP), 10,736 ha in extent, is located between Batang Tinjar and Sungai Teru in the upper reaches of the Baram river basin in northern Sarawak and was gazetted on 1st July 1990. LBNP is one of the nine national parks under the jurisdiction of SARAWAK FORESTRY Corporation (SFC), Miri Region. The park supports three major ecosystems: Peat Swamp Forest (PSF) (73.98%), including Mixed Peat Swamp Forest, Alan Batu Forest and Alan Bunga Forest; Mixed Dipterocarp Forest (15.73%); and Lake and Rivers (10.29%). Three ethnic communities, the Berawan, Iban and Penan, have a close association with the park and of these, the Berawan have been granted special privileges to utilize park resources. A total of 14 longhouses / villages are located either within the park or close to its boundary. Several oil palm estates lie in close proximity with the park's boundary and logging concessions are also located in the surroundings. The park's biodiversity experiences negative effects and stresses due to land clearing for settlements and cultivation and also due to commercial logging and plantation activities. The state government has taken steps to protect and conserve the forest. One initiative was through the Asean Peatland Forests Project (APFP), implemented by the Government of Malaysia. This project concerns the rehabilitation and sustainable use of peatlands in Southeast Asia. Similar projects have been implemented in Indonesia, Vietnam and the Philippines under an agreement with the International Fund for Agriculture Development / Global Environment Facility between 2010 and 2014, with the Forest Department of Peninsular Malaysia as the National Project Executing Agency. The main objective of the APFP project is to enhance the management of Peat Swamp Forest not only for its important ecological functions including hydrology, but also its role in climate change and, when forest fires occur, the serious annual trans-boundary haze.

PROJECT ACTIVITIES

1. A field study on best management practices on peatland at Loagan Bunut National Park

The purpose of this activity was to document and promote best management practices at a demonstration site (Loagan Bunut National Park) and to upscale good management practices for peatlands. The two main focus areas were: to understand the potential of local communities' sustainable use of non-timber forest products and to develop Standard Operating Practices for use by the park management team. The study was led by a team of 17 experts from FRIM and SFC.

Image 1:

2. A community/stakeholder outreach

Park management conducts regular education and awareness campaigns for all stakeholders including school students with the support of the Special Parks Committee and local Fisheries Management Committee. Under the APFP a one day awareness programme was conducted for selected local community members and oil palm plantation representatives. The objectives were to enhance levels of awareness on (i) the functions of LBNP, (ii) conservation and the importance of conserving peatlands and (iii) associated threats. A total of 31 local community representatives (heads of communities and committee members) and ten representatives from oil palm plantations attended. The local communities involved were: Kpg Loagan Bunut, Rh Jungan, Rh Jengging, Rh Long Akoi, Rh Kajan and Rh Paking while the oil palm estates were Loagan Bunut Estate and Lelak Estate.

A two day road show cum exhibition was conducted at Pustaka Miri (the Miri regional branch of Sarawak State Library) to inform the public about the existence of Loagan Bunut National Park, the importance of Peat Swamp Forest and the reasons why it should be protected and how it may be protected, and how conserving peatland can help save the park. The road show was targeted at tourism industry players, students and the general public. Briefings were also conducted to further garner support towards efforts to raise awareness on the importance of Loagan Bunut National Park and Peat Swamp Forest conservation.

Image 1: A composite showing

2. A community enhancement program

Two activities were initiated under the community enhancement program: the *Selambau* adoption Program and a site visit to *Sahabat Hutan Gambut Selangor Utara*

Fishing is one of the main sources of income for the local communities located around the park. One local community, the Berawan, use a unique traditional fishing method called '*Selambau*' which is also an important tourist attraction at the park. A selambu is ... However, most of the nine *selambau* that remain in the area are dilapidated. To ensure that this tradition is not lost the project embarked on a pilot project to adopt and refurbish an active *selambau* belonging to En. Jalin Junta. The refurbished *selambau* is expected to boost En Jalin's income from both fishing and tourism.

Before After

Image 2:

Selected local community members and stakeholders were taken on a site visit to the established Peat Swamp Forest site *Sahabat Hutan Gambut Selangor Utara* in Selangor, Peninsular Malaysia. The main objective of the visit was to further enhance participants' knowledge of potential economic activities in such forest and to help them appreciate peatland management.

3. The erection of signage

Fifteen (15) signs showing the park rules and regulations were erected at strategic locations along the park boundary lines to inform stakeholders.

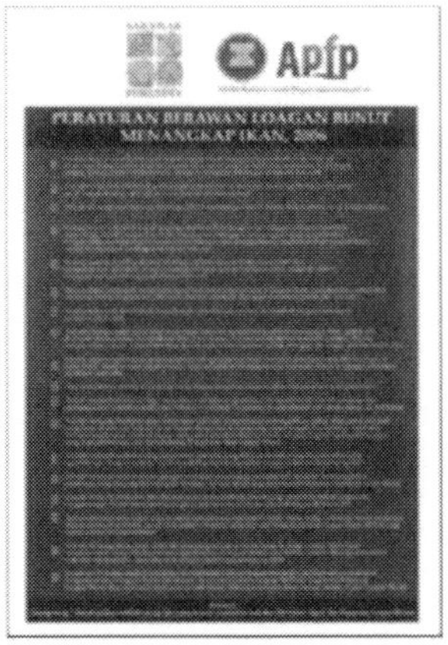

Image 3:

DISCUSSION

Peat Swamp Forests once represented 1,140,744 ha (about 9%) of Sarawak's landmass of 12,264,830 ha, Sarawak's Peat Swamp Forests have been subjected to intervention since the mid-1900s. Vast expanses of PSF, including that at LBNP, have been exploited for timber and/or converted into oil palm plantations. Forest fires pose a threat to PSF especially in areas that agricultural practices have caused to become dry. Due to forest conversion and fires the extent of PSF in Sarawak has declined from *c.* 700,000 ha in the 1960s and 1970s to only *c.* 612,400 ha (Chai 1999). The decline in expanse of PSF in Sarawak has had serious impacts on PSF biodiversity and ecological functions, not to mention ecosystem services. Annual fires on peatland throughout Southeast Asia cause serious transboundary haze problems. As such, any initiatives, such as those described in this paper, to conserve peatlands and get local communities, the general public and the government to value them are of immeasurable value.

CONCLUSION

All activities were successfully implemented with the support of all parties. The communities were happy with the government's support in conserving the Peat Swamp Forest and indirectly assisting them to improve their livelihoods. We hope similar support will be made available to expand the programs to other communities. Park management now has fewer issues since the stakeholders are better informed about the park's importance.

ACKNOWLEDGEMENT

The authors gratefully acknowledge the International Fund for Agriculture Development and the Global Environment Facility for funding this project through the AFPF initiatives. Many thanks are also due to Mr Wong Ting Chung, CEO of SARAWAK FORESTRY Corporation, Mr Oswald Braken Tisen, Deputy General Manager of Protected Areas and Biodiversity Conservation, SFC and En Abang Arabi Abang Aimran, SFC Regional Manager (Miri) for their guidance and support. We would also like to thank Dr Khali and his team from Forest Research Institute of Malaysia (FRIM) and all SFC staff who were involved in the project.

REFERENCE

Chai 1999

Abstract No: A-056

Fishing Communities of Sebangau, Borneo: Knowledges, Practices and Values

Sara A. Thornton[1,2], Dudin[2], Suwido H. Limin[3], Susan E. Page[1,2], Caroline Upton[1] and Mark E. Harrison[1,2]

[1]*Department of Geography, University of Leicester, UK*
[2]*The Orangutan Tropical Peatland Project (OuTrop), UK*
[3]*Center for International Cooperation in Sustainable Management of Tropical Peatland (CIMTROP),*
[4]*University of Palangka Raya, Indonesia*

**Corresponding author: sat32@le.ac.uk*

SUMMARY

Fishing is one of the main sources of livelihood and dietary protein in villages in tropical peatland areas, yet peatland rivers remain at high risk from human disturbance, making assessments of fish biodiversity and monitoring of water quality a high priority. This project has completed some of the first in-depth assessments of local fish biodiversity of both tropical peat-swamp forest (TPSF) standing water and blackwater river habitats in the Sabangau catchment in Central Kalimantan, Borneo. Monthly environmental and fish data were collected over a 13-month period. These form the baseline for future monitoring projects and also allows an evaluation of locally initiated sustainable livelihood projects (such as the use of fish ponds) which have been piloted in this location. In the long-term this information will be vital to improved understanding of these wetland habitats, their importance for community livelihoods, and ultimately to finding ways of promoting ecosystem conservation alongside community development.

***Keywords**: fish, peat, Borneo, monitoring, livelihoods*

INTRODUCTION

Due to the unique characteristics of the tropical peat swamp forest (TPSF) habitat, including their acidic waters, Indonesia's peatland rivers are important fish habitats that often have a higher degree of endemism than other rivers (Ng *et al.*, 1994; Noor *et al.*, 2005). Fishing is one of the main sources of livelihood for the communities living along the rivers and forests in Central Kalimantan (Lyons, 2003). However, with ever-increasing human populations, alarming deforestation rates throughout Indonesia, and ongoing pollution and habitat degradation, the prognosis for water habitats throughout Asia is a matter of growing concern (Dudgeon, 2000). There have been few studies of fish in this region, but one by Giam *et al.* (2012) found that if TPSF deforestation continues, 77% of fish species are likely to become extinct in Sundaland, with Central Kalimantan being most heavily impacted. This would have severe implications for the wetland ecosystems as well as the local communities depending on the forest and water habitats for their livelihoods. It is therefore vital to understand these wetland habitats, their importance for community livelihoods and cultures, and ultimately to find ways of promoting conservation alongside community development.

The results presented in this paper are part of a larger interdisciplinary project that is evaluating broader values related to fishing and the importance of fish for local communities. The ecological element of this project reported here was focused on sampling the local fish to add to our understanding of TPSF fish ecology and biodiversity in this region. Therefore, this project involved monthly fish and water quality surveys in the Sabangau Forest and River, including measurements of water pH, turbidity, oxygen saturation, nutrient levels and other environmental variables. The research methodology was also designed to identify appropriate approaches for fish population sampling to form the basis of future monitoring and sampling strategies.

The results of 13 months of fish and water surveys in the Sabangau river and 5 months of surveys in the forest are presented followed by discussion of the implications of the results for future fish and river water quality monitoring.

METHODS

The Sabangau River was sampled from September 2014 to September 2015, and the Sabangau Forest from January 2015 to August 2015. A shorter sample period was used in the forest due to insufficient water to set traps (a minimum of 10cm water depth is needed) during the other months. Traditional wire traps, *tampirai*, were used to sample fish, with a mesh size of 0.6 cm and dimensions of approximately 89 x 38 x 38 cm (length x width x height). The bait used was a mixture of *tempeh* and *terasi* (fermented soya bean with fermented shrimp paste). This bait is commonly used by local fishermen and was recommended for use in this project by them.

Every month, a total of 5 sampling days were completed. Traps were set up on alternating sides of the river over a 7km stretch. Kereng Bangkirai, the nearest village, is located in the middle of this sampling area. Twenty traps were used, with a distance of 400 m between each trap. In the forest, the traps were placed in standing water pools and small canals (max width 2.5m). Two canals were used where seven traps were placed in each canal, 50m away from each other. The further 6 traps were placed in standing water pools.

Traps were set the day before the first sampling day. Each trap was then checked and emptied daily, with all fish caught identified and their standard length (SL) measured to the nearest mm. If a large number of fish was caught (over 100 individuals), a sample of 20 individuals of each species were measured with the rest counted. Mortality was noted. Environmental measurements were taken at each site, including: weather conditions, pH, surface water temperature, dissolved oxygen content of the surface water (% and mg/L) and Secchi depth (as a proxy for turbidity). On the final sampling day, samples were taken of the surface water and brought to the University of Palangka Raya laboratory to be tested for NH_3, NO_2 and NO_3.

The river and forest surveys had some variations in terms of the environmental data that were gathered. In the river, the water depths (from middle of the river as well as trap locations) were measured. In the forest, Secchi depth data were not obtained due to the pools and canals in the forest being too shallow. Lastly, flow measurements were not taken in the river, but were taken in the forest where surface water flow in the canals was measured using a stopwatch and a floating ping-pong ball.

Fish catch per unit effort (CPUE) was calculated using the following formula (Merilä, 2015):

$$CPUE = N_{catch}/(N_{traps}*N_{nights})$$

where N_{catch} = Number of fish trapped, N_{traps} = Number of traps set, N_{nights} = Number of nights set

RESULTS

In the river, a total of 55,147 fish were trapped and counted from September 2014 to September 2015 over 1,300 trap nights, with 22,917 fish measured. In the forest, a total of 3,938 fish were trapped and counted from February to July 2016 over 600 trap nights, with 3,905 fish measured. In the river 39 different species were trapped, and in the forest 27 species were trapped. *Rasbora kalbarensis* was added to the list following observations in the river. This species is too small to be trapped using the methods used. This addition leads to a final count of 47 different species from 15 different families (Table 1).

Table 1: Fish species found in the Sabangau River and Forest between September 2015 and September 2016

Family	Latin Name
Osphronemidae	*Betta anabatoides, Betta foerschi, Luciocephalus pulcher, Luciocephalus aura, Belontia hasselti, Sphaerichtys osphromenoides, Sphaerichtys acrostoma, Trichopodus pectoralis*
Cyprinidae	*Cyclocheilichthys janthochir, Osteochilus spilurus, Desmopuntius foerschi, D. hexazona, D. rhoboocellatus, D. johorensis, Eirmotus sp., Rasbora kalochroma, R. cephalotaenia, R. dorciocellata, R. kalbarensis, Osteochilus melanopleura, Trigonopoma gracile, Striuntius lineatus*
Channidae	*Channa pleurophthalmus, C. micropeltes, C. lucius, C. bankanensis, C. sp.*
Siluridae	*Silurichtys hasseltii, Kryptopterus macrocephalus, Ompok leiacanthus, Wallago leeri*
Helostomatidae	*Helostoma temminickii*
Hemiramphidae	*Hemirhamphodon chrysopunctatus*
Mastacembelidae	*Macrognathus maculatus, M. aculeatus*
Clariidae	*Clarias sp., Clarias sp., Enchelochlarias tapeinopterus*
Bagridae	*Mystus olyroides, Leiocassis micropogon, Leiocassis sp.*
Pristolepididae	*Pristolepsis grooti*
Anabantidae	*Anabas testudineus*
Nandidae	*Nandus nebulosus*
Horabagridae	*Pseudeutropius moolenburghae*
Chacidae	*Chaca bankanensis*
Synbranchidae	*Monopterus sp.*

Table 2 illustrates the species richness, total number of fish trapped, Catch Per Unit Effort (CPUE) and the inverse of Simpson's diversity index.

Table 2: Species richness, number of fish trapped and calculated inverse Simpson's diversity for each habitat

Habitat	*Species richness*	*Number of fish trapped*	*Average CPUE*	*Simpsons 1-D*
River	39	55145	8.44	0.82
Forest	27	3938	1.22	0.70

Figure 1: Monthly CPUE in the river and forest

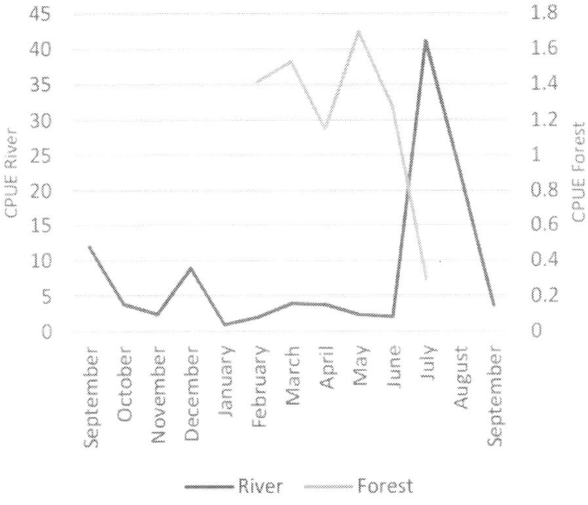

Figure 2: Average rainfall (mm) per month and river and forest water depth (m) from September 2014 to September 2015

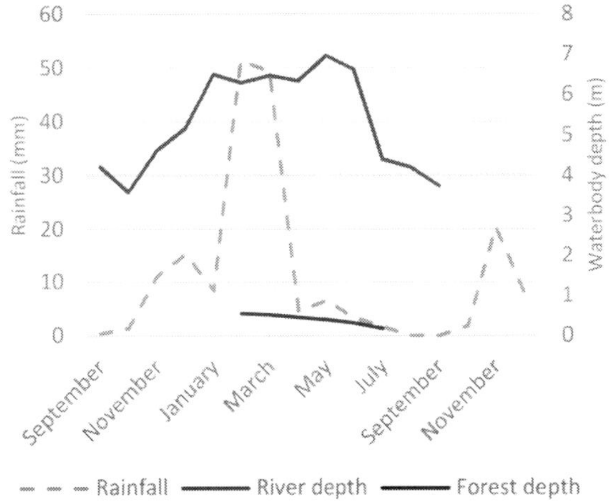

Figure 1 illustrates the calculated CPUE for each month from September 2014 to September 2015 in the Sabangau River and from February to July 2016 in the forest. In the river, the two increases in CPUE in December and July are related to the changing seasons from dry season to wet season (December) and wet season to dry season (July). During these months, large changes in environmental conditions occurred in, for example, rainfall and water depth (Figure 2). These months also coincide with the main fishing seasons in the area, when increased numbers of local villagers are seen fishing on the river. Percent mortality was calculated for each month of trapping and Figure 3 illustrates the mortality rates of the river surveys. In October 2014 we had the maximum level of fish mortality in our traps, reaching 50%. This then dropped to less than 10% for the majority of the wet season when dissolved oxygen levels were also higher. We see an increasing trend of mortality rates after July (with the onset of the dry season) where there is also a corresponding decrease in dissolved oxygen levels.

oxygen levels (mg/L) in the Sabangau river

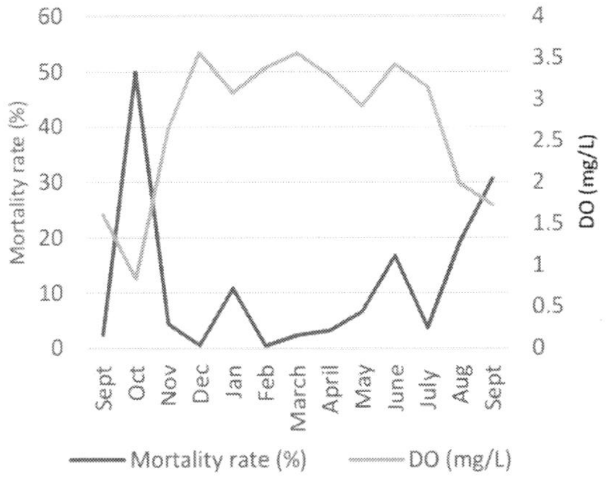

DISCUSSION

The sampling programme produced a species list comprising 47 fish species across both the Sabangau river and forest habitats. Giam *et al.* (2012) projected that Central Kalimantan had 45 different species in its TPSF habitats, and so our results are supportive of and add to this projection. As with any fauna trapping methods, our fish traps have limitations including being selective against certain fish sizes, being dependent on fish behaviour and potentially being selective against certain species. With the use of a wider range of sampling methods this species list could be added to in the future. On the other hand, sampling was carried out over a much longer period than in most other surveys in this region. The species total is comparable to and at times higher than those from other surveys in peat-swamp environments. In Batang Kerang in Balai Ringin, Sarawak, 12 species were found in the black water habitat (Rahim *et al.*, 2009). In the North Selangor PSF 48 different species were recorded (Ng *et al.*,

1992, 1994) and in Raja Musa PSF 22 species were recorded (Norhisyam *et al.*, 2012). Sabangau is therefore a notable area for peat-swamp forest fish diversity.

A greater total number and diversity of fish were caught in the river than in the forest, thus the river has a higher diversity index than the forest. While the forest was sampled for fewer months and further sampling might encounter more species, this difference in diversity is also likely due to the river providing a greater range of habitats than the forest in terms of, for example, greater range of water depths and vegetation densities and types. In order to continue to build a complete fish species list for the area, the use of additional fishing methods, including nets and rod fishing, would be necessary. When designing future sampling programmes, it is also recommended to take into consideration the perspectives of the local community members and fisherpeople: fishing methods with high mortality rates should not only be avoided to limit fish deaths while sampling, but also to avoid fisherpeople perceiving the researcher as fishing for consumption and taking fish from the river. This could potentially have negative implications for local perceptions of fish research and, thus, for conservation efforts.

Due to the limitations of the trapping method and its selectivity in terms of fish capture, it is not possible to produce absolute population estimates for the various species that were identified during the study. However, the same traps used in this research could be used in the future to monitor catch trends and population dynamics e.g. decreasing catch trends are a likely sign of decreasing fish populations in the area.

In addition to dissolved oxygen, this project is also investigating the other environmental variables that may contribute to fish mortality. A drop in dissolved oxygen levels in the river during October could have played a significant role in the increase in mortality seen in that month, but other factors may also have an influence. Based on correlations between environmental data and fish mortality, the project aims to provide guidelines for future monitoring of the river, by recommending time periods and environmental conditions that minimise mortality and are therefore most appropriate for fish surveys to be undertaken.

CONCLUSION

This project identified 47 fish species in the Sabangau peatland, with 39 species found in the Sabangau river and 27 in the peat swamp forest. Local trapping methods (*tampirai*) were used, with trapping in the river undertaken on a monthly basis over the period of 13 months, while the forest habitat was sampled over a 5-month period. Environmental variables including dissolved oxygen, water temperature, pH, turbidity and nutrient levels were also measured in both locations monthly. Fish mortality data were obtained which along with the environmental data, will be used to inform appropriate sampling strategies for future monitoring in order to minimise fish mortality. The traps employed in this study were shown to be an effective sampling tool since they trapped fish according to a consistent and reasonably well understood bias, were available locally and required little expertise in deployment. These were important considerations for a baseline study that is anticipated to be continued by local staff in future years. In addition, the data from sampling in both the forest and river will be compared to data from traditional fish ponds that have been built as a sustainable livelihood initiative at the forest edge in order to better understand the potential of these artificial fish habitats for local livelihood support.

Continued monitoring in the sample locations is highly recommended in order to collect longer-term data on fish catch, and hence population, trends and water quality to facilitate on-going evaluation of river health. Fishing is an important source of protein and income locally and therefore surveys of fish populations and river health are vital not only to understand the TPSF environment but also the implications of environmental changes on local human communities. These data also provide essential information by which to evaluate local sustainable livelihood projects such as the use of fish ponds. While fish may not be the most charismatic of peat swamp forest species, like great-apes or felids, they provide one of the clearest faunal links between people, livelihoods and their natural environment. In areas with high dependence on fish for livelihoods, fish research and conservation projects could be a great opportunity to increase the relevance of environmental research to local communities and to potentially increase local support for conservation projects, as well as providing improved knowledge and understanding of livelihood strategies.

ACKNOWLEDGEMENTS

Many thanks to the research assistants who have supported this research in the field; Iwan, Amat, Krisyoyo, Karno and Unyil. Thanks are given to CIMTROP, the local counterpart who supported the project, as well as OuTrop and their staff and volunteers for their helped with logistics and fieldwork. Finally, thanks to the Rufford Foundation and the International Peat Society for their vital funding.

REFERENCES

1. Dudgeon D, Choowaew S, Ho SC. (2000). *River conservation in Southeast Asia: Conflicts, constraints and compromise.* Pages 279–308 in Boon PJ, Davies BR, Petts GE, eds. Global Perspectives on River Conservation: Science, Policy and Practice. Chichester (UK): John Wiley & Sons.
2. Giam, H., Koh, L.P., Tan, H.H., Miettinen, J., Tan, H.T.W. and Ng, P.K.L. (2012) *Global extinctions of freshwater fishes follow peatland converstion in Sundaland.* Frontiers in Ecology and the Environment, 10:465-470.
3. Merilä, J. (2015). *Baiting improves CPUE in nine-spined stickleback (Pungitius pungitius) minnow trap fishery.* Ecology and evolution, 5(17):3737-42.
4. Ng, P. K. L., J. B. Tay, K. K. P. Lim & Yang, C.M. (1992) *The conservation of the fish and other aquatic fauna of the North Selangor Peat Swamp Forest and adjacent areas.* AWB Publication No. 81, Kuala Lumpur, Malaysia, pp. I-iv, 1-90, figs. 1-110.
5. Ng, P. K. L., J. B. Tay & Lim, K. K. P. (1994) *Diversity and conservation of blackwater fishes in Peninsular Malaysia, particularly in the North Selangor peat swamp forest.* Hydrobiologia, 285, 203-218.
6. Noor, Y. R., Heyde, J., & Suryadiputra, I. N. (2005). *Community-based approach to peatland adaptation and management in Central Kalimantan, Jambi, South Sumatra, Indonesia.* In D. Murdiyarso & H.
7. Norhisyam, M.S., Roshani, O., Zuhairi, A.N.M., Akmal, S.N., Mohd M.Z., Syahril, Ainil Hawa, S., Wahidah, M.N., Harmin, S.A. (2012) *Water Quality, Diversity and Distribution of Blackwater Fishes in Selected Locations of Raja Musa Peat Swamp Forest Reserve.* Malaysian Sciences and Technology Congress 2012

Abstract No: A-145

RECREATION IMPACT ON THE SOIL OF TROPICAL RAIN FOREST IN MALIAU BASIN CONSERVATION AREA (MBCA), SABAH, MALAYSIA

Wilter A. Malandi[1*], Ian D. Rotherham[2] and Siti Rahayu M.Hashim[3]

[1]*Faculty of Development and Society, University of Sheffield Hallam, Sheffield, United Kingdom*
[2]*Faculty of Development and Society, University of Sheffield Hallam, Sheffield, United Kingdom*
[3]*Faculty of Science and Natural Resources University Malaysia Sabah, Jalan UMS, 88400 Kota Kinabalu, Sabah, Malaysia*

**Corresponding author: wilaz08@yahoo.co.uk*

Assessing recreation impacts to the soil in MBCA was conducted on long-established trails using convenient point sampling. Five (5) trails with different usage rate were selected. On trails, transect line located at most attracted point and alienated perpendicular to the trail as a basic line. Five (5) plots systematically located fairly along the transect and each plot size is 1m2 with interval distance of 2.5m apart. One plot located on the trail as comparison while another 2 plots located both sides of the trail for fair impact assessment. The outer last plots were located beyond 5m off-trail for control purpose. Comparison of soil compaction, soil organic matter and moisture content were conducted in the trailside and control quadrate. The result indicated that soil moisture content (%) and organic matter content (SOM) were lower on trails subjected to high visitor use than that on trails under low use. However, soil compaction and moisture content on high-use trails were higher than that on low use. The rate of change in each of the Soil properties moving outwards from the centre of the trail towards the undamaged area on its margins and beyond was higher on trails under high visitor use than on low-use trails. The impact of low-visitor use is localized and limited to the trail boundaries and their immediate surroundings (5 m axis perpendicular to the trails), while the effected on high-use trails is dispersed over a larger area. The conclusion derived from this study is that the spatial damage caused to area in numerous low-use trails and high visitor use is significantly different particularly the occurrence of soil organic matter. Thus, there is a need to reduce the number of visitation and to rehabilitate them.

Keywords: *soil, recreation impact, compaction, organic matter*

Abstract No: A-191

SUSTAINABILITY-EDU CAMPAIGN FOR THE PEATLAND: AN EARLY PREVENTION ACTION OF FUTURE INDONESIA

Nina Yulianti[1, 2*], Betrixia Barbara[3], Rony Teguh[4], Eritha Kristiana Firdara[5] and Muliatie[1]

[1]*Division of Agrotechnology, Faculty of Agriculture, University of Palangka Raya, Indonesia*
[2]*Division of Management of Natural Resources and Environmental, Graduate School of University of Palangka Raya, Indonesia*
[3]*Division of Social Economics Agricultural, Faculty of Agriculture, University of Palangka Raya, Indonesia*
[4]*Division of Informatics, Faculty of Engineering, University of Palangka Raya, Indonesia*
[5]*Division of Forestry, Faculty of Agriculture, University of Palangka Raya, Indonesia*

**Corresponding author: ninyulianti.unpar@gmail.com, nina@kaltengpeatlandfire.org*

SUMMARY

Peatland fires in Kalimantan (Indonesia's Borneo) occur almost every year, which is with an average of hotspot (NASA source) reaching 15,000 or more than fifty percent of total fires in Indonesia (Yulianti et al, 2012). In 2015, the peak of fires occurred in October with 400 hotspots/day on peatlands. Previous study has categorized peatland fire as human-made disaster. However, it should be more appropriately categorized as an environmental disaster due to its huge impact not only on the local, but also extends towards global environments. This study aims to promote sustainable peatland and fire early warning towards Sustainable Development Goals (SDGs) particularly in Central Kalimantan, with the pilot province of REDD+ in Indonesia. The pilot site was located in four villages and capital city, and was conducted from pre-fire season 2014 to fire season 2015. In order to improve the awareness of the local community, this study applied 5 (five) learning methods such as class lectures, trainings, audio-visual media, dialogue and e-learning. The selection of a suitable method was dependent on the knowledge and the skill of the audiences. The result of this study shows that the effectiveness of the learning method was difficult to measure. From the comparison of the five learning methods, most numbers of 'physical' audience was obtainable during the audio-visual media activity. The audiences in these sessions were mostly undergraduate degree and student. There were three documentary films used: namely, "The lands above the cloud", "There is no place we rather be", and "Fight against the haze". The films' contents explain the difficulty of the firefighting work, the bad effect of fire and the social activity in the community. The main focus is the understanding of the audience on how to sustain the peatlands by reducing fires and haze crisis.

***Keyword**: Central Kalimantan, learning, peat fire, sustainability, tropical peatland*

INTRODUCTION

Previous studies in Kalimantan showed the most fire prone area was part of Central Kalimantan Province. The studies mostly investigated the relationship of degraded peatland, weather factors (precipitation patterns and El Niño) and agriculture activities particularly areas with the most prolific cultivation of palm oil (Yulianti and Hayasaka, 2013). These severe fires have many serious negative impacts on human health, local economies, and global climate change (Limin et al., 2007; Yulianti, 2011). Indonesia has been positioned as one of the country emitters of carbon and great exporter of trans-boundary haze among the countries of Southeast Asia.

The common question revolves around, "Who is the culprit behind the forests and land wildfire?" In the current state of law enforcement related to this disaster, the public assumes that the culprit would be difficult to be apprehended. Proactive steps are required, so that recurrent and future fires can be prevented or at least reduced. One approach is by creating public awareness through education among the public and related industries. This strategy is expected to develop the knowledge and values that drive behavior in support of a sustainable environment.

METHODS

The five learning activities applied were (1) lectures, (2) training, (3) audio-visual media, (4) dialogue and (5) e-learning. Simple methods such as lectures and dialogues are intended for villagers where simple and easily understood practical presentations were utilized. Training on the use of appropriate fire monitoring applications was carried out with policy makers and students. In addition, the audio-visual media (three documentary films) was shown to high school students, university students and lecturers. The e-learning method was targeted towards the online community, which includes other researchers. The online material includes the documentary videos and data related fires.

RESULTS AND DISCUSSION

1) Lectures

Presentation of these methods was assisted by visual tools in the form of slide presentations and merchandise. The following are the lecture activities that had been carried out:

- Workshop and Meeting of the Parties Peatland Fires Research (Peatland Fire Research Workshop and Stakeholder Meeting) on March 11, 2015 in Kuala Kapuas, Central Kalimantan, with the main audience from Kapuas district government and NGOs (~ 30 participants).
- Satellite Imagery Analysis Training and Monitoring Spot Sample on June 8, 2015, in Palangka Raya with the main audience from the Local Government Unit of Central Kalimantan and Central Kalimantan UPT KLHK (~ 20 participants).
- Workshop on "Forest and Peatland Fires in Central Kalimantan and Its Impact on Humans and the Environment" on October 3, 2015, at the University of Palangka Raya (UPR) with the University of Palangka Raya and high school students (~30 participants).
- Workshop and the Third Meeting of the Parties Peatland Fires Research (Third Peatland Fire Research Workshop and Stakeholder Meeting) on October 27, 2015 in Palangka Raya, Central Kalimantan, the main audience from the Local Government Unit of Central Kalimantan and NGOs in Central Kalimantan (~50 participants).

2) Training

This activity was divided into two objectives: (i) the demonstration process to understand step by step; and (ii) the demonstration of results to show or demonstrate the result of a process. Below are the activities that have been performed:

- Methods based fire monitoring online on August 1, 2015 in Tumbang Nusa, District Pisau the main audience of local villagers and foreign students from OUTROP (Orangutan Tropical Peatland Project) totaling 45 people.

- The introduction of the website and android applications related fires in Central Kalimantan, on October 3, 2015 at the University of Palangka Raya with the main audience of high school students and Students Se-city of Palangka Raya which numbered about 30 people.
- REDD + Training Academy's expert staff of Parliament on 7 November 2015 in the Office UNORCID (The United Nations Office for REDD+ Coordination in Indonesia) with the main audience of expert staff of Parlementaria of Commission IV, VII and VIII which numbered about 30 people.

3) Audio-visual media,

Audio-visual media is an intermediary or use of the motion materials such as documentary movie from various perspectives. Last year (27 October 2015), the screenings of Forest and Peatland, was conducted at the University of Palangka Raya. The audiences included academicians from the Faculty of Agriculture (~200 participants), as well as the Vice Rector II UPR, the Mayor and Vice Mayor of Palangka Raya.

4) Dialogue

The advantage of this method is that it helps the growth of the attention of participants to the material presented and to develop their ability to use their knowledge and experience, so that knowledge becomes functional. These activities are conducted with several sources that was initiated by UNORCID as a response to a fire in 2015 at the event of Dialogue Series event entitled "El Niño: Advancing coordination to address haze impacts and sub-national response systems" on 7 October 2015 in the Office UNORCID, Jakarta main audience is INGOs and national private sector which numbered about 35 people.

5) E-learning

The advantage of this method is it time and cost effective. The audiences can be reached without being physically present, making it a time saving learning process. There is no travel cost incurred, and the cost of infrastructure, equipment, books, etc. can be cut back. The audiences are not limited by any geographical area and more independent learners can be reached this way. The number of visitor can be tracked by online statistics. The following are media had been designed and used in this activity:

- Central Kalimantan Peatland Fire website (http://www.kaltengpeatlandfire.org) (134 visitors)
- Kalteng Peatland Fire Facebook page (https://www.facebook.com/Kalteng-Peatland-Fire-447212238737160/?ref=bookmarks) (100 liqueur)
- Kalteng Peatlanfd Fire videos on Youtube (https://www.youtube.com/channel/UCIZLjNg9ZgkUuSGA5M-0yQQ) (viewer)

CONCLUSIONS

Learning methods of Sustainability-Edu Campaign are lectures, training, audio-visual media directly, dialogue and e-learning for early prevention action of future Indonesian's fire and haze crisis. The numbers of audiences in these activities ranged from 20 to 200 with the highest number achieved during the audio-visual method with a documentary film. E-Learning material received the most hits. To date ( ), the Facebook page has 414 likes, the website has at least 200 visitors daily, and the YouTube videos has from 21 to 148 views.

ACKNOWLEDGEMENT

This study was conducted as a part of research that was supported by the Indonesia Ministry of Research,

Technology, and Higher Education (MP3EI Scheme) on *"Development of Integrated Fire Early Warning Systems for Sustainable Palm Oil Agro-ecosistem in Peatlands"* for FY 2014-2015. The authors would like to thank the students from the Division of Agrotechnology, Division of Social Economics and Division of Informatics, University of Palangka Raya for their help in the field work study. The authors also acknowledge the beneficial support provided by the village chiefs in Pulang Pisau, Luwuk Kanan, Dadahup, Beaming Hulu and Kalampangan.

REFERENCES

1. Limin, S, H., Hidenori Takahashi, Aswin Dj Usup, Hiroshi Hayasaka, Mitsuhiko Kamiya and Naoto Murao. 2007. Impacts of haze in 2002 on social activity and human health in Palangka Raya. Tropics Vol.16: 275-282.
2. Yulianti, N. 2011. The health effect of smoke and haze from tropical forest-peat fires. In: *Textbook for summer school 2011 in Indonesia "Management strategy of tropical peatland: development and conservation"*, Nov. 8-19, 2011. Integrated field environmental science global center of excellent (IFES-GCOE) Indonesia liason office, Bogor, Indonesia. pp. 114-115.
3. Yulianti, N., H. Hayasaka and A.Usup. 2012. Recent forest and peat fire trends in Indonesia, the latest decade by MODIS hotspot data. *Global Environmental Research* 16, 1, 105-116.
4. Yulianti, N., Hayasaka, H., Usup, A., and Sepriando, A. 2013. Recent Trends of Fire Occurrence in Sumatra (Analysis using MODIS Hotspots Data): a comparison with Fire Occurrence in Kalimantan. Open Journal of Forestry Vol. 3 No.4, p.129-137.

Abstract No: A-165

USEFUL PLANTS FROM THE PEAT SWAMP FOREST: DOCUMENTING TRADITIONAL KNOWLEDGE OF THE MELANAU COMMUNITY OF KAMPUNG JEMORENG MATU, SARAWAK

Jovita Elderson Ripen*, Arlene Alicia and Tu Chu Lee

Sarawak Biodiversity Centre, Malaysia

Corresponding author email address: jovitaelderson@sbc.org.my

SUMMARY

The biodiversity of natural habitats in Peat Swamp Forests (PSFs) offers many benefits to local communities. This paper shares the experience of the Sarawak Biodiversity Centre in documenting useful plants that benefit the Melanau Community in Kampung Jemoreng, Matu, a village close to peat swamp forests. A total of 16 species of indigenous plants belonging to 13 families were identified and documented. Of these, 5 species of plants were recorded for food, 3 species for headache, 2 species for skin diseases, and 1 species each for use as an insect repellent, a food supplement, and as building material. The single species each was also identified for the treatment of wounds, hypertension, and fever. The plant family with the largest number of useful species is the Clusiaceae, with three species that had practical applications; one species in each of the families Annonaceae, Euphorbiaceae, Fabaceae, Flagerelliaceae, Schizaceae, Melastomataceae, Moraceae, Rubiaceae, Sapotaceae, Sapindaceae, Simaroubiaceae and Zingiberaceae was also found useful.

Keywords: ***Peat swamp forest, Melanau communnity, Kampung Jemoreng, Matu***

INTRODUCTION

Traditional medicine continues to play a major role among the people in Sarawak and it is expected to gain more prominence in the future. The importance of ethno botanical resources to the native communities of Sarawak is one of the driving forces behind the current trend of community-based resource management. For the Melanau community, medicinal plants are used as a therapeutic agent because they are easy to obtain and cheap as compared with modern medicine.

The use of plants for medicinal purposes has not been formally documented in Sarawak although the practice may have dated back to as early as the first existence of the nomadic tribes on the island. More contemporary records on the use of wild plants for medicinal purposes have been written for the Kedayan communities in Sarawak by Ahmad (1993), and for the Iban communities in Batang Ai areas and the Kelabit communities in Pa Dalih, Bario by Christensen (2002). Khamisiyah (2006) has similarly documented the traditional herbal medicines of the Bidayuh-Selako communities in Lundu areas of Sarawak. As part of a comprehensive documentation on the ethno botany of the Lanjak-Entimau Wildlife Sanctuary area in Sarawak, Chai (2000) identified and documented many more applications of wild plants for consumption and medicinal uses; wild vegetables, wild fruits and edible oil were consumed as food, while others were used as traditional medicine, firewood, materials for arts and crafts, and construction materials.

The more recent studies on medicinal plants of the state have been reported in Medicinal Plants of Sarawak (Chai, 2006). Chai's study recorded a total of 608 species of medicinal plants used by various communities of Sarawak. Another study on the useful plants of the state appears in The Flora of Pulong Tau National Park (Pearce, 2006). This study recorded 27 plant species with 40 medicinal uses based on information from the local communities. Unfortunately, no study has been carried out on the systematic documentation of medicinal plants used by the Melanau community of Jemoreng Matu, Mukah district.

This paper shares the experience of the Sarawak Biodiversity Centre (SBC) in documenting useful plants that have benefited the Melanau Community in Kampung Jemoreng, Matu. The village is well known for Jemoreng Ketiau oil. Ketiau is moderately hard reddish timber, suitable for making solid doors, cabinet and furniture. The seeds produce Ketiau fat, used by the local people for cooking and lighting. However, the production of Ketiau oil is diminishing due to deforestation. Ketiau seeds from Kampung Jemoreng were brought back to SBC and oil was extracted. The oil producing seeds showed that it has the potential in food flavoring and cosmetic industries.

OBJECTIVE

The objective of the study is to document beneficial plants used by the Melanau Community in Kampung Jemoreng, Matu.

Study location

The study was carried out with the Melanau community at Kampung Jemoreng, Matu, Mukah District of Sarawak, approximately 8km from Matu. The Melanau community in the area practiced traditional medicine using plants found in the forest. Most members of the community worked in the city while others were paddy farmers. Most of the area had been developed for crop plantation and only a few areas remains as undisturbed environments with clean rivers and jungle streams amidst the peat swamp forest.

METHODOLOGY

Documentation

The documentation of useful plants was carried out on 27 and 28 November 2011, and 4 February 2014. The local community leader was approached to help identify residents knowledgeable with the use of traditional medicinal plants. They were incorporated into the study as knowledge holders and field guides. For this study, plant collections were carried out with the assistance of the same knowledge holders to identify plants and to ensure consistency information. Vernacular plant names, their uses and methods of preparing the herbs were recorded during the plant collection sessions. In the study, the field parameters recorded included details on the location, habitat, and all related information concerning the use of the plant.

Plant Collection and Specimen Identification

Plant samples were collected for herbarium, research, and propagation purposes. The specimens of each species were brought to the Sarawak Herbarium (SAR) for identification and deposited at the SBC herbarium. All plant samples were processed at SBC for further research and selected plant samples were propagated at SBC.

RESULTS AND DISCUSSION

Plants Documented

A total of 16 species of wild indigenous plants belonging to 13 families were identified and documented. The plant family with the highest number of useful species was the Clusiaceae, with three species that had practical applications. Each of the following families has a species that has a useful function: Annonaceae, Euphorbiaceae, Fabaceae, Flagerelliaceae, Schizaceae, Melastomataceae, Moraceae, Rubiaceae, Sapotaceae, Sapindaceae, Simaroubiaceae, and Zingiberaceae. Some of these plants were available at the local market. In this study, the local community mostly used plants as food (refer to Chart 1). This showed that they have the knowledge in edible plants and still depending on the forest resources to supplement their livelihood.

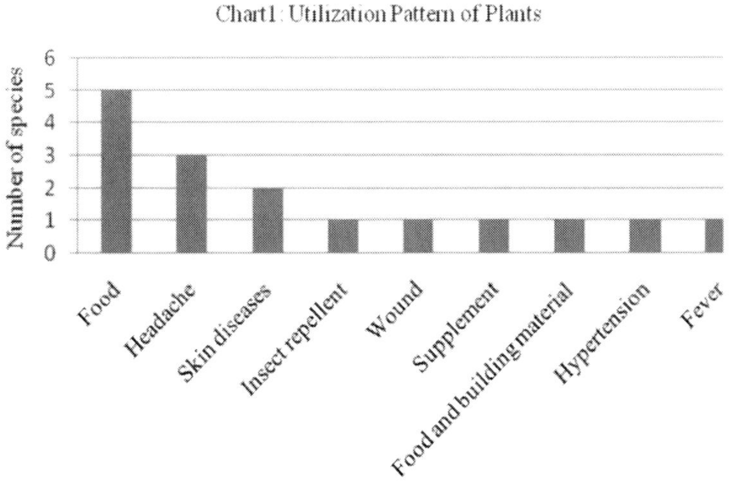

Pattern of Utilization

Chart 1 shows the number of uses for the plants under different categories of utilization, according to the selected villagers who had wide knowledge of useful plants in Kampung Jemoreng. Follow up visits are required to document these plants further, especially plants that are indigenous to Sarawak.

This study revealed that out of 16 species, the most frequently utilized plant part was the fruits with 5 species, followed by leaves with 4 species, bark with 2 species, latex with 2 species and rhizome with 1 species. In another 2 species, the entire plant was utilized. The record on the fruits is higher than the other plant parts due to the documentations were conducted coincided with the fruiting season.

The herbal preparations were for internal and external use. 8 species were for internal use while the other 8 species were for external use. For internal use, the plant part was boiled and drunk. For external use, the plant part was pounded and applied on the affected area.

Chart 2: Number of plant species from which various plant parts were used

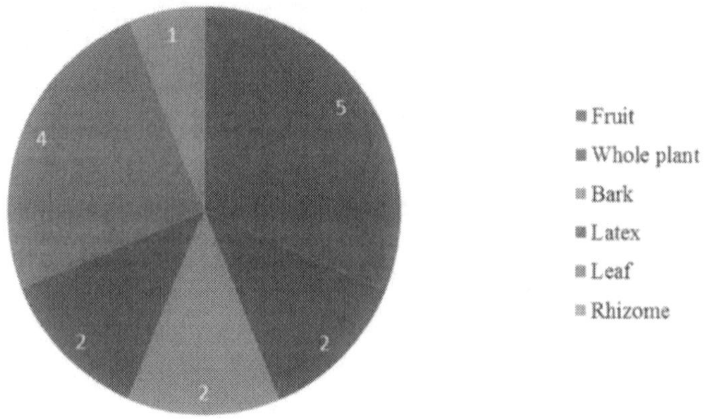

CONCLUSION

A total of 16 species of wild indigenous plants belonging to 13 families were identified and documented for their utility value as medicines, food, and construction material. Most of the species were documented for medicinal and food purposes. This study provides information on the plants useful to the Melanau Community in Kampung Jemoreng, Matu. The results, though preliminary, contribute to a broader understanding of the utilization pattern of plant resources, whether as medicine, food and other purposes by the Melanau community. This knowledge should be documented and preserved before it disappears. Plant conservation measures such as propagating selected species in the community nursery should be taken to conserve useful plants. In this regard, raising awareness among the local people on sustainable utilization and management of plant resources would be a step in the right direction. The government should also empower the local community through capacity building so that they can generate revenue from traditional knowledge and improve their socio-economic wellbeing.

ACKNOWLEDGMENT

The authors wish to acknowledge Sarawak Biodiversity Centre for the financial and technical support provided. The Sarawak Forest Department is also acknowledged for the use of its herbarium. Special thanks go to the Melanau community in Kampung Jemoreng, Matu for their assistance and their imparting for valuable knowledge on useful plants.

REFERENCES

1. Ahmad, F. B. 1993. Medicinal plants used by the Kadayan community in Sarawak. *Sarawak Museum Journal* 44 (65), pp. 45-57.
2. Chai, P. 2000. Ethnobotany. In E. Soepardmo and Paul P.K. Chai (Eds), Development of Lanjak-Entimau Wikdlife Sanctuary as a Totally Protected Area – Phase I & Phase II, Scientific Report, Forest Department Sarawak and International Tropical Timber Organization, Kuching, pp 175-188.
3. Christensen, H. 2002. *Ethnobotany of the Iban & the Kelabit.* Forest Department Sarawak, Malaysia.

4. Khamisiyah, S. 2006. *Medicinal plants of the Selako-Bidayuh community at Sematan, Lundu, Sarawak*. Kota Samarahan: Universiti Malaysia Sarawak.
5. Meer Der, P.J, San, T.K, Chiew, C.Y and J. Liam. 2004. Ramin (*Gonystylus bancanus*) Regeneration and growth in Sarawak's Peat Swamp Forests. Joining Working Group Malaysia-Netherlands.
6. Noweg, T., A. M. Razip, E. Tipot, and J. Liam. 2005. Medicinal plants of Loagan Bunut National Park. *In*: Scientific Journey Through Borneo: Loagan Bunut. A. A. Tuen, A.K. Sayok, E. Efransjah and G.T. Noweg (Eds). Pp. 202-207. Institute of Biodiversity and Environmental Conservation, Universiti Malaysia Sarawak, Kota Samarahan and UNDP-GEF Peatswamp Project, Forest Research Institute of Malaysia, Selangor.
7. Pearce, K.G. 2006. *The flora of Pulong Tau National Park. ITTO Project PD 224/03 Rev.1 (F) Transboundary biodiversity conservation-The Pulong Tau National Park, Sarawak, Malaysia*. Yokohama: International Timber Organisation, Malaysia: Japan & Sarawak Forest Department.
8. Truong, P. 2004. Regeneration of Mixed Swamp Foret of Sarawak (Malaysia) Study Based on Six Typical Mixed Swamp Forest Species. Joining Working Group Malaysia-Netherlands.

APPENDIX 1: List of plants and their method of preparation

Family	Species	Local Name	Part of plant	Method of Preparation
Annonaceae	*Goniothalamus malayanus* Hook.f. & Thiomson	Semangun	Bark	The bark is burned to produce smoke
Clusiaceae	*Calophyllum* sp.1	Bintangor	Latex	The latex applied on the affected area
Clusiaceae	*Garcinia caudiculata* Ridl.	Kandis	Fruit	The fruit is edible
Clusiaceae	*Cinnamomum* sp.	Kayu manat	Latex	The latex applied on the affected area
Euphorbiaceae	*Baccaurea* sp.	Keliben	Fruit	The fruit is edible
Fabaceae	*Archidendron ellipticum* (Blume) J.C. Nielson	Baso	Leaf	The leaf cooked as vegetable
Flagellariaceae	*Flagellaria indica* L.	Kerutung	Whole plant	The leaf crushed and applied on head
Melastomataceae	*Dissochaeta divaricata* G. Don	Kerab	Leaf	The leaf crushed and applied on head
Moraceae	*Ficus deltoidea* Jack	Tebat Melinto (Daun Kecil)	Leaf	The leaf is boiled and drink
Myrtaceae	*Melaleuca cajuputi* Powell	Gelam	Bark	The bark is pounded and applied on the affected area
Rubiaceae	*Nauclea perduncularis* Wall	Tepong	Fruit	The fruit is edible
Sapindaceae	*Nephelium cf. Maingayi*	Buah Kaup	Fruit	The fruit is edible
Sapotaceae	*Madhuca motleyana* J.F. Macbr.	Ketiau	Fruit	The oil was extracted for cooking oil. The stem is used for building material
Schizaceae	*Lygodium microphyllum* R.Br.	Kelkaat	Whole plant	The whole plant is crushed and applied on head
Simaroubaceae	*Quassia indica* (Gaertn.)Noot	Kelpait	leaf	The leaf is boiled and drink
Zingiberaceae	*Alpinia* sp.	Upak	Rhizome	The rhizome is boiled and drank

THEME 7

SPECIAL SESSION

SPECIAL SESSION 2: PEAT FOR HORTICULTURE & ENERGY

Abstract No: A-045

DEVELOPMENT OF BIOLOGICAL SUBSTRATE AND INDUSTRIAL EXPLOITATION

Xia Jiang Ping

Xiamen Jiangping Biology Substrate Technology Co., Ltd., China

**Corresponding author: 984910143@qq.com*

SUMMARY

With the mushroom residue, such as coconut chaff of agriculture and forestry waste as the main raw material, supplemented by peat, vermiculite and perlite as the auxiliary raw materials. Our company has developed exclusive seedling substrate and growing media according to objective requirements of target crop plants and cultivating objectives, so that the orientated cultivation management can be carried out smoothly.

Keywords: *Biology, substrate, technology, development, ecology*

COMPANY INTRODUCTION

Xiamen Jiangping Biology Substrate Technology Company is dedicated to the development, production and sales of biological substrates for 13 years. The company pays more attention to understanding industrial development trends, learning and introducing biological substrate developments and production technologies by following the pace of developed regions in horticulture such as Netherlands and Israel.

Our company has automated production lines and substrate packing machinery. We produce more than 30 types of products that have precise proportions and balanced mixtures and are of stable quality. Our products include biology substrates, environmental restoration materials, soil improvers which are widely used in the fields of growing vegetables, flowers,, forestry seedlings, tree cultivation, home gardening, soil improvement and ecological remediation of high and steep slopes.

With the rapid development of facility agriculture, it has been widely used in soil-less culture technology and plug seedling production techniques. Solid biological substrate in demand has been increasing. Solid substrate is taken as a principal factor in agricultural facility cultivation. Traditionally, there are ten types of solid substrates including rock wool, sand, gravel, roseite, perlite, swollen ceramsite, furnace slag, peat, bits of wood and the like, the peat has been employed most widely among them, and it is recognized that the peat is one of the most frequently-used gardening facility substrates worldwide. With the awareness of sustainable development and environmental and ecological demand have been gradually increasing in China, meanwhile, as people's awareness of environmental protection is increasingly growing, more and more people are paying attentions to agriculture and forestry production, a great mount of by-products have been recycled when processing.

It is renewable, short regeneration cycle, biodegradable, environmental friendly, etc., namely, By-products have been processed into substrates, organic fertilizers and organic mulch by resource utilization of organic wastes of agriculture and forestry. Organic wastes of agriculture and forestry mainly include bark, fruit and rice shell, sawdust, straw, bagasse and coco coir and so forth.

Module and Method

In terms of fermentation technology of agriculture and forestry waste substrate, our company has independently researched and developed fermentation technology of agriculture and forestry waste substrate, namely, controllable fermentation degree of fermentation technology, by which organic growing media has been produced. According to the different c/n rate, particle size, water content of agriculture and forestry waste, add different organic C, N source accordingly. Under the particular combined condition of photosynthetic bacteria, saccharomycetes, lactic acid bacteria which are interacted, apply the oxygen saturation, temperature of waste dumping and water content to conduct fermentation degree control in order to achieve surface fermentation and degradation, then give rise to small particle matter of the second fermentation and to remove the worm egg and non-purpose floras, and attaining high-efficient substrate material. Its primary technology is to rapidly speed to ferment decomposable small particles and half lignin and to ensure that the matters do not hurt seedlings when using. Decomposition can remove hazardous substance such as phenols and eradicate pathogenic bacteria, worm egg, and weed seedling, etc.

To inoculate is beneficial for preventing microorganism and biology from plant diseases. Xiamen Jiangping Company has successfully employed the technology to substrate fermentation in edible fungi cultivation waste, oil camellia crust, conifer bark and ecological breeding padding of livestock, at the same time, formulate equipment selection, technological parameter, and standard technological processing. After fermenting, ratio of obtaining and physical and medical indexes all meet the related production standards.

For Slow release EC method, as long as most agriculture and forestry waste material starts fermenting, there will be exiting the problem of the high EC value. It may hurt the plant growth if the problem is neglected. On that account, our company independently developed slow release EC technology, working method and equipment after agriculture and forestry substrate fermenting, and the EC value of fermentation is controlled in the range of safety.

By the treatment of the substrate fermentation and slow release EC, agriculture and forestry waste can form solid biology substrate with loosen texture and good ventilation which is rich in organic substance and beneficial microorganism. It provides good environment for root growth. The solid biology substrate becomes main raw material for developing and producing flowers and pants substrate including gardening cultivation substrate, vegetable seedling substrate, rhododendron substrate, wild nursery-grown plant transplanting substrate, forestry seedling substrate, slope ecological restoration substrate and soil improvement, and facilitate integrated utilization of agriculture and forestry waste and contribute to the society.

RESULT

Application practice in agriculture and forestry waste material as main raw material, take substrate material as main material and mix peat moss, perlite, organic fertilizer, inorganic fertilizer, and developed biology substrate with functional properties which embody the rest of characters of soil-less culture substrates except for the soil-less culture substrates with general features, increase the quality and output of plants, prevent them from continuous cropping obstacles, soil spreading diseases, and reduce the usage amount of inorganic fertilizer.

There are other four functions of biology substrate below:

One, nutrition management is very simple, and reduces the usage amount of inorganic fertilizer because of agriculture and forestry waste materials are organic raw materials with nutrient elements, it greatly simplifies nutrient management process and sharply reduces usage amount of inorganic fertilizer.

Two, plunge less fund to equipment and easily promote for use. Except for nutrient solution needed to add fertilizer, organic solid fertilizer can also be used, no need to put refined nutrient solution for formulating and test supply system.

Three, biology substrate with beneficial microorganism can not only enhance plant resistance and adjust the root environment of plant, but also advance utilization rate of fertilizer and strengthen disease resistance of plant.

Four, take organic material as principal thing to implement the organic cultivation management for producing organic.

DISCUSSION

It is estimated that annual quantity demand for solid biology substrate nationwide may reach 450 million cubic meters by 2025. So far, China is rapidly growing in the substrate industry, however, it is still in the low level in the research and development of biology substrate, formula development and processing and production, compared with international developed countries in which China still lags behind. As China is a big country in agriculture and edible mushrooms production, and has a great deal of organic waste of agriculture and forestry. Xiamen Jiangping Biology Substrate Technology Company has been dedicating to give full play to resource strengths, using organic waste of agriculture and forestry for research and development and producing different types of biology substrate so as to better serve to customers.

At present, the company mainly applies forestry and agricultural residue as principal raw materials such as mushroom residue, coco coir and peat moss, vermiculite and pearlite as auxiliary materials. Compound exclusive grow seedlings used in production and growing media based on purpose plant and cultivated aim in order to implement of oriented cultivation and management.

By the use of automated mixed-substrate production line for manufacturing and packaging, the composition of products in proportion is not only more precise, but also the products can be mixed evenly, which can keep products stable in quality.

The biological substrates manufactured by Xiamen Jingping Biology Substrate Technology Company are mainly used in the fields of vegetables, flowers, forestry, home gardening, soil improvement and high, steep slope ecological restoration and water pollution control of livestock breeding and so forth. Our development, production and marketing has been ranking of the first class nationwide.

At present, agriculture and forestry waste our company uses a lot includes edible fungi cultivation salvaged material, oil camellia crust, conifer bark, ecological breeding padding of livestock(coco fiber padding), and coco coir which are mainly used in sea mushroom, pleurotus eryngii and so on. By controllable fermentation degree of fermentation technology, slow-release EC method, useless sections in agriculture and forestry waste can be effectively degraded, and reuse them to reproduce biology substrate.

CONCLUSION

After agriculture and forestry waste material is fermented and degrade EC value, its physical and chemical properties can be improved well, it is widely used in the large-scale and industrial production. In recent years, our company has developed and promoted different series of products.

Xiamen Jiangping Biology Substrate Technology Company has been dedicating to give full play to resource strengths, using organic waste of agriculture and forestry for research and development and producing different types of biology substrate so as to better serve to customers.

Abstract No: A-260

EFFECT OF HORTICULTURE AND FLORICULTURE BIONIC PEAT ON THE ATMOSPHERIC ENVIRONMENT

Lina Wang, Ping Zhouxia, Jie Wang, Fang Dongdong

East China University of Science and Technology, Shanghai 200237, China

**Corresponding author: wanglina@ecust.edu.cn*

Horticultural bionic peat (HBP) is based on corn stover biomass as an alternative raw material to peat, and its parameters are natural peat density (specific surface area), porosity, humic acid etc., HBP can be derived from local materials of which there is a large amount of resources. The HBP is made by biological oxygen solution and biological fermentation. It is used in floriculture to grow *Sansevieria, Clivia, Phalaenopsis, Azalea*, rose, Milan etc. Improved efficiency of atmospheric environmental monitoring is reaching 50-90% of the degree of purification estimated by unit area

Keywords: *peat; horticulture bionic peat, floriculture*

Abstract No: A-264

EFFECTS OF PEAT APPLICATION AS ORGANIC SOIL CONDITIONER TO PROMOTE FERTILIZATION EFFICIENCY ON KOREAN THISTLE AND CHINESE CABBAGE CULTIVATION

Se-Won Kim[1*], Yong-Bok Kim[1], Byoung-Gon Choi[1], Dong-Geun Shin[1], Dae-Jin Kim[1], Young-Ho Seo[1], Soo-Jeong Lim[1], Seung-Chul Choi[1], Dae-Ki Hong[1], In-Jong Kim[1] and Chang-Su Park[2]

[1]*Researcher in Gangwondo Agricultural Research & Extension Services, Korea*
[2]*Director of Marketing Department Product Team, CHOBI CO., LTD., Korea*

[*]*Corresponding Author: gurbong@korea.kr; Tel. 82-33-339-8801*

SUMMARY

Peat application as a soil amendment is very effective to reduce chemical fertilizer usage. Peat treatment (2ton/ha) in cultivation of Korean thistle increased yield 31% compared to chemical fertilizer application alone. Even when reducing 50% of fertilizer amounts, co-application of peat and fertilizer resulted in thistle yields similar to standard fertilizer usage with high efficiency of nitrogen fertilizer, about 77%. As a result of treatment with the functional complex fertilizer containing peat 'Mi-Rae-Ro'^{R} in Chinese cabbage cultivation, yield increased by 44% in the standard amount of the complex fertilizer treatments, and by 35% in 20% reduced amount of the complex fertilizer compared with conventional chemical fertilizer. Therefore many kinds of fertilizer containing peat material are developing now in South Korea.

Keywords: *peat, soil amendment, fertilizer containing peat, Korean thistle, Chinese cabbage*

INTRODUCTION

Fertilizer consumption in Korea is very high being about 258 kg/ha in 2014 (MAFRA, 2015). To reduce the use of chemical fertilizer it is common to use a variety of organic materials including Legume green manure crops, compost and organic fertilizer, earthworm cast. Recently, agricultural utilization of peat resources has been expanded. Peat is largely divided into raised bog peat formed in the highlands and low moors peat formed in rainforest regions (Park, 1990). Carbon content in the peat is less than 60% and the organic matter level is 60 to 90%. Most peats are showing acidic (Jo, 1996). There are two important aspects of resource use and conservation of peatlands worldwide. So it is emphasized to preserve peatlands which have the role of carbon storage and to respond to climate change (IMCG, 2002). From the past to today peat has been used for various purposes, such as fuel, poultry excrement absorbent, soil amendment and substrate in horticulture.(Park, 1990; IMCG 2002) Peatland area in South Korea is only 0.1%(Lim, 1983), so eutrophic peat is imported from large highland area such as China, Canada and Russia. Depending on quality, the price of imported peat is \$200~\$600/ton, which is processed and formulated in the local plant. The exact total amount of imported peat is unknown because of the utilization of peat for various purposes. CHOBI, a domestic fertilizer company, imports about 700 tons per year from Jiansu Province in China, and sells the raw material itself or in combination with other marketed fertilizers with improved functionality.(FACT, 2015) In Korea, there are about 290 ha of peatlands classified as 'Yong-Ho' in eastern coastal area in Gangwon province and it has been attempted to mine for domestic production and application in blueberry culitivation suitable for acidic soil and to restore disturbed greenhaouse soils (Lim, 1983; Choi, 2012).

This study was performed following two steps. First, we compared the effects of the soil amendment treatment including peat material to establish appropriate criteria and effective verification. This field test was carried out with Korean thistle which is one of the popular wild vegetables in Korea (Lee, 2000). In case of wild vegetable cultivation, improper use of chemical fertilizers and non-composted manure cause many physiological disorders. Second, we investigated the effects of eco-friendly fertilizer products containing peat with humus and some kinds of beneficial microorganisms as additives by conducting Chinese cabbage field trials.

METHODS

Promoting fertilizer efficiency by three kinds of soil amendments including Peat in Korean thistle (Cirsium setidens Nakai.) cultivation

The test was carried out as a field trial at the Wild Vegetable Research Centre located in Pyeongchang-gun Gangwo-do in 2015. The initial soil chemical properties are shown in Table 1. The tested soil conditioners were fermented oil dregs (FOD), vermicompost (VC) and formulated commercial peat which was registered in the list of legal organic material licensed by RDA.(Kim, 2014; GWARES, 2015)(Table 2) We treated those soil conditioners with fertilizers 7 days before Korean thistle transplanting. Treatments were 600 kg/ha of FOD and peat and 2000 kg/ha of VC. At the same time we treated with fertilizer according to standard criteria N-P-K = 200-100-120 kg/ha. We also prepared 50% treatments compared to standard fertilizer usage and divided basal and top dressing amounts into 50% treatments each. Seedlings of Korean thistle were transplanted on May 28 spaced at 30×25cm after film mulching. We harvested Korean thistle leaves three times at intervals of 20 days from July 4 and determined the yield. Plants were analyzed to determine the total nitrogen content and fertilization efficiency. Chemical analysis of soil and plant components was carried out according to standard methods of RDA (2010).

Table 1: Soil chemical properties before the experiment

pH (1:5)	EC (dS/m)	OM (g/kg)	NH4-N (mg/kg)	NO3-N (mg/kg)	Av.P2O5 (mg/kg)	LR (kg/10a)	Ex. Cations(cmol+/kg)		
							K	Ca	Mg
6.8	0.18	10.7	2.6	28.9	339	133	0.35	6.13	0.92

Table 2: Chemical properties of tested soil conditioners

Soil conditioner	OM (%)	T-N (%)	P2O5 (%)	K_2O (%)	Characteristics
Fermented Oil Dregs (FOD) (Alive310 R)	66.5	4.49	2.18	1.28	Guaranteed Content(%) - OM 70, N 3.7, P_2O_5 2.2, K_2O 1.1 Mixed dregs from various oil plants
Commercial Peat (Nutri-save R)	34.4	0.59	0.83	0.78	imported material, peat100%
Vermicompost (VC)	24.7	0.71	0.86	0.46	OM10%<, made of earthworm cast

Effects of functional fertilizer containing Peat in chinese cabbage (Brassica campestris L.) cultivation and more effective fertilizer product development

This experiment was conducted to develop the complex fertilizers 'Mi-Rae-Ro'R with high humus containing peat and microbial agents in Chinese cabbage(CR Var. Syngenta) cultivation.(Kim, 2010) The test was carried out at the field of Gangwon ARES located in Chuncheon city Gangwo-do in 2010. The soil chemical properties before the experiment are shown in Table 3.

Table 3: Chemical characteristics of experimental soil

pH (1:5)	EC (dS/m)	OM (g/kg)	NH_4-N (mg/kg)	NO_3-N (mg/kg)	Av.P_2O_5 (mg/kg)	LR (kg/10a)	Ex. Cations (cmol+/kg)		
							K	Ca	Mg
6.95	0.30	21.1	14.9	16.6	960	256	0.60	3.91	0.67

Assurance components of the test fertilizer are NPK = 110-80-110 kg/ha for basal dressing and NPK = 150-0-80kg/ha for top dressing, MgO 10kg/ha and B_2O_3 1kg/ha.(Table 4) It was physically compounded with 20% additives(Nutri-SaveR). As peat additives, Nutri-save has Leonadite 95~97%, starch(formulated material) 2~3% and microorganism such as live yeast. After spraying lime and compost each 2 tons / ha, we treated test fertilizers. Seedlings of Chinese cabbage were transplanted on Apr. 26 at the planting distance of 70×35cm after film mulching.(RDA, 2002) We harvested on Jun. 29 to survey growth characteristics yield, fertilizer efficiency and change of soil physio-chemical properties.

Table 4: Component amount of tested fertilizers in each treatment

Treatment	Component amount ($N-P_2O_5-K_2O$ kg/ha)		
	Basal dressing	Top dressing	Total
CF-100	110-78-110	210-0-88	320-78-198
CF-80	88-62- 88	168-0-70	256-62-158
PCF-80	88-62- 88	168-0-70	256-62-158
PCF-100	110-78-110	210-0-88	320-78-198
Control(None)	0-0-0	0-0-0	0-0-0

* CF-80 (Conventional Fertilizer, lowering NPK components to 80% level), PCF (Peat Compounded Fertilizer)
* Top dressing date : May 25 (1st), Jun. 15 (2nd)

RESULTS

Promoting fertilizer efficiency by three kinds of soil amendments including Peat in Korea thistle cultivation

As a result of surveying Korean thistle growth, FOD and half of fertilizer treatment resulted in increased leaf length and leaf number. VC increased stem number compared to conventional treatment.(Table 5)

Table 5: Characteristics of Korean thistle growth before first top dressing depending on treatments

Treatment		Survival Rate	Plant Length	No. of stem	Leaf color
Soil conditioner	NPK(kg/ha)	(%)	(cm)	(ea)	(SPAD)
None	0-0-0	94.4±2.4	25.7±3.1	1.6±0.5	27.4±1.8
	200-100-120	97.2±4.8	35.6±0.7	2.4±0.5	34.0±1.1
FOD	100- 50- 60	98.6±2.4	37.4±1.7	3.4±0.5	36.2±2.4
	200-100-120	97.2±2.4	36.5±0.3	3.6±0.5	33.7±1.5
Peat	100- 50- 60	98.6±2.4	36.0±1.7	2.8±0.4	31.5±2.4
	200-100-120	97.2±4.8	37.3±4.3	3.2±0.8	32.8±1.3
VC	100- 50- 60	94.4±2.4	36.5±0.5	3.8±0.4	30.4±1.1
	200-100-120	95.8±4.2	36.1±2.3	3.0±0.7	33.1±1.5

Generally Korean thistle shoots can be harvested 4~5 times from May to August. The products were made by boiling, frozen and drying (Lee, 2000). As a result of three times harvesting, all tested soil amendments increased yields of shoots compared to fertilizer alone treatment. FOD (high nutrient contents) 50% reduced fertilizer and peat-standard fertilizer increased by 11% and 31%, respectively (Table 6).

Table 6: Yield of harvested Korean thistles depending on soil conditioners

Treatment		Yields in each harvesting time (g/2m²)			Sum of yield(g/2m²)		Drying rate (%)
Soil Conditioner	NPK (kg/ha)	1st(Jul. 4)	2nd(Jul. 21)	3rd(Aug. 8)	Wet wt. (Index)	Dried wt. (Index)	
None	0-0-0	391±125c	638±139c	883±95c	1,912e (52)	221 (54)	11.6
	200-100-120	785±92b	1,193±43b	1,687±197ab	3,665cd (100)	411 (100)	11.2
FOD	100- 50-60	802±78b	1,421±157ab	1,860±226ab	4,083b (111)	467 (113)	11.4
	200-100-120	772±34b	1,428±162ab	1,587±201b	3,787bcd (103)	430 (105)	11.3
Peat	100- 50-60	945±112b	1,188±84b	1,493±194b	3,626d (99)	413 (100)	11.4
	200-100-120	1207±180a	1,599±221a	2,013±189a	4,819a (131)	521 (127)	10.9
VC	100- 50-60	798±63b	1,337±210ab	1,647±223b	3,782bcd (103)	415 (101)	11.0
	200-100-120	842±199b	1,544±176a	1,587±180b	3,973bc (108)	440 (107)	11.1

* Mean in each columns by Duncan's multiple range test at 5% level(SAS 9.1)

Nitrogen uptake of Korean thistle is considered to be relatively high compared to other crops because of frequent harvests. Even if for the diet of 50% of the fertilizer, soil amendments significantly increased uptake of nitrogen. It is expected that soil improving agent can hold nutrient effectively and reduce the remnant nutrients as shown in Table 7.

Table 7: Nitrogen uptake and using rate depending on soil conditioners

Treatment		N uptake (kg/ha)					N utilizing rate (%)
Soil Conditioner	NPK (kg/ha)	1st (Jul. 4)	2nd (Jul. 21)	3rd (Aug. 8)	Remained stubble	Total	
None	0-0-0	5.7±1.8	6.3±1.7	8.3±0.9	32.1±9.0	52.4±11.4	-
	200-100-120	14.2±1.6	16.6±0.8	25.2±2.6	112.3±16.4	168.3±16.7	57.9± 8.3
FOD	100- 50- 60	12.8±1.4	19.0±2.3	29.0±4.9	88.1±22.8	148.9±19.4	76.0±15.3
	200-100-120	15.5±0.5	23.5±2.9	27.9±2.2	110.5±31.5	177.4±30.3	55.1±13.4
Peat	100- 50- 60	15.2±1.7	15.0±1.6	18.8±2.6	83.3±15.8	132.3±16.8	76.9±16.1
	200-100-120	20.2±3.1	20.3±3.3	26.0±1.6	105.3±11.2	171.8±15.8	58.5± 7.7
VC	100- 50- 60	14.3±1.1	18.2±3.1	22.6±2.7	82.2±10.8	137.3±11.2	74.5± 9.8
	200-100-120	13.3±2.8	21.4±2.9	23.4±2.3	105.0±17.7	163.1±16.4	51.8± 7.7

Soil EC and nitrate-N after the test was reduced significantly, indicating that soil conditioner could promote utilizing efficiency of nutrients. The effects were particularly good in the peat treatment because of many humus with high cation exchange capacity (Table 8).

Table 8: Soil chemical properties after the experiment

Treatment										
Soil Conditioner	NPK (kg/ha)	pH (1:5)	EC (dS/m)	OM (g/kg)	P2O5 (mg/kg)	K	Ca	Mg	NO_3-N (mg/kg)
						(cmol(+)/kg)			
None	0-0-0	6.6	0.20	12.0	326	0.34	6.30	1.01	5.9
	200-100-120	6.9	2.24	11.8	514	0.40	6.48	1.12	127.9
FOD	200-100-120	6.6	1.81	12.5	396	0.15	8.14	1.39	78.9
Peat	200-100-120	6.7	1.36	15.3	546	0.31	6.46	1.60	30.7
VC	200-100-120	6.5	1.76	13.3	459	0.17	6.89	1.37	91.3

Effects of functional fertilizer containing peat in Chinese cabbage cultivation and more effective fertilizer product development

Excessive fertilization generally increased the plant disease of horticultural crops. In this results, a fertilizer containing peat was effective to reduce soft rot and black rot in Chinese cabbage. In addition, the leaf number, weight of head and marketable rate of Chinese cabbage was improved (Table 9).

Table 9: Growth and yield characteristics of Chinese cabbage

Treatment	Leaf color (Spad)	Bacterial soft rot (%)	Bacterial leaf rot (0~9)	No. of leaf (ea)	Weight of head (g)	Marketable rate (%)
CF-100	43.3a	15.4a	6.0b	64.0ab	1,988ab	75.0a
CF-80	40.6a	12.5ab	6.0b	63.4ab	1,689ab	78.9a
PCF-80	44.5a	7.5bc	1.8a	67.5a	2,507a	81.4a
PCF-100	46.3a	8.9b	0.8a	67.7a	2,712a	80.7a
Control	29.8b	1.8c	1.3a	59.1b	1,287b	9.3b

* Bacterial disease outbreak by *Pectobacterium carotovorum* and *Pseudomonas syringae* (KSPP, 2009)

Peat-containing compounded fertilizer made 35% yields increase even in NPK 80% level compared with conventional fertilizer treatment. Nitrogen and potassium utilizing rates improved up to 72.6% and 87.9%, respectively.(Table 10) As a result of the analysis of soil physio-chemical properties after experiment, peat-containing fertilizer(PCF) lowered EC and ammonium-N (Table 11) But there were no significant differences in water holding capacity, porosity and water-resistant aggregate rate.

Table 10: Nutrients uptake and utilizing rate of applied fertilizer

Treatment	Marketable yield (ton/ha, Index)	NPK Uptake (kg/ha)			Utilizing rate (%)		
		N	P_2O_5	K_2O	N	P_2O_5	K_2O
CF-100	60.2(100)ab	151ab	22.9a	112a	44.5b	26.7ns	51.9b
CF-80	53.4(88.8)b	131b	22.1a	110a	47.9b	32.3	60.7ab
PCF-80	81.3(135)ab	195a	27.1a	149a	72.6a	33.2	87.9a
PCF-100	86,9(144)a	202a	22.7a	159a	60.4ab	31.9	75.5ab
Control	5.4(9.0)c	8.9c	2.1b	9.0b	-	-	-

C.V.(%) ------ 32.6

Table 11: Soil chemical properties after the experiment

Treatment	pH (1:5)	EC (dS/m)	OM (g/kg)	NH_4-N (mg/kg)	NO_3-N (mg/kg)	P2O5 (mg/kg)	CEC (cmol/kg)	Ex. Cations (cmol/kg) K	Ca	Mg
CF-100	6.0ns	1.06a	20.9ns	20.1a	101.7a	1219a	11.3ns	0.74ns	4.13ns	0.84ns
CF-80	5.8	0.92ab	21.2	15.7ab	69.0b	1180ab	11.5	0.55	3.77	0.73
PCF-80	5.9	0.72b	22.0	10.3b	56.4b	1215a	11.7	0.50	3.81	0.78
PCF-100	6.3	0.66b	21.8	11.4b	42.4b	1198a	12.6	0.59	4.22	0.88
Control	6.4	0.24c	21.8	8.2c	28.3c	1082b	11.5	0.52	4.96	0.95

CONCLUSION

Effects of peat treatment as a soil amendment in Korean thistle cultivation

All tested soil amendments increased yields of Korean thistle shoots compared to fertilizer alone treatment. FOD (high nutrient contents) 50% reduced fertilizer and peat-standard fertilizer increased by 11% and 31%, respectively. Soil EC and nitrate-N after the test reduced significantly, indicating that soil conditioner could promote using efficiency of nutrients.

Effects of functional fertilizer containing peat in chinese cabbage cultivation and more effective fertilizer product development

Fertilizer containing peat was effective to reduce soft rot and black rot in Chinese cabbage. In addition, the leaf number, weight of head and marketable rate of Chinese cabbage was improved. Peat-containing compounded fertilizer made 35% increase of yields even in NPK 80% level compared with conventional fertilizer treatment, in addition to improve nitrogen and potassium utilizing rates. Currently many kinds of compounded fertilizers containing peat (NS, Nutri-save) have been developed and produced in CHOBI. LTD. It is expected to be used as an effective agricultural fertilizer.

ACKNOWLEDGEMENTS

This study was carried out with the support of "Cooperative Research Program for Agricultural Science & Technology Development (Project No. PJ0105092016), Rural Development Administration, Republic of Korea.

REFERENCES

1. Choi SS, Choi KS, Park YS (2012) Peat application in blueberry soil management in Gangwon eastern coast peatland(Korean). RDA report
2. Foundation of AG. Tech, Commercialization and Transfer(FACT) (2015) Statistics of peat import as soil amendment
3. Joosten, H. & Clarke, D. (2002) Wise use of mires and peatlands. ISBN951-97744-8-3, Chapter 3. pp. 45-100
4. Jo Guk-Hyun (1996) Physio-chemical characteristics and agricultural use of tropical peat soil(Korean). *Journal of Agro-engineering and technology* 524: 157-166
5. Kim SW (2010) Report of Eco-friendly functional complex fertilizer development to lower application in chinese cabbage cultivation(Korean). Gangwondo ARES
6. Kim SW, Lim SJ, Seo YH, Cho BU, Choi SC, Heo SJ, Kim JR, Kim IJ, Seo GC (2014) Chemical characteristics of earthworm vermicompost and its application effects on soil properties to produce organic vegetables. ELS2014-14. EGU-SSS Conference
7. KSPP (2009) List of plant disease in Korea. ISBN : 978-89-963306-0-8-91520. pp. 106-107
8. Lee KG, Hong JK, Ahn MH, Bang SB, Park YH, Kywon SB, Jang GJ (2000) New economic crop wild vegetable cultivation(1st edition, Korean). ISBN 89-7947-022-3, pp. 206-214
9. Lim SU, Moon MS (1983) Composition and nitrogen distribution of peat and organic matter from paddy soil in Korea. *Journal of Korean Society of Soil Science and Fertilizer* 16(3): 266-273
10. MAFRA (2015) Statistics of pesticide and fertilizer use in Korea. http://www.index.go.kr(online)
11. Park H. (1990) Present and prospect of peat research (Korean). *Journal of Korean Society of Soil Science and Fertilizer* 23(4): 302-309

12. Rural Development Administration (2002) Cultivartion technique of highland vegetables. Chapter of Chinese cabbage(Korean). pp 49-86
13. Rural Development Administration (2010) Methods of soil chemical analysis. ISBN 978-89-480-0913-2

Abstract No: A-050

HEAVY METAL CONTENT IN FUEL PEAT

Niklas Vähä-Savo[1], Minna Salonen[2] and Jaakko Lehtovaara[1]

[1]*Vapo Oy, Yrjönkatu, Finland,*
[2]*Labtium Oy, Koivurannantie, Finland*

**Corresponding Author: niklas.vaha-savo@vapo.fi; minna.salonen@labtium.fi; jaakko.lehtovaara@vapo.fi*

SUMMARY

In this study, the heavy metal content in fuel peat delivered to 33 powers and heating plants, located in different parts of Finland, during 2014 was studied. From the delivered fuel peat (dark, highly decomposed peat, v. Post 4-7), combined samples each representing half of the year were prepared and analyzed for ash and heavy metal content. From one plant only a first half year combined sample was received, thus a total of 65 samples were analyzed. The results show that in average fuel peat in Finland contains small amounts of heavy metals, and there is no significant difference in heavy metal content in fuel peat harvested from different parts of Finland. Peat contains slightly more heavy metals than woody biomass fuels, due to the fact that heavy metals have been concentrated in peat due to the decomposition of organic material. Compared to coal, peat contains clearly smaller amounts of heavy metals.

***Keywords**: fuel, peat, heavy metal content*

INTRODUCTION

In Europe, peat is used as fuel for energy production only in few countries (Finland, Sweden, Ireland, and Estonia). Milled peat is mainly used for heat and power production in circulating fluidized bed boilers (CFB), bubbling fluidized bed boiler (BFB boilers), and pulverized firing boiler (PF boilers), while sod peat is mainly used in grate firing boilers.

Due to growing environmental and health concerns, the more precise knowledge on the chemical composition of solid fuels is of great interest. These concerns include solid, gaseous, and liquid emissions from solid fuel combustion plants as well as utilization of the solid ash from the combustion plants. At the moment in Europe, the new large combustion plant best available technology reference document (LCP Bref) is being updated. This update will most likely result in e.g. emission limits for mercury in the flue gas.

In this work, the heavy metal content of energy peat (milled and sod peat) delivered to 33 plants during 2014 was studied. The main focus was to determine the average heavy metal content in Finnish energy peat, and also to determine if there are regional variations in the heavy metal content of energy peat.

MATERIALS AND METHODS

For this study, 33 heat and power plants located in different parts of Finland were selected, Figure 1. The plants or Vapo delivered weekly or monthly combined peat samples to Labtium Oy in Jyväskylä for fuel analysis. For this study Labtium prepared from the weekly or monthly combined peat samples a 6 month combined sample for heavy metal content analysis. The combined peat samples were prepared based on the delivered dry tons of peat. Thus, from every plant a 6 month spring sample (January-June, 2014) and a fall (July-December, 2014) were prepared, except from one plant only a spring sample was obtained.

The 6 month combined samples were analyzed at Labtium Oy, Jyväskylä for ash content 550 °C (SFS-EN 14775) and 815 °C (ISO 1171) with accredited methods. The samples were decomposed according to SFS-EN ISO 15290 method A and analyzed for minor elements according to SFS-EN ISO 17294-2:2005 (mod.) method. The content of following elements were determined: arsenic (As), cadmium (Cd), chromium (Cr), copper (Cu), mercury (Hg), molybdenum (Mo), nickel (Ni), lead (Pb), vanadium (V), and zinc (Zn).

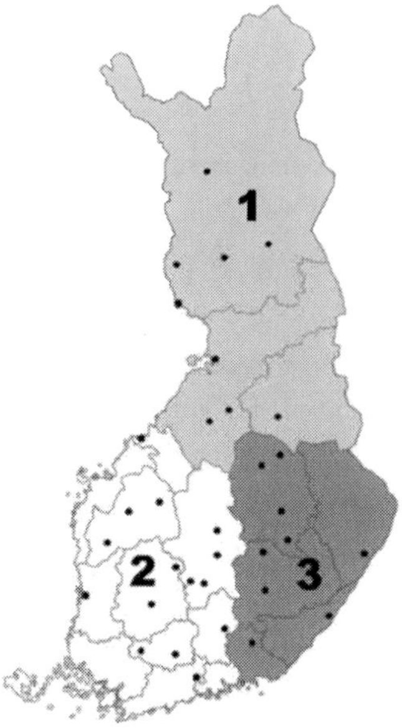

Figure 1: Locations and regions of the heat and power plants from where samples were obtained.

RESULTS AND DISCUSSION

The frequency and cumulative distribution (in percent) of the contents of different elements from the collected 65 fuel peat samples around Finland is shown in Figure 2. Some of the analyzed element contents were below the detection limit the analysis instrument. This was seen especially in the distribution of mercury, where the detection limit of the analysis was 0,05 mg/kg d.b., and 37 of the 65 samples were below this limit. Also some arsenic, lead and molybdenum concentrations were below the detection limit. One exceptionally high mercury content was also found during this study, 0,2 mg/kg d.b. No clear reason for this exceptionally high mercury content was found.

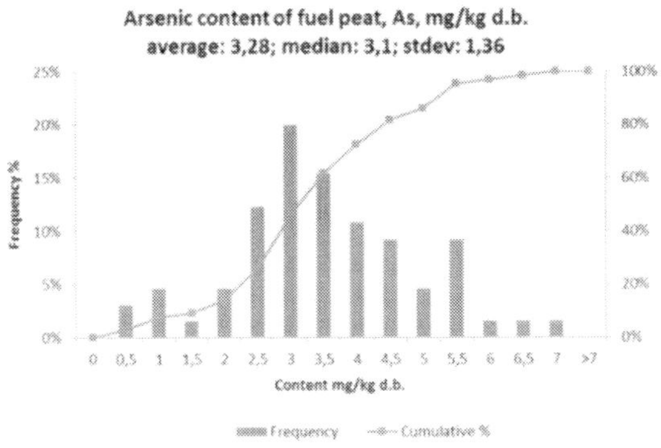
Arsenic content of fuel peat, As, mg/kg d.b.
average: 3,28; median: 3,1; stdev: 1,36
Frequency %
Content mg/kg d.b.
0 0,5 1 1,5 2 2,5 3 3,5 4 4,5 5 5,5 6 6,5 7 >7
Frequency
Cumulative %

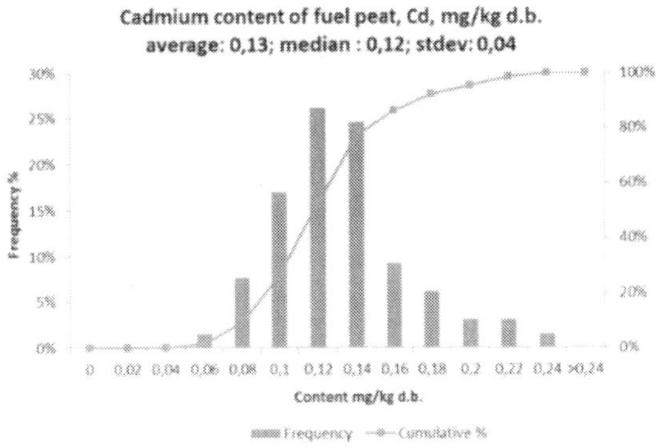
Cadmium content of fuel peat, Cd, mg/kg d.b.
average: 0,13; median : 0,12; stdev: 0,04
Frequency %
Content mg/kg d.b.
0 0,02 0,04 0,06 0,08 0,1 0,12 0,14 0,16 0,18 0,2 0,22 0,24 >0,24
Frequency
Cumulative %

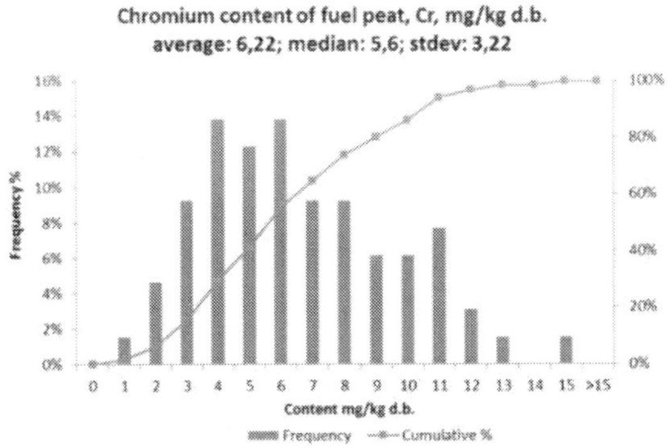
Chromium content of fuel peat, Cr, mg/kg d.b.
average: 6,22; median: 5,6; stdev: 3,22
Frequency %
Content mg/kg d.b.
0 1 2 3 4 5 6 7 8 9 10 11 12 13 14 15 >15
Frequency
Cumulative %

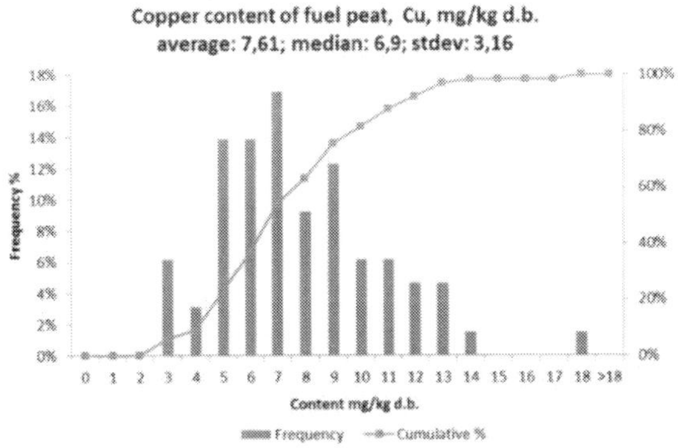
Copper content of fuel peat, Cu, mg/kg d.b.
average: 7,61; median: 6,9; stdev: 3,16
Frequency %
Content mg/kg d.b.
0 1 2 3 4 5 6 7 8 9 10 11 12 13 14 15 16 17 18 >18
Frequency
Cumulative %

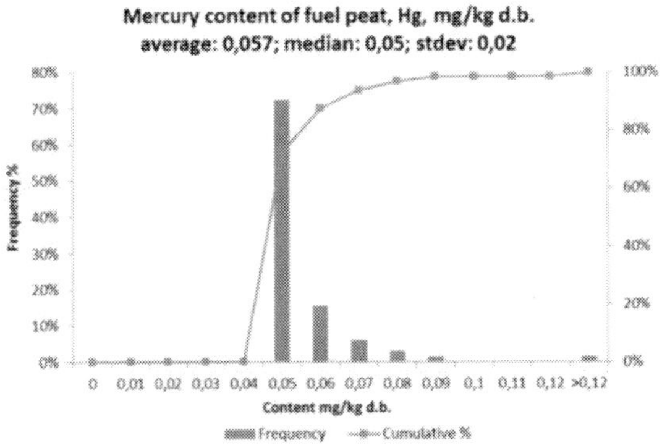
Mercury content of fuel peat, Hg, mg/kg d.b.
average: 0,057; median: 0,05; stdev: 0,02
Frequency %
Content mg/kg d.b.
0 0,01 0,02 0,03 0,04 0,05 0,06 0,07 0,08 0,09 0,1 0,11 0,12 >0,12
Frequency
Cumulative %

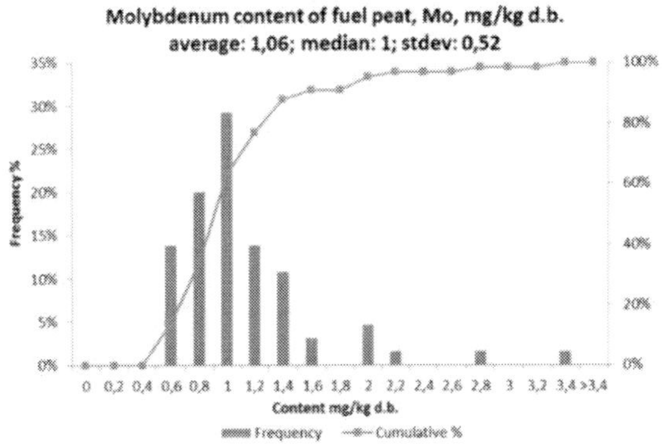
Molybdenum content of fuel peat, Mo, mg/kg d.b.
average: 1,06; median: 1; stdev: 0,52
Frequency %
Content mg/kg d.b.
0 0,2 0,4 0,6 0,8 1 1,2 1,4 1,6 1,8 2 2,2 2,4 2,6 2,8 3 3,2 3,4 >3,4
Frequency
Cumulative %

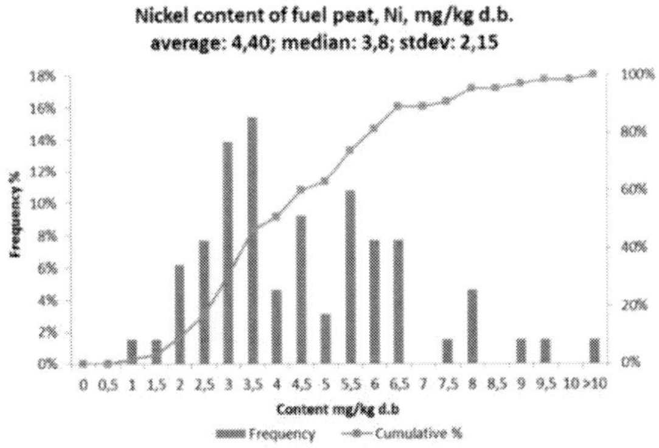
Nickel content of fuel peat, Ni, mg/kg d.b.
average: 4,40; median: 3,8; stdev: 2,15
Frequency %
Content mg/kg d.b
0 0,5 1 1,5 2 2,5 3 3,5 4 4,5 5 5,5 6 6,5 7 7,5 8 8,5 9 9,5 10 >10
Frequency
Cumulative %

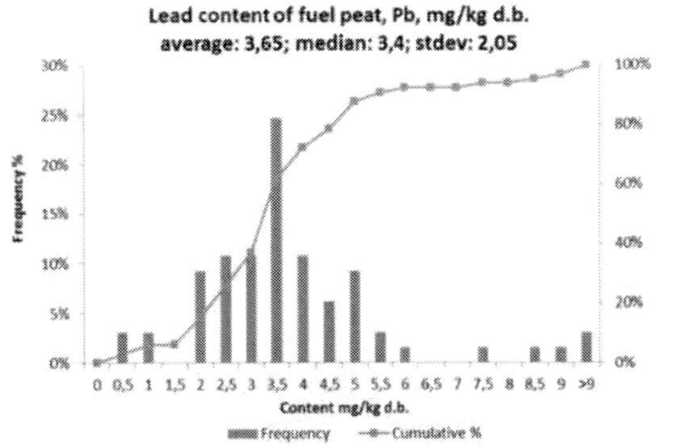
Lead content of fuel peat, Pb, mg/kg d.b.
average: 3,65; median: 3,4; stdev: 2,05
Frequency %
Content mg/kg d.b.
0 0,5 1 1,5 2 2,5 3 3,5 4 4,5 5 5,5 6 6,5 7 7,5 8 8,5 9 >9
Frequency
Cumulative %

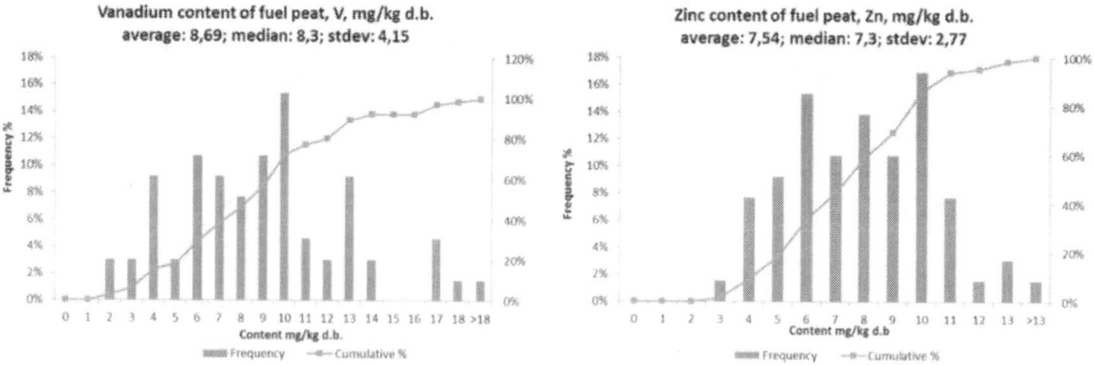

Figure 2: Frequency and cumulative distribution of heavy metals in fuel peat.

The ash content of the samples correlated with cadmium, chromium, copper, nickel, and vanadium content, shown in Table 1. Also, content of elements with similar oxidation states correlated with each other: e.g. chromium-copper, chromium-nickel, chromium-vanadium nickel-copper, and lead-cadmium.

Table 1: Spearman rank correlation of ash content and the heavy metals

	Ash content (815 °C)	As	Cd	Cr	Cu	Hg	Mo	Ni	Pb	V	Zn
Ash content(815 °C)	1	,238	,520**	,866**	,673**	,112	,340**	,744**	,084	,803**	,144
As	,238	1	,483**	,135	,367**	,339**	,277*	,006	,361**	,454**	,190
Cd	,520**	,483**	1	,385**	,494**	,434**	,359**	,218	,606**	,633**	,376**
Cr	,866**	,135	,385**	1	,660**	,171	,300*	,825**	-,005	,740**	,173
Cu	,673**	,367**	,494**	,660**	1	,073	,392**	,762**	-,123	,656**	,248*
Hg	,112	,339**	,434**	,171	,073	1	,191	-,022	,498**	,206	,375**
Mo	,340**	,277*	,359**	,300*	,392**	,191	1	,254*	,194	,424**	,262*
Ni	,744**	,006	,218	,825**	,762**	-,022	,254*	1	-,291*	,537**	,128
Pb	,084	,361**	,606**	-,005	-,123	,498**	,194	-,291*	1	,241	,345**
V	,803**	,454**	,633**	,740**	,656**	,206	,424**	,537**	,241	1	,174
Zn	,144	,190	,376**	,173	,248*	,375**	,262*	,128	,345**	,174	1

**. Correlation is significant at the 0.01 level (2-tailed).
*. Correlation is significant at the 0.05 level (2-tailed).

The fuel peat heavy metal content in Finland in average and in the different regions presented in Figure 1 is shown in Table 2. The average arsenic and lead contents were lower in Northern Finland than in Finland in average, while average chromium, copper, nickel, and vanadium contents were higher than in Finland in average. In Western Finland, the average arsenic and lead contents were higher than in Finland in average; while the rest of the heavy metal contents were at similar levels or slightly lower than in Finland in average. In Eastern Finland, the heavy metal contents were slightly lower or at similar level than in Finland in average.

Table 2: Fuel peat heavy metal content in different regions of Finland

	Finland		Region 1 Northern Finland		Region 2 Western Finland		Region 3 Eastern Finland	
n	65		18		30		17	
	Average w-% d.b.	Stdev w-% d.b.	Average w-% d.b.	Stdev w-% d.b.	Average w-% d.b.	Stdev w-% d.b.	Average w-% d.b.	Stdev w-% d.b.
Ash content (815 °C)	5,6	2,2	6,7	1,5	5,6	2,4	4,6	2,1
Ash content (550 °C)	5,8	2,2	6,8	1,5	5,7	2,4	4,7	2,1
	Average mg/kg d.b.	Stdev mg/kg d.b.	Average mg/kg d.b.	Stdev mg/kg d.b.	Average mg/kg d.b.	Stdev mg/kg d.b.	Average mg/kg d.b.	Stdev mg/kg d.b.
As	3,28	1,38	2,78	1,64	3,58	1,05	3,30	1,51
Cd	0,13	0,04	0,13	0,04	0,13	0,03	0,12	0,04
Cr	6,22	3,22	9,24	2,53	5,26	2,48	4,70	3,02
Cu	7,41	3,16	8,46	3,54	6,82	2,60	7,33	3,55
Hg	0,057	0,020	0,056	0,011	0,057	0,027	0,056	0,011
Mo	1,06	0,52	1,10	0,36	1,13	0,66	0,89	0,32
Ni	4,40	2,15	6,29	2,25	3,56	1,44	3,90	1,93
Pb	3,65	2,05	2,81	1,74	4,09	1,87	3,75	2,47
V	8,69	4,15	10,80	5,32	8,16	3,03	7,37	3,84
Zn	7,54	2,77	7,95	2,88	7,25	2,68	7,63	2,90

The average lead and zinc content in fuel peat analyzed during this study was lower than in previous studies, while copper, nickel, and vanadium contents were slightly higher, Table 3. Previous study by Imatran Voima (Lehtovaara *et al.*, 1989) showed considerably higher mercury, cadmium, and arsenic contents in fuel peat. The study was conducted in 1989, and thus analytical methods used then could be the reason for the high contents. The fuel peat studied during the Optimiturve study (Siltaloppi *et al.*, 1992) had a higher cadmium, lead, and vanadium content than the fuel peat in this study.
Merja Tolvanen (2004) studied the composition of trace elements in fuel peat in three different boilers in Finland, and the nickel and cadmium content in fuel peat was similar to this study. In her study, the arsenic content in fuel peat varied between 0, 89-15,3 mg/kg d.b, and the highest values were found in central Finland. One reason for the high variation could be that the fuel peat samples were collected during a few day mass balance test period at the power plants. During this study the samples consisted of fuel samples collected during a far longer period.

According to the Official Statistics of Finland in 2014, 4% of the total energy consumed originated from peat, 9% from coal, and 25% from wood based fuels. When compared to other fuels used in Finland for heat and power generation, peat contains less heavy metal than coal, Table 3. Also, wood based solid biofuels can contain considerable amounts of certain heavy metals, e.g. zinc, nickel, and copper.

Table 3: Heavy content in fuel peat and other fuels

	Average heavy metal contents (mg/kg d.b.)									
Fuel Peat in Finland	**As**	**Cd**	**Cr**	**Cu**	**Hg**	**Mo**	**Ni**	**Pb**	**V**	**Zn**
Vapo 1990-2013 [1]	2,38	0,11	5,19	5,76	0,06	1,22	3,87	4,14	7,85	9,38
Optimiturve [2]	2,6	0,14	5,7	5,8	-	-	3,7	5,3	-	12,2
Imatran Voima [3]	4,5	0,46	6,36	4,4	0,35	-	3,2	6,3	-	9,1
This study	**3,28**	**0,13**	**6,22**	**7,41**	**0,06**	**1,06**	**4,40**	**3,65**	**8,69**	**7,54**
Other Fuels used in Finland										
Coal [4]	5,10	-	17,10	15,50	0,10	8,20	20,80	10,30	26,50	34,80
Coniferous wood [5]	< 0,1	0,10	1,0	2,0	0,02	-	0,5	2,0	< 2	10
Logging residue, conferous wood	0,6	0,2	1,0	10,0	0,03	-	1,6	1,3	0,6	20
Bark from conferous wood [5]	1,0	0,5	5,0	5,0	0,05	-	10	4,0	1,0	100

[1] Vapon unpublished data
[2] Siltaloppi et al., 1992
[3] Lehtovaara et al., 1989
[4] Alakangas et al., 2016
[5] SFS-EN ISO 17225-1

CONCLUSIONS

The study showed that 95% or more of the collected fuel peat samples had mercury and cadmium contents below 0,25mg/kg; arsenic, molybdenum, nickel, and lead contents below 9 mg/kg; chromium, copper, and zinc contents below 13 mg/kg; and vanadium content below 17 mg/kg (all d.b.). The mercury content in fuel peat was extremely low. In over 55% of the analyzed samples the mercury content was below the detection limit, which was 0.05 mg/kg dry fuel. Ash content correlated with cadmium, chromium, copper, nickel, and vanadium content. Also, concentration of heavy metals with similar oxidation numbers correlated with each other. In northern Finland, the average arsenic and lead contents in fuel peat were slightly lower and the average zinc and nickel contents were slightly higher than in Finland in average.

Peat contains slightly more heavy metals than biomass fuels, due to the fact that heavy metals have been concentrated in peat due to the decomposition of organic material. In other words, peat is a slowly renewable fuel, which contains far less heavy metals than coal, making it a more environmentally sound fuel than coal.

ACKNOWLEDGEMENTS

The authors wish to thank Mrs Anneli Wichmann for calculating the Spearman rank correlation and employees at Labtium Oy Jyväskylä for conducting the fuel analysis.

REFERENCES

1. Alakangas E., Hurskainen M., Laatikainen-Luntama J., and Korhonen, J. *Suomessa käytettävien polttoaineiden ominaisuuksia [Properties of fuels used in Finland]* (in Finnish), VTT Technology, 2016
2. Lehtovaara J., Mustonen R., Penttilä R., Dernjatin P., and Uotila I. (1989) *Heavy Metal Contents and Natural Radioactivity of Fuel Peat (In Finnish)* Imatran Voima Oy R&D-notes, Helsinki 1989, 42 p., ISBN 951-8928-10-X
3. Official Statistics of Finland (OSF): Energy supply and consumption [e-publication]. ISSN=1799-7976. 2014, Appendix figure 1. Total energy consumption 2014. Helsinki: Statistics Finland [referred: 19.2.2016].
4. Siltaloppi L., Laitinen L., Lehtovaara J., Hakkarainen P., and Herranen M. (1992) *Optimiturve Research Program Reports 48: Analytical Methods of Peat in the Point of View of Environmental Protection (in Finnish),* Jyväskylä 1992, 61p p. + app. 15 p., ISBN 952-9500-46-7
5. Tolvanen M. Mass Balance *Determination for trace elements at coal-, peat- and bark-fired power plants* PhD Thesis, VTT Technical Research Center of Finland, 2004, 253 p.
6. SFS-EN ISO 17225-1:2014 *Solid biofuels. Fuel Specifications and classes. Part 1: General requirements*

Abstract No: A-087

TROPICAL PEAT GRANULATION AND LABORATORY TESTING

Aleksandr Mikhailov

National Mineral Resources University, Saint Petersburg, Russia

**Corresponding author: malpar5@yandex.ru*

SUMMARY

In Malaysia peat can uses for household heating and for cooking but the most important use of peat is as a fuel and energy generation. The effect of the tropical peat extrusion granulation has been investigated in this study. The purpose of this study was to definition of peat samples granulation possibility for receiving of agglomerating production (granulated peat fuel, granulated peat fertilizers). Granulation runs have been performed on natural tropical peat from a Paya Indah Wetland in Kuala Langat district, Selangor, Malaysia. The peat was mix and the resulting well mixed mass was then pelletizing by the application of pressure in conventional equipment – stiff extrusion. The granules were formed in the cylindrical mold. The extrusion experiment of peat was carried out with a piston press, established by universal Zwick/Roell Z100 Machine. Breakdown of mix via dies with a length of calibrating part of 60 mm and with a diameter of 15 mm at a speed of 0.0125 m/s. A suite of tests, which showed, characterized these granules: - dry granule strength measurements show that, these peat granules have sufficient strength for production. The normal dry granule strength is 3.0–6.0 MPa to crush the granules. - experiments on mechanical strength of granules were made, when granules could be dropped from a height of 2.0 m on a concrete floor and survive. The mechanical strength of cylindrical granules made 92.5%. A fine colloidal particle of peat promotes process of granules consolidation. The great influence on physico-mechanical properties of granules from black high-moor peat is exerted by group structure. Humic acids and easily hydrolyzable connections exert the greatest impact on durability of granules.

***Keywords**: peat, extrusion, granules, laboratory testing.*

INTRODUCTION

Fuel peat is a local, solid fuel, which is used in the form of milled peat, sod peat, peat briquettes or pellets. Fuel peat is used mainly in combined heat and power production, but peat briquettes, pellets and sod peat are also used in household appliances (Quality 2005). In Malaysia peat can uses for household heating and for cooking but the most important use of peat is as a fuel and energy generation. Granulation method can be broadly classified into two types: Wet granulation and Dry granulation. The effect of the tropical wet peat extrusion granulation has been investigated in this study. The purpose of this study was to definition of peat samples granulation possibility for receiving of agglomerating production (granulated peat fuel, granulated peat fertilizers). Granulation runs have been performed on natural tropical peat from a Paya Indah Wetland in Kuala Langat district, Selangor, Malaysia.

All materials have different properties that result in advantages and disadvantages. Study and understanding of these properties is critical to the design of a mechanical system and the selection of the correct materials for a given part. The purpose of this study is to definition of peat samples granulation possibility for receiving of agglomerating production (granulated peat fuel, granulated peat fertilizers) (Mikhailov *et al.*, 2012).

Wet granulation using high shear mixers is a widespread technique applied in fields such as peat industry and various branches of the chemical industry. Formulations are usually developed at small scale and following validation are scaled-up to production units (Benbow 1989).

MATERIALS AND METHODS

For carrying out experimental works on a peat granulation the pilot batch of peat samples raw materials from a peat deposit Paya Indah wetland Malaysia was received. Some relevant properties for peat materials are presented in Table 1. Total weight of samples – 7 kg

Table 1: Peat Sample's parameters

Sample Number	Sampling depth, m	Total Moisture (ARB), %	Ash, (DB), %	Total Sulphur, (DB), %	Fixed Carbon (DB), %	Gross Calorific Value, (DAF), kcal/kg
SG1A	0-1.0	80.3	20.2	0.19	28.6	5598
SG3A	0-1.2	88.8	20.8	0.20	28.5	5547
SG5A	0-2.0	94.0	7.8	0.19	33.3	6505
SG7A	0-2.0	92.2	12.9	0.26	30.9	5692
SG8A	0-1.25	92.5	21.6	0.13	28.9	5258
SG12A	0-2.5	84.0	24.2	0.15	25.7	5784
SG14A	0-2.05	92.0	7.3	0.14	32.3	5505

The each peat bag was opened and dumped on a plastic sheet, and thoroughly mixed by hand. A portion was removed and placed in a plastic bag for Peat Botanical Analysis and Decomposition degree of peat. The remainder (approximately 0.7 kg) was placed in a plastic bag for granulating experiments. After preliminary separation were removed large wood inclusions from peat samples. Preliminary dewatering of peat was carried out on a fabric filter press.

The separated and dehydrated peat were subjected to mechanical processing – attritioning. Attritioning of peat raw materials is carried out for the purpose of preliminary mechanical processing on laboratory chopper for a further extrusioning and nodulizing.

The moisture content was obtained on the AnD MX-50 Moisture Analyzer. Extrusion of peat was carried out on a piston press with a diameter of 32 mm and 300 mm long, established by universal Zwick/Roell Z100 Machine, by breakdown of peat via dies with a length of calibrating part of 60 mm and with a diameter of 15 mm at a speed of 0,0125 m/s and ambient temperature – 20 °C. The scheme of experimental installation is submitted in figure 1. Nodulizing of peat was seen off on the laboratory granulator OVP-020.

Figure 1: Experimental installation on universal Zwick/Roell Z100 Machine. Granulation process

Experiment on granules drying is made on experimental drying installation in a motionless layer with a constant speed and air temperature (+35 °C) with an atmospheric pressure. Air in a drying chamber moved an electric fan heater. The drying chamber 300 mm high and with a diameter of 85 mm was also isolated 10 mm by a layer of mineral wool and wrapped up by aluminum foil, for elimination of radial temperature gradients. Air temperature in a drying chamber was taken by the thermometer with an accuracy of ±1 °C. Experiments on drying were made at relative humidity of air of 30% and atmospheric pressure of 758 mm of mercury column and temperature of air of +23 °C.

Damp granules kept within the cartridge, which was suspended in a drying chamber at the height of 100 mm from an output nozzle of a fan heater. The area of the cartridge is 0.08 m^2. The mass of granules before drying, and also the mass of container decided on laboratory scales of VLKT-500 on accuracy ± 0.01 g.
Granule strength was evaluated by single granule compression tests using a «Tinius Olsen» Universal Testing Machine. The «Tinius Olsen» Universal Testing Machine allows recording a maximum force, sufficient to break all of the tested granules. Fixation of the loading operating on a sample and the deformation arising thus was carried out in the automatic mode.

RESULTS AND DISCUSSION

In Test Centre of Peat of All-Russian Research Institute of Peat Industry were carried out laboratory analyses by definition of Peat Botanical Content and Decomposition degree of Peat by GOST 28245-89 (table 2).

Table 2: Peat Botanical Analysis and Decomposition degree (GOST 28245-89)

Sample	Sampling depth, m	Peat-forming plants	Content, %	Type of peat	Decomposition degree, %/von Post Scale
SG1A	0-1.0	Blackamoor (*Typha latifolia*) Narrow-leaved cat's-tail (*Typha angustifolia*) Ferns (*Polypodiophyta*) Miscellaneous herbs Bark and wood of deciduous trees Bog undershrub	20 15 10 15 25 15	Woody grass peat	25-28/H4
SG3A	0-1.2	Blackamoor (*Typha latifolia*) Bark and wood of deciduous trees Miscellaneous herbs Bog undershrub	15 65 10 10	Woody peat	30-32/H4
SG5A	0-2.0	Blackamoor (*Typha latifolia*) Narrow-leaved cat's-tail (*Typha angustifolia*) Cereal grass family *(Gramineae) including reed* Bark and wood of deciduous trees Bog undershrub	10 10 25 35 20	Woody grass peat	30/H4
SG7A	0-2.0	Narrow-leaved cat's-tail (*Typha angustifolia*) Ferns (*Polypodiophyta*) Sedge (*Carex*) Miscellaneous herbs Bark and wood of deciduous trees Bog undershrub	20 25 5 15 25 10	Woody grass peat	25-28/H4
SG8A	0-1.25	Blackamoor (*Typha latifolia*) Narrow-leaved cat's-tail (*Typha angustifolia*) Reed (*Phragmites)* Sedge (*Carex*) Miscellaneous herbs Bark and wood of deciduous trees Bog undershrub	15 10 10 10 25 15 15	Grass peat	25-30/H4
SG12A	0-2.5	Ferns (*Polypodiophyta*) Blackamoor (*Typha latifolia*) Narrow-leaved cat's-tail (*Typha angustifolia*) Miscellaneous herbs Bark and wood of deciduous trees Bog undershrub	25 15 15 15 15 15	Grass peat	25-30/H4

Sample	Sampling depth, m	Peat-forming plants	Content, %	Type of peat	Decomposition degree, %/von Post Scale
SG14A	0-2.05	Bluejoint (*Calamagrostis*), Blackamoor (*Typha latifolia*) Ferns (*Polypodiophyta*) Miscellaneous herbs Bark and wood of deciduous trees Bog undershrub	10 15 10 15 40 10	Woody grass peat	28-30/H4

Table 2: Peat Botanical Analysis and Decomposition degree (GOST 28245-89)

Sample	Sampling depth, m	Peat-forming plants	Content, %	Type of peat	Decomposition degree, %/von Post Scale
SG1A	0-1.0	Blackamoor (*Typha latifolia*) Narrow-leaved cat's-tail (*Typha angustifolia*) Ferns (*Polypodiophyta*) Miscellaneous herbs Bark and wood of deciduous trees Bog undershrub	20 15 10 15 25 15	Woody grass peat	25-28/H4
SG3A	0-1.2	Blackamoor (*Typha latifolia*) Bark and wood of deciduous trees Miscellaneous herbs Bog undershrub	15 65 10 10	Woody peat	30-32/H4
SG5A	0-2.0	Blackamoor (*Typha latifolia*) Narrow-leaved cat's-tail (*Typha angustifolia*) Cereal grass family *(Gramineae) including reed* Bark and wood of deciduous trees Bog undershrub	10 10 25 35 20	Woody grass peat	30/H4
SG7A	0-2.0	Narrow-leaved cat's-tail (*Typha angustifolia*) Ferns (*Polypodiophyta*) Sedge (*Carex*) Miscellaneous herbs Bark and wood of deciduous trees Bog undershrub	20 25 5 15 25 10	Woody grass peat	25-28/H4
SG8A	0-1.25	Blackamoor (*Typha latifolia*) Narrow-leaved cat's-tail (*Typha angustifolia*) Reed (*Phragmites)* Sedge (*Carex*) Miscellaneous herbs Bark and wood of deciduous trees Bog undershrub	15 10 10 10 25 15 15	Grass peat	25-30/H4
SG12A	0-2.5	Ferns (*Polypodiophyta*) Blackamoor (*Typha latifolia*) Narrow-leaved cat's-tail (*Typha angustifolia*) Miscellaneous herbs Bark and wood of deciduous trees Bog undershrub	25 15 15 15 15 15	Grass peat	25-30/H4

Sample	Sampling depth, m	Peat-forming plants	Content, %	Type of peat	Decomposition degree, %/von Post Scale
SG14A	0-2.05	Bluejoint (*Calamagrostis*), Blackamoor (*Typha latifolia*) Ferns (*Polypodiophyta*) Miscellaneous herbs Bark and wood of deciduous trees Bog undershrub	10 15 10 15 40 10	Woody grass peat	28-30/H4

Extent of decomposition and botanical content considerably influence properties of peat therefore are used as universal indicators for calculation of parameters of technological processes of production and processing of peat raw materials.

From factors of group composition of peat humic acids (HA) and the highly hydrolyzable (HH) have the greatest impact on strength of granules (Lishtvan 2010). Based on these conclusions the table of peat samples on strength of granules (table 3) was made.

Table 3: Classification of peat raw materials by strength of peat granules

Sample	Ash, (DB), %	Decomposition degree *R*, %/von Post Scale	Type of peat	Moisture, %	Strength category	Humic acid-highly hydrolysable ratio HA/HH
SG1A	20.2	25-28/H4	Woody grass peat pH= 3,8 – 5,0; 20≤ *R*≤ 30	76.17	medium	1,5 – 2,0
SG3A	20.8	30-32/H4	Woody peat pH= 4,5 – 5,5; *R*≥ 30	81.80	low	2,0
SG5A	7.8	30/H4	Woody grass peat pH= 4,5 – 5,5; *R*≥ 30	79.24	low	2,0
SG7A	12.9	25-28/H4	Woody grass peat pH= 3,8 – 5,0; 20≤ *R*≤ 30	77.85	medium	1,5 – 2,0
SG8A	21.6	25-30/H4	Grass peat pH= 3,8 – 5,0; 20≤ *R*≤ 30	81.30	medium	1,5 – 2,0
SG12A	24.2	25-30/H4	Grass peat pH= 3,8 – 5,0; 20≤ *R*≤ 30	76.60	medium	1,5 – 2,0
SG14A	7.3	28-30/H4	Woody grass peat pH= 3,8 – 5,0; 20≤ *R*≤ 30	80.93	medium	1,5 – 2,0

The jointing and density which in turn depend on extent of mechanical processing of material, and also technological indicators of processes of formation and drying has essential impact on strength properties of peat granules.

Laboratory peat granules (figure 2) of Ø15 mm from wet peat (after single attrition in laboratory chopper): extrusion method; nodulizing method.

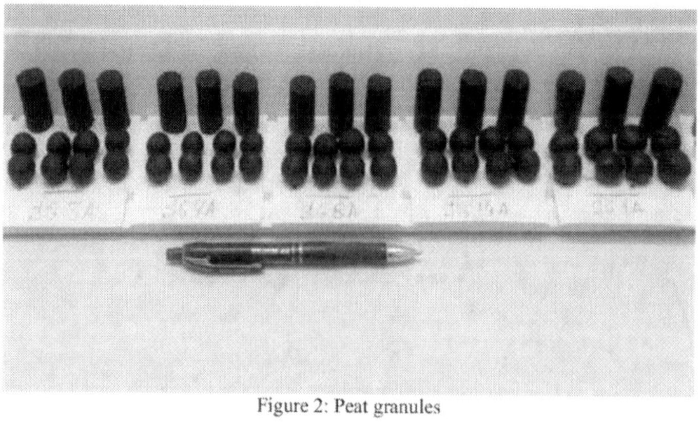

Figure 2: Peat granules

In Tables 4 and 5, the experimental results are summarized.

Table 4: Shrinkage of granules after drying (extrusion)

Sample	D_w, mm	L_w, mm	V_w, m^3 10^{-6}	w_w, %	M_{pw}, g	D_d, mm	L_d, mm	M_{pd}, g	V_d, m^3 10^{-6}	Density, kg/m^3	Drying shrinkage, %
SG1A	15.0	33.0	5.83	76.17	7.05	11.0	22.8	1.77	2.17	815	62,8
SG3A	15.0	33.2	5.87	81.80	6.46	11.8	24.2	1.58	2.65	596	54.9
SG5A	15.0	36.4	6.43	79.24	6.29	12.3	25.9	1.55	3.08	503	52.1
SG7A	15.0	34.0	6.01	77.85	6.28	12.2	24.8	1.52	2.90	524	51.8
SG8A	15.0	35.1	6.20	81.30	6.40	12.5	23.0	1.50	2.82	532	54.5
SG12A	15.0	33.3	5.89	76.60	7.04	12.0	25.0	1.74	2.83	615	51.9
SG14A	15.0	33.0	5.83	80.93	6.81	12.4	25.1	1.51	3.03	498	48.0

D_w – wet diameter; L_w - wet length; V_w – wet volume; w_w – moisture of wet granules; M_{pw} – mass of wet granules; D_d – dry diameter; L_d - dry length; V_d – dry volume; w_d – moisture of dry granules; M_{pd} – mass of dry granules. Moisture content for dry samples w_d was not measured.

Table 5: Shrinkage of granules after drying (nodulizing)

Sample	D_w, mm	V_w, m^3 10^{-6}	w_w, %	M_w, kg 10^{-3}	M_d, kg 10^{-3}	D_d, mm	V_d, m^3 10^{-7}	Density, kg/m^3	Drying shrinkage, %
SG1A	15.0	1.76	76.17	2.68	0.79	11.1	7.16	895	59.3
SG3A	15.0	1.76	81.80	2.42	0.50	11.5	7.96	628	54.8
SG5A	15.0	1.76	79.24	1.94	0.40	11.4	7.76	515	55.9
SG7A	15.0	1.76	77.85	1.92	0.45	11.2	7.36	611	58.2
SG8A	15.3	1.85	81.30	2.51	0.54	11.8	8.60	613	53.5
SG12A	16.5	2.35	76.60	3.02	0,76	12.8	10.98	692	53.3
SG14A	15.9	2.10	80.93	2.86	0.56	12.5	10.23	547	51.3

D_w – wet diameter; V_w – wet volume; w_w – moisture of wet granules; M_w – mass of wet granules; D_d – dry diameter; V_d – dry volume; M_d – mass of dry granules. Moisture content for dry samples w_d was not measured.

Dry granule strength measurements show that, these peat granules have sufficient strength for production. The normal peat dry granule strength is 3.0-6.0 MPa. Volume shrinkage of peat granules after drying makes 50-60%.

Experiments on mechanical strength of peat granules made when falling samples in height of 2 m on a concrete floor. The mechanical strength of cylindrical granules made 92.5%. The mechanical strength of spherical granules made 90.1%.

Peat granules have to have a cylindrical or spherical form (Quality, 2005). Diameter and length of cylindrical and diameter of spherical granules has to have the following sizes in mm:
diameter d – from 5 to 25; length L – from 10 mm to 7,5 d.

On quality indicators peat granules have to conform to the requirements specified in table 6.

Table 6: Quality rating (GOST 54248—2010. Peat briquettes and pellets (granules) for heating purposes

Parameter	Value of a quantity*		Test method
	Class I	Class II	
Moisture content, % no more than	16	20	GOST 11305
Ash content (DB), % no more than	15	15	GOST 11306
Net calorific value as received ($q_{p,net,ar}$), MJ/kg (kcal/kg) not less	15,0 (3600)	12,5 (3000)	GOST 147
Bulk density, kg/m^3 not less	600	450	GOST 13673
Mechanical strength, %	95	90	GOST 18132
Amount of fines, %	5	10	GOST 11130

*Class I – dry peat forming. Peat pellets. High energy Press forming process.
Class II – wet peat forming. Peat granules. Low energy Extrusion process

CONCLUSION

The conducted researches are based on the experimental laboratory modeling of preparation processes of peat, its agglomeration and drying of peat granules and prove correctness of the chosen direction of researches and possibility of practical implementation of the proposed technical and technological solutions.

The peat sample was from Paya Indah Wetland in Kuala Langat district, Selangor, Malaysia. On Humic acid - highly hydrolysable relation peat samples of SG3A and SG5A belong to low-strength category. Samples of SG1A, SG7A, SG8A, SG12A, SG14A belong to medium-strength category. The present research analyzes the possibility of peat high shear wet granulation process. The granulation of peat is carried out by extrusion method and nebulizing method. The received peat granules of two types (the cylinder and sphere) showed sufficient strength after a granulation and drying. Appearance of granules - without noticeable cracks.

Volume shrinkage of peat granules after drying makes 50-60%. Granules have close indicators to the standard, except an ash-content. Tropical Peat granulation is the promising technology to reduce transport cost and improve the fuel quality for peat fuels production.

REFERENCES

1. Mikhailov, A., Bolshunov, A., Kremcheev, E., Epifantsev, K. 2012. Requirements to peat for production of granulating fuel. *Mining Informational and Analytical Bulletin*. Vol. 4, pp. 59-63.
2. Benbow J.J., Lawsow T.A., Oxley E.W., Bridgwater J. 1989. Prediction of paste extrusion pressure. *Ceramic Bull*. Vol. 68, No 10. P. 1821-1824.
3. Lishtvan, I. 2010. Physicochemical properties of peat and their transformation when using peat deposits. *Fossil fuel chemistry*, Vol. 6, pp. 3–10.
4. *Quality guidelines for fuel peat: fuel classification and quality assurance, sampling and analysis of properties*. NT Envir. 009, Nordic Innovation Centre, Approved 2005-11. p. 24.
5. GOST 54248—2010. Peat briquettes and pellets (granules) for heating purposes. Specifications.

SPECIAL SESSION 4: TROPICAL PEATLAND BIODIVERSITY & CONSERVATION IN SOUTHEAST ASIA

Abstract No: A-314

DIVERSITY AND POPULATION DENSITY OF MESOFAUNA IN *ACACIA* PLANTATION VS CONSERVATION FOREST IN PEATLAND OF TELUK MERANTI AREA

Gunawan Djajakirana[1], Angga Iman Syah[2], and Marissa Permatasari Jayaputra[3]

[1]*Teaching Staff of Department of Soil Science and Land Resources, Faculty of Agriculture, Bogor Agricultural Institute. Wing 21 Level 4, Building of Faculty of Agriculture, IPB Campus, Darmaga-Bogor, Indonesia*
[2]*Students of Department of Soil Science and Land Resources, Faculty of Agriculture, Bogor Agricultural Institute, Indonesia*
[3]*Alumny of Department of Soil Science and Land Resources, Faculty of Agriculture, Bogor Agricultural Institute, Indonesia*

**Corresponding author: -*

SUMMARY

Peatland in Indonesia is a unique ecosystem. The peat is mostly oligotrophic peat formed from woody materials. This peat is quite poor in term of fertility; however this peatland can thrive into a dense forest due to nutrients recycling process of the litter from the trees. In the dome area, the trees are smaller than the surrounding. Most of the peatland could not support the large amount of population of the living organisms, although there is a possibility of having high diversity of organisms. Therefore, the aim of this study was to determine the population and diversity of meso fauna in peat land that was converted to forest plantation.

This study was conducted in tropical peatland both in conservation forest and industrial forest plantation of 6 and 36 months old of *Acacia* trees at Teluk Meranti, Riau Province. Kempson methods was used to count the population and the identification of meso fauna until sub order a normal light stereo microscope was used. The diversity of soil meso fauna was calculated using Shannon diversity index.

It was found that the population in the 36 months old of *Acacia* plantation was larger compared to the two other locations. This was caused by more litter produced in the 36 months old of *Acacia* as a source of food for the growth of meso fauna. Total population density in the 36 months old of *Acacia* plantation, conservation forest, and 6 months old of *Acacia* plantation were 580 indv/m^2, 470 indv/m^2, and 263 indv/m^2, respectively. The value of diversity in the forest conservation was the highest but not significantly different with the 36 months old of *Acacia*, which amounted 2.17 and 2.13, respectively.

In the conservation forest, it was found 11 sub order of meso fauna, whereas in the 36 months old *Acacia* plantation was found 13 sub order. The result suggests that the recovery condition of the diversity and population of mesofauna can be reached due to the peatland condition of long terms cultivation of *Acacia* plantation that improved the organic matter quality of the peat land.

Keywords: *oligotropic, litter, organic matter quality*

INTRODUCTION

Peatland in Indonesia is a unique ecosystem. The peat is mostly oligotrophic peat formed from woody materials. This peat is quiet poor in term of soil fertility, however this peat land can thrive into a dense forest due to nutrients recycling process of the litter from the trees. By regulation, Indonesian peatland can be used both as agricultural area or non-agricultural area. Non-agricultural area is destined to maintain its sustainability of natural environment of peatland ecosystem such as conservation forest and protected forest. Meanwhile, agricultural area is to utilize the potential of natural resources from peatland to be converted into more economic land, namely agricultural field, plantation, and industrial forest plantation.

The utilization of peatland to support sustainable development needs careful and precise planning, application of appropriate technology and accurate management also needed to be included in the planning. If managements not met with peatland capabilities and requirements, then a declined of its function in physical, chemical, biological will likely become a problem for further development. Biological function is an important key in the soil ecosystem especially in the tropic area, declined of this function will result the decreasing of soil organism and may disrupt the whole soil process (Lavelle *et al.*, 1994). Soil fauna consists of an organism that plays an important role in the decomposition of organic matter in the soil ecosystem, their activities are determined by the source of its energy and nutrients from organic matter. According to Setiadi (1989) soil fauna has an important function as an organic matter decomposer in soil ecosystem. Buckman and Brady (1982) reported that soil fauna also important in acceleration of nutrients supply in the soil. A number of soil fauna plays an important role in transforming soil organic matter of crop residue into smaller fractions and release the nutrients which able to absorb by plants, these process are result from decomposition process further lead to the formation of humus.

Soil fauna identification is important in relation with organic matter decomposition process in soil and peatland. On the basis of their body size, soil fauna possess small and simple body size. According to Wood (1989), soil fauna can be classified into three categories based on their body size. Micro fauna, possess a body size <100 microns, meso fauna possess a body sizes of 100 microns – 2 mm, and macro fauna possess a body size of 2 – 20 mm. The number of individuals and diversity of soil meso fauna is one of the biological parameter that can be used to assess the ecosystem characteristic. Soil meso fauna has an important role to transform litter and other organic materials such as woods and roots into small fragments then can be further modified and used by other soil microbes. Most of the peatland could not support the large amount of population of the living organisms, although there is a possibility of having high diversity of organisms. Therefore, the aim of this study was to determine the population and diversity of meso fauna in peatland that was converted into forest plantation.

METHODOLOGY

This study was conducted in tropical peatland both in conservation forest and industrial forest plantation of 6 and 36 months old of *Acacia* trees at Teluk Meranti, Riau Province. Soil samples were collected using a 10 cm x 10 cm x 10 cm sample box. Then, soil samples were transferred into Kempson extractor where a container of 70% of alcohol was placed at the bottom of the extractor to collect the meso fauna for 7 days (Fig. 1). The collection of meso fauna was further observed by a stereo microscope to count the population and to identify the soil meso fauna. The diversity of soil meso fauna was calculated using Shannon diversity index

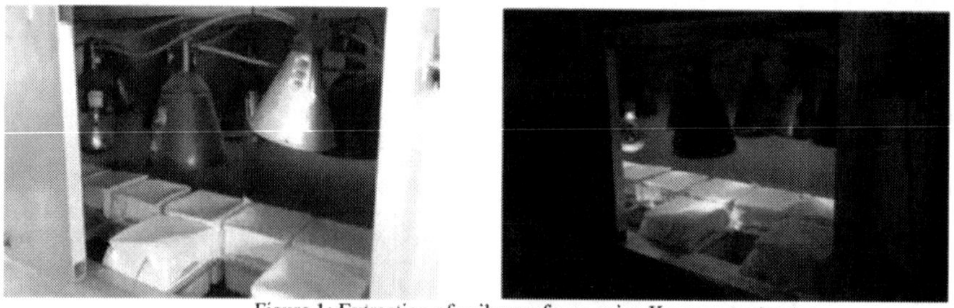

Figure 1: Extraction of soil mesofauna using Kempson extractor

RESULTS

According to identification results, it appears that there was difference in the number of individuals and number of sub order of soil meso fauna in the three different land use. Total population of meso fauna from three different land use were presented in table 1. Based on data of Table 1, it clearly showed that *Acacia* 36 months old had the greatest abundance of individuals and sub order.

Table 1: Total population of Mesofauna in 3 different land use

Ordo	Sub Ordo	*Acacia* 6 months	*Acacia* 36 months	Conservation Forest
Acari	Oribatida	43	157	130
	Mesostigmata	43	60	40
	Prostigmata	17	47	17
Araneae	Ortognatha	0	23	17
	Labidognatha	0	17	10
Coleoptera	Adephaga	0	17	7
	Polyphaga	3	50	27
Collembola	Arthropleona	60	97	107
	Symphyleona	0	3	10
Diplopoda	Polydesmida	3	3	0
Diptera	Nematocera	0	3	30
Hemiptera	Cimicimorpha	0	3	0
	Pentatomorpha	10	0	0
Hymenoptera	Aprocita	73	90	23
Isopoda	-	0	3	0
Pseudoscorpiones	-	7	3	30
Symphilla	-	0	3	23
Thysanoptera	-	3	0	0
Total		263 ± 11	580 ± 12	470 ± 3

The diversity index of observed meso fauna was calculated using Shannon diversity index formula. According to Maguran (1987), the value of diversity index is range from 1.5 – 3.5. Value of < 1.5 indicates a low diversity index, the value between 1.5 – 3.5 indicates moderate, and value of > 3.5 indicates a high diversity. Figure 2 shows the diversity of mesofauna in three different land use. Similar value of diversity index was obtained both by *Acacia* 36 months and conservation forest, which amounted 2.13 and 2.17, respectively.

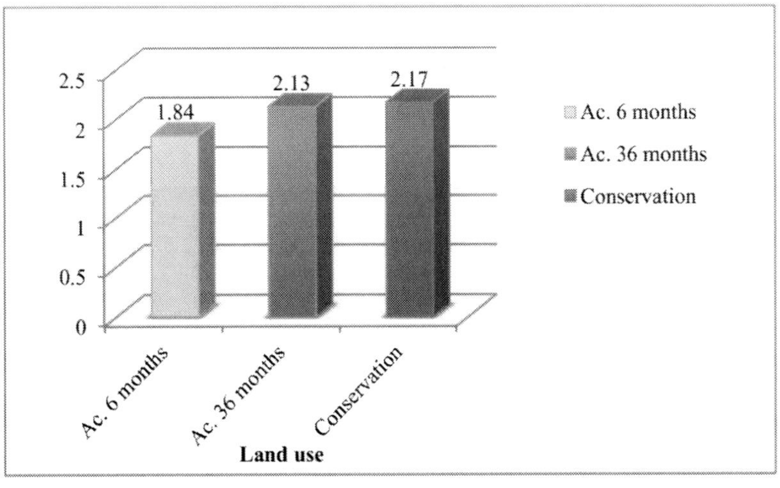

Figure 2: Diversity Index of Mesofauna in 3 different land use

DISCUSSION

Based on the table, the greatest number of individuals of soil meso fauna being found was from the order *Acari* and *Collembola*. This great number of individuals being recorded due to the availability of organic matter as a food source to give nutrition for these orders. According to Lavelle and Spain (2001) *Acari* have a high resistance to water and temperature stress condition, the structure had been designed to withstand water pressure up to -6.0 MPa (pF 5) at a high temperature before moving to the lower temperature condition. In its ecosystem, the abundance of *Acari* and *Collembola* is an important component in several soil processes such as soil formation and has a great impact in nutrient cycling processes (Manh Vu and Nguyen, 2000).

The greatest abundance of soil meso fauna population was obtained from 36 months old of *Acacia* (580 indv/m^2), followed by conservation forest (470 indv/m^2) and 6 months old of *Acacia* (263 indv/m^2). The 36 months old of *Acacia* plantation had the highest number of individuals due to the number of litter produced by *Acacia* tree as a food source, which can enhance the presence of soil meso fauna. The utilization of peatland as *Acacia crassicarpa* plantation can produce high amount of litter that reached 9.2 ton/ha/y (Suwardi *et al*, 2011). Compared to the *Acacia* plantation, no proper management such as maintain the water level and addition of fertilizer were done in conservation forest, these factors will affect the availability of food source for soil meso fauna. Only small amount of litter was produced by 6 months old *Acacia* plantation thus reduce the availability of food source for soil organism, the tree is also relatively young and small which increasing the temperature of soil surface and inhibit the growth of soil meso fauna especially the non resistant one. Table 1 also shows the number of sub order was obtained in three different land use. The number of sub order was found at 8, 13, and 11 sub orders in 6 months old *Acacia*, 36 months old *Acacia*, and conservation forest, respectively.

Mercianto *et al* (1998) reported the value of diversity is affected by different land use. The diversity index of observed meso fauna was calculated using Shannon diversity index formula. The greatest value of diversity index was found in conservation forest with the value of 2.17, a similar value of 2.13 was obtained by 36 months old *Acacia* plantation, whilst 6 months old *Acacia* plantation had the lowest value of diversity index namely 1.84 but still can be categorized as moderate. The value of diversity was influenced by the number of individuals (total population) and the number of sub order, also the amount and variety of organic materials available in the soil. High value of diversity index in forest conservation was caused by the variety of vegetation and organic materials enhance the availability of food source for the growth of soil meso fauna. Other factor that may influence the diversity is disturbance of the ecosystem. No disturbance or relatively small disturbance of human activity can be found in the conservation forest, whereas in the 6 months old of *Acacia* plantation, preparation and maintenance activities still need to be done in the field such as fertilizer application, pest and disease control, and other management to support the growth of young *Acacia* trees. These fieldwork managements may disrupt the activities of organism in the soil ecosystem. The 36 months old of *Acacia* plantation had a similar condition as conservation forest namely minimum disturbance. Thus, the diversity index between the 36 months *Acacia* plantation and conservation forest had a similar value (2.13 *vs* 2.17).

CONCLUSION

The greatest number of individuals and diversity were acquired from 36 months old of *Acacia*. *Acari* and *Collembola* were occupied as the order of soil meso fauna which comprised high number of individuals in the three different land use. The result suggests that the recovery condition of the diversity and population of mesofauna can be reached due to the peatland condition of long terms cultivation of *Acacia* plantation that improved the organic matter quality of the peat land. Utilization of peatland as *Acacia* plantation after three years did not change much of the population and diversity of meso fauna found in the soil.

ACKNOWLEDGEMENT

The authors thank to RAPP for providing the research facilities and Dr. Darmawan as the project leader of the broader research project for the collaboration in this research

REFERENCE

1. Buckman H O and N C Brady. (1982). "The Nature and Properties of Soils" 8th ed., Mac millan Company: New York.
2. Cover TM and JA Thomas. 1991. Elements of Information Theory. John Wiley and Sons Inc. New York.

3. Lavelle P and AV Spain. 2001. Soil Ecology. Kluwer Acad. Publ., Dordrecht. Lavelle P, Dangerfield M, Fragoso C, Eschenbrenner V, Lopez, D Hernandez, Pashanasi B, dan Brussard L. 1994. The Relationship Between Soil Macrofauna and Tropical Soil Fertility. In: Woomer Pl dan MJ Swift (Eds). The Biological Management of Tropical Soil Fertility. John Wiley and Sons.
4. Baffins Lane, Chichester, West Sussex Lavelle P, Dangerfield M, Fragoso C, Eschenbrenner V, Lopez, D Hernandez, Pashanasi B, dan Brussard L. 1994. The Relationship Between Soil Macrofauna and Tropical Soil Fertility. In: Woomer Pl dan MJ Swift (Eds). The Biological Management of Tropical Soil Fertility. John Wiley and Sons.
5. Baffins Lane, Chichester, West Sussex Lavelle P, Dangerfield M, Fragoso C, Eschenbrenner V, Lopez, D Hernandez, Pashanasi B, dan Brussard L. 1994. The Relationship Between Soil Macrofauna and Tropical Soil Fertility. In: Woomer Pl dan MJ Swift (Eds). The Biological Management of Tropical Soil Fertility. John Wiley and Sons.
6. Baffins Lane, Chichester, West Sussex Lavelle P, Dangerfield M, Fragoso C, Eschenbrenner V, Lopez, D Hernandez, Pashanasi B, dan Brussard L. 1994. The Relationship between Soil Macrofauna and Tropical Soil Fertility. In: Woomer Pl dan MJ Swift (Eds). *The Biological Management of Tropical Soil Fertility*. John Wiley and Sons. Baffins Lane, Chichester, West Sussex.
7. Manh Vu Q and TT Nguyen. 2000. Microarthropods community structures (Oribatei and Collembola) in Tam Dao National Park, Vietnam. *Journal of Biosciences*. 25:379-386.
8. Magurran AE. 1987. Ecological Diversity and its Measurement. Chapman and Hall. London.
9. Mercianto Y, Yayuk R Ludwig JA and JF Reynolds. 1988. Statistical Ecology: *Primer Methods and Computing. John Wiley and Sons Inc*. New York. 337 p.
10. Setiadi Y.1989. Utilization of Micro-Organisms in Forestry. Department of Education and Culture. Directorate General of Higher Education. Centre of Biotechnology University. Bogor Agricultural Institute, Bogor. p.38-39 (Indonesian)
11. Suwardi, Djajakirana G, Sumawinata B, Baskoro DPT, Munoz C, Hatano R. 2011. Nutrient Cycle in *Acacia crassicarpa* Plantation on Deep Tropical Peatland at Bukitbatu, Bengkalis, Indonesia. Proceeding of The 10th International Conference of The East and Southeast Asia Federation of Soil Science Societies. 227-228. Colombo-Sri Lanka 10-13 October 2011.
12. Wood M. 1989. Soil Biology. Chapman and Hall. New York.

Abstract No: A-190

MACROINVERTEBRATES OF THE TROPICAL PEAT SWAMP FOREST: A CASE STUDY FROM MALUDAM NATIONAL PARK

Ella Michael Dosi[1], Lee Nyanti[2], Jongkar Grinang[3], Khalid Haron[1] and Mohd Haniff Harun[1]

[1]Malaysian Palm Oil Board, Malaysia
[2]Department of Aquatic Science, Faculty of Resource Science and Technology, Universiti Malaysia Sarawak, Malaysia
[3]Institute of Biodiversity and Environmental Conservation, Malaysia

**Corresponding author: ellamichael@mpob.gov.my*

SUMMARY

Macroinvertebrates are important components in ecological processes of aquatic ecosystems. Nonetheless, roles and functions of the fauna in peat swamp habitat have not been well documented in particular from Borneo. This study aims to document the diversity and composition of macroinvertebrates in the peat swamp forest of Maludam National Park. Collection of macroinvertebrates was made from three stations at Maludam River between November 2011 and July 2013. A total of 2,344 individuals of macroinvertebrates representing 33 species, 18 families and eight orders were caught. About 47% of the total individuals are order Coleoptera, and followed by Hemiptera (24.7%), Odonata (12.3%), Diptera (5.7%), Ephemeroptera (5.5%), Decapoda (4.0%), Blattoidea (0.8%) and Lepidoptera (0.1%). The dominant species was *Dineutus unidentatus* with 774 individuals or 33.0 % of the total individuals caught. Coleoptera (water beetles) represents more than half of the total samples caught, and this implies that the insect serves as a good indicator of peat swamp habitat. The findings are useful information for biodiversity conservation in tropical peat swamp forest.

Keywords: *biodiversity, macroinvertebrates, tropical peat swamp forest, aquatic ecosystem*

INTRODUCTION

Macroinvertebrates are important in regulating food webs in aquatic ecosystems through their functional feeding mechanisms as predators, prey and processors of organic materials. Macroinvertebrates are often being use to assess the functional health of stream water quality. Nutrient enrichment due to anthropogenic activities is known to have significant impacts on the health of aquatic ecosystems (Wang *et al.*, 2007). Nutrient enrichment was reported to alter the relative and absolute abundance of periphyton and macroinvertebrates (Dudley *et al.*, 1986). The sensitivity of Plecoptera, Emphemeroptera, Trichoptera and Diptera to many insecticides (Schulz & Liess, 1999; Leonard, *et al.*, 2000; Berenzen *et al.*, 2005) could be attributed to the differences in physiology, generation cycle and the mobility of the species (Mercer *et al.*, 2013). Thus, their presence can be used as an indicator of the water body status. Tropical region are inhabited by numerous endemic tropical stream macroinvertebrates in which many have not been catalogued to genus and species level (Mattson *et al.*, 1999; Jacobsen *et al.*, 2008). In addition, the freshwater macroinvertebrates of Malaysia are poorly known and few species have been described (Morse *et al.*, 2007) especially from the peat swamp habitats. According to Yule (2010), many aquatic invertebrates species are restricted to peat swamp forest, which subjected to extinction when the peat swamps are destroyed. This study aims to document species richness and composition of macroinvertebrates in tropical peat swamp ecosystem. This study is expected to produce information that needed for conserving freshwater peat swamp.

MATERIAL AND METHODS

Study Site

Maludam National Park is located in central of Sarawak, Malaysia, comprises a single largest peat dome in the Northern Borneo, and the park covers an area of 43,147 hectares. Three sampling stations were selected at Maludam National Park namely Stations 1 (N01°34.894' E111°05.086'), Station 2 (N01°35.799'E111°04.415') and Station 3 (N01°37.043'E111°03.746'). The stations are located at upper reaches of Sungai Maludam, which classified as mixed peat swamp forest. The water of all stations was slow flowing and black in appearance. The bottom substrate was mainly peat with submerged logs, leaves and branches. There are also submerged vegetations at shallow area of the stream channel. Water depths of the stream were ranging from 1.1 m during dry season to 6.2 m during wet season.

Macroinvertebrates Sampling

Sampling of macroinvertebrates was conducted every three months between November 2011 and July 2013. Macroinvertebrates were sampled using a scoop net (frame size = 40 cm x 32 cm, mesh size = 400 micromn). The specimens were put into the plastic bottle containing 85% alcohol and brought back to laboratory for sorting and identification.

Biological Indices

Species diversity, species evenness and species richness for macroinvertebrates at each sampling site was determined using Shannon's Diversity Index (H), Pielou Evenness Index (J), and Margalef Richness Index (D).

RESULTS

Macroinvertebrates Diversity and Composition

A total of 2,344 macroinvertebrates were collected from three stations in Maludam National Park. The samples represent 33 species from 18 families and eight orders. In terms of the total individuals recorded, the dominant species was *Dineutus unidentatus* with 774 individuals, which is 33.0 % of the total individual recorded. In terms of diversity indices, Species Diversity (H') ranged from 1.935 to 2.473. Species Richness (D) ranged from 4.248 to 4.484. Species Evenness (J) ranged from 0.569 to 0.655. Based on the functional feeding group, 84.6% of the macroinvertebrates caught were predators, 11.2% were gathering collector and 4.1% were shredders.

In terms of order, the macroinvertebrate community constituted of order Coleoptera (46.8%), followed by Hemiptera (24.7%), Odonata (12.3%), Diptera (5.7%), Ephemeroptera (5.5%), Decapoda (4.0%), Blattodea (0.8% and Lepidoptera (0.1%). In terms of family, the community was represented by Gyrinidae (46.5%), Gerridae (14.7%), Libellulidae (7.1%), Nepidae (7.0%), Chironomidae (5.7%), Baetidae (5.5%), Palaemonidae (4.0%), Coenagrionidae (3.7%), Belostomatidae (1.2%), Gomphidae (1.0%), Notonectidae (1.0%), Blaberidae (0.8%), Hydrometridae (0.8%), Aeshnidae (0.5%), Dytiscidae (0.3%), Helotrephidae (0.1 %), Pyralidae (0.1 %) and Corduliidae (< 0.1 %). The dominant family, Gyrinidae was represented by two species namely *Dineutus unidentatus* and *Orectochilus* sp..

In terms of macroinvertebrates composition at each station, a total of 644 individuals and 30 species from 17 families belonging to 8 orders were recorded from Station 1. Station 1 was inhabited by Coleoptera (56.8%), Hemiptera (15.8%), Odonata (13.2%), Ephemeroptera (8.2%), Decapoda (4.5%), Blattodea (0.6%), Diptera (0.6%) and Lepidoptera (0.2%). Coleoptera was represented by Gyrinidae which comprise of two species *Dineutus unidentatus* and *Orectochilus* sp.. *Dineutus unidentatus* was the dominant species at Station 1 with 56.1% of the total individual recorded. Station 2 recorded a total of 971 individuals and 31 species from 17 families belonging to 8 orders. Macroinvertebrates compositions consisted of Hemiptera (36.1%), Coleoptera (28.9%), Odonata (12.5%), Diptera (11.5%), Ephemeroptera (5.7%), Decapoda (4.3%), Blattodea (0.8%) and Lepidoptera (0.2%). Hemiptera which was the biggest order inhabiting Station 2 was represented by Gerridae (74.0%), Nepidae (19.1%), Belostomatidae (2.6%), Notonectidae (2.3%), Hydrometridae (1.7%) and Helotrephidae (0.3%). In terms of species, 24.9% of the macroinvertebrates was represented by the dominant species, *Limnometra octopunctata*. In Station 3, 729 individuals and 29 species from 16 families belonging to 7 orders were recorded. Macroinvertebrates compositions consisted of Coleoptera (61.6%), Hemiptera (17.6%), Odonata (11.4%), Decapoda (3.2%), Ephemeroptera (2.9%), Diptera (2.5%) and Blattodea (1.0%). Coleoptera was the dominant inhabitants of Station 3 and was mainly represented by Gyrinidae (99.6%) and Dytiscidae (0.5%). Gyrinidae was represented by *Dineutus unidentatus* and *Orectochilus* sp. whereby both species were present in high abundance with 32.1% and 29.2% of the total individuals recorded, respectively. Overall, Coleoptera and Hemiptera were the two major orders recorded at each station.

Environmental Parameters

Environmental parameters measured were water temperature, dissolved oxygen, pH and turbidity. Water temperature ranged from 26.14 to 26.59°C, which considered as low due to the partially shaded river. Dissolved oxygen ranged from 1.65 to 2.65 mg/L, a natural characteristic of peat water. Water was acidic as reflected by low reading of pH ranging from 4.05 to 4.10. Low turbidity recorded at all stations ranged from 3.59 to 3.79 NTU.

DISCUSSION

Macroinvertebrates are often being used as bioindicators of stream health (Azrina *et al.*, 2005) due to their ubiquitous distribution, measurable duration of their lifecycle, sedentary nature which makes them constantly encounter the environmental changes of the habitat they lived in (Rosenberg and Resh, 1993). In Maludam National Park, Coleoptera (water beetles) represents more than half of the population. High presence of Coleoptera which mainly represented by Gyrinidae was related with the slow running waters (Ward, 1992) which are the general habitat of Gyrinidae. Since they are predators which prey on other invertebrates, their presences are dependent on the habitat of sufficient quality to support their prey. Thus, predatory bugs were generally observed to be more common in forest stream of good quality (OPIC, 2007). Moreover, predator represents more than half of the macroinvertebrates recorded. The presence of Chironomidae which is one of the taxa-specific indicators for very poor water quality (Xu *et al.*, 2014) was low in Maludam National Park. According to Acharyya and Mitsch (2000), high presence of chironomids in the aquatic ecosystems often indicates a high pollution load, low level of dissolved oxygen and over enriched condition. In addition, numerous presence of highly tolerant organism usually indicates poor water quality (Hynes, 1998). It was also reported that the abundance of tolerant species, mainly *Chironomus* spp. was increased in the water with high concentrations of organic and/or inorganic pollutants (Al-Shami *et al.*, 2010).

CONCLUSION

This study provides information on the macroinvertebrates composition in the tropical peat swamp forest of Maludam National Park. The peat swamp stream of Maludam National Park supports diverse species of macroinvertebrates, which mainly represented by Coleoptera.

ACKNOWLEDGEMENTS

The authors would like to acknowledge Director General of Malaysian Palm Oil Board (MPOB) for allowing us to present this study at International Peat Congress 2016 (IPC 2016). Thank you also goes to the Director of Biological Research of MPOB for the support and the staff of Tropical Peat Research Institute of MPOB and Universiti Malaysia Sarawak (UNIMAS) for the logistics supports. Last but not least, the appreciation goes to the MPOB Peat Manuscript Review Committee for their comments in improving this paper.

REFERENCES

1. Acharyya, S. and Mitsch, W.J. (2000). Macroinvertebrate diversity and its ecological implication in two created wetland ecosystems. Annual Report (Olentangy River Wetland Research Park). The Ohio State University.
2. Al-Shami, S.A., Rawi, C.S., Hassan Ahmad, A., and Nor, S.A. (2010). Distribution of chironomidae (Insect: Diptera) in polluted rivers of the Juru Basin, Penang, Malaysia. *Journal of Environmental Science (China)*, 22 (11): 1718-27
3. Azrina, M.Z., Yap, C.K., Ismail, A.R., Ismail, A., and Tan, S.G. (2005). Anthropogenic impacts on the distribution and biodiversity of benthic macroinvertebrates and water quality of the Langat River Peninsular Malaysia. *Ecotoxicology and Environmental Safety*, 64: 337-347.
4. Berenzen, N., Kumke, T., Schulz, H., & Schulz, R. (2005). Macroinvertebrate community structure in agricultural streams: Impact of runoff-related pesticide contamination. *Ecotoxicology and Environmental Safety*, 60: 37–46.
5. Dudley T.L., Cooper,S.D., Hemphill, N. (1986). Effects of macroalgae on a stream invertebrate community. *Journal of the North American Benthological Society*, Vol.5 No.2 pp.93–106.
6. Hynes, K.E. (1998). Benthic Macroinvertebrate Diversity and Biotic Indices for Monitoring of 5 Urban and Urbanizing Lakes within the Halifax Regional Municipality (HRM), Nova Scotia, Canada. Soil & Water Conservation Society of Metro Halifax. xiv, 114p.
7. Jacobsen, D., Cressa, C., Mathooko, J., & Dudgeon, D. (2008). Macroinvertebrates: Composition, Life Histories and Production. In: D. Dudgeon (Ed.), *Tropical Stream Ecology* (pp. 66–106). London: Elsevier.
8. Leonard, A., Hyne, R., Lim, R., Pablo, F., & Van den Brink, P. (2000). Riverine endosulfan concentrations in the Namoi River, Australia: Link to cotton field runoff and macroinvertebrate population densities. *Environmental Toxicology Chemistry*, 19: 1540–1551.
9. Margalef, R. (1968). *Perspective in Ecological Theory*. Chigago: University of Chigago Press.
10. Mattson, B., Cederberg, G., & Blix, L. (1999). Agricultural land use in life cycle assessment (LCA): Case studies of three vegetable oil crops. *Journal of Cleaner Production*, *8*: 283–292.

11. Mercer, E.V., Mercer, T.G. and Sayok, A.K. (2013). Effects of forest conversions to oil palm plantations on freshwater macroinvertebrates: a case study from Sarawak, Malaysia. *Journal of Land Use Science*, DOI:10.1080/1747423X.2013.786149.
12. Morse, J.C., Bae, Y.J., Munkhjargal, G., Sangpradub, N., Tanida, K., Vshivkova, T.S., Wang, B., Yang, L. and Yule, C.M. (2007). Freshwater biomonitoring with macroinvertebrates in East Asia. *Frontiers in Ecology and the Environment,* 5 (1): 33–42.
13. Oil Palm Industry Corporation, OPIC. (2007). Impact of Oil Palm on Freshwater Streams in Oro and West New Britain Provinces. Oil Palm Industry Corporation, OPIC.
14. Pielou, E. C. J. (1966). The measurement of diversity in different types of biological collections. *Journal of Theoretical Biology*, *13*, 131-144.
15. Rosenberg, D.M. and Resh, V.H. (1993). *Freshwater Biomonitoring and Benthic Macroinvertebrates.* Chapman and Hall, New York, USA, 488 pp.
16. Schulz, R., & Liess, M. (1999). A field study of the effects of agriculturally derived insecticide input on stream macroinvertebrate dynamics. *Aquatic Toxicology*, *46*: 155–176.
17. Shannon, C. E., & Weaver, W. (1963). *The Mathematical Theory of Communication* (pp. 144). Illinois, Urbana: University of Illinois Press.
18. Wang, L.Z., D.M. Robertson, and P.J. Garrison. (2007). Linkages between nutrients and macroinvertebrate and fish assemblages in wadeable streams: Implication to nutrient criteria development. *Environmental Management.* 39:194–212.
19. Ward, J.V. (1992). *Aquatic Insect Ecology, 1. Biology and Habitat.* New York, John Wiley & Sons, Inc.
20. Yule, C.M. (2010) Loss of biodiversity and ecosystems functioning in Indo-Malayan peat swamp forest. *Biodiversity Conservation*, 19: 393-409.

Abstract No: A-438

MICRODISTRIBUTION AND COMMUNITY STRUCTURE OF AQUATIC MACROINVERTEBRATES IN THE LARGEST PEAT BOG IN CROATIA

Sanja Gottstein[1], Andreja Brigić[1*], Ana Previšić[1], Marina Vilenica[2], Mladen Kerovec[1] and Ivančica Ternjej[1]

[1]*Division of Zoology, Department of Biology, Faculty of Science, University of Zagreb, Croatia*
[2]*Faculty of Teacher Education, Department in Petrinja, University of Zagreb, Croatia*

**Corresponding author: andreja.brigic@biol.pmf.hr*

SUMMARY

Peat bogs are generally characterised by great internal diversity that provides a plethora of various aquatic and semiaquatic habitats. Data on microdistribution and ecology of aquatic macroinvertebrates from the Southern Europe, including the Western Balkan peat bogs, are very scarce. The current study was conducted at the largest peat bog in Croatia influenced by the rapid successional changes causing its area to decrease significantly. Aquatic macroinvertebrates were sampled at four main habitat types: lake, hollow, ditch and pool. Sampling was conducted monthly during one vegetation season, from April to October 2015, using a 25x25 cm benthos net. In total, we recorded taxa from 18 different taxonomic groups, with aquatic insect orders and Crustaceans having the highest richness. Crustaceans, Diptera and Coleoptera were the groups recorded in the highest densities. However, our study shows that the aquatic macroinvertebrate assemblages in the Đon močvar peat bog differ between studied microhabitats, most probably related to differences in physico-chemical water properties of studied habitats. Among the environmental variables analysed, physical water properties (such as temperature, depth and habitat size) were the most important in affecting the spatial distribution of aquatic macroinvertebrates at this peat bog. Our study supports the view that the peat bogs in Croatia are extremely endangered habitats. With the current trends of decreasing traditional agricultural activities, it is of a crucial importance to protect Croatian largest remaining peat bog from rapid successional changes.

Keywords: *biodiversity, physico-chemical water properties, species richness, peatland, microhabitats*

INTRODUCTION

Climate change, agricultural activities (i.e. drainage and peat extraction), as well as secondary succession (i.e. soil formation and vegetation colonisation) are the main factors involved in surface modification of peatlands (Więcek *et al.*, 2013). They are amongst the most fragile and endangered ecosystems worldwide (Langheinrich *et al.*, 2004). The biodiversity of the peatlands in South-Eastern Europe is generally poorly understood even though they are clearly distinctive parts of the landscape (Topić & Stančić 2006). The studies of the microdistribution and ecology of aquatic macroinvertebrates were mainly conducted in the area of Northern and Central Europe (e.g. van Kleef *et al.*, 2012, Svobodova *et al.*, 2013), while the data from the Southern Europe, including the Western Balkan peat bogs are very scarce (e.g. Previšić *et al.*, 2013). Accordingly, no previous study has dealt with diversity and ecology of aquatic macroinvertebrates of peat bogs in Croatia.

Peat bogs are characterised by great internal diversity that provides a plethora of various aquatic and semiaquatic habitats. These habitats differ in water level, chemistry and vegetation composition and structure. That is way they are areas of high interests to study the relationship between aquatic macroinvertebrates and their microhabitats. Thus, the aims of this study were to: (1) describe the density and diversity of aquatic macroinvertebrate assemblages at different habitat types in the peat bog and (2) analyse environmental variables that affect spatial distribution of aquatic macroinvertebrates.

METHODS

Study area

The study was conducted in the Đon močvar bog located in the Central Croatia (N 45; E 15), at 130 m a.s.l. It spreads over an area of 10 ha, representing one of the largest and oldest peat bogs in Croatia. Moreover, it is a complex ecosystem, encompassing a mosaic of different habitats from open woodless *Sphagnum* L. sites, deep hollows, and small ponds, to swampy areas dominated by *Phragmites* Adans. Abandonment of traditional land-management practices, such as mowing and grazing, has led to a severe process of succession.

Consequently, its area decreased from 40 ha to 10 ha by the beginning of the 20th century. However, the bog and surrounding area are protected as a Botanical Reserve and it is a potential NATURA 2000 site (Alegro & Šegota 2008).

Macroinvertebrate sampling & water properties measurements

Aquatic macroinvertebrates were sampled at four main habitat types: lake, hollow, ditch and pool. The study sites differed in physico-chemical water properties, size and vegetation composition (Table 1). The triplicate samples of macrozoobenthos were collected at each site, once a month, using a benthos net (25×25 cm = 0.0625 m^2; mesh size = 500 μm) for a total of 24 samples. The samples were collected during one vegetation season, from the end of April to the end of October 2015. The specimens were sorted, counted and identified to the lowest possible taxonomic level.

The physico-chemical water properties (temperature, pH, dissolved O_2, and conductivity) were measured at each site, with a multiparameter probe (WTW Multi 3430). Alkalinity, as a concentration of calcium carbonate (mg/L), was measured using Standard Analytical Procedure (APHA).

Data analysis

In order to compare physico-chemical water properties, one-way ANOVA or Kruskal-Wallis H tests were used, followed by post hoc Fischer LSD or Multiple comparison tests. The selection of parametric or non-parametric tests depended on the normality of the data, which were tested using a Shapiro-Wilk W test. These tests were performed using Statistica 12.0 software package (StatSoft Inc. 2013). Shannon diversity index (H') was calculated based on order taxa level, using PRIMER 6 software package (Clarke & Gorley 2006).

RESULTS

Majority of physico-chemical water properties differed significantly between studied habitats (Table 1). Microclimatic conditions were more stable in deep hollows and lake, while in shallow pools of *Rhynchosporetum albae* association and small and shallow ditches were highly prone to oscillations. Moreover, some values exceeded the biological limits for some macroinvertebrate taxa. For example, during the summer in unshaded ditches the water temperature was elevated (28.6 °C), while in the hollows pH values decreased (5.02) due to low groundwater level. Values of majority of other measured physico-chemical water properties in hollows surrounded by trees of *Alnus glutinosa* were stable, except the values of dissolved oxygen concentration that markedly fluctuated during the study period.

Table 1: Comparison of different habitat types using 1-way ANOVA or Kruskal Wallis sum rank tests and the values (mean ± SD) of measured physico-chemical water properties (N=7, per site) in the peat bog Đon močvar.

Microhabitats	Lake	Hollows	Ditches	Pools	Anova/Kruskal Wallis	Comparisons ($p < 0.05$)
Main vegetation	*Carex acutiformis*, *Typha latifolia*	*Sphagnum* spp., *Alnus glutinosa*	*Sphagnum* spp., *Carex echinata*	*Rhynchospora alba*, *Sphagnum* spp.		
Vegetation coverage	medium	high	medium	low		
Water depth, range (cm)	60 ± 0.90	100 ± 0.6	22.5 ± 0.08	20 ± 0.03	15,01	H>P>D=L
Width of microhabitat (m)	0.3 ± 1.15	0.2 ± 0.8	0.1 ± 0.21	20 ± 1.77	24,09	P>H>D=L
Length of microhabitat (m)	0.4 ± 1.52	5 ± 0.5	10 ± 0	10 ± 1.76	27,88	P>H>L; L=H
Water temperature (°C)	14.2 ± 6.7	11 ± 0.7	14.9 ± 6.6	18.7 ± 8.5	2,21	P>H=D=L
Oxygen (mg/L)	5.4 ± 3.3	6.6 ± 3	6.1 ± 3.2	7.2 ± 1.8	0,91	ns
pH	5.5 ± 0.3	5.5 ± 0.2	5.5 ± 0.3	5.8 ± 0.4	1,17	ns
Conductivity (μS/cm)	33.5 ± 5.4	22.35 ± 8.4	28 ± 45	31.5 ± 64	4,53	ns
CaCO3 (mg/L)	16.2 ± 3.5	15 ± 2.3	15 ± 4	16.2 ± 3.52	5,41	ns

In total, we recorded taxa from 18 different groups at the Đon močvar bog, with aquatic insect orders and Crustaceans having the highest richness (Figure 1). The dominant taxa in ditches and hollowes were

Amphipoda, while Diptera prevailed in pools. The majority of Ostracoda and Copepoda were recorded from the lake and Isopoda from the hollows. The relative frequency of Oligochaeta was the highest in ditches. Ephemeroptera occurred rarely in the lake and sporadically in pools (Figure 1).

The values of Shannon diversity index (H') were as it follows: lake (2.05 bits/ind.), ditches (1.80 bits/ind.), hollows (1.42 bits/ind.) and pools (1.34 bits/ind.; Figure 2). The highest macroinvertebrate density was recorded in hollows surrounded by *A. glutinosa* trees, followed by ditches. The lowest macroinvertebrate density was recorded in the lake and pools (Figure 3). Additionally, the density differed between the seasons, being the highest in spring (May and June) and the lowest during the summer (July and August).

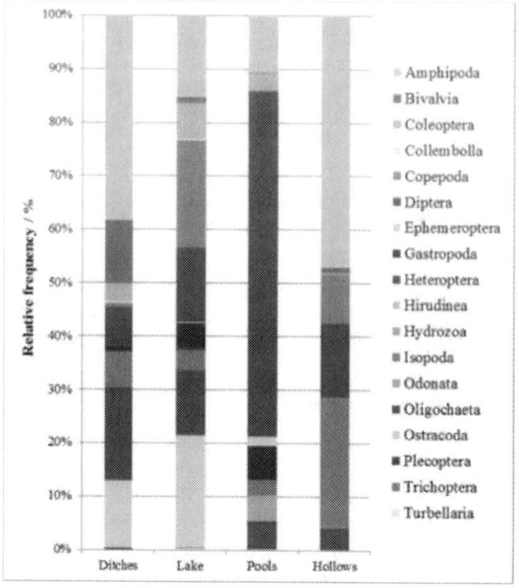

Figure 1: Relative frequency of aquatic macroinvertebrates at the study sites (ditches, lake, pools and hollows) in the Đon močvar peat bog.

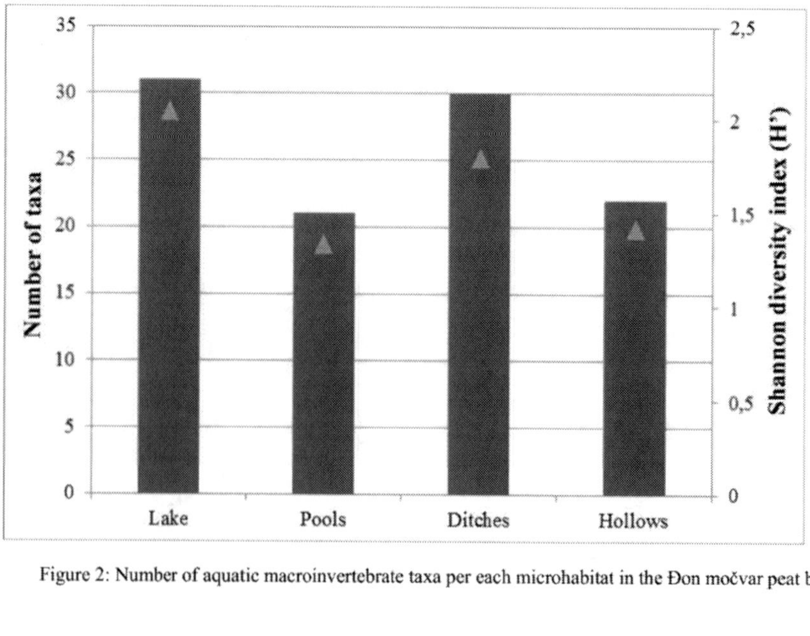

Figure 2: Number of aquatic macroinvertebrate taxa per each microhabitat in the Đon močvar peat bog.

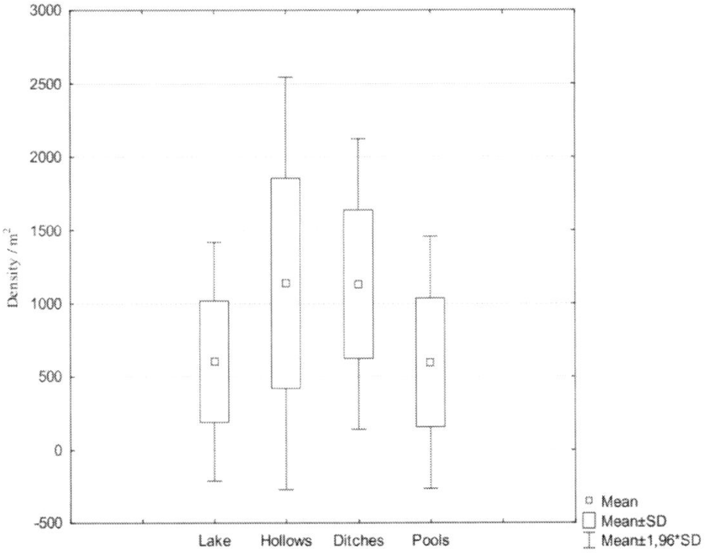

Figure 3: The range of aquatic macroinvertebrate density (m^2) at the study sites (ditches, lake, pools and hollows) in the Đon močvar peat bog during the study period between April and October 2015.

DISCUSSION

Wheeler and Proctor (2000) divided peatlands into two disctinct types: bogs having pH below 5.0 and fens having pH above 5.5, rather than into minerothrophic fens and ombrothrophic bogs. In the review of Hájek *et al.*, (2006) the peatland subdivision has been made based on the pH/calcium (poor-rich) gradient and in the light of the studies of the biodiversity of various aquatic macroinvertebrate taxa, especially molluscs. Based on the aquatic macroinvertebrate community composition and the measured physico-chemical water properties, the peat bog Đon močvar cannot be classified as a true ombrothrophic (mineral poor) peat bog according to Hájek *et al.*, (2006).

Our study shows that the aquatic macroinvertebrate assemblages in the Đon močvar peat bog differ between studied microhabitat, which is most probably related to differences in physical water properties of studied habitats, such as temperature, depth and the habitat size. The water in this peat bog originates from both, the rainfall and from the groundwater, in many ways causing the differences between the small shallow pools and permanent deep water sites. Although vegetation composition and structure at each study site played an important role in physico-chemical water properties in the studied peat bog, it is also possible that seasonal influence of groundwater could be more intensive. Consequently, the particular microhabitats with specific peat bog invertebrate species have not been recorded. On the other hand, depressions at the peat substrates surrounded by hummocks rich in *Sphagnum* spp. and *Rhynchosporetum albae* association had higher fluctuations of physico-chemical water properties, especially pH values which even dropped below 5.1. The acidic aquatic habitats of peatland pools are poor in inorganic ions (Ca^{2+}, Cl^-, SO_4^{2-}), which could have caused low values of conductivity in the most of the microhabitat exposed to the moss cushions in the peat bog Đon Močvar (Wheeler & Proctor 2000, Horsák 2006).

In this study, we found high density of Crustaceans, Diptera and Coleoptera, which is in accordance with studies conducted in Canadian and North European peatlands (Danks & Rosenberg 1987, Rydin & Jeglum 2006). Crustaceans and Diptera are overall very important components of aquatic fauna, crucial to peat bog food webs. Taxa recorded at this peat bog are mostly common at peatlands, but due to overall rareness of such habitats in the Southern Europe these are also rare in this region, including Croatia (e.g. Previšić *et al.*, 2013). Seasonal variations in density and richness of macroinvertebrates recorded here are in line with those observed in other peatlands, e.g. in small peatland lakes in Ireland Baars *et al.*, (2014) recorded highest taxa richness during the spring. Taxa richness and diversity of macroinvertebrates were quite similar among different habitat types, with the lake having the highest values. Habitat permanency was identified as important in structuring the invertebrate assemblages of aquatic peatland habitats with larger pools hosting higher abundance and different community composition than smaller habitats more at risk of drying out (Baars *et al.*, 2014). Since diversity presented here is based on the taxa order level, the real diversity in this peat bog is much higher than the presented. The highest macroinvertebrate density was recorded in the hollows, mainly due to higher density of Crustaceans (Amphipoda and Isopoda), most likely related to the relatively stable conditions and dependence on groundwater levels. Oscillations in water temperature, depth and the pH value most likely play an important role as an environmental barrier for species occurrence in shallow water microhabitats (Baars *et al.*, 2014).

CONCLUSION

Biodiversity of aquatic macroinvertebrates in the peat bog Đon močvar in Croatia is shaped by the taxonomic group, environmental conditions and microhabitat specificity. Due to the presence of numerous rare species, the peat bog habitats in Croatia are considered to be extremely endangered habitats. With the current trends of decreasing traditional agricultural activities, it is of a crucial importance to protect Croatian largest remaining peat bog from rapid successional changes.

REFERENCES

1. Alegro A, Šegota V. 2008. Florističke i vegetacijske značajke botaničkog rezervata „Đon močvar" u Blatuši. General technical report. State Institute for Nature Protection, Zagreb, Croatia.
2. Baars J.-R., Murray D.A., Hannigan, E., Kelly-Quinn M. 2014. Macroinvertebrate assemblages of small upland peatland lakes in Ireland. Biology and Environment: Proceedings of the Royal Irish Academy, Vol. 114B, No. 3, Small Water Bodies: Importance, Threats and Knowledge Gaps, pp. 233-248.
3. Clarke KR, Gorley RN. 2006. PRIMER v6: User Manual/Tutorial. PRIMER-E, Plymouth.
4. Hájek M., Horsák M., Hájková P., Dítě D. 2006. Habitat diversity of central European fens in relation to environmental gradients and an effort to standardize fen terminology in ecological studies. *Perspectives in Plant Ecology, Evolution and Systematics* 8: 97-114.
5. Horsák M. 2006. Mollusc community patterns and species response curves along a mineral richness gradient: a case study in fens. *Journal of Biogeography* 33: 98–107.
6. Langheinrich U., Tischew S., Gersberg R.M., Lüderitz V. 2004. Ditches and canals in management of fens: opportunity or risk? A case study in th Drömling Natural Park, Germany. *Wetlands Ecology and Management* 12: 429-445.
7. Previšić A., Brigić A., Sedlar Z., Šoštarić R. 2013. First data on caddisfly (Insecta, Trichoptera) fauna of peatlands in Croatia. *Natura Croatica* 22 (2): 235-242.
8. Svobodová J., Matěna J., Kopáček J., Poláková S., Vrba J. 2013. Spatial and temporal changes of benthic macroinvertebrate assemblagesin acidified streams in the Bohemian Forest (Czech Republic). Aquatic Insects: International Journal of Freshwater Entomology, 34:sup1, 157–172.
9. van Kleef H.H., van Duinen G.-J.A. Verberk, W.C.E.P., Leuven R.S.E.W., van der Velde G., Esselink H. 2012. Moorland pools as refugia for endangered species characteristic of raised bog gradients. Journal for Nature Conservation 20: 255–263.
10. Topić J, Stančić Z. 2006. Extinction of fen and bog plants and their habitats in Croatia. *Biodiversity and Conservation* 15: 3371-3381.
11. Verhoeven J.T.A., Setter T.L. 2010. Agricultural use of wetlands: opportunities and limitations. Annals of Botany 105 (1): 155-163.
12. Wheeler B.D., Proctor M.C.F. 2000. Ecological gradients, subdivisions and terminology of north-west European mires. *Journal of Ecology* 88:187–203.
13. Więcek M., Martin P., Gąnka M. 2013. Distribution patterns and environmental correlates of water mites (Hydrachnidia, Acari) in peatland microhabitats. *Experimental & Applied Acarology* 61 (2): 147-160.

AUTHOR INDEX

AUTHOR INDEX

AUTHOR INDEX

AUTHOR INDEX

AUTHOR INDEX

International Peatland Society (IPS)
Vapaudenkatu 12
40100 Jyvaskyla Finland

ISBN 978-1-5108-6213-5

9 781510 862135

CURRAN ASSOCIATES INC.
proceedings
.com